RSMeans®

Building Construction Cost Data

59th Annual Edition

D1561069

2001

Senior Editor
Phillip R. Waier, PE

Contributing Editors
Barbara Balboni
Robert A. Bastoni
Howard M. Chandler
John H. Chiang, PE
Paul C. Crosscup
Jennifer L. Curran
Stephen E. Donnelly
J. Robert Lang
Robert C. McNichols
Melville J. Mossman, PE
John J. Moylan
Jeannene D. Murphy
Peter T. Nightingale
Stephen C. Plotner
Michael J. Regan
Stephen J. Sechovicz

Manager, Engineering Operations
John H. Ferguson, PE

Group Vice President
Durwood S. Snead

Vice President and General Manager
Roger J. Grant

Vice President, Sales and Marketing
John M. Shea

Production Manager
Michael Kokernak

Production Coordinator
Marion E. Schofield

Technical Support
Thomas J. Dion
Michael H. Donelan
Jonathan Forgit
Mary Lou Geary
Gary L. Hoitt
Paula Reale-Camelio
Robin Richardson
Kathryn S. Rodriguez
Sheryl A. Rose
Elizabeth A. Ryan
James N. Wills

Book & Cover Design
Norman R. Forgit

First Printing

Foreword

R.S. Means Co., Inc. is a subsidiary of CMD Group (Construction Market Data), a leading provider of construction information, products, and services in North America and globally. CMD's flagship product line includes more than 100 regional editions, national construction project information, sales leads, and over 70 local plan room/libraries in major business centers. CMD also publishes ProFile, a directory of more than 20,000 architectural firms in the U.S. Architect's First Source (AFS) provides Publishers First Source for Products, CSI's SPEC-DATA® and CSI's MANU-SPEC® building product directories for the selection of nationally available building products. R.S. Means provides Construction cost data and training, and consulting services in print, CD-ROM and online. Associated Construction Publications (ACP) provides regional magazines covering the U.S. highways heavy construction, and heavy equipment trader. Manufacturers' Survey Associates (MSA) provides surveys, plans, and specifications. CMD Group is headquartered in Atlanta and has 1,400 employees worldwide. CMD Group is owned by Cahners Business Information (www.cahners.com), a member of the Reed Elsevier plc group (NYSE: RUK and ENL). Cahners is the leading U.S. provider of business information to 16 vertical markets, including building & construction, entertainment, manufacturing, and retail. Cahners' content portfolio encompasses 140 Web sites as well as *Variety, Publishers Weekly, Design News* and 127 other market-leading business-to-business magazines. Cahners developed the leading business-to-business Web portals e-inSITE in the electronics industry, Manufacturing.net in manufacturing as well as Buildingteam.com and HousingZone.com in construction, and maintains an active program of Internet and print launches.

Our Mission

Since 1942, R.S. Means Company, Inc. has been actively engaged in construction cost publishing and consulting throughout North America.

Today, over 50 years after the company began, our primary objective remains the same: to provide you, the construction and facilities professional, with the most current and comprehensive construction cost data possible.

Whether you are a contractor, an owner, an architect, an engineer, a facilities manager, or anyone else who needs a fast and reliable construction cost estimate, you'll find this publication to be a highly useful and necessary tool.

Today, with the constant flow of new construction methods and materials, it's difficult to find the time to look at and evaluate all the different construction cost possibilities. In addition, because labor and material costs keep changing, last year's cost information is not a reliable basis for today's estimate or budget.

That's why so many construction professionals turn to R.S. Means. We keep track of the costs for you, along with a wide range of other key information, from city cost indexes . . . to productivity rates . . . to crew composition . . . to contractor's overhead and profit rates.

R.S. Means performs these functions by collecting data from all facets of the industry, and organizing it in a format that is instantly accessible to you. From the preliminary budget to the detailed unit price estimate, you'll find the data in this book useful for all phases of construction cost determination.

The Staff, the Organization, and Our Services

When you purchase one of R.S. Means' publications, you are in effect hiring the services of a full-time staff of construction and engineering professionals.

Our thoroughly experienced and highly qualified staff works daily at collecting, analyzing, and disseminating comprehensive cost information for your needs. These staff members have years of practical construction experience and engineering training prior to joining the firm. As a result, you can count on them not only for the cost figures, but also for additional background reference information that will help you create a realistic estimate.

The Means organization is always prepared to help you solve construction problems through its five major divisions: Construction and Cost Data Publishing, Electronic Products and Services, Consulting Services, Insurance Division, and Educational Services.

Besides a full array of construction cost estimating books, Means also publishes a number of other reference works for the construction industry. Subjects include construction estimating and project and business management; special topics such as HVAC, roofing, plumbing, and hazardous waste remediation; and a library of facility management references.

In addition, you can access all of our construction cost data through your computer with Means CostWorks 2000 CD-ROM, an electronic tool that offers over 50,000 lines of Means detailed construction cost data, along with assembly and whole building cost data. You can also access Means cost information from our Web site at www.rsmeans.com

What's more, you can increase your knowledge and improve your construction estimating and management performance with a Means Construction Seminar or In-House Training Program. These two-day seminar programs offer unparalleled opportunities for everyone in your organization to get updated on a wide variety of construction-related issues.

Means also is a worldwide provider of construction cost management and analysis services for commercial and government owners and of claims and valuation services for insurers.

In short, R.S. Means can provide you with the tools and expertise for constructing accurate and dependable construction estimates and budgets in a variety of ways.

Robert Snow Means Established a Tradition of Quality That Continues Today

Robert Snow Means spent years building his company, making certain he always delivered a quality product.

Today, at R.S. Means, we do more than talk about the quality of our data and the usefulness of our books. We stand behind all of our data, from historical cost indexes... to construction materials and techniques... to current costs.

If you have any questions about our products or services, please call us toll-free at 1-800-334-3509. Our customer service representatives will be happy to assist you or visit our Web site at www.rsmeans.com

Table of Contents

UNIT PRICES

GENERAL REQUIREMENTS	1
SITE CONSTRUCTION	2
CONCRETE	3
MASONRY	4
METALS	5
WOOD & PLASTICS	6
THERMAL & MOISTURE PROTECTION	7
DOORS & WINDOWS	8
FINISHES	9
SPECIALTIES	10
EQUIPMENT	11
FURNISHINGS	12
SPECIAL CONSTRUCTION	13
CONVEYING SYSTEMS	14
MECHANICAL	15
ELECTRICAL	16
SQUARE FOOT	17

REFERENCE INFORMATION

REFERENCE NUMBERS

CREWS

COST INDEXES

INDEX

How the Book Is Built: An Overview

A Powerful Construction Tool

You have in your hands one of the most powerful construction tools available today. A successful project is built on the foundation of an accurate and dependable estimate. This book will enable you to construct just such an estimate.

For the casual user the book is designed to be:

- quickly and easily understood so you can get right to your estimate
- filled with valuable information so you can understand the necessary factors that go into the cost estimate

For the regular user, the book is designed to be:

- a handy desk reference that can be quickly referred to for key costs
- a comprehensive, fully reliable source of current construction costs and productivity rates, so you'll be prepared to estimate any project
- a source book for preliminary project cost, product selections, and alternate materials and methods

To meet all of these requirements we have organized the book into the following clearly defined sections.

Quick Start

This one-page section (see following page) can quickly get you started on your estimate.

How To Use the Book: The Details

This section contains an in-depth explanation of how the book is arranged . . . and how you can use it to determine a reliable construction cost estimate. It includes information about how we develop our cost figures and how to completely prepare your estimate.

Unit Price Section

All cost data has been divided into the 16 divisions according to the MasterFormat system of classification and numbering as developed by the Construction Specifications Institute (CSI) and Construction Specifications Canada (CSC). For a listing of these divisions and an outline of their subdivisions, see the Unit Price Section Table of Contents.

Estimating tips are included at the beginning of each division.

Division 17: Quick Project Estimates:

In addition to the 16 Unit Price Divisions there is a S.F. (Square Foot) and C.F. (Cubic Foot) Cost Division, Division 17. It contains costs for 58 different building types that allow you to make a rough estimate for the overall cost of a project or its major components.

Reference Section

This section includes information on Reference Numbers, Change Orders, Crew Listings, Historical Cost Indexes, City Cost Indexes, Location Factors and a listing of Abbreviations. It is visually identified by a vertical gray bar on the edge of pages.

Reference Numbers: At the beginning of selected major classifications in the Unit Price Section are "reference numbers" shown in bold squares. These numbers refer you to related information in the Reference Section.

In this section, you'll find reference tables, explanations, and estimating information that support how we develop the unit price data. Also included are alternate pricing methods, technical data, and estimating procedures, along with information on design and economy in construction. You'll also find helpful tips on what to expect and what to avoid when estimating and constructing your project.

It is recommended that you refer to the Reference Section if a "reference number" appears within the section you are estimating.

Change Orders: This section includes information on the factors that influence the pricing of change orders.

Crew Listings: This section lists all the crews referenced in the book. For the purposes of this book, a crew is composed of more than one trade classification and/or the addition of power equipment to any trade classification. Power equipment is included in the cost of the crew. Costs are shown both with bare labor rates and with the installing contractor's overhead and profit added. For each, the total crew cost per eight-hour day and the composite cost per labor-hour are listed.

Historical Cost Indexes: These indexes provide you with data to adjust construction costs over time. If you know costs for a project completed in the past, you can use these indexes to calculate a rough estimate of what it would cost to construct the same project today.

City Cost Indexes: Obviously, costs vary depending on the regional economy. You can adjust the "national average" costs in this book to over 930 locations throughout the U.S. and Canada by using the data in this section. How to use information is included.

Location Factors, to quickly adjust the data to over 930 zip code areas, are included.

Abbreviations: A listing of abbreviations used throughout this book, along with the terms they represent, is included.

Index

A comprehensive listing of all terms and subjects in this book to help you find what you need quickly when you are not sure where it falls in MasterFormat.

The Scope of This Book

This book is designed to be as comprehensive and as easy to use as possible. To that end we have made certain assumptions and limited its scope in three key ways:

1. We have established material prices based on a "national average."
2. We have computed labor costs based on a 30-city "national average" of union wage rates.
3. We have targeted the data for projects of a certain size range.

For a more detailed explanation of how the cost data is developed, see "How To Use the Book: The Details."

Project Size

This book is aimed primarily at commercial and industrial projects costing $1,000,000 and up, or large multi-family housing projects. Costs are primarily for new construction or major renovation of buildings rather than repairs or minor alterations.

With reasonable exercise of judgment the figures can be used for any building work. *For civil engineering structures such as bridges, dams, highways, or the like, please refer to **Means Heavy Construction Cost Data.***

Quick Start

If you feel you are ready to use this book and don't think you need the detailed instructions that begin on the following page, this Quick Start section is for you.

These steps will allow you to get started estimating in a matter of minutes.

1 Find each cost data section you need in the Unit Price Section Table of Contents.

The cost data has been divided into 16 divisions according to the CSI MasterFormat.

2 Turn to the indicated section and locate the line item you need for your estimate. Portions of a sample page layout appear here.

• If there is a reference number listed at the beginning of a section, for example, R03110-050, it refers to additional information you may find useful. See the Reference Section for detailed information.

• Note the crew code designation. You'll find full descriptions of crews in the Crews Section, including labor-hour and equipment costs.

3 Determine the total number of units your job will require. Note that the unit of measure for the material you're using is listed under "UNIT."

• Bare Costs: These figures show unit costs for materials and installation. Labor and equipment costs are calculated according to crew costs and average daily output. Bare costs do not contain allowances for overhead, profit, or taxes.

• "Labor-hours" allows you to calculate the total labor-hours to complete that task. Just multiply the quantity of work by this figure for an estimate of activity duration.

4 Then multiply the total units by the "Total Incl. O&P," which stands for the total cost including the installing contractor's overhead and profit. (See the next pages for a complete explanation.)

• If the work is to be subcontracted, add the general contractor's markup, approximately 10%.

5 The price you calculate will be an estimate for a completed item of work.

6 Compile a list of all items included in the total project. Summarize cost information, and add project overhead.

Localize costs by using the City Cost Indexes or Location Factors found in the Reference Section.

For a more complete explanation of the way costs are derived, please see the following section.

Commonly Used Abbreviations

R.S. Means utilizes standard industry abbreviations. There is a complete glossary of abbreviations in the reference section. The following are a few of the most commonly used abbreviations you'll find in the book:

B.F.	Board Feet
C	Hundred; Centigrade
C.Y.	Cubic Yard (27 Cubic Feet)
Cwt	100 Pounds
Ea.	Each
Flr.	Floor
L.F.	Linear Foot
Lb.	Pound
MBF	Thousand Board Feet
Opng.	Opening
S.F.	Square Foot
SFCA	Square Foot Contact Area
S.Y.	Square Yard
Sq.	Square; 100 Square Feet
Sty.	Story
Surf.	Surface
V.L.F.	Vertical Linear Foot

Editors' Note: We urge you to spend time reading and understanding the supporting material. An accurate estimate requires experience, knowledge, and careful calculation. The more you know about how we at R.S. Means developed the data, the more accurate your estimate will be. In addition, it's important to take into consideration some of the reference material such as Crews Listing and the "reference numbers."

03400 | Precast Concrete

03410 | Plant Precast

			CREW	DAILY OUTPUT	LABOR-HOURS	UNIT	2001 BARE COSTS MAT.	LABOR	EQUIP.	TOTAL	TOTAL INCL O&P	
400	0010	**JOISTS** 40 psf L.L., 6″ deep for 12′ spans	C-12	600	.080	L.F.	5.70	2.30	.86	8.86	10.75	400
	0050	8″ deep for 16′ spans		575	.083		6.70	2.40	.90	10	12.05	
620	0010	**SLABS** Prestressed roof/floor members, solid, grouted, 4″ thick R03410-030	C-11	3,600	.020	S.F.	4.90	.64	.41	5.95	7.00	620
	0050	6″ thick		4,500	.016		4.73	.51	.33	5.57	6.45	
	0100	8″ thick, hollow **CN**		5,600	.013		5.25	.41	.26	5.92	6.80	
	0150	10″ thick		8,800	.008		5.95	.26	.17	6.38	7.20	
	0200	12″ thick		8,000	.009		6.15	.29	.18	6.62	7.45	
650	0010	**PRESTRESSED CONCRETE** pretensioned, see division 03400 R03410-030										650
	0020	See also division 03230-600										
	0100	Post-tensioned in place, small job R03410-090	C-17B	8.50	9.647	C.Y.	215	292	40.50	547.50	740	
	0200	Large job	″	10	8.200	″	161	248	34.50	443.50	605	

How to Use the Book: The Details

What's Behind the Numbers? The Development of Cost Data

The staff at R.S. Means continuously monitors developments in the construction industry in order to ensure reliable, thorough and up-to-date cost information.

While *overall* construction costs may vary relative to general economic conditions, price fluctuations within the industry are dependent upon many factors. Individual price variations may, in fact, be opposite to overall economic trends. Therefore, costs are continually monitored and complete updates are published yearly. Also, new items are frequently added in response to changes in materials and methods.

Costs—$ (U.S.)

All costs represent U.S. national averages and are given in U.S. dollars. The Means City Cost Indexes can be used to adjust costs to a particular location. The City Cost Indexes for Canada can be used to adjust U.S. national averages to local costs in Canadian dollars.

Material Costs

The R.S. Means staff contacts manufacturers, dealers, distributors, and contractors all across the U.S. and Canada to determine national average material costs. If you have access to current material costs for your specific location, you may wish to make adjustments to reflect differences from the national average. Included within material costs are fasteners for a normal installation. R.S. Means engineers use manufacturers' recommendations, written specifications and/or standard construction practice for size and spacing of fasteners. Adjustments to material costs may be required for your specific application or location. Material costs do not include sales tax.

Labor Costs

Labor costs are based on the average of wage rates from 30 major U.S. cities. Rates are determined from labor union agreements or prevailing wages for construction trades for the current year. Rates along with overhead and profit markups are listed on the inside back cover of this book.

- If wage rates in your area vary from those used in this book, or if rate increases are expected within a given year, labor costs should be adjusted accordingly.

Labor costs reflect productivity based on actual working conditions. These figures include time spent during a normal workday on tasks other than actual installation, such as material receiving and handling, mobilization at site, site movement, breaks, and cleanup.

Productivity data is developed over an extended period so as not to be influenced by abnormal variations and reflects a typical average.

Equipment Costs

Equipment costs include not only rental, but also operating costs for equipment under normal use. The operating costs include parts and labor for routine servicing such as repair and replacement of pumps, filters and worn lines. Normal operating expendables such as fuel, lubricants, tires and electricity (where applicable) are also included. Extraordinary operating expendables with highly variable wear patterns such as diamond bits and blades are excluded. These costs are included under materials. Equipment rental rates are obtained from industry sources throughout North America—contractors, suppliers, dealers, manufacturers, and distributors.

Crew Equipment Cost/Day—The power equipment required for each crew is included in the crew cost. The daily cost for crew equipment is based on dividing the weekly bare rental rate by 5 (number of working days per week), and then adding the hourly operating cost times 8 (hours per day). This "Crew Equipment Cost/Day" is listed in Subdivision 01590.

General Conditions

Cost data in this book is presented in two ways: Bare Costs and Total Cost including O&P (Overhead and Profit). General Conditions, when applicable, should also be added to the Total Cost including O&P. The costs for General Conditions are listed in Division 1 and the Reference Section of this book. General Conditions for the *Installing Contractor* may range from 0% to 10% of the Total Cost including O&P. For the *General* or *Prime Contractor*, costs for General Conditions may range from 5% to 15% of the Total Cost including O&P, with a figure of 10% as the most typical allowance.

Overhead and Profit

Total Cost including O&P for the *Installing Contractor* is shown in the last column on the Unit Price pages of this book. This figure is the sum of the bare material cost plus 10% for profit, the base labor cost plus total overhead and profit, and the bare equipment cost plus 10% for profit. Details for the calculation of Overhead and Profit on labor are shown on the inside back cover and in the Reference Section of this book. (See the "How To Use the Unit Price Pages" for an example of this calculation.)

Factors Affecting Costs

Costs can vary depending upon a number of variables. Here's how we have handled the main factors affecting costs.

Quality—The prices for materials and the workmanship upon which productivity is based represent sound construction work. They are also in line with U.S. government specifications.

Overtime—We have made no allowance for overtime. If you anticipate premium time or work beyond normal working hours, be sure to make an appropriate adjustment to your labor costs.

Productivity—The productivity, daily output, and labor-hour figures for each line item are based on working an eight-hour day in daylight hours in moderate temperatures. For work that extends beyond normal work hours or is performed under adverse conditions, productivity may decrease. (See the section in "How To Use the Unit Price Pages" for more on productivity.)

Size of Project—The size, scope of work, and type of construction project will have a significant impact on cost. Economies of scale can reduce costs for large projects. Unit costs can often run higher for small projects. Costs in this book are intended for the size and type of project as previously described in "How the Book Is Built: An Overview." Costs for projects of a significantly different size or type should be adjusted accordingly.

Location—Material prices in this book are for metropolitan areas. However, in dense urban areas, traffic and site storage limitations may increase costs. Beyond a 20-mile radius of large cities, extra trucking or transportation charges may also increase the material costs slightly. On the other hand, lower wage rates may be in effect. Be sure to consider both these factors when preparing an estimate, particularly if the job site is located in a central city or remote rural location.

In addition, highly specialized subcontract items may require travel and per diem expenses for mechanics.

Other factors—
- season of year
- contractor management
- weather conditions
- local union restrictions
- building code requirements
- availability of:
  - adequate energy
  - skilled labor
  - building materials
- owner's special requirements/restrictions
- safety requirements
- environmental considerations

Unpredictable Factors—General business conditions influence "in-place" costs of all items. Substitute materials and construction methods may have to be employed. These may affect the installed cost and/or life cycle costs. Such factors may be difficult to evaluate and cannot necessarily be predicted on the basis of the job's location in a particular section of the country. Thus, where these factors apply, you may find significant, but unavoidable cost variations for which you will have to apply a measure of judgment to your estimate.

Rounding of Costs

In general, all unit prices in excess of $5.00 have been rounded to make them easier to use and still maintain adequate precision of the results. The rounding rules we have chosen are in the following table.

Prices from . . .	Rounded to the nearest . . .
$.01 to $5.00	$.01
$5.01 to $20.00	$.05
$20.01 to $100.00	$.50
$100.01 to $300.00	$1.00
$300.01 to $1,000.00	$5.00
$1,000.01 to $10,000.00	$25.00
$10,000.01 to $50,000.00	$100.00
$50,000.01 and above	$500.00

Final Checklist

Estimating can be a straightforward process provided you remember the basics. Here's a checklist of some of the items you should remember to do before completing your estimate.

Did you remember to . . .
- factor in the City Cost Index for your locale
- take into consideration which items have been marked up and by how much
- mark up the entire estimate sufficiently for your purposes
- read the background information on techniques and technical matters that could impact your project time span and cost
- include all components of your project in the final estimate
- double check your figures to be sure of your accuracy
- call R.S. Means if you have any questions about your estimate or the data you've found in our publications

Remember, R.S. Means stands behind its publications. If you have any questions about your estimate . . . about the costs you've used from our books . . . or even about the technical aspects of the job that may affect your estimate, feel free to call the R.S. Means editors at 1-800-334-3509.

Unit Price Section

Table of Contents

How to Use the Unit Price Pages

The following is a detailed explanation of a sample entry in the Unit Price Section. Next to each bold number below is the item being described with appropriate component of the sample entry following in parenthesis. Some prices are listed as bare costs, others as costs that include overhead and profit of the installing contractor. In most cases, if the work is to be subcontracted, the general contractor will need to add an additional markup (R.S. Means suggests using 10%) to the figures in the column "Total Incl. O&P."

1 Division Number/Title (03400/Precast Concrete)

Use the Unit Price Section Table of Contents to locate specific items. The sections are classified according to the CSI MasterFormat (1995 Edition).

2 Line Numbers (03410 620 0100)

Each unit price line item has been assigned a unique 12-digit code based on the CSI MasterFormat classification.

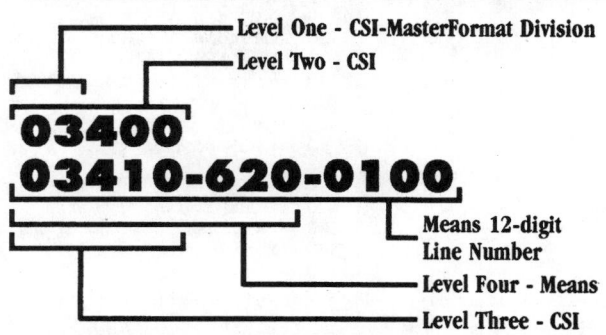

- Level One - CSI-MasterFormat Division
- Level Two - CSI

03400
03410-620-0100

- Means 12-digit Line Number
- Level Four - Means
- Level Three - CSI

3 Description (SLABS, etc.)

Each line item is described in detail. Sub-items and additional sizes are indented beneath the appropriate line items. The first line or two after the main item (in boldface) may contain descriptive information that pertains to all line items beneath this boldface listing.

Items which include the symbol **CN** are updated in the Key Material Price Section of the *DesignBuildIntelligence* quarterly publication.

4 Reference Number Information

R03410 -030 You'll see reference numbers shown in bold rectangles at the beginning of some sections. These refer to related items in the Reference Section, visually identified by a vertical gray bar on the edge of pages.

The relation may be: (1) an estimating procedure that should be read before estimating, (2) an alternate pricing method, or (3) technical information.

The "R" designates the Reference Section. The numbers refer to the MasterFormat classification system.

It is strongly recommended that you review all reference numbers that appear within the section in which you are working.

Example: The rectangle number above is directing you to refer to the reference number R03410-030. This particular reference number shows delivered and erected costs for standard prestressed, precast concrete shapes and other detail information.

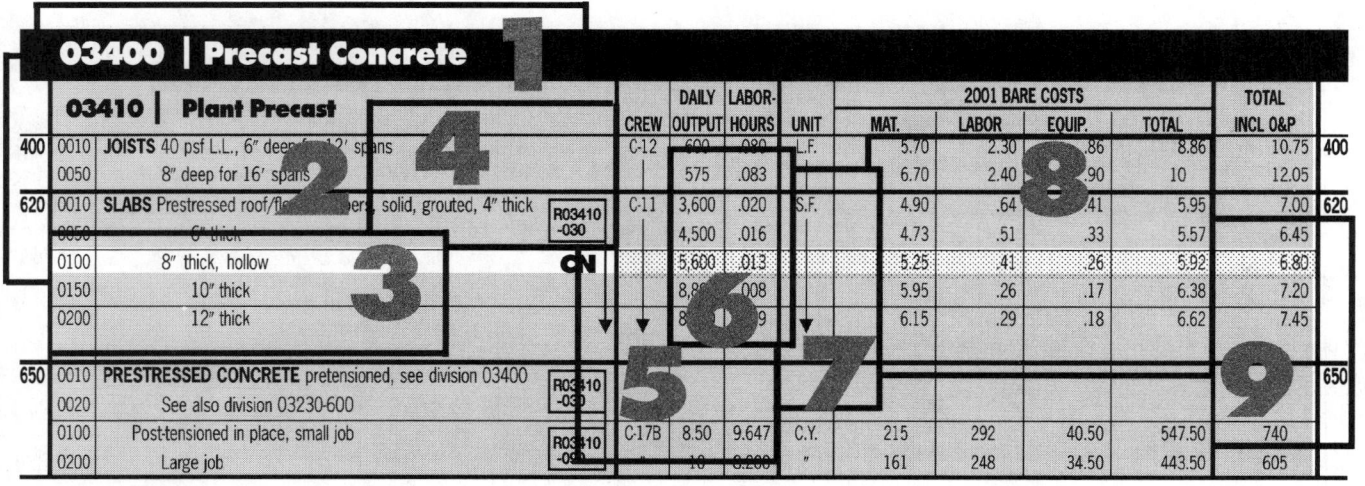

03400 | Precast Concrete

		03410 Plant Precast		CREW	DAILY OUTPUT	LABOR-HOURS	UNIT	2001 BARE COSTS MAT.	LABOR	EQUIP.	TOTAL	TOTAL INCL O&P	
400	0010	**JOISTS** 40 psf L.L., 6" deep for 12' spans		C-12	600	.080	L.F.	5.70	2.30	.86	8.86	10.75	400
	0050	8" deep for 16' spans			575	.083		6.70	2.40	.90	10	12.05	
620	0010	**SLABS** Prestressed roof/floor members, solid, grouted, 4" thick	R03410 -030	C-11	3,600	.020	S.F.	4.90	.64	.41	5.95	7.00	620
	0050	6" thick			4,500	.016		4.73	.51	.33	5.57	6.45	
	0100	8" thick, hollow	CN		5,600	.013		5.25	.41	.26	5.92	6.80	
	0150	10" thick			8,800	.008		5.95	.26	.17	6.38	7.20	
	0200	12" thick			8,000	.009		6.15	.29	.18	6.62	7.45	
650	0010	**PRESTRESSED CONCRETE** pretensioned, see division 03400	R03410 -030										650
	0020	See also division 03230-600											
	0100	Post-tensioned in place, small job	R03410 -090	C-17B	8.50	9.647	C.Y.	215	292	40.50	547.50	740	
	0200	Large job			10	8.200	"	161	248	34.50	443.50	605	

2

Crew (C-11)

The "Crew" column designates the typical trade or crew used to install the item. If an installation can be accomplished by one trade and requires no power equipment, that trade and the number of workers are listed (for example, "2 Struc. Steel Workers"). If an installation requires a composite crew, a crew code designation is listed (for example, "C-11"). You'll find full details on all composite crews in the Crew Listings.

* For a complete list of all trades utilized in this book and their abbreviations, see the inside back cover.

	Bare Costs		Incl. Subs O & P		Cost Per Labor-Hour	
Crew C-11	Hr.	Daily	Hr.	Daily	Bare Costs	Incl. O&P
1 Struc. Steel Foreman	$34.85	$278.80	$63.20	$505.60	$32.09	$56.33
6 Struc. Steel Workers	32.85	1576.80	59.60	2860.80		
1 Equip. Oper. (crane)	31.15	249.20	47.15	377.20		
1 Equip. Oper. Oiler	25.75	206.00	39.00	312.00		
1 Truck Crane, 150 Ton		1478.00		1625.80	20.53	22.58
72 L.H., Daily Totals		$3788.80		$5681.40	$52.62	$78.91

Productivity: Daily Output (5600)/Labor-Hours (.013)

The "Daily Output" represents the typical number of units the designated crew will install in a normal 8-hour day. To find out the number of days the given crew would require to complete the installation, divide your quantity by the daily output. For example:

Quantity	÷	Daily Output	=	Duration
15,000 S.F.	÷	5600 S.F./ Crew Day	=	2.68 Crew Days

The "Labor-Hours" figure represents the number of labor-hours required to install one unit of work. To find out the number of labor-hours required for your particular task, multiply the quantity of the item times the number of labor-hours shown. For example:

Quantity	x	Productivity Rate	=	Duration
15,000 S.F.	x	.013 Labor-Hours/ S.F.	=	195 Labor-Hours

Unit (S.F.)

The abbreviated designation indicates the unit of measure upon which the price, production, and crew are based (S.F. = Square Foot). For a complete listing of abbreviations refer to the Abbreviations Listing in the Reference Section of this book.

Bare Costs:

Mat. (Bare Material Cost) (5.25)

The unit material cost is the "bare" material cost with no overhead and profit included. *Costs shown reflect national average material prices for January of the current year and include delivery to the job site. No sales taxes are included.*

Labor (.41)

The unit labor cost is derived by multiplying bare labor-hour costs for Crew C-11 by labor-hour units. The bare labor-hour cost is found in the Crew Section under C-11. (If a trade is listed, the hourly labor cost—the wage rate—is found on the inside back cover.)

Labor-Hour Cost Crew C-11	x	Labor-Hour Units	=	Labor
$32.09	x	.013	=	$.41

Equip. (Equipment) (.26)

Equipment costs for each crew are listed in the description of each crew. Tools or equipment whose value justifies purchase or ownership by a contractor are considered overhead as shown on the inside back cover. The unit equipment cost is derived by multiplying the bare equipment hourly cost by the labor-hour units.

Equipment Cost Crew C-11	x	Labor-Hour Units	=	Equip.
$20.53	x	.013	=	$.26

Total (5.92)

The total of the bare costs is the arithmetic total of the three previous columns: mat., labor, and equip.

Material	+	Labor	+	Equip.	=	Total
$5.25	+	$.41	+	$.26	=	$5.92

Total Costs Including O&P

This figure is the sum of the bare material cost plus 10% for profit; the bare labor cost plus total overhead and profit (per the inside back cover or, if a crew is listed, from the crew listings); and the bare equipment cost plus 10% for profit.

Material is Bare Material Cost + 10% = 5.25 + .53	=	$5.78
Labor for Crew C-11 = Labor-Hour Cost (56.33) x Labor-Hour Units (.013)	=	$ .73
Equip. is Bare Equip. Cost + 10% = .26 + .03	=	$ .29
Total	=	$6.80

Division 1
General Requirements

Estimating Tips

The General Requirements of any contract are very important to both the bidder and the owner. These lay the ground rules under which the contract will be executed and have a significant influence on the cost of operations. Therefore, it is extremely important to thoroughly read and understand the General Requirements both before preparing an estimate and when the estimate is complete, to ascertain that nothing in the contract is overlooked. Caution should be exercised when applying items listed in Division 1 to an estimate. Many of the items are included in the unit prices listed in the other divisions such as mark-ups on labor and company overhead.

01300 Administrative Requirements

- Before determining a final cost estimate, it is a good practice to review all the items listed in subdivision 01300 to make final adjustments for items that may need customizing to specific job conditions.

01330 Submittal Procedures

- Requirements for initial and periodic submittals can represent a significant cost to the General Requirements of a job. Thoroughly check the submittal specifications when estimating a project to determine any costs that should be included.

01400 Quality Requirements

- All projects will require some degree of Quality Control. This cost is not included in the unit cost of construction listed in each division. Depending upon the terms of the contract, the various costs of inspection and testing can be the responsibility of either the owner or the contractor. Be sure to include the required costs in your estimate.

01500 Temporary Facilities & Controls

- Barricades, access roads, safety nets, scaffolding, security and many more requirements for the execution of a safe project are elements of direct cost. These costs can easily be overlooked when preparing an estimate. When looking through the major classifications of this subdivision, determine which items apply to each division in your estimate.

01590 Equipment Rental

- This subdivision contains transportation, handling, storage, protection and product options and substitutions. Listed in this cost manual are average equipment rental rates for all types of equipment. This is useful information when estimating the time and materials requirement of any particular operation in order to establish a unit or total cost.
- A good rule of thumb is that weekly rental is 3 times daily rental and that monthly rental is 3 times weekly rental.

- The figures in the column for Crew Equipment Cost represent the rental rate used in determining the daily cost of equipment in a crew. It is calculated by dividing the weekly rate by 5 days and adding the hourly operating cost times 8 hours.

01770 Closeout Procedures

- When preparing an estimate, read the specifications to determine the requirements for Contract Closeout thoroughly. Final cleaning, record documentation, operation and maintenance data, warranties and bonds, and spare parts and maintenance materials can all be elements of cost for the completion of a contract. Do not overlook these in your estimate.

01830 Operations & Maintenance

- If maintenance and repair are included in your contract, they require special attention. To estimate the cost to remove and replace any unit usually requires a site visit to determine the accessibility and the specific difficulty at that location. Obstructions, dust control, safety, and often overtime hours must be considered when preparing your estimate.

Reference Numbers

Reference numbers are shown in bold squares at the beginning of some major classifications. These numbers refer to related items in the Reference Section. The reference information may be an estimating procedure, an alternate pricing method or technical information.

Note: Not all subdivisions listed here necessarily appear in this publication.

01103 | Models & Renderings

		CREW	DAILY OUTPUT	LABOR-HOURS	UNIT	2001 BARE COSTS MAT.	LABOR	EQUIP.	TOTAL	TOTAL INCL O&P	
200	0010	**MODELS** Cardboard & paper, 1 building, minimum				Ea.	560			560	615	**200**
	0050	Maximum					1,275			1,275	1,400	
	0100	2 buildings, minimum					750			750	825	
	0150	Maximum				↓	1,700			1,700	1,875	
	0200	Plexiglass and metal, basic layout				SF Flr.	.06			.06	.07	
	0210	Including equipment and personnel				"	.25			.25	.28	
	0300	Site plan layout, minimum				Ea.	1,075			1,075	1,175	
	0350	Maximum				"	1,800			1,800	1,975	
500	0010	**RENDERINGS** Color, matted, 20" x 30", eye level,										**500**
	0020	1 building, minimum				Ea.	1,675			1,675	1,850	
	0050	Average					2,800			2,800	3,075	
	0100	Maximum					3,950			3,950	4,350	
	1000	5 buildings, minimum					3,400			3,400	3,750	
	1100	Maximum					6,700			6,700	7,375	
	2000	Aerial perspective, color, 1 building, minimum					2,800			2,800	3,075	
	2100	Maximum					6,700			6,700	7,375	
	3000	5 buildings, minimum					3,375			3,375	3,725	
	3100	Maximum				↓	11,200			11,200	12,300	

01107 | Professional Consultant

		CREW	DAILY OUTPUT	LABOR-HOURS	UNIT	MAT.	LABOR	EQUIP.	TOTAL	TOTAL INCL O&P	
100	0011	**ARCHITECTURAL FEES**	R01107 -010								**100**
	0020	For new construction									
	0060	Minimum				Project					4.90%
	0090	Maximum									16%
	0100	For alteration work, to $500,000, add to fee									50%
	0150	Over $500,000, add to fee				↓					25%
200	0010	**CONSTRUCTION MANAGEMENT FEES** $1,000,000 job, minimum				Project					4.50%	**200**
	0050	Maximum									7.50%
	0300	$5,000,000 job, minimum									2.50%
	0350	Maximum				↓					4%
300	0010	**ENGINEERING FEES**	R01107 -030								**300**
	0020	Educational planning consultant, minimum				Project					.50%
	0100	Maximum				"					2.50%
	0200	Electrical, minimum				Contrct					4.10%
	0300	Maximum									10.10%
	0400	Elevator & conveying systems, minimum									2.50%
	0500	Maximum									5%
	0600	Food service & kitchen equipment, minimum									8%
	0700	Maximum									12%
	0800	Landscaping & site development, minimum									2.50%
	0900	Maximum									6%
	1000	Mechanical (plumbing & HVAC), minimum									4.10%
	1100	Maximum				↓					10.10%
	1200	Structural, minimum				Project					1%
	1300	Maximum				"					2.50%
700	0010	**SURVEYING** Conventional, topographical, minimum	A-7	3.30	7.273	Acre	16	225		241	370	**700**
	0100	Maximum	A-8	.60	53.333		48	1,625		1,673	2,550	
	0300	Lot location and lines, minimum, for large quantities	A-7	2	12		25	370		395	610	
	0320	Average	"	1.25	19.200		45	595		640	975	
	0400	Maximum, for small quantities	A-8	1	32	↓	72	970		1,042	1,575	
	0600	Monuments, 3' long	A-7	10	2.400	Ea.	19	74.50		93.50	137	
	0800	Property lines, perimeter, cleared land	"	1,000	.024	L.F.	.03	.74		.77	1.19	
	0900	Wooded land	A-8	875	.037	"	.05	1.11		1.16	1.78	
	1100	Crew for building layout, 2 person crew	A-6	1	16	Day		515		515	815	
	1200	3 person crew	A-7	1	24	↓		745		745	1,150	

Important: See the Reference Section for critical supporting data - Reference Nos., Crews, & City Cost Indexes

01100 | Summary

01107 | Professional Consultant

			DAILY OUTPUT	LABOR-HOURS	UNIT	2001 BARE COSTS				TOTAL INCL O&P	
						MAT.	LABOR	EQUIP.	TOTAL		
700	1300	4 person crew	A-8	1	32	Day		970		970	1,500	700
	1500	Aerial surveying, including ground control, minimum fee, 10 acres				Total					5,500	
	1510	100 acres									9,100	
	1550	From existing photography, deduct				↓					1,340	
	1600	2' contours, 10 acres				Acre					440	
	1650	20 acres									300	
	1800	50 acres									90	
	1850	100 acres									80	
	2000	1000 acres									17.01	
	2050	10,000 acres				↓					11.01	
	2150	For 1' contours and										
	2160	dense urban areas, add to above				Acre					40%	
	3000	Inertial guidance system for										
	3010	locating coordinates, rent per day				Ea.					4,000	

01200 | Price & Payment Procedures

01250 | Contract Modification Procedures

			CREW	DAILY OUTPUT	LABOR-HOURS	UNIT	2001 BARE COSTS				TOTAL INCL O&P	
							MAT.	LABOR	EQUIP.	TOTAL		
200	0010	**CONTINGENCIES** for estimate at conceptual stage				Project					20%	200
	0050	Schematic stage									15%	
	0100	Preliminary working drawing stage (Design Dev.)									10%	
	0150	Final working drawing stage				↓					3%	
300	0010	**CREWS** For building construction, see How To Use This Book										300
500	0010	**JOB CONDITIONS** Modifications to total										500
	0020	project cost summaries										
	0100	Economic conditions, favorable, deduct				Project					2%	
	0200	Unfavorable, add									5%	
	0300	Hoisting conditions, favorable, deduct									2%	
	0400	Unfavorable, add									5%	
	0500	General Contractor management, experienced, deduct									2%	
	0600	Inexperienced, add									10%	
	0700	Labor availability, surplus, deduct									1%	
	0800	Shortage, add									10%	
	0900	Material storage area, available, deduct									1%	
	1000	Not available, add									2%	
	1100	Subcontractor availability, surplus, deduct									5%	
	1200	Shortage, add									12%	
	1300	Work space, available, deduct									2%	
	1400	Not available, add				↓					5%	
600	0010	**OVERTIME** For early completion of projects or where	R01100 -110									600
	0020	labor shortages exist, add to usual labor, up to				Costs		100%				

01255 | Cost Indexes

			CREW	DAILY OUTPUT	LABOR-HOURS	UNIT	2001 BARE COSTS				TOTAL INCL O&P	
							MAT.	LABOR	EQUIP.	TOTAL		
200	0010	**CONSTRUCTION COST INDEX** (Reference) over 930 zip code locations in										200
	0020	The U.S. and Canada, total bldg cost, min. (Clarksdale, MS)				%					66.80%	
	0050	Average									100%	
	0100	Maximum (New York, NY)				↓					134.50%	
400	0010	**HISTORICAL COST INDEXES** (Reference) Back to 1951										400

01200 | Price & Payment Procedures

01255		Cost Indexes		CREW	DAILY OUTPUT	LABOR-HOURS	UNIT	2001 BARE COSTS MAT.	LABOR	EQUIP.	TOTAL	TOTAL INCL O&P	
500	0010	**LABOR INDEX** (Reference) For over 930 zip code locations in											500
	0020	the U.S. and Canada, minimum (Clarksdale, MS)					%		35%				
	0050	Average					↓		100%				
	0100	Maximum (New York, NY)							161.90%				
600	0010	**MATERIAL INDEX** (Reference) For over 930 zip code locations in											600
	0020	the U.S. and Canada, minimum (Elizabethtown, KY)					%	92.20%					
	0040	Average					↓	100%					
	0060	Maximum (Ketchikan, AK)						144.20%					

01290 | Payment Procedures

				CREW	DAILY OUTPUT	LABOR-HOURS	UNIT	MAT.	LABOR	EQUIP.	TOTAL	INCL O&P	
800	0010	**TAXES** Sales tax, State, average	R01100 -090				%	4.71%					800
	0050	Maximum						7.25%					
	0200	Social Security, on first $76,200 of wages	R01100 -100						7.65%				
	0300	Unemployment, MA, combined Federal and State, minimum							2.10%				
	0350	Average					↓		7%				
	0400	Maximum							8%				

01300 | Administrative Requirements

01310		Project Management/Coordination		CREW	DAILY OUTPUT	LABOR-HOURS	UNIT	2001 BARE COSTS MAT.	LABOR	EQUIP.	TOTAL	TOTAL INCL O&P	
150	0010	**PERMITS** Rule of thumb, most cities, minimum					Job					.50%	150
	0100	Maximum					"					2%	
200	0010	**PERFORMANCE BOND** For buildings, minimum	R01100 -080				Job					.60%	200
	0100	Maximum					"					2.50%	
300	0010	**CONSTRUCTION TIME** Requirements	R01100 -020										300
350	0010	**INSURANCE** Builders risk, standard, minimum	R01100 -040				Job					.22%	350
	0050	Maximum					↓					.59%	
	0200	All-risk type, minimum	R01100 -050									.25%	
	0250	Maximum					↓					.62%	
	0400	Contractor's equipment floater, minimum	R01100 -060				Value					.50%	
	0450	Maximum					"					1.50%	
	0600	Public liability, average					Job					1.55%	
	0800	Workers' compensation & employer's liability, average											
	0850	by trade, carpentry, general					Payroll		19.01%				
	0900	Clerical							.47%				
	0950	Concrete							17.82%				
	1000	Electrical							6.79%				
	1050	Excavation							10.93%				
	1100	Glazing							14.08%				
	1150	Insulation							17.65%				
	1200	Lathing							11.76%				
	1250	Masonry							17.04%				
	1300	Painting & decorating							14.81%				
	1350	Pile driving							27.68%				
	1400	Plastering							15.71%				
	1450	Plumbing							8.47%				
	1500	Roofing							34.33%				
	1550	Sheet metal work (HVAC)							11.93%				
	1600	Steel erection, structural					↓		40.87%				

Important: See the Reference Section for critical supporting data - Reference Nos., Crews, & City Cost Indexes

		01310	Project Management/Coordination		CREW	DAILY OUTPUT	LABOR-HOURS	UNIT	2001 BARE COSTS				TOTAL INCL O&P	
									MAT.	LABOR	EQUIP.	TOTAL		
350	1650		Tile work, interior ceramic	R01100 -040				Payroll		10.30%				**350**
	1700		Waterproofing, brush or hand caulking							8.04%				
	1800		Wrecking	R01100 -050						42.15%				
	2000		Range of 35 trades in 50 states, excl. wrecking, min							2%				
	2100		Average	R01100 -060						17.50%				
	2200		Maximum							132.92%				
400	0010	**MAIN OFFICE EXPENSE** Average for General Contractors		R01100 -050										**400**
	0020	As a percentage of their annual volume												
	0125	Annual volume under 1 million dollars						% Vol.				13.60%		
	0145	Up to 2.5 million dollars										8%		
	0150	Up to 4.0 million dollars										6.80%		
	0200	Up to 7.0 million dollars										5.60%		
	0250	Up to 10 million dollars										5.10%		
	0300	Over 10 million dollars										3.90%		
500	0010	**MARK-UP** For General Contractors for change		R01100 -070										**500**
	0100	of scope of job as bid												
	0200	Extra work, by subcontractors, add						%					10%	
	0250	By General Contractor, add											15%	
	0400	Omitted work, by subcontractors, deduct all but											5%	
	0450	By General Contractor, deduct all but											7.50%	
	0600	Overtime work, by subcontractors, add											15%	
	0650	By General Contractor, add											10%	
	1000	Installing contractors, on his own labor, minimum								47.80%				
	1100	Maximum								87.50%				
600	0010	**OVERHEAD** As percent of direct costs, minimum		R01100 -050				%				5%		**600**
	0050	Average										13%		
	0100	Maximum		R01100 -070								30%		
620	0010	**OVERHEAD & PROFIT** Allowance to add to items in this												**620**
	0020	book that do not include Subs O&P, average						%				25%		
	0100	Allowance to add to items in this book that												
	0110	do include Subs O&P, minimum						%					5%	
	0150	Average											10%	
	0200	Maximum											15%	
	0300	Typical, by size of project, under $100,000										30%		
	0350	$500,000 project										25%		
	0400	$2,000,000 project										20%		
	0450	Over $10,000,000 project										15%		
700	0010	**FIELD PERSONNEL** Clerk average						Week	280			280	440	**700**
	0100	Field engineer, minimum							675			675	1,060	
	0120	Average							875			875	1,375	
	0140	Maximum							1,005			1,005	1,580	
	0160	General purpose laborer, average							925			925	1,450	
	0180	Project manager, minimum							1,265			1,265	1,985	
	0200	Average							1,420			1,420	2,230	
	0220	Maximum							1,605			1,605	2,520	
	0240	Superintendent, minimum							1,210			1,210	1,900	
	0260	Average							1,340			1,340	2,105	
	0280	Maximum							1,510			1,510	2,370	
	0290	Timekeeper, average							780			780	1,225	

		01320	Construction Progress Documents											
200	0010	**SCHEDULING** Critical path, as % of architectural fee, minimum						%				.50%		**200**
	0100	Maximum						"				1%		
	0300	Computer-update, micro, no plots, minimum						Ea.				450		
	0400	Including plots, maximum						"				1,550		

01300 | Administrative Requirements

		01320	**Construction Progress Documents**	CREW	DAILY OUTPUT	LABOR-HOURS	UNIT	2001 BARE COSTS				TOTAL INCL O&P	
								MAT.	LABOR	EQUIP.	TOTAL		
200	0600		Rule of thumb, CPM scheduling, small job ($10 Million)				Job					.05%	**200**
	0650		Large job ($50 Million +)									.03%	
	0700		Including cost control, small job									.08%	
	0750		Large job									.04%	

01321 | Construction Photos

				CREW	DAILY OUTPUT	LABOR-HOURS	UNIT	MAT.	LABOR	EQUIP.	TOTAL	TOTAL INCL O&P	
500	0010		**PHOTOGRAPHS** 8″ x 10″, 4 shots, 2 prints ea., std. mounting				Set	263			263	289	**500**
	0100		Hinged linen mounts					290			290	320	
	0200		8″ x 10″, 4 shots, 2 prints each, in color					310			310	340	
	0300		For I.D. slugs, add to all above					3.75			3.75	4.13	
	0500		Aerial photos, initial fly-over, 6 shots, 1 print ea., 8″ x 10″					650			650	715	
	0550		11″ x 14″ prints					720			720	795	
	0600		16″ x 20″ prints					930			930	1,025	
	0700		For full color prints, add					40%				40%	
	0750		Add for traffic control area					263			263	289	
	0900		For over 30 miles from airport, add per				Mile	4.83			4.83	5.30	
	1000		Vertical photography, 4 to 6 shots with				Set	1,000			1,000	1,100	
	1010		different scales, 1 print each										
	1500		Time lapse equipment, camera and projector, buy					3,575			3,575	3,925	
	1550		Rent per month					530			530	585	
	1700		Cameraman and film, including processing, B.&W.				Day	1,225			1,225	1,350	
	1720		Color				″	1,225			1,225	1,350	

01400 | Quality Requirements

		01450	**Quality Control**	CREW	DAILY OUTPUT	LABOR-HOURS	UNIT	2001 BARE COSTS				TOTAL INCL O&P	
								MAT.	LABOR	EQUIP.	TOTAL		
500	0010		**FIELD TESTING**										**500**
	0015		For concrete building costing $1,000,000, minimum				Project					5,000	
	0020		Maximum									40,000	
	0050		Steel building, minimum									5,000	
	0070		Maximum									15,000	
	0100		For building costing, $10,000,000, minimum									32,000	
	0150		Maximum									50,000	
	0200		Asphalt testing, compressive strength Marshall stability, set of 3				Ea.					165	
	0220		Density, set of 3									87	
	0250		Extraction, individual tests on sample									120	
	0300		Penetration									35	
	0350		Mix design, 5 specimens									200	
	0360		Additional specimen									40	
	0400		Specific gravity									45	
	0420		Swell test									70	
	0450		Water effect and cohesion, set of 6									200	
	0470		Water effect and plastic flow									70	
	0600		Concrete testing, aggregates, abrasion									120	
	0650		Absorption									46	
	0800		Petrographic analysis									850	
	0900		Specific gravity									45	
	1000		Sieve analysis, washed									65	
	1050		Unwashed									65	
	1200		Sulfate soundness									125	

Important: See the Reference Section for critical supporting data - Reference Nos., Crews, & City Cost Indexes

	01450	Quality Control	CREW	DAILY OUTPUT	LABOR-HOURS	UNIT	MAT.	LABOR	EQUIP.	TOTAL	TOTAL INCL O&P	
500	1300	Weight per cubic foot				Ea.					40	500
	1500	Cement, physical tests									300	
	1600	Chemical tests									270	
	1800	Compressive strength test, cylinder, delivered to lab/cyl									13	
	1900	Picked up by lab, minimum									15	
	1950	Average									20	
	2000	Maximum									30	
	2200	Compressive strength, cores (not incl. drilling)									40	
	2250	Core drilling, 4" diameter (plus technician)				Inch					25	
	2260	Technician for core drilling				Hr.					50	
	2300	Patching core holes				Ea.					24	
	2400	Drying shrinkage at 28 days									260	
	2500	Flexural test beams									65	
	2600	Mix design, one batch mix									285	
	2650	Added trial batches									132	
	2800	Modulus of elasticity									150	
	2900	Tensile test, cylinders									50	
	3000	Water-Cement ratio curve, 3 batches									155	
	3100	4 batches									205	
	3300	Masonry testing, absorption, per 5 brick									50	
	3350	Chemical resistance, per 2 brick									55	
	3400	Compressive strength, per 5 brick									70	
	3420	Efflorescence, per 5 brick									50	
	3440	Imperviousness, per 5 brick									96	
	3470	Modulus of rupture, per 5 brick									55	
	3500	Moisture, block only									35	
	3550	Mortar, compressive strength, set of 3									25	
	4100	Reinforcing steel, bend test									61	
	4200	Tensile test, up to #8 bar									35	
	4220	#9 to #11 bar									40	
	4240	#14 bar and larger									50	
	4400	Soil testing, Atterberg limits, liquid and plastic limits									61	
	4510	Hydrometer analysis									120	
	4530	Specific gravity									48	
	4600	Sieve analysis, washed									56.67	
	4700	Unwashed									65	
	4710	Consolidation test (ASTM D2435), minimum									320	
	4715	Maximum									475	
	4720	Density and classification of undisturbed sample									75	
	4735	Soil density, nuclear method, ASTM D2922-71									38.67	
	4740	Sand cone method ASTM D1556064									30.17	
	4750	Moisture content									5.33	
	4780	Permeability test, double ring infiltrometer									550	
	4800	Permeability, variable or constant head, undisturbed									205	
	4850	Recompacted									233.33	
	4900	Proctor compaction, 4" standard mold									125	
	4950	6" modified mold									75	
	5100	Shear tests, triaxial, minimum									450	
	5150	Maximum									600	
	5300	Direct shear, minimum									250	
	5350	Maximum									300	
	5550	Technician for inspection, per day, earthwork									215	
	5650	Bolting									270	
	5750	Roofing									250	
	5790	Welding									260	
	5820	Non-destructive testing, dye penetrant				Day					320	

01400 | Quality Requirements

01450 | Quality Control

		CREW	DAILY OUTPUT	LABOR-HOURS	UNIT	2001 BARE COSTS				TOTAL INCL O&P	
						MAT.	LABOR	EQUIP.	TOTAL		
500	5840	Magnetic particle				Day					320	**500**
	5860	Radiography									480	
	5880	Ultrasonic				↓					330	
	6000	Welding certification, minimum				Ea.					100	
	6100	Maximum				"					275	
	7000	Underground storage tank										
	7500	Volumetric tightness test , <=12,000 gal				Ea.					350	
	7510	<=30,000 gal				"					605	
	7600	Vadose zone (soil gas) sampling, 10-40 samples, min.				Day					1,500	
	7610	Maximum				"					2,500	
	7700	Ground water monitoring incl. drilling 3 wells, min.				Total					5,000	
	7710	Maximum				"					7,000	
	8000	X-ray concrete slabs				Ea.					200	

01500 | Temporary Facilities & Controls

01510 | Temporary Utilities

			CREW	DAILY OUTPUT	LABOR-HOURS	UNIT	2001 BARE COSTS				TOTAL INCL O&P	
							MAT.	LABOR	EQUIP.	TOTAL		
800	0010	**TEMPORARY UTILITIES**										**800**
	0100	Heat, incl. fuel and operation, per week, 12 hrs. per day	1 Skwk	100	.080	CSF Flr	5.10	2.39		7.49	9.40	
	0200	24 hrs. per day	"	60	.133		7.70	3.98		11.68	14.70	
	0350	Lighting, incl. service lamps, wiring & outlets, minimum	1 Elec	34	.235		2.07	8.05		10.12	14.35	
	0360	Maximum	"	17	.471		4.51	16.15		20.66	29	
	0400	Power for temp lighting only, per month, min/month 6.6 KWH								.75	1.18	
	0450	Maximum/month 23.6 KWH								2.85	3.14	
	0600	Power for job duration incl. elevator, etc., minimum								47	51.70	
	0650	Maximum				↓				110	121	
	1000	Toilet, portable, see division 01590-400										

01520 | Construction Facilities

			CREW	DAILY OUTPUT	LABOR-HOURS	UNIT	2001 BARE COSTS				TOTAL INCL O&P	
							MAT.	LABOR	EQUIP.	TOTAL		
500	0010	**OFFICE** Trailer, furnished, no hookups, 20' x 8', buy	2 Skwk	1	16	Ea.	5,325	480		5,805	6,625	**500**
	0250	Rent per month					150			150	165	
	0300	32' x 8', buy	2 Skwk	.70	22.857		7,825	680		8,505	9,700	
	0350	Rent per month					165			165	182	
	0400	50' x 10', buy	2 Skwk	.60	26.667		13,400	795		14,195	16,000	
	0450	Rent per month					295			295	325	
	0500	50' x 12', buy	2 Skwk	.50	32		15,800	955		16,755	18,900	
	0550	Rent per month					345			345	380	
	0700	For air conditioning, rent per month, add				↓	35.50			35.50	39	
	0800	For delivery, add per mile				Mile	1.50			1.50	1.65	
	1000	Portable buildings, prefab, on skids, economy, 8' x 8'	2 Carp	265	.060	S.F.	80	1.76		81.76	91	
	1100	Deluxe, 8' x 12'	"	150	.107	"	87	3.11		90.11	100	
	1200	Storage boxes, 20' x 8', buy	2 Skwk	1.80	8.889	Ea.	3,300	265		3,565	4,050	
	1250	Rent per month					72.50			72.50	80	
	1300	40' x 8', buy	2 Skwk	1.40	11.429		3,950	340		4,290	4,875	
	1350	Rent per month				↓	103			103	113	
	5000	Air supported structures, see division 13011-200										
550	0010	**FIELD OFFICE EXPENSE**										**550**
	0100	Field office expense, office equipment rental average				Month	136			136	150	

Important: See the Reference Section for critical supporting data - Reference Nos., Crews, & City Cost Indexes

		01520 | Construction Facilities	CREW	DAILY OUTPUT	LABOR-HOURS	UNIT	MAT.	LABOR	EQUIP.	TOTAL	TOTAL INCL O&P	
							\multicolumn{4}{c}{2001 BARE COSTS}			
550	0120	Office supplies, average				Month	82			82	90	**550**
	0125	Office trailer rental, see division 01520-500										
	0140	Telephone bill; avg. bill/month incl. long dist.				Month	200			200	220	
	0160	Field office lights & HVAC				"	92			92	101	
900	0010	**WEATHER STATION** Remote recording, minimum				Ea.	5,350			5,350	5,875	**900**
	0100	Maximum				"	25,000			25,000	27,500	

01530 | Temporary Construction

			CREW	DAILY OUTPUT	LABOR-HOURS	UNIT	MAT.	LABOR	EQUIP.	TOTAL	TOTAL INCL O&P	
700	0010	**PROTECTION** Stair tread, 2" x 12" planks, 1 use	1 Carp	75	.107	Tread	4.43	3.11		7.54	9.75	**700**
	0100	Exterior plywood, 1/2" thick, 1 use		65	.123		1.48	3.59		5.07	7.25	
	0200	3/4" thick, 1 use	↓	60	.133	↓	2.25	3.89		6.14	8.55	
900	0010	**WINTER PROTECTION** Reinforced plastic on wood										**900**
	0100	framing to close openings	2 Clab	750	.021	S.F.	.35	.49		.84	1.15	
	0200	Tarpaulins hung over scaffolding, 8 uses, not incl. scaffolding		1,500	.011		.16	.24		.40	.56	
	0250	Tarpaulin polyester reinf. w/ integral fastening system 11 mils thick		1,600	.010		.73	.23		.96	1.16	
	0300	Prefab fiberglass panels, steel frame, 8 uses	↓	1,200	.013	↓	.70	.30		1	1.25	

01540 | Construction Aids

			CREW	DAILY OUTPUT	LABOR-HOURS	UNIT	MAT.	LABOR	EQUIP.	TOTAL	TOTAL INCL O&P	
500	0010	**PERSONNEL PROTECTIVE EQUIPMENT**										**500**
	0015	Hazardous waste protection										
	0020	Respirator mask only, full face, silicone				Ea.	209			209	230	
	0030	Half face, silicone					30.50			30.50	33.50	
	0040	Respirator cartridges, 2 reg'd/mask, dust or asbestos					4.38			4.38	4.81	
	0050	Chemical vapor					4.02			4.02	4.42	
	0060	Combination vapor and dust					8.55			8.55	9.40	
	0100	Emergency escape breathing apparatus, 5 min					430			430	475	
	0110	10 min					485			485	535	
	0150	Self contained breathing apparatus with full face piece, 30 min					1,850			1,850	2,025	
	0160	60 min					2,725			2,725	3,000	
	0200	Encapsulating suits, limited use, level A					695			695	765	
	0210	Level B				↓	164			164	180	
	0300	Over boots, latex				Pr.	5.05			5.05	5.55	
	0310	PVC					9.50			9.50	10.45	
	0320	Neoprene					46.50			46.50	51	
	0400	Gloves, nitrile/PVC					5.35			5.35	5.85	
	0410	Neoprene coated				↓	28			28	31	
550	0010	**PUMP STAGING**, Aluminum R01540-200										**550**
	0200	24' long pole section, buy				Ea.	335			335	365	
	0300	18' long pole section, buy					258			258	284	
	0400	12' long pole section, buy					174			174	192	
	0500	6' long pole section, buy					92			92	101	
	0600	6' long splice joint section, buy					68			68	75	
	0700	Pump jack					111			111	123	
	0900	Foldable brace					48.50			48.50	53	
	1000	Workbench/back safety rail support					59			59	64.50	
	1100	Scaffolding planks/workbench, 14" wide x 24' long					545			545	600	
	1200	Plank end safety rail					183			183	202	
	1250	Safety net, 22' long				↓	267			267	294	
	1300	System in place, 50' working height, per use based on 50 uses	2 Carp	84.80	.189	C.S.F.	4.95	5.50		10.45	14.05	
	1400	100 uses		84.80	.189		2.48	5.50		7.98	11.30	
	1500	150 uses	↓	84.80	.189	↓	1.66	5.50		7.16	10.40	
700	0010	**SAFETY NETS** No supports, stock sizes, nylon, 4" mesh				S.F.	1			1	1.10	**700**
	0100	Polypropylene, 6" mesh				↓	1.55			1.55	1.71	

13

GENERAL REQUIREMENTS

01540	Construction Aids	CREW	DAILY OUTPUT	LABOR-HOURS	UNIT	2001 BARE COSTS				TOTAL INCL O&P	
						MAT.	LABOR	EQUIP.	TOTAL		
700 0200	Small mesh debris nets, 1/4" & 3/4" mesh, stock sizes				S.F.	.72			.72	.79	**700**
0220	Combined 4" mesh and 1/4" mesh, stock sizes					2			2	2.20	
0300	Monthly rental, 4" mesh, stock sizes, 1st month					.19			.19	.21	
0320	2nd month rental					.15			.15	.17	
0340	Maximum rental/year				↓	.75			.75	.83	
750 0010	**SCAFFOLDING**										**750**
0015	Steel tubular, rent, 1 use/mo, no plank, erect & dismantle R01540 -100										
0090	Building exterior, wall face, 1 to 5 stories	3 Carp	24	1	C.S.F.	24.50	29		53.50	72	
0200	6 to 12 stories	4 Carp	21.20	1.509		24.50	44		68.50	95.50	
0310	13 to 20 stories	5 Carp	20	2		24.50	58.50		83	118	
0460	Building interior, wall face area, up to 16' high	3 Carp	25	.960	↓	24.50	28		52.50	70.50	
0560	16' to 40' high		23	1.043		24.50	30.50		55	74	
0800	Building interior floor area, up to 30' high		312	.077	C.C.F.	1.87	2.24		4.11	5.55	
0900	Over 30' high	4 Carp	275	.116	"	1.87	3.39		5.26	7.35	
0910	Steel tubular, heavy duty shoring, buy										
0920	Frames 5' high 2' wide				Ea.	75			75	82.50	
0925	5' high 4' wide					85			85	93.50	
0930	6' high 2' wide					86			86	94.50	
0935	6' high 4' wide				↓	101			101	111	
0940	Accessories										
0945	Cross braces				Ea.	16			16	17.60	
0950	U-head, 8" x 8"					16			16	17.60	
0955	J-head, 4" x 8"					12			12	13.20	
0960	Base plate, 8" x 8"					13			13	14.30	
0965	Leveling jack				↓	30.50			30.50	33.50	
1000	Steel tubular, regular, buy										
1100	Frames 3' high 5' wide				Ea.	58			58	64	
1150	5' high 5' wide					67			67	73.50	
1200	6'-4" high 5' wide					84			84	92.50	
1350	7'-6" high 6' wide					145			145	160	
1500	Accessories cross braces					15			15	16.50	
1550	Guardrail post					15			15	16.50	
1600	Guardrail 7' section					7.25			7.25	8	
1650	Screw jacks & plates					24			24	26.50	
1700	Sidearm brackets					28			28	31	
1750	8" casters					33			33	36.50	
1800	Plank 2" x 10" x 16'-0"					42.50			42.50	47	
1900	Stairway section					235			235	259	
1910	Stairway starter bar					21			21	23.50	
1920	Stairway inside handrail					53			53	58.50	
1930	Stairway outside handrail					73			73	80.50	
1940	Walk-thru frame guardrail				↓	28			28	31	
2000	Steel tubular, regular, rent/mo.										
2100	Frames 3' high 5' wide				Ea.	3.75			3.75	4.13	
2150	5' high 5' wide					3.75			3.75	4.13	
2200	6'-4" high 5' wide					3.75			3.75	4.13	
2250	7'-6" high 6' wide					7			7	7.70	
2500	Accessories, cross braces					.60			.60	.66	
2550	Guardrail post					1			1	1.10	
2600	Guardrail 7' section					.75			.75	.83	
2650	Screw jacks & plates					1.50			1.50	1.65	
2700	Sidearm brackets					1.50			1.50	1.65	
2750	8" casters					6			6	6.60	
2800	Outrigger for rolling tower					3			3	3.30	
2850	Plank 2" x 10" x 16'-0"				↓	5			5	5.50	

Important: See the Reference Section for critical supporting data - Reference Nos., Crews, & City Cost Indexes

01540 | Construction Aids

		Description	CREW	DAILY OUTPUT	LABOR-HOURS	UNIT	MAT.	LABOR	EQUIP.	TOTAL	TOTAL INCL O&P	
750	2900	Stairway section				Ea.	10			10	11	**750**
	2910	Stairway starter bar R01540 -100					.10			.10	.11	
	2920	Stairway inside handrail					5			5	5.50	
	2930	Stairway outside handrail					5			5	5.50	
	2940	Walk-thru frame guardrail					2			2	2.20	
	3000	Steel tubular, heavy duty shoring, rent/mo.										
	3250	5' high 2' & 4' wide				Ea.	5			5	5.50	
	3300	6' high 2' & 4' wide					5			5	5.50	
	3500	Accessories, cross braces					1			1	1.10	
	3600	U - head, 8" x 8"					1			1	1.10	
	3650	J - head, 4" x 8"					1			1	1.10	
	3700	Base plate, 8" x 8"					1			1	1.10	
	3750	Leveling jack					2			2	2.20	
	5700	Planks, 2"x10"x16'-0" in place, up to 50' high	3 Carp	144	.167			4.86		4.86	7.60	
	5800	In place over 50' high	4 Carp	160	.200			5.85		5.85	9.10	
	6000	Heavy duty shoring for elevated slab forms to 8'-2" high, floor area										
	6010	Set up and take down										
	6100	1 use/month	4 Carp	36	.889	C.S.F.	29.50	26		55.50	73	
	6150	2 uses/month	"	36	.889	"	14.80	26		40.80	57	
	6500	To 14'-8" high										
	6600	1 use/month	4 Carp	18	1.778	C.S.F.	43	52		95	129	
	6650	2 uses/month	"	18	1.778	"	21.50	52		73.50	105	
755	0011	**SCAFFOLDING SPECIALTIES**										**755**
	1200	Sidewalk bridge, heavy duty steel posts & beams, including										
	1210	parapet protection & waterproofing										
	1220	8' to 10' wide, 2 posts	3 Carp	15	1.600	L.F.	42	46.50		88.50	119	
	1230	3 posts	"	10	2.400	"	63	70		133	179	
	1500	Sidewalk bridge using tubular steel										
	1510	scaffold frames, including planking	3 Carp	45	.533	L.F.	4.72	15.55		20.27	29.50	
	1600	For 2 uses per month, deduct from all above					50%					
	1700	For 1 use every 2 months, add to all above					100%					
	1900	Catwalks, 32" wide, no guardrails, 6' span, buy				Ea.	120			120	132	
	2000	10' span, buy				"	190			190	209	
	2800	Hand winch-operated masons										
	2810	scaffolding, no plank moving required										
	2900	98' long, 10'-6" high, buy				Ea.	19,700			19,700	21,700	
	3000	Rent per month					790			790	865	
	3100	28'-6" high, buy					25,700			25,700	28,200	
	3200	Rent per month					1,025			1,025	1,125	
	3400	196' long, 28'-6" high, buy					49,700			49,700	54,500	
	3500	Rent per month					2,000			2,000	2,175	
	3600	64'-6" high, buy					73,000			73,000	80,000	
	3700	Rent per month					2,900			2,900	3,200	
	3720	Putlog, standard, 8' span, with hangers, buy					61			61	67	
	3730	Rent per month					10			10	11	
	3750	12' span, buy					92			92	101	
	3755	Rent per month					15			15	16.50	
	3760	Trussed type, 16' span, buy					210			210	231	
	3770	Rent per month					20			20	22	
	3790	22' span, buy					252			252	277	
	3795	Rent per month					30			30	33	
	3800	Rolling ladders with handrails, 30" wide, buy, 2 step					144			144	158	
	4000	7 step					430			430	475	
	4050	10 step					645			645	710	
	4100	Rolling towers, buy, 5' wide, 7' long, 10' high					1,150			1,150	1,250	
	4200	For 5' high added sections, to buy, add					188			188	207	

1

GENERAL REQUIREMENTS

01540	Construction Aids	CREW	DAILY OUTPUT	LABOR-HOURS	UNIT	2001 BARE COSTS				TOTAL INCL O&P	
						MAT.	LABOR	EQUIP.	TOTAL		
755 4300	Complete incl. wheels, railings, outriggers,										**755**
4350	21' high, to buy				Ea.	1,925			1,925	2,125	
4400	Rent/month				"	138			138	152	
760 0010	**STAGING AIDS** and fall protection equipment										**760**
0100	Sidewall staging bracket, tubular, buy				Ea.	29			29	31.50	
0110	Cost each per day, based on 250 days use				Day	.12			.12	.13	
0200	Guard post, buy				Ea.	15			15	16.50	
0210	Cost each per day, based on 250 days use				Day	.06			.06	.07	
0300	End guard chains, buy per set				Ea.	25			25	27.50	
0310	Cost per set per day, based on 250 days use				Day	.12			.12	.13	
1000	Roof shingling bracket, steel, buy				Ea.	5.75			5.75	6.30	
1010	Cost each per day, based on 250 days use				Day	.02			.02	.03	
1100	Wood bracket, buy				Ea.	11			11	12.10	
1110	Cost each per day, based on 250 days use				Day	.04			.04	.05	
2000	Ladder jack, aluminum, buy per pair				Pair	76.50			76.50	84	
2010	Cost per pair per day, based on 250 days use				Day	.31			.31	.34	
2100	Steel siderail jack, buy per pair				Pair	69			69	76	
2110	Cost per pair per day, based on 250 days use				Day	.28			.28	.30	
3000	Laminated wood plank, 2x10x16', buy				Ea.	42.50			42.50	47	
3010	Cost each per day, based on 250 days use				Day	.17			.17	.19	
3100	Aluminum scaffolding plank, 20" wide x 24' long, buy				Ea.	660			660	730	
3110	Cost each per day, based on 250 days use				Day	2.65			2.65	2.91	
4000	Nylon full body harness, lanyard and rope grab				Ea.	225			225	248	
4010	Cost each per day, based on 250 days use				Day	.90			.90	.99	
4100	Rope for safety line, 5/8" x 100' nylon, buy				Ea.	35			35	38.50	
4110	Cost each per day, based on 250 days use				Day	.14			.14	.15	
4200	Permanent U-Bolt roof anchor, buy				Ea.	29.50			29.50	32.50	
4300	Temporary (one use) roof ridge anchor, buy				"	18.60			18.60	20.50	
5000	Installation (setup and removal) of staging aids										
5010	Sidewall staging bracket	2 Carp	64	.250	Ea.		7.30		7.30	11.40	
5020	Guard post with 2 wood rails	"	64	.250			7.30		7.30	11.40	
5030	End guard chains, set	1 Carp	64	.125			3.64		3.64	5.70	
5100	Roof shingling bracket		96	.083			2.43		2.43	3.80	
5200	Ladder jack		64	.125			3.64		3.64	5.70	
5300	Wood plank, 2x10x16'	2 Carp	80	.200			5.85		5.85	9.10	
5310	Aluminum scaffold plank, 20" x 24'	"	40	.400			11.65		11.65	18.25	
5410	Safety rope	1 Carp	40	.200			5.85		5.85	9.10	
5420	Permanent U-Bolt roof anchor (install only)	2 Carp	40	.400			11.65		11.65	18.25	
5430	Temporary roof ridge anchor (install only)	1 Carp	64	.125			3.64		3.64	5.70	
780 0010	**SWING STAGING**, 500 lb cap., 2' wide to 24' long, hand operated hoist										**780**
0020	steel cable type, with 60' cables, buy				Ea.	3,650			3,650	4,000	
0030	Rent per month				"	450			450	495	
0600	Lightweight (not for masons) 24' long for 150' height.										
0610	manual type, buy				Ea.	3,900			3,900	4,300	
0620	Rent per month					520			520	575	
0700	Powered, electric or air, to 150' high, buy					13,500			13,500	14,800	
0710	Rent per month					840			840	925	
0780	To 300' high, buy					14,300			14,300	15,700	
0800	Rent per month					910			910	1,000	
1000	Bosun's chair or work basket 3' x 3.5', to 300' high, electric, buy					7,250			7,250	7,975	
1010	Rent per month					450			450	495	
2200	Move swing staging (setup and remove)	E-4	2	16	Move		535	42	577	1,025	
790 0010	**SURVEYOR STAKES** Hardwood, 1" x 1" x 48" long				C	42			42	46	**790**
0100	2" x 2" x 18" long					50.50			50.50	55.50	

Important: See the Reference Section for critical supporting data - Reference Nos., Crews, & City Cost Indexes

01540 | Construction Aids

		CREW	DAILY OUTPUT	LABOR-HOURS	UNIT	MAT.	LABOR	EQUIP.	TOTAL	TOTAL INCL O&P	
790	0150	2" x 2" x 24" long				C	63			63	69.50	**790**
	0200	2" x 2" x 30" long				↓	71			71	78	
800	0010	**TARPAULINS** Cotton duck, 10 oz. to 13.13 oz. per S.Y., minimum				S.F.	.46			.46	.51	**800**
	0050	Maximum					.55			.55	.61	
	0100	Polyvinyl coated nylon, 14 oz. to 18 oz., minimum					.45			.45	.50	
	0150	Maximum					.65			.65	.72	
	0200	Reinforced polyethylene 3 mils thick, white					.10			.10	.11	
	0300	4 mils thick, white, clear or black					.12			.12	.13	
	0400	5.5 mils thick, clear					.09			.09	.10	
	0500	White, fire retardant					.16			.16	.18	
	0600	7.5 mils, oil resistant, fire retardant					.17			.17	.19	
	0700	8.5 mils, black					.22			.22	.24	
	0710	Woven polyethylene, 6 mils thick					.45			.45	.50	
	0730	Polyester reinforced w/ integral fastening system 11 mils thick					1			1	1.10	
	0740	Mylar polyester, non-reinforced, 7 mils thick				↓	1.10			1.10	1.21	
820	0010	**SMALL TOOLS** As % of contractor's work, minimum R01100 -050				Total					.50%	**820**
	0100	Maximum				"					2%	

01550 | Vehicular Access & Parking

		CREW	DAILY OUTPUT	LABOR-HOURS	UNIT	MAT.	LABOR	EQUIP.	TOTAL	TOTAL INCL O&P	
700	0010	**ROADS AND SIDEWALKS** Temporary										**700**
	0050	Roads, gravel fill, no surfacing, 4" gravel depth	B-14	715	.067	S.Y.	2.72	1.62	.25	4.59	5.80	
	0100	8" gravel depth	"	615	.078	"	5.45	1.89	.29	7.63	9.25	
	1000	Ramp, 3/4" plywood on 2" x 6" joists, 16" O.C.	2 Carp	300	.053	S.F.	1.34	1.55		2.89	3.90	
	1100	On 2" x 10" joists, 16" O.C.	"	275	.058		1.96	1.70		3.66	4.81	
	2200	Sidewalks, 2" x 12" planks, 2 uses	1 Carp	350	.023		.74	.67		1.41	1.85	
	2300	Exterior plywood, 2 uses, 1/2" thick		750	.011		.25	.31		.56	.76	
	2400	5/8" thick		650	.012		.31	.36		.67	.90	
	2500	3/4" thick	↓	600	.013	↓	.37	.39		.76	1.02	

01560 | Barriers & Enclosures

		CREW	DAILY OUTPUT	LABOR-HOURS	UNIT	MAT.	LABOR	EQUIP.	TOTAL	TOTAL INCL O&P	
100	0010	**BARRICADES** 5' high, 3 rail @ 2" x 8", fixed	2 Carp	30	.533	L.F.	10.80	15.55		26.35	36.50	**100**
	0150	Movable	"	20	.800	"	10.80	23.50		34.30	48.50	
	0300	Stock units, 6' high, 8' wide, plain, buy				Ea.	430			430	475	
	0350	With reflective tape, buy				"	525			525	580	
	0400	Break-a-way 3" PVC pipe barricade										
	0410	with 3 ea. 1' x 4' reflectorized panels, buy				Ea.	305			305	335	
	0500	Plywood with steel legs, 32" wide					70			70	77	
	0600	Telescoping Christmas tree, 9' high, 5 flags, buy					121			121	133	
	0800	Traffic cones, PVC, 18" high					5.80			5.80	6.40	
	0850	28" high				↓	18.15			18.15	20	
	1000	Guardrail, wooden, 3' high, 1" x 6", on 2" x 4" posts	2 Carp	200	.080	L.F.	1.05	2.33		3.38	4.80	
	1100	2" x 6", on 4" x 4" posts	"	165	.097		1.65	2.83		4.48	6.25	
	1200	Portable metal with base pads, buy					15			15	16.50	
	1250	Typical installation, assume 10 reuses	2 Carp	600	.027	↓	1.58	.78		2.36	2.96	
	1300	Barricade tape, polyethelyne, 7 mil, 3" wide x 500' long roll				Ea.	25			25	27.50	
	5000	Barricades, see also division 01590-400										
250	0010	**FENCING** Chain link, 11 ga, 5' high	2 Clab	100	.160	L.F.	3.58	3.66		7.24	9.65	**250**
	0100	6' high		75	.213		3.28	4.87		8.15	11.25	
	0200	Rented chain link, 6' high, to 500' (up to 12 mo.)		100	.160		2.26	3.66		5.92	8.20	
	0250	Over 1000' (up to 12 mo.)	↓	110	.145		1.64	3.32		4.96	7	
	0350	Plywood, painted, 2" x 4" frame, 4' high	A-4	135	.178		4.44	5		9.44	12.65	
	0400	4" x 4" frame, 8' high	"	110	.218		7.90	6.15		14.05	18.20	
	0500	Wire mesh on 4" x 4" posts, 4' high	2 Carp	100	.160		6	4.66		10.66	13.85	
	0550	8' high	"	80	.200	↓	9	5.85		14.85	19	

01560		Barriers & Enclosures	CREW	DAILY OUTPUT	LABOR-HOURS	UNIT	2001 BARE COSTS				TOTAL INCL O&P	
							MAT.	LABOR	EQUIP.	TOTAL		
400	0010	TEMPORARY CONSTRUCTION See also division 01530										400
800	0010	WATCHMAN Service, monthly basis, uniformed person, minimum				Hr.					7.80	800
	0100	Maximum									14.15	
	0200	Person and command dog, minimum									10.30	
	0300	Maximum				↓					15.30	
	0500	Sentry dog, leased, with job patrol (yard dog), 1 dog				Week					195	
	0600	2 dogs				"					275	
	0800	Purchase, trained sentry dog, minimum				Ea.					800	
	0900	Maximum				"					2,000	
01580		**Project Signs**										
700	0010	SIGNS Hi-intensity reflectorized, no posts, buy				S.F.	14			14	15.40	700

GENERAL REQUIREMENTS 1

01590 | Equipment Rental

				UNIT	HOURLY OPER. COST	RENT PER DAY	RENT PER WEEK	RENT PER MONTH	CREW EQUIPMENT COST/DAY	
100	0010	**CONCRETE EQUIPMENT RENTAL**	R01590 -100							100
	0100	without operators								
	0200	Bucket, concrete lightweight, 1/2 C.Y.	R03310 -090	Ea.	.15	28.50	85	255	18.20	
	0300	1 C.Y.			.20	43.50	130	390	27.60	
	0400	1-1/2 C.Y.			.25	45	135	405	29	
	0500	2 C.Y.			.30	57.50	173	520	37	
	0600	Cart, concrete, self propelled, operator walking, 10 C.F.			1.10	69.50	209	625	50.60	
	0700	Operator riding, 18 C.F.			1.50	107	320	960	76	
	0800	Conveyer for concrete, portable, gas, 16" wide, 26' long			4.45	187	560	1,675	147.60	
	0900	46' long			4.70	240	720	2,150	181.60	
	1000	56' long			4.75	253	760	2,275	190	
	1100	Core drill, electric, 2-1/2 H.P., 1" to 8" bit diameter			1.71	71.50	215	645	56.70	
	1150	11 H.P., 8" to 18" cores			5.93	90	270	810	101.45	
	1200	Finisher, concrete floor, gas, riding trowel, 48" diameter			2.70	108	325	975	86.60	
	1300	Gas, manual, 3 blade, 36" trowel			2	53.50	160	480	48	
	1400	4 blade, 48" trowel			2.25	58.50	175	525	53	
	1500	Float, hand-operated (Bull float) 48" wide			.08	10	30	90	6.65	
	1570	Curb builder, 14 H.P., gas, single screw			5.20	66.50	200	600	81.60	
	1590	Double screw			11.15	83.50	250	750	139.20	
	1600	Grinder, concrete and terrazzo, electric, floor			1.81	76.50	230	690	60.50	
	1700	Wall grinder			.91	38.50	115	345	30.30	
	1800	Mixer, powered, mortar and concrete, gas, 6 C.F., 18 H.P.			3	58.50	175	525	59	
	1900	10 C.F., 25 H.P.			4.20	53.50	160	480	65.60	
	2000	16 C.F.			4.40	75	225	675	80.20	
	2100	Concrete, stationary, tilt drum, 2 C.Y.			7.75	267	800	2,400	222	
	2120	Pump, concrete, truck mounted, 4" line, 80' boom			12	805	2,420	7,250	580	
	2140	5" line, 110' boom			17.75	1,250	3,775	11,300	897	
	2160	Mud jack, 50 C.F. per hr.			3.46	93.50	280	840	83.70	
	2180	225 C.F. per hr.			5.40	315	950	2,850	233.20	
	2600	Saw, concrete, manual, gas, 18 H.P.			2.10	80	240	720	64.80	
	2650	Self-propelled, gas, 30 H.P.			4.30	107	320	960	98.40	
	2700	Vibrators, concrete, electric, 60 cycle, 2 H.P.			.80	28.50	85	255	23.40	
	2800	3 H.P.			1.14	40	120	360	33.10	
	2900	Gas engine, 5 H.P.			.65	40	120	360	29.20	
	3000	8 H.P.			1	50	150	450	38	
	3100	Concrete transit mixer, hydraulic drive								
	3120	6 x 4, 250 H.P., 8 C.Y., rear discharge			23.25	900	2,700	8,100	726	
	3200	Front discharge			23.25	985	2,950	8,850	776	
	3300	6 x 6, 285 H.P., 12 C.Y., rear discharge			25.25	1,025	3,100	9,300	822	
	3400	Front discharge			25.25	1,075	3,200	9,600	842	
200	0010	**EARTHWORK EQUIPMENT RENTAL** Without operators	R01590 -100							200
	0040	Aggregate spreader, push type 8' to 12' wide		Ea.	1	108	325	975	73	
	0050	Augers for truck or trailer mounting, vertical drilling	R02315 -300							
	0055	Fence post auger, truck mounted		Ea.	5.50	530	1,595	4,775	363	
	0060	4" to 36" diam., 54 H.P., gas, 10' spindle travel	R02315 -400		16.30	650	1,945	5,825	519.40	
	0070	14' spindle travel			18.75	810	2,430	7,300	636	
	0075	Auger, truck mounted, vertical drilling, to 25' depth	R02315 -450		63.15	2,275	6,825	20,500	1,870	
	0080	Auger, horizontal boring machine, 12" to 36" diameter, 45 H.P.			6.90	335	1,000	3,000	255.20	
	0090	12" to 48" diameter, 65 H.P.	R02455 -900		10.40	735	2,200	6,600	523.20	
	0100	Excavator, diesel hydraulic, crawler mounted, 1/2 C.Y. cap.			8.80	415	1,240	3,725	318.40	
	0120	5/8 C.Y. capacity			10.50	460	1,380	4,150	360	
	0140	3/4 C.Y. capacity			12.95	515	1,550	4,650	413.60	
	0150	1 C.Y. capacity			16.35	600	1,800	5,400	490.80	
	0200	1-1/2 C.Y. capacity			19.40	730	2,190	6,575	593.20	
	0300	2 C.Y. capacity			26.85	1,075	3,200	9,600	854.80	
	0320	2-1/2 C.Y. capacity			49.60	1,925	5,800	17,400	1,557	
	0340	3-1/2 C.Y. capacity			61.75	2,475	7,400	22,200	1,974	
	0341	Attachments								

01590 | Equipment Rental

GENERAL REQUIREMENTS 1

200

	Description	Ref	UNIT	HOURLY OPER. COST	RENT PER DAY	RENT PER WEEK	RENT PER MONTH	CREW EQUIPMENT COST/DAY	
0342	Bucket thumbs	R01590 -100	Ea.	1.10	172	515	1,550	111.80	**200**
0345	Grapples			1	202	605	1,825	129	
0350	Gradall type, truck mounted, 3 ton @ 15' radius, 5/8 C.Y.	R02315 -300		21.05	800	2,400	7,200	648.40	
0370	1 C.Y. capacity			24.60	965	2,890	8,675	774.80	
0400	Backhoe-loader, 40 to 45 H.P., 5/8 C.Y. capacity	R02315 -400		4.60	220	660	1,975	168.80	
0450	45 H.P. to 60 H.P., 3/4 C.Y. capacity			5.50	228	685	2,050	181	
0460	80 H.P., 1-1/4 C.Y. capacity	R02315 -450		6.30	297	890	2,675	228.40	
0470	112 H.P., 1-1/2 C.Y. capacity			10.30	370	1,105	3,325	303.40	
0480	Attachments	R02455 -900							
0482	Compactor, 20,000 lb			1.75	196	588	1,775	131.60	
0485	Hydraulic hammer, 750 ft-lbs			1.30	243	729	2,175	156.20	
0486	Hydraulic hammer, 1200 ft-lbs			1.75	294	882	2,650	190.40	
0500	Brush chipper, gas engine, 6" cutter head, 35 H.P.			3.10	167	500	1,500	124.80	
0550	12" cutter head, 130 H.P.			5.70	242	725	2,175	190.60	
0600	15" cutter head, 165 H.P.			9.10	267	800	2,400	232.80	
0750	Bucket, clamshell, general purpose, 3/8 C.Y.			.75	61.50	185	555	43	
0800	1/2 C.Y.			.75	70	210	630	48	
0850	3/4 C.Y.			.85	80	240	720	54.80	
0900	1 C.Y.			.90	106	319	955	71	
0950	1-1/2 C.Y.			1.45	133	400	1,200	91.60	
1000	2 C.Y.			1.55	167	500	1,500	112.40	
1010	Bucket, dragline, medium duty, 1/2 C.Y.			.40	28.50	85	255	20.20	
1020	3/4 C.Y.			.40	30	90	270	21.20	
1030	1 C.Y.			.40	33.50	100	300	23.20	
1040	1-1/2 C.Y.			.65	50	150	450	35.20	
1050	2 C.Y.			.65	66.50	200	600	45.20	
1070	3 C.Y.			1	110	330	990	74	
1200	Compactor, roller, 2 drum, 2000 lb., operator walking			3.75	135	405	1,225	111	
1250	Rammer compactor, gas, 1000 lb. blow			.75	46.50	140	420	34	
1300	Vibratory plate, gas, 13" plate, 1000 lb. blow			.75	43.50	130	390	32	
1350	24" plate, 5000 lb. blow			1.95	75	225	675	60.60	
1370	Curb builder/extruder, 14 H.P., gas, single screw			5.20	50	150	450	71.60	
1390	Double screw			11.15	91.50	275	825	144.20	
1750	Extractor, piling, see lines 2500 to 2750								
1860	Grader, self-propelled, 25,000 lb.		Ea.	12.45	555	1,658	4,975	431.20	
1910	30,000 lb.			14.05	580	1,735	5,200	459.40	
1920	40,000 lb.			21.75	800	2,400	7,200	654	
1930	55,000 lb.			29.30	1,400	4,183	12,500	1,071	
1950	Hammer, pavement demo., hyd., gas, self-prop., 1000 to 1250 lb.			10.45	400	1,195	3,575	322.60	
2000	Diesel 1300 to 1500 lb.			15.60	480	1,440	4,325	412.80	
2050	Pile driving hammer, steam or air, 4150 ft.-lb. @ 225 BPM			1.40	270	810	2,425	173.20	
2100	8750 ft.-lb. @ 145 BPM			1.85	425	1,270	3,800	268.80	
2150	15,000 ft.-lb. @ 60 BPM			2.05	495	1,485	4,450	313.40	
2200	24,450 ft.-lb. @ 111 BPM			2.65	535	1,605	4,825	342.20	
2250	Leads, 15,000 ft.-lb. hammers		L.F.	.40	3.33	10	30	5.20	
2300	24,450 ft.-lb. hammers and heavier		"	.60	4	12	36	7.20	
2350	Diesel type hammer, 22,400 ft.-lb.		Ea.	10.55	515	1,550	4,650	394.40	
2400	41,300 ft.-lb.			15.50	675	2,025	6,075	529	
2450	141,000 ft.-lb.			26.15	1,525	4,565	13,700	1,122	
2500	Vib. elec. hammer/extractor, 200 KW diesel generator, 34 H.P.			16.50	690	2,065	6,200	545	
2550	80 H.P.			29.95	1,025	3,075	9,225	854.60	
2600	150 H.P.			43.50	1,550	4,675	14,000	1,283	
2700	Extractor, steam or air, 700 ft.-lb.			1.60	187	560	1,675	124.80	
2750	1000 ft.-lb.			1.85	283	850	2,550	184.80	
3000	Roller, tandem, gas, 3 to 5 ton			4.15	167	500	1,500	133.20	
3050	Diesel, 8 to 12 ton			3.80	300	900	2,700	210.40	
3100	Towed type, vibratory, gas 12.5 H.P., 2 ton			2.30	250	750	2,250	168.40	
3150	Sheepsfoot, double 60" x 60"			.85	105	315	945	69.80	

Important: See the Reference Section for critical supporting data - Reference Nos., Crews, & City Cost Indexes

01590 | Equipment Rental

			UNIT	HOURLY OPER. COST	RENT PER DAY	RENT PER WEEK	RENT PER MONTH	CREW EQUIPMENT COST/DAY	
200	3200	Pneumatic tire diesel roller, 12 ton	R01590 -100	Ea.	4.95	293	880	2,650	215.60	**200**
	3250	21 to 25 ton			8.55	390	1,170	3,500	302.40	
	3300	Sheepsfoot roller, self-propelled, 4 wheel, 130 H.P.	R02315 -300		24.50	700	2,100	6,300	616	
	3320	300 H.P.			34.15	840	2,520	7,550	777.20	
	3350	Vibratory steel drum & pneumatic tire, diesel, 18,000 lb.	R02315 -400		10.15	460	1,380	4,150	357.20	
	3400	29,000 lb.			16.40	535	1,600	4,800	451.20	
	3450	Scrapers, towed type, 9 to 12 C.Y. capacity	R02315 -450		3.37	161	482	1,450	123.35	
	3500	12 to 17 C.Y. capacity			3.58	214	643	1,925	157.25	
	3550	Scrapers, self-propelled, 4 x 4 drive, 2 engine, 14 C.Y. capacity	R02455 -900		56.90	1,900	5,710	17,100	1,597	
	3600	2 engine, 24 C.Y. capacity			84.50	2,100	6,280	18,800	1,932	
	3650	Self-loading, 11 C.Y. capacity			26.70	760	2,275	6,825	668.60	
	3700	22 C.Y. capacity			52.25	1,275	3,800	11,400	1,178	
	3710	Screening plant 110 hp. w / 5' x 10'screen			13	415	1,250	3,750	354	
	3720	5' x 16' screen			14.30	495	1,480	4,450	410.40	
	3850	Shovels, see Cranes division 01590-600								
	3860	Shovel/backhoe bucket, 1/2 C.Y.		Ea.	.75	51.50	155	465	37	
	3870	3/4 C.Y.			.75	56.50	170	510	40	
	3880	1 C.Y.			.80	63.50	190	570	44.40	
	3890	1-1/2 C.Y.			.90	212	635	1,900	134.20	
	3910	3 C.Y.			1.05	400	1,200	3,600	248.40	
	4110	Tractor, crawler, with bulldozer, torque converter, diesel 75 H.P.			9.75	315	940	2,825	266	
	4150	105 H.P.			13.90	480	1,440	4,325	399.20	
	4200	140 H.P.			15.90	610	1,830	5,500	493.20	
	4260	200 H.P.			24.25	900	2,705	8,125	735	
	4310	300 H.P.			32.10	1,275	3,850	11,600	1,027	
	4360	410 H.P.			44.65	1,600	4,830	14,500	1,323	
	4380	700 H.P.			91.85	3,150	9,470	28,400	2,629	
	4400	Loader, crawler, torque conv., diesel, 1-1/2 C.Y., 80 H.P.			8.65	395	1,190	3,575	307.20	
	4450	1-1/2 to 1-3/4 C.Y., 95 H.P.			9.85	465	1,400	4,200	358.80	
	4510	1-3/4 to 2-1/4 C.Y., 130 H.P.			13.25	585	1,755	5,275	457	
	4530	2-1/2 to 3-1/4 C.Y., 190 H.P.			19.50	1,025	3,070	9,200	770	
	4560	3-1/2 to 5 C.Y., 275 H.P.			26.35	1,300	3,900	11,700	990.80	
	4610	Tractor loader, wheel, torque conv., 4 x 4, 1 to 1-1/4 C.Y., 65 H.P.			8.20	270	810	2,425	227.60	
	4620	1-1/2 to 1-3/4 C.Y., 80 H.P.			8.80	355	1,070	3,200	284.40	
	4650	1-3/4 to 2 C.Y., 100 H.P.			9.35	385	1,150	3,450	304.80	
	4710	2-1/2 to 3-1/2 C.Y., 130 H.P.			11.60	500	1,495	4,475	391.80	
	4730	3 to 4-1/2 C.Y., 170 H.P.			14.85	665	2,000	6,000	518.80	
	4760	5-1/4 to 5-3/4 C.Y., 270 H.P.			27.45	990	2,975	8,925	814.60	
	4810	7 to 8 C.Y., 375 H.P.			39.60	1,400	4,170	12,500	1,151	
	4870	12-1/2 C.Y., 690 H.P.			80.40	2,425	7,275	21,800	2,098	
	4880	Wheeled, skid steer, 10 C.F., 30 H.P. gas			4.75	127	380	1,150	114	
	4890	1 C.Y., 78 H.P., diesel			6	287	860	2,575	220	
	4891	Attachments for all skid steer loaders								
	4892	Auger		Ea.	.49	81.50	245	735	52.90	
	4893	Backhoe			.63	105	314	940	67.85	
	4894	Broom			.62	103	309	925	66.75	
	4895	Forks			.20	33.50	101	305	21.80	
	4896	Grapple			.47	78	234	700	50.55	
	4897	Concrete hammer			1.02	171	512	1,525	110.55	
	4898	Tree spade			.92	153	460	1,375	99.35	
	4899	Trencher			.73	121	364	1,100	78.65	
	4900	Trencher, chain, boom type, gas, operator walking, 12 H.P.			1.60	140	420	1,250	96.80	
	4910	Operator riding, 40 H.P.			4.55	267	800	2,400	196.40	
	5000	Wheel type, diesel, 4' deep, 12" wide			10.60	565	1,700	5,100	424.80	
	5100	Diesel, 6' deep, 20" wide			19.10	805	2,420	7,250	636.80	
	5150	Ladder type, diesel, 5' deep, 8" wide			9.15	425	1,275	3,825	328.20	
	5200	Diesel, 8' deep, 16" wide			27.05	825	2,475	7,425	711.40	
	5250	Truck, dump, tandem, 12 ton payload			18.05	375	1,130	3,400	370.40	

GENERAL REQUIREMENTS 1

01590 | Equipment Rental

GENERAL REQUIREMENTS

			UNIT	HOURLY OPER. COST	RENT PER DAY	RENT PER WEEK	RENT PER MONTH	CREW EQUIPMENT COST/DAY	
200	5300	Three axle dump, 16 ton payload	R01590 -100	Ea.	24.85	475	1,420	4,250	482.80	**200**
	5350	Dump trailer only, rear dump, 16-1/2 C.Y.			4	180	540	1,625	140	
	5400	20 C.Y.	R02315 -300		4.45	183	550	1,650	145.60	
	5450	Flatbed, single axle, 1-1/2 ton rating			9.75	133	400	1,200	158	
	5500	3 ton rating	R02315 -400		12.40	142	425	1,275	184.20	
	5550	Off highway rear dump, 25 ton capacity			37.80	1,000	2,995	8,975	901.40	
	5600	35 ton capacity	R02315 -450		38.80	1,325	3,950	11,900	1,100	
400	0010	**GENERAL EQUIPMENT RENTAL** Without operators	R02250 -450							**400**
	0150	Aerial lift, scissor type, to 15' high, 1000 lb. cap., electric		Ea.	1.15	83.50	250	750	59.20	
	0160	To 25' high, 2000 lb. capacity	R02250 -400		2	128	385	1,150	93	
	0170	Telescoping boom to 40' high, 750 lb. capacity, gas			6.50	265	795	2,375	211	
	0180	1000 lb. capacity	R02315 -300		8.20	390	1,175	3,525	300.60	
	0190	To 60' high, 750 lb. capacity			8.30	405	1,220	3,650	310.40	
	0195	Air compressor, portable, 6.5 CFM, electric			.70	33.50	100	300	25.60	
	0196	gasoline			.80	43.50	130	390	32.40	
	0200	Air compressor, portable, gas engine, 60 C.F.M.			5.41	58.50	175	525	78.30	
	0300	160 C.F.M.			6.80	73.50	220	660	98.40	
	0400	Diesel engine, rotary screw, 250 C.F.M.			6.90	117	350	1,050	125.20	
	0500	365 C.F.M.			8.10	150	450	1,350	154.80	
	0600	600 C.F.M.			13.25	242	725	2,175	251	
	0700	750 C.F.M.			17.40	258	775	2,325	294.20	
	0800	For silenced models, small sizes, add			3%	5%	5%	5%		
	0900	Large sizes, add			5%	7%	7%	7%		
	0920	Air tools and accessories								
	0930	Breaker, pavement, 60 lb.		Ea.	.20	30	90	270	19.60	
	0940	80 lb.			.20	40	120	360	25.60	
	0950	Drills, hand (jackhammer) 65 lb.			.20	26.50	80	240	17.60	
	0960	Track or wagon, swing boom, 4" drifter			25.70	415	1,250	3,750	455.60	
	0970	5" drifter			34.40	745	2,230	6,700	721.20	
	0980	Dust control per drill			1.10	16	48	144	18.40	
	0990	Hammer, chipping, 12 lb.			.20	26.50	80	240	17.60	
	1000	Hose, air with couplings, 50' long, 3/4" diameter			.02	5	15	45	3.15	
	1100	1" diameter			.03	5.65	17	51	3.65	
	1200	1-1/2" diameter			.04	9.35	28	84	5.90	
	1300	2" diameter			.11	17.65	53	159	11.50	
	1400	2-1/2" diameter			.12	20.50	62	186	13.35	
	1410	3" diameter			.16	26.50	80	240	17.30	
	1450	Drill, steel, 7/8" x 2'			.04	4.33	13	39	2.90	
	1460	7/8" x 6'			.04	5.35	16	48	3.50	
	1520	Moil points			.03	4.33	13	39	2.85	
	1525	Pneumatic nailer w/accessories			.42	28	84	252	20.15	
	1530	Sheeting driver for 60 lb. breaker			.10	11.65	35	105	7.80	
	1540	For 90 lb. breaker			.24	17.65	53	159	12.50	
	1550	Spade, 25 lb.			.15	7.65	23	69	5.80	
	1560	Tamper, single, 35 lb.			.45	29.50	89	267	21.40	
	1570	Triple, 140 lb.			.90	46.50	140	420	35.20	
	1580	Wrenches, impact, air powered, up to 3/4" bolt			.10	21.50	65	195	13.80	
	1590	Up to 1-1/4" bolt			.15	40	120	360	25.20	
	1600	Barricades, barrels, reflectorized, 1 to 50 barrels			.02	2.58	7.75	23.50	1.70	
	1610	100 to 200 barrels			.01	1.93	5.80	17.40	1.25	
	1620	Barrels with flashers, 1 to 50 barrels			.02	3.25	9.75	29.50	2.10	
	1630	100 to 200 barrels			.02	2.60	7.80	23.50	1.70	
	1640	Barrels with steady burn type C lights			.03	4.33	13	39	2.85	
	1650	Illuminated board, trailer mounted, with generator			.30	107	320	960	66.40	
	1670	Portable, stock, with flashers, 1 to 6 units			.02	3.25	9.75	29.50	2.10	
	1680	25 to 50 units			.02	3.03	9.10	27.50	2	
	1690	Butt fusion machine, electric			10.40	365	1,095	3,275	302.20	

Important: See the Reference Section for critical supporting data - Reference Nos., Crews, & City Cost Indexes

01590 | Equipment Rental

			UNIT	HOURLY OPER. COST	RENT PER DAY	RENT PER WEEK	RENT PER MONTH	CREW EQUIPMENT COST/DAY	
400	1695	Electro fusion machine	Ea.	4.20	142	425	1,275	118.60	400
	1700	Carts, brick, hand powered, 1000 lb. capacity		.13	21	63	189	13.65	
	1800	Gas engine, 1500 lb., 7-1/2' lift		2.73	106	319	955	85.65	
	1830	Distributor, asphalt, trailer mtd, 2000 gal., 38 H.P. diesel		3.10	485	1,450	4,350	314.80	
	1840	3000 gal., 38 H.P. diesel		3.60	500	1,500	4,500	328.80	
	1850	Drill, rotary hammer, electric, 1-1/2" diameter		.41	25.50	76	228	18.50	
	1860	Carbide bit for above		.03	5.35	16	48	3.45	
	1870	Emulsion sprayer, 65 gal., 5 H.P. gas engine		1.41	55	165	495	44.30	
	1880	200 gal., 5 H.P. engine		2.05	66.50	200	600	56.40	
	1900	Fencing, see division 01560-250 & 02820							
	1920	Floodlight, mercury, vapor or quartz, on tripod							
	1930	1000 watt	Ea.	.25	25	75	225	17	
	1940	2000 watt		.44	43.50	130	390	29.50	
	1960	Floodlights, trailer mounted with generator, 2-1000 watt lights		1.70	103	310	930	75.60	
	2020	Forklift, wheeled, for brick, 18', 3000 lb., 2 wheel drive, gas		10.75	172	515	1,550	189	
	2040	28', 4000 lb., 4 wheel drive, diesel		8.40	218	655	1,975	198.20	
	2100	Generator, electric, gas engine, 1.5 KW to 3 KW		1.13	40	120	360	33.05	
	2200	5 KW		1.49	58.50	175	525	46.90	
	2300	10 KW		2.40	133	400	1,200	99.20	
	2400	25 KW		6.80	153	460	1,375	146.40	
	2500	Diesel engine, 20 KW		4.35	117	350	1,050	104.80	
	2600	50 KW		6.90	133	400	1,200	135.20	
	2700	100 KW		11.88	193	580	1,750	211.05	
	2800	250 KW		29.05	335	1,000	3,000	432.40	
	2850	Hammer, hydraulic, for mounting on boom, to 500 ft.-lb.		.95	130	390	1,175	85.60	
	2860	500 to 1200 ft.-lb.		2.10	260	780	2,350	172.80	
	2900	Heaters, space, oil or electric, 50 MBH		.59	27.50	82	246	21.10	
	3000	100 MBH		1.06	35	105	315	29.50	
	3100	300 MBH		3.41	53.50	160	480	59.30	
	3150	500 MBH		6.77	70	210	630	96.15	
	3200	Hose, water, suction with coupling, 20' long, 2" diameter		.06	10	30	90	6.50	
	3210	3" diameter		.06	15	45	135	9.50	
	3220	4" diameter		.06	20	60	180	12.50	
	3230	6" diameter		.06	36.50	110	330	22.50	
	3240	8" diameter		.36	59.50	178	535	38.50	
	3250	Discharge hose with coupling, 50' long, 2" diameter		.05	8.35	25	75	5.40	
	3260	3" diameter		.05	10	30	90	6.40	
	3270	4" diameter		.06	13.35	40	120	8.50	
	3280	6" diameter		.07	33.50	100	300	20.55	
	3290	8" diameter		.33	54.50	163	490	35.25	
	3300	Ladders, extension type, 16' to 36' long		.14	18.35	55	165	12.10	
	3400	40' to 60' long		.18	29.50	89	267	19.25	
	3410	Level, laser type, for pipe laying, self leveling		1.41	93.50	281	845	67.50	
	3430	Manual leveling		.66	63.50	190	570	43.30	
	3440	Rotary beacon with rod and sensor		1.04	90	270	810	62.30	
	3460	Builders level with tripod and rod		.08	26.50	80	240	16.65	
	3500	Light towers, towable, with diesel generator, 2000 watt		1.50	108	325	975	77	
	3600	4000 watt		1.70	130	390	1,175	91.60	
	3700	Mixer, powered, plaster and mortar, 6 C.F., 7 H.P.		.90	65	195	585	46.20	
	3800	10 C.F., 9 H.P.		1.05	91.50	275	825	63.40	
	3850	Nailer, pneumatic		.42	28	84	252	20.15	
	3900	Paint sprayers complete, 8 CFM		.29	40	120	360	26.30	
	4000	17 CFM		.68	56.50	170	510	39.45	
	4020	Pavers, bituminous, rubber tires, 8' wide, 52 H.P., gas		12.25	635	1,900	5,700	478	
	4030	8' wide, 64 H.P., diesel		19	1,075	3,220	9,650	796	
	4050	Crawler, 10' wide, 78 H.P., gas		22.10	1,375	4,100	12,300	996.80	
	4060	10' wide, 87 H.P., diesel		27.60	1,425	4,300	12,900	1,081	
	4070	Concrete paver, 12' to 24' wide, 250 H.P.		29	1,525	4,550	13,700	1,142	

Reference notes: R02250-450, R02250-400, R02315-300

GENERAL REQUIREMENTS 1

01590 | Equipment Rental

		UNIT	HOURLY OPER. COST	RENT PER DAY	RENT PER WEEK	RENT PER MONTH	CREW EQUIPMENT COST/DAY
400								**400**
4080	Placer-spreader-trimmer, 24' wide, 300 H.P.	Ea.	36.40	1,800	5,400	16,200	1,371
4100	Pump, centrifugal gas pump, 1-1/2", 4 MGPH	R02250 -450	.85	31.50	95	285	25.80
4200	2", 8 MGPH	R02250 -400	1.20	33.50	100	300	29.60
4300	3", 15 MGPH		1.40	46.50	140	420	39.20
4400	6", 90 MGPH	R02315 -300	9.30	150	450	1,350	164.40
4500	Submersible electric pump, 1-1/4", 55 GPM		.35	36.50	110	330	24.80
4600	1-1/2", 83 GPM		.41	40	120	360	27.30
4700	2", 120 GPM		.42	46.50	140	420	31.35
4800	3", 300 GPM		.75	58.50	175	525	41
4900	4", 560 GPM		5.30	82	246	740	91.60
5000	6", 1590 GPM		8	233	700	2,100	204
5100	Diaphragm pump, gas, single, 1-1/2" diameter		.52	29.50	88	264	21.75
5200	2" diameter		.80	40.50	122	365	30.80
5300	3" diameter		.75	47.50	143	430	34.60
5400	Double, 4" diameter		1.75	80	240	720	62
5500	Trash pump, self-priming, gas, 2" diameter		1.65	40.50	122	365	37.60
5600	Diesel, 4" diameter		2.65	73.50	220	660	65.20
5650	Diesel, 6" diameter		6.40	122	365	1,100	124.20
5660	Rollers, see division 01590-200						
5700	Salamanders, L.P. gas fired, 100,000 B.T.U.	Ea.	1.06	20	60	180	20.50
5705	50,000 BTU		.79	13.35	40	120	14.30
5720	Sandblaster, portable, open top, 3 C.F. capacity		.15	53.50	160	480	33.20
5730	6 C.F. capacity		.20	78	234	700	48.40
5740	Accessories for above		.10	17	51	153	11
5750	Sander, floor		.69	40	120	360	29.50
5760	Edger		.56	25	75	225	19.50
5800	Saw, chain, gas engine, 18" long		.15	41.50	125	375	26.20
5900	36" long		.15	70	210	630	43.20
5950	60" long		.15	83.50	250	750	51.20
6000	Masonry, table mounted, 14" diameter, 5 H.P.		1.30	57	171	515	44.60
6050	Saw, portable cut-off, 8 H.P.		.85	56.50	170	510	40.80
6100	Circular, hand held, electric, 7-1/4" diameter		.16	23.50	70	210	15.30
6200	12" diameter		.25	33.50	100	300	22
6275	Shot blaster, walk behind, 20" wide		1.05	230	690	2,075	146.40
6300	Steam cleaner, 100 gallons per hour		.95	63.50	190	570	45.60
6310	200 gallons per hour		1.35	68.50	205	615	51.80
6340	Tar Kettle/Pot, 400 gallon		2.12	73.50	220	660	60.95
6350	Torch, cutting, acetylene-oxygen, 150' hose		1.50	33.50	100	300	32
6360	Hourly operating cost includes tips and gas		7.80				62.40
6410	Toilet, portable chemical		.10	16.35	49	147	10.60
6420	Recycle flush type		.12	20.50	61	183	13.15
6430	Toilet, fresh water flush, garden hose,		.14	23	69	207	14.90
6440	Hoisted, non-flush, for high rise		.12	20	60	180	12.95
6450	Toilet, trailers, minimum		.20	34	102	305	22
6460	Maximum		.61	102	306	920	66.10
6470	Trailer, office, see division 01520-500						
6500	Trailers, platform, flush deck, 2 axle, 25 ton capacity	Ea.	3.35	123	370	1,100	100.80
6600	40 ton capacity		4.55	223	670	2,000	170.40
6700	3 axle, 50 ton capacity		5	247	740	2,225	188
6800	75 ton capacity		6.45	325	975	2,925	246.60
6850	Trailer, storage, see division 01520-500						
6900	Water tank, engine driven discharge, 5000 gallons	Ea.	5.50	233	700	2,100	184
7000	10,000 gallons		7.75	330	990	2,975	260
7020	Transit (builder's level) with tripod		.08	25	75	225	15.65
7030	Trench box, 3000 lbs. 6'x8'		.54	90	270	810	58.30
7040	7200 lbs. 6'x20'		1.07	179	537	1,600	115.95
7050	8000 lbs., 8' x 16'		.82	167	500	1,500	106.55
7060	9500 lbs., 8'x20'		1.47	200	600	1,800	131.75

Important: See the Reference Section for critical supporting data - Reference Nos., Crews, & City Cost Indexes

01500 | Temporary Facilities & Controls

01590 | Equipment Rental

			UNIT	HOURLY OPER. COST	RENT PER DAY	RENT PER WEEK	RENT PER MONTH	CREW EQUIPMENT COST/DAY
400	7065	11,000 lbs., 8'x24'	R02250 -450	Ea.	1.37	237	710	2,125	152.95
	7070	12,000 lbs., 10' x 20'			1.80	300	900	2,700	194.40
	7100	Truck, pickup, 3/4 ton, 2 wheel drive	R02250 -400		4.75	75	225	675	83
	7200	4 wheel drive			4.90	83.50	250	750	89.20
	7250	Crew carrier, 9 passenger	R02315 -300		3.80	100	300	900	90.40
	7290	Tool van, 24,000 G.V.W.			6.49	103	310	930	113.90
	7300	Tractor, 4 x 2, 30 ton capacity, 195 H.P.			12.55	365	1,100	3,300	320.40
	7410	250 H.P.			17.20	435	1,300	3,900	397.60
	7500	6 x 2, 40 ton capacity, 240 H.P.			16	475	1,425	4,275	413
	7600	6 x 4, 45 ton capacity, 240 H.P.			19.20	585	1,750	5,250	503.60
	7620	Vacuum truck, hazardous material, 2500 gallon			7.10	305	920	2,750	240.80
	7625	5,000 gallon			7.15	410	1,225	3,675	302.20
	7650	Vacuum, H.E.P.A., 16 gal., wet/dry			.27	53.50	160	480	34.15
	7655	55 gal, wet/dry			.59	46.50	140	420	32.70
	7690	Large production vacuum loader, 3150 CFM			13.85	685	2,050	6,150	520.80
	7700	Welder, electric, 200 amp			4.97	43.50	130	390	65.75
	7800	300 amp			7.83	63.50	190	570	100.65
	7900	Gas engine, 200 amp			4.40	55	165	495	68.20
	8000	300 amp			5.25	70	210	630	84
	8100	Wheelbarrow, any size			.06	9.65	29	87	6.30
	8200	Wrecking ball, 4000 lb.			.50	68.50	205	615	45
600	0010	**LIFTING AND HOISTING EQUIPMENT RENTAL**	R01590 -150						
	0100	without operators							
	0150	Crane, flatbed mntd, 3 ton cap.	R01590 -100	Ea.	7.55	270	810	2,425	222.40
	0200	Crane, climbing, 106' jib, 6000 lb. capacity, 410 FPM			38.75	1,250	3,750	11,300	1,060
	0300	101' jib, 10,250 lb. capacity, 270 FPM	R02315 -450		43.75	1,575	4,750	14,300	1,300
	0400	Tower, static, 130' high, 106' jib,							
	0500	6200 lb. capacity at 400 FPM		Ea.	41.73	1,450	4,345	13,000	1,203
	0600	Crawler, cable, 1/2 C.Y., 15 tons at 12' radius			4.97	530	1,590	4,775	357.75
	0700	3/4 C.Y., 20 tons at 12' radius			18.55	540	1,625	4,875	473.40
	0800	1 C.Y., 25 tons at 12' radius			25.90	565	1,700	5,100	547.20
	0900	Crawler mounted, lattice boom, 1-1/2 C.Y., 40 tons at 12' radius			27	835	2,500	7,500	716
	1000	2 C.Y., 50 tons at 12' radius			36.35	990	2,975	8,925	885.80
	1100	3 C.Y., 75 tons at 12' radius			39.15	1,025	3,100	9,300	933.20
	1200	100 ton capacity, standard boom			47.35	1,375	4,150	12,500	1,209
	1300	165 ton capacity, standard boom			71.50	2,225	6,700	20,100	1,912
	1400	200 ton capacity, 150' boom			73.25	2,575	7,700	23,100	2,126
	1500	450' boom			105.30	3,550	10,680	32,000	2,978
	1600	Truck mounted, lattice boom, 6 x 4, 20 tons at 10' radius			18.10	685	2,050	6,150	554.80
	1700	25 tons at 10' radius			23.15	1,050	3,150	9,450	815.20
	1800	8 x 4, 30 tons at 10' radius			25.95	650	1,950	5,850	597.60
	1900	40 tons at 12' radius			31.45	835	2,500	7,500	751.60
	2000	8 x 4, 60 tons at 15' radius			38.65	1,000	3,000	9,000	909.20
	2050	82 tons at 15' radius			41.57	1,525	4,600	13,800	1,253
	2100	90 tons at 15' radius			43.08	1,575	4,725	14,200	1,290
	2200	115 tons at 15' radius			45.40	1,800	5,400	16,200	1,443
	2300	150 tons at 18' radius			46	1,850	5,550	16,700	1,478
	2350	165 tons at 18' radius			51.75	2,175	6,500	19,500	1,714
	2400	Truck mounted, hydraulic, 12 ton capacity			27.35	495	1,480	4,450	514.80
	2500	25 ton capacity			28.70	665	2,000	6,000	629.60
	2550	33 ton capacity			31.85	915	2,750	8,250	804.80
	2600	55 ton capacity			38.95	985	2,950	8,850	901.60
	2700	80 ton capacity			56.80	1,450	4,355	13,100	1,325
	2800	Self-propelled, 4 x 4, with telescoping boom, 5 ton			11.50	320	960	2,875	284
	2900	12-1/2 ton capacity			17.15	480	1,440	4,325	425.20
	3000	15 ton capacity			19.45	600	1,800	5,400	515.60
	3050	20 ton capacity			20.05	630	1,885	5,650	537.40

GENERAL REQUIREMENTS 1

25

01590 | Equipment Rental

GENERAL REQUIREMENTS

			UNIT	HOURLY OPER. COST	RENT PER DAY	RENT PER WEEK	RENT PER MONTH	CREW EQUIPMENT COST/DAY	
600	3100	25 ton capacity	Ea.	22.25	705	2,120	6,350	602	600
	3200	Derricks, guy, 20 ton capacity, 60' boom, 75' mast		11.44	305	920	2,750	275.50	
	3300	100' boom, 115' mast		18.63	530	1,590	4,775	467.05	
	3400	Stiffleg, 20 ton capacity, 70' boom, 37' mast		13.30	395	1,185	3,550	343.40	
	3500	100' boom, 47' mast		20.98	640	1,925	5,775	552.85	
	3550	Helicopter, small, lift to 1250 lbs. maximum, w/pilot		62.12	2,475	7,445	22,300	1,986	
	3600	Hoists, chain type, overhead, manual, 3/4 ton		.06	6.65	20	60	4.50	
	3900	10 ton		.25	28.50	85	255	19	
	4000	Hoist and tower, 5000 lb. cap., portable electric, 40' high		3.75	177	530	1,600	136	
	4100	For each added 10' section, add		.08	13.65	41	123	8.85	
	4200	Hoist and single tubular tower, 5000 lb. electric, 100' high		5.08	247	740	2,225	188.65	
	4300	For each added 6'-6" section, add		.14	23.50	71	213	15.30	
	4400	Hoist and double tubular tower, 5000 lb., 100' high		5.45	272	815	2,450	206.60	
	4500	For each added 6'-6" section, add		.15	25.50	77	231	16.60	
	4550	Hoist and tower, mast type, 6000 lb., 100' high		5.88	282	845	2,525	216.05	
	4570	For each added 10' section, add		.10	17	51	153	11	
	4600	Hoist and tower, personnel, electric, 2000 lb., 100' @ 125 FPM		12.33	750	2,245	6,725	547.65	
	4700	3000 lb., 100' @ 200 FPM		14.13	850	2,550	7,650	623.05	
	4800	3000 lb., 150' @ 300 FPM		15.65	950	2,855	8,575	696.20	
	4900	4000 lb., 100' @ 300 FPM		16.20	970	2,910	8,725	711.60	
	5000	6000 lb., 100' @ 275 FPM		17.50	1,025	3,060	9,175	752	
	5100	For added heights up to 500', add	L.F.	.01	1.70	5.10	15.30	1.10	
	5200	Jacks, hydraulic, 20 ton	Ea.	.15	14.65	44	132	10	
	5500	100 ton	"	.20	40.50	122	365	26	
	6000	Jacks, hydraulic, climbing with 50' jackrods							
	6010	and control consoles, minimum 3 mo. rental							
	6100	30 ton capacity	Ea.	1.53	102	305	915	73.25	
	6150	For each added 10' jackrod section, add		.05	3.33	10	30	2.40	
	6300	50 ton capacity		2.45	163	490	1,475	117.60	
	6350	For each added 10' jackrod section, add		.06	4	12	36	2.90	
	6500	125 ton capacity		6.38	425	1,275	3,825	306.05	
	6550	For each added 10' jackrod section, add		.44	29	87	261	20.90	
	6600	Cable jack, 10 ton capacity with 200' cable		1.28	85	255	765	61.25	
	6650	For each added 50' of cable, add		.13	8.65	26	78	6.25	
700	0010	**WELLPOINT EQUIPMENT RENTAL** See also division 02240							700
	0020	Based on 2 months rental							
	0100	Combination jetting & wellpoint pump, 60 H.P. diesel	Ea.	8.29	252	755	2,275	217.30	
	0200	High pressure gas jet pump, 200 H.P., 300 psi	"	14.52	215	645	1,925	245.15	
	0300	Discharge pipe, 8" diameter	L.F.	.01	.41	1.22	3.66	.30	
	0350	12" diameter		.01	.60	1.80	5.40	.45	
	0400	Header pipe, flows up to 150 G.P.M., 4" diameter		.01	.37	1.12	3.36	.30	
	0500	400 G.P.M., 6" diameter		.01	.43	1.30	3.90	.35	
	0600	800 G.P.M., 8" diameter		.01	.60	1.80	5.40	.45	
	0700	1500 G.P.M., 10" diameter		.01	.63	1.90	5.70	.45	
	0800	2500 G.P.M., 12" diameter		.02	1.20	3.60	10.80	.90	
	0900	4500 G.P.M., 16" diameter		.02	1.53	4.60	13.80	1.10	
	0950	For quick coupling aluminum and plastic pipe, add		.02	1.58	4.75	14.25	1.10	
	1100	Wellpoint, 25' long, with fittings & riser pipe, 1-1/2" or 2" diameter	Ea.	.05	3.17	9.50	28.50	2.30	
	1200	Wellpoint pump, diesel powered, 4" diameter, 20 H.P.		4.05	145	435	1,300	119.40	
	1300	6" diameter, 30 H.P.		5.28	180	540	1,625	150.25	
	1400	8" suction, 40 H.P.		7.18	247	740	2,225	205.45	
	1500	10" suction, 75 H.P.		9.81	288	865	2,600	251.50	
	1600	12" suction, 100 H.P.		14.70	460	1,385	4,150	394.60	
	1700	12" suction, 175 H.P.		19.46	510	1,530	4,600	461.70	

Reference boxes: R01590-150, R01590-100, R02315-450, R02240-900

			CREW	DAILY OUTPUT	LABOR-HOURS	UNIT	2001 BARE COSTS				TOTAL INCL O&P	
	01740	Cleaning					MAT.	LABOR	EQUIP.	TOTAL		
500	0010	**CLEANING UP** After job completion, allow, minimum				Job					.30%	500
	0040	Maximum				"					1%	
	0050	Cleanup of floor area, continuous, per day	A-5	24	.750	M.S.F.	1.65	17.20	1.64	20.49	30.50	
	0100	Final	"	11.50	1.565	"	2.63	36	3.43	42.06	62.50	
	0200	Rubbish removal, see division 02225-730										

01800 | Facility Operation

			CREW	DAILY OUTPUT	LABOR-HOURS	UNIT	2001 BARE COSTS				TOTAL INCL O&P	
	01810	Commissioning					MAT.	LABOR	EQUIP.	TOTAL		
100	0010	**COMMISSIONING**										100
	0100	As-built drawings, punchlist, training, manuals, minimum				Project					.50%	
	0150	Maximum				"					2%	

For information about Means Estimating Seminars, see yellow pages 11 and 12 in back of book

GENERAL REQUIREMENTS 1

		CREW	DAILY OUTPUT	LABOR-HOURS	UNIT	2001 BARE COSTS				TOTAL INCL O&P
						MAT.	LABOR	EQUIP.	TOTAL	

Division 2
Site Construction

Estimating Tips

02200 Site Preparation

- If possible visit the site and take an inventory of the type, quantity and size of the trees. Certain trees may have a landscape resale value or firewood value. Stump disposal can be very expensive, particularly if they cannot be buried at the site. Consider using a bulldozer in lieu of hand cutting trees.
- Estimators should visit the site to determine the need for haul road, access, storage of materials, and security considerations. When estimating for access roads on unstable soil, consider using a geotextile stabilization fabric. It can greatly reduce the quantity of crushed stone or gravel. Sites of limited size and access can cause cost overruns due to lost productivity. Theft and damage is another consideration if the location is isolated. A temporary fence or security guards may be required. Investigate the site thoroughly.

02210 Subsurface Investigation

In preparing estimates on structures involving earthwork or foundations, all information concerning soil characteristics should be obtained. Look particularly for hazardous waste, evidence of prior dumping of debris, and previous stream beds.

- The costs shown for selective demolition do not include rubbish handling or disposal. These items should be estimated separately using Means data or other sources.

02300 Earthwork

- Estimating the actual cost of performing earthwork requires careful consideration of the variables involved. This includes items such as type of soil, whether or not water will be encountered, dewatering, whether or not banks need bracing, disposal of excavated earth, length of haul to fill or spoil sites, etc. If the project has large quantities of cut or fill, consider raising or lowering the site to reduce costs while paying close attention to the effect on site drainage and utilities if doing this.
- If the project has large quantities of fill, creating a borrow pit on the site can significantly lower the costs. It is very important to consider what time of year the project is scheduled for completion. Bad weather can create large cost overruns from dewatering, site repair and lost productivity from cold weather.

02700 Bases, Ballasts, Pavements/Appurtenances

- When estimating paving, keep in mind the project schedule. If an asphaltic paving project is in a colder climate and runs through to the spring, consider placing the base course in the autumn, then topping it in the spring just prior to completion. This could save considerable costs in spring repair. Keep in mind that prices for asphalt and concrete are generally higher in the cold seasons.

02500 Utility Services
02600 Drainage & Containment

- Never assume that the water, sewer and drainage lines will go in at the early stages of the project. Consider the site access needs before dividing the site in half with open trenches, loose pipe, and machinery obstructions. Always inspect the site to establish that the site drawings are complete. Check off all existing utilities on your drawing as you locate them. If you find any discrepancies, mark up the site plan for further research. Differing site conditions can be very costly if discovered later in the project.

02900 Planting

- The timing of planting and guarantee specifications often dictate the costs for establishing tree and shrub growth and a stand of grass or ground cover. Establish the work performance schedule to coincide with the local planting season. Maintenance and growth guarantees can add from 20% to 100% to the total landscaping cost. The cost to replace trees and shrubs can be as high as 5% of the total cost depending on the planting zone, soil conditions and time of year.

Reference Numbers

Reference numbers are shown in bold squares at the beginning of some major classifications. These numbers refer to related items in the Reference Section. The reference information may be an estimating procedure, an alternate pricing method or technical information.

Note: Not all subdivisions listed here necessarily appear in this publication.

2 SITE CONSTRUCTION

		02060	Aggregate		CREW	DAILY OUTPUT	LABOR-HOURS	UNIT	2001 BARE COSTS				TOTAL INCL O&P	
									MAT.	LABOR	EQUIP.	TOTAL		
150	0010	**BORROW**		R02315 -400										**150**
	0020		and spread, with 200 H.P. dozer, no compaction											
	0100		Bank run gravel	CN	B-15	600	.047	C.Y.	13.60	1.20	2.83	17.63	19.90	
	0200		Common borrow			600	.047		5	1.20	2.83	9.03	10.45	
	0300		Crushed stone, (1.40 tons per CY), 1-1/2"			600	.047		18.80	1.20	2.83	22.83	25.50	
	0320		3/4"	CN		600	.047		20.50	1.20	2.83	24.53	28	
	0340		1/2"			600	.047		18.25	1.20	2.83	22.28	25	
	0360		3/8"			600	.047		13.20	1.20	2.83	17.23	19.50	
	0400		Sand, washed, concrete			600	.047		13.40	1.20	2.83	17.43	19.70	
	0500		Dead or bank sand			600	.047		3.55	1.20	2.83	7.58	8.85	
	0600		Select structural fill			600	.047		7.60	1.20	2.83	11.63	13.30	
	0700		Screened loam	CN		600	.047		15.35	1.20	2.83	19.38	22	
	0800		Topsoil, weed free			600	.047		11.15	1.20	2.83	15.18	17.20	
	0900		For 5 mile haul, add		B-34B	200	.040			.96	2.41	3.37	4.12	

02065 | Cement & Concrete

					CREW	DAILY OUTPUT	LABOR-HOURS	UNIT	MAT.	LABOR	EQUIP.	TOTAL	TOTAL INCL O&P	
300	0010	**ASPHALTIC CONCRETE** plant mix (145 lb. per C.F.)	CN	R02065 -300				Ton	33			33	36.50	**300**
	0200	All weather patching mix, hot							31.50			31.50	34.50	
	0250	Cold patch							36			36	39.50	
	0300	Berm mix							31.50			31.50	34.50	

02080 | Utility Materials

				CREW	DAILY OUTPUT	LABOR-HOURS	UNIT	MAT.	LABOR	EQUIP.	TOTAL	TOTAL INCL O&P	
400	0010	**FIRE HYDRANTS**, Mech. joints unless noted											**400**
	1000	Fire hydrants, two way; excavation and backfill not incl.											
	1100	4-1/2" valve size, depth 2'-0"		B-21	10	2.800	Ea.	660	74.50	14.20	748.70	860	
	1120	2'-6"			10	2.800		700	74.50	14.20	788.70	900	
	1140	3'-0"			10	2.800		740	74.50	14.20	828.70	945	
	1300	7'-0"			6	4.667		895	124	23.50	1,042.50	1,200	
	2400	Lower barrel extensions with stems, 1'-0"		B-20	14	1.714		290	44.50		334.50	390	
	2480	3'-0"		"	12	2		820	51.50		871.50	980	
790	0010	**UNDERGROUND MARKING TAPE**											**790**
	0400	Underground tape, detectable aluminum, 2"		1 Clab	150	.053	C.L.F.	3.70	1.22		4.92	6	
	0500	6"		"	140	.057	"	9.25	1.31		10.56	12.25	
800	0010	**UTILITY VAULTS** Precast concrete, 6" thick											**800**
	0050	5' x 10' x 6' high, I.D.		B-13	2	28	Ea.	1,350	695	315	2,360	2,925	
	0100	6' x 10' x 6' high, I.D.			2	28		1,400	695	315	2,410	2,975	
	0150	5' x 12' x 6' high, I.D.			2	28		1,500	695	315	2,510	3,075	
	0200	6' x 12' x 6' high, I.D.			1.80	31.111		1,675	770	350	2,795	3,400	
	0250	6' x 13' x 6' high, I.D.			1.50	37.333		2,200	925	420	3,545	4,275	
	0300	8' x 14' x 7' high, I.D.			1	56		2,375	1,375	630	4,380	5,450	
	0350	Hand hole, precast concrete, 1-1/2" thick											
	0400	1'-0" x 2'-0" x 1'-9", I.D., light duty		B-1	4	6	Ea.	235	141		376	480	
	0450	4'-6" x 3'-2" x 2'-0", O.D., heavy duty		B-6	3	8	"	545	199	60.50	804.50	970	

02100 | Site Remediation

		02110	Excavation, Removal & Handling	CREW	DAILY OUTPUT	LABOR-HOURS	UNIT	2001 BARE COSTS				TOTAL INCL O&P	
								MAT.	LABOR	EQUIP.	TOTAL		
300	0010		**HAZARDOUS WASTE CLEANUP/PICKUP/DISPOSAL**										**300**
	0100		For contractor equipment, i.e. dozer,										

02110 | Excavation, Removal & Handling

		CREW	DAILY OUTPUT	LABOR-HOURS	UNIT	2001 BARE COSTS MAT.	LABOR	EQUIP.	TOTAL	TOTAL INCL O&P	
300	0110	Front end loader, dump truck, etc., see div. 01590-200										**300**
	1000	Solid pickup									
	1100	55 gal. drums				Ea.					200
	1120	Bulk material, minimum				Ton					150
	1130	Maximum				"					500
	1200	Transportation to disposal site									
	1220	Truckload = 80 drums or 25 C.Y. or 18 tons									
	1260	Minimum				Mile					2.30
	1270	Maximum				"					4
	3000	Liquid pickup, vacuum truck, stainless steel tank									
	3100	Minimum charge, 4 hours									
	3110	1 compartment, 2200 gallon				Hr.					100
	3120	2 compartment, 5000 gallon				"					100
	3400	Transportation in 6900 gallon bulk truck				Mile					4.30
	3410	In teflon lined truck				"					5
	5000	Heavy sludge or dry vacuumable material				Hr.					100
	6000	Dumpsite disposal charge, minimum				Ton					100
	6020	Maximum				"					400

02115 | Underground Tank Removal

		CREW	DAILY OUTPUT	LABOR-HOURS	UNIT	2001 BARE COSTS MAT.	LABOR	EQUIP.	TOTAL	TOTAL INCL O&P	
200	0010	**REMOVAL OF UNDERGROUND STORAGE TANKS** R02115 -200										**200**
	0011	Petroleum storage tanks, non-leaking									
	0100	Excavate & load onto trailer									
	0110	3000 gal. to 5000 gal. tank	B-14	4	12	Ea.		290	45	335	500
	0120	6000 gal to 8000 gal tank	B-3A	3	13.333			325	198	523	720
	0130	9000 gal to 12000 gal tank	"	2	20	↓		485	297	782	1,075
	0190	Known leaking tank add				%				100%	100%
	0200	Remove sludge, water and remaining product from tank bottom									
	0201	of tank with vacuum truck									
	0300	3000 gal to 5000 gal tank	A-13	5	1.600	Ea.		46	104	150	185
	0310	6000 gal to 8000 gal tank	↓	4	2			57.50	130	187.50	230
	0320	9000 gal to 12000 gal tank	↓	3	2.667	↓		76.50	174	250.50	305
	0390	Dispose of sludge off-site, average				Gal.					4
	0400	Insert inert solid CO2 "dry ice" into tank									
	0401	For cleaning/transporting tanks (1.5 lbs./100 gal. cap)	1 Clab	500	.016	Lb.	1.20	.37		1.57	1.89
	1020	Haul tank to certified salvage dump, 100 miles round trip									
	1023	3000 gal. to 5000 gal. tank				Ea.				550	630
	1026	6000 gal. to 8000 gal. tank								650	750
	1029	9,000 gal. to 12,000 gal. tank				↓				875	1,000
	1100	Disposal of contaminated soil to landfill									
	1110	Minimum				C.Y.					100
	1111	Maximum				"					300
	1120	Disposal of contaminated soil to									
	1121	bituminous concrete batch plant									
	1130	Minimum				C.Y.					50
	1131	Maximum				"					100
	2010	Decontamination of soil on site incl poly tarp on top/bottom									
	2011	Soil containment berm, and chemical treatment									
	2020	Minimum	B-11C	100	.160	C.Y.	5.60	4.26	1.81	11.67	14.70
	2021	Maximum	"	100	.160		7.25	4.26	1.81	13.32	16.55
	2050	Disposal of decontaminated soil, minimum									60
	2055	Maximum				↓					125

SITE CONSTRUCTION 2

02210	Subsurface Investigation	CREW	DAILY OUTPUT	LABOR-HOURS	UNIT	2001 BARE COSTS				TOTAL INCL O&P	
						MAT.	LABOR	EQUIP.	TOTAL		
310	**0010** **BORINGS** Initial field stake out and determination of elevations	A-6	1	16	Day		515		515	815	**310**
	0100 Drawings showing boring details				Total		170		170	245	
	0200 Report and recommendations from P.E.						375		375	540	
	0300 Mobilization and demobilization, minimum	B-55	4	6	↓		138	176	314	410	
	0350 For over 100 miles, per added mile		450	.053	Mile		1.23	1.56	2.79	3.63	
	0600 Auger holes in earth, no samples, 2-1/2" diameter		78.60	.305	L.F.		7.05	8.95	16	21	
	0650 4" diameter		67.50	.356			8.20	10.45	18.65	24	
	0800 Cased borings in earth, with samples, 2-1/2" diameter		55.50	.432		12.35	9.95	12.70	35	43	
	0850 4" diameter	↓	32.60	.736		19.75	16.95	21.50	58.20	71.50	
	1000 Drilling in rock, "BX" core, no sampling	B-56	34.90	.458			11.85	20.50	32.35	41	
	1050 With casing & sampling		31.70	.505		12.35	13	23	48.35	58.50	
	1200 "NX" core, no sampling		25.92	.617			15.95	28	43.95	55	
	1250 With casing and sampling	↓	25	.640	↓	15.30	16.50	29	60.80	74.50	
	1400 Drill rig and crew with truck mounted auger	B-55	1	24	Day		555	705	1,260	1,625	
	1450 With crawler type drill	B-56	1	16	"		415	725	1,140	1,425	
	1500 For inner city borings add, minimum									10%	
	1510 Maximum									20%	
320	**0010** **DRILLING, CORE** Reinforced concrete slab, up to 6" thick slab										**320**
	0020 Including bit, layout and set up										
	0100 1" diameter core	B-89A	28	.571	Ea.	2.30	15.05	3.62	20.97	30	
	0150 Each added inch thick, add		300	.053		.41	1.41	.34	2.16	3.02	
	0300 3" diameter core		23	.696		5.10	18.35	4.41	27.86	39	
	0350 Each added inch thick, add		186	.086		.92	2.27	.55	3.74	5.15	
	0500 4" diameter core		19	.842		5.10	22	5.35	32.45	46.50	
	0550 Each added inch thick, add		170	.094		1.17	2.48	.60	4.25	5.85	
	0700 6" diameter core		14	1.143		8.45	30	7.25	45.70	64.50	
	0750 Each added inch thick, add		140	.114		1.43	3.01	.72	5.16	7.10	
	0900 8" diameter core		11	1.455		11.55	38.50	9.20	59.25	83	
	0950 Each added inch thick, add		95	.168		1.94	4.44	1.07	7.45	10.25	
	1100 10" diameter core		10	1.600		15.40	42	10.15	67.55	94	
	1150 Each added inch thick, add		80	.200		2.55	5.25	1.27	9.07	12.45	
	1300 12" diameter core		9	1.778		18.45	47	11.25	76.70	106	
	1350 Each added inch thick, add		68	.235		3.06	6.20	1.49	10.75	14.70	
	1500 14" diameter core		7	2.286		22.50	60	14.50	97	135	
	1550 Each added inch thick, add		55	.291		3.88	7.65	1.84	13.37	18.30	
	1700 18" diameter core		4	4		29	105	25.50	159.50	225	
	1750 Each added inch thick, add	↓	28	.571		5.10	15.05	3.62	23.77	33	
	1760 For horizontal holes, add to above				↓				30%	30%	
	1770 Prestressed hollow core plank, 6" thick										
	1780 1" diameter core	B-89A	52	.308	Ea.	1.53	8.10	1.95	11.58	16.50	
	1790 Each added inch thick, add		350	.046		.26	1.20	.29	1.75	2.50	
	1800 3" diameter core		50	.320		3.37	8.45	2.03	13.85	19.15	
	1810 Each added inch thick, add		240	.067		.56	1.76	.42	2.74	3.83	
	1820 4" diameter core		48	.333		4.49	8.80	2.11	15.40	21	
	1830 Each added inch thick, add		216	.074		.77	1.95	.47	3.19	4.43	
	1840 6" diameter core		44	.364		5.55	9.60	2.31	17.46	23.50	
	1850 Each added inch thick, add		175	.091		.92	2.41	.58	3.91	5.45	
	1860 8" diameter core		32	.500		7.45	13.20	3.17	23.82	32	
	1870 Each added inch thick, add		118	.136		1.28	3.57	.86	5.71	7.95	
	1880 10" diameter core		28	.571		10.05	15.05	3.62	28.72	38.50	
	1890 Each added inch thick, add		99	.162		1.38	4.26	1.02	6.66	9.30	
	1900 12" diameter core		22	.727		12.25	19.15	4.61	36.01	48.50	
	1910 Each added inch thick, add		85	.188	↓	2.04	4.96	1.19	8.19	11.30	
	1950 Minimum charge for above, 3" diameter core		7	2.286	Total		60	14.50	74.50	110	
	2000 4" diameter core	↓	6.80	2.353	↓		62	14.90	76.90	113	

Important: See the Reference Section for critical supporting data - Reference Nos., Crews, & City Cost Indexes

02210	Subsurface Investigation	CREW	DAILY OUTPUT	LABOR-HOURS	UNIT	2001 BARE COSTS				TOTAL INCL O&P	
						MAT.	LABOR	EQUIP.	TOTAL		
320 2050	6" diameter core	B-89A	6	2.667	Total		70.50	16.90	87.40	129	**320**
2100	8" diameter core		5.50	2.909			76.50	18.45	94.95	141	
2150	10" diameter core		4.75	3.368			89	21.50	110.50	163	
2200	12" diameter core		3.90	4.103			108	26	134	198	
2250	14" diameter core		3.38	4.734			125	30	155	229	
2300	18" diameter core		3.15	5.079			134	32	166	246	
3010	Bits for core drill, diamond, premium, 1" diameter				Ea.	91.50			91.50	101	
3020	3" diameter					228			228	251	
3040	4" diameter					254			254	279	
3050	6" diameter					405			405	445	
3080	8" diameter					555			555	610	
3120	12" diameter					885			885	970	
3180	18" diameter					1,875			1,875	2,050	
3240	24" diameter					2,500			2,500	2,725	
900 0010	**TEST PITS** Hand digging, light soil	1 Clab	4.50	1.778	C.Y.		40.50		40.50	63.50	**900**
0100	Heavy soil	"	2.50	3.200			73		73	114	
0120	Loader-backhoe, light soil	B-11M	28	.571			15.20	8.15	23.35	32.50	
0130	Heavy soil	"	20	.800			21.50	11.40	32.90	45	
1000	Subsurface exploration, mobilization				Mile				5	5.75	
1010	Difficult access for rig, add				Hr.				100	115	
1020	Auger borings, drill rig, incl. samples				L.F.				11.50	13.25	
1030	Hand auger								17	19.55	
1050	Drill and sample every 5', split spoon								15	17.25	
1060	Extra samples				Ea.				20	23	

02220	Site Demolition										
100 0010	**BUILDING DEMOLITION** Large urban projects, incl. 20 Mi. haul										**100**
0012	No foundation or dump fees, C.F. is volume of building standing, steel	B-8	21,500	.003	C.F.		.08	.11	.19	.24	
0050	Concrete		15,300	.004			.11	.15	.26	.33	
0080	Masonry		20,100	.003			.08	.12	.20	.26	
0100	Mixture of types, average		20,100	.003			.08	.12	.20	.26	
0500	Small bldgs, or single bldgs, no salvage included, steel	B-3	14,800	.003			.08	.12	.20	.25	
0600	Concrete		11,300	.004			.11	.15	.26	.33	
0650	Masonry		14,800	.003			.08	.12	.20	.25	
0700	Wood		14,800	.003			.08	.12	.20	.25	
1000	Single family, one story house, wood, minimum				Ea.				2,300	2,700	
1020	Maximum								4,000	4,800	
1200	Two family, two story house, wood, minimum								3,000	3,600	
1220	Maximum								5,800	7,000	
1300	Three family, three story house, wood, minimum								4,000	4,800	
1320	Maximum								7,000	8,400	
5000	For buildings with no interior walls, deduct								50%		
400 0010	**EXPLOSIVE/IMPLOSIVE DEMOLITION** Large projects, no disposal/fee										**400**
0020	based on building volume, steel building	B-5B	16,900	.003	C.F.		.08	.12	.20	.25	
0100	Concrete building		16,900	.003			.08	.12	.20	.25	
0200	Masonry building		16,900	.003			.08	.12	.20	.25	
0400	Disposal of material, minimum	B-3	445	.108	C.Y.		2.68	3.90	6.58	8.40	
0500	Maximum	"	365	.132	"		3.26	4.76	8.02	10.30	
550 0010	**FOOTINGS AND FOUNDATIONS DEMOLITION**										**550**
0200	Floors, concrete slab on grade,										
0240	4" thick, plain concrete	B-9C	500	.080	S.F.		1.86	.35	2.21	3.30	
0280	Reinforced, wire mesh		470	.085			1.98	.38	2.36	3.51	
0300	Rods		400	.100			2.33	.44	2.77	4.13	
0400	6" thick, plain concrete		375	.107			2.48	.47	2.95	4.40	
0420	Reinforced, wire mesh		340	.118			2.74	.52	3.26	4.85	
0440	Rods		300	.133			3.10	.59	3.69	5.50	

SITE CONSTRUCTION 2

		02220	Site Demolition	CREW	DAILY OUTPUT	LABOR-HOURS	UNIT	2001 BARE COSTS MAT.	LABOR	EQUIP.	TOTAL	TOTAL INCL O&P	
550	1000		Footings, concrete, 1' thick, 2' wide	B-5	300	.187	L.F.		4.72	3.15	7.87	10.75	550
	1080		1'-6" thick, 2' wide		250	.224			5.65	3.79	9.44	12.90	
	1120		3' wide		200	.280			7.10	4.73	11.83	16.15	
	1140		2' thick, 3' wide		175	.320			8.10	5.40	13.50	18.45	
	1200		Average reinforcing, add								10%	10%	
	1220		Heavy reinforcing, add								20%	20%	
	2000		Walls, block, 4" thick	1 Clab	180	.044	S.F.		1.02		1.02	1.59	
	2040		6" thick		170	.047			1.08		1.08	1.68	
	2080		8" thick		150	.053			1.22		1.22	1.91	
	2100		12" thick		150	.053			1.22		1.22	1.91	
	2200		For horizontal reinforcing, add								10%	10%	
	2220		For vertical reinforcing, add								20%	20%	
	2400		Concrete, plain concrete, 6" thick	B-9	160	.250			5.80	1.10	6.90	10.30	
	2420		8" thick		140	.286			6.65	1.26	7.91	11.80	
	2440		10" thick		120	.333			7.75	1.47	9.22	13.75	
	2500		12" thick		100	.400			9.30	1.76	11.06	16.50	
	2600		For average reinforcing, add								10%	10%	
	2620		For heavy reinforcing, add								20%	20%	
	4000		For congested sites or small quantities, add up to								200%	200%	
	4200		Add for disposal, on site	B-11A	232	.069	C.Y.		1.83	3.17	5	6.30	
	4250		To five miles	B-30	220	.109	"		2.85	7.10	9.95	12.15	
575	0010		**HYDRODEMOLITION**, concrete pavement, 4000 PSI, 2" depth	B-5	500	.112	S.F.		2.83	1.89	4.72	6.45	575
	0120		4" depth		450	.124			3.15	2.10	5.25	7.20	
	0130		6" depth		400	.140			3.54	2.37	5.91	8.10	
	0410		6000 PSI, 2" depth		410	.137			3.45	2.31	5.76	7.90	
	0420		4" depth		350	.160			4.04	2.70	6.74	9.20	
	0430		6" depth		300	.187			4.72	3.15	7.87	10.75	
	0510		8000 PSI, 2" depth		330	.170			4.29	2.87	7.16	9.80	
	0520		4" depth		280	.200			5.05	3.38	8.43	11.50	
	0530		6" depth		240	.233			5.90	3.94	9.84	13.50	
875	0010		**SITE DEMOLITION** No hauling, abandon catch basin or manhole	B-6	7	3.429	Ea.		85	26	111	160	875
	0020		Remove existing catch basin or manhole, masonry		4	6			149	45	194	280	
	0030		Catch basin or manhole frames and covers, stored		13	1.846			46	13.90	59.90	86.50	
	0040		Remove and reset		7	3.429			85	26	111	160	
	0100		Roadside delineators, remove only	B-80	175	.183			4.56	3.13	7.69	10.50	
	0110		Remove and reset	"	100	.320			8	5.45	13.45	18.30	
	0600		Fencing, barbed wire, 3 strand	2 Clab	430	.037	L.F.		.85		.85	1.33	
	0650		5 strand	"	280	.057			1.31		1.31	2.04	
	0700		Chain link, posts & fabric, remove only, 8' to 10' high	B-6	445	.054			1.34	.41	1.75	2.52	
	0750		Remove and reset		70	.343			8.50	2.59	11.09	16	
	0800		Guiderail, corrugated steel, remove only	B-80A	100	.240			5.50	1.84	7.34	10.65	
	0850		Remove and reset	"	40	.600			13.70	4.61	18.31	26.50	
	0860		Guide posts, remove only	B-80B	120	.267	Ea.		6.50	1.85	8.35	12.10	
	0870		Remove and reset	B-55	50	.480			11.05	14.05	25.10	32.50	
	0900		Hydrants, fire, remove only	B-21A	5	8			225	85	310	440	
	0950		Remove and reset	"	2	20			565	213	778	1,100	
	1000		Masonry walls, block or tile, solid, remove	B-5	1,800	.031	C.F.		.79	.53	1.32	1.80	
	1100		Cavity wall		2,200	.025			.64	.43	1.07	1.47	
	1200		Brick, solid		900	.062			1.57	1.05	2.62	3.59	
	1300		With block back-up		1,130	.050			1.25	.84	2.09	2.86	
	1400		Stone, with mortar		900	.062			1.57	1.05	2.62	3.59	
	1500		Dry set		1,500	.037			.94	.63	1.57	2.15	
	1600		Median barrier, precast concrete, remove and store	B-3	430	.112	L.F.		2.77	4.04	6.81	8.70	
	1610		Remove and reset	"	390	.123	"		3.05	4.45	7.50	9.60	

2 SITE CONSTRUCTION

Important: See the Reference Section for critical supporting data - Reference Nos., Crews, & City Cost Indexes

02220 | Site Demolition

			CREW	DAILY OUTPUT	LABOR-HOURS	UNIT	2001 BARE COSTS				TOTAL INCL O&P	
							MAT.	LABOR	EQUIP.	TOTAL		
875	1710	Pavement removal, bituminous roads, 3" thick	B-38	690	.058	S.Y.		1.50	1.36	2.86	3.81	875
	1750	4" to 6" thick		420	.095			2.47	2.23	4.70	6.25	
	1800	Bituminous driveways		640	.063			1.62	1.46	3.08	4.11	
	1900	Concrete to 6" thick, hydraulic hammer, mesh reinforced		255	.157			4.07	3.67	7.74	10.30	
	2000	Rod reinforced		200	.200	▼		5.20	4.68	9.88	13.15	
	2100	Concrete, 7" to 24" thick, plain		33	1.212	C.Y.		31.50	28.50	60	79.50	
	2200	Reinforced	▼	24	1.667	"		43	39	82	110	
	2300	With hand held air equipment, bituminous, to 6" thick	B-39	1,900	.025	S.F.		.61	.09	.70	1.05	
	2320	Concrete to 6" thick, no reinforcing		1,200	.040			.97	.15	1.12	1.66	
	2340	Mesh reinforced		1,400	.034			.83	.13	.96	1.43	
	2360	Rod reinforced	▼	765	.063	▼		1.52	.23	1.75	2.61	
	2400	Curbs, concrete, plain	B-6	360	.067	L.F.		1.65	.50	2.15	3.11	
	2500	Reinforced		275	.087			2.17	.66	2.83	4.07	
	2600	Granite		360	.067			1.65	.50	2.15	3.11	
	2700	Bituminous		528	.045			1.13	.34	1.47	2.12	
	2900	Pipe removal, sewer/water, no excavation, 12" diameter		175	.137			3.40	1.03	4.43	6.40	
	2930	15" diameter		150	.160			3.97	1.21	5.18	7.50	
	2960	24" diameter		120	.200			4.96	1.51	6.47	9.30	
	3000	36" diameter		90	.267			6.60	2.01	8.61	12.45	
	3200	Steel, welded connections, 4" diameter		160	.150			3.72	1.13	4.85	7	
	3300	10" diameter	▼	80	.300	▼		7.45	2.26	9.71	14	
	3500	Railroad track removal, ties and track	B-13	330	.170	▼		4.20	1.91	6.11	8.60	
	3600	Ballast	B-14	500	.096	C.Y.		2.32	.36	2.68	4.01	
	3700	Remove and re-install, ties & track using new bolts & spikes		50	.960	L.F.		23	3.62	26.62	40	
	3800	Turnouts using new bolts and spikes	▼	1	48	Ea.		1,150	181	1,331	2,000	
	4000	Sidewalk removal, bituminous, 2-1/2" thick	B-6	325	.074	S.Y.		1.83	.56	2.39	3.44	
	4050	Brick, set in mortar		185	.130			3.22	.98	4.20	6.05	
	4100	Concrete, plain, 4"		160	.150			3.72	1.13	4.85	7	
	4200	Mesh reinforced	▼	150	.160	▼		3.97	1.21	5.18	7.50	
	5000	Slab on grade removal, plain	B-5	45	1.244	C.Y.		31.50	21	52.50	71.50	
	5100	Mesh reinforced		33	1.697			43	28.50	71.50	98	
	5200	Rod reinforced	▼	25	2.240			56.50	38	94.50	129	
	5500	For congested sites or small quantities, add up to								200%	200%	
	5550	For disposal on site, add	B-11A	232	.069			1.83	3.17	5	6.30	
	5600	To 5 miles, add	B-34D	76	.105	▼		2.52	7.35	9.87	11.95	

02225 | Selective Demolition

			CREW	DAILY OUTPUT	LABOR-HOURS	UNIT	MAT.	LABOR	EQUIP.	TOTAL	TOTAL INCL O&P	
310	0010	**CEILING DEMOLITION**										310
	0200	Drywall, furred and nailed	2 Clab	800	.020	S.F.		.46		.46	.72	
	0220	On metal frame		760	.021			.48		.48	.75	
	0240	On suspension system, including system		720	.022			.51		.51	.79	
	1000	Plaster, lime and horse hair, on wood lath, incl. lath		700	.023			.52		.52	.82	
	1020	On metal lath		570	.028			.64		.64	1	
	1100	Gypsum, on gypsum lath		720	.022			.51		.51	.79	
	1120	On metal lath		500	.032			.73		.73	1.14	
	1200	Suspended ceiling, mineral fiber, 2'x2' or 2'x4'		1,500	.011			.24		.24	.38	
	1250	On suspension system, incl. system		1,200	.013			.30		.30	.48	
	1500	Tile, wood fiber, 12" x 12", glued		900	.018			.41		.41	.64	
	1540	Stapled		1,500	.011			.24		.24	.38	
	1580	On suspension system, incl. system		760	.021			.48		.48	.75	
	2000	Wood, tongue and groove, 1" x 4"		1,000	.016			.37		.37	.57	
	2040	1" x 8"		1,100	.015			.33		.33	.52	
	2400	Plywood or wood fiberboard, 4' x 8' sheets	▼	1,200	.013	▼		.30		.30	.48	
320	0010	**CUTOUT DEMOLITION** Conc., elev. slab, light reinf., under 6 C.F.	B-9C	65	.615	C.F.		14.30	2.71	17.01	25.50	320
	0050	Light reinforcing, over 6 C.F.	"	75	.533	"		12.40	2.35	14.75	22	

2 SITE CONSTRUCTION

		02225	Selective Demolition	CREW	DAILY OUTPUT	LABOR-HOURS	UNIT	MAT.	2001 BARE COSTS LABOR	EQUIP.	TOTAL	TOTAL INCL O&P	
320	0200		Slab on grade to 6" thick, not reinforced, under 8 S.F.	B-9	85	.471	S.F.		10.95	2.08	13.03	19.40	320
	0250		Not reinforced, over 8 S.F.		175	.229	"		5.30	1.01	6.31	9.40	
	0600		Walls, not reinforced, under 6 C.F.		60	.667	C.F.		15.50	2.94	18.44	27.50	
	0650		Not reinforced, over 6 C.F.		65	.615			14.30	2.71	17.01	25.50	
	1000		Concrete, elevated slab, bar reinforced, under 6 C.F.	B-9C	45	.889			20.50	3.92	24.42	37	
	1050		Bar reinforced, over 6 C.F.	"	50	.800			18.60	3.53	22.13	33	
	1200		Slab on grade to 6" thick, bar reinforced, under 8 S.F.	B-9	75	.533	S.F.		12.40	2.35	14.75	22	
	1250		Bar reinforced, over 8 S.F.	"	105	.381	"		8.85	1.68	10.53	15.70	
	1400		Walls, bar reinforced, under 6 C.F.	B-9C	50	.800	C.F.		18.60	3.53	22.13	33	
	1450		Bar reinforced, over 6 C.F.	"	55	.727	"		16.90	3.21	20.11	30	
	2000		Brick, to 4 S.F. opening, not including toothing										
	2040		4" thick	B-9C	30	1.333	Ea.		31	5.90	36.90	55	
	2060		8" thick		18	2.222			51.50	9.80	61.30	92	
	2080		12" thick		10	4			93	17.65	110.65	165	
	2400		Concrete block, to 4 S.F. opening, 2" thick		35	1.143			26.50	5.05	31.55	47	
	2420		4" thick		30	1.333			31	5.90	36.90	55	
	2440		8" thick		27	1.481			34.50	6.55	41.05	61	
	2460		12" thick		24	1.667			39	7.35	46.35	68.50	
	2600		Gypsum block, to 4 S.F. opening, 2" thick	B-9	80	.500			11.65	2.21	13.86	20.50	
	2620		4" thick		70	.571			13.30	2.52	15.82	24	
	2640		8" thick		55	.727			16.90	3.21	20.11	30	
	2800		Terra cotta, to 4 S.F. opening, 4" thick		70	.571			13.30	2.52	15.82	24	
	2840		8" thick		65	.615			14.30	2.71	17.01	25.50	
	2880		12" thick		50	.800			18.60	3.53	22.13	33	
	3000		Toothing masonry cutouts, brick, soft old mortar	1 Brhe	40	.200	V.L.F.		4.59		4.59	7.10	
	3100		Hard mortar		30	.267			6.10		6.10	9.45	
	3200		Block, soft old mortar		70	.114			2.62		2.62	4.05	
	3400		Hard mortar		50	.160			3.67		3.67	5.65	
	6000		Walls, interior, not including re-framing,										
	6010		openings to 5 S.F.										
	6100		Drywall to 5/8" thick	A-1	24	.333	Ea.		7.60	2.70	10.30	14.85	
	6200		Paneling to 3/4" thick		20	.400			9.15	3.24	12.39	17.85	
	6300		Plaster, on gypsum lath		20	.400			9.15	3.24	12.39	17.85	
	6340		On wire lath		14	.571			13.05	4.63	17.68	25.50	
	7000		Wood frame, not including re-framing, openings to 5 S.F.										
	7200		Floors, sheathing and flooring to 2" thick	A-1	5	1.600	Ea.		36.50	12.95	49.45	71.50	
	7310		Roofs, sheathing to 1" thick, not including roofing		6	1.333			30.50	10.80	41.30	59.50	
	7410		Walls, sheathing to 1" thick, not including siding		7	1.143			26	9.25	35.25	51	
340	0010		**DOOR DEMOLITION**										340
	0200		Doors, exterior, 1-3/4" thick, single, 3' x 7' high	1 Clab	16	.500	Ea.		11.45		11.45	17.90	
	0220		Double, 6' x 7' high		12	.667			15.25		15.25	24	
	0500		Interior, 1-3/8" thick, single, 3' x 7' high		20	.400			9.15		9.15	14.30	
	0520		Double, 6' x 7' high		16	.500			11.45		11.45	17.90	
	0700		Bi-folding, 3' x 6'-8" high		20	.400			9.15		9.15	14.30	
	0720		6' x 6'-8" high		18	.444			10.15		10.15	15.90	
	0900		Bi-passing, 3' x 6'-8" high		16	.500			11.45		11.45	17.90	
	0940		6' x 6'-8" high		14	.571			13.05		13.05	20.50	
	1500		Remove and reset, minimum	1 Carp	8	1			29		29	45.50	
	1520		Maximum	"	6	1.333			39		39	61	
	2000		Frames, including trim, metal	A-1	8	1			23	8.10	31.10	45	
	2200		Wood	2 Carp	32	.500			14.60		14.60	23	
	3000		Special doors, counter doors		6	2.667			77.50		77.50	122	
	3100		Double acting		10	1.600			46.50		46.50	73	
	3200		Floor door (trap type)		8	2			58.50		58.50	91	
	3300		Glass, sliding, including frames		12	1.333			39		39	61	
	3400		Overhead, commercial, 12' x 12' high		4	4			117		117	182	

Important: See the Reference Section for critical supporting data - Reference Nos., Crews, & City Cost Indexes

02200 | Site Preparation

		02225	Selective Demolition	CREW	DAILY OUTPUT	LABOR-HOURS	UNIT	2001 BARE COSTS				TOTAL INCL O&P		
								MAT.	LABOR	EQUIP.	TOTAL			
340	3440		20' x 16' high	2 Carp	3	5.333	Ea.		155		155	243	**340**	
	3500		Residential, 9' x 7' high		8	2			58.50		58.50	91		
	3540		16' x 7' high		7	2.286			66.50		66.50	104		
	3600		Remove and reset, minimum		4	4			117		117	182		
	3620		Maximum		2.50	6.400			187		187	292		
	3700		Roll-up grille		5	3.200			93.50		93.50	146		
	3800		Revolving door		2	8			233		233	365		
	3900		Storefront swing door	↓	3	5.333	↓		155		155	243		
380	0010	**FLOORING DEMOLITION**											**380**	
	0200		Brick with mortar	2 Clab	475	.034	S.F.		.77		.77	1.20		
	0400	Carpet, bonded, including surface scraping			2,000	.008			.18		.18	.29		
	0440		Scrim applied		8,000	.002			.05		.05	.07		
	0480		Tackless		9,000	.002			.04		.04	.06		
	0600	Composition, acrylic or epoxy		↓	400	.040			.91		.91	1.43		
	0700	Concrete, scarify skin		A-1	225	.036			.81	.29	1.10	1.59		
	0800	Resilient, sheet goods		2 Clab	1,400	.011			.26		.26	.41		
	0820		For gym floors		900	.018			.41		.41	.64		
	0900	Vinyl composition tile, 12" x 12"			1,000	.016			.37		.37	.57		
	2000	Tile, ceramic, thin set			675	.024			.54		.54	.85		
	2020		Mud set		625	.026			.59		.59	.92		
	2200		Marble, slate, thin set		675	.024			.54		.54	.85		
	2220		Mud set		625	.026			.59		.59	.92		
	2600		Terrazzo, thin set		450	.036			.81		.81	1.27		
	2620		Mud set		425	.038			.86		.86	1.35		
	2640		Cast in place	↓	300	.053			1.22		1.22	1.91		
	3000	Wood, block, on end		1 Carp	400	.020			.58		.58	.91		
	3200		Parquet		450	.018			.52		.52	.81		
	3400		Strip flooring, interior, 2-1/4" x 25/32" thick		325	.025			.72		.72	1.12		
	3500		Exterior, porch flooring, 1" x 4"		220	.036			1.06		1.06	1.66		
	3800		Subfloor, tongue and groove, 1" x 6"		325	.025			.72		.72	1.12		
	3820		1" x 8"		430	.019			.54		.54	.85		
	3840		1" x 10"		520	.015			.45		.45	.70		
	4000		Plywood, nailed		600	.013			.39		.39	.61		
	4100		Glued and nailed	↓	400	.020			.58		.58	.91		
	8000	Remove flooring, bead blast, minimum		A-1A	1,000	.008			.24	.15	.39	.53		
	8100		Maximum		400	.020			.60	.37	.97	1.34		
	8150		Mastic only	↓	1,500	.005	↓		.16	.10	.26	.36		
390	0010	**FRAMING DEMOLITION**											**390**	
	1020	Concrete, average reinforcing, beams, 8" x 10"		B-9	120	.333	L.F.		7.75	1.47	9.22	13.75		
	1040		10" x 12"		110	.364			8.45	1.60	10.05	15		
	1060		12" x 14"		90	.444			10.35	1.96	12.31	18.30		
	1200		Columns, 8" x 8"		120	.333			7.75	1.47	9.22	13.75		
	1240		10" x 10"		120	.333			7.75	1.47	9.22	13.75		
	1280		12" x 12"		110	.364			8.45	1.60	10.05	15		
	1320		14" x 14"		100	.400			9.30	1.76	11.06	16.50		
	1400		Girders, 14" x 16"		55	.727			16.90	3.21	20.11	30		
	1440		16" x 18"		40	1	↓		23.50	4.41	27.91	41.50		
	1600		Slabs, elevated, 6" thick		600	.067	S.F.		1.55	.29	1.84	2.75		
	1640		8" thick		450	.089			2.07	.39	2.46	3.66		
	1680		10" thick	↓	360	.111			2.58	.49	3.07	4.58		
	1900		Add for heavy reinforcement				↓					25%		
	2000	Steel framing, beams, 4" x 6"		B-13	500	.112	L.F.		2.77	1.26	4.03	5.70		
	2020		4" x 8"		400	.140			3.46	1.57	5.03	7.10		
	2080		8" x 12"		250	.224			5.55	2.52	8.07	11.35		
	2200		Columns, 6" x 6"	↓	400	.140	↓		3.46	1.57	5.03	7.10		

SITE CONSTRUCTION | 2

		CREW	DAILY OUTPUT	LABOR-HOURS	UNIT	MAT.	LABOR	EQUIP.	TOTAL	TOTAL INCL O&P	
	**02225	Selective Demolition**					2001 BARE COSTS					
390	2240	8" x 8"	B-13	350	.160	L.F.		3.96	1.80	5.76	8.15	**390**
	2280	10" x 10"		320	.175			4.33	1.97	6.30	8.85	
	2400	Girders, 10" x 12"		225	.249			6.15	2.80	8.95	12.65	
	2440	10" x 14"		200	.280			6.95	3.15	10.10	14.15	
	2480	10" x 16"		165	.339			8.40	3.81	12.21	17.20	
	2520	10" x 24"	▼	125	.448			11.10	5.05	16.15	22.50	
	3000	Wood framing, beams, 6" x 8"	B-2	275	.145			3.38		3.38	5.30	
	3040	6" x 10"		220	.182			4.23		4.23	6.60	
	3080	6" x 12"		185	.216			5.05		5.05	7.85	
	3120	8" x 12"		140	.286			6.65		6.65	10.40	
	3160	10" x 12"	▼	110	.364			8.45		8.45	13.25	
	3400	Fascia boards, 1" x 6"	1 Clab	500	.016			.37		.37	.57	
	3440	1" x 8"		450	.018			.41		.41	.64	
	3480	1" x 10"		400	.020			.46		.46	.72	
	3800	Headers over openings, 2 @ 2" x 6"		110	.073			1.66		1.66	2.60	
	3840	2 @ 2" x 8"		100	.080			1.83		1.83	2.86	
	3880	2 @ 2" x 10"	▼	90	.089			2.03		2.03	3.18	
	4230	Joists, 2" x 6"	2 Clab	970	.016			.38		.38	.59	
	4240	2" x 8"		940	.017			.39		.39	.61	
	4250	2" x 10"		910	.018			.40		.40	.63	
	4280	2" x 12"		880	.018			.42		.42	.65	
	5400	Posts, 4" x 4"		800	.020			.46		.46	.72	
	5440	6" x 6"		400	.040			.91		.91	1.43	
	5480	8" x 8"		300	.053			1.22		1.22	1.91	
	5500	10" x 10"		240	.067			1.52		1.52	2.38	
	5800	Rafters, ordinary, 2" x 6"		850	.019			.43		.43	.67	
	5840	2" x 8"		837	.019	▼		.44		.44	.68	
	6200	Stairs and stringers, minimum		40	.400	Riser		9.15		9.15	14.30	
	6240	Maximum		26	.615	"		14.05		14.05	22	
	6600	Studs, 2" x 4"		2,000	.008	L.F.		.18		.18	.29	
	6640	2" x 6"	▼	1,600	.010	"		.23		.23	.36	
	9500	See Div. 02225-730 for rubbish handling										
400	0010	**GUTTING** Building interior, including disposal, dumpster fees not included										**400**
	0500	Residential building										
	0560	Minimum	B-16	400	.080	SF Flr.		1.89	1.21	3.10	4.27	
	0580	Maximum	"	360	.089	"		2.10	1.34	3.44	4.75	
	0900	Commercial building										
	1000	Minimum	B-16	350	.091	SF Flr.		2.16	1.38	3.54	4.88	
	1020	Maximum	"	250	.128	"		3.02	1.93	4.95	6.80	
610	0010	**MASONRY DEMOLITION**										**610**
	1000	Chimney, 16" x 16", soft old mortar	A-1	24	.333	V.L.F.		7.60	2.70	10.30	14.85	
	1020	Hard mortar		18	.444			10.15	3.60	13.75	19.85	
	1080	20" x 20", soft old mortar		12	.667			15.25	5.40	20.65	30	
	1100	Hard mortar		10	.800			18.30	6.50	24.80	35.50	
	1140	20" x 32", soft old mortar		10	.800			18.30	6.50	24.80	35.50	
	1160	Hard mortar		8	1			23	8.10	31.10	45	
	1200	48" x 48", soft old mortar		5	1.600			36.50	12.95	49.45	71.50	
	1220	Hard mortar		4	2			45.50	16.20	61.70	89.50	
	2000	Columns, 8" x 8", soft old mortar		48	.167			3.81	1.35	5.16	7.45	
	2020	Hard mortar		40	.200			4.57	1.62	6.19	8.95	
	2060	16" x 16", soft old mortar		16	.500			11.45	4.05	15.50	22.50	
	2100	Hard mortar		14	.571			13.05	4.63	17.68	25.50	
	2140	24" x 24", soft old mortar		8	1			23	8.10	31.10	45	
	2160	Hard mortar		6	1.333			30.50	10.80	41.30	59.50	
	2200	36" x 36", soft old mortar	▼	4	2	▼		45.50	16.20	61.70	89.50	

Important: See the Reference Section for critical supporting data - Reference Nos., Crews, & City Cost Indexes

2

SITE CONSTRUCTION

02225 | Selective Demolition

			CREW	DAILY OUTPUT	LABOR-HOURS	UNIT	2001 BARE COSTS MAT.	LABOR	EQUIP.	TOTAL	TOTAL INCL O&P	
610	2220	Hard mortar	A-1	3	2.667	V.L.F.		61	21.50	82.50	120	**610**
	3000	Copings, precast or masonry, to 8″ wide										
	3020	Soft old mortar	A-1	180	.044	L.F.		1.02	.36	1.38	1.99	
	3040	Hard mortar	″	160	.050	″		1.14	.41	1.55	2.24	
	3100	To 12″ wide										
	3120	Soft old mortar	A-1	160	.050	L.F.		1.14	.41	1.55	2.24	
	3140	Hard mortar	″	140	.057	″		1.31	.46	1.77	2.55	
	4000	Fireplace, brick, 30″ x 24″ opening										
	4020	Soft old mortar	A-1	2	4	Ea.		91.50	32.50	124	179	
	4040	Hard mortar		1.25	6.400			146	52	198	286	
	4100	Stone, soft old mortar		1.50	5.333			122	43	165	239	
	4120	Hard mortar		1	8	↓		183	65	248	360	
	5000	Veneers, brick, soft old mortar		140	.057	S.F.		1.31	.46	1.77	2.55	
	5020	Hard mortar		125	.064			1.46	.52	1.98	2.86	
	5100	Granite and marble, 2″ thick		180	.044			1.02	.36	1.38	1.99	
	5120	4″ thick		170	.047			1.08	.38	1.46	2.10	
	5140	Stone, 4″ thick		180	.044			1.02	.36	1.38	1.99	
	5160	8″ thick		175	.046	↓		1.04	.37	1.41	2.04	
	5400	Alternate pricing method, stone, 4″ thick		60	.133	C.F.		3.05	1.08	4.13	5.95	
	5420	8″ thick	↓	85	.094	″		2.15	.76	2.91	4.20	
620	0010	**MILLWORK AND TRIM DEMOLITION**										**620**
	1000	Cabinets, wood, base cabinets	2 Clab	80	.200	L.F.		4.57		4.57	7.15	
	1020	Wall cabinets	″	80	.200	″		4.57		4.57	7.15	
	1060	Remove and reset, base cabinets	2 Carp	18	.889	Ea.		26		26	40.50	
	1070	Wall cabinets	″	20	.800	″		23.50		23.50	36.50	
	1100	Steel, painted, base cabinets	2 Clab	60	.267	L.F.		6.10		6.10	9.55	
	1120	Wall cabinets		60	.267	″		6.10		6.10	9.55	
	1200	Casework, large area		320	.050	S.F.		1.14		1.14	1.79	
	1220	Selective		200	.080	″		1.83		1.83	2.86	
	1500	Counter top, minimum		200	.080	L.F.		1.83		1.83	2.86	
	1510	Maximum	↓	120	.133			3.05		3.05	4.77	
	1550	Remove and reset, minimum	2 Carp	50	.320			9.35		9.35	14.60	
	1560	Maximum	″	40	.400	↓		11.65		11.65	18.25	
	2000	Paneling, 4′ x 8′ sheets, 1/4″ thick	2 Clab	2,000	.008	S.F.		.18		.18	.29	
	2100	Boards, 1″ x 4″		700	.023			.52		.52	.82	
	2120	1″ x 6″		750	.021			.49		.49	.76	
	2140	1″ x 8″		800	.020	↓		.46		.46	.72	
	3000	Trim, baseboard, to 6″ wide		1,200	.013	L.F.		.30		.30	.48	
	3040	12″ wide	↓	1,000	.016			.37		.37	.57	
	3080	Remove and reset, minimum	2 Carp	400	.040			1.17		1.17	1.82	
	3090	Maximum	″	300	.053			1.55		1.55	2.43	
	3100	Ceiling trim	2 Clab	1,000	.016			.37		.37	.57	
	3120	Chair rail		1,200	.013			.30		.30	.48	
	3140	Railings with balusters		240	.067	↓		1.52		1.52	2.38	
	3160	Wainscoting	↓	700	.023	S.F.		.52		.52	.82	
690	0010	**ROOFING AND SIDING DEMOLITION**										**690**
	1000	Deck, roof, concrete plank	B-13	1,680	.033	S.F.		.82	.37	1.19	1.69	
	1100	Gypsum plank		3,900	.014			.36	.16	.52	.73	
	1150	Metal decking	↓	3,500	.016			.40	.18	.58	.81	
	1200	Wood, boards, tongue and groove, 2″ x 6″	2 Clab	960	.017			.38		.38	.60	
	1220	2″ x 10″		1,040	.015			.35		.35	.55	
	1280	Standard planks, 1″ x 6″		1,080	.015			.34		.34	.53	
	1320	1″ x 8″		1,160	.014			.32		.32	.49	
	1340	1″ x 12″		1,200	.013			.30		.30	.48	
	1350	Plywood, to 1″ thick	↓	2,000	.008	↓		.18		.18	.29	

2 SITE CONSTRUCTION

			CREW	DAILY OUTPUT	LABOR-HOURS	UNIT	2001 BARE COSTS				TOTAL INCL O&P	
	02225	Selective Demolition					MAT.	LABOR	EQUIP.	TOTAL		
690	2000	Gutters, aluminum or wood, edge hung	1 Clab	240	.033	L.F.		.76		.76	1.19	690
	2100	Built-in		100	.080	"		1.83		1.83	2.86	
	2500	Roof accessories, plumbing vent flashing		14	.571	Ea.		13.05		13.05	20.50	
	2600	Adjustable metal chimney flashing		9	.889	"		20.50		20.50	32	
	2650	Coping, sheet metal, up to 12" wide		240	.033	L.F.		.76		.76	1.19	
	2660	Concrete, up to 12" wide	2 Clab	160	.100	"		2.29		2.29	3.58	
	3000	Roofing, built-up, 5 ply roof, no gravel	B-2	1,600	.025	S.F.		.58		.58	.91	
	3001	Including gravel		890	.045			1.04		1.04	1.63	
	3100	Gravel removal, minimum		5,000	.008			.19		.19	.29	
	3120	Maximum		2,000	.020			.47		.47	.73	
	3400	Roof insulation board, up to 2" thick		3,900	.010			.24		.24	.37	
	3450	Roll roofing, cold adhesive	1 Clab	12	.667	Sq.		15.25		15.25	24	
	4000	Shingles, asphalt strip, 1 layer	B-2	3,500	.011	S.F.		.27		.27	.42	
	4100	Slate		2,500	.016			.37		.37	.58	
	4300	Wood		2,200	.018			.42		.42	.66	
	4500	Skylight to 10 S.F.	1 Clab	8	1	Ea.		23		23	36	
	5000	Siding, metal, horizontal		444	.018	S.F.		.41		.41	.64	
	5020	Vertical		400	.020			.46		.46	.72	
	5200	Wood, boards, vertical		400	.020			.46		.46	.72	
	5220	Clapboards, horizontal		380	.021			.48		.48	.75	
	5240	Shingles		350	.023			.52		.52	.82	
	5260	Textured plywood		725	.011			.25		.25	.39	
720	0010	**DISPOSAL ONLY** Urban buildings with salvage value allowed										720
	0020	Including loading and 5 mile haul to dump										
	0200	Steel frame	B-3	430	.112	C.Y.		2.77	4.04	6.81	8.70	
	0300	Concrete frame		365	.132			3.26	4.76	8.02	10.30	
	0400	Masonry construction		445	.108			2.68	3.90	6.58	8.40	
	0500	Wood frame		247	.194			4.82	7.05	11.87	15.20	
730	0010	**RUBBISH HANDLING** The following are to be added to the										730
	0020	demolition prices										
	0400	Chute, circular, prefabricated steel, 18" diameter	B-1	40	.600	L.F.	19.60	14.10		33.70	43.50	
	0440	30" diameter	"	30	.800	"	26.50	18.80		45.30	59	
	0725	Dumpster, weekly rental, 1 dump/week, 20C.Y. capacity (8Tons)				Week					425	
	0800	30 C.Y. capacity (10 Tons)									640	
	0840	40 C.Y. capacity (13 Tons)									775	
	1000	Dust partition, 6 mil polyethylene, 4' x 8' panels, 1" x 3" frame	2 Carp	2,000	.008	S.F.	.17	.23		.40	.54	
	1080	2" x 4" frame	"	2,000	.008	"	.33	.23		.56	.72	
	2000	Load, haul to chute & dumping into chute, 50' haul	2 Clab	24	.667	C.Y.		15.25		15.25	24	
	2040	100' haul		16.50	.970			22		22	34.50	
	2080	Over 100' haul, add per 100 L.F.		35.50	.451			10.30		10.30	16.10	
	2120	In elevators, per 10 floors, add		140	.114			2.61		2.61	4.09	
	3000	Loading & trucking, including 2 mile haul, chute loaded	B-16	45	.711			16.80	10.75	27.55	38	
	3040	Hand loading truck, 50' haul	"	48	.667			15.75	10.05	25.80	35.50	
	3080	Machine loading truck	B-17	120	.267			6.55	4.59	11.14	15.15	
	5000	Haul, per mile, up to 8 C.Y. truck	B-34B	1,165	.007			.16	.41	.57	.71	
	5100	Over 8 C.Y. truck	"	1,550	.005			.12	.31	.43	.53	
740	0010	**DUMP CHARGES** Typical urban city, tipping fees only										740
	0100	Building construction materials				Ton					55	
	0200	Trees, brush, lumber									45	
	0300	Rubbish only									50	
	0500	Reclamation station, usual charge									80	
760	0010	**SAW CUTTING**, Asphalt, up to 3" deep	B-89	1,050	.015	L.F.	.24	.40	.28	.92	1.17	760
	0020	Each additional inch of depth		1,800	.009		.06	.23	.16	.45	.60	
	0400	Concrete slabs, mesh reinforcing, up to 3" deep		980	.016		.33	.43	.30	1.06	1.34	
	0420	Each additional inch of depth		1,600	.010		.44	.26	.19	.89	1.08	

Important: See the Reference Section for critical supporting data - Reference Nos., Crews, & City Cost Indexes

SITE CONSTRUCTION | **2**

02225	Selective Demolition	CREW	DAILY OUTPUT	LABOR-HOURS	UNIT	2001 BARE COSTS				TOTAL INCL O&P	
						MAT.	LABOR	EQUIP.	TOTAL		
760	0800	Concrete walls, hydraulic saw, plain, per inch of depth	B-89B	250	.064	L.F.	.30	1.67	2.06	4.03	5.15	**760**
	0820	Rod reinforcing, per inch of depth		150	.107		.42	2.78	3.43	6.63	8.45	
	1200	Masonry walls, hydraulic saw, brick, per inch of depth		300	.053		.30	1.39	1.72	3.41	4.33	
	1220	Block walls, solid, per inch of depth	↓	250	.064		.31	1.67	2.06	4.04	5.15	
	2000	Brick or masonry w/hand held saw, per inch of depth	A-1	125	.064		.25	1.46	.52	2.23	3.13	
	5000	Wood sheathing to 1" thick, on walls	1 Carp	200	.040			1.17		1.17	1.82	
	5020	On roof	"	250	.032	↓		.93		.93	1.46	
	9950	See also div. 02210-320 core drilling										
790	0010	**TORCH CUTTING** Steel, 1" thick plate	1 Clab	32	.250	L.F.		5.70		5.70	8.95	**790**
	0040	1" diameter bar	"	210	.038	Ea.		.87		.87	1.36	
	1000	Oxygen lance cutting, reinforced concrete walls										
	1040	12" to 16" thick walls	1 Clab	10	.800	L.F.		18.30		18.30	28.50	
	1080	24" thick walls	"	6	1.333	"		30.50		30.50	47.50	
840	0010	**WALLS AND PARTITIONS DEMOLITION**										**840**
	0100	Brick, 4" to 12" thick	B-9C	220	.182	C.F.		4.23	.80	5.03	7.50	
	0200	Concrete block, 4" thick		1,000	.040	S.F.		.93	.18	1.11	1.65	
	0280	8" thick	↓	810	.049			1.15	.22	1.37	2.04	
	0300	Exterior stucco 1" thick over netting	B-9	3,200	.013			.29	.06	.35	.51	
	1000	Drywall, nailed	1 Clab	1,000	.008			.18		.18	.29	
	1020	Glued and nailed		900	.009			.20		.20	.32	
	1500	Fiberboard, nailed		900	.009			.20		.20	.32	
	1520	Glued and nailed		800	.010			.23		.23	.36	
	2000	Movable walls, metal, 5' high		300	.027			.61		.61	.95	
	2020	8' high	↓	400	.020			.46		.46	.72	
	2200	Metal or wood studs, finish 2 sides, fiberboard	B-1	520	.046			1.09		1.09	1.70	
	2250	Lath and plaster		260	.092			2.17		2.17	3.40	
	2300	Plasterboard (drywall)		520	.046			1.09		1.09	1.70	
	2350	Plywood	↓	450	.053			1.25		1.25	1.96	
	3000	Plaster, lime and horsehair, on wood lath	1 Clab	400	.020			.46		.46	.72	
	3020	On metal lath		335	.024			.55		.55	.85	
	3400	Gypsum or perlite, on gypsum lath		410	.020			.45		.45	.70	
	3420	On metal lath	↓	300	.027			.61		.61	.95	
	3600	Plywood, one side	B-1	1,500	.016			.38		.38	.59	
	3750	Terra cotta block and plaster, to 6" thick	"	175	.137	↓		3.23		3.23	5.05	
	3800	Toilet partitions, slate or marble	1 Clab	5	1.600	Ea.		36.50		36.50	57	
	3820	Hollow metal	"	8	1	"		23		23	36	
	5000	Wallcovering, vinyl	1 Pape	700	.011	S.F.		.30		.30	.46	
	5040	Designer	"	480	.017	"		.44		.44	.67	
850	0010	**WINDOW DEMOLITION**										**850**
	0200	Aluminum, including trim, to 12 S.F.	1 Clab	16	.500	Ea.		11.45		11.45	17.90	
	0240	To 25 S.F.		11	.727			16.60		16.60	26	
	0280	To 50 S.F.		5	1.600			36.50		36.50	57	
	0320	Storm windows, to 12 S.F.		27	.296			6.75		6.75	10.60	
	0360	To 25 S.F.		21	.381			8.70		8.70	13.60	
	0400	To 50 S.F.		16	.500	↓		11.45		11.45	17.90	
	0600	Glass, minimum		200	.040	S.F.		.91		.91	1.43	
	0620	Maximum		150	.053	"		1.22		1.22	1.91	
	1000	Steel, including trim, to 12 S.F.		13	.615	Ea.		14.05		14.05	22	
	1020	To 25 S.F.		9	.889			20.50		20.50	32	
	1040	To 50 S.F.		4	2			45.50		45.50	71.50	
	2000	Wood, including trim, to 12 S.F.		22	.364			8.30		8.30	13	
	2020	To 25 S.F.		18	.444			10.15		10.15	15.90	
	2060	To 50 S.F.	↓	13	.615			14.05		14.05	22	
	5020	Remove and reset window, minimum	1 Carp	6	1.333	↓		39		39	61	

02225 | Selective Demolition

			CREW	DAILY OUTPUT	LABOR-HOURS	UNIT	2001 BARE COSTS				TOTAL INCL O&P	
							MAT.	LABOR	EQUIP.	TOTAL		
850	5040	Average	1 Carp	4	2	Ea.		58.50		58.50	91	850
	5080	Maximum	↓	2	4	↓		117		117	182	

02230 | Site Clearing

			CREW	DAILY OUTPUT	LABOR-HOURS	UNIT	MAT.	LABOR	EQUIP.	TOTAL	TOTAL INCL O&P	
200	0010	**CLEAR AND GRUB** Cut & chip light, trees to 6" diam.	B-7	1	48	Acre		1,175	1,050	2,225	2,975	200
	0150	Grub stumps and remove	B-30	2	12			315	780	1,095	1,325	
	0200	Cut & chip medium, trees to 12" diam.	B-7	.70	68.571			1,675	1,500	3,175	4,250	
	0250	Grub stumps and remove	B-30	1	24			625	1,550	2,175	2,675	
	0300	Cut & chip heavy, trees to 24" diam.	B-7	.30	160			3,900	3,500	7,400	9,925	
	0350	Grub stumps and remove	B-30	.50	48			1,250	3,125	4,375	5,325	
	0400	If burning is allowed, reduce cut & chip				↓					40%	
	3000	Chipping stumps, to 18" deep, 12" diam.	B-86	20	.400	Ea.		12.15	8.35	20.50	27.50	
	3040	18" diameter		16	.500			15.20	10.40	25.60	34.50	
	3080	24" diameter		14	.571			17.35	11.90	29.25	39.50	
	3100	30" diameter		12	.667			20	13.90	33.90	46	
	3120	36" diameter		10	.800			24.50	16.65	41.15	55.50	
	3160	48" diameter	↓	8	1	↓		30.50	21	51.50	69	
	5000	Tree thinning, feller buncher, conifer										
	5080	Up to 8" diameter	B-93	240	.033	Ea.		1.01	1.55	2.56	3.24	
	5120	12" diameter		160	.050			1.52	2.33	3.85	4.86	
	5240	Hardwood, up to 4" diameter		240	.033			1.01	1.55	2.56	3.24	
	5280	8" diameter		180	.044			1.35	2.07	3.42	4.32	
	5320	12" diameter	↓	120	.067	↓		2.02	3.11	5.13	6.50	
	7000	Tree removal, congested area, aerial lift truck										
	7040	8" diameter	B-85	7	5.714	Ea.		140	106	246	335	
	7080	12" diameter		6	6.667			164	124	288	390	
	7120	18" diameter		5	8			197	149	346	470	
	7160	24" diameter		4	10			246	186	432	585	
	7240	36" diameter		3	13.333			330	248	578	780	
	7280	48" diameter	↓	2	20	Acre		490	370	860	1,175	
220	0010	**CLEARING** Brush with brush saw	A-1	.25	32	Acre		730	259	989	1,425	220
	0100	By hand	"	.12	66.667			1,525	540	2,065	2,975	
	0300	With dozer, ball and chain, light clearing	B-11A	2	8			213	370	583	730	
	0400	Medium clearing		1.50	10.667			284	490	774	975	
	0500	With dozer and brush rake, light		10	1.600			42.50	73.50	116	147	
	0550	Medium brush to 4" diameter		8	2			53	92	145	183	
	0600	Heavy brush to 4" diameter	↓	6.40	2.500	↓		66.50	115	181.50	228	
	1000	Brush mowing, tractor w/rotary mower, no removal										
	1020	Light density	B-84	2	4	Acre		121	89.50	210.50	283	
	1040	Medium density		1.50	5.333			162	119	281	375	
	1080	Heavy density	↓	1	8	↓		243	179	422	565	
250	0010	**FELLING TREES & PILING** With tractor, large tract, firm										250
	0020	level terrain, no boulders, less than 12" diam. trees										
	0300	300 HP dozer, up to 400 trees/acre, 0 to 25% hardwoods	B-10M	.75	16	Acre		445	1,375	1,820	2,175	
	0340	25% to 50% hardwoods		.60	20			555	1,700	2,255	2,725	
	0370	75% to 100% hardwoods		.45	26.667			745	2,275	3,020	3,625	
	0400	500 trees/acre, 0% to 25% hardwoods		.60	20			555	1,700	2,255	2,725	
	0440	25% to 50% hardwoods		.48	25			695	2,150	2,845	3,425	
	0470	75% to 100% hardwoods		.36	33.333			930	2,850	3,780	4,575	
	0500	More than 600 trees/acre, 0 to 25% hardwoods		.52	23.077			645	1,975	2,620	3,150	
	0540	25% to 50% hardwoods		.42	28.571			795	2,450	3,245	3,925	
	0570	75% to 100% hardwoods	↓	.31	38.710	↓		1,075	3,325	4,400	5,300	
	0900	Large tract clearing per tree										
	1500	300 HP dozer, to 12" diameter, softwood	B-10M	320	.037	Ea.		1.04	3.21	4.25	5.15	
	1550	Hardwood	↓	100	.120	↓		3.34	10.25	13.59	16.40	

Important: See the Reference Section for critical supporting data - Reference Nos., Crews, & City Cost Indexes

		02230	Site Clearing	CREW	DAILY OUTPUT	LABOR-HOURS	UNIT	2001 BARE COSTS MAT.	LABOR	EQUIP.	TOTAL	TOTAL INCL O&P	
250	1600		12" to 24" diameter, softwood	B-10M	200	.060	Ea.		1.67	5.15		6.82	8.20	250
	1650		Hardwood		80	.150			4.18	12.85		17.03	20.50	
	1700		24" to 36" diameter, softwood		100	.120			3.34	10.25		13.59	16.40	
	1750		Hardwood		50	.240			6.70	20.50		27.20	32.50	
	1800		36" to 48" diameter, softwood		70	.171			4.77	14.65		19.42	23.50	
	1850		Hardwood		35	.343			9.55	29.50		39.05	47	
280	0010	**SELECTIVE CLEARING**											280
	1000		Stump removal on site by hydraulic backhoe, 1-1/2 C.Y.										
	1040		4" to 6" diameter	B-17	60	.533	Ea.		13.10	9.20		22.30	30	
	1050		8" to 12" diameter	B-30	33	.727			18.95	47		65.95	81	
	1100		14" to 24" diameter		25	.960			25	62.50		87.50	107	
	1150		26" to 36" diameter		16	1.500			39	97.50		136.50	167	
	2000		Remove selective trees, on site using chain saws and chipper,										
	2050		not incl. stumps, up to 6" diameter	B-7	18	2.667	Ea.		65	58		123	165	
	2100		8" to 12" diameter		12	4			97.50	87		184.50	248	
	2150		14" to 24" diameter		10	4.800			117	105		222	297	
	2200		26" to 36" diameter		8	6			147	131		278	370	
	2300		Machine load, 2 mile haul to dump, 12" diam. tree, add									150	225	
880	0010	**STRIPPING** Topsoil, and stockpiling, sandy loam												880
	0020		200 H.P. dozer, ideal conditions	B-10B	2,300	.005	C.Y.		.15	.32		.47	.57	
	0100		Adverse conditions	"	1,150	.010			.29	.64		.93	1.14	
	0200		300 HP dozer, ideal conditions	B-10M	3,000	.004			.11	.34		.45	.55	
	0300		Adverse conditions	"	1,650	.007			.20	.62		.82	.99	
	0400		400 HP dozer, ideal conditions	B-10X	3,900	.003			.09	.34		.43	.50	
	0500		Adverse conditions	"	2,000	.006			.17	.66		.83	.99	
	0600		Clay, dry and soft, 200 HP dozer, ideal conditions	B-10B	1,600	.007			.21	.46		.67	.83	
	0601		Strip topsoil, clay, dry & soft, 200 HP dozer, ideal conditions		1,600	.007			.21	.46		.67	.83	
	0700		Adverse conditions		800	.015			.42	.92		1.34	1.65	
	1000		Medium hard, 300 HP dozer, ideal conditions	B-10M	2,000	.006			.17	.51		.68	.82	
	1100		Adverse conditions		1,100	.011			.30	.93		1.23	1.49	
	1200		Very hard, 400 HP dozer, ideal conditions	B-10X	2,600	.005			.13	.51		.64	.76	
	1300		Adverse conditions	"	1,340	.009			.25	.99		1.24	1.47	

		02240	**Dewatering**										
500	0010	**DEWATERING** Excavate drainage trench, 2' wide, 2' deep		B-11C	90	.178	C.Y.		4.73	2.01		6.74	9.45	500
	0100		2' wide, 3' deep, with backhoe loader	"	135	.119			3.15	1.34		4.49	6.30	
	0200		Excavate sump pits by hand, light soil	1 Clab	7.10	1.127			26			26	40.50	
	0300		Heavy soil	"	3.50	2.286			52			52	81.50	
	0500		Pumping 8 hr., attended 2 hrs. per day, including 20 L.F.										
	0550		of suction hose & 100 L.F. discharge hose										
	0600		2" diaphragm pump used for 8 hours	B-10H	4	3	Day		83.50	12.05		95.55	141	
	0650		4" diaphragm pump used for 8 hours	B-10I	4	3			83.50	23		106.50	153	
	0800		8 hrs. attended, 2" diaphragm pump	B-10H	1	12			335	48		383	565	
	0900		3" centrifugal pump	B-10J	1	12			335	61.50		396.50	580	
	1000		4" diaphragm pump	B-10I	1	12			335	91.50		426.50	610	
	1100		6" centrifugal pump	B-10K	1	12			335	228		563	760	
	1300		CMP, incl. excavation 3' deep, 12" diameter	B-6	115	.209	L.F.	6.35	5.20	1.57		13.12	16.70	
	1400		18" diameter		100	.240	"	7.90	5.95	1.81		15.66	19.90	
	1600		Sump hole construction, incl. excavation and gravel, pit		1,250	.019	C.F.	.67	.48	.14		1.29	1.63	
	1700		With 12" gravel collar, 12" pipe, corrugated, 16 ga.		70	.343	L.F.	12.10	8.50	2.59		23.19	29.50	
	1800		15" pipe, corrugated, 16 ga.		55	.436		15.45	10.85	3.29		29.59	37.50	
	1900		18" pipe, corrugated, 16 ga.		50	.480		18.15	11.90	3.62		33.67	42.50	
	2000		24" pipe, corrugated, 14 ga.		40	.600		22	14.90	4.52		41.42	52	
	2200		Wood lining, up to 4' x 4', add		300	.080	SFCA	12.30	1.99	.60		14.89	17.25	
	9950		See div. 02240-900 for wellpoints										
	9960		See div. 02240-700 for deep well systems										

SITE CONSTRUCTION **2**

For expanded coverage of these items see *Means Heavy Construction Cost Data 2001*

2

SITE CONSTRUCTION

02240	Dewatering		CREW	DAILY OUTPUT	LABOR-HOURS	UNIT	2001 BARE COSTS				TOTAL INCL O&P
							MAT.	LABOR	EQUIP.	TOTAL	
700	0010	**WELLS** For dewatering 10' to 20' deep, 2' diameter										**700**
	0020	with steel casing, minimum	B-6	165	.145	V.L.F.	2	3.61	1.10	6.71	9
	0050	Average		98	.245		4	6.10	1.85	11.95	15.85
	0100	Maximum		49	.490		10	12.15	3.69	25.84	34
	0300	For pumps for dewatering, see division 01590-400-4100 to 4400									
	0500	For domestic water wells, see division 02520-900									
900	0010	**WELLPOINTS** For wellpoint equipment rental, see div. 01590-700 R02240-900										**900**
	0100	Installation and removal of single stage system									
	0110	Labor only, .75 labor-hours per L.F., minimum	1 Clab	10.70	.748	LF Hdr		17.10		17.10	26.50
	0200	2.0 labor-hours per L.F., maximum	"	4	2	"		45.50		45.50	71.50
	0400	Pump operation, 4 @ 6 hr. shifts									
	0410	Per 24 hour day	4 Eqlt	1.27	25.197	Day		725		725	1,100
	0500	Per 168 hour week, 160 hr. straight, 8 hr. double time		.18	177	Week		5,100		5,100	7,750
	0550	Per 4.3 week month		.04	800	Month		23,000		23,000	34,800
	0600	Complete installation, operation, equipment rental, fuel &									
	0610	removal of system with 2" wellpoints 5' O.C.									
	0700	100' long header, 6" diameter, first month	4 Eqlt	3.23	9.907	LF Hdr	112	285		397	555
	0800	Thereafter, per month		4.13	7.748		89.50	223		312.50	435
	1000	200' long header, 8" diameter, first month		6	5.333		100	153		253	340
	1100	Thereafter, per month		8.39	3.814		50.50	110		160.50	222
	1300	500' long header, 8" diameter, first month		10.63	3.010		39	86.50		125.50	174
	1400	Thereafter, per month		20.91	1.530		28	44		72	97
	1600	1,000' long header, 10" diameter, first month		11.62	2.754		33.50	79		112.50	157
	1700	Thereafter, per month		41.81	.765		16.75	22		38.75	52
	1900	Note: above figures include pumping 168 hrs. per week									
	1910	and include the pump operator and one stand-by pump.									

02250 | Shoring & Underpinning

			CREW	DAILY OUTPUT	LABOR-HOURS	UNIT	MAT.	LABOR	EQUIP.	TOTAL	TOTAL INCL O&P
050	0010	**GROUTING, PRESSURE** Cement and sand, 1:1 mix, minimum	B-61	124	.323	Bag	8.65	7.90	2.58	19.13	24.50	**050**
	0100	Maximum		51	.784	"	8.65	19.15	6.30	34.10	46.50
	0200	Cement and sand, 1:1 mix, minimum		250	.160	C.F.	17.25	3.91	1.28	22.44	26.50
	0300	Maximum		100	.400		26	9.75	3.20	38.95	47
	0400	Epoxy cement grout, minimum		137	.292		100	7.15	2.34	109.49	124
	0500	Maximum		57	.702		100	17.15	5.60	122.75	143
	0600	Structural epoxy grout				Gal.	45			45	49.50
	0700	Alternate pricing method: (Add for materials)									
	0710	5 person crew and equipment	B-61	1	40	Day		975	320	1,295	1,875
100	0010	**UNDERPINNING FOUNDATIONS** Including excavation,										**100**
	0020	forming, reinforcing, concrete and equipment									
	0100	5' to 16' below grade, 100 to 500 C.Y.	B-52	2.30	24.348	C.Y.	183	655	168	1,006	1,400
	0200	Over 500 C.Y.		2.50	22.400		164	605	154	923	1,300
	0400	16' to 25' below grade, 100 to 500 C.Y.		2	28		201	755	193	1,149	1,600
	0500	Over 500 C.Y.		2.10	26.667		190	720	183	1,093	1,525
	0700	26' to 40' below grade, 100 to 500 C.Y.		1.60	35		219	940	241	1,400	1,975
	0800	Over 500 C.Y.		1.80	31.111		201	835	214	1,250	1,750
	0900	For under 50 C.Y., add					10%	40%			
	1000	For 50 C.Y. to 100 C.Y., add					5%	20%			
400	0010	**SHEET PILING** Steel, not incl. wales, 22 psf, 15' excav., left in place	B-40	10.81	5.920	Ton	810	173	185	1,168	1,375	**400**
	0100	Drive, extract & salvage		6	10.667		340	310	335	985	1,250
	0300	20' deep excavation, 27 psf, left in place R02250-450		12.95	4.942		810	145	154	1,109	1,300
	0400	Drive, extract & salvage		6.55	9.771		340	286	305	931	1,175
	0600	25' deep excavation, 38 psf, left in place R02250-400		19	3.368		810	98.50	105	1,013.50	1,175
	0700	Drive, extract & salvage		10.50	6.095		340	178	190	708	875
	0900	40' deep excavation, 38 psf, left in place **CN**		21.20	3.019		810	88.50	94.50	993	1,150
	1000	Drive, extract & salvage		12.25	5.224		340	153	163	656	805

		02250	Shoring & Underpinning		CREW	DAILY OUTPUT	LABOR-HOURS	UNIT	2001 BARE COSTS				TOTAL INCL O&P	
									MAT.	LABOR	EQUIP.	TOTAL		
400	1200		15' deep excavation, 22 psf, left in place	R02250 -450	B-40	983	.065	S.F.	9.45	1.91	2.03	13.39	15.75	400
	1300		Drive, extract & salvage			656	.098		3.84	2.85	3.05	9.74	12.20	
	1500		20' deep excavation, 27 psf, left in place	R02250 -400		960	.067		11.85	1.95	2.08	15.88	18.50	
	1600		Drive, extract & salvage			640	.100		4.99	2.93	3.12	11.04	13.70	
	1800		25' deep excavation, 38 psf, left in place			1,000	.064		17.45	1.87	2	21.32	24.50	
	1900		Drive, extract & salvage			670	.096		6.85	2.79	2.98	12.62	15.35	
	2100		Rent steel sheet piling and wales, first month					Ton	180			180	198	
	2200		Per added month						18			18	19.80	
	2300		Rental piling left in place, add to rental						580			580	635	
	2500		Wales, connections & struts, 2/3 salvage						187			187	206	
	2700		High strength piling, 50,000 psi, add						40.50			40.50	44.50	
	2800		55,000 psi, add						43			43	47.50	
	3000		Tie rod, not upset, 1-1/2" to 4" diameter with turnbuckle						1,325			1,325	1,450	
	3100		No turnbuckle						1,050			1,050	1,150	
	3300		Upset, 1-3/4" to 4" diameter with turnbuckle						1,525			1,525	1,675	
	3400		No turnbuckle						1,325			1,325	1,450	
	3600		Lightweight, 18" to 28" wide, 7 ga., 9.22 psf, and											
	3610		9 ga., 8.6 psf, minimum					Lb.	.56			.56	.62	
	3700		Average						.61			.61	.67	
	3750		Maximum						.70			.70	.77	
	3900		Wood, solid sheeting, incl. wales, braces and spacers,											
	3910		drive, extract & salvage, 8' deep excavation		B-31	330	.121	S.F.	1.73	2.97	.45	5.15	7.05	
	4000		10' deep, 50 S.F./hr. in & 150 S.F./hr. out			300	.133		1.78	3.27	.50	5.55	7.60	
	4100		12' deep, 45 S.F./hr. in & 135 S.F./hr. out			270	.148		1.83	3.63	.55	6.01	8.30	
	4200		14' deep, 42 S.F./hr. in & 126 S.F./hr. out			250	.160		1.88	3.92	.60	6.40	8.90	
	4300		16' deep, 40 S.F./hr. in & 120 S.F./hr. out			240	.167		1.94	4.09	.62	6.65	9.25	
	4400		18' deep, 38 S.F./hr. in & 114 S.F./hr. out			230	.174		2.01	4.26	.65	6.92	9.55	
	4500		20' deep, 35 S.F./hr. in & 105 S.F./hr. out			210	.190		2.07	4.67	.71	7.45	10.35	
	4520		Left in place, 8' deep, 55 S.F./hr.			440	.091		3.11	2.23	.34	5.68	7.30	
	4540		10' deep, 50 S.F./hr.			400	.100		3.27	2.45	.37	6.09	7.85	
	4560		12' deep, 45 S.F./hr.			360	.111		3.46	2.72	.42	6.60	8.50	
	4565		14' deep, 42 S.F./hr.			335	.119		3.66	2.93	.45	7.04	9.10	
	4570		16' deep, 40 S.F./hr.			320	.125		3.89	3.06	.47	7.42	9.60	
	4580		18' deep, 38 S.F./hr.			305	.131		4.15	3.21	.49	7.85	10.15	
	4590		20' deep, 35 S.F./hr.			280	.143		4.44	3.50	.53	8.47	11	
	4700		Alternate pricing, left in place, 8' deep			1.76	22.727	M.B.F.	700	555	85	1,340	1,725	
	4800		Drive, extract and salvage, 8' deep			1.32	30.303	"	620	745	113	1,478	1,950	
	5000		For treated lumber add cost of treatment to lumber											
	5010		See division 06073-400											
500	0010		**SHORING** Existing building, with timber, no salvage allowance		B-51	2.20	21.818	M.B.F.	740	510	72	1,322	1,675	500
	1000		On cribbing with 35 ton screw jacks, per box and jack		"	3.60	13.333	Jack	41	310	44	395	580	
900	0010		**VIBROFLOTATION**	R02250 -900										900
	0900		Vibroflotation compacted sand cylinder, minimum		B-60	750	.075	V.L.F.		1.97	1.51	3.48	4.69	
	0950		Maximum			325	.172			4.55	3.48	8.03	10.85	
	1100		Vibro replacement compacted stone cylinder, minimum			500	.112			2.96	2.26	5.22	7.05	
	1150		Maximum			250	.224			5.90	4.52	10.42	14.10	
	1300		Mobilization and demobilization, minimum			.47	119	Total		3,150	2,400	5,550	7,475	
	1400		Maximum			.14	400	"		10,600	8,075	18,675	25,100	

02260 | Excavation Support/Protection

700	0010		**SLURRY TRENCH** Excavated slurry trench in wet soils											700
	0020		backfilled with 3000 PSI concrete, no reinforcing steel											
	0050		Minimum		C-7	333	.216	C.F.	4.80	5.35	3.02	13.17	16.85	
	0100		Maximum			200	.360	"	8.05	8.90	5.05	22	28	

SITE CONSTRUCTION 2

02200 | Site Preparation

02260 | Excavation Support/Protection

			CREW	DAILY OUTPUT	LABOR-HOURS	UNIT	2001 BARE COSTS MAT.	LABOR	EQUIP.	TOTAL	TOTAL INCL O&P	
700	0200	Alternate pricing method, minimum	C-7	150	.480	S.F.	9.60	11.90	6.70	28.20	36.50	700
	0300	Maximum	↓	120	.600		14.40	14.85	8.40	37.65	48	
	0500	Reinforced slurry trench, minimum	B-48	177	.316		7.20	8.10	11.75	27.05	33.50	
	0600	Maximum	"	69	.812	↓	24	21	30	75	91.50	
	0800	Haul for disposal, 2 mile haul, excavated material, add	B-34B	99	.081	C.Y.		1.94	4.88	6.82	8.30	
	0900	Haul bentonite castings for disposal, add	"	40	.200	"		4.79	12.05	16.84	20.50	
850	0010	**SOLDIER BEAMS & LAGGING** H piles with 3" wood sheeting										850
	0020	horizontal between piles, including removal of wales & braces										
	0100	No hydrostatic head, 15' deep, 1 line of braces, minimum	B-50	545	.205	S.F.	7.40	5.75	3.06	16.21	21	
	0200	Maximum		495	.226		8.20	6.30	3.37	17.87	23	
	0400	15' to 22' deep with 2 lines of braces, 10" H, minimum		360	.311		8.70	8.70	4.64	22.04	29	
	0500	Maximum		330	.339		9.85	9.50	5.05	24.40	32	
	0700	23' to 35' deep with 3 lines of braces, 12" H, minimum		325	.345		11.35	9.65	5.15	26.15	34	
	0800	Maximum		295	.380		12.30	10.60	5.65	28.55	37	
	1000	36' to 45' deep with 4 lines of braces, 14" H, minimum		290	.386		12.70	10.80	5.75	29.25	38	
	1100	Maximum		265	.423		13.40	11.80	6.30	31.50	41	
	1300	No hydrostatic head, left in place, 15' dp., 1 line of braces, min.		635	.176		9.85	4.93	2.63	17.41	21.50	
	1400	Maximum		575	.195		10.55	5.45	2.90	18.90	23.50	
	1600	15' to 22' deep with 2 lines of braces, minimum		455	.246		14.75	6.90	3.67	25.32	31.50	
	1700	Maximum		415	.270		16.40	7.55	4.02	27.97	35	
	1900	23' to 35' deep with 3 lines of braces, minimum		420	.267		17.55	7.45	3.98	28.98	36	
	2000	Maximum		380	.295		19.40	8.25	4.39	32.04	40	
	2200	36' to 45' deep with 4 lines of braces, minimum		385	.291		21	8.15	4.34	33.49	41	
	2300	Maximum	↓	350	.320		24.50	8.95	4.77	38.22	47	
	2350	Lagging only, 3" thick wood between piles 8' O.C., minimum	B-46	400	.120		1.64	3.14	.11	4.89	7.05	
	2370	Maximum		250	.192		2.46	5	.17	7.63	11.15	
	2400	Open sheeting no bracing, for trenches to 10' deep, min.		1,736	.028		.74	.72	.02	1.48	2.03	
	2450	Maximum	↓	1,510	.032		.82	.83	.03	1.68	2.30	
	2500	Tie-back method, add to open sheeting, add, minimum								20%	20%	
	2550	Maximum				↓				60%	60%	
	2700	Tie-backs only, based on tie-backs total length, minimum	B-46	86.80	.553	L.F.	8.60	14.45	.50	23.55	34	
	2750	Maximum		38.50	1.247	"	15.10	32.50	1.12	48.72	71.50	
	3500	Tie-backs only, typical average, 25' long		2	24	Ea.	380	630	21.50	1,031.50	1,475	
	3600	35' long	↓	1.58	30.380	"	505	795	27.50	1,327.50	1,875	

02300 | Earthwork

02305 | Equipment

			CREW	DAILY OUTPUT	LABOR-HOURS	UNIT	2001 BARE COSTS MAT.	LABOR	EQUIP.	TOTAL	TOTAL INCL O&P	
250	0010	**MOBILIZATION OR DEMOBILIZATION** Up to 50 miles [R01590-100]										250
	0020	Dozer, loader, backhoe or excavator, 70 H.P.- 250 H.P.	B-34K	6	1.333	Ea.		32	132	164	194	
	0100	Above 250 H.P		4	2			48	198	246	290	
	0300	Scraper, towed type (incl. tractor), 6 C.Y. capacity		3.75	2.133			51	211	262	310	
	0400	10 C.Y.		3.50	2.286			54.50	226	280.50	330	
	0600	Self-propelled scraper, 15 C.Y.		3.30	2.424			58	239	297	350	
	0700	24 C.Y.		3	2.667			64	263	327	390	
	0900	Shovel or dragline, 3/4 C.Y.		3.60	2.222			53	220	273	325	
	1000	1-1/2 C.Y.	↓	3	2.667			64	263	327	390	
	1100	Delivery charge for small equipment on flatbed trailer, minimum									40	
	1150	Maximum				↓					100	
	3000	For large pieces of equipment, allow for knockdown,										

			CREW	DAILY OUTPUT	LABOR-HOURS	UNIT	2001 BARE COSTS				TOTAL INCL O&P	
		02305 | Equipment					MAT.	LABOR	EQUIP.	TOTAL		
250	3001	assembly and lead and tail vehicles for highway transport R01590 -100										250

02310 | Grading

			CREW	DAILY OUTPUT	LABOR-HOURS	UNIT	MAT.	LABOR	EQUIP.	TOTAL	TOTAL INCL O&P	
440	0010	**FINE GRADE** Area to be paved with grader, small area	B-11L	400	.040	S.Y.		1.06	1.15	2.21	2.89	440
	0100	Large area		2,000	.008			.21	.23	.44	.58	
	1100	Fine grade for slab on grade, machine	↓	1,040	.015			.41	.44	.85	1.12	
	1150	Hand grading	B-18	700	.034	↓		.81	.09	.90	1.36	
460	0010	**LOAM OR TOPSOIL** Remove and stockpile on site										460
	0020	6" deep, 200' haul	B-10B	865	.014	C.Y.		.39	.85	1.24	1.52	
	0100	300' haul		520	.023			.64	1.41	2.05	2.54	
	0150	500' haul		225	.053	↓		1.49	3.27	4.76	5.85	
	0200	Alternate method: 6" deep, 200' haul		5,090	.002	S.Y.		.07	.14	.21	.26	
	0250	500' haul	↓	1,325	.009	"		.25	.55	.80	1	
	0400	Spread from pile to rough finish grade, F.E. loader, 1.5 C.Y.	B-10S	200	.060	C.Y.		1.67	1.42	3.09	4.11	
	0500	Up to 200' radius, by hand	1 Clab	14	.571	↓		13.05		13.05	20.50	
	0600	Top dress by hand, 1 C.Y. for 600 S.F.	"	11.50	.696	↓	15.35	15.90		31.25	42	
	0700	Furnish and place, truck dumped, screened, 4" deep	B-10S	1,300	.009	S.Y.	1.92	.26	.22	2.40	2.74	
	0800	6" deep	"	820	.015	"	2.46	.41	.35	3.22	3.71	

02315 | Excavation and Fill

			CREW	DAILY OUTPUT	LABOR-HOURS	UNIT	MAT.	LABOR	EQUIP.	TOTAL	TOTAL INCL O&P	
100	0010	**BACKFILL** By hand, no compaction, light soil R02315 -300	1 Clab	14	.571	C.Y.		13.05		13.05	20.50	100
	0100	Heavy soil		11	.727			16.60		16.60	26	
	0300	Compaction in 6" layers, hand tamp, add to above	↓	20.60	.388			8.85		8.85	13.90	
	0400	Roller compaction operator walking, add	B-10A	100	.120			3.34	1.11	4.45	6.30	
	0500	Air tamp, add	B-9C	190	.211			4.89	.93	5.82	8.65	
	0600	Vibrating plate, add	A-1	60	.133			3.05	1.08	4.13	5.95	
	0800	Compaction in 12" layers, hand tamp, add to above	1 Clab	34	.235			5.40		5.40	8.40	
	0900	Roller compaction operator walking, add	B-10A	150	.080			2.23	.74	2.97	4.21	
	1000	Air tamp, add	B-9	285	.140			3.26	.62	3.88	5.80	
	1100	Vibrating plate, add	A-1	90	.089			2.03	.72	2.75	3.97	
	1300	Dozer backfilling, bulk, up to 300' haul, no compaction	B-10B	1,200	.010			.28	.61	.89	1.10	
	1400	Air tamped	B-11B	240	.067			1.77	3.85	5.62	6.95	
	1600	Compacting backfill, 6" to 12" lifts, vibrating roller	B-10C	800	.015			.42	1.13	1.55	1.88	
	1700	Sheepsfoot roller	B-10D	750	.016			.45	1.07	1.52	1.86	
	1900	Dozer backfilling, trench, up to 300' haul, no compaction	B-10B	900	.013			.37	.82	1.19	1.47	
	2000	Air tamped	B-11B	235	.068			1.81	3.93	5.74	7.10	
	2200	Compacting backfill, 6" to 12" lifts, vibrating roller	B-10C	700	.017			.48	1.29	1.77	2.15	
	2300	Sheepsfoot roller	B-10D	650	.018			.51	1.24	1.75	2.15	
	2350	Spreading in 8" layers, small dozer	B-10B	1,060	.011	↓		.32	.69	1.01	1.24	
120	0010	**BACKFILL, STRUCTURAL** Dozer or F.E. loader										120
	0020	From existing stockpile, no compaction										
	2000	75 H.P., 50' haul, sand & gravel	B-10L	1,100	.011	C.Y.		.30	.24	.54	.73	
	2020	Common earth		975	.012			.34	.27	.61	.82	
	2040	Clay		850	.014			.39	.31	.70	.94	
	2400	300' haul, sand & gravel		370	.032			.90	.72	1.62	2.17	
	2420	Common earth		330	.036			1.01	.81	1.82	2.44	
	2440	Clay	↓	290	.041			1.15	.92	2.07	2.77	
	3000	105 H.P., 50' haul, sand & gravel	B-10W	1,350	.009			.25	.30	.55	.71	
	3020	Common earth		1,225	.010			.27	.33	.60	.78	
	3040	Clay		1,100	.011			.30	.36	.66	.86	
	3300	300' haul, sand & gravel		465	.026			.72	.86	1.58	2.04	
	3320	Common earth		415	.029			.81	.96	1.77	2.29	
	3340	Clay	↓	370	.032	↓		.90	1.08	1.98	2.57	

For expanded coverage of these items see *Means Heavy Construction Cost Data 2001*

SITE CONSTRUCTION 2

SITE CONSTRUCTION | **2**

02315 | Excavation and Fill

			CREW	DAILY OUTPUT	LABOR-HOURS	UNIT	MAT.	LABOR	EQUIP.	TOTAL	TOTAL INCL O&P	
120	4000	200 H.P., 50' haul, sand & gravel	B-10B	2,500	.005	C.Y.		.13	.29	.42	.52	120
	4020	Common earth		2,200	.005			.15	.33	.48	.60	
	4040	Clay		1,950	.006			.17	.38	.55	.67	
	4400	300' haul, sand & gravel		805	.015			.42	.91	1.33	1.63	
	4420	Common earth		735	.016			.45	1	1.45	1.79	
	4440	Clay		660	.018			.51	1.11	1.62	2	
	5000	300 H.P., 50' haul, sand & gravel	B-10M	3,170	.004			.11	.32	.43	.52	
	5020	Common earth		2,900	.004			.12	.35	.47	.57	
	5040	Clay		2,700	.004			.12	.38	.50	.61	
	5400	300' haul, sand & gravel		1,500	.008			.22	.68	.90	1.09	
	5420	Common earth		1,350	.009			.25	.76	1.01	1.22	
	5440	Clay		1,225	.010			.27	.84	1.11	1.34	
	6010	For trench backfill, see div. 02315-900 & 02315-940										
	6100	For compaction, see div. 02315-320										
130	0010	**BEDDING** For pipe and conduit, not incl. compaction										130
	0050	Crushed or screened bank run gravel	B-6	150	.160	C.Y.	17	3.97	1.21	22.18	26	
	0100	Crushed stone 3/4" to 1/2"		150	.160		18.80	3.97	1.21	23.98	28	
	0200	Sand, dead or bank		150	.160		3.55	3.97	1.21	8.73	11.40	
	0500	Compacting bedding in trench	A-1	90	.089			2.03	.72	2.75	3.97	
320	0010	**COMPACTION, STRUCTURAL** Steel wheel tandem roller, 5 tons `R02315 -300`	B-10E	8	1.500	Hr.		42	16.65	58.65	82.50	320
	0100	10 tons	B-10F	8	1.500	"		42	26.50	68.50	93	
	0300	Sheepsfoot or wobbly wheel roller, 8" lifts, common fill	B-10G	1,300	.009	C.Y.		.26	.47	.73	.91	
	0400	Select fill	"	1,500	.008			.22	.41	.63	.79	
	0600	Vibratory plate, 8" lifts, common fill	A-1	200	.040			.91	.32	1.23	1.79	
	0700	Select fill	"	216	.037			.85	.30	1.15	1.65	
340	0010	**DRILLING AND BLASTING** Only, rock, open face, under 1500 C.Y.	B-47	225	.107	C.Y.	1.80	2.72	3.29	7.81	9.80	340
	0100	Over 1500 C.Y.		300	.080		1.80	2.04	2.47	6.31	7.85	
	0200	Areas where blasting mats are required, under 1500 C.Y.		175	.137		1.80	3.49	4.23	9.52	12.05	
	0250	Over 1500 C.Y.		250	.096		1.80	2.45	2.96	7.21	9	
	0300	Bulk drilling and blasting, can vary greatly, average									5	
	0500	Pits, average									20	
	1300	Deep hole method, up to 1500 C.Y.	B-47	50	.480		1.80	12.25	14.80	28.85	37	
	1400	Over 1500 C.Y.		66	.364		1.80	9.25	11.25	22.30	28.50	
	1900	Restricted areas, up to 1500 C.Y.		13	1.846		1.80	47	57	105.80	137	
	2000	Over 1500 C.Y.		20	1.200		1.80	30.50	37	69.30	90.50	
	2200	Trenches, up to 1500 C.Y.		22	1.091		5.20	28	33.50	66.70	86	
	2300	Over 1500 C.Y.		26	.923		5.20	23.50	28.50	57.20	74	
	2500	Pier holes, up to 1500 C.Y.		22	1.091		1.80	28	33.50	63.30	82	
	2600	Over 1500 C.Y.		31	.774		1.80	19.75	24	45.55	59	
	2800	Boulders under 1/2 C.Y., loaded on truck, no hauling	B-100	80	.150			4.18	5.70	9.88	12.70	
	2900	Boulders, drilled, blasted	B-47	100	.240		1.80	6.10	7.40	15.30	19.60	
	3100	Jackhammer operators with foreman compressor, air tools	B-9	1	40	Day		930	176	1,106	1,650	
	3300	Track drill, compressor, operator and foreman	B-47	1	24	"		610	740	1,350	1,750	
	3500	Blasting caps				Ea.	3.10			3.10	3.41	
	3700	Explosives					.25			.25	.28	
	3900	Blasting mats, rent, for first day					90			90	99	
	4000	Per added day					30			30	33	
	4200	Preblast survey for 6 room house, individual lot, minimum	A-6	2.40	6.667			215		215	340	
	4300	Maximum	"	1.35	11.852			380		380	600	
	4500	City block within zone of influence, minimum	A-8	25,200	.001	S.F.		.04		.04	.06	
	4600	Maximum	"	15,100	.002	"		.06		.06	.10	
345	0010	**DRILLING ONLY** 2" hole for rock bolts, average	B-47	316	.076	L.F.		1.94	2.35	4.29	5.55	345
	0800	2-1/2" hole for pre-splitting, average		600	.040			1.02	1.24	2.26	2.94	
	1600	Quarry operations, 2-1/2" to 3-1/2" diameter		715	.034			.86	1.04	1.90	2.46	

Important: See the Reference Section for critical supporting data - Reference Nos., Crews, & City Cost Indexes

02315 | Excavation and Fill

		CREW	DAILY OUTPUT	LABOR-HOURS	UNIT	2001 BARE COSTS MAT.	LABOR	EQUIP.	TOTAL	TOTAL INCL O&P	
400	0010	**EXCAVATING, BULK BANK MEASURE** Common earth piled R02315 -400									**400**
	0020	For loading onto trucks, add								15%	15%	
	0050	For mobilization and demobilization, see division 02305-250 R02315 -450									
	0100	For hauling, see division 02320-200									
	0200	Backhoe, hydraulic, crawler mtd., 1 C.Y. cap. = 75 C.Y./hr.	B-12A	600	.027	C.Y.		.76	.82	1.58	2.05
	0250	1-1/2 C.Y. cap. = 100 C.Y./hr.	B-12B	800	.020			.57	.74	1.31	1.68
	0260	2 C.Y. cap. = 130 C.Y./hr.	B-12C	1,040	.015			.44	.82	1.26	1.56
	0300	3 C.Y. cap. = 160 C.Y./hr.	B-12D	1,280	.013			.36	1.54	1.90	2.24
	0310	Wheel mounted, 1/2 C.Y. cap. = 30 C.Y./hr.	B-12E	240	.067			1.90	1.33	3.23	4.33
	0360	3/4 C.Y. cap. = 45 C.Y./hr.	B-12F	360	.044			1.26	1.15	2.41	3.17
	0500	Clamshell, 1/2 C.Y. cap. = 20 C.Y./hr.	B-12G	160	.100			2.85	2.42	5.27	7
	0550	1 C.Y. cap. = 35 C.Y./hr.	B-12H	280	.057			1.63	2.21	3.84	4.89
	0950	Dragline, 1/2 C.Y. cap. = 30 C.Y./hr.	B-12I	240	.067			1.90	2.06	3.96	5.15
	1000	3/4 C.Y. cap. = 35 C.Y./hr.	"	280	.057			1.63	1.77	3.40	4.40
	1050	1-1/2 C.Y. cap. = 65 C.Y./hr.	B-12P	520	.031			.88	1.44	2.32	2.92
	1200	Front end loader, track mtd., 1-1/2 C.Y. cap. = 70 C.Y./hr.	B-10N	560	.021			.60	.55	1.15	1.51
	1250	2-1/2 C.Y. cap. = 95 C.Y./hr.	B-100	760	.016			.44	.60	1.04	1.33
	1300	3 C.Y. cap. = 130 C.Y./hr.	B-10P	1,040	.012			.32	.74	1.06	1.30
	1350	5 C.Y. cap. = 160 C.Y./hr.	B-10Q	1,280	.009			.26	.77	1.03	1.25
	1500	Wheel mounted, 3/4 C.Y. cap. = 45 C.Y./hr.	B-10R	360	.033			.93	.63	1.56	2.12
	1550	1-1/2 C.Y. cap. = 80 C.Y./hr.	B-10S	640	.019			.52	.44	.96	1.29
	1600	2-1/4 C.Y. cap. = 100 C.Y./hr.	B-10T	800	.015			.42	.49	.91	1.18
	1650	5 C.Y. cap. = 185 C.Y./hr.	B-10U	1,480	.008			.23	.55	.78	.96
	1800	Hydraulic excavator, truck mtd, 1/2 C.Y. = 30 C.Y./hr.	B-12J	240	.067			1.90	2.70	4.60	5.85
	1850	48 inch bucket, 1 C.Y. = 45 C.Y./hr.	B-12K	360	.044			1.26	2.15	3.41	4.28
	3700	Shovel, 1/2 C.Y. capacity = 55 C.Y./hr.	B-12L	440	.036			1.03	.86	1.89	2.51
	3750	3/4 C.Y. capacity = 85 C.Y./hr.	B-12M	680	.024			.67	.76	1.43	1.84
	3800	1 C.Y. capacity = 120 C.Y./hr.	B-12N	960	.017			.47	.62	1.09	1.40
	3850	1-1/2 C.Y. capacity = 160 C.Y./hr.	B-120	1,280	.013			.36	.66	1.02	1.27
	3900	3 C.Y. cap. = 250 C.Y./hr.	B-12T	2,000	.008			.23	.59	.82	.99
	4000	For soft soil or sand, deduct								15%	15%
	4100	For heavy soil or stiff clay, add								60%	60%
	4200	For wet excavation with clamshell or dragline, add								100%	100%
	4250	All other equipment, add								50%	50%
	4400	Clamshell in sheeting or cofferdam, minimum	B-12H	160	.100			2.85	3.86	6.71	8.55
	4450	Maximum	"	60	.267			7.60	10.30	17.90	23
	8000	For hauling excavated material, see div. 02320-200									
410	0010	**EXCAVATING, BULK, DOZER** Open site										**410**
	2000	75 H.P., 50' haul, sand & gravel	B-10L	460	.026	C.Y.		.73	.58	1.31	1.75
	2020	Common earth		400	.030			.84	.67	1.51	2.01
	2040	Clay		250	.048			1.34	1.06	2.40	3.21
	2200	150' haul, sand & gravel		230	.052			1.45	1.16	2.61	3.49
	2220	Common earth		200	.060			1.67	1.33	3	4.01
	2240	Clay		125	.096			2.67	2.13	4.80	6.40
	2400	300' haul, sand & gravel		120	.100			2.79	2.22	5.01	6.70
	2420	Common earth		100	.120			3.34	2.66	6	8.05
	2440	Clay		65	.185			5.15	4.09	9.24	12.35
	3000	105 H.P., 50' haul, sand & gravel	B-10W	700	.017			.48	.57	1.05	1.36
	3020	Common earth		610	.020			.55	.65	1.20	1.56
	3040	Clay		385	.031			.87	1.04	1.91	2.47
	3200	150' haul, sand & gravel		310	.039			1.08	1.29	2.37	3.07
	3220	Common earth		270	.044			1.24	1.48	2.72	3.52
	3240	Clay		170	.071			1.97	2.35	4.32	5.60
	3300	300' haul, sand & gravel		140	.086			2.39	2.85	5.24	6.80
	3320	Common earth		120	.100			2.79	3.33	6.12	7.90

SITE CONSTRUCTION | 2

2 SITE CONSTRUCTION

			CREW	DAILY OUTPUT	LABOR-HOURS	UNIT	2001 BARE COSTS				TOTAL INCL O&P
		02315 | Excavation and Fill					MAT.	LABOR	EQUIP.	TOTAL	
410	3340	Clay	B-10W	100	.120	C.Y.		3.34	3.99	7.33	9.50	410
	4000	200 H.P., 50' haul, sand & gravel	B-10B	1,400	.009			.24	.52	.76	.94
	4020	Common earth		1,230	.010			.27	.60	.87	1.08
	4040	Clay		770	.016			.43	.95	1.38	1.71
	4200	150' haul, sand & gravel		595	.020			.56	1.24	1.80	2.22
	4220	Common earth		516	.023			.65	1.42	2.07	2.56
	4240	Clay		325	.037			1.03	2.26	3.29	4.06
	4400	300' haul, sand & gravel		310	.039			1.08	2.37	3.45	4.26
	4420	Common earth		270	.044			1.24	2.72	3.96	4.88
	4440	Clay		170	.071			1.97	4.32	6.29	7.75
	5000	300 H.P., 50' haul, sand & gravel	B-10M	1,900	.006			.18	.54	.72	.87
	5020	Common earth		1,650	.007			.20	.62	.82	.99
	5040	Clay		1,025	.012			.33	1	1.33	1.60
	5200	150' haul, sand & gravel		920	.013			.36	1.12	1.48	1.78
	5220	Common earth		800	.015			.42	1.28	1.70	2.05
	5240	Clay		500	.024			.67	2.05	2.72	3.28
	5400	300' haul, sand & gravel		470	.026			.71	2.18	2.89	3.49
	5420	Common earth		410	.029			.82	2.50	3.32	4.01
	5440	Clay		250	.048			1.34	4.11	5.45	6.55
	5500	460 H.P., 50' haul, sand & gravel	B-10X	1,930	.006			.17	.69	.86	1.01
	5510	Common earth		1,680	.007			.20	.79	.99	1.17
	5520	Clay		1,050	.011			.32	1.26	1.58	1.88
	5530	150' haul, sand & gravel		1,290	.009			.26	1.03	1.29	1.53
	5540	Common earth		1,120	.011			.30	1.18	1.48	1.76
	5550	Clay		700	.017			.48	1.89	2.37	2.81
	5560	300' haul, sand & gravel		660	.018			.51	2	2.51	2.97
	5570	Common earth		575	.021			.58	2.30	2.88	3.42
	5580	Clay		350	.034			.96	3.78	4.74	5.60
	6000	700 H.P., 50' haul, sand & gravel	B-10V	3,500	.003			.10	.75	.85	.98
	6010	Common earth		3,035	.004			.11	.87	.98	1.12
	6020	Clay		1,925	.006			.17	1.36	1.53	1.77
	6030	150' haul, sand & gravel		2,025	.006			.17	1.30	1.47	1.68
	6040	Common earth		1,750	.007			.19	1.50	1.69	1.94
	6050	Clay		1,100	.011			.30	2.39	2.69	3.09
	6060	300' haul, sand & gravel		1,030	.012			.32	2.55	2.87	3.31
	6070	Common earth		900	.013			.37	2.92	3.29	3.78
	6080	Clay		550	.022			.61	4.78	5.39	6.20
430	0010	**EXCAVATION, BULK, SCRAPERS** R02315 -400										430
	0100	Elevating scraper 11 C.Y., sand & gravel 1500' haul	B-33F	690	.020	C.Y.		.57	1.34	1.91	2.35
	0150	3000' haul		610	.023			.65	1.52	2.17	2.66
	0200	5000' haul		505	.028			.78	1.83	2.61	3.21
	0300	Common earth, 1500' haul		600	.023			.66	1.54	2.20	2.70
	0350	3000' haul		530	.026			.75	1.75	2.50	3.06
	0400	5000' haul		440	.032			.90	2.10	3	3.68
	0500	Clay, 1500' haul		375	.037			1.05	2.47	3.52	4.32
	0550	3000' haul		330	.042			1.20	2.80	4	4.91
	0600	5000' haul		275	.051			1.44	3.37	4.81	5.90
	1000	Self propelled scraper, 14 C.Y. 1/4 push dozer, sand									
	1050	and gravel, 1500' haul	B-33D	920	.015	C.Y.		.43	2.02	2.45	2.88
	1100	3000' haul		805	.017			.49	2.30	2.79	3.28
	1200	5000' haul		645	.022			.61	2.87	3.48	4.09
	1300	Common earth, 1500' haul		800	.017			.49	2.32	2.81	3.30
	1350	3000' haul		700	.020			.56	2.65	3.21	3.77
	1400	5000' haul		560	.025			.71	3.31	4.02	4.72
	1500	Clay, 1500' haul		500	.028			.79	3.71	4.50	5.30

Important: See the Reference Section for critical supporting data - Reference Nos., Crews, & City Cost Indexes

02315 | Excavation and Fill

					CREW	DAILY OUTPUT	LABOR-HOURS	UNIT	2001 BARE COSTS MAT.	LABOR	EQUIP.	TOTAL	TOTAL INCL O&P	
430	1550	3000' haul		R02315 -400	B-33D	440	.032	C.Y.		.90	4.21	5.11	6	**430**
	1600	5000' haul			↓	350	.040			1.13	5.30	6.43	7.55	
	2000	21 C.Y., 1/4 push dozer, sand & gravel, 1500' haul			B-33E	1,180	.012			.33	1.85	2.18	2.55	
	2100	3000' haul				910	.015			.43	2.40	2.83	3.30	
	2200	5000' haul				750	.019			.53	2.92	3.45	4.01	
	2300	Common earth, 1500' haul				1,030	.014			.38	2.12	2.50	2.92	
	2350	3000' haul				790	.018			.50	2.77	3.27	3.81	
	2400	5000' haul				650	.022			.61	3.37	3.98	4.63	
	2500	Clay, 1500' haul				645	.022			.61	3.39	4	4.66	
	2550	3000' haul				495	.028			.80	4.42	5.22	6.10	
	2600	5000' haul			↓	405	.035			.98	5.40	6.38	7.45	
	2700	Towed, 10 C.Y., 1/4 push dozer, sand & gravel, 1500' haul			B-33B	560	.025			.71	2.57	3.28	3.91	
	2720	3000' haul				450	.031			.88	3.20	4.08	4.86	
	2730	5000' haul				365	.038			1.08	3.95	5.03	6	
	2750	Common earth, 1500' haul				420	.033			.94	3.43	4.37	5.20	
	2770	3000' haul				400	.035			.99	3.60	4.59	5.45	
	2780	5000' haul				310	.045			1.27	4.65	5.92	7.05	
	2800	Clay, 1500' haul				315	.044			1.25	4.57	5.82	6.95	
	2820	3000' haul				300	.047			1.32	4.80	6.12	7.30	
	2840	5000' haul			↓	225	.062			1.76	6.40	8.16	9.75	
	2900	15 C.Y., 1/4 push dozer, sand & gravel, 1500' haul			B-33C	800	.017			.49	1.80	2.29	2.73	
	2920	3000' haul				640	.022			.62	2.25	2.87	3.42	
	2940	5000' haul				520	.027			.76	2.77	3.53	4.21	
	2960	Common earth, 1500' haul				600	.023			.66	2.40	3.06	3.64	
	2980	3000' haul				560	.025			.71	2.57	3.28	3.91	
	3000	5000' haul				440	.032			.90	3.28	4.18	4.97	
	3020	Clay, 1500' haul				450	.031			.88	3.20	4.08	4.86	
	3040	3000' haul				420	.033			.94	3.43	4.37	5.20	
	3060	5000' haul			↓	↓	320	.044	↓		1.23	4.50	5.73	6.85	
440	0010	**EXCAVATING, STRUCTURAL** Hand, pits to 6' deep, sandy soil			1 Clab	8	1	C.Y.	23			23	36	**440**
	0100	Heavy soil or clay				4	2		45.50			45.50	71.50	
	0300	Pits 6' to 12' deep, sandy soil				5	1.600		36.50			36.50	57	
	0500	Heavy soil or clay				3	2.667		61			61	95.50	
	0700	Pits 12' to 18' deep, sandy soil				4	2		45.50			45.50	71.50	
	0900	Heavy soil or clay				2	4		91.50			91.50	143	
	1100	Hand loading trucks from stock pile, sandy soil				12	.667		15.25			15.25	24	
	1300	Heavy soil or clay			↓	8	1	↓	23			23	36	
	1500	For wet or muck hand excavation, add to above						%				50%	50%	
	2000	Machine excavation, for spread and mat footings, elevator pits,												
	2001	and small building foundations												
	2035	Common earth, hydraulic backhoe, 3/4 C.Y. bucket			B-12F	90	.178	C.Y.		5.05	4.60	9.65	12.70	
	2040	1 C.Y. bucket			B-12A	108	.148			4.21	4.55	8.76	11.40	
	2050	1-1/2 C.Y. bucket			B-12B	144	.111			3.16	4.12	7.28	9.30	
	2060	2 C.Y. bucket			B-12C	200	.080			2.28	4.27	6.55	8.15	
	2070	Sand and gravel, 3/4 C.Y. bucket			B-12F	100	.160			4.55	4.14	8.69	11.45	
	2080	1 C.Y. bucket			B-12A	120	.133			3.79	4.09	7.88	10.25	
	2090	1-1/2 C.Y. bucket			B-12B	160	.100			2.85	3.71	6.56	8.40	
	3000	2 C.Y. bucket			B-12C	220	.073			2.07	3.89	5.96	7.40	
	3010	Clay, till, or blasted rock, 3/4 C.Y. bucket			B-12F	80	.200			5.70	5.15	10.85	14.30	
	3020	1 C.Y. bucket			B-12A	95	.168			4.79	5.15	9.94	12.95	
	3030	1-1/2 C.Y. bucket			B-12B	130	.123			3.50	4.56	8.06	10.30	
	3040	2 C.Y. bucket			B-12C	175	.091	↓		2.60	4.89	7.49	9.30	
	9010	For mobilization or demobilization, see div. 02305-250												
	9020	For dewatering, see div. 02240-500												
	9022	For larger structures, see Bulk Excavation, div. 02315-400												

2 SITE CONSTRUCTION

			CREW	DAILY OUTPUT	LABOR-HOURS	UNIT	2001 BARE COSTS				TOTAL INCL O&P	
	02315	**Excavation and Fill**					MAT.	LABOR	EQUIP.	TOTAL		
440	9024	For loading onto trucks, add								15%		**440**
	9026	For hauling, see div. 02320-200										
	9030	For sheeting or soldier beams/lagging, see div. 02250 & 02260										
	9040	For trench excavation of strip footings, see div. 02315-900										
500	0010	**FILL** Borrow, load, 1 mile haul, spread with dozer										**500**
	0020	for embankments	B-15	1,200	.023	C.Y.	5	.60	1.42	7.02	7.95	
	0100	Select fill for shoulders & embankments	"	1,200	.023	"	7.60	.60	1.42	9.62	10.80	
	0201	For hauling over 1 mile, add to above per C.Y., div. 02320-200				Mile				.62	.82	
505	0010	**FILL** Spread dumped material, by dozer, no compaction	B-10B	1,000	.012	C.Y.		.33	.74	1.07	1.32	**505**
	0100	By hand	1 Clab	12	.667	"		15.25		15.25	24	
	0500	Gravel fill, compacted, under floor slabs, 4" deep	B-37	10,000	.005	S.F.	.15	.12	.01	.28	.36	
	0600	6" deep		8,600	.006		.23	.13	.02	.38	.48	
	0700	9" deep		7,200	.007		.38	.16	.02	.56	.69	
	0800	12" deep		6,000	.008		.53	.19	.02	.74	.90	
	1000	Alternate pricing method, 4" deep		120	.400	C.Y.	11.35	9.65	1.11	22.11	29	
	1100	6" deep		160	.300		11.35	7.25	.83	19.43	24.50	
	1200	9" deep		200	.240		11.35	5.80	.67	17.82	22	
	1300	12" deep		220	.218		11.35	5.25	.61	17.21	21.50	
	1500	For fill under exterior paving, see division 02720-200										
	1600	For flowable fill, see division 03310-220										
900	0010	**EXCAVATING, TRENCH** or continuous footing, common earth										**900**
	0020	No sheeting or dewatering included										
	0050	1' to 4' deep, 3/8 C.Y. tractor loader/backhoe	B-11C	150	.107	C.Y.		2.84	1.21	4.05	5.70	
	0060	1/2 C.Y. tractor loader/backhoe	B-11M	200	.080			2.13	1.14	3.27	4.53	
	0090	4' to 6' deep, 1/2 C.Y. tractor loader/backhoe	"	200	.080			2.13	1.14	3.27	4.53	
	0100	5/8 C.Y. hydraulic backhoe	B-12Q	250	.064			1.82	1.44	3.26	4.34	
	0110	3/4 C.Y. hydraulic backhoe	B-12F	300	.053			1.52	1.38	2.90	3.82	
	0300	1/2 C.Y. hydraulic excavator, truck mounted	B-12J	200	.080			2.28	3.24	5.52	7	
	0500	6' to 10' deep, 3/4 C.Y. hydraulic backhoe, 6' to 10' deep	B-12F	225	.071			2.02	1.84	3.86	5.10	
	0510	1 C.Y. hydraulic backhoe	B-12A	400	.040			1.14	1.23	2.37	3.07	
	0600	1 C.Y. hydraulic excavator, truck mounted	B-12K	400	.040			1.14	1.94	3.08	3.85	
	0610	1-1/2 C.Y. hydraulic backhoe	B-12B	600	.027			.76	.99	1.75	2.24	
	0900	10' to 14' deep, 3/4 C.Y. hydraulic backhoe	B-12F	200	.080			2.28	2.07	4.35	5.75	
	0910	1 C.Y. hydraulic backhoe	B-12A	360	.044			1.26	1.36	2.62	3.41	
	1000	1-1/2 C.Y. hydraulic backhoe	B-12B	540	.030			.84	1.10	1.94	2.49	
	1300	14' to 20' deep, 1 C.Y. hydraulic backhoe	B-12A	320	.050			1.42	1.53	2.95	3.84	
	1310	1-1/2 C.Y. hydraulic backhoe	B-12B	480	.033			.95	1.24	2.19	2.80	
	1320	2-1/2 C.Y. hydraulic backhoe	B-12S	850	.019			.54	1.83	2.37	2.82	
	1400	By hand with pick and shovel 2' to 6' deep, light soil	1 Clab	8	1			23		23	36	
	1500	Heavy soil	"	4	2			45.50		45.50	71.50	
	1700	For tamping backfilled trenches, air tamp, add	A-1	100	.080			1.83	.65	2.48	3.57	
	1900	Vibrating plate, add	B-18	230	.104			2.45	.26	2.71	4.13	
	2100	Trim sides and bottom for concrete pours, common earth		1,500	.016	S.F.		.38	.04	.42	.63	
	2300	Hardpan		600	.040	"		.94	.10	1.04	1.58	
	2400	Pier and spread footing excavation, add to above				C.Y.				30%	30%	
	3000	Backfill trench, F.E. loader, wheel mtd., 1 C.Y. bucket										
	3020	Minimal haul	B-10R	400	.030	C.Y.		.84	.57	1.41	1.91	
	3040	100' haul	"	200	.060			1.67	1.14	2.81	3.80	
	3080	2-1/4 C.Y. bucket, minimum haul	B-10T	600	.020			.56	.65	1.21	1.57	
	3090	100' haul	"	300	.040			1.11	1.31	2.42	3.14	
940	0010	**EXCAVATING, UTILITY TRENCH** Common earth										**940**
	0050	Trenching with chain trencher, 12 H.P., operator walking										
	0100	4" wide trench, 12" deep	B-53	800	.010	L.F.		.29	.12	.41	.57	
	0150	18" deep		750	.011			.31	.13	.44	.60	
	0200	24" deep		700	.011			.33	.14	.47	.65	
	0300	6" wide trench, 12" deep		650	.012			.35	.15	.50	.70	

Important: See the Reference Section for critical supporting data - Reference Nos., Crews, & City Cost Indexes

02315 | Excavation and Fill

			CREW	DAILY OUTPUT	LABOR-HOURS	UNIT	2001 BARE COSTS				TOTAL INCL O&P
							MAT.	LABOR	EQUIP.	TOTAL	
940	0350	18" deep	B-53	600	.013	L.F.		.38	.16	.54	.76	940
	0400	24" deep		550	.015			.42	.18	.60	.82	
	0450	36" deep		450	.018			.51	.22	.73	1.01	
	0600	8" wide trench, 12" deep		475	.017			.48	.20	.68	.95	
	0650	18" deep		400	.020			.58	.24	.82	1.14	
	0700	24" deep		350	.023			.66	.28	.94	1.30	
	0750	36" deep	▼	300	.027	▼		.77	.32	1.09	1.52	
	1000	Backfill by hand including compaction, add										
	1050	4" wide trench, 12" deep	A-1	800	.010	L.F.		.23	.08	.31	.45	
	1100	18" deep		530	.015			.34	.12	.46	.67	
	1150	24" deep		400	.020			.46	.16	.62	.90	
	1300	6" wide trench, 12" deep		540	.015			.34	.12	.46	.66	
	1350	18" deep		405	.020			.45	.16	.61	.89	
	1400	24" deep		270	.030			.68	.24	.92	1.32	
	1450	36" deep		180	.044			1.02	.36	1.38	1.99	
	1600	8" wide trench, 12" deep		400	.020			.46	.16	.62	.90	
	1650	18" deep		265	.030			.69	.24	.93	1.35	
	1700	24" deep		200	.040			.91	.32	1.23	1.79	
	1750	36" deep	▼	135	.059	▼		1.35	.48	1.83	2.65	
	2000	Chain trencher, 40 H.P. operator riding										
	2050	6" wide trench and backfill, 12" deep	B-54	1,200	.007	L.F.		.19	.16	.35	.47	
	2100	18" deep		1,000	.008			.23	.20	.43	.57	
	2150	24" deep		975	.008			.24	.20	.44	.58	
	2200	36" deep		900	.009			.26	.22	.48	.63	
	2250	48" deep		750	.011			.31	.26	.57	.75	
	2300	60" deep		650	.012			.35	.30	.65	.87	
	2400	8" wide trench and backfill, 12" deep		1,000	.008			.23	.20	.43	.57	
	2450	18" deep		950	.008			.24	.21	.45	.60	
	2500	24" deep		900	.009			.26	.22	.48	.63	
	2550	36" deep		800	.010			.29	.25	.54	.71	
	2600	48" deep		650	.012			.35	.30	.65	.87	
	2700	12" wide trench and backfill, 12" deep		975	.008			.24	.20	.44	.58	
	2750	18" deep		860	.009			.27	.23	.50	.66	
	2800	24" deep		800	.010			.29	.25	.54	.71	
	2850	36" deep		725	.011			.32	.27	.59	.78	
	3000	16" wide trench and backfill, 12" deep		835	.010			.28	.24	.52	.68	
	3050	18" deep		750	.011			.31	.26	.57	.75	
	3100	24" deep	▼	700	.011	▼		.33	.28	.61	.81	
	3200	Compaction with vibratory plate, add									50%	50%	
	5100	Hand excavate and trim for pipe bells after trench excavation										
	5200	8" pipe	1 Clab	155	.052	L.F.		1.18		1.18	1.85	
	5300	18" pipe	"	130	.062	"		1.41		1.41	2.20	

02320 | Hauling

			CREW	DAILY OUTPUT	LABOR-HOURS	UNIT	MAT.	LABOR	EQUIP.	TOTAL	TOTAL INCL O&P
200	0011	HAULING Excavated or borrow material, loose cubic yards										200
	0015	no loading included, highway haulers										
	0020	6 C.Y. dump truck, 1/4 mile round trip, 5.0 loads/hr.	B-34A	195	.041	C.Y.		.98	1.90	2.88	3.59	
	0030	1/2 mile round trip, 4.1 loads/hr.		160	.050			1.20	2.32	3.52	4.38	
	0040	1 mile round trip, 3.3 loads/hr.		130	.062			1.47	2.85	4.32	5.40	
	0100	2 mile round trip, 2.6 loads/hr.		100	.080			1.92	3.70	5.62	7	
	0150	3 mile round trip, 2.1 loads/hr.		80	.100			2.40	4.63	7.03	8.75	
	0200	4 mile round trip, 1.8 loads/hr.	▼	70	.114			2.74	5.30	8.04	10	
	0310	12 C.Y. dump truck, 1/4 mile round trip 3.7 loads/hr.	B-34B	288	.028			.67	1.68	2.35	2.86	
	0320	1/2 mile round trip, 3.2 loads/hr.		250	.032			.77	1.93	2.70	3.29	
	0330	1 mile round trip 2.7, loads/hr.		210	.038			.91	2.30	3.21	3.92	
	0400	2 mile round trip, 2.2 loads/hr.	▼	180	.044	▼		1.06	2.68	3.74	4.58	

Note: R02315-400 reference appears near item 0011.

02320 | Hauling

			CREW	DAILY OUTPUT	LABOR-HOURS	UNIT	MAT.	LABOR	EQUIP.	TOTAL	TOTAL INCL O&P	
200	0450	3 mile round trip, 1.9 loads/hr.	B-34B	170	.047	C.Y.		1.13	2.84	3.97	4.84	200
	0500	4 mile round trip, 1.6 loads/hr.		125	.064			1.53	3.86	5.39	6.60	
	0540	5 mile round trip, 1 load/hr.		78	.103			2.46	6.20	8.66	10.55	
	0550	10 mile round trip, 0.60 load/hr.		58	.138			3.30	8.30	11.60	14.20	
	0560	20 mile round trip, 0.4 load/hr.		39	.205			4.91	12.40	17.31	21	
	0600	16.5 C.Y. dump trailer, 1 mile round trip, 2.6 loads/hr.	B-34C	280	.029			.68	1.98	2.66	3.22	
	0700	2 mile round trip, 2.1 loads/hr.		225	.036			.85	2.46	3.31	4	
	1000	3 mile round trip, 1.8 loads/hr.		193	.041			.99	2.87	3.86	4.67	
	1100	4 mile round trip, 1.6 loads/hr.		172	.047			1.11	3.22	4.33	5.25	
	1110	5 mile round trip, 1 load/hr.		108	.074			1.77	5.10	6.87	8.35	
	1120	10 mile round trip, .60 load/hr.		80	.100			2.40	6.90	9.30	11.25	
	1130	20 mile round trip, .4 load/hr.		54	.148			3.55	10.25	13.80	16.65	
	1150	20 C.Y. dump trailer, 1 mile round trip, 2.5 loads/hr.	B-34D	325	.025			.59	1.72	2.31	2.79	
	1200	2 mile round trip, 2 loads/hr.		260	.031			.74	2.15	2.89	3.49	
	1220	3 mile round trip, 1.7 loads/hr.		221	.036			.87	2.53	3.40	4.10	
	1240	4 mile round trip, 1.5 loads/hr.		195	.041			.98	2.87	3.85	4.65	
	1245	5 mile round trip, 1.1 load/hr.		143	.056			1.34	3.91	5.25	6.35	
	1250	10 mile round trip, .75 load/hr.		110	.073			1.74	5.10	6.84	8.25	
	1255	20 mile round trip, .5 load/hr.		78	.103			2.46	7.15	9.61	11.65	
	1300	Hauling in medium traffic, add								20%	20%	
	1400	Heavy traffic, add								30%	30%	
	1600	Grading at dump, or embankment if required, by dozer	B-10B	1,000	.012			.33	.74	1.07	1.32	
	1800	Spotter at fill or cut, if required	1 Clab	8	1	Hr.		23		23	36	

R02315 -400

02325 | Dredging

			CREW	DAILY OUTPUT	LABOR-HOURS	UNIT	MAT.	LABOR	EQUIP.	TOTAL	TOTAL INCL O&P	
250	0010	**DREDGING** Mobilization and demobilization., add to below, minimum	B-8	.53	120	Total	3,100	4,475		7,575	9,650	250
	0100	Maximum	"	.10	640	"	16,400	23,700		40,100	51,000	
	0300	Barge mounted clamshell excavation into scows,										
	0310	Dumped 20 miles at sea, minimum	B-57	310	.155	C.Y.		4.03	3.92	7.95	10.50	
	0400	Maximum	"	213	.225	"		5.85	5.70	11.55	15.30	
	0500	Barge mounted dragline or clamshell, hopper dumped,										
	0510	pumped 1000' to shore dump, minimum	B-57	340	.141	C.Y.		3.67	3.58	7.25	9.60	
	0525	All pumping uses 2000 gallons of water per cubic yard										
	0600	Maximum	B-57	243	.198	C.Y.		5.15	5	10.15	13.40	
	1000	Hydraulic method, pumped 1000' to shore dump, minimum		460	.104			2.72	2.64	5.36	7.10	
	1100	Maximum		310	.155			4.03	3.92	7.95	10.50	
	1400	Into scows dumped 20 miles, minimum		425	.113			2.94	2.86	5.80	7.65	
	1500	Maximum		243	.198			5.15	5	10.15	13.40	
	1600	For inland rivers and canals in South, deduct								30%	30%	

02340 | Soil Stabilization

			CREW	DAILY OUTPUT	LABOR-HOURS	UNIT	MAT.	LABOR	EQUIP.	TOTAL	TOTAL INCL O&P	
160	0010	**CALCIUM CHLORIDE** Delivered, 100 lb. bags, truckload lots				Ton	415			415	460	160
	0200	Solution, 4 lb. flake per gallon, tank truck delivery				Gal.	.88			.88	.97	

02360 | Soil Treatment

			CREW	DAILY OUTPUT	LABOR-HOURS	UNIT	MAT.	LABOR	EQUIP.	TOTAL	TOTAL INCL O&P	
800	0010	**TERMITE PRETREATMENT**										800
	0020	Slab and walls, residential	1 Skwk	1,200	.007	SF Flr.	.24	.20		.44	.57	
	0100	Commercial, minimum		2,496	.003		.26	.10		.36	.44	
	0200	Maximum		1,645	.005		.39	.15		.54	.66	
	0400	Insecticides for termite control, minimum		14.20	.563	Gal.	10.60	16.80		27.40	38	
	0500	Maximum		11	.727	"	18.10	21.50		39.60	54	

02370 | Erosion & Sedimentation Control

			CREW	DAILY OUTPUT	LABOR-HOURS	UNIT	MAT.	LABOR	EQUIP.	TOTAL	TOTAL INCL O&P	
300	0010	**RIP-RAP** Random, broken stone										300
	0100	Machine placed for slope protection	B-12G	62	.258	C.Y.	18.80	7.35	6.25	32.40	38.50	

02370 | Erosion & Sedimentation Control

			CREW	DAILY OUTPUT	LABOR-HOURS	UNIT	2001 BARE COSTS				TOTAL INCL O&P	
							MAT.	LABOR	EQUIP.	TOTAL		
300	0110	3/8 to 1/4 C.Y. pieces, grouted	B-13	80	.700	S.Y.	33.50	17.30	7.85	58.65	72.50	300
	0200	18" minimum thickness, not grouted	"	53	1.057	"	19.70	26	11.90	57.60	75	
	0300	Dumped, 50 lb. average	B-11A	800	.020	Ton	10.50	.53	.92	11.95	13.40	
	0350	100 lb. average		700	.023		15	.61	1.05	16.66	18.60	
	0370	300 lb. average		600	.027		17.50	.71	1.23	19.44	21.50	
	0400	Gabions, galvanized steel mesh mats or boxes, stone filled, 6" deep	B-13	200	.280	S.Y.	13.35	6.95	3.15	23.45	29	
	0500	9" deep		163	.344		17.20	8.50	3.86	29.56	36.50	
	0600	12" deep		153	.366		20.50	9.05	4.11	33.66	41	
	0700	18" deep		102	.549		23.50	13.60	6.15	43.25	53.50	
	0800	36" deep		60	.933		40	23	10.50	73.50	91	
550	0010	EROSION CONTROL Jute mesh, 100 S.Y. per roll, 4' wide, stapled	B-80A	2,400	.010	S.Y.	.58	.23	.08	.89	1.08	550
	0100	Plastic netting, stapled, 2" x 1" mesh, 20 mil	B-1	2,500	.010		.42	.23		.65	.81	
	0200	Polypropylene mesh, stapled, 6.5 oz./S.Y.		2,500	.010		1	.23		1.23	1.45	
	0300	Tobacco netting, or jute mesh #2, stapled		2,500	.010		.07	.23		.30	.43	
	1000	Silt fence, polypropylene, 3' high, ideal conditions	2 Clab	1,600	.010	L.F.	.30	.23		.53	.69	
	1100	Adverse conditions	"	950	.017	"	.30	.38		.68	.93	
	1200	Place and remove hay bales	A-2	3	8	Ton	51	184	52.50	287.50	400	
	1250	Hay bales, staked	"	2,500	.010	L.F.	2.04	.22	.06	2.32	2.65	

02390 | Shore Protect/Mooring Structures

			CREW	DAILY OUTPUT	LABOR-HOURS	UNIT	MAT.	LABOR	EQUIP.	TOTAL	INCL O&P	
220	0010	DOCKS Floating, recreational, prefabricated galvanized steel with										220
	0020	polyethylene encased polystyrene, no pilings included	F-3	330	.121	S.F.	23	3.58	1.56	28.14	33	
	0200	Pile supported, shore constructed, bare, 3" decking		130	.308		17.25	9.10	3.96	30.31	37.50	
	0250	4" decking		120	.333		16.45	9.85	4.29	30.59	38	
	0400	Floating, small boat, prefab, no shore facilities, minimum		250	.160		8.35	4.73	2.06	15.14	18.80	
	0500	Maximum		150	.267		23	7.90	3.43	34.33	41.50	
	0700	Per slip, minimum (180 S.F. each)		1.59	25.157	Ea.	1,275	745	325	2,345	2,900	
	0800	Maximum		1.40	28.571	"	5,350	845	370	6,565	7,575	

02400 | Tunneling, Boring & Jacking

02420 | Initial Tunnel Support Systems

			CREW	DAILY OUTPUT	LABOR-HOURS	UNIT	2001 BARE COSTS				TOTAL INCL O&P	
							MAT.	LABOR	EQUIP.	TOTAL		
700	0011	ROCK BOLTS										700
	2020	Hollow core, prestressable anchor, 1" diameter, 5' long	2 Skwk	32	.500	Ea.	72	14.95		86.95	103	
	2025	10' long		24	.667		135	19.90		154.90	179	
	2060	2" diameter, 5' long		32	.500		269	14.95		283.95	320	
	2065	10' long		24	.667		520	19.90		539.90	600	
	2100	Super high-tensile, 3/4" diameter, 5' long		32	.500		15.75	14.95		30.70	41	
	2105	10' long		24	.667		29	19.90		48.90	63	
	2160	2" diameter, 5' long		32	.500		139	14.95		153.95	177	
	2165	10' long		24	.667		250	19.90		269.90	305	
	4400	Drill hole for rock bolt, 1-3/4" diam., 5' long (for 3/4" bolt)	B-56	17	.941			24.50	42.50	67	84.50	
	4405	10' long		9	1.778			46	80.50	126.50	159	
	4420	2" diameter, 5' long (for 1" bolt)		13	1.231			32	55.50	87.50	111	
	4425	10' long		7	2.286			59	103	162	205	
	4460	3-1/2" diameter, 5' long (for 2" bolt)		10	1.600			41.50	72.50	114	143	
	4465	10' long		5	3.200			82.50	145	227.50	286	

SITE CONSTRUCTION 2

02400 | Tunneling, Boring & Jacking

02441 | Microtunneling

		CREW	DAILY OUTPUT	LABOR-HOURS	UNIT	2001 BARE COSTS				TOTAL INCL O&P
						MAT.	LABOR	EQUIP.	TOTAL	
400	0010	**MICROTUNNELING** Not including excavation, backfill, shoring,									400
	0020	or dewatering, average 50'/day, slurry method									
	0100	24" to 48" outside diameter, minimum				L.F.					600
	0110	Adverse conditions, add				%					50%
	1000	Rent microtunneling machine, average monthly lease				Month					80,000
	1010	Operating technician				Day					600
	1100	Mobilization and demobilization, minimum				Job					40,000
	1110	Maximum				"					400,000

02445 | Boring or Jacking Conduits

		CREW	DAILY OUTPUT	LABOR-HOURS	UNIT	2001 BARE COSTS				TOTAL INCL O&P
						MAT.	LABOR	EQUIP.	TOTAL	
300	0010	**HORIZONTAL BORING** Casing only, 100' minimum,									300
	0020	not incl. jacking pits or dewatering									
	0100	Roadwork, 1/2" thick wall, 24" diameter casing	B-42	20	3.200	L.F.	47.50	82.50	62	192	251
	0200	36" diameter		16	4		75	103	77.50	255.50	330
	0300	48" diameter		15	4.267		110	110	82.50	302.50	385
	0500	Railroad work, 24" diameter		15	4.267		47.50	110	82.50	240	320
	0600	36" diameter		14	4.571		75	118	88.50	281.50	365
	0700	48" diameter	▼	12	5.333		110	137	103	350	450
	0900	For ledge, add				▼				145	175

02450 | Foundation & Load Bearing Elements

02455 | Driven Piles

		CREW	DAILY OUTPUT	LABOR-HOURS	UNIT	2001 BARE COSTS				TOTAL INCL O&P
						MAT.	LABOR	EQUIP.	TOTAL	
220	0010	**PILES, CONCRETE** 200 piles, 60' long									220
	0020	unless specified otherwise, not incl. pile caps or mobilization									
	0050	Cast in place augered piles, no casing or reinforcing									
	0060	8" diameter	B-43	540	.089	V.L.F.	2.10	2.23	3.46	7.79	9.55
	0065	10" diameter		480	.100		3.34	2.51	3.90	9.75	11.85
	0070	12" diameter		420	.114		4.70	2.86	4.45	12.01	14.50
	0075	14" diameter		360	.133		6.35	3.34	5.20	14.89	17.85
	0080	16" diameter		300	.160		8.55	4.01	6.25	18.81	22.50
	0085	18" diameter	▼	240	.200	▼	10.60	5	7.80	23.40	28
	0100	Cast in place, thin wall shell pile, straight sided,									
	0110	not incl. reinforcing, 8" diam., 16 ga., 5.8 lb./L.F.	B-19	700	.091	V.L.F.	3.94	2.68	2.32	8.94	11.25
	0200	10" diameter, 16 ga. corrugated, 7.3 lb./L.F.		650	.098		5.15	2.88	2.50	10.53	13.15
	0300	12" diameter, 16 ga. corrugated, 8.7 lb./L.F.		600	.107		6.70	3.12	2.71	12.53	15.45
	0400	14" diameter, 16 ga. corrugated, 10.0 lb./L.F.		550	.116		7.90	3.40	2.96	14.26	17.45
	0500	16" diameter, 16 ga. corrugated, 11.6 lb./L.F.	▼	500	.128	▼	9.65	3.75	3.25	16.65	20.50
	0800	Cast in place friction pile, 50' long, fluted,									
	0810	tapered steel, 4000 psi concrete, no reinforcing									
	0900	12" diameter, 7 ga.	B-19	600	.107	V.L.F.	12.10	3.12	2.71	17.93	21.50
	1000	14" diameter, 7 ga.		560	.114		13.15	3.34	2.91	19.40	23
	1100	16" diameter, 7 ga.		520	.123		15.45	3.60	3.13	22.18	26.50
	1200	18" diameter, 7 ga.	▼	480	.133	▼	18.10	3.90	3.39	25.39	30
	1300	End bearing, fluted, constant diameter,									
	1320	4000 psi concrete, no reinforcing									
	1340	12" diameter, 7 ga.	B-19	600	.107	V.L.F.	12.60	3.12	2.71	18.43	22
	1360	14" diameter, 7 ga.		560	.114		15.75	3.34	2.91	22	26
	1380	16" diameter, 7 ga.	▼	520	.123		18.30	3.60	3.13	25.03	29.50

Important: See the Reference Section for critical supporting data - Reference Nos., Crews, & City Cost Indexes

02455 | Driven Piles

		CREW	DAILY OUTPUT	LABOR-HOURS	UNIT	MAT.	LABOR	EQUIP.	TOTAL	TOTAL INCL O&P	
220	1400	18" diameter, 7 ga.	B-19	480	.133	V.L.F.	20	3.90	3.39	27.29	32	220
	1500	For reinforcing steel, add				Lb.	.54			.54	.59	
	1700	For ball or pedestal end, add	B-19	11	5.818	C.Y.	79	170	148	397	530	
	1900	For lengths above 60', concrete, add	"	11	5.818	"	82	170	148	400	530	
	2000	For steel thin shell, pipe only				Lb.	.52			.52	.57	
	2200	Precast, prestressed, 50' long, 12" diam., 2-3/8" wall	B-19	720	.089	V.L.F.	9.90	2.60	2.26	14.76	17.65	
	2300	14" diameter, 2-1/2" wall	↓	680	.094		13	2.75	2.39	18.14	21.50	
	2500	16" diameter, 3" wall	↓	640	.100		18	2.93	2.54	23.47	27.50	
	2600	18" diameter, 3" wall	B-19A	600	.107		22.50	3.12	2.88	28.50	33.50	
	2800	20" diameter, 3-1/2" wall		560	.114		26	3.34	3.09	32.43	38	
	2900	24" diameter, 3-1/2" wall	↓	520	.123		32	3.60	3.32	38.92	44.50	
	3100	Precast, prestressed, 40' long, 10" thick, square	B-19	700	.091		6.80	2.68	2.32	11.80	14.40	
	3200	12" thick, square		680	.094		8.65	2.75	2.39	13.79	16.65	
	3400	14" thick, square		600	.107		10.50	3.12	2.71	16.33	19.65	
	3500	Octagonal		640	.100		14	2.93	2.54	19.47	23	
	3700	16" thick, square		560	.114		16.35	3.34	2.91	22.60	26.50	
	3800	Octagonal	↓	600	.107		16.80	3.12	2.71	22.63	26.50	
	4000	18" thick, square	B-19A	520	.123		19.50	3.60	3.32	26.42	31	
	4100	Octagonal	B-19	560	.114		19.90	3.34	2.91	26.15	30.50	
	4300	20" thick, square	B-19A	480	.133		25	3.90	3.60	32.50	38	
	4400	Octagonal	B-19	520	.123		22	3.60	3.13	28.73	33.50	
	4600	24" thick, square	B-19A	440	.145		35	4.26	3.93	43.19	50	
	4700	Octagonal	B-19	480	.133		31.50	3.90	3.39	38.79	45	
	4750	Mobilization for 10,000 L.F. pile job, add	↓	3,300	.019			.57	.49	1.06	1.47	
	4800	25,000 L.F. pile job, add	↓	8,500	.008	↓		.22	.19	.41	.57	
350	0011	**PILING SPECIAL COSTS** pile caps, see Division 03310-240										350
	0500	Cutoffs, concrete piles, plain	1 Pile	5.50	1.455	Ea.		42		42	71.50	
	0600	With steel thin shell, add		38	.211			6.05		6.05	10.30	
	0700	Steel pile or "H" piles		19	.421			12.15		12.15	20.50	
	0800	Wood piles	↓	38	.211	↓		6.05		6.05	10.30	
	0900	Pre-augering up to 30' deep, average soil, 24" diameter	B-43	180	.267	L.F.		6.70	10.40	17.10	22	
	0920	36" diameter		115	.417			10.45	16.25	26.70	34	
	0960	48" diameter		70	.686			17.20	26.50	43.70	56	
	0980	60" diameter	↓	50	.960	↓		24	37.50	61.50	78	
	1000	Testing, any type piles, test load is twice the design load										
	1050	50 ton design load, 100 ton test				Ea.				14,000	15,000	
	1100	100 ton design load, 200 ton test								18,000	19,000	
	1150	150 ton design load, 300 ton test								22,500	24,000	
	1200	200 ton design load, 400 ton test								24,500	27,000	
	1250	400 ton design load, 800 ton test				↓				28,350	31,500	
	1500	Wet conditions, soft damp ground										
	1600	Requiring mats for crane, add								40%	40%	
	1700	Barge mounted driving rig, add								30%	30%	
500	0010	**MOBILIZATION** Set up & remove, air compressor, 600 C.F.M. [R02455 -900]	A-5	3.30	5.455	Ea.		125	11.95	136.95	208	500
	0100	1200 C.F.M.	"	2.20	8.182			187	17.90	204.90	315	
	0200	Crane, with pile leads and pile hammer, 75 ton	B-19	.60	106			3,125	2,700	5,825	8,075	
	0300	150 ton	"	.36	177			5,200	4,525	9,725	13,500	
	0500	Drill rig, for caissons, to 36", minimum	B-43	2	24			600	935	1,535	1,950	
	0600	Up to 84"	"	1	48			1,200	1,875	3,075	3,900	
	0800	Auxiliary boiler, for steam small	A-5	1.66	10.843			248	24	272	415	
	0900	Large	"	.83	21.687			495	47.50	542.50	830	
	1100	Rule of thumb: complete pile driving set up, small	B-19	.45	142			4,150	3,625	7,775	10,800	
	1200	Large	"	.27	237	↓		6,925	6,025	12,950	17,900	
850	0010	**PILES, STEEL** Not including mobilization or demobilization										850
	0100	Step tapered, round, concrete filled										

SITE CONSTRUCTION **2**

			DAILY	LABOR-		\multicolumn{4}{c}{2001 BARE COSTS}			TOTAL	
02455	**Driven Piles**	**CREW**	**OUTPUT**	**HOURS**	**UNIT**	**MAT.**	**LABOR**	**EQUIP.**	**TOTAL**	**INCL O&P**	
850	0110	8" tip, 60 ton capacity, 30' depth	B-19	760	.084	V.L.F.	5	2.46	2.14	9.60	11.85	850
	0120	60' depth		740	.086		5.65	2.53	2.20	10.38	12.75	
	0130	80' depth		700	.091		5.85	2.68	2.32	10.85	13.35	
	0150	10" tip, 90 ton capacity, 30' depth		700	.091		6.15	2.68	2.32	11.15	13.65	
	0160	60' depth		690	.093		6.35	2.71	2.36	11.42	13.95	
	0170	80' depth		670	.096		6.85	2.79	2.43	12.07	14.75	
	0190	12" tip, 120 ton capacity, 30' depth		660	.097		8.85	2.84	2.47	14.16	17.10	
	0200	60' depth, 12" diameter		630	.102		8.80	2.97	2.58	14.35	17.35	
	0210	80' depth		590	.108		7.75	3.17	2.76	13.68	16.75	
	0250	"H" Sections, 50' long, HP8 x 36		640	.100		9	2.93	2.54	14.47	17.45	
	0400	HP10 X 42		610	.105		10.50	3.07	2.67	16.24	19.50	
	0500	HP10 X 57		610	.105		14.25	3.07	2.67	19.99	23.50	
	0700	HP12 X 53		590	.108		13.25	3.17	2.76	19.18	23	
	0800	HP12 X 74	B-19A	590	.108		18.50	3.17	2.93	24.60	29	
	1000	HP14 X 73		540	.119		18.25	3.47	3.20	24.92	29	
	1100	HP14 X 89		540	.119		22.50	3.47	3.20	29.17	33.50	
	1300	HP14 X 102		510	.125		25.50	3.67	3.39	32.56	37.50	
	1400	HP14 X 117		510	.125		29.50	3.67	3.39	36.56	42	
	1600	Splice on standard points, not in leads, 8" or 10"	1 Sswl	5	1.600	Ea.	55	52.50		107.50	156	
	1700	12" or 14"		4	2		80	65.50		145.50	207	
	1900	Heavy duty points, not in leads, 10" wide		4	2		85	65.50		150.50	213	
	2100	14" wide		3.50	2.286		110	75		185	257	
	2600	Pipe piles, 50' lg. 8" diam., 29 lb. per L.F., no concrete	B-19	500	.128	V.L.F.	9	3.75	3.25	16	19.60	
	2700	Concrete filled		460	.139		9.65	4.07	3.54	17.26	21	
	2900	10" diameter, 34 lb. per L.F., no concrete		500	.128		11.25	3.75	3.25	18.25	22	
	3000	Concrete filled		450	.142		12.55	4.16	3.62	20.33	24.50	
	3200	12" diameter, 44 lb. per L.F., no concrete		475	.135		13.90	3.94	3.43	21.27	25.50	
	3300	Concrete filled		415	.154		15.20	4.51	3.92	23.63	28.50	
	3500	14" diameter, 46 lb. per L.F., no concrete		430	.149		14.90	4.36	3.78	23.04	27.50	
	3600	Concrete filled		355	.180		16.85	5.30	4.58	26.73	32	
	3800	16" diameter, 52 lb. per L.F., no concrete		385	.166		16.55	4.86	4.23	25.64	31	
	3900	Concrete filled		335	.191		19.45	5.60	4.86	29.91	36	
	4100	18" diameter, 59 lb. per L.F., no concrete		355	.180		21.50	5.30	4.58	31.38	37.50	
	4200	Concrete filled		310	.206		23	6.05	5.25	34.30	40.50	
	4400	Splices for pipe piles, not in leads, 8" diameter	1 Sswl	4.67	1.713	Ea.	33	56.50		89.50	138	
	4500	14" diameter		3.79	2.111		43	69.50		112.50	174	
	4600	16" diameter		3.03	2.640		53.50	86.50		140	216	
	4800	Points, standard, 8" diameter		4.61	1.735		28	57		85	134	
	4900	14" diameter		4.05	1.975		39	65		104	161	
	5000	16" diameter		3.37	2.374		47.50	78		125.50	193	
	5200	Points, heavy duty, 10" diameter		2.89	2.768		33.50	91		124.50	202	
	5300	14" or 16" diameter		2.02	3.960		53	130		183	295	
	5500	For reinforcing steel, add		1,150	.007	Lb.	.40	.23		.63	.85	
	5700	For thick wall sections, add				"	.45			.45	.50	
900	0010	**PILES, WOOD** Friction or end bearing, not including	R02455									900
	0050	mobilization or demobilization	-900									
	0100	Untreated piles, up to 30' long, 12" butts, 8" points	B-19	625	.102	V.L.F.	5.70	3	2.60	11.30	14.05	
	0200	30' to 39' long, 12" butts, 8" points		700	.091		5.70	2.68	2.32	10.70	13.20	
	0300	40' to 49' long, 12" butts, 7" points		720	.089		5.70	2.60	2.26	10.56	13.05	
	0400	50' to 59' long, 13"butts, 7" points		800	.080		5.80	2.34	2.03	10.17	12.40	
	0500	60' to 69' long, 13" butts, 7" points		840	.076		6.50	2.23	1.94	10.67	12.90	
	0600	70' to 80' long, 13" butts, 6" points		840	.076		7.25	2.23	1.94	11.42	13.70	
	0800	Treated piles, 12 lb. per C.F.,										
	0810	friction or end bearing, ASTM class B										
	1000	Up to 30' long, 12" butts, 8" points	B-19	625	.102	V.L.F.	8.90	3	2.60	14.50	17.55	
	1100	30' to 39' long, 12" butts, 8" points		700	.091		9.10	2.68	2.32	14.10	16.90	

2 SITE CONSTRUCTION

02455 | Driven Piles

			CREW	DAILY OUTPUT	LABOR-HOURS	UNIT	2001 BARE COSTS				TOTAL INCL O&P
							MAT.	LABOR	EQUIP.	TOTAL	
900	1200	40' to 49' long, 12" butts, 7" points R02455-900	B-19	720	.089	V.L.F.	9.05	2.60	2.26	13.91	16.70	900
	1300	50' to 59' long, 13" butts, 7" points	↓	800	.080		8.75	2.34	2.03	13.12	15.70
	1400	60' to 69' long, 13" butts, 6" points	B-19A	840	.076		13.15	2.23	2.06	17.44	20.50
	1500	70' to 80' long, 13" butts, 6" points	"	840	.076	↓	16.85	2.23	2.06	21.14	24.50
	1600	Treated piles, C.C.A., 2.5# per C.F.									
	1610	8" butts, 10' long	B-19	400	.160	V.L.F.	6.20	4.68	4.07	14.95	18.95
	1620	11' to 16' long		500	.128		6.20	3.75	3.25	13.20	16.55
	1630	17' to 20' long		575	.111		6.20	3.26	2.83	12.29	15.25
	1640	10" butts, 10' to 16' long		500	.128		7.10	3.75	3.25	14.10	17.50
	1650	17' to 20' long		575	.111		7.10	3.26	2.83	13.19	16.20
	1660	21' to 40' long		700	.091		7.10	2.68	2.32	12.10	14.70
	1670	12" butts, 10' to 20' long		575	.111		7.65	3.26	2.83	13.74	16.80
	1680	21' to 35' long		650	.098		7.65	2.88	2.50	13.03	15.85
	1690	36' to 40' long		700	.091		7.65	2.68	2.32	12.65	15.30
	1695	14" butts. to 40' long	↓	700	.091	↓	10.95	2.68	2.32	15.95	18.95
	1700	Boot for pile tip, minimum	1 Pile	27	.296	Ea.	17.45	8.55		26	33.50
	1800	Maximum		21	.381		52.50	10.95		63.45	76
	2000	Point for pile tip, minimum		20	.400		17.45	11.50		28.95	39
	2100	Maximum		15	.533		63	15.35		78.35	95
	2300	Splice for piles over 50' long, minimum	B-46	35	1.371		43.50	36	1.23	80.73	108
	2400	Maximum		20	2.400	↓	52.50	63	2.16	117.66	163
	2600	Concrete encasement with wire mesh and tube		331	.145	V.L.F.	8.20	3.79	.13	12.12	15.40
	2700	Mobilization for 10,000 L.F. pile job, add	B-19	3,300	.019			.57	.49	1.06	1.47
	2800	25,000 L.F. pile job, add	"	8,500	.008	↓		.22	.19	.41	.57

02465 | Bored Piles

			CREW	DAILY OUTPUT	LABOR-HOURS	UNIT	MAT.	LABOR	EQUIP.	TOTAL	TOTAL INCL O&P
600	0010	CAISSONS Incl. excav., concrete, 50 lbs. reinf. per C.Y., not R02465-600										600
	0020	incl. mobilization, boulder removal, disposal									
	0100	Open style, machine drilled, to 50' deep, in stable ground, no									
	0110	casings or ground water, 18" diam., 0.065 C.Y./L.F.	B-43	200	.240	V.L.F.	5.10	6	9.35	20.45	25
	0200	24" diameter, 0.116 C.Y./L.F.		190	.253		9.10	6.35	9.85	25.30	30.50
	0300	30" diameter, 0.182 C.Y./L.F.		150	.320		14.25	8	12.45	34.70	42
	0400	36" diameter, 0.262 C.Y./L.F.		125	.384		20.50	9.60	14.95	45.05	54
	0500	48" diameter, 0.465 C.Y./L.F.		100	.480		36.50	12	18.70	67.20	79
	0600	60" diameter, 0.727 C.Y./L.F.		90	.533		57	13.35	21	91.35	107
	0700	72" diameter, 1.05 C.Y./L.F.		80	.600		82.50	15.05	23.50	121.05	139
	0800	84" diameter, 1.43 C.Y./L.F.	↓	75	.640	↓	112	16.05	25	153.05	177
	1000	For bell excavation and concrete, add									
	1020	4' bell diameter, 24" shaft, 0.444 C.Y.	B-43	20	2.400	Ea.	29	60	93.50	182.50	228
	1040	6' bell diameter, 30" shaft, 1.57 C.Y.		5.70	8.421		102	211	330	643	795
	1060	8' bell diameter, 36" shaft, 3.72 C.Y.		2.40	20		241	500	780	1,521	1,900
	1080	9' bell diameter, 48" shaft, 4.48 C.Y.		2	24		290	600	935	1,825	2,275
	1100	10' bell diameter, 60" shaft, 5.24 C.Y.		1.70	28.235		340	705	1,100	2,145	2,675
	1120	12' bell diameter, 72" shaft, 8.74 C.Y.		1	48		565	1,200	1,875	3,640	4,525
	1140	14' bell diameter, 84" shaft, 13.6 C.Y.	↓	.70	68.571	↓	880	1,725	2,675	5,280	6,575
	1200	Open style, machine drilled, to 50' deep, in wet ground, pulled									
	1300	casing and pumping, 18" diameter, 0.065 C.Y./L.F.	B-48	160	.350	V.L.F.	5.10	8.95	13	27.05	33.50
	1400	24" diameter, 0.116 C.Y./L.F.		125	.448		9.10	11.45	16.60	37.15	46
	1500	30" diameter, 0.182 C.Y./L.F.		85	.659		14.25	16.85	24.50	55.60	68.50
	1600	36" diameter, 0.262 C.Y./L.F.	↓	60	.933		20.50	24	34.50	79	97.50
	1700	48" diameter, 0.465 C.Y./L.F.	B-49	55	1.600		36.50	42.50	49	128	161
	1800	60" diameter, 0.727 C.Y./L.F.		35	2.514		57	67	77.50	201.50	253
	1900	72" diameter, 1.05 C.Y./L.F.		30	2.933		82.50	78.50	90	251	315
	2000	84" diameter, 1.43 C.Y./L.F.	↓	25	3.520	↓	112	94	108	314	390
	2100	For bell excavation and concrete, add									
	2120	4' bell diameter, 24" shaft, 0.444 C.Y.	B-48	19.80	2.828	Ea.	29	72.50	105	206.50	258

SITE CONSTRUCTION

02465		Bored Piles		CREW	DAILY OUTPUT	LABOR-HOURS	UNIT	2001 BARE COSTS MAT.	LABOR	EQUIP.	TOTAL	TOTAL INCL O&P	
600	2140	6' bell diameter, 30" shaft, 1.57 C.Y.	R02465 -600	B-48	5.70	9.825	Ea.	102	251	365	718	895	**600**
	2160	8' bell diameter, 36" shaft, 3.72 C.Y.	↓	↓	2.40	23.333	↓	241	595	865	1,701	2,125	
	2180	9' bell diameter, 48" shaft, 4.48 C.Y.		B-49	3.30	26.667		290	710	820	1,820	2,350	
	2200	10' bell diameter, 60" shaft, 5.24 C.Y.			2.80	31.429		340	840	965	2,145	2,775	
	2220	12' bell diameter, 72" shaft, 8.74 C.Y.			1.60	55		565	1,475	1,700	3,740	4,775	
	2240	14' bell diameter, 84" shaft, 13.6 C.Y.		↓	1	88	↓	880	2,350	2,700	5,930	7,625	
	2300	Open style, machine drilled, to 50' deep, in soft rocks and											
	2400	medium hard shales, 18" diameter, 0.065 C.Y./L.F.		B-49	50	1.760	V.L.F.	5.10	47	54	106.10	139	
	2500	24" diameter, 0.116 C.Y./L.F.			30	2.933		9.10	78.50	90	177.60	233	
	2600	30" diameter, 0.182 C.Y./L.F.			20	4.400		14.25	117	135	266.25	350	
	2700	36" diameter, 0.262 C.Y./L.F.			15	5.867		20.50	157	180	357.50	465	
	2800	48" diameter, 0.465 C.Y./L.F.			10	8.800		36.50	235	271	542.50	710	
	2900	60" diameter, 0.727 C.Y./L.F.			7	12.571		57	335	385	777	1,025	
	3000	72" diameter, 1.05 C.Y./L.F.			6	14.667		82.50	390	450	922.50	1,200	
	3100	84" diameter, 1.43 C.Y./L.F.		↓	5	17.600	↓	112	470	540	1,122	1,450	
	3200	For bell excavation and concrete, add											
	3220	4' bell diameter, 24" shaft, 0.444 C.Y.		B-49	10.90	8.073	Ea.	29	215	248	492	645	
	3240	6' bell diameter, 30" shaft, 1.57 C.Y.			3.10	28.387		102	760	875	1,737	2,250	
	3260	8' bell diameter, 36" shaft, 3.72 C.Y.			1.30	67.692		241	1,800	2,075	4,116	5,400	
	3280	9' bell diameter, 48" shaft, 4.48 C.Y.			1.10	80		290	2,125	2,450	4,865	6,375	
	3300	10' bell diameter, 60" shaft, 5.24 C.Y.			.90	97.778		340	2,600	3,000	5,940	7,775	
	3320	12' bell diameter, 72" shaft, 8.74 C.Y.			.60	146		565	3,925	4,500	8,990	11,700	
	3340	14' bell diameter, 84" shaft, 13.6 C.Y.			.40	220	↓	880	5,875	6,775	13,530	17,600	
	3600	For rock excavation, sockets, add, minimum			120	.733	C.F.		19.55	22.50	42.05	55.50	
	3650	Average			95	.926			24.50	28.50	53	70	
	3700	Maximum		↓	48	1.833	↓		49	56.50	105.50	139	
	3900	For 50' to 100' deep, add					V.L.F.				7%	7%	
	4000	For 100' to 150' deep, add									25%	25%	
	4100	For 150' to 200' deep, add					↓				30%	30%	
	4200	For casings left in place, add					Lb.	.54			.54	.59	
	4300	For other than 50 lb. reinf. per C.Y., add or deduct					"	.54			.54	.59	
	4400	For steel "I" beam cores, add		B-49	8.30	10.602	Ton	980	283	325	1,588	1,875	
	4500	Load and haul excess excavation, 2 miles		B-34B	178	.045	C.Y.		1.08	2.71	3.79	4.62	
	4600	For mobilization, 50 mile radius, rig to 36"		B-43	2	24	Ea.		600	935	1,535	1,950	
	4650	Rig to 84"		B-48	1.75	32			820	1,175	1,995	2,550	
	4700	For low headroom, add									50%		
	5000	Bottom inspection		1 Skwk	1.20	6.667	↓		199		199	310	
800	0010	**PRESSURE INJECTED FOOTINGS** or Displacement Caissons	R02465 -800										**800**
	0100	incl. mobilization and demobilization, up to 50 miles											
	0200	Uncased shafts, 30 to 80 tons cap., 17" diam., 10' depth		B-44	88	.727	V.L.F.	12.95	21	10.80	44.75	60.50	
	0300	25' depth			165	.388		9.25	11.20	5.75	26.20	35	
	0400	80-150 ton capacity, 22" diameter, 10' depth			80	.800		16.20	23	11.85	51.05	69	
	0500	20' depth			130	.492		12.95	14.20	7.30	34.45	46	
	0700	Cased shafts, 10 to 30 ton capacity, 10-5/8" diam., 20' depth			175	.366		9.25	10.55	5.45	25.25	33.50	
	0800	30' depth			240	.267		8.65	7.70	3.96	20.31	26.50	
	0850	30 to 60 ton capacity, 12" diameter, 20' depth			160	.400		12.95	11.55	5.95	30.45	39.50	
	0900	40' depth			230	.278		9.95	8.05	4.13	22.13	28.50	
	1000	80 to 100 ton capacity, 16" diameter, 20' depth			160	.400		18.50	11.55	5.95	36	46	
	1100	40' depth			230	.278		17.25	8.05	4.13	29.43	36.50	
	1200	110 to 140 ton capacity, 17-5/8" diameter, 20' depth			160	.400		19.90	11.55	5.95	37.40	47.50	
	1300	40' depth			230	.278		18.50	8.05	4.13	30.68	38	
	1400	140 to 175 ton capacity, 19" diameter, 20' depth			130	.492		21.50	14.20	7.30	43	55	
	1500	40' depth		↓	210	.305	↓	19.90	8.80	4.52	33.22	41.50	
	1700	Over 30' long, L.F. cost tends to be lower											
	1900	Maximum depth is about 90'		↓									

02510 | Water Distribution

		CREW	DAILY OUTPUT	LABOR-HOURS	UNIT	2001 BARE COSTS				TOTAL INCL O&P
						MAT.	LABOR	EQUIP.	TOTAL	
800	0010 **PIPING, WATER DISTRIBUTION SYSTEMS** Pipe, laid										800
	0020 in trench, excavation and backfill not included R02510 -800									
	1400 Ductile Iron, cement lined, class 50 water pipe, 18' lengths									
	1410 Mechanical joint, 4" diameter	B-20	144	.167	L.F.	8.75	4.31		13.06	16.40
	1420 6" diameter		126	.190		9.10	4.92		14.02	17.70
	1430 8" diameter		108	.222		11.65	5.75		17.40	22
	1440 10" diameter		90	.267		15.15	6.90		22.05	27.50
	1450 12" diameter CN	B-21	72	.389		19.35	10.35	1.97	31.67	40
	1460 14" diameter		54	.519		24	13.80	2.63	40.43	50.50
	1470 16" diameter		46	.609		26	16.20	3.09	45.29	57
	1480 18" diameter		42	.667		34.50	17.75	3.38	55.63	68.50
	1490 24" diameter		35	.800		51	21.50	4.06	76.56	94
	1550 Push on joint, 4" diameter	B-20	155	.155		6.45	4		10.45	13.35
	1560 6" diameter		135	.178		7.45	4.60		12.05	15.35
	1570 8" diameter		115	.209		10.50	5.40		15.90	20
	1580 10" diameter		98	.245		15.95	6.35		22.30	27.50
	1590 12" diameter		78	.308		16.80	7.95		24.75	31
	1600 14" diameter	B-21	58	.483		18.50	12.85	2.45	33.80	43
	1610 16" diameter		52	.538		26	14.35	2.73	43.08	54
	1620 18" diameter		43	.651		29	17.35	3.30	49.65	62.50
	1630 20" diameter		41	.683		32	18.15	3.46	53.61	67.50
	1640 24" diameter		40	.700		41	18.65	3.55	63.20	78
	1950 Butterfly valves with boxes, cast iron									
	1970 4" diameter	B-20	6	4	Ea.	360	103		463	555
	1990 6" diameter	"	5	4.800		485	124		609	730
	2010 8" diameter	B-21	4	7		725	186	35.50	946.50	1,125
	2030 10" diameter		3.50	8		955	213	40.50	1,208.50	1,425
	2050 12" diameter		3	9.333		1,325	248	47.50	1,620.50	1,875
	2070 14" diameter		2	14		1,800	375	71	2,246	2,625
	2090 16" diameter		2	14		2,225	375	71	2,671	3,100
	2650 Polyvinyl chloride pipe, class 160, S.D.R.-26, 1-1/2" diameter	B-20	300	.080	L.F.	.59	2.07		2.66	3.89
	2700 2" diameter		250	.096		.89	2.48		3.37	4.87
	2750 2-1/2" diameter		250	.096		1.32	2.48		3.80	5.35
	2800 3" diameter		200	.120		1.89	3.10		4.99	6.95
	2850 4" diameter		200	.120		3.09	3.10		6.19	8.25
	2900 6" diameter		180	.133		6.65	3.45		10.10	12.75
	2950 8" diameter	B-21	160	.175		11.30	4.66	.89	16.85	20.50
	8000 Fittings, ductile iron, mechanical joint									
	8010 90° bend 4" diameter	B-20	37	.649	Ea.	145	16.75		161.75	187
	8020 6" diameter		25	.960		195	25		220	253
	8040 8" diameter		21	1.143		275	29.50		304.50	350
	8060 10" diameter	B-21	21	1.333		435	35.50	6.75	477.25	545
	8080 12" diameter		18	1.556		595	41.50	7.90	644.40	730
	8100 14" diameter		16	1.750		610	46.50	8.85	665.35	750
	8120 16" diameter		14	2		660	53	10.15	723.15	825
	8140 18" diameter		10	2.800		1,525	74.50	14.20	1,613.70	1,800
	8160 20" diameter		8	3.500		2,300	93	17.75	2,410.75	2,700
	8180 24" diameter		6	4.667		2,600	124	23.50	2,747.50	3,075
	8200 Wye or tee, 4" diameter	B-20	25	.960		213	25		238	273
	8220 6" diameter		17	1.412		160	36.50		196.50	233
	8240 8" diameter		14	1.714		234	44.50		278.50	330
	8260 10" diameter	B-21	14	2		800	53	10.15	863.15	975
	8280 12" diameter		12	2.333		975	62	11.85	1,048.85	1,175
	8300 14" diameter		10	2.800		910	74.50	14.20	998.70	1,125
	8320 16" diameter		8	3.500		1,050	93	17.75	1,160.75	1,325
	8340 18" diameter		6	4.667		1,975	124	23.50	2,122.50	2,400

SITE CONSTRUCTION 2

02510	Water Distribution	CREW	DAILY OUTPUT	LABOR-HOURS	UNIT	2001 BARE COSTS				TOTAL INCL O&P	
						MAT.	LABOR	EQUIP.	TOTAL		
800 8360	20" diameter	B-21	4	7	Ea.	2,600	186	35.50	2,821.50	3,175	**800**
8380	24" diameter	↓	3	9.333	↓	3,025	248	47.50	3,320.50	3,750	

R02510 -800

02520 | Wells

		CREW	DAILY OUTPUT	LABOR-HOURS	UNIT	MAT.	LABOR	EQUIP.	TOTAL	TOTAL INCL O&P	
900 0010	**WELLS** Domestic water										**900**
0100	Drilled, 4" to 6" diameter	B-23	120	.333	L.F.		7.75	17.10	24.85	31	
0200	8" diameter	"	95.20	.420	"		9.75	21.50	31.25	39	
0400	Gravel pack well, 40' deep, incl. gravel & casing, complete										
0500	24" diameter casing x 18" diameter screen	B-23	.13	307	Total	21,000	7,150	15,800	43,950	51,500	
0600	36" diameter casing x 18" diameter screen		.12	333	"	22,600	7,750	17,100	47,450	55,500	
0800	Observation wells, 1-1/4" riser pipe	↓	163	.245	V.L.F.	11.55	5.70	12.60	29.85	35.50	
0900	For flush Buffalo roadway box, add	1 Skwk	16.60	.482	Ea.	31.50	14.40		45.90	57	
1200	Test well, 2-1/2" diameter, up to 50' deep (15 to 50 GPM)	B-23	1.51	26.490	"	475	615	1,350	2,440	2,975	
1300	Over 50' deep, add	"	121.80	.328	L.F.	12.60	7.65	16.85	37.10	44.50	
1500	Pumps, installed in wells to 100' deep, 4" submersible										
1510	1/2 H.P.	Q-1	3.22	4.969	Ea.	355	154		509	625	
1520	3/4 H.P.		2.66	6.015		425	186		611	750	
1600	1 H.P.	↓	2.29	6.987		480	217		697	850	
1700	1-1/2 H.P.	Q-22	1.60	10		620	310	320	1,250	1,500	
1800	2 H.P.		1.33	12.030		840	375	385	1,600	1,925	
1900	3 H.P.		1.14	14.035		1,050	435	450	1,935	2,300	
2000	5 H.P.		1.14	14.035		1,550	435	450	2,435	2,850	
3000	Pump, 6" submersible, 25' to 150' deep, 25 H.P., 249 to 297 GPM		.89	17.978		3,900	555	580	5,035	5,775	
3100	25' to 500' deep, 30 H.P., 100 to 300 GPM	↓	.73	21.918	↓	3,950	680	705	5,335	6,125	
8000	Steel well casing	B-23A	3,020	.008	Lb.	.40	.21	.65	1.26	1.47	
9950	See div. 02240-900 for wellpoints										
9960	See div. 02240-700 for drainage wells										
910 0010	**PUMPS, WELL** Water system, with pressure control										**910**
1000	Deep well, jet, 42 gal. galvanized tank										
1040	3/4 HP	1 Plum	.80	10	Ea.	545	345		890	1,125	
3000	Shallow well, jet, 30 gal. galvanized tank										
3040	1/2 HP	1 Plum	2	4	Ea.	550	138		688	815	

02530 | Sanitary Sewerage

		CREW	DAILY OUTPUT	LABOR-HOURS	UNIT	MAT.	LABOR	EQUIP.	TOTAL	TOTAL INCL O&P	
100 0010	**SEWAGE TREATMENT** Plant, not incl. fencing or external piping										**100**
0020	Steel packaged, blown air aeration plants										
0100	1,000 GPD				Gal.				15	17.25	
0200	5,000 GPD								10	11.50	
0300	15,000 GPD								5.50	6.30	
0400	30,000 GPD								5.20	6	
0500	50,000 GPD								4	4.60	
0600	100,000 GPD								3.50	4	
0700	200,000 GPD								2.50	2.88	
0800	500,000 GPD				↓				2.45	2.80	
1000	Concrete, extended aeration, primary and secondary treatment										
1010	10,000 GPD				Gal.				11	12.65	
1100	30,000 GPD								5.50	6.35	
1200	50,000 GPD								4.50	5.18	
1400	100,000 GPD								3.50	4.05	
1500	500,000 GPD				↓				2.50	2.90	
1700	Municipal wastewater treatment facility										
1720	1.0 MGD				Gal.				4.30	4.95	
1740	1.5 MGD								4.25	4.90	
1760	2.0 MGD				↓				3.65	4.20	

02530	Sanitary Sewerage		CREW	DAILY OUTPUT	LABOR-HOURS	UNIT	2001 BARE COSTS				TOTAL INCL O&P
							MAT.	LABOR	EQUIP.	TOTAL	
100	1780	3.0 MGD				Gal.				2.85	3.30	**100**
	1800	5.0 MGD				↓				2.60	3
	2000	Holding tank system, not incl. excavation or backfill									
	2010	Recirculating chemical water closet	2 Plum	4	4	Ea.	700	138		838	980
	2100	For voltage converter, add	"	16	1		186	34.50		220.50	256
	2200	For high level alarm, add	1 Plum	7.80	1.026	↓	106	35.50		141.50	171
730	0010	**PIPING, DRAINAGE & SEWAGE, CONCRETE** R02510 -810										**730**
	0020	Not including excavation or backfill									
	1000	Non-reinforced pipe, extra strength, B&S or T&G joints									
	1010	6" diameter	B-14	265.04	.181	L.F.	3.48	4.38	.68	8.54	11.40
	1020	8" diameter		224	.214		3.83	5.20	.81	9.84	13.15
	1030	10" diameter		216	.222		4.25	5.35	.84	10.44	13.95
	1040	12" diameter		200	.240		5.20	5.80	.90	11.90	15.75
	1050	15" diameter		180	.267		6.10	6.45	1.01	13.56	17.80
	1060	18" diameter		144	.333		7.50	8.05	1.26	16.81	22
	1070	21" diameter		112	.429		9.20	10.35	1.62	21.17	28
	1080	24" diameter	↓	100	.480	↓	11.30	11.60	1.81	24.71	32.50
	2000	Reinforced culvert, class 3, no gaskets									
	2010	12" diameter	B-14	210	.229	L.F.	9.80	5.50	.86	16.16	20.50
	2020	15" diameter		175	.274		12.10	6.65	1.03	19.78	24.50
	2030	18" diameter		130	.369		12.20	8.90	1.39	22.49	29
	2035	21" diameter		120	.400		14.85	9.65	1.51	26.01	33
	2040	24" diameter **CN**	↓	100	.480		17.80	11.60	1.81	31.21	39.50
	2045	27" diameter	B-13	92	.609		21.50	15.05	6.85	43.40	54.50
	2050	30" diameter		88	.636		24.50	15.75	7.15	47.40	59.50
	2060	36" diameter	↓	72	.778		35	19.25	8.75	63	78
	2070	42" diameter	B-13B	72	.778		47.50	19.25	12.50	79.25	96.50
	2080	48" diameter		64	.875		59.50	21.50	14.10	95.10	115
	2090	60" diameter		48	1.167		95	29	18.80	142.80	170
	2100	72" diameter		40	1.400		135	34.50	22.50	192	227
	2120	84" diameter		32	1.750		245	43.50	28	316.50	365
	2140	96" diameter	↓	24	2.333		294	57.50	37.50	389	455
	2200	With gaskets, class 3, 12" diameter	B-21	168	.167		10.80	4.44	.85	16.09	19.75
	2220	15" diameter		160	.175		12.95	4.66	.89	18.50	22.50
	2230	18" diameter		152	.184		16.20	4.90	.93	22.03	26.50
	2240	24" diameter	↓	136	.206		24.50	5.50	1.04	31.04	36.50
	2260	30" diameter	B-13	88	.636		32.50	15.75	7.15	55.40	68
	2270	36" diameter	"	72	.778		48.50	19.25	8.75	76.50	93
	2290	48" diameter	B-13B	64	.875		79.50	21.50	14.10	115.10	137
	2310	72" diameter	"	40	1.400		205	34.50	22.50	262	305
	2330	Flared ends, 6'-1" long, 12" diameter	B-21	190	.147		37	3.92	.75	41.67	47.50
	2340	15" diameter		155	.181		43	4.81	.92	48.73	55.50
	2400	6'-2" long, 18" diameter		122	.230		45.50	6.10	1.16	52.76	61
	2420	24" diameter	↓	88	.318		55	8.45	1.61	65.06	75.50
	2440	36" diameter	B-13	60	.933	↓	84	23	10.50	117.50	140
	3040	Vitrified plate lined, add to above, 30" to 36" diameter				SFCA	3.18			3.18	3.50
	3050	42" to 54" diameter, add					3.40			3.40	3.74
	3060	60" to 72" diameter, add					3.98			3.98	4.38
	3070	Over 72" diameter, add				↓	4.24			4.24	4.66
	3080	Radius pipe, add to pipe prices, 12" to 60" diameter				L.F.	50%				
	3090	Over 60" diameter, add				"	20%				
	3500	Reinforced elliptical, 8' lengths, C507 class 3									
	3520	14" x 23" inside, round equivalent 18" diameter	B-21	82	.341	L.F.	22.50	9.10	1.73	33.33	40.50
	3530	24" x 38" inside, round equivalent 30" diameter	B-13	58	.966		41	24	10.85	75.85	94
	3540	29" x 45" inside, round equivalent 36" diameter		52	1.077		50.50	26.50	12.10	89.10	110
	3550	38" x 60" inside, round equivalent 48" diameter	↓	38	1.474	↓	77.50	36.50	16.55	130.55	160

02530	Sanitary Sewerage		CREW	DAILY OUTPUT	LABOR-HOURS	UNIT	2001 BARE COSTS				TOTAL INCL O&P	
							MAT.	LABOR	EQUIP.	TOTAL		
730	3560	48" x 76" inside, round equivalent 60" diameter	R02510 -810	B-13	26	2.154	L.F.	139	53.50	24	216.50	262	**730**
	3570	58" x 91" inside, round equivalent 72" diameter		↓	22	2.545	↓	187	63	28.50	278.50	335	
	3780	Concrete slotted pipe, class 4 mortar joint											
	3800	12" diameter		B-21	168	.167	L.F.	11.15	4.44	.85	16.44	20	
	3840	18" diameter		"	152	.184	"	17.25	4.90	.93	23.08	27.50	
	3900	Class 4 O-ring											
	3940	12" diameter		B-21	168	.167	L.F.	11.75	4.44	.85	17.04	20.50	
	3960	18" diameter		"	152	.184	"	16.45	4.90	.93	22.28	26.50	
780	0010	**PIPING, DRAINAGE & SEWAGE, POLYVINYL CHLORIDE**											**780**
	0020	Not including excavation or backfill											
	2000	10' lengths, S.D.R. 35, B&S, 4" diameter		B-20	375	.064	L.F.	1.41	1.65		3.06	4.14	
	2040	6" diameter			350	.069		2.41	1.77		4.18	5.45	
	2080	8" diameter		↓	335	.072		4.40	1.85		6.25	7.75	
	2120	10" diameter		B-21	330	.085		6.55	2.26	.43	9.24	11.20	
	2160	12" diameter			320	.087		7.35	2.33	.44	10.12	12.20	
	2200	15" diameter		↓	190	.147		11.15	3.92	.75	15.82	19.20	
790	0010	**PIPING, DRAINAGE & SEWAGE, VITRIFIED CLAY** C700											**790**
	0020	Not including excavation or backfill,											
	4030	Extra strength, compression joints, C425											
	5000	4" diameter x 4' long		B-20	265	.091	L.F.	1.54	2.34		3.88	5.35	
	5020	6" diameter x 5' long		"	200	.120		2.61	3.10		5.71	7.75	
	5040	8" diameter x 5' long		B-21	200	.140		3.70	3.73	.71	8.14	10.65	
	5060	10" diameter x 5' long			190	.147		6.20	3.92	.75	10.87	13.70	
	5080	12" diameter x 6' long			150	.187		8.25	4.97	.95	14.17	17.90	
	5100	15" diameter x 7' long			110	.255		14.45	6.75	1.29	22.49	28	
	5120	18" diameter x 7' long			88	.318		21.50	8.45	1.61	31.56	38.50	
	5140	24" diameter x 7' long		↓	45	.622		39	16.55	3.15	58.70	72.50	
	5160	30" diameter x 7' long		B-22	31	.968		72.50	26	6.85	105.35	128	
	5180	36" diameter x 7' long		"	20	1.500		113	40.50	10.65	164.15	200	
	6000	For 3' lengths, add						30%	30%				
	6020	For 2' lengths, add						40%	60%				
	6060	For plain joints, deduct						25%					
	7060	2' lengths, add to above					↓	40%					

02540	Septic Tank Systems	CREW	DAILY OUTPUT	LABOR-HOURS	UNIT	MAT.	LABOR	EQUIP.	TOTAL	TOTAL INCL O&P	
700	0010	**SEPTIC TANKS** Not incl. excav. or piping, precast, 1,000 gallon	B-21	8	3.500	Ea.	490	93	17.75	600.75	700	**700**
	0100	2,000 gallon	"	5	5.600		980	149	28.50	1,157.50	1,350	
	0200	5,000 gallon	B-13	3.50	16		4,925	395	180	5,500	6,250	
	0300	15,000 gallon, 4 piece	B-13B	1.70	32.941		11,800	815	530	13,145	14,700	
	0400	25,000 gallon, 4 piece		1.10	50.909		25,900	1,250	820	27,970	31,400	
	0500	40,000 gallon, 4 piece	↓	.80	70		31,800	1,725	1,125	34,650	38,900	
	0520	50,000 gallon, 5 piece	B-13C	.60	93.333		36,600	2,300	2,025	40,925	46,000	
	0540	75,000 gallon, cast in place	C-14C	.25	448		44,500	12,500	152	57,152	69,000	
	0560	100,000 gallon	"	.15	746		55,000	20,800	254	76,054	94,000	
	0600	High density polyethylene, 1,000 gallon	B-21	6	4.667		800	124	23.50	947.50	1,100	
	0700	1,500 gallon	"	4	7		1,000	186	35.50	1,221.50	1,425	
	1000	Distribution boxes, concrete, 7 outlets	2 Clab	16	1		89	23		112	134	
	1100	9 outlets	"	8	2		232	45.50		277.50	325	
	1150	Leaching field chambers, 13' x 3'-7" x 1'-4", standard	B-13	16	3.500		665	86.50	39.50	791	910	
	1200	Heavy duty, 8' x 4' x 1'-6"		14	4		330	99	45	474	570	
	1300	13' x 3'-9" x 1'-6"		12	4.667		1,050	115	52.50	1,217.50	1,375	
	1350	20' x 4' x 1'-6"	↓	5	11.200		775	277	126	1,178	1,425	
	1400	Leaching pit, precast concrete, 3' diameter, 3' deep	B-21	8	3.500		305	93	17.75	415.75	500	
	1500	6' diameter, 3' section		4.70	5.957		535	159	30	724	870	
	2000	Velocity reducing pit, precast conc., 6' diameter, 3' deep	↓	4.70	5.957	↓	232	159	30	421	535	

2 SITE CONSTRUCTION

02540 | Septic Tank Systems

			DAILY OUTPUT	LABOR-HOURS	UNIT	2001 BARE COSTS				TOTAL INCL O&P	
			CREW			MAT.	LABOR	EQUIP.	TOTAL		
700	2200	Excavation for septic tank, 3/4 C.Y. backhoe	B-12F	145	.110	C.Y.		3.14	2.85	5.99	7.90	700
	2400	4' trench for disposal field, 3/4 C.Y. backhoe	"	335	.048	L.F.		1.36	1.23	2.59	3.42	
	2600	Gravel fill, run of bank	B-6	150	.160	C.Y.	13.60	3.97	1.21	18.78	22.50	
	2800	Crushed stone, 3/4"	"	150	.160	"	21.50	3.97	1.21	26.68	31	

02550 | Piped Energy Distribution

			CREW	DAILY OUTPUT	LABOR-HOURS	UNIT	MAT.	LABOR	EQUIP.	TOTAL	TOTAL INCL O&P	
450	0010	**GAS STATION PRODUCT LINE**										450
	0020	Primary containment pipe, fiberglass-reinforced										
	0030	Plastic pipe 15' & 30' lengths										
	0040	2" diameter	Q-6	425	.056	L.F.	2.91	1.84		4.75	5.95	
	0050	3" diameter		400	.060		3.92	1.95		5.87	7.25	
	0060	4" diameter	↓	375	.064	↓	5.05	2.08		7.13	8.70	
	0100	Fittings										
	0110	Elbows, 90° & 45°, bell-ends, 2"	Q-6	24	1	Ea.	29.50	32.50		62	81.50	
	0120	3" diameter		22	1.091		31.50	35.50		67	88.50	
	0130	4" diameter		20	1.200		42	39		81	105	
	0200	Tees, bell ends, 2"		21	1.143		36.50	37		73.50	96.50	
	0210	3" diameter		18	1.333		37	43.50		80.50	106	
	0220	4" diameter		15	1.600		48.50	52		100.50	132	
	0230	Flanges bell ends, 2"		24	1		8.65	32.50		41.15	58.50	
	0240	3" diameter		22	1.091		10.90	35.50		46.40	65.50	
	0250	4" diameter		20	1.200		14.85	39		53.85	75.50	
	0260	Sleeve couplings, 2"		21	1.143		7.45	37		44.45	64	
	0270	3" diameter		18	1.333		10.30	43.50		53.80	77	
	0280	4" diameter		15	1.600		14.25	52		66.25	94	
	0290	Threaded adapters 2"		21	1.143		10.15	37		47.15	67	
	0300	3" diameter		18	1.333		14.80	43.50		58.30	82	
	0310	4" diameter		15	1.600		21.50	52		73.50	102	
	0320	Reducers, 2"		27	.889		12.50	29		41.50	57.50	
	0330	3" diameter		22	1.091		14.80	35.50		50.30	70	
	0340	4" diameter	↓	20	1.200	↓	21.50	39		60.50	82.50	
	1010	Gas station product line for secondary containment (double wall)										
	1100	Fiberglass reinforced plastic pipe 25' lengths										
	1120	Pipe, plain end, 3"	Q-6	375	.064	L.F.	4.04	2.08		6.12	7.60	
	1130	4" diameter		350	.069		5.05	2.23		7.28	8.90	
	1140	5" diameter		325	.074		7	2.40		9.40	11.35	
	1150	6" diameter	↓	300	.080	↓	8.90	2.60		11.50	13.75	
	1200	Fittings										
	1230	Elbows, 90° & 45°, 3"	Q-6	18	1.333	Ea.	36	43.50		79.50	105	
	1240	4" diameter		16	1.500		64.50	49		113.50	145	
	1250	5" diameter		14	1.714		149	56		205	248	
	1260	6" diameter		12	2		151	65		216	264	
	1270	Tees, 3"		15	1.600		54.50	52		106.50	139	
	1280	4" diameter		12	2		80.50	65		145.50	187	
	1290	5" diameter		9	2.667		163	87		250	310	
	1300	6" diameter		6	4		170	130		300	385	
	1310	Couplings, 3"		18	1.333		25	43.50		68.50	93	
	1320	4" diameter		16	1.500		67	49		116	147	
	1330	5" diameter		14	1.714		139	56		195	237	
	1340	6" diameter		12	2		144	65		209	257	
	1350	Cross-over nipples, 3"		18	1.333		5.90	43.50		49.40	72	
	1360	4" diameter		16	1.500		6.95	49		55.95	81	
	1370	5" diameter		14	1.714		10.30	56		66.30	95.50	
	1380	6" diameter		12	2		10.80	65		75.80	110	
	1400	Telescoping, reducers, concentric 4" x 3"		18	1.333		19.75	43.50		63.25	87	
	1410	5" x 4"	↓	17	1.412	↓	51.50	46		97.50	126	

For expanded coverage of these items see *Means Heavy Construction Cost Data 2001*

		02550	Piped Energy Distribution	CREW	DAILY OUTPUT	LABOR-HOURS	UNIT	2001 BARE COSTS				TOTAL INCL O&P	
								MAT.	LABOR	EQUIP.	TOTAL		
450	1420		6" x 5"	Q-6	16	1.500	Ea.	124	49		173	210	**450**
464	0010		**PIPING, GAS SERVICE & DISTRIBUTION, POLYETHYLENE**										**464**
	0020		not including excavation or backfill										
	1000		60 psi coils, comp cplg @ 100', 1/2" diameter, SDR 9.3	B-20A	608	.053	L.F.	.38	1.44		1.82	2.63	
	1040		1-1/4" diameter, SDR 11		544	.059		.65	1.61		2.26	3.18	
	1100		2" diameter, SDR 11		488	.066		.80	1.80		2.60	3.63	
	1160		3" diameter, SDR 11	↓	408	.078		1.68	2.15		3.83	5.15	
	1500		60 PSI 40' joints with coupling, 3" diameter, SDR 11	B-21A	408	.098		1.74	2.76	1.04	5.54	7.30	
	1540		4" diameter, SDR 11		352	.114		3.84	3.20	1.21	8.25	10.45	
	1600		6" diameter, SDR 11		328	.122		11.95	3.44	1.30	16.69	19.85	
	1640		8" diameter, SDR 11	↓	272	.147	↓	16.30	4.14	1.56	22	26	

02580 | Elec/Communication Structures

				CREW	DAILY OUTPUT	LABOR-HOURS	UNIT	MAT.	LABOR	EQUIP.	TOTAL	TOTAL INCL O&P	
300	0010		**ELECTRIC & TELEPHONE SITE WORK** Not including excavation										**300**
	0200		backfill and cast in place concrete										
	0400		Hand holes, precast concrete, with concrete cover										
	0600		2' x 2' x 3' deep	R-3	2.40	8.333	Ea.	237	282	59	578	745	
	0800		3' x 3' x 3' deep		1.90	10.526		310	355	74.50	739.50	955	
	1000		4' x 4' x 4' deep	↓	1.40	14.286	↓	590	485	101	1,176	1,475	
	1200		Manholes, precast with iron racks & pulling irons, C.I. frame										
	1400		and cover, 4' x 6' x 7' deep	B-13	2	28	Ea.	1,150	695	315	2,160	2,700	
	1600		6' x 8' x 7' deep		1.90	29.474		1,425	730	330	2,485	3,075	
	1800		6' x 10' x 7' deep	↓	1.80	31.111		1,600	770	350	2,720	3,325	
	2000		Poles, wood, preservative treatment, see also div. 16520, 20' high	R-3	3.10	6.452		236	219	46	501	635	
	2400		25' high		2.90	6.897		250	234	49	533	680	
	2600		30' high		2.60	7.692		270	261	54.50	585.50	745	
	2800		35' high		2.40	8.333		350	282	59	691	870	
	3000		40' high		2.30	8.696		430	295	61.50	786.50	985	
	3200		45' high	↓	1.70	11.765	↓	525	400	83.50	1,008.50	1,275	
	3400		Cross arms with hardware & insulators										
	3600		4' long	1 Elec	2.50	3.200	Ea.	110	110		220	285	
	3800		5' long		2.40	3.333		128	114		242	310	
	4000		6' long	↓	2.20	3.636	↓	147	125		272	350	
	4200		Underground duct, banks ready for concrete fill, min. of 7.5"										
	4400		between conduits, ctr. to ctr.(for wire & cable see div. 16120)										
	4580		PVC, type EB, 1 @ 2" diameter	2 Elec	480	.033	L.F.	.66	1.14		1.80	2.44	
	4600		2 @ 2" diameter		240	.067		1.33	2.29		3.62	4.87	
	4800		4 @ 2" diameter		120	.133		2.65	4.57		7.22	9.75	
	5000		2 @ 3" diameter		200	.080		1.82	2.74		4.56	6.10	
	5200		4 @ 3" diameter		100	.160		3.63	5.50		9.13	12.20	
	5400		2 @ 4" diameter		160	.100		2.80	3.43		6.23	8.20	
	5600		4 @ 4" diameter		80	.200		5.60	6.85		12.45	16.40	
	5800		6 @ 4" diameter		54	.296		8.40	10.15		18.55	24.50	
	6200		Rigid galvanized steel, 2 @ 2" diameter		180	.089		9.60	3.05		12.65	15.15	
	6400		4 @ 2" diameter		90	.178		19.25	6.10		25.35	30	
	6800		2 @ 3" diameter		100	.160		21	5.50		26.50	31.50	
	7000		4 @ 3" diameter		50	.320		42.50	11		53.50	63	
	7200		2 @ 4" diameter		70	.229		30.50	7.85		38.35	45	
	7400		4 @ 4" diameter		34	.471		61	16.15		77.15	91	
	7600		6 @ 4" diameter	↓	22	.727	↓	91.50	25		116.50	137	
890	0010		**RADIO TOWERS** Guyed, 50'h, 40 lb. sec., 70MPH basic wind spd.	2 Sswk	1	16	Ea.	1,575	525		2,100	2,675	**890**
	0100		Wind load 90 MPH basic wind speed	"	1	16		1,575	525		2,100	2,675	
	0300		190' high, 40 lb. section, wind load 70 MPH basic wind speed	K-2	.33	72.727		4,225	2,200	560	6,985	9,125	
	0400		200' high, 70 lb. section, wind load 90 MPH basic wind speed		.33	72.727	↓	8,525	2,200	560	11,285	13,800	

Important: See the Reference Section for critical supporting data - Reference Nos., Crews, & City Cost Indexes

02500 | Utility Services

02580 | Elec/Communication Structures

			DAILY OUTPUT	LABOR-HOURS	UNIT	2001 BARE COSTS				TOTAL INCL O&P	
			CREW			MAT.	LABOR	EQUIP.	TOTAL		
890	0600	300' high, 70 lb. section, wind load 70 MPH basic wind speed	K-2	.20	120	Ea.	12,100	3,650	920	16,670	20,700	890
	0700	270' high, 90 lb. section, wind load 90 MPH basic wind speed		.20	120		14,000	3,650	920	18,570	22,800	
	0800	400' high, 100 lb. section, wind load 70 MPH basic wind speed		.14	171		20,400	5,200	1,325	26,925	32,900	
	0900	Self-supporting, 60' high, wind load 70 MPH basic wind speed		.80	30		3,275	910	230	4,415	5,425	
	0910	60' high, wind load 90MPH basic wind speed		.45	53.333		5,875	1,625	410	7,910	9,750	
	1000	120' high, wind load 70MPH basic wind speed		.40	60		8,025	1,825	460	10,310	12,500	
	1200	190' high, wind load 90 MPH basic wind speed		.20	120		19,500	3,650	920	24,070	28,800	
	2000	For states west of Rocky Mountains, add for shipping					10%					

02600 | Drainage & Containment

02620 | Subdrainage

			DAILY OUTPUT	LABOR-HOURS	UNIT	2001 BARE COSTS				TOTAL INCL O&P	
			CREW			MAT.	LABOR	EQUIP.	TOTAL		
210	0010	**PIPING, SUBDRAINAGE, CONCRETE**										210
	0021	Not including excavation and backfill R02510 -810										
	3000	Porous wall concrete underdrain, std. strength, 4" diameter	B-20	335	.072	L.F.	1.78	1.85		3.63	4.86	
	3020	6" diameter	"	315	.076		2.31	1.97		4.28	5.65	
	3040	8" diameter	B-21	310	.090		2.86	2.40	.46	5.72	7.40	
	3060	12" diameter		285	.098		6.05	2.61	.50	9.16	11.25	
	3080	15" diameter		230	.122		6.95	3.24	.62	10.81	13.40	
	3100	18" diameter		165	.170		9.15	4.52	.86	14.53	18.10	
	4000	Extra strength, 6" diameter	B-20	315	.076		2.36	1.97		4.33	5.70	
	4020	8" diameter	B-21	310	.090		3.54	2.40	.46	6.40	8.15	
	4040	10" diameter		285	.098		7.10	2.61	.50	10.21	12.40	
	4060	12" diameter		230	.122		7.65	3.24	.62	11.51	14.20	
	4080	15" diameter		200	.140		8.50	3.73	.71	12.94	15.95	
	4100	18" diameter		165	.170		12.40	4.52	.86	17.78	21.50	
240	0010	**PIPING, SUBDRAINAGE, CORRUGATED METAL**										240
	0021	Not including excavation and backfill										
	2010	Aluminum, perforated										
	2020	6" diameter, 18 ga.	B-14	380	.126	L.F.	2.62	3.05	.48	6.15	8.15	
	2200	8" diameter, 16 ga.		370	.130		3.81	3.14	.49	7.44	9.60	
	2220	10" diameter, 16 ga.		360	.133		4.76	3.22	.50	8.48	10.80	
	2240	12" diameter, 16 ga.		285	.168		5.35	4.07	.63	10.05	12.90	
	2260	18" diameter, 16 ga.		205	.234		8	5.65	.88	14.53	18.55	
	3000	Uncoated galvanized, perforated										
	3020	6" diameter, 18 ga.	B-20	380	.063	L.F.	4.08	1.63		5.71	7.05	
	3200	8" diameter, 16 ga.	"	370	.065		5.60	1.68		7.28	8.80	
	3220	10" diameter, 16 ga.	B-21	360	.078		8.40	2.07	.39	10.86	12.90	
	3240	12" diameter, 16 ga.		285	.098		8.80	2.61	.50	11.91	14.30	
	3260	18" diameter, 16 ga.		205	.137		13.45	3.63	.69	17.77	21	
	4000	Steel, perforated, asphalt coated										
	4020	6" diameter 18 ga.	B-20	380	.063	L.F.	3.26	1.63		4.89	6.15	
	4030	8" diameter 18 ga	"	370	.065		5.10	1.68		6.78	8.25	
	4040	10" diameter 16 ga	B-21	360	.078		5.85	2.07	.39	8.31	10.10	
	4050	12" diameter 16 ga		285	.098		6.75	2.61	.50	9.86	12	
	4060	18" diameter 16 ga		205	.137		9.20	3.63	.69	13.52	16.50	
270	0010	**PIPING, SUBDRAINAGE, POLYVINYL CHLORIDE**										270
	0020	Perforated, price as solid pipe, division 02530-780										
280	0010	**PIPING, SUBDRAINAGE, VITRIFIED CLAY**										280
	0020	Not including excavation and backfill										

2 SITE CONSTRUCTION

02620 | Subdrainage

			CREW	DAILY OUTPUT	LABOR-HOURS	UNIT	MAT.	LABOR	EQUIP.	TOTAL	TOTAL INCL O&P	
280	3000	Perforated, 5' lengths, C700, 4" diameter	B-14	400	.120	L.F.	1.91	2.90	.45	5.26	7.10	**280**
	3020	6" diameter		315	.152		3.25	3.68	.57	7.50	9.95	
	3040	8" diameter		290	.166		4.62	4	.62	9.24	12	
	3060	12" diameter		275	.175		9.60	4.22	.66	14.48	17.80	
	4000	Channel pipe, 4" diameter	B-20	430	.056		1.79	1.44		3.23	4.23	
	4020	6" diameter		335	.072		3.15	1.85		5	6.35	
	4060	8" diameter		295	.081		4.81	2.10		6.91	8.60	
	4080	12" diameter	B-21	280	.100		10.50	2.66	.51	13.67	16.25	

02630 | Storm Drainage

			CREW	DAILY OUTPUT	LABOR-HOURS	UNIT	MAT.	LABOR	EQUIP.	TOTAL	TOTAL INCL O&P	
100	0010	**PIPING, STORM DRAINAGE, CORRUGATED METAL**										**100**
	0020	Not including excavation or backfill										
	2000	Corrugated metal pipe, galvanized and coated										
	2020	Bituminous coated with paved invert, 20' lengths										
	2040	8" diameter, 16 ga.	B-14	330	.145	L.F.	5.85	3.52	.55	9.92	12.50	
	2060	10" diameter, 16 ga.		260	.185		7	4.46	.70	12.16	15.40	
	2080	12" diameter, 16 ga.		210	.229		8.45	5.50	.86	14.81	18.85	
	2100	15" diameter, 16 ga.		200	.240		10.25	5.80	.90	16.95	21.50	
	2120	18" diameter, 16 ga.		190	.253		13.15	6.10	.95	20.20	25	
	2140	24" diameter, 14 ga. CN		160	.300		16.15	7.25	1.13	24.53	30.50	
	2160	30" diameter, 14 ga.	B-13	120	.467		21	11.55	5.25	37.80	46.50	
	2180	36" diameter, 12 ga.		120	.467		31	11.55	5.25	47.80	57.50	
	2200	48" diameter, 12 ga.		100	.560		47	13.85	6.30	67.15	80.50	
	2220	60" diameter, 10 ga.	B-13B	75	.747		61	18.45	12	91.45	109	
	2240	72" diameter, 8 ga.	"	45	1.244		93	31	20	144	172	
	2500	Galvanized, uncoated, 20' lengths										
	2520	8" diameter, 16 ga.	B-14	355	.135	L.F.	4.61	3.27	.51	8.39	10.70	
	2540	10" diameter, 16 ga.		280	.171		5.10	4.14	.65	9.89	12.75	
	2560	12" diameter, 16 ga.		220	.218		5.75	5.25	.82	11.82	15.45	
	2580	15" diameter, 16 ga.		220	.218		7.65	5.25	.82	13.72	17.50	
	2600	18" diameter, 16 ga.		205	.234		10.30	5.65	.88	16.83	21	
	2620	24" diameter, 14 ga.		175	.274		14.10	6.65	1.03	21.78	27	
	2640	30" diameter, 14 ga.	B-13	130	.431		17.90	10.65	4.84	33.39	41.50	
	2660	36" diameter, 12 ga.		130	.431		29.50	10.65	4.84	44.99	54.50	
	2680	48" diameter, 12 ga.		110	.509		39.50	12.60	5.70	57.80	69.50	
	2690	60" diameter, 10 ga.	B-13B	78	.718		62	17.75	11.55	91.30	108	
	2780	End sections, 8" diameter	B-14	24	2	Ea.	55	48.50	7.55	111.05	144	
	2785	10" diameter		22	2.182		56.50	52.50	8.25	117.25	153	
	2790	12" diameter		35	1.371		42.50	33	5.15	80.65	104	
	2800	18" diameter		30	1.600		65.50	38.50	6.05	110.05	139	
	2810	24" diameter	B-13	25	2.240		95.50	55.50	25	176	219	
	2820	30" diameter		25	2.240		181	55.50	25	261.50	315	
	2825	36" diameter		20	2.800		240	69.50	31.50	341	405	
	2830	48" diameter		10	5.600		495	139	63	697	830	
	2835	60" diameter	B-13B	5	11.200		650	277	180	1,107	1,350	
	2840	72" diameter	"	4	14		1,175	345	225	1,745	2,050	
	3000	Corrugated galvanized or alum. oval arch culverts, coated & paved										
	3020	17" x 13", 16 ga., 15" equivalent	B-14	200	.240	L.F.	17.35	5.80	.90	24.05	29	
	3040	21" x 15", 16 ga., 18" equivalent		150	.320		22.50	7.75	1.21	31.46	38	
	3060	28" x 20", 14 ga., 24" equivalent		125	.384		32	9.30	1.45	42.75	51.50	
	3080	35" x 24", 14 ga., 30" equivalent		100	.480		39.50	11.60	1.81	52.91	63.50	
	3100	42" x 29", 12 ga., 36" equivalent	B-13	100	.560		58.50	13.85	6.30	78.65	92.50	
	3120	49" x 33", 12 ga., 42" equivalent		90	.622		70.50	15.40	7	92.90	109	
	3140	57" x 38", 12 ga., 48" equivalent		75	.747		79.50	18.45	8.40	106.35	125	
	3160	Steel, plain oval arch culverts, plain										
	3180	17" x 13", 16 ga., 15" equivalent	B-14	225	.213	L.F.	9.55	5.15	.80	15.50	19.40	

		02630	Storm Drainage	CREW	DAILY OUTPUT	LABOR-HOURS	UNIT	2001 BARE COSTS MAT.	LABOR	EQUIP.	TOTAL	TOTAL INCL O&P	
100	3200		21" x 15", 16 ga., 18" equivalent	B-14	175	.274	L.F.	11.30	6.65	1.03	18.98	24	100
	3220		28" x 20", 14 ga., 24" equivalent	↓	150	.320		18.15	7.75	1.21	27.11	33.50	
	3240		35" x 24", 14 ga., 30" equivalent	B-13	108	.519		23	12.85	5.85	41.70	51.50	
	3260		42" x 29", 12 ga., 36" equivalent		108	.519		37.50	12.85	5.85	56.20	68	
	3280		49" x 33", 12 ga., 42" equivalent		92	.609		44.50	15.05	6.85	66.40	80	
	3300		57" x 38", 12 ga., 48" equivalent		75	.747	↓	39	18.45	8.40	65.85	81	
	3320		End sections, 17" x 13"		22	2.545	Ea.	52	63	28.50	143.50	187	
	3340		42" x 29"	↓	17	3.294	"	214	81.50	37	332.50	405	
	3360		Multi-plate arch, steel	B-20	1,690	.014	Lb.	.60	.37		.97	1.24	
200	0010		**CATCH BASINS OR MANHOLES** not including footing, excavation,										200
	0020		backfill, frame and cover										
	0050		Brick, 4' inside diameter, 4' deep	D-1	1	16	Ea.	271	420		691	950	
	0100		6' deep		.70	22.857		380	600		980	1,350	
	0150		8' deep		.50	32	↓	485	840		1,325	1,825	
	0200		For depths over 8', add		4	4	V.L.F.	105	105		210	278	
	0400		Concrete blocks (radial), 4' I.D., 4' deep		1.50	10.667	Ea.	225	280		505	680	
	0500		6' deep		1	16		298	420		718	980	
	0600		8' deep		.70	22.857		370	600		970	1,350	
	0700		For depths over 8', add	↓	5.50	2.909	V.L.F.	38.50	76.50		115	160	
	0800		Concrete, cast in place, 4' x 4', 8" thick, 4' deep	C-14H	2	24	Ea.	345	690	18.95	1,053.95	1,500	
	0900		6' deep		1.50	32		500	925	25.50	1,450.50	2,025	
	1000		8' deep		1	48	↓	715	1,375	38	2,128	3,000	
	1100		For depths over 8', add	↓	8	6	V.L.F.	85.50	173	4.74	263.24	375	
	1110		Precast, 4' I.D., 4' deep	B-22	4.10	7.317	Ea.	305	197	52	554	695	
	1120		6' deep		3	10		425	269	71	765	965	
	1130		8' deep		2	15	↓	455	405	107	967	1,250	
	1140		For depths over 8', add	↓	16	1.875	V.L.F.	78.50	50.50	13.30	142.30	180	
	1150		5' I.D., 4' deep	B-6	3	8	Ea.	445	199	60.50	704.50	860	
	1160		6' deep		2	12		605	298	90.50	993.50	1,225	
	1170		8' deep		1.50	16		760	395	121	1,276	1,575	
	1180		For depths over 8', add		12	2	V.L.F.	99	49.50	15.10	163.60	202	
	1190		6' I.D., 4' deep		2	12	Ea.	730	298	90.50	1,118.50	1,375	
	1200		6' deep		1.50	16		950	395	121	1,466	1,800	
	1210		8' deep		1	24	↓	1,175	595	181	1,951	2,400	
	1220		For depths over 8', add	↓	8	3	V.L.F.	153	74.50	22.50	250	310	
	1250		Slab tops, precast, 8" thick										
	1300		4' diameter manhole	B-6	8	3	Ea.	156	74.50	22.50	253	310	
	1400		5' diameter manhole		7.50	3.200		275	79.50	24	378.50	450	
	1500		6' diameter manhole		7	3.429		335	85	26	446	530	
	1600		Frames & covers, C.I., 24" square, 500 lb.		7.80	3.077		214	76.50	23	313.50	380	
	1700		26" D shape, 600 lb.		7	3.429		340	85	26	451	535	
	1800		Light traffic, 18" diameter, 100 lb.		10	2.400		114	59.50	18.10	191.60	238	
	1900		24" diameter, 300 lb.		8.70	2.759		138	68.50	21	227.50	280	
	2000		36" diameter, 900 lb.		5.80	4.138		385	103	31	519	615	
	2100		Heavy traffic, 24" diameter, 400 lb.		7.80	3.077		158	76.50	23	257.50	320	
	2200		36" diameter, 1150 lb.		3	8		460	199	60.50	719.50	875	
	2300		Mass. State standard, 26" diameter, 475 lb.		7	3.429		275	85	26	386	465	
	2400		30" diameter, 620 lb.		7	3.429		300	85	26	411	490	
	2500		Watertight, 24" diameter, 350 lb.		7.80	3.077		260	76.50	23	359.50	430	
	2600		26" diameter, 500 lb.		7	3.429		261	85	26	372	445	
	2700		32" diameter, 575 lb.	↓	6	4	↓	500	99.50	30	629.50	735	
	2800		3 piece cover & frame, 10" deep,										
	2900		1200 lbs., for heavy equipment	B-6	3	8	Ea.	795	199	60.50	1,054.50	1,250	
	3000		Raised for paving 1-1/4" to 2" high,										
	3100		4 piece expansion ring										

SITE CONSTRUCTION **2**

For expanded coverage of these items see *Means Heavy Construction Cost Data 2001*

02630 | Storm Drainage

		CREW	DAILY OUTPUT	LABOR-HOURS	UNIT	MAT.	LABOR	EQUIP.	TOTAL	TOTAL INCL O&P	
						2001 BARE COSTS					
200	3200	20" to 26" diameter	1 Clab	3	2.667	Ea.	105	61		166	212	**200**
	3300	30" to 36" diameter	"	3	2.667	"	147	61		208	258	
	3320	Frames and covers, existing, raised for paving, 2", including										
	3340	row of brick, concrete collar, up to 12" wide frame	B-6	18	1.333	Ea.	32	33	10.05	75.05	97.50	
	3360	20" to 26" wide frame		11	2.182		42	54	16.45	112.45	148	
	3380	30" to 36" wide frame		9	2.667		52.50	66	20	138.50	182	
	3400	Inverts, single channel brick	D-1	3	5.333		59	140		199	282	
	3500	Concrete		5	3.200		46	84		130	181	
	3600	Triple channel, brick		2	8		89.50	210		299.50	425	
	3700	Concrete		3	5.333		61.50	140		201.50	285	
	3800	Steps, heavyweight cast iron, 7" x 9"	1 Bric	40	.200		9.45	5.90		15.35	19.55	
	3900	8" x 9"		40	.200		14.20	5.90		20.10	25	
	3928	12" x 10-1/2"		40	.200		13	5.90		18.90	23.50	
	4000	Standard sizes, galvanized steel		40	.200		11.75	5.90		17.65	22	
	4100	Aluminum		40	.200		15	5.90		20.90	25.50	

02720 | Unbound Base Courses & Ballasts

		CREW	DAILY OUTPUT	LABOR-HOURS	UNIT	MAT.	LABOR	EQUIP.	TOTAL	TOTAL INCL O&P	
						2001 BARE COSTS					
200	0010	**BASE COURSE** For roadways and large paved areas										**200**
	0050	Crushed 3/4" stone base, compacted, 3" deep	B-36B	5,200	.012	S.Y.	2.01	.33	.57	2.91	3.35	
	0100	6" deep		5,000	.013		4.03	.35	.60	4.98	5.60	
	0200	9" deep		4,600	.014		6.05	.38	.65	7.08	7.95	
	0300	12" deep		4,200	.015		8.05	.41	.71	9.17	10.25	
	0301	Crushed 1-1/2" stone base, compacted to 4" deep		6,000	.011		4.05	.29	.50	4.84	5.45	
	0302	6" deep		5,400	.012		6.05	.32	.55	6.92	7.80	
	0303	8" deep		4,500	.014		8.10	.38	.66	9.14	10.20	
	0304	12" deep		3,800	.017		12.15	.45	.79	13.39	14.90	
	0350	Bank run gravel, spread and compacted										
	0370	6" deep	B-32	6,000	.005	S.Y.	7.30	.15	.23	7.68	8.50	
	0390	9" deep		4,900	.007		10.90	.19	.29	11.38	12.60	
	0400	12" deep		4,200	.008		14.55	.22	.33	15.10	16.70	
	0700	Liquid application to gravel base, asphalt emulsion	B-45	6,000	.003	Gal.	2.60	.07	.12	2.79	3.10	
	0800	Prime and seal, cut back asphalt		6,000	.003	"	3.07	.07	.12	3.26	3.61	
	1000	Macadam penetration crushed stone, 2 gal. per S.Y., 4" thick		6,000	.003	S.Y.	5.20	.07	.12	5.39	5.95	
	1100	6" thick, 3 gal. per S.Y.		4,000	.004		7.80	.11	.18	8.09	8.95	
	1200	8" thick, 4 gal. per S.Y.		3,000	.005		10.40	.14	.24	10.78	11.95	
	6000	Stabilization fabric, polypropylene, 6 oz./S.Y.	B-6	10,000	.002		.84	.06	.02	.92	1.03	
	8900	For small and irregular areas, add						50%	50%			
215	0010	**BASE** Prepare and roll sub-base, small areas to 2500 S.Y.	B-32A	1,500	.016	S.Y.		.45	.61	1.06	1.35	**215**
	0100	Large areas over 2500 S.Y.	B-32	3,700	.009	"		.25	.38	.63	.80	

02740 | Flexible Pavement

		CREW	DAILY OUTPUT	LABOR-HOURS	UNIT	MAT.	LABOR	EQUIP.	TOTAL	TOTAL INCL O&P	
						2001 BARE COSTS					
300	0010	**ASPHALTIC CONCRETE PAVEMENT** for highways										**300**
	0020	and large paved areas [R02065 -300]										
	0080	Binder course, 1-1/2" thick	B-25	7,725	.011	S.Y.	1.97	.29	.22	2.48	2.85	
	0120	2" thick		6,345	.014		2.63	.35	.27	3.25	3.73	
	0160	3" thick		4,905	.018		3.90	.45	.35	4.70	5.35	
	0200	4" thick		4,140	.021		5.20	.53	.41	6.14	7.05	

Important: See the Reference Section for critical supporting data - Reference Nos., Crews, & City Cost Indexes

02740 | Flexible Pavement

			CREW	DAILY OUTPUT	LABOR-HOURS	UNIT	MAT.	LABOR	EQUIP.	TOTAL	TOTAL INCL O&P	
300	0300	Wearing course, 1" thick [R02065-300]	B-25B	10,575	.009	S.Y.	1.54	.23	.18	1.95	2.25	300
	0340	1-1/2" thick		7,725	.012		2.34	.32	.25	2.91	3.33	
	0380	2" thick		6,345	.015		3.14	.39	.30	3.83	4.39	
	0420	2-1/2" thick		5,480	.018		3.88	.45	.35	4.68	5.35	
	0460	3" thick		4,900	.020		4.62	.50	.39	5.51	6.30	
	0800	Alternate method of figuring paving costs										
	0810	Binder course, 1-1/2" thick	B-25	630	.140	Ton	26	3.50	2.71	32.21	37	
	0811	2" thick		690	.128		26	3.20	2.47	31.67	36	
	0812	3" thick		800	.110		26	2.76	2.13	30.89	35	
	0813	4" thick		850	.104		26	2.60	2.01	30.61	34.50	
	0850	Wearing course, 1" thick	B-25B	575	.167		28.50	4.26	3.33	36.09	42	
	0851	1-1/2" thick		630	.152		28.50	3.89	3.04	35.43	41	
	0852	2" thick		690	.139		28.50	3.55	2.78	34.83	40	
	0853	2-1/2" thick		745	.129		28.50	3.29	2.57	34.36	39.50	
	0854	3" thick		800	.120		28.50	3.06	2.40	33.96	39	
	1000	Pavement replacement over trench, 2" thick	B-37	90	.533	S.Y.	3.20	12.90	1.48	17.58	25	
	1050	4" thick		70	.686		6.35	16.55	1.91	24.81	35	
	1080	6" thick		55	.873		10.05	21	2.43	33.48	47	
315	0011	PAVING Asphaltic concrete, parking lots & driveways										315
	0020	6" stone base, 2" binder course, 1" topping	B-25C	9,000	.005	S.F.	1.13	.14	.17	1.44	1.63	
	0300	Binder course, 1-1/2" thick		35,000	.001		.30	.04	.04	.38	.43	
	0400	2" thick		25,000	.002		.39	.05	.06	.50	.58	
	0500	3" thick		15,000	.003		.60	.08	.10	.78	.90	
	0600	4" thick		10,800	.004		.79	.11	.14	1.04	1.19	
	0800	Sand finish course, 3/4" thick		41,000	.001		.17	.03	.04	.24	.27	
	0900	1" thick		34,000	.001		.21	.04	.04	.29	.34	
	1000	Fill pot holes, hot mix, 2" thick	B-16	4,200	.008		.39	.18	.12	.69	.83	
	1100	4" thick		3,500	.009		.56	.22	.14	.92	1.11	
	1120	6" thick		3,100	.010		.76	.24	.16	1.16	1.38	
	1140	Cold patch, 2" thick	B-51	3,000	.016		.45	.37	.05	.87	1.14	
	1160	4" thick		2,700	.018		.86	.41	.06	1.33	1.65	
	1180	6" thick		1,900	.025		1.33	.59	.08	2	2.48	

02750 | Rigid Pavement

			CREW	DAILY OUTPUT	LABOR-HOURS	UNIT	MAT.	LABOR	EQUIP.	TOTAL	TOTAL INCL O&P	
100	0010	CONCRETE PAVEMENT Including joints, finishing, and curing										100
	0020	Fixed form, 12' pass, unreinforced, 6" thick	B-26	3,000	.029	S.Y.	16.25	.76	.61	17.62	19.75	
	0100	8" thick		2,750	.032		22.50	.82	.67	23.99	27	
	0200	9" thick		2,500	.035		26	.91	.73	27.64	31	
	0300	10" thick		2,100	.042		28.50	1.08	.87	30.45	33.50	
	0400	12" thick		1,800	.049		30.50	1.26	1.02	32.78	36.50	
	0500	15" thick		1,500	.059		34	1.51	1.22	36.73	41	
	0510	For small irregular areas, add						100%				
	0700	Finishing, broom finish small areas	2 Cefi	120	.133	S.Y.		3.73		3.73	5.55	
	1000	Curing, with sprayed membrane by hand	2 Clab	1,500	.011	"	.32	.24		.56	.73	
	1650	For integral coloring, see div. 03310-220										

02766 | Pavement Markings

			CREW	DAILY OUTPUT	LABOR-HOURS	UNIT	MAT.	LABOR	EQUIP.	TOTAL	TOTAL INCL O&P	
550	0010	LINES ON PAV'T Acrylic waterborne, white or yellow, 4" wide	B-78	20,000	.002	L.F.	.11	.06	.02	.19	.24	550
	0200	6" wide		11,000	.004		.10	.10	.04	.24	.32	
	0500	8" wide		10,000	.005		.14	.11	.05	.30	.38	
	0600	12" wide		4,000	.012		.26	.28	.12	.66	.86	
	0620	Arrows or gore lines		2,300	.021	S.F.	.50	.49	.20	1.19	1.53	
	0640	Temporary paint, white or yellow		15,000	.003	L.F.	.15	.07	.03	.25	.32	
	0660	Removal	1 Clab	300	.027			.61		.61	.95	
	0680	Temporary tape	2 Clab	1,500	.011		1.38	.24		1.62	1.90	

For expanded coverage of these items see *Means Heavy Construction Cost Data 2001*

SITE CONSTRUCTION 2

2 SITE CONSTRUCTION

			DAILY	LABOR-		2001 BARE COSTS				TOTAL	
02766	**Pavement Markings**	CREW	OUTPUT	HOURS	UNIT	MAT.	LABOR	EQUIP.	TOTAL	INCL O&P	
550	0710	Thermoplastic, white or yellow, 4" wide	B-79	15,000	.003	L.F.	.56	.06	.05	.67	.77	**550**
	0730	6" wide		14,000	.003		.81	.07	.05	.93	1.05	
	0740	8" wide		12,000	.003		1.09	.08	.06	1.23	1.39	
	0750	12" wide		6,000	.007		1.62	.16	.12	1.90	2.17	
	0760	Arrows		660	.061	S.F.	1.50	1.42	1.12	4.04	5.10	
	0770	Gore lines		2,500	.016		1	.37	.30	1.67	2.01	
	0780	Letters		660	.061		1.25	1.42	1.12	3.79	4.82	
	0790	Layout of pavement marking	A-2	25,000	.001	L.F.		.02	.01	.03	.04	
	0800	Parking stall, paint, white	B-78	440	.109	Stall	2.60	2.54	1.07	6.21	8	
	1000	Street letters and numbers	"	1,600	.030	S.F.	.50	.70	.29	1.49	1.96	

			DAILY	LABOR-		2001 BARE COSTS				TOTAL	
02770	**Curbs and Gutters**	CREW	OUTPUT	HOURS	UNIT	MAT.	LABOR	EQUIP.	TOTAL	INCL O&P	
225	0010	**CURBS** Asphaltic, machine formed, 8" wide, 6" high, 40 L.F./ton	B-27	1,000	.032	L.F.	.57	.75	.14	1.46	1.96	**225**
	0100	8" wide, 8" high, 30 L.F. per ton		900	.036		.66	.83	.16	1.65	2.20	
	0150	Asphaltic berm, 12" W, 3"-6" H, 35 L.F./ton, before pavement		700	.046		.81	1.07	.21	2.09	2.79	
	0200	12" W, 1-1/2" to 4" H, 60 L.F. per ton, laid with pavement	B-2	1,050	.038		.49	.89		1.38	1.93	
	0300	Concrete, wood forms, 6" x 18", straight	C-2A	500	.096		2.18	2.71		4.89	6.60	
	0400	6" x 18", radius		200	.240		2.30	6.80		9.10	13.05	
	0410	Steel forms, 6" x 18", straight		700	.069		2.69	1.94		4.63	5.95	
	0411	6" x 18", radius		400	.120		3.47	3.39		6.86	9.05	
	0415	Machine formed, 6" x 18", straight	B-69A	2,000	.024		3.04	.61	.22	3.87	4.51	
	0416	6" x 18", radius	"	900	.053		3.17	1.35	.49	5.01	6.10	
	0421	Curb and gutter, straight										
	0422	with 6" high curb and 6" thick gutter, wood forms										
	0430	24" wide, .055 C.Y. per L.F.	C-2A	375	.128	L.F.	10.70	3.61		14.31	17.35	
	0435	30" wide, .066 C.Y. per L.F.		340	.141		11.60	3.99		15.59	19	
	0440	Steel forms, 24" wide, straight		700	.069		4.95	1.94		6.89	8.45	
	0441	Radius		300	.160		4.95	4.52		9.47	12.45	
	0442	30" wide, straight		700	.069		5.95	1.94		7.89	9.55	
	0443	Radius		300	.160		5.95	4.52		10.47	13.55	
	0445	Machine formed, 24" wide, straight	B-69A	2,000	.024		4.95	.61	.22	5.78	6.60	
	0446	Radius		900	.053		4.95	1.35	.49	6.79	8.05	
	0447	30" wide, straight		2,000	.024		5.95	.61	.22	6.78	7.70	
	0448	Radius		900	.053		5.95	1.35	.49	7.79	9.15	
	0550	Precast, 6" x 18", straight	B-29	700	.080		6.60	1.98	.93	9.51	11.35	
	0600	6" x 18", radius	"	325	.172		7.50	4.26	2	13.76	17.05	
	1000	Granite, split face, straight, 5" x 16"	D-13	500	.096		9.10	2.68	.85	12.63	15.05	
	1100	6" x 18"	"	450	.107		11.95	2.98	.95	15.88	18.75	
	1300	Radius curbing, 6" x 18", over 10' radius	B-29	260	.215		14.60	5.35	2.49	22.44	27	
	1400	Corners, 2' radius		80	.700	Ea.	49	17.30	8.10	74.40	90	
	1600	Edging, 4-1/2" x 12", straight		300	.187	L.F.	4.54	4.62	2.16	11.32	14.50	
	1800	Curb inlets, (guttermouth) straight		41	1.366	Ea.	109	34	15.80	158.80	190	
	2000	Indian granite (belgian block)										
	2100	Jumbo, 10-1/2" x 7-1/2" x 4", grey	D-1	150	.107	L.F.	1.54	2.80		4.34	6.05	
	2150	Pink		150	.107		2.06	2.80		4.86	6.60	
	2200	Regular, 9" x 4-1/2" x 4-1/2", grey		160	.100		1.42	2.63		4.05	5.60	
	2250	Pink		160	.100		2	2.63		4.63	6.25	
	2300	Cubes, 4" x 4" x 4", grey		175	.091		1.40	2.40		3.80	5.25	
	2350	Pink		175	.091		1.48	2.40		3.88	5.35	
	2400	6" x 6" x 6", pink		155	.103		3.60	2.71		6.31	8.15	
	2500	Alternate pricing method for indian granite										
	2550	Jumbo, 10-1/2" x 7-1/2" x 4" (30lb), grey				Ton	88			88	97	
	2600	Pink					120			120	132	
	2650	Regular, 9" x 4-1/2" x 4-1/2" (20lb), grey					100			100	110	
	2700	Pink					140			140	154	
	2750	Cubes, 4" x 4" x 4" (5lb), grey					170			170	187	

02770 | Curbs and Gutters

			CREW	DAILY OUTPUT	LABOR-HOURS	UNIT	2001 BARE COSTS				TOTAL INCL O&P	
							MAT.	LABOR	EQUIP.	TOTAL		
225	2800	Pink				Ton	190			190	209	225
	2850	6" x 6" x 6" (25lb), pink					140			140	154	
	2900	For pallets, add				▼	15			15	16.50	

02775 | Sidewalks

			CREW	DAILY OUTPUT	LABOR-HOURS	UNIT	MAT.	LABOR	EQUIP.	TOTAL	TOTAL INCL O&P	
275	0010	**SIDEWALKS, DRIVEWAYS, & PATIOS** No base R02065 -300										275
	0020	Asphaltic concrete, 2" thick	B-37	720	.067	S.Y.	3.49	1.61	.19	5.29	6.55	
	0100	2-1/2" thick	"	660	.073	"	4.43	1.76	.20	6.39	7.85	
	0300	Concrete, 3000 psi, CIP, 6 x 6 - W1.4 x W1.4 mesh,										
	0310	broomed finish, no base, 4" thick	B-24	600	.040	S.F.	1.08	1.07		2.15	2.83	
	0350	5" thick		545	.044		1.44	1.17		2.61	3.38	
	0400	6" thick	▼	510	.047		1.68	1.25		2.93	3.78	
	0450	For bank run gravel base, 4" thick, add	B-18	2,500	.010		.35	.23	.02	.60	.76	
	0520	8" thick, add	"	1,600	.015		.70	.35	.04	1.09	1.36	
	0550	Exposed aggregate finish, add to above, minimum	B-24	1,875	.013		.07	.34		.41	.60	
	0600	Maximum	"	455	.053		.24	1.41		1.65	2.43	
	1000	Crushed stone, 1" thick, white marble	2 Clab	1,700	.009		.21	.22		.43	.57	
	1050	Bluestone	"	1,700	.009		.19	.22		.41	.55	
	1700	Redwood, prefabricated, 4' x 4' sections	2 Carp	316	.051		7.15	1.48		8.63	10.15	
	1750	Redwood planks, 1" thick, on sleepers	"	240	.067	▼	4.99	1.94		6.93	8.55	

02778 | Steps

			CREW	DAILY OUTPUT	LABOR-HOURS	UNIT	MAT.	LABOR	EQUIP.	TOTAL	TOTAL INCL O&P	
280	0010	**STEPS** Incl. excav., borrow & concrete base, where applicable										280
	0100	Brick steps	B-24	35	.686	LF Riser	7.85	18.25		26.10	36.50	
	0200	Railroad ties	2 Clab	25	.640		2.75	14.60		17.35	26	
	0300	Bluestone treads, 12" x 2" or 12" x 1-1/2"	B-24	30	.800	▼	19.45	21.50		40.95	54.50	
	0500	Concrete, cast in place, see division 03310-240										
	0600	Precast concrete, see division 03480-800										

02780 | Unit Pavers

			CREW	DAILY OUTPUT	LABOR-HOURS	UNIT	MAT.	LABOR	EQUIP.	TOTAL	TOTAL INCL O&P	
100	0010	**ASPHALT BLOCKS**, 6"x12"x1-1/4", w/bed & neopr. adhesive	D-1	135	.119	S.F.	3.75	3.11		6.86	8.95	100
	0100	3" thick		130	.123		5.25	3.23		8.48	10.80	
	0300	Hexagonal tile, 8" wide, 1-1/4" thick		135	.119		3.75	3.11		6.86	8.95	
	0400	2" thick		130	.123		5.25	3.23		8.48	10.80	
	0500	Square, 8" x 8", 1-1/4" thick		135	.119		3.75	3.11		6.86	8.95	
	0600	2" thick	▼	130	.123		5.25	3.23		8.48	10.80	
	0900	For exposed aggregate (ground finish) add					.25			.25	.28	
	0910	For colors, add				▼	.20			.20	.22	
200	0010	**BRICK PAVING** 4" x 8" x 1-1/2", without joints (4.5 brick/S.F.)	D-1	110	.145	S.F.	2.10	3.82		5.92	8.20	200
	0100	Grouted, 3/8" joint (3.9 brick/S.F.)		90	.178		2.43	4.67		7.10	9.85	
	0200	4" x 8" x 2-1/4", without joints (4.5 bricks/S.F.)		110	.145		2.69	3.82		6.51	8.85	
	0300	Grouted, 3/8" joint (3.9 brick/S.F.)	▼	90	.178		2.48	4.67		7.15	9.95	
	0500	Bedding, asphalt, 3/4" thick	B-25	5,130	.017		.33	.43	.33	1.09	1.40	
	0540	Course washed sand bed, 1" thick	B-18	5,000	.005		.14	.11	.01	.26	.35	
	0580	Mortar, 1" thick	D-1	300	.053		.26	1.40		1.66	2.46	
	0620	2" thick		200	.080		.52	2.10		2.62	3.82	
	1500	Brick on 1" thick sand bed laid flat, 4.5 per S.F.		100	.160		2.07	4.20		6.27	8.80	
	2000	Brick pavers, laid on edge, 7.2 per S.F.		70	.229		2.04	6		8.04	11.55	
	2500	For 4" thick concrete bed and joints, add	▼	595	.027		.78	.71		1.49	1.95	
	2800	For steam cleaning, add	A-1	950	.008	▼	.05	.19	.07	.31	.44	
600	0010	**PRECAST CONCRETE PAVING SLABS**										600
	0710	Precast concrete patio blocks, 2-3/8" thick, colors, 8" x 16"	D-1	265	.060	S.F.	1.04	1.59		2.63	3.59	
	0750	Exposed local aggregate, natural	2 Bric	250	.064		4.68	1.89		6.57	8.10	
	0800	Colors	▼	250	.064	▼	5	1.89		6.89	8.45	

SITE CONSTRUCTION 2

2 SITE CONSTRUCTION

			CREW	DAILY OUTPUT	LABOR-HOURS	UNIT	2001 BARE COSTS				TOTAL INCL O&P	
		02780 | Unit Pavers					MAT.	LABOR	EQUIP.	TOTAL		
600	0850	Exposed granite or limestone aggregate	2 Bric	250	.064	S.F.	5.65	1.89		7.54	9.15	600
	0900	Exposed white tumblestone aggregate	↓	250	.064	↓	3.19	1.89		5.08	6.45	
650	0010	**PLANTER BLOCKS** Precast concrete, interlocking										650
	0020	"V" blocks for retaining soil	D-1	205	.078	S.F.	3.94	2.05		5.99	7.50	
800	0010	**STONE PAVERS**										800
	1100	Flagging, bluestone, irregular, 1" thick,	D-1	81	.198	S.F.	4	5.20		9.20	12.40	
	1150	Snapped random rectangular, 1" thick		92	.174		6.05	4.57		10.62	13.70	
	1200	1-1/2" thick		85	.188		7.30	4.95		12.25	15.65	
	1250	2" thick		83	.193		8.50	5.05		13.55	17.20	
	1300	Slate, natural cleft, irregular, 3/4" thick		92	.174		4.25	4.57		8.82	11.75	
	1350	Random rectangular, gauged, 1/2" thick		105	.152		9.20	4		13.20	16.30	
	1400	Random rectangular, butt joint, gauged, 1/4" thick	↓	150	.107	↓	9.90	2.80		12.70	15.25	
	1500	For interior setting, add								25%	25%	
	1550	Granite blocks, 3-1/2" x 3-1/2" x 3-1/2"	D-1	92	.174	S.F.	5.85	4.57		10.42	13.50	
	1600	4" to 12" long, 3" to 5" wide, 3" to 5" thick		98	.163		4.88	4.29		9.17	12	
	1650	6" to 15" long, 3" to 6" wide, 3" to 5" thick	↓	105	.152	↓	2.60	4		6.60	9.05	
		02785 | Flexible Pavement Coating										
800	0010	**SEALCOATING** 2 coat coal tar pitch emulsion over 10,000 S.Y.	B-45	5,000	.003	S.Y.	.45	.09	.15	.69	.79	800
	0030	1000 to 10,000 S.Y.	"	3,000	.005		.45	.14	.24	.83	.99	
	0100	Under 1000 S.Y.	B-1	1,050	.023		.45	.54		.99	1.34	
	0300	Petroleum resistant, over 10,000 S.Y.	B-45	5,000	.003		.52	.09	.15	.76	.86	
	0320	1000 to 10,000 S.Y.	"	3,000	.005		.52	.14	.24	.90	1.06	
	0400	Under 1000 S.Y.	B-1	1,050	.023		.52	.54		1.06	1.41	
	0600	Non-skid pavement renewal, over 10,000 S.Y.	B-45	5,000	.003		.62	.09	.15	.86	.97	
	0620	1000 to 10,000 S.Y.	"	3,000	.005		.62	.14	.24	1	1.17	
	0700	Under 1000 S.Y.	B-1	1,050	.023		.62	.54		1.16	1.52	
	0800	Prepare and clean surface for above	A-2	8,545	.003	↓		.06	.02	.08	.12	
	1000	Hand seal asphalt curbing	B-1	4,420	.005	L.F.	.31	.13		.44	.54	
	1900	Asphalt surface treatment, single course, small area										
	1901	0.30 gal/S.Y. asphalt material, 20#/S.Y. aggregate	B-91	5,000	.013	S.Y.	.73	.35	.28	1.36	1.63	
	1910	Roadway or large area		10,000	.006		.67	.17	.14	.98	1.15	
	1950	Asphalt surface treatment, dbl. course for small area		3,000	.021		1.35	.58	.46	2.39	2.88	
	1960	Roadway or large area		6,000	.011		1.22	.29	.23	1.74	2.03	
	1980	Asphalt surface treatment, single course, for shoulders		7,500	.009		.78	.23	.18	1.19	1.41	
	2080	Sand sealing, sharp sand, asphalt emulsion, small area		10,000	.006		.52	.17	.14	.83	.98	
	2120	Roadway or large area	↓	18,000	.004	↓	.45	.10	.08	.63	.72	
		02790 | Athletic/Recreational Surfaces										
400	0010	**TURF, ARTIFICIAL** Not including asphalt base or drainage, but										400
	0020	including cushion pad, over 50,000 S.F.										
	0200	1/2" pile and 5/16" cushion pad, standard	C-17	3,200	.025	S.F.	5.85	.76		6.61	7.60	
	0300	Deluxe		2,560	.031		6.90	.95		7.85	9.10	
	0500	1/2" pile and 5/8" cushion pad, standard		2,844	.028		8.50	.85		9.35	10.70	
	0600	Deluxe	↓	2,327	.034	↓	9.30	1.04		10.34	11.85	
	0800	For asphaltic concrete base, 2-1/2" thick,										
	0900	with 6" crushed stone sub-base, add	B-25	12,000	.007	S.F.	1	.18	.14	1.32	1.54	
850	0010	**TENNIS COURT** Asphalt, incl. base, 2-1/2" thick, one court	B-37	450	.107	S.Y.	12.35	2.58	.30	15.23	17.95	850
	0200	Two courts		675	.071		7.35	1.72	.20	9.27	11	
	0300	Clay courts		360	.133		28	3.22	.37	31.59	36.50	
	0400	Pulverized natural greenstone with 4" base, fast dry		250	.192		26	4.64	.53	31.17	36.50	
	0800	Rubber-acrylic base resilient pavement	↓	600	.080		27	1.93	.22	29.15	33	
	1000	Colored sealer, acrylic emulsion, 3 coats	2 Clab	800	.020		3.41	.46		3.87	4.47	
	1100	3 coat, 2 colors	"	900	.018		5.05	.41		5.46	6.20	
	1200	For preparing old courts, add	1 Clab	825	.010	↓		.22		.22	.35	

Important: See the Reference Section for critical supporting data - Reference Nos., Crews, & City Cost Indexes

02700 | Bases, Ballasts, Pavements & Appurtenances

02790 | Athletic/Recreational Surfaces

			CREW	DAILY OUTPUT	LABOR-HOURS	UNIT	2001 BARE COSTS MAT.	LABOR	EQUIP.	TOTAL	TOTAL INCL O&P	
850	1400	Posts for nets, 3-1/2" diameter with eye bolts	B-1	3.40	7.059	Pr.	140	166		306	415	850
	1500	With pulley & reel		3.40	7.059	"	200	166		366	480	
	1700	Net, 42' long, nylon thread with binder		50	.480	Ea.	179	11.30		190.30	215	
	1800	All metal		6.50	3.692	"	315	87		402	480	
	2000	Paint markings on asphalt, 2 coats	1 Pord	1.78	4.494	Court	58.50	117		175.50	243	
	2200	Complete court with fence, etc., asphaltic conc., minimum	B-37	.20	240		12,000	5,800	665	18,465	23,000	
	2300	Maximum		.16	300		14,900	7,250	835	22,985	28,600	
	2800	Clay courts, minimum		.20	240		14,300	5,800	665	20,765	25,600	
	2900	Maximum		.16	300		17,600	7,250	835	25,685	31,600	
900	0010	**RUNNING TRACK** Asphalt, incl base, 3" thick	B-37	300	.160	S.Y.	10.40	3.87	.44	14.71	17.95	900
	0100	Surface, latex rubber system, 3/8" thick, black	B-20	125	.192		4.68	4.96		9.64	12.95	
	0150	Colors		125	.192		8.30	4.96		13.26	16.95	
	0300	Urethane rubber system, 3/8" thick, black		120	.200		12.50	5.15		17.65	22	
	0400	Color coating		115	.209		16.25	5.40		21.65	26.50	

SITE CONSTRUCTION **2**

02800 | Site Improvements and Amenities

02810 | Irrigation System

			CREW	DAILY OUTPUT	LABOR-HOURS	UNIT	2001 BARE COSTS MAT.	LABOR	EQUIP.	TOTAL	TOTAL INCL O&P	
800	0010	**SPRINKLER IRRIGATION SYSTEM** For lawns										800
	0100	Golf course with fully automatic system	C-17	.05	1,600	9 holes	79,000	48,400		127,400	162,500	
	0200	24' diam. head at 15' O.C. incl. piping, auto oper., minimum	B-20	70	.343	Head	17.35	8.85		26.20	33	
	0300	Maximum		40	.600		40	15.50		55.50	68.50	
	0500	60' diam. head at 40' O.C. incl. piping, auto oper., minimum		28	.857		52.50	22		74.50	92.50	
	0600	Maximum		23	1.043		147	27		174	205	
	0800	Residential system, custom, 1" supply		2,000	.012	S.F.	.26	.31		.57	.78	
	0900	1-1/2" supply		1,800	.013	"	.29	.34		.63	.86	
	1020	Pop up spray head w/risers, hi-pop, full circle pattern, 4"	2 Skwk	76	.211	Ea.	3.24	6.30		9.54	13.40	
	1030	1/2 circle pattern		76	.211		3.31	6.30		9.61	13.50	
	1040	6", full circle pattern		76	.211		7.75	6.30		14.05	18.40	
	1050	1/2 circle pattern		76	.211		7.75	6.30		14.05	18.40	
	1060	12", full circle pattern		76	.211		9.65	6.30		15.95	20.50	
	1070	1/2 circle pattern		76	.211		9.70	6.30		16	20.50	
	1080	Pop up bubbler head w/risers, hi-pop bubbler head, 4"		76	.211		3.40	6.30		9.70	13.60	
	1090	6"		76	.211		7.75	6.30		14.05	18.40	
	1100	12"		76	.211		9.65	6.30		15.95	20.50	
	1110	Impact full/part circle sprinklers, 28'-54' 25-60 PSI		37	.432		9.15	12.90		22.05	30.50	
	1120	Spaced 37'-49' @ 25-50 PSI		37	.432		21	12.90		33.90	44	
	1130	Spaced 43'-61' @ 30-60 PSI		37	.432		44	12.90		56.90	69	
	1140	Spaced 54'-78' @ 40-80 PSI		37	.432		96.50	12.90		109.40	127	
	1145	Impact rotor pop-up full/part commercial circle sprinklers										
	1150	Spaced 42'-65' 35-80 PSI	2 Skwk	25	.640	Ea.	21.50	19.10		40.60	53.50	
	1160	Spaced 48'-76' 45-85 PSI	"	25	.640	"	6.50	19.10		25.60	37	
	1165	Impact rotor pop-up part. circle comm., 53'-75', 55-100 PSI, w/ acc										
	1170	Plastic case, metal cover	2 Skwk	25	.640	Ea.	139	19.10		158.10	183	
	1180	Rubber cover		25	.640		106	19.10		125.10	147	
	1190	Iron case, metal cover		22	.727		132	21.50		153.50	179	
	1200	Rubber cover		22	.727		139	21.50		160.50	187	
	1250	Plastic case, 2 nozzle, metal cover		25	.640		105	19.10		124.10	146	

	02810	Irrigation System	CREW	DAILY OUTPUT	LABOR-HOURS	UNIT	MAT.	LABOR	EQUIP.	TOTAL	TOTAL INCL O&P	
							\multicolumn{4}{c|}{2001 BARE COSTS}			

800	1260	Rubber cover	2 Skwk	25	.640	Ea.	111	19.10		130.10	152	800
	1270	Iron case, 2 nozzle, metal cover		22	.727		149	21.50		170.50	198	
	1280	Rubber cover	↓	22	.727	↓	158	21.50		179.50	208	
	1282	Impact rotor pop-up full circle comm., 39'-99', 30-100 PSI										
	1284	Plastic case, metal cover	2 Skwk	25	.640	Ea.	105	19.10		124.10	146	
	1286	Rubber cover		25	.640		115	19.10		134.10	157	
	1288	Iron case, metal cover		22	.727		155	21.50		176.50	204	
	1290	Rubber cover		22	.727		161	21.50		182.50	211	
	1292	Plastic case, 2 nozzle, metal cover		22	.727		112	21.50		133.50	157	
	1294	Rubber cover		22	.727		117	21.50		138.50	163	
	1296	Iron case, 2 nozzle, metal cover		20	.800		149	24		173	202	
	1298	Rubber cover		20	.800		158	24		182	212	
	1305	Electric remote control valve, plastic, 3/4"		18	.889		16.20	26.50		42.70	59.50	
	1310	1"		18	.889		24	26.50		50.50	68	
	1320	1-1/2"	↓	18	.889	↓	51.50	26.50		78	98	
	1335	Quick coupling valves, brass, locking cover										
	1340	Inlet coupling valve, 3/4"	2 Skwk	18.75	.853	Ea.	40	25.50		65.50	84	
	1350	1"		18.75	.853		49.50	25.50		75	94.50	
	1360	Controller valve boxes, 6" round boxes		18.75	.853		3.41	25.50		28.91	44	
	1370	10" round boxes		14.25	1.123		7.50	33.50		41	61	
	1380	12" square box	↓	9.75	1.641	↓	14.50	49		63.50	93	
	1388	Electromech. control, 14 day 3-60 min, auto start to 23/day										
	1390	4 station	2 Skwk	1.04	15.385	Ea.	167	460		627	905	
	1400	7 station		.64	25		166	745		911	1,350	
	1410	12 station		.40	40		254	1,200		1,454	2,150	
	1420	Dual programs, 18 station		.24	66.667		1,250	2,000		3,250	4,500	
	1430	23 station	↓	.16	100	↓	1,625	2,975		4,600	6,475	
	1435	Backflow preventer, bronze, 0-175 PSI, w/valves, test cocks										
	1440	3/4"	2 Skwk	2	8	Ea.	101	239		340	485	
	1450	1"		2	8		103	239		342	490	
	1460	1-1/2"		2	8		208	239		447	605	
	1470	2"	↓	2	8	↓	223	239		462	620	
	1475	Pressure vacuum breaker, brass, 15-150 PSI										
	1480	3/4"	2 Skwk	2	8	Ea.	60	239		299	440	
	1490	1"		2	8		82	239		321	465	
	1500	1-1/2"		2	8		162	239		401	555	
	1510	2"	↓	2	8	↓	150	239		389	540	

	02815	Fountains										
225	0010	**FOUNTAINS/AERATORS**										225
	0100	Pump w/controls										
	0200	Single phase, 100' chord, 1/2 H.P. pump	2 Skwk	4.40	3.636	Ea.	2,550	109		2,659	3,000	
	0300	3/4 H.P. pump		4.30	3.721		2,925	111		3,036	3,375	
	0400	1 H.P. pump		4.20	3.810		2,950	114		3,064	3,425	
	0500	1-1/2 H.P. pump		4.10	3.902		3,050	116		3,166	3,525	
	0600	2 H.P. pump		4	4		3,100	119		3,219	3,575	
	0700	Three phase, 200' chord, 5 H.P. pump		3.90	4.103		7,475	122		7,597	8,425	
	0800	7-1/2 H.P. pump		3.80	4.211		8,450	126		8,576	9,500	
	0900	10 H.P. pump		3.70	4.324		9,425	129		9,554	10,600	
	1000	15 H.P. pump		3.60	4.444		11,200	133		11,333	12,500	
	1100	Nozzles, minimum		8	2		187	59.50		246.50	300	
	1200	Maximum		8	2		246	59.50		305.50	365	
	1300	Lights w/mounting kits, 200 watt		18	.889		310	26.50		336.50	380	
	1400	300 watt		18	.889		345	26.50		371.50	415	
	1500	500 watt	↓	18	.889	↓	375	26.50		401.50	455	

Important: See the Reference Section for critical supporting data - Reference Nos., Crews, & City Cost Indexes

SITE CONSTRUCTION **2**

02815	Fountains	CREW	DAILY OUTPUT	LABOR-HOURS	UNIT	2001 BARE COSTS MAT.	LABOR	EQUIP.	TOTAL	TOTAL INCL O&P	
225	1600 Color blender	2 Skwk	12	1.333	Ea.	292	40		332	385	225

	02820	Fences & Gates										
500	0010	**FENCE, MISC. METAL** Chicken wire, posts @ 4', 1" mesh, 4' high	B-80	410	.078	L.F.	1.14	1.95	1.33	4.42	5.70	500
	0100	2" mesh, 6' high		350	.091		1.04	2.28	1.56	4.88	6.40	
	0200	Galv. steel, 12 ga., 2" x 4" mesh, posts 5' O.C., 3' high		300	.107		1.56	2.66	1.82	6.04	7.85	
	0300	5' high		300	.107		2.08	2.66	1.82	6.56	8.40	
	0400	14 ga., 1" x 2" mesh, 3' high		300	.107		1.66	2.66	1.82	6.14	7.95	
	0500	5' high		300	.107		2.29	2.66	1.82	6.77	8.65	
	1000	Kennel fencing, 1-1/2" mesh, 6' long, 3'-6" wide, 6'-2" high	2 Clab	4	4	Ea.	260	91.50		351.50	430	
	1050	12' long		4	4		310	91.50		401.50	490	
	1200	Top covers, 1-1/2" mesh, 6' long		15	1.067		53	24.50		77.50	96	
	1250	12' long		12	1.333		84.50	30.50		115	141	
	1300	For kennel doors, see division 08344-350										
	4500	Security fence, prison grade, set in concrete, 12' high	B-80	25	1.280	L.F.	21.50	32	22	75.50	97	
	4600	16' high		20	1.600		25.50	40	27.50	93	120	
	5300	Tubular picket, steel, 6' sections, 1-9/16" posts, 4' high		300	.107		16.15	2.66	1.82	20.63	24	
	5400	2" posts, 5' high		240	.133		22.50	3.33	2.28	28.11	32	
	5600	2" posts, 6' high		200	.160		25.50	3.99	2.74	32.23	37	
	5700	Staggered picket 1-9/16" posts, 4' high		300	.107		14.55	2.66	1.82	19.03	22	
	5800	2" posts, 5' high		240	.133		24	3.33	2.28	29.61	34	
	5900	2" posts, 6' high		200	.160		25	3.99	2.74	31.73	36	
	6200	Gates, 4' high, 3' wide	B-1	10	2.400	Ea.	140	56.50		196.50	243	
	6300	5' high, 3' wide		10	2.400		182	56.50		238.50	289	
	6400	6' high, 3' wide		10	2.400		187	56.50		243.50	295	
	6500	4' wide		10	2.400		218	56.50		274.50	330	
528	0010	**FENCE, CHAIN LINK INDUSTRIAL**, schedule 40										528
	0020	3 strands barb wire, 2" post @ 10' O.C., set in concrete, 6' H										
	0200	9 ga. wire, galv. steel	B-80	240	.133	L.F.	7.50	3.33	2.28	13.11	15.90	
	0300	Aluminized steel		240	.133		9.65	3.33	2.28	15.26	18.25	
	0500	6 ga. wire, galv. steel		240	.133		12.15	3.33	2.28	17.76	21	
	0600	Aluminized steel		240	.133		13.95	3.33	2.28	19.56	23	
	0800	6 ga. wire, 6' high but omit barbed wire, galv. steel		250	.128		11.80	3.19	2.19	17.18	20.50	
	0900	Aluminized steel		250	.128		16.50	3.19	2.19	21.88	25.50	
	0920	8' H, 6 ga. wire, 2-1/2" line post, galv. steel		180	.178		19.20	4.44	3.04	26.68	31	
	0940	Aluminized steel		180	.178		23.50	4.44	3.04	30.98	36	
	1100	Add for corner posts, 3" diam., galv. steel		40	.800	Ea.	57	19.95	13.70	90.65	109	
	1200	Aluminized steel		40	.800		68.50	19.95	13.70	102.15	122	
	1300	Add for braces, galv. steel		80	.400		15.60	10	6.85	32.45	40	
	1350	Aluminized steel		80	.400		21	10	6.85	37.85	46	
	1400	Gate for 6' high fence, 1-5/8" frame, 3' wide, galv. steel		10	3.200		94.50	80	54.50	229	287	
	1500	Aluminized steel		10	3.200		115	80	54.50	249.50	310	
	2000	5'-0" high fence, 9 ga., no barbed wire, 2" line post,										
	2010	10' O.C., 1-5/8" top rail										
	2100	Galvanized steel	B-80	300	.107	L.F.	6.25	2.66	1.82	10.73	12.95	
	2200	Aluminized steel		300	.107	"	7.55	2.66	1.82	12.03	14.40	
	2400	Gate, 4' wide, 5' high, 2" frame, galv. steel		10	3.200	Ea.	104	80	54.50	238.50	297	
	2500	Aluminized steel		10	3.200	"	114	80	54.50	248.50	310	
	3100	Overhead slide gate, chain link, 6' high, to 18' wide		38	.842	L.F.	92.50	21	14.40	127.90	150	
	3110	Cantilever type		48	.667		39.50	16.65	11.40	67.55	81.50	
	3120	8' high		24	1.333		57	33.50	23	113.50	140	
	3130	10' high		18	1.778		67.50	44.50	30.50	142.50	177	
	5000	Double swing gates, incl. posts & hardware										
	5010	5' high, 12' opening	B-80	3.40	9.412	Opng.	275	235	161	671	840	

SITE CONSTRUCTION **2**

	02820	Fences & Gates	CREW	DAILY OUTPUT	LABOR-HOURS	UNIT	MAT.	LABOR	EQUIP.	TOTAL	TOTAL INCL O&P	
								2001 BARE COSTS				
528	5020	20' opening	B-80	2.80	11.429	Opng.	375	285	195	855	1,075	**528**
	5060	6' high, 12' opening		3.20	10		480	250	171	901	1,100	
	5070	20' opening		2.60	12.308		655	305	210	1,170	1,425	
	5080	8' high, 12' opening		2.13	15.002		710	375	257	1,342	1,625	
	5090	20' opening		1.45	22.069		945	550	375	1,870	2,325	
	5100	10' high, 12' opening		1.31	24.427		830	610	420	1,860	2,325	
	5110	20' opening		1.03	31.068		1,250	775	530	2,555	3,150	
	5120	12' high, 12' opening		1.05	30.476		1,225	760	520	2,505	3,100	
	5130	20' opening	↓	.85	37.647	↓	1,550	940	645	3,135	3,875	
	5190	For aluminized steel add					20%					
	7001	Snow fence on steel posts 10' O.C., 4' high	B-1	500	.048	L.F.	1.57	1.13		2.70	3.49	
530	0010	**FENCE, CHAIN LINK RESIDENTIAL,** sch. 20, 11 ga. wire, 1-5/8" post										**530**
	0020	10' O.C., 1-3/8" top rail, 2" corner post, galv. stl. 3' high	B-1	500	.048	L.F.	2.52	1.13		3.65	4.54	
	0050	4' high		400	.060		2.85	1.41		4.26	5.35	
	0100	6' high		200	.120	↓	3.47	2.82		6.29	8.25	
	0150	Add for gate 3' wide, 1-3/8" frame, 3' high		12	2	Ea.	37.50	47		84.50	115	
	0170	4' high		10	2.400		43.50	56.50		100	136	
	0190	6' high		10	2.400		59.50	56.50		116	154	
	0200	Add for gate 4' wide, 1-3/8" frame, 3' high		9	2.667		42.50	62.50		105	145	
	0220	4' high		9	2.667		48	62.50		110.50	151	
	0240	6' high		8	3	↓	56	70.50		126.50	172	
	0350	Aluminized steel, 11 ga. wire, 3' high		500	.048	L.F.	3.26	1.13		4.39	5.35	
	0380	4' high		400	.060		4.18	1.41		5.59	6.80	
	0400	6' high		200	.120	↓	5.90	2.82		8.72	10.90	
	0450	Add for gate 3' wide, 1-3/8" frame, 3' high		12	2	Ea.	45	47		92	123	
	0470	4' high		10	2.400		74	56.50		130.50	170	
	0490	6' high		10	2.400		93	56.50		149.50	191	
	0500	Add for gate 4' wide, 1-3/8" frame, 3' high		10	2.400		51	56.50		107.50	145	
	0520	4' high		9	2.667		56.50	62.50		119	161	
	0540	6' high		8	3	↓	65.50	70.50		136	182	
	0620	Vinyl covered, 9 ga. wire, 3' high		500	.048	L.F.	2.72	1.13		3.85	4.76	
	0640	4' high		400	.060		3.17	1.41		4.58	5.70	
	0660	6' high		200	.120	↓	4.02	2.82		6.84	8.85	
	0720	Add for gate 3' wide, 1-3/8" frame, 3' high		12	2	Ea.	52.50	47		99.50	131	
	0740	4' high		10	2.400		59.50	56.50		116	154	
	0760	6' high		10	2.400		92	56.50		148.50	190	
	0780	Add for gate 4' wide, 1-3/8" frame, 3' high		10	2.400		60	56.50		116.50	155	
	0800	4' high		9	2.667		65.50	62.50		128	170	
	0820	6' high	↓	8	3	↓	74	70.50		144.50	192	
	0860	Tennis courts, 11 ga. wire, 2-1/2" post 10' O.C., 1-5/8" top rail										
	0900	10' high	B-1	155	.155	L.F.	7.15	3.64		10.79	13.55	
	0920	12' high		130	.185	"	8.70	4.34		13.04	16.35	
	1000	Add for gate 4' wide, 1-5/8" frame 7' high		10	2.400	Ea.	75.50	56.50		132	172	
	1040	Aluminized steel, 11 ga. wire 10' high		155	.155	L.F.	8.85	3.64		12.49	15.45	
	1100	12' high		130	.185	"	11.10	4.34		15.44	19	
	1140	Add for gate 4' wide, 1-5/8" frame, 7' high		10	2.400	Ea.	86.50	56.50		143	184	
	1250	Vinyl covered, 9 ga. wire, 10' high		155	.155	L.F.	8.80	3.64		12.44	15.35	
	1300	12' high		130	.185	"	15.10	4.34		19.44	23.50	
	1400	Add for gate 4' wide, 1-5/8" frame, 7' high	↓	10	2.400	Ea.	89	56.50		145.50	186	
890	0005	**WIRE FENCING**										**890**
	0010	Barbed wire, galvanized, domestic steel, hi-tensile 15-1/2 ga.				M.L.F.	25			25	27.50	
	0020	standard, 12-3/4 ga.					34			34	37.50	
	0210	Barbless wire, 2-strand galvanized, 12-1/2 ga.				↓	33			33	36.50	
	0500	Helical razor ribbon, stainless steel, 18" dia x 18" spacing				C.L.F.	97.50			97.50	107	
	0600	Hardware cloth galv., 1/4" mesh, 23 ga., 2' wide				C.S.F.	45			45	49.50	

Important: See the Reference Section for critical supporting data - Reference Nos., Crews, & City Cost Indexes

02820 | Fences & Gates

			CREW	DAILY OUTPUT	LABOR-HOURS	UNIT	MAT.	LABOR	EQUIP.	TOTAL	TOTAL INCL O&P	
890	0700	3' wide				C.S.F.	44			44	48	**890**
	0900	1/2" mesh, 19 ga., 2' wide					38.50			38.50	42.50	
	1000	4' wide					38			38	41.50	
	1200	Chain link fabric, steel, 2" mesh, 6 ga, galvanized					113			113	125	
	1300	9 ga, galvanized					56			56	61.50	
	1350	Vinyl coated					47			47	51.50	
	1360	Aluminized					72.50			72.50	80	
	1400	2-1/4" mesh, 11.5 ga, galvanized					37.50			37.50	41.50	
	1600	1-3/4" mesh (tennis courts), 11.5 ga (core), vinyl coated					49.50			49.50	54	
	1700	9 ga, galvanized					64			64	70.50	
	2100	Welded wire fabric, galvanized, 1" x 2", 14 ga.					32			32	35	
	2200	2" x 4", 12-1/2 ga.				↓	21.50			21.50	23.50	
925	0010	**FENCE, RAIL** Picket, No. 2 cedar, Gothic, 2 rail, 3' high	B-1	160	.150	L.F.	4.58	3.53		8.11	10.55	**925**
	0050	Gate, 3'-6" wide		9	2.667	Ea.	39.50	62.50		102	142	
	0400	3 rail, 4' high		150	.160	L.F.	5.25	3.76		9.01	11.70	
	0500	Gate, 3'-6" wide		9	2.667	Ea.	47.50	62.50		110	150	
	0600	Open rail, rustic, No. 1 cedar, 2 rail, 3' high		160	.150	L.F.	4.11	3.53		7.64	10	
	0650	Gate, 3' wide		9	2.667	Ea.	45.50	62.50		108	149	
	0700	3 rail, 4' high		150	.160	L.F.	4.69	3.76		8.45	11.05	
	0900	Gate, 3' wide		9	2.667	Ea.	59	62.50		121.50	163	
	1200	Stockade, No. 2 cedar, treated wood rails, 6' high		160	.150	L.F.	5.70	3.53		9.23	11.80	
	1250	Gate, 3' wide		9	2.667	Ea.	47	62.50		109.50	150	
	1300	No. 1 cedar, 3-1/4" cedar rails, 6' high		160	.150	L.F.	13.80	3.53		17.33	20.50	
	1500	Gate, 3' wide		9	2.667	Ea.	110	62.50		172.50	219	
	1520	Open rail, split, No. 1 cedar, 2 rail, 3' high		160	.150	L.F.	4.17	3.53		7.70	10.10	
	1540	3 rail, 4'-0" high		150	.160		5.40	3.76		9.16	11.85	
	3300	Board, shadow box, 1" x 6", treated pine, 6' high		160	.150		8.45	3.53		11.98	14.80	
	3400	No. 1 cedar, 6' high		150	.160		16.65	3.76		20.41	24.50	
	3900	Basket weave, No. 1 cedar, 6' high		160	.150	↓	16.50	3.53		20.03	23.50	
	3950	Gate, 3'-6" wide		8	3	Ea.	106	70.50		176.50	226	
	4000	Treated pine, 6' high		150	.160	L.F.	8.90	3.76		12.66	15.70	
	4200	Gate, 3'-6" wide		9	2.667	Ea.	49.50	62.50		112	152	
	5000	Fence rail, redwood, 2" x 4", merch grade 8'		2,400	.010	L.F.	.89	.24		1.13	1.35	
	5050	Select grade, 8'		2,400	.010	"	2.77	.24		3.01	3.42	
	6000	Fence post, select redwood, earthpacked & treated, 4" x 4" x 6'		96	.250	Ea.	8.90	5.90		14.80	18.95	
	6010	4" x 4" x 8'		96	.250		10.55	5.90		16.45	21	
	6020	Set in concrete, 4" x 4" x 6'		50	.480		11.45	11.30		22.75	30	
	6030	4" x 4" x 8'		50	.480		13.65	11.30		24.95	32.50	
	6040	Wood post, 4' high, set in concrete, incl. concrete		50	.480		6.65	11.30		17.95	25	
	6050	Earth packed		96	.250		4.55	5.90		10.45	14.20	
	6060	6' high, set in concrete, incl. concrete		50	.480		8.55	11.30		19.85	27	
	6070	Earth packed	↓	96	.250	↓	6.20	5.90		12.10	16.05	

02830 | Retaining Walls

			CREW	DAILY OUTPUT	LABOR-HOURS	UNIT	MAT.	LABOR	EQUIP.	TOTAL	TOTAL INCL O&P	
100	0010	**RETAINING WALLS** Aluminized steel bin, excavation										**100**
	0020	and backfill not included, 10' wide										
	0100	4' high, 5.5' deep	B-13	650	.086	S.F.	12.80	2.13	.97	15.90	18.40	
	0200	8' high, 5.5' deep		615	.091		14.70	2.25	1.02	17.97	21	
	0300	10' high, 7.7' deep		580	.097		15.50	2.39	1.09	18.98	22	
	0400	12' high, 7.7' deep		530	.106		16.70	2.61	1.19	20.50	24	
	0500	16' high, 7.7' deep		515	.109		17.65	2.69	1.22	21.56	25	
	0600	16' high, 9.9' deep		500	.112		18.60	2.77	1.26	22.63	26	
	0700	20' high, 9.9' deep		470	.119		21	2.95	1.34	25.29	29	
	0800	20' high, 12.1' deep		460	.122		22.50	3.01	1.37	26.88	30.50	
	0900	24' high, 12.1' deep		455	.123		24	3.05	1.38	28.43	32	
	1000	24' high, 14.3' deep	↓	450	.124	↓	25	3.08	1.40	29.48	34	

SITE CONSTRUCTION 2

2 SITE CONSTRUCTION

02830	Retaining Walls		CREW	DAILY OUTPUT	LABOR-HOURS	UNIT	2001 BARE COSTS				TOTAL INCL O&P	
							MAT.	LABOR	EQUIP.	TOTAL		
100	1100	28' high, 14.3' deep	B-13	440	.127	S.F.	25.50	3.15	1.43	30.08	35	100
	1300	For plain galvanized bin type walls, deduct					10%					
	1800	Concrete gravity wall with vertical face including excavation & backfill										
	1850	No reinforcing										
	1900	6' high, level embankment	C-17C	36	2.306	L.F.	46	70	13.80	129.80	175	
	2000	33° slope embankment		32	2.594		43	78.50	15.55	137.05	188	
	2200	8' high, no surcharge		27	3.074		59	93	18.40	170.40	232	
	2300	33° slope embankment		24	3.458		71	105	20.50	196.50	266	
	2500	10' high, level embankment		19	4.368		84	132	26	242	330	
	2600	33° slope embankment		18	4.611		117	140	27.50	284.50	380	
	2800	Reinforced concrete cantilever, incl. excavation, backfill & reinf.										
	2900	6' high, 33° slope embankment	C-17C	35	2.371	L.F.	43	72	14.20	129.20	176	
	3000	8' high, 33° slope embankment		29	2.862		50	86.50	17.15	153.65	210	
	3100	10' high, 33° slope embankment		20	4.150		65	126	25	216	296	
	3200	20' high, 500 lb. per L.F. surcharge		7.50	11.067		194	335	66.50	595.50	810	
	3500	Concrete cribbing, incl. excavation and backfill										
	3700	12' high, open face	B-13	210	.267	S.F.	21.50	6.60	3	31.10	37	
	3900	Closed face	"	210	.267	"	20	6.60	3	29.60	36	
	4100	Concrete filled slurry trench, see division 02260-700										
	4300	Stone filled gabions, not incl. excavation,										
	4310	Stone, delivered, 3' wide										
	4350	Galvanized, 6' high, 33° slope embankment	B-13	49	1.143	L.F.	14	28.50	12.85	55.35	73.50	
	4500	Highway surcharge		27	2.074		28	51.50	23.50	103	136	
	4600	9' high, up to 33° slope embankment		24	2.333		31.50	57.50	26	115	153	
	4700	Highway surcharge		16	3.500		49	86.50	39.50	175	232	
	4900	12' high, up to 33° slope embankment		14	4		49	99	45	193	257	
	5000	Highway surcharge		11	5.091		70	126	57	253	335	
	5950	For PVC coating, add					20%					
	7100	Segmental Retaining Wall system, incl pins, and void fill										
	7120	base not included										
	7140	Large unit, 8" high x 18" wide x 20" deep, 3 plane split	B-62	300	.080	S.F.	8.40	1.99	.38	10.77	12.75	
	7150	straight split		300	.080		8.40	1.99	.38	10.77	12.75	
	7160	Medium, ltwt, 8" high x 18" wide x 12" deep, 3 plane split		400	.060		7.40	1.49	.29	9.18	10.75	
	7170	straight split		400	.060		7.40	1.49	.29	9.18	10.75	
	7180	Small unit, 4" x 18" x 10" deep, 3 plane split		400	.060		6.80	1.49	.29	8.58	10.10	
	7190	straight split		400	.060		6.80	1.49	.29	8.58	10.10	
	7200	Cap unit, 3 plane split		300	.080		6.40	1.99	.38	8.77	10.55	
	7210	Cap unit, st split		300	.080		6.40	1.99	.38	8.77	10.55	
	7260	For reinforcing, add								2	2.50	
	8000	For higher walls, add components as necessary										
400	0010	**STONE WALL** Including excavation, concrete footing and										400
	0020	stone 3' below grade. Price is exposed face area.										
	0200	Decorative random stone, to 6' high, 1'-6" thick, dry set	D-1	35	.457	S.F.	7.60	12		19.60	27	
	0300	Mortar set		40	.400		9.25	10.50		19.75	26.50	
	0500	Cut stone, to 6' high, 1'-6" thick, dry set		35	.457		11.50	12		23.50	31	
	0600	Mortar set		40	.400		13.50	10.50		24	31	
	0800	Retaining wall, random stone, 6' to 10' high, 2' thick, dry set		45	.356		9.50	9.35		18.85	25	
	0900	Mortar set		50	.320		11.50	8.40		19.90	25.50	
	1100	Cut stone, 6' to 10' high, 2' thick, dry set		45	.356		14.50	9.35		23.85	30.50	
	1200	Mortar set		50	.320		15.75	8.40		24.15	30.50	

02840 | Walk/Road/Parking Appurtenances

			CREW	DAILY OUTPUT	LABOR-HOURS	UNIT	MAT.	LABOR	EQUIP.	TOTAL	TOTAL INCL O&P	
155	0010	**BUMPER RAILS** For garages, 12 ga. rail, 6" wide, with steel										155
	0020	posts 12'-6" O.C., Minimum	E-4	190	.168	L.F.	8.60	5.60	.44	14.64	20	
	0030	Average		165	.194		10.75	6.45	.51	17.71	24	
	0100	Maximum		140	.229		12.90	7.60	.60	21.10	28.50	

Important: See the Reference Section for critical supporting data - Reference Nos., Crews, & City Cost Indexes

		02840 | Walk/Road/Parking Appurtenances	CREW	DAILY OUTPUT	LABOR-HOURS	UNIT	MAT.	2001 BARE COSTS LABOR	EQUIP.	TOTAL	TOTAL INCL O&P	
155	0300	12" channel rail, minimum	E-4	160	.200	L.F.	10.75	6.65	.53	17.93	24.50	155
	0400	Maximum	↓	120	.267	↓	16.15	8.90	.70	25.75	34.50	
200	0010	**TRAFFIC CONTROL DEVICES**										200
	0100	Traffic channelizing pavement markers, layout only	A-7	2,000	.012	Ea.		.37		.37	.58	
	0110	13" x 7-1/2" x 2-1/2" high, non-plowable install	2 Clab	96	.167		16.50	3.81		20.31	24	
	0200	8" x 8"x 3-1/4" high, non-plowable, install		96	.167		15	3.81		18.81	22.50	
	0230	4" x 4" x 3/4" high, non-plowable, install	↓	120	.133		2	3.05		5.05	6.95	
	0240	9-1/4" x 5-7/8" x 1/4" high, plowable, concrete pav't	A-2A	70	.343		12	7.90	3.66	23.56	29.50	
	0250	9-1/4" x 5-7/8" x 1/4" high, plowable, asphalt pav't	"	120	.200		2.30	4.61	2.14	9.05	12.05	
	0300	Barrier and curb delineators,reflectorized, 2" x 4"	2 Clab	150	.107		1.30	2.44		3.74	5.25	
	0310	3" x 5"	"	150	.107	↓	2.65	2.44		5.09	6.75	
	0500	Rumble strip, polycarbonate										
	0510	24" x 3-1/2" x 1/2" high	2 Clab	50	.320	Ea.	5	7.30		12.30	16.95	
500	0010	**GUIDE/GUARD RAIL** Corrugated steel, galv. steel posts, 6'-3" O.C.	B-80	850	.038	L.F.	10.75	.94	.64	12.33	14	500
	0200	End sections, galvanized, flared		50	.640	Ea.	44	15.95	10.95	70.90	85	
	0300	Wrap around end		50	.640	"	66	15.95	10.95	92.90	109	
	0400	Timber guide rail, 4" x 8" with 6" x 8" wood posts, treated		960	.033	L.F.	14	.83	.57	15.40	17.30	
	0600	Cable guide rail, 3 at 3/4" cables, steel posts, single face		900	.036		5.20	.89	.61	6.70	7.80	
	0700	Wood posts		950	.034		6.65	.84	.58	8.07	9.30	
	0900	Guide rail, steel box beam, 6" x 6"		120	.267		17.10	6.65	4.56	28.31	34	
	1100	Median barrier, steel box beam, 6" x 8"	↓	215	.149	↓	20.50	3.72	2.55	26.77	31	
	1200	Impact barrier, UTMCD, barrel type	B-16	30	1.067	Ea.	252	25	16.10	293.10	335	
	1400	Resilient guide fence and light shield, 6' high	B-2	130	.308	L.F.	18.05	7.15		25.20	31	
	1500	Concrete posts, individual, 6'-5", triangular	B-80	110	.291	Ea.	35	7.25	4.97	47.22	55	
	1550	Square	"	110	.291	"	34.50	7.25	4.97	46.72	54.50	
	2000	Median, precast concrete, 3'-6" high, 2' wide, single face	B-29	380	.147	L.F.	33.50	3.65	1.71	38.86	44.50	
	2200	Double face	"	340	.165	"	31	4.07	1.91	36.98	42.50	
	2400	Speed bumps, thermoplastic, 10-1/2" x 2-1/4" x 48" long	B-2	120	.333	Ea.	81	7.75		88.75	102	
600	0010	**HIGHWAY SOUND BARRIERS**, not including footing										600
	0100	Precast concrete, concrete columns @ 30' OC, 8" T, 8' H	C-12	400	.120	L.F.	66	3.45	1.29	70.74	79.50	
	0110	12' H		265	.181		99	5.20	1.94	106.14	119	
	0120	16' H		200	.240		132	6.90	2.58	141.48	159	
	0130	20' H	↓	160	.300		165	8.65	3.22	176.87	199	
	0400	Lt. Wt. composite panel, cementitious face, St. posts @ 12' OC, 8' H	B-80B	190	.168		73	4.10	1.17	78.27	87.50	
	0410	12' H		125	.256		109	6.25	1.78	117.03	132	
	0420	16' H		95	.337		145	8.20	2.34	155.54	175	
	0430	20' H	↓	75	.427	↓	182	10.40	2.97	195.37	219	
700	0010	**PARKING BARRIERS** Timber with saddles, treated type										700
	0100	4" x 4" for cars	B-2	520	.077	L.F.	2.73	1.79		4.52	5.80	
	0200	6" x 6" for trucks		520	.077	"	5.90	1.79		7.69	9.25	
	0400	Folding with individual padlocks		50	.800	Ea.	345	18.60		363.60	410	
	0600	Flexible fixed stanchion, 2' high, 3" diameter		100	.400		17.75	9.30		27.05	34	
	1000	Wheel stops, precast concrete incl. dowels, 6" x 10" x 6'-0"		120	.333		28.50	7.75		36.25	43	
	1100	8" x 13" x 6'-0"		120	.333		34	7.75		41.75	49.50	
	1200	Thermoplastic, 6" x 10" x 6'-0"	↓	120	.333		52.50	7.75		60.25	70	
	1300	Pipe bollards, conc filled/paint, 8' L x 4' D hole, 6" diam.	B-6	20	1.200		173	30	9.05	212.05	247	
	1400	8" diam.		15	1.600		263	39.50	12.05	314.55	365	
	1500	12" diam.	↓	12	2	↓	340	49.50	15.10	404.60	470	
	9000	Parking lot control, see division 11156-600										

02850 | Prefabricated Bridges

210	0010	**BRIDGES** Pedestrian, spans over streams, roadways, etc.										210
	0020	including erection, not including foundations										

SITE CONSTRUCTION 2

		02850	Prefabricated Bridges	CREW	DAILY OUTPUT	LABOR-HOURS	UNIT	MAT.	LABOR	EQUIP.	TOTAL	TOTAL INCL O&P	
210	0050		Precast concrete, complete in place, 8' wide, 60' span	E-2	215	.260	S.F.	33.50	8.30	6	47.80	58	210
	0100		100' span		185	.303		37	9.65	6.95	53.60	65	
	0150		120' span		160	.350		40	11.15	8.05	59.20	72.50	
	0200		150' span		145	.386		41.50	12.30	8.90	62.70	77	
	0300		Steel, trussed or arch spans, compl. in place, 8' wide, 40' span		320	.175		45	5.60	4.03	54.63	63.50	
	0400		50' span		395	.142		40.50	4.52	3.27	48.29	56	
	0500		60' span		465	.120		40.50	3.84	2.77	47.11	54	
	0600		80' span		570	.098		48	3.13	2.26	53.39	61	
	0700		100' span		465	.120		67.50	3.84	2.77	74.11	84	
	0800		120' span		365	.153		85.50	4.89	3.53	93.92	106	
	0900		150' span		310	.181		91	5.75	4.16	100.91	115	
	1000		160' span		255	.220		91	7	5.05	103.05	118	
	1100		10' wide, 80' span		640	.087		50	2.79	2.02	54.81	62	
	1200		120' span		415	.135		65	4.30	3.11	72.41	82.50	
	1300		150' span		445	.126		73	4.01	2.90	79.91	90	
	1400		200' span		205	.273		77.50	8.70	6.30	92.50	108	
	1600		Wood, laminated type, complete in place, 80' span	C-12	203	.236		40.50	6.80	2.54	49.84	58	
	1700		130' span	"	153	.314		42	9.05	3.37	54.42	64	

		02870	Site Furnishings										
610	0010		BENCHES Park, precast concrete, w/backs,wood rails, 4' long	2 Clab	5	3.200	Ea.	385	73		458	540	610
	0100		8' long		4	4		640	91.50		731.50	845	
	0300		Fiberglass, without back, one piece, 4' long		10	1.600		405	36.50		441.50	505	
	0400		8' long		7	2.286		840	52		892	1,000	
	0500		Steel barstock pedestals w/backs, 2" x 3" wood rails, 4' long		10	1.600		755	36.50		791.50	885	
	0510		8' long		7	2.286		895	52		947	1,075	
	0520		3" x 8" wood plank, 4' long		10	1.600		760	36.50		796.50	895	
	0530		8' long		7	2.286		770	52		822	925	
	0540		Backless, 4" x 4" wood plank, 4' square		10	1.600		740	36.50		776.50	865	
	0550		8' long		7	2.286		700	52		752	850	
	0600		Aluminum pedestals, with backs, aluminum slats, 8' long		8	2		420	45.50		465.50	530	
	0610		15' long		5	3.200		355	73		428	505	
	0620		Portable, aluminum slats, 8' long		8	2		330	45.50		375.50	435	
	0630		15' long		5	3.200		460	73		533	625	
	0800		Cast iron pedestals, back & arms, wood slats, 4' long		8	2		310	45.50		355.50	410	
	0820		8' long		5	3.200		795	73		868	985	
	0840		Backless, wood slats, 4' long		8	2		495	45.50		540.50	615	
	0860		8' long		5	3.200		535	73		608	700	
	1700		Steel frame, fir seat, 10' long		10	1.600		150	36.50		186.50	222	

800	0010		TRASH RECEPTACLE Fiberglass, 2' square, 18" high	2 Clab	30	.533	Ea.	214	12.20		226.20	255	800
	0100		2' square, 2'-6" high		30	.533		300	12.20		312.20	350	
	0300		Circular , 2' diameter, 18" high		30	.533		193	12.20		205.20	231	
	0400		2' diameter, 2'-6" high		30	.533		257	12.20		269.20	300	
815	0010		TRASH CLOSURE Steel with pullover cover										815
	0020		2'-3" wide, 4'-7" high, 6'-2" long	2 Clab	5	3.200	Ea.	715	73		788	900	
	0100		10'-1" long		4	4		945	91.50		1,036.50	1,200	
	0300		Wood, 10' wide, 6' high, 10' long		1.20	13.333		745	305		1,050	1,300	

		02880	Playfield Equipment										
100	0010		BLEACHERS Outdoor, portable, 3 to 5 tiers, to 300' long, min.	2 Sswk	120	.133	Seat	29	4.38		33.38	40	100
	0100		Maximum, less than 15' long, prefabricated		80	.200		38	6.55		44.55	54	
	0200		6 to 20 tiers, minimum, up to 300' long		120	.133		34.50	4.38		38.88	45.50	
	0300		Max., under 15', (highly prefabricated, on wheels)		80	.200		50	6.55		56.55	67	
	0500		Permanent grandstands, wood seat, steel frame, 24" row										
	0600		3 to 15 tiers, minimum	2 Sswk	60	.267	Seat	87.50	8.75		96.25	112	

Important: See the Reference Section for critical supporting data - Reference Nos., Crews, & City Cost Indexes

02880 | Playfield Equipment

			CREW	DAILY OUTPUT	LABOR-HOURS	UNIT	2001 BARE COSTS MAT.	LABOR	EQUIP.	TOTAL	TOTAL INCL O&P	
100	0700	Maximum	2 Sswk	48	.333	Seat	98	10.95		108.95	128	**100**
	0900	16 to 30 tiers, minimum		60	.267		103	8.75		111.75	129	
	0950	Average		55	.291		129	9.55		138.55	159	
	1000	Maximum		48	.333		155	10.95		165.95	190	
	1200	Seat backs only, 30" row, fiberglass		160	.100		18.20	3.29		21.49	26	
	1300	Steel and wood		160	.100		22.50	3.29		25.79	31	
	1400	NOTE: average seating is 1.5' in width										
140	0010	**BACKSTOPS** Baseball, prefabricated, 30' wide, 12' high & 1 overhang	B-1	1	24	Ea.	1,900	565		2,465	2,975	**140**
	0100	40' wide, 12' high & 2 overhangs	"	.75	32		2,400	755		3,155	3,800	
	0300	Basketball, steel, single goal	B-13	3.04	18.421		735	455	207	1,397	1,750	
	0400	Double goal	"	1.92	29.167		510	720	330	1,560	2,050	
	0600	Tennis, wire mesh with pair of ends	B-1	2.48	9.677	Set	1,125	228		1,353	1,600	
	0700	Enclosed court	"	1.30	18.462	Ea.	3,200	435		3,635	4,200	
	0900	Handball or squash court, outdoor, wood	2 Carp	.50	32		2,750	935		3,685	4,475	
	1000	Masonry handball/squash court	D-1	.30	53.333		21,300	1,400		22,700	25,700	
225	0010	**GOAL POSTS** Steel, football, double post	B-1	1.50	16	Pr.	1,175	375		1,550	1,900	**225**
	0100	Deluxe, single post		1.50	16		1,875	375		2,250	2,650	
	0300	Football, convertible to soccer		1.50	16		1,850	375		2,225	2,650	
	0500	Soccer, regulation		2	12		1,500	282		1,782	2,100	
700	0010	**PLAYGROUND EQUIPMENT** See also individual items										**700**
	0200	Bike rack, 10' long, permanent	B-1	12	2	Ea.	390	47		437	505	
	0400	Horizontal monkey ladder, 14' long		4	6		525	141		666	800	
	0590	Parallel bars, 10' long		4	6		224	141		365	465	
	0600	Posts, tether ball set, 2-3/8" O.D.		12	2		150	47		197	238	
	0800	Poles, multiple purpose, 10'-6" long		12	2	Pr.	110	47		157	195	
	1000	Ground socket for movable posts, 2-3/8" post		10	2.400		76	56.50		132.50	173	
	1100	3-1/2" post		10	2.400		104	56.50		160.50	204	
	1300	See-saw, steel, 2 units		6	4	Ea.	730	94		824	950	
	1400	4 units		4	6		915	141		1,056	1,225	
	1500	6 units		3	8		1,925	188		2,113	2,425	
	1700	Shelter, fiberglass golf tee, 3 person		4.60	5.217		2,150	123		2,273	2,575	
	1900	Slides, stainless steel bed, 12' long, 6' high		3	8		1,700	188		1,888	2,150	
	2000	20' long, 10' high		2	12		1,975	282		2,257	2,625	
	2200	Swings, plain seats, 8' high, 4 seats		2	12		820	282		1,102	1,350	
	2300	8 seats		1.30	18.462		1,475	435		1,910	2,300	
	2500	12' high, 4 seats		2	12		1,075	282		1,357	1,625	
	2600	8 seats		1.30	18.462		1,500	435		1,935	2,325	
	2800	Whirlers, 8' diameter		3	8		1,625	188		1,813	2,075	
	2900	10' diameter		3	8		2,350	188		2,538	2,875	
710	0010	**MODULAR PLAYGROUND** Basic components										**710**
	0100	Deck, square, steel	B-1	1	24	Ea.	565	565		1,130	1,500	
	0110	Polyurethane		1	24		500	565		1,065	1,425	
	0120	Triangular, steel		1	24		415	565		980	1,350	
	0130	Post, steel, 5" square		18	1.333		17.50	31.50		49	68.50	
	0140	Aluminum, 2-3/8" square		20	1.200		16.25	28		44.25	62	
	0150	5" square		18	1.333	L.F.	21	31.50		52.50	72	
	0160	Roof, square poly, 54" side		18	1.333	Ea.	810	31.50		841.50	940	
	0170	Transfer module		3	8	"	1,850	188		2,038	2,325	
	0180	Guardrail, pipe		60	.400	L.F.	205	9.40		214.40	241	
	0190	Steps, deck-to-deck		8	3	Ea.	1,025	70.50		1,095.50	1,225	
	0200	Activity panel, minimum		2	12		325	282		607	795	
	0210	Maximum		2	12		620	282		902	1,125	
	0360	With guardrails		3	8		1,750	188		1,938	2,225	
	0370	Crawl tunnel, straight, 56" long		4	6		990	141		1,131	1,325	
	0380	90°		4	6		1,250	141		1,391	1,600	

SITE CONSTRUCTION **2**

02880 | Playfield Equipment

			CREW	DAILY OUTPUT	LABOR-HOURS	UNIT	MAT.	LABOR	EQUIP.	TOTAL	TOTAL INCL O&P	
710	1200	Slide, tunnel	B-1	8	3	Ea.	1,400	70.50		1,470.50	1,625	710
	1210	Straight, poly		8	3		197	70.50		267.50	325	
	1220	Stainless steel, 54" high		6	4		204	94		298	370	
	1230	Curved, poly, 40" high		6	4		1,025	94		1,119	1,275	
	1240	Spyroslide, 56" - 72" high		5	4.800		3,425	113		3,538	3,950	
	1300	Ladder, vertical		5	4.800		475	113		588	700	
	1310	Horizontal, 8' long		5	4.800		635	113		748	875	
	1320	Corkscrew climber		3	8		525	188		713	870	
	1330	Fire pole		6	4		230	94		324	400	
	1340	Bridge, ring		4	6		935	141		1,076	1,250	
	1350	Clatter		4	6	L.F.	267	141		408	515	
880	0010	**PLATFORM/PADDLE TENNIS COURT** Complete with lighting, etc.										880
	0100	Aluminum slat deck with aluminum frame	B-1	.08	300	Court	37,000	7,050		44,050	51,500	
	0500	Aluminum slat deck and wood frame	C-1	.12	266		37,000	7,350		44,350	52,000	
	0800	Aluminum deck heater, add	B-1	1.18	20.339		3,600	480		4,080	4,700	
	0900	Douglas fir planking and wood frame 2" x 6" x 30'	C-1	.12	266		37,000	7,350		44,350	52,000	
	1000	Plywood deck with steel frame		.12	266		37,000	7,350		44,350	52,000	
	1100	Steel slat deck with wood frame		.12	266		26,000	7,350		33,350	40,100	

02890 | Traffic Signs & Signals

			CREW	DAILY OUTPUT	LABOR-HOURS	UNIT	MAT.	LABOR	EQUIP.	TOTAL	TOTAL INCL O&P	
700	0010	**SIGNS** Stock, 24" x 24", no posts, .080" alum. reflectorized	B-80	70	.457	Ea.	37	11.40	7.80	56.20	66.50	700
	0100	High intensity		70	.457		37	11.40	7.80	56.20	66.50	
	0300	30" x 30", reflectorized		70	.457		57	11.40	7.80	76.20	88.50	
	0400	High intensity		70	.457		65	11.40	7.80	84.20	97.50	
	0600	Guide and directional signs, 12" x 18", reflectorized		70	.457		17.25	11.40	7.80	36.45	45	
	0700	High intensity		70	.457		28	11.40	7.80	47.20	57	
	0900	18" x 24", stock signs, reflectorized		70	.457		31	11.40	7.80	50.20	60	
	1000	High intensity		70	.457		31	11.40	7.80	50.20	60	
	1200	24" x 24", stock signs, reflectorized		70	.457		29	11.40	7.80	48.20	58	
	1300	High intensity		70	.457		29	11.40	7.80	48.20	58	
	1500	Add to above for steel posts, galvanized, 10'-0" upright, bolted		200	.160		13.90	3.99	2.74	20.63	24.50	
	1600	12'-0" upright, bolted		140	.229		16.85	5.70	3.91	26.46	31.50	
	1800	Highway road signs, aluminum, over 20 S. F., reflectorized		350	.091	S.F.	12.20	2.28	1.56	16.04	18.65	
	2000	High intensity		350	.091		15.25	2.28	1.56	19.09	22	
	2200	Highway, suspended over road, 80 S.F. min., reflectorized		165	.194		15.25	4.84	3.32	23.41	28	
	2300	High intensity		165	.194		20.50	4.84	3.32	28.66	33.50	
900	0010	**TRAFFIC SIGNALS** Mid block pedestrian crosswalk,										900
	0020	with pushbutton and mast arms	R-2	.30	186	Total	11,500	5,675	945	18,120	22,400	
	0100	Intersection, 8 signals w/three sect. (2 each direction), programmed	"	.15	373		26,800	11,400	1,900	40,100	48,800	
	0120	For each additional traffic phase controller, add	L-9	1.20	30		1,500	795		2,295	2,950	
	0200	Semi-actuated, detectors in side street only, add		.81	44.444		2,400	1,175		3,575	4,550	
	0300	Fully-actuated, detectors in all streets, add		.49	73.469		6,750	1,950		8,700	10,600	
	0400	For pedestrian pushbutton, add		.70	51.429		3,275	1,350		4,625	5,800	
	0500	Optically programmed signal only, add per head		1.64	21.951		2,500	580		3,080	3,700	
	0600	School flashing system, programmed		.41	87.805	Signal	6,000	2,325		8,325	10,400	

Important: See the Reference Section for critical supporting data - Reference Nos., Crews, & City Cost Indexes

02900 | Planting

02905 | Transplanting

			CREW	DAILY OUTPUT	LABOR-HOURS	UNIT	MAT.	LABOR	EQUIP.	TOTAL	TOTAL INCL O&P	
725	0010	**PLANTING** Moving shrubs on site, 12" ball	B-62	28	.857	Ea.		21.50	4.07	25.57	37.50	725
	0100	24" ball	"	22	1.091			27	5.20	32.20	47.50	
	0300	Moving trees on site, 36" ball	B-6	3.75	6.400			159	48.50	207.50	298	
	0400	60" ball	"	1	24			595	181	776	1,125	

(note box: R02930 -900)

02910 | Plant Preparation

			CREW	DAILY OUTPUT	LABOR-HOURS	UNIT	MAT.	LABOR	EQUIP.	TOTAL	TOTAL INCL O&P	
500	0010	**MULCH**										500
	0100	Aged barks, 3" deep, hand spread	1 Clab	100	.080	S.Y.	2.06	1.83		3.89	5.15	
	0150	Skid steer loader	B-63	13.50	2.963	M.S.F.	227	71	8.45	306.45	370	
	0200	Hay, 1" deep, hand spread	1 Clab	475	.017	S.Y.	.26	.38		.64	.89	
	0250	Power mulcher, small	B-64	180	.089	M.S.F.	19.05	2.06	1.57	22.68	26	
	0350	Large	B-65	530	.030	"	19.05	.70	.74	20.49	23	
	0400	Humus peat, 1" deep, hand spread	1 Clab	700	.011	S.Y.	1.15	.26		1.41	1.67	
	0450	Push spreader	A-1	2,500	.003	"	1.43	.07	.03	1.53	1.72	
	0550	Tractor spreader	B-66	700	.011	M.S.F.	107	.33	.24	107.57	119	
	0600	Oat straw, 1" deep, hand spread	1 Clab	475	.017	S.Y.	.29	.38		.67	.92	
	0650	Power mulcher, small	B-64	180	.089	M.S.F.	26	2.06	1.57	29.63	33.50	
	0700	Large	B-65	530	.030	"	26	.70	.74	27.44	30.50	
	0750	Add for asphaltic emulsion	B-45	1,770	.009	Gal.	1.65	.25	.41	2.31	2.64	
	0800	Peat moss, 1" deep, hand spread	1 Clab	900	.009	S.Y.	1.55	.20		1.75	2.03	
	0850	Push spreader	A-1	2,500	.003	"	1.65	.07	.03	1.75	1.96	
	0950	Tractor spreader	B-66	700	.011	M.S.F.	180	.33	.24	180.57	199	
	1000	Polyethylene film, 6 mil.	2 Clab	2,000	.008	S.Y.	.15	.18		.33	.46	
	1100	Redwood nuggets, 3" deep, hand spread	1 Clab	150	.053	"	6.20	1.22		7.42	8.70	
	1150	Skid steer loader	B-63	13.50	2.963	M.S.F.	620	71	8.45	699.45	800	
	1200	Stone mulch, hand spread, ceramic chips, economy	1 Clab	125	.064	S.Y.	5.75	1.46		7.21	8.65	
	1250	Deluxe	"	95	.084	"	8.85	1.92		10.77	12.75	
	1300	Granite chips	B-1	10	2.400	C.Y.	29	56.50		85.50	120	
	1400	Marble chips		10	2.400		108	56.50		164.50	208	
	1500	Onyx gemstone		10	2.400		315	56.50		371.50	440	
	1600	Pea gravel		28	.857		30	20		50	64	
	1700	Quartz		10	2.400		139	56.50		195.50	242	
	1800	Tar paper, 15 Lb. felt	1 Clab	800	.010	S.Y.	.41	.23		.64	.81	
	1900	Wood chips, 2" deep, hand spread	"	220	.036	"	1.65	.83		2.48	3.12	
	1950	Skid steer loader	B-63	20.30	1.970	M.S.F.	111	47.50	5.60	164.10	202	

02912 | General Planting

			CREW	DAILY OUTPUT	LABOR-HOURS	UNIT	MAT.	LABOR	EQUIP.	TOTAL	TOTAL INCL O&P	
275	0010	**GROUND COVER** Plants, pachysandra, in prepared beds	B-1	15	1.600	C	15	37.50		52.50	75.50	275
	0200	Vinca minor, 1 yr, bare root		12	2	"	19	47		66	94.50	
	0600	Stone chips, in 50 lb. bags, Georgia marble		520	.046	Bag	4.30	1.09		5.39	6.45	
	0700	Onyx gemstone		260	.092		15.80	2.17		17.97	21	
	0800	Quartz		260	.092		5.75	2.17		7.92	9.75	
	0900	Pea gravel, truckload lots		28	.857	Ton	17.15	20		37.15	50.50	

02920 | Lawns & Grasses

			CREW	DAILY OUTPUT	LABOR-HOURS	UNIT	MAT.	LABOR	EQUIP.	TOTAL	TOTAL INCL O&P	
500	0010	**SEEDING** Mechanical seeding, 215 lb./acre	B-66	1.50	5.333	Acre	485	153	113	751	890	500
	0100	44 lb./M.S.Y.	"	2,500	.003	S.Y.	.15	.09	.07	.31	.38	
	0300	Fine grading and seeding incl. lime, fertilizer & seed,										
	0310	with equipment	B-14	1,000	.048	S.Y.	.16	1.16	.18	1.50	2.18	
	0600	Limestone hand push spreader, 50 lbs. per M.S.F.	1 Clab	180	.044	M.S.F.	3.25	1.02		4.27	5.15	
	0800	Grass seed hand push spreader, 4.5 lbs. per M.S.F.	"	180	.044	"	10	1.02		11.02	12.60	
	1000	Hydro or air seeding for large areas, incl. seed and fertilizer	B-81	8,900	.003	S.Y.	.15	.07	.07	.29	.35	
	1100	With wood fiber mulch added	"	8,900	.003	"	.25	.07	.07	.39	.46	
	1300	Seed only, over 100 lbs., field seed, minimum				Lb.	1			1	1.10	
	1400	Maximum					3.50			3.50	3.85	

(note box: R02920 -500)

SITE CONSTRUCTION — 2

For expanded coverage of these items see *Means Site Work and Landscape Cost Data 2001*

2 SITE CONSTRUCTION

			CREW	DAILY OUTPUT	LABOR-HOURS	UNIT	2001 BARE COSTS				TOTAL INCL O&P	
	02920	**Lawns & Grasses**					MAT.	LABOR	EQUIP.	TOTAL		
500	1500	Lawn seed, minimum R02920 -500				Lb.	1.50			1.50	1.65	**500**
	1600	Maximum				↓	4.25			4.25	4.68	
	1800	Aerial operations, seeding only, field seed	B-58	50	.480	Acre	350	11.90	43.50	405.40	450	
	1900	Lawn seed		50	.480		510	11.90	43.50	565.40	625	
	2100	Seed and liquid fertilizer, field seed		50	.480		400	11.90	43.50	455.40	505	
	2200	Lawn seed		50	.480	↓	550	11.90	43.50	605.40	670	
600	0010	**SODDING** 1″ deep, bluegrass sod, on level ground, over 8 M.S.F.	B-63	22	1.818	M.S.F.	155	43.50	5.20	203.70	245	**600**
	0200	4 M.S.F.		17	2.353		230	56.50	6.70	293.20	350	
	0300	1000 S.F.		3.50	11.429		250	275	32.50	557.50	735	
	0500	Sloped ground, over 8 M.S.F.		6	6.667		155	160	19	334	440	
	0600	4 M.S.F.		5	8		230	192	23	445	575	
	0700	1000 S.F.		4	10		250	240	28.50	518.50	680	
	1000	Bent grass sod, on level ground, over 6 M.S.F.		20	2		460	48	5.70	513.70	585	
	1100	3 M.S.F.		18	2.222		570	53.50	6.35	629.85	715	
	1200	Sodding 1000 S.F. or less		14	2.857		655	68.50	8.15	731.65	835	
	1500	Sloped ground, over 6 M.S.F.		15	2.667		460	64	7.60	531.60	615	
	1600	3 M.S.F.		13.50	2.963		570	71	8.45	649.45	745	
	1700	1000 S.F.	↓	12	3.333	↓	655	80	9.50	744.50	855	
	02930	**Exterior Plants**										
050	0010	**SHRUBS AND TREES** Evergreen, in prepared beds, B & B										**050**
	0100	Arborvitae pyramidal, 4′-5′	B-17	30	1.067	Ea.	35	26	18.40	79.40	99	
	0150	Globe, 12″-15″	B-1	96	.250		10.35	5.90		16.25	20.50	
	0300	Cedar, blue, 8′-10′	B-17	18	1.778		111	43.50	30.50	185	223	
	0500	Hemlock, canadian, 2-1/2′-3′	B-1	36	.667		14.25	15.70		29.95	40	
	0550	Holly, Savannah, 8′ - 10′ H		9.68	2.479		500	58.50		558.50	640	
	0600	Juniper, andorra, 18″-24″		80	.300		14.55	7.05		21.60	27	
	0620	Wiltoni, 15″-18″		80	.300		15.10	7.05		22.15	27.50	
	0640	Skyrocket, 4-1/2′-5′	B-17	55	.582		40	14.30	10	64.30	77	
	0660	Blue pfitzer, 2′-2-1/2′	B-1	44	.545		16.65	12.85		29.50	38.50	
	0680	Ketleerie, 2-1/2′-3′		50	.480		29	11.30		40.30	49.50	
	0700	Pine, black, 2-1/2′-3′		50	.480		30.50	11.30		41.80	51	
	0720	Mugo, 18″-24″		60	.400		31	9.40		40.40	49	
	0740	White, 4′-5′	B-17	75	.427		41.50	10.50	7.35	59.35	70.50	
	0800	Spruce, blue, 18″-24″	B-1	60	.400		28	9.40		37.40	45.50	
	0840	Norway, 4′-5′	B-17	75	.427		56	10.50	7.35	73.85	86	
	0900	Yew, denisforma, 12″-15″	B-1	60	.400		22.50	9.40		31.90	39.50	
	1000	Capitata, 18″-24″		30	.800		16.45	18.80		35.25	47.50	
	1100	Hicksi, 2′-2-1/2′	↓	30	.800	↓	27	18.80		45.80	59	
410	0010	**SHRUBS** Broadleaf evergreen, planted in prepared beds										**410**
	0100	Andromeda, 15″-18″, container	B-1	96	.250	Ea.	14	5.90		19.90	24.50	
	0200	Azalea, 15″ - 18″, container		96	.250		19	5.90		24.90	30	
	0300	Barberry, 9″-12″, container		130	.185		11.45	4.34		15.79	19.40	
	0400	Boxwood, 15″-18″, B & B		96	.250		17.50	5.90		23.40	28.50	
	0500	Euonymus, emerald gaiety, 12″ to 15″, container		115	.209		12.25	4.91		17.16	21	
	0600	Holly, 15″-18″, B & B		96	.250		17	5.90		22.90	28	
	0900	Mount laurel, 18″ - 24″, B & B		80	.300		75	7.05		82.05	93.50	
	1000	Paxistema, 9 - 12″ high		130	.185		15	4.34		19.34	23.50	
	1100	Rhododendron, 18″-24″, container		48	.500		37.50	11.75		49.25	60	
	1200	Rosemary, 1 gal container		600	.040		35	.94		35.94	40	
	2000	Deciduous, amelanchier, 2′-3′, B & B		57	.421		55	9.90		64.90	76	
	2100	Azalea, 15″-18″, B & B		96	.250		19.80	5.90		25.70	31	
	2300	Bayberry, 2′-3′, B & B		57	.421		23.50	9.90		33.40	41	
	2600	Cotoneaster, 15″-18″, B & B	↓	80	.300		18	7.05		25.05	31	
	2800	Dogwood, 3′-4′, B & B	B-17	40	.800	↓	21	19.70	13.80	54.50	68.50	

Important: See the Reference Section for critical supporting data - Reference Nos., Crews, & City Cost Indexes

02930	Exterior Plants	CREW	DAILY OUTPUT	LABOR-HOURS	UNIT	2001 BARE COSTS MAT.	LABOR	EQUIP.	TOTAL	TOTAL INCL O&P	
410	2900	Euonymus, alatus compacta, 15" to 18", container	B-1	80	.300	Ea.	33	7.05		40.05	47.50	410
	3200	Forsythia, 2'-3', container	"	60	.400		27	9.40		36.40	44	
	3300	Hibiscus, 3'-4', B & B	B-17	75	.427		28.50	10.50	7.35	46.35	56	
	3400	Honeysuckle, 3'-4', B & B	B-1	60	.400		24	9.40		33.40	41	
	3500	Hydrangea, 2'-3', B & B	"	57	.421		30	9.90		39.90	48.50	
	3600	Lilac, 3'-4', B & B	B-17	40	.800		39	19.70	13.80	72.50	88.50	
	3900	Privet, bare root, 18"-24"	B-1	80	.300		7.50	7.05		14.55	19.30	
	4100	Quince, 2'-3', B & B	"	57	.421		24.50	9.90		34.40	42.50	
	4200	Russian olive, 3'-4', B & B	B-17	75	.427		19	10.50	7.35	36.85	45.50	
	4400	Spirea, 3'-4', B & B	B-1	70	.343		42	8.05		50.05	58.50	
	4500	Viburnum, 3'-4', B & B	B-17	40	.800		24.50	19.70	13.80	58	72.50	
680	0010	**PLANT BED PREPARATION**										680
	0100	Backfill planting pit, by hand, on site topsoil	2 Clab	18	.889	C.Y.		20.50		20.50	32	
	0200	Prepared planting mix	"	24	.667			15.25		15.25	24	
	0300	Skid steer loader, on site topsoil	B-62	340	.071			1.75	.34	2.09	3.08	
	0400	Prepared planting mix	"	410	.059			1.45	.28	1.73	2.56	
	1000	Excavate planting pit, by hand, sandy soil	2 Clab	16	1			23		23	36	
	1100	Heavy soil or clay	"	8	2			45.50		45.50	71.50	
	1200	1/2 C.Y. backhoe, sandy soil	B-11C	150	.107			2.84	1.21	4.05	5.70	
	1300	Heavy soil or clay	"	115	.139			3.70	1.57	5.27	7.45	
	2000	Mix planting soil, incl. loam, manure, peat, by hand	2 Clab	60	.267		19.50	6.10		25.60	31	
	2100	Skid steer loader	B-62	150	.160		19.50	3.97	.76	24.23	28.50	
	3000	Pile sod, skid steer loader	"	2,800	.009	S.Y.		.21	.04	.25	.37	
	3100	By hand	2 Clab	400	.040			.91		.91	1.43	
	4000	Remove sod, F.E. loader	B-10S	2,000	.006			.17	.14	.31	.42	
	4100	Sod cutter	B-12K	3,200	.005			.14	.24	.38	.49	
	4200	By hand	2 Clab	240	.067			1.52		1.52	2.38	
900	0010	**TREES** Deciduous, in prep. beds, balled & burlapped (B&B)										900
	0100	Ash, 2" caliper	B-17	8	4	Ea.	103	98.50	69	270.50	340	
	0200	Beech, 5'-6'		50	.640		206	15.75	11.05	232.80	264	
	0300	Birch, 6'-8', 3 stems		20	1.600		210	39.50	27.50	277	320	
	0500	Crabapple, 6'-8'		20	1.600		150	39.50	27.50	217	256	
	0600	Dogwood, 4'-5'		40	.800		61	19.70	13.80	94.50	113	
	0700	Eastern redbud 4'-5'		40	.800		122	19.70	13.80	155.50	180	
	0800	Elm, 8'-10'		20	1.600		87	39.50	27.50	154	187	
	0900	Ginkgo, 6'-7'		24	1.333		100	33	23	156	186	
	1000	Hawthorn, 8'-10', 1" caliper		20	1.600		107	39.50	27.50	174	209	
	1100	Honeylocust, 10'-12', 1-1/2" caliper		10	3.200		142	78.50	55	275.50	340	
	1300	Larch, 8'		32	1		60.50	24.50	17.25	102.25	123	
	1400	Linden, 8'-10', 1" caliper		20	1.600		101	39.50	27.50	168	202	
	1500	Magnolia, 4'-5'		20	1.600		59.50	39.50	27.50	126.50	157	
	1600	Maple, red, 8'-10', 1-1/2" caliper		10	3.200		137	78.50	55	270.50	330	
	1700	Mountain ash, 8'-10', 1" caliper		16	2		127	49	34.50	210.50	254	
	1800	Oak, 2-1/2"-3" caliper		6	5.333		207	131	92	430	530	
	2100	Planetree, 9'-11', 1-1/4" caliper		10	3.200		92.50	78.50	55	226	284	
	2200	Plum, 6'-8', 1" caliper		20	1.600		75	39.50	27.50	142	174	
	2300	Poplar, 9'-11', 1-1/4" caliper		10	3.200		42.50	78.50	55	176	229	
	2500	Sumac, 2'-3'		75	.427		27	10.50	7.35	44.85	54	
	2700	Tulip, 5'-6'		40	.800		41	19.70	13.80	74.50	90.50	
	2800	Willow, 6'-8', 1" caliper		20	1.600		63	39.50	27.50	130	160	
910	0010	**TRAVEL** To all nursery items, for 10 to 20 miles, add				All					5%	910
	0100	30 to 50 miles, add				"					10%	

R02930 -900

SITE CONSTRUCTION 2

02945 | Planting Accessories

		CREW	DAILY OUTPUT	LABOR-HOURS	UNIT	2001 BARE COSTS				TOTAL INCL O&P	
						MAT.	LABOR	EQUIP.	TOTAL		
310	**0010**	**EDGING**									**310**
	0050	Aluminum alloy, including stakes, 1/8" x 4", mill finish	B-1	390	.062	L.F.	1.87	1.45		3.32	4.32
	0051	Black paint		390	.062		2.17	1.45		3.62	4.65
	0052	Black anodized	↓	390	.062		2.51	1.45		3.96	5
	0100	Brick, set horizontally, 1-1/2 bricks per L.F.	D-1	370	.043		.63	1.14		1.77	2.45
	0150	Set vertically, 3 bricks per L.F.	"	135	.119		2.52	3.11		5.63	7.60
	0200	Corrugated aluminum, roll, 4" wide	1 Carp	650	.012		.29	.36		.65	.88
	0250	6" wide	"	550	.015		.36	.42		.78	1.06
	0600	Railroad ties, 6" x 8"	2 Carp	170	.094		2.37	2.74		5.11	6.90
	0650	7" x 9"		136	.118		2.63	3.43		6.06	8.25
	0750	2" x 4"	↓	330	.048		2.67	1.41		4.08	5.15
	0800	Steel edge strips, incl. stakes, 1/4" x 5"	B-1	390	.062		2.83	1.45		4.28	5.35
	0850	3/16" x 4"	"	390	.062	↓	2.24	1.45		3.69	4.72
500	**0010**	**PLANTERS** Concrete, sandblasted, precast, 48" diameter, 24" high	2 Clab	15	1.067	Ea.	480	24.50		504.50	565	**500**
	0100	Fluted, precast, 7' diameter, 36" high		10	1.600		875	36.50		911.50	1,025
	0300	Fiberglass, circular, 36" diameter, 24" high		15	1.067		385	24.50		409.50	460
	0400	60" diameter, 24" high		10	1.600		605	36.50		641.50	720
	0600	Square, 24" side, 36" high		15	1.067		475	24.50		499.50	565
	0700	48" side, 36" high		15	1.067		880	24.50		904.50	1,000
	0900	Planter/bench, 72" square, 36" high		5	3.200		1,400	73		1,473	1,650
	1000	96" square, 27" high		5	3.200		2,600	73		2,673	2,975
	1200	Wood, square, 48" side, 24" high		15	1.067		880	24.50		904.50	1,000
	1300	Circular, 48" diameter, 30" high		10	1.600		675	36.50		711.50	800
	1500	72" diameter, 30" high		10	1.600		1,125	36.50		1,161.50	1,275
	1600	Planter/bench, 72"	↓	5	3.200	↓	2,575	73		2,648	2,950
775	**0010**	**TREE GUYING** Including stakes, guy wire and wrap										**775**
	0100	Less than 3" caliper, 2 stakes	2 Clab	35	.457	Ea.	14.90	10.45		25.35	33
	0200	3" to 4" caliper, 3 stakes	"	21	.762	"	16.70	17.40		34.10	45.50
	1000	Including arrowhead anchor, cable, turnbuckles and wrap									
	1100	Less than 3" caliper, 3" anchors	2 Clab	20	.800	Ea.	45	18.30		63.30	78
	1200	3" to 6" caliper, 4" anchors		15	1.067		52.50	24.50		77	96
	1300	6" caliper, 6" anchors		12	1.333		80	30.50		110.50	136
	1400	8" caliper, 8" anchors	↓	9	1.778	↓	87.50	40.50		128	160

02950 | Site Restoration & Rehabilitation

02955 | Restoration of Underground Piping

		CREW	DAILY OUTPUT	LABOR-HOURS	UNIT	2001 BARE COSTS				TOTAL INCL O&P	
						MAT.	LABOR	EQUIP.	TOTAL		
700	**0010**	**LINING PIPE** with cement, incl. bypass and cleaning										**700**
	0020	Less than 10,000 L.F., urban, 6" to 10"	C-17E	130	.615	L.F.	6	18.60	.57	25.17	36
	0200	24" to 36"		90	.889		9.55	27	.82	37.37	53.50
	0300	48" to 72"	↓	80	1	↓	15.25	30.50	.92	46.67	65.50
800	**0010**	**CORROSION RESISTANCE** Wrap & coat, add to pipe, 4" dia.				L.F.	1.35			1.35	1.49	**800**
	0040	6" diameter					1.42			1.42	1.56
	0060	8" diameter					2.19			2.19	2.41
	0100	12" diameter					3.27			3.27	3.60
	0200	24" diameter					6.20			6.20	6.80
	0500	Coating, bituminous, per diameter inch, 1 coat, add					.24			.24	.26
	0540	3 coat					.38			.38	.42
	0560	Coal tar epoxy, per diameter inch, 1 coat, add				↓	.15			.15	.17

Important: See the Reference Section for critical supporting data - Reference Nos., Crews, & City Cost Indexes

2 SITE CONSTRUCTION

		02955	Restoration of Underground Piping	CREW	DAILY OUTPUT	LABOR-HOURS	UNIT	2001 BARE COSTS				TOTAL INCL O&P	
								MAT.	LABOR	EQUIP.	TOTAL		
800	0600		3 coat				L.F.	.30			.30	.33	800

		02990	Structure Moving										
300	0010		**MOVING BUILDINGS** One day move, up to 24' wide										300
	0020		Reset on new foundation, patch & hook-up, average move				Total					8,700	
	0040		Wood or steel frame bldg., based on ground floor area	B-4	185	.259	S.F.		6.05	2.65	8.70	12.35	
	0060		Masonry bldg., based on ground floor area	"	137	.350	↓		8.20	3.58	11.78	16.70	
	0200		For 24' to 42' wide, add				↓					15%	
	0220		For each additional day on road, add	B-4	1	48	Day		1,125	490	1,615	2,300	
	0240		Construct new basement, move building, 1 day										
	0300		move, patch & hook-up, based on ground floor area	B-3	155	.310	S.F.	6	7.70	11.20	24.90	31	

SITE CONSTRUCTION 2

Division Notes

		CREW	DAILY OUTPUT	LABOR-HOURS	UNIT	2001 BARE COSTS				TOTAL INCL O&P
						MAT.	LABOR	EQUIP.	TOTAL	

Division 3
Concrete

Estimating Tips

General

- Carefully check all the plans and specifications. Concrete often appears on drawings other than structural drawings, including mechanical and electrical drawings for equipment pads. The cost of cutting and patching is often difficult to estimate. See Subdivision 02225 for demolition costs.
- Always obtain concrete prices from suppliers near the job site. A volume discount can often be negotiated depending upon competition in the area. Remember to add for waste, particularly for slabs and footings on grade.

03100 Concrete Forms & Accessories

- A primary cost for concrete construction is forming. Most jobs today are constructed with prefabricated forms. The selection of the forms best suited for the job and the total square feet of forms required for efficient concrete forming and placing are key elements in estimating concrete construction. Enough forms must be available for erection to make efficient use of the concrete placing equipment and crew.
- Concrete accessories for forming and placing depend upon the systems used. Study the plans and specifications to assure that all special accessory requirements have been included in the cost estimate such as anchor bolts, inserts and hangers.

03200 Concrete Reinforcement

- Ascertain that the reinforcing steel supplier has included all accessories, cutting, bending and an allowance for lapping, splicing and waste. A good rule of thumb is 10% for lapping, splicing and waste. Also, 10% waste should be allowed for welded wire fabric.

03300 Cast-in-Place Concrete

- When estimating structural concrete, pay particular attention to requirements for concrete additives, curing methods and surface treatments. Special consideration for climate, hot or cold, must be included in your estimate. Be sure to include requirements for concrete placing equipment and concrete finishing.

03400 Precast Concrete
03500 Cementitious Decks & Toppings

- The cost of hauling precast concrete structural members is often an important factor. For this reason, it is important to get a quote from the nearest supplier. It may become economically feasible to set up precasting beds on the site if the hauling costs are prohibitive.

Reference Numbers

Reference numbers are shown in bold squares at the beginning of some major classifications. These numbers refer to related items in the Reference Section. The reference information may be an estimating procedure, an alternate pricing method or technical information.

Note: Not all subdivisions listed here necessarily appear in this publication.

3 CONCRETE

03060	Basic Concrete Materials	CREW	DAILY OUTPUT	LABOR-HOURS	UNIT	2001 BARE COSTS				TOTAL INCL O&P	
						MAT.	LABOR	EQUIP.	TOTAL		
100	**0010**	**CONCRETE ADMIXTURES & SURFACE TREATMENTS**									**100**
0040	Abrasives, aluminum oxide, over 20 tons				Lb.	.95			.95	1.05	
0070	Under 1 ton					1			1	1.10	
0100	Silicon carbide, black, over 20 tons					1.30			1.30	1.43	
0120	Under 1 ton				↓	1.35			1.35	1.49	
0200	Air entraining agent, .7 to 1.5 oz. per bag, 55 gallon lots				Gal.	8.50			8.50	9.35	
0220	5 gallon lots					8.75			8.75	9.65	
0300	Bonding agent, acrylic latex (200-250 S.F. per gallon)					26.50			26.50	29	
0320	Epoxy resin (70-80 S.F. per gallon)				↓	51			51	56	
0400	Calcium chloride, 100 lb. bags, FOB plant, truckload lots				Ton	340			340	375	
0420	Less than truckload lots				Bag	29			29	31.50	
0500	Carbon black, liquid, 2 to 8 lbs. per bag of cement				Lb.	3			3	3.30	
0600	Colors, integral, 2 to 10 lb. per bag of cement, minimum					1.38			1.38	1.52	
0610	Average					2.17			2.17	2.39	
0620	Maximum				↓	3.97			3.97	4.37	
0700	Curing compound, (200 to 400 S.F. per gallon), 55 gal. lots				Gal.	7.50			7.50	8.25	
0720	5 gallon lots					9.95			9.95	10.95	
0800	Premium grade, (450 S.F. per gallon), 55 gallon lots					11.50			11.50	12.65	
0820	5 gallon lots					12.75			12.75	14.05	
0900	Dustproofing compound, (200-600 S.F./gal.), 55 gallon lots					8.40			8.40	9.25	
0920	5 gallon lots				↓	9.95			9.95	10.95	
1000	Epoxy dustproof coating, colors, (300-400 S.F. per coat),										
1010	or transparent, (400-600 S.F. per coat)				Gal.	58			58	64	
1100	Hardeners, metallic, 55 lb. bags, natural (grey)				Lb.	.77			.77	.85	
1200	Colors, average					1			1	1.10	
1300	Non-metallic, 55 lb. bags, natural (grey), minimum					.35			.35	.39	
1310	Maximum					.38			.38	.42	
1320	Non-metallic, colors, minimum					.45			.45	.50	
1340	Maximum					.72			.72	.79	
1400	Non-metallic, non-slip, 100 lb. bags, minimum					.45			.45	.50	
1420	Maximum				↓	.90			.90	.99	
1500	Solution type, (300 to 400 S.F. per gallon)				Gal.	6			6	6.60	
1550	Release agent, for tilt slabs					6.75			6.75	7.45	
1570	For forms, average					4.50			4.50	4.95	
1600	Sealer, hardener and dustproofer, clear, 450 S.F., minimum					6.90			6.90	7.60	
1620	Maximum					14.25			14.25	15.70	
1700	Colors (300-400 S.F. per gallon)					37			37	40.50	
1800	Set accelerator for below freezing, 1 to 1-1/2 gal. per C.Y.					5.35			5.35	5.90	
1900	Set retarder, 2 to 4 fl. oz. per bag of cement				↓	9.85			9.85	10.80	
2000	Waterproofing, integral 1 lb. per bag of cement				Lb.	.80			.80	.88	
2100	Powdered metallic, 40 lbs. per 100 S.F., minimum					1			1	1.10	
2120	Maximum				↓	2			2	2.20	
2200	Water reducing admixture, average				Gal.	9			9	9.90	
110	**0010**	**AGGREGATE** Expanded shale, C.L. lots, 52 lb. per C.F., minimum [R03310-020]				Ton	36			36	39.50	**110**
0050	Maximum				"	48			48	53	
0100	Lightweight vermiculite or perlite, 4 C.F. bag, C.L. lots [R03310-030]				Bag	5.60			5.60	6.15	
0150	L.C.L. lots				"	6.15			6.15	6.80	
0250	Sand & stone, loaded at pit, crushed bank gravel [R03310-050]				Ton	10.20			10.20	11.20	
0350	Sand, washed, for concrete					9.50			9.50	10.45	
0400	For plaster or brick					11.25			11.25	12.35	
0450	Stone, 3/4" to 1-1/2"					13.75			13.75	15.15	
0500	3/8" roofing stone & 1/2" pea stone					13.50			13.50	14.85	
0550	For trucking 10 miles, add to the above					4			4	4.40	
0600	30 miles, add to the above				↓	8.50			8.50	9.35	
0850	Sand & stone, loaded at pit, crushed bank gravel				C.Y.	16.10			16.10	17.70	

Important: See the Reference Section for critical supporting data - Reference Nos., Crews, & City Cost Indexes

	03060	Basic Concrete Materials		CREW	DAILY OUTPUT	LABOR-HOURS	UNIT	2001 BARE COSTS MAT.	LABOR	EQUIP.	TOTAL	TOTAL INCL O&P	
110	0950	Sand, washed, for concrete	R03310 -020				C.Y.	11.40			11.40	12.55	110
	1000	For plaster or brick						17.35			17.35	19.10	
	1050	Stone, 3/4″ to 1-1/2″	R03310 -030					21.50			21.50	24	
	1100	3/8″ roofing stone & 1/2″ pea stone						17			17	18.70	
	1150	For trucking 10 miles, add to the above	R03310 -050					5.60			5.60	6.15	
	1200	30 miles, add to the above						11.90			11.90	13.10	
	1310	Quartz chips, 50 lb. bags					Cwt.	15.70			15.70	17.30	
	1330	Silica chips, 50 lb. bags						8.60			8.60	9.50	
	1410	White marble, 3/8″ to 1/2″, 50 lb. bags						13			13	14.30	
	1430	3/4″					Ton	26.50			26.50	29	
200	0010	**CEMENT** Material only	R03310 -020										200
	0050	Masonry, gray, T.L. or C.L. lots					Bag	5.95			5.95	6.55	
	0060	L.T.L. or L.C.L. lots	R03310 -060					5.75			5.75	6.35	
	0100	Masonry, white, T.L. or C.L. lots						16.20			16.20	17.80	
	0120	L.T.L. or L.C.L. lots						16.75			16.75	18.45	
	0240	Portland, type I, plain/air entrained, TL lots, 94 lb bags						7.20			7.20	7.90	
	0300	Trucked in bulk, per cwt	CN				Cwt.	4.10			4.10	4.51	
	0400	Type III, high early strength, TL lots, 94 lb bags	CN				Bag	8.65			8.65	9.50	
	0420	L.T.L. or L.C.L. lots						9.10			9.10	10	
	0500	White high early strength, T.L. or C.L. lots, bags						19			19	21	
	0520	L.T.L. or L.C.L. lots						21			21	23	
	0600	White, T.L. or C.L. lots, bags						18			18	19.80	
	0620	L.T.L. or L.C.L. lots						17.45			17.45	19.20	
210	0010	**CRIBBING** See under Retaining Walls, division 02370-700											210
220	0010	**CUTTING** Concrete see division 02225-760											220
250	0010	**DAMPPROOFING** See division 07110											250
300	0010	**EQUIPMENT** For placing conc. see div. 01590-100	R01590 -100										300
400	0010	**LIFT SLAB** See division 03310-240	R03310 -120										400
700	0010	**SAWING CONCRETE** See division 02225-760											700
850	0010	**WATERPROOFING AND DAMPPROOFING** See division 07110											850
	0050	Integral waterproofing, add to cost of regular concrete						4.25			4.25	4.68	
870	0010	**WINTER PROTECTION** For heated ready mix, add, minimum					C.Y.	3.90			3.90	4.29	870
	0050	Maximum						5			5	5.50	
	0100	Protecting concrete and temporary heat, add, minimum		2 Clab	6,000	.003	S.F.	.16	.06		.22	.28	
	0150	Maximum, see also division 01510-800		″	2,000	.008	″	.66	.18		.84	1.02	
	0200	Temporary shelter for slab on grade, wood frame and polyethylene											
	0201	sheeting, minimum		2 Carp	10	1.600	M.S.F.	296	46.50		342.50	400	
	0210	Maximum		″	3	5.333	″	360	155		515	640	
	0300	See also Division 03390-200											

			DAILY	LABOR-			2001 BARE COSTS				TOTAL	
03110	**Structural C.I.P. Forms**	CREW	OUTPUT	HOURS	UNIT	MAT.	LABOR	EQUIP.	TOTAL	INCL O&P	
300	0010	**EXPANSION JOINT** See division 03150-250										300
405	0010	**FORMS IN PLACE, BEAMS AND GIRDERS** R03110 -040										405
	0020	See also Elevated Slabs, division 03310-240										
	0500	Beams & girders, exterior spandrel, plywood, 12" wide, 1 use R03110 -050	C-2	225	.213	SFCA	2.43	6.05		8.48	12.15	
	0550	2 use		275	.175		1.26	4.96		6.22	9.15	
	0600	3 use R03110 -060		295	.163		.97	4.63		5.60	8.30	
	0650	4 use		310	.155		.79	4.40		5.19	7.75	
	1000	Exterior spandrel, 18" wide, 1 use		250	.192		2.19	5.45		7.64	10.95	
	1050	2 use		275	.175		1.20	4.96		6.16	9.05	
	1100	3 use		305	.157		.87	4.47		5.34	7.95	
	1150	4 use		315	.152		.72	4.33		5.05	7.60	
	1500	Exterior spandrel, 24" wide, 1 use		265	.181		1.98	5.15		7.13	10.25	
	1550	2 use		290	.166		1.12	4.71		5.83	8.60	
	1600	3 use		315	.152		.79	4.33		5.12	7.65	
	1650	4 use		325	.148		.64	4.20		4.84	7.25	
	2000	Interior beam, 12" wide, 1 use		300	.160		2.35	4.55		6.90	9.70	
	2050	2 use		340	.141		1.33	4.01		5.34	7.75	
	2100	3 use		364	.132		.94	3.75		4.69	6.90	
	2150	4 use		377	.127		.76	3.62		4.38	6.50	
	2500	Interior beam, 24" wide, 1 use		320	.150		2.04	4.26		6.30	8.90	
	2550	2 use		365	.132		1.15	3.74		4.89	7.10	
	2600	3 use		385	.125		.81	3.54		4.35	6.45	
	2650	4 use		395	.122		.66	3.45		4.11	6.10	
	3000	Beam and Girder, encasing steel frame, hung, plywood, 1 use		325	.148		2.35	4.20		6.55	9.15	
	3050	2 use		390	.123		1.29	3.50		4.79	6.85	
	3100	3 use		415	.116		.94	3.29		4.23	6.20	
	3150	4 use		430	.112		.76	3.17		3.93	5.80	
	3500	Beam bottoms only, to 30" wide, plywood, 1 use		230	.209		3.56	5.95		9.51	13.20	
	3550	2 use		265	.181		1.99	5.15		7.14	10.25	
	3600	3 use		280	.171		1.42	4.87		6.29	9.20	
	3650	4 use		290	.166		1.16	4.71		5.87	8.60	
	4000	Beam sides only, vertical, 36" high, plywood, 1 use		335	.143		3.57	4.07		7.64	10.25	
	4050	2 use		405	.119		1.96	3.37		5.33	7.40	
	4100	3 use		430	.112		1.43	3.17		4.60	6.55	
	4150	4 use		445	.108		1.16	3.07		4.23	6.05	
	4500	Sloped sides, 36" high, plywood, 1 use		305	.157		3.54	4.47		8.01	10.90	
	4550	2 use		370	.130		1.97	3.69		5.66	7.90	
	4600	3 use		405	.119		1.41	3.37		4.78	6.80	
	4650	4 use		425	.113		1.15	3.21		4.36	6.25	
	5000	Upstanding beams, 36" high, plywood, 1 use		225	.213		4.17	6.05		10.22	14.10	
	5050	2 use		255	.188		2.32	5.35		7.67	10.90	
	5100	3 use		275	.175		1.69	4.96		6.65	9.60	
	5150	4 use		280	.171		1.37	4.87		6.24	9.15	
410	0010	**FORMS IN PLACE, COLUMNS** R03110 -040										410
	0500	Round fiberglass, 4 use per mo., rent, 12" diameter	C-1	160	.200	L.F.	2.15	5.50		7.65	11	
	0550	16" diameter R03110 -050		150	.213		2.30	5.90		8.20	11.75	
	0600	18" diameter		140	.229		2.55	6.30		8.85	12.65	
	0650	24" diameter R03110 -060		135	.237		3.25	6.55		9.80	13.85	
	0700	28" diameter		130	.246		3.60	6.80		10.40	14.55	
	0800	30" diameter		125	.256		4.20	7.05		11.25	15.65	
	0850	36" diameter		120	.267		4.75	7.35		12.10	16.75	
	1500	Round fiber tube, 1 use, 8" diameter		155	.206		2.03	5.70		7.73	11.15	
	1550	10" diameter		155	.206		2.83	5.70		8.53	12	
	1600	12" diameter		150	.213		3.68	5.90		9.58	13.25	
	1650	14" diameter		145	.221		4.43	6.10		10.53	14.35	

3 CONCRETE

			CREW	DAILY OUTPUT	LABOR-HOURS	UNIT	2001 BARE COSTS				TOTAL INCL O&P	
		**03110	Structural C.I.P. Forms**						MAT.	LABOR	EQUIP.	TOTAL		
410	1700	16" diameter		C-1	140	.229	L.F.	5.95	6.30		12.25	16.40	**410**
	1750	20" diameter			135	.237		9.20	6.55		15.75	20.50	
	1800	24" diameter			130	.246		10.75	6.80		17.55	22.50	
	1850	30" diameter			125	.256		15.55	7.05		22.60	28	
	1900	36" diameter			115	.278		21.50	7.65		29.15	35.50	
	1950	42" diameter			100	.320		41	8.80		49.80	59.50	
	2000	48" diameter			85	.376		53	10.40		63.40	75	
	2200	For seamless type, add						15%					
	3000	Round, steel, 4 use per mo., rent, regular duty, 12" diameter		C-1	145	.221	L.F.	2.75	6.10		8.85	12.55	
	3050	16" diameter			125	.256		3	7.05		10.05	14.35	
	3100	Heavy duty, 20" diameter			105	.305		3.25	8.40		11.65	16.75	
	3150	24" diameter			85	.376		3.35	10.40		13.75	19.95	
	3200	30" diameter			70	.457		3.60	12.60		16.20	23.50	
	3250	36" diameter			60	.533		4.15	14.70		18.85	27.50	
	3300	48" diameter			50	.640		6.15	17.65		23.80	34.50	
	3350	60" diameter			45	.711		7.50	19.60		27.10	39	
	4000	Column capitals, steel, 4 uses/mo., 24" col, 4' cap diameter			12	2.667	Ea.	18.25	73.50		91.75	135	
	4050	5' cap diameter			11	2.909		19.80	80		99.80	148	
	4100	6' cap diameter			10	3.200		22.50	88		110.50	163	
	4150	7' cap diameter			9	3.556		25	98		123	181	
	4500	For second and succeeding months, deduct						50%					
	5000	Plywood, 8" x 8" columns, 1 use		C-1	165	.194	SFCA	1.68	5.35		7.03	10.20	
	5050	2 use			195	.164		.97	4.52		5.49	8.15	
	5100	3 use			210	.152		.67	4.20		4.87	7.30	
	5150	4 use			215	.149		.55	4.10		4.65	7	
	5500	12" x 12" columns, 1 use			180	.178		1.69	4.90		6.59	9.50	
	5550	2 use			210	.152		.93	4.20		5.13	7.55	
	5600	3 use			220	.145		.67	4.01		4.68	7	
	5650	4 use			225	.142		.55	3.92		4.47	6.75	
	6000	16" x 16" columns, 1 use			185	.173		1.73	4.77		6.50	9.35	
	6050	2 use			215	.149		.93	4.10		5.03	7.40	
	6100	3 use			230	.139		.69	3.84		4.53	6.75	
	6150	4 use			235	.136		.56	3.75		4.31	6.45	
	6500	24" x 24" columns, 1 use			190	.168		1.86	4.64		6.50	9.30	
	6550	2 use			216	.148		1.02	4.08		5.10	7.50	
	6600	3 use			230	.139		.70	3.84		4.54	6.75	
	6650	4 use			238	.134		.60	3.71		4.31	6.45	
	7000	36" x 36" columns, 1 use			200	.160		1.82	4.41		6.23	8.90	
	7050	2 use			230	.139		1.02	3.84		4.86	7.10	
	7100	3 use			245	.131		.73	3.60		4.33	6.45	
	7150	4 use			250	.128		.59	3.53		4.12	6.15	
	7500	Steel framed plywood, 4 use per mo., rent, 8" x 8"			340	.094		2.62	2.59		5.21	6.95	
	7550	10" x 10"			350	.091		2.36	2.52		4.88	6.55	
	7600	12" x 12"			370	.086		2.38	2.38		4.76	6.35	
	7650	16" x 16"			400	.080		2.44	2.21		4.65	6.15	
	7700	20" x 20"			420	.076		2.39	2.10		4.49	5.90	
	7750	24" x 24"			440	.073		2.64	2.01		4.65	6.05	
	7755	30" x 30"			440	.073		3.33	2.01		5.34	6.80	
415	0010	**FORMS IN PLACE, CULVERT** 5' to 8' square or rectangular, 1 use		C-1	170	.188	SFCA	2.73	5.20		7.93	11.10	**415**
	0050	2 use			180	.178		1.46	4.90		6.36	9.25	
	0100	3 use			190	.168		1.14	4.64		5.78	8.50	
	0150	4 use			200	.160		.98	4.41		5.39	8	
420	0010	**FORMS IN PLACE, ELEVATED SLABS**											**420**
	0050	See also corrugated form deck, division 05310-300											
	1000	Flat plate plywood to 15' high, 1 use		C-2	470	.102	S.F.	2.61	2.90		5.51	7.40	
	1050	2 use			520	.092		1.44	2.62		4.06	5.70	

Reference codes in column: 1750 R03110-040; 1850 R03110-050; 1950 R03110-060; 0100 R03110-050; 0050 R03110-020; 1000 R03110-050.

			CREW	DAILY OUTPUT	LABOR-HOURS	UNIT	2001 BARE COSTS				TOTAL INCL O&P
	03110	**Structural C.I.P. Forms**					MAT.	LABOR	EQUIP.	TOTAL	
420	1100	3 use	C-2	545	.088	S.F.	1.04	2.50		3.54	5.05
	1150	4 use		560	.086		.85	2.44		3.29	4.74
	1500	15' to 20' high ceilings, 4 use		495	.097		1.07	2.76		3.83	5.50
	1600	21' to 35' high ceilings, 4 use		450	.107		1.25	3.03		4.28	6.10
	2000	Flat slab with drop panels, to 15' high, 1 use		449	.107		2.75	3.04		5.79	7.80
	2050	2 use		509	.094		1.70	2.68		4.38	6.05
	2100	3 use		532	.090		1.40	2.57		3.97	5.55
	2150	4 use		544	.088		1.23	2.51		3.74	5.25
	2250	15' to 20' high ceilings, 4 use		480	.100		1.43	2.84		4.27	6
	2350	20' to 35' high ceilings, 4 use		435	.110		1.57	3.14		4.71	6.65
	3000	Floor slab hung from steel beams, 1 use		485	.099		1.59	2.81		4.40	6.15
	3050	2 use		535	.090		1.14	2.55		3.69	5.25
	3100	3 use		550	.087		.99	2.48		3.47	4.96
	3150	4 use		565	.085		.91	2.42		3.33	4.78
	3500	Floor slab, with 20" metal pans, 1 use		415	.116		3.60	3.29		6.89	9.10
	3550	2 use		445	.108		1.80	3.07		4.87	6.80
	3600	3 use		475	.101		1.20	2.87		4.07	5.80
	3650	4 use		500	.096		1.25	2.73		3.98	5.65
	3700	Floor slab with 30" pans, 1 use		418	.115		7.50	3.26		10.76	13.35
	3720	2 use		455	.105		3.92	3		6.92	9
	3740	3 use		470	.102		3.26	2.90		6.16	8.10
	3760	4 use		480	.100		2.78	2.84		5.62	7.50
	4000	Floor slab with 19" metal domes, 1 use		405	.119		3.60	3.37		6.97	9.20
	4050	2 use		435	.110		2.40	3.14		5.54	7.55
	4100	3 use		465	.103		2	2.93		4.93	6.80
	4150	4 use		495	.097		1.25	2.76		4.01	5.70
	4500	With 30" fiberglass domes, 1 use		405	.119		4.57	3.37		7.94	10.30
	4520	2 use		450	.107		3.19	3.03		6.22	8.25
	4530	3 use		460	.104		2.62	2.97		5.59	7.50
	4550	4 use		470	.102		2.22	2.90		5.12	7
	5000	Box out for slab openings, over 16" deep, 1 use		190	.253	SFCA	3.27	7.20		10.47	14.85
	5050	2 use		240	.200	"	1.80	5.70		7.50	10.90
	5500	Shallow slab box outs, to 10 S.F.		42	1.143	Ea.	10.95	32.50		43.45	63
	5550	Over 10 S.F. (use perimeter)		600	.080	L.F.	1.46	2.27		3.73	5.15
	6000	Bulkhead forms for slab, with keyway, 1 use, 2 piece		500	.096		1.76	2.73		4.49	6.20
	6100	3 piece (see also edge forms)		460	.104		2.33	2.97		5.30	7.20
	6200	Bulkhead forms for slab, w/keyway expanded metal									
	6210	In lieu of 2 piece form	C-1	1,100	.029	L.F.	.72	.80		1.52	2.04
	6215	In lieu of 3 piece form		960	.033		.72	.92		1.64	2.23
	6220	6" high, 4 uses		1,100	.029		.88	.80		1.68	2.22
	6500	Curb forms, wood, 6" to 12" high, on elevated slabs, 1 use		180	.178	SFCA	1.61	4.90		6.51	9.40
	6550	2 use		205	.156		1.29	4.30		5.59	8.15
	6600	3 use		220	.145		.94	4.01		4.95	7.30
	6650	4 use		225	.142		.76	3.92		4.68	7
	7000	Edge forms to 6" high, on elevated slab, 4 use		500	.064	L.F.	.40	1.76		2.16	3.19
	7500	Depressed area forms to 12" high, 4 use		300	.107		.73	2.94		3.67	5.40
	7550	12" to 24" high, 4 use		175	.183		.99	5.05		6.04	9
	8000	Perimeter deck and rail for elevated slabs, straight		90	.356		9.55	9.80		19.35	26
	8050	Curved		65	.492		13.10	13.55		26.65	35.50
	8500	Void forms, round fiber, 3" diameter		450	.071		1.15	1.96		3.11	4.34
	8550	4" diameter		425	.075		1.46	2.08		3.54	4.86
	8600	6" diameter		400	.080		2.22	2.21		4.43	5.90
	8650	8" diameter		375	.085		3.58	2.35		5.93	7.60
	8700	10" diameter		350	.091		4.28	2.52		6.80	8.65
	8750	12" diameter		300	.107		5.20	2.94		8.14	10.30
	8800	Metal end closures, loose, minimum				C	30			30	33

(Reference: R03110-060)

Important: See the Reference Section for critical supporting data - Reference Nos., Crews, & City Cost Indexes

		03110	Structural C.I.P. Forms	CREW	DAILY OUTPUT	LABOR-HOURS	UNIT	2001 BARE COSTS MAT.	LABOR	EQUIP.	TOTAL	TOTAL INCL O&P	
420	8850		Maximum — R03110-020				C	155			155	171	**420**
425	0010	**FORMS IN PLACE, EQUIPMENT FOUNDATIONS** 1 use		C-2	160	.300	SFCA	2.57	8.55		11.12	16.20	**425**
	0050		2 use		190	.253		1.42	7.20		8.62	12.80	
	0100		3 use		200	.240		1.03	6.80		7.83	11.85	
	0150		4 use		205	.234		.84	6.65		7.49	11.30	
430	0010	**FORMS IN PLACE, FOOTINGS** Continuous wall, plywood, 1 use R03110-050		C-1	375	.085	SFCA	2.40	2.35		4.75	6.30	**430**
	0050		2 use		440	.073		1.32	2.01		3.33	4.59	
	0100		3 use R03110-060		470	.068		.96	1.88		2.84	4	
	0150		4 use		485	.066		.78	1.82		2.60	3.71	
	0500	Dowel supports for footings or beams, 1 use			500	.064	L.F.	.90	1.76		2.66	3.75	
	1000	Integral starter wall, to 4" high, 1 use			400	.080		.89	2.21		3.10	4.42	
	1500	Keyway, 4 use, tapered wood, 2" x 4"		1 Carp	530	.015		.22	.44		.66	.93	
	1550	2" x 6"			500	.016		.30	.47		.77	1.05	
	2000	Tapered plastic, 2" x 3"			530	.015		.52	.44		.96	1.26	
	2050	2" x 4"			500	.016		.67	.47		1.14	1.47	
	2250	For keyway hung from supports, add			150	.053		.90	1.55		2.45	3.42	
	3000	Pile cap, square or rectangular, plywood, 1 use		C-1	290	.110	SFCA	1.95	3.04		4.99	6.90	
	3050	2 use			346	.092		1.07	2.55		3.62	5.15	
	3100	3 use			371	.086		.78	2.38		3.16	4.58	
	3150	4 use			383	.084		.64	2.30		2.94	4.30	
	4000	Triangular or hexagonal caps, plywood, 1 use			225	.142		2.31	3.92		6.23	8.70	
	4050	2 use			280	.114		1.27	3.15		4.42	6.35	
	4100	3 use			305	.105		.92	2.89		3.81	5.55	
	4150	4 use			315	.102		.75	2.80		3.55	5.20	
	5000	Spread footings, plywood, 1 use			305	.105		1.84	2.89		4.73	6.55	
	5050	2 use			371	.086		1.01	2.38		3.39	4.83	
	5100	3 use			401	.080		.73	2.20		2.93	4.25	
	5150	4 use			414	.077		.60	2.13		2.73	3.99	
	6000	Supports for dowels, plinths or templates, 2' x 2'			25	1.280	Ea.	3.46	35.50		38.96	59	
	6050	4' x 4' footing			22	1.455		6.90	40		46.90	70.50	
	6100	8' x 8' footing			20	1.600		13.80	44		57.80	84	
	6150	12' x 12' footing			17	1.882		24	52		76	108	
	7000	Plinths, 1 use			250	.128	SFCA	2.50	3.53		6.03	8.25	
	7100	4 use			270	.119	"	.82	3.27		4.09	6	
435	0010	**FORMS IN PLACE, GRADE BEAM** Plywood, 1 use R03110-050		C-2	530	.091	SFCA	1.69	2.57		4.26	5.90	**435**
	0050		2 use		580	.083		.93	2.35		3.28	4.70	
	0100		3 use R03110-060		600	.080		.67	2.27		2.94	4.30	
	0150		4 use		605	.079		.55	2.26		2.81	4.13	
440	0010	**FORMS IN PLACE, MAT FOUNDATION** 1 use		C-2	290	.166	SFCA	1.84	4.71		6.55	9.35	**440**
	0050		2 use		310	.155		1.01	4.40		5.41	8	
	0100		3 use		330	.145		.72	4.14		4.86	7.25	
	0120		4 use		350	.137		.60	3.90		4.50	6.75	
445	0010	**FORMS IN PLACE, SLAB ON GRADE**											**445**
	1000	Bulkhead forms with keyway, wood, 1 use, 2 piece		C-1	510	.063	L.F.	.70	1.73		2.43	3.48	
	1050	3 piece			400	.080		.85	2.21		3.06	4.39	
	1100	4 piece			350	.091		1.18	2.52		3.70	5.25	
	1400	Bulkhead forms w/keyway, 1 piece expanded metal, left in place											
	1410	In lieu of 2 piece form		C-1	1,375	.023	L.F.	1.15	.64		1.79	2.27	
	1420	In lieu of 3 piece form			1,200	.027		1.15	.74		1.89	2.42	
	1430	In lieu of 4 piece form			1,050	.030		1.15	.84		1.99	2.58	
	2000	Curb forms, wood, 6" to 12" high, on grade, 1 use		C-1	215	.149	SFCA	1.86	4.10		5.96	8.45	
	2050	2 use			250	.128		1.03	3.53		4.56	6.65	
	2100	3 use			265	.121		.75	3.33		4.08	6	
	2150	4 use			275	.116		.61	3.21		3.82	5.65	

3

CONCRETE

3 CONCRETE

	03110	Structural C.I.P. Forms		CREW	DAILY OUTPUT	LABOR-HOURS	UNIT	MAT.	LABOR	EQUIP.	TOTAL	TOTAL INCL O&P	
445	3000	Edge forms, wood, 4 use, on grade, to 6" high		C-1	600	.053	L.F.	.48	1.47		1.95	2.83	445
	3050	7" to 12" high			435	.074	SFCA	.99	2.03		3.02	4.25	
	3500	For depressed slabs, 4 use, to 12" high			300	.107	L.F.	.69	2.94		3.63	5.35	
	3550	To 24" high			175	.183		.90	5.05		5.95	8.90	
	4000	For slab blockouts, to 12" high, 1 use			200	.160		.70	4.41		5.11	7.65	
	4050	To 24" high, 1 use			120	.267		.89	7.35		8.24	12.50	
	4100	Plastic (extruded), to 6" high, multiple use, on grade			800	.040		.23	1.10		1.33	1.98	
	5000	Screed, 24 ga. metal key joint, see Div 03150-250											
	5020	Wood, incl. wood stakes, 1" x 3"		C-1	900	.036	L.F.	.45	.98		1.43	2.03	
	5050	2" x 4"			900	.036	"	1.27	.98		2.25	2.93	
	6000	Trench forms in floor, wood, 1 use			160	.200	SFCA	2.27	5.50		7.77	11.15	
	6050	2 use			175	.183		1.27	5.05		6.32	9.30	
	6100	3 use			180	.178		.92	4.90		5.82	8.65	
	6150	4 use			185	.173		.75	4.77		5.52	8.30	
450	0010	**FORMS IN PLACE, STAIRS** (Slant length x width), 1 use	R03110-050	C-2	165	.291	S.F.	3.68	8.25		11.93	17	450
	0050	2 use			170	.282		2.02	8.05		10.07	14.80	
	0100	3 use	R03110-060		180	.267		1.47	7.60		9.07	13.45	
	0150	4 use			190	.253		1.03	7.20		8.23	12.40	
	1000	Alternate pricing method (0.7 L.F./S.F.), 1 use			100	.480	LF Rsr	4.90	13.65		18.55	27	
	1050	2 use			105	.457		2.70	13		15.70	23.50	
	1100	3 use			110	.436		1.96	12.40		14.36	21.50	
	1150	4 use			115	.417		1.62	11.85		13.47	20.50	
	2000	Stairs, cast on sloping ground (length x width), 1 use			220	.218	S.F.	2.50	6.20		8.70	12.45	
	2100	4 use			240	.200	"	.83	5.70		6.53	9.80	
455	0010	**FORMS IN PLACE, WALLS**	R03110-010										455
	0100	Box out for wall openings, to 16" thick, to 10 S.F.		C-2	24	2	Ea.	23	57		80	115	
	0150	Over 10 S.F. (use perimeter)	R03110-050	"	280	.171	L.F.	2.05	4.87		6.92	9.90	
	0250	Brick shelf, 4" w, add to wall forms, use wall area abv shelf											
	0260	1 use	R03110-060	C-2	240	.200	SFCA	2.27	5.70		7.97	11.40	
	0300	2 use			275	.175		1.25	4.96		6.21	9.15	
	0350	4 use			300	.160		.91	4.55		5.46	8.10	
	0500	Bulkhead forms, with keyway, 1 use, 2 piece			265	.181	L.F.	2.50	5.15		7.65	10.80	
	0550	3 piece			175	.274	"	3.10	7.80		10.90	15.60	
	0600	Bulkhead forms w/keyway, 1 piece expanded metal, left in place											
	0610	In lieu of 2 piece form		C-1	800	.040	L.F.	1.20	1.10		2.30	3.05	
	0620	In lieu of 3 piece form		"	525	.061	"	1.20	1.68		2.88	3.95	
	0700	Buttress forms, to 8' high, 1 use		C-2	350	.137	SFCA	3.08	3.90		6.98	9.50	
	0750	2 use			430	.112		1.70	3.17		4.87	6.85	
	0800	3 use			460	.104		1.24	2.97		4.21	6	
	0850	4 use			480	.100		1.02	2.84		3.86	5.55	
	1000	Corbel (haunch) forms, to 12" wide, add to wall forms, 1 use			150	.320	L.F.	1.69	9.10		10.79	16.10	
	1050	2 use			170	.282		.93	8.05		8.98	13.55	
	1100	3 use			175	.274		.68	7.80		8.48	12.95	
	1150	4 use			180	.267		.55	7.60		8.15	12.45	
	2000	Job built plywood wall forms, to 8' high, 1 use, below grade			300	.160	SFCA	2.31	4.55		6.86	9.65	
	2050	2 use, below grade			365	.132		1.29	3.74		5.03	7.25	
	2100	3 use, below grade			425	.113		.92	3.21		4.13	6	
	2150	4 use, below grade			435	.110		.76	3.14		3.90	5.75	
	2400	Over 8' to 16' high, 1 use			280	.171		3.76	4.87		8.63	11.80	
	2450	2 use			345	.139		1.15	3.96		5.11	7.45	
	2500	3 use			375	.128		.82	3.64		4.46	6.60	
	2550	4 use			395	.122		.67	3.45		4.12	6.15	
	2700	Over 16' high, 1 use			235	.204		2.35	5.80		8.15	11.70	
	2750	2 use			290	.166		1.29	4.71		6	8.75	
	2800	3 use			315	.152		.94	4.33		5.27	7.85	
	2850	4 use			330	.145		.76	4.14		4.90	7.30	

03110	Structural C.I.P. Forms		CREW	DAILY OUTPUT	LABOR-HOURS	UNIT	2001 BARE COSTS				TOTAL INCL O&P	
							MAT.	LABOR	EQUIP.	TOTAL		
455	3000	For architectural finish, add	R03110 -010	C-2	1,820	.026	SFCA	.62	.75		1.37	1.85	455
	3500	Polystyrene (expanded) wall forms											
	3510	To 8' high, 1 use, left in place	R03110 -050	1 Carp	295	.027	SFCA	1.65	.79		2.44	3.06	
	4000	Radial wall forms, plywood, smooth curved, 1 use		C-2	245	.196		2.08	5.55		7.63	11	
	4050	2 use	R03110 -060		300	.160		1.14	4.55		5.69	8.35	
	4100	3 use			325	.148		.83	4.20		5.03	7.45	
	4150	4 use			335	.143		.68	4.07		4.75	7.10	
	4200	Wall forms, smooth curved, below grade, job built plywood, 1 use			225	.213		2.81	6.05		8.86	12.60	
	4210	2 use			225	.213		1.55	6.05		7.60	11.20	
	4220	3 use			225	.213		1.27	6.05		7.32	10.90	
	4230	4 use			225	.213		.91	6.05		6.96	10.50	
	4300	Curved, plywood, with 2' chords, 1 use			290	.166		1.86	4.71		6.57	9.40	
	4350	2 use			355	.135		1.02	3.84		4.86	7.10	
	4400	3 use			385	.125		.74	3.54		4.28	6.35	
	4450	4 use			400	.120		.60	3.41		4.01	6	
	4500	Over 8' high, 1 use			290	.166		.75	4.71		5.46	8.15	
	4525	2 use			355	.135		.41	3.84		4.25	6.45	
	4550	3 use			385	.125		.30	3.54		3.84	5.90	
	4575	4 use			400	.120		.25	3.41		3.66	5.60	
	4600	Retaining wall forms, plywood, battered, to 8' high, 1 use			300	.160		1.74	4.55		6.29	9	
	4650	2 use			355	.135		.95	3.84		4.79	7.05	
	4700	3 use			375	.128		.69	3.64		4.33	6.45	
	4750	4 use			390	.123		.53	3.50		4.03	6.05	
	4900	Over 8' to 16' high, 1 use			240	.200		1.92	5.70		7.62	11	
	4950	2 use			295	.163		1.05	4.63		5.68	8.40	
	5000	3 use			305	.157		.77	4.47		5.24	7.85	
	5050	4 use		▼	320	.150		.62	4.26		4.88	7.35	
	5500	For gang wall forming, 192 S.F. sections, deduct						10%	10%				
	5550	384 S.F. sections, deduct					▼	20%	20%				
	5750	Liners for forms (add to wall forms), A.B.S. plastic											
	5800	Aged wood, 4" wide, 1 use		1 Carp	250	.032	SFCA	5	.93		5.93	6.95	
	5820	2 use			400	.020		2.75	.58		3.33	3.94	
	5840	4 use			750	.011		1.70	.31		2.01	2.36	
	5900	Fractured rope rib, 1 use			250	.032		7.65	.93		8.58	9.85	
	6000	4 use			750	.011		2.45	.31		2.76	3.19	
	6100	Ribbed look, 1/2" & 3/4" deep, 1 use			300	.027		5.20	.78		5.98	6.90	
	6200	4 use			800	.010		1.65	.29		1.94	2.28	
	6300	Rustic brick pattern, 1 use			250	.032		4.80	.93		5.73	6.75	
	6400	4 use			750	.011		1.60	.31		1.91	2.25	
	6500	Striated, random, 3/8" x 3/8" deep, 1 use			300	.027		5.10	.78		5.88	6.80	
	6600	4 use		▼	800	.010	▼	1.65	.29		1.94	2.28	
	6800	Rustication strips, A.B.S. plastic, 2 piece snap-on											
	6850	1" deep x 1-3/8" wide, 1 use		C-2	400	.120	L.F.	3.75	3.41		7.16	9.50	
	6900	2 use			600	.080		2.10	2.27		4.37	5.85	
	6950	4 use			800	.060		1.25	1.71		2.96	4.05	
	7050	Wood, beveled edge, 3/4" deep, 1 use			600	.080		.23	2.27		2.50	3.81	
	7100	1" deep, 1 use			450	.107	▼	.35	3.03		3.38	5.15	
	7200	For solid board finish, uniform, 1 use, add to wall forms			300	.160	SFCA	.75	4.55		5.30	7.95	
	7300	Non-uniform finish		▼	250	.192		.66	5.45		6.11	9.30	
	7500	Lintel or sill forms, 1 use		1 Carp	30	.267		2.44	7.75		10.19	14.85	
	7520	2 use			34	.235		1.34	6.85		8.19	12.25	
	7540	3 use			36	.222		.98	6.50		7.48	11.25	
	7560	4 use		▼	37	.216		.79	6.30		7.09	10.70	
	7800	Modular prefabricated plywood, to 8' high, 1 use per month		C-2	1,180	.041		1.43	1.16		2.59	3.38	
	7820	2 use per month			1,200	.040		.79	1.14		1.93	2.65	
	7840	3 use per month			1,240	.039		.57	1.10		1.67	2.35	

		03110	Structural C.I.P. Forms	CREW	DAILY OUTPUT	LABOR-HOURS	UNIT	2001 BARE COSTS				TOTAL INCL O&P	
								MAT.	LABOR	EQUIP.	TOTAL		
455	7860		4 use per month	C-2	1,260	.038	SFCA	.47	1.08		1.55	2.21	455
	8000		To 16' high, 1 use per month		715	.067		1.79	1.91		3.70	4.96	
	8020		2 use per month		740	.065		.98	1.84		2.82	3.97	
	8040		3 use per month		770	.062		.72	1.77		2.49	3.56	
	8060		4 use per month		790	.061		.59	1.73		2.32	3.35	
	8100		Over 16' high, 1 use per month		715	.067		2.15	1.91		4.06	5.35	
	8120		2 use per month		740	.065		1.18	1.84		3.02	4.19	
	8140		3 use per month		770	.062		.86	1.77		2.63	3.72	
	8160		4 use per month		790	.061		.72	1.73		2.45	3.49	
	8600		Pilasters, 1 use		270	.178		2.33	5.05		7.38	10.45	
	8620		2 use		330	.145		1.28	4.14		5.42	7.85	
	8640		3 use		370	.130		.93	3.69		4.62	6.80	
	8660		4 use		385	.125		.76	3.54		4.30	6.40	
	9000		Steel framed plywood, to 8' high, 1 use per month		600	.080		1.80	2.27		4.07	5.55	
	9020		2 use per month		640	.075		.99	2.13		3.12	4.43	
	9040		3 use per month		655	.073		.72	2.08		2.80	4.05	
	9060		4 use per month		665	.072		.59	2.05		2.64	3.86	
	9200		Over 8' to 16' high, 1 use per month		455	.105		2.50	3		5.50	7.45	
	9220		2 use per month		505	.095		1.38	2.70		4.08	5.75	
	9240		3 use per month		525	.091		1	2.60		3.60	5.15	
	9260		4 use per month		530	.091		.83	2.57		3.40	4.94	
	9400		Over 16' to 20' high, 1 use per month		425	.113		2.06	3.21		5.27	7.25	
	9420		2 use per month		435	.110		1.13	3.14		4.27	6.15	
	9440		3 use per month		455	.105		.82	3		3.82	5.60	
	9460		4 use per month	↓	465	.103	↓	.68	2.93		3.61	5.35	
	9475		For elevated walls, add						10%				
	9480		For battered walls, 1 side battered, add					10%	10%				
	9485		For battered walls, 2 sides battered, add	↓				15%	15%				
460	0010	**FORMS IN PLACE, INSULATING CONCRETE**											460
	0020	Forms left in place, S.F. is for both sides											
	1000	Panel system, flat cavity, minimum		2 Carp	960	.017	S.F.	1.80	.49		2.29	2.74	
	1010	Maximum			960	.017		2.70	.49		3.19	3.73	
	1020	Grid cavity, minimum			960	.017		2	.49		2.49	2.96	
	1030	Maximum			960	.017		3	.49		3.49	4.06	
	1040	Post and beam cavity, minimum			960	.017		2.20	.49		2.69	3.18	
	1050	Maximum			960	.017		3.30	.49		3.79	4.39	
	1060	Plank system, flat cavity, minimum			1,920	.008		1.60	.24		1.84	2.14	
	1070	Maximum			1,920	.008		2.40	.24		2.64	3.02	
	1120	Block system, flat cavity, minimum			480	.033		1.80	.97		2.77	3.50	
	1130	Maximum			480	.033		2.70	.97		3.67	4.49	
	1140	Grid cavity, minimum			480	.033		2	.97		2.97	3.72	
	1150	Maximum			480	.033		3	.97		3.97	4.82	
	1160	Post and beam cavity, minimum			480	.033		2.20	.97		3.17	3.94	
	1170	Maximum		↓	480	.033	↓	3.30	.97		4.27	5.15	
500	0010	**GAS STATION FORMS** Curb fascia, with template,											500
	0050	12 ga. steel, left in place, 9" high		1 Carp	50	.160	L.F.	6.95	4.66		11.61	14.95	
	1000	Sign or light bases, 18" diameter, 9" high			9	.889	Ea.	39	26		65	83.50	
	1050	30" diameter, 13" high		↓	8	1		66	29		95	118	
	2000	Island forms, 10' long, 9" high, 3'-6" wide		C-1	10	3.200		180	88		268	335	
	2050	4' wide			9	3.556		195	98		293	370	
	2500	20' long, 9" high, 4' wide			6	5.333		315	147		462	575	
	2550	5' wide		↓	5	6.400	↓	330	176		506	640	
750	0010	**REGLET** See division 07710-750											750
800	0010	**SCAFFOLDING** See division 01540-750											800

R03110-010
R03110-050
R03110-060

Important: See the Reference Section for critical supporting data - Reference Nos., Crews, & City Cost Indexes

CONCRETE 3

		03110	Structural C.I.P. Forms	CREW	DAILY OUTPUT	LABOR-HOURS	UNIT	2001 BARE COSTS				TOTAL INCL O&P	
								MAT.	LABOR	EQUIP.	TOTAL		
820	0010	SLIPFORMS Silos, minimum	R03110 -030	C-17E	3,885	.021	SFCA	1.10	.62	.02	1.74	2.21	820
	0050	Maximum			1,095	.073		1.55	2.21	.07	3.83	5.25	
	1000	Buildings, minimum			3,660	.022		1.27	.66	.02	1.95	2.46	
	1050	Maximum			875	.091		2.25	2.77	.08	5.10	6.90	

		03150	Concrete Accessories										
080	0010	ACCESSORIES, ANCHOR BOLTS J-type, incl. nut and washer											080
	0020	1/2" diameter, 6" long		1 Carp	90	.089	Ea.	.95	2.59		3.54	5.10	
	0050	10" long			85	.094		1.05	2.74		3.79	5.45	
	0100	12" long			85	.094		1.15	2.74		3.89	5.55	
	0200	5/8" diameter, 12" long			80	.100		1.27	2.92		4.19	5.95	
	0250	18" long			70	.114		1.50	3.33		4.83	6.85	
	0300	24" long			60	.133		1.73	3.89		5.62	8	
	0350	3/4" diameter, 8" long			80	.100		1.48	2.92		4.40	6.20	
	0400	12" long			70	.114		1.88	3.33		5.21	7.25	
	0450	18" long			60	.133		2.40	3.89		6.29	8.75	
	0500	24" long			50	.160		3.19	4.66		7.85	10.80	
	0600	7/8" diameter, 12" long			60	.133		2.07	3.89		5.96	8.35	
	0650	18" long			50	.160		2.76	4.66		7.42	10.35	
	0700	24" long			40	.200		2.88	5.85		8.73	12.25	
	0800	1" diameter, 12" long			55	.145		2.98	4.24		7.22	9.95	
	0850	18" long			45	.178		3.62	5.20		8.82	12.10	
	0900	24" long			35	.229		4.41	6.65		11.06	15.25	
	0950	36" long			25	.320		6.05	9.35		15.40	21.50	
	1200	1-1/2" diameter, 18" long			22	.364		8.80	10.60		19.40	26.50	
	1250	24" long			18	.444		10.45	12.95		23.40	32	
	1300	36" long			12	.667		10.10	19.45		29.55	41.50	
	1350	Larger sizes			200	.040	Lb.	.79	1.17		1.96	2.69	
	8000	Sleeves, see Division 03150-620											
085	0013	ANCHOR BOLTS See divisions 04080-070 and 05090-080											085
160	0010	ACCESSORIES, CHAMFER STRIPS											160
	2000	Polyvinyl chloride, 1/2" wide with leg		1 Carp	535	.015	L.F.	.30	.44		.74	1.01	
	2200	3/4" wide with leg			525	.015		.39	.44		.83	1.12	
	2400	1" radius with leg			515	.016		.51	.45		.96	1.27	
	2800	1-1/2" radius with leg			500	.016		1.75	.47		2.22	2.66	
	5000	Wood, 1/2" wide			535	.015		.12	.44		.56	.81	
	5200	3/4" wide			525	.015		.30	.44		.74	1.02	
	5400	1" wide			515	.016		.42	.45		.87	1.17	
170	0010	ACCESSORIES, COLUMN FORM											170
	1000	Column clamps, adjustable to 24" x 24", buy					Set	73			73	80.50	
	1100	Rent per month						7.75			7.75	8.55	
	1300	For sizes to 30" x 30", buy						84			84	92.50	
	1400	Rent per month						6.50			6.50	7.15	
	1600	For sizes to 36" x 36", buy						103			103	113	
	1700	Rent per month						10.25			10.25	11.30	
	2000	Bull winch (band iron) 36" x 36", buy						47.50			47.50	52.50	
	2100	Rent per month						4.35			4.35	4.79	
	2300	48" x 48", buy						49			49	54	
	2400	Rent per month						5.50			5.50	6.05	
	3000	Chain & wedge type 36" x 36", buy						67			67	73.50	
	3100	Rent per month						7.50			7.50	8.25	
	3300	60" x 60", buy						90			90	99	
	3400	Rent per month						10.50			10.50	11.55	
	4000	Friction collars 2'-6" dia., buy						680			680	750	

3 CONCRETE

03150	Concrete Accessories	CREW	DAILY OUTPUT	LABOR-HOURS	UNIT	2001 BARE COSTS MAT.	LABOR	EQUIP.	TOTAL	TOTAL INCL O&P	
170 4100	Rent per month				Set	67			67	73.50	**170**
4300	4'-0" dia., buy					775			775	855	
4400	Rent per month				↓	85			85	93.50	
200 0010	**ACCESSORIES, DOVETAIL ANCHOR SYSTEM**										**200**
0500	Anchor slot, galv., filled, 24 ga.	1 Carp	425	.019	L.F.	.62	.55		1.17	1.54	
0600	20 ga.		400	.020		.76	.58		1.34	1.75	
0800	16 oz. copper, foam filled		375	.021		1.68	.62		2.30	2.82	
0900	26 ga. stainless steel, foam filled	↓	375	.021	↓	1.20	.62		1.82	2.29	
1200	Brick anchor, corr., galv., 3-1/2" long, 16 ga.	1 Bric	10.50	.762	C	18.75	22.50		41.25	55.50	
1300	12 ga.		10.50	.762		26	22.50		48.50	63.50	
1500	Flat, galv., 3-1/2" long, 16 ga.		10.50	.762		24	22.50		46.50	61	
1600	12 ga.		10.50	.762		46	22.50		68.50	85.50	
2000	Cavity wall, corr., galv., 5" long, 16 ga.		10.50	.762		25	22.50		47.50	62.50	
2100	12 ga.		10.50	.762		36	22.50		58.50	74.50	
3000	Furring anchors, corr., galv., 1-1/2" long, 16 ga.		10.50	.762		9.50	22.50		32	45.50	
3100	12 ga.		10.50	.762		16	22.50		38.50	52.50	
6000	Stone anchors, 3-1/2" long, galv., 1/8" x 1" wide		10.50	.762		78.50	22.50		101	122	
6100	1/4" x 1" wide	↓	10.50	.762	↓	122	22.50		144.50	170	
250 0010	**EXPANSION JOINT** Keyed, cold, 24 ga, incl. stakes, 3-1/2" high	1 Carp	200	.040	L.F.	.53	1.17		1.70	2.40	**250**
0050	4-1/2" high		200	.040		.66	1.17		1.83	2.55	
0100	5-1/2" high		195	.041		.72	1.20		1.92	2.66	
0150	7-1/2" high	↓	190	.042		.88	1.23		2.11	2.89	
0300	Poured asphalt, plain, 1/2" x 1"	1 Clab	450	.018		.34	.41		.75	1.01	
0350	1" x 2"		400	.020		1.20	.46		1.66	2.04	
0500	Neoprene, liquid, cold applied, 1/2" x 1"		450	.018		1.57	.41		1.98	2.37	
0550	1" x 2"		400	.020		6.10	.46		6.56	7.40	
0700	Polyurethane, poured, 2 part, 1/2" x 1"		400	.020		1.88	.46		2.34	2.79	
0750	1" x 2"		350	.023		7.35	.52		7.87	8.90	
0900	Rubberized asphalt, hot or cold applied, 1/2" x 1"		450	.018		.68	.41		1.09	1.39	
0950	1" x 2"		400	.020		1.27	.46		1.73	2.12	
1100	Hot applied, fuel resistant, 1/2" x 1"		450	.018		1.05	.41		1.46	1.80	
1150	1" x 2"	↓	400	.020		1.46	.46		1.92	2.33	
2000	Premolded, bituminous fiber, 1/2" x 6"	1 Carp	375	.021		.36	.62		.98	1.37	
2050	1" x 12"		300	.027		.69	.78		1.47	1.98	
2250	Cork with resin binder, 1/2" x 6"		375	.021		1.44	.62		2.06	2.55	
2300	1" x 12"		300	.027		5.15	.78		5.93	6.85	
2500	Neoprene sponge, closed cell, 1/2" x 6"		375	.021		1.29	.62		1.91	2.39	
2550	1" x 12"		300	.027		5.85	.78		6.63	7.60	
2750	Polyethylene foam, 1/2" x 6"		375	.021		.49	.62		1.11	1.51	
2800	1" x 12"		300	.027		1.32	.78		2.10	2.67	
3000	Polyethylene backer rod, 3/8" diameter		460	.017		.03	.51		.54	.82	
3050	3/4" diameter		460	.017		.06	.51		.57	.86	
3100	1" diameter		460	.017		.11	.51		.62	.91	
3500	Polyurethane foam, with polybutylene, 1/2" x 1/2"		475	.017		.49	.49		.98	1.31	
3550	1" x 1"		450	.018		1.47	.52		1.99	2.43	
3750	Polyurethane foam, regular, closed cell, 1/2" x 6"		375	.021		1.14	.62		1.76	2.22	
3800	1" x 12"		300	.027		1.83	.78		2.61	3.23	
4000	Polyvinyl chloride foam, closed cell, 1/2" x 6"		375	.021		1.68	.62		2.30	2.82	
4050	1" x 12"		300	.027		5.20	.78		5.98	6.95	
4250	Rubber, gray sponge, 1/2" x 6"		375	.021		2.34	.62		2.96	3.54	
4300	1" x 12"	↓	300	.027	↓	9.15	.78		9.93	11.30	
4500	Lead wool for joints, 1 ton lots				Lb.	2.18			2.18	2.40	
4550	Retail				"	2.33			2.33	2.56	
5000	For installation in walls, add						75%				

Important: See the Reference Section for critical supporting data - Reference Nos., Crews, & City Cost Indexes

		03150	Concrete Accessories	CREW	DAILY OUTPUT	LABOR-HOURS	UNIT	2001 BARE COSTS MAT.	LABOR	EQUIP.	TOTAL	TOTAL INCL O&P	
250	5250		For installation in boxouts, add						25%				250
350	0010	**ACCESSORIES, HANGERS**											350
	0020		Slab and beam form										
	0500		Banding iron, 3/4" x 22 ga, 14 L.F. per lb or										
	0550		1/2" x 14 ga, 7 L.F. per lb.				Lb.	.95			.95	1.05	
	1000		Fascia ties, coil type add to frame ties below				C	58			58	64	
	1500		Frame ties to 8-1/8"					148			148	163	
	1550		8-1/8" to 10-1/8"					155			155	171	
	5000		Snap tie hanger, to 30" overall length, 4000 #					320			320	355	
	5050		30" to 36" overall length					350			350	385	
	5100		42" to 48" overall length					390			390	425	
	5500		Steel beam hanger										
	5600		Flange to 8-1/8"				C	282			282	310	
	5650		8-1/8" to 10-1/8"					235			235	258	
	6000		Tie hangers to 24" overall length, 6000 #					325			325	360	
	6100		30" to 36" overall length					380			380	415	
	6500		Tie back hanger, up to 12-1/8" flange					310			310	340	
	8500		Wire, black annealed, 9 ga				Cwt.	85			85	93.50	
	8600		16 ga				"	90			90	99	
400	0010	**ACCESSORIES, INSERTS**											400
	1000		All size nut insert, 5/8" & 3/4", incl. nut	1 Carp	84	.095	Ea.	3.10	2.78		5.88	7.75	
	2000		Continuous slotted, 1-5/8" x 1-3/8"										
	2100		3" long, 12 ga.	1 Carp	65	.123	Ea.	2.80	3.59		6.39	8.70	
	2150		6" long		65	.123		3.65	3.59		7.24	9.60	
	2200		12" long, 8 ga.		65	.123		8.90	3.59		12.49	15.40	
	2250		24" long		65	.123		14.50	3.59		18.09	21.50	
	2300		36" long		60	.133		20	3.89		23.89	28	
	2350		60" long		55	.145		31	4.24		35.24	40.50	
	7000		Threaded cast										
	7100		1/4" diameter bolt	1 Carp	84	.095	Ea.	4.55	2.78		7.33	9.35	
	7350		7/8" diameter bolt	"	84	.095	"	7.60	2.78		10.38	12.70	
	9000		Wedge										
	9050		For 5/8" diameter bolt	1 Carp	60	.133	Ea.	3.30	3.89		7.19	9.75	
	9100		For 3/4" diameter bolt	"	60	.133	"	7.20	3.89		11.09	14	
	9800		Cut washers, "Black"										
	9850		5/8" bolt				Ea.	.21			.21	.23	
	9950		For galvanized inserts, add					30%					
600	0010	**SHORES** Erect and strip, by hand, horizontal members											600
	0500		Aluminum joists and stringers	2 Carp	60	.267	Ea.		7.75		7.75	12.15	
	0600		Steel, adjustable beams		45	.356			10.35		10.35	16.20	
	0700		Wood joists		50	.320			9.35		9.35	14.60	
	0800		Wood stringers		30	.533			15.55		15.55	24.50	
	1000		Vertical members to 10' high		55	.291			8.50		8.50	13.25	
	1050		To 13' high		50	.320			9.35		9.35	14.60	
	1100		To 16' high		45	.356			10.35		10.35	16.20	
	1500		Reshoring		1,400	.011	S.F.	.18	.33		.51	.72	
	1600		Flying truss system	C-17D	9,600	.009	SFCA		.27	.07	.34	.50	
	1760		Horizontal, aluminum joists, 6' to 30' spans, buy				L.F.	24.50			24.50	27	
	1770		Aluminum stringers, 12' & 16' spans				"	34			34	37	
	1810		Horizontal, steel beam, adjustable, 4' to 7' span				Ea.	112			112	123	
	1830		6' to 10' span					143			143	157	
	1920		9' to 15' span					265			265	292	
	1940		12' to 20' span					305			305	335	
	1970		Steel stringer, 6' to 15' span				L.F.	8			8	8.80	
	3000		Rent for job duration, aluminum, first month				SF Flr.	.27			.27	.30	

CONCRETE 3

		03150 Concrete Accessories	CREW	DAILY OUTPUT	LABOR-HOURS	UNIT	2001 BARE COSTS				TOTAL INCL O&P	
							MAT.	LABOR	EQUIP.	TOTAL		
600	3050	Steel				SF Flr.	.20			.20	.22	600
	3500	Vertical, adjustable steel, 5'-7" to 9'-6" high, 10,000# cap., buy				Ea.	59			59	65	
	3550	7'-3" to 12'-10" high, 7800# capacity					71			71	78	
	3600	8'-10" to 12'-4" high, 10,000# capacity					79			79	87	
	3650	8'-10" to 16'-1" high, 3800# capacity					88			88	97	
	4000	Frame shoring systems, aluminum, 10,000# per leg,										
	4050	6' wide, 5' & 6' high				Ea.	240			240	264	
	4100	5' to 7' post with base, jack screw & top plate				Set	53			53	58.50	
	5010	Steel, 10,000# per leg										
	5040	2' & 4' wide, 3', 4', 5' & 6' high				Ea.	97			97	107	
	5250	6' extension tube with adjusting collar					91			91	100	
	5550	Base plate					9.75			9.75	10.75	
	5600	12" adjustable leg					39			39	43	
	5650	Top plate					21			21	23	
	5750	Flying truss system				SFCA	9			9	9.90	
620	0010	ACCESSORIES, SLEEVES AND CHASES										620
	0100	Plastic, 1 use, 9" long, 2" diameter	1 Carp	100	.080	Ea.	.53	2.33		2.86	4.23	
	0150	4" diameter		90	.089		1.56	2.59		4.15	5.75	
	0200	6" diameter		75	.107		2.75	3.11		5.86	7.90	
	0250	12" diameter		60	.133		18.05	3.89		21.94	26	
640	0010	ACCESSORIES, SNAP TIES, FLAT WASHER, 4-3/4" L&W										640
	0100	3000 lb., to 8"				C	76.50			76.50	84.50	
	0200	11" & 12"					92			92	101	
	0250	16"					97.50			97.50	107	
	0300	18"					100			100	110	
	0500	With plastic cone, to 8"					64			64	70.50	
	0600	11" & 12"					88			88	97	
	0650	16"					91			91	100	
	0700	18"					94.50			94.50	104	
	1000	5000 lb., to 8"					100			100	110	
	1150	11" & 12"					117			117	129	
	1200	16"					128			128	141	
	1250	18"					125			125	137	
	1500	With plastic cone, to 8"					109			109	120	
	1600	11" & 12"					142			142	157	
	1650	16"					157			157	172	
	1700	18"					162			162	179	
660	0010	STAIR TREAD INSERTS Cast iron, abrasive, 3" wide	1 Carp	90	.089	L.F.	5.75	2.59		8.34	10.40	660
	0020	4" wide		80	.100		7	2.92		9.92	12.25	
	0040	6" wide		75	.107		8.65	3.11		11.76	14.35	
	0050	9" wide		70	.114		12.75	3.33		16.08	19.25	
	0100	12" wide		65	.123		19.15	3.59		22.74	26.50	
	0300	Cast aluminum, compared to cast iron, deduct					10%					
	0500	Extruded aluminum safety tread, 3" wide	1 Carp	75	.107		4.85	3.11		7.96	10.20	
	0550	4" wide		75	.107		6.55	3.11		9.66	12.05	
	0600	6" wide		75	.107		10.95	3.11		14.06	16.90	
	0650	9" wide to resurface stairs		70	.114		15.45	3.33		18.78	22	
	1700	Cement filled pan type, plain	1 Cefi	115	.070	S.F.	2.25	1.94		4.19	5.35	
	1750	Non-slip	"	100	.080	"	3.38	2.24		5.62	7.05	
850	0010	ACCESSORIES, WALL AND FOUNDATION										850
	2000	Footings, form braces, solid steel, adjustable				Ea.	12.30			12.30	13.55	
	2050	Spreaders for footer, adjustable				"	4.08			4.08	4.49	
	3000	Form oil, coverage varies greatly, minimum				Gal.	5.15			5.15	5.65	

Important: See the Reference Section for critical supporting data - Reference Nos., Crews, & City Cost Indexes

03100 | Concrete Forms & Accessories

		03150	Concrete Accessories	CREW	DAILY OUTPUT	LABOR-HOURS	UNIT	2001 BARE COSTS				TOTAL INCL O&P	
								MAT.	LABOR	EQUIP.	TOTAL		
850	3050		Maximum				Gal.	7.15			7.15	7.85	850
	3500		Form patches, 1-3/4" diameter				C	61.50			61.50	68	
	3550		2-3/4" diameter				"	78.50			78.50	86	
	4000		Nail stakes, 3/4" diameter, 18" long				Ea.	2.62			2.62	2.88	
	4050		24" long					2.91			2.91	3.20	
	4200		30" long					3.35			3.35	3.69	
	4250		36" long					3.73			3.73	4.10	
860	0010		**WATERSTOP** PVC, ribbed 3/16" thick, 4" wide	1 Carp	155	.052	L.F.	.56	1.50		2.06	2.97	860
	0050		6" wide		145	.055		1.21	1.61		2.82	3.85	
	0500		Ribbed, PVC, with center bulb, 9" wide, 3/16" thick		135	.059		2.23	1.73		3.96	5.15	
	0550		3/8" thick		130	.062		2.59	1.79		4.38	5.65	
	0800		Dumbbell type, PVC, 6" wide, 3/16" thick		150	.053		1	1.55		2.55	3.53	
	0850		3/8" thick		145	.055		1.40	1.61		3.01	4.06	
	1000		9" wide, 3/8" thick, PVC, plain		130	.062		2.76	1.79		4.55	5.85	
	1050		Center bulb		130	.062		5.75	1.79		7.54	9.15	
	1250		Split PVC, 3/8" thick, 6" wide		145	.055		3.85	1.61		5.46	6.75	
	1300		9" wide		130	.062		4.43	1.79		6.22	7.70	
	2000		Rubber, flat dumbbell, 3/8" thick, 6" wide		145	.055		4.83	1.61		6.44	7.80	
	2050		9" wide		135	.059		7.95	1.73		9.68	11.40	
	2500		Flat dumbbell split, 3/8" thick, 6" wide		145	.055		6.90	1.61		8.51	10.10	
	2550		9" wide		135	.059		10.20	1.73		11.93	13.90	
	3000		Center bulb, 1/4" thick, 6" wide		145	.055		4.62	1.61		6.23	7.60	
	3050		9" wide		135	.059		9.10	1.73		10.83	12.70	
	3500		Center bulb split, 3/8" thick, 6" wide		145	.055		5.55	1.61		7.16	8.65	
	3550		9" wide		135	.059		9.70	1.73		11.43	13.35	
	5000		Waterstop fittings, rubber, flat										
	5010		Dumbbell or center bulb, 3/8" thick,										
	5200		Field union, 6" wide	1 Carp	50	.160	Ea.	9.55	4.66		14.21	17.80	
	5250		9" wide		50	.160		13.75	4.66		18.41	22.50	
	5500		Flat cross, 6" wide		30	.267		35	7.75		42.75	50.50	
	5550		9" wide		30	.267		58.50	7.75		66.25	76.50	
	6000		Flat tee, 6" wide		30	.267		34.50	7.75		42.25	50	
	6050		9" wide		30	.267		49	7.75		56.75	66	
	6500		Flat ell, 6" wide		40	.200		30.50	5.85		36.35	42.50	
	6550		9" wide		40	.200		46	5.85		51.85	59.50	
	7000		Vertical tee, 6" wide		25	.320		28.50	9.35		37.85	46	
	7050		9" wide		25	.320		43	9.35		52.35	61.50	
	7500		Vertical ell, 6" wide		35	.229		26	6.65		32.65	39	
	7550		9" wide		35	.229		43	6.65		49.65	57.50	

03200 | Concrete Reinforcement

		03210	Reinforcing Steel	CREW	DAILY OUTPUT	LABOR-HOURS	UNIT	2001 BARE COSTS				TOTAL INCL O&P	
								MAT.	LABOR	EQUIP.	TOTAL		
100	0010		**ACCESSORIES** Materials only										100
	0020		See also Form Accessories, division 03150										
	0100		Beam bolsters, (BB) standard, lower, up to 1-1/2" high, plain				C.L.F.	37			37	40.50	
	0102		Galvanized					57			57	62.50	
	0104		Stainless					108			108	119	
	0106		Plastic					65			65	71.50	

For expanded coverage of these items see *Means Concrete & Masonry Cost Data 2001*

			DAILY OUTPUT	LABOR-HOURS	UNIT	2001 BARE COSTS				TOTAL INCL O&P	
03210		Reinforcing Steel	CREW			MAT.	LABOR	EQUIP.	TOTAL		
100	0108	Epoxy			C.L.F.	89			89	98	100
	0110	2-1/2" to 3" high, plain				49			49	54	
	0120	Galvanized				65			65	71.50	
	0140	Stainless				148			148	163	
	0160	Plastic				68			68	75	
	0162	Epoxy				94			94	103	
	0200	Upper, standard (BBU) to 1-1/2" high, plain				107			107	118	
	0210	2-1/2" to 3" high				193			193	212	
	0300	Beam bolster with plate (BBP) to 1-1/2" high, plain				123			123	135	
	0310	2-1/2" to 3" high				246			246	271	
	0500	Slab bolsters, continuous, plain (SB) 3/4" to 1" high, plain				32			32	35	
	0502	Galvanized				37			37	40.50	
	0504	Stainless				60			60	66	
	0506	Plastic				45			45	49.50	
	0510	1" to 2" high, plain				38			38	42	
	0515	Galvanized				45			45	49.50	
	0520	Stainless				85			85	93.50	
	0525	Plastic				50			50	55	
	0530	For bolsters with wire runners (SBR), add				45			45	49.50	
	0540	For bolsters with plates (SBP), add			↓	109			109	120	
	0700	Clip or bar ties, 16 ga., plain, 3" long			C	8.90			8.90	9.80	
	0710	4" long				9.40			9.40	10.35	
	0720	6" long				11			11	12.10	
	0730	8" long			↓	11.50			11.50	12.65	
	0900	Flange clips, expandable flanges, 10 ga., 12" O.C., continuous,									
	0910	galvanized, over 500 L.F., 4" to 8"			C.L.F.	33			33	36.50	
	0920	9" to 12"				45			45	49.50	
	0930	17" to 24"			↓	46			46	50.50	
	1200	High chairs, individual, no plates (1 HC), to 3" high, plain			C	46			46	50.50	
	1202	Galvanized				64			64	70.50	
	1204	Stainless				131			131	144	
	1206	Plastic				61			61	67	
	1210	5" high, plain				70			70	77	
	1212	Galvanized				88			88	97	
	1214	Stainless				190			190	209	
	1216	Plastic				85.50			85.50	94	
	1220	8" high, plain				152			152	167	
	1222	Galvanized				194			194	213	
	1224	Stainless				320			320	350	
	1226	Plastic				191			191	210	
	1230	12" high, plain				315			315	350	
	1232	Galvanized				385			385	425	
	1234	Stainless				580			580	640	
	1236	Plastic				355			355	390	
	1240	15" high, plain				590			590	650	
	1242	Galvanized				655			655	725	
	1244	Stainless				970			970	1,075	
	1246	Plastic				640			640	705	
	1250	For each added 1" up to 24" high, plain, add				42			42	46	
	1252	Galvanized, add				49			49	54	
	1254	Stainless, add				54			54	59.50	
	1256	Plastic, add				49			49	54	
	1400	Individual high chairs, with plates, (HCP), to 5" high, add				192			192	211	
	1410	Over 5" high, add				234			234	257	
	1500	Bar chair (BC) for up to 1-3/4" high, plain				25			25	27.50	
	1520	Galvanized			↓	29			29	32	

Important: See the Reference Section for critical supporting data - Reference Nos., Crews, & City Cost Indexes

		CREW	DAILY OUTPUT	LABOR-HOURS	UNIT	2001 BARE COSTS MAT.	LABOR	EQUIP.	TOTAL	TOTAL INCL O&P	
03210	**Reinforcing Steel**										
100 1530	Stainless				C	76			76	83.50	100
1540	Plastic					50			50	55	
1550	Joist chair (JC), joists up to 6", plain					31			31	34	
1580	Galvanized					38			38	42	
1600	Stainless					54			54	59.50	
1620	Plastic					54			54	59.50	
1630	Epoxy					126			126	139	
1700	Continuous high chairs, legs 8" O.C. (CHC) to 4" high, plain				C.L.F.	61			61	67	
1705	Galvanized					71			71	78	
1710	Stainless					152			152	167	
1715	Plastic					75			75	82.50	
1718	Epoxy					109			109	120	
1720	6" high, plain					88			88	97	
1725	Galvanized					120			120	132	
1730	Stainless					177			177	195	
1735	Plastic					120			120	132	
1738	Epoxy					146			146	161	
1740	8" high, plain					128			128	141	
1745	Galvanized					169			169	186	
1750	Stainless					210			210	231	
1755	Plastic					167			167	184	
1758	Epoxy					220			220	242	
1760	12" high, plain					315			315	345	
1765	Galvanized					360			360	395	
1770	Stainless					500			500	550	
1775	Plastic					355			355	395	
1778	Epoxy					520			520	575	
1780	15" high, plain					350			350	385	
1785	Galvanized					405			405	445	
1790	Stainless					400			400	440	
1795	Plastic					400			400	440	
1798	Epoxy					685			685	755	
1800	For each added 1" up to 24" high, plain, add					29			29	32	
1820	Galvanized, add					35			35	38.50	
1840	Stainless, add					31			31	34	
1860	Plastic, add					31			31	34	
1900	For continuous bottom plate, (CHCP), add					137			137	151	
1940	For upper continuous high chairs, (CHCU), add					137			137	151	
1960	For galvanized wire runners, add					130			130	143	
2100	Paper tubing, 4' lengths, for #2 & #3 bar					53			53	58.50	
2120	For #6 bar					66			66	72.50	
2200	Screed base, 1/2" diameter, 2-1/2" high, plain				C	137			137	151	
2210	Galvanized					142			142	156	
2220	5-1/2" high, plain					165			165	182	
2250	Galvanized					175			175	193	
2300	3/4" diameter, 2-1/2" high, plain					170			170	187	
2310	Galvanized					180			180	198	
2320	5-1/2" high, plain					210			210	231	
2350	Galvanized					225			225	248	
2400	Screed holder, 1/2" diam. for 1" I.D. pipe, plain, 6" long					142			142	156	
2420	12" long					235			235	259	
2500	3/4" diameter, for 1-1/2" I.D. pipe, 6" long					255			255	281	
2520	12" long					420			420	460	
2700	Screw anchor for bolts, plain, 1/2" diameter					93			93	102	
2720	1" diameter					278			278	305	
2740	1-1/2" diameter					460			460	505	

3

CONCRETE

3 CONCRETE

03210	Reinforcing Steel		CREW	DAILY OUTPUT	LABOR-HOURS	UNIT	2001 BARE COSTS MAT.	LABOR	EQUIP.	TOTAL	TOTAL INCL O&P	
100	2800	Screw eye bolts, 1/2" x 5" long					C	106			106	117	100
	2820	1" x 9" long						420			420	460	
	2840	1-1/2" x 14" long						1,025			1,025	1,125	
	2900	Screw anchor bolts, 1/2" x up to 7" long						425			425	470	
	2920	1" x up to 12" long						1,375			1,375	1,525	
	3000	Slab lifting inserts, single, 3/4" dia., galv., 4" high						285			285	315	
	3010	6" high						350			350	385	
	3030	7" high						400			400	440	
	3100	1" diameter, 5" high						450			450	495	
	3120	7" high						475			475	525	
	3200	Double lifting inserts, 1" diameter, 5" high						890			890	980	
	3220	7" high						940			940	1,025	
	3330	1-1/4" diameter, 5" high						975			975	1,075	
	3500	Sleeper clips for wood sleepers, 20 ga., galv., 2" wide					M	340			340	375	
	3520	4" wide						420			420	460	
	3600	Spacers, plastic for 1" bar clearance, average						52			52	57	
	3620	For 2" bar clearance, average						63			63	69.50	
	3800	Subgrade chairs, 1/2" diameter, 3-1/2" high					C	280			280	310	
	3850	12" high						780			780	860	
	3900	3/4" diameter, 3-1/2" high						360			360	395	
	3950	12" high						850			850	935	
	4200	Subgrade stakes, 3/4" diameter, 12" long						290			290	320	
	4250	24" long						390			390	430	
	4300	1" diameter, 12" long						435			435	480	
	4350	24" long						640			640	705	
	4500	Tie wire, 16 ga. annealed steel, under 500 lbs.					Cwt.	84			84	92.50	
	4520	2,000 to 4,000 lbs.					"	79			79	87	
	4550	Tie wire holder, plastic case					Ea.	33			33	36.50	
	4600	Aluminum case					"	40			40	44	
200	0010	**COATED REINFORCING** Add to material											200
	0100	Epoxy coated, A775					Cwt.	25			25	27.50	
	0150	Galvanized, #3						33			33	36.50	
	0200	#4						33			33	36.50	
	0250	#5						32.50			32.50	35.50	
	0300	#6 or over						32.50			32.50	35.50	
	1000	For over 20 tons, #6 or larger, minimum						30			30	33	
	1500	Maximum						36			36	39.50	
600	0010	**REINFORCING IN PLACE** A615 Grade 60	CN										600
	0100	Beams & Girders, #3 to #7	R03210 -010	4 Rodm	1.60	20	Ton	555	655		1,210	1,700	
	0150	#8 to #18			2.70	11.852		530	390		920	1,250	
	0200	Columns, #3 to #7	R03210 -020		1.50	21.333		555	700		1,255	1,775	
	0250	#8 to #18			2.30	13.913		530	455		985	1,350	
	0300	Spirals, hot rolled, 8" to 15" diameter	R03210 -040		2.20	14.545		935	475		1,410	1,825	
	0320	15" to 24" diameter			2.20	14.545		910	475		1,385	1,800	
	0330	24" to 36" diameter	R03210 -050		2.30	13.913		890	455		1,345	1,750	
	0340	36" to 48" diameter			2.40	13.333		870	435		1,305	1,700	
	0360	48" to 64" diameter	R03210 -060		2.50	12.800		955	420		1,375	1,750	
	0380	64" to 84" diameter			2.60	12.308		1,000	405		1,405	1,775	
	0390	84" to 96" diameter	R03210 -080		2.70	11.852		1,000	390		1,390	1,750	
	0400	Elevated slabs, #4 to #7			2.90	11.034		585	360		945	1,250	
	0500	Footings, #4 to #7			2.10	15.238		525	500		1,025	1,425	
	0550	#8 to #18			3.60	8.889		500	291		791	1,050	
	0600	Slab on grade, #3 to #7			2.30	13.913		525	455		980	1,350	
	0700	Walls, #3 to #7			3	10.667		525	350		875	1,175	
	0750	#8 to #18			4	8		525	262		787	1,025	

Important: See the Reference Section for critical supporting data - Reference Nos., Crews, & City Cost Indexes

	03210	Reinforcing Steel		CREW	DAILY OUTPUT	LABOR-HOURS	UNIT	2001 BARE COSTS				TOTAL INCL O&P	
								MAT.	LABOR	EQUIP.	TOTAL		
600	1000	Typical in place, 10 ton lots, average	R03210 -010	4 Rodm	1.70	18.824	Ton	555	615		1,170	1,650	600
	1100	Over 50 ton lots, average		↓	2.30	13.913		530	455		985	1,350	
	1200	High strength steel, Grade 75, #14 bars only, add	R03210 -020					60			60	66	
	2000	Unloading & sorting, add to above		C-5	100	.560			17.80	6.30	24.10	36.50	
	2200	Crane cost for handling, add to above, minimum	R03210 -040		135	.415			13.20	4.66	17.86	27	
	2210	Average			92	.609			19.35	6.85	26.20	39.50	
	2220	Maximum	R03210 -050	↓	35	1.600	↓		51	18	69	104	
	2400	Dowels, 2 feet long, deformed, #3		2 Rodm	520	.031	Ea.	.23	1.01		1.24	1.96	
	2410	#4	R03210 -060		480	.033		.41	1.09		1.50	2.30	
	2420	#5			435	.037		.64	1.20		1.84	2.76	
	2430	#6	R03210 -080		360	.044	↓	.92	1.46		2.38	3.48	
	2450	Longer and heavier dowels			725	.022	Lb.	.40	.72		1.12	1.67	
	2500	Smooth dowels, 12" long, 1/4" or 3/8" diameter			140	.114	Ea.	.61	3.74		4.35	7	
	2520	5/8" diameter			125	.128		1.06	4.19		5.25	8.25	
	2530	3/4" diameter			110	.145		1.32	4.76		6.08	9.55	
	2700	Dowel caps, 5" long, 1/2" to 3/4" diameter			800	.020		.14	.66		.80	1.26	
	2720	1-1/4" diameter		↓	750	.021	↓	.34	.70		1.04	1.57	
700	0010	**SPLICING REINFORCING BARS** Incl. holding bars in	R03210 -070										700
	0020	place while splicing											
	0100	Butt weld columns #4 bars		C-5	190	.295	Ea.	1.10	9.40	3.31	13.81	20.50	
	0110	#6 bars			150	.373		1.55	11.90	4.20	17.65	26	
	0130	#10 bars			95	.589		2.10	18.75	6.65	27.50	40.50	
	0150	#14 bars		↓	65	.862	↓	2.60	27.50	9.70	39.80	58.50	
	0280	Column splice clamps, sleeve & wedge, or end bearing											
	0300	#7 or #8 bars		C-5	190	.295	Ea.	3.25	9.40	3.31	15.96	22.50	
	0310	#9 or #10 bars			170	.329		3.30	10.50	3.70	17.50	25	
	0320	#11 bars			160	.350		4.50	11.15	3.93	19.58	27.50	
	0330	#14 bars			150	.373		5.75	11.90	4.20	21.85	30.50	
	0340	#18 bars		↓	140	.400		8.50	12.70	4.50	25.70	35.50	
	0500	Reducer inserts for above, #14 to #18 bar						3.25			3.25	3.58	
	0520	#14 to #11 bar						2.90			2.90	3.19	
	0550	#10 to #9 bar						.90			.90	.99	
	0560	#9 to #8 bar						.95			.95	1.05	
	0580	#8 to #7 bar						.90			.90	.99	
	0600	For bolted speed sleeve type, deduct					↓	15%					
	0800	Mechanical butt splice, sleeve type with filler metal, compression											
	0810	only, all grades, columns only #11 bars		C-5	68	.824	Ea.	13.50	26	9.25	48.75	68	
	0900	#14 bars			62	.903		15	28.50	10.15	53.65	75	
	0920	#18 bars			62	.903		18	28.50	10.15	56.65	78.50	
	1000	125% yield point, grade 60, columns only, #6 bars			68	.824		19	26	9.25	54.25	74	
	1020	#7 or #8 bars			68	.824		16.50	26	9.25	51.75	71.50	
	1030	#9 bars			68	.824		16.50	26	9.25	51.75	71.50	
	1040	#10 bars			68	.824		17.50	26	9.25	52.75	72.50	
	1050	#11 bars			68	.824		22	26	9.25	57.25	77	
	1060	#14 bars			62	.903		28	28.50	10.15	66.65	89.50	
	1070	#18 bars		↓	62	.903	↓	40	28.50	10.15	78.65	103	
	1200	Full tension, grade 60 steel, columns,											
	1220	slabs or beams, #6, #7, #8 bars		C-5	68	.824	Ea.	16	26	9.25	51.25	71	
	1230	#9 bars			68	.824		17.50	26	9.25	52.75	72.50	
	1240	#10 bars			68	.824		19.50	26	9.25	54.75	74.50	
	1250	#11 bars			68	.824		23	26	9.25	58.25	78.50	
	1260	#14 bars			62	.903		31	28.50	10.15	69.65	92.50	
	1270	#18 bars		↓	62	.903	↓	52	28.50	10.15	90.65	116	
	1400	If equipment handling not required, deduct							50%				
	1600	Mechanical threaded type, bar threading not included,		↓									

CONCRETE **3**

3 CONCRETE

		03210	Reinforcing Steel		CREW	DAILY OUTPUT	LABOR-HOURS	UNIT	MAT.	LABOR	EQUIP.	TOTAL	TOTAL INCL O&P	
									2001 BARE COSTS					
700	1700		Straight bars, #10 & #11	R03210 -070	C-5	140	.400	Ea.	16.75	12.70	4.50	33.95	44.50	700
	1750		#14 bars			130	.431		19.50	13.70	4.84	38.04	49.50	
	1800		#18 bars			75	.747		31	24	8.40	63.40	82.50	
	2100		#11 to #18 & #14 to #18 transition			75	.747		33	24	8.40	65.40	85	
	2400		Bent bars, #10 & #11			105	.533		29	16.95	6	51.95	66.50	
	2500		#14			90	.622		38	19.80	7	64.80	82	
	2600		#18			70	.800		55	25.50	9	89.50	112	
	2800		#11 to #14 transition			75	.747		40	24	8.40	72.40	92.50	
	2900		#11 to #18 & #14 to #18 transition			70	.800		55	25.50	9	89.50	112	

		03220	Welded Wire Fabric		CREW	DAILY OUTPUT	LABOR-HOURS	UNIT	MAT.	LABOR	EQUIP.	TOTAL	TOTAL INCL O&P	
200	0010		WELDED WIRE FABRIC ASTM A185	R03220 -030										200
	0050		Sheets											
	0100		6 x 6 - W1.4 x W1.4 (10 x 10) 21 lb. per C.S.F.		2 Rodm	35	.457	C.S.F.	7.20	14.95		22.15	33.50	
	0200		6 x 6 - W2.1 x W2.1 (8 x 8) 30 lb. per C.S.F.			31	.516		9.20	16.90		26.10	38.50	
	0300		6 x 6 - W2.9 x W2.9 (6 x 6) 42 lb. per C.S.F.			29	.552		12.20	18.05		30.25	44	
	0400		6 x 6 - W4 x W4 (4 x 4) 58 lb. per C.S.F.			27	.593		17.30	19.40		36.70	52	
	0500		4 x 4 - W1.4 x W1.4 (10 x 10) 31 lb. per C.S.F.			31	.516		11.15	16.90		28.05	41	
	0600		4 x 4 - W2.1 x W2.1 (8 x 8) 44 lb. per C.S.F.			29	.552		13.55	18.05		31.60	45.50	
	0650		4 x 4 - W2.9 x W2.9 (6 x 6) 61 lb. per C.S.F.			27	.593		20.50	19.40		39.90	55.50	
	0700		4 x 4 - W4 x W4 (4 x 4) 85 lb. per C.S.F.			25	.640		27.50	21		48.50	65.50	
	0750		Rolls											
	0800		2 x 2 - #14 galv., 21 lb/C.S.F., beam & column wrap		2 Rodm	6.50	2.462	C.S.F.	15.15	80.50		95.65	154	
	0900		2 x 2 - #12 galv. for gunite reinforcing		"	6.50	2.462		21	80.50		101.50	160	
	1000		Specially fabricated heavier gauges in sheets		4 Rodm	50	.640			21		21	35.50	
	1010		Material only, minimum					Ton	525			525	580	
	1020		Average						725			725	800	
	1030		Maximum						950			950	1,050	

		03230	Stressing Tendons		CREW	DAILY OUTPUT	LABOR-HOURS	UNIT	MAT.	LABOR	EQUIP.	TOTAL	TOTAL INCL O&P	
600	0010		PRESTRESSING STEEL Post-tensioned in field	R03410 -090										600
	0100		Grouted strand, 50' span, 100 kip		C-3	1,200	.053	Lb.	2.58	1.60	.16	4.34	5.65	
	0150		300 kip			2,700	.024		2.11	.71	.07	2.89	3.57	
	0300		100' span, 100 kip			1,700	.038		2.58	1.13	.11	3.82	4.84	
	0350		300 kip			3,200	.020		2.47	.60	.06	3.13	3.78	
	0500		200' span, 100 kip			2,700	.024		2.58	.71	.07	3.36	4.09	
	0550		300 kip			3,500	.018		2.47	.55	.06	3.08	3.68	
	0800		Grouted bars, 50' span, 42 kip			2,600	.025		.45	.74	.07	1.26	1.80	
	0850		143 kip			3,200	.020		.43	.60	.06	1.09	1.53	
	1000		75' span, 42 kip			3,200	.020		.46	.60	.06	1.12	1.56	
	1050		143 kip			4,200	.015		.39	.46	.05	.90	1.24	
	1200		Ungrouted strand, 50' span, 100 kip		C-4	1,275	.025		1.92	.83	.06	2.81	3.60	
	1250		300 kip			1,475	.022		2.10	.72	.05	2.87	3.59	
	1400		100' span, 100 kip			1,500	.021		1.95	.71	.05	2.71	3.41	
	1450		300 kip			1,650	.019		2.10	.64	.05	2.79	3.45	
	1600		200' span, 100 kip			1,500	.021		1.95	.71	.05	2.71	3.41	
	1650		300 kip			1,700	.019		2.10	.63	.05	2.78	3.42	
	1800		Ungrouted bars, 50' span, 42 kip			1,400	.023		.28	.76	.06	1.10	1.65	
	1850		143 kip			1,700	.019		.27	.63	.05	.95	1.40	
	2000		75' span, 42 kip			1,800	.018		.28	.59	.04	.91	1.35	
	2050		143 kip			2,200	.015		.27	.48	.04	.79	1.15	
	2220		Ungrouted single strand, 100' slab, 25 kip			1,200	.027		2.09	.89	.07	3.05	3.88	
	2250		35 kip			1,475	.022		1.95	.72	.05	2.72	3.43	

Important: See the Reference Section for critical supporting data - Reference Nos., Crews, & City Cost Indexes

03200 | Concrete Reinforcement

03240 | Fibrous Reinforcing

		CREW	DAILY OUTPUT	LABOR-HOURS	UNIT	2001 BARE COSTS MAT.	LABOR	EQUIP.	TOTAL	TOTAL INCL O&P	
300	0010	**FIBROUS REINFORCING**										300
	0100	Synthetic fibers, add to concrete				Lb.	3.79			3.79	4.17	
	0110	1-1/2 lb. per C.Y.				C.Y.	5.85			5.85	6.45	
	0150	Steel fibers, add to concrete				Lb.	.48			.48	.53	
	0155	25 lb. per C.Y.				C.Y.	12			12	13.20	
	0160	50 lb. per C.Y.					24			24	26.50	
	0170	75 lb. per C.Y.					37			37	40.50	
	0180	100 lb. per C.Y.					48			48	53	

03300 | Cast-In-Place Concrete

03310 | Structural Concrete

			CREW	DAILY OUTPUT	LABOR-HOURS	UNIT	2001 BARE COSTS MAT.	LABOR	EQUIP.	TOTAL	TOTAL INCL O&P	
200	0010	**CONCRETE, FIELD MIX** FOB forms 2250 psi	R03310-080			C.Y.	65			65	71.50	200
	0020	3000 psi				"	68			68	75	
220	0010	**CONCRETE, READY MIX** Regular weight	R03310-040									220
	0020	2000 psi				C.Y.	62.50			62.50	69	
	0100	2500 psi	R03310-050				61.50			61.50	67.50	
	0150	3000 psi **CN**					65			65	71	
	0200	3500 psi	R03310-070				66			66	72.50	
	0300	4000 psi					68.50			68.50	75.50	
	0350	4500 psi					70.50			70.50	78	
	0400	5000 psi **CN**					73			73	80.50	
	0411	6000 psi					83			83	91.50	
	0412	8000 psi					136			136	149	
	0413	10,000 psi					193			193	212	
	0414	12,000 psi					233			233	256	
	1000	For high early strength cement, add					10%					
	1010	For structural lightweight with regular sand, add					25%					
	2000	For all lightweight aggregate, add					45%					
	3000	For integral colors, 2500 psi, 5 bag mix										
	3100	Red, yellow or brown, 1.8 lb. per bag, add				C.Y.	13.85			13.85	15.25	
	3200	9.4 lb. per bag, add					75			75	82	
	3400	Black, 1.8 lb. per bag, add					16.45			16.45	18.10	
	3500	7.5 lb. per bag, add					69			69	76	
	3700	Green, 1.8 lb. per bag, add					32.50			32.50	36	
	3800	7.5 lb. per bag, add					157			157	173	
240	0010	**CONCRETE IN PLACE** Including forms (4 uses), reinforcing	R03310-010									240
	0050	steel, including finishing unless otherwise indicated										
	0300	Beams, 5 kip per L.F., 10' span	R03310-100	C-14A	15.62	12.804	C.Y.	215	375	39.50	629.50	875
	0350	25' span		"	18.55	10.782		199	315	33.50	547.50	755
	0500	Chimney foundations, industrial, minimum	R03350-130	C-14C	32.22	3.476		133	97	1.18	231.18	300
	0510	Maximum		"	23.71	4.724		155	132	1.61	288.61	380
	0700	Columns, square, 12" x 12", minimum reinforcing	R04210-055	C-14A	11.96	16.722		232	490	51.50	773.50	1,075
	0720	Average reinforcing			10.13	19.743		325	580	61	966	1,325
	0740	Maximum reinforcing			9.03	22.148		405	650	68.50	1,123.50	1,550
	0800	16" x 16", minimum reinforcing			16.22	12.330		187	360	38	585	815
	0820	Average reinforcing			12.57	15.911		299	465	49	813	1,125
	0840	Maximum reinforcing			10.25	19.512		410	570	60.50	1,040.50	1,425
	0900	24" x 24", minimum reinforcing			23.66	8.453		157	248	26	431	590
	0920	Average reinforcing			17.71	11.293		247	330	35	612	835

3

CONCRETE

03310	Structural Concrete		CREW	DAILY OUTPUT	LABOR-HOURS	UNIT	2001 BARE COSTS				TOTAL INCL O&P
							MAT.	LABOR	EQUIP.	TOTAL	
240	0940	Maximum reinforcing		C-14A	14.15	14.134	C.Y.	340	415	43.50	798.50	1,075	240
	1000	36" x 36", minimum reinforcing			33.69	5.936		144	174	18.35	336.35	455
	1020	Average reinforcing			23.32	8.576		229	251	26.50	506.50	680
	1040	Maximum reinforcing			17.82	11.223		315	330	34.50	679.50	905
	1100	Columns, round, tied, 12" diameter, minimum reinforcing			20.97	9.537		243	279	29.50	551.50	740
	1120	Average reinforcing			15.27	13.098		360	385	40.50	785.50	1,050
	1140	Maximum reinforcing			12.11	16.515		470	485	51	1,006	1,325
	1200	16" diameter, minimum reinforcing			31.49	6.351		227	186	19.65	432.65	565
	1220	Average reinforcing			19.12	10.460		355	305	32.50	692.50	910
	1240	Maximum reinforcing			13.77	14.524		480	425	45	950	1,250
	1300	20" diameter, minimum reinforcing			41.04	4.873		220	143	15.05	378.05	485
	1320	Average reinforcing			24.05	8.316		330	244	25.50	599.50	780
	1340	Maximum reinforcing			17.01	11.758		445	345	36.50	826.50	1,075
	1400	24" diameter, minimum reinforcing			51.85	3.857		201	113	11.90	325.90	415
	1420	Average reinforcing			27.06	7.391		315	217	23	555	715
	1440	Maximum reinforcing			18.29	10.935		430	320	34	784	1,025
	1500	36" diameter, minimum reinforcing			75.04	2.665		190	78	8.25	276.25	340
	1520	Average reinforcing			37.49	5.335		276	156	16.50	448.50	570
	1540	Maximum reinforcing		▼	22.84	8.757		385	257	27	669	860
	1900	Elevated slabs, flat slab, 125 psf Sup. Load, 20' span		C-14B	38.45	5.410		147	158	16.05	321.05	430
	1950	30' span			50.99	4.079		135	119	12.10	266.10	350
	2100	Flat plate, 125 psf Sup. Load, 15' span			30.24	6.878		156	201	20.50	377.50	515
	2150	25' span			49.60	4.194		129	123	12.45	264.45	350
	2300	Waffle const., 30" domes, 125 psf Sup. Load, 20' span			37.07	5.611		190	164	16.65	370.65	485
	2350	30' span			44.07	4.720		173	138	14	325	425
	2500	One way joists, 30" pans, 125 psf Sup. Load, 15' span			27.38	7.597		222	222	22.50	466.50	620
	2550	25' span			31.15	6.677		208	195	19.85	422.85	560
	2700	One way beam & slab, 125 psf Sup. Load, 15' span			20.59	10.102		178	295	30	503	695
	2750	25' span			28.36	7.334		163	215	22	400	545
	2900	Two way beam & slab, 125 psf Sup. Load, 15' span			24.04	8.652		168	253	25.50	446.50	615
	2950	25' span		▼	35.87	5.799	▼	142	170	17.20	329.20	445
	3100	Elevated slabs including finish, not										
	3110	including forms or reinforcing										
	3150	Regular concrete, 4" slab		C-8	2,613	.021	S.F.	.86	.55	.22	1.63	2.02
	3200	6" slab			2,585	.022		1.34	.56	.22	2.12	2.57
	3250	2-1/2" thick floor fill			2,685	.021		.58	.54	.22	1.34	1.70
	3300	Lightweight, 110# per C.F., 2-1/2" thick floor fill			2,585	.022		.69	.56	.22	1.47	1.86
	3400	Cellular concrete, 1-5/8" fill, under 5000 S.F.			2,000	.028		.47	.72	.29	1.48	1.94
	3450	Over 10,000 S.F.			2,200	.025		.37	.65	.26	1.28	1.70
	3500	Add per floor for 3 to 6 stories high			31,800	.002			.05	.02	.07	.09
	3520	For 7 to 20 stories high		▼	21,200	.003	▼		.07	.03	.10	.13
	3800	Footings, spread under 1 C.Y.		C-14C	38.07	2.942	C.Y.	96	82	1	179	237
	3850	Over 5 C.Y.			81.04	1.382		87	38.50	.47	125.97	158
	3900	Footings, strip, 18" x 9", plain			41.04	2.729		86	76	.93	162.93	216
	3950	36" x 12", reinforced			61.55	1.820		88	51	.62	139.62	178
	4000	Foundation mat, under 10 C.Y.			38.67	2.896		118	81	.98	199.98	259
	4050	Over 20 C.Y.		▼	56.40	1.986		105	55.50	.68	161.18	204
	4200	Grade walls, 8" thick, 8' high		C-14D	45.83	4.364		115	127	13.50	255.50	340
	4250	14' high			27.26	7.337		143	213	22.50	378.50	520
	4260	12" thick, 8' high			64.32	3.109		102	90	9.60	201.60	265
	4270	14' high			40.01	4.999		114	145	15.45	274.45	370
	4300	15" thick, 8' high			80.02	2.499		96	72.50	7.70	176.20	229
	4350	12' high			51.26	3.902		101	113	12.05	226.05	300
	4500	18' high		▼	48.85	4.094	▼	111	119	12.65	242.65	325
	4520	Handicap access ramp, railing both sides, 3' wide		C-14H	14.58	3.292	L.F.	104	95	2.60	201.60	267
	4525	5' wide		▼	12.22	3.928	▼	115	113	3.10	231.10	310

Reference notes in column: R03310-010, R03310-100, R03350-130, R04210-055

Important: See the Reference Section for critical supporting data - Reference Nos., Crews, & City Cost Indexes

		03310	Structural Concrete		CREW	DAILY OUTPUT	LABOR-HOURS	UNIT	2001 BARE COSTS				TOTAL INCL O&P	
									MAT.	LABOR	EQUIP.	TOTAL		
240	4530		With 6" curb and rails both sides, 3' wide	R03310 -010	C-14H	8.55	5.614	L.F.	106	162	4.44	272.44	375	**240**
	4535		5' wide		↓	7.31	6.566	↓	106	189	5.20	300.20	420	
	4650		Slab on grade, not including finish, 4" thick	R03310 -100	C-14E	60.75	1.449	C.Y.	79.50	41.50	.62	121.62	155	
	4700		6" thick		"	92	.957	"	76	27.50	.41	103.91	128	
	4751		Slab on grade, incl. troweled finish, not incl. forms	R03350 -130										
	4760		or reinforcing, over 10,000 S.F., 4" thick slab		C-14F	3,425	.021	S.F.	.86	.56	.01	1.43	1.79	
	4820		6" thick slab	R04210 -055		3,350	.021		1.25	.57	.01	1.83	2.25	
	4840		8" thick slab			3,184	.023		1.72	.60	.01	2.33	2.80	
	4900		12" thick slab			2,734	.026		2.57	.70	.01	3.28	3.90	
	4950		15" thick slab		↓	2,505	.029	↓	3.23	.76	.02	4.01	4.73	
	5000		Slab on grade, incl. textured finish, not incl. forms											
	5001		or reinforcing, 4" thick slab		C-14G	2,873	.019	S.F.	.84	.51	.01	1.36	1.71	
	5010		6" thick			2,590	.022		1.32	.56	.01	1.89	2.32	
	5020		8" thick		↓	2,320	.024	↓	1.72	.63	.02	2.37	2.86	
	5200		Lift slab in place above the foundation, incl. forms,											
	5210		reinforcing, concrete and columns, minimum		C-14B	2,113	.098	S.F.	4.83	2.88	.29	8	10.15	
	5250		Average			1,650	.126		5.45	3.69	.37	9.51	12.20	
	5300		Maximum		↓	1,500	.139	↓	6.20	4.06	.41	10.67	13.70	
	5500		Lightweight, ready mix, including screed finish only,											
	5510		not including forms or reinforcing											
	5550		1:4 for structural roof decks		C-14B	260	.800	C.Y.	97	23.50	2.38	122.88	147	
	5600		1:6 for ground slab with radiant heat		C-14F	92	.783		92	20.50	.41	112.91	133	
	5650		1:3:2 with sand aggregate, roof deck		C-14B	260	.800		96	23.50	2.38	121.88	146	
	5700		Ground slab		C-14F	107	.673		96	17.80	.36	114.16	133	
	5900		Pile caps, incl. forms and reinf., sq. or rect., under 5 C.Y.		C-14C	54.14	2.069		80.50	58	.70	139.20	181	
	5950		Over 10 C.Y.			75	1.493		83	41.50	.51	125.01	158	
	6000		Triangular or hexagonal, under 5 C.Y.			53	2.113		78	59	.72	137.72	180	
	6050		Over 10 C.Y.		↓	85	1.318		86	37	.45	123.45	153	
	6200		Retaining walls, gravity, 4' high see division 02370-700		C-14D	66.20	3.021		88	87.50	9.35	184.85	245	
	6250		10' high			125	1.600		77	46.50	4.94	128.44	163	
	6300		Cantilever, level backfill loading, 8' high			70	2.857		99	83	8.85	190.85	249	
	6350		16' high		↓	91	2.198	↓	93	64	6.80	163.80	209	
	6800		Stairs, not including safety treads, free standing, 3'-6" wide		C-14H	83	.578	LF Nose	6.10	16.65	.46	23.21	33.50	
	6850		Cast on ground			125	.384	"	4.25	11.05	.30	15.60	22.50	
	7000		Stair landings, free standing			200	.240	S.F.	2.35	6.90	.19	9.44	13.70	
	7050		Cast on ground		↓	475	.101	"	1.40	2.91	.08	4.39	6.25	
450	0010	**INSULATING CONCRETE** See division 03310 and 03500												**450**
700	0010	**PLACING CONCRETE** and vibrating, including labor & equipment	R03310 -090										**700**
	0050		Beams, elevated, small beams, pumped		C-20	60	1.067	C.Y.		26.50	10.95	37.45	52.50	
	0100		With crane and bucket		C-7	45	1.600			39.50	22.50	62	85.50	
	0200		Large beams, pumped		C-20	90	.711			17.55	7.30	24.85	35	
	0250		With crane and bucket		C-7	65	1.108			27.50	15.45	42.95	59.50	
	0400		Columns, square or round, 12" thick, pumped		C-20	60	1.067			26.50	10.95	37.45	52.50	
	0450		With crane and bucket		C-7	40	1.800			44.50	25	69.50	96.50	
	0600		18" thick, pumped		C-20	90	.711			17.55	7.30	24.85	35	
	0650		With crane and bucket		C-7	55	1.309			32.50	18.25	50.75	70	
	0800		24" thick, pumped		C-20	92	.696			17.15	7.15	24.30	34.50	
	0850		With crane and bucket		C-7	70	1.029			25.50	14.35	39.85	55.50	
	1000		36" thick, pumped		C-20	140	.457			11.30	4.69	15.99	22.50	
	1050		With crane and bucket		C-7	100	.720			17.85	10.05	27.90	38.50	
	1400		Elevated slabs, less than 6" thick, pumped		C-20	140	.457			11.30	4.69	15.99	22.50	
	1450		With crane and bucket		C-7	95	.758			18.80	10.60	29.40	40.50	
	1500		6" to 10" thick, pumped		C-20	160	.400			9.85	4.10	13.95	19.75	
	1550		With crane and bucket		C-7	110	.655			16.25	9.15	25.40	35	
	1600		Slabs over 10" thick, pumped		C-20	180	.356	↓		8.80	3.64	12.44	17.55	

CONCRETE 3

			DAILY	LABOR-			2001 BARE COSTS			TOTAL	
03310		**Structural Concrete**								INCL O&P	
			CREW	OUTPUT	HOURS	UNIT	MAT.	LABOR	EQUIP.	TOTAL	
700	1650	With crane and bucket R03310 -090	C-7	130	.554	C.Y.		13.75	7.75	21.50	29.50	**700**
	1900	Footings, continuous, shallow, direct chute	C-6	120	.400			9.60	.63	10.23	15.60	
	1950	Pumped	C-20	150	.427			10.55	4.37	14.92	21	
	2000	With crane and bucket	C-7	90	.800			19.85	11.15	31	43	
	2100	Footings, continuous, deep, direct chute	C-6	140	.343			8.25	.54	8.79	13.35	
	2150	Pumped	C-20	160	.400			9.85	4.10	13.95	19.75	
	2200	With crane and bucket	C-7	110	.655			16.25	9.15	25.40	35	
	2400	Footings, spread, under 1 C.Y., direct chute	C-6	55	.873			21	1.38	22.38	34	
	2450	Pumped	C-20	65	.985			24.50	10.10	34.60	48.50	
	2500	With crane and bucket	C-7	45	1.600			39.50	22.50	62	85.50	
	2600	Footings, spread, over 5 C.Y., direct chute	C-6	120	.400			9.60	.63	10.23	15.60	
	2650	Pumped	C-20	150	.427			10.55	4.37	14.92	21	
	2700	With crane and bucket	C-7	100	.720			17.85	10.05	27.90	38.50	
	2900	Foundation mats, over 20 C.Y., direct chute	C-6	350	.137			3.30	.22	3.52	5.35	
	2950	Pumped	C-20	400	.160			3.95	1.64	5.59	7.90	
	3000	With crane and bucket	C-7	300	.240			5.95	3.35	9.30	12.90	
	3200	Grade beams, direct chute	C-6	150	.320			7.70	.51	8.21	12.45	
	3250	Pumped	C-20	180	.356			8.80	3.64	12.44	17.55	
	3300	With crane and bucket	C-7	120	.600			14.85	8.40	23.25	32	
	3500	High rise, for more than 5 stories, pumped, add per story	C-20	2,100	.030			.75	.31	1.06	1.50	
	3510	With crane and bucket, add per story	C-7	2,100	.034			.85	.48	1.33	1.84	
	3700	Pile caps, under 5 C.Y., direct chute	C-6	90	.533			12.80	.84	13.64	21	
	3750	Pumped	C-20	110	.582			14.35	5.95	20.30	28.50	
	3800	With crane and bucket	C-7	80	.900			22.50	12.55	35.05	48.50	
	3850	Pile cap, 5 C.Y. to 10 C.Y., direct chute	C-6	175	.274			6.60	.43	7.03	10.70	
	3900	Pumped	C-20	200	.320			7.90	3.28	11.18	15.80	
	3950	With crane and bucket	C-7	150	.480			11.90	6.70	18.60	25.50	
	4000	Over 10 C.Y., direct chute	C-6	215	.223			5.35	.35	5.70	8.70	
	4050	Pumped	C-20	240	.267			6.60	2.73	9.33	13.15	
	4100	With crane and bucket	C-7	185	.389			9.65	5.45	15.10	21	
	4300	Slab on grade, 4" thick, direct chute	C-6	110	.436			10.50	.69	11.19	17	
	4350	Pumped	C-20	130	.492			12.15	5.05	17.20	24.50	
	4400	With crane and bucket	C-7	110	.655			16.25	9.15	25.40	35	
	4600	Over 6" thick, direct chute	C-6	165	.291			7	.46	7.46	11.35	
	4650	Pumped	C-20	185	.346			8.55	3.55	12.10	17.10	
	4700	With crane and bucket	C-7	145	.497			12.30	6.95	19.25	26.50	
	4900	Walls, 8" thick, direct chute	C-6	90	.533			12.80	.84	13.64	21	
	4950	Pumped	C-20	100	.640			15.80	6.55	22.35	31.50	
	5000	With crane and bucket	C-7	80	.900			22.50	12.55	35.05	48.50	
	5050	12" thick, direct chute	C-6	100	.480			11.55	.76	12.31	18.75	
	5100	Pumped	C-20	110	.582			14.35	5.95	20.30	28.50	
	5200	With crane and bucket	C-7	90	.800			19.85	11.15	31	43	
	5300	15" thick, direct chute	C-6	105	.457			11	.72	11.72	17.80	
	5350	Pumped	C-20	120	.533			13.15	5.45	18.60	26.50	
	5400	With crane and bucket	C-7	95	.758	▼		18.80	10.60	29.40	40.50	
	5600	Wheeled concrete dumping, add to placing costs above										
	5610	Walking cart, 50' haul, add	C-18	32	.281	C.Y.		6.50	1.58	8.08	11.90	
	5620	150' haul, add		24	.375			8.65	2.11	10.76	15.85	
	5700	250' haul, add		18	.500			11.55	2.81	14.36	21	
	5800	Riding cart, 50' haul, add	C-19	80	.112			2.60	.95	3.55	5.10	
	5810	150' haul, add		60	.150			3.46	1.27	4.73	6.80	
	5900	250' haul, add	▼	45	.200	▼		4.61	1.69	6.30	9.05	

	03350		**Concrete Finishing**									
300	0010	**FINISHING FLOORS** Monolithic, screed finish R03350 -130	1 Cefi	900	.009	S.F.		.25		.25	.37	**300**
	0100	Screed and bull float (darby) finish	"	725	.011	"		.31		.31	.46	

		03350	Concrete Finishing	CREW	DAILY OUTPUT	LABOR-HOURS	UNIT	MAT.	LABOR	EQUIP.	TOTAL	TOTAL INCL O&P	
								\multicolumn{4}{c}{2001 BARE COSTS}				
300	0150		Screed, float, and broom finish	1 Cefi	630	.013	S.F.		.36		.36	.53	**300**
	0200		Screed, float, and hand trowel		600	.013			.37		.37	.55	
	0250		Machine trowel		550	.015			.41		.41	.60	
	0400		Integral topping and finish, using 1:1:2 mix, 3/16" thick	C-10	1,000	.024		.06	.63		.69	1.01	
	0450		1/2" thick		950	.025		.15	.66		.81	1.17	
	0500		3/4" thick		850	.028		.23	.74		.97	1.38	
	0600		1" thick		750	.032		.31	.84		1.15	1.61	
	0800		Granolithic topping, laid after, 1:1:1-1/2 mix, 1/2" thick		590	.041		.16	1.07		1.23	1.79	
	0820		3/4" thick		580	.041		.24	1.09		1.33	1.91	
	0850		1" thick		575	.042		.33	1.10		1.43	2.01	
	0950		2" thick		500	.048		.65	1.26		1.91	2.62	
	1200		Heavy duty, 1:1:2, 3/4" thick, preshrunk, gray, 20 MSF		320	.075		2.10	1.97		4.07	5.30	
	1300		100 MSF		380	.063		2.10	1.66		3.76	4.81	
	1350		For colors, .50 psf, add, minimum		1,650	.015		.30	.38		.68	.91	
	1400		Maximum		1,500	.016		.60	.42		1.02	1.29	
	1600		Exposed local aggregate finish, minimum	1 Cefi	625	.013		3.60	.36		3.96	4.49	
	1650		Maximum		465	.017		11.40	.48		11.88	13.25	
	1800		Floor abrasives, .25 psf, add to above, aluminum oxide		850	.009		.15	.26		.41	.56	
	1850		Silicon carbide		850	.009		.18	.26		.44	.59	
	2000		Floor hardeners, metallic, light service, .50 psf, add		850	.009		.15	.26		.41	.56	
	2050		Medium service, .75 psf, add		750	.011		.22	.30		.52	.68	
	2100		Heavy service, 1.0 psf, add		650	.012		.30	.34		.64	.84	
	2150		Extra heavy, 1.5 psf, add		575	.014		.34	.39		.73	.96	
	2300		Non-metallic, light service, .50 psf, add		850	.009		.17	.26		.43	.58	
	2350		Medium service, .75 psf, add		750	.011		.24	.30		.54	.70	
	2400		Heavy service, 1.00 psf, add		650	.012		.31	.34		.65	.85	
	2450		Extra heavy, 1.50 psf, add		575	.014		.48	.39		.87	1.10	
	2600		Add for colored hardeners, metallic					50%					
	2650		Non-metallic					25%					
	2800		Trap rock wearing surface for monolithic floors										
	2810		2.0 psf, add to above	C-10	1,250	.019	S.F.	.78	.50		1.28	1.62	
	3000		Floor coloring, dusted on, 0.5 psf per S.F., add to above, min.	1 Cefi	1,300	.006		.58	.17		.75	.90	
	3050		Maximum	"	625	.013		2.03	.36		2.39	2.76	
	3100		Colors only, minimum				Lb.	.98			.98	1.08	
	3120		Maximum				"	3.43			3.43	3.77	
	3200		Integral colors, see division 03310-220										
	3600		1/2" topping using 5 lb. per bag, regular colors	C-10	590	.041	S.F.	.19	1.07		1.26	1.82	
	3650		Blue or green	"	590	.041		.19	1.07		1.26	1.82	
	3800		Dustproofing, silicate liquids, 1 coat	1 Cefi	1,900	.004		.07	.12		.19	.25	
	3850		2 coats		1,300	.006		.13	.17		.30	.40	
	4000		Epoxy coating, 1 coat, clear		1,500	.005		.38	.15		.53	.64	
	4050		Colors		1,500	.005		.38	.15		.53	.64	
	4400		Stair finish, float		275	.029			.81		.81	1.21	
	4500		Steel trowel finish		200	.040			1.12		1.12	1.66	
	4600		Silicon carbide finish, .25 psf		150	.053		.52	1.49		2.01	2.79	
350	0010	**FINISHING WALLS** Break ties and patch voids		1 Cefi	540	.015	S.F.	.03	.41		.44	.65	**350**
	0050		Burlap rub with grout		450	.018		.03	.50		.53	.77	
	0100		Carborundum rub, dry		270	.030		.03	.83		.86	1.26	
	0150		Wet rub		175	.046		.03	1.28		1.31	1.93	
	0300		Bush hammer, green concrete	B-39	1,000	.048		.03	1.16	.18	1.37	2.02	
	0350		Cured concrete	"	650	.074		.03	1.79	.27	2.09	3.11	
	0600		Float finish, 1/16" thick	1 Cefi	300	.027		.01	.75		.76	1.12	
	0700		Sandblast, light penetration	C-10	1,100	.022		.21	.57		.78	1.09	
	0750		Heavy penetration	"	375	.064		.42	1.68		2.10	3	
	0800		Board finish, see division 03110-455										

(R03350 -140 reference noted at line 0150)

CONCRETE 3

		03350	Concrete Finishing	CREW	DAILY OUTPUT	LABOR-HOURS	UNIT	2001 BARE COSTS				TOTAL INCL O&P	
								MAT.	LABOR	EQUIP.	TOTAL		
350	0850		Rustication strips, see division 03110-455										350
600	0010		**SLAB TEXTURE STAMPING,** buy										600
	0020		Approx. 3 S.F.- 5 S.F. each, minimum				Ea.	41			41	45	
	0030		Average				"	45			45	49.50	
	0120		Per S.F. of tool, average				S.F.	49			49	54	
	0200		Commonly used chemicals for texture systems										
	0210		Hardeners w/colors average				S.F.	.41			.41	.45	
	0220		Release agents w/colors, average					.16			.16	.18	
	0225		Clear, average					.12			.12	.13	
	0230		Sealers, clear, average					.11			.11	.12	
	0240		Colors, average					.13			.13	.14	
		03370	**Specially Placed Concrete**										
300	0010		**GUNITE,** dry mix										300
	0020		Applied in 1" layers, no mesh included	C-8	2,000	.028	S.F.	.94	.72	.29	1.95	2.45	
	0100		Mesh for gunite 2 x 2, #12, to 3" thick	2 Rodm	800	.020		.17	.66		.83	1.30	
	0150		Over 3" thick	"	500	.032		.21	1.05		1.26	2.02	
	0300		Typical in place, including mesh, 2" thick, minimum	C-16	1,000	.072		1.75	1.96	.58	4.29	5.65	
	0350		Maximum		500	.144		2.71	3.92	1.16	7.79	10.45	
	0500		4" thick, minimum		750	.096		2.59	2.62	.77	5.98	7.80	
	0550		Maximum		350	.206		4.03	5.60	1.66	11.29	15.10	
	0900		Prepare old walls, no scaffolding, minimum	C-10	1,000	.024		.60	.63		1.23	1.61	
	0950		Maximum	"	275	.087		1.92	2.29		4.21	5.55	
	1100		For high finish requirement or close tolerance, add, minimum						50%				
	1150		Maximum						110%				
		03390	**Concrete Curing**										
200	0010		**CURING** Burlap, 4 uses assumed, 7.5 oz.	2 Clab	55	.291	C.S.F.	5.95	6.65		12.60	16.90	200
	0100		12 oz.		55	.291		11.25	6.65		17.90	23	
	0200		Waterproof curing paper, 2 ply, reinforced		70	.229		4.94	5.20		10.14	13.60	
	0300		Sprayed membrane curing compound		95	.168		3.52	3.85		7.37	9.85	
	0400		Curing blankets, 1" to 2" thick, buy, minimum				S.F.	1.10			1.10	1.21	
	0450		Maximum					2.75			2.75	3.03	
	0500		Electrically heated pads, 110 volts, 15 watts per S.F., buy					4.50			4.50	4.95	
	0600		20 watts per S.F., buy					6			6	6.60	
	0710		Electrically, heated pads, 15 watts/S.F., 20 uses, minimum					.16			.16	.18	
	0800		Maximum					.27			.27	.29	

03400 | Precast Concrete

		03410	Plant Precast	CREW	DAILY OUTPUT	LABOR-HOURS	UNIT	2001 BARE COSTS				TOTAL INCL O&P	
								MAT.	LABOR	EQUIP.	TOTAL		
100	0011		**BEAMS,** "L" shaped, 20' span, 12" x 20"	C-11	32	2.250	Ea.	1,350	72	46	1,468	1,675	100
	1000		Inverted tee beams, add to above, small beams	*R03410 -030*			L.F.	15%					
	1050		Large beams				"	5.55			5.55	6.10	
	1200		Rectangular, 20' span, 12" x 20"	C-11	32	2.250	Ea.	925	72	46	1,043	1,200	
	1250		18" x 36"		24	3		1,700	96.50	61.50	1,858	2,100	
	1300		24" x 44"		22	3.273		2,450	105	67	2,622	2,950	
	1400		30' span, 12" x 36"		24	3		2,175	96.50	61.50	2,333	2,600	
	1450		18" x 44"		20	3.600		3,050	116	74	3,240	3,625	

Important: See the Reference Section for critical supporting data - Reference Nos., Crews, & City Cost Indexes

03410 | Plant Precast

			CREW	DAILY OUTPUT	LABOR-HOURS	UNIT	MAT.	LABOR	EQUIP.	TOTAL	TOTAL INCL O&P	
100	1500	24" x 52"	C-11	16	4.500	Ea.	4,325	144	92.50	4,561.50	5,100	**100**
	1600	40' span, 12" x 52" [R03410-030]		20	3.600		4,025	116	74	4,215	4,700	
	1650	18" x 52"		16	4.500		4,900	144	92.50	5,136.50	5,750	
	1700	24" x 52"		12	6		6,000	193	123	6,316	7,075	
	2000	"T" shaped, 20' span, 12" x 20"		32	2.250		1,600	72	46	1,718	1,950	
	2050	18" x 36"		24	3		2,550	96.50	61.50	2,708	3,050	
	2100	24" x 44"		22	3.273		3,600	105	67	3,772	4,200	
	2200	30' span, 12" x 36"		24	3		3,650	96.50	61.50	3,808	4,225	
	2250	18" x 44"		20	3.600		4,975	116	74	5,165	5,750	
	2300	24" x 52"		16	4.500		5,150	144	92.50	5,386.50	6,000	
	2500	40' span, 12" x 52"		20	3.600		6,850	116	74	7,040	7,825	
	2550	18" x 52"		16	4.500		7,500	144	92.50	7,736.50	8,600	
	2600	24" x 52"		12	6		9,150	193	123	9,466	10,600	
210	0010	**COLUMNS** Rectangular to 12' high, small columns	C-11	120	.600	L.F.	66.50	19.25	12.30	98.05	121	**210**
	0050	Large columns		96	.750		105	24	15.40	144.40	175	
	0300	24' high, small columns		192	.375		99	12.05	7.70	118.75	138	
	0350	Large columns		144	.500		132	16.05	10.25	158.30	184	
400	0010	**JOISTS** 40 psf L.L., 6" deep for 12' spans	C-12	600	.080	L.F.	5.70	2.30	.86	8.86	10.75	**400**
	0050	8" deep for 16' spans		575	.083		6.70	2.40	.90	10	12.05	
	0100	10" deep for 20' spans		550	.087		7.50	2.51	.94	10.95	13.20	
	0150	12" deep for 24' spans		525	.091		10.25	2.63	.98	13.86	16.45	
620	0010	**SLABS** Prestressed roof/floor members, solid, grouted, 4" thick [R03410-030]	C-11	3,600	.020	S.F.	4.90	.64	.41	5.95	7.00	**620**
	0050	6" thick		4,500	.016		4.73	.51	.33	5.57	6.45	
	0100	8" thick, hollow **CN**		5,600	.013		5.25	.41	.26	5.92	6.80	
	0150	10" thick		8,800	.008		5.95	.26	.17	6.38	7.20	
	0200	12" thick		8,000	.009		6.15	.29	.18	6.62	7.45	
650	0010	**PRESTRESSED CONCRETE** pretensioned, see division 03400 [R03410-030]										**650**
	0020	See also division 03230-600										
	0100	Post-tensioned in place, small job [R03410-090]	C-17B	8.50	9.647	C.Y.	215	292	40.50	547.50	740	
	0200	Large job	"	10	8.200	"	161	248	34.50	443.50	605	
660	0010	**PRESTRESSED** Roof and floor members, see division 03400 [R03410-030]										**660**
750	0010	**TEES** Prestressed [R03410-030]										**750**
	0020	Quad tee, short spans, roof	C-11	7,200	.010	S.F.	4.35	.32	.21	4.88	5.60	
	0050	Floor		7,200	.010		4.35	.32	.21	4.88	5.60	
	0200	Double tee, floor members, 60' span		8,400	.009		6.10	.28	.18	6.56	7.35	
	0250	80' span		8,000	.009		7.30	.29	.18	7.77	8.70	
	0300	Roof members, 30' span		4,800	.015		4.65	.48	.31	5.44	6.30	
	0350	50' span		6,400	.011		5.50	.36	.23	6.09	6.95	
	0400	Wall members, up to 55' high		3,600	.020		6.25	.64	.41	7.30	8.45	
	0500	Single tee roof members, 40' span		3,200	.023		5.75	.72	.46	6.93	8.10	
	0550	80' span		5,120	.014		7.15	.45	.29	7.89	8.95	
	0600	100' span		6,000	.012		11	.39	.25	11.64	13.05	
	0650	120' span		6,000	.012		11.50	.39	.25	12.14	13.60	
	1000	Double tees, floor members										
	1100	Lightweight, 20" x 8' wide, 45' span	C-11	20	3.600	Ea.	1,875	116	74	2,065	2,325	
	1150	24" x 8' wide, 50' span		18	4		2,025	128	82	2,235	2,550	
	1200	32" x 10' wide, 60' span		16	4.500		3,425	144	92.50	3,661.50	4,125	
	1250	Standard weight, 12" x 8' wide, 20' span		22	3.273		700	105	67	872	1,025	
	1300	16" x 8' wide, 25' span		20	3.600		930	116	74	1,120	1,300	
	1350	18" x 8' wide, 30' span **CN**		20	3.600		1,175	116	74	1,365	1,575	
	1400	20" x 8' wide, 45' span		18	4		1,325	128	82	1,535	1,800	
	1450	24" x 8' wide, 50' span		16	4.500		1,725	144	92.50	1,961.50	2,250	
	1500	32" x 10' wide, 60' span		14	5.143		3,150	165	106	3,421	3,875	

3 CONCRETE

03410 | Plant Precast

			CREW	DAILY OUTPUT	LABOR-HOURS	UNIT	MAT.	LABOR	EQUIP.	TOTAL	TOTAL INCL O&P	
750	2000	Roof members	R03410 -030									750
	2050	Lightweight, 20" x 8' wide, 40' span		C-11	20	3.600	Ea.	1,425	116	74	1,615	1,850
	2100	24" x 8' wide, 50' span			18	4		1,900	128	82	2,110	2,425
	2150	32" x 10' wide, 60' span			16	4.500		3,150	144	92.50	3,386.50	3,825
	2200	Standard weight, 12" x 8' wide, 30' span			22	3.273		955	105	67	1,127	1,300
	2250	16" x 8' wide, 30' span			20	3.600		1,000	116	74	1,190	1,375
	2300	18" x 8' wide, 30' span			20	3.600		1,125	116	74	1,315	1,500
	2350	20" x 8' wide, 40' span			18	4		1,150	128	82	1,360	1,575
	2400	24" x 8' wide, 50' span			16	4.500		1,525	144	92.50	1,761.50	2,025
	2450	32" x 10' wide, 60' span			14	5.143		2,675	165	106	2,946	3,350

03450 | Architectural Precast

			CREW	DAILY OUTPUT	LABOR-HOURS	UNIT	MAT.	LABOR	EQUIP.	TOTAL	TOTAL INCL O&P	
850	0011	**WALL PANELS**	R03450 -010									850
	0150	Low rise, 4' x 8'x 4" thick		C-11	320	.225	S.F.	8.70	7.20	4.62	20.52	27.50
	0200	8'x 8' x 4" thick			576	.125		8.60	4.01	2.57	15.18	19.30
	0250	8'x 16'x 4" thick			1,024	.070		8.55	2.26	1.44	12.25	14.95
	0400	8'x 8', 4" thick, smooth gray			576	.125		8.60	4.01	2.57	15.18	19.30
	0500	Exposed aggregate			576	.125		9.50	4.01	2.57	16.08	20.50
	0600	High rise, 4' x 8' x 4" thick			288	.250		8.70	8	5.15	21.85	29.50
	0650	8' x 8'x 4" thick			512	.141		8.60	4.51	2.89	16	20.50
	0700	8' x 16' x 4" thick			768	.094		8.55	3.01	1.92	13.48	16.80
	0800	Insulated panel, 2" polystyrene, add						1.60			1.60	1.76
	0850	2" urethane, add						2.10			2.10	2.31
	1000	20' x 10', 6" thick, smooth gray **CN**		C-11	1,800	.040		11	1.28	.82	13.10	15.25
	1100	Exposed aggregate		"	1,800	.040		12	1.28	.82	14.10	16.35
	1200	Finishes, white, add						1.70			1.70	1.87
	1250	Exposed aggregate, add						.80			.80	.88
	1300	Granite faced, domestic, add						27			27	29.50
	2200	Fiberglass reinforced cement with urethane core											
	2210	R20, 8' x 8', minimum		E-2	750	.075	S.F.	8.30	2.38	1.72	12.40	15.20
	2220	Maximum		"	600	.093	"	15.50	2.98	2.15	20.63	24.50

03470 | Tilt-Up Precast

			CREW	DAILY OUTPUT	LABOR-HOURS	UNIT	MAT.	LABOR	EQUIP.	TOTAL	TOTAL INCL O&P	
600	0010	**TILT-UP** Wall panel construction, walls only, 5-1/2" thick	R03470 -020	C-14	1,600	.090	S.F.	2.87	2.56	.83	6.26	8.15	600
	0100	7-1/2" thick			1,550	.093		3.08	2.64	.85	6.57	8.50
	0500	Walls and columns, 5-1/2" thick walls, 12" x 12" columns			1,565	.092		3	2.62	.85	6.47	8.40
	0550	7-1/2" thick wall, 12" x 12" columns			1,370	.105		4	2.99	.97	7.96	10.20
	0800	Columns only, site precast, minimum			200	.720	L.F.	24	20.50	6.60	51.10	66.50
	0850	Maximum			105	1.371	"	44	39	12.60	95.60	124

03480 | Precast Specialties

			CREW	DAILY OUTPUT	LABOR-HOURS	UNIT	MAT.	LABOR	EQUIP.	TOTAL	TOTAL INCL O&P	
200	0010	**CURBS** Roadway type, see division 02770-225											200
400	0010	**LINTELS**											400
	0800	Precast concrete, 4" wide, 8" high, to 5' long		D-1	175	.091	L.F.	4.25	2.40		6.65	8.40
	0850	5'-12' long		D-4	190	.168		4.62	4.39	.67	9.68	12.60
	1000	6" wide, 8" high, to 5' long			185	.173		5.40	4.51	.69	10.60	13.65
	1050	5'-12' long			190	.168		5.90	4.39	.67	10.96	14
	1200	8" wide, 8" high, to 5' long			185	.173		3.47	4.51	.69	8.67	11.55
	1250	5'-12' long			190	.168		4.11	4.39	.67	9.17	12
	1400	10" wide, 8" high, to 14' long			180	.178		35.50	4.63	.71	40.84	47
	1450	12" wide, 8" high, to 19' long			185	.173		38	4.51	.69	43.20	49
800	0010	**STAIRS**, Precast concrete treads on steel stringers, 3' wide		C-12	75	.640	Riser	54	18.40	6.85	79.25	95.50	800
	0300	Front entrance, 5' wide with 48" platform, 2 risers			16	3	Flight	275	86.50	32	393.50	475

Important: See the Reference Section for critical supporting data - Reference Nos., Crews, & City Cost Indexes

03480 | Precast Specialties

			CREW	DAILY OUTPUT	LABOR-HOURS	UNIT	2001 BARE COSTS				TOTAL INCL O&P	
							MAT.	LABOR	EQUIP.	TOTAL		
800	0350	5 risers	C-12	12	4	Flight	315	115	43	473	570	800
	0500	6' wide, 2 risers		15	3.200		315	92	34.50	441.50	525	
	0550	5 risers		11	4.364		340	126	47	513	620	
	0700	7' wide, 2 risers		14	3.429		380	98.50	37	515.50	615	
	0750	5 risers	↓	10	4.800		415	138	51.50	604.50	725	
	1200	Basement entrance stairs, steel bulkhead doors, minimum	B-51	22	2.182		460	51	7.20	518.20	590	
	1250	Maximum	"	11	4.364	↓	800	102	14.35	916.35	1,050	

03500 | Cementitious Decks & Underlayments

03510 | Cementitious Roof Deck

			CREW	DAILY OUTPUT	LABOR-HOURS	UNIT	2001 BARE COSTS				TOTAL INCL O&P	
							MAT.	LABOR	EQUIP.	TOTAL		
200	0010	**WOOD FIBER** Lightweight cement system	R05120-250									200
	0050	Plank, beveled, 1" thick	2 Carp	1,000	.016	S.F.	2	.47		2.47	2.93	
	0100	Plank, T & G, 1-1/2" thick		975	.016		2.25	.48		2.73	3.23	
	0150	2" thick		950	.017		3.15	.49		3.64	4.24	
	0200	2-1/2" thick		925	.017		3.30	.50		3.80	4.42	
	0250	3" thick		900	.018		3.75	.52		4.27	4.94	
	0300	3-1/2" thick		875	.018		5.50	.53		6.03	6.90	
	0350	4" thick	↓	850	.019		6.05	.55		6.60	7.50	
	1000	Bulb tee, sub-purlin and grout, 6' span, add	E-1	5,000	.005		1.63	.15	.02	1.80	2.09	
	1100	8' span	"	4,200	.006	↓	1.68	.18	.02	1.88	2.19	
250	0010	**CONCRETE CHANNEL SLABS** 2-3/4" or 3-1/2" thick, straight	C-12	1,575	.030	S.F.	3.61	.88	.33	4.82	5.70	250
	0050	Chopped up		785	.061		3.21	1.76	.66	5.63	7	
	0200	6" thick, span to 20'		1,300	.037		3.75	1.06	.40	5.21	6.20	
	0300	8" thick, span to 24'	↓	1,100	.044	↓	4.28	1.26	.47	6.01	7.20	
270	0010	**CONCRETE PLANK** Lightweight, nailable, T&G, 2" thick	C-12	1,800	.027	S.F.	2.61	.77	.29	3.67	4.37	270
	0050	2-3/4" thick		1,575	.030		3.10	.88	.33	4.31	5.15	
	0100	3-3/4" thick	↓	1,375	.035		3.80	1	.37	5.17	6.15	
	0150	For premium ceiling finish, add				↓	.35			.35	.39	
	0200	For sloping roofs, slope over 4 in 12, add						25%				
	0250	Slope over 6 in 12, add						150%				
350	0010	**FORMBOARD** Including sub-purlins	R05120-250									350
	0050	Non-asbestos fiber cement, 1/8" thick	C-13	2,950	.008	S.F.	2.10	.26	.03	2.39	2.79	
	0070	1/4" thick		2,950	.008		3.75	.26	.03	4.04	4.61	
	0100	Fiberglass, 1" thick, economy	↓	2,700	.009		.95	.28	.03	1.26	1.57	
	1000	Poured gypsum, 2" thick, add to formboard above	C-8	6,000	.009		.75	.24	.10	1.09	1.31	
	1100	3" thick	"	4,800	.012	↓	1.05	.30	.12	1.47	1.75	
900	0010	**WOOD PLANK** Roof decks, see division 06170-600 & 06170-550										900

03520 | Lightweight Concrete Roof Insul

			CREW	DAILY OUTPUT	LABOR-HOURS	UNIT	2001 BARE COSTS				TOTAL INCL O&P	
							MAT.	LABOR	EQUIP.	TOTAL		
250	0010	**INSULATING** Lightweight cellular concrete roof fill	R03520-010									250
	0020	Portland cement and foaming agent	C-8	50	1.120	C.Y.	72	28.50	11.60	112.10	136	
	0100	Poured vermiculite or perlite, field mix,										
	0110	1:6 field mix	C-8	50	1.120	C.Y.	78	28.50	11.60	118.10	143	
	0200	Ready mix, 1:6 mix, roof fill, 2" thick	↓	10,000	.006	S.F.	.43	.14	.06	.63	.76	
	0250	3" thick		7,700	.007		.65	.19	.08	.92	1.09	
	0400	Expanded volcanic glass rock, with binder, minimum	2 Carp	1,500	.011		.25	.31		.56	.77	
	0450	Maximum	"	1,200	.013	↓	.75	.39		1.14	1.44	

03610	Construction Grout	CREW	DAILY OUTPUT	LABOR-HOURS	UNIT	2001 BARE COSTS				TOTAL INCL O&P	
						MAT.	LABOR	EQUIP.	TOTAL		
400	0010 **GROUT** Column & machine bases, non-shrink, metallic, 1" deep	1 Cefi	35	.229	S.F.	8.75	6.40		15.15	19.15	**400**
	0050 2" deep		25	.320		17.55	8.95		26.50	32.50	
	0300 Non-shrink, non-metallic, 1" deep		35	.229		20	6.40		26.40	31.50	
	0350 2" deep		25	.320		39.50	8.95		48.45	57	

3 CONCRETE

03900 | Concrete Restoration & Cleaning

03920	Concrete Resurfacing	CREW	DAILY OUTPUT	LABOR-HOURS	UNIT	2001 BARE COSTS				TOTAL INCL O&P	
						MAT.	LABOR	EQUIP.	TOTAL		
600	0010 **PATCHING CONCRETE**										**600**
	0100 Floors, 1/4" thick, small areas, regular grout	1 Cefi	170	.047	S.F.	.06	1.32		1.38	2.03	
	0150 Epoxy grout	"	100	.080	"	3.19	2.24		5.43	6.85	
	0300 Slab on Grade, cut outs, up to 50 C.F.	2 Cefi	50	.320	C.F.	4.80	8.95		13.75	18.60	
	2000 Walls, including chipping, cleaning and epoxy grout										
	2100 Minimum	1 Cefi	65	.123	S.F.	3.19	3.44		6.63	8.60	
	2150 Average		50	.160		4.79	4.47		9.26	11.90	
	2200 Maximum		40	.200		6.40	5.60		12	15.30	
	2510 Underlayment, P.C. based self-leveling, 4100 psi, pumped, 1/4"	C-8	20,000	.003		1.20	.07	.03	1.30	1.46	
	2520 1/2"		19,000	.003		2.16	.08	.03	2.27	2.53	
	2530 3/4"		18,000	.003		3.36	.08	.03	3.47	3.86	
	2540 1"		17,000	.003		4.56	.08	.03	4.67	5.15	
	2550 1-1/2"		15,000	.004		6.95	.10	.04	7.09	7.85	
	2560 Hand mix, 1/2"	C-18	4,000	.002		2.16	.05	.01	2.22	2.47	
	2610 Topping, P.C. based self-level/dry 6100 psi, pumped, 1/4"	C-8	20,000	.003		1.80	.07	.03	1.90	2.12	
	2620 1/2"		19,000	.003		3.24	.08	.03	3.35	3.71	
	2630 3/4"		18,000	.003		5.05	.08	.03	5.16	5.70	
	2660 1"		17,000	.003		6.85	.08	.03	6.96	7.65	
	2670 1-1/2"		15,000	.004		10.45	.10	.04	10.59	11.70	
	2680 Hand mix, 1/2"	C-18	4,000	.002		3.24	.05	.01	3.30	3.65	

For information about Means Estimating Seminars, see yellow pages 11 and 12 in back of book

Division 4
Masonry

Estimating Tips

04050 Basic Masonry Materials & Methods

- The terms *mortar* and *grout* are often used interchangeably, and incorrectly. Mortar is used to bed masonry units, seal the entry of air and moisture, provide architectural appearance, and allow for size variations in the units. Grout is used primarily in reinforced masonry construction and is used to bond the masonry to the reinforcing steel. Common mortar types are M(2500 psi), S(1800 psi), N(750 psi), and O(350 psi), and conform to ASTM C270. Grout is either fine or coarse, conforms to ASTM C476, and in-place strengths generally exceed 2500 psi. Mortar and grout are different components of masonry construction and are placed by entirely different methods. An estimator should be aware of their unique uses and costs.

04200 Masonry Units

- The most common types of unit masonry are brick and concrete masonry. The major classifications of brick are building brick (ASTM C62), facing brick (ASTM C216) and glazed brick, fire brick and pavers. Many varieties of texture and appearance can exist within these classifications, and the estimator would be wise to check local custom and availability within the project area. On repair and remodeling jobs, matching the existing brick may be the most important criteria.
- Brick and concrete block are priced by the piece and then converted into a price per square foot of wall. Openings less than two square feet are generally ignored by the estimator because any savings in units used is offset by the cutting and trimming required.

- All masonry walls, whether interior or exterior, require bracing. The cost of bracing walls during construction should be included by the estimator and this bracing must remain in place until permanent bracing is complete. Permanent bracing of masonry walls is accomplished by masonry itself, in the form of pilasters or abutting wall corners, or by anchoring the walls to the structural frame. Accessories in the form of anchors, anchor slots and ties are used, but their supply and installation can be by different trades. For instance, anchor slots on spandrel beams and columns are supplied and welded in place by the steel fabricator, but the ties from the slots into the masonry are installed by the bricklayer. Regardless of the installation method the estimator must be certain that these accessories are accounted for in pricing.

Reference Numbers

Reference numbers are shown in bold squares at the beginning of some major classifications. These numbers refer to related items in the Reference Section. The reference information may be an estimating procedure, an alternate pricing method or technical information.

Note: Not all subdivisions listed here necessarily appear in this publication.

			DAILY OUTPUT	LABOR-HOURS	UNIT	2001 BARE COSTS				TOTAL INCL O&P	
		**04060	Masonry Mortar**	CREW			MAT.	LABOR	EQUIP.	TOTAL		
200	0010	**CEMENT** Gypsum 80 lb. bag, T.L. lots				Bag	11.50			11.50	12.65	200
	0050	L.T.L. lots					12			12	13.20	
	0100	Masonry, 70 lb. bag, T.L. lots **CN**					5.95			5.95	6.55	
	0150	L.T.L. lots					5.75			5.75	6.35	
	0200	White, 70 lb. bag, T.L. lots					16.20			16.20	17.80	
	0250	L.T.L. lots					16.75			16.75	18.45	
400	0010	**LIME** Masons, hydrated, 50 lb. bag, T.L. lots **CN**				Bag	5.65			5.65	6.20	400
	0050	L.T.L. lots					5.90			5.90	6.50	
	0200	Finish, double hydrated, 50 lb. bag, T.L. lots					6.90			6.90	7.60	
	0250	L.T.L. lots					7.60			7.60	8.35	
500	0010	**MORTAR** R04060-100										500
	0020	With masonry cement										
	0100	Type M, 1:1:6 mix R04060-200	1 Brhe	143	.056	C.F.	3.05	1.28		4.33	5.35	
	0200	Type N, 1:3 mix	"	143	.056	"	2.83	1.28		4.11	5.10	
	2000	With portland cement and lime										
	2100	Type M, 1:1/4:3 mix	1 Brhe	143	.056	C.F.	3.79	1.28		5.07	6.15	
	2200	Type N, 1:1:6 mix, 750 psi		143	.056		3.06	1.28		4.34	5.35	
	2300	Type O, 1:2:9 mix (Pointing Mortar)		143	.056		2.97	1.28		4.25	5.25	
	2700	Mortar for glass block		143	.056		6.60	1.28		7.88	9.25	
	2800	Gypsum cement mortar					5.70			5.70	6.25	
	2900	Mortar for Fire Brick, 80 lb. bag, T.L. Lots				Bag	12.75			12.75	14.05	
520	0010	**POINTING MORTAR** See also Division 04060-500				Lb.	.90			.90	.99	520
	0050	White				"	1.05			1.05	1.16	
540	0010	**COLORS** 50 lb. bags (2 bags per M bricks), R04060-100										540
	0020	range 2 to 10 lb. per bag of cement, minimum				Lb.	1.50			1.50	1.65	
	0050	Average					2.50			2.50	2.75	
	0100	Maximum					5			5	5.50	
750	0010	**SAND** For mortar, screened and washed, at the pit **CN**				Ton	10.95			10.95	12.05	750
	0050	With 10 mile haul					11.95			11.95	13.15	
	0100	With 30 mile haul					13			13	14.30	
	0200	Screened and washed, at the pit				C.Y.	15.20			15.20	16.70	
	0250	With 10 mile haul					16.60			16.60	18.25	
	0300	With 30 mile haul				*	18.05			18.05	19.85	
770	0010	**SURFACE BONDING** CMU walls with fiberglass mortar,										770
	0020	gray or white colors, not incl. block work	1 Bric	540	.015	S.F.	.52	.44		.96	1.25	
900	0010	**WATERPROOFING** Admixture, 1 qt. to 2 bags of masonry cement				Qt.	6			6	6.60	900

		**04070	Masonry Grout**									
420	0010	**GROUTING** Bond bms. & lintels, 8" dp., pumped, not incl. block R04060-100										420
	0020	8" thick, 0.2 C.F. per L.F.	D-4	1,400	.023	L.F.	.69	.60	.09	1.38	1.78	
	0050	10" thick, 0.25 C.F. per L.F.		1,200	.027		.87	.70	.11	1.68	2.14	
	0060	12" thick, 0.3 C.F. per L.F.		1,040	.031		1.04	.80	.12	1.96	2.52	
	0200	Concrete block cores, solid, 4" thk., by hand, 0.067 C.F./S.F. of wall	D-8	1,100	.036	S.F.	.24	.98		1.22	1.78	
	0210	6" thick, pumped, 0.175 C.F. per S.F.	D-4	720	.044		.59	1.16	.18	1.93	2.63	
	0250	8" thick, pumped, 0.258 C.F. per S.F.		680	.047		.90	1.23	.19	2.32	3.08	
	0300	10" thick, pumped, 0.340 C.F. per S.F.		660	.048		1.18	1.26	.19	2.63	3.45	
	0350	12" thick, pumped, 0.422 C.F. per S.F.		640	.050		1.46	1.30	.20	2.96	3.82	
	0500	Cavity walls, 2" space, pumped, no shoring, 0.167 C.F./S.F. of wall		1,700	.019		.59	.49	.08	1.16	1.48	
	0550	3" space, 0.250 C.F./S.F.		1,200	.027		.87	.70	.11	1.68	2.14	
	0600	4" space, 0.333 C.F. per S.F.		1,150	.028		1.15	.73	.11	1.99	2.49	
	0700	6" space, 0.500 C.F. per S.F.		800	.040		1.74	1.04	.16	2.94	3.69	
	0800	Door frames, 3' x 7' opening, 2.5 C.F. per opening		60	.533	Opng.	8.70	13.90	2.13	24.73	33.50	
	0850	6' x 7' opening, 3.5 C.F. per opening		45	.711	"	12.15	18.55	2.84	33.54	45	
	2000	Grout, C476, for bond beams, lintels and CMU cores		350	.091	C.F.	3.47	2.38	.37	6.22	7.90	

Important: See the Reference Section for critical supporting data - Reference Nos., Crews, & City Cost Indexes

4 MASONRY

04080 | Masonry Anchor & Reinforcement

			CREW	DAILY OUTPUT	LABOR-HOURS	UNIT	2001 BARE COSTS				TOTAL INCL O&P	
							MAT.	LABOR	EQUIP.	TOTAL		
070	0010	**ANCHOR BOLTS** Hooked type with nut and washer, 1/2" diam., 8" long	1 Bric	200	.040	Ea.	.48	1.18		1.66	2.36	070
	0030	12" long		190	.042		1.05	1.25		2.30	3.08	
	0040	5/8" diameter, 8" long		180	.044		1.30	1.32		2.62	3.46	
	0050	12" long		170	.047		1.43	1.39		2.82	3.72	
	0060	3/4" diameter, 8" long		160	.050		1.48	1.48		2.96	3.92	
	0070	12" long		150	.053		1.88	1.58		3.46	4.51	
200	0010	**REINFORCING** Steel bars A615, placed horiz., #3 & #4 bars	1 Bric	450	.018	Lb.	.28	.53		.81	1.11	200
	0020	#5 & #6 bars [R04080-500]		800	.010		.28	.30		.58	.76	
	0050	Placed vertical, #3 & #4 bars		350	.023		.28	.68		.96	1.35	
	0060	#5 & #6 bars		650	.012		.28	.36		.64	.86	
	0200	Joint reinforcing, regular truss, to 6" wide, mill std galvanized		30	.267	C.L.F.	11.05	7.90		18.95	24.50	
	0250	12" wide		20	.400		11.75	11.85		23.60	31.50	
	0400	Cavity truss with drip section, to 6" wide		30	.267		9.70	7.90		17.60	23	
	0450	12" wide		20	.400		11.05	11.85		22.90	30.50	
650	0010	**WALL TIES** To brick veneer, galv., corrugated, 7/8" x 7", 22 Ga.	1 Bric	10.50	.762	C	4.47	22.50		26.97	40	650
	0100	24 Ga.		10.50	.762		3.97	22.50		26.47	39.50	
	0150	16 Ga.		10.50	.762		13.45	22.50		35.95	50	
	0200	Buck anchors, galv., corrugated, 16 gauge, 2" bend. 8" x 2"		10.50	.762		93	22.50		115.50	137	
	0250	8" x 3"		10.50	.762		99	22.50		121.50	144	
	0600	Cavity wall, Z type, galvanized, 6" long, 1/4" diameter		10.50	.762		20	22.50		42.50	57	
	0650	3/16" diameter		10.50	.762		9.50	22.50		32	45.50	
	0800	8" long, 1/4" diameter		10.50	.762		24	22.50		46.50	61.50	
	0850	3/16" diameter		10.50	.762		10.45	22.50		32.95	46.50	
	1000	Rectangular type, galvanized, 1/4" diameter, 2" x 6"		10.50	.762		25.50	22.50		48	63.50	
	1050	2" x 8" or 4" x 6"		10.50	.762		29	22.50		51.50	66.50	
	1100	3/16" diameter, 2" x 6"		10.50	.762		16.95	22.50		39.45	53.50	
	1150	2" x 8" or 4" x 6"		10.50	.762		19.40	22.50		41.90	56.50	
	1500	Rigid partition anchors, plain, 8" long, 1" x 1/8"		10.50	.762		48	22.50		70.50	88	
	1550	1" x 1/4"		10.50	.762		94	22.50		116.50	138	
	1580	1-1/2" x 1/8"		10.50	.762		66.50	22.50		89	108	
	1600	1-1/2" x 1/4"		10.50	.762		158	22.50		180.50	208	
	1650	2" x 1/8"		10.50	.762		83	22.50		105.50	127	
	1700	2" x 1/4"		10.50	.762		225	22.50		247.50	283	

04090 | Masonry Accessories

			CREW	DAILY OUTPUT	LABOR-HOURS	UNIT	MAT.	LABOR	EQUIP.	TOTAL	TOTAL INCL O&P	
150	0010	**CAULKING** See division 07920-800										150
170	0010	**CONTROL JOINT** Rubber, 4" and wider wall	1 Bric	400	.020	L.F.	2.58	.59		3.17	3.76	170
	0050	PVC, 4" wall		400	.020		1.77	.59		2.36	2.87	
	0100	Rubber, 6" wall		320	.025		4.68	.74		5.42	6.30	
	0120	PVC, 6" wall		320	.025		1.55	.74		2.29	2.85	
	0140	Rubber, 8" and wider wall		280	.029		5.35	.85		6.20	7.20	
	0160	PVC, 8" wall		280	.029		1.81	.85		2.66	3.30	
	0180	12" wall		240	.033		2.66	.99		3.65	4.45	
420	0010	**INSULATION** See also division 07210-550										420
	0100	Inserts, styrofoam, plant installed, add to block prices										
	0200	8" x 16" units, 6" thick				S.F.	.80			.80	.88	
	0250	8" thick					.80			.80	.88	
	0300	10" thick					.95			.95	1.05	
	0350	12" thick					1			1	1.10	
	0500	8" x 8" units, 8" thick					.65			.65	.72	
	0550	12" thick					.80			.80	.88	
650	0010	**PARGETING** Regular Portland cement, 1/2" thick	D-1	2.50	6.400	C.S.F.	12.70	168		180.70	274	650
	5100	Waterproof Portland cement	"	2.50	6.400	"	14.10	168		182.10	276	

MASONRY 4

04090	Masonry Accessories	CREW	DAILY OUTPUT	LABOR-HOURS	UNIT	2001 BARE COSTS MAT.	LABOR	EQUIP.	TOTAL	TOTAL INCL O&P	
700	**0010** SCAFFOLDING & SWING STAGING See division 01540 `R01540 -100`										**700**
850	**0010** VENT BOX See division 04090-860										**850**
860	**0010** VENT BOX Extruded aluminum, 4" deep, 2-3/8" x 8-1/8"	1 Bric	30	.267	Ea.	30.50	7.90		38.40	45.50	**860**
	0050 5" x 8-1/8"		25	.320		42.50	9.45		51.95	61	
	0100 2-1/4" x 25"		25	.320		60	9.45		69.45	80.50	
	0150 5" x 16-1/2"		22	.364		44	10.75		54.75	65	
	0200 6" x 16-1/2"		22	.364		85	10.75		95.75	110	
	0250 7-3/4" x 16-1/2"		20	.400		80	11.85		91.85	106	
	0400 For baked enamel finish, add					35%					
	0500 For cast aluminum, painted, add					60%					
	1000 Stainless steel ventilators, 6" x 6"	1 Bric	25	.320		90	9.45		99.45	114	
	1050 8" x 8"		24	.333		95	9.85		104.85	120	
	1100 12" x 12"		23	.348		110	10.30		120.30	137	
	1150 12" x 6"		24	.333		95	9.85		104.85	120	
	1200 Foundation block vent, galv., 1-1/4" thk, 8" high, 16" long, no damper		30	.267		16	7.90		23.90	30	
	1250 For damper, add					5			5	5.50	
900	**0010** WALL PLUGS For nailing to brickwork, 26 ga., galvanized, plain	1 Bric	10.50	.762	C	24	22.50		46.50	61.50	**900**
	0050 Wood filled	"	10.50	.762	"	82	22.50		104.50	125	

04210	Clay Masonry Units	CREW	DAILY OUTPUT	LABOR-HOURS	UNIT	2001 BARE COSTS MAT.	LABOR	EQUIP.	TOTAL	TOTAL INCL O&P	
100	**0010** COMMON BUILDING BRICK C62, TL lots, material only `R04210 -120`										**100**
	0020 Standard, minimum				M	258			258	283	
	0050 Average (select)				"	310			310	340	
120	**0010** BRICK VENEER Scaffolding not included, truck load lots `R04210 -120`										**120**
	0015 Material costs incl. 3% brick and 25% mortar waste										
	0020 Standard, select common, 4" x 2-2/3" x 8" (6.75/S.F.) `R04210 -180`	D-8	1.50	26.667	M	355	720		1,075	1,500	
	0050 Red, 4" x 2-2/3" x 8", running bond		1.50	26.667		430	720		1,150	1,575	
	0100 Full header every 6th course (7.88/S.F.) `R04210 -500`		1.45	27.586		430	745		1,175	1,625	
	0150 English, full header every 2nd course (10.13/S.F.)		1.40	28.571		430	770		1,200	1,675	
	0200 Flemish, alternate header every course (9.00/S.F.) `R04210 -550`		1.40	28.571		430	770		1,200	1,675	
	0250 Flemish, alt. header every 6th course (7.13/S.F.)		1.45	27.586		430	745		1,175	1,625	
	0300 Full headers throughout (13.50/S.F.)		1.40	28.571		430	770		1,200	1,675	
	0350 Rowlock course (13.50/S.F.)		1.35	29.630		430	800		1,230	1,700	
	0400 Rowlock stretcher (4.50/S.F.)		1.40	28.571		435	770		1,205	1,675	
	0450 Soldier course (6.75/S.F.)		1.40	28.571		430	770		1,200	1,675	
	0500 Sailor course (4.50/S.F.)		1.30	30.769		435	830		1,265	1,750	
	0601 Buff or gray face, running bond, (6.75/S.F.)		1.50	26.667		430	720		1,150	1,575	
	0700 Glazed face, 4" x 2-2/3" x 8", running bond		1.40	28.571		1,500	770		2,270	2,850	
	0750 Full header every 6th course (7.88/S.F.)		1.35	29.630		1,475	800		2,275	2,825	
	1000 Jumbo, 6" x 4" x 12",(3.00/S.F.)		1.30	30.769		1,250	830		2,080	2,650	
	1051 Norman, 4" x 2-2/3" x 12" (4.50/S.F.)		1.45	27.586		735	745		1,480	1,950	
	1100 Norwegian, 4" x 3-1/5" x 12" (3.75/S.F.)		1.40	28.571		570	770		1,340	1,825	
	1150 Economy, 4" x 4" x 8" (4.50 per S.F.)		1.40	28.571		560	770		1,330	1,825	
	1201 Engineer, 4" x 3-1/5" x 8", (5.63/S.F.)		1.45	27.586		365	745		1,110	1,550	
	1251 Roman, 4" x 2" x 12", (6.00/S.F.)		1.50	26.667		760	720		1,480	1,950	

4

MASONRY

		04210	Clay Masonry Units		CREW	DAILY OUTPUT	LABOR-HOURS	UNIT	2001 BARE COSTS				TOTAL INCL O&P	
									MAT.	LABOR	EQUIP.	TOTAL		
120	1300	S.C.R. 6" x 2-2/3" x 12" (4.50/S.F.)		R04210 -120	D-8	1.40	28.571	M	900	770		1,670	2,200	120
	1350	Utility, 4" x 4" x 12" (3.00/S.F.)			↓	1.35	29.630	↓	1,075	800		1,875	2,425	
	1360	For less than truck load lots, add		R04210 -180				↓	10					
	1400	For battered walls, add								30%				
	1450	For corbels, add		R04210 -500						75%				
	1500	For curved walls, add								30%				
	1550	For pits and trenches, deduct		R04210 -550						20%				
	1999	Alternate method of figuring by square foot												
	2000	Standard, sel. common, 4" x 2-2/3" x 8", (6.75/S.F.)			D-8	230	.174	S.F.	2.90	4.69		7.59	10.45	
	2020	Standard, red, 4" x 2-2/3" x 8", running bond (6.75/SF)				220	.182		2.90	4.90		7.80	10.75	
	2050	Full header every 6th course (7.88/S.F.)				185	.216		3.38	5.85		9.23	12.70	
	2100	English, full header every 2nd course (10.13/S.F.)				140	.286		4.34	7.70		12.04	16.65	
	2150	Flemish, alternate header every course (9.00/S.F.)				150	.267		3.86	7.20		11.06	15.35	
	2200	Flemish, alt. header every 6th course (7.13/S.F.)				205	.195		3.06	5.25		8.31	11.45	
	2250	Full headers throughout (13.50/S.F.)				105	.381		5.75	10.25		16	22	
	2300	Rowlock course (13.50/S.F.)				100	.400		5.75	10.80		16.55	23	
	2350	Rowlock stretcher (4.50/S.F.)				310	.129		1.95	3.48		5.43	7.50	
	2400	Soldier course (6.75/S.F.)				200	.200		2.90	5.40		8.30	11.55	
	2450	Sailor course (4.50/S.F.)				290	.138		1.95	3.72		5.67	7.90	
	2600	Buff or gray face, running bond, (6.75/S.F.)				220	.182		3.08	4.90		7.98	10.95	
	2700	Glazed face brick, running bond				210	.190		9.90	5.15		15.05	18.80	
	2750	Full header every 6th course (7.88/S.F.)				170	.235		11.55	6.35		17.90	22.50	
	3000	Jumbo, 6" x 4" x 12" running bond (3.00/S.F.)				435	.092		3.53	2.48		6.01	7.70	
	3050	Norman, 4" x 2-2/3" x 12" running bond, (4.5/S.F.)				320	.125		3.42	3.37		6.79	8.95	
	3100	Norwegian, 4" x 3-1/5" x 12" (3.75/S.F.)				375	.107		2.09	2.87		4.96	6.75	
	3150	Economy, 4" x 4" x 8" (4.50/S.F.)				310	.129		2.50	3.48		5.98	8.10	
	3200	Engineer, 4" x 3-1/5" x 8" (5.63/S.F.)				260	.154		2.04	4.14		6.18	8.65	
	3250	Roman, 4" x 2" x 12" (6.00/S.F.)				250	.160		4.52	4.31		8.83	11.60	
	3300	SCR, 6" x 2-2/3" x 12" (4.50/S.F.)				310	.129		4.14	3.48		7.62	9.90	
	3350	Utility, 4" x 4" x 12" (3.00/S.F.)			↓	450	.089	↓	3.20	2.39		5.59	7.20	
	3400	For cavity wall construction, add								15%				
	3450	For stacked bond, add								10%				
	3500	For interior veneer construction, add								15%				
	3550	For curved walls, add			↓					30%				
200	0011	**CAST CERAMIC FLOORING** See division 09600												200
300	0010	**FACE BRICK** C216, TL lots, material only		R04210 -120										300
	0300	Standard modular, 4" x 2-2/3" x 8", minimum						M	380			380	420	
	0350	Maximum	**CN**						315			315	345	
	0450	Economy, 4" x 4" x 8", minimum							500			500	550	
	0500	Maximum							530			530	585	
	0510	Economy, 4" x 4" x 12", minimum							500			500	550	
	0520	Maximum							530			530	585	
	0550	Jumbo, 6" x 4" x 12", minimum							1,100			1,100	1,200	
	0600	Maximum							1,400			1,400	1,550	
	0610	Jumbo, 8" x 4" x 12", minimum							1,100			1,100	1,200	
	0620	Maximum							1,400			1,400	1,550	
	0650	Norwegian, 4" x 3-1/5" x 12", minimum							500			500	550	
	0700	Maximum							700			700	770	
	0710	Norwegian, 6" x 3-1/5" x 12", minimum							500			500	550	
	0720	Maximum							700			700	770	
	0850	Standard glazed, plain colors, 4" x 2-2/3" x 8", minimum							1,375			1,375	1,525	
	0900	Maximum							1,100			1,100	1,200	
	1000	Deep trim shades, 4" x 2-2/3" x 8", minimum							1,125			1,125	1,250	
	1050	Maximum							1,250			1,250	1,375	
	1080	Jumbo utility, 4" x 4" x 1			↓			↓	995			995	1,100	

MASONRY 4

			DAILY OUTPUT	LABOR-HOURS	UNIT	2001 BARE COSTS				TOTAL INCL O&P	
04210		**Clay Masonry Units**	CREW			MAT.	LABOR	EQUIP.	TOTAL		
300	1120	4" x 8" x 8" R04210-120			M	1,050			1,050	1,150	**300**
	1140	4" x 8" x 16"				2,200			2,200	2,425	
	1260	Engineer, 4" x 3-1/5" x 8", minimum 2"				315			315	345	
	1270	Maximum				475			475	525	
	1350	King, 4" x 2-3/4" x 10", minimum				420			420	460	
	1360	Maximum				450			450	495	
	1400	Norman, 4" x 2-3/4" x 12"				420			420	460	
	1450	Roman, 4" x 2" x 12"				420			420	460	
	1500	SCR, 6" x 2-2/3" x 12"				420			420	460	
	1550	Double, 4" x 5-1/3" x 8"				420			420	460	
	1600	Triple, 4" x 5-1/3" x 12"				420			420	460	
	1770	Standard modular, double glazed, 4" x 2-2/3" x 8"				950			950	1,050	
	1850	Jumbo, colored glazed ceramic, 6" x 4" x 12"				1,400			1,400	1,550	
	2050	Jumbo utility, glazed, 4" x 4" x 12"				1,050			1,050	1,150	
	2100	4" x 8" x 8"				1,450			1,450	1,600	
	2150	4" x 16" x 8"				2,500			2,500	2,750	
	2160	Fire Brick, 2" x 2-2/3" x 9", minimum									
	2165	Maximum			M	900			900	990	
	2170	For less than truck load lots, add				10					
	2180	For buff or gray brick, add				15					
320	0010	**STRUCTURAL BRICK** C652, Grade SW, incl mortar, scaffolding not incl									**320**
	0100	Standard unit, 4-5/8" x 2-3/4" x 9-5/8"	D-8	245	.163	S.F.	3.58	4.40		7.98	10.75	
	0120	Bond beam		225	.178		6.90	4.79		11.69	15	
	0140	V cut bond beam		225	.178		6.60	4.79		11.39	14.70	
	0160	Stretcher quoin, 5-5/8" x 2-3/4" x 9-5/8"		245	.163		6.40	4.40		10.80	13.80	
	0180	Corner quoin		245	.163		6.95	4.40		11.35	14.45	
	0200	Corner, 45 deg, 4-5/8" x 2-3/4" x 10-7/16"		235	.170		7.20	4.59		11.79	15	
350	0010	**STRUCTURAL FACING TILE** Scaffolding not incl, standard colors									**350**
	0020	6T series, 5-1/3" x 12", 2.3 pieces per S.F., glazed 1 side, 2" thick	D-8	225	.178	S.F.	4.72	4.79		9.51	12.60	
	0100	4" thick		220	.182		5.55	4.90		10.45	13.65	
	0150	Glazed 2 sides		195	.205		9.05	5.55		14.60	18.50	
	0250	6" thick		210	.190		9.10	5.15		14.25	17.95	
	0300	Glazed 2 sides		185	.216		12.80	5.85		18.65	23	
	0400	8" thick		180	.222		11.75	6		17.75	22	
	0500	Special shapes, group 1		400	.100	Ea.	4.34	2.69		7.03	8.95	
	0550	Group 2		375	.107		6.50	2.87		9.37	11.60	
	0600	Group 3		350	.114		8.65	3.08		11.73	14.25	
	0650	Group 4		325	.123		13.75	3.32		17.07	20.50	
	0700	Group 5		300	.133		20.50	3.59		24.09	28	
	0750	Group 6		275	.145		28.50	3.92		32.42	37.50	
	1000	Fire rated, 4" thick, 1 hr. rating		210	.190	S.F.	12.35	5.15		17.50	21.50	
	1300	Acoustic, 4" thick		210	.190	"	14.75	5.15		19.90	24	
	1400	For designer colors, add					25%					
	2000	8W series, 8" x 16", 1.125 pieces per S.F.										
	2050	2" thick, glazed 1 side	D-8	360	.111	S.F.	5.35	2.99		8.34	10.50	
	2100	4" thick, glazed 1 side		345	.116		6.05	3.12		9.17	11.50	
	2150	Glazed 2 sides		325	.123		9.45	3.32		12.77	15.50	
	2200	6" thick, glazed 1 side		330	.121		9.25	3.27		12.52	15.25	
	2250	8" thick, glazed 1 side		310	.129		10.30	3.48		13.78	16.70	
	2500	Special shapes, group 1		300	.133	Ea.	7.10	3.59		10.69	13.35	
	2550	Group 2		280	.143		9.30	3.85		13.15	16.20	
	2600	Group 3		260	.154		9.85	4.14		13.99	17.25	
	2650	Group 4		250	.160		14	4.31		18.31	22	
	2700	Group 5		240	.167		36.50	4.49		40.99	47.50	
	2750	Group 6		230	.174		46.50	4.69		51.19	58.50	

Important: See the Reference Section for critical supporting data - Reference Nos., Crews, & City Cost Indexes

		04210	Clay Masonry Units	CREW	DAILY OUTPUT	LABOR-HOURS	UNIT	2001 BARE COSTS MAT.	LABOR	EQUIP.	TOTAL	TOTAL INCL O&P	
350	3000		4" thick, glazed 1 side	D-8	345	.116	S.F.	9.50	3.12		12.62	15.30	350
	3100		Acoustic, 4" thick	↓	345	.116	"	9.60	3.12		12.72	15.40	
	3120		4W series, 8" x 8", 2.25 pieces per S.F.										
	3125		2" thick, glazed 1 side	D-8	360	.111	S.F.	5.25	2.99		8.24	10.40	
	3130		4" thick, glazed 1 side		345	.116		6.40	3.12		9.52	11.90	
	3135		Glazed 2 sides		325	.123		8.55	3.32		11.87	14.55	
	3140		6" thick, glazed 1 side		330	.121		8.40	3.27		11.67	14.30	
	3150		8" thick, glazed 1 side		310	.129	↓	12.60	3.48		16.08	19.25	
	3155		Special shapes, group I		300	.133	Ea.	4.07	3.59		7.66	10.05	
	3160		Group II	↓	280	.143	"	4.93	3.85		8.78	11.35	
	3200		For designer colors, add					25%					
	3300		For epoxy mortar joints, add				S.F.	1.10			1.10	1.21	
810	0010		**TERRA COTTA** Coping, split type, not glazed, 9" wide	D-1	90	.178	L.F.	5.10	4.67		9.77	12.80	810
	0100		13" wide		80	.200		8.10	5.25		13.35	17	
	0200		Split type, glazed, 9" wide		90	.178		9.75	4.67		14.42	17.95	
	0250		13" wide	↓	80	.200	↓	13	5.25		18.25	22.50	
	0500		Partition or back-up blocks, scored, in C.L. lots										
	0700		Non-load bearing 12" x 12", 3" thick, special order	D-8	550	.073	S.F.	4.45	1.96		6.41	7.95	
	0750		4" thick, standard		500	.080		3.75	2.16		5.91	7.45	
	0800		6" thick		450	.089		3.80	2.39		6.19	7.90	
	0850		8" thick		400	.100		5	2.69		7.69	9.65	
	1000		Load bearing, 12" x 12", 4" thick, in walls		500	.080		4.13	2.16		6.29	7.85	
	1050		In floors		750	.053		4.13	1.44		5.57	6.75	
	1200		6" thick, in walls		450	.089		3.80	2.39		6.19	7.90	
	1250		In floors		675	.059		3.80	1.60		5.40	6.65	
	1400		8" thick, in walls		400	.100		5	2.69		7.69	9.65	
	1450		In floors		575	.070		5	1.87		6.87	8.40	
	1600		10" thick, in walls, special order		350	.114		5.45	3.08		8.53	10.75	
	1650		In floors, special order		500	.080		5.45	2.16		7.61	9.35	
	1800		12" thick, in walls, special order		300	.133		6.50	3.59		10.09	12.70	
	1850		In floors, special order	↓	450	.089		6.50	2.39		8.89	10.85	
	2000		For reinforcing with steel rods, add to above					15%	5%				
	2100		For smooth tile instead of scored, add					1.50			1.50	1.65	
	2200		For L.C.L. quantities, add				↓	10%	10%				
820	0010		**TERRA COTTA TILE** On walls, dry set, 1/2" thick										820
	0100		Square, hexagonal or lattice shapes, unglazed	1 Tilf	135	.059	S.F.	4.25	1.67		5.92	7.15	
	0300		Glazed, plain colors		130	.062		5.75	1.73		7.48	8.90	
	0400		Intense colors	↓	125	.064		8.90	1.80		10.70	12.45	

		04220	Concrete Masonry Units										
180	0010		**AUTOCLAVED AERATED CONCRETE BLOCK** Scaffolding not incl										180
	0050		Solid, 4" x 12" x 24", incl mortar	D-8	600	.067	S.F.	1.23	1.80		3.03	4.14	
	0060		6" x 12" x 24"		600	.067		1.85	1.80		3.65	4.81	
	0070		8" x 8" x 24"		575	.070		2.47	1.87		4.34	5.60	
	0080		10" x 12" x 24"		575	.070		3.08	1.87		4.95	6.30	
	0090		12" x 12" x 24"	↓	550	.073	↓	3.70	1.96		5.66	7.10	
200	0010		**CHIMNEY BLOCK** Scaffolding not included										200
	0220		1 piece, with 8" x 8" flue, 16" x 16"	D-1	28	.571	V.L.F.	12.70	15		27.70	37	
	0230		2 piece, 16" x 16"		26	.615		14.30	16.15		30.45	41	
	0240		2 piece, with 8" x 12" flue, 16" x 20"	↓	24	.667	↓	18.70	17.50		36.20	47.50	
220	0010		**CONCRETE BLOCK, BACK-UP** Scaffolding not included										220
	0020		Sand aggregate, 8" x 16" units, tooled joint 1 side [R04220 -200]										
	1000		Reinforced, alternate courses, 4" thick	D-8	435	.092	S.F.	.97	2.48		3.45	4.90	
	1100		6" thick		415	.096		1.43	2.60		4.03	5.60	
	1150		8" thick		395	.101		1.53	2.73		4.26	5.90	
	1200		10" thick	↓	385	.104	↓	2.12	2.80		4.92	6.65	

MASONRY 4

04220	Concrete Masonry Units		CREW	DAILY OUTPUT	LABOR-HOURS	UNIT	2001 BARE COSTS				TOTAL INCL O&P	
							MAT.	LABOR	EQUIP.	TOTAL		
220	1250	12" thick	R04220 -200	D-9	365	.132	S.F.	2.21	3.46		5.67	7.80	220
230	0010	**CONCRETE BLOCK BOND BEAM** Scaffolding not included											230
	0020	Not including grout or reinforcing											
	0100	Regular block, 8" high, 8" thick		D-8	565	.071	L.F.	1.46	1.91		3.37	4.55	
	0150	12" thick		D-9	510	.094		2.25	2.47		4.72	6.30	
	0500	Lightweight, 8" high, 8" thick		D-8	575	.070		1.39	1.87		3.26	4.43	
	0550	12" thick		D-9	520	.092	↓	2.76	2.43		5.19	6.80	
	2000	Including grout and 2 #5 bars											
	2100	Regular block, 8" high, 8" thick		D-8	300	.133	L.F.	2.85	3.59		6.44	8.70	
	2150	12" thick		D-9	250	.192		4.09	5.05		9.14	12.30	
	2500	Lightweight, 8" high, 8" thick		D-8	305	.131		3.11	3.53		6.64	8.85	
	2550	12" thick		D-9	255	.188	↓	4.60	4.95		9.55	12.70	
240	0010	**CONCRETE BLOCK, DECORATIVE** Scaffolding not included											240
	0020	Embossed, simulated brick face											
	0100	8" x 16" units, 4" thick		D-8	400	.100	S.F.	2.15	2.69		4.84	6.50	
	0200	8" thick			340	.118		2.93	3.17		6.10	8.10	
	0250	12" thick		↓	300	.133	↓	3.78	3.59		7.37	9.70	
	0400	Embossed both sides											
	0500	8" thick		D-8	300	.133	S.F.	3.27	3.59		6.86	9.15	
	0550	12" thick		"	275	.145	"	4.28	3.92		8.20	10.75	
	1000	Fluted high strength											
	1100	8" x 16" x 4" thick, flutes 1 side,		D-8	345	.116	S.F.	2.60	3.12		5.72	7.70	
	1150	Flutes 2 sides			335	.119		3.16	3.22		6.38	8.45	
	1200	8" thick		↓	300	.133		4.06	3.59		7.65	10	
	1250	For special colors, add					↓	.24			.24	.26	
	1400	Deep grooved, smooth face											
	1450	8" x 16" x 4" thick		D-8	345	.116	S.F.	1.63	3.12		4.75	6.65	
	1500	8" thick		"	300	.133	"	2.80	3.59		6.39	8.65	
	2000	Formblock, incl. inserts & reinforcing											
	2100	8" x 16" x 8" thick		D-8	345	.116	S.F.	2.93	3.12		6.05	8.05	
	2150	12" thick		"	310	.129	"	3.60	3.48		7.08	9.30	
	2500	Ground face											
	2600	8" x 16" x 4" thick		D-8	345	.116	S.F.	3.72	3.12		6.84	8.95	
	2650	6" thick			310	.129		4.09	3.48		7.57	9.85	
	2700	8" thick		↓	290	.138		4.76	3.72		8.48	11	
	2750	12" thick		D-9	265	.181	↓	5.70	4.76		10.46	13.60	
	2900	For special colors, add, minimum						15%					
	2950	For special colors, add, maximum						45%					
	4000	Slump block											
	4100	4" face height x 16" x 4" thick		D-1	165	.097	S.F.	3.87	2.55		6.42	8.20	
	4150	6" thick			160	.100		4.79	2.63		7.42	9.30	
	4200	8" thick			155	.103		6.45	2.71		9.16	11.30	
	4250	10" thick			140	.114		9.55	3		12.55	15.20	
	4300	12" thick			130	.123		10.20	3.23		13.43	16.20	
	4400	6" face height x 16" x 6" thick			155	.103		3.89	2.71		6.60	8.45	
	4450	8" thick			150	.107		5.05	2.80		7.85	9.90	
	4500	10" thick			130	.123		7.70	3.23		10.93	13.50	
	4550	12" thick		↓	120	.133	↓	8	3.50		11.50	14.20	
	5000	Split rib profile units, 1" deep ribs, 8 ribs											
	5100	8" x 16" x 4" thick		D-8	345	.116	S.F.	1.88	3.12		5	6.90	
	5150	6" thick			325	.123		2.36	3.32		5.68	7.70	
	5200	8" thick		↓	305	.131		2.88	3.53		6.41	8.60	
	5250	12" thick		D-9	275	.175		3.61	4.59		8.20	11.05	
	5400	For special deeper colors, 4" thick, add					↓	.18			.18	.20	

Important: See the Reference Section for critical supporting data - Reference Nos., Crews, & City Cost Indexes

04220	Concrete Masonry Units		CREW	DAILY OUTPUT	LABOR-HOURS	UNIT	2001 BARE COSTS				TOTAL INCL O&P	
							MAT.	LABOR	EQUIP.	TOTAL		
240	5450	12" thick, add				S.F.	.35			.35	.39	**240**
	5600	For white, 4" thick, add					.72			.72	.80	
	5650	6" thick, add					.95			.95	1.04	
	5700	8" thick, add					1.18			1.18	1.29	
	5750	12" thick, add					1.64			1.64	1.80	
	6000	Split face or scored split face										
	6100	8" x 16" x 4" thick	D-8	350	.114	S.F.	2.19	3.08		5.27	7.15	
	6150	6" thick		315	.127		2.45	3.42		5.87	8	
	6200	8" thick		295	.136		4.43	3.65		8.08	10.50	
	6250	12" thick	D-9	270	.178		5.80	4.67		10.47	13.55	
	6400	For special deeper colors, 4" thick, add					.24			.24	.26	
	6450	6" thick, add					.24			.24	.26	
	6500	8" thick, add					.25			.25	.27	
	6550	12" thick, add					.43			.43	.47	
	6650	For white, 4" thick, add					.79			.79	.87	
	6700	6" thick, add					.79			.79	.87	
	6750	8" thick, add					.73			.73	.81	
	6800	12" thick, add					.68			.68	.75	
	7000	Scored ground face, 2 to 5 scores										
	7100	8" x 16" x 4" thick	D-8	345	.116	S.F.	3.60	3.12		6.72	8.80	
	7150	6" thick		310	.129		4.36	3.48		7.84	10.15	
	7200	8" thick		290	.138		4.88	3.72		8.60	11.10	
	7250	12" thick	D-9	265	.181		6.10	4.76		10.86	14.05	
	8000	Hexagonal face profile units, 8" x 16" units										
	8100	4" thick, hollow	D-8	345	.116	S.F.	1.99	3.12		5.11	7	
	8200	Solid		345	.116		2.83	3.12		5.95	7.95	
	8300	6" thick, hollow		310	.129		2.39	3.48		5.87	8	
	8350	8" thick, hollow		290	.138		3.29	3.72		7.01	9.35	
	8500	For stacked bond, add						26%				
	8550	For high rise construction, add per story	D-8	67.80	.590	M.S.F.		15.90		15.90	24.50	
	8600	For scored block, add					10%					
	8650	For honed or ground face, per face, add				Ea.	.26			.26	.29	
	8700	For honed or ground end, per end, add				"	2.54			2.54	2.80	
	8750	For bullnose block, add					10%					
	8800	For special color, add					13%					
250	0010	**CONCRETE BLOCK, EXTERIOR** Not including scaffolding										**250**
	0020	Reinforced alt courses, tooled joints 2 sides, foam inserts										
	0100	Regular, 8" x 16" x 6" thick	D-8	390	.103	S.F.	1.61	2.76		4.37	6.05	
	0200	8" thick		365	.110		2.39	2.95		5.34	7.20	
	0250	10" thick		355	.113		2.79	3.04		5.83	7.75	
	0300	12" thick	D-9	330	.145		2.89	3.82		6.71	9.10	
	0500	Lightweight, 8" x 16" x 6" thick	D-8	410	.098		1.63	2.63		4.26	5.85	
	0600	8" thick		385	.104		2.20	2.80		5	6.75	
	0650	10" thick		370	.108		2.86	2.91		5.77	7.65	
	0700	12" thick	D-9	350	.137		4.13	3.60		7.73	10.10	
260	0010	**CONCRETE BLOCK FOUNDATION WALL** Scaffolding not included										**260**
	0050	Normal-weight, trowel cut joints, parged 1/2" thick, no reinforcing										
	0200	Hollow, 8" x 16" x 6" thick	D-8	450	.089	S.F.	1.55	2.39		3.94	5.40	
	0250	8" thick		430	.093		1.65	2.51		4.16	5.70	
	0300	10" thick		420	.095		2.25	2.57		4.82	6.45	
	0350	12" thick	D-9	395	.122		2.34	3.19		5.53	7.50	
	0500	Solid, 8" x 16" block, 6" thick	D-8	440	.091		1.65	2.45		4.10	5.60	
	0550	8" thick	"	415	.096		2.41	2.60		5.01	6.65	
	0600	12" thick	D-9	380	.126		3.51	3.32		6.83	9	

MASONRY 4

MASONRY **4**

04220	Concrete Masonry Units	CREW	DAILY OUTPUT	LABOR-HOURS	UNIT	2001 BARE COSTS				TOTAL INCL O&P
						MAT.	LABOR	EQUIP.	TOTAL	
270	**0010 CONCRETE BLOCK, HIGH STRENGTH** Scaffolding not included									**270**
0050	Hollow, reinforced alternate courses, 8" x 16" units									
0200	3500 psi, 4" thick	D-8	430	.093	S.F.	1.16	2.51		3.67	5.15
0250	6" thick		400	.100		1.58	2.69		4.27	5.90
0300	8" thick	▼	375	.107		2.35	2.87		5.22	7.05
0350	12" thick	D-9	340	.141		2.85	3.71		6.56	8.90
0500	5000 psi, 4" thick	D-8	430	.093		1.29	2.51		3.80	5.30
0550	6" thick		400	.100		1.96	2.69		4.65	6.30
0600	8" thick	▼	375	.107		2.67	2.87		5.54	7.35
0650	12" thick	D-9	340	.141	▼	3.96	3.71		7.67	10.10
1000	For 75% solid block, add					30%				
1050	For 100% solid block, add					50%				
280	**0010 CONCRETE BLOCK, LINTELS** Scaffolding not included									**280**
0100	Including grout and horizontal reinforcing									
0200	8" x 8" x 8", 1 #4 bar	D-4	300	.107	L.F.	3.43	2.78	.43	6.64	8.50
0250	2 #4 bars		295	.108		3.55	2.83	.43	6.81	8.75
0400	8" x 16" x 8", 1 #4 bar		275	.116		6.05	3.03	.47	9.55	11.80
0450	2 #4 bars		270	.119		6.15	3.09	.47	9.71	12.05
1000	12" x 8" x 8", 1 #4 bar		275	.116		4.90	3.03	.47	8.40	10.55
1100	2 #4 bars		270	.119		5	3.09	.47	8.56	10.80
1150	2 #5 bars		270	.119		5.15	3.09	.47	8.71	10.90
1200	2 #6 bars		265	.121		5.30	3.15	.48	8.93	11.20
1500	12" x 16" x 8", 1 #4 bar		250	.128		8	3.34	.51	11.85	14.50
1600	2 #3 bars		245	.131		8	3.40	.52	11.92	14.60
1650	2 #4 bars		245	.131		8.10	3.40	.52	12.02	14.75
1700	2 #5 bars	▼	240	.133	▼	8.25	3.47	.53	12.25	15.05
300	**0010 CONCRETE BRICK** C55, grade N, type I, scaffolding not included									**300**
0100	Regular, 4 x 2-1/4 x 8	D-8	220	.182	Ea.	.30	4.90		5.20	7.90
0125	Rusticated, 4 x 2-1/4 x 8		220	.182		.34	4.90		5.24	7.90
0150	Frog, 4 x 2-1/4 x 8		220	.182		.32	4.90		5.22	7.90
0200	Double, 4 x 4-7/8 x 8	▼	180	.222	▼	.53	6		6.53	9.85
320	**0010 CONCRETE SCREEN BLOCK** Scaffolding not included									**320**
0200	8" x 16", 4" thick	D-8	180	.222	S.F.	1.57	6		7.57	11
0300	8" thick		270	.148		2.29	3.99		6.28	8.65
0350	12" x 12", 4" thick		300	.133		1.90	3.59		5.49	7.65
0500	8" thick	▼	330	.121	▼	2.35	3.27		5.62	7.65
340	**0010 COPING** Stock units									**340**
0050	Precast concrete, 10" wide, 4" tapers to 3-1/2", 8" wall	D-1	75	.213	L.F.	14.15	5.60		19.75	24
0100	12" wide, 3-1/2" tapers to 3", 10" wall		70	.229		10.10	6		16.10	20.50
0110	14" wide, 4" tapers to 3-1/2", 12" wall		65	.246		15.15	6.45		21.60	26.50
0150	16" wide, 4" tapers to 3-1/2", 14" wall		60	.267	▼	13.90	7		20.90	26
0250	Precast concrete corners		40	.400	Ea.	23.50	10.50		34	42.50
0300	Limestone for 12" wall, 4" thick		90	.178	L.F.	13.25	4.67		17.92	22
0350	6" thick		80	.200		15.50	5.25		20.75	25
0500	Marble, to 4" thick, no wash, 9" wide		90	.178		19	4.67		23.67	28
0550	12" wide		80	.200		28.50	5.25		33.75	39.50
0700	Terra cotta, 9" wide		90	.178		4.60	4.67		9.27	12.25
0750	12" wide		80	.200		7.65	5.25		12.90	16.50
0800	Aluminum, for 12" wall	▼	80	.200	▼	11	5.25		16.25	20
500	**0010 CONCRETE BLOCK, INTERLOCKING** Scaffolding not incl., mortar incl.									**500**
0100	Not including grout or reinforcing									
0200	8" x 16" units, 2,000 psi, 8" thick R04220 -220	D-1	245	.065	S.F.	1.70	1.72		3.42	4.52
0300	12" thick	▼	220	.073	▼	2.54	1.91		4.45	5.75

Important: See the Reference Section for critical supporting data - Reference Nos., Crews, & City Cost Indexes

04200 | Masonry Units

04220 | Concrete Masonry Units

			CREW	DAILY OUTPUT	LABOR-HOURS	UNIT	MAT.	LABOR	EQUIP.	TOTAL	TOTAL INCL O&P	
500	0350	16" thick	D-1	185	.086	S.F.	3.86	2.27		6.13	7.75	500
	0400	Including grout & reinforcing, 8" thick [R04220-220]	D-4	245	.131		5.35	3.40	.52	9.27	11.65	
	0450	12" thick		220	.145		6.30	3.79	.58	10.67	13.40	
	0500	16" thick		185	.173		7.70	4.51	.69	12.90	16.20	
700	0010	**GLAZED CONCRETE BLOCK** No scaffolding or reinforcing incl.										700
	0100	Single face, 8" x 16" units, 2" thick	D-8	360	.111	S.F.	6.05	2.99		9.04	11.30	
	0200	4" thick		345	.116		6.30	3.12		9.42	11.75	
	0250	6" thick		330	.121		6.65	3.27		9.92	12.35	
	0300	8" thick		310	.129		6.95	3.48		10.43	13	
	0350	10" thick		295	.136		8.30	3.65		11.95	14.75	
	0400	12" thick	D-9	280	.171		8.55	4.51		13.06	16.35	
	0700	Double face, 8" x 16" units, 4" thick	D-8	310	.129		10.25	3.48		13.73	16.60	
	0750	6" thick		290	.138		10.55	3.72		14.27	17.40	
	0800	8" thick		270	.148		10.95	3.99		14.94	18.20	
	1000	Jambs, bullnose or square, single face, 8" x 16", 2" thick		315	.127	Ea.	10	3.42		13.42	16.30	
	1050	4" thick		285	.140	"	11.35	3.78		15.13	18.35	
	1200	Caps, bullnose or square, 8" x 16", 2" thick		420	.095	L.F.	9.80	2.57		12.37	14.70	
	1250	4" thick		380	.105		12.60	2.84		15.44	18.25	
	1500	Cove base, 8" x 16", 2" thick		315	.127		6.70	3.42		10.12	12.65	
	1550	4" thick		285	.140		6.75	3.78		10.53	13.30	
	1600	6" thick		265	.151		6.90	4.07		10.97	13.90	
	1650	8" thick		245	.163		7.30	4.40		11.70	14.85	

04270 | Glass Masonry Units

			CREW	DAILY OUTPUT	LABOR-HOURS	UNIT	MAT.	LABOR	EQUIP.	TOTAL	TOTAL INCL O&P	
200	0010	**GLASS BLOCK** Scaffolding not included										200
	0100	Plain, 4" thick, under 1,000 S.F., 6" x 6" block [R04270-700]	D-8	115	.348	S.F.	12.70	9.35		22.05	28.50	
	0150	8" x 8" block		160	.250		8.85	6.75		15.60	20	
	0200	12" x 12" block		175	.229		10.85	6.15		17	21.50	
	0300	1,000 to 5,000 S.F., 6" x 6" block		135	.296		12.90	8		20.90	26.50	
	0350	8" x 8" block		190	.211		8.80	5.65		14.45	18.45	
	0400	12" x 12" block		215	.186		10.95	5		15.95	19.80	
	0500	Over 5,000 S.F., 6" x 6" block		145	.276		12.35	7.45		19.80	25	
	0550	8" x 8" block		215	.186		8	5		13	16.55	
	0600	12" x 12" block		240	.167		10.15	4.49		14.64	18.15	
	0700	For solar reflective blocks, add					100%					
	0800	Under 1,000 S.F., 4" x 8" blocks	D-8	145	.276	S.F.	13.05	7.45		20.50	26	
	0850	Over 5,000 S.F.		170	.235		13.95	6.35		20.30	25	
	1000	Thinline, plain, 3-1/8" thick, under 1,000 S.F., 6" x 6" block		115	.348		10.85	9.35		20.20	26.50	
	1050	8" x 8" block		160	.250		6.10	6.75		12.85	17.10	
	1200	Over 5,000 S.F., 6" x 6" block		145	.276		9.45	7.45		16.90	22	
	1250	8" x 8" block		215	.186		5.85	5		10.85	14.20	
	1400	For cleaning block after installation (both sides), add		1,000	.040		.10	1.08		1.18	1.78	

04290 | Adobe Masonry Units

			CREW	DAILY OUTPUT	LABOR-HOURS	UNIT	MAT.	LABOR	EQUIP.	TOTAL	TOTAL INCL O&P	
100	0010	**ADOBE BRICK** Semi-stabilized, with cement mortar										100
	0060	Brick, 10" x 4" x 14", 2.6/S.F.	D-8	560	.071	S.F.	1.89	1.92		3.81	5.05	
	0080	12" x 4" x 16", 2.3/S.F.		580	.069		2.67	1.86		4.53	5.80	
	0100	10" x 4" x 16", 2.3/S.F.		590	.068		2.16	1.83		3.99	5.20	
	0120	8" x 4" x 16", 2.3/S.F.		560	.071		1.85	1.92		3.77	5	
	0140	4" x 4" x 16", 2.3/S.F.		540	.074		1.73	2		3.73	4.98	
	0160	6" x 4" x 16", 2.3/S.F.		540	.074		1.48	2		3.48	4.71	
	0180	4" x 4" x 12", 3.0/S.F.		520	.077		2.08	2.07		4.15	5.50	
	0200	8" x 4" x 12", 3.0/S.F.		520	.077		2.12	2.07		4.19	5.55	

MASONRY 4

04412 | Bluestone

		CREW	DAILY OUTPUT	LABOR-HOURS	UNIT	MAT.	LABOR	EQUIP.	TOTAL	TOTAL INCL O&P	
100	0010	**BLUESTONE** Cut to size										100
	0500	Sills, natural cleft, 10" wide to 6' long, 1-1/2" thick	D-11	70	.343	L.F.	9.85	9.60		19.45	25.50	
	0550	2" thick	"	63	.381		11.70	10.70		22.40	29.50	
	1000	Stair treads, natural cleft, 12" wide, 6' long, 1-1/2" thick	D-10	115	.348		14.85	9.60	3.70	28.15	35	
	1050	2" thick		105	.381		16.65	10.55	4.05	31.25	39	
	1100	Smooth finish, 1-1/2" thick		115	.348		19.50	9.60	3.70	32.80	40.50	
	1300	Thermal finish		115	.348		22	9.60	3.70	35.30	43	
	1350	2" thick		105	.381		24.50	10.55	4.05	39.10	47.50	
800	0010	**WINDOW SILL** Bluestone, thermal top, 10" wide, 1-1/2" thick	D-1	85	.188	S.F.	12.75	4.95		17.70	21.50	800
	0050	2" thick		75	.213	"	14.75	5.60		20.35	25	
	0100	Cut stone, 5" x 8" plain		48	.333	L.F.	10	8.75		18.75	24.50	
	0200	Face brick on edge, brick, 8" wide		80	.200		2	5.25		7.25	10.30	
	0400	Marble, 9" wide, 1" thick		85	.188		7.25	4.95		12.20	15.65	
	0600	Precast concrete, 4" tapers to 3", 9" wide		70	.229		9.05	6		15.05	19.25	
	0650	11" wide		60	.267		15.50	7		22.50	28	
	0700	13" wide, 3 1/2" tapers to 2 1/2", 12" wall		50	.320		12.15	8.40		20.55	26.50	
	0900	Slate, colored, unfading, honed, 12" wide, 1" thick		85	.188		15	4.95		19.95	24	
	0950	2" thick		70	.229		21	6		27	32.50	

04413 | Granite

		CREW	DAILY OUTPUT	LABOR-HOURS	UNIT	MAT.	LABOR	EQUIP.	TOTAL	TOTAL INCL O&P	
300	0010	**GRANITE** Cut to size										300
	0050	Veneer, polished face, 3/4" to 1-1/2" thick										
	0150	Low price, gray, light gray, etc. **CN**	D-10	130	.308	S.F.	18.75	8.50	3.27	30.52	37	
	0220	High price, red, black, etc. **CN**	"	130	.308	"	32	8.50	3.27	43.77	51.50	
	0300	1-1/2" to 2-1/2" thick, veneer										
	0350	Low price, gray, light gray, etc.	D-10	130	.308	S.F.	21	8.50	3.27	32.77	39.50	
	0550	High price, red, black, etc.	"	130	.308	"	36.50	8.50	3.27	48.27	56.50	
	0700	2-1/2" to 4" thick, veneer										
	0750	Low price, gray, light gray, etc.	D-10	110	.364	S.F.	26	10.05	3.87	39.92	48	
	0950	High price, red, black, etc.	"	110	.364		41.50	10.05	3.87	55.42	65.50	
	1000	For bush hammered finish, deduct					5%					
	1050	Coarse rubbed finish, deduct					10%					
	1100	Honed finish, deduct					5%					
	1150	Thermal finish, deduct					18%					
	2450	For radius under 5', add				L.F.	100%					
	2500	Steps, copings, etc., finished on more than one surface										
	2550	Minimum	D-10	50	.800	C.F.	73	22	8.50	103.50	123	
	2600	Maximum	"	50	.800	"	109	22	8.50	139.50	163	
	2800	Pavers, 4" x 4" x 4" blocks, split face and joints										
	2850	Minimum	D-11	80	.300	S.F.	10.40	8.40		18.80	24.50	
	2900	Maximum	"	80	.300	"	20.50	8.40		28.90	35.50	
	3500	Curbing, city street type, See Division 02770-225										
	4000	Soffits, 2" thick, minimum	D-13	35	1.371	S.F.	31	38.50	12.15	81.65	107	
	4100	Maximum		35	1.371		62.50	38.50	12.15	113.15	141	
	4200	4" thick, minimum		35	1.371		42.50	38.50	12.15	93.15	119	
	4300	Maximum		35	1.371		80	38.50	12.15	130.65	160	

04414 | Limestone

		CREW	DAILY OUTPUT	LABOR-HOURS	UNIT	MAT.	LABOR	EQUIP.	TOTAL	TOTAL INCL O&P	
400	0010	**LIMESTONE** See also Ashlar Veneer, division 04414-400										400
	0020	Veneer facing panels										
	0500	Texture finish, light stick, 4-1/2" thick, 5' x 12'	D-4	300	.107	S.F.	20	2.78	.43	23.21	26.50	
	0750	5" thick, 5' x 14' panels	D-10	275	.145		24	4.02	1.55	29.57	34.50	
	1000	Sugarcube finish, 2" Thick, 3' x 5' panels		275	.145		11.90	4.02	1.55	17.47	21	
	1050	3" Thick, 4' x 9' panels		275	.145		12.40	4.02	1.55	17.97	21.50	
	1200	4" Thick, 5' x 11' panels		275	.145		16.55	4.02	1.55	22.12	26	
	1400	Sugarcube, textured finish, 4-1/2" thick, 5' x 12'		275	.145		21.50	4.02	1.55	27.07	31.50	

4 MASONRY

Important: See the Reference Section for critical supporting data - Reference Nos., Crews, & City Cost Indexes

04414 | Limestone

			CREW	DAILY OUTPUT	LABOR-HOURS	UNIT	2001 BARE COSTS				TOTAL INCL O&P
							MAT.	LABOR	EQUIP.	TOTAL	
400	1450	5" thick, 5' x 14' panels	D-10	275	.145	S.F.	25	4.02	1.55	30.57	35.50	400
	2000	Coping, sugarcube finish, top & 2 sides		30	1.333	C.F.	55	37	14.15	106.15	133	
	2100	Sills, lintels, jambs, trim, stops, sugarcube finish, average		20	2		49.50	55.50	21.50	126.50	163	
	2150	Detailed		20	2	↓	65.50	55.50	21.50	142.50	181	
	2300	Steps, extra hard, 14" wide, 6" rise	↓	50	.800	L.F.	45	22	8.50	75.50	93	
	3000	Quoins, plain finish, 6"x12"x12"	D-12	25	1.280	Ea.	108	34.50		142.50	172	
	3050	6"x16"x24"	"	25	1.280	"	144	34.50		178.50	211	

04415 | Marble

			CREW	DAILY OUTPUT	LABOR-HOURS	UNIT	2001 BARE COSTS				TOTAL INCL O&P
							MAT.	LABOR	EQUIP.	TOTAL	
500	0011	**MARBLE** Ashlar, split face, 4" + or - thick, random										500
	0040	lengths 1' to 4' & heights 2" to 7-1/2", average	D-8	175	.229	S.F.	13.45	6.15		19.60	24.50	
	0100	Base, polished, 3/4" or 7/8" thick, polished, 6" high	D-10	65	.615	L.F.	12.25	17	6.55	35.80	46.50	
	0300	Carvings or bas relief, from templates, average		80	.500	S.F.	109	13.85	5.30	128.15	147	
	0350	Maximum	↓	80	.500	"	255	13.85	5.30	274.15	305	
	0600	Columns, cornices, mouldings, etc.										
	0650	Hand or special machine cut, average	D-10	35	1.143	C.F.	109	31.50	12.15	152.65	182	
	0700	Maximum	"	35	1.143	"	234	31.50	12.15	277.65	320	
	1000	Facing, polished finish, cut to size, 3/4" to 7/8" thick										
	1050	Average	D-10	130	.308	S.F.	17.95	8.50	3.27	29.72	36.50	
	1100	Maximum		130	.308		41.50	8.50	3.27	53.27	62.50	
	1300	1-1/4" thick, average		125	.320		26	8.85	3.40	38.25	46	
	1350	Maximum		125	.320		52	8.85	3.40	64.25	74.50	
	1500	2" thick, average		120	.333		30	9.20	3.54	42.74	51	
	1550	Maximum	↓	120	.333	↓	52	9.20	3.54	64.74	75.50	
	2200	Window sills, 6" x 3/4" thick	D-1	85	.188	L.F.	6.75	4.95		11.70	15.10	
	2500	Flooring, polished tiles, 12" x 12" x 3/8" thick										
	2510	Thin set, average	D-11	90	.267	S.F.	8.30	7.50		15.80	20.50	
	2600	Maximum		90	.267		30	7.50		37.50	44.50	
	2700	Mortar bed, average		65	.369		8.45	10.35		18.80	25.50	
	2740	Maximum	↓	65	.369		27.50	10.35		37.85	46.50	
	2780	Travertine, 3/8" thick, average	D-10	130	.308		11.50	8.50	3.27	23.27	29.50	
	2790	Maximum	"	130	.308		28	8.50	3.27	39.77	47.50	
	2800	Patio tile, non-slip, 1/2" thick, flame finish	D-11	75	.320	↓	11.70	9		20.70	27	
	2900	Shower or toilet partitions, 7/8" thick partitions										
	3050	3/4" or 1-1/4" thick stiles, polished 2 sides, average	D-11	75	.320	S.F.	35	9		44	52.50	
	3201	Soffits, add to above prices				"	20%	100%				
	3210	Stairs, risers, 7/8" thick x 6" high	D-10	115	.348	L.F.	11.75	9.60	3.70	25.05	32	
	3360	Treads, 12" wide x 1-1/4" thick	"	115	.348	"	17.15	9.60	3.70	30.45	38	
	3500	Thresholds, 3' long, 7/8" thick, 4" to 5" wide, plain	D-12	24	1.333	Ea.	12.95	35.50		48.45	69.50	
	3550	Beveled		24	1.333	"	15.10	35.50		50.60	71.50	
	3700	Window stools, polished, 7/8" thick, 5" wide	↓	85	.376	L.F.	12.10	10.10		22.20	29	

04417 | Sandstone

			CREW	DAILY OUTPUT	LABOR-HOURS	UNIT	2001 BARE COSTS				TOTAL INCL O&P
							MAT.	LABOR	EQUIP.	TOTAL	
700	0011	**SANDSTONE OR BROWNSTONE**										700
	0100	Sawed face veneer, 2-1/2" thick, to 2' x 4' panels	D-10	130	.308	S.F.	15.65	8.50	3.27	27.42	34	
	0150	4" thick, to 3'-6" x 8'panels		100	.400		15.65	11.05	4.25	30.95	39	
	0300	Split face, random sizes	↓	100	.400	↓	9.20	11.05	4.25	24.50	32	
	0350	Cut stone trim (limestone)										
	0360	Ribbon stone, 4" thick, 5' pieces	D-8	120	.333	Ea.	113	9		122	138	
	0370	Cove stone, 4" thick, 5' pieces		105	.381		113	10.25		123.25	141	
	0380	Cornice stone, 10" to 12" wide		90	.444		140	11.95		151.95	173	
	0390	Band stone, 4" thick, 5' pieces		145	.276		72.50	7.45		79.95	91	
	0410	Window and door trim, 3" to 4" wide		160	.250		61.50	6.75		68.25	78	
	0420	Key stone, 18" long	↓	60	.667	↓	64.50	17.95		82.45	99	

MASONRY **4**

04418	Slate	CREW	DAILY OUTPUT	LABOR-HOURS	UNIT	2001 BARE COSTS				TOTAL INCL O&P
						MAT.	LABOR	EQUIP.	TOTAL	
800	0010 **SLATE** Pennsylvania, blue gray to gray black; Vermont,									800
	0050 Unfading green, mottled green & purple, gray & purple									
	0100 Virginia, blue black									
	0200 Exterior paving, natural cleft, 1" thick									
	0500 24" x 24", Pennsylvania	D-12	120	.267	S.F.	8.90	7.15		16.05	21
	0550 Vermont		120	.267		11.65	7.15		18.80	24
	0600 Virginia		120	.267		13.05	7.15		20.20	25.50
	1000 Interior flooring, natural cleft, 1/2" thick									
	1300 24" x 24" Pennsylvania	D-12	120	.267	S.F.	6.10	7.15		13.25	17.80
	1350 Vermont		120	.267		9.15	7.15		16.30	21
	1400 Virginia		120	.267		9.45	7.15		16.60	21.50
	2000 Facing panels, 1-1/4" thick, to 4' x 4' panels									
	2100 Natural cleft finish, Pennsylvania	D-10	180	.222	S.F.	18.15	6.15	2.36	26.66	32
	2110 Vermont		180	.222		18.90	6.15	2.36	27.41	33
	2120 Virginia		180	.222		21	6.15	2.36	29.51	35.50
	2150 Sand rubbed finish, surface, add					1.97			1.97	2.17
	2200 Honed finish, add					3.88			3.88	4.27
	2500 Ribbon, natural cleft finish, 1" thick, to 9 S.F.	D-10	80	.500		8.35	13.85	5.30	27.50	36.50
	2700 1-1/2" thick		78	.513		10.85	14.20	5.45	30.50	40
	2850 2" thick		76	.526		13.10	14.55	5.60	33.25	43
	3000 Roofing, see division 07310-800									
	3500 Stair treads, sand finish, 1" thick x 12" wide									
	3600 3 L.F. to 6 L.F.	D-10	120	.333	L.F.	15	9.20	3.54	27.74	34.50
	3700 Ribbon, sand finish, 1" thick x 12" wide									
	3750 To 6 L.F.	D-10	120	.333	L.F.	10.05	9.20	3.54	22.79	29
	4000 Stools or sills, sand finish, 1" thick, 6" wide	D-12	160	.200		7.25	5.35		12.60	16.25
	4200 10" wide		90	.356		11	9.50		20.50	27
	4400 2" thick, 6" wide		140	.229		11.70	6.10		17.80	22.50
	4600 10" wide		90	.356		17.50	9.50		27	34
	4800 For lengths over 3', add					25%				

04420	Collected Stone									
500	0011 **LIGHTWEIGHT NATURAL STONE** Lava type									500
	0100 Veneer, rubble face, sawed back, irregular shapes	D-10	130	.308	S.F.	5.25	8.50	3.27	17.02	22.50
	0200 Sawed face and back, irregular shapes	"	130	.308	"	5.25	8.50	3.27	17.02	22.50
750	0011 **ROUGH STONE WALL**, Dry									750
	0100 Random fieldstone, under 18" thick	D-12	60	.533	C.F.	10.25	14.30		24.55	33.50
	0150 Over 18" thick	"	63	.508	"	12.50	13.60		26.10	35

04430	Quarried Stone									
100	0011 **ASHLAR VENEER** 4" + or - thk, random or random rectangular [R04430-500]									100
	0150 Sawn face, split joints, low priced stone	D-8	140	.286	S.F.	4.98	7.70		12.68	17.40
	0200 Medium priced stone		130	.308		7.50	8.30		15.80	21
	0300 High priced stone		120	.333		10	9		19	25
	0600 Seam face, split joints, medium price stone		125	.320		8.50	8.60		17.10	22.50
	0700 High price stone		120	.333		10.75	9		19.75	26
	1000 Split or rock face, split joints, medium price stone		125	.320		8.50	8.60		17.10	22.50
	1100 High price stone		120	.333		11	9		20	26

4 MASONRY

Important: See the Reference Section for critical supporting data - Reference Nos., Crews, & City Cost Indexes

04500 | Refractories

04550 | Flue Liners

			CREW	DAILY OUTPUT	LABOR-HOURS	UNIT	2001 BARE COSTS MAT.	LABOR	EQUIP.	TOTAL	TOTAL INCL O&P	
250	0010	**FLUE LINING** Including mortar joints, 8" x 8"	D-1	125	.128	V.L.F.	2.98	3.36		6.34	8.50	250
	0100	8" x 12"		103	.155		3.88	4.08		7.96	10.55	
	0200	12" x 12"		93	.172		5.95	4.52		10.47	13.50	
	0300	12" x 18"		84	.190		9.10	5		14.10	17.75	
	0400	18" x 18"		75	.213		12.55	5.60		18.15	22.50	
	0500	20" x 20"		66	.242		17.85	6.35		24.20	29.50	
	0600	24" x 24"		56	.286		22.50	7.50		30	36	
	1000	Round, 18" diameter		66	.242		23.50	6.35		29.85	36	
	1100	24" diameter	↓	47	.340	↓	16.55	8.95		25.50	32	

04580 | Refractory Brick

			CREW	DAILY OUTPUT	LABOR-HOURS	UNIT	2001 BARE COSTS MAT.	LABOR	EQUIP.	TOTAL	TOTAL INCL O&P	
250	0010	**FIRE BRICK** 9" x 2-1/2" x 4-1/2", low duty, 2000° F	D-1	.60	26.667	M	815	700		1,515	1,975	250
	0050	High duty, 3000° F	"	.60	26.667	"	1,500	700		2,200	2,725	
260	0010	**FIRE CLAY** Gray, high duty, 100 lb. bag				Bag	42			42	46	260
	0050	100 lb. drum, premixed (400 brick per drum)				Drum	52			52	57	
270	0010	**FIREPLACE** For prefabricated fireplace, see div. 10305-100										270
	0100	Brick fireplace, not incl. foundations or chimneys										
	0110	30" x 29" opening, incl. chamber, plain brickwork	D-1	.40	40	Ea.	375	1,050		1,425	2,050	
	0200	Fireplace box only (110 brick)	"	2	8	"	120	210		330	455	
	0300	For elaborate brickwork and details, add					35%	35%				
	0400	For hearth, brick & stone, add	D-1	2	8	Ea.	135	210		345	475	
	0410	For steel angle, damper, cleanouts, add		4	4		97	105		202	269	
	0600	Plain brickwork, incl. metal circulator		.50	32	↓	725	840		1,565	2,100	
	0800	Face brick only, standard size, 8" x 2-2/3" x 4"	↓	.30	53.333	M	380	1,400		1,780	2,600	

04700 | Simulated Masonry

04710 | Simulated Brick

			CREW	DAILY OUTPUT	LABOR-HOURS	UNIT	2001 BARE COSTS MAT.	LABOR	EQUIP.	TOTAL	TOTAL INCL O&P	
600	0010	**SIMULATED BRICK** Aluminum, baked on colors	1 Carp	200	.040	S.F.	2.25	1.17		3.42	4.30	600
	0050	Fiberglass panels		200	.040		2.35	1.17		3.52	4.41	
	0100	Urethane pieces cemented in mastic		150	.053		4.50	1.55		6.05	7.40	
	0150	Vinyl siding panels	↓	200	.040		1.80	1.17		2.97	3.80	
	0160	Cement base, brick, incl. mastic	D-1	100	.160	↓	3	4.20		7.20	9.80	
	0170	Corner		50	.320	V.L.F.	7.25	8.40		15.65	21	
	0180	Stone face, incl. mastic		100	.160	S.F.	7	4.20		11.20	14.20	
	0190	Corner	↓	50	.320	V.L.F.	7.75	8.40		16.15	21.50	

04730 | Simulated Stone

			CREW	DAILY OUTPUT	LABOR-HOURS	UNIT	2001 BARE COSTS MAT.	LABOR	EQUIP.	TOTAL	TOTAL INCL O&P	
600	0010	**SIMULATED STONE**										600
	0100	Insulated fiberglass panels, 5/8" ply backer	L-4	200	.120	S.F.	9	3.27		12.27	15.05	

04810 | Unit Masonry Assemblies

		CREW	DAILY OUTPUT	LABOR-HOURS	UNIT	2001 BARE COSTS MAT.	LABOR	EQUIP.	TOTAL	TOTAL INCL O&P	
160	0010	**CHIMNEY** See Div. 03310 for foundation, add to prices below R04210-050									**160**
	0100	Brick, 16" x 16", 8" flue, scaff. not incl.	D-1	18.20	.879	V.L.F.	16.50	23		39.50	53.50
	0150	16" x 20" with one 8" x 12" flue		16	1		20	26.50		46.50	62.50
	0200	16" x 24" with two 8" x 8" flues		14	1.143		28.50	30		58.50	78
	0250	20" x 20" with one 12" x 12" flue		13.70	1.168		19.95	30.50		50.45	69.50
	0300	20" x 24" with two 8" x 12" flues		12	1.333		32.50	35		67.50	89.50
	0350	20" x 32" with two 12" x 12" flues	↓	10	1.600		33	42		75	102
	1800	Metal, high temp. steel jacket, factory lining, 24" diam.	E-2	65	.862		174	27.50	19.85	221.35	261
	1900	60" diameter	"	30	1.867		630	59.50	43	732.50	845
	2100	Poured concrete, brick lining, 200' high x 10' diam.					5,450			5,450	6,000
	2200	200' high x 18' diameter									4,995
	2400	250' high x 9' diameter									3,920
	2500	300' x 14' diameter									4,690
	2700	400' high x 18' diameter									5,255
	2800	500' x 20' diameter	↓			↓	9,700			9,700	10,700
170	0010	**COLUMNS** Brick, scaffolding not included R04210-100									**170**
	0050	8" x 8", 9 brick	D-1	56	.286	V.L.F.	3.79	7.50		11.29	15.75
	0100	12" x 8", 13.5 brick		37	.432		5.70	11.35		17.05	24
	0200	12" x 12", 20 brick		25	.640		8.40	16.80		25.20	35.50
	0300	16" x 12", 27 brick		19	.842		11.35	22		33.35	46.50
	0400	16" x 16", 36 brick		14	1.143		15.15	30		45.15	63
	0500	20" x 16", 45 brick		11	1.455		18.95	38		56.95	80
	0600	20" x 20", 56 brick		9	1.778		23.50	46.50		70	98
	0700	24" x 20", 68 brick		7	2.286		28.50	60		88.50	125
	0800	24" x 24", 81 brick		6	2.667		34	70		104	146
	1000	36" x 36", 182 brick	↓	3	5.333	↓	76.50	140		216.50	300
180	0010	**CONCRETE BLOCK COLUMN** or pilaster. Scaffolding not included.									**180**
	0050	Including vertical reinforcing (4-#4 bars) and grout									
	0160	1 piece unit, 16" x 16"	D-1	26	.615	V.L.F.	8.90	16.15		25.05	35
	0170	2 piece units, 16" x 20"		24	.667		12.05	17.50		29.55	40.50
	0180	20" x 20"		22	.727		17.65	19.10		36.75	49
	0190	22" x 24"		18	.889		21.50	23.50		45	60
	0200	20" x 32"	↓	14	1.143	↓	22	30		52	71
210	0010	**CONCRETE BLOCK, PARTITIONS** Scaffolding not included R04220-200									**210**
	0100	Acoustical slotted block									
	0200	NRC .50, type A, 4" thick	D-8	315	.127	S.F.	2.37	3.42		5.79	7.90
	0210	NRC .65 type R, 4" thick		315	.127		2.85	3.42		6.27	8.45
	0250	NRC .50, type A, 6" thick		290	.138		2.67	3.72		6.39	8.70
	0260	NRC .65 type R, 6" thick		290	.138		3.63	3.72		7.35	9.75
	0400	NRC .45 type A-1, 8" thick		265	.151		4.59	4.07		8.66	11.35
	0410	NRC .55, type Q, 8" thick		265	.151		5.25	4.07		9.32	12.05
	0500	NRC .60 type R, 8" thick		265	.151		3.74	4.07		7.81	10.40
	0600	NRC .65 type RR, 8" thick		265	.151		10.70	4.07		14.77	18.05
	0700	NRC .65 type 4R-RF, 8" thick		265	.151		5.10	4.07		9.17	11.95
	0710	NRC .70 type R, 12" thick	↓	245	.163	↓	5.60	4.40		10	13
	1000	Lightweight block, tooled joints, 2 sides, hollow									
	1100	Not reinforced, 8" x 16" x 4" thick	D-8	440	.091	S.F.	.99	2.45		3.44	4.87
	1150	6" thick		410	.098		1.38	2.63		4.01	5.60
	1200	8" thick		385	.104		1.72	2.80		4.52	6.20
	1250	10" thick	↓	370	.108		2.26	2.91		5.17	7
	1300	12" thick	D-9	350	.137		2.73	3.60		6.33	8.55
	2000	Not reinforced, 8" x 24" x 4" thick, hollow		460	.104		.70	2.74		3.44	5
	2100	6" thick	↓	440	.109	↓	.97	2.87		3.84	5.50

Important: See the Reference Section for critical supporting data - Reference Nos., Crews, & City Cost Indexes

04810 | Unit Masonry Assemblies

			CREW	DAILY OUTPUT	LABOR-HOURS	UNIT	2001 BARE COSTS				TOTAL INCL O&P	
							MAT.	LABOR	EQUIP.	TOTAL		
210	2150	8" thick — R04220-200	D-9	415	.116	S.F.	1.22	3.04		4.26	6.05	**210**
	2200	10" thick		385	.125		1.60	3.28		4.88	6.80	
	2250	12" thick	↓	365	.132		1.92	3.46		5.38	7.45	
	2800	Solid, not reinforced, 8" x 16" x 2" thick	D-8	440	.091		.83	2.45		3.28	4.70	
	2900	4" thick		420	.095		1.14	2.57		3.71	5.20	
	2950	6" thick		390	.103		1.57	2.76		4.33	6	
	3000	8" thick		365	.110		2.14	2.95		5.09	6.90	
	3050	10" thick	↓	350	.114		2.79	3.08		5.87	7.85	
	3100	12" thick	D-9	330	.145	↓	4.06	3.82		7.88	10.35	
	4000	Regular block, tooled joints, 2 sides, hollow										
	4100	Not reinforced, 8" x 16" x 4" thick	D-8	430	.093	S.F.	.86	2.51		3.37	4.81	
	4150	6" thick		400	.100		1.31	2.69		4	5.60	
	4200	8" thick **CN**		375	.107		1.41	2.87		4.28	6	
	4250	10" thick	↓	360	.111		2	2.99		4.99	6.85	
	4300	12" thick	D-9	340	.141		2.09	3.71		5.80	8.05	
	4500	Reinforced alternate courses, 8" x 16" x 4" thick	D-8	425	.094		.93	2.54		3.47	4.95	
	4550	6" thick		395	.101		1.39	2.73		4.12	5.75	
	4600	8" thick		370	.108		1.49	2.91		4.40	6.15	
	4650	10" thick	↓	355	.113		2.12	3.04		5.16	7	
	4700	12" thick	D-9	335	.143		2.17	3.77		5.94	8.20	
	4900	Solid, not reinforced, 2" thick	D-8	435	.092		.75	2.48		3.23	4.65	
	5000	3" thick		430	.093		.86	2.51		3.37	4.82	
	5050	4" thick		415	.096		1.21	2.60		3.81	5.35	
	5100	6" thick		385	.104		1.41	2.80		4.21	5.90	
	5150	8" thick	↓	360	.111		2.17	2.99		5.16	7	
	5200	12" thick	D-9	325	.148		3.26	3.88		7.14	9.60	
	5500	Solid, reinforced alternate courses, 4" thick	D-8	420	.095		1.26	2.57		3.83	5.35	
	5550	6" thick		380	.105		1.47	2.84		4.31	6	
	5600	8" thick	↓	355	.113		2.23	3.04		5.27	7.15	
	5650	12" thick	D-9	320	.150	↓	2.84	3.94		6.78	9.25	
300	0010	**FACING PANELS** Stone aggregate mounted on plywood,										**300**
	0020	See division 07440-200										
400	0010	**LINTELS** See division 05120-480										**400**
540	0010	**WALLS** Cavity, brick and CMU, no scaffolding										**540**
	0200	4" face brick, 4" block	D-8	165	.242	S.F.	3.85	6.55		10.40	14.35	
	0400	6" block		145	.276		4.27	7.45		11.72	16.20	
	0600	8" block	↓	125	.320	↓	4.33	8.60		12.93	18.05	
650	0010	**WALLS** Building brick, including mortar — R04210-120										**650**
	0060	Includes 3% brick waste and 25% mortar waste										
	0140	4" thick, facing, 4" x 2-2/3" x 8" — R04210-180	D-8	1.45	27.586	M	297	745		1,042	1,475	
	0150	4" thick, as back-up, 6.75 bricks per S.F.		1.60	25		297	675		972	1,375	
	0204	8" thick, 13.50 bricks per S.F. — R04210-185		1.80	22.222		305	600		905	1,250	
	0250	12" thick, 20.25 bricks per S.F.		1.90	21.053		305	565		870	1,200	
	0304	16" thick, 27.00 bricks per S.F.		2	20		310	540		850	1,175	
	0500	Reinforced, 4" wall, 4" x 2-2/3" x 8"		1.40	28.571		310	770		1,080	1,550	
	0550	8" thick, 13.50 bricks per S.F.		1.75	22.857		370	615		985	1,350	
	0600	12" thick, 20.25 bricks per S.F.		1.85	21.622		375	580		955	1,300	
	0650	16" thick, 27.00 bricks per S.F.	↓	1.95	20.513	↓	375	555		930	1,275	
	0790	Alternate method of figuring by square foot										
	0800	4" wall, face, 4" x 2-2/3" x 8"	D-8	215	.186	S.F.	2.87	5		7.87	10.90	
	0850	4" thick, as back up, 6.75 bricks per S.F.		240	.167		2.01	4.49		6.50	9.15	
	0900	8" thick wall, 13.50 brick per S.F.		135	.296		4.10	8		12.10	16.85	
	1000	12" thick wall, 20.25 bricks per S.F.		95	.421		6.15	11.35		17.50	24.50	
	1050	16" thick wall, 27.00 bricks per S.F.		75	.533		8.30	14.35		22.65	31	
	1200	Reinforced, 4" x 2-2/3" x 8" , 4" wall	↓	205	.195	↓	2.02	5.25		7.27	10.30	

04810 | Unit Masonry Assemblies

			CREW	DAILY OUTPUT	LABOR-HOURS	UNIT	MAT.	LABOR	EQUIP.	TOTAL	TOTAL INCL O&P	
							2001 BARE COSTS					
650	1250	8" thick wall, 13.50 brick per S.F. [R04210-120]	D-8	130	.308	S.F.	4.12	8.30		12.42	17.35	**650**
	1300	12" thick wall, 20.25 bricks per S.F.		90	.444		6.20	11.95		18.15	25.50	
	1350	16" thick wall, 27.00 bricks per S.F. [R04210-180]	↓	70	.571	↓	8.35	15.40		23.75	33	
670	0010	**STEPS** With select common	D-1	.30	53.333	M	310	1,400		1,710	2,525	**670**

04840 | Prefabricated Masonry Panels

			CREW	DAILY OUTPUT	LABOR-HOURS	UNIT	MAT.	LABOR	EQUIP.	TOTAL	TOTAL INCL O&P	
900	0010	**WALL PANELS** Prefabricated, 4" thick, minimum	C-11	775	.093	S.F.	4.82	2.98	1.91	9.71	12.65	**900**
	0100	Maximum	"	500	.144		7	4.62	2.96	14.58	19.05	
	0200	4" brick & 2" concrete back-up, add					50%					
	0300	4" brick & 1" urethane & 3" concrete back-up, add				↓	70%					

04900 | Masonry Restoration & Cleaning

04910 | Unit Masonry Restoration

			CREW	DAILY OUTPUT	LABOR-HOURS	UNIT	MAT.	LABOR	EQUIP.	TOTAL	TOTAL INCL O&P	
							2001 BARE COSTS					
600	0010	**NEEDLE BEAM MASONRY** Incl. shoring 10' x 10' opening										**600**
	0400	Block, concrete, 8" thick	B-9	7.10	5.634	Ea.	30	131	25	186	266	
	0420	12" thick		6.70	5.970		44	139	26.50	209.50	295	
	0800	Brick, 4" thick with 8" backup block		5.70	7.018		44	163	31	238	340	
	1000	Brick, solid, 8" thick		6.20	6.452		30	150	28.50	208.50	300	
	1040	12" thick		4.90	8.163		44	190	36	270	385	
	1080	16" thick	↓	4.50	8.889		72.50	207	39	318.50	450	
	2000	Add for additional floors of shoring	B-1	6	4	↓	30	94		124	180	
750	0010	**SAWING** Brick or block by hand, per inch depth	D-5	300	.027	L.F.		.79		.79	1.22	**750**

04930 | Unit Masonry Cleaning

			CREW	DAILY OUTPUT	LABOR-HOURS	UNIT	MAT.	LABOR	EQUIP.	TOTAL	TOTAL INCL O&P	
200	0010	**CLEAN AND POINT** Smooth brick	1 Bric	300	.027	S.F.	.19	.79		.98	1.43	**200**
	0100	Rough brick	"	265	.030	"	.20	.89		1.09	1.60	
220	0010	**CLEANING MASONRY** No staging included, unless noted										**220**
	0200	Chemical cleaning, brush and wash, minimum	D-1	800	.020	S.F.	.04	.53		.57	.85	
	0220	Average		400	.040		.05	1.05		1.10	1.68	
	0240	Maximum	↓	330	.048		.07	1.27		1.34	2.05	
	0400	High pressure water only, minimum	B-9	2,000	.020			.47	.09	.56	.83	
	0420	Average		1,500	.027			.62	.12	.74	1.10	
	0440	Maximum		1,000	.040			.93	.18	1.11	1.65	
	2000	Steam cleaning, minimum		3,000	.013			.31	.06	.37	.54	
	2020	Average		2,500	.016			.37	.07	.44	.66	
	2040	Maximum	↓	1,500	.027			.62	.12	.74	1.10	
	4000	Add for masking doors and windows				↓					.80	
	4200	Add for pedestrian protection				Job					10%	
750	0010	**STEAM CLEAN** Building, not incl. scaffolding, minimum	B-9	3,000	.013	S.F.		.31	.06	.37	.54	**750**
	0100	Maximum		1,500	.027			.62	.12	.74	1.10	
	0300	Common face brick		1,750	.023			.53	.10	.63	.94	
	0400	Wire cut face brick	↓	1,250	.032	↓		.74	.14	.88	1.32	
900	0010	**WASHING BRICK** Acid wash, smooth brick [R04930-100]	1 Bric	560	.014	S.F.	.02	.42		.44	.67	**900**
	0050	Rough brick		400	.020		.03	.59		.62	.95	
	0060	Stone, acid wash	↓	600	.013	↓	.04	.39		.43	.65	
	1000	Muriatic acid, price per gallon in 5 gallon lots				Gal.	4.50			4.50	4.95	

For information about Means Estimating Seminars, see yellow pages 11 and 12 in back of book

Important: See the Reference Section for critical supporting data - Reference Nos., Crews, & City Cost Indexes

Division 5
Metals

Estimating Tips

05050 Basic Metal Materials & Methods

- Nuts, bolts, washers, connection angles and plates can add a significant amount to both the tonnage of a structural steel job as well as the estimated cost. As a rule of thumb add 10% to the total weight to account for these accessories.

- Type 2 steel construction, commonly referred to as "simple construction," consists generally of field bolted connections with lateral bracing supplied by other elements of the building, such as masonry walls or x-bracing. The estimator should be aware, however, that shop connections may be accomplished by welding or bolting. The method may be particular to the fabrication shop and may have an impact on the estimated cost.

05200 Metal Joists

- In any given project the total weight of open web steel joists is determined by the loads to be supported and the design. However, economies can be realized in minimizing the amount of labor used to place the joists. This is done by maximizing the joist spacing and therefore minimizing the number of joists required to be installed on the job. Certain spacings and locations may be required by the design, but in other cases maximizing the spacing and keeping it as uniform as possible will keep the costs down.

05300 Metal Deck

- The takeoff and estimating of metal deck involves more than simply the area of the floor or roof and the type of deck specified or shown on the drawings. Many different sizes and types of openings may exist. Small openings for individual pipes or conduits may be drilled after the floor/roof is installed, but larger openings may require special deck lengths as well as reinforcing or structural support. The estimator should determine who will be supplying this reinforcing. Additionally, some deck terminations are part of the deck package, such as screed angles and pour stops, and others will be part of the steel contract, such as angles attached to structural members and cast-in-place angles and plates. The estimator must ensure that all pieces are accounted for in the complete estimate.

05500 Metal Fabrications

- The most economical steel stairs are those that use common materials, standard details and most importantly, a uniform and relatively simple method of field assembly. Commonly available A36 channels and plates are very good choices for the main stringers of the stairs, as are angles and tees for the carrier members. Risers and treads are usually made by specialty shops, and it is most economical to use a typical detail in as many places as possible. The stairs should be pre-assembled and shipped directly to the site. The field connections should be simple and straightforward to be accomplished efficiently and with a minimum of equipment and labor.

Reference Numbers

Reference numbers are shown in bold squares at the beginning of some major classifications. These numbers refer to related items in the Reference Section. The reference information may be an estimating procedure, an alternate pricing method or technical information.

Note: Not all subdivisions listed here necessarily appear in this publication.

			DAILY	LABOR-			2001 BARE COSTS			TOTAL	
05090	**Metal Fastenings**	CREW	OUTPUT	HOURS	UNIT	MAT.	LABOR	EQUIP.	TOTAL	INCL O&P	
080	0010	**ANCHOR BOLTS**										080
	0020	See also divisions 03150 and 04080										
	0100	J-type, incl. nut, washer, 1/2" diameter x 6" long	2 Carp	70	.229	Ea.	.95	6.65		7.60	11.45	
	0110	12" long		65	.246		1.15	7.20		8.35	12.45	
	0120	18" long		60	.267		1.49	7.75		9.24	13.80	
	0130	3/4" diameter x 8" long		50	.320		1.48	9.35		10.83	16.25	
	0140	12" long		45	.356		1.88	10.35		12.23	18.25	
	0150	18" long		40	.400		2.40	11.65		14.05	21	
	0160	1" diameter x 12" long		35	.457		2.98	13.35		16.33	24.50	
	0170	18" long		30	.533		3.62	15.55		19.17	28.50	
	0180	24" long		25	.640		4.41	18.65		23.06	34	
	0190	36" long		20	.800		6.05	23.50		29.55	43	
	0200	1-1/2" diameter x 18" long		22	.727		8.80	21		29.80	42.50	
	0210	24" long		16	1		10.45	29		39.45	57	
	0300	L-type, incl. hex nuts, 3/4" diameter x 12" long		45	.356		1	10.35		11.35	17.30	
	0310	18" long		40	.400		1.28	11.65		12.93	19.65	
	0320	24" long		35	.457		1.56	13.35		14.91	22.50	
	0330	30" long		30	.533		1.98	15.55		17.53	26.50	
	0340	36" long		25	.640		2.26	18.65		20.91	31.50	
	0350	1" diameter x 12" long		35	.457		1.93	13.35		15.28	23	
	0360	18" long		30	.533		2.43	15.55		17.98	27	
	0370	24" long		25	.640		2.99	18.65		21.64	32.50	
	0380	30" long		23	.696		3.52	20.50		24.02	35.50	
	0390	36" long		20	.800		4.04	23.50		27.54	41	
	0400	42" long		18	.889		4.89	26		30.89	46	
	0410	48" long		15	1.067		5.50	31		36.50	54.50	
	0420	1-1/4" diameter x 18" long		25	.640		4.26	18.65		22.91	33.50	
	0430	24" long		20	.800		5.10	23.50		28.60	42	
	0440	30" long		20	.800		5.90	23.50		29.40	43	
	0450	36" long		18	.889		6.70	26		32.70	48	
	0460	42" long		16	1		7.60	29		36.60	54	
	0470	48" long		14	1.143		8.65	33.50		42.15	61.50	
	0480	54" long		12	1.333		10.20	39		49.20	72.50	
	0490	60" long		10	1.600		11.20	46.50		57.70	85.50	
	0500	1-1/2" diameter x 18" long		22	.727		6.65	21		27.65	40.50	
	0510	24" long		19	.842		7.75	24.50		32.25	47	
	0520	30" long		17	.941		8.80	27.50		36.30	52.50	
	0530	36" long		16	1		10.10	29		39.10	56.50	
	0540	42" long		15	1.067		11.55	31		42.55	61	
	0550	48" long		13	1.231		12.95	36		48.95	70.50	
	0560	54" long		11	1.455		15.80	42.50		58.30	84	
	0570	60" long		9	1.778		17.30	52		69.30	100	
	0580	1-3/4" diameter x 18" long		20	.800		10.75	23.50		34.25	48.50	
	0590	24" long		18	.889		12.50	26		38.50	54.50	
	0600	30" long		17	.941		14.60	27.50		42.10	59	
	0610	36" long		16	1		16.65	29		45.65	64	
	0620	42" long		14	1.143		18.65	33.50		52.15	72.50	
	0630	48" long		12	1.333		20.50	39		59.50	83.50	
	0640	54" long		10	1.600		25.50	46.50		72	101	
	0650	60" long		8	2		27.50	58.50		86	121	
	0660	2" diameter x 24" long		17	.941		16.90	27.50		44.40	61.50	
	0670	30" long		15	1.067		19.10	31		50.10	69.50	
	0680	36" long		13	1.231		21	36		57	79	
	0690	42" long		11	1.455		23.50	42.50		66	92.50	
	0700	48" long		10	1.600		27	46.50		73.50	103	
	0710	54" long		9	1.778		32	52		84	117	

5 METALS

Important: See the Reference Section for critical supporting data - Reference Nos., Crews, & City Cost Indexes

		05090	Metal Fastenings	CREW	DAILY OUTPUT	LABOR-HOURS	UNIT	2001 BARE COSTS				TOTAL INCL O&P	
								MAT.	LABOR	EQUIP.	TOTAL		
080	0720		60" long	2 Carp	8	2	Ea.	34.50	58.50		93	129	**080**
	0730		66" long		7	2.286		37	66.50		103.50	145	
	0740		72" long		6	2.667		40.50	77.50		118	167	
150	0010	**BOLTS & HEX NUTS** Steel, A307											**150**
	0100		1/4" diameter, 1/2" long				Ea.	.04			.04	.04	
	0200		1" long					.05			.05	.06	
	0300		2" long					.07			.07	.08	
	0400		3" long					.11			.11	.12	
	0500		4" long					.16			.16	.18	
	0600		3/8" diameter, 1" long					.10			.10	.11	
	0700		2" long					.13			.13	.14	
	0800		3" long					.18			.18	.20	
	0900		4" long					.24			.24	.26	
	1000		5" long					.25			.25	.28	
	1100		1/2" diameter, 1-1/2" long					.21			.21	.23	
	1200		2" long					.24			.24	.26	
	1300		4" long					.38			.38	.42	
	1400		6" long					.43			.43	.47	
	1500		8" long					.64			.64	.70	
	1600		5/8" diameter, 1-1/2" long					.33			.33	.36	
	1700		2" long					.37			.37	.41	
	1800		4" long					.50			.50	.55	
	1900		6" long					.62			.62	.68	
	2000		8" long					1.02			1.02	1.12	
	2100		10" long					1.27			1.27	1.40	
	2200		3/4" diameter, 2" long					.48			.48	.53	
	2300		4" long					.78			.78	.86	
	2400		6" long					.99			.99	1.09	
	2500		8" long					1.46			1.46	1.61	
	2600		10" long					1.90			1.90	2.09	
	2700		12" long					2.19			2.19	2.41	
	2800		1" diameter, 3" long					1.31			1.31	1.44	
	2900		6" long					1.96			1.96	2.16	
	3000		12" long					3.68			3.68	4.05	
	3100		For galvanized, add					75%					
	3200		For stainless, add					350%					
340	0010	**DRILLING** For anchors, up to 4" deep, incl. bit and layout											**340**
	0050		in concrete or brick walls and floors, no anchor										
	0100		Holes, 1/4" diameter	1 Carp	75	.107	Ea.	.09	3.11		3.20	4.96	
	0150		For each additional inch of depth, add		430	.019		.02	.54		.56	.87	
	0200		3/8" diameter		63	.127		.08	3.70		3.78	5.90	
	0250		For each additional inch of depth, add		340	.024		.02	.69		.71	1.09	
	0300		1/2" diameter		50	.160		.07	4.66		4.73	7.40	
	0350		For each additional inch of depth, add		250	.032		.02	.93		.95	1.48	
	0400		5/8" diameter		48	.167		.14	4.86		5	7.75	
	0450		For each additional inch of depth, add		240	.033		.03	.97		1	1.56	
	0500		3/4" diameter		45	.178		.14	5.20		5.34	8.25	
	0550		For each additional inch of depth, add		220	.036		.04	1.06		1.10	1.70	
	0600		7/8" diameter		43	.186		.18	5.40		5.58	8.70	
	0650		For each additional inch of depth, add		210	.038		.04	1.11		1.15	1.79	
	0700		1" diameter		40	.200		.21	5.85		6.06	9.35	
	0750		For each additional inch of depth, add		190	.042		.05	1.23		1.28	1.98	
	0800		1-1/4" diameter		38	.211		.30	6.15		6.45	9.95	
	0850		For each additional inch of depth, add		180	.044		.08	1.30		1.38	2.11	

5

METALS

		05090	Metal Fastenings	CREW	DAILY OUTPUT	LABOR-HOURS	UNIT	\multicolumn{4}{c}{2001 BARE COSTS}	TOTAL INCL O&P	
								MAT.	LABOR	EQUIP.	TOTAL		
340	0900		1-1/2" diameter	1 Carp	35	.229	Ea.	.48	6.65		7.13	10.95	340
	0950		For each additional inch of depth, add	↓	165	.048	↓	.12	1.41		1.53	2.34	
	1000		For ceiling installations, add						40%				
	1100		Drilling & layout for drywall or plaster walls, no anchor										
	1200		Holes, 1/4" diameter	1 Carp	150	.053	Ea.	.01	1.55		1.56	2.44	
	1300		3/8" diameter		140	.057		.01	1.67		1.68	2.62	
	1400		1/2" diameter		130	.062		.01	1.79		1.80	2.82	
	1500		3/4" diameter		120	.067		.02	1.94		1.96	3.06	
	1600		1" diameter		110	.073		.03	2.12		2.15	3.35	
	1700		1-1/4" diameter		100	.080		.04	2.33		2.37	3.69	
	1800		1-1/2" diameter	↓	90	.089		.06	2.59		2.65	4.12	
	1900		For ceiling installations, add				↓		40%				
380	0010	**EXPANSION ANCHORS** & shields											380
	0100		Bolt anchors for concrete, brick or stone, no layout and drilling										
	0200		Expansion shields, zinc, 1/4" diameter, 1" long, single	1 Carp	90	.089	Ea.	.92	2.59		3.51	5.05	
	0300		1-3/8" long, double		85	.094		1.01	2.74		3.75	5.40	
	0400		3/8" diameter, 2" long, single		85	.094		1.52	2.74		4.26	5.95	
	0500		2" long, double		80	.100		1.88	2.92		4.80	6.65	
	0600		1/2" diameter, 2-1/2" long, single		80	.100		2.51	2.92		5.43	7.30	
	0700		2-1/2" long, double		75	.107		2.43	3.11		5.54	7.55	
	0800		5/8" diameter, 2-5/8" long, single		75	.107		3.59	3.11		6.70	8.80	
	0900		3" long, double		70	.114		3.59	3.33		6.92	9.15	
	1000		3/4" diameter, 2-3/4" long, single		70	.114		5.35	3.33		8.68	11.05	
	1100		4" long, double	↓	65	.123		7.15	3.59		10.74	13.45	
	1410		Concrete anchor, w/rod & epoxy cartridge, 1-3/4" diameter x 15" long	E-22	20	1.200		77	36.50		113.50	143	
	1415		18" long		17	1.412		92.50	43		135.50	170	
	1420		2" diameter x 18" long		16	1.500		118	46		164	202	
	1425		24" long		15	1.600		154	49		203	247	
	1430		Chemical anchor, w/rod & epoxy cartridge, 3/4" diam. x 9-1/2" long		27	.889		11.35	27		38.35	55	
	1435		1" diameter x 11-3/4" long		24	1		21.50	30.50		52	71.50	
	1440		1-1/4" diameter x 14" long	↓	21	1.143		41	35		76	99.50	
	1500		Self drilling anchor, snap-off, for 1/4" diameter bolt	1 Carp	26	.308		.93	8.95		9.88	15.05	
	1600		3/8" diameter bolt		23	.348		1.39	10.15		11.54	17.40	
	1700		1/2" diameter bolt		20	.400		2.09	11.65		13.74	20.50	
	1800		5/8" diameter bolt		18	.444		3.57	12.95		16.52	24.50	
	1900		3/4" diameter bolt	↓	16	.500	↓	6.35	14.60		20.95	30	
	2100		Hollow wall anchors for gypsum wall board, plaster or tile										
	2300		1/8" diameter, short	1 Carp	160	.050	Ea.	.26	1.46		1.72	2.57	
	2400		Long		160	.050		.29	1.46		1.75	2.60	
	2500		3/16" diameter, short		150	.053		.60	1.55		2.15	3.09	
	2600		Long		150	.053		.66	1.55		2.21	3.16	
	2700		1/4" diameter, short		140	.057		.80	1.67		2.47	3.49	
	2800		Long		140	.057		.89	1.67		2.56	3.59	
	3000		Toggle bolts, bright steel, 1/8" diameter, 2" long		85	.094		.21	2.74		2.95	4.52	
	3100		4" long		80	.100		.33	2.92		3.25	4.92	
	3200		3/16" diameter, 3" long		80	.100		.34	2.92		3.26	4.93	
	3300		6" long		75	.107		.49	3.11		3.60	5.40	
	3400		1/4" diameter, 3" long		75	.107		.37	3.11		3.48	5.25	
	3500		6" long		70	.114		.53	3.33		3.86	5.80	
	3600		3/8" diameter, 3" long		70	.114		.66	3.33		3.99	5.95	
	3700		6" long		60	.133		1.20	3.89		5.09	7.40	
	3800		1/2" diameter, 4" long		60	.133		1.91	3.89		5.80	8.20	
	3900		6" long	↓	50	.160	↓	3.89	4.66		8.55	11.60	
	4000		Nailing anchors										
	4100		Nylon nailing anchor, 1/4" diameter, 1" long	1 Carp	320	.025	C	16.20	.73		16.93	18.95	
	4200		1-1/2" long		280	.029		21	.83		21.83	24.50	

5 METALS

Important: See the Reference Section for critical supporting data - Reference Nos., Crews, & City Cost Indexes

05090	Metal Fastenings		CREW	DAILY OUTPUT	LABOR-HOURS	UNIT	2001 BARE COSTS				TOTAL INCL O&P	
							MAT.	LABOR	EQUIP.	TOTAL		
380	4300	2" long		1 Carp	240	.033	C	34.50	.97		35.47	39.50	**380**
	4400	Metal nailing anchor, 1/4" diameter, 1" long			320	.025		22.50	.73		23.23	25.50	
	4500	1-1/2" long			280	.029		30.50	.83		31.33	35	
	4600	2" long	↓		240	.033	↓	39	.97		39.97	44	
	5000	Screw anchors for concrete, masonry,											
	5100	stone & tile, no layout or drilling included											
	5200	Jute fiber, #6, #8, & #10, 1" long		1 Carp	240	.033	Ea.	.20	.97		1.17	1.74	
	5300	#12, 1-1/2" long			200	.040		.29	1.17		1.46	2.14	
	5400	#14, 2" long			160	.050		.46	1.46		1.92	2.79	
	5500	#16, 2" long			150	.053		.48	1.55		2.03	2.96	
	5600	#20, 2" long			140	.057		.77	1.67		2.44	3.46	
	5700	Lag screw shields, 1/4" diameter, short			90	.089		.40	2.59		2.99	4.49	
	5800	Long			85	.094		.45	2.74		3.19	4.79	
	5900	3/8" diameter, short			85	.094		.65	2.74		3.39	5	
	6000	Long			80	.100		.80	2.92		3.72	5.45	
	6100	1/2" diameter, short			80	.100		1.11	2.92		4.03	5.80	
	6200	Long			75	.107		1.25	3.11		4.36	6.25	
	6300	3/4" diameter, short			70	.114		2.47	3.33		5.80	7.90	
	6400	Long			65	.123		3.16	3.59		6.75	9.10	
	6600	Lead, #6 & #8, 3/4" long			260	.031		.18	.90		1.08	1.60	
	6700	#10 - #14, 1-1/2" long			200	.040		.28	1.17		1.45	2.13	
	6800	#16 & #18, 1-1/2" long			160	.050		.38	1.46		1.84	2.70	
	6900	Plastic, #6 & #8, 3/4" long			260	.031		.04	.90		.94	1.44	
	7000	#8 & #10, 7/8" long			240	.033		.04	.97		1.01	1.56	
	7100	#10 & #12, 1" long			220	.036		.05	1.06		1.11	1.72	
	7200	#14 & #16, 1-1/2" long	↓		160	.050	↓	.07	1.46		1.53	2.36	
	8000	Wedge anchors, not including layout or drilling											
	8050	Carbon steel, 1/4" diameter, 1-3/4" long		1 Carp	150	.053	Ea.	.32	1.55		1.87	2.78	
	8100	3 1/4" long			145	.055		.42	1.61		2.03	2.98	
	8150	3/8" diameter, 2-1/4" long			150	.053		.60	1.55		2.15	3.09	
	8200	5" long			145	.055		1.06	1.61		2.67	3.69	
	8250	1/2" diameter, 2-3/4" long			140	.057		.84	1.67		2.51	3.53	
	8300	7" long			130	.062		1.44	1.79		3.23	4.39	
	8350	5/8" diameter, 3-1/2" long			130	.062		1.55	1.79		3.34	4.52	
	8400	8-1/2" long			115	.070		3.29	2.03		5.32	6.80	
	8450	3/4" diameter, 4-1/4" long			115	.070		1.99	2.03		4.02	5.35	
	8500	10" long			100	.080		4.50	2.33		6.83	8.60	
	8550	1" diameter, 6" long			100	.080		6.80	2.33		9.13	11.15	
	8575	9" long			80	.100		8.80	2.92		11.72	14.20	
	8600	12" long			80	.100		9.50	2.92		12.42	15	
	8650	1-1/4" diameter, 9" long			70	.114		13.25	3.33		16.58	19.80	
	8700	12" long	↓		60	.133	↓	13.30	3.89		17.19	21	
	8750	For type 303 stainless steel, add						350%					
	8800	For type 316 stainless steel, add						450%					
420	0010	**HIGH STRENGTH BOLTS**	R05090 -510										**420**
	0020	A325 Type 1, structural steel, bolt-nut-washer set											
	0100	1/2" diameter x 1-1/2" long		1 Sswk	120	.067	Ea.	.26	2.19		2.45	4.26	
	0120	2" long			120	.067		.26	2.19		2.45	4.26	
	0150	3" long			120	.067		.34	2.19		2.53	4.34	
	0170	5/8" diameter x 1-1/2" long			120	.067		.41	2.19		2.60	4.42	
	0180	2" long			120	.067		.44	2.19		2.63	4.45	
	0190	3" long			120	.067		.53	2.19		2.72	4.55	
	0200	3/4" diameter x 2" long			120	.067		.61	2.19		2.80	4.64	
	0220	3" long			115	.070		.70	2.29		2.99	4.92	
	0250	4" long			110	.073		.83	2.39		3.22	5.25	
	0300	6" long	↓	↓	105	.076	↓	1.03	2.50		3.53	5.65	

METALS | **5**

143

05090 | Metal Fastenings

			DAILY OUTPUT	LABOR-HOURS	UNIT	2001 BARE COSTS				TOTAL INCL O&P	
			CREW			MAT.	LABOR	EQUIP.	TOTAL		
420	0350	8" long	1 Sswk	95	.084	Ea.	1.64	2.77		4.41	6.80	**420**
	0360	7/8" diameter x 2" long R05090-510		115	.070		.88	2.29		3.17	5.10	
	0365	3" long		110	.073		1.01	2.39		3.40	5.45	
	0370	4" long		105	.076		1.17	2.50		3.67	5.85	
	0380	6" long		100	.080		1.43	2.63		4.06	6.35	
	0390	8" long		90	.089		2.16	2.92		5.08	7.70	
	0400	1" diameter x 2" long		105	.076		1.21	2.50		3.71	5.85	
	0420	3" long		105	.076		1.37	2.50		3.87	6.05	
	0450	4" long		105	.076		1.52	2.50		4.02	6.20	
	0500	6" long		90	.089		1.87	2.92		4.79	7.35	
	0550	8" long		85	.094		2.97	3.09		6.06	8.85	
	0600	1-1/4" diameter x 3" long		85	.094		2.82	3.09		5.91	8.70	
	0650	4" long		80	.100		3.03	3.29		6.32	9.30	
	0700	6" long		75	.107		3.94	3.50		7.44	10.70	
	0750	8" long	▼	70	.114	▼	4.80	3.75		8.55	12.10	
	1020	A490, bolt-nut-washer set										
	1100	1/2" diameter x 1-1/2" long	1 Sswk	120	.067	Ea.	.30	2.19		2.49	4.30	
	1120	2" long		120	.067		.35	2.19		2.54	4.36	
	1150	3" long		120	.067		.41	2.19		2.60	4.42	
	1170	5/8" diameter x 1-1/2" long		120	.067		.42	2.19		2.61	4.43	
	1180	2" long		120	.067		.46	2.19		2.65	4.48	
	1190	3" long		120	.067		.56	2.19		2.75	4.59	
	1200	3/4" diameter x 2" long		120	.067		.73	2.19		2.92	4.77	
	1220	3" long		115	.070		.99	2.29		3.28	5.25	
	1250	4" long		110	.073		.93	2.39		3.32	5.35	
	1300	6" long		105	.076		1.29	2.50		3.79	5.95	
	1350	8" long		95	.084		1.86	2.77		4.63	7.05	
	1360	7/8" diameter x 2" long		115	.070		1.04	2.29		3.33	5.30	
	1365	3" long		110	.073		1.14	2.39		3.53	5.60	
	1370	4" long		105	.076		1.36	2.50		3.86	6.05	
	1380	6" long		100	.080		1.81	2.63		4.44	6.75	
	1390	8" long		90	.089		2.61	2.92		5.53	8.15	
	1400	1" diameter x 2" long		105	.076		1.36	2.50		3.86	6.05	
	1420	3" long		105	.076		1.62	2.50		4.12	6.30	
	1450	4" long		105	.076		1.99	2.50		4.49	6.75	
	1500	6" long		90	.089		2.30	2.92		5.22	7.85	
	1550	8" long		85	.094		3.42	3.09		6.51	9.35	
	1600	1-1/4" diameter x 3" long		85	.094		3.32	3.09		6.41	9.25	
	1650	4" long		80	.100		3.68	3.29		6.97	10	
	1700	6" long		75	.107		4.75	3.50		8.25	11.60	
	1750	8" long	▼	70	.114	▼	5.95	3.75		9.70	13.30	
460	0005	**LAG SCREWS**										**460**
	0010	Steel, 1/4" diameter, 2" long	1 Carp	200	.040	Ea.	.05	1.17		1.22	1.88	
	0100	3/8" diameter, 3" long		150	.053		.15	1.55		1.70	2.60	
	0200	1/2" diameter, 3" long		130	.062		.25	1.79		2.04	3.09	
	0300	5/8" diameter, 3" long	▼	120	.067	▼	.62	1.94		2.56	3.72	
500	0005	**MACHINE SCREWS**										**500**
	0010	Steel, round head, #8 x 1" long				C	1.85			1.85	2.04	
	0110	#8 x 2" long					4.39			4.39	4.83	
	0200	#10 x 1" long					2.79			2.79	3.07	
	0300	#10 x 2" long				▼	5.30			5.30	5.85	
540	0010	**MACHINERY ANCHORS**, heavy duty, incl. sleeve, floating base nut,										**540**
	0020	lower stud & coupling nut, fiber plug, connecting stud, washer & nut.										

Important: See the Reference Section for critical supporting data - Reference Nos., Crews, & City Cost Indexes

05090 | Metal Fastenings

			CREW	DAILY OUTPUT	LABOR-HOURS	UNIT	2001 BARE COSTS				TOTAL INCL O&P	
							MAT.	LABOR	EQUIP.	TOTAL		
540	0030	For flush mounted embedment in poured concrete heavy equip. pads.										**540**
	0200	Material only, 1/2" diameter stud & bolt				Ea.	45			45	49.50	
	0300	5/8" diameter					50			50	55	
	0500	3/4" diameter					57.50			57.50	63	
	0600	7/8" diameter					62.50			62.50	69	
	0800	1" diameter					66			66	72.50	
	0900	1-1/4" diameter				▼	87.50			87.50	96.50	
580	0005	**POWDER ACTUATED** Tools & fasteners										**580**
	0010	Stud driver, .22 caliber, buy, minimum				Ea.	310			310	340	
	0100	Maximum				"	540			540	595	
	0300	Powder charges for above, low velocity				C	16.55			16.55	18.20	
	0400	Standard velocity					25			25	27.50	
	0600	Drive pins & studs, 1/4" & 3/8" diam., to 3" long, minimum					21.50			21.50	24	
	0700	Maximum				▼	53			53	58.50	
	0800	Pneumatic stud driver for 1/8" diameter studs				Ea.	1,875			1,875	2,050	
	0900	Drive pins for above, 1/2" to 3/4" long				M	410			410	450	
600	0010	**RIVETS**										**600**
	0100	Aluminum rivet & mandrel, 1/2" grip length x 1/8" diameter				C	4.53			4.53	4.98	
	0200	3/16" diameter					7			7	7.70	
	0300	Aluminum rivet, steel mandrel, 1/8" diameter					4.23			4.23	4.65	
	0400	3/16" diameter					8.90			8.90	9.80	
	0500	Copper rivet, steel mandrel, 1/8" diameter					5.50			5.50	6.05	
	0600	Monel rivet, steel mandrel, 1/8" diameter					19.30			19.30	21	
	0700	3/16" diameter					55.50			55.50	61	
	0800	Stainless rivet & mandrel, 1/8" diameter					12			12	13.20	
	0900	3/16" diameter					18.20			18.20	20	
	1000	Stainless rivet, steel mandrel, 1/8" diameter					7.65			7.65	8.40	
	1100	3/16" diameter					13.75			13.75	15.10	
	1200	Steel rivet and mandrel, 1/8" diameter					4.74			4.74	5.20	
	1300	3/16" diameter				▼	7.15			7.15	7.85	
	1400	Hand riveting tool, minimum				Ea.	88.50			88.50	97.50	
	1500	Maximum					465			465	510	
	1600	Power riveting tool, minimum					880			880	965	
	1700	Maximum				▼	2,000			2,000	2,200	
820	0010	**VIBRATION PADS**										**820**
	0300	Laminated synthetic rubber impregnated cotton duck, 1/2" thick	2 Sswk	20	.800	S.F.	50	26.50		76.50	103	
	0400	1" thick		20	.800		101	26.50		127.50	159	
	0600	Neoprene bearing pads, 1/2" thick		24	.667		18.90	22		40.90	60.50	
	0700	1" thick		20	.800		39	26.50		65.50	90	
	0900	Fabric reinforced neoprene, 5000 psi, 1/2" thick		24	.667		8.50	22		30.50	49	
	1000	1" thick		20	.800		17	26.50		43.50	66	
	1200	Felt surfaced vinyl pads, cork and sisal, 5/8" thick		24	.667		22	22		44	64	
	1300	1" thick		20	.800		40.50	26.50		67	92	
	1500	Teflon bonded to 10 ga. carbon steel, 1/32" layer		24	.667		36	22		58	79	
	1600	3/32" layer		24	.667		54	22		76	99	
	1800	Bonded to 10 ga. stainless steel, 1/32" layer		24	.667		65	22		87	111	
	1900	3/32" layer	▼	24	.667	▼	83	22		105	131	
	2100	Circular machine leveling pad & stud				Kip	5.30			5.30	5.80	
840	0005	**WELD SHEAR CONNECTORS**										**840**
	0010	3/4" diameter, 3-3/16" long	E-10	1,030	.016	Ea.	.34	.53	.50	1.37	1.88	
	0020	3-3/8" long		1,030	.016		.58	.53	.50	1.61	2.14	
	0200	3-7/8" long		1,030	.016		.38	.53	.50	1.41	1.93	
	0300	4-3/16" long		1,030	.016		.39	.53	.50	1.42	1.94	
	0500	4-7/8" long	▼	1,030	.016	▼	.44	.53	.50	1.47	1.99	

METALS

5

		05090	Metal Fastenings	CREW	DAILY OUTPUT	LABOR-HOURS	UNIT	2001 BARE COSTS				TOTAL INCL O&P	
								MAT.	LABOR	EQUIP.	TOTAL		
840	0600		5-3/16" long	E-10	1,030	.016	Ea.	.46	.53	.50	1.49	2.02	**840**
	0800		5-3/8" long		1,030	.016		.46	.53	.50	1.49	2.02	
	0900		6-3/16" long		1,000	.016		.50	.54	.52	1.56	2.10	
	1000		7-3/16" long		1,000	.016		.63	.54	.52	1.69	2.24	
	1100		8-3/16" long		1,000	.016		.69	.54	.52	1.75	2.31	
	1500		7/8" diameter, 3-11/16" long		1,030	.016		.53	.53	.50	1.56	2.09	
	1600		4-3/16" long		1,030	.016		.57	.53	.50	1.60	2.14	
	1700		5-3/16" long		1,030	.016		.64	.53	.50	1.67	2.21	
	1800		6-3/16" long		1,000	.016		.71	.54	.52	1.77	2.33	
	1900		7-3/16" long		1,000	.016		.80	.54	.52	1.86	2.43	
	2000		8-3/16" long	▼	1,000	.016	▼	.87	.54	.52	1.93	2.51	
860	0005	**WELD STUDS**											**860**
	0010		1/4" diameter, 2-11/16" long	E-10	1,030	.016	Ea.	.21	.53	.50	1.24	1.74	
	0100		4-1/8" long		1,030	.016		.20	.53	.50	1.23	1.73	
	0200		3/8" diameter, 4-1/8" long		1,030	.016		.23	.53	.50	1.26	1.76	
	0300		6-1/8" long		1,030	.016		.29	.53	.50	1.32	1.83	
	0400		1/2" diameter, 2-1/8" long		1,030	.016		.22	.53	.50	1.25	1.75	
	0500		3-1/8" long		1,030	.016		.27	.53	.50	1.30	1.81	
	0600		4-1/8" long		1,030	.016		.32	.53	.50	1.35	1.86	
	0700		5-5/16" long		1,030	.016		.39	.53	.50	1.42	1.94	
	0800		6-1/8" long		1,000	.016		.42	.54	.52	1.48	2.01	
	0900		8-1/8" long		1,000	.016		.59	.54	.52	1.65	2.20	
	1000		5/8" diameter, 2-11/16" long		1,030	.016		.38	.53	.50	1.41	1.93	
	1010		4-3/16" long		1,030	.016		.46	.53	.50	1.49	2.02	
	1100		6-9/16" long		1,000	.016		.60	.54	.52	1.66	2.21	
	1200		8-3/16" long	▼	1,000	.016	▼	.81	.54	.52	1.87	2.44	
880	0005	**WELD ROD**											**880**
	0010		Steel, type E6011 (all purpose), 1/8" dia, less than 500#				Lb.	1.34			1.34	1.47	
	0100		500# to 2,000#					1.21			1.21	1.33	
	0200		2,000# to 5,000#					1.14			1.14	1.25	
	0300		5/32" diameter, less than 500#					1.28			1.28	1.41	
	0310		500# to 2,000#					1.16			1.16	1.28	
	0320		2,000# to 5,000#					1.09			1.09	1.20	
	0400		3/16" dia, less than 500#					1.28			1.28	1.41	
	0500		500# to 2,000#					1.16			1.16	1.28	
	0600		2,000# to 5,000#					1.09			1.09	1.20	
	0620		Steel, type E6010 (pipe), 1/8" dia, less than 500#					1.47			1.47	1.62	
	0630		500# to 2,000#					1.31			1.31	1.44	
	0640		2,000# to 5,000#					1.22			1.22	1.34	
	0650		Steel, type E7018 (low hydrogen), 1/8" dia, less than 500#					1.26			1.26	1.39	
	0660		500# to 2,000# **CN**					1.14			1.14	1.25	
	0670		2,000# to 5,000#					1.08			1.08	1.19	
	0700		Steel, type E7024 (jet weld), 1/8" dia, less than 500#					1.34			1.34	1.47	
	0710		500# to 2,000#					1.21			1.21	1.33	
	0720		2,000# to 5,000#					1.14			1.14	1.25	
	1550		Aluminum, type 4043, 1/8" dia, less than 10#					5.15			5.15	5.65	
	1560		10# to 60#					4.42			4.42	4.86	
	1570		Over 60#					4.42			4.42	4.86	
	1600		Aluminum, type 5356, 1/8" dia, less than 10#					5.65			5.65	6.25	
	1610		10# to 60#					5.25			5.25	5.80	
	1620		Over 60#					5.25			5.25	5.80	
	1900		Cast iron (cold welding), 1/8" dia, less than 500#					16.25			16.25	17.90	
	1910		500# to 1,000#					14.20			14.20	15.65	
	1920		Over 1,000#				▼	14			14	15.40	

5 METALS

05050 | Basic Materials & Methods

05090 | Metal Fastenings

			CREW	DAILY OUTPUT	LABOR-HOURS	UNIT	MAT.	LABOR	EQUIP.	TOTAL	TOTAL INCL O&P	
							2001 BARE COSTS					
880	2000	Stainless steel, type 308-16, 1/8" dia, less than 500#				Lb.	5.45			5.45	5.95	**880**
	2100	500# to 1000#					4.92			4.92	5.40	
	2220	Over 1000#				↓	4.83			4.83	5.30	
900	0005	**WELDING STRUCTURAL**										**900**
	0010	Field welding, 1/8" E6011, cost per welder, no oper. engr R05090-520	E-14	8	1	Hr.	2.68	35	10.50	48.18	77.50	
	0200	With 1/2 operating engineer	E-13	8	1.500		2.68	49	10.50	62.18	99.50	
	0300	With 1 operating engineer	E-12	8	2	↓	2.68	63.50	10.50	76.68	122	
	0500	With no operating engineer, 2# weld rod per ton	E-14	8	1	Ton	2.68	35	10.50	48.18	77.50	
	0600	8# E6011 per ton	"	2	4		10.70	139	42	191.70	310	
	0800	With one operating engineer per welder, 2# E6011 per ton	E-12	8	2		2.68	63.50	10.50	76.68	122	
	0900	8# E6011 per ton	"	2	8	↓	10.70	254	42	306.70	485	
	1200	Continuous fillet, stick welding, incl. equipment										
	1300	Single pass, 1/8" thick, 0.1#/L.F.	E-14	150	.053	L.F.	.13	1.86	.56	2.55	4.14	
	1400	3/16" thick, 0.2#/L.F.		75	.107		.27	3.72	1.12	5.11	8.25	
	1500	1/4" thick, 0.3#/L.F.		50	.160		.40	5.60	1.68	7.68	12.40	
	1610	5/16" thick, 0.4#/L.F.		38	.211		.54	7.35	2.21	10.10	16.30	
	1800	3 passes, 3/8" thick, 0.5#/L.F.		30	.267		.67	9.30	2.80	12.77	20.50	
	2010	4 passes, 1/2" thick, 0.7#/L.F.		22	.364		.94	12.65	3.82	17.41	28	
	2200	5 to 6 passes, 3/4" thick, 1.3#/L.F.		12	.667		1.74	23	7	31.74	51.50	
	2400	8 to 11 passes, 1" thick, 2.4#/L.F.	↓	6	1.333		3.22	46.50	14	63.72	103	
	2600	For all position welding, add, minimum						20%				
	2700	Maximum						300%				
	2900	For semi-automatic welding, deduct, minimum						5%				
	3000	Maximum				↓		15%				
	4000	Cleaning and welding plates, bars, or rods										
	4010	to existing beams, columns, or trusses	E-14	12	.667	L.F.	.67	23	7	30.67	50.50	
920	0010	**STEEL CUTTING**										**920**
	0020	Hand burning, incl. preparation, torch cutting & grinding, no staging										
	0100	Steel to 1/2" thick	E-14	70	.114	L.F.		3.98	1.20	5.18	8.50	
	0150	3/4" thick		50	.160			5.60	1.68	7.28	11.95	
	0200	1" thick	↓	45	.178	↓		6.20	1.87	8.07	13.30	

05100 | Structural Metal Framing

05120 | Structural Steel

			CREW	DAILY OUTPUT	LABOR-HOURS	UNIT	MAT.	LABOR	EQUIP.	TOTAL	TOTAL INCL O&P	
							2001 BARE COSTS					
140	0005	**SUBPURLINS**										**140**
	0006	Bulb tees, painted, 32-5/8" O.C., 40 psf L.L. R05120-250										
	0010	Up to 5'-6" span, 1.48 plf	E-1	5,900	.004	S.F.	.28	.13	.01	.42	.56	
	0050	6'-4" span, 1.68 plf		5,200	.005		.28	.15	.02	.45	.59	
	0060	7'-8" span, 1.87 plf		4,700	.005		.30	.16	.02	.48	.63	
	0100	8'-9" span, 2.15 plf		4,200	.006		.33	.18	.02	.53	.70	
	0200	10'-2" span, 3.19 plf		3,100	.008		.41	.25	.03	.69	.91	
	0300	12'-0" span, 3.87 plf	↓	2,700	.009	↓	.52	.29	.03	.84	1.10	
	0600	For galvanizing, add				Lb.	.21			.21	.23	
	1420	For 24-5/8" spacing, add				S.F.	33%	33%				
	1430	For 48-5/8" spacing, deduct	↓			"	50%	50%				

5 METALS

147

			DAILY	LABOR-		2001 BARE COSTS				TOTAL	
05120	**Structural Steel**	CREW	OUTPUT	HOURS	UNIT	MAT.	LABOR	EQUIP.	TOTAL	INCL O&P	
180	**0005**	**CANOPY FRAMING**										**180**
	0010	6" and 8" members	E-4	3,000	.011	Lb.	.74	.36	.03	1.13	1.49	
220	**0010**	**CEILING SUPPORTS**										**220**
	1000	Entrance door/folding partition supports	E-4	60	.533	L.F.	12.25	17.80	1.40	31.45	47.50	
	1100	Linear accelerator door supports		14	2.286		55.50	76	6	137.50	206	
	1200	Lintels or shelf angles, hung, exterior hot dipped galv.		267	.120		8.35	4	.32	12.67	16.80	
	1250	Two coats primer paint instead of galv.		267	.120		7.25	4	.32	11.57	15.55	
	1400	Monitor support, ceiling hung, expansion bolted		4	8	Ea.	194	267	21	482	720	
	1450	Hung from pre-set inserts		6	5.333		209	178	14.05	401.05	570	
	1600	Motor supports for overhead doors		4	8		98.50	267	21	386.50	615	
	1700	Partition support for heavy folding partitions, without pocket		24	1.333	L.F.	28	44.50	3.51	76.01	115	
	1750	Supports at pocket only		12	2.667		55.50	89	7	151.50	230	
	2000	Rolling grilles & fire door supports		34	.941		24	31.50	2.48	57.98	86	
	2100	Spider-leg light supports, expansion bolted to ceiling slab		8	4	Ea.	79.50	133	10.50	223	340	
	2150	Hung from pre-set inserts		12	2.667	"	86	89	7	182	263	
	2400	Toilet partition support		36	.889	L.F.	28	29.50	2.34	59.84	87	
	2500	X-ray travel gantry support		12	2.667	"	95.50	89	7	191.50	274	
260	**0005**	**COLUMNS**										**260**
	0010	Aluminum, extruded, stock units, no cap or base, 6" diameter [R05120-210]	E-4	240	.133	L.F.	8	4.45	.35	12.80	17.25	
	0100	8" diameter		170	.188		10.60	6.30	.50	17.40	23.50	
	0200	10" diameter		150	.213		13.95	7.10	.56	21.61	29	
	0300	12" diameter		140	.229		22.50	7.60	.60	30.70	39	
	0400	15" diameter		120	.267		29	8.90	.70	38.60	49	
	0410	Caps and bases, plain, 6" diameter				Set	17.05			17.05	18.75	
	0420	8" diameter					21			21	23	
	0430	10" diameter					28			28	31	
	0440	12" diameter					66.50			66.50	73	
	0450	15" diameter					121			121	133	
	0460	Caps, ornamental, minimum					157			157	172	
	0470	Maximum					780			780	860	
	0500	For square columns, add to column prices above				L.F.	50%					
	0700	Residential, flat, 8' high, plain	E-4	20	1.600	Ea.	59.50	53.50	4.21	117.21	167	
	0720	Fancy		20	1.600		121	53.50	4.21	178.71	235	
	0740	Corner type, plain		20	1.600		106	53.50	4.21	163.71	218	
	0760	Fancy		20	1.600		213	53.50	4.21	270.71	335	
	0800	Steel (lally), concrete filled, extra strong pipe, 3-1/2" diameter	E-2	660	.085	L.F.	20	2.71	1.95	24.66	29	
	0930	6" diameter		1,200	.047		35.50	1.49	1.08	38.07	43	
	1000	Lightweight units, 3-1/2" diameter		780	.072		2.33	2.29	1.65	6.27	8.35	
	1050	4" diameter		900	.062		3.44	1.98	1.43	6.85	8.80	
	1100	For galvanizing, add				Lb.	.15			.15	.17	
	1300	For web ties, angles, etc., add per added lb.	1 Sswk	945	.008		.61	.28		.89	1.17	
	1500	Steel pipe, extra strong, no concrete, 3" to 5" diameter	E-2	16,000	.003		.86	.11	.08	1.05	1.23	
	1600	6" to 12" diameter		14,000	.004		.94	.13	.09	1.16	1.35	
	1700	Steel pipe, extra strong, no concrete, 3" diameter x 12'-0"		60	.933	Ea.	116	30	21.50	167.50	203	
	1750	4" diameter x 12'-0"		58	.966		172	31	22.50	225.50	267	
	1800	6" diameter x 12'-0"		54	1.037		360	33	24	417	485	
	1850	8" diameter x 14'-0"		50	1.120		640	35.50	26	701.50	795	
	1900	10" diameter x 16'-0"		48	1.167		925	37	27	989	1,125	
	1950	12" diameter x 18'-0"		45	1.244		1,250	39.50	28.50	1,318	1,475	
	3300	Structural tubing, square, A500GrB, 4" to 6" square, light section		11,270	.005	Lb.	.53	.16	.11	.80	.99	
	3600	Heavy section		32,000	.002	"	.68	.06	.04	.78	.89	
	4000	Concrete filled, add				L.F.	3.01			3.01	3.31	
	4500	Structural tubing, sq, 4" x 4" x 1/4" x 12'-0"	E-2	58	.966	Ea.	87.50	31	22.50	141	174	
	4550	6" x 6" x 1/4" x 12'-0"		54	1.037		143	33	24	200	241	
	4600	8" x 8" x 3/8" x 14'-0"		50	1.120		400	35.50	26	461.50	530	

Important: See the Reference Section for critical supporting data - Reference Nos., Crews, & City Cost Indexes

5 METALS

05120 | Structural Steel

		Description	CREW	DAILY OUTPUT	LABOR-HOURS	UNIT	MAT.	LABOR	EQUIP.	TOTAL	TOTAL INCL O&P	
260	4650	10" x 10" x 1/2" x 16'-0"	E-2	48	1.167	Ea.	740	37	27	804	905	260
	5100	Structural tubing, rect, 5" to 6" wide, light section		8,000	.007	Lb.	.53	.22	.16	.91	1.15	
	5200	Heavy section		12,000	.005		.63	.15	.11	.89	1.07	
	5300	7" to 10" wide, light section		15,000	.004		.58	.12	.09	.79	.94	
	5400	Heavy section		18,000	.003		.68	.10	.07	.85	1	
	5500	Structural tubing, rect, 5" x 3" x 1/4" x 12'-0"		58	.966	Ea.	85	31	22.50	138.50	172	
	5550	6" x 4" x 5/16" x 12'-0"		54	1.037		158	33	24	215	257	
	5600	8" x 4" x 3/8" x 12'-0"		54	1.037		212	33	24	269	315	
	5650	10" x 6" x 3/8" x 14'-0"		50	1.120		340	35.50	26	401.50	465	
	5700	12" x 8" x 1/2" x 16'-0"		48	1.167		735	37	27	799	905	
	5800	Adjustable jack post, 8' maximum height, 2-3/4" diameter					22			22	24	
	5850	4" diameter					35.50			35.50	39	
	6000	Prefabricated, fireproof, with steel jackets and one coat										
	6100	shop paint, 2 to 4 hour rated, minimum	E-2	27,000	.002	Lb.	.46	.07	.05	.58	.67	
	6200	Average		35,000	.002		.61	.05	.04	.70	.80	
	6250	Maximum		43,000	.001		1.08	.04	.03	1.15	1.29	
	6400	Mild steel, flat, 9" wide, stock units, painted, plain	E-4	160	.200	L.F.	4.84	6.65	.53	12.02	18	
	6450	Fancy		160	.200		9.55	6.65	.53	16.73	23	
	6500	Corner columns, painted, plain		160	.200		7.70	6.65	.53	14.88	21	
	6550	Fancy		160	.200		15.05	6.65	.53	22.23	29	
	6800	W Shape, A36 steel, 2 tier, W8 x 24	E-2	1,080	.052		21	1.65	1.19	23.84	27	
	6850	W8 x 31		1,080	.052		27	1.65	1.19	29.84	34	
	6900	W8 x 48		1,032	.054		42	1.73	1.25	44.98	51	
	6950	W8 x 67		984	.057		58.50	1.81	1.31	61.62	69	
	7000	W10 x 45		1,032	.054		39.50	1.73	1.25	42.48	48	
	7050	W10 x 68		984	.057		59.50	1.81	1.31	62.62	70	
	7100	W10 x 112		960	.058		98	1.86	1.34	101.20	113	
	7150	W12 x 50		1,032	.054		44	1.73	1.25	46.98	52.50	
	7200	W12 x 87		984	.057		76	1.81	1.31	79.12	88.50	
	7250	W12 x 120		960	.058		105	1.86	1.34	108.20	121	
	7300	W12 x 190		912	.061		166	1.96	1.41	169.37	188	
	7350	W14 x 74		984	.057		65	1.81	1.31	68.12	76	
	7400	W14 x 120		960	.058		105	1.86	1.34	108.20	121	
	7450	W14 x 176		912	.061		154	1.96	1.41	157.37	175	
300	0005	**CURB EDGING**										300
	0010	Steel angle w/anchors, on forms, 1" x 1", 0.8#/L.F.	E-4	350	.091	L.F.	1.25	3.05	.24	4.54	7.20	
	0100	2" x 2" angles, 3.92#/L.F.		330	.097		3.54	3.23	.26	7.03	10.05	
	0200	3" x 3" angles, 6.1#/L.F.		300	.107		5.70	3.56	.28	9.54	13	
	0300	4" x 4" angles, 8.2#/L.F.		275	.116		7.25	3.88	.31	11.44	15.35	
	1000	6" x 4" angles, 12.3#/L.F.		250	.128		10.25	4.27	.34	14.86	19.35	
	1050	Steel channels with anchors, on forms, 3" channel, 5#/L.F.		290	.110		4.34	3.68	.29	8.31	11.80	
	1100	4" channel, 5.4#/L.F.		270	.119		4.63	3.95	.31	8.89	12.60	
	1200	6" channel, 8.2#/L.F.		255	.125		7.25	4.19	.33	11.77	15.90	
	1300	8" channel, 11.5#/L.F.		225	.142		9.65	4.74	.37	14.76	19.60	
	1400	10" channel, 15.3#/L.F.		180	.178		12.45	5.95	.47	18.87	25	
	1500	12" channel, 20.7#/L.F.		140	.229		16.40	7.60	.60	24.60	32.50	
	2000	For curved edging, add					35%	10%				
440	0010	**LIGHTWEIGHT FRAMING**										440
	0200	For load-bearing steel studs see division 05410-400										
	0400	Angle framing, field fabricated, 4" and larger	E-3	440	.055	Lb.	.36	1.83	.19	2.38	3.92	
	0450	Less than 4" angles		265	.091	"	.37	3.04	.32	3.73	6.25	
	0460	1/2" x 1/2" x 1/8"		200	.120	L.F.	.07	4.02	.42	4.51	7.85	
	0462	3/4" x 3/4" x 1/8"		160	.150		.21	5.05	.53	5.79	9.90	
	0464	1" x 1" x 1/8"		135	.178		.29	5.95	.62	6.86	11.80	
	0466	1-1/4" x 1-1/4" x 3/16"		115	.209		.54	7	.73	8.27	14.10	

R05120-210

R05120-240

METALS 5

	05120	Structural Steel		CREW	DAILY OUTPUT	LABOR-HOURS	UNIT	2001 BARE COSTS				TOTAL INCL O&P
								MAT.	LABOR	EQUIP.	TOTAL	
440	0468	1-1/2" x 1-1/2" x 3/16"	R05120 -240	E-3	100	.240	L.F.	.66	8.05	.84	9.55	16.25	440
	0470	2" x 2" x 1/4"			90	.267		1.17	8.95	.93	11.05	18.50
	0472	2-1/2" x 2-1/2" x 1/4"			72	.333		1.51	11.15	1.17	13.83	23.50
	0474	3" x 2" x 3/8"			65	.369		2.17	12.40	1.29	15.86	26.50
	0476	3" x 3" x 3/8"			57	.421		2.65	14.10	1.47	18.22	30
	0600	Channel framing, field fabricated, 8" and larger			500	.048	Lb.	.37	1.61	.17	2.15	3.50
	0650	Less than 8" channels			335	.072	"	.37	2.40	.25	3.02	5.05
	0660	C2 x 1.78			115	.209	L.F.	.65	7	.73	8.38	14.20
	0662	C3 x 4.1			80	.300		1.51	10.05	1.05	12.61	21
	0664	C4 x 5.4			66	.364		1.98	12.20	1.27	15.45	25.50
	0666	C5 x 6.7			57	.421		2.46	14.10	1.47	18.03	30
	0668	C6 x 8.2			55	.436		2.91	14.65	1.53	19.09	31.50
	0670	C7 x 9.8			40	.600		3.60	20	2.10	25.70	43
	0672	C8 x 11.5			36	.667		4.23	22.50	2.33	29.06	47.50
	0710	Structural bar tee, field fabricated, 3/4" x 3/4" x 1/8"			160	.150		.21	5.05	.53	5.79	9.90
	0712	1" x 1" x 1/8"			135	.178		.29	5.95	.62	6.86	11.80
	0714	1-1/2" x 1-1/2" x 1/4"			114	.211		.86	7.05	.74	8.65	14.55
	0716	2" x 2" x 1/4"			89	.270		1.17	9.05	.94	11.16	18.75
	0718	2-1/2" x 2-1/2" x 3/8"			72	.333		2.17	11.15	1.17	14.49	24
	0720	3" x 3" x 3/8"			57	.421		2.65	14.10	1.47	18.22	30
	0730	Structural zee, field fabricated, 1-1/4" x 1-3/4" x 1-3/4"			114	.211		.28	7.05	.74	8.07	13.90
	0732	2-11/16" x 3" x 2-11/16"			114	.211		.65	7.05	.74	8.44	14.35
	0734	3-1/16" x 4" x 3-1/16"			133	.180		.99	6.05	.63	7.67	12.75
	0736	3-1/4" x 5" x 3-1/4"			133	.180		1.35	6.05	.63	8.03	13.10
	0738	3-1/2" x 6" x 3-1/2"			160	.150		2.03	5.05	.53	7.61	11.90
	0740	Junior beam, field fabricated, 3"			80	.300		2.09	10.05	1.05	13.19	21.50
	0742	4"			72	.333		2.83	11.15	1.17	15.15	25
	0744	5"			67	.358		3.68	12	1.25	16.93	27.50
	0746	6"			62	.387		4.59	13	1.35	18.94	30
	0748	7"			57	.421		5.60	14.10	1.47	21.17	33.50
	0750	8"			53	.453		6.75	15.20	1.58	23.53	36.50
	1000	Continuous slotted channel framing system, minimum		2 Sswk	220	.073	Lb.	1.90	2.39		4.29	6.40
	1200	Maximum		"	135	.119		2.14	3.89		6.03	9.40
	1300	Cross bracing, rods, 3/4" diameter		E-3	700	.034		.74	1.15	.12	2.01	3.02
	1310	7/8" diameter			850	.028		.74	.95	.10	1.79	2.64
	1320	1" diameter			1,000	.024		.74	.80	.08	1.62	2.36
	1330	Angle, 5" x 5" x 3/8"			440	.055		.74	1.83	.19	2.76	4.34
	1350	Hanging lintels, average			350	.069		.74	2.30	.24	3.28	5.25
	1380	Roof frames, 3'-0" square, 5' span		E-2	4,200	.013		.74	.43	.31	1.48	1.89
	1400	Tie rod, not upset, 1-1/2" to 4" diameter, with turnbuckle		2 Sswk	800	.020		.80	.66		1.46	2.07
	1420	No turnbuckle			700	.023		.77	.75		1.52	2.20
	1500	Upset, 1-3/4" to 4" diameter, with turnbuckle			800	.020		.80	.66		1.46	2.07
	1520	No turnbuckle			700	.023		.77	.75		1.52	2.20
480	0005	**LINTELS**											480
	0010	Plain steel angles, under 500 lb.		1 Bric	550	.015	Lb.	.47	.43		.90	1.19
	0100	500 to 1000 lb. **CN**			640	.013		.46	.37		.83	1.08
	0200	1,000 to 2,000 lb.			640	.013		.45	.37		.82	1.06
	0300	2,000 to 4,000 lb.			640	.013		.43	.37		.80	1.05
	0500	For built-up angles and plates, add to above						.15			.15	.17
	0700	For engineering, add to above						.06			.06	.07
	0900	For galvanizing, add to above, under 500 lb.						.37			.37	.40
	0950	500 to 2,000 lb.						.36			.36	.39
	1000	Over 2,000 lb.						.34			.34	.37
	2000	Steel angles, 3-1/2" x 3", 1/4" thick, 2'-6" long		1 Bric	47	.170	Ea.	6.60	5.05		11.65	15.10
	2100	4'-6" long			26	.308		11.90	9.10		21	27

Important: See the Reference Section for critical supporting data - Reference Nos., Crews, & City Cost Indexes

				DAILY	LABOR-		2001 BARE COSTS				TOTAL	
05120		**Structural Steel**	CREW	OUTPUT	HOURS	UNIT	MAT.	LABOR	EQUIP.	TOTAL	INCL O&P	
480	2600	4" x 3-1/2", 1/4" thick, 5'-0" long	1 Bric	21	.381	Ea.	15.20	11.30		26.50	34	480
	2700	9'-0" long	↓	12	.667	↓	27.50	19.75		47.25	60.50	
	3500	For precast concrete lintels, see div. 03480-400										
520	0005	**PIPE SUPPORT FRAMING**										520
	0010	Under 10#/L.F.	E-4	3,900	.008	Lb.	.82	.27	.02	1.11	1.42	
	0200	10.1 to 15#/L.F.		4,300	.007		.81	.25	.02	1.08	1.36	
	0400	15.1 to 20#/L.F.		4,800	.007		.80	.22	.02	1.04	1.30	
	0600	Over 20#/L.F.	↓	5,400	.006	↓	.78	.20	.02	1	1.24	
560	0010	**PLATES** Structural steel										560
	2010	48"-60" wide, 10'-60' long, 5-50 tons, mill prices										
	2100	1/4" thick				Cwt.	37.50			37.50	41.50	
	2150	5/16" thick					37.50			37.50	41.50	
	2200	3/8" thick					35.50			35.50	39	
	2250	1/2" thick					35.50			35.50	39	
	2300	3/4" thick					35.50			35.50	39	
	2350	1" thick					35.50			35.50	39	
	2400	2" thick					36.50			36.50	40.50	
	2450	4" thick					38.50			38.50	42.50	
	2500	6" thick					40.50			40.50	44.50	
	2550	8" thick				↓	40.50			40.50	44.50	
600	0005	**STRESSED SKIN** Roof & ceiling system										600
	0010	Double panel flat roof, spans to 100'	E-2	1,150	.049	S.F.	4.90	1.55	1.12	7.57	9.35	
	0100	Double panel convex roof, spans to 200'		960	.058		7.95	1.86	1.34	11.15	13.45	
	0200	Double panel arched roof, spans to 300'	↓	760	.074	↓	12.25	2.35	1.70	16.30	19.45	
640	0010	**STRUCTURAL STEEL MEMBERS**										640
	0020	Shop fabricated for 1-2 story bldg., bolted conn's., 100 tons										
	0100	W 6 x 9	E-2	600	.093	L.F.	5.60	2.98	2.15	10.73	13.70	
	0120	x 16		600	.093		10	2.98	2.15	15.13	18.50	
	0140	x 20		600	.093		12.50	2.98	2.15	17.63	21.50	
	0300	W 8 x 10		600	.093		6.25	2.98	2.15	11.38	14.35	
	0320	x 15		600	.093		9.35	2.98	2.15	14.48	17.80	
	0350	x 21		600	.093		13.10	2.98	2.15	18.23	22	
	0360	x 24		550	.102		15	3.25	2.35	20.60	24.50	
	0370	x 28		550	.102		17.50	3.25	2.35	23.10	27.50	
	0500	x 31		550	.102		19	3.25	2.35	24.60	29	
	0520	x 35		550	.102		21.50	3.25	2.35	27.10	31.50	
	0540	x 48		550	.102		29.50	3.25	2.35	35.10	40.50	
	0600	W 10 x 12		600	.093		7.50	2.98	2.15	12.63	15.75	
	0620	x 15		600	.093		9.35	2.98	2.15	14.48	17.80	
	0700	x 22		600	.093		13.75	2.98	2.15	18.88	22.50	
	0720	x 26		600	.093		16.25	2.98	2.15	21.38	25.50	
	0740	x 33		550	.102		20	3.25	2.35	25.60	30	
	0900	x 49		550	.102		30	3.25	2.35	35.60	41	
	1100	W 12 x 14		880	.064		8.75	2.03	1.47	12.25	14.75	
	1300	x 22		880	.064		13.75	2.03	1.47	17.25	20	
	1500	x 26		880	.064		16.25	2.03	1.47	19.75	23	
	1520	x 35		810	.069		21.50	2.20	1.59	25.29	29	
	1560	x 50		750	.075		30.50	2.38	1.72	34.60	39.50	
	1580	x 58		750	.075		35.50	2.38	1.72	39.60	45	
	1700	x 72		640	.087		43	2.79	2.02	47.81	54.50	
	1740	x 87		640	.087		52	2.79	2.02	56.81	64.50	
	1900	W 14 x 26		990	.057		16.25	1.80	1.30	19.35	22.50	
	2100	x 30		900	.062		18.75	1.98	1.43	22.16	25.50	
	2300	x 34	↓	810	.069	↓	21	2.20	1.59	24.79	28.50	

R05120 -210

R05120 -240

METALS **5**

05120 | Structural Steel

		CREW	DAILY OUTPUT	LABOR-HOURS	UNIT	MAT.	LABOR	EQUIP.	TOTAL	TOTAL INCL O&P	
640	2320	x 43	E-2	810	.069	L.F.	26.50	2.20	1.59	30.29	34.50	640
2340	x 53		800	.070		32.50	2.23	1.61	36.34	41
2360	x 74		760	.074		44.50	2.35	1.70	48.55	55
2380	x 90		740	.076		54	2.41	1.74	58.15	65.50
2500	x 120		720	.078		70.50	2.48	1.79	74.77	84
2700	W 16 x 26		1,000	.056		16.25	1.79	1.29	19.33	22.50
2900	x 31		900	.062		19	1.98	1.43	22.41	26
3100	x 40		800	.070		24.50	2.23	1.61	28.34	32.50
3120	x 50		800	.070		30.50	2.23	1.61	34.34	39
3140	x 67		760	.074		40	2.35	1.70	44.05	50
3300	W 18 x 35	E-5	960	.083		21.50	2.70	1.43	25.63	30
3500	x 40		960	.083		24.50	2.70	1.43	28.63	33.50
3520	x 46		960	.083		28	2.70	1.43	32.13	37.50
3700	x 50		912	.088		30.50	2.84	1.51	34.85	40
3900	x 55		912	.088		33.50	2.84	1.51	37.85	43.50
3920	x 65		900	.089		40	2.88	1.53	44.41	50.50
3940	x 76		900	.089		45.50	2.88	1.53	49.91	56.50
3960	x 86		900	.089		51.50	2.88	1.53	55.91	63.50
3980	x 106		900	.089		62.50	2.88	1.53	66.91	75
4100	W 21 x 44		1,064	.075		27	2.43	1.29	30.72	35
4300	x 50		1,064	.075		30.50	2.43	1.29	34.22	39
4500	x 62		1,036	.077		38	2.50	1.33	41.83	48
4700	x 68		1,036	.077		41	2.50	1.33	44.83	51
4720	x 83		1,000	.080		50	2.59	1.37	53.96	61
4740	x 93		1,000	.080		56	2.59	1.37	59.96	67.50
4760	x 101		1,000	.080		59.50	2.59	1.37	63.46	71.50
4780	x 122		1,000	.080		71.50	2.59	1.37	75.46	85
4900	W 24 x 55		1,110	.072		33.50	2.33	1.24	37.07	42.50
5100	x 62		1,110	.072		38	2.33	1.24	41.57	47.50
5300	x 68		1,110	.072		41	2.33	1.24	44.57	50.50
5500	x 76		1,110	.072		45.50	2.33	1.24	49.07	55.50
5700	x 84		1,080	.074		50.50	2.40	1.27	54.17	61
5720	x 94		1,080	.074		56.50	2.40	1.27	60.17	67.50
5740	x 104		1,050	.076		61	2.47	1.31	64.78	73.50
5760	x 117		1,050	.076		69	2.47	1.31	72.78	81.50
5780	x 146		1,050	.076		86	2.47	1.31	89.78	100
5800	W 27 x 84		1,190	.067		50.50	2.18	1.16	53.84	60.50
5900	x 94		1,190	.067		56.50	2.18	1.16	59.84	67
5920	x 114		1,150	.070		67	2.25	1.20	70.45	79
5940	x 146		1,150	.070		86	2.25	1.20	89.45	100
5960	x 161		1,150	.070		94.50	2.25	1.20	97.95	109
6100	W 30 x 99		1,200	.067		59.50	2.16	1.15	62.81	70.50
6300	x 108		1,200	.067		63.50	2.16	1.15	66.81	75
6500	x 116		1,160	.069		68	2.23	1.18	71.41	80
6520	x 132		1,160	.069		77.50	2.23	1.18	80.91	90.50
6540	x 148		1,160	.069		87	2.23	1.18	90.41	101
6560	x 173		1,120	.071		102	2.31	1.23	105.54	117
6580	x 191		1,120	.071		112	2.31	1.23	115.54	129
6700	W 33 x 118		1,176	.068		69.50	2.20	1.17	72.87	81.50
6900	x 130		1,134	.071		76.50	2.28	1.21	79.99	89.50
7100	x 141		1,134	.071		83	2.28	1.21	86.49	96.50
7120	x 169		1,100	.073		99.50	2.35	1.25	103.10	115
7140	x 201		1,100	.073		118	2.35	1.25	121.60	136
7300	W 36 x 135		1,170	.068		79.50	2.21	1.17	82.88	92.50
7500	x 150		1,170	.068		88	2.21	1.17	91.38	102
7600	x 170		1,150	.070		100	2.25	1.20	103.45	115

Reference boxes: R05120-210, R05120-240

5 METALS

05120 | Structural Steel

			CREW	DAILY OUTPUT	LABOR-HOURS	UNIT	2001 BARE COSTS				TOTAL INCL O&P	
							MAT.	LABOR	EQUIP.	TOTAL		
640	7700	x 194	E-5	1,125	.071	L.F.	114	2.30	1.22	117.52	130	**640**
	7900	x 230		1,125	.071		135	2.30	1.22	138.52	154	
	7920	x 260		1,035	.077		153	2.50	1.33	156.83	174	
	8100	x 300		1,035	.077		176	2.50	1.33	179.83	200	
	8490	For jobs less than 100 tons, add				Ton	10%					
680	0010	**STRUCTURAL STEEL PROJECTS** Bolted, unless noted otherwise										**680**
	0200	Apartments, nursing homes, etc., 1 to 2 stories	E-5	10.30	7.767	Ton	1,225	251	133	1,609	1,950	
	0300	3 to 6 stories	"	10.10	7.921		1,250	256	136	1,642	1,975	
	0400	7 to 15 stories	E-6	14.20	9.014		1,275	292	107	1,674	2,025	
	0500	Over 15 stories	"	13.90	9.209		1,325	299	110	1,734	2,100	
	0700	Offices, hosp., etc., steel bearing, 1 to 2 stories **CN**	E-5	10.30	7.767		1,225	251	133	1,609	1,950	
	0800	3 to 6 stories	E-6	14.40	8.889		1,250	288	106	1,644	2,000	
	0900	7 to 15 stories		14.20	9.014		1,275	292	107	1,674	2,025	
	1000	Over 15 stories		13.90	9.209		1,325	299	110	1,734	2,100	
	1100	For multi-story masonry wall bearing construction, add						30%				
	1300	Industrial bldgs., 1 story, beams & girders, steel bearing	E-5	12.90	6.202		1,225	201	107	1,533	1,825	
	1400	Masonry bearing	"	10	8		1,225	259	137	1,621	1,950	
	1500	Industrial bldgs., 1 story, under 10 tons,										
	1510	steel from warehouse, trucked	E-2	7.50	7.467	Ton	1,475	238	172	1,885	2,225	
	1600	1 story with roof trusses, steel bearing	E-5	10.60	7.547		1,450	244	130	1,824	2,175	
	1700	Masonry bearing	"	8.30	9.639		1,450	310	166	1,926	2,325	
	1900	Monumental structures, banks, stores, etc., minimum	E-6	13	9.846		1,225	320	117	1,662	2,050	
	2000	Maximum	"	9	14.222		2,025	460	169	2,654	3,225	
	2200	Churches, minimum	E-5	11.60	6.897		1,150	223	118	1,491	1,775	
	2300	Maximum	"	5.20	15.385		1,525	500	264	2,289	2,850	
	2800	Power stations, fossil fuels, minimum	E-6	11	11.636		1,225	375	138	1,738	2,175	
	2900	Maximum		5.70	22.456		1,850	730	267	2,847	3,600	
	2950	Nuclear fuels, non-safety steel, minimum		7	18.286		1,225	595	218	2,038	2,650	
	3000	Maximum		5.50	23.273		1,850	755	277	2,882	3,650	
	3040	Safety steel, minimum		2.50	51.200		1,800	1,650	610	4,060	5,575	
	3070	Maximum		1.50	85.333		2,350	2,775	1,025	6,150	8,575	
	3100	Roof trusses, minimum	E-5	13	6.154		1,725	199	106	2,030	2,350	
	3200	Maximum		8.30	9.639		2,075	310	166	2,551	3,025	
	3210	Schools, minimum		14.50	5.517		1,225	179	95	1,499	1,775	
	3220	Maximum		8.30	9.639		1,800	310	166	2,276	2,700	
	3400	Welded construction, simple commercial bldgs., 1 to 2 stories	E-7	7.60	10.526		1,250	340	192	1,782	2,175	
	3500	7 to 15 stories	E-9	8.30	15.422		1,450	500	206	2,156	2,700	
	3700	Welded rigid frame, 1 story, minimum	E-7	15.80	5.063		1,275	164	92.50	1,531.50	1,800	
	3800	Maximum	"	5.50	14.545		1,650	470	265	2,385	2,950	
	4000	High strength steels, add to A36 price, minimum					10			10	11	
	4100	Maximum					60			60	66	
	4300	Column base plates, light, up to 150 lb	2 Sswk	2,000	.008	Lb.	.67	.26		.93	1.22	
	4400	Heavy, over 150 lb	E-2	7,500	.007	"	.70	.24	.17	1.11	1.37	
	4600	Castellated beams, light sections, to 50#/L.F., minimum		10.70	5.234	Ton	1,275	167	121	1,563	1,850	
	4700	Maximum		7	8		1,400	255	184	1,839	2,200	
	4900	Heavy sections, over 50# per L.F., minimum		11.70	4.786		1,350	153	110	1,613	1,850	
	5000	Maximum		7.80	7.179		1,475	229	165	1,869	2,200	
	5500	Steel domes - see R13128-310										
	5700	Steel estimating weights per S.F. - see R05120-220										
	5900	Galvanizing structural steel in shop, under 1 ton, add to above				Ton	400			400	440	
	5950	1 ton to 20 tons					350			350	385	
	6000	Over 20 tons					250			250	275	
	6100	Cold galvanizing, brush	1 Psst	1,100	.007	S.F.	.06	.20		.26	.44	
	6125	Steel surface treatments										
	6170	Wire brush, hand	1 Psst	240	.033	S.F.	.02	.90		.92	1.72	

Reference numbers in column: R05120-210, R05120-240, R05080-310, R05090-510, R05120-210, R05120-220, R05120-230, R05120-240

METALS **5**

05120	Structural Steel		CREW	DAILY OUTPUT	LABOR-HOURS	UNIT	MAT.	LABOR	EQUIP.	TOTAL	TOTAL INCL O&P	
680	6180	Power tool	1 Psst	600	.013	S.F.	.05	.36		.41	.74	**680**
	6215	Pressure washing, 2800-6000 S.F./day	1 Pord	3,500	.002			.06		.06	.09	
	6220	Steam cleaning, 2800-4000 S.F./day		2,400	.003			.09		.09	.13	
	6225	Water blasting		3,200	.002			.07		.07	.10	
	6230	Brush-off blast	E-11	6,000	.005		.07	.14	.03	.24	.35	
	6235	Com'l blast (SSPC-6), loose scale, fine pwder rust, 2.0 #/S.F.		4,000	.008		.14	.21	.04	.39	.56	
	6240	Tight mill scale, little/no rust, 3.0 #/S.F.		3,200	.010		.21	.26	.05	.52	.74	
	6245	Exist coat blistered/pitted, 4.0 #/S.F.		2,100	.015		.28	.40	.08	.76	1.09	
	6250	Exist coat badly pitted/nodules, 6.7 #/S.F.		1,300	.025		.47	.65	.13	1.25	1.76	
	6255	Near white blast (SSPC-10), loose scale, fine rust, 5.6 #/S.F.		1,700	.019		.39	.50	.10	.99	1.39	
	6260	Tight mill scale, little/no rust, 6.9 #/S.F.		1,400	.023		.48	.61	.12	1.21	1.70	
	6265	Exist coat blistered/pitted, 9.0 #/S.F.		1,100	.029		.63	.77	.15	1.55	2.18	
	6270	Exist coat badly pitted/nodules, 11.3 #/S.F.		800	.040		.79	1.06	.21	2.06	2.91	
	6510	Paints & protective coatings, sprayed										
	6520	Alkyds, primer	2 Psst	3,600	.004	S.F.	.06	.12		.18	.29	
	6540	Gloss topcoats		3,200	.005		.05	.14		.19	.30	
	6560	Silicone alkyd		3,200	.005		.09	.14		.23	.35	
	6610	Epoxy, primer		3,000	.005		.16	.14		.30	.44	
	6630	Intermediate or topcoat		2,800	.006		.13	.16		.29	.43	
	6650	Enamel coat		2,800	.006		.16	.16		.32	.46	
	6700	Epoxy ester, primer		2,800	.006		.33	.16		.49	.65	
	6720	Topcoats		2,800	.006		.11	.16		.27	.41	
	6810	Latex primer		3,600	.004		.05	.12		.17	.28	
	6830	Topcoats		3,200	.005		.05	.14		.19	.31	
	6910	Universal primers, one part, phenolic, modified alkyd		2,000	.008		.08	.22		.30	.50	
	6940	Two part, epoxy spray		2,000	.008		.19	.22		.41	.62	
	7000	Zinc rich primers, self cure, spray, inorganic		1,800	.009		.48	.24		.72	.98	
	7010	Epoxy, spray, organic		1,800	.009		.13	.24		.37	.59	
	7020	Above one story, spray painting simple structures, add						25%				
	7030	Intricate structures, add						50%				

05140 | Structural Aluminum

080	0005	**ALUMINUM**										**080**
	0010	Structural shapes, 1" to 10" members, under 1 ton	E-2	1,050	.053	Lb.	2.21	1.70	1.23	5.14	6.75	
	0050	1 to 5 tons		1,330	.042		2.03	1.34	.97	4.34	5.65	
	0100	Over 5 tons **CN**		1,330	.042		1.90	1.34	.97	4.21	5.50	
	0300	Extrusions, over 5 tons, stock shapes		1,330	.042		1.94	1.34	.97	4.25	5.55	
	0400	Custom shapes		1,330	.042		2.16	1.34	.97	4.47	5.80	

05150 | Wire Rope Assemblies

800	0005	**STEEL WIRE ROPE**										**800**
	0010	6 x 19, bright, fiber core, 5000' rolls, 1/2" diameter				L.F.	.66			.66	.73	
	0050	Steel core					.84			.84	.92	
	0100	Fiber core, 1" diameter					2.19			2.19	2.41	
	0150	Steel core					2.48			2.48	2.73	
	0300	6 x 19, galvanized, fiber core, 1/2" diameter					.95			.95	1.05	
	0350	Steel core					1.09			1.09	1.20	
	0400	Fiber core, 1" diameter					2.78			2.78	3.06	
	0450	Steel core					2.92			2.92	3.21	
	0500	6 x 7, bright, IPS, fiber core, <500 L.F. w/acc., 1/4" diameter	E-17	6,400	.002		.66	.08		.74	.88	
	0510	1/2" diameter		2,100	.008		1.62	.26		1.88	2.25	
	0520	3/4" diameter		960	.017		2.92	.56		3.48	4.23	
	0550	6 x 19, bright, IPS, IWRC, <500 L.F. w/acc., 1/4" diameter		5,760	.003		.62	.09		.71	.85	
	0560	1/2" diameter		1,730	.009		1.06	.31		1.37	1.74	
	0570	3/4" diameter		770	.021		1.83	.70		2.53	3.29	
	0580	1" diameter		420	.038		3.40	1.29	.01	4.70	6.10	

05100 | Structural Metal Framing

05150 | Wire Rope Assemblies

		CREW	DAILY OUTPUT	LABOR-HOURS	UNIT	MAT.	LABOR	EQUIP.	TOTAL	TOTAL INCL O&P	
							2001 BARE COSTS				
800	0590	1-1/4" diameter	E-17	290	.055	L.F.	4.91	1.87	.01	6.79	8.80	**800**
	0600	1-1/2" diameter	↓	192	.083		7.10	2.82	.02	9.94	12.95	
	0610	1-3/4" diameter	E-18	240	.167		10.95	5.45	2.31	18.71	24	
	0620	2" diameter		160	.250		14.15	8.20	3.47	25.82	34	
	0630	2-1/4" diameter	↓	160	.250		19	8.20	3.47	30.67	39	
	0650	6 x 37, bright, IPS, IWRC, <500 L.F. w/acc., 1/4" diameter	E-17	6,400	.002		.74	.08		.82	.96	
	0660	1/2" diameter		1,730	.009		1.25	.31		1.56	1.95	
	0670	3/4" diameter		770	.021		2.09	.70		2.79	3.58	
	0680	1" diameter		430	.037		3.33	1.26	.01	4.60	5.95	
	0690	1-1/4" diameter		290	.055		5.15	1.87	.01	7.03	9.05	
	0700	1-1/2" diameter	↓	190	.084		7.25	2.85	.02	10.12	13.15	
	0710	1-3/4" diameter	E-18	260	.154		10.85	5.05	2.13	18.03	23	
	0720	2" diameter		200	.200		14	6.55	2.77	23.32	30	
	0730	2-1/4" diameter	↓	160	.250		18.20	8.20	3.47	29.87	38	
	0800	6 x 19 & 6 x 37, swaged, 1/2" diameter	E-17	1,220	.013		2.48	.44		2.92	3.54	
	0810	9/16" diameter		1,120	.014		2.72	.48		3.20	3.87	
	0820	5/8" diameter		930	.017		3.31	.58		3.89	4.70	
	0830	3/4" diameter		640	.025		4.13	.85		4.98	6.10	
	0840	7/8" diameter		480	.033		5.05	1.13	.01	6.19	7.60	
	0850	1" diameter		350	.046		6.10	1.55	.01	7.66	9.50	
	0860	1-1/8" diameter		288	.056		7.85	1.88	.01	9.74	12.05	
	0870	1-1/4" diameter		230	.070		9.35	2.35	.01	11.71	14.55	
	0880	1-3/8" diameter	↓	192	.083		10.80	2.82	.02	13.64	17	
	0890	1-1/2" diameter	E-18	300	.133	↓	13.05	4.37	1.85	19.27	24	

05160 | Metal Framing Systems

		CREW	DAILY OUTPUT	LABOR-HOURS	UNIT	MAT.	LABOR	EQUIP.	TOTAL	TOTAL INCL O&P	
							2001 BARE COSTS				
800	0005	**SPACE FRAME**										**800**
	0010	Steel collars and channel members, 4' modules, minimum	E-2	1,200	.047	S.F.	15.75	1.49	1.08	18.32	21	
	0200	Maximum		900	.062		31.50	1.98	1.43	34.91	39.50	
	0400	5' modules, minimum		1,300	.043		13.65	1.37	.99	16.01	18.50	
	0500	Maximum		1,000	.056		19.95	1.79	1.29	23.03	26.50	
	0600	Steel collars and square tubular members, 5' modules, minimum		1,200	.047		15.75	1.49	1.08	18.32	21	
	0650	Maximum		1,000	.056		23	1.79	1.29	26.08	30	
	0700	4' modules, minimum		1,100	.051		16.80	1.62	1.17	19.59	22.50	
	0800	Maximum		900	.062		26.50	1.98	1.43	29.91	34	
	0900	Steel nodes & tubular members, 7' to 10' modules, minimum		1,650	.034		21	1.08	.78	22.86	25.50	
	0950	Maximum		825	.068		52.50	2.16	1.56	56.22	63.50	
	1100	Less than 7' modules, minimum		1,200	.047		34.50	1.49	1.08	37.07	42	
	1200	Less than 7' modules, maximum	↓	600	.093	↓	68.50	2.98	2.15	73.63	82.50	

05200 | Metal Joists

05210 | Steel Joists

		CREW	DAILY OUTPUT	LABOR-HOURS	UNIT	MAT.	LABOR	EQUIP.	TOTAL	TOTAL INCL O&P	
							2001 BARE COSTS				
600	0010	**OPEN WEB JOISTS**, Truckload lots										**600**
	0020	K series, horizontal bridging, spans up to 30', minimum	E-7	15	5.333	Ton	815	173	97	1,085	1,300	
	0050	Average		12	6.667		920	216	122	1,258	1,525	
	0080	Maximum	↓	9	8.889	↓	1,100	288	162	1,550	1,875	
	0130	8K1, 5.1 Lb/LF		1,200	.067	L.F.	2.34	2.16	1.22	5.72	7.70	
	0140	10K1, 5.0 Lb/LF	↓	1,200	.067	↓	2.30	2.16	1.22	5.68	7.65	

	05210	Steel Joists	CREW	DAILY OUTPUT	LABOR-HOURS	UNIT	MAT.	LABOR	EQUIP.	TOTAL	TOTAL INCL O&P	
								2001 BARE COSTS				
600	0160	12K3, 5.7 Lb/LF	E-7	1,500	.053	L.F.	2.62	1.73	.97	5.32	7	**600**
	0180	14K3, 6.0 Lb/LF		1,500	.053		2.76	1.73	.97	5.46	7.15	
	0200	16K3, 6.3 Lb/LF		1,800	.044		2.90	1.44	.81	5.15	6.60	
	0220	16K6, 8.1 Lb/LF		1,800	.044		3.72	1.44	.81	5.97	7.50	
	0240	18K5, 7.7 Lb/LF		2,000	.040		3.54	1.29	.73	5.56	6.95	
	0260	18K9, 10.2 Lb/LF		2,000	.040	▼	4.69	1.29	.73	6.71	8.25	
	0410	Span 30' to 50', minimum		17	4.706	Ton	805	152	86	1,043	1,250	
	0440	Average CN		17	4.706		905	152	86	1,143	1,350	
	0460	Maximum		10	8	▼	960	259	146	1,365	1,675	
	0500	20K5, 8.2 Lb/LF		2,000	.040	L.F.	3.71	1.29	.73	5.73	7.15	
	0520	20K9, 10.8 Lb/LF		2,000	.040		4.89	1.29	.73	6.91	8.50	
	0540	22K5, 8.8 Lb/LF		2,000	.040		3.98	1.29	.73	6	7.45	
	0560	22K9, 11.3 Lb/LF		2,000	.040		5.10	1.29	.73	7.12	8.70	
	0580	24K6, 9.7 Lb/LF		2,200	.036		4.39	1.18	.66	6.23	7.65	
	0600	24K10, 13.1 Lb/LF		2,200	.036		5.95	1.18	.66	7.79	9.30	
	0620	26K6, 10.6 Lb/LF		2,200	.036		4.80	1.18	.66	6.64	8.10	
	0640	26K10, 13.8 Lb/LF		2,200	.036		6.25	1.18	.66	8.09	9.65	
	0660	28K8, 12.7 Lb/LF		2,400	.033		5.75	1.08	.61	7.44	8.85	
	0680	28K12, 17.1 Lb/LF		2,400	.033		7.75	1.08	.61	9.44	11.05	
	0700	30K8, 13.2 Lb/LF		2,400	.033		5.95	1.08	.61	7.64	9.10	
	0720	30K12, 17.6 Lb/LF	▼	2,400	.033	▼	7.95	1.08	.61	9.64	11.30	
	1010	CS series, horizontal bridging										
	1020	Spans to 30', minimum	E-7	15	5.333	Ton	840	173	97	1,110	1,325	
	1040	Average		12	6.667		935	216	122	1,273	1,550	
	1060	Maximum		9	8.889	▼	1,000	288	162	1,450	1,775	
	1100	10CS2, 7.5 Lb/LF		1,200	.067	L.F.	3.51	2.16	1.22	6.89	9	
	1120	12CS2, 8.0 Lb/LF		1,500	.053		3.74	1.73	.97	6.44	8.25	
	1140	14CS2, 8.0Lb/LF		1,500	.053		3.74	1.73	.97	6.44	8.25	
	1160	16CS2, 8.5 Lb/LF		1,800	.044		3.98	1.44	.81	6.23	7.80	
	1180	16CS4, 14.5 Lb/LF		1,800	.044		6.80	1.44	.81	9.05	10.85	
	1200	18CS2, 9.0 Lb/LF		2,000	.040		4.21	1.29	.73	6.23	7.70	
	1220	18CS4, 15.0 Lb/LF		2,000	.040		7	1.29	.73	9.02	10.80	
	1240	20CS2, 9.5 Lb/LF		2,000	.040		4.45	1.29	.73	6.47	7.95	
	1260	20CS4, 16.5 Lb/LF		2,000	.040		7.70	1.29	.73	9.72	11.60	
	1280	22CS2, 10.0 Lb/LF		2,000	.040		4.68	1.29	.73	6.70	8.25	
	1300	22CS4, 16.5 Lb/LF		2,000	.040		7.70	1.29	.73	9.72	11.60	
	1320	24CS2, 10.0 Lb/LF		2,200	.036		4.68	1.18	.66	6.52	7.95	
	1340	24CS4, 16.5 Lb/LF		2,200	.036		7.70	1.18	.66	9.54	11.30	
	1360	26CS2, 10.0 Lb/LF		2,200	.036		4.68	1.18	.66	6.52	7.95	
	1380	26CS4, 16.5 Lb/LF		2,200	.036		7.70	1.18	.66	9.54	11.30	
	1400	28CS2, 10.5 Lb/LF		2,400	.033		4.91	1.08	.61	6.60	7.95	
	1420	28CS4, 16.5 Lb/LF		2,400	.033		7.70	1.08	.61	9.39	11.05	
	1440	30CS2, 11.0 Lb/LF		2,400	.033		5.15	1.08	.61	6.84	8.20	
	1460	30CS4, 16.5 Lb/LF	▼	2,400	.033	▼	7.70	1.08	.61	9.39	11.05	
	2000	LH series, bolted cross bridging										
	2020	Spans to 96', minimum	E-7	16	5	Ton	905	162	91	1,158	1,375	
	2040	Average		13	6.154		995	199	112	1,306	1,575	
	2080	Maximum		11	7.273	▼	1,175	235	133	1,543	1,850	
	2200	18LH04, 12 Lb/LF		1,400	.057	L.F.	5.95	1.85	1.04	8.84	10.95	
	2220	18LH08, 19 Lb/LF		1,400	.057		9.45	1.85	1.04	12.34	14.80	
	2240	20LH04, 12 Lb/LF		1,400	.057		5.95	1.85	1.04	8.84	10.95	
	2260	20LH08, 19 Lb/LF		1,400	.057		9.45	1.85	1.04	12.34	14.80	
	2280	24LH05, 13 Lb/LF		1,400	.057		6.45	1.85	1.04	9.34	11.50	
	2300	24LH10, 23 Lb/LF		1,400	.057		11.45	1.85	1.04	14.34	17	
	2320	28LH06, 16 Lb/LF		1,800	.044		7.95	1.44	.81	10.20	12.15	
	2340	28LH11, 25 Lb/LF	▼	1,800	.044	▼	12.45	1.44	.81	14.70	17.10	

05210	Steel Joists	CREW	DAILY OUTPUT	LABOR-HOURS	UNIT	2001 BARE COSTS				TOTAL INCL O&P
						MAT.	LABOR	EQUIP.	TOTAL	
600										**600**
2360	32LH08, 17 Lb/LF	E-7	1,800	.044	L.F.	8.45	1.44	.81	10.70	12.70
2380	32LH13, 30 Lb/LF		1,800	.044		14.90	1.44	.81	17.15	19.80
2400	36LH09, 21 Lb/LF		1,800	.044		10.45	1.44	.81	12.70	14.90
2420	36LH14, 36 Lb/LF		1,800	.044		17.90	1.44	.81	20.15	23
2440	40LH10, 21 Lb/LF		2,200	.036		10.45	1.18	.66	12.29	14.30
2460	40LH15, 36 Lb/LF		2,200	.036		17.90	1.18	.66	19.74	22.50
2480	44LH11, 22 Lb/LF		2,200	.036		10.95	1.18	.66	12.79	14.85
2500	44LH16, 42 Lb/LF		2,200	.036		21	1.18	.66	22.84	26
2520	48LH11, 22 Lb/LF		2,200	.036		10.95	1.18	.66	12.79	14.85
2540	48LH16, 42 Lb/LF		2,200	.036		21	1.18	.66	22.84	26
3010	DLH series, bolted cross bridging									
3020	Spans to 144' (shipped in 2 pieces), minimum	E-7	16	5	Ton	1,000	162	91	1,253	1,475
3040	Average		13	6.154		1,075	199	112	1,386	1,650
3100	Maximum		11	7.273		1,300	235	133	1,668	2,000
3200	52DLH11, 26 Lb/LF		2,000	.040	L.F.	13.30	1.29	.73	15.32	17.75
3220	52DLH16, 45 Lb/LF		2,000	.040		24	1.29	.73	26.02	29.50
3240	56DLH11, 26 Lb/LF		2,000	.040		13.85	1.29	.73	15.87	18.35
3260	56DLH16, 46 Lb/LF		2,000	.040		24.50	1.29	.73	26.52	30
3280	60DLH12, 29 Lb/LF		2,000	.040		15.45	1.29	.73	17.47	20
3300	60DLH17, 52 Lb/LF		2,000	.040		27.50	1.29	.73	29.52	33.50
3320	64DLH12, 31 Lb/LF		2,200	.036		16.50	1.18	.66	18.34	21
3340	64DLH17, 52 Lb/LF		2,200	.036		27.50	1.18	.66	29.34	33.50
3360	68DLH13, 37 Lb/LF		2,200	.036		19.70	1.18	.66	21.54	24.50
3380	68DLH18, 61 Lb/LF		2,200	.036		32.50	1.18	.66	34.34	38.50
3400	72DLH14, 41 Lb/LF		2,200	.036		22	1.18	.66	23.84	27
3420	72DLH19, 70 Lb/LF		2,200	.036		37.50	1.18	.66	39.34	44
4010	SLH series, bolted cross bridging									
4020	Spans to 200', minimum	E-7	16	5	Ton	1,050	162	91	1,303	1,525
4040	Average		13	6.154		1,175	199	112	1,486	1,775
4060	Maximum		11	7.273		1,400	235	133	1,768	2,100
4200	80SLH15, 40 Lb/LF		1,500	.053	L.F.	23.50	1.73	.97	26.20	30
4220	80SLH20, 75 Lb/LF		1,500	.053		44	1.73	.97	46.70	52.50
4240	88SLH16, 46 Lb/LF		1,500	.053		27	1.73	.97	29.70	33.50
4260	88SLH21, 89 Lb/LF		1,500	.053		52	1.73	.97	54.70	61.50
4280	96SLH17, 52 Lb/LF		1,500	.053		30.50	1.73	.97	33.20	37.50
4300	96SLH22, 102 Lb/LF		1,500	.053		59.50	1.73	.97	62.20	69.50
4320	104SLH18, 59 Lb/LF		1,800	.044		34.50	1.44	.81	36.75	41.50
4340	104SLH23, 109 Lb/LF		1,800	.044		64	1.44	.81	66.25	73.50
4360	112SLH19, 67 Lb/LF		1,800	.044		39	1.44	.81	41.25	46.50
4380	112SLH24, 131 Lb/LF		1,800	.044		76.50	1.44	.81	78.75	88
4400	120SLH20, 77 Lb/LF		1,800	.044		45	1.44	.81	47.25	53
4420	120SLH25, 152 Lb/LF		1,800	.044		89	1.44	.81	91.25	101
6000	For welded cross bridging, add						30%			
6100	For L.T.L. lots, add					10%	15%			
6200	For shop prime paint other than mfrs. standard, add					20%				
6300	For bottom chord extensions, add per chord				Ea.	24.50			24.50	26.50
7000	Joist girders, minimum	E-5	15	5.333	Ton	850	173	91.50	1,114.50	1,350
7020	Average		13	6.154		935	199	106	1,240	1,500
7040	Maximum		11	7.273		980	235	125	1,340	1,625
8000	Trusses, factory fabricated WT chords, average		11	7.273		2,800	235	125	3,160	3,625

5

METALS

05310	Steel Deck	CREW	DAILY OUTPUT	LABOR-HOURS	UNIT	MAT.	LABOR	EQUIP.	TOTAL	TOTAL INCL O&P
							2001 BARE COSTS			
300	0010 **METAL DECKING** Steel decking									300
	0200 Cellular units, galvanized, 2" deep, 20-20 gauge, over 15 squares	E-4	1,460	.022	S.F.	3	.73	.06	3.79	4.69
	0250 18-20 gauge		1,420	.023		3	.75	.06	3.81	4.73
	0300 18-18 gauge		1,390	.023		3.50	.77	.06	4.33	5.30
	0320 16-18 gauge		1,360	.024		4.20	.78	.06	5.04	6.10
	0340 16-16 gauge		1,330	.024		5	.80	.06	5.86	7.05
	0400 3" deep, galvanized, 20-20 gauge		1,375	.023		3	.78	.06	3.84	4.78
	0500 18-20 gauge		1,350	.024		3.50	.79	.06	4.35	5.35
	0600 18-18 gauge		1,290	.025		4	.83	.07	4.90	5.95
	0700 16-18 gauge		1,230	.026		4	.87	.07	4.94	6.05
	0800 16-16 gauge		1,150	.028		5	.93	.07	6	7.25
	1000 4-1/2" deep, galvanized, 20-18 gauge		1,100	.029		5.40	.97	.08	6.45	7.80
	1100 18-18 gauge		1,040	.031		5.95	1.03	.08	7.06	8.50
	1200 16-18 gauge		980	.033		6.75	1.09	.09	7.93	9.45
	1300 16-16 gauge	▼	935	.034	▼	6.95	1.14	.09	8.18	9.80
	1500 For acoustical deck, add					15%				
	1700 For cells used for ventilation, add					15%				
	1900 For multi-story or congested site, add						50%			
	2100 Open type, galv., 1-1/2" deep wide rib, 22 gauge, under 50 squares	E-4	4,500	.007	S.F.	.84	.24	.02	1.10	1.38
	2200 50-500 squares **CN**		4,900	.007		.70	.22	.02	.94	1.19
	2400 Over 500 squares		5,100	.006		.63	.21	.02	.86	1.09
	2600 20 gauge, under 50 squares		3,865	.008		.98	.28	.02	1.28	1.60
	2650 50-500 squares		4,170	.008		.83	.26	.02	1.11	1.40
	2700 Over 500 squares		4,300	.007		.73	.25	.02	1	1.27
	2900 18 gauge, under 50 squares		3,800	.008		1.32	.28	.02	1.62	1.98
	2950 50-500 squares		4,100	.008		1.08	.26	.02	1.36	1.68
	3000 Over 500 squares		4,300	.007		.95	.25	.02	1.22	1.51
	3050 16 gauge, under 50 squares		3,700	.009		1.66	.29	.02	1.97	2.37
	3060 50-500 squares		4,000	.008		1.33	.27	.02	1.62	1.96
	3100 Over 500 squares	▼	4,200	.008		1.24	.25	.02	1.51	1.84
	3150 For intermediate rib instead of wide rib, deduct					.01			.01	.01
	3160 For narrow rib instead of wide rib, add					.26			.26	.28
	3200 3" deep, 22 gauge, under 50 squares	E-4	3,600	.009		1.35	.30	.02	1.67	2.05
	3250 50-500 squares		3,800	.008		1.07	.28	.02	1.37	1.71
	3260 over 500 squares		4,000	.008		.90	.27	.02	1.19	1.49
	3300 20 gauge, under 50 squares		3,400	.009		1.52	.31	.02	1.85	2.28
	3350 50-500 squares		3,600	.009		1.22	.30	.02	1.54	1.91
	3360 over 500 squares		3,800	.008		1.04	.28	.02	1.34	1.67
	3400 18 gauge, under 50 squares		3,200	.010		1.92	.33	.03	2.28	2.75
	3450 50-500 squares		3,400	.009		1.62	.31	.02	1.95	2.38
	3460 over 500 squares		3,600	.009		1.41	.30	.02	1.73	2.12
	3500 16 gauge, under 50 squares		3,000	.011		2.37	.36	.03	2.76	3.29
	3550 50-500 squares		3,200	.010		1.90	.33	.03	2.26	2.72
	3560 over 500 squares		3,400	.009		1.79	.31	.02	2.12	2.57
	3700 4-1/2" deep, long span roof, over 50 squares, 20 gauge		2,700	.012		2.21	.40	.03	2.64	3.18
	3800 18 gauge		2,460	.013		2.73	.43	.03	3.19	3.83
	3900 16 gauge		2,350	.014		3.44	.45	.04	3.93	4.64
	4100 6" deep, long span, 18 gauge		2,000	.016		3.87	.53	.04	4.44	5.30
	4200 16 gauge		1,930	.017		4.57	.55	.04	5.16	6.10
	4300 14 gauge		1,860	.017		4.68	.57	.05	5.30	6.25
	4500 7-1/2" deep, long span, 18 gauge		1,690	.019		4.24	.63	.05	4.92	5.85
	4600 16 gauge		1,590	.020		5.15	.67	.05	5.87	6.95
	4700 14 gauge	▼	1,490	.021	▼	5.45	.72	.06	6.23	7.35
	4800 For painted instead of galvanized, deduct					2%				
	5000 For acoustical perforated, with fiberglass, add				S.F.	1.01			1.01	1.11
	5200 Non-cellular composite deck, galv., 2" deep, 22 gauge	E-4	3,860	.008	▼	.80	.28	.02	1.10	1.40

05300 | Metal Decking

05310 | Steel Deck

		CREW	DAILY OUTPUT	LABOR-HOURS	UNIT	MAT.	LABOR	EQUIP.	TOTAL	TOTAL INCL O&P	
300	5300	20 gauge	E-4	3,600	.009	S.F.	.93	.30	.02	1.25	1.59	**300**
	5400	18 gauge		3,380	.009		1.25	.32	.02	1.59	1.98	
	5500	16 gauge		3,200	.010		1.68	.33	.03	2.04	2.49	
	5700	3" deep, galv., 22 gauge		3,200	.010		.87	.33	.03	1.23	1.60	
	5800	20 gauge		3,000	.011		1.02	.36	.03	1.41	1.80	
	5900	18 gauge **CN**		2,850	.011		1.34	.37	.03	1.74	2.18	
	6000	16 gauge		2,700	.012		1.91	.40	.03	2.34	2.85	
	6100	Slab form, steel, 28 gauge, 9/16" deep, uncoated		4,000	.008		.49	.27	.02	.78	1.04	
	6200	Galvanized		4,000	.008		.52	.27	.02	.81	1.07	
	6220	24 gauge, 1" deep, uncoated		3,900	.008		.71	.27	.02	1	1.30	
	6240	Galvanized		3,900	.008		.74	.27	.02	1.03	1.33	
	6300	24 gauge, 1-5/16" deep, uncoated		3,800	.008		.73	.28	.02	1.03	1.33	
	6400	Galvanized		3,800	.008		.86	.28	.02	1.16	1.48	
	6500	22 gauge, 1-5/16" deep, uncoated		3,700	.009		.84	.29	.02	1.15	1.47	
	6600	Galvanized		3,700	.009		.93	.29	.02	1.24	1.57	
	6700	22 gauge, 2" deep uncoated		3,600	.009		.92	.30	.02	1.24	1.58	
	6800	Galvanized		3,600	.009		.90	.30	.02	1.22	1.56	
	7000	Sheet metal edge closure form, 12" wide with 2 bends										
	7100	18 gauge	E-14	360	.022	L.F.	1.89	.77	.23	2.89	3.74	
	7200	16 gauge	"	360	.022	"	2.59	.77	.23	3.59	4.51	
	8000	Metal deck and trench, 2" thick, 20 gauge, combination										
	8010	60% cellular, 40% non-cellular, inserts and trench	R-4	1,100	.036	S.F.	5.60	1.22	.08	6.90	8.40	

5

METALS

05400 | Cold Formed Metal Framing

05410 | Load-Bearing Metal Studs

		CREW	DAILY OUTPUT	LABOR-HOURS	UNIT	MAT.	LABOR	EQUIP.	TOTAL	TOTAL INCL O&P	
100	0010	**BRACING,** shear wall X-bracing, per 10' x 10' bay, one face										**100**
	0120	Metal strap, 20 ga x 4" wide	2 Carp	18	.889	Ea.	10.80	26		36.80	52.50	
	0130	6" wide		18	.889		17.10	26		43.10	59.50	
	0160	18 ga x 4" wide		16	1		15.75	29		44.75	63	
	0170	6" wide		16	1		23.50	29		52.50	71	
	0410	Continuous strap bracing, per horizontal row on both faces										
	0420	Metal strap, 20 ga x 2" wide, studs 12" O.C.	1 Carp	7	1.143	C.L.F.	28.50	33.50		62	83.50	
	0430	16" O.C.		8	1		28.50	29		57.50	77	
	0440	24" O.C.		10	.800		28.50	23.50		52	68	
	0450	18 ga x 2" wide, studs 12" O.C.		6	1.333		39.50	39		78.50	105	
	0460	16" O.C.		7	1.143		39.50	33.50		73	95.50	
	0470	24" O.C.		8	1		39.50	29		68.50	89	
120	0010	**BRIDGING,** solid between studs w/ 1-1/4" leg track, per stud bay										**120**
	0200	Studs 12" O.C., 18 ga x 2-1/2" wide	1 Carp	125	.064	Ea.	.48	1.87		2.35	3.44	
	0210	3-5/8" wide		120	.067		.57	1.94		2.51	3.66	
	0220	4" wide		120	.067		.60	1.94		2.54	3.71	
	0230	6" wide		115	.070		.79	2.03		2.82	4.03	
	0240	8" wide		110	.073		1	2.12		3.12	4.42	
	0300	16 ga x 2-1/2" wide		115	.070		.59	2.03		2.62	3.82	
	0310	3-5/8" wide		110	.073		.72	2.12		2.84	4.11	
	0320	4" wide		110	.073		.77	2.12		2.89	4.17	
	0330	6" wide		105	.076		.99	2.22		3.21	4.56	
	0340	8" wide		100	.080		1.26	2.33		3.59	5.05	
	1200	Studs 16" O.C., 18 ga x 2-1/2" wide		125	.064		.61	1.87		2.48	3.59	

			DAILY OUTPUT	LABOR-HOURS	UNIT	2001 BARE COSTS				TOTAL INCL O&P	
05410	**Load-Bearing Metal Studs**		CREW			MAT.	LABOR	EQUIP.	TOTAL		
120	1210	3-5/8" wide	1 Carp	120	.067	Ea.	.73	1.94		2.67	3.84	**120**
	1220	4" wide		120	.067		.78	1.94		2.72	3.89	
	1230	6" wide		115	.070		1.01	2.03		3.04	4.28	
	1240	8" wide		110	.073		1.29	2.12		3.41	4.74	
	1300	16 ga x 2-1/2" wide		115	.070		.76	2.03		2.79	4	
	1310	3-5/8" wide		110	.073		.92	2.12		3.04	4.34	
	1320	4" wide		110	.073		.99	2.12		3.11	4.41	
	1330	6" wide		105	.076		1.27	2.22		3.49	4.87	
	1340	8" wide		100	.080		1.62	2.33		3.95	5.45	
	2200	Studs 24" O.C., 18 ga x 2-1/2" wide		125	.064		.88	1.87		2.75	3.89	
	2210	3-5/8" wide		120	.067		1.05	1.94		2.99	4.20	
	2220	4" wide		120	.067		1.12	1.94		3.06	4.27	
	2230	6" wide		115	.070		1.46	2.03		3.49	4.77	
	2240	8" wide		110	.073		1.86	2.12		3.98	5.35	
	2300	16 ga x 2-1/2" wide		115	.070		1.10	2.03		3.13	4.38	
	2310	3-5/8" wide		110	.073		1.34	2.12		3.46	4.79	
	2320	4" wide		110	.073		1.43	2.12		3.55	4.90	
	2330	6" wide		105	.076		1.84	2.22		4.06	5.50	
	2340	8" wide	▼	100	.080	▼	2.34	2.33		4.67	6.20	
	3000	Continuous bridging, per row										
	3100	16 ga x 1-1/2" channel thru studs 12" O.C.	1 Carp	6	1.333	C.L.F.	26.50	39		65.50	90	
	3110	16" O.C.		7	1.143		26.50	33.50		60	81	
	3120	24" O.C.		8.80	.909		26.50	26.50		53	70.50	
	4100	2" x 2" angle x 18 ga, studs 12" O.C.		7	1.143		38.50	33.50		72	94.50	
	4110	16" O.C.		9	.889		38.50	26		64.50	83	
	4120	24" O.C.		12	.667		38.50	19.45		57.95	73	
	4200	16 ga, studs 12" O.C.		5	1.600		49.50	46.50		96	128	
	4210	16" O.C.		7	1.143		49.50	33.50		83	107	
	4220	24" O.C.	▼	10	.800	▼	49.50	23.50		73	91	
300	0010	**FRAMING,** boxed headers/beams										**300**
	0200	Double, 18 ga x 6" deep	2 Carp	220	.073	L.F.	2.75	2.12		4.87	6.35	
	0210	8" deep		210	.076		3.05	2.22		5.27	6.80	
	0220	10" deep		200	.080		3.70	2.33		6.03	7.70	
	0230	12" deep		190	.084		4.06	2.45		6.51	8.30	
	0300	16 ga x 8" deep		180	.089		3.51	2.59		6.10	7.90	
	0310	10" deep		170	.094		4.20	2.74		6.94	8.90	
	0320	12" deep		160	.100		4.58	2.92		7.50	9.60	
	0400	14 ga x 10" deep		140	.114		4.90	3.33		8.23	10.60	
	0410	12" deep		130	.123		5.40	3.59		8.99	11.50	
	1210	Triple, 18 ga x 8" deep		170	.094		4.41	2.74		7.15	9.15	
	1220	10" deep		165	.097		5.30	2.83		8.13	10.25	
	1230	12" deep		160	.100		5.85	2.92		8.77	11	
	1300	16 ga x 8" deep		145	.110		5.10	3.22		8.32	10.65	
	1310	10" deep		140	.114		6.05	3.33		9.38	11.85	
	1320	12" deep		135	.119		6.65	3.45		10.10	12.70	
	1400	14 ga x 10" deep		115	.139		6.70	4.06		10.76	13.70	
	1410	12" deep	▼	110	.145	▼	7.40	4.24		11.64	14.80	
400	0010	**FRAMING, STUD WALLS** w/ top & bottom track, no openings,										**400**
	0020	headers, beams, bridging or bracing										
	4100	8' high walls, 18 ga x 2-1/2" wide, studs 12" O.C.	2 Carp	54	.296	L.F.	4.59	8.65		13.24	18.55	
	4110	16" O.C.		77	.208		3.67	6.05		9.72	13.55	
	4120	24" O.C.		107	.150		2.75	4.36		7.11	9.80	
	4130	3-5/8" wide, studs 12" O.C.		53	.302		5.50	8.80		14.30	19.80	
	4140	16" O.C.		76	.211		4.38	6.15		10.53	14.40	
	4150	24" O.C.	▼	105	.152	▼	3.28	4.44		7.72	10.55	

5 METALS

05410	Load-Bearing Metal Studs	CREW	DAILY OUTPUT	LABOR-HOURS	UNIT	2001 BARE COSTS				TOTAL INCL O&P	
						MAT.	LABOR	EQUIP.	TOTAL		
400 4160	4" wide, studs 12" O.C.	2 Carp	52	.308	L.F.	5.70	8.95		14.65	20.50	**400**
4170	16" O.C.		74	.216		4.57	6.30		10.87	14.90	
4180	24" O.C.		103	.155		3.43	4.53		7.96	10.85	
4190	6" wide, studs 12" O.C.		51	.314		7.25	9.15		16.40	22.50	
4200	16" O.C.		73	.219		5.80	6.40		12.20	16.40	
4210	24" O.C.		101	.158		4.37	4.62		8.99	12	
4220	8" wide, studs 12" O.C.		50	.320		8.95	9.35		18.30	24.50	
4230	16" O.C.		72	.222		7.20	6.50		13.70	18.05	
4240	24" O.C.		100	.160		5.45	4.66		10.11	13.25	
4300	16 ga x 2-1/2" wide, studs 12" O.C.		47	.340		5.40	9.90		15.30	21.50	
4310	16" O.C.		68	.235		4.27	6.85		11.12	15.45	
4320	24" O.C.		94	.170		3.15	4.96		8.11	11.20	
4330	3-5/8" wide, studs 12" O.C.		46	.348		6.50	10.15		16.65	23	
4340	16" O.C.		66	.242		5.15	7.05		12.20	16.70	
4350	24" O.C.		92	.174		3.80	5.05		8.85	12.15	
4360	4" wide, studs 12" O.C.		45	.356		6.85	10.35		17.20	23.50	
4370	16" O.C.		65	.246		5.40	7.20		12.60	17.15	
4380	24" O.C.		90	.178		3.99	5.20		9.19	12.50	
4390	6" wide, studs 12" O.C.		44	.364		8.60	10.60		19.20	26	
4400	16" O.C.		64	.250		6.85	7.30		14.15	18.90	
4410	24" O.C.		88	.182		5.05	5.30		10.35	13.85	
4420	8" wide, studs 12" O.C.		43	.372		10.55	10.85		21.40	28.50	
4430	16" O.C.		63	.254		8.40	7.40		15.80	21	
4440	24" O.C.		86	.186		6.25	5.40		11.65	15.35	
5100	10' high walls, 18 ga x 2-1/2" wide, studs 12" O.C.		54	.296		5.50	8.65		14.15	19.55	
5110	16" O.C.		77	.208		4.36	6.05		10.41	14.30	
5120	24" O.C.		107	.150		3.21	4.36		7.57	10.35	
5130	3-5/8" wide, studs 12" O.C.		53	.302		6.60	8.80		15.40	21	
5140	16" O.C.		76	.211		5.20	6.15		11.35	15.30	
5150	24" O.C.		105	.152		3.83	4.44		8.27	11.15	
5160	4" wide, studs 12" O.C.		52	.308		6.85	8.95		15.80	21.50	
5170	16" O.C.		74	.216		5.45	6.30		11.75	15.80	
5180	24" O.C.		103	.155		4	4.53		8.53	11.50	
5190	6" wide, studs 12" O.C.		51	.314		8.70	9.15		17.85	24	
5200	16" O.C.		73	.219		6.90	6.40		13.30	17.60	
5210	24" O.C.		101	.158		5.10	4.62		9.72	12.80	
5220	8" wide, studs 12" O.C.		50	.320		10.70	9.35		20.05	26.50	
5230	16" O.C.		72	.222		8.50	6.50		15	19.50	
5240	24" O.C.		100	.160		6.30	4.66		10.96	14.25	
5300	16 ga x 2-1/2" wide, studs 12" O.C.		47	.340		6.50	9.90		16.40	22.50	
5310	16" O.C.		68	.235		5.10	6.85		11.95	16.35	
5320	24" O.C.		94	.170		3.71	4.96		8.67	11.85	
5330	3-5/8" wide, studs 12" O.C.		46	.348		7.90	10.15		18.05	24.50	
5340	16" O.C.		66	.242		6.20	7.05		13.25	17.85	
5350	24" O.C.		92	.174		4.48	5.05		9.53	12.90	
5360	4" wide, studs 12" O.C.		45	.356		8.25	10.35		18.60	25.50	
5370	16" O.C.		65	.246		6.50	7.20		13.70	18.30	
5380	24" O.C.		90	.178		4.70	5.20		9.90	13.25	
5390	6" wide, studs 12" O.C.		44	.364		10.40	10.60		21	28	
5400	16" O.C.		64	.250		8.15	7.30		15.45	20.50	
5410	24" O.C.		88	.182		5.95	5.30		11.25	14.85	
5420	8" wide, studs 12" O.C.		43	.372		12.70	10.85		23.55	31	
5430	16" O.C.		63	.254		10	7.40		17.40	22.50	
5440	24" O.C.		86	.186		7.30	5.40		12.70	16.55	
6190	12' high walls, 18 ga x 6" wide, studs 12" O.C.		41	.390		10.15	11.40		21.55	29	
6200	16" O.C.		58	.276		7.95	8.05		16	21.50	

5

METALS

05410	Load-Bearing Metal Studs	CREW	DAILY OUTPUT	LABOR-HOURS	UNIT	2001 BARE COSTS				TOTAL INCL O&P
						MAT.	LABOR	EQUIP.	TOTAL	
400 6210	24" O.C.	2 Carp	81	.198	L.F.	5.80	5.75		11.55	15.40 **400**
6220	8" wide, studs 12" O.C.		40	.400		12.45	11.65		24.10	32
6230	16" O.C.		57	.281		9.85	8.20		18.05	23.50
6240	24" O.C.		80	.200		7.20	5.85		13.05	17
6390	16 ga x 6" wide, studs 12" O.C.		35	.457		12.15	13.35		25.50	34.50
6400	16" O.C.		51	.314		9.50	9.15		18.65	25
6410	24" O.C.		70	.229		6.85	6.65		13.50	17.90
6420	8" wide, studs 12" O.C.		34	.471		14.85	13.70		28.55	38
6430	16" O.C.		50	.320		11.65	9.35		21	27.50
6440	24" O.C.		69	.232		8.40	6.75		15.15	19.80
6530	14 ga x 3-5/8" wide, studs 12" O.C.		34	.471		11.55	13.70		25.25	34.50
6540	16" O.C.		48	.333		9	9.70		18.70	25
6550	24" O.C.		65	.246		6.45	7.20		13.65	18.30
6560	4" wide, studs 12" O.C.		33	.485		12.15	14.15		26.30	35.50
6570	16" O.C.		47	.340		9.50	9.90		19.40	26
6580	24" O.C.		64	.250		6.80	7.30		14.10	18.90
6730	12 ga x 3-5/8" wide, studs 12" O.C.		31	.516		15.90	15.05		30.95	41
6740	16" O.C.		43	.372		12.25	10.85		23.10	30.50
6750	24" O.C.		59	.271		8.65	7.90		16.55	22
6760	4" wide, studs 12" O.C.		30	.533		17.05	15.55		32.60	43.50
6770	16" O.C.		42	.381		13.15	11.10		24.25	32
6780	24" O.C.		58	.276		9.25	8.05		17.30	23
7390	16' high walls, 16 ga x 6" wide, studs 12" O.C.		33	.485		15.75	14.15		29.90	39.50
7400	16" O.C.		48	.333		12.15	9.70		21.85	28.50
7410	24" O.C.		67	.239		8.60	6.95		15.55	20.50
7420	8" wide, studs 12" O.C.		32	.500		19.20	14.60		33.80	44
7430	16" O.C.		47	.340		14.85	9.90		24.75	32
7440	24" O.C.		66	.242		10.55	7.05		17.60	22.50
7560	14 ga x 4" wide, studs 12" O.C.		31	.516		15.70	15.05		30.75	41
7570	16" O.C.		45	.356		12.15	10.35		22.50	29.50
7580	24" O.C.		61	.262		8.60	7.65		16.25	21.50
7590	6" wide, studs 12" O.C.		30	.533		19.80	15.55		35.35	46.50
7600	16" O.C.		44	.364		15.35	10.60		25.95	33.50
7610	24" O.C.		60	.267		10.85	7.75		18.60	24
7760	12 ga x 4" wide, studs 12" O.C.		29	.552		22.50	16.10		38.60	49.50
7770	16" O.C.		40	.400		17.05	11.65		28.70	37
7780	24" O.C.		55	.291		11.85	8.50		20.35	26.50
7790	6" wide, studs 12" O.C.		28	.571		28	16.65		44.65	57
7800	16" O.C.		39	.410		21.50	11.95		33.45	42
7810	24" O.C.		54	.296		15	8.65		23.65	30
8590	20' high walls, 14 ga x 6" wide, studs 12" O.C.		29	.552		24.50	16.10		40.60	51.50
8600	16" O.C.		42	.381		18.70	11.10		29.80	38
8610	24" O.C.		57	.281		13.10	8.20		21.30	27
8620	8" wide, studs 12" O.C.		28	.571		30	16.65		46.65	59
8630	16" O.C.		41	.390		23	11.40		34.40	43.50
8640	24" O.C.		56	.286		16.10	8.35		24.45	31
8790	12 ga x 6" wide, studs 12" O.C.		27	.593		34.50	17.25		51.75	65
8800	16" O.C.		37	.432		26.50	12.60		39.10	48.50
8810	24" O.C.		51	.314		18.30	9.15		27.45	34.50
8820	8" wide, studs 12" O.C.		26	.615		42	17.95		59.95	74.50
8830	16" O.C.		36	.444		32.50	12.95		45.45	56
8840	24" O.C.	2 Carp	50	.320	L.F.	22.50	9.35		31.85	39

05420	Cold-Formed Metal Joists									
100 0010	**BRACING**, continuous, per row, top & bottom									**100**
0120	Flat strap, 20 ga x 2" wide, joists at 12" O.C.	1 Carp	4.67	1.713	C.L.F.	30	50		80	111

		05420	Cold-Formed Metal Joists	CREW	DAILY OUTPUT	LABOR-HOURS	UNIT	2001 BARE COSTS MAT.	LABOR	EQUIP.	TOTAL	TOTAL INCL O&P	
100	0130		16" O.C.	1 Carp	5.33	1.501	C.L.F.	29	44		73	101	**100**
	0140		24" O.C.		6.66	1.201		28	35		63	85.50	
	0150		18 ga x 2" wide, joists at 12" O.C.		4	2		39	58.50		97.50	134	
	0160		16" O.C.		4.67	1.713		38.50	50		88.50	121	
	0170		24" O.C.	↓	5.33	1.501	↓	38	44		82	110	
120	0010		**BRIDGING**, solid between joists w/ 1-1/4" leg track, per joist bay										**120**
	0230		Joists 12" O.C., 18 ga track x 6" wide	1 Carp	80	.100	Ea.	.79	2.92		3.71	5.40	
	0240		8" wide		75	.107		1	3.11		4.11	5.95	
	0250		10" wide		70	.114		1.24	3.33		4.57	6.55	
	0260		12" wide		65	.123		1.43	3.59		5.02	7.15	
	0330		16 ga track x 6" wide		70	.114		.99	3.33		4.32	6.30	
	0340		8" wide		65	.123		1.26	3.59		4.85	7	
	0350		10" wide		60	.133		1.54	3.89		5.43	7.80	
	0360		12" wide		55	.145		1.79	4.24		6.03	8.60	
	0440		14 ga track x 8" wide		60	.133		1.58	3.89		5.47	7.85	
	0450		10" wide		55	.145		1.94	4.24		6.18	8.80	
	0460		12" wide		50	.160		2.25	4.66		6.91	9.80	
	0550		12 ga track x 10" wide		45	.178		2.86	5.20		8.06	11.25	
	0560		12" wide		40	.200		3.24	5.85		9.09	12.65	
	1230		16" O.C., 18 ga track x 6" wide		80	.100		1.01	2.92		3.93	5.65	
	1240		8" wide		75	.107		1.29	3.11		4.40	6.30	
	1250		10" wide		70	.114		1.58	3.33		4.91	6.95	
	1260		12" wide		65	.123		1.83	3.59		5.42	7.60	
	1330		16 ga track x 6" wide		70	.114		1.27	3.33		4.60	6.60	
	1340		8" wide		65	.123		1.62	3.59		5.21	7.40	
	1350		10" wide		60	.133		1.98	3.89		5.87	8.30	
	1360		12" wide		55	.145		2.29	4.24		6.53	9.15	
	1440		14 ga track x 8" wide		60	.133		2.03	3.89		5.92	8.35	
	1450		10" wide		55	.145		2.49	4.24		6.73	9.40	
	1460		12" wide		50	.160		2.89	4.66		7.55	10.50	
	1550		12 ga track x 10" wide		45	.178		3.66	5.20		8.86	12.15	
	1560		12" wide		40	.200		4.16	5.85		10.01	13.65	
	2230		24" O.C., 18 ga track x 6" wide		80	.100		1.46	2.92		4.38	6.15	
	2240		8" wide		75	.107		1.86	3.11		4.97	6.90	
	2250		10" wide		70	.114		2.29	3.33		5.62	7.70	
	2260		12" wide		65	.123		2.65	3.59		6.24	8.50	
	2330		16 ga track x 6" wide		70	.114		1.84	3.33		5.17	7.20	
	2340		8" wide		65	.123		2.34	3.59		5.93	8.15	
	2350		10" wide		60	.133		2.86	3.89		6.75	9.25	
	2360		12" wide		55	.145		3.32	4.24		7.56	10.30	
	2440		14 ga track x 8" wide		60	.133		2.94	3.89		6.83	9.35	
	2450		10" wide		55	.145		3.60	4.24		7.84	10.60	
	2460		12" wide		50	.160		4.18	4.66		8.84	11.90	
	2550		12 ga track x 10" wide		45	.178		5.30	5.20		10.50	13.95	
	2560		12" wide	↓	40	.200	↓	6	5.85		11.85	15.70	
200	0010		**FRAMING, BAND JOIST** (track) fastened to bearing wall										**200**
	0220		18 ga track x 6" deep	2 Carp	1,000	.016	L.F.	.64	.47		1.11	1.43	
	0230		8" deep		920	.017		.82	.51		1.33	1.69	
	0240		10" deep		860	.019		1.01	.54		1.55	1.96	
	0320		16 ga track x 6" deep		900	.018		.81	.52		1.33	1.70	
	0330		8" deep		840	.019		1.03	.56		1.59	2	
	0340		10" deep		780	.021		1.26	.60		1.86	2.33	
	0350		12" deep		740	.022		1.46	.63		2.09	2.60	
	0430		14 ga track x 8" deep		750	.021		1.29	.62		1.91	2.39	
	0440		10" deep	↓	720	.022	↓	1.59	.65		2.24	2.75	

5

METALS

			DAILY	LABOR-		2001 BARE COSTS				TOTAL	
05420	**Cold-Formed Metal Joists**	CREW	OUTPUT	HOURS	UNIT	MAT.	LABOR	EQUIP.	TOTAL	INCL O&P	
200	0450	12" deep	2 Carp	700	.023	L.F.	1.84	.67		2.51	3.06	**200**
	0540	12 ga track x 10" deep		670	.024		2.33	.70		3.03	3.65	
	0550	12" deep	↓	650	.025	↓	2.65	.72		3.37	4.03	
300	0010	**FRAMING, BOXED HEADERS/BEAMS**										**300**
	0200	Double, 18 ga x 6" deep	2 Carp	220	.073	L.F.	2.75	2.12		4.87	6.35	
	0210	8" deep		210	.076		3.05	2.22		5.27	6.80	
	0220	10" deep		200	.080		3.70	2.33		6.03	7.70	
	0230	12" deep		190	.084		4.06	2.45		6.51	8.30	
	0300	16 ga x 8" deep		180	.089		3.51	2.59		6.10	7.90	
	0310	10" deep		170	.094		4.20	2.74		6.94	8.90	
	0320	12" deep		160	.100		4.58	2.92		7.50	9.60	
	0400	14 ga x 10" deep		140	.114		4.90	3.33		8.23	10.60	
	0410	12" deep		130	.123		5.40	3.59		8.99	11.50	
	0500	12 ga x 10" deep		110	.145		6.50	4.24		10.74	13.80	
	0510	12" deep		100	.160		7.20	4.66		11.86	15.20	
	1210	Triple, 18 ga x 8" deep		170	.094		4.41	2.74		7.15	9.15	
	1220	10" deep		165	.097		5.30	2.83		8.13	10.25	
	1230	12" deep		160	.100		5.85	2.92		8.77	11	
	1300	16 ga x 8" deep		145	.110		5.10	3.22		8.32	10.65	
	1310	10" deep		140	.114		6.05	3.33		9.38	11.85	
	1320	12" deep		135	.119		6.65	3.45		10.10	12.70	
	1400	14 ga x 10" deep		115	.139		7.10	4.06		11.16	14.20	
	1410	12" deep		110	.145		7.85	4.24		12.09	15.25	
	1500	12 ga x 10" deep		90	.178		9.50	5.20		14.70	18.55	
	1510	12" deep	↓	85	.188	↓	10.55	5.50		16.05	20	
410	0010	**FRAMING, JOISTS**, no band joists (track), web stiffeners, headers,										**410**
	0020	beams, bridging or bracing										
	0030	Joists (2" flange) and fasteners, materials only										
	0220	18 ga x 6" deep				L.F.	.85			.85	.94	
	0230	8" deep					1.01			1.01	1.11	
	0240	10" deep					1.19			1.19	1.31	
	0320	16 ga x 6" deep					1.04			1.04	1.14	
	0330	8" deep					1.25			1.25	1.37	
	0340	10" deep					1.45			1.45	1.59	
	0350	12" deep					1.65			1.65	1.81	
	0430	14 ga x 8" deep					1.58			1.58	1.73	
	0440	10" deep					1.82			1.82	2	
	0450	12" deep					2.07			2.07	2.28	
	0540	12 ga x 10" deep					2.65			2.65	2.91	
	0550	12" deep				↓	3.01			3.01	3.31	
	1010	Installation of joists to band joists, beams & headers, labor only										
	1220	18 ga x 6" deep	2 Carp	110	.145	Ea.		4.24		4.24	6.65	
	1230	8" deep		90	.178			5.20		5.20	8.10	
	1240	10" deep		80	.200			5.85		5.85	9.10	
	1320	16 ga x 6" deep		95	.168			4.91		4.91	7.70	
	1330	8" deep		70	.229			6.65		6.65	10.40	
	1340	10" deep		60	.267			7.75		7.75	12.15	
	1350	12" deep		55	.291			8.50		8.50	13.25	
	1430	14 ga x 8" deep		65	.246			7.20		7.20	11.20	
	1440	10" deep		45	.356			10.35		10.35	16.20	
	1450	12" deep		35	.457			13.35		13.35	21	
	1540	12 ga x 10" deep		40	.400			11.65		11.65	18.25	
	1550	12" deep	↓	30	.533	↓		15.55		15.55	24.50	
500	0010	**FRAMING, WEB STIFFENERS** at joist bearing, fabricated from										**500**
	0020	stud piece (1-5/8" flange) to stiffen joist (2" flange)										

Important: See the Reference Section for critical supporting data - Reference Nos., Crews, & City Cost Indexes

05420	Cold-Formed Metal Joists	CREW	DAILY OUTPUT	LABOR-HOURS	UNIT	2001 BARE COSTS				TOTAL INCL O&P	
						MAT.	LABOR	EQUIP.	TOTAL		
500 2120	For 6" deep joist, with 18 ga x 2-1/2" stud	1 Carp	120	.067	Ea.	1.01	1.94		2.95	4.15	**500**
2130	3-5/8" stud		110	.073		1.13	2.12		3.25	4.56	
2140	4" stud		105	.076		1.08	2.22		3.30	4.66	
2150	6" stud		100	.080		1.19	2.33		3.52	4.96	
2160	8" stud		95	.084		1.23	2.45		3.68	5.20	
2220	8" deep joist, with 2-1/2" stud		120	.067		1.11	1.94		3.05	4.26	
2230	3-5/8" stud		110	.073		1.22	2.12		3.34	4.66	
2240	4" stud		105	.076		1.18	2.22		3.40	4.77	
2250	6" stud		100	.080		1.30	2.33		3.63	5.10	
2260	8" stud		95	.084		1.42	2.45		3.87	5.40	
2320	10" deep joist, with 2-1/2" stud		110	.073		1.57	2.12		3.69	5.05	
2330	3-5/8" stud		100	.080		1.73	2.33		4.06	5.55	
2340	4" stud		95	.084		1.70	2.45		4.15	5.70	
2350	6" stud		90	.089		1.85	2.59		4.44	6.10	
2360	8" stud		85	.094		1.90	2.74		4.64	6.40	
2420	12" deep joist, with 2-1/2" stud		110	.073		1.66	2.12		3.78	5.15	
2430	3-5/8" stud		100	.080		1.82	2.33		4.15	5.65	
2440	4" stud		95	.084		1.77	2.45		4.22	5.80	
2450	6" stud		90	.089		1.94	2.59		4.53	6.20	
2460	8" stud		85	.094		2.11	2.74		4.85	6.60	
3130	For 6" deep joist, with 16 ga x 3-5/8" stud		100	.080		1.19	2.33		3.52	4.96	
3140	4" stud		95	.084		1.17	2.45		3.62	5.15	
3150	6" stud		90	.089		1.29	2.59		3.88	5.45	
3160	8" stud		85	.094		1.35	2.74		4.09	5.80	
3230	8" deep joist, with 3-5/8" stud		100	.080		1.32	2.33		3.65	5.10	
3240	4" stud		95	.084		1.28	2.45		3.73	5.25	
3250	6" stud		90	.089		1.43	2.59		4.02	5.60	
3260	8" stud		85	.094		1.52	2.74		4.26	5.95	
3330	10" deep joist, with 3-5/8" stud		85	.094		1.81	2.74		4.55	6.30	
3340	4" stud		80	.100		1.83	2.92		4.75	6.55	
3350	6" stud		75	.107		1.99	3.11		5.10	7.05	
3360	8" stud		70	.114		2.06	3.33		5.39	7.45	
3430	12" deep joist, with 3-5/8" stud		85	.094		1.97	2.74		4.71	6.45	
3440	4" stud		80	.100		1.92	2.92		4.84	6.65	
3450	6" stud		75	.107		2.14	3.11		5.25	7.20	
3460	8" stud		70	.114		2.27	3.33		5.60	7.70	
4230	For 8" deep joist, with 14 ga x 3-5/8" stud		90	.089		1.71	2.59		4.30	5.95	
4240	4" stud		85	.094		1.73	2.74		4.47	6.20	
4250	6" stud		80	.100		1.88	2.92		4.80	6.60	
4260	8" stud		75	.107		2.02	3.11		5.13	7.10	
4330	10" deep joist, with 3-5/8" stud		75	.107		2.40	3.11		5.51	7.50	
4340	4" stud		70	.114		2.36	3.33		5.69	7.80	
4350	6" stud		65	.123		2.60	3.59		6.19	8.45	
4360	8" stud		60	.133		2.73	3.89		6.62	9.10	
4430	12" deep joist, with 3-5/8" stud		75	.107		2.55	3.11		5.66	7.65	
4440	4" stud		70	.114		2.58	3.33		5.91	8.05	
4450	6" stud		65	.123		2.80	3.59		6.39	8.70	
4460	8" stud		60	.133		3.01	3.89		6.90	9.40	
5330	For 10" deep joist, with 12 ga x 3-5/8" stud		65	.123		2.51	3.59		6.10	8.35	
5340	4" stud		60	.133		2.59	3.89		6.48	8.95	
5350	6" stud		55	.145		2.86	4.24		7.10	9.80	
5360	8" stud		50	.160		3.14	4.66		7.80	10.75	
5430	12" deep joist, with 3-5/8" stud		65	.123		2.78	3.59		6.37	8.65	
5440	4" stud		60	.133		2.73	3.89		6.62	9.10	
5450	6" stud		55	.145		3.12	4.24		7.36	10.10	
5460	8" stud		50	.160		3.58	4.66		8.24	11.25	

METALS **5**

05460	Cold-Formed Roof Framing	CREW	DAILY OUTPUT	LABOR-HOURS	UNIT	2001 BARE COSTS				TOTAL INCL O&P	
						MAT.	LABOR	EQUIP.	TOTAL		
100	**0010**	**FRAMING, BRACING**									**100**
	0020	Continuous bracing, per row									
	0100	16 ga x 1-1/2" channel thru rafters/trusses @ 16" O.C.	1 Carp	4.50	1.778	C.L.F.	26.50	52		78.50	110
	0120	24" O.C.		6	1.333		26.50	39		65.50	90
	0300	2" x 2" angle x 18 ga, rafters/trusses @ 16" O.C.		6	1.333		38.50	39		77.50	104
	0320	24" O.C.		8	1		38.50	29		67.50	88
	0400	16 ga, rafters/trusses @ 16" O.C.		4.50	1.778		49.50	52		101.50	136
	0420	24" O.C.	↓	6.50	1.231	↓	49.50	36		85.50	111
200	**0010**	**FRAMING, BRIDGING**									**200**
	0020	Solid, between rafters w/ 1-1/4" leg track, per rafter bay									
	1200	Rafters 16" O.C., 18 ga x 4" deep	1 Carp	60	.133	Ea.	.78	3.89		4.67	6.95
	1210	6" deep		57	.140		1.01	4.09		5.10	7.50
	1220	8" deep		55	.145		1.29	4.24		5.53	8.05
	1230	10" deep		52	.154		1.58	4.48		6.06	8.75
	1240	12" deep		50	.160		1.83	4.66		6.49	9.30
	2200	24" O.C., 18 ga x 4" deep		60	.133		1.12	3.89		5.01	7.35
	2210	6" deep		57	.140		1.46	4.09		5.55	8
	2220	8" deep		55	.145		1.86	4.24		6.10	8.70
	2230	10" deep		52	.154		2.29	4.48		6.77	9.50
	2240	12" deep	↓	50	.160	↓	2.65	4.66		7.31	10.20
500	**0010**	**FRAMING, PARAPETS**									**500**
	0100	3' high installed on 1st story, 18 ga x 4" wide studs, 12" O.C.	2 Carp	100	.160	L.F.	2.86	4.66		7.52	10.45
	0110	16" O.C.		150	.107		2.43	3.11		5.54	7.55
	0120	24" O.C.		200	.080		2.01	2.33		4.34	5.85
	0200	6" wide studs, 12" O.C.		100	.160		3.65	4.66		8.31	11.30
	0210	16" O.C.		150	.107		3.11	3.11		6.22	8.30
	0220	24" O.C.		200	.080		2.57	2.33		4.90	6.50
	1100	Installed on 2nd story, 18 ga x 4" wide studs, 12" O.C.		95	.168		2.86	4.91		7.77	10.85
	1110	16" O.C.		145	.110		2.43	3.22		5.65	7.75
	1120	24" O.C.		190	.084		2.01	2.45		4.46	6.05
	1200	6" wide studs, 12" O.C.		95	.168		3.65	4.91		8.56	11.70
	1210	16" O.C.		145	.110		3.11	3.22		6.33	8.50
	1220	24" O.C.		190	.084		2.57	2.45		5.02	6.65
	2100	Installed on gable, 18 ga x 4" wide studs, 12" O.C.		85	.188		2.86	5.50		8.36	11.75
	2110	16" O.C.		130	.123		2.43	3.59		6.02	8.30
	2120	24" O.C.		170	.094		2.01	2.74		4.75	6.50
	2200	6" wide studs, 12" O.C.		85	.188		3.65	5.50		9.15	12.60
	2210	16" O.C.		130	.123		3.11	3.59		6.70	9.05
	2220	24" O.C.	↓	170	.094	↓	2.57	2.74		5.31	7.10
550	**0010**	**FRAMING, ROOF RAFTERS**									**550**
	0100	Boxed ridge beam, double, 18 ga x 6" deep	2 Carp	160	.100	L.F.	2.75	2.92		5.67	7.60
	0110	8" deep		150	.107		3.05	3.11		6.16	8.20
	0120	10" deep		140	.114		3.70	3.33		7.03	9.25
	0130	12" deep		130	.123		4.06	3.59		7.65	10.05
	0200	16 ga x 6" deep		150	.107		3.11	3.11		6.22	8.30
	0210	8" deep		140	.114		3.51	3.33		6.84	9.05
	0220	10" deep		130	.123		4.20	3.59		7.79	10.20
	0230	12" deep	↓	120	.133		4.58	3.89		8.47	11.15
	1100	Rafters, 2" flange, material only, 18 ga x 6" deep					.85			.85	.94
	1110	8" deep					1.01			1.01	1.11
	1120	10" deep					1.19			1.19	1.31
	1130	12" deep					1.38			1.38	1.51
	1200	16 ga x 6" deep					1.04			1.04	1.14
	1210	8" deep					1.25			1.25	1.37
	1220	10" deep				↓	1.45			1.45	1.59

		05460	Cold-Formed Roof Framing	CREW	DAILY OUTPUT	LABOR-HOURS	UNIT	MAT.	LABOR	EQUIP.	TOTAL	TOTAL INCL O&P	
								2001 BARE COSTS					
550	1230		12" deep				L.F.	1.65			1.65	1.81	550
	2100		Installation only, ordinary rafter to 4:12 pitch, 18 ga x 6" deep	2 Carp	35	.457	Ea.		13.35		13.35	21	
	2110		8" deep		30	.533			15.55		15.55	24.50	
	2120		10" deep		25	.640			18.65		18.65	29	
	2130		12" deep		20	.800			23.50		23.50	36.50	
	2200		16 ga x 6" deep		30	.533			15.55		15.55	24.50	
	2210		8" deep		25	.640			18.65		18.65	29	
	2220		10" deep		20	.800			23.50		23.50	36.50	
	2230		12" deep		15	1.067			31		31	48.50	
	8100		Add to labor, ordinary rafters on steep roofs						25%				
	8110		Dormers & complex roofs						50%				
	8200		Hip & valley rafters to 4:12 pitch						25%				
	8210		Steep roofs						50%				
	8220		Dormers & complex roofs						75%				
	8300		Hip & valley jack rafters to 4:12 pitch						50%				
	8310		Steep roofs						75%				
	8320		Dormers & complex roofs						100%				
600	0010		**FRAMING, ROOF TRUSSES**										600
	0020		Fabrication of trusses on-site, Fink (W) or King Post, to 4:12 pitch										
	0120		18 ga x 4" chords, 16' span	2 Carp	12	1.333	Ea.	32	39		71	96	
	0130		20' span		11	1.455		40	42.50		82.50	111	
	0140		24' span		11	1.455		48	42.50		90.50	119	
	0150		28' span		10	1.600		56	46.50		102.50	135	
	0160		32' span		10	1.600		64	46.50		110.50	143	
	0250		6" chords, 28' span		9	1.778		70.50	52		122.50	159	
	0260		32' span		9	1.778		80.50	52		132.50	170	
	0270		36' span		8	2		90.50	58.50		149	191	
	0280		40' span		8	2		101	58.50		159.50	202	
	1120		5:12 to 8:12 pitch, 18 ga x 4" chords, 16' span		10	1.600		36.50	46.50		83	113	
	1130		20' span		9	1.778		45.50	52		97.50	131	
	1140		24' span		9	1.778		54.50	52		106.50	141	
	1150		28' span		8	2		64	58.50		122.50	161	
	1160		32' span		8	2		73	58.50		131.50	172	
	1250		6" chords, 28' span		7	2.286		80.50	66.50		147	193	
	1260		32' span		7	2.286		92	66.50		158.50	205	
	1270		36' span		6	2.667		104	77.50		181.50	236	
	1280		40' span		6	2.667		115	77.50		192.50	249	
	2120		9:12 to 12:12 pitch, 18 ga x 4" chords, 16' span		8	2		45.50	58.50		104	141	
	2130		20' span		7	2.286		57	66.50		123.50	167	
	2140		24' span		7	2.286		68.50	66.50		135	179	
	2150		28' span		6	2.667		80	77.50		157.50	210	
	2160		32' span		6	2.667		91	77.50		168.50	222	
	2250		6" chords, 28' span		5	3.200		101	93.50		194.50	257	
	2260		32' span		5	3.200		115	93.50		208.50	273	
	2270		36' span		4	4		130	117		247	325	
	2280		40' span		4	4		144	117		261	340	
650	0010		**FRAMING, SOFFITS & CANOPIES**										650
	0130		Continuous ledger track @ wall, studs @ 16" O.C., 18 ga x 4" wide	2 Carp	535	.030	L.F.	.52	.87		1.39	1.93	
	0140		6" wide		500	.032		.67	.93		1.60	2.20	
	0150		8" wide		465	.034		.86	1		1.86	2.51	
	0160		10" wide		430	.037		1.06	1.08		2.14	2.86	
	0230		Studs @ 24" O.C., 18 ga x 4" wide		800	.020		.49	.58		1.07	1.45	
	0240		6" wide		750	.021		.64	.62		1.26	1.67	
	0250		8" wide		700	.023		.82	.67		1.49	1.94	

METALS **5**

05400 | Cold Formed Metal Framing

05460 | Cold-Formed Roof Framing

		CREW	DAILY OUTPUT	LABOR-HOURS	UNIT	2001 BARE COSTS MAT.	LABOR	EQUIP.	TOTAL	TOTAL INCL O&P	
650	0260	10" wide	2 Carp	650	.025	L.F.	1.01	.72		1.73	2.23	650
	1000	Horizontal soffit and canopy members, material only										
	1030	1-5/8" flange studs, 18 ga x 4" deep				L.F.	.68			.68	.75	
	1040	6" deep					.86			.86	.95	
	1050	8" deep					1.06			1.06	1.16	
	1140	2" flange joists, 18 ga x 6" deep					.97			.97	1.07	
	1150	8" deep					1.15			1.15	1.27	
	1160	10" deep					1.36			1.36	1.49	
	4030	Installation only, 18 ga, 1-5/8" flange x 4" deep	2 Carp	130	.123	Ea.		3.59		3.59	5.60	
	4040	6" deep		110	.145			4.24		4.24	6.65	
	4050	8" deep		90	.178			5.20		5.20	8.10	
	4140	2" flange, 18 ga x 6" deep		110	.145			4.24		4.24	6.65	
	4150	8" deep		90	.178			5.20		5.20	8.10	
	4160	10" deep		80	.200			5.85		5.85	9.10	
	6010	Clips to attach facia to rafter tails, 2" x 2" x 18 ga angle	1 Carp	120	.067		.46	1.94		2.40	3.54	
	6020	16 ga angle	"	100	.080		.59	2.33		2.92	4.29	

05500 | Metal Fabrications

05514 | Ladders

		CREW	DAILY OUTPUT	LABOR-HOURS	UNIT	2001 BARE COSTS MAT.	LABOR	EQUIP.	TOTAL	TOTAL INCL O&P	
500	0005	**LADDER**										500
	0010	Steel, 20" wide, bolted to concrete, with cage	E-4	50	.640	V.L.F.	54.50	21.50	1.68	77.68	100	
	0100	Without cage		85	.376		25.50	12.55	.99	39.04	52	
	0300	Aluminum, bolted to concrete, with cage		50	.640		92	21.50	1.68	115.18	141	
	0400	Without cage		85	.376		47	12.55	.99	60.54	75.50	
	1350	Alternating tread stair, 56/68°, steel, standard paint color	2 Sswk	50	.320		132	10.50		142.50	164	
	1360	Non-standard paint color		50	.320		149	10.50		159.50	183	
	1370	Galvanized steel		50	.320		149	10.50		159.50	183	
	1380	Stainless steel		50	.320		221	10.50		231.50	262	
	1390	68°, aluminum		50	.320		165	10.50		175.50	200	

05517 | Metal Stairs

		CREW	DAILY OUTPUT	LABOR-HOURS	UNIT	2001 BARE COSTS MAT.	LABOR	EQUIP.	TOTAL	TOTAL INCL O&P	
300	0010	**FIRE ESCAPE**										300
	0200	2' wide balcony, 1" x 1/4" bars 1-1/2" O.C.	1 Sswk	5	1.600	L.F.	36	52.50		88.50	135	
	0400	1st story cantilevered stair, standard		.09	88.889	Ea.	1,500	2,925		4,425	6,950	
	0700	Platform & fixed stair, 36" x 40"		.17	47.059	Flight	660	1,550		2,210	3,525	
	0900	For 3'-6" wide escapes, add to above					100%	150%				
350	0005	**FIRE ESCAPE STAIRS**										350
	0010	One story, disappearing, stainless steel	2 Sswk	20	.800	V.L.F.	149	26.50		175.50	211	
	0100	Portable ladder				Ea.	50			50	55	
700	0010	**STAIR** Steel, safety nosing, steel stringers										700
	0020	Grating tread and pipe railing, 3'-6" wide	E-4	35	.914	Riser	105	30.50	2.40	137.90	174	
	0100	4'-0" wide		30	1.067		137	35.50	2.81	175.31	218	
	0200	Cement fill metal pan, picket rail, 3'-6" wide		35	.914		158	30.50	2.40	190.90	231	
	0300	4'-0" wide		30	1.067		179	35.50	2.81	217.31	264	
	0350	Wall rail, both sides, 3'-6" wide CN		53	.604		120	20	1.59	141.59	170	
	0400	Cast iron tread and pipe rail, 3'-6" wide		35	.914		168	30.50	2.40	200.90	243	
	0500	Checkered plate tread, industrial, 3'-6" wide		28	1.143		105	38	3.01	146.01	188	

5
METALS

05517 | Metal Stairs

		CREW	DAILY OUTPUT	LABOR-HOURS	UNIT	2001 BARE COSTS MAT.	LABOR	EQUIP.	TOTAL	TOTAL INCL O&P	
700	**0550**	Circular, for tanks, 3'-0" wide	E-4	33	.970	Riser	116	32.50	2.55	151.05	188	**700**
	0600	For isolated stairs, add						100%				
	0800	Custom steel stairs, 3'-6" wide, minimum	E-4	35	.914		158	30.50	2.40	190.90	231	
	0810	Average		30	1.067		210	35.50	2.81	248.31	299	
	0900	Maximum	↓	20	1.600		263	53.50	4.21	320.71	390	
	1100	For 4' wide stairs, add					5%	5%				
	1300	For 5' wide stairs, add				↓	10%	10%				
	1500	Landing, steel pan, conventional	E-4	160	.200	S.F.	21	6.65	.53	28.18	35.50	
	1600	Pre-erected	"	255	.125	"	37	4.19	.33	41.52	48.50	
	1700	Pre-erected, steel pan tread, 3'-6" wide, 2 line pipe rail	E-2	87	.644	Riser	173	20.50	14.85	208.35	243	
	1810	Spiral aluminum, 5'-0" diameter, stock units	E-4	45	.711		194	23.50	1.87	219.37	259	
	1820	Custom units		45	.711		370	23.50	1.87	395.37	450	
	1900	Spiral, cast iron, 4'-0" diameter, ornamental, minimum		45	.711		173	23.50	1.87	198.37	236	
	1920	Maximum		25	1.280		236	42.50	3.37	281.87	340	
	2000	Spiral, steel, industrial checkered plate, 4' diameter		45	.711		173	23.50	1.87	198.37	236	
	2200	Stock units, 6'-0" diameter	↓	40	.800	↓	210	26.50	2.10	238.60	282	
	3110	Spiral steel, stock units, primed, flat metal tread, 3'-6" dia	2 Carp	1.60	10	Flight	840	292		1,132	1,375	
	3120	4'-0" dia		1.45	11.034		965	320		1,285	1,550	
	3130	4'-6" dia		1.35	11.852		1,050	345		1,395	1,725	
	3140	5'-0" dia		1.25	12.800		1,150	375		1,525	1,850	
	3210	Galvanized, 3'-6" dia		1.60	10		1,425	292		1,717	2,025	
	3220	4'-0" dia		1.45	11.034		1,600	320		1,920	2,275	
	3230	4'-6" dia		1.35	11.852		1,750	345		2,095	2,475	
	3240	5'-0" dia		1.25	12.800		1,900	375		2,275	2,650	
	3310	Checkered plate tread, 3'-6" dia		1.45	11.034		1,025	320		1,345	1,625	
	3320	4'-0" dia		1.35	11.852		1,175	345		1,520	1,850	
	3330	4'-6" dia		1.25	12.800		1,275	375		1,650	1,975	
	3340	5'-0" dia		1.15	13.913		1,375	405		1,780	2,150	
	3410	Galvanized, 3'-6" dia		1.45	11.034		1,625	320		1,945	2,300	
	3420	4'-0" dia		1.35	11.852		1,825	345		2,170	2,575	
	3430	4'-6" dia		1.25	12.800		2,000	375		2,375	2,775	
	3440	5'-0" dia		1.15	13.913		2,150	405		2,555	3,000	
	3510	Red oak tread on flat metal, 3'-6" dia		1.35	11.852		1,400	345		1,745	2,100	
	3520	4'-0" dia		1.25	12.800		1,550	375		1,925	2,275	
	3530	4'-6" dia		1.15	13.913		1,700	405		2,105	2,475	
	3540	5'-0" dia	↓	1.05	15.238	↓	1,825	445		2,270	2,700	
	3900	Industrial ships ladder, 3' W, grating treads, 2 line pipe rail	E-4	30	1.067	Riser	68.50	35.50	2.81	106.81	143	
	4000	Aluminum	"	30	1.067	"	105	35.50	2.81	143.31	184	

05520 | Handrails & Railings

		CREW	DAILY OUTPUT	LABOR-HOURS	UNIT	2001 BARE COSTS MAT.	LABOR	EQUIP.	TOTAL	TOTAL INCL O&P	
700	**0005**	**RAILING, PIPE**										**700**
	0010	Aluminum, 2 rail, satin finish, 1-1/4" diameter	E-4	160	.200	L.F.	13.65	6.65	.53	20.83	27.50	
	0030	Clear anodized		160	.200		16.90	6.65	.53	24.08	31	
	0040	Dark anodized		160	.200		19.05	6.65	.53	26.23	33.50	
	0080	1-1/2" diameter, satin finish		160	.200		16.35	6.65	.53	23.53	30.50	
	0090	Clear anodized		160	.200		18.20	6.65	.53	25.38	32.50	
	0100	Dark anodized		160	.200		20	6.65	.53	27.18	34.50	
	0140	Aluminum, 3 rail, 1-1/4" diam., satin finish		137	.234		21	7.80	.61	29.41	38	
	0150	Clear anodized		137	.234		26	7.80	.61	34.41	44	
	0160	Dark anodized		137	.234		29	7.80	.61	37.41	47	
	0200	1-1/2" diameter, satin finish		137	.234		25	7.80	.61	33.41	42.50	
	0210	Clear anodized		137	.234		28.50	7.80	.61	36.91	46.50	
	0220	Dark anodized		137	.234		31	7.80	.61	39.41	49.50	
	0500	Steel, 2 rail, on stairs, primed, 1-1/4" diameter		160	.200		9.85	6.65	.53	17.03	23.50	
	0520	1-1/2" diameter		160	.200		10.80	6.65	.53	17.98	24.50	
	0540	Galvanized, 1-1/4" diameter	↓	160	.200	↓	13.65	6.65	.53	20.83	27.50	

		CREW	DAILY OUTPUT	LABOR-HOURS	UNIT	2001 BARE COSTS				TOTAL INCL O&P	
05520	**Handrails & Railings**					MAT.	LABOR	EQUIP.	TOTAL		
700	0560	1-1/2" diameter	E-4	160	.200	L.F.	15.30	6.65	.53	22.48	29.50	**700**
	0580	Steel, 3 rail, primed, 1-1/4" diameter		137	.234		14.65	7.80	.61	23.06	31	
	0600	1-1/2" diameter		137	.234		15.55	7.80	.61	23.96	32	
	0620	Galvanized, 1-1/4" diameter		137	.234		20.50	7.80	.61	28.91	37.50	
	0640	1-1/2" diameter **CN**		137	.234		24	7.80	.61	32.41	41.50	
	0700	Stainless steel, 2 rail, 1-1/4" diam. #4 finish		137	.234		33.50	7.80	.61	41.91	52	
	0720	High polish		137	.234		54	7.80	.61	62.41	74.50	
	0740	Mirror polish		137	.234		67.50	7.80	.61	75.91	89.50	
	0760	Stainless steel, 3 rail, 1-1/2" diam., #4 finish		120	.267		50.50	8.90	.70	60.10	72.50	
	0770	High polish		120	.267		83.50	8.90	.70	93.10	109	
	0780	Mirror finish		120	.267		102	8.90	.70	111.60	129	
	0900	Wall rail, alum. pipe, 1-1/4" diam., satin finish		213	.150		7.80	5	.40	13.20	18.15	
	0905	Clear anodized		213	.150		9.50	5	.40	14.90	20	
	0910	Dark anodized		213	.150		11.55	5	.40	16.95	22	
	0915	1-1/2" diameter, satin finish		213	.150		8.65	5	.40	14.05	19.05	
	0920	Clear anodized		213	.150		10.85	5	.40	16.25	21.50	
	0925	Dark anodized		213	.150		13.40	5	.40	18.80	24.50	
	0930	Steel pipe, 1-1/4" diameter, primed		213	.150		5.95	5	.40	11.35	16.10	
	0935	Galvanized		213	.150		8.65	5	.40	14.05	19.05	
	0940	1-1/2" diameter		176	.182		6.15	6.05	.48	12.68	18.30	
	0945	Galvanized		213	.150		8.70	5	.40	14.10	19.10	
	0955	Stainless steel pipe, 1-1/2" diam., #4 finish		107	.299		26.50	9.95	.79	37.24	48.50	
	0960	High polish		107	.299		54.50	9.95	.79	65.24	79	
	0965	Mirror polish		107	.299		64	9.95	.79	74.74	89.50	
780	0005	**RAILINGS, INDUSTRIAL** Welded										**780**
	0010	2 rail, 3'-6" high, 1-1/2" pipe	E-4	255	.125	L.F.	14.40	4.19	.33	18.92	24	
	0100	2" angle rail	"	255	.125		13.15	4.19	.33	17.67	22.50	
	0200	For 4" high kick plate, 10 gauge, add					3			3	3.30	
	0300	1/4" thick, add					3.85			3.85	4.24	
	0500	For curved rails, add					30%	30%				

05530 | Gratings

		CREW	DAILY OUTPUT	LABOR-HOURS	UNIT	MAT.	LABOR	EQUIP.	TOTAL	TOTAL INCL O&P	
300	0010	**FLOOR GRATING, ALUMINUM**										**300**
	0200	For straight cuts, add				L.F.	2.13			2.13	2.34	
	0300	For curved cuts, add					2.83			2.83	3.11	
	0400	For straight banding, add					2.52			2.52	2.77	
	0500	For curved banding, add					3.46			3.46	3.81	
	0600	For aluminum checkered plate nosings, add					3.55			3.55	3.91	
	0700	For straight toe plate, add					6.05			6.05	6.65	
	0800	For curved toe plate, add					7.55			7.55	8.30	
	1000	For cast aluminum abrasive nosings, add					4			4	4.40	
	1200	Expanded aluminum, .65# per S.F.	E-4	1,050	.030	S.F.	3.76	1.02	.08	4.86	6.05	
	1400	Extruded I bars are 10% less than 3/16" bars										
	1600	Heavy duty, all extruded plank, 3/4" deep, 1.8 # per S.F.	E-4	1,100	.029	S.F.	10.55	.97	.08	11.60	13.45	
	1700	1-1/4" deep, 2.9# per S.F.		1,000	.032		11.20	1.07	.08	12.35	14.40	
	1800	1-3/4" deep, 4.2# per S.F.		925	.035		13.40	1.15	.09	14.64	16.90	
	1900	2-1/4" deep, 5.0# per S.F.		875	.037		15.30	1.22	.10	16.62	19.15	
	2100	For safety serrated surface, add					15%					
320	0010	**FLOOR GRATING PLANKS**										**320**
	0020	Aluminum, 9-1/2" wide, 14 ga., 2" rib	E-4	950	.034	L.F.	9.90	1.12	.09	11.11	13	
	0200	Galvanized steel, 9-1/2" wide, 14 ga., 2-1/2" rib		950	.034		5.75	1.12	.09	6.96	8.50	
	0300	4" rib		950	.034		6.95	1.12	.09	8.16	9.75	
	0500	12 gauge, 2-1/2" rib		950	.034		7.35	1.12	.09	8.56	10.20	
	0600	3" rib		950	.034		8.25	1.12	.09	9.46	11.20	
	0800	Stainless steel, type 304, 16 ga., 2" rib		950	.034		17.30	1.12	.09	18.51	21	
	0900	Type 316		950	.034		21	1.12	.09	22.21	25	

5 METALS

Important: See the Reference Section for critical supporting data - Reference Nos., Crews, & City Cost Indexes

05530 | Gratings

		CREW	DAILY OUTPUT	LABOR-HOURS	UNIT	2001 BARE COSTS				TOTAL INCL O&P
						MAT.	LABOR	EQUIP.	TOTAL	
340	**0010**	**FLOOR GRATING, STEEL**									**340**
	0050	Labor for installing, from ground/floor	E-4	845	.038	S.F.		1.26	.10	1.36	2.40
	0100	Elevated		460	.070	"		2.32	.18	2.50	4.41
	0300	Platforms, to 12' high, rectangular		3,150	.010	Lb.	1.12	.34	.03	1.49	1.87
	0400	Circular	↓	2,300	.014	"	1.24	.46	.04	1.74	2.24
	0800	For straight cuts, add				L.F.	2.24			2.24	2.46
	0900	For curved cuts, add					3.03			3.03	3.33
	1000	For straight banding, add					2.32			2.32	2.55
	1100	For curved banding, add					3.50			3.50	3.85
	1200	For checkered plate nosings, add					4.24			4.24	4.66
	1300	For straight toe or kick plate, add					5.55			5.55	6.15
	1400	For curved toe or kick plate, add					6.75			6.75	7.40
	1500	For abrasive nosings, add				↓	4.48			4.48	4.93
	1510	For stair treads, see division 05550-700									
	1600	For safety serrated surface, minimum, add					15%				
	1700	Maximum, add					25%				
	2000	Stainless steel gratings, close spaced, 1" x 1/8" bars, up to 300 S.F.	E-4	450	.071	S.F.	21	2.37	.19	23.56	27.50
	2100	Standard spacing, 3/4" x 1/8" bars		500	.064		21	2.13	.17	23.30	27
	2200	1-1/4" x 3/16" bars		400	.080		24.50	2.67	.21	27.38	32
	2400	Expanded steel grating, at ground, 3.0# per S.F.		900	.036		2	1.19	.09	3.28	4.45
	2500	3.14# per S.F.		900	.036		2.09	1.19	.09	3.37	4.55
	2600	4.0# per S.F.		850	.038		2.58	1.26	.10	3.94	5.25
	2650	4.27# per S.F.		850	.038		2.80	1.26	.10	4.16	5.45
	2700	5.0# per S.F.		800	.040		3.33	1.33	.11	4.77	6.20
	2800	6.25# per S.F.		750	.043		4.10	1.42	.11	5.63	7.20
	2900	7.0# per S.F.	↓	700	.046		4.72	1.52	.12	6.36	8.10
	3100	For flattened expanded steel grating, add					8%				
	3300	For elevated installation above 15', add				↓		15%			
360	**0005**	**GRATING FRAME**									**360**
	0010	Aluminum, for gratings 1" to 1-1/2" deep	1 Sswk	70	.114	L.F.	6.55	3.75		10.30	14
	0100	For each corner, add				Ea.	5.15			5.15	5.65

05540 | Floor Plates

		CREW	DAILY OUTPUT	LABOR-HOURS	UNIT	MAT.	LABOR	EQUIP.	TOTAL	TOTAL INCL O&P
200	**0005**	**CHECKERED PLATE**									**200**
	0010	1/4" & 3/8", 2000 to 5000 S.F., bolted	E-4	2,900	.011	Lb.	.62	.37	.03	1.02	1.38
	0100	Welded		4,400	.007	"	.58	.24	.02	.84	1.10
	0300	Pit or trench cover and frame, 1/4" plate, 2' to 3' wide	↓	100	.320	S.F.	16.25	10.65	.84	27.74	38
	0400	For galvanizing, add				Lb.	.36			.36	.40
	0500	Platforms, 1/4" plate, no handrails included, rectangular	E-4	4,200	.008		.98	.25	.02	1.25	1.56
	0600	Circular	"	2,500	.013	↓	1.37	.43	.03	1.83	2.32
700	**0010**	**TRENCH COVER**									**700**
	0020	Cast iron grating with bar stops and angle frame, to 18" wide	1 Sswk	20	.400	L.F.	43	13.15		56.15	71.50
	0100	Frame only (both sides of trench), 1" grating		45	.178		9.45	5.85		15.30	21
	0150	2" grating	↓	35	.229	↓	14.70	7.50		22.20	30
	0200	Aluminum, stock units, including frames and									
	0210	3/8" plain cover plate, 4" opening	E-4	205	.156	L.F.	31	5.20	.41	36.61	44
	0300	6" opening		185	.173		38	5.75	.45	44.20	53
	0400	10" opening		170	.188		52.50	6.30	.50	59.30	70
	0500	16" opening	↓	155	.206		72	6.90	.54	79.44	92.50
	0700	Add per inch for additional widths to 24"					2.87			2.87	3.16
	0900	For custom fabrication, add					50%				
	1100	For 1/4" plain cover plate, deduct					12%				
	1500	For cover recessed for tile, 1/4" thick, deduct					12%				
	1600	3/8" thick, add				↓	5%				

5 METALS

05540 | Floor Plates

		CREW	DAILY OUTPUT	LABOR-HOURS	UNIT	MAT.	LABOR	EQUIP.	TOTAL	TOTAL INCL O&P	
700	1800	For checkered plate cover, 1/4" thick, deduct				L.F.	12%					**700**
	1900	3/8" thick, add					2%					
	2100	For slotted or round holes in cover, 1/4" thick, add					3%					
	2200	3/8" thick, add					4%					
	2300	For abrasive cover, add					12%					

05550 | Stair Treads & Nosings

		CREW	DAILY OUTPUT	LABOR-HOURS	UNIT	MAT.	LABOR	EQUIP.	TOTAL	TOTAL INCL O&P	
700	0005	**STAIR TREADS**										**700**
	0010	Aluminum grating, 3' long, 1-1/2" x 3/16" rect. bars, 6" wide	1 Sswk	24	.333	Ea.	28	10.95		38.95	51	
	0100	12" wide		22	.364		47	11.95		58.95	73	
	0200	1-1/2" x 3/16" I-bars, 6" wide		24	.333		33	10.95		43.95	56.50	
	0300	12" wide		22	.364		53.50	11.95		65.45	80.50	
	0400	For abrasive nosings, add					11.25			11.25	12.35	
	0500	For narrow mesh, add					60%					
	0600	Treads, 12" x 3'-6", not incl. stringers. See also div. 03150-660										
	0700	Cast aluminum, abrasive, 3' long x 12" wide, 5/16" thick	1 Sswk	15	.533	Ea.	103	17.50		120.50	146	
	0800	3/8" thick		15	.533		108	17.50		125.50	151	
	0900	1/2" thick		15	.533		123	17.50		140.50	167	
	1000	Cast bronze, abrasive, 3/8" thick		8	1		420	33		453	520	
	1100	1/2" thick		8	1		550	33		583	665	
	1200	Cast iron, abrasive, 3' long x 12" wide, 3/8" thick		15	.533		90.50	17.50		108	132	
	1300	1/2" thick		15	.533		107	17.50		124.50	150	
	1400	Fiberglass reinforced plastic with safety nosing,										
	1500	1-1/2" thick, 12" wide, 24" long	1 Sswk	22	.364	Ea.	92	11.95		103.95	123	
	1600	30" long		22	.364		96	11.95		107.95	128	
	1700	36" long		22	.364		105	11.95		116.95	137	
	2000	Steel grating, painted, 3' long, 1-1/4" x 3/16" bars, 6" wide		20	.400		25.50	13.15		38.65	52	
	2010	12" wide		18	.444		28.50	14.60		43.10	58	
	2100	Add for abrasive nosing, 3' long, painted					10.55			10.55	11.65	
	2200	Galvanized					14.60			14.60	16.05	
	2300	Painting 3' treads, in shop, nonstandard paint					1.74			1.74	1.91	
	2400	Added coats, standard paint					.75			.75	.83	
	2500	Expanded steel, 2-1/2" deep, 9" x 3' long, 18 gauge	1 Sswk	20	.400		18.65	13.15		31.80	44.50	
	2600	14 gauge	"	20	.400		23	13.15		36.15	49	

05560 | Metal Castings

		CREW	DAILY OUTPUT	LABOR-HOURS	UNIT	MAT.	LABOR	EQUIP.	TOTAL	TOTAL INCL O&P	
200	0010	**CONSTRUCTION CASTINGS**										**200**
	0020	Manhole covers and frames see Division 02630-200										
	0100	Column bases, cast iron, 16" x 16", approx. 65 lbs.	E-4	46	.696	Ea.	83	23	1.83	107.83	136	
	0200	32" x 32", approx. 256 lbs.	"	23	1.391		310	46.50	3.66	360.16	430	
	0400	Cast aluminum for wood columns, 8" x 8"	1 Carp	32	.250		29	7.30		36.30	43.50	
	0500	12" x 12"	"	32	.250		63	7.30		70.30	81	
	0600	Miscellaneous C.I. castings, light sections, less than 150 lbs	E-4	3,200	.010	Lb.	1.27	.33	.03	1.63	2.04	
	1100	Heavy sections, more than 150 lb		4,200	.008		.63	.25	.02	.90	1.17	
	1300	Special low volume items		3,200	.010		2.23	.33	.03	2.59	3.09	
	1500	For ductile iron, add					100%					

05580 | Formed Metal Fabrications

		CREW	DAILY OUTPUT	LABOR-HOURS	UNIT	MAT.	LABOR	EQUIP.	TOTAL	TOTAL INCL O&P	
150	0005	**ALLOY STEEL CHAIN**, Grade 80										**150**
	0010	Self-colored, cut lengths, w/accessories, 1/4"	E-17	4	4	C.L.F.	330	135	.72	465.72	605	
	0020	3/8"		2	8		430	271	1.44	702.44	960	
	0030	1/2"		1.20	13.333		635	450	2.40	1,087.40	1,525	
	0040	5/8"		.72	22.222		1,225	750	4	1,979	2,725	
	0050	3/4"		.48	33.333		1,700	1,125	6	2,831	3,925	

Important: See the Reference Section for critical supporting data - Reference Nos., Crews, & City Cost Indexes

05500 | Metal Fabrications

		05580	Formed Metal Fabrications	CREW	DAILY OUTPUT	LABOR-HOURS	UNIT	2001 BARE COSTS MAT.	LABOR	EQUIP.	TOTAL	TOTAL INCL O&P	
150	0060		7/8"	E-17	.40	40	C.L.F.	2,575	1,350	7.20	3,932.20	5,300	**150**
	0070		1"		.35	45.714		3,900	1,550	8.25	5,458.25	7,100	
	0080		1-1/4"	↓	.24	66.667	↓	7,000	2,250	12	9,262	11,800	
	0110		Clevis slip hook, 1/4"				Ea.	7.70			7.70	8.45	
	0120		3/8"					11.15			11.15	12.25	
	0130		1/2"					20.50			20.50	22.50	
	0140		5/8"					36.50			36.50	40	
	0150		3/4"					76.50			76.50	84	
	0160		Eye/sling hook w/ hammerlock coupling, 7/8"					189			189	207	
	0170		1"					315			315	345	
	0180		1-1/4"				↓	505			505	560	
600	0005	**LAMP POSTS**											**600**
	0010		Aluminum, 7' high, stock units, post only	1 Carp	16	.500	Ea.	68	14.60		82.60	98	
	0100		Mild steel, plain	"	16	.500	"	41	14.60		55.60	68	
900	0005	**WINDOW GUARDS**											**900**
	0010		Expanded metal, steel angle frame, permanent	E-4	350	.091	S.F.	15.05	3.05	.24	18.34	22.50	
	0020		Steel bars, 1/2" x 1/2", spaced 5" O.C.	"	290	.110	"	10.40	3.68	.29	14.37	18.45	
	0030		Hinge mounted, add				Opng.	30			30	33	
	0040		Removable type, add				"	19.15			19.15	21	
	0050		For galvanized guards, add				S.F.	35%					
	0070		For pivoted or projected type, add					105%	40%				
	0100		Mild steel, stock units, economy	E-4	405	.079		4.08	2.64	.21	6.93	9.50	
	0200		Deluxe		405	.079	↓	8.40	2.64	.21	11.25	14.25	
	0400		Woven wire, stock units, 3/8" channel frame, 3' x 5' opening		40	.800	Opng.	110	26.50	2.10	138.60	172	
	0500		4' x 6' opening	↓	38	.842		177	28	2.21	207.21	247	
	0800		Basket guards for above, add					151			151	166	
	1000		Swinging guards for above, add				↓	52			52	57	

05650 | Railroad Track & Accessories

		05655	Railroad Trackwork		CREW	DAILY OUTPUT	LABOR-HOURS	UNIT	2001 BARE COSTS MAT.	LABOR	EQUIP.	TOTAL	TOTAL INCL O&P	
700	0010	**RAILROAD** Car bumpers, standard		R05650 -100	B-14	2	24	Ea.	2,050	580	90.50	2,720.50	3,275	**700**
	0100		Heavy duty			2	24		3,900	580	90.50	4,570.50	5,300	
	0200		Derails hand throw (sliding)	R05650 -200		10	4.800	↓	720	116	18.10	854.10	995	
	0300		Hand throw with standard timbers, open stand & target			8	6		780	145	22.50	947.50	1,100	
	0400		Resurface and realign existing track			200	.240	L.F.		5.80	.90	6.70	10	
	0600		For crushed stone ballast, add			500	.096	"	9.05	2.32	.36	11.73	13.95	
	0800		Siding, yard spur, level grade											
	0810		100 lb. rail, new material on wood ties		B-14	57	.842	L.F.	57	20.50	3.17	80.67	97.50	
	1000		Steel ties in concrete w/100# rail, fasteners & plates			22	2.182	"	101	52.50	8.25	161.75	202	
	1200		Switch timber, for a #8 switch, pressure treated			3.70	12.973	M.B.F.	620	315	49	984	1,225	
	1300		Complete set of timbers, 3.7 M.B.F. for #8 switch			1	48	Total	2,675	1,150	181	4,006	4,950	
	1400		Ties, concrete, 8'-6" long, 30" O.C.			80	.600	Ea.	70	14.50	2.26	86.76	102	
	1600		Wood, pressure treated, 6" x 8" x 8'-6", C.L. lots			90	.533		28.50	12.90	2.01	43.41	53	
	1700		L.C.L. lots			90	.533		29.50	12.90	2.01	44.41	54.50	
	1900		Heavy duty, 7" x 9" x 8'-6", C.L. lots			70	.686	↓	31	16.55	2.59	50.14	63	
	2000		L.C.L. lots			70	.686		29	16.55	2.59	48.14	61	

05650 | Railroad Track & Accessories

05655 | Railroad Trackwork

			CREW	DAILY OUTPUT	LABOR-HOURS	UNIT	2001 BARE COSTS				TOTAL INCL O&P
							MAT.	LABOR	EQUIP.	TOTAL	
700	2200	Turnouts, #8, incl. 100 lb. rails, plates, bars, frog, switch pt. R05650 -100									**700**
	2300	Timbers and ballast 6″ below bottom of tie	B-14	.50	96	Ea.	18,800	2,325	360	21,485	24,600
	2400	Wheel stops, fixed R05650 -200	↓	18	2.667	Pr.	460	64.50	10.05	534.55	615
	2450	Hinged		14	3.429	″	505	83	12.95	600.95	700
750	0005	**RAILROAD TRACK** R05650 -100									**750**
	0010	Track bolts				Ea.	1.73			1.73	1.90
	0100	Joint bars				Pr.	26			26	28.50
	0200	Spikes				Ea.	.41			.41	.45
	0300	Tie plates	↓			″	1.50			1.50	1.65

05700 | Ornamental Metal

05720 | Ornamental Railings

			CREW	DAILY OUTPUT	LABOR-HOURS	UNIT	2001 BARE COSTS				TOTAL INCL O&P
							MAT.	LABOR	EQUIP.	TOTAL	
700	0005	**RAILINGS, ORNAMENTAL**									**700**
	0010	Aluminum, bronze or stainless, minimum	1 Sswk	24	.333	L.F.	46.50	10.95		57.45	71
	0100	Maximum		9	.889		575	29		604	685
	0200	Aluminum ornamental rail, minimum		15	.533		33.50	17.50		51	69
	0300	Maximum		8	1		72	33		105	139
	0400	Hand-forged wrought iron, minimum		12	.667		99.50	22		121.50	150
	0500	Maximum		8	1		425	33		458	525
	0550	Steel, minimum		12	.667		45	22		67	89
	0560	Maximum		8	1		198	33		231	278
	0600	Composite metal and wood or glass, minimum		6	1.333		52.50	44		96.50	138
	0700	Maximum	↓	5	1.600	↓	158	52.50		210.50	269

05800 | Expansion Control

05810 | Exp. Joint Cover Assemblies

			CREW	DAILY OUTPUT	LABOR-HOURS	UNIT	2001 BARE COSTS				TOTAL INCL O&P
							MAT.	LABOR	EQUIP.	TOTAL	
350	0010	**EXPANSION JOINT ASSEMBLIES** Custom units									**350**
	0200	Floor cover assemblies, 1″ space, aluminum	1 Sswk	38	.211	L.F.	14	6.90		20.90	28
	0300	Bronze		38	.211		27	6.90		33.90	42.50
	0500	2″ space, aluminum		38	.211		16.95	6.90		23.85	31
	0600	Bronze		38	.211		29	6.90		35.90	44.50
	0800	Wall and ceiling assemblies, 1″ space, aluminum		38	.211		8.35	6.90		15.25	22
	0900	Bronze		38	.211		25.50	6.90		32.40	40.50
	1100	2″ space, aluminum		38	.211		14.15	6.90		21.05	28
	1200	Bronze		38	.211		31	6.90		37.90	47
	1400	Floor to wall assemblies, 1″ space, aluminum		38	.211		12.75	6.90		19.65	26.50
	1500	Bronze or stainless		38	.211		30.50	6.90		37.40	46.50
	1700	Gym floor angle covers, aluminum, 3″ x 3″ angle		46	.174		11.05	5.70		16.75	22.50
	1800	3″ x 4″ angle		46	.174		13	5.70		18.70	24.50
	2000	Roof closures, aluminum, flat roof, low profile, 1″ space	↓	57	.140	↓	25.50	4.61		30.11	36.50

Important: See the Reference Section for critical supporting data - Reference Nos., Crews, & City Cost Indexes

			CREW	DAILY OUTPUT	LABOR-HOURS	UNIT	2001 BARE COSTS				TOTAL INCL O&P	
05810		**Exp. Joint Cover Assemblies**					MAT.	LABOR	EQUIP.	TOTAL		
350	2100	High profile	1 Sswk	57	.140	L.F.	31.50	4.61		36.11	43	**350**
	2300	Roof to wall, low profile, 1" space	↓	57	.140	↓	14.10	4.61		18.71	24	
	2400	High profile		57	.140		18.15	4.61		22.76	28.50	

For information about Means Estimating Seminars, see yellow pages 11 and 12 in back of book

METALS **5**

Division Notes

	CREW	DAILY OUTPUT	LABOR-HOURS	UNIT	2001 BARE COSTS				TOTAL INCL O&P
					MAT.	LABOR	EQUIP.	TOTAL	

Division 6
Wood & Plastics

Estimating Tips

06050 Basic Wood & Plastic Materials & Methods

- Common to any wood framed structure are the accessory connector items such as screws, nails, adhesives, hangers, connector plates, straps, angles and holdowns. For typical wood framed buildings, such as residential projects, the aggregate total for these items can be significant, especially in areas where seismic loading is a concern. For floor and wall framing, nail quantities can be figured on a "pounds per thousand board feet basis", with 10 to 25 lbs. per MBF the range. Holdowns, hangers and other connectors should be taken off by the piece.

06100 Rough Carpentry

- Lumber is a traded commodity and therefore sensitive to supply and demand in the marketplace. Even in "budgetary" estimating of wood framed projects, it is advisable to call local suppliers for the latest market pricing.
- Common quantity units for wood framed projects are "thousand board feet" (MBF). A board foot is a volume of wood, 1" x 1' x 1', or 144 cubic inches. Board foot quantities are generally calculated using nominal material dimensions—dressed sizes are ignored. Board foot per lineal foot of any stick of lumber can be calculated by dividing the nominal cross sectional area by 12. As an example, 2,000 lineal feet of 2 x 12 equates to 4 MBF by dividing the nominal area, 2 x 12, by 12, which equals 2, and multiplying by 2,000 to give 4,000 board feet. This simple rule applies to all nominal dimensioned lumber.
- Waste is an issue of concern at the quantity takeoff for any area of construction. Framing lumber is sold in even foot lengths, i.e., 10', 12', 14', 16', and depending on spans, wall heights and the grade of lumber, waste is inevitable. A rule of thumb for lumber waste is 5% to 10% depending on material quality and the complexity of the framing.
- Wood in various forms and shapes is used in many projects, even where the main structural framing is steel, concrete or masonry. Plywood as a back-up partition material and 2x boards used as blocking and cant strips around roof edges are two common examples. The estimator should ensure that the costs of all wood materials are included in the final estimate.

06200 Finish Carpentry

- It is necessary to consider the grade of workmanship when estimating labor costs for erecting millwork and interior finish. In practice, there are three grades: premium, custom and economy. The Means daily output for base and case moldings is in the range of 200 to 250 L.F. per carpenter per day. This is appropriate for most average custom grade projects. For premium projects an adjustment to productivity of 25% to 50% should be made depending on the complexity of the job.

Reference Numbers

Reference numbers are shown in bold squares at the beginning of some major classifications. These numbers refer to related items in the Reference Section. The reference information may be an estimating procedure, an alternate pricing method or technical information.

Note: Not all subdivisions listed here necessarily appear in this publication.

	06055	Wood & Plastic Laminate	CREW	DAILY OUTPUT	LABOR-HOURS	UNIT	2001 BARE COSTS				TOTAL INCL O&P	
							MAT.	LABOR	EQUIP.	TOTAL		
720	0010	**CONVECTOR COVERS** Laminated plastic on 3/4"										**720**
	0020	thick particle board, 12" wide, minimum	1 Carp	16	.500	L.F.	20	14.60		34.60	45	
	0050	Average		13	.615		25.50	17.95		43.45	56	
	0100	Maximum		13	.615		35	17.95		52.95	66.50	
	0300	Add to above for grille, minimum		150	.053	S.F.	1.60	1.55		3.15	4.19	
	0400	Maximum		75	.107	"	4.50	3.11		7.61	9.80	
740	0010	**COUNTER TOP** Stock, plastic lam., 24" wide w/backsplash, min.	1 Carp	30	.267	L.F.	4.89	7.75		12.64	17.55	**740**
	0100	Maximum		25	.320		14.25	9.35		23.60	30.50	
	0300	Custom plastic, 7/8" thick, aluminum molding, no splash		30	.267		15.70	7.75		23.45	29.50	
	0400	Cove splash		30	.267		20.50	7.75		28.25	34.50	
	0600	1-1/4" thick, no splash		28	.286		18.50	8.35		26.85	33.50	
	0700	Square splash		28	.286		23	8.35		31.35	38.50	
	0900	Square edge, plastic face, 7/8" thick, no splash		30	.267		19.80	7.75		27.55	34	
	1000	With splash		30	.267		26	7.75		33.75	40.50	
	1200	For stainless channel edge, 7/8" thick, add					2.21			2.21	2.43	
	1300	1-1/4" thick, add					2.58			2.58	2.84	
	1500	For solid color suede finish, add					1.96			1.96	2.16	
	1700	For end splash, add				Ea.	12.35			12.35	13.60	
	1900	For cut outs, standard, add, minimum	1 Carp	32	.250		2.63	7.30		9.93	14.30	
	2000	Maximum		8	1		3.14	29		32.14	49	
	2100	Postformed, including backsplash and front edge		30	.267	L.F.	8.55	7.75		16.30	21.50	
	2110	Mitred, add		12	.667	Ea.		19.45		19.45	30.50	
	2200	Built-in place, 25" wide, plastic laminate		25	.320	L.F.	10.80	9.35		20.15	26.50	
	2300	Ceramic tile mosaic		25	.320		24.50	9.35		33.85	41.50	
	2500	Marble, stock, with splash, 1/2" thick, minimum	1 Bric	17	.471		30	13.95		43.95	54.50	
	2700	3/4" thick, maximum	"	13	.615		76	18.20		94.20	112	
	2900	Maple, solid, laminated, 1-1/2" thick, no splash	1 Carp	28	.286		31	8.35		39.35	47	
	3000	With square splash		28	.286		35	8.35		43.35	51.50	
	3200	Stainless steel		24	.333	S.F.	73	9.70		82.70	95.50	
	3400	Recessed cutting block with trim, 16" x 20" x 1"		8	1	Ea.	41	29		70	91	
	3600	Table tops, plastic laminate, square edge, 7/8" thick		45	.178	S.F.	7.15	5.20		12.35	15.95	
	3700	1-1/8" thick		40	.200	"	7.35	5.85		13.20	17.20	

	06073	**Wood Treatment**										
400	0011	**LUMBER TREATMENT**										**400**
	0400	Fire retardant, wet				M.B.F.	282			282	310	
	0500	KDAT					255			255	281	
	0700	Salt treated, water borne, .40 lb. retention					122			122	134	
	0800	Oil borne, 8 lb. retention					143			143	157	
	1000	Kiln dried lumber, 1" & 2" thick, softwoods					81.50			81.50	90	
	1100	Hardwoods					87			87	95.50	
	1500	For small size 1" stock, add					11			11	12.10	
	1700	For full size rough lumber, add					20%					
600	0010	**PLYWOOD TREATMENT** Fire retardant, 1/4" thick				M.S.F.	204			204	224	**600**
	0030	3/8" thick					224			224	246	
	0050	1/2" thick					240			240	264	
	0070	5/8" thick					255			255	281	
	0100	3/4" thick					280			280	310	
	0200	For KDAT, add					61			61	67	
	0500	Salt treated water borne, .25 lb., wet, 1/4" thick					112			112	123	
	0530	3/8" thick					117			117	129	
	0550	1/2" thick					122			122	134	
	0570	5/8" thick					133			133	146	
	0600	3/4" thick					138			138	152	
	0800	For KDAT add					61			61	67	

6 WOOD & PLASTICS

Important: See the Reference Section for critical supporting data - Reference Nos., Crews, & City Cost Indexes

06073 | Wood Treatment

			CREW	DAILY OUTPUT	LABOR-HOURS	UNIT	2001 BARE COSTS				TOTAL INCL O&P	
							MAT.	LABOR	EQUIP.	TOTAL		
600	0900	For .40 lb., per C.F. retention, add				M.S.F.	51			51	56	**600**
	1000	For certification stamp, add				↓	30			30	33	

06090 | Wood & Plastic Fastenings

			CREW	DAILY OUTPUT	LABOR-HOURS	UNIT	MAT.	LABOR	EQUIP.	TOTAL	TOTAL INCL O&P	
600	0010	**NAILS** Prices of material only, based on 50# box purchase, copper, plain				Lb.	8.35			8.35	9.15	**600**
	0400	Stainless steel, plain					4.87			4.87	5.35	
	0500	Box, 3d to 20d, bright					1.13			1.13	1.24	
	0520	Galvanized					1.34			1.34	1.47	
	0600	Common, 3d to 60d, plain					.77			.77	.85	
	0700	Galvanized					1.18			1.18	1.30	
	0800	Aluminum					3.31			3.31	3.64	
	1000	Annular or spiral thread, 4d to 60d, plain					1.67			1.67	1.84	
	1200	Galvanized					1.67			1.67	1.84	
	1400	Drywall nails, plain					1.33			1.33	1.46	
	1600	Galvanized					1.33			1.33	1.46	
	1800	Finish nails, 4d to 10d, plain					.94			.94	1.03	
	2000	Galvanized					1.04			1.04	1.14	
	2100	Aluminum					4.85			4.85	5.35	
	2300	Flooring nails, hardened steel, 2d to 10d, plain					1.22			1.22	1.34	
	2400	Galvanized					2.17			2.17	2.39	
	2500	Gypsum lath nails, 1-1/8", 13 ga. flathead, blued					1.33			1.33	1.46	
	2600	Masonry nails, hardened steel, 3/4" to 3" long, plain					1.71			1.71	1.88	
	2700	Galvanized					1.71			1.71	1.88	
	2900	Roofing nails, threaded, galvanized					1.30			1.30	1.43	
	3100	Aluminum					4.70			4.70	5.15	
	3300	Compressed lead head, threaded, galvanized					1.44			1.44	1.58	
	3600	Siding nails, plain shank, galvanized					1.33			1.33	1.46	
	3800	Aluminum					4			4	4.40	
	5000	Add to prices above for cement coating					.07			.07	.08	
	5200	Zinc or tin plating					.12			.12	.13	
	5500	Vinyl coated sinkers, 8d to 16d				↓	.55			.55	.61	
650	0010	**NAILS** mat. only, for pneumatic tools, framing, per carton of 5000, 2"				Ea.	36.50			36.50	40	**650**
	0100	2-3/8"					41.50			41.50	45.50	
	0200	Per carton of 4000, 3"					37			37	40.50	
	0300	3-1/4"					39			39	43	
	0400	Per carton of 5000, 2-3/8", galv.					56.50			56.50	62	
	0500	Per carton of 4000, 3", galv.					63.50			63.50	70	
	0600	3-1/4", galv.					79			79	87	
	0700	Roofing, per carton of 7200, 1"					34.50			34.50	38	
	0800	1-1/4"					32			32	35.50	
	0900	1-1/2"					37			37	40.50	
	1000	1-3/4"				↓	44.50			44.50	49	
700	0010	**SHEET METAL SCREWS** Steel, standard, #8 x 3/4", plain				C	2.69			2.69	2.96	**700**
	0100	Galvanized					3.37			3.37	3.71	
	0300	#10 x 1", plain					3.69			3.69	4.06	
	0400	Galvanized					4.26			4.26	4.69	
	0600	With washers, #14 x 1", plain					10			10	11	
	0700	Galvanized					10			10	11	
	0900	#14 x 2", plain					10			10	11	
	1000	Galvanized					17.80			17.80	19.55	
	1500	Self-drilling, with washers, (pinch point) #8 x 3/4", plain					6			6	6.60	
	1600	Galvanized					6			6	6.60	
	1800	#10 x 3/4", plain					6			6	6.60	
	1900	Galvanized				↓	6			6	6.60	

6

WOOD & PLASTICS

6 WOOD & PLASTICS

06090	Wood & Plastic Fastenings	CREW	DAILY OUTPUT	LABOR-HOURS	UNIT	2001 BARE COSTS MAT.	LABOR	EQUIP.	TOTAL	TOTAL INCL O&P	
700 3000	Stainless steel w/aluminum or neoprene washers, #14 x 1", plain				C	18			18	19.80	**700**
3100	#14 x 2", plain				↓	24.50			24.50	27	
750 0010	**WOOD SCREWS** #8, 1" long, steel				C	3.29			3.29	3.62	**750**
0100	Brass					11			11	12.10	
0200	#8, 2" long, steel					3.69			3.69	4.06	
0300	Brass					11.50			11.50	12.65	
0400	#10, 1" long, steel					4.22			4.22	4.64	
0500	Brass					22.50			22.50	24.50	
0600	#10, 2" long, steel					7.50			7.50	8.25	
0700	Brass					39.50			39.50	43.50	
0800	#10, 3" long, steel					11.75			11.75	12.90	
1000	#12, 2" long, steel					4.79			4.79	5.25	
1100	Brass					16			16	17.60	
1500	#12, 3" long, steel					15.90			15.90	17.50	
2000	#12, 4" long, steel				↓	28.50			28.50	31	
800 0010	**TIMBER CONNECTORS** Add up cost of each part for total										**800**
0020	cost of connection										
0100	Connector plates, steel, with bolts, straight	2 Carp	75	.213	Ea.	16.35	6.20		22.55	28	
0110	Tee		50	.320		24	9.35		33.35	41	
0120	T- Strap, 14 gauge 12" x 8" x 2"		50	.320		24	9.35		33.35	41	
0150	Anchor plate, 7 gauge, 9" x 7"	↓	75	.213		16.35	6.20		22.55	28	
0200	Bolts, machine, sq. hd. with nut & washer, 1/2" diameter, 4" long	1 Carp	140	.057		.75	1.67		2.42	3.44	
0300	7-1/2" long		130	.062		.95	1.79		2.74	3.86	
0500	3/4" diameter, 7-1/2" long		130	.062		1.71	1.79		3.50	4.69	
0600	15" long		95	.084	↓	2.18	2.45		4.63	6.25	
0800	Drilling bolt holes in timber, 1/2" diameter		450	.018	Inch		.52		.52	.81	
0900	1" diameter		350	.023	"		.67		.67	1.04	
1100	Framing anchors, 2 or 3 dimensional, 10 gauge, no nails incl.		175	.046	Ea.	.41	1.33		1.74	2.53	
1150	Framing anchors, 18 gauge, 4 1/2" x 2 3/4"		175	.046		.41	1.33		1.74	2.53	
1160	Framing anchors, 18 gauge, 4 1/2" x 3"		175	.046		.41	1.33		1.74	2.53	
1170	Clip anchors plates, 18 gauge, 12" x 1 1/8"		175	.046		.41	1.33		1.74	2.53	
1250	Holdowns, 3 gauge base, 10 gauge body		8	1		13.60	29		42.60	60.50	
1260	Holdowns, 7 gauge 11 1/16" x 3 1/4"		8	1		13.60	29		42.60	60.50	
1270	Holdowns, 7 gauge 14 3/8" x 3 1/8"		8	1		13.60	29		42.60	60.50	
1275	Holdowns, 12 gauge 8" x 2 1/2"		8	1		13.60	29		42.60	60.50	
1300	Joist and beam hangers, 18 ga. galv., for 2" x 4" joist		175	.046		.51	1.33		1.84	2.64	
1400	2" x 6" to 2" x 10" joist		165	.048		.43	1.41		1.84	2.68	
1600	16 ga. galv., 3" x 6" to 3" x 10" joist		160	.050		2.31	1.46		3.77	4.82	
1700	3" x 10" to 3" x 14" joist		160	.050		2.67	1.46		4.13	5.20	
1800	4" x 6" to 4" x 10" joist		155	.052		2.03	1.50		3.53	4.58	
1900	4" x 10" to 4" x 14" joist		155	.052		2.74	1.50		4.24	5.35	
2000	Two-2" x 6" to two-2" x 10" joists		150	.053		2.20	1.55		3.75	4.85	
2100	Two-2" x 10" to two-2" x 14" joists		150	.053		2.20	1.55		3.75	4.85	
2300	3/16" thick, 6" x 8" joist		145	.055		4.81	1.61		6.42	7.80	
2400	6" x 10" joist		140	.057		5.65	1.67		7.32	8.85	
2500	6" x 12" joist		135	.059		6.80	1.73		8.53	10.20	
2700	1/4" thick, 6" x 14" joist		130	.062		8.45	1.79		10.24	12.10	
2800	Joist anchors, 1/4" x 1-1/4" x 18"	↓	140	.057		3.30	1.67		4.97	6.25	
2900	Plywood clips, extruded aluminum H clip, for 3/4" panels					.13			.13	.14	
3000	Galvanized 18 ga. back-up clip					.12			.12	.13	
3200	Post framing, 16 ga. galv. for 4" x 4" base, 2 piece	1 Carp	130	.062		4.75	1.79		6.54	8.05	
3300	Cap		130	.062		2.33	1.79		4.12	5.35	
3500	Rafter anchors, 18 ga. galv., 1-1/2" wide, 5-1/4" long		145	.055		.40	1.61		2.01	2.96	
3600	10-3/4" long		145	.055		.79	1.61		2.40	3.39	
3800	Shear plates, 2-5/8" diameter	↓	120	.067	↓	1.42	1.94		3.36	4.60	

06090	Wood & Plastic Fastenings	CREW	DAILY OUTPUT	LABOR-HOURS	UNIT	2001 BARE COSTS				TOTAL INCL O&P
						MAT.	LABOR	EQUIP.	TOTAL	
800										**800**
3900	4" diameter	1 Carp	115	.070	Ea.	3.27	2.03		5.30	6.75
4000	Sill anchors, embedded in concrete or block, 18-5/8" long		115	.070		.96	2.03		2.99	4.23
4100	Spike grids, 4" x 4", flat or curved		120	.067		.35	1.94		2.29	3.43
4400	Split rings, 2-1/2" diameter		120	.067		1.16	1.94		3.10	4.32
4500	4" diameter		110	.073		1.78	2.12		3.90	5.30
4550	Tie plate, 20 gauge, 7" x 3 1/8"		110	.073		1.78	2.12		3.90	5.30
4560	Tie plate, 20 gauge, 5" x 4 1/8"		110	.073		1.78	2.12		3.90	5.30
4575	Twist straps, 18 gauge, 12" x 1 1/4"		110	.073		1.78	2.12		3.90	5.30
4580	Twist straps, 18 gauge, 16" x 1 1/4"		110	.073		1.78	2.12		3.90	5.30
4600	Strap ties, 20 ga., 2 -1/16" wide, 12 13/16" long		180	.044		1.04	1.30		2.34	3.17
4700	Strap ties, 16 ga., 1-3/8" wide, 12" long		180	.044		1.04	1.30		2.34	3.17
4800	24" long		160	.050		1.43	1.46		2.89	3.85
5000	Toothed rings, 2-5/8" or 4" diameter		90	.089		.97	2.59		3.56	5.10
5200	Truss plates, nailed, 20 gauge, up to 32' span		17	.471	Truss	7	13.70		20.70	29
5400	Washers, 2" x 2" x 1/8"				Ea.	.23			.23	.25
5500	3" x 3" x 3/16"				"	.58			.58	.64
6101	Beam hangers, polymer painted									
6102	Bolted, 3 ga., (W x H x L)									
6104	3-1/4" x 9" x 12" top flange	1 Carp	1	8	C	5,575	233		5,808	6,500
6106	5-1/4" x 9" x 12" top flange		1	8		5,800	233		6,033	6,750
6108	5-1/4" x 11" x 11-3/4" top flange		1	8		13,000	233		13,233	14,700
6110	6-7/8" x 9" x 12" top flange		1	8		5,975	233		6,208	6,950
6112	6-7/8" x 11" x 13-1/2" top flange		1	8		13,700	233		13,933	15,500
6114	8-7/8" x 11" x 15-1/2" top flange		1	8		14,600	233		14,833	16,500
6116	Nailed, 3 ga., (W x H x L)									
6118	3-1/4" x 10-1/2" x 10" top flange	1 Carp	1.80	4.444	C	3,850	130		3,980	4,425
6120	3-1/4" x 10-1/2" x 12" top flange		1.80	4.444		4,450	130		4,580	5,100
6122	5-1/4" x 9-1/2" x 10" top flange		1.80	4.444		4,150	130		4,280	4,750
6124	5-1/4" x 9-1/2" x 12" top flange		1.80	4.444		4,700	130		4,830	5,375
6126	5-1/2" x 9-1/2" x 12" top flange		1.80	4.444		4,150	130		4,280	4,750
6128	6-7/8" x 8-1/2" x 12" top flange		1.80	4.444		4,275	130		4,405	4,925
6130	7-1/2" x 8-1/2" x 12" top flange		1.80	4.444		4,425	130		4,555	5,075
6132	8-7/8" x 7-1/2" x 14" top flange		1.80	4.444		4,900	130		5,030	5,575
6201	Beam and purlin hangers, galvanized, 12 ga.									
6202	Purlin or joist size, 3" x 8"	1 Carp	1.70	4.706	C	705	137		842	990
6204	3" x 10"		1.70	4.706		790	137		927	1,075
6206	3" x 12"		1.65	4.848		935	141		1,076	1,250
6208	3" x 14"		1.65	4.848		1,100	141		1,241	1,425
6210	3" x 16"		1.65	4.848		1,250	141		1,391	1,600
6212	4" x 8"		1.65	4.848		705	141		846	995
6214	4" x 10"		1.65	4.848		820	141		961	1,125
6216	4" x 12"		1.60	5		880	146		1,026	1,200
6218	4" x 14"		1.60	5		955	146		1,101	1,275
6220	4" x 16"		1.60	5		1,100	146		1,246	1,425
6224	6" x 10"		1.55	5.161		1,200	150		1,350	1,550
6226	6" x 12"		1.55	5.161		1,275	150		1,425	1,650
6228	6" x 14"		1.50	5.333		1,400	155		1,555	1,775
6230	6" x 16"		1.50	5.333		1,575	155		1,730	2,000
6300	Column bases									
6302	4 x 4, 16 ga.	1 Carp	1.80	4.444	C	980	130		1,110	1,275
6306	7 ga.		1.80	4.444		1,825	130		1,955	2,200
6314	6 x 6, 16 ga.		1.75	4.571		1,250	133		1,383	1,575
6318	7 ga.		1.75	4.571		2,550	133		2,683	3,000
6326	8 x 8, 7 ga.		1.65	4.848		4,250	141		4,391	4,900
6330	8 x 10, 7 ga.		1.65	4.848		4,550	141		4,691	5,225
6590	Joist hangers, heavy duty 12 ga., galvanized									

06090 | Wood & Plastic Fastenings

		CREW	DAILY OUTPUT	LABOR-HOURS	UNIT	2001 BARE COSTS MAT.	LABOR	EQUIP.	TOTAL	TOTAL INCL O&P	
800	6592	2" x 4"	1 Carp	1.75	4.571	C	800	133		933	1,100	**800**
	6594	2" x 6"		1.65	4.848		855	141		996	1,150	
	6595	2" x 6", 16 gauge		1.65	4.848		855	141		996	1,150	
	6596	2" x 8"		1.65	4.848		910	141		1,051	1,225	
	6597	2" x 8", 16 gauge		1.65	4.848		910	141		1,051	1,225	
	6598	2" x 10"		1.65	4.848		975	141		1,116	1,300	
	6600	2" x 12"		1.65	4.848		1,100	141		1,241	1,425	
	6622	(2) 2" x 6"		1.60	5		1,075	146		1,221	1,400	
	6624	(2) 2" x 8"		1.60	5		1,150	146		1,296	1,500	
	6626	(2) 2" x 10"		1.55	5.161		1,300	150		1,450	1,650	
	6628	(2) 2" x 12"		1.55	5.161		1,575	150		1,725	1,950	
	6890	Purlin hangers, painted										
	6892	12 ga., 2" x 6"	1 Carp	1.80	4.444	C	975	130		1,105	1,275	
	6894	2" x 8"		1.80	4.444		1,025	130		1,155	1,325	
	6896	2" x 10"		1.80	4.444		1,050	130		1,180	1,350	
	6898	2" x 12"		1.75	4.571		1,150	133		1,283	1,450	
	6934	(2) 2" x 6"		1.70	4.706		985	137		1,122	1,300	
	6936	(2) 2" x 8"		1.70	4.706		1,075	137		1,212	1,425	
	6938	(2) 2" x 10"		1.70	4.706		1,200	137		1,337	1,550	
	6940	(2) 2" x 12"		1.65	4.848		1,275	141		1,416	1,625	
825	0010	**ROUGH HARDWARE** Average % of carpentry material, minimum					.50%					**825**
	0200	Maximum					1.50%					
850	0010	**BRACING**										**850**
	0300	Let-in, "T" shaped, 22 ga. galv. steel, studs at 16" O.C.	1 Carp	5.80	1.379	C.L.F.	40	40		80	107	
	0400	Studs at 24" O.C.		6	1.333		40	39		79	105	
	0500	16 ga. galv. steel straps, studs at 16" O.C.		6	1.333		60	39		99	127	
	0600	Studs at 24" O.C.		6.20	1.290		60	37.50		97.50	125	

06100 | Rough Carpentry

06110 | Wood Framing

		CREW	DAILY OUTPUT	LABOR-HOURS	UNIT	2001 BARE COSTS MAT.	LABOR	EQUIP.	TOTAL	TOTAL INCL O&P	
100	0010	**BLOCKING**										**100**
	2600	Miscellaneous, to wood construction										
	2620	2" x 4"	1 Carp	.17	47.059	M.B.F.	600	1,375		1,975	2,800	
	2625	Pneumatic nailed		.21	38.095		600	1,100		1,700	2,375	
	2660	2" x 8"		.27	29.630		620	865		1,485	2,025	
	2665	Pneumatic nailed		.33	24.242		620	705		1,325	1,775	
	2720	To steel construction										
	2740	2" x 4"	1 Carp	.14	57.143	M.B.F.	600	1,675		2,275	3,250	
	2780	2" x 8"	"	.21	38.095	"	620	1,100		1,720	2,400	
150	0010	**BRACING** Let-in, with 1" x 6" boards, studs @ 16" O.C.	1 Carp	1.50	5.333	C.L.F.	52.50	155		207.50	300	**150**
	0200	Studs @ 24" O.C.	"	2.30	3.478	"	52.50	101		153.50	217	
200	0010	**BRIDGING** Wood, for joists 16" O.C., 1" x 3"	1 Carp	1.30	6.154	C.Pr.	28.50	179		207.50	315	**200**
	0015	Pneumatic nailed		1.70	4.706		28.50	137		165.50	247	
	0100	2" x 3" bridging		1.30	6.154		41.50	179		220.50	325	
	0105	Pneumatic nailed		1.70	4.706		41.50	137		178.50	261	
	0300	Steel, galvanized, 18 ga., for 2" x 10" joists at 12" O.C.		1.30	6.154		58.50	179		237.50	345	
	0400	24" O.C.		1.40	5.714		220	167		387	505	

Important: See the Reference Section for critical supporting data - Reference Nos., Crews, & City Cost Indexes

		06110	Wood Framing	CREW	DAILY OUTPUT	LABOR-HOURS	UNIT	2001 BARE COSTS MAT.	LABOR	EQUIP.	TOTAL	TOTAL INCL O&P	
200	0600		For 2" x 14" joists at 16" O.C.	1 Carp	1.30	6.154	C.Pr.	54.50	179		233.50	340	**200**
	0700		24" O.C.		1.40	5.714		54.50	167		221.50	320	
	0900		Compression type, 16" O.C., 2" x 8" joists		2	4		126	117		243	320	
	1000		2" x 12" joists		2	4		141	117		258	335	
505	0010	**FRAMING, BEAMS & GIRDERS**	R06100 -010										**505**
	3500		Single, 2" x 6"	2 Carp	.70	22.857	M.B.F.	590	665		1,255	1,700	
	3505		Pneumatic nailed	R06110 -030	.81	19.704		590	575		1,165	1,550	
	3520		2" x 8"		.86	18.605		620	540		1,160	1,525	
	3525		Pneumatic nailed		1	16.048		620	470		1,090	1,425	
	3540		2" x 10"		1	16		730	465		1,195	1,525	
	3545		Pneumatic nailed		1.16	13.793		730	400		1,130	1,425	
	3560		2" x 12"		1.10	14.545		740	425		1,165	1,475	
	3565		Pneumatic nailed		1.28	12.539		740	365		1,105	1,375	
	3580		2" x 14"		1.17	13.675		760	400		1,160	1,475	
	3585		Pneumatic nailed		1.36	11.791		760	345		1,105	1,375	
	3600		3" x 8"		1.10	14.545		1,125	425		1,550	1,900	
	3620		3" x 10"		1.25	12.800		1,125	375		1,500	1,800	
	3640		3" x 12"		1.35	11.852		1,125	345		1,470	1,775	
	3660		3" x 14"		1.40	11.429		1,125	335		1,460	1,750	
	3680		4" x 8"	F-3	2.66	15.038		1,275	445	194	1,914	2,300	
	3700		4" x 10"		3.16	12.658		1,275	375	163	1,813	2,150	
	3720		4" x 12"		3.60	11.111		1,275	330	143	1,748	2,075	
	3740		4" x 14"		3.96	10.101		1,275	298	130	1,703	2,000	
	4000		Double, 2" x 6"	2 Carp	1.25	12.800		590	375		965	1,225	
	4005		Pneumatic nailed		1.45	11.034		590	320		910	1,150	
	4020		2" x 8"		1.60	10		620	292		912	1,150	
	4025		Pneumatic nailed		1.86	8.621		620	251		871	1,075	
	4040		2" x 10"		1.92	8.333		730	243		973	1,175	
	4045		Pneumatic nailed		2.23	7.185		730	209		939	1,125	
	4060		2" x 12"		2.20	7.273		740	212		952	1,150	
	4065		Pneumatic nailed		2.55	6.275		740	183		923	1,100	
	4080		2" x 14"		2.45	6.531		760	190		950	1,150	
	4085		Pneumatic nailed		2.84	5.634		760	164		924	1,100	
	5000		Triple, 2" x 6"		1.65	9.697		590	283		873	1,100	
	5005		Pneumatic nailed		1.91	8.377		590	244		834	1,025	
	5020		2" x 8"		2.10	7.619		620	222		842	1,025	
	5025		Pneumatic nailed		2.44	6.568		620	191		811	985	
	5040		2" x 10"		2.50	6.400		730	187		917	1,100	
	5045		Pneumatic nailed		2.90	5.517		730	161		891	1,050	
	5060		2" x 12"		2.85	5.614		740	164		904	1,075	
	5065		Pneumatic nailed		3.31	4.840		740	141		881	1,025	
	5080		2" x 14"		3.15	5.079		760	148		908	1,075	
	5085		Pneumatic nailed		3.35	4.770		760	139		899	1,050	
510	0010	**FRAMING, CEILINGS**											**510**
	6400		Suspended, 2" x 3"	2 Carp	.50	32	M.B.F.	555	935		1,490	2,050	
	6450		2" x 4"		.59	27.119		600	790		1,390	1,875	
	6500		2" x 6"		.80	20		590	585		1,175	1,550	
	6550		2" x 8"		.86	18.605		620	540		1,160	1,525	
515	0010	**FRAMING, COLUMNS**											**515**
	0400		4" x 4"	2 Carp	.52	30.769	M.B.F.	755	895		1,650	2,225	
	0420		4" x 6"		.55	29.091		1,275	850		2,125	2,725	
	0440		4" x 8"		.59	27.119		1,275	790		2,065	2,625	
	0460		6" x 6"		.65	24.615		1,775	720		2,495	3,075	
	0480		6" x 8"		.70	22.857		2,300	665		2,965	3,575	

WOOD & PLASTICS | **6**

		06110	Wood Framing	CREW	DAILY OUTPUT	LABOR-HOURS	UNIT	2001 BARE COSTS				TOTAL INCL O&P	
								MAT.	LABOR	EQUIP.	TOTAL		
515	0500		6" x 10"	2 Carp	.75	21.333	M.B.F.	1,850	620		2,470	3,000	515
520	0010	**FRAMING, HEAVY** Mill timber, beams, single 6" x 10"		2 Carp	1.10	14.545	M.B.F.	1,825	425		2,250	2,675	520
	0100		Single 8" x 16"		1.20	13.333		1,800	390		2,190	2,575	
	0200		Built from 2" lumber, multiple 2" x 14"		.90	17.778		760	520		1,280	1,650	
	0210		Built from 3" lumber, multiple 3" x 6"		.70	22.857		1,125	665		1,790	2,275	
	0220		Multiple 3" x 8"		.80	20		1,125	585		1,710	2,125	
	0230		Multiple 3" x 10"		.90	17.778		1,125	520		1,645	2,025	
	0240		Multiple 3" x 12"		1	16		1,125	465		1,590	1,950	
	0250		Built from 4" lumber, multiple 4" x 6"		.80	20		1,275	585		1,860	2,300	
	0260		Multiple 4" x 8"		.90	17.778		1,275	520		1,795	2,200	
	0270		Multiple 4" x 10"		1	16		1,275	465		1,740	2,125	
	0280		Multiple 4" x 12"		1.10	14.545		1,275	425		1,700	2,075	
	0290		Columns, structural grade, 1500f, 4" x 4"		.60	26.667		1,525	775		2,300	2,900	
	0300		6" x 6"		.65	24.615		1,750	720		2,470	3,050	
	0400		8" x 8"		.70	22.857		1,950	665		2,615	3,200	
	0500		10" x 10"		.75	21.333		1,900	620		2,520	3,050	
	0600		12" x 12"		.80	20		1,900	585		2,485	3,000	
	0800		Floor planks, 2" thick, T & G, 2" x 6"		1.05	15.238		1,600	445		2,045	2,450	
	0900		2" x 10"		1.10	14.545		760	425		1,185	1,500	
	1100		3" thick, 3" x 6"		1.05	15.238		1,150	445		1,595	1,975	
	1200		3" x 10"		1.10	14.545		1,150	425		1,575	1,950	
	1400		Girders, structural grade, 12" x 12"		.80	20		1,650	585		2,235	2,725	
	1500		10" x 16"	▼	1	16	▼	1,600	465		2,065	2,500	
	2050	Roof planks, see division 06150-600											
	2300	Roof purlins, 4" thick, structural grade		2 Carp	1.05	15.238	M.B.F.	1,125	445		1,570	1,950	
	2500	Roof trusses, add timber connectors, division 06090-800		"	.45	35.556	"	1,100	1,025		2,125	2,825	
530	0010	**FRAMING, JOISTS**											530
	2650	Joists, 2" x 4"	R06100 -010	2 Carp	.83	19.277	M.B.F.	600	560		1,160	1,550	
	2655		Pneumatic nailed		.96	16.667		600	485		1,085	1,425	
	2680		2" x 6"	R06110 -030	1.25	12.800		590	375		965	1,225	
	2685		Pneumatic nailed		1.44	11.111		590	325		915	1,150	
	2700		2" x 8"		1.46	10.959		620	320		940	1,175	
	2705		Pneumatic nailed		1.68	9.524		620	278		898	1,125	
	2720		2" x 10"		1.49	10.738		730	315		1,045	1,300	
	2725		Pneumatic nailed		1.71	9.357		730	273		1,003	1,225	
	2740		2" x 12"		1.75	9.143		740	267		1,007	1,225	
	2745		Pneumatic nailed		2.01	7.960		740	232		972	1,175	
	2760		2" x 14"		1.79	8.939		760	261		1,021	1,250	
	2765		Pneumatic nailed		2.06	7.767		760	226		986	1,200	
	2780		3" x 6"		1.39	11.511		1,125	335		1,460	1,750	
	2790		3" x 8"		1.90	8.421		1,125	245		1,370	1,600	
	2800		3" x 10"		1.95	8.205		1,125	239		1,364	1,600	
	2820		3" x 12"		1.80	8.889		1,125	259		1,384	1,625	
	2840		4" x 6"	▼	1.60	10		1,275	292		1,567	1,850	
	2850		4" x 8"	F-3	4.15	9.639		1,275	285	124	1,684	1,975	
	2860		4" x 10"	2 Carp	2	8		1,275	233		1,508	1,775	
	2880		4" x 12"		1.80	8.889	▼	1,275	259		1,534	1,800	
	3000		Composite wood joist 9-1/2" deep		.90	17.778	M.L.F.	1,350	520		1,870	2,275	
	3010		11-1/2" deep		.88	18.182		1,450	530		1,980	2,425	
	3020		14" deep		.82	19.512		1,650	570		2,220	2,700	
	3030		16" deep		.78	20.513		2,150	600		2,750	3,275	
	4000		Open web joist 12" deep		.88	18.182		1,500	530		2,030	2,475	
	4010		14" deep		.82	19.512		1,750	570		2,320	2,825	
	4020		16" deep	▼	.78	20.513	▼	1,825	600		2,425	2,925	

Important: See the Reference Section for critical supporting data - Reference Nos., Crews, & City Cost Indexes

	06110	Wood Framing	CREW	DAILY OUTPUT	LABOR-HOURS	UNIT	MAT.	LABOR	EQUIP.	TOTAL	TOTAL INCL O&P	
530	4030	18" deep	2 Carp	.74	21.622	M.L.F.	1,875	630		2,505	3,050	**530**
	6000	Composite rim joist, 1-1/4" x 9-1/2"	R06100 -010	90	.178		1,625	5.20		1,630.20	1,775	
	6010	1-1/4" x 11-1/2"		.88	18.182		1,775	530		2,305	2,775	
	6020	1-1/4" x 14-1/2"	R06110 -030	.82	19.512		2,125	570		2,695	3,225	
	6030	1-1/4" x 16-1/2"		.78	20.513		2,250	600		2,850	3,400	
545	0010	**FRAMING, MISCELLANEOUS**										**545**
	8500	Firestops, 2" x 4"	2 Carp	.51	31.373	M.B.F.	600	915		1,515	2,075	
	8505	Pneumatic nailed		.62	25.806		600	750		1,350	1,825	
	8520	2" x 6"		.60	26.667		590	775		1,365	1,875	
	8525	Pneumatic nailed		.73	21.858		590	635		1,225	1,650	
	8540	2" x 8"		.60	26.667		620	775		1,395	1,900	
	8560	2" x 12"		.70	22.857		740	665		1,405	1,850	
	8600	Nailers, treated, wood construction, 2" x 4"		.53	30.189		785	880		1,665	2,250	
	8605	Pneumatic nailed		.64	25.157		785	735		1,520	2,025	
	8620	2" x 6"		.75	21.333		895	620		1,515	1,950	
	8625	Pneumatic nailed		.90	17.778		895	520		1,415	1,800	
	8640	2" x 8"		.93	17.204		870	500		1,370	1,750	
	8645	Pneumatic nailed		1.12	14.337		870	420		1,290	1,600	
	8660	Steel construction, 2" x 4"		.50	32		785	935		1,720	2,325	
	8680	2" x 6"		.70	22.857		895	665		1,560	2,025	
	8700	2" x 8"		.87	18.391		870	535		1,405	1,800	
	8760	Rough bucks, treated, for doors or windows, 2" x 6"		.40	40		895	1,175		2,070	2,800	
	8765	Pneumatic nailed		.48	33.333		895	970		1,865	2,500	
	8780	2" x 8"		.51	31.373		870	915		1,785	2,375	
	8785	Pneumatic nailed		.61	26.144		870	760		1,630	2,150	
	8800	Stair stringers, 2" x 10"		.22	72.727		730	2,125		2,855	4,125	
	8820	2" x 12"		.26	61.538		740	1,800		2,540	3,600	
	8840	3" x 10"		.31	51.613		1,125	1,500		2,625	3,575	
	8860	3" x 12"		.38	42.105		1,125	1,225		2,350	3,150	
	8870	Composite LSL, 1-1/4" x 11-1/2"		130	.123	L.F.	1.81	3.59		5.40	7.60	
	8880	1-1/4" x 14-1/2"		130	.123	"	2.17	3.59		5.76	8	
550	0010	**PARTITIONS** Wood stud with single bottom plate and										**550**
	0020	double top plate, no waste, std. & better lumber										
	0180	2" x 4" studs, 8' high, studs 12" O.C.	2 Carp	80	.200	L.F.	4.41	5.85		10.26	13.95	
	0185	12" O.C., pneumatic nailed		96	.167		4.41	4.86		9.27	12.45	
	0200	16" O.C.		100	.160		3.61	4.66		8.27	11.25	
	0205	16" O.C., pneumatic nailed		120	.133		3.61	3.89		7.50	10.05	
	0300	24" O.C.		125	.128		2.81	3.73		6.54	8.95	
	0305	24" O.C., pneumatic nailed		150	.107		2.81	3.11		5.92	7.95	
	0380	10' high, studs 12" O.C.		80	.200		5.20	5.85		11.05	14.85	
	0385	12" O.C., pneumatic nailed		96	.167		5.20	4.86		10.06	13.35	
	0400	16" O.C.		100	.160		4.21	4.66		8.87	11.95	
	0405	16" O.C., pneumatic nailed		120	.133		4.21	3.89		8.10	10.75	
	0500	24" O.C.		125	.128		3.21	3.73		6.94	9.40	
	0505	24" O.C., pneumatic nailed		150	.107		3.21	3.11		6.32	8.40	
	0580	12' high, studs 12" O.C.		65	.246		6	7.20		13.20	17.80	
	0585	12" O.C., pneumatic nailed		78	.205		6	6		12	15.95	
	0600	16" O.C.		80	.200		4.82	5.85		10.67	14.40	
	0605	16" O.C., pneumatic nailed		96	.167		4.82	4.86		9.68	12.90	
	0700	24" O.C.		100	.160		3.61	4.66		8.27	11.25	
	0705	24" O.C., pneumatic nailed		120	.133		3.61	3.89		7.50	10.05	
	0780	2" x 6" studs, 8' high, studs 12" O.C.		70	.229		6.50	6.65		13.15	17.55	
	0785	12" O.C., pneumatic nailed		84	.190		6.50	5.55		12.05	15.85	
	0800	16" O.C.		90	.178		5.30	5.20		10.50	13.95	
	0805	16" O.C., pneumatic nailed		108	.148		5.30	4.32		9.62	12.60	

WOOD & PLASTICS **6**

For expanded coverage of these items see *Means Interior Cost Data 2001*

06110 | Wood Framing

		CREW	DAILY OUTPUT	LABOR-HOURS	UNIT	2001 BARE COSTS				TOTAL INCL O&P
						MAT.	LABOR	EQUIP.	TOTAL	
550 0900	24" O.C.	2 Carp	115	.139	L.F.	4.13	4.06		8.19	10.90
0905	24" O.C., pneumatic nailed		138	.116		4.13	3.38		7.51	9.85
0980	10' high, studs 12" O.C.		70	.229		7.65	6.65		14.30	18.85
0985	12" O.C., pneumatic nailed		84	.190		7.65	5.55		13.20	17.15
1000	16" O.C.		90	.178		6.20	5.20		11.40	14.90
1005	16" O.C., pneumatic nailed		108	.148		6.20	4.32		10.52	13.55
1100	24" O.C.		115	.139		4.72	4.06		8.78	11.55
1105	24" O.C., pneumatic nailed		138	.116		4.72	3.38		8.10	10.50
1180	12' high, studs 12" O.C.		55	.291		8.85	8.50		17.35	23
1185	12" O.C., pneumatic nailed		66	.242		8.85	7.05		15.90	21
1200	16" O.C.		70	.229		7.10	6.65		13.75	18.20
1205	16" O.C., pneumatic nailed		84	.190		7.10	5.55		12.65	16.50
1300	24" O.C.		90	.178		5.30	5.20		10.50	13.95
1305	24" O.C., pneumatic nailed		108	.148		5.30	4.32		9.62	12.60
1400	For horizontal blocking, 2" x 4", add		600	.027		.40	.78		1.18	1.66
1500	2" x 6", add		600	.027		.59	.78		1.37	1.87
1600	For openings, add		250	.064			1.87		1.87	2.92
1700	Headers for above openings, material only, add				M.B.F.	620			620	685
555 0010	**FRAMING, ROOFS**									
5250	Composite rafter, 9-1/2" deep	2 Carp	575	.028	L.F.	1.49	.81		2.30	2.91
5260	11-1/2" deep		575	.028	"	1.61	.81		2.42	3.04
6070	Fascia boards, 2" x 8"		.30	53.333	M.B.F.	620	1,550		2,170	3,100
6080	2" x 10"		.30	53.333		730	1,550		2,280	3,225
7000	Rafters, to 4 in 12 pitch, 2" x 6"		1	16		590	465		1,055	1,375
7060	2" x 8"		1.26	12.698		620	370		990	1,275
7300	Hip and valley rafters, 2" x 6"		.76	21.053		590	615		1,205	1,600
7360	2" x 8"		.96	16.667		620	485		1,105	1,450
7540	Hip and valley jacks, 2" x 6"		.60	26.667		590	775		1,365	1,875
7600	2" x 8"		.65	24.615		620	720		1,340	1,800
7780	For slopes steeper than 4 in 12, add						30%			
7790	For dormers or complex roofs, add						50%			
7800	Rafter tie, 1" x 4", #3	2 Carp	.27	59.259	M.B.F.	1,100	1,725		2,825	3,900
7820	Ridge board, #2 or better, 1" x 6" **CN**		.30	53.333		1,800	1,550		3,350	4,400
7840	1" x 8"		.37	43.243		1,800	1,250		3,050	3,950
7860	1" x 10"		.42	38.095		1,800	1,100		2,900	3,700
7880	2" x 6"		.50	32		590	935		1,525	2,100
7900	2" x 8"		.60	26.667		620	775		1,395	1,900
7920	2" x 10"		.66	24.242		730	705		1,435	1,900
7940	Roof cants, split, 4" x 4"		.86	18.605		755	540		1,295	1,675
7960	6" x 6"		1.80	8.889		1,775	259		2,034	2,350
7980	Roof curbs, untreated, 2" x 6"		.52	30.769		590	895		1,485	2,050
8000	2" x 12"		.80	20		740	585		1,325	1,725
560 0010	**FRAMING, SILLS**									
4482	Ledgers, nailed, 2" x 4"	2 Carp	.50	32	M.B.F.	600	935		1,535	2,100
4484	2" x 6"		.60	26.667		590	775		1,365	1,875
4486	Bolted, not including bolts, 3" x 8"		.65	24.615		1,125	720		1,845	2,350
4488	3" x 12"		.70	22.857		1,125	665		1,790	2,275
4490	Mud sills, redwood, construction grade, 2" x 4"		.59	27.119		4,000	790		4,790	5,625
4492	2" x 6"		.78	20.513		4,000	600		4,600	5,325
4500	Sills, 2" x 4"		.40	40		600	1,175		1,775	2,475
4520	2" x 6"		.55	29.091		590	850		1,440	1,975
4540	2" x 8"		.67	23.881		620	695		1,315	1,775
4600	Treated, 2" x 4"		.36	44.444		785	1,300		2,085	2,900
4620	2" x 6"		.50	32		895	935		1,830	2,425
4640	2" x 8"		.60	26.667		870	775		1,645	2,175
4700	4" x 4"		.60	26.667		1,025	775		1,800	2,350

6 WOOD & PLASTICS

Important: See the Reference Section for critical supporting data - Reference Nos., Crews, & City Cost Indexes

		06110	Wood Framing		CREW	DAILY OUTPUT	LABOR-HOURS	UNIT	MAT.	LABOR	EQUIP.	TOTAL	TOTAL INCL O&P	
										2001 BARE COSTS				
560	4720		4" x 6"		2 Carp	.70	22.857	M.B.F.	1,050	665		1,715	2,200	560
	4740		4" x 8"			.80	20		1,050	585		1,635	2,075	
	4760		4" x 10"		↓	.87	18.391	↓	975	535		1,510	1,925	
565	0010	**FRAMING, SLEEPERS**												565
	0300		On concrete, treated, 1" x 2"		2 Carp	.39	41.026	M.B.F.	590	1,200		1,790	2,525	
	0320		1" x 3"			.50	32		740	935		1,675	2,250	
	0340		2" x 4"			.99	16.162		785	470		1,255	1,600	
	0360		2" x 6"		↓	1.30	12.308	↓	895	360		1,255	1,550	
570	0010	**FRAMING, SOFFITS & CANOPIES**												570
	1300		Canopy or soffit framing, 1" x 4"		2 Carp	.30	53.333	M.B.F.	1,800	1,550		3,350	4,400	
	1340		1" x 8"			.50	32		1,800	935		2,735	3,425	
	1360		2" x 4"			.41	39.024		600	1,150		1,750	2,425	
	1400		2" x 8"			.67	23.881		620	695		1,315	1,775	
	1420		3" x 4"			.50	32		1,125	935		2,060	2,675	
	1460		3" x 8"		↓	.60	26.667	↓	1,125	775		1,900	2,450	
575	0010	**FRAMING, TREATED LUMBER**												575
	0020		Water-borne salt, C.C.A., A.C.A., wet, .40 P.C.F. retention											
	0100		2" x 4"					M.B.F.	785			785	865	
	0110		2" x 6"						895			895	985	
	0120		2" x 8"						870			870	955	
	0130		2" x 10"						855			855	940	
	0140		2" x 12"						980			980	1,075	
	0200		4" x 4"						1,025			1,025	1,125	
	0210		4" x 6"						1,050			1,050	1,150	
	0220		4" x 8"					↓	1,050			1,050	1,175	
	0250		Add for .60 P.C.F. retention						40%					
	0260		Add for 2.5 P.C.F. retention						200%					
	0270		Add for K.D.A.T.						20%					
590	0010	**FRAMING, WALLS**		R06100 -010										590
	5860		Headers over openings, 2" x 6"		2 Carp	.36	44.444	M.B.F.	590	1,300		1,890	2,675	
	5865		2" x 6", pneumatic nailed	R06110 -030			.43	37.209		590	1,075		1,665	2,350	
	5880		2" x 8"				.45	35.556		620	1,025		1,645	2,300	
	5885		2" x 8", pneumatic nailed				.54	29.630		620	865		1,485	2,025	
	5900		2" x 10"				.53	30.189		730	880		1,610	2,175	
	5905		2" x 10", pneumatic nailed				.67	23.881		730	695		1,425	1,900	
	5920		2" x 12"				.60	26.667		740	775		1,515	2,025	
	5925		2" x 12", pneumatic nailed				.72	22.222		740	650		1,390	1,825	
	5940		4" x 12"				.76	21.053		1,275	615		1,890	2,350	
	5945		4" x 12", pneumatic nailed				.92	17.391		1,275	505		1,780	2,200	
	5960		6" x 12"				.84	19.048		2,125	555		2,680	3,200	
	5965		6" x 12", pneumatic nailed				1.01	15.873		2,125	465		2,590	3,050	
	6000		Plates, untreated, 2" x 3"				.43	37.209		555	1,075		1,630	2,300	
	6005		2" x 3", pneumatic nailed				.52	30.769		555	895		1,450	2,000	
	6020		2" x 4"	CN			.53	30.189		600	880		1,480	2,025	
	6025		2" x 4", pneumatic nailed				.67	23.881		600	695		1,295	1,750	
	6040		2" x 6"				.75	21.333		590	620		1,210	1,625	
	6045		2" x 6", pneumatic nailed				.90	17.778		590	520		1,110	1,450	
	6120		Studs, 8' high wall, 2" x 3"				.60	26.667		555	775		1,330	1,825	
	6125		2" x 3", pneumatic nailed				.72	22.222		555	650		1,205	1,625	
	6140		2" x 4"				.92	17.391		600	505		1,105	1,450	
	6145		2" x 4", pneumatic nailed				1.10	14.493		600	420		1,020	1,325	
	6160		2" x 6"		↓	↓	1	16	↓	590	465		1,055	1,375	

WOOD & PLASTICS 6

06110 | Wood Framing

		CREW	DAILY OUTPUT	LABOR-HOURS	UNIT	2001 BARE COSTS				TOTAL INCL O&P	
						MAT.	LABOR	EQUIP.	TOTAL		
590	6165	2" x 6", pneumatic nailed	2 Carp	1.20	13.333	M.B.F.	590	390		980	1,250	**590**
	6180	3" x 4"		.80	20		1,125	585		1,710	2,125	
	6185	3" x 4", pneumatic nailed		.96	16.667		1,125	485		1,610	1,975	
	8200	For 12' high walls, deduct						5%				
	8220	For stub wall, 6' high, add						20%				
	8240	3' high, add						40%				
	8250	For second story & above, add						5%				
	8300	For dormer & gable, add						15%				
600	0010	**FURRING** Wood strips, 1" x 2", on walls, on wood	1 Carp	550	.015	L.F.	.21	.42		.63	.89	**600**
	0015	On wood, pneumatic nailed		710	.011		.21	.33		.54	.74	
	0300	On masonry		495	.016		.21	.47		.68	.97	
	0400	On concrete		260	.031		.21	.90		1.11	1.63	
	0600	1" x 3", on walls, on wood		550	.015		.19	.42		.61	.87	
	0605	On wood, pneumatic nailed		710	.011		.19	.33		.52	.72	
	0700	On masonry		495	.016		.19	.47		.66	.95	
	0800	On concrete		260	.031		.19	.90		1.09	1.61	
	0850	On ceilings, on wood		350	.023		.19	.67		.86	1.25	
	0855	On wood, pneumatic nailed		450	.018		.19	.52		.71	1.02	
	0900	On masonry		320	.025		.19	.73		.92	1.35	
	0950	On concrete		210	.038		.19	1.11		1.30	1.95	
700	0010	**GROUNDS** For casework, 1" x 2" wood strips, on wood	1 Carp	330	.024	L.F.	.21	.71		.92	1.34	**700**
	0100	On masonry		285	.028		.21	.82		1.03	1.51	
	0200	On concrete		250	.032		.21	.93		1.14	1.69	
	0400	For plaster, 3/4" deep, on wood		450	.018		.21	.52		.73	1.04	
	0500	On masonry		225	.036		.21	1.04		1.25	1.85	
	0600	On concrete		175	.046		.21	1.33		1.54	2.31	
	0700	On metal lath		200	.040		.21	1.17		1.38	2.05	

06120 | Structural Panels

		CREW	DAILY OUTPUT	LABOR-HOURS	UNIT	MAT.	LABOR	EQUIP.	TOTAL	TOTAL INCL O&P	
200	0010	**MINERAL FIBER CEMENT PANELS** Including panels, fasteners,										**200**
	0100	accessories, trim & sealant										
	0130	Architectural, textured finish, 1/8" thick, minimum	G-3	500	.064	S.F.	5.75	1.80		7.55	9.15	
	0140	Maximum		500	.064		7.25	1.80		9.05	10.80	
	0150	1/4" thick, minimum		500	.064		6.75	1.80		8.55	10.25	
	0200	Maximum		500	.064		8.85	1.80		10.65	12.55	
	0250	3/8" thick, minimum		500	.064		8.90	1.80		10.70	12.60	
	0300	Maximum		500	.064		11.75	1.80		13.55	15.75	
	0350	5/8" thick, minimum		300	.107		11.75	3.01		14.76	17.60	
	0400	Maximum		300	.107		17.10	3.01		20.11	23.50	
	2000	Flat sheets, 1/8" thick		1,200	.027		4.05	.75		4.80	5.65	
	2100	1/4" thick		1,020	.031		5.80	.88		6.68	7.75	
	2200	3/8" thick		885	.036		7.30	1.02		8.32	9.65	
	2300	5/8" thick		795	.040		9.95	1.14		11.09	12.70	
	3000	Glasweld, mineral enamel coating, 1/8" thick		600	.053		3.50	1.50		5	6.20	
	3100	1/4" thick		322	.099		4.45	2.80		7.25	9.25	
	4000	Sandwich panel, Glasweld face and back										
	4100	1" thick, perlite core	G-3	322	.099	S.F.	7.25	2.80		10.05	12.35	
	4200	Polyurethane core		322	.099		7.65	2.80		10.45	12.75	
	4500	2" thick, perlite core		322	.099		7.95	2.80		10.75	13.10	
	4600	Polyurethane core		322	.099		8.35	2.80		11.15	13.55	
800	0010	**STRESSED SKIN PLYWOOD ROOF PANELS** 3/8" group 1 top										**800**
	0020	skin, 3/8" exterior AD bottom skin										
	0030	1150f stringers, 4' x 8' panels	F-3	2,075	.019	SF Roof	3.10	.57	.25	3.92	4.57	
	0100	4-1/4" deep										

Left margin: 6 WOOD & PLASTICS

R06100-010, R06110-030

06120 | Structural Panels

			CREW	DAILY OUTPUT	LABOR-HOURS	UNIT	MAT.	LABOR	EQUIP.	TOTAL	TOTAL INCL O&P	
							2001 BARE COSTS					
800	0200	6-1/8" deep	F-3	1,725	.023	SF Roof	3.36	.69	.30	4.35	5.10	800
	0300	8-1/8" deep		1,475	.027		3.89	.80	.35	5.04	5.90	
	0500	3/8" top skin, no bottom skin, 5-3/4" deep		1,725	.023		2.94	.69	.30	3.93	4.62	
	0600	7-3/4" deep		1,475	.027		3.36	.80	.35	4.51	5.35	
	0800	For 3-1/2" factory fiberglass insulation, add					.36			.36	.40	
	1000	For 1/2" thick top skin, add					.36			.36	.40	
	1500	Floor panels, substitute 5/8" underlayment as										
	1510	top skin, add to roof panels above				SF Flr.	.42			.42	.46	
	2000	Curved roof panels, 3/8" structural 1 top skin,										
	2010	3/8" exterior AC bottom skin, laminated ribs										
	2200	8' radius, 2-1/4" deep, tie rods not req'd.	F-3	1,150	.035	SF Flr.	5.80	1.03	.45	7.28	8.50	
	2400	10' radius, 1-1/2" deep, tie rods are included		950	.042		4.57	1.24	.54	6.35	7.60	
	2600	10' radius, 3-3/8" deep, tie rods not req'd.		1,150	.035		7.95	1.03	.45	9.43	10.85	
	2800	12' radius, 2" deep, tie rods are included		950	.042		4.72	1.24	.54	6.50	7.75	
	3000	12' radius, 4-1/2" deep, tie rods not req'd.		1,150	.035		8.25	1.03	.45	9.73	11.15	
	4000	Folded plate roofs, structural 1 top skin with intermediate										
	4010	rafters and end chord. Cost of tie rods included										
	4200	Slope 7 in 12, 4' fold, 2" thick, 32' span	F-3	850	.047	SF Flr.	3.78	1.39	.61	5.78	7	
	4400	Slope 8-1/2 in 12, 5' fold, 4" thick, 56' span		950	.042		7.40	1.24	.54	9.18	10.70	
	4600	Slope 10 in 12, 8' fold, 4" thick, 52' span		950	.042		4.43	1.24	.54	6.21	7.40	
	4800	Slope 10 in 12, 8' fold, 4" thick, 72' span		1,025	.039		7.80	1.15	.50	9.45	10.90	
	6000	Box beams, structural 1 web										
	6200	24" deep, 2-2" x 4" flanges, 2 webs @ 3/8"	F-3	295	.136	L.F.	8.90	4.01	1.75	14.66	17.90	
	6400	24" deep, 3-2" x 4" flanges, 2 webs @ 1/2"		260	.154		11.05	4.55	1.98	17.58	21.50	
	6600	48" deep, 3-2" x 6" flanges, 2 webs @ 3/4"		140	.286		19.15	8.45	3.68	31.28	38	
	6800	48" deep, 6-2" x 6" flanges, 4 webs @ 3/8",										
	6810	including 2 interior webs	F-3	115	.348	L.F.	39	10.30	4.48	53.78	64	
	7000	For exterior AC outer webs, add					1.03			1.03	1.13	
	7200	For medium density overlaid outer webs, add					1.54			1.54	1.69	

06150 | Wood Decking

			CREW	DAILY OUTPUT	LABOR-HOURS	UNIT	MAT.	LABOR	EQUIP.	TOTAL	TOTAL INCL O&P	
600	0010	**ROOF DECKS**										600
	0020	For laminated decks, see division 06170-550										
	0200	For cementitious decks, see division 03450-000										
	0400	Cedar planks, 3" thick	2 Carp	320	.050	S.F.	5.65	1.46		7.11	8.55	
	0500	4" thick		250	.064		7.65	1.87		9.52	11.30	
	0700	Douglas fir, 3" thick		320	.050		2.12	1.46		3.58	4.61	
	0800	4" thick		250	.064		2.84	1.87		4.71	6.05	
	1000	Hemlock, 3" thick		320	.050		2.12	1.46		3.58	4.61	
	1100	4" thick		250	.064		2.83	1.87		4.70	6.05	
	1300	Western white spruce, 3" thick		320	.050		2.05	1.46		3.51	4.54	
	1400	4" thick		250	.064		2.73	1.87		4.60	5.90	

06160 | Sheathing

				CREW	DAILY OUTPUT	LABOR-HOURS	UNIT	MAT.	LABOR	EQUIP.	TOTAL	TOTAL INCL O&P	
800	0010	**SHEATHING** Plywood on roof, CDX	R06160 -020										800
	0030	5/16" thick		2 Carp	1,600	.010	S.F.	.33	.29		.62	.83	
	0035	Pneumatic nailed	R06110 -030		1,952	.008		.33	.24		.57	.74	
	0050	3/8" thick			1,525	.010		.38	.31		.69	.89	
	0055	Pneumatic nailed			1,860	.009		.38	.25		.63	.80	
	0100	1/2" thick **CN**			1,400	.011		.49	.33		.82	1.06	
	0105	Pneumatic nailed			1,708	.009		.49	.27		.76	.97	
	0200	5/8" thick			1,300	.012		.62	.36		.98	1.24	
	0205	Pneumatic nailed			1,586	.010		.62	.29		.91	1.14	
	0300	3/4" thick			1,200	.013		.75	.39		1.14	1.43	

6

WOOD & PLASTICS

For expanded coverage of these items see Means Interior Cost Data 2001

06160 | Sheathing

			CREW	DAILY OUTPUT	LABOR HOURS	UNIT	MAT.	LABOR	EQUIP.	TOTAL	TOTAL INCL O&P	
800	0305	Pneumatic nailed		2 Carp	1,464	.011	S.F.	.75	.32		1.07	1.32	800
	0500	Plywood on walls with exterior CDX, 3/8" thick			1,200	.013		.38	.39		.77	1.02	
	0505	Pneumatic nailed	R06160-020		1,488	.011		.38	.31		.69	.90	
	0600	1/2" thick			1,125	.014		.49	.41		.90	1.19	
	0605	Pneumatic nailed	R06110-030		1,395	.011		.49	.33		.82	1.06	
	0700	5/8" thick			1,050	.015		.62	.44		1.06	1.37	
	0705	Pneumatic nailed			1,302	.012		.62	.36		.98	1.24	
	0800	3/4" thick			975	.016		.75	.48		1.23	1.57	
	0805	Pneumatic nailed			1,209	.013		.75	.39		1.14	1.42	
	1000	For shear wall construction, add							20%				
	1200	For structural 1 exterior plywood, add					S.F.	10%					
	1400	With boards, on roof 1" x 6" boards, laid horizontal		2 Carp	725	.022		1.30	.64		1.94	2.44	
	1500	Laid diagonal			650	.025		1.30	.72		2.02	2.55	
	1700	1" x 8" boards, laid horizontal			875	.018		1.30	.53		1.83	2.26	
	1800	Laid diagonal			725	.022		1.30	.64		1.94	2.44	
	2000	For steep roofs, add							40%				
	2200	For dormers, hips and valleys, add						5%	50%				
	2400	Boards on walls, 1" x 6" boards, laid regular		2 Carp	650	.025		1.30	.72		2.02	2.55	
	2500	Laid diagonal			585	.027		1.30	.80		2.10	2.68	
	2700	1" x 8" boards, laid regular			765	.021		1.30	.61		1.91	2.38	
	2800	Laid diagonal			650	.025		1.30	.72		2.02	2.55	
	2850	Gypsum, weatherproof, 1/2" thick			1,125	.014		.28	.41		.69	.96	
	2900	Sealed, 4/10" thick			1,100	.015		.44	.42		.86	1.14	
	3000	Wood fiber, regular, no vapor barrier, 1/2" thick			1,200	.013		.53	.39		.92	1.19	
	3100	5/8" thick			1,200	.013		.71	.39		1.10	1.39	
	3300	No vapor barrier, in colors, 1/2" thick			1,200	.013		.77	.39		1.16	1.46	
	3400	5/8" thick			1,200	.013		.95	.39		1.34	1.66	
	3600	With vapor barrier one side, white, 1/2" thick			1,200	.013		.54	.39		.93	1.20	
	3700	Vapor barrier 2 sides, 1/2" thick			1,200	.013		.82	.39		1.21	1.51	
	3800	Asphalt impregnated, 25/32" thick			1,200	.013		.35	.39		.74	1	
	3850	Intermediate, 1/2" thick			1,200	.013		.29	.39		.68	.93	
850	0010	**SUBFLOOR** Plywood, CDX, 1/2" thick	R06160-020	2 Carp	1,500	.011	SF Flr.	.49	.31		.80	1.03	850
	0015	Pneumatic nailed			1,860	.009		.49	.25		.74	.93	
	0100	5/8" thick			1,350	.012		.62	.35		.97	1.22	
	0105	Pneumatic nailed			1,674	.010		.62	.28		.90	1.12	
	0200	3/4" thick			1,250	.013		.75	.37		1.12	1.40	
	0205	Pneumatic nailed			1,550	.010		.75	.30		1.05	1.29	
	0300	1-1/8" thick, 2-4-1 including underlayment			1,050	.015		2	.44		2.44	2.89	
	0500	With boards, 1" x 10" S4S, laid regular			1,100	.015		1.01	.42		1.43	1.77	
	0600	Laid diagonal			900	.018		1.02	.52		1.54	1.93	
	0800	1" x 8" S4S, laid regular			1,000	.016		.91	.47		1.38	1.73	
	0900	Laid diagonal			850	.019		.91	.55		1.46	1.86	
	1100	Wood fiber, T&G, 2' x 8' planks, 1" thick			1,000	.016		1.26	.47		1.73	2.12	
	1200	1-3/8" thick			900	.018		1.55	.52		2.07	2.52	
900	0010	**UNDERLAYMENT** Plywood, underlayment grade, 3/8" thick	R06160-020	2 Carp	1,500	.011	SF Flr.	.58	.31		.89	1.13	900
	0015	Pneumatic nailed			1,860	.009		.58	.25		.83	1.03	
	0100	1/2" thick			1,450	.011		.74	.32		1.06	1.31	
	0105	Pneumatic nailed			1,798	.009		.74	.26		1	1.22	
	0200	5/8" thick			1,400	.011		.70	.33		1.03	1.29	
	0205	Pneumatic nailed			1,736	.009		.70	.27		.97	1.19	
	0300	3/4" thick			1,300	.012		.90	.36		1.26	1.55	
	0305	Pneumatic nailed			1,612	.010		.90	.29		1.19	1.44	
	0500	Particle board, 3/8" thick			1,500	.011		.38	.31		.69	.91	
	0505	Pneumatic nailed			1,860	.009		.38	.25		.63	.81	

Important: See the Reference Section for critical supporting data - Reference Nos., Crews, & City Cost Indexes

6 WOOD & PLASTICS

06160 | Sheathing

			CREW	DAILY OUTPUT	LABOR-HOURS	UNIT	2001 BARE COSTS				TOTAL INCL O&P	
							MAT.	LABOR	EQUIP.	TOTAL		
900	0600	1/2" thick	2 Carp	1,450	.011	SF Flr.	.40	.32		.72	.94	900
	0605	Pneumatic nailed R06160-020		1,798	.009		.40	.26		.66	.85	
	0800	5/8" thick		1,400	.011		.54	.33		.87	1.11	
	0805	Pneumatic nailed		1,736	.009		.54	.27		.81	1.01	
	0900	3/4" thick		1,300	.012		.58	.36		.94	1.20	
	0905	Pneumatic nailed		1,612	.010		.58	.29		.87	1.09	
	1100	Hardboard, underlayment grade, 4' x 4', .215" thick	↓	1,500	.011	↓	.41	.31		.72	.94	

06170 | Prefabricated Structural Wood

			CREW	DAILY OUTPUT	LABOR-HOURS	UNIT	MAT.	LABOR	EQUIP.	TOTAL	TOTAL INCL O&P	
550	0010	LAMINATED ROOF DECK Pine or hemlock, 3" thick	2 Carp	425	.038	S.F.	2.83	1.10		3.93	4.83	550
	0100	4" thick		325	.049		3.76	1.44		5.20	6.40	
	0300	Cedar, 3" thick		425	.038		3.45	1.10		4.55	5.50	
	0400	4" thick		325	.049		4.40	1.44		5.84	7.10	
	0600	Fir, 3" thick		425	.038		2.88	1.10		3.98	4.89	
	0700	4" thick	↓	325	.049	↓	3.61	1.44		5.05	6.20	
600	0010	STRUCTURAL JOISTS Fabricated "I" joists with wood flanges,										600
	0100	Plywood webs, incl. bridging & blocking, panels 24" O.C.										
	1200	15' to 24' span, 50 psf live load	F-5	2,400	.013	SF Flr.	1.44	.40		1.84	2.20	
	1300	55 psf live load		2,250	.014		1.55	.42		1.97	2.37	
	1400	24' to 30' span, 45 psf live load		2,600	.012		1.80	.37		2.17	2.55	
	1500	55 psf live load	↓	2,400	.013		1.80	.40		2.20	2.60	
	1600	Tubular steel open webs, 45 psf, 24" O.C., 40' span	F-3	6,250	.006		1.80	.19	.08	2.07	2.36	
	1700	55' span		7,750	.005		1.75	.15	.07	1.97	2.24	
	1800	70' span		9,250	.004		2.27	.13	.06	2.46	2.76	
	1900	85 psf live load, 26' span	↓	2,300	.017	↓	2.11	.51	.22	2.84	3.37	
980	0010	ROOF TRUSSES										980
	0020	For timber connectors, see div. 06090-800 R06170-100										
	0100	Fink (W) or King post type, 2'-0" O.C.										
	0200	Metal plate connected, 4 in 12 slope										
	0210	24' to 29' span	F-3	3,000	.013	SF Flr.	1.39	.39	.17	1.95	2.33	
	0300	30' to 43' span		3,000	.013		1.54	.39	.17	2.10	2.49	
	0400	44' to 60' span	↓	3,000	.013		1.70	.39	.17	2.26	2.67	
	0600	For change in roof pitch, subtract					.06			.06	.07	
	0700	Glued and nailed, add	↓			↓	50%					

06180 | Glued-Laminated Construction

			CREW	DAILY OUTPUT	LABOR-HOURS	UNIT	MAT.	LABOR	EQUIP.	TOTAL	TOTAL INCL O&P	
400	0010	LAMINATED FRAMING Not including decking										400
	0020	30 lb., short term live load, 15 lb. dead load										
	0200	Straight roof beams, 20' clear span, beams 8' O.C.	F-3	2,560	.016	SF Flr.	1.44	.46	.20	2.10	2.52	
	0300	Beams 16' O.C.		3,200	.013		1.05	.37	.16	1.58	1.91	
	0500	40' clear span, beams 8' O.C.		3,200	.013		2.78	.37	.16	3.31	3.81	
	0600	Beams 16' O.C.	↓	3,840	.010		2.27	.31	.13	2.71	3.13	
	0800	60' clear span, beams 8' O.C.	F-4	2,880	.017		4.77	.48	.31	5.56	6.35	
	0900	Beams 16' O.C.	"	3,840	.013		3.55	.36	.23	4.14	4.73	
	1100	Tudor arches, 30' to 40' clear span, frames 8' O.C.	F-3	1,680	.024		6.20	.70	.31	7.21	8.30	
	1200	Frames 16' O.C.	"	2,240	.018		4.87	.53	.23	5.63	6.40	
	1400	50' to 60' clear span, frames 8' O.C.	F-4	2,200	.022		6.70	.63	.41	7.74	8.85	
	1500	Frames 16' O.C.		2,640	.018		5.70	.53	.34	6.57	7.45	
	1700	Radial arches, 60' clear span, frames 8' O.C.		1,920	.025		6.25	.72	.47	7.44	8.55	
	1800	Frames 16' O.C.		2,880	.017		4.82	.48	.31	5.61	6.40	
	2000	100' clear span, frames 8' O.C.		1,600	.030		6.50	.87	.56	7.93	9.10	
	2100	Frames 16' O.C.		2,400	.020		5.70	.58	.38	6.66	7.55	
	2300	120' clear span, frames 8' O.C.		1,440	.033		8.65	.96	.63	10.24	11.70	
	2400	Frames 16' O.C.	↓	1,920	.025	↓	7.85	.72	.47	9.04	10.30	

WOOD & PLASTICS **6**

06180	Glued-Laminated Construction	CREW	DAILY OUTPUT	LABOR-HOURS	UNIT	2001 BARE COSTS				TOTAL INCL O&P
						MAT.	LABOR	EQUIP.	TOTAL	
400 2600	Bowstring trusses, 20' O.C., 40' clear span	F-3	2,400	.017	SF Flr.	3.89	.49	.21	4.59	5.30	400
2700	60' clear span	F-4	3,600	.013		3.49	.39	.25	4.13	4.72
2800	100' clear span		4,000	.012		4.95	.35	.23	5.53	6.25
2900	120' clear span	▼	3,600	.013		5.30	.39	.25	5.94	6.75
3000	For less than 1000 B.F., add					20%				
3050	For over 5000 B.F., deduct					10%				
3100	For premium appearance, add to S.F. prices					5%				
3300	For industrial type, deduct					15%				
3500	For stain and varnish, add					5%				
3900	For 3/4" laminations, add to straight					25%				
4100	Add to curved				▼	15%				
4300	Alternate pricing method: (use nominal footage of									
4310	components). Straight beams, camber less than 6"	F-3	3.50	11.429	M.B.F.	2,150	340	147	2,637	3,050
4400	Columns, including hardware		2	20		2,325	590	257	3,172	3,750
4600	Curved members, radius over 32'		2.50	16		2,375	475	206	3,056	3,550
4700	Radius 10' to 32'	▼	3	13.333		2,350	395	172	2,917	3,375
4900	For complicated shapes, add maximum					100%				
5100	For pressure treating, add to straight					35%				
5200	Add to curved				▼	45%				
6000	Laminated veneer members, southern pine or western species									
6050	1-3/4" wide x 5-1/2" deep	2 Carp	480	.033	L.F.	3.67	.97		4.64	5.55
6100	9-1/2" deep		480	.033		3.84	.97		4.81	5.75
6150	14" deep		450	.036		5.50	1.04		6.54	7.65
6200	18" deep	▼	450	.036	▼	7.10	1.04		8.14	9.45
6300	Parallel strand members, southern pine or western species									
6350	1-3/4" wide x 9-1/4" deep	2 Carp	480	.033	L.F.	4.42	.97		5.39	6.40
6400	11-1/4" deep		450	.036		5.45	1.04		6.49	7.55
6450	14" deep		400	.040		6.45	1.17		7.62	8.90
6500	3-1/2" wide x 9-1/4" deep		480	.033		8.60	.97		9.57	10.95
6550	11-1/4" deep		450	.036		10.60	1.04		11.64	13.25
6600	14" deep		400	.040		12.65	1.17		13.82	15.70
6650	7" wide x 9-1/4" deep		450	.036		16.95	1.04		17.99	20.50
6700	11-1/4" deep		420	.038		21	1.11		22.11	24.50
6750	14" deep	▼	400	.040	▼	25	1.17		26.17	29.50

06220	Millwork	CREW	DAILY OUTPUT	LABOR-HOURS	UNIT	2001 BARE COSTS				TOTAL INCL O&P
						MAT.	LABOR	EQUIP.	TOTAL	
200 0010	**MOLDINGS, BASE**										200
0500	Base, stock pine, 9/16" x 3-1/2"	1 Carp	240	.033	L.F.	1.02	.97		1.99	2.64
0550	9/16" x 4-1/2"		200	.040		1.29	1.17		2.46	3.24
0561	Base shoe, oak, 3/4" x 1"	▼	240	.033	▼	.77	.97		1.74	2.37
400 0010	**MOLDINGS, CASINGS**										400
0090	Apron, stock pine, 5/8" x 2"	1 Carp	250	.032	L.F.	.97	.93		1.90	2.53
0110	5/8" x 3-1/2"		220	.036		1.41	1.06		2.47	3.21
0300	Band, stock pine, 11/16" x 1-1/8"		270	.030		.39	.86		1.25	1.78
0350	11/16" x 1-3/4"		250	.032		.61	.93		1.54	2.13
0700	Casing, stock pine, 11/16" x 2-1/2"		240	.033		.78	.97		1.75	2.38
0750	11/16" x 3-1/2"	▼	215	.037	▼	1.49	1.08		2.57	3.34

6 WOOD & PLASTICS

06220 | Millwork

		CREW	DAILY OUTPUT	LABOR-HOURS	UNIT	2001 BARE COSTS				TOTAL INCL O&P
						MAT.	LABOR	EQUIP.	TOTAL	
450	**0010 MOLDINGS, CEILINGS**									**450**
0600	Bed, stock pine, 9/16" x 1-3/4"	1 Carp	270	.030	L.F.	.59	.86		1.45	2
0650	9/16" x 2"		240	.033		.71	.97		1.68	2.30
1200	Cornice molding, stock pine, 9/16" x 1-3/4"		330	.024		.63	.71		1.34	1.80
1300	9/16" x 2-1/4"		300	.027		.86	.78		1.64	2.17
2400	Cove scotia, stock pine, 9/16" x 1-3/4"		270	.030		.55	.86		1.41	1.96
2500	11/16" x 2-3/4"		255	.031		1.16	.91		2.07	2.71
2600	Crown, stock pine, 9/16" x 3-5/8"		250	.032		1.52	.93		2.45	3.13
2700	11/16" x 4-5/8"	▼	220	.036	▼	1.92	1.06		2.98	3.77
500	**0010 MOLDINGS, EXTERIOR**									**500**
1500	Cornice, boards, pine, 1" x 2"	1 Carp	330	.024	L.F.	.24	.71		.95	1.37
1700	1" x 6"		250	.032		.86	.93		1.79	2.41
2000	1" x 12"		180	.044		1.14	1.30		2.44	3.28
2200	Three piece, built-up, pine, minimum		80	.100		1.47	2.92		4.39	6.20
2300	Maximum		65	.123		5.05	3.59		8.64	11.15
3000	Corner board, sterling pine, 1" x 4"		200	.040		.66	1.17		1.83	2.55
3100	1" x 6"		200	.040		.96	1.17		2.13	2.88
3350	Fascia, sterling pine, 1" x 6"		250	.032		.96	.93		1.89	2.52
3370	1" x 8"		225	.036		1.50	1.04		2.54	3.27
3400	Trim, exterior, sterling pine, back band		250	.032		.57	.93		1.50	2.09
3500	Casing		250	.032		.60	.93		1.53	2.12
3600	Crown		250	.032		1.20	.93		2.13	2.78
3700	Porch rail with balusters		22	.364		9	10.60		19.60	26.50
3800	Screen		395	.020		.32	.59		.91	1.27
4100	Verge board, sterling pine, 1" x 4"		200	.040		.47	1.17		1.64	2.34
4200	1" x 6"		200	.040		.72	1.17		1.89	2.61
4300	2" x 6"		165	.048		1.40	1.41		2.81	3.75
4400	2" x 8"	▼	165	.048	▼	1.86	1.41		3.27	4.26
4700	For redwood trim, add					200%				
700	**0010 MOLDINGS, TRIM**									**700**
0200	Astragal, stock pine, 11/16" x 1-3/4"	1 Carp	255	.031	L.F.	.79	.91		1.70	2.30
0250	1-5/16" x 2-3/16"		240	.033		2.74	.97		3.71	4.53
0800	Chair rail, stock pine, 5/8" x 2-1/2"		270	.030		.85	.86		1.71	2.29
0900	5/8" x 3-1/2"		240	.033		1.27	.97		2.24	2.92
1000	Closet pole, stock pine, 1-1/8" diameter		200	.040		.80	1.17		1.97	2.70
1100	Fir, 1-5/8" diameter		200	.040		1.20	1.17		2.37	3.14
3300	Half round, stock pine, 1/4" x 1/2"		270	.030		.20	.86		1.06	1.57
3350	1/2" x 1"	▼	255	.031	▼	.35	.91		1.26	1.82
3400	Handrail, fir, single piece, stock, hardware not included									
3450	1-1/2" x 1-3/4"	1 Carp	80	.100	L.F.	1.22	2.92		4.14	5.90
3470	Pine, 1-1/2" x 1-3/4"		80	.100		1.07	2.92		3.99	5.75
3500	1-1/2" x 2-1/2"		76	.105		1.44	3.07		4.51	6.40
3600	Lattice, stock pine, 1/4" x 1-1/8"		270	.030		.33	.86		1.19	1.71
3700	1/4" x 1-3/4"		250	.032		.36	.93		1.29	1.86
3800	Miscellaneous, custom, pine, 1" x 1"		270	.030		.99	.86		1.85	2.44
3900	1" x 3"		240	.033		.79	.97		1.76	2.39
4100	Birch or oak, nominal 1" x 1"		240	.033		.47	.97		1.44	2.04
4200	Nominal 1" x 3"		215	.037		1.60	1.08		2.68	3.46
4400	Walnut, nominal 1" x 1"		215	.037		.77	1.08		1.85	2.55
4500	Nominal 1" x 3"		200	.040		2.30	1.17		3.47	4.35
4700	Teak, nominal 1" x 1"		215	.037		1.09	1.08		2.17	2.90
4800	Nominal 1" x 3"		200	.040		3.10	1.17		4.27	5.25
4900	Quarter round, stock pine, 1/4" x 1/4"		275	.029		.22	.85		1.07	1.57
4950	3/4" x 3/4"		255	.031	▼	.42	.91		1.33	1.89
5600	Wainscot moldings, 1-1/8" x 9/16", 2' high, minimum	▼	76	.105	S.F.	5.90	3.07		8.97	11.30

WOOD & PLASTICS **6**

6 WOOD & PLASTICS

06220	Millwork	CREW	DAILY OUTPUT	LABOR-HOURS	UNIT	MAT.	LABOR	EQUIP.	TOTAL	TOTAL INCL O&P	
700 5700	Maximum	1 Carp	65	.123	S.F.	13.50	3.59		17.09	20.50	700
800 0010	**MOLDINGS, WINDOW AND DOOR**										800
2800	Door moldings, stock, decorative, 1-1/8" wide, plain	1 Carp	17	.471	Set	28.50	13.70		42.20	52.50	
2900	Detailed		17	.471	"	68	13.70		81.70	96.50	
3150	Door trim set, 1 head and 2 sides, pine, 2-1/2 wide		5.90	1.356	Opng.	12.70	39.50		52.20	76	
3170	4-1/2" wide		5.30	1.509	"	24	44		68	95	
3200	Glass beads, stock pine, 1/4" x 11/16"		285	.028	L.F.	.30	.82		1.12	1.61	
3250	3/8" x 1/2"		275	.029		.36	.85		1.21	1.73	
3270	3/8" x 7/8"		270	.030		.40	.86		1.26	1.79	
4850	Parting bead, stock pine, 3/8" x 3/4"		275	.029		.29	.85		1.14	1.65	
4870	1/2" x 3/4"		255	.031		.36	.91		1.27	1.83	
5000	Stool caps, stock pine, 11/16" x 3-1/2"		200	.040		1.31	1.17		2.48	3.26	
5100	1-1/16" x 3-1/4"		150	.053		1.97	1.55		3.52	4.60	
5300	Threshold, oak, 3' long, inside, 5/8" x 3-5/8"		32	.250	Ea.	6.20	7.30		13.50	18.25	
5400	Outside, 1-1/2" x 7-5/8"		16	.500	"	25	14.60		39.60	50.50	
5900	Window trim sets, including casings, header, stops,										
5910	stool and apron, 2-1/2" wide, minimum	1 Carp	13	.615	Opng.	15.30	17.95		33.25	45	
5950	Average		10	.800		26.50	23.50		50	65.50	
6000	Maximum		6	1.333		38	39		77	103	
900 0010	**SOFFITS** Wood fiber, no vapor barrier, 15/32" thick	2 Carp	525	.030	S.F.	.75	.89		1.64	2.22	900
0100	5/8" thick		525	.030		.81	.89		1.70	2.28	
0300	As above, 5/8" thick, with factory finish		525	.030		.83	.89		1.72	2.30	
0500	Hardboard, 3/8" thick, slotted		525	.030		1	.89		1.89	2.49	
1000	Exterior AC plywood, 1/4" thick		420	.038		.70	1.11		1.81	2.51	
1100	1/2" thick		420	.038		.97	1.11		2.08	2.81	
1150	For aluminum soffit, see division 07460-750										

06250	Prefinished Paneling	CREW	DAILY OUTPUT	LABOR-HOURS	UNIT	MAT.	LABOR	EQUIP.	TOTAL	TOTAL INCL O&P	
200 0010	**PANELING, HARDBOARD**										200
0050	Not incl. furring or trim, hardboard, tempered, 1/8" thick	2 Carp	500	.032	S.F.	.31	.93		1.24	1.80	
0100	1/4" thick		500	.032		.39	.93		1.32	1.89	
0300	Tempered pegboard, 1/8" thick		500	.032		.39	.93		1.32	1.89	
0400	1/4" thick		500	.032		.42	.93		1.35	1.92	
0600	Untempered hardboard, natural finish, 1/8" thick		500	.032		.33	.93		1.26	1.82	
0700	1/4" thick		500	.032		.32	.93		1.25	1.81	
0900	Untempered pegboard, 1/8" thick		500	.032		.33	.93		1.26	1.82	
1000	1/4" thick		500	.032		.37	.93		1.30	1.87	
1200	Plastic faced hardboard, 1/8" thick		500	.032		.54	.93		1.47	2.05	
1300	1/4" thick		500	.032		.72	.93		1.65	2.25	
1500	Plastic faced pegboard, 1/8" thick		500	.032		.51	.93		1.44	2.02	
1600	1/4" thick		500	.032		.63	.93		1.56	2.15	
1800	Wood grained, plain or grooved, 1/4" thick, minimum		500	.032		.48	.93		1.41	1.99	
1900	Maximum		425	.038		1.01	1.10		2.11	2.83	
2100	Moldings for hardboard, wood or aluminum, minimum		500	.032	L.F.	.33	.93		1.26	1.82	
2200	Maximum		425	.038	"	.91	1.10		2.01	2.72	
500 0010	**PANELING, PLYWOOD**										500
2400	Plywood, prefinished, 1/4" thick, 4' x 8' sheets										
2410	with vertical grooves. Birch faced, minimum	2 Carp	500	.032	S.F.	.74	.93		1.67	2.27	
2420	Average		420	.038		1.12	1.11		2.23	2.97	
2430	Maximum		350	.046		1.64	1.33		2.97	3.88	
2600	Mahogany, African		400	.040		2.10	1.17		3.27	4.13	
2700	Philippine (Lauan)		500	.032		.90	.93		1.83	2.45	
2900	Oak or Cherry, minimum		500	.032		1.76	.93		2.69	3.40	

Note at 2400: R06160 -020

Important: See the Reference Section for critical supporting data - Reference Nos., Crews, & City Cost Indexes

06250 | Prefinished Paneling

			CREW	DAILY OUTPUT	LABOR-HOURS	UNIT	2001 BARE COSTS				TOTAL INCL O&P	
							MAT.	LABOR	EQUIP.	TOTAL		
500	3000	Maximum	2 Carp	400	.040	S.F.	2.70	1.17		3.87	4.79	**500**
	3200	Rosewood R06160 -020		320	.050		3.83	1.46		5.29	6.50	
	3400	Teak		400	.040		2.70	1.17		3.87	4.79	
	3600	Chestnut		375	.043		3.99	1.24		5.23	6.35	
	3800	Pecan		400	.040		1.72	1.17		2.89	3.71	
	3900	Walnut, minimum		500	.032		2.30	.93		3.23	3.99	
	3950	Maximum		400	.040		4.36	1.17		5.53	6.60	
	4000	Plywood, prefinished, 3/4" thick, stock grades, minimum		320	.050		1.05	1.46		2.51	3.44	
	4100	Maximum		224	.071		4.50	2.08		6.58	8.20	
	4300	Architectural grade, minimum		224	.071		3.32	2.08		5.40	6.90	
	4400	Maximum		160	.100		5.05	2.92		7.97	10.15	
	4600	Plywood, "A" face, birch, V.C., 1/2" thick, natural		450	.036		1.57	1.04		2.61	3.35	
	4700	Select		450	.036		1.72	1.04		2.76	3.51	
	4900	Veneer core, 3/4" thick, natural		320	.050		1.66	1.46		3.12	4.11	
	5000	Select		320	.050		1.87	1.46		3.33	4.34	
	5200	Lumber core, 3/4" thick, natural		320	.050		2.49	1.46		3.95	5	
	5500	Plywood, knotty pine, 1/4" thick, A2 grade		450	.036		1.36	1.04		2.40	3.12	
	5600	A3 grade		450	.036		1.72	1.04		2.76	3.51	
	5800	3/4" thick, veneer core, A2 grade		320	.050		1.77	1.46		3.23	4.23	
	5900	A3 grade		320	.050		1.98	1.46		3.44	4.46	
	6100	Aromatic cedar, 1/4" thick, plywood		400	.040		1.74	1.17		2.91	3.73	
	6200	1/4" thick, particle board		400	.040		.85	1.17		2.02	2.76	

06260 | Board Paneling

			CREW	DAILY OUTPUT	LABOR-HOURS	UNIT	MAT.	LABOR	EQUIP.	TOTAL	TOTAL INCL O&P	
400	0010	**PANELING, BOARDS**										**400**
	6400	Wood board paneling, 3/4" thick, knotty pine	2 Carp	300	.053	S.F.	1.26	1.55		2.81	3.82	
	6500	Rough sawn cedar		300	.053		1.61	1.55		3.16	4.20	
	6700	Redwood, clear, 1" x 4" boards		300	.053		3.76	1.55		5.31	6.55	
	6900	Aromatic cedar, closet lining, boards		275	.058		2.90	1.70		4.60	5.85	

06270 | Closet/Utility Wood Shelving

			CREW	DAILY OUTPUT	LABOR-HOURS	UNIT	MAT.	LABOR	EQUIP.	TOTAL	TOTAL INCL O&P	
200	0010	**SHELVING** Pine, clear grade, no edge band, 1" x 8"	1 Carp	115	.070	L.F.	1.71	2.03		3.74	5.05	**200**
	0100	1" x 10"		110	.073		2.31	2.12		4.43	5.85	
	0200	1" x 12"		105	.076		4.18	2.22		6.40	8.05	
	0400	For lumber edge band, by hand, add					1.46			1.46	1.61	
	0420	By machine, add					.94			.94	1.03	
	0600	Plywood, 3/4" thick with lumber edge, 12" wide	1 Carp	75	.107		1.24	3.11		4.35	6.20	
	0700	24" wide		70	.114		2.35	3.33		5.68	7.80	
	0900	Bookcase, clear grade pine, shelves 12" O.C., 8" deep, /SF shelf		70	.114	S.F.	3.35	3.33		6.68	8.90	
	1000	12" deep shelves		65	.123	"	4.19	3.59		7.78	10.20	
	1200	Adjustable closet rod and shelf, 12" wide, 3' long		20	.400	Ea.	40.50	11.65		52.15	63	
	1300	8' long		15	.533	"	57	15.55		72.55	87	
	1500	Prefinished shelves with supports, stock, 8" wide		75	.107	L.F.	3.65	3.11		6.76	8.90	
	1600	10" wide		70	.114	"	4.07	3.33		7.40	9.70	
	1800	Custom, high quality dadoed pine shelving units, minimum				S.F.					28	
	1900	Maximum				"					40	

06410 | Custom Cabinets

		CREW	DAILY OUTPUT	LABOR-HOURS	UNIT	MAT.	LABOR	EQUIP.	TOTAL	TOTAL INCL O&P
100										**100**
0010	**CABINETS** Corner china cabinets, stock pine,									
0020	80" high, unfinished, minimum	2 Carp	6.60	2.424	Ea.	430	70.50		500.50	580
0100	Maximum	"	4.40	3.636	"	950	106		1,056	1,225
0300	Built-in drawer units, pine, 18" deep, 32" high, unfinished									
0400	Minimum	2 Carp	53	.302	L.F.	109	8.80		117.80	134
0500	Maximum	"	40	.400	"	138	11.65		149.65	170
0700	Kitchen base cabinets, hardwood, not incl. counter tops,									
0710	24" deep, 35" high, prefinished									
0800	One top drawer, one door below, 12" wide	2 Carp	24.80	.645	Ea.	126	18.80		144.80	168
0840	18" wide		23.30	.687		186	20		206	236
0880	24" wide		22.30	.717		220	21		241	275
1000	Four drawers, 12" wide		24.80	.645		300	18.80		318.80	360
1040	18" wide		23.30	.687		325	20		345	385
1060	24" wide		22.30	.717		350	21		371	420
1200	Two top drawers, two doors below, 27" wide		22	.727		262	21		283	320
1260	36" wide		20.30	.788		300	23		323	365
1300	48" wide		18.90	.847		335	24.50		359.50	410
1500	Range or sink base, two doors below, 30" wide		21.40	.748		219	22		241	275
1540	36" wide		20.30	.788		246	23		269	305
1580	48" wide	↓	18.90	.847		277	24.50		301.50	345
1800	For sink front units, deduct					53			53	58.50
2000	Corner base cabinets, 36" wide, standard	2 Carp	18	.889		192	26		218	252
2100	Lazy Susan with revolving door	"	16.50	.970	↓	315	28.50		343.50	390
4000	Kitchen wall cabinets, hardwood, 12" deep with two doors									
4050	12" high, 30" wide	2 Carp	24.80	.645	Ea.	121	18.80		139.80	163
4100	36" wide		24	.667		142	19.45		161.45	187
4400	15" high, 30" wide		24	.667		142	19.45		161.45	187
4440	36" wide		22.70	.705		155	20.50		175.50	202
4700	24" high, 30" wide		23.30	.687		163	20		183	212
4720	36" wide		22.70	.705		180	20.50		200.50	230
5000	30" high, one door, 12" wide		22	.727		106	21		127	149
5040	18" wide		20.90	.766		137	22.50		159.50	186
5060	24" wide		20.30	.788		150	23		173	201
5300	Two doors, 27" wide		19.80	.808		169	23.50		192.50	223
5340	36" wide		18.80	.851		208	25		233	268
5380	48" wide		18.40	.870		257	25.50		282.50	320
6000	Corner wall, 30" high, 24" wide		18	.889		131	26		157	185
6050	30" wide		17.20	.930		163	27		190	222
6100	36" wide		16.50	.970		176	28.50		204.50	238
6500	Revolving Lazy Susan		15.20	1.053		248	30.50		278.50	320
7000	Broom cabinet, 84" high, 24" deep, 18" wide		10	1.600		350	46.50		396.50	460
7500	Oven cabinets, 84" high, 24" deep, 27" wide		8	2	↓	530	58.50		588.50	675
7750	Valance board trim	↓	396	.040	L.F.	7.60	1.18		8.78	10.20
9000	For deluxe models of all cabinets, add					40%				
9500	For custom built in place, add					25%	10%			
9550	Rule of thumb, kitchen cabinets not including									
9560	appliances & counter top, minimum	2 Carp	30	.533	L.F.	80.50	15.55		96.05	113
9600	Maximum	"	25	.640	"	225	18.65		243.65	277
9610	For metal cabinets, see division 12310-750									
210										**210**
0010	**CASEWORK, FRAMES**									
0050	Base cabinets, counter storage, 36" high, one bay									
0100	18" wide	1 Carp	2.70	2.963	Ea.	91	86.50		177.50	235
0400	Two bay, 36" wide		2.20	3.636		139	106		245	320
1100	Three bay, 54" wide		1.50	5.333		165	155		320	425
2800	Book cases, one bay, 7' high, 18" wide	↓	2.40	3.333	↓	107	97		204	270

Important: See the Reference Section for critical supporting data - Reference Nos., Crews, & City Cost Indexes

		06410	Custom Cabinets	CREW	DAILY OUTPUT	LABOR-HOURS	UNIT	\multicolumn{4}{c}{2001 BARE COSTS}	TOTAL INCL O&P	
								MAT.	LABOR	EQUIP.	TOTAL		
210	3500		Two bay, 36" wide	1 Carp	1.60	5	Ea.	155	146		301	400	210
	4100		Three bay, 54" wide		1.20	6.667		257	194		451	590	
	5100		Coat racks, one bay, 7' high, 24" wide		4.50	1.778		107	52		159	199	
	5300		Two bay, 48" wide		2.75	2.909		149	85		234	297	
	5800		Three bay, 72" wide		2.10	3.810		219	111		330	415	
	6100		Wall mounted cabinet, one bay, 24" high, 18" wide		3.60	2.222		59	65		124	166	
	6800		Two bay, 36" wide		2.20	3.636		86	106		192	261	
	7400		Three bay, 54" wide		1.70	4.706		107	137		244	335	
	8400		30" high, one bay, 18" wide		3.60	2.222		64	65		129	172	
	9000		Two bay, 36" wide		2.15	3.721		85	108		193	264	
	9400		Three bay, 54" wide		1.60	5		106	146		252	345	
	9800		Wardrobe, 7' high, single, 24" wide		2.70	2.963		118	86.50		204.50	265	
	9880		Partition & adjustable shelves, 48" wide		1.70	4.706		150	137		287	380	
	9950		Partition, adjustable shelves & drawers, 48" wide		1.40	5.714		225	167		392	510	
220	0010	**CABINET DOORS**											220
	2000		Glass panel, hardwood frame										
	2200		12" wide, 18" high	1 Carp	34	.235	Ea.	15.50	6.85		22.35	28	
	2600		30" high		32	.250		25.50	7.30		32.80	39.50	
	4450		18" wide, 18" high		32	.250		16	7.30		23.30	29	
	4550		30" high		29	.276		25.50	8.05		33.55	40.50	
	5000		Hardwood, raised panel										
	5100		12" wide, 18" high	1 Carp	16	.500	Ea.	21.50	14.60		36.10	46.50	
	5200		30" high		15	.533		34	15.55		49.55	62	
	5500		18" wide, 18" high		15	.533		31	15.55		46.55	58.50	
	5600		30" high		14	.571		52.50	16.65		69.15	83.50	
	6000		Plastic laminate on particle board										
	6100		12" wide, 18" high	1 Carp	25	.320	Ea.	13.60	9.35		22.95	29.50	
	6140		30" high		23	.348		22	10.15		32.15	40	
	6500		18" wide, 18" high		24	.333		19.85	9.70		29.55	37	
	6600		30" high		22	.364		33.50	10.60		44.10	53.50	
	7000		Plywood, with edge band										
	7010		12" wide, 18" high	1 Carp	27	.296	Ea.	18.30	8.65		26.95	33.50	
	7120		30" high		25	.320		31.50	9.35		40.85	49	
	7650		18" wide, 18" high		26	.308		26.50	8.95		35.45	43.50	
	7750		30" high		24	.333		46	9.70		55.70	65.50	
230	0010	**CABINET HARDWARE**											230
	1000		Catches, minimum	1 Carp	235	.034	Ea.	.72	.99		1.71	2.34	
	1040		Maximum	"	80	.100	"	4.19	2.92		7.11	9.15	
	2000		Door/drawer pulls, handles										
	2200		Handles and pulls, projecting, metal, minimum	1 Carp	160	.050	Ea.	1.54	1.46		3	3.97	
	2240		Maximum		68	.118		7.35	3.43		10.78	13.45	
	2300		Wood, minimum		160	.050		1.54	1.46		3	3.97	
	2340		Maximum		68	.118		4.20	3.43		7.63	9.95	
	2600		Flush, metal, minimum		160	.050		1.47	1.46		2.93	3.90	
	2640		Maximum		68	.118		10.50	3.43		13.93	16.90	
	3000		Drawer tracks/glides, minimum		48	.167	Pr.	5.75	4.86		10.61	13.95	
	3040		Maximum		24	.333		16.80	9.70		26.50	33.50	
	4000		Cabinet hinges, minimum		160	.050		1.43	1.46		2.89	3.85	
	4040		Maximum		68	.118		6.30	3.43		9.73	12.30	
240	0010	**DRAWERS**											240
	0100		Solid hardwood front										
	1000		4" high, 12" wide	1 Carp	17	.471	Ea.	19.10	13.70		32.80	42.50	
	1200		18" wide	"	16	.500	"	25	14.60		39.60	50.50	
	2800		Plastic laminate on particle board front										
	3000		4" high, 12" wide	1 Carp	17	.471	Ea.	19.95	13.70		33.65	43.50	

WOOD & PLASTICS 6

		06410	Custom Cabinets	CREW	DAILY OUTPUT	LABOR-HOURS	UNIT	2001 BARE COSTS				TOTAL INCL O&P	
								MAT.	LABOR	EQUIP.	TOTAL		
240	3200		18" wide	1 Carp	16	.500	Ea.	23	14.60		37.60	48.50	**240**
	5400		Plywood, flush panel front										
	6000		4" high, 12" wide	1 Carp	17	.471	Ea.	20.50	13.70		34.20	44	
	6200		18" wide	"	16	.500	"	25	14.60		39.60	50.50	
400	0010	**VANITIES**											**400**
	8000		Vanity bases, 2 doors, 30" high, 21" deep, 24" wide	2 Carp	20	.800	Ea.	124	23.50		147.50	173	
	8050		30" wide		16	1		130	29		159	189	
	8100		36" wide		13.33	1.200		146	35		181	215	
	8150		48" wide	↓	11.43	1.400		184	41		225	266	
	9000	For deluxe models of all vanities, add to above						40%					
	9500	For custom built in place, add to above					↓	25%	10%				
500	0010	**RAILING** Custom design, architectural grade, hardwood, minimum	1 Carp	38	.211	L.F.	12	6.15		18.15	23	**500**
	0100	Maximum		30	.267		46	7.75		53.75	63	
	0300	Stock interior railing with spindles 6" O.C., 4' long		40	.200		29	5.85		34.85	40.50	
	0400	8' long	↓	48	.167	↓	27	4.86		31.86	37	
505	0010	**DECK, WOOD, PRESSURE TREATED LUMBER**											**505**
	0100	Railings and trim , 1" x 4"	1 Carp	300	.027	L.F.	.62	.78		1.40	1.90	
	0200	2" x 4"		300	.027		.64	.78		1.42	1.92	
	0300	2" x 6"		300	.027	↓	.85	.78		1.63	2.16	
	0400	Decking, 1" x 4"		275	.029	S.F.	1.56	.85		2.41	3.05	
	0500	2" x 4"		300	.027		1.62	.78		2.40	3	
	0600	2" x 6"		320	.025		1.61	.73		2.34	2.91	
	0650	5/4" x 6"		320	.025		1.68	.73		2.41	2.99	
	0700	Redwood decking, 1" x 4"		275	.029		4	.85		4.85	5.75	
	0800	2" x 6"		340	.024		11.40	.69		12.09	13.60	
	0900	5/4" x 6"	↓	320	.025	↓	7.15	.73		7.88	9	
620	0011	**STAIRS, PREFABRICATED**											**620**
	0100	Box stairs, prefabricated, 3'-0" wide											
	0110	Oak treads, no handrails, 2' high	2 Carp	5	3.200	Flight	216	93.50		309.50	385	
	0200	4' high		4	4		430	117		547	655	
	0300	6' high		3.50	4.571		620	133		753	890	
	0400	8' high		3	5.333		775	155		930	1,100	
	0600	With pine treads for carpet, 2' high		5	3.200		88.50	93.50		182	243	
	0700	4' high		4	4		164	117		281	360	
	0800	6' high		3.50	4.571		240	133		373	470	
	0900	8' high	↓	3	5.333		274	155		429	545	
	1100	For 4' wide stairs, add				↓	25%					
	1500	Prefabricated stair rail with balusters, 5 risers	2 Carp	15	1.067	Ea.	229	31		260	300	
	1700	Basement stairs, prefabricated, soft wood,										
	1710	open risers, 3' wide, 8' high	2 Carp	4	4	Flight	575	117		692	810	
	1900	Open stairs, prefabricated prefinished poplar, metal stringers,										
	1910	treads 3'-6" wide, no railings										
	2000	3' high	2 Carp	5	3.200	Flight	229	93.50		322.50	400	
	2100	4' high		4	4		485	117		602	715	
	2200	6' high		3.50	4.571		555	133		688	825	
	2300	8' high	↓	3	5.333	↓	730	155		885	1,050	
	2500	For prefab. 3 piece wood railings & balusters, add for										
	2600	3' high stairs	2 Carp	15	1.067	Ea.	31.50	31		62.50	83	
	2700	4' high stairs		14	1.143		51	33.50		84.50	109	
	2800	6' high stairs		13	1.231		63	36		99	126	
	2900	8' high stairs		12	1.333		96.50	39		135.50	167	
	3100	For 3'-6" x 3'-6" platform, add	↓	4	4	↓	72.50	117		189.50	262	

Heading block: **06430 | Stairs & Railings** appears above the 500 section.

Side margin: **6 WOOD & PLASTICS**

Important: See the Reference Section for critical supporting data - Reference Nos., Crews, & City Cost Indexes

		06430	Stairs & Railings	CREW	DAILY OUTPUT	LABOR-HOURS	UNIT	2001 BARE COSTS				TOTAL INCL O&P	
								MAT.	LABOR	EQUIP.	TOTAL		
620	3300		Curved stairways, 3'-3" wide, prefabricated, oak, unfinished,										620
	3310		incl. curved balustrade system, open one side										
	3400		9' high	2 Carp	.70	22.857	Flight	6,375	665		7,040	8,075	
	3500		10' high		.70	22.857		7,200	665		7,865	8,975	
	3700		Open two sides, 9' high		.50	32		10,000	935		10,935	12,500	
	3800		10' high		.50	32		10,800	935		11,735	13,400	
	4000		Residential, wood, oak treads, prefabricated		1.50	10.667		930	310		1,240	1,500	
	4200		Built in place		.44	36.364		1,325	1,050		2,375	3,100	
	4400		Spiral, oak, 4'-6" diameter, unfinished, prefabricated,										
	4500		incl. railing, 9' high	2 Carp	1.50	10.667	Flight	4,000	310		4,310	4,875	
630	0010		STAIR PARTS Balusters, turned, 30" high, pine, minimum R06430 -100	1 Carp	28	.286	Ea.	4.11	8.35		12.46	17.55	630
	0100		Maximum		26	.308		9	8.95		17.95	24	
	0300		30" high birch balusters, minimum		28	.286		6.30	8.35		14.65	20	
	0400		Maximum		26	.308		10.20	8.95		19.15	25.50	
	0600		42" high, pine balusters, minimum		27	.296		6	8.65		14.65	20	
	0700		Maximum		25	.320		13	9.35		22.35	29	
	0900		42" high birch balusters, minimum		27	.296		7.65	8.65		16.30	22	
	1000		Maximum		25	.320		27	9.35		36.35	44	
	1050		Baluster, stock pine, 1-1/16" x 1-1/16"		240	.033	L.F.	1.98	.97		2.95	3.70	
	1100		1-5/8" x 1-5/8"		220	.036	"	2.19	1.06		3.25	4.07	
	1200		Newels, 3-1/4" wide, starting, minimum		7	1.143	Ea.	33.50	33.50		67	89	
	1300		Maximum		6	1.333		126	39		165	200	
	1500		Landing, minimum		5	1.600		73.50	46.50		120	154	
	1600		Maximum		4	2		179	58.50		237.50	287	
	1800		Railings, oak, built-up, minimum		60	.133	L.F.	5.55	3.89		9.44	12.25	
	1900		Maximum		55	.145		15.75	4.24		19.99	24	
	2100		Add for sub rail		110	.073		4.21	2.12		6.33	7.95	
	2300		Risers, beech, 3/4" x 7-1/2" high		64	.125		5.80	3.64		9.44	12.05	
	2400		Fir, 3/4" x 7-1/2" high		64	.125		1.59	3.64		5.23	7.45	
	2600		Oak, 3/4" x 7-1/2" high		64	.125		5	3.64		8.64	11.20	
	2800		Pine, 3/4" x 7-1/2" high		66	.121		1.58	3.53		5.11	7.30	
	2850		Skirt board, pine, 1" x 10"		55	.145		1.74	4.24		5.98	8.55	
	2900		1" x 12"		52	.154		2.11	4.48		6.59	9.30	
	3000		Treads, 1-1/16" x 9-1/2" wide, 3' long, oak		18	.444	Ea.	23	12.95		35.95	46	
	3100		4' long, oak		17	.471		29	13.70		42.70	53.50	
	3300		1-1/16" x 11-1/2" wide, 3' long, oak		18	.444		23.50	12.95		36.45	46.50	
	3400		6' long, oak		14	.571		56	16.65		72.65	87.50	
	3600		Beech treads, add					40%					
	3800		For mitered return nosings, add				L.F.	8.40			8.40	9.25	

				CREW	DAILY OUTPUT	LABOR-HOURS	UNIT	MAT.	LABOR	EQUIP.	TOTAL	TOTAL INCL O&P	
150	0010		BEAMS, DECORATIVE Rough sawn cedar, non-load bearing, 4" x 4"	2 Carp	180	.089	L.F.	1.30	2.59		3.89	5.50	150
	0100		4" x 6"		170	.094		2.50	2.74		5.24	7.05	
	0200		4" x 8"		160	.100		3.21	2.92		6.13	8.10	
	0300		4" x 10"		150	.107		4.46	3.11		7.57	9.75	
	0400		4" x 12"		140	.114		5.40	3.33		8.73	11.15	
	0500		8" x 8"		130	.123		7.55	3.59		11.14	13.90	
	1100		Beam connector plates see div. 06090-800										
350	0010		GRILLES and panels, hardwood, sanded										350
	0020		2' x 4' to 4' x 8', custom designs, unfinished, minimum	1 Carp	38	.211	S.F.	12	6.15		18.15	23	
	0050		Average		30	.267		26	7.75		33.75	40.50	
	0100		Maximum		19	.421		40	12.25		52.25	63	
	0300		As above, but prefinished, minimum		38	.211		12	6.15		18.15	23	
	0400		Maximum		19	.421		45	12.25		57.25	68.50	

WOOD & PLASTICS 6

For expanded coverage of these items see *Means Interior Cost Data 2001*

	06440	Wood Ornaments	CREW	DAILY OUTPUT	LABOR-HOURS	UNIT	2001 BARE COSTS MAT.	LABOR	EQUIP.	TOTAL	TOTAL INCL O&P	
400	0010	**LOUVERS** Redwood, 2'-0" diameter, full circle	1 Carp	16	.500	Ea.	105	14.60		119.60	139	**400**
	0100	Half circle		16	.500		104	14.60		118.60	137	
	0200	Octagonal		16	.500		86	14.60		100.60	118	
	0300	Triangular, 5/12 pitch, 5'-0" at base		16	.500		180	14.60		194.60	221	
500	0010	**FIREPLACE MANTELS** 6" molding, 6' x 3'-6" opening, minimum	1 Carp	5	1.600	Opng.	130	46.50		176.50	215	**500**
	0100	Maximum		5	1.600		157	46.50		203.50	246	
	0300	Prefabricated pine, colonial type, stock, deluxe		2	4		760	117		877	1,025	
	0400	Economy		3	2.667		256	77.50		333.50	405	
550	0010	**FIREPLACE MANTEL BEAMS** Rough texture wood, 4" x 8"	1 Carp	36	.222	L.F.	4.24	6.50		10.74	14.80	**550**
	0100	4" x 10"		35	.229	"	5.30	6.65		11.95	16.25	
	0300	Laminated hardwood, 2-1/4" x 10-1/2" wide, 6' long		5	1.600	Ea.	95.50	46.50		142	178	
	0400	8' long		5	1.600	"	133	46.50		179.50	219	
	0600	Brackets for above, rough sawn		12	.667	Pr.	8.75	19.45		28.20	40	
	0700	Laminated		12	.667	"	13.25	19.45		32.70	45	
700	0010	**COLUMNS** For base plates, see division 05560-200										**700**
	0050	Aluminum, round colonial, 6" diameter	2 Carp	80	.200	V.L.F.	16	5.85		21.85	26.50	
	0100	8" diameter		62.25	.257		19	7.50		26.50	32.50	
	0200	10" diameter		55	.291		23.50	8.50		32	39.50	
	0250	Fir, stock units, hollow round, 6" diameter		80	.200		13	5.85		18.85	23.50	
	0300	8" diameter		80	.200		15	5.85		20.85	25.50	
	0350	10" diameter		70	.229		19	6.65		25.65	31.50	
	0400	Solid turned, to 8' high, 3-1/2" diameter		80	.200		7	5.85		12.85	16.80	
	0500	4-1/2" diameter		75	.213		10	6.20		16.20	21	
	0600	5-1/2" diameter		70	.229		14	6.65		20.65	26	
	0800	Square columns, built-up, 5" x 5"		65	.246		13	7.20		20.20	25.50	
	0900	Solid, 3-1/2" x 3-1/2"		130	.123		6	3.59		9.59	12.20	
	1600	Hemlock, tapered, T & G, 12" diam, 10' high		100	.160		30	4.66		34.66	40.50	
	1700	16' high		65	.246		53	7.20		60.20	69.50	
	1900	10' high, 14" diameter		100	.160		77	4.66		81.66	92	
	2000	18' high		65	.246		73	7.20		80.20	91.50	
	2200	18" diameter, 12' high		65	.246		103	7.20		110.20	124	
	2300	20' high		50	.320		99	9.35		108.35	124	
	2500	20" diameter, 14' high		40	.400		122	11.65		133.65	152	
	2600	20' high		35	.457		126	13.35		139.35	160	
	2800	For flat pilasters, deduct					33%					
	3000	For splitting into halves, add				Ea.	60			60	66	
	4000	Rough sawn cedar posts, 4" x 4"	2 Carp	250	.064	V.L.F.	2.43	1.87		4.30	5.60	
	4100	4" x 6"		235	.068		3.62	1.98		5.60	7.10	
	4200	6" x 6"		220	.073		5.45	2.12		7.57	9.30	
	4300	8" x 8"		200	.080		5.60	2.33		7.93	9.80	

	06445	Simulated Wood Ornaments										
100	0010	**MILLWORK, HIGH DENSITY POLYMER**										**100**
	0100	Base, 9/16" x 3-3/16"	1 Carp	230	.035	L.F.	1.28	1.01		2.29	3	
	0200	Casing, fluted, 5/8" x 3-1/4"		215	.037		3.59	1.08		4.67	5.65	
	0300	Chair rail, 9/16" x 2-1/4"		260	.031		1.87	.90		2.77	3.46	
	0600	Cove, 13/16" x 3-3/4"		260	.031		3.75	.90		4.65	5.55	
	0700	Crown, 3/4" x 3-13/16"		260	.031		5.30	.90		6.20	7.25	
	0800	Half round, 15/16" x 2"		240	.033		14.75	.97		15.72	17.70	

	06470	Screen, Blinds & Shutters										
100	0010	**SHUTTERS, EXTERIOR** Aluminum, louvered, 1'-4" wide, 3'-0" long	1 Carp	10	.800	Pr.	39.50	23.50		63	80	**100**
	0400	6'-8" long		9	.889		79.50	26		105.50	128	
	1000	Pine, louvered, primed, each 1'-2" wide, 3'-3" long		10	.800		75	23.50		98.50	119	
	1001	Pine, louvered, primed, each 1'-2" wide, 3'-3" long		20	.400	Ea.	35.50	11.65		47.15	57.50	

6 WOOD & PLASTICS

06400 | Architectural Woodwork

06470 | Screen, Blinds & Shutters

			CREW	DAILY OUTPUT	LABOR-HOURS	UNIT	2001 BARE COSTS				TOTAL INCL O&P
							MAT.	LABOR	EQUIP.	TOTAL	
100	1100	4'-7" long	1 Carp	10	.800	Pr.	101	23.50		124.50	148
	1101	4'-7" long		20	.400	Ea.	97.50	11.65		109.15	125
	1500	Each 1'-6" wide, 3'-3" long		10	.800	Pr.	79.50	23.50		103	124
	1600	4'-7" long		10	.800	"	112	23.50		135.50	160
	1601	4'-7" long		20	.400	Ea.	106	11.65		117.65	134
	1620	Hemlock, louvered, 1'-2" wide, 5'-7" long		10	.800	Pr.	123	23.50		146.50	172
	1630	Each 1'-4" wide, 2'-2" long		10	.800		76.50	23.50		100	121
	1670	4'-3" long		10	.800		91.50	23.50		115	138
	1690	5'-11" long		10	.800		129	23.50		152.50	179
	1700	Door blinds, 6'-9" long, each 1'-3" wide		9	.889		130	26		156	184
	1710	1'-6" wide		9	.889		140	26		166	194
	1720	Hemlock, solid raised panel, each 1'-4" wide, 3'-3" long		10	.800		124	23.50		147.50	173
	1740	4'-3" long		10	.800		157	23.50		180.50	209
	1770	5'-11" long		10	.800		209	23.50		232.50	267
	1800	Door blinds, 6'-9" long, each 1'-3" wide		9	.889		236	26		262	300
	1900	1'-6" wide		9	.889		257	26		283	325
	2500	Polystyrene, solid raised panel, each 1'-4" wide, 3'-3" long		10	.800		52	23.50		75.50	93.50
	2700	4'-7" long		10	.800		62.50	23.50		86	106
	4500	Polystyrene, louvered, each 1'-2" wide, 3'-3" long		10	.800		40	23.50		63.50	80.50
	4750	5'-3" long		10	.800		53	23.50		76.50	95
	6000	Vinyl, louvered, each 1'-2" x 4'-7" long		10	.800		52	23.50		75.50	93.50
	6200	Each 1'-4" x 6'-8" long		9	.889		79	26		105	128

06500 | Structural Plastics

06510 | Struct Plastic Shapes & Plates

			CREW	DAILY OUTPUT	LABOR-HOURS	UNIT	2001 BARE COSTS				TOTAL INCL O&P
							MAT.	LABOR	EQUIP.	TOTAL	
400	0010	**CASTINGS, FIBERGLASS**									
	0100	Angle, 1" x 1" x 1/8" thick	2 Sswk	240	.067	L.F.	1.04	2.19		3.23	5.10
	0120	3" x 3" x 1/4" thick		200	.080		4.32	2.63		6.95	9.50
	0140	4" x 4" x 1/4" thick		200	.080		5.55	2.63		8.18	10.85
	0160	4" x 4" x 3/8" thick		200	.080		8.65	2.63		11.28	14.25
	0180	6" x 6" x 1/2" thick		160	.100		16.90	3.29		20.19	24.50
	1000	Flat sheet, 1/8" thick		140	.114	S.F.	4.40	3.75		8.15	11.65
	1020	1/4" thick		120	.133		8.45	4.38		12.83	17.25
	1040	3/8" thick		100	.160		14.60	5.25		19.85	25.50
	1060	1/2" thick		80	.200		18.75	6.55		25.30	32.50
	2000	Handrail, 42" high, 2" diam. rails pickets 5' O.C.		32	.500	L.F.	43	16.45		59.45	77.50
	3000	Round bar, 1/4" diam.		240	.067		.48	2.19		2.67	4.50
	3020	1/2" diam.		200	.080		1.14	2.63		3.77	6
	3040	3/4" diam.		200	.080		1.65	2.63		4.28	6.60
	3060	1" diam.		160	.100		2.93	3.29		6.22	9.15
	3080	1-1/4" diam.		160	.100		3.47	3.29		6.76	9.75
	3100	1-1/2" diam.		140	.114		4.25	3.75		8	11.50
	3500	Round tube, 1" diam. x 1/8" thick		240	.067		1.88	2.19		4.07	6.05
	3520	2" diam. x 1/4" thick		200	.080		4.61	2.63		7.24	9.80
	3540	3" diam. x 1/4" thick		160	.100		8.95	3.29		12.24	15.75
	4000	Square bar, 1/2" square		240	.067		3.68	2.19		5.87	8
	4020	1" square		200	.080		3.85	2.63		6.48	9
	4040	1-1/2" square		160	.100		7.10	3.29		10.39	13.75
	4500	Square tube, 1" x 1" x 1/8" thick		240	.067		1.67	2.19		3.86	5.80

For expanded coverage of these items see *Means Interior Cost Data 2001*

201

06500 | Structural Plastics

06510 | Struct Plastic Shapes & Plates

		CREW	DAILY OUTPUT	LABOR-HOURS	UNIT	2001 BARE COSTS MAT.	LABOR	EQUIP.	TOTAL	TOTAL INCL O&P	
400	4520	2" x 2" x 1/8" thick	2 Sswk	200	.080	L.F.	3.14	2.63		5.77	8.20	**400**
	4540	3" x 3" x 1/4" thick		160	.100		8.60	3.29		11.89	15.40	
	5000	Threaded rod, 3/8" diam.		320	.050		2.90	1.64		4.54	6.15	
	5020	1/2" diam.		320	.050		3.42	1.64		5.06	6.75	
	5040	5/8" diam.		280	.057		3.78	1.88		5.66	7.55	
	5060	3/4" diam.		280	.057		4.30	1.88		6.18	8.15	
	6000	Wide flange beam, 4" x 4" x 1/4" thick		120	.133		7.75	4.38		12.13	16.50	
	6020	6" x 6" x 1/4" thick		100	.160		14.05	5.25		19.30	25	
	6040	8" x 8" x 3/8" thick	↓	80	.200	↓	27	6.55		33.55	41.50	

06520 | Plastic Struct Assemblies

		CREW	DAILY OUTPUT	LABOR-HOURS	UNIT	2001 BARE COSTS MAT.	LABOR	EQUIP.	TOTAL	TOTAL INCL O&P	
100	0010	**STAIR TREAD, FIBERGLASS** Isophthalic Resin, 10-1/2" deep										**100**
	0100	24" wide	2 Sswk	52	.308	Ea.	33.50	10.10		43.60	55	
	0140	30" wide		52	.308		39.50	10.10		49.60	62	
	0180	36" wide		52	.308		46.50	10.10		56.60	69.50	
	0220	42" wide	↓	52	.308	↓	54.50	10.10		64.60	78.50	

06600 | Plastic Fabrications

06610 | Fiberglass

		CREW	DAILY OUTPUT	LABOR-HOURS	UNIT	2001 BARE COSTS MAT.	LABOR	EQUIP.	TOTAL	TOTAL INCL O&P	
300	0010	**GRATING, FIBERGLASS**										**300**
	0100	Molded, green (for mod. corrosive environment)										
	0140	1" x 4" mesh, 1" thick	2 Sswk	400	.040	S.F.	10.50	1.31		11.81	13.95	
	0180	1-1/2" square mesh, 1" thick		400	.040		15.60	1.31		16.91	19.55	
	0220	1-1/4" thick		400	.040		12.30	1.31		13.61	15.90	
	0260	1-1/2" thick		400	.040		22	1.31		23.31	27	
	0300	2" square mesh, 2" thick	↓	320	.050	↓	21	1.64		22.64	26	
	1000	Orange (for highly corrosive environment)										
	1040	1" x 4" mesh, 1" thick	2 Sswk	400	.040	S.F.	13.05	1.31		14.36	16.75	
	1080	1-1/2" square mesh, 1" thick		400	.040		17.45	1.31		18.76	21.50	
	1120	1-1/4" thick		400	.040		17.85	1.31		19.16	22	
	1160	1-1/2" thick		400	.040		19.30	1.31		20.61	23.50	
	1200	2" square mesh, 2" thick	↓	320	.050	↓	23	1.64		24.64	28.50	
	3000	Pultruded, green (for mod. corrosive environment)										
	3040	1" O.C. bar spacing, 1" thick	2 Sswk	400	.040	S.F.	15.60	1.31		16.91	19.55	
	3080	1-1/2" thick		320	.050		17.15	1.64		18.79	22	
	3120	1-1/2" O.C. bar spacing, 1" thick		400	.040		12.45	1.31		13.76	16.10	
	3160	1-1/2" thick	↓	400	.040	↓	14.05	1.31		15.36	17.85	
	4000	Grating support legs, fixed height, no base				Ea.	40.50			40.50	44.50	
	4040	With base					36			36	39.50	
	4080	Adjustable to 60"				↓	54			54	59.50	

06620 | Non-Structural Plastics

		CREW	DAILY OUTPUT	LABOR-HOURS	UNIT	2001 BARE COSTS MAT.	LABOR	EQUIP.	TOTAL	TOTAL INCL O&P	
200	0010	**FLOOR GRATING, FIBERGLASS**										**200**
	0100	Reinforced polyester, fire retardant, 1" x 4" grid, 1" thick	E-4	510	.063	S.F.	14.45	2.09	.17	16.71	19.90	
	0200	1-1/2" x 6" mesh, 1-1/2" thick		500	.064		17.70	2.13	.17	20	23.50	
	0300	With grit surface, 1-1/2" x 64" grid, 1-1/2" thick	↓	500	.064	↓	18.60	2.13	.17	20.90	24.50	

Important: See the Reference Section for critical supporting data - Reference Nos., Crews, & City Cost Indexes

6

WOOD & PLASTICS

06620 | Non-Structural Plastics

		CREW	DAILY OUTPUT	LABOR-HOURS	UNIT	2001 BARE COSTS MAT.	LABOR	EQUIP.	TOTAL	TOTAL INCL O&P	
600	**0010** **NETTING, FLEXIBLE PLASTIC** 1/8" square mesh	4 Clab	4,000	.008	S.F.	.38	.18		.56	.71	**600**
	0100 1/4" square mesh		4,000	.008		.22	.18		.40	.53	
	0120 1/2" square mesh		4,000	.008		.33	.18		.51	.65	
	0140 5/8" x 3/4" mesh		4,000	.008		.28	.18		.46	.60	
	0160 1-1/4" x 1-1/2" mesh		4,000	.008		.16	.18		.34	.47	
	0200 4" square mesh		4,000	.008		.05	.18		.23	.35	
	1000 Poly clips				Ea.	.35			.35	.39	
810	**0010** **SOLID SURFACE COUNTERTOPS,** Acrylic polymer										**810**
	0020 Pricing for orders of 100 L.F. or greater										
	0100 25" wide, solid colors	2 Carp	28	.571	L.F.	43	16.65		59.65	73	
	0200 Patterned colors		28	.571		54.50	16.65		71.15	86	
	0300 Premium patterned colors		28	.571		68	16.65		84.65	101	
	0400 With silicone attached 4" backsplash, solid colors		27	.593		47	17.25		64.25	79	
	0500 Patterned colors		27	.593		59.50	17.25		76.75	92.50	
	0600 Premium patterned colors		27	.593		74	17.25		91.25	109	
	0700 With hard seam attached 4" backsplash, solid colors		23	.696		47	20.50		67.50	83.50	
	0800 Patterned colors		23	.696		59.50	20.50		80	97	
	0900 Premium patterned colors		23	.696		74	20.50		94.50	113	
	1000 Pricing for order of 51 - 99 L.F.										
	1100 25" wide, solid colors	2 Carp	24	.667	L.F.	49.50	19.45		68.95	84.50	
	1200 Patterned colors		24	.667		62.50	19.45		81.95	99.50	
	1300 Premium patterned colors		24	.667		78	19.45		97.45	117	
	1400 With silicone attached 4" backsplash, solid colors		23	.696		54	20.50		74.50	91	
	1500 Patterned colors		23	.696		68.50	20.50		89	107	
	1600 Premium patterned colors		23	.696		85.50	20.50		106	126	
	1700 With hard seam attached 4" backsplash, solid colors		20	.800		54	23.50		77.50	96	
	1800 Patterned colors		20	.800		68.50	23.50		92	112	
	1900 Premium patterned colors		20	.800		85.50	23.50		109	131	
	2000 Pricing for order of 1 - 50 L.F.										
	2100 25" wide, solid colors	2 Carp	20	.800	L.F.	58	23.50		81.50	100	
	2200 Patterned colors		20	.800		73.50	23.50		97	117	
	2300 Premium patterned colors		20	.800		92	23.50		115.50	138	
	2400 With silicone attached 4" backsplash, solid colors		19	.842		63.50	24.50		88	109	
	2500 Patterned colors		19	.842		80.50	24.50		105	127	
	2600 Premium patterned colors		19	.842		100	24.50		124.50	149	
	2700 With hard seam attached 4" backsplash, solid colors		4	4		63.50	117		180.50	252	
	2800 Patterned colors		15	1.067		80.50	31		111.50	137	
	2900 Premium patterned colors		15	1.067		100	31		131	159	
	3000 Sinks, pricing for order of 100 or greater units										
	3100 Single bowl, hard seamed, solid colors, 13" x 17"	1 Carp	3	2.667	Ea.	290	77.50		367.50	440	
	3200 10" x 15"		7	1.143		134	33.50		167.50	199	
	3300 Cutouts for sinks		8	1			29		29	45.50	
	3400 Sinks, pricing for order of 51 - 99 units										
	3500 Single bowl, hard seamed, solid colors, 13" x 17"	1 Carp	2.55	3.137	Ea.	335	91.50		426.50	510	
	3600 10" x 15"		6	1.333		154	39		193	230	
	3700 Cutouts for sinks		7	1.143			33.50		33.50	52	
	3800 Sinks, pricing for order of 1 - 50 units										
	3900 Single bowl, hard seamed, solid colors, 13" x 17"	1 Carp	2	4	Ea.	390	117		507	610	
	4000 10" x 15"		4.55	1.758		181	51.50		232.50	279	
	4100 Cutouts for sinks		5.25	1.524			44.50		44.50	69.50	
	4200 Cooktop cutouts, pricing for 100 or greater units		4	2		21	58.50		79.50	114	
	4300 51 - 99 units		3.40	2.353		24	68.50		92.50	134	
	4400 1 - 50 units		3	2.667		28	77.50		105.50	153	
850	**0010** **VANITY TOPS**										**850**
	0015 Solid surface, center bowl, 17" x 19"	1 Carp	12	.667	Ea.	177	19.45		196.45	225	

For expanded coverage of these items see Means Interior Cost Data 2001

WOOD & PLASTICS 6

06620	Non-Structural Plastics	CREW	DAILY OUTPUT	LABOR-HOURS	UNIT	2001 BARE COSTS				TOTAL INCL O&P	
						MAT.	LABOR	EQUIP.	TOTAL		
850 0020	19" x 25"	1 Carp	12	.667	Ea.	213	19.45		232.45	266	**850**
0030	19" x 31"		12	.667		259	19.45		278.45	315	
0040	19" x 37"		12	.667		300	19.45		319.45	360	
0050	22" x 25"		10	.800		240	23.50		263.50	300	
0060	22" x 31"		10	.800		280	23.50		303.50	345	
0070	22" x 37"		10	.800		325	23.50		348.50	395	
0080	22" x 43"		10	.800		370	23.50		393.50	445	
0090	22" x 49"		10	.800		410	23.50		433.50	490	
0110	22" x 55"		8	1		465	29		494	560	
0120	22" x 61"		8	1		535	29		564	630	
0130	22" x 68"		8	1		685	29		714	800	
0140	22" x 73"		8	1		770	29		799	895	
0150	22" x 85"		8	1		890	29		919	1,025	
0160	Offset bowl, left or right, 22" x 49"		10	.800		490	23.50		513.50	575	
0170	22" x 55"		8	1		560	29		589	660	
0180	22" x 61"		8	1		635	29		664	745	
0190	22" x 68"		8	1		745	29		774	865	
0200	22" x 73"		8	1		920	29		949	1,050	
0210	22" x 85"		8	1		1,075	29		1,104	1,225	
0220	Double bowl, 22" x 61"		8	1		585	29		614	690	
0230	Corner top/bowl, 22" x 49"	▼	8	1	▼	455	29		484	545	
0240	For aggregate colors, add					35%					
0250	For faucets and fittings see 15410-300										

For information about Means Estimating Seminars, see yellow pages 11 and 12 in back of book

Division 7
Thermal & Moisture Protection

Estimating Tips

07100 Dampproofing & Waterproofing

- Be sure of the job specifications before pricing this subdivision. The difference in cost between waterproofing and dampproofing can be great. Waterproofing will hold back standing water. Dampproofing prevents the transmission of water vapor. Also included in this section are vapor retarding membranes.

07200 Thermal Protection

- Insulation and fireproofing products are measured by area, thickness, volume or R value. Specifications may only give what the specific R value should be in a certain situation. The estimator may need to choose the type of insulation to meet that R value.

07300 Shingles, Roof Tiles & Roof Coverings
07400 Roofing & Siding Panels

- Many roofing and siding products are bought and sold by the square. One square is equal to an area that measures 100 square feet.

This simple change in unit of measure could create a large error if the estimator is not observant. Accessories and fasteners necessary for a complete installation must be figured into any calculations for both material and labor.

07500 Membrane Roofing
07600 Flashing & Sheet Metal
07700 Roof Specialties & Accessories

- The items in these subdivisions compose a roofing system. No one component completes the installation and all must be estimated. Built-up or single ply membrane roofing systems are made up of many products and installation trades. Wood blocking at roof perimeters or penetrations, parapet coverings, reglets, roof drains, gutters, downspouts, sheet metal flashing, skylights, smoke vents or roof hatches all need to be considered along with the roofing material. Several different installation trades will need to work together on the roofing system. Inherent difficulties in the scheduling and coordination of various trades must be accounted for when estimating labor costs.

07900 Joint Sealers

- To complete the weather-tight shell the sealants and caulkings must be estimated. Where different materials meet—at expansion joints, at flashing penetrations, and at hundreds of other locations throughout a construction project—they provide another line of defense against water penetration. Often, an entire system is based on the proper location and placement of caulking or sealants. The detail drawings that are included as part of a set of architectural plans, show typical locations for these materials. When caulking or sealants are shown at typical locations, this means the estimator must include them for all the locations where this detail is applicable. Be careful to keep different types of sealants separate, and remember to consider backer rods and primers if necessary.

Reference Numbers

Reference numbers are shown in bold squares at the beginning of some major classifications. These numbers refer to related items in the Reference Section. The reference information may be an estimating procedure, an alternate pricing method or technical information.

Note: Not all subdivisions listed here necessarily appear in this publication.

7 THERMAL & MOISTURE PROTECTION

07110	Dampproofing	CREW	DAILY OUTPUT	LABOR-HOURS	UNIT	MAT.	LABOR	EQUIP.	TOTAL	TOTAL INCL O&P	
						2001 BARE COSTS					
100	0010 **BITUMINOUS ASPHALT COATING** For foundation										100
	0030 Brushed on, below grade, 1 coat	1 Rofc	665	.012	S.F.	.06	.31		.37	.60	
	0100 2 coat		500	.016		.10	.41		.51	.82	
	0300 Sprayed on, below grade, 1 coat, 25.6 S.F./gal.		830	.010		.07	.25		.32	.51	
	0400 2 coat, 20.5 S.F./gal.		500	.016		.14	.41		.55	.87	
	0500 Asphalt coating, with fibers				Gal.	3.68			3.68	4.05	
	0600 Troweled on, asphalt with fibers, 1/16" thick	1 Rofc	500	.016	S.F.	.15	.41		.56	.88	
	0700 1/8" thick		400	.020		.28	.51		.79	1.19	
	1000 1/2" thick		350	.023		.92	.59		1.51	2.02	
200	0010 **CEMENT PARGING** 2 coats, 1/2" thick, regular P.C. [R07110 -010]	D-1	250	.064	S.F.	.15	1.68		1.83	2.77	200
	0100 Waterproofed Portland cement	"	250	.064	"	.18	1.68		1.86	2.80	

07130	Sheet Waterproofing	CREW	DAILY OUTPUT	LABOR-HOURS	UNIT	MAT.	LABOR	EQUIP.	TOTAL	TOTAL INCL O&P	
200	0010 **ELASTOMERIC WATERPROOFING**										200
	0050 Acrylic rubber, fluid applied, 20 mils thick	3 Rofc	1,000	.024	S.F.	1.57	.62		2.19	2.79	
	0060 50 mil, reinforced, stucco texture	"	600	.040		2.53	1.03		3.56	4.55	
	0090 EPDM, plain, 45 mils thick	2 Rofc	580	.028		.76	.71		1.47	2.06	
	0100 60 mils thick		570	.028		1.11	.72		1.83	2.46	
	0300 Nylon reinforced sheets, 45 mils thick		580	.028		1.08	.71		1.79	2.41	
	0400 60 mils thick		570	.028		1.50	.72		2.22	2.89	
	0600 Vulcanizing splicing tape for above, 2" wide				C.L.F.	33.50			33.50	36.50	
	0700 4" wide				"	67			67	73.50	
	0900 Adhesive, bonding, 60 SF per gal				Gal.	13.60			13.60	14.95	
	1000 Splicing, 75 SF per gal				"	21			21	23	
	1200 Neoprene sheets, plain, 45 mils thick	2 Rofc	580	.028	S.F.	1.02	.71		1.73	2.34	
	1300 60 mils thick		570	.028		1.73	.72		2.45	3.14	
	1500 Nylon reinforced, 45 mils thick		580	.028		1.26	.71		1.97	2.61	
	1600 60 mils thick		570	.028		1.28	.72		2	2.65	
	1800 120 mils thick		500	.032		2.54	.82		3.36	4.20	
	1900 Adhesive, splicing, 150 S.F. per gal. per coat				Gal.	18.15			18.15	19.95	
	2100 Fiberglass reinforced, fluid applied, 1/8" thick	2 Rofc	500	.032	S.F.	1.50	.82		2.32	3.06	
	2200 Polyethylene and rubberized asphalt sheets, 1/8" thick		550	.029		.54	.75		1.29	1.87	
	2210 Asphaltic hardboard protection board, 1/8" thick		500	.032		.30	.82		1.12	1.74	
	2220 Asphaltic hardboard protection board, 1/4" thick		450	.036		.52	.91		1.43	2.14	
	2400 Polyvinyl chloride sheets, plain, 10 mils thick		580	.028		.14	.71		.85	1.37	
	2500 20 mils thick		570	.028		.22	.72		.94	1.48	
	2700 30 mils thick		560	.029		.30	.73		1.03	1.59	
	3000 Adhesives, trowel grade, 40-100 SF per gal				Gal.	20			20	22	
	3100 Brush grade, 100-250 SF per gal.				"	20			20	22	
	3300 Bitumen modified polyurethane, fluid applied, 55 mils thick	2 Rofc	665	.024	S.F.	.65	.62		1.27	1.78	
	3600 Vinyl plastic, sprayed on, 25 to 40 mils thick	"	475	.034	"	.98	.87		1.85	2.57	
500	0010 **MEMBRANE WATERPROOFING** On slabs, 1 ply, felt	G-1	3,000	.019	S.F.	.16	.45	.11	.72	1.06	500
	0100 Glass fiber fabric		2,100	.027		.17	.64	.16	.97	1.46	
	0300 2 ply, felt		2,500	.022		.31	.54	.13	.98	1.42	
	0400 Glass fiber fabric		1,650	.034		.38	.82	.20	1.40	2.05	
	0600 3 ply, felt		2,100	.027		.47	.64	.16	1.27	1.78	
	0700 Glass fiber fabric		1,550	.036		.51	.87	.22	1.60	2.30	
	0900 For installation on walls, add						15%				
	1000 For adhered 1/4" EPS protection board, add	2 Rofc	3,500	.005		.14	.12		.26	.35	
	1050 3/8" thick, add		3,500	.005		.16	.12		.28	.38	
	1060 1/2" thick, add		3,500	.005		.18	.12		.30	.40	
	1070 Fiberglass fabric, black, 20/10 mesh		116	.138	Sq.	9.95	3.54		13.49	17.05	
	1080 White, 20/10 mesh		116	.138	"	10.25	3.54		13.79	17.40	
	1100 1/16" urethane, troweled		200	.080	S.F.	.64	2.06		2.70	4.23	
	1200 Roller applied		120	.133	"	.58	3.43		4.01	6.55	

Important: See the Reference Section for critical supporting data - Reference Nos., Crews, & City Cost Indexes

07100 | Dampproofing & Waterproofing

07160 | Cementitious Waterproofing

			CREW	DAILY OUTPUT	LABOR-HOURS	UNIT	MAT.	LABOR	EQUIP.	TOTAL	TOTAL INCL O&P	
150	0010	**CEMENTITIOUS WATERPROOFING** One coat cement base										150
	0020	1/8" application, sprayed on	G-2	1,000	.024	S.F.	1.50	.59	.23	2.32	2.82	
	0030	2 coat, cementitious/metallic slurry, troweled, 1/4" thick	1 Cefi	2.48	3.226	C.S.F.	35	90		125	173	
	0040	3 coat, 3/8" thick	↓	1.84	4.348	↓	52.50	122		174.50	239	
	0050	4 coat, 1/2" thick	↓	1.20	6.667	↓	70	186		256	355	

07170 | Bentonite Waterproofing

			CREW	DAILY OUTPUT	LABOR-HOURS	UNIT	MAT.	LABOR	EQUIP.	TOTAL	TOTAL INCL O&P	
700	0010	**BENTONITE**, Panels, 4' x 4', 3/16" thick	1 Rofc	625	.013	S.F.	.84	.33		1.17	1.49	700
	0100	Rolls, 3/8" thick, with geotextile fabric both sides	"	550	.015	"	.92	.37		1.29	1.65	
	0300	Granular bentonite, 50 lb. bags (.625 C.F.)				Bag	12.85			12.85	14.10	
	0400	3/8" thick, troweled on	1 Rofc	475	.017	S.F.	.64	.43		1.07	1.45	
	0500	Drain board, expanded polystyrene, binder encapsulated, 1-1/2" thick	1 Rohe	1,600	.005		1.02	.10		1.12	1.28	
	0510	2" thick		1,600	.005		1.35	.10		1.45	1.65	
	0520	3" thick		1,600	.005		2.03	.10		2.13	2.39	
	0530	4" thick		1,600	.005		2.70	.10		2.80	3.13	
	0600	With filter fabric, 1-1/2" thick		1,600	.005		1.23	.10		1.33	1.51	
	0625	2" thick		1,600	.005		1.62	.10		1.72	1.94	
	0650	3" thick		1,600	.005		2.29	.10		2.39	2.68	
	0675	4" thick	↓	1,600	.005	↓	2.97	.10		3.07	3.43	
	0700	Vapor retarder, see polyethelene, 07260-100										

07190 | Water Repellents

			CREW	DAILY OUTPUT	LABOR-HOURS	UNIT	MAT.	LABOR	EQUIP.	TOTAL	TOTAL INCL O&P	
700	0010	**RUBBER COATING** Water base liquid, roller applied	2 Rofc	7,000	.002	S.F.	.55	.06		.61	.71	700
	0200	Silicone or stearate, sprayed on CMU, 1 coat	1 Rofc	4,000	.002		.27	.05		.32	.39	
	0300	2 coats	"	3,000	.003	↓	.54	.07		.61	.72	

07200 | Thermal Protection

07210 | Building Insulation

			CREW	DAILY OUTPUT	LABOR-HOURS	UNIT	MAT.	LABOR	EQUIP.	TOTAL	TOTAL INCL O&P	
150	0010	**BLOWN-IN INSULATION** Ceilings, with open access										150
	0020	Cellulose, 3-1/2" thick, R13	G-4	5,000	.005	S.F.	.13	.11	.05	.29	.38	
	0030	5-3/16" thick, R19		3,800	.006		.20	.15	.07	.42	.52	
	0050	6-1/2" thick, R22		3,000	.008		.25	.19	.09	.53	.66	
	0100	8-11/16" thick, R30		2,600	.009		.33	.22	.10	.65	.81	
	0120	10-7/8" thick, R38		1,800	.013		.42	.31	.14	.87	1.11	
	1000	Fiberglass, 5" thick, R11		3,800	.006		.16	.15	.07	.38	.48	
	1050	6" thick, R13		3,000	.008		.19	.19	.09	.47	.59	
	1100	8-1/2" thick, R19		2,200	.011		.26	.26	.12	.64	.82	
	1200	10" thick, R22		1,800	.013		.32	.31	.14	.77	1	
	1300	12" thick, R26		1,500	.016		.38	.38	.17	.93	1.20	
	2000	Mineral wool, 4" thick, R12		3,500	.007		.17	.16	.07	.40	.52	
	2050	6" thick, R17		2,500	.010		.19	.23	.10	.52	.67	
	2100	9" thick, R23	↓	1,750	.014	↓	.28	.32	.15	.75	.97	
	2500	Wall installation, incl. drilling & patching from outside, two 1"										
	2510	diam. holes @ 16" O.C., top & mid-point of wall, add to above										
	2700	For masonry	G-4	415	.058	S.F.	.06	1.36	.62	2.04	2.88	
	2800	For wood siding	↓	840	.029	↓	.06	.67	.31	1.04	1.46	

7

THERMAL & MOISTURE PROTECTION

207

		07210	Building Insulation	CREW	DAILY OUTPUT	LABOR-HOURS	UNIT	2001 BARE COSTS				TOTAL INCL O&P	
								MAT.	LABOR	EQUIP.	TOTAL		
150	2900		For stucco/plaster	G-4	665	.036	S.F.	.06	.85	.39	1.30	1.82	150
400	0010	**INSULATION FASTENERS**											400
	0050		Clips, galv, 1" or 2" insulation				C	17.50			17.50	19.25	
	0100		6" insulation					30			30	33	
	0300		Screws with plates, galv, for 1" or 2" insulation					15.75			15.75	17.35	
	0500		For 6" insulation					28.50			28.50	31.50	
500	0010	**POURED INSULATION** Cellulose fiber, R3.8 per inch		1 Carp	200	.040	C.F.	.47	1.17		1.64	2.34	500
	0040		Ceramic type (perlite), R3.2 per inch		200	.040		1.59	1.17		2.76	3.57	
	0080		Fiberglass wool, R4 per inch		200	.040		.36	1.17		1.53	2.22	
	0100		Mineral wool, R3 per inch		200	.040		.32	1.17		1.49	2.17	
	0300		Polystyrene, R4 per inch		200	.040		2.12	1.17		3.29	4.15	
	0400		Vermiculite or perlite, R2.7 per inch		200	.040		1.59	1.17		2.76	3.57	
	0700		Wood fiber, R3.85 per inch		200	.040		.59	1.17		1.76	2.47	
550	0010	**MASONRY INSULATION** Vermiculite or perlite, poured											550
	0100		In cores of concrete block, 4" thick wall, .115 CF/SF	D-1	4,800	.003	S.F.	.18	.09		.27	.34	
	0200		6" thick wall, .175 CF/SF		3,000	.005		.28	.14		.42	.53	
	0300		8" thick wall, .258 CF/SF		2,400	.007		.41	.18		.59	.72	
	0400		10" thick wall, .340 CF/SF		1,850	.009		.54	.23		.77	.94	
	0500		12" thick wall, .422 CF/SF		1,200	.013		.67	.35		1.02	1.28	
	0550		For sand fill, deduct from above					70%					
	0600		Poured cavity wall, vermiculite or perlite, water repellant	D-1	250	.064	C.F.	1.59	1.68		3.27	4.35	
	0700		Foamed in place, urethane in 2-5/8" cavity	G-2	1,035	.023	S.F.	.39	.57	.23	1.19	1.55	
	0800		For each 1" added thickness, add	"	2,372	.010	"	.12	.25	.10	.47	.62	
600	0600	**PERIMETER INSULATION**, polystyrene, expanded, 1" thick, R4		1 Carp	680	.012	S.F.	.18	.34		.52	.74	600
	0700		2" thick, R8		675	.012	"	.34	.35		.69	.91	
700	0010	**REFLECTIVE INSULATION**, aluminum foil on reinforced scrim			19	.421	C.S.F.	13.90	12.25		26.15	34.50	700
	0100		Reinforced with woven polyolefin		19	.421		16.90	12.25		29.15	38	
	0500		With single bubble air space, R8.8		15	.533		27	15.55		42.55	54	
	0600		With double bubble air space, R9.8		15	.533		29	15.55		44.55	56.50	
800	0010	**SPRAYED** Fibrous/cementitious, finished wall, 1" thick, R3.7		G-2	2,050	.012	S.F.	.22	.29	.11	.62	.81	800
	0100		Attic, 5.2" thick, R19	"	1,550	.015	"	.36	.38	.15	.89	1.15	
	0300		Foam type, incl. preparation										
	0600		3 #/CF, 1" thick, R3.8	G-2	770	.031	S.F.	.47	.76	.30	1.53	2.03	
	0700		2" thick, R7.5	"	475	.051	"	.93	1.24	.49	2.66	3.47	
900	0010	**WALL INSULATION, RIGID**											900
	0040		Fiberglass, 1.5#/CF, unfaced, 1" thick, R4.1	1 Carp	1,000	.008	S.F.	.27	.23		.50	.66	
	0060		1-1/2" thick, R6.2		1,000	.008		.40	.23		.63	.80	
	0080		2" thick, R8.3		1,000	.008		.43	.23		.66	.83	
	0120		3" thick, R12.4		800	.010		.54	.29		.83	1.05	
	0370		3#/CF, unfaced, 1" thick, R4.3		1,000	.008		.33	.23		.56	.72	
	0390		1-1/2" thick, R6.5		1,000	.008		.65	.23		.88	1.08	
	0400		2" thick, R8.7		890	.009		.79	.26		1.05	1.28	
	0420		2-1/2" thick, R10.9		800	.010		.99	.29		1.28	1.55	
	0440		3" thick, R13		800	.010		1.17	.29		1.46	1.75	
	0520		Foil faced, 1" thick, R4.3		1,000	.008		.78	.23		1.01	1.22	
	0540		1-1/2" thick, R6.5		1,000	.008		1.05	.23		1.28	1.52	
	0560		2" thick, R8.7		890	.009		1.31	.26		1.57	1.85	
	0580		2-1/2" thick, R10.9		800	.010		1.55	.29		1.84	2.17	
	0600		3" thick, R13		800	.010		1.69	.29		1.98	2.32	
	0670		6#/CF, unfaced, 1" thick, R4.3		1,000	.008		.75	.23		.98	1.19	
	0690		1-1/2" thick, R6.5		890	.009		1.16	.26		1.42	1.69	
	0700		2" thick, R8.7		800	.010		1.63	.29		1.92	2.25	

Important: See the Reference Section for critical supporting data - Reference Nos., Crews, & City Cost Indexes

7 THERMAL & MOISTURE PROTECTION

07210 | Building Insulation

			DAILY OUTPUT	LABOR-HOURS	UNIT	2001 BARE COSTS				TOTAL INCL O&P
						MAT.	LABOR	EQUIP.	TOTAL	
900	0721	2-1/2" thick, R10.9	1 Carp 800	.010	S.F.	1.79	.29		2.08	2.43	**900**
	0741	3" thick, R13	730	.011		2.14	.32		2.46	2.85
	0821	Foil faced, 1" thick, R4.3	1,000	.008		1.06	.23		1.29	1.53
	0840	1-1/2" thick, R6.5	890	.009		1.52	.26		1.78	2.08
	0850	2" thick, R8.7	800	.010		1.99	.29		2.28	2.65
	0880	2-1/2" thick, R10.9	800	.010		2.39	.29		2.68	3.09
	0900	3" thick, R13	730	.011		2.85	.32		3.17	3.64
	1500	Foamglass, 1-1/2" thick, R4.5	800	.010		1.53	.29		1.82	2.14
	1550	3" thick, R9	730	.011		2.71	.32		3.03	3.48
	1600	Isocyanurate, 4' x 8' sheet, foil faced, both sides								
	1610	1/2" thick, R3.9	1 Carp 800	.010	S.F.	.28	.29		.57	.77
	1620	5/8" thick, R4.5	800	.010		.29	.29		.58	.78
	1630	3/4" thick, R5.4	800	.010		.30	.29		.59	.79
	1640	1" thick, R7.2	800	.010		.33	.29		.62	.82
	1650	1-1/2" thick, R10.8	730	.011		.37	.32		.69	.91
	1660	2" thick, R14.4 CN	730	.011		.46	.32		.78	1.01
	1670	3" thick, R21.6	730	.011		1.08	.32		1.40	1.69
	1680	4" thick, R28.8	730	.011		1.33	.32		1.65	1.96
	1700	Perlite, 1" thick, R2.77	800	.010		.25	.29		.54	.74
	1750	2" thick, R5.55	730	.011		.49	.32		.81	1.04
	1900	Extruded polystyrene, 25 PSI compressive strength, 1" thick, R5	800	.010		.32	.29		.61	.81
	1940	2" thick R10	730	.011		.64	.32		.96	1.20
	1960	3" thick, R15	730	.011		.91	.32		1.23	1.50
	2100	Expanded polystyrene, 1" thick, R3.85	800	.010		.13	.29		.42	.60
	2120	2" thick, R7.69	730	.011		.35	.32		.67	.89
	2140	3" thick, R11.49	730	.011		.50	.32		.82	1.05
950	0010	**WALL OR CEILING INSUL., NON-RIGID**									**950**
	0040	Fiberglass, kraft faced, batts or blankets								
	0060	3-1/2" thick, R11, 11" wide	1 Carp 1,150	.007	S.F.	.22	.20		.42	.56
	0080	15" wide CN	1,600	.005		.22	.15		.37	.47
	0100	23" wide	1,600	.005		.22	.15		.37	.47
	0140	6" thick, R19, 11" wide	1,000	.008		.32	.23		.55	.71
	0160	15" wide	1,350	.006		.32	.17		.49	.62
	0180	23" wide	1,600	.005		.32	.15		.47	.58
	0200	9" thick, R30, 15" wide	1,150	.007		.58	.20		.78	.96
	0220	23" wide	1,350	.006		.58	.17		.75	.91
	0240	12" thick, R38, 15" wide	1,000	.008		.74	.23		.97	1.17
	0260	23" wide	1,350	.006		.74	.17		.91	1.08
	0400	Fiberglass, foil faced, batts or blankets								
	0420	3-1/2" thick, R11, 15" wide	1 Carp 1,600	.005	S.F.	.33	.15		.48	.59
	0440	23" wide	1,600	.005		.33	.15		.48	.59
	0460	6" thick, R19, 15" wide	1,350	.006		.40	.17		.57	.71
	0480	23" wide	1,600	.005		.40	.15		.55	.67
	0500	9" thick, R30, 15" wide	1,150	.007		.69	.20		.89	1.08
	0550	23" wide	1,350	.006		.69	.17		.86	1.03
	0800	Fiberglass, unfaced, batts or blankets								
	0820	3-1/2" thick, R11, 15" wide	1 Carp 1,350	.006	S.F.	.20	.17		.37	.49
	0830	23" wide	1,600	.005		.20	.15		.35	.45
	0860	6" thick, R19, 15" wide	1,150	.007		.33	.20		.53	.68
	0880	23" wide	1,350	.006		.33	.17		.50	.63
	0900	9" thick, R30, 15" wide	1,000	.008		.58	.23		.81	1
	0920	23" wide	1,150	.007		.58	.20		.78	.96
	0940	12" thick, R38, 15" wide	1,000	.008		.74	.23		.97	1.17
	0960	23" wide	1,150	.007		.74	.20		.94	1.13
	1300	Mineral fiber batts, kraft faced								
	1320	3-1/2" thick, R12	1 Carp 1,600	.005	S.F.	.25	.15		.40	.51

07200 | Thermal Protection

07210	Building Insulation	CREW	DAILY OUTPUT	LABOR-HOURS	UNIT	MAT.	LABOR	EQUIP.	TOTAL	TOTAL INCL O&P	
950	1340	6" thick, R19	1 Carp	1,600	.005	S.F.	.38	.15		.53	.65	950
	1380	10" thick, R30		1,350	.006	↓	.60	.17		.77	.93	
	1850	Friction fit wire insulation supports, 16" O.C.	↓	960	.008	Ea.	.05	.24		.29	.44	
	1900	For foil backing, add				S.F.	.04			.04	.04	

07220 | Roof & Deck Insulation

			CREW	DAILY OUTPUT	LABOR-HOURS	UNIT	MAT.	LABOR	EQUIP.	TOTAL	TOTAL INCL O&P	
700	0010	**ROOF DECK INSULATION**										700
	0020	Fiberboard low density, 1/2" thick R1.39	1 Rofc	1,000	.008	S.F.	.18	.21		.39	.55	
	0030	1" thick R2.78		800	.010		.33	.26		.59	.80	
	0080	1 1/2" thick R4.17		800	.010		.49	.26		.75	.98	
	0100	2" thick R5.56		800	.010		.66	.26		.92	1.17	
	0110	Fiberboard high density, 1/2" thick R1.3		1,000	.008		.19	.21		.40	.56	
	0120	1" thick R2.5		800	.010		.35	.26		.61	.83	
	0130	1-1/2" thick R3.8		800	.010		.57	.26		.83	1.07	
	0200	Fiberglass, 3/4" thick R2.78		1,000	.008		.45	.21		.66	.85	
	0400	15/16" thick R3.70		1,000	.008		.59	.21		.80	1	
	0460	1-1/16" thick R4.17		1,000	.008		.74	.21		.95	1.16	
	0600	1-5/16" thick R5.26		1,000	.008		1.02	.21		1.23	1.47	
	0650	2-1/16" thick R8.33		800	.010		1.09	.26		1.35	1.64	
	0700	2-7/16" thick R10		800	.010		1.24	.26		1.50	1.80	
	1500	Foamglass, 1-1/2" thick R4.5		800	.010		1.42	.26		1.68	2	
	1530	3" thick R9		700	.011	↓	2.94	.29		3.23	3.73	
	1600	Tapered for drainage		600	.013	B.F.	.91	.34		1.25	1.59	
	1650	Perlite, 1/2" thick R1.32		1,050	.008	S.F.	.26	.20		.46	.63	
	1655	3/4" thick R2.08		800	.010		.32	.26		.58	.79	
	1660	1" thick R2.78		800	.010		.27	.26		.53	.74	
	1670	1-1/2" thick R4.17		800	.010		.38	.26		.64	.86	
	1680	2" thick R5.56		700	.011		.54	.29		.83	1.09	
	1685	2-1/2" thick R6.67		700	.011	↓	.75	.29		1.04	1.33	
	1690	Tapered for drainage		800	.010	B.F.	.57	.26		.83	1.07	
	1700	Polyisocyanurate, 2#/CF density, 3/4" thick, R5.1		1,500	.005	S.F.	.30	.14		.44	.57	
	1705	1" thick R7.14		1,400	.006		.31	.15		.46	.59	
	1715	1-1/2" thick R10.87		1,250	.006		.34	.16		.50	.65	
	1725	2" thick R14.29		1,100	.007		.44	.19		.63	.80	
	1735	2-1/2" thick R16.67		1,050	.008		.49	.20		.69	.88	
	1745	3" thick R21.74		1,000	.008		.69	.21		.90	1.11	
	1755	3-1/2" thick R25		1,000	.008	↓	.72	.21		.93	1.14	
	1765	Tapered for drainage	↓	1,400	.006	B.F.	.37	.15		.52	.66	
	1900	Extruded Polystyrene										
	1910	15 PSI compressive strength, 1" thick, R5	1 Rofc	1,500	.005	S.F.	.22	.14		.36	.48	
	1920	2" thick, R10		1,250	.006		.34	.16		.50	.65	
	1930	3" thick R15		1,000	.008		.75	.21		.96	1.18	
	1932	4" thick R20		1,000	.008	↓	1.04	.21		1.25	1.49	
	1934	Tapered for drainage		1,500	.005	B.F.	.34	.14		.48	.61	
	1940	25 PSI compressive strength, 1" thick R5		1,500	.005	S.F.	.35	.14		.49	.63	
	1942	2" thick R10		1,250	.006		.69	.16		.85	1.04	
	1944	3" thick R15		1,000	.008		1.04	.21		1.25	1.49	
	1946	4" thick R20		1,000	.008	↓	1.08	.21		1.29	1.54	
	1948	Tapered for drainage		1,500	.005	B.F.	.39	.14		.53	.67	
	1950	40 psi compressive strength, 1" thick R5		1,500	.005	S.F.	.34	.14		.48	.61	
	1952	2" thick R10		1,250	.006		.67	.16		.83	1.02	
	1954	3" thick R15		1,000	.008		.98	.21		1.19	1.43	
	1956	4" thick R20		1,000	.008	↓	1.31	.21		1.52	1.79	
	1958	Tapered for drainage		1,400	.006	B.F.	.49	.15		.64	.79	
	1960	60 PSI compressive strength, 1" thick R5		1,450	.006	S.F.	.41	.14		.55	.69	
	1962	2" thick R10	↓	1,200	.007	↓	.73	.17		.90	1.09	

7 THERMAL & MOISTURE PROTECTION

07220 | Roof & Deck Insulation

		CREW	DAILY OUTPUT	LABOR-HOURS	UNIT	2001 BARE COSTS				TOTAL INCL O&P
						MAT.	LABOR	EQUIP.	TOTAL	
700	1964	3" thick R15	1 Rofc	975	.008	S.F.	1.09	.21		1.30	1.56	700
1966	4" thick R20		950	.008	↓	1.51	.22		1.73	2.03
1968	Tapered for drainage		1,400	.006	B.F.	.59	.15		.74	.90
2010	Expanded polystyrene, 1#/CF density, 3/4" thick R2.89		1,500	.005	S.F.	.18	.14		.32	.44
2020	1" thick R3.85		1,500	.005		.18	.14		.32	.44
2100	2" thick R7.69		1,250	.006		.34	.16		.50	.65
2110	3" thick R11.49		1,250	.006		.53	.16		.69	.86
2120	4" thick R15.38		1,200	.007		.55	.17		.72	.90
2130	5" thick R19.23		1,150	.007		.69	.18		.87	1.07
2140	6" thick R23.26		1,150	.007	↓	.81	.18		.99	1.20
2150	Tapered for drainage	↓	1,500	.005	B.F.	.33	.14		.47	.60
2400	Composites with 2" EPS									
2410	1" fiberboard	1 Rofc	950	.008	S.F.	.76	.22		.98	1.21
2420	7/16" oriented strand board		800	.010		.90	.26		1.16	1.43
2430	1/2" plywood		800	.010		.97	.26		1.23	1.51
2440	1" perlite	↓	800	.010	↓	.80	.26		1.06	1.32
2450	Composites with 1 1/2" polyisocyanurate									
2460	1" fiberboard	1 Rofc	800	.010	S.F.	.82	.26		1.08	1.34
2470	1" perlite		850	.009		.85	.24		1.09	1.36
2480	7/16" oriented strand board	↓	800	.010	↓	.98	.26		1.24	1.52

07240 | Ext. Insulation/Finish Systems

		CREW	DAILY OUTPUT	LABOR-HOURS	UNIT	MAT.	LABOR	EQUIP.	TOTAL	TOTAL INCL O&P
100	0010	**EXTERIOR INSULATION FINISH SYSTEM**										100
0095	Field applied, 1" EPS insulation	J-1	295	.136	S.F.	1.74	3.48	.20	5.42	7.50
0100	With 1/2" cement board sheathing		220	.182		2.77	4.67	.27	7.71	10.50
0105	2" EPS insulation		295	.136		1.96	3.48	.20	5.64	7.70
0110	With 1/2" cement board sheathing		220	.182		2.99	4.67	.27	7.93	10.75
0115	3" EPS insulation		295	.136		2.11	3.48	.20	5.79	7.90
0120	With 1/2" cement board sheathing		220	.182		3.14	4.67	.27	8.08	10.90
0125	4" EPS insulation		295	.136		2.31	3.48	.20	5.99	8.10
0130	With 1/2" cement board sheathing		220	.182		4.38	4.67	.27	9.32	12.25
0140	Premium finish add		1,265	.032		.27	.81	.05	1.13	1.59
0150	Heavy duty reinforcement add	↓	914	.044	↓	1.65	1.12	.06	2.83	3.61
0160	2.5#/S.Y. metal lath substrate add	1 Lath	75	.107	S.Y.	2.12	3.01		5.13	6.80
0170	3.4#/S.Y. metal lath substrate add	"	75	.107	"	2.21	3.01		5.22	6.90
0180	Color or texture change,	J-1	1,265	.032	S.F.	.72	.81	.05	1.58	2.08
0190	With substrate leveling base coat	1 Plas	530	.015		.72	.41		1.13	1.42
0210	With substrate sealing base coat	1 Pord	1,224	.007		.07	.17		.24	.34
0220	Prefab. panels, with hat channels 2 1/2" x 3/4", 2" EPS insul.	L-5	1,800	.031		7.70	1.02	.35	9.07	10.65
0240	3" EPS insulation		1,800	.031		8.55	1.02	.35	9.92	11.60
0250	4" EPS insulation		1,800	.031		9.55	1.02	.35	10.92	12.70
0260	1-1/2" profile lightweight metal backing, 1" EPS insulation		1,800	.031		11.75	1.02	.35	13.12	15.15
0270	2" EPS insulation		1,800	.031		13.10	1.02	.35	14.47	16.65
0280	3" EPS insulation		1,800	.031		14.65	1.02	.35	16.02	18.30
0290	4" EPS insulation		1,800	.031		16.35	1.02	.35	17.72	20
0310	6"-16 Ga. steel stud back-up, 1" EPS insulation		1,800	.031		13.55	1.02	.35	14.92	17.10
0320	2" EPS insulation		1,800	.031		15.15	1.02	.35	16.52	18.85
0330	3" EPS insulation		1,800	.031		16.85	1.02	.35	18.22	21
0340	4" EPS insulation	↓	1,800	.031		18.85	1.02	.35	20.22	22.50
0350	Premium finish add	J-1	1,265	.032		.27	.81	.05	1.13	1.59
0360	Heavy duty reinforcement add	"	914	.044	↓	1.65	1.12	.06	2.83	3.61
0370	V groove shape in panel face				L.F.	.52			.52	.57
0380	U groove shape in panel face				"	.69			.69	.76
0390	Architectural features,									
0410	Crown moulding 8" high x 4" wide	1 Plas	150	.053	L.F.	1.15	1.46		2.61	3.50
0420	Crown moulding 12" high x 6" wide	↓	150	.053	↓	2.15	1.46		3.61	4.60

7 THERMAL & MOISTURE PROTECTION

07240 | Ext. Insulation/Finish Systems

		CREW	DAILY OUTPUT	LABOR-HOURS	UNIT	2001 BARE COSTS MAT.	LABOR	EQUIP.	TOTAL	TOTAL INCL O&P	
100	0430 Crown moulding 16" high x 12" wide	1 Plas	150	.053	L.F.	5.65	1.46		7.11	8.50	100
	0440 For higher than one story, add						25%				

07260 | Vapor Retarders

		CREW	DAILY OUTPUT	LABOR-HOURS	UNIT	2001 BARE COSTS MAT.	LABOR	EQUIP.	TOTAL	TOTAL INCL O&P	
100	0010 **BUILDING PAPER** Aluminum and kraft laminated, foil 1 side	1 Carp	37	.216	Sq.	3.55	6.30		9.85	13.75	100
	0100 Foil 2 sides		37	.216		5.70	6.30		12	16.10	
	0300 Asphalt, two ply, 30#, for subfloors		19	.421		9.85	12.25		22.10	30	
	0400 Asphalt felt sheathing paper, 15#		37	.216		2.13	6.30		8.43	12.20	
	0450 Housewrap, exterior, spun bonded polypropylene										
	0470 Small roll	1 Carp	3,800	.002	S.F.	.10	.06		.16	.21	
	0480 Large roll	"	4,000	.002	"	.09	.06		.15	.19	
	0500 Material only, 3' x 111.1' roll				Ea.	33			33	36.50	
	0520 9' x 111.1' roll				"	94			94	103	
	0600 Polyethylene vapor barrier, standard, .002" thick	1 Carp	37	.216	Sq.	1.09	6.30		7.39	11.05	
	0700 .004" thick		37	.216		2.14	6.30		8.44	12.20	
	0900 .006" thick		37	.216		2.87	6.30		9.17	13	
	1200 .010" thick		37	.216		5.60	6.30		11.90	16.05	
	1300 Clear reinforced, fire retardant, .008" thick		37	.216		8.40	6.30		14.70	19.10	
	1350 Cross laminated type, .003" thick		37	.216		6.50	6.30		12.80	17	
	1400 .004" thick		37	.216		7.25	6.30		13.55	17.85	
	1500 Red rosin paper, 5 sq rolls, 4 lb per square		37	.216		1.55	6.30		7.85	11.55	
	1600 5 lbs. per square		37	.216		2	6.30		8.30	12.05	
	1800 Reinf. waterproof, .002" polyethylene backing, 1 side		37	.216		4.92	6.30		11.22	15.25	
	1900 2 sides		37	.216		6.50	6.30		12.80	17	
	2100 Roof deck vapor barrier, class 1 metal decks	1 Rofc	37	.216		8.40	5.55		13.95	18.75	
	2200 For all other decks	"	37	.216		6.25	5.55		11.80	16.45	
	2400 Waterproofed kraft with sisal or fiberglass fibers, minimum	1 Carp	37	.216		5.30	6.30		11.60	15.70	
	2500 Maximum	"	37	.216		13.25	6.30		19.55	24.50	

07300 | Shingles, Roof Tiles & Roof Coverings

07310 | Shingles

		CREW	DAILY OUTPUT	LABOR-HOURS	UNIT	2001 BARE COSTS MAT.	LABOR	EQUIP.	TOTAL	TOTAL INCL O&P	
050	0010 **ALUMINUM** Shingles, mill finish, .019" thick	1 Carp	5	1.600	Sq.	150	46.50		196.50	238	050
	0100 .020" thick	"	5	1.600		148	46.50		194.50	235	
	0300 For colors, add					15.15			15.15	16.65	
	0600 Ridge cap, .024" thick	1 Carp	170	.047	L.F.	1.66	1.37		3.03	3.98	
	0700 End wall flashing, .024" thick		170	.047		1.29	1.37		2.66	3.57	
	0900 Valley section, .024" thick		170	.047		2.08	1.37		3.45	4.44	
	1000 Starter strip, .024" thick		400	.020		1.12	.58		1.70	2.14	
	1200 Side wall flashing, .024" thick		170	.047		1.28	1.37		2.65	3.56	
	1500 Gable flashing, .024" thick		400	.020		1.20	.58		1.78	2.23	
100	0010 **ASPHALT SHINGLES**										100
	0100 Standard strip shingles										
	0150 Inorganic, class A, 210-235 lb/sq **CN**	1 Rofc	5.50	1.455	Sq.	27.50	37.50		65	94	
	0155 Pneumatic nailed		7	1.143		27.50	29.50		57	80.50	
	0200 Organic, class C, 235-240 lb/sq		5	1.600		35.50	41		76.50	110	
	0205 Pneumatic nailed		6.25	1.280		35.50	33		68.50	95.50	
	0250 Standard, laminated multi-layered shingles										
	0300 Class A, 240-260 lb/sq	1 Rofc	4.50	1.778	Sq.	39	45.50		84.50	121	

Important: See the Reference Section for critical supporting data - Reference Nos., Crews, & City Cost Indexes

		07310	Shingles	CREW	DAILY OUTPUT	LABOR-HOURS	UNIT	2001 BARE COSTS				TOTAL INCL O&P	
								MAT.	LABOR	EQUIP.	TOTAL		
100	0305		Pneumatic nailed	1 Rofc	5.63	1.422	Sq.	39	36.50		75.50	106	**100**
	0350		Class C, 260-300 lb/square, 4 bundles/square		4	2		49	51.50		100.50	143	
	0355		Pneumatic nailed	↓	5	1.600	↓	49	41		90	125	
	0400		Premium, laminated multi-layered shingles										
	0450		Class A, 260-300 lb, 4 bundles/sq	1 Rofc	3.50	2.286	Sq.	48.50	58.50		107	155	
	0455		Pneumatic nailed		4.37	1.831		48.50	47		95.50	135	
	0500		Class C, 300-385 lb/square, 5 bundles/square		3	2.667		65.50	68.50		134	190	
	0505		Pneumatic nailed		3.75	2.133		65.50	55		120.50	166	
	0800		#15 felt underlayment		64	.125		2.13	3.21		5.34	7.85	
	0825		#30 felt underlayment		58	.138		4.92	3.54		8.46	11.50	
	0850		Self adhering polyethylene and rubberized asphalt underlayment		22	.364	↓	37	9.35		46.35	57	
	0900		Ridge shingles		330	.024	L.F.	.72	.62		1.34	1.86	
	0905		Pneumatic nailed	↓	412.50	.019	"	.72	.50		1.22	1.65	
	1000		For steep roofs (7 to 12 pitch or greater), add						50%				
500	0010		**FIBER CEMENT** shingles, 16" x 9.35", 500 lb per square	1 Carp	4	2	Sq.	244	58.50		302.50	360	**500**
	0110		Starters, 16" x 9.35"		3	2.667	C.L.F.	83	77.50		160.50	213	
	0120		Hip & ridge, 4.75" x 14"		1	8	"	600	233		833	1,025	
	0200		Shakes, 16" x 9.35", 550 lb per square		2.20	3.636	Sq.	221	106		327	410	
	0300		Hip & ridge, 4.75 x 14"		1	8	C.L.F.	600	233		833	1,025	
	0400		Hexagonal, 16" x 16"		3	2.667	Sq.	165	77.50		242.50	305	
	0500		Square, 16" x 16"	↓	3	2.667	"	148	77.50		225.50	285	
800	0010		**SLATE**, Buckingham, Virginia, black										**800**
	0100		3/16" - 1/4" thick	1 Rots	1.75	4.571	Sq.	540	119		659	800	
	0200		1/4" thick		1.75	4.571		720	119		839	995	
	0900		Pennsylvania black, Bangor, #1 clear		1.75	4.571		435	119		554	685	
	1200		Vermont, unfading, green, mottled green		1.75	4.571		425	119		544	670	
	1300		Semi-weathering green & gray		1.75	4.571		296	119		415	530	
	1400		Purple		1.75	4.571		390	119		509	635	
	1500		Black or gray		1.75	4.571		345	119		464	585	
	1600		Red		1.75	4.571		1,125	119		1,244	1,425	
	1700		Variegated purple		1.75	4.571		375	119		494	615	
900	0010		**STEEL** Shingles, galvanized, 26 gauge	1 Rots	2.20	3.636	Sq.	152	94.50		246.50	330	**900**
	0200		24 gauge	"	2.20	3.636		160	94.50		254.50	340	
	0300		For colored galvanized shingles, add					41.50			41.50	46	
	0500		For 1" factory applied polystyrene insulation, add	↓				30.50			30.50	33.50	
980	0010		**WOOD** 16" No. 1 red cedar shingles, 5" exposure, on roof	1 Carp	2.50	3.200	Sq.	151	93.50		244.50	310	**980**
	0015		Pneumatic nailed		3.25	2.462		151	72		223	278	
	0200		7-1/2" exposure, on walls		2.05	3.902		101	114		215	289	
	0205		Pneumatic nailed		2.67	2.996		101	87.50		188.50	248	
	0300		18" No. 1 red cedar perfections, 5-1/2" exposure, on roof		2.75	2.909		160	85		245	310	
	0305		Pneumatic nailed		3.57	2.241		160	65.50		225.50	278	
	0500		7-1/2" exposure, on walls		2.25	3.556		118	104		222	291	
	0505		Pneumatic nailed		2.92	2.740		118	80		198	254	
	0600		Resquared, and rebutted, 5-1/2" exposure, on roof		3	2.667		199	77.50		276.50	340	
	0605		Pneumatic nailed		3.90	2.051		199	60		259	315	
	0900		7-1/2" exposure, on walls		2.45	3.265		146	95		241	310	
	0905		Pneumatic nailed	↓	3.18	2.516		146	73.50		219.50	276	
	1000		Add to above for fire retardant shingles, 16" long					30			30	33	
	1050		18" long				↓	28.50			28.50	31.50	
	1060		Preformed ridge shingles	1 Carp	400	.020	L.F.	1.65	.58		2.23	2.73	
	1100		Hand-split red cedar shakes, 1/2" thick x 24" long, 10" exp. on roof		2.50	3.200	Sq.	138	93.50		231.50	298	
	1105		Pneumatic nailed		3.25	2.462		138	72		210	264	
	1110		3/4" thick x 24" long, 10" exp. on roof		2.25	3.556		138	104		242	315	
	1115		Pneumatic nailed		2.92	2.740		138	80		218	277	
	1200		1/2" thick, 18" long, 8-1/2" exp. on roof	↓	2	4	↓	97.50	117		214.50	289	

R07310 -020

7 THERMAL & MOISTURE PROTECTION

			DAILY OUTPUT	LABOR-HOURS	UNIT	2001 BARE COSTS				TOTAL INCL O&P	
	07310	**Shingles**	CREW			MAT.	LABOR	EQUIP.	TOTAL		
980	1205	Pneumatic nailed	1 Carp	2.60	3.077	Sq.	97.50	89.50		187	247	980
	1210	3/4" thick x 18" long, 8 1/2" exp. on roof		1.80	4.444		97.50	130		227.50	310	
	1215	Pneumatic nailed		2.34	3.419		97.50	99.50		197	263	
	1255	10" exp. on walls		2	4		110	117		227	305	
	1260	10" exposure on walls, pneumatic nailed		2.60	3.077		110	89.50		199.50	261	
	1700	Add to above for fire retardant shakes, 24" long					30			30	33	
	1800	18" long					30			30	33	
	1810	Ridge shakes	1 Carp	350	.023	L.F.	2.35	.67		3.02	3.63	
	2000	White cedar shingles, 16" long, extras, 5" exposure, on roof		2.40	3.333	Sq.	112	97		209	275	
	2005	Pneumatic nailed		3.12	2.564		112	74.50		186.50	240	
	2050	5" exposure on walls		2	4		112	117		229	305	
	2055	Pneumatic nailed		2.60	3.077		112	89.50		201.50	263	
	2100	7-1/2" exposure, on walls		2	4		80	117		197	270	
	2105	Pneumatic nailed		2.60	3.077		80	89.50		169.50	228	
	2150	"B" grade, 5" exposure on walls		2	4		110	117		227	305	
	2155	Pneumatic nailed		2.60	3.077		110	89.50		199.50	261	
	2300	For 15# organic felt underlayment on roof, 1 layer, add		64	.125		2.13	3.64		5.77	8.05	
	2400	2 layers, add		32	.250		4.26	7.30		11.56	16.10	
	2600	For steep roofs (7/12 pitch or greater), add to above						50%				
	2700	Panelized systems, No.1 cedar shingles on 5/16" CDX plywood										
	2800	On walls, 8' strips, 7" or 14" exposure	2 Carp	700	.023	S.F.	3.20	.67		3.87	4.56	
	3500	On roofs, 8' strips, 7" or 14" exposure	1 Carp	3	2.667	Sq.	320	77.50		397.50	470	
	3505	Pneumatic nailed	"	4	2	"	320	58.50		378.50	440	
	07320	**Roof Tiles**										
100	0010	**ALUMINUM** Tiles with accessories, .032" thick, mission tile	1 Carp	2.50	3.200	Sq.	425	93.50		518.50	615	100
	0200	Spanish tiles	"	3	2.667	"	365	77.50		442.50	525	
200	0010	**CLAY TILE** ASTM C1167, GR 1, severe weathering, acces. incl.										200
	0200	Lanai tile or Classic tile, 158 pc per sq	1 Rots	1.65	4.848	Sq.	395	126		521	650	
	0300	Americana, 158 pc per sq, most colors		1.65	4.848		520	126		646	785	
	0350	Green, gray or brown		1.65	4.848		490	126		616	755	
	0400	Blue		1.65	4.848		490	126		616	755	
	0600	Spanish tile, 171 pc per sq, red		1.80	4.444		300	116		416	530	
	0800	Blend		1.80	4.444		420	116		536	660	
	0900	Glazed white		1.80	4.444		500	116		616	750	
	1100	Mission tile, 192 pc per sq, machine scored finish, red		1.15	6.957		635	181		816	1,000	
	1700	French tile, 133 pc per sq, smooth finish, red		1.35	5.926		575	154		729	895	
	1750	Blue or green		1.35	5.926		685	154		839	1,025	
	1800	Norman black 317 pc per sq		1	8		845	208		1,053	1,275	
	2200	Williamsburg tile, 158 pc per sq, aged cedar		1.35	5.926		490	154		644	805	
	2250	Gray or green		1.35	5.926		490	154		644	805	
	2510	One piece mission tile, natural red, 75 pc per square		1.65	4.848		133	126		259	360	
	2530	Mission Tile, 134 pc per square		1.15	6.957		178	181		359	505	
300	0010	**CONCRETE TILE** Including installation of accessories										300
	0020	Corrugated, 13" x 16-1/2", 90 per sq, 950 lb per sq										
	0050	Earthtone colors, nailed to wood deck	1 Rots	1.35	5.926	Sq.	100	154		254	375	
	0150	Blues		1.35	5.926		108	154		262	385	
	0200	Greens		1.35	5.926		108	154		262	385	
	0250	Premium colors		1.35	5.926		153	154		307	435	
	0500	Shakes, 13" x 16-1/2", 90 per sq, 950 lb per sq										
	0600	All colors, nailed to wood deck	1 Rots	1.50	5.333	Sq.	185	139		324	440	
	1500	Accessory pieces, ridge & hip, 10" x 16-1/2", 8 lbs. each				Ea.	2.25			2.25	2.48	
	1700	Rake, 6-1/2" x 16-3/4", 9 lbs. each					2.25			2.25	2.48	
	1800	Mansard hip, 10" x 16-1/2", 9.2 lbs. each					2.25			2.25	2.48	
	1900	Hip starter, 10" x 16-1/2", 10.5 lbs. each					9.50			9.50	10.45	

Important: See the Reference Section for critical supporting data - Reference Nos., Crews, & City Cost Indexes

07300 | Shingles, Roof Tiles & Roof Coverings

	07320	**Roof Tiles**	CREW	DAILY OUTPUT	LABOR-HOURS	UNIT	2001 BARE COSTS				TOTAL INCL O&P	
							MAT.	LABOR	EQUIP.	TOTAL		
300	2000	3 or 4 way apex, 10" each side, 11.5 lbs. each				Ea.	10.25			10.25	11.30	**300**

07400 | Roofing & Siding Panels

	07410	**Metal Roof & Wall Panels**	CREW	DAILY OUTPUT	LABOR-HOURS	UNIT	2001 BARE COSTS				TOTAL INCL O&P	
							MAT.	LABOR	EQUIP.	TOTAL		
100	0010	**ALUMINUM ROOFING** Corrugated or ribbed, .0155" thick, natural	G-3	1,200	.027	S.F.	.62	.75		1.37	1.85	**100**
	0300	Painted		1,200	.027		.89	.75		1.64	2.15	
	0400	Corrugated, .018" thick, on steel frame, natural finish		1,200	.027		.80	.75		1.55	2.05	
	0600	Painted		1,200	.027		.99	.75		1.74	2.26	
	0700	Corrugated, on steel frame, natural, .024" thick		1,200	.027		1.16	.75		1.91	2.45	
	0800	Painted, .024" thick		1,200	.027		1.40	.75		2.15	2.71	
	0900	.032" thick, natural		1,200	.027		1.19	.75		1.94	2.48	
	1200	painted		1,200	.027		1.64	.75		2.39	2.97	
	1300	V-Beam, on steel frame construction, .032" thick, natural		1,200	.027		1.40	.75		2.15	2.71	
	1500	Painted		1,200	.027		1.83	.75		2.58	3.18	
	1600	.040" thick, natural		1,200	.027		1.70	.75		2.45	3.04	
	1800	Painted		1,200	.027		2.19	.75		2.94	3.58	
	1900	.050" thick, natural		1,200	.027		2.17	.75		2.92	3.56	
	2100	Painted		1,200	.027		2.63	.75		3.38	4.06	
	2200	For roofing on wood frame, deduct		4,600	.007		.05	.20		.25	.36	
	2400	Ridge cap, .032" thick, natural		800	.040	L.F.	1.77	1.13		2.90	3.70	
500	0010	**MANSARD** Colored aluminum, with battens, .032" thick										**500**
	0600	Stock units, straight surfaces	1 Shee	115	.070	S.F.	2.13	2.33		4.46	5.95	
	0700	Concave or convex surfaces		75	.107	"	2.35	3.58		5.93	8.15	
	0800	For framing, to 5' high, add		115	.070	L.F.	2.35	2.33		4.68	6.20	
	0900	Soffits, to 1' wide		125	.064	S.F.	1.16	2.15		3.31	4.60	
690	0010	**METAL FACING PANELS**										**690**
	0400	Textured aluminum, 4' x 8' x 5/16" plywood backing, single face	2 Shee	375	.043	S.F.	2.18	1.43		3.61	4.61	
	0600	Double face		375	.043		3.29	1.43		4.72	5.85	
	0700	4' x 10' x 5/16" plywood backing, single face		375	.043		2.32	1.43		3.75	4.76	
	0900	Double face		375	.043		3.41	1.43		4.84	5.95	
	1000	4' x 12' x 5/15" plywood backing, single face		375	.043		2.99	1.43		4.42	5.50	
	1300	Smooth al, 1/4" panel, fluoropolymer finish, double face		375	.043		5.35	1.43		6.78	8.10	
	1350	Clear anodized finish, double face		375	.043		5.95	1.43		7.38	8.75	
	1400	Double face textured aluminum, structural panel, 1" EPS insulation		375	.043		3.60	1.43		5.03	6.15	
	1500	Accessories, outside corner	1 Shee	175	.046	L.F.	1.54	1.53		3.07	4.06	
	1600	Inside corner		175	.046		1.04	1.53		2.57	3.51	
	1800	Batten mounting clip		200	.040		.35	1.34		1.69	2.46	
	1900	Low profile batten		480	.017		.72	.56		1.28	1.65	
	2100	High profile batten		480	.017		1.21	.56		1.77	2.19	
	2200	Water table		200	.040		1.28	1.34		2.62	3.48	
	2400	Horizontal joint connector		200	.040		1.05	1.34		2.39	3.23	
	2500	Corner cap		200	.040		1.28	1.34		2.62	3.48	
	2700	H - moulding		480	.017		.76	.56		1.32	1.70	
700	0010	**STEEL ROOFING** on steel frame, corrugated or ribbed, 30 ga galv	G-3	1,100	.029	S.F.	.77	.82		1.59	2.12	**700**
	0100	28 ga		1,050	.030		.81	.86		1.67	2.22	
	0300	26 ga		1,000	.032		.90	.90		1.80	2.39	
	0400	24 ga		950	.034		1.05	.95		2	2.63	

THERMAL & MOISTURE PROTECTION 7

07400 | Roofing & Siding Panels

07410 | Metal Roof & Wall Panels

			CREW	DAILY OUTPUT	LABOR-HOURS	UNIT	MAT.	LABOR	EQUIP.	TOTAL	TOTAL INCL O&P	
700	0600	Colored, 28 ga	G-3	1,050	.030	S.F.	1.08	.86		1.94	2.52	700
	0700	26 ga		1,000	.032		1.15	.90		2.05	2.67	
	0710	Flat profile, 1-3/4" standing seams, 10" wide, standard finish. 26 ga		1,000	.032		2.37	.90		3.27	4.01	
	0715	24 ga		950	.034		2.75	.95		3.70	4.50	
	0720	22 ga		900	.036		3.39	1		4.39	5.30	
	0725	Zinc aluminum alloy finish, 26 ga		1,000	.032		1.85	.90		2.75	3.44	
	0730	24 ga		950	.034		2.21	.95		3.16	3.90	
	0735	22 ga		900	.036		2.54	1		3.54	4.35	
	0740	12" wide, standard finish, 26 ga		1,000	.032		2.36	.90		3.26	4	
	0745	24 ga		950	.034		2.74	.95		3.69	4.48	
	0750	Zinc aluminum alloy finish, 26 ga		1,000	.032		1.75	.90		2.65	3.33	
	0755	24 ga		950	.034		2.09	.95		3.04	3.77	
	0840	Flat profile, 1" x 3/8" batten, 12" wide, standard finish, 26 ga		1,000	.032		1.84	.90		2.74	3.42	
	0845	24 ga		950	.034		2.16	.95		3.11	3.85	
	0850	22 ga		900	.036		2.60	1		3.60	4.42	
	0855	Zinc aluminum alloy finish, 26 ga		1,000	.032		1.56	.90		2.46	3.12	
	0860	24 ga		950	.034		1.73	.95		2.68	3.37	
	0865	22 ga		900	.036		2.01	1		3.01	3.77	
	0870	16-1/2" wide, standard finish, 24 ga		950	.034		2.19	.95		3.14	3.88	
	0875	22 ga		900	.036		2.46	1		3.46	4.27	
	0880	Zinc aluminum alloy finish, 24 ga		950	.034		1.65	.95		2.60	3.29	
	0885	22 ga		900	.036		1.83	1		2.83	3.57	
	0890	Flat profile, 2" x 2" batten, 12" wide, standard finish, 26 ga		1,000	.032		2.11	.90		3.01	3.72	
	0895	24 ga		950	.034		2.52	.95		3.47	4.24	
	0900	22 ga		900	.036		3.09	1		4.09	4.96	
	0905	Zinc aluminum alloy finish, 26 ga		1,000	.032		1.74	.90		2.64	3.31	
	0910	24 ga		950	.034		1.88	.95		2.83	3.54	
	0915	22 ga		900	.036		2.32	1		3.32	4.11	
	0920	16-1/2" wide, standard finish, 24 ga		950	.034		2.34	.95		3.29	4.04	
	0925	22 ga		900	.036		2.72	1		3.72	4.55	
	0930	Zinc aluminum alloy finish, 24 ga		950	.034		1.85	.95		2.80	3.51	
	0935	22 ga		900	.036		2.11	1		3.11	3.88	
	1200	Ridge, galvanized, 10" wide		800	.040	L.F.	1.73	1.13		2.86	3.65	
	1210	20" wide		750	.043	"	3.04	1.20		4.24	5.20	

07420 | Plastic Roof & Wall Panels

			CREW	DAILY OUTPUT	LABOR-HOURS	UNIT	MAT.	LABOR	EQUIP.	TOTAL	TOTAL INCL O&P	
770	0010	**FIBERGLASS** Corrugated panels, roofing, 8 oz per SF	G-3	1,000	.032	S.F.	2.24	.90		3.14	3.86	770
	0100	12 oz per SF		1,000	.032		5.15	.90		6.05	7.05	
	0300	Corrugated siding, 6 oz per SF		880	.036		1.94	1.03		2.97	3.72	
	0400	8 oz per SF		880	.036		2.24	1.03		3.27	4.05	
	0500	Fire retardant		880	.036		3.09	1.03		4.12	4.99	
	0600	12 oz. siding, textured		880	.036		5.05	1.03		6.08	7.15	
	0700	Fire retardant		880	.036		4.14	1.03		5.17	6.15	
	0900	Flat panels, 6 oz per SF, clear or colors		880	.036		1.73	1.03		2.76	3.49	
	1100	Fire retardant, class A		880	.036		3	1.03		4.03	4.89	
	1300	8 oz per SF, clear or colors		880	.036		2.24	1.03		3.27	4.05	
	1700	Sandwich panels, fiberglass, 1-9/16" thick, panels to 20 SF		180	.178		21.50	5		26.50	32	
	1900	As above, but 2-3/4" thick, panels to 100 SF		265	.121		16.10	3.41		19.51	23	

07440 | Faced Panels

			CREW	DAILY OUTPUT	LABOR-HOURS	UNIT	MAT.	LABOR	EQUIP.	TOTAL	TOTAL INCL O&P	
200	0010	**EXPOSED AGGREGATE PANELS**										200
	1400	Fiberglass polymer back-up,										
	1500	Small size aggregate	F-3	445	.090	S.F.	4.62	2.66	1.16	8.44	10.50	
	1600	Medium size aggregate		445	.090		5.20	2.66	1.16	9.02	11.10	
	1700	Large size aggregate		445	.090		5.35	2.66	1.16	9.17	11.30	

Vertical side text: 7 — THERMAL & MOISTURE PROTECTION

216 **Important: See the Reference Section for critical supporting data - Reference Nos., Crews, & City Cost Indexes**

07460 | Siding

		CREW	DAILY OUTPUT	LABOR-HOURS	UNIT	2001 BARE COSTS				TOTAL INCL O&P
						MAT.	LABOR	EQUIP.	TOTAL	
100 0010	**ALUMINUM SIDING** .019" thick, on steel construction, natural	G-3	775	.041	S.F.	.66	1.16		1.82	2.54 **100**
0100	Painted		775	.041		.86	1.16		2.02	2.76
0400	Farm type, .021" thick on steel frame, natural		775	.041		.77	1.16		1.93	2.66
0600	Painted		775	.041		.94	1.16		2.10	2.84
0700	Industrial type, corrugated, on steel, .024" thick, mill		775	.041		.97	1.16		2.13	2.88
0900	Painted		775	.041		1.17	1.16		2.33	3.10
1000	.032" thick, mill		775	.041		1.33	1.16		2.49	3.27
1200	Painted		775	.041		1.67	1.16		2.83	3.65
1300	V-Beam, on steel frame, .032" thick, mill		775	.041		1.53	1.16		2.69	3.49
1500	Painted		775	.041		1.80	1.16		2.96	3.79
1600	.040" thick, mill		775	.041		1.86	1.16		3.02	3.86
1800	Painted		775	.041		2.19	1.16		3.35	4.22
1900	.050" thick, mill		775	.041		2.20	1.16		3.36	4.23
2100	Painted		775	.041		2.63	1.16		3.79	4.70
2200	Ribbed, 3" profile, on steel frame, .032" thick, natural		775	.041		1.38	1.16		2.54	3.33
2400	Painted		775	.041		1.68	1.16		2.84	3.66
2500	.040" thick, natural		775	.041		1.63	1.16		2.79	3.60
2700	Painted		775	.041		1.91	1.16		3.07	3.91
2750	.050" thick, natural		775	.041		1.88	1.16		3.04	3.88
2760	Painted		775	.041		2.14	1.16		3.30	4.16
3300	For siding on wood frame, deduct from above	↓	2,800	.011	↓	.06	.32		.38	.57
3400	Screw fasteners, aluminum, self tapping, neoprene washer, 1"				M	125			125	138
3600	Stitch screws, self tapping, with neoprene washer, 5/8"				"	94			94	104
3630	Flashing, sidewall, .032" thick	G-3	800	.040	L.F.	1.79	1.13		2.92	3.72
3650	End wall, .040" thick		800	.040		2.09	1.13		3.22	4.05
3670	Closure strips, corrugated, .032" thick		800	.040		.53	1.13		1.66	2.33
3680	Ribbed, 4" or 8", .032" thick		800	.040		.53	1.13		1.66	2.33
3690	V-beam, .040" thick	↓	800	.040	↓	.72	1.13		1.85	2.54
3800	Horizontal, colored clapboard, 8" wide, plain	2 Carp	515	.031	S.F.	1.23	.91		2.14	2.77
3900	Insulated		515	.031		1.52	.91		2.43	3.09
4000	Vertical board & batten, colored, non-insulated	↓	515	.031		1.08	.91		1.99	2.61
4200	For simulated wood design, add				↓	.08			.08	.09
4300	Corners for above, outside	2 Carp	515	.031	V.L.F.	1.70	.91		2.61	3.29
4500	Inside corners	"	515	.031	"	.96	.91		1.87	2.48
4600	Sandwich panels, 1" insulation, single story	G-3	395	.081	S.F.	4.61	2.28		6.89	8.60
4900	Multi-story	"	345	.093		6.45	2.62		9.07	11.15
5100	For baked enamel finish 1 side, add				↓	.24			.24	.26
5200	See also Metal Facing Panels, division 07410-690									
300 0010	**FASCIA** Aluminum, reverse board and batten,									**300**
0100	.032" thick, colored, no furring included	1 Shee	145	.055	S.F.	2.14	1.85		3.99	5.20
0300	Steel, galv and enameled, stock, no furring, long panels		145	.055		2.23	1.85		4.08	5.30
0600	Short panels	↓	115	.070	↓	3.38	2.33		5.71	7.30
500 0010	**FIBER CEMENT SIDING**									**500**
0020	Lap siding, 5/16" thick, 6" wide, smooth texture	2 Carp	415	.039	S.F.	.93	1.12		2.05	2.79
0025	Woodgrain texture		415	.039		.93	1.12		2.05	2.79
0030	7-1/2" wide, smooth texture		425	.038		.88	1.10		1.98	2.69
0035	Woodgrain texture		425	.038		.88	1.10		1.98	2.69
0040	8" wide, smooth texture		425	.038		.87	1.10		1.97	2.68
0045	Roughsawn texture		425	.038		.87	1.10		1.97	2.68
0050	9-1/2" wide, smooth texture		440	.036		.84	1.06		1.90	2.59
0055	Woodgrain texture		440	.036		.84	1.06		1.90	2.59
0060	12" wide, smooth texture		455	.035		.81	1.02		1.83	2.50
0065	Woodgrain texture		455	.035		.81	1.02		1.83	2.50
0070	Panel siding, 5/16" thick, smooth texture		750	.021		.73	.62		1.35	1.77
0075	Stucco texture		750	.021		.73	.62		1.35	1.77
0080	Grooved woodgrain texture	↓	750	.021	↓	.73	.62		1.35	1.77

			DAILY	LABOR-			2001 BARE COSTS			TOTAL	
07460		**Siding**	CREW	OUTPUT	HOURS	UNIT	MAT.	LABOR	EQUIP.	TOTAL	INCL O&P
500	0085	V - grooved woodgrain texture	2 Carp	750	.021	S.F.	.73	.62		1.35	1.77	**500**
	0090	Wood starter strip	↓	400	.040	L.F.	.18	1.17		1.35	2.02
600	0010	**VINYL SIDING** Solid PVC panels, 8" to 10" wide, plain	1 Carp	255	.031	S.F.	.69	.91		1.60	2.19	**600**
	0100	with 3/8" insulation		255	.031		.76	.91		1.67	2.27
	0200	Soffit and fascia		205	.039	↓	1.40	1.14		2.54	3.32
	0300	Window and door trim moldings		185	.043	L.F.	.36	1.26		1.62	2.37
	0500	Corner posts, outside corner		205	.039		1.15	1.14		2.29	3.05
	0600	Inside corner	↓	205	.039	↓	.59	1.14		1.73	2.43
750	0010	**SOFFIT** Aluminum, residential, stock units, .020" thick	1 Carp	210	.038	S.F.	.99	1.11		2.10	2.83	**750**
	0100	Baked enamel on steel, 16 or 18 gauge		105	.076		3.74	2.22		5.96	7.60
	0300	Polyvinyl chloride, white, solid		230	.035		.65	1.01		1.66	2.31
	0400	Perforated	↓	230	.035		.65	1.01		1.66	2.31
	0500	For colors, add				↓	.06			.06	.07
800	0010	**STEEL SIDING**, Beveled, vinyl coated, 8" wide, including fasteners	1 Carp	265	.030	S.F.	1.15	.88		2.03	2.65	**800**
	0050	10" wide	"	275	.029		1.23	.85		2.08	2.68
	0080	Galv, corrugated or ribbed, on steel frame, 30 gauge	G-3	800	.040		.77	1.13		1.90	2.60
	0100	28 gauge		795	.040		.81	1.14		1.95	2.65
	0300	26 gauge		790	.041		.88	1.14		2.02	2.74
	0400	24 gauge		785	.041		1.06	1.15		2.21	2.95
	0600	22 gauge		770	.042		1.21	1.17		2.38	3.15
	0700	Colored, corrugated/ribbed, on steel frame, 10 yr fnsh, 28 ga.		800	.040		1.11	1.13		2.24	2.97
	0900	26 gauge		795	.040		1.06	1.14		2.20	2.93
	1000	24 gauge		790	.041		1.24	1.14		2.38	3.13
	1020	20 gauge		785	.041		1.42	1.15		2.57	3.34
	1200	Factory sandwich panel, 26 ga., 1" insulation, galvanized		380	.084		2.58	2.37		4.95	6.55
	1300	Colored 1 side		380	.084		3.61	2.37		5.98	7.65
	1500	Galvanized 2 sides		380	.084		4.48	2.37		6.85	8.60
	1600	Colored 2 sides		380	.084		4.64	2.37		7.01	8.80
	1800	Acrylic paint face, regular paint liner	↓	380	.084		3.50	2.37		5.87	7.55
	1900	For 2" thick polystyrene, add					.54			.54	.59
	2000	22 ga, galv, 2" insulation, baked enamel exterior	G-3	360	.089		6.85	2.51		9.36	11.45
	2100	P.V.F. exterior finish	"	360	.089	↓	7.20	2.51		9.71	11.85
900	0010	**WOOD SIDING, BOARDS**										**900**
	3200	Wood, cedar bevel, A grade, 1/2" x 6"	1 Carp	250	.032	S.F.	1.65	.93		2.58	3.28
	3300	1/2" x 8"		275	.029		1.90	.85		2.75	3.42
	3500	3/4" x 10", clear grade		300	.027		3.49	.78		4.27	5.05
	3600	"B" grade		300	.027		2.80	.78		3.58	4.30
	3800	Cedar, rough sawn, 1" x 4", A grade, natural		240	.033		2.67	.97		3.64	4.46
	3900	Stained		240	.033		3.01	.97		3.98	4.83
	4100	1" x 12", board & batten, #3 & Btr., natural		260	.031		2.02	.90		2.92	3.62
	4200	Stained		260	.031		2.35	.90		3.25	3.99
	4400	1" x 8" channel siding, #3 & Btr., natural		250	.032		1.96	.93		2.89	3.62
	4500	Stained		250	.032		2.23	.93		3.16	3.91
	4700	Redwood, clear, beveled, vertical grain, 1/2" x 4"		200	.040		3.12	1.17		4.29	5.25
	4750	1/2" x 6"		225	.036		2.62	1.04		3.66	4.50
	4800	1/2" x 8"		250	.032		2.12	.93		3.05	3.79
	5000	3/4" x 10"		300	.027		3.46	.78		4.24	5.05
	5200	Channel siding, 1" x 10", B grade	↓	285	.028		2.23	.82		3.05	3.73
	5250	Redwood, T&G boards, B grade, 1" x 4"	2 Carp	300	.053		2.66	1.55		4.21	5.35
	5270	1" x 8"	"	375	.043		2.29	1.24		3.53	4.47
	5400	White pine, rough sawn, 1" x 8", natural	1 Carp	275	.029		.67	.85		1.52	2.07
	5500	Stained	"	275	.029	↓	.99	.85		1.84	2.42
950	0010	**WOOD PRODUCT SIDING**										**950**
	0030	Lap siding, hardboard, 7/16" x 8", primed									

07400 | Roofing & Siding Panels

07460 | Siding

			CREW	DAILY OUTPUT	LABOR-HOURS	UNIT	2001 BARE COSTS				TOTAL INCL O&P	
							MAT.	LABOR	EQUIP.	TOTAL		
950	0051	Wood grain texture finish	L-2	552	.029	S.F.	1.04	.74		1.78	2.30	950
	0100	Panels, 7/16" thick, smooth, textured or grooved, primed	2 Carp	700	.023		.73	.67		1.40	1.84	
	0200	Stained		700	.023		.88	.67		1.55	2.01	
	0700	Particle board, overlaid, 3/8" thick		750	.021		.63	.62		1.25	1.66	
	0900	Plywood, medium density overlaid, 3/8" thick		750	.021		1.02	.62		1.64	2.09	
	1000	1/2" thick		700	.023		1.19	.67		1.86	2.35	
	1100	3/4" thick		650	.025		1.56	.72		2.28	2.84	
	1600	Texture 1-11, cedar, 5/8" thick, natural		675	.024		1.53	.69		2.22	2.76	
	1700	Factory stained		675	.024		1.74	.69		2.43	2.99	
	1900	Texture 1-11, fir, 5/8" thick, natural		675	.024		.86	.69		1.55	2.03	
	2000	Factory stained		675	.024		1.08	.69		1.77	2.27	
	2050	Texture 1-11, S.Y.P., 5/8" thick, natural		675	.024		.81	.69		1.50	1.97	
	2100	Factory stained		675	.024		.88	.69		1.57	2.05	
	2200	Rough sawn cedar, 3/8" thick, natural		675	.024		1.08	.69		1.77	2.27	
	2300	Factory stained		675	.024		1.20	.69		1.89	2.40	
	2500	Rough sawn fir, 3/8" thick, natural		675	.024		.58	.69		1.27	1.72	
	2600	Factory stained		675	.024		.65	.69		1.34	1.80	
	2800	Redwood, textured siding, 5/8" thick		675	.024		1.80	.69		2.49	3.06	
	3000	Polyvinyl chloride coated, 3/8" thick	▼	750	.021	▼	.88	.62		1.50	1.94	

07500 | Membrane Roofing

07510 | Built-Up Bituminous Roofing

			CREW	DAILY OUTPUT	LABOR-HOURS	UNIT	2001 BARE COSTS				TOTAL INCL O&P	
							MAT.	LABOR	EQUIP.	TOTAL		
050	0010	**ASPHALT** Coated felt, #30, 2 sq per roll, not mopped	1 Rofc	58	.138	Sq.	4.92	3.54		8.46	11.50	050
	0200	#15, 4 sq per roll, plain or perforated, not mopped		58	.138		2.13	3.54		5.67	8.45	
	0300	Roll roofing, smooth, #65		15	.533		12	13.70		25.70	36.50	
	0500	#90		15	.533		14.85	13.70		28.55	40	
	0520	Mineralized		15	.533		14.75	13.70		28.45	40	
	0540	D.C. (Double coverage), 19" selvage edge	▼	10	.800	▼	27	20.50		47.50	65.50	
	0580	Adhesive (lap cement)				Gal.	3.68			3.68	4.05	
	0600	Steep, flat or dead level asphalt, 10 ton lots, bulk				Ton	260			260	286	
	0800	Packaged				"	345			345	380	
300	0010	**BUILT-UP ROOFING** R07510 -020										300
	0120	Asphalt flood coat with gravel/slag surfacing, not including										
	0140	Insulation, flashing or wood nailers										
	0200	Asphalt base sheet, 3 plies #15 asphalt felt, mopped	G-1	22	2.545	Sq.	41	61.50	15.15	117.65	167	
	0350	On nailable decks		21	2.667		44.50	64.50	15.85	124.85	176	
	0500	4 plies #15 asphalt felt, mopped		20	2.800		57.50	67.50	16.65	141.65	197	
	0550	On nailable decks		19	2.947		51.50	71	17.55	140.05	198	
	0700	Coated glass base sheet, 2 plies glass (type IV), mopped		22	2.545		45	61.50	15.15	121.65	171	
	0850	3 plies glass, mopped		20	2.800		53	67.50	16.65	137.15	193	
	0950	On nailable decks		19	2.947		50	71	17.55	138.55	196	
	1100	4 plies glass fiber felt (type IV), mopped		20	2.800		64	67.50	16.65	148.15	205	
	1150	On nailable decks		19	2.947		58.50	71	17.55	147.05	205	
	1200	Coated & saturated base sheet, 3 plies #15 asph. felt, mopped		20	2.800		47.50	67.50	16.65	131.65	186	
	1250	On nailable decks		19	2.947		44.50	71	17.55	133.05	190	
	1300	4 plies #15 asphalt felt, mopped	▼	22	2.545	▼	54	61.50	15.15	130.65	181	
	2000	Asphalt flood coat, smooth surface										

07510 | Built-Up Bituminous Roofing

			CREW	DAILY OUTPUT	LABOR-HOURS	UNIT	2001 BARE COSTS				TOTAL INCL O&P
							MAT.	LABOR	EQUIP.	TOTAL	
300	2200	Asphalt base sheet & 3 plies #15 asphalt felt, mopped R07510-020	G-1	24	2.333	Sq.	42.50	56	13.90	112.40	158	300
	2400	On nailable decks		23	2.435		39.50	58.50	14.50	112.50	160	
	2600	4 plies #15 asphalt felt, mopped		24	2.333		49.50	56	13.90	119.40	166	
	2700	On nailable decks		23	2.435		46.50	58.50	14.50	119.50	168	
	2900	Coated glass fiber base sheet, mopped, and 2 plies of	G-1	25	2.240	Sq.	40	54	13.35	107.35	151	
	2910	glass fiber felt (type IV)										
	3100	On nailable decks		24	2.333		37.50	56	13.90	107.40	153	
	3200	3 plies, mopped		23	2.435		48	58.50	14.50	121	169	
	3300	On nailable decks		22	2.545		45	61.50	15.15	121.65	171	
	3800	4 plies glass fiber felt (type IV), mopped		23	2.435		56	58.50	14.50	129	178	
	3900	On nailable decks		22	2.545		53.50	61.50	15.15	130.15	180	
	4000	Coated & saturated base sheet, 3 plies #15 asph. felt, mopped		24	2.333		42	56	13.90	111.90	158	
	4200	On nailable decks		23	2.435		39.50	58.50	14.50	112.50	160	
	4300	4 plies #15 organic felt, mopped		22	2.545		49	61.50	15.15	125.65	176	
	4500	Coal tar pitch with gravel/slag surfacing										
	4600	4 plies #15 tarred felt, mopped	G-1	21	2.667	Sq.	101	64.50	15.85	181.35	238	
	4800	3 plies glass fiber felt (type IV), mopped	"	19	2.947	"	83	71	17.55	171.55	232	
	5000	Coated glass fiber base sheet, and 2 plies of										
	5010	glass fiber felt, (type IV), mopped	G-1	19	2.947	Sq.	83.50	71	17.55	172.05	233	
	5300	On nailable decks		18	3.111		74	75	18.50	167.50	231	
	5600	4 plies glass fiber felt (type IV), mopped		21	2.667		114	64.50	15.85	194.35	252	
	5800	On nailable decks		20	2.800		104	67.50	16.65	188.15	249	
400	0010	CANTS 4" x 4", treated timber, cut diagonally	1 Rofc	325	.025	L.F.	1.24	.63		1.87	2.45	400
	0100	Foamglass		325	.025		1.99	.63		2.62	3.28	
	0300	Mineral or fiber, trapezoidal, 1"x 4" x 48"		325	.025		.17	.63		.80	1.28	
	0400	1-1/2" x 5-5/8" x 48"		325	.025		.29	.63		.92	1.41	
700	0010	FELT Glass fibered, #15, no mopping	1 Rofc	58	.138	Sq.	3.38	3.54		6.92	9.80	700
	0300	Base sheet, #45, channel vented		58	.138		16.50	3.54		20.04	24.50	
	0400	#50, coated		58	.138		8.50	3.54		12.04	15.45	
	0500	Cap, mineral surfaced		58	.138		16.50	3.54		20.04	24.50	
	0600	Flashing membrane, #65		16	.500		22	12.85		34.85	46	
	0800	Coal tar fibered, #15, no mopping		58	.138		7.50	3.54		11.04	14.35	
	0900	Asphalt felt, #15, 4 sq per roll, no mopping CN		58	.138		2.13	3.54		5.67	8.45	
	1100	#30, 2 sq per roll		58	.138		4.92	3.54		8.46	11.50	
	1200	Double coated, #33		58	.138		5.90	3.54		9.44	12.60	
	1400	#40, base sheet		58	.138		6.70	3.54		10.24	13.50	
	1450	Coated and saturated		58	.138		6.45	3.54		9.99	13.20	
	1500	Tarred felt, organic, #15, 4 sq rolls		58	.138		7.80	3.54		11.34	14.70	
	1550	#30, 2 sq roll		58	.138		15.60	3.54		19.14	23.50	
	1700	Add for mopping above felts, per ply, asphalt, 24 lb per sq	G-1	192	.292		4.12	7.05	1.74	12.91	18.55	
	1800	Coal tar mopping, 30 lb per sq		186	.301		8.50	7.25	1.79	17.54	24	
	1900	Flood coat, with asphalt, 60 lb per sq		60	.933		10.30	22.50	5.55	38.35	56	
	2000	With coal tar, 75 lb per sq		56	1		21.50	24	5.95	51.45	71.50	

07520 | Cold Applied Bituminous Roofing

			CREW	DAILY OUTPUT	LABOR-HOURS	UNIT	MAT.	LABOR	EQUIP.	TOTAL	TOTAL INCL O&P
200	0010	COLD APPLIED 3-ply system (components listed below)	G-5	50	.800	Sq.		18.75	3.63	22.38	36	200
	0100	Spunbond poly. fabric, 1.35 oz/SY, 36"W, 10.8 Sq/roll				Ea.	123			123	135	
	0200	49" wide, 14.6 Sq./roll					169			169	186	
	0300	2.10 oz./S.Y., 36" wide, 10.8 Sq./roll					185			185	203	
	0400	49" wide, 14.6 Sq./roll					250			250	275	
	0500	Base & finish coat, 3 gal./Sq., 5 gal./can				Gal.	3.25			3.25	3.58	
	0600	Coating, ceramic granules, 1/2 Sq./bag				Ea.	11.50			11.50	12.65	
	0700	Aluminum, 2 gal./Sq.				Gal.	9.25			9.25	10.20	
	0800	Emulsion, fibered or non-fibered, 4 gal./Sq.				"	4.25			4.25	4.68	

Important: See the Reference Section for critical supporting data - Reference Nos., Crews, & City Cost Indexes

07530 | Elastomeric Membrane Roofing

		CREW	DAILY OUTPUT	LABOR-HOURS	UNIT	2001 BARE COSTS				TOTAL INCL O&P
						MAT.	LABOR	EQUIP.	TOTAL	
350	0010	**ELASTOMERIC ROOFING**									**350**
	0100	For Elastomeric waterproofing, see division 07130-200									
	0110	Acrylic rubber, fluid applied, 20 mils thick	G-5	2,000	.020	S.F.	1.80	.47	.09	2.36	2.89
	0120	50 mils, reinforced		1,200	.033		2.80	.78	.15	3.73	4.59
	0130	For walking surface, add	↓	900	.044		.85	1.04	.20	2.09	2.95
	0300	Hypalon neoprene, fluid applied, 20 mil thick, not-reinforced	G-1	1,135	.049		2.05	1.19	.29	3.53	4.62
	0600	Non-woven polyester, reinforced		960	.058		2.07	1.41	.35	3.83	5.05
	0700	5 coat neoprene deck, 60 mil thick, under 10,000 SF		325	.172		4.56	4.15	1.03	9.74	13.30
	0900	Over 10,000 SF		625	.090		4.25	2.16	.53	6.94	9
	1300	Vinyl plastic traffic deck, sprayed, 2 to 4 mils thick		625	.090		1.33	2.16	.53	4.02	5.75
	1500	Vinyl and neoprene membrane traffic deck	↓	1,550	.036	↓	1.41	.87	.22	2.50	3.29
	1600	Polyurethane spray-on with 20 mil silicone rubber coating applied									
	1700	1″ thick, R7, minimum	G-2	875	.027	S.F.	1.34	.67	.27	2.28	2.79
	1800	Maximim		805	.030		1.80	.73	.29	2.82	3.42
	1900	2″ thick, R14, minimum		685	.035		1.90	.86	.34	3.10	3.78
	2000	Maximum		575	.042		2.41	1.02	.41	3.84	4.67
	2100	3″ thick, R21, minimum		500	.048		2.50	1.17	.47	4.14	5.05
	2200	Maximum	↓	440	.055	↓	3.20	1.33	.53	5.06	6.15
800	0010	**SINGLE-PLY MEMBRANE**									**800**
	0800	Chlorosulfonated polyethylene-hypalon (CSPE), 45 mils,									
	0900	0.29 P.S.F., fully adhered	G-5	26	1.538	Sq.	123	36	7	166	206
	1100	Loose-laid & ballasted with stone (10 P.S.F.)		51	.784		130	18.40	3.56	151.96	178
	1200	Partially adhered with fastening strips		35	1.143		125	27	5.20	157.20	190
	1300	Plates with adhesive attachment	↓	35	1.143	↓	123	27	5.20	155.20	188
	3500	Ethylene propylene diene monomer (EPDM), 45 mils, 0.28 P.S.F.									
	3600	Loose-laid & ballasted with stone (10 P.S.F.)	G-5	51	.784	Sq.	63.50	18.40	3.56	85.46	105
	3700	Partially adhered		35	1.143		55.50	27	5.20	87.70	113
	3800	Fully adhered with adhesive	↓	26	1.538	↓	80.50	36	7	123.50	158
	4500	60 mils, 0.40 P.S.F.									
	4600	Loose-laid & ballasted with stone (10 P.S.F.)	G-5	51	.784	Sq.	76	18.40	3.56	97.96	119
	4700	Partially adhered		35	1.143		67	27	5.20	99.20	125
	4800	Fully adhered with adhesive	↓	26	1.538	↓	92	36	7	135	171
	4810	45 mil, .28 PSF, membrane only **CN**					35.50			35.50	39
	4820	60 mil, .40 PSF, membrane only				↓	46			46	50.50
	4850	Seam tape for membrane, 4″ x 100′ roll				Ea.	67.50			67.50	74
	4900	Batten strips, 10′ sections					2.47			2.47	2.72
	4910	Cover tape for batten strips, 6″ x 100′ roll				↓	127			127	140
	4930	Plate anchors				M	124			124	137
	4970	Adhesive for fully adhered systems, 60 S.F./gal.				Gal.	15			15	16.50
	7500	Polyisobutylene (PIB), 100 mils, 0.57 P.S.F.									
	7600	Loose-laid & ballasted with stone/gravel (10 P.S.F.)	G-5	51	.784	Sq.	124	18.40	3.56	145.96	172
	7700	Partially adhered with adhesive		35	1.143		156	27	5.20	188.20	223
	7800	Hot asphalt attachment		35	1.143		148	27	5.20	180.20	215
	7900	Fully adhered with contact cement	↓	26	1.538	↓	161	36	7	204	247
	8200	Polyvinyl chloride (PVC), heat welded seams									
	8700	Reinforced, 48 mils, 0.33 P.S.F.									
	8750	Loose-laid & ballasted with stone/gravel (12 P.S.F.)	G-5	51	.784	Sq.	93.50	18.40	3.56	115.46	138
	8800	Partially adhered with mechanical fasteners		35	1.143		85	27	5.20	117.20	145
	8850	Fully adhered with adhesive	↓	26	1.538	↓	117	36	7	160	198
	8860	Reinforced, 60 mils, .40 P.S.F.									
	8870	Loose-laid & ballasted with stone/gravel (12 P.S.F.)	G-5	51	.784	Sq.	91.50	18.40	3.56	113.46	136
	8880	Partially adhered with mechanical fasteners		35	1.143		83	27	5.20	115.20	143
	8890	Fully adhered with adhesive	↓	26	1.538	↓	115	36	7	158	196

THERMAL & MOISTURE PROTECTION **7**

07550	Modified Bit. Membrane Roofing	CREW	DAILY OUTPUT	LABOR-HOURS	UNIT	2001 BARE COSTS				TOTAL INCL O&P
						MAT.	LABOR	EQUIP.	TOTAL	
500	0010 **MODIFIED BITUMEN ROOFING** R07550-030										500
	0020 Base sheet, #15 glass fiber felt, nailed to deck	1 Rofc	58	.138	Sq.	4.11	3.54		7.65	10.60
	0030 Spot mopped to deck	G-1	295	.190		5.45	4.57	1.13	11.15	15.10
	0040 Fully mopped to deck	"	192	.292		7.50	7.05	1.74	16.29	22.50
	0050 #15 organic felt, nailed to deck	1 Rofc	58	.138		2.86	3.54		6.40	9.25
	0060 Spot mopped to deck	G-1	295	.190		4.19	4.57	1.13	9.89	13.70
	0070 Fully mopped to deck	"	192	.292		6.25	7.05	1.74	15.04	21
	0080 SBS modified, granule surf cap sheet, polyester rein., mopped									
	0600 150 mils	G-1	2,000	.028	S.F.	.44	.67	.17	1.28	1.82
	1100 160 mils		2,000	.028		.62	.67	.17	1.46	2.02
	1500 Glass fiber reinforced, mopped, 160 mils		2,000	.028		.41	.67	.17	1.25	1.79
	1600 Smooth surface cap sheet, mopped, 145 mils		2,100	.027		.41	.64	.16	1.21	1.72
	1700 Smooth surface flashing, 145 mils		1,260	.044		.41	1.07	.26	1.74	2.58
	1800 150 mils		1,260	.044		.40	1.07	.26	1.73	2.57
	1900 Granular surface flashing, 150 mils		1,260	.044		.44	1.07	.26	1.77	2.61
	2000 160 mils		1,260	.044		.62	1.07	.26	1.95	2.81
	2100 APP mod., smooth surf. cap sheet, poly. reinf., torched, 160 mils	G-5	2,100	.019		.40	.45	.09	.94	1.31
	2150 170 mils		2,100	.019		.45	.45	.09	.99	1.37
	2200 Granule surface cap sheet, poly. reinf., torched, 180 mils		2,000	.020		.49	.47	.09	1.05	1.45
	2250 Smooth surface flashing, torched, 160 mils		1,260	.032		.40	.74	.14	1.28	1.88
	2300 170 mils		1,260	.032		.45	.74	.14	1.33	1.94
	2350 Granule surface flashing, torched, 180 mils		1,260	.032		.49	.74	.14	1.37	1.98
	2400 Fibrated aluminum coating	1 Rofc	3,800	.002		.09	.05		.14	.19

07580	Roll Roofing									
200	0010 **ROLL ROOFING**										200
	0100 Asphalt, mineral surface									
	0200 1 ply #15 organic felt, 1 ply mineral surfaced									
	0300 Selvage roofing, lap 19", nailed & mopped	G-1	27	2.074	Sq.	35.50	50	12.35	97.85	139
	0400 3 plies glass fiber felt (type IV), 1 ply mineral surfaced									
	0500 Selvage roofing, lapped 19", mopped	G-1	25	2.240	Sq.	54	54	13.35	121.35	166
	0600 Coated glass fiber base sheet, 2 plies of glass fiber									
	0700 Felt (type IV), 1 ply mineral surfaced selvage									
	0800 Roofing, lapped 19", mopped	G-1	25	2.240	Sq.	59	54	13.35	126.35	172
	0900 On nailable decks	"	24	2.333	"	55	56	13.90	124.90	172
	1000 3 plies glass fiber felt (type III), 1 ply mineral surfaced									
	1100 Selvage roofing, lapped 19", mopped	G-1	25	2.240	Sq.	54	54	13.35	121.35	166

07590	Roof Maintenance & Repairs									
300	0010 **ROOF COATINGS** Asphalt CN				Gal.	2.95			2.95	3.25	300
	0200 Asphalt base, fibered aluminum coating					9.20			9.20	10.10
	0300 Asphalt primer, 5 gallon					3.27			3.27	3.60
	0600 Coal tar pitch, 200 lb. barrels				Ton	565			565	625
	0700 Tar roof cement, 5 gal. lots				Gal.	5.85			5.85	6.45
	0800 Glass fibered roof & patching cement, 5 gallon				"	3.50			3.50	3.85
	0900 Reinforcing glass membrane, 450 S.F./roll				Ea.	45.50			45.50	50
	1000 Neoprene roof coating, 5 gal, 2 gal/sq				Gal.	21			21	23
	1100 Roof patch & flashing cement, 5 gallon					15.95			15.95	17.55
	1200 Roof resaturant, glass fibered, 3 gal/sq					7.30			7.30	8.05
	1300 Mineral rubber, 3 gal/sq					4.71			4.71	5.20

Important: See the Reference Section for critical supporting data - Reference Nos., Crews, & City Cost Indexes

7 THERMAL & MOISTURE PROTECTION

07610 | Sheet Metal Roofing

		CREW	DAILY OUTPUT	LABOR-HOURS	UNIT	MAT.	LABOR	EQUIP.	TOTAL	TOTAL INCL O&P	
						2001 BARE COSTS					
300	0010	**COPPER ROOFING** Batten seam, over 10 sq, 16 oz, 130 lb/sq	1 Shee	1.10	7.273	Sq.	405	244		649	820	**300**
	0200	18 oz, 145 lb per sq		1	8		450	268		718	910	
	0300	20 oz, 160 lb per sq		1	8		500	268		768	965	
	0400	Standing seam, over 10 squares, 16 oz, 125 lb per sq		1.30	6.154		390	206		596	745	
	0600	18 oz, 140 lb per sq		1.20	6.667		435	224		659	825	
	0700	20 oz, 150 lb per sq		1.10	7.273		465	244		709	890	
	0900	Flat seam, over 10 squares, 16 oz, 115 lb per sq		1.20	6.667		355	224		579	740	
	1000	20 oz, 145 lb per sq		1.10	7.273		450	244		694	870	
	1200	For abnormal conditions or small areas, add					25%	100%				
	1300	For lead-coated copper, add					25%					
500	0010	**LEAD ROOFING** 5 lb. per SF, batten seam	1 Shee	1.20	6.667	Sq.	385	224		609	765	**500**
	0100	Flat seam	"	1.30	6.154	"	385	206		591	740	
700	0010	**STAINLESS STEEL ROOFING** Type 304, batten seam, 28 gauge	1 Shee	1.20	6.667	Sq.	305	224		529	685	**700**
	0100	26 gauge	"	1.15	6.957		380	233		613	780	
	0200	For standing seam construction, deduct					2%					
	0500	For flat seam construction, deduct					3%					
	0800	For lead or terne coated stainless, 28 gauge, add					70			70	77	
	0900	For 26 gauge, add					92.50			92.50	102	
900	0010	**ZINC** Copper alloy roofing, batten seam, .020" thick	1 Shee	1.20	6.667	Sq.	520	224		744	915	**900**
	0100	.027" thick		1.15	6.957		630	233		863	1,050	
	0300	.032" thick		1.10	7.273		710	244		954	1,150	
	0400	.040" thick		1.05	7.619		835	256		1,091	1,325	
	0600	For standing seam construction, deduct					2%					
	0700	For flat seam construction, deduct					3%					

07650 | Flexible Flashing

		CREW	DAILY OUTPUT	LABOR-HOURS	UNIT	MAT.	LABOR	EQUIP.	TOTAL	TOTAL INCL O&P	
600	0010	**FLASHING** Aluminum, mill finish, .013" thick	1 Shee	145	.055	S.F.	.35	1.85		2.20	3.25	**600**
	0030	.016" thick		145	.055		.51	1.85		2.36	3.42	
	0060	.019" thick		145	.055		.77	1.85		2.62	3.71	
	0100	.032" thick		145	.055		1.04	1.85		2.89	4	
	0200	.040" thick		145	.055		1.45	1.85		3.30	4.46	
	0300	.050" thick		145	.055		1.84	1.85		3.69	4.88	
	0325	Mill finish 5" x 7" step flashing, .016" thick		1,920	.004	Ea.	.10	.14		.24	.33	
	0350	Mill finish 12" x 12" step flashing, .016" thick		1,600	.005	"	.40	.17		.57	.70	
	0400	Painted finish, add				S.F.	.24			.24	.26	
	0500	Fabric-backed 2 sides, .004" thick	1 Shee	330	.024		.93	.81		1.74	2.28	
	0700	.005" thick		330	.024		1.09	.81		1.90	2.46	
	0750	Mastic-backed, self adhesive		460	.017		2.26	.58		2.84	3.39	
	0800	Mastic-coated 2 sides, .004" thick		330	.024		.93	.81		1.74	2.28	
	1000	.005" thick		330	.024		1.09	.81		1.90	2.46	
	1100	.016" thick		330	.024		1.20	.81		2.01	2.58	
	1300	Asphalt flashing cement, 5 gallon				Gal.	3.34			3.34	3.67	
	1600	Copper, 16 oz, sheets, under 1000 lbs.	1 Shee	115	.070	S.F.	2.18	2.33		4.51	6	
	1700	Over 4000 lbs.		155	.052		2.91	1.73		4.64	5.85	
	1900	20 oz sheets, under 1000 lbs.		110	.073		3.90	2.44		6.34	8.05	
	2000	Over 4000 lbs.		145	.055		3.62	1.85		5.47	6.85	
	2200	24 oz sheets, under 1000 lbs.		105	.076		4.69	2.56		7.25	9.10	
	2300	Over 4000 lbs.		135	.059		4.34	1.99		6.33	7.85	
	2500	32 oz sheets, under 1000 lbs.		100	.080		6.20	2.68		8.88	11	
	2600	Over 4000 lbs.		130	.062		5.80	2.06		7.86	9.60	
	2700	W shape for valleys, 16 oz, 24" wide		100	.080	L.F.	5.90	2.68		8.58	10.65	
	2800	Copper, paperbacked 1 side, 2 oz		330	.024	S.F.	.86	.81		1.67	2.21	
	2900	3 oz		330	.024		1.12	.81		1.93	2.49	
	3100	Paperbacked 2 sides, 2 oz		330	.024		.86	.81		1.67	2.21	
	3150	3 oz		330	.024		1.11	.81		1.92	2.48	
	3200	5 oz		330	.024		1.67	.81		2.48	3.10	

THERMAL & MOISTURE PROTECTION 7

07650	Flexible Flashing	CREW	DAILY OUTPUT	LABOR-HOURS	UNIT	2001 BARE COSTS				TOTAL INCL O&P	
						MAT.	LABOR	EQUIP.	TOTAL		
600	3250	7 oz	1 Shee	330	.024	S.F.	2.72	.81		3.53	4.25	600
	3400	Mastic-backed 2 sides, copper, 2 oz		330	.024		1.02	.81		1.83	2.38
	3500	3 oz		330	.024		1.25	.81		2.06	2.64
	3700	5 oz		330	.024		1.85	.81		2.66	3.30
	3800	Fabric-backed 2 sides, copper, 2 oz		330	.024		1.09	.81		1.90	2.46
	4000	3 oz		330	.024		1.40	.81		2.21	2.80
	4100	5 oz		330	.024		1.90	.81		2.71	3.35
	4300	Copper-clad stainless steel, .015" thick, under 500 lbs.		115	.070		3.16	2.33		5.49	7.10
	4400	Over 2000 lbs.		155	.052		3.05	1.73		4.78	6.05
	4600	.018" thick, under 500 lbs.		100	.080		4.18	2.68		6.86	8.75
	4700	Over 2000 lbs.	▼	145	.055	▼	3.06	1.85		4.91	6.25
	4900	Fabric, asphalt-saturated cotton, specification grade	1 Rofc	35	.229	S.Y.	1.93	5.85		7.78	12.20
	5000	Utility grade		35	.229		1.22	5.85		7.07	11.45
	5200	Open-mesh fabric, saturated, 40 oz per S.Y.		35	.229		1.35	5.85		7.20	11.60
	5300	Close-mesh fabric, saturated, 17 oz per S.Y.		35	.229		1.42	5.85		7.27	11.65
	5500	Fiberglass, resin-coated		35	.229		1.16	5.85		7.01	11.40
	5600	Asphalt-coated, 40 oz per S.Y.		35	.229	▼	7.90	5.85		13.75	18.80
	5800	Lead, 2.5 lb. per SF, up to 12" wide		135	.059	S.F.	2.80	1.52		4.32	5.70
	5900	Over 12" wide	▼	135	.059		3.25	1.52		4.77	6.20
	6100	Lead-coated copper, fabric-backed, 2 oz	1 Shee	330	.024		1.41	.81		2.22	2.81
	6200	5 oz		330	.024		1.62	.81		2.43	3.04
	6400	Mastic-backed 2 sides, 2 oz		330	.024		1.10	.81		1.91	2.47
	6500	5 oz		330	.024		1.36	.81		2.17	2.76
	6700	Paperbacked 1 side, 2 oz		330	.024		.95	.81		1.76	2.31
	6800	3 oz		330	.024		1.12	.81		1.93	2.49
	7000	Paperbacked 2 sides, 2 oz		330	.024		.98	.81		1.79	2.34
	7100	5 oz	▼	330	.024		1.56	.81		2.37	2.98
	7300	Polyvinyl chloride, black, .010" thick	1 Rofc	285	.028		.14	.72		.86	1.39
	7400	.020" thick		285	.028		.22	.72		.94	1.48
	7600	.030" thick		285	.028		.29	.72		1.01	1.56
	7700	.056" thick		285	.028		.69	.72		1.41	2
	7900	Black or white for exposed roofs, .060" thick	▼	285	.028	▼	1.55	.72		2.27	2.95
	8060	PVC tape, 5" x 45 mils, for joint covers, 100 L.F./roll				Ea.	79.50			79.50	87
	8100	Rubber, butyl, 1/32" thick	1 Rofc	285	.028	S.F.	.70	.72		1.42	2.01
	8200	1/16" thick		285	.028		1.05	.72		1.77	2.40
	8300	Neoprene, cured, 1/16" thick		285	.028		1.48	.72		2.20	2.87
	8400	1/8" thick	▼	285	.028		2.99	.72		3.71	4.53
	8500	Shower pan, bituminous membrane, 7 oz	1 Shee	155	.052		1.08	1.73		2.81	3.86
	8550	3 ply copper and fabric, 3 oz		155	.052		1.60	1.73		3.33	4.43
	8600	7 oz		155	.052		3.30	1.73		5.03	6.30
	8650	Copper, 16 oz		100	.080		3.05	2.68		5.73	7.50
	8700	Lead on copper and fabric, 5 oz		155	.052		1.62	1.73		3.35	4.45
	8800	7 oz		155	.052		2.87	1.73		4.60	5.85
	8850	Polyvinyl chloride, .030" thick		160	.050		.30	1.68		1.98	2.92
	8900	Stainless steel sheets, 32 ga, .010" thick		155	.052		2.16	1.73		3.89	5.05
	9000	28 ga, .015" thick		155	.052		1.52	1.73		3.25	4.34
	9100	26 ga, .018" thick		155	.052		3.25	1.73		4.98	6.25
	9200	24 ga, .025" thick	▼	155	.052	▼	4.22	1.73		5.95	7.30
	9290	For mechanically keyed flashing, add					40%				
	9300	Stainless steel, paperbacked 2 sides, .005" thick	1 Shee	330	.024	S.F.	1.87	.81		2.68	3.32
	9400	Terne coated stainless steel, .015" thick, 28 ga		155	.052		4.05	1.73		5.78	7.15
	9500	.018" thick, 26 ga		155	.052		4.57	1.73		6.30	7.70
	9600	Zinc and copper alloy (brass), .020" thick		155	.052		3.26	1.73		4.99	6.25
	9700	.027" thick		155	.052		4.37	1.73		6.10	7.50
	9800	.032" thick		155	.052		5.10	1.73		6.83	8.25
	9900	.040" thick	▼	155	.052	▼	6.20	1.73		7.93	9.50

7

THERMAL & MOISTURE PROTECTION

07710 | Manufactured Roof Specialties

		CREW	DAILY OUTPUT	LABOR-HOURS	UNIT	MAT.	LABOR	EQUIP.	TOTAL	TOTAL INCL O&P	
						2001 BARE COSTS					
400	0010	**DOWNSPOUTS** Aluminum 2" x 3", .020" thick, embossed	1 Shee	190	.042	L.F.	.74	1.41		2.15	2.99	400
	0100	Enameled		190	.042		.90	1.41		2.31	3.17	
	0300	Enameled, .024" thick, 2" x 3"		180	.044		1.09	1.49		2.58	3.50	
	0400	3" x 4"		140	.057		1.57	1.92		3.49	4.69	
	0600	Round, corrugated aluminum, 3" diameter, .020" thick		190	.042		.79	1.41		2.20	3.05	
	0700	4" diameter, .025" thick		140	.057		1.51	1.92		3.43	4.62	
	0900	Wire strainer, round, 2" diameter		155	.052	Ea.	1.75	1.73		3.48	4.60	
	1000	4" diameter		155	.052		1.82	1.73		3.55	4.67	
	1200	Rectangular, perforated, 2" x 3"		145	.055		2.15	1.85		4	5.25	
	1300	3" x 4"		145	.055		3.10	1.85		4.95	6.25	
	1500	Copper, round, 16 oz., stock, 2" diameter		190	.042	L.F.	4.11	1.41		5.52	6.70	
	1600	3" diameter		190	.042		3.91	1.41		5.32	6.50	
	1800	4" diameter		145	.055		4.69	1.85		6.54	8	
	1900	5" diameter		130	.062		6.55	2.06		8.61	10.40	
	2100	Rectangular, corrugated copper, stock, 2" x 3"		190	.042		3.18	1.41		4.59	5.70	
	2200	3" x 4"		145	.055		4.73	1.85		6.58	8.05	
	2400	Rectangular, plain copper, stock, 2" x 3"		190	.042		4.78	1.41		6.19	7.45	
	2500	3" x 4"		145	.055		6.30	1.85		8.15	9.75	
	2700	Wire strainers, rectangular, 2" x 3"		145	.055	Ea.	2.80	1.85		4.65	5.95	
	2800	3" x 4"		145	.055		4.44	1.85		6.29	7.75	
	3000	Round, 2" diameter		145	.055		2.63	1.85		4.48	5.75	
	3100	3" diameter		145	.055		3.67	1.85		5.52	6.90	
	3300	4" diameter		145	.055		5.70	1.85		7.55	9.10	
	3400	5" diameter		115	.070		8.20	2.33		10.53	12.65	
	3600	Lead-coated copper, round, stock, 2" diameter		190	.042	L.F.	5.65	1.41		7.06	8.40	
	3700	3" diameter		190	.042		4.87	1.41		6.28	7.55	
	3900	4" diameter		145	.055		6.50	1.85		8.35	10	
	4200	6" diameter, corrugated		105	.076		10.65	2.56		13.21	15.65	
	4300	Rectangular, corrugated, stock, 2" x 3"		190	.042		4.86	1.41		6.27	7.55	
	4500	Plain, stock, 2" x 3"		190	.042		7.05	1.41		8.46	10	
	4600	3" x 4"		145	.055		7.65	1.85		9.50	11.30	
	4800	Steel, galvanized, round, corrugated, 2" or 3" diam, 28 ga		190	.042		.73	1.41		2.14	2.98	
	4900	4" diameter, 28 gauge		145	.055		1.07	1.85		2.92	4.04	
	5100	5" diameter, 28 gauge		130	.062		1.40	2.06		3.46	4.73	
	5200	26 gauge		130	.062		1.36	2.06		3.42	4.69	
	5400	6" diameter, 28 gauge		105	.076		1.94	2.56		4.50	6.10	
	5500	26 gauge		105	.076		1.42	2.56		3.98	5.50	
	5700	Rectangular, corrugated, 28 gauge, 2" x 3"		190	.042		.54	1.41		1.95	2.77	
	5800	3" x 4"		145	.055		1.50	1.85		3.35	4.51	
	6000	Rectangular, plain, 28 gauge, galvanized, 2" x 3"		190	.042		.63	1.41		2.04	2.87	
	6100	3" x 4"		145	.055		1.23	1.85		3.08	4.21	
	6300	Epoxy painted, 24 gauge, corrugated, 2" x 3"		190	.042		1.01	1.41		2.42	3.29	
	6400	3" x 4"		145	.055		1.67	1.85		3.52	4.70	
	6600	Wire strainers, rectangular, 2" x 3"		145	.055	Ea.	1.62	1.85		3.47	4.64	
	6700	3" x 4"		145	.055		2.61	1.85		4.46	5.75	
	6900	Round strainers, 2" or 3" diameter		145	.055		1.20	1.85		3.05	4.18	
	7000	4" diameter		145	.055		1.42	1.85		3.27	4.42	
	7200	5" diameter		145	.055		2.20	1.85		4.05	5.30	
	7300	6" diameter		115	.070		2.63	2.33		4.96	6.50	
	7500	Steel pipe, black, extra heavy, 4" diameter		20	.400	L.F.	4.48	13.40		17.88	25.50	
	7600	6" diameter		18	.444		7.60	14.90		22.50	31.50	
	7800	Stainless steel tubing, schedule 5, 2" x 3" or 3" diameter		190	.042		16	1.41		17.41	19.80	
	7900	3" x 4" or 4" diameter		145	.055		20.50	1.85		22.35	25.50	
	8100	4" x 5" or 5" diameter		135	.059		42	1.99		43.99	49	
	8200	Vinyl, rectangular, 2" x 3"		210	.038		.72	1.28		2	2.76	
	8300	Round, 2-1/2"		220	.036		.72	1.22		1.94	2.67	

7 THERMAL & MOISTURE PROTECTION

07710		Manufactured Roof Specialties	CREW	DAILY OUTPUT	LABOR-HOURS	UNIT	MAT.	LABOR	EQUIP.	TOTAL	TOTAL INCL O&P	
450	0010	**DRIP EDGE**, aluminum, .016" thick, 5" wide, mill finish	1 Carp	400	.020	L.F.	.20	.58		.78	1.13	**450**
	0100	White finish		400	.020		.22	.58		.80	1.15	
	0200	8" wide, mill finish		400	.020		.30	.58		.88	1.24	
	0300	Ice belt, 28" wide, mill finish		100	.080		3.42	2.33		5.75	7.40	
	0310	Vented, mill finish		400	.020		1.38	.58		1.96	2.43	
	0320	Painted finish		400	.020		1.50	.58		2.08	2.56	
	0400	Galvanized, 5" wide		400	.020		.22	.58		.80	1.15	
	0500	8" wide, mill finish		400	.020		.33	.58		.91	1.27	
	0510	Rake edge, aluminum, 1-1/2" x 1-1/2"		400	.020		.13	.58		.71	1.05	
	0520	3-1/2" x 1-1/2"		400	.020		.19	.58		.77	1.12	
500	0010	**ELBOWS** Aluminum, 2" x 3", embossed	1 Shee	100	.080	Ea.	.91	2.68		3.59	5.15	**500**
	0100	Enameled		100	.080		1.65	2.68		4.33	5.95	
	0200	3" x 4", .025" thick, embossed		100	.080		3.20	2.68		5.88	7.65	
	0300	Enameled		100	.080		3.20	2.68		5.88	7.65	
	0400	Round corrugated, 3", embossed, .020" thick		100	.080		1.98	2.68		4.66	6.30	
	0500	4", .025" thick		100	.080		2.99	2.68		5.67	7.45	
	0600	Copper, 16 oz. round, 2" diameter		100	.080		11.15	2.68		13.83	16.45	
	0700	3" diameter		100	.080		6.10	2.68		8.78	10.85	
	0800	4" diameter		100	.080		10.40	2.68		13.08	15.55	
	1000	2" x 3" corrugated		100	.080		5.10	2.68		7.78	9.80	
	1100	3" x 4" corrugated		100	.080		9.35	2.68		12.03	14.40	
	1300	Vinyl, 2-1/2" diameter, 45° or 75°		100	.080		2	2.68		4.68	6.35	
	1400	Tee Y junction		75	.107		8.50	3.58		12.08	14.90	
550	0010	**GRAVEL STOP** Aluminum, .050" thick, 4" face height, mill finish	1 Shee	145	.055	L.F.	3.22	1.85		5.07	6.40	**550**
	0080	Duranodic finish		145	.055		3.69	1.85		5.54	6.90	
	0100	Painted		145	.055		4.26	1.85		6.11	7.55	
	0300	6" face height		135	.059		3.84	1.99		5.83	7.30	
	0350	Duranodic finish		135	.059		4.35	1.99		6.34	7.85	
	0400	Painted		135	.059		5.05	1.99		7.04	8.60	
	0600	8" face height		125	.064		4.49	2.15		6.64	8.25	
	0650	Duranodic finish		125	.064		4.98	2.15		7.13	8.80	
	0700	Painted		125	.064		5.05	2.15		7.20	8.90	
	0900	12" face height, .080 thick, 2 piece		100	.080		6.20	2.68		8.88	10.95	
	0950	Duranodic finish		100	.080		6.30	2.68		8.98	11.05	
	1000	Painted		100	.080		7.40	2.68		10.08	12.30	
	1350	Galv steel, 24 ga., 4" leg, plain, with continuous cleat, 4" face		145	.055		1.50	1.85		3.35	4.51	
	1360	6" face height		145	.055		2.27	1.85		4.12	5.35	
	1500	Polyvinyl chloride, 6" face height		135	.059		3.28	1.99		5.27	6.70	
	1600	9" face height		125	.064		3.87	2.15		6.02	7.60	
	1800	Stainless steel, 24 ga., 6" face height		135	.059		7.15	1.99		9.14	10.90	
	1900	12" face height		100	.080		15	2.68		17.68	20.50	
	2100	20 ga., 6" face height		135	.059		8.10	1.99		10.09	11.95	
	2200	12" face height		100	.080		17.10	2.68		19.78	23	
650	0010	**GUTTERS** Aluminum, stock units, 5" box, .027" thick, plain	1 Shee	120	.067	L.F.	1.18	2.24		3.42	4.75	**650**
	0100	Enameled		120	.067		1.09	2.24		3.33	4.65	
	0300	5" box type, .032" thick, plain		120	.067		1.14	2.24		3.38	4.70	
	0400	Enameled		120	.067		1.24	2.24		3.48	4.81	
	0600	5" x 6" combination fascia & gutter, .032" thick, enameled		60	.133		3.52	4.47		7.99	10.75	
	0700	Copper, half round, 16 oz, stock units, 4" wide		120	.067		3.43	2.24		5.67	7.20	
	0900	5" wide		120	.067		2.96	2.24		5.20	6.70	
	1000	6" wide		115	.070		4.82	2.33		7.15	8.90	
	1200	K type, 16 oz, stock, 4" wide		120	.067		3.46	2.24		5.70	7.25	
	1300	5" wide		120	.067		3.08	2.24		5.32	6.85	
	1500	Lead coated copper, half round, stock, 4" wide		120	.067		4.67	2.24		6.91	8.60	
	1600	6" wide		115	.070		6.60	2.33		8.93	10.85	

Important: See the Reference Section for critical supporting data - Reference Nos., Crews, & City Cost Indexes

			CREW	DAILY OUTPUT	LABOR-HOURS	UNIT	2001 BARE COSTS				TOTAL INCL O&P	
		**07710	Manufactured Roof Specialties**					MAT.	LABOR	EQUIP.	TOTAL		
650	1800	K type, stock, 4" wide	1 Shee	120	.067	L.F.	7.10	2.24		9.34	11.25	**650**
	1900	5" wide		120	.067		5.50	2.24		7.74	9.50	
	2100	Stainless steel, half round or box, stock, 4" wide		120	.067		4.65	2.24		6.89	8.55	
	2200	5" wide		120	.067		5	2.24		7.24	8.95	
	2400	Steel, galv, half round or box, 28 ga, 5" wide, plain		120	.067		.90	2.24		3.14	4.44	
	2500	Enameled		120	.067		1.04	2.24		3.28	4.59	
	2700	26 ga, stock, 5" wide		120	.067		.95	2.24		3.19	4.50	
	2800	6" wide	▼	120	.067		1.41	2.24		3.65	5	
	3000	Vinyl, O.G., 4" wide	1 Carp	110	.073		.85	2.12		2.97	4.26	
	3100	5" wide		110	.073		1	2.12		3.12	4.42	
	3200	4" half round, stock units	▼	110	.073	▼	.68	2.12		2.80	4.07	
	3250	Joint connectors				Ea.	1.36			1.36	1.50	
	3300	Wood, clear treated cedar, fir or hemlock, 3" x 4"	1 Carp	100	.080	L.F.	6.30	2.33		8.63	10.55	
	3400	4" x 5"	"	100	.080	"	7.30	2.33		9.63	11.65	
700	0010	**GUTTER GUARD** 6" wide strip, aluminum mesh	1 Carp	500	.016	L.F.	.37	.47		.84	1.14	**700**
	0100	Vinyl mesh		500	.016	"	.22	.47		.69	.97	
750	0010	**REGLET** Aluminum, .025" thick, in concrete parapet		225	.036	L.F.	.94	1.04		1.98	2.65	**750**
	0100	Copper, 10 oz.		225	.036		1.62	1.04		2.66	3.40	
	0300	16 oz.		225	.036		2.16	1.04		3.20	4	
	0400	Galvanized steel, 24 gauge		225	.036		.71	1.04		1.75	2.40	
	0600	Stainless steel, .020" thick		225	.036		1.60	1.04		2.64	3.38	
	0700	Zinc and copper alloy, 20 oz.	▼	225	.036		1.79	1.04		2.83	3.59	
	0900	Counter flashing for above, 12" wide, .032" aluminum	1 Shee	150	.053		1.21	1.79		3	4.09	
	1000	Copper, 10 oz.		150	.053		3.39	1.79		5.18	6.50	
	1200	16 oz.		150	.053		3.77	1.79		5.56	6.90	
	1300	Galvanized steel, .020" thick		150	.053		.63	1.79		2.42	3.45	
	1500	Stainless steel, .020" thick		150	.053		2.82	1.79		4.61	5.85	
	1600	Zinc and copper alloy, 20 oz.	▼	150	.053	▼	3.17	1.79		4.96	6.25	
800	0010	**EXPANSION JOINT**										**800**
	0300	Butyl or neoprene center with foam insulation, metal flanges										
	0400	Aluminum, .032" thick for openings to 2-1/2"	1 Rofc	165	.048	L.F.	7.55	1.25		8.80	10.45	
	0600	For joint openings to 3-1/2"		165	.048		8.80	1.25		10.05	11.85	
	0610	For joint openings to 5"		165	.048		10.60	1.25		11.85	13.80	
	0620	For joint openings to 8"		165	.048		16.75	1.25		18	20.50	
	0700	Copper, 16 oz. for openings to 2-1/2"		165	.048		10.60	1.25		11.85	13.80	
	0900	For joint openings to 3-1/2"		165	.048		12.20	1.25		13.45	15.55	
	0910	For joint openings to 5"		165	.048		14.30	1.25		15.55	17.85	
	0920	For joint openings to 8"		165	.048		21.50	1.25		22.75	25.50	
	1000	Galvanized steel, 26 ga. for openings to 2-1/2"		165	.048		6.40	1.25		7.65	9.15	
	1200	For joint openings to 3-1/2"		165	.048		7.55	1.25		8.80	10.45	
	1210	For joint openings to 5"		165	.048		9.45	1.25		10.70	12.55	
	1220	For joint openings to 8"		165	.048		16.05	1.25		17.30	19.85	
	1300	Lead-coated copper, 16 oz. for openings to 2-1/2"		165	.048		18.85	1.25		20.10	23	
	1500	For joint openings to 3-1/2"		165	.048		22.50	1.25		23.75	26.50	
	1600	Stainless steel, .018", for openings to 2-1/2"		165	.048		9.45	1.25		10.70	12.55	
	1800	For joint openings to 3-1/2"		165	.048		10.75	1.25		12	14	
	1810	For joint openings to 5"		165	.048		13.30	1.25		14.55	16.80	
	1820	For joint openings to 8"		165	.048		20.50	1.25		21.75	24.50	
	1900	Neoprene, double-seal type with thick center, 4-1/2" wide		125	.064		9.10	1.64		10.74	12.85	
	1950	Polyethylene bellows, with galv steel flat flanges		100	.080		3.52	2.06		5.58	7.40	
	1960	With galvanized angle flanges	▼	100	.080		3.88	2.06		5.94	7.80	
	2000	Roof joint with extruded aluminum cover, 2"	1 Shee	115	.070		24.50	2.33		26.83	30	
	2100	Roof joint, plastic curbs, foam center, standard	1 Rofc	100	.080		8.85	2.06		10.91	13.30	
	2200	Large		100	.080	▼	11.85	2.06		13.91	16.55	
	2300	Transitions, regular, minimum		10	.800	Ea.	76.50	20.50		97	120	
	2350	Maximum	▼	4	2	▼	97.50	51.50		149	196	

7

THERMAL & MOISTURE PROTECTION

			CREW	DAILY OUTPUT	LABOR-HOURS	UNIT	2001 BARE COSTS				TOTAL INCL O&P	
	07710	**Manufactured Roof Specialties**					MAT.	LABOR	EQUIP.	TOTAL		
800	2400	Large, minimum	1 Rofc	9	.889	Ea.	112	23		135	162	**800**
	2450	Maximum	↓	3	2.667	↓	117	68.50		185.50	247	
	2500	Roof to wall joint with extruded aluminum cover	1 Shee	115	.070	L.F.	20.50	2.33		22.83	26	
	2600	See also divisions 03150 & 05810										
	2700	Wall joint, closed cell foam on PVC cover, 9" wide	1 Rofc	125	.064	L.F.	3.16	1.64		4.80	6.30	
	2800	12" wide	"	115	.070	"	3.57	1.79		5.36	7	
	07720	**Roof Accessories**										
480	0010	**PITCH POCKETS**										**480**
	0100	Adjustable, 4" to 7", welded corners, 4" deep	1 Rofc	48	.167	Ea.	10.50	4.28		14.78	18.90	
	0200	Side extenders, 6"	"	240	.033	"	1.70	.86		2.56	3.34	
500	0010	**ROOF VENTS** Mushroom for built-up roofs, aluminum	1 Rofc	30	.267	Ea.	24	6.85		30.85	38.50	**500**
	0100	PVC, 6" high	"	30	.267		27.50	6.85		34.35	42.50	
550	0010	**RIDGE VENT**										**550**
	0100	Aluminum strips, mill finish	1 Rofc	160	.050	L.F.	1.15	1.29		2.44	3.48	
	0150	Painted finish		160	.050	"	2.12	1.29		3.41	4.55	
	0200	Connectors		48	.167	Ea.	1.88	4.28		6.16	9.40	
	0300	End caps		48	.167	"	.79	4.28		5.07	8.20	
	0400	Galvanized strips, with damper and bird screen		160	.050	L.F.	20.50	1.29		21.79	25	
	0430	Molded polyethylene, shingles not included		160	.050	"	2.50	1.29		3.79	4.96	
	0440	End plugs		48	.167	Ea.	.79	4.28		5.07	8.20	
	0450	Flexible roll, shingles not included	↓	160	.050	L.F.	1.95	1.29		3.24	4.35	
700	0010	**ROOF HATCHES** With curb, 1" fiberglass insulation, 2'-6" x 3'-0"										**700**
	0500	Aluminum curb and cover	G-3	10	3.200	Ea.	395	90		485	575	
	0520	Galvanized steel curb and aluminum cover **CN**		10	3.200		340	90		430	515	
	0540	Galvanized steel curb and cover		10	3.200		355	90		445	530	
	0600	2'-6" x 4'-6", aluminum curb and cover		9	3.556		570	100		670	780	
	0800	Galvanized steel curb and aluminum cover		9	3.556		475	100		575	680	
	0900	Galvanized steel curb and cover		9	3.556		550	100		650	765	
	1200	2'-6" x 8'-0", aluminum curb and cover		6.60	4.848		1,100	137		1,237	1,400	
	1400	Galvanized steel curb and aluminum cover		6.60	4.848		920	137		1,057	1,200	
	1500	Galvanized steel curb and cover	↓	6.60	4.848		900	137		1,037	1,200	
	1800	For plexiglass panels, 2'-6" x 3'-0", add to above				↓	345			345	380	
800	0010	**WALKWAY** For built-up roofs, asphalt impregnated, 3' x 6' x 1/2" thk	1 Rofc	400	.020	S.F.	.99	.51		1.50	1.97	**800**
	0100	3' x 3' x 3/4" thick	"	400	.020		1.55	.51		2.06	2.59	
	0300	Concrete patio blocks, 2" thick, natural	1 Clab	115	.070		1.39	1.59		2.98	4.02	
	0400	Colors	"	115	.070	↓	1.75	1.59		3.34	4.42	
850	0010	**SMOKE HATCHES** Unlabeled, not including hand winch operator										**850**
	0200	For 3'-0" long, add to roof hatches from division 07720-700				Ea.	25%	5%				
	0300	For 8'-0" long, add to roof hatches from division 07720-700				"	10%	5%				
860	0010	**SMOKE VENT**, insulated, 4' x 4'										**860**
	0100	Aluminum cover and frame	G-3	13	2.462	Ea.	1,050	69.50		1,119.50	1,250	
	0200	Galvanized steel cover and frame		13	2.462		950	69.50		1,019.50	1,150	
	0300	4' x 8' aluminum cover and frame		8	4		1,425	113		1,538	1,750	
	0400	Galvanized steel cover and frame	↓	8	4	↓	1,250	113		1,363	1,550	
870	0010	**VENTS, ONE-WAY** For insul. decks, 1 per M.S.F., plastic, min.	1 Rofc	40	.200	Ea.	12.50	5.15		17.65	22.50	**870**
	0100	Maximum		20	.400		28.50	10.30		38.80	49	
	0300	Aluminum	↓	30	.267		12.50	6.85		19.35	25.50	
	0800	Polystyrene baffles, 12" wide for 16" O.C. rafter spacing	1 Carp	90	.089		.45	2.59		3.04	4.55	
	0900	For 24" O.C. rafter spacing	"	110	.073	↓	1.05	2.12		3.17	4.48	

Important: See the Reference Section for critical supporting data - Reference Nos., Crews, & City Cost Indexes

THERMAL & MOISTURE PROTECTION **7**

			CREW	DAILY OUTPUT	LABOR-HOURS	UNIT	2001 BARE COSTS				TOTAL INCL O&P
		07812	**Cementitious Fireproofing**				MAT.	LABOR	EQUIP.	TOTAL	
600	0010	**SPRAYED** Mineral fiber or cementitious for fireproofing,										600
	0050	not incl tamping or canvas protection									
	0100	1" thick, on flat plate steel	G-2	3,000	.008	S.F.	.40	.20	.08	.68	.83
	0200	Flat decking		2,400	.010		.40	.24	.10	.74	.93
	0400	Beams		1,500	.016		.40	.39	.16	.95	1.21
	0500	Corrugated or fluted decks		1,250	.019		.61	.47	.19	1.27	1.60
	0700	Columns, 1-1/8" thick		1,100	.022		.45	.53	.21	1.19	1.55
	0800	2-3/16" thick	↓	700	.034	↓	.88	.84	.33	2.05	2.63
	0850	For tamping, add						10%			
	0900	For canvas protection, add	G-2	5,000	.005	S.F.	.06	.12	.05	.23	.30
	1000	Acoustical sprayed, 1" thick, finished, straight work, minimum		520	.046		.44	1.13	.45	2.02	2.71
	1100	Maximum		200	.120		.47	2.94	1.17	4.58	6.35
	1300	Difficult access, minimum		225	.107		.47	2.61	1.04	4.12	5.70
	1400	Maximum	↓	130	.185	↓	.51	4.52	1.79	6.82	9.50
	1500	Intumescent epoxy fireproofing on wire mesh, 3/16" thick									
	1550	1 hour rating, exterior use	G-2	136	.176	S.F.	5.40	4.32	1.72	11.44	14.50
	1600	Magnesium oxychloride, 35# to 40# density, 1/4" thick		3,000	.008		1.14	.20	.08	1.42	1.64
	1650	1/2" thick		2,000	.012		2.28	.29	.12	2.69	3.09
	1700	60# to 70# density, 1/4" thick		3,000	.008		1.50	.20	.08	1.78	2.04
	1750	1/2" thick		2,000	.012		3.03	.29	.12	3.44	3.91
	2000	Vermiculite cement, troweled or sprayed, 1/4" thick		3,000	.008		1.03	.20	.08	1.31	1.52
	2050	1/2" thick	↓	2,000	.012	↓	2.04	.29	.12	2.45	2.82
		07840	**Firestopping**								
100	0010	**FIRESTOPPING**	R07800 -030								100
	0100	Metallic piping, non insulated									
	0110	Through walls, 2" diameter	1 Carp	16	.500	Ea.	9.60	14.60		24.20	33.50
	0120	4" diameter		14	.571		14.65	16.65		31.30	42
	0130	6" diameter		12	.667		19.70	19.45		39.15	52
	0140	12" diameter		10	.800		35	23.50		58.50	75
	0150	Through floors, 2" diameter		32	.250		5.80	7.30		13.10	17.80
	0160	4" diameter		28	.286		8.35	8.35		16.70	22.50
	0170	6" diameter		24	.333		11	9.70		20.70	27.50
	0180	12" diameter	↓	20	.400	↓	18.50	11.65		30.15	39
	0190	Metallic piping, insulated									
	0200	Through walls, 2" diameter	1 Carp	16	.500	Ea.	13.60	14.60		28.20	38
	0210	4" diameter		14	.571		18.65	16.65		35.30	46.50
	0220	6" diameter		12	.667		23.50	19.45		42.95	56.50
	0230	12" diameter		10	.800		39	23.50		62.50	79
	0240	Through floors, 2" diameter		32	.250		9.80	7.30		17.10	22
	0250	4" diameter		28	.286		12.35	8.35		20.70	26.50
	0260	6" diameter		24	.333		15	9.70		24.70	31.50
	0270	12" diameter	↓	20	.400		18.50	11.65		30.15	39
	0280	Non metallic piping, non insulated									
	0290	Through walls, 2" diameter	1 Carp	12	.667	Ea.	39.50	19.45		58.95	74
	0300	4" diameter		10	.800		49.50	23.50		73	91
	0310	6" diameter		8	1		69	29		98	122
	0330	Through floors, 2" diameter		16	.500		31	14.60		45.60	57
	0340	4" diameter		6	1.333		38.50	39		77.50	103
	0350	6" diameter	↓	6	1.333	↓	46	39		85	112
	0370	Ductwork, insulated & non insulated, round									
	0380	Through walls, 6" diameter	1 Carp	12	.667	Ea.	20	19.45		39.45	52.50
	0390	12" diameter		10	.800		40	23.50		63.50	80.50
	0400	18" diameter		8	1		65	29		94	117
	0410	Through floors, 6" diameter		16	.500		11	14.60		25.60	35
	0420	12" diameter	↓	14	.571	↓	20	16.65		36.65	48

		CREW	DAILY OUTPUT	LABOR-HOURS	UNIT	2001 BARE COSTS				TOTAL INCL O&P	
07840	**Firestopping**					MAT.	LABOR	EQUIP.	TOTAL		
100	0430	18" diameter [R07800-030]	1 Carp	12	.667	Ea.	35	19.45		54.45	69	100
	0440	Ductwork, insulated & non insulated, rectangular										
	0450	With stiffener/closure angle, through walls, 6" x 12"	1 Carp	8	1	Ea.	16.65	29		45.65	64	
	0460	12" x 24"		6	1.333		22	39		61	85.50	
	0470	24" x 48"		4	2		63	58.50		121.50	161	
	0480	With stiffener/closure angle, through floors, 6" x 12"		10	.800		9	23.50		32.50	46.50	
	0490	12" x 24"		8	1		16.20	29		45.20	63.50	
	0500	24" x 48"		6	1.333		32	39		71	96	
	0510	Multi trade openings										
	0520	Through walls, 6" x 12"	1 Carp	2	4	Ea.	35	117		152	221	
	0530	12" x 24"	"	1	8		141	233		374	520	
	0540	24" x 48"	2 Carp	1	16		565	465		1,030	1,350	
	0550	48" x 96"	"	.75	21.333		2,275	620		2,895	3,475	
	0560	Through floors, 6" x 12"	1 Carp	2	4		35	117		152	221	
	0570	12" x 24"	"	1	8		141	233		374	520	
	0580	24" x 48"	2 Carp	.75	21.333		565	620		1,185	1,600	
	0590	48" x 96"	"	.50	32		2,275	935		3,210	3,950	
	0600	Structural penetrations, through walls										
	0610	Steel beams, W8 x 10	1 Carp	8	1	Ea.	22	29		51	69.50	
	0620	W12 x 14		6	1.333		35	39		74	99.50	
	0630	W21 x 44		5	1.600		70	46.50		116.50	150	
	0640	W36 x 135		3	2.667		170	77.50		247.50	310	
	0650	Bar joists, 18" deep		6	1.333		32	39		71	96	
	0660	24" deep		6	1.333		40	39		79	105	
	0670	36" deep		5	1.600		60	46.50		106.50	139	
	0680	48" deep		4	2		70	58.50		128.50	168	
	0690	Construction joints, floor slab at exterior wall										
	0700	Precast, brick, block or drywall exterior										
	0710	2" wide joint	1 Carp	125	.064	L.F.	5	1.87		6.87	8.40	
	0720	4" wide joint	"	75	.107	"	10	3.11		13.11	15.85	
	0730	Metal panel, glass or curtain wall exterior										
	0740	2" wide joint	1 Carp	40	.200	L.F.	11.85	5.85		17.70	22	
	0750	4" wide joint	"	25	.320	"	16.15	9.35		25.50	32.50	
	0760	Floor slab to drywall partition										
	0770	Flat joint	1 Carp	100	.080	L.F.	4.90	2.33		7.23	9.05	
	0780	Fluted joint		50	.160		10	4.66		14.66	18.30	
	0790	Etched fluted joint		75	.107		6.50	3.11		9.61	12	
	0800	Floor slab to concrete/masonry partition										
	0810	Flat joint	1 Carp	75	.107	L.F.	11	3.11		14.11	16.95	
	0820	Fluted joint	"	50	.160	"	13	4.66		17.66	21.50	
	0830	Concrete/CMU wall joints										
	0840	1" wide	1 Carp	100	.080	L.F.	6	2.33		8.33	10.25	
	0850	2" wide		75	.107		11	3.11		14.11	16.95	
	0860	4" wide		50	.160		21	4.66		25.66	30.50	
	0870	Concrete/CMU floor joints										
	0880	1" wide	1 Carp	200	.040	L.F.	3	1.17		4.17	5.10	
	0890	2" wide		150	.053		5.50	1.55		7.05	8.50	
	0900	4" wide		100	.080		10.50	2.33		12.83	15.20	

Important: See the Reference Section for critical supporting data - Reference Nos., Crews, & City Cost Indexes

7
THERMAL & MOISTURE PROTECTION

07920	Joint Sealants	CREW	DAILY OUTPUT	LABOR-HOURS	UNIT	2001 BARE COSTS				TOTAL INCL O&P
						MAT.	LABOR	EQUIP.	TOTAL	
800	0010	**CAULKING AND SEALANTS**									800
	0020	Acoustical sealant, elastomeric, cartridges				Ea.	2.05			2.05	2.26
	0030	Backer rod, polyethylene, 1/4" diameter	1 Bric	4.60	1.739	C.L.F.	1.28	51.50		52.78	81
	0050	1/2" diameter		4.60	1.739		2.62	51.50		54.12	82.50
	0070	3/4" diameter		4.60	1.739		5.05	51.50		56.55	85
	0090	1" diameter	↓	4.60	1.739	↓	8	51.50		59.50	88.50
	0100	Acrylic latex caulk, white									
	0200	11 fl. oz cartridge				Ea.	1.80			1.80	1.98
	0500	1/4" x 1/2"	1 Bric	248	.032	L.F.	.15	.95		1.10	1.64
	0600	1/2" x 1/2"		250	.032		.29	.95		1.24	1.78
	0800	3/4" x 3/4"		230	.035		.66	1.03		1.69	2.32
	0900	3/4" x 1"		200	.040		.88	1.18		2.06	2.80
	1000	1" x 1"	↓	180	.044	↓	1.10	1.32		2.42	3.24
	1400	Butyl based, bulk				Gal.	22			22	24
	1500	Cartridges				"	26.50			26.50	29.50
	1700	Bulk, in place 1/4" x 1/2", 154 L.F./gal.	1 Bric	230	.035	L.F.	.14	1.03		1.17	1.75
	1800	1/2" x 1/2", 77 L.F./gal.	"	180	.044	"	.29	1.32		1.61	2.34
	2000	Latex acrylic based, bulk				Gal.	23			23	25.50
	2100	Cartridges					26			26	28.50
	2300	Polysulfide compounds, 1 component, bulk				↓	43.50			43.50	47.50
	2600	1 or 2 component, in place, 1/4" x 1/4", 308 L.F./gal.	1 Bric	145	.055	L.F.	.14	1.63		1.77	2.67
	2700	1/2" x 1/4", 154 L.F./gal.		135	.059		.28	1.75		2.03	3.02
	2900	3/4" x 3/8", 68 L.F./gal.		130	.062		.64	1.82		2.46	3.52
	3000	1" x 1/2", 38 L.F./gal.	↓	130	.062	↓	1.14	1.82		2.96	4.07
	3200	Polyurethane, 1 or 2 component				Gal.	47			47	51.50
	3500	Bulk, in place, 1/4" x 1/4"	1 Bric	150	.053	L.F.	.15	1.58		1.73	2.61
	3600	1/2" x 1/4"		145	.055		.31	1.63		1.94	2.86
	3800	3/4" x 3/8", 68 L.F./gal.		130	.062		.69	1.82		2.51	3.58
	3900	1" x 1/2"	↓	110	.073	↓	1.22	2.15		3.37	4.67
	4100	Silicone rubber, bulk				Gal.	34			34	37.50
	4200	Cartridges				"	40			40	44
	4400	Neoprene gaskets, closed cell, adhesive, 1/8" x 3/8"	1 Bric	240	.033	L.F.	.20	.99		1.19	1.74
	4500	1/4" x 3/4"		215	.037		.48	1.10		1.58	2.23
	4700	1/2" x 1"		200	.040		1.40	1.18		2.58	3.37
	4800	3/4" x 1-1/2"	↓	165	.048	↓	2.91	1.44		4.35	5.40
	5500	Resin epoxy coating, 2 component, heavy duty				Gal.	26			26	28.50
	5800	Tapes, sealant, P.V.C. foam adhesive, 1/16" x 1/4"				C.L.F.	4.60			4.60	5.05
	5900	1/16" x 1/2"					6.80			6.80	7.50
	5950	1/16" x 1"					11.30			11.30	12.45
	6000	1/8" x 1/2"				↓	7.65			7.65	8.40
	6200	Urethane foam, 2 component, handy pack, 1 C.F.				Ea.	27.50			27.50	30.50
	6300	50.0 C.F. pack				C.F.	14.05			14.05	15.45

For information about Means Estimating Seminars, see yellow pages 11 and 12 in back of book

THERMAL & MOISTURE PROTECTION **7**

		CREW	DAILY OUTPUT	LABOR-HOURS	UNIT	2001 BARE COSTS				TOTAL INCL O&P
						MAT.	LABOR	EQUIP.	TOTAL	

Division 8
Doors & Windows

Estimating Tips

08100 Metal Doors & Frames

- Most metal doors and frames look alike, but there may be significant differences among them. When estimating these items be sure to choose the line item that most closely compares to the specification or door schedule requirements regarding:
  - type of metal
  - metal gauge
  - door core material
  - fire rating
  - finish

08200 Wood & Plastic Doors

- Wood and plastic doors vary considerably in price. The primary determinant is the veneer material. Lauan, birch and oak are the most common veneers. Other variables include the following:
  - hollow or solid core
  - fire rating
  - flush or raised panel
  - finish
- If the specifications require compliance with AWI (Architectural Woodwork Institute) standards or acoustical standards, the cost of the door may increase substantially. All wood doors are priced pre-mortised for hinges and predrilled for cylindrical locksets.

08300 Specialty Doors

- There are many varieties of special doors, and they are usually priced per each. Add frames, hardware or operators required for a complete installation.

08510 Steel Windows

- Most metal windows are delivered preglazed. However, some metal windows are priced without glass. Refer to 08800 Glazing for glass pricing. The grade C indicates commercial grade windows, usually ASTM C-35.

08550 Wood Windows

- All wood windows are priced preglazed. The two glazing options priced are single pane float glass and insulating glass 1/2" thick. Add the cost of screens and grills if required.

08700 Hardware

- Hardware costs add considerably to the cost of a door. The most efficient method to determine the hardware requirements for a project is to review the door schedule. This schedule, in conjunction with the specifications, is all you should need to take off the door hardware.
- Door hinges are priced by the pair, with most doors requiring 1-1/2 pairs per door. The hinge prices do not include installation labor because it is included in door installation. Hinges are classified according to the frequency of use.

08800 Glazing

- Different openings require different types of glass. The three most common types are:
  - float
  - tempered
  - insulating
- Most exterior windows are glazed with insulating glass. Entrance doors and window walls, where the glass is less than 18" from the floor, are generally glazed with tempered glass. Interior windows and some residential windows are glazed with float glass.

08900 Glazed Curtain Wall

- Glazed curtain walls consist of the metal tube framing and the glazing material. The cost data in this subdivision is presented for the metal tube framing alone or the composite wall. If your estimate requires a detailed takeoff of the framing, be sure to add the glazing cost.

Reference Numbers

Reference numbers are shown in bold squares at the beginning of some major classifications. These numbers refer to related items in the Reference Section. The reference information may be an estimating procedure, an alternate pricing method or technical information.

Note: Not all subdivisions listed here necessarily appear in this publication.

08110	Steel Doors & Frames	CREW	DAILY OUTPUT	LABOR-HOURS	UNIT	MAT.	LABOR	EQUIP.	TOTAL	TOTAL INCL O&P
							2001 BARE COSTS			

200	0010	**COMMERCIAL STEEL DOORS** R08110-120										200
	0015	Flush, full panel, hollow core									
	0020	1-3/8" thick, 20 ga., 2'-0" x 6'-8"	2 Carp	20	.800	Ea.	153	23.50		176.50	206
	0040	2'-8" x 6'-8"		18	.889		157	26		183	214
	0060	3'-0" x 6'-8"		17	.941		160	27.50		187.50	219
	0100	3'-0" x 7'-0"		17	.941		167	27.50		194.50	227
	0120	For vision lite, add					38			38	42
	0140	For narrow lite, add					63			63	69.50
	0160	For bottom louver, add					78			78	86
	0230	For baked enamel finish, add					30%	15%			
	0260	For galvanizing, add					15%				
	0320	Half glass, 20 ga., 2'-0" x 6'-8"	2 Carp	20	.800	Ea.	205	23.50		228.50	262
	0340	2'-8" x 6'-8"		18	.889		210	26		236	272
	0360	3'-0" x 6'-8"		17	.941		212	27.50		239.50	276
	0400	3'-0" x 7'-0"		17	.941		221	27.50		248.50	286
	0500	Hollow core, 1-3/4" thick, full panel, 20 ga., 2'-8" x 6'-8"		18	.889		160	26		186	217
	0520	3'-0" x 6'-8"		17	.941		160	27.50		187.50	219
	0640	3'-0" x 7'-0"		17	.941		168	27.50		195.50	227
	0680	4'-0" x 7'-0"		15	1.067		232	31		263	305
	0700	4'-0" x 8'-0"		13	1.231		270	36		306	355
	1000	18 ga., 2'-8" x 6'-8"		17	.941		184	27.50		211.50	246
	1020	3'-0" x 6'-8"		16	1		179	29		208	243
	1120	3'-0" x 7'-0" **CN**		17	.941		188	27.50		215.50	249
	1180	4'-0" x 7'-0"		14	1.143		250	33.50		283.50	330
	1200	4'-0" x 8'-0"		17	.941		297	27.50		324.50	370
	1230	Half glass, 20 ga., 2'-8" x 6'-8"		20	.800		246	23.50		269.50	310
	1240	3'-0" x 6'-8"		18	.889		242	26		268	305
	1260	3'-0" x 7'-0"		18	.889		248	26		274	315
	1280	4'-0" x 7'-0"		16	1		315	29		344	390
	1300	4'-0" x 8'-0"		13	1.231		360	36		396	450
	1320	18 ga., 2'-8" x 6'-8"		18	.889		244	26		270	310
	1340	3'-0" x 6'-8"		17	.941		242	27.50		269.50	310
	1360	3'-0" x 7'-0"		17	.941		248	27.50		275.50	315
	1380	4'-0" x 7'-0"		15	1.067		300	31		331	380
	1400	4'-0" x 8'-0"		14	1.143		350	33.50		383.50	435
	1720	Insulated, 1-3/4" thick, full panel, 18 ga., 3'-0" x 6'-8"		15	1.067		245	31		276	320
	1740	2'-8" x 7'-0"		16	1		248	29		277	320
	1760	3'-0" x 7'-0"		15	1.067		245	31		276	320
	1800	4'-0" x 8'-0"		13	1.231		355	36		391	445
	1820	Half glass, 18 ga., 3'-0" x 6'-8"		16	1		290	29		319	365
	1840	2'-8" x 7'-0"		17	.941		300	27.50		327.50	375
	1860	3'-0" x 7'-0"		16	1		294	29		323	370
	1900	4'-0" x 8'-0"		14	1.143		410	33.50		443.50	500

250	0010	**DOOR FRAMES**										250
	0020	Steel channels with anchors and bar stops									
	0100	6" channel @ 8.2#/L.F., 3' x 7' door, weighs 150#	E-4	13	2.462	Ea.	110	82	6.45	198.45	277
	0200	8" channel @ 11.5#/L.F., 6' x 8' door, weighs 275#		9	3.556		202	119	9.35	330.35	445
	0300	8' x 12' door, weighs 400#		6.50	4.923		294	164	12.95	470.95	635
	0400	10" channel @ 15.3#/L.F., 10' x 10' door, weighs 500# **CN**		6	5.333		370	178	14.05	562.05	745
	0500	12' x 12' door, weighs 600#		5.50	5.818		440	194	15.30	649.30	850
	0600	12" channel @ 20.7#/L.F., 12' x 12' door, weighs 825#		4.50	7.111		605	237	18.70	860.70	1,125
	0700	12' x 16' door, weighs 1000#		4	8		735	267	21	1,023	1,325
	0800	For frames without bar stops, light sections, deduct					15%				
	0900	Heavy sections, deduct					10%				

Important: See the Reference Section for critical supporting data - Reference Nos., Crews, & City Cost Indexes

8 DOORS & WINDOWS

08110 | Steel Doors & Frames

			CREW	DAILY OUTPUT	LABOR-HOURS	UNIT	MAT.	LABOR	EQUIP.	TOTAL	TOTAL INCL O&P	
300	0010	**FIRE DOOR**										**300**
	0015	Steel, flush, "B" label, 90 minute	R08110 -120									
	0020	Full panel, 20 ga., 2'-0" x 6'-8"	2 Carp	20	.800	Ea.	166	23.50		189.50	219	
	0040	2'-8" x 6'-8"		18	.889		173	26		199	231	
	0060	3'-0" x 6'-8"		17	.941		173	27.50		200.50	233	
	0080	3'-0" x 7'-0"		17	.941		180	27.50		207.50	241	
	0140	18 ga., 3'-0" x 6'-8"		16	1		192	29		221	257	
	0160	2'-8" x 7'-0"		17	.941		204	27.50		231.50	268	
	0180	3'-0" x 7'-0"		16	1		199	29		228	265	
	0200	4'-0" x 7'-0"		15	1.067		263	31		294	340	
	0220	For "A" label, 3 hour, 18 ga., use same price as "B" label										
	0240	For vision lite, add				Ea.	18			18	19.80	
	0520	Flush, "B" label 90 min., composite, 20 ga., 2'-0" x 6'-8"	2 Carp	18	.889		224	26		250	288	
	0540	2'-8" x 6'-8"		17	.941		228	27.50		255.50	294	
	0560	3'-0" x 6'-8"		16	1		231	29		260	300	
	0580	3'-0" x 7'-0"		16	1		239	29		268	310	
	0640	Flush, "A" label 3 hour, composite, 18 ga., 3'-0" x 6'-8"		15	1.067		250	31		281	325	
	0660	2'-8" x 7'-0"		16	1		261	29		290	335	
	0680	3'-0" x 7'-0"		15	1.067		257	31		288	330	
	0700	4'-0" x 7'-0"		14	1.143		320	33.50		353.50	405	
600	0010	**RESIDENTIAL STEEL DOOR**										**600**
	0020	Prehung, insulated, exterior										
	0030	Embossed, full panel, 2'-8" x 6'-8"	2 Carp	17	.941	Ea.	178	27.50		205.50	239	
	0040	3'-0" x 6'-8"		15	1.067		179	31		210	246	
	0060	3'-0" x 7'-0"		15	1.067		233	31		264	305	
	0070	5'-4" x 6'-8", double		8	2		315	58.50		373.50	440	
	0220	Half glass, 2'-8" x 6'-8"		17	.941		226	27.50		253.50	291	
	0240	3'-0" x 6'-8"		16	1		229	29		258	298	
	0260	3'-0" x 7'-0"		16	1		277	29		306	350	
	0270	5'-4" x 6'-8", double		8	2		485	58.50		543.50	620	
	0720	Raised plastic face, full panel, 2'-8" x 6'-8"		16	1		221	29		250	289	
	0740	3'-0" x 6'-8"		15	1.067		225	31		256	296	
	0760	3'-0" x 7'-0"		15	1.067		239	31		270	310	
	0780	5'-4" x 6'-8", double		8	2		440	58.50		498.50	575	
	0820	Half glass, 2'-8" x 6'-8"		17	.941		263	27.50		290.50	330	
	0840	3'-0" x 6'-8"		16	1		266	29		295	340	
	0860	3'-0" x 7'-0"		16	1		291	29		320	365	
	0880	5'-4" x 6'-8", double		8	2		550	58.50		608.50	695	
	1320	Flush face, full panel, 2'-6" x 6'-8"		16	1		200	29		229	266	
	1340	3'-0" x 6'-8"		15	1.067		202	31		233	272	
	1360	3'-0" x 7'-0"		15	1.067		256	31		287	330	
	1380	5'-4" x 6'-8", double		8	2		400	58.50		458.50	530	
	1420	Half glass, 2'-8" x 6'-8"		17	.941		247	27.50		274.50	315	
	1440	3'-0" x 6'-8"		16	1		250	29		279	320	
	1460	3'-0" x 7'-0"		16	1		305	29		334	380	
	1480	5'-4" x 6'-8", double		8	2		495	58.50		553.50	635	
	2300	Interior, residential, closet, bi-fold, 6'-8" x 2'-0" wide		16	1		128	29		157	187	
	2330	3'-0" wide		16	1		144	29		173	204	
	2360	4'-0" wide		15	1.067		218	31		249	289	
	2400	5'-0" wide		14	1.143		253	33.50		286.50	330	
	2420	6'-0" wide		13	1.231		283	36		319	365	
820	0010	**STEEL FRAMES, KNOCK DOWN**	R08110 -100									**820**
	0020	16 ga., up to 5-3/4 deep										
	0025	6'-8" high, 3'-0" wide, single	2 Carp	16	1	Ea.	63.50	29		92.50	116	
	0040	6'-0" wide, double		14	1.143		80.50	33.50		114	141	

08100 | Metal Doors & Frames

08110 | Steel Doors & Frames

				CREW	DAILY OUTPUT	LABOR-HOURS	UNIT	2001 BARE COSTS				TOTAL INCL O&P
								MAT.	LABOR	EQUIP.	TOTAL	
820	0100	7'-0" high, 3'-0" wide, single	R08110 -100	2 Carp	16	1	Ea.	65	29		94	117	**820**
	0140	6'-0" wide, double			14	1.143		82	33.50		115.50	143	
	1000	16 ga., up to 4-7/8" deep, 7'-0" H, 3'-0" W, single	CN		16	1		71	29		100	124	
	1140	6'-0" wide, double			14	1.143		85.50	33.50		119	146	
	2800	14 ga., up to 3-7/8" deep, 7'-0" high, 3'-0" wide, single			16	1		74.50	29		103.50	128	
	2840	6'-0" wide, double			14	1.143		89.50	33.50		123	151	
	3600	5-3/4" deep, 7'-0" high, 4'-0" wide, single			15	1.067		63.50	31		94.50	119	
	3640	8'-0" wide, double			12	1.333		101	39		140	172	
	3700	8'-0" high, 4'-0" wide, single			15	1.067		94	31		125	152	
	3740	8'-0" wide, double			12	1.333		116	39		155	189	
	4000	6-3/4" deep, 7'-0" high, 4'-0" wide, single			15	1.067		90	31		121	148	
	4040	8'-0"			12	1.333		112	39		151	184	
	4100	8'-0" high, 4'-0" wide, single			15	1.067		106	31		137	165	
	4140	8'-0" wide, double			12	1.333		130	39		169	204	
	4400	8-3/4" deep, 7'-0" high, 4'-0" wide, single			15	1.067		101	31		132	161	
	4440	8'-0" wide, double			12	1.333		126	39		165	199	
	4500	8'-0" high, 4'-0" wide, single			15	1.067		114	31		145	174	
	4540	8'-0" wide, double			12	1.333		140	39		179	215	
	4900	For welded frames, add						26			26	29	
	5400	14 ga., "B" label, up to 5-3/4" deep, 7'-0" high, 4'-0" wide, single		2 Carp	15	1.067		87	31		118	144	
	5440	8'-0" wide, double			12	1.333		106	39		145	178	
	5800	6-3/4" deep, 7'-0" high, 4'-0" wide, single			15	1.067		96	31		127	155	
	5840	8'-0" wide, double			12	1.333		118	39		157	191	
	6200	8-3/4" deep, 7'-0" high, 4'-0" wide, single			15	1.067		108	31		139	167	
	6240	8'-0" wide, double			12	1.333		132	39		171	207	
	6300	For "A" label use same price as "B" label											
	6400	For baked enamel finish, add						30%	15%				
	6500	For galvanizing, add						15%					
	7900	Transom lite frames, fixed, add		2 Carp	155	.103	S.F.	25	3.01		28.01	32	
	8000	Movable, add		"	130	.123	"	30	3.59		33.59	38.50	

08160 | Sliding Metal Doors & Grilles

			CREW	DAILY OUTPUT	LABOR-HOURS	UNIT	MAT.	LABOR	EQUIP.	TOTAL	TOTAL INCL O&P	
300	0010	**STEEL, SLIDING**										**300**
	0020	Up to 50' x 18', electric, standard duty, minimum	L-5	360	.156	S.F.	18.15	5.10	1.75	25	31	
	0100	Maximum		340	.165		30.50	5.40	1.85	37.75	45	
	0500	Heavy duty, minimum		297	.189		24.50	6.20	2.12	32.82	40.50	
	0600	Maximum		277	.202		65	6.65	2.27	73.92	86	

08200 | Wood & Plastic Doors

08210 | Wood Doors

				CREW	DAILY OUTPUT	LABOR-HOURS	UNIT	2001 BARE COSTS				TOTAL INCL O&P	
								MAT.	LABOR	EQUIP.	TOTAL		
450	0010	**KALAMEIN**											**450**
	0020	Interior, flush type, 3' x 7'		2 Carp	4.30	3.721	Opng.	170	108		278	355	
720	0010	**PRE-HUNG DOORS**	R08210 -110										**720**
	0300	Exterior, wood, comb. storm & screen, 6'-9" x 2'-6" wide		2 Carp	15	1.067	Ea.	240	31		271	315	
	0320	2'-8" wide			15	1.067		240	31		271	315	
	0340	3'-0" wide			15	1.067		247	31		278	320	
	0360	For 7'-0" high door, add						23.50			23.50	25.50	
	0370	For aluminum storm doors, see division 08280-800											

8 DOORS & WINDOWS

Important: See the Reference Section for critical supporting data - Reference Nos., Crews, & City Cost Indexes

		08210 | Wood Doors	CREW	DAILY OUTPUT	LABOR-HOURS	UNIT	MAT.	LABOR	EQUIP.	TOTAL	TOTAL INCL O&P	
							2001 BARE COSTS					
720	1600	Entrance door, flush, birch, solid core										**720**
	1620	4-5/8" solid jamb, 1-3/4" x 6'-8" x 2'-8" wide R08210 -110	2 Carp	16	1	Ea.	191	29		220	256	
	1640	3'-0" wide	"	16	1		199	29		228	264	
	1680	For 7'-0" high door, add					9.35			9.35	10.30	
	2000	Entrance door, colonial, 6 panel pine										
	2020	4-5/8" solid jamb, 1-3/4" x 6'-8" x 2'-8" wide	2 Carp	16	1	Ea.	445	29		474	535	
	2040	3'-0" wide	"	16	1		470	29		499	560	
	2060	For 7'-0" high door, add					19.50			19.50	21.50	
	2200	For 5-5/8" solid jamb, add					22.50			22.50	25	
	4000	Interior, passage door, 4-5/8" solid jamb										
	4400	Lauan, flush, solid core, 1-3/8" x 6'-8" x 2'-6" wide	2 Carp	20	.800	Ea.	135	23.50		158.50	185	
	4420	2'-8" wide		20	.800		148	23.50		171.50	200	
	4440	3'-0" wide		19	.842		153	24.50		177.50	207	
	4600	Hollow core, 1-3/8" x 6'-8" x 2'-6" wide		20	.800		110	23.50		133.50	158	
	4620	2'-8" wide		20	.800		110	23.50		133.50	159	
	4640	3'-0" wide		19	.842		112	24.50		136.50	163	
	4700	For 7'-0" high door, add					15.60			15.60	17.15	
	5000	Birch, flush, solid core, 1-3/8" x 6'-8" x 2'-6" wide	2 Carp	20	.800		153	23.50		176.50	205	
	5020	2'-8" wide		20	.800		156	23.50		179.50	208	
	5040	3'-0" wide		19	.842		162	24.50		186.50	218	
	5200	Hollow core, 1-3/8" x 6'-8" x 2'-6" wide		20	.800		122	23.50		145.50	171	
	5220	2'-8" wide		20	.800		125	23.50		148.50	175	
	5240	3'-0" wide		19	.842		127	24.50		151.50	179	
	5280	For 7'-0" high door, add					15.60			15.60	17.15	
	5500	Hardboard paneled, 1-3/8" x 6'-8" x 2'-6" wide	2 Carp	20	.800		124	23.50		147.50	174	
	5520	2'-8" wide		20	.800		127	23.50		150.50	176	
	5540	3'-0" wide		19	.842		129	24.50		153.50	181	
	6000	Pine paneled, 1-3/8" x 6'-8" x 2'-6" wide		20	.800		213	23.50		236.50	271	
	6020	2'-8" wide		20	.800		224	23.50		247.50	283	
	6040	3'-0" wide		19	.842		232	24.50		256.50	295	
	6500	For 5-5/8" solid jamb, add					7.85			7.85	8.65	
	6520	For split jamb, deduct					12.20			12.20	13.40	
850	0010	**TIN CLAD** R08110 -100										**850**
	0020	3 ply, 6' x 7', double sliding, manual with hardware	2 Carp	1	16	Opng.	1,350	465		1,815	2,200	
	1000	For electric operator, add	1 Elec	2	4	"	2,375	137		2,512	2,800	
900	0010	**WOOD DOOR, ARCHITECTURAL** R08210 -100										**900**
	0015	Flush, int., 1-3/4", 7 ply, hollow core,										
	0020	Lauan face, 2'-0" x 6'-8"	2 Carp	17	.941	Ea.	25.50	27.50		53	71	
	0040	2'-6" x 6'-8"		17	.941		28.50	27.50		56	74.50	
	0080	3'-0" x 6'-8"		17	.941		36.50	27.50		64	83.50	
	0100	4'-0" x 6'-8"		16	1		57.50	29		86.50	109	
	0120	Birch face, 2'-0" x 6'-8"		17	.941		37.50	27.50		65	84	
	0140	2'-6" x 6'-8"		17	.941		59	27.50		86.50	108	
	0180	3'-0" x 6'-8"		17	.941		62	27.50		89.50	111	
	0200	4'-0" x 6'-8"		16	1		79	29		108	132	
	0220	Oak face, 2'-0" x 6'-8"		17	.941		60.50	27.50		88	110	
	0240	2'-6" x 6'-8"		17	.941		64.50	27.50		92	114	
	0280	3'-0" x 6'-8"		17	.941		69	27.50		96.50	119	
	0300	4'-0" x 6'-8"		16	1		87	29		116	142	
	0320	Walnut face, 2'-0" x 6'-8"		17	.941		122	27.50		149.50	177	
	0340	2'-6" x 6'-8"		17	.941		124	27.50		151.50	180	
	0380	3'-0" x 6'-8"		17	.941		129	27.50		156.50	185	
	0400	4'-0" x 6'-8"		16	1		146	29		175	207	
	0430	For 7'-0" high, add					13.80			13.80	15.15	
	0440	For 8'-0" high, add					19.30			19.30	21	

DOORS & WINDOWS | **8**

			DAILY	LABOR-		2001 BARE COSTS				TOTAL	
08210	**Wood Doors**	CREW	OUTPUT	HOURS	UNIT	MAT.	LABOR	EQUIP.	TOTAL	INCL O&P	
900	0460	For 8'-0" high walnut, add	R08210 -100			Ea.	11.55			11.55	12.70	**900**
	0480	For prefinishing, clear, add					30.50			30.50	33.50	
	0500	For prefinishing, stain, add					41.50			41.50	45.50	
	1320	M.D. overlay on hardboard, 2'-0" x 6'-8"	2 Carp	17	.941		85.50	27.50		113	137	
	1340	2'-6" x 6'-8"		17	.941		85.50	27.50		113	137	
	1380	3'-0" x 6'-8"		17	.941		101	27.50		128.50	154	
	1400	4'-0" x 6'-8"	▼	16	1		131	29		160	190	
	1420	For 7'-0" high, add					7.60			7.60	8.35	
	1440	For 8'-0" high, add					20			20	22	
	1720	H.P. plastic laminate, 2'-0" x 6'-8"	2 Carp	16	1		191	29		220	256	
	1740	2'-6" x 6'-8"		16	1		191	29		220	256	
	1780	3'-0" x 6'-8"		15	1.067		217	31		248	288	
	1800	4'-0" x 6'-8"	▼	14	1.143		305	33.50		338.50	385	
	1820	For 7'-0" high, add					7.60			7.60	8.35	
	1840	For 8'-0" high, add					19.30			19.30	21	
	2020	5 ply particle core, lauan face, 2'-6" x 6'-8"	2 Carp	15	1.067		67.50	31		98.50	123	
	2040	3'-0" x 6'-8"		14	1.143		74	33.50		107.50	134	
	2080	3'-0" x 7'-0"		13	1.231		77	36		113	141	
	2100	4'-0" x 7'-0"		12	1.333		95.50	39		134.50	166	
	2120	Birch face, 2'-6" x 6'-8"		15	1.067		81	31		112	138	
	2140	3'-0" x 6'-8"		14	1.143		88.50	33.50		122	150	
	2180	3'-0" x 7'-0"		13	1.231		90.50	36		126.50	156	
	2200	4'-0" x 7'-0"		12	1.333		110	39		149	182	
	2220	Oak face, 2'-6" x 6'-8"		15	1.067		89	31		120	147	
	2240	3'-0" x 6'-8"		14	1.143		98	33.50		131.50	160	
	2280	3'-0" x 7'-0"		13	1.231		101	36		137	167	
	2300	4'-0" x 7'-0"		12	1.333		123	39		162	197	
	2320	Walnut face, 2'-0" x 6'-8"		15	1.067		98.50	31		129.50	158	
	2340	2'-6" x 6'-8"		14	1.143		113	33.50		146.50	176	
	2380	3'-0" x 6'-8"		13	1.231		127	36		163	196	
	2400	4'-0" x 6'-8"	▼	12	1.333		158	39		197	235	
	2440	For 8'-0" high, add					23			23	25.50	
	2460	For 8'-0" high walnut, add					13.50			13.50	14.85	
	2480	For solid wood core, add					30			30	33	
	2720	For prefinishing, clear, add					19.70			19.70	21.50	
	2740	For prefinishing, stain, add					41			41	45	
	3320	M.D. overlay on hardboard, 2'-6" x 6'-8"	2 Carp	14	1.143		74.50	33.50		108	134	
	3340	3'-0" x 6'-8"		13	1.231		81.50	36		117.50	146	
	3380	3'-0" x 7'-0"		12	1.333		83.50	39		122.50	153	
	3400	4'-0" x 7'-0"	▼	10	1.600		102	46.50		148.50	185	
	3440	For 8'-0" height, add					23			23	25.50	
	3460	For solid wood core, add					30			30	33	
	3720	H.P. plastic laminate, 2'-6" x 6'-8"	2 Carp	13	1.231		114	36		150	182	
	3740	3'-0" x 6'-8"		12	1.333		129	39		168	203	
	3780	3'-0" x 7'-0"		11	1.455		134	42.50		176.50	215	
	3800	4'-0" x 7'-0"	▼	8	2		163	58.50		221.50	271	
	3840	For 8'-0" height, add					23			23	25.50	
	3860	For solid wood core, add					28.50			28.50	31	
	4000	Exterior, flush, solid wood stave core, birch, 1-3/4" x 7'-0" x 2'-6"	2 Carp	15	1.067		143	31		174	206	
	4020	2'-8" wide		15	1.067		150	31		181	213	
	4040	3'-0" wide		14	1.143		158	33.50		191.50	226	
	4100	Oak faced 1-3/4" x 7'-0" x 2'-6" wide		15	1.067		157	31		188	222	
	4120	2'-8" wide		15	1.067		168	31		199	234	
	4140	3'-0" wide		14	1.143		180	33.50		213.50	250	
	4200	Walnut faced, 1-3/4" x 7'-0" x 2'-6" wide		15	1.067		231	31		262	305	
	4220	2'-8" wide	▼	15	1.067	▼	242	31		273	315	

Section label (vertical, left margin): **8 DOORS & WINDOWS**

Important: See the Reference Section for critical supporting data - Reference Nos., Crews, & City Cost Indexes

08210		Wood Doors		CREW	DAILY OUTPUT	LABOR-HOURS	UNIT	2001 BARE COSTS				TOTAL INCL O&P	
								MAT.	LABOR	EQUIP.	TOTAL		
900	4240	3'-0" wide	R08210 -100	2 Carp	14	1.143	Ea.	252	33.50		285.50	330	**900**
	4300	For 6'-8" high door, deduct from 7'-0" door						12.90			12.90	14.15	
910	0010	**WOOD DOORS, DECORATOR**											**910**
	3000	Solid wood, 1-3/4" thick stile and rail											
	3020	Mahogany, 3'-0" x 7'-0", minimum		2 Carp	14	1.143	Ea.	445	33.50		478.50	540	
	3030	Maximum			10	1.600		650	46.50		696.50	790	
	3040	3'-6" x 8'-0", minimum			10	1.600		655	46.50		701.50	795	
	3050	Maximum			8	2		755	58.50		813.50	925	
	3100	Pine, 3'-0" x 7'-0", minimum			14	1.143		291	33.50		324.50	370	
	3110	Maximum			10	1.600		525	46.50		571.50	650	
	3120	3'-6" x 8'-0", minimum			10	1.600		580	46.50		626.50	710	
	3130	Maximum			8	2		960	58.50		1,018.50	1,150	
	3200	Red oak, 3'-0" x 7'-0", minimum			14	1.143		655	33.50		688.50	770	
	3210	Maximum			10	1.600		1,175	46.50		1,221.50	1,350	
	3220	3'-6" x 8'-0", minimum			10	1.600		830	46.50		876.50	990	
	3230	Maximum			8	2		1,375	58.50		1,433.50	1,600	
	4000	Hand carved door, mahogany											
	4020	3'-0" x 7'-0", minimum		2 Carp	14	1.143	Ea.	650	33.50		683.50	765	
	4030	Maximum			11	1.455		1,550	42.50		1,592.50	1,800	
	4040	3'-6" x 8'-0", minimum			10	1.600		1,050	46.50		1,096.50	1,250	
	4050	Maximum			8	2		2,225	58.50		2,283.50	2,550	
	4200	Red oak, 3'-0" x 7'-0", minimum			14	1.143		1,275	33.50		1,308.50	1,450	
	4210	Maximum			11	1.455		3,000	42.50		3,042.50	3,375	
	4220	3'-6" x 8'-0", minimum			10	1.600		2,575	46.50		2,621.50	2,925	
	4280	For 6'-8" high door, deduct from 7'-0" door						23.50			23.50	25.50	
	4400	For custom finish, add						103			103	113	
	4600	Side light, mahogany, 7'-0" x 1'-6" wide, minimum		2 Carp	18	.889		258	26		284	325	
	4610	Maximum			14	1.143		700	33.50		733.50	820	
	4620	8'-0" x 1'-6" wide, minimum			14	1.143		320	33.50		353.50	400	
	4630	Maximum			10	1.600		810	46.50		856.50	970	
	4640	Side light, oak, 7'-0" x 1'-6" wide, minimum			18	.889		345	26		371	420	
	4650	Maximum			14	1.143		805	33.50		838.50	935	
	4660	8'-0" x 1-6" wide, minimum			14	1.143		420	33.50		453.50	510	
	4670	Maximum			10	1.600		945	46.50		991.50	1,125	
	6520	Interior cafe doors, 2'-6" opening, stock, panel pine			16	1		150	29		179	211	
	6540	3'-0" opening			16	1		156	29		185	217	
	6550	Louvered pine											
	6560	2'-6" opening		2 Carp	16	1	Ea.	131	29		160	190	
	8000	3'-0" opening			16	1		139	29		168	199	
	8010	2'-6" opening, hardwood			16	1		173	29		202	236	
	8020	3'-0" opening			16	1		203	29		232	269	
	8800	Pre-hung doors, see division 08210-720											
920	0010	**WOOD DOORS, PANELED**											**920**
	0020	Interior, six panel, hollow core, 1-3/8" thick											
	0040	Molded hardboard, 2'-0" x 6'-8"		2 Carp	17	.941	Ea.	41.50	27.50		69	88.50	
	0060	2'-6" x 6'-8"			17	.941		44.50	27.50		72	92	
	0080	3'-0" x 6'-8"			17	.941		49.50	27.50		77	97	
	0140	Embossed print, molded hardboard, 2'-0" x 6'-8"			17	.941		44.50	27.50		72	92	
	0160	2'-6" x 6'-8"			17	.941		44.50	27.50		72	92	
	0180	3'-0" x 6'-8"			17	.941		49.50	27.50		77	97	
	0540	Six panel, solid, 1-3/8" thick, pine, 2'-0" x 6'-8"			15	1.067		108	31		139	168	
	0560	2'-6" x 6'-8"			14	1.143		122	33.50		155.50	186	
	0580	3'-0" x 6'-8"			13	1.231		140	36		176	210	
	1020	Two panel, bored rail, solid, 1-3/8" thick, pine, 1'-6" x 6'-8"			16	1		197	29		226	263	
	1040	2'-0" x 6'-8"			15	1.067		259	31		290	335	
	1060	2'-6" x 6'-8"			14	1.143		296	33.50		329.50	375	

DOORS & WINDOWS **8**

		08210	Wood Doors	CREW	DAILY OUTPUT	LABOR-HOURS	UNIT	2001 BARE COSTS				TOTAL INCL O&P	
								MAT.	LABOR	EQUIP.	TOTAL		
920	1340		Two panel, solid, 1-3/8" thick, fir, 2'-0" x 6'-8"	2 Carp	15	1.067	Ea.	108	31		139	168	**920**
	1360		2'-6" x 6'-8"		14	1.143		122	33.50		155.50	186	
	1380		3'-0" x 6'-8"		13	1.231		296	36		332	380	
	1740		Five panel, solid, 1-3/8" thick, fir, 2'-0" x 6'-8"		15	1.067		194	31		225	262	
	1760		2'-6" x 6'-8"		14	1.143		296	33.50		329.50	375	
	1780		3'-0" x 6'-8"	↓	13	1.231	↓	296	36		332	380	
930	0010	**WOOD DOORS, RESIDENTIAL**											**930**
	0200		Exterior, combination storm & screen, pine										
	0260		2'-8" wide	2 Carp	10	1.600	Ea.	220	46.50		266.50	315	
	0280		3'-0" wide		9	1.778		228	52		280	330	
	0300		7'-1" x 3'-0" wide		9	1.778		248	52		300	355	
	0400		Full lite, 6'-9" x 2'-6" wide		11	1.455		220	42.50		262.50	310	
	0420		2'-8" wide		10	1.600		220	46.50		266.50	315	
	0440		3'-0" wide		9	1.778		228	52		280	330	
	0500		7'-1" x 3'-0" wide		9	1.778		251	52		303	355	
	0700		Dutch door, pine, 1-3/4" x 6'-8" x 2'-8" wide, minimum		12	1.333		585	39		624	705	
	0720		Maximum		10	1.600		620	46.50		666.50	760	
	0800		3'-0" wide, minimum		12	1.333		615	39		654	735	
	0820		Maximum		10	1.600		665	46.50		711.50	810	
	1000		Entrance door, colonial, 1-3/4" x 6'-8" x 2'-8" wide		16	1		320	29		349	395	
	1020		6 panel pine, 3'-0" wide		15	1.067		345	31		376	430	
	1100		8 panel pine, 2'-8" wide		16	1		475	29		504	565	
	1120		3'-0" wide	↓	15	1.067		515	31		546	615	
	1200		For tempered safety glass lites, add					24			24	26.50	
	1300		Flush, birch, solid core, 1-3/4" x 6'-8" x 2'-8" wide	2 Carp	16	1		74	29		103	127	
	1320		3'-0" wide		15	1.067		81	31		112	138	
	1350		7'-0" x 2'-8" wide		16	1		82.50	29		111.50	136	
	1360		3'-0" wide	↓	15	1.067		90	31		121	148	
	1380		For tempered safety glass lites, add				↓	50.50			50.50	55.50	
	2700		Interior, closet, bi-fold, w/hardware, no frame or trim incl.										
	2720		Flush, birch, 6'-6" or 6'-8" x 2'-6" wide	2 Carp	13	1.231	Ea.	44.50	36		80.50	105	
	2740		3'-0" wide		13	1.231		44.50	36		80.50	105	
	2760		4'-0" wide		12	1.333		81.50	39		120.50	151	
	2780		5'-0" wide		11	1.455		88.50	42.50		131	164	
	2800		6'-0" wide		10	1.600		97	46.50		143.50	179	
	3000		Raised panel pine, 6'-6" or 6'-8" x 2'-6" wide		13	1.231		122	36		158	190	
	3020		3'-0" wide		13	1.231		136	36		172	205	
	3040		4'-0" wide		12	1.333		217	39		256	299	
	3060		5'-0" wide		11	1.455		250	42.50		292.50	340	
	3080		6'-0" wide		10	1.600		280	46.50		326.50	385	
	3200		Louvered, pine 6'-6" or 6'-8" x 2'-6" wide		13	1.231		101	36		137	167	
	3220		3'-0" wide		13	1.231		113	36		149	180	
	3240		4'-0" wide		12	1.333		176	39		215	255	
	3260		5'-0" wide		11	1.455		200	42.50		242.50	287	
	3280		6'-0" wide	↓	10	1.600	↓	222	46.50		268.50	315	
	4400		Bi-passing closet, incl. hardware and frame, no trim incl.										
	4420		Flush, lauan, 6'-8" x 4'-0" wide	2 Carp	12	1.333	Opng.	156	39		195	232	
	4440		5'-0" wide		11	1.455		169	42.50		211.50	253	
	4460		6'-0" wide		10	1.600		181	46.50		227.50	272	
	4600		Flush, birch, 6'-8" x 4'-0" wide		12	1.333		176	39		215	255	
	4620		5'-0" wide		11	1.455		195	42.50		237.50	282	
	4640		6'-0" wide		10	1.600		212	46.50		258.50	305	
	4800		Louvered, pine, 6'-8" x 4'-0" wide		12	1.333		355	39		394	450	
	4820		5'-0" wide		11	1.455		385	42.50		427.50	490	
	4840		6'-0" wide		10	1.600		435	46.50		481.50	550	
	5000		Paneled, pine, 6'-8" x 4'-0" wide	↓	12	1.333	↓	340	39		379	430	

8

DOORS & WINDOWS

Important: See the Reference Section for critical supporting data - Reference Nos., Crews, & City Cost Indexes

08210 | Wood Doors

			CREW	DAILY OUTPUT	LABOR-HOURS	UNIT	MAT.	LABOR	EQUIP.	TOTAL	TOTAL INCL O&P	
								2001 BARE COSTS				
930	5020	5'-0" wide	2 Carp	11	1.455	Opng.	370	42.50		412.50	475	930
	5040	6'-0" wide	↓	10	1.600	↓	415	46.50		461.50	535	
	6100	Folding accordion, closet, including track and frame										
	6120	Vinyl, 2 layer, stock (see also division 10651-100)	2 Carp	400	.040	S.F.	2.91	1.17		4.08	5	
	6140	Woven mahogany and vinyl, stock		400	.040		1.56	1.17		2.73	3.54	
	6160	Wood slats with vinyl overlay, stock		400	.040		9.35	1.17		10.52	12.10	
	6180	Economy vinyl, stock		400	.040		1.59	1.17		2.76	3.57	
	6200	Rigid PVC	↓	400	.040	↓	4.37	1.17		5.54	6.65	
	6220	For custom partition, add					25%	10%				
	7310	Passage doors, flush, no frame included										
	7320	Hardboard, hollow core, 1-3/8" x 6'-8" x 1'-6" wide	2 Carp	18	.889	Ea.	37	26		63	81	
	7330	2'-0" wide		18	.889		39	26		65	83	
	7340	2'-6" wide		18	.889		43	26		69	87.50	
	7350	2'-8" wide		18	.889		45	26		71	90	
	7360	3'-0" wide		17	.941		47	27.50		74.50	94.50	
	7420	Lauan, hollow core, 1-3/8" x 6'-8" x 1'-6" wide		18	.889		23	26		49	66	
	7440	2'-0" wide		18	.889		25	26		51	68	
	7450	2'-4" wide		18	.889		28	26		54	71.50	
	7460	2'-6" wide		18	.889		28	26		54	71.50	
	7480	2'-8" wide		18	.889		29.50	26		55.50	73	
	7500	3'-0" wide		17	.941		31.50	27.50		59	77.50	
	7700	Birch, hollow core, 1-3/8" x 6'-8" x 1'-6" wide		18	.889		30	26		56	73.50	
	7720	2'-0" wide		18	.889		36.	26		62	80	
	7740	2'-6" wide		18	.889		41.50	26		67.50	86.50	
	7760	2'-8" wide		18	.889		41.50	26		67.50	86.50	
	7780	3'-0" wide **CN**		17	.941		47	27.50		74.50	95	
	8000	Pine louvered, 1-3/8" x 6'-8" x 1'-6" wide		19	.842		90.50	24.50		115	138	
	8020	2'-0" wide		18	.889		114	26		140	166	
	8040	2'-6" wide		18	.889		124	26		150	177	
	8060	2'-8" wide		18	.889		131	26		157	185	
	8080	3'-0" wide		17	.941		140	27.50		167.50	197	
	8300	Pine paneled, 1-3/8" x 6'-8" x 1'-6" wide		19	.842		101	24.50		125.50	150	
	8320	2'-0" wide		18	.889		116	26		142	169	
	8330	2'-4" wide		18	.889		128	26		154	182	
	8340	2'-6" wide		18	.889		130	26		156	184	
	8360	2'-8" wide		18	.889		141	26		167	196	
	8380	3'-0" wide	↓	17	.941	↓	150	27.50		177.50	208	
	8550	For over 20 doors, deduct					15%					
950	0010	**WOOD FIRE DOORS** R08210 -100										950
	0020	Particle core, 7 face plys, "B" label,										
	0040	1 hour, birch face, 1-3/4" x 2'-6" x 6'-8"	2 Carp	14	1.143	Ea.	217	33.50		250.50	290	
	0080	3'-0" x 6'-8"		13	1.231		224	36		260	300	
	0090	3'-0" x 7'-0"		12	1.333		234	39		273	320	
	0100	4'-0" x 7'-0"		12	1.333		310	39		349	400	
	0140	Oak face, 2'-6" x 6'-8"		14	1.143		217	33.50		250.50	290	
	0180	3'-0" x 6'-8"		13	1.231		224	36		260	305	
	0190	3'-0" x 7'-0"		12	1.333		234	39		273	320	
	0200	4'-0" x 7'-0"		12	1.333		305	39		344	395	
	0240	Walnut face, 2'-6" x 6'-8"		14	1.143		285	33.50		318.50	365	
	0280	3'-0" x 6'-8"		13	1.231		291	36		327	375	
	0290	3'-0" x 7'-0"		12	1.333		305	39		344	395	
	0300	4'-0" x 7'-0"		12	1.333		410	39		449	510	
	0440	M.D. overlay on hardboard, 2'-6" x 6'-8"		15	1.067		190	31		221	258	
	0480	3'-0" x 6'-8"		14	1.143		198	33.50		231.50	270	
	0490	3'-0" x 7'-0"		13	1.231		209	36		245	286	
	0500	4'-0" x 7'-0"	↓	12	1.333	↓	255	39		294	340	

DOORS & WINDOWS | **8**

		08210	Wood Doors	CREW	DAILY OUTPUT	LABOR-HOURS	UNIT	2001 BARE COSTS				TOTAL INCL O&P	
								MAT.	LABOR	EQUIP.	TOTAL		
950	0540		H.P. plastic laminate, 2'-6" x 6'-8" R08210-100	2 Carp	13	1.231	Ea.	254	36		290	335	950
	0580		3'-0" x 6'-8"		12	1.333		267	39		306	355	
	0590		3'-0" x 7'-0"		11	1.455		270	42.50		312.50	365	
	0600		4'-0" x 7'-0"		10	1.600		345	46.50		391.50	455	
	0740		90 minutes, birch face, 1-3/4" x 2'-6" x 6'-8"		14	1.143		215	33.50		248.50	288	
	0780		3'-0" x 6'-8"		13	1.231		220	36		256	298	
	0790		3'-0" x 7'-0"		12	1.333		231	39		270	315	
	0800		4'-0" x 7'-0"		12	1.333		315	39		354	405	
	0840		Oak face, 2'-6" x 6'-8"		14	1.143		203	33.50		236.50	275	
	0880		3'-0" x 6'-8"		13	1.231		211	36		247	288	
	0890		3'-0" x 7'-0"		12	1.333		221	39		260	305	
	0900		4'-0" x 7'-0"		12	1.333		305	39		344	395	
	0940		Walnut face, 2'-6" x 6'-8"		14	1.143		279	33.50		312.50	355	
	0980		3'-0" x 6'-8"		13	1.231		286	36		322	370	
	0990		3'-0" x 7'-0"		12	1.333		300	39		339	390	
	1000		4'-0" x 7'-0"		12	1.333		430	39		469	535	
	1140		M.D. overlay on hardboard, 2'-6" x 6'-8"		15	1.067		221	31		252	292	
	1180		3'-0" x 6'-8"		14	1.143		227	33.50		260.50	300	
	1190		3'-0" x 7'-0"		13	1.231		236	36		272	315	
	1200		4'-0" x 7'-0"		12	1.333		320	39		359	415	
	1240		For 8'-0" height, add					40.50			40.50	44.50	
	1260		For 8'-0" height walnut, add					53.50			53.50	59	
	1340		H.P. plastic laminate, 2'-6" x 6'-8"	2 Carp	13	1.231		275	36		311	360	
	1380		3'-0" x 6'-8"		12	1.333		289	39		328	380	
	1390		3'-0" x 7'-0"		11	1.455		292	42.50		334.50	385	
	1400		4'-0" x 7'-0"		10	1.600		380	46.50		426.50	490	
	2200		Custom architectural "B" label, flush, 1-3/4" thick, birch,										
	2210		Solid core										
	2220		2'-6" x 7'-0"	2 Carp	15	1.067	Ea.	330	31		361	415	
	2260		3'-0" x 7'-0"		14	1.143		335	33.50		368.50	420	
	2300		4'-0" x 7'-0"		13	1.231		460	36		496	560	
	2420		4'-0" x 8'-0"		11	1.455		535	42.50		577.50	655	
	2460		For 6'-8" high door, deduct from 7'-0" door					13.25			13.25	14.60	
	2480		For oak veneer, add					50%					
	2500		For walnut veneer, add					75%					
960	0010		**WOOD FRAMES**										960
	0400		Exterior frame, incl. ext. trim, pine, 5/4 x 4-9/16" deep	2 Carp	375	.043	L.F.	3.92	1.24		5.16	6.25	
	0420		5-3/16" deep		375	.043		6.70	1.24		7.94	9.30	
	0440		6-9/16" deep		375	.043		8.75	1.24		9.99	11.60	
	0600		Oak, 5/4 x 4-9/16" deep		350	.046		8.40	1.33		9.73	11.35	
	0620		5-3/16" deep		350	.046		9.50	1.33		10.83	12.55	
	0640		6-9/16" deep		350	.046		10.55	1.33		11.88	13.70	
	0800		Walnut, 5/4 x 4-9/16" deep		350	.046		9.90	1.33		11.23	13	
	0820		5-3/16" deep		350	.046		14.35	1.33		15.68	17.90	
	0840		6-9/16" deep		350	.046		16.95	1.33		18.28	20.50	
	1000		Sills, 8/4 x 8" deep, oak, no horns		100	.160		11.95	4.66		16.61	20.50	
	1020		2" horns		100	.160		13.30	4.66		17.96	22	
	1040		3" horns		100	.160		15.35	4.66		20.01	24	
	1100		8/4 x 10" deep, oak, no horns		90	.178		16.10	5.20		21.30	26	
	1120		2" horns		90	.178		17.95	5.20		23.15	28	
	1140		3" horns		90	.178		19.50	5.20		24.70	29.50	
	2000		Exterior, colonial, frame & trim, 3' opng., in-swing, minimum		22	.727	Ea.	278	21		299	340	
	2010		Average		21	.762		415	22		437	490	
	2020		Maximum		20	.800		935	23.50		958.50	1,050	
	2100		5'-4" opening, in-swing, minimum		17	.941		315	27.50		342.50	390	

Important: See the Reference Section for critical supporting data - Reference Nos., Crews, & City Cost Indexes

8 DOORS & WINDOWS

08210 | Wood Doors

			CREW	DAILY OUTPUT	LABOR-HOURS	UNIT	2001 BARE COSTS				TOTAL INCL O&P	
							MAT.	LABOR	EQUIP.	TOTAL		
960	2120	Maximum	2 Carp	15	1.067	Ea.	935	31		966	1,075	960
	2140	Out-swing, minimum		17	.941		325	27.50		352.50	400	
	2160	Maximum		15	1.067		975	31		1,006	1,125	
	2400	6'-0" opening, in-swing, minimum		16	1		300	29		329	375	
	2420	Maximum		10	1.600		975	46.50		1,021.50	1,150	
	2460	Out-swing, minimum		16	1		325	29		354	400	
	2480	Maximum		10	1.600	↓	1,200	46.50		1,246.50	1,400	
	2600	For two sidelights, add, minimum		30	.533	Opng.	310	15.55		325.55	370	
	2620	Maximum		20	.800	"	995	23.50		1,018.50	1,125	
	2700	Custom birch frame, 3'-0" opening		16	1	Ea.	179	29		208	242	
	2750	6'-0" opening		16	1		254	29		283	325	
	2900	Exterior, modern, plain trim, 3' opng., in-swing, minimum		26	.615		27	17.95		44.95	57.50	
	2920	Average		24	.667		34	19.45		53.45	68	
	2940	Maximum		22	.727	↓	39	21		60	76	
	3000	Interior frame, pine, 11/16" x 3-5/8" deep		375	.043	L.F.	3.85	1.24		5.09	6.20	
	3020	4-9/16" deep		375	.043		5.15	1.24		6.39	7.65	
	3200	Oak, 11/16" x 3-5/8" deep		350	.046		4.77	1.33		6.10	7.35	
	3220	4-9/16" deep		350	.046		5.15	1.33		6.48	7.75	
	3240	5-3/16" deep		350	.046		5.30	1.33		6.63	7.95	
	3400	Walnut, 11/16" x 3-5/8" deep		350	.046		8.05	1.33		9.38	10.95	
	3420	4-9/16" deep		350	.046		8.50	1.33		9.83	11.45	
	3440	5-3/16" deep		350	.046	↓	8.80	1.33		10.13	11.80	
	3600	Pocket door frame		16	1	Ea.	71.50	29		100.50	124	
	3800	Threshold, oak, 5/8" x 3-5/8" deep		200	.080	L.F.	3.10	2.33		5.43	7.05	
	3820	4-5/8" deep		190	.084		3.94	2.45		6.39	8.15	
	3840	5-5/8" deep	↓	180	.089	↓	4.74	2.59		7.33	9.25	
	4000	For casing see division 06220-400										

08260 | Sliding Wood & Plastic Doors

			CREW	DAILY OUTPUT	LABOR-HOURS	UNIT	MAT.	LABOR	EQUIP.	TOTAL	TOTAL INCL O&P	
700	0010	**GLASS, SLIDING**										700
	0012	Vinyl clad, 1" insul. glass, 6'-0" x 6'-10" high	2 Carp	4	4	Opng.	755	117		872	1,025	
	0030	6'-0" x 8'-0" high		4	4	Ea.	1,600	117		1,717	1,925	
	0100	8'-0" x 6'-10" high		4	4	Opng.	1,700	117		1,817	2,025	
	0500	3 leaf, 9'-0" x 6'-10" high		3	5.333		1,525	155		1,680	1,950	
	0600	12'-0" x 6'-10" high	↓	3	5.333	↓	1,900	155		2,055	2,350	

08280 | Wood/Plastic Storm/Screen Doors

			CREW	DAILY OUTPUT	LABOR-HOURS	UNIT	MAT.	LABOR	EQUIP.	TOTAL	TOTAL INCL O&P	
800	0010	**STORM DOORS & FRAMES** Aluminum, residential,										800
	0020	combination storm and screen										
	0400	Clear anodic coating, 6'-8" x 2'-6" wide	2 Carp	15	1.067	Ea.	139	31		170	202	
	0420	2'-8" wide		14	1.143		166	33.50		199.50	235	
	0440	3'-0" wide	↓	14	1.143	↓	166	33.50		199.50	235	
	0500	For 7' door height, add					5%					
	1000	Mill finish, 6'-8" x 2'-6" wide	2 Carp	15	1.067	Ea.	196	31		227	264	
	1020	2'-8" wide		14	1.143		196	33.50		229.50	267	
	1040	3'-0" wide	↓	14	1.143		212	33.50		245.50	285	
	1100	For 7'-0" door, add					5%					
	1500	White painted, 6'-8" x 2'-6" wide	2 Carp	15	1.067		191	31		222	259	
	1520	2'-8" wide		14	1.143		198	33.50		231.50	270	
	1540	3'-0" wide	↓	14	1.143		204	33.50		237.50	277	
	1600	For 7'-0" door, add				↓	5%					
	2000	Wood door & screen, see division 08210-930										
	2020											

8

DOORS & WINDOWS

08310 | Access Doors & Panels

		CREW	DAILY OUTPUT	LABOR-HOURS	UNIT	2001 BARE COSTS				TOTAL INCL O&P
						MAT.	LABOR	EQUIP.	TOTAL	
100	0010	**ACCESS DOORS**									**100**
	1000	Fire rated door with lock								
	1100	Metal, 12" x 12"	1 Carp	10	.800	Ea.	107	23.50		130.50	155
	1150	18" x 18"		9	.889		135	26		161	190
	1200	24" x 24"		9	.889		162	26		188	220
	1250	24" x 36"		8	1		214	29		243	281
	1300	24" x 48"		8	1		261	29		290	335
	1350	36" x 36"		7.50	1.067		320	31		351	400
	1400	48" x 48"		7.50	1.067		380	31		411	465
	1600	Stainless steel, 12" x 12"		10	.800		172	23.50		195.50	227
	1650	18" x 18"		9	.889		250	26		276	315
	1700	24" x 24"		9	.889		300	26		326	370
	1750	24" x 36"	↓	8	1	↓	365	29		394	445
	2000	Flush door for finishing									
	2100	Metal 8" x 8"	1 Carp	10	.800	Ea.	32.50	23.50		56	72
	2150	12" x 12"	"	10	.800	"	35	23.50		58.50	75
	3000	Recessed door for acoustic tile									
	3100	Metal, 12" x 12"	1 Carp	4.50	1.778	Ea.	40.50	52		92.50	126
	3150	12" x 24"		4.50	1.778		56.50	52		108.50	143
	3200	24" x 24"		4	2		72.50	58.50		131	171
	3250	24" x 36"	↓	4	2	↓	92.50	58.50		151	192
	4000	Recessed door for drywall									
	4100	Metal 12" x 12"	1 Carp	6	1.333	Ea.	47	39		86	113
	4150	12" x 24"		5.50	1.455		66	42.50		108.50	140
	4200	24" x 36"	↓	5	1.600	↓	101	46.50		147.50	185
	6000	Standard door									
	6100	Metal, 8" x 8"	1 Carp	10	.800	Ea.	28.50	23.50		52	67.50
	6150	12" x 12"		10	.800		31	23.50		54.50	70.50
	6200	18" x 18"		9	.889		39	26		65	83.50
	6250	24" x 24"		9	.889		51	26		77	96.50
	6300	24" x 36"		8	1		71	29		100	124
	6350	36" x 36"		8	1		87	29		116	142
	6500	Stainless steel, 8" x 8"		10	.800		54	23.50		77.50	96
	6550	12" x 12"		10	.800		69	23.50		92.50	113
	6600	18" x 18"		9	.889		120	26		146	173
	6650	24" x 24"	↓	9	.889	↓	156	26		182	212
150	0010	**BULKHEAD CELLAR DOORS**									**150**
	0020	Steel, not incl. sides, 44" x 62"	1 Carp	5.50	1.455	Ea.	189	42.50		231.50	275
	0100	52" x 73"		5.10	1.569		210	45.50		255.50	305
	0500	With sides and foundation plates, 57" x 45" x 24"		4.70	1.702		247	49.50		296.50	350
	0600	42" x 49" x 51"	↓	4.30	1.860	↓	297	54		351	410
300	0010	**FLOOR, COMMERCIAL**									**300**
	0020	Aluminum tile, steel frame, one leaf, 2' x 2' opng.	2 Sswk	3.50	4.571	Opng.	355	150		505	660
	0050	3'-6" x 3'-6" opening		3.50	4.571		640	150		790	975
	0500	Double leaf, 4' x 4' opening		3	5.333		940	175		1,115	1,350
	0550	5' x 5' opening	↓	3	5.333	↓	1,375	175		1,550	1,850
350	0010	**FLOOR, INDUSTRIAL**									**350**
	0020	Steel 300 psf L.L., single leaf, 2' x 2', 175#	2 Sswk	6	2.667	Opng.	470	87.50		557.50	675
	0050	3' x 3' opening, 300#		5.50	2.909		645	95.50		740.50	885
	0300	Double leaf, 4' x 4' opening, 455#		5	3.200		970	105		1,075	1,275
	0350	5' x 5' opening, 645#		4.50	3.556		1,275	117		1,392	1,600
	1000	Aluminum, 300 psf L.L., single leaf, 2' x 2', 60#		6	2.667		460	87.50		547.50	665
	1050	3' x 3' opening, 100#		5.50	2.909		715	95.50		810.50	965
	1500	Double leaf, 4' x 4' opening, 160#	↓	5	3.200	↓	1,125	105		1,230	1,450

Important: See the Reference Section for critical supporting data - Reference Nos., Crews, & City Cost Indexes

8 DOORS & WINDOWS

08310 | Access Doors & Panels

			CREW	DAILY OUTPUT	LABOR-HOURS	UNIT	2001 BARE COSTS				TOTAL INCL O&P	
							MAT.	LABOR	EQUIP.	TOTAL		
350	1550	5' x 5' opening, 235#	2 Sswk	4.50	3.556	Opng.	1,500	117		1,617	1,850	350
	2000	Aluminum, 150 psf L.L., single leaf, 2' x 2', 60#		6	2.667		420	87.50		507.50	625	
	2050	3' x 3' opening, 95#		5.50	2.909		625	95.50		720.50	860	
	2500	Double leaf, 4' x 4' opening, 150#		5	3.200		1,000	105		1,105	1,300	
	2550	5' x 5' opening, 230#	↓	4.50	3.556	↓	1,350	117		1,467	1,675	

08320 | Detention Doors & Frames

			CREW	DAILY OUTPUT	LABOR-HOURS	UNIT	MAT.	LABOR	EQUIP.	TOTAL	TOTAL INCL O&P	
900	0010	**SECURITY GATES** See division 10610-100										900
950	0010	**VAULT FRONT**										950
	0020	Door and frame, 32" x 78", clear opening										
	0100	1 hour test, 32" door, weighs 750 lbs.	2 Sswk	1.50	10.667	Opng.	2,675	350		3,025	3,550	
	0200	2 hour test, 32" door, weighs 950 lbs.		1.30	12.308		3,175	405		3,580	4,225	
	0250	40" door, weighs 1130 lbs.		1	16		3,325	525		3,850	4,625	
	0300	4 hour test, 32" door, weighs 1025 lbs.		1.20	13.333		3,200	440		3,640	4,325	
	0350	40" door, weighs 1140 lbs.	↓	.90	17.778		3,725	585		4,310	5,150	
	0500	For stainless steel front, including frame, add to above					1,650			1,650	1,825	
	0550	Back, add				↓	1,650			1,650	1,825	
	0600	For time lock, two movement, add	1 Elec	2	4	Ea.	1,300	137		1,437	1,650	
	0650	Three movement, add	"	2	4		1,725	137		1,862	2,100	
	0800	Day gate, painted, steel, 32" wide	2 Sswk	1.50	10.667		1,500	350		1,850	2,275	
	0850	40" wide		1.40	11.429		1,650	375		2,025	2,500	
	0900	Aluminum, 32" wide		1.50	10.667		2,275	350		2,625	3,125	
	0950	40" wide	↓	1.40	11.429	↓	2,525	375		2,900	3,450	
	2050	Security vault door, class I, 3' wide, 3 1/2" thick	E-24	.19	166	Opng.	13,600	5,375	3,275	22,250	28,000	
	2100	Class II, 3' wide, 7" thick		.19	166		16,200	5,375	3,275	24,850	30,900	
	2150	Class III, 9R, 3' wide, 10" thick, minimum		.13	250	↓	22,100	8,050	4,925	35,075	43,800	
	2160	Class V, type 1, 40" door		2.48	12.903	Ea.	4,900	415	254	5,569	6,400	
	2170	Class V, type 2, 40" door	↓	2.48	12.903		4,925	415	254	5,594	6,425	
	2180	Day gate for class V vault	2 Sswk	2	8	↓	965	263		1,228	1,525	

08330 | Coiling Doors & Grilles

			CREW	DAILY OUTPUT	LABOR-HOURS	UNIT	MAT.	LABOR	EQUIP.	TOTAL	TOTAL INCL O&P	
130	0010	**COUNTER DOORS**										130
	0020	Manual, incl. frm and hdwe, galv. stl., 4' roll-up, 6' long	2 Carp	2	8	Opng.	645	233		878	1,075	
	0300	Galvanized steel, UL label		1.80	8.889		775	259		1,034	1,250	
	0600	Stainless steel, 4' high roll-up, 6' long		2	8		1,050	233		1,283	1,550	
	0700	10' long		1.80	8.889		1,550	259		1,809	2,100	
	2000	Aluminum, 4' high, 4' long		2.20	7.273		710	212		922	1,100	
	2020	6' long		2	8		785	233		1,018	1,225	
	2040	8' long		1.90	8.421		900	245		1,145	1,375	
	2060	10' long		1.80	8.889		1,075	259		1,334	1,600	
	2080	14' long		1.40	11.429		1,575	335		1,910	2,250	
	2100	6' high, 4' long		2	8		785	233		1,018	1,225	
	2120	6' long		1.60	10		920	292		1,212	1,450	
	2140	10' long	↓	1.40	11.429	↓	1,250	335		1,585	1,900	
640	0010	**COILING GRILLE**										640
	0015	Aluminum, manual, incl. frame, mill finish										
	0020	Top coiling, 4' high, 4' long	2 Sswk	3.20	5	Opng.	1,000	164		1,164	1,400	
	0030	6' long		3.20	5		1,050	164		1,214	1,450	
	0040	8' long		2.40	6.667		1,200	219		1,419	1,700	
	0050	12' long		2.40	6.667		1,400	219		1,619	1,925	
	0060	16' long		1.60	10		1,725	330		2,055	2,500	
	0070	6' high, 4' long	↓	3.20	5	↓	1,075	164		1,239	1,475	

DOORS & WINDOWS **8**

8
DOORS & WINDOWS

08330 | Coiling Doors & Grilles

		CREW	DAILY OUTPUT	LABOR-HOURS	UNIT	MAT.	LABOR	EQUIP.	TOTAL	TOTAL INCL O&P	
640	0080	6' long	2 Sswk	3.20	5	Opng.	1,100	164		1,264	1,525	**640**
	0090	8' long		2.40	6.667		1,250	219		1,469	1,775	
	0100	12' long		1.60	10		1,450	330		1,780	2,200	
	0110	16' long		1.20	13.333		1,875	440		2,315	2,850	
	0200	Side coiling, 8' high, 12' long		.60	26.667		1,450	875		2,325	3,200	
	0220	18' long		.50	32		2,125	1,050		3,175	4,225	
	0240	24' long		.40	40		2,900	1,325		4,225	5,575	
	0260	12' high, 12' long		.50	32		2,125	1,050		3,175	4,225	
	0280	18' long		.40	40		3,125	1,325		4,450	5,800	
	0300	24' long		.28	57.143		4,250	1,875		6,125	8,075	
700	0010	ROLLING GRILLE SUPPORTS Overhead framed	E-4	36	.889	L.F.	16.85	29.50	2.34	48.69	75	**700**
720	0010	ROLLING SERVICE DOORS Steel, manual, 20 ga., incl. hardware										**720**
	0050	8' x 8' high	2 Sswk	1.60	10	Ea.	695	330		1,025	1,350	
	0100	10' x 10' high		1.40	11.429		920	375		1,295	1,675	
	0200	20' x 10' high		1	16		1,875	525		2,400	3,025	
	0300	12' x 12' high		1.20	13.333		1,200	440		1,640	2,125	
	0400	20' x 12' high		.90	17.778		1,950	585		2,535	3,175	
	0500	14' x 14' high		.80	20		1,575	655		2,230	2,950	
	0600	20' x 16' high		.60	26.667		2,250	875		3,125	4,075	
	0700	10' x 20' high		.50	32		1,350	1,050		2,400	3,400	
	1000	12' x 12', crank operated, crank on door side		.80	20		1,050	655		1,705	2,375	
	1100	Crank thru wall		.70	22.857		1,175	750		1,925	2,650	
	1300	For vision panel, add					194			194	213	
	1400	For 22 ga., deduct				S.F.	.66			.66	.73	
	1600	3' x 7' pass door within rolling steel door, new construction				Ea.	1,050			1,050	1,150	
	1700	Existing construction	2 Sswk	2	8		1,050	263		1,313	1,625	
	2000	Class A fire doors, manual, 20 ga., 8' x 8' high		1.40	11.429		915	375		1,290	1,675	
	2100	10' x 10' high		1.10	14.545		1,225	480		1,705	2,200	
	2200	20' x 10' high		.80	20		2,425	655		3,080	3,875	
	2300	12' x 12' high		1	16		1,625	525		2,150	2,725	
	2400	20' x 12' high		.80	20		2,800	655		3,455	4,275	
	2500	14' x 14' high		.60	26.667		2,100	875		2,975	3,900	
	2600	20' x 16' high		.50	32		3,500	1,050		4,550	5,750	
	2700	10' x 20' high		.40	40		2,200	1,325		3,525	4,800	
	3000	For 18 ga. doors, add				S.F.	.69			.69	.76	
	3300	For enamel finish, add				"	.82			.82	.90	
	3600	For safety edge bottom bar, pneumatic, add				L.F.	10.75			10.75	11.85	
	3700	Electric, add					20			20	22.50	
	4000	For weatherstripping, extruded rubber, jambs, add					6.95			6.95	7.65	
	4100	Hood, add					4.43			4.43	4.87	
	4200	Sill, add					2.53			2.53	2.78	
	4500	Motor operators, to 14' x 14' opening	2 Sswk	5	3.200	Ea.	670	105		775	930	
	4600	Over 14' x 14', jack shaft type	"	5	3.200		640	105		745	890	
	4700	For fire door, additional fusible link, add					12.65			12.65	13.90	

08341 | Cold Storage Doors

		CREW	DAILY OUTPUT	LABOR-HOURS	UNIT	MAT.	LABOR	EQUIP.	TOTAL	TOTAL INCL O&P	
200	0010	COLD STORAGE										**200**
	0020	Single, 20 ga. galvanized steel										
	0300	Horizontal sliding, 5' x 7', manual operation, 2" thick	2 Carp	2	8	Ea.	2,075	233		2,308	2,650	
	0400	4" thick		2	8		2,725	233		2,958	3,375	
	0500	6" thick		2	8		2,650	233		2,883	3,300	
	0800	5' x 7', power operation, 2" thick		1.90	8.421		4,425	245		4,670	5,225	
	0900	4" thick		1.90	8.421		4,475	245		4,720	5,300	
	1000	6" thick		1.90	8.421		5,100	245		5,345	6,000	

Important: See the Reference Section for critical supporting data - Reference Nos., Crews, & City Cost Indexes

08341 | Cold Storage Doors

			CREW	DAILY OUTPUT	LABOR-HOURS	UNIT	MAT.	LABOR	EQUIP.	TOTAL	TOTAL INCL O&P	
200	1300	9' x 10', manual operation, 2" insulation	2 Carp	1.70	9.412	Ea.	3,575	274		3,849	4,350	**200**
	1400	4" insulation		1.70	9.412		3,675	274		3,949	4,475	
	1500	6" insulation		1.70	9.412		4,425	274		4,699	5,300	
	1800	Power operation, 2" insulation		1.60	10		6,125	292		6,417	7,200	
	1900	4" insulation		1.60	10		6,275	292		6,567	7,350	
	2000	6" insulation		1.70	9.412		7,125	274		7,399	8,250	
	2300	For stainless steel face, add					20%					
	3000	Hinged, lightweight, 3' x 7'-0", galvanized 1 face, 2" thick	2 Carp	2	8	Ea.	1,025	233		1,258	1,500	
	3050	4" thick		1.90	8.421		1,175	245		1,420	1,650	
	3300	Aluminum doors, 3' x 7'-0", 4" thick		1.90	8.421		1,050	245		1,295	1,525	
	3350	6" thick		1.40	11.429		1,875	335		2,210	2,575	
	3600	Stainless steel, 3' x 7'-0", 4" thick		1.90	8.421		1,350	245		1,595	1,850	
	3650	6" thick		1.40	11.429		2,275	335		2,610	3,025	
	3900	Painted, 3' x 7'-0", 4" thick		1.90	8.421		965	245		1,210	1,425	
	3950	6" thick		1.40	11.429		1,850	335		2,185	2,550	
	5000	Bi-parting, electric operated										
	5010	6' x 8' opening, galv. faces, 4" thick for cooler	2 Carp	.80	20	Opng.	5,775	585		6,360	7,250	
	5050	For freezer, 4" thick		.80	20		6,350	585		6,935	7,900	
	5300	For door buck framing and door protection, add		2.50	6.400		470	187		657	810	
	6000	Galvanized batten door, galvanized hinges, 4' x 7'		2	8		1,425	233		1,658	1,925	
	6050	6' x 8'		1.80	8.889		1,950	259		2,209	2,525	
	6500	Fire door, 3 hr., 6' x 8', single slide		.80	20		6,675	585		7,260	8,225	
	6550	Double, bi-parting		.70	22.857		8,650	665		9,315	10,600	

08343 | Hangar Doors

			CREW	DAILY OUTPUT	LABOR-HOURS	UNIT	MAT.	LABOR	EQUIP.	TOTAL	TOTAL INCL O&P	
400	0010	**HANGAR DOOR**										**400**
	0020	Bi-fold, ovhd., 20 PSF wind load, incl. elec. oper.										
	0100	Without sheeting, 12' high x 40'	2 Sswk	240	.067	S.F.	9.50	2.19		11.69	14.40	
	0200	16' high x 60'		230	.070		17.20	2.29		19.49	23	
	0300	20' high x 80'		220	.073		19.50	2.39		21.89	26	

08344 | Industrial Doors

			CREW	DAILY OUTPUT	LABOR-HOURS	UNIT	MAT.	LABOR	EQUIP.	TOTAL	TOTAL INCL O&P	
120	0010	**AIR CURTAINS** Incl. motor starters, transformers,										**120**
	0050	door switches & temperature controls										
	0100	Shipping and receiving doors, unheated, minimal wind stoppage										
	0150	8' high, multiples of 3' wide	2 Shee	3.60	4.444	L.F.	175	149		324	420	
	0160	5' wide		5	3.200		186	107		293	370	
	0210	10' high, multiples of 4' wide		3.60	4.444		174	149		323	420	
	0250	12' high, 3'-6" wide		3.30	4.848		172	163		335	440	
	0260	12' wide		3.30	4.848		203	163		366	475	
	0350	16' high, 3'-6" wide		3.30	4.848		335	163		498	620	
	0360	12' wide		3.30	4.848		168	163		331	435	
	0500	Maximum wind stoppage										
	0550	10' high, multiples of 4' wide	2 Shee	4.40	3.636	L.F.	129	122		251	330	
	0650	14' high, multiples of 4' wide		3.25	4.923		168	165		333	440	
	0750	20' high, multiples of 8' wide		3	5.333		365	179		544	675	
	1100	Heated, maximum wind stoppage, steam heat										
	1150	10' high, multiples of 4' wide	2 Shee	3	5.333	L.F.	470	179		649	790	
	1250	14' high, multiples of 4' wide		2.80	5.714		570	192		762	925	
	1350	20' high, multiples of 8' wide		2.60	6.154		570	206		776	950	
	1500	Customer entrance doors, unheated, minimal wind stoppage										
	1550	10' high, multiples of 3' wide	2 Shee	3.30	4.848	L.F.	175	163		338	445	
	1560	5' wide		5	3.200		189	107		296	375	
	1650	Maximum wind stoppage, 12' high, multiples of 4' wide		3.30	4.848		187	163		350	455	

DOORS & WINDOWS 8

08344 | Industrial Doors

			CREW	DAILY OUTPUT	LABOR-HOURS	UNIT	2001 BARE COSTS				TOTAL INCL O&P
							MAT.	LABOR	EQUIP.	TOTAL	
120	1700	Heated, minimal wind stoppage, electric heat										120
	1750	8' high, multiples of 3' wide	2 Shee	3.10	5.161	L.F.	480	173		653	790
	1760	Multiples of 5' wide		3.10	5.161		360	173		533	665
	1850	10' high, multiples of 3' wide		3.10	5.161		460	173		633	770
	1860	Multiples of 5' wide	↓	3.10	5.161	↓	365	173		538	665
	1950	Maximum wind stoppage, steam heat									
	1960	12' high, multiples of 4' wide	2 Shee	2.80	5.714	L.F.	291	192		483	615
	2000	Walk-in coolers and freezers, ambient air, minimal wind stoppage									
	2050	8' high, multiples of 3' wide	2 Shee	3.60	4.444	L.F.	156	149		305	400
	2060	Multiples of 5' wide		3.60	4.444		156	149		305	400
	2250	Maximum wind stoppage, 12' high, multiples of 3' wide		3.30	4.848		167	163		330	435
	2450	Conveyor openings or service windows, unheated, 5' high		4	4		202	134		336	430
	2460	Heated, electric, 5' high, 2'-6" wide	↓	3.30	4.848	↓	207	163		370	480
	2700	Entrance with recirculating system, unheated, add					175			175	193
	2800	Installation of each doorway	2 Shee	.10	160	Total		5,375		5,375	8,300
200	0010	**DOUBLE ACTING, SWING**										200
	1000	.063" aluminum, 7'-0" high, 4'-0" wide	2 Carp	4.20	3.810	Pr.	355	111		466	565
	1050	6'-8" wide	"	4	4	"	490	117		607	720
	2000	Solid core wood, 3/4" thick, metal frame, stainless steel									
	2010	base plate, 7' high opening, 4' wide	2 Carp	4	4	Pr.	725	117		842	980
	2050	7' wide	"	3.80	4.211	"	1,025	123		1,148	1,325
300	0010	**GLASS DOOR, SWING**										300
	0020	Including hardware, 1/2" thick, tempered, 3' x 7' opening	2 Glaz	2	8	Opng.	1,575	228		1,803	2,100
	0100	6' x 7' opening	"	1.40	11.429	"	3,200	325		3,525	4,025
350	0010	**KENNEL DOORS**										350
	0020	2 way, swinging type, 13" x 19" opening	2 Carp	11	1.455	Opng.	199	42.50		241.50	286
	0100	17" x 29" opening	"	11	1.455	"	214	42.50		256.50	305
600	0010	**SHOCK ABSORBING DOORS**										600
	0020	Rigid, no frame, 1-1/2" thick, 5' x 7'	2 Sswk	1.90	8.421	Opng.	1,150	277		1,427	1,750
	0100	8' x 8'		1.80	8.889		1,600	292		1,892	2,300
	0500	Flexible, no frame, insulated, .16" thick, economy, 5' x 7'		2	8		1,400	263		1,663	2,000
	0600	Deluxe		1.90	8.421		2,125	277		2,402	2,825
	1000	8' x 8' opening, economy		2	8		2,175	263		2,438	2,875
	1100	Deluxe	↓	1.90	8.421	↓	2,800	277		3,077	3,575
650	0010	**TUBULAR STEEL SWING DOORS**										650
	0020	Tubular steel, 7' high, single, 3'-4" opening	2 Sswk	2.50	6.400	Ea.	470	210		680	895
	0100	Double, 6'-0" opening	"	2	8	Pr.	595	263		858	1,125

08348 | Sound Control Doors

			CREW	DAILY OUTPUT	LABOR-HOURS	UNIT	MAT.	LABOR	EQUIP.	TOTAL	TOTAL INCL O&P
100	0010	**ACOUSTICAL DOORS**										100
	0020	Including framed seals, 3' x 7', wood, 27 STC rating	2 Carp	1.50	10.667	Ea.	335	310		645	855
	0100	Steel, 40 STC rating		1.50	10.667		1,300	310		1,610	1,900
	0200	45 STC rating		1.50	10.667		1,700	310		2,010	2,350
	0300	48 STC rating		1.50	10.667		2,150	310		2,460	2,850
	0400	52 STC rating	↓	1.50	10.667	↓	2,575	310		2,885	3,300

08360 | Overhead Doors

			CREW	DAILY OUTPUT	LABOR-HOURS	UNIT	MAT.	LABOR	EQUIP.	TOTAL	TOTAL INCL O&P
550	0010	**OVERHEAD, COMMERCIAL** Frames not included										550
	1000	Stock, sectional, heavy duty, wood, 1-3/4" thick, 8' x 8' high	2 Carp	2	8	Ea.	465	233		698	875
	1100	10' x 10' high		1.80	8.889		695	259		954	1,175
	1200	12' x 12' high	↓	1.50	10.667	↓	1,000	310		1,310	1,575

8 DOORS & WINDOWS

08360 | Overhead Doors

		CREW	DAILY OUTPUT	LABOR-HOURS	UNIT	MAT.	LABOR	EQUIP.	TOTAL	TOTAL INCL O&P	
								2001 BARE COSTS			
550	1300	Chain hoist, 14' x 14' high	2 Carp	1.30	12.308	Ea.	1,550	360		1,910	2,250	**550**
	1400	12' x 16' high		1	16		1,375	465		1,840	2,225	
	1500	20' x 8' high		1.30	12.270		1,275	360		1,635	1,950	
	1600	20' x 16' high		.65	24.615		3,175	720		3,895	4,625	
	1800	Center mullion openings, 8' high		4	4		495	117		612	725	
	1900	20' high	▼	2	8	▼	925	233		1,158	1,400	
	2100	For medium duty custom door, deduct					5%	5%				
	2150	For medium duty stock doors, deduct					10%	5%				
	2300	Fiberglass and aluminum, heavy duty, sectional, 12' x 12' high	2 Carp	1.50	10.667	Ea.	1,300	310		1,610	1,900	
	2450	Chain hoist, 20' x 20' high		.50	32		4,450	935		5,385	6,325	
	2600	Steel, 24 ga. sectional, manual, 8' x 8' high		2	8		375	233		608	780	
	2650	10' x 10' high		1.80	8.889		520	259		779	975	
	2700	12' x 12' high		1.50	10.667		700	310		1,010	1,250	
	2800	Chain hoist, 20' x 14' high	▼	.70	22.857	▼	1,650	665		2,315	2,850	
	2850	For 1-1/4" rigid insulation and 26 ga. galv.										
	2860	back panel, add				S.F.	1.80			1.80	1.98	
	2900	For electric trolley operator, 1/3 H.P., to 12' x 12', add	1 Carp	2	4	Ea.	475	117		592	700	
	2950	Over 12' x 12', 1/2 H.P., add	"	1	8	"	635	233		868	1,075	
600	0010	**RESIDENTIAL GARAGE DOORS** Including hardware, no frame										**600**
	0050	Hinged, wood, custom, double door, 9' x 7'	2 Carp	4	4	Ea.	310	117		427	525	
	0070	16' x 7'		3	5.333		530	155		685	830	
	0200	Overhead, sectional, incl. hardware, fiberglass, 9' x 7', standard		5.28	3.030		515	88.50		603.50	705	
	0220	Deluxe		5.28	3.030		600	88.50		688.50	800	
	0300	16' x 7', standard		6	2.667		795	77.50		872.50	995	
	0320	Deluxe		6	2.667		995	77.50		1,072.50	1,225	
	0500	Hardboard, 9' x 7', standard		8	2		330	58.50		388.50	450	
	0520	Deluxe		8	2		395	58.50		453.50	525	
	0600	16' x 7', standard		6	2.667		580	77.50		657.50	755	
	0620	Deluxe		6	2.667		675	77.50		752.50	860	
	0700	Metal, 9' x 7', standard		5.28	3.030		259	88.50		347.50	425	
	0720	Deluxe		8	2		515	58.50		573.50	655	
	0800	16' x 7', standard		3	5.333		510	155		665	805	
	0820	Deluxe		6	2.667		705	77.50		782.50	900	
	0900	Wood, 9' x 7', standard		8	2		365	58.50		423.50	490	
	0920	Deluxe		8	2		1,050	58.50		1,108.50	1,250	
	1000	16' x 7', standard		6	2.667		735	77.50		812.50	925	
	1020	Deluxe	▼	6	2.667		1,525	77.50		1,602.50	1,800	
	1800	Door hardware, sectional	1 Carp	4	2		161	58.50		219.50	268	
	1810	Door tracks only		4	2		75	58.50		133.50	174	
	1820	One side only	▼	7	1.143		52	33.50		85.50	109	
	3000	Swing-up, including hardware, fiberglass, 9' x 7', standard	2 Carp	8	2		505	58.50		563.50	645	
	3020	Deluxe		8	2		600	58.50		658.50	750	
	3100	16' x 7', standard		6	2.667		635	77.50		712.50	820	
	3120	Deluxe		6	2.667		740	77.50		817.50	935	
	3200	Hardboard, 9' x 7', standard		8	2		261	58.50		319.50	380	
	3220	Deluxe		8	2		345	58.50		403.50	470	
	3300	16' x 7', standard		6	2.667		365	77.50		442.50	520	
	3320	Deluxe		6	2.667		540	77.50		617.50	715	
	3400	Metal, 9' x 7', standard		8	2		286	58.50		344.50	405	
	3420	Deluxe		8	2		450	58.50		508.50	580	
	3500	16' x 7', standard		6	2.667		450	77.50		527.50	610	
	3520	Deluxe		6	2.667		720	77.50		797.50	915	
	3600	Wood, 9' x 7', standard		8	2		315	58.50		373.50	435	
	3620	Deluxe		8	2		500	58.50		558.50	640	
	3700	16' x 7', standard		6	2.667		545	77.50		622.50	720	
	3720	Deluxe	▼	6	2.667	▼	765	77.50		842.50	965	

DOORS & WINDOWS **8**

08360 | Overhead Doors

		CREW	DAILY OUTPUT	LABOR-HOURS	UNIT	2001 BARE COSTS				TOTAL INCL O&P	
						MAT.	LABOR	EQUIP.	TOTAL		
600	3900	Door hardware only, swing up	1 Carp	4	2	Ea.	79	58.50		137.50	178	600
	3920	One side only		7	1.143		51	33.50		84.50	108	
	4000	For electric operator, economy, add		8	1		210	29		239	277	
	4100	Deluxe, including remote control		8	1		300	29		329	375	
	4500	For transmitter/receiver control , add to operator				Total	70.50			70.50	77.50	
	4600	Transmitters, additional				"	22.50			22.50	25	
800	0010	TELESCOPING STEEL DOORS Baked enamel finish										800
	1000	Overhead, .03" thick, electric operated, 10' x 10'	E-3	.80	30	Ea.	8,925	1,000	105	10,030	11,700	
	2000	20' x 10'		.60	40		11,900	1,350	140	13,390	15,600	
	3000	20' x 16'		.40	60		13,700	2,000	210	15,910	18,900	

08370 | Vertical Lift Doors

		CREW	DAILY OUTPUT	LABOR-HOURS	UNIT	MAT.	LABOR	EQUIP.	TOTAL	TOTAL INCL O&P	
950	0010	VERTICAL LIFT DOORS										950
	0020	Motorized, 14 ga. stl, incl., frm and ctrl pnl										
	0050	16' x 16' high	L-10	.50	48	Ea.	15,300	1,575	1,025	17,900	20,800	
	0100	10' x 20' high		1.30	18.462		17,200	610	395	18,205	20,400	
	0120	15' x 20' high		1.30	18.462		21,300	610	395	22,305	24,900	
	0140	20' x 20' high		1	24		25,700	790	515	27,005	30,200	
	0160	25' x 20' high		1	24		29,000	790	515	30,305	33,800	
	0170	32' x 24' high		.75	32		30,100	1,050	685	31,835	35,700	
	0180	20' x 25' high		1	24		30,500	790	515	31,805	35,500	
	0200	25' x 25' high		.70	34.286		34,600	1,125	735	36,460	40,800	
	0220	25' x 30' high		.70	34.286		37,100	1,125	735	38,960	43,600	
	0240	30' x 30' high		.70	34.286		42,600	1,125	735	44,460	49,600	
	0260	35' x 30' high		.70	34.286		47,100	1,125	735	48,960	55,000	

08380 | Traffic Doors

		CREW	DAILY OUTPUT	LABOR-HOURS	UNIT	MAT.	LABOR	EQUIP.	TOTAL	TOTAL INCL O&P	
480	0010	FLEXIBLE TRANSPARENT STRIP ENTRANCE										480
	0100	12" strip width, 2/3 overlap	3 Shee	135	.178	SF Surf	3.76	5.95		9.71	13.35	
	0200	Full overlap		115	.209		4.65	7		11.65	15.90	
	0220	8" strip width, 1/2 overlap		140	.171		2.76	5.75		8.51	11.95	
	0240	Full overlap		120	.200		3.66	6.70		10.36	14.40	
	0300	Add for suspension system, header mount				L.F.	7.30			7.30	8	
	0400	Wall mount				"	7.35			7.35	8.10	

08400 | Entrances & Storefronts

08411 | Aluminum Framed Storefront

		CREW	DAILY OUTPUT	LABOR-HOURS	UNIT	2001 BARE COSTS				TOTAL INCL O&P	
						MAT.	LABOR	EQUIP.	TOTAL		
100	0010	ALUMINUM FRAMES										100
	0020	Entrance, 3' x 7' opening, clear anodized finish	2 Sswk	7	2.286	Opng.	176	75		251	330	
	0040	Bronze finish		7	2.286		275	75		350	440	
	0060	Black finish		7	2.286		310	75		385	480	
	0500	6' x 7' opening, clear finish		6	2.667		275	87.50		362.50	465	
	0520	Bronze finish		6	2.667		310	87.50		397.50	505	
	0540	Black finish		6	2.667		365	87.50		452.50	565	
	1000	With 3' high transoms, 3' x 10' opening, clear finish		6.50	2.462		335	81		416	515	
	1050	Bronze finish		6.50	2.462		370	81		451	555	
	1100	Black finish		6.50	2.462		440	81		521	625	

8

DOORS & WINDOWS

		08411	Aluminum Framed Storefront	CREW	DAILY OUTPUT	LABOR-HOURS	UNIT	2001 BARE COSTS MAT.	LABOR	EQUIP.	TOTAL	TOTAL INCL O&P	
100	1500		With 3' high transoms, 6' x 10' opening, clear finish	2 Sswk	5.50	2.909	Opng.	410	95.50		505.50	625	100
	1550		Bronze finish		5.50	2.909		440	95.50		535.50	655	
	1600		Black finish	↓	5.50	2.909	↓	520	95.50		615.50	745	
120	0010	**ALUMINUM DOORS** Commercial entrance											120
	0800		Narrow stile, no glazing, standard hardware, pair of 2'-6" x 7'-0"	2 Carp	1.70	9.412	Pr.	645	274		919	1,150	
	1000		3'-0" x 7'-0", single		3	5.333	Ea.	425	155		580	715	
	1200		Pair of 3'-0" x 7'-0"		1.70	9.412	Pr.	855	274		1,129	1,375	
	1500		3'-6" x 7'-0", single		3	5.333	Ea.	460	155		615	750	
	2000		Medium stile, pair of 2'-6" x 7'-0"		1.70	9.412	Pr.	705	274		979	1,200	
	2100		3'-0" x 7'-0", single		3	5.333	Ea.	560	155		715	860	
	2200		Pair of 3'-0" x 7'-0"		1.70	9.412	Pr.	1,075	274		1,349	1,600	
	2300		3'-6" x 7'-0", single	↓	5.33	3.002	Ea.	660	87.50		747.50	860	
	5000		Flush panel doors, pair of 2'-6" x 7'-0"	2 Sswk	2	8	Pr.	860	263		1,123	1,425	
	5050		3'-0" x 7'-0", single		2.50	6.400	Ea.	430	210		640	855	
	5100		Pair of 3'-0" x 7'-0"		2	8	Pr.	890	263		1,153	1,450	
	5150		3'-6" x 7'-0", single	↓	2.50	6.400	Ea.	530	210		740	960	
140	0010	**ALUMINUM DOORS & FRAMES** Entrance, narrow stile, including											140
	0015		hardware & closer, clear finish, not incl. glass, 2'-6" x 7'-0" opng.	2 Sswk	2	8	Ea.	420	263		683	940	
	0020		3'-0" x 7'-0" opening		2	8		425	263		688	940	
	0030		3'-6" x 7'-0" opening		2	8		435	263		698	955	
	0100		3'-0" x 10'-0" opening, 3' high transom		1.80	8.889		690	292		982	1,300	
	0200		3'-6" x 10'-0" opening, 3' high transom		1.80	8.889		680	292		972	1,275	
	0280		5'-0" x 7'-0" opening		2	8	↓	725	263		988	1,275	
	0300		6'-0" x 7'-0" opening		1.30	12.308	Pr.	705	405		1,110	1,500	
	0400		6'-0" x 10'-0" opening, 3' high transom		1.10	14.545		630	480		1,110	1,550	
	0420		7'-0" x 7'-0" opening		1	16		765	525		1,290	1,800	
	0500		Wide stile, 2'-6" x 7'-0" opening		2	8	Ea.	645	263		908	1,175	
	0520		3'-0" x 7'-0" opening		2	8		635	263		898	1,175	
	0540		3'-6" x 7'-0" opening		2	8		665	263		928	1,200	
	0560		5'-0" x 7'-0" opening		2	8	↓	1,025	263		1,288	1,600	
	0580		6'-0" x 7'-0" opening		1.30	12.308	Pr.	980	405		1,385	1,800	
	0600		7'-0" x 7'-0" opening	↓	1	16	"	1,100	525		1,625	2,175	
	1100		For full vision doors, with 1/2" glass, add				Leaf	55%					
	1200		For non-standard size, add					67%					
	1300		Light bronze finish, add					36%					
	1400		Dark bronze finish, add					18%					
	1500		For black finish, add				↓	36%					
	1600		Concealed panic device, add					905			905	995	
	1700		Electric striker release, add				Opng.	233			233	256	
	1800		Floor check, add				Leaf	690			690	760	
	1900		Concealed closer, add				"	460			460	505	
	2000		Flush 3' x 7' Insulated, 12"x 12" lite, clear finish	2 Sswk	2	8	Ea.	870	263		1,133	1,425	
600	0010	**STAINLESS STEEL AND GLASS** Entrance unit, narrow stiles											600
	0020		3' x 7' opening, including hardware, minimum	2 Sswk	1.60	10	Opng.	4,475	330		4,805	5,525	
	0050		Average		1.40	11.429		4,850	375		5,225	6,000	
	0100		Maximum	↓	1.20	13.333		5,200	440		5,640	6,500	
	1000		For solid bronze entrance units, statuary finish, add					60%					
	1100		Without statuary finish, add				↓	45%					
	2000		Balanced doors, 3' x 7', economy	2 Sswk	.90	17.778	Ea.	6,050	585		6,635	7,725	
	2100		Premium	"	.70	22.857	"	10,400	750		11,150	12,900	
650	0010	**STOREFRONT SYSTEMS** Aluminum frame, clear 3/8" plate glass,											650
	0020		incl. 3' x 7' door with hardware (400 sq. ft. max. wall)										
	0500		Wall height to 12' high, commercial grade	2 Glaz	150	.107	S.F.	11.65	3.05		14.70	17.45	
	0600		Institutional grade	↓	130	.123		15.55	3.51		19.06	22.50	

DOORS & WINDOWS 8

08400 | Entrances & Storefronts

08411 | Aluminum Framed Storefront

		CREW	DAILY OUTPUT	LABOR-HOURS	UNIT	2001 BARE COSTS MAT.	LABOR	EQUIP.	TOTAL	TOTAL INCL O&P	
650	0700	Monumental grade	2 Glaz	115	.139	S.F.	22	3.97		25.97	30.50	650
	1000	6' x 7' door with hardware, commercial grade		135	.119		11.90	3.38		15.28	18.25	
	1100	Institutional grade		115	.139		16.35	3.97		20.32	24	
	1200	Monumental grade		100	.160		30	4.57		34.57	40.50	
	1500	For bronze anodized finish, add					15%					
	1600	For black anodized finish, add					30%					
	1700	For stainless steel framing, add to monumental					75%					

08460 | Automatic Entrance Doors

		CREW	DAILY OUTPUT	LABOR-HOURS	UNIT	MAT.	LABOR	EQUIP.	TOTAL	TOTAL INCL O&P	
600	0010	**SLIDING ENTRANCE** 12' x 7'-6" opng., 5' x 7' door, 2 way traf.,										600
	0020	mat activated, panic pushout, incl. operator & hardware,										
	0030	not including glass or glazing	2 Glaz	.70	22.857	Opng.	5,725	655		6,380	7,300	
650	0010	**SLIDING PANELS**										650
	0020	Mall fronts, aluminum & glass, 15' x 9' high	2 Glaz	1.30	12.308	Opng.	2,250	350		2,600	3,000	
	0100	24' x 9' high		.70	22.857		3,250	655		3,905	4,600	
	0200	48' x 9' high, with fixed panels		.90	17.778		6,075	510		6,585	7,450	
	0500	For bronze finish, add					17%					

08470 | Revolving Entrance Doors

		CREW	DAILY OUTPUT	LABOR-HOURS	UNIT	MAT.	LABOR	EQUIP.	TOTAL	TOTAL INCL O&P	
600	0010	**REVOLVING DOORS** Aluminum, 6'-6" to 7'-0" diameter,										600
	0020	6'-10" to 7' high, stock units, minimum	4 Sswk	.75	42.667	Opng.	14,800	1,400		16,200	18,900	
	0050	Average		.60	53.333		18,300	1,750		20,050	23,300	
	0100	Maximum		.45	71.111		24,100	2,325		26,425	30,800	
	1000	Stainless steel		.30	106		26,900	3,500		30,400	36,000	
	1100	Solid bronze		.15	213		31,400	7,000		38,400	47,300	
	1500	For automatic controls, add	2 Elec	2	8		10,800	274		11,074	12,300	

08480 | Balanced Entrance Doors

		CREW	DAILY OUTPUT	LABOR-HOURS	UNIT	MAT.	LABOR	EQUIP.	TOTAL	TOTAL INCL O&P	
150	0010	**BALANCED DOORS**										150
	0020	Hardware & frame, alum. & glass, 3' x 7', econ.	2 Sswk	.90	17.778	Ea.	4,625	585		5,210	6,150	
	0150	Premium	"	.70	22.857	"	5,775	750		6,525	7,700	

08500 | Windows

08510 | Steel Windows

		CREW	DAILY OUTPUT	LABOR-HOURS	UNIT	2001 BARE COSTS MAT.	LABOR	EQUIP.	TOTAL	TOTAL INCL O&P	
700	0010	**SCREENS**										700
	0020	For metal sash, aluminum or bronze mesh, flat screen	2 Sswk	1,200	.013	S.F.	3	.44		3.44	4.09	
	0500	Wicket screen, inside window		1,000	.016		4.58	.53		5.11	6	
	0800	Security screen, aluminum frame with stainless steel cloth		1,200	.013		16.15	.44		16.59	18.60	
	0900	Steel grate, painted, on steel frame		1,600	.010		8.70	.33		9.03	10.15	
	1000	For solar louvers, add		160	.100		16.75	3.29		20.04	24.50	
	4000	See also division 05580-900										
750	0010	**STEEL SASH** Custom units, glazing and trim not included R08510-100										750
	0100	Casement, 100% vented	2 Sswk	200	.080	S.F.	34.50	2.63		37.13	43	

Important: See the Reference Section for critical supporting data - Reference Nos., Crews, & City Cost Indexes

08510 | Steel Windows

			CREW	DAILY OUTPUT	LABOR-HOURS	UNIT	MAT.	LABOR	EQUIP.	TOTAL	TOTAL INCL O&P	
750	0200	50% vented	2 Sswk	200	.080	S.F.	29.50	2.63		32.13	37.50	**750**
	0300	Fixed		200	.080		19.75	2.63		22.38	26.50	
	1000	Projected, commercial, 40% vented		200	.080		36	2.63		38.63	44.50	
	1100	Intermediate, 50% vented		200	.080		37.50	2.63		40.13	46	
	1500	Industrial, horizontally pivoted		200	.080		38.50	2.63		41.13	47.50	
	1600	Fixed		200	.080		21.50	2.63		24.13	28.50	
	2000	Industrial security sash, 50% vented		200	.080		40	2.63		42.63	49	
	2100	Fixed		200	.080		33	2.63		35.63	41.50	
	2500	Picture window		200	.080		20.50	2.63		23.13	28	
	3000	Double hung		200	.080		39	2.63		41.63	48	
	5000	Mullions for above, open interior face		240	.067	L.F.	7.05	2.19		9.24	11.70	
	5100	With interior cover		240	.067	"	11.90	2.19		14.09	17	
770	0010	**STEEL WINDOWS** Stock, including frame, trim and insul. glass										**770**
	0020	See also division 13128										
	1000	Custom units, double hung, 2'-8" x 4'-6" opening	2 Sswk	12	1.333	Ea.	495	44		539	625	
	1100	2'-4" x 3'-9" opening		12	1.333		410	44		454	530	
	1500	Commercial projected, 3'-9" x 5'-5" opening		10	1.600		865	52.50		917.50	1,050	
	1600	6'-9" x 4'-1" opening		7	2.286		1,150	75		1,225	1,375	
	2000	Intermediate projected, 2'-9" x 4'-1" opening		12	1.333		485	44		529	615	
	2100	4'-1" x 5'-5" opening		10	1.600		980	52.50		1,032.50	1,175	

08520 | Aluminum Windows

			CREW	DAILY OUTPUT	LABOR-HOURS	UNIT	MAT.	LABOR	EQUIP.	TOTAL	TOTAL INCL O&P	
100	0010	**ALUMINUM SASH**										**100**
	0020	Stock, grade C, glaze & trim not incl., casement	2 Sswk	200	.080	S.F.	27	2.63		29.63	34.50	
	0050	Double hung		200	.080		26	2.63		28.63	33.50	
	0100	Fixed casement		200	.080		9.85	2.63		12.48	15.60	
	0150	Picture window		200	.080		11.35	2.63		13.98	17.25	
	0200	Projected window		200	.080		22.50	2.63		25.13	30	
	0250	Single hung		200	.080		11.70	2.63		14.33	17.65	
	0300	Sliding		200	.080		15.15	2.63		17.78	21.50	
	1000	Mullions for above, tubular		240	.067	L.F.	4.02	2.19		6.21	8.40	
	2000	Custom aluminum sash, grade HC, glazing not included, minimum		200	.080	S.F.	28	2.63		30.63	36	
	2100	Maximum		85	.188	"	36.50	6.20		42.70	51.50	
120	0010	**ALUMINUM WINDOWS** Incl. frame and glazing, Commercial grade										**120**
	0020	See also division 05120-440										
	1000	Stock units, casement, 3'-1" x 3'-2" opening	2 Sswk	10	1.600	Ea.	263	52.50		315.50	385	
	1050	Add for storms					53			53	58	
	1600	Projected, with screen, 3'-1" x 3'-2" opening	2 Sswk	10	1.600		188	52.50		240.50	305	
	1700	Add for storms					50			50	55	
	2000	4'-5" x 5'-3" opening	2 Sswk	8	2		265	65.50		330.50	410	
	2100	Add for storms					69			69	76	
	2500	Enamel finish windows, 3'-1" x 3'-2"	2 Sswk	10	1.600		169	52.50		221.50	282	
	2600	4'-5" x 5'-3"		8	2		253	65.50		318.50	395	
	3000	Single hung, 2' x 3' opening, enameled, standard glazed		10	1.600		126	52.50		178.50	235	
	3100	Insulating glass		10	1.600		153	52.50		205.50	264	
	3300	2'-8" x 6'-8" opening, standard glazed		8	2		268	65.50		333.50	415	
	3400	Insulating glass		8	2		345	65.50		410.50	500	
	3700	3'-4" x 5'-0" opening, standard glazed		9	1.778		173	58.50		231.50	296	
	3800	Insulating glass		9	1.778		243	58.50		301.50	375	
	3890	Awning type, 3' x 3' opening standard glass		14	1.143		310	37.50		347.50	410	
	3900	Insulating glass		14	1.143		330	37.50		367.50	435	
	3910	3' x 4' opening, standard glass		10	1.600		360	52.50		412.50	495	
	3920	Insulating glass		10	1.600		420	52.50		472.50	555	
	3930	3' x 5'-4" opening, standard glass		10	1.600		435	52.50		487.50	575	
	3940	Insulating glass		10	1.600		515	52.50		567.50	660	

DOORS & WINDOWS 8

08520 | Aluminum Windows

			CREW	DAILY OUTPUT	LABOR-HOURS	UNIT	2001 BARE COSTS				TOTAL INCL O&P	
							MAT.	LABOR	EQUIP.	TOTAL		
120	3950	4' x 5'-4" opening, standard glass	2 Sswk	9	1.778	Ea.	480	58.50		538.50	635	120
	3960	Insulating glass		9	1.778		575	58.50		633.50	740	
	4000	Sliding aluminum, 3' x 2' opening, standard glazed		10	1.600		142	52.50		194.50	252	
	4100	Insulating glass		10	1.600		158	52.50		210.50	269	
	4300	5' x 3' opening, standard glazed		9	1.778		180	58.50		238.50	305	
	4400	Insulating glass		9	1.778		252	58.50		310.50	385	
	4600	8' x 4' opening, standard glazed		6	2.667		260	87.50		347.50	445	
	4700	Insulating glass		6	2.667		415	87.50		502.50	620	
	5000	9' x 5' opening, standard glazed		4	4		395	131		526	670	
	5100	Insulating glass		4	4		630	131		761	930	
	5500	Sliding, with thermal barrier and screen, 6' x 4', 2 track		8	2		535	65.50		600.50	710	
	5700	4 track	▼	8	2		655	65.50		720.50	840	
	6000	For above units with bronze finish, add					12%					
	6200	For installation in concrete openings, add				▼	5%					
500	0010	**JALOUSIES**										500
	0020	Aluminum incl. glazing & screens, stock, 1'-7" x 3'-2"	2 Sswk	10	1.600	Ea.	115	52.50		167.50	223	
	0100	2'-3" x 4'-0"		10	1.600		165	52.50		217.50	277	
	0200	3'-1" x 2'-0"		10	1.600		130	52.50		182.50	239	
	0300	3'-1" x 5'-3"		10	1.600		235	52.50		287.50	355	
	1000	Mullions for above, 2'-0" long		80	.200		8.85	6.55		15.40	21.50	
	1100	5'-3" long	▼	80	.200	▼	15.15	6.55		21.70	28.50	
600	0010	**LOUVERS** See division 06440 & 10210										600

08550 | Wood Windows

			CREW	DAILY OUTPUT	LABOR-HOURS	UNIT	2001 BARE COSTS				TOTAL INCL O&P	
							MAT.	LABOR	EQUIP.	TOTAL		
100	0010	**AWNING WINDOW** Including frame, screens and grills										100
	0100	Average quality, builders model, 34" x 22", double insulated glass	1 Carp	10	.800	Ea.	197	23.50		220.50	253	
	0200	Low E glass		10	.800		208	23.50		231.50	265	
	0300	40" x 28", double insulated glass		9	.889		250	26		276	315	
	0400	Low E Glass		9	.889		264	26		290	330	
	0500	48" x 36", double insulated glass		8	1		385	29		414	465	
	0600	Low E glass		8	1		400	29		429	485	
	1000	34" x 22"		10	.800		207	23.50		230.50	264	
	1100	40" x 22"		10	.800		227	23.50		250.50	287	
	1200	36" x 28"		9	.889		242	26		268	310	
	1300	36" x 36"		9	.889		263	26		289	330	
	1400	48" x 28"		8	1		287	29		316	360	
	1500	60" x 36"		8	1		460	29		489	550	
	2000	Metal clad, deluxe, double insulated glass, 34" x 22"		10	.800		184	23.50		207.50	240	
	2100	40" x 22"		10	.800		228	23.50		251.50	288	
	2200	36" x 25"		9	.889		217	26		243	280	
	2300	40" x 30"		9	.889		271	26		297	340	
	2400	48" x 28"		8	1		277	29		306	350	
	2500	60" x 36"	▼	8	1	▼	295	29		324	370	
150	0010	**BOW-BAY WINDOW** Including frame, screens and grills,										150
	0020	end panels operable										
	1000	Bow type, casement, wood, bldrs mdl, 8' x 5' dbl insltd glass, 4 panel	2 Carp	10	1.600	Ea.	875	46.50		921.50	1,025	
	1050	Low E glass		10	1.600		1,125	46.50		1,171.50	1,300	
	1100	10'-0" x 5'-0" , double insulated glass, 6 panels		6	2.667		1,175	77.50		1,252.50	1,400	
	1200	Low E glass, 6 panels		6	2.667		1,225	77.50		1,302.50	1,475	
	1300	Vinyl clad, bldrs model, double insulated glass, 6'-0" x 4'-0", 3 panel		10	1.600		950	46.50		996.50	1,125	
	1340	9'-0" x 4'-0", 4 panel		8	2		1,250	58.50		1,308.50	1,475	
	1380	10'-0" x 6'-0", 5 panels		7	2.286		2,125	66.50		2,191.50	2,450	
	1420	12'-0" x 6'-0", 6 panels	▼	6	2.667	▼	2,725	77.50		2,802.50	3,100	

08550 | Wood Windows

			CREW	DAILY OUTPUT	LABOR-HOURS	UNIT	2001 BARE COSTS				TOTAL INCL O&P	
							MAT.	LABOR	EQUIP.	TOTAL		
150	1600	Metal clad, casement, bldrs mdl, 6'-0" x 4'-0", dbl insltd gls, 3 panels	2 Carp	10	1.600	Ea.	785	46.50		831.50	940	150
	1640	9'-0" x 4'-0" , 4 panels		8	2		1,100	58.50		1,158.50	1,300	
	1680	10'-0" x 5'-0", 5 panels		7	2.286		1,525	66.50		1,591.50	1,775	
	1720	12'-0" x 6'-0", 6 panels		6	2.667		2,125	77.50		2,202.50	2,450	
	2000	Bay window, casement, builders model, 8' x 5' dbl insul glass, 4 panels		10	1.600		1,325	46.50		1,371.50	1,550	
	2050	Low E glass,		10	1.600		1,625	46.50		1,671.50	1,850	
	2100	12'-0" x 6'-0" , double insulated glass, 6 panels		6	2.667		1,675	77.50		1,752.50	1,950	
	2200	Low E glass		6	2.667		1,725	77.50		1,802.50	2,025	
	2280	6'-0" x 4'-0"		11	1.455		975	42.50		1,017.50	1,150	
	2300	Vinyl clad, premium, double insulated glass, 8'-0" x 5'-0"		10	1.600		1,150	46.50		1,196.50	1,325	
	2340	10'-0" x 5'-0"		8	2		1,625	58.50		1,683.50	1,875	
	2380	10'-0" x 6'-0"		7	2.286		1,700	66.50		1,766.50	1,975	
	2420	12'-0" x 6'-0"		6	2.667		2,025	77.50		2,102.50	2,350	
	2600	Metal clad, deluxe, dbl insul. glass, 8'-0" x 5'-0" high, 4 panels		10	1.600		1,175	46.50		1,221.50	1,375	
	2640	10'-0" x 5'-0" high, 5 panels		8	2		1,275	58.50		1,333.50	1,500	
	2680	10'-0" x 6'-0" high, 5 panels		7	2.286		1,500	66.50		1,566.50	1,750	
	2720	12'-0" x 6'-0" high, 6 panels		6	2.667		2,075	77.50		2,152.50	2,425	
	3000	Double hung, bldrs. model, bay, 8' x 4' high, dbl insulated glass		10	1.600		935	46.50		981.50	1,100	
	3050	Low E glass		10	1.600		1,000	46.50		1,046.50	1,175	
	3100	9'-0" x 5'-0" high, doublel insulated glass		6	2.667		1,000	77.50		1,077.50	1,225	
	3200	Low E glass		6	2.667		1,075	77.50		1,152.50	1,300	
	3300	Vinyl clad, premium, double insulated glass, 7'-0" x 4'-6"		10	1.600		970	46.50		1,016.50	1,150	
	3340	8'-0" x 4'-6"		8	2		990	58.50		1,048.50	1,200	
	3380	8'-0" x 5'-0"		7	2.286		1,025	66.50		1,091.50	1,250	
	3420	9'-0" x 5'-0"		6	2.667		1,075	77.50		1,152.50	1,300	
	3600	Metal clad, deluxe, dbl insul. glass, 7'-0" x 4'-0" high		10	1.600		900	46.50		946.50	1,075	
	3640	8'-0" x 4'-0" high		8	2		930	58.50		988.50	1,125	
	3680	8'-0" x 5'-0" high		7	2.286		965	66.50		1,031.50	1,150	
	3720	9'-0" x 5'-0" high		6	2.667		1,025	77.50		1,102.50	1,250	
200	0010	**CASEMENT WINDOW** Including frame, screen, and grills										200
	0100	Avg. quality, bldrs. model, 2'-0" x 3'-0" H, double insulated glass	1 Carp	10	.800	Ea.	162	23.50		185.50	215	
	0150	Low E glass **CN**		10	.800		204	23.50		227.50	261	
	0200	2'-0" x 4'-6" high, double insulated glass		9	.889		211	26		237	273	
	0250	Low E glass		9	.889		278	26		304	345	
	0300	2'-3" x 6'-0" high, double insulated glass		8	1		235	29		264	305	
	0350	Low E glass		8	1		310	29		339	385	
	0522	Vinyl clad, premium, double insulated glass, 2'-0" x 3'-0"		10	.800		212	23.50		235.50	270	
	0524	2'-0" x 4'-0"		9	.889		251	26		277	315	
	0525	2'-0" x 5'-0"		8	1		272	29		301	345	
	0528	2'-0" x 6'-0"		8	1		345	29		374	425	
	8000	Solid vinyl, premium, double insulated glass, 2'-0" x 3'-0" high		10	.800		166	23.50		189.50	219	
	8020	2'-0" x 4'-0" high		9	.889		203	26		229	264	
	8040	2'-0" x 5'-0" high		8	1		234	29		263	305	
	8100	Metal clad, deluxe, double insulated glass, 2'-0" x 3'-0" high		10	.800		165	23.50		188.50	219	
	8120	2'-0" x 4'-0" high		9	.889		199	26		225	260	
	8140	2'-0" x 5'-0" high		8	1		226	29		255	294	
	8160	2'-0" x 6'-0" high		8	1		259	29		288	330	
	8200	For multiple leaf units, deduct for stationary sash										
	8220	2' high				Ea.	17.15			17.15	18.90	
	8240	4'-6" high					19.80			19.80	22	
	8260	6' high					26.50			26.50	29	
	8300	For installation, add per leaf						15%				
250	0010	**DOUBLE HUNG** Including frame, screens, and grills R08550 -010										250
	0100	Avg. quality, bldrs. model, 2'-0" x 3'-0" high, dbl insul. glass	1 Carp	10	.800	Ea.	203	23.50		226.50	260	

8

DOORS & WINDOWS

		08550 **Wood Windows**	CREW	DAILY OUTPUT	LABOR-HOURS	UNIT	2001 BARE COSTS MAT.	LABOR	EQUIP.	TOTAL	TOTAL INCL O&P	
250	0150	Low E glass R08550-010	1 Carp	10	.800	Ea.	213	23.50		236.50	271	**250**
	0200	3'-0" x 4'-0" high, double insulated glass		9	.889		277	26		303	345	
	0250	Low E glass		9	.889		289	26		315	355	
	0300	4'-0" x 4'-6" high, double insulated glass		8	1		310	29		339	385	
	0350	Low E glass		8	1		320	29		349	400	
	1000	Vinyl clad, premium, double insulated glass, 2'-6" x 3'-0"		10	.800		211	23.50		234.50	270	
	1100	3'-0" x 3'-6"		10	.800		253	23.50		276.50	315	
	1200	3'-0" x 4'-0"		9	.889		277	26		303	345	
	1300	3'-0" x 4'-6"		9	.889		292	26		318	360	
	1400	3'-0" x 5'-0"		8	1		305	29		334	380	
	1500	3'-6" x 6'-0"		8	1		370	29		399	455	
	1540	Solid vinyl, average quality, double insulated glass, 2'-0" x 3'-0"		10	.800		123	23.50		146.50	172	
	1542	3'-0" x 4'-0"		9	.889		149	26		175	205	
	1544	4'-0" x 4'-6"		8	1		179	29		208	243	
	1560	Premium, double insulated glass, 2'-6" x 3'-0"		10	.800		140	23.50		163.50	191	
	1562	3'-0" x 3'-6"		9	.889		162	26		188	219	
	1564	3'-0" x 4'-0"		9	.889		172	26		198	231	
	1566	3'-0" x 4'-6"		9	.889		177	26		203	235	
	1568	3'-0" x 5'-0"		8	1		181	29		210	245	
	1570	3'-6" x 6'-0"		8	1		199	29		228	265	
	2000	Metal clad, deluxe, double insulated glass, 2'-6" x 3'-0" high		10	.800		175	23.50		198.50	229	
	2100	3'-0" x 3'-6" high		10	.800		207	23.50		230.50	265	
	2200	3'-0" x 4'-0" high		9	.889		220	26		246	283	
	2300	3'-0" x 4'-6" high		9	.889		238	26		264	305	
	2400	3'-0" x 5'-0" high		8	1		255	29		284	325	
	2500	3'-6" x 6'-0" high		8	1		310	29		339	385	
650	0010	**PALLADIAN WINDOWS**										**650**
	0020	Aluminum clad, double insulated glass, including frame and grills										
	0040	3'-2" x 2'-0" high	2 Carp	11	1.455	Ea.	970	42.50		1,012.50	1,150	
	0060	3'-2" x 4'-10"		11	1.455		1,100	42.50		1,142.50	1,275	
	0080	3'-2" x 6'-4"		10	1.600		1,300	46.50		1,346.50	1,500	
	0100	4'-0" x 4'-0"		10	1.600		1,075	46.50		1,121.50	1,250	
	0120	4'-0" x 5'-4"	3 Carp	10	2.400		1,250	70		1,320	1,450	
	0140	4'-0" x 6'-0"		9	2.667		1,300	77.50		1,377.50	1,550	
	0160	4'-0" x 7'-4"		9	2.667		1,425	77.50		1,502.50	1,675	
	0180	5'-5" x 4'-10"		9	2.667		1,400	77.50		1,477.50	1,650	
	0200	5'-5" x 6'-10"		9	2.667		1,650	77.50		1,727.50	1,950	
	0220	5'-5" x 7'-9"		9	2.667		1,800	77.50		1,877.50	2,100	
	0240	6'-0" x 7'-11"		8	3		2,400	87.50		2,487.50	2,750	
	0260	8'-0" x 6'-0"		8	3		2,050	87.50		2,137.50	2,375	
670	0010	**PICTURE WINDOW** Including frame and grills										**670**
	0100	Average quality, bldrs. model, 3'-6" x 4'-0" high, dbl insulated glass	2 Carp	12	1.333	Ea.	243	39		282	330	
	0150	Low E glass		12	1.333		265	39		304	355	
	0200	4'-0" x 4'-6" high, double insulated glass		11	1.455		260	42.50		302.50	355	
	0250	Low E glass		11	1.455		285	42.50		327.50	380	
	0300	5'-0" x 4'-0" high, double insulated glass		11	1.455		320	42.50		362.50	415	
	0350	Low E glass		11	1.455		360	42.50		402.50	460	
	0400	6'-0" x 4'-6" high, double insulated glass		10	1.600		410	46.50		456.50	525	
	0450	Low E glass		10	1.600		460	46.50		506.50	580	
	1000	Vinyl clad, premium, dbl. insult. glass, 4'-0" x 4'-0"		12	1.333		430	39		469	535	
	1100	4'-0" x 6'-0"		11	1.455		595	42.50		637.50	715	
	1200	5'-0" x 6'-0"		10	1.600		770	46.50		816.50	920	
	1300	6'-0" x 6'-0"		10	1.600		785	46.50		831.50	940	
	2000	Metal clad, deluxe, double insulated glass, 4'-0" x 4'-0" high		12	1.333		259	39		298	345	
	2100	4'-0" x 6'-0" high		11	1.455		385	42.50		427.50	485	
	2200	5'-0" x 6'-0" high		10	1.600		420	46.50		466.50	540	

Important: See the Reference Section for critical supporting data - Reference Nos., Crews, & City Cost Indexes

08550 | Wood Windows

			CREW	DAILY OUTPUT	LABOR-HOURS	UNIT	2001 BARE COSTS MAT.	LABOR	EQUIP.	TOTAL	TOTAL INCL O&P	
670	2300	6'-0" x 6'-0" high	2 Carp	10	1.600	Ea.	485	46.50		531.50	605	670
750	0010	**SLIDING WINDOW** Including frame, screen, and grills										750
	0100	Average quality, bldrs. model, 3'-0" x 3'-0" high, double insulated	1 Carp	10	.800	Ea.	131	23.50		154.50	181	
	0120	Low E glass		10	.800		166	23.50		189.50	219	
	0200	4'-0" x 3'-6" high, double insulated		9	.889		156	26		182	213	
	0220	Low E glass		9	.889		195	26		221	256	
	0300	6'-0" x 5'-0" high, double insulated		8	1		286	29		315	360	
	0320	Low E glass		8	1		340	29		369	420	
	1000	Vinyl clad, premium, dbl. insult. glass, 3'-0" x 3'-0"		10	.800		480	23.50		503.50	560	
	1050	4'-0" x 3'-6"		9	.889		575	26		601	670	
	1100	5'-0" x 4'-0"		9	.889		665	26		691	770	
	1150	6'-0" x 5'-0"		8	1		825	29		854	955	
	2000	Metal clad, deluxe, double insulated glass, 3'-0" x 3'-0" high		10	.800		267	23.50		290.50	330	
	2050	4'-0" x 3'-6" high		9	.889		325	26		351	400	
	2100	5'-0" x 4'-0" high		9	.889		395	26		421	475	
	2150	6'-0" x 5'-0" high		8	1		480	29		509	575	
770	0010	**WEATHERSTRIPPING** See division 08720										770
800	0010	**WINDOW GRILLE OR MUNTIN** Snap-in type										800
	0020	Standard pattern interior grills										
	2000	Wood, awning window, glass size 28" x 16" high	1 Carp	30	.267	Ea.	17.15	7.75		24.90	31	
	2060	44" x 24" high		32	.250		25	7.30		32.30	39	
	2100	Casement, glass size, 20" x 36" high		30	.267		21	7.75		28.75	35	
	2180	20" x 56" high		32	.250		30.50	7.30		37.80	45	
	2200	Double hung, glass size, 16" x 24" high		24	.333	Set	37.50	9.70		47.20	56	
	2280	32" x 32" high		34	.235	"	105	6.85		111.85	126	
	2500	Picture, glass size, 48" x 48" high		30	.267	Ea.	120	7.75		127.75	144	
	2580	60" x 68" high		28	.286	"	132	8.35		140.35	158	
	2600	Sliding, glass size, 14" x 36" high		24	.333	Set	20.50	9.70		30.20	37.50	
	2680	36" x 36" high		22	.364	"	42	10.60		52.60	63	
820	0010	**WOOD SASH** Including glazing but not including trim										820
	0050	Custom, 5'-0" x 4'-0", 1" dbl. glazed, 3/16" thick lites	2 Carp	3.20	5	Ea.	191	146		337	440	
	0100	1/4" thick lites		5	3.200		195	93.50		288.50	360	
	0200	1" thick, triple glazed		5	3.200		450	93.50		543.50	640	
	0300	7'-0" x 4'-6" high, 1" double glazed, 3/16" thick lites		4.30	3.721		455	108		563	670	
	0400	1/4" thick lites		4.30	3.721		515	108		623	735	
	0500	1" thick, triple glazed		4.30	3.721		585	108		693	815	
	0600	8'-6" x 5'-0" high, 1" double glazed, 3/16" thick lites		3.50	4.571		615	133		748	885	
	0700	1/4" thick lites		3.50	4.571		670	133		803	950	
	0800	1" thick, triple glazed		3.50	4.571		680	133		813	955	
	0900	Window frames only, based on perimeter length				L.F.	3.76			3.76	4.14	
	1200	Window sill, stock, per lineal foot					8.60			8.60	9.45	
	1250	Casing, stock					2.99			2.99	3.29	
	3000	Replacement sash, double hung, double glazing, to 12 S.F.	1 Carp	64	.125	S.F.	18.60	3.64		22.24	26	
	3100	12 S.F. to 20 S.F.		94	.085		15.50	2.48		17.98	21	
	3200	20 S.F. and over		106	.075		13.55	2.20		15.75	18.35	
	3800	Triple glazing for above, add					2.76			2.76	3.04	
	7000	Sash, single lite, 2'-0" x 2'-0" high	1 Carp	20	.400	Ea.	36.50	11.65		48.15	58.50	
	7050	2'-6" x 2'-0" high		19	.421		39	12.25		51.25	62	
	7100	2'-6" x 2'-6" high		18	.444		41.50	12.95		54.45	66	
	7150	3'-0" x 2'-0" high		17	.471		52.50	13.70		66.20	79.50	
840	0010	**WOOD SCREENS**										840
	0020	Over 3 S.F., 3/4" frames	2 Carp	375	.043	S.F.	3.09	1.24		4.33	5.35	

8

DOORS & WINDOWS

For expanded coverage of these items see *Means Interior Cost Data 2001*

08500 | Windows

		08550	Wood Windows	CREW	DAILY OUTPUT	LABOR-HOURS	UNIT	2001 BARE COSTS				TOTAL INCL O&P	
								MAT.	LABOR	EQUIP.	TOTAL		
840	0100		1-1/8" frames	2 Carp	375	.043	S.F.	3.04	1.24		4.28	5.30	840

		08580	Special Function Windows										
900	0010		**STORM WINDOWS** Aluminum, residential										900
	0300		Basement, mill finish, incl. fiberglass screen										
	0320		1'-10" x 1'-0" high	2 Carp	30	.533	Ea.	25	15.55		40.55	52.50	
	0340		2'-9" x 1'-6" high	"	30	.533	"	27.50	15.55		43.05	55	
	1600		Double-hung, combination, storm & screen										
	2000		Average quality, clear anodic coating, 2'-0" x 3'-5" high	2 Carp	30	.533	Ea.	66.50	15.55		82.05	97.50	
	2020		2'-6" x 5'-0" high		28	.571		83.50	16.65		100.15	118	
	2040		4'-0" x 6'-0" high		25	.640		98.50	18.65		117.15	137	
	2400		White painted, 2'-0" x 3'-5" high		30	.533		65.50	15.55		81.05	96.50	
	2420		2'-6" x 5'-0" high		28	.571		72	16.65		88.65	106	
	2440		4'-0" x 6'-0" high		25	.640		79	18.65		97.65	116	
	2600		Mill finish, 2'-0" x 3'-5" high		30	.533		59.50	15.55		75.05	90	
	2620		2'-6" x 5'-0" high		28	.571		66.50	16.65		83.15	99	
	2640		4'-0" x 6-8" high		25	.640		74.50	18.65		93.15	111	

08600 | Skylights

		08620	Unit Skylights	CREW	DAILY OUTPUT	LABOR-HOURS	UNIT	2001 BARE COSTS				TOTAL INCL O&P	
								MAT.	LABOR	EQUIP.	TOTAL		
400	0010		**PREFABRICATED** Glass block with metal frame, minimum	G-3	265	.121	S.F.	39.50	3.41		42.91	49	400
	0100		Maximum	"	160	.200	"	79.50	5.65		85.15	96	
800	0010		**SKYLIGHT** Plastic domes, flush or curb mounted, ten or										800
	0100		more units, curb not included										
	0300		Nominal size under 10 S.F., double	G-3	130	.246	S.F.	18.50	6.95		25.45	31.50	
	0400		Single		160	.200		12.30	5.65		17.95	22.50	
	0600		10 S.F. to 20 S.F., double		315	.102		14.35	2.86		17.21	20	
	0700		Single		395	.081		7.15	2.28		9.43	11.40	
	0900		20 S.F. to 30 S.F., double		395	.081		13.20	2.28		15.48	18.05	
	1000		Single		465	.069		9.10	1.94		11.04	13	
	1200		30 S.F. to 65 S.F., double		465	.069		9.65	1.94		11.59	13.65	
	1300		Single		610	.052		13.15	1.48		14.63	16.75	
	1500		For insulated 4" curbs, double, add					25%					
	1600		Single, add					30%					
	1800		For integral insulated 9" curbs, double, add					30%					
	1900		Single, add					40%					
	2120		Ventilating insulated plexiglass dome with										
	2130		curb mounting, 36" x 36"	G-3	12	2.667	Ea.	340	75		415	490	
	2150		52" x 52"		12	2.667		510	75		585	680	
	2160		28" x 52"		10	3.200		400	90		490	580	
	2170		36" x 52"		10	3.200		430	90		520	615	
	2180		For electric opening system, add					256			256	281	
	2200		Field fabricated, factory type, aluminum and wire glass	G-3	120	.267	S.F.	13.20	7.50		20.70	26	
	2300		Insulated safety glass with aluminum frame		160	.200		78.50	5.65		84.15	95.50	
	2400		Sandwich panels, fiberglass, for walls, 1-9/16" thick, to 250 SF		200	.160		13.95	4.51		18.46	22.50	
	2500		250 SF and up		265	.121		12.50	3.41		15.91	19.05	
	2700		As above, but for roofs, 2-3/4" thick, to 250 SF		295	.108		20	3.06		23.06	27	
	2800		250 SF and up		330	.097		16.50	2.73		19.23	22.50	

8

DOORS & WINDOWS

258   **Important: See the Reference Section for critical supporting data - Reference Nos., Crews, & City Cost Indexes**

		08710 | Door Hardware	CREW	DAILY OUTPUT	LABOR-HOURS	UNIT	2001 BARE COSTS				TOTAL INCL O&P	
							MAT.	LABOR	EQUIP.	TOTAL		
100	0010	**AUTOMATIC OPENERS COMMERCIAL** Swing doors, single	2 Skwk	.80	20	Ea.	2,725	595		3,320	3,900	**100**
	0100	Single operating pair		.50	32	Pr.	4,100	955		5,055	6,025	
	0400	For double simultaneous doors, one way, add		1.20	13.333		345	400		745	1,000	
	0500	Two way, add		.90	17.778		430	530		960	1,300	
	1000	Sliding doors, 3' wide, including track & hanger, single		.60	26.667	Opng.	3,775	795		4,570	5,425	
	1300	Bi-parting		.50	32		4,575	955		5,530	6,525	
	1450	Activating carpet, single door, one way add		2.20	7.273		700	217		917	1,100	
	1550	Two way, add		1.30	12.308		1,000	365		1,365	1,675	
	1750	Handicap opener, button operating	1 Carp	1.50	5.333	Ea.	1,300	155		1,455	1,675	
	1775	For wall mounted actuator button, add				"	1,300			1,300	1,425	
120	0010	**AUTOMATIC OPENERS INDUSTRIAL**, sliding doors, to 6' wide	2 Skwk	.60	26.667	Opng.	4,550	795		5,345	6,250	**120**
	0200	To 12' wide	"	.40	40	"	5,550	1,200		6,750	7,975	
	0400	Over 12' wide, add per L.F. of excess				L.F.	605			605	670	
	1000	Swing doors, to 5' wide	2 Skwk	.80	20	Ea.	2,650	595		3,245	3,850	
	1860	Add for controls, wall pushbutton, 3 button		4	4		162	119		281	365	
	1870	Ceiling pull cord		4.30	3.721		139	111		250	325	
150	0010	**AVERAGE** Percentage for hardware, total job cost, minimum									.75%	**150**
	0050	Maximum									3.50%	
	0500	Total hardware for building, average distribution					85%	15%				
	1000	Door hardware, apartment, interior				Door	107			107	118	
	1500	Hospital bedroom, minimum					243			243	268	
	2000	Maximum					535			535	585	
	2100	Pocket door				Ea.	109			109	120	
	2250	School, single exterior, incl. lever, not incl. panic device				Door	360			360	395	
	2500	Single interior, regular use, no lever included					240			240	264	
	2550	Including handicap lever					325			325	360	
	2600	Heavy use, incl. lever and closer					420			420	460	
	2850	Stairway, single interior					600			600	660	
	3100	Double exterior, with panic device				Pr.	845			845	930	
	3600	Toilet, public, single interior				Door	132			132	145	
200	0010	**BOLTS, FLUSH**										**200**
	0020	Standard, concealed	1 Carp	7	1.143	Ea.	17.55	33.50		51.05	71.50	
	0800	Automatic fire exit	"	5	1.600		273	46.50		319.50	375	
	1600	For electric release, add	1 Elec	3	2.667		94	91.50		185.50	240	
	3000	Barrel, brass, 2" long	1 Carp	40	.200		2.16	5.85		8.01	11.50	
	3020	4" long		40	.200		2.35	5.85		8.20	11.70	
	3060	6" long		40	.200		4.78	5.85		10.63	14.35	
220	0010	**BUMPER PLATES**										**220**
	0020	1-1/2" x 3/4" U channel	2 Carp	80	.200	L.F.	3.15	5.85		9	12.55	
	1000	Tear drop, spring-steel, 4" high		15	1.067	Ea.	40.50	31		71.50	93	
	1100	8" high		15	1.067		81	31		112	138	
	1200	10" high		15	1.067		101	31		132	161	
300	0010	**DOOR CLOSER** Rack and pinion	1 Carp	6.50	1.231	Ea.	108	36		144	175	**300**
	0020	Adjustable backcheck, 3 way mount, all sizes, regular arm		6	1.333		114	39		153	187	
	0040	Hold open arm		6	1.333		125	39		164	198	
	0100	Fusible link		6.50	1.231		97	36		133	163	
	0200	Non sized, regular arm		6	1.333		108	39		147	180	
	0240	Hold open arm		6	1.333		135	39		174	209	
	0400	4 way mount, non sized, regular arm		6	1.333		148	39		187	224	
	0440	Hold open arm		6	1.333		160	39		199	237	
	2000	Backcheck and adjustable power, hinge face mount										
	2010	All sizes, regular arm	1 Carp	6.50	1.231	Ea.	137	36		173	206	
	2040	Hold open arm		6.50	1.231		147	36		183	217	
	2400	Top jamb mount, all sizes, regular arm		6	1.333		137	39		176	211	

DOORS & WINDOWS | 8

	08710	Door Hardware	CREW	DAILY OUTPUT	LABOR-HOURS	UNIT	2001 BARE COSTS				TOTAL INCL O&P	
							MAT.	LABOR	EQUIP.	TOTAL		
300	2440	Hold open arm	1 Carp	6	1.333	Ea.	147	39		186	223	300
	2800	Top face mount, all sizes, regular arm		6.50	1.231		136	36		172	206	
	2840	Hold open arm		6.50	1.231		147	36		183	217	
	4000	Backcheck, overhead concealed, all sizes, regular arm		5.50	1.455		144	42.50		186.50	226	
	4040	Concealed arm		5	1.600		154	46.50		200.50	242	
	4400	Compact overhead, concealed, all sizes, regular arm		5.50	1.455		263	42.50		305.50	355	
	4440	Concealed arm		5	1.600		274	46.50		320.50	375	
	4800	Concealed in door, all sizes, regular arm		5.50	1.455		97.50	42.50		140	174	
	4840	Concealed arm		5	1.600		105	46.50		151.50	188	
	4900	Floor concealed, all sizes, single acting		2.20	3.636		124	106		230	300	
	4940	Double acting	▼	2.20	3.636		159	106		265	340	
	5000	For cast aluminum cylinder, deduct					13.10			13.10	14.40	
	5040	For delayed action, add					23			23	25	
	5080	For fusible link arm, add					9.50			9.50	10.45	
	5120	For shock absorbing arm, add					28.50			28.50	31	
	5160	For spring power adjustment, add					22			22	24	
	6000	Closer-holder, hinge face mount, all sizes, exposed arm	1 Carp	6.50	1.231		100	36		136	167	
	7000	Electronic closer-holder, hinge facemount, concealed arm		5	1.600		153	46.50		199.50	241	
	7400	With built-in detector	▼	5	1.600	▼	460	46.50		506.50	580	
320	0010	DEADLOCKS Mortise, heavy duty, outside key	1 Carp	9	.889	Ea.	112	26		138	164	320
	0020	Double cylinder		9	.889		124	26		150	177	
	0100	Medium duty, outside key		10	.800		87	23.50		110.50	132	
	0110	Double cylinder		10	.800		109	23.50		132.50	157	
	1000	Tubular, standard duty, outside key		10	.800		47	23.50		70.50	88	
	1010	Double cylinder		10	.800		60	23.50		83.50	103	
	1200	Night latch, outside key	▼	10	.800	▼	59	23.50		82.50	102	
340	0010	DOORSTOPS Holder and bumper, floor or wall	1 Carp	32	.250	Ea.	27	7.30		34.30	41.50	340
	1300	Wall bumper, 4" diameter, with rubber pad, aluminum		32	.250		6.60	7.30		13.90	18.65	
	1600	Door bumper, floor type, aluminum		32	.250		3.77	7.30		11.07	15.55	
	1900	Plunger type, door mounted	▼	32	.250	▼	23	7.30		30.30	37	
400	0010	ENTRANCE LOCKS Cylinder, grip handle, deadlocking latch	1 Carp	9	.889	Ea.	103	26		129	154	400
	0020	Deadbolt		8	1		125	29		154	183	
	0100	Push and pull plate, dead bolt	▼	8	1		119	29		148	177	
	0900	For handicapped lever, add				▼	130			130	143	
450	0010	FLOOR CHECKS For over 3' wide doors, single acting	1 Carp	2.50	3.200	Ea.	400	93.50		493.50	585	450
	0500	Double acting	"	2.50	3.200	"	505	93.50		598.50	705	
500	0010	HASP Steel, 3" assembly	1 Carp	26	.308	Ea.	2.39	8.95		11.34	16.70	500
	0020	4-1/2"		13	.615		3.04	17.95		20.99	31.50	
	0040	6"	▼	12.50	.640	▼	4.81	18.65		23.46	34.50	
520	0010	HINGES Full mortise, avg. freq., steel base, 4-1/2" x 4-1/2", USP				Pr.	17.90			17.90	19.70	520
	0100	5" x 5", USP					29			29	32	
	0200	6" x 6", USP					60.50			60.50	67	
	0400	Brass base, 4-1/2" x 4-1/2", US10					37			37	40.50	
	0500	5" x 5", US10					52.50			52.50	57.50	
	0600	6" x 6", US10					87			87	96	
	0800	Stainless steel base, 4-1/2" x 4-1/2", US32				▼	61			61	67.50	
	0900	For non removable pin, add				Ea.	2.14			2.14	2.35	
	0910	For floating pin, driven tips, add					3.03			3.03	3.33	
	0930	For hospital type tip on pin, add					6.05			6.05	6.65	
	0940	For steeple type tip on pin, add				▼	6.55			6.55	7.25	
	0950	Full mortise, high frequency, steel base, 3-1/2" x 3-1/2", US26D				Pr.	19.40			19.40	21.50	
	1000	4-1/2" x 4-1/2", USP					37.50			37.50	41.50	
	1100	5" x 5", USP					40			40	44	

(Note at row 0400: R08700 -100)

Important: See the Reference Section for critical supporting data - Reference Nos., Crews, & City Cost Indexes

08710 | Door Hardware

			CREW	DAILY OUTPUT	LABOR-HOURS	UNIT	2001 BARE COSTS				TOTAL INCL O&P	
							MAT.	LABOR	EQUIP.	TOTAL		
520	1200	6" x 6", USP				Pr.	97			97	107	**520**
	1400	Brass base, 3-1/2" x 3-1/2", US4 R08700-100					35			35	38.50	
	1430	4-1/2" x 4-1/2", US10					41.50			41.50	46	
	1500	5" x 5", US10					74.50			74.50	82	
	1600	6" x 6", US10					124			124	136	
	1800	Stainless steel base, 4-1/2" x 4-1/2", US32					94.50			94.50	104	
	1930	For hospital type tip on pin, add				Ea.	6.55			6.55	7.25	
	1950	Full mortise, low frequency, steel base, 3-1/2" x 3-1/2", US26D				Pr.	12.25			12.25	13.45	
	2000	4-1/2" x 4-1/2", USP					13.45			13.45	14.80	
	2100	5" x 5", USP					21.50			21.50	23.50	
	2200	6" x 6", USP					42			42	46.50	
	2300	4-1/2" x 4-1/2", US3					9.85			9.85	10.80	
	2310	5" x 5", US3					30.50			30.50	33.50	
	2400	Brass bass, 4-1/2" x 4-1/2", US10					30.50			30.50	34	
	2500	5" x 5", US10					46			46	50.50	
	2800	Stainless steel base, 4-1/2" x 4-1/2", US32					51			51	56	
550	0010	**KICK PLATE** 6" high, for 3' door, stainless steel	1 Carp	15	.533	Ea.	14.25	15.55		29.80	40	**550**
	0500	Bronze		15	.533		20	15.55		35.55	46.50	
	2000	Aluminum, .050, with 3 beveled edges, 10" x 28"		15	.533		14.70	15.55		30.25	40.50	
	2010	10" x 30"		15	.533		15.75	15.55		31.30	42	
	2020	10" x 34"		15	.533		17.80	15.55		33.35	44	
	2040	10" x 38"		15	.533		19.65	15.55		35.20	46	
650	0010	**LOCKSET** Standard duty, cylindrical, with sectional trim										**650**
	0020	Non-keyed, passage	1 Carp	12	.667	Ea.	37	19.45		56.45	71.50	
	0100	Privacy		12	.667		45	19.45		64.45	80.50	
	0400	Keyed, single cylinder function **CN**		10	.800		66	23.50		89.50	110	
	0420	Hotel		8	1		90	29		119	145	
	0500	Lever handled, keyed, single cylinder function		10	.800		91	23.50		114.50	137	
	1000	Heavy duty with sectional trim, non-keyed, passages		12	.667		105	19.45		124.45	146	
	1100	Privacy		12	.667		132	19.45		151.45	177	
	1400	Keyed, single cylinder function		10	.800		156	23.50		179.50	209	
	1420	Hotel		8	1		233	29		262	300	
	1600	Communicating		10	.800		185	23.50		208.50	240	
	1690	For re-core cylinder, add					26.50			26.50	29	
	1700	Residential, interior door, minimum	1 Carp	16	.500		12.60	14.60		27.20	37	
	1720	Maximum		8	1		33.50	29		62.50	82.50	
	1800	Exterior, minimum		14	.571		28	16.65		44.65	57	
	1810	Average		8	1		59.50	29		88.50	111	
	1820	Maximum		8	1		118	29		147	176	
700	0010	**MORTISE LOCKSET** Comm., wrought knobs & full escutcheon trim										**700**
	0020	Non-keyed, passage, minimum	1 Carp	9	.889	Ea.	139	26		165	194	
	0030	Maximum		8	1		225	29		254	293	
	0040	Privacy, minimum		9	.889		148	26		174	204	
	0050	Maximum		8	1		243	29		272	315	
	0100	Keyed, office/entrance/apartment, minimum		8	1		170	29		199	233	
	0110	Maximum		7	1.143		292	33.50		325.50	370	
	0120	Single cylinder, typical, minimum		8	1		146	29		175	207	
	0130	Maximum		7	1.143		270	33.50		303.50	350	
	0200	Hotel, minimum		7	1.143		176	33.50		209.50	245	
	0210	Maximum		6	1.333		286	39		325	375	
	0300	Communication, double cylinder, minimum		8	1		176	29		205	239	
	0310	Maximum		7	1.143		227	33.50		260.50	300	
	1000	Wrought knobs and sectional trim, non-keyed, passage, minimum		10	.800		92.50	23.50		116	139	
	1010	Maximum		9	.889		182	26		208	242	
	1040	Privacy, minimum		10	.800		108	23.50		131.50	156	

DOORS & WINDOWS   **8**

			DAILY	LABOR-		2001 BARE COSTS				TOTAL	
08710		**Door Hardware**	CREW	OUTPUT	HOURS	UNIT	MAT.	LABOR	EQUIP.	TOTAL	INCL O&P
700	1050	Maximum	1 Carp	9	.889	Ea.	195	26		221	255	**700**
	1100	Keyed, entrance,office/apartment, minimum		9	.889		160	26		186	217
	1110	Maximum		8	1		232	29		261	300
	1120	Single cylinder, typical, minimum		9	.889		154	26		180	211
	1130	Maximum		8	1		225	29		254	293
	2000	Cast knobs and full escutcheon trim									
	2010	Non-keyed, passage, minimum	1 Carp	9	.889	Ea.	196	26		222	257
	2020	Maximum		8	1		320	29		349	395
	2040	Privacy, minimum		9	.889		236	26		262	300
	2050	Maximum		8	1		345	29		374	420
	2120	Keyed, single cylinder, typical, minimum		8	1		236	29		265	305
	2130	Maximum		7	1.143		375	33.50		408.50	460
	2200	Hotel, minimum		7	1.143		271	33.50		304.50	350
	2210	Maximum		6	1.333		505	39		544	615
	3000	Cast knob and sectional trim, non-keyed, passage, minimum		10	.800		153	23.50		176.50	205
	3010	Maximum		10	.800		305	23.50		328.50	370
	3040	Privacy, minimum		10	.800		174	23.50		197.50	228
	3050	Maximum		10	.800		305	23.50		328.50	370
	3100	Keyed, office/entrance/apartment, minimum		9	.889		197	26		223	258
	3110	Maximum		9	.889		310	26		336	380
	3120	Single cylinder, typical, minimum		9	.889		197	26		223	258
	3130	Maximum		9	.889		380	26		406	460
	3190	For re-core cylinder, add					26.50			26.50	29.50
	3800	Cipher lockset	1 Carp	13	.615		640	17.95		657.95	735
	3900	Keyless, pushbutton type									
	4000	Residential/light commercial, deadbolt, standard	1 Carp	9	.889	Ea.	89	26		115	139
	4010	Heavy duty		9	.889		106	26		132	157
	4020	Industrial, heavy duty, with deadbolt		9	.889		221	26		247	284
	4030	Key override		9	.889		245	26		271	310
	4040	Lever activated handle		9	.889		268	26		294	335
	4050	Key override		9	.889		297	26		323	365
	4060	Double sided pushbutton type		8	1		490	29		519	585
	4070	Key override		8	1		530	29		559	625
750	0010	**PANIC DEVICE** For rim locks, single door, exit only	1 Carp	6	1.333	Ea.	330	39		369	425	**750**
	0020	Outside key and pull		5	1.600		380	46.50		426.50	495
	0200	Bar and vertical rod, exit only		5	1.600		485	46.50		531.50	610
	0210	Outside key and pull		4	2		580	58.50		638.50	730
	0400	Bar and concealed rod		4	2		490	58.50		548.50	630
	0600	Touch bar, exit only		6	1.333		390	39		429	490
	0610	Outside key and pull		5	1.600		470	46.50		516.50	590
	0700	Touch bar and vertical rod, exit only		5	1.600		530	46.50		576.50	660
	0710	Outside key and pull		4	2		620	58.50		678.50	770
	1000	Mortise, bar, exit only		4	2		435	58.50		493.50	570
	1600	Touch bar, exit only		4	2		500	58.50		558.50	640
	2000	Narrow stile, rim mounted, bar, exit only		6	1.333		525	39		564	640
	2010	Outside key and pull		5	1.600		570	46.50		616.50	700
	2200	Bar and vertical rod, exit only		5	1.600		540	46.50		586.50	670
	2210	Outside key and pull		4	2		540	58.50		598.50	685
	2400	Bar and concealed rod, exit only		3	2.667		630	77.50		707.50	810
	3000	Mortise, bar, exit only		4	2		440	58.50		498.50	575
	3600	Touch bar, exit only		4	2		645	58.50		703.50	795
780	0010	**PUSH-PULL PLATE**										**780**
	0100	Push plate, .050 thick, 4" x 16", aluminum	1 Carp	12	.667	Ea.	5.05	19.45		24.50	36
	0500	Bronze		12	.667		11.30	19.45		30.75	43
	1500	Pull handle and push bar, aluminum		11	.727		108	21		129	152

Important: See the Reference Section for critical supporting data - Reference Nos., Crews, & City Cost Indexes

		08710	Door Hardware	CREW	DAILY OUTPUT	LABOR-HOURS	UNIT	2001 BARE COSTS MAT.	LABOR	EQUIP.	TOTAL	TOTAL INCL O&P	
780	2000		Bronze	1 Carp	10	.800	Ea.	140	23.50		163.50	191	780
	3000		Push plate both sides, aluminum		14	.571		13.25	16.65		29.90	40.50	
	3500		Bronze		13	.615		33.50	17.95		51.45	64.50	
	4000		Door pull, designer style, cast aluminum, minimum		12	.667		61	19.45		80.45	97.50	
	5000		Maximum		8	1		282	29		311	355	
	6000		Cast bronze, minimum		12	.667		65.50	19.45		84.95	103	
	7000		Maximum		8	1		305	29		334	380	
	8000		Walnut, minimum		12	.667		50	19.45		69.45	85.50	
	9000		Maximum	▼	8	1	▼	281	29		310	355	
800	0010	**SPECIAL HINGES**											800
	0015		Paumelle, high frequency										
	0020		Steel base, 6" x 4-1/2", US10				Pr.	107			107	118	
	0100		Bronze base, 5" x 4-1/2", US10					144			144	158	
	0200		Paumelle, average frequency, steel base, 4-1/2" x 3-1/2", US10					72.50			72.50	79.50	
	0400		Olive knuckle, low frequency, brass base, 6" x 4-1/2", US10				▼	131			131	145	
	1000		Electric hinge with concealed conductor, average frequency										
	1010		Steel base, 4-1/2" x 4-1/2", US26D				Pr.	240			240	264	
	1100		Bronze base, 4-1/2" x 4-1/2", US26D				"	249			249	274	
	1200		Electric hinge with concealed conductor, high frequency										
	1210		Steel base, 4-1/2" x 4-1/2", US26D				Pr.	179			179	197	
	1600		Double weight, 800 lb., steel base, removable pin, 5" x 6", USP					112			112	124	
	1700		Steel base-welded pin, 5" x 6", USP					124			124	137	
	1800		Triple weight, 2000 lb., steel base, welded pin, 5" x 6", USP					130			130	142	
	2000		Pivot reinf., high frequency, steel base, 7-3/4" door plate, USP					144			144	159	
	2200		Bronze base, 7-3/4" door plate, US10				▼	175			175	192	
	3000		Swing clear, full mortise, full or half surface, high frequency,										
	3010		Steel base, 5" high, USP				Pr.	121			121	133	
	3200		Swing clear, full mortise, average frequency										
	3210		Steel base, 4-1/2" high, USP				Pr.	96			96	106	
	4000		Wide throw, average frequency, steel base, 4-1/2" x 6", USP					73.50			73.50	81	
	4200		High frequency, steel base, 4-1/2" x 6", USP				▼	112			112	124	
	4600		Spring hinge, single acting, 6" flange, steel				Ea.	41.50			41.50	45.50	
	4700		Brass					73			73	80.50	
	4900		Double acting, 6" flange, steel					75.50			75.50	83	
	4950		Brass				▼	123			123	136	
	9000		Continuous hinge, steel, full mortise, heavy duty	2 Carp	64	.250	L.F.	10.40	7.30		17.70	23	
		08720	**Weatherstripping & Seals**										
100	0010	**ASTRAGALS** One piece overlapping											100
	0400		Cadmium plated steel, flat, 3/16" x 2"	1 Carp	90	.089	L.F.	2.59	2.59		5.18	6.90	
	0600		Prime coated steel, flat, 1/8" x 3"		90	.089		3.60	2.59		6.19	8	
	0800		Stainless steel, flat, 3/32" x 1-5/8"		90	.089		13.50	2.59		16.09	18.90	
	1000		Aluminum, flat, 1/8" x 2"		90	.089		2.60	2.59		5.19	6.90	
	1200		Nail on, "T" extrusion		120	.067		.57	1.94		2.51	3.67	
	1300		Vinyl bulb insert		105	.076		.93	2.22		3.15	4.49	
	1600		Screw on, "T" extrusion		90	.089		3.79	2.59		6.38	8.20	
	1700		Vinyl insert		75	.107		2.55	3.11		5.66	7.65	
	2000		"L" extrusion, neoprene bulbs		75	.107		1.48	3.11		4.59	6.50	
	2100		Neoprene sponge insert		75	.107		4.49	3.11		7.60	9.80	
	2200		Magnetic		75	.107		7.40	3.11		10.51	13	
	2400		Spring hinged security seal, with cam		75	.107		4.76	3.11		7.87	10.10	
	2600		Spring loaded locking bolt, vinyl insert		45	.178		6.50	5.20		11.70	15.25	
	2800		Neoprene sponge strip, "Z" shaped, aluminum		60	.133		3.08	3.89		6.97	9.50	
	2900		Solid neoprene strip, nail on aluminum strip	▼	90	.089	▼	2.58	2.59		5.17	6.90	

DOORS & WINDOWS | **8**

08720	Weatherstripping & Seals	CREW	DAILY OUTPUT	LABOR-HOURS	UNIT	2001 BARE COSTS				TOTAL INCL O&P
						MAT.	LABOR	EQUIP.	TOTAL	
100	3000	One piece stile protection									**100**
	3020	Neoprene fabric loop, nail on aluminum strips	1 Carp	60	.133	L.F.	.49	3.89		4.38	6.65
	3110	Flush mounted aluminum extrusion, 1/2" x 1-1/4"		60	.133		2.46	3.89		6.35	8.80
	3140	3/4" x 1-3/8"		60	.133		3.11	3.89		7	9.50
	3160	1-1/8" x 1-3/4"		60	.133		4.97	3.89		8.86	11.55
	3300	Mortise, 9/16" x 3/4"		60	.133		2.64	3.89		6.53	9
	3320	13/16" x 1-3/8"		60	.133		2.86	3.89		6.75	9.25
	3600	Spring bronze strip, nail on type		105	.076		2.25	2.22		4.47	5.95
	3620	Screw on, with retainer		75	.107		1.84	3.11		4.95	6.90
	3800	Flexible stainless steel housing, pile insert, 1/2" door		105	.076		5.10	2.22		7.32	9.05
	3820	3/4" door		105	.076		5.75	2.22		7.97	9.75
	4000	Extruded aluminum retainer, flush mount, pile insert		105	.076		1.78	2.22		4	5.45
	4080	Mortise, felt insert		90	.089		3.17	2.59		5.76	7.55
	4160	Mortise with spring, pile insert		90	.089		2.48	2.59		5.07	6.80
	4400	Rigid vinyl retainer, mortise, pile insert		105	.076		1.77	2.22		3.99	5.40
	4600	Wool pile filler strip, aluminum backing		105	.076		1.78	2.22		4	5.45
	5000	Two piece overlapping astragal, extruded aluminum retainer									
	5010	Pile insert	1 Carp	60	.133	L.F.	2.31	3.89		6.20	8.65
	5020	Vinyl bulb insert		60	.133		1.49	3.89		5.38	7.75
	5040	Vinyl flap insert		60	.133		4.63	3.89		8.52	11.20
	5060	Solid neoprene flap insert		60	.133		4.58	3.89		8.47	11.15
	5080	Hypalon rubber flap insert		60	.133		4.68	3.89		8.57	11.25
	5090	Snap on cover, pile insert		60	.133		5.35	3.89		9.24	12
	5400	Magnetic aluminum, surface mounted		60	.133		18.10	3.89		21.99	26
	5500	Interlocking aluminum, 5/8" x 1" neoprene bulb insert		45	.178		2.87	5.20		8.07	11.25
	5600	Adjustable aluminum, 9/16" x 21/32", pile insert		45	.178		13.65	5.20		18.85	23
	5790	For vinyl bulb, deduct					.37			.37	.41
	5800	Magnetic, adjustable, 9/16" x 21/32"	1 Carp	45	.178		17.50	5.20		22.70	27.50
	6000	Two piece stile protection									
	6010	Cloth backed rubber loop, 1" gap, nail on aluminum strips	1 Carp	45	.178	L.F.	2.94	5.20		8.14	11.35
	6040	Screw on aluminum strips		45	.178		4.58	5.20		9.78	13.15
	6100	1-1/2" gap, screw on aluminum extrusion		45	.178		4.12	5.20		9.32	12.65
	6240	Vinyl fabric loop, slotted aluminum extrusion, 1" gap		45	.178		1.46	5.20		6.66	9.70
	6300	1-1/4" gap		45	.178		4.34	5.20		9.54	12.85
300	0010	**WEATHERSTRIPPING** Window, double hung, 3' x 5', zinc	1 Carp	7.20	1.111	Opng.	10.70	32.50		43.20	62.50	**300**
	0100	Bronze		7.20	1.111		19.45	32.50		51.95	72
	0500	As above but heavy duty, zinc		4.60	1.739		13	50.50		63.50	94
	0600	Bronze		4.60	1.739		22.50	50.50		73	105
	1000	Doors, wood frame, interlocking, for 3' x 7' door, zinc		3	2.667		11.65	77.50		89.15	135
	1100	Bronze		3	2.667		18.35	77.50		95.85	142
	1300	6' x 7' opening, zinc		2	4		12.75	117		129.75	196
	1400	Bronze		2	4		24	117		141	209
	1700	Wood frame, spring type, bronze									
	1800	3' x 7' door	1 Carp	7.60	1.053	Opng.	15.45	30.50		45.95	65
	1900	6' x 7' door	"	7	1.143	"	16.45	33.50		49.95	70
	2200	Metal frame, spring type, bronze									
	2300	3' x 7' door	1 Carp	3	2.667	Opng.	25.50	77.50		103	150
	2400	6' x 7' door	"	2.50	3.200	"	35	93.50		128.50	184
	2500	For stainless steel, spring type, add					133%				
	2700	Metal frame, extruded sections, 3' x 7' door, aluminum	1 Carp	2	4	Opng.	34	117		151	219
	2800	Bronze		2	4		85.50	117		202.50	276
	3100	6' x 7' door, aluminum		1.20	6.667		43	194		237	355
	3200	Bronze		1.20	6.667		101	194		295	415
	3500	Threshold weatherstripping									
	3650	Door sweep, flush mounted, aluminum	1 Carp	25	.320	Ea.	10	9.35		19.35	25.50
	3700	Vinyl		25	.320		11.85	9.35		21.20	27.50

08700 | Hardware

08720 | Weatherstripping & Seals

			CREW	DAILY OUTPUT	LABOR-HOURS	UNIT	2001 BARE COSTS				TOTAL INCL O&P	
							MAT.	LABOR	EQUIP.	TOTAL		
300	5000	Garage door bottom weatherstrip, 12' aluminum, clear	1 Carp	14	.571	Ea.	16.05	16.65		32.70	43.50	300
	5010	Bronze		14	.571		61	16.65		77.65	93.50	
	5050	Bottom protection, 12' aluminum, clear		14	.571		19.45	16.65		36.10	47.50	
	5100	Bronze		14	.571		76	16.65		92.65	110	
800	0010	THRESHOLD 3' long door saddles, aluminum	1 Carp	48	.167	L.F.	3.38	4.86		8.24	11.30	800
	0100	Aluminum, 8" wide, 1/2" thick		12	.667	Ea.	29	19.45		48.45	62.50	
	0500	Bronze		60	.133	L.F.	27.50	3.89		31.39	36	
	0600	Bronze, panic threshold, 5" wide, 1/2" thick		12	.667	Ea.	57	19.45		76.45	93	
	0700	Rubber, 1/2" thick, 5-1/2" wide		20	.400		28.50	11.65		40.15	50	
	0800	2-3/4" wide		20	.400		13.25	11.65		24.90	33	

08770 | Door/Window Accessories

			CREW	DAILY OUTPUT	LABOR-HOURS	UNIT	2001 BARE COSTS				TOTAL INCL O&P	
							MAT.	LABOR	EQUIP.	TOTAL		
100	0010	AREA WALL Galvanized steel, 20 ga., 3'-2" wide, 1' deep	1 Sswk	29	.276	Ea.	12.20	9.05		21.25	30	100
	0100	2' deep		23	.348		21.50	11.45		32.95	44.50	
	0300	16 ga., galv., 3'-2" wide, 1' deep		29	.276		17.20	9.05		26.25	35.50	
	0400	3' deep		23	.348		35	11.45		46.45	59	
	0600	Welded grating for above, 15 lbs., painted		45	.178		33	5.85		38.85	47	
	0700	Galvanized		45	.178		63	5.85		68.85	80	
	0900	Translucent plastic cap for above		60	.133		12.65	4.38		17.03	22	
200	0010	DOOR PROTECTION Acrylic and neoprene cover for door										200
	0020	frame, high impact type	1 Carp	100	.080	L.F.	7.05	2.33		9.38	11.45	
550	0010	DETECTION SYSTEMS See division 13851-065										550

08800 | Glazing

08810 | Glass

			CREW	DAILY OUTPUT	LABOR-HOURS	UNIT	2001 BARE COSTS				TOTAL INCL O&P	
							MAT.	LABOR	EQUIP.	TOTAL		
100	0010	ACOUSTICAL GLASS UNITS 1 lite at 3/8", 1 lite at 3/16", for 1" thick	2 Glaz	100	.160	S.F.	18.80	4.57		23.37	27.50	100
	0100	For 4" thick	"	80	.200	"	32	5.70		37.70	44	
160	0010	BEVELED GLASS With design patterns, 1/4" thick, 1/2" bevel, minimum	2 Glaz	150	.107	S.F.	32	3.05		35.05	40	160
	0050	Average		125	.128		75.50	3.65		79.15	88.50	
	0100	Maximum		100	.160		133	4.57		137.57	154	
205	0010	CURTAIN WALL See division 08900										205
250	0010	FACETED Color tinted glass, 3/4" thick, minimum	2 Glaz	95	.168	S.F.	27	4.81		31.81	37.50	250
	0100	Maximum	"	75	.213	"	47.50	6.10		53.60	62	
260	0010	FLOAT GLASS 3/16" thick, clear, plain	2 Glaz	130	.123	S.F.	3.62	3.51		7.13	9.35	260
	0200	Tempered, clear		130	.123		4.32	3.51		7.83	10.10	
	0300	Tinted		130	.123		5.40	3.51		8.91	11.30	
	0600	1/4" thick, clear, plain		120	.133		4.55	3.81		8.36	10.75	
	0700	Tinted		120	.133		4.32	3.81		8.13	10.50	
	0800	Tempered, clear		120	.133		5.40	3.81		9.21	11.70	
	0900	Tinted		120	.133		7.50	3.81		11.31	14	
	1600	3/8" thick, clear, plain		75	.213		7.15	6.10		13.25	17.15	
	1700	Tinted		75	.213		8.65	6.10		14.75	18.75	
	1800	Tempered, clear		75	.213		10.80	6.10		16.90	21	
	1900	Tinted		75	.213		13.45	6.10		19.55	24	
	2200	1/2" thick, clear, plain		55	.291		14.05	8.30		22.35	28	

Note for 0600 row: R08810-010, CN

For expanded coverage of these items see *Means Interior Cost Data 2001*

265

08810 | Glass

			CREW	DAILY OUTPUT	LABOR-HOURS	UNIT	2001 BARE COSTS MAT.	LABOR	EQUIP.	TOTAL	TOTAL INCL O&P	
260	2300	Tinted · R08810-010	2 Glaz	55	.291	S.F.	15.10	8.30		23.40	29.50	**260**
	2400	Tempered, clear		55	.291		16.20	8.30		24.50	30.50	
	2500	Tinted		55	.291		20	8.30		28.30	34.50	
	2800	5/8" thick, clear, plain		45	.356		15.10	10.15		25.25	32	
	2900	Tempered, clear		45	.356		17.30	10.15		27.45	34.50	
	3200	3/4" thick, clear, plain		35	.457		19.45	13.05		32.50	41.50	
	3300	Tempered, clear		35	.457		22.50	13.05		35.55	45	
	3600	1" thick, clear, plain		30	.533		32.50	15.25		47.75	58.50	
	8900	For low emissivity coating for 3/16" and 1/4" only, add to above					15%					
270	0010	**FULL VISION** Window system with 3/4" glass mullions, 10' high	H-2	130	.185	S.F.	42.50	4.92		47.42	54.50	**270**
	0100	10' to 20' high, minimum		110	.218		45	5.80		50.80	58.50	
	0150	Average		100	.240		48.50	6.40		54.90	63.50	
	0200	Maximum		80	.300		54.50	8		62.50	72.50	
280	0010	**GLASS BLOCK** See division 04270-200 · R04270-700										**280**
300	0010	**GLAZING VARIABLES** · R08810-010										**300**
	0500	For high rise glazing, exterior, add per S.F. per story				S.F.					.09	
	0600	For glass replacement, add				"		100%				
	0700	For gasket settings, add				L.F.	3.24			3.24	3.56	
	0800	For concrete reglet settings, add				S.F.	20%	25%				
	0900	For sloped glazing, add				"		25%				
	2000	Fabrication, polished edges, 1/4" thick				Inch	.27			.27	.30	
	2100	1/2" thick					.71			.71	.78	
	2500	Mitered edges, 1/4" thick					.71			.71	.78	
	2600	1/2" thick					1.14			1.14	1.25	
460	0010	**INSULATING GLASS** 2 lites 1/8" float, 1/2" thk, under 15 S.F.										**460**
	0020	Clear	2 Glaz	95	.168	S.F.	6.30	4.81		11.11	14.20	
	0100	Tinted · R08810-010		95	.168		9.30	4.81		14.11	17.55	
	0200	2 lites 3/16" float, for 5/8" thk unit, 15 to 30 S.F., clear		90	.178		7.55	5.10		12.65	16	
	0300	Tinted		90	.178		7.80	5.10		12.90	16.25	
	0400	1" thk, dbl. glazed, 1/4" float, 30-70 S.F., clear **CN**		75	.213		10.70	6.10		16.80	21	
	0500	Tinted		75	.213		12.95	6.10		19.05	23.50	
	0600	1" thick double glazed, 1/4" float, 1/4" wire		75	.213		16.20	6.10		22.30	27	
	0700	1/4" float, 1/4" tempered		75	.213		15.70	6.10		21.80	26.50	
	0800	1/4" wire, 1/4" tempered		75	.213		22	6.10		28.10	33.50	
	0900	Both lites, 1/4" wire		75	.213		20.50	6.10		26.60	32	
	2000	Both lites, light & heat reflective		85	.188		17.30	5.35		22.65	27	
	2500	Heat reflective, film inside, 1" thick unit, clear		85	.188		15.10	5.35		20.45	25	
	2600	Tinted		85	.188		16.30	5.35		21.65	26	
	3000	Film on weatherside, clear, 1/2" thick unit		95	.168		10.80	4.81		15.61	19.20	
	3100	5/8" thick unit		90	.178		13.70	5.10		18.80	23	
	3200	1" thick unit		85	.188		14.90	5.35		20.25	24.50	
500	0010	**LAMINATED GLASS** Clear float, .03" vinyl, 1/4" thick	2 Glaz	90	.178	S.F.	7.30	5.10		12.40	15.70	**500**
	0100	3/8" thick		78	.205		11.80	5.85		17.65	22	
	0200	.06" vinyl, 1/2" thick		65	.246		13.80	7.05		20.85	26	
	1000	5/8" thick		90	.178		16.20	5.10		21.30	25.50	
	2000	Bullet-resisting, 1-3/16" thick, to 15 S.F.		16	1		41	28.50		69.50	88.50	
	2100	Over 15 S.F.		16	1		36.50	28.50		65	84	
	2500	2-1/4" thick, to 15 S.F.		12	1.333		52	38		90	115	
	2600	Over 15 S.F.		12	1.333		46.50	38		84.50	109	
550	0010	**LEAD GLASS** For X-ray, see division 13091-600										**550**
600	0010	**OBSCURE GLASS** 1/8" thick, minimum	2 Glaz	140	.114	S.F.	6	3.26		9.26	11.55	**600**
	0100	Maximum		125	.128		7.20	3.65		10.85	13.45	

Important: See the Reference Section for critical supporting data - Reference Nos., Crews, & City Cost Indexes

		08810 | Glass	CREW	DAILY OUTPUT	LABOR-HOURS	UNIT	2001 BARE COSTS MAT.	LABOR	EQUIP.	TOTAL	TOTAL INCL O&P	
600	0300	7/32" thick, minimum	2 Glaz	120	.133	S.F.	6.65	3.81		10.46	13.05	600
	0400	Maximum	↓	105	.152	↓	8.50	4.35		12.85	15.95	
650	0010	**PATTERNED GLASS** Colored, 1/8" thick, minimum	2 Glaz	140	.114	S.F.	7.05	3.26		10.31	12.75	650
	0100	Maximum		125	.128		8.35	3.65		12	14.75	
	0300	7/32" thick, minimum		120	.133		8.25	3.81		12.06	14.80	
	0400	Maximum	↓	105	.152	↓	9	4.35		13.35	16.50	
675	0010	**REFLECTIVE GLASS** 1/4" float with fused metallic oxide, tinted	2 Glaz	115	.139	S.F.	9	3.97		12.97	15.90	675
	0500	1/4" float glass with reflective applied coating		115	.139		7.50	3.97		11.47	14.25	
	2000	Solar film on glass, not including glass, minimum		180	.089		3.62	2.54		6.16	7.85	
	2050	Maximum	↓	225	.071	↓	8.35	2.03		10.38	12.30	
740	0010	**SANDBLASTED GLASS** Float glass, 1/8" thick	2 Glaz	160	.100	S.F.	6	2.86		8.86	10.95	740
	0100	3/16" thick		130	.123		6.65	3.51		10.16	12.65	
	0500	Plate glass, 1/4" thick		120	.133		6.90	3.81		10.71	13.35	
	0600	3/8" thick	↓	75	.213	↓	7.50	6.10		13.60	17.50	
760	0010	**SHEET GLASS** Gray, 1/8" thick	2 Glaz	160	.100	S.F.	2.97	2.86		5.83	7.60	760
	0200	1/4" thick		130	.123	"	3.90	3.51		7.41	9.65	
780	0010	**SPANDREL GLASS** 1/4" thick, standard colors, up to 1,000 S.F.		110	.145	S.F.	10.20	4.15		14.35	17.55	780
	0200	1,000 to 2,000 S.F.	↓	120	.133	"	9.55	3.81		13.36	16.25	
	0300	For custom colors, add				Total	10%					
	0500	For 3/8" thick, add				S.F.	6.20			6.20	6.85	
	1000	For double coated, 1/4" thick, add					2.32			2.32	2.55	
	1200	For insulation on panels, add					3.83			3.83	4.21	
	2000	Panels, insulated, with aluminum backed fiberglass, 1" thick	2 Glaz	120	.133		9.25	3.81		13.06	15.90	
	2100	2" thick	"	120	.133		10.75	3.81		14.56	17.60	
	2500	With galvanized steel backing, add				↓	3.19			3.19	3.51	
850	0010	**WINDOW GLASS** Clear float, stops, putty bed, 1/8" thick [R08810-100]	2 Glaz	480	.033	S.F.	2.97	.95		3.92	4.71	850
	0500	3/16" thick, clear		480	.033		3.67	.95		4.62	5.50	
	0600	Tinted		480	.033		4.16	.95		5.11	6	
	0700	Tempered	↓	480	.033	↓	5.05	.95		6	7	
860	0010	**WINDOW WALL** See division 08911-900										860
900	0010	**WIRE GLASS** 1/4" thick, rough obscure (chicken wire)	2 Glaz	135	.119	S.F.	10.15	3.38		13.53	16.30	900
	1000	Polished wire, 1/4" thick, diamond, clear		135	.119		13.10	3.38		16.48	19.55	
	1500	Pinstripe, obscure	↓	135	.119	↓	12.30	3.38		15.68	18.65	

08830 | Mirrors

			CREW	DAILY OUTPUT	LABOR-HOURS	UNIT	MAT.	LABOR	EQUIP.	TOTAL	TOTAL INCL O&P	
100	0010	**MIRRORS** No frames, wall type, 1/4" plate glass, polished edge										100
	0100	Up to 5 S.F.	2 Glaz	125	.128	S.F.	5.95	3.65		9.60	12.10	
	0200	Over 5 S.F.		160	.100		5.75	2.86		8.61	10.70	
	0500	Door type, 1/4" plate glass, up to 12 S.F.		160	.100		6.20	2.86		9.06	11.15	
	1000	Float glass, up to 10 S.F., 1/8" thick		160	.100		3.63	2.86		6.49	8.30	
	1100	3/16" thick		150	.107		4.23	3.05		7.28	9.25	
	1500	12" x 12" wall tiles, square edge, clear		195	.082		1.55	2.34		3.89	5.25	
	1600	Veined		195	.082		3.95	2.34		6.29	7.90	
	2000	1/4" thick, stock sizes, one way transparent		125	.128		13.45	3.65		17.10	20.50	
	2010	Bathroom, unframed, laminated	↓	160	.100	↓	10.30	2.86		13.16	15.65	

08840 | Plastic Glazing

			CREW	DAILY OUTPUT	LABOR-HOURS	UNIT	MAT.	LABOR	EQUIP.	TOTAL	TOTAL INCL O&P	
600	0010	**PLEXIGLASS ACRYLIC** Clear, masked, 1/8" thick, cut sheets	2 Glaz	170	.094	S.F.	2.98	2.69		5.67	7.35	600
	0200	Full sheets		195	.082		1.56	2.34		3.90	5.25	
	0500	1/4" thick, cut sheets		165	.097		5.25	2.77		8.02	10	
	0600	Full sheets		185	.086		2.87	2.47		5.34	6.90	
	0900	3/8" thick, cut sheets		155	.103		9.65	2.95		12.60	15.10	
	1000	Full sheets	↓	180	.089	↓	5.20	2.54		7.74	9.60	

DOORS & WINDOWS **8**

			DAILY	LABOR-		2001 BARE COSTS				TOTAL	
08840		**Plastic Glazing**	CREW	OUTPUT	HOURS	UNIT	MAT.	LABOR	EQUIP.	TOTAL	INCL O&P
600	1300	1/2″ thick, cut sheets	2 Glaz	135	.119	S.F.	11.10	3.38		14.48	17.40	**600**
	1400	Full sheets		150	.107		10.80	3.05		13.85	16.45
	1700	3/4″ thick, cut sheets		115	.139		39.50	3.97		43.47	49.50
	1800	Full sheets		130	.123		23	3.51		26.51	30.50
	2100	1″ thick, cut sheets		105	.152		44.50	4.35		48.85	55.50
	2200	Full sheets		125	.128		27.50	3.65		31.15	36
	3000	Colored, 1/8″ thick, cut sheets		170	.094		9.20	2.69		11.89	14.20
	3200	Full sheets		195	.082		5.95	2.34		8.29	10.10
	3500	1/4″ thick, cut sheets		165	.097		10.25	2.77		13.02	15.50
	3600	Full sheets		185	.086		7	2.47		9.47	11.45
	4000	Mirrors, untinted, cut sheets, 1/8″ thick		185	.086		4.32	2.47		6.79	8.50
	4200	1/4″ thick		180	.089		7.85	2.54		10.39	12.45
650	0010	**POLYCARBONATE** Clear, masked, cut sheets, 1/8″ thick	2 Glaz	170	.094	S.F.	5.20	2.69		7.89	9.80	**650**
	0500	3/16″ thick		165	.097		6.25	2.77		9.02	11.10
	1000	1/4″ thick		155	.103		6.90	2.95		9.85	12.05
	1500	3/8″ thick		150	.107		12.75	3.05		15.80	18.65
900	0010	**VINYL GLASS** Steel mesh reinforced, stock sizes, .090″ thick	2 Glaz	170	.094	S.F.	7.15	2.69		9.84	12	**900**
	0500	.120″ thick		170	.094		9.05	2.69		11.74	14.10
	1000	.250″ thick		155	.103		12.65	2.95		15.60	18.40
	1500	For non-standard sizes, add					15%				

			DAILY	LABOR-		2001 BARE COSTS				TOTAL	
08911		**Glazed Aluminum Curtain Wall**	CREW	OUTPUT	HOURS	UNIT	MAT.	LABOR	EQUIP.	TOTAL	INCL O&P
200	0010	**CURTAIN WALLS** Aluminum, stock, including glazing, minimum	H-1	205	.156	S.F.	19.30	4.79		24.09	29	**200**
	0050	Average, single glazed		195	.164		26	5.05		31.05	37.50
	0150	Average, double glazed		180	.178		36.50	5.45		41.95	49.50
	0200	Maximum		160	.200		98.50	6.15		104.65	118
700	0010	**TUBE FRAMING** For window walls and store fronts, aluminum, stock										**700**
	0050	Plain tube frame, mill finish, 1-3/4″ x 1-3/4″	2 Glaz	103	.155	L.F.	6.05	4.44		10.49	13.40
	0150	1-3/4″ x 4″		98	.163		7.60	4.66		12.26	15.40
	0200	1-3/4″ x 4-1/2″		95	.168		8.40	4.81		13.21	16.55
	0250	2″ x 6″		89	.180		12.75	5.15		17.90	22
	0350	4″ x 4″		87	.184		12.45	5.25		17.70	21.50
	0400	4-1/2″ x 4-1/2″		85	.188		13.95	5.35		19.30	23.50
	0450	Glass bead		240	.067		1.61	1.90		3.51	4.66
	1000	Flush tube frame, mill finish, 1/4″ glass, 1-3/4″ x 4″, open header		80	.200		7.45	5.70		13.15	16.85
	1050	Open sill		82	.195		6.50	5.55		12.05	15.60
	1100	Closed back header		83	.193		10.45	5.50		15.95	19.80
	1150	Closed back sill		85	.188		9.90	5.35		15.25	19.05
	1200	Vertical mullion, one piece		75	.213		11.05	6.10		17.15	21.50
	1250	Two piece		73	.219		11.85	6.25		18.10	22.50
	1300	90° or 180° vertical corner post		75	.213		18.60	6.10		24.70	30
	1400	1-3/4″ x 4-1/2″, open header		80	.200		9.10	5.70		14.80	18.65
	1450	Open sill		82	.195		7.50	5.55		13.05	16.70
	1500	Closed back header		83	.193		11.50	5.50		17	21
	1550	Closed back sill		85	.188		10.70	5.35		16.05	19.90
	1600	Vertical mullion, one piece		75	.213		11.95	6.10		18.05	22.50
	1650	Two piece		73	.219		12.65	6.25		18.90	23.50
	1700	90° or 180° vertical corner post		75	.213		12.95	6.10		19.05	23.50

8

DOORS & WINDOWS

08911 | Glazed Aluminum Curtain Wall

		CREW	DAILY OUTPUT	LABOR-HOURS	UNIT	2001 BARE COSTS				TOTAL INCL O&P	
						MAT.	LABOR	EQUIP.	TOTAL		
700	2000	Flush tube frame, mill fin. for ins. glass, 2" x 4-1/2", open header	2 Glaz	75	.213	L.F.	10.60	6.10		16.70	21	700
	2050	Open sill		77	.208		9.30	5.95		15.25	19.20	
	2100	Closed back header		78	.205		11.55	5.85		17.40	21.50	
	2150	Closed back sill		80	.200		11.40	5.70		17.10	21	
	2200	Vertical mullion, one piece		70	.229		12.80	6.55		19.35	24	
	2250	Two piece		68	.235		13.70	6.70		20.40	25.50	
	2300	90° or 180° vertical corner post		70	.229		12.95	6.55		19.50	24	
	5000	Flush tube frame, mill fin., thermal brk., 2-1/4"x 4-1/2", open header		74	.216		11.70	6.15		17.85	22	
	5050	Open sill		75	.213		10.20	6.10		16.30	20.50	
	5100	Vertical mullion, one piece		69	.232		14.10	6.60		20.70	25.50	
	5150	Two piece		67	.239		15.05	6.80		21.85	27	
	5200	90° or 180° vertical corner post		69	.232		13.55	6.60		20.15	25	
	6980	Door stop (snap in)	↓	380	.042	↓	2.18	1.20		3.38	4.22	
	7000	For joints, 90°, clip type, add				Ea.	18.65			18.65	20.50	
	7050	Screw spline joint, add					14.05			14.05	15.45	
	7100	For joint other than 90°, add				↓	29.50			29.50	32.50	
	8000	For bronze anodized aluminum, add					15%					
	8020	For black finish, add					27%					
	8050	For stainless steel materials, add					350%					
	8100	For monumental grade, add					50%					
	8150	For steel stiffener, add	2 Glaz	200	.080	L.F.	7.15	2.28		9.43	11.35	
	8200	For 2 to 5 stories, add per story				Story		5%				
900	0010	**WINDOW WALLS** Aluminum, stock, including glazing, minimum	H-2	160	.150	S.F.	25	4		29	33.50	900
	0050	Average		140	.171	"	30.50	4.57		35.07	40.50	
	0100	Maximum	↓	110	.218	S.F.	95.50	5.80		101.30	114	
	0500	For translucent sandwich wall systems, see div. 07420-770										
	0850	Cost of the above walls depends on material,										
	0860	finish, repetition, and size of units.										
	0870	The larger the opening, the lower the S.F. cost										
	1200	Double glazed acoustical window wall for airports,										
	1220	including 1" thick glass with 2" x 4-1/2" tube frame	H-2	40	.600	S.F.	62.50	16		78.50	93	

08950 | Translucent Wall/Roof Assemblies

		CREW	DAILY OUTPUT	LABOR-HOURS	UNIT	MAT.	LABOR	EQUIP.	TOTAL	TOTAL INCL O&P	
100	0010	**SKYROOFS** Translucent panels, 2-3/4" thick, under 5000 SF	G-3	395	.081	SF Hor.	18.95	2.28		21.23	24.50	100
	0100	Over 5000 SF		465	.069		16.90	1.94		18.84	21.50	
	0300	Continuous vaulted, semi-circular, to 8' wide, double glazed		145	.221		43	6.20		49.20	56.50	
	0400	Single glazed		160	.200		28.50	5.65		34.15	40.50	
	0600	To 20' wide, single glazed		175	.183		31.50	5.15		36.65	42.50	
	0700	Over 20' wide, single glazed		200	.160		36.50	4.51		41.01	47	
	0900	Motorized opening type, single glazed, 1/3 opening		145	.221		38	6.20		44.20	51	
	1000	Full opening	↓	130	.246	↓	43.50	6.95		50.45	58.50	
	1200	Pyramid type units, self-supporting, to 30' clear opening,										
	1300	square or circular, single glazed, minimum	G-3	200	.160	SF Hor.	21	4.51		25.51	30	
	1310	Average		165	.194		29.50	5.45		34.95	41	
	1400	Maximum		130	.246		42.50	6.95		49.45	57.50	
	1500	Grid type, 4' to 10' modules, single glass glazed, minimum		200	.160		26.50	4.51		31.01	36.50	
	1550	Maximum		128	.250		43.50	7.05		50.55	59	
	1600	Preformed acrylic, minimum		300	.107		31.50	3.01		34.51	39.50	
	1650	Maximum	↓	175	.183	↓	44.50	5.15		49.65	57	
	1800	Skyroofs, dome type, self-supporting, to 100' clear opening, circular										
	1900	Rise to span ratio = 0.20										
	1920	Minimum	G-3	197	.162	SF Hor.	13	4.58		17.58	21.50	
	1950	Maximum		113	.283		43.50	8		51.50	60	
	2100	Rise to span ratio = 0.33, minimum		169	.189		26	5.35		31.35	37	
	2150	Maximum	↓	101	.317	↓	51	8.95		59.95	70.50	

DOORS & WINDOWS **8**

08950	Translucent Wall/Roof Assemblies	CREW	DAILY OUTPUT	LABOR-HOURS	UNIT	2001 BARE COSTS				TOTAL INCL O&P	
						MAT.	LABOR	EQUIP.	TOTAL		
100	2200	Rise to span ratio = 0.50, minimum	G-3	148	.216	SF Hor.	39	6.10		45.10	52.50	100
	2250	Maximum		87	.368		57	10.35		67.35	78.50	
	2400	Ridge units, continuous, to 8' wide, double		130	.246		99.50	6.95		106.45	120	
	2500	Single		200	.160		68	4.51		72.51	82	
	2700	Ridge and furrow units, over 4' O.C., double, minimum		200	.160		21.50	4.51		26.01	30.50	
	2750	Maximum		120	.267		39.50	7.50		47	55	
	2800	Single, minimum		214	.150		18.20	4.22		22.42	26.50	
	2850	Maximum		153	.209		38.50	5.90		44.40	51.50	
	3000	Rolling roof, translucent panels, flat roof, residential, mininum		253	.126	S.F.	16.50	3.57		20.07	23.50	
	3030	Maximum		160	.200		33	5.65		38.65	45.50	
	3100	Lean-to skyroof, long span, double, minimum		197	.162		22	4.58		26.58	31.50	
	3150	Maximum		101	.317		44	8.95		52.95	62.50	
	3300	Single, minimum		321	.100		16.55	2.81		19.36	22.50	
	3350	Maximum		160	.200		27.50	5.65		33.15	39.50	

For information about Means Estimating Seminars, see yellow pages 11 and 12 in back of book

8 DOORS & WINDOWS

Division 9
Finishes

Estimating Tips

General

- Room Finish Schedule: A complete set of plans should contain a room finish schedule. If one is not available, it would be well worth the time and effort to put one together. A room finish schedule should contain the room number, room name (for clarity), floor materials, base materials, wainscot materials, wainscot height, wall materials (for each wall), ceiling materials, ceiling height and special instructions.

- Surplus Finishes: Review the specifications to determine if there is any requirement to provide certain amounts of extra materials for the owner's maintenance department. In some cases the owner may require a substantial amount of materials, especially when it is a special order item or long lead time item.

09200 Plaster & Gypsum Board

- Lath is estimated by the square yard for both gypsum and metal lath, plus usually 5% allowance for waste. Furring, channels and accessories are measured by the linear foot. An extra foot should be allowed for each accessory miter or stop.

- Plaster is also estimated by the square yard. Deductions for openings vary by preference, from zero deduction to 50% of all openings over 2 feet in width. Some estimators deduct a percentage of the total yardage for openings. The estimator should allow one extra square foot for each linear foot of horizontal interior or exterior angle located below the ceiling level. Also, double the areas of small radius work.

- Each room should be measured, perimeter times maximum wall height. Ceiling areas are equal to length times width.

- Drywall accessories, studs, track, and acoustical caulking are all measured by the linear foot. Drywall taping is figured by the square foot. Gypsum wallboard is estimated by the square foot. No material deductions should be made for door or window openings under 32 S.F. Coreboard can be obtained in a 1″ thickness for solid wall and shaft work. Additions should be made to price out the inside or outside corners.

- Different types of partition construction should be listed separately on the quantity sheets. There may be walls with studs of various widths, double studded, and similar or dissimilar surface materials. Shaft work is usually different construction from surrounding partitions requiring separate quantities and pricing of the work.

09300 Tile
09400 Terrazzo

- Tile and terrazzo areas are taken off on a square foot basis. Trim and base materials are measured by the linear foot. Accent tiles are listed per each. Two basic methods of installation are used. Mud set is approximately 30% more expensive than the thin set. In terrazzo work, be sure to include the linear footage of embedded decorative strips, grounds, machine rubbing and power cleanup.

09600 Flooring

- Wood flooring is available in strip, parquet, or block configuration. The latter two types are set in adhesives with quantities estimated by the square foot. The laying pattern will influence labor costs and material waste. In addition to the material and labor for laying wood floors, the estimator must make allowances for sanding and finishing these areas unless the flooring is prefinished.

- Most of the various types of flooring are all measured on a square foot basis. Base is measured by the linear foot. If adhesive materials are to be quantified, they are estimated at a specified coverage rate by the gallon depending upon the specified type and the manufacturer's recommendations.

- Sheet flooring is measured by the square yard. Roll widths vary, so consideration should be given to use the most economical width, as waste must be figured into the total quantity. Consider also the installation methods available, direct glue down or stretched .

09700 Wall Finishes

- Wall coverings are estimated by the square foot. The area to be covered is measured, length by height of wall above baseboards, to calculate the square footage of each wall. This figure is divided by the number of square feet in the single roll which is being used. Deduct, in full, the areas of openings such as doors and windows. Where a pattern match is required allow 25%-30% waste. One gallon of paste should be sufficient to hang 12 single rolls of light to medium weight paper.

09800 Acoustical Treatment

- Acoustical systems fall into several categories. The takeoff of these materials is by the square foot of area with a 5% allowance for waste. Do not forget about scaffolding, if applicable, when estimating these systems.

09900 Paints & Coatings

- Painting is one area where bids vary to a greater extent than almost any other section of a project. This arises from the many methods of measuring surfaces to be painted. The estimator should check the plans and specifications carefully to be sure of the required number of coats.

- Protection of adjacent surfaces is not included in painting costs. When considering the method of paint application, an important factor is the amount of protection and masking required. These must be estimated separately and may be the determining factor in choosing the method of application.

Reference Numbers

Reference numbers are shown in bold squares at the beginning of some major classifications. These numbers refer to related items in the Reference Section. The reference information may be an estimating procedure, an alternate pricing method or technical information.

Note: Not all subdivisions listed here necessarily appear in this publication.

09100 | Metal Support Assemblies

09110 | Non-Load Bearing Wall Framing

		CREW	DAILY OUTPUT	LABOR-HOURS	UNIT	2001 BARE COSTS MAT.	LABOR	EQUIP.	TOTAL	TOTAL INCL O&P	
100	0010	**METAL STUDS, PARTITIONS,** 10' high, with runners R09110-610										100
	0050	See also Studding, division 05120-440										
	2000	Non-load bearing, galvanized, 25 ga. 1-5/8" wide, 16" O.C.	1 Carp	495	.016	S.F.	.15	.47		.62	.91	
	2100	24" O.C.		760	.011		.11	.31		.42	.60	
	2200	2-1/2" wide, 16" O.C.		490	.016		.17	.48		.65	.92	
	2250	24" O.C.		750	.011		.12	.31		.43	.62	
	2300	3-5/8" wide, 16" O.C.		480	.017		.19	.49		.68	.97	
	2350	24" O.C.		740	.011		.14	.32		.46	.65	
	2400	4" wide, 16" O.C.		475	.017		.23	.49		.72	1.03	
	2450	24" O.C.		740	.011		.17	.32		.49	.68	
	2500	6" wide, 16" O.C.		470	.017		.30	.50		.80	1.11	
	2550	24" O.C.		725	.011		.22	.32		.54	.75	
	2600	20 ga. studs, 1-5/8" wide, 16" O.C.		395	.020		.26	.59		.85	1.20	
	2650	24" O.C.		610	.013		.19	.38		.57	.81	
	2700	2-1/2" wide, 16" O.C.		390	.021		.27	.60		.87	1.24	
	2750	24" O.C.		600	.013		.20	.39		.59	.83	
	2800	3-5/8" wide, 16" O.C. **CN**		385	.021		.29	.61		.90	1.27	
	2850	24" O.C.		590	.014		.22	.40		.62	.86	
	2900	4" wide, 16" O.C.		380	.021		.37	.61		.98	1.36	
	2950	24" O.C.		590	.014		.27	.40		.67	.92	
	3000	6" wide, 16" O.C.		375	.021		.43	.62		1.05	1.44	
	3050	24" O.C.		580	.014		.31	.40		.71	.98	
	5000	Load bearing studs, see division 05410-400										

09130 | Acoustical Suspension

		CREW	DAILY OUTPUT	LABOR-HOURS	UNIT	2001 BARE COSTS MAT.	LABOR	EQUIP.	TOTAL	TOTAL INCL O&P	
100	0010	**CEILING SUSPENSION SYSTEMS** For boards and tile										100
	0050	Class A suspension system, 15/16" T bar, 2' x 4' grid **CN**	1 Carp	800	.010	S.F.	.33	.29		.62	.82	
	0300	2' x 2' grid	"	650	.012		.40	.36		.76	1	
	0350	For 9/16" grid, add					.13			.13	.14	
	0360	For fire rated grid, add					.07			.07	.08	
	0370	For colored grid, add					.15			.15	.17	
	0400	Concealed Z bar suspension system, 12" module	1 Carp	520	.015		.36	.45		.81	1.10	
	0600	1-1/2" carrier channels, 4' O.C., add	"	470	.017		.22	.50		.72	1.02	
	0700	Carrier channels for ceilings with										
	0900	recessed lighting fixtures, add	1 Carp	460	.017	S.F.	.34	.51		.85	1.16	
	1040	Hanging wire, 12 ga., 4' long		65	.123	C.S.F.	.72	3.59		4.31	6.40	
	1080	8' long		65	.123	"	3.05	3.59		6.64	8.95	
	1200	Seismic bracing, 2-1/2" compression post with four bracing wires		50	.160	Ea.	2.16	4.66		6.82	9.70	

09200 | Plaster & Gypsum Board

09205 | Furring & Lathing

		CREW	DAILY OUTPUT	LABOR-HOURS	UNIT	2001 BARE COSTS MAT.	LABOR	EQUIP.	TOTAL	TOTAL INCL O&P	
530	0010	**FURRING** Beams & columns, 7/8" galvanized channels,										530
	0030	12" O.C.	1 Lath	155	.052	S.F.	.18	1.46		1.64	2.36	
	0050	16" O.C.		170	.047		.14	1.33		1.47	2.14	
	0070	24" O.C.		185	.043		.10	1.22		1.32	1.93	
	0100	Ceilings, on steel, 7/8" channels, galvanized, 12" O.C.		210	.038		.16	1.07		1.23	1.78	
	0300	16" O.C.		290	.028		.14	.78		.92	1.32	

Important: See the Reference Section for critical supporting data - Reference Nos., Crews, & City Cost Indexes

09205 | Furring & Lathing

			DAILY OUTPUT	LABOR-HOURS	UNIT	MAT.	LABOR	EQUIP.	TOTAL	TOTAL INCL O&P	
							2001 BARE COSTS				
			CREW								
530	0400	24" O.C.	1 Lath 420	.019	S.F.	.10	.54		.64	.91	530
	0600	1-5/8" channels, galvanized, 12" O.C.	190	.042		.25	1.19		1.44	2.04	
	0700	16" O.C.	260	.031		.22	.87		1.09	1.54	
	0900	24" O.C.	390	.021		.15	.58		.73	1.02	
	1000	Walls, 7/8" channels, galvanized, 12" O.C.	235	.034		.16	.96		1.12	1.61	
	1200	16" O.C.	265	.030		.14	.85		.99	1.43	
	1300	24" O.C.	350	.023		.10	.64		.74	1.07	
	1500	1-5/8" channels, galvanized, 12" O.C.	210	.038		.25	1.07		1.32	1.87	
	1600	16" O.C.	240	.033		.22	.94		1.16	1.64	
	1800	24" O.C.	305	.026		.15	.74		.89	1.26	
	8000	Suspended ceilings, including carriers									
	8200	1-1/2" carriers, 24" O.C. with:									
	8300	7/8" channels, 16" O.C.	1 Lath 165	.048	S.F.	.58	1.37		1.95	2.68	
	8320	24" O.C.	200	.040		.54	1.13		1.67	2.27	
	8400	1-5/8" channels, 16" O.C.	155	.052		.66	1.46		2.12	2.90	
	8420	24" O.C.	190	.042		.59	1.19		1.78	2.42	
	8600	2" carriers, 24" O.C. with:									
	8700	7/8" channels, 16" O.C.	1 Lath 155	.052	S.F.	.14	1.46		1.60	2.33	
	8720	24" O.C.	190	.042		.10	1.19		1.29	1.88	
	8800	1-5/8" channels, 16" O.C.	145	.055		.60	1.56		2.16	2.98	
	8820	24" O.C.	180	.044		.53	1.25		1.78	2.45	
540	0010	GYPSUM LATH Plain or perforated, nailed, 3/8" thick R09205-050	1 Lath 85	.094	S.Y.	3.51	2.65		6.16	7.80	540
	0100	1/2" thick, nailed	80	.100		3.51	2.82		6.33	8.05	
	0300	Clipped to steel studs, 3/8" thick	75	.107		3.60	3.01		6.61	8.45	
	0400	1/2" thick	70	.114		3.60	3.22		6.82	8.75	
	0600	Firestop gypsum base, to steel studs, 3/8" thick	70	.114		3.51	3.22		6.73	8.65	
	0700	1/2" thick	65	.123		3.96	3.47		7.43	9.55	
	0900	Foil back, to steel studs, 3/8" thick	75	.107		3.60	3.01		6.61	8.45	
	1000	1/2" thick	70	.114		3.96	3.22		7.18	9.15	
	1500	For ceiling installations, add	216	.037			1.04		1.04	1.56	
	1600	For columns and beams, add	170	.047			1.33		1.33	1.98	
560	0010	METAL LATH Diamond, expanded, 2.5 lb. per S.Y., painted R09205-060			S.Y.	1.50			1.50	1.65	560
	0100	Galvanized, 2.5 lb. per S.Y.				1.43			1.43	1.57	
	0300	3.4 lb. per S.Y., painted				2.27			2.27	2.50	
	0400	Galvanized				2.05			2.05	2.26	
	0600	For 15# asphalt sheathing paper, add				.19			.19	.21	
	0900	Flat rib, 1/8" high, 2.75 lb., painted				2.25			2.25	2.48	
	1000	Foil backed				2.70			2.70	2.97	
	1200	3.4 lb. per S.Y., painted				2.26			2.26	2.49	
	1300	Galvanized				3.06			3.06	3.37	
	1500	For 15# asphalt sheating paper, add				.19			.19	.21	
	1800	High rib, 3/8" high, 3.4 lb. per S.Y., painted				3.26			3.26	3.59	
	1900	Galvanized				2.72			2.72	2.99	
	2400	High rib, 3/4" high, painted, .60 lb. per S.F.			S.F.	.31			.31	.34	
	2500	.75 lb. per S.F.			"	.67			.67	.74	
	2800	Stucco mesh, painted, 3.6 lb.			S.Y.	1.62			1.62	1.78	
	3000	K-lath, perforated, absorbent paper, regular				2.38			2.38	2.62	
	3100	Heavy duty				2.81			2.81	3.09	
	3300	Waterproof, heavy duty, grade B backing				2.75			2.75	3.03	
	3400	Fire resistant backing				3.04			3.04	3.34	
	3600	2.5 lb. diamond painted, on wood framing, on walls	1 Lath 85	.094		1.50	2.65		4.15	5.60	
	3700	On ceilings	75	.107		1.50	3.01		4.51	6.15	
	3900	3.4 lb. diamond painted, on wood framing, on walls	80	.100		2.26	2.82		5.08	6.70	
	4000	On ceilings	70	.114		2.26	3.22		5.48	7.30	
	4200	3.4 lb. diamond painted, wired to steel framing	75	.107		2.26	3.01		5.27	7	

FINISHES 9

09205 | Furring & Lathing

		CREW	DAILY OUTPUT	LABOR-HOURS	UNIT	MAT.	LABOR	EQUIP.	TOTAL	TOTAL INCL O&P
						\[2001 BARE COSTS\]				
560 4300	On ceilings R09205-060	1 Lath	60	.133	S.Y.	2.26	3.76		6.02	8.10
4500	Columns and beams, wired to steel		40	.200		2.26	5.65		7.91	10.90
4600	Cornices, wired to steel		35	.229		2.26	6.45		8.71	12.10
4800	Screwed to steel studs, 2.5 lb.		80	.100		1.50	2.82		4.32	5.85
4900	3.4 lb.		75	.107		2.27	3.01		5.28	7
5100	Rib lath, painted, wired to steel, on walls, 2.5 lb.		75	.107		2.25	3.01		5.26	6.95
5200	3.4 lb.		70	.114		3.26	3.22		6.48	8.40
5400	4.0 lb.		65	.123		3.35	3.47		6.82	8.90
5500	For self-furring lath, add					.06			.06	.07
5700	Suspended ceiling system, incl. 3.4 lb. diamond lath, painted	1 Lath	15	.533		8.80	15.05		23.85	32
5800	Galvanized	"	15	.533		9.10	15.05		24.15	32.50
6000	Hollow metal stud partitions, 3.4 lb. painted lath both sides									
6010	Non-load bearing, 25 ga., w/rib lath 2-1/2" studs, 12" O.C.	1 Lath	20.30	.394	S.Y.	8.45	11.10		19.55	26
6300	16" O.C.		21.10	.379		7.95	10.70		18.65	24.50
6350	24" O.C.		22.70	.352		7.60	9.95		17.55	23
6400	3-5/8" studs, 16" O.C.		19.50	.410		8.30	11.55		19.85	26.50
6600	24" O.C.		20.40	.392		7.85	11.05		18.90	25
6700	4" studs, 16" O.C.		20.40	.392		9.15	11.05		20.20	26.50
6900	24" O.C.		21.60	.370		8	10.45		18.45	24.50
7000	6" studs, 16" O.C.		19.50	.410		9.15	11.55		20.70	27.50
7100	24" O.C.		21.10	.379		8.50	10.70		19.20	25.50
7200	L.B. partitions, 16 ga., w/rib lath, 2-1/2" studs, 16" O.C.		20	.400		7.60	11.30		18.90	25
7300	3-5/8" studs, 16 ga.		19.70	.406		8.65	11.45		20.10	26.50
7500	4" studs, 16 ga.		19.50	.410		9.10	11.55		20.65	27.50
7600	6" studs, 16 ga.		18.70	.428		10.45	12.05		22.50	29.50
700 0010	**ACCESSORIES, PLASTER** Casing bead, expanded flange, galvanized	1 Lath	2.70	2.963	C.L.F.	27	83.50		110.50	155
0900	Channels, cold rolled, 16 ga., 3/4" deep, galvanized					15.95			15.95	17.55
1200	1-1/2" deep, 16 ga., galvanized					24.50			24.50	27
1620	Corner bead, expanded bullnose, 3/4" radius, #10, galvanized	1 Lath	2.60	3.077		20	87		107	152
1650	#1, galvanized		2.55	3.137		35	88.50		123.50	171
1670	Expanded wing, 2-3/4" wide, galv. #1		2.65	3.019		20	85		105	149
1700	Inside corner, (corner rite) 3" x 3", painted		2.60	3.077		17.65	87		104.65	149
1750	Strip-ex, 4" wide, painted		2.55	3.137		14.75	88.50		103.25	148
1800	Expansion joint, 3/4" grounds, limited expansion, galv., 1 piece		2.70	2.963		65	83.50		148.50	197
2100	Extreme expansion, galvanized, 2 piece		2.60	3.077		120	87		207	262

09210 | Gypsum Plaster

		CREW	DAILY OUTPUT	LABOR-HOURS	UNIT	MAT.	LABOR	EQUIP.	TOTAL	TOTAL INCL O&P
100 0010	**GYPSUM PLASTER** 80# bag, less than 1 ton R09210-105				Bag	14.10			14.10	15.50
0100	Over 1 ton				"	12.80			12.80	14.10
0300	2 coats, no lath included, on walls	J-1	105	.381	S.Y.	3.42	9.80	.56	13.78	19.40
0400	On ceilings	"	92	.435		3.42	11.15	.64	15.21	21.50
0600	2 coats on and incl. 3/8" gypsum lath on steel, on walls	J-2	97	.495		7	12.90	.61	20.51	28
0700	On ceilings	"	83	.578		7	15.10	.71	22.81	31.50
0900	3 coats, no lath included, on walls	J-1	87	.460		4.77	11.80	.68	17.25	24
1000	On ceilings	"	78	.513		4.77	13.15	.76	18.68	26
1200	3 coats on and including painted metal lath, on wood studs	J-2	86	.558		7.95	14.55	.69	23.19	31.50
1300	On ceilings	"	76.50	.627		7.95	16.40	.77	25.12	34.50
1600	For irregular or curved surfaces, add						30%			
1800	For columns & beams, add						50%			
200 0010	**GAUGING PLASTER** 100 lb. bags, less than 1 ton				Bag	21.50			21.50	23.50
0100	Over 1 ton				"	20.50			20.50	22.50
300 0010	**KEENES CEMENT** In 100 lb. bags, less than 1 ton				Bag	23.50			23.50	25.50
0100	Over 1 ton				"	22.50			22.50	25
0300	Finish only, add to plaster prices, standard	J-1	215	.186	S.Y.	2.19	4.78	.28	7.25	10
0400	High quality	"	144	.278	"	2.21	7.15	.41	9.77	13.80

9 FINISHES

Important: See the Reference Section for critical supporting data - Reference Nos., Crews, & City Cost Indexes

09210 | Gypsum Plaster

		CREW	DAILY OUTPUT	LABOR-HOURS	UNIT	2001 BARE COSTS				TOTAL INCL O&P	
						MAT.	LABOR	EQUIP.	TOTAL		
500	0010	**PERLITE OR VERMICULITE PLASTER** 100 lb. bags Under 200 bags				Bag	13			13	14.30	**500**
	0100	Over 200 bags				"	12.05			12.05	13.25	
	0300	2 coats, no lath included, on walls R09210-115	J-1	92	.435	S.Y.	3.24	11.15	.64	15.03	21.50	
	0400	On ceilings	"	79	.506		3.24	13	.75	16.99	24.50	
	0600	2 coats, on and incl. 3/8" gypsum lath, on metal studs	J-2	84	.571		5.95	14.90	.70	21.55	30	
	0700	On ceilings	"	70	.686		5.95	17.90	.84	24.69	35	
	0900	3 coats, no lath included, on walls	J-1	74	.541		5.40	13.90	.80	20.10	28.50	
	1000	On ceilings	"	63	.635		5.40	16.30	.94	22.64	32	
	1200	3 coats, on and incl. painted metal lath, on metal studs	J-2	72	.667		8.65	17.40	.82	26.87	37	
	1300	On ceilings		61	.787		8.65	20.50	.97	30.12	42	
	1500	3 coats, on and incl. suspended metal lath ceiling	↓	37	1.297		14.20	34	1.60	49.80	69	
	1700	For irregular or curved surfaces, add to above						30%				
	1800	For columns and beams, add to above						50%				
	1900	For soffits, add to ceiling prices						40%				
650	0010	**PLASTER PARTITION WALL**										**650**
	0400	Stud walls, 3.4 lb. metal lath, 3 coat gypsum plaster, 2 sides										
	0600	2" x 4" wood studs, 16" O.C.	J-2	315	.152	S.F.	2.98	3.98	.19	7.15	9.55	
	0700	2-1/2" metal studs, 25 ga., 12" O.C.		325	.148		2.76	3.85	.18	6.79	9.15	
	0800	3-5/8" metal studs, 25 ga., 16" O.C.	↓	320	.150	↓	2.78	3.92	.18	6.88	9.20	
	0900	Gypsum lath, 2 coat vermiculite plaster, 2 sides										
	1000	2" x 4" wood studs, 16" O.C.	J-2	355	.135	S.F.	3.32	3.53	.17	7.02	9.25	
	1200	2-1/2" metal studs, 25 ga., 12" O.C.		365	.132		2.94	3.43	.16	6.53	8.65	
	1300	3-5/8" metal studs, 25 ga., 16" O.C.	↓	360	.133		3.03	3.48	.16	6.67	8.80	
900	0010	**THIN COAT** Plaster, 1 coat veneer, not incl. lath	J-1	3,600	.011	S.F.	.07	.29	.02	.38	.54	**900**
	1000	In 50 lb. bags				Bag	8.80			8.80	9.65	

09220 | Portland Cement Plaster

		CREW	DAILY OUTPUT	LABOR-HOURS	UNIT	MAT.	LABOR	EQUIP.	TOTAL	TOTAL INCL O&P	
200	0010	**STUCCO**, 3 coats 1" thick, float finish, with mesh, on wood frame R09220-300	J-2	63	.762	S.Y.	3.65	19.90	.94	24.49	35.50	**200**
	0100	On masonry construction, no mesh incl.	J-1	67	.597		2.03	15.35	.88	18.26	26.50	
	0300	For trowel finish, add	1 Plas	170	.047			1.28		1.28	1.97	
	0400	For 3/4" thick, on masonry, deduct	J-1	880	.045		.56	1.17	.07	1.80	2.48	
	0600	For coloring and special finish, add, minimum		685	.058		.36	1.50	.09	1.95	2.79	
	0700	Maximum	↓	200	.200		1.26	5.15	.30	6.71	9.55	
	0900	For soffits, add	J-2	155	.310		1.94	8.10	.38	10.42	14.85	
	1000	Exterior stucco, with bonding agent, 3 coats, on walls, no mesh incl.	J-1	200	.200		3.25	5.15	.30	8.70	11.75	
	1200	Ceilings		180	.222		3.25	5.70	.33	9.28	12.70	
	1300	Beams		80	.500		3.25	12.85	.74	16.84	24	
	1500	Columns	↓	100	.400		3.25	10.25	.59	14.09	20	
	1600	Mesh, painted, nailed to wood, 1.8 lb.	1 Lath	60	.133		3.09	3.76		6.85	9	
	1800	3.6 lb.		55	.145		1.62	4.10		5.72	7.90	
	1900	Wired to steel, painted, 1.8 lb.		53	.151		3.09	4.26		7.35	9.75	
	2100	3.6 lb.	↓	50	.160	↓	1.62	4.51		6.13	8.55	

09250 | Gypsum Board

		CREW	DAILY OUTPUT	LABOR-HOURS	UNIT	MAT.	LABOR	EQUIP.	TOTAL	TOTAL INCL O&P	
200	0010	**CEMENTITIOUS BACKERBOARD**										**200**
	0070	Cementitious backerboard, on floor, 3' x 4'x 1/2" sheets	2 Carp	525	.030	S.F.	1.04	.89		1.93	2.54	
	0080	3' x 5' x 1/2" sheets		525	.030		1.04	.89		1.93	2.54	
	0090	3' x 6' x 1/2" sheets		525	.030		1.04	.89		1.93	2.53	
	0100	3' x 4'x 5/8" sheets		525	.030		1.08	.89		1.97	2.58	
	0110	3' x 5' x 5/8" sheets		525	.030		1.06	.89		1.95	2.56	
	0120	3' x 6' x 5/8" sheets		525	.030		1.07	.89		1.96	2.56	
	0150	On wall, 3' x 4'x 1/2" sheets		350	.046		1.04	1.33		2.37	3.23	
	0160	3' x 5' x 1/2" sheets		350	.046		1.04	1.33		2.37	3.23	
	0170	3' x 6' x 1/2" sheets	↓	350	.046	↓	1.04	1.33		2.37	3.22	

FINISHES 9

9 FINISHES

	09250	**Gypsum Board**	CREW	DAILY OUTPUT	LABOR-HOURS	UNIT	2001 BARE COSTS MAT.	2001 BARE COSTS LABOR	2001 BARE COSTS EQUIP.	2001 BARE COSTS TOTAL	TOTAL INCL O&P	
200	0180	3' x 4'x 5/8" sheets	2 Carp	350	.046	S.F.	1.08	1.33		2.41	3.27	**200**
	0190	3' x 5' x 5/8" sheets		350	.046		1.06	1.33		2.39	3.25	
	0200	3' x 6' x 5/8" sheets		350	.046		1.07	1.33		2.40	3.25	
	0250	On counter, 3' x 4'x 1/2" sheets		180	.089		1.04	2.59		3.63	5.20	
	0260	3' x 5' x 1/2" sheets		180	.089		1.04	2.59		3.63	5.20	
	0270	3' x 6' x 1/2" sheets		180	.089		1.04	2.59		3.63	5.20	
	0300	3' x 4'x 5/8" sheets		180	.089		1.08	2.59		3.67	5.25	
	0310	3' x 5' x 5/8" sheets		180	.089		1.06	2.59		3.65	5.20	
	0320	3' x 6' x 5/8" sheets	▼	180	.089	▼	1.07	2.59		3.66	5.20	
300	0010	**BLUEBOARD** For use with thin coat										**300**
	0100	plaster application (see division 09210-900)										
	1000	3/8" thick, on walls or ceilings, standard, no finish included	2 Carp	1,900	.008	S.F.	.26	.25		.51	.67	
	1100	With thin coat plaster finish		875	.018		.33	.53		.86	1.19	
	1400	On beams, columns, or soffits, standard, no finish included		675	.024		.30	.69		.99	1.41	
	1450	With thin coat plaster finish		475	.034		.38	.98		1.36	1.96	
	3000	1/2" thick, on walls or ceilings, standard, no finish included		1,900	.008		.26	.25		.51	.67	
	3100	With thin coat plaster finish		875	.018		.33	.53		.86	1.19	
	3300	Fire resistant, no finish included		1,900	.008		.26	.25		.51	.67	
	3400	With thin coat plaster finish		875	.018		.33	.53		.86	1.19	
	3450	On beams, columns, or soffits, standard, no finish included		675	.024		.30	.69		.99	1.41	
	3500	With thin coat plaster finish		475	.034		.38	.98		1.36	1.96	
	3700	Fire resistant, no finish included		675	.024		.30	.69		.99	1.41	
	3800	With thin coat plaster finish		475	.034		.38	.98		1.36	1.96	
	5000	5/8" thick, on walls or ceilings, fire resistant, no finish included		1,900	.008		.30	.25		.55	.71	
	5100	With thin coat plaster finish		875	.018		.37	.53		.90	1.24	
	5500	On beams, columns, or soffits, no finish included		675	.024		.35	.69		1.04	1.46	
	5600	With thin coat plaster finish		475	.034		.43	.98		1.41	2.01	
	6000	For high ceilings, over 8' high, add		3,060	.005			.15		.15	.24	
	6500	For over 3 stories high, add per story	▼	6,100	.003	▼		.08		.08	.12	
500	0010	**CEILINGS** Gypsum drywall, fire rated, finished										**500**
	0100	Screwed to grid, channel or joists, 1/2" thick	2 Carp	765	.021	S.F.	.24	.61		.85	1.21	
	0200	5/8" thick		765	.021		.29	.61		.90	1.27	
	0300	Over 8' high, 1/2" thick		615	.026		.24	.76		1	1.45	
	0400	5/8" thick	▼	615	.026	▼	.29	.76		1.05	1.51	
	0600	Grid suspension system, direct hung										
	0700	1-1/2" C.R.C., with 7/8" hi hat furring channel, 16" O.C.	2 Carp	600	.027	S.F.	.84	.78		1.62	2.14	
	0800	24" O.C.		900	.018		.77	.52		1.29	1.66	
	0900	3-5/8" C.R.C., with 7/8" hi hat furring channel, 16" O.C.		600	.027		.89	.78		1.67	2.20	
	1000	24" O.C.	▼	900	.018	▼	.78	.52		1.30	1.67	
700	0010	**DRYWALL** Gypsum plasterboard, nailed or screwed	R09250 -100									**700**
	0100	to studs unless otherwise noted										
	0150	3/8" thick, on walls, standard, no finish included	2 Carp	2,000	.008	S.F.	.26	.23		.49	.65	
	0200	On ceilings, standard, no finish included		1,800	.009		.26	.26		.52	.70	
	0250	On beams, columns, or soffits, no finish included		675	.024		.30	.69		.99	1.41	
	0300	1/2" thick, on walls, standard, no finish included **CN**		2,000	.008		.26	.23		.49	.65	
	0350	Taped and finished (level 4 finish)		965	.017		.30	.48		.78	1.09	
	0390	With compound skim coat (level 5 finish)		775	.021		.32	.60		.92	1.29	
	0400	Fire resistant, no finish included		2,000	.008		.24	.23		.47	.62	
	0450	Taped and finished (level 4 finish)		965	.017		.28	.48		.76	1.07	
	0490	With compound skim coat (level 5 finish)		775	.021		.30	.60		.90	1.27	
	0500	Water resistant, no finish included		2,000	.008		.34	.23		.57	.73	
	0550	Taped and finished (level 4 finish)		965	.017		.38	.48		.86	1.18	
	0590	With compound skim coat (level 5 finish)		775	.021		.40	.60		1	1.38	
	0600	Prefinished, vinyl, clipped to studs		900	.018		.56	.52		1.08	1.43	
	1000	On ceilings, standard, no finish included	▼ ▼	1,800	.009	▼	.26	.26		.52	.70	

Important: See the Reference Section for critical supporting data - Reference Nos., Crews, & City Cost Indexes

		09250	Gypsum Board	CREW	DAILY OUTPUT	LABOR-HOURS	UNIT	2001 BARE COSTS				TOTAL INCL O&P	
								MAT.	LABOR	EQUIP.	TOTAL		
700	1050		Taped and finished (level 4 finish) R09250-100	2 Carp	765	.021	S.F.	.30	.61		.91	1.28	700
	1090		With compound skim coat (level 5 finish)		610	.026		.32	.76		1.08	1.55	
	1100		Fire resistant, no finish included		1,800	.009		.24	.26		.50	.67	
	1150		Taped and finished (level 4 finish)		765	.021		.28	.61		.89	1.26	
	1195		With compound skim coat (level 5 finish)		610	.026		.30	.76		1.06	1.53	
	1200		Water resistant, no finish included		1,800	.009		.34	.26		.60	.78	
	1250		Taped and finished (level 4 finish)		765	.021		.38	.61		.99	1.37	
	1290		With compound skim coat (level 5 finish)		610	.026		.40	.76		1.16	1.64	
	1500		On beams, columns, or soffits, standard, no finish included		675	.024		.30	.69		.99	1.41	
	1550		Taped and finished (level 4 finish)		475	.034		.35	.98		1.33	1.92	
	1590		With compound skim coat (level 5 finish)		540	.030		.37	.86		1.23	1.75	
	1600		Fire resistant, no finish included		675	.024		.28	.69		.97	1.38	
	1650		Taped and finished (level 4 finish)		475	.034		.32	.98		1.30	1.89	
	1690		With compound skim coat (level 5 finish)		540	.030		.35	.86		1.21	1.73	
	1700		Water resistant, no finish included		675	.024		.39	.69		1.08	1.51	
	1750		Taped and finished (level 4 finish)		475	.034		.44	.98		1.42	2.02	
	1790		With compound skim coat (level 5 finish)		540	.030		.46	.86		1.32	1.86	
	2000		5/8" thick, on walls, standard, no finish included		2,000	.008		.29	.23		.52	.68	
	2050		Taped and finished (level 4 finish)		965	.017		.33	.48		.81	1.12	
	2090		With compound skim coat (level 5 finish)		775	.021		.35	.60		.95	1.33	
	2100		Fire resistant, no finish included		2,000	.008		.29	.23		.52	.68	
	2150		Taped and finished (level 4 finish)		965	.017		.33	.48		.81	1.12	
	2195		With compound skim coat (level 5 finish)		775	.021		.35	.60		.95	1.33	
	2200		Water resistant, no finish included		2,000	.008		.43	.23		.66	.83	
	2250		Taped and finished (level 4 finish)		965	.017		.47	.48		.95	1.28	
	2290		With compound skim coat (level 5 finish)		775	.021		.49	.60		1.09	1.48	
	2300		Prefinished, vinyl, clipped to studs		900	.018		.65	.52		1.17	1.53	
	3000		On ceilings, standard, no finish included		1,800	.009		.29	.26		.55	.73	
	3050		Taped and finished (level 4 finish)		765	.021		.33	.61		.94	1.31	
	3090		With compound skim coat (level 5 finish)		615	.026		.35	.76		1.11	1.58	
	3100		Fire resistant, no finish included		1,800	.009		.29	.26		.55	.73	
	3150		Taped and finished (level 4 finish)		765	.021		.33	.61		.94	1.31	
	3190		With compound skim coat (level 5 finish)		615	.026		.35	.76		1.11	1.58	
	3200		Water resistant, no finish included		1,800	.009		.43	.26		.69	.88	
	3250		Taped and finished (level 4 finish)		765	.021		.47	.61		1.08	1.47	
	3290		With compound skim coat (level 5 finish)		615	.026		.49	.76		1.25	1.73	
	3500		On beams, columns, or soffits, no finish included		675	.024		.33	.69		1.02	1.45	
	3550		Taped and finished (level 4 finish)		475	.034		.38	.98		1.36	1.96	
	3590		With compound skim coat (level 5 finish)		380	.042		.40	1.23		1.63	2.36	
	3600		Fire resistant, no finish included		675	.024		.33	.69		1.02	1.45	
	3650		Taped and finished (level 4 finish)		475	.034		.38	.98		1.36	1.96	
	3690		With compound skim coat (level 5 finish)		380	.042		.40	1.23		1.63	2.36	
	3700		Water resistant, no finish included		675	.024		.49	.69		1.18	1.62	
	3750		Taped and finished (level 4 finish)		475	.034		.54	.98		1.52	2.13	
	3790		With compound skim coat (level 5 finish)		380	.042		.56	1.23		1.79	2.54	
	4000		Fireproofing, beams or columns, 2 layers, 1/2" thick, incl finish		330	.048		.52	1.41		1.93	2.78	
	4050		5/8" thick		300	.053		.66	1.55		2.21	3.16	
	4100		3 layers, 1/2" thick		225	.071		.84	2.07		2.91	4.16	
	4150		5/8" thick		210	.076		.99	2.22		3.21	4.56	
	5050		For 1" thick coreboard on columns		480	.033		.45	.97		1.42	2.02	
	5100		For foil-backed board, add					.10			.10	.11	
	5200		For high ceilings, over 8' high, add	2 Carp	3,060	.005			.15		.15	.24	
	5270		For textured spray, add	2 Lath	1,600	.010		.05	.28		.33	.48	
	5300		For over 3 stories high, add per story	2 Carp	6,100	.003			.08		.08	.12	
	5350		For finishing corners, inside or outside, add	"	1,100	.015	L.F.	.06	.42		.48	.73	
	5500		For acoustical sealant, add per bead	1 Carp	500	.016	"	.03	.47		.50	.76	

09250 | Gypsum Board

			DAILY OUTPUT	LABOR-HOURS	UNIT	2001 BARE COSTS				TOTAL INCL O&P	
			CREW			MAT.	LABOR	EQUIP.	TOTAL		
700	5550	Sealant, 1 quart tube R09250-100			Ea.	4.89			4.89	5.40	**700**
	5600	Sound deadening board, 1/4" gypsum	2 Carp	1,800	.009	S.F.	.24	.26		.50	.67	
	5650	1/2" wood fiber	"	1,800	.009	"	.34	.26		.60	.78	
800	0010	**HIGH ABUSE GYPSUM BOARD**, fiber reinforced, nailed or										**800**
	0100	screwed to studs unless otherwise noted										
	0110	1/2" thick, on walls, no finish included	2 Carp	1,800	.009	S.F.	.41	.26		.67	.86	
	0120	Taped and finished (level 4 finish)		870	.018		.45	.54		.99	1.34	
	0130	With compound skim coat (level 5 finish)		700	.023		.47	.67		1.14	1.56	
	0150	On ceilings, no finish included		1,620	.010		.41	.29		.70	.90	
	0160	Taped and finished (level 4 finish)		690	.023		.45	.68		1.13	1.56	
	0170	With compound skim coat (level 5 finish)		550	.029		.47	.85		1.32	1.85	
	0210	5/8" thick, on walls, no finish included		1,800	.009		.56	.26		.82	1.03	
	0220	Taped and finished (level 4 finish)		870	.018		.60	.54		1.14	1.50	
	0230	With compound skim coat (level 5 finish)		700	.023		.62	.67		1.29	1.72	
	0250	On ceilings, no finish included		1,620	.010		.56	.29		.85	1.07	
	0260	Taped and finished (level 4 finish)		690	.023		.60	.68		1.28	1.72	
	0270	With compound skim coat (level 5 finish)		550	.029		.62	.85		1.47	2.01	
	0310	5/8" thick, on walls, very high impact, no finish included		1,800	.009		.60	.26		.86	1.07	
	0320	Taped and finished (level 4 finish)		870	.018		.64	.54		1.18	1.54	
	0330	With compound skim coat (level 5 finish)		700	.023		.66	.67		1.33	1.77	
	0350	On ceilings, no finish included		1,620	.010		.60	.29		.89	1.11	
	0360	Taped and finished (level 4 finish)		690	.023		.64	.68		1.32	1.76	
	0370	With compound skim coat (level 5 finish)		550	.029		.66	.85		1.51	2.06	
	0400	High abuse, gypsum core, paper face										
	0410	1/2" thick, on walls, no finish included	2 Carp	1,800	.009	S.F.	.40	.26		.66	.85	
	0420	Taped and finished (level 4 finish)		870	.018		.44	.54		.98	1.32	
	0430	With compound skim coat (level 5 finish)		700	.023		.46	.67		1.13	1.55	
	0450	On ceilings, no finish included		1,620	.010		.40	.29		.69	.89	
	0460	Taped and finished (level 4 finish)		690	.023		.44	.68		1.12	1.54	
	0470	With compound skim coat (level 5 finish)		550	.029		.46	.85		1.31	1.84	
	0510	5/8" thick, on walls, no finish included		1,800	.009		.44	.26		.70	.89	
	0520	Taped and finished (level 4 finish)		870	.018		.48	.54		1.02	1.37	
	0530	With compound skim coat (level 5 finish)		700	.023		.50	.67		1.17	1.59	
	0550	On ceilings, no finish included		1,620	.010		.44	.29		.73	.93	
	0560	Taped and finished (level 4 finish)		690	.023		.48	.68		1.16	1.59	
	0570	With compound skim coat (level 5 finish)		550	.029		.50	.85		1.35	1.88	
	1000	For high ceilings, over 8' high, add		2,750	.006			.17		.17	.27	
	1010	For over 3 stories high, add per story		5,500	.003			.08		.08	.13	

09260 | Gypsum Board Systems

			DAILY OUTPUT	LABOR-HOURS	UNIT	2001 BARE COSTS				TOTAL INCL O&P	
			CREW			MAT.	LABOR	EQUIP.	TOTAL		
100	0010	**PARTITION WALL** Stud wall, 8' to 12' high										**100**
	0050	1/2", interior, gypsum drywall, standard, taped both sides										
	0500	Installed on and incl., 2" x 4" wood studs, 16" O.C.	2 Carp	310	.052	S.F.	1.05	1.50		2.55	3.51	
	1000	Metal studs, NLB, 25 ga., 16" O.C., 3-5/8" wide		350	.046		.80	1.33		2.13	2.96	
	1200	6" wide		330	.048		.89	1.41		2.30	3.19	
	1400	Water resistant, on 2" x 4" wood studs, 16" O.C.		310	.052		1.21	1.50		2.71	3.68	
	1600	Metal studs, NLB, 25 ga., 16" O.C., 3-5/8" wide		350	.046		.96	1.33		2.29	3.14	
	1800	6" wide		330	.048		1.05	1.41		2.46	3.37	
	2000	Fire res., 2 layers, 1-1/2 hr., on 2" x 4" wood studs, 16" O.C.		210	.076		1.49	2.22		3.71	5.10	
	2200	Metal studs, NLB, 25 ga., 16" O.C., 3-5/8" wide		250	.064		1.24	1.87		3.11	4.28	
	2400	6" wide		230	.070		1.33	2.03		3.36	4.63	
	2600	Fire & water res., 2 layers, 1-1/2 hr., 2"x4" studs, 16" O.C.		210	.076		1.49	2.22		3.71	5.10	
	2800	Metal studs, NLB, 25 ga., 16" O.C., 3-5/8" wide		250	.064		1.24	1.87		3.11	4.28	
	3000	6" wide		230	.070		1.33	2.03		3.36	4.63	

9 FINISHES

Important: See the Reference Section for critical supporting data - Reference Nos., Crews, & City Cost Indexes

09260 | Gypsum Board Systems

		CREW	DAILY OUTPUT	LABOR-HOURS	UNIT	2001 BARE COSTS				TOTAL INCL O&P
						MAT.	LABOR	EQUIP.	TOTAL	
100	3200	5/8", interior, gypsum drywall, standard, taped both sides									100
	3400	Installed on and including 2" x 4" wood studs, 16" O.C.	2 Carp	300	.053	S.F.	1.11	1.55		2.66	3.65
	3600	24" O.C.		330	.048		1.01	1.41		2.42	3.32
	3800	Metal studs, NLB, 25 ga., 16" O.C., 3-5/8" wide		340	.047		.86	1.37		2.23	3.10
	4000	6" wide		320	.050		.95	1.46		2.41	3.33
	4200	24" O.C., 3-5/8" wide		360	.044		.86	1.30		2.16	2.98
	4400	6" wide		340	.047		.95	1.37		2.32	3.20
	4800	Water resistant, on 2" x 4" wood studs, 16" O.C.		300	.053		1.39	1.55		2.94	3.96
	5000	24" O.C.		330	.048		1.29	1.41		2.70	3.63
	5200	Metal studs, NLB, 25 ga. 16" O.C., 3-5/8" wide		340	.047		1.14	1.37		2.51	3.40
	5400	6" wide		320	.050		1.23	1.46		2.69	3.63
	5600	24" O.C., 3-5/8" wide		360	.044		1.14	1.30		2.44	3.28
	5800	6" wide		340	.047		1.23	1.37		2.60	3.50
	6000	Fire res., 2 layers, 2 hr., on 2" x 4" wood studs, 16" O.C.		205	.078		1.59	2.28		3.87	5.30
	6200	24" O.C.		235	.068		1.59	1.98		3.57	4.85
	6400	Metal studs, NLB, 25 ga., 16" O.C., 3-5/8" wide		245	.065		1.44	1.90		3.34	4.56
	6600	6" wide		225	.071		1.53	2.07		3.60	4.92
	6800	24" O.C., 3-5/8" wide		265	.060		1.44	1.76		3.20	4.33
	7000	6" wide		245	.065		1.53	1.90		3.43	4.66
	7200	Fire & water res., 2 layers, 2 hr., 2" x 4" studs, 16" O.C.		205	.078		1.69	2.28		3.97	5.40
	7400	24" O.C.		235	.068		1.59	1.98		3.57	4.85
	7600	Metal studs, NLB, 25 ga., 16" O.C., 3-5/8" wide		245	.065		1.44	1.90		3.34	4.56
	7800	6" wide		225	.071		1.53	2.07		3.60	4.92
	8000	24" O.C., 3-5/8" wide		265	.060		1.44	1.76		3.20	4.33
	8200	6" wide	▼	245	.065	▼	1.53	1.90		3.43	4.66
	8600	1/2" blueboard, mesh tape both sides									
	8620	Installed on and including 2" x 4" wood studs, 16" O.C.	2 Carp	300	.053	S.F.	1.13	1.55		2.68	3.67
	8640	Metal studs, NLB, 25 ga., 16" O.C., 3-5/8" wide		340	.047		.88	1.37		2.25	3.12
	8660	6" wide	▼	320	.050	▼	.97	1.46		2.43	3.35
	9000	Exterior, 1/2" gypsum sheathing, 1/2" gypsum finished, interior,									
	9100	including foil faced insulation, metal studs, 20 ga.									
	9200	16" O.C., 3-5/8" wide	2 Carp	290	.055	S.F.	1.45	1.61		3.06	4.12
	9400	6" wide	"	270	.059	"	1.45	1.73		3.18	4.30
800	0010	**SHAFT WALL** Cavity type on 25 ga. J track & C-H studs, 24" O.C.									800
	0030	1" thick coreboard wall liner on shaft side									
	0040	2-hour assembly with double layer									
	0060	5/8" fire rated gypsum board on room side	2 Carp	220	.073	S.F.	1.03	2.12		3.15	4.45
	0100	3-hour assembly with triple layer									
	0300	5/8" fire rated gypsum board on room side	2 Carp	180	.089	S.F.	1.32	2.59		3.91	5.50
	0400	4-hour assembly, 1" coreboard, 5/8" fire rated gypsum board									
	0600	and 3/4" galv. metal furring channels, 24" O.C., with									
	0700	Double layer 5/8" fire rated gypsum board on room side	2 Carp	110	.145	S.F.	1.13	4.24		5.37	7.90
	0900	For taping & finishing, add per side	1 Carp	1,050	.008	"	.04	.22		.26	.39
	1000	For insulation, see div. 07210-000									

09270 | Drywall Accessories

				CREW	DAILY OUTPUT	LABOR-HOURS	UNIT	MAT.	LABOR	EQUIP.	TOTAL	TOTAL INCL O&P
100	0010	**ACCESSORIES, DRYWALL** Casing bead, galvanized steel	R09110 -610	1 Carp	2.90	2.759	C.L.F.	13.80	80.50		94.30	141	100
	0100	Vinyl			3	2.667		15.85	77.50		93.35	139
	0300	Corner bead, galvanized steel, 1" x 1"			4	2		10.30	58.50		68.80	102
	0400	Corner bead, galvanized steel, 1-1/4" x 1-1/4"			3.50	2.286		9.25	66.50		75.75	114
	0600	Vinyl corner bead			4	2		20.50	58.50		79	114
	0900	Furring channel, galv. steel, 7/8" deep, standard			2.60	3.077		17.35	89.50		106.85	159
	1000	Resilient			2.55	3.137		18.50	91.50		110	164
	1100	J trim, galvanized steel, 1/2" wide			3	2.667		11.85	77.50		89.35	135

FINISHES **9**

09270 | Drywall Accessories

			CREW	DAILY OUTPUT	LABOR-HOURS	UNIT	MAT.	LABOR	EQUIP.	TOTAL	TOTAL INCL O&P	
							2001 BARE COSTS					
100	1120	5/8" wide	1 Carp	2.95	2.712	C.L.F.	12.40	79		91.40	138	100
	1140	L trim, galvanized		3	2.667		15	77.50		92.50	139	
	1150	U trim, galvanized		2.95	2.712		15.65	79		94.65	141	
	1160	Screws #6 x 1" A				M	6.65			6.65	7.30	
	1170	#6 x 1-5/8" A				"	8.65			8.65	9.55	
	1200	Studs and runners for partitions, see also div. 05120-440										
	1500	Z stud, galvanized steel, 1-1/2" wide	1 Carp	2.60	3.077	C.L.F.	24	89.50		113.50	166	
	1600	2" wide	"	2.55	3.137	"	28.50	91.50		120	175	

(Note: row 1120 references R09110-610)

09310 | Ceramic Tile

			CREW	DAILY OUTPUT	LABOR-HOURS	UNIT	MAT.	LABOR	EQUIP.	TOTAL	TOTAL INCL O&P	
							2001 BARE COSTS					
100	0010	**CERAMIC TILE**										100
	0050	Base, using 1' x 4" high pc. with 1" x 1" tiles, mud set	D-7	82	.195	L.F.	3.99	4.96		8.95	11.75	
	0100	Thin set	"	128	.125		3.79	3.18		6.97	8.85	
	0300	For 6" high base, 1" x 1" tile face, add					.63			.63	.69	
	0400	For 2" x 2" tile face, add to above					.33			.33	.36	
	0600	Cove base, 4-1/4" x 4-1/4" high, mud set	D-7	91	.176		2.94	4.47		7.41	9.85	
	0700	Thin set		128	.125		2.96	3.18		6.14	7.95	
	0900	6" x 4-1/4" high, mud set		100	.160		2.54	4.07		6.61	8.80	
	1000	Thin set		137	.117		2.64	2.97		5.61	7.30	
	1200	Sanitary cove base, 6" x 4-1/4" high, mud set		93	.172		3.45	4.38		7.83	10.25	
	1300	Thin set		124	.129		3.50	3.28		6.78	8.70	
	1500	6" x 6" high, mud set		84	.190		3	4.84		7.84	10.45	
	1600	Thin set		117	.137		3.04	3.48		6.52	8.50	
	1800	Bathroom accessories, average		82	.195	Ea.	9.50	4.96		14.46	17.80	
	1900	Bathtub, 5', rec. 4-1/4" x 4-1/4" tile wainscot, adhesive set 6' high		2.90	5.517		140	140		280	360	
	2100	7' high wainscot		2.50	6.400		160	163		323	415	
	2200	8' high wainscot		2.20	7.273		170	185		355	460	
	2400	Bullnose trim, 4-1/4" x 4-1/4", mud set		82	.195	L.F.	2.77	4.96		7.73	10.40	
	2500	Thin set		128	.125		2.71	3.18		5.89	7.70	
	2700	6" x 4-1/4" bullnose trim, mud set		84	.190		2.30	4.84		7.14	9.70	
	2800	Thin set		124	.129		2.30	3.28		5.58	7.40	
	3000	Floors, natural clay, random or uniform, thin set, color group 1		183	.087	S.F.	3.62	2.22		5.84	7.25	
	3100	Color group 2		183	.087		3.90	2.22		6.12	7.60	
	3300	Porcelain type, 1 color, color group 2, 1" x 1"		183	.087		4.19	2.22		6.41	7.90	
	3400	2" x 2" or 2" x 1", thin set		190	.084		3.90	2.14		6.04	7.45	
	3600	For random blend, 2 colors, add					.77			.77	.85	
	3700	4 colors, add					1.10			1.10	1.21	
	3900	For color group 3, add					.45			.45	.50	
	4000	For abrasive non-slip tile, add					.44			.44	.48	
	4300	Specialty tile, 4-1/4" x 4-1/4" x 1/2", decorator finish	D-7	183	.087		8.95	2.22		11.17	13.15	
	4500	Add for epoxy grout, 1/16" joint, 1" x 1" tile		800	.020		.54	.51		1.05	1.34	
	4600	2" x 2" tile		820	.020		.50	.50		1	1.28	
	4800	Pregrouted sheets, walls, 4-1/4" x 4-1/4", 6" x 4-1/4"										
	4810	and 8-1/2" x 4-1/4", 4 S.F. sheets, silicone grout	D-7	240	.067	S.F.	4.15	1.70		5.85	7.10	
	5100	Floors, unglazed, 2 S.F. sheets,										
	5110	urethane adhesive	D-7	180	.089	S.F.	4.13	2.26		6.39	7.90	
	5400	Walls, interior, thin set, 4-1/4" x 4-1/4" tile **CN**		190	.084		2.09	2.14		4.23	5.45	
	5500	6" x 4-1/4" tile		190	.084		2.30	2.14		4.44	5.70	

Important: See the Reference Section for critical supporting data - Reference Nos., Crews, & City Cost Indexes

9 FINISHES

09310 | Ceramic Tile

			CREW	DAILY OUTPUT	LABOR-HOURS	UNIT	2001 BARE COSTS MAT.	LABOR	EQUIP.	TOTAL	TOTAL INCL O&P	
100	5700	8-1/2" x 4-1/4" tile	D-7	190	.084	S.F.	3.25	2.14		5.39	6.75	100
	5800	6" x 6" tile		200	.080		2.53	2.03		4.56	5.80	
	5810	8" x 8" tile		225	.071		3.05	1.81		4.86	6.05	
	5820	12" x 12" tile		300	.053		2.98	1.36		4.34	5.30	
	5830	16" x 16" tile		500	.032		3.23	.81		4.04	4.75	
	6000	Decorated wall tile, 4-1/4" x 4-1/4", minimum		270	.059		3.50	1.51		5.01	6.10	
	6100	Maximum		180	.089		39	2.26		41.26	46	
	6300	Exterior walls, frostproof, mud set, 4-1/4" x 4-1/4"		102	.157		4.02	3.99		8.01	10.30	
	6400	1-3/8" x 1-3/8"		93	.172		3.78	4.38		8.16	10.60	
	6600	Crystalline glazed, 4-1/4" x 4-1/4", mud set, plain		100	.160		3.15	4.07		7.22	9.45	
	6700	4-1/4" x 4-1/4", scored tile		100	.160		4.05	4.07		8.12	10.45	
	6900	6"x 6" plain		93	.172		3.88	4.38		8.26	10.70	
	7000	For epoxy grout, 1/16" joints, 4-1/4" tile, add		800	.020		.33	.51		.84	1.11	
	7200	For tile set in dry mortar, add		1,735	.009			.23		.23	.35	
	7300	For tile set in portland cement mortar, add	▼	290	.055			1.40		1.40	2.07	
	9000	Regrout tile 4-1/2 x 4-1/2, or larger, wall	1 Tilf	100	.080		.13	2.25		2.38	3.47	
	9220	Floor	"	125	.064	▼	.14	1.80		1.94	2.81	
300	0010	**CERAMIC TILE PANELS** Insulated, over 1000 S.F., 1-1/2" thick	D-7	220	.073	S.F.	8.65	1.85		10.50	12.30	300
	0100	2-1/2" thick	"	220	.073	"	9.30	1.85		11.15	12.95	

09330 | Quarry Tile

			CREW	DAILY OUTPUT	LABOR-HOURS	UNIT	MAT.	LABOR	EQUIP.	TOTAL	TOTAL INCL O&P	
100	0010	**QUARRY TILE** Base, cove or sanitary, 2" or 5" high, mud set										100
	0100	1/2" thick	D-7	110	.145	L.F.	3.76	3.70		7.46	9.60	
	0300	Bullnose trim, red, mud set, 6" x 6" x 1/2" thick		120	.133		4.04	3.39		7.43	9.45	
	0400	4" x 4" x 1/2" thick		110	.145		3.98	3.70		7.68	9.85	
	0600	4" x 8" x 1/2" thick, using 8" as edge		130	.123	▼	3.78	3.13		6.91	8.80	
	0700	Floors, mud set, 1,000 S.F. lots, red, 4" x 4" x 1/2" thick		120	.133	S.F.	3.81	3.39		7.20	9.20	
	0900	6" x 6" x 1/2" thick		140	.114		2.87	2.91		5.78	7.45	
	1000	4" x 8" x 1/2" thick	▼	130	.123		3.81	3.13		6.94	8.80	
	1300	For waxed coating, add					.61			.61	.67	
	1500	For colors other than green, add					.36			.36	.40	
	1600	For abrasive surface, add					.43			.43	.47	
	1800	Brown tile, imported, 6" x 6" x 3/4"	D-7	120	.133		4.53	3.39		7.92	10	
	1900	8" x 8" x 1"		110	.145		5.15	3.70		8.85	11.10	
	2100	For thin set mortar application, deduct		700	.023			.58		.58	.86	
	2200	For epoxy grout & mortar, 6" x 6" x 1/2", add		350	.046		1.59	1.16		2.75	3.47	
	2700	Stair tread, 6" x 6" x 3/4", plain		50	.320		4.10	8.15		12.25	16.55	
	2800	Abrasive		47	.340		4.68	8.65		13.33	17.95	
	3000	Wainscot, 6" x 6" x 1/2", thin set, red		105	.152		3.49	3.88		7.37	9.60	
	3100	Colors other than green		105	.152	▼	3.89	3.88		7.77	10.05	
	3300	Window sill, 6" wide, 3/4" thick		90	.178	L.F.	4.47	4.52		8.99	11.60	
	3400	Corners	▼	80	.200	Ea.	4.91	5.10		10.01	12.90	

09350 | Glass Mosaics

			CREW	DAILY OUTPUT	LABOR-HOURS	UNIT	MAT.	LABOR	EQUIP.	TOTAL	TOTAL INCL O&P	
100	0010	**GLASS MOSAICS** 3/4" tile on 12" sheets, standard grout										100
	0300	Color group 1 & 2	D-7	73	.219	S.F.	15.25	5.55		20.80	25	
	0350	Color group 3		73	.219		16.05	5.55		21.60	26	
	0400	Color group 4		73	.219		22	5.55		27.55	32.50	
	0450	Color group 5		73	.219		24.50	5.55		30.05	35.50	
	0500	Color group 6		73	.219		30	5.55		35.55	41.50	
	0600	Color group 7		73	.219		34.50	5.55		40.05	46.50	
	0700	Color group 8, golds, silvers & specialties	▼	64	.250	▼	50	6.35		56.35	64.50	

9 FINISHES

09370	Metal Tile	CREW	DAILY OUTPUT	LABOR-HOURS	UNIT	2001 BARE COSTS				TOTAL INCL O&P	
						MAT.	LABOR	EQUIP.	TOTAL		
100	0010	**METAL TILE** 4' x 4' sheet, 24 ga., tile pattern, nailed										100
	0200	Stainless steel	2 Carp	512	.031	S.F.	22	.91		22.91	26	
	0400	Aluminized steel	"	512	.031	"	11.90	.91		12.81	14.55	

09420	Precast Terrazzo	CREW	DAILY OUTPUT	LABOR-HOURS	UNIT	2001 BARE COSTS				TOTAL INCL O&P	
						MAT.	LABOR	EQUIP.	TOTAL		
900	0010	**TERRAZZO, PRECAST** Base, 6" high, straight	1 Mstz	35	.229	L.F.	8.80	6.45		15.25	19.25	900
	0100	Cove		30	.267		9.50	7.55		17.05	21.50	
	0300	8" high base, straight		30	.267		8.50	7.55		16.05	20.50	
	0400	Cove		25	.320		12.50	9.05		21.55	27	
	0600	For white cement, add					.35			.35	.39	
	0700	For 16 ga. zinc toe strip, add					1.25			1.25	1.38	
	0900	Curbs, 4" x 4" high	1 Mstz	19	.421		24	11.90		35.90	44	
	1000	8" x 8" high	"	15	.533		25.50	15.10		40.60	50.50	
	1200	Floor tiles, non-slip, 1" thick, 12" x 12"	D-1	29	.552	S.F.	14.70	14.50		29.20	38.50	
	1300	1-1/4" thick, 12" x 12"		29	.552		17.05	14.50		31.55	41.50	
	1500	16" x 16"		23	.696		18.55	18.30		36.85	48.50	
	1600	1-1/2" thick, 16" x 16"		21	.762		16.95	20		36.95	49.50	
	1800	For Venetian terrazzo, add					5.10			5.10	5.60	
	1900	For white cement, add					.48			.48	.53	
	2400	Stair treads, 1-1/2" thick, non-slip, three line pattern	2 Mstz	70	.229	L.F.	34.50	6.45		40.95	47	
	2500	Nosing and two lines		70	.229		34.50	6.45		40.95	47	
	2700	2" thick treads, straight		60	.267		33.50	7.55		41.05	48	
	2800	Curved		50	.320		44	9.05		53.05	62	
	3000	Stair risers, 1" thick, to 6" high, straight sections		60	.267		7.65	7.55		15.20	19.55	
	3100	Cove		50	.320		11.55	9.05		20.60	26	
	3300	Curved, 1" thick, to 6" high, vertical		48	.333		15.75	9.45		25.20	31.50	
	3400	Cove		38	.421		30	11.90		41.90	50.50	
	3600	Stair tread and riser, single piece, straight, minimum		60	.267		43.50	7.55		51.05	59	
	3700	Maximum		40	.400		56.50	11.30		67.80	79	
	3900	Curved tread and riser, minimum		40	.400		61	11.30		72.30	84	
	4000	Maximum		32	.500		77	14.15		91.15	106	
	4200	Stair stringers, notched, 1" thick		25	.640		25	18.10		43.10	54.50	
	4300	2" thick		22	.727		29.50	20.50		50	63	
	4500	Stair landings, structural, non-slip, 1-1/2" thick		85	.188	S.F.	27	5.35		32.35	38	
	4600	3" thick		75	.213		38.50	6.05		44.55	51.50	
	4800	Wainscot, 12" x 12" x 1" tiles	1 Mstz	12	.667		5.10	18.85		23.95	33.50	
	4900	16" x 16" x 1-1/2" tiles	"	8	1		11.95	28.50		40.45	55	

09450	Cast-in-Place Terrazzo										
100	0010	**TERRAZZO, CAST IN PLACE** Cove base, 6" high, 16ga. zinc [R09400-100]	1 Mstz	20	.400	L.F.	2.78	11.30		14.08	19.80	100
	0100	Curb, 6" high and 6" wide		6	1.333		4.57	37.50		42.07	61	
	0300	Divider strip for floors, 14 ga., 1-1/4" deep, zinc		375	.021		.94	.60		1.54	1.92	
	0400	Brass		375	.021		1.67	.60		2.27	2.73	
	0600	Heavy top strip 1/4" thick, 1-1/4" deep, zinc		300	.027		1.50	.75		2.25	2.77	
	0900	Galv. bottoms, brass		300	.027		2.64	.75		3.39	4.02	
	1200	For thin set floors, 16 ga., 1/2" x 1/2", zinc		350	.023		.83	.65		1.48	1.87	
	1300	Brass		350	.023		1.56	.65		2.21	2.68	

9 FINISHES

09400 | Terrazzo

09450 | Cast-in-Place Terrazzo

			CREW	DAILY OUTPUT	LABOR-HOURS	UNIT	2001 BARE COSTS				TOTAL INCL O&P
							MAT.	LABOR	EQUIP.	TOTAL	
100	1500	Floor, bonded to concrete, 1-3/4" thick, gray cement R09400-100	J-3	130	.123	S.F.	2.44	3.16	1.08	6.68	8.55	100
	1600	White cement, mud set		130	.123		2.78	3.16	1.08	7.02	8.95
	1800	Not bonded, 3" total thickness, gray cement		115	.139		3.05	3.58	1.22	7.85	10
	1900	White cement, mud set	↓	115	.139	↓	3.33	3.58	1.22	8.13	10.30
	2100	For Venetian terrazzo, 1" topping, add					50%	50%			
	2200	For heavy duty abrasive terrazzo, add					50%	50%			
	2400	Bonded conductive floor for hospitals	J-3	90	.178	S.F.	3.33	4.57	1.56	9.46	12.15
	2500	Epoxy terrazzo, 1/4" thick, minimum		100	.160		3.77	4.11	1.41	9.29	11.80
	2550	Average		75	.213		4.16	5.50	1.88	11.54	14.75
	2600	Maximum	↓	60	.267	↓	4.55	6.85	2.34	13.74	17.75
	2700	Monolithic terrazzo, 1/2" thick									
	2710	10' panels	J-3	125	.128	S.F.	2.22	3.29	1.13	6.64	8.55
	3000	Stairs, cast in place, pan filled treads		30	.533	L.F.	2.16	13.70	4.69	20.55	28
	3100	Treads and risers	↓	14	1.143	"	4.52	29.50	10.05	44.07	59.50
	3300	For stair landings, add to floor prices						50%			
	3400	Stair stringers and fascia	J-3	30	.533	S.F.	3.71	13.70	4.69	22.10	29.50
	3600	For abrasive metal nosings on stairs, add		150	.107	L.F.	6.20	2.74	.94	9.88	11.95
	3700	For abrasive surface finish, add		600	.027	S.F.	.85	.69	.23	1.77	2.21
	3900	For raised abrasive strips, add		150	.107	L.F.	.81	2.74	.94	4.49	5.95
	4000	Wainscot, bonded, 1-1/2" thick		30	.533	S.F.	2.76	13.70	4.69	21.15	28.50
	4200	Epoxy terrazzo, 1/4" thick	↓	40	.400	"	4.15	10.30	3.52	17.97	23.50
200	0010	**TILE OR TERRAZZO BASE** Scratch coat only	1 Mstz	150	.053	S.F.	.31	1.51		1.82	2.57	200
	0500	Scratch and brown coat only	"	75	.107	"	.56	3.02		3.58	5.10

09500 | Ceilings

09510 | Acoustical Ceilings

			CREW	DAILY OUTPUT	LABOR-HOURS	UNIT	2001 BARE COSTS				TOTAL INCL O&P
							MAT.	LABOR	EQUIP.	TOTAL	
700	0010	**SUSPENDED ACOUSTIC CEILING TILES**, Not including										700
	0100	suspension system									
	0300	Fiberglass boards, film faced, 2' x 2' or 2' x 4', 5/8" thick	1 Carp	625	.013	S.F.	.52	.37		.89	1.15
	0400	3/4" thick		600	.013		1.13	.39		1.52	1.85
	0500	3" thick, thermal, R11		450	.018		1.25	.52		1.77	2.19
	0600	Glass cloth faced fiberglass, 3/4" thick		500	.016		1.68	.47		2.15	2.58
	0700	1" thick		485	.016		1.81	.48		2.29	2.74
	0820	1-1/2" thick, nubby face		475	.017		2.21	.49		2.70	3.20
	1110	Mineral fiber tile, lay-in, 2' x 2' or 2' x 4', 5/8" thick, fine texture		625	.013		.43	.37		.80	1.05
	1115	Rough textured		625	.013		1.05	.37		1.42	1.74
	1125	3/4" thick, fine textured		600	.013		1.16	.39		1.55	1.89
	1130	Rough textured		600	.013		1.46	.39		1.85	2.22
	1135	Fissured		600	.013		1.72	.39		2.11	2.50
	1150	Tegular, 5/8" thick, fine textured		470	.017		1.03	.50		1.53	1.91
	1155	Rough textured		470	.017		1.34	.50		1.84	2.25
	1165	3/4" thick, fine textured		450	.018		1.46	.52		1.98	2.42
	1170	Rough textured		450	.018		1.64	.52		2.16	2.61
	1175	Fissured	↓	450	.018		2.56	.52		3.08	3.63
	1180	For aluminum face, add					4.67			4.67	5.15
	1185	For plastic film face, add					.69			.69	.76
	1190	For fire rating, add					.35			.35	.39
	1300	Mirror faced panels, 15/16" thick, 2' x 2'	1 Carp	500	.016	↓	9.65	.47		10.12	11.35

For expanded coverage of these items see *Means Interior Cost Data 2001*

FINISHES **9**

09510	Acoustical Ceilings	CREW	DAILY OUTPUT	LABOR-HOURS	UNIT	MAT.	LABOR	EQUIP.	TOTAL	TOTAL INCL O&P	
						2001 BARE COSTS					
700 1900	Eggcrate, acrylic, 1/2" x 1/2" x 1/2" cubes	1 Carp	500	.016	S.F.	1.41	.47		1.88	2.28	**700**
2100	Polystyrene eggcrate, 3/8" x 3/8" x 1/2" cubes		510	.016		1.18	.46		1.64	2.02	
2200	1/2" x 1/2" x 1/2" cubes		500	.016		1.58	.47		2.05	2.47	
2400	Luminous panels, prismatic, acrylic		400	.020		1.71	.58		2.29	2.79	
2500	Polystyrene		400	.020		.87	.58		1.45	1.87	
2700	Flat white acrylic		400	.020		2.98	.58		3.56	4.19	
2800	Polystyrene		400	.020		2.04	.58		2.62	3.15	
3000	Drop pan, white, acrylic		400	.020		4.37	.58		4.95	5.70	
3100	Polystyrene		400	.020		3.65	.58		4.23	4.93	
3600	Perforated aluminum sheets, .024" thick, corrugated, painted		490	.016		1.74	.48		2.22	2.65	
3700	Plain		500	.016		2.16	.47		2.63	3.11	
3720	Mineral fiber, 24" x 24" or 48", reveal edge, painted, 5/8" thick		600	.013		.97	.39		1.36	1.68	
3740	3/4" thick	↓	575	.014	↓	1.58	.41		1.99	2.37	
760 0010	**SUSPENDED CEILINGS, COMPLETE** Including standard										**760**
0100	suspension system but not incl. 1-1/2" carrier channels										
0600	Fiberglass ceiling board, 2' x 4' x 5/8", plain faced,	1 Carp	500	.016	S.F.	1.06	.47		1.53	1.90	
0700	Offices, 2' x 4' x 3/4"		380	.021		1.18	.61		1.79	2.26	
0800	Mineral fiber, on 15/16" T bar susp. 2' x 2' x 3/4" lay-in board		345	.023		1.67	.68		2.35	2.90	
0810	2' x 4' x 5/8" tile		380	.021		1.47	.61		2.08	2.58	
0820	Tegular, 2' x 2' x 5/8" tile on 9/16" grid		250	.032		1.98	.93		2.91	3.64	
0830	2' x 4' x 3/4" tile		225	.036		2.06	1.04		3.10	3.89	
0900	Luminous panels, prismatic, acrylic		255	.031		2.64	.91		3.55	4.33	
1200	Metal pan with acoustic pad, steel		75	.107		3.42	3.11		6.53	8.60	
1300	Painted aluminum		75	.107		6.05	3.11		9.16	11.55	
1500	Aluminum, degreased finish		75	.107		3.94	3.11		7.05	9.20	
1600	Stainless steel		75	.107		7.25	3.11		10.36	12.85	
1800	Tile, Z bar suspension, 5/8" mineral fiber tile		150	.053		1.53	1.55		3.08	4.11	
1900	3/4" mineral fiber tile	↓	150	.053	↓	1.63	1.55		3.18	4.22	
2400	For strip lighting, see division 16510-440										
2500	For rooms under 500 S.F., add				S.F.		25%				
900 0010	**CEILING TILE**, Stapled or cemented										**900**
0100	12" x 12" or 12" x 24", not including furring										
0600	Mineral fiber, vinyl coated, 5/8" thick **CN**	1 Carp	1,000	.008	S.F.	.76	.23		.99	1.20	
0700	3/4" thick		1,000	.008		1.21	.23		1.44	1.69	
0900	Fire rated, 3/4" thick, plain faced		1,000	.008		1.03	.23		1.26	1.49	
1000	Plastic coated face		1,000	.008		1.09	.23		1.32	1.56	
1200	Aluminum faced, 5/8" thick, plain		1,000	.008		1.12	.23		1.35	1.59	
3700	Wall application of above, add	↓	3,100	.003	↓		.08		.08	.12	
3900	For ceiling primer, add					.12			.12	.13	
4000	For ceiling cement, add					.33			.33	.36	

09631	Brick Flooring	CREW	DAILY OUTPUT	LABOR-HOURS	UNIT	MAT.	LABOR	EQUIP.	TOTAL	TOTAL INCL O&P	
						2001 BARE COSTS					
100 0010	**FLOORING**										**100**
0020	Acid proof shales, red, 8" x 3-3/4" x 1-1/4" thick	D-7	.43	37.209	M	695	945		1,640	2,175	
0050	2-1/4" thick	D-1	.40	40	↓	755	1,050		1,805	2,450	
0200	Acid proof clay brick, 8" x 3-3/4" x 2-1/4" thick	"	.40	40		755	1,050		1,805	2,450	

Important: See the Reference Section for critical supporting data - Reference Nos., Crews, & City Cost Indexes

			DAILY	LABOR-			2001 BARE COSTS				TOTAL	
		09631	**Brick Flooring**	CREW	OUTPUT	HOURS	UNIT	MAT.	LABOR	EQUIP.	TOTAL	INCL O&P	
100	0260	Cast ceramic, pressed, 4" x 8" x 1/2", unglazed	D-7	100	.160	S.F.	4.94	4.07		9.01	11.45	100
	0270	Glazed		100	.160		6.60	4.07		10.67	13.25	
	0280	Hand molded flooring, 4" x 8" x 3/4", unglazed		95	.168		6.55	4.28		10.83	13.55	
	0290	Glazed		95	.168		8.20	4.28		12.48	15.35	
	0300	8" hexagonal, 3/4" thick, unglazed		85	.188		7.15	4.79		11.94	14.95	
	0310	Glazed		85	.188		12.95	4.79		17.74	21.50	
	0400	Heavy duty industrial, cement mortar bed, 2" thick, not incl. brick	D-1	80	.200		.66	5.25		5.91	8.85	
	0450	Acid proof joints, 1/4" wide	"	65	.246		1.13	6.45		7.58	11.25	
	0500	Pavers, 8" x 4", 1" to 1-1/4" thick, red	D-7	95	.168		2.88	4.28		7.16	9.50	
	0510	Ironspot	"	95	.168		4.07	4.28		8.35	10.85	
	0540	1-3/8" to 1-3/4" thick, red	D-1	95	.168		2.78	4.43		7.21	9.90	
	0560	Ironspot		95	.168		4.02	4.43		8.45	11.25	
	0580	2-1/4" thick, red		90	.178		2.83	4.67		7.50	10.30	
	0590	Ironspot		90	.178		4.38	4.67		9.05	12	
	0800	For sidewalks and patios with pavers, see division 02780-200										
	0870	For epoxy joints, add	D-1	600	.027	S.F.	2.15	.70		2.85	3.45	
	0880	For Furan underlayment, add	"	600	.027		1.78	.70		2.48	3.04	
	0890	For waxed surface, steam cleaned, add	D-5	1,000	.008		.15	.24		.39	.54	
		09635	**Marble Flooring**										
100	0010	MARBLE Thin gauge tile, 12" x 6", 3/8", White Carara	D-7	60	.267	S.F.	8.75	6.80		15.55	19.65	100
	0100	Travertine		60	.267		9.65	6.80		16.45	20.50	
	0200	12" x 12" x 3/8", thin set, floors		60	.267		8.75	6.80		15.55	19.65	
	0300	On walls		52	.308		8.90	7.80		16.70	21.50	
		09637	**Stone Flooring**										
100	0010	SLATE TILE Vermont, 6" x 6" x 1/4" thick, thin set	D-7	180	.089	S.F.	4.14	2.26		6.40	7.90	100
	0200	See also division 02775-275										
200	0010	SLATE & STONE FLOORS See division 02780-800										200
300	0010	CONCRETE FLOORS And toppings, see division 03350-300										300
		09643	**Wood Block Flooring**										
100	0010	WOOD BLOCK FLOORING End grain flooring, coated, 2" thick	1 Carp	295	.027	S.F.	2.81	.79		3.60	4.33	100
	0400	Natural finish, 1" thick, fir		125	.064		2.91	1.87		4.78	6.10	
	0600	1-1/2" thick, pine		125	.064		2.86	1.87		4.73	6.05	
	0700	2" thick, pine		125	.064		2.90	1.87		4.77	6.10	
		09644	**Wood Comp. Flooring**										
100	0010	WOOD COMPOSITION Gym floors										100
	0100	2-1/4" x 6-7/8" x 3/8", on 2" grout setting bed	D-7	150	.107	S.F.	4.78	2.71		7.49	9.25	
	0200	Thin set, on concrete	"	250	.064		4.37	1.63		6	7.20	
	0300	Sanding and finishing, add	1 Carp	200	.040		.64	1.17		1.81	2.52	
		09648	**Wood Strip Flooring**										
100	0010	WOOD Fir, vertical grain, 1" x 4", not incl. finish, B & better	1 Carp	255	.031	S.F.	2.30	.91		3.21	3.96	100
	0100	C grade & better	"	255	.031	"	2.16	.91		3.07	3.81	
	0600	Gym floor, in mastic, over 2 ply felt, #2 & better										
	0700	25/32" thick maple	1 Carp	100	.080	S.F.	3.25	2.33		5.58	7.25	
	0900	33/32" thick maple		98	.082		3.75	2.38		6.13	7.85	
	1000	For 1/2" corkboard underlayment, add		750	.011		.73	.31		1.04	1.29	
	1300	For #1 grade maple, add					.40			.40	.44	
	1600	Maple flooring, over sleepers, #2 & better										
	1700	25/32" thick	1 Carp	85	.094	S.F.	3.35	2.74		6.09	8	
	1900	33/32" thick	"	83	.096		3.90	2.81		6.71	8.70	

9

FINISHES

		09648	Wood Strip Flooring	CREW	DAILY OUTPUT	LABOR-HOURS	UNIT	2001 BARE COSTS				TOTAL INCL O&P	
								MAT.	LABOR	EQUIP.	TOTAL		
100	2000		For #1 grade, add				S.F.	.40			.40	.44	100
	2200		For 3/4" subfloor, add	1 Carp	350	.023		.87	.67		1.54	2	
	2300		With two 1/2" subfloors, 25/32" thick	"	69	.116		4.20	3.38		7.58	9.90	
	2500		Maple, incl. finish, #2 & btr., 25/32" thick, on rubber										
	2600		Sleepers, with two 1/2" subfloors	1 Carp	76	.105	S.F.	4.50	3.07		7.57	9.75	
	2800		With steel spline, double connection to channels	"	73	.110		4.80	3.19		7.99	10.30	
	2900		For 33/32" maple, add					.52			.52	.57	
	3100		For #1 grade maple, add					.40			.40	.44	
	3500		For termite proofing all of the above, add					.20			.20	.22	
	3700		Portable hardwood, prefinished panels	1 Carp	83	.096		6	2.81		8.81	11	
	3720		Insulated with polystyrene, 1" thick, add		165	.048		.52	1.41		1.93	2.78	
	3750		Running tracks, Sitka spruce surface, 25/32" x 2-1/4"		62	.129		11	3.76		14.76	18	
	3770		3/4" plywood surface, finished		100	.080		2.60	2.33		4.93	6.50	
	3800		See also resilient gym floors, division 09658-100										
	4000		Maple, strip, 25/32" x 2-1/4", not incl. finish, select	1 Carp	170	.047	S.F.	3.20	1.37		4.57	5.65	
	4100		#2 & better		170	.047		2.65	1.37		4.02	5.05	
	4300		33/32" x 3-1/4", not incl. finish, #1 grade		170	.047		3.25	1.37		4.62	5.75	
	4400		#2 & better		170	.047		2.90	1.37		4.27	5.35	
	4600		Oak, white or red, 25/32" x 2-1/4", not incl. finish										
	4700	CN	#1 common	1 Carp	170	.047	S.F.	2.70	1.37		4.07	5.10	
	4900		Select quartered, 2-1/4" wide		170	.047		2.91	1.37		4.28	5.35	
	5000		Clear		170	.047		3.50	1.37		4.87	6	
	5200		Parquetry, standard, 5/16" thick, not incl. finish, oak, minimum		160	.050		2.27	1.46		3.73	4.78	
	5300		Maximum		100	.080		5.10	2.33		7.43	9.30	
	5500		Teak, minimum		160	.050		4.15	1.46		5.61	6.85	
	5600		Maximum		100	.080		7.25	2.33		9.58	11.65	
	5650		13/16" thick, select grade oak, minimum		160	.050		8	1.46		9.46	11.10	
	5700		Maximum		100	.080		12.15	2.33		14.48	17	
	5800		Custom parquetry, including finish, minimum		100	.080		13.40	2.33		15.73	18.40	
	5900		Maximum		50	.160		17.75	4.66		22.41	27	
	6100		Prefinished, white oak, prime grade, 2-1/4" wide		170	.047		5.85	1.37		7.22	8.60	
	6200		3-1/4" wide		185	.043		7.50	1.26		8.76	10.20	
	6400		Ranch plank		145	.055		7.25	1.61		8.86	10.50	
	6500		Hardwood blocks, 9" x 9", 25/32" thick		160	.050		4.85	1.46		6.31	7.65	
	6700		Parquetry, 5/16" thick, oak, minimum		160	.050		3.30	1.46		4.76	5.90	
	6800		Maximum		100	.080		8.10	2.33		10.43	12.55	
	7000		Walnut or teak, parquetry, minimum		160	.050		4.50	1.46		5.96	7.25	
	7100		Maximum		100	.080		7.85	2.33		10.18	12.30	
	7200		Acrylic wood parquet blocks, 12" x 12" x 5/16",										
	7210		irradiated, set in epoxy	1 Carp	160	.050	S.F.	6.55	1.46		8.01	9.50	
	7400		Yellow pine, 3/4" x 3-1/8", T & G, C & better, not incl. finish	"	200	.040		2.15	1.17		3.32	4.19	
	7500		Refinish wood floor, sand, 2 cts poly, wax, soft wood, min.	1 Clab	400	.020		.65	.46		1.11	1.44	
	7600		Hard wood, max		130	.062		.98	1.41		2.39	3.28	
	7800		Sanding and finishing, 2 coats polyurethane		295	.027		.65	.62		1.27	1.69	
	7900		Subfloor and underlayment, see division 06160										
	8015		Transition molding, 2 1/4" wide, 5' long	1 Carp	19.20	.417	Ea.	10.35	12.15		22.50	30.50	
	8300		Floating floor, wood composition strip, complete.	1 Clab	133	.060	S.F.	3.79	1.37		5.16	6.30	
	8310		Floating floor components, T & G wood composite strips					3.48			3.48	3.82	
	8320		Film					.09			.09	.10	
	8330		Foam					.21			.21	.23	
	8340		Adhesive					.07			.07	.08	
	8350		Installation kit					.16			.16	.18	
	8360		Trim, 2" wide x 3' long				L.F.	2.05			2.05	2.26	
	8370		Reducer moulding				"	4.15			4.15	4.57	

Important: See the Reference Section for critical supporting data - Reference Nos., Crews, & City Cost Indexes

9 FINISHES

09651 | Resilient Base & Access.

		CREW	DAILY OUTPUT	LABOR-HOURS	UNIT	2001 BARE COSTS				TOTAL INCL O&P
						MAT.	LABOR	EQUIP.	TOTAL	
100	0010	**STAIR TREADS AND RISERS** See index for materials other									100
	0100	than rubber and vinyl									
	0300	Rubber, molded tread, 12" wide, 5/16" thick, black	1 Tilf	115	.070	L.F.	7.35	1.96		9.31	11
	0400	Colors		115	.070		7.75	1.96		9.71	11.45
	0600	1/4" thick, black		115	.070		7.50	1.96		9.46	11.15
	0700	Colors		115	.070		7.75	1.96		9.71	11.45
	0900	Grip strip safety tread, colors, 5/16" thick		115	.070		10.30	1.96		12.26	14.25
	1000	3/16" thick		120	.067	↓	7.80	1.88		9.68	11.30
	1200	Landings, smooth sheet rubber, 1/8" thick		120	.067	S.F.	3.50	1.88		5.38	6.60
	1300	3/16" thick		120	.067	"	4.50	1.88		6.38	7.70
	1500	Nosings, 3" wide, 3/16" thick, black		140	.057	L.F.	2.59	1.61		4.20	5.25
	1600	Colors		140	.057		2.53	1.61		4.14	5.15
	1800	Risers, 7" high, 1/8" thick, flat		250	.032		2.90	.90		3.80	4.52
	1900	Coved		250	.032		2.09	.90		2.99	3.63
	2100	Vinyl, molded tread, 12" wide, colors, 1/8" thick		115	.070		2.95	1.96		4.91	6.15
	2200	1/4" thick		115	.070	↓	4.75	1.96		6.71	8.15
	2300	Landing material, 1/8" thick		200	.040	S.F.	3.25	1.13		4.38	5.25
	2400	Riser, 7" high, 1/8" thick, coved		175	.046	L.F.	1.90	1.29		3.19	3.99
	2500	Tread and riser combined, 1/8" thick	↓	80	.100	"	5.50	2.82		8.32	10.20

09658 | Resilient Tile Flooring

		CREW	DAILY OUTPUT	LABOR-HOURS	UNIT	MAT.	LABOR	EQUIP.	TOTAL	TOTAL INCL O&P
100	0010	**RESILIENT FLOORING**									100
	0800	Base, cove, rubber or vinyl, .080" thick [R09658-600]									
	1100	Standard colors, 2-1/2" high	1 Tilf	315	.025	L.F.	.41	.72		1.13	1.51
	1150	4" high		315	.025		.47	.72		1.19	1.58
	1200	6" high		315	.025		.75	.72		1.47	1.89
	1450	1/8" thick, standard colors, 2-1/2" high		315	.025		.46	.72		1.18	1.57
	1500	4" high **CN**		315	.025	↓	.63	.72		1.35	1.75
	1600	Corners, 2-1/2" high		315	.025	Ea.	1.05	.72		1.77	2.22
	1630	4" high		315	.025		1.10	.72		1.82	2.27
	1660	6" high		315	.025	↓	1.42	.72		2.14	2.62
	1700	Conductive flooring, rubber tile, 1/8" thick		315	.025	S.F.	2.58	.72		3.30	3.90
	1800	Homogeneous vinyl tile, 1/8" thick		315	.025		3.52	.72		4.24	4.93
	2200	Cork tile, standard finish, 1/8" thick		315	.025		3.45	.72		4.17	4.86
	2250	3/16" thick		315	.025		3.43	.72		4.15	4.83
	2300	5/16" thick		315	.025		4.62	.72		5.34	6.15
	2350	1/2" thick		315	.025		5.50	.72		6.22	7.10
	2500	Urethane finish, 1/8" thick		315	.025		4.38	.72		5.10	5.90
	2550	3/16" thick		315	.025		5.25	.72		5.97	6.80
	2600	5/16" thick		315	.025		6.15	.72		6.87	7.80
	2650	1/2" thick		315	.025		8.25	.72		8.97	10.10
	3700	Polyethylene, in rolls, no base incl., landscape surfaces		275	.029		2.31	.82		3.13	3.75
	3800	Nylon action surface, 1/8" thick		275	.029		2.48	.82		3.30	3.94
	3900	1/4" thick		275	.029		3.57	.82		4.39	5.15
	4000	3/8" thick		275	.029		4.49	.82		5.31	6.15
	4100	Golf tee surface with foam back		235	.034		4.44	.96		5.40	6.30
	4200	Practice putting, knitted nylon surface	↓	235	.034	↓	3.77	.96		4.73	5.55
	4400	Polyurethane, thermoset, prefabricated in place, indoor									
	4500	3/8" thick for basketball, gyms, etc.	1 Tilf	100	.080	S.F.	3.55	2.25		5.80	7.25
	4600	1/2" thick for professional sports		95	.084		4.15	2.37		6.52	8.05
	4700	Outdoor, 1/4" thick, smooth, for tennis		100	.080		3.18	2.25		5.43	6.85
	4800	Rough, for track, 3/8" thick		95	.084		3.69	2.37		6.06	7.55
	5000	Poured in place, indoor, with finish, 1/4" thick		80	.100		2.62	2.82		5.44	7.05
	5050	3/8" thick		65	.123		3.18	3.46		6.64	8.60
	5100	1/2" thick	↓	50	.160	↓	4.22	4.50		8.72	11.30

FINISHES 9

9 FINISHES

	09658	Resilient Tile Flooring		CREW	DAILY OUTPUT	LABOR-HOURS	UNIT	2001 BARE COSTS MAT.	LABOR	EQUIP.	TOTAL	TOTAL INCL O&P	
100	5500	Polyvinyl chloride, sheet goods for gyms, 1/4" thick	R09658-600	1 Tilf	80	.100	S.F.	3.63	2.82		6.45	8.15	100
	5600	3/8" thick			60	.133		4.09	3.75		7.84	10.05	
	5900	Rubber, sheet goods, 36" wide, 1/8" thick			120	.067		3.18	1.88		5.06	6.25	
	5950	3/16" thick			100	.080		4.52	2.25		6.77	8.30	
	6000	1/4" thick			90	.089		5.20	2.50		7.70	9.45	
	6050	Tile, marbleized colors, 12" x 12", 1/8" thick			400	.020		3.56	.56		4.12	4.75	
	6100	3/16" thick			400	.020		4.89	.56		5.45	6.25	
	6300	Special tile, plain colors, 1/8" thick			400	.020		3.94	.56		4.50	5.15	
	6350	3/16" thick			400	.020		5.30	.56		5.86	6.70	
	6410	Raised, radial or square, minimum			400	.020		6.20	.56		6.76	7.65	
	6430	Maximum			400	.020		6.15	.56		6.71	7.65	
	6450	For golf course, skating rink, etc., 1/4" thick			275	.029		6.05	.82		6.87	7.85	
	6700	Synthetic turf, 3/8" thick		▼	90	.089	▼	3.25	2.50		5.75	7.30	
	6750	Interlocking 2' x 2' squares, 1/2" thick, not											
	6810	cemented, for playgrounds, minimum		1 Tilf	210	.038	S.F.	2.69	1.07		3.76	4.55	
	6850	Maximum			190	.042		6.90	1.19		8.09	9.35	
	7000	Vinyl composition tile, 12" x 12", 1/16" thick			500	.016		.71	.45		1.16	1.45	
	7050	Embossed			500	.016		.89	.45		1.34	1.65	
	7100	Marbleized			500	.016		.89	.45		1.34	1.65	
	7150	Solid			500	.016		1	.45		1.45	1.77	
	7200	3/32" thick, embossed			500	.016		.92	.45		1.37	1.68	
	7250	Marbleized			500	.016		1.01	.45		1.46	1.78	
	7300	Solid			500	.016		1.47	.45		1.92	2.29	
	7350	1/8" thick, marbleized **CN**			500	.016		.97	.45		1.42	1.74	
	7400	Solid			500	.016		2.04	.45		2.49	2.91	
	7450	Conductive			500	.016		3.69	.45		4.14	4.73	
	7500	Vinyl tile, 12" x 12", .050" thick, minimum			500	.016		1.59	.45		2.04	2.42	
	7550	Maximum			500	.016		3.10	.45		3.55	4.08	
	7600	1/8" thick, minimum			500	.016		2	.45		2.45	2.87	
	7650	Solid colors			500	.016		4.48	.45		4.93	5.60	
	7700	Marbleized or Travertine pattern			500	.016		3.20	.45		3.65	4.19	
	7750	Florentine pattern			500	.016		3.68	.45		4.13	4.72	
	7800	Maximum			500	.016		7.55	.45		8	8.95	
	8000	Vinyl sheet goods, backed, .065" thick, minimum			250	.032		1.85	.90		2.75	3.37	
	8050	Maximum			200	.040		2.51	1.13		3.64	4.42	
	8100	.080" thick, minimum			230	.035		2	.98		2.98	3.65	
	8150	Maximum			200	.040		2.85	1.13		3.98	4.80	
	8200	.125" thick, minimum			230	.035		2.25	.98		3.23	3.93	
	8250	Maximum		▼	200	.040	▼	3.57	1.13		4.70	5.60	
	8700	Adhesive cement, 1 gallon does 200 to 300 S.F.					Gal.	15			15	16.50	
	8800	Asphalt primer, 1 gallon per 300 S.F.						8.65			8.65	9.55	
	8900	Emulsion, 1 gallon per 140 S.F.						11			11	12.10	
	8950	Latex underlayment, liquid, fortified		▼			▼	30			30	33	

	09673	Composition Flooring		CREW	DAILY OUTPUT	LABOR-HOURS	UNIT	MAT.	LABOR	EQUIP.	TOTAL	INCL O&P	
100	0010	**COMPOSITION FLOORING** Acrylic, 1/4" thick		C-6	520	.092	S.F.	1.24	2.22	.15	3.61	4.96	100
	0100	3/8" thick			450	.107		1.63	2.56	.17	4.36	5.95	
	0300	Cupric oxychloride, on bond coat, minimum			480	.100		2.77	2.40	.16	5.33	6.95	
	0400	Maximum			420	.114		4.63	2.75	.18	7.56	9.55	
	0600	Epoxy, with colored quartz chips, broadcast, minimum			675	.071		2.19	1.71	.11	4.01	5.20	
	0700	Maximum			490	.098		2.66	2.35	.15	5.16	6.75	
	0900	Trowelled, minimum			560	.086		2.83	2.06	.14	5.03	6.45	
	1000	Maximum		▼	480	.100	▼	4.12	2.40	.16	6.68	8.40	
	1200	Heavy duty epoxy topping, 1/4" thick,											
	1300	500 to 1,000 S.F.		C-6	420	.114	S.F.	4.40	2.75	.18	7.33	9.30	

Important: See the Reference Section for critical supporting data - Reference Nos., Crews, & City Cost Indexes

09673 | Composition Flooring

			CREW	DAILY OUTPUT	LABOR-HOURS	UNIT	MAT.	LABOR	EQUIP.	TOTAL	TOTAL INCL O&P	
							2001 BARE COSTS					
100	1500	1,000 to 2,000 S.F.	C-6	450	.107	S.F.	3.19	2.56	.17	5.92	7.65	**100**
	1600	Over 10,000 S.F.	↓	480	.100		2.99	2.40	.16	5.55	7.20	
	1800	Epoxy terrazzo, 1/4" thick, chemical resistant, minimum	J-3	200	.080		4.44	2.06	.70	7.20	8.70	
	1900	Maximum		150	.107		7.25	2.74	.94	10.93	13.10	
	2100	Conductive, minimum		210	.076		5.60	1.96	.67	8.23	9.80	
	2200	Maximum	↓	160	.100		7.85	2.57	.88	11.30	13.35	
	2400	Mastic, hot laid, 2 coat, 1-1/2" thick, standard, minimum	C-6	690	.070		3.21	1.67	.11	4.99	6.25	
	2500	Maximum		520	.092		4.12	2.22	.15	6.49	8.15	
	2700	Acidproof, minimum		605	.079		4.12	1.91	.13	6.16	7.60	
	2800	Maximum		350	.137		5.70	3.30	.22	9.22	11.65	
	3000	Neoprene, trowelled on, 1/4" thick, minimum		545	.088		3.16	2.12	.14	5.42	6.90	
	3100	Maximum		430	.112		4.35	2.68	.18	7.21	9.15	
	3150	Polyacrylate terrazzo, 1/4" thick, minimum		735	.065		2.47	1.57	.10	4.14	5.25	
	3170	Maximum		480	.100		3.27	2.40	.16	5.83	7.50	
	3200	3/8" thick, minimum		620	.077		3	1.86	.12	4.98	6.30	
	3220	Maximum		480	.100		4.79	2.40	.16	7.35	9.15	
	3300	Conductive terrazzo, 1/4" thick, minimum		450	.107		5.90	2.56	.17	8.63	10.65	
	3330	Maximum		305	.157		7.60	3.78	.25	11.63	14.50	
	3350	3/8" thick, minimum		365	.132		8	3.16	.21	11.37	13.95	
	3370	Maximum		255	.188		10.15	4.52	.30	14.97	18.55	
	3450	Granite, conductive, 1/4" thick, minimum		695	.069		6.25	1.66	.11	8.02	9.55	
	3470	Maximum		420	.114		8.20	2.75	.18	11.13	13.45	
	3500	3/8" thick, minimum		695	.069		9.20	1.66	.11	10.97	12.80	
	3520	Maximum		380	.126		11.20	3.04	.20	14.44	17.20	
	3600	Polyester, with colored quartz chips, 1/16" thick, minimum		1,065	.045		2.40	1.08	.07	3.55	4.40	
	3700	Maximum		560	.086		3.42	2.06	.14	5.62	7.10	
	3900	1/8" thick, minimum		810	.059		2.86	1.42	.09	4.37	5.45	
	4000	Maximum		675	.071		4.03	1.71	.11	5.85	7.20	
	4200	Polyester, heavy duty, compared to epoxy, add		2,590	.019		1	.45	.03	1.48	1.82	
	4300	Polyurethane, with suspended vinyl chips, minimum		1,065	.045		6.15	1.08	.07	7.30	8.55	
	4500	Maximum	↓	860	.056	↓	8.85	1.34	.09	10.28	11.95	

09680 | Carpet

			CREW	DAILY OUTPUT	LABOR-HOURS	UNIT	MAT.	LABOR	EQUIP.	TOTAL	TOTAL INCL O&P	
800	0010	**CARPET** Commercial grades, direct cement										**800**
	0700	Nylon, level loop, 26 oz., light to medium traffic **CN**	1 Tilr	75	.107	S.Y.	13.95	3		16.95	19.80	
	0720	28 oz., light to medium traffic		75	.107		15.20	3		18.20	21	
	0900	32 oz., medium traffic		75	.107		19.75	3		22.75	26	
	1100	40 oz., medium to heavy traffic		75	.107		29.50	3		32.50	37	
	2920	Nylon plush, 30 oz., medium traffic		57	.140		14.60	3.95		18.55	22	
	3000	36 oz., medium traffic		75	.107		18.40	3		21.40	24.50	
	3100	42 oz., medium to heavy traffic		70	.114		19.25	3.22		22.47	26	
	3200	46 oz., medium to heavy traffic		70	.114		25.50	3.22		28.72	33	
	3300	54 oz., heavy traffic		70	.114		28.50	3.22		31.72	36.50	
	3340	60 oz., heavy traffic		70	.114		40.50	3.22		43.72	49.50	
	3665	Olefin, 24 oz., light to medium traffic		75	.107		8.50	3		11.50	13.80	
	3670	26 oz., medium traffic		75	.107		9.20	3		12.20	14.55	
	3680	28 oz., medium to heavy traffic		75	.107		10.30	3		13.30	15.80	
	3700	32 oz., medium to heavy traffic		75	.107		12.70	3		15.70	18.40	
	3730	42 oz., heavy traffic		70	.114		18.70	3.22		21.92	25.50	
	4110	Wool, level loop, 40 oz., medium traffic		75	.107		63.50	3		66.50	74	
	4500	50 oz., medium to heavy traffic		75	.107		65	3		68	75.50	
	4700	Patterned, 32 oz., medium to heavy traffic		70	.114		64	3.22		67.22	75.50	
	4900	48 oz., heavy traffic	↓	70	.114	↓	65	3.22		68.22	76.50	
	5000	For less than full roll, add					25%					
	5100	For small rooms, less than 12' wide, add						25%				

FINISHES 9

		09680	Carpet	CREW	DAILY OUTPUT	LABOR-HOURS	UNIT	2001 BARE COSTS				TOTAL INCL O&P	
								MAT.	LABOR	EQUIP.	TOTAL		
800	5200	For large open areas (no cuts), deduct							25%				800
	5600	For bound carpet baseboard, add		1 Tilf	300	.027	L.F.	1.02	.75		1.77	2.23	
	5610	For stairs, not incl. price of carpet, add		"	30	.267	Riser		7.50		7.50	11.10	
	5620	For borders and patterns, add to labor							18%				
	8950	For tackless, stretched installation, add padding to above											
	9000	Sponge rubber pad, minimum		1 Tilf	150	.053	S.Y.	2.74	1.50		4.24	5.25	
	9100	Maximum			150	.053		7.65	1.50		9.15	10.60	
	9200	Felt pad, minimum			150	.053		3.25	1.50		4.75	5.80	
	9300	Maximum			150	.053		5.90	1.50		7.40	8.70	
	9400	Bonded urethane pad, minimum			150	.053		3.47	1.50		4.97	6.05	
	9500	Maximum			150	.053		5.95	1.50		7.45	8.75	
	9600	Prime urethane pad, minimum			150	.053		2	1.50		3.50	4.42	
	9700	Maximum			150	.053		3.69	1.50		5.19	6.30	
	9850	For "branded" fiber, add						25%					
900	0010	**CARPET TILE**											900
	0100	Tufted nylon, 18" x 18", hard back, 20 oz.		1 Tilf	150	.053	S.Y.	18.50	1.50		20	22.50	
	0110	26 oz.			150	.053		31.50	1.50		33	37	
	0200	Cushion back, 20 oz.			150	.053		23.50	1.50		25	27.50	
	0210	26 oz.			150	.053		36.50	1.50		38	42	
910	0010	**CARPET MAINTENANCE** Steam clean, per cleaning, minimum		1 Clab	3,000	.003	S.F.	.07	.06		.13	.18	910
	0500	Maximum		"	2,000	.004	"	.10	.09		.19	.25	

		09720	Wall Coverings	CREW	DAILY OUTPUT	LABOR-HOURS	UNIT	2001 BARE COSTS				TOTAL INCL O&P	
								MAT.	LABOR	EQUIP.	TOTAL		
100	0010	**WALL COVERING** Including sizing, add 10%-30% waste at takeoff	R09700 -700										100
	0050	Aluminum foil		1 Pape	275	.029	S.F.	.80	.76		1.56	2.04	
	0100	Copper sheets, .025" thick, vinyl backing			240	.033		4.27	.87		5.14	6.05	
	0300	Phenolic backing			240	.033		5.55	.87		6.42	7.45	
	0600	Cork tiles, light or dark, 12" x 12" x 3/16"			240	.033		2.44	.87		3.31	4.01	
	0700	5/16" thick			235	.034		2.84	.89		3.73	4.48	
	0900	1/4" basketweave			240	.033		4.36	.87		5.23	6.15	
	1000	1/2" natural, non-directional pattern			240	.033		6.15	.87		7.02	8.10	
	1100	3/4" natural, non-directional pattern			240	.033		9.10	.87		9.97	11.35	
	1200	Granular surface, 12" x 36", 1/2" thick			385	.021		.94	.55		1.49	1.86	
	1300	1" thick			370	.022		1.22	.57		1.79	2.20	
	1500	Polyurethane coated, 12" x 12" x 3/16" thick			240	.033		2.94	.87		3.81	4.56	
	1600	5/16" thick			235	.034		4.18	.89		5.07	5.95	
	1800	Cork wallpaper, paperbacked, natural			480	.017		1.67	.44		2.11	2.51	
	1900	Colors			480	.017		2.07	.44		2.51	2.95	
	2100	Flexible wood veneer, 1/32" thick, plain woods			100	.080		1.76	2.10		3.86	5.15	
	2200	Exotic woods			95	.084		2.67	2.21		4.88	6.30	
	2400	Gypsum-based, fabric-backed, fire											
	2500	resistant for masonry walls, minimum, 21 oz./S.Y.		1 Pape	800	.010	S.F.	.65	.26		.91	1.12	
	2700	Maximum, (small quantities)		"	640	.013		1.07	.33		1.40	1.68	
	2750	Acrylic, modified, semi-rigid PVC, .028" thick		2 Carp	330	.048		.88	1.41		2.29	3.18	
	2800	.040" thick		"	320	.050		1.16	1.46		2.62	3.56	
	3000	Vinyl wall covering, fabric-backed, lightweight, (12-15 oz./S.Y.)		1 Pape	640	.013		.54	.33		.87	1.09	
	3300	Medium weight, type 2, (20-24 oz./S.Y.)			480	.017		.67	.44		1.11	1.41	

Important: See the Reference Section for critical supporting data - Reference Nos., Crews, & City Cost Indexes

09720 | Wall Coverings

			CREW	DAILY OUTPUT	LABOR-HOURS	UNIT	MAT.	LABOR	EQUIP.	TOTAL	TOTAL INCL O&P	
100	3400	Heavy weight, type 3, (28 oz./S.Y.) R09700-700	1 Pape	435	.018	S.F.	1.08	.48		1.56	1.93	**100**
	3600	Adhesive, 5 gal. lots, (18SY/Gal.)				Gal.	8.60			8.60	9.45	
	3700	Wallpaper, average workmanship, solid pattern, low cost paper	1 Pape	640	.013	S.F.	.28	.33		.61	.81	
	3900	basic patterns (matching required), avg. cost paper		535	.015		.61	.39		1	1.27	
	4000	Paper at $50 per double roll, quality workmanship	↓	435	.018	↓	1.46	.48		1.94	2.35	
	4100	Linen wall covering, paper backed										
	4150	Flame treatment, minimum				S.F.	.64			.64	.70	
	4180	Maximum					1.21			1.21	1.33	
	4200	Grass cloths with lining paper, minimum	1 Pape	400	.020		.61	.53		1.14	1.47	
	4300	Maximum	"	350	.023	↓	1.95	.60		2.55	3.06	

09770 | Special Wall Surfaces

			CREW	DAILY OUTPUT	LABOR-HOURS	UNIT	MAT.	LABOR	EQUIP.	TOTAL	TOTAL INCL O&P	
400	0010	**FIBERGLASS REINFORCED PLASTIC** panels, .090" thick, on walls										**400**
	0020	Adhesive mounted, embossed surface	2 Carp	640	.025	S.F.	1.21	.73		1.94	2.47	
	0030	Smooth surface		640	.025		1.43	.73		2.16	2.71	
	0040	Fire rated, embossed surface		640	.025		1.59	.73		2.32	2.89	
	0050	Nylon rivet mounted, on drywall, embossed surface		480	.033		1.13	.97		2.10	2.76	
	0060	Smooth surface		480	.033		1.33	.97		2.30	2.98	
	0070	Fire rated, embossed surface		480	.033		1.49	.97		2.46	3.16	
	0080	On masonry, embossed surface		320	.050		1.13	1.46		2.59	3.52	
	0090	Smooth surface		320	.050		1.43	1.46		2.89	3.85	
	0100	Fire rated, embossed surface		320	.050		1.50	1.46		2.96	3.93	
	0110	Nylon rivet and adhesive mounted, on drywall, embossed surface		240	.067		1.33	1.94		3.27	4.50	
	0120	Smooth surface		240	.067		1.50	1.94		3.44	4.69	
	0130	Fire rated, embossed surface		240	.067		1.68	1.94		3.62	4.89	
	0140	On masonry, embossed surface		190	.084		1.33	2.45		3.78	5.30	
	0150	Smooth surface		190	.084		1.50	2.45		3.95	5.50	
	0160	Fire rated, embossed surface	↓	190	.084	↓	1.68	2.45		4.13	5.70	
	0170	For moldings add	1 Carp	250	.032	L.F.	.22	.93		1.15	1.70	
	0180	On ceilings, for lay in grid system, embossed surface		400	.020	S.F.	1.21	.58		1.79	2.24	
	0190	Smooth surface		400	.020		1.43	.58		2.01	2.48	
	0200	Fire rated, embossed surface	↓	400	.020	↓	1.59	.58		2.17	2.66	
700	0010	**RAISED PANEL SYSTEM,** 3/4" MDO										**700**
	0100	Standard, paint grade	2 Carp	300	.053	S.F.	8.05	1.55		9.60	11.30	
	0110	Oak veneer		300	.053		13.80	1.55		15.35	17.60	
	0120	Maple veneer		300	.053		19.65	1.55		21.20	24	
	0130	Cherry veneer		300	.053		24.50	1.55		26.05	29.50	
	0300	Class I fire rated, paint grade		300	.053		14.10	1.55		15.65	17.95	
	0310	Oak veneer		300	.053		22	1.55		23.55	27	
	0320	Maple veneer		300	.053		30	1.55		31.55	35.50	
	0330	Cherry veneer	↓	300	.053	↓	34.50	1.55		36.05	40.50	
	5000	For prefinished paneling, see division 06250-500 & 06250-200										
750	0010	**SLATWALL PANELS AND ACCESSORIES**										**750**
	0100	Slatwall panel, 4' x 8' x 3/4" T, MDF, paint grade	1 Carp	500	.016	S.F.	1.20	.47		1.67	2.05	
	0110	Melamine finish		500	.016		1.82	.47		2.29	2.73	
	0120	High pressure plastic laminate finish	↓	500	.016		2.90	.47		3.37	3.92	
	0130	Aluminum channel inserts, add				↓	2.18			2.18	2.40	
	0200	Accessories, corner forms, 8' L				L.F.	3.10			3.10	3.41	
	0210	T-connector, 8' L					4.50			4.50	4.95	
	0220	J-mold, 8' L					1.15			1.15	1.27	
	0230	Edge cap, 8' L					.75			.75	.83	
	0240	Finish end cap, 8' L				↓	2.75			2.75	3.03	
	0300	Display hook, 4" L				Ea.	.85			.85	.94	
	0310	6" L					.90			.90	.99	
	0320	8" L					1			1	1.10	
	0330	10" L				↓	1.10			1.10	1.21	

9

FINISHES

09770	Special Wall Surfaces	CREW	DAILY OUTPUT	LABOR-HOURS	UNIT	2001 BARE COSTS				TOTAL INCL O&P	
						MAT.	LABOR	EQUIP.	TOTAL		
750	0340	12" L				Ea.	1.20			1.20	1.32	750
	0350	Acrylic, 4" L					.70			.70	.77	
	0360	6" L					.80			.80	.88	
	0370	8" L					.85			.85	.94	
	0380	10" L					.95			.95	1.05	
	0400	Waterfall hanger, metal, 12" - 16"					5.40			5.40	5.95	
	0410	Acrylic					7.70			7.70	8.45	
	0500	Shelf bracket, metal, 8"					4.20			4.20	4.62	
	0510	10"					4.50			4.50	4.95	
	0520	12"					4.80			4.80	5.30	
	0530	14"					5.40			5.40	5.95	
	0540	16"					6			6	6.60	
	0550	Acrylic, 8"					2.50			2.50	2.75	
	0560	10"					2.80			2.80	3.08	
	0570	12"					3.10			3.10	3.41	
	0580	14"					3.50			3.50	3.85	
	0600	Shelf, acrylic, 12" x 16" x 1/4"					21			21	23	
	0610	12" x 24" x 1/4"					35			35	38.50	

09820	Acoustical Insul/Sealants	CREW	DAILY OUTPUT	LABOR-HOURS	UNIT	2001 BARE COSTS				TOTAL INCL O&P	
						MAT.	LABOR	EQUIP.	TOTAL		
500	0010	**SOUND ATTENUATION** Blanket, 1" thick	1 Carp	925	.009	S.F.	.24	.25		.49	.65	500
	0500	1-1/2" thick		920	.009		.24	.25		.49	.66	
	1000	2" thick		915	.009		.31	.25		.56	.74	
	1500	3" thick		910	.009		.40	.26		.66	.84	
	3000	Thermal or acoustical batt above ceiling, 2" thick		900	.009		.42	.26		.68	.87	
	3100	3" thick		900	.009		.63	.26		.89	1.10	
	3200	4" thick		900	.009		.77	.26		1.03	1.26	
	3400	Urethane plastic foam, open cell, on wall, 2" thick	2 Carp	2,050	.008		2.56	.23		2.79	3.18	
	3500	3" thick		1,550	.010		3.40	.30		3.70	4.21	
	3600	4" thick		1,050	.015		4.77	.44		5.21	5.95	
	3700	On ceiling, 2" thick		1,700	.009		2.55	.27		2.82	3.24	
	3800	3" thick		1,300	.012		3.40	.36		3.76	4.30	
	3900	4" thick		900	.018		4.77	.52		5.29	6.05	
	4000	Nylon matting 0.4" thick, with carbon black spinerette										
	4010	plus polyester fabric, on floor	J-4	4,000	.004	S.F.	1.90	.10		2	2.24	
	4200	Fiberglass reinf. backer board underlayment, 7/16" thick, on floor	"	800	.020	"	1.59	.51		2.10	2.50	

09830	Acoustical Barriers	CREW	DAILY OUTPUT	LABOR-HOURS	UNIT	2001 BARE COSTS				TOTAL INCL O&P	
						MAT.	LABOR	EQUIP.	TOTAL		
100	0011	**BARRIERS** Plenum										100
	0600	Aluminum foil, fiberglass reinf., parallel with joists	1 Carp	275	.029	S.F.	.72	.85		1.57	2.12	
	0700	Perpendicular to joists		180	.044		.73	1.30		2.03	2.83	
	0900	Aluminum mesh, kraft paperbacked		275	.029		.69	.85		1.54	2.09	
	0970	Fiberglass batts, kraft faced, 3-1/2" thick		1,400	.006		.25	.17		.42	.54	
	0980	6" thick		1,300	.006		.42	.18		.60	.74	
	1000	Sheet lead, 1 lb., 1/64" thick, perpendicular to joists		150	.053		1.97	1.55		3.52	4.60	
	1100	Vinyl foam reinforced, 1/8" thick, 1.0 lb. per S.F.		150	.053		2.84	1.55		4.39	5.55	

Important: See the Reference Section for critical supporting data - Reference Nos., Crews, & City Cost Indexes

09800 | Acoustical Treatment

09840 | Acoustical Wall Treatment

			CREW	DAILY OUTPUT	LABOR-HOURS	UNIT	2001 BARE COSTS				TOTAL INCL O&P
							MAT.	LABOR	EQUIP.	TOTAL	
100	0010	**SOUND ABSORBING PANELS** Perforated steel facing, painted with										100
	0100	fiberglass or mineral filler, no backs, 2-1/4" thick, modular									
	0200	space units, ceiling or wall hung, white or colored	1 Carp	100	.080	S.F.	8.85	2.33		11.18	13.35
	0300	Fiberboard sound deadening panels, 1/2" thick	"	600	.013	"	.29	.39		.68	.93
	0500	Fiberglass panels, 4' x 8' x 1" thick, with									
	0600	glass cloth face for walls, cemented	1 Carp	155	.052	S.F.	6.80	1.50		8.30	9.80
	0700	1-1/2" thick, dacron covered, inner aluminum frame,									
	0710	wall mounted	1 Carp	300	.027	S.F.	7.35	.78		8.13	9.30
	0900	Mineral fiberboard panels, fabric covered, 30"x 108",									
	1000	3/4" thick, concealed spline, wall mounted	1 Carp	150	.053	S.F.	5.30	1.55		6.85	8.30

09900 | Paints & Coatings

09910 | Paints & Coatings

				CREW	DAILY OUTPUT	LABOR-HOURS	UNIT	2001 BARE COSTS				TOTAL INCL O&P
								MAT.	LABOR	EQUIP.	TOTAL	
100	0010	**CABINETS AND CASEWORK**	R09910 -100									100
	1000	Primer coat, oil base, brushwork		1 Pord	650	.012	S.F.	.05	.32		.37	.54
	2000	Paint, oil base, brushwork, 1 coat	R09910 -220		650	.012		.06	.32		.38	.56
	3000	Stain, brushwork, wipe off			650	.012		.05	.32		.37	.54
	4000	Shellac, 1 coat, brushwork			650	.012		.05	.32		.37	.55
	4500	Varnish, 3 coats, brushwork, sand after 1st coat			325	.025		.17	.64		.81	1.16
	5000	For latex paint, deduct						10%				
300	0010	**DOORS AND WINDOWS, EXTERIOR**	R09910 -100									300
	0100	Door frames & trim, only										
	0110	Brushwork, primer	R09910 -220	1 Pord	512	.016	L.F.	.05	.41		.46	.67
	0120	Finish coat, exterior latex			512	.016		.06	.41		.47	.68
	0130	Primer & 1 coat, exterior latex			300	.027		.11	.70		.81	1.18
	0140	Primer & 2 coats, exterior latex			265	.030		.16	.79		.95	1.38
	0150	Doors, flush, both sides, incl. frame & trim										
	0160	Roll & brush, primer		1 Pord	10	.800	Ea.	3.75	21		24.75	36
	0170	Finish coat, exterior latex			10	.800		4.27	21		25.27	36.50
	0180	Primer & 1 coat, exterior latex			7	1.143		8	30		38	54.50
	0190	Primer & 2 coats, exterior latex			5	1.600		12.30	42		54.30	77
	0200	Brushwork, stain, sealer & 2 coats polyurethane			4	2		15.25	52		67.25	96.50
	0210	Doors, French, both sides, 10-15 lite, incl. frame & trim										
	0220	Brushwork, primer		1 Pord	6	1.333	Ea.	1.88	35		36.88	55
	0230	Finish coat, exterior latex			6	1.333		2.13	35		37.13	55.50
	0240	Primer & 1 coat, exterior latex			3	2.667		4.01	69.50		73.51	110
	0250	Primer & 2 coats, exterior latex			2	4		6	104		110	166
	0260	Brushwork, stain, sealer & 2 coats polyurethane			2.50	3.200		5.45	83.50		88.95	133
	0270	Doors, louvered, both sides, incl. frame & trim										
	0280	Brushwork, primer		1 Pord	7	1.143	Ea.	3.75	30		33.75	49.50
	0290	Finish coat, exterior latex			7	1.143		4.27	30		34.27	50
	0300	Primer & 1 coat, exterior latex			4	2		8	52		60	88.50
	0310	Primer & 2 coats, exterior latex			3	2.667		12.05	69.50		81.55	119
	0320	Brushwork, stain, sealer & 2 coats polyurethane			4.50	1.778		15.25	46.50		61.75	87.50
	0330	Doors, panel, both sides, incl. frame & trim										
	0340	Roll & brush, primer		1 Pord	6	1.333	Ea.	3.75	35		38.75	57
	0350	Finish coat, exterior latex			6	1.333		4.27	35		39.27	57.50
	0360	Primer & 1 coat, exterior latex			3	2.667		8	69.50		77.50	115

For expanded coverage of these items see *Means Interior Cost Data 2001*

FINISHES **9**

	09910	Paints & Coatings		CREW	DAILY OUTPUT	LABOR-HOURS	UNIT	2001 BARE COSTS MAT.	LABOR	EQUIP.	TOTAL	TOTAL INCL O&P	
300	0370	Primer & 2 coats, exterior latex	R09910 -100	1 Pord	2.50	3.200	Ea.	12.05	83.50		95.55	140	300
	0380	Brushwork, stain, sealer & 2 coats polyurethane		↓	3	2.667	↓	15.25	69.50		84.75	123	
	0400	Windows, per ext. side, based on 15 SF	R09910 -220										
	0410	1 to 6 lite											
	0420	Brushwork, primer		1 Pord	13	.615	Ea.	.74	16.05		16.79	25.50	
	0430	Finish coat, exterior latex			13	.615		.84	16.05		16.89	25.50	
	0440	Primer & 1 coat, exterior latex			8	1		1.58	26		27.58	41.50	
	0450	Primer & 2 coats, exterior latex			6	1.333		2.38	35		37.38	55.50	
	0460	Stain, sealer & 1 coat varnish		↓	7	1.143	↓	2.16	30		32.16	48	
	0470	7 to 10 lite											
	0480	Brushwork, primer		1 Pord	11	.727	Ea.	.74	19		19.74	30	
	0490	Finish coat, exterior latex			11	.727		.84	19		19.84	30	
	0500	Primer & 1 coat, exterior latex			7	1.143		1.58	30		31.58	47	
	0510	Primer & 2 coats, exterior latex			5	1.600		2.38	42		44.38	66	
	0520	Stain, sealer & 1 coat varnish		↓	6	1.333	↓	2.16	35		37.16	55.50	
	0530	12 lite											
	0540	Brushwork, primer		1 Pord	10	.800	Ea.	.74	21		21.74	33	
	0550	Finish coat, exterior latex			10	.800		.84	21		21.84	33	
	0560	Primer & 1 coat, exterior latex			6	1.333		1.58	35		36.58	54.50	
	0570	Primer & 2 coats, exterior latex			5	1.600		2.38	42		44.38	66	
	0580	Stain, sealer & 1 coat varnish		↓	6	1.333	↓	2.15	35		37.15	55.50	
	0590	For oil base paint, add		▼			▼	10%					
310	0010	**DOORS & WINDOWS, INTERIOR LATEX**	R09910 -100										310
	0100	Doors flush, both sides, incl. frame & trim											
	0110	Roll & brush, primer	R09910 -220	1 Pord	10	.800	Ea.	3.26	21		24.26	35.50	
	0120	Finish coat, latex			10	.800		3.53	21		24.53	36	
	0130	Primer & 1 coat latex			7	1.143		6.80	30		36.80	53	
	0140	Primer & 2 coats latex			5	1.600		10.10	42		52.10	74.50	
	0160	Spray, both sides, primer			20	.400		3.44	10.45		13.89	19.70	
	0170	Finish coat, latex			20	.400		3.70	10.45		14.15	19.95	
	0180	Primer & 1 coat latex			11	.727		7.20	19		26.20	37	
	0190	Primer & 2 coats latex		↓	8	1	↓	10.70	26		36.70	52	
	0200	Doors, French, both sides, 10-15 lite, incl. frame & trim											
	0210	Roll & brush, primer		1 Pord	6	1.333	Ea.	1.63	35		36.63	55	
	0220	Finish coat, latex			6	1.333		1.77	35		36.77	55	
	0230	Primer & 1 coat latex			3	2.667		3.40	69.50		72.90	110	
	0240	Primer & 2 coats latex		↓	2	4	↓	5.05	104		109.05	165	
	0260	Doors, louvered, both sides, incl. frame & trim											
	0270	Roll & brush, primer		1 Pord	7	1.143	Ea.	3.26	30		33.26	49	
	0280	Finish coat, latex			7	1.143		3.53	30		33.53	49.50	
	0290	Primer & 1 coat, latex			4	2		6.60	52		58.60	87	
	0300	Primer & 2 coats, latex			3	2.667		10.30	69.50		79.80	117	
	0320	Spray, both sides, primer			20	.400		3.44	10.45		13.89	19.70	
	0330	Finish coat, latex			20	.400		3.70	10.45		14.15	19.95	
	0340	Primer & 1 coat, latex			11	.727		7.20	19		26.20	37	
	0350	Primer & 2 coats, latex		↓	8	1	↓	10.95	26		36.95	52	
	0360	Doors, panel, both sides, incl. frame & trim											
	0370	Roll & brush, primer		1 Pord	6	1.333	Ea.	3.44	35		38.44	57	
	0380	Finish coat, latex			6	1.333		3.53	35		38.53	57	
	0390	Primer & 1 coat, latex			3	2.667		6.80	69.50		76.30	113	
	0400	Primer & 2 coats, latex			2.50	3.200		10.30	83.50		93.80	138	
	0420	Spray, both sides, primer			10	.800		3.44	21		24.44	36	
	0430	Finish coat, latex			10	.800		3.70	21		24.70	36	
	0440	Primer & 1 coat, latex			5	1.600		7.20	42		49.20	71.50	
	0450	Primer & 2 coats, latex		↓	4	2	↓	10.95	52		62.95	91.50	
	0460	Windows, per interior side, base on 15 SF		▼									

Important: See the Reference Section for critical supporting data - Reference Nos., Crews, & City Cost Indexes

		09910	Paints & Coatings	CREW	DAILY OUTPUT	LABOR-HOURS	UNIT	2001 BARE COSTS				TOTAL INCL O&P	
								MAT.	LABOR	EQUIP.	TOTAL		
310	0470		1 to 6 lite										310
	0480		Brushwork, primer	1 Pord	13	.615	Ea.	.64	16.05		16.69	25	
	0490		Finish coat, enamel		13	.615		.70	16.05		16.75	25.50	
	0500		Primer & 1 coat enamel		8	1		1.34	26		27.34	41.50	
	0510		Primer & 2 coats enamel		6	1.333		2.04	35		37.04	55	
	0530		7 to 10 lite										
	0540		Brushwork, primer	1 Pord	11	.727	Ea.	.64	19		19.64	29.50	
	0550		Finish coat, enamel		11	.727		.70	19		19.70	30	
	0560		Primer & 1 coat enamel		7	1.143		1.34	30		31.34	47	
	0570		Primer & 2 coats enamel		5	1.600		2.04	42		44.04	65.50	
	0590		12 lite										
	0600		Brushwork, primer	1 Pord	10	.800	Ea.	.64	21		21.64	32.50	
	0610		Finish coat, enamel		10	.800		.70	21		21.70	33	
	0620		Primer & 1 coat enamel		6	1.333		1.34	35		36.34	54.50	
	0630		Primer & 2 coats enamel		5	1.600		2.04	42		44.04	65.50	
	0650		For oil base paint, add					10%					
320	0010		**DOORS AND WINDOWS, INTERIOR ALKYD (OIL BASE)**										320
	0500		Flush door & frame, 3' x 7', oil, primer, brushwork	1 Pord	10	.800	Ea.	2.05	21		23.05	34.50	
	1000		Paint, 1 coat		10	.800		1.97	21		22.97	34	
	1400		Stain, brushwork, wipe off		18	.444		.98	11.60		12.58	18.75	
	1600		Shellac, 1 coat, brushwork		25	.320		1.14	8.35		9.49	13.95	
	1800		Varnish, 3 coats, brushwork, sand after 1st coat		9	.889		3.47	23		26.47	39.50	
	2000		Panel door & frame, 3' x 7', oil, primer, brushwork		6	1.333		1.82	35		36.82	55	
	2200		Paint, 1 coat		6	1.333		1.97	35		36.97	55	
	2600		Stain, brushwork, panel door, 3' x 7', not incl. frame		16	.500		.98	13.05		14.03	21	
	2800		Shellac, 1 coat, brushwork		22	.364		1.14	9.50		10.64	15.70	
	3000		Varnish, 3 coats, brushwork, sand after 1st coat		7.50	1.067		3.47	28		31.47	46.50	
	4400		Windows, including frame and trim, per side										
	4600		Colonial type, 6/6 lites, 2' x 3', oil, primer, brushwork	1 Pord	14	.571	Ea.	.29	14.90		15.19	23	
	5800		Paint, 1 coat		14	.571		.31	14.90		15.21	23	
	6200		3' x 5' opening, 6/6 lites, primer coat, brushwork		12	.667		.72	17.40		18.12	27.50	
	6400		Paint, 1 coat		12	.667		.78	17.40		18.18	27.50	
	6800		4' x 8' opening, 6/6 lites, primer coat, brushwork		8	1		1.54	26		27.54	41.50	
	7000		Paint, 1 coat		8	1		1.66	26		27.66	42	
	8000		Single lite type, 2' x 3', oil base, primer coat, brushwork		33	.242		.29	6.35		6.64	9.95	
	8200		Paint, 1 coat		33	.242		.31	6.35		6.66	10	
	8600		3' x 5' opening, primer coat, brushwork		20	.400		.72	10.45		11.17	16.70	
	8800		Paint, 1 coat		20	.400		.78	10.45		11.23	16.75	
	9200		4' x 8' opening, primer coat, brushwork		14	.571		1.54	14.90		16.44	24	
	9400		Paint, 1 coat		14	.571		1.66	14.90		16.56	24.50	
400	0010		**FENCES**										400
	0100		Chain link or wire metal, one side, water base										
	0110		Roll & brush, first coat	1 Pord	960	.008	S.F.	.06	.22		.28	.39	
	0120		Second coat		1,280	.006		.05	.16		.21	.31	
	0130		Spray, first coat		2,275	.004		.06	.09		.15	.20	
	0140		Second coat		2,600	.003		.06	.08		.14	.18	
	0150		Picket, water base										
	0160		Roll & brush, first coat	1 Pord	865	.009	S.F.	.06	.24		.30	.44	
	0170		Second coat		1,050	.008		.06	.20		.26	.37	
	0180		Spray, first coat		2,275	.004		.06	.09		.15	.21	
	0190		Second coat		2,600	.003		.06	.08		.14	.19	
	0200		Stockade, water base										
	0210		Roll & brush, first coat	1 Pord	1,040	.008	S.F.	.06	.20		.26	.38	
	0220		Second coat		1,200	.007		.06	.17		.23	.34	
	0230		Spray, first coat		2,275	.004		.06	.09		.15	.21	
	0240		Second coat		2,600	.003		.06	.08		.14	.19	

R09910-100
R09910-220

FINISHES **9**

09910	Paints & Coatings	CREW	DAILY OUTPUT	LABOR-HOURS	UNIT	MAT.	LABOR	EQUIP.	TOTAL	TOTAL INCL O&P	
						2001 BARE COSTS					
500	**0010**	**FLOORS, INTERIOR**									**500**
	0100	Concrete									
	0110	Brushwork, latex, block filler									
	0120	1st coat	1 Pord	975	.008	S.F.	.11	.21		.32	.45
	0130	2nd coat		1,150	.007		.07	.18		.25	.36
	0140	3rd coat	↓	1,300	.006	↓	.06	.16		.22	.30
	0150	Roll, latex, block filler									
	0160	1st coat	1 Pord	2,600	.003	S.F.	.14	.08		.22	.28
	0170	2nd coat		3,250	.002		.09	.06		.15	.19
	0180	3rd coat	↓	3,900	.002	↓	.06	.05		.11	.15
	0190	Spray, latex, block filler									
	0200	1st coat	1 Pord	2,600	.003	S.F.	.12	.08		.20	.26
	0210	2nd coat		3,250	.002		.07	.06		.13	.17
	0220	3rd coat	↓	3,900	.002	↓	.05	.05		.10	.14
620	**0010**	**MISCELLANEOUS, EXTERIOR**	R09910 -110								**620**
	0015	For painting metals, see Div. 05120-680									
	0100	Railing, ext., decorative wood, incl. cap & baluster	R09910 -220								
	0110	newels & spindles @ 12" O.C.									
	0120	Brushwork, stain, sand, seal & varnish									
	0130	First coat	1 Pord	90	.089	L.F.	.43	2.32		2.75	4.01
	0140	Second coat	"	120	.067	"	.43	1.74		2.17	3.13
	0150	Rough sawn wood, 42" high, 2"x2" verticals, 6" O.C.									
	0160	Brushwork, stain, each coat	1 Pord	90	.089	L.F.	.14	2.32		2.46	3.68
	0170	Wrought iron, 1" rail, 1/2" sq. verticals									
	0180	Brushwork, zinc chromate, 60" high, bars 6" O.C.									
	0190	Primer	1 Pord	130	.062	L.F.	.48	1.61		2.09	2.98
	0200	Finish coat		130	.062		.15	1.61		1.76	2.62
	0210	Additional coat	↓	190	.042	↓	.18	1.10		1.28	1.86
	0220	Shutters or blinds, single panel, 2'x4', paint all sides									
	0230	Brushwork, primer	1 Pord	20	.400	Ea.	.54	10.45		10.99	16.50
	0240	Finish coat, exterior latex		20	.400		.45	10.45		10.90	16.40
	0250	Primer & 1 coat, exterior latex		13	.615		.87	16.05		16.92	25.50
	0260	Spray, primer		35	.229		.79	5.95		6.74	9.95
	0270	Finish coat, exterior latex		35	.229		.95	5.95		6.90	10.15
	0280	Primer & 1 coat, exterior latex	↓	20	.400	↓	.85	10.45		11.30	16.85
	0290	For louvered shutters, add				S.F.	10%				
	0300	Stair stringers, exterior, metal									
	0310	Roll & brush, zinc chromate, to 14", each coat	1 Pord	320	.025	L.F.	.05	.65		.70	1.05
	0320	Rough sawn wood, 4" x 12"									
	0330	Roll & brush, exterior latex, each coat	1 Pord	215	.037	L.F.	.07	.97		1.04	1.55
	0340	Trellis/lattice, 2"x2" @ 3" O.C. with 2"x8" supports									
	0350	Spray, latex, per side, each coat	1 Pord	475	.017	S.F.	.07	.44		.51	.74
	0450	Decking, Ext., sealer, alkyd, brushwork, sealer coat		1,140	.007		.05	.18		.23	.33
	0460	1st coat		1,140	.007		.05	.18		.23	.34
	0470	2nd coat		1,300	.006		.04	.16		.20	.28
	0500	Paint, alkyd, brushwork, primer coat		1,140	.007		.07	.18		.25	.36
	0510	1st coat		1,140	.007		.07	.18		.25	.35
	0520	2nd coat		1,300	.006		.05	.16		.21	.29
	0600	Sand paint, alkyd, brushwork, 1 coat	↓	150	.053	↓	.09	1.39		1.48	2.21
630	**0010**	**MISCELLANEOUS, INTERIOR**	R09910 -100								**630**
	2400	Floors, conc./wood, oil base, primer/sealer coat, brushwork	2 Pord	1,950	.008	S.F.	.06	.21		.27	.39
	2450	Roller	R09910 -220	5,200	.003		.06	.08		.14	.18
	2600	Spray		6,000	.003		.06	.07		.13	.17
	2650	Paint 1 coat, brushwork		1,950	.008		.05	.21		.26	.39
	2800	Roller	↓	5,200	.003	↓	.05	.08		.13	.18

Important: See the Reference Section for critical supporting data - Reference Nos., Crews, & City Cost Indexes

9 FINISHES

09910 | Paints & Coatings

			CREW	DAILY OUTPUT	LABOR-HOURS	UNIT	2001 BARE COSTS MAT.	LABOR	EQUIP.	TOTAL	TOTAL INCL O&P	
630	2850	Spray	2 Pord	6,000	.003	S.F.	.06	.07		.13	.17	**630**
	3000	Stain, wood floor, brushwork, 1 coat	R09910 -100	4,550	.004		.05	.09		.14	.19	
	3200	Roller		5,200	.003		.05	.08		.13	.17	
	3250	Spray	R09910 -220	6,000	.003		.05	.07		.12	.16	
	3400	Varnish, wood floor, brushwork		4,550	.004		.06	.09		.15	.20	
	3450	Roller		5,200	.003		.06	.08		.14	.18	
	3600	Spray		6,000	.003		.06	.07		.13	.18	
	3650	For dust proofing or anti skid, see division 03350-300										
	3800	Grilles, per side, oil base, primer coat, brushwork	1 Pord	520	.015	S.F.	.10	.40		.50	.72	
	3850	Spray		1,140	.007		.10	.18		.28	.39	
	3920	Paint 2 coats, brushwork		325	.025		.20	.64		.84	1.20	
	3940	Spray		650	.012		.23	.32		.55	.74	
	5000	Pipe, to 4" diameter, primer or sealer coat, oil base, brushwork	2 Pord	1,250	.013	L.F.	.06	.33		.39	.57	
	5100	Spray		2,165	.007		.06	.19		.25	.35	
	5350	Paint 2 coats, brushwork		775	.021		.11	.54		.65	.94	
	5400	Spray		1,240	.013		.12	.34		.46	.64	
	6300	To 16" diameter, primer or sealer coat, brushwork		310	.052		.23	1.35		1.58	2.31	
	6350	Spray		540	.030		.26	.77		1.03	1.47	
	6500	Paint 2 coats, brushwork		195	.082		.44	2.14		2.58	3.74	
	6550	Spray		310	.052		.49	1.35		1.84	2.59	
	7000	Trim, wood, incl. puttying, under 6" wide										
	7200	Primer coat, oil base, brushwork	1 Pord	650	.012	L.F.	.02	.32		.34	.52	
	7250	Paint, 1 coat, brushwork		650	.012		.03	.32		.35	.52	
	7450	3 coats		325	.025		.07	.64		.71	1.06	
	7500	Over 6" wide, primer coat, brushwork		650	.012		.05	.32		.37	.54	
	7550	Paint, 1 coat, brushwork		650	.012		.05	.32		.37	.55	
	7650	3 coats		325	.025		.15	.64		.79	1.14	
	8000	Cornice, simple design, primer coat, oil base, brushwork		650	.012	S.F.	.05	.32		.37	.54	
	8250	Paint, 1 coat		650	.012		.05	.32		.37	.55	
	8350	Ornate design, primer coat		350	.023		.05	.60		.65	.96	
	8400	Paint, 1 coat		350	.023		.05	.60		.65	.97	
	8600	Balustrades, primer coat, oil base, brushwork		520	.015		.05	.40		.45	.66	
	8650	Paint, 1 coat		520	.015		.05	.40		.45	.67	
	8900	Trusses and wood frames, primer coat, oil base, brushwork		800	.010		.05	.26		.31	.45	
	8950	Spray		1,200	.007		.05	.17		.22	.33	
	9220	Paint 2 coats, brushwork		500	.016		.10	.42		.52	.75	
	9240	Spray		600	.013		.11	.35		.46	.65	
	9260	Stain, brushwork, wipe off		600	.013		.05	.35		.40	.58	
	9280	Varnish, 3 coats, brushwork		275	.029		.17	.76		.93	1.34	
	9350	For latex paint, deduct					10%					
700	0010	**SIDING EXTERIOR**, Alkyd (oil base)	R09910 -100									**700**
	0500	Spray	2 Pord	4,550	.004	S.F.	.08	.09		.17	.23	
	0800	Paint 2 coats, brushwork	R09910 -220	1,300	.012		.11	.32		.43	.61	
	1000	Spray		4,550	.004		.14	.09		.23	.29	
	1200	Stucco, rough, oil base, paint 2 coats, brushwork		1,300	.012		.11	.32		.43	.61	
	1400	Roller		1,625	.010		.11	.26		.37	.51	
	1600	Spray		2,925	.005		.12	.14		.26	.35	
	1800	Texture 1-11 or clapboard, oil base, primer coat, brushwork		1,300	.012		.09	.32		.41	.59	
	2000	Spray		4,550	.004		.09	.09		.18	.24	
	2400	Paint 2 coats, brushwork		810	.020		.15	.52		.67	.96	
	2600	Spray		2,600	.006		.17	.16		.33	.43	
	3400	Stain 2 coats, brushwork		950	.017		.09	.44		.53	.77	
	4000	Spray		3,050	.005		.10	.14		.24	.32	
	4200	Wood shingles, oil base primer coat, brushwork		1,300	.012		.08	.32		.40	.58	
	4400	Spray		3,900	.004		.08	.11		.19	.24	
	5000	Paint 2 coats, brushwork		810	.020		.13	.52		.65	.93	

FINISHES 9

09910 | Paints & Coatings

			CREW	DAILY OUTPUT	LABOR-HOURS	UNIT	2001 BARE COSTS MAT.	LABOR	EQUIP.	TOTAL	TOTAL INCL O&P	
700	5200	Spray	2 Pord	2,275	.007	S.F.	.12	.18		.30	.41	**700**
	6500	Stain 2 coats, brushwork		950	.017		.09	.44		.53	.77	
	7000	Spray		2,660	.006		.13	.16		.29	.38	
	8000	For latex paint, deduct					10%					
	8100	For work over 12' H, from pipe scaffolding, add						15%				
	8200	For work over 12' H, from extension ladder, add						25%				
	8300	For work over 12' H, from swing staging, add						35%				
710	0010	**SIDING, MISC.**										**710**
	0100	Aluminum siding										
	0110	Brushwork, primer	2 Pord	2,275	.007	S.F.	.05	.18		.23	.33	
	0120	Finish coat, exterior latex		2,275	.007		.04	.18		.22	.32	
	0130	Primer & 1 coat exterior latex		1,300	.012		.09	.32		.41	.59	
	0140	Primer & 2 coats exterior latex		975	.016		.13	.43		.56	.80	
	0150	Mineral Fiber shingles										
	0160	Brushwork, primer	2 Pord	1,495	.011	S.F.	.09	.28		.37	.53	
	0170	Finish coat, industrial enamel		1,495	.011		.10	.28		.38	.54	
	0180	Primer & 1 coat enamel		810	.020		.19	.52		.71	1	
	0190	Primer & 2 coats enamel		540	.030		.29	.77		1.06	1.49	
	0200	Roll, primer		1,625	.010		.10	.26		.36	.50	
	0210	Finish coat, industrial enamel		1,625	.010		.11	.26		.37	.51	
	0220	Primer & 1 coat enamel		975	.016		.21	.43		.64	.88	
	0230	Primer & 2 coats enamel		650	.025		.31	.64		.95	1.32	
	0240	Spray, primer		3,900	.004		.08	.11		.19	.24	
	0250	Finish coat, industrial enamel		3,900	.004		.09	.11		.20	.26	
	0260	Primer & 1 coat enamel		2,275	.007		.17	.18		.35	.46	
	0270	Primer & 2 coats enamel		1,625	.010		.25	.26		.51	.67	
	0280	Waterproof sealer, first coat		4,485	.004		.06	.09		.15	.21	
	0290	Second coat		5,235	.003		.06	.08		.14	.19	
	0300	Rough wood incl. shingles, shakes or rough sawn siding										
	0310	Brushwork, primer	2 Pord	1,280	.013	S.F.	.11	.33		.44	.62	
	0320	Finish coat, exterior latex		1,280	.013		.07	.33		.40	.57	
	0330	Primer & 1 coat exterior latex		960	.017		.18	.44		.62	.85	
	0340	Primer & 2 coats exterior latex		700	.023		.24	.60		.84	1.18	
	0350	Roll, primer		2,925	.005		.15	.14		.29	.38	
	0360	Finish coat, exterior latex		2,925	.005		.08	.14		.22	.31	
	0370	Primer & 1 coat exterior latex		1,790	.009		.23	.23		.46	.61	
	0380	Primer & 2 coats exterior latex		1,300	.012		.31	.32		.63	.83	
	0390	Spray, primer		3,900	.004		.12	.11		.23	.30	
	0400	Finish coat, exterior latex		3,900	.004		.06	.11		.17	.23	
	0410	Primer & 1 coat exterior latex		2,600	.006		.19	.16		.35	.44	
	0420	Primer & 2 coats exterior latex		2,080	.008		.25	.20		.45	.58	
	0430	Waterproof sealer, first coat		4,485	.004		.11	.09		.20	.26	
	0440	Second coat		4,485	.004		.06	.09		.15	.21	
	0450	Smooth wood incl. butt, T&G, beveled, drop or B&B siding										
	0460	Brushwork, primer	2 Pord	2,325	.007	S.F.	.08	.18		.26	.36	
	0470	Finish coat, exterior latex		1,280	.013		.07	.33		.40	.57	
	0480	Primer & 1 coat exterior latex		800	.020		.15	.52		.67	.96	
	0490	Primer & 2 coats exterior latex		630	.025		.21	.66		.87	1.24	
	0500	Roll, primer		2,275	.007		.09	.18		.27	.38	
	0510	Finish coat, exterior latex		2,275	.007		.07	.18		.25	.36	
	0520	Primer & 1 coat exterior latex		1,300	.012		.16	.32		.48	.67	
	0530	Primer & 2 coats exterior latex		975	.016		.23	.43		.66	.91	
	0540	Spray, primer		4,550	.004		.07	.09		.16	.21	
	0550	Finish coat, exterior latex		4,550	.004		.06	.09		.15	.21	
	0560	Primer & 1 coat exterior latex		2,600	.006		.13	.16		.29	.38	

The reference notes R09910-100 and R09910-220 appear next to rows 5200, 7000, 0100, and 0120.

9 FINISHES

Important: See the Reference Section for critical supporting data - Reference Nos., Crews, & City Cost Indexes

09910	Paints & Coatings		CREW	DAILY OUTPUT	LABOR-HOURS	UNIT	2001 BARE COSTS				TOTAL INCL O&P	
							MAT.	LABOR	EQUIP.	TOTAL		
710	0570	Primer & 2 coats exterior latex	2 Pord	1,950	.008	S.F.	.19	.21		.40	.54	**710**
	0580	Waterproof sealer, first coat		5,230	.003		.06	.08		.14	.19	
	0590	Second coat		5,980	.003		.06	.07		.13	.18	
	0600	For oil base paint, add					10%					
800	0010	**TRIM, EXTERIOR**										**800**
	0100	Door frames & trim (see Doors, interior or exterior)										
	0110	Fascia, latex paint, one coat coverage										
	0120	1" x 4", brushwork	1 Pord	640	.013	L.F.	.02	.33		.35	.52	
	0130	Roll		1,280	.006		.02	.16		.18	.27	
	0140	Spray		2,080	.004		.01	.10		.11	.17	
	0150	1" x 6" to 1" x 10", brushwork		640	.013		.06	.33		.39	.57	
	0160	Roll		1,230	.007		.06	.17		.23	.33	
	0170	Spray		2,100	.004		.05	.10		.15	.20	
	0180	1" x 12", brushwork		640	.013		.06	.33		.39	.57	
	0190	Roll		1,050	.008		.06	.20		.26	.37	
	0200	Spray		2,200	.004		.05	.10		.15	.19	
	0210	Gutters & downspouts, metal, zinc chromate paint										
	0220	Brushwork, gutters, 5", first coat	1 Pord	640	.013	L.F.	.05	.33		.38	.56	
	0230	Second coat		960	.008		.05	.22		.27	.39	
	0240	Third coat		1,280	.006		.04	.16		.20	.29	
	0250	Downspouts, 4", first coat		640	.013		.05	.33		.38	.56	
	0260	Second coat		960	.008		.05	.22		.27	.39	
	0270	Third coat		1,280	.006		.04	.16		.20	.29	
	0280	Gutters & downspouts, wood										
	0290	Brushwork, gutters, 5", primer	1 Pord	640	.013	L.F.	.05	.33		.38	.55	
	0300	Finish coat, exterior latex		640	.013		.05	.33		.38	.56	
	0310	Primer & 1 coat exterior latex		400	.020		.11	.52		.63	.92	
	0320	Primer & 2 coats exterior latex		325	.025		.16	.64		.80	1.16	
	0330	Downspouts, 4", primer		640	.013		.05	.33		.38	.55	
	0340	Finish coat, exterior latex		640	.013		.05	.33		.38	.56	
	0350	Primer & 1 coat exterior latex		400	.020		.11	.52		.63	.92	
	0360	Primer & 2 coats exterior latex		325	.025		.08	.64		.72	1.07	
	0370	Molding, exterior, up to 14" wide										
	0380	Brushwork, primer	1 Pord	640	.013	L.F.	.06	.33		.39	.57	
	0390	Finish coat, exterior latex		640	.013		.06	.33		.39	.57	
	0400	Primer & 1 coat exterior latex		400	.020		.13	.52		.65	.94	
	0410	Primer & 2 coats exterior latex		315	.025		.13	.66		.79	1.15	
	0420	Stain & fill		1,050	.008		.06	.20		.26	.36	
	0430	Shellac		1,850	.004		.07	.11		.18	.24	
	0440	Varnish		1,275	.006		.07	.16		.23	.32	
910	0350	**WALLS, MASONRY (CMU), EXTERIOR**										**910**
	0360	Concrete masonry units (CMU), smooth surface										
	0370	Brushwork, latex, first coat	1 Pord	640	.013	S.F.	.03	.33		.36	.54	
	0380	Second coat		960	.008		.03	.22		.25	.36	
	0390	Waterproof sealer, first coat		736	.011		.07	.28		.35	.50	
	0400	Second coat		1,104	.007		.05	.19		.24	.34	
	0410	Roll, latex, paint, first coat		1,465	.005		.04	.14		.18	.26	
	0420	Second coat		1,790	.004		.03	.12		.15	.21	
	0430	Waterproof sealer, first coat		1,680	.005		.07	.12		.19	.26	
	0440	Second coat		2,060	.004		.05	.10		.15	.20	
	0450	Spray, latex, paint, first coat		1,950	.004		.03	.11		.14	.19	
	0460	Second coat		2,600	.003		.03	.08		.11	.15	
	0470	Waterproof sealer, first coat		2,245	.004		.08	.09		.17	.23	
	0480	Second coat		2,990	.003		.03	.07		.10	.15	
	0490	Concrete masonry unit (CMU), porous										
	0500	Brushwork, latex, first coat	1 Pord	640	.013	S.F.	.07	.33		.40	.57	

R09910 -100
R09910 -220

9

FINISHES

			CREW	DAILY OUTPUT	LABOR-HOURS	UNIT	2001 BARE COSTS				TOTAL INCL O&P	
							MAT.	LABOR	EQUIP.	TOTAL		
910	0510	Second coat	1 Pord	960	.008	S.F.	.03	.22		.25	.37	**910**
	0520	Waterproof sealer, first coat		736	.011		.08	.28		.36	.52	
	0530	Second coat		1,104	.007		.04	.19		.23	.34	
	0540	Roll latex, first coat		1,465	.005		.05	.14		.19	.28	
	0550	Second coat		1,790	.004		.03	.12		.15	.22	
	0560	Waterproof sealer, first coat		1,680	.005		.08	.12		.20	.28	
	0570	Second coat		2,060	.004		.05	.10		.15	.20	
	0580	Spray latex, first coat		1,950	.004		.04	.11		.15	.20	
	0590	Second coat		2,600	.003		.03	.08		.11	.15	
	0600	Waterproof sealer, first coat		2,245	.004		.07	.09		.16	.21	
	0610	Second coat	↓	2,990	.003	↓	.04	.07		.11	.15	
920	0010	**WALLS AND CEILINGS,** Interior										**920**
	0100	Concrete, dry wall or plaster, oil base, primer or sealer coat										
	0200	Smooth finish, brushwork	1 Pord	1,150	.007	S.F.	.05	.18		.23	.33	
	0240	Roller		2,040	.004		.05	.10		.15	.21	
	0300	Sand finish, brushwork		975	.008		.05	.21		.26	.38	
	0340	Roller		1,150	.007		.05	.18		.23	.34	
	0380	Spray		2,275	.004		.04	.09		.13	.18	
	0800	Paint 2 coats, smooth finish, brushwork		680	.012		.09	.31		.40	.57	
	0840	Roller		800	.010		.09	.26		.35	.50	
	0880	Spray		1,625	.005		.08	.13		.21	.29	
	0900	Sand finish, brushwork		605	.013		.09	.35		.44	.63	
	0940	Roller		1,020	.008		.09	.20		.29	.41	
	0980	Spray		1,700	.005		.08	.12		.20	.28	
	1200	Paint 3 coats, smooth finish, brushwork		510	.016		.13	.41		.54	.76	
	1240	Roller		650	.012		.14	.32		.46	.64	
	1280	Spray		1,625	.005		.12	.13		.25	.33	
	1600	Glaze coating, 5 coats, spray, clear		900	.009		.60	.23		.83	1.01	
	1640	Multicolor	↓	900	.009		.83	.23		1.06	1.26	
	1700	For latex paint, deduct					10%					
	1800	For ceiling installations, add				↓		25%				
	2000	Masonry or concrete block, oil base, primer or sealer coat										
	2100	Smooth finish, brushwork	1 Pord	1,224	.007	S.F.	.05	.17		.22	.31	
	2180	Spray		2,400	.003		.07	.09		.16	.20	
	2200	Sand finish, brushwork		1,089	.007		.07	.19		.26	.37	
	2280	Spray		2,400	.003		.07	.09		.16	.20	
	2800	Paint 2 coats, smooth finish, brushwork		756	.011		.14	.28		.42	.57	
	2880	Spray		1,360	.006		.13	.15		.28	.37	
	2900	Sand finish, brushwork		672	.012		.14	.31		.45	.62	
	2980	Spray		1,360	.006		.13	.15		.28	.37	
	3600	Glaze coating, 5 coats, spray, clear		900	.009		.60	.23		.83	1.01	
	3620	Multicolor		900	.009		.83	.23		1.06	1.26	
	4000	Block filler, 1 coat, brushwork		425	.019		.12	.49		.61	.88	
	4100	Silicone, water repellent, 2 coats, spray	↓	2,000	.004		.24	.10		.34	.42	
	4120	For latex paint, deduct					10%					
	8200	For work 8 - 15' H, add						10%				
	8300	For work over 15' H, add	↓			↓		20%				

09930 | Stains/Transp. Finishes

			CREW	DAILY OUTPUT	LABOR-HOURS	UNIT	MAT.	LABOR	EQUIP.	TOTAL	TOTAL INCL O&P	
100	0010	**VARNISH** 1 coat + sealer, on wood trim, no sanding included	1 Pord	400	.020	S.F.	.06	.52		.58	.87	**100**
	0100	Hardwood floors, 2 coats, no sanding included, roller	"	1,890	.004	"	.12	.11		.23	.30	

09963 | Glazed Coatings

			CREW	DAILY OUTPUT	LABOR-HOURS	UNIT	MAT.	LABOR	EQUIP.	TOTAL	TOTAL INCL O&P	
200	0010	**WALL COATINGS**										**200**
	0100	Acrylic glazed coatings, minimum	1 Pord	525	.015	S.F.	.25	.40		.65	.89	

Important: See the Reference Section for critical supporting data - Reference Nos., Crews, & City Cost Indexes

09963 | Glazed Coatings

			CREW	DAILY OUTPUT	LABOR-HOURS	UNIT	MAT.	LABOR	EQUIP.	TOTAL	TOTAL INCL O&P	
								2001 BARE COSTS				
200	0200	Maximum	1 Pord	305	.026	S.F.	.52	.68		1.20	1.61	200
	0300	Epoxy coatings, minimum		525	.015		.32	.40		.72	.96	
	0400	Maximum		170	.047		.99	1.23		2.22	2.96	
	0600	Exposed aggregate, troweled on, 1/16" to 1/4", minimum		235	.034		.49	.89		1.38	1.89	
	0700	Maximum (epoxy or polyacrylate)		130	.062		1.06	1.61		2.67	3.62	
	0900	1/2" to 5/8" aggregate, minimum		130	.062		.98	1.61		2.59	3.53	
	1000	Maximum		80	.100		1.67	2.61		4.28	5.80	
	1500	Exposed aggregate, sprayed on, 1/8" aggregate, minimum		295	.027		.46	.71		1.17	1.59	
	1600	Maximum		145	.055		.84	1.44		2.28	3.11	
	1800	High build epoxy, 50 mil, minimum		390	.021		.54	.54		1.08	1.41	
	1900	Maximum		95	.084		.93	2.20		3.13	4.37	
	2100	Laminated epoxy with fiberglass, minimum		295	.027		.59	.71		1.30	1.73	
	2200	Maximum		145	.055		1.05	1.44		2.49	3.35	
	2400	Sprayed perlite or vermiculite, 1/16" thick, minimum		2,935	.003		.21	.07		.28	.34	
	2500	Maximum		640	.013		.60	.33		.93	1.16	
	2700	Vinyl plastic wall coating, minimum		735	.011		.27	.28		.55	.73	
	2800	Maximum		240	.033		.66	.87		1.53	2.05	
	3000	Urethane on smooth surface, 2 coats, minimum		1,135	.007		.20	.18		.38	.50	
	3100	Maximum		665	.012		.45	.31		.76	.98	
	3600	Ceramic-like glazed coating, cementitious, minimum		440	.018		.39	.47		.86	1.15	
	3700	Maximum		345	.023		.65	.61		1.26	1.64	
	3900	Resin base, minimum		640	.013		.27	.33		.60	.80	
	4000	Maximum	▼	330	.024	▼	.44	.63		1.07	1.44	

09990 | Paint Restoration

			CREW	DAILY OUTPUT	LABOR-HOURS	UNIT	MAT.	LABOR	EQUIP.	TOTAL	TOTAL INCL O&P	
800	0010	**SANDING** and puttying interior trim, compared to										800
	0100	Painting 1 coat, on quality work				L.F.		100%				
	0300	Medium work						50%				
	0400	Industrial grade				▼		25%				
	0500	Surface protection, placement and removal										
	0510	Basic drop cloths	1 Pord	6,400	.001	S.F.		.03		.03	.05	
	0520	Masking with paper		800	.010		.03	.26		.29	.43	
	0530	Volume cover up (using plastic sheathing, or building paper)	▼	16,000	.001	▼		.01		.01	.02	
900	0010	**SURFACE PREPARATION, EXTERIOR**										900
	0015	Doors, per side, not incl. frames or trim										
	0020	Scrape & sand										
	0030	Wood, flush	1 Pord	616	.013	S.F.		.34		.34	.52	
	0040	Wood, detail		496	.016			.42		.42	.64	
	0050	Wood, louvered		280	.029			.75		.75	1.14	
	0060	Wood, overhead	▼	616	.013	▼		.34		.34	.52	
	0070	Wire brush										
	0080	Metal, flush	1 Pord	640	.013	S.F.		.33		.33	.50	
	0090	Metal, detail		520	.015			.40		.40	.61	
	0100	Metal, louvered		360	.022			.58		.58	.88	
	0110	Metal or fibr., overhead		640	.013			.33		.33	.50	
	0120	Metal, roll up		560	.014			.37		.37	.57	
	0130	Metal, bulkhead	▼	640	.013	▼		.33		.33	.50	
	0140	Power wash, based on 2500 lb. operating pressure										
	0150	Metal, flush	B-9	2,240	.018	S.F.		.42	.08	.50	.74	
	0160	Metal, detail		2,120	.019			.44	.08	.52	.78	
	0170	Metal, louvered		2,000	.020			.47	.09	.56	.83	
	0180	Metal or fibr., overhead		2,400	.017			.39	.07	.46	.69	
	0190	Metal, roll up		2,400	.017			.39	.07	.46	.69	
	0200	Metal, bulkhead	▼	2,200	.018	▼		.42	.08	.50	.75	
	0400	Windows, per side, not incl. trim										

9

FINISHES

09990		Paint Restoration	CREW	DAILY OUTPUT	LABOR-HOURS	UNIT	2001 BARE COSTS				TOTAL INCL O&P
							MAT.	LABOR	EQUIP.	TOTAL	
900	0410	Scrape & sand									**900**
	0420	Wood, 1-2 lite	1 Pord	320	.025	S.F.		.65		.65	.99
	0430	Wood, 3-6 lite		280	.029			.75		.75	1.14
	0440	Wood, 7-10 lite		240	.033			.87		.87	1.32
	0450	Wood, 12 lite		200	.040			1.04		1.04	1.59
	0460	Wood, Bay / Bow	↓	320	.025	↓		.65		.65	.99
	0470	Wire brush									
	0480	Metal, 1-2 lite	1 Pord	480	.017	S.F.		.44		.44	.66
	0490	Metal, 3-6 lite		400	.020			.52		.52	.80
	0500	Metal, Bay / Bow	↓	480	.017	↓		.44		.44	.66
	0510	Power wash, based on 2500 lb. operating pressure									
	0520	1-2 lite	B-9	4,400	.009	S.F.		.21	.04	.25	.37
	0530	3-6 lite		4,320	.009			.22	.04	.26	.38
	0540	7-10 lite		4,240	.009			.22	.04	.26	.39
	0550	12 lite		4,160	.010			.22	.04	.26	.40
	0560	Bay / Bow	↓	4,400	.009	↓		.21	.04	.25	.37
	0600	Siding, scrape and sand, light=10-30%, med.=30-70%									
	0610	Heavy=70-100%, % of surface to sand									
	0650	Texture 1-11, light	1 Pord	480	.017	S.F.		.44		.44	.66
	0660	Med.		440	.018			.47		.47	.72
	0670	Heavy		360	.022			.58		.58	.88
	0680	Wood shingles, shakes, light		440	.018			.47		.47	.72
	0690	Med.		360	.022			.58		.58	.88
	0700	Heavy		280	.029			.75		.75	1.14
	0710	Clapboard, light		520	.015			.40		.40	.61
	0720	Med.		480	.017			.44		.44	.66
	0730	Heavy	↓	400	.020	↓		.52		.52	.80
	0740	Wire brush									
	0750	Aluminum, light	1 Pord	600	.013	S.F.		.35		.35	.53
	0760	Med.		520	.015			.40		.40	.61
	0770	Heavy	↓	440	.018	↓		.47		.47	.72
	0780	Pressure wash, based on 2500 lb.. operating pressure									
	0790	Stucco	B-9	3,080	.013	S.F.		.30	.06	.36	.53
	0800	Aluminum or vinyl		3,200	.013			.29	.06	.35	.51
	0810	Siding, masonry, brick & block	↓	2,400	.017	↓		.39	.07	.46	.69
	1300	Miscellaneous, wire brush									
	1310	Metal, pedestrian gate	1 Pord	100	.080	S.F.		2.09		2.09	3.18
	8000	For Chemical Washing, see Division 04930-900									
	8010	For Steam Cleaning, see Division 04930-750									
	8020	For Sand Blasting, see Division 05120-680 and 03350-350									
910	0010	**SURFACE PREPARATION, INTERIOR**									**910**
	0020	Doors									
	0030	Scrape & sand									
	0040	Wood, flush	1 Pord	616	.013	S.F.		.34		.34	.52
	0050	Wood, detail		496	.016			.42		.42	.64
	0060	Wood, louvered	↓	280	.029	↓		.75		.75	1.14
	0070	Wire brush									
	0080	Metal, flush	1 Pord	640	.013	S.F.		.33		.33	.50
	0090	Metal, detail		520	.015			.40		.40	.61
	0100	Metal, louvered	↓	360	.022	↓		.58		.58	.88
	0110	Hand wash									
	0120	Wood, flush	1 Pord	2,160	.004	S.F.		.10		.10	.15
	0130	Wood, detailed		2,000	.004			.10		.10	.16
	0140	Wood, louvered		1,360	.006			.15		.15	.23
	0150	Metal, flush		2,160	.004			.10		.10	.15
	0160	Metal, detail	↓	2,000	.004	↓		.10		.10	.16

9

FINISHES

09990	Paint Restoration	CREW	DAILY OUTPUT	LABOR-HOURS	UNIT	2001 BARE COSTS				TOTAL INCL O&P	
						MAT.	LABOR	EQUIP.	TOTAL		
910 0170	Metal, louvered	1 Pord	1,360	.006	S.F.		.15		.15	.23	**910**
0400	Windows, per side, not incl. trim										
0410	Scrape & sand										
0420	Wood, 1-2 lite	1 Pord	360	.022	S.F.		.58		.58	.88	
0430	Wood, 3-6 lite		320	.025			.65		.65	.99	
0440	Wood, 7-10 lite		280	.029			.75		.75	1.14	
0450	Wood, 12 lite		240	.033			.87		.87	1.32	
0460	Wood, Bay / Bow	↓	360	.022	↓		.58		.58	.88	
0470	Wire brush										
0480	Metal, 1-2 lite	1 Pord	520	.015	S.F.		.40		.40	.61	
0490	Metal, 3-6 lite		440	.018			.47		.47	.72	
0500	Metal, Bay / Bow	↓	520	.015	↓		.40		.40	.61	
0600	Walls, sanding, light=10-30%										
0610	Med.=30-70%, heavy=70-100%, % of surface to sand										
0650	Walls, sand										
0660	Drywall, gypsum, plaster, light	1 Pord	3,077	.003	S.F.		.07		.07	.10	
0670	Drywall, gypsum, plaster, med.		2,160	.004			.10		.10	.15	
0680	Drywall, gypsum, plaster, heavy		923	.009			.23		.23	.34	
0690	Wood, T&G, light		2,400	.003			.09		.09	.13	
0700	Wood, T&G, med.		1,600	.005			.13		.13	.20	
0710	Wood, T&G, heavy	↓	800	.010	↓		.26		.26	.40	
0720	Walls, wash										
0730	Drywall, gypsum, plaster	1 Pord	3,200	.002	S.F.		.07		.07	.10	
0740	Wood, T&G		3,200	.002			.07		.07	.10	
0750	Masonry, brick & block, smooth		2,800	.003			.07		.07	.11	
0760	Masonry, brick & block, coarse	↓	2,000	.004	↓		.10		.10	.16	
8000	For Chemical Washing, see Division 04930-900										
8010	For Steam Cleaning, see Division 04930-750										
8020	For Sand Blasting, see Division 04930-700										

FINISHES 9

For information about Means Estimating Seminars, see yellow pages 11 and 12 in back of book

For expanded coverage of these items see Means Interior Cost Data 2001

Division Notes

		CREW	DAILY OUTPUT	LABOR-HOURS	UNIT	2001 BARE COSTS				TOTAL INCL O&P
						MAT.	LABOR	EQUIP.	TOTAL	

Division 10
Specialties

Estimating Tips
General
- The items in this division are usually priced per square foot or each.
- Many items in Division 10 require some type of support system that is not usually furnished with the item. Examples of these systems include blocking for the attachment of grab bars and support angles for ceiling hung toilet partitions. The required blocking or supports must be added to the estimate in the appropriate division.
- Some items in Division 10, such as lockers, may require assembly before installation. Verify the amount of assembly required. Assembly can often exceed installation time.

10100 Visual Display Boards
- Toilet partitions are priced by the stall. A stall consists of a side wall, pilaster and door with hardware. Toilet tissue holders and grab bars are extra.

10600 Partitions
- The required acoustical rating of a folding partition can have a significant impact on costs. Verify the sound transmission coefficient rating of the panel priced to the specification requirements.

Reference Numbers
Reference numbers are shown in bold squares at the beginning of some major classifications. These numbers refer to related items in the Reference Section. The reference information may be an estimating procedure, an alternate pricing method or technical information.

Note: Not all subdivisions listed here necessarily appear in this publication.

10110	Chalkboards	CREW	DAILY OUTPUT	LABOR-HOURS	UNIT	2001 BARE COSTS				TOTAL INCL O&P
						MAT.	LABOR	EQUIP.	TOTAL	
0010	**CHALKBOARDS** Porcelain enamel steel									240
0100	Freestanding, reversible									
0120	Economy, wood frame, 4' x 6'									
0140	Chalkboard both sides				Ea.	294			294	325
0160	Chalkboard one side, cork other side				"	360			360	400
0200	Standard, lightweight satin finished aluminum, 4' x 6'									
0220	Chalkboard both sides				Ea.	294			294	325
0240	Chalkboard one side, cork other side				"	360			360	400
0300	Deluxe, heavy duty extruded aluminum, 4' x 6'									
0320	Chalkboard both sides				Ea.	1,050			1,050	1,150
0340	Chalkboard one side, cork other side				"	1,025			1,025	1,150
0400	Sliding chalkboards									
0450	Vertical, one sliding board with back panel, wall mounted									
0500	8' x 4'	2 Carp	8	2	Ea.	1,275	58.50		1,333.50	1,500
0520	8' x 8'		7.50	2.133		1,775	62		1,837	2,050
0540	8' x 12'	↓	7	2.286	↓	2,225	66.50		2,291.50	2,525
0600	Two sliding boards, with back panel									
0620	8' x 4'	2 Carp	8	2	Ea.	1,950	58.50		2,008.50	2,250
0640	8' x 8'		7.50	2.133		2,725	62		2,787	3,100
0660	8' x 12'	↓	7	2.286	↓	3,375	66.50		3,441.50	3,800
0700	Horizontal, two track									
0800	4' x 8', 2 sliding panels	2 Carp	8	2	Ea.	1,175	58.50		1,233.50	1,375
0820	4' x 12', 2 sliding panels		7.50	2.133		1,675	62		1,737	1,950
0840	4' x 16', 4 sliding panels	↓	7	2.286	↓	2,250	66.50		2,316.50	2,575
0900	Four track, four sliding panels									
0920	4' x 8'	2 Carp	8	2	Ea.	1,875	58.50		1,933.50	2,150
0940	4' x 12'		7.50	2.133		2,725	62		2,787	3,100
0960	4' x 16'	↓	7	2.286	↓	3,425	66.50		3,491.50	3,875
1200	Vertical, motor operated									
1400	One sliding panel with back panel									
1450	10' x 4'	2 Carp	4	4	Ea.	4,975	117		5,092	5,650
1500	10' x 10'		3.75	4.267		5,750	124		5,874	6,525
1550	10' x 16'	↓	3.50	4.571	↓	6,525	133		6,658	7,400
1700	Two sliding panels with back panel									
1750	10' x 4'	2 Carp	4	4	Ea.	8,050	117		8,167	9,025
1800	10' x 10'		3.75	4.267		9,100	124		9,224	10,200
1850	10' x 16'	↓	3.50	4.571	↓	10,200	133		10,333	11,400
2000	Three sliding panels with back panel									
2100	10' x 4'	2 Carp	4	4	Ea.	10,600	117		10,717	11,900
2150	10' x 10'		3.75	4.267		12,300	124		12,424	13,700
2200	10' x 16'	↓	3.50	4.571	↓	13,800	133		13,933	15,400
2400	For projection screen, glass beaded, add				S.F.	4.50			4.50	4.95
2500	For remote control, 1 panel control, add				Ea.	405			405	445
2600	2 panel control, add				"	705			705	775
2800	For units without back panels, deduct				S.F.	4.91			4.91	5.40
2850	For liquid chalk porcelain panels, add				"	3.64			3.64	4
3000	Swing leaf, any comb. of chalkboard & cork, aluminum frame									
3100	Floor style, 5 panels									
3150	30" x 40" panels				Ea.	1,250			1,250	1,375
3200	48" x 40" panels				"	1,450			1,450	1,575
3300	Wall mounted, 5 panels									
3400	30" x 40" panels	2 Carp	16	1	Ea.	1,250	29		1,279	1,425
3450	48" x 40" panels	"	16	1	"	1,450	29		1,479	1,625
3600	Extra panels for swing leaf units									
3700	30" x 40" panels				Ea.	206			206	226
3750	48" x 40" panels				"	243			243	267

Important: See the Reference Section for critical supporting data - Reference Nos., Crews, & City Cost Indexes

10 SPECIALTIES

10110 | Chalkboards

			CREW	DAILY OUTPUT	LABOR-HOURS	UNIT	MAT.	LABOR	EQUIP.	TOTAL	TOTAL INCL O&P	
240	3900	Wall hung										**240**
	4000	Aluminum frame and chalktrough										
	4200	3' x 4'	2 Carp	16	1	Ea.	141	29		170	201	
	4300	3' x 5'		15	1.067		191	31		222	259	
	4500	4' x 8'		14	1.143		257	33.50		290.50	335	
	4600	4' x 12'		13	1.231		350	36		386	440	
	4700	Wood frame and chalktrough										
	4800	3' x 4'	2 Carp	16	1	Ea.	134	29		163	193	
	5000	3' x 5'		15	1.067		189	31		220	256	
	5100	4' x 5'		14	1.143		195	33.50		228.50	267	
	5300	4' x 8'		13	1.231		233	36		269	310	
	5400	Liquid chalk, white porcelain enamel, wall hung										
	5420	Deluxe units, aluminum trim and chalktrough										
	5450	4' x 4'	2 Carp	16	1	Ea.	176	29		205	240	
	5500	4' x 8'		14	1.143		310	33.50		343.50	390	
	5550	4' x 12'		12	1.333		465	39		504	570	
	5700	Wood trim and chalktrough										
	5900	4' x 4'	2 Carp	16	1	Ea.	375	29		404	460	
	6000	4' x 6'		15	1.067		455	31		486	550	
	6200	4' x 8'		14	1.143		535	33.50		568.50	635	
	6300	Liquid chalk, felt tip markers					1.34			1.34	1.47	
	6500	Erasers					1.37			1.37	1.51	
	6600	Board cleaner, 8 oz. bottle					4.18			4.18	4.60	

10120 | Tack & Visual Aid Boards

			CREW	DAILY OUTPUT	LABOR-HOURS	UNIT	MAT.	LABOR	EQUIP.	TOTAL	TOTAL INCL O&P	
350	0010	**CONTROL BOARDS** Magnetic, porcelain finish, 18" x 24", framed	2 Carp	8	2	Ea.	145	58.50		203.50	251	**350**
	0100	24" x 36"		7.50	2.133		236	62		298	360	
	0200	36" x 48"		7	2.286		440	66.50		506.50	590	
	0300	48" x 72"		6	2.667		670	77.50		747.50	855	
	0400	48" x 96"		5	3.200		785	93.50		878.50	1,000	
940	0010	**BULLETIN BOARD** Cork sheets, unbacked, no frame, 1/4" thick	2 Carp	290	.055	S.F.	5.85	1.61		7.46	8.90	**940**
	0100	1/2" thick		290	.055		2.52	1.61		4.13	5.30	
	0300	Fabric-face, no frame, on 7/32" cork underlay		290	.055		4.50	1.61		6.11	7.45	
	0400	On 1/4" cork on 1/4" hardboard		290	.055		5.65	1.61		7.26	8.75	
	0600	With edges wrapped		290	.055		6	1.61		7.61	9.10	
	0700	On 7/16" fire retardant core		290	.055		4.20	1.61		5.81	7.15	
	0900	With edges wrapped		290	.055		4.51	1.61		6.12	7.50	
	1000	Designer fabric only, cut to size					1.87			1.87	2.06	
	1200	1/4" vinyl cork, on 1/4" hardboard, no frame	2 Carp	290	.055		6.15	1.61		7.76	9.25	
	1300	On 1/4" coreboard		290	.055		6	1.61		7.61	9.10	
	2000	For map and display rail, economy, add		385	.042	L.F.	1.48	1.21		2.69	3.53	
	2100	Deluxe, add		350	.046	"	2.81	1.33		4.14	5.15	
	2120	Prefabricated, 1/4" cork, 3' x 5' with aluminum frame		16	1	Ea.	106	29		135	162	
	2140	Wood frame		16	1		129	29		158	188	
	2160	4' x 4' with aluminum frame		16	1		121	29		150	179	
	2180	Wood frame		16	1		203	29		232	269	
	2200	4' x 8' with aluminum frame		14	1.143		210	33.50		243.50	283	
	2210	With wood frame		14	1.143		177	33.50		210.50	247	
	2220	4' x 12' with aluminum frame		12	1.333		290	39		329	380	
	2230	Bulletin board case, single glass door, with lock										
	2240	36" x 24", economy	2 Carp	12	1.333	Ea.	179	39		218	258	
	2250	Deluxe		12	1.333		385	39		424	485	
	2260	42" x 30", economy		12	1.333		282	39		321	370	
	2270	Deluxe		12	1.333		390	39		429	490	

SPECIALTIES 10

10120 | Tack & Visual Aid Boards

		CREW	DAILY OUTPUT	LABOR-HOURS	UNIT	2001 BARE COSTS MAT.	LABOR	EQUIP.	TOTAL	TOTAL INCL O&P
940										**940**
2300	Glass enclosed cabinets, alum., cork panel, hinged doors									
2400	3' x 3', 1 door	2 Carp	12	1.333	Ea.	430	39		469	535
2500	4' x 4', 2 door		11	1.455		715	42.50		757.50	855
2600	4' x 7', 3 door		10	1.600		1,175	46.50		1,221.50	1,375
2800	4' x 10', 4 door		8	2		1,475	58.50		1,533.50	1,700
2900	For lights, add per door opening	1 Elec	13	.615		148	21		169	194
3100	Horizontal sliding units, 4 doors, 4' x 8' 8' x 4'	2 Carp	9	1.778		1,675	52		1,727	1,900
3200	4' x 12'		7	2.286		2,050	66.50		2,116.50	2,375
3400	8 doors, 4' x 16'		5	3.200		3,325	93.50		3,418.50	3,800
3500	4' x 24'		4	4		4,125	117		4,242	4,700

10 SPECIALTIES

10155 | Toilet Compartments

		CREW	DAILY OUTPUT	LABOR-HOURS	UNIT	2001 BARE COSTS MAT.	LABOR	EQUIP.	TOTAL	TOTAL INCL O&P
100										**100**
0010	**PARTITIONS, TOILET**									
0100	Cubicles, ceiling hung, marble	2 Marb	2	8	Ea.	1,325	234		1,559	1,800
0200	Painted metal	2 Carp	4	4		365	117		482	580
0250	Phenolic		4	4		730	117		847	980
0300	Plastic laminate on particle board		4	4		500	117		617	725
0500	Stainless steel		4	4		995	117		1,112	1,275
0600	For handicap units, incl. 52" grab bars, add					293			293	320
0800	Floor & ceiling anchored, marble	2 Marb	2.50	6.400		1,450	187		1,637	1,875
1000	Painted metal	2 Carp	5	3.200		365	93.50		458.50	550
1050	Phenolic		5	3.200		810	93.50		903.50	1,025
1100	Plastic laminate on particle board		5	3.200		470	93.50		563.50	660
1300	Stainless steel		5	3.200		1,150	93.50		1,243.50	1,425
1400	For handicap units, incl. 52" grab bars, add					253			253	278
1600	Floor mounted, marble	2 Marb	3	5.333		850	156		1,006	1,175
1700	Painted metal	2 Carp	7	2.286		340	66.50		406.50	480
1750	Phenolic		7	2.286		730	66.50		796.50	905
1800	Plastic laminate on particle board		7	2.286		465	66.50		531.50	615
2000	Stainless steel		7	2.286		1,175	66.50		1,241.50	1,400
2100	For handicap units, incl. 52" grab bars, add					253			253	278
2200	For juvenile units, deduct					35			35	38.50
2400	Floor mounted, headrail braced, marble	2 Marb	3	5.333		820	156		976	1,150
2500	Painted metal	2 Carp	6	2.667		365	77.50		442.50	525
2550	Phenolic		6	2.667		785	77.50		862.50	980
2600	Plastic laminate on particle board **CN**		6	2.667		630	77.50		707.50	815
2800	Stainless steel		6	2.667		1,150	77.50		1,227.50	1,375
2900	For handicap units, incl. 52" grab bars, add					253			253	278
3000	Wall hung partitions, painted metal	2 Carp	7	2.286		465	66.50		531.50	615
3300	Stainless steel	"	7	2.286		1,125	66.50		1,191.50	1,325
3400	For handicap units, incl. 52" grab bars, add					253			253	278
4000	Screens, entrance, floor mounted, 58" high, 48" wide									
4100	Marble	2 Marb	9	1.778	Ea.	535	52		587	665
4200	Painted metal	2 Carp	15	1.067		166	31		197	231
4300	Plastic laminate on particle board		15	1.067		294	31		325	375
4500	Stainless steel		15	1.067		610	31		641	720
4600	Urinal screen, 18" wide, ceiling braced, marble	D-1	6	2.667		540	70		610	705
4700	Painted metal	2 Carp	8	2		126	58.50		184.50	230

10155 | Toilet Compartments

		CREW	DAILY OUTPUT	LABOR-HOURS	UNIT	MAT.	LABOR	EQUIP.	TOTAL	TOTAL INCL O&P	
100	4800	Plastic laminate on particle board	2 Carp	8	2	Ea.	252	58.50		310.50	370	100
	5000	Stainless steel	↓	8	2	↓	435	58.50		493.50	570	
	5100	Floor mounted, head rail braced										
	5200	Marble	D-1	6	2.667	Ea.	475	70		545	630	
	5300	Painted metal	2 Carp	8	2		168	58.50		226.50	276	
	5400	Plastic laminate on particle board		8	2		211	58.50		269.50	325	
	5600	Stainless steel	↓	8	2		485	58.50		543.50	620	
	5700	Pilaster, flush, marble	D-1	9	1.778		605	46.50		651.50	735	
	5800	Painted metal	2 Carp	10	1.600		219	46.50		265.50	315	
	5900	Plastic laminate on particle board		10	1.600		288	46.50		334.50	390	
	6100	Stainless steel	↓	10	1.600		385	46.50		431.50	495	
	6200	Post braced, marble	D-1	9	1.778		595	46.50		641.50	725	
	6300	Painted metal	2 Carp	10	1.600		229	46.50		275.50	325	
	6400	Plastic laminate on particle board		10	1.600		288	46.50		334.50	390	
	6600	Stainless steel	↓	10	1.600	↓	380	46.50		426.50	495	
	6700	Wall hung, bracket supported										
	6800	Painted metal	2 Carp	10	1.600	Ea.	231	46.50		277.50	325	
	6900	Plastic laminate on particle board		10	1.600		113	46.50		159.50	197	
	7100	Stainless steel		10	1.600		350	46.50		396.50	460	
	7400	Flange supported, painted metal		10	1.600		170	46.50		216.50	260	
	7500	Plastic laminate on particle board		10	1.600		232	46.50		278.50	330	
	7700	Stainless steel		10	1.600		405	46.50		451.50	520	
	7800	Wedge type, painted metal		10	1.600		201	46.50		247.50	294	
	8100	Stainless steel	↓	10	1.600	↓	415	46.50		461.50	530	

10185 | Shower/Dressing Compartments

		CREW	DAILY OUTPUT	LABOR-HOURS	UNIT	MAT.	LABOR	EQUIP.	TOTAL	TOTAL INCL O&P	
100	0010	**PARTITIONS, SHOWER** Floor mounted, no plumbing										100
	0100	Cabinet, incl. base, no door, painted steel, 1" thick walls	2 Shee	5	3.200	Ea.	625	107		732	850	
	0300	With door, fiberglass		4.50	3.556		510	119		629	745	
	0600	Galvanized and painted steel, 1" thick walls		5	3.200		665	107		772	895	
	0800	Stall, 1" thick wall, no base, enameled steel		5	3.200		635	107		742	865	
	1200	Stainless steel	↓	5	3.200		1,125	107		1,232	1,400	
	1400	For double entry type, no doors, deduct					10%					
	1500	Circular fiberglass, cabinet 36" diameter,	2 Shee	4	4		525	134		659	780	
	1700	One piece, 36" diameter, less door		4	4		450	134		584	700	
	1800	With door		3.50	4.571		725	153		878	1,025	
	2000	Curved shell shower, no door needed	↓	3	5.333		665	179		844	1,000	
	2300	For fiberglass seat, add to both above					94			94	103	
	2400	Glass stalls, with doors, no receptors, chrome on brass	2 Shee	3	5.333		1,075	179		1,254	1,475	
	2700	Anodized aluminum	"	4	4		750	134		884	1,025	
	2900	Marble shower stall, stock design, with shower door	2 Marb	1.20	13.333		1,675	390		2,065	2,425	
	3000	With curtain		1.30	12.308		1,475	360		1,835	2,175	
	3200	Receptors, precast terrazzo, 32" x 32"		14	1.143		272	33.50		305.50	350	
	3300	48" x 34"		9.50	1.684		400	49		449	515	
	3500	Plastic, simulated terrazzo receptor, 32" x 32"		14	1.143		89	33.50		122.50	150	
	3600	32" x 48"		12	1.333		128	39		167	201	
	3800	Precast concrete, colors, 32" x 32"		14	1.143		158	33.50		191.50	226	
	3900	48" x 48"	↓	8	2		194	58.50		252.50	305	
	4100	Shower doors, economy plastic, 24" wide	1 Shee	9	.889		94	30		124	149	
	4200	Tempered glass door, economy		8	1		181	33.50		214.50	251	
	4400	Folding, tempered glass, aluminum frame		6	1.333		298	44.50		342.50	400	
	4500	Sliding, tempered glass, 48" opening		6	1.333		188	44.50		232.50	275	
	4700	Deluxe, tempered glass, chrome on brass frame, minimum		8	1		229	33.50		262.50	305	
	4800	Maximum		1	8		615	268		883	1,100	
	4850	On anodized aluminum frame, minimum		2	4		107	134		241	325	
	4900	Maximum	↓	1	8	↓	360	268		628	815	

SPECIALTIES 10

	10185	Shower/Dressing Compartments	CREW	DAILY OUTPUT	LABOR-HOURS	UNIT	2001 BARE COSTS				TOTAL INCL O&P	
							MAT.	LABOR	EQUIP.	TOTAL		
100	5100	Shower enclosure, tempered glass, anodized alum. frame										100
	5120	2 panel & door, corner unit, 32" x 32"	1 Shee	2	4	Ea.	360	134		494	605	
	5140	Neo-angle corner unit, 16" x 24" x 16"	"	2	4		665	134		799	935	
	5200	Shower surround, 3 wall, polypropylene, 32" x 32"	1 Carp	4	2		233	58.50		291.50	345	
	5220	PVC, 32" x 32"		4	2		235	58.50		293.50	350	
	5240	Fiberglass		4	2		277	58.50		335.50	395	
	5250	2 wall, polypropylene, 32" x 32"		4	2		194	58.50		252.50	305	
	5270	PVC		4	2		235	58.50		293.50	350	
	5290	Fiberglass	↓	4	2		261	58.50		319.50	380	
	5300	Tub doors, tempered glass & frame, minimum	1 Shee	8	1		154	33.50		187.50	222	
	5400	Maximum		6	1.333		355	44.50		399.50	460	
	5600	Chrome plated, brass frame, minimum		8	1		201	33.50		234.50	273	
	5700	Maximum		6	1.333		400	44.50		444.50	510	
	5900	Tub/shower enclosure, temp. glass, alum. frame, minimum		2	4		275	134		409	505	
	6200	Maximum		1.50	5.333		535	179		714	865	
	6500	On chrome-plated brass frame, minimum		2	4		380	134		514	625	
	6600	Maximum	↓	1.50	5.333		785	179		964	1,150	
	6800	Tub surround, 3 wall, polypropylene	1 Carp	4	2		154	58.50		212.50	261	
	6900	PVC		4	2		235	58.50		293.50	350	
	7000	Fiberglass, minimum		4	2		261	58.50		319.50	380	
	7100	Maximum	↓	3	2.667	↓	450	77.50		527.50	615	

10190 | Cubicles

			CREW	DAILY OUTPUT	LABOR-HOURS	UNIT	MAT.	LABOR	EQUIP.	TOTAL	TOTAL INCL O&P	
200	0010	**PARTITIONS, HOSPITAL** Curtain track, box channel, ceiling mounted	1 Carp	135	.059	L.F.	4.20	1.73		5.93	7.30	200
	0100	Suspended	"	100	.080	"	5.60	2.33		7.93	9.80	
	0300	Curtains, nylon mesh tops, fire resistant, 11 oz. per lineal yard										
	0310	Polyester oxford cloth, 9' ceiling height	1 Carp	425	.019	L.F.	9.10	.55		9.65	10.85	
	0500	8' ceiling height		425	.019		7.70	.55		8.25	9.30	
	0700	Designer oxford cloth	↓	425	.019	↓	19.50	.55		20.05	22.50	
	0800	I.V. track systems										
	0820	I.V. track, oval	1 Carp	135	.059	L.F.	4	1.73		5.73	7.10	
	0830	I.V. trolley		32	.250	Ea.	27.50	7.30		34.80	42	
	0840	I.V. pendent, (tree, 5 hook)	↓	32	.250	"	98	7.30		105.30	119	

	10210	Wall Louvers	CREW	DAILY OUTPUT	LABOR-HOURS	UNIT	2001 BARE COSTS				TOTAL INCL O&P	
							MAT.	LABOR	EQUIP.	TOTAL		
800	0010	**LOUVERS** Aluminum with screen, residential, 8" x 8"	1 Carp	38	.211	Ea.	6.85	6.15		13	17.15	800
	0100	12" x 12"		38	.211		8.20	6.15		14.35	18.60	
	0200	12" x 18"		35	.229		12	6.65		18.65	23.50	
	0250	14" x 24"		30	.267		15.50	7.75		23.25	29	
	0300	18" x 24"		27	.296		18	8.65		26.65	33.50	
	0500	24" x 30"		24	.333		25	9.70		34.70	42.50	
	0700	Triangle, adjustable, small		20	.400	↓	22	11.65		33.65	42.50	
	0800	Large	↓	15	.533		39.50	15.55		55.05	68	
	1200	Extruded aluminum, see division 15850-600										
	2100	Midget, aluminum, 3/4" deep, 1" diameter	1 Carp	85	.094	Ea.	.63	2.74		3.37	4.98	
	2150	3" diameter		60	.133		1.32	3.89		5.21	7.55	
	2200	4" diameter	↓	50	.160	↓	1.89	4.66		6.55	9.40	

10 SPECIALTIES

Important: See the Reference Section for critical supporting data - Reference Nos., Crews, & City Cost Indexes

10200 | Louvers & Vents

10210 | Wall Louvers

			CREW	DAILY OUTPUT	LABOR-HOURS	UNIT	2001 BARE COSTS MAT.	LABOR	EQUIP.	TOTAL	TOTAL INCL O&P	
800	2250	6" diameter	1 Carp	30	.267	Ea.	2.25	7.75		10	14.65	800
	2300	Ridge vent strip, mill finish	1 Shee	155	.052	L.F.	2.14	1.73		3.87	5	
	2330	Soffit vent, continuous, 3" wide, aluminum, mill finish	1 Carp	200	.040	↓	.43	1.17		1.60	2.29	
	2340	Baked enamel finish		200	.040		.46	1.17		1.63	2.33	
	2400	Under eaves vent, aluminum, mill finish, 16" x 4"		48	.167	Ea.	1.24	4.86		6.10	8.95	
	2500	16" x 8"		48	.167		1.69	4.86		6.55	9.45	
	7000	Vinyl gable vent, 8" x 8"		38	.211		8.95	6.15		15.10	19.45	
	7020	12" x 12"		38	.211		17	6.15		23.15	28.50	
	7080	12" x 18"		35	.229		22	6.65		28.65	34.50	
	7200	18" x 24"	↓	30	.267	↓	26	7.75		33.75	40.50	

10260 | Wall & Corner Guards

10265 | Wall & Corner Guards

			CREW	DAILY OUTPUT	LABOR-HOURS	UNIT	2001 BARE COSTS MAT.	LABOR	EQUIP.	TOTAL	TOTAL INCL O&P	
200	0010	**CORNER GUARDS** Steel angle w/anchors, 1" x 1" x 1/4", 1.5#/L.F.	2 Carp	160	.100	L.F.	3.55	2.92		6.47	8.45	200
	0100	2" x 2" x 1/4" angles, 3.2#/L.F.		150	.107		6.50	3.11		9.61	12	
	0200	3" x 3" x 5/16" angles, 6.1#/L.F.		140	.114		10.50	3.33		13.83	16.75	
	0300	4" x 4" x 5/16" angles, 8.2#/L.F.	↓	120	.133		14	3.89		17.89	21.50	
	0350	For angles drilled and anchored to masonry, add					15%	120%				
	0370	Drilled and anchored to concrete, add				↓	20%	170%				
	0400	For galvanized angles, add					35%					
	0450	For stainless steel angles, add				L.F.	100%					
	0500	Steel door track/wheel guards, 4'-0" high	E-4	22	1.455	Ea.	118	48.50	3.83	170.33	222	
	0800	Pipe bumper for truck doors, 8' long, 6" diameter, filled	↓	20	1.600	↓	188	53.50	4.21	245.71	310	
	0900	8" diameter	↓	20	1.600	↓	289	53.50	4.21	346.71	420	
250	0010	**CORNER PROTECTION**										250
	0100	Stainless steel, 16 ga., adhesive mount, 3-1/2" leg	1 Sswk	80	.100	L.F.	13.75	3.29		17.04	21	
	0200	12 ga. stainless, adhesive mount	"	80	.100		24.50	3.29		27.79	33	
	0300	For screw mount, add						10%				
	0500	Vinyl acrylic, adhesive mount, 3" leg	1 Carp	128	.063		4.92	1.82		6.74	8.25	
	0550	1-1/2" leg		160	.050		3.80	1.46		5.26	6.45	
	0600	Screw mounted, 3" leg		80	.100		5.90	2.92		8.82	11	
	0650	1-1/2" leg		100	.080		3.93	2.33		6.26	7.95	
	0700	Clear plastic, screw mounted, 2-1/2"		60	.133		2.70	3.89		6.59	9.05	
	1000	Vinyl cover, alum. retainer, surface mount, 3" x 3"		48	.167		6.15	4.86		11.01	14.35	
	1050	2" x 2"		48	.167		4.45	4.86		9.31	12.50	
	1100	Flush mounted, 3" x 3"		32	.250		12.35	7.30		19.65	25	
	1150	2" x 2"	↓	32	.250	↓	9.10	7.30		16.40	21.50	
500	0010	**WALLGUARD**										500
	0400	Rub rail, vinyl, adhesive mounted	1 Carp	185	.043	L.F.	3.60	1.26		4.86	5.95	
	0500	Neoprene, aluminum backing, 1-1/2" x 2"		110	.073		6.15	2.12		8.27	10.05	
	1000	Trolley rail, PVC, clipped to wall, 5" high		185	.043		5.65	1.26		6.91	8.15	
	1050	8" high		180	.044	↓	7.10	1.30		8.40	9.85	
	1200	Bed bumper, vinyl acrylic, alum. retainer, 21" long		10	.800	Ea.	33.50	23.50		57	73.50	
	1300	53" long with aligner		9	.889	"	100	26		126	151	
	1400	Bumper, vinyl cover, alum. retain., cush. mnt., 1-1/2" x 2-3/4"		80	.100	L.F.	10.10	2.92		13.02	15.65	
	1500	2" x 4-1/4"		80	.100		13.50	2.92		16.42	19.40	
	1600	Surface mounted, 1-3/4" x 3-5/8"	↓	80	.100	↓	9.10	2.92		12.02	14.55	

SPECIALTIES 10

10260 | Wall & Corner Guards

10265	Wall & Corner Guards	CREW	DAILY OUTPUT	LABOR-HOURS	UNIT	2001 BARE COSTS				TOTAL INCL O&P
						MAT.	LABOR	EQUIP.	TOTAL	
500										**500**
2000	Crash rail, vinyl cover, alum. retainer, 1" x 4"	1 Carp	110	.073	L.F.	10	2.12		12.12	14.30
2100	1" x 8"		90	.089		12.50	2.59		15.09	17.80
2150	Vinyl inserts, aluminum plate, 1" x 2-1/2"		110	.073		10.05	2.12		12.17	14.40
2200	1" x 5"		90	.089		14.50	2.59		17.09	20
3000	Handrail/bumper, vinyl cover, alum. retainer									
3010	Bracket mounted, flat rail, 5-1/2"	1 Carp	80	.100	L.F.	12.70	2.92		15.62	18.50
3100	6-1/2"		80	.100		19.05	2.92		21.97	25.50
3200	Bronze bracket, 1-3/4" diam. rail		80	.100		15.50	2.92		18.42	21.50

10270 | Access Flooring

10275	Access Flooring	CREW	DAILY OUTPUT	LABOR-HOURS	UNIT	2001 BARE COSTS				TOTAL INCL O&P
						MAT.	LABOR	EQUIP.	TOTAL	
150										**150**
0010	**PEDESTAL ACCESS FLOORS** Computer room application, metal									
0020	Particle board or steel panels, no covering, under 6,000 S.F.	2 Carp	400	.040	S.F.	6.25	1.17		7.42	8.70
0300	Metal covered, over 6,000 S.F.		450	.036		6.20	1.04		7.24	8.40
0400	Aluminum, 24" panels		500	.032		21	.93		21.93	24.50
0600	For carpet covering, add					4.44			4.44	4.88
0700	For vinyl floor covering, add					4.30			4.30	4.73
0900	For high pressure laminate covering, add					3.01			3.01	3.31
0910	For snap on stringer system, add	2 Carp	1,000	.016		1.02	.47		1.49	1.85
0950	Office applications, to 8" high, steel panels,									
0960	no covering, over 6,000 S.F.	2 Carp	500	.032	S.F.	6.55	.93		7.48	8.70
1000	Machine cutouts after initial installation	1 Carp	10	.800	Ea.	33.50	23.50		57	73.50
1050	Pedestals, 6" to 12"	2 Carp	85	.188		6.35	5.50		11.85	15.55
1100	Air conditioning grilles, 4" x 12"	1 Carp	17	.471		42	13.70		55.70	67.50
1150	4" x 18"	"	14	.571		57.50	16.65		74.15	89
1200	Approach ramps, minimum	2 Carp	85	.188	S.F.	17.45	5.50		22.95	28
1300	Maximum	"	60	.267	"	26.50	7.75		34.25	41
1500	Handrail, 2 rail, aluminum	1 Carp	15	.533	L.F.	75	15.55		90.55	107

10300 | Fireplaces & Stoves

10305	Manufactured Fireplaces	CREW	DAILY OUTPUT	LABOR-HOURS	UNIT	2001 BARE COSTS				TOTAL INCL O&P
						MAT.	LABOR	EQUIP.	TOTAL	
100										**100**
0010	**FIREPLACE, PREFABRICATED** Free standing or wall hung									
0100	with hood & screen, minimum	1 Carp	1.30	6.154	Ea.	960	179		1,139	1,325
0150	Average		1	8		1,150	233		1,383	1,650
0200	Maximum		.90	8.889		2,775	259		3,034	3,450
0500	Chimney dbl. wall, all stainless, over 8'-6", 7" diam., add		33	.242	V.L.F.	46	7.05		53.05	62
0600	10" diameter, add		32	.250		46	7.30		53.30	62.50
0700	12" diameter, add		31	.258		60.50	7.50		68	78.50
0800	14" diameter, add		30	.267		76.50	7.75		84.25	96
1000	Simulated brick chimney top, 4' high, 16" x 16"		10	.800	Ea.	164	23.50		187.50	218
1100	24" x 24"		7	1.143	"	305	33.50		338.50	390

312   **Important: See the Reference Section for critical supporting data - Reference Nos., Crews, & City Cost Indexes**

10300 | Fireplaces & Stoves

10305 | Manufactured Fireplaces

			CREW	DAILY OUTPUT	LABOR-HOURS	UNIT	2001 BARE COSTS				TOTAL INCL O&P	
							MAT.	LABOR	EQUIP.	TOTAL		
100	1500	Simulated logs, gas fired, 40,000 BTU, 2' long, minimum	1 Carp	7	1.143	Set	420	33.50		453.50	510	100
	1600	Maximum		6	1.333		590	39		629	710	
	1700	Electric, 1,500 BTU, 1'-6" long, minimum		7	1.143		114	33.50		147.50	177	
	1800	11,500 BTU, maximum		6	1.333		246	39		285	330	
	2000	Fireplace, built-in, 36" hearth, radiant		1.30	6.154	Ea.	490	179		669	820	
	2100	Recirculating, small fan		1	8		705	233		938	1,150	
	2150	Large fan		.90	8.889		1,300	259		1,559	1,850	
	2200	42" hearth, radiant		1.20	6.667		630	194		824	995	
	2300	Recirculating, small fan		.90	8.889		825	259		1,084	1,300	
	2350	Large fan		.80	10		1,575	292		1,867	2,175	
	2400	48" hearth, radiant		1.10	7.273		1,175	212		1,387	1,625	
	2500	Recirculating, small fan		.80	10		1,450	292		1,742	2,050	
	2550	Large fan		.70	11.429		2,250	335		2,585	3,000	
	3000	See through, including doors		.80	10		1,850	292		2,142	2,500	
	3200	Corner (2 wall)		1	8		920	233		1,153	1,375	

10310 | Fireplace Specialties & Accessories

			CREW	DAILY OUTPUT	LABOR-HOURS	UNIT	MAT.	LABOR	EQUIP.	TOTAL	TOTAL INCL O&P	
100	0010	FIREPLACE ACCESSORIES Chimney screens, galv., 13" x 13" flue	1 Bric	8	1	Ea.	33.50	29.50		63	83	100
	0050	Galv., 24" x 24" flue		5	1.600		100	47.50		147.50	183	
	0200	Stainless steel, 13" x 13" flue		8	1		264	29.50		293.50	335	
	0250	20" x 20" flue		5	1.600		360	47.50		407.50	470	
	0400	Cleanout doors and frames, cast iron, 8" x 8"		12	.667		24	19.75		43.75	56.50	
	0450	12" x 12"		10	.800		33.50	23.50		57	73	
	0500	18" x 24"		8	1		105	29.50		134.50	161	
	0550	Cast iron frame, steel door, 24" x 30"		5	1.600		227	47.50		274.50	320	
	0800	Damper, rotary control, steel, 30" opening		6	1.333		64	39.50		103.50	131	
	0850	Cast iron, 30" opening		6	1.333		71	39.50		110.50	139	
	0880	36" opening		6	1.333		77	39.50		116.50	146	
	0900	48" opening		6	1.333		110	39.50		149.50	182	
	0920	60" opening		6	1.333		247	39.50		286.50	330	
	0950	72" opening		5	1.600		297	47.50		344.50	400	
	1000	84" opening, special order		5	1.600		635	47.50		682.50	775	
	1050	96" opening, special order		4	2		645	59		704	800	
	1200	Steel plate, poker control, 60" opening		8	1		225	29.50		254.50	294	
	1250	84" opening, special opening		5	1.600		410	47.50		457.50	525	
	1400	"Universal" type, chain operated, 32" x 20" opening		8	1		156	29.50		185.50	217	
	1450	48" x 24" opening		5	1.600		261	47.50		308.50	360	
	1600	Dutch Oven door and frame, cast iron, 12" x 15" opening		13	.615		92	18.20		110.20	129	
	1650	Copper plated, 12" x 15" opening		13	.615		177	18.20		195.20	222	
	1800	Fireplace forms, no accessories, 32" opening		3	2.667		480	79		559	650	
	1900	36" opening		2.50	3.200		580	94.50		674.50	785	
	2000	40" opening		2	4		700	118		818	955	
	2100	78" opening		1.50	5.333		1,000	158		1,158	1,350	
	2400	Squirrel and bird screens, galvanized, 8" x 8" flue		16	.500		36	14.80		50.80	63	
	2450	13" x 13" flue		12	.667		41.50	19.75		61.25	76	

10320 | Stoves

			CREW	DAILY OUTPUT	LABOR-HOURS	UNIT	MAT.	LABOR	EQUIP.	TOTAL	TOTAL INCL O&P	
100	0010	WOODBURNING STOVES Cast iron, minimum	2 Carp	1.30	12.308	Ea.	725	360		1,085	1,350	100
	0020	Average		1	16		1,150	465		1,615	2,000	
	0030	Maximum		.80	20		2,175	585		2,760	3,300	
	0050	For gas log lighter, add					36			36	39.50	

SPECIALTIES 10

313

			DAILY	LABOR-			2001 BARE COSTS			TOTAL	
	10342	**Cupolas**	CREW	OUTPUT	HOURS	UNIT	MAT.	LABOR	EQUIP.	TOTAL	INCL O&P
100	0010	**CUPOLA** Stock units, pine, painted, 18" sq., 28" high, alum. roof	1 Carp	4.10	1.951	Ea.	138	57		195	241	**100**
	0100	Copper roof		3.80	2.105		141	61.50		202.50	251
	0300	23" square, 33" high, aluminum roof		3.70	2.162		232	63		295	355
	0400	Copper roof		3.30	2.424		233	70.50		303.50	370
	0600	30" square, 37" high, aluminum roof		3.70	2.162		355	63		418	490
	0700	Copper roof		3.30	2.424		365	70.50		435.50	510
	0900	Hexagonal, 31" wide, 46" high, copper roof		4	2		530	58.50		588.50	670
	1000	36" wide, 50" high, copper roof		3.50	2.286		565	66.50		631.50	725
	1200	For deluxe stock units, add to above					25%				
	1400	For custom built units, add to above					50%	50%			

10 **SPECIALTIES**

			DAILY	LABOR-			2001 BARE COSTS			TOTAL	
	10355	**Flagpoles**	CREW	OUTPUT	HOURS	UNIT	MAT.	LABOR	EQUIP.	TOTAL	INCL O&P
400	0010	**FLAGPOLE**, Ground set										**400**
	0050	Not including base or foundation									
	0100	Aluminum, tapered, ground set 20' high	K-1	2	8	Ea.	595	210	92	897	1,075
	0200	25' high		1.70	9.412		710	247	108	1,065	1,275
	0300	30' high		1.50	10.667		745	280	123	1,148	1,400
	0400	35' high		1.40	11.429		1,175	300	132	1,607	1,900
	0500	40' high		1.20	13.333		1,800	350	153	2,303	2,675
	0600	50' high		1	16		2,175	420	184	2,779	3,225
	0700	60' high		.90	17.778		4,000	465	205	4,670	5,350
	0800	70' high		.80	20		6,525	525	230	7,280	8,250
	1100	Counterbalanced, internal halyard, 20' high		1.80	8.889		1,050	234	102	1,386	1,625
	1200	30' high		1.50	10.667		1,550	280	123	1,953	2,300
	1300	40' high		1.30	12.308		2,625	325	142	3,092	3,525
	1400	50' high		1	16		4,100	420	184	4,704	5,350
	2820	Aluminum, electronically operated, 30' high		1.40	11.429		3,450	300	132	3,882	4,375
	2840	35' high		1.30	12.308		3,525	325	142	3,992	4,525
	2860	39' high		1.10	14.545		3,850	380	167	4,397	5,000
	2880	45' high		1	16		4,925	420	184	5,529	6,250
	2900	50' high		.90	17.778		5,225	465	205	5,895	6,700
	3000	Fiberglass, tapered, ground set, 23' high		2	8		880	210	92	1,182	1,400
	3100	29"-7' high		1.50	10.667		1,175	280	123	1,578	1,875
	3200	36'-1" high		1.40	11.429		1,575	300	132	2,007	2,350
	3300	39'-5" high		1.20	13.333		2,050	350	153	2,553	2,950
	3400	49'-2" high		1	16		3,475	420	184	4,079	4,675
	3500	59' high		.90	17.778		5,775	465	205	6,445	7,300
	4300	Concrete, direct imbedded installation									
	4400	Internal halyard, 20' high	K-1	2.50	6.400	Ea.	1,175	168	73.50	1,416.50	1,625
	4500	25' high		2.50	6.400		1,300	168	73.50	1,541.50	1,775
	4600	30' high		2.30	6.957		1,525	183	80	1,788	2,075
	4700	40' high		2.10	7.619		2,275	200	87.50	2,562.50	2,900
	4800	50' high		1.90	8.421		3,375	221	97	3,693	4,150
	5000	60' high		1.80	8.889		5,100	234	102	5,436	6,075
	5100	70' high		1.60	10		6,225	263	115	6,603	7,375
	5200	80' high		1.40	11.429		8,200	300	132	8,632	9,625
	5300	90' high		1.20	13.333		11,200	350	153	11,703	13,000
	5500	100' high		1	16		11,600	420	184	12,204	13,700

10350 | Flagpoles

10355 | Flagpoles

		Description	CREW	DAILY OUTPUT	LABOR-HOURS	UNIT	2001 BARE COSTS				TOTAL INCL O&P	
							MAT.	LABOR	EQUIP.	TOTAL		
400	6400	Wood poles, tapered, clear vertical grain fir with tilting										**400**
	6410	base, not incl. foundation, 4" butt, 25' high	K-1	1.90	8.421	Ea.	500	221	97	818	995	
	6800	6" butt, 30' high	"	1.30	12.308	"	620	325	142	1,087	1,350	
	7300	Foundations for flagpoles, including										
	7400	excavation and concrete, to 35' high poles	C-1	10	3.200	Ea.	400	88		488	580	
	7600	40' to 50' high	↓	3.50	9.143	↓	730	252		982	1,200	
	7700	Over 60' high	▼	2	16	▼	815	440		1,255	1,575	
900	0010	**FLAGPOLE**, Structure mounted										**900**
	0100	Fiberglass, vertical wall set, 19'-8" long	K-1	1.50	10.667	Ea.	1,025	280	123	1,428	1,700	
	0200	23' long		1.40	11.429		1,000	300	132	1,432	1,700	
	0300	26'-3" long		1.30	12.308		1,475	325	142	1,942	2,250	
	0800	19'-8" long outrigger		1.30	12.308		1,125	325	142	1,592	1,900	
	1300	Aluminum, vertical wall set, tapered, with base, 20' high		1.20	13.333		795	350	153	1,298	1,575	
	1400	29'-6" high		1	16		2,000	420	184	2,604	3,050	
	2400	Outrigger poles with base, 12' long		1.30	12.308		1,125	325	142	1,592	1,900	
	2500	14' long	▼	1	16	▼	1,200	420	184	1,804	2,175	

10400 | Identification Devices

10410 | Directories

		Description	CREW	DAILY OUTPUT	LABOR-HOURS	UNIT	2001 BARE COSTS				TOTAL INCL O&P	
							MAT.	LABOR	EQUIP.	TOTAL		
100	0010	**DIRECTORY BOARDS**										**100**
	0050	Plastic, glass covered, 30" x 20"	2 Carp	3	5.333	Ea.	289	155		444	565	
	0100	36" x 48"		2	8		600	233		833	1,025	
	0300	Grooved cork, 30" x 20"		3	5.333		300	155		455	575	
	0400	36" x 48"		2	8		223	233		456	610	
	0600	Black felt, 30" x 20"		3	5.333		315	155		470	590	
	0700	36" x 48"		2	8		505	233		738	920	
	0900	Outdoor, weatherproof, black plastic, 36" x 24"		2	8		315	233		548	710	
	1000	36" x 36"		1.50	10.667		660	310		970	1,200	
	1800	Indoor, economy, open face, 18" x 24"		7	2.286		122	66.50		188.50	239	
	1900	24" x 36"		7	2.286		151	66.50		217.50	270	
	2000	36" x 24"		6	2.667		151	77.50		228.50	288	
	2100	36" x 48"		6	2.667		216	77.50		293.50	360	
	2400	Building directory, alum., black felt panels, 1 door, 24" x 18"		4	4		220	117		337	425	
	2500	36" x 24"		3.50	4.571		295	133		428	535	
	2600	48" x 32"		3	5.333		455	155		610	745	
	2700	36" x 48", 2 door		2.50	6.400		565	187		752	915	
	2800	36" x 60"		2	8		720	233		953	1,150	
	2900	48" x 60"	▼	1	16		790	465		1,255	1,600	
	3100	For bronze enamel finish, add					15%					
	3200	For bronze anodized finish, add					25%					
	3400	For illuminated directory, single door unit, add				↓	148			148	163	
	3500	For 6" header panel, 6 letters per foot, add				L.F.	24			24	26.50	

10430 | Exterior Signage

		Description	CREW	DAILY OUTPUT	LABOR-HOURS	UNIT	2001 BARE COSTS				TOTAL INCL O&P	
							MAT.	LABOR	EQUIP.	TOTAL		
200	0010	**SIGNS** Letters, 2" high, 3/8" deep, cast bronze	1 Carp	24	.333	Ea.	14.05	9.70		23.75	30.50	**200**
	0140	1/2" deep, cast aluminum	↓	18	.444	↓	14.05	12.95		27	36	

SPECIALTIES 10

315

			DAILY	LABOR-			2001 BARE COSTS			TOTAL	
10430		**Exterior Signage**	CREW	OUTPUT	HOURS	UNIT	MAT.	LABOR	EQUIP.	TOTAL	INCL O&P
200	0160	Cast bronze	1 Carp	32	.250	Ea.	23	7.30		30.30	36.50	**200**
	0300	6" high, 5/8" deep, cast aluminum		24	.333		16.50	9.70		26.20	33.50
	0400	Cast bronze		24	.333		35.50	9.70		45.20	54.50
	0600	8" high, 3/4" deep, cast aluminum		14	.571		29	16.65		45.65	57.50
	0700	Cast bronze		20	.400		62	11.65		73.65	86.50
	0900	10" high, 1" deep, cast aluminum		18	.444		29.50	12.95		42.45	53
	1000	Bronze		18	.444		80	12.95		92.95	109
	1200	12" high, 1-1/4" deep, cast aluminum		12	.667		36.50	19.45		55.95	71
	1500	Cast bronze		18	.444		105	12.95		117.95	137
	1600	14" high, 2-5/16" deep, cast aluminum		12	.667		60	19.45		79.45	96.50
	1800	Fabricated stainless steel, 6" high, 2" deep		20	.400		94	11.65		105.65	121
	1900	12" high, 3" deep		18	.444		111	12.95		123.95	144
	2100	18" high, 3" deep		12	.667		163	19.45		182.45	211
	2200	24" high, 4" deep		10	.800		228	23.50		251.50	288
	2700	Acrylic, on high density foam,		20	.400		18.70	11.65		30.35	39
	2800	12" high, 2" deep		18	.444		44	12.95		56.95	69
	3900	Plaques, custom, 20" x 30", for up to 450 letters, cast aluminum	2 Carp	4	4		775	117		892	1,025
	4000	Cast bronze		4	4		1,025	117		1,142	1,300
	4200	30" x 36", up to 900 letters cast aluminum		3	5.333		1,550	155		1,705	1,975
	4300	Cast bronze		3	5.333		2,000	155		2,155	2,450
	4500	36" x 48", for up to 1300 letters, cast bronze		2	8		3,050	233		3,283	3,725
	4800	Signs, reflective alum. street signs, dbl. face, 2-way, w/bracket		30	.533		65.50	15.55		81.05	96.50
	4900	4-way		30	.533		105	15.55		120.55	141
	5100	Exit signs, 24 ga. alum., 14" x 12" surface mounted	1 Carp	30	.267		11.85	7.75		19.60	25
	5200	10" x 7"		20	.400		9.65	11.65		21.30	29
	5400	Bracket mounted, double face, 12" x 10"		30	.267		33	7.75		40.75	48.50
	5500	Sticky back, stock decals, 14" x 10"	1 Clab	50	.160		4.70	3.66		8.36	10.85
	6000	Interior elec., wall mount, fiberglass panels, 2 lamps, 6"	1 Elec	8	1		53.50	34.50		88	110
	6100	8"	"	8	1		46	34.50		80.50	102
	6400	Replacement sign faces, 6" or 8"	1 Clab	50	.160		21	3.66		24.66	29

			DAILY	LABOR-			2001 BARE COSTS			TOTAL	
10455		**Turnstiles**	CREW	OUTPUT	HOURS	UNIT	MAT.	LABOR	EQUIP.	TOTAL	INCL O&P
900	0010	**TURNSTILES** One way, 4 arm, 46" diameter, economy, manual	2 Carp	5	3.200	Ea.	254	93.50		347.50	425	**900**
	0100	Electric		1.20	13.333		850	390		1,240	1,550
	0300	High security, galv., 5'-5" diameter, 7' high, manual		1	16		2,200	465		2,665	3,150
	0350	Electric		.60	26.667		2,875	775		3,650	4,375
	0420	Three arm, 24" opening, light duty, manual		2	8		820	233		1,053	1,275
	0450	Heavy duty		1.50	10.667		2,225	310		2,535	2,925
	0460	Manual, with registering & controls, light duty		2	8		1,775	233		2,008	2,325
	0470	Heavy duty		1.50	10.667		2,175	310		2,485	2,850
	0480	Electric, heavy duty		1.10	14.545		2,550	425		2,975	3,475
	0500	For coin or token operating, add					340			340	370
	1200	One way gate with horizontal bars, 5'-5" diameter									
	1300	7' high, recreation or transit type	2 Carp	.80	20	Ea.	2,875	585		3,460	4,050
	1500	For electronic counter, add				"	167			167	183

Important: See the Reference Section for critical supporting data - Reference Nos., Crews, & City Cost Indexes

10 SPECIALTIES

		10505 | Metal Lockers	CREW	DAILY OUTPUT	LABOR-HOURS	UNIT	2001 BARE COSTS MAT.	LABOR	EQUIP.	TOTAL	TOTAL INCL O&P	
500	0011	**LOCKERS** Steel, baked enamel										500
	0110	Single tier box locker, 12″ x 15″ x 72″ [R10505-050]	1 Shee	8	1	Ea.	130	33.50		163.50	195	
	0120	18″ x 15″ x 72″		8	1		157	33.50		190.50	225	
	0130	12″ x 18″ x 72″		8	1		137	33.50		170.50	203	
	0140	18″ x 18″ x 72″		8	1		163	33.50		196.50	231	
	0410	Double tier, 12″ x 15″ x 36″		21	.381		142	12.80		154.80	176	
	0420	18″ x 15″ x 36″		21	.381		123	12.80		135.80	155	
	0430	12″ x 18″ x 36″		21	.381		148	12.80		160.80	183	
	0440	18″ x 18″ x 36″		21	.381		116	12.80		128.80	147	
	0500	Two person, 18″ x 15″ x 72″		8	1		210	33.50		243.50	283	
	0510	18″ x 18″ x 72″		8	1		206	33.50		239.50	279	
	0520	Duplex, 15″ x 15″ x 72″		8	1		196	33.50		229.50	268	
	0530	15″ x 21″ x 72″		8	1	▼	264	33.50		297.50	340	
	0600	5 tier box lockers, minimum		30	.267	Opng.	24	8.95		32.95	40.50	
	0700	Maximum		24	.333		39	11.20		50.20	60.50	
	0900	6 tier box lockers, minimum		36	.222		24.50	7.45		31.95	38.50	
	1000	Maximum		30	.267	▼	29	8.95		37.95	46	
	1100	Wire meshed wardrobe, floor. mtd., open front varsity type		7.50	1.067	Ea.	134	36		170	203	
	2100	Locker bench, laminated maple, top only		100	.080	L.F.	12.65	2.68		15.33	18.05	
	2200	Pedestals, steel pipe	▼	25	.320	Ea.	38	10.75		48.75	58.50	
	2400	16-person locker unit with clothing rack										
	2500	72 wide x 15″ deep x 72″ high	1 Shee	8	1	Ea.	375	33.50		408.50	460	
	2550	18″ deep	″	8	1	″	360	33.50		393.50	445	
	3000	Wall mounted lockers, 4 person, with coat bar										
	3100	48″ wide x 18″ deep x 12″ high	1 Shee	8	1	Ea.	182	33.50		215.50	252	
	3250	Rack w/ 24 wire mesh baskets		1.50	5.333	Set	270	179		449	575	
	3260	30 baskets		1.25	6.400		232	215		447	585	
	3270	36 baskets		.95	8.421		325	283		608	795	
	3280	42 baskets	▼	.80	10	▼	365	335		700	925	
	3300	For built-in lock with 2 keys, add				Ea.	6.10			6.10	6.70	
	3600	For hanger rods, add	▼			″	1.65			1.65	1.82	

		10525 |Fire Prot. Specialties	CREW	DAILY OUTPUT	LABOR-HOURS	UNIT	2001 BARE COSTS MAT.	LABOR	EQUIP.	TOTAL	TOTAL INCL O&P	
200	0010	**FIRE EQUIPMENT CABINETS** Not equipped, 20 ga. steel box,										200
	0040	recessed, D.S. glass in door, box size given										
	1000	Portable extinguisher, single, 8″ x 12″ x 27″, alum. door & frame	Q-12	8	2	Ea.	74.50	62		136.50	176	
	1100	Steel door and frame	″	8	2	″	56	62		118	156	
	3000	Hose rack assy., 1-1/2″ valve & 100′ hose, 24″ x 40″ x 5-1/2″										
	3100	Aluminum door and frame	Q-12	6	2.667	Ea.	183	82.50		265.50	325	
	3200	Steel door and frame		6	2.667		121	82.50		203.50	258	
	3300	Stainless steel door and frame	▼	6	2.667	▼	238	82.50		320.50	385	
	4000	Hose rack assy., 2-1/2″ x 1-1/2″ valve, 100′ hose, 24″ x 40″ x 8″										
	4100	Aluminum door and frame	Q-12	6	2.667	Ea.	185	82.50		267.50	330	
	4200	Steel door and frame	▼	6	2.667	▼	125	82.50		207.50	262	
	4300	Stainless steel door and frame	▼	6	2.667	▼	240	82.50		322.50	390	
	5000	Hose rack assy., 2-1/2″ x 1-1/2″ valve, 100′ hose										
	5100	Aluminum door and frame	Q-12	5	3.200	Ea.	235	99		334	410	

		CREW	DAILY OUTPUT	LABOR-HOURS	UNIT	2001 BARE COSTS				TOTAL INCL O&P	
10525	**Fire Prot. Specialties**					MAT.	LABOR	EQUIP.	TOTAL		
200 5200	Steel door and frame	Q-12	5	3.200	Ea.	156	99		255	320	**200**
5300	Stainless steel door and frame	↓	5	3.200	↓	278	99		377	455	
8000	Valve cabinet for 2-1/2" FD angle valve, 18" x 18" x 8"										
8100	Aluminum door and frame	Q-12	12	1.333	Ea.	81.50	41.50		123	153	
8200	Steel door and frame	↓	12	1.333		61.50	41.50		103	130	
8300	Stainless steel door and frame	↓	12	1.333	↓	107	41.50		148.50	181	
300 0010	**FIRE EXTINGUISHERS**										**300**
0120	CO2, portable with swivel horn, 5 lb.				Ea.	101			101	111	
0140	With hose and "H" horn, 10 lb.					150			150	165	
0160	15 lb.					172			172	189	
0180	20 lb.					207			207	228	
0360	Wheeled type, cart mounted, 50 lb.				↓	1,200			1,200	1,325	
1000	Dry chemical, pressurized										
1040	Standard type, portable, painted, 2-1/2 lb.				Ea.	27.50			27.50	30.50	
1060	5 lb.					40			40	44	
1080	10 lb.					67			67	73.50	
1100	20 lb.					90			90	99	
1120	30 lb.					145			145	160	
1300	Standard type, wheeled, 150 lb.					1,400			1,400	1,550	
2000	ABC all purpose type, portable, 2-1/2 lb.					27.50			27.50	30.50	
2060	5 lb.					40			40	44	
2080	9-1/2 lb.					60			60	66	
2100	20 lb.					85			85	93.50	
2300	Wheeled, 45 lb.					650			650	715	
2360	150 lb.					1,450			1,450	1,600	
3000	Dry chemical, outside cartridge to -65°F, painted, 9 lb.					200			200	220	
3060	26 lb.					250			250	275	
5000	Pressurized water, 2-1/2 gallon, stainless steel					75			75	82.50	
5060	With anti-freeze					110			110	121	
6000	Soda & acid, 2-1/2 gallon, stainless steel					75			75	82.50	
9400	Installation of extinguishers, 12 or more, on wood	1 Carp	30	.267			7.75		7.75	12.15	
9420	On masonry or concrete	"	15	.533	↓		15.55		15.55	24.50	

		CREW	DAILY OUTPUT	LABOR-HOURS	UNIT	2001 BARE COSTS				TOTAL INCL O&P	
10535	**Awning & Canopies**					MAT.	LABOR	EQUIP.	TOTAL		
200 0010	**CANOPIES** Wall hung, .032", aluminum, prefinished, 8' x 10'	K-2	1.30	18.462	Ea.	1,375	560	142	2,077	2,650	**200**
0300	8' x 20'		1.10	21.818		2,750	665	168	3,583	4,350	
0500	10' x 10'		1.30	18.462		1,550	560	142	2,252	2,825	
0700	10' x 20'		1.10	21.818		2,875	665	168	3,708	4,475	
1000	12' x 20'		1	24		3,525	730	184	4,439	5,350	
1360	12' x 30'		.80	30		5,175	910	230	6,315	7,525	
1700	12' x 40'	↓	.60	40		5,525	1,225	305	7,055	8,550	
1900	For free standing units, add				↓	20%	10%				
2300	Aluminum entrance canopies, flat soffit, .032"										
2500	3'-6" x 4'-0", clear anodized	2 Carp	4	4	Ea.	580	117		697	815	
2700	Bronze anodized		4	4		1,025	117		1,142	1,300	
3000	Polyurethane painted		4	4		825	117		942	1,100	
3300	4'-6" x 10'-0", clear anodized		2	8		1,600	233		1,833	2,125	
3500	Bronze anodized	↓	2	8	↓	2,050	233		2,283	2,625	

Important: See the Reference Section for critical supporting data - Reference Nos., Crews, & City Cost Indexes

10535 | Awning & Canopies

			CREW	DAILY OUTPUT	LABOR-HOURS	UNIT	2001 BARE COSTS MAT.	LABOR	EQUIP.	TOTAL	TOTAL INCL O&P	
200	3700	Polyurethane painted	2 Carp	2	8	Ea.	1,700	233		1,933	2,250	200
	4000	Wall downspout, 10 L.F., clear anodized	1 Carp	7	1.143		99	33.50		132.50	161	
	4300	Bronze anodized		7	1.143		173	33.50		206.50	242	
	4500	Polyurethane painted	↓	7	1.143	↓	149	33.50		182.50	216	
	4710	Canvas awnings, including acrylic canvas and frame, standard design										
	4720	Door and window, slope, 3' high, 4' wide	1 Carp	4.50	1.778	Ea.	495	52		547	625	
	4730	6' wide		3.50	2.286		635	66.50		701.50	805	
	4740	8' wide		3	2.667		775	77.50		852.50	975	
	4810	Waterfall, 4' wide		3	2.667		765	77.50		842.50	965	
	4820	6' wide		2.25	3.556		995	104		1,099	1,250	
	4830	8' wide		1.80	4.444		1,225	130		1,355	1,550	
	4910	Dome, 4' wide		7.50	1.067		296	31		327	375	
	4920	6' wide		3.50	2.286		665	66.50		731.50	835	
	4930	8' wide	↓	2	4		1,175	117		1,292	1,475	
	5010	Entry or walkway, peak, 12' long, 4' wide	2 Carp	.90	17.778		3,500	520		4,020	4,650	
	5020	6' wide		.60	26.667		5,400	775		6,175	7,175	
	5030	8' wide		.40	40		7,450	1,175		8,625	10,000	
	5060	Radius with dome end, 4' wide		1.10	14.545		2,650	425		3,075	3,600	
	5070	6' wide		.70	22.857		4,275	665		4,940	5,750	
	5080	8' wide	↓	.50	32		6,075	935		7,010	8,125	
	5110	For fire retardant canvas, add					7%					
	5120	For lettering or graphics, add					35%					
	5130	For painted or coated acrylic canvas, deduct					8%					
	5140	For translucent or opaque vinyl canvas, add					10%					
	5150	For 6 or more units, deduct				↓	20%	15%				
	7000	Carport, baked vinyl finish, .032", 20' x 10', no foundations, min.	K-2	4	6	Car	2,475	182	46	2,703	3,100	
	7250	Maximum		2	12	"	5,900	365	92	6,357	7,225	
	7500	Walkway cover, to 12' wide, stl., vinyl finish, .032",no fndtns., min.		250	.096	S.F.	14.55	2.92	.74	18.21	22	
	7750	Maximum	↓	200	.120	"	15.80	3.64	.92	20.36	25	

10555 | Mail Delivery Systems

			CREW	DAILY OUTPUT	LABOR-HOURS	UNIT	2001 BARE COSTS MAT.	LABOR	EQUIP.	TOTAL	TOTAL INCL O&P	
600	0010	**MAIL BOXES** Horiz., key lock, 5"H x 6"W x 15"D, alum., rear load	1 Carp	34	.235	Ea.	30.50	6.85		37.35	44.50	600
	0100	Front loading		34	.235		34	6.85		40.85	48.50	
	0200	Double, 5"H x 12"W x 15"D, rear loading		26	.308		58	8.95		66.95	78	
	0300	Front loading		26	.308		61.50	8.95		70.45	82	
	0500	Quadruple, 10"H x 12"W x 15"D, rear loading		20	.400		108	11.65		119.65	137	
	0600	Front loading		20	.400		106	11.65		117.65	134	
	0800	Vertical, front load, 15"H x 5"W x 6"D, alum., per compartment		34	.235		23.50	6.85		30.35	36.50	
	0900	Bronze, duranodic finish		34	.235		43	6.85		49.85	58.50	
	1000	Steel, enameled		34	.235		26	6.85		32.85	39.50	
	1700	Alphabetical directories, 120 names		10	.800		108	23.50		131.50	156	
	1800	Letter collection box		6	1.333		575	39		614	695	
	1900	Letter slot, residential		20	.400		54.50	11.65		66.15	78.50	
	2000	Post office type		8	1		191	29		220	256	
	2200	Post office counter window, with grille		2	4		515	117		632	745	
	2250	Key keeper, single key, aluminum		26	.308		34.50	8.95		43.45	51.50	
	2300	Steel, enameled	↓	26	.308	↓	70	8.95		78.95	91	

SPECIALTIES 10

10550 | Postal Specialties

		10555	Mail Delivery Systems	CREW	DAILY OUTPUT	LABOR-HOURS	UNIT	2001 BARE COSTS				TOTAL INCL O&P	
								MAT.	LABOR	EQUIP.	TOTAL		
700	0010		**MAIL CHUTES** Aluminum & glass, 14-1/4" wide, 4-5/8" deep	2 Shee	4	4	Floor	650	134		784	920	700
	0100		8-5/8" deep		3.80	4.211		720	141		861	1,000	
	0300		8-3/4" x 3-1/2", aluminum		5	3.200		550	107		657	770	
	0400		Bronze or stainless		4.50	3.556		855	119		974	1,125	
	0600		Lobby collection boxes, aluminum		5	3.200	Ea.	1,750	107		1,857	2,100	
	0700		Bronze or stainless		4.50	3.556	"	2,150	119		2,269	2,550	

10600 | Partitions

		10605	Wire Mesh Partitions	CREW	DAILY OUTPUT	LABOR-HOURS	UNIT	2001 BARE COSTS				TOTAL INCL O&P	
								MAT.	LABOR	EQUIP.	TOTAL		
100	0010		**PARTITIONS, WOVEN WIRE** For tool or stockroom enclosures										100
	0100		Channel frame, 1-1/2" diamond mesh, 10 ga. wire, painted										
	0300		Wall panels, 4'-0" wide, 7' high	2 Carp	25	.640	Ea.	91.50	18.65		110.15	130	
	0400		8' high		23	.696		98	20.50		118.50	140	
	0600		10' high		18	.889		113	26		139	165	
	0700		For 5' wide panels, add					5%					
	0900		Ceiling panels, 10' long, 2' wide	2 Carp	25	.640		82.50	18.65		101.15	120	
	1000		4' wide		15	1.067		99	31		130	158	
	1200		Panel with service window & shelf, 5' wide, 7' high		20	.800		268	23.50		291.50	330	
	1300		8' high		15	1.067		281	31		312	360	
	1500		Sliding doors, full height, 3' wide, 7' high		6	2.667		258	77.50		335.50	405	
	1600		10' high		5	3.200		291	93.50		384.50	465	
	1800		6' wide sliding door, 7' full height		5	3.200		320	93.50		413.50	495	
	1900		10' high		4	4		370	117		487	590	
	2100		Swinging doors, 3' wide, 7' high, no transom		6	2.667		170	77.50		247.50	310	
	2200		7' high, 3' transom		5	3.200		213	93.50		306.50	380	

		10610	Folding Gates	CREW	DAILY OUTPUT	LABOR-HOURS	UNIT	MAT.	LABOR	EQUIP.	TOTAL	TOTAL INCL O&P	
100	0010		**SECURITY GATES** For roll up type, see division 08330-130										100
	0300		Scissors type folding gate, ptd. steel, single, 6' high, 5-1/2'wide	2 Sswk	4	4	Opng.	114	131		245	365	
	0350		6-1/2' wide		4	4		140	131		271	395	
	0400		7-1/2' wide		4	4		202	131		333	460	
	0600		Double gate, 7-1/2' high, 8' wide		2.50	6.400		248	210		458	650	
	0650		10' wide		2.50	6.400		284	210		494	690	
	0700		12' wide		2	8		350	263		613	860	
	0750		14' wide		2	8		405	263		668	920	
	0900		Door gate, folding steel, 4' wide, 61" high		4	4		59	131		190	305	
	1000		71" high		4	4		61	131		192	305	
	1200		81" high		4	4		66.50	131		197.50	310	
	1300		Window gates, 2' to 4' wide, 31" high		4	4		32.50	131		163.50	274	
	1500		55" high		3.75	4.267		43.50	140		183.50	300	
	1600		79" high		3.50	4.571		54	150		204	330	

		10615	Demountable Partitions	CREW	DAILY OUTPUT	LABOR-HOURS	UNIT	MAT.	LABOR	EQUIP.	TOTAL	TOTAL INCL O&P	
100	0010		**PARTITIONS, MOVABLE OFFICE** Demountable, add for doors										100
	0100		Do not deduct door openings from total L.F.										
	0900		Demountable gypsum system on 2" to 2-1/2"										
	1000		steel studs, 9' high, 3" to 3-3/4" thick										
	1200		Vinyl clad gypsum **CN**	2 Carp	48	.333	L.F.	36.50	9.70		46.20	55	
	1300		Fabric clad gypsum		44	.364		91	10.60		101.60	117	

Important: See the Reference Section for critical supporting data - Reference Nos., Crews, & City Cost Indexes

10615	Demountable Partitions	CREW	DAILY OUTPUT	LABOR-HOURS	UNIT	2001 BARE COSTS				TOTAL INCL O&P
						MAT.	LABOR	EQUIP.	TOTAL	
100	1500	Steel clad gypsum	2 Carp	40	.400	L.F.	98.50	11.65		110.15	126	100
1600	1.75 system, aluminum framing, vinyl clad hardboard,									
1800	paper honeycomb core panel, 1-3/4" to 2-1/2" thick									
1900	9' high	2 Carp	48	.333	L.F.	61.50	9.70		71.20	82.50
2100	7' high		60	.267		55	7.75		62.75	72.50
2200	5' high		80	.200		46.50	5.85		52.35	60
2250	Unitized gypsum system									
2300	Unitized panel, 9' high, 2" to 2-1/2" thick									
2350	Vinyl clad gypsum	2 Carp	48	.333	L.F.	79	9.70		88.70	102
2400	Fabric clad gypsum	"	44	.364	"	130	10.60		140.60	160
2500	Unitized mineral fiber system									
2510	Unitized panel, 9' high, 2-1/4" thick, aluminum frame									
2550	Vinyl clad mineral fiber	2 Carp	48	.333	L.F.	78.50	9.70		88.20	102
2600	Fabric clad mineral fiber	"	44	.364	"	117	10.60		127.60	146
2800	Movable steel walls, modular system									
2900	Unitized panels, 9' high, 48" wide									
3100	Baked enamel, pre-finished	2 Carp	60	.267	L.F.	89	7.75		96.75	110
3200	Fabric clad steel		56	.286	"	129	8.35		137.35	154
5310	Trackless wall, cork finish, semi-acoustic, 1-5/8" thick, minimum		325	.049	S.F.	26	1.44		27.44	30.50
5320	Maximum		190	.084		24.50	2.45		26.95	31
5330	Acoustic, 2" thick, minimum		305	.052		21	1.53		22.53	25.50
5340	Maximum		225	.071		36	2.07		38.07	43
5500	For acoustical partitions, add, minimum					1.50			1.50	1.65
5550	Maximum					7			7	7.70
5700	For doors, see div. 08100 & 08200									
5800	For door hardware, see div. 08700									
6100	In-plant modular office system, w/prehung hollow core door									
6200	3" thick polystyrene core panels									
6250	12' x 12', 2 wall	2 Clab	3.80	4.211	Ea.	2,700	96		2,796	3,100
6300	4 wall		1.90	8.421		3,750	192		3,942	4,425
6350	16' x 16', 2 wall		3.60	4.444		3,775	102		3,877	4,300
6400	4 wall		1.80	8.889		5,225	203		5,428	6,050

10630	Port. Partitions/Screens/Panels	CREW	DAILY OUTPUT	LABOR-HOURS	UNIT	MAT.	LABOR	EQUIP.	TOTAL	TOTAL INCL O&P
100	0010	PARTITIONS, PORTABLE Divider panels, free standing, fiber core										100
0020	Fabric face straight									
0100	3'-0" long, 4'-0" high	2 Carp	100	.160	L.F.	95.50	4.66		100.16	112
0200	5'-0" high		90	.178		96.50	5.20		101.70	114
0500	6'-0" high		75	.213		109	6.20		115.20	130
0900	5'-0" long, 4'-0" high		175	.091		72	2.67		74.67	83.50
1000	5'-0" high		150	.107		88.50	3.11		91.61	102
1500	6'-0" high		125	.128		85	3.73		88.73	99.50
1600	6'-0" long, 5'-0" high		162	.099		71	2.88		73.88	82.50
3100	Curved, 3'-0" long, 5'-0" high		90	.178		85	5.20		90.20	102
3150	6'-0" high		75	.213		98.50	6.20		104.70	118
3200	Economical panels, fabric face, 4'-0" long, 5'-0" high		132	.121		126	3.53		129.53	145
3250	6'-0" high		112	.143		24	4.16		28.16	33
3300	5'-0" long, 5'-0" high		150	.107		26.50	3.11		29.61	34
3350	6'-0" high		125	.128		31	3.73		34.73	40.50
3380	3'-0" curved, 5'-0" high		90	.178		85	5.20		90.20	102
3390	6'-0" high		75	.213		98.50	6.20		104.70	118
3450	Acoustical panels, 60 to 90 NRC, 3'-0" long, 5'-0" high		90	.178		82.50	5.20		87.70	99
3550	6'-0" high		75	.213		80.50	6.20		86.70	98.50
3600	5'-0" long, 5'-0" high		150	.107		57.50	3.11		60.61	68.50
3650	6'-0" high		125	.128		64	3.73		67.73	76.50
3700	6'-0" long, 5'-0" high		162	.099		56	2.88		58.88	66

SPECIALTIES 10

			DAILY	LABOR-		2001 BARE COSTS				TOTAL	
		10630 | **Port. Partitions/Screens/Panels**	CREW	OUTPUT	HOURS	UNIT	MAT.	LABOR	EQUIP.	TOTAL	INCL O&P
100	3750	6'-0" high	2 Carp	138	.116	L.F.	58.50	3.38		61.88	69.50	100
	3800	Economy acoustical panels, 40 NRC, 4'-0" long, 5'-0" high		132	.121		31.50	3.53		35.03	40
	3850	6'-0" high		112	.143		36	4.16		40.16	46.50
	3900	5'-0" long, 6'-0" high		125	.128		31	3.73		34.73	40.50
	3950	6'-0" long, 5'-0" high		162	.099		31	2.88		33.88	38.50
	4000	Metal chalkboard, 6'-6" high, chalkboard, 1 side		125	.128		82	3.73		85.73	96.50
	4100	Metal chalkboard, 2 sides		120	.133		93.50	3.89		97.39	109
	4300	Tackboard, both sides	▼	123	.130	▼	74	3.79		77.79	87.50

		10651 | **Accordion Folding Partitions**									
100	0010	**PARTITIONS, FOLDING ACCORDION**										100
	0100	Vinyl covered, over 150 S.F., frame not included									
	0300	Residential, 1.25 lb. per S.F., 8' maximum height	2 Carp	300	.053	S.F.	13.50	1.55		15.05	17.30
	0400	Commercial, 1.75 lb. per S.F., 8' maximum height		225	.071		13.50	2.07		15.57	18.10
	0600	2 lb. per S.F., 17' maximum height		150	.107		14.50	3.11		17.61	21
	0700	Industrial, 4 lb. per S.F., 20' maximum height		75	.213		24.50	6.20		30.70	37
	0900	Acoustical, 3 lb. per S.F., 17' maximum height		100	.160		19.50	4.66		24.16	29
	1200	5 lb. per S.F., 20' maximum height		95	.168		27	4.91		31.91	37
	1300	5.5 lb. per S.F., 17' maximum height		90	.178		30	5.20		35.20	41
	1400	Fire rated, 4.5 psf, 20' maximum height		160	.100		30	2.92		32.92	37.50
	1500	Vinyl clad wood or steel, electric operation, 5.0 psf		160	.100		35	2.92		37.92	43
	1900	Wood, non-acoustic, birch or mahogany, to 10' high	▼	300	.053	▼	18	1.55		19.55	22

		10653 | **Folding Panel Partitions**									
200	0010	**PARTITIONS, FOLDING LEAF** Acoustic, wood										200
	0100	Vinyl faced, to 18' high, 6 psf, minimum	2 Carp	60	.267	S.F.	37.50	7.75		45.25	53.50
	0150	Average		45	.356		45	10.35		55.35	65.50
	0200	Maximum		30	.533		58	15.55		73.55	88.50
	0400	Formica or hardwood finish, minimum		60	.267		39	7.75		46.75	54.50
	0500	Maximum		30	.533		41.50	15.55		57.05	70
	0600	Wood, low acoustical type, 4.5 psf, to 14' high		50	.320		28	9.35		37.35	45.50
	1100	Steel, acoustical, 9 to 12 lb. per S.F., vinyl faced, minimum		60	.267		40	7.75		47.75	56
	1200	Maximum		30	.533		49	15.55		64.55	78.50
	1700	Aluminum framed, acoustical, to 12' high, 5.5 psf, minimum		60	.267		27	7.75		34.75	41.50
	1800	Maximum		30	.533		32.50	15.55		48.05	60.50
	2000	6.5 lb. per S.F., minimum		60	.267		28.50	7.75		36.25	43.50
	2100	Maximum	▼	30	.533	▼	35	15.55		50.55	63

		10658 | **Acoustic Air Wall**									
100	0010	**PARTITIONS, OPERABLE** Acoustic air wall, 1-5/8" thick, minimum	2 Carp	375	.043	S.F.	23	1.24		24.24	27.50	100
	0100	Maximum		365	.044		39.50	1.28		40.78	45.50
	0300	2-1/4" thick, minimum		360	.044		26	1.30		27.30	30.50
	0400	Maximum	▼	330	.048	▼	45	1.41		46.41	51.50
	0600	For track type, add to above				L.F.	84			84	92.50
	0700	Overhead track type, acoustical, 3" thick, 11 psf, minimum	2 Carp	350	.046	S.F.	58	1.33		59.33	66
	0800	Maximum	"	300	.053	"	70	1.55		71.55	79.50

10 SPECIALTIES

10670 | Storage Shelving

10674 | Storage Shelving

			DAILY OUTPUT	LABOR-HOURS	UNIT	2001 BARE COSTS				TOTAL INCL O&P	
						MAT.	LABOR	EQUIP.	TOTAL		
500	0010	**SHELVING** Metal, industrial, cross-braced, 3' wide, 12" deep	1 Sswk	175	.046	SF Shlf	9.25	1.50		10.75	12.90	**500**
	0100	24" deep		330	.024		7.20	.80		8	9.40	
	0300	4' wide, 12" deep		185	.043		6.95	1.42		8.37	10.25	
	0400	24" deep		380	.021		7.15	.69		7.84	9.10	
	1200	Enclosed sides, cross-braced back, 3' wide, 12" deep		175	.046		13.50	1.50		15	17.55	
	1300	24" deep		290	.028		8.55	.91		9.46	11.05	
	1500	Fully enclosed, sides and back, 3' wide, 12" deep		150	.053		15.80	1.75		17.55	20.50	
	1600	24" deep		255	.031		9.95	1.03		10.98	12.80	
	1800	4' wide, 12" deep		150	.053		15	1.75		16.75	19.70	
	1900	24" deep		290	.028		9.65	.91		10.56	12.25	
	2200	Wide span, 1600 lb. capacity per shelf, 6' wide, 24" deep		380	.021		6.75	.69		7.44	8.65	
	2400	36" deep		440	.018		5.95	.60		6.55	7.65	
	2600	8' wide, 24" deep		440	.018		6.15	.60		6.75	7.85	
	2800	36" deep	▼	520	.015	▼	5.15	.51		5.66	6.55	
	4000	Pallet racks, steel frame 5,000 lb. capacity, 8' long, 36" deep	2 Sswk	450	.036		4.36	1.17		5.53	6.90	
	4200	42" deep		500	.032		3.82	1.05		4.87	6.10	
	4400	48" deep	▼	520	.031	▼	3.40	1.01		4.41	5.55	
600	0010	**PARTS BINS** Metal, gray baked enamel finish										**600**
	0100	6'-3" high, 3' wide										
	0300	12 bins, 18" wide x 12" high, 12" deep	2 Clab	10	1.600	Ea.	226	36.50		262.50	305	
	0400	24" deep		10	1.600		287	36.50		323.50	370	
	0600	72 bins, 6" wide x 6" high, 12" deep		8	2		375	45.50		420.50	480	
	0700	24" deep	▼	8	2	▼	775	45.50		820.50	920	
	1000	7'-3" high, 3' wide										
	1200	14 bins, 18" wide x 12" high, 12" deep	2 Clab	10	1.600	Ea.	256	36.50		292.50	340	
	1300	24" deep		10	1.600		330	36.50		366.50	420	
	1500	84 bins, 6" wide x 6" high, 12" deep		8	2		610	45.50		655.50	740	
	1600	24" deep	▼	8	2		860	45.50		905.50	1,025	

10750 | Telephone Specialties

10755 | Telephone Enclosures

			DAILY OUTPUT	LABOR-HOURS	UNIT	2001 BARE COSTS				TOTAL INCL O&P	
						MAT.	LABOR	EQUIP.	TOTAL		
400	0010	**TELEPHONE ENCLOSURE**										**400**
	0300	Shelf type, wall hung, minimum	2 Carp	5	3.200	Ea.	940	93.50		1,033.50	1,175	
	0400	Maximum		5	3.200		2,425	93.50		2,518.50	2,825	
	0600	Booth type, painted steel, indoor or outdoor, minimum		1.50	10.667		2,975	310		3,285	3,750	
	0700	Maximum (stainless steel)		1.50	10.667		9,850	310		10,160	11,300	
	1300	Outdoor, acoustical, on post		3	5.333		1,300	155		1,455	1,675	
	1400	Phone carousel, pedestal mounted with dividers		.60	26.667		4,950	775		5,725	6,675	
	1900	Outdoor, drive-up type, wall mounted		4	4		775	117		892	1,025	
	2000	Post mounted, stainless steel posts	▼	3	5.333	▼	1,225	155		1,380	1,600	
	2200	Directory shelf, wall mounted, stainless steel										
	2300	3 binders	2 Carp	8	2	Ea.	950	58.50		1,008.50	1,150	
	2500	4 binders		7	2.286		1,075	66.50		1,141.50	1,300	
	2600	5 binders		6	2.667		1,400	77.50		1,477.50	1,650	
	2800	Table type, stainless steel, 4 binders		8	2		1,125	58.50		1,183.50	1,325	
	2900	7 binders	▼	7	2.286	▼	1,400	66.50		1,466.50	1,625	

10820	Bath Accessories	CREW	DAILY OUTPUT	LABOR-HOURS	UNIT	2001 BARE COSTS				TOTAL INCL O&P
						MAT.	LABOR	EQUIP.	TOTAL	
100	0010	**BATH ACCESSORIES**										100
	0200	Curtain rod, stainless steel, 5' long, 1" diameter	1 Carp	13	.615	Ea.	24	17.95		41.95	54.50
	0300	1-1/4" diameter	"	13	.615	"	22.50	17.95		40.45	53
	0500	Dispenser units, combined soap & towel dispensers,									
	0510	mirror and shelf, flush mounted	1 Carp	10	.800	Ea.	268	23.50		291.50	330
	0600	Towel dispenser and waste receptacle,									
	0610	18 gallon capacity	1 Carp	10	.800	Ea.	310	23.50		333.50	375
	0800	Grab bar, straight, 1-1/4" diameter, stainless steel, 18" long		24	.333		20	9.70		29.70	37
	0900	24" long		23	.348		23.50	10.15		33.65	42
	1000	30" long		22	.364		23.50	10.60		34.10	42.50
	1100	36" long		20	.400		25.50	11.65		37.15	46.50
	1200	1-1/2" diameter, 24" long		23	.348		44.50	10.15		54.65	65
	1300	36" long		20	.400		50	11.65		61.65	73.50
	1500	Tub bar, 1-1/4" diameter, 24" x 36"		14	.571		75.50	16.65		92.15	109
	1600	Plus vertical arm		12	.667		83	19.45		102.45	122
	1900	End tub bar, 1" diameter, 90° angle, 16" x 32"		12	.667		116	19.45		135.45	158
	2300	Hand dryer, surface mounted, electric, 115 volt, 20 amp		4	2		530	58.50		588.50	675
	2400	230 volt, 10 amp		4	2		535	58.50		593.50	675
	2600	Hat and coat strip, stainless steel, 4 hook, 36" long		24	.333		51	9.70		60.70	71
	2700	6 hook, 60" long		20	.400		79.50	11.65		91.15	106
	3000	Mirror, with stainless steel 3/4" square frame, 18" x 24"		20	.400		61	11.65		72.65	85.50
	3100	36" x 24"		15	.533		104	15.55		119.55	139
	3200	48" x 24"		10	.800		141	23.50		164.50	192
	3300	72" x 24"		6	1.333		216	39		255	298
	3500	With 5" stainless steel shelf, 18" x 24"		20	.400		94.50	11.65		106.15	122
	3600	36" x 24"		15	.533		132	15.55		147.55	170
	3700	48" x 24"		10	.800		153	23.50		176.50	205
	3800	72" x 24"		6	1.333		252	39		291	340
	4100	Mop holder strip, stainless steel, 5 holders, 48" long		20	.400		56.50	11.65		68.15	80.50
	4200	Napkin/tampon dispenser, recessed		15	.533		350	15.55		365.55	410
	4300	Robe hook, single, regular		36	.222		4.84	6.50		11.34	15.45
	4400	Heavy duty, concealed mounting		36	.222		15.60	6.50		22.10	27.50
	4600	Soap dispenser, chrome, surface mounted, liquid		20	.400		41	11.65		52.65	63.50
	4700	Powder		20	.400		41	11.65		52.65	63.50
	5000	Recessed stainless steel, liquid		10	.800		141	23.50		164.50	192
	5100	Powder		10	.800		255	23.50		278.50	320
	5300	Soap tank, stainless steel, 1 gallon		10	.800		159	23.50		182.50	212
	5400	5 gallon		5	1.600		219	46.50		265.50	315
	5600	Shelf, stainless steel, 5" wide, 18 ga., 24" long		24	.333		36.50	9.70		46.20	55
	5700	48" long		16	.500		54.50	14.60		69.10	83
	5800	8" wide shelf, 18 ga., 24" long		22	.364		45	10.60		55.60	66
	5900	48" long		14	.571		77.50	16.65		94.15	111
	6000	Toilet seat cover dispenser, stainless steel, recessed		20	.400		87.50	11.65		99.15	115
	6050	Surface mounted		15	.533		23.50	15.55		39.05	50.50
	6100	Toilet tissue dispenser, surface mounted, SS, single roll		30	.267		11.30	7.75		19.05	24.50
	6200	Double roll		24	.333		15.75	9.70		25.45	32.50
	6400	Towel bar, stainless steel, 18" long		23	.348		30.50	10.15		40.65	49.50
	6500	30" long		21	.381		49	11.10		60.10	71.50
	6700	Towel dispenser, stainless steel, surface mounted		16	.500		36	14.60		50.60	63
	6800	Flush mounted, recessed		10	.800		157	23.50		180.50	210
	7000	Towel holder, hotel type, 2 guest size		20	.400		13.20	11.65		24.85	33
	7200	Towel shelf, stainless steel, 24" long, 8" wide		20	.400		45.50	11.65		57.15	68.50
	7400	Tumbler holder, tumbler only		30	.267		24	7.75		31.75	38
	7500	Soap, tumbler & toothbrush		30	.267		24	7.75		31.75	38
	7700	Wall urn ash receiver, surface mount, 11" long		12	.667		97.50	19.45		116.95	138
	7800	7-1/2", long		18	.444		71	12.95		83.95	98.50

Important: See the Reference Section for critical supporting data - Reference Nos., Crews, & City Cost Indexes

10 SPECIALTIES

10820 | Bath Accessories

			CREW	DAILY OUTPUT	LABOR-HOURS	UNIT	2001 BARE COSTS				TOTAL INCL O&P	
							MAT.	LABOR	EQUIP.	TOTAL		
100	8000	Waste receptacles, stainless steel, with top, 13 gallon	1 Carp	10	.800	Ea.	157	23.50		180.50	210	100
	8100	36 gallon	↓	8	1	↓	249	29		278	320	
400	0010	**MEDICINE CABINETS** With mirror, st. st. frame, 16" x 22", unlighted	1 Carp	14	.571	Ea.	68.50	16.65		85.15	102	400
	0100	Wood frame		14	.571		95	16.65		111.65	131	
	0300	Sliding mirror doors, 20" x 16" x 4-3/4", unlighted		7	1.143		85	33.50		118.50	146	
	0400	24" x 19" x 8-1/2", lighted		5	1.600		134	46.50		180.50	220	
	0600	Triple door, 30" x 32", unlighted, plywood body		7	1.143		211	33.50		244.50	284	
	0700	Steel body		7	1.143		278	33.50		311.50	355	
	0900	Oak door, wood body, beveled mirror, single door		7	1.143		124	33.50		157.50	188	
	1000	Double door		6	1.333		315	39		354	405	
	1200	Hotel cabinets, stainless, with lower shelf, unlighted		10	.800		170	23.50		193.50	224	
	1300	Lighted	↓	5	1.600	↓	252	46.50		298.50	350	

10880 | Scales

10885 | Scales

			CREW	DAILY OUTPUT	LABOR-HOURS	UNIT	2001 BARE COSTS				TOTAL INCL O&P	
							MAT.	LABOR	EQUIP.	TOTAL		
100	0010	**SCALES** Built-in floor scale, not incl. foundations										100
	0100	Dial type, 5 ton capacity, 8' x 6' platform	3 Carp	.50	48	Ea.	5,475	1,400		6,875	8,225	
	0300	9' x 7' platform		.40	60		7,700	1,750		9,450	11,200	
	0400	10 ton capacity, steel platform, 8' x 6' platform		.40	60		8,600	1,750		10,350	12,200	
	0600	9' x 7' platform	↓	.35	68.571	↓	8,750	2,000		10,750	12,800	
	0700	Truck scales, incl. steel weigh bridge,										
	0800	not including foundation, pits										
	1550	Digital, electronic, 100 ton capacity, steel deck 12' x 10' platform	3 Carp	.20	120	Ea.	9,375	3,500		12,875	15,800	
	1600	40' x 10' platform		.14	171		19,100	5,000		24,100	28,800	
	1640	60' x 10' platform		.13	184		23,600	5,375		28,975	34,300	
	1680	70' x 10' platform	↓	.12	200		26,300	5,825		32,125	38,100	
	2000	For standard automatic printing device, add					1,900			1,900	2,075	
	2100	For remote reading electronic system, add					2,025			2,025	2,225	
	2300	Concrete foundation pits for above, 8' x 6', 5 C.Y. required	C-1	.50	64		715	1,775		2,490	3,550	
	2400	14' x 6' platform, 10 C.Y. required		.35	91.429		1,050	2,525		3,575	5,100	
	2600	50' x 10' platform, 30 C.Y. required		.25	128		1,425	3,525		4,950	7,075	
	2700	70' x 10' platform, 40 C.Y. required	↓	.15	213		3,100	5,875		8,975	12,600	
	2750	Crane scales, dial, 1 ton capacity					795			795	875	
	2780	5 ton capacity					925			925	1,025	
	2800	Digital, 1 ton capacity					1,900			1,900	2,100	
	2850	10 ton capacity				↓	3,450			3,450	3,800	
	2900	Low profile electronic warehouse scale,										
	3000	not incl. printer, 4' x 4' platform, 10,000 lb. capacity	2 Carp	.30	53.333	Ea.	1,850	1,550		3,400	4,450	
	3300	5' x 7' platform, 10,000 lb. capacity		.25	64		3,100	1,875		4,975	6,325	
	3400	20,000 lb. capacity	↓	.20	80		4,000	2,325		6,325	8,050	
	3500	For printers, incl. time, date & numbering, add					1,900			1,900	2,075	
	3800	Portable, beam type, capacity 1000#, platform 18" x 24"					625			625	690	
	3900	Dial type, capacity 2000#, platform 24" x 24"					995			995	1,100	
	4000	Digital type, capacity 1000#, platform 24" x 30"					1,600			1,600	1,750	
	4100	Portable contractor truck scales, 50 ton cap., 40' x 10' platform					26,800			26,800	29,500	
	4200	60' x 10' platform				↓	22,200			22,200	24,400	

SPECIALTIES 10

500		10905	Coat Racks/Wardrobes	CREW	DAILY OUTPUT	LABOR-HOURS	UNIT	2001 BARE COSTS				TOTAL INCL O&P	500
								MAT.	LABOR	EQUIP.	TOTAL		
	0010	**COAT RACKS & WARDROBES**											
	0020	Floor model hat & coat racks, 6 hangers										
	0050	Standing, beech wood, 21" x 21" x 72", chrome				Ea.	196			196	216	
	0100	18 gauge tubular steel, 21" x 21" x 69", wood walnut				"	224			224	246	
	0500	16 gauge steel frame, 22 gauge steel shelves										
	0650	Single pedestal, 30" x 18" x 63"				Ea.	139			139	153	
	0800	Single face rack, 29" x 18-1/2" x 62"					160			160	176	
	0900	51" x 18-1/2" x 70"					277			277	305	
	0910	Double face rack, 39" x 26" x 70"					186			186	204	
	0920	63" x 26" x 70"					330			330	360	
	0940	For 2" ball casters, add				Set	47.50			47.50	52.50	
	1400	Utility hook strips, 3/8" x 2-1/2" x 18", 6 hooks	1 Carp	48	.167	Ea.	63	4.86		67.86	77	
	1500	34" long, 12 hooks	"	48	.167	"	47	4.86		51.86	59	
	1650	Wall mounted racks, 16 gauge steel frame, 22 gauge steel shelves										
	1850	12" x 15" x 26", 6 hangers	1 Carp	32	.250	Ea.	113	7.30		120.30	135	
	2000	12" x 15" x 50", 12 hangers	"	32	.250	"	171	7.30		178.30	199	
	2150	Wardrobe cabinet, steel, baked enamel finish										
	2300	36" x 21" x 78", incl. top shelf & hanger rod				Ea.	375			375	410	

For information about Means Estimating Seminars, see yellow pages 11 and 12 in back of book

10 SPECIALTIES

Important: See the Reference Section for critical supporting data - Reference Nos., Crews, & City Cost Indexes

Division 11
Equipment

Estimating Tips

General

- The items in this division are usually priced per square foot or each. Many of these items are purchased by the owner for installation by the contractor. Check the specifications for responsibilities, and include time for receiving, storage, installation and mechanical and electrical hook-ups in the appropriate divisions.

- Many items in Division 11 require some type of support system that is not usually furnished with the item. Examples of these systems include blocking for the attachment of casework and support angles for ceiling hung projection screens. The required blocking or supports must be added to the estimate in the appropriate division.

- Some items in Division 11 may require assembly or electrical hook-ups. Verify the amount of assembly required or the need for a hard electrical connection and add the appropriate costs.

Reference Numbers

Reference numbers are shown in bold squares at the beginning of some major classifications. These numbers refer to related items in the Reference Section. The reference information may be an estimating procedure, an alternate pricing method or technical information.

Note: Not all subdivisions listed here necessarily appear in this publication.

11010 | Maintenance Equipment

11012 | Contractor Equipment

		CREW	DAILY OUTPUT	LABOR-HOURS	UNIT	2001 BARE COSTS				TOTAL INCL O&P	
						MAT.	LABOR	EQUIP.	TOTAL		
100	0010	CONTRACTOR EQUIPMENT See division 01590 [R01590 -100]										100

11013 | Floor/Wall Cleaning Equipment

		CREW	DAILY OUTPUT	LABOR-HOURS	UNIT	MAT.	LABOR	EQUIP.	TOTAL	TOTAL INCL O&P	
800	0010	**VACUUM CLEANING**										800
	0020	Central, 3 inlet, residential	1 Skwk	.90	8.889	Total	555	265		820	1,025	
	0200	Commercial		.70	11.429		960	340		1,300	1,575	
	0400	5 inlet system, residential		.50	16		840	480		1,320	1,675	
	0600	7 inlet system, commercial		.40	20		1,050	595		1,645	2,075	
	0800	9 inlet system, residential	↓	.30	26.667		1,200	795		1,995	2,575	
	4010	Rule of thumb: First 1200 S.F., installed				↓					1,044	
	4020	For each additional S.F., add				S.F.					.17	

11020 | Security & Vault Equipment

11021 | Safes

		CREW	DAILY OUTPUT	LABOR-HOURS	UNIT	2001 BARE COSTS				TOTAL INCL O&P	
						MAT.	LABOR	EQUIP.	TOTAL		
600	0010	**SAFE**										600
	0015	Office, 4 hr. rating, 30" x 18" x 18" inside				Ea.	2,850			2,850	3,125	
	0100	60" x 36" x 18"					6,175			6,175	6,775	
	0200	1 hr. rating, 30" x 18" x 18"					1,425			1,425	1,575	
	0250	40" x 18" x 18"					1,625			1,625	1,775	
	0300	60" x 36" x 18", double door					4,075			4,075	4,500	
	0400	Data, 4 hr. rating, 23-1/2" x 19-1/2" x 17" inside					2,250			2,250	2,475	
	0450	52" x 19" x 17"					5,500			5,500	6,050	
	0500	63" x 34" x 16", double door					8,525			8,525	9,375	
	0550	52" x 34" x 16", inside					8,000			8,000	8,800	
	0600	1 hr. rating, 27" x 19" x 16"					4,200			4,200	4,625	
	0700	63" x 34" x 16"					7,250			7,250	7,975	
	0750	Diskette, 1 hr., 14" x 12" x 11", inside					2,175			2,175	2,375	
	0800	Money, "B" label, 9" x 14" x 14"					445			445	490	
	0900	Tool resistive, 24" x 24" x 20"					2,500			2,500	2,750	
	1050	Tool and torch resistive, 24" x 24" x 20"					6,350			6,350	7,000	
	1150	Jewelers, 23" x 20" x 18"					8,125			8,125	8,925	
	1200	63" x 25" x 18"					14,600			14,600	16,000	
	1300	For handling into building, add, minimum	A-2	8.50	2.824	↓		65	18.60	83.60	122	
	1400	Maximum	"	.78	30.769	↓		710	202	912	1,325	

11030 | Teller & Service Equipment

11038 | Bank Equipment

		CREW	DAILY OUTPUT	LABOR-HOURS	UNIT	2001 BARE COSTS				TOTAL INCL O&P	
						MAT.	LABOR	EQUIP.	TOTAL		
150	0010	**BANK EQUIPMENT**										150
	0020	Alarm system, police	2 Elec	1.60	10	Ea.	3,600	345		3,945	4,450	
	0100	With vault alarm	"	.40	40		14,300	1,375		15,675	17,800	
	0400	Bullet resistant teller window, 44" x 60"	1 Glaz	.60	13.333	↓	2,375	380		2,755	3,175	

11030 | Teller & Service Equipment

150	11038	Bank Equipment	CREW	DAILY OUTPUT	LABOR-HOURS	UNIT	2001 BARE COSTS MAT.	LABOR	EQUIP.	TOTAL	TOTAL INCL O&P	150
	0500	48" x 60"	1 Glaz	.60	13.333	Ea.	3,275	380		3,655	4,175	
	3000	Counters for banks, frontal only	2 Carp	1	16	Station	1,350	465		1,815	2,200	
	3100	Complete with steel undercounter	"	.50	32	"	2,625	935		3,560	4,325	
	4600	Door and frame, bullet-resistant, with vision panel, minimum	2 Sswk	1.10	14.545	Ea.	2,550	480		3,030	3,675	
	4700	Maximum		1.10	14.545		3,450	480		3,930	4,675	
	4800	Drive-up window, drawer & mike, not incl. glass, minimum		1	16		3,675	525		4,200	4,975	
	4900	Maximum		.50	32		6,925	1,050		7,975	9,525	
	5000	Night depository, with chest, minimum		1	16		6,175	525		6,700	7,750	
	5100	Maximum		.50	32		9,775	1,050		10,825	12,700	
	5200	Package receiver, painted		3.20	5		1,000	164		1,164	1,400	
	5300	Stainless steel		3.20	5		1,700	164		1,864	2,175	
	5400	Partitions, bullet-resistant, 1-3/16" glass, 8' high	2 Carp	10	1.600	L.F.	145	46.50		191.50	233	
	5450	Acrylic	"	10	1.600	"	275	46.50		321.50	380	
	5500	Pneumatic tube systems, 2 lane drive-up, complete	L-3	.25	64	Total	18,900	2,025		20,925	23,900	
	5550	With T.V. viewer	"	.20	80	"	36,600	2,525		39,125	44,200	
	5570	Safety deposit boxes, minimum	1 Sswk	44	.182	Opng.	42	5.95		47.95	57	
	5580	Maximum, 10" x 15" opening		19	.421		89	13.85		102.85	123	
	5590	Teller locker, average		15	.533		1,150	17.50		1,167.50	1,300	
	5600	Pass thru, bullet-res. window, painted steel, 24" x 36"	2 Sswk	1.60	10	Ea.	1,375	330		1,705	2,100	
	5700	48" x 48"		1.20	13.333		1,950	440		2,390	2,950	
	5800	72" x 40"		.80	20		2,525	655		3,180	3,975	
	5900	For stainless steel frames, add					20%					
	6000	Surveillance system, 16 mm film camera, complete	2 Elec	1	16	Ea.	3,700	550		4,250	4,900	
	6010	For each additional camera, add					1,575			1,575	1,725	
	6100	Surveillance system, video camera, complete	2 Elec	1	16		11,800	550		12,350	13,800	
	6110	For each additional camera, add					725			725	800	
	6200	Twenty-four hour teller, single unit,										
	6300	automated deposit, cash and memo	L-3	.25	64	Ea.	35,600	2,025		37,625	42,300	
	7000	Vault front, see division 08320-950										

11040 | Ecclesiastical Equipment

250	11041	Ecclesiastical Equipment	CREW	DAILY OUTPUT	LABOR-HOURS	UNIT	2001 BARE COSTS MAT.	LABOR	EQUIP.	TOTAL	TOTAL INCL O&P	250
	0010	**CHURCH EQUIPMENT**										
	0020	Altar, wood, custom design, plain	1 Carp	1.40	5.714	Ea.	1,675	167		1,842	2,075	
	0050	Deluxe	"	.20	40		8,050	1,175		9,225	10,700	
	0070	Granite or marble, average	2 Marb	.50	32		6,475	935		7,410	8,575	
	0090	Deluxe	"	.20	80		21,200	2,325		23,525	26,900	
	0100	Arks, prefabricated, plain	2 Carp	.80	20		6,350	585		6,935	7,900	
	0130	Deluxe, maximum	"	.20	80		79,500	2,325		81,825	91,000	
	0150	Baptistry, fiberglass, 3'-6" deep, x 13'-7" long,										
	0160	steps at both ends, incl. plumbing, minimum	L-8	1	20	Ea.	2,450	605		3,055	3,625	
	0200	Maximum	"	.70	28.571		4,775	865		5,640	6,600	
	0250	Add for filter, heater and lights					1,050			1,050	1,150	
	0300	Carillon, 4 octave (48 bells), with keyboard				System	500,000			500,000	550,000	
	0320	2 octave (24 bells)					200,000			200,000	220,000	
	0340	3 to 4 bell peal, minimum					45,000			45,000	49,500	
	0360	Maximum					300,000			300,000	330,000	
	0380	Cast bronze bell, average				Ea.	60,000			60,000	66,000	

EQUIPMENT 11

11041	Ecclesiastical Equipment	CREW	DAILY OUTPUT	LABOR-HOURS	UNIT	2001 BARE COSTS				TOTAL INCL O&P	
						MAT.	LABOR	EQUIP.	TOTAL		
250	0400	Electronic, digital, minimum				Ea.	11,500			11,500	12,700	250
	0410	With keyboard, maximum					39,000			39,000	42,900	
	0500	Reconciliation room, wood, prefabricated, single, plain	1 Carp	.60	13.333		2,125	390		2,515	2,925	
	0550	Deluxe		.40	20		5,825	585		6,410	7,325	
	0650	Double, plain		.40	20		4,250	585		4,835	5,575	
	0700	Deluxe		.20	40		13,300	1,175		14,475	16,400	
	1000	Lecterns, wood, plain		5	1.600		475	46.50		521.50	600	
	1100	Deluxe		2	4		2,500	117		2,617	2,925	
	1500	Pews, bench type, hardwood, minimum		20	.400	L.F.	58.50	11.65		70.15	82.50	
	1550	Maximum		15	.533		117	15.55		132.55	153	
	1570	For kneeler, add					13.25			13.25	14.60	
	2000	Pulpits, hardwood, prefabricated, plain	1 Carp	2	4	Ea.	1,050	117		1,167	1,350	
	2100	Deluxe		1.60	5	"	7,000	146		7,146	7,925	
	2500	Railing, hardwood, average		25	.320	L.F.	133	9.35		142.35	161	
	2700	Safes, see division 11021-600										
	3000	Seating, individual, oak, contour, laminated	1 Carp	21	.381	Person	117	11.10		128.10	145	
	3100	Cushion seat		21	.381		106	11.10		117.10	134	
	3200	Fully upholstered		21	.381		95.50	11.10		106.60	122	
	3300	Combination, self-rising		21	.381		292	11.10		303.10	335	
	3500	For cherry, add					30%					
	4000	Steeples, translucent fiberglass, 30" square, 15' high	F-3	2	20	Ea.	3,175	590	257	4,022	4,700	
	4150	25' high		1.80	22.222		3,700	655	286	4,641	5,425	
	4350	Opaque fiberglass, 24" square, 14' high		2	20		2,650	590	257	3,497	4,125	
	4500	28' high		1.80	22.222		3,075	655	286	4,016	4,750	
	4600	Aluminum, baked finish, 14' high, 16" square					1,575			1,575	1,750	
	4620	20' high, 3'-6" base					4,225			4,225	4,650	
	4640	35' high, 8' base					16,000			16,000	17,600	
	4660	60' high, 14' base					36,100			36,100	39,700	
	4680	152' high, custom					355,500			355,500	391,000	
	4700	Porcelain enamel steeples, custom, 40' high	F-3	.50	80		10,400	2,375	1,025	13,800	16,200	
	4800	60' high	"	.30	133		18,000	3,950	1,725	23,675	27,800	
	5000	Wall cross, aluminum, extruded, 2" x 2" section	1 Carp	34	.235	L.F.	34	6.85		40.85	48.50	
	5150	4" x 4" section		29	.276		49	8.05		57.05	66	
	5300	Bronze, extruded, 1" x 2" section		31	.258		67	7.50		74.50	85.50	
	5350	2-1/2" x 2-1/2" section		34	.235		101	6.85		107.85	122	
	5450	Solid bar stock, 1/2" x 3" section		29	.276		133	8.05		141.05	159	
	5600	Fiberglass, stock		34	.235		27.50	6.85		34.35	41	
	5700	Stainless steel, 4" deep, channel section		29	.276		107	8.05		115.05	131	
	5800	4" deep box section		29	.276		133	8.05		141.05	159	

11051	Library Equipment	CREW	DAILY OUTPUT	LABOR-HOURS	UNIT	2001 BARE COSTS				TOTAL INCL O&P	
						MAT.	LABOR	EQUIP.	TOTAL		
400	0010	**LIBRARY EQUIPMENT**										400
	0020	Bookshelf, mtl, 90" high, 10" shelf, dbl face	1 Carp	11.50	.696	L.F.	93.50	20.50		114	135	
	0300	Single face	"	12	.667	"	150	19.45		169.45	196	
	0600	For 8" shelving, subtract from above					10%					
	0700	For 12" shelving, add to above					10%					
	0800	For 42" high with countertop, subtract from above					20%					

Important: See the Reference Section for critical supporting data - Reference Nos., Crews, & City Cost Indexes

11 EQUIPMENT

11050 | Library Equipment

11051 | Library Equipment

		CREW	DAILY OUTPUT	LABOR-HOURS	UNIT	2001 BARE COSTS MAT.	LABOR	EQUIP.	TOTAL	TOTAL INCL O&P	
400	**1100** Magazine shelving, 90" high, 12" deep, single face	1 Carp	11.50	.696	L.F.	94	20.50		114.50	136	**400**
	1400 Double face		11.50	.696	"	169	20.50		189.50	218	
	2500 Carrels, hardwood, 36" x 24", minimum		5	1.600	Ea.	590	46.50		636.50	725	
	2650 Maximum	↓	4	2		770	58.50		828.50	940	
	2700 Card catalog file, 60 trays, complete					5,675			5,675	6,225	
	2720 Alternate method: each tray					94.50			94.50	104	
	3100 Chairs, wood			↓	↓	121			121	133	
	3500 Charging desk, built-in, with counter, plastic laminated top	1 Carp	7	1.143	L.F.	415	33.50		448.50	505	
	3700 Reading table, laminated top, 60" x 36"				Ea.	630			630	690	
	3800 Mobile compacted shelving, hand crank, 9'-0" high										
	3820 Double face, including track, 3' section				Ea.	860			860	945	
	3840 For electrical operation, add					25%					

11060 | Theater & Stage Equipment

11063 | Stage Equipment

		CREW	DAILY OUTPUT	LABOR-HOURS	UNIT	2001 BARE COSTS MAT.	LABOR	EQUIP.	TOTAL	TOTAL INCL O&P	
600	**0010 STAGE EQUIPMENT**										**600**
	0050 Control boards with dimmers and breakers, minimum	1 Elec	1	8	Ea.	6,500	274		6,774	7,550	
	0100 Average		.50	16		19,000	550		19,550	21,700	
	0150 Maximum	↓	.20	40	↓	70,000	1,375		71,375	79,000	
	0500 Curtain track, straight, light duty	2 Carp	20	.800	L.F.	18.35	23.50		41.85	56.50	
	0600 Heavy duty		18	.889		37.50	26		63.50	82	
	0700 Curved sections		12	1.333	↓	110	39		149	182	
	1000 Curtains, velour, medium weight		600	.027	S.F.	6	.78		6.78	7.80	
	1150 Silica based yarn, fireproof	↓	50	.320		12	9.35		21.35	28	
	1500 Flooring, portable oak parquet, 3' x 3' sections				↓	10.05			10.05	11.05	
	1600 Cart to carry 225 S.F. of flooring				Ea.	305			305	335	
	2000 Lights, border, quartz, reflector, vented,										
	2100 colored or white	1 Elec	20	.400	L.F.	138	13.70		151.70	173	
	2500 Spotlight, follow spot, with transformer, 2,100 watt	"	4	2	Ea.	1,325	68.50		1,393.50	1,550	
	2600 For no transformer, deduct					475			475	525	
	3000 Stationary spot, fresnel quartz, 6" lens	1 Elec	4	2		115	68.50		183.50	229	
	3100 8" lens		4	2		181	68.50		249.50	300	
	3500 Ellipsoidal quartz, 1,000W, 6" lens		4	2		239	68.50		307.50	365	
	3600 12" lens		4	2		420	68.50		488.50	560	
	4000 Strobe light, 1 to 15 flashes per second, quartz		3	2.667		540	91.50		631.50	730	
	4500 Color wheel, portable, five hole, motorized	↓	4	2	↓	115	68.50		183.50	229	
	5000 Stages, portable with steps, folding legs, stock, 8" high				SF Stg.	15.15			15.15	16.70	
	5100 16" high					20			20	22	
	5200 32" high					22.50			22.50	25	
	5300 40" high					45			45	49.50	
	6000 Telescoping platforms, extruded alum., straight, minimum	4 Carp	157	.204		19.85	5.95		25.80	31.50	
	6100 Maximum		77	.416		27	12.10		39.10	49	
	6500 Pie-shaped, minimum		150	.213		37.50	6.20		43.70	51.50	
	6600 Maximum	↓	70	.457		40.50	13.35		53.85	65.50	
	6800 For 3/4" plywood covered deck, deduct					2.73			2.73	3	
	7000 Band risers, steel frame, plywood deck, minimum	4 Carp	275	.116		23	3.39		26.39	31	
	7100 Maximum	"	138	.232	↓	43.50	6.75		50.25	58.50	
	7500 Chairs for above, self-storing, minimum	2 Carp	43	.372	Ea.	78	10.85		88.85	102	
	7600 Maximum	"	40	.400	"	124	11.65		135.65	155	

11060 | Theater & Stage Equipment

11063	Stage Equipment	CREW	DAILY OUTPUT	LABOR-HOURS	UNIT	2001 BARE COSTS				TOTAL INCL O&P	
						MAT.	LABOR	EQUIP.	TOTAL		
600	8000	Rule of thumb: total stage equipment, minimum	4 Carp	100	.320	SF Stg.	72.50	9.35		81.85	94	**600**
	8100	Maximum	"	25	1.280	"	400	37.50		437.50	500	

11100 | Mercantile Equipment

11102	Barber Shop Equipment	CREW	DAILY OUTPUT	LABOR-HOURS	UNIT	2001 BARE COSTS				TOTAL INCL O&P	
						MAT.	LABOR	EQUIP.	TOTAL		
150	0010	**BARBER EQUIPMENT**										**150**
	0020	Chair, hydraulic, movable, minimum	1 Carp	24	.333	Ea.	410	9.70		419.70	465	
	0050	Maximum	"	16	.500		2,700	14.60		2,714.60	3,000	
	0200	Wall hung styling station with mirrors, minimum	L-2	8	2		315	51.50		366.50	425	
	0300	Maximum	"	4	4		1,800	103		1,903	2,125	
	0500	Sink, hair washing basin, rough plumbing not incl.	1 Plum	8	1		273	34.50		307.50	350	
	1000	Sterilizer, liquid solution for tools					125			125	138	
	1100	Total equipment, rule of thumb, per chair, minimum	L-8	1	20		1,475	605		2,080	2,575	
	1150	Maximum	"	1	20		4,000	605		4,605	5,350	

11103	Cash Register/Checking	CREW	DAILY OUTPUT	LABOR-HOURS	UNIT	2001 BARE COSTS				TOTAL INCL O&P	
						MAT.	LABOR	EQUIP.	TOTAL		
200	0010	**CHECKOUT COUNTER**										**200**
	0020	Supermarket conveyor, single belt	2 Clab	10	1.600	Ea.	1,975	36.50		2,011.50	2,225	
	0100	Double belt, power take-away		9	1.778		3,400	40.50		3,440.50	3,825	
	0400	Double belt, power take-away, incl. side scanning		7	2.286		4,225	52		4,277	4,725	
	0800	Warehouse or bulk type		6	2.667		4,950	61		5,011	5,550	
	1000	Scanning system, 2 lanes, w/registers, scan gun & memory				System	12,400			12,400	13,600	
	1100	10 lanes, single processor, full scan, with scales				"	117,500			117,500	129,000	
	2000	Register, restaurant, minimum				Ea.	515			515	565	
	2100	Maximum					2,275			2,275	2,500	
	2150	Store, minimum					515			515	565	
	2200	Maximum					2,275			2,275	2,500	

11104	Display Cases & Systems	CREW	DAILY OUTPUT	LABOR-HOURS	UNIT	2001 BARE COSTS				TOTAL INCL O&P	
						MAT.	LABOR	EQUIP.	TOTAL		
700	0010	**REFRIGERATED FOOD CASES**										**700**
	0030	Dairy, multi-deck, 12' long	Q-5	3	5.333	Ea.	7,075	167		7,242	8,025	
	0100	For rear sliding doors, add					1,000			1,000	1,100	
	0200	Delicatessen case, service deli, 12' long, single deck	Q-5	3.90	4.103		4,750	129		4,879	5,425	
	0300	Multi-deck, 18 S.F. shelf display		3	5.333		5,825	167		5,992	6,650	
	0400	Freezer, self-contained, chest-type, 30 C.F.		3.90	4.103		3,475	129		3,604	4,025	
	0500	Glass door, upright, 78 C.F.		3.30	4.848		6,600	152		6,752	7,500	
	0600	Frozen food, chest type, 12' long		3.30	4.848		4,775	152		4,927	5,475	
	0700	Glass door, reach-in, 5 door		3	5.333		9,150	167		9,317	10,400	
	0800	Island case, 12' long, single deck		3.30	4.848		5,400	152		5,552	6,175	
	0900	Multi-deck		3	5.333		11,400	167		11,567	12,900	
	1000	Meat case, 12' long, single deck		3.30	4.848		3,925	152		4,077	4,550	
	1050	Multi-deck		3.10	5.161		6,775	162		6,937	7,700	
	1100	Produce, 12' long, single deck		3.30	4.848		5,200	152		5,352	5,950	
	1200	Multi-deck		3.10	5.161		5,800	162		5,962	6,625	

Important: See the Reference Section for critical supporting data - Reference Nos., Crews, & City Cost Indexes

11110 | Commercial Laundry & Dry Cleaning Equipment

11119	Laundry Cleaning	CREW	DAILY OUTPUT	LABOR-HOURS	UNIT	2001 BARE COSTS				TOTAL INCL O&P
						MAT.	LABOR	EQUIP.	TOTAL	
450	**0010**	**LAUNDRY EQUIPMENT** Not incl. rough-in									**450**
0500	Dryers, gas fired residential, 16 lb. capacity, average	1 Plum	3	2.667	Ea.	520	92		612	710
1000	Commercial, 30 lb. capacity, coin operated, single		3	2.667		2,375	92		2,467	2,775
1100	Double stacked		2	4		5,100	138		5,238	5,800
1500	Industrial, 30 lb. capacity		2	4		2,025	138		2,163	2,425
1600	50 lb. capacity		1.70	4.706		2,650	162		2,812	3,175
2000	Dry cleaners, electric, 20 lb. capacity	L-1	.20	80		27,900	2,750		30,650	34,800
2050	25 lb. capacity		.17	94.118		36,300	3,225		39,525	44,900
2100	30 lb. capacity		.15	106		38,300	3,675		41,975	47,600
2150	60 lb. capacity		.09	177		60,000	6,100		66,100	75,000
3500	Folders, blankets & sheets, minimum	1 Elec	.17	47.059		25,600	1,625		27,225	30,500
3700	King size with automatic stacker		.10	80		44,100	2,750		46,850	52,500
3800	For conveyor delivery, add		.45	17.778		5,250	610		5,860	6,675
4500	Ironers, institutional, 110", single roll		.20	40		24,200	1,375		25,575	28,700
4700	Lint collector, ductwork not included, 8,000 to 10,000 C.F.M.	Q-10	.30	80		6,925	2,500		9,425	11,500
4800	Pressers, low capacity air operated	L-6	1.75	6.857		7,400	236		7,636	8,500
4820	Hand operated		1.75	6.857		6,375	236		6,611	7,375
4830	Extractor, low capacity		1.75	6.857		5,450	236		5,686	6,325
4840	Ironer 48", 240V		3.50	3.429		85,000	118		85,118	93,500
4860	Coin dry cleaner 20 lb.		1.75	6.857		21,200	236		21,436	23,700
4900	Spreader feeders, 240V, 2 station		.70	17.143		41,400	590		41,990	46,400
4920	4 station		.35	34.286		51,000	1,175		52,175	58,000
5000	Washers, residential, 4 cycle, average	1 Plum	3	2.667		595	92		687	795
5300	Commercial, coin operated, average	"	3	2.667		955	92		1,047	1,200
6000	Combination washer/extractor, 20 lb. capacity	L-6	1.50	8		3,425	275		3,700	4,175
6100	30 lb. capacity		.80	15		6,600	515		7,115	8,025
6200	50 lb. capacity		.68	17.647		8,225	605		8,830	9,975
6300	75 lb. capacity		.30	40		17,000	1,375		18,375	20,800
6350	125 lb. capacity		.16	75		20,600	2,575		23,175	26,500
6380	Washer extractor/dryer, 110 lb., 240V		1	12		6,600	415		7,015	7,875
6400	Washer extractor, 135 lb, 240V		1	12		19,800	415		20,215	22,400
6450	Pass through		1	12		52,000	415		52,415	58,000
6500	200 lb.		1	12		51,000	415		51,415	56,500
6550	Pass through		1	12		55,000	415		55,415	61,000
6600	Hand operated presser		.70	17.143		4,775	590		5,365	6,125
6620	Mushroom press 115V		.70	17.143		5,650	590		6,240	7,100

11130 | Audio-Visual Equipment

11136	Projection Screens	CREW	DAILY OUTPUT	LABOR-HOURS	UNIT	2001 BARE COSTS				TOTAL INCL O&P
						MAT.	LABOR	EQUIP.	TOTAL	
500	**0010**	**PROJECTION SCREENS** Wall or ceiling hung, matte white									**500**
0100	Manually operated, economy	2 Carp	500	.032	S.F.	4.41	.93		5.34	6.30
0300	Intermediate		450	.036		5.15	1.04		6.19	7.25
0400	Deluxe		400	.040		7.15	1.17		8.32	9.65
0600	Electric operated, matte white, 25 S.F., economy		5	3.200	Ea.	645	93.50		738.50	855
0700	Deluxe		4	4		1,450	117		1,567	1,750
0900	50 S.F., economy		3	5.333		325	155		480	600
1000	Deluxe		2	8		1,500	233		1,733	2,025
1200	Heavy duty, electric operated, 200 S.F.		1.50	10.667		2,950	310		3,260	3,725
1300	400 S.F.		1	16		3,650	465		4,115	4,725

EQUIPMENT 11

11136	Projection Screens	CREW	DAILY OUTPUT	LABOR-HOURS	UNIT	2001 BARE COSTS				TOTAL INCL O&P	
						MAT.	LABOR	EQUIP.	TOTAL		
500 1500	Rigid acrylic in wall, for rear projection, 1/4" thick	2 Glaz	30	.533	S.F.	35.50	15.25		50.75	62.50	**500**
1600	1/2" thick (maximum size 10' x 20')	"	25	.640	"	63	18.25		81.25	97	
600 0010	**MOVIE EQUIPMENT**										**600**
0020	Changeover, minimum				Ea.	350			350	385	
0100	Maximum					685			685	750	
0400	Film transport, incl. platters and autowind, minimum					3,800			3,800	4,175	
0500	Maximum					10,800			10,800	11,900	
0800	Lamphouses, incl. rectifiers, xenon, 1,000 watt	1 Elec	2	4		4,800	137		4,937	5,475	
0900	1,600 watt		2	4		5,100	137		5,237	5,800	
1000	2,000 watt		1.50	5.333		5,500	183		5,683	6,325	
1100	4,000 watt		1.50	5.333		6,800	183		6,983	7,750	
1400	Lenses, anamorphic, minimum					920			920	1,000	
1500	Maximum					2,100			2,100	2,300	
1800	Flat 35 mm, minimum					800			800	880	
1900	Maximum					1,250			1,250	1,375	
2200	Pedestals, for projectors					1,125			1,125	1,225	
2300	Console type					8,100			8,100	8,900	
2600	Projector mechanisms, incl. soundhead, 35 mm, minimum					8,400			8,400	9,250	
2700	Maximum					11,500			11,500	12,700	
3000	Projection screens, rigid, in wall, acrylic, 1/4" thick	2 Glaz	195	.082	S.F.	31.50	2.34		33.84	38.50	
3100	1/2" thick	"	130	.123	"	36.50	3.51		40.01	46	
3300	Electric operated, heavy duty, 400 S.F.	2 Carp	1	16	Ea.	2,225	465		2,690	3,175	
3320	Theatre projection screens, matte white, including frames	"	200	.080	S.F.	5	2.33		7.33	9.15	
3400	Also see division 11136-500										
3700	Sound systems, incl. amplifier, mono, minimum	1 Elec	.90	8.889	Ea.	2,500	305		2,805	3,200	
3800	Dolby/Super Sound, maximum		.40	20		13,700	685		14,385	16,000	
4100	Dual system, 2 channel, front surround, minimum		.70	11.429		3,500	390		3,890	4,425	
4200	Dolby/Super Sound, 4 channel, maximum		.40	20		12,500	685		13,185	14,800	
4500	Sound heads, 35 mm					4,000			4,000	4,400	
4900	Splicer, wet type, minimum					560			560	615	
5000	Tape type, maximum					1,000			1,000	1,100	
5300	Speakers, recessed behind screen, minimum	1 Elec	2	4		800	137		937	1,075	
5400	Maximum	"	1	8		2,325	274		2,599	2,975	
5700	Seating, painted steel, upholstered, minimum	2 Carp	35	.457		100	13.35		113.35	131	
5800	Maximum	"	28	.571		320	16.65		336.65	375	
6100	Rewind tables, minimum					2,000			2,000	2,200	
6200	Maximum					3,550			3,550	3,900	
7000	For automation, varying sophistication, minimum	1 Elec	1	8	System	1,800	274		2,074	2,375	
7100	Maximum	2 Elec	.30	53.333	"	4,200	1,825		6,025	7,350	

11141	Service Station Equipment	CREW	DAILY OUTPUT	LABOR-HOURS	UNIT	2001 BARE COSTS				TOTAL INCL O&P	
						MAT.	LABOR	EQUIP.	TOTAL		
150 0010	**AUTOMOTIVE**										**150**
0030	Compressors, electric, 1-1/2 H.P., standard controls	L-4	1.50	16	Ea.	315	435		750	1,025	
0550	Dual controls		1.50	16		460	435		895	1,200	
0600	5 H.P., 115/230 volt, standard controls		1	24		1,525	655		2,180	2,725	
0650	Dual controls		1	24		1,625	655		2,280	2,825	
1100	Product dispenser with vapor recovery for 6 nozzles, installed, not										

11140 | Vehicle Service Equipment

11141 | Service Station Equipment

		CREW	DAILY OUTPUT	LABOR-HOURS	UNIT	2001 BARE COSTS				TOTAL INCL O&P	
						MAT.	LABOR	EQUIP.	TOTAL		
150	**1110**	including piping to storage tanks				Ea.	15,000			15,000	16,500	**150**
	2200	Hoists, single post, 8,000# capacity, swivel arms	L-4	.40	60		3,500	1,625		5,125	6,425	
	2400	Two posts, adjustable frames, 11,000# capacity		.25	96		4,500	2,625		7,125	9,050	
	2500	24,000# capacity		.15	160		6,000	4,375		10,375	13,500	
	2700	7,500# capacity, frame supports		.50	48		5,000	1,300		6,300	7,550	
	2800	Four post, roll on ramp		.50	48		4,500	1,300		5,800	7,000	
	2810	Hydraulic lifts, above ground, 2 post, clear floor, 6000 lb cap		2.67	8.989		4,700	245		4,945	5,550	
	2815	9000 lb capacity		2.29	10.480		11,200	286		11,486	12,800	
	2820	15,000 lb capacity		2	12		12,600	325		12,925	14,400	
	2825	30,000 lb capacity		1.60	15		27,900	410		28,310	31,200	
	2830	4 post, ramp style, 25,000 lb capacity		2	12		10,900	325		11,225	12,500	
	2835	35,000 lb capacity		1	24		51,000	655		51,655	57,000	
	2840	50,000 lb capacity		1	24		57,000	655		57,655	63,500	
	2845	75,000 lb capacity	↓	1	24		66,000	655		66,655	73,500	
	2850	For drive thru tracks, add, minimum					700			700	770	
	2855	Maximum					1,200			1,200	1,325	
	2860	Ramp extensions, 3'(set of 2)					575			575	635	
	2865	Rolling jack platform					2,000			2,000	2,200	
	2870	Elec/hyd jacking beam					5,350			5,350	5,875	
	2880	Scissor lift, portable, 6000 lb capacity				↓	5,250			5,250	5,775	
	3000	Lube equipment, 3 reel type, with pumps, not including piping	L-4	.50	48	Set	6,000	1,300		7,300	8,650	
	4000	Spray painting booth, 26' long, complete	"	.40	60	Ea.	12,000	1,625		13,625	15,800	

EQUIPMENT 11

11150 | Parking Control Equipment

11156 | Parking Equipment

		CREW	DAILY OUTPUT	LABOR-HOURS	UNIT	2001 BARE COSTS				TOTAL INCL O&P	
						MAT.	LABOR	EQUIP.	TOTAL		
600	**0010**	**PARKING EQUIPMENT**										**600**
	5000	Barrier gate with programmable controller	2 Elec	3	5.333	Ea.	2,475	183		2,658	3,000	
	5020	Industrial	"	3	5.333		3,525	183		3,708	4,150	
	5100	Card reader	1 Elec	2	4		2,175	137		2,312	2,575	
	5120	Proximity with customer display	2 Elec	1	16		4,500	550		5,050	5,775	
	5200	Cashier booth, average	B-22	1	30		9,250	805	213	10,268	11,700	
	5300	Collector station, pay on foot	2 Elec	.20	80		97,500	2,750		100,250	111,500	
	5320	Credit card only	↓	.50	32		18,000	1,100		19,100	21,500	
	5500	Exit verifier	↓	1	16		15,500	550		16,050	17,900	
	5600	Fee computer	1 Elec	1.50	5.333		13,700	183		13,883	15,300	
	5700	Full sign, 4" letters	"	2	4		1,075	137		1,212	1,400	
	5800	Inductive loop	2 Elec	4	4		150	137		287	370	
	5900	Ticket spitter with time/date stamp, standard		2	8		6,000	274		6,274	7,000	
	5920	Mag stripe encoding	↓	2	8		16,500	274		16,774	18,600	
	5950	Vehicle detector, microprocessor based	1 Elec	3	2.667		375	91.50		466.50	550	
	6000	Parking control software, minimum		.50	16		19,500	550		20,050	22,200	
	6020	Maximum	↓	.20	40	↓	81,000	1,375		82,375	91,000	

335

11161	Loading Dock Equipment	CREW	DAILY OUTPUT	LABOR-HOURS	UNIT	2001 BARE COSTS				TOTAL INCL O&P	
						MAT.	LABOR	EQUIP.	TOTAL		
200	0010 **DOCK BUMPERS** Bolts not included										200
	0020 2" x 6" to 4" x 8", average	1 Carp	.30	26.667	M.B.F.	930	775		1,705	2,250	
400	0010 **LOADING DOCK**										400
	0020 Bumpers, rubber blocks 4-1/2" thk, 10" H, 14" long	1 Carp	26	.308	Ea.	38	8.95		46.95	55.50	
	0200 24" long		22	.364		67.50	10.60		78.10	90.50	
	0300 36" long		17	.471		72	13.70		85.70	101	
	0500 12" high, 14" long		25	.320		71	9.35		80.35	93	
	0550 24" long		20	.400		78.50	11.65		90.15	105	
	0600 36" long		15	.533		87.50	15.55		103.05	121	
	0800 Rubber blocks 6" thick, 10" high, 14" long		22	.364		63	10.60		73.60	85.50	
	0850 24" long		18	.444		86	12.95		98.95	116	
	0900 36" long		13	.615		102	17.95		119.95	140	
	0910 20" high, 11" long		13	.615		104	17.95		121.95	143	
	0920 Extruded rubber bumpers, T section, 22" x 22" x 3" thick		41	.195		40	5.70		45.70	53	
	0940 Molded rubber bumpers, 24" x 12" x 3" thick		20	.400		38	11.65		49.65	60.50	
	1000 Welded installation of above bumpers	E-14	8	1		2.65	35	10.50	48.15	77.50	
	1100 For drilled anchors, add per anchor	1 Carp	36	.222		4.76	6.50		11.26	15.40	
	1300 Steel bumpers, see division 10265 & 08770										
	1350 Wood bumpers, see division 11161-200										
	2200 Dock boards, heavy duty, 60" x 60", aluminum, 5,000 lb. cap.				Ea.	1,050			1,050	1,150	
	2700 9,000 lb. capacity					1,075			1,075	1,175	
	3200 15,000 lb. capacity					1,200			1,200	1,325	
	3600 Door seal for door perimeter, 12" x 12", vinyl covered	1 Carp	26	.308	L.F.	18.55	8.95		27.50	34.50	
	3900 Folding gates, see division 10610-100										
	4200 Platform lifter, 6' x 6', portable, 3,000 lb. capacity				Ea.	6,500			6,500	7,150	
	4250 4,000 lb. capacity					8,000			8,000	8,800	
	4400 Fixed, 6' x 8', 5,000 lb. capacity	E-16	.70	22.857		7,000	775	120	7,895	9,225	
	4500 Levelers, hinged for trucks, 10 ton capacity, 6' x 8'		1.08	14.815		3,525	500	78	4,103	4,900	
	4650 7' x 8'		1.08	14.815		3,375	500	78	3,953	4,725	
	4670 Air bag power operated, 10 ton cap., 6'x8'		1.08	14.815		4,100	500	78	4,678	5,525	
	4680 7' x 8'		1.08	14.815		4,125	500	78	4,703	5,525	
	4700 Hydraulic, 10 ton capacity, 6' x 8' **CN**		1.08	14.815		6,150	500	78	6,728	7,775	
	4800 7' x 8'		1.08	14.815		6,625	500	78	7,203	8,275	
	5000 Lights for loading docks, single arm, 24" long	1 Elec	3.80	2.105		99	72		171	217	
	5700 Double arm, 60" long	"	3.80	2.105		130	72		202	251	
	5800 Loading dock safety restraints, manual style	E-16	1.08	14.815		2,250	500	78	2,828	3,475	
	5900 Automatic style	"	1.08	14.815		3,800	500	78	4,378	5,175	
	6200 Shelters, fabric, for truck or train, scissor arms, minimum	1 Carp	1	8		1,050	233		1,283	1,525	
	6300 Maximum	"	.50	16		1,550	465		2,015	2,425	

11179	Waste Handling Equipment	CREW	DAILY OUTPUT	LABOR-HOURS	UNIT	2001 BARE COSTS				TOTAL INCL O&P	
						MAT.	LABOR	EQUIP.	TOTAL		
150	0010 **WASTE HANDLING**										150
	0020 Compactors, 115 volt, 250#/hr., chute fed	L-4	1	24	Ea.	8,225	655		8,880	10,100	
	0100 Hand fed		2.40	10		5,675	273		5,948	6,675	
	0300 Multi-bag, 230 volt, 600#/hr, chute fed		1	24		7,025	655		7,680	8,750	
	0400 Hand fed		1	24		6,375	655		7,030	8,050	
	0500 Containerized, hand fed, 2 to 6 C.Y. containers, 250#/hr.		1	24		7,475	655		8,130	9,250	

EQUIPMENT 11

11179	Waste Handling Equipment	CREW	DAILY OUTPUT	LABOR-HOURS	UNIT	2001 BARE COSTS MAT.	LABOR	EQUIP.	TOTAL	TOTAL INCL O&P	
150											**150**
0550	For chute fed, add per floor	L-4	1	24	Ea.	860	655		1,515	1,975	
1000	Heavy duty industrial compactor, 0.5 C.Y. capacity		1	24		5,050	655		5,705	6,575	
1050	1.0 C.Y. capacity		1	24		7,525	655		8,180	9,300	
1100	3 C.Y. capacity		.50	48		10,500	1,300		11,800	13,700	
1150	5.0 C.Y. capacity		.50	48		14,000	1,300		15,300	17,500	
1200	Combination shredder/compactor (5,000 lbs./hr.)		.50	48		25,200	1,300		26,500	29,800	
1400	For handling hazardous waste materials, 55 gallon drum packer, std.					11,700			11,700	12,900	
1410	55 gallon drum packer w/HEPA filter					14,900			14,900	16,400	
1420	55 gallon drum packer w/charcoal & HEPA filter					19,000			19,000	20,900	
1430	All of the above made explosion proof, add					9,075			9,075	9,975	
1500	Crematory, not including building, 1 place	Q-3	.20	160		42,400	5,250		47,650	54,500	
1750	2 place		.10	320		60,500	10,500		71,000	82,500	
4400	Incinerator, gas, not incl. chimney, elec. or pipe, 50#/hr., minimum		.80	40		16,200	1,325		17,525	19,800	
4420	Maximum		.70	45.714		21,100	1,500		22,600	25,500	
4440	200 lb. per hr., minimum (batch type)		.60	53.333		21,100	1,750		22,850	25,900	
4460	Maximum (with feeder)		.50	64		41,100	2,100		43,200	48,400	
4480	400 lb. per hr., minimum (batch type)		.30	106		25,000	3,500		28,500	32,800	
4500	Maximum (with feeder)		.25	128		47,200	4,200		51,400	58,500	
4520	800 lb. per hr., with feeder, minimum		.20	160		61,500	5,250		66,750	75,500	
4540	Maximum		.17	188		84,000	6,175		90,175	102,000	
4560	1,200 lb. per hr., with feeder, minimum		.15	213		89,000	7,000		96,000	108,500	
4580	Maximum		.11	290		107,000	9,550		116,550	132,000	
4600	2,000 lb. per hr., with feeder, minimum		.10	320		155,500	10,500		166,000	187,000	
4620	Maximum		.05	640		261,500	21,000		282,500	319,000	
4700	For heat recovery system, add, minimum		.25	128		50,500	4,200		54,700	62,000	
4710	Add, maximum		.11	290		161,500	9,550		171,050	192,000	
4720	For automatic ash conveyer, add		.50	64		20,200	2,100		22,300	25,400	
4750	Large municipal incinerators, incl. stack, minimum		.25	128	Ton/day	12,900	4,200		17,100	20,600	
4850	Maximum		.10	320	"	34,300	10,500		44,800	53,500	
5500	Shredder, municipal use, 35 ton per hour				Ea.	192,000			192,000	211,000	
5600	60 ton per hour					409,000			409,000	450,000	
5750	Shredder & baler, 50 ton per day					383,500			383,500	422,000	
5800	Shredder, industrial, minimum					15,100			15,100	16,600	
5850	Maximum					81,000			81,000	89,000	
5900	Baler, industrial, minimum					6,050			6,050	6,650	
5950	Maximum					353,500			353,500	389,000	
6000	Transfer station compactor, with power unit										
6050	and pedestal, not including pit, 50 ton per hour				Ea.	121,000			121,000	133,000	

EQUIPMENT 11

11191	Detention Equipment	CREW	DAILY OUTPUT	LABOR-HOURS	UNIT	2001 BARE COSTS MAT.	LABOR	EQUIP.	TOTAL	TOTAL INCL O&P	
150	0010 **DETENTION EQUIPMENT**										**150**
0500	Bar front, rolling, 7/8" bars, 4" O.C., 7' high, 5' wide, with hardware	E-4	2	16	Ea.	4,175	535	42	4,752	5,625	
1000	Doors & frames, 3' x 7', complete, with hardware, single plate		4	8		3,100	267	21	3,388	3,925	
1650	Double plate		4	8		3,850	267	21	4,138	4,725	
2000	Cells, prefab., 5' to 6' wide, 7' to 8' high, 7' to 8' deep,										
2010	bar front, cot, not incl. plumbing	E-4	1.50	21.333	Ea.	7,400	710	56	8,166	9,500	
2500	Cot, bolted, single, painted steel		20	1.600		279	53.50	4.21	336.71	405	
2700	Stainless steel		20	1.600		725	53.50	4.21	782.71	900	

11190 | Detention Equipment

		11191	Detention Equipment	CREW	DAILY OUTPUT	LABOR-HOURS	UNIT	2001 BARE COSTS MAT.	LABOR	EQUIP.	TOTAL	TOTAL INCL O&P	
150	3000		Toilet apparatus including wash basin, average	L-8	1.50	13.333	Ea.	2,075	405		2,480	2,900	150
	4000		Visitor cubicle, vision panel, no intercom	E-4	2	16	↓	2,350	535	42	2,927	3,625	

11300 | Fluid Waste Treatment & Disposal Equipment

		11310	Sewage & Sludge Pumps	CREW	DAILY OUTPUT	LABOR-HOURS	UNIT	2001 BARE COSTS MAT.	LABOR	EQUIP.	TOTAL	TOTAL INCL O&P	
700	0010		SEWAGE PUMPING STATIONS Prefabricated steel, concrete										700
	0020		or fiberglass, 200 GPM	C-17D	.17	494	Total	28,600	15,000	3,900	47,500	59,500	
	0200		1,000 GPM		.07	1,200		42,400	36,300	9,475	88,175	114,000	
	0500		Add for generator unit, 200 GPM, steel		.34	247		21,700	7,475	1,950	31,125	37,800	
	0600		Concrete		.51	164		13,800	5,000	1,300	20,100	24,500	
	1000		Add for generator unit, 1,000 GPM, steel		.30	280		23,100	8,475	2,200	33,775	41,100	
	1200		Concrete	↓	.38	221		19,500	6,700	1,750	27,950	33,900	
	1500		For drilled water well, if required, add	B-23	.50	80	↓	5,625	1,850	4,100	11,575	13,600	

		11390	Pkg Sewage Treat Plants	CREW	DAILY OUTPUT	LABOR-HOURS	UNIT	2001 BARE COSTS MAT.	LABOR	EQUIP.	TOTAL	TOTAL INCL O&P	
900	0010		WASTEWATER TREATMENT SYSTEM Fiberglass, 1,000 gallon	B-21	1.29	21.705	Ea.	2,750	580	110	3,440	4,050	900
	0100		1,500 gallon	"	1.03	27.184	"	6,025	725	138	6,888	7,900	

11400 | Food Service Equipment

		11405	Food Storage Equipment	CREW	DAILY OUTPUT	LABOR-HOURS	UNIT	2001 BARE COSTS MAT.	LABOR	EQUIP.	TOTAL	TOTAL INCL O&P	
800	0010		WINE CELLAR, refrigerated, Redwood interior, carpeted, walk-in type										800
	0020		6'-8" high, including racks										
	0200		80"W x 48"D for 900 bottles	2 Carp	1.50	10.667	Ea.	2,600	310		2,910	3,325	
	0250		80" W x 72" D for 1300 bottles		1.33	12.030		3,425	350		3,775	4,325	
	0300		80" W x 94" D for 1900 bottles		1.17	13.675		4,450	400		4,850	5,525	
	0400		80" W x 124" D for 2500 bottles	↓	1	16	↓	5,400	465		5,865	6,650	
	0600		Portable cabinets, red oak, reach-in temp.& humidity controlled										
	0650		26-5/8"W x 26-1/2"D x 68"H for 235 bottles				Ea.	2,350			2,350	2,575	
	0660		32"W x 21-1/2"D x 73-1/2"H for 144 bottles					2,725			2,725	3,000	
	0670		32"W x 29-1/2"D x 73-1/2"H for 288 bottles					2,750			2,750	3,025	
	0680		39-1/2"W x 29-1/2"D x 86-1/2"H for 440 bottles					3,125			3,125	3,425	
	0690		52-1/2"W x 29-1/2"D x 73-1/2"H for 468 bottles					3,575			3,575	3,950	
	0700		52-1/2"W x 29-1/2"D x 86-1/2"H for 572 bottles				↓	3,775			3,775	4,150	
	0730		Portable, red oak, can be built-in with glass door										
	0750		23-7/8"W x 24"D x 34-1/2"H for 50 bottles				Ea.	855			855	945	

		11410	Food Prep Equipment	CREW	DAILY OUTPUT	LABOR-HOURS	UNIT	2001 BARE COSTS MAT.	LABOR	EQUIP.	TOTAL	TOTAL INCL O&P	
150	0010		COMMERCIAL KITCHEN EQUIPMENT										150
	0020		Bake oven, gas, one section	Q-1	8	2	Ea.	3,750	62		3,812	4,225	
	0300		Two sections		7	2.286		7,475	71		7,546	8,325	
	0600		Three sections	↓	6	2.667	↓	10,700	82.50		10,782.50	11,800	

11410	Food Prep Equipment	CREW	DAILY OUTPUT	LABOR-HOURS	UNIT	2001 BARE COSTS				TOTAL INCL O&P	
						MAT.	LABOR	EQUIP.	TOTAL		
150 0900	Electric convection, single deck	L-7	4	7	Ea.	5,075	197		5,272	5,875	**150**
1050	Butter pat dispenser	1 Clab	13	.615		420	14.05		434.05	480	
1100	Bread dispenser, counter top	"	13	.615		490	14.05		504.05	560	
1300	Broiler, without oven, standard	Q-1	8	2		3,600	62		3,662	4,050	
1550	Infra-red	L-7	4	7		4,600	197		4,797	5,375	
1650	Cabinet, heated, 1 compartment, reach-in	R-18	5.60	4.643		2,225	125		2,350	2,650	
1655	Pass-thru roll-in		5.60	4.643		3,100	125		3,225	3,625	
1660	2 compartment, reach-in	↓	4.80	5.417		4,675	145		4,820	5,350	
1670	Mobile					2,200			2,200	2,425	
1700	Choppers, 5 pounds	R-18	7	3.714		1,575	100		1,675	1,875	
1720	16 pounds		5	5.200		1,975	140		2,115	2,400	
1740	35 to 40 pounds	↓	4	6.500		3,875	175		4,050	4,525	
1840	Coffee brewer, 5 burners	1 Plum	3	2.667		970	92		1,062	1,225	
1850	Coffee urn, twin 6 gallon urns		2	4		6,150	138		6,288	6,975	
1860	Single, 3 gallon	↓	3	2.667		4,500	92		4,592	5,100	
1900	Cup and glass dispenser, drop in	1 Clab	4	2		870	45.50		915.50	1,025	
1920	Disposable cup, drop in	"	16	.500		245	11.45		256.45	288	
2350	Cooler, reach-in, beverage, 6' long	Q-1	6	2.667		2,800	82.50		2,882.50	3,200	
2650	Dish dispenser, drop in, 12"	1 Clab	11	.727		1,025	16.60		1,041.60	1,150	
2660	Mobile	"	10	.800	↓	1,725	18.30		1,743.30	1,925	
2700	Dishwasher, commercial, rack type										
2720	10 to 12 racks per hour	Q-1	3.20	5	Ea.	2,550	155		2,705	3,050	
2750	Semi-automatic 38 to 50 racks per hour	"	1.30	12.308		5,375	380		5,755	6,475	
2800	Automatic, 190 to 230 racks per hour	Q-2	.70	34.286		11,000	1,100		12,100	13,800	
2820	235 to 275 racks per hour		.50	48		22,200	1,550		23,750	26,700	
2840	8,750 to 12,500 dishes per hour	↓	.20	120	↓	41,700	3,850		45,550	51,500	
2950	Dishwasher hood, canopy type	L-3A	10	1.200	L.F.	410	38.50		448.50	510	
2960	Pant leg type	"	2.50	4.800	Ea.	4,925	153		5,078	5,675	
2970	Exhaust hood, sst, gutter on all sides, 4' x 4' x 2'	1 Carp	1.80	4.444		2,700	130		2,830	3,175	
2980	4' x 4' x 7'	"	1.60	5		4,250	146		4,396	4,900	
3000	Fast food equipment, total package, minimum	6 Skwk	.08	600		116,000	17,900		133,900	155,500	
3100	Maximum	"	.07	685		157,500	20,500		178,000	205,500	
3300	Food warmer, counter, 1.2 KW					650			650	715	
3550	1.6 KW					830			830	915	
3600	Well, hot food, built-in, rectangular, 12" x 20"	R-30	10	2.600		264	71.50		335.50	400	
3610	Circular, 7 qt		10	2.600		221	71.50		292.50	350	
3620	Refrigerated, 2 compartments		10	2.600		1,600	71.50		1,671.50	1,850	
3630	3 compartments		9	2.889		1,575	79		1,654	1,850	
3640	4 compartments	↓	8	3.250		2,175	89		2,264	2,525	
3800	Food mixers, 20 quarts	L-7	7	4		3,250	112		3,362	3,750	
3850	40 quarts		5.40	5.185		7,350	146		7,496	8,300	
3900	60 quarts		5	5.600		10,000	157		10,157	11,200	
4040	80 quarts		3.90	7.179		11,400	202		11,602	12,900	
4080	130 quarts		2.20	12.727		16,900	360		17,260	19,200	
4100	Floor type, 20 quarts		15	1.867		3,125	52.50		3,177.50	3,500	
4120	60 quarts		14	2		8,800	56		8,856	9,775	
4140	80 quarts		12	2.333		11,400	65.50		11,465.50	12,600	
4160	140 quarts	↓	8.60	3.256		20,400	91.50		20,491.50	22,500	
4300	Freezers, reach-in, 44 C.F.	Q-1	4	4		7,400	124		7,524	8,325	
4500	68 C.F.	"	3	5.333		8,725	165		8,890	9,825	
4600	Freezer, pre-fab, 8' x 8' w/refrigeration	2 Carp	.45	35.556		6,525	1,025		7,550	8,800	
4620	8' x 12'		.35	45.714		8,200	1,325		9,525	11,100	
4640	8' x 16'		.25	64		9,450	1,875		11,325	13,300	
4660	8' x 20'	↓	.17	94.118		13,400	2,750		16,150	19,100	
4680	Reach-in, 1 compartment	Q-1	4	4		1,975	124		2,099	2,350	
4700	2 compartment	"	3	5.333	↓	3,275	165		3,440	3,850	

EQUIPMENT 11

		Food Prep Equipment	CREW	DAILY OUTPUT	LABOR-HOURS	UNIT	2001 BARE COSTS				TOTAL INCL O&P	
	11410						MAT.	LABOR	EQUIP.	TOTAL		
150	4720	Frost cold plate	R-30	9	2.889	Ea.	10,800	79		10,879	12,000	**150**
	4750	Fryer, with twin baskets, modular model	Q-1	7	2.286		2,900	71		2,971	3,300	
	5000	Floor model on 6" legs	"	5	3.200		3,950	99		4,049	4,475	
	5100	Extra single basket, large					89.50			89.50	98.50	
	5200	Garbage disposal 1.5 HP, 100 GPH	L-1	4.80	3.333		1,600	115		1,715	1,950	
	5210	3 HP, 120 GPH		4.60	3.478		2,575	120		2,695	3,000	
	5220	5 HP, 250 GPH	↓	4.50	3.556		3,175	122		3,297	3,675	
	5300	3' Long SST griddle, 24" plate dp w/4" legs, elec, 208V 3Ph.	Q-1	7	2.286		1,725	71		1,796	2,000	
	5550	4' long	"	6	2.667		2,925	82.50		3,007.50	3,325	
	5700	Hot chocolate dispenser	1 Plum	4	2		735	69		804	910	
	5800	Ice cube maker, 50 pounds per day	Q-1	6	2.667		1,525	82.50		1,607.50	1,800	
	5900	250 pounds per day		1.20	13.333		1,950	415		2,365	2,750	
	6050	500 pounds per day		4	4		2,825	124		2,949	3,300	
	6060	With bin		1.20	13.333		3,625	415		4,040	4,625	
	6090	1000 pounds per day, with bin		1	16		6,850	495		7,345	8,275	
	6100	Ice flakers, 300 pounds per day		1.60	10		3,850	310		4,160	4,700	
	6120	600 pounds per day		.95	16.842		4,025	520		4,545	5,225	
	6130	1000 pounds per day		.75	21.333		6,475	660		7,135	8,100	
	6140	2000 pounds per day	↓	.65	24.615		12,100	765		12,865	14,500	
	6160	Ice storage bin, 500 pound capacity	Q-5	1	16		1,550	500		2,050	2,450	
	6180	1000 pound	"	.56	28.571		2,250	895		3,145	3,825	
	6200	Iced tea brewer	1 Plum	3.44	2.326		650	80		730	835	
	6250	Jet spray dispenser	R-18	4.50	5.778		2,225	155		2,380	2,650	
	6300	Juice dispenser, concentrate	"	4.50	5.778		825	155		980	1,150	
	6350	20 Gal kettle w/steam jacket, tilting w/positive lock, S/S	L-7	7	4		5,675	112		5,787	6,400	
	6600	60 gallons	"	6	4.667		6,350	131		6,481	7,175	
	6690	Milk dispenser, bulk, 2 flavor	R-30	8	3.250		1,025	89		1,114	1,250	
	6695	3 flavor	"	8	3.250		1,425	89		1,514	1,675	
	6700	Peelers, small	R-18	8	3.250		1,750	87.50		1,837.50	2,050	
	6720	Large	"	6	4.333	↓	3,075	116		3,191	3,550	
	6750	Pot sink, 3 compartment	1 Plum	7.25	1.103	L.F.	440	38		478	545	
	6760	Pot washer, small		1.60	5	Ea.	12,900	172		13,072	14,500	
	6770	Large		1.20	6.667		32,300	230		32,530	35,800	
	6800	Pulper/extractor, close coupled, 5 HP	↓	1.90	4.211		2,825	145		2,970	3,350	
	6850	Mobile rack w/pan slide					865			865	955	
	6900	Range, restaurant type, 6 burners and 1 standard oven, 36" wide	Q-1	7	2.286		2,100	71		2,171	2,400	
	6950	Convection		7	2.286		2,825	71		2,896	3,225	
	7150	2 standard ovens, 24" griddle, 60" wide		6	2.667		4,450	82.50		4,532.50	5,025	
	7200	1 standard, 1 convection oven		6	2.667		5,725	82.50		5,807.50	6,425	
	7450	Heavy duty, single 34" standard oven, open top		5	3.200		3,875	99		3,974	4,425	
	7500	Convection oven		5	3.200		5,175	99		5,274	5,825	
	7700	Griddle top		6	2.667		4,575	82.50		4,657.50	5,175	
	7750	Convection oven		6	2.667		5,625	82.50		5,707.50	6,325	
	7950	Hood fire protection system, minimum		3	5.333		2,900	165		3,065	3,425	
	8050	Maximum		1	16		21,100	495		21,595	24,000	
	8300	Refrigerators, reach-in type, 44 C.F.		5	3.200		5,075	99		5,174	5,725	
	8310	With glass doors, 68 C.F.	↓	4	4		6,450	124		6,574	7,275	
	8320	Refrigerator, reach-in, 1 compartment	R-18	7.80	3.333		1,825	89.50		1,914.50	2,125	
	8330	2 compartment		6.20	4.194		2,425	113		2,538	2,825	
	8340	3 compartment	↓	5.60	4.643		3,300	125		3,425	3,825	
	8350	Pre-fab, with refrigeration, 8' x 8'	2 Carp	.45	35.556		5,000	1,025		6,025	7,125	
	8360	8' x 12'		.35	45.714		6,900	1,325		8,225	9,675	
	8370	8' x 16'		.25	64		7,300	1,875		9,175	11,000	
	8380	8' x 20'	↓	.17	94.118		8,975	2,750		11,725	14,200	
	8390	Pass-thru/roll-in, 1 compartment	R-18	7.80	3.333		2,900	89.50		2,989.50	3,300	
	8400	2 compartment		6.24	4.167	↓	4,125	112		4,237	4,725	

		CREW	DAILY OUTPUT	LABOR-HOURS	UNIT	2001 BARE COSTS				TOTAL INCL O&P
11410	**Food Prep Equipment**					MAT.	LABOR	EQUIP.	TOTAL	
150 8410	3 compartment	R-18	5.60	4.643	Ea.	5,225	125		5,350	5,950 **150**
8420	Walk-in, alum, door & floor only, no refrig, 6' x 6' x 7'-6"	2 Carp	1.40	11.429		5,650	335		5,985	6,750
8430	10' x 6' x 7'-6"		.55	29.091		8,100	850		8,950	10,300
8440	12' x 14' x 7'-6"		.25	64		11,300	1,875		13,175	15,300
8450	12' x 20' x 7'-6"	↓	.17	94.118		13,800	2,750		16,550	19,500
8460	Refrigerated cabinets, mobile					2,225			2,225	2,425
8470	Refrigerator/freezer, reach-in, 1 compartment	R-18	5.60	4.643		3,725	125		3,850	4,300
8480	2 compartment		4.80	5.417		5,350	145		5,495	6,125
8580	Slicer with table	↓	9	2.889		2,950	77.50		3,027.50	3,375
8600	Stainless steel shelving, louvered 4-tier, 20" x 3'	1 Clab	6	1.333		1,050	30.50		1,080.50	1,225
8605	20" x 4'		6	1.333		1,250	30.50		1,280.50	1,425
8610	20" x 6'		6	1.333		1,725	30.50		1,755.50	1,950
8615	24" x 3'		6	1.333		1,100	30.50		1,130.50	1,275
8620	24" x 4'		6	1.333		1,325	30.50		1,355.50	1,500
8625	24" x 6'		6	1.333		1,825	30.50		1,855.50	2,075
8630	Flat 4-tier, 20" x 3'		6	1.333		980	30.50		1,010.50	1,125
8635	20" x 4'		6	1.333		1,200	30.50		1,230.50	1,350
8640	20" x 5'		6	1.333		1,350	30.50		1,380.50	1,550
8645	24" x 3'		6	1.333		1,050	30.50		1,080.50	1,200
8650	24" x 4'		6	1.333		1,300	30.50		1,330.50	1,475
8655	24" x 6'		6	1.333		2,475	30.50		2,505.50	2,775
8700	Galvanized shelving, louvered 4-tier, 20" x 3'		6	1.333		375	30.50		405.50	460
8705	20" x 4'		6	1.333		425	30.50		455.50	515
8710	20" x 6'		6	1.333		510	30.50		540.50	615
8715	24" x 3'		6	1.333		410	30.50		440.50	500
8720	24" x 4'		6	1.333		465	30.50		495.50	560
8725	24" x 6'		6	1.333		640	30.50		670.50	750
8730	Flat 4-tier, 20" x 3'		6	1.333		300	30.50		330.50	385
8735	20" x 4'		6	1.333		345	30.50		375.50	430
8740	20" x 6'		6	1.333		480	30.50		510.50	580
8745	24" x 3'		6	1.333		286	30.50		316.50	365
8750	24" x 4'		6	1.333		320	30.50		350.50	400
8755	24" x 6'		6	1.333		525	30.50		555.50	630
8760	Stainless steel dunnage rack, 24" x 3'		8	1		475	23		498	560
8765	24" x 4'		8	1		545	23		568	635
8770	Galvanized dunnage rack, 24" x 3'		8	1		130	23		153	179
8775	24" x 4'	↓	8	1	↓	148	23		171	198
8800	Serving counter, straight	1 Carp	40	.200	L.F.	435	5.85		440.85	490
8820	Curved section	"	30	.267	"	625	7.75		632.75	695
8825	Solid surface, see section 06610-810									
8830	Soft serve ice cream machine, medium	R-18	11	2.364	Ea.	6,625	63.50		6,688.50	7,400
8840	Large	"	9	2.889		9,975	77.50		10,052.50	11,100
8850	Steamer, electric 27 KW	L-7	7	4		7,900	112		8,012	8,875
9100	Electric, 10 KW or gas 100,000 BTU	"	5	5.600		3,600	157		3,757	4,200
9150	Toaster, conveyor type, 16-22 slices per minute					935			935	1,025
9160	Pop-up, 2 slot					475			475	520
9170	Trash compactor, small, up to 125 lb. compacted weight	L-4	4	6		14,700	164		14,864	16,500
9175	Large, up to 175 lb. compacted weight	"	3	8		17,900	218		18,118	20,000
9180	Tray and silver dispenser, mobile	1 Clab	16	.500	↓	645	11.45		656.45	730
9200	For deluxe models of above equipment, add					75%				
9400	Rule of thumb: Equipment cost based									
9410	on kitchen work area									
9420	Office buildings, minimum	L-7	77	.364	S.F.	50.50	10.20		60.70	71.50
9450	Maximum		58	.483		85.50	13.55		99.05	115
9550	Public eating facilities, minimum		77	.364		66.50	10.20		76.70	89
9600	Maximum	↓	46	.609	↓	108	17.10		125.10	146

EQUIPMENT 11

11410	Food Prep Equipment	CREW	DAILY OUTPUT	LABOR-HOURS	UNIT	2001 BARE COSTS				TOTAL INCL O&P
						MAT.	LABOR	EQUIP.	TOTAL	
150	9750	Hospitals, minimum	L-7	58	.483	S.F.	68	13.55		81.55	96	150
	9800	Maximum	↓	39	.718	↓	114	20		134	157	

11454	Residential Appliances		CREW	DAILY OUTPUT	LABOR-HOURS	UNIT	2001 BARE COSTS				TOTAL INCL O&P	
							MAT.	LABOR	EQUIP.	TOTAL		
500	0010	**RESIDENTIAL APPLIANCES**										500
	0020	Cooking range, 30" free standing, 1 oven, minimum	2 Clab	10	1.600	Ea.	249	36.50		285.50	330	
	0050	Maximum		4	4		1,200	91.50		1,291.50	1,475	
	0150	2 oven, minimum		10	1.600		1,300	36.50		1,336.50	1,475	
	0200	Maximum	↓	10	1.600		1,425	36.50		1,461.50	1,600	
	0350	Built-in, 30" wide, 1 oven, minimum	1 Elec	6	1.333		315	45.50		360.50	415	
	0400	Maximum	2 Carp	2	8		1,050	233		1,283	1,550	
	0500	2 oven, conventional, minimum		4	4		920	117		1,037	1,200	
	0550	1 conventional, 1 microwave, maximum	↓	2	8		1,525	233		1,758	2,050	
	0700	Free-standing, 1 oven, 21" wide range, minimum	2 Clab	10	1.600		281	36.50		317.50	365	
	0750	21" wide, maximum	"	4	4		465	91.50		556.50	660	
	0900	Counter top cook tops, 4 burner, standard, minimum	1 Elec	6	1.333		190	45.50		235.50	277	
	0950	Maximum		3	2.667		430	91.50		521.50	610	
	1050	As above, but with grille and griddle attachment, minimum		6	1.333		395	45.50		440.50	500	
	1100	Maximum		3	2.667		525	91.50		616.50	715	
	1200	Induction cooktop, 30" wide		3	2.667		495	91.50		586.50	680	
	1250	Microwave oven, minimum		4	2		85.50	68.50		154	196	
	1300	Maximum	↓	2	4		385	137		522	630	
	1500	Combination range, refrigerator and sink, 30" wide, minimum	L-1	2	8		700	275		975	1,175	
	1550	Maximum		1	16		1,400	550		1,950	2,375	
	1570	60" wide, average		1.40	11.429		2,325	395		2,720	3,150	
	1590	72" wide, average		1.20	13.333		2,625	460		3,085	3,575	
	1600	Office model, 48" wide **CN**		2	8		1,975	275		2,250	2,600	
	1620	Refrigerator and sink only	↓	2.40	6.667	↓	1,975	229		2,204	2,525	
	1640	Combination range, refrigerator, sink, microwave										
	1660	oven and ice maker	L-1	.80	20	Ea.	3,875	690		4,565	5,275	
	1750	Compactor, residential size, 4 to 1 compaction, minimum	1 Carp	5	1.600		350	46.50		396.50	460	
	1800	Maximum	"	3	2.667		380	77.50		457.50	540	
	2000	Deep freeze, 15 to 23 C.F., minimum	2 Clab	10	1.600		410	36.50		446.50	510	
	2050	Maximum		5	3.200		530	73		603	700	
	2200	30 C.F., minimum		8	2		770	45.50		815.50	915	
	2250	Maximum	↓	3	5.333		895	122		1,017	1,175	
	2450	Dehumidifier, portable, automatic, 15 pint					195			195	214	
	2550	40 pint					226			226	249	
	2750	Dishwasher, built-in, 2 cycles, minimum	L-1	4	4		246	138		384	475	
	2800	Maximum		2	8		271	275		546	715	
	2950	4 or more cycles, minimum		4	4		242	138		380	475	
	2960	Average		4	4		320	138		458	560	
	3000	Maximum	↓	2	8		510	275		785	975	
	3200	Dryer, automatic, minimum	L-2	3	5.333		251	137		388	490	
	3250	Maximum	"	2	8		555	205		760	930	
	3300	Garbage disposer, sink type, minimum	L-1	10	1.600		37.50	55		92.50	124	
	3350	Maximum	"	10	1.600		178	55		233	279	
	3550	Heater, electric, built-in, 1250 watt, ceiling type, minimum	1 Elec	4	2	↓	68	68.50		136.50	177	

Important: See the Reference Section for critical supporting data - Reference Nos., Crews, & City Cost Indexes

11454	Residential Appliances	CREW	DAILY OUTPUT	LABOR-HOURS	UNIT	2001 BARE COSTS				TOTAL INCL O&P	
						MAT.	LABOR	EQUIP.	TOTAL		
500 3600	Maximum	1 Elec	3	2.667	Ea.	111	91.50		202.50	259	**500**
3700	Wall type, minimum		4	2		96.50	68.50		165	208	
3750	Maximum		3	2.667		128	91.50		219.50	278	
3900	1500 watt wall type, with blower		4	2		119	68.50		187.50	233	
3950	3000 watt	▼	3	2.667		244	91.50		335.50	405	
4150	Hood for range, 2 speed, vented, 30" wide, minimum	L-3	5	3.200		35.50	101		136.50	194	
4200	Maximum		3	5.333		445	168		613	750	
4300	42" wide, minimum		5	3.200		168	101		269	340	
4330	Custom		5	3.200		600	101		701	815	
4350	Maximum	▼	3	5.333		730	168		898	1,050	
4500	For ventless hood, 2 speed, add					14.05			14.05	15.50	
4650	For vented 1 speed, deduct from maximum					27			27	30	
4850	Humidifier, portable, 8 gallons per day					97.50			97.50	107	
5000	15 gallons per day					157			157	173	
5200	Icemaker, automatic, 20 lb. per day	1 Plum	7	1.143		530	39.50		569.50	645	
5350	51 lb. per day	"	2	4		790	138		928	1,075	
5500	Refrigerator, no frost, 10 C.F. to 12 C.F. minimum	2 Clab	10	1.600		425	36.50		461.50	520	
5600	Maximum		6	2.667		670	61		731	830	
5750	14 C.F. to 16 C.F., minimum		9	1.778		470	40.50		510.50	585	
5800	Maximum		5	3.200		530	73		603	700	
5950	18 C.F. to 20 C.F., minimum		8	2		495	45.50		540.50	615	
6000	Maximum		4	4		710	91.50		801.50	930	
6150	21 C.F. to 29 C.F., minimum		7	2.286		705	52		757	855	
6200	Maximum	▼	3	5.333		2,675	122		2,797	3,150	
6400	Sump pump cellar drainer, pedestal, 1/3 H.P., molded PVC base	1 Plum	3	2.667		86.50	92		178.50	234	
6450	Solid brass	"	2	4	▼	179	138		317	405	
6460	Sump pump, see also division 15440-940										
6650	Washing machine, automatic, minimum	1 Plum	3	2.667	Ea.	325	92		417	500	
6700	Maximum	"	1	8		640	276		916	1,125	
6900	Water heater, electric, glass lined, 30 gallon, minimum	L-1	5	3.200		221	110		331	410	
6950	Maximum		3	5.333		305	183		488	615	
7100	80 gallon, minimum		2	8		420	275		695	875	
7150	Maximum	▼	1	16		580	550		1,130	1,475	
7180	Water heater, gas, glass lined, 30 gallon, minimum	2 Plum	5	3.200		298	110		408	495	
7220	Maximum		3	5.333		415	184		599	730	
7260	50 gallon, minimum		2.50	6.400		430	220		650	810	
7300	Maximum	▼	1.50	10.667	▼	600	365		965	1,225	
7310	Water heater, see also division 15480-200										
7350	Water softener, automatic, to 30 grains per gallon	2 Plum	5	3.200	Ea.	420	110		530	625	
7400	To 100 grains per gallon	"	4	4		550	138		688	815	
7450	Vent kits for dryers	1 Carp	10	.800	▼	10.30	23.50		33.80	48	
550 0010	**DISAPPEARING STAIRWAY** No trim included										**550**
0100	Custom grade, pine, 8'-6" ceiling, minimum	1 Carp	4	2	Ea.	96.50	58.50		155	197	
0150	Average		3.50	2.286		97.50	66.50		164	211	
0200	Maximum		3	2.667		161	77.50		238.50	299	
0500	Heavy duty, pivoted, from 7'-7" to 12'-10" floor to floor		3	2.667		315	77.50		392.50	470	
0600	16'-0" ceiling		2	4		1,050	117		1,167	1,325	
0800	Economy folding, pine, 8'-6" ceiling		4	2		88	58.50		146.50	188	
0900	9'-6" ceiling	▼	4	2		95.50	58.50		154	196	
1000	Fire escape, galvanized steel, 8'-0" to 10'-4" ceiling	2 Carp	1	16		1,125	465		1,590	1,950	
1010	10'-6" to 13'-6" ceiling		1	16		1,400	465		1,865	2,275	
1100	Automatic electric, aluminum, floor to floor height, 8' to 9'		1	16		5,500	465		5,965	6,800	
1400	11' to 12'		.90	17.778		5,925	520		6,445	7,325	
1700	14' to 15'	▼	.70	22.857	▼	6,325	665		6,990	8,000	

EQUIPMENT 11

11471 | Darkroom Processing

		CREW	DAILY OUTPUT	LABOR-HOURS	UNIT	2001 BARE COSTS				TOTAL INCL O&P
						MAT.	LABOR	EQUIP.	TOTAL	
700	0010	**DARKROOM EQUIPMENT**									700
	0020	Developing sink, 5" deep, 24" x 48"	Q-1	2	8	Ea.	3,950	248		4,198	4,725
	0050	48" x 52"		1.70	9.412		4,000	292		4,292	4,850
	0200	10" deep, 24" x 48"		1.70	9.412		4,975	292		5,267	5,925
	0250	24" x 108"	▼	1.50	10.667		1,800	330		2,130	2,475
	0500	Dryers, dehumidified filtered air, 36" x 25" x 68" high	L-7	6	4.667		3,825	131		3,956	4,425
	0550	48" x 25" x 68" high		5	5.600		7,100	157		7,257	8,075
	2000	Processors, automatic, color print, minimum		4	7		10,100	197		10,297	11,400
	2050	Maximum		.60	46.667		10,100	1,300		11,400	13,100
	2300	Black and white print, minimum		2	14		7,650	395		8,045	9,000
	2350	Maximum		.80	35		49,900	985		50,885	56,500
	2600	Manual processor, 16" x 20" maximum print size		2	14		7,700	395		8,095	9,050
	2650	20" x 24" maximum print size		1	28		7,250	785		8,035	9,200
	3000	Viewing lites, 20" x 24"		6	4.667		310	131		441	545
	3100	20" x 24" with color correction	▼	6	4.667		435	131		566	685
	3500	Washers, round, minimum sheet 11" x 14"	Q-1	2	8		2,425	248		2,673	3,050
	3550	Maximum sheet 20" x 24"		1	16		2,825	495		3,320	3,850
	3800	Square, minimum sheet 20" x 24"		1	16		2,525	495		3,020	3,525
	3900	Maximum sheet 50" x 56"	▼	.80	20	▼	3,950	620		4,570	5,275
	4500	Combination tank sink, tray sink, washers, with									
	4510	dry side tables, average	Q-1	.45	35.556	Ea.	7,575	1,100		8,675	10,000

11472 | Revolving Darkroom Doors

		CREW	DAILY OUTPUT	LABOR-HOURS	UNIT	2001 BARE COSTS				TOTAL INCL O&P
						MAT.	LABOR	EQUIP.	TOTAL	
370	0010	**DARKROOM DOORS**									370
	0015	Revolving, standard, 2 way, 36" diameter	2 Carp	3.10	5.161	Opng.	1,625	150		1,775	2,025
	0020	41" diameter		3.10	5.161		1,775	150		1,925	2,175
	0050	3 way, 51" diameter		1.40	11.429		2,225	335		2,560	2,975
	1000	4 way, 49" diameter		1.40	11.429		2,625	335		2,960	3,425
	2000	Hinged safety, 2 way, 41" diameter		2.30	6.957		2,075	203		2,278	2,600
	2500	3 way, 51" diameter		1.40	11.429		2,625	335		2,960	3,400
	3000	Pop out safety, 2 way, 41" diameter		3.10	5.161		2,625	150		2,775	3,100
	4000	3 way, 51" diameter		1.40	11.429		2,650	335		2,985	3,450
	5000	Wheelchair-type, pop out, 51" diameter		1.40	11.429		2,575	335		2,910	3,350
	5020	72" diameter	▼	.90	17.778	▼	5,325	520		5,845	6,675
	9300	For complete dark rooms, see division 13035-300									

11480 | Athletic Recreational & Therapeutic Equipment

11483 | Bowling Alleys

		CREW	DAILY OUTPUT	LABOR-HOURS	UNIT	2001 BARE COSTS				TOTAL INCL O&P
						MAT.	LABOR	EQUIP.	TOTAL	
150	0010	**BOWLING ALLEYS** Including alley, pinsetter, scorer,									150
	0020	counters and misc. supplies, minimum	4 Carp	.20	160	Lane	32,200	4,675		36,875	42,800
	0150	Average		.19	168		34,500	4,900		39,400	45,700
	0300	Maximum	▼	.18	177		36,700	5,175		41,875	48,500
	0400	Combo table ball rack, add					550			550	605
	0600	For automatic scorer, add, minimum					6,000			6,000	6,600
	0700	Maximum				▼	6,800			6,800	7,475

Important: See the Reference Section for critical supporting data - Reference Nos., Crews, & City Cost Indexes

11484 | Exercise Equipment

		CREW	DAILY OUTPUT	LABOR-HOURS	UNIT	2001 BARE COSTS				TOTAL INCL O&P
						MAT.	LABOR	EQUIP.	TOTAL	
400	0010	**HEALTH CLUB EQUIPMENT**									400
	0020	Abdominal rack, 2 board capacity				Ea.	380			380	415
	0050	Abdominal board, upholstered					425			425	465
	0200	Bicycle trainer, minimum					665			665	730
	0300	Deluxe, electric					3,375			3,375	3,725
	0400	Bar bell set, chrome plated steel, 25 lbs.					199			199	219
	0420	100 lbs.					300			300	330
	0450	200 lbs.					580			580	640
	0500	Weight plates, cast iron, per lb.				Lb.	4.08			4.08	4.49
	0520	Storage rack, 10 station				Ea.	645			645	705
	0600	Circuit training apparatus, 12 machines minimum	2 Clab	1.25	12.800	Set	22,400	292		22,692	25,200
	0700	Average		1	16		27,500	365		27,865	30,900
	0800	Maximum		.75	21.333		32,600	485		33,085	36,700
	0820	Dumbbell set, cast iron, with rack and 5 pair					630			630	695
	0900	Squat racks	2 Clab	5	3.200	Ea.	620	73		693	800
	1200	Multi-station gym machine, 5 station					6,475			6,475	7,125
	1250	9 station					9,075			9,075	9,975
	1280	Rowing machine, hydraulic					1,200			1,200	1,325
	1300	Treadmill, manual					1,175			1,175	1,300
	1320	Motorized					3,525			3,525	3,875
	1340	Electronic					4,425			4,425	4,875
	1360	Cardio-testing					6,325			6,325	6,950
	1400	Treatment/massage tables, minimum					425			425	465
	1420	Deluxe, with accessories					630			630	695
	1600	For saunas, see division 13035-800									
	1640	For steam baths, see division 13035-940									
	1680	For whirlpool baths, see division 15418-100									
	1720	For additional exercise equipment, see div. 11486-700									

11486 | Gymnasium Equipment

		CREW	DAILY OUTPUT	LABOR-HOURS	UNIT	2001 BARE COSTS				TOTAL INCL O&P
700	0010	**SCHOOL EQUIPMENT**									700
	0200	For exterior equipment, see division 02800									
	0201	For chairs & desks, see division 12560-200									
	0300	For chalkboards & bulletin boards, see div. 10110-940 & 10110-240									
	0400	For lockers, see division 10505-500									
	1000	Basketball backstops, wall mtd., 6' extended, fixed, minimum	L-2	1	16	Ea.	900	410		1,310	1,625
	1100	Maximum		1	16		1,325	410		1,735	2,125
	1200	Swing up, minimum		1	16		1,075	410		1,485	1,825
	1250	Maximum		1	16		1,925	410		2,335	2,750
	1300	Portable, manual, heavy duty, spring operated		1.90	8.421		9,000	216		9,216	10,200
	1400	Ceiling suspended, stationary, minimum		.78	20.513		1,600	525		2,125	2,575
	1450	Fold up, with accessories, maximum		.40	40		4,825	1,025		5,850	6,900
	1600	For electrically operated, add	1 Elec	1	8		1,575	274		1,849	2,150
	2000	Benches, folding, in wall, 14' table, 2 benches	L-4	2	12	Set	510	325		835	1,075
	3000	Bleachers, telescoping, manual to 15 tier, minimum	F-5	65	.492	Seat	51	14.60		65.60	79
	3100	Maximum		60	.533		76.50	15.80		92.30	109
	3300	16 to 20 tier, minimum		60	.533		122	15.80		137.80	160
	3400	Maximum		55	.582		153	17.25		170.25	195
	3600	21 to 30 tier, minimum		50	.640		128	19		147	170
	3700	Maximum		40	.800		153	23.50		176.50	205
	3900	For integral power operation, add, minimum	2 Elec	300	.053		25.50	1.83		27.33	30.50
	4000	Maximum	"	250	.064		41	2.20		43.20	48.50
	4100	Boxing ring, elevated, 22' x 22'	L-4	.10	240	Ea.	9,000	6,550		15,550	20,200
	4110	For cellular plastic foam padding, add		.10	240		3,900	6,550		10,450	14,600
	4120	Floor level, including posts and ropes only, 20' x 20'		.80	30		1,175	820		1,995	2,575
	4130	Canvas, 30' x 30'		5	4.800		1,075	131		1,206	1,400

EQUIPMENT 11

11486 | Gymnasium Equipment

		CREW	DAILY OUTPUT	LABOR-HOURS	UNIT	2001 BARE COSTS				TOTAL INCL O&P	
						MAT.	LABOR	EQUIP.	TOTAL		
700	4150	Exercise equipment, bicycle trainer				Ea.	360			360	395	700
	4180	Chinning bar, adjustable, wall mounted	1 Carp	5	1.600		255	46.50		301.50	355	
	4200	Exercise ladder, 16' x 1'-7", suspended	L-2	3	5.333		1,100	137		1,237	1,425	
	4210	High bar, floor plate attached	1 Carp	4	2		935	58.50		993.50	1,125	
	4240	Parallel bars, adjustable		4	2		2,050	58.50		2,108.50	2,375	
	4270	Uneven parallel bars, adjustable		4	2		2,450	58.50		2,508.50	2,800	
	4280	Wall mounted, adjustable	L-2	1.50	10.667	Set	705	274		979	1,200	
	4300	Rope, ceiling mounted, 18' long	1 Carp	3.66	2.186	Ea.	183	63.50		246.50	300	
	4330	Side horse, vaulting		5	1.600		1,500	46.50		1,546.50	1,725	
	4360	Treadmill, motorized, deluxe, training type		5	1.600		4,850	46.50		4,896.50	5,400	
	4390	Weight lifting multi-station, minimum	2 Clab	1	16		2,275	365		2,640	3,075	
	4450	Maximum	"	.50	32		12,600	730		13,330	15,100	
	4480	For additional exercise equipment, see div. 11484-400										
	4500	Gym divider curtain, mesh top, vinyl bottom, manual	L-4	500	.048	S.F.	6.55	1.31		7.86	9.25	
	4700	Electric roll up	L-7	400	.070		9.60	1.97		11.57	13.60	
	5500	Gym mats, 2" thick, naugahyde covered					3.14			3.14	3.45	
	5600	Vinyl/nylon covered					4.62			4.62	5.10	
	5800	Wall pads, 1-1/2" thick	2 Carp	640	.025		5.05	.73		5.78	6.70	
	6000	Wrestling mats, 1" thick, heavy duty					4.20			4.20	4.62	
	7000	Scoreboards, baseball, minimum	R-3	1.30	15.385	Ea.	2,575	520	109	3,204	3,725	
	7200	Maximum		.05	400		14,000	13,500	2,850	30,350	38,700	
	7300	Football, minimum		.86	23.256		3,525	790	165	4,480	5,225	
	7400	Maximum		.20	100		12,000	3,375	710	16,085	19,200	
	7500	Basketball (one side), minimum		2.07	9.662		1,975	325	68.50	2,368.50	2,750	
	7600	Maximum		.30	66.667		12,200	2,250	475	14,925	17,300	
	7700	Hockey-basketball (four sides), minimum		.25	80		5,550	2,700	570	8,820	10,800	
	7800	Maximum		.15	133		21,800	4,525	945	27,270	31,800	

11488 | Shooting Ranges

		CREW	DAILY OUTPUT	LABOR-HOURS	UNIT	2001 BARE COSTS				TOTAL INCL O&P	
						MAT.	LABOR	EQUIP.	TOTAL		
700	0010	**SHOOTING RANGE** Incl. bullet traps, target provisions, controls,										700
	0100	separators, ceiling system, etc. Not incl. structural shell										
	0200	Commercial	L-9	.64	56.250	Point	7,850	1,500		9,350	11,100	
	0300	Law enforcement		.28	128		16,700	3,400		20,100	23,800	
	0400	National Guard armories		.71	50.704		4,100	1,350		5,450	6,700	
	0500	Reserve training centers		.71	50.704		4,300	1,350		5,650	6,900	
	0600	Schools and colleges		.32	112		11,100	2,975		14,075	17,000	
	0700	Major acadamies		.19	189		19,900	5,025		24,925	30,000	
	0800	For acoustical treatment, add					10%	10%				
	0900	For lighting, add					28%	25%				
	1000	For plumbing, add					5%	5%				
	1100	For ventilating system, add, minimum					40%	40%				
	1200	Add, average					25%	25%				
	1300	Add, maximum					35%	35%				

11500 | Industrial & Process Equipment

11520 | Industrial Equipment

		CREW	DAILY OUTPUT	LABOR-HOURS	UNIT	2001 BARE COSTS				TOTAL INCL O&P	
						MAT.	LABOR	EQUIP.	TOTAL		
250	0010	**DUST COLLECTION SYSTEMS** Commercial / industrial										250
	0120	Central vacuum units										

11520	Industrial Equipment	CREW	DAILY OUTPUT	LABOR-HOURS	UNIT	2001 BARE COSTS				TOTAL INCL O&P
						MAT.	LABOR	EQUIP.	TOTAL	
250	0130	Includes stand, filters and motorized shaker									250
0200	500 CFM, 10" inlet, 2 HP	Q-20	2.40	8.333	Ea.	3,075	259		3,334	3,800
0220	1000 CFM, 10" inlet, 3 HP		2.20	9.091		3,225	282		3,507	3,975
0240	1500 CFM, 10" inlet, 5 HP		2	10		3,375	310		3,685	4,200
0260	3000 CFM, 13" inlet, 10 HP		1.50	13.333		8,625	415		9,040	10,100
0280	5000 CFM, 16" inlet, 2 @ 10 HP		1	20		9,125	620		9,745	11,000
1000	Vacuum tubing, galvanized									
1100	2-1/8" OD, 16 ga.	Q-9	440	.036	L.F.	1.76	1.10		2.86	3.64
1110	2-1/2" OD, 16 ga.		420	.038		2.04	1.15		3.19	4.02
1120	3" OD, 16 ga.		400	.040		2.59	1.21		3.80	4.72
1130	3-1/2" OD, 16 ga.		380	.042		3.68	1.27		4.95	6
1140	4" OD, 16 ga.		360	.044		3.76	1.34		5.10	6.20
1150	5" OD, 14 ga.		320	.050		6.95	1.51		8.46	10
1160	6" OD, 14 ga.		280	.057		7.80	1.73		9.53	11.25
1170	8" OD, 14 ga.		200	.080		11.80	2.42		14.22	16.75
1180	10" OD, 12 ga.		160	.100		11.80	3.02		14.82	17.65
1190	12" OD, 12 ga.		120	.133		34	4.03		38.03	43
1200	14" OD, 12 ga.		80	.200		37.50	6.05		43.55	50.50
1940	Hose, flexible wire reinforced rubber									
1956	3" dia.	Q-9	400	.040	L.F.	5.25	1.21		6.46	7.60
1960	4" dia.		360	.044		7.10	1.34		8.44	9.85
1970	5" dia.		320	.050		8.15	1.51		9.66	11.30
1980	6" dia.		280	.057		9.50	1.73		11.23	13.10
2000	90° Elbow, slip fit									
2110	2-1/8" dia.	Q-9	70	.229	Ea.	7.35	6.90		14.25	18.75
2120	2-1/2" dia.		65	.246		10.30	7.45		17.75	23
2130	3" dia.		60	.267		13.95	8.05		22	28
2140	3-1/2" dia.		55	.291		17.25	8.80		26.05	32.50
2150	4" dia.		50	.320		21.50	9.65		31.15	38.50
2160	5" dia.		45	.356		40.50	10.75		51.25	61
2170	6" dia.		40	.400		56	12.10		68.10	80
2180	8" dia.		30	.533		106	16.10		122.10	142
2400	45° Elbow, slip fit									
2410	2-1/8" dia.	Q-9	70	.229	Ea.	6.45	6.90		13.35	17.75
2420	2-1/2" dia.		65	.246		9.50	7.45		16.95	22
2430	3" dia.		60	.267		11.45	8.05		19.50	25
2440	3-1/2" dia.		55	.291		14.40	8.80		23.20	29.50
2450	4" dia.		50	.320		18.70	9.65		28.35	35.50
2460	5" dia.		45	.356		31.50	10.75		42.25	51
2470	6" dia.		40	.400		42.50	12.10		54.60	65.50
2480	8" dia.		35	.457		83.50	13.80		97.30	114
2800	90° TY, slip fit thru 6" dia									
2810	2-1/8" dia.	Q-9	42	.381	Ea.	14.40	11.50		25.90	33.50
2820	2-1/2" dia.		39	.410		18.70	12.40		31.10	39.50
2830	3" dia.		36	.444		24.50	13.40		37.90	47.50
2840	3-1/2" dia.		33	.485		31.50	14.65		46.15	57
2850	4" dia.		30	.533		45.50	16.10		61.60	75
2860	5" dia.		27	.593		86	17.90		103.90	122
2870	6" dia.		24	.667		117	20		137	160
2880	8" dia., butt end					249			249	274
2890	10" dia., butt end					450			450	495
2900	12" dia., butt end					450			450	495
2910	14" dia., butt end					815			815	895
2920	6 x 4" dia., butt end					71.50			71.50	78.50
2930	8" x 4" dia., butt end					135			135	149
2940	10" x 4" dia., butt end					177			177	195

EQUIPMENT 11

11520	Industrial Equipment	CREW	DAILY OUTPUT	LABOR-HOURS	UNIT	2001 BARE COSTS				TOTAL INCL O&P
						MAT.	LABOR	EQUIP.	TOTAL	
250										**250**
2950	12" x 4" dia., butt end				Ea.	204			204	224
3100	90° Elbow, butt end segmented									
3110	8" dia., butt end, segmented				Ea.	161			161	177
3120	10" dia., butt end, segmented					264			264	291
3130	12" dia., butt end, segmented					335			335	370
3140	14" dia., butt end, segmented					420			420	460
3200	45° Elbow, butt end segmented									
3210	8" dia., butt end, segmented				Ea.	137			137	151
3220	10" dia., butt end, segmented					191			191	210
3230	12" dia., butt end, segmented					195			195	215
3240	14" dia., butt end, segmented					240			240	264
3400	All butt end fittings require one coupling per joint.									
3410	Labor for fitting included with couplings.									
3460	Compression coupling, galvanized, neoprene gasket									
3470	2-1/8" dia.	Q-9	44	.364	Ea.	11.20	11		22.20	29.50
3480	2-1/2" dia.		44	.364		11.20	11		22.20	29.50
3490	3" dia.		38	.421		14.70	12.70		27.40	36
3500	3-1/2" dia.		35	.457		16.45	13.80		30.25	39.50
3510	4" dia.		33	.485		17.90	14.65		32.55	42
3520	5" dia.		29	.552		20.50	16.65		37.15	48
3530	6" dia.		26	.615		24	18.60		42.60	54.50
3540	8" dia.		22	.727		43.50	22		65.50	81.50
3550	10" dia.		20	.800		63.50	24		87.50	108
3560	12" dia.		18	.889		79	27		106	129
3570	14" dia.		16	1		112	30		142	170
3800	Air gate valves, galvanized									
3810	2-1/8" dia.	Q-9	30	.533	Ea.	85	16.10		101.10	119
3820	2-1/2" dia.		28	.571		89.50	17.25		106.75	125
3830	3" dia.		26	.615		104	18.60		122.60	143
3840	4" dia.		23	.696		136	21		157	183
3850	6" dia.		18	.889		188	27		215	248
300	**0010**	**EQUIPMENT INSTALLATION**								**300**
0020	Industrial equipment, minimum	E-2	12	4.667	Ton		149	108	257	375
0200	Maximum	"	2	28	"		895	645	1,540	2,250
850	**0010**	**VOCATIONAL SHOP EQUIPMENT**								**850**
0020	Benches, work, wood, average	2 Carp	5	3.200	Ea.	400	93.50		493.50	585
0100	Metal, average		5	3.200		225	93.50		318.50	395
0400	Combination belt & disc sander, 6"		4	4		745	117		862	1,000
0700	Drill press, floor mounted, 12", 1/2 H.P.		4	4		430	117		547	650
0800	Dust collector, not incl. ductwork, 6" diameter	1 Shee	1.10	7.273		2,475	244		2,719	3,100
1000	Grinders, double wheel, 1/2 H.P.	2 Carp	5	3.200		224	93.50		317.50	390
1300	Jointer, 4", 3/4 H.P.		4	4		1,075	117		1,192	1,375
1600	Kilns, 16 C.F., to 2000°		4	4		2,175	117		2,292	2,550
1900	Lathe, woodworking, 10", 1/2 H.P.		4	4		500	117		617	730
2200	Planer, 13" x 6"		4	4		1,200	117		1,317	1,475
2500	Potter's wheel, motorized		4	4		540	117		657	775
2800	Saws, band, 14", 3/4 H.P.		4	4		495	117		612	725
3100	Metal cutting band saw, 14"		4	4		840	117		957	1,100
3400	Radial arm saw, 10", 2 H.P.		4	4		800	117		917	1,050
3700	Scroll saw, 24"		4	4		1,400	117		1,517	1,700
4000	Table saw, 10", 3 H.P.		4	4		1,600	117		1,717	1,925
4300	Welder AC arc, 30 amp capacity		4	4		2,025	117		2,142	2,400

11 EQUIPMENT

Important: See the Reference Section for critical supporting data - Reference Nos., Crews, & City Cost Indexes

		11620	Laboratory Equipment	CREW	DAILY OUTPUT	LABOR- HOURS	UNIT	MAT.	LABOR	EQUIP.	TOTAL	TOTAL INCL O&P	
								2001 BARE COSTS					
350	0010		**LABORATORY EQUIPMENT**										350
	0020		Cabinets, base, door units, metal	2 Carp	18	.889	L.F.	127	26		153	181	
	0300		Drawer units		18	.889		275	26		301	345	
	0700		Tall storage cabinets, open, 7' high		20	.800		278	23.50		301.50	340	
	0900		With glazed doors		20	.800		350	23.50		373.50	420	
	1300		Wall cabinets, metal, 12-1/2" deep, open		20	.800		88.50	23.50		112	134	
	1500		With doors		20	.800	▼	183	23.50		206.50	239	
	1550		Counter tops, not incl. base cabinets, acidproof, minimum		82	.195	S.F.	20.50	5.70		26.20	31.50	
	1600		Maximum		70	.229		33	6.65		39.65	46.50	
	1650		Stainless steel	▼	82	.195	▼	66	5.70		71.70	81.50	
	2000		Fume hood, with countertop & base, not including HVAC										
	2020		Simple, minimum	2 Carp	5.40	2.963	L.F.	505	86.50		591.50	690	
	2050		Complex, including fixtures		2.40	6.667		1,200	194		1,394	1,600	
	2100		Special, maximum	▼	1.70	9.412	▼	1,250	274		1,524	1,800	
	2200		Ductwork, minimum	2 Shee	1	16	Hood	835	535		1,370	1,750	
	2250		Maximum	"	.50	32	"	4,225	1,075		5,300	6,300	
	2300		Service fixtures, average				Ea.	43			43	47	
	2500		For sink assembly with hot and cold water, add	1 Plum	1.40	5.714		525	197		722	870	
	2550		Glassware washer, undercounter, minimum	L-1	1.80	8.889		6,200	305		6,505	7,275	
	2600		Maximum	"	1	16		7,525	550		8,075	9,100	
	2650		Glove box, fiberglass, bacteriological					11,000			11,000	12,100	
	2700		Controlled atmosphere					8,500			8,500	9,350	
	2750		Radioisotope					11,000			11,000	12,100	
	2770		Carcinogenic					11,000			11,000	12,100	
	2800		Sink, one piece plastic, flask wash, hose, free standing	1 Plum	1.60	5		1,325	172		1,497	1,700	
	2850		Epoxy resin sink, 25" x 16" x 10"	"	2	4	▼	147	138		285	370	
	3000		Utility table, acid resistant top with drawers	2 Carp	30	.533	L.F.	109	15.55		124.55	145	
	3800		Titration unit, four 2000 ml reservoirs				Ea.	8,350			8,350	9,200	
	4200		Alternate pricing method: as percent of lab furniture										
	4400		Installation, not incl. plumbing & duct work				% Furn.					22%	
	4800		Plumbing, final connections, simple system									10%	
	5000		Moderately complex system									15%	
	5200		Complex system									20%	
	5400		Electrical, simple system									10%	
	5600		Moderately complex system									20%	
	5800		Complex system				▼					35%	
	6000		Safety equipment, eye wash, hand held				Ea.	210			210	231	
	6200		Deluge shower				"	500			500	550	
	6300		Rule of thumb: lab furniture including installation & connection										
	6320		High school				S.F.					29	
	6340		College									42.75	
	6360		Clinical, health care									36.75	
	6380		Industrial				▼					59.25	

11700 | Medical Equipment

		11710	Medical Equipment	CREW	DAILY OUTPUT	LABOR- HOURS	UNIT	MAT.	LABOR	EQUIP.	TOTAL	TOTAL INCL O&P	
								2001 BARE COSTS					
500	0010		**MEDICAL EQUIPMENT**										500
	0015		Autopsy table, standard	1 Plum	1	8	Ea.	6,500	276		6,776	7,575	

EQUIPMENT 11

11710	Medical Equipment	CREW	DAILY OUTPUT	LABOR-HOURS	UNIT	2001 BARE COSTS				TOTAL INCL O&P	
						MAT.	LABOR	EQUIP.	TOTAL		
500	0020	Deluxe	1 Plum	.60	13.333	Ea.	13,000	460		13,460	15,100	500
	0300	Blood pressure unit, mercurial, wall					160			160	176
	0400	Diagnostic set, wall					475			475	525
	0700	Distiller, water, steam heated, 50 gal. capacity	1 Plum	1.40	5.714		13,500	197		13,697	15,200
	0750	Exam room furnishings, average per room					4,725			4,725	5,200
	1800	Heat therapy unit, humidified, 26″ x 78″ x 28″					2,475			2,475	2,725
	2100	Hubbard tank with accessories, stainless steel,									
	2110	125 GPM at 45 psi water pressure				Ea.	19,300			19,300	21,200
	2150	For electric overhead hoist, add					2,100			2,100	2,325
	2500	Incubators, minimum					2,650			2,650	2,925
	2600	Maximum					14,700			14,700	16,200
	2900	K-Module for heat therapy, 20 oz. capacity, 75° to 110°F					297			297	325
	3200	Mortuary refrigerator, end operated, 2 capacity					10,300			10,300	11,400
	3300	6 capacity					19,200			19,200	21,100
	3600	Paraffin bath, 126°F, auto controlled					1,125			1,125	1,250
	3900	Parallel bars for walking training, 12′-0″					925			925	1,025
	4200	Refrigerator, blood bank, 28.6 C.F. emergency signal					5,775			5,775	6,350
	4210	Reach-in, 16.9 C.F.					6,175			6,175	6,775
	4400	Scale, physician's, with height rod					253			253	279
	4600	Station, dietary, medium, with ice					11,900			11,900	13,100
	4700	Medicine					5,375			5,375	5,925
	5000	Scrub, surgical, stainless steel, single station, minimum	1 Plum	3	2.667		970	92		1,062	1,225
	5100	Maximum					5,825			5,825	6,400
	5600	Sterilizers, floor loading, 26″ x 62″ x 42″, single door, steam					118,000			118,000	129,500
	5650	Double door, steam					151,500			151,500	166,500
	5800	General purpose, 20″ x 20″ x 38″, single door					11,400			11,400	12,500
	6000	Portable, counter top, steam, minimum					2,825			2,825	3,100
	6020	Maximum					4,425			4,425	4,850
	6050	Portable, counter top, gas, 17″x15″x32-1/2″					29,200			29,200	32,100
	6150	Manual washer/sterilizer, 16″x16″x26″	1 Plum	2	4		40,000	138		40,138	44,200
	6200	Steam generators, electric 10 KW to 180 KW, freestanding									
	6250	Minimum	1 Elec	3	2.667	Ea.	5,950	91.50		6,041.50	6,675
	6300	Maximum	″	.70	11.429		21,400	390		21,790	24,200
	6500	Surgery table, minor minimum	1 Sswk	.70	11.429		10,300	375		10,675	12,000
	6520	Maximum		.50	16		19,400	525		19,925	22,300
	6550	Major surgery table, minimum		.50	16		23,400	525		23,925	26,700
	6570	Maximum		.50	16		77,000	525		77,525	86,000
	6700	Surgical lights, doctor's office, single arm	2 Elec	2	8		1,100	274		1,374	1,600
	6750	Dual arm		1	16		4,100	550		4,650	5,350
	6800	Major operating room, dual head, minimum		1	16		13,000	550		13,550	15,100
	6850	Maximum		1	16		21,600	550		22,150	24,600
	7000	Tables, physical therapy, walk off, electric	2 Carp	3	5.333		2,375	155		2,530	2,875
	7150	Standard, vinyl top with base cabinets, minimum		3	5.333		970	155		1,125	1,325
	7200	Maximum		2	8		2,875	233		3,108	3,525
	7500	Thermometer, electric, portable					294			294	325
	8100	Utensil washer-sanitizer	1 Plum	2	4		8,100	138		8,238	9,125
	8200	Bed pan washer-sanitizer	″	2	4		5,300	138		5,438	6,025
	8400	Whirlpool bath, mobile, sst, 18″ x 24″ x 60″					3,500			3,500	3,850
	8450	Fixed, incl. mixing valves	1 Plum	2	4		6,850	138		6,988	7,725
	8700	X-ray, mobile, minimum					9,950			9,950	10,900
	8750	Maximum					56,000			56,000	61,500
	8900	Stationary, minimum					31,100			31,100	34,200
	8950	Maximum					161,500			161,500	178,000
	9150	Developing processors, minimum					8,650			8,650	9,525
	9200	Maximum					22,700			22,700	25,000
	9800	For hospital partitions, see division 10190-200									

Important: See the Reference Section for critical supporting data - Reference Nos., Crews, & City Cost Indexes

11710 | Medical Equipment

		CREW	DAILY OUTPUT	LABOR-HOURS	UNIT	2001 BARE COSTS				TOTAL INCL O&P	
						MAT.	LABOR	EQUIP.	TOTAL		
500	9900	For casework & furniture, see division 12310-750 & 12560-400									500

11740 | Dental Equipment

			CREW	DAILY OUTPUT	LABOR-HOURS	UNIT	MAT.	LABOR	EQUIP.	TOTAL	TOTAL INCL O&P	
200	0010	**DENTAL EQUIPMENT**										200
	0020	Central suction system, minimum	1 Plum	1.20	6.667	Ea.	2,700	230		2,930	3,325	
	0100	Maximum	"	.90	8.889		20,900	305		21,205	23,500	
	0300	Air compressor, minimum	1 Skwk	.80	10		2,975	299		3,274	3,750	
	0400	Maximum		.50	16		20,600	480		21,080	23,500	
	0600	Chair, electric or hydraulic, minimum		.50	16		3,400	480		3,880	4,500	
	0700	Maximum	▼	.25	32		7,200	955		8,155	9,425	
	0800	Doctor's/assistant's stool, minimum					385			385	425	
	0850	Maximum					755			755	835	
	1000	Drill console with accessories, minimum	1 Skwk	1.60	5		3,075	149		3,224	3,600	
	1100	Maximum		1.60	5		8,750	149		8,899	9,850	
	2000	Light, ceiling mounted, minimum		8	1		1,775	30		1,805	2,000	
	2100	Maximum	▼	8	1		3,575	30		3,605	3,975	
	2200	Unit light, minimum	2 Skwk	5.33	3.002		1,325	89.50		1,414.50	1,600	
	2210	Maximum		5.33	3.002		4,325	89.50		4,414.50	4,900	
	2220	Track light, minimum		3.20	5		2,350	149		2,499	2,800	
	2230	Maximum	▼	3.20	5		5,150	149		5,299	5,900	
	2300	Sterilizers, steam portable, minimum					2,975			2,975	3,275	
	2350	Maximum					10,300			10,300	11,300	
	2600	Steam, institutional					12,800			12,800	14,100	
	2650	Dry heat, electric, portable, 3 trays					1,000			1,000	1,100	
	2700	Ultra-sonic cleaner, portable, minimum					810			810	890	
	2750	Maximum (institutional)					1,800			1,800	2,000	
	3000	X-ray unit, wall, minimum	1 Skwk	4	2		4,100	59.50		4,159.50	4,600	
	3010	Maximum		4	2		7,725	59.50		7,784.50	8,600	
	3100	Panoramic unit	▼	.60	13.333		18,500	400		18,900	21,000	
	3105	Deluxe, minimum	2 Skwk	1.60	10		26,800	299		27,099	30,000	
	3110	Maximum	"	1.60	10		62,000	299		62,299	68,500	
	3500	Developers, X-ray, average	1 Plum	5.33	1.501		3,600	51.50		3,651.50	4,050	
	3600	Maximum	"	5.33	1.501	▼	6,700	51.50		6,751.50	7,450	

For information about Means Estimating Seminars, see yellow pages 11 and 12 in back of book

EQUIPMENT **11**

	CREW	DAILY OUTPUT	LABOR-HOURS	UNIT	2001 BARE COSTS				TOTAL INCL O&P
					MAT.	LABOR	EQUIP.	TOTAL	

Division 12
Furnishings

Estimating Tips

General

- The items in this division are usually priced per square foot or each. Most of these items are purchased by the owner and placed by the supplier. Do not assume the items in Division 12 will be purchased and installed by the supplier. Check the specifications for responsibilities and include receiving, storage, installation and mechanical and electrical hook-ups in the appropriate divisions.

- Some items in this division require some type of support system that is not usually furnished with the item. Examples of these systems include blocking for the attachment of casework and heavy drapery rods. The required blocking must be added to the estimate in the appropriate division.

Reference Numbers

Reference numbers are shown in bold squares at the beginning of some major classifications. These numbers refer to related items in the Reference Section. The reference information may be an estimating procedure, an alternate pricing method or technical information.

Note: Not all subdivisions listed here necessarily appear in this publication.

		12310 | Metal Casework	CREW	DAILY OUTPUT	LABOR-HOURS	UNIT	2001 BARE COSTS				TOTAL INCL O&P	
							MAT.	LABOR	EQUIP.	TOTAL		
100	0010	**KEY CABINETS**										**100**
	0020	Wall mounted, 60 key capacity	1 Carp	20	.400	Ea.	167	11.65		178.65	201	
	0200	Drawer type, 600 key capacity	1 Clab	15	.533		2,125	12.20		2,137.20	2,350	
	0300	2,400 key capacity		20	.400		4,775	9.15		4,784.15	5,275	
	0400	Tray type, 20 key capacity		50	.160		96.50	3.66		100.16	112	
	0500	50 key capacity		40	.200		129	4.57		133.57	149	
200	0010	**DISPLAY CASES** Free standing, all glass										**200**
	0020	Aluminum frame, 42" high x 36" x 12" deep	2 Carp	8	2	Ea.	415	58.50		473.50	545	
	0100	70" high x 48" x 18" deep	"	6	2.667		1,200	77.50		1,277.50	1,450	
	0500	For wood bases, add					9%					
	0600	For hardwood frames, deduct					8%					
	0700	For bronze, baked enamel finish, add					10%					
	2000	Wall mounted, glass front, aluminum frame										
	2010	Non-illuminated, one section 3' x 4' x 1'-4"	2 Carp	5	3.200	Ea.	1,000	93.50		1,093.50	1,250	
	2100	5' x 4' x 1'-4"		5	3.200		1,200	93.50		1,293.50	1,475	
	2200	6' x 4' x 1'-4"		4	4		1,275	117		1,392	1,575	
	2500	Two sections, 8' x 4' x 1'-4"		2	8		1,700	233		1,933	2,250	
	2600	10' x 4' x 1'-4"		2	8		1,750	233		1,983	2,300	
	3000	Three sections, 16' x 4' x 1'-4"		1.50	10.667	Section	2,900	310		3,210	3,675	
	3500	For fluorescent lights, add					223			223	245	
	4000	Table exhibit cases, 2' wide, 3' high, 4' long, flat top	2 Carp	5	3.200	Ea.	715	93.50		808.50	930	
	4100	3' wide, 3' high, 4' long, sloping top	"	3	5.333	"	1,050	155		1,205	1,400	
560	0010	**IRONING CENTER**										**560**
	0020	Including cabinet, board & light, minimum	1 Carp	2	4	Ea.	247	117		364	455	
	0100	Maximum, see also division 11119-450	"	1.50	5.333	"	565	155		720	865	
750	0010	**CASEWORK**										**750**
	0500	Hospital, base cabinets, laminated plastic	2 Carp	10	1.600	L.F.	189	46.50		235.50	281	
	1000	Stainless steel	"	10	1.600		237	46.50		283.50	335	
	1200	For all drawers, add					9.65			9.65	10.60	
	1300	Cabinet base trim, 4" high, enameled steel	2 Carp	200	.080		29	2.33		31.33	35	
	1400	Stainless steel		200	.080		43	2.33		45.33	51	
	1450	Counter top, laminated plastic, no backsplash		40	.400		32.50	11.65		44.15	54.50	
	1650	With backsplash		40	.400		40.50	11.65		52.15	63	
	1800	For sink cutout, add		12.20	1.311	Ea.		38		38	60	
	1900	Stainless steel counter top		40	.400	L.F.	90.50	11.65		102.15	118	
	2000	For drop-in stainless 43" x 21" sink, add				Ea.	460			460	505	
	2050	For solid surface countertops see 06610-810										
	2100	Nurses station, door type, laminated plastic	2 Carp	10	1.600	L.F.	219	46.50		265.50	315	
	2200	Enameled steel		10	1.600		190	46.50		236.50	282	
	2300	Stainless steel		10	1.600		253	46.50		299.50	350	
	2400	For drawer type, add					89			89	98	
	2500	Wall cabinets, laminated plastic	2 Carp	15	1.067		142	31		173	205	
	2600	Enameled steel		15	1.067		158	31		189	223	
	2700	Stainless steel		15	1.067		246	31		277	320	
	2800	For glass doors, add					22.50			22.50	25	
	3500	Kitchen, base cabinets, metal, minimum	2 Carp	30	.533		46.50	15.55		62.05	75.50	
	3600	Maximum		25	.640		118	18.65		136.65	159	
	3700	Wall cabinets, metal, minimum		30	.533		46.50	15.55		62.05	75.50	
	3800	Maximum		25	.640		106	18.65		124.65	146	
	5000	School, 24" deep, metal, 84" high units		15	1.067		232	31		263	305	
	5150	Counter height units		20	.800		180	23.50		203.50	235	
	5450	Wood, custom fabricated, 32" high counter		20	.800		150	23.50		173.50	202	
	5600	Add for counter top		56	.286		17.55	8.35		25.90	32.50	
	5800	84" high wall units		15	1.067		157	31		188	221	
	6000	Laminated plastic finish is same price as wood										

Important: See the Reference Section for critical supporting data - Reference Nos., Crews, & City Cost Indexes

12 FURNISHINGS

12460 | Furnishing Accessories

		CREW	DAILY OUTPUT	LABOR-HOURS	UNIT	MAT.	LABOR	EQUIP.	TOTAL	TOTAL INCL O&P	
						2001 BARE COSTS					
900	**0010 ASH/TRASH RECEIVERS**										**900**
1000	Ash urn, cylindrical metal										
1020	8" diameter, 20" high	1 Clab	60	.133	Ea.	110	3.05		113.05	126	
1060	10" diameter, 26" high	"	60	.133	"	155	3.05		158.05	175	
2000	Combination ash/trash urn, metal										
2020	8" diameter, 20" high	1 Clab	60	.133	Ea.	102	3.05		105.05	117	
2050	10" diameter, 26" high	"	60	.133	"	174	3.05		177.05	196	
4000	Trash receptacle, metal										
4020	8" diameter, 15" high	1 Clab	60	.133	Ea.	58	3.05		61.05	69	
4040	10" diameter, 18" high		60	.133		100	3.05		103.05	115	
5040	16" x 8" x 14" high	↓	60	.133	↓	29	3.05		32.05	37	
5500	Trash receptacle, plastic, with lid										
5520	35 gallon	1 Clab	60	.133	Ea.	121	3.05		124.05	139	
5540	45 gallon	"	60	.133	"	149	3.05		152.05	169	

12483 | Floor Mats & Frames

		CREW	DAILY OUTPUT	LABOR-HOURS	UNIT	MAT.	LABOR	EQUIP.	TOTAL	TOTAL INCL O&P	
200	**0010 FLOOR MATS**										**200**
0020	Recessed, in-laid black rubber, 3/8" thick, solid	1 Clab	155	.052	S.F.	19.55	1.18		20.73	23.50	
0050	Perforated		155	.052		25	1.18		26.18	29.50	
0100	1/2" thick, solid		155	.052		20.50	1.18		21.68	24.50	
0150	Perforated		155	.052		23	1.18		24.18	27	
0200	In colors, 3/8" thick, solid		155	.052		22	1.18		23.18	26	
0250	Perforated		155	.052		24.50	1.18		25.68	29	
0300	1/2" thick, solid		155	.052		30.50	1.18		31.68	35.50	
0350	Perforated		155	.052		31.50	1.18		32.68	37	
0500	Link mats, including nosings, aluminum, 3/8" thick **CN**		155	.052		16.85	1.18		18.03	20.50	
0550	Black rubber with galvanized tie rods		155	.052		13.25	1.18		14.43	16.45	
0600	Steel, galvanized, 3/8" thick		155	.052		6.40	1.18		7.58	8.90	
0650	Vinyl, in colors	↓	155	.052	↓	17.15	1.18		18.33	21	
0750	Add for nosings, rubber				L.F.	6.15			6.15	6.75	
0850	Recess frames for above mats, aluminum	1 Carp	100	.080		3.81	2.33		6.14	7.85	
0870	Bronze	"	100	.080	↓	8.05	2.33		10.38	12.50	
0900	Skate lock tile, 24" x 24" x 1/2" thick, rubber, black	1 Clab	125	.064	S.F.	12.85	1.46		14.31	16.45	
0950	Color		125	.064	"	14.75	1.46		16.21	18.55	
1000	12" x 24" border, black		75	.107	L.F.	21.50	2.44		23.94	27.50	
1100	Color		75	.107	"	26	2.44		28.44	32.50	
1150	12" x 12" outside corner, black		100	.080	S.F.	20.50	1.83		22.33	26	
1200	Color		100	.080		24	1.83		25.83	29.50	
1500	Duckboard, aluminum slats		155	.052		17.80	1.18		18.98	21.50	
1700	Hardwood strips on rubber base, to 54" wide		155	.052		12.50	1.18		13.68	15.60	
1800	Assembled with brass rods and vinyl spacers, to 48" wide		155	.052		16.65	1.18		17.83	20	
1850	Tire fabric, 3/4" thick		155	.052		10.25	1.18		11.43	13.15	
1900	Vinyl, 36" wide, in colors, hollow top & bottoms		155	.052		4.24	1.18		5.42	6.50	
1950	Solid top & bottom members	↓	155	.052	↓	7.75	1.18		8.93	10.40	

12492 | Blinds and Shades

		CREW	DAILY OUTPUT	LABOR-HOURS	UNIT	MAT.	LABOR	EQUIP.	TOTAL	TOTAL INCL O&P	
100	**0010 BLINDS, INTERIOR**										**100**
0020	Horizontal, 1" aluminum slats, solid color, stock	1 Carp	590	.014	S.F.	2.63	.40		3.03	3.51	
0090	Custom, minimum		590	.014		1.89	.40		2.29	2.70	
0100	Maximum		440	.018		6.60	.53		7.13	8.10	
0250	2" aluminum slats, custom, minimum		590	.014		2.74	.40		3.14	3.63	
0350	Maximum		440	.018		6.95	.53		7.48	8.50	
0450	Stock, minimum		590	.014		2.70	.40		3.10	3.59	
0500	Maximum		440	.018		5	.53		5.53	6.35	
0600	2" steel slats, stock, minimum		590	.014		1.52	.40		1.92	2.29	
0630	Maximum	↓	440	.018	↓	4.24	.53		4.77	5.50	

FURNISHINGS 12

For expanded coverage of these items see *Means Interior Cost Data 2001*

12492 | Blinds and Shades

		CREW	DAILY OUTPUT	LABOR-HOURS	UNIT	2001 BARE COSTS				TOTAL INCL O&P	
						MAT.	LABOR	EQUIP.	TOTAL		
100	0750	Custom, minimum	1 Carp	590	.014	S.F.	1.37	.40		1.77	2.13	100
	0850	Maximum		400	.020		6.80	.58		7.38	8.40	
	1500	Vertical, 3" to 5" PVC or cloth strips, minimum **CN**		460	.017		6.65	.51		7.16	8.10	
	1600	Maximum		400	.020		8.85	.58		9.43	10.65	
	1800	4" aluminum slats, minimum		460	.017		2.97	.51		3.48	4.06	
	1900	Maximum		400	.020		7.05	.58		7.63	8.65	
	1950	Mylar mirror-finish strips, to 8" wide, minimum		460	.017		11.75	.51		12.26	13.75	
	1970	Maximum		400	.020		17.65	.58		18.23	20.50	
	3000	Wood folding panels with movable louvers, 7" x 20" each		17	.471	Pr.	38	13.70		51.70	63	
	3300	8" x 28" each		17	.471		54.50	13.70		68.20	81.50	
	3450	9" x 36" each		17	.471		65	13.70		78.70	93	
	3600	10" x 40" each		17	.471		73.50	13.70		87.20	103	
	4000	Fixed louver type, stock units, 8" x 20" each		17	.471		56.50	13.70		70.20	84	
	4150	10" x 28" each		17	.471		77.50	13.70		91.20	107	
	4300	12" x 36" each		17	.471		98.50	13.70		112.20	131	
	4450	18" x 40" each		17	.471		118	13.70		131.70	151	
	5000	Insert panel type, stock, 7" x 20" each		17	.471		14.35	13.70		28.05	37.50	
	5150	8" x 28" each		17	.471		26.50	13.70		40.20	50.50	
	5300	9" x 36" each		17	.471		33.50	13.70		47.20	58.50	
	5450	10" x 40" each		17	.471		36	13.70		49.70	61	
	5600	Raised panel type, stock, 10" x 24" each		17	.471		97.50	13.70		111.20	129	
	5650	12" x 26" each		17	.471		113	13.70		126.70	147	
	5700	14" x 30" each		17	.471		128	13.70		141.70	163	
	5750	16" x 36" each		17	.471		144	13.70		157.70	180	
	6000	For custom built pine, add					22%					
	6500	For custom built hardwood blinds, add					42%					
600	0010	**SHADES**										600
	0020	Basswood, roll-up, stain finish, 3/8" slats	1 Carp	300	.027	S.F.	9.10	.78		9.88	11.20	
	0200	7/8" slats		300	.027		8.60	.78		9.38	10.65	
	0300	Vertical side slide, stain finish, 3/8" slats		300	.027		13.75	.78		14.53	16.35	
	0400	7/8" slats		300	.027		13.75	.78		14.53	16.35	
	0500	For fire retardant finishes, add					16%					
	0600	For "B" rated finishes, add					20%					
	0900	Mylar, single layer, non-heat reflective	1 Carp	685	.012		5.10	.34		5.44	6.15	
	1000	Double layered, heat reflective		685	.012		6.90	.34		7.24	8.15	
	1100	Triple layered, heat reflective		685	.012		6.90	.34		7.24	8.15	
	1200	For metal roller instead of wood, add per				Shade	2.63			2.63	2.89	
	1300	Vinyl coated cotton, standard	1 Carp	685	.012	S.F.	1.54	.34		1.88	2.22	
	1400	Lightproof decorator shades		685	.012		1.39	.34		1.73	2.06	
	1500	Vinyl, lightweight, 4 gauge		685	.012		.38	.34		.72	.95	
	1600	Heavyweight, 6 gauge		685	.012		1.20	.34		1.54	1.85	
	1700	Vinyl laminated fiberglass, 6 ga., translucent		685	.012		1.79	.34		2.13	2.50	
	1800	Lightproof		685	.012		2.74	.34		3.08	3.54	
	3000	Woven aluminum, 3/8" thick, lightproof and fireproof		350	.023		3.94	.67		4.61	5.35	

12493 | Curtains and Drapes

		CREW	DAILY OUTPUT	LABOR-HOURS	UNIT	2001 BARE COSTS				TOTAL INCL O&P	
200	0010	**DRAPERY HARDWARE**										200
	0030	Standard traverse, per foot, minimum	1 Carp	59	.136	L.F.	1.45	3.95		5.40	7.80	
	0100	Maximum		51	.157	"	8.05	4.57		12.62	16	
	4000	Traverse rods, adjustable, 28" to 48"		22	.364	Ea.	15.35	10.60		25.95	33.50	
	4020	48" to 84"		20	.400		24.50	11.65		36.15	45.50	
	4040	66" to 120"		18	.444		25.50	12.95		38.45	48.50	
	4060	84" to 156"		16	.500		29.50	14.60		44.10	55.50	
	4080	100" to 180"		14	.571		31	16.65		47.65	60	
	4090	156" to 228"		13	.615		40	17.95		57.95	72	
	4100	228" to 312"		13	.615		47	17.95		64.95	79.50	

Important: See the Reference Section for critical supporting data - Reference Nos., Crews, & City Cost Indexes

12 FURNISHINGS

12493	Curtains and Drapes	CREW	DAILY OUTPUT	LABOR-HOURS	UNIT	2001 BARE COSTS				TOTAL INCL O&P	
						MAT.	LABOR	EQUIP.	TOTAL		
200	4200	Double rods, adjustable, 30" to 48"	1 Carp	9	.889	Ea.	34	26		60	78	200
	4220	48" to 86"		9	.889		45	26		71	89.50	
	4240	86" to 150"		8	1		60.50	29		89.50	112	
	4260	100" to 180"		7	1.143		69	33.50		102.50	128	
	4300	Tray and curtain rod, adjustable, 30" to 48"		9	.889		26.50	26		52.50	70	
	4320	48" to 86"		9	.889		35.50	26		61.50	79.50	
	4340	86" to 150"		8	1		45	29		74	95	
	4360	100" to 180"		7	1.143		46	33.50		79.50	103	
	4600	Valance, pinch pleated fabric, 12" deep, up to 54" long, minimum					29			29	31.50	
	4610	Maximum					72			72	79.50	
	4620	Up to 77" long, minimum					44.50			44.50	48.50	
	4630	Maximum					116			116	128	
	5000	Stationary rods, first 2 feet					7.15			7.15	7.85	
	5020	Each additional foot, add				L.F.	2.87			2.87	3.16	

12510	Office Furniture	CREW	DAILY OUTPUT	LABOR-HOURS	UNIT	2001 BARE COSTS				TOTAL INCL O&P	
						MAT.	LABOR	EQUIP.	TOTAL		
580	0010	**MULTI-MEDIA BOARDS** See division 10110-240										580
600	0010	**OFFICE CASE GOODS**										600
	0020	Desks, 29" high, double pedestal, 30" x 60", metal, minimum				Ea.	355			355	395	
	0030	Maximum					1,000			1,000	1,100	
	0160	Wood, minimum					445			445	490	
	0180	Maximum					1,825			1,825	2,025	
	0600	Desks, single pedestal, 30" x 60", metal, minimum					296			296	325	
	0620	Maximum					765			765	845	
	0640	Wood, minimum					385			385	420	
	0650	Maximum					575			575	630	
	0670	Executive return, 24" x 42", with box, file, wood, minimum					263			263	289	
	0680	Maximum					575			575	630	
	0720	Desks, secretarial, 30" x 60", metal, minimum					203			203	223	
	0730	Maximum					575			575	630	
	0740	Return, 20" x 42", minimum					192			192	211	
	0750	Maximum					385			385	420	
	0800	Wood, minimum					530			530	585	
	0810	Maximum					1,850			1,850	2,050	
	0820	Return, 20" x 42", minimum					340			340	375	
	0830	Maximum					985			985	1,075	
	0900	Desktop organizer, 72" x 14" x 36" high, wood, minimum					110			110	120	
	0920	Maximum					246			246	271	
	0940	59" x 12" x 23" high, steel, minimum					142			142	157	
	0960	Maximum					219			219	241	
	2000	Chairs, office type, executive, minimum					263			263	289	
	2150	Maximum					1,675			1,675	1,850	
	2200	Management, minimum					219			219	241	
	2250	Maximum					1,250			1,250	1,375	
	2280	Task, minimum					142			142	157	
	2290	Maximum					485			485	535	
	2300	Arm kit, minimum					45.50			45.50	50	

FURNISHINGS 12

For expanded coverage of these items see *Means Interior Cost Data 2001*

12510 | Office Furniture

			CREW	DAILY OUTPUT	LABOR-HOURS	UNIT	MAT.	LABOR	EQUIP.	TOTAL	TOTAL INCL O&P	
600	2320	Maximum				Ea.	93			93	102	**600**
	6000	Table, conference										
	6050	Boat, 96" x 42", minimum				Ea.	590			590	650	
	6150	Maximum					3,200			3,200	3,525	
	6720	Rectangle, 96" x 42", minimum					645			645	710	
	6740	Maximum				↓	2,650			2,650	2,900	
675	0010	**POSTS**										**675**
	0020	Portable for pedestrian traffic control, standard, minimum				Ea.	90			90	98.50	
	0100	Maximum					138			138	152	
	0300	Deluxe posts, minimum					162			162	179	
	0400	Maximum				↓	285			285	315	
	0600	Ropes for above posts, plastic covered, 1-1/2" diameter				L.F.	7.50			7.50	8.25	
	0700	Chain core				"	6.80			6.80	7.50	

12520 | Seating

			CREW	DAILY OUTPUT	LABOR-HOURS	UNIT	MAT.	LABOR	EQUIP.	TOTAL	TOTAL INCL O&P	
550	0010	**SEATING**										**550**
	0100	Bleachers, See div. 02880 & 11486										
	0101	Benches, See 02880, 10505 & 11486										
	0500	Classroom, movable chair & desk type, minimum				Set					65	
	0600	Maximum				"					120	
	1000	Lecture hall, pedestal type, minimum	2 Carp	22	.727	Ea.	108	21		129	152	
	1200	Maximum		14.50	1.103		385	32		417	470	
	2000	Auditorium chair, all veneer construction		22	.727		121	21		142	166	
	2200	Veneer back, padded seat		22	.727		153	21		174	201	
	2350	Fully upholstered, spring seat	↓	22	.727		154	21		175	203	
	2450	For tablet arms, add					40			40	44	
	2500	For fire retardancy, CATB-133, add				↓	16.15			16.15	17.75	

12540 | Hospitality Furniture

			CREW	DAILY OUTPUT	LABOR-HOURS	UNIT	MAT.	LABOR	EQUIP.	TOTAL	TOTAL INCL O&P	
100	0010	**TABLES, FOLDING** Laminated plastic tops										**100**
	1000	Tubular steel legs with glides										
	1020	18" x 60", minimum				Ea.	173			173	190	
	1040	Maximum					580			580	640	
	1840	36" x 96", minimum					281			281	310	
	1860	Maximum					1,175			1,175	1,300	
	2000	Round, wood stained, plywood top, 60" diameter, minimum					259			259	285	
	2020	Maximum				↓	1,350			1,350	1,500	
500	0010	**FURNITURE, HOTEL**										**500**
	0020	Standard quality set, minimum				Room	1,475			1,475	1,625	
	0200	Maximum				"	7,300			7,300	8,025	
700	0010	**FURNITURE, RESTAURANT**										**700**
	0020	Bars, built-in, front bar	1 Carp	5	1.600	L.F.	193	46.50		239.50	285	
	0200	Back bar	"	5	1.600	"	140	46.50		186.50	227	
	0300	Booth seating see division 12640-150										
	2000	Chair, bentwood side chair, metal, minimum				Ea.	68			68	74.50	
	2020	Maximum					86.50			86.50	95.50	
	2600	Upholstered seat & back, arms, minimum					193			193	213	
	2620	Maximum				↓	500			500	550	

12560 | Institutional Furniture

			CREW	DAILY OUTPUT	LABOR-HOURS	UNIT	MAT.	LABOR	EQUIP.	TOTAL	TOTAL INCL O&P	
100	0010	**BANK FURNITURE** See division 12510-600										**100**
150	0010	**CHURCH FURNITURE** See division 11041-250										**150**

12 FURNISHINGS

12560	Institutional Furniture	CREW	DAILY OUTPUT	LABOR-HOURS	UNIT	2001 BARE COSTS				TOTAL INCL O&P	
						MAT.	LABOR	EQUIP.	TOTAL		
200	**0010**	**FURNITURE, SCHOOL**										**200**
1000	Chair, molded plastic,										
1100	Integral tablet arm, minimum				Ea.	53.50			53.50	59	
1150	Maximum					222			222	244	
2000	Desk, single pedestal, top book compartment, minimum					49			49	54	
2020	Maximum					53.50			53.50	58.50	
2200	Flip top, minimum					63			63	69.50	
2220	Maximum				↓	68.50			68.50	75	
300	**0010**	**FURNITURE, DORMITORY**										**300**
1000	Chest, four drawer, minimum				Ea.	355			355	395	
1020	Maximum				"	480			480	525	
1050	Built-in, minimum	2 Carp	13	1.231	L.F.	107	36		143	174	
1150	Maximum		10	1.600		212	46.50		258.50	305	
1200	Desk top, built-in, laminated plastic, 24" deep, minimum		50	.320		23.50	9.35		32.85	40.50	
1300	Maximum		40	.400		70.50	11.65		82.15	96.50	
1450	30" deep, minimum		50	.320		29.50	9.35		38.85	47	
1550	Maximum		40	.400		131	11.65		142.65	162	
1750	Dressing unit, built-in, minimum		12	1.333		175	39		214	254	
1850	Maximum	↓	8	2	↓	525	58.50		583.50	665	
8000	Rule of thumb: total cost for furniture, minimum				Student					1,900	
8050	Maximum				"					3,600	
400	**0010**	**FURNITURE, HOSPITAL**										**400**
0020	Beds, manual, minimum				Ea.	825			825	910	
0100	Maximum					1,450			1,450	1,575	
0300	Manual and electric beds, minimum					1,025			1,025	1,150	
0400	Maximum					2,225			2,225	2,450	
0600	All electric hospital beds, minimum					1,375			1,375	1,525	
0700	Maximum					3,425			3,425	3,775	
0900	Manual, nursing home beds, minimum					655			655	720	
1000	Maximum					1,350			1,350	1,500	
1020	Overbed table, laminated top, minimum					278			278	305	
1040	Maximum				↓	690			690	760	
1100	Patient wall systems, not incl. plumbing, minimum				Room	830			830	910	
1200	Maximum				"	1,525			1,525	1,675	
2000	Geriatric chairs, minimum				Ea.	268			268	295	
2020	Maximum				"	625			625	690	
700	**0010**	**FURNITURE, LIBRARY**										**700**
0100	Attendant desk, 36" x 62" x 29" high	1 Carp	16	.500	Ea.	2,275	14.60		2,289.60	2,525	
0200	Book display, "A" frame display, both sides, 42" x 42" x 60" high		16	.500		2,450	14.60		2,464.60	2,725	
0220	Table with bulletin board, 42" x 24" x 49" high		16	.500		1,250	14.60		1,264.60	1,400	
0800	Card catalogue, 30 tray unit		16	.500		2,475	14.60		2,489.60	2,750	
0840	60 tray unit	↓	16	.500		4,250	14.60		4,264.60	4,675	
0880	72 tray unit	2 Carp	16	1		4,600	29		4,629	5,125	
1000	Carrels, single face, initial unit	1 Carp	16	.500		755	14.60		769.60	855	
1500	Double face, initial unit	2 Carp	16	1		1,150	29		1,179	1,300	
4000	Dictionary stand, stationary	1 Carp	16	.500		700	14.60		714.60	795	
4020	Revolving		16	.500		243	14.60		257.60	290	
4200	Exhibit case, table style, 60" x 28" x 36"		11	.727		3,450	21		3,471	3,825	
7000	Tables, card catalog reference, 24" x 60" x 42"	↓	16	.500	↓	780	14.60		794.60	885	

FURNISHINGS **12**

12640	Booths & Tables	CREW	DAILY OUTPUT	LABOR-HOURS	UNIT	2001 BARE COSTS				TOTAL INCL O&P
						MAT.	LABOR	EQUIP.	TOTAL	
150	0010 **BOOTHS**									150
	1000 Banquet, upholstered seat and back, custom									
	1500 Straight, minimum	2 Carp	40	.400	L.F.	114	11.65		125.65	144
	1520 Maximum		36	.444		222	12.95		234.95	265
	1600 "L" or "U" shape, minimum		35	.457		116	13.35		129.35	149
	1620 Maximum	↓	30	.533	↓	207	15.55		222.55	252
	1800 Upholstered outside finished backs for									
	1810 single booths and custom banquets									
	1820 Minimum	2 Carp	44	.364	L.F.	13.15	10.60		23.75	31
	1840 Maximum	"	40	.400	"	39.50	11.65		51.15	62
	3000 Fixed seating, one piece plastic chair and									
	3010 plastic laminate table top									
	3100 Two seat, 24" x 24" table, minimum	F-7	30	1.067	Ea.	460	27.50		487.50	550
	3120 Maximum		26	1.231		655	32		687	770
	3200 Four seat, 24" x 48" table, minimum		28	1.143		455	29.50		484.50	545
	3220 Maximum	↓	24	1.333	↓	780	34.50		814.50	910
	5000 Mount in floor, wood fiber core with									
	5010 plastic laminate face, single booth									
	5050 24" wide	F-7	30	1.067	Ea.	176	27.50		203.50	238
	5100 48" wide	"	28	1.143	"	224	29.50		253.50	294

12830	Interior Planters	CREW	DAILY OUTPUT	LABOR-HOURS	UNIT	2001 BARE COSTS				TOTAL INCL O&P
						MAT.	LABOR	EQUIP.	TOTAL	
600	0010 **PLANTERS**									600
	1000 Fiberglass, hanging, 12" diameter, 7" high				Ea.	34.50			34.50	38
	1500 Rectangular, 48" long, 16" high x 15" wide					194			194	214
	1650 60" long, 30" high, 28" wide					495			495	545
	2000 Round, 12" diameter, 13" high					70			70	76.50
	2050 25" high					76			76	84
	5000 Square, 10" side, 20" high					100			100	110
	5100 14" side, 15" high					97			97	107
	6000 Metal bowl, 32" diameter, 8" high, minimum					274			274	300
	6050 Maximum				↓	365			365	405
	8750 Wood, fiberglass liner, square									
	8780 14" square, 15" high, minimum				Ea.	192			192	211
	8800 Maximum					236			236	259
	9400 Plastic cylinder, molded, 10" diameter, 10" high					7.75			7.75	8.55
	9500 11" diameter, 11" high				↓	24.50			24.50	27

12 FURNISHINGS

Important: See the Reference Section for critical supporting data - Reference Nos., Crews, & City Cost Indexes

Division 13
Special Construction

Estimating Tips

General

- The items and systems in this division are usually estimated, purchased, supplied and installed as a unit by one or more subcontractors. The estimator must ensure that all parties are operating from the same set of specifications and assumptions and that all necessary items are estimated and will be provided. Many times the complex items and systems are covered but the more common ones such as excavation or a crane are overlooked for the very reason that everyone assumes nobody could miss them. The estimator should be the central focus and be able to ensure that all systems are complete.

- Another area where problems can develop in this division is at the interface between systems. The estimator must ensure, for instance, that anchor bolts, nuts and washers are estimated and included for the air-supported structures and pre-engineered buildings to be bolted to their foundations.

Utility supply is a common area where essential items or pieces of equipment can be missed or overlooked due to the fact that each subcontractor may feel it is the others' responsibility. The estimator should also be aware of certain items which may be supplied as part of a package but installed by others, and ensure that the installing contractor's estimate includes the cost of installation. Conversely, the estimator must also ensure that items are not costed by two different subcontractors, resulting in an inflated overall estimate.

13120 Pre-Engineered Structures

- The foundations and floor slab, as well as rough mechanical and electrical, should be estimated, as this work is required for the assembly and erection of the structure. Generally, as noted in the book, the pre-engineered building comes as a shell and additional features must be included by the estimator. Here again, the estimator must have a clear understanding of the scope of each portion of the work and all the necessary interfaces.

13200 Storage Tanks

- The prices in this subdivision for above and below ground storage tanks do not include foundations or hold-down slabs. The estimator should refer to Divisions 2 and 3 for foundation system pricing. In addition to the foundations, required tank accessories such as tank gauges, leak detection devices, and additional manholes and piping must be added to the tank prices.

Reference Numbers

Reference numbers are shown in bold squares at the beginning of some major classifications. These numbers refer to related items in the Reference Section. The reference information may be an estimating procedure, an alternate pricing method or technical information.

Note: Not all subdivisions listed here necessarily appear in this publication.

		CREW	DAILY OUTPUT	LABOR-HOURS	UNIT	MAT.	LABOR	EQUIP.	TOTAL	TOTAL INCL O&P	
13011	**Air Supported Structures**					2001 BARE COSTS					
100	**0010 AIR SUPPORTED STORAGE TANK COVERS** Vinyl polyester										**100**
0100	scrim, double layer, with hardware, blower, standby & controls										
0200	Round, 75' diameter	B-2	4,500	.009	S.F.	6.10	.21		6.31	7	
0300	100' diameter		5,000	.008		5.50	.19		5.69	6.35	
0400	150' diameter		5,000	.008		4.15	.19		4.34	4.86	
0500	Rectangular, 20' x 20'		4,500	.009		13.50	.21		13.71	15.15	
0600	30' x 40'		4,500	.009		13.50	.21		13.71	15.15	
0700	50' x 60'		4,500	.009		13.50	.21		13.71	15.15	
0800	For single wall construction, deduct, minimum					.39			.39	.43	
0900	Maximum					1.28			1.28	1.41	
1000	For maximum resistance to atmosphere or cold, add					.54			.54	.59	
1100	For average shipping charges, add				Total	1,050			1,050	1,150	
200	**0010 AIR SUPPORTED STRUCTURES**	R13011 -110									**200**
0020	Site preparation, incl. anchor placement and utilities	B-11B	2,000	.008	SF Flr.	.71	.21	.46	1.38	1.62	
0030	For concrete curb, see division 03310-240										
0050	Warehouse, polyester/vinyl fabric, 28 oz., over 10 yr. life, welded										
0060	Seams, tension cables, primary & auxiliary inflation system,										
0070	airlock, personnel doors and liner										
0100	5000 S.F.	4 Clab	5,000	.006	SF Flr.	15	.15		15.15	16.75	
0250	12,000 S.F.	"	6,000	.005		10.85	.12		10.97	12.15	
0400	24,000 S.F.	8 Clab	12,000	.005		7.95	.12		8.07	8.95	
0500	50,000 S.F.	"	12,500	.005		6.85	.12		6.97	7.75	
0700	12 oz. reinforced vinyl fabric, 5 yr. life, sewn seams,										
0710	accordian door, including liner										
0750	3000 S.F.	4 Clab	3,000	.011	SF Flr.	7.85	.24		8.09	9	
0800	12,000 S.F.	"	6,000	.005		5.80	.12		5.92	6.60	
0850	24,000 S.F.	8 Clab	12,000	.005		5.75	.12		5.87	6.55	
0950	Deduct for single layer					.62			.62	.68	
1000	Add for welded seams					.90			.90	.99	
1050	Add for double layer, welded seams included					1.85			1.85	2.04	
1250	Tedlar/vinyl fabric, 28 oz., with liner, over 10 yr. life,										
1260	incl. overhead and personnel doors										
1300	3000 S.F.	4 Clab	3,000	.011	SF Flr.	14.55	.24		14.79	16.40	
1450	12,000 S.F.	"	6,000	.005		10.25	.12		10.37	11.45	
1550	24,000 S.F.	8 Clab	12,000	.005		7.95	.12		8.07	8.95	
1700	Deduct for single layer					1.29			1.29	1.42	
2250	Greenhouse/shelter, woven polyethylene with liner, 2 yr. life,										
2260	sewn seams, including doors										
2300	3000 S.F.	4 Clab	3,000	.011	SF Flr.	5.90	.24		6.14	6.90	
2350	12,000 S.F.	"	6,000	.005		6	.12		6.12	6.80	
2450	24,000 S.F.	8 Clab	12,000	.005		5	.12		5.12	5.70	
2550	Deduct for single layer					.56			.56	.62	
2600	Tennis/gymnasium, polyester/vinyl fabric, 28 oz., over 10 yr. life,										
2610	including thermal liner, heat and lights										
2650	7200 S.F.	4 Clab	6,000	.005	SF Flr.	14	.12		14.12	15.60	
2750	13,000 S.F.	"	6,500	.005		10.50	.11		10.61	11.75	
2850	Over 24,000 S.F.	8 Clab	12,000	.005		9.50	.12		9.62	10.65	
2860	For low temperature conditions, add					.64			.64	.70	
2870	For average shipping charges, add				Total	2,800			2,800	3,075	
2900	Thermal liner, translucent reinforced vinyl				SF Flr.	.88			.88	.97	
2950	Metalized mylar fabric and mesh, double liner				"	1.40			1.40	1.54	
3050	Stadium/convention center, teflon coated fiberglass, heavy weight,										
3060	over 20 yr. life, incl. thermal liner and heating system										
3100	Minimum	9 Clab	26,000	.003	SF Flr.	36	.06		36.06	39.50	
3110	Maximum	"	19,000	.004	"	42	.09		42.09	46	
3400	Doors, air lock, 15' long, 10' x 10'	2 Carp	.80	20	Ea.	13,200	585		13,785	15,400	

13 SPECIAL CONSTRUCTION

13010 | Air Supported Structures

13011 | Air Supported Structures

		CREW	DAILY OUTPUT	LABOR-HOURS	UNIT	MAT.	LABOR	EQUIP.	TOTAL	TOTAL INCL O&P	
200						2001 BARE COSTS					**200**
3600	15' x 15'	2 Carp	.50	32	Ea.	19,100	935		20,035	22,500	
3700	For each added 5' length, add [R13011-110]					2,750			2,750	3,025	
3900	Revolving personnel door, 6' diameter, 6'-6" high	2 Carp	.80	20	↓	9,650	585		10,235	11,500	
4200	Double wall, self supporting, shell only, minimum				SF Flr.					21	
4300	Maximum	▼			"					39	

13030 | Special Purpose Rooms

13035 | Special Purpose Rooms

		CREW	DAILY OUTPUT	LABOR-HOURS	UNIT	MAT.	LABOR	EQUIP.	TOTAL	TOTAL INCL O&P	
100						2001 BARE COSTS					**100**
0010	**INTEGRATED CEILINGS** Lighting, ventilating & acoustical										
0100	Luminaire, incl. connections, 5' x 5' modules, 50% lighted	L-3	90	.178	S.F.	3.53	5.60		9.13	12.55	
0200	100% lighted	"	50	.320		5.25	10.10		15.35	21.50	
0400	For ventilating capacity with perforations, add				↓					.27	
0600	For supply air diffuser, add				Ea.					64	
0700	Dimensionaire, 2' x 4' board system, see also div. 09510-760	L-3	50	.320	L.F.	8.20	10.10		18.30	24.50	
0900	Tile system	1 Carp	250	.032	S.F.	2.14	.93		3.07	3.81	
1000	For air bar suspension, add, minimum				↓					.61	
1100	Maximum				▼					1.05	
1200	For vaulted coffer, including fixture, stock, add				Ea.	80			80	88	
1300	Custom, add, minimum									133	
1400	Average									345	
1500	Maximum				▼					575	
1600	Grid sys. & ceil. tile only, flat profile, 5'x5' mod., 50% lghtd.										
1620	Mineral fiber panels	1 Carp	700	.011	S.F.	3.23	.33		3.56	4.07	
1630	Glass fiber panels	"	700	.011		3.47	.33		3.80	4.34	
1640	100% lighted, add					1.68			1.68	1.85	
1650	For supply air linear diffuser, add					.53			.53	.58	
1660	For vaulted coffer, 5' x 5' modules, 50% lighted	1 Carp	493	.016	▼	4.12	.47		4.59	5.25	
1800	Radiant hot water system with finished acoustic ceiling,										
1810	not including supply piping. Heating only (gross S.F.)										
2100	Elementary schools, minimum				S.F.					5.30	
2200	Maximum									6.65	
2400	High schools and colleges, minimum									4.75	
2500	Maximum									6.65	
2700	Libraries, minimum									4.80	
2800	Maximum									5.75	
3000	Hospitals, minimum									6.50	
3100	Maximum									8.15	
3300	Office buildings, minimum									4.60	
3400	Maximum									6.15	
3600	For combined heating and cooling, add, minimum									30%	
3700	Maximum									40%	
4000	Radiant electric ceiling board, strapped between joists	1 Elec	250	.032	▼	1.74	1.10		2.84	3.55	
4100	2' x 4' heating panel for grid system, manila finish		25	.320	Ea.	80	11		91	104	
4200	Textured epoxy finish		22	.364		82	12.45		94.45	109	
4300	Vinyl finish		19	.421		84	14.45		98.45	114	
4400	Hair cell, ABS plastic finish	▼	13	.615	▼	94	21		115	135	
4500	2' x 4' alternate blank panel, for use with above										
4600	Manila finish	1 Elec	50	.160	Ea.	25	5.50		30.50	35.50	

SPECIAL CONSTRUCTION **13**

13035		Special Purpose Rooms	CREW	DAILY OUTPUT	LABOR-HOURS	UNIT	2001 BARE COSTS				TOTAL INCL O&P	
							MAT.	LABOR	EQUIP.	TOTAL		
100	4700	Textured epoxy finish	1 Elec	45	.178	Ea.	30	6.10		36.10	42	**100**
	4800	Vinyl finish		40	.200		32	6.85		38.85	45.50	
	4900	Hair cell, ABS plastic finish	↓	25	.320	↓	64	11		75	87	
150	0010	**ANECHOIC CHAMBERS** Standard units, 7' ceiling heights										**150**
	0100	Area for pricing is net inside dimensions										
	0300	200 cycles per second cutoff, 25 S.F. floor area				SF Flr.					1,375	
	0400	50 S.F.									1,100	
	0600	75 S.F.									1,050	
	0700	100 S.F.									1,025	
	0900	For 150 cycles per second cutoff, add					30%	30%				
	1000	For 100 cycles per second cutoff, add				↓	45%	45%				
180	0010	**AUDIOMETRIC ROOMS** Under 500 S.F. surface	4 Carp	98	.327	SF Surf	40	9.50		49.50	59	**180**
	0100	Over 500 S.F. surface	"	120	.267	"	38	7.75		45.75	54	
200	0010	**CLEAN ROOMS**										**200**
	1100	Clean room, soft wall, 12' x 12', Class 100	1 Carp	.18	44.444	Ea.	12,200	1,300		13,500	15,400	
	1110	Class 1,000		.18	44.444		9,450	1,300		10,750	12,400	
	1120	Class 10,000		.21	38.095		8,050	1,100		9,150	10,600	
	1130	Class 100,000	↓	.21	38.095	↓	8,050	1,100		9,150	10,600	
	2800	Ceiling grid support, slotted channel struts 4'-0" O.C., ea. way				S.F.					6.50	
	3000	Ceiling panel, vinyl coated foil on mineral substrate										
	3020	Sealed, non-perforated				S.F.					1.40	
	4000	Ceiling panel seal, silicone sealant, 150 L.F./gal.	1 Carp	150	.053	L.F.	.22	1.55		1.77	2.67	
	4100	Two sided adhesive tape	"	240	.033	"	.10	.97		1.07	1.63	
	4200	Clips, one per panel				Ea.	.85			.85	.94	
	6000	HEPA filter,2'x4',99.97% eff.,3" dp beveled frame(silicone seal)					260			260	286	
	6040	6" deep skirted frame (channel seal)					300			300	330	
	6100	99.99% efficient, 3" deep beveled frame (silicone seal)					280			280	310	
	6140	6" deep skirted frame (channel seal)					320			320	350	
	6200	99.999% efficient, 3" deep beveled frame (silicone seal)					320			320	350	
	6240	6" deep skirted frame (channel seal)				↓	360			360	395	
	7000	Wall panel systems, including channel strut framing										
	7020	Polyester coated aluminum, particle board				S.F.					20	
	7100	Porcelain coated aluminum, particle board									35	
	7400	Wall panel support, slotted channel struts, to 12' high				↓					18	
300	0010	**DARKROOMS** Shell, complete except for door, 64 S.F., 8' high	2 Carp	128	.125	SF Flr.	65.50	3.64		69.14	77.50	**300**
	0100	12' high		64	.250		78.50	7.30		85.80	98	
	0500	120 S.F. floor, 8' high		120	.133		48	3.89		51.89	59	
	0600	12' high		60	.267		59	7.75		66.75	77	
	0800	240 S.F. floor, 8' high		120	.133	↓	34	3.89		37.89	43.50	
	0900	12' high		60	.267		47	7.75		54.75	63.50	
	1200	Mini-cylindrical, revolving, unlined, 4' diameter	↓	3.50	4.571	Ea.	3,250	133		3,383	3,775	
	1400	5'-6" diameter	↓	2.50	6.400		5,125	187		5,312	5,950	
	1600	Add for lead lining, inner cylinder, 1/32" thick					1,300			1,300	1,450	
	1700	1/16" thick					1,525			1,525	1,675	
	1800	Add for lead lining, inner and outer cylinder, 1/32" thick					2,425			2,425	2,675	
	1900	1/16" thick				↓	2,525			2,525	2,800	
	2000	For darkroom door, see division 11472-370										
500	0010	**MUSIC** Practice room, modular, perforated steel, under 500 S.F.	2 Carp	70	.229	SF Surf	24	6.65		30.65	37	**500**
	0100	Over 500 S.F.	"	80	.200	"	21	5.85		26.85	32	
700	0010	**REFRIGERATION** Curbs, 12" high, 4" thick, concrete	2 Carp	58	.276	L.F.	3.02	8.05		11.07	15.90	**700**
	1000	Doors, see division 08341-200										
	2400	Finishes, 2 coat portland cement plaster, 1/2" thick	1 Plas	48	.167	S.F.	.83	4.55		5.38	7.85	
	2500	For galvanized reinforcing mesh, add	1 Lath	335	.024	↓	.56	.67		1.23	1.63	

T3 SPECIAL CONSTRUCTION

Important: See the Reference Section for critical supporting data - Reference Nos., Crews, & City Cost Indexes

			CREW	DAILY OUTPUT	LABOR-HOURS	UNIT	MAT.	LABOR	EQUIP.	TOTAL	TOTAL INCL O&P	
700	2700	3/16" thick latex cement	1 Plas	88	.091	S.F.	1.42	2.48		3.90	5.35	**700**
	2900	For glass cloth reinforced ceilings, add	"	450	.018		.34	.49		.83	1.11	
	3100	Fiberglass panels, 1/8" thick	1 Carp	149.45	.054		1.88	1.56		3.44	4.51	
	3200	Polystyrene, plastic finish ceiling, 1" thick		274	.029		1.74	.85		2.59	3.24	
	3400	2" thick		274	.029		1.97	.85		2.82	3.50	
	3500	4" thick		219	.037		2.20	1.06		3.26	4.09	
	3800	Floors, concrete, 4" thick	1 Cefi	93	.086		.82	2.40		3.22	4.47	
	3900	6" thick	"	85	.094		1.24	2.63		3.87	5.25	
	4000	Insulation, 1" to 6" thick, cork				B.F.	.80			.80	.88	
	4100	Urethane					.79			.79	.87	
	4300	Polystyrene, regular					.54			.54	.59	
	4400	Bead board					.41			.41	.45	
	4600	Installation of above, add per layer	2 Carp	657.60	.024	S.F.	.25	.71		.96	1.39	
	4700	Wall and ceiling juncture		298.90	.054	L.F.	1.28	1.56		2.84	3.85	
	4900	Partitions, galvanized sandwich panels, 4" thick, stock		219.20	.073	S.F.	5.40	2.13		7.53	9.30	
	5000	Aluminum or fiberglass		219.20	.073	"	5.95	2.13		8.08	9.85	
	5200	Prefab walk-in, 7'-6" high, aluminum, incl. door & floors,										
	5210	not incl. partitions or refrigeration, 6' x 6' O.D. nominal	2 Carp	54.80	.292	SF Flr.	97	8.50		105.50	120	
	5500	10' x 10' O.D. nominal		82.20	.195		78	5.65		83.65	95	
	5700	12' x 14' O.D. nominal		109.60	.146		70	4.26		74.26	83.50	
	5800	12' x 20' O.D. nominal		109.60	.146		61	4.26		65.26	73.50	
	6100	For 8'-6" high, add					5%					
	6300	Rule of thumb for complete units, w/o doors & refrigeration, cooler	2 Carp	146	.110		88	3.19		91.19	102	
	6400	Freezer		109.60	.146		104	4.26		108.26	121	
	6600	Shelving, plated or galvanized, steel wire type		360	.044	SF Hor.	7.70	1.30		9	10.50	
	6700	Slat shelf type		375	.043		9.50	1.24		10.74	12.40	
	6900	For stainless steel shelving, add					300%					
	7000	Vapor barrier, on wood walls	2 Carp	1,644	.010	S.F.	.11	.28		.39	.56	
	7200	On masonry walls	"	1,315	.012	"	.29	.35		.64	.88	
	7500	For air curtain doors, see division 08344-120										
800	0010	**SAUNA** Prefabricated, incl. heater & controls, 7' high, 6' x 4', C/C	L-7	2.20	12.727	Ea.	3,200	360		3,560	4,075	**800**
	0050	6' x 4', C/P		2	14		2,525	395		2,920	3,375	
	0400	6' x 5', C/C		2	14		3,225	395		3,620	4,125	
	0450	6' x 5', C/P		2	14		2,875	395		3,270	3,750	
	0600	6' x 6', C/C		1.80	15.556		3,800	435		4,235	4,850	
	0650	6' x 6', C/P		1.80	15.556		3,000	435		3,435	3,975	
	0800	6' x 9', C/C		1.60	17.500		4,175	490		4,665	5,350	
	0850	6' x 9', C/P		1.60	17.500		4,175	490		4,665	5,350	
	1000	8' x 12', C/C		1.10	25.455		7,350	715		8,065	9,175	
	1050	8' x 12', C/P		1.10	25.455		5,775	715		6,490	7,450	
	1200	8' x 8', C/C		1.40	20		4,925	560		5,485	6,300	
	1250	8' x 8', C/P		1.40	20		4,350	560		4,910	5,650	
	1400	8' x 10', C/C		1.20	23.333		5,400	655		6,055	6,950	
	1450	8' x 10', C/P		1.20	23.333		4,725	655		5,380	6,225	
	1600	10' x 12', C/C		1	28		7,200	785		7,985	9,125	
	1650	10' x 12', C/P		1	28		6,375	785		7,160	8,250	
	1700	Door only, cedar, 2'x6', with tempered insulated glass window	2 Carp	3.40	4.706		267	137		404	510	
	1800	Prehung, incl. jambs, pulls & hardware	"	12	1.333		305	39		344	400	
	2500	Heaters only (incl. above), wall mounted, to 200 C.F.					505			505	555	
	2750	To 300 C.F.					530			530	580	
	3000	Floor standing, to 720 C.F., 10,000 watts, w/controls	1 Elec	3	2.667		925	91.50		1,016.50	1,150	
	3250	To 1,000 C.F., 16,000 watts	"	3	2.667		1,575	91.50		1,666.50	1,850	
900	0010	**SPORT COURT** Floors, No. 2 & better maple, 25/32" thick				SF Flr.					6.65	**900**
	0100	Walls, laminated plastic bonded to galv. steel studs				SF Wall					8.45	
	0150	Laminated fiberglass surfacing, minimum									2.10	
	0180	Maximum									2.37	

		13035	Special Purpose Rooms	CREW	DAILY OUTPUT	LABOR-HOURS	UNIT	2001 BARE COSTS				TOTAL INCL O&P	
								MAT.	LABOR	EQUIP.	TOTAL		
900	0300		Squash, regulation court in existing building, minimum				Court					14,500	900
	0400		Maximum				"					27,100	
	0450		Rule of thumb for components:										
	0470		Walls	3 Carp	.15	160	Court	10,100	4,675		14,775	18,400	
	0500		Floor	"	.25	96		4,525	2,800		7,325	9,350	
	0550		Lighting	2 Elec	.60	26.667		1,425	915		2,340	2,950	
	0600		Handball, racquetball court in existing building, minimum	C-1	.20	160		1,750	4,400		6,150	8,825	
	0800		Maximum	"	.10	320		23,400	8,825		32,225	39,500	
	0900		Rule of thumb for components: walls	3 Carp	.12	200		9,225	5,825		15,050	19,200	
	1000		Floor		.25	96		4,800	2,800		7,600	9,650	
	1100		Ceiling	▼	.33	72.727		2,000	2,125		4,125	5,525	
	1200		Lighting	2 Elec	.60	26.667	▼	2,475	915		3,390	4,100	
940	0010		STEAM BATH Heater, timer & head, single, to 140 C.F.	1 Plum	1.20	6.667	Ea.	840	230		1,070	1,275	940
	0500		To 300 C.F.	"	1.10	7.273		970	251		1,221	1,450	
	1000		Commercial size, with blow-down assembly, to 800 C.F.	1 Plum	.90	8.889		3,800	305		4,105	4,625	
	1500		To 2500 C.F.	"	.80	10		4,000	345		4,345	4,925	
	2000		Multiple, motels, apts., 2 baths, w/ blow-down assm., 500 C.F.	Q-1	1.30	12.308		3,025	380		3,405	3,900	
	2500		4 baths	"	.70	22.857		3,675	710		4,385	5,100	
	2700		Conversion unit for residential tub, including door				▼	1,775			1,775	1,950	

		13039	Vaults										
900	0010		VAULT FRONT See division 08320-950										900

		13081	Sound Control	CREW	DAILY OUTPUT	LABOR-HOURS	UNIT	2001 BARE COSTS				TOTAL INCL O&P	
								MAT.	LABOR	EQUIP.	TOTAL		
100	0010		ACOUSTICAL Enclosure, 4" thick wall and ceiling panels										100
	0020		8# per S.F., up to 12' span	3 Carp	72	.333	SF Surf	25	9.70		34.70	42	
	0300		Better quality panels, 10.5# per S.F.		64	.375		28	10.95		38.95	48	
	0400		Reverb-chamber, 4" thick, parallel walls		60	.400		35	11.65		46.65	57	
	0600		Skewed wall, parallel roof, 4" thick panels		55	.436		40	12.70		52.70	64	
	0700		Skewed walls, skewed roof, 4" layers, 4" air space		48	.500		45	14.60		59.60	72.50	
	0900		Sound-absorbing panels, pntd mtl, 2'-6" x 8', under 1,000 S.F.		215	.112		9.05	3.25		12.30	15.05	
	1100		Over 1000 S.F.		240	.100		8.70	2.92		11.62	14.10	
	1200		Fabric faced	▼	240	.100		7.25	2.92		10.17	12.55	
	1500		Flexible transparent curtain, clear	3 Shee	215	.112		5.60	3.75		9.35	11.95	
	1600		50% foam		215	.112		7.85	3.75		11.60	14.40	
	1700		75% foam		215	.112		7.85	3.75		11.60	14.40	
	1800		100% foam	▼	215	.112	▼	7.85	3.75		11.60	14.40	
	3100		Audio masking system, including speakers, amplification										
	3110		and signal generator										
	3200		Ceiling mounted, 5,000 S.F.	2 Elec	2,400	.007	S.F.	.96	.23		1.19	1.40	
	3300		10,000 S.F.		2,800	.006		.78	.20		.98	1.15	
	3400		Plenum mounted, 5,000 S.F.		3,800	.004		.81	.14		.95	1.11	
	3500		10,000 S.F.	▼	4,400	.004	▼	.54	.12		.66	.78	

Important: See the Reference Section for critical supporting data - Reference Nos., Crews, & City Cost Indexes

13091	X-Ray/Radio Freq Protection	CREW	DAILY OUTPUT	LABOR-HOURS	UNIT	2001 BARE COSTS				TOTAL INCL O&P
						MAT.	LABOR	EQUIP.	TOTAL	
600	**0010** **SHIELDING LEAD**									**600**
0100	Laminated lead in wood doors, 1/16" thick, no hardware				S.F.	26			26	28.50
0200	Lead lined door frame, not incl. hardware,									
0210	1/16" thick lead, butt prepared for hardware	1 Lath	2.40	3.333	Ea.	299	94		393	470
0300	Lead sheets, 1/16" thick	2 Lath	135	.119	S.F.	4.57	3.34		7.91	10.05
0400	1/8" thick		120	.133		9.55	3.76		13.31	16.10
0500	Lead shielding, 1/4" thick		135	.119		15.25	3.34		18.59	22
0550	1/2" thick		120	.133		30.50	3.76		34.26	39
0600	Lead glass, 1/4" thick, 2.0 mm LE, 12" x 16"	2 Glaz	13	1.231	Ea.	247	35		282	325
0700	24" x 36"		8	2		970	57		1,027	1,150
0800	36" x 60"		2	8		1,850	228		2,078	2,375
0850	Window frame with 1/16" lead and voice passage, 36" x 60"		2	8		380	228		608	760
0870	24" x 36" frame		8	2		288	57		345	400
0900	Lead gypsum board, 5/8" thick with 1/16" lead		160	.100	S.F.	4.78	2.86		7.64	9.60
0910	1/8" lead **CN**		140	.114		9.75	3.26		13.01	15.70
0930	1/32" lead	2 Lath	200	.080		2.94	2.26		5.20	6.60
0950	Lead headed nails (average 1 lb. per sheet)				Lb.	5.25			5.25	5.80
1000	Butt joints in 1/8" lead or thicker, 2" batten strip x 7' long	2 Lath	240	.067	Ea.	13.15	1.88		15.03	17.25
1200	X-ray protection, average radiography or fluoroscopy									
1210	room, up to 300 S.F. floor, 1/16" lead, minimum	2 Lath	.25	64	Total	4,600	1,800		6,400	7,750
1500	Maximum, 7'-0" walls	"	.15	106	"	6,000	3,000		9,000	11,100
1600	Deep therapy X-ray room, 250 KV capacity,									
1800	up to 300 S.F. floor, 1/4" lead, minimum	2 Lath	.08	200	Total	15,500	5,650		21,150	25,500
1900	Maximum, 7'-0" walls	"	.06	266	"	21,000	7,525		28,525	34,300
2000	X-ray viewing panels, clear lead plastic									
2010	7 mm thick, 0.3 mm LE, 2.3 lbs/S.F.	H-3	139	.115	S.F.	122	2.92		124.92	138
2020	12 mm thick, 0.5 mm LE, 3.9 lbs/S.F.		82	.195		165	4.95		169.95	190
2030	18 mm thick, 0.8mm LE, 5.9 lbs/S.F.		54	.296		179	7.50		186.50	209
2040	22 mm thick, 1.0 mm LE, 7.2 lbs/S.F.		44	.364		183	9.20		192.20	215
2050	35 mm thick, 1.5 mm LE, 11.5 lbs/S.F.		28	.571		205	14.50		219.50	249
2060	46 mm thick, 2.0 mm LE, 15.0 lbs/S.F.		21	.762		270	19.30		289.30	325
2090	For panels 12 S.F. to 48 S.F., add crating charge				Ea.					50
4000	X-ray barriers, modular, panels mounted within framework for									
4002	attaching to floor, wall or ceiling, upper portion is clear lead									
4005	plastic window panels 48"H, lower portion is opaque leaded									
4008	steel panels 36"H, structural supports not incl.									
4010	1-section barrier, 36"W x 84"H overall									
4020	0.5 mm LE panels	H-3	6.40	2.500	Ea.	2,750	63.50		2,813.50	3,125
4030	0.8 mm LE panels		6.40	2.500		2,925	63.50		2,988.50	3,325
4040	1.0 mm LE panels		5.33	3.002		3,025	76		3,101	3,450
4050	1.5 mm LE panels		5.33	3.002		3,225	76		3,301	3,675
4060	2-section barrier, 72"W x 84"H overall									
4070	0.5 mm LE panels	H-3	4	4	Ea.	5,700	101		5,801	6,425
4080	0.8 mm LE panels		4	4		6,025	101		6,126	6,775
4090	1.0 mm LE panels		3.56	4.494		6,150	114		6,264	6,950
5000	1.5 mm LE panels		3.20	5		6,650	127		6,777	7,525
5010	3-section barrier, 108"W x 84"H overall									
5020	0.5 mm LE panels	H-3	3.20	5	Ea.	8,150	127		8,277	9,175
5030	0.8 mm LE panels		3.20	5		8,550	127		8,677	9,600
5040	1.0 mm LE panels		2.67	5.993		8,750	152		8,902	9,850
5050	1.5 mm LE panels		2.46	6.504		9,500	165		9,665	10,800
7000	X-ray barriers, mobile, mounted within framework w/casters on									
7005	bottom, clear lead plastic window panels on upper portion,									
7010	opaque on lower, 30"W x 75"H overall, incl. framework									
7020	24"H upper w/0.5 mm LE, 48"H lower w/0.8 mm LE	1 Carp	16	.500	Ea.	1,875	14.60		1,889.60	2,075
7030	48"W x 75"H overall, incl. framework									

SPECIAL CONSTRUCTION **13**

13090 | Radiation Protection

13091 | X-Ray/Radio Freq Protection

			CREW	DAILY OUTPUT	LABOR-HOURS	UNIT	2001 BARE COSTS MAT.	LABOR	EQUIP.	TOTAL	TOTAL INCL O&P	
600	7040	36"H upper w/0.5 mm LE, 36"H lower w/0.8 mm LE	1 Carp	16	.500	Ea.	3,300	14.60		3,314.60	3,650	600
	7050	36"H upper w/1.0 mm LE, 36"H lower w/1.5 mm LE	"	16	.500	"	4,000	14.60		4,014.60	4,425	
	7060	72"W x 75"H overall, incl. framework										
	7070	36"H upper w/0.5 mm LE, 36"H lower w/0.8 mm LE	1 Carp	16	.500	Ea.	3,925	14.60		3,939.60	4,325	
	7080	36"H upper w/1.0 mm LE, 36"H lower w/1.5 mm LE	"	16	.500	"	4,950	14.60		4,964.60	5,475	
700	0010	**SHIELDING, RADIO FREQUENCY**										700
	0020	Prefabricated or screen-type copper or steel, minimum	2 Carp	180	.089	SF Surf	24	2.59		26.59	30.50	
	0100	Average	↓	155	.103		26	3.01		29.01	33	
	0150	Maximum	↓	145	.110	↓	31	3.22		34.22	39	

13120 | Pre-Engineered Structures

13128 | Pre-Eng. Structures

			CREW	DAILY OUTPUT	LABOR-HOURS	UNIT	2001 BARE COSTS MAT.	LABOR	EQUIP.	TOTAL	TOTAL INCL O&P	
060	0010	**PORTABLE BOOTHS** Prefab aluminum with doors, windows, ext. roof										060
	0100	lights wiring & insulation, 15 S.F. building, O.D., painted, minimum				S.F.	255			255	281	
	0300	30 S.F. building, minimum					175			175	193	
	0400	50 S.F. building, minimum					130			130	143	
	0600	80 S.F. building, minimum					105			105	116	
	0700	100 S.F. building, minimum				↓	97			97	107	
	0900	Acoustical booth, 27 Db @ 1,000 Hz, 15 S.F. floor				Ea.	2,875			2,875	3,175	
	1000	7' x 7'-6", including light & ventilation					5,900			5,900	6,500	
	1200	Ticket booth, galv. steel, not incl. foundations., 4' x 4'					4,425			4,425	4,875	
	1300	4' x 6'				↓	5,175			5,175	5,700	
070	0010	**CONTROL TOWERS**, 12' x 10', incl. instruments, min.				Ea.					450,000	070
	0100	Maximum				↓					1,000,000	
	0500	With standard 40' tower, average				↓					600,000	
	1000	Temporary portable control towers, 8' x 12',										
	1010	complete with one position communications, minimum				Ea.					275,000	
	2000	For fixed facilities, depending on height, minimum									50,000	
	2010	Maximum				↓					100,000	
160	0010	**TENSION STRUCTURES** Rigid steel/alum. frame, vyl. coated polyester										160
	0100	fabric shell, 60' clear span, not incl. foundations or floors										
	0200	6,000 S.F.	B-41	1,000	.044	SF Flr.	10.55	1.04	.18	11.77	13.45	
	0300	12,000 S.F.		1,100	.040		8.95	.95	.16	10.06	11.50	
	0400	80' clear span, 20,800 S.F.	↓	1,220	.036		9.40	.86	.15	10.41	11.85	
	0410	100' clear span, 10,000 S.F.	L-5	2,175	.026		10.40	.85	.29	11.54	13.25	
	0430	26,000 S.F.		2,300	.024		8.80	.80	.27	9.87	11.40	
	0450	36,000 S.F.		2,500	.022		8.55	.74	.25	9.54	11	
	0460	120' clear span, 24,000 S.F.		3,000	.019		11.50	.61	.21	12.32	13.95	
	0470	150' clear span, 30,000 S.F.	↓	6,000	.009		11.20	.31	.10	11.61	13	
	0480	200' clear span, 40,000 S.F.	E-6	8,000	.016	↓	14.40	.52	.19	15.11	17	
	0500	For roll-up door, 12' x 14', add	L-2	1	16	Ea.	3,675	410		4,085	4,675	
	0600	For personnel doors, add, minimum				SF Flr.	5%					
	0700	Add, maximum					15%					
	0800	For site work, simple foundation, etc., add, minimum								1.25	1.95	
	0900	Add, maximum				↓				2.75	3.05	
200	0010	**COMFORT STATIONS** Prefab., stock, w/doors, windows & fixt.										200
	0100	Not incl. interior finish or electrical										

Important: See the Reference Section for critical supporting data - Reference Nos., Crews, & City Cost Indexes

			DAILY	LABOR-		2001 BARE COSTS				TOTAL	
13128	**Pre-Eng. Structures**	CREW	OUTPUT	HOURS	UNIT	MAT.	LABOR	EQUIP.	TOTAL	INCL O&P	
200	0300	Mobile, on steel frame, minimum				S.F.	37.50			37.50	41	**200**
	0350	Maximum					62.50			62.50	69	
	0400	Permanent, including concrete slab, minimum	B-12J	50	.320		138	9.10	12.95	160.05	180	
	0500	Maximum	"	43	.372		200	10.60	15.10	225.70	253	
	0600	Alternate pricing method, mobile, minimum				Fixture	1,725			1,725	1,900	
	0650	Maximum					2,575			2,575	2,825	
	0700	Permanent, minimum	B-12J	.70	22.857		9,900	650	925	11,475	12,900	
	0750	Maximum	"	.50	32		16,500	910	1,300	18,710	21,000	
300	0010	**DOMES**										**300**
	0020	Revolv alum, elec drv for astronomy observation, shell only, stk units										
	0600	10'-0" diameter, 800#, dome	2 Carp	.25	64	Ea.	9,400	1,875		11,275	13,200	
	0700	Base		.67	23.881		3,250	695		3,945	4,675	
	0900	18'-0" diameter, 2,500#, dome		.17	94.118		27,500	2,750		30,250	34,600	
	1000	Base		.33	48.485		9,100	1,425		10,525	12,200	
	1200	24'-0" diameter, 4,500#, dome		.08	200		51,000	5,825		56,825	65,000	
	1300	Base		.25	64		16,400	1,875		18,275	20,900	
	1500	Bulk storage, shell only, dual radius hemispher. arch, steel										
	1600	framing, corrugated steel covering, 150' diameter	E-2	550	.102	SF Flr.	27	3.25	2.35	32.60	37.50	
	1700	400' diameter	"	720	.078		22	2.48	1.79	26.27	30.50	
	1800	Wood framing, wood decking, to 400' diameter	F-4	400	.120		20	3.47	2.25	25.72	30	
	1900	Radial framed wood (2" x 6"), 1/2" thick										
	2000	plywood, asphalt shingles, 50' diameter	F-3	2,000	.020	SF Flr.	25	.59	.26	25.85	28.50	
	2100	60' diameter		1,900	.021		19	.62	.27	19.89	22.50	
	2200	72' diameter		1,800	.022		17	.66	.29	17.95	20	
	2300	116' diameter		1,730	.023		15	.68	.30	15.98	17.90	
	2400	150' diameter		1,500	.027		13	.79	.34	14.13	15.90	
340	0010	**GEODESIC DOME** Shell only, interlocking plywood panels `R13128 -310`										**340**
	0400	30' diameter	F-5	1.60	20	Ea.	11,600	595		12,195	13,700	
	0500	34' diameter		1.14	28.070		14,300	830		15,130	17,000	
	0600	39' diameter		1	32		16,100	950		17,050	19,200	
	0700	45' diameter	F-3	1.13	35.556		19,800	1,050	460	21,310	23,900	
	0750	55' diameter		1	40		28,400	1,175	515	30,090	33,700	
	0800	60' diameter		1	40		37,000	1,175	515	38,690	43,100	
	0850	65' diameter		.80	50		43,900	1,475	645	46,020	51,500	
	1100	Aluminum panel, with 6" insulation										
	1200	100' diameter				SF Flr.					30	
	1300	500' diameter				"					25	
	1600	Aluminum framed, plexiglass closure panels										
	1700	40' diameter				SF Flr.					82.50	
	1800	200' diameter				"					77	
	2100	Aluminum framed, aluminum closure panels										
	2200	40' diameter				SF Flr.					55	
	2300	100' diameter									31	
	2400	200' diameter									33	
	2500	For VRP faced bonded fiberglass insulation, add									10	
	2700	Aluminum framed, fiberglass sandwich panel closure										
	2800	6' diameter	2 Carp	150	.107	SF Flr.	33	3.11		36.11	41.50	
	2900	28' diameter	"	350	.046	"	25	1.33		26.33	29.50	
360	0010	**GARAGE COSTS** `R13128 -910`										**360**
	0020	Public parking, average				Car					10,500	
	0100	See also division 17100-410										
	0300	Residential, prefab shell, stock, wood, single car, minimum	2 Carp	1	16	Total	2,550	465		3,015	3,525	
	0350	Maximum		.67	23.881		5,775	695		6,470	7,450	
	0400	Two car, minimum		.67	23.881		3,825	695		4,520	5,300	
	0450	Maximum		.50	32		7,625	935		8,560	9,850	

		CREW	DAILY OUTPUT	LABOR-HOURS	UNIT	2001 BARE COSTS				TOTAL INCL O&P
13128	**Pre-Eng. Structures**					MAT.	LABOR	EQUIP.	TOTAL	
380											**380**
0010	**GARDEN HOUSE** Prefab wood, no floors or foundations									
0100	32 to 200 S.F., minimum	2 Carp	200	.080	SF Flr.	15.25	2.33		17.58	20.50
0300	Maximum	"	48	.333	"	27.50	9.70		37.20	45.50
500											**500**
0010	**GRANDSTANDS** Permanent, municipal, including foundation									
0050	Steel understructure w/aluminum closed deck, minimum				Seat					130
0100	Maximum									225
0300	Steel, minimum									33
0400	Maximum									88
0600	Aluminum, extruded, stock design, minimum									70
0700	Maximum									115
0900	Composite, steel, wood and plastic, stock design, minimum									82.50
1000	Maximum				▼					154
540											**540**
0010	**GREENHOUSE** Shell only, stock units, not incl. 2' stub walls,									
0020	foundation, floors, heat or compartments									
0300	Residential type, free standing, 8'-6" long x 7'-6" wide	2 Carp	59	.271	SF Flr.	35	7.90		42.90	51
0400	10'-6" wide		85	.188		27	5.50		32.50	38
0600	13'-6" wide		108	.148		24	4.32		28.32	33.50
0700	17'-0" wide		160	.100		27	2.92		29.92	34
0900	Lean-to type, 3'-10" wide		34	.471		31	13.70		44.70	55.50
1000	6'-10" wide	▼	58	.276	▼	24	8.05		32.05	39
1500	Commercial, custom, truss frame, incl. equip., plumbing, elec.,									
1510	benches and controls, under 2,000 S.F., minimum				SF Flr.					30
1550	Maximum									38
1700	Over 5,000 S.F., minimum									23
1750	Maximum				▼					30
2000	Institutional, custom, rigid frame, including compartments and									
2010	multi-controls, under 500 S.F., minimum				SF Flr.					77
2050	Maximum									99
2150	Over 2,000 S.F., minimum									39
2200	Maximum									65
2400	Concealed rigid frame, under 500 S.F., minimum									90
2450	Maximum									110
2550	Over 2,000 S.F., minimum									68
2600	Maximum									79
2800	Lean-to type, under 500 S.F., minimum									80
2850	Maximum									120
3000	Over 2,000 S.F., minimum				▼					44
3050	Maximum									73
3600	For 1/4" clear plate glass, add				SF Surf	1.40			1.40	1.54
3700	For 1/4" tempered glass, add				"	3.15			3.15	3.47
3900	For cooling, add, minimum				SF Flr.	2.10			2.10	2.31
4000	Maximum					5.20			5.20	5.70
4200	For heaters, 13.6 MBH, add					4			4	4.40
4300	60 MBH, add				▼	1.50			1.50	1.65
4500	For benches, 2' x 3'-6", add				SF Hor.	17.90			17.90	19.70
4600	3' x 10', add				S.F.	9.70			9.70	10.65
4800	For controls, add, minimum				Total	1,800			1,800	1,975
4900	Maximum				"	10,700			10,700	11,800
5100	For humidification equipment, add				M.C.F.	4.60			4.60	5.05
5200	For vinyl shading, add				S.F.	.97			.97	1.07
6000	Geodesic hemisphere, 1/8" plexiglass glazing									
6050	8' diameter	2 Carp	2	8	Ea.	2,025	233		2,258	2,600
6150	24' diameter	▼	.35	45.714		10,400	1,325		11,725	13,500
6250	48' diameter	▼	.20	80	▼	28,200	2,325		30,525	34,700

Important: See the Reference Section for critical supporting data - Reference Nos., Crews, & City Cost Indexes

13 **SPECIAL CONSTRUCTION**

13128	Pre-Eng. Structures	CREW	DAILY OUTPUT	LABOR-HOURS	UNIT	2001 BARE COSTS MAT.	LABOR	EQUIP.	TOTAL	TOTAL INCL O&P	
580	0010	**HANGARS** Prefabricated steel T hangars, Galv. steel roof &										**580**
	0100	walls, incl. electric bi-folding doors, 4 or more units,										
	0110	not including floors or foundations, minimum	E-2	1,275	.044	SF Flr.	8.85	1.40	1.01	11.26	13.30	
	0130	Maximum		1,063	.053		9.50	1.68	1.21	12.39	14.70	
	0900	With bottom rolling doors, minimum		1,386	.040		8.05	1.29	.93	10.27	12.10	
	1000	Maximum		966	.058		9.50	1.85	1.34	12.69	15.15	
	1200	Alternate pricing method:										
	1300	Galv. roof and walls, electric bi-folding doors, minimum	E-2	1.06	52.830	Plane	10,600	1,675	1,225	13,500	15,900	
	1500	Maximum		.91	61.538		11,700	1,950	1,425	15,075	17,900	
	1600	With bottom rolling doors, minimum		1.25	44.800		8,400	1,425	1,025	10,850	12,900	
	1800	Maximum		.97	57.732		10,000	1,850	1,325	13,175	15,700	
	2000	Circular type, prefab., steel frame, plastic skin, electric										
	2010	door, including foundations, 80' diameter,										
	2020	for up to 5 light planes, minimum	E-2	.50	112	Total	81,000	3,575	2,575	87,150	98,000	
	2200	Maximum	"	.25	224	"	91,000	7,150	5,150	103,300	118,500	
600	0010	**KIOSKS** Round, 5' diameter, 8' high, 1/4" fiberglass wall				Ea.	5,500			5,500	6,050	**600**
	0100	1" insulated double wall, fiberglass					6,250			6,250	6,875	
	0500	Rectangular, 5' x 9', 7'-6" high, 1/4" fiberglass wall					8,000			8,000	8,800	
	0600	1" insulated double wall, fiberglass					9,500			9,500	10,500	
700	0010	**PRE-ENGINEERED STEEL BUILDINGS** R13128-210										**700**
	0100	Clear span rigid frame, 26 ga. colored roofing and siding										
	0200	30' to 40' wide, 10' eave height	E-2	1,800	.031	SF Flr.	4.08	.99	.72	5.79	7	
	0300	14' eave height		1,800	.031		4.32	.99	.72	6.03	7.25	
	0400	16' eave height		1,400	.040		4.51	1.28	.92	6.71	8.20	
	0500	20' eave height		1,000	.056		4.93	1.79	1.29	8.01	9.90	
	0600	24' eave height		1,000	.056		5.55	1.79	1.29	8.63	10.60	
	0700	50' to 100' wide, 10' eave height		1,800	.031		3.55	.99	.72	5.26	6.40	
	0800	14' eave height		1,800	.031		3.77	.99	.72	5.48	6.65	
	0900	16' eave height		1,400	.040		3.99	1.28	.92	6.19	7.60	
	1000	20' eave height		1,000	.056		4.24	1.79	1.29	7.32	9.20	
	1100	24' eave height		1,000	.056		4.63	1.79	1.29	7.71	9.60	
	1200	Clear span tapered beam frame, 26 ga. colored roofing and siding										
	1300	30' wide, 10' eave height	E-2	1,800	.031	SF Flr.	4.56	.99	.72	6.27	7.50	
	1400	14' eave height		1,800	.031		5.05	.99	.72	6.76	8.05	
	1500	16' eave height		1,400	.040		5.40	1.28	.92	7.60	9.20	
	1600	20' eave height		1,000	.056		5.95	1.79	1.29	9.03	11.05	
	1700	40' wide, 10' eave height		1,800	.031		4.18	.99	.72	5.89	7.10	
	1800	14' eave height		1,800	.031		4.51	.99	.72	6.22	7.45	
	1900	16' eave height		1,400	.040		4.72	1.28	.92	6.92	8.45	
	2000	20' eave height		1,000	.056		5.15	1.79	1.29	8.23	10.20	
	2100	50' to 80' wide, 10' eave height		1,800	.031		3.94	.99	.72	5.65	6.85	
	2200	14' eave height		1,800	.031		4.26	.99	.72	5.97	7.20	
	2300	16' eave height		1,400	.040		4.45	1.28	.92	6.65	8.15	
	2400	20' eave height		1,000	.056		4.94	1.79	1.29	8.02	9.95	
	2500	Single post 2-span frame, 26 ga. colored roofing and siding										
	2600	80' wide, 14' eave height	E-2	1,800	.031	SF Flr.	3.36	.99	.72	5.07	6.20	
	2700	16' eave height		1,400	.040		3.58	1.28	.92	5.78	7.15	
	2800	20' eave height		1,000	.056		3.89	1.79	1.29	6.97	8.80	
	2900	24' eave height		1,000	.056		4.20	1.79	1.29	7.28	9.15	
	3000	100' wide, 14' eave height		1,800	.031		3.25	.99	.72	4.96	6.10	
	3100	16' eave height		1,400	.040		3.42	1.28	.92	5.62	7	
	3200	20' eave height		1,000	.056		3.73	1.79	1.29	6.81	8.60	
	3300	24' eave height		1,000	.056		4.01	1.79	1.29	7.09	8.95	
	3400	120' wide, 14' eave height		1,800	.031		3.22	.99	.72	4.93	6.05	
	3500	16' eave height		1,400	.040		3.35	1.28	.92	5.55	6.90	

SPECIAL CONSTRUCTION 13

		CREW	DAILY OUTPUT	LABOR-HOURS	UNIT	MAT.	LABOR	EQUIP.	TOTAL	TOTAL INCL O&P	
13128	**Pre-Eng. Structures**					2001 BARE COSTS					
700	3600	20' eave height R13128-210	E-2	1,000	.056	SF Flr.	3.63	1.79	1.29	6.71	8.50	700
	3700	24' eave height	↓	1,000	.056	↓	3.94	1.79	1.29	7.02	8.85	
	3800	Double post 3-span frame, 26 ga. colored roofing and siding										
	3900	150' wide, 14' eave height	E-2	1,800	.031	SF Flr.	2.97	.99	.72	4.68	5.80	
	4000	16' eave height		1,400	.040		3.07	1.28	.92	5.27	6.60	
	4100	20' eave height		1,000	.056		3.28	1.79	1.29	6.36	8.15	
	4200	24' eave height	↓	1,000	.056	↓	3.84	1.79	1.29	6.92	8.75	
	4300	Triple post 4-span frame, 26 ga. colored roofing and siding										
	4400	160' wide, 14' eave height	E-2	1,800	.031	SF Flr.	2.88	.99	.72	4.59	5.70	
	4500	16' eave height		1,400	.040		3.01	1.28	.92	5.21	6.55	
	4600	20' eave height		1,000	.056		3.20	1.79	1.29	6.28	8.05	
	4700	24' eave height		1,000	.056		3.72	1.79	1.29	6.80	8.60	
	4800	200' wide, 14' eave height		1,800	.031		2.90	.99	.72	4.61	5.70	
	4900	16' eave height		1,400	.040		2.97	1.28	.92	5.17	6.50	
	5000	20' eave height		1,000	.056		3.20	1.79	1.29	6.28	8.05	
	5100	24' eave height	↓	1,000	.056	↓	3.73	1.79	1.29	6.81	8.60	
	5200	Accessory items: add to the basic building cost above										
	5250	Eave overhang, 2' wide, 26 ga., with soffit	E-2	360	.156	L.F.	13.90	4.96	3.58	22.44	28	
	5300	4' wide, without soffit		300	.187		14	5.95	4.30	24.25	30.50	
	5350	With soffit		250	.224		19.40	7.15	5.15	31.70	39.50	
	5400	6' wide, without soffit		250	.224		18.45	7.15	5.15	30.75	38.50	
	5450	With soffit		200	.280	↓	25	8.95	6.45	40.40	50	
	5500	Entrance canopy, incl. frame, 4' x 4'		25	2.240	Ea.	130	71.50	51.50	253	325	
	5550	4' x 8'		19	2.947	"	233	94	68	395	495	
	5600	End wall roof overhang, 4' wide, without soffit		850	.066	L.F.	9.45	2.10	1.52	13.07	15.65	
	5650	With soffit	↓	500	.112	"	13.60	3.57	2.58	19.75	24	
	5700	Doors, H.M. self-framing, incl. butts, lockset and trim										
	5750	Single leaf, 3070 (3' x 7'), economy	2 Sswk	5	3.200	Opng.	233	105		338	445	
	5800	Deluxe		4	4		310	131		441	580	
	5825	Glazed		4	4		315	131		446	585	
	5850	3670 (3'-6" x 7')		4	4		295	131		426	565	
	5900	4070 (4' x 7')		3	5.333		350	175		525	705	
	5950	Double leaf, 6070 (6' x 7')		2	8		425	263		688	945	
	6000	Glazed	↓	2	8		585	263		848	1,125	
	6050	Framing only, for openings, 3' x 7'	E-2	25	2.240		85.50	71.50	51.50	208.50	275	
	6100	10' x 10'		21	2.667		281	85	61.50	427.50	525	
	6150	For windows below, 2020 (2' x 2')		25	2.240		90.50	71.50	51.50	213.50	281	
	6200	4030 (4' x 3')	↓	22	2.545	↓	111	81	58.50	250.50	330	
	6250	Flashings, 26 ga., corner or eave, painted	2 Sswk	240	.067	L.F.	2.45	2.19		4.64	6.65	
	6300	Galvanized		240	.067		1.65	2.19		3.84	5.80	
	6350	Rake flashing, painted		240	.067		2.45	2.19		4.64	6.65	
	6400	Galvanized		240	.067		1.85	2.19		4.04	6	
	6450	Ridge flashing, 18" wide, painted		240	.067		2.75	2.19		4.94	7	
	6500	Galvanized		240	.067		1.75	2.19		3.94	5.90	
	6550	Gutter, eave type, 26 ga., painted		320	.050		3.18	1.64		4.82	6.50	
	6600	Galvanized		320	.050		1.75	1.64		3.39	4.91	
	6650	Valley type, between buildings, painted		120	.133		5.90	4.38		10.28	14.45	
	6700	Galvanized	↓	120	.133	↓	5.20	4.38		9.58	13.65	
	6750	Insulation, rated .6 lb density, vinyl faced										
	6800	1-1/2" thick, R5	2 Carp	2,300	.007	S.F.	.19	.20		.39	.53	
	6850	3" thick, R10		2,300	.007		.24	.20		.44	.58	
	6900	4" thick, R13		2,300	.007		.32	.20		.52	.67	
	6950	Foil/scrim/kraft (FSK) faced, 1-1/2" thick, R5		2,300	.007		.21	.20		.41	.55	
	7000	2" thick, R6		2,300	.007		.25	.20		.45	.60	
	7050	3" thick, R10		2,300	.007		.30	.20		.50	.65	
	7100	4" thick, R13	↓	2,300	.007	↓	.37	.20		.57	.73	

Important: See the Reference Section for critical supporting data - Reference Nos., Crews, & City Cost Indexes

T3 SPECIAL CONSTRUCTION

		13128	**Pre-Eng. Structures**	CREW	DAILY OUTPUT	LABOR-HOURS	UNIT	MAT.	LABOR	EQUIP.	TOTAL	TOTAL INCL O&P	
700	7150		Met polyester/scrim/kraft (PSK) facing,1-1/2" thk,R5 R13128-210	2 Carp	2,300	.007	S.F.	.32	.20		.52	.67	**700**
	7200		2" thick, R6		2,300	.007		.37	.20		.57	.73	
	7250		3" thick, R11		2,300	.007		.38	.20		.58	.74	
	7300		4" thick, R13		2,300	.007		.45	.20		.65	.82	
	7350		Vinyl/scrim/foil (VSF), 1-1/2" thick, R5		2,300	.007		.29	.20		.49	.64	
	7400		2" thick, R6		2,300	.007		.35	.20		.55	.71	
	7450		3" thick, R10		2,300	.007		.43	.20		.63	.79	
	7500		4" thick, R13		2,300	.007		.49	.20		.69	.86	
	7650		Sash, single slide, glazed, with screens, 2020 (2'x 2')	E-1	22	1.091	Opng.	72.50	35	3.82	111.32	144	
	7700		3030 (3' x 3')		14	1.714		163	55	6	224	281	
	7750		4030 (4' x 3')		13	1.846		217	59.50	6.45	282.95	350	
	7800		6040 (6' x 4')		12	2		435	64.50	7	506.50	600	
	7850		Double slide sash, 3030 (3' x 3')		14	1.714		139	55	6	200	255	
	7900		6040 (6' x 4')		12	2		370	64.50	7	441.50	525	
	7950		Fixed glass, no screens, 3030 (3' x 3')		14	1.714		128	55	6	189	243	
	8000		6040 (6' x 4')		12	2		340	64.50	7	411.50	495	
	8050		Prefinished storm sash, 3030 (3' x 3')		70	.343		55.50	11	1.20	67.70	82	
	8100		Siding and roofing, see division 07300 & 07400										
	8200		Skylight, fiberglass panels, to 30 S.F.	E-1	10	2.400	Ea.	154	77	8.40	239.40	310	
	8250		Larger sizes, add for excess over 30 S.F.	"	300	.080	S.F.	5.15	2.57	.28	8	10.40	
	8300		Roof vents, circular with damper, birdscreen										
	8350		and operator hardware, painted										
	8400		26 ga., 12" diameter	1 Sswk	4	2	Ea.	72	65.50		137.50	198	
	8450		20" diameter		3	2.667		148	87.50		235.50	320	
	8500		24 ga., 24" diameter		2	4		293	131		424	560	
	8550		Galvanized		2	4		245	131		376	510	
	8600		Continuous, 26 ga., 10' long, 9" wide	2 Sswk	4	4		207	131		338	465	
	8650		12" wide		4	4		248	131		379	510	
800	0010		**SHELTERS** Aluminum frame, acrylic glazing, 3' x 9' x 8' high		1.14	14.035	Ea.	2,550	460		3,010	3,625	**800**
	0100		9' x 12' x 8' high		.73	21.918	"	4,250	720		4,970	5,975	
840	0010		**SILOS** Concrete stave industrial, not incl. foundations, conical or										**840**
	0100		sloping bottoms, 12' diameter, 35' high	D-8	.11	363	Ea.	15,700	9,800		25,500	32,400	
	0200		16' diameter, 45' high		.08	500		21,000	13,500		34,500	43,900	
	0400		25' diameter, 75' high		.05	800		51,500	21,600		73,100	90,000	
	0500		Steel, factory fab., 30,000 gallon cap., painted, minimum	L-5	1	56		11,000	1,850	630	13,480	16,100	
	0700		Maximum		.50	112		17,500	3,675	1,250	22,425	27,200	
	0800		Epoxy lined, minimum		1	56		18,000	1,850	630	20,480	23,800	
	1000		Maximum		.50	112		22,800	3,675	1,250	27,725	33,000	
880	0010		**SWIMMING POOL ENCLOSURE** Translucent, free standing,										**880**
	0020		not including foundations, heat or light										
	0200		Economy, minimum	2 Carp	200	.080	SF Hor.	11	2.33		13.33	15.75	
	0300		Maximum		100	.160		23	4.66		27.66	33	
	0400		Deluxe, minimum		100	.160		25.50	4.66		30.16	35.50	
	0600		Maximum		70	.229		275	6.65		281.65	315	
	0700		For motorized roof, 40% opening, solid roof, add					3.30			3.30	3.63	
	0800		Skylight type roof, add					4.95			4.95	5.45	
	0900		Air-inflated, including blowers and heaters, minimum									3.50	
	1000		Maximum									6.70	

SPECIAL CONSTRUCTION 13

			DAILY	LABOR-			2001 BARE COSTS			TOTAL	
13151	**Swimming Pools**	CREW	OUTPUT	HOURS	UNIT	MAT.	LABOR	EQUIP.	TOTAL	INCL O&P	
200	0010	**SWIMMING POOLS** Residential in-ground, vinyl lined, concrete sides										**200**
	0020	Sides including equipment, sand bottom	B-52	300	.187	SF Surf	10.40	5	1.28	16.68	20.50	
	0100	Metal or polystyrene sides R13128-520	B-14	410	.117		8.70	2.83	.44	11.97	14.45	
	0200	Add for vermiculite bottom					.67			.67	.74	
	0500	Gunite bottom and sides, white plaster finish										
	0600	12' x 30' pool	B-52	145	.386	SF Surf	17.25	10.40	2.66	30.31	38	
	0720	16' x 32' pool		155	.361		15.50	9.70	2.49	27.69	35	
	0750	20' x 40' pool		250	.224		13.85	6.05	1.54	21.44	26.50	
	0810	Concrete bottom and sides, tile finish										
	0820	12' x 30' pool	B-52	80	.700	SF Surf	17.40	18.85	4.82	41.07	54	
	0830	16' x 32' pool		95	.589		14.40	15.85	4.06	34.31	45.50	
	0840	20' x 40' pool		130	.431		11.45	11.60	2.96	26.01	34	
	1100	Motel, gunite with plaster finish, incl. medium										
	1150	capacity filtration & chlorination	B-52	115	.487	SF Surf	21	13.10	3.35	37.45	47.50	
	1200	Municipal, gunite with plaster finish, incl. high										
	1250	capacity filtration & chlorination	B-52	100	.560	SF Surf	27.50	15.05	3.85	46.40	57.50	
	1350	Add for formed gutters				L.F.	47.50			47.50	52.50	
	1360	Add for stainless steel gutters				"	141			141	155	
	1600	For water heating system, see division 15510-880										
	1700	Filtration and deck equipment only, as % of total				Total				20%	20%	
	1800	Deck equipment, rule of thumb, 20' x 40' pool				SF Pool					1.30	
	1900	5000 S.F. pool				"					1.90	
	3000	Painting pools, preparation + 3 coats, 20' x 40' pool, epoxy	2 Pord	.33	48.485	Total	595	1,275		1,870	2,575	
	3100	Rubber base paint, 18 gallons	"	.33	48.485		450	1,275		1,725	2,425	
	3500	42' x 82' pool, 75 gallons, epoxy paint	3 Pord	.14	171		2,500	4,475		6,975	9,575	
	3600	Rubber base paint	"	.14	171		1,925	4,475		6,400	8,950	
700	0010	**SWIMMING POOL EQUIPMENT** Diving stand, stainless steel, 3 meter	2 Carp	.40	40	Ea.	4,625	1,175		5,800	6,925	**700**
	0300	1 meter		2.70	5.926		3,750	173		3,923	4,400	
	0600	Diving boards, 16' long, aluminum		2.70	5.926		1,475	173		1,648	1,875	
	0700	Fiberglass		2.70	5.926		1,075	173		1,248	1,475	
	0900	Filter system, sand or diatomite type, incl. pump, 6,000 gal./hr.	2 Plum	1.80	8.889	Total	1,050	305		1,355	1,600	
	1020	Add for chlorination system, 800 S.F. pool		3	5.333	Ea.	196	184		380	495	
	1040	5,000 S.F. pool		3	5.333	"	1,150	184		1,334	1,525	
	1100	Gutter system, stainless steel, with grating, stock,										
	1110	contains supply and drainage system	E-1	20	1.200	L.F.	160	38.50	4.20	202.70	247	
	1120	Integral gutter and 5' high wall system, stainless steel	"	10	2.400	"	240	77	8.40	325.40	405	
	1200	Ladders, heavy duty, stainless steel, 2 tread	2 Carp	7	2.286	Ea.	410	66.50		476.50	555	
	1500	4 tread		6	2.667		465	77.50		542.50	630	
	1800	Lifeguard chair, stainless steel, fixed		2.70	5.926		1,275	173		1,448	1,675	
	1900	Portable					1,675			1,675	1,825	
	2100	Lights, underwater, 12 volt, with transformer, 300 watt	1 Elec	.40	20		116	685		801	1,150	
	2200	110 volt, 500 watt, standard		.40	20		124	685		809	1,150	
	2400	Low water cutoff type		.40	20		128	685		813	1,175	
	2800	Heaters, see division 15510-880										
	3000	Pool covers, reinforced vinyl	3 Clab	1,800	.013	S.F.	.26	.30		.56	.77	
	3050	Automatic, electric									9.65	
	3100	Vinyl water tube	3 Clab	3,200	.007		.20	.17		.37	.49	
	3200	Maximum	"	3,000	.008		.45	.18		.63	.79	
	3250	Sealed air bubble polyethylene solar blanket					.19			.19	.21	
	3300	Slides, tubular, fiberglass, aluminum handrails & ladder, 5'-0", straight	2 Carp	1.60	10	Ea.	2,150	292		2,442	2,800	
	3320	8'-0", curved		3	5.333		7,425	155		7,580	8,425	
	3400	10'-0", curved		1	16		16,600	465		17,065	18,900	
	3420	12'-0", straight with platform		1.20	13.333		1,400	390		1,790	2,150	
	4500	Hydraulic lift, movable pool bottom, single ram										
	4520	Under 1,000 S.F. area	L-9	.03	1,200	Ea.	80,000	31,800		111,800	139,500	
	4600	Four ram lift, over 1,000 S.F.	"	.02	1,800		96,500	47,600		144,100	183,500	

13 SPECIAL CONSTRUCTION

13150 | Swimming Pools

		13151	Swimming Pools	CREW	DAILY OUTPUT	LABOR-HOURS	UNIT	2001 BARE COSTS MAT.	LABOR	EQUIP.	TOTAL	TOTAL INCL O&P	
700	5000		Removable access ramp, stainless steel	2 Clab	2	8	Ea.	6,175	183		6,358	7,075	700
	5500		Removable stairs, stainless steel, collapsible	"	2	8	↓	2,400	183		2,583	2,925	

13170 | Tubs & Pools

		13171	Therapeutic Pools	CREW	DAILY OUTPUT	LABOR-HOURS	UNIT	2001 BARE COSTS MAT.	LABOR	EQUIP.	TOTAL	TOTAL INCL O&P	
800	0010	**THERAPEUTIC POOLS** See division 15418											800

13175 | Ice Rinks

		13176	Ice Rinks	CREW	DAILY OUTPUT	LABOR-HOURS	UNIT	2001 BARE COSTS MAT.	LABOR	EQUIP.	TOTAL	TOTAL INCL O&P	
500	0010	**ICE SKATING** Equipment incl. refrigeration, plumbing & cooling											500
	0020	coils & concrete slab, 85' x 200' rink											
	0300	55° system, 5 mos., 100 ton				Total					451,000	
	0700	90° system, 12 mos., 135 ton				"					500,500	
	1000	Dasher boards, 1/2" H.D. polyethylene faced steel frame, 3' acrylic										
	1020	screen at sides, 5' acrylic ends, 85' x 200'	F-5	.06	533	Ea.	115,000	15,800		130,800	151,000	
	1100	Fiberglass & aluminum construction, same sides and ends	"	.06	533		160,000	15,800		175,800	200,500	
	1200	Subsoil heating system (recycled from compressor), 85' x 200'	Q-7	.27	118		25,000	3,950		28,950	33,500	
	1300	Subsoil insulation, 2 lb. polystyrene with vapor barrier, 85' x 200'	2 Carp	.14	114	↓	30,000	3,325		33,325	38,200	

13200 | Storage Tanks

		13201	Storage Tanks	CREW	DAILY OUTPUT	LABOR-HOURS	UNIT	2001 BARE COSTS MAT.	LABOR	EQUIP.	TOTAL	TOTAL INCL O&P	
200	0010	**ELEVATED STORAGE TANKS** Not incl. pipe or pumps											200
	3000	Elevated water tanks, 100' to bottom capacity line, incl painting										
	3010	50,000 gallons				Ea.					166,000	
	3300	100,000 gallons									229,000	
	3400	250,000 gallons									316,000	
	3600	500,000 gallons									510,000	
	3700	750,000 gallons									703,000	
	3900	1,000,000 gallons				↓					812,000	
300	0010	**GROUND TANKS** Not incl. pipe or pumps, prestress conc., 250,000 gal.				Ea.					280,000	300
	0100	500,000 gallons									380,000	
	0300	1,000,000 gallons									540,000	
	0400	2,000,000 gallons				↓					816,000	

SPECIAL CONSTRUCTION 13

375

	13201	Storage Tanks	CREW	DAILY OUTPUT	LABOR-HOURS	UNIT	2001 BARE COSTS MAT.	LABOR	EQUIP.	TOTAL	TOTAL INCL O&P	
300	0600	4,000,000 gallons				Ea.					1,290,000	300
	0700	6,000,000 gallons									1,760,000	
	0750	8,000,000 gallons									2,240,000	
	0800	10,000,000 gallons									2,700,000	
	0900	Steel, ground level, ht/dia less than 1, not incl. fdn, 100,000 gallons									98,000	
	1000	250,000 gallons									137,000	
	1200	500,000 gallons									209,000	
	1250	750,000 gallons									249,000	
	1300	1,000,000 gallons									336,000	
	1500	2,000,000 gallons									615,000	
	1600	4,000,000 gallons									955,000	
	1800	6,000,000 gallons									1,325,000	
	1850	8,000,000 gallons									1,735,000	
	1900	10,000,000 gallons				▼					1,937,500	
	2100	Steel standpipes, hgt/dia more than 1, 100' to overflow, no fdn										
	2200	500,000 gallons				Ea.					275,000	
	2400	750,000 gallons									335,000	
	2500	1,000,000 gallons									408,000	
	2700	1,500,000 gallons									570,000	
	2800	2,000,000 gallons				▼					700,000	
	3000	Steel, storage, above ground, including cradles, coating,										
	3020	fittings, not including fdn, pumps or piping										
	3040	Single wall, interior, 275 gallon	Q-5	5	3.200	Ea.	236	100		336	410	
	3060	550 gallon	"	2.70	5.926		825	186		1,011	1,175	
	3080	1,000 gallon	Q-7	5	6.400		1,050	213		1,263	1,475	
	3100	1,500 gallon		4.75	6.737		1,975	224		2,199	2,525	
	3120	2,000 gallon		4.60	6.957		2,000	231		2,231	2,550	
	3140	5,000 gallon		3.20	10		4,200	330		4,530	5,125	
	3150	10,000 gallon		2	16		6,900	530		7,430	8,400	
	3160	15,000 gallon		1.70	18.824		9,650	625		10,275	11,500	
	3170	20,000 gallon		1.45	22.069		11,300	735		12,035	13,500	
	3180	25,000 gallon capacity		1.30	24.615		14,100	820		14,920	16,700	
	3190	30,000 gallon	▼	1.10	29.091		17,000	965		17,965	20,200	
	3320	Double wall, 500 gallon capacity	Q-5	2.40	6.667		2,625	209		2,834	3,200	
	3330	2000 gallon capacity	Q-7	4.15	7.711		4,800	256		5,056	5,650	
	3340	4000 gallon capacity		3.60	8.889		8,525	295		8,820	9,825	
	3350	6000 gallon capacity		2.40	13.333		10,200	445		10,645	11,900	
	3360	8000 gallon capacity		2	16		11,600	530		12,130	13,600	
	3370	10000 gallon capacity		1.80	17.778		12,800	590		13,390	15,000	
	3380	15000 gallon capacity		1.50	21.333		19,100	710		19,810	22,100	
	3390	20000 gallon capacity		1.30	24.615		21,700	820		22,520	25,100	
	3400	25000 gallon capacity		1.15	27.826		26,400	925		27,325	30,400	
	3410	30000 gallon capacity	▼	1	32	▼	28,900	1,075		29,975	33,400	
	4000	Fixed roof oil storage tanks, steel, (1 BBL=42 GAL w/ fdn 3'D x 1'W)										
	4200	5,000 barrels				Ea.					144,000	
	4300	25,000 barrels									202,000	
	4500	55,000 barrels									342,000	
	4600	100,000 barrels									550,000	
	4800	150,000 barrels									775,000	
	4900	225,000 barrels									1,168,000	
	5100	Floating roof gasoline tanks, steel, 5,000 barrels									122,000	
	5200	25,000 barrels									273,000	
	5400	55,000 barrels									413,000	
	5500	100,000 barrels									625,000	
	5700	150,000 barrels									846,000	
	5800	225,000 barrels				▼					1,173,000	

Important: See the Reference Section for critical supporting data - Reference Nos., Crews, & City Cost Indexes

13 SPECIAL CONSTRUCTION

			CREW	DAILY OUTPUT	LABOR-HOURS	UNIT	2001 BARE COSTS				TOTAL INCL O&P	
		13201 Storage Tanks					MAT.	LABOR	EQUIP.	TOTAL		
300	6000	Wood tanks, ground level, 2" cypress, 3,000 gallons	C-1	.19	168	Ea.	5,775	4,650		10,425	13,600	300
	6100	2-1/2" cypress, 10,000 gallons		.12	266		15,600	7,350		22,950	28,700	
	6300	3" redwood or 3" fir, 20,000 gallons		.10	320		23,800	8,825		32,625	40,000	
	6400	30,000 gallons		.08	400		29,500	11,000		40,500	49,700	
	6600	45,000 gallons		.07	457		44,600	12,600		57,200	69,000	
	6700	Larger sizes, minimum				Gal.					.66	
	6900	Maximum				"					.81	
	7000	Vinyl coated fabric pillow tanks, freestanding, 5,000 gallons	4 Clab	4	8	Ea.	1,900	183		2,083	2,375	
	7100	Supporting embankment not included, 25,000 gallons	6 Clab	2	24		6,700	550		7,250	8,225	
	7200	50,000 gallons	8 Clab	1.50	42.667		9,750	975		10,725	12,200	
	7300	100,000 gallons	9 Clab	.90	80		15,100	1,825		16,925	19,500	
	7400	150,000 gallons		.50	144		19,100	3,300		22,400	26,200	
	7500	200,000 gallons		.40	180		22,300	4,125		26,425	30,900	
	7600	250,000 gallons		.30	240		26,800	5,475		32,275	38,100	
800	0010	**UNDERGROUND STORAGE TANKS**										800
	0210	Fiberglass, underground, single wall, U.L. listed, not including										
	0220	manway or hold-down strap										
	0240	2,000 gallon capacity	Q-7	4.57	7.002	Ea.	2,375	233		2,608	2,950	
	0250	4,000 gallon capacity		3.55	9.014		3,425	300		3,725	4,225	
	0260	6,000 gallon capacity		2.67	11.985		3,825	400		4,225	4,800	
	0280	10,000 gallon capacity		2	16		5,200	530		5,730	6,525	
	0284	15,000 gallon capacity		1.68	19.048		7,575	635		8,210	9,300	
	0290	20,000 gallon capacity		1.45	22.069		10,500	735		11,235	12,600	
	0500	For manway, fittings and hold-downs, add					20%	15%				
	1020	Fiberglass, underground, double wall, U.L. listed										
	1030	includes manways, not incl. hold-down straps										
	1040	600 gallon capacity	Q-5	2.42	6.612	Ea.	3,200	207		3,407	3,825	
	1050	1,000 gallon capacity	"	2.25	7.111		4,250	223		4,473	5,000	
	1060	2,500 gallon capacity	Q-7	4.16	7.692		6,050	256		6,306	7,025	
	1070	3,000 gallon capacity		3.90	8.205		6,500	273		6,773	7,550	
	1080	4,000 gallon capacity		3.64	8.791		7,100	292		7,392	8,250	
	1090	6,000 gallon capacity		2.42	13.223		8,225	440		8,665	9,725	
	1100	8,000 gallon capacity **CN**		2.08	15.385		10,400	510		10,910	12,200	
	1110	10,000 gallon capacity		1.82	17.582		10,800	585		11,385	12,800	
	1120	12,000 gallon capacity		1.70	18.824		13,200	625		13,825	15,400	
	2210	Fiberglass, underground, single wall, U.L. listed, including										
	2220	hold-down straps, no manways										
	2240	2,000 gallon capacity	Q-7	3.55	9.014	Ea.	2,525	300		2,825	3,225	
	2250	4,000 gallon capacity		2.90	11.034		3,600	365		3,965	4,500	
	2260	6,000 gallon capacity		2	16		4,150	530		4,680	5,350	
	2280	10,000 gallon capacity		1.60	20		5,525	665		6,190	7,075	
	2284	15,000 gallon capacity		1.39	23.022		7,900	765		8,665	9,850	
	2290	20,000 gallon capacity		1.14	28.070		11,000	935		11,935	13,500	
	3020	Fiberglass, underground, double wall, U.L. listed										
	3030	includes manways and hold-down straps										
	3040	600 gallon capacity	Q-5	1.86	8.602	Ea.	3,350	270		3,620	4,075	
	3050	1,000 gallon capacity	"	1.70	9.412		4,425	295		4,720	5,300	
	3060	2,500 gallon capacity	Q-7	3.29	9.726		6,225	325		6,550	7,325	
	3070	3,000 gallon capacity		3.13	10.224		6,675	340		7,015	7,875	
	3080	4,000 gallon capacity		2.93	10.921		7,275	365		7,640	8,550	
	3090	6,000 gallon capacity		1.86	17.204		8,550	570		9,120	10,300	
	3100	8,000 gallon capacity		1.65	19.394		10,700	645		11,345	12,800	
	3110	10,000 gallon capacity		1.48	21.622		11,100	720		11,820	13,300	
	3120	12,000 gallon capacity		1.40	22.857		13,500	760		14,260	16,100	
	5000	Steel underground, sti-P3, set in place, not incl. hold-down bars.										
	5500	Excavation, pad, pumps and piping not included										

SPECIAL CONSTRUCTION 13

13201	Storage Tanks	CREW	DAILY OUTPUT	LABOR-HOURS	UNIT	2001 BARE COSTS				TOTAL INCL O&P
						MAT.	LABOR	EQUIP.	TOTAL	
800 5510	Single wall, 500 gallon capacity, 7 gauge shell	Q-5	2.70	5.926	Ea.	820	186		1,006	1,175	800
5520	1,000 gallon capacity, 7 gauge shell	"	2.50	6.400		1,425	201		1,626	1,875
5530	2,000 gallon capacity, 1/4" thick shell	Q-7	4.60	6.957		2,300	231		2,531	2,875
5535	2,500 gallon capacity, 7 gauge shell	Q-5	3	5.333		2,500	167		2,667	3,000
5540	5,000 gallon capacity, 1/4" thick shell	Q-7	3.20	10		4,675	330		5,005	5,650
5580	15,000 gallon capacity, 5/16" thick shell		1.70	18.824		10,200	625		10,825	12,200
5600	20,000 gallon capacity, 5/16" thick shell		1.50	21.333		14,700	710		15,410	17,200
5610	25,000 gallon capacity, 3/8" thick shell		1.30	24.615		17,600	820		18,420	20,600
5620	30,000 gallon capacity, 3/8" thick shell		1.10	29.091		21,500	965		22,465	25,100
5630	40,000 gallon capacity, 3/8" thick shell		.90	35.556		30,700	1,175		31,875	35,500
5640	50,000 gallon capacity, 3/8" thick shell		.80	40		38,300	1,325		39,625	44,200

13281	Hazardous Material Remediation	CREW	DAILY OUTPUT	LABOR-HOURS	UNIT	2001 BARE COSTS				TOTAL INCL O&P
						MAT.	LABOR	EQUIP.	TOTAL	
120 0010	**BULK ASBESTOS REMOVAL**										120
0020	Includes disposable tools and 1 suit and respirator/day/worker									
0100	Beams, W 10 x 19	A-9	235	.272	L.F.		8.75		8.75	14.05
0110	W 12 x 22		210	.305			9.80		9.80	15.75
0120	W 14 x 26		180	.356			11.45		11.45	18.35
0130	W 16 x 31		160	.400			12.90		12.90	20.50
0140	W 18 x 40		140	.457			14.70		14.70	23.50
0150	W 24 x 55		110	.582			18.75		18.75	30
0160	W 30 x 108		85	.753			24.50		24.50	39
0170	W 36 x 150		72	.889			28.50		28.50	46
0200	Boiler insulation		480	.133	S.F.	.06	4.29		4.35	6.95
0210	With metal lath add				%				50%	
0300	Boiler breeching or flue insulation	A-9	520	.123	S.F.		3.96		3.96	6.35
0310	For active boiler, add				%				100%	
0400	Duct or AHU insulation	A-10B	440	.073	S.F.		2.35		2.35	3.76
0500	Duct vibration isolation joints, up to 24 Sq. In. duct	A-9	56	1.143	Ea.		37		37	59
0520	25 Sq. In. to 48 Sq. In. duct		48	1.333			43		43	69
0530	49 Sq. In. to 76 Sq. In. duct		40	1.600			51.50		51.50	82.50
0600	Pipe insulation, air cell type, up to 4" diameter pipe		900	.071	L.F.		2.29		2.29	3.67
0610	4" to 8" diameter pipe		800	.080			2.58		2.58	4.13
0620	10" to 12" diameter pipe		700	.091			2.95		2.95	4.72
0630	14" to 16" diameter pipe		550	.116			3.75		3.75	6
0650	Over 16" diameter pipe		650	.098	S.F.		3.17		3.17	5.10
0700	With glove bag up to 3" diameter pipe		100	.640	L.F.	3.15	20.50		23.65	36.50
1000	Pipe fitting insulation up to 4" diameter pipe		320	.200	Ea.		6.45		6.45	10.30
1100	6" to 8" diameter pipe		304	.211			6.80		6.80	10.85
1110	10" to 12" diameter pipe		192	.333			10.75		10.75	17.20
1120	14" to 16" diameter pipe		128	.500			16.10		16.10	26
1130	Over 16" diameter pipe		176	.364	S.F.		11.70		11.70	18.75
1200	With glove bag, up to 8" diameter pipe		40	1.600	Ea.	6.55	51.50		58.05	89.50
2000	Scrape foam fireproofing from flat surface		2,400	.027	S.F.		.86		.86	1.38
2100	Irregular surfaces		1,200	.053			1.72		1.72	2.75
3000	Remove cementitious material from flat surface		1,800	.036			1.15		1.15	1.83
3100	Irregular surface		1,400	.046			1.47		1.47	2.36

T3 SPECIAL CONSTRUCTION

			DAILY	LABOR-			2001 BARE COSTS				TOTAL	
13281	**Hazardous Material Remediation**	CREW	OUTPUT	HOURS	UNIT	MAT.	LABOR	EQUIP.	TOTAL	INCL O&P	
120	4000	Scrape acoustical coating/fireproofing, from ceiling	A-9	3,200	.020	S.F.		.64		.64	1.03	**120**
	5000	Remove VAT from floor by hand	↓	2,400	.027			.86		.86	1.38	
	5100	By machine	A-11	4,800	.013	↓		.43	.01	.44	.70	
	5150	For 2 layers, add				%				50%		
	6000	Remove contaminated soil from crawl space by hand	A-9	400	.160	C.F.		5.15		5.15	8.25	
	6100	With large production vacuum loader	A-12	700	.091	"		2.95	.74	3.69	5.55	
	7000	Radiator backing, not including radiator removal	A-9	1,200	.053	S.F.		1.72		1.72	2.75	
	8000	Cement-asbestos transite board	2 Asbe	2,000	.008		.08	.26		.34	.50	
	8100	Transite shingle siding	A-10D	750	.043		.08	1.29	1.07	2.44	3.29	
	8200	Shingle roofing	A-10B	2,000	.016		.07	.52		.59	.91	
	8250	Built-up, no gravel, non-friable	B-2	1,400	.029		.07	.66		.73	1.12	
	8300	Asbestos millboard	2 Asbe	1,000	.016	↓	.08	.51		.59	.91	
	9000	For type C (supplied air) respirator equipment, add				%					10%	
125	0010	**ASBESTOS ABATEMENT WORK AREA** Containment and preparation.										**125**
	0100	Pre-cleaning, HEPA vacuum and wet wipe, flat surfaces	A-10	12,000	.005	S.F.		.17		.17	.28	
	0200	Protect carpeted area, 2 layers 6 mil poly on 3/4" plywood	"	1,000	.064		1.50	2.06		3.56	4.95	
	0300	Separation barrier, 2" x 4" @ 16", 1/2" plywood ea. side, 8' high	2 Carp	400	.040		1.25	1.17		2.42	3.20	
	0310	12' high		320	.050		1.40	1.46		2.86	3.82	
	0320	16' high		200	.080		1.50	2.33		3.83	5.30	
	0400	Personnel decontam. chamber, 2" x 4" @ 16", 3/4" ply ea. side		280	.057		2.50	1.67		4.17	5.35	
	0450	Waste decontam. chamber, 2" x 4" studs @ 16", 3/4" ply ea. side	↓	360	.044	↓	3	1.30		4.30	5.35	
	0500	Cover surfaces with polyethelene sheeting										
	0501	Including glue and tape										
	0550	Floors, each layer, 6 mil	A-10	8,000	.008	S.F.	.10	.26		.36	.52	
	0551	4 mil		9,000	.007		.06	.23		.29	.44	
	0560	Walls, each layer, 6 mil		6,000	.011		.09	.34		.43	.65	
	0561	4 mil	↓	7,000	.009		.07	.29		.36	.55	
	0570	For heights above 12', add						20%				
	0575	For heights above 20', add						30%				
	0580	For fire retardant poly, add					100%					
	0590	For large open areas, deduct					10%	20%				
	0600	Seal floor penetrations with foam firestop to 36 Sq. In.	2 Carp	200	.080	Ea.	6.25	2.33		8.58	10.55	
	0610	36 Sq. In. to 72 Sq. In.		125	.128		12.50	3.73		16.23	19.60	
	0615	72 Sq. In. to 144 Sq. In.		80	.200		25	5.85		30.85	36.50	
	0620	Wall penetrations, to 36 square inches		180	.089		6.25	2.59		8.84	10.95	
	0630	36 Sq. In. to 72 Sq. In.		100	.160		12.50	4.66		17.16	21	
	0640	72 Sq. In. to 144 Sq. In.	↓	60	.267	↓	25	7.75		32.75	39.50	
	0800	Caulk seams with latex	1 Carp	230	.035	L.F.	.15	1.01		1.16	1.76	
	0900	Set up neg. air machine, 1-2k C.F.M. /25 M.C.F. volume	1 Asbe	4.30	1.860	Ea.		60		60	96	
130	0010	**DEMOLITION IN ASBESTOS CONTAMINATED AREA**										**130**
	0200	Ceiling, including suspension system, plaster and lath	A-9	2,100	.030	S.F.		.98		.98	1.57	
	0210	Finished plaster, leaving wire lath		585	.109			3.52		3.52	5.65	
	0220	Suspended acoustical tile		3,500	.018			.59		.59	.94	
	0230	Concealed tile grid system		3,000	.021			.69		.69	1.10	
	0240	Metal pan grid system		1,500	.043			1.37		1.37	2.20	
	0250	Gypsum board		2,500	.026	↓		.82		.82	1.32	
	0260	Lighting fixtures up to 2' x 4'	↓	72	.889	Ea.		28.50		28.50	46	
	0400	Partitions, non load bearing										
	0410	Plaster, lath, and studs	A-9	690	.093	S.F.	.55	2.99		3.54	5.40	
	0450	Gypsum board and studs	"	1,390	.046	"		1.48		1.48	2.38	
	9000	For type C (supplied air) respirator equipment, add				%					10%	
135	0010	**ASBESTOS ABATEMENT EQUIPMENT** and supplies, buy [R13281 -120]										**135**
	0200	Air filtration device, 2000 C.F.M.				Ea.	2,500			2,500	2,750	
	0250	Large volume air sampling pump, minimum					450			450	495	
	0260	Maximum	↓			↓	1,000			1,000	1,100	

SPECIAL CONSTRUCTION 13

13281	Hazardous Material Remediation	CREW	DAILY OUTPUT	LABOR-HOURS	UNIT	MAT.	LABOR	EQUIP.	TOTAL	TOTAL INCL O&P	
135	0300	Airless sprayer unit, 2 gun				Ea.	2,000			2,000	2,200	135
	0350	Light stand, 500 watt	R13281 -120			↓	250			250	275	
	0400	Personal respirators										
	0410	Negative pressure, 1/2 face, dual operation, min.				Ea.	22.50			22.50	25	
	0420	Maximum					24			24	26.50	
	0450	P.A.P.R., full face, minimum					400			400	440	
	0460	Maximum					700			700	770	
	0470	Supplied air, full face, incl. air line, minimum					450			450	495	
	0480	Maximum					600			600	660	
	0500	Personnel sampling pump, minimum					450			450	495	
	0510	Maximum					750			750	825	
	1500	Power panel, 20 unit, incl. G.F.I.					1,800			1,800	1,975	
	1600	Shower unit, including pump and filters					1,125			1,125	1,250	
	1700	Supplied air system (type C)					10,000			10,000	11,000	
	1750	Vacuum cleaner, HEPA, 16 gal., stainless steel, wet/dry					1,000			1,000	1,100	
	1760	55 gallon					2,200			2,200	2,425	
	1800	Vacuum loader, 9-18 ton/hr					90,000			90,000	99,000	
	1900	Water atomizer unit, including 55 gal. drum					230			230	253	
	2000	Worker protection, whole body, foot, head cover & gloves, plastic					30			30	33	
	2500	Respirator, single use					10.50			10.50	11.55	
	2550	Cartridge for respirator					37.50			37.50	41.50	
	2570	Glove bag, 7 mil, 50" x 64"					8.50			8.50	9.35	
	2580	10 mil, 44" x 60"					8.40			8.40	9.25	
	3000	HEPA vacuum for work area, minimun					1,000			1,000	1,100	
	3050	Maximum					2,775			2,775	3,050	
	6000	Disposable polyethelene bags, 6 mil, 3 C.F.					1.15			1.15	1.27	
	6300	Disposable fiber drums, 3 C.F.					6.50			6.50	7.15	
	6400	Pressure sensitive caution lables, 3" x 5"					8.90			8.90	9.80	
	6450	11" x 17"					6.50			6.50	7.15	
	6500	Negative air machine, 1800 C.F.M.	↓			↓	775			775	855	
140	0010	**DECONTAMINATION CONTAINMENT AREA DEMOLITION** and clean-up										140
	0100	Spray exposed substrate with surfactant (bridging)										
	0200	Flat surfaces	A-9	6,000	.011	S.F.	.35	.34		.69	.94	
	0250	Irregular surfaces		4,000	.016	"	.30	.52		.82	1.16	
	0300	Pipes, beams, and columns		2,000	.032	L.F.	.55	1.03		1.58	2.26	
	1000	Spray encapsulate polyethelene sheeting		8,000	.008	S.F.	.30	.26		.56	.74	
	1100	Roll down polyethelene sheeting		8,000	.008	"		.26		.26	.41	
	1500	Bag polyethelene sheeting		400	.160	Ea.	.75	5.15		5.90	9.10	
	2000	Fine clean exposed substrate, with nylon brush		2,400	.027	S.F.		.86		.86	1.38	
	2500	Wet wipe substrate		4,800	.013			.43		.43	.69	
	2600	Vacuum surfaces, fine brush	↓	6,400	.010	↓		.32		.32	.52	
	3000	Structural demolition										
	3100	Wood stud walls	A-9	2,800	.023	S.F.		.74		.74	1.18	
	3500	Window manifolds, not incl. window replacement		4,200	.015			.49		.49	.79	
	3600	Plywood carpet protection	↓	2,000	.032	↓		1.03		1.03	1.65	
	4000	Remove custom decontamination facility	A-10A	8	3	Ea.	15	97		112	172	
	4100	Remove portable decontamination facility	3 Asbe	12	2	"	12.50	64.50		77	117	
	5000	HEPA vacuum, shampoo carpeting	A-9	4,800	.013	S.F.	.05	.43		.48	.75	
	9000	Final cleaning of protected surfaces	A-10A	8,000	.003	"		.10		.10	.16	
145	0010	**OSHA TESTING**										145
	0100	Certified technician, minimum				Day					300	
	0110	Maximum				"					500	
	0200	Personal sampling, PCM analysis, minimum	1 Asbe	8	1	Ea.	2.75	32		34.75	54.50	
	0210	Maximum	"	4	2	"	3	64.50		67.50	106	
	0300	Industrial hygienist, minimum				Day					400	

Important: See the Reference Section for critical supporting data - Reference Nos., Crews, & City Cost Indexes

		13281	Hazardous Material Remediation	CREW	DAILY OUTPUT	LABOR-HOURS	UNIT	MAT.	LABOR	EQUIP.	TOTAL	TOTAL INCL O&P	
									2001 BARE COSTS				
145	0310		Maximum				Day					550	**145**
	1000		Cleaned area samples	1 Asbe	8	1	Ea.	2.63	32		34.63	54.50	
	1100		PCM air sample analysis, minimum		8	1		30	32		62	84.50	
	1110		Maximum	↓	4	2		3.09	64.50		67.59	106	
	1200		TEM air sample analysis, minimum								100	125	
	1210		Maximum				↓				400	500	
150	0010	**ENCAPSULATION WITH SEALANTS**											**150**
	0100		Ceilings and walls, minimum	A-9	21,000	.003	S.F.	.25	.10		.35	.44	
	0110		Maximum		10,600	.006		.40	.19		.59	.75	
	0200		Columns and beams, minimum		13,300	.005		.25	.15		.40	.53	
	0210		Maximum		5,325	.012	↓	.45	.39		.84	1.12	
	0300		Pipes to 12" diameter including minor repairs, minimum		800	.080	L.F.	.35	2.58		2.93	4.52	
	0310		Maximum	↓	400	.160	"	1	5.15		6.15	9.35	
155	0010	**WASTE PACKAGING, HANDLING, & DISPOSAL**											**155**
	0100		Collect and bag bulk material, 3 C.F. bags, by hand	A-9	400	.160	Ea.	1.15	5.15		6.30	9.50	
	0200		Large production vacuum loader	A-12	880	.073		.80	2.34	.59	3.73	5.30	
	1000		Double bag and decontaminate	A-9	960	.067		2.30	2.15		4.45	5.95	
	2000		Containerize bagged material in drums, per 3 C.F. drum	"	800	.080		6.50	2.58		9.08	11.30	
	3000		Cart bags 50' to dumpster	2 Asbe	400	.040	↓		1.29		1.29	2.06	
	5000		Disposal charges, not including haul, minimum				C.Y.					50	
	5020		Maximum				"					175	
	5100		Remove refrigerant from system	1 Plum	40	.200	Lb.		6.90		6.90	10.40	
	9000		For type C (supplied air) respirator equipment, add				%					10%	
440	0010	**REMOVAL** Existing lead paint, by chemicals, per application											**440**
	0020		See also, Div. 13280, Haz. Mat'l. Abatement	R13281 -460									
	0050		Baseboard, to 6" wide	1 Pord	64	.125	L.F.	1.47	3.26		4.73	6.60	
	0070		To 12" wide		32	.250	"	2.88	6.55		9.43	13.10	
	0200		Balustrades, one side		28	.286	S.F.	3.27	7.45		10.72	14.95	
	1400		Cabinets, simple design		32	.250		2.86	6.55		9.41	13.10	
	1420		Ornate design		25	.320		3.67	8.35		12.02	16.75	
	1600		Cornice, simple design		60	.133		1.53	3.48		5.01	7	
	1620		Ornate design		20	.400		4.52	10.45		14.97	21	
	2800		Doors, one side, flush		84	.095		1.11	2.49		3.60	5	
	2820		Two panel		80	.100		1.15	2.61		3.76	5.25	
	2840		Four panel		45	.178	↓	2.03	4.64		6.67	9.30	
	2880		For trim, one side, add		64	.125	L.F.	1.47	3.26		4.73	6.60	
	3000		Fence, picket, one side		30	.267	S.F.	3.07	6.95		10.02	14	
	3200		Grilles, one side, simple design		30	.267		3.07	6.95		10.02	14	
	3220		Ornate design		25	.320	↓	3.67	8.35		12.02	16.75	
	4400		Pipes, to 4" diameter		90	.089	L.F.	1.05	2.32		3.37	4.69	
	4420		To 8" diameter		50	.160		1.82	4.18		6	8.35	
	4440		To 12" diameter		36	.222		2.55	5.80		8.35	11.65	
	4460		To 16" diameter		20	.400	↓	4.55	10.45		15	21	
	4500		For hangers, add		40	.200	Ea.	2.29	5.20		7.49	10.45	
	4800		Siding		90	.089	S.F.	1.05	2.32		3.37	4.69	
	5000		Trusses, open		55	.145	SF Face	1.67	3.80		5.47	7.65	
	6200		Windows, one side only, double hung, 1/1 light, 24" x 48" high		4	2	Ea.	23	52		75	105	
	6220		30" x 60" high		3	2.667		30.50	69.50		100	140	
	6240		36" x 72" high		2.50	3.200		37	83.50		120.50	168	
	6280		40" x 80" high		2	4		46	104		150	210	
	6400		Colonial window, 6/6 light, 24" x 48" high		2	4		46	104		150	210	
	6420		30" x 60" high		1.50	5.333		61.50	139		200.50	280	
	6440		36" x 72" high		1	8		92	209		301	420	
	6480		40" x 80" high		1	8		92	209		301	420	
	6600		8/8 light, 24" x 48" high	↓	2	4	↓	46	104		150	210	

SPECIAL CONSTRUCTION 13

		13281	Hazardous Material Remediation	CREW	DAILY OUTPUT	LABOR-HOURS	UNIT	2001 BARE COSTS				TOTAL INCL O&P	
								MAT.	LABOR	EQUIP.	TOTAL		
440	6620		40" x 80" high R13281-460	1 Pord	1	8	Ea.	92	209		301	420	**440**
	6800		12/12 light, 24" x 48" high		1	8		92	209		301	420	
	6820		40" x 80" high	↓	.75	10.667	↓	123	278		401	560	
	6840		Window frame & trim items, included in pricing above	↓									
460	0010		**LEAD PAINT ENCAPSULATION**, water based polymer coating,14 mil DFT										**460**
	0020		Interior, brushwork, trim, under 6"	1 Pord	240	.033	L.F.	2.16	.87		3.03	3.70	
	0030		6" to 12" wide		180	.044		2.87	1.16		4.03	4.93	
	0040		Balustrades		300	.027		1.73	.70		2.43	2.96	
	0050		Pipe to 4" diameter		500	.016		1.04	.42		1.46	1.78	
	0060		To 8" diameter		375	.021		1.38	.56		1.94	2.37	
	0070		To 12" diameter		250	.032	↓	2.07	.84		2.91	3.55	
	0080		To 16" diameter		170	.047	↓	3.04	1.23		4.27	5.20	
	0090		Cabinets, ornate design		200	.040	S.F.	2.59	1.04		3.63	4.44	
	0100		Simple design	↓	250	.032	"	2.07	.84		2.91	3.55	
	0110		Doors, 3' x 7', both sides, incl. frame & trim										
	0120		Flush	1 Pord	6	1.333	Ea.	26.50	35		61.50	82	
	0130		French, 10-15 lite		3	2.667		5.30	69.50		74.80	112	
	0140		Panel		4	2		32	52		84	115	
	0150		Louvered	↓	2.75	2.909	↓	29	76		105	148	
	0160		Windows, per interior side, per 15 S.F.										
	0170		1 to 6 lite	1 Pord	14	.571	Ea.	18.30	14.90		33.20	42.50	
	0180		7 to 10 lite		7.50	1.067		20	28		48	64.50	
	0190		12 lite		5.75	1.391		27	36.50		63.50	85.50	
	0200		Radiators		8	1	↓	64.50	26		90.50	111	
	0210		Grilles, vents		275	.029	S.F.	1.88	.76		2.64	3.23	
	0220		Walls, roller, drywall or plaster		1,000	.008		.51	.21		.72	.88	
	0230		With spunbonded reinforcing fabric		720	.011		.58	.29		.87	1.08	
	0240		Wood		800	.010		.64	.26		.90	1.10	
	0250		Ceilings, roller, drywall or plaster		900	.009	↓	.58	.23		.81	.99	
	0260		Wood		700	.011	↓	.73	.30		1.03	1.25	
	0270		Exterior, brushwork, gutters and downspouts		300	.027	L.F.	1.73	.70		2.43	2.96	
	0280		Columns		400	.020	S.F.	1.29	.52		1.81	2.22	
	0290		Spray, siding	↓	600	.013	"	.86	.35		1.21	1.48	
	0300		Miscellaneous										
	0310		Electrical conduit, brushwork, to 2" diameter	1 Pord	500	.016	L.F.	1.04	.42		1.46	1.78	
	0320		Brick, block or concrete, spray		500	.016	S.F.	1.04	.42		1.46	1.78	
	0330		Steel, flat surfaces and tanks to 12"		500	.016		1.04	.42		1.46	1.78	
	0340		Beams, brushwork		400	.020		1.29	.52		1.81	2.22	
	0350		Trusses	↓	400	.020	↓	1.29	.52		1.81	2.22	

		13630	Solar Collector Components	CREW	DAILY OUTPUT	LABOR-HOURS	UNIT	2001 BARE COSTS				TOTAL INCL O&P	
								MAT.	LABOR	EQUIP.	TOTAL		
200	0010		**SOLAR ENERGY** R13600-610										**200**
	0020		System/Package prices, not including connecting										
	0030		pipe, insulation, or special heating/plumbing fixtures										
	0500		Hot water, standard package, low temperature										
	0540		1 collector, circulator, fittings, 65 gal. tank	Q-1	.50	32	Ea.	1,350	990		2,340	3,000	
	0580		2 collectors, circulator, fittings, 120 gal. tank	↓	.40	40	↓	1,925	1,250		3,175	4,000	

Important: See the Reference Section for critical supporting data - Reference Nos., Crews, & City Cost Indexes

T3 SPECIAL CONSTRUCTION

13630	Solar Collector Components		CREW	DAILY OUTPUT	LABOR-HOURS	UNIT	2001 BARE COSTS				TOTAL INCL O&P	
							MAT.	LABOR	EQUIP.	TOTAL		
200	0620	3 collectors, circulator, fittings, 120 gal. tank	R13600 -610	Q-1	.40	40	Ea.	2,350	1,250		3,600	4,450	**200**
	0700	Medium temperature package											
	0720	1 collector, circulator, fittings, 80 gal. tank		Q-1	.50	32	Ea.	1,450	990		2,440	3,100	
	0740	2 collectors, circulator, fittings, 120 gal. tank			.40	40		2,075	1,250		3,325	4,175	
	0780	3 collectors, circulator, fittings, 120 gal. tank		↓	.30	53.333		3,775	1,650		5,425	6,650	
	0980	For each additional 120 gal. tank, add					↓	660			660	730	
	2300	Circulators, air											
	2310	Blowers											
	2400	Reversible fan, 20" diameter, 2 speed		Q-9	18	.889	Ea.	102	27		129	154	
	2520	Space & DHW system, less duct work		"	.50	32		1,400	965		2,365	3,050	
	2870	1/12 HP, 30 GPM		Q-1	10	1.600	↓	315	49.50		364.50	420	
	3000	Collector panels, air with aluminum absorber plate											
	3010	Wall or roof mount											
	3040	Flat black, plastic glazing											
	3080	4' x 8'		Q-9	6	2.667	Ea.	600	80.50		680.50	785	
	3200	Flush roof mount, 10' to 16' x 22" wide		"	96	.167	L.F.	146	5.05		151.05	169	
	3300	Collector panels, liquid with copper absorber plate											
	3330	Alum. frame, 4' x 8', 5/32" single glazing		Q-1	9.50	1.684	Ea.	545	52		597	680	
	3390	Alum. frame, 4' x 10', 5/32" single glazing		"	6	2.667	"	650	82.50		732.50	835	
	3440	Flat black											
	3450	Alum. frame, 3' x 8'		Q-1	9	1.778	Ea.	430	55		485	560	
	3500	Alum. frame, 4' x 8.5'			5.50	2.909		490	90		580	675	
	3520	Alum. frame, 4' x 10.5'			10	1.600		595	49.50		644.50	730	
	3540	Alum. frame, 4' x 12.5'			5	3.200		735	99		834	960	
	3600	Liquid, full wetted, plastic, alum. frame, 3' x 10'			5	3.200		195	99		294	365	
	3650	Collector panel mounting, flat roof or ground rack			7	2.286	↓	64.50	71		135.50	178	
	3670	Roof clamps		↓	70	.229	Set	1.61	7.10		8.71	12.45	
	3700	Roof strap, teflon		1 Plum	205	.039	L.F.	9.50	1.34		10.84	12.50	
	3900	Differential controller with two sensors											
	3930	Thermostat, hard wired		1 Plum	8	1	Ea.	92	34.50		126.50	153	
	4100	Five station with digital read-out		"	3	2.667	"	202	92		294	360	
	4300	Heat exchanger											
	4580	Fluid to fluid package includes two circulating pumps											
	4590	expansion tank, check valve, relief valve											
	4600	controller, high temperature cutoff and sensors		Q-1	2.50	6.400	Ea.	695	198		893	1,075	
	4650	Heat transfer fluid											
	4700	Propylene glycol, inhibited anti-freeze		1 Plum	28	.286	Gal.	8.80	9.85		18.65	24.50	
	8250	Water storage tank with heat exchanger and electric element											
	8300	80 gal. with 2" x 2 lb. density insulation		1 Plum	1.60	5	Ea.	745	172		917	1,075	
	8380	120 gal. with 2" x 2 lb. density insulation		↓	1.40	5.714	↓	840	197		1,037	1,225	
	8400	120 gal. with 2" x 2 lb. density insul., 40 S.F. heat coil		↓	1.40	5.714		965	197		1,162	1,375	

13710	Security Access	CREW	DAILY OUTPUT	LABOR-HOURS	UNIT	2001 BARE COSTS				TOTAL INCL O&P	
						MAT.	LABOR	EQUIP.	TOTAL		
300	0010	**ACCESS CONTROL**										**300**
	0020	Card type, 1 time zone, minimum				Ea.	300			300	330	
	0040	Maximum				↓	1,025			1,025	1,125	
	0060	3 time zones, minimum				↓	740			740	815	

SPECIAL CONSTRUCTION 13

13700 | Security Access and Surveillance

		13710	Security Access	CREW	DAILY OUTPUT	LABOR-HOURS	UNIT	2001 BARE COSTS MAT.	LABOR	EQUIP.	TOTAL	TOTAL INCL O&P	
300	0080		Maximum				Ea.	1,700			1,700	1,875	300
	0100		System with printer, and control console, 3 zones				Total	8,300			8,300	9,125	
	0120		6 zones				"	10,900			10,900	12,000	
	0140		For each door, minimum, add				Ea.	1,225			1,225	1,350	
	0160		Maximum, add				"	1,800			1,800	2,000	

13800 | Building Automation & Control

		13834	Electric/Electronic Control	CREW	DAILY OUTPUT	LABOR-HOURS	UNIT	2001 BARE COSTS MAT.	LABOR	EQUIP.	TOTAL	TOTAL INCL O&P	
200	0010		**CONTROL SYSTEMS, ELECTRONIC**										200
	0020		For electronic costs, add to division 13836-200				Ea.					15%	

		13836	**Pneumatic Controls**	CREW	DAILY OUTPUT	LABOR-HOURS	UNIT	2001 BARE COSTS MAT.	LABOR	EQUIP.	TOTAL	TOTAL INCL O&P	
200	0010		**CONTROL SYSTEMS, PNEUMATIC** (Sub's quote incl. mat. & labor)										200
	0011		and nominal 50 Ft. of tubing. Add control panelboard if req'd.										
	0100		Heating and Ventilating, split system										
	0200		Mixed air control, economizer cycle, panel readout, tubing										
	0220		Up to 10 tons	Q-19	.68	35.294	Ea.	2,750	1,150		3,900	4,775	
	0240		For 10 to 20 tons		.63	37.915		2,950	1,225		4,175	5,100	
	0260		For over 20 tons	↓	.58	41.096	↓	3,200	1,325		4,525	5,525	
	0300		Heating coil, hot water, 3 way valve,										
	0320		Freezestat, limit control on discharge, readout	Q-5	.69	23.088	Ea.	2,050	725		2,775	3,350	
	0500		Cooling coil, chilled water, room										
	0520		Thermostat, 3 way valve	Q-5	2	8	Ea.	915	251		1,166	1,375	
	0600		Cooling tower, fan cycle, damper control,										
	0620		Control system including water readout in/out at panel	Q-19	.67	35.821	Ea.	3,625	1,150		4,775	5,750	
	1000		Unit ventilator, day/night operation,										
	1100		freezestat, ASHRAE, cycle 2	Q-19	.91	26.374	Ea.	2,000	855		2,855	3,500	
	2000		Compensated hot water from boiler, valve control,										
	2100		readout and reset at panel, up to 60 GPM	Q-19	.55	43.956	Ea.	3,750	1,425		5,175	6,275	
	2120		For 120 GPM		.51	47.059		4,025	1,525		5,550	6,725	
	2140		For 240 GPM		.49	49.180		4,225	1,600		5,825	7,025	
	3000		Boiler room combustion air, damper to 5 SF, controls		1.36	17.582		1,825	570		2,395	2,850	
	3500		Fan coil, heating and cooling valves, 4 pipe control system		3	8		820	259		1,079	1,300	
	3600		Heat exchanger system controls	↓	.86	27.907		1,775	905		2,680	3,300	
	4000		Pneumatic thermostat, including controlling room radiator valve	Q-5	2.43	6.593		545	207		752	910	
	4060		Pump control system	Q-19	3	8	↓	840	259		1,099	1,325	
	4500		Air supply for pneumatic control system										
	4600		Tank mounted duplex compressor, starter, alternator,										
	4620		piping, dryer, PRV station and filter										
	4630		1/2 HP	Q-19	.68	35.139	Ea.	6,750	1,125		7,875	9,125	
	4660		1-1/2 HP		.57	41.739		8,225	1,350		9,575	11,100	
	4690		5 HP	↓	.42	57.143	↓	19,600	1,850		21,450	24,300	

Important: See the Reference Section for critical supporting data - Reference Nos., Crews, & City Cost Indexes

T3 SPECIAL CONSTRUCTION

13851	Detection & Alarm	CREW	DAILY OUTPUT	LABOR-HOURS	UNIT	2001 BARE COSTS				TOTAL INCL O&P	
						MAT.	LABOR	EQUIP.	TOTAL		
050	**0010**	**CLOCKS**									**050**
	0080	12" diameter, single face	1 Elec	8	1	Ea.	75.50	34.50		110	134
	0100	Double face	"	6.20	1.290	"	144	44.50		188.50	224
055	**0010**	**CLOCK SYSTEMS**, not including wires & conduits									**055**
	0100	Time system components, master controller	1 Elec	.33	24.242	Ea.	1,625	830		2,455	3,050
	0200	Program bell		8	1		53.50	34.50		88	110
	0400	Combination clock & speaker		3.20	2.500		189	86		275	335
	0600	Frequency generator		2	4		6,350	137		6,487	7,175
	0800	Job time automatic stamp recorder, minimum		4	2		445	68.50		513.50	590
	1000	Maximum		4	2		680	68.50		748.50	850
	1200	Time stamp for correspondence, hand operated					340			340	375
	1400	Fully automatic					495			495	545
	1600	Master time clock system, clocks & bells, 20 room	4 Elec	.20	160		4,075	5,500		9,575	12,700
	1800	50 room	"	.08	400		9,400	13,700		23,100	30,800
	2000	Time clock, 100 cards in & out, 1 color	1 Elec	3.20	2.500		950	86		1,036	1,175
	2200	2 colors		3.20	2.500		1,025	86		1,111	1,250
	2400	With 3 circuit program device, minimum		2	4		375	137		512	620
	2600	Maximum		2	4		545	137		682	805
	2800	Metal rack for 25 cards		7	1.143		60	39		99	125
	3000	Watchman's tour station		8	1		63	34.50		97.50	121
	3200	Annunciator with zone indication		1	8		230	274		504	665
	3400	Time clock with tape		1	8		610	274		884	1,075
065	**0010**	**DETECTION SYSTEMS**, not including wires & conduits									**065**
	0100	Burglar alarm, battery operated, mechanical trigger	1 Elec	4	2	Ea.	249	68.50		317.50	375
	0200	Electrical trigger		4	2		297	68.50		365.50	425
	0400	For outside key control, add		8	1		70.50	34.50		105	129
	0600	For remote signaling circuitry, add		8	1		112	34.50		146.50	174
	0800	Card reader, flush type, standard		2.70	2.963		835	102		937	1,075
	1000	Multi-code		2.70	2.963		1,075	102		1,177	1,325
	1200	Door switches, hinge switch		5.30	1.509		52.50	52		104.50	136
	1400	Magnetic switch		5.30	1.509		62	52		114	146
	1600	Exit control locks, horn alarm		4	2		310	68.50		378.50	440
	1800	Flashing light alarm		4	2		350	68.50		418.50	485
	2000	Indicating panels, 1 channel		2.70	2.963		330	102		432	515
	2200	10 channel	2 Elec	3.20	5		1,125	172		1,297	1,500
	2400	20 channel		2	8		2,200	274		2,474	2,825
	2600	40 channel		1.14	14.035		4,000	480		4,480	5,125
	2800	Ultrasonic motion detector, 12 volt	1 Elec	2.30	3.478		206	119		325	405
	3000	Infrared photoelectric detector	"	2.30	3.478		170	119		289	365
	3594	Fire, alarm control panel									
	3600	4 zone	2 Elec	2	8	Ea.	920	274		1,194	1,400
	3800	8 zone		1	16		1,400	550		1,950	2,375
	4000	12 zone		.67	23.988		1,825	825		2,650	3,225
	4020	Alarm device	1 Elec	8	1		122	34.50		156.50	185
	4050	Actuating device		8	1		292	34.50		326.50	370
	4200	Battery and rack		4	2		690	68.50		758.50	860
	4400	Automatic charger		8	1		445	34.50		479.50	540
	4600	Signal bell		8	1		49.50	34.50		84	106
	4800	Trouble buzzer or manual station		8	1		37	34.50		71.50	91.50
	5000	Detector, rate of rise		8	1		33.50	34.50		68	88
	5200	Smoke detector, ceiling type		6.20	1.290		75	44.50		119.50	149
	5400	Duct type		3.20	2.500		250	86		336	405
	5600	Strobe and horn		5.30	1.509		95	52		147	183
	5800	Fire alarm horn		6.70	1.194		36.50	41		77.50	101

SPECIAL CONSTRUCTION 13

385

13851	Detection & Alarm		CREW	DAILY OUTPUT	LABOR-HOURS	UNIT	2001 BARE COSTS				TOTAL INCL O&P	
							MAT.	LABOR	EQUIP.	TOTAL		
065	6000	Door holder, electro-magnetic	1 Elec	4	2	Ea.	77.50	68.50		146	188	065
	6200	Combination holder and closer		3.20	2.500		430	86		516	605	
	6400	Code transmitter		4	2		690	68.50		758.50	860	
	6600	Drill switch		8	1		86.50	34.50		121	146	
	6800	Master box		2.70	2.963		3,100	102		3,202	3,550	
	7000	Break glass station		8	1		50	34.50		84.50	106	
	7800	Remote annunciator, 8 zone lamp		1.80	4.444		175	152		327	420	
	8000	12 zone lamp	2 Elec	2.60	6.154		300	211		511	645	
	8200	16 zone lamp	"	2.20	7.273		300	249		549	700	
350	0010	**TANK LEAK DETECTION SYSTEMS** Liquid and vapor										350
	0100	For hydrocarbons and hazardous liquids/vapors										
	0120	Controller, data acquisition, incl. printer, modem, RS232 port										
	0140	24 channel, for use with all probes				Ea.	2,050			2,050	2,250	
	0160	9 channel, for external monitoring				"	1,575			1,575	1,750	
	0200	Probes										
	0210	Well monitoring										
	0220	Liquid phase detection				Ea.	710			710	785	
	0230	Hydrocarbon vapor, fixed position					655			655	720	
	0240	Hydrocarbon vapor, float mounted					580			580	640	
	0250	Both liquid and vapor hydrocarbon					880			880	970	
	0300	Secondary containment, liquid phase										
	0310	Pipe trench/manway sump				Ea.	320			320	350	
	0320	Double wall pipe and manual sump					310			310	340	
	0330	Double wall fiberglass annular space					286			286	315	
	0340	Double wall steel tank annular space					286			286	315	
	0500	Accessories										
	0510	Modem, non-dedicated phone line				Ea.	256			256	282	
	0600	Monitoring, internal										
	0610	Automatic tank gauge, incl. overfill				Ea.	1,025			1,025	1,125	
	0620	Product line				"	1,100			1,100	1,200	
	0700	Monitoring, special										
	0710	Cathodic protection				Ea.	610			610	670	
	0720	Annular space chemical monitor				"	830			830	915	

13910	Basic Fire Protection Matl/Methd		CREW	DAILY OUTPUT	LABOR-HOURS	UNIT	2001 BARE COSTS				TOTAL INCL O&P	
							MAT.	LABOR	EQUIP.	TOTAL		
400	0010	**FIRE HOSE AND EQUIPMENT**										400
	0200	Adapters, rough brass, straight hose threads										
	0220	One piece, female to male, rocker lugs										
	0240	1" x 1"				Ea.	20.50			20.50	22.50	
	2200	Hose, less couplings										
	2260	Synthetic jacket, lined, 300 lb. test, 1-1/2" diameter	Q-12	2,600	.006	L.F.	1.44	.19		1.63	1.87	
	2280	2-1/2" diameter		2,200	.007		2.40	.23		2.63	2.98	
	2360	High strength, 500 lb. test, 1-1/2" diameter		2,600	.006		1.49	.19		1.68	1.93	
	2380	2-1/2" diameter		2,200	.007		2.59	.23		2.82	3.19	
	2600	Hose rack, swinging, for 1-1/2" diameter hose,										
	2620	Enameled steel, 50' & 75' lengths of hose	Q-12	20	.800	Ea.	32.50	25		57.50	73	
	2640	100' and 125' lengths of hose	"	20	.800	"	32.50	25		57.50	73	

Important: See the Reference Section for critical supporting data - Reference Nos., Crews, & City Cost Indexes

			DAILY	LABOR-		2001 BARE COSTS				TOTAL	
	13910	**Basic Fire Protection Matl/Methd**	CREW	OUTPUT	HOURS	UNIT	MAT.	LABOR	EQUIP.	TOTAL	INCL O&P
400	3750	Hydrants, wall, w/caps, single, flush, polished brass										**400**
	3800	2-1/2" x 2-1/2"	Q-12	5	3.200	Ea.	105	99		204	266
	3840	2-1/2" x 3"	"	5	3.200	"	141	99		240	305
	3950	Double, flush, polished brass									
	4000	2-1/2" x 2-1/2" x 4"	Q-12	5	3.200	Ea.	282	99		381	460
	4040	2-1/2" x 2-1/2" x 6"	"	4.60	3.478		405	108		513	615
	4200	For polished chrome, add				↓	10%				
	4350	Double, projecting, polished brass									
	4400	2-1/2" x 2-1/2" x 4"	Q-12	5	3.200	Ea.	130	99		229	293
	4450	2-1/2" x 2-1/2" x 6"	"	4.60	3.478	"	251	108		359	440
	4460	Valve control, dbl. flush/projecting hydrant, cap &									
	4470	chain, ext. rod & cplg., escutcheon, polished brass	Q-12	8	2	Ea.	154	62		216	263
	5600	Nozzles, brass									
	5620	Adjustable fog, 3/4" booster line				Ea.	69			69	76
	5630	1" booster line					80.50			80.50	88.50
	5640	1-1/2" leader line					84.50			84.50	93
	5660	2-1/2" direct connection				↓	165			165	182
	5780	For chrome plated, add					8%				
	5850	Electrical fire, adjustable fog, no shock									
	5900	1-1/2"				Ea.	263			263	289
	5920	2-1/2"					360			360	395
	5980	For polished chrome, add				↓	6%				
	6200	Heavy duty, comb. adj. fog and str. stream, with handle									
	6210	1" booster line				Ea.	251			251	277
	7140	Standpipe connections, wall, w/plugs & chains									
	7160	Single, flush, brass, 2-1/2" x 2-1/2"	Q-12	5	3.200	Ea.	78.50	99		177.50	237
	7180	2-1/2" x 3"	"	5	3.200	"	82	99		181	240
	7240	For polished chrome, add					15%				
	7280	Double, flush, polished brass									
	7300	2-1/2" x 2-1/2" x 4"	Q-12	5	3.200	Ea.	265	99		364	440
	7330	2-1/2" x 2-1/2" x 6"	"	4.60	3.478	"	360	108		468	560
	7400	For polished chrome, add					15%				
	7440	For sill cock combination, add				Ea.	45			45	49.50
	7900	Three way, flush, polished brass									
	7920	2-1/2" (3) x 4"	Q-12	4.80	3.333	Ea.	825	103		928	1,075
	7930	2-1/2" (3) x 6"	"	4.80	3.333	↓	835	103		938	1,075
	8000	For polished chrome, add				↓	9%				
	8020	Three way, projecting, polished brass									
	8040	2-1/2" (3) x 4"	Q-12	4.80	3.333	Ea.	580	103		683	795
800	0010	**FIRE VALVES**										**800**
	0080	Wheel handle, 300 lb., 1-1/2"	1 Spri	12	.667	Ea.	26.50	23		49.50	63.50
	0090	2-1/2"	"	7	1.143	"	46	39.50		85.50	110
	0100	For polished brass, add					35%				
	0110	For polished chrome, add					50%				
	13920	**Fire Pumps**									
400	0010	**FIRE PUMPS** Including controller, fittings and relief valve										**400**
	0030	Diesel									
	0050	500 GPM, 50 psi, 27 HP, 4" pump	Q-13	.64	50	Ea.	46,600	1,650		48,250	54,000
	0200	750 GPM, 50 psi, 44 HP, 5" pump	↓	.60	53.333		49,700	1,750		51,450	57,000
	0400	1000 GPM, 100 psi, 89 HP, 4" pump		.56	57.143		53,500	1,875		55,375	61,500
	0700	2,000 GPM, 100 psi, 167 HP, 6" pump		.34	94.118		56,500	3,100		59,600	66,500
	0950	3500 GPM, 100 psi, 300 HP, 10" pump	↓	.24	133	↓	99,500	4,375		103,875	116,000
	3000	Electric									

13920 | Fire Pumps

		CREW	DAILY OUTPUT	LABOR-HOURS	UNIT	2001 BARE COSTS				TOTAL INCL O&P	
						MAT.	LABOR	EQUIP.	TOTAL		
400	3100	250 GPM, 55 psi, 15 HP, 3,550 RPM, 2" pump	Q-13	.70	45.714	Ea.	10,900	1,500		12,400	14,300	400
	3200	500 GPM, 50 psi, 27 HP, 1770 RPM, 4" pump		.68	47.059		13,500	1,550		15,050	17,300	
	3350	750 GPM, 50 psi, 44 HP, 1,770 RPM, 5" pump		.64	50		19,800	1,650		21,450	24,300	
	3400	750 GPM, 100 psi, 66 HP, 3550 RPM, 4" pump		.58	55.172		17,500	1,800		19,300	22,100	
	5000	For jockey pump 1", 3 HP, with control, add	Q-12	2	8		2,425	248		2,673	3,050	

13930 | Wet-Pipe Fire Supp. Sprinklers

		CREW	DAILY OUTPUT	LABOR-HOURS	UNIT	2001 BARE COSTS				TOTAL INCL O&P	
						MAT.	LABOR	EQUIP.	TOTAL		
400	0010	**SPRINKLER SYSTEM COMPONENTS**										400
	0600	Accelerator	1 Spri	8	1	Ea.	335	34.50		369.50	420	
	2600	Sprinkler heads, not including supply piping										
	2640	Dry, pendent, 1/2" orifice, 3/4" or 1" NPT										
	2700	15-1/4" to 18" length	1 Spri	14	.571	Ea.	44.50	19.70		64.20	79	
	2710	18-1/4" to 21" length		13	.615		47	21		68	83.50	
	2720	21-1/4" to 24" length		13	.615		49.50	21		70.50	86.50	
	2730	24-1/4" to 27" length		13	.615		52	21		73	89	
	3600	Foam-water, pendent or upright, 1/2" NPT		12	.667		50	23		73	89.50	
	3700	Standard spray, pendent or upright, brass, 135° to 286°F										
	3730	1/2" NPT, 7/16" orifice	1 Spri	16	.500	Ea.	6	17.25		23.25	32.50	
	3740	1/2" NPT, 1/2" orifice **CN**	"	16	.500		4.13	17.25		21.38	30.50	
	3860	For wax and lead coating, add					5.50			5.50	6.05	
	3880	For wax coating, add					2.50			2.50	2.75	
	3900	For lead coating, add					3			3	3.30	
	3920	For 360°F, same cost										
	3930	For 400°F, add				Ea.	5.50			5.50	6.05	
	3940	For 500°F, add				"	5.50			5.50	6.05	
	4500	Sidewall, horizontal, brass, 135° to 286°F										
	4520	1/2" NPT, 1/2" orifice	1 Spri	16	.500	Ea.	6	17.25		23.25	32.50	
	4540	For 360°F, same cost										
	4800	Recessed pendent, brass, 135° to 286°F										
	4820	1/2" NPT, 3/8" orifice	1 Spri	10	.800	Ea.	14.50	27.50		42	57.50	
	4830	1/2" NPT, 7/16" orifice		10	.800		10.25	27.50		37.75	53	
	4840	1/2" NPT, 1/2" orifice		10	.800		12	27.50		39.50	54.50	
	6200	Valves										
	6500	Check, swing, C.I. body, brass fittings, auto. ball drip										
	6520	4" size	Q-12	3	5.333	Ea.	141	165		306	405	
	6800	Check, wafer, butterfly type, C.I. body, bronze fittings										
	6820	4" size	Q-12	4	4	Ea.	152	124		276	355	
	7000	Deluge, assembly, incl. trim, pressure										
	7020	operated relief, emergency release, gauges										
	7040	2" size	Q-12	2	8	Ea.	1,000	248		1,248	1,475	
	7060	3" size	"	1.50	10.667	"	1,175	330		1,505	1,800	

13960 | CO2 Fire Extinguishing

		CREW	DAILY OUTPUT	LABOR-HOURS	UNIT	2001 BARE COSTS				TOTAL INCL O&P	
						MAT.	LABOR	EQUIP.	TOTAL		
200	0010	**AUTOMATIC FIRE SUPPRESSION SYSTEMS**										200
	0040	For detectors and control stations, see division 13850										
	1000	Dispersion nozzle, CO2, 3" x 5"	1 Plum	18	.444	Ea.	50	15.30		65.30	78	
	1100	FM200, 1-1/2"	"	14	.571		50	19.70		69.70	84.50	
	2000	Extinguisher, CO2 system, high pressure, 75 lb. cylinder	Q-1	6	2.667		950	82.50		1,032.50	1,175	
	2400	FM200 system, filled, with mounting bracket										
	2540	196 lb. container	Q-1	4	4	Ea.	5,800	124		5,924	6,550	
	3000	Electro/mechanical release	L-1	4	4		125	138		263	345	
	3400	Manual pull station	1 Plum	6	1.333		45	46		91	119	
	6000	Average FM200 system, minimum				C.F.	1.25			1.25	1.38	
	6020	Maximum				"	2.50			2.50	2.75	

For information about Means Estimating Seminars, see yellow pages 11 and 12 in back of book

T3 SPECIAL CONSTRUCTION

Division 14
Conveying Systems

Estimating Tips

General

- Many products in Division 14 will require some type of support or blocking for installation not included with the item itself. Examples are supports for conveyors or tube systems, attachment points for lifts, and footings for hoists or cranes. Add these supports in the appropriate division.

14100 Dumbwaiters
14200 Elevators

- Dumbwaiters and elevators are estimated and purchased in a method similar to buying a car. The manufacturer has a base unit with standard features. Added to this base unit price will be whatever options the owner or specifications require. Increased load capacity, additional vertical travel, additional stops, higher speed, and cab finish options are items to be considered. When developing an estimate for dumbwaiters and elevators, remember that some items needed by the installers may have to be included as part of the general contract.

Examples are:
- shaftway
- rail support brackets
- machine room
- electrical supply
- sill angles
- electrical connections
- pits
- roof penthouses
- pit ladders

Check the job specifications and drawings before pricing.

14300 Escalators & Moving Walks

- Escalators and moving walks are specialty items installed by specialty contractors. There are numerous options associated with these items. For specific options contact a manufacturer or contractor. In a method similar to estimating dumbwaiters and elevators, you should verify the extent of general contract work and add items as necessary.

14400 Lifts
14500 Material Handling
14600 Hoists & Cranes

- Products such as correspondence lifts, conveyors, chutes, pneumatic tube systems, material handling cranes and hoists as well as other items specified in this subdivision may require trained installers. The general contractor might not have any choice as to who will perform the installation or when it will be performed. Long lead times are often required for these products, making early decisions in scheduling necessary.

Reference Numbers

Reference numbers are shown in bold squares at the beginning of some major classifications. These numbers refer to related items in the Reference Section. The reference information may be an estimating procedure, an alternate pricing method or technical information.

Note: Not all subdivisions listed here necessarily appear in this publication.

14100 | Dumbwaiters

14110 | Manual Dumbwaiters

			CREW	DAILY OUTPUT	LABOR-HOURS	UNIT	2001 BARE COSTS				TOTAL INCL O&P	
							MAT.	LABOR	EQUIP.	TOTAL		
400	0010	**DUMBWAITERS** 2 stop, hand, minimum	2 Elev	.75	21.333	Ea.	2,275	760		3,035	3,650	400
	0100	Maximum		.50	32	"	5,200	1,150		6,350	7,425	
	0300	For each additional stop, add	↓	.75	21.333	Stop	825	760		1,585	2,050	

14120 | Electric Dumbwaiters

			CREW	DAILY OUTPUT	LABOR-HOURS	UNIT	2001 BARE COSTS				TOTAL INCL O&P	
							MAT.	LABOR	EQUIP.	TOTAL		
400	0010	**DUMBWAITERS** 2 stop, electric, minimum	2 Elev	.13	123	Ea.	5,775	4,400		10,175	13,000	400
	0100	Maximum		.11	145	"	17,300	5,175		22,475	26,800	
	0600	For each additional stop, add	↓	.54	29.630	Stop	2,550	1,050		3,600	4,400	

14200 | Elevators

14210 | Electric Traction Elevators

				CREW	DAILY OUTPUT	LABOR-HOURS	UNIT	2001 BARE COSTS				TOTAL INCL O&P	
								MAT.	LABOR	EQUIP.	TOTAL		
100	0012	**ELEVATORS OR LIFTS**											100
	7000	Residential, cab type, 1 floor, 2 stop, minimum		2 Elev	.20	80	Ea.	7,850	2,850		10,700	12,900	
	7100	Maximum			.10	160		13,300	5,700		19,000	23,200	
	7200	2 floor, 3 stop, minimum			.12	133		11,700	4,750		16,450	20,000	
	7300	Maximum			.06	266		19,000	9,500		28,500	35,200	
	7700	Stair climber (chair lift), single seat, minimum			1	16		3,800	570		4,370	5,025	
	7800	Maximum			.20	80		5,225	2,850		8,075	10,100	
	8000	Wheelchair lift, minimum			1	16		5,200	570		5,770	6,575	
	8500	Maximum			.50	32		12,300	1,150		13,450	15,300	
	8700	Stair lift, minimum			1	16		10,300	570		10,870	12,200	
	8900	Maximum		↓	.20	80	↓	16,300	2,850		19,150	22,200	
200	0010	**ELEVATORS**											200
	0020	For multi-story buildings, housing project, minimum	R14200 -100				% total					2.50%	
	0100	Maximum										4.50%	
	0300	Office building, minimum	R14200 -200									2.50%	
	0400	Maximum					↓					10%	
	0410	Holeless hydraulic passenger, 2000 lb capacity, 2 story	R14200 -300	2 Elev	.10	160	Ea.	27,600	5,700		33,300	38,900	
	0420	2500 lb capacity			.10	160		30,300	5,700		36,000	42,000	
	0425	Electric freight, base unit, 4000 lb, 200 fpm, 4 stop, std. fin.	R14200 -400	↓	.05	320		64,000	11,400		75,400	87,500	
	0450	For 5000 lb capacity, add						4,600			4,600	5,075	
	0500	For 6000 lb capacity, add						8,125			8,125	8,925	
	0525	For 7000 lb capacity, add						10,900			10,900	12,000	
	0550	For 8000 lb capacity, add						15,300			15,300	16,800	
	0575	For 10000 lb capacity, add						18,200			18,200	20,100	
	0600	For 12000 lb capacity, add						22,300			22,300	24,500	
	0625	For 16000 lb capacity, add						26,700			26,700	29,400	
	0650	For 20000 lb capacity, add						29,500			29,500	32,400	
	0675	For increased speed, 250 fpm, add						8,800			8,800	9,700	
	0700	300 fpm, geared electric, add						11,000			11,000	12,100	
	0725	350 fpm, geared electric, add						13,000			13,000	14,300	
	0750	400 fpm, geared electric, add						14,700			14,700	16,100	
	0775	500 fpm, gearless electric, add						18,500			18,500	20,300	
	0800	600 fpm, gearless electric, add						20,400			20,400	22,400	
	0825	700 fpm, gearless electric, add						23,800			23,800	26,100	
	0850	800 fpm, gearless electric, add						26,400			26,400	29,100	

14 CONVEYING SYSTEMS

Important: See the Reference Section for critical supporting data - Reference Nos., Crews, & City Cost Indexes

14210	Electric Traction Elevators		CREW	DAILY OUTPUT	LABOR-HOURS	UNIT	2001 BARE COSTS				TOTAL INCL O&P	
							MAT.	LABOR	EQUIP.	TOTAL		
200	0875	For class "B" loading, add	R14200 -100				Ea.	1,600			1,600	1,750	**200**
	0900	For class "C-1" loading, add						3,950			3,950	4,350	
	0925	For class "C-2" loading, add	R14200 -200					4,725			4,725	5,175	
	0950	For class "C-3" loading, add						6,475			6,475	7,125	
	0975	For travel over 40 V.L.F., add	R14200 -300	2 Elev	7.25	2.207	V.L.F.	94	78.50		172.50	222	
	1000	For number of stops over 4, add			.27	59.259	Stop	1,675	2,125		3,800	5,050	
	1025	Hydraulic freight, base unit, 2000 lb, 50 fpm, 2 stop, std. fin.	R14200 -400		.10	160	Ea.	32,400	5,700		38,100	44,200	
	1050	For 2500 lb capacity, add						2,100			2,100	2,300	
	1075	For 3000 lb capacity, add						3,600			3,600	3,975	
	1100	For 3500 lb capacity, add						5,450			5,450	6,000	
	1125	For 4000 lb capacity, add						5,825			5,825	6,425	
	1150	For 4500 lb capacity, add						6,925			6,925	7,625	
	1175	For 5000 lb capacity, add						9,450			9,450	10,400	
	1200	For 6000 lb capacity, add						9,975			9,975	11,000	
	1225	For 7000 lb capacity, add						15,700			15,700	17,200	
	1250	For 8000 lb capacity, add						17,100			17,100	18,800	
	1275	For 10000 lb capacity, add						18,100			18,100	19,900	
	1300	For 12000 lb capacity, add						21,900			21,900	24,100	
	1325	For 16000 lb capacity, add						28,600			28,600	31,400	
	1350	For 20000 lb capacity, add						31,700			31,700	34,900	
	1375	For increased speed, 100 fpm, add						680			680	745	
	1400	125 fpm, add						1,250			1,250	1,375	
	1425	150 fpm, add						2,375			2,375	2,625	
	1450	175 fpm, add						3,725			3,725	4,100	
	1475	For class "B" loading, add						1,550			1,550	1,725	
	1500	For class "C-1" loading, add						3,900			3,900	4,300	
	1525	For class "C-2" loading, add						4,675			4,675	5,150	
	1550	For class "C-3" loading, add						6,425			6,425	7,075	
	1575	For travel over 20 V.L.F., add		2 Elev	7.25	2.207	V.L.F.	206	78.50		284.50	345	
	1600	For number of stops over 2, add			.27	59.259	Stop	430	2,125		2,555	3,675	
	1625	Electric pass., base unit, 2000 lb, 200 fpm, 4 stop, std. fin.			.05	320	Ea.	61,500	11,400		72,900	84,500	
	1650	For 2500 lb capacity, add						2,525			2,525	2,775	
	1675	For 3000 lb capacity, add						3,850			3,850	4,225	
	1700	For 3500 lb capacity, add						5,475			5,475	6,025	
	1725	For 4000 lb capacity, add						5,600			5,600	6,150	
	1750	For 4500 lb capacity, add						7,350			7,350	8,100	
	1775	For 5000 lb capacity, add						9,350			9,350	10,300	
	1800	For increased speed, 250 fpm, geared electric, add						2,075			2,075	2,275	
	1825	300 fpm, geared electric, add						4,250			4,250	4,675	
	1850	350 fpm, geared electric, add						5,050			5,050	5,550	
	1875	400 fpm, geared electric, add						7,175			7,175	7,900	
	1900	500 fpm, gearless electric, add						33,700			33,700	37,100	
	1925	600 fpm, gearless electric, add						35,600			35,600	39,200	
	1950	700 fpm, gearless electric, add						39,000			39,000	42,900	
	1975	800 fpm, gearless electric, add						42,900			42,900	47,200	
	2000	For travel over 40 V.L.F., add		2 Elev	7.25	2.207	V.L.F.	94	78.50		172.50	222	
	2025	For number of stops over 4, add			.27	59.259	Stop	2,100	2,125		4,225	5,500	
	2050	Hyd. pass., base unit, 1500 lb, 100 fpm, 2 stop, std. fin.			.10	160	Ea.	27,000	5,700		32,700	38,300	
	2075	For 2000 lb capacity, add						485			485	535	
	2100	For 2500 lb capacity, add						1,050			1,050	1,175	
	2125	For 3000 lb capacity, add						2,700			2,700	2,950	
	2150	For 3500 lb capacity, add						4,550			4,550	5,000	
	2175	For 4000 lb capacity, add						5,250			5,250	5,775	
	2200	For 4500 lb capacity, add						6,350			6,350	7,000	
	2225	For 5000 lb capacity, add						8,875			8,875	9,750	
	2250	For increased speed, 125 fpm, add						725			725	800	

14210	Electric Traction Elevators	CREW	DAILY OUTPUT	LABOR-HOURS	UNIT	MAT.	2001 BARE COSTS LABOR	EQUIP.	TOTAL	TOTAL INCL O&P	
200	2275	150 fpm, add				Ea.	1,575			1,575	1,725	**200**
	2300	175 fpm, add					2,775			2,775	3,050	
	2325	200 fpm, add					4,475			4,475	4,925	
	2350	For travel over 12 V.L.F., add	2 Elev	7.25	2.207	V.L.F.	206	78.50		284.50	345	
	2375	For number of stops over 2, add		.27	59.259	Stop	415	2,125		2,540	3,650	
	2400	Electric hospital, base unit, 4000 lb, 200 fpm, 4 stop, std fin.		.05	320	Ea.	66,000	11,400		77,400	89,500	
	2425	For 4500 lb capacity, add					4,550			4,550	5,025	
	2450	For 5000 lb capacity, add					5,950			5,950	6,550	
	2475	For increased speed, 250 fpm, geared electric, add					2,225			2,225	2,450	
	2500	300 fpm, geared electric, add					4,225			4,225	4,650	
	2525	350 fpm, geared electric, add					5,150			5,150	5,675	
	2550	400 fpm, geared electric, add					7,175			7,175	7,900	
	2575	500 fpm, gearless electric, add					32,200			32,200	35,400	
	2600	600 fpm, gearless electric, add					35,600			35,600	39,200	
	2625	700 fpm, gearless electric, add					38,900			38,900	42,700	
	2650	800 fpm, gearless electric, add					42,900			42,900	47,200	
	2675	For travel over 40 V.L.F., add	2 Elev	7.25	2.207	V.L.F.	94	78.50		172.50	222	
	2700	For number of stops over 4, add		.27	59.259	Stop	2,625	2,125		4,750	6,075	
	2725	Hydraulic hospital, base unit, 4000 lb, 100 fpm, 2 stop, std. fin.		.10	160	Ea.	37,400	5,700		43,100	49,700	
	2750	For 4000 lb capacity, add					4,500			4,500	4,950	
	2775	For 4500 lb capacity, add					5,300			5,300	5,825	
	2800	For 5000 lb capacity, add					7,725			7,725	8,475	
	2825	For increased speed, 125 fpm, add					1,250			1,250	1,375	
	2850	150 fpm, add					2,125			2,125	2,325	
	2875	175 fpm, add					3,400			3,400	3,750	
	2900	200 fpm, add					4,975			4,975	5,450	
	2925	For travel over 12 V.L.F., add	2 Elev	7.25	2.207	V.L.F.	206	78.50		284.50	345	
	2950	For number of stops over 2, add	"	.27	59.259	Stop	2,600	2,125		4,725	6,075	
	2975	Passenger elevator options										
	3000	2 car group automatic controls	2 Elev	.66	24.242	Ea.	2,150	865		3,015	3,650	
	3025	3 car group automatic controls		.44	36.364		3,225	1,300		4,525	5,500	
	3050	4 car group automatic controls		.33	48.485		5,350	1,725		7,075	8,475	
	3075	5 car group automatic controls		.26	61.538		7,275	2,200		9,475	11,300	
	3100	6 car group automatic controls		.22	72.727		11,000	2,600		13,600	16,000	
	3125	Intercom service		3	5.333		285	190		475	600	
	3150	Duplex car selective collective		.66	24.242		2,375	865		3,240	3,900	
	3175	Center opening 1 speed doors		2	8		1,225	285		1,510	1,775	
	3200	Center opening 2 speed doors		2	8		1,625	285		1,910	2,225	
	3225	Rear opening doors (opposite front)		2	8		3,425	285		3,710	4,200	
	3250	Side opening 2 speed doors		2	8		5,200	285		5,485	6,150	
	3275	Automatic emergency power switching		.66	24.242		770	865		1,635	2,150	
	3300	Manual emergency power switching		8	2		295	71.50		366.50	435	
	3325	Cab finishes (based on 3500 lb cab size)										
	3350	Acrylic panel ceiling				Ea.	390			390	430	
	3375	Aluminum eggcrate ceiling					450			450	495	
	3400	Stainless steel doors					815			815	900	
	3425	Carpet flooring					325			325	360	
	3450	Epoxy flooring					267			267	294	
	3475	Quarry tile flooring					410			410	455	
	3500	Slate flooring					575			575	635	
	3525	Textured rubber flooring					105			105	116	
	3550	Stainless steel walls					2,350			2,350	2,575	
	3575	Stainless steel returns at door					490			490	540	
	3625	Hall finishes, stainless steel doors					815			815	900	
	3650	Stainless steel frames					815			815	900	
	3675	12 month maintenance contract									2,640	

Reference boxes: R14200 -100, R14200 -200, R14200 -300, R14200 -400

Important: See the Reference Section for critical supporting data - Reference Nos., Crews, & City Cost Indexes

14 CONVEYING SYSTEMS

14210 | Electric Traction Elevators

		CREW	DAILY OUTPUT	LABOR-HOURS	UNIT	2001 BARE COSTS MAT.	LABOR	EQUIP.	TOTAL	TOTAL INCL O&P	
200	3700	Signal devices, hall lanterns	2 Elev	8	2	Ea.	300	71.50		371.50	440	**200**
	3725	Position indicators, up to 3		9.40	1.702		210	60.50		270.50	325	
	3750	Position indicators, per each over 3	↓	32	.500		58	17.85		75.85	91	
	3775	High speed heavy duty door opener					1,475			1,475	1,625	
	3800	Variable voltage, O.H. gearless machine, min.	2 Elev	.16	100		21,700	3,575		25,275	29,200	
	3815	Maximum		.07	228		47,800	8,150		55,950	65,000	
	3825	Basement installed geared machine	↓	.33	48.485	↓	10,700	1,725		12,425	14,400	
	3850	Freight elevator options										
	3875	Doors, bi-parting	2 Elev	.66	24.242	Ea.	3,675	865		4,540	5,350	
	3900	Power operated door and gate	"	.66	24.242		14,900	865		15,765	17,700	
	3925	Finishes, steel plate floor					645			645	710	
	3950	14 ga. 1/4" x 4' steel plate walls					1,575			1,575	1,725	
	3975	12 month maintenance contract									1,992	
	4000	Signal devices, hall lanterns	2 Elev	8	2		300	71.50		371.50	440	
	4025	Position indicators, up to 3	↓	9.40	1.702		210	60.50		270.50	325	
	4050	Position indicators, per each over 3		32	.500		58	17.85		75.85	91	
	4075	Variable voltage basement installed geared machine	↓	.66	24.242	↓	12,000	865		12,865	14,400	
	4100	Hospital elevator options										
	4125	2 car group automatic controls	2 Elev	.66	24.242	Ea.	2,150	865		3,015	3,650	
	4150	3 car group automatic controls		.44	36.364		3,225	1,300		4,525	5,500	
	4175	4 car group automatic controls		.33	48.485		5,350	1,725		7,075	8,500	
	4200	5 car group automatic controls		.26	61.538		7,300	2,200		9,500	11,300	
	4225	6 car group automatic controls		.22	72.727		11,000	2,600		13,600	16,000	
	4250	Intercom service		3	5.333		285	190		475	600	
	4275	Duplex car selective collective		.66	24.242		2,375	865		3,240	3,900	
	4300	Center opening 1 speed doors		2	8		1,225	285		1,510	1,775	
	4325	Center opening 2 speed doors		2	8		1,625	285		1,910	2,225	
	4350	Rear opening doors (opposite front)		2	8		3,425	285		3,710	4,200	
	4375	Side opening 2 speed doors		2	8		5,200	285		5,485	6,150	
	4400	Automatic emergency power switching		.66	24.242		770	865		1,635	2,150	
	4425	Manual emergency power switching	↓	8	2	↓	295	71.50		366.50	435	
	4450	Cab finishes (based on 3500# cab size)										
	4475	Aluminum eggcrate ceiling				Ea.	450			450	495	
	4500	Stainless steel doors					815			815	900	
	4525	Epoxy flooring					267			267	294	
	4550	Quarry tile flooring					415			415	455	
	4575	Textured rubber flooring					105			105	116	
	4600	Stainless steel walls					2,350			2,350	2,575	
	4625	Stainless steel returns at door					490			490	540	
	4675	Hall finishes, stainless steel doors					815			815	900	
	4700	Stainless steel frames					815			815	900	
	4725	12 month maintenance contract									3,985	
	4750	Signal devices, hall lanterns	2 Elev	8	2		300	71.50		371.50	440	
	4775	Position indicators, up to 3		9.40	1.702		210	60.50		270.50	325	
	4800	Position indicators, per each over 3	↓	32	.500		58	17.85		75.85	91	
	4825	High speed heavy duty door opener					1,475			1,475	1,625	
	4850	Variable voltage, O.H. gearless machine, min.	2 Elev	.16	100		21,700	3,575		25,275	29,200	
	4865	Maximum	↓	.07	228		47,800	8,150		55,950	65,000	
	4875	Basement installed geared machine	↓	.33	48.485	↓	10,700	1,725		12,425	14,400	
	5000	Drilling for piston, casing included, 18" diameter	B-48	80	.700	V.L.F.	25.50	17.90	26	69.40	84	

Reference boxes: R14200-100, R14200-200, R14200-300, R14200-400

	14320	Escalators		CREW	DAILY OUTPUT	LABOR-HOURS	UNIT	2001 BARE COSTS				TOTAL INCL O&P	
								MAT.	LABOR	EQUIP.	TOTAL		
300	0010	**ESCALATORS**	R14320 -100										300
	1000	Glass, 32" wide x 10' floor to floor height		M-1	.07	457	Ea.	56,500	15,500	1,350	73,350	87,000	
	1010	48" wide x 10' floor to floor height			.07	457		62,000	15,500	1,350	78,850	93,000	
	1020	32" wide x 15' floor to floor height			.06	533		59,000	18,100	1,575	78,675	94,000	
	1030	48" wide x 15' floor to floor height			.06	533		62,500	18,100	1,575	82,175	98,000	
	1040	32" wide x 20' floor to floor height			.05	653		61,000	22,100	1,950	85,050	102,500	
	1050	48" wide x 20' floor to floor height			.05	653		65,000	22,100	1,950	89,050	107,000	
	1060	32" wide x 25' floor to floor height			.04	800		65,500	27,100	2,375	94,975	115,500	
	1070	48" wide x 25' floor to floor height			.04	800		70,000	27,100	2,375	99,475	120,500	
	1080	Enameled steel, 32" wide x 10' floor to floor height			.07	457		58,000	15,500	1,350	74,850	88,500	
	1090	48" wide x 10' floor to floor height			.07	457		62,000	15,500	1,350	78,850	93,000	
	1110	32" wide x 15' floor to floor height			.06	533		59,000	18,100	1,575	78,675	94,000	
	1120	48" wide x 15' floor to floor height			.06	533		62,500	18,100	1,575	82,175	98,000	
	1130	32" wide x 20' floor to floor height			.05	653		61,000	22,100	1,950	85,050	102,500	
	1140	48" wide x 20' floor to floor height			.05	653		65,000	22,100	1,950	89,050	107,000	
	1150	32" wide x 25' floor to floor height			.04	800		65,500	27,100	2,375	94,975	115,500	
	1160	48" wide x 25' floor to floor height			.04	800		70,000	27,100	2,375	99,475	120,500	
	1170	Stainless steel, 32" wide x 10' floor to floor height			.07	457		63,500	15,500	1,350	80,350	94,500	
	1180	48" wide x 10' floor to floor height			.07	457		66,000	15,500	1,350	82,850	98,000	
	1500	32" wide x 15' floor to floor height			.06	533		64,500	18,100	1,575	84,175	100,000	
	1700	48" wide x 15' floor to floor height			.06	533		67,500	18,100	1,575	87,175	103,000	
	2300	32" wide x 25' floor to floor height			.04	800		73,000	27,100	2,375	102,475	124,000	
	2500	48" wide x 25' floor to floor height		↓	.04	800	↓	77,500	27,100	2,375	106,975	128,500	

	14360	Moving Walks		CREW	DAILY OUTPUT	LABOR-HOURS	UNIT	MAT.	LABOR	EQUIP.	TOTAL	TOTAL INCL O&P	
500	0010	**MOVING RAMPS AND WALKS** Walk, 27" tread width, minimum	R14360 -200	M-1	6.50	4.923	L.F.	690	167	14.60	871.60	1,025	500
	0100	300' to 500', maximum			4.43	7.223		955	245	21.50	1,221.50	1,450	
	0300	48" tread width walk, minimum			4.43	7.223		1,550	245	21.50	1,816.50	2,100	
	0400	100' to 350', maximum			3.82	8.377		1,825	284	25	2,134	2,450	
	0600	Ramp, 12° incline, 36" tread width, minimum			5.27	6.072		1,275	206	18.05	1,499.05	1,725	
	0700	70' to 90' maximum			3.82	8.377		1,825	284	25	2,134	2,450	
	0900	48" tread width, minimum			3.57	8.964		1,850	305	26.50	2,181.50	2,550	
	1000	40' to 70', maximum		↓	2.91	10.997	↓	2,350	370	32.50	2,752.50	3,175	

14400 | Lifts

	14460	Correspondence & Parcel Lifts	CREW	DAILY OUTPUT	LABOR-HOURS	UNIT	2001 BARE COSTS				TOTAL INCL O&P	
							MAT.	LABOR	EQUIP.	TOTAL		
200	0010	**CORRESPONDENCE LIFT** 1 floor 2 stop, 25 lb capacity, electric	2 Elev	.20	80	Ea.	4,825	2,850		7,675	9,600	200
	0100	Hand, 5 lb capacity	"	.20	80	"	1,825	2,850		4,675	6,300	
600	0010	**PARCEL LIFT** 20" x 20", 100 lb capacity, electric, per floor	2 Mill	.25	64	Ea.	7,475	1,950		9,425	11,100	600

		14510	Material Handling	CREW	DAILY OUTPUT	LABOR-HOURS	UNIT	2001 BARE COSTS				TOTAL INCL O&P	
								MAT.	LABOR	EQUIP.	TOTAL		
900	0010		**MOTORIZED CAR** Distribution systems, single track,										900
	0100		20 lb. per car capacity, material handling										
	0200		Minimum, 50' to 100'	4 Mill	.19	168	Station	23,000	5,150		28,150	33,000	
	0300		Maximum, 100' to 200'	"	.15	213	"	31,000	6,525		37,525	43,800	
	0400		Larger system, incl. hospital transport, track type,										
	0500		fully automated material handling system										
	0600		Minimum, complete system	4 Mill	.05	640	Ea.	102,000	19,600		121,600	141,000	
	0700		Maximum, with several stations	E-6	.05	2,560	"	594,500	83,000	30,500	708,000	834,000	

		14550	Conveyors										
350	0010		**MATERIAL HANDLING** Conveyors, gravity type 2" rollers, 3" O.C.										350
	0050		10' sections with 2 supports, 600 lb. capacity, 18" wide				Ea.	355			355	390	
	0100		24" wide					410			410	450	
	0150		1400 lb. capacity, 18" wide					325			325	360	
	0200		24" wide					365			365	400	
	0350		Horizontal belt, center drive and takeup, 60 fpm										
	0400		16" belt, 26.5' length	2 Mill	.50	32	Ea.	2,500	980		3,480	4,200	
	0450		24" belt, 41.5' length		.40	40		3,700	1,225		4,925	5,900	
	0500		61.5' length		.30	53.333		4,800	1,625		6,425	7,700	
	0600		Inclined belt, 10' rise with horizontal loader and										
	0620		End idler assembly, 27.5' length, 18" belt	2 Mill	.30	53.333	Ea.	7,300	1,625		8,925	10,500	
	0700		24" belt	"	.15	106	"	8,200	3,250		11,450	13,900	
	3600		Monorail, overhead, manual, channel type										
	3700		125 lb. per L.F.	1 Mill	26	.308	L.F.	8.10	9.40		17.50	23	
	3900		500 lb. per L.F.	"	21	.381	"	7.35	11.65		19	25.50	
	4000		Trolleys for above, 2 wheel, 125 lb. capacity				Ea.	45			45	49.50	
	4200		4 wheel, 250 lb. capacity					165			165	181	
	4300		8 wheel, 1,000 lb. capacity					360			360	395	
900	0010		**VERTICAL CONVEYOR** Automatic selective										900
	0100		to 10 floors, base price	2 Mill	.13	120	Floor	22,900	3,675		26,575	30,700	
	0200		Add for electrical hook-up and testing	2 Elec	.50	32	"		1,100		1,100	1,650	

		14560	Chutes										
250	0010		**CHUTES** Linen or refuse, incl. sprinklers, 12' floor height										250
	0050		Aluminized steel, 16 ga., 18" diameter	2 Shee	3.50	4.571	Floor	710	153		863	1,025	
	0100		24" diameter		3.20	5		755	168		923	1,100	
	0200		30" diameter		3	5.333		870	179		1,049	1,225	
	0300		36" diameter		2.80	5.714		1,000	192		1,192	1,400	
	0400		Galvanized steel, 16 ga., 18" diameter		3.50	4.571		700	153		853	1,000	
	0500		24" diameter		3.20	5		790	168		958	1,125	
	0600		30" diameter		3	5.333		885	179		1,064	1,250	
	0700		36" diameter		2.80	5.714		1,050	192		1,242	1,450	
	0800		Stainless steel, 18" diameter		3.50	4.571		1,300	153		1,453	1,675	
	0900		24" diameter		3.20	5		1,350	168		1,518	1,750	
	1000		30" diameter		3	5.333		1,700	179		1,879	2,150	
	1005		36" diameter		2.80	5.714		1,725	192		1,917	2,200	
	1200		Linen chute bottom collector, aluminized steel		4	4	Ea.	980	134		1,114	1,275	
	1300		Stainless steel		4	4		1,250	134		1,384	1,575	
	1500		Refuse, bottom hopper, aluminized steel, 18" diameter		3	5.333		600	179		779	935	
	1600		24" diameter		3	5.333		665	179		844	1,000	
	1800		36" diameter		3	5.333		1,125	179		1,304	1,500	
	2900		Package chutes, spiral type, minimum		4.50	3.556	Floor	1,700	119		1,819	2,050	
	3000		Maximum		1.50	10.667	"	4,425	360		4,785	5,425	

CONVEYING SYSTEMS 14

14580 | Pneumatic Tube Systems

		CREW	DAILY OUTPUT	LABOR-HOURS	UNIT	2001 BARE COSTS				TOTAL INCL O&P	
						MAT.	LABOR	EQUIP.	TOTAL		
800	0010	**PNEUMATIC TUBE SYSTEM** Single tube, 2 stations, blower										800
	0020	100' long, stock										
	0100	3" diameter	2 Stpi	.12	133	Total	4,800	4,650		9,450	12,300	
	0300	4" diameter	"	.09	177	"	5,400	6,200		11,600	15,300	
	0400	Twin tube, two stations or more, conventional system										
	0600	2-1/2" round	2 Stpi	62.50	.256	L.F.	9.65	8.90		18.55	24	
	0700	3" round		46	.348		11.10	12.10		23.20	30.50	
	0900	4" round		49.60	.323		12.30	11.25		23.55	30.50	
	1000	4" x 7" oval		37.60	.426		17.90	14.85		32.75	42	
	1050	Add for blower		2	8	System	3,775	279		4,054	4,600	
	1110	Plus for each round station, add		7.50	2.133	Ea.	425	74.50		499.50	580	
	1150	Plus for each oval station, add		7.50	2.133	"	425	74.50		499.50	580	
	1200	Alternate pricing method: base cost, minimum		.75	21.333	Total	4,650	745		5,395	6,225	
	1300	Maximum		.25	64	"	9,200	2,225		11,425	13,500	
	1500	Plus total system length, add, minimum		93.40	.171	L.F.	5.95	5.95		11.90	15.55	
	1600	Maximum		37.60	.426	"	17.65	14.85		32.50	42	
	1800	Completely automatic system, 4" round, 15 to 50 stations		.29	55.172	Station	14,600	1,925		16,525	19,000	
	2200	51 to 144 stations		.32	50		11,300	1,750		13,050	15,100	
	2400	6" round or 4" x 7" oval, 15 to 50 stations		.24	66.667		18,300	2,325		20,625	23,600	
	2800	51 to 144 stations		.23	69.565		15,400	2,425		17,825	20,600	

14600 | Hoists & Cranes

14610 | Fixed Hoists

		CREW	DAILY OUTPUT	LABOR-HOURS	UNIT	2001 BARE COSTS				TOTAL INCL O&P	
						MAT.	LABOR	EQUIP.	TOTAL		
500	0010	**MATERIAL HANDLING**										500
	1500	Cranes, portable hydraulic, floor type, 2,000 lb capacity				Ea.	1,800			1,800	1,975	
	1600	4,000 lb capacity					3,100			3,100	3,425	
	1800	Movable gantry type, 12' to 15' range, 2,000 lb capacity					2,775			2,775	3,050	
	1900	6,000 lb capacity					4,025			4,025	4,425	
	2100	Hoists, electric overhead, chain, hook hung, 15' lift, 1 ton cap.					1,800			1,800	1,975	
	2200	3 ton capacity					2,250			2,250	2,475	
	2500	5 ton capacity					5,000			5,000	5,500	
	2600	For hand-pushed trolley, add					15%					
	2700	For geared trolley, add					30%					
	2800	For motor trolley, add					75%					
	3000	For lifts over 15', 1 ton, add				L.F.	17.10			17.10	18.80	
	3100	5 ton, add				"	40			40	43.50	
	3300	Lifts, scissor type, portable, electric, 36" high, 2,000 lb				Ea.	3,150			3,150	3,475	
	3400	48" high, 4,000 lb				"	3,600			3,600	3,950	

14630 | Bridge Cranes

		CREW	DAILY OUTPUT	LABOR-HOURS	UNIT	2001 BARE COSTS				TOTAL INCL O&P	
						MAT.	LABOR	EQUIP.	TOTAL		
300	0010	**CRANE RAIL** Box beam bridge, no equipment included	E-4	3,400	.009	Lb.	.87	.31	.02	1.20	1.56	300
	0200	Running track only, 104 lb per yard	"	5,600	.006	"	.46	.19	.02	.67	.88	
700	0010	**OVERHEAD BRIDGE CRANES**										700
	0100	1 girder, 20' span, 3 ton	M-3	1	34	Ea.	15,300	1,050	134	16,484	18,600	
	0125	5 ton		1	34		16,800	1,050	134	17,984	20,200	
	0150	7.5 ton		1	34		20,000	1,050	134	21,184	23,700	
	0175	10 ton		.80	42.500		26,400	1,300	168	27,868	31,200	
	0200	15 ton		.80	42.500		33,900	1,300	168	35,368	39,400	

Important: See the Reference Section for critical supporting data - Reference Nos., Crews, & City Cost Indexes

14 CONVEYING SYSTEMS

	14630	Bridge Cranes	CREW	DAILY OUTPUT	LABOR-HOURS	UNIT	2001 BARE COSTS				TOTAL INCL O&P	
							MAT.	LABOR	EQUIP.	TOTAL		
700	0225	30' span, 3 ton	M-3	1	34	Ea.	15,900	1,050	134	17,084	19,200	700
	0250	5 ton		1	34		17,500	1,050	134	18,684	21,000	
	0275	7.5 ton		1	34		21,000	1,050	134	22,184	24,800	
	0300	10 ton		.80	42.500		27,300	1,300	168	28,768	32,200	
	0325	15 ton		.80	42.500		35,400	1,300	168	36,868	41,100	
	0350	2 girder, 40' span, 3 ton	M-4	.50	72		26,400	2,200	435	29,035	32,800	
	0375	5 ton		.50	72		27,600	2,200	435	30,235	34,200	
	0400	7.5 ton		.50	72		30,300	2,200	435	32,935	37,100	
	0425	10 ton		.40	90		35,300	2,750	545	38,595	43,600	
	0450	15 ton		.40	90		48,000	2,750	545	51,295	58,000	
	0475	25 ton		.30	120		57,000	3,675	725	61,400	69,000	
	0500	50' span, 3 ton		.50	72		30,000	2,200	435	32,635	36,800	
	0525	5 ton		.50	72		31,200	2,200	435	33,835	38,100	
	0550	7.5 ton		.50	72		33,400	2,200	435	36,035	40,500	
	0575	10 ton		.40	90		38,400	2,750	545	41,695	47,100	
	0600	15 ton		.40	90		50,500	2,750	545	53,795	60,500	
	0625	25 ton		.30	120		59,500	3,675	725	63,900	72,000	

For information about Means Estimating Seminars, see yellow pages 11 and 12 in back of book

CONVEYING SYSTEMS 14

Division Notes

	CREW	DAILY OUTPUT	LABOR-HOURS	UNIT	2001 BARE COSTS				TOTAL INCL O&P
					MAT.	LABOR	EQUIP.	TOTAL	

Division 15
Mechanical

Estimating Tips

15100 Building Services Piping
This subdivision is primarily basic pipe and related materials. The pipe may be used by any of the mechanical disciplines, i.e., plumbing, fire protection, heating, and air conditioning.

- The piping section lists the add to labor for elevated pipe installation. These adds apply to all elevated pipe, fittings, valves, insulation, etc., that are placed above 10' high. CAUTION: the correct percentage may vary for the same pipe. For example, the percentage add for the basic pipe installation should be based on the maximum height that the craftsman must install for that particular section. If the pipe is to be located 14' above the floor but it is suspended on threaded rod from beams, the bottom flange of which is 18' high (4' rods), then the height is actually 18' and the add is 20%. The pipe coverer, however, does not have to go above the 14' and so his add should be 10%.

- Most pipe is priced first as straight pipe with a joint (coupling, weld, etc.) every 10' and a hanger usually every 10'. There are exceptions with hanger spacing such as: for cast iron pipe (5') and plastic pipe (3 per 10'). Following each type of pipe there are several lines listing sizes and the amount to be subtracted to delete couplings and hangers. This is for pipe that is to be buried or supported together on trapeze hangers. The reason that the couplings are deleted is that these runs are usually long and frequently longer lengths of pipe are used. By deleting the couplings the estimator is expected to look up and add back the correct reduced number of couplings.

- When preparing an estimate it may be necessary to approximate the fittings. Fittings usually run between 25% and 50% of the cost of the pipe. The lower percentage is for simpler runs, and the higher number is for complex areas like mechanical rooms.

15400 Plumbing Fixtures & Equipment
- Plumbing fixture costs usually require two lines, the fixture itself and its "rough-in, supply and waste".
- Remember that gas and oil fired units need venting.

15500 Heat Generation Equipment
- When estimating the cost of an HVAC system, check to see who is responsible for providing and installing the temperature control system. It is possible to overlook controls, assuming that they would be included in the electrical estimate.
- When looking up a boiler be careful on specified capacity. Some manufacturers rate their products on output while others use input.
- Include HVAC insulation for pipe, boiler and duct (wrap and liner).
- Be careful when looking up mechanical items to get the correct pressure rating and connection type (thread, weld, flange).

15700 Heating/Ventilation/ Air Conditioning Equipment
- Combination heating and cooling units are sized by the air conditioning requirements. (See Reference No. R15710-020 for preliminary sizing guide.)
- A ton of air conditioning is nominally 400 CFM.

- Rectangular duct is taken off by the linear foot for each size, but its cost is usually estimated by the pound. Remember that SMACNA standards now base duct on internal pressure.
- Prefabricated duct is estimated and purchased like pipe: straight sections and fittings.
- Note that cranes or other lifting equipment are not included on any lines in Division 15. For example, if a crane is required to lift a heavy piece of pipe into place high above a gym floor, or to put a rooftop unit on the roof of a four-story building, etc., it must be added. Due to the potential for extreme variation—from nothing additional required, to a major crane or helicopter—we feel that including a nominal amount for "lifting contingency" would be useless and detract from the accuracy of the estimate. When using equipment rental from Means do not forget to include the cost of the operator(s).

Reference Numbers
Reference numbers are shown in bold squares at the beginning of some major classifications. These numbers refer to related items in the Reference Section. The reference information may be an estimating procedure, an alternate pricing method or technical information.

Note: Not all subdivisions listed here necessarily appear in this publication.

15051	Mechanical General	CREW	DAILY OUTPUT	LABOR-HOURS	UNIT	2001 BARE COSTS				TOTAL INCL O&P
						MAT.	LABOR	EQUIP.	TOTAL	
100	**0010** **BOILERS, GENERAL** Prices do not include flue piping, elec. wiring,									**100**
	0020 gas or oil piping, boiler base, pad, or tankless unless noted									
	0100 Boiler H.P.: 10 KW = 34 lbs/steam/hr = 33,475 BTU/hr.	R15500-050								
	0120									
	0150 To convert SFR to BTU rating: Hot water, 150 x SFR;									
	0160 Forced hot water, 180 x SFR; steam, 240 x SFR									
700	**0010** **PIPING** See also divisions 02500 & 02600 for site work									**700**
	1000 Add to labor for elevated installation									
	1080 10' to 15' high						10%			
	1100 15' to 20' high						20%			
	1120 20' to 25' high						25%			
	1140 25' to 30' high						35%			
	1160 30' to 35' high						40%			
	1180 35' to 40' high						50%			
	1200 Over 40' high						55%			

15055	Selective Mech Demolition	CREW	DAILY OUTPUT	LABOR-HOURS	UNIT	MAT.	LABOR	EQUIP.	TOTAL	TOTAL INCL O&P
300	**0010** **HVAC DEMOLITION**									**300**
	0100 Air conditioner, split unit, 3 ton	Q-5	2	8	Ea.		251		251	380
	0150 Package unit, 3 ton	Q-6	3	8			260		260	395
	0200 Air conditioner, rooftop, gas heat, remove & reset, 10 ton		.30	80			2,600		2,600	3,925
	0240 Remove & reset, 20 ton	↓	.15	160			5,200		5,200	7,850
	0300 Boiler, electric	Q-19	2	12			390		390	585
	0340 Gas or oil, steel, under 150 MBH	Q-6	3	8			260		260	395
	0380 Over 150 MBH	"	2	12	↓		390		390	590
	1000 Ductwork, 4" high, 8" wide	1 Clab	200	.040	L.F.		.91		.91	1.43
	1100 6" high, 8" wide		165	.048			1.11		1.11	1.73
	1200 10" high, 12" wide		125	.064			1.46		1.46	2.29
	1300 12"-14" high, 16"-18" wide		85	.094			2.15		2.15	3.36
	1400 18" high, 24" wide		67	.119			2.73		2.73	4.27
	1500 30" high, 36" wide		56	.143			3.26		3.26	5.10
	1540 72" wide	↓	50	.160	↓		3.66		3.66	5.70
	3000 Mechanical equipment, light items. Unit is weight, not cooling.	Q-5	.90	17.778	Ton		560		560	840
	3600 Heavy items	"	1.10	14.545	"		455		455	690
	3700 Deduct for salvage (when applicable), minimum				Job					52
	3750 Maximum				"					420
600	**0010** **PLUMBING DEMOLITION**									**600**
	1020 Fixtures, including 10' piping									
	1100 Bath tubs, cast iron	1 Plum	4	2	Ea.		69		69	104
	1120 Fiberglass		6	1.333			46		46	69.50
	1140 Steel		5	1.600			55		55	83
	1200 Lavatory, wall hung		10	.800			27.50		27.50	41.50
	1220 Counter top		8	1			34.50		34.50	52
	1300 Sink, steel or cast iron, single		8	1			34.50		34.50	52
	1320 Double		7	1.143			39.50		39.50	59.50
	1400 Water closet, floor mounted		8	1			34.50		34.50	52
	1420 Wall mounted		7	1.143			39.50		39.50	59.50
	1500 Urinal, floor mounted		4	2			69		69	104
	1520 Wall mounted		7	1.143			39.50		39.50	59.50
	1600 Water fountains, free standing		8	1			34.50		34.50	52
	1620 Recessed		6	1.333	↓		46		46	69.50
	2000 Piping, metal, to 1-1/2" diameter		200	.040	L.F.		1.38		1.38	2.08
	2050 2" to 3-1/2" diameter	↓	150	.053			1.84		1.84	2.77
	2100 4" to 6" diameter	2 Plum	100	.160	↓		5.50		5.50	8.30

15 MECHANICAL

15050 | Basic Materials & Methods

15055 | Selective Mech Demolition

			DAILY	LABOR-		2001 BARE COSTS				TOTAL	
		CREW	OUTPUT	HOURS	UNIT	MAT.	LABOR	EQUIP.	TOTAL	INCL O&P	
600	2150	8" to 14" diameter	2 Plum	60	.267	L.F.		9.20		9.20	13.85	**600**
	2153	16" diameter	↓	55	.291	↓		10		10	15.15	
	2160	Deduct for salvage, aluminum scrap				Ton					525	
	2170	Brass scrap									420	
	2180	Copper scrap									1,025	
	2200	Lead scrap									235	
	2220	Steel scrap				↓					65	
	2250	Water heater, 40 gal.	1 Plum	6	1.333	Ea.		46		46	69.50	

15082 | Duct Insulation

			DAILY	LABOR-		2001 BARE COSTS				TOTAL	
		CREW	OUTPUT	HOURS	UNIT	MAT.	LABOR	EQUIP.	TOTAL	INCL O&P	
200	0010	**INSULATION**										**200**
	0100	Rule of thumb, as a percentage of total mechanical costs				Job				10%		
	0110	Insulation req'd is based on the surface size/area to be covered										
	1000	Boiler, 1-1/2" calcium silicate, 1/2" cement finish	Q-14	50	.320	S.F.	2.53	9.25		11.78	17.65	
	1020	2" fiberglass	"	80	.200	"	1.49	5.80		7.29	10.90	
	2000	Breeching, 2" calcium silicate with 1/2" cement finish, no lath										
	2020	Rectangular	Q-14	42	.381	S.F.	2.86	11		13.86	21	
	2040	Round	"	38.70	.413	"	3.21	11.95		15.16	22.50	
	3000	Ductwork										
	3020	Blanket type, fiberglass, flexible										
	3030	Fire resistant liner, black coating one side										
	3050	1/2" thick, 2 lb. density	Q-14	380	.042	S.F.	.29	1.22		1.51	2.27	
	3060	1" thick, 1-1/2 lb. density		350	.046		.39	1.32		1.71	2.55	
	3070	1-1/2" thick, 1-1/2 lb. density		320	.050		.68	1.45		2.13	3.07	
	3080	2" thick, 1-1/2 lb. density	↓	300	.053	↓	.80	1.54		2.34	3.35	
	3140	FRK vapor barrier wrap, .75 lb. density										
	3160	1" thick	Q-14	350	.046	S.F.	.27	1.32		1.59	2.42	
	3170	1-1/2" thick		320	.050		.24	1.45		1.69	2.58	
	3180	2" thick		300	.053		.29	1.54		1.83	2.79	
	3190	3" thick		260	.062		.43	1.78		2.21	3.32	
	3200	4" thick	↓	242	.066	↓	.58	1.91		2.49	3.70	
	3210	Vinyl jacket, same as FRK										
	3280	Unfaced, 1 lb. density										
	3310	1" thick	Q-14	360	.044	S.F.	.24	1.29		1.53	2.32	
	3320	1-1/2" thick		330	.048		.33	1.40		1.73	2.61	
	3330	2" thick	↓	310	.052		.39	1.49		1.88	2.82	
	3490	Board type, fiberglass liner, 3 lb. density										
	3500	Fire resistant, black pigmented, 1 side										
	3520	1" thick	Q-14	150	.107	S.F.	1.16	3.09		4.25	6.20	
	3540	1-1/2" thick		130	.123		1.43	3.56		4.99	7.25	
	3560	2" thick	↓	120	.133	↓	1.72	3.86		5.58	8.10	
	3600	FRK vapor barrier										
	3620	1" thick	Q-14	150	.107	S.F.	1.27	3.09		4.36	6.35	
	3630	1-1/2" thick		130	.123		1.64	3.56		5.20	7.50	
	3640	2" thick	↓	120	.133	↓	1.99	3.86		5.85	8.40	
	3680	No finish										
	3700	1" thick	Q-14	170	.094	S.F.	.68	2.72		3.40	5.10	
	3710	1-1/2" thick		140	.114		1.02	3.31		4.33	6.40	
	3720	2" thick		130	.123		1.30	3.56		4.86	7.15	
	3800	1/2" cement over 1" wire mesh, incl. corner bead		100	.160		1.23	4.63		5.86	8.75	
	3820	Glass cloth, pasted on		170	.094	↓	2	2.72		4.72	6.55	
	3900	Weatherproof, non-metallic, 2 lb. per S.F.	↓	100	.160		2.86	4.63		7.49	10.55	
	4000	Pipe covering (price copper tube one size less than IPS)										
	6600	Fiberglass, with all service jacket										
	6840	1" wall, 1/2" iron pipe size	Q-14	240	.067	L.F.	1.06	1.93		2.99	4.26	
	6870	1" iron pipe size	↓	220	.073	↓	1.24	2.10		3.34	4.73	

For expanded coverage of these items see *Means Mechanical or Plumbing Cost Data 2001*

15082 | Duct Insulation

		CREW	DAILY OUTPUT	LABOR-HOURS	UNIT	2001 BARE COSTS				TOTAL INCL O&P
						MAT.	LABOR	EQUIP.	TOTAL	
6900	2" iron pipe size	Q-14	200	.080	L.F.	1.65	2.31		3.96	5.55
6920	3" iron pipe size		180	.089		2.05	2.57		4.62	6.40
6940	4" iron pipe size		150	.107		2.64	3.09		5.73	7.85
7320	2" wall, 1/2" iron pipe size		220	.073		3.49	2.10		5.59	7.20
7440	6" iron pipe size		100	.160		6.65	4.63		11.28	14.75
7460	8" iron pipe size		80	.200		8.25	5.80		14.05	18.35
7480	10" iron pipe size		70	.229		9.85	6.60		16.45	21.50
7490	12" iron pipe size	▼	65	.246	▼	10.85	7.10		17.95	23.50
7600	For fiberglass with standard canvas jacket, deduct					5%				
7660	For fittings, add 3 L.F. for each fitting									
7680	plus 4 L.F. for each flange of the fitting									
7700	For equipment or congested areas, add						20%			
7720	Finishes, for .010" aluminum jacket, add	Q-14	200	.080	S.F.	.31	2.31		2.62	4.05
7740	For .016" aluminum jacket, add		200	.080		.40	2.31		2.71	4.15
7760	For .010" stainless steel, add	▼	160	.100	▼	1.20	2.89		4.09	5.95
7780	For single layer of felt, add					10%	10%			
7879	Rubber tubing, flexible closed cell foam									
7880	3/8" wall, 1/4" iron pipe size	1 Asbe	120	.067	L.F.	.28	2.14		2.42	3.74
7910	1/2" iron pipe size		115	.070		.36	2.24		2.60	3.98
7920	3/4" iron pipe size		115	.070		.34	2.24		2.58	3.95
7930	1" iron pipe size		110	.073		.49	2.34		2.83	4.29
7950	1-1/2" iron pipe size		110	.073		.72	2.34		3.06	4.54
8100	1/2" wall, 1/4" iron pipe size		90	.089		.58	2.86		3.44	5.20
8130	1/2" iron pipe size		89	.090		.45	2.89		3.34	5.15
8140	3/4" iron pipe size		89	.090		.51	2.89		3.40	5.20
8150	1" iron pipe size		88	.091		.55	2.92		3.47	5.30
8170	1-1/2" iron pipe size		87	.092		.83	2.96		3.79	5.65
8180	2" iron pipe size		86	.093		1.59	2.99		4.58	6.55
8200	3" iron pipe size		85	.094		1.66	3.03		4.69	6.70
8300	3/4" wall, 1/4" iron pipe size		90	.089		.65	2.86		3.51	5.30
8330	1/2" iron pipe size		89	.090		.78	2.89		3.67	5.50
8340	3/4" iron pipe size		89	.090		.86	2.89		3.75	5.60
8350	1" iron pipe size		88	.091		1.14	2.92		4.06	5.95
8370	1-1/2" iron pipe size		87	.092		1.76	2.96		4.72	6.70
8380	2" iron pipe size		86	.093		2.34	2.99		5.33	7.35
8400	3" iron pipe size		85	.094		3.19	3.03		6.22	8.35
8444	1" wall, 1/2" iron pipe size		86	.093		1.63	2.99		4.62	6.60
8445	3/4" iron pipe size		84	.095		1.82	3.06		4.88	6.90
8446	1" iron pipe size		84	.095		2.21	3.06		5.27	7.35
8447	1-1/4" iron pipe size		82	.098		2.57	3.14		5.71	7.85
8448	1-1/2" iron pipe size		82	.098		3.38	3.14		6.52	8.70
8449	2" iron pipe size		80	.100		4.51	3.22		7.73	10.10
8450	2-1/2" iron pipe size	▼	80	.100	▼	5.90	3.22		9.12	11.60
8456	Rubber insulation tape, 1/8" x 2" x 30'				Ea.	10.90			10.90	12

15106 | Glass Pipe & Fittings

		CREW	DAILY OUTPUT	LABOR-HOURS	UNIT	2001 BARE COSTS				TOTAL INCL O&P
						MAT.	LABOR	EQUIP.	TOTAL	
0010	**PIPE, GLASS** Borosilicate, couplings & hangers 10' O.C.									
0020	Drainage									

Important: See the Reference Section for critical supporting data - Reference Nos., Crews, & City Cost Indexes

15106	Glass Pipe & Fittings	CREW	DAILY OUTPUT	LABOR-HOURS	UNIT	2001 BARE COSTS				TOTAL INCL O&P	
						MAT.	LABOR	EQUIP.	TOTAL		
120	1100	1-1/2" diameter	Q-1	52	.308	L.F.	8.35	9.55		17.90	23.50	**120**
	1120	2" diameter		44	.364		10.95	11.25		22.20	29	
	1140	3" diameter		39	.410		14.55	12.70		27.25	35	
	1160	4" diameter		30	.533		26	16.55		42.55	53.50	
	1180	6" diameter	▼	26	.615	▼	47	19.10		66.10	80.50	

15107	Metal Pipe & Fittings	CREW	DAILY OUTPUT	LABOR-HOURS	UNIT	MAT.	LABOR	EQUIP.	TOTAL	TOTAL INCL O&P	
220	0010	**PIPE, BRASS** Plain end,										**220**
	0900	Field threaded, coupling & clevis hanger 10' O.C.										
	0920	Regular weight										
	0980	1/8" diameter	1 Plum	62	.129	L.F.	2.55	4.45		7	9.50	
	1120	1/2" diameter		48	.167		4.51	5.75		10.26	13.60	
	1140	3/4" diameter		46	.174		6	6		12	15.65	
	1160	1" diameter	▼	43	.186		8.50	6.40		14.90	19	
	1180	1-1/4" diameter	Q-1	72	.222		12.70	6.90		19.60	24.50	
	1200	1-1/2" diameter		65	.246		14.95	7.65		22.60	28	
	1220	2" diameter	▼	53	.302	▼	20	9.35		29.35	36	
320	0010	**PIPE, CAST IRON** Soil, on hangers 5' O.C.										**320**
	0020	Single hub, service wt., lead & oakum joints 10' O.C.										
	2120	2" diameter	Q-1	63	.254	L.F.	4.71	7.85		12.56	17.10	
	2140	3" diameter		60	.267		4.64	8.25		12.89	17.60	
	2160	4" diameter **CN**	▼	55	.291		7.95	9		16.95	22.50	
	2180	5" diameter	Q-2	76	.316		10.60	10.15		20.75	27	
	2200	6" diameter	"	73	.329		9.15	10.55		19.70	26	
	2220	8" diameter	Q-3	59	.542		20	17.80		37.80	49	
	2240	10" diameter		54	.593		33.50	19.45		52.95	66.50	
	2260	12" diameter	▼	48	.667		47	22		69	84.50	
	2320	For service weight, double hub, add					10%					
	2340	For extra heavy, single hub, add					48%	4%				
	2360	For extra heavy, double hub, add				▼	71%	4%				
	2400	Lead for caulking, (1#/dia in)				Lb.	.98			.98	1.08	
	2420	Oakum for caulking, (1/8#/dia in)				"	4.66			4.66	5.15	
	4000	No hub, couplings 10' O.C.										
	4100	1-1/2" diameter	Q-1	71	.225	L.F.	5.05	7		12.05	16.10	
	4120	2" diameter		67	.239		5.10	7.40		12.50	16.80	
	4160	4" diameter	▼	58	.276	▼	8.15	8.55		16.70	22	
420	0010	**PIPE, COPPER** Solder joints										**420**
	1000	Type K tubing, couplings & clevis hangers 10' O.C.										
	1100	1/4" diameter	1 Plum	84	.095	L.F.	1.15	3.28		4.43	6.20	
	1200	1" diameter		66	.121		2.40	4.18		6.58	8.95	
	1260	2" diameter	▼	40	.200	▼	5.25	6.90		12.15	16.15	
	2000	Type L tubing, couplings & hangers 10' O.C.										
	2100	1/4" diameter	1 Plum	88	.091	L.F.	.97	3.13		4.10	5.80	
	2120	3/8" diameter		84	.095		1.13	3.28		4.41	6.20	
	2140	1/2" diameter **CN**		81	.099		1.25	3.40		4.65	6.55	
	2160	5/8" diameter		79	.101		1.60	3.49		5.09	7	
	2180	3/4" diameter		76	.105		1.59	3.63		5.22	7.20	
	2200	1" diameter		68	.118		2.02	4.05		6.07	8.35	
	2220	1-1/4" diameter		58	.138		2.54	4.75		7.29	9.95	
	2240	1-1/2" diameter		52	.154		3.07	5.30		8.37	11.35	
	2260	2" diameter	▼	42	.190		4.47	6.55		11.02	14.80	
	2280	2-1/2" diameter	Q-1	62	.258		6.50	8		14.50	19.25	
	2300	3" diameter		56	.286		8.65	8.85		17.50	23	
	2320	3-1/2" diameter	▼	43	.372	▼	11.05	11.55		22.60	29.50	

MECHANICAL 15

			DAILY	LABOR-		2001 BARE COSTS				TOTAL	
15107	**Metal Pipe & Fittings**	CREW	OUTPUT	HOURS	UNIT	MAT.	LABOR	EQUIP.	TOTAL	INCL O&P	
420	2340	4" diameter	Q-1	39	.410	L.F.	13.55	12.70		26.25	34	**420**
	2360	5" diameter	↓	34	.471		38	14.60		52.60	63.50	
	2380	6" diameter	Q-2	40	.600		47.50	19.30		66.80	81	
	2400	8" diameter	"	36	.667		82	21.50		103.50	123	
	2410	For other than full hard temper, add				↓	21%					
	2590	For silver solder, add						15%				
	4000	Type DWV tubing, couplings & hangers 10' O.C.										
	4100	1-1/4" diameter	1 Plum	60	.133	L.F.	2.14	4.59		6.73	9.30	
	4120	1-1/2" diameter		54	.148		2.54	5.10		7.64	10.50	
	4140	2" diameter	↓	44	.182		3.19	6.25		9.44	12.95	
	4160	3" diameter	Q-1	58	.276		5.25	8.55		13.80	18.65	
	4180	4" diameter		40	.400		8.95	12.40		21.35	28.50	
	4200	5" diameter	↓	36	.444		26	13.80		39.80	49.50	
	4220	6" diameter	Q-2	42	.571	↓	36.50	18.35		54.85	67.50	
500	0010	**PIPE, CORROSION RESISTANT** No couplings or hangers										**500**
	0020	Iron alloy, drain, mechanical joint										
	1000	1-1/2" diameter	Q-1	70	.229	L.F.	22.50	7.10		29.60	35.50	
	1100	2" diameter		66	.242		26	7.50		33.50	40	
	1120	3" diameter		60	.267		36	8.25		44.25	52.50	
	1140	4" diameter	↓	52	.308	↓	46.50	9.55		56.05	65.50	
	2980	Plastic, epoxy, fiberglass filament wound										
	3000	2" diameter	Q-1	62	.258	L.F.	5.20	8		13.20	17.80	
	3100	3" diameter		51	.314		7.10	9.75		16.85	22.50	
	3120	4" diameter		45	.356		9.40	11		20.40	27	
	3140	6" diameter	↓	32	.500	↓	14.40	15.50		29.90	39.50	
	3980	Polyester, fiberglass filament wound										
	4000	2" diameter	Q-1	62	.258	L.F.	9.85	8		17.85	23	
	4100	3" diameter		51	.314		13.20	9.75		22.95	29	
	4120	4" diameter		45	.356		14.90	11		25.90	33	
	4140	6" diameter	↓	32	.500	↓	23.50	15.50		39	49.50	
	4980	Polypropylene, acid resistant, fire retardant, schedule 40										
	5000	1-1/2" diameter	Q-1	68	.235	L.F.	.95	7.30		8.25	12.05	
	5100	2" diameter		62	.258		1.29	8		9.29	13.50	
	5120	3" diameter		51	.314		2.70	9.75		12.45	17.65	
	5140	4" diameter	↓	45	.356	↓	3.83	11		14.83	21	
	5980	Proxylene, fire retardant, Schedule 40										
	6000	1-1/2" diameter	Q-1	68	.235	L.F.	3.21	7.30		10.51	14.55	
	6100	2" diameter		62	.258		4.40	8		12.40	16.95	
	6120	3" diameter		51	.314		7.95	9.75		17.70	23.50	
	6140	4" diameter	↓	45	.356		11.30	11		22.30	29	
620	0010	**PIPE, STEEL**										**620**
	0012	The steel pipe in this section does not include fittings such as ells, tees										
	0014	For fittings either add a % (usually 25 to 35%) or see										
	0015	the Mechanical or Plumbing Cost Data										
	0020	All pipe sizes are to Spec. A-53 unless noted otherwise										
	0050	Schedule 40, threaded, with couplings, and clevis type										
	0060	hangers sized for covering, 10' O.C.										
	0540	Black, 1/4" diameter	1 Plum	66	.121	L.F.	1.29	4.18		5.47	7.70	
	0550	3/8" diameter		65	.123		1.40	4.24		5.64	7.95	
	0560	1/2" diameter		63	.127		1.22	4.37		5.59	7.95	
	0570	3/4" diameter		61	.131		1.36	4.52		5.88	8.30	
	0580	1" diameter	↓	53	.151		1.73	5.20		6.93	9.75	
	0590	1-1/4" diameter	Q-1	89	.180		2.04	5.55		7.59	10.65	
	0600	1-1/2" diameter		80	.200		2.29	6.20		8.49	11.85	
	0610	2" diameter		64	.250		2.89	7.75		10.64	14.90	
	0620	2-1/2" diameter	↓	50	.320	↓	4.59	9.90		14.49	20	

R15100 -050

CN

Important: See the Reference Section for critical supporting data - Reference Nos., Crews, & City Cost Indexes

		CREW	DAILY OUTPUT	LABOR-HOURS	UNIT	MAT.	LABOR	EQUIP.	TOTAL	TOTAL INCL O&P	
620	0630	3" diameter	Q-1	43	.372	L.F.	5.80	11.55		17.35	24	**620**
	0640	3-1/2" diameter		40	.400		7.70	12.40		20.10	27	
	0650	4" diameter		36	.444		8.55	13.80		22.35	30.50	
	0660	5" diameter		26	.615		12.55	19.10		31.65	43	
	0670	6" diameter	Q-2	31	.774		16.50	25		41.50	55.50	
	1290	Galvanized, 1/4" diameter	1 Plum	66	.121		1.49	4.18		5.67	7.95	
	1300	3/8" diameter		65	.123		1.60	4.24		5.84	8.15	
	1310	1/2" diameter		63	.127		1.37	4.37		5.74	8.10	
	1320	3/4" diameter		61	.131		1.53	4.52		6.05	8.50	
	1330	1" diameter		53	.151		1.81	5.20		7.01	9.85	
	1340	1-1/4" diameter	Q-1	89	.180		2.16	5.55		7.71	10.75	
	1350	1-1/2" diameter		80	.200		2.39	6.20		8.59	12	
	1360	2" diameter		64	.250		3.03	7.75		10.78	15.05	
	1370	2-1/2" diameter		50	.320		4.52	9.90		14.42	19.95	
	1380	3" diameter		43	.372		5.60	11.55		17.15	23.50	
	1390	3-1/2" diameter		40	.400		7.10	12.40		19.50	26.50	
	1400	4" diameter		36	.444		8.05	13.80		21.85	30	
	1410	5" diameter		26	.615		14.90	19.10		34	45.50	
	1420	6" diameter	Q-2	31	.774		20.50	25		45.50	60	
	1430	8" diameter		27	.889		33	28.50		61.50	79.50	
	1440	10" diameter		23	1.043		48.50	33.50		82	104	
	1450	12" diameter		18	1.333		66.50	43		109.50	138	
	2000	Welded, sch. 40, on yoke & roll hangers, sized for covering,										
	2010	10' O.C. (no hangers incl. for 14" diam. and up)										
	2040	Black, 1" diameter	Q-15	93	.172	L.F.	2.60	5.35	1.08	9.03	12.10	
	2070	2" diameter		61	.262		3.88	8.15	1.65	13.68	18.40	
	2090	3" diameter		43	.372		5.45	11.55	2.34	19.34	26	
	2110	4" diameter		37	.432		7.90	13.40	2.72	24.02	31.50	
	2120	5" diameter		32	.500		13.10	15.50	3.15	31.75	41.50	
	2130	6" diameter	Q-16	36	.667		16.80	21.50	2.79	41.09	54	
	2140	8" diameter		29	.828		24.50	26.50	3.47	54.47	71	
	2150	10" diameter		24	1		43	32	4.19	79.19	101	
	2160	12" diameter		19	1.263		53	40.50	5.30	98.80	125	
690	0010	**PIPE, GROOVED-JOINT STEEL FITTINGS & VALVES**										**690**
	0020	Pipe includes coupling & clevis type hanger 10' O.C.										
	1000	Schedule 40, black										
	1040	3/4" diameter	1 Plum	71	.113	L.F.	1.92	3.88		5.80	7.95	
	1050	1" diameter		63	.127		2.03	4.37		6.40	8.85	
	1060	1-1/4" diameter		58	.138		2.51	4.75		7.26	9.90	
	1070	1-1/2" diameter		51	.157		2.79	5.40		8.19	11.20	
	1080	2" diameter		40	.200		3.21	6.90		10.11	13.95	
	1090	2-1/2" diameter	Q-1	57	.281		4.71	8.70		13.41	18.35	
	1100	3" diameter		50	.320		5.30	9.90		15.20	21	
	1110	4" diameter		45	.356		7.55	11		18.55	25	
	1120	5" diameter		37	.432		12.75	13.40		26.15	34	
	1130	6" diameter	Q-2	42	.571		16.55	18.35		34.90	45.50	
	1800	Galvanized										
	1840	3/4" diameter	1 Plum	71	.113	L.F.	2.11	3.88		5.99	8.15	
	1850	1" diameter		63	.127		2.17	4.37		6.54	9	
	1860	1-1/4" diameter		58	.138		2.69	4.75		7.44	10.10	
	1870	1-1/2" diameter		51	.157		3.01	5.40		8.41	11.45	
	1880	2" diameter		40	.200		3.51	6.90		10.41	14.25	
	1890	2-1/2" diameter	Q-1	57	.281		4.87	8.70		13.57	18.50	
	1900	3" diameter		50	.320		5.90	9.90		15.80	21.50	
	1910	4" diameter		45	.356		8.20	11		19.20	25.50	

15107	Metal Pipe & Fittings	CREW	DAILY OUTPUT	LABOR-HOURS	UNIT	2001 BARE COSTS				TOTAL INCL O&P
						MAT.	LABOR	EQUIP.	TOTAL	
690										**690**
1920	5" diameter	Q-1	37	.432	L.F.	15.65	13.40		29.05	37.50
1930	6" diameter	Q-2	42	.571	↓	20.50	18.35		38.85	50
3990	Fittings: cplg. & labor required at joints not incl. in fitting									
3994	price. Add 1 per joint for installed price.									
4000	Elbow, 90° or 45°, painted									
4030	3/4" diameter	1 Plum	50	.160	Ea.	13.65	5.50		19.15	23.50
4040	1" diameter		50	.160		13.65	5.50		19.15	23.50
4050	1-1/4" diameter		40	.200		13.65	6.90		20.55	25.50
4060	1-1/2" diameter		33	.242		13.65	8.35		22	27.50
4070	2" diameter	↓	25	.320		13.65	11		24.65	31.50
4080	2-1/2" diameter	Q-1	40	.400		13.65	12.40		26.05	33.50
4090	3" diameter		33	.485		24.50	15.05		39.55	49
4100	4" diameter		25	.640		26.50	19.85		46.35	59
4110	5" diameter	↓	20	.800		64	25		89	108
4120	6" diameter	Q-2	25	.960		75	31		106	129
4250	For galvanized elbows, add				↓	26%				
4690	Tee, painted									
4700	3/4" diameter	1 Plum	38	.211	Ea.	21	7.25		28.25	34
4740	1" diameter		33	.242		21	8.35		29.35	35.50
4750	1-1/4" diameter		27	.296		21	10.20		31.20	38.50
4760	1-1/2" diameter		22	.364		21	12.55		33.55	42
4770	2" diameter	↓	17	.471		21	16.20		37.20	47.50
4780	2-1/2" diameter	Q-1	27	.593		21	18.35		39.35	50.50
4790	3" diameter		22	.727		29.50	22.50		52	66.50
4800	4" diameter		17	.941		45	29		74	93.50
4810	5" diameter	↓	13	1.231		105	38		143	174
4820	6" diameter	Q-2	17	1.412		122	45.50		167.50	203
4900	For galvanized tees, add				↓	24%				
4906	Couplings, rigid style, painted									
4908	1" diameter	1 Plum	100	.080	Ea.	9.90	2.76		12.66	15.05
4909	1-1/4" diameter		100	.080		9.90	2.76		12.66	15.05
4910	1-1/2" diameter		67	.119		9.90	4.11		14.01	17.10
4912	2" diameter	↓	50	.160		10.15	5.50		15.65	19.50
4914	2-1/2" diameter	Q-1	80	.200		11.70	6.20		17.90	22
4916	3" diameter		67	.239		13.65	7.40		21.05	26.50
4918	4" diameter		50	.320		19.35	9.90		29.25	36.50
4920	5" diameter	↓	40	.400		25	12.40		37.40	46
4922	6" diameter	Q-2	50	.480	↓	33.50	15.45		48.95	60.50
4940	Flexible, standard, painted									
4950	3/4" diameter	1 Plum	100	.080	Ea.	7.10	2.76		9.86	12
4960	1" diameter		100	.080		7.10	2.76		9.86	12
4970	1-1/4" diameter		80	.100		9.45	3.45		12.90	15.60
4980	1-1/2" diameter		67	.119		10.35	4.11		14.46	17.55
4990	2" diameter	↓	50	.160		10.90	5.50		16.40	20.50
5000	2-1/2" diameter	Q-1	80	.200		13.05	6.20		19.25	24
5010	3" diameter		67	.239		14.45	7.40		21.85	27
5020	3-1/2" diameter		57	.281		21	8.70		29.70	36
5030	4" diameter		50	.320		21	9.90		30.90	38
5040	5" diameter	↓	40	.400		32.50	12.40		44.90	54
5050	6" diameter	Q-2	50	.480	↓	38	15.45		53.45	65.50
920	0010 **PIPE, STAINLESS STEEL**									**920**
3500	Threaded, couplings and hangers 10' O.C.									
3520	Schedule 40, type 304									
3540	1/4" diameter	1 Plum	54	.148	L.F.	4.87	5.10		9.97	13.05
3550	3/8" diameter		53	.151		5.55	5.20		10.75	13.95
3560	1/2" diameter	↓	52	.154	↓	6.55	5.30		11.85	15.25

Important: See the Reference Section for critical supporting data - Reference Nos., Crews, & City Cost Indexes

15107 | Metal Pipe & Fittings

			CREW	DAILY OUTPUT	LABOR-HOURS	UNIT	2001 BARE COSTS				TOTAL INCL O&P	
							MAT.	LABOR	EQUIP.	TOTAL		
920	3580	1" diameter	1 Plum	45	.178	L.F.	10.70	6.10		16.80	21	920
	3610	2" diameter	Q-1	57	.281		19.35	8.70		28.05	34.50	
	3640	4" diameter	Q-2	51	.471		55	15.15		70.15	84	
	3740	For small quantities, add					10%					
	4250	Schedule 40, type 316										
	4290	1/4" diameter	1 Plum	54	.148	L.F.	5.80	5.10		10.90	14.05	
	4300	3/8" diameter		53	.151		7.50	5.20		12.70	16.10	
	4310	1/2" diameter		52	.154		8.25	5.30		13.55	17.05	
	4320	3/4" diameter		51	.157		10.35	5.40		15.75	19.50	
	4330	1" diameter		45	.178		13.60	6.10		19.70	24	
	4360	2" diameter	Q-1	57	.281		25	8.70		33.70	40.50	
	4390	4" diameter	Q-2	51	.471		73.50	15.15		88.65	104	
	4490	For small quantities, add					10%					

15108 | Plastic Pipe & Fittings

			CREW	DAILY OUTPUT	LABOR-HOURS	UNIT	MAT.	LABOR	EQUIP.	TOTAL	TOTAL INCL O&P	
520	0010	**PIPE, PLASTIC**										520
	0020	Fiberglass reinforced, couplings 10' O.C., hangers 3 per 10'										
	0200	High strength										
	0240	2" diameter	Q-1	58	.276	L.F.	10.45	8.55		19	24.50	
	0260	3" diameter		51	.314		14.70	9.75		24.45	31	
	0280	4" diameter		47	.340		17.40	10.55		27.95	35	
	0300	6" diameter		38	.421		26.50	13.05		39.55	48.50	
	0320	8" diameter	Q-2	48	.500		41	16.10		57.10	69.50	
	1800	PVC, couplings 10' O.C., hangers 3 per 10'										
	1820	Schedule 40										
	1860	1/2" diameter	1 Plum	54	.148	L.F.	2.23	5.10		7.33	10.15	
	1870	3/4" diameter		51	.157		2.28	5.40		7.68	10.65	
	1880	1" diameter		46	.174		2.48	6		8.48	11.75	
	1890	1-1/4" diameter		42	.190		2.72	6.55		9.27	12.90	
	1900	1-1/2" diameter		36	.222		2.85	7.65		10.50	14.70	
	1910	2" diameter **CN**	Q-1	59	.271		3.17	8.40		11.57	16.20	
	1920	2-1/2" diameter		56	.286		3.97	8.85		12.82	17.70	
	1930	3" diameter		53	.302		4.96	9.35		14.31	19.60	
	1940	4" diameter		48	.333		6.05	10.35		16.40	22.50	
	1950	5" diameter		43	.372		7.75	11.55		19.30	26	
	1960	6" diameter		39	.410		10.10	12.70		22.80	30.50	
	4100	DWV type, schedule 40, couplings 10' O.C., hangers 3 per 10'										
	4120	ABS										
	4140	1-1/4" diameter	1 Plum	42	.190	L.F.	2.33	6.55		8.88	12.45	
	4150	1-1/2" diameter	"	36	.222		2.36	7.65		10.01	14.15	
	4160	2" diameter	Q-1	59	.271		2.49	8.40		10.89	15.45	
	4400	PVC										
	4410	1-1/4" diameter	1 Plum	42	.190	L.F.	2.33	6.55		8.88	12.45	
	4420	1-1/2" diameter	"	36	.222		2.44	7.65		10.09	14.25	
	4460	2" diameter	Q-1	59	.271		2.51	8.40		10.91	15.45	
	4470	3" diameter		53	.302		4.34	9.35		13.69	18.95	
	4480	4" diameter		48	.333		4.74	10.35		15.09	21	
	4490	6" diameter		39	.410		8.15	12.70		20.85	28	
	5360	CPVC, couplings 10' O.C., hangers 3 per 10'										
	5380	Schedule 40										
	5460	1/2" diameter	1 Plum	54	.148	L.F.	2.88	5.10		7.98	10.85	
	5470	3/4" diameter		51	.157		3.18	5.40		8.58	11.65	
	5480	1" diameter		46	.174		3.75	6		9.75	13.15	
	5490	1-1/4" diameter		42	.190		4.35	6.55		10.90	14.70	
	5500	1-1/2" diameter		36	.222		5.35	7.65		13	17.45	

MECHANICAL 15

			DAILY	LABOR-				2001 BARE COSTS			TOTAL	
15108	**Plastic Pipe & Fittings**	CREW	OUTPUT	HOURS	UNIT	MAT.	LABOR	EQUIP.	TOTAL		**INCL O&P**	
520	5510	2" diameter	Q-1	59	.271	L.F.	6.20	8.40		14.60	19.55	**520**
	5520	2-1/2" diameter		56	.286		9.95	8.85		18.80	24.50	
	5530	3" diameter	▼	53	.302	▼	12	9.35		21.35	27.50	

15110 | Valves

			CREW	DAILY OUTPUT	LABOR-HOURS	UNIT	MAT.	LABOR	EQUIP.	TOTAL	INCL O&P	
100	0010	**VALVES, BRASS**										**100**
	0500	Gas cocks, threaded										
	0530	1/2" size	1 Plum	24	.333	Ea.	7.65	11.50		19.15	26	
	0540	3/4" size		22	.364		10.30	12.55		22.85	30.50	
	0550	1" size		19	.421		12.60	14.50		27.10	36	
	0560	1-1/4" size	▼	15	.533	▼	36	18.35		54.35	67	
160	0010	**VALVES, BRONZE**										**160**
	1020	Angle, 150 lb., rising stem, threaded										
	1030	1/8" size	1 Plum	24	.333	Ea.	42	11.50		53.50	63.50	
	1040	1/4" size		24	.333		42	11.50		53.50	63.50	
	1050	3/8" size		24	.333		42	11.50		53.50	63.50	
	1060	1/2" size		22	.364		42	12.55		54.55	65	
	1070	3/4" size		20	.400		56.50	13.80		70.30	83	
	1080	1" size		19	.421		81	14.50		95.50	111	
	1100	1-1/2" size		13	.615		135	21		156	181	
	1110	2" size	▼	11	.727	▼	219	25		244	279	
	1380	Ball, 150 psi, threaded										
	1400	1/4" size	1 Plum	24	.333	Ea.	6.40	11.50		17.90	24.50	
	1430	3/8" size		24	.333		6.40	11.50		17.90	24.50	
	1450	1/2" size		22	.364		6.40	12.55		18.95	26	
	1460	3/4" size		20	.400		10.60	13.80		24.40	32.50	
	1470	1" size		19	.421		13.30	14.50		27.80	36.50	
	1480	1-1/4" size		15	.533		22.50	18.35		40.85	52.50	
	1490	1-1/2" size		13	.615		28.50	21		49.50	63.50	
	1500	2" size	▼	11	.727	▼	35.50	25		60.50	77.50	
	1750	Check, swing, class 150, regrinding disc, threaded										
	1800	1/8" size	1 Plum	24	.333	Ea.	22.50	11.50		34	42.50	
	1830	1/4" size		24	.333		22.50	11.50		34	42.50	
	1840	3/8" size		24	.333		22.50	11.50		34	42.50	
	1850	1/2" size		24	.333		22.50	11.50		34	42.50	
	1860	3/4" size		20	.400		30	13.80		43.80	54	
	1870	1" size		19	.421		45	14.50		59.50	71.50	
	1880	1-1/4" size		15	.533		62.50	18.35		80.85	96	
	1890	1-1/2" size		13	.615		73.50	21		94.50	113	
	1900	2" size	▼	11	.727		108	25		133	157	
	1910	2-1/2" size	Q-1	15	1.067	▼	179	33		212	247	
	2000	For 200 lb, add					5%	10%				
	2040	For 300 lb, add					15%	15%				
	2850	Gate, N.R.S., soldered, 125 psi										
	2900	3/8" size	1 Plum	24	.333	Ea.	16.85	11.50		28.35	36	
	2920	1/2" size		24	.333		14.75	11.50		26.25	33.50	
	2940	3/4" size		20	.400		16.85	13.80		30.65	39.50	
	2950	1" size		19	.421		24	14.50		38.50	48.50	
	2960	1-1/4" size		15	.533		40	18.35		58.35	71	
	2970	1-1/2" size		13	.615		45	21		66	81.50	
	2980	2" size	▼	11	.727		57.50	25		82.50	102	
	2990	2-1/2" size	Q-1	15	1.067		145	33		178	209	
	3000	3" size	"	13	1.231	▼	189	38		227	266	
	3850	Rising stem, soldered, 300 psi										
	3950	1" size	1 Plum	19	.421	Ea.	55	14.50		69.50	82.50	

Important: See the Reference Section for critical supporting data - Reference Nos., Crews, & City Cost Indexes

15110	Valves	CREW	DAILY OUTPUT	LABOR-HOURS	UNIT	2001 BARE COSTS				TOTAL INCL O&P
						MAT.	LABOR	EQUIP.	TOTAL	
160 3980	2" size	1 Plum	11	.727	Ea.	137	25		162	189	**160**
4000	3" size	Q-1	13	1.231	↓	385	38		423	485
4250	Threaded, class 150									
4310	1/4" size	1 Plum	24	.333	Ea.	21.50	11.50		33	41.50
4320	3/8" size		24	.333		21.50	11.50		33	41.50
4330	1/2" size		24	.333		20.50	11.50		32	40
4340	3/4" size		20	.400		24	13.80		37.80	47.50
4350	1" size		19	.421		32	14.50		46.50	57
4360	1-1/4" size		15	.533		43	18.35		61.35	75
4370	1-1/2" size		13	.615		54	21		75	91.50
4380	2" size	↓	11	.727		73.50	25		98.50	119
4390	2-1/2" size	Q-1	15	1.067		171	33		204	238
4400	3" size	"	13	1.231		240	38		278	320
4500	For 300 psi, threaded, add					100%	15%			
4540	For chain operated type, add				↓	15%				
4850	Globe, class 150, rising stem, threaded									
4920	1/4" size	1 Plum	24	.333	Ea.	31.50	11.50		43	52
4940	3/8" size		24	.333		31.50	11.50		43	52
4950	1/2" size		24	.333		31.50	11.50		43	52
4960	3/4" size		20	.400		43	13.80		56.80	68
4970	1" size		19	.421		67	14.50		81.50	95.50
4980	1-1/4" size		15	.533		105	18.35		123.35	144
4990	1-1/2" size		13	.615		128	21		149	172
5000	2" size	↓	11	.727		191	25		216	248
5010	2-1/2" size	Q-1	15	1.067		385	33		418	475
5020	3" size	"	13	1.231	↓	550	38		588	660
5120	For 300 lb threaded, add					50%	15%			
5600	Relief, pressure & temperature, self-closing, ASME, threaded									
5640	3/4" size	1 Plum	28	.286	Ea.	65	9.85		74.85	86.50
5650	1" size		24	.333		94.50	11.50		106	121
5660	1-1/4" size		20	.400		189	13.80		202.80	229
5670	1-1/2" size		18	.444		360	15.30		375.30	425
5680	2" size	↓	16	.500	↓	395	17.25		412.25	460
5950	Pressure, poppet type, threaded									
6000	1/2" size	1 Plum	30	.267	Ea.	13.15	9.20		22.35	28.50
6040	3/4" size	"	28	.286	"	44	9.85		53.85	63.50
6400	Pressure, water, ASME, threaded									
6440	3/4" size	1 Plum	28	.286	Ea.	43	9.85		52.85	62.50
6450	1" size		24	.333		91	11.50		102.50	117
6460	1-1/4"size		20	.400		149	13.80		162.80	185
6470	1-1/2" size		18	.444		206	15.30		221.30	249
6480	2" size		16	.500		298	17.25		315.25	350
6490	2-1/2" size	↓	15	.533	↓	875	18.35		893.35	990
6900	Reducing, water pressure									
6920	300 psi to 25-75 psi, threaded or sweat									
6940	1/2" size	1 Plum	24	.333	Ea.	108	11.50		119.50	136
6950	3/4" size ze		20	.400		108	13.80		121.80	140
6960	1" si		19	.421		167	14.50		181.50	206
6970	1-1/4" size		15	.533		300	18.35		318.35	360
6980	1-1/2" size	↓	13	.615	↓	450	21		471	530
8350	Tempering, water, sweat connections									
8400	1/2" size	1 Plum	24	.333	Ea.	40	11.50		51.50	61.50
8440	3/4" size	"	20	.400	"	49	13.80		62.80	75
8650	Threaded connections									
8700	1/2" size	1 Plum	24	.333	Ea.	49	11.50		60.50	71.50
8740	3/4" size	↓	20	.400	↓	187	13.80		200.80	227

MECHANICAL 15

		**15110	Valves**	CREW	DAILY OUTPUT	LABOR-HOURS	UNIT	2001 BARE COSTS				TOTAL INCL O&P	
							MAT.	LABOR	EQUIP.	TOTAL		
160	8750	1" size	1 Plum	19	.421	Ea.	206	14.50		220.50	249	**160**
	8760	1-1/4" size		15	.533		330	18.35		348.35	390	
	8770	1-1/2" size		13	.615		355	21		376	425	
	8780	2" size	↓	11	.727	↓	540	25		565	630	
200	0010	**VALVES, IRON BODY**										**200**
	1020	Butterfly, wafer type, gear actuator, 200 lb.										
	1030	2" size	1 Plum	14	.571	Ea.	109	19.70		128.70	149	
	1040	2-1/2" size	Q-1	9	1.778		112	55		167	206	
	1050	3" size		8	2		116	62		178	222	
	1060	4" size	↓	5	3.200		145	99		244	310	
	1070	5" size	Q-2	5	4.800		175	154		329	425	
	1080	6" size	"	5	4.800	↓	198	154		352	450	
	1650	Gate, 125 lb., N.R.S.										
	2150	Flanged										
	2200	2" size	1 Plum	5	1.600	Ea.	276	55		331	390	
	2240	2-1/2" size	Q-1	5	3.200		284	99		383	460	
	2260	3" size		4.50	3.556		320	110		430	515	
	2280	4" size	↓	3	5.333		455	165		620	750	
	2300	6" size	Q-2	3	8	↓	775	257		1,032	1,250	
	3550	OS&Y, 125 lb., flanged										
	3600	2" size	1 Plum	5	1.600	Ea.	209	55		264	310	
	3660	3" size	Q-1	4.50	3.556		243	110		353	435	
	3680	4" size	"	3	5.333		345	165		510	630	
	3700	6" size	Q-2	3	8	↓	570	257		827	1,025	
	3900	For 250 lb, flanged, add					200%	10%				
	5450	Swing check, 125 lb., threaded										
	5500	2" size	1 Plum	11	.727	Ea.	340	25		365	415	
	5540	2-1/2" size	Q-1	15	1.067		400	33		433	490	
	5550	3" size		13	1.231		445	38		483	550	
	5560	4" size	↓	10	1.600	↓	710	49.50		759.50	860	
	5950	Flanged										
	6000	2" size	1 Plum	5	1.600	Ea.	144	55		199	241	
	6040	2-1/2" size	Q-1	5	3.200		174	99		273	340	
	6050	3" size		4.50	3.556		187	110		297	370	
	6060	4" size	↓	3	5.333		294	165		459	575	
	6070	6" size	Q-2	3	8	↓	505	257		762	945	
500	0010	**VALVES, PLASTIC**										**500**
	1100	Angle, PVC, threaded										
	1110	1/4" size	1 Plum	26	.308	Ea.	47.50	10.60		58.10	68	
	1120	1/2" size		26	.308		47.50	10.60		58.10	68	
	1130	3/4" size		25	.320		55.50	11		66.50	77.50	
	1140	1" size	↓	23	.348	↓	66.50	12		78.50	91	
	1150	Ball, PVC, socket or threaded, single union										
	1200	1/4" size	1 Plum	26	.308	Ea.	24	10.60		34.60	42.50	
	1220	3/8" size		26	.308		24	10.60		34.60	42.50	
	1230	1/2" size		26	.308		24	10.60		34.60	42.50	
	1240	3/4" size		25	.320		28.50	11		39.50	48	
	1250	1" size		23	.348		34	12		46	55.50	
	1260	1-1/4" size		21	.381		45	13.10		58.10	69.50	
	1270	1-1/2" size		20	.400		57	13.80		70.80	83.50	
	1280	2" size	↓	17	.471	↓	81.50	16.20		97.70	114	
	1360	For PVC, flanged, add					100%	15%				
	1650	CPVC, socket or threaded, single union										
	1700	1/2" size	1 Plum	26	.308	Ea.	33.50	10.60		44.10	52.50	
	1720	3/4" size		25	.320		42	11		53	62.50	
	1730	1" size	↓	23	.348	↓	50	12		62	73	

15 MECHANICAL

Important: See the Reference Section for critical supporting data - Reference Nos., Crews, & City Cost Indexes

		15110	Valves	CREW	DAILY OUTPUT	LABOR-HOURS	UNIT	2001 BARE COSTS				TOTAL INCL O&P	
								MAT.	LABOR	EQUIP.	TOTAL		
500	1750		1-1/4" size	1 Plum	21	.381	Ea.	83.50	13.10		96.60	112	**500**
	1760		1-1/2" size	↓	20	.400		83.50	13.80		97.30	113	
	1840		For CPVC, flanged, add					65%	15%				
	1880		For true union, socket or threaded, add				↓	50%	5%				
	2050		Polypropylene, threaded										
	2100		1/4" size	1 Plum	26	.308	Ea.	30	10.60		40.60	49	
	2120		3/8" size		26	.308		30	10.60		40.60	49	
	2130		1/2" size		26	.308		30	10.60		40.60	49	
	2140		3/4" size		25	.320		37.50	11		48.50	57.50	
	2150		1" size		23	.348		44.50	12		56.50	67	
	2160		1-1/4" size		21	.381		64.50	13.10		77.60	91	
	2170		1-1/2" size		20	.400		74	13.80		87.80	103	
	2180		2" size	↓	17	.471	↓	101	16.20		117.20	136	
	4850		Foot valve, PVC, socket or threaded										
	4900		1/2" size	1 Plum	34	.235	Ea.	40.50	8.10		48.60	57	
	4930		3/4" size		32	.250		46	8.60		54.60	64	
	4940		1" size		28	.286		60	9.85		69.85	81	
	4950		1-1/4" size		27	.296		115	10.20		125.20	142	
	4960		1-1/2" size	↓	26	.308	↓	115	10.60		125.60	143	
	6350		Y sediment strainer, PVC, socket or threaded										
	6400		1/2" size	1 Plum	26	.308	Ea.	29.50	10.60		40.10	48.50	
	6440		3/4" size		24	.333		32	11.50		43.50	53	
	6450		1" size		23	.348		39	12		51	61	
	6460		1-1/4" size		21	.381		64.50	13.10		77.60	91	
	6470		1-1/2" size	↓	20	.400	↓	67.50	13.80		81.30	95.50	
700	0010	**VALVES, STEEL**											**700**
	0800	Cast											
	1350		Check valve, swing type, 150 lb., flanged										
	1400		2" size	1 Plum	8	1	Ea.	465	34.50		499.50	565	
	1440		2-1/2" size	Q-1	5	3.200		595	99		694	805	
	1450		3" size		4.50	3.556		595	110		705	820	
	1460		4" size	↓	3	5.333		875	165		1,040	1,200	
	1540		For 300 lb., flanged, add					50%	15%				
	1548		For 600 lb., flanged, add				↓	110%	20%				
	1950		Gate valve, 150 lb., flanged										
	2000		2" size	1 Plum	8	1	Ea.	540	34.50		574.50	645	
	2040		2-1/2"size	Q-1	5	3.200		765	99		864	990	
	2050		3" size		4.50	3.556		765	110		875	1,000	
	2060		4" size	↓	3	5.333		930	165		1,095	1,275	
	2070		6" size	Q-2	3	8	↓	1,475	257		1,732	2,025	
	3650		Globe valve, 150 lb., flanged										
	3700		2" size	1 Plum	8	1	Ea.	675	34.50		709.50	795	
	3740		2-1/2" size	Q-1	5	3.200		850	99		949	1,075	
	3750		3" size		4.50	3.556		850	110		960	1,100	
	3760		4" size	↓	3	5.333		1,250	165		1,415	1,625	
	3770		6" size	Q-2	3	8	↓	1,950	257		2,207	2,550	
	5150	Forged											
	5650		Check valve, class 800, horizontal, socket										
	5698		Threaded										
	5700		1/4" size	1 Plum	24	.333	Ea.	41	11.50		52.50	62.50	
	5720		3/8" size		24	.333		41	11.50		52.50	62.50	
	5730		1/2" size		24	.333		41	11.50		52.50	62.50	
	5740		3/4" size		20	.400		44.50	13.80		58.30	70	
	5750		1" size		19	.421		52	14.50		66.50	79	
	5760		1-1/4" size	↓	15	.533	↓	99.50	18.35		117.85	137	

MECHANICAL 15

15120 | Piping Specialties

		CREW	DAILY OUTPUT	LABOR-HOURS	UNIT	2001 BARE COSTS MAT.	LABOR	EQUIP.	TOTAL	TOTAL INCL O&P	
120	0010	**AIR CONTROL**									**120**
	0030	Air separator, with strainer									
	0040	2" diameter	Q-5	6	2.667	Ea.	515	83.50		598.50	695
	0080	2-1/2" diameter		5	3.200		585	100		685	795
	0100	3" diameter		4	4		890	126		1,016	1,175
	0120	4" diameter	↓	3	5.333		1,300	167		1,467	1,675
	0130	5" diameter	Q-6	3.60	6.667		1,650	217		1,867	2,125
	0140	6" diameter	"	3.40	7.059	↓	1,975	230		2,205	2,525
160	0010	**AUTOMATIC AIR VENT**									**160**
	0020	Cast iron body, stainless steel internals, float type									
	0060	1/2" NPT inlet, 300 psi	1 Stpi	12	.667	Ea.	78.50	23		101.50	121
	0220	3/4" NPT inlet, 250 psi	"	10	.800		251	28		279	320
	0340	1-1/2" NPT inlet, 250 psi	Q-5	12	1.333	↓	780	42		822	925
300	0010	**EXPANSION JOINTS**									**300**
	0100	Bellows type, neoprene cover, flanged spool									
	0120	6" face to face, 1" diameter	1 Stpi	13	.615	Ea.	158	21.50		179.50	207
	0140	1-1/4" diameter		11	.727		161	25.50		186.50	216
	0160	1-1/2" diameter	↓	10.60	.755		161	26.50		187.50	217
	0180	2" diameter	Q-5	13.30	1.203		163	38		201	236
	0190	2-1/2" diameter		12.40	1.290		170	40.50		210.50	248
	0200	3" diameter		11.40	1.404		193	44		237	279
	0480	10" face to face, 2" diameter		13	1.231		240	38.50		278.50	325
	0500	2-1/2" diameter		12	1.333		253	42		295	340
	0520	3" diameter		11	1.455		257	45.50		302.50	350
	0540	4" diameter		8	2		287	63		350	410
	0560	5" diameter		7	2.286		390	71.50		461.50	540
	0580	6" diameter	↓	6	2.667	↓	355	83.50		438.50	520
320	0010	**EXPANSION TANKS**									**320**
	1505	Fiberglass and steel single / double wall storage, see Div 13201									
	1510	Tank leak detection systems, see Div 13851-350									
	2000	Steel, liquid expansion, ASME, painted, 15 gallon capacity	Q-5	17	.941	Ea.	340	29.50		369.50	415
	2020	24 gallon capacity		14	1.143		340	36		376	430
	2040	30 gallon capacity		12	1.333		375	42		417	480
	2060	40 gallon capacity		10	1.600		430	50		480	550
	2080	60 gallon capacity		8	2		515	63		578	660
	2100	80 gallon capacity		7	2.286		530	71.50		601.50	690
	2120	100 gallon capacity		6	2.667		685	83.50		768.50	875
	3000	Steel ASME expansion, rubber diaphragm, 19 gal. cap. accept.		12	1.333		1,275	42		1,317	1,475
	3020	31 gallon capacity		8	2		1,425	63		1,488	1,650
	3040	61 gallon capacity		6	2.667		2,000	83.50		2,083.50	2,300
	3080	119 gallon capacity		4	4		2,250	126		2,376	2,675
	3100	158 gallon capacity		3.80	4.211		3,150	132		3,282	3,675
	3140	317 gallon capacity		2.80	5.714		4,750	179		4,929	5,500
	3180	528 gallon capacity	↓	2.40	6.667	↓	7,700	209		7,909	8,800
	5950										
350	0010	**FLEXIBLE CONNECTORS**, Corrugated, 7/8" O.D., 1/2" I.D.									**350**
	0050	Gas, seamless brass, steel fittings									
	0200	12" long	1 Plum	36	.222	Ea.	9.95	7.65		17.60	22.50
	0220	18" long		36	.222		12.35	7.65		20	25
	0240	24" long		34	.235		14.60	8.10		22.70	28.50
	0280	36" long		32	.250		17.40	8.60		26	32
	0340	60" long	↓	30	.267	↓	26.50	9.20		35.70	43
	2000	Water, copper tubing, dielectric separators									
	2100	12" long	1 Plum	36	.222	Ea.	8.50	7.65		16.15	21
	2260	24" long	"	34	.235	"	12.65	8.10		20.75	26

Important: See the Reference Section for critical supporting data - Reference Nos., Crews, & City Cost Indexes

		15120	Piping Specialties	CREW	DAILY OUTPUT	LABOR-HOURS	UNIT	2001 BARE COSTS				TOTAL INCL O&P	
								MAT.	LABOR	EQUIP.	TOTAL		
370	0010	**FLEXIBLE METAL HOSE** Connectors, standard lengths											370
	0100	Bronze braided, bronze ends											
	0120	3/8″ diameter x 12″	1 Stpi	26	.308	Ea.	14.40	10.70		25.10	32	
	0160	3/4″ diameter x 12″		20	.400		20	13.95		33.95	43	
	0180	1″ diameter x 18″		19	.421		26	14.65		40.65	50.50	
	0200	1-1/2″ diameter x 18″		13	.615		41	21.50		62.50	77.50	
	0220	2″ diameter x 18″		11	.727		49.50	25.50		75	93	
520	0010	**HYDRONIC HEATING CONTROL VALVES**											520
	0100	Radiator supply, 1/2″ diameter	1 Stpi	24	.333	Ea.	36	11.60		47.60	57	
	0120	3/4″ diameter		20	.400		36.50	13.95		50.45	61.50	
	0140	1″ diameter		19	.421		45.50	14.65		60.15	72	
	0160	1-1/4″ diameter		15	.533		64	18.60		82.60	98.50	
	0500	For low pressure steam, add					25%					
670	0010	**PRESSURE REGULATOR**											670
	3000	Steam, high capacity, bronze body, stainless steel trim											
	3020	Threaded, 1/2″ diameter	1 Stpi	24	.333	Ea.	705	11.60		716.60	795	
	3030	3/4″ diameter		24	.333		705	11.60		716.60	795	
	3040	1″ diameter		19	.421		790	14.65		804.65	890	
	3060	1-1/4″ diameter		15	.533		870	18.60		888.60	990	
	3080	1-1/2″ diameter		13	.615		995	21.50		1,016.50	1,125	
	3100	2″ diameter		11	.727		1,225	25.50		1,250.50	1,400	
	3120	2-1/2″ diameter	Q-5	12	1.333		1,525	42		1,567	1,750	
	3140	3″ diameter	″	11	1.455		1,750	45.50		1,795.50	2,000	
	3500	Flanged connection, iron body, 125 lb. W.S.P.										
	3520	3″ diameter	Q-5	11	1.455	Ea.	1,900	45.50		1,945.50	2,175	
	3540	4″ diameter	″	5	3.200	″	2,400	100		2,500	2,800	
760	0010	**STEAM TRAP**											760
	0030	Cast iron body, threaded										
	0040	Inverted bucket										
	0050	1/2″ pipe size	1 Stpi	12	.667	Ea.	100	23		123	145	
	0070	3/4″ pipe size		10	.800		172	28		200	231	
	0100	1″ pipe size		9	.889		265	31		296	340	
	0120	1-1/4″ pipe size		8	1		400	35		435	495	
	1000	Float & thermostatic, 15 psi										
	1010	3/4″ pipe size	1 Stpi	16	.500	Ea.	96	17.45		113.45	133	
	1020	1″ pipe size		15	.533		115	18.60		133.60	155	
	1040	1-1/2″ pipe size		9	.889		254	31		285	325	
	1060	2″ pipe size		6	1.333		470	46.50		516.50	590	
820	0010	**STRAINERS, Y TYPE** Bronze body											820
	0050	Screwed, 150 lb., 1/4″ pipe size	1 Stpi	24	.333	Ea.	11.40	11.60		23	30	
	0070	3/8″ pipe size		24	.333		15.90	11.60		27.50	35	
	0100	1/2″ pipe size		20	.400		15.90	13.95		29.85	38.50	
	0140	1″ pipe size		17	.471		18.70	16.40		35.10	45.50	
	0160	1-1/2″ pipe size		14	.571		40.50	19.90		60.40	74.50	
	0180	2″ pipe size		13	.615		53.50	21.50		75	91.50	
	0182	3″ pipe size		12	.667		286	23		309	350	
	0200	300 lb., 2-1/2″ pipe size	Q-5	17	.941		286	29.50		315.50	360	
	0220	3″ pipe size		16	1		565	31.50		596.50	675	
	0240	4″ pipe size		15	1.067		1,300	33.50		1,333.50	1,475	
	0500	For 300 lb rating 1/4″ thru 2″, add					15%					
	1000	Flanged, 150 lb., 1-1/2″ pipe size	1 Stpi	11	.727	Ea.	305	25.50		330.50	375	
	1020	2″ pipe size	″	8	1		390	35		425	485	
	1030	2-1/2″ pipe size	Q-5	5	3.200		505	100		605	705	
	1040	3″ pipe size		4.50	3.556		620	112		732	855	

MECHANICAL 15

For expanded coverage of these items see *Means Mechanical or Plumbing Cost Data 2001*

15120		Piping Specialties	CREW	DAILY OUTPUT	LABOR-HOURS	UNIT	MAT.	LABOR	EQUIP.	TOTAL	TOTAL INCL O&P	
820	1060	4" pipe size	Q-5	3	5.333	Ea.	945	167		1,112	1,275	820
	1100	6" pipe size	Q-6	3	8		2,500	260		2,760	3,150	
	1106	8" pipe size	"	2.60	9.231	↓	3,900	300		4,200	4,750	
	1500	For 300 lb rating, add					40%					
840	0010	**STRAINERS, Y TYPE** Iron body										840
	0050	Screwed, 250 lb., 1/4" pipe size	1 Stpi	20	.400	Ea.	6.65	13.95		20.60	28.50	
	0070	3/8" pipe size		20	.400		6.30	13.95		20.25	28	
	0100	1/2" pipe size		20	.400		6.65	13.95		20.60	28.50	
	0140	1" pipe size		16	.500		10.75	17.45		28.20	38.50	
	0160	1-1/2" pipe size		12	.667		17.75	23		40.75	54.50	
	0180	2" pipe size	↓	8	1		27.50	35		62.50	82.50	
	0220	3" pipe size	Q-5	11	1.455		151	45.50		196.50	235	
	0240	4" pipe size	"	5	3.200	↓	255	100		355	430	
	0500	For galvanized body, add					50%					
	1000	Flanged, 125 lb., 1-1/2" pipe size	1 Stpi	11	.727	Ea.	86	25.50		111.50	133	
	1020	2" pipe size	"	8	1		64	35		99	123	
	1040	3" pipe size	Q-5	4.50	3.556		84.50	112		196.50	261	
	1060	4" pipe size	"	3	5.333		155	167		322	425	
	1080	5" pipe size	Q-6	3.40	7.059		242	230		472	610	
	1100	6" pipe size	"	3	8	↓	295	260		555	720	
	1500	For 250 lb rating, add					20%					
	2000	For galvanized body, add					50%					
	2500	For steel body, add					40%					
920	0010	**VENTURI FLOW** Measuring device										920
	0050	1/2" diameter	1 Stpi	24	.333	Ea.	105	11.60		116.60	134	
	0120	1" diameter		19	.421		94	14.65		108.65	125	
	0140	1-1/4" diameter		15	.533		134	18.60		152.60	175	
	0160	1-1/2" diameter		13	.615		140	21.50		161.50	187	
	0180	2" diameter	↓	11	.727		166	25.50		191.50	222	
	0220	3" diameter	Q-5	14	1.143		335	36		371	425	
	0240	4" diameter	"	11	1.455		375	45.50		420.50	485	
	0280	6" diameter	Q-6	3.50	6.857		660	223		883	1,050	
	0500	For meter, add				↓	1,175			1,175	1,300	
940	0010	**WATER SUPPLY METERS**										940
	2000	Domestic/commercial, bronze										
	2020	Threaded										
	2060	5/8" diameter, to 20 GPM	1 Plum	16	.500	Ea.	55.50	17.25		72.75	87	
	2080	3/4" diameter, to 30 GPM		14	.571		96	19.70		115.70	136	
	2100	1" diameter, to 50 GPM	↓	12	.667	↓	131	23		154	179	
	2300	Threaded/flanged										
	2340	1-1/2" diameter, to 100 GPM	1 Plum	8	1	Ea.	405	34.50		439.50	495	
	2360	2" diameter, to 160 GPM	"	6	1.333	"	535	46		581	660	
	2600	Flanged, compound										
	2640	3" diameter, 320 GPM	Q-1	3	5.333	Ea.	2,425	165		2,590	2,900	
	2660	4" diameter, to 500 GPM		1.50	10.667		3,775	330		4,105	4,650	
	2680	6" diameter, to 1,000 GPM		1	16		5,425	495		5,920	6,725	
	2700	8" diameter, to 1,800 GPM	↓	.80	20	↓	10,700	620		11,320	12,700	

15140 | Domestic Water Piping

100	0010	**BACKFLOW PREVENTER** Includes valves										100
	0020	and four test cocks, corrosion resistant, automatic operation										
	4000	Reduced pressure principle										
	4100	Threaded, valves are ball										
	4120	3/4" pipe size	1 Plum	16	.500	Ea.	685	17.25		702.25	780	
	4140	1" pipe size	↓	14	.571	↓	730	19.70		749.70	830	

15140 | Domestic Water Piping

			DAILY OUTPUT	LABOR-HOURS	UNIT	2001 BARE COSTS				TOTAL INCL O&P	
			CREW			MAT.	LABOR	EQUIP.	TOTAL		
100	4150	1-1/4" pipe size	1 Plum	12	.667	Ea.	1,025	23		1,048	1,150	100
	4160	1-1/2" pipe size		10	.800		1,025	27.50		1,052.50	1,175	
	4180	2" pipe size	↓	7	1.143	↓	1,050	39.50		1,089.50	1,200	
	5000	Flanged, bronze, valves are OS&Y										
	5060	2-1/2" pipe size	Q-1	5	3.200	Ea.	2,725	99		2,824	3,150	
	5080	3" pipe size		4.50	3.556		3,375	110		3,485	3,900	
	5100	4" pipe size		3	5.333		4,800	165		4,965	5,525	
	5120	6" pipe size	Q-2	3	8	↓	10,200	257		10,457	11,600	
	5600	Flanged, iron, valves are OS&Y										
	5660	2-1/2" pipe size	Q-1	5	3.200	Ea.	1,825	99		1,924	2,150	
	5680	3" pipe size		4.50	3.556		1,950	110		2,060	2,300	
	5700	4" pipe size	↓	3	5.333		2,575	165		2,740	3,075	
	5720	6" pipe size	Q-2	3	8		4,050	257		4,307	4,850	
	5740	8" pipe size		2	12		8,175	385		8,560	9,575	
	5760	10" pipe size	↓	1	24	↓	11,200	770		11,970	13,500	
600	0010	**VACUUM BREAKERS** Hot or cold water										600
	1030	Anti-siphon, brass										
	1040	1/4" size	1 Plum	24	.333	Ea.	18.65	11.50		30.15	38	
	1050	3/8" size		24	.333		18.65	11.50		30.15	38	
	1060	1/2" size		24	.333		21	11.50		32.50	41	
	1080	3/4" size		20	.400		25	13.80		38.80	48.50	
	1100	1" size		19	.421		39	14.50		53.50	65	
	1120	1-1/4" size		15	.533		68.50	18.35		86.85	103	
	1140	1-1/2" size		13	.615		80.50	21		101.50	121	
	1160	2" size	↓	11	.727	↓	125	25		150	176	
	1300	For polished chrome, (1/4" thru 1"), add					50%					
	1900	Vacuum relief, water service, bronze										
	2000	1/2" size	1 Plum	30	.267	Ea.	17.70	9.20		26.90	33.50	
800	0010	**WATER HAMMER ARRESTORS / SHOCK ABSORBERS**										800
	0490	Copper										
	0500	3/4" male I.P.S. For 1 to 11 fixtures	1 Plum	12	.667	Ea.	16.05	23		39.05	52	
	0600	1" male I.P.S., For 12 to 32 fixtures		8	1		41	34.50		75.50	97	
	0700	1-1/4" male I.P.S. For 33 to 60 fixtures		8	1		47.50	34.50		82	105	
	0800	1-1/2" male I.P.S. For 61 to 113 fixtures		8	1		65	34.50		99.50	124	
	0900	2" male I.P.S.For 114 to 154 fixtures		8	1		104	34.50		138.50	166	
	1000	2-1/2" male I.P.S. For 155 to 330 fixtures	↓	4	2	↓	231	69		300	360	

15155 | Drainage Specialties

			CREW	DAILY OUTPUT	LABOR-HOURS	UNIT	MAT.	LABOR	EQUIP.	TOTAL	TOTAL INCL O&P	
160	0010	**CLEANOUTS**										160
	0060	Floor type										
	0080	Round or square, scoriated nickel bronze top										
	0100	2" pipe size	1 Plum	10	.800	Ea.	73.50	27.50		101	123	
	0120	3" pipe size		8	1		110	34.50		144.50	173	
	0140	4" pipe size	↓	6	1.333	↓	110	46		156	191	
	0980	Round top, recessed for terrazzo										
	1000	2" pipe size	1 Plum	9	.889	Ea.	73.50	30.50		104	127	
	1080	3" pipe size		6	1.333		110	46		156	191	
	1100	4" pipe size		4	2		110	69		179	225	
	1120	5" pipe size	Q-1	6	2.667		140	82.50		222.50	279	
170	0010	**CLEANOUT TEE**										170
	0100	Cast iron, B&S, with countersunk plug										
	0200	2" pipe size	1 Plum	4	2	Ea.	100	69		169	214	
	0220	3" pipe size	↓	3.60	2.222	↓	110	76.50		186.50	237	

15155	Drainage Specialties	CREW	DAILY OUTPUT	LABOR-HOURS	UNIT	MAT.	LABOR	EQUIP.	TOTAL	TOTAL INCL O&P	
170							**2001 BARE COSTS**				**170**
0240	4" pipe size	1 Plum	3.30	2.424	Ea.	136	83.50		219.50	276	
0280	6" pipe size	Q-1	5	3.200		365	99		464	555	
0500	For round smooth access cover, same price				▼						
4000	Plastic, tees and adapters. Add plugs										
4010	ABS, DWW										
4020	Cleanout tee, 1-1/2" pipe size	1 Plum	15	.533	Ea.	3.82	18.35		22.17	31.50	
4030	2" pipe size	Q-1	27	.593		5.05	18.35		23.40	33	
4040	3" pipe size		21	.762		10.10	23.50		33.60	46.50	
4050	4" pipe size	▼	16	1		18.85	31		49.85	68	
4100	Cleanout plug, 1-1/2" pipe size	1 Plum	32	.250		.79	8.60		9.39	13.85	
4110	2" pipe size	Q-1	56	.286		.92	8.85		9.77	14.35	
4120	3" pipe size		36	.444		1.54	13.80		15.34	22.50	
4130	4" pipe size	▼	30	.533		3.23	16.55		19.78	28.50	
4180	Cleanout adapter fitting, 1-1/2" pipe size	1 Plum	32	.250		1.24	8.60		9.84	14.35	
4190	2" pipe size	Q-1	56	.286		1.73	8.85		10.58	15.25	
4200	3" pipe size		36	.444		4.91	13.80		18.71	26.50	
4210	4" pipe size	▼	30	.533	▼	8.05	16.55		24.60	34	
5000	PVC, DWV										
5010	Cleanout tee, 1-1/2" pipe size	1 Plum	15	.533	Ea.	1.24	18.35		19.59	29	
5020	2" pipe size	Q-1	27	.593		2.37	18.35		20.72	30	
5030	3" pipe size		21	.762		4.65	23.50		28.15	40.50	
5040	4" pipe size	▼	16	1		8.90	31		39.90	57	
5090	Cleanout plug, 1-1/2" pipe size	1 Plum	32	.250		.72	8.60		9.32	13.80	
5100	2" pipe size	Q-1	56	.286		.89	8.85		9.74	14.35	
5110	3" pipe size		36	.444		1.89	13.80		15.69	23	
5120	4" pipe size		30	.533		2.79	16.55		19.34	28	
5130	6" pipe size	▼	24	.667		8.55	20.50		29.05	40.50	
5170	Cleanout adapter fitting, 1-1/2" pipe size	1 Plum	32	.250		1.07	8.60		9.67	14.20	
5180	2" pipe size	Q-1	56	.286		1.50	8.85		10.35	15	
5190	3" pipe size		36	.444		4.25	13.80		18.05	25.50	
5200	4" pipe size		30	.533		6.95	16.55		23.50	32.50	
5210	6" pipe size	▼	24	.667	▼	15.60	20.50		36.10	48	
300	**DRAINS**										**300**
0010											
0140	Cornice, C.I., 45° or 90° outlet										
0180	1-1/2" & 2" pipe size	Q-1	14	1.143	Ea.	91	35.50		126.50	154	
0200	3" and 4" pipe size	"	12	1.333		124	41.50		165.50	199	
0260	For galvanized body, add					24.50			24.50	27	
0280	For polished bronze dome, add				▼	21			21	23	
0400	Deck, auto park, C.I., 13" top										
0440	3", 4", 5", and 6" pipe size	Q-1	8	2	Ea.	540	62		602	685	
0480	For galvanized body, add				"	255			255	281	
2000	Floor, medium duty, C.I., deep flange, 7" dia top										
2040	2" and 3" pipe size	Q-1	12	1.333	Ea.	75.50	41.50		117	146	
2080	For galvanized body, add					31.50			31.50	35	
2120	For polished bronze top, add				▼	38			38	42	
2400	Heavy duty, with sediment bucket, C.I., 12" dia. loose grate										
2420	2", 3", 4", 5", and 6" pipe size	Q-1	9	1.778	Ea.	259	55		314	370	
2460	For polished bronze top, add				"	107			107	118	
2500	Heavy duty, cleanout & trap w/bucket, C.I., 15" top										
2540	2", 3", and 4" pipe size	Q-1	6	2.667	Ea.	1,975	82.50		2,057.50	2,300	
2560	For galvanized body, add					555			555	610	
2580	For polished bronze top, add				▼	615			615	675	
2780	Shower, with strainer, uniform diam. trap, bronze top										
2800	1-1/2", 2" and 3" pipe size	Q-1	8	2	Ea.	159	62		221	269	
2820	4" pipe size	"	7	2.286		175	71		246	300	
2840	For galvanized body, add					62			62	68.50	

15 MECHANICAL

15155 | Drainage Specialties

			CREW	DAILY OUTPUT	LABOR-HOURS	UNIT	2001 BARE COSTS MAT.	LABOR	EQUIP.	TOTAL	TOTAL INCL O&P	
300	3860	Roof, flat metal deck, C.I. body, 12" C.I. dome										300
	3890	3" pipe size	Q-1	14	1.143	Ea.	147	35.50		182.50	216	
	3920	6" pipe size	"	10	1.600	"	255	49.50		304.50	355	
	4620	Main, all aluminum, 12" low profile dome										
	4640	2", 3" and 4" pipe size	Q-1	14	1.143	Ea.	164	35.50		199.50	234	
	4980	Scupper floor, oblique strainer, C.I.										
	5000	6" x 7" top, 2", 3" and 4" pipe size	Q-1	16	1	Ea.	106	31		137	164	
	5100	8" x 12" top, 5" and 6" pipe size	"	14	1.143		206	35.50		241.50	281	
	5160	For galvanized body, add					40%					
	5200	For polished bronze strainer, add					85%					
	5980	Trench, floor, hvy duty, modular, C.I., 12" x 12" top										
	6000	2", 3", 4", 5", & 6" pipe size	Q-1	8	2	Ea.	335	62		397	465	
	6100	For polished bronze top, add				"	164			164	181	
	6960	Backwater valve, soil pipe, C.I. body										
	6980	Bronze gate and automatic flapper valves										
	7000	3" and 4" pipe size	Q-1	13	1.231	Ea.	665	38		703	790	
	7100	5" and 6" pipe size	"	13	1.231	"	1,075	38		1,113	1,225	
	7240	Bronze flapper valve, bolted cover										
	7260	2" pipe size	Q-1	16	1	Ea.	224	31		255	293	
	7300	4" pipe size	"	13	1.231		430	38		468	535	
	7340	6" pipe size	Q-2	17	1.412		620	45.50		665.50	750	
400	0010	**INTERCEPTORS**										**400**
	0150	Grease, cast iron, 4 GPM, 8 lb. fat capacity	1 Plum	4	2	Ea.	445	69		514	595	
	0200	7 GPM, 14 lb. fat capacity		4	2		615	69		684	785	
	1000	10 GPM, 20 lb. fat capacity		4	2		725	69		794	905	
	1040	15 GPM, 30 lb. fat capacity		4	2		1,075	69		1,144	1,275	
	1060	20 GPM, 40 lb. fat capacity		3	2.667		1,325	92		1,417	1,600	
	1120	Fabricated steel, 50 GPM, 100 lb. fat capacity	Q-1	2	8		2,425	248		2,673	3,025	
	1160	100 GPM, 200 lb. fat capacity	"	2	8		5,475	248		5,723	6,400	
	1560	For chemical add-port, add					97			97	106	
	1580	For seepage pan, add					7%					
	3000	Hair, cast iron, 1-1/4" and 1-1/2" pipe connection	1 Plum	8	1	Ea.	165	34.50		199.50	234	
	3100	For chrome-plated cast iron, add					103			103	113	
	4000	Oil, fabricated steel, 10 GPM, 2" pipe size	1 Plum	4	2		990	69		1,059	1,200	
	4100	15 GPM, 2" or 3" pipe size		4	2		1,350	69		1,419	1,600	
	4120	20 GPM, 2" or 3" pipe size		3	2.667		1,650	92		1,742	1,950	
	4220	100 GPM, 3" pipe size	Q-1	2	8		5,475	248		5,723	6,400	
	6000	Solids, precious metals recovery, C.I., 1-1/4" to 2" pipe	1 Plum	4	2		251	69		320	380	
	6100	Dental Lab., large, C.I., 1-1/2" to 2" pipe	"	3	2.667		880	92		972	1,100	
780	0010	**TRAPS**										**780**
	0030	Cast iron, service weight										
	0050	Running P trap, without vent										
	1100	2"	Q-1	16	1	Ea.	17.85	31		48.85	66.50	
	1140	3"		14	1.143		29	35.50		64.50	85.50	
	1150	4"		13	1.231		52.50	38		90.50	116	
	1160	6"	Q-2	17	1.412		243	45.50		288.50	335	
	1180	Running trap, single hub, with vent										
	2080	3" pipe size, 3" vent	Q-1	14	1.143	Ea.	44	35.50		79.50	102	
	2120	4" pipe size, 4" vent	"	13	1.231		60	38		98	124	
	2300	For double hub, vent, add					10%	20%				
	3000	P trap, B&S, 2" pipe size	Q-1	16	1		13.20	31		44.20	61.50	
	3040	3" pipe size	"	14	1.143		19.50	35.50		55	75	
	3350	Deep seal trap, B&S										
	3400	1-1/4" pipe size	Q-1	14	1.143	Ea.	17.10	35.50		52.60	72.50	
	3410	1-1/2" pipe size		14	1.143		17.10	35.50		52.60	72.50	

MECHANICAL 15

For expanded coverage of these items see *Means Mechanical or Plumbing Cost Data 2001*

15155 | Drainage Specialties

			CREW	DAILY OUTPUT	LABOR-HOURS	UNIT	MAT.	LABOR	EQUIP.	TOTAL	TOTAL INCL O&P	
							\multicolumn{4}{c}{2001 BARE COSTS}			
780	3420	2" pipe size	Q-1	14	1.143	Ea.	17.05	35.50		52.55	72.50	**780**
	3440	3" pipe size	↓	12	1.333		27.50	41.50		69	93	
	3800	Drum trap, 4" x 5", 1-1/2" tapping	Q-2	17	1.412		13.50	45.50		59	83.50	
	3820	2" tapping	"	17	1.412		13.50	45.50		59	83.50	
	3840	For galvanized, add				↓	60%					
	4700	Copper, drainage, drum trap										
	4800	3" x 5" solid, 1-1/2" pipe size	1 Plum	16	.500	Ea.	16.70	17.25		33.95	44.50	
	4840	3" x 6" swivel, 1-1/2" pipe size	"	16	.500	"	24.50	17.25		41.75	53	
	5100	P trap, standard pattern										
	5200	1-1/4" pipe size	1 Plum	18	.444	Ea.	11.90	15.30		27.20	36	
	5240	1-1/2" pipe size		17	.471		11.90	16.20		28.10	37.50	
	5260	2" pipe size		15	.533		18.35	18.35		36.70	47.50	
	5280	3" pipe size	↓	11	.727	↓	44.50	25		69.50	87	
	5340	With cleanout and slip joint										
	5360	1-1/4" pipe size	1 Plum	18	.444	Ea.	16.85	15.30		32.15	41.50	
	5400	1-1/2" pipe size	"	17	.471	"	17.20	16.20		33.40	43.50	
940	0010	**VENT FLASHING**										**940**
	1000	Aluminum with lead ring										
	1020	1-1/4" pipe	1 Plum	20	.400	Ea.	6.40	13.80		20.20	28	
	1030	1-1/2" pipe		20	.400		6.40	13.80		20.20	28	
	1040	2" pipe		18	.444		6.85	15.30		22.15	30.50	
	1050	3" pipe		17	.471		7.60	16.20		23.80	33	
	1060	4" pipe	↓	16	.500	↓	9.15	17.25		26.40	36	
	1350	Copper with neoprene ring										
	1400	1-1/4" pipe	1 Plum	20	.400	Ea.	14.05	13.80		27.85	36.50	
	1430	1-1/2" pipe		20	.400		14.05	13.80		27.85	36.50	
	1440	2" pipe		18	.444		14.85	15.30		30.15	39.50	
	1450	3" pipe		17	.471		17.40	16.20		33.60	43.50	
	1460	4" pipe	↓	16	.500	↓	19.20	17.25		36.45	47	

15180 | Heating and Cooling Piping

			CREW	DAILY OUTPUT	LABOR-HOURS	UNIT	MAT.	LABOR	EQUIP.	TOTAL	TOTAL INCL O&P	
200	0010	**PUMPS, CIRCULATING** Heated or chilled water application										**200**
	0600	Bronze, sweat connections, 1/40 HP, in line										
	0640	3/4" size	Q-1	16	1	Ea.	114	31		145	172	
	1000	Flange connection, 3/4" to 1-1/2" size										
	1040	1/12 HP	Q-1	6	2.667	Ea.	310	82.50		392.50	465	
	1060	1/8 HP		6	2.667		535	82.50		617.50	710	
	1100	1/3 HP		6	2.667		595	82.50		677.50	780	
	1140	2" size, 1/6 HP		5	3.200		765	99		864	990	
	1180	2-1/2" size, 1/4 HP	↓	5	3.200	↓	995	99		1,094	1,250	
	2000	Cast iron, flange connection										
	2040	3/4" to 1-1/2" size, in line, 1/12 HP	Q-1	6	2.667	Ea.	202	82.50		284.50	345	
	2100	1/3 HP		6	2.667		380	82.50		462.50	540	
	2140	2" size, 1/6 HP		5	3.200		415	99		514	605	
	2180	2-1/2" size, 1/4 HP		5	3.200		540	99		639	745	
	2220	3" size, 1/4 HP	↓	4	4	↓	550	124		674	790	
	2600	For non-ferrous impeller, add					3%					
300	0010	**PUMPS, CONDENSATE RETURN SYSTEM**										**300**
	0200	Simplex, 3/4 H.P. mtr, float switch, controls, 10 Gal. C.I. rcvr, 6-15GPM	Q-1	1	16	Ea.	1,300	495		1,795	2,175	
	1000	Duplex, 2 pumps, 3/4 H.P. motors, float switch,										
	1060	alternator asssembly, 15 Gal. C.I. receiver	Q-1	.50	32	Ea.	1,800	990		2,790	3,475	
800	0010	**STEAM CONDENSATE METER**										**800**
	0100	500 lb. per hour	1 Stpi	14	.571	Ea.	2,300	19.90		2,319.90	2,550	
	0140	1500 lb. per hour	"	7	1.143	"	2,475	40		2,515	2,775	

Important: See the Reference Section for critical supporting data - Reference Nos., Crews, & City Cost Indexes

15 MECHANICAL

15230	**Industrial Process Piping**	CREW	DAILY OUTPUT	LABOR-HOURS	UNIT	2001 BARE COSTS				TOTAL INCL O&P	
						MAT.	LABOR	EQUIP.	TOTAL		
500	0010	**PUMPS, GENERAL UTILITY** With motor										**500**
	0200	Multi-stage, horizontal split, for boiler feed applications										
	0300	Two stage, 3" discharge x 4" suction, 75 HP	Q-7	.30	106	Ea.	14,900	3,550		18,450	21,800	
	0340	Four stage, 3" discharge x 4" suction, 150 HP	"	.18	177	"	24,500	5,900		30,400	35,900	
	2000	Single stage										
	2060	End suction, 1"D. x 2"S., 3 HP	Q-1	.50	32	Ea.	3,650	990		4,640	5,500	
	2100	1-1/2"D. x 3"S., 10 HP	"	.40	40		3,925	1,250		5,175	6,200	
	2140	2"D. x 3"S., 15 HP	Q-2	.60	40		4,275	1,275		5,550	6,650	
	3000	Double suction, 2"D. x 2-1/2"S., 10 HP	Q-1	.30	53.333		5,050	1,650		6,700	8,050	
	3060	3"D. x 4"S., 15 HP	Q-2	.46	52.174		5,200	1,675		6,875	8,250	
	3180	6"D. x 8"S., 60 HP	Q-3	.30	106		8,475	3,500		11,975	14,600	
	3190	75 HP, to 2500 GPM		.28	114		10,500	3,750		14,250	17,200	
	3220	100 HP, to 3000 GPM		.26	123		13,300	4,050		17,350	20,800	
	3240	150 HP, to 4000 GPM		.24	133		17,900	4,375		22,275	26,300	

15410	**Plumbing Fixtures**	CREW	DAILY OUTPUT	LABOR-HOURS	UNIT	2001 BARE COSTS				TOTAL INCL O&P	
						MAT.	LABOR	EQUIP.	TOTAL		
040	0010	**FIXTURES** Includes trim fittings unless otherwise noted	R15100 -420									**040**
	0080	For rough-in, supply, waste, and vent, see add for each type										
	0120	For electric water coolers, see division 15413										
	0160	For color, unless otherwise noted, add				Ea.	20%					
200	0010	**CARRIERS/SUPPORTS** For plumbing fixtures										**200**
	0500	Drinking fountain, wall mounted										
	0600	Plate type with studs, top back plate	1 Plum	7	1.143	Ea.	26.50	39.50		66	88.50	
	0700	Top front and back plate		7	1.143		33	39.50		72.50	95.50	
	0800	Top & bottom, front & back plates, w/bearing jacks		7	1.143		47.50	39.50		87	112	
	3000	Lavatory, concealed arm										
	3050	Floor mounted, single										
	3100	High back fixture	1 Plum	6	1.333	Ea.	161	46		207	247	
	3200	Flat slab fixture		6	1.333		188	46		234	276	
	3220	Paraplegic		6	1.333		136	46		182	220	
	3250	Floor mounted, back to back										
	3300	High back fixtures	1 Plum	5	1.600	Ea.	230	55		285	335	
	3400	Flat slab fixtures		5	1.600		282	55		337	395	
	3430	Paraplegic		5	1.600		191	55		246	293	
	3500	Wall mounted, in stud or masonry										
	3600	High back fixture	1 Plum	6	1.333	Ea.	75.50	46		121.50	153	
	3700	Flat slab fixture	"	6	1.333	"	122	46		168	204	
	4600	Sink, floor mounted										
	4650	Exposed arm system										
	4700	Single heavy fixture	1 Plum	5	1.600	Ea.	298	55		353	410	
	4750	Single heavy sink with slab		5	1.600		201	55		256	305	
	4800	Back to back, standard fixtures		5	1.600		230	55		285	335	
	4850	Back to back, heavy fixtures		5	1.600		268	55		323	380	
	4900	Back to back, heavy sink with slab		5	1.600		268	55		323	380	
	4950	Exposed offset arm system										
	5000	Single heavy deep fixture	1 Plum	5	1.600	Ea.	256	55		311	365	
	5100	Plate type system										
	5200	With bearing jacks, single fixture	1 Plum	5	1.600	Ea.	271	55		326	380	

MECHANICAL 15

For expanded coverage of these items see *Means Mechanical or Plumbing Cost Data 2001*

	15410	Plumbing Fixtures	CREW	DAILY OUTPUT	LABOR-HOURS	UNIT	2001 BARE COSTS				TOTAL INCL O&P	
							MAT.	LABOR	EQUIP.	TOTAL		
200	5300	With exposed arms, single heavy fixture	1 Plum	5	1.600	Ea.	350	55		405	465	200
	5400	Wall mounted, exposed arms, single heavy fixture		5	1.600		126	55		181	222	
	6000	Urinal, floor mounted, 2″ or 3″ coupling, blowout type		6	1.333		171	46		217	258	
	6100	With fixture or hanger bolts, blowout or washout		6	1.333		122	46		168	204	
	6200	With bearing plate		6	1.333		136	46		182	220	
	6300	Wall mounted, plate type system		6	1.333		97	46		143	176	
	6980	Water closet, siphon jet										
	7000	Horizontal, adjustable, caulk										
	7040	Single, 4″ pipe size	1 Plum	6	1.333	Ea.	205	46		251	296	
	7050	4″ pipe size, paraplegic		6	1.333		205	46		251	296	
	7060	5″ pipe size		6	1.333		271	46		317	370	
	7100	Double, 4″ pipe size		5	1.600		385	55		440	505	
	7110	4″ pipe size, paraplegic		5	1.600		205	55		260	310	
	7120	5″ pipe size		5	1.600		271	55		326	380	
	7160	Horizontal, adjustable, extended, caulk										
	7180	Single, 4″ pipe size	1 Plum	6	1.333	Ea.	205	46		251	296	
	7200	5″ pipe size		6	1.333		365	46		411	475	
	7240	Double, 4″ pipe size		5	1.600		277	55		332	390	
	7260	5″ pipe size		5	1.600		365	55		420	490	
	7400	Vertical, adjustable, caulk or thread										
	7440	Single, 4″ pipe size	1 Plum	6	1.333	Ea.	242	46		288	335	
	7460	5″ pipe size		6	1.333		305	46		351	405	
	7480	6″ pipe size		5	1.600		360	55		415	480	
	7520	Double, 4″ pipe size		5	1.600		420	55		475	550	
	7540	5″ pipe size		5	1.600		485	55		540	620	
	7560	6″ pipe size		4	2		535	69		604	695	
	7600	Vertical, adjustable, extended, caulk										
	7620	Single, 4″ pipe size	1 Plum	6	1.333	Ea.	242	46		288	335	
	7640	5″ pipe size		6	1.333		305	46		351	405	
	7680	6″ pipe size		5	1.600		360	55		415	480	
	7720	Double, 4″ pipe size		5	1.600		420	55		475	550	
	7740	5″ pipe size		5	1.600		485	55		540	620	
	7760	6″ pipe size		4	2		535	69		604	695	
	7780	Water closet, blow out										
	7800	Vertical offset, caulk or thread										
	7820	Single, 4″ pipe size	1 Plum	6	1.333	Ea.	232	46		278	325	
	7840	Double, 4″ pipe size	″	5	1.600	″	395	55		450	520	
	7880	Vertical offset, extended, caulk										
	7900	Single, 4″ pipe size	1 Plum	6	1.333	Ea.	291	46		337	390	
	7920	Double, 4″ pipe size	″	5	1.600	″	455	55		510	585	
	7960	Vertical, for floor mounted back-outlet										
	7980	Single, 4″ thread, 2″ vent	1 Plum	6	1.333	Ea.	187	46		233	276	
	8000	Double, 4″ thread, 2″ vent	″	6	1.333	″	335	46		381	440	
	8040	Vertical, for floor mounted back-outlet, extended										
	8060	Single, 4″ caulk, 2″ vent	1 Plum	6	1.333	Ea.	179	46		225	267	
	8080	Double, 4″ caulk, 2″ vent	″	6	1.333	″	278	46		324	375	
	8200	Water closet, residential										
	8220	Vertical centerline, floor mount										
	8240	Single, 3″ caulk, 2″ or 3″ vent	1 Plum	6	1.333	Ea.	185	46		231	274	
	8260	4″ caulk, 2″ or 4″ vent		6	1.333		233	46		279	325	
	8280	3″ copper sweat, 3″ vent		6	1.333		185	46		231	274	
	8300	4″ copper sweat, 4″ vent		6	1.333		233	46		279	325	
	8400	Vertical offset, floor mount										
	8420	Single, 3″ or 4″ caulk, vent	1 Plum	4	2	Ea.	232	69		301	360	
	8440	3″ or 4″ copper sweat, vent		5	1.600		232	55		287	340	
	8460	Double, 3″ or 4″ caulk, vent		4	2		395	69		464	540	

   Important: See the Reference Section for critical supporting data - Reference Nos., Crews, & City Cost Indexes

		15410	Plumbing Fixtures	CREW	DAILY OUTPUT	LABOR-HOURS	UNIT	2001 BARE COSTS				TOTAL INCL O&P	
								MAT.	LABOR	EQUIP.	TOTAL		
200	8480		3" or 4" copper sweat, vent	1 Plum	5	1.600	Ea.	395	55		450	520	200
	9000		Water cooler (electric), floor mounted										
	9100		Plate type with bearing plate, single	1 Plum	6	1.333	Ea.	108	46		154	189	
300	0010	**FAUCETS/FITTINGS**											300
	0150		Bath, faucets, diverter spout combination, sweat	1 Plum	8	1	Ea.	102	34.50		136.50	164	
	0200		For integral stops, IPS unions, add					68.50			68.50	75.50	
	0420		Bath, press-bal mix valve w/diverter, spout, shower hd, arm/flange	1 Plum	8	1	↓	102	34.50		136.50	164	
	0810		Bidet										
	0812		Fitting, over the rim, swivel spray/pop-up drain	1 Plum	8	1	Ea.	126	34.50		160.50	190	
	0840		Flush valves, with vacuum breaker										
	0850		Water closet										
	0860		Exposed, rear spud	1 Plum	8	1	Ea.	106	34.50		140.50	169	
	0920		Urinal										
	0930		Exposed, stall	1 Plum	8	1	Ea.	97.50	34.50		132	159	
	0940		Wall, (washout)		8	1		97.50	34.50		132	159	
	0950		Pedestal, top spud		8	1		99	34.50		133.50	161	
	0960		Concealed, stall		8	1		112	34.50		146.50	175	
	0970		Wall (washout)	↓	8	1	↓	115	34.50		149.50	179	
	0971		Automatic flush sensor and operator for										
	0972		urinals or water closets	1 Plum	16	.500	Ea.	320	17.25		337.25	375	
	1000		Kitchen sink faucets, top mount, cast spout		10	.800		48	27.50		75.50	94.50	
	1100		For spray, add		24	.333		12	11.50		23.50	30.50	
	2000		Laundry faucets, shelf type, IPS or copper unions		12	.667		39.50	23		62.50	78	
	2100		Lavatory faucet, centerset, without drain		10	.800		35	27.50		62.50	79.50	
	2810		Automatic sensor and operator, with faucet head		6.15	1.301		284	45		329	385	
	3000		Service sink faucet, cast spout, pail hook, hose end		14	.571		67.50	19.70		87.20	104	
	4000		Shower by-pass valve with union		18	.444		47.50	15.30		62.80	75	
	4200		Shower thermostatic mixing valve, concealed		8	1		226	34.50		260.50	300	
	5000		Sillcock, compact, brass, IPS or copper to hose	↓	24	.333	↓	4.94	11.50		16.44	23	
		15411	Commercial/Indust Fixtures										
400	0010	**HOT WATER DISPENSERS**											400
	0160		Commercial, 100 cup, 11.3 amp	1 Plum	14	.571	Ea.	305	19.70		324.70	365	
	3180		Household, 60 cup	"	14	.571	"	154	19.70		173.70	199	
500	0010	**HYDRANTS**											500
	0050		Wall type, moderate climate, bronze, encased										
	0200		3/4" IPS connection	1 Plum	16	.500	Ea.	226	17.25		243.25	275	
	0300		1" IPS connection	"	14	.571		226	19.70		245.70	279	
	0500		Anti-siphon type				↓	30.50			30.50	33.50	
	1000		Non-freeze, bronze, exposed										
	1100		3/4" IPS connection, 4" to 9" thick wall	1 Plum	14	.571	Ea.	153	19.70		172.70	199	
	1120		10" to 14" thick wall		12	.667		166	23		189	218	
	1140		15" to 19" thick wall		12	.667		185	23		208	239	
	1160		20" to 24" thick wall	↓	10	.800	↓	201	27.50		228.50	263	
	1200		For 1" IPS connection, add					15%	10%				
	1240		For 3/4" adapter type vacuum breaker, add				Ea.	19.25			19.25	21	
	1280		For anti-siphon type				"	40.50			40.50	44.50	
	2000		Non-freeze bronze, encased										
	2100		3/4" IPS connection, 5" to 9" thick wall	1 Plum	14	.571	Ea.	264	19.70		283.70	320	
	2140		15" to 19" thick wall	"	12	.667	↓	297	23		320	360	
	2280		Anti-siphon type				↓	124			124	136	
	3000		Ground box type, bronze frame, 3/4" IPS connection										
	3080		Non-freeze, all bronze, polished face, set flush										
	3100		2 feet depth of bury	1 Plum	8	1	Ea.	282	34.50		316.50	360	

MECHANICAL 15

15411	Commercial/Indust Fixtures		CREW	DAILY OUTPUT	LABOR-HOURS	UNIT	2001 BARE COSTS				TOTAL INCL O&P	
							MAT.	LABOR	EQUIP.	TOTAL		
500	3180	6 feet depth of bury	1 Plum	7	1.143	Ea.	370	39.50		409.50	465	500
	3220	8 feet depth of bury	↓	5	1.600		415	55		470	540	
	3400	For 1" IPS connection, add					15%	10%				
	3550	For 2" connection, add					445%	24%				
	3600	For tapped drain port in box, add				↓	25.50			25.50	28.50	
	5000	Moderate climate, all bronze, polished face										
	5020	and scoriated cover, set flush										
	5100	3/4" IPS connection	1 Plum	16	.500	Ea.	201	17.25		218.25	247	
	5120	1" IPS connection	"	14	.571		200	19.70		219.70	250	
	5200	For tapped drain port in box, add				↓	25.50			25.50	28.50	
700	0010	**URINALS**										700
	3000	Wall hung, vitreous china, with hanger & self-closing valve										
	3100	Siphon jet type	Q-1	3	5.333	Ea.	279	165		444	555	
	3120	Blowout type		3	5.333		320	165		485	600	
	3300	Rough-in, supply, waste & vent		2.83	5.654		80.50	175		255.50	355	
	5000	Stall type, vitreous china, includes valve		2.50	6.400		450	198		648	795	
	5100	3" seam cover, add		12	1.333		118	41.50		159.50	193	
	5200	6" seam cover, add		12	1.333		164	41.50		205.50	243	
	6980	Rough-in, supply, waste and vent	↓	1.99	8.040	↓	99	249		348	485	
840	0010	**WASH FOUNTAINS** Rigging not included										840
	1900	Group, foot control										
	2000	Precast terrazzo, circular, 36" diam., 5 or 6 persons	Q-2	3	8	Ea.	2,275	257		2,532	2,900	
	2100	54" diameter for 8 or 10 persons		2.50	9.600		2,750	310		3,060	3,500	
	2400	Semi-circular, 36" diam. for 3 persons		3	8		2,050	257		2,307	2,650	
	2500	54" diam. for 4 or 5 persons		2.50	9.600		2,525	310		2,835	3,250	
	2700	Quarter circle (corner), 54" for 3 persons		3.50	6.857		2,525	220		2,745	3,100	
	3000	Stainless steel, circular, 36" diameter		3.50	6.857		2,650	220		2,870	3,225	
	3100	54" diameter		2.80	8.571		3,475	276		3,751	4,250	
	3400	Semi-circular, 36" diameter		3.50	6.857		2,275	220		2,495	2,825	
	3500	54" diameter	↓	2.80	8.571	↓	3,000	276		3,276	3,725	
	5610	Group, infrared control, barrier free										
	5614	Precast terrazzo										
	5620	Semi-circular 36" diam. for 3 persons	Q-2	3	8	Ea.	3,000	257		3,257	3,700	
	5630	46" diam. for 4 persons		2.80	8.571		3,350	276		3,626	4,125	
	5640	Circular, 54" diam. for 8 persons, button control	↓	2.50	9.600		5,150	310		5,460	6,150	
	5700	Rough-in, supply, waste and vent for above wash fountains	Q-1	1.82	8.791		82.50	273		355.50	500	
	6200	Duo for small washrooms, stainless steel		2	8		1,550	248		1,798	2,100	
	6500	Rough-in, supply, waste & vent for duo fountains	↓	2.02	7.921	↓	46	246		292	420	

15412	Drinking Fountains											
200	0010	**DRINKING FOUNTAIN** For connection to cold water supply										200
	1000	Wall mounted, non-recessed										
	1400	Bronze, with no back	1 Plum	4	2	Ea.	990	69		1,059	1,200	
	1800	Cast aluminum, enameled, for correctional institutions [R15100 -420]		4	2		595	69		664	760	
	2000	Fiberglass, 12" back, single bubbler unit		4	2		530	69		599	690	
	2040	Dual bubbler		3.20	2.500		770	86		856	975	
	2400	Precast stone, no back		4	2		480	69		549	635	
	2700	Stainless steel, single bubbler, no back		4	2		795	69		864	980	
	2740	With back		4	2		945	69		1,014	1,150	
	2780	Dual handle & wheelchair projection type		4	2		495	69		564	650	
	2820	Dual level for handicapped type	↓	3.20	2.500	↓	1,000	86		1,086	1,225	
	3300	Vitreous china										
	3340	7" back	1 Plum	4	2	Ea.	405	69		474	550	
	3940	For vandal-resistant bottom plate, add	↓			↓	50.50			50.50	56	

15412 | Drinking Fountains

			CREW	DAILY OUTPUT	LABOR-HOURS	UNIT	MAT.	LABOR	EQUIP.	TOTAL	TOTAL INCL O&P	
							\multicolumn{4}{c}{2001 BARE COSTS}			
200	3960	For freeze-proof valve system, add	1 Plum	2	4	Ea.	400	138		538	650	**200**
	3980	For rough-in, supply and waste, add	"	2.21	3.620	↓	35	125		160	227	
	4000	Wall mounted, semi-recessed										
	4200	Poly-marble, single bubbler	1 Plum	4	2	Ea.	645	69		714	815	
	4600	Stainless steel, satin finish, single bubbler		4	2		755	69		824	935	
	4900	Vitreous china, single bubbler		4	2		435	69		504	580	
	5980	For rough-in, supply and waste, add	↓	1.83	4.372	↓	35	151		186	266	
	6000	Wall mounted, fully recessed										
	6400	Poly-marble, single bubbler	1 Plum	4	2	Ea.	725	69		794	905	
	6800	Stainless steel, single bubbler		4	2		635	69		704	800	
	7560	For freeze-proof valve system, add		2	4		495	138		633	755	
	7580	For rough-in, supply and waste, add	↓	1.83	4.372	↓	35	151		186	266	
	7600	Floor mounted, pedestal type										
	7700	Aluminum, architectural style, C.I. base	1 Plum	2	4	Ea.	440	138		578	690	
	7780	Wheelchair handicap unit		2	4		1,025	138		1,163	1,350	
	8400	Stainless steel, architectural style		2	4		1,125	138		1,263	1,450	
	8600	Enameled iron, heavy duty service, 2 bubblers		2	4		1,050	138		1,188	1,350	
	8660	4 bubblers		2	4		1,125	138		1,263	1,425	
	8880	For freeze-proof valve system, add		2	4		320	138		458	560	
	8900	For rough-in, supply and waste, add	↓	1.83	4.372	↓	35	151		186	266	
	9100	Deck mounted										
	9500	Stainless steel, circular receptor	1 Plum	4	2	Ea.	281	69		350	415	
	9760	White enameled steel, 14" x 9" receptor		4	2		240	69		309	370	
	9860	White enameled cast iron, 24" x 16" receptor		3	2.667		230	92		322	390	
	9980	For rough-in, supply and waste, add	↓	1.83	4.372	↓	35	151		186	266	

R15100 -420

15413 | Electric Water Coolers

			CREW	DAILY OUTPUT	LABOR-HOURS	UNIT	MAT.	LABOR	EQUIP.	TOTAL	TOTAL INCL O&P	
900	0010	**WATER COOLER**										**900**
	0030	See line 15413-900-9800 for rough-in, waste & vent										
	0040	for all water coolers										
	0100	Wall mounted, non-recessed										
	0140	4 GPH	Q-1	4	4	Ea.	475	124		599	705	
	0160	8 GPH, barrier free, sensor operated		4	4		620	124		744	870	
	0180	8.2 GPH	↓	4	4		540	124		664	775	
	0600	For hot and cold water, add					138			138	151	
	0640	For stainless steel cabinet, add					67			67	74	
	1000	Dual height, 8.2 GPH	Q-1	3.80	4.211		780	131		911	1,050	
	1040	14.3 GPH	"	3.80	4.211		815	131		946	1,100	
	1240	For stainless steel cabinet, add					112			112	123	
	2600	Wheelchair type, 8 GPH	Q-1	4	4		1,375	124		1,499	1,700	
	3300	Semi-recessed, 8.1 GPH		4	4		785	124		909	1,050	
	3320	12 GPH	↓	4	4	↓	830	124		954	1,100	
	4600	Floor mounted, flush-to-wall										
	4640	4 GPH	1 Plum	3	2.667	Ea.	480	92		572	670	
	4680	8.2 GPH		3	2.667		540	92		632	730	
	4720	14.3 GPH	↓	3	2.667		565	92		657	765	
	4960	For hot and cold water, add					250			250	275	
	4980	For stainless steel cabinet, add					96			96	106	
	5000	Dual height, 8.2 GPH	1 Plum	2	4		845	138		983	1,150	
	5040	14.3 GPH	"	2	4		860	138		998	1,150	
	5120	For stainless steel cabinet, add					144			144	158	
	9800	For supply, waste & vent, all coolers	1 Plum	2.21	3.620	↓	35	125		160	227	

R15100 -430

MECHANICAL 15

15414	Emergency Fixtures	CREW	DAILY OUTPUT	LABOR-HOURS	UNIT	2001 BARE COSTS				TOTAL INCL O&P	
						MAT.	LABOR	EQUIP.	TOTAL		
200	0010	**INDUSTRIAL SAFETY FIXTURES** Rough-in not included									200
	1000	Eye wash fountain									
	1400	Plastic bowl, pedestal mounted	Q-1	4	4	Ea.	182	124		306	390
	1600	Unmounted		4	4		131	124		255	330
	1800	Wall mounted		4	4		134	124		258	335
	2000	Stainless steel, pedestal mounted		4	4		273	124		397	485
	2200	Unmounted		4	4		182	124		306	390
	2400	Wall mounted		4	4		174	124		298	380
	3000	Eye wash, portable, self-contained					375			375	410
	4000	Eye and face wash, combination fountain									
	4200	Stainless steel, pedestal mounted	Q-1	4	4	Ea.	390	124		514	615
	4400	Unmounted		4	4		294	124		418	510
	4600	Wall mounted		4	4		300	124		424	515
	5000	Shower, single head, drench, ball valve, pull, freestanding		4	4		255	124		379	465
	5200	Horizontal or vertical supply		4	4		232	124		356	445
	6000	Multi-nozzle, eye/face wash combination		4	4		480	124		604	715
	6400	Multi-nozzle, 12 spray, shower only		4	4		1,100	124		1,224	1,375
	6600	For freeze-proof, add		6	2.667		268	82.50		350.50	420

15418	Resi/Comm/Industrial Fixtures	CREW	DAILY OUTPUT	LABOR-HOURS	UNIT	MAT.	LABOR	EQUIP.	TOTAL	TOTAL INCL O&P	
100	0010	**BATHS**									100
	0100	Tubs, recessed porcelain enamel on cast iron, with trim									
	0140	42" x 37"	Q-1	5	3.200	Ea.	710	99		809	930
	0180	48" x 42"		4	4		1,050	124		1,174	1,325
	0220	72" x 36"		3	5.333		1,175	165		1,340	1,550
	2000	Enameled formed steel, 4'-6" long		5.80	2.759		277	85.50		362.50	435
	2200	5' long		5.50	2.909		261	90		351	425
	4000	Soaking, acrylic with pop-up drain, 60" x 32" x 21" deep		5.50	2.909		730	90		820	940
	4100	60" x 48" x 18-1/2" deep		5	3.200		590	99		689	800
	6000	Whirlpool, bath with vented overflow, molded fiberglass									
	6100	66" x 48" x 24"	Q-1	1	16	Ea.	2,050	495		2,545	3,000
	9600	Rough-in, supply, waste and vent, for all above tubs, add	"	2.07	7.729	"	101	240		341	470
400	0010	**LAUNDRY SINKS** With trim									400
	0020	Porcelain enamel on cast iron, black iron frame									
	0050	24" x 20", single compartment	Q-1	6	2.667	Ea.	340	82.50		422.50	495
	0100	24" x 23", single compartment	"	6	2.667	"	365	82.50		447.50	530
	2000	Molded stone, on wall hanger or legs									
	2020	22" x 23", single compartment	Q-1	6	2.667	Ea.	117	82.50		199.50	254
	2100	45" x 21", double compartment	"	5	3.200	"	243	99		342	415
	3000	Plastic, on wall hanger or legs									
	3020	18" x 23", single compartment	Q-1	6.50	2.462	Ea.	82	76.50		158.50	206
	3300	40" x 24", double compartment		5.50	2.909		187	90		277	340
	5000	Stainless steel, counter top, 22" x 17" single compartment		6	2.667		270	82.50		352.50	420
	5100	22" x 22", single compartment		6	2.667		340	82.50		422.50	500
	5200	33" x 22", double compartment		5	3.200		315	99		414	495
	9600	Rough-in, supply, waste and vent, for all laundry sinks		2.14	7.477		63	232		295	420
450	0010	**LAVATORIES** With trim, white unless noted otherwise									450
	0500	Vanity top, porcelain enamel on cast iron [R15100-420]									
	0600	20" x 18"	Q-1	6.40	2.500	Ea.	156	77.50		233.50	289
	0640	33" x 19" oval		6.40	2.500		335	77.50		412.50	485
	0720	19" round		6.40	2.500		144	77.50		221.50	276
	0860	For color, add					25%				
	1000	Cultured marble, 19" x 17", single bowl	Q-1	6.40	2.500	Ea.	101	77.50		178.50	228
	1040	25" x 19", single bowl	"	6.40	2.500	"	128	77.50		205.50	258
	1580	For color, same price									
	1900	Stainless steel, self-rimming, 25" x 22", single bowl, ledge	Q-1	6.40	2.500	Ea.	162	77.50		239.50	295

15 MECHANICAL

15418	Resi/Comm/Industrial Fixtures	CREW	DAILY OUTPUT	LABOR-HOURS	UNIT	2001 BARE COSTS				TOTAL INCL O&P	
						MAT.	LABOR	EQUIP.	TOTAL		
450	1960	17" x 22", single bowl R15100-420	Q-1	6.40	2.500	Ea.	157	77.50		234.50	290	**450**
	2600	Steel, enameled, 20" x 17", single bowl		5.80	2.759		84.50	85.50		170	222
	2660	19" round		5.80	2.759		82.50	85.50		168	220
	2900	Vitreous china, 20" x 16", single bowl		5.40	2.963		168	92		260	325
	2960	20" x 17", single bowl		5.40	2.963		102	92		194	252
	3020	19" round, single bowl		5.40	2.963		101	92		193	250
	3200	22" x 13", single bowl		5.40	2.963		176	92		268	335
	3560	For color, add					50%				
	3580	Rough-in, supply, waste and vent for all above lavatories	Q-1	2.30	6.957	Ea.	55.50	216		271.50	385
	4000	Wall hung									
	4040	Porcelain enamel on cast iron, 16" x 14", single bowl	Q-1	8	2	Ea.	273	62		335	395
	4180	20" x 18", single bowl		8	2		184	62		246	296
	4240	22" x 19", single bowl		8	2		335	62		397	465
	4580	For color, add					30%				
	6000	Vitreous china, 18" x 15", single bowl with backsplash	Q-1	7	2.286	Ea.	136	71		207	256
	6180	19" x 19", corner style	"	8	2	"	360	62		422	495
	6500	For color, add					30%				
	6960	Rough-in, supply, waste and vent for above lavatories	Q-1	1.66	9.639	Ea.	187	299		486	655
500	0010	**SHOWERS**										**500**
	1500	Stall, with drain only. Add for valve and door/curtain									
	3000	Fiberglass, one piece, with 3 walls, 32" x 32" square	Q-1	2.40	6.667	Ea.	291	207		498	630
	3100	36" x 36" square		2.40	6.667		335	207		542	675
	3250	64" x 65-3/4" x 81-1/2" fold. seat, whlchr.		1.80	8.889		2,675	276		2,951	3,375
	4000	Polypropylene, with molded-stone floor, 30" x 30"		2	8		370	248		618	785
	4200	Rough-in, supply, waste and vent for above showers		2.05	7.805		58	242		300	430
	4520	Showers, fiberglass receptor only	1 Plum	8	1		155	34.50		189.50	223
	5000	Built-in, head, arm, 4 GPM valve		4	2		73.50	69		142.50	185
	5200	Head, arm, by-pass, integral stops, handles		3.60	2.222		189	76.50		265.50	325
	6000	Group, w/pressure balancing valve, rough-in and rigging not included									
	6800	Column, 6 heads, no receptors, less partitions	Q-1	3	5.333	Ea.	1,450	165		1,615	1,825
	6900	With stainless steel partitions		1	16		3,350	495		3,845	4,450
	7600	5 heads, no receptors, less partitions		3	5.333		1,200	165		1,365	1,575
	7700	With stainless steel partitions		1	16		1,200	495		1,695	2,075
	8000	Wall, 2 heads, no receptors, less partitions		4	4		720	124		844	975
	8100	With stainless steel partitions		2	8		1,675	248		1,923	2,225
600	0010	**SINKS** With faucets and drain										**600**
	2000	Kitchen, counter top style, P.E. on C.I., 24" x 21" single bowl	Q-1	5.60	2.857	Ea.	186	88.50		274.50	340
	2100	31" x 22" single bowl R15100-420		5.60	2.857		325	88.50		413.50	495
	2200	32" x 21" double bowl		4.80	3.333		267	103		370	450
	2300	42" x 21" double bowl		4.80	3.333		440	103		543	640
	3000	Stainless steel, self rimming, 19" x 18" single bowl		5.60	2.857		280	88.50		368.50	445
	3100	25" x 22" single bowl		5.60	2.857		310	88.50		398.50	475
	4000	Steel, enameled, with ledge, 24" x 21" single bowl		5.60	2.857		99.50	88.50		188	243
	4100	32" x 21" double bowl		4.80	3.333		126	103		229	294
	4960	For color sinks except stainless steel, add					10%				
	4980	For rough-in, supply, waste and vent, counter top sinks	Q-1	2.14	7.477		63	232		295	420
	5000	Kitchen, raised deck, P.E. on C.I.									
	5100	32" x 21", dual level, double bowl	Q-1	2.60	6.154	Ea.	360	191		551	685
	5700	For color, add					20%				
	5790	For rough-in, supply, waste & vent, sinks	Q-1	1.85	8.649		63	268		331	475
	6650	Service, floor, corner, P.E. on C.I., 28" x 28"		4.40	3.636		475	113		588	690
	6790	For rough-in, supply, waste & vent, floor service sinks		1.64	9.756		127	300		427	595
	7000	Service, wall, P.E. on C.I., roll rim, 22" x 18"		4	4		405	124		529	630
	7100	24" x 20"		4	4		445	124		569	675
	8600	Vitreous china, 22" x 20"		4	4		380	124		504	605

MECHANICAL 15

15418 | Resi/Comm/Industrial Fixtures

			DAILY OUTPUT	LABOR-HOURS	UNIT	2001 BARE COSTS				TOTAL INCL O&P	
			CREW			MAT.	LABOR	EQUIP.	TOTAL		
600	8960	For stainless steel rim guard, front or side, add				Ea.	31			31	34	**600**
	8980	For rough-in, supply, waste & vent, wall service sinks	Q-1	1.30	12.308	↓	245	380		625	845	
900	0010	**WATER CLOSETS**										**900**
	0030	For automatic flush, see 15410-300-0972										
	0150	Tank type, vitreous china, incl. seat, supply pipe w/stop										
	0200	Wall hung, one piece	Q-1	5.30	3.019	Ea.	425	93.50		518.50	610	
	0400	Two piece, close coupled		5.30	3.019		480	93.50		573.50	665	
	0960	For rough-in, supply, waste, vent and carrier		2.73	5.861		251	182		433	550	
	1000	Floor mounted, one piece		5.30	3.019		480	93.50		573.50	670	
	1100	Two piece, close coupled, water saver **CN**	↓	5.30	3.019	↓	133	93.50		226.50	288	
	1960	For color, add					30%					
	1980	For rough-in, supply, waste and vent	Q-1	3.05	5.246	Ea.	114	163		277	370	
	3000	Bowl only, with flush valve, seat										
	3100	Wall hung	Q-1	5.80	2.759	Ea.	335	85.50		420.50	500	
	3200	For rough-in, supply, waste and vent, single WC		2.56	6.250		258	194		452	575	
	3300	Floor mounted		5.80	2.759		300	85.50		385.50	460	
	3350	With wall outlet		5.80	2.759		450	85.50		535.50	625	
	3390	Water closet bowl w/auto self flush, self clean, self sanitizing		4.70	3.404		1,500	106		1,606	1,800	
	3400	For rough-in, supply, waste and vent, single WC	↓	2.84	5.634	↓	120	175		295	395	

15440 | Plumbing Pumps

			DAILY OUTPUT	LABOR-HOURS	UNIT	2001 BARE COSTS				TOTAL INCL O&P	
			CREW			MAT.	LABOR	EQUIP.	TOTAL		
240	0010	**PUMPS, PRESSURE BOOSTER SYSTEM**										**240**
	0200	Pump system, with diaphragm tank, control, press. switch										
	0300	1 HP pump	Q-1	1.30	12.308	Ea.	3,050	380		3,430	3,925	
	0400	1-1/2 HP pump		1.25	12.800		3,075	395		3,470	3,975	
	0420	2 HP pump		1.20	13.333		3,150	415		3,565	4,075	
	0440	3 HP pump	↓	1.10	14.545		3,200	450		3,650	4,175	
	0460	5 HP pump	Q-2	1.50	16		3,525	515		4,040	4,650	
	0480	7-1/2 HP pump		1.42	16.901		3,925	545		4,470	5,150	
	0500	10 HP pump	↓	1.34	17.910	↓	4,125	575		4,700	5,400	
	1000	Pump/ energy storage system, diaphragm tank, 3 HP pump										
	1100	motor, PRV, switch, gauge, control center, flow switch										
	1200	125 lb. working pressure	Q-2	.70	34.286	Ea.	8,850	1,100		9,950	11,400	
	1300	250 lb. working pressure	"	.64	37.500	"	9,675	1,200		10,875	12,400	
400	0010	**PUMPS, GRINDER SYSTEM** Complete, incl. check valve, tank, std.										**400**
	0020	controls incl. alarm/disconnect panel w/wire. Excavation not included										
	0260	Simplex, 9 GPM at 60 PSIG, 70 gal. tank				Ea.	2,150			2,150	2,375	
	0300	For manway, 26" I.D., 18" high, add					405			405	445	
	0340	26" I.D., 36" high, add					475			475	525	
	0380	43" I.D., 4' high, add				↓	525			525	575	
800	0010	**PUMPS, SEWAGE EJECTOR** With operating and level controls										**800**
	0100	Simplex system incl. tank, cover, pump 15' head										
	0500	37 gal PE tank, 12 GPM, 1/2 HP, 2" discharge	Q-1	3.20	5	Ea.	365	155		520	635	
	0510	3" discharge		3.10	5.161		390	160		550	670	
	0530	87 GPM, .7 HP, 2" discharge		3.20	5		560	155		715	850	
	0540	3" discharge		3.10	5.161		610	160		770	910	
	0600	45 gal. coated stl tank, 12 GPM, 1/2 HP, 2" discharge		3	5.333		645	165		810	960	
	0610	3" discharge		2.90	5.517		675	171		846	1,000	
	0630	87 GPM, .7 HP, 2" discharge		3	5.333		830	165		995	1,150	
	0640	3" discharge		2.90	5.517		875	171		1,046	1,225	
	0660	134 GPM, 1 HP, 2" discharge		2.80	5.714		895	177		1,072	1,250	
	0680	3" discharge		2.70	5.926		945	184		1,129	1,325	
	0700	70 gal. PE tank, 12 GPM, 1/2 HP, 2" discharge		2.60	6.154		730	191		921	1,100	
	0710	3" discharge	↓	2.40	6.667	↓	780	207		987	1,175	

15 MECHANICAL

15400 | Plumbing Fixtures & Equipment

15440 | Plumbing Pumps

			CREW	DAILY OUTPUT	LABOR-HOURS	UNIT	2001 BARE COSTS MAT.	LABOR	EQUIP.	TOTAL	TOTAL INCL O&P	
800	0730	87 GPM, 0.7 HP, 2" discharge	Q-1	2.50	6.400	Ea.	980	198		1,178	1,375	800
	0740	3" discharge		2.30	6.957		1,000	216		1,216	1,425	
	0760	134 GPM, 1 HP, 2" discharge		2.20	7.273		1,025	225		1,250	1,475	
	0770	3" discharge	↓	2	8	↓	1,100	248		1,348	1,575	
900	0010	**PUMPS, PEDESTAL SUMP** With float control										900
	0400	Molded PVC base, 21 GPM at 15' head, 1/3 HP	1 Plum	5	1.600	Ea.	86.50	55		141.50	178	
	0800	Iron base, 21 GPM at 15' head, 1/3 HP		5	1.600		110	55		165	204	
	1200	Solid brass, 21 GPM at 15' head, 1/3 HP	↓	5	1.600	↓	179	55		234	280	
940	0010	**PUMPS, SUBMERSIBLE** Sump										940
	7000	Sump pump, automatic										
	7100	Plastic, 1-1/4" discharge, 1/4 HP	1 Plum	6	1.333	Ea.	105	46		151	186	
	7140	1/3 HP		5	1.600		127	55		182	223	
	7160	1/2 HP		5	1.600		153	55		208	251	
	7180	1-1/2" discharge, 1/2 HP		4	2		171	69		240	292	
	7500	Cast iron, 1-1/4" discharge, 1/4 HP		6	1.333		125	46		171	207	
	7540	1/3 HP		6	1.333		140	46		186	224	
	7560	1/2 HP	↓	5	1.600	↓	176	55		231	276	

15460 | Domestic Water Cond Equipment

			CREW	DAILY OUTPUT	LABOR-HOURS	UNIT	MAT.	LABOR	EQUIP.	TOTAL	TOTAL INCL O&P	
900	0010	**WATER SOFTENER**										900
	5800	Softener systems, automatic, intermediate sizes										
	5820	available, may be used in multiples.										
	6000	Hardness capacity between regenerations and flow										
	6100	150,000 grains, 37 GPM cont., 51 GPM peak	Q-1	1.20	13.333	Ea.	3,575	415		3,990	4,550	
	6200	300,000 grains, 81 GPM cont., 113 GPM peak		1	16		5,300	495		5,795	6,575	
	6300	750,000 grains, 160 GPM cont., 230 GPM peak		.80	20		6,900	620		7,520	8,500	
	6400	900,000 grains, 185 GPM cont., 270 GPM peak	↓	.70	22.857	↓	11,100	710		11,810	13,300	

15480 | Domestic Water Heaters

			CREW	DAILY OUTPUT	LABOR-HOURS	UNIT	MAT.	LABOR	EQUIP.	TOTAL	TOTAL INCL O&P	
200	0010	**WATER HEATERS**										200
	0020	For solar, see division 13600										
	1000	Residential, electric, glass lined tank, 5 yr, 10 gal., single element	1 Plum	2.30	3.478	Ea.	195	120		315	395	
	1040	20 gallon, single element		2.20	3.636		228	125		353	440	
	1060	30 gallon, double element		2.20	3.636		246	125		371	460	
	1080	40 gallon, double element		2	4		265	138		403	500	
	1100	52 gallon, double element		2	4		300	138		438	545	
	1180	120 gallon, double element		1.40	5.714		680	197		877	1,050	
	2000	Gas fired, glass lined tank, 5 yr, vent not incl., 20 gallon		2.10	3.810		188	131		319	405	
	2040	30 gallon		2	4		330	138		468	575	
	2100	75 gallon		1.50	5.333		525	184		709	855	
	2120	100 gallon		1.30	6.154		790	212		1,002	1,175	
	3000	Oil fired, glass lined tank, 5 yr, vent not included, 30 gallon		2	4		760	138		898	1,050	
	3040	50 gallon		1.80	4.444		1,025	153		1,178	1,350	
	3060	70 gallon		1.50	5.333		1,350	184		1,534	1,775	
	3080	85 gallon	↓	1.40	5.714	↓	3,425	197		3,622	4,075	
	4000	Commercial, 100° rise. NOTE: for each size tank, a range of										
	4010	heaters between the ones shown are available										
	4020	Electric										
	4100	5 gal., 3 kW, 12 GPH, 208V	1 Plum	2	4	Ea.	1,300	138		1,438	1,625	
	4120	10 gal., 6 kW, 25 GPH, 208V		2	4		1,425	138		1,563	1,775	
	4140	50 gal., 9 kW, 37 GPH, 208V		1.80	4.444		1,975	153		2,128	2,400	
	4160	50 gal., 36 kW, 148 GPH, 208V	↓	1.80	4.444		3,000	153		3,153	3,550	
	4300	200 gal., 15 kW, 61 GPH, 480V	Q-1	1.70	9.412		9,275	292		9,567	10,600	
	4320	200 gal., 120 kW, 490 GPH, 480V		1.70	9.412		12,700	292		12,992	14,400	
	4460	400 gal., 30 kW, 123 GPH, 480V	↓	1	16	↓	12,600	495		13,095	14,700	

MECHANICAL 15

15480	Domestic Water Heaters		CREW	DAILY OUTPUT	LABOR-HOURS	UNIT	2001 BARE COSTS				TOTAL INCL O&P	
							MAT.	LABOR	EQUIP.	TOTAL		
200 5400	Modulating step control, 2-5 steps		1 Elec	5.30	1.509	Ea.	1,125	52		1,177	1,325	**200**
5440	6-10 steps			3.20	2.500		1,450	86		1,536	1,725	
5460	11-15 steps			2.70	2.963		1,775	102		1,877	2,100	
5480	16-20 steps		↓	1.60	5	↓	2,075	172		2,247	2,550	
6000	Gas fired, flush jacket, std. controls, vent not incl.											
6040	75 MBH input, 73 GPH		1 Plum	1.40	5.714	Ea.	1,250	197		1,447	1,675	
6060	98 MBH input, 95 GPH			1.40	5.714		2,175	197		2,372	2,700	
6080	120 MBH input, 110 GPH	**CN**		1.20	6.667		2,375	230		2,605	2,950	
6180	200 MBH input, 192 GPH			.60	13.333		2,600	460		3,060	3,550	
6200	250 MBH input, 245 GPH			.50	16		2,750	550		3,300	3,850	
6900	For low water cutoff, add			8	1		198	34.50		232.50	270	
6960	For bronze body hot water circulator, add		↓	4	2	↓	1,100	69		1,169	1,300	
8000	Oil fired, flush jacket, std. controls, vent not incl.											
8060	103 MBH gross output, 116 GPH		1 Plum	1.10	7.273	Ea.	895	251		1,146	1,375	
8080	122 MBH gross output, 141 GPH			1	8		1,400	276		1,676	1,975	
8100	137 MBH gross output, 161 GPH		↓	.80	10		1,500	345		1,845	2,175	
8160	225 MBH gross output, 256 GPH		Q-1	.80	20		2,125	620		2,745	3,275	
8180	262 MBH gross output, 315 GPH			.70	22.857		2,225	710		2,935	3,525	
8280	735 MBH gross output, 880 GPH			.40	40		4,975	1,250		6,225	7,350	
8300	840 MBH gross output, 1000 GPH		↓	.40	40		5,725	1,250		6,975	8,175	
8900	For low water cutoff, add		1 Plum	8	1		198	34.50		232.50	270	
8960	For bronze body hot water circulator, add		"	4	2	↓	745	69		814	920	
900 0010	**HEAT TRANSFER PACKAGES** Complete, controls,											**900**
0020	expansion tank, converter, air separator											
1000	Hot water, 180°F enter, 200°F leaving, 15# steam											
1010	One pump system, 28 GPM		Q-6	.75	32	Ea.	10,700	1,050		11,750	13,400	
1020	35 GPM			.70	34.286		11,800	1,125		12,925	14,700	
1040	55 GPM			.65	36.923		13,500	1,200		14,700	16,700	
1060	130 GPM			.55	43.636		16,700	1,425		18,125	20,600	
1080	255 GPM			.40	60		23,000	1,950		24,950	28,300	
1100	550 GPM		↓	.30	80	↓	29,200	2,600		31,800	36,100	

15510	Heating Boilers and Accessories	CREW	DAILY OUTPUT	LABOR-HOURS	UNIT	2001 BARE COSTS				TOTAL INCL O&P	
						MAT.	LABOR	EQUIP.	TOTAL		
300 0010	**BOILERS, ELECTRIC, ASME** Standard controls and trim										**300**
1000	Steam, 6 KW, 20.5 MBH	Q-19	1.20	20	Ea.	7,900	645		8,545	9,675	
1160	60 KW, 205 MBH		1	24		9,775	775		10,550	11,900	
1220	112 KW, 382 MBH		.75	32		11,200	1,025		12,225	13,900	
1280	222 KW, 758 MBH	↓	.55	43.636		15,300	1,400		16,700	18,900	
1380	518 KW, 1768 MBH	Q-21	.36	88.889		20,600	2,925		23,525	27,000	
1480	814 KW, 2778 MBH		.25	128		31,500	4,225		35,725	41,100	
1600	2,340 KW, 7984 MBH	↓	.16	200		60,000	6,600		66,600	75,500	
2000	Hot water, 6 KW, 20.5 MBH	Q-19	1.30	18.462		3,400	595		3,995	4,625	
2100	74 KW, 253 MBH		1.10	21.818		4,725	705		5,430	6,250	
2220	296 KW, 1010 MBH	↓	.55	43.636		10,600	1,400		12,000	13,800	
2500	1,036 KW, 3536 MBH	Q-21	.34	94.118		33,600	3,100		36,700	41,700	
2680	2,400 KW, 8191 MBH		.25	128		57,500	4,225		61,725	69,500	
2820	3,600 KW, 12,283 MBH	↓	.16	200		72,000	6,600		78,600	89,500	

15 **MECHANICAL**

		15510	Heating Boilers and Accessories	CREW	DAILY OUTPUT	LABOR-HOURS	UNIT	2001 BARE COSTS MAT.	LABOR	EQUIP.	TOTAL	TOTAL INCL O&P	
400	0010		**BOILERS, GAS FIRED** Natural or propane, standard controls										**400**
	1000		Cast iron, with insulated jacket										
	2000		Steam, gross output, 81 MBH	Q-7	1.40	22.857	Ea.	1,125	760		1,885	2,400	
	2080		203 MBH		.90	35.556		1,900	1,175		3,075	3,875	
	2180		400 MBH		.56	56.838		3,175	1,900		5,075	6,350	
	2240		765 MBH		.43	74.419		5,075	2,475		7,550	9,300	
	2320		1,875 MBH		.30	106		10,700	3,550		14,250	17,200	
	2440		4,720 MBH		.15	207		20,500	6,900		27,400	33,000	
	2480		6,100 MBH		.13	246		49,000	8,175		57,175	66,500	
	2540		6,970 MBH		.10	320		55,000	10,600		65,600	76,500	
	3000		Hot water, gross output, 80 MBH		1.46	21.918		1,000	730		1,730	2,225	
	3140	CN	320 MBH		.80	40		2,475	1,325		3,800	4,700	
	3260		1,088 MBH		.40	80		6,375	2,650		9,025	11,100	
	3380		3,264 MBH		.18	179		16,100	5,975		22,075	26,700	
	3480		6,100 MBH		.13	250		50,000	8,300		58,300	67,500	
	3540		6,970 MBH		.09	359		56,000	12,000		68,000	79,500	
	4000		Steel, insulating jacket										
	4500		Steam, not including burner, gross output										
	5500		1,440 MBH	Q-6	.35	68.571	Ea.	15,300	2,225		17,525	20,200	
	5580		3,065 MBH	"	.18	133		21,900	4,325		26,225	30,600	
	5640		7,200 MBH	Q-7	.18	177		40,100	5,900		46,000	53,000	
	5720		17,990 MBH	"	.10	320		75,000	10,600		85,600	98,500	
	6000		Hot water, including burner & one zone valve, gross output										
	6020		72 MBH	Q-6	2	12	Ea.	1,750	390		2,140	2,525	
	6120		227 MBH		1.30	18.462		4,050	600		4,650	5,350	
	6180		480 MBH		.70	34.286		6,600	1,125		7,725	8,950	
	6240		960 MBH		.45	53.333		11,400	1,725		13,125	15,100	
	6340		3,000 MBH		.15	160		31,600	5,200		36,800	42,600	
	7000		For tankless water heater on smaller gas units, add					10%					
460	0010		**BOILERS, GAS/OIL** Combination with burners and controls										**460**
	1000		Cast iron with insulated jacket										
	2000		Steam, gross output, 720 MBH	Q-7	.43	74.074	Ea.	6,375	2,450		8,825	10,800	
	2080		1,600 MBH		.30	107		9,825	3,550		13,375	16,200	
	2140		2,700 MBH		.19	165		14,600	5,500		20,100	24,400	
	2280		5,520 MBH		.14	235		52,000	7,825		59,825	69,000	
	2340		6,390 MBH		.11	296		55,500	9,850		65,350	76,000	
	2380		6,970 MBH		.09	372		59,000	12,400		71,400	83,500	
	2900		Hot water, gross output										
	2910		200 MBH	Q-6	.61	39.024	Ea.	4,325	1,275		5,600	6,675	
	2920		300 MBH		.49	49.080		4,325	1,600		5,925	7,150	
	2930		400 MBH		.41	57.971		5,050	1,875		6,925	8,400	
	2940		500 MBH		.36	67.039		5,450	2,175		7,625	9,275	
	3000		584 MBH	Q-7	.44	72.072		5,900	2,400		8,300	10,100	
	3060		1,460 MBH		.28	113		15,300	3,750		19,050	22,500	
	3160		4,088 MBH		.16	195		56,000	6,475		62,475	71,500	
	3300		13,500 MBH, 403.3 BHP		.04	727		91,000	24,200		115,200	137,000	
	4000		Steel, insulated jacket, skid base, tubeless										
	4500		Steam, 150 psi gross output, 335 MBH, 10 BHP	Q-6	.54	44.037	Ea.	9,425	1,425		10,850	12,600	
	4560		670 MBH, 20 BHP		.36	65.934		11,700	2,150		13,850	16,200	
	4640		1,339 MBH, 40 BHP		.29	81.911		18,500	2,675		21,175	24,400	
	4720		2,511 MBH, 75 BHP		.17	141		25,200	4,600		29,800	34,700	
	5000		Hot water, gross output, 525 MBH		.45	52.980		9,500	1,725		11,225	13,100	
	5080		1,050 MBH		.35	67.989		15,300	2,200		17,500	20,300	
	5140		2,310 MBH		.20	120		28,500	3,900		32,400	37,300	
	5180		3,150 MBH		.16	146		37,900	4,750		42,650	48,900	

MECHANICAL 15

15510	Heating Boilers and Accessories	CREW	DAILY OUTPUT	LABOR-HOURS	UNIT	2001 BARE COSTS				TOTAL INCL O&P
						MAT.	LABOR	EQUIP.	TOTAL	
500	0010	**BOILERS, OIL FIRED** Standard controls, flame retention burner									**500**
	1000	Cast iron, with insulated flush jacket								
	2000	Steam, gross output, 109 MBH	Q-7	1.20	26.667	Ea.	1,375	885		2,260	2,875
	2060	207 MBH		.90	35.556		1,875	1,175		3,050	3,850
	2180	1,084 MBH		.38	85.106		6,350	2,825		9,175	11,300
	2280	3,000 MBH		.19	170		14,400	5,650		20,050	24,400
	2380	5,520 MBH		.14	235		43,100	7,825		50,925	59,000
	2460	6,970 MBH		.09	363		55,500	12,100		67,600	79,500
	3000	Hot water, same price as steam								
	4000	For tankless coil in smaller sizes, add					15%			
	5000	Steel, insulated jacket, burner								
	6000	Steam, full water leg construction, gross output								
	6020	144 MBH	Q-6	1.33	18.045	Ea.	3,275	585		3,860	4,475
	6120	468 MBH		.70	34.483		6,025	1,125		7,150	8,325
	6180	1,008 MBH		.39	61.381		9,325	2,000		11,325	13,300
	6280	2,400 MBH		.19	125		17,800	4,075		21,875	25,800
	6400	Larger sizes are same as steel, gas fired								
	7000	Hot water, gross output, 103 MBH	Q-6	1.60	15	Ea.	965	490		1,455	1,800
	7120	420 MBH		.70	34.483		4,175	1,125		5,300	6,275
	7200	840 MBH		.43	55.172		10,200	1,800		12,000	13,900
	7260	1,680 MBH		.29	83.624		11,600	2,725		14,325	16,900
	7320	3,150 MBH		.13	184		18,000	6,000		24,000	28,900
	7340	For tankless coil in steam or hot water, add					7%			
880	0010	**SWIMMING POOL HEATERS** Not including wiring, external									**880**
	0020	piping, base or pad,								
	0060	Gas fired, input, 115 MBH	Q-6	3	8	Ea.	1,525	260		1,785	2,075
	0100	135 MBH		2	12		1,725	390		2,115	2,475
	0160	155 MBH		1.50	16		1,825	520		2,345	2,775
	0200	190 MBH		1	24		2,350	780		3,130	3,775
	0280	500 MBH		.40	60		5,700	1,950		7,650	9,225
	0400	1,800 MBH		.14	171		15,900	5,575		21,475	25,900
	0440	3,750 MBH		.09	266		32,100	8,675		40,775	48,400
	2000	Electric, 12 KW, 4,800 gallon pool	Q-19	3	8		1,525	259		1,784	2,075
	2020	15 KW, 7,200 gallon pool		2.80	8.571		1,525	277		1,802	2,100
	2040	24 KW, 9,600 gallon pool		2.40	10		2,050	325		2,375	2,725
	2100	55 KW, 24,000 gallon pool		1.20	20		2,900	645		3,545	4,175

15530	Furnaces									
400	0010	**FURNACES** Hot air heating, blowers, standard controls									**400**
	0020	not including gas, oil or flue piping								
	1000	Electric, UL listed								
	1020	10.2 MBH	Q-20	5	4	Ea.	315	124		439	535
	1040	17.1 MBH		4.80	4.167		330	129		459	560
	1060	27.3 MBH		4.60	4.348		395	135		530	640
	1100	34.1 MBH		4.40	4.545		405	141		546	660
	3000	Gas, AGA certified, upflow, direct drive models								
	3020	45 MBH input	Q-9	4	4	Ea.	435	121		556	665
	3040	60 MBH input		3.80	4.211		580	127		707	835
	3060	75 MBH input		3.60	4.444		615	134		749	885
	3100	100 MBH input		3.20	5		655	151		806	955
	6000	Oil, UL listed, atomizing gun type burner								
	6020	56 MBH output	Q-9	3.60	4.444	Ea.	745	134		879	1,025
	6030	84 MBH output		3.50	4.571		775	138		913	1,075
	6040	95 MBH output		3.40	4.706		790	142		932	1,100

Important: See the Reference Section for critical supporting data - Reference Nos., Crews, & City Cost Indexes

15 MECHANICAL

15530	Furnaces	CREW	DAILY OUTPUT	LABOR-HOURS	UNIT	2001 BARE COSTS				TOTAL INCL O&P	
						MAT.	LABOR	EQUIP.	TOTAL		
400 6060	134 MBH output	Q-9	3.20	5	Ea.	1,100	151		1,251	1,425	**400**
6080	151 MBH output	↓	3	5.333	↓	1,225	161		1,386	1,575	

15540 | Fuel-Fired Heaters

		CREW	DAILY OUTPUT	LABOR-HOURS	UNIT	MAT.	LABOR	EQUIP.	TOTAL	TOTAL INCL O&P	
300 0010	**DUCT FURNACES** Includes burner, controls, stainless steel										**300**
0020	heat exchanger. Gas fired, electric ignition										
0030	Indoor installation										
0100	120 MBH output	Q-5	4	4	Ea.	1,175	126		1,301	1,475	
0130	200 MBH output		2.70	5.926		1,625	186		1,811	2,050	
0140	240 MBH output		2.30	6.957		1,625	218		1,843	2,125	
0180	320 MBH output	↓	1.60	10	↓	2,050	315		2,365	2,725	
0300	For powered venter and adapter, add					277			277	305	
0500	For required flue pipe, see 15550										
1000	Outdoor installation, with vent cap										
1020	75 MBH output	Q-5	4	4	Ea.	1,600	126		1,726	1,975	
1060	120 MBH output		4	4		1,975	126		2,101	2,375	
1100	187 MBH output		3	5.333		2,825	167		2,992	3,375	
1140	300 MBH output		1.80	8.889		3,700	279		3,979	4,500	
1180	450 MBH output	↓	1.40	11.429		4,250	360		4,610	5,225	
1400	For powered venter, add				↓	10%					
900 0010	**SPACE HEATERS** Cabinet, grilles, fan, controls, burner,										**900**
0020	thermostat, no piping. For flue see 15550										
1000	Gas fired, floor mounted										
1100	60 MBH output	Q-5	10	1.600	Ea.	530	50		580	660	
1140	100 MBH output		8	2		580	63		643	730	
1180	180 MBH output		6	2.667		790	83.50		873.50	995	
2000	Suspension mounted, propeller fan, 20 MBH output		8.50	1.882		410	59		469	540	
2040	60 MBH output		7	2.286		505	71.50		576.50	665	
2060	80 MBH output		6	2.667		560	83.50		643.50	740	
2100	130 MBH output		5	3.200		745	100		845	970	
2240	320 MBH output	↓	2	8		1,550	251		1,801	2,075	
2500	For powered venter and adapter, add					248			248	272	
5000	Wall furnace, 17.5 MBH output	Q-5	6	2.667		495	83.50		578.50	670	
5020	24 MBH output		5	3.200		510	100		610	715	
5040	35 MBH output		4	4		690	126		816	950	
6000	Oil fired, suspension mounted, 94 MBH output		4	4		1,925	126		2,051	2,325	
6040	140 MBH output		3	5.333		2,050	167		2,217	2,500	
6060	184 MBH output	↓	3	5.333	↓	2,200	167		2,367	2,675	

15550 | Breechings, Chimneys & Stacks

		CREW	DAILY OUTPUT	LABOR-HOURS	UNIT	MAT.	LABOR	EQUIP.	TOTAL	TOTAL INCL O&P	
440 0010	**VENT CHIMNEY** Prefab metal, U.L. listed										**440**
0020	Gas, double wall, galvanized steel										
0080	3" diameter	Q-9	72	.222	V.L.F.	3.48	6.70		10.18	14.20	
0100	4" diameter		68	.235		4.35	7.10		11.45	15.75	
0120	5" diameter		64	.250		5.05	7.55		12.60	17.25	
0140	6" diameter		60	.267		6.25	8.05		14.30	19.30	
0160	7" diameter		56	.286		8.65	8.65		17.30	23	
0180	8" diameter		52	.308		9.65	9.30		18.95	25	
0200	10" diameter		48	.333		20.50	10.05		30.55	38	
0220	12" diameter		44	.364		27	11		38	47	
0260	16" diameter	↓	40	.400		62	12.10		74.10	86.50	
0300	20" diameter	Q-10	36	.667		94.50	21		115.50	136	
0480	38" diameter	"	24	1		300	31.50		331.50	380	
7800	All fuel, double wall, stainless steel, 6" diameter	Q-9	60	.267		28.50	8.05		36.55	44	
7802	7" diameter		56	.286		37	8.65		45.65	54	
7804	8" diameter	↓	52	.308	↓	43	9.30		52.30	62	

MECHANICAL 15

15550	Breechings, Chimneys & Stacks	CREW	DAILY OUTPUT	LABOR-HOURS	UNIT	2001 BARE COSTS				TOTAL INCL O&P	
						MAT.	LABOR	EQUIP.	TOTAL		
440 7806	10" diameter	Q-9	48	.333	V.L.F.	63	10.05		73.05	85	**440**
7808	12" diameter		44	.364		84.50	11		95.50	110	
7810	14" diameter	↓	42	.381	↓	111	11.50		122.50	140	
9000	High temp. (2000° F), steel jacket, acid resist. refractory lining										
9010	11 ga. galvanized jacket, U.L. listed										
9020	Straight section, 48" long, 10" diameter	Q-10	13.30	1.805	Ea.	335	56.50		391.50	455	
9040	18" diameter		7.40	3.243		510	102		612	715	
9070	36" diameter	↓	2.70	8.889		1,075	278		1,353	1,625	
9090	48" diameter	Q-11	2.70	11.852		1,575	380		1,955	2,325	
9120	Tee section, 10" diameter	Q-10	4.40	5.455		705	171		876	1,050	
9140	18" diameter		2.40	10		1,000	315		1,315	1,575	
9170	36" diameter	↓	.80	30		3,300	940		4,240	5,075	
9190	48" diameter	Q-11	.90	35.556		5,600	1,150		6,750	7,925	
9220	Cleanout pier section, 10" diameter	Q-10	3.50	6.857		545	215		760	930	
9240	18" diameter		1.90	12.632		730	395		1,125	1,425	
9270	36" diameter	↓	.75	32		1,350	1,000		2,350	3,025	
9290	48" diameter	Q-11	.75	42.667		2,050	1,375		3,425	4,350	
9320	For drain, add					53%					
9330	Elbow, 30° and 45°, 10" diameter	Q-10	6.60	3.636		460	114		574	680	
9350	18" diameter		3.70	6.486		745	203		948	1,125	
9380	36" diameter	↓	1.30	18.462		1,850	580		2,430	2,925	
9400	48" diameter	Q-11	1.35	23.704		3,225	760		3,985	4,725	
9430	For 60° and 90° elbow, add					112%					
9440	End cap, 10" diameter	Q-10	26	.923		790	29		819	910	
9460	18" diameter		15	1.600		1,125	50		1,175	1,300	
9490	36" diameter	↓	5	4.800		1,950	150		2,100	2,375	
9510	48" diameter	Q-11	5.30	6.038		2,875	193		3,068	3,450	
9540	Increaser (1 diameter), 10" diameter	Q-10	6.60	3.636		390	114		504	605	
9560	18" diameter		3.70	6.486		610	203		813	985	
9590	36" diameter	↓	1.30	18.462		1,200	580		1,780	2,225	
9592	42" diameter	Q-11	1.60	20		1,325	640		1,965	2,450	
9594	48" diameter		1.35	23.704		1,575	760		2,335	2,925	
9596	54" diameter	↓	1.10	29.091	↓	1,925	930		2,855	3,525	
9600	For expansion joints, add to straight section					7%					
9610	For 1/4" hot rolled steel jacket, add					157%					
9620	For 2950°F very high temperature, add					89%					
9630	26 ga. aluminized jacket, straight section, 48" long										
9640	10" diameter	Q-10	15.30	1.569	V.L.F.	197	49		246	292	
9660	18" diameter		8.50	2.824	↓	300	88.50		388.50	465	
9690	36" diameter		3.10	7.742	↓	695	242		937	1,150	
9810	Draw band, galv. stl., 11 gauge, 10" diameter		32	.750	Ea.	53	23.50		76.50	95	
9820	12" diameter		30	.800		57	25		82	101	
9830	18" diameter		26	.923		71.50	29		100.50	123	
9860	36" diameter	↓	18	1.333		121	42		163	198	
9880	48" diameter	Q-11	20	1.600	↓	207	51		258	305	
600 0010	**INDUCED DRAFT FANS**										**600**
1000	Breeching installation										
1800	Hot gas, 600°F, variable pitch pulley and motor										
1860	8" diam. inlet, 1/4 H.P., 1phase, 1120 CFM	Q-9	4	4	Ea.	1,575	121		1,696	1,900	
1900	12" diam. inlet, 3/4 H.P., 3 phase, 2960 CFM		3	5.333		2,150	161		2,311	2,600	
1940	18" diam. inlet, 3 H.P., 3 phase, 9120 CFM		2	8		3,325	242		3,567	4,025	
1980	24" diam. inlet, 7-1/2 H.P., 3 phase, 17,760 CFM	↓	.80	20	↓	5,200	605		5,805	6,650	
2300	For multi-blade damper at fan inlet, add					20%					

15 MECHANICAL

Important: See the Reference Section for critical supporting data - Reference Nos., Crews, & City Cost Indexes

15620 | Packaged Water Chillers

		CREW	DAILY OUTPUT	LABOR-HOURS	UNIT	2001 BARE COSTS				TOTAL INCL O&P	
						MAT.	LABOR	EQUIP.	TOTAL		
100	0010	**ABSORPTION WATER CHILLERS**									**100**
	0020	Steam or hot water, water cooled									
	0050	100 ton	Q-7	.13	240	Ea.	110,500	7,975		118,475	133,500
	0400	420 ton	"	.10	323	"	190,500	10,700		201,200	225,500
600	0010	**CENTRIFUGAL/RECIP. WATER CHILLERS,** With standard controls									**600**
	0020	Centrifugal liquid chiller, water cooled									
	0030	not including water tower									
	0100	Open drive, 2000 ton	Q-7	.07	477	Ea.	483,500	15,900		499,400	555,500
	0490	Reciprocating, packaged w/integral air cooled condenser, 15 ton cool		.37	86.486		12,300	2,875		15,175	17,900
	0500	20 ton cooling		.34	94.955		15,500	3,150		18,650	21,900
	0520	40 ton cooling		.30	108		24,900	3,600		28,500	32,800
	0600	100 ton cooling		.25	129		53,000	4,300		57,300	64,500
	0680	Water cooled, single compressor, semi-hermetic, tower not incl.									
	0700	2 to 5 ton cooling	Q-5	.57	28.021	Ea.	5,850	880		6,730	7,750
	0740	8 ton cooling	"	.31	52.117		9,825	1,625		11,450	13,300
	0760	10 ton cooling	Q-6	.36	67.039		10,400	2,175		12,575	14,700
	0800	20 ton cooling	Q-7	.38	83.989		12,800	2,800		15,600	18,200
	0820	30 ton cooling	"	.33	96.096		15,400	3,200		18,600	21,700
	0980	Water cooled, multiple compress., semi-hermetic, tower not incl.									
	1000	15 ton cooling	Q-6	.36	65.934	Ea.	16,000	2,150		18,150	20,800
	1020	20 ton cooling	Q-7	.41	78.049		17,400	2,600		20,000	23,100
	1060	30 ton cooling		.31	101		19,900	3,400		23,300	27,000
	1100	50 ton cooling		.28	113		25,100	3,775		28,875	33,300
	1160	100 ton cooling		.18	179		48,700	5,975		54,675	62,500
	1180	120 ton cooling		.16	196		52,000	6,525		58,525	67,000
	1200	140 ton cooling		.16	202		56,500	6,725		63,225	72,000
	1450	Water cooled, dual compressors, direct drive, tower not incl.									
	1500	80 ton cooling	Q-7	.14	222	Ea.	46,400	7,375		53,775	62,000
	1520	100 ton cooling		.14	228		54,000	7,600		61,600	71,000
	1540	120 ton cooling		.14	231		59,500	7,700		67,200	77,000
	1580	150 ton cooling		.13	240		72,500	8,000		80,500	91,500
	1620	200 ton cooling		.13	250		88,500	8,300		96,800	109,500
	1660	250 ton cooling		.12	260		102,000	8,650		110,650	125,000

15640 | Packaged Cooling Towers

		CREW	DAILY OUTPUT	LABOR-HOURS	UNIT	MAT.	LABOR	EQUIP.	TOTAL	TOTAL INCL O&P	
400	0010	**COOLING TOWERS** Packaged units									**400**
	0070	Galvanized steel									
	0080	Draw thru, single flow									
	0100	Belt drive, 60 tons	Q-6	90	.267	TonAC	78.50	8.65		87.15	99
	0150	95 tons		100	.240		69	7.80		76.80	88
	0200	110 tons		109	.220		67.50	7.15		74.65	85.50
	0250	125 tons		120	.200		65.50	6.50		72	82
	1500	Induced air, double flow									
	1900	Gear drive, 150 ton	Q-6	126	.190	TonAC	91	6.20		97.20	109
	2000	300 ton		129	.186		62	6.05		68.05	77
	2100	600 ton		132	.182		58.50	5.90		64.40	73
	2150	840 ton		142	.169		47	5.50		52.50	60
	2200	Up to 1,000 tons		150	.160		43.50	5.20		48.70	56
	3000	For higher capacities, use multiples									
	3500	For pumps and piping, add	Q-6	38	.632	TonAC	39	20.50		59.50	74
	4000	For absorption systems, add				"	75%	75%			
	4500	For rigging, see division 01559									
	5000	Fiberglass									
	5010	Draw thru									
	5100	60 tons	Q-6	1.50	16	Ea.	2,775	520		3,295	3,825

MECHANICAL 15

15640 | Packaged Cooling Towers

		CREW	DAILY OUTPUT	LABOR-HOURS	UNIT	MAT.	LABOR	EQUIP.	TOTAL	TOTAL INCL O&P	
400	**5120**	125 tons	Q-6	.99	24.242	Ea.	5,675	790		6,465	7,450	**400**
	5140	300 tons		.43	55.814		13,300	1,825		15,125	17,400	
	5160	600 tons		.22	109		24,200	3,550		27,750	32,000	
	5180	1000 tons		.15	160		41,500	5,200		46,700	53,500	
	6000	Stainless steel										
	6010	Draw thru										
	6100	60 tons	Q-6	1.50	16	Ea.	7,575	520		8,095	9,100	
	6120	110 tons		.99	24.242		12,100	790		12,890	14,500	
	6140	300 tons		.43	55.814		33,500	1,825		35,325	39,700	
	6160	600 tons		.22	109		52,000	3,550		55,550	62,500	
	6180	1000 tons		.15	160		84,500	5,200		89,700	101,000	

15660 | Liquid Coolers/Evap Condensers

			CREW	DAILY OUTPUT	LABOR-HOURS	UNIT	MAT.	LABOR	EQUIP.	TOTAL	TOTAL INCL O&P	
100	**0010**	**CONDENSERS** Ratings are for 30°F TD, R-22										**100**
	0080	Air cooled, belt drive, propeller fan										
	0240	50 ton	Q-6	.69	34.985	Ea.	10,400	1,150		11,550	13,200	
	0280	59 ton		.58	41.308		11,500	1,350		12,850	14,600	
	0320	73 ton		.47	51.173		13,400	1,675		15,075	17,200	
	0360	86 ton		.40	60.302		16,700	1,950		18,650	21,400	
	0380	88 ton		.39	61.697		17,800	2,000		19,800	22,600	
	1550	Air cooled, direct drive, propeller fan										
	1590	1 ton	Q-5	3.80	4.211	Ea.	545	132		677	800	
	1600	1-1/2 ton		3.60	4.444		650	139		789	925	
	1620	2 ton		3.20	5		715	157		872	1,025	
	1640	5 ton		2	8		1,450	251		1,701	1,975	
	1660	10 ton		1.40	11.429		2,250	360		2,610	3,025	
	1690	16 ton		1.10	14.545		3,175	455		3,630	4,175	
	1720	26 ton		.84	19.002		4,125	595		4,720	5,425	
	1760	41 ton	Q-6	.77	31.008		7,525	1,000		8,525	9,800	
	1800	63 ton	"	.54	44.037		11,900	1,425		13,325	15,300	

15710 | Heat Exchangers

			CREW	DAILY OUTPUT	LABOR-HOURS	UNIT	MAT.	LABOR	EQUIP.	TOTAL	TOTAL INCL O&P	
900	**0010**	**HEAT EXCHANGERS**										**900**
	0016	Shell & tube type, 4 pass, 3/4" O.D. copper tubes,										
	0020	C.I. heads, C.I. tube sheet, steel shell										
	0100	Hot water 40°F to 180°F, by steam at 10 PSI										
	0120	8 GPM	Q-5	6	2.667	Ea.	895	83.50		978.50	1,100	
	0140	10 GPM		5	3.200		1,350	100		1,450	1,625	
	0160	40 GPM		4	4		2,075	126		2,201	2,500	
	0180	64 GPM		2	8		3,200	251		3,451	3,875	
	0200	96 GPM		1	16		4,225	500		4,725	5,400	
	0220	120 GPM	Q-6	1.50	16		5,550	520		6,070	6,875	
	1000	Hot water 40°F to 140°F, by water at 200°F										
	1020	7 GPM	Q-5	6	2.667	Ea.	1,100	83.50		1,183.50	1,325	
	1040	16 GPM		5	3.200		1,550	100		1,650	1,850	
	1060	34 GPM		4	4		2,350	126		2,476	2,800	

15 MECHANICAL

			DAILY	LABOR-		2001 BARE COSTS				TOTAL	
15710		**Heat Exchangers**	CREW	OUTPUT	HOURS	UNIT	MAT.	LABOR	EQUIP.	TOTAL	INCL O&P
900	1100	74 GPM	Q-5	1.50	10.667	Ea.	4,225	335		4,560	5,150	**900**
	3000	Plate type,									
	3100	400 GPM	Q-6	.80	30	Ea.	24,500	975		25,475	28,500
	3120	800 GPM	"	.50	48		43,100	1,550		44,650	49,800
	3140	1200 GPM	Q-7	.34	94.118		88,500	3,125		91,625	102,000
	3160	1800 GPM	"	.24	133	↓	133,000	4,425		137,425	152,500

15720		**Air Handling Units**										
200	0010	**CENTRAL STATION AIR-HANDLING UNIT** Chilled water										**200**
	1000	Modular, capacity at 700 FPM face velocity									
	1100	1300 CFM	Q-5	1.20	13.333	Ea.	2,325	420		2,745	3,200
	1300	3200 CFM	"	.80	20		3,075	630		3,705	4,350
	1500	8000 CFM	Q-6	.60	40		5,425	1,300		6,725	7,925
	1700	20,000 CFM		.31	77.419		11,100	2,525		13,625	16,000
	1900	33,500 CFM	↓	.19	126		19,200	4,100		23,300	27,400
	2100	63,000 CFM	Q-7	.13	246		37,400	8,175		45,575	53,500
	2200	For hot water heating coil, add				↓	21%	5%			

500	0010	**MAKE-UP AIR UNIT**										**500**
	0020	Indoor suspension, natural/LP gas, direct fired,									
	0030	standard control. For flue see division 15550-440									
	0040	70°F temperature rise, MBH is input									
	0100	2000 CFM, 168 MBH	Q-6	3	8	Ea.	4,800	260		5,060	5,700
	0160	6000 CFM, 502 MBH		1.50	16		6,050	520		6,570	7,450
	0220	12,000 CFM, 1005 MBH	↓	1	24		7,550	780		8,330	9,475
	0300	24,000 CFM, 2007 MBH	Q-7	1	32		9,825	1,075		10,900	12,400
	0400	50,000 CFM, 4180 MBH	"	.80	40		13,500	1,325		14,825	16,800
	0600	For discharge louver assembly, add					10%				
	0700	For filters, add					20%				
	0800	For air shut-off damper section, add					10%				
	0900	For vertical unit, add				↓	10%				

15730		**Unitary Air Conditioning Equip**										
200	0010	**COMPUTER ROOM UNITS**										**200**
	1000	Air cooled, includes remote condenser but not									
	1020	interconnecting tubing or refrigerant									
	1080	3 ton	Q-5	.50	32	Ea.	7,025	1,000		8,025	9,250
	1120	5 ton		.45	35.556		9,400	1,125		10,525	12,000
	1160	6 ton		.30	53.333		17,300	1,675		18,975	21,600
	1200	8 ton		.27	59.259		19,600	1,850		21,450	24,400
	1240	10 ton		.25	64		20,400	2,000		22,400	25,400
	1280	15 ton		.22	72.727		22,800	2,275		25,075	28,500
	1290	18 ton	↓	.20	80		25,900	2,500		28,400	32,300
	1320	20 ton	Q-6	.29	82.759		27,200	2,700		29,900	34,000
	1360	23 ton	"	.28	85.714	↓	28,600	2,800		31,400	35,600
500	0010	**PACKAGED TERMINAL AIR CONDITIONER** Cabinet, wall sleeve,										**500**
	0100	louver, electric heat, thermostat, manual changeover, 208 V									
	0200	6,000 BTUH cooling, 8800 BTU heat	Q-5	6	2.667	Ea.	915	83.50		998.50	1,125
	0220	9,000 BTUH cooling, 13,900 BTU heat		5	3.200		935	100		1,035	1,175
	0240	12,000 BTUH cooling, 13,900 BTU heat		4	4		970	126		1,096	1,275
	0260	15,000 BTUH cooling, 13,900 BTU heat	↓	3	5.333		1,050	167		1,217	1,400
	0500	For hot water coil, increase heat by 10%, add					5%	10%			
	1000	For steam, increase heat output by 30%, add				↓	8%	10%			
600	0010	**ROOF TOP AIR CONDITIONERS** Standard controls, curb, economizer										**600**
	1000	Single zone, electric cool, gas heat									

MECHANICAL 15

		15730	Unitary Air Conditioning Equip	CREW	DAILY OUTPUT	LABOR-HOURS	UNIT	MAT.	LABOR	EQUIP.	TOTAL	TOTAL INCL O&P	
									2001 BARE COSTS				
600	1090		2 ton cooling, 55 MBH heating R15700-010	Q-5	.93	17.204	Ea.	4,050	540		4,590	5,275	**600**
	1100		3 ton cooling, 60 MBH heating		.70	22.857		4,225	715		4,940	5,700	
	1120		4 ton cooling, 95 MBH heating R15700-020		.61	26.403		4,500	830		5,330	6,200	
	1140		5 ton cooling, 112 MBH heating		.56	28.520		4,675	895		5,570	6,500	
	1145		6 ton cooling, 140 MBH heating		.52	30.769		5,350	965		6,315	7,350	
	1150		7.5 ton cooling, 170 MBH heating		.50	32.258		7,325	1,000		8,325	9,575	
	1160		10 ton cooling, 200 MBH heating	Q-6	.67	35.982		9,500	1,175		10,675	12,200	
	1170		12.5 ton cooling, 230 MBH heating		.63	37.975		10,800	1,225		12,025	13,800	
	1190		18 ton cooling, 330 MBH heating		.52	45.889		15,100	1,500		16,600	18,900	
	1200		20 ton cooling, 360 MBH heating	Q-7	.67	47.976		20,600	1,600		22,200	25,000	
	1210		25 ton cooling, 450 MBH heating		.56	57.554		24,600	1,925		26,525	30,000	
	1220		30 ton cooling, 540 MBH heating		.47	68.376		29,100	2,275		31,375	35,400	
	1260		50 ton cooling, 810 MBH heating		.28	113		46,000	3,775		49,775	56,000	
	1265		60 ton cooling, 900 MBH heating		.23	136		52,000	4,550		56,550	64,500	
	2000		Multizone, electric cool, gas heat, economizer										
	2100		15 ton cooling, 360 MBH heating	Q-7	.61	52.545	Ea.	39,900	1,750		41,650	46,500	
	2120		20 ton cooling, 360 MBH heating **CN**		.53	60.038		45,500	2,000		47,500	53,000	
	2200		40 ton cooling, 540 MBH heating		.28	113		66,500	3,775		70,275	79,000	
	2210		50 ton cooling, 540 MBH heating		.22	142		85,000	4,725		89,725	100,500	
	2220		70 ton cooling, 1500 MBH heating		.16	198		105,000	6,600		111,600	125,500	
	2240		80 ton cooling, 1500 MBH heating		.14	228		120,000	7,600		127,600	143,500	
	2260		90 ton cooling, 1500 MBH heating		.13	256		126,000	8,500		134,500	151,500	
	2280		105 ton cooling, 1500 MBH heating		.11	290		147,000	9,675		156,675	176,000	
	2400		For hot water heat coil, deduct					5%					
	2500		For steam heat coil, deduct					2%					
	2600		For electric heat, deduct					3%	5%				
840	0010	**SELF-CONTAINED SINGLE PACKAGE**											**840**
	0100		Air cooled, for free blow or duct, not incl. remote condenser										
	0200		3 ton cooling	Q-5	1	16	Ea.	4,400	500		4,900	5,575	
	0220		5 ton cooling	Q-6	1.20	20		5,525	650		6,175	7,050	
	0240		10 ton cooling	Q-7	1	32		9,400	1,075		10,475	11,900	
	0260		20 ton cooling		.90	35.556		15,300	1,175		16,475	18,600	
	0280		30 ton cooling		.80	40		19,300	1,325		20,625	23,200	
	0340		60 ton cooling	Q-8	.40	80		38,400	2,650	252	41,302	46,500	
	0490		For duct mounting no price change										
	0500		For hot water or steam heating coils, add				Ea.	10%	10%				
	1000		Water cooled for free blow or duct, not including tower										
	1010		Constant volume										
	1100		3 ton cooling	Q-6	1	24	Ea.	3,075	780		3,855	4,550	
	1120		5 ton cooling	"	1	24		3,650	780		4,430	5,200	
	1140		10 ton cooling	Q-7	.90	35.556		7,425	1,175		8,600	9,950	
	1160		20 ton cooling		.80	40		13,300	1,325		14,625	16,600	
	1180		30 ton cooling		.70	45.714		17,600	1,525		19,125	21,700	

		15740	Heat Pumps										
100	0010	**HEAT PUMPS** (Not including interconnecting tubing)											**100**
	1000		Air to air, split system, not including curbs, pads, or ductwork										
	1020		2 ton cooling, 8.5 MBH heat @ 0°F	Q-5	1.20	13.333	Ea.	2,100	420		2,520	2,925	
	1060		5 ton cooling, 27 MBH heat @ 0°F		.50	32		4,275	1,000		5,275	6,225	
	1080		7.5 ton cooling, 33 MBH heat @ 0°F		.30	53.333		6,575	1,675		8,250	9,750	
	1100		10 ton cooling, 50 MBH heat @ 0°F	Q-6	.38	63.158		8,500	2,050		10,550	12,500	
	1120		15 ton cooling, 64 MBH heat @ 0°F	"	.26	92.308		11,700	3,000		14,700	17,400	
	1180		40 ton cooling, 193 MBH heat @ 0°F	Q-7	.12	266		33,900	8,875		42,775	50,500	
	1300		Supplementary electric heat coil, included										
	1500		Single package, not including curbs, pads, or plenums										

Important: See the Reference Section for critical supporting data - Reference Nos., Crews, & City Cost Indexes

15740 | Heat Pumps

			CREW	DAILY OUTPUT	LABOR-HOURS	UNIT	2001 BARE COSTS				TOTAL INCL O&P	
							MAT.	LABOR	EQUIP.	TOTAL		
100	1520	2 ton cooling, 6.5 MBH heat @ 0°F	Q-5	1.50	10.667	Ea.	2,525	335		2,860	3,275	100
	1580	4 ton cooling, 13 MBH heat @ 0°F		.96	16.667		3,800	525		4,325	4,975	
	1640	7.5 ton cooling, 35 MBH heat @ 0°F	↓	.40	40	↓	8,225	1,250		9,475	11,000	
	2000	Water source to air, single package										
	2100	1 ton cooling, 13 MBH heat @ 75°F	Q-5	2	8	Ea.	965	251		1,216	1,450	
	2140	2 ton cooling, 19 MBH heat @ 75°F		1.70	9.412		1,225	295		1,520	1,775	
	2220	5 ton cooling, 29 MBH heat @ 75°F	↓	.90	17.778	↓	2,125	560		2,685	3,200	
	3960	For supplementary heat coil, add					10%					
	4000	For increase in capacity thru use										
	4020	of solar collector, size boiler at 60%										

15750 | Humidity Control Equipment

			CREW	DAILY OUTPUT	LABOR-HOURS	UNIT	MAT.	LABOR	EQUIP.	TOTAL	TOTAL INCL O&P	
500	0010	**HUMIDIFIERS**										500
	0520	Steam, room or duct, filter, regulators, auto. controls, 220 V										
	0540	11 lb. per hour	Q-5	6	2.667	Ea.	2,000	83.50		2,083.50	2,325	
	0560	22 lb. per hour		5	3.200		2,200	100		2,300	2,575	
	0580	33 lb. per hour		4	4		2,250	126		2,376	2,675	
	0600	50 lb. per hour		4	4		2,750	126		2,876	3,225	
	0620	100 lb. per hour	↓	3	5.333	↓	3,300	167		3,467	3,900	

15761 | Air Coils

			CREW	DAILY OUTPUT	LABOR-HOURS	UNIT	MAT.	LABOR	EQUIP.	TOTAL	TOTAL INCL O&P	
200	0010	**DUCT HEATERS** Electric, 480 V, 3 Ph										200
	0020	Finned tubular insert, 500°F										
	0100	8" wide x 6" high, 4.0 kW	Q-20	16	1.250	Ea.	525	39		564	640	
	0120	12" high, 8.0 kW		15	1.333		840	41.50		881.50	990	
	0140	18" high, 12.0 kW		14	1.429		1,175	44.50		1,219.50	1,375	
	0160	24" high, 16.0 kW		13	1.538		1,525	47.50		1,572.50	1,750	
	0180	30" high, 20.0 kW		12	1.667		1,850	51.50		1,901.50	2,125	
	0300	12" wide x 6" high, 6.7 kW		15	1.333		540	41.50		581.50	655	
	0360	24" high, 26.7 kW		12	1.667		1,575	51.50		1,626.50	1,800	
	0700	24" wide x 6" high, 17.8 kW		13	1.538		650	47.50		697.50	790	
	0760	24" high, 71.1 kW	↓	10	2	↓	1,950	62		2,012	2,250	
	8000	To obtain BTU multiply kW by 3413										
700	0010	**COILS, FLANGED**										700
	0500	Chilled water cooling, 6 rows, 24" x 48"	Q-5	3.20	5	Ea.	2,600	157		2,757	3,075	
	1000	Direct expansion cooling, 6 rows, 24" x 48"		2.80	5.714		2,825	179		3,004	3,375	
	1500	Hot water heating, 1 row, 24" x 48"		4	4		1,050	126		1,176	1,350	
	2000	Steam heating, 1 row, 24" x 48"	↓	3.06	5.229	↓	1,475	164		1,639	1,875	

15765 | Fan Coil Unit/Unit Ventilators

			CREW	DAILY OUTPUT	LABOR-HOURS	UNIT	MAT.	LABOR	EQUIP.	TOTAL	TOTAL INCL O&P	
200	0010	**FAN COIL AIR CONDITIONING** Cabinet mounted, filters, controls										200
	0100	Chilled water, 1/2 ton cooling	Q-5	8	2	Ea.	730	63		793	900	
	0120	1 ton cooling		6	2.667		830	83.50		913.50	1,050	
	0180	3 ton cooling	↓	4	4		1,675	126		1,801	2,025	
	0200	10 ton cooling	Q-6	2.80	8.571		2,400	279		2,679	3,075	
	0220	15 ton cooling		1.50	16		3,350	520		3,870	4,450	
	0240	20 ton cooling		.80	30		4,300	975		5,275	6,200	
	0260	30 ton cooling	↓	.60	40		6,350	1,300		7,650	8,975	
	0940	Direct expansion, for use w/air cooled condensing, 1.5 ton cooling	Q-5	5	3.200		440	100		540	635	
	1000	5 ton cooling	"	3	5.333		1,000	167		1,167	1,350	
	1040	10 ton cooling	Q-6	2.60	9.231		2,250	300		2,550	2,925	
	1060	20 ton cooling		.70	34.286		4,175	1,125		5,300	6,275	
	1100	40 ton cooling	↓	.45	53.333	↓	8,775	1,725		10,500	12,300	
	1510	For condensing unit add see division 15670.										

MECHANICAL 15

15765	Fan Coil Unit/Unit Ventilators	CREW	DAILY OUTPUT	LABOR-HOURS	UNIT	2001 BARE COSTS				TOTAL INCL O&P
						MAT.	LABOR	EQUIP.	TOTAL	
600 0010	**HEATING & VENTILATING UNITS** Classroom									**600**
0020	Includes filter, heating/cooling coils, standard controls									
0080	750 CFM, 2 tons cooling	Q-6	2	12	Ea.	3,000	390		3,390	3,900
0120	1250 CFM, 3 tons cooling	↓	1.40	17.143		3,650	560		4,210	4,875
0140	1500 CFM, 4 tons cooling	↓	.80	30		3,900	975		4,875	5,775
0500	For electric heat, add					35%				
1000	For no cooling, deduct				↓	25%	10%			

15766	Fin Tube Radiation									
190 0010	**HYDRONIC HEATING** Terminal units, not incl. main supply pipe									**190**
1000	Radiation									
1100	Panel, baseboard, C.I., including supports, no covers	Q-5	46	.348	L.F.	21	10.90		31.90	39.50
1150	Fin tube, wall hung, 14" slope top cover, with damper									
1200	1-1/4" copper tube, 4-1/4" alum. fin	Q-5	38	.421	L.F.	26	13.20		39.20	48.50
1250	1-1/4" steel tube, 4-1/4" steel fin	"	36	.444	"	23.50	13.95		37.45	46.50
1500	Note: fin tube may also require corners, caps, etc.									
1990	Convector unit, floor recessed, flush, with trim									
2000	for under large glass wall areas, no damper	Q-5	20	.800	L.F.	24.50	25		49.50	65
2100	For unit with damper, add				"	9.95			9.95	10.95
3000	Radiators, cast iron									
3100	Free standing or wall hung, 6 tube, 25" high	Q-5	96	.167	Section	21.50	5.25		26.75	31.50
3200	4 tube, 19" high	"	96	.167	"	14.80	5.25		20.05	24
3250	Adj. brackets, 2 per wall radiator up to 30 sections	1 Stpi	32	.250	Ea.	32	8.70		40.70	48
3950	Unit heaters, propeller, 115 V 2 psi steam, 60°F entering air									
4000	Horizontal, 12 MBH	Q-5	12	1.333	Ea.	266	42		308	355
4060	43.9 MBH		8	2		440	63		503	580
4140	96.8 MBH		6	2.667		560	83.50		643.50	740
4180	157.6 MBH		4	4		720	126		846	980
4240	286.9 MBH		2	8		1,250	251		1,501	1,750
4250	326.0 MBH		1.90	8.421		1,325	264		1,589	1,850
4260	364 MBH		1.80	8.889		1,475	279		1,754	2,050
4270	404 MBH	↓	1.60	10		1,925	315		2,240	2,600
4300	For vertical diffuser, add					136			136	149
4310	Vertical flow, 40 MBH	Q-5	11	1.455		420	45.50		465.50	530
4314	58.5 MBH		8	2		430	63		493	565
4326	131.0 MBH		4	4		675	126		801	930
4346	297.0 MBH	↓	1.80	8.889		1,400	279		1,679	1,975
4354	420 MBH, (460 V)	Q-6	1.80	13.333		1,925	435		2,360	2,775
4358	500 MBH, (460 V)		1.71	14.035		2,375	455		2,830	3,325
4362	570 MBH, (460 V)		1.40	17.143		2,850	560		3,410	4,000
4366	620 MBH, (460 V)		1.30	18.462		3,275	600		3,875	4,500
4370	960 MBH, (460 V)	↓	1.10	21.818	↓	5,750	710		6,460	7,400
9500	To convert SFR to BTU rating: Hot water, 150 x SFR									
9510	Forced hot water, 180 x SFR; steam, 240 x SFR									

15768	Infrared Heaters									
600 0010	**INFRA-RED UNIT**									**600**
0020	Gas fired, unvented, electric ignition, 100% shutoff. Piping and									
0030	wiring not included									
0060	Input, 15 MBH	Q-5	7	2.286	Ea.	310	71.50		381.50	450
0120	45 MBH	↓	5	3.200		390	100		490	575
0160	60 MBH		4	4		455	126		581	690
0240	120 MBH	↓	2	8	↓	805	251		1,056	1,275

15770 | Floor-Heating & Snow-Melting Eq.

		CREW	DAILY OUTPUT	LABOR-HOURS	UNIT	2001 BARE COSTS				TOTAL INCL O&P
						MAT.	LABOR	EQUIP.	TOTAL	
200	0010	**ELECTRIC HEATING**, equipments are not including wires & conduits									200
	0200	Snow melting for paved surface embedded mat heaters & controls	1 Elec	130	.062	S.F.	6.10	2.11		8.21	9.85
	0400	Cable heating, radiant heat plaster, no controls, in South		130	.062		7.25	2.11		9.36	11.15
	0600	In North		90	.089		7.25	3.05		10.30	12.55
	0800	Cable on 1/2" board not incl. controls, tract housing		90	.089		6.10	3.05		9.15	11.25
	1000	Custom housing		80	.100		7.10	3.43		10.53	12.90
	1100	Rule of thumb: Baseboard units, including control		4.40	1.818	kW	75	62.50		137.50	176
	1200	Duct heaters, including controls		5.30	1.509	"	61.50	52		113.50	146
	1300	Baseboard heaters, 2' long, 375 watt		8	1	Ea.	34	34.50		68.50	88.50
	1400	3' long, 500 watt		8	1		41	34.50		75.50	96
	1600	4' long, 750 watt		6.70	1.194		48	41		89	114
	1800	5' long, 935 watt		5.70	1.404		57	48		105	135
	2000	6' long, 1125 watt		5	1.600		65	55		120	154
	2400	8' long, 1500 watt		4	2		81	68.50		149.50	191
	2950	Wall heaters with fan, 120 to 277 volt									
	2970	surface mounted, residential, 750 watt	1 Elec	7	1.143	Ea.	105	39		144	175
	3000	1500 watt		5	1.600		120	55		175	214
	3040	2250 watt		4	2		255	68.50		323.50	385
	3070	4000 watt		3.50	2.286		260	78.50		338.50	405
	3600	Thermostats, integral		16	.500		25	17.15		42.15	53
	3800	Line voltage, 1 pole		8	1		25	34.50		59.50	78.50

15780 | Energy Recovery Equipment

		CREW	DAILY OUTPUT	LABOR-HOURS	UNIT	2001 BARE COSTS				TOTAL INCL O&P
						MAT.	LABOR	EQUIP.	TOTAL	
100	0010	**HEAT RECOVERY PACKAGES**									100
	0100	Air to air									
	2000	Kitchen exhaust, commercial, heat pipe exchanger									
	2040	Combined supply/exhaust air volume									
	2080	2.5 to 6.0 MCFM	Q-10	2.80	8.571	MCFM	4,725	268		4,993	5,625
	2120	6 to 16 MCFM		5	4.800		2,900	150		3,050	3,400
	2160	16 to 22 MCFM		6	4		2,250	125		2,375	2,700
	7950										

15800 | Air Distribution

15810 | Ducts

		CREW	DAILY OUTPUT	LABOR-HOURS	UNIT	2001 BARE COSTS				TOTAL INCL O&P
						MAT.	LABOR	EQUIP.	TOTAL	
600	0010	**DUCTWORK** R15810 -050									600
	0020	Fabricated rectangular, includes fittings, joints, supports,									
	0030	allowance for flexible connections, no insulation									
	0031	NOTE: Fabrication and installation are combined									
	0040	as LABOR cost. Approx. 25% fittings assumed.									
	0100	Aluminum, alloy 3003-H14, under 100 lb.	Q-10	75	.320	Lb.	3.23	10		13.23	19
	0110	100 to 500 lb.		80	.300		2.23	9.40		11.63	16.95
	0120	500 to 1,000 lb.		95	.253		1.73	7.90		9.63	14.10
	0140	1,000 to 2,000 lb.		120	.200		1.33	6.25		7.58	11.10
	0150	2,000 to 5,000 lb. **CN**		130	.185		1.28	5.80		7.08	10.35
	0160	Over 5,000 lb.		145	.166		1.23	5.20		6.43	9.35
	0500	Galvanized steel, under 200 lb.		235	.102		1.32	3.20		4.52	6.40
	0520	200 to 500 lb.		245	.098		.82	3.07		3.89	5.65
	0540	500 to 1,000 lb.		255	.094		.57	2.95		3.52	5.20

	15810	Ducts	CREW	DAILY OUTPUT	LABOR-HOURS	UNIT	2001 BARE COSTS				TOTAL INCL O&P	
							MAT.	LABOR	EQUIP.	TOTAL		
600	0560	1,000 to 2,000 lb. R15810-050	Q-10	265	.091	Lb.	.42	2.84		3.26	4.84	**600**
	0570	2,000 to 5,000 lb.		275	.087		.37	2.73		3.10	4.63	
	0580	Over 5,000 lb. **CN**		285	.084		.32	2.64		2.96	4.42	
	1000	Stainless steel, type 304, under 100 lb.		165	.145		3.37	4.56		7.93	10.75	
	1020	100 to 500 lb.		175	.137		2.37	4.30		6.67	9.25	
	1030	500 to 1,000 lb.		190	.126		1.87	3.96		5.83	8.15	
	1040	1,000 to 2,000 lb.		200	.120		1.47	3.76		5.23	7.40	
	1050	2,000 to 5,000 lb.		225	.107		1.42	3.34		4.76	6.70	
	1060	Over 5,000 lb.		235	.102		1.37	3.20		4.57	6.45	
	1100	For medium pressure ductwork, add						15%				
	1200	For high pressure ductwork, add						40%				
	1300	Flexible, coated fiberglass fabric on corr. resist. metal helix										
	1400	pressure to 12" (WG) UL-181										
	1500	Non-insulated, 3" diameter	Q-9	400	.040	L.F.	.95	1.21		2.16	2.92	
	1540	5" diameter		320	.050		1.11	1.51		2.62	3.55	
	1560	6" diameter		280	.057		1.25	1.73		2.98	4.04	
	1580	7" diameter		240	.067		1.64	2.01		3.65	4.91	
	1600	8" diameter		200	.080		1.69	2.42		4.11	5.60	
	1640	10" diameter		160	.100		2.17	3.02		5.19	7.05	
	1660	12" diameter		120	.133		2.57	4.03		6.60	9.05	
	1900	Insulated, 1" thick with 3/4 lb., PE jacket, 3" diameter		380	.042		1.64	1.27		2.91	3.76	
	1910	4" diameter		340	.047		1.92	1.42		3.34	4.30	
	1920	5" diameter		300	.053		1.92	1.61		3.53	4.60	
	1940	6" diameter		260	.062		2.15	1.86		4.01	5.25	
	1960	7" diameter		220	.073		2.57	2.20		4.77	6.20	
	1980	8" diameter		180	.089		2.63	2.68		5.31	7.05	
	2020	10" diameter		140	.114		3.42	3.45		6.87	9.10	
	2040	12" diameter		100	.160		3.98	4.83		8.81	11.85	
	3490	Rigid fiberglass duct board, foil reinf. kraft facing										
	3500	Rectangular, 1" thick, alum. faced, (FRK), std. weight	Q-10	350	.069	SF Surf	.83	2.15		2.98	4.23	

	15820	Duct Accessories										
300	0010	**DUCT ACCESSORIES**										**300**
	0050	Air extractors, 12" x 4"	1 Shee	24	.333	Ea.	14.75	11.20		25.95	33.50	
	0100	8" x 6"		22	.364		14.75	12.20		26.95	35	
	0200	20" x 8"		16	.500		33.50	16.80		50.30	62.50	
	0280	24" x 12"		10	.800		45.50	27		72.50	91.50	
	1000	Duct access door, insulated, 6" x 6"		14	.571		13.65	19.15		32.80	44.50	
	1020	10" x 10"		11	.727		16.25	24.50		40.75	55.50	
	1040	12" x 12"		10	.800		17.55	27		44.55	61	
	1050	12" x 18"		9	.889		27.50	30		57.50	76	
	1070	18" x 18"		8	1		31	33.50		64.50	86.50	
	1074	24" x 18"		8	1		37	33.50		70.50	93	
	2000	Fabrics for flexible connections, with metal edge		100	.080	L.F.	1.55	2.68		4.23	5.85	
	2100	Without metal edge		160	.050	"	1.17	1.68		2.85	3.88	
	3000	Fire damper, curtain type, 1-1/2 hr rated, vertical, 6" x 6"		24	.333	Ea.	19.70	11.20		30.90	39	
	3020	8" x 6"		22	.364		19.70	12.20		31.90	40.50	
	3240	16" x 14"		18	.444		31.50	14.90		46.40	57.50	
	3400	24" x 20"		8	1		39.50	33.50		73	95.50	
	5990	Multi-blade dampers, opposed blade, 8" x 6"		24	.333		18.40	11.20		29.60	37.50	
	5994	8" x 8"		22	.364		19.20	12.20		31.40	40	
	5996	10" x 10"		21	.381		21.50	12.80		34.30	44	
	6000	12" x 12"		21	.381		25	12.80		37.80	47.50	
	6020	12" x 18"		18	.444		33.50	14.90		48.40	60	
	6030	14" x 10"		20	.400		21.50	13.40		34.90	44.50	
	6031	14" x 14"		17	.471		29.50	15.80		45.30	57	

Important: See the Reference Section for critical supporting data - Reference Nos., Crews, & City Cost Indexes

15820 | Duct Accessories

		CREW	DAILY OUTPUT	LABOR-HOURS	UNIT	2001 BARE COSTS MAT.	LABOR	EQUIP.	TOTAL	TOTAL INCL O&P	
300	6033	16" x 12"	1 Shee	17	.471	Ea.	29.50	15.80		45.30	57	300
	6035	16" x 16"		16	.500		37	16.80		53.80	66.50	
	6037	18" x 14"		16	.500		37	16.80		53.80	66.50	
	6038	18" x 18"		15	.533		44	17.90		61.90	76	
	6070	20" x 16"		14	.571		44	19.15		63.15	78	
	6072	20" x 20"		13	.615		53	20.50		73.50	90	
	6074	22" x 18"		14	.571		53	19.15		72.15	87.50	
	6076	24" x 16"		11	.727		52	24.50		76.50	94.50	
	6078	24" x 20"		8	1		61.50	33.50		95	120	
	6080	24" x 24"		8	1		72	33.50		105.50	131	
	6110	26" x 26"		6	1.333		84.50	44.50		129	162	
	6133	30" x 30"	Q-9	6.60	2.424		112	73		185	237	
	6135	32" x 32"		6.40	2.500		128	75.50		203.50	258	
	6180	48" x 36"		5.60	2.857		215	86.50		301.50	370	
	7000	Splitter damper assembly, self-locking, 1' rod	1 Shee	24	.333		15.80	11.20		27	34.50	
	7020	3' rod		22	.364		20.50	12.20		32.70	41.50	
	7040	4' rod		20	.400		22.50	13.40		35.90	45.50	
	7060	6' rod		18	.444		27.50	14.90		42.40	53.50	
	8000	Multi-blade dampers, parallel blade										
	8100	8" x 8"	1 Shee	24	.333	Ea.	52.50	11.20		63.70	75.50	
	8140	16" x 10"		20	.400		55.50	13.40		68.90	81.50	
	8200	24" x 16"		11	.727		74	24.50		98.50	119	
	8260	30" x 18"		7	1.143		86	38.50		124.50	154	
	9000	Silencers, noise control for air flow, duct				MCFM	41.50			41.50	45.50	
	9100	Louvers, galvanized				"	60			60	66	
	9200	Plenums, measured by panel surface				S.F.	8.25			8.25	9.10	
	9300	Vent, air transfer				Ea.	139			139	153	

15830 | Fans

		CREW	DAILY OUTPUT	LABOR-HOURS	UNIT	MAT.	LABOR	EQUIP.	TOTAL	TOTAL INCL O&P	
100	0010 **FANS**										100
	0020 Air conditioning and process air handling										
	0030 Axial flow, compact, low sound, 2.5" S.P.										
	0050 3,800 CFM, 5 HP	Q-20	3.40	5.882	Ea.	3,500	182		3,682	4,125	
	0080 6,400 CFM, 5 HP		2.80	7.143		3,900	222		4,122	4,650	
	0100 10,500 CFM, 7-1/2 HP		2.40	8.333		4,875	259		5,134	5,750	
	0120 15,600 CFM, 10 HP		1.60	12.500		6,125	390		6,515	7,350	
	0200 In-line centrifugal, supply/exhaust booster										
	0220 aluminum wheel/hub, disconnect switch, 1/4" S.P.										
	0240 500 CFM, 10" diameter connection	Q-20	3	6.667	Ea.	700	207		907	1,075	
	0260 1,380 CFM, 12" diameter connection		2	10		800	310		1,110	1,350	
	0280 1,520 CFM, 16" diameter connection		2	10		915	310		1,225	1,475	
	0300 2,560 CFM, 18" diameter connection		1	20		1,000	620		1,620	2,050	
	0320 3,480 CFM, 20" diameter connection		.80	25		1,200	775		1,975	2,525	
	0326 5,080 CFM, 20" diameter connection		.75	26.667		1,325	825		2,150	2,750	
	1500 Vaneaxial, low pressure, 2000 CFM, 1/2 HP		3.60	5.556		1,575	172		1,747	2,025	
	1520 4,000 CFM, 1 HP		3.20	6.250		1,625	194		1,819	2,075	
	1540 8,000 CFM, 2 HP		2.80	7.143		1,900	222		2,122	2,450	
	2500 Ceiling fan, right angle, extra quiet, 0.10" S.P.										
	2520 95 CFM	Q-20	20	1	Ea.	110	31		141	169	
	2540 210 CFM		19	1.053		130	32.50		162.50	193	
	2560 385 CFM		18	1.111		165	34.50		199.50	235	
	2580 885 CFM		16	1.250		325	39		364	420	
	2600 1,650 CFM		13	1.538		450	47.50		497.50	570	
	2620 2,960 CFM		11	1.818		600	56.50		656.50	745	
	2640 For wall or roof cap, add	1 Shee	16	.500		110	16.80		126.80	147	

R15700 -040

MECHANICAL 15

15830 | Fans

		CREW	DAILY OUTPUT	LABOR-HOURS	UNIT	2001 BARE COSTS				TOTAL INCL O&P
						MAT.	LABOR	EQUIP.	TOTAL	
100 2660	For straight thru fan, add [R15700 -040]				Ea.	10%					**100**
2680	For speed control switch, add	1 Elec	16	.500	↓	60	17.15		77.15	91.50
3000	Paddle blade air circulator, 3 speed switch									
3020	42", 5,000 CFM high, 3000 CFM low	1 Elec	2.40	3.333	Ea.	73	114		187	251
3040	52", 6,500 CFM high, 4000 CFM low	"	2.20	3.636	"	74	125		199	268
3100	For antique white motor, same cost									
3200	For brass plated motor, same cost									
3300	For light adaptor kit, add				Ea.	26			26	29
3500	Centrifugal, airfoil, motor and drive, complete									
3520	1000 CFM, 1/2 HP	Q-20	2.50	8	Ea.	870	248		1,118	1,350
3540	2,000 CFM, 1 HP		2	10		935	310		1,245	1,500
3560	4,000 CFM, 3 HP		1.80	11.111		1,200	345		1,545	1,850
3580	8,000 CFM, 7-1/2 HP		1.40	14.286		1,775	445		2,220	2,625
3600	12,000 CFM, 10 HP	↓	1	20	↓	2,600	620		3,220	3,800
4500	Corrosive fume resistant, plastic									
4600	roof ventilators, centrifugal, V belt drive, motor									
4620	1/4" S.P., 250 CFM, 1/4 HP	Q-20	6	3.333	Ea.	2,350	103		2,453	2,725
4640	895 CFM, 1/3 HP		5	4		2,550	124		2,674	3,000
4660	1630 CFM, 1/2 HP		4	5		3,000	155		3,155	3,550
4680	2240 CFM, 1 HP	↓	3	6.667	↓	3,150	207		3,357	3,775
5000	Utility set, centrifugal, V belt drive, motor									
5020	1/4" S.P., 1200 CFM, 1/4 HP	Q-20	6	3.333	Ea.	2,300	103		2,403	2,675
5040	1520 CFM, 1/3 HP		5	4		2,300	124		2,424	2,725
5060	1850 CFM, 1/2 HP		4	5		2,300	155		2,455	2,775
5080	2180 CFM, 3/4 HP		3	6.667		2,325	207		2,532	2,875
5100	1/2" S.P., 3600 CFM, 1 HP		2	10		3,375	310		3,685	4,175
5120	4250 CFM, 1-1/2 HP		1.60	12.500		3,425	390		3,815	4,350
5140	4800 CFM, 2 HP	↓	1.40	14.286	↓	3,450	445		3,895	4,475
6000	Propeller exhaust, wall shutter, 1/4" S.P.									
6020	Direct drive, two speed									
6100	375 CFM, 1/10 HP	Q-20	10	2	Ea.	198	62		260	310
6120	730 CFM, 1/7 HP		9	2.222		220	69		289	350
6140	1000 CFM, 1/8 HP		8	2.500		305	77.50		382.50	455
6200	4720 CFM, 1 HP	↓	5	4	↓	490	124		614	730
6300	V-belt drive, 3 phase									
6320	6175 CFM, 3/4 HP	Q-20	5	4	Ea.	410	124		534	640
6340	7500 CFM, 3/4 HP		5	4		435	124		559	665
6360	10,100 CFM, 1 HP		4.50	4.444		530	138		668	790
6380	14,300 CFM, 1-1/2 HP	↓	4	5	↓	620	155		775	925
6650	Residential, bath exhaust, grille, back draft damper									
6660	50 CFM	Q-20	24	.833	Ea.	28.50	26		54.50	71
6670	110 CFM		22	.909		47	28		75	95
6680	Light combination, squirrel cage, 100 watt, 70 CFM	↓	24	.833	↓	58	26		84	104
6700	Light/heater combination, ceiling mounted									
6710	70 CFM, 1450 watt	Q-20	24	.833	Ea.	70.50	26		96.50	117
6800	Heater combination, recessed, 70 CFM		24	.833		33.50	26		59.50	76
6820	With 2 infrared bulbs		23	.870		50.50	27		77.50	97
6900	Kitchen exhaust, grille, complete, 160 CFM		22	.909		58.50	28		86.50	108
6910	180 CFM		20	1		49.50	31		80.50	102
6920	270 CFM		18	1.111		91	34.50		125.50	153
6930	350 CFM	↓	16	1.250	↓	70	39		109	137
6940	Residential roof jacks and wall caps									
6944	Wall cap with back draft damper									
6946	3" & 4" dia. round duct	1 Shee	11	.727	Ea.	12.05	24.50		36.55	51
6948	6" dia. round duct	"	11	.727	"	29	24.50		53.50	69.50
6958	Roof jack with bird screen and back draft damper	↓								

Important: See the Reference Section for critical supporting data - Reference Nos., Crews, & City Cost Indexes

15 MECHANICAL

15800 | Air Distribution

15830 | Fans

		CREW	DAILY OUTPUT	LABOR-HOURS	UNIT	MAT.	LABOR	EQUIP.	TOTAL	TOTAL INCL O&P	
100	6960	3" & 4" dia. round duct	1 Shee	11	.727	Ea.	11.60	24.50		36.10	50.50	100
	6962	3-1/4" x 10" rectangular duct	"	10	.800	"	21.50	27		48.50	65	
	6980	Transition										
	6982	3-1/4" x 10" to 6" dia. round	1 Shee	20	.400	Ea.	13.05	13.40		26.45	35	
	7000	Roof exhauster, centrifugal, aluminum housing, 12" galvanized										
	7020	curb, bird screen, back draft damper, 1/4" S.P.										
	7100	Direct drive, 320 CFM, 11" sq. damper	Q-20	7	2.857	Ea.	287	88.50		375.50	450	
	7120	600 CFM, 11" sq. damper		6	3.333		291	103		394	480	
	7140	815 CFM, 13" sq. damper		5	4		291	124		415	510	
	7160	1450 CFM, 13" sq. damper		4.20	4.762		375	148		523	635	
	7180	2050 CFM, 16" sq. damper		4	5		375	155		530	650	
	7200	V-belt drive, 1650 CFM, 12" sq. damper		6	3.333		655	103		758	880	
	7220	2750 CFM, 21" sq. damper		5	4		760	124		884	1,025	
	7230	3500 CFM, 21" sq. damper		4.50	4.444		840	138		978	1,125	
	7240	4910 CFM, 23" sq. damper		4	5		1,050	155		1,205	1,400	
	7260	8525 CFM, 28" sq. damper		3	6.667		1,300	207		1,507	1,750	
	7280	13,760 CFM, 35" sq. damper		2	10		1,800	310		2,110	2,450	
	7300	20,558 CFM, 43" sq. damper		1	20		3,800	620		4,420	5,125	
	7320	For 2 speed winding, add					15%					
	7340	For explosionproof motor, add				Ea.	282			282	310	
	7360	For belt driven, top discharge, add					15%					
	7500	Utility set, steel construction, pedestal, 1/4" S.P.										
	7520	Direct drive, 150 CFM, 1/8 HP	Q-20	6.40	3.125	Ea.	585	97		682	795	
	7540	485 CFM, 1/6 HP		5.80	3.448		740	107		847	980	
	7560	1950 CFM, 1/2 HP		4.80	4.167		865	129		994	1,150	
	7580	2410 CFM, 3/4 HP		4.40	4.545		1,600	141		1,741	1,975	
	7600	3328 CFM, 1-1/2 HP		3	6.667		1,775	207		1,982	2,275	
	7680	V-belt drive, drive cover, 3 phase										
	7700	800 CFM, 1/4 HP	Q-20	6	3.333	Ea.	415	103		518	615	
	7720	1,300 CFM, 1/3 HP		5	4		435	124		559	670	
	7740	2,000 CFM, 1 HP		4.60	4.348		515	135		650	770	
	7760	2,900 CFM, 3/4 HP		4.20	4.762		695	148		843	990	
	8500	Wall exhausters, centrifugal, auto damper, 1/8" S.P.										
	8520	Direct drive, 610 CFM, 1/20 HP	Q-20	14	1.429	Ea.	160	44.50		204.50	244	
	8540	796 CFM, 1/12 HP		13	1.538		165	47.50		212.50	255	
	8560	822 CFM, 1/6 HP		12	1.667		261	51.50		312.50	365	
	8580	1,320 CFM, 1/4 HP		12	1.667		263	51.50		314.50	370	
	9500	V-belt drive, 3 phase										
	9520	2,800 CFM, 1/4 HP	Q-20	9	2.222	Ea.	725	69		794	905	
	9540	3,740 CFM, 1/2 HP	"	8	2.500	"	755	77.50		832.50	950	

15850 | Air Outlets & Inlets

		CREW	DAILY OUTPUT	LABOR-HOURS	UNIT	MAT.	LABOR	EQUIP.	TOTAL	TOTAL INCL O&P	
300	0010	DIFFUSERS Aluminum, opposed blade damper unless noted										300
	0100	Ceiling, linear, also for sidewall										
	0500	Perforated, 24" x 24" lay-in panel size, 6" x 6"	1 Shee	16	.500	Ea.	79.50	16.80		96.30	113	
	0520	8" x 8"		15	.533		82	17.90		99.90	118	
	0530	9" x 9"		14	.571		84	19.15		103.15	122	
	0540	10" x 10"		14	.571		86	19.15		105.15	124	
	0560	12" x 12"		12	.667		86	22.50		108.50	129	
	0590	16" x 16"		11	.727		107	24.50		131.50	156	
	0600	18" x 18"		10	.800		114	27		141	168	
	0610	20" x 20"		10	.800		130	27		157	185	
	0620	24" x 24"		9	.889		163	30		193	225	
	1000	Rectangular, 1 to 4 way blow, 6" x 6"		16	.500		46	16.80		62.80	77	
	1010	8" x 8"		15	.533		54	17.90		71.90	87	
	1014	9" x 9"		15	.533		56	17.90		73.90	89	

R15700 -040

MECHANICAL 15

			DAILY	LABOR-		2001 BARE COSTS				TOTAL	
15850	**Air Outlets & Inlets**		CREW	OUTPUT	HOURS	UNIT	MAT.	LABOR	EQUIP.	TOTAL	INCL O&P
300	1016	10" x 10"	1 Shee	15	.533	Ea.	67	17.90		84.90	101	**300**
	1020	12" x 6"		15	.533		57	17.90		74.90	90
	1040	12" x 9"		14	.571		69.50	19.15		88.65	106
	1060	12" x 12"		12	.667		82	22.50		104.50	125
	1070	14" x 6"		13	.615		61	20.50		81.50	99.50
	1074	14" x 14"		12	.667		101	22.50		123.50	146
	1150	18" x 18"		9	.889		149	30		179	210
	1160	21" x 21"		8	1		189	33.50		222.50	259
	1170	24" x 12"		10	.800		134	27		161	190
	1500	Round, butterfly damper, 6" diameter		18	.444		15.90	14.90		30.80	40.50
	1520	8" diameter		16	.500		16.85	16.80		33.65	44.50
	1540	10" diameter		14	.571		21	19.15		40.15	52.50
	1560	12" diameter		12	.667		27.50	22.50		50	65
	1580	14" diameter		10	.800		34.50	27		61.50	79.50
	2000	T bar mounting, 24" x 24" lay-in frame, 6" x 6"		16	.500		75.50	16.80		92.30	109
	2020	9" x 9"		14	.571		84	19.15		103.15	122
	2040	12" x 12"		12	.667		111	22.50		133.50	157
	2060	15" x 15"		11	.727		143	24.50		167.50	195
	2080	18" x 18"		10	.800		149	27		176	206
	6000	For steel diffusers instead of aluminum, deduct					10%				
500	0010	**GRILLES**										**500**
	0020	Aluminum									
	1000	Air return, 6" x 6"	1 Shee	26	.308	Ea.	12.35	10.30		22.65	29.50
	1020	10" x 6"		24	.333		14.95	11.20		26.15	33.50
	1080	16" x 8"		22	.364		21.50	12.20		33.70	42.50
	1100	12" x 12"		22	.364		21.50	12.20		33.70	42.50
	1120	24" x 12"		18	.444		38.50	14.90		53.40	65
	1220	24" x 18"		16	.500		45.50	16.80		62.30	76
	1280	36" x 24"		14	.571		90.50	19.15		109.65	129
	3000	Filter grille with filter, 12" x 12"		24	.333		35	11.20		46.20	56
	3020	18" x 12"		20	.400		51.50	13.40		64.90	77
	3040	24" x 18"		18	.444		74	14.90		88.90	105
	3060	24" x 24"		16	.500		97	16.80		113.80	133
	6000	For steel grilles instead of aluminum in above, deduct					10%				
600	0010	**LOUVERS**										**600**
	0100	Aluminum, extruded, with screen, mill finish									
	1000	Brick vent, (see also division 04090)									
	1100	Standard, 4" deep, 8" wide, 5" high	1 Shee	24	.333	Ea.	23	11.20		34.20	43
	1200	Modular, 4" deep, 7-3/4" wide, 5" high		24	.333		24	11.20		35.20	44
	1300	Speed brick, 4" deep, 11-5/8" wide, 3-7/8" high		24	.333		24	11.20		35.20	44
	1400	Fuel oil brick, 4" deep, 8" wide, 5" high		24	.333		42	11.20		53.20	63.50
	2000	Cooling tower and mechanical equip., screens, light weight		40	.200	S.F.	9.95	6.70		16.65	21.50
	2020	Standard weight		35	.229		27.50	7.65		35.15	42.50
	2500	Dual combination, automatic, intake or exhaust		20	.400		38	13.40		51.40	62.50
	2520	Manual operation		20	.400		28	13.40		41.40	51.50
	2540	Electric or pneumatic operation		20	.400		28	13.40		41.40	51.50
	2560	Motor, for electric or pneumatic		14	.571	Ea.	330	19.15		349.15	395
	3000	Fixed blade, continuous line									
	3100	Mullion type, stormproof	1 Shee	28	.286	S.F.	28	9.60		37.60	46
	3200	Stormproof		28	.286		28	9.60		37.60	46
	3300	Vertical line		28	.286		37	9.60		46.60	56
	3500	For damper to use with above, add					50%	30%			
	3520	Motor, for damper, electric or pneumatic	1 Shee	14	.571	Ea.	330	19.15		349.15	395
	4000	Operating, 45°, manual, electric or pneumatic		24	.333	S.F.	28	11.20		39.20	48.50
	4100	Motor, for electric or pneumatic		14	.571	Ea.	330	19.15		349.15	395
	4200	Penthouse, roof		56	.143	S.F.	16.30	4.79		21.09	25.50

Important: See the Reference Section for critical supporting data - Reference Nos., Crews, & City Cost Indexes

15850	Air Outlets & Inlets	CREW	DAILY OUTPUT	LABOR-HOURS	UNIT	2001 BARE COSTS				TOTAL INCL O&P	
						MAT.	LABOR	EQUIP.	TOTAL		
600	4300	Walls	1 Shee	40	.200	S.F.	39.50	6.70		46.20	53.50	**600**
	5000	Thinline, under 4" thick, fixed blade	↓	40	.200	↓	15.80	6.70		22.50	28	
	5010	Finishes, applied by mfr. at additional cost, available in colors										
	5020	Prime coat only, add				S.F.	2.30			2.30	2.53	
	5040	Baked enamel finish coating, add					4.23			4.23	4.65	
	5060	Anodized finish, add					4.59			4.59	5.05	
	5080	Duranodic finish, add					8.30			8.30	9.15	
	5100	Fluoropolymer finish coating, add					13			13	14.30	
	9980	For small orders (under 10 pieces), add				↓	25%					
700	0010	**REGISTERS**										**700**
	0980	Air supply										
	1000	Ceiling/wall, O.B. damper, anodized aluminum										
	1010	One or two way deflection, adj. curved face bars										
	1020	8" x 4"	1 Shee	26	.308	Ea.	18.55	10.30		28.85	36.50	
	1120	12" x 12"	↓	18	.444		34	14.90		48.90	60.50	
	1240	20" x 6"		18	.444		30.50	14.90		45.40	56.50	
	1340	24" x 8"		13	.615		41	20.50		61.50	77	
	1350	24" x 18"	↓	12	.667		76	22.50		98.50	119	
	2700	Above registers in steel instead of aluminum, deduct				↓	10%					
	4000	Floor, toe operated damper, enameled steel										
	4020	4" x 8"	1 Shee	32	.250	Ea.	16.35	8.40		24.75	31	
	4100	8" x 10"		22	.364		19.45	12.20		31.65	40.50	
	4140	10" x 10"		20	.400		23.50	13.40		36.90	46	
	4220	14" x 14"		16	.500		77.50	16.80		94.30	112	
	4240	14" x 20"	↓	15	.533	↓	103	17.90		120.90	142	
	4980	Air return										
	5000	Ceiling or wall, fixed 45° face blades										
	5010	Adjustable O.B. damper, anodized aluminum										
	5020	4" x 8"	1 Shee	26	.308	Ea.	21.50	10.30		31.80	39.50	
	5060	6" x 10"		19	.421		24	14.15		38.15	48.50	
	5280	24" x 24"		11	.727		103	24.50		127.50	151	
	5300	24" x 36"	↓	8	1	↓	159	33.50		192.50	227	
	6000	For steel construction instead of aluminum, deduct					10%					

15854 | Ventilators

			CREW	DAILY OUTPUT	LABOR-HOURS	UNIT	MAT.	LABOR	EQUIP.	TOTAL	INCL O&P	
300	0010	**VENTILATORS** Base, damper & bird screen, CFM in 5 MPH wind										**300**
	0500	Rotary syphon, galvanized, 6" neck diameter, 185 CFM	Q-9	16	1	Ea.	51	30		81	103	
	0560	12" neck diameter, 310 CFM		10	1.600		72	48.50		120.50	154	
	0660	24" neck diameter, 1,530 CFM		8	2		293	60.50		353.50	415	
	0700	36" neck diameter, 3,800 CFM		6	2.667		800	80.50		880.50	1,000	
	0720	42" neck diameter, 4,500 CFM	↓	4	4	↓	1,300	121		1,421	1,600	
	1280	Spinner ventilators, wind driven, galvanized										
	1300	4" neck diameter, 180 CFM	Q-9	20	.800	Ea.	52	24		76	95	
	1340	6" neck diameter, 250 CFM		16	1		58	30		88	111	
	1400	12" neck diameter, 770 CFM		10	1.600		84.50	48.50		133	167	
	1500	24" neck diameter, 3,100 CFM		8	2		245	60.50		305.50	365	
	1540	36" neck diameter, 5,500 CFM	↓	6	2.667	↓	720	80.50		800.50	915	
	2000	Stationary, gravity, syphon, galvanized										
	2160	6" neck diameter, 66 CFM	Q-9	16	1	Ea.	45	30		75	96	
	2240	12" neck diameter, 160 CFM		10	1.600		94.50	48.50		143	179	
	2340	24" neck diameter, 900 CFM		8	2		257	60.50		317.50	375	
	2380	36" neck diameter, 2,000 CFM		6	2.667		805	80.50		885.50	1,000	
	4200	Stationary mushroom, aluminum, 16" orifice diameter		10	1.600		246	48.50		294.50	345	
	4220	26" orifice diameter		6.15	2.602		365	78.50		443.50	520	
	4230	30" orifice diameter	↓	5.71	2.802	↓	530	84.50		614.50	715	

(note: R15700 -040 reference box near item 0560/0660)

MECHANICAL 15

15854 | Ventilators

			CREW	DAILY OUTPUT	LABOR-HOURS	UNIT	MAT.	LABOR	EQUIP.	TOTAL	TOTAL INCL O&P	
								2001 BARE COSTS				
300	4240	38" orifice diameter	Q-9	5	3.200	Ea.	760	96.50		856.50	985	**300**
	4250	42" orifice diameter R15700-040		4.70	3.404		1,000	103		1,103	1,250	
	4260	50" orifice diameter	↓	4.44	3.604	↓	1,200	109		1,309	1,500	
	5000	Relief vent										
	5500	Rectangular, aluminum, galvanized curb										
	5510	intake/exhaust, 0.05" SP										
	5600	500 CFM, 12" x 16"	Q-9	8	2	Ea.	365	60.50		425.50	495	
	5640	1000 CFM, 12" x 24"		6.60	2.424		435	73		508	590	
	5680	3000 CFM, 20" x 42"	↓	4	4	↓	750	121		871	1,000	

15860 | Air Cleaning Devices

			CREW	DAILY OUTPUT	LABOR-HOURS	UNIT	MAT.	LABOR	EQUIP.	TOTAL	TOTAL INCL O&P	
								2001 BARE COSTS				
100	0010	**AIR FILTERS**										**100**
	0050	Activated charcoal type, full flow				MCFM	600			600	660	
	2000	Electronic air cleaner, duct mounted										
	2150	400 - 1000 CFM	1 Shee	2.30	3.478	Ea.	545	117		662	775	
	2200	1000 - 1400 CFM		2.20	3.636		700	122		822	955	
	2250	1400 - 2000 CFM	↓	2.10	3.810	↓	760	128		888	1,025	
	2950	Mechanical media filtration units										
	3000	High efficiency type, with frame, non-supported				MCFM	45			45	49.50	
	3100	Supported type					55			55	60.50	
	4000	Medium efficiency, extended surface					5			5	5.50	
	4500	Permanent washable					20			20	22	
	5000	Renewable disposable roll				↓	120			120	132	
	5500	Throwaway glass or paper media type				Ea.	4.60			4.60	5.05	

15950 | Testing/Adjusting/Balancing

15955 | HVAC Test/Adjust/Balance

			CREW	DAILY OUTPUT	LABOR-HOURS	UNIT	MAT.	LABOR	EQUIP.	TOTAL	TOTAL INCL O&P	
								2001 BARE COSTS				
100	0010	**BALANCING, AIR** (Subcontractor's quote incl. material & labor)										**100**
	0900	Heating and ventilating equipment										
	1000	Centrifugal fans, utility sets				Ea.					248.64	
	1100	Heating and ventilating unit									372.96	
	1200	In-line fan									372.96	
	1300	Propeller and wall fan									70.45	
	1400	Roof exhaust fan									165.76	
	2000	Air conditioning equipment, central station									538.72	
	2100	Built-up low pressure unit									497.28	
	2200	Built-up high pressure unit									580.16	
	2500	Multi-zone A.C. and heating unit									372.96	
	2600	For each zone over one, add									82.88	
	2700	Package A.C. unit									207.20	
	2800	Rooftop heating and cooling unit									290.08	
	3000	Supply, return, exhaust, registers & diffusers, avg. height ceiling									49.73	
	3100	High ceiling									74.59	
	3200	Floor height				↓					41.44	
900	0010	**BALANCING, WATER** (Subcontractor's quote incl. material & labor)										**900**
	0050	Air cooled condenser				Ea.					147.28	

Important: See the Reference Section for critical supporting data - Reference Nos., Crews, & City Cost Indexes

15 MECHANICAL

15955		HVAC Test/Adjust/Balance	CREW	DAILY OUTPUT	LABOR-HOURS	UNIT	2001 BARE COSTS				TOTAL INCL O&P	
							MAT.	LABOR	EQUIP.	TOTAL		
900	0100	Cabinet unit heater				Ea.					50.50	900
	0200	Chiller									357.68	
	0300	Convector									42.08	
	0500	Cooling tower									273.52	
	0600	Fan coil unit, unit ventilator									75.74	
	0700	Fin tube and radiant panels									84.16	
	0800	Main and duct re-heat coils									77.85	
	0810	Heat exchanger									77.85	
	1000	Pumps									185.15	
	1100	Unit heater									58.91	

For information about Means Estimating Seminars, see yellow pages 11 and 12 in back of book

MECHANICAL 15

Division Notes

	CREW	DAILY OUTPUT	LABOR-HOURS	UNIT	2001 BARE COSTS				TOTAL INCL O&P
					MAT.	LABOR	EQUIP.	TOTAL	

Division 16
Electrical

Estimating Tips

16060 Grounding & Bonding
- When taking off grounding system, identify separately the type and size of wire and list each unique type of ground connection.

16100 Wiring Methods
- Conduit should be taken off in three main categories: power distribution, branch power, and branch lighting, so the estimator can concentrate on systems and components, therefore making it easier to ensure all items have been accounted for.
- For cost modifications for elevated conduit installation, add the percentages to labor according to the height of installation and only the quantities exceeding the different height levels, not to the total conduit quantities.
- Remember that aluminum wiring of equal ampacity is larger in diameter than copper and may require larger conduit.
- If more than three wires at a time are being pulled, deduct percentages from the labor hours of that grouping of wires.

- The estimator should take the weights of materials into consideration when completing a takeoff. Topics to consider include: How will the materials be supported? What methods of support are available? How high will the support structure have to reach? Will the final support structure be able to withstand the total burden? Is the support material included or separate from the fixture, equipment and material specified?

16200 Electrical Power
- Do not overlook the costs for equipment used in the installation. If scaffolding or highlifts are available in the field, contractors may use them in lieu of the proposed ladders and rolling staging.

16400 Low-Voltage Distribution
- Supports and concrete pads may be shown on drawings for the larger equipment, or the support system may be just a piece of plywood for the back of a panelboard. In either case, it must be included in the costs.

16500 Lighting
- Fixtures should be taken off room by room, using the fixture schedule, specifications, and the ceiling plan. For large concentrations of lighting fixtures in the same area deduct the percentages from labor hours.

16700 Communications
16800 Sound & Video
- When estimating material costs for special systems, it is always prudent to obtain manufacturers' quotations for equipment prices and special installation requirements which will affect the total costs.

Reference Numbers
Reference numbers are shown in bold squares at the beginning of some major classifications. These numbers refer to related items in the Reference Section. The reference information may be an estimating procedure, an alternate pricing method or technical information.

Note: Not all subdivisions listed here necessarily appear in this publication.

16055	Selective Demolition	CREW	DAILY OUTPUT	LABOR-HOURS	UNIT	2001 BARE COSTS				TOTAL INCL O&P
						MAT.	LABOR	EQUIP.	TOTAL	
300	0010	**ELECTRICAL DEMOLITION**									300
0020	Conduit to 15' high, including fittings & hangers									
0100	Rigid galvanized steel, 1/2" to 1" diameter	1 Elec	242	.033	L.F.		1.13		1.13	1.69
0120	1-1/4" to 2"		200	.040			1.37		1.37	2.05
0140	2" to 4"		151	.053			1.82		1.82	2.71
0160	4" to 6"		80	.100			3.43		3.43	5.10
0200	Electric metallic tubing (EMT) 1/2" to 1"		394	.020			.70		.70	1.04
0220	1-1/4" to 1-1/2"		326	.025			.84		.84	1.26
0260	3-1/2" to 4"	▼	155	.052	▼		1.77		1.77	2.64
0270	Armored cable, (BX) avg. 50' runs									
0280	#14, 2 wire	1 Elec	690	.012	L.F.		.40		.40	.59
0290	#14, 3 wire		571	.014			.48		.48	.72
0300	#12, 2 wire		605	.013			.45		.45	.68
0310	#12, 3 wire		514	.016			.53		.53	.80
0320	#10, 2 wire		514	.016			.53		.53	.80
0330	#10, 3 wire		425	.019			.65		.65	.96
0340	#8, 3 wire	▼	342	.023	▼		.80		.80	1.20
0350	Non metallic sheathed cable (Romex)									
0360	#14, 2 wire	1 Elec	720	.011	L.F.		.38		.38	.57
0370	#14, 3 wire		657	.012			.42		.42	.62
0380	#12, 2 wire		629	.013			.44		.44	.65
0390	#10, 3 wire	▼	450	.018	▼		.61		.61	.91
0400	Wiremold raceway, including fittings & hangers									
0420	No. 3000	1 Elec	250	.032	L.F.		1.10		1.10	1.64
0440	No. 4000		217	.037			1.26		1.26	1.89
0460	No. 6000	▼	166	.048	▼		1.65		1.65	2.47
0500	Channels, steel, including fittings & hangers									
0520	3/4" x 1-1/2"	1 Elec	308	.026	L.F.		.89		.89	1.33
0540	1-1/2" x 1-1/2"		269	.030			1.02		1.02	1.52
0560	1-1/2" x 1-7/8"	▼	229	.035	▼		1.20		1.20	1.79
0600	Copper bus duct, indoor, 3 phase									
0610	Including hangers & supports									
0620	225 amp	2 Elec	135	.119	L.F.		4.07		4.07	6.05
0640	400 amp		106	.151			5.20		5.20	7.75
0660	600 amp		86	.186			6.40		6.40	9.55
0680	1000 amp		60	.267			9.15		9.15	13.65
0700	1600 amp		40	.400			13.70		13.70	20.50
0720	3000 amp	▼	10	1.600	▼		55		55	82
1300	Transformer, dry type, 1 ph, incl. removal of									
1320	supports, wire & pipe terminations									
1340	1 kVA	1 Elec	7.70	1.039	Ea.		35.50		35.50	53
1420	75 kVA	"	1.25	6.400	"		220		220	330
1440	3 Phase to 600V, primary									
1460	3 kVA	1 Elec	3.85	2.078	Ea.		71.50		71.50	106
1520	75 kVA	"	1.35	5.926			203		203	305
1550	300 kVA	R-3	1.80	11.111			375	79	454	650
1570	750 kVA	"	1.10	18.182	▼		615	129	744	1,050
1800	Wire, THW-THWN-THHN, removed from									
1810	in place conduit, to 15' high									
1830	#14	1 Elec	65	.123	C.L.F.		4.22		4.22	6.30
1840	#12		55	.145			4.99		4.99	7.45
1850	#10		45.50	.176			6.05		6.05	9
1860	#8		40.40	.198			6.80		6.80	10.15
1870	#6	▼	32.60	.245			8.40		8.40	12.55
1880	#4	2 Elec	53	.302	▼		10.35		10.35	15.45
1890	#3	▼	50	.320	▼		11		11	16.40

Important: See the Reference Section for critical supporting data - Reference Nos., Crews, & City Cost Indexes

16 ELECTRICAL

16050 | Basic Electrical Materials & Methods

16055	Selective Demolition	CREW	DAILY OUTPUT	LABOR-HOURS	UNIT	MAT.	LABOR	EQUIP.	TOTAL	TOTAL INCL O&P
1900	#2	2 Elec	44.60	.359	C.L.F.		12.30		12.30	18.35
1910	1/0		33.20	.482			16.55		16.55	24.50
1920	2/0		29.20	.548			18.80		18.80	28
1930	3/0		25	.640			22		22	33
1940	4/0		22	.727			25		25	37
1950	250 kcmil		20	.800			27.50		27.50	41
1960	300 kcmil		19	.842			29		29	43
1970	350 kcmil		18	.889			30.50		30.50	45.50
1980	400 kcmil		17	.941			32.50		32.50	48
1990	500 kcmil		16.20	.988			34		34	50.50
2000	Interior fluorescent fixtures, incl. supports									
2010	& whips, to 15' high									
2100	Recessed drop-in 2' x 2', 2 lamp	2 Elec	35	.457	Ea.		15.70		15.70	23.50
2120	2' x 4', 2 lamp		33	.485			16.65		16.65	25
2140	2' x 4', 4 lamp		30	.533			18.30		18.30	27.50
2160	4' x 4', 4 lamp		20	.800			27.50		27.50	41
2180	Surface mount, acrylic lens & hinged frame									
2200	1' x 4', 2 lamp	2 Elec	44	.364	Ea.		12.45		12.45	18.60
2220	2' x 2', 2 lamp		44	.364			12.45		12.45	18.60
2260	2' x 4', 4 lamp		33	.485			16.65		16.65	25
2280	4' x 4', 4 lamp		40	.400			13.70		13.70	20.50
2300	Strip fixtures, surface mount									
2320	4' long, 1 lamp	2 Elec	53	.302	Ea.		10.35		10.35	15.45
2340	4' long, 2 lamp		50	.320			11		11	16.40
2360	8' long, 1 lamp		42	.381			13.05		13.05	19.50
2380	8' long, 2 lamp		40	.400			13.70		13.70	20.50
2400	Pendant mount, industrial, incl. removal									
2410	of chain or rod hangers, to 15' high									
2420	4' long, 2 lamp	2 Elec	35	.457	Ea.		15.70		15.70	23.50
2440	8' long, 2 lamp	"	27	.593	"		20.50		20.50	30.50

16060 | Grounding & Bonding

	GROUNDING	CREW	DAILY OUTPUT	LABOR-HOURS	UNIT	MAT.	LABOR	EQUIP.	TOTAL	TOTAL INCL O&P
0010	**GROUNDING**									
0030	Rod, copper clad, 8' long, 1/2" diameter	1 Elec	5.50	1.455	Ea.	15.85	50		65.85	92
0050	3/4" diameter		5.30	1.509		30	52		82	111
0080	10' long, 1/2" diameter		4.80	1.667		17.50	57		74.50	105
0100	3/4" diameter		4.40	1.818		29.50	62.50		92	126
0130	15' long, 3/4" diameter		4	2		79	68.50		147.50	189
0390	Bare copper wire, #8 stranded		11	.727	C.L.F.	14.10	25		39.10	52.50
0400	#6		10	.800		23.50	27.50		51	66.50
0600	#2	2 Elec	10	1.600		54.50	55		109.50	142
0800	3/0		6.60	2.424		132	83		215	269
1000	4/0		5.70	2.807		164	96.50		260.50	325
1200	250 kcmil	3 Elec	7.20	3.333		194	114		308	385
1800	Water pipe ground clamps, heavy duty									
2000	Bronze, 1/2" to 1" diameter	1 Elec	8	1	Ea.	11.70	34.50		46.20	64
2100	1-1/4" to 2" diameter		8	1		15.30	34.50		49.80	68
2200	2-1/2" to 3" diameter		6	1.333		41	45.50		86.50	114
2800	Brazed connections, #6 wire		12	.667		10.75	23		33.75	46
3000	#2 wire		10	.800		14.40	27.50		41.90	57
3100	3/0 wire		8	1		21.50	34.50		56	75
3200	4/0 wire		7	1.143		24.50	39		63.50	85.50
3400	250 kcmil wire		5	1.600		29	55		84	114
3600	500 kcmil wire		4	2		35.50	68.50		104	141

			DAILY	LABOR-		2001 BARE COSTS				TOTAL
16120	**Conductors & Cables**	CREW	OUTPUT	HOURS	UNIT	MAT.	LABOR	EQUIP.	TOTAL	INCL O&P
120	0010	**ARMORED CABLE**									120
0050	600 volt, copper (BX), #14, 2 conductor, solid	1 Elec	2.40	3.333	C.L.F.	47.50	114		161.50	224
0100	3 conductor, solid		2.20	3.636		62.50	125		187.50	255
0150	#12, 2 conductor, solid		2.30	3.478		49	119		168	232
0200	3 conductor, solid		2	4		74	137		211	287
0250	#10, 2 conductor, solid		2	4		87.50	137		224.50	300
0300	3 conductor, solid		1.60	5		116	172		288	385
0350	#8, 3 conductor, solid		1.30	6.154		189	211		400	525
0400	3 conductor with PVC jacket, in cable tray, #6		3.10	2.581		254	88.50		342.50	410
0450	#4	2 Elec	5.40	2.963		330	102		432	510
0500	#2		4.60	3.478		435	119		554	660
0550	#1		4	4		590	137		727	855
0600	1/0		3.60	4.444		695	152		847	995
0650	2/0		3.40	4.706		840	161		1,001	1,175
0700	3/0		3.20	5		985	172		1,157	1,325
0750	4/0		3	5.333		1,125	183		1,308	1,525
0800	250 kcmil	3 Elec	3.60	6.667		1,275	229		1,504	1,750
0850	350 kcmil		3.30	7.273		1,700	249		1,949	2,225
0900	500 kcmil		3	8		2,200	274		2,474	2,825
1050	5 kV, copper, 3 conductor with PVC jacket,									
1060	non-shielded, in cable tray, #4	2 Elec	380	.042	L.F.	5	1.44		6.44	7.65
1100	#2		360	.044		6.50	1.52		8.02	9.45
1200	#1		300	.053		8.25	1.83		10.08	11.85
1400	1/0		290	.055		9.55	1.89		11.44	13.30
1600	2/0		260	.062		11.05	2.11		13.16	15.30
2000	4/0		240	.067		14.75	2.29		17.04	19.65
2100	250 kcmil	3 Elec	330	.073		20	2.49		22.49	25.50
2150	350 kcmil		315	.076		25	2.61		27.61	31.50
2200	500 kcmil		270	.089		30.50	3.05		33.55	38
2400	15 kV, copper, 3 conductor with PVC jacket galv steel armored									
2500	grounded neutral, in cable tray, #2	2 Elec	300	.053	L.F.	10.50	1.83		12.33	14.30
2600	#1		280	.057		11.20	1.96		13.16	15.25
2800	1/0		260	.062		12.90	2.11		15.01	17.30
2900	2/0		220	.073		17	2.49		19.49	22.50
3000	4/0		190	.084		19.30	2.89		22.19	25.50
3100	250 kcmil	3 Elec	270	.089		21.50	3.05		24.55	28
3150	350 kcmil		240	.100		25.50	3.43		28.93	33
3200	500 kcmil		210	.114		34	3.92		37.92	43.50
3400	15 kV, copper, 3 conductor with PVC jacket,									
3450	ungrounded neutral, in cable tray, #2	2 Elec	260	.062	L.F.	11.30	2.11		13.41	15.60
3500	#1		230	.070		12.55	2.39		14.94	17.35
3600	1/0		200	.080		14.35	2.74		17.09	19.90
3700	2/0		190	.084		17.65	2.89		20.54	23.50
3800	4/0		160	.100		21.50	3.43		24.93	28.50
4000	250 kcmil	3 Elec	210	.114		25	3.92		28.92	33.50
4050	350 kcmil		195	.123		32.50	4.22		36.72	42.50
4100	500 kcmil		180	.133		39.50	4.57		44.07	50.50
9010	600 volt, copper (MC) steel clad, #14, 2 wire	1 Elec	2.40	3.333	C.L.F.	47	114		161	223
9020	3 wire		2.20	3.636		61.50	125		186.50	254
9040	#12, 2 wire		2.30	3.478		50.50	119		169.50	234
9050	3 wire		2	4		75	137		212	288
9070	#10, 2 wire		2	4		87	137		224	300
9080	3 wire		1.60	5		133	172		305	400
9100	#8, 2 wire, stranded		1.80	4.444		166	152		318	410
9110	3 wire, stranded		1.30	6.154		238	211		449	575
9200	600 volt, copper (MC) alum. clad, #14, 2 wire		2.65	3.019		47	104		151	207

Important: See the Reference Section for critical supporting data - Reference Nos., Crews, & City Cost Indexes

		16120	Conductors & Cables	CREW	DAILY OUTPUT	LABOR-HOURS	UNIT	2001 BARE COSTS				TOTAL INCL O&P	
								MAT.	LABOR	EQUIP.	TOTAL		
120	9210		3 wire	1 Elec	2.45	3.265	C.L.F.	61.50	112		173.50	235	120
	9220		4 wire		2.20	3.636		86.50	125		211.50	281	
	9230		#12, 2 wire		2.55	3.137		50.50	108		158.50	217	
	9240		3 wire		2.20	3.636		75	125		200	269	
	9250		4 wire		2	4		98.50	137		235.50	315	
	9260		#10, 2 wire		2.20	3.636		87	125		212	282	
	9270		3 wire		1.80	4.444		133	152		285	375	
	9280		4 wire		1.55	5.161		206	177		383	490	
230	0010	**CABLE TERMINATIONS**											230
	0015		Wire connectors, screw type, #22 to #14	1 Elec	260	.031	Ea.	.06	1.06		1.12	1.65	
	0020		#18 to #12		240	.033		.06	1.14		1.20	1.78	
	0025		#18 to #10		240	.033		.09	1.14		1.23	1.81	
	0030		Screw-on connectors, insulated, #18 to #12		240	.033		.08	1.14		1.22	1.80	
	0035		#16 to #10		230	.035		.10	1.19		1.29	1.89	
	0040		#14 to #8		210	.038		.22	1.31		1.53	2.19	
	0045		#12 to #6		180	.044		.35	1.52		1.87	2.67	
	0050		Terminal lugs, solderless, #16 to #10		50	.160		.44	5.50		5.94	8.70	
	0100		#8 to #4		30	.267		.57	9.15		9.72	14.30	
	0150		#2 to #1		22	.364		.77	12.45		13.22	19.45	
	0200		1/0 to 2/0		16	.500		2.15	17.15		19.30	28	
	0250		3/0		12	.667		2.62	23		25.62	37	
	0300		4/0		11	.727		2.62	25		27.62	40	
	0350		250 kcmil		9	.889		2.62	30.50		33.12	48.50	
	0400		350 kcmil		7	1.143		3.39	39		42.39	62	
	0450		500 kcmil		6	1.333		6.60	45.50		52.10	76	
	1600		Crimp 1 hole lugs, copper or aluminum, 600 volt										
	1620		#14	1 Elec	60	.133	Ea.	.29	4.57		4.86	7.15	
	1630		#12		50	.160		.41	5.50		5.91	8.65	
	1640		#10		45	.178		.41	6.10		6.51	9.55	
	1780		#8		36	.222		1.56	7.60		9.16	13.10	
	1800		#6		30	.267		2.50	9.15		11.65	16.40	
	2000		#4		27	.296		2.80	10.15		12.95	18.25	
	2200		#2		24	.333		3.70	11.45		15.15	21	
	2400		#1		20	.400		4.15	13.70		17.85	25	
	2600		2/0		15	.533		5.10	18.30		23.40	33	
	2800		3/0		12	.667		6	23		29	40.50	
	3000		4/0		11	.727		6.50	25		31.50	44	
	3200		250 kcmil		9	.889		7.90	30.50		38.40	54	
	3400		300 kcmil		8	1		8.80	34.50		43.30	60.50	
	3500		350 kcmil		7	1.143		9	39		48	68.50	
	3600		400 kcmil		6.50	1.231		10.65	42		52.65	74.50	
	3800		500 kcmil		6	1.333		12.90	45.50		58.40	82.50	
280	0010	**CONTROL CABLE**											280
	0020		600 volt, copper, #14 THWN wire with PVC jacket, 2 wires	1 Elec	9	.889	C.L.F.	13	30.50		43.50	60	
	0100		4 wires		7	1.143		20.50	39		59.50	81	
	0200		6 wires		6	1.333		33	45.50		78.50	105	
	0300		8 wires		5.30	1.509		39	52		91	121	
	0400		10 wires		4.80	1.667		47	57		104	137	
	0500		12 wires		4.30	1.860		53	64		117	154	
	0600		14 wires		3.80	2.105		65	72		137	180	
	0700		16 wires		3.50	2.286		76	78.50		154.50	201	
	0800		18 wires		3.30	2.424		79	83		162	211	
	0900		20 wires		3	2.667		97	91.50		188.50	244	
	1000		22 wires		2.80	2.857		99	98		197	255	
400	0010	**FIBER OPTICS**											400
	0020		Fiber optics cable only. Added costs depend on the type of fiber										

ELECTRICAL 16

16120		Conductors & Cables	CREW	DAILY OUTPUT	LABOR-HOURS	UNIT	2001 BARE COSTS				TOTAL INCL O&P
							MAT.	LABOR	EQUIP.	TOTAL	
400	0030	special connectors, optical modems, and networking parts.										400
	0040	Specialized tools & techniques cause installation costs to vary.									
	0070	Cable, minimum, bulk simplex	1 Elec	8	1	C.L.F.	24	34.50		58.50	77.50
	0080	Cable, maximum, bulk plenum quad	"	2.29	3.493	"	117	120		237	310
	0150	Fiber optic jumper				Ea.	55.50			55.50	61
	0200	Fiber optic pigtail					30			30	33
	0300	Fiber optic connector	1 Elec	24	.333		16.90	11.45		28.35	35.50
	0350	Fiber optic finger splice		32	.250		32	8.60		40.60	48
	0400	Transceiver (low cost bi-directional)		8	1		425	34.50		459.50	520
	0450	Multi-channel rack enclosure (10 modules)		2	4		475	137		612	730
	0500	Fiber optic patch panel (12 ports)	▼	6	1.333	▼	178	45.50		223.50	265
500	0010	**MINERAL INSULATED CABLE** 600 volt										500
	0100	1 conductor, #12	1 Elec	1.60	5	C.L.F.	195	172		367	470
	0200	#10		1.60	5		255	172		427	535
	0400	#8		1.50	5.333		299	183		482	605
	0500	#6	▼	1.40	5.714		335	196		531	665
	0600	#4	2 Elec	2.40	6.667		465	229		694	850
	0800	#2		2.20	7.273		620	249		869	1,050
	0900	#1		2.10	7.619		710	261		971	1,175
	1000	1/0		2	8		815	274		1,089	1,300
	1100	2/0		1.90	8.421		975	289		1,264	1,500
	1200	3/0		1.80	8.889		1,150	305		1,455	1,725
	1400	4/0	▼	1.60	10		1,325	345		1,670	1,950
	1410	250 kcmil	3 Elec	2.40	10		1,500	345		1,845	2,150
	1420	350 kcmil		1.95	12.308		1,675	420		2,095	2,475
	1430	500 kcmil	▼	1.95	12.308	▼	2,100	420		2,520	2,925
550	0010	**NON-METALLIC SHEATHED CABLE** 600 volt										550
	0100	Copper with ground wire, (Romex)									
	0150	#14, 2 conductor	1 Elec	2.70	2.963	C.L.F.	14.45	102		116.45	168
	0200	3 conductor		2.40	3.333		26.50	114		140.50	200
	0250	#12, 2 conductor		2.50	3.200		21	110		131	187
	0300	3 conductor		2.20	3.636		37	125		162	227
	0350	#10, 2 conductor		2.20	3.636		40.50	125		165.50	231
	0400	3 conductor		1.80	4.444		53.50	152		205.50	287
	0450	#8, 3 conductor		1.50	5.333		113	183		296	395
	0500	#6, 3 conductor	▼	1.40	5.714	▼	176	196		372	485
	0550	SE type SER aluminum cable, 3 RHW and									
	0600	1 bare neutral, 3 #8 & 1 #8	1 Elec	1.60	5	C.L.F.	93	172		265	360
	0650	3 #6 & 1 #6	"	1.40	5.714		105	196		301	410
	0700	3 #4 & 1 #6	2 Elec	2.40	6.667		118	229		347	470
	0750	3 #2 & 1 #4		2.20	7.273		174	249		423	560
	0800	3 #1/0 & 1 #2		2	8		263	274		537	700
	0850	3 #2/0 & 1 #1		1.80	8.889		310	305		615	795
	0900	3 #4/0 & 1 #2/0	▼	1.60	10	▼	440	345		785	995
700	0010	**SHIELDED CABLE** Splicing & terminations not included										700
	0040	Copper, XLP shielding, 5 kV, #6	2 Elec	4.40	3.636	C.L.F.	86.50	125		211.50	282
	0050	#4		4.40	3.636		112	125		237	310
	0100	#2		4	4		133	137		270	350
	0200	#1		4	4		153	137		290	375
	0400	1/0		3.80	4.211		168	144		312	400
	0600	2/0		3.60	4.444		209	152		361	460
	0800	4/0	▼	3.20	5		275	172		447	560
	1000	250 kcmil	3 Elec	4.50	5.333		330	183		513	640
	1200	350 kcmil	▼	3.90	6.154	▼	430	211		641	785

16 ELECTRICAL

Important: See the Reference Section for critical supporting data - Reference Nos., Crews, & City Cost Indexes

16120 | Conductors & Cables

		CREW	DAILY OUTPUT	LABOR-HOURS	UNIT	2001 BARE COSTS				TOTAL INCL O&P	
						MAT.	LABOR	EQUIP.	TOTAL		
700	1400	500 kcmil	3 Elec	3.60	6.667	C.L.F.	530	229		759	925	**700**
	1600	15 KV, ungrounded neutral, #1	2 Elec	4	4		188	137		325	410	
	1800	1/0		3.80	4.211		224	144		368	460	
	2000	2/0		3.60	4.444		255	152		407	510	
	2200	4/0		3.20	5		335	172		507	625	
	2400	250 kcmil	3 Elec	4.50	5.333		370	183		553	685	
	2600	350 kcmil		3.90	6.154		470	211		681	830	
	2800	500 kcmil		3.60	6.667		580	229		809	980	
900	0010	**WIRE**										**900**
	0020	600 volt type THW, copper, solid, #14 R16120-910	1 Elec	13	.615	C.L.F.	4.13	21		25.13	36	
	0030	#12		11	.727		5.85	25		30.85	43.50	
	0040	#10		10	.800		9.45	27.50		36.95	51.50	
	0050	Stranded, #14 R16132-210		13	.615		4.55	21		25.55	36.50	
	0100	#12		11	.727		6.45	25		31.45	44	
	0120	#10		10	.800		9.90	27.50		37.40	52	
	0140	#8		8	1		17.05	34.50		51.55	70	
	0160	#6		6.50	1.231		27.50	42		69.50	93	
	0180	#4	2 Elec	10.60	1.509		42	52		94	124	
	0200	#3		10	1.600		51.50	55		106.50	139	
	0220	#2		9	1.778		65.50	61		126.50	163	
	0240	#1		8	2		83	68.50		151.50	194	
	0260	1/0		6.60	2.424		98	83		181	232	
	0280	2/0		5.80	2.759		123	94.50		217.50	276	
	0300	3/0		5	3.200		151	110		261	330	
	0350	4/0		4.40	3.636		189	125		314	395	
	0400	250 kcmil	3 Elec	6	4		228	137		365	455	
	0420	300 kcmil		5.70	4.211		270	144		414	515	
	0450	350 kcmil		5.40	4.444		315	152		467	575	
	0480	400 kcmil		5.10	4.706		360	161		521	635	
	0490	500 kcmil		4.80	5		440	172		612	740	
	0530	Aluminum, stranded, #8	1 Elec	9	.889		12.25	30.50		42.75	59	
	0540	#6	"	8	1		15.60	34.50		50.10	68	
	0560	#4	2 Elec	13	1.231		19.35	42		61.35	84.50	
	0580	#2		10.60	1.509		26	52		78	107	
	0600	#1		9	1.778		38.50	61		99.50	133	
	0620	1/0		8	2		45.50	68.50		114	152	
	0640	2/0		7.20	2.222		54	76		130	174	
	0680	3/0		6.60	2.424		67.50	83		150.50	198	
	0700	4/0		6.20	2.581		75	88.50		163.50	215	
	0720	250 kcmil	3 Elec	8.70	2.759		91.50	94.50		186	242	
	0740	300 kcmil		8.10	2.963		126	102		228	291	
	0760	350 kcmil		7.50	3.200		128	110		238	305	
	0780	400 kcmil		6.90	3.478		150	119		269	345	
	0800	500 kcmil		6	4		165	137		302	385	
	0850	600 kcmil		5.70	4.211		209	144		353	445	
	0880	700 kcmil		5.10	4.706		242	161		403	505	
	0900	750 kcmil		4.80	5		244	172		416	525	
	0920	Type THWN-THHN, copper, solid, #14	1 Elec	13	.615		4.13	21		25.13	36	
	0940	#12		11	.727		5.85	25		30.85	43.50	
	0960	#10		10	.800		9.45	27.50		36.95	51.50	
	1000	Stranded, #14		13	.615		4.55	21		25.55	36.50	
	1200	#12		11	.727		6.45	25		31.45	44	
	1250	#10 **CN**		10	.800		9.90	27.50		37.40	52	
	1300	#8		8	1		17.05	34.50		51.55	70	
	1350	#6		6.50	1.231		27.50	42		69.50	93	
	1400	#4	2 Elec	10.60	1.509		42	52		94	124	

ELECTRICAL 16

16131 | Cable Trays

		CREW	DAILY OUTPUT	LABOR-HOURS	UNIT	2001 BARE COSTS				TOTAL INCL O&P
						MAT.	LABOR	EQUIP.	TOTAL	
105	0010	**CABLE TRAY LADDER TYPE** w/ ftngs & supports, 4" dp., to 15' elev.										105
	0160	Galvanized steel tray									
	0170	4" rung spacing, 6" wide	2 Elec	98	.163	L.F.	8.15	5.60		13.75	17.30
	0200	12" wide		86	.186		9.80	6.40		16.20	20.50
	0400	18" wide		82	.195		11.40	6.70		18.10	22.50
	0600	24" wide		78	.205		13.10	7.05		20.15	25
	3200	Aluminum tray, 4" deep, 6" rung spacing, 6" wide		134	.119		10.25	4.10		14.35	17.35
	3220	12" wide		124	.129		11.45	4.43		15.88	19.20
	3230	18" wide		114	.140		12.75	4.81		17.56	21.50
	3240	24" wide	▼	106	.151	▼	14.90	5.20		20.10	24
	9980	Allow. for tray ftngs., 5% min.-20% max.									

16132 | Conduit & Tubing

		CREW	DAILY OUTPUT	LABOR-HOURS	UNIT	2001 BARE COSTS				TOTAL INCL O&P
						MAT.	LABOR	EQUIP.	TOTAL	
205	0010	**CONDUIT** To 15' high, includes 2 terminations, 2 elbows and										205
	0020	11 beam clamps per 100 L.F. R16132 -210									
	0300	Aluminum, 1/2" diameter	1 Elec	100	.080	L.F.	1.21	2.74		3.95	5.45
	0500	3/4" diameter		90	.089		1.62	3.05		4.67	6.35
	0700	1" diameter		80	.100		2.20	3.43		5.63	7.50
	1000	1-1/4" diameter		70	.114		2.84	3.92		6.76	8.95
	1030	1-1/2" diameter		65	.123		3.51	4.22		7.73	10.15
	1050	2" diameter		60	.133		4.65	4.57		9.22	11.95
	1070	2-1/2" diameter	▼	50	.160		7.25	5.50		12.75	16.15
	1100	3" diameter	2 Elec	90	.178		9.70	6.10		15.80	19.75
	1130	3-1/2" diameter		80	.200		12	6.85		18.85	23.50
	1140	4" diameter	▼	70	.229		14.55	7.85		22.40	27.50
	1750	Rigid galvanized steel, 1/2" diameter	1 Elec	90	.089		1.58	3.05		4.63	6.30
	1770	3/4" diameter		80	.100		1.87	3.43		5.30	7.15
	1800	1" diameter		65	.123		2.62	4.22		6.84	9.20
	1830	1-1/4" diameter		60	.133		3.49	4.57		8.06	10.70
	1850	1-1/2" diameter		55	.145		4.16	4.99		9.15	12
	1870	2" diameter		45	.178		5.55	6.10		11.65	15.20
	1900	2-1/2" diameter	▼	35	.229		9.20	7.85		17.05	22
	1930	3" diameter	2 Elec	50	.320		11.65	11		22.65	29
	1950	3-1/2" diameter		44	.364		14.25	12.45		26.70	34.50
	1970	4" diameter	▼	40	.400		17.05	13.70		30.75	39.50
	2500	Steel, intermediate conduit (IMC), 1/2" diameter	1 Elec	100	.080		1.25	2.74		3.99	5.50
	2530	3/4" diameter		90	.089		1.49	3.05		4.54	6.20
	2550	1" diameter		70	.114		2.06	3.92		5.98	8.10
	2570	1-1/4" diameter		65	.123		2.69	4.22		6.91	9.25
	2600	1-1/2" diameter		60	.133		3.09	4.57		7.66	10.25
	2630	2" diameter		50	.160		4	5.50		9.50	12.60
	2650	2-1/2" diameter	▼	40	.200		7.90	6.85		14.75	18.95
	2670	3" diameter	2 Elec	60	.267		10.20	9.15		19.35	25
	2700	3-1/2" diameter		54	.296		12.50	10.15		22.65	29
	2730	4" diameter	▼	50	.320		14.50	11		25.50	32.50
	5000	Electric metallic tubing (EMT), 1/2" diameter	1 Elec	170	.047		.36	1.61		1.97	2.81
	5020	3/4" diameter **CN**		130	.062		.56	2.11		2.67	3.76
	5040	1" diameter		115	.070		.94	2.39		3.33	4.60
	5060	1-1/4" diameter		100	.080		1.41	2.74		4.15	5.65
	5080	1-1/2" diameter		90	.089		1.80	3.05		4.85	6.55
	5100	2" diameter		80	.100		2.29	3.43		5.72	7.60
	5120	2-1/2" diameter	▼	60	.133		5.45	4.57		10.02	12.85
	5140	3" diameter	2 Elec	100	.160		5.90	5.50		11.40	14.70
	5160	3-1/2" diameter		90	.178		7.45	6.10		13.55	17.30
	5180	4" diameter	▼	80	.200	▼	8.35	6.85		15.20	19.45

16 ELECTRICAL

16132 | Conduit & Tubing

		CREW	DAILY OUTPUT	LABOR-HOURS	UNIT	MAT.	LABOR	EQUIP.	TOTAL	TOTAL INCL O&P	
205	9900	Add to labor for higher elevated installation										**205**
	9910	15' to 20' high, add	R16132-210					10%				
	9920	20' to 25' high, add						20%				
	9930	25' to 30' high, add						25%				
	9940	30' to 35' high, add						30%				
	9950	35' to 40' high, add						35%				
	9960	Over 40' high, add						40%				
	9980	Allow. for cond. ftngs., 5% min.-20% max.										
230	0010	**CONDUIT IN CONCRETE SLAB** Including terminations,										**230**
	0020	fittings and supports										
	3230	PVC, schedule 40, 1/2" diameter	1 Elec	270	.030	L.F.	.40	1.02		1.42	1.96	
	3250	3/4" diameter		230	.035		.48	1.19		1.67	2.31	
	3270	1" diameter		200	.040		.64	1.37		2.01	2.76	
	3300	1-1/4" diameter		170	.047		.91	1.61		2.52	3.41	
	3330	1-1/2" diameter		140	.057		1.10	1.96		3.06	4.14	
	3350	2" diameter		120	.067		1.40	2.29		3.69	4.95	
	4350	Rigid galvanized steel, 1/2" diameter		200	.040		1.32	1.37		2.69	3.50	
	4400	3/4" diameter		170	.047		1.60	1.61		3.21	4.17	
	4450	1" diameter		130	.062		2.36	2.11		4.47	5.75	
	4500	1-1/4" diameter		110	.073		3.04	2.49		5.53	7.05	
	4600	1-1/2" diameter		100	.080		3.71	2.74		6.45	8.20	
	4800	2" diameter		90	.089		4.94	3.05		7.99	10	
240	0010	**CONDUIT IN TRENCH** Includes terminations and fittings										**240**
	0020	Does not include excavation or backfill, see div. 02315										
	0200	Rigid galvanized steel, 2" diameter	1 Elec	150	.053	L.F.	4.77	1.83		6.60	8	
	0400	2-1/2" diameter	"	100	.080		8.30	2.74		11.04	13.25	
	0600	3" diameter	2 Elec	160	.100		10.75	3.43		14.18	16.95	
	0800	3-1/2" diameter		140	.114		13.65	3.92		17.57	21	
	1000	4" diameter		100	.160		15.65	5.50		21.15	25.50	
	1200	5" diameter		80	.200		32.50	6.85		39.35	46.50	
	1400	6" diameter		60	.267		46.50	9.15		55.65	64.50	

16133 | Multi-outlet Assemblies

		CREW	DAILY OUTPUT	LABOR-HOURS	UNIT	MAT.	LABOR	EQUIP.	TOTAL	TOTAL INCL O&P	
540	0010	**TRENCH DUCT** Steel with cover										**540**
	0020	Standard adjustable, depths to 4"										
	0100	Straight, single compartment, 9" wide	2 Elec	40	.400	L.F.	67.50	13.70		81.20	95	
	0200	12" wide		32	.500		76.50	17.15		93.65	110	
	0400	18" wide		26	.615		102	21		123	144	
	0600	24" wide		22	.727		131	25		156	181	
	0800	30" wide		20	.800		158	27.50		185.50	215	
	1000	36" wide		16	1		190	34.50		224.50	260	
	1200	Horizontal elbow, 9" wide		5.40	2.963	Ea.	250	102		352	425	
	1400	12" wide		4.60	3.478		288	119		407	495	
	1600	18" wide		4	4		370	137		507	610	
	1800	24" wide		3.20	5		520	172		692	825	
	2000	30" wide		2.60	6.154		695	211		906	1,075	
	2200	36" wide		2.40	6.667		910	229		1,139	1,350	
	2400	Vertical elbow, 9" wide		5.40	2.963		86.50	102		188.50	248	
	2600	12" wide		4.60	3.478		95	119		214	283	
	2800	18" wide		4	4		109	137		246	325	
	3000	24" wide		3.20	5		135	172		307	405	
	3200	30" wide		2.60	6.154		150	211		361	480	
	3400	36" wide		2.40	6.667		164	229		393	520	
	3600	Cross, 9" wide		4	4		410	137		547	655	
	3800	12" wide		3.20	5		435	172		607	730	

ELECTRICAL 16

For expanded coverage of these items see *Means Electrical Cost Data 2001*

16133	Multi-outlet Assemblies	CREW	DAILY OUTPUT	LABOR-HOURS	UNIT	MAT.	LABOR	EQUIP.	TOTAL	TOTAL INCL O&P	
540						**2001 BARE COSTS**					**540**
4000	18" wide	2 Elec	2.60	6.154	Ea.	520	211		731	885	
4200	24" wide		2.20	7.273		660	249		909	1,100	
4400	30" wide		2	8		855	274		1,129	1,350	
4600	36" wide		1.80	8.889		1,075	305		1,380	1,625	
4800	End closure, 9" wide		14.40	1.111		25.50	38		63.50	85	
5000	12" wide		12	1.333		29.50	45.50		75	101	
5200	18" wide		10	1.600		45	55		100	132	
5400	24" wide		8	2		59	68.50		127.50	167	
5600	30" wide		6.60	2.424		73.50	83		156.50	205	
5800	36" wide		5.80	2.759		88	94.50		182.50	238	
6000	Tees, 9" wide		4	4		249	137		386	480	
6200	12" wide		3.60	4.444		290	152		442	550	
6400	18" wide		3.20	5		370	172		542	660	
6600	24" wide		3	5.333		530	183		713	860	
6800	30" wide		2.60	6.154		695	211		906	1,075	
7000	36" wide		2	8		910	274		1,184	1,400	
7200	Riser, and cabinet connector, 9" wide		5.40	2.963		109	102		211	272	
7400	12" wide		4.60	3.478		127	119		246	320	
7600	18" wide		4	4		156	137		293	375	
7800	24" wide		3.20	5		188	172		360	465	
8000	30" wide		2.60	6.154		217	211		428	555	
8200	36" wide		2	8		253	274		527	690	
8400	Insert assembly, cell to conduit adapter, 1-1/4"	1 Elec	16	.500		43	17.15		60.15	73	
560	**0010**	**UNDERFLOOR DUCT**									**560**
0100	Duct, 1-3/8" x 3-1/8" blank, standard	2 Elec	160	.100	L.F.	7.70	3.43		11.13	13.55	
0200	1-3/8" x 7-1/4" blank, super duct		120	.133		15.40	4.57		19.97	24	
0400	7/8" or 1-3/8" insert type, 24" O.C., 1-3/8" x 3-1/8", std.		140	.114		10.30	3.92		14.22	17.20	
0600	1-3/8" x 7-1/4", super duct		100	.160		18	5.50		23.50	28	
0800	Junction box, single duct, 1 level, 3-1/8"	1 Elec	4	2	Ea.	232	68.50		300.50	355	
1000	Junction box, single duct, 1 level, 7-1/4"		2.70	2.963		270	102		372	450	
1200	1 level, 2 duct, 3-1/8"		3.20	2.500		310	86		396	470	
1400	Junction box, 1 level, 2 duct, 7-1/4"		2.30	3.478		795	119		914	1,050	
1600	Triple duct, 3-1/8"		2.30	3.478		525	119		644	760	
1800	Insert to conduit adapter, 3/4" & 1"		32	.250		18.95	8.60		27.55	34	
2000	Support, single cell		27	.296		28.50	10.15		38.65	46.50	
2200	Super duct		16	.500		28.50	17.15		45.65	57	
2400	Double cell		16	.500		28.50	17.15		45.65	57	
2600	Triple cell		11	.727		28.50	25		53.50	68.50	
2800	Vertical elbow, standard duct		10	.800		51	27.50		78.50	97	
3000	Super duct		8	1		51	34.50		85.50	107	
3200	Cabinet connector, standard duct		32	.250		38.50	8.60		47.10	55.50	
3400	Super duct		27	.296		38.50	10.15		48.65	57.50	
3600	Conduit adapter, 1" to 1-1/4"		32	.250		38.50	8.60		47.10	55.50	
3800	2" to 1-1/4"		27	.296		46	10.15		56.15	66	
4000	Outlet, low tension (tele, computer, etc.)		8	1		54	34.50		88.50	111	
4200	High tension, receptacle (120 volt)		8	1		54	34.50		88.50	111	
800	**0010**	**SURFACE RACEWAY**									**800**
0090	Metal, straight section										
0100	No. 500	1 Elec	100	.080	L.F.	.63	2.74		3.37	4.79	
0110	No. 700		100	.080		.71	2.74		3.45	4.88	
0400	No. 1500, small pancake		90	.089		1.33	3.05		4.38	6	
0600	No. 2000, base & cover, blank		90	.089		1.29	3.05		4.34	5.95	
0800	No. 3000, base & cover, blank		75	.107		2.53	3.66		6.19	8.25	
1000	No. 4000, base & cover, blank		65	.123		4.30	4.22		8.52	11.05	

16 ELECTRICAL

Important: See the Reference Section for critical supporting data - Reference Nos., Crews, & City Cost Indexes

16133 | Multi-outlet Assemblies

			DAILY OUTPUT	LABOR-HOURS	UNIT	2001 BARE COSTS				TOTAL INCL O&P	
						MAT.	LABOR	EQUIP.	TOTAL		
			CREW								
800	1200	No. 6000, base & cover, blank	1 Elec	50	.160	L.F.	7.05	5.50		12.55	15.95	800
	2400	Fittings, elbows, No. 500		40	.200	Ea.	1.14	6.85		7.99	11.50	
	2800	Elbow cover, No. 2000		40	.200		2.30	6.85		9.15	12.80	
	2880	Tee, No. 500		42	.190		2.21	6.55		8.76	12.20	
	2900	No. 2000		27	.296		7.05	10.15		17.20	23	
	3000	Switch box, No. 500		16	.500		8.10	17.15		25.25	34.50	
	3400	Telephone outlet, No. 1500		16	.500		8.60	17.15		25.75	35	
	3600	Junction box, No. 1500		16	.500		6	17.15		23.15	32	
	3800	Plugmold wired sections, No. 2000										
	4000	1 circuit, 6 outlets, 3 ft. long	1 Elec	8	1	Ea.	21.50	34.50		56	74.50	
	4100	2 circuits, 8 outlets, 6 ft. long	"	5.30	1.509	"	36	52		88	117	

16134 | Wireway & Aux Gutters

			CREW	DAILY OUTPUT	LABOR-HOURS	UNIT	MAT.	LABOR	EQUIP.	TOTAL	INCL O&P	
150	0010	**WIREWAY** to 15' high										150
	0100	Screw cover, with fittings and supports, 2-1/2" x 2-1/2"	1 Elec	45	.178	L.F.	8.85	6.10		14.95	18.80	
	0200	4" x 4"	"	40	.200		9.70	6.85		16.55	21	
	0400	6" x 6"	2 Elec	60	.267		16.55	9.15		25.70	32	
	0600	8" x 8"	"	40	.400		28	13.70		41.70	51.50	
	9980	Allow. for wireway ftngs., 5% min.-20% max.										

16136 | Boxes

			CREW	DAILY OUTPUT	LABOR-HOURS	UNIT	MAT.	LABOR	EQUIP.	TOTAL	INCL O&P	
600	0010	**OUTLET BOXES**										600
	0020	Pressed steel, octagon, 4"	1 Elec	20	.400	Ea.	1.44	13.70		15.14	22	
	0060	Covers, blank		64	.125		.59	4.29		4.88	7.05	
	0100	Extension		40	.200		2.29	6.85		9.14	12.75	
	0150	Square, 4"		20	.400		2.05	13.70		15.75	23	
	0200	Extension		40	.200		2.41	6.85		9.26	12.90	
	0250	Covers, blank		64	.125		.68	4.29		4.97	7.15	
	0300	Plaster rings		64	.125		1.09	4.29		5.38	7.60	
	0650	Switchbox		27	.296		2.26	10.15		12.41	17.65	
	1100	Concrete, floor, 1 gang		5.30	1.509		57.50	52		109.50	141	
	2000	Poke-thru fitting, fire rated, for 3-3/4" floor		6.80	1.176		90	40.50		130.50	159	
	2040	For 7" floor		6.80	1.176		90	40.50		130.50	159	
	2100	Pedestal, 15 amp, duplex receptacle & blank plate		5.25	1.524		93	52.50		145.50	180	
	2120	Duplex receptacle and telephone plate		5.25	1.524		93.50	52.50		146	181	
	2140	Pedestal, 20 amp, duplex recept. & phone plate		5	1.600		94	55		149	185	
	2200	Abandonment plate		32	.250		27.50	8.60		36.10	43	
700	0010	**PULL BOXES & CABINETS**										700
	0100	Sheet metal, pull box, NEMA 1, type SC, 6" W x 6" H x 4" D	1 Elec	8	1	Ea.	8.35	34.50		42.85	60	
	0200	8" W x 8" H x 4" D		8	1		11.45	34.50		45.95	63.50	
	0300	10" W x 12" H x 6" D		5.30	1.509		20	52		72	99.50	
	0400	16" W x 20" H x 8" D		4	2		76	68.50		144.50	186	
	0500	20" W x 24" H x 8" D		3.20	2.500		89	86		175	226	
	0600	24" W x 36" H x 8" D		2.70	2.963		125	102		227	290	
	0650	Hinged cabinets, NEMA 1, 6" W x 6" H x 4" D		8	1		8.50	34.50		43	60.50	
	0800	12" W x 16" H x 6" D		4.70	1.702		28	58.50		86.50	118	
	1000	20" W x 20" H x 6" D		3.60	2.222		56	76		132	176	
	1200	20" W x 20" H x 8" D		3.20	2.500		113	86		199	252	
	1400	24" W x 36" H x 8" D		2.70	2.963		180	102		282	350	
	1600	24" W x 42" H x 8" D		2	4		273	137		410	505	
	2100	Pull box, NEMA 3R, type SC, raintight & weatherproof										
	2150	6" L x 6" W x 6	1 Elec	10	.800	Ea.	14.30	27.50		41.80	57	
	2200	8" L x 6" W x 6" D		8	1		17.85	34.50		52.35	70.50	
	2250	10" L x 6" W x 6" D		7	1.143		23.50	39		62.50	84.50	
	2300	12" L x 12" W x 6" D		5	1.600		33.50	55		88.50	119	

ELECTRICAL 16

16136 | Boxes

		CREW	DAILY OUTPUT	LABOR-HOURS	UNIT	2001 BARE COSTS				TOTAL INCL O&P	
						MAT.	LABOR	EQUIP.	TOTAL		
700	2350	16" L x 16" W x 6" D " D	1 Elec	4.50	1.778	Ea.	67	61		128	165	700
	2400	20" L x 20" W x 6" D		4	2		92	68.50		160.50	203	
	2450	24" L x 18" W x 8" D		3	2.667		100	91.50		191.50	247	
	2500	24" L x 24" W x 10" D		2.50	3.200		239	110		349	425	
	2550	30" L x 24" W x 12" D		2	4		246	137		383	475	
	2600	36" L x 36" W x 12" D		1.50	5.333		325	183		508	630	
	2800	Cast iron, pull boxes for surface mounting										
	3000	NEMA 4, watertight & dust tight										
	3050	6" L x 6" W x 6" D	1 Elec	4	2	Ea.	146	68.50		214.50	263	
	3100	8" L x 6" W x 6" D		3.20	2.500		198	86		284	345	
	3150	10" L x 6" W x 6" D		2.50	3.200		246	110		356	435	
	3200	12" L x 12" W x 6" D		2.30	3.478		415	119		534	640	
	3250	16" L x 16" W x 6" D		1.30	6.154		850	211		1,061	1,250	
	3300	20" L x 20" W x 6" D		.80	10		1,575	345		1,920	2,250	
	3350	24" L x 18" W x 8" D		.70	11.429		1,675	390		2,065	2,400	
	3400	24" L x 24" W x 10" D		.50	16		2,550	550		3,100	3,625	
	3450	30" L x 24" W x 12" D		.40	20		4,275	685		4,960	5,725	
	3500	36" L x 36" W x 12" D		.20	40		5,275	1,375		6,650	7,875	
	6000	J.I.C. wiring boxes, NEMA 12, dust tight & drip tight										
	6050	6" L x 8" W x 4" D	1 Elec	10	.800	Ea.	33	27.50		60.50	77	
	6100	8" L x 10" W x 4" D		8	1		41	34.50		75.50	96	
	6150	12" L x 14" W x 6" D		5.30	1.509		67	52		119	151	
	6200	14" L x 16" W x 6" D		4.70	1.702		79.50	58.50		138	175	
	6250	16" L x 20" W x 6" D		4.40	1.818		170	62.50		232.50	280	
	6300	24" L x 30" W x 6" D		3.20	2.500		250	86		336	405	
	6350	24" L x 30" W x 8" D		2.90	2.759		267	94.50		361.50	435	
	6400	24" L x 36" W x 8" D		2.70	2.963		295	102		397	475	
	6450	24" L x 42" W x 8" D		2.30	3.478		320	119		439	535	
	6500	24" L x 48" W x 8" D		2	4		350	137		487	590	
	7000	Cabinets, current transformer										
	7050	Single door, 24" H x 24" W x 10" D	1 Elec	1.60	5	Ea.	107	172		279	375	
	7100	30" H x 24" W x 10" D		1.30	6.154		120	211		331	445	
	7150	36" H x 24" W x 10" D		1.10	7.273		134	249		383	515	
	7200	30" H x 30" W x 10" D		1	8		140	274		414	565	
	7250	36" H x 30" W x 10" D		.90	8.889		189	305		494	665	
	7300	36" H x 36" W x 10" D		.80	10		206	345		551	735	
	7500	Double door, 48" H x 36" W x 10" D		.60	13.333		370	455		825	1,100	
	7550	24" H x 24" W x 12" D		1	8		193	274		467	620	

16139 | Residential Wiring

		CREW	DAILY OUTPUT	LABOR-HOURS	UNIT	MAT.	LABOR	EQUIP.	TOTAL	TOTAL INCL O&P	
700	0010	**RESIDENTIAL WIRING**									700
	0020	20' avg. runs and #14/2 wiring incl. unless otherwise noted										
	1000	Service & panel, includes 24' SE-AL cable, service eye, meter,										
	1010	Socket, panel board, main bkr., ground rod, 15 or 20 amp										
	1020	1-pole circuit breakers, and misc. hardware										
	1100	100 amp, with 10 branch breakers	1 Elec	1.19	6.723	Ea.	395	231		626	780	
	1110	With PVC conduit and wire		.92	8.696		430	298		728	915	
	1120	With RGS conduit and wire		.73	10.959		550	375		925	1,175	
	1150	150 amp, with 14 branch breakers		1.03	7.767		615	266		881	1,075	
	1170	With PVC conduit and wire		.82	9.756		680	335		1,015	1,250	
	1180	With RGS conduit and wire		.67	11.940		895	410		1,305	1,600	
	1200	200 amp, with 18 branch breakers	2 Elec	1.80	8.889		805	305		1,110	1,350	
	1220	With PVC conduit and wire		1.46	10.959		870	375		1,245	1,525	
	1230	With RGS conduit and wire		1.24	12.903		1,150	445		1,595	1,925	
	1800	Lightning surge suppressor for above services, add	1 Elec	32	.250		39.50	8.60		48.10	56.50	
	2000	Switch devices										

Important: See the Reference Section for critical supporting data - Reference Nos., Crews, & City Cost Indexes

16 ELECTRICAL

			DAILY	LABOR-		2001 BARE COSTS				TOTAL	
16139	**Residential Wiring**	CREW	OUTPUT	HOURS	UNIT	MAT.	LABOR	EQUIP.	TOTAL	INCL O&P	
700	2100	Single pole, 15 amp, Ivory, with a 1-gang box, cover plate,										**700**
	2110	Type NM (Romex) cable	1 Elec	17.10	.468	Ea.	6.85	16.05		22.90	31.50	
	2120	Type MC (BX) cable		14.30	.559		16.95	19.20		36.15	47	
	2130	EMT & wire		5.71	1.401		17.65	48		65.65	91	
	2150	3-way, #14/3, type NM cable		14.55	.550		10.80	18.85		29.65	40	
	2170	Type MC cable		12.31	.650		21.50	22.50		44	57	
	2180	EMT & wire		5	1.600		20	55		75	104	
	2200	4-way, #14/3, type NM cable		14.55	.550		23.50	18.85		42.35	54	
	2220	Type MC cable		12.31	.650		34	22.50		56.50	71	
	2230	EMT & wire		5	1.600		32.50	55		87.50	118	
	2250	S.P., 20 amp, #12/2, type NM cable		13.33	.600		12.05	20.50		32.55	44	
	2270	Type MC cable		11.43	.700		21	24		45	59	
	2280	EMT & wire		4.85	1.649		23.50	56.50		80	111	
	2290	S.P. rotary dimmer, 600W, no wiring		17	.471		15.70	16.15		31.85	41.50	
	2300	S.P. rotary dimmer, 600W, type NM cable		14.55	.550		18.60	18.85		37.45	48.50	
	2320	Type MC cable		12.31	.650		28.50	22.50		51	65	
	2330	EMT & wire		5	1.600		30	55		85	116	
	2350	3-way rotary dimmer, type NM cable		13.33	.600		16	20.50		36.50	48	
	2370	Type MC cable		11.43	.700		26	24		50	64.50	
	2380	EMT & wire	▼	4.85	1.649	▼	27.50	56.50		84	115	
	2400	Interval timer wall switch, 20 amp, 1-30 min., #12/2										
	2410	Type NM cable	1 Elec	14.55	.550	Ea.	29.50	18.85		48.35	60.50	
	2420	Type MC cable		12.31	.650		36	22.50		58.50	73.50	
	2430	EMT & wire	▼	5	1.600	▼	41	55		96	127	
	2500	Decorator style										
	2510	S.P., 15 amp, type NM cable	1 Elec	17.10	.468	Ea.	10.40	16.05		26.45	35.50	
	2520	Type MC cable		14.30	.559		20.50	19.20		39.70	51	
	2530	EMT & wire		5.71	1.401		21	48		69	95	
	2550	3-way, #14/3, type NM cable		14.55	.550		14.35	18.85		33.20	44	
	2570	Type MC cable		12.31	.650		25	22.50		47.50	61	
	2580	EMT & wire		5	1.600		23.50	55		78.50	108	
	2600	4-way, #14/3, type NM cable		14.55	.550		27	18.85		45.85	57.50	
	2620	Type MC cable		12.31	.650		37.50	22.50		60	75	
	2630	EMT & wire		5	1.600		36	55		91	122	
	2650	S.P., 20 amp, #12/2, type NM cable		13.33	.600		15.60	20.50		36.10	47.50	
	2670	Type MC cable		11.43	.700		24.50	24		48.50	63	
	2680	EMT & wire		4.85	1.649		27	56.50		83.50	114	
	2700	S.P., slide dimmer, type NM cable		17.10	.468		25.50	16.05		41.55	52.50	
	2720	Type MC cable		14.30	.559		36	19.20		55.20	68	
	2730	EMT & wire		5.71	1.401		37.50	48		85.50	113	
	2750	S.P., touch dimmer, type NM cable		17.10	.468		21.50	16.05		37.55	47.50	
	2770	Type MC cable		14.30	.559		31.50	19.20		50.70	63.50	
	2780	EMT & wire		5.71	1.401		33	48		81	108	
	2800	3-way touch dimmer, type NM cable		13.33	.600		39	20.50		59.50	73.50	
	2820	Type MC cable		11.43	.700		49	24		73	90	
	2830	EMT & wire	▼	4.85	1.649	▼	50.50	56.50		107	141	
	3000	Combination devices										
	3100	S.P. switch/15 amp recpt., Ivory, 1-gang box, plate										
	3110	Type NM cable	1 Elec	11.43	.700	Ea.	14.65	24		38.65	52	
	3120	Type MC cable		10	.800		25	27.50		52.50	68	
	3130	EMT & wire		4.40	1.818		26.50	62.50		89	122	
	3150	S.P. switch/pilot light, type NM cable		11.43	.700		15.30	24		39.30	53	
	3170	Type MC cable		10	.800		25.50	27.50		53	69	
	3180	EMT & wire		4.43	1.806		27	62		89	122	
	3190	2-S.P. switches, 2-#14/2, no wiring		14	.571		5.45	19.60		25.05	35.50	
	3200	2-S.P. switches, 2-#14/2, type NM cables	▼	10	.800	▼	16.85	27.50		44.35	59.50	

ELECTRICAL 16

16139	Residential Wiring	CREW	DAILY OUTPUT	LABOR-HOURS	UNIT	MAT.	2001 BARE COSTS LABOR	EQUIP.	TOTAL	TOTAL INCL O&P	
3220	Type MC cable	1 Elec	8.89	.900	Ea.	33.50	31		64.50	83	700
3230	EMT & wire		4.10	1.951		28	67		95	131	
3250	3-way switch/15 amp recpt., #14/3, type NM cable		10	.800		21.50	27.50		49	64.50	
3270	Type MC cable		8.89	.900		32	31		63	81	
3280	EMT & wire		4.10	1.951		30.50	67		97.50	134	
3300	2-3 way switches, 2-#14/3, type NM cables		8.89	.900		28.50	31		59.50	77.50	
3320	Type MC cable		8	1		46.50	34.50		81	102	
3330	EMT & wire		4	2		35	68.50		103.50	141	
3350	S.P. switch/20 amp recpt., #12/2, type NM cable		10	.800		25.50	27.50		53	69	
3370	Type MC cable		8.89	.900		32	31		63	81.50	
3380	EMT & wire	↓	4.10	1.951	↓	37	67		104	141	
3400	Decorator style										
3410	S.P. switch/15 amp recpt., type NM cable	1 Elec	11.43	.700	Ea.	18.20	24		42.20	56	
3420	Type MC cable		10	.800		28.50	27.50		56	72	
3430	EMT & wire		4.40	1.818		30	62.50		92.50	126	
3450	S.P. switch/pilot light, type NM cable		11.43	.700		18.85	24		42.85	56.50	
3470	Type MC cable		10	.800		29	27.50		56.50	73	
3480	EMT & wire		4.40	1.818		30.50	62.50		93	127	
3500	2-S.P. switches, 2-#14/2, type NM cables		10	.800		20.50	27.50		48	63.50	
3520	Type MC cable		8.89	.900		37	31		68	87	
3530	EMT & wire		4.10	1.951		31.50	67		98.50	135	
3550	3-way/15 amp recpt., #14/3, type NM cable		10	.800		25	27.50		52.50	68.50	
3570	Type MC cable		8.89	.900		35.50	31		66.50	85	
3580	EMT & wire		4.10	1.951		34	67		101	138	
3650	2-3 way switches, 2-#14/3, type NM cables		8.89	.900		32	31		63	81.50	
3670	Type MC cable		8	1		50	34.50		84.50	106	
3680	EMT & wire		4	2		38.50	68.50		107	145	
3700	S.P. switch/20 amp recpt., #12/2, type NM cable		10	.800		29	27.50		56.50	73	
3720	Type MC cable		8.89	.900		36	31		67	85.50	
3730	EMT & wire	↓	4.10	1.951	↓	40.50	67		107.50	145	
4000	Receptacle devices										
4010	Duplex outlet, 15 amp recpt., Ivory, 1-gang box, plate										
4015	Type NM cable	1 Elec	14.55	.550	Ea.	5.40	18.85		24.25	34	
4020	Type MC cable		12.31	.650		15.50	22.50		38	50.50	
4030	EMT & wire		5.33	1.501		16.20	51.50		67.70	95	
4050	With #12/2, type NM cable		12.31	.650		6.70	22.50		29.20	41	
4070	Type MC cable		10.67	.750		15.75	25.50		41.25	56	
4080	EMT & wire		4.71	1.699		18.05	58.50		76.55	107	
4100	20 amp recpt., #12/2, type NM cable		12.31	.650		9.95	22.50		32.45	44.50	
4120	Type MC cable		10.67	.750		19	25.50		44.50	59.50	
4130	EMT & wire	↓	4.71	1.699	↓	21.50	58.50		80	111	
4140	For GFI see line 4300 below										
4150	Decorator style, 15 amp recpt., type NM cable	1 Elec	14.55	.550	Ea.	8.95	18.85		27.80	38	
4170	Type MC cable		12.31	.650		19.05	22.50		41.55	54.50	
4180	EMT & wire		5.33	1.501		19.75	51.50		71.25	98.50	
4200	With #12/2, type NM cable		12.31	.650		10.25	22.50		32.75	45	
4220	Type MC cable		10.67	.750		19.30	25.50		44.80	60	
4230	EMT & wire		4.71	1.699		21.50	58.50		80	111	
4250	20 amp recpt. #12/2, type NM cable		12.31	.650		13.50	22.50		36	48.50	
4270	Type MC cable		10.67	.750		22.50	25.50		48	63.50	
4280	EMT & wire		4.71	1.699		25	58.50		83.50	115	
4300	GFI, 15 amp recpt., type NM cable		12.31	.650		33	22.50		55.50	70	
4320	Type MC cable		10.67	.750		43	25.50		68.50	86	
4330	EMT & wire		4.71	1.699		44	58.50		102.50	136	
4350	GFI with #12/2, type NM cable		10.67	.750		34.50	25.50		60	76.50	
4370	Type MC cable	↓	9.20	.870	↓	43.50	30		73.50	92.50	

Important: See the Reference Section for critical supporting data - Reference Nos., Crews, & City Cost Indexes

16139	Residential Wiring	CREW	DAILY OUTPUT	LABOR-HOURS	UNIT	2001 BARE COSTS				TOTAL INCL O&P	
						MAT.	LABOR	EQUIP.	TOTAL		
700	4380	EMT & wire	1 Elec	4.21	1.900	Ea.	45.50	65		110.50	148	700
	4400	20 amp recpt., #12/2 type NM cable		10.67	.750		36	25.50		61.50	78
	4420	Type MC cable		9.20	.870		45	30		75	94
	4430	EMT & wire		4.21	1.900		47.50	65		112.50	150
	4500	Weather-proof cover for above receptacles, add	↓	32	.250	↓	4.40	8.60		13	17.65
	4550	Air conditioner outlet, 20 amp-240 volt recpt.									
	4560	30' of #12/2, 2 pole circuit breaker									
	4570	Type NM cable	1 Elec	10	.800	Ea.	40.50	27.50		68	85.50
	4580	Type MC cable		9	.889		52	30.50		82.50	103
	4590	EMT & wire		4	2		51.50	68.50		120	159
	4600	Decorator style, type NM cable		10	.800		44	27.50		71.50	89.50
	4620	Type MC cable		9	.889		56	30.50		86.50	107
	4630	EMT & wire	↓	4	2	↓	55	68.50		123.50	163
	4650	Dryer outlet, 30 amp-240 volt recpt., 20' of #10/3									
	4660	2 pole circuit breaker									
	4670	Type NM cable	1 Elec	6.41	1.248	Ea.	47.50	43		90.50	117
	4680	Type MC cable		5.71	1.401		56	48		104	134
	4690	EMT & wire	↓	3.48	2.299	↓	53	79		132	176
	4700	Range outlet, 50 amp-240 volt recpt., 30' of #8/3									
	4710	Type NM cable	1 Elec	4.21	1.900	Ea.	74	65		139	179
	4720	Type MC cable		4	2		101	68.50		169.50	213
	4730	EMT & wire		2.96	2.703		69	92.50		161.50	214
	4750	Central vacuum outlet, Type NM cable		6.40	1.250		43.50	43		86.50	112
	4770	Type MC cable		5.71	1.401		59	48		107	137
	4780	EMT & wire	↓	3.48	2.299	↓	53.50	79		132.50	177
	4800	30 amp-110 volt locking recpt., #10/2 circ. bkr.									
	4810	Type NM cable	1 Elec	6.20	1.290	Ea.	51.50	44.50		96	123
	4820	Type MC cable		5.40	1.481		71	51		122	155
	4830	EMT & wire	↓	3.20	2.500	↓	62.50	86		148.50	197
	4900	Low voltage outlets									
	4910	Telephone recpt., 20' of 4/C phone wire	1 Elec	26	.308	Ea.	6.70	10.55		17.25	23
	4920	TV recpt., 20' of RG59U coax wire, F type connector	"	16	.500	"	11.15	17.15		28.30	38
	4950	Door bell chime, transformer, 2 buttons, 60' of bellwire									
	4970	Economy model	1 Elec	11.50	.696	Ea.	48.50	24		72.50	89
	4980	Custom model		11.50	.696		83.50	24		107.50	128
	4990	Luxury model, 3 buttons	↓	9.50	.842	↓	228	29		257	294
	6000	Lighting outlets									
	6050	Wire only (for fixture), type NM cable	1 Elec	32	.250	Ea.	3.77	8.60		12.37	16.95
	6070	Type MC cable		24	.333		11.60	11.45		23.05	30
	6080	EMT & wire		10	.800		11.40	27.50		38.90	53.50
	6100	Box (4"), and wire (for fixture), type NM cable		25	.320		7.65	11		18.65	25
	6120	Type MC cable		20	.400		15.50	13.70		29.20	37.50
	6130	EMT & wire	↓	11	.727	↓	15.30	25		40.30	54
	6200	Fixtures (use with lines 6050 or 6100 above)									
	6210	Canopy style, economy grade	1 Elec	40	.200	Ea.	25.50	6.85		32.35	38.50
	6220	Custom grade		40	.200		46	6.85		52.85	61
	6250	Dining room chandelier, economy grade		19	.421		76	14.45		90.45	105
	6260	Custom grade		19	.421		225	14.45		239.45	270
	6270	Luxury grade		15	.533		495	18.30		513.30	575
	6310	Kitchen fixture (fluorescent), economy grade		30	.267		51.50	9.15		60.65	70
	6320	Custom grade		25	.320		161	11		172	193
	6350	Outdoor, wall mounted, economy grade		30	.267		27	9.15		36.15	43
	6360	Custom grade		30	.267		101	9.15		110.15	125
	6370	Luxury grade		25	.320		227	11		238	266
	6410	Outdoor PAR floodlights, 1 lamp, 150 watt		20	.400		20	13.70		33.70	42.50
	6420	2 lamp, 150 watt each	↓	20	.400	↓	33.50	13.70		47.20	57.50

ELECTRICAL 16

16139	Residential Wiring	CREW	DAILY OUTPUT	LABOR-HOURS	UNIT	MAT.	LABOR	EQUIP.	TOTAL	TOTAL INCL O&P	
700	6430	For infrared security sensor, add	1 Elec	32	.250	Ea.	87	8.60		95.60	109	700
	6450	Outdoor, quartz-halogen, 300 watt flood		20	.400		38	13.70		51.70	62.50	
	6600	Recessed downlight, round, pre-wired, 50 or 75 watt trim		30	.267		35	9.15		44.15	52	
	6610	With shower light trim		30	.267		42	9.15		51.15	59.50	
	6620	With wall washer trim		28	.286		52.50	9.80		62.30	72.50	
	6630	With eye-ball trim		28	.286		49	9.80		58.80	68.50	
	6640	For direct contact with insulation, add					1.60			1.60	1.76	
	6700	Porcelain lamp holder	1 Elec	40	.200		3.50	6.85		10.35	14.10	
	6710	With pull switch		40	.200		3.75	6.85		10.60	14.40	
	6750	Fluorescent strip, 1-20 watt tube, wrap around diffuser, 24"		24	.333		51.50	11.45		62.95	73.50	
	6760	1-40 watt tube, 48"		24	.333		65	11.45		76.45	88.50	
	6770	2-40 watt tubes, 48"		20	.400		78	13.70		91.70	107	
	6780	With residential ballast		20	.400		89.50	13.70		103.20	119	
	6800	Bathroom heat lamp, 1-250 watt		28	.286		30.50	9.80		40.30	48	
	6810	2-250 watt lamps		28	.286		51	9.80		60.80	70.50	
	6820	For timer switch, see line 2400										
	6900	Outdoor post lamp, incl. post, fixture, 35' of #14/2										
	6910	Type NMC cable	1 Elec	3.50	2.286	Ea.	181	78.50		259.50	315	
	6920	Photo-eye, add		27	.296		29	10.15		39.15	47	
	6950	Clock dial time switch, 24 hr., w/enclosure, type NM cable		11.43	.700		51	24		75	92	
	6970	Type MC cable		11	.727		61	25		86	104	
	6980	EMT & wire		4.85	1.649		61.50	56.50		118	152	
	7000	Alarm systems										
	7050	Smoke detectors, box, #14/3, type NM cable	1 Elec	14.55	.550	Ea.	28.50	18.85		47.35	59.50	
	7070	Type MC cable		12.31	.650		37	22.50		59.50	74	
	7080	EMT & wire		5	1.600		35.50	55		90.50	121	
	7090	For relay output to security system, add					11.75			11.75	12.95	
	8000	Residential equipment										
	8050	Disposal hook-up, incl. switch, outlet box, 3' of flex										
	8060	20 amp-1 pole circ. bkr., and 25' of #12/2										
	8070	Type NM cable	1 Elec	10	.800	Ea.	19.70	27.50		47.20	62.50	
	8080	Type MC cable		8	1		30	34.50		64.50	84	
	8090	EMT & wire		5	1.600		32.50	55		87.50	118	
	8100	Trash compactor or dishwasher hook-up, incl. outlet box,										
	8110	3' of flex, 15 amp-1 pole circ. bkr., and 25' of #14/2										
	8120	Type NM cable	1 Elec	10	.800	Ea.	13.70	27.50		41.20	56	
	8130	Type MC cable		8	1		26	34.50		60.50	79.50	
	8140	EMT & wire		5	1.600		26.50	55		81.50	112	
	8150	Hot water sink dispensor hook-up, use line 8100										
	8200	Vent/exhaust fan hook-up, type NM cable	1 Elec	32	.250	Ea.	3.77	8.60		12.37	16.95	
	8220	Type MC cable		24	.333		11.60	11.45		23.05	30	
	8230	EMT & wire		10	.800		11.40	27.50		38.90	53.50	
	8250	Bathroom vent fan, 50 CFM (use with above hook-up)										
	8260	Economy model	1 Elec	15	.533	Ea.	21.50	18.30		39.80	51	
	8270	Low noise model		15	.533		30	18.30		48.30	60.50	
	8280	Custom model		12	.667		111	23		134	156	
	8300	Bathroom or kitchen vent fan, 110 CFM										
	8310	Economy model	1 Elec	15	.533	Ea.	56	18.30		74.30	89	
	8320	Low noise model	"	15	.533	"	75	18.30		93.30	110	
	8350	Paddle fan, variable speed (w/o lights)										
	8360	Economy model (AC motor)	1 Elec	10	.800	Ea.	100	27.50		127.50	151	
	8370	Custom model (AC motor)		10	.800		173	27.50		200.50	231	
	8380	Luxury model (DC motor)		8	1		340	34.50		374.50	425	
	8390	Remote speed switch for above, add		12	.667		23	23		46	59.50	
	8500	Whole house exhaust fan, ceiling mount, 36", variable speed										
	8510	Remote switch, incl. shutters, 20 amp-1 pole circ. bkr.										

Important: See the Reference Section for critical supporting data - Reference Nos., Crews, & City Cost Indexes

16139	Residential Wiring	CREW	DAILY OUTPUT	LABOR-HOURS	UNIT	MAT.	LABOR	EQUIP.	TOTAL	TOTAL INCL O&P	
								2001 BARE COSTS			
700											**700**
8520	30' of #12/2, type NM cable	1 Elec	4	2	Ea.	550	68.50		618.50	705	
8530	Type MC cable		3.50	2.286		560	78.50		638.50	735	
8540	EMT & wire		3	2.667		565	91.50		656.50	755	
8600	Whirlpool tub hook-up, incl. timer switch, outlet box										
8610	3' of flex, 20 amp-1 pole GFI circ. bkr.										
8620	30' of #12/2, type NM cable	1 Elec	5	1.600	Ea.	75.50	55		130.50	165	
8630	Type MC cable		4.20	1.905		82.50	65.50		148	188	
8640	EMT & wire		3.40	2.353		84.50	80.50		165	213	
8650	Hot water heater hook-up, incl. 1-2 pole circ. bkr., box;										
8660	3' of flex, 20' of #10/2, type NM cable	1 Elec	5	1.600	Ea.	21	55		76	105	
8670	Type MC cable		4.20	1.905		34	65.50		99.50	135	
8680	EMT & wire		3.40	2.353		28.50	80.50		109	152	
9000	Heating/air conditioning										
9050	Furnace/boiler hook-up, incl. firestat, local on-off switch										
9060	Emergency switch, and 40' of type NM cable	1 Elec	4	2	Ea.	43	68.50		111.50	150	
9070	Type MC cable		3.50	2.286		59.50	78.50		138	183	
9080	EMT & wire		1.50	5.333		61	183		244	340	
9100	Air conditioner hook-up, incl. local 60 amp disc. switch										
9110	3' sealtite, 40 amp, 2 pole circuit breaker										
9130	40' of #8/2, type NM cable	1 Elec	3.50	2.286	Ea.	140	78.50		218.50	271	
9140	Type MC cable		3	2.667		185	91.50		276.50	340	
9150	EMT & wire		1.30	6.154		148	211		359	480	
9200	Heat pump hook-up, 1-40 & 1-100 amp 2 pole circ. bkr.										
9210	Local disconnect switch, 3' sealtite										
9220	40' of #8/2 & 30' of #3/2										
9230	Type NM cable	1 Elec	1.30	6.154	Ea.	345	211		556	695	
9240	Type MC cable		1.08	7.407		455	254		709	880	
9250	EMT & wire		.94	8.511		345	292		637	815	
9500	Thermostat hook-up, using low voltage wire										
9520	Heating only	1 Elec	24	.333	Ea.	5.70	11.45		17.15	23.50	
9530	Heating/cooling	"	20	.400	"	7.05	13.70		20.75	28.50	

16140	Wiring Devices										
500	0010	**LOW VOLTAGE SWITCHING**									**500**
	3600	Relays, 120 V or 277 V standard	1 Elec	12	.667	Ea.	26	23		49	62.50
	3800	Flush switch, standard		40	.200		9.05	6.85		15.90	20
	4000	Interchangeable		40	.200		11.80	6.85		18.65	23.50
	4100	Surface switch, standard		40	.200		6.60	6.85		13.45	17.55
	4200	Transformer 115 V to 25 V		12	.667		93	23		116	136
	4400	Master control, 12 circuit, manual		4	2		94	68.50		162.50	205
	4500	25 circuit, motorized		4	2		102	68.50		170.50	214
	4600	Rectifier, silicon		12	.667		30.50	23		53.50	67.50
	4800	Switchplates, 1 gang, 1, 2 or 3 switch, plastic		80	.100		3	3.43		6.43	8.40
	5000	Stainless steel		80	.100		8.10	3.43		11.53	14
	5400	2 gang, 3 switch, stainless steel		53	.151		15.65	5.20		20.85	25
	5500	4 switch, plastic		53	.151		6.70	5.20		11.90	15.10
	5800	3 gang, 9 switch, stainless steel		32	.250		50	8.60		58.60	68
910	0010	**WIRING DEVICES**									**910**
	0200	Toggle switch, quiet type, single pole, 15 amp **CN**	1 Elec	40	.200	Ea.	4.70	6.85		11.55	15.40
	0600	3 way, 15 amp		23	.348		6.70	11.95		18.65	25
	0900	4 way, 15 amp		15	.533		19.40	18.30		37.70	49
	1650	Dimmer switch, 120 volt, incandescent, 600 watt, 1 pole		16	.500		10.80	17.15		27.95	37.50
	2460	Receptacle, duplex, 120 volt, grounded, 15 amp		40	.200		1.14	6.85		7.99	11.50
	2470	20 amp		27	.296		9.95	10.15		20.10	26
	2490	Dryer, 30 amp		15	.533		10.20	18.30		28.50	38.50

ELECTRICAL 16

16100 | Wiring Methods

16140 | Wiring Devices

		CREW	DAILY OUTPUT	LABOR-HOURS	UNIT	2001 BARE COSTS				TOTAL INCL O&P	
						MAT.	LABOR	EQUIP.	TOTAL		
910	2500	Range, 50 amp	1 Elec	11	.727	Ea.	10.75	25		35.75	49	910
	2600	Wall plates, stainless steel, 1 gang		80	.100		1.80	3.43		5.23	7.10	
	2800	2 gang		53	.151		4.10	5.20		9.30	12.25	
	3200	Lampholder, keyless		26	.308		9.20	10.55		19.75	26	
	3400	Pullchain with receptacle	▼	22	.364	▼	8.90	12.45		21.35	28.50	

16150 | Wiring Connections

		CREW	DAILY OUTPUT	LABOR-HOURS	UNIT	2001 BARE COSTS				TOTAL INCL O&P	
						MAT.	LABOR	EQUIP.	TOTAL		
275	0010	**MOTOR CONNECTIONS**										275
	0020	Flexible conduit and fittings, 115 volt, 1 phase, up to 1 HP motor	1 Elec	8	1	Ea.	4.39	34.50		38.89	56	
	0200	25 HP motor		2.70	2.963		17.75	102		119.75	172	
	0400	50 HP motor		2.20	3.636		46.50	125		171.50	238	
	0600	100 HP motor	▼	1.50	5.333	▼	117	183		300	400	

16200 | Electrical Power

16220 | Motors & Generators

		CREW	DAILY OUTPUT	LABOR-HOURS	UNIT	2001 BARE COSTS				TOTAL INCL O&P	
						MAT.	LABOR	EQUIP.	TOTAL		
610	0010	**MOTORS** 230/460 volts, 60 HZ										610
	0050	Dripproof, premium efficiency, 1.15 service factor										
	0060	1800 RPM, 1/4 HP	1 Elec	5.33	1.501	Ea.	116	51.50		167.50	205	
	0070	1/3 HP		5.33	1.501		127	51.50		178.50	217	
	0080	1/2 HP		5.33	1.501		149	51.50		200.50	241	
	0090	3/4 HP		5.33	1.501		167	51.50		218.50	261	
	0100	1 HP		4.50	1.778		175	61		236	284	
	0250	5 HP		4.50	1.778		267	61		328	385	
	0350	10 HP	▼	4	2		475	68.50		543.50	620	
	0450	20 HP	**CN** 2 Elec	5.20	3.077	▼	760	106		866	995	

16230 | Generator Assemblies

		CREW	DAILY OUTPUT	LABOR-HOURS	UNIT	2001 BARE COSTS				TOTAL INCL O&P	
						MAT.	LABOR	EQUIP.	TOTAL		
450	0010	**GENERATOR SET**										450
	0020	Gas or gasoline operated, includes battery,										
	0050	charger, muffler & transfer switch										
	0200	3 phase 4 wire, 277/480 volt, 7.5 kW	R-3	.83	24.096	Ea.	6,000	815	171	6,986	8,025	
	0300	11.5 kW		.71	28.169		8,500	955	200	9,655	11,000	
	0400	20 kW		.63	31.746		10,000	1,075	225	11,300	12,800	
	0500	35 kW		.55	36.364		12,000	1,225	258	13,483	15,300	
	0600	80 kW		.40	50		20,500	1,700	355	22,555	25,500	
	0700	100 kW		.33	60.606		22,500	2,050	430	24,980	28,400	
	0800	125 kW		.28	71.429		46,000	2,425	505	48,930	54,500	
	0900	185 kW	▼	.25	80	▼	61,000	2,700	570	64,270	71,500	
	2000	Diesel engine, including battery, charger,										
	2010	muffler, automatic transfer switch & day tank, 30 kW	R-3	.55	36.364	Ea.	16,000	1,225	258	17,483	19,700	
	2100	50 kW		.42	47.619		19,700	1,625	340	21,665	24,500	
	2200	75 kW		.35	57.143		25,700	1,925	405	28,030	31,600	
	2300	100 kW		.31	64.516		28,500	2,175	460	31,135	35,200	
	2400	125 kW		.29	68.966		30,000	2,325	490	32,815	37,000	
	2500	150 kW		.26	76.923		34,400	2,600	545	37,545	42,300	
	2600	175 kW		.25	80		37,500	2,700	570	40,770	46,000	
	2700	200 kW	▼	.24	83.333	▼	38,700	2,825	590	42,115	47,500	

Important: See the Reference Section for critical supporting data - Reference Nos., Crews, & City Cost Indexes

16230	Generator Assemblies	CREW	DAILY OUTPUT	LABOR-HOURS	UNIT	2001 BARE COSTS				TOTAL INCL O&P	
						MAT.	LABOR	EQUIP.	TOTAL		
450 2800	250 kW	R-3	.23	86.957	Ea.	45,600	2,950	615	49,165	55,000	**450**
2900	300 kW		.22	90.909		49,300	3,075	645	53,020	59,500	
3000	350 kW		.20	100		55,500	3,375	710	59,585	67,500	
3100	400 kW		.19	105		69,000	3,575	745	73,320	81,500	
3200	500 kW	↓	.18	111	↓	86,500	3,775	790	91,065	101,500	

16270 | Transformers

		CREW	DAILY OUTPUT	LABOR-HOURS	UNIT	MAT.	LABOR	EQUIP.	TOTAL	TOTAL INCL O&P	
200 0010	**DRY TYPE TRANSFORMER**										**200**
0050	Single phase, 240/480 volt primary, 120/240 volt secondary										
0100	1 kVA	1 Elec	2	4	Ea.	153	137		290	375	
0300	2 kVA		1.60	5		230	172		402	510	
0500	3 kVA		1.40	5.714		285	196		481	610	
0700	5 kVA	↓	1.20	6.667		395	229		624	770	
0900	7.5 kVA	2 Elec	2.20	7.273		545	249		794	970	
1100	10 kVA		1.60	10		700	345		1,045	1,275	
1300	15 kVA		1.20	13.333		950	455		1,405	1,725	
1500	25 kVA		1	16		1,225	550		1,775	2,175	
1700	37.5 kVA		.80	20		1,575	685		2,260	2,775	
1900	50 kVA		.70	22.857		1,875	785		2,660	3,250	
2100	75 kVA		.65	24.615		2,500	845		3,345	3,975	
2190	480V primary 120/240V secondary, nonvent., 15 kVA		1.20	13.333		855	455		1,310	1,625	
2200	25 kVA		.90	17.778		1,350	610		1,960	2,400	
2210	37 kVA		.75	21.333		1,625	730		2,355	2,875	
2220	50 kVA	↓	.65	24.615	↓	1,925	845		2,770	3,375	
2300	3 phase, 480 volt primary 120/208 volt secondary										
2310	Ventilated, 3 kVA	1 Elec	1	8	Ea.	425	274		699	880	
2700	6 kVA		.80	10		665	345		1,010	1,250	
2900	9 kVA	↓	.70	11.429		755	390		1,145	1,425	
3100	15 kVA	2 Elec	1.10	14.545		1,000	500		1,500	1,850	
3300	30 kVA		.90	17.778		1,175	610		1,785	2,200	
3500	45 kVA		.80	20		1,375	685		2,060	2,550	
3700	75 kVA	↓	.70	22.857		2,125	785		2,910	3,525	
3900	112.5 kVA	R-3	.90	22.222		2,825	755	158	3,738	4,425	
4100	150 kVA		.85	23.529		3,700	795	167	4,662	5,450	
4300	225 kVA		.65	30.769		5,000	1,050	218	6,268	7,325	
4500	300 kVA		.55	36.364		6,325	1,225	258	7,808	9,100	
4700	500 kVA		.45	44.444		10,500	1,500	315	12,315	14,100	
4800	750 kVA	↓	.35	57.143	↓	18,400	1,925	405	20,730	23,500	
600 0010	**OIL FILLED TRANSFORMER** Pad mounted, primary delta or Y,										**600**
0050	5 kV or 15 kV, with taps, 277/480 V secondary, 3 phase										
0100	150 kVA	R-3	.65	30.769	Ea.	6,150	1,050	218	7,418	8,575	
0200	300 kVA		.45	44.444		8,275	1,500	315	10,090	11,700	
0300	500 kVA		.40	50		12,300	1,700	355	14,355	16,400	
0400	750 kVA		.38	52.632		14,900	1,775	375	17,050	19,500	
0500	1000 kVA		.26	76.923		17,600	2,600	545	20,745	23,900	
0600	1500 kVA		.23	86.957		21,000	2,950	615	24,565	28,100	
0700	2000 kVA		.20	100		26,500	3,375	710	30,585	35,000	
0800	3750 kVA	↓	.16	125	↓	49,600	4,225	890	54,715	62,000	

16280 | Power Filters & Conditioners

		CREW	DAILY OUTPUT	LABOR-HOURS	UNIT	MAT.	LABOR	EQUIP.	TOTAL	TOTAL INCL O&P	
300 0010	**CAPACITORS** Indoor										**300**
0020	240 volts, single & 3 phase, 0.5 kVAR	1 Elec	2.70	2.963	Ea.	270	102		372	450	
0100	1.0 kVAR		2.70	2.963		325	102		427	510	
0150	2.5 kVAR	↓	2	4	↓	385	137		522	630	

ELECTRICAL 16

For expanded coverage of these items see *Means Electrical Cost Data 2001*

16200 | Electrical Power

16280 | Power Filters & Conditioners

		CREW	DAILY OUTPUT	LABOR-HOURS	UNIT	2001 BARE COSTS MAT.	LABOR	EQUIP.	TOTAL	TOTAL INCL O&P	
300	0200	5.0 kVAR	1 Elec	1.80	4.444	Ea.	450	152		602	725	**300**
	0250	7.5 kVAR		1.60	5		515	172		687	820	
	0300	10 kVAR		1.50	5.333		615	183		798	955	
	0350	15 kVAR		1.30	6.154		850	211		1,061	1,250	
	0400	20 kVAR		1.10	7.273		1,050	249		1,299	1,550	
	0450	25 kVAR		1	8		1,250	274		1,524	1,775	
	1000	480 volts, single & 3 phase, 1 kVAR		2.70	2.963		246	102		348	425	
	1050	2 kVAR		2.70	2.963		283	102		385	460	
	1100	5 kVAR		2	4		360	137		497	600	
	1150	7.5 kVAR		2	4		390	137		527	635	
	1200	10 kVAR		2	4		430	137		567	680	
	1250	15 kVAR		2	4		535	137		672	790	
	1300	20 kVAR		1.60	5		595	172		767	910	
	1350	30 kVAR		1.50	5.333		745	183		928	1,100	
	1400	40 kVAR		1.20	6.667		945	229		1,174	1,400	
	1450	50 kVAR		1.10	7.273		1,075	249		1,324	1,550	

16290 | Power Measure & Control

		CREW	DAILY OUTPUT	LABOR-HOURS	UNIT	2001 BARE COSTS MAT.	LABOR	EQUIP.	TOTAL	TOTAL INCL O&P	
800	0010	**SWITCHBOARD INSTRUMENTS** 3 phase, 4 wire										**800**
	0100	AC indicating, ammeter & switch	1 Elec	8	1	Ea.	1,200	34.50		1,234.50	1,350	
	0200	Voltmeter & switch		8	1		1,200	34.50		1,234.50	1,350	
	0300	Wattmeter		8	1		2,350	34.50		2,384.50	2,650	
	0400	AC recording, ammeter		4	2		4,200	68.50		4,268.50	4,725	
	0500	Voltmeter		4	2		4,200	68.50		4,268.50	4,725	
	0600	Ground fault protection, zero sequence		2.70	2.963		3,700	102		3,802	4,225	
	0700	Ground return path		2.70	2.963		3,700	102		3,802	4,225	
	0800	3 current transformers, 5 to 800 amp		2	4		1,550	137		1,687	1,900	
	0900	1000 to 1500 amp		1.30	6.154		2,225	211		2,436	2,775	
	1200	2000 to 4000 amp		1	8		2,625	274		2,899	3,300	
	1300	Fused potential transformer, maximum 600 volt		8	1		705	34.50		739.50	825	

16400 | Low-Voltage Distribution

16410 | Encl Switches & Circuit Breakers

		CREW	DAILY OUTPUT	LABOR-HOURS	UNIT	2001 BARE COSTS MAT.	LABOR	EQUIP.	TOTAL	TOTAL INCL O&P	
200	0010	**CIRCUIT BREAKERS** (in enclosure)										**200**
	0100	Enclosed (NEMA 1), 600 volt, 3 pole, 30 amp	1 Elec	3.20	2.500	Ea.	380	86		466	545	
	0200	60 amp		2.80	2.857		380	98		478	560	
	0400	100 amp		2.30	3.478		435	119		554	655	
	0600	225 amp		1.50	5.333		1,000	183		1,183	1,375	
	0700	400 amp	2 Elec	1.60	10		1,700	345		2,045	2,375	
	0800	600 amp		1.20	13.333		2,475	455		2,930	3,400	
	1000	800 amp		.94	17.021		3,225	585		3,810	4,425	
800	0010	**SAFETY SWITCHES**										**800**
	0100	General duty 240 volt, 3 pole NEMA 1, fusible, 30 amp	1 Elec	3.20	2.500	Ea.	67.50	86		153.50	203	
	0200	60 amp		2.30	3.478		114	119		233	305	
	0300	100 amp		1.90	4.211		197	144		341	435	
	0400	200 amp		1.30	6.154		425	211		636	780	
	0500	400 amp	2 Elec	1.80	8.889		1,075	305		1,380	1,625	
	0600	600 amp	"	1.20	13.333		2,000	455		2,455	2,875	
	2900	Heavy duty, 240 volt, 3 pole NEMA 1 fusible										

16 ELECTRICAL

16410 | Encl Switches & Circuit Breakers

			CREW	DAILY OUTPUT	LABOR-HOURS	UNIT	MAT.	LABOR	EQUIP.	TOTAL	TOTAL INCL O&P	
800	2910	30 amp	1 Elec	3.20	2.500	Ea.	109	86		195	248	800
	3000	60 amp		2.30	3.478		185	119		304	380	
	3300	100 amp		1.90	4.211		291	144		435	535	
	3500	200 amp	↓	1.30	6.154		500	211		711	865	
	3700	400 amp	2 Elec	1.80	8.889		1,150	305		1,455	1,725	
	3900	600 amp	"	1.20	13.333	↓	2,100	455		2,555	2,975	

16420 | Enclosed Controllers

			CREW	DAILY OUTPUT	LABOR-HOURS	UNIT	MAT.	LABOR	EQUIP.	TOTAL	TOTAL INCL O&P	
220	0010	**CONTROL STATIONS**										220
	0050	NEMA 1, heavy duty, stop/start	1 Elec	8	1	Ea.	113	34.50		147.50	175	
	0100	Stop/start, pilot light		6.20	1.290		153	44.50		197.50	234	
	0200	Hand/off/automatic		6.20	1.290		83.50	44.50		128	158	
	0400	Stop/start/reverse	↓	5.30	1.509	↓	153	52		205	246	

16440 | Swbds, Panels & Cont Centers

			CREW	DAILY OUTPUT	LABOR-HOURS	UNIT	MAT.	LABOR	EQUIP.	TOTAL	TOTAL INCL O&P	
660	0010	**MOTOR STARTERS & CONTROLS**										660
	0050	Magnetic, FVNR, with enclosure and heaters, 480 volt [R16220-610]										
	0100	5 HP, size 0	1 Elec	2.30	3.478	Ea.	202	119		321	400	
	0200	10 HP, size 1	"	1.60	5		227	172		399	505	
	0300	25 HP, size 2	2 Elec	2.20	7.273		425	249		674	840	
	0400	50 HP, size 3		1.80	8.889		695	305		1,000	1,225	
	0500	100 HP, size 4		1.20	13.333		1,550	455		2,005	2,375	
	0600	200 HP, size 5	↓	.90	17.778		3,600	610		4,210	4,875	
	0700	Combination, with motor circuit protectors, 5 HP, size 0	1 Elec	1.80	4.444		655	152		807	950	
	0800	10 HP, size 1	"	1.30	6.154		680	211		891	1,075	
	0900	25 HP, size 2	2 Elec	2	8		955	274		1,229	1,450	
	1000	50 HP, size 3		1.32	12.121		1,375	415		1,790	2,150	
	1200	100 HP, size 4	↓	.80	20		3,000	685		3,685	4,325	
	1400	Combination, with fused switch, 5 HP, size 0	1 Elec	1.80	4.444		500	152		652	780	
	1600	10 HP, size 1	"	1.30	6.154		535	211		746	905	
	1800	25 HP, size 2	2 Elec	2	8		870	274		1,144	1,375	
	2000	50 HP, size 3		1.32	12.121		1,475	415		1,890	2,250	
	2200	100 HP, size 4	↓	.80	20	↓	2,575	685		3,260	3,850	
700	0010	**PANELBOARD & LOAD CENTER CIRCUIT BREAKERS**										700
	0050	Bolt-on, 10,000 amp IC, 120 volt, 1 pole										
	0100	15 to 50 amp	1 Elec	10	.800	Ea.	10	27.50		37.50	52	
	0200	60 amp		8	1		10	34.50		44.50	62	
	0300	70 amp	↓	8	1	↓	19	34.50		53.50	72	
	0350	240 volt, 2 pole										
	0400	15 to 50 amp	1 Elec	8	1	Ea.	22	34.50		56.50	75	
	0500	60 amp		7.50	1.067		22	36.50		58.50	78.50	
	0600	80 to 100 amp		5	1.600		56.50	55		111.50	144	
	0700	3 pole, 15 to 60 amp		6.20	1.290		69.50	44.50		114	143	
	0800	70 amp		5	1.600		87.50	55		142.50	179	
	0900	80 to 100 amp		3.60	2.222		99.50	76		175.50	223	
	1000	22,000 amp I.C., 240 volt, 2 pole, 70 - 225 amp		2.70	2.963		430	102		532	620	
	1100	3 pole, 70 - 225 amp		2.30	3.478		475	119		594	705	
	1200	14,000 amp I.C., 277 volts, 1 pole, 15 - 30 amp		8	1		26.50	34.50		61	80	
	1300	22,000 amp I.C., 480 volts, 2 pole, 70 - 225 amp		2.70	2.963		430	102		532	620	
	1400	3 pole, 70 - 225 amp	↓	2.30	3.478	↓	475	119		594	705	
720	0010	**PANELBOARDS** (Commercial use)										720
	0050	NQOD, w/20 amp 1 pole bolt-on circuit breakers										
	0100	3 wire, 120/240 volts, 100 amp main lugs										
	0150	10 circuits	1 Elec	1	8	Ea.	390	274		664	835	

ELECTRICAL 16

16440 | Swbds, Panels & Cont Centers

		CREW	DAILY OUTPUT	LABOR-HOURS	UNIT	MAT.	LABOR	EQUIP.	TOTAL	TOTAL INCL O&P	
720							2001 BARE COSTS				**720**
0200	14 circuits	1 Elec	.88	9.091	Ea.	455	310		765	965	
0250	18 circuits		.75	10.667		500	365		865	1,100	
0300	20 circuits		.65	12.308		560	420		980	1,250	
0350	225 amp main lugs, 24 circuits	2 Elec	1.20	13.333		635	455		1,090	1,375	
0400	30 circuits		.90	17.778		740	610		1,350	1,725	
0450	36 circuits		.80	20		845	685		1,530	1,950	
0500	38 circuits		.72	22.222		910	760		1,670	2,150	
0550	42 circuits		.66	24.242		950	830		1,780	2,300	
0600	4 wire, 120/208 volts, 100 amp main lugs, 12 circuits	1 Elec	1	8		440	274		714	895	
0650	16 circuits		.75	10.667		505	365		870	1,100	
0700	20 circuits		.65	12.308		590	420		1,010	1,275	
0750	24 circuits CN		.60	13.333		640	455		1,095	1,400	
0800	30 circuits		.53	15.094		740	520		1,260	1,575	
0850	225 amp main lugs, 32 circuits	2 Elec	.90	17.778		830	610		1,440	1,825	
0900	34 circuits		.84	19.048		850	655		1,505	1,900	
0950	36 circuits		.80	20		870	685		1,555	1,975	
1000	42 circuits		.68	23.529		975	805		1,780	2,275	
1200	NEHB, w/20 amp, 1 pole bolt-on circuit breakers										
1250	4 wire, 277/480 volts, 100 amp main lugs, 12 circuits	1 Elec	.88	9.091	Ea.	840	310		1,150	1,400	
1300	20 circuits	"	.60	13.333		1,250	455		1,705	2,050	
1350	225 amp main lugs, 24 circuits	2 Elec	.90	17.778		1,425	610		2,035	2,475	
1400	30 circuits		.80	20		1,725	685		2,410	2,925	
1450	36 circuits		.72	22.222		2,000	760		2,760	3,350	
1600	NQOD panel, w/20 amp, 1 pole, circuit breakers										
1650	3 wire, 120/240 volt with main circuit breaker										
1700	100 amp main, 12 circuits	1 Elec	.80	10	Ea.	540	345		885	1,100	
1750	20 circuits	"	.60	13.333		690	455		1,145	1,450	
1800	225 amp main, 30 circuits	2 Elec	.68	23.529		1,325	805		2,130	2,650	
1850	42 circuits		.52	30.769		1,525	1,050		2,575	3,250	
1900	400 amp main, 30 circuits		.54	29.630		1,825	1,025		2,850	3,550	
1950	42 circuits		.50	32		2,050	1,100		3,150	3,900	
2000	4 wire, 120/208 volts with main circuit breaker										
2050	100 amp main, 24 circuits	1 Elec	.47	17.021	Ea.	805	585		1,390	1,750	
2100	30 circuits	"	.40	20		910	685		1,595	2,025	
2200	225 amp main, 32 circuits	2 Elec	.72	22.222		1,550	760		2,310	2,850	
2250	42 circuits		.56	28.571		1,675	980		2,655	3,325	
2300	400 amp main, 42 circuits		.48	33.333		2,275	1,150		3,425	4,200	
2350	600 amp main, 42 circuits		.40	40		3,375	1,375		4,750	5,775	
2400	NEHB, with 20 amp, 1 pole circuit breaker										
2450	4 wire, 277/480 volts with main circuit breaker										
2500	100 amp main, 24 circuits	1 Elec	.42	19.048	Ea.	1,650	655		2,305	2,800	
2550	30 circuits	"	.38	21.053		1,950	720		2,670	3,200	
2600	225 amp main, 30 circuits	2 Elec	.72	22.222		2,450	760		3,210	3,850	
2650	42 circuits	"	.56	28.571		3,025	980		4,005	4,800	
800	0010	**SWITCHBOARDS** distribution section									**800**
	0100	Aluminum bus bars, not including breakers									
	0200	120/208 or 277/480 volt, 4 wire, 600 amp	2 Elec	1	16	Ea.	1,225	550		1,775	2,175
	0300	800 amp		.88	18.182		1,550	625		2,175	2,625
	0400	1000 amp		.80	20		1,775	685		2,460	2,975
	0500	1200 amp		.72	22.222		2,425	760		3,185	3,825
	0600	1600 amp		.66	24.242		2,850	830		3,680	4,375
	0700	2000 amp		.62	25.806		3,325	885		4,210	4,975
	0800	2500 amp		.60	26.667		3,750	915		4,665	5,500
	0900	3000 amp		.56	28.571		4,550	980		5,530	6,475
	0950	4000 amp		.52	30.769		6,650	1,050		7,700	8,875

16 ELECTRICAL

Important: See the Reference Section for critical supporting data - Reference Nos., Crews, & City Cost Indexes

16440 | Swbds, Panels & Cont Centers

		CREW	DAILY OUTPUT	LABOR-HOURS	UNIT	2001 BARE COSTS				TOTAL INCL O&P
						MAT.	LABOR	EQUIP.	TOTAL	
820	0010 **SWITCHBOARDS** feeder section group mounted devices									**820**
	0030 Circuit breakers									
	0160 FA frame, 15 to 60 amp, 240 volt, 1 pole	1 Elec	8	1	Ea.	67	34.50		101.50	125
	0280 FA frame, 70 to 100 amp, 240 volt, 1 pole		7	1.143		88.50	39		127.50	156
	0420 KA frame, 70 to 225 amp		3.20	2.500		740	86		826	945
	0430 LA frame, 125 to 400 amp		2.30	3.478		1,675	119		1,794	2,025
	0460 MA frame, 450 to 600 amp		1.60	5		2,775	172		2,947	3,300
	0470 700 to 800 amp		1.30	6.154		3,600	211		3,811	4,275
	0480 MAL frame, 1000 amp		1	8		3,725	274		3,999	4,500
	0490 PA frame, 1200 amp		.80	10		7,575	345		7,920	8,825
	0500 Branch circuit, fusible switch, 600 volt, double 30/30 amp		4	2		740	68.50		808.50	915
	0550 60/60 amp		3.20	2.500		755	86		841	960
	0600 100/100 amp		2.70	2.963		1,050	102		1,152	1,300
	0650 Single, 30 amp		5.30	1.509		485	52		537	615
	0700 60 amp		4.70	1.702		485	58.50		543.50	620
	0750 100 amp		4	2		705	68.50		773.50	875
	0800 200 amp		2.70	2.963		1,050	102		1,152	1,300
	0850 400 amp		2.30	3.478		1,975	119		2,094	2,350
	0900 600 amp		1.80	4.444		2,350	152		2,502	2,800
	0950 800 amp		1.30	6.154		3,825	211		4,036	4,525
	1000 1200 amp		.80	10		4,575	345		4,920	5,525
840	0010 **SWITCHBOARDS** Incoming main service section									**840**
	0100 Aluminum bus bars, not including CT's or PT's									
	0200 No main disconnect, includes CT compartment									
	0300 120/208 volt, 4 wire, 600 amp	2 Elec	1	16	Ea.	2,650	550		3,200	3,750
	0400 800 amp		.88	18.182		2,650	625		3,275	3,850
	0500 1000 amp		.80	20		3,175	685		3,860	4,525
	0600 1200 amp		.72	22.222		3,175	760		3,935	4,650
	0700 1600 amp		.66	24.242		3,175	830		4,005	4,750
	0800 2000 amp		.62	25.806		3,425	885		4,310	5,100
	1000 3000 amp		.56	28.571		4,525	980		5,505	6,450
	2000 Fused switch & CT compartment									
	2100 120/208 volt, 4 wire, 400 amp	2 Elec	1.12	14.286	Ea.	3,550	490		4,040	4,625
	2200 600 amp		.94	17.021		4,200	585		4,785	5,500
	2300 800 amp		.84	19.048		7,175	655		7,830	8,850
	2400 1200 amp		.68	23.529		9,325	805		10,130	11,500
	2900 Pressure switch & CT compartment									
	3000 120/208 volt, 4 wire, 800 amp	2 Elec	.80	20	Ea.	6,450	685		7,135	8,100
	3100 1200 amp		.66	24.242		12,500	830		13,330	15,000
	3200 1600 amp		.62	25.806		13,300	885		14,185	15,900
	3300 2000 amp		.56	28.571		14,100	980		15,080	17,000
	4400 Circuit breaker, molded case & CT compartment									
	4600 3 pole, 4 wire, 600 amp	2 Elec	.94	17.021	Ea.	5,550	585		6,135	6,975
	4800 800 amp		.84	19.048		6,650	655		7,305	8,275
	5000 1200 amp		.68	23.529		9,050	805		9,855	11,200
	5100 Copper bus bars, not incl. CT's or PT's, add, minimum					15%				

16450 | Enclosed Bus Assemblies

		CREW	DAILY OUTPUT	LABOR-HOURS	UNIT	MAT.	LABOR	EQUIP.	TOTAL	TOTAL INCL O&P
320	0010 **COPPER BUS DUCT** 10 ft long									**320**
	0050 3 pole 4 wire, plug-in/indoor, straight section, 225 amp	2 Elec	40	.400	L.F.	136	13.70		149.70	171
	1000 400 amp		32	.500		136	17.15		153.15	176
	1500 600 amp		26	.615		136	21		157	182
	2400 800 amp		20	.800		162	27.50		189.50	219
	2450 1000 amp		18	.889		179	30.50		209.50	242

16450	Enclosed Bus Assemblies	CREW	DAILY OUTPUT	LABOR-HOURS	UNIT	MAT.	LABOR	EQUIP.	TOTAL	TOTAL INCL O&P
							2001 BARE COSTS			
320											320
2500	1350 amp	2 Elec	16	1	L.F.	255	34.50		289.50	330
2510	1600 amp		12	1.333		289	45.50		334.50	390
2520	2000 amp		10	1.600		365	55		420	480
2550	Feeder, 600 amp		28	.571		119	19.60		138.60	161
2600	800 amp		22	.727		145	25		170	196
2700	1000 amp		20	.800		162	27.50		189.50	219
2800	1350 amp		18	.889		238	30.50		268.50	310
2900	1600 amp		14	1.143		272	39		311	360
3000	2000 amp		12	1.333		350	45.50		395.50	455
3100	Elbows, 225 amp		4	4	Ea.	805	137		942	1,100
3200	400 amp		3.60	4.444		805	152		957	1,125
3300	600 amp		3.20	5		805	172		977	1,150
3400	800 amp		2.80	5.714		875	196		1,071	1,250
3500	1000 amp		2.60	6.154		975	211		1,186	1,400
3600	1350 amp		2.40	6.667		1,150	229		1,379	1,600
3700	1600 amp		2.20	7.273		1,250	249		1,499	1,750
3800	2000 amp		1.80	8.889		1,550	305		1,855	2,150
4000	End box, 225 amp		34	.471		109	16.15		125.15	144
4100	400 amp		32	.500		109	17.15		126.15	146
4200	600 amp		28	.571		109	19.60		128.60	150
4300	800 amp		26	.615		109	21		130	152
4400	1000 amp		24	.667		109	23		132	154
4500	1350 amp		22	.727		109	25		134	157
4600	1600 amp		20	.800		109	27.50		136.50	161
4700	2000 amp		18	.889		133	30.50		163.50	193
4800	Cable tap box end, 225 amp		3.20	5		780	172		952	1,100
5000	400 amp		2.60	6.154		780	211		991	1,175
5100	600 amp		2.20	7.273		780	249		1,029	1,225
5200	800 amp		2	8		875	274		1,149	1,375
5300	1000 amp		1.60	10		960	345		1,305	1,550
5400	1350 amp		1.40	11.429		1,150	390		1,540	1,850
5500	1600 amp		1.20	13.333		1,300	455		1,755	2,100
5600	2000 amp		1	16		1,475	550		2,025	2,450
5700	Switchboard stub, 225 amp		5.40	2.963		815	102		917	1,050
5800	400 amp		4.60	3.478		815	119		934	1,075
5900	600 amp		4	4		815	137		952	1,100
6000	800 amp		3.20	5		985	172		1,157	1,325
6100	1000 amp		3	5.333		1,150	183		1,333	1,525
6200	1350 amp		2.60	6.154		1,475	211		1,686	1,950
6300	1600 amp		2.40	6.667		1,650	229		1,879	2,175
6400	2000 amp		2	8		2,025	274		2,299	2,625
6490	Tee fittings, 225 amp		2.40	6.667		1,100	229		1,329	1,575
6500	400 amp		2	8		1,100	274		1,374	1,625
6600	600 amp		1.80	8.889		1,100	305		1,405	1,675
6700	800 amp		1.60	10		1,275	345		1,620	1,900
6800	1350 amp		1.20	13.333		1,850	455		2,305	2,700
7000	1600 amp		1	16		2,100	550		2,650	3,125
7100	2000 amp		.80	20		2,475	685		3,160	3,750
7200	Plug-in fusible switches w/3 fuses, 600 volt, 3 pole, 30 amp	1 Elec	4	2		360	68.50		428.50	495
7300	60 amp		3.60	2.222		390	76		466	545
7400	100 amp		2.70	2.963		830	102		932	1,075
7500	200 amp	2 Elec	3.20	5		985	172		1,157	1,325
7600	400 amp		1.40	11.429		2,575	390		2,965	3,400
7700	600 amp		.90	17.778		3,350	610		3,960	4,600
7800	800 amp		.66	24.242		6,175	830		7,005	8,025
7900	1200 amp		.50	32		11,600	1,100		12,700	14,400

Important: See the Reference Section for critical supporting data - Reference Nos., Crews, & City Cost Indexes

16400 | Low-Voltage Distribution

		16450	Enclosed Bus Assemblies	CREW	DAILY OUTPUT	LABOR-HOURS	UNIT	2001 BARE COSTS				TOTAL INCL O&P	
								MAT.	LABOR	EQUIP.	TOTAL		
320	8000		Plug-in circuit breakers, molded case, 15 to 50 amp	1 Elec	4.40	1.818	Ea.	460	62.50		522.50	600	320
	8100		70 to 100 amp	"	3.10	2.581		510	88.50		598.50	690	
	8200		150 to 225 amp	2 Elec	3.40	4.706		1,375	161		1,536	1,775	
	8300		250 to 400 amp		1.40	11.429		2,425	390		2,815	3,250	
	8400		500 to 600 amp		1	16		3,275	550		3,825	4,425	
	8500		700 to 800 amp		.64	25		4,025	860		4,885	5,725	
	8600		900 to 1000 amp		.56	28.571		5,775	980		6,755	7,825	
	8700		1200 amp	↓	.44	36.364	↓	6,950	1,250		8,200	9,475	

16500 | Lighting

		16510	Interior Luminaires	CREW	DAILY OUTPUT	LABOR-HOURS	UNIT	2001 BARE COSTS				TOTAL INCL O&P	
								MAT.	LABOR	EQUIP.	TOTAL		
440	0010	**INTERIOR LIGHTING FIXTURES** Including lamps, mounting											440
	0030		hardware and connections										
	0100		Fluorescent, C.W. lamps, troffer, recess mounted in grid, RS										
	0200		Acrylic lens, 1'W x 4'L, two 40 watt	1 Elec	5.70	1.404	Ea.	46.50	48		94.50	123	
	0210		1'W x 4'L, three 40 watt		5.40	1.481		52.50	51		103.50	134	
	0300		2'W x 2'L, two U40 watt		5.70	1.404		50.50	48		98.50	128	
	0400		2'W x 4'L, two 40 watt		5.30	1.509		50.50	52		102.50	133	
	0500		2'W x 4'L, three 40 watt		5	1.600		53.50	55		108.50	141	
	0600		2'W x 4'L, four 40 watt **CN**	↓	4.70	1.702		56.50	58.50		115	149	
	0700		4'W x 4'L, four 40 watt	2 Elec	6.40	2.500		288	86		374	445	
	0800		4'W x 4'L, six 40 watt		6.20	2.581		298	88.50		386.50	460	
	0900		4'W x 4'L, eight 40 watt	↓	5.80	2.759		310	94.50		404.50	480	
	0910		Acrylic lens, 1'W x 4'L, two 32 watt	1 Elec	5.70	1.404		55.50	48		103.50	133	
	0930		2'W x 2'L, two U32 watt		5.70	1.404		76	48		124	156	
	0940		2'W x 4'L, two 32 watt		5.30	1.509		68	52		120	153	
	0950		2'W x 4'L, three 32 watt		5	1.600		73	55		128	163	
	0960		2'W x 4'L, four 32 watt	↓	4.70	1.702	↓	76	58.50		134.50	171	
	1000		Surface mounted, RS										
	1030		Acrylic lens with hinged & latched door frame										
	1100		1'W x 4'L, two 40 watt	1 Elec	7	1.143	Ea.	71	39		110	137	
	1110		1'W x 4'L, three 40 watt		6.70	1.194		81	41		122	150	
	1200		2'W x 2'L, two U40 watt		7	1.143		86	39		125	153	
	1300		2'W x 4'L, two 40 watt		6.20	1.290		79	44.50		123.50	153	
	1400		2'W x 4'L, three 40 watt		5.70	1.404		89	48		137	170	
	1500		2'W x 4'L, four 40 watt	↓	5.30	1.509		91	52		143	178	
	1600		4'W x 4'L, four 40 watt	2 Elec	7.20	2.222		390	76		466	545	
	1700		4'W x 4'L, six 40 watt		6.60	2.424		425	83		508	595	
	1800		4'W x 4'L, eight 40 watt		6.20	2.581		435	88.50		523.50	610	
	1900		2'W x 8'L, four 40 watt		6.40	2.500		141	86		227	283	
	2000		2'W x 8'L, eight 40 watt	↓	6.20	2.581	↓	172	88.50		260.50	320	
	2100		Strip fixture										
	2130		Surface mounted										
	2200		4' long, one 40 watt RS	1 Elec	8.50	.941	Ea.	26.50	32.50		59	77	
	2300		4' long, two 40 watt RS		8	1		28.50	34.50		63	82	
	2400		4' long, one 40 watt, SL		8	1		38.50	34.50		73	93.50	
	2500		4' long, two 40 watt, SL	↓	7	1.143		52.50	39		91.50	117	
	2600		8' long, one 75 watt, SL	2 Elec	13.40	1.194		39.50	41		80.50	105	
	2700		8' long, two 75 watt, SL	"	12.40	1.290	↓	47.50	44.50		92	119	

ELECTRICAL 16

For expanded coverage of these items see *Means Electrical Cost Data 2001*

440		16510	Interior Luminaires	CREW	DAILY OUTPUT	LABOR-HOURS	UNIT	2001 BARE COSTS				TOTAL INCL O&P	
								MAT.	LABOR	EQUIP.	TOTAL		
440	2800		4' long, two 60 watt, HO	1 Elec	6.70	1.194	Ea.	77	41		118	146	**440**
	2900		8' long, two 110 watt, HO	2 Elec	10.60	1.509	↓	81	52		133	167	
	3000		Pendent mounted, industrial, white porcelain enamel										
	3100		4' long, two 40 watt, RS	1 Elec	5.70	1.404	Ea.	43.50	48		91.50	120	
	3200		4' long, two 60 watt, HO	"	5	1.600		69	55		124	158	
	3300		8' long, two 75 watt, SL	2 Elec	8.80	1.818		82	62.50		144.50	183	
	3400		8' long, two 110 watt, HO	"	8	2		105	68.50		173.50	218	
	3470		Troffer, air handling, 2'W x 4'L with four 40 watt, RS	1 Elec	4	2		77	68.50		145.50	187	
	3480		2'W x 2'L with two U40 watt RS		5.50	1.455		67	50		117	148	
	3490		Air connector insulated, 5" diameter		20	.400		52.50	13.70		66.20	78.50	
	3500		6" diameter	↓	20	.400	↓	53.50	13.70		67.20	79.50	
	3580		Mercury vapor, integral ballast, ceiling, recess mounted,										
	3590		prismatic glass lens, floating door										
	3600		2'W x 2'L, 250 watt DX lamp	1 Elec	3.20	2.500	Ea.	263	86		349	415	
	3700		2'W x 2'L, 400 watt DX lamp		2.90	2.759		268	94.50		362.50	435	
	3800		Surface mtd., prismatic lens, 2'W x 2'L, 250 watt DX lamp		2.70	2.963		263	102		365	440	
	3900		2'W x 2'L, 400 watt DX lamp	↓	2.40	3.333	↓	297	114		411	495	
	4000		High bay, aluminum reflector										
	4030		Single unit, 400 watt DX lamp	2 Elec	4.60	3.478	Ea.	260	119		379	465	
	4100		Single unit, 1000 watt DX lamp		4	4		410	137		547	655	
	4200		Twin unit, two 400 watt DX lamps	↓	3.20	5	↓	440	172		612	740	
	4450		Incandescent, high hat can, round alzak reflector, prewired										
	4470		100 watt	1 Elec	8	1	Ea.	55.50	34.50		90	112	
	4480		150 watt		8	1		81	34.50		115.50	140	
	4500		300 watt	↓	6.70	1.194	↓	184	41		225	263	
	4600		Square glass lens with metal trim, prewired										
	4630		100 watt	1 Elec	6.70	1.194	Ea.	42	41		83	107	
	4700		200 watt		6.70	1.194		61	41		102	128	
	4800		300 watt		5.70	1.404		90	48		138	171	
	4900		Ceiling/wall, surface mounted, metal cylinder, 75 watt		10	.800		36	27.50		63.50	80.50	
	4920		150 watt	↓	10	.800	↓	56	27.50		83.50	103	
	5200		Ceiling, surface mounted, opal glass drum										
	5300		8", one 60 watt lamp	1 Elec	10	.800	Ea.	34	27.50		61.50	78.50	
	5400		10", two 60 watt lamps		8	1		38	34.50		72.50	93	
	5500		12", four 60 watt lamps		6.70	1.194		55	41		96	122	
	6010		Vapor tight, incandescent, ceiling mounted, 200 watt		6.20	1.290		46	44.50		90.50	117	
	6100		Fluorescent, surface mounted, 2 lamps, 4'L, RS, 40 watt		3.20	2.500		90	86		176	227	
	6200		Mercury vapor with ballast, 175 watt	↓	3.20	2.500	↓	272	86		358	425	
	6300		Explosionproof										
	6510		Incandescent, ceiling mounted, 200 watt	1 Elec	4	2	Ea.	630	68.50		698.50	795	
	6600		Fluorescent, RS, 4' long, ceiling mounted, two 40 watt		2.70	2.963		1,575	102		1,677	1,900	
	6700		Mercury vapor with ballast, surface mounted, 175 watt		2.70	2.963		525	102		627	730	
	6850		Vandalproof, surface mounted, fluorescent, two 40 watt		3.20	2.500		171	86		257	315	
	6860		Incandescent, one 150 watt	↓	8	1	↓	53	34.50		87.50	109	
	7500		Ballast replacement, by weight of ballast, to 15' high										
	7520		Indoor fluorescent, less than 2 lbs.	1 Elec	10	.800	Ea.		27.50		27.50	41	
	7540		Two 40W, watt reducer, 2 to 5 lbs.		9.40	.851		18.90	29		47.90	64.50	
	7560		Two F96 slimline, over 5 lbs.		8	1		32.50	34.50		67	87	
	7580		Vaportite ballast, less than 2 lbs.		9.40	.851			29		29	43.50	
	7600		2 lbs. to 5 lbs.		8.90	.899			31		31	46	
	7620		Over 5 lbs.		7.60	1.053			36		36	54	
	7630		Electronic ballast for two tubes		8	1		32.50	34.50		67	87	
	7640		Dimmable ballast one lamp		8	1		45	34.50		79.50	101	
	7650		Dimmable ballast two-lamp	↓	7.60	1.053	↓	70	36		106	131	

16 ELECTRICAL

Important: See the Reference Section for critical supporting data - Reference Nos., Crews, & City Cost Indexes

16520 | Exterior Luminaires

		CREW	DAILY OUTPUT	LABOR-HOURS	UNIT	2001 BARE COSTS				TOTAL INCL O&P
						MAT.	LABOR	EQUIP.	TOTAL	
300	**0010**	**EXTERIOR FIXTURES** With lamps									**300**
	0200	Wall mounted, incandescent, 100 watt	1 Elec	8	1	Ea.	28	34.50		62.50	82
	0400	Quartz, 500 watt		5.30	1.509		53.50	52		105.50	137
	0600	Mercury vapor, 100 watt		5.30	1.509		229	52		281	330
	0800	Wall pack, mercury vapor, 175 watt		4	2		221	68.50		289.50	345
	1000	250 watt		4	2		213	68.50		281.50	335
	1100	Low pressure sodium, 35 watt		4	2		208	68.50		276.50	330
	1150	55 watt		4	2		280	68.50		348.50	410
	1200	Floodlights with ballast and lamp,									
	1400	pole mounted, pole not included									
	1500	Mercury vapor, 250 watt	1 Elec	2.40	3.333	Ea.	200	114		314	390
	1600	400 watt	2 Elec	4.40	3.636		278	125		403	490
	1800	1000 watt	"	4	4		365	137		502	605
	1950	Metal halide, 175 watt	1 Elec	2.70	2.963		285	102		387	465
	2000	400 watt	2 Elec	4.40	3.636		350	125		475	570
	2200	1000 watt	"	4	4		450	137		587	700
	2340	High pressure sodium, 70 watt	1 Elec	2.70	2.963		193	102		295	365
	2400	400 watt	2 Elec	4.40	3.636		335	125		460	555
	2600	1000 watt	"	4	4		500	137		637	755
	2650	Roadway area luminaire, low pressure sodium, 135 watt	1 Elec	2	4		535	137		672	795
	2700	180 watt	"	2	4		565	137		702	825
	2720	Mercury vapor, 400 watt	2 Elec	4.40	3.636		340	125		465	560
	2730	1000 watt		4	4		425	137		562	675
	2750	Metal halide, 400 watt		4.40	3.636		445	125		570	670
	2760	1000 watt		4	4		530	137		667	785
	2780	High pressure sodium, 400 watt		4.40	3.636		500	125		625	735
	2790	1000 watt		4	4		555	137		692	815
	2800	Light poles, anchor base									
	2820	not including concrete bases									
	2840	Aluminum pole, 8' high	1 Elec	4	2	Ea.	470	68.50		538.50	620
	3000	20' high	R-3	2.90	6.897		615	234	49	898	1,075
	3200	30' high		2.60	7.692		1,200	261	54.50	1,515.50	1,775
	3400	35' high		2.30	8.696		1,300	295	61.50	1,656.50	1,925
	3600	40' high		2	10		1,475	340	71	1,886	2,200
	3800	Bracket arms, 1 arm	1 Elec	8	1		80.50	34.50		115	140
	4000	2 arms		8	1		162	34.50		196.50	229
	4200	3 arms		5.30	1.509		243	52		295	345
	4400	4 arms		5.30	1.509		325	52		377	435
	4500	Steel pole, galvanized, 8' high		3.80	2.105		420	72		492	570
	4600	20' high	R-3	2.60	7.692		745	261	54.50	1,060.50	1,275
	4800	30' high		2.30	8.696		875	295	61.50	1,231.50	1,475
	5000	35' high		2.20	9.091		960	310	64.50	1,334.50	1,575
	5200	40' high		1.70	11.765		1,175	400	83.50	1,658.50	1,975
	5400	Bracket arms, 1 arm	1 Elec	8	1		122	34.50		156.50	185
	5600	2 arms		8	1		189	34.50		223.50	259
	5800	3 arms		5.30	1.509		205	52		257	305
	6000	4 arms		5.30	1.509		285	52		337	395

16530 | Emergency Lighting

		CREW	DAILY OUTPUT	LABOR-HOURS	UNIT	2001 BARE COSTS				TOTAL INCL O&P
320	**0010**	**EXIT AND EMERGENCY LIGHTING**									**320**
	0080	Exit light ceiling or wall mount, incandescent, single face	1 Elec	8	1	Ea.	37.50	34.50		72	92.50
	0100	Double face		6.70	1.194		44	41		85	110
	0200	L.E.D. standard, single face		8	1		62	34.50		96.50	119
	0220	double face		6.70	1.194		65	41		106	133
	0240	L.E.D. w/ battery unit, single face		4.40	1.818		105	62.50		167.50	209

ELECTRICAL 16

16500 | Lighting

16530 | Emergency Lighting

		CREW	DAILY OUTPUT	LABOR-HOURS	UNIT	MAT.	2001 BARE COSTS LABOR	EQUIP.	TOTAL	TOTAL INCL O&P	
320	0260	double face	1 Elec	4	2	Ea.	107	68.50		175.50	220	320
	0300	Emergency light units, battery operated										
	0350	Twin sealed beam light, 25 watt, 6 volt each										
	0500	Lead battery operated	1 Elec	4	2	Ea.	170	68.50		238.50	289	
	0700	Nickel cadmium battery operated		4	2		505	68.50		573.50	655	
	0900	Self-contained fluorescent lamp pack	↓	10	.800	↓	117	27.50		144.50	169	

16585 | Lamps

		CREW	DAILY OUTPUT	LABOR-HOURS	UNIT	MAT.	2001 BARE COSTS LABOR	EQUIP.	TOTAL	TOTAL INCL O&P	
600	0010	**LAMPS**										600
	0080	Fluorescent, rapid start, cool white, 2' long, 20 watt	1 Elec	1	8	C	287	274		561	725	
	0100	4' long, 40 watt		.90	8.889		266	305		571	750	
	0200	Slimline, 4' long, 40 watt		.90	8.889		870	305		1,175	1,425	
	0400	High output, 4' long, 60 watt		.90	8.889		1,025	305		1,330	1,575	
	0500	8' long, 110 watt		.80	10		950	345		1,295	1,550	
	0560	Twin tube compact lamp		.90	8.889		425	305		730	925	
	0570	Double twin tube compact lamp		.80	10		925	345		1,270	1,525	
	0600	Mercury vapor, mogul base, deluxe white, 100 watt		.30	26.667		3,500	915		4,415	5,225	
	0700	250 watt		.30	26.667		4,600	915		5,515	6,450	
	0800	400 watt		.30	26.667		3,700	915		4,615	5,450	
	0900	1000 watt		.20	40		8,600	1,375		9,975	11,500	
	1000	Metal halide, mogul base, 175 watt		.30	26.667		4,450	915		5,365	6,250	
	1200	400 watt		.30	26.667		4,700	915		5,615	6,525	
	1300	1000 watt		.20	40		12,900	1,375		14,275	16,300	
	1350	High pressure sodium, 70 watt		.30	26.667		4,425	915		5,340	6,250	
	1380	250 watt		.30	26.667		5,050	915		5,965	6,925	
	1400	400 watt		.30	26.667		5,175	915		6,090	7,075	
	1450	1000 watt		.20	40		18,500	1,375		19,875	22,500	
	3000	Guards, fluorescent lamp, 4' long		1	8		610	274		884	1,075	
	3200	8' long	↓	.90	8.889	↓	870	305		1,175	1,425	

16700 | Communications

16720 | Tel and Intercomm Equipment

		CREW	DAILY OUTPUT	LABOR-HOURS	UNIT	MAT.	2001 BARE COSTS LABOR	EQUIP.	TOTAL	TOTAL INCL O&P	
300	0010	**DOCTORS IN-OUT REGISTER**										300
	0050	Register, 200 names	4 Elec	.64	50	Ea.	9,475	1,725		11,200	13,000	
	0100	Combination control and recall, 200 names	"	.64	50		12,400	1,725		14,125	16,200	
	0200	Recording register	1 Elec	.50	16		4,825	550		5,375	6,125	
	0300	Transformers	"	4	2		162	68.50		230.50	280	
	0400	Pocket pages				↓	835			835	920	
600	0010	**NURSE CALL SYSTEMS**										600
	0100	Single bedside call station	1 Elec	8	1	Ea.	170	34.50		204.50	237	
	0200	Ceiling speaker station		8	1		49	34.50		83.50	105	
	0400	Emergency call station		8	1		83	34.50		117.50	143	
	0600	Pillow speaker		8	1		153	34.50		187.50	219	
	0800	Double bedside call station		4	2		258	68.50		326.50	385	
	1000	Duty station		4	2		128	68.50		196.50	243	
	1200	Standard call button		8	1		56.50	34.50		91	113	
	1400	Lights, corridor, dome or zone indicator	↓	8	1	↓	52.50	34.50		87	109	
	1600	Master control station for 20 stations	2 Elec	.65	24.615	Total	3,000	845		3,845	4,550	

Important: See the Reference Section for critical supporting data - Reference Nos., Crews, & City Cost Indexes

16800 | Sound & Video

16820 | Sound Reinforcement

		CREW	DAILY OUTPUT	LABOR-HOURS	UNIT	2001 BARE COSTS				TOTAL INCL O&P	
						MAT.	LABOR	EQUIP.	TOTAL		
300	0010 **DOORBELL SYSTEM** Incl. transformer, button & signal										300
	0100 6" bell	1 Elec	4	2	Ea.	55.50	68.50		124	163	
	0200 Buzzer	"	4	2	"	54.50	68.50		123	162	
800	0010 **PUBLIC ADDRESS SYSTEM**										800
	0100 Conventional, office	1 Elec	5.33	1.501	Speaker	95.50	51.50		147	182	
	0200 Industrial	"	2.70	2.963	"	185	102		287	355	
	0400 Explosionproof system is 3 times cost of central control										
	0600 Installation costs run about 120% of material cost										
840	0010 **SOUND SYSTEM** not including rough-in wires, cables & conduits										840
	0100 Components, outlet, projector	1 Elec	8	1	Ea.	44	34.50		78.50	99.50	
	0200 Microphone		4	2		49	68.50		117.50	156	
	0400 Speakers, ceiling or wall		8	1		85	34.50		119.50	145	
	0600 Trumpets		4	2		154	68.50		222.50	271	
	0800 Privacy switch		8	1		60.50	34.50		95	118	
	1000 Monitor panel		4	2		276	68.50		344.50	405	
	1200 Antenna, AM/FM		4	2		154	68.50		222.50	271	
	1400 Volume control		8	1		61.50	34.50		96	119	
	1600 Amplifier, 250 watts		1	8		1,150	274		1,424	1,650	
	1800 Cabinets	▼	1	8		600	274		874	1,075	
	2000 Intercom, 25 station capacity, master station	2 Elec	2	8		1,450	274		1,724	2,000	
	2200 Remote station	1 Elec	8	1		116	34.50		150.50	178	
	2400 Intercom outlets		8	1		68	34.50		102.50	126	
	2600 Handset		4	2		210	68.50		278.50	335	
	2800 Emergency call system, 12 zones, annunciator		1.30	6.154		680	211		891	1,050	
	3000 Bell		5.30	1.509		70	52		122	155	
	3200 Light or relay		8	1		35	34.50		69.50	89.50	
	3400 Transformer		4	2		154	68.50		222.50	271	
	3600 House telephone, talking station		1.60	5		330	172		502	620	
	3800 Press to talk, release to listen	▼	5.30	1.509		77	52		129	162	
	4000 System-on button					46			46	50.50	
	4200 Door release	1 Elec	4	2		82	68.50		150.50	192	
	4400 Combination speaker and microphone		8	1		140	34.50		174.50	205	
	4600 Termination box		3.20	2.500		44	86		130	177	
	4800 Amplifier or power supply		5.30	1.509	▼	505	52		557	640	
	5000 Vestibule door unit		16	.500	Name	93	17.15		110.15	128	
	5200 Strip cabinet		27	.296	Ea.	176	10.15		186.15	209	
	5400 Directory	▼	16	.500	"	83	17.15		100.15	117	

16850 | Television Equipment

		CREW	DAILY OUTPUT	LABOR-HOURS	UNIT	2001 BARE COSTS				TOTAL INCL O&P	
						MAT.	LABOR	EQUIP.	TOTAL		
600	0010 **T.V. SYSTEMS** not including rough-in wires, cables & conduits										600
	0100 Master TV antenna system										
	0200 VHF reception & distribution, 12 outlets	1 Elec	6	1.333	Outlet	152	45.50		197.50	236	
	0400 30 outlets		10	.800		100	27.50		127.50	151	
	0600 100 outlets		13	.615		102	21		123	144	
	0800 VHF & UHF reception & distribution, 12 outlets		6	1.333		151	45.50		196.50	235	
	1000 30 outlets		10	.800		100	27.50		127.50	151	
	1200 100 outlets		13	.615		102	21		123	144	
	1400 School and deluxe systems, 12 outlets		2.40	3.333		199	114		313	390	
	1600 30 outlets		4	2		175	68.50		243.50	295	
	1800 80 outlets	▼	5.30	1.509	▼	168	52		220	263	
	2000 Closed circuit, surveillance, one station (camera & monitor)	2 Elec	2.60	6.154	Total	965	211		1,176	1,375	
	2200 For additional camera stations, add	1 Elec	2.70	2.963	Ea.	540	102		642	745	
	2400 Industrial quality, one station (camera & monitor)	2 Elec	2.60	6.154	Total	2,000	211		2,211	2,525	

16850	**Television Equipment**	CREW	DAILY OUTPUT	LABOR-HOURS	UNIT	2001 BARE COSTS				TOTAL INCL O&P	
						MAT.	LABOR	EQUIP.	TOTAL		
600 2600	For additional camera stations, add	1 Elec	2.70	2.963	Ea.	1,225	102		1,327	1,500	**600**
2610	For low light, add		2.70	2.963		985	102		1,087	1,225	
2620	For very low light, add		2.70	2.963		7,250	102		7,352	8,125	
2800	For weatherproof camera station, add		1.30	6.154		755	211		966	1,150	
3000	For pan and tilt, add		1.30	6.154		1,950	211		2,161	2,475	
3200	For zoom lens - remote control, add, minimum		2	4		1,800	137		1,937	2,175	
3400	Maximum		2	4		6,575	137		6,712	7,425	
3410	For automatic iris for low light, add	▼	2	4	▼	1,575	137		1,712	1,925	
3600	Educational T.V. studio, basic 3 camera system, black & white,										
3800	electrical & electronic equip. only, minimum	4 Elec	.80	40	Total	9,350	1,375		10,725	12,400	
4000	Maximum (full console)		.28	114		39,800	3,925		43,725	49,700	
4100	As above, but color system, minimum		.28	114		52,500	3,925		56,425	64,000	
4120	Maximum	▼	.12	266	▼	229,000	9,150		238,150	265,500	
4200	For film chain, black & white, add	1 Elec	1	8	Ea.	10,700	274		10,974	12,200	
4250	Color, add		.25	32		13,000	1,100		14,100	16,000	
4400	For video tape recorders, add, minimum	▼	1	8	▼	2,250	274		2,524	2,875	
4600	Maximum	4 Elec	.40	80	▼	18,700	2,750		21,450	24,700	

For information about Means Estimating Seminars, see yellow pages 11 and 12 in back of book

16 ELECTRICAL

Division 17
Square Foot & Cubic Foot Costs

Estimating Tips

- The cost figures in Division 17 were derived from approximately 10,200 projects contained in the Means database of completed construction projects, and include the contractor's overhead and profit, but do not generally include architectural fees or land costs. The figures have been adjusted to January of the current year. New projects are added to our files each year, and outdated projects are discarded. For this reason, certain costs may not show a uniform annual progression. In no case are all subdivisions of a project listed.

- These projects were located throughout the U.S. and reflect a tremendous variation in square foot (S.F.) and cubic foot (C.F.) costs. This is due to differences, not only in labor and material costs, but also in individual owners' requirements. For instance, a bank in a large city would have different features than one in a rural area. This is true of all the different types of buildings analyzed. Therefore, caution should be exercised when using Division 17 costs. For example, for court houses, costs in the database are local court house costs and will not apply to the larger, more elaborate federal court houses. As a general rule, the projects in the 1/4 column do not include any site work or equipment, while the projects in the 3/4 column may include both equipment and site work. The median figures do not generally include site work.

- None of the figures "go with" any others. All individual cost items were computed and tabulated separately. Thus the sum of the median figures for Plumbing, HVAC and Electrical will not normally total up to the total Mechanical and Electrical costs arrived at by separate analysis and tabulation of the projects.

- Each building was analyzed as to total and component costs and percentages. The figures were arranged in ascending order with the results tabulated as shown. The 1/4 column shows that 25% of the projects had lower costs, 75% higher. The 3/4 column shows that 75% of the projects had lower costs, 25% had higher. The median column shows that 50% of the projects had lower costs, 50% had higher.

- There are two times when square foot costs are useful. The first is in the conceptual stage when no details are available. Then square foot costs make a useful starting point. The second is after the bids are in and the costs can be worked back into their appropriate units for information purposes. As soon as details become available in the project design, the square foot approach should be discontinued and the project priced as to its particular components. When more precision is required or for estimating the replacement cost of specific buildings, the current edition of *Means Square Foot Costs* should be used.

- In using the figures in Division 17, it is recommended that the median column be used for preliminary figures if no additional information is available. The median figures, when multiplied by the total city construction cost index figures (see City Cost Indexes) and then multiplied by the project size modifier in Reference Number R17100-100, should present a fairly accurate base figure, which would then have to be adjusted in view of the estimator's experience, local economic conditions, code requirements and the owner's particular requirements. There is no need to factor the percentage figures, as these should remain constant from city to city. All tabulations mentioning air conditioning had at least partial air conditioning.

- The editors of this book would greatly appreciate receiving cost figures on one or more of your recent projects which would then be included in the averages for next year. All cost figures received will be kept confidential except that they will be averaged with other similar projects to arrive at S.F. and C.F. cost figures for next year's book. See the last page of the book for details and the discount available for submitting one or more of your projects.

17100 | S.F. & C.F. Costs

			UNIT	UNIT COSTS			% OF TOTAL		
				1/4	MEDIAN	3/4	1/4	MEDIAN	3/4
010	0010	**APARTMENTS** Low Rise (1 to 3 story) R17100-100	S.F.	43.95	55.05	73.60				**010**
	0020	Total project cost	C.F.	3.94	5.25	6.45			
	0100	Site work	S.F.	4.02	5.50	8.70	6.80%	11%	14.10%
	0500	Masonry		.82	2.13	3.50	1.50%	4%	6.50%
	1500	Finishes		4.62	6.05	7.80	9%	10.70%	12.90%
	1800	Equipment		1.43	2.17	3.15	2.70%	4.10%	6.20%
	2720	Plumbing		3.39	4.40	5.55	6.70%	9%	10.10%
	2770	Heating, ventilating, air conditioning		2.18	2.69	3.95	4.20%	5.80%	7.70%
	2900	Electrical		2.53	3.30	4.52	5.20%	6.70%	8.40%
	3100	Total: Mechanical & Electrical		8.75	11.15	14	16%	18.20%	23%
	9000	Per apartment unit, total cost	Apt.	40,500	61,700	92,200			
	9500	Total: Mechanical & Electrical	"	7,700	12,200	15,900			
020	0010	**APARTMENTS** Mid Rise (4 to 7 story)	S.F.	57.15	69.50	85				**020**
	0020	Total project costs	C.F.	4.55	6.30	8.60			
	0100	Site work	S.F.	2.33	4.62	8.30	5.20%	6.70%	9.10%
	0500	Masonry		3.87	5.35	7.60	5.90%	7.60%	10.60%
	1500	Finishes		7.35	9.35	11.90	10.50%	13.10%	17.70%
	1800	Equipment		1.91	2.73	3.50	2.80%	3.50%	4.70%
	2500	Conveying equipment		1.32	1.63	1.99	2%	2.30%	2.70%
	2720	Plumbing		3.42	5.45	6.05	6.30%	7.40%	10%
	2900	Electrical		4.02	5.50	6.40	6.70%	7.50%	8.90%
	3100	Total: Mechanical & Electrical		11.60	15.70	19.25	18.80%	21.60%	25.10%
	9000	Per apartment unit, total cost	Apt.	65,900	77,800	128,700			
	9500	Total: Mechanical & Electrical	"	12,400	14,400	18,200			
030	0010	**APARTMENTS** High Rise (8 to 24 story)	S.F.	66.05	79.70	97.40				**030**
	0020	Total project costs	C.F.	5.62	7.85	9.55			
	0100	Site work	S.F.	2.02	3.87	5.40	2.60%	4.80%	6.20%
	0500	Masonry		3.82	6.95	8.85	4.70%	9.60%	11.10%
	1500	Finishes		7.35	9.15	10.80	9.70%	11.80%	13.70%
	1800	Equipment		2.13	2.67	3.46	2.80%	3.50%	4.30%
	2500	Conveying equipment		1.50	2.28	3.25	2.20%	2.80%	3.40%
	2720	Plumbing		4.87	5.75	7.05	7%	9.10%	10.60%
	2900	Electrical		4.54	5.75	7.75	6.40%	7.70%	8.90%
	3100	Total: Mechanical & Electrical		13.60	17.35	20.90	18%	22.30%	24.40%
	9000	Per apartment unit, total cost	Apt.	68,400	74,200	104,900			
	9500	Total: Mechanical & Electrical	"	14,800	16,900	18,000			
040	0010	**AUDITORIUMS**	S.F.	67.95	92.05	124				**040**
	0020	Total project costs	C.F.	4.30	6	9			
	2720	Plumbing	S.F.	4.35	6	7.60	6.30%	7.20%	9.05%
	2900	Electrical		5.55	7.65	9.55	6.80%	9%	10.60%
	3100	Total: Mechanical & Electrical		10.60	14.25	24.80	14.40%	18.50%	23.60%
050	0010	**AUTOMOTIVE SALES**	S.F.	49.50	56.95	83.85				**050**
	0020	Total project costs	C.F.	3.30	4.02	5.20			
	2720	Plumbing	S.F.	2.48	4.02	4.39	4.70%	6.50%	7%
	2770	Heating, ventilating, air conditioning		3.58	5.55	5.99	6.40%	10.30%	10.40%
	2900	Electrical		3.94	6.13	6.95	7.30%	10%	12.40%
	3100	Total: Mechanical & Electrical		8.90	12.85	16.05	17%	20.40%	26%
060	0010	**BANKS**	S.F.	98.60	123	156				**060**
	0020	Total project costs	C.F.	7.10	9.65	12.65			
	0100	Site work	S.F.	10.70	18.35	26.85	7.50%	13.90%	17.60%
	0500	Masonry		5.05	8.55	18.70	2.90%	6.20%	11.40%
	1500	Finishes		8.50	11.75	15.20	5.50%	7.70%	10.30%
	1800	Equipment		3.98	8.25	18.45	3.30%	7.70%	12.50%
	2720	Plumbing		3.14	4.49	6.50	2.80%	3.90%	4.90%
	2770	Heating, ventilating, air conditioning		6.10	7.95	10.55	5%	7.20%	8.50%
	2900	Electrical		9.55	12.60	16.40	8.30%	10.30%	12.20%
	3100	Total: Mechanical & Electrical		22.65	30.50	37	16.60%	20.40%	24.40%
	3500	See also division 11020 & 11030							

SQUARE FOOT 17

17100	S.F. & C.F. Costs			UNIT COSTS			% OF TOTAL		
		UNIT	1/4	MEDIAN	3/4	1/4	MEDIAN	3/4	
130	0010	**CHURCHES**	S.F.	66.20	83.15	108				**130**
	0020	Total project costs [R17100 -100]	C.F.	4.16	5.25	6.90				
	1800	Equipment	S.F.	.80	1.91	4.21	1%	2.20%	4.70%	
	2720	Plumbing		2.61	3.65	5.40	3.60%	5%	6.30%	
	2770	Heating, ventilating, air conditioning		6.10	7.95	11.70	7.60%	10%	12.20%	
	2900	Electrical		5.50	7.60	9.85	7.30%	8.80%	10.90%	
	3100	Total: Mechanical & Electrical	↓	14.30	21.45	31.15	19.60%	22.90%	25.40%	
	3500	See also division 11040								
150	0010	**CLUBS, COUNTRY**	S.F.	69.85	82.85	109				**150**
	0020	Total project costs	C.F.	5.80	7.05	9.75				
	2720	Plumbing	S.F.	4.62	6.45	14.70	6.40%	9.60%	10%	
	2900	Electrical	↓	5.65	8.10	10.65	7%	9.30%	11.40%	
	3100	Total: Mechanical & Electrical	↓	12.20	15.70	29.20	16.10%	22.30%	30.90%	
170	0010	**CLUBS, SOCIAL** Fraternal	S.F.	56.45	80.65	106				**170**
	0020	Total project costs	C.F.	3.39	5.45	6.30				
	2720	Plumbing	S.F.	3.25	4.50	5.45	5.20%	6.80%	8.30%	
	2770	Heating, ventilating, air conditioning		5.20	6.30	8.10	8.70%	11%	14.40%	
	2900	Electrical		4.55	7.10	8.60	7.30%	9.50%	11.40%	
	3100	Total: Mechanical & Electrical	↓	12.15	16.50	23.60	19.30%	23%	33.10%	
180	0010	**CLUBS, Y.M.C.A.**	S.F.	65.80	83.10	111				**180**
	0020	Total project costs	C.F.	3.32	5.55	8.30				
	2720	Plumbing	S.F.	4.79	9.05	10.15	6%	9.70%	16%	
	2900	Electrical		5.45	7.20	10.60	6.40%	9.20%	10.80%	
	3100	Total: Mechanical & Electrical	↓	11.95	17.10	25.50	16.20%	21.90%	28.50%	
190	0010	**COLLEGES** Classrooms & Administration	S.F.	82.30	109	146				**190**
	0020	Total project costs	C.F.	6	8.35	13.55				
	0500	Masonry	S.F.	5.25	10.50	11.70	5.10%	11.90%	12.10%	
	2720	Plumbing		4.03	7.90	14.65	4.80%	8.90%	11.80%	
	2900	Electrical		6.75	10.40	12.80	8.40%	10%	12.10%	
	3100	Total: Mechanical & Electrical	↓	14.50	26.40	40.85	14.20%	24.70%	32.50%	
210	0010	**COLLEGES** Science, Engineering, Laboratories	S.F.	131	159	193				**210**
	0020	Total project costs	C.F.	7.75	11.35	12.85				
	1800	Equipment	S.F.	7.55	17.10	18.65	5.30%	9.70%	15%	
	2900	Electrical		11.20	16.15	24.35	7.10%	9.60%	15.40%	
	3100	Total: Mechanical & Electrical	↓	41.30	49.20	76.15	28%	31.60%	39.80%	
	3500	See also division 11600								
230	0010	**COLLEGES** Student Unions	S.F.	86.30	121	142				**230**
	0020	Total project costs	C.F.	4.82	6.30	8.15				
	3100	Total: Mechanical & Electrical	S.F.	22.70	32.45	35.15	17.40%	23.90%	28.90%	
250	0010	**COMMUNITY CENTERS**	"	64.50	86.60	115				**250**
	0020	Total project costs	C.F.	4.65	6.65	8.60				
	1800	Equipment	S.F.	1.79	3.05	4.95	2%	3.30%	6.40%	
	2720	Plumbing		3.46	5.90	8.60	4.90%	7.10%	9.50%	
	2770	Heating, ventilating, air conditioning		5.70	8.20	11.30	7.70%	10.80%	13%	
	2900	Electrical		5.70	7.70	11.70	7.40%	9.40%	11.50%	
	3100	Total: Mechanical & Electrical	↓	21.15	25.25	36.40	25.10%	27.90%	34.40%	
280	0010	**COURT HOUSES**	S.F.	102	118	136				**280**
	0020	Total project costs	C.F.	7.80	9.45	13.10				
	2720	Plumbing	S.F.	4.89	6.82	9.80	5.90%	7.40%	9.60%	
	2900	Electrical		9	10.95	14.35	8.40%	9.80%	11.60%	
	3100	Total: Mechanical & Electrical	↓	20.20	27.70	35.55	20.10%	25.70%	28.70%	
300	0010	**DEPARTMENT STORES**	S.F.	38.05	51.45	64.95				**300**
	0020	Total project costs	C.F.	2	2.64	3.59				
	2720	Plumbing	S.F.	1.24	1.50	2.27	3.10%	4.20%	5.90%	
	2770	Heating, ventilating, air conditioning	↓	3.46	5.35	8.05	8.30%	12.40%	14.80%	

SQUARE FOOT **17**

17100 | S.F. & C.F. Costs

			UNIT	UNIT COSTS			% OF TOTAL			
				1/4	MEDIAN	3/4	1/4	MEDIAN	3/4	
300	2900	Electrical	S.F.	4.37	6	7.05	9.10%	12.20%	14.90%	300
	3100	Total: Mechanical & Electrical		7.70	9.95	16.10	20%	19%	26.50%	
310	0010	**DORMITORIES** Low Rise (1 to 3 story)	S.F.	62.20	88.75	107				310
	0020	Total project costs	C.F.	4.31	6.60	9.90				
	2720	Plumbing	S.F.	4.34	5.80	7.35	8%	9%	9.60%	
	2770	Heating, ventilating, air conditioning		4.59	5.50	7.30	4.60%	8%	10%	
	2900	Electrical		4.59	7	8.75	6.60%	8.90%	9.60%	
	3100	Total: Mechanical & Electrical		24.10	25.25	26.30	22.50%	24.10%	29.10%	
	9000	Per bed, total cost	Bed	30,600	33,900	72,800				
320	0010	**DORMITORIES** Mid Rise (4 to 8 story)	S.F.	88.60	116	143				320
	0020	Total project costs	C.F.	9.75	10.70	12.85				
	2900	Electrical	S.F.	6.55	10.30	13.15	7.40%	8.90%	10.40%	
	3100	Total: Mechanical & Electrical	"	19.65	26.30	34.40	18.10%	19.50%	30.60%	
	9000	Per bed, total cost	Bed	12,600	28,800	59,200				
340	0010	**FACTORIES**	S.F.	33.80	49.85	77.15				340
	0020	Total project costs	C.F.	2.15	3.19	5.30				
	0100	Site work	S.F.	3.75	7.05	11.45	5.80%	9.90%	14.10%	
	2720	Plumbing		1.99	3.36	5.70	4.60%	6.20%	8.70%	
	2770	Heating, ventilating, air conditioning		3.52	5.05	6.80	5.20%	8.50%	11.40%	
	2900	Electrical		4.11	6.55	10.05	8.10%	10.50%	14.20%	
	3100	Total: Mechanical & Electrical		9.90	15.90	24.15	20.40%	28.10%	34.50%	
360	0010	**FIRE STATIONS**	S.F.	64.80	87.05	112				360
	0020	Total project costs	C.F.	3.89	5.30	7.05				
	0500	Masonry	S.F.	9.75	17.55	23.20	8.70%	14.10%	19.30%	
	1140	Roofing		2.17	5.85	6.70	1.90%	4.90%	5%	
	1580	Painting		1.68	2.51	2.57	1.40%	2.10%	2.20%	
	1800	Equipment		1.43	2	4.79	1.10%	2.50%	4.80%	
	2720	Plumbing		4.21	6.20	9.15	6.20%	7.70%	9.70%	
	2770	Heating, ventilating, air conditioning		3.63	5.95	9.10	4.90%	7.50%	9.30%	
	2900	Electrical		4.61	7.95	10.70	7%	9.20%	11%	
	3100	Total: Mechanical & Electrical		20.45	25.25	29.95	18.80%	23.80%	27.30%	
370	0010	**FRATERNITY HOUSES** and Sorority Houses	S.F.	66.50	85.65	121				370
	0020	Total project costs	C.F.	6.35	6.90	8.85				
	2720	Plumbing	S.F.	4.98	5.75	10.55	5.20%	8%	10.90%	
	2900	Electrical		4.39	9.50	11.60	6.60%	9.90%	10.70%	
	3100	Total: Mechanical & Electrical		12.15	17.25	20.75	14.60%	19.90%	20.70%	
380	0010	**FUNERAL HOMES**	S.F.	69.80	95.70	174				380
	0020	Total project costs	C.F.	7.15	7.95	15.30				
	2900	Electrical	S.F.	3.10	5.70	6.70	3.60%	4.40%	11%	
	3100	Total: Mechanical & Electrical	"	11.15	16.65	21.55	12.90%	17.80%	18.80%	
390	0010	**GARAGES, COMMERCIAL** (Service)	S.F.	38.30	60.80	83.60				390
	0020	Total project costs	C.F.	2.43	3.64	5.25				
	1800	Equipment	S.F.	2.30	5.05	7.90	3.70%	6.80%	8.40%	
	2720	Plumbing		2.58	3.88	7.60	4.70%	7.40%	11%	
	2730	Heating & ventilating		3.61	4.92	6.80	5.30%	6.90%	9.60%	
	2900	Electrical		3.65	5.60	7.75	7.20%	9%	11.20%	
	3100	Total: Mechanical & Electrical		8.55	15.95	23.55	14.10%	22.50%	26.90%	
400	0010	**GARAGES, MUNICIPAL** (Repair)	S.F.	58.40	77.75	111				400
	0020	Total project costs	C.F.	3.65	4.63	7.55				
	0500	Masonry	S.F.	5.50	10.70	16.60	6%	10%	15.50%	
	2720	Plumbing		2.62	5.05	9.50	3.60%	6.70%	8%	
	2730	Heating & ventilating		4.48	6.50	12.50	6.20%	7.40%	13.50%	
	2900	Electrical		4.31	6.35	9.80	6.30%	8%	11.70%	
	3100	Total: Mechanical & Electrical		11	19.75	32.55	15.20%	25.50%	32.70%	

(Note: R17100-100 reference appears at row 3100 of line 300)

17 SQUARE FOOT

17100 | S.F. & C.F. Costs

				UNIT	UNIT COSTS			% OF TOTAL			
					1/4	MEDIAN	3/4	1/4	MEDIAN	3/4	
410	0010	**GARAGES, PARKING**	R17100 -100	S.F.	22	31.90	56.95				410
	0020	Total project costs		C.F.	2.13	2.90	4.22				
	2720	Plumbing		S.F.	.59	1	1.54	2.60%	3.40%	3.90%	
	2900	Electrical			.93	1.41	2.07	4.30%	5.20%	6.30%	
	3100	Total: Mechanical & Electrical		↓	1.24	3.64	4.67	6.50%	9.40%	12.80%	
	3200										
	9000	Per car, total cost		Car	9,600	12,000	15,600				
430	0010	**GYMNASIUMS**		S.F.	63	80.45	103				430
	0020	Total project costs		C.F.	3.15	4	5.25				
	1800	Equipment		S.F.	1.33	2.71	5.40	2.10%	3.40%	6.70%	
	2720	Plumbing			4	4.93	5.90	5.40%	7.30%	7.90%	
	2770	Heating, ventilating, air conditioning			4.30	6.55	13.15	9%	11.10%	22.60%	
	2900	Electrical			4.79	6	8.05	6.60%	8.30%	10.70%	
	3100	Total: Mechanical & Electrical		↓	14.80	20.40	27.35	20.60%	26.20%	29.40%	
	3500	See also division 11480									
460	0010	**HOSPITALS**		S.F.	130	152	225				460
	0020	Total project costs		C.F.	9.20	11.35	16.35				
	1800	Equipment		S.F.	3.16	5.90	10.20	2.50%	3.80%	6%	
	2720	Plumbing			10.85	14.60	18.80	7.80%	9.40%	11.80%	
	2770	Heating, ventilating, air conditioning			15.35	20.35	27.40	8.40%	14.60%	17%	
	2900	Electrical			13.05	16.95	26.70	9.90%	12%	14.50%	
	3100	Total: Mechanical & Electrical		↓	37.15	49.25	80.70	26.60%	33.10%	39%	
	9000	Per bed or person, total cost		Bed	46,800	99,300	156,600				
	9900	See also division 11700 & 11780									
480	0010	**HOUSING** For the Elderly		S.F.	59.65	75.25	92.45				480
	0020	Total project costs		C.F.	4.23	5.90	7.55				
	0100	Site work		S.F.	4.16	6.70	9.45	5.10%	8.20%	12.10%	
	0500	Masonry			1.82	6.80	9.90	2.10%	7.10%	12.20%	
	1800	Equipment			1.43	1.95	3.15	1.90%	3.20%	4.40%	
	2510	Conveying systems			1.45	1.95	2.65	1.80%	2.30%	2.90%	
	2720	Plumbing			4.43	5.80	7.75	8.10%	9.70%	10.90%	
	2730	Heating, ventilating, air conditioning			2.27	3.22	4.81	3.30%	5.60%	7.20%	
	2900	Electrical			4.44	6	7.70	7.30%	8.50%	10.50%	
	3100	Total: Mechanical & Electrical		↓	15.30	17.95	23.75	18.10%	22%	29.10%	
	9000	Per rental unit, total cost		Unit	55,500	64,500	72,100				
	9500	Total: Mechanical & Electrical		"	12,200	14,200	16,600				
500	0010	**HOUSING** Public (Low Rise)		S.F.	51.85	69.70	90.60				500
	0020	Total project costs		C.F.	3.98	5.55	6.90				
	0100	Site work		S.F.	6.40	9.20	14.90	8.40%	11.70%	16.50%	
	1800	Equipment			1.36	2.22	3.64	2.30%	3%	5.10%	
	2720	Plumbing			3.40	4.78	6.05	6.80%	9%	11.60%	
	2730	Heating, ventilating, air conditioning			1.82	3.53	3.86	4.20%	6%	6.40%	
	2900	Electrical			3.03	4.52	6.25	5.10%	6.60%	8.30%	
	3100	Total: Mechanical & Electrical		↓	14.40	18.55	20.75	14.50%	17.60%	26.50%	
	9000	Per apartment, total cost		Apt.	55,000	62,600	78,600				
	9500	Total: Mechanical & Electrical		"	10,000	13,000	15,000				
510	0010	**ICE SKATING RINKS**		S.F.	44.60	77.40	110				510
	0020	Total project costs		C.F.	3.15	3.22	3.71				
	2720	Plumbing		S.F.	1.60	3	3.07	3.10%	5.60%	6.70%	
	2900	Electrical			4.59	7.04	7.45	6.70%	15%	15.80%	
	3100	Total: Mechanical & Electrical		↓	7.70	11.10	13.85	9.90%	25.90%	29.80%	
520	0010	**JAILS**		S.F.	132	168	217				520
	0020	Total project costs		C.F.	12.30	15.10	19.25				
	1800	Equipment		S.F.	5.45	15.05	25.60	4%	9.40%	15.20%	
	2720	Plumbing			13.30	16.85	22.25	7%	8.90%	13.80%	
	2770	Heating, ventilating, air conditioning			11.75	15.71	30.35	7.50%	9.40%	17.70%	
	2900	Electrical		↓	14.35	18.45	22.80	8.10%	11.40%	12.40%	

SQUARE FOOT 17

		17100 | S.F. & C.F. Costs	UNIT	UNIT COSTS			% OF TOTAL			
				1/4	MEDIAN	3/4	1/4	MEDIAN	3/4	
520	3100	Total: Mechanical & Electrical R17100-100	S.F.	36.65	65	76.90	29.20%	31.10%	34.10%	520
530	0010	**LIBRARIES**	S.F.	77.80	99.15	127				530
	0020	Total project costs	C.F.	5.45	6.80	8.85				
	0500	Masonry	S.F.	4.45	9.95	17.10	5.80%	9.50%	11.90%	
	1800	Equipment		1.13	3.03	4.75	1.20%	2.80%	4.50%	
	2720	Plumbing		3.15	4.45	6	3.60%	4.90%	5.70%	
	2770	Heating, ventilating, air conditioning		6.75	11.40	14.85	8%	11%	14.60%	
	2900	Electrical		8	10.25	12.85	8.30%	11%	12.10%	
	3100	Total: Mechanical & Electrical		23.05	31.55	39.50	18.90%	25.30%	27.60%	
550	0010	**MEDICAL CLINICS**	S.F.	76.55	94.80	119				550
	0020	Total project costs	C.F.	5.70	7.40	9.85				
	1800	Equipment	S.F.	2.10	4.41	6.85	1.80%	5.20%	7.40%	
	2720	Plumbing		5.15	7.25	9.70	6.10%	8.40%	10%	
	2770	Heating, ventilating, air conditioning		6.25	8.05	11.85	6.70%	9%	11.30%	
	2900	Electrical		6.50	9.30	12.30	8.10%	10%	12.20%	
	3100	Total: Mechanical & Electrical		20.45	28.80	40.25	22%	27.60%	34.30%	
	3500	See also division 11700								
570	0010	**MEDICAL OFFICES**	S.F.	71.85	89.05	110				570
	0020	Total project costs	C.F.	5.35	7.35	10.05				
	1800	Equipment	S.F.	2.55	4.85	6.80	3%	5.80%	7.20%	
	2720	Plumbing		4.03	6.20	8.45	5.70%	6.80%	8.60%	
	2770	Heating, ventilating, air conditioning		4.87	7.15	9.30	6.20%	8%	9.70%	
	2900	Electrical		5.70	8.30	11.60	7.60%	9.80%	11.40%	
	3100	Total: Mechanical & Electrical		14.20	20.35	30.25	18.50%	22%	24.90%	
590	0010	**MOTELS**	S.F.	46.10	68.25	88				590
	0020	Total project costs	C.F.	4.02	5.65	9.25				
	2720	Plumbing	S.F.	4.67	5.95	7.10	9.40%	10.60%	12.50%	
	2770	Heating, ventilating, air conditioning		2.85	4.24	7.60	5.60%	5.60%	10%	
	2900	Electrical		4.35	5.55	7.25	7.10%	8.20%	10.40%	
	3100	Total: Mechanical & Electrical		14.80	18.50	31.75	18.50%	21%	24.40%	
	5000									
	9000	Per rental unit, total cost	Unit	23,500	44,600	48,200				
	9500	Total: Mechanical & Electrical	"	4,600	6,900	8,000				
600	0010	**NURSING HOMES**	S.F.	69.25	91.55	112				600
	0020	Total project costs	C.F.	5.55	7.10	9.70				
	1800	Equipment	S.F.	2.32	3.10	5	2.40%	3.70%	6%	
	2720	Plumbing		6.50	8.30	11.50	9.40%	10.70%	14.20%	
	2770	Heating, ventilating, air conditioning		6.45	9.30	11.50	9.30%	11.40%	11.80%	
	2900	Electrical		7.15	8.95	12	9.70%	11%	13%	
	3100	Total: Mechanical & Electrical		17.05	23.85	34.95	26%	29.90%	30.50%	
	3200									
	9000	Per bed or person, total cost	Bed	30,000	36,900	49,100				
610	0010	**OFFICES** Low Rise (1 to 4 story)	S.F.	58.35	74.30	98.95				610
	0020	Total project costs	C.F.	4.22	5.90	8				
	0100	Site work	S.F.	4.40	7.50	11.60	5.30%	9.70%	14%	
	0500	Masonry		2.03	4.75	8.95	2.90%	5.80%	8.70%	
	1800	Equipment		.73	1.32	3.64	1.20%	1.50%	4%	
	2720	Plumbing		2.22	3.36	4.76	3.70%	4.50%	6.10%	
	2770	Heating, ventilating, air conditioning		4.80	6.65	9.80	7.20%	10.50%	11.90%	
	2900	Electrical		4.94	6.85	9.55	7.50%	9.60%	11.10%	
	3100	Total: Mechanical & Electrical		11.65	16.15	23.60	18%	21.80%	26.50%	
620	0010	**OFFICES** Mid Rise (5 to 10 story)	S.F.	64.35	78.05	106				620
	0020	Total project costs	C.F.	4.50	5.70	8.25				
	2720	Plumbing	S.F.	1.95	3.02	4.34	2.80%	3.70%	4.50%	
	2770	Heating, ventilating, air conditioning		4.90	7	11.15	7.60%	9.40%	11%	

See R17100-100 and City Cost Indexes in the Reference Section

17 SQUARE FOOT

17100 | S.F. & C.F. Costs		UNIT	UNIT COSTS			% OF TOTAL		
			1/4	MEDIAN	3/4	1/4	MEDIAN	3/4
620	2900	Electrical	S.F.	4.78	6.10	9.25	6.50%	8.20%	10%
	3100	Total: Mechanical & Electrical	↓	12.20	15.60	30.95	17.90%	22.30%	29.90%
630	0010	**OFFICES** High Rise (11 to 20 story)	S.F.	77.90	99.85	123			
	0020	Total project costs	C.F.	4.98	6.90	9.90			
	2900	Electrical	S.F.	3.98	5.75	8.70	5.80%	7%	10.50%
	3100	Total: Mechanical & Electrical	"	14.55	18.60	34.10	15.40%	17%	34.10%
640	0010	**POLICE STATIONS**	S.F.	93.30	125	157			
	0020	Total project costs	C.F.	7.55	9.15	12.70			
	0500	Masonry	S.F.	11.10	16.35	19.75	7.80%	10.60%	11.30%
	1800	Equipment		1.54	6.65	10.65	2.10%	5.20%	9.80%
	2720	Plumbing		5.30	8.55	11.95	5.60%	6.90%	11.30%
	2770	Heating, ventilating, air conditioning		8.30	11	14.95	7%	10.70%	12%
	2900	Electrical		10.35	15.50	19.65	9.70%	11.90%	14.90%
	3100	Total: Mechanical & Electrical	↓	32.95	39.35	55.40	25.10%	31.30%	36.40%
650	0010	**POST OFFICES**	S.F.	72.70	92	115			
	0020	Total project costs	C.F.	4.44	5.70	6.75			
	2720	Plumbing	S.F.	3.37	4.33	5.25	4.40%	5.60%	5.60%
	2770	Heating, ventilating, air conditioning		5.30	6.50	7.25	7%	8.40%	10.20%
	2900	Electrical		6.15	8.55	10.10	7.20%	9.60%	11%
	3100	Total: Mechanical & Electrical	↓	10.85	21	26.50	16.40%	20.40%	22.30%
660	0010	**POWER PLANTS**	S.F.	542	691	1,264			
	0020	Total project costs	C.F.	14.31	28.95	66.70			
	2900	Electrical	S.F.	36.70	77.90	116	9.50%	12.80%	18.40%
	8100	Total: Mechanical & Electrical	"	91.47	298	667	32.50%	32.60%	52.60%
670	0010	**RELIGIOUS EDUCATION**	S.F.	58.75	76.25	88.90			
	0020	Total project costs	C.F.	3.35	4.80	6.20			
	2720	Plumbing	S.F.	2.51	3.57	5.03	4.30%	4.90%	8.40%
	2770	Heating, ventilating, air conditioning		5.90	6.65	7.35	9.80%	10%	11.80%
	2900	Electrical		4.79	6.35	8.35	7.90%	9.10%	10.30%
	3100	Total: Mechanical & Electrical	↓	12.40	21.50	25.55	17.60%	20.50%	22%
690	0010	**RESEARCH** Laboratories and facilities	S.F.	90.25	130	189			
	0020	Total project costs	C.F.	6.75	11.30	15.20			
	1800	Equipment	S.F.	4.01	7.90	19.25	1.60%	5.20%	9.30%
	2720	Plumbing		9.05	11.85	18.65	7.30%	9.20%	13.30%
	2770	Heating, ventilating, air conditioning		8.13	27.30	32.30	7.20%	16.50%	17.50%
	2900	Electrical		10.40	17.45	29.70	9.60%	12%	15.80%
	3100	Total: Mechanical & Electrical	↓	24	45.55	86.75	23.90%	35.60%	41.70%
700	0010	**RESTAURANTS**	S.F.	86.90	112	145			
	0020	Total project costs	C.F.	7.25	9.60	12.65			
	1800	Equipment	S.F.	5.20	13.90	21	6.10%	13.40%	15.60%
	2720	Plumbing		6.90	8.40	12	6.10%	8.30%	9.10%
	2770	Heating, ventilating, air conditioning		9.15	12.20	15.90	9.40%	12.20%	13%
	2900	Electrical		9.25	11.45	14.85	8.50%	10.60%	11.60%
	3100	Total: Mechanical & Electrical	↓	28.95	30.20	38.20	21.10%	24%	29.50%
	5000								
	9000	Per seat unit, total cost	Seat	3,200	4,300	5,400			
	9500	Total: Mechanical & Electrical	"	675	960	1,263			
720	0010	**RETAIL STORES**	S.F.	40.55	54.65	71.85			
	0020	Total project costs	C.F.	2.76	3.94	5.45			
	2720	Plumbing	S.F.	1.48	2.48	4.25	3.20%	4.60%	6.80%
	2770	Heating, ventilating, air conditioning		3.20	4.39	6.60	6.70%	8.70%	10.10%
	2900	Electrical		3.66	4.96	7.20	7.30%	9.90%	11.60%
	3100	Total: Mechanical & Electrical	↓	9.80	12.55	16.30	17.10%	21.40%	23.80%
740	0010	**SCHOOLS** Elementary	S.F.	64.55	79.60	96			
	0020	Total project costs	C.F.	4.37	5.60	7.25			
	0500	Masonry	S.F.	6	9.40	13.20	7.10%	10.50%	15.20%
	1800	Equipment		2.05	3.44	6.10	2.50%	4.20%	7.60%
	2720	Plumbing		3.74	5.40	7.25	5.70%	7.10%	9.40%
	2730	Heating, ventilating, air conditioning	↓	5.75	9.15	12.80	8.10%	10.80%	15.20%

(R17100-100 reference appears at row 620)

For expanded coverage of these items see *Means Square Foot Costs 2001*

SQUARE FOOT 17

17100 | S.F. & C.F. Costs

			UNIT	UNIT COSTS			% OF TOTAL		
				1/4	MEDIAN	3/4	1/4	MEDIAN	3/4
740	2900	Electrical	S.F.	6	7.65	9.80	8.40%	10%	11.60%	740
	3100	Total: Mechanical & Electrical *(R17100 -100)*	↓	20.80	23.05	32.55	22.20%	28%	30.40%
	9000	Per pupil, total cost	Ea.	6,400	10,700	34,700			
	9500	Total: Mechanical & Electrical	"	2,175	2,750	11,000			
760	0010	**SCHOOLS** Junior High & Middle	S.F.	65.55	81.10	95				760
	0020	Total project costs	C.F.	4.31	5.65	6.35			
	0500	Masonry	S.F.	7.40	9.85	12.15	8.80%	11.10%	14%
	1800	Equipment		2.20	3.54	5.50	2.60%	4.30%	5.90%
	2720	Plumbing		4.35	4.84	6.40	5.60%	6.90%	8.10%
	2770	Heating, ventilating, air conditioning		5.05	9.70	13.55	8.70%	12.70%	17.40%
	2900	Electrical		6.35	7.95	9.60	7.80%	9.40%	10.60%
	3100	Total: Mechanical & Electrical	↓	18.30	23	30.55	23.30%	25.70%	27.30%
	9000	Per pupil, total cost	Ea.	8,300	9,500	11,800			
780	0010	**SCHOOLS** Senior High	S.F.	70.80	81.10	114				780
	0020	Total project costs	C.F.	4.54	5.90	8.30			
	1800	Equipment	S.F.	1.88	4.45	6.55	2.30%	3.70%	5.40%
	2720	Plumbing		3.66	6.70	11	5%	6.90%	12%
	2770	Heating, ventilating, air conditioning		8.20	9.30	17.90	8.90%	11%	15%
	2900	Electrical		6.95	9.15	15.25	8.30%	10.10%	12.60%
	3100	Total: Mechanical & Electrical	↓	19	25.05	46.85	19.80%	23.10%	27.80%
	9000	Per pupil, total cost	Ea.	6,800	11,500	17,200			
800	0010	**SCHOOLS** Vocational	S.F.	57.80	80.75	103				800
	0020	Total project costs	C.F.	3.54	5.10	7.15			
	0500	Masonry	S.F.	3.40	8.40	12.85	4%	10.90%	19.90%
	1800	Equipment	"	1.81	2.46	6.25	2.90%	3.40%	4.70%
	2720	Plumbing	S.F.	3.71	5.65	8.15	5.40%	7%	8.50%
	2770	Heating, ventilating, air conditioning		5.20	9.65	16.15	8.80%	11.90%	14.60%
	2900	Electrical		5.95	8.25	11.65	8.40%	11.20%	13.80%
	3100	Total: Mechanical & Electrical	↓	15.65	20.95	39.80	21.70%	27.30%	33.10%
	9000	Per pupil, total cost	Ea.	8,100	21,600	32,300			
830	0010	**SPORTS ARENAS**	S.F.	49.25	67.70	99.35				830
	0020	Total project costs	C.F.	2.75	4.88	6.35			
	2720	Plumbing	S.F.	2.62	4.36	8.20	4.50%	6.30%	9.40%
	2770	Heating, ventilating, air conditioning		5.35	7.50	9.75	5.80%	10.20%	13.50%
	2900	Electrical		4.35	6.85	8.60	7.70%	9.80%	12.30%
	3100	Total: Mechanical & Electrical	↓	12.80	22.75	29.35	13.40%	22.50%	30.80%
850	0010	**SUPERMARKETS**	S.F.	46.75	54.85	63.65				850
	0020	Total project costs	C.F.	2.61	3.15	4.77			
	2720	Plumbing	S.F.	2.61	3.29	3.83	5.40%	6%	7.50%
	2770	Heating, ventilating, air conditioning		3.85	4.72	5.60	8.60%	8.60%	9.60%
	2900	Electrical		5.45	6.75	8	10.40%	12.40%	13.60%
	3100	Total: Mechanical & Electrical	↓	15.30	16.50	22.85	17.40%	20.40%	28.40%
860	0010	**SWIMMING POOLS**	S.F.	82.65	127	177				860
	0020	Total project costs	C.F.	6.10	7.55	8.25			
	2720	Plumbing	S.F.	7	8	11.15	9.70%	12.30%	12.30%
	2900	Electrical		5.70	8.85	11.50	7.50%	8%	8%
	3100	Total: Mechanical & Electrical	↓	12.05	25.60	47.40	17.70%	24.90%	31.60%
870	0010	**TELEPHONE EXCHANGES**	S.F.	101	147	187				870
	0020	Total project costs	C.F.	6.22	9.55	13.55			
	2720	Plumbing	S.F.	4.25	6.55	9.60	4.50%	5.80%	6.90%
	2770	Heating, ventilating, air conditioning		8.65	19.45	24.65	11.80%	11.80%	18.40%
	2900	Electrical		10.25	15.85	28.75	10.90%	14%	17.80%
	3100	Total: Mechanical & Electrical	↓	22	30.25	75	27.30%	33.40%	44.40%
910	0010	**THEATERS**	S.F.	63.30	81.20	120				910
	0020	Total project costs	C.F.	2.92	4.32	6.35			
	2720	Plumbing	S.F.	1.97	2.30	6.85	2.90%	4.70%	6.80%
	2770	Heating, ventilating, air conditioning	↓	6.15	7.45	9.20	8%	12.20%	13.40%

17 SQUARE FOOT

See R17100-100 and City Cost Indexes in the Reference Section

		17100 | S.F. & C.F. Costs	UNIT	UNIT COSTS			% OF TOTAL			
				1/4	MEDIAN	3/4	1/4	MEDIAN	3/4	
910	2900	Electrical	S.F.	5.55	7.45	15.20	8%	10%	12.40%	910
	3100	Total: Mechanical & Electrical	↓	14.25	21.30	43.70	22.90%	26.60%	27.50%	
940	0010	**TOWN HALLS** City Halls & Municipal Buildings	S.F.	70.65	89.30	117				940
	0020	Total project costs	C.F.	5.30	7.40	9.90				
	2720	Plumbing	S.F.	2.51	5.20	8.60	4.20%	6.10%	7.90%	
	2770	Heating, ventilating, air conditioning		5.35	10.60	15.45	7%	9%	13.50%	
	2900	Electrical		6.35	8.55	12.10	8.20%	9.50%	11.70%	
	3100	Total: Mechanical & Electrical	↓	22.40	23.25	29.50	22%	25.10%	30.40%	
970	0010	**WAREHOUSES** And Storage Buildings	S.F.	26.35	36.80	56.70				970
	0020	Total project costs	C.F.	1.33	2.16	3.58				
	0100	Site work	S.F.	2.64	5.40	8.15	6%	12.80%	19.80%	
	0500	Masonry		1.64	3.74	8.10	5%	7.70%	13.20%	
	1800	Equipment		.43	.91	5.10	1%	2.40%	6.50%	
	2720	Plumbing		.88	1.58	2.95	2.90%	4.80%	6.60%	
	2730	Heating, ventilating, air conditioning		1	2.83	3.80	2.40%	5%	8.90%	
	2900	Electrical		1.56	2.94	4.86	5%	7.30%	10%	
	3100	Total: Mechanical & Electrical	↓	4.35	6.40	14.60	12.80%	18.40%	26.20%	
990	0010	**WAREHOUSE & OFFICES** Combination	S.F.	31.70	42.50	56.40				990
	0020	Total project costs	C.F.	1.64	2.41	3.56				
	1800	Equipment	S.F.	.58	1.09	1.68	1.20%	2.40%	2.70%	
	2720	Plumbing		1.23	2.11	3.33	3.60%	4.70%	6.30%	
	2770	Heating, ventilating, air conditioning		1.95	3.08	4.35	5%	5.60%	9.60%	
	2900	Electrical		2.15	3.17	4.97	5.70%	7.70%	10%	
	3100	Total: Mechanical & Electrical	↓	5.05	8.40	10.50	13.80%	18.60%	23%	

(R17100 -100)

For information about Means Estimating Seminars, see yellow pages 11 and 12 in back of book

SQUARE FOOT 17

	CREW	DAILY OUTPUT	LABOR-HOURS	UNIT	2001 BARE COSTS				TOTAL INCL O&P
					MAT.	LABOR	EQUIP.	TOTAL	

Reference Section

All the reference information is in one section making it easy to find what you need to know . . . and easy to use the book on a daily basis. This section is visually identified by a vertical gray bar on the edge of pages.

In the reference number information that follows, you'll see the background that relates to the "reference numbers" that appeared in the Unit Price Sections. You'll find reference tables, explanations and estimating information that support how we arrived at the unit price data. Also included are alternate pricing methods, technical data and estimating procedures along with information on design and economy in construction.

Also in this Reference Section, we've included Change Orders, information on pricing changes to contract documents; Crew Listings, a full listing of all the crews, equipment and their costs; Historical Cost Indexes for cost comparisons over time; City Cost Indexes and Location Factors for adjusting costs to the region you are in; and an explanation of all Abbreviations used in the book.

Table of Contents

R01100-005 Tips for Accurate Estimating

1. Use pre-printed or columnar forms for orderly sequence of dimensions and locations and for recording telephone quotations.

2. Use only the front side of each paper or form except for certain pre-printed summary forms.

3. Be consistent in listing dimensions: For example, length x width x height. This helps in rechecking to ensure that, the total length of partitions is appropriate for the building area.

4. Use printed (rather than measured) dimensions where given.

5. Add up multiple printed dimensions for a single entry where possible.

6. Measure all other dimensions carefully.

7. Use each set of dimensions to calculate multiple related quantities.

8. Convert foot and inch measurements to decimal feet when listing. Memorize decimal equivalents to .01 parts of a foot (1/8″ equals approximately .01′).

9. Do not "round off" quantities until the final summary.

10. Mark drawings with different colors as items are taken off.

11. Keep similar items together, different items separate.

12. Identify location and drawing numbers to aid in future checking for completeness.

13. Measure or list everything on the drawings or mentioned in the specifications.

14. It may be necessary to list items not called for to make the job complete.

15. Be alert for: Notes on plans such as N.T.S. (not to scale); changes in scale throughout the drawings; reduced size drawings; discrepancies between the specifications and the drawings.

16. Develop a consistent pattern of performing an estimate. For example:
    a. Start the quantity takeoff at the lower floor and move to the next higher floor.
    b. Proceed from the main section of the building to the wings.
    c. Proceed from south to north or vice versa, clockwise or counterclockwise.
    d. Take off floor plan quantities first, elevations next, then detail drawings.

17. List all gross dimensions that can be either used again for different quantities, or used as a rough check of other quantities for verification (exterior perimeter, gross floor area, individual floor areas, etc.).

18. Utilize design symmetry or repetition (repetitive floors, repetitive wings, symmetrical design around a center line, similar room layouts, etc.). Note: Extreme caution is needed here so as not to omit or duplicate an area.

19. Do not convert units until the final total is obtained. For instance, when estimating concrete work, keep all units to the nearest cubic foot, then summarize and convert to cubic yards.

20. When figuring alternatives, it is best to total all items involved in the basic system, then total all items involved in the alternates. Therefore you work with positive numbers in all cases. When adds and deducts are used, it is often confusing whether to add or subtract a portion of an item; especially on a complicated or involved alternate.

R01100-020 Construction Time Requirements

Table at left is average construction time in months for different types of building projects. Table at right is the construction time in months for different size projects. Design time runs 25% to 40% of construction time.

Type Building	Construction Time	Project Value	Construction Time
Industrial Buildings	12 Months	Under $1,400,000	10 Months
Commercial Buildings	15 Months	Up to $3,800,000	15 Months
Research & Development	18 Months	Up to $19,000,000	21 Months
Institutional Buildings	20 Months	over $19,000,000	28 Months

R01100-040 Builder's Risk Insurance

Builder's Risk Insurance is insurance on a building during construction. Premiums are paid by the owner or the contractor. Blasting, collapse and underground insurance would raise total insurance costs above those listed. Floater policy for materials delivered to the job runs $.75 to $1.25 per $100 value. Contractor equipment insurance runs $.50 to $1.50 per $100 value. Insurance for miscellaneous tools to $1,500 value runs from $3.00 to $7.50 per $100 value.

Tabulated below are New England Builder's Risk insurance rates in dollars per $100 value for $1,000 deductible. For $25,000 deductible, rates can be reduced 13% to 34%. On contracts over $1,000,000, rates may be lower than those tabulated. Policies are written annually for the total completed value in place. For "all risk" insurance (excluding flood, earthquake and certain other perils) add $.025 to total rates below.

Coverage	Frame Construction (Class 1) Range		Average	Brick Construction (Class 4) Range		Average	Fire Resistive (Class 6) Range		Average
Fire Insurance	$.300 to	$.420	$.394	$.132 to	$.189	$.174	$.052 to	$.080	$.070
Extended Coverage	.115 to	.150	.144	.080 to	.105	.101	.081 to	.105	.100
Vandalism	.012 to	.016	.015	.008 to	.011	.011	.008 to	.011	.010
Total Annual Rate	$.427 to	$.586	$.553	$.220 to	$.305	$.286	$.141 to	$.196	$.180

R01100-050   General Contractor's Overhead

The table below shows a contractor's overhead as a percentage of direct cost in two ways. The figures on the right are for the overhead, markup based on both material and labor. The figures on the left are based on the entire overhead applied only to the labor. This figure would be used if the owner supplied the materials or if a contract is for labor only. Note: Some of these markups are included in the labor rates shown on Reference Table R01100-070.

Items of General Contractor's Indirect Costs	% of Direct Costs	
	As a Markup of Labor Only	As a Markup of Both Material and Labor
Field Supervision	6.0%	2.9%
Main Office Expense (see details below)	16.2	7.7
Tools and Minor Equipment	1.0	0.5
Workers' Compensation & Employers' Liability. See R01100-060	17.5	8.3
Field Office, Sheds, Photos, Etc.	1.5	0.7
Performance and Payment Bond, 0.7% to 1.5%. See R01100-080	2.3	1.1
Unemployment Tax See R01100-100 (Combined Federal and State)	7.0	3.3
Social Security and Medicare, See R01100-100	7.7	3.7
Sales Tax — add if applicable 42/80 x % as markup of total direct costs including both material and labor. See R01100-090		
Sub Total	59.2%	28.2%
*Builder's Risk Insurance ranges from 0.141% to 0.586%. See R01100-040	0.6	0.3
*Public Liability Insurance	3.2	1.5
Grand Total	63.0%	30.0%

*Paid by Owner or Contractor

Main Office Expense

A General Contractor's main office expense consists of many items not detailed in the front portion of the book. The percentage of main office expense declines with increased annual volume of the contractor. Typical main office expense ranges from 2% to 20% with the median about 7.2% of total volume. This equals about 7.7% of direct costs. The following are approximate percentages of total overhead for different items usually included in a General Contractor's main office overhead. With different accounting procedures, these percentages may vary.

Item	Typical Range		Average
Managers', clerical and estimators' salaries	40 % to	55 %	48%
Profit sharing, pension and bonus plans	2 to	20	12
Insurance	5 to	8	6
Estimating and project management (not including salaries)	5 to	9	7
Legal, accounting and data processing	0.5 to	5	3
Automobile and light truck expense	2 to	8	5
Depreciation of overhead capital expenditures	2 to	6	4
Maintenance of office equipment	0.1 to	1.5	1
Office rental	3 to	5	4
Utilities including phone and light	1 to	3	2
Miscellaneous	5 to	15	8
Total			100%

R01100-060 Workers' Compensation Insurance Rates by Trade

The table below tabulates the national averages for Workers' Compensation insurance rates by trade and type of building. The average "Insurance Rate" is multiplied by the "% of Building Cost" for each trade. This produces the "Workers' Compensation Cost" by % of total labor cost, to be added for each trade by building type to determine the weighted average Workers' Compensation rate for the building types analyzed.

Trade	Insurance Rate (% Labor Cost) Range		Average	% of Building Cost Office Bldgs.	Schools & Apts.	Mfg.	Workers' Compensation Office Bldgs.	Schools & Apts.	Mfg.
Excavation, Grading, etc.	3.8 % to	26.6%	10.9%	4.8%	4.9%	4.5%	.52%	.53%	.49%
Piles & Foundations	5.9 to	80.1	27.7	7.1	5.2	8.7	1.97	1.44	2.41
Concrete	5.9 to	35.5	17.8	5.0	14.8	3.7	.89	2.63	.66
Masonry	5.3 to	48.6	17.0	6.9	7.5	1.9	1.17	1.28	.32
Structural Steel	5.9 to	132.9	40.9	10.7	3.9	17.6	4.38	1.60	7.20
Miscellaneous & Ornamental Metals	4.9 to	34.0	13.2	2.8	4.0	3.6	.37	.53	.48
Carpentry & Millwork	5.9 to	49.9	19.0	3.7	4.0	0.5	.70	.76	.10
Metal or Composition Siding	5.9 to	36.7	17.6	2.3	0.3	4.3	.40	.05	.76
Roofing	5.9 to	88.8	34.3	2.3	2.6	3.1	.79	.89	1.06
Doors & Hardware	4.1 to	28.8	11.4	0.9	1.4	0.4	.10	.16	.05
Sash & Glazing	5.7 to	32.4	14.1	3.5	4.0	1.0	.49	.56	.14
Lath & Plaster	5.2 to	44.6	15.7	3.3	6.9	0.8	.52	1.08	.13
Tile, Marble & Floors	3.7 to	29.5	10.3	2.6	3.0	0.5	.27	.31	.05
Acoustical Ceilings	3.5 to	26.7	11.8	2.4	0.2	0.3	.28	.02	.04
Painting	5.9 to	41.1	14.8	1.5	1.6	1.6	.22	.24	.24
Interior Partitions	5.9 to	49.9	19.0	3.9	4.3	4.4	.74	.82	.84
Miscellaneous Items	2.6 to	128.0	18.5	5.2	3.7	9.7	.96	.68	1.79
Elevators	2.0 to	18.9	8.4	2.1	1.1	2.2	.18	.09	.18
Sprinklers	3.0 to	20.6	8.8	0.5	—	2.0	.04	—	.18
Plumbing	3.0 to	15.9	8.5	4.9	7.2	5.2	.42	.61	.44
Heat., Vent., Air Conditioning	3.5 to	32.5	11.9	13.5	11.0	12.9	1.61	1.31	1.54
Electrical	2.7 to	11.0	6.8	10.1	8.4	11.1	.69	.57	.75
Total	2.0 % to	132.9%	—	100.0%	100.0%	100.0%	17.71%	16.16%	19.85%
			Overall Weighted Average	17.91%					

Workers' Compensation Insurance Rates by States

The table below lists the weighted average Workers' Compensation base rate for each state with a factor comparing this with the national average of 17.5%.

State	Weighted Average	Factor	State	Weighted Average	Factor	State	Weighted Average	Factor
Alabama	30.5%	174	Kentucky	19.8%	113	North Dakota	15.0%	86
Alaska	11.1	63	Louisiana	27.3	156	Ohio	19.1	109
Arizona	12.5	71	Maine	21.8	125	Oklahoma	21.9	125
Arkansas	14.2	81	Maryland	11.9	68	Oregon	19.2	110
California	18.6	106	Massachusetts	17.5	100	Pennsylvania	22.9	131
Colorado	26.5	151	Michigan	20.6	118	Rhode Island	20.9	119
Connecticut	19.4	111	Minnesota	37.7	215	South Carolina	13.8	79
Delaware	12.3	70	Mississippi	22.8	130	South Dakota	14.6	83
District of Columbia	21.4	122	Missouri	15.8	90	Tennessee	13.0	74
Florida	28.0	160	Montana	37.3	213	Texas	16.4	94
Georgia	24.9	142	Nebraska	15.7	90	Utah	12.9	74
Hawaii	16.7	95	Nevada	19.4	111	Vermont	14.9	85
Idaho	10.8	62	New Hampshire	23.2	133	Virginia	10.9	62
Illinois	23.3	133	New Jersey	11.0	63	Washington	10.0	57
Indiana	7.2	41	New Mexico	23.1	132	West Virginia	14.3	82
Iowa	12.1	69	New York	16.4	94	Wisconsin	13.7	78
Kansas	9.6	55	North Carolina	13.3	76	Wyoming	6.5	37
			Weighted Average for U.S. is	17.9% of payroll = 100%				

Rates in the following table are the base or manual costs per $100 of payroll for Workers' Compensation in each state. Rates are usually applied to straight time wages only and not to premium time wages and bonuses.

The weighted average skilled worker rate for 35 trades is 17.5%. For bidding purposes, apply the full value of Workers' Compensation directly to total labor costs, or if labor is 38%, materials 42% and overhead and profit 20% of total cost, carry 38/80 x 17.5% =8.3% of cost (before overhead and profit) into overhead. Rates vary not only from state to state but also with the experience rating of the contractor.

Rates are the most current available at the time of publication.

R01100-060 Workers' Compensation Insurance Rates by Trade and State (cont.)

State	Carpentry — 3 stories or less	Carpentry — interior cab. work	Carpentry — general	Concrete Work — NOC	Concrete Work — flat (flr, sdwk.)	Electrical Wiring — inside	Excavation — earth NOC	Excavation — rock	Glaziers	Insulation Work	Lathing	Masonry	Painting & Decorating	Pile Driving	Plastering	Plumbing	Roofing	Sheet Metal Work (HVAC)	Steel Erection — door & sash	Steel Erection — inter, ornam.	Steel Erection — structure	Steel Erection — NOC	Tile Work — (interior ceramic)	Waterproofing	Wrecking
	5651	5437	5403	5213	5221	5190	6217	6217	5462	5479	5443	5022	5474	6003	5480	5183	5551	5538	5102	5102	5040	5057	5348	9014	5701
AL	29.00	14.42	30.31	23.87	18.39	10.36	19.14	19.14	32.36	21.66	14.63	25.12	19.63	49.29	44.55	12.07	75.95	30.15	17.28	17.28	52.35	65.34	20.31	7.12	54.68
AK	8.81	8.42	9.30	9.30	5.59	5.67	8.82	8.82	9.10	10.01	5.64	10.99	8.49	29.93	9.97	5.25	17.33	6.01	9.40	9.40	17.20	17.20	6.23	6.38	25.07
AZ	12.94	7.31	23.11	11.90	7.03	5.46	7.53	7.53	11.21	13.57	6.80	11.90	8.89	17.26	10.66	6.75	17.09	8.80	8.71	8.71	31.81	20.24	6.29	4.29	50.31
AR	16.12	10.60	15.38	16.45	5.97	7.93	9.21	9.21	12.58	15.29	12.66	9.32	11.10	19.14	13.01	6.58	30.74	10.28	8.19	8.19	27.11	25.39	7.80	4.58	27.11
CA	28.28	9.07	28.28	13.18	13.18	9.93	7.88	7.88	16.37	23.34	10.90	14.55	19.45	21.18	18.12	11.59	39.79	15.33	13.55	13.55	23.93	21.91	7.74	19.45	21.91
CO	32.22	13.54	20.95	20.96	15.13	9.20	15.99	15.99	15.98	21.31	14.68	31.06	21.85	41.53	37.40	14.50	59.10	12.54	11.83	11.83	73.46	43.49	15.04	12.26	73.46
CT	22.88	13.79	21.35	15.44	13.85	5.94	8.19	8.19	21.67	26.13	8.60	23.82	16.74	20.45	16.66	9.16	29.83	9.89	11.52	11.52	66.97	27.81	11.14	5.71	50.86
DE	13.83	13.83	11.56	9.28	6.29	5.82	8.54	8.54	11.18	11.56	10.51	9.85	13.41	11.64	10.51	5.41	22.89	10.29	10.21	10.21	26.69	10.21	7.54	9.85	25.69
DC	16.64	7.93	16.96	29.16	16.85	7.03	12.07	12.07	21.57	18.23	11.28	25.62	14.04	32.48	18.37	10.51	23.16	11.62	24.74	24.74	60.38	32.31	17.92	4.39	66.43
FL	36.73	23.28	29.09	29.92	16.15	10.51	15.27	15.27	17.81	25.18	24.27	28.72	28.92	49.35	28.79	13.37	53.20	17.12	18.67	18.67	43.71	50.61	12.56	7.89	43.71
GA	31.04	16.02	32.71	20.67	15.12	9.82	19.55	19.55	21.97	19.15	26.66	23.03	21.20	40.88	19.50	11.14	40.72	18.65	13.74	13.74	36.03	53.09	13.08	10.16	36.03
HI	17.38	11.62	28.20	13.74	12.27	7.10	7.73	7.73	20.55	21.19	10.94	17.87	11.33	20.15	15.61	6.06	33.24	8.02	11.11	11.11	31.71	21.70	9.78	11.54	31.71
ID	8.79	6.95	14.19	10.28	10.45	4.56	6.41	6.41	6.96	10.12	7.12	7.92	7.51	14.30	8.97	3.95	20.53	5.87	8.05	8.05	27.60	20.85	4.78	6.59	26.68
IL	20.76	12.31	21.64	35.48	12.83	8.86	8.69	8.69	23.09	24.90	14.24	20.34	13.15	37.63	13.78	11.68	35.88	14.58	21.53	21.53	58.63	52.47	13.87	6.26	58.63
IN	7.08	4.06	7.07	6.68	3.23	3.00	3.79	3.79	5.72	7.01	3.48	5.32	5.94	9.68	5.16	3.00	11.87	4.29	4.92	4.92	28.84	13.32	3.69	3.26	27.19
IA	10.22	5.19	12.01	9.18	6.42	3.84	5.56	5.56	11.62	16.49	5.95	10.93	7.58	16.30	9.26	5.01	17.38	6.09	9.80	9.80	45.02	27.20	5.60	4.16	45.02
KS	12.10	7.50	9.17	10.12	6.55	4.01	5.02	5.02	7.59	13.37	5.73	9.94	7.28	12.42	8.78	4.96	20.54	5.93	5.93	5.93	19.14	17.05	4.16	3.66	16.49
KY	16.47	15.26	24.34	22.12	9.53	8.95	13.67	13.67	15.96	14.68	10.62	22.00	19.83	30.44	13.94	10.38	32.83	15.92	13.21	13.21	66.41	36.94	12.82	8.85	66.41
LA	29.63	22.95	26.01	20.86	14.80	10.48	24.73	24.73	23.88	20.82	14.00	21.27	27.63	54.39	21.42	13.78	49.11	21.35	15.51	15.51	37.84	61.81	11.66	10.26	37.84
ME	13.43	10.42	43.59	24.29	11.12	10.02	14.75	14.75	13.35	15.39	14.03	17.26	16.07	31.44	17.95	11.12	32.07	17.70	15.08	15.08	37.84	61.81	11.66	9.37	37.84
MD	10.55	5.95	10.55	11.35	5.05	5.15	9.25	9.25	13.20	13.05	6.45	11.35	6.75	27.45	6.65	5.55	22.80	7.00	9.15	9.15	26.80	18.50	6.35	3.50	26.80
MA	11.05	7.61	13.61	22.12	9.81	3.69	5.91	5.91	9.92	18.24	8.84	17.55	9.04	17.59	7.39	5.69	67.48	7.65	11.96	11.96	50.78	46.56	10.48	3.89	34.86
MI	16.08	9.61	17.85	24.50	12.37	5.71	10.99	10.99	9.62	20.95	11.61	19.18	17.86	64.20	18.33	8.19	43.08	10.91	14.52	14.52	36.41	31.20	13.08	10.42	41.58
MN	27.66	28.76	49.94	30.20	22.59	8.28	19.73	19.73	30.01	37.20	23.93	29.89	19.91	80.08	23.93	15.88	88.83	13.91	27.21	27.21	132.92	31.83	29.54	8.71	132.92
MS	24.99	20.10	26.38	17.69	10.13	9.84	15.53	15.53	18.15	21.31	11.97	19.52	16.75	55.90	22.89	10.23	33.43	21.81	12.10	12.10	46.09	36.57	12.26	9.38	37.42
MO	18.72	7.52	11.84	13.28	10.66	5.79	11.05	11.05	8.97	19.99	9.54	13.57	11.77	16.88	14.22	7.10	25.74	9.76	13.82	13.82	47.98	31.96	5.83	5.71	47.98
MT	30.63	15.19	47.53	32.78	24.74	11.01	26.63	26.63	25.04	38.54	19.54	48.55	41.06	53.68	27.00	15.03	85.06	16.93	33.95	33.95	86.98	55.25	13.30	12.10	86.98
NE	16.19	9.23	15.94	17.31	12.73	5.43	10.19	10.19	12.36	16.79	9.34	18.07	11.58	22.01	14.62	9.06	33.91	13.86	10.75	10.75	25.03	26.96	7.88	5.47	25.03
NV	19.86	10.88	14.94	14.89	11.46	9.64	9.26	9.26	13.64	22.78	14.60	14.48	16.01	27.25	17.93	10.76	33.53	18.03	16.53	16.53	45.36	32.56	18.03	7.43	45.36
NH	16.38	9.82	19.68	28.99	9.29	7.10	13.87	13.87	12.87	43.98	10.90	25.97	17.94	28.09	17.33	9.74	58.76	12.48	13.27	13.27	55.90	49.67	12.82	7.37	55.90
NJ	10.40	8.85	10.40	10.83	8.37	4.23	7.95	7.95	7.36	12.78	7.88	10.77	11.49	11.32	7.88	5.48	29.41	6.20	8.03	8.03	22.52	12.96	5.74	5.37	29.92
NM	25.35	13.09	20.45	19.66	13.39	6.34	10.95	10.95	14.58	31.49	16.25	26.97	16.87	33.27	15.64	12.10	43.41	16.46	21.26	21.26	67.82	29.91	9.67	10.65	67.82
NY	15.13	6.82	14.34	22.04	15.14	6.77	8.75	8.75	16.13	11.09	14.58	21.00	13.37	29.90	11.57	8.49	32.78	15.10	14.46	14.46	21.93	20.26	12.11	5.85	32.53
NC	13.08	11.23	15.08	16.19	6.34	7.36	9.18	9.18	8.25	12.80	6.49	11.00	10.42	18.01	15.63	6.06	29.08	10.36	10.19	10.19	29.07	15.79	7.44	3.74	39.03
ND	12.70	12.70	12.70	9.80	9.80	5.57	9.09	9.06	8.83	12.70	11.94	10.99	9.02	25.96	11.94	7.26	28.69	7.26	12.70	12.70	25.96	25.96	8.80	28.69	20.13
OH	17.06	17.06	17.06	15.16	15.16	9.12	15.16	15.16	22.67	17.90	17.90	20.44	22.67	15.16	17.90	10.47	33.45	32.47	15.16	15.16	15.16	15.16	13.22	15.16	15.16
OK	26.16	11.79	19.33	15.51	11.50	7.41	18.45	18.45	13.55	18.00	12.05	16.80	17.10	36.26	18.29	8.72	42.26	12.45	11.17	11.17	69.45	46.76	11.42	8.20	69.45
OR	29.51	9.28	20.03	16.50	10.61	6.63	12.94	12.94	14.95	19.68	12.27	12.43	19.83	22.05	13.85	8.38	38.11	11.85	11.01	11.01	61.69	25.54	9.92	12.10	61.69
PA	15.80	15.80	19.85	28.18	11.84	7.80	12.74	12.74	15.69	19.85	18.94	18.96	22.05	32.12	18.94	11.57	43.30	12.58	24.71	24.71	59.05	24.71	11.83	18.96	81.34
RI	19.53	11.65	18.07	18.23	16.24	4.43	10.38	10.38	12.85	22.78	11.97	25.11	24.13	37.66	17.25	8.52	33.92	10.29	14.07	14.07	59.49	37.50	14.36	7.70	78.79
SC	19.10	13.03	19.24	12.88	6.19	7.02	8.32	8.32	12.22	10.69	7.27	9.55	11.19	16.64	18.89	6.88	28.98	11.42	9.49	9.49	21.80	23.66	6.23	4.65	21.80
SD	13.70	6.67	17.59	16.61	6.07	5.60	9.23	9.23	11.50	15.30	7.77	10.02	12.97	31.49	12.79	8.27	20.70	7.55	9.64	9.64	45.63	21.23	6.90	4.75	46.57
TN	13.22	9.52	11.99	12.39	7.53	5.00	8.68	8.68	8.96	15.04	8.51	12.73	10.88	15.62	12.19	5.91	24.81	8.76	7.36	7.36	45.06	13.95	5.89	4.98	45.06
TX	16.89	12.49	16.89	18.90	10.64	8.69	11.28	11.28	11.91	14.50	12.98	16.51	11.74	22.91	20.99	8.82	27.56	15.13	11.85	11.85	27.79	21.44	9.25	7.91	28.44
UT	11.17	11.17	11.17	17.68	7.99	7.05	6.38	6.38	9.55	10.95	12.32	13.75	15.29	17.24	10.60	6.41	26.27	6.30	8.99	8.99	23.51	23.51	6.06	5.83	26.53
VT	11.93	7.61	14.88	34.92	9.35	4.51	7.91	7.91	11.95	11.32	8.84	13.76	7.82	19.81	10.86	6.71	24.32	10.29	10.29	10.29	32.12	35.79	6.45	8.56	32.12
VA	10.00	6.46	8.65	9.29	5.47	3.45	6.13	6.13	10.17	8.77	7.59	8.07	8.11	24.38	8.20	5.60	17.80	6.74	10.42	10.42	19.28	30.25	6.78	2.57	19.28
WA	7.57	7.57	7.57	6.22	6.22	2.71	7.32	7.32	9.42	7.30	7.57	9.87	8.81	14.33	10.96	4.47	19.48	3.47	12.96	12.96	12.96	12.96	8.93	10.23	12.96
WV	14.98	14.98	14.98	26.36	26.36	5.02	9.10	9.10	6.96	6.96	16.88	14.51	16.81	10.03	16.81	6.65	12.47	6.96	14.98	14.98	11.89	15.59	16.02	4.67	13.27
WI	10.31	8.30	19.64	9.42	8.44	5.53	6.39	6.39	10.37	12.12	13.99	15.11	10.03	18.39	11.59	5.53	32.21	8.32	12.89	12.89	32.11	16.18	10.39	3.63	36.51
WY	5.94	5.94	5.94	5.94	5.94	5.94	5.94	5.94	5.94	5.94	5.94	5.94	5.94	5.94	5.94	5.94	5.94	5.94	5.94	5.94	5.94	5.94	5.94	5.94	5.94
AVG.	17.57	11.40	19.01	17.82	11.14	6.79	10.93	10.93	14.08	17.65	11.76	17.04	14.81	27.68	15.71	8.47	34.33	11.93	13.21	13.21	40.87	29.19	10.30	8.04	42.15

R01100-060 Workers' Compensation (cont.) (Canada in Canadian dollars)

Province		Alberta	British Columbia	Manitoba	Ontario	New Brunswick	Newfndld. & Labrador	Northwest Territories	Nova Scotia	Prince Edward Island	Quebec	Saskat-chewan	Yukon
Carpentry—3 stories or less	Rate	2.53	5.20	5.35	6.66	3.76	6.00	2.50	6.96	5.96	13.01	5.38	2.35
	Code	40400	721028	40102	723	422	403	4-41	4022	401	80110	B12-02	4-042
Carpentry—interior cab. work	Rate	1.70	5.44	5.35	6.66	3.85	6.00	2.50	6.96	3.64	13.01	3.86	2.35
	Code	42133	721021	40102	723	427	403	4-41	4022	402	80110	B11-25	4-042
CARPENTRY—general	Rate	2.53	5.20	5.35	6.66	3.76	6.00	2.50	6.96	5.96	13.01	5.38	2.35
	Code	40400	721028	40102	723	422	403	4-41	4022	401	80110	B12-02	4-042
CONCRETE WORK—NOC	Rate	3.63	7.33	6.72	15.22	3.76	6.00	2.50	6.31	5.96	15.31	7.99	3.25
	Code	42104	721010	40110	745	422	403	4-41	4224	401	80100	B14-04	2-032
CONCRETE WORK—flat (flr. sidewalk)	Rate	3.63	7.33	6.72	15.22	3.76	6.00	2.50	6.31	5.96	15.31	7.99	3.25
	Code	42104	721010	40110	745	422	403	4-41	4224	401	80100	B14-04	2-032
ELECTRICAL Wiring—inside	Rate	1.73	3.93	3.50	3.20	1.49	4.83	2.00	2.70	3.64	6.97	3.86	2.35
	Code	42124	721019	40203	704	426	400	4-46	4261	402	80170	B11-05	4-041
EXCAVATION—earth NOC	Rate	2.19	4.03	5.35	4.54	2.72	6.00	2.50	3.64	3.76	7.40	4.69	3.25
	Code	40604	721031	40706	711	421	403	4-43	4214	404	80030	R11-06	2-016
EXCAVATION—rock	Rate	2.19	4.03	5.35	4.54	2.72	6.00	2.50	3.64	3.76	7.40	4.69	3.25
	Code	40604	721031	40706	711	421	403	4-43	4214	404	80030	R11-06	2-016
GLAZIERS	Rate	2.14	3.37	3.50	8.82	3.85	4.55	2.50	9.30	3.64	16.25	7.99	2.35
	Code	42121	715020	40109	751	423	402	4-41	4233	402	80150	B13-04	4-042
INSULATION WORK	Rate	2.53	6.46	5.35	8.82	3.85	4.55	2.50	9.30	5.96	14.15	5.38	3.25
	Code	42184	721029	40102	751	423	402	4-41	4234	401	80120	B12-07	2-035
LATHING	Rate	4.58	8.12	5.35	6.66	3.85	4.55	2.50	6.34	3.64	14.15	7.99	3.25
	Code	42135	721033	40102	723	427	402	4-41	4271	402	80120	B13-02	2-036
MASONRY	Rate	3.63	8.12	5.35	14.22	3.85	6.00	2.50	9.30	5.96	15.31	7.99	3.25
	Code	42102	721037	40102	741	423	403	4-41	4231	401	80100	B15-01	2-032
PAINTING & DECORATING	Rate	2.93	6.46	6.72	8.87	3.85	4.55	2.50	6.34	3.64	14.15	5.38	3.25
	Code	42111	721041	40105	719	427	402	4-41	4275	402	80120	B12-01	2-036
PILE DRIVING	Rate	3.63	14.60	5.35	5.27	3.76	9.60	2.50	6.31	5.96	7.40	5.38	3.25
	Code	42159	722004	40706	732	422	404	4-43	4221	401	80030	B12-10	2-030
PLASTERING	Rate	4.58	8.12	6.72	8.87	3.85	4.55	2.50	6.34	3.64	14.15	7.99	3.25
	Code	42135	721042	40108	719	427	402	4-41	4271	402	80120	B13-02	2-036
PLUMBING	Rate	1.73	4.30	3.50	4.04	1.88	3.88	2.00	3.64	3.64	7.55	3.86	2.35
	Code	42122	721043	40204	707	424	401	4-46	4241	402	80160	B11-01	4-039
ROOFING	Rate	7.69	10.43	6.72	12.45	7.72	6.00	2.50	9.30	5.96	21.16	7.99	3.25
	Code	42118	721036	40403	728	430	403	4-41	4236	401	80130	B15-02	2-031
SHEET METAL WORK (HVAC)	Rate	1.73	4.30	5.35	4.04	1.88	3.88	2.00	3.64	3.64	7.55	3.86	2.35
	Code	42117	721043	40402	707	424	401	4-46	4244	402	80160	B11-07	4-040
STEEL ERECTION—door & sash	Rate	2.53	14.60	5.35	18.61	3.76	9.60	2.50	9.33	5.96	30.77	7.99	3.25
	Code	42106	722005	40502	748	422	404	4-41	4227	401	80080	B15-03	2-012
STEEL ERECTION—inter., ornam.	Rate	2.53	14.60	5.35	18.61	3.76	6.00	2.50	9.33	5.96	30.77	7.99	3.25
	Code	42106	722005	40502	748	422	403	4-41	4227	401	80080	B15-03	2-012
STEEL ERECTION—structure	Rate	2.53	14.60	5.35	18.61	3.76	9.60	2.50	9.33	5.96	30.77	7.99	3.25
	Code	42106	722005	40502	748	422	404	4-41	4227	401	80080	B15-04	2-012
STEEL ERECTION—NOC	Rate	2.53	14.60	5.35	18.61	3.76	9.60	2.50	9.33	5.96	30.77	7.99	3.25
	Code	42106	722005	40502	748	422	404	4-41	4227	401	80080	B15-03	2-012
TILE WORK—inter. (ceramic)	Rate	2.56	3.57	2.31	8.87	3.85	4.55	2.50	6.34	3.64	14.15	7.99	3.25
	Code	42113	721054	40103	719	427	402	4-41	4276	402	80120	B13-01	2-034
WATERPROOFING	Rate	2.93	6.46	5.35	6.66	3.85	6.00	2.50	9.30	3.64	21.16	3.86	3.25
	Code	42139	721016	40102	723	423	403	4-41	4239	402	80130	B11-17	2-030
WRECKING	Rate	12.86	6.75	6.72	18.61	2.72	6.00	2.50	3.64	5.96	25.35	7.99	3.25
	Code	42108	721005	40106	748	421	403	4-43	4211	401	80220	B14-07	2-030

GENERAL REQUIREMENTS 1

R01100-070   Contractor's Overhead & Profit

Below are the **average** installing contractor's percentage mark-ups applied to base labor rates to arrive at typical billing rates.

Column A: Labor rates are based on union wages averaged for 30 major U.S. cities. Base rates including fringe benefits are listed hourly and daily. These figures are the sum of the wage rate and employer-paid fringe benefits such as vacation pay, employer-paid health and welfare costs, pension costs, plus appropriate training and industry advancement funds costs.

Column B: Workers' Compensation rates are the national average of state rates established for each trade.

Column C: Column C lists average fixed overhead figures for all trades. Included are Federal and State Unemployment costs set at 7.0%; Social Security Taxes (FICA) set at 7.65%; Builder's Risk Insurance costs set at 0.34%; and Public Liability costs set at 1.55%. All the percentages except those for Social Security Taxes vary from state to state as well as from company to company.

Columns D and E: Percentages in Columns D and E are based on the presumption that the installing contractor has annual billing of $1,500,000 and up. Overhead percentages may increase with smaller annual billing. The overhead percentages for any given contractor may vary greatly and depend on a number of factors, such as the contractor's annual volume, engineering and logistical support costs, and staff requirements. The figures for overhead and profit will also vary depending on the type of job, the job location, and the prevailing economic conditions. All factors should be examined very carefully for each job.

Column F: Column F lists the total of Columns B, C, D, and E.

Column G: Column G is Column A (hourly base labor rate) multiplied by the percentage in Column F (O&P percentage).

Column H: Column H is the total of Column A (hourly base labor rate) plus Column G (Total O&P).

Column I: Column I is Column H multiplied by eight hours.

		A		B	C	D	E	F	G	H	I
		Base Rate Incl. Fringes		Workers' Comp. Ins.	Average Fixed Over-head	Over-head	Profit	Total Overhead & Profit		Rate with O & P	
Abbr.	Trade	Hourly	Daily					%	Amount	Hourly	Daily
Skwk	Skilled Workers Average (35 trades)	$29.85	$238.80	17.5%	16.5%	13.0%	10.0%	57.0%	$17.00	$46.85	$374.80
	Helpers Average (5 trades)	22.15	177.20	19.3		11.0		56.8	12.55	34.70	277.60
	Foreman Average, Inside ($.50 over trade)	30.35	242.80	17.5		13.0		57.0	17.30	47.65	381.20
	Foreman Average, Outside ($2.00 over trade)	31.85	254.80	17.5		13.0		57.0	18.15	50.00	400.00
Clab	Common Building Laborers	22.85	182.80	19.0		11.0		56.5	12.90	35.75	286.00
Asbe	Asbestos/Insulation Workers/Pipe Coverers	32.15	257.20	17.7		16.0		60.2	19.35	51.50	412.00
Boil	Boilermakers	34.55	276.40	15.9		16.0		58.4	20.20	54.75	438.00
Bric	Bricklayers	29.60	236.80	17.0		11.0		54.5	16.15	45.75	366.00
Brhe	Bricklayer Helpers	22.95	183.60	17.0		11.0		54.5	12.50	35.45	283.60
Carp	Carpenters	29.15	233.20	19.0		11.0		56.5	16.45	45.60	364.80
Cefi	Cement Finishers	27.95	223.60	11.1		11.0		48.6	13.60	41.55	332.40
Elec	Electricians	34.30	274.40	6.8		16.0		49.3	16.90	51.20	409.60
Elev	Elevator Constructors	35.65	285.20	8.4		16.0		50.9	18.15	53.80	430.40
Eqhv	Equipment Operators, Crane or Shovel	31.15	249.20	10.9		14.0		51.4	16.00	47.15	377.20
Eqmd	Equipment Operators, Medium Equipment	30.35	242.80	10.9		14.0		51.4	15.60	45.95	367.60
Eqlt	Equipment Operators, Light Equipment	28.75	230.00	10.9		14.0		51.4	14.80	43.55	348.40
Eqol	Equipment Operators, Oilers	25.75	206.00	10.9		14.0		51.4	13.25	39.00	312.00
Eqmm	Equipment Operators, Master Mechanics	31.80	254.40	10.9		14.0		51.4	16.35	48.15	385.20
Glaz	Glaziers	28.55	228.40	14.1		11.0		51.6	14.75	43.30	346.40
Lath	Lathers	28.20	225.60	11.8		11.0		49.3	13.90	42.10	336.80
Marb	Marble Setters	29.20	233.60	17.0		11.0		54.5	15.90	45.10	360.80
Mill	Millwrights	30.55	244.40	11.2		11.0		48.7	14.90	45.45	363.60
Mstz	Mosaic and Terrazzo Workers	28.30	226.40	10.3		11.0		47.8	13.55	41.85	334.80
Pord	Painters, Ordinary	26.10	208.80	14.8		11.0		52.3	13.65	39.75	318.00
Psst	Painters, Structural Steel	27.15	217.20	50.0		11.0		87.5	23.75	50.90	407.20
Pape	Paper Hangers	26.25	210.00	14.8		11.0		52.3	13.75	40.00	320.00
Pile	Pile Drivers	28.80	230.40	27.7		16.0		70.2	20.20	49.00	392.00
Plas	Plasterers	27.30	218.40	15.7		11.0		53.2	14.50	41.80	334.40
Plah	Plasterer Helpers	23.25	186.00	15.7		11.0		53.2	12.35	35.60	284.80
Plum	Plumbers	34.45	275.60	8.5		16.0		51.0	17.55	52.00	416.00
Rodm	Rodmen (Reinforcing)	32.75	262.00	29.2		14.0		69.7	22.85	55.60	444.80
Rofc	Roofers, Composition	25.70	205.60	34.3		11.0		71.8	18.45	44.15	353.20
Rots	Roofers, Tile and Slate	26.00	208.00	34.3		11.0		71.8	18.65	44.65	357.20
Rohe	Roofer Helpers (Composition)	19.10	152.80	34.3		11.0		71.8	13.70	32.80	262.40
Shee	Sheet Metal Workers	33.55	268.40	11.9		16.0		54.4	18.25	51.80	414.40
Spri	Sprinkler Installers	34.45	275.60	8.8		16.0		51.3	17.65	52.10	416.80
Stpi	Steamfitters or Pipefitters	34.85	278.80	8.5		16.0		51.0	17.75	52.60	420.80
Ston	Stone Masons	29.75	238.00	17.0		11.0		54.5	16.20	45.95	367.60
Sswk	Structural Steel Workers	32.85	262.80	40.9		14.0		81.4	26.75	59.60	476.80
Tilf	Tile Layers	28.15	225.20	10.3		11.0		47.8	13.45	41.60	332.80
Tilh	Tile Layer Helpers	22.70	181.60	10.3		11.0		47.8	10.85	33.55	268.40
Trlt	Truck Drivers, Light	23.40	187.20	15.3		11.0		52.8	12.35	35.75	286.00
Trhv	Truck Drivers, Heavy	23.95	191.60	15.3		11.0		52.8	12.65	36.60	292.80
Sswl	Welders, Structural Steel	32.85	262.80	40.9		14.0		81.4	26.75	59.60	476.80
Wrck	*Wrecking	22.85	182.80	42.2	▼	11.0	▼	79.7	18.20	41.05	328.40

*Not included in Averages.

REFERENCE NOS.

495

R01100-080   Performance Bond

This table shows the cost of a Performance Bond for a construction job scheduled to be completed in 12 months. Add 1% of the premium cost per month for jobs requiring more than 12 months to complete. The rates are "standard" rates offered to contractors that the bonding company considers financially sound and capable of doing the work. Preferred rates are offered by some bonding companies based upon financial strength of the contractor. Actual rates vary from contractor to contractor and from bonding company to bonding company. Contractors should prequalify through a bonding agency before submitting a bid on a contract that requires a bond.

Contract Amount	Building Construction Class B Projects			Highways & Bridges					
				Class A New Construction			Class A-1 Highway Resurfacing		
First $ 100,000 bid	$25.00 per M			$15.00 per M			$9.40 per M		
Next 400,000 bid	$ 2,500	plus	$15.00 per M	$ 1,500	plus	$10.00 per M	$ 940	plus	$7.20 per M
Next 2,000,000 bid	8,500	plus	10.00 per M	5,500	plus	7.00 per M	3,820	plus	5.00 per M
Next 2,500,000 bid	28,500	plus	7.50 per M	19,500	plus	5.50 per M	15,820	plus	4.50 per M
Next 2,500,000 bid	47,250	plus	7.00 per M	33,250	plus	5.00 per M	28,320	plus	4.50 per M
Over 7,500,000 bid	64,750	plus	6.00 per M	45,750	plus	4.50 per M	39,570	plus	4.00 per M

R01100-090   Sales Tax by State

State sales tax on materials is tabulated below (5 states have no sales tax). Many states allow local jurisdictions, such as a county or city, to levy additional sales tax.

Some projects may be sales tax exempt, particularly those constructed with public funds.

State	Tax (%)	State	Tax (%)	State	Tax (%)	State	Tax (%)
Alabama	4	Illinois	6.25	Montana	0	Rhode Island	7
Alaska	0	Indiana	5	Nebraska	4.5	South Carolina	5
Arizona	5	Iowa	5	Nevada	6.875	South Dakota	4
Arkansas	4.625	Kansas	4.9	New Hampshire	0	Tennessee	6
California	7.25	Kentucky	6	New Jersey	6	Texas	6.25
Colorado	3	Louisiana	4	New Mexico	5	Utah	4.75
Connecticut	6	Maine	6	New York	4	Vermont	5
Delaware	0	Maryland	5	North Carolina	4	Virginia	4.5
District of Columbia	5.75	Massachusetts	5	North Dakota	5	Washington	6.5
Florida	6	Michigan	6	Ohio	5	West Virginia	6
Georgia	4	Minnesota	6.5	Oklahoma	4.5	Wisconsin	5
Hawaii	4	Mississippi	7	Oregon	0	Wyoming	4
Idaho	5	Missouri	4.225	Pennsylvania	6	Average	4.71 %

Sales Tax by Province (Canada)

GST - a value-added tax, which the federal government imposes on most goods and services provided in or imported into Canada.
PST - a retail sales tax, which five of the provinces impose on the price of most goods and some services.

QST - a value-added tax, similar to the federal GST, which Quebec imposes.
HST - Three provinces have combined their retail sales tax with the federal GST into one harmonized tax.

Province	PST (%)	QST (%)	GST(%)	HST(%)
Alberta	0	0	7	0
British Columbia	7	0	7	0
Manitoba	7	0	7	0
New Brunswick	0	0	0	15
Newfoundland	0	0	0	15
Northwest Territories	0	0	7	0
Nova Scotia	0	0	0	15
Ontario	8	0	7	0
Prince Edward Island	10.7	0	7	0
Quebec	0	8.02	7	0
Saskatchewan	6	0	7	0
Yukon	0	0	7	0

R01100-100   Unemployment Taxes and Social Security Taxes

Mass. State Unemployment tax ranges from 1.325% to 7.225% plus an experience rating assessment the following year, on the first $10,800 of wages. Federal Unemployment tax is 6.2% of the first $7,000 of wages. This is reduced by a credit for payment to the state. The minimum Federal Unemployment is .8% after all credits.

Combined rates in Mass. thus vary from 2.125% to 8.025% of the first $10,800 of wages. Combined average U.S. rate is about 7.0% of the first $7,000. Contractors with permanent workers will pay less since the average annual

wages for skilled workers is $29.85 x 2,000 hours or about $59,700 per year. The average combined rate for U.S. would thus be 7.0% x $7,000 ÷ $59,700 = 0.8% of total wages for permanent employees.

Rates vary not only from state to state but also with the experience rating of the contractor.

Social Security (FICA) for 2001 is estimated at time of publication to be 7.65% of wages up to $76,200.

R01100-110 Overtime

One way to improve the completion date of a project or eliminate negative float from a schedule is to compress activity duration times. This can be achieved by increasing the crew size or working overtime with the proposed crew.

To determine the costs of working overtime to compress activity duration times, consider the following examples. Below is an overtime efficiency and cost chart based on a five, six, or seven day week with an eight through twelve hour day. Payroll percentage increases for time and one half and double time are shown for the various working days.

Days per Week	Hours per Day	Production Efficiency					Payroll Cost Factors	
		1 Week	2 Weeks	3 Weeks	4 Weeks	Average 4 Weeks	@ 1-1/2 Times	@ 2 Times
5	8	100%	100%	100%	100%	100 %	100 %	100 %
	9	100	100	95	90	96.25	105.6	111.1
	10	100	95	90	85	91.25	110.0	120.0
	11	95	90	75	65	81.25	113.6	127.3
	12	90	85	70	60	76.25	116.7	133.3
6	8	100	100	95	90	96.25	108.3	116.7
	9	100	95	90	85	92.50	113.0	125.9
	10	95	90	85	80	87.50	116.7	133.3
	11	95	85	70	65	78.75	119.7	139.4
	12	90	80	65	60	73.75	122.2	144.4
7	8	100	95	85	75	88.75	114.3	128.6
	9	95	90	80	70	83.75	118.3	136.5
	10	90	85	75	65	78.75	121.4	142.9
	11	85	80	65	60	72.50	124.0	148.1
	12	85	75	60	55	68.75	126.2	152.4

R01107-010   Architectural Fees

Tabulated below are typical percentage fees by project size, for good professional architectural service. Fees may vary from those listed depending upon degree of design difficulty and economic conditions in any particular area.

Rates can be interpolated horizontally and vertically. Various portions of the same project requiring different rates should be adjusted

proportionately. For alterations, add 50% to the fee for the first $500,000 of project cost and add 25% to the fee for project cost over $500,000.

Architectural fees tabulated below include Structural, Mechanical and Electrical Engineering Fees. They do not include the fees for special consultants such as kitchen planning, security, acoustical, interior design, etc.

Building Types	Total Project Size in Thousands of Dollars						
	100	250	500	1,000	5,000	10,000	50,000
Factories, garages, warehouses, repetitive housing	9.0%	8.0%	7.0%	6.2%	5.3%	4.9%	4.5%
Apartments, banks, schools, libraries, offices, municipal buildings	12.2	12.3	9.2	8.0	7.0	6.6	6.2
Churches, hospitals, homes, laboratories, museums, research	15.0	13.6	12.7	11.9	9.5	8.8	8.0
Memorials, monumental work, decorative furnishings	—	16.0	14.5	13.1	10.0	9.0	8.3

R01107-030   Engineering Fees

Typical **Structural Engineering Fees** based on type of construction and total project size. These fees are included in Architectural Fees.

Type of Construction	Total Project Size (in thousands of dollars)			
	$500	$500-$1,000	$1,000-$5,000	Over $5000
Industrial buildings, factories & warehouses	Technical payroll times 2.0 to 2.5	1.60%	1.25%	1.00%
Hotels, apartments, offices, dormitories, hospitals, public buildings, food stores		2.00%	1.70%	1.20%
Museums, banks, churches and cathedrals		2.00%	1.75%	1.25%
Thin shells, prestressed concrete, earthquake resistive		2.00%	1.75%	1.50%
Parking ramps, auditoriums, stadiums, convention halls, hangars & boiler houses		2.50%	2.00%	1.75%
Special buildings, major alterations, underpinning & future expansion		Add to above 0.5%	Add to above 0.5%	Add to above 0.5%

For complex reinforced concrete or unusually complicated structures, add 20% to 50%.

Typical **Mechanical and Electrical Engineering Fees** are based on the size of the subcontract. The fee structure for Mechanical Engineering is shown below; Electrical Engineering fees range from 2 to 5%. These fees are included in Architectural Fees.

Type of Construction	Subcontract Size							
	$25,000	$50,000	$100,000	$225,000	$350,000	$500,000	$750,000	$1,000,000
Simple structures	6.4%	5.7%	4.8%	4.5%	4.4%	4.3%	4.2%	4.1%
Intermediate structures	8.0	7.3	6.5	5.6	5.1	5.0	4.9	4.8
Complex structures	12.0	9.0	9.0	8.0	7.5	7.5	7.0	7.0

For renovations, add 15% to 25% to applicable fee.

R01540-100   Steel Tubular Scaffolding

On new construction, tubular scaffolding is efficient up to 60' high or five stories. Above this it is usually better to use a hung scaffolding if construction permits. Swing scaffolding operations may interfere with tenants. In this case, the tubular is more practical at all heights.

In repairing or cleaning the front of an existing building the cost of tubular scaffolding per S.F. of building front increases as the height increases above the first tier. The first tier cost is relatively high due to leveling and alignment.

The minimum efficient crew for erection is three workers. For heights over 50', a crew of four is more efficient. Use two or more on top and two at the bottom for handing up or hoisting. Four workers can erect and dismantle about nine frames per hour up to five stories. From five to eight stories they will average six frames per hour. With 7' horizontal spacing

this will run about 400 S.F. and 265 S.F. of wall surface, respectively. Time for placing planks must be added to the above. On heights above 50', five planks can be placed per labor-hour.

The cost per 1,000 S.F. of building front in the table below was developed by pricing the materials required for a typical tubular scaffolding system eleven frames long and two frames high. Planks were figured five wide for standing plus two wide for materials.

Frames are 5' wide and usually spaced 7' O.C. horizontally. Sidewalk frames are 6' wide. Rental rates will be lower for jobs over three months duration.

For jobs under twenty-five frames, add 50% to rental cost. These figures do not include accessories which are listed separately below. Large quantities for long periods can reduce rental rates by 20%.

Item	Unit	Monthly Rent	Per 1,000 S. F. of Building Front	
			No. of Pieces	Rental per Month
5' Wide Standard Frame, 6'-4" High	Ea.	$ 3.75	24	$ 90.00
Leveling Jack & Plate		1.50	24	36.00
Cross Brace		.60	44	26.40
Side Arm Bracket, 21"		1.50	12	18.00
Guardrail Post		1.00	12	12.00
Guardrail, 7' section		.75	22	16.50
Stairway Section		10.00	2	20.00
Stairway Starter Bar		.10	1	.10
Stairway Inside Handrail		5.00	2	10.00
Stairway Outside Handrail		5.00	2	10.00
Walk-Thru Frame Guardrail		2.00	2	4.00
			Total	$243.00
			Per C.S.F., 1 Use/Mo.	$ 24.30

Scaffolding is often used as falsework over 15' high during construction of cast-in-place concrete beams and slabs. Two foot wide scaffolding is generally used for heavy beam construction. The span between frames depends upon the load to be carried with a maximum span of 5'.

Heavy duty shoring frames with a capacity of 10,000#/leg can be spaced up to 10' O. C. depending upon form support design and loading.

Scaffolding used as horizontal shoring requires less than half the material required with conventional shoring.

On new construction, erection is done by carpenters.

Rolling towers supporting horizontal shores can reduce labor and speed the job. For maintenance work, catwalks with spans up to 70' can be supported by the rolling towers.

R01540-200   Pump Staging

Pump staging is generally not available for rent. Purchase prices for individual items are shown in the chart below.

Item	Unit	Purchase, Each	Per 2,400 S.F. of Building Front	
			No. of Pieces	Cost to Buy
Aluminum pole section, 24' long	Ea.	$335.00	6	$2,010.00
Aluminum splice joint, 6' long		68.00	3	204.00
Aluminum foldable brace		48.50	3	145.50
Aluminum pump jack		111.00	3	333.00
Aluminum support for workbench/back safety rail		59.00	3	177.00
Aluminum scaffold plank/workbench, 14" wide x 24' long		545.00	4	2,180.00
Safety net, 22' long		267.00	2	534.00
Aluminum plank end safety rail		183.00	2	366.00
			Total System	$5,949.50
			Per C.S.F., 1 Use	$247.90

This system in place will cover up to 2,400 square feet of wall area. The cost in place will depend on how many uses are realized during the life of the equipment. Several options are given in Division 01540-550. The above prices are bare costs.

R01590-100   Contractor Equipment

Rental Rates shown in the front of the book pertain to late model high quality machines in excellent working condition, rented from equipment dealers. Rental rates from contractors may be substantially lower than the rental rates from equipment dealers depending upon economic conditions. For older, less productive machines, reduce rates by a maximum of 15%. Any overtime must be added to the base rates. For shift work, rates are lower. Usual rule of thumb is 150% of one shift rate for two shifts; 200% for three shifts.

For periods of less than one week, operated equipment is usually more economical to rent than renting bare equipment and hiring an operator.

Equipment moving and mobilization costs must be added to rental rates where applicable. A large crane, for instance, may take two days to erect and two days to dismantle.

Rental rates vary throughout the country with larger cities generally having lower rates. Lease plans for new equipment are available for periods in excess of six months with a percentage of payments applying toward purchase.

Monthly rental rates vary from 2% to 5% of the cost of the equipment

depending on the anticipated life of the equipment and its wearing parts. Weekly rates are about 1/3 the monthly rates and daily rental rates about 1/3 the weekly rate.

The hourly operating costs for each piece of equipment include costs to the user such as fuel, oil, lubrication, normal expendables for the equipment, and a percentage of mechanic's wages chargeable to maintenance. The hourly operating costs listed do not include the operator's wages.

The daily cost for equipment used in the standard crews is figured by dividing the weekly rate by five, then adding eight times the hourly operating cost to give the total daily equipment cost, not including the operator. This figure is in the right hand column of Division 01590 under Crew Equipment Cost/Day.

Pile Driving rates shown for pile hammer and extractor do not include leads, crane, boiler or compressor. Vibratory pile driving requires an added field specialist during set-up and pile driving operation for the electric model. The hydraulic model requires a field specialist for set-up only. Up to 125 reuses of sheet piling are possible using vibratory drivers. For normal conditions, crane capacity for hammer type and size are as follows.

Crane Capacity	Hammer Type and Size		
	Air or Steam	Diesel	Vibratory
25 ton	to 8,750 ft.-lb.		70 H.P.
40 ton	15,000 ft.-lb.	to 32,000 ft.-lb.	170 H.P.
60 ton	25,000 ft.-lb.		300 H.P.
100 ton		112,000 ft.-lb.	

Cranes should be specified for the job by size, building and site characteristics, availability, performance characteristics, and duration of time required.

Backhoes & Shovels rent for about the same as equivalent size cranes but maintenance and operating expense is higher. Crane operators rate must

be adjusted for high boom heights. Average adjustments: for 150' boom add $.80 per hour; over 185', add $1.40 per hour; over 210', add $1.85 per hour; over 250', add $2.65 per hour and over 295', add $4.20 per hour.

Tower Cranes

Capacity In Kip-Feet	Typical Jib Length in Feet	Speed at Maximum Reach and Load	Purchase Price (New)		Monthly Rental, to 6 mo.	
			Crane & 80' Mast	Mast Sections	Crane & 80' Mast	Mast Sections
725	100	350 FPM	$ 256,000	$ 670 /L.F.	$ 6,400	$16.80 /L.F.
900	100	500	303,000	790	7,600	19.60
*1100	130	1000	418,000	910	10,400	22.70
1450	150	1000	580,000	1,300	14,500	32.40
2150	200	1000	729,000	1,480	18,200	37.00
3000	200	1000	1,018,000	1,510	25,500	37.70

*Most widely used.

Tower Cranes of the climbing or static type have jibs from 50' to 200' and capacities at maximum reach range from 4,000 to 14,000 pounds. Lifting capacities increase up to maximum load as the hook radius decreases.

Typical rental rates, based on purchase price are about 2% to 3% per month.

Erection and dismantling runs between $13,000 and $82,000. Climbing operation takes ten labor hours per 20' climb. Crane dead time is about five hours per 40' climb. If crane is bolted to side of the building add cost of ties and extra mast sections. Mast sections cost $600 to $1,500 per vertical foot or can be rented at 2% to 3% of purchase price per month. Contractors using climbers claim savings of $1.50 per C.Y. of concrete placed, plus $.21 per S.F. of formwork. Climbing cranes have from 80' to 180' of mast while static cranes have 80' to 800' of mast.

Truck Cranes can be converted to tower cranes by using tower attachments. Mast heights over 400' have been used. See Division 01590-600 for rental rates of high boom cranes.

A single 100' high material **Hoist and Tower** can be erected and dismantled for about $15,600; a double 100' high hoist and tower for about $20,700. Erection costs for additional heights are $100 and $130 per vertical foot respectively up to 150' and $100 to $165 per vertical foot over 150' high. A 40' high portable Buck hoist costs about $5,300 to erect and dismantle. Additional heights run $80 per vertical foot to 80' and $100 per vertical foot for the next 100'. Most material hoists do not meet local code requirements for carrying personnel.

A 150' high **Personnel Hoist** requires about 500 to 800 labor hours to erect and dismantle with costs ranging from $16,400 to $26,300. Budget erection cost is $165 per vertical foot for all trades. Local code requirements or labor scarcity requiring overtime can add up to 50% to any of the above erection costs.

Earthmoving Equipment: The selection of earthmoving equipment depends upon the type and quantity of material, moisture content, haul distance, haul road, time available, and equipment available. Short haul cut and fill operations may require dozers only, while another operation may require excavators, a fleet of trucks, and spreading and compaction equipment. Stockpiled material and granular material are easily excavated with front end loaders. Scrapers are most economically used with hauls between 300' and 1-1/2 miles if adequate haul roads can be maintained. Shovels are often used for blasted rock and any material where a vertical face of 8' or more can be excavated. Special conditions may dictate the use of draglines, clamshells, or backhoes. Spreading and compaction equipment must be matched to the soil characteristics, the compaction required and the rate the fill is being supplied.

R01590-150   Heavy Lifting

Hydraulic Climbing Jacks

The use of hydraulic heavy lift systems is an alternative to conventional type crane equipment. The lifting, lowering, pushing, or pulling mechanism is a hydraulic climbing jack moving on a square steel jackrod from 1-5/8" to 4" square, or a steel cable. The jackrod or cable can be vertical or horizontal, stationary or movable, depending on the individual application. When the jackrod is stationary, the climbing jack will climb the rod and push or pull the load along with itself. When the climbing jack is stationary, the jackrod is movable with the load attached to the end and the climbing jack will lift or lower the jackrod with the attached load. The heavy lift system is normally operated by a single control lever located at the hydraulic pump.

The system is flexible in that one or more climbing jacks can be applied wherever a load support point is required, and the rate of lift synchronized.

Economic benefits have been demonstrated on projects such as: erection of ground assembled roofs and floors, complete bridge spans, girders and trusses, towers, chimney liners and steel vessels, storage tanks, and heavy machinery. Other uses are raising and lowering offshore work platforms, caissons, tunnel sections and pipelines.

R02065-300   Bituminous Paving

City	Bituminous Asphalt per Ton*	Pavement (3") 6.13 S.Y./ton				Sidewalks (2") 9.2 S.Y./ton			
		Cost per S.Y.			Per Ton	Cost per S.Y.			Per Ton
		Material*	Installation	Total	Total	Material*	Installation	Total	Total
Atlanta	$26.75	$4.36	$ .71	$5.07	$31.06	$2.91	$1.19	$4.10	$37.72
Baltimore	34.00	5.55	.76	6.31	38.69	3.70	1.33	5.03	46.28
Boston	43.00	7.01	1.05	8.06	49.39	4.67	2.29	6.96	64.03
Buffalo	31.00	5.06	1.02	6.08	37.28	3.37	2.20	5.57	51.24
Chicago	29.75	4.85	1.07	5.92	36.26	3.23	2.37	5.60	51.52
Cincinnati	34.25	5.59	.90	6.49	39.78	3.72	1.80	5.52	50.78
Cleveland	32.00	5.22	.97	6.19	37.97	3.48	2.12	5.60	51.52
Columbus	25.00	4.08	.88	4.96	30.42	2.72	1.73	4.45	40.94
Dallas	25.00	4.08	.70	4.78	29.29	2.72	1.13	3.85	35.42
Denver	32.00	5.22	.76	5.98	36.64	3.48	1.36	4.84	44.53
Detroit	32.00	5.22	1.00	6.22	38.11	3.48	2.16	5.64	51.89
Houston	29.75	4.85	.74	5.59	34.26	3.23	1.29	4.52	41.58
Indianapolis	30.00	4.89	.86	5.75	35.28	3.26	1.70	4.96	45.63
Kansas City	28.00	4.57	.90	5.47	33.54	3.04	1.87	4.91	45.17
Los Angeles	30.50	4.98	1.01	5.99	36.71	3.32	2.17	5.49	50.51
Memphis	31.00	5.06	.68	5.74	35.17	3.37	1.08	4.45	40.94
Milwaukee	30.50	4.98	.99	5.97	36.58	3.32	2.10	5.42	49.86
Minneapolis	27.50	4.49	.98	5.47	33.54	2.99	2.14	5.13	47.20
Nashville	30.75	5.02	.71	5.73	35.10	3.34	1.18	4.52	41.58
New Orleans	39.00	6.36	.67	7.03	43.09	4.24	1.07	5.31	48.85
New York City	43.50	7.10	1.28	8.38	51.37	4.73	3.09	7.82	71.94
Philadelphia	32.00	5.22	1.00	6.22	38.16	3.48	2.27	5.75	52.90
Phoenix	27.00	4.40	.76	5.16	31.65	2.93	1.37	4.30	39.56
Pittsburgh	32.50	5.30	.90	6.20	38.01	3.53	1.79	5.32	48.94
St. Louis	28.50	4.65	.99	5.64	34.59	3.10	2.15	5.25	48.30
San Antonio	28.50	4.65	.71	5.36	32.85	3.10	1.15	4.25	39.10
San Diego	33.00	5.38	1.01	6.39	39.16	3.59	2.17	5.76	52.99
San Francisco	30.00	4.89	1.01	5.90	36.19	3.26	2.18	5.44	50.05
Seattle	34.50	5.63	.97	6.60	40.48	3.75	2.12	5.87	54.00
Washington, D.C.	40.00	6.53	.75	7.28	44.63	4.35	1.32	5.67	52.16
Average	$31.70	$5.17	$ .89	$6.06	$37.17	$3.45	$1.80	$5.24	$48.24

Assumed density is 145 lb. per C.F.
*Includes delivery within 20 miles

Table below shows quantities and bare costs for 1000 S.Y. of Bituminous Paving.

Item	Roads and Parking Areas, 3" Thick (02740-300-0460)			Sidewalks, 2" Thick (02775-275-0010)		
	Quantities		Cost	Quantities		Cost
Bituminous asphalt	163 tons @ $31.70	per ton	$5,167.10	109 tons @ $31.70	per ton	$3,455.30
Installation using	Crew B-25B @ $4,367.00	/4900SY/ day x 1000	891.22	Crew B-37 @ $1,293.20	/720 SY/day x 1000	1,796.11
Total per 1000 S.Y.			$6,058.32			$5,251.41
Total per S.Y.			$ 6.06			$ 5.25
Total per Ton			$ 37.17			$ 48.18

R02115-200 Underground Storage Tank Removal

Underground Storage Tank Removal can be divided into two categories: Non-Leaking and Leaking. Prior to removing an underground storage tank, tests should be made, with the proper authorities present, to determine whether a tank has been leaking or the surrounding soil has been contaminated.

To safely remove Liquid Underground Storage Tanks:
1. Excavate to the top of the tank.
2. Disconnect all piping.
3. Open all tank vents and access ports.

4. Remove all liquids and/or sludge.
5. Purge the tank with an inert gas.
6. Provide access to the inside of the tank and clean out the interior using proper personal protective equipment (PPE).
7. Excavate soil surrounding the tank using proper PPE for on-site personnel.
8. Pull and properly dispose of the tank.
9. Clean up the site of all contaminated material.
10. Install new tanks or close the excavation.

R02240-900 Wellpoints

A single stage wellpoint system is usually limited to dewatering an average 15' depth below normal ground water level. Multi-stage systems are employed for greater depth with the pumping equipment installed only at the lowest header level. Ejectors, with unlimited lift capacity, can be economical when two or more stages of wellpoints can be replaced or when horizontal clearance is restricted, such as in deep trenches or tunneling projects, and where low water flows are expected. Wellpoints are usually spaced on 2-1/2' to 10' centers along a header pipe. Wellpoint spacing, header size, and pump size are all determined by the expected flow, as dictated by soil conditions.

In almost all soils encountered in wellpoint dewatering, the wellpoints may be jetted into place. Cemented soils and stiff clays may require sand wicks about 12" in diameter around each wellpoint to increase efficiency and eliminate weeping into the excavation. These sand wicks require 1/2 to 3 C.Y. of washed filter sand and are installed by using a 12" diameter steel casing and hole puncher jetted into the ground 2' deeper than the wellpoint. Rock may require predrilled holes.

Labor required for the complete installation and removal of a single stage wellpoint system is in the range of 3/4 to 2 labor-hours per linear foot of header, depending upon jetting conditions, wellpoint spacing, etc.

Continuous pumping is necessary except in some free draining soil where temporary flooding is permissible (as in trenches which are backfilled after each day's work). Good practice requires provision of a stand-by pump during the continuous pumping operation.

Systems for continuous trenching below the water table should be installed three to four times the length of expected daily progress to insure uninterrupted digging, and header pipe size should not be changed during the job.

For pervious free draining soils, deep wells in place of wellpoints may be economical because of lower installation and maintenance costs. Daily production ranges between two to three wells per day, for 25' to 40' depths, to one well per day for depths over 50'.

Detailed analysis and estimating for any dewatering problem is available at no cost from wellpoint manufacturers. Major firms will quote "sufficient equipment" quotes or their affiliates offer lump sum proposals to cover complete dewatering responsibility.

	Description for 200' System with 8" Header	Quantities	1st Month Unit	1st Month Total	Thereafter Unit	Thereafter Total
	Wellpoints 25' long, 2" diameter @ 5' O.C.	40 Each	$ 28.50	$ 1,140.00	$ 21.38	$ 855.00
	Header pipe, 8" diameter	200 L.F.	5.40	1,080.00	2.70	540.00
	Discharge pipe, 8" diameter	100 L.F.	3.66	366.00	2.38	238.00
	8" valves	3 Each	140.00	420.00	91.00	273.00
Equipment & Material	Combination Jetting & Wellpoint pump (standby)	1 Each	2,275.00	2,275.00	1,592.50	1,592.50
	Wellpoint pump, 8" diameter	1 Each	2,225.00	2,225.00	1,557.50	1,557.50
	Transportation to and from site	1 Day	674.40	674.40	—	—
	Fuel 30 days x 60 gal./day	1800 Gallons	1.05	1,890.00	1.05	1,890.00
	Lubricants for 30 days x 16 lbs./day	480 Lbs.	1.10	528.00	1.10	528.00
	Sand for points	40 C.Y.	16.60	664.00	—	—
	Equipment & Materials Subtotal			$11,262.40		$ 7,474.00
	Technician to supervise installation	1 Week	$ 31.80	$ 1,272.00	—	—
Labor	Labor for installation and removal of system	300 Labor-hours	22.85	6,855.00	—	—
	4 Operators straight time 40 hrs./wk. for 4.33 wks.	693 Hrs.	28.75	19,923.75	$ 28.75	$19,923.75
	4 Operators overtime 2 hrs./wk. for 4.33 wks.	35 Hrs.	57.50	2,012.50	57.50	2,012.50
	Labor Subtotal			$30,063.25		$21,936.25
	Total Cost			$41,325.65		$29,410.25
	Monthly Cost/L.F. Header			$ 206.63		$ 147.05

R02250-400 Wood Sheet Piling

Wood sheet piling may be used for depths to 20' where there is no ground water. If moderate ground water is encountered Tongue & Groove sheeting will help to keep it out. When considerable ground water is present, steel sheeting must be used.

For estimating purposes on trench excavation, sizes are as follows:

Depth	Sheeting	Wales	Braces	B.F. per S.F.
To 8'	3 x 12's	6 x 8's, 2 line	6 x 8's, @ 10'	4.0 @ 8'
8' x 12'	3 x 12's	10 x 10's, 2 line	10 x 10's, @ 9'	5.0 average
12' to 20'	3 x 12's	12 x 12's, 3 line	12 x 12's, @ 8'	7.0 average

Sheeting to be toed in at least 2' depending upon soil conditions. A five person crew with an air compressor and sheeting driver can drive and brace 440 SF/day at 8' deep, 360 SF/day at 12' deep, and 320 SF/day at 16' deep. For normal soils, piling can be pulled in 1/3 the time to install. Pulling difficulty increases with the time in the ground. Production can be increased by high pressure jetting. Figures below assume 50% of lumber is salvaged and includes pulling costs. Some jurisdictions require an equipment operator in addition to Crew B-31.

Sheeting Pulled

Daily Cost Crew B-31	L.H./ Day	Hourly Cost	Daily Cost	8' Depth, 440 S.F./Day		16' Depth, 320 S.F./Day	
				To Drive (1 Day)	To Pull (1/3 Day)	To Drive (1 Day)	To Pull (1/3 Day)
1 Foreman	8	$24.85	$ 198.80	$ 198.80	$ 66.20	$ 198.80	$ 66.20
3 Laborers	24	22.85	548.40	548.40	182.62	548.40	182.62
1 Carpenter	8	29.15	233.20	233.20	77.66	233.20	77.66
1 Air Compressor			125.20	125.20	41.69	125.20	41.69
1 Sheeting Driver			12.50	12.50	4.16	12.50	4.16
2 -50 Ft. Air Hoses, 1-1/2" Diam.			11.80	11.80	3.93	11.80	3.93
Lumber (50% salvage)				1.76 MBF	559.68	2.24 MBF	712.32
Total			$1,129.90	$1,689.58	$376.26	$1,842.22	$376.26
Total/S.F.				$ 3.84	$ .86	$ 5.76	$ 1.18
Total (Drive and Pull)/S.F.				$ 4.70		$ 6.93	

Sheeting Left in Place

Daily Cost	8' Depth 440 S.F./Day		10' Depth 400 S.F./Day		12' Depth 360 S.F./Day		16' Depth 320 S.F./Day		18' Depth 305 S.F./Day		20' Depth 280 S.F./Day	
Crew B-31		$1,129.90		$1,129.90		$1,129.90		$1,129.90		$1,129.90		$1,129.90
Lumber	1.76 M	1,119.36	1.8 M	1,144.80	1.8 M	1,144.80	2.24 M	1,424.64	2.1 M	1,335.60	1.9 M	1,208.40
Total in Place		$2,249.26		$2,274.70		$2,274.70		$2,554.54		$2,465.50		$2,338.30
Total/S.F.		$ 5.11		$ 5.69		$ 6.32		$ 7.98		$ 8.08		$ 8.35
Total/M.B.F.		$1,277.99		$1,263.72		$1,263.72		$1,140.42		$1,174.05		$1,230.68

R02250-450 Steel Sheet Piling

Limiting weights are 22 to 38#/S.F. of wall surface with 27#/S.F. average for usual types and sizes. (Weights of piles themselves are from 30.7#/L.F. to 57#/L.F. but they are 15" to 21" wide.) Lightweight sections 12" to 28" wide from 3 ga. to 12 ga. thick are also available for shallow excavations. Piles may be driven two at a time with an impact or vibratory hammer (use vibratory to pull) hung from a crane without leads. A reasonable estimate of the life of steel sheet piling is 10 uses with up to 125 uses possible if a vibratory hammer is used. Used piling costs from 50% to 80% of new piling depending on location and market conditions. Sheet piling and H piles can be rented for about 30% of the delivered mill price for the first month and 5% per month thereafter. Allow 1 labor-hour per pile for cleaning and trimming after driving. These costs increase with depth and hydrostatic head. Vibratory drivers are faster in wet granular soils and are excellent for pile extraction. Pulling difficulty increases with the time in the ground and may cost more than driving. It is often economical to abandon the sheet piling, especially if it can be used as the outer wall form. Allow about 1/3 additional length or more, for toeing into ground. Add bracing, waler and strut costs. Waler costs can equal the cost per ton of sheeting.

Cost of Sheet Piling & Production Rate by Ton & S.F.

Depth of Excavation	15' Depth		20' Depth		25' Depth	
Description of Pile	22 psf = 90.9 S.F./Ton		27 psf = 74 S.F./Ton		38 psf = 52.6 S.F./Ton	
Type of operation:	Drive &	Drive &	Drive &	Drive &	Drive &	Drive &
Left in Place or Removed	Left	Extract*	Left	Extract*	Left	Extract*
Labor & Equip. to Drive 1 ton	$ 358.13	$536.20	$ 298.72	$448.08	$ 203.76	$304.12
Piling (75% Salvage)	812.00	203.00	812.00	203.00	812.00	203.00
Cost/Ton in Place	$1,170.13	$739.20	$1,110.72	$651.08	$1,015.76	$507.12
Production Rate, Tons/Day	10.81	7.22	12.96	8.64	19.00	12.73
Cost, S.F. in Place (incl. 33% toe in)	$ 12.87	$ 8.13	$ 15.01	$ 8.80	$ 19.31	$ 9.64
Production Rate, S.F./Day (incl. 33% toe in)	983	656	960	640	1,000	670

Crew B-40	Bare Costs		Inc. Subs O&P		Installation Cost per Ton
	Hr.	Daily	Hr.	Daily	
1 Pile Driver Foreman	$30.80	$ 246.40	$52.40	$ 419.20	for 15' Deep Excavation plus 33% toe-in
4 Pile Drivers	28.80	921.60	49.00	1,568.00	$3,871.40 per day/10.81 tons = $358.13 per ton
1 Equip. Oper. Oiler	25.75	206.00	39.00	312.00	Installation Cost per S.F.
2 Equip. Oper. (crane)	31.15	498.40	47.15	754.40	$\dfrac{2000\#}{22\#/S.F.}$ = 90.9 S.F. x 10.81 tons = 983 S.F. per day
1 Crane, 40 Ton		716.00		787.60	
Vibratory Hammer & Gen.		1,283.00		1,411.30	$3,871.40 / 983 S.F. per day = $3.94 per S.F.
64 L.H., Daily Totals		$3,871.40		$5,252.50	

*For driving & extracting, two mobilizations & demobilizations will be necessary

R02250-900   Vibroflotation and Vibro Replacement Soil Compaction

Vibroflotation is a proprietary system of compacting sandy soils in place to increase relative density to about 70%. Typical bearing capacities attained will be 6000 psf for saturated sand and 12,000 psf for dry sand. Usual range is 4000 to 8000 psf capacity. Costs in the front of the book are for a vertical foot of compacted cylinder 6' to 10' in diameter.

Vibro replacement is a proprietary system of improving cohesive soils in place to increase bearing capacity. Most silts and clays above or below the water table can be strengthened by installation of stone columns.

The process consists of radial displacement of the soil by vibration. The created hole is then backfilled in stages with coarse granular fill which is thoroughly compacted and displaced into the surrounding soil in the form of a column.

The total project cost would depend on the number and depth of the compacted cylinders. The installing company guarantees relative soil density of the sand cylinders after compaction and the bearing capacity of the soil after the replacement process. Detailed estimating information is available from the installer at no cost.

R02315-300   Compacting Backfill

Compaction of fill in embankments, around structures, in trenches, and under slabs is important to control settlement. Factors affecting compaction are:

1. Soil gradation
2. Moisture content
3. Equipment used
4. Depth of fill per lift
5. Density required

The costs for testing and soil analyses are listed in Division 01450-500. Also, see Division 02315 for further backfill, borrow, and compaction costs.

Example:

Compact granular fill around a building foundation using a 21" wide x 24" vibratory plate in 8" lifts. Operator moves at 50 FPM working a 50 minute hour to develop 95% Modified Proctor Density with 4 passes.

Production Rate:

$$\frac{1.75' \text{ plate width x 50 F.P.M. x 50 min./hr. x .67' lift}}{27 \text{ C.F. per C.Y.}} = 108.5 \text{ C.Y./hr.}$$

Production Rate for 4 Passes:

$$\frac{108.5 \text{ C.Y.}}{4 \text{ passes}} = 27.125 \text{ C.Y./hr. x 8 hrs.} = 217 \text{ C.Y./day}$$

Compacting 217 C.Y. with 21" Wide Vibratory Plate		L.H./ Day	Hourly Cost	Daily Cost	C.Y. Cost
1	Laborer	8	$22.85	$182.80	$ .84
1	Vibratory Plate Compactor			60.60	.28
Total for 217 C.Y./day				$243.40	$1.12

R02315-400 Excavating

The selection of equipment used for structural excavation and bulk excavation or for grading is determined by the following factors.
1. Quantity of material.
2. Type of material.
3. Depth or height of cut.
4. Length of haul.
5. Condition of haul road.
6. Accessibility of site.
7. Moisture content and dewatering requirements.
8. Availability of excavating and hauling equipment.

Some additional costs must be allowed for hand trimming the sides and bottom of concrete pours and other excavation below the general excavation.

When planning excavation and fill, the following should also be considered.
1. Swell factor.
2. Compaction factor.
3. Moisture content.
4. Density requirements.

A typical example for scheduling and estimating the cost of excavation of a 15′ deep basement on a dry site when the material must be hauled off the site, is outlined below.

Assumptions:
1. Swell factor, 18%.
2. No mobilization or demobilization.
3. Allowance included for idle time and moving on job.
4. No dewatering, sheeting, or bracing.
5. No truck spotter or hand trimming.

Number of B.C.Y. per truck = 1.5 C.Y. bucket x 8 passes = 12 loose C.Y.

$$= 12 \times \frac{100}{118} = 10.2 \text{ B.C.Y. per truck}$$

Truck Haul Cycle:

Load truck 8 passes	=	4 minutes
Haul distance 1 mile	=	9 minutes
Dump time	=	2 minutes
Return 1 mile	=	7 minutes
Spot under machine	=	1 minute
		23 minute cycle

Fleet Haul Production per day in B.C.Y.

$$4 \text{ trucks} \times \frac{50 \text{ min. hour}}{23 \text{ min. haul cycle}} \times 8 \text{ hrs.} \times 10.2 \text{ B.C.Y.}$$

$$= 4 \times 2.2 \times 8 \times 10.2 = 718 \text{ B.C.Y./day}$$

Excavating Cost with a 1-1/2 C.Y. Hydraulic Excavator 15′ Deep, 2 Mile Round Trip Haul		L.H./Day	Hourly Cost	Daily Cost	Subtotal	Unit Price
1	Equipment Operator	8	$31.15	$ 249.20		
1	Oiler	8	25.75	206.00		
4	Truck Drivers	32	23.95	766.40	$1,221.60	$1.70
1	Hydraulic Excavator			593.20		
4	Dump Trucks			1,931.20	2,524.40	3.51
Total for 720 B.C.Y.				$3,746.00	$3,746.00	$5.20

Description		1-1/2 C.Y. Hyd. Backhoe 15′ Deep		1-1/2 C.Y. Power Shovel 7′ Bank		1-1/2 C.Y. Dragline 7′ Deep		2-1/2 C.Y. Trackloader Stockpile
Operator (and Oiler, if required)		$ 455.20		$ 455.20		$ 455.20		$ 455.20
Truck Drivers	3 Ea.	574.80	4 Ea.	766.40	3 Ea.	574.80	4 Ea.	766.40
Equipment Rental		593.20		850.20		921.00		770.00
20 C.Y. Trailer Dump Trucks	3 Ea.	1,448.40	4 Ea.	1,931.20	3 Ea.	1,448.40	4 Ea.	1,931.20
Total Cost per Day		$3,071.60		$4,003.00		$3,399.40		$3,922.80
Daily Production, C.Y. Bank Measure		720.00		960.00		640.00		1000.00
Cost per C.Y.		$ 4.27		$ 4.17		$ 5.31		$ 3.92

Add the mobilization and demobilization costs to the total excavation costs. When equipment is rented for more than three days, there is often no mobilization charge by the equipment dealer. On larger jobs outside of urban areas, scrapers can move earth economically provided a dump site or fill area and adequate haul roads are available. Excavation within sheeting bracing or cofferdam bracing is usually done with a clamshell and production is low, since the clamshell may have to be guided by hand between the bracing. When excavating or filling an area enclosed with a wellpoint system, add 10% to 15% to the cost to allow for restricted access. When estimating earth excavation quantities for structures, allow work space outside the building footprint for construction of the foundation, and a slope of 1:1 unless sheeting is used.

R02315-450　Excavating Equipment

The table below lists THEORETICAL hourly production in C.Y./hr. bank measure for some typical excavation equipment. Figures assume 50 minute hours, 83% job efficiency, 100% operator efficiency, 90° swing and properly sized hauling units, which must be modified for adverse digging and loading conditions. Actual production costs in the front of the book average about 50% of the theoretical values listed here.

Equipment	Soil Type	B.C.Y. Weight	% Swell	1 C.Y.	1-1/2 C.Y	2 C.Y.	2-1/2 C.Y.	3 C.Y.	3-1/2 C.Y.	4 C.Y.
Hydraulic Excavator	Moist loam, sandy clay	3400 lb.	40%	85	125	175	220	275	330	380
"Backhoe"	Sand and gravel	3100	18	80	120	160	205	260	310	365
15' Deep Cut	Common earth	2800	30	70	105	150	190	240	280	330
	Clay, hard, dense	3000	33	65	100	130	170	210	255	300
	Moist loam, sandy clay	3400	40	170 (6.0)	245 (7.0)	295 (7.8)	335 (8.4)	385 (8.8)	435 (9.1)	475 (9.4)
Power Shovel	Sand and gravel	3100	18	165 (6.0)	225 (7.0)	275 (7.8)	325 (8.4)	375 (8.8)	420 (9.1)	460 (9.4)
Optimum Cut (Ft.)	Common earth	2800	30	145 (7.8)	200 (9.2)	250 (10.2)	295 (11.2)	335 (12.1)	375 (13.0)	425 (13.8)
	Clay, hard, dense	3000	33	120 (9.0)	175 (10.7)	220 (12.2)	255 (13.3)	300 (14.2)	335 (15.1)	375 (16.0)
	Moist loam, sandy clay	3400	40	130 (6.6)	180 (7.4)	220 (8.0)	250 (8.5)	290 (9.0)	325 (9.5)	385 (10.0)
Drag Line	Sand and gravel	3100	18	130 (6.6)	175 (7.4)	210 (8.0)	245 (8.5)	280 (9.0)	315 (9.5)	375 (10.0)
Optimum Cut (Ft.)	Common earth	2800	30	110 (8.0)	160 (9.0)	190 (9.9)	220 (10.5)	250 (11.0)	280 (11.5)	310 (12.0)
	Clay, hard, dense	3000	33	90 (9.3)	130 (10.7)	160 (11.8)	190 (12.3)	225 (12.8)	250 (13.3)	280 (12.0)

Equipment	Soil Type	B.C.Y. Weight	% Swell	Wheel Loaders				Track Loaders		
				3 C.Y.	4 C.Y.	6 C.Y.	8 C.Y.	2-1/4 C.Y.	3 C.Y.	4 C.Y.
	Moist loam, sandy clay	3400	40	260	340	510	690	135	180	250
	Sand and gravel	3100	18	245	320	480	650	130	170	235
Loading Tractors	Common earth	2800	30	230	300	460	620	120	155	220
	Clay, hard, dense	3000	33	200	270	415	560	110	145	200
	Rock, well-blasted	4000	50	180	245	380	520	100	130	180

R02455-900   Wood Bearing Piles

Untreated Southern Yellow Pine is most generally used for pile foundations cut off below the low water line. These are driven with the bark on. All piles cut off above the low water line should be treated with a preservative or encased in concrete for the section above water.

Item	Unit Cost	Units	Quantity	Total Cost	Cost/Pile	Cost/L.F.
50' Treated Piles, 13" Butt, 7" Tip	$ 9.20	L.F.	200	$ 92,000.00	$460.00	$ 9.20
Installation, Crew B-19	3,499.40	Day	13	45,492.20	227.46	4.55
Mobilization & Demobilization, Crew B-19	3,499.40	Day	3	10,498.20	52.49	1.05
Transportation of Equip. One Way	981.80	Day	1	981.80	4.91	.10
Totals				$148,972.20	$744.86	$14.90

The above figures are based on driving 800 L.F. daily which can be considered average. Time is included for moving rig, cutoff & ordinary delays. A general observation is that the cost of a pile in place complete is about two times the cost of pile only. See also equipment rental division 01590 and R01590-100 for equipment capacities.

R02465-600   Caissons

The three principal types of cassions are:

(1) Belled Caissons, which except for shallow depths and poor soil conditions, are generally recommended. They provide more bearing than shaft area. Because of its conical shape, no horizontal reinforcement of the bell is required.

(2) Straight Shaft Caissons are used where relatively light loads are to be supported by caissons that rest on high value bearing strata. While the shaft is larger in diameter than for belled types this is more than offset by the saving in time and labor.

(3) Keyed Caissons are used when extremely heavy loads are to be carried. A keyed or socketed caisson transfers its load into rock by a combination of end-bearing and shear reinforcing of the shaft. The most economical shaft often consists of a steel casing, a steel wide flange core and concrete. Allowable compressive stresses of .225 f'c for concrete, 16,000 psi for the wide flange core, and 9,000 psi for the steel casing are commonly used. The usual range of shaft diameter is 18" to 84". The number of sizes specified for any one project should be limited due to the problems of casing and auger storage. When hand work is to be performed, shaft diameters should not be less than 32". When inspection of borings is required a minimum shaft diameter of 30" is recommended. Concrete caissons are intended to be poured against earth excavation so permanent forms which add to cost should not be used if the excavation is clean and the earth sufficiently impervious to prevent excessive loss of concrete.

Soil Conditions for Belling		
Good	**Requires Handwork**	**Not Recommended**
Clay	Hard Shale	Silt
Sandy Clay	Limestone	Sand
Silty Clay	Sandstone	Gravel
Clayey Silt	Weathered Mica	Igneous Rock
Hard-pan		
Soft Shale		
Decomposed Rock		

R02465-800   Pressure Injected Footings

Pressure Injected Footings are end bearing foundation units consisting of expanded bulbous bases formed by high energy blows, and concrete shafts either cased or uncased, to transfer the load.

The bulb must be formed in granular, rock or hardpan soils. Bearing is achieved at a predetermined depth so that the length of the shaft is usually less than for friction piles. High load capacity reduces the number of units and caps required.

Mobilization and demobilization costs below assume maximum distance of 50 miles.

100 Uncased Pressure Injected Footings 25' Long	Quantity Unit	Unit Cost	Total	Cost/Pile	Cost/L.F.
Crew B-44, 8 piles/day	13 Days	$2,799.20	$36,389.60	$363.90	$14.56
Mobilization & Demobilization	2 Days	2,799.20	5,598.40	55.98	2.24
Transportation one way	1.5 Days	981.80	1,472.70	14.73	.59
Total Installation			$43,460.70	$434.61	$17.38
Shafts: 100 ea. 17" diam., 25' deep	155 C.Y.	$ 107.20	$16,616.00	$166.16	$ 6.65
Pressure Bulbs: 100 ea. @ .75 C.Y.	75 C.Y.	107.20	8,040.00	80.40	3.22
Waste: 15% of above	35 C.Y.	107.20	3,752.00	37.52	1.50
Total Material Cost			$28,408.00	$284.08	$11.37
Total Cost in Place			$71,868.70	$718.69	$28.75

R02510-800   Piping Designations

There are several systems currently in use to describe pipe and fittings. The following paragraphs will help to identify and clarify classifications of piping systems used for water distribution.

Piping may be classified by schedule. Piping schedules include 5S, 10S, 10, 20, 30, Standard, 40, 60, Extra Strong, 80, 100, 120, 140, 160 and Double Extra Strong. These schedules are dependent upon the pipe wall thickness. The wall thickness of a particular schedule may vary with pipe size.

Ductile iron pipe for water distribution is classified by Pressure Classes such as Class 150, 200, 250, 300 and 350. These classes are actually the rated water working pressure of the pipe in pounds per square inch (psi). The pipe in these pressure classes is designed to withstand the rated water working pressure plus a surge allowance of 100 psi.

The American Water Works Association (AWWA) provides standards for various types of **plastic pipe.** C-900 is the specification for polyvinyl chloride (PVC) piping used for water distribution in sizes ranging from 4″ through 12″. C-901 is the specification for polyethylene (PE) pressure pipe, tubing and fittings used for water distribution in sizes ranging from 1/2″ through 3″. C-905 is the specification for PVC piping sizes 14″ and greater.

PVC pressure-rated pipe is identified using the standard dimensional ratio (SDR) method. This method is defined by the American Society for Testing and Materials (ASTM) Standard D 2241. This pipe is available in SDR numbers 64, 41, 32.5, 26, 21, 17, and 13.5. Pipe with an SDR of 64 will have the thinnest wall while pipe with an SDR of 13.5 will have the thickest wall. When the pressure rating (PR) of a pipe is given in psi, it is based on a line supplying water at 73 degrees F.

The National Sanitation Foundation (NSF) seal of approval is applied to products that can be used with potable water. These products have been tested to ANSI/NSF Standard 14.

Valves and strainers are classified by American National Standards Institute (ANSI) Classes. These Classes are 125, 150, 200, 250, 300, 400, 600, 900, 1500 and 2500. Within each class there is an operating pressure range dependent upon temperature. Design parameters should be compared to the appropriate material dependent, pressure-temperature rating chart for accurate valve selection.

R02510-810   Concrete Pipe

Prices given are for inside 20 mile delivery zone. Add $1.75 per ton of pipe for each additional 10 miles. Minimum truckload is 10 tons. The non-reinforced pipe listed in the front of the book is designation ASTM

C14-59 extra strength. The reinforced pipe listed is ASTM C76-65T class 3, no gaskets. The installation cost given includes shaping bottom of the trench, placing the pipe, and backfilling and tamping to the top of the pipe only.

R02920-500   Seeding

The type of grass is determined by light, shade and moisture content of soil plus intended use. Fertilizer should be disked 4″ before seeding. For steep slopes disk five tons of mulch and lay two tons of hay or straw on surface per acre after seeding. Surface mulch can be staked, lightly disked or tar emulsion sprayed. Material for mulch can be wood chips, peat moss, partially

rotted hay or straw, wood fibers and sprayed emulsions. Hemp seed blankets with fertilizer are also available. For spring seeding, watering is necessary. Late fall seeding may have to be reseeded in the spring. Hydraulic seeding, power mulching, and aerial seeding can be used on large areas.

R02930-900   Cost of Trees: Based on Pin Oak (Quercus palustris)

Tree Diameter	Normal Height	Catalog List Price of Tree	Guying Material	Equipment Charge	Installation Labor	Total
2 to 3 inch	14 feet	$ 140	$15.00	$ 55.14	$ 78.72	$ 288.86
3 to 4 inch	16 feet	235	18.00	91.90	131.20	476.10
4 to 5 inch	18 feet	405	75.50	110.28	157.44	748.22
6 to 7 inch	22 feet	825	80.00	137.85	196.80	1,239.65
8 to 9 inch	26 feet	1,060	90.00	183.80	262.40	1,596.20

Installation Time & Cost for Planting Trees, Bare Costs													
Ball Size Diam. X Depth	Soil in Ball	Weight of Ball	Hole Diam. Req'd	Hole Excavation	Amount of Soil Displ.	Topsoil Handled	Time Required in Labor-Hours					Cost	
							Dig & Lace	Handle Ball	Dig Hole	Plant & Prune	Water & Guy	Total L.H.	Crew	Total per Tree
Inches	C.F.	Lbs.	Feet	C.F.	C.F.	C.F.								
12 x 12	.70	56.00	2.00	4.00	3.00	11.00	.25	.17	.33	.25	.07	1.10	1 Clab	$ 25.14
18 x 16	2.00	160.00	2.50	8.00	6.00	21.00	.50	.33	.47	.35	.08	1.70	2 Clab	38.85
24 x 18	4.00	320.00	3.00	13.00	9.00	38.00	1.00	.67	1.08	.82	.20	3.80	3 Clab	86.83
30 x 21	7.50	600.00	4.00	27.00	19.50	76.00	.82	.71	.79	1.22	.26	3.80		122.97
36 x 24	12.50	980.00	4.50	38.00	25.50	114.00	1.08	.95	1.11	1.32	.30	4.76		154.03
42 x 27	19.00	1,520.00	5.50	64.00	45.00	185.00	1.90	1.27	1.87	1.43	.34	6.80	B-6	220.05
48 x 30	28.00	2,040.00	6.00	85.00	57.00	254.00	2.41	1.60	2.06	1.55	.39	8.00	@	258.88
54 x 33	38.50	3,060.00	7.00	127.00	88.50	370.00	2.86	1.90	2.39	1.76	.45	9.40	$32.36	304.18
60 x 36	52.00	4,160.00	7.50	159.00	107.00	474.00	3.26	2.17	2.73	2.00	.51	10.70	per	346.25
66 x 39	68.00	5,440.00	8.00	196.00	128.00	596.00	3.61	2.41	3.07	2.26	.58	11.90	Labor-	385.08
72 x 42	87.00	7,160.00	9.00	267.00	180.00	785.00	3.90	2.60	3.71	2.78	.70	13.70	hour	443.33

R03110-010   Wall Form Materials

Aluminum Forms

Approximate weight is 3 lbs. per S.F.C.A. Standard widths are available from 4″ to 36″ with 36″ most common. Standard lengths of 2′, 4′, 6′ to 8′ are available. Forms are lightweight and fewer ties are needed with the wider widths. The form face is either smooth or textured.

Cost of bare forms per S.F.C.A. with different facing surface is listed below. Forms may also be rented.

Purchase Cost Per S.F.								
Finish	3′ x 8′	2′ x 8′	12″ x 8′	6″ x 8′	3′ x 4′	2′ x 4′	12″ x 4′	6″ x 4′
Smooth Aluminum (.096″ Face Sheet)	$13.15	$16.25	$22.00	$36.50	$14.10	$19.40	$25.50	$39.80
Textured Brick Aluminum	$15.35	$19.50	$26.30	$41.90	$17.60	$23.25	$29.80	$47.50

Metal Framed Plywood Forms

Manufacturers claim over 75 reuses of plywood and over 300 reuses of steel frames. Sale price for steel framed forms is from $8.75 per S.F. for 2′ x 8′ to $12.75 per S.F. for 2′ x 3′. Narrower forms range between $12.00 per S.F. to $23.00 per S.F. for 1′ x 3′. Many specials such as corners, fillers, pilasters, etc. are available. Monthly rental is generally about 15% of purchase price for first month and 9% per month thereafter with 90% of rental applied to purchase for the first month and decreasing percentages thereafter. Aluminum framed forms cost 25% to 30% more than steel framed.

Rule of thumb purchase price including corners, specials, etc.; steel framed $13.00 per S.F.; aluminum framed $18.00 per S.F.

Reconditioned steel framed forms are rented for an average of $1.35 per S.F per month. Aluminum framed forms are rented for $2.25 per S.F. for the first month and $1.50 per S.F. per month thereafter.

After the first month, extra days may be prorated from the monthly charge. Rental rates do not include ties, accessories, cleaning, loss of hardware or freight in and out. Approximate weight is 5 lbs. per S.F. for steel; 3 lbs. per S.F. for aluminum.

Forms can be rented with option to buy.

Plywood Forms, Job Fabricated

There are two types of plywood used for concrete forms.
1. Exterior plyform which is completely waterproof. This is face oiled to facilitate stripping. Ten reuses can be expected with this type with 25 reuses possible.
2. An overlaid type consists of a resin fiber fused to exterior plyform. No oiling is required except to facilitate cleaning. This is available in both high density (HDO) and medium density overlaid (MDO). Using HDO, 50 reuses can be expected with 200 possible.

Plyform is available in 5/8″ and 3/4″ thickness. High density overlaid is available in 3/8″, 1/2″, 5/8″ and 3/4″ thickness.

5/8″ thick is sufficient for most building forms, while 3/4″ is best on heavy construction.

For prices on plywood and framing lumber see R06100-010 and R06160-020.

Plywood Forms, Modular, Prefabricated

There are many plywood forming systems without frames. Most of these are manufactured from 1-1/8″ (HDO) plywood and have some hardware attached. These are used principally for foundation walls 8′ or less high. With care and maintenance, 100 reuses can be attained with decreasing quality of surface finish. Sale price of 2′ x 8′ panels is $6.75 per S.F. with 4″ x 8′ fillers costing $25.00 per S.F. Typical forms and accessories for 1000 S.F. of form area cost $7200 not including form ties.

Steel Forms

Approximate weight is 6-1/2 lbs. per S.F.C.A. including accessories. Standard widths are available from 2″ to 24″, with 24″ most common. Standard lengths are from 2′ to 8′, with 4′ the most common. Forms are easily ganged into modular units.

Sale price for typical hand set job is $12.50 per S.F.C.A. including all usual accessories, specials, corners, etc., but not including ties or freight. Cost of bare forms runs from $10.00 for wide forms to over $22.00 per S.F.C.A. for narrow widths and/or short lengths. Forms are usually leased for 15% of the purchase price per month prorated daily over 30 days. Standard 6000 lb. wall ties for 12″ walls cost $85 per hundred and 24″ long ties cost $125 per hundred.

Rental may be applied to sale price and usually rental forms are bought. With careful handling and cleaning 200 to 400 reuses are possible.

Straight wall gang forms up to 12′ x 20′ or 8′ x 30′ can be fabricated. These crane handled forms usually cost from $21.00 to $28.00 per S.F.C.A. or can be leased for approx. 9% per month. Straight wall gang forms utilizing 40,000 lb. and 60,000 lb. ties with sizes from 24′ x 10′ to 24′ x 24′ cost from $22.00 to $30.00 per S.F. including all accessories and taper ties. Rental rates on these gang forms run from $.30 to $.75 per week per S.F.C.A.

Individual job analysis is available from the manufacturer at no charge.

R03110-020   Floor Pans and Domes

For 8' to 15' Ceiling Heights Using Crew C-2 at $28.43 per Labor-Hour	20" Pans (03110-420)				19" Domes (03110-420)			
		1 Use		4 Use		1 Use		4 Use
Rent 20" pans or 19" domes		$ 86.00		$ 26.50		$ 86.00		$ 26.50
Adjustable shores and accessories		48.00		26.00		48.00		26.00
110 S.F. 3/4" plyform at $987 per M.S.F.		108.57		35.29		108.57		35.29
210 B.F. supporting joists, girts and braces at $600 per MBF		126.00		40.95		126.00		40.95
Labor handle, place, strip, oil and clean pans and domes	1.5 L.H.	42.65	1.0 L.H.	28.43	1.8 L.H.	51.17	1.2 L.H.	34.12
Make up, erect, remove wood decking	10 L.H.	284.30	8.5 L.H.	241.66	10.0 L.H.	284.30	8.5 L.H.	241.66
Total per 100 S.F. of floor area		$695.52		$398.83		$704.04		$404.52

The figures above are for closed deck forming. For open deck forming deduct $25 per 100 S.F. for four uses. For pan rental, figure $.85 per S.F. of total area for one use; $.42 for two uses; $.30 for three uses; and $.25 for four uses, which is about the most that can be expected for any one project. The purchase price of fiberglass long pans is $6.00 per S.F.C.A. or an average $12.00 per S.F. of floor area.*

For two-way grid system, 19" steel domes are leased for $.25 to $.75 and 30" fiberglass domes are leased for $.50 to $2.25 per S.F. of floor area.

The purchase price of custom size fiberglass forms runs from $6.00 to $18.00 per S.F.C.A.*

For slab height from 15' to 20' add $55 per 100 S.F. and for 20' to 35' add $75 per 100 S.F., both for four uses.

*It is necessary to divide the purchase cost by the number of expected uses to determine the cost per use.

R03110-030   Slipforms

The slipform method of forming may be used for forming circular silo and multi-celled storage bin type structures over 30' high, and building core shear walls over eight stories high. The shear walls, usually enclose elevator shafts, stairwells, mechanical spaces, and toilet rooms. Reuse of the form on duplicate structures will reduce the height necessary and spread the cost of building the form. Slipform systems can be used to cast chimneys, towers, piers, dams, underground shafts or other structures capable of being extruded.

Slipforms are usually 4' high and are raised semi-continuously by jacks climbing on rods which are embedded in the concrete. The jacks are powered by a hydraulic, pneumatic, or electric source and are available in 3, 6, and 22 ton capacities. Interior work decks and exterior scaffolds must be provided for placing inserts, embedded items, reinforcing steel, and concrete. Scaffolds below the form for finishers may be required. The interior work decks are often used as roof slab forms on silos and bin work. Form raising rates will range from 6" to 20" per hour for silos; 6" to 30" per hour for buildings; and 6" to 48" per hour for shaft work.

Reinforcing bars and stressing strands are usually hoisted by crane or gin pole and the concrete material can be hoisted by crane, winch-powered skip, or pumps. The slipform system is operated on a continuous 24 hour day when a monolithic structure is desired. For least cost, the system is operated only during normal working hours.

The cost of the form, including equipment setting, will range from $8.00 to $20 per square foot of actual form built. The cost of work decks and scaffolds will range from $2.50 to $10 per square foot of total deck area. Slipform equipment rental will range from $.20 to $.60 per S.F. of surface formed. Operating costs of slipform systems will range from $.10 to $.50 per S.F. of surface formed.

Placing concrete will range from 0.5 to 1.5 labor-hours per C.Y. Finishing (if required) and curing costs will range from $.08 to $.35 per S.F. of surface. Bucks, blockouts, keyways, weldplates, etc. are extra. In-place total costs can range from $300 to over $900 per C.Y.

R03110-040 Forms for Reinforced Concrete

Design Economy

Avoid many sizes in proportioning beams and columns.

From story to story avoid changing column dimensions. Gain strength by adding steel or using a richer mix. If a change in size of column is necessary, vary one dimension only to minimize form alterations. Keep beams and columns the same width.

From floor to floor in a multi-story building vary beam depth, not width, as that will leave slab panel form unchanged. It is cheaper to vary the strength of a beam from floor to floor by means of steel area than by 2″ changes in either width or depth.

Cost Factors

Material includes the cost of lumber, cost of rent for metal pans or forms if used, nails, form ties, form oil, bolts and accessories.

Labor includes the cost of carpenters to make up, erect, remove and repair, plus common labor to clean and move. Having carpenters remove forms minimizes repairs.

Improper alignment and condition of forms will increase finishing cost. When forms are heavily oiled, concrete surfaces must be neutralized before finishing. Special curing compounds will cause spillages to spall off in first frost. Gang forming methods will reduce costs on large projects.

Materials Used

Boards are seldom used unless their architectural finish is required. Generally, steel, fiberglass and plywood are used for contact surfaces. Labor on plywood is 10% less than with boards. The plywood is backed up with

2 x 4's at 12″ to 32″ O.C. Walers are generally 2 - 2 x 4's. Column forms are held together with steel yokes or bands. Shoring is with adjustable shoring or scaffolding for high ceilings.

Reuse

Floor and column forms can be reused four or possibly five times without excessive repair. Remember to allow for 10% waste on each reuse.

When modular sized wall forms are made, up to twenty uses can be expected with exterior plyform.

When forms are reused, the cost to erect, strip, clean and move will not be affected. 10% replacement of lumber should be included and about one hour of carpenter time for repairs on each reuse per 100 S.F.

The reuse cost for certain accessory items normally rented on a monthly basis will be lower than the cost for the first use.

After fifth use, new material required plus time needed for repair prevent form cost from dropping further and it may go up. Much depends on care in stripping, the number of special bays, changes in beam or column sizes and other factors.

Costs for multiple use of formwork may be developed as follows:

2 Uses
$$\frac{(1st\ Use + Reuse)}{2} = avg.\ cost/2\ uses$$

3 Uses
$$\frac{(1st\ Use + 2\ Reuse)}{3} = avg.\ cost/3\ uses$$

4 Uses
$$\frac{(1st\ use + 3\ Reuse)}{4} = avg.\ cost/4\ uses$$

R03110-050 Forms In Place

This section assumes that all cuts are made with power saws, that adjustable shores are employed and that maximum use is made of commercial form ties and accessories. Bare costs are used in the table below.

BEAM AND GIRDER, INTERIOR, 12″ Wide (Line 03110-405-2000)			First Use			Reuse		
Item	Cost	Unit	Quantity	Material	Installation	Quantity	Material	Installation
5/8″ exterior plyform	$875.00	M.S.F.	115 S.F.	$100.65		11.5 S.F.	$10.05	
Lumber	600.00	M.B.F.	200 B.F.	120.00		20.0 B.F.	12.00	
Accessories, incl. adjustable shores			Allow	24.00		Allow	24.00	
Make up, crew C-2	28.43	L.H.	6.4 L.H.		$181.95	1.0 L.H.		$ 28.45
Erect and strip			8.3 L.H.		235.95	8.3 L.H.		235.95
Clean and move			1.3 L.H.		36.95	1.3 L.H.		36.95
Total per 100 S.F.C.A.			16.0 L.H.	$244.65	$454.85	10.6 L.H.	$46.05	$301.35

For structural steel frame with beams encased, subtract 1.2 labor-hours, and 50 B.F. lumber or about $55.00 per 100 S.F.C.A. for the first use and $32 for each reuse.

BOX CULVERT, 5′ to 8′ Square or Rectangular (Line 03110-415-0010)			First Use			Reuse		
Item	Cost	Unit	Quantity	Material	Installation	Quantity	Material	Installation
3/4″ exterior plyform	$987.00	M.S.F.	110 S.F.	$108.55		11.0 S.F.	$10.85	
Lumber	600.00	M.B.F.	170 B.F.	102.00		17.0 B.F.	10.20	
Accessories			Allow	19.00		Allow	19.00	
Build in place, crew C-1	27.57	L.H.	14.5 L.H.		$399.75	14.5 L.H.		$399.75
Strip and salvage			4.3 L.H.		118.55	4.3 L.H.		118.55
Total per 100 S.F.C.A.			18.8 L.H.	$229.55	$518.30	18.8 L.H.	$40.05	$518.30

R03110-050 Forms in Place (cont.)

COLUMNS, 24″ x 24″ (Line 03110-410-6500)

Item	Cost	Unit	First Use Quantity	Material	Installation	Reuse Quantity	Material	Installation
5/8″ exterior plyform	$875.00	M.S.F.	120 S.F.	$105.00		12.0 S.F.	$10.50	
Lumber	600.00	M.B.F.	125 B.F.	75.00		12.5 B.F.	7.50	
Clamps, chamfer strips and accessories			Allow	24.00		Allow	24.00	
Make up, crew C-1	27.57	L.H.	5.8 L.H.		$159.90	1.0 L.H.		$ 27.55
Erect and strip			9.8 L.H.		270.20	9.8 L.H.		270.20
Clean and move			1.2 L.H.		33.10	1.2 L.H.		33.10
Total per 100 S.F.C.A.			16.8 L.H.	$204.00	$463.20	12.0 L.H.	$42.00	$330.85

FLAT SLAB WITH DROP PANELS (Line 03110-420-2000)

Item	Cost	Unit	First Use Quantity	Material	Installation	Reuse Quantity	Material	Installation
5/8″ exterior plyform	$875.00	M.S.F.	115 S.F.	$100.65		11.5 S.F.	$10.05	
Lumber	600.00	M.B.F.	210 B.F.	126.00		21.0 B.F.	12.60	
Accessories, incl. adjustable shores			Allow	24.00		Allow	24.00	
Make up, crew C-2	28.43	L.H.	3.5 L.H.		$ 99.50	1.0 L.H.		$ 28.45
Erect and strip			6.0 L.H.		170.60	6.0 L.H.		170.60
Clean and move			1.2 L.H.		34.10	1.2 L.H.		34.10
Total per 100 S.F.C.A.			10.7 L.H.	$250.65	$304.20	8.2 L.H.	$46.65	$233.15

Drop panels included but column caps figure with columns.

FOOTINGS, SPREAD (Line 03110-430-5000)

Item	Cost	Unit	First Use Quantity	Materials	Installation	Reuse Quantity	Material	Installation
Lumber	$600.00	M.B.F.	260 B.F.	$156.00		26 B.F.	$15.60	
Accessories			Allow	7.65		Allow	7.65	
Make up, crew C-1	27.57	L.H.	4.7 L.H.		$129.60	1.0 L.H.		$ 27.55
Erect and strip			4.2 L.H.		115.80	4.2 L.H.		115.80
Clean and move			1.6 L.H.		44.10	1.6 L.H.		44.10
Total per 100 S.F.C.A.			10.5 L.H.	$163.65	$289.50	6.8 L.H.	$23.25	$187.45

FOUNDATION WALL, 8′ High (Line 03110-455-2000)

Item	Cost	Unit	First Use Quantity	Material	Installation	Reuse Quantity	Material	Installation
5/8″ exterior plyform	$875.00	M.S.F.	110 S.F.	$ 96.25		11.0 S.F.	$ 9.65	
Lumber	600.00	M.B.F.	140 B.F.	84.00		14.0 B.F.	8.40	
Accessories			Allow	24.00		Allow	24.00	
Make up, crew C-2	28.43	L.H.	5.0 L.H.		$142.15	1.0 L.H.		$ 28.45
Erect and strip			6.5 L.H.		184.80	6.5 L.H.		184.80
Clean and move			1.5 L.H.		42.65	1.5 L.H.		42.65
Total per 100 S.F.C.A.			13.0 L.H.	$204.25	$369.60	9.0 L.H.	$42.05	$255.90

PILE CAPS, Square or Rectangular (Line 03110-430-3000)

Item	Cost	Unit	First Use Quantity	Material	Installation	Reuse Quantity	Material	Installation
5/8″ exterior plyform	$875.00	M.S.F.	110 S.F.	$ 96.25		11.0 S.F.	$ 9.65	
Lumber	600.00	M.B.F.	160 B.F.	96.00		16.0 B.F.	9.60	
Accessories			Allow	7.28		Allow	7.28	
Make up, crew C-1	27.57	L.H.	4.5 L.H.		$124.05	1.0 L.H.		$ 27.55
Erect and strip			5.0 L.H.		137.85	5.0 L.H.		137.85
Clean and move			1.5 L.H.		41.35	1.5 L.H.		41.35
Total per 100 S.F.C.A.			11.0 L.H.	$199.53	$303.25	7.5 L.H.	$26.53	$206.75

STAIRS, Average Run (Inclined Length x Width) (Line 03110-450-0010)

Item	Cost	Unit	First Use Quantity	Materials	Installation	Reuse Quantity	Material	Installation
5/8″ exterior plyform	$875.00	M.S.F.	110 S.F.	$ 96.25		11.0 S.F.	$ 9.65	
Lumber	600.00	M.B.F.	425 B.F.	255.00		42.5 B.F.	25.50	
Accessories			Allow	19.00		Allow	19.00	
Build in place, crew C-2	28.43	L.H.	25.0 L.H.		$710.75	25.0 L.H.		$710.75
Strip and salvage			4.0 L.H.		113.70	4.0 L.H.		113.70
Total per 100 S.F.			29.0 L.H.	$370.25	$824.45	29.0 L.H.	$54.15	$824.45

R03110-060 Formwork Labor Hours

Item	Unit	Hours Required			Total Hours	Multiple Use		
		Fabricate	Erect & Strip	Clean & Move	1 Use	2 Use	3 Use	4 Use
Beam and Girder, interior beams, 12" wide	100 S.F.	6.4	8.3	1.3	16.0	13.3	12.4	12.0
Hung from steel beams		5.8	7.7	1.3	14.8	12.4	11.6	11.2
Beam sides only, 36" high		5.8	7.2	1.3	14.3	11.9	11.1	10.7
Beam bottoms only, 24" wide		6.6	13.0	1.3	20.9	18.1	17.2	16.7
Box out for openings		9.9	10.0	1.1	21.0	16.6	15.1	14.3
Buttress forms, to 8' high		6.0	6.5	1.2	13.7	11.2	10.4	10.0
Centering, steel, 3/4" rib lath			1.0		1.0			
3/8" rib lath or slab form			0.9		0.9			
Chamfer strip or keyway	100 L.F.		1.5		1.5	1.5	1.5	1.5
Columns, fiber tube 8" diameter			20.6		20.6			
12"			21.3		21.3			
16"			22.9		22.9			
20"			23.7		23.7			
24"			24.6		24.6			
30"			25.6		25.6			
Round Steel, 12" diameter			22.0		22.0	22.0	22.0	22.0
16"			25.6		25.6	25.6	25.6	25.6
20"			30.5		30.5	30.5	30.5	30.5
24"			37.7		37.7	37.7	37.7	37.7
Plywood 8" x 8"	100 S.F.	7.0	11.0	1.2	19.2	16.2	15.2	14.7
12" x 12"		6.0	10.5	1.2	17.7	15.2	14.4	14.0
16" x 16"		5.9	10.0	1.2	17.1	14.7	13.8	13.4
24" x 24"		5.8	9.8	1.2	16.8	14.4	13.6	13.2
Steel framed plywood 8" x 8"			10.0	1.0	11.0	11.0	11.0	11.0
12" x 12"			9.3	1.0	10.3	10.3	10.3	10.3
16" x 16"			8.5	1.0	9.5	9.5	9.5	9.5
24" x 24"			7.8	1.0	8.8	8.8	8.8	8.8
Drop head forms, plywood		9.0	12.5	1.5	23.0	19.0	17.7	17.0
Coping forms		8.5	15.0	1.5	25.0	21.3	20.0	19.4
Culvert, box			14.5	4.3	18.8	18.8	18.8	18.8
Curb forms, 6" to 12" high, on grade		5.0	8.5	1.2	14.7	12.7	12.1	11.7
On elevated slabs		6.0	10.8	1.2	18.0	15.5	14.7	14.3
Edge forms to 6" high, on grade	100 L.F.	2.0	3.5	0.6	6.1	5.6	5.4	5.3
7" to 12" high	100 S.F.	2.5	5.0	1.0	8.5	7.8	7.5	7.4
Equipment foundations		10.0	18.0	2.0	30.0	25.5	24.0	23.3
Flat slabs, including drops		3.5	6.0	1.2	10.7	9.5	9.0	8.8
Hung from steel		3.0	5.5	1.2	9.7	8.7	8.4	8.2
Closed deck for domes		3.0	5.8	1.2	10.0	9.0	8.7	8.5
Open deck for pans		2.2	5.3	1.0	8.5	7.9	7.7	7.6
Footings, continuous, 12" high		3.5	3.5	1.5	8.5	7.3	6.8	6.6
Spread, 12" high		4.7	4.2	1.6	10.5	8.7	8.0	7.7
Pile caps, square or rectangular		4.5	5.0	1.5	11.0	9.3	8.7	8.4
Grade beams, 24" deep		2.5	5.3	1.2	9.0	8.3	8.0	7.9
Lintel or Sill forms		8.0	17.0	2.0	27.0	23.5	22.3	21.8
Spandrel beams, 12" wide		9.0	11.2	1.3	21.5	17.5	16.2	15.5
Stairs			25.0	4.0	29.0	29.0	29.0	29.0
Trench forms in floor		4.5	14.0	1.5	20.0	18.3	17.7	17.4
Walls, Plywood, at grade, to 8' high		5.0	6.5	1.5	13.0	11.0	9.7	9.5
8' to 16'		7.5	8.0	1.5	17.0	13.8	12.7	12.1
16' to 20'		9.0	10.0	1.5	20.5	16.5	15.2	14.5
Foundation walls, to 8' high		4.5	6.5	1.0	12.0	10.3	9.7	9.4
8' to 16' high		5.5	7.5	1.0	14.0	11.8	11.0	10.6
Retaining wall to 12' high, battered		6.0	8.5	1.5	16.0	13.5	12.7	12.3
Radial walls to 12' high, smooth		8.0	9.5	2.0	19.5	16.0	14.8	14.3
2' chords		7.0	8.0	1.5	16.5	13.5	12.5	12.0
Prefabricated modular, to 8' high		—	4.3	1.0	5.3	5.3	5.3	5.3
Steel, to 8' high		—	6.8	1.2	8.0	8.0	8.0	8.0
8' to 16' high		—	9.1	1.5	10.6	10.3	10.2	10.2
Steel framed plywood to 8' high		—	6.8	1.2	8.0	7.5	7.3	7.2
8' to 16' high		—	9.3	1.2	10.5	9.5	9.2	9.0

R03210-010 Reinforcing Steel Weights and Measures

Bar Designation No.**	Nominal Weight Lb./Ft.	U.S. Customary Units Nominal Dimensions*			SI Units Nominal Dimensions*			
		Diameter in.	Cross Sectional Area, in.²	Perimeter in.	Nominal Weight kg/m	Diameter mm	Cross Sectional Area, cm²	Perimeter mm
3	.376	.375	.11	1.178	.560	9.52	.71	29.9
4	.668	.500	.20	1.571	.994	12.70	1.29	39.9
5	1.043	.625	.31	1.963	1.552	15.88	2.00	49.9
6	1.502	.750	.44	2.356	2.235	19.05	2.84	59.8
7	2.044	.875	.60	2.749	3.042	22.22	3.87	69.8
8	2.670	1.000	.79	3.142	3.973	25.40	5.10	79.8
9	3.400	1.128	1.00	3.544	5.059	28.65	6.45	90.0
10	4.303	1.270	1.27	3.990	6.403	32.26	8.19	101.4
11	5.313	1.410	1.56	4.430	7.906	35.81	10.06	112.5
14	7.650	1.693	2.25	5.320	11.384	43.00	14.52	135.1
18	13.600	2.257	4.00	7.090	20.238	57.33	25.81	180.1

* The nominal dimensions of a deformed bar are equivalent to those of a plain round bar having the same weight per foot as the deformed bar.
** Bar numbers are based on the number of eighths of an inch included in the nominal diameter of the bars.

R03210-020 Metric Rebar Specification - ASTM A615-81

Grade 300 (300 MPa* = 43,560 psi; +8.7% vs. Grade 40)				
Grade 400 (400 MPa* = 58,000 psi; −3.4% vs. Grade 60)				
Bar No.	Diameter mm	Area mm²	Equivalent in.²	Comparison with U.S. Customary Bars
10	11.3	100	.16	Between #3 & #4
15	16.0	200	.31	#5 (.31 in.²)
20	19.5	300	.47	#6 (.44 in.²)
25	25.2	500	.78	#8 (.79 in.²)
30	29.9	700	1.09	#9 (1.00 in.²)
35	35.7	1000	1.55	#11 (1.56 in.²)
45	43.7	1500	2.33	#14 (2.25 in.²)
55	56.4	2500	3.88	#18 (4.00 in.²)

* MPa = megapascals

R03210-040 Weight of Steel Reinforcing Per Square Foot of Wall (PSF)

Reinforced Weights: The table below suggests the weights per square foot for reinforcing steel in walls. Weights are approximate and will be the same for all grades of steel bars. For bars in two directions, add weights for each size and spacing.

C/C Spacing in Inches	#3 Wt. (PSF)	#4 Wt. (PSF)	#5 Wt. (PSF)	#6 Wt. (PSF)	#7 Wt. (PSF)	#8 Wt. (PSF)	#9 Wt. (PSF)	#10 Wt. (PSF)	#11 Wt. (PSF)
2″	2.26	4.01	6.26	9.01	12.27				
3″	1.50	2.67	4.17	6.01	8.18	10.68	13.60	17.21	21.25
4″	1.13	2.01	3.13	4.51	6.13	8.10	10.20	12.91	15.94
5″	.90	1.60	2.50	3.60	4.91	6.41	8.16	10.33	12.75
6″	.752	1.34	2.09	3.00	4.09	5.34	6.80	8.61	10.63
8″	.564	1.00	1.57	2.25	3.07	4.01	5.10	6.46	7.97
10″	.451	.802	1.25	1.80	2.45	3.20	4.08	5.16	6.38
12″	.376	.668	1.04	1.50	2.04	2.67	3.40	4.30	5.31
18″	.251	.445	.695	1.00	1.32	1.78	2.27	2.86	3.54
24″	.188	.334	.522	.751	1.02	1.34	1.70	2.15	2.66
30″	.150	.267	.417	.600	.817	1.07	1.36	1.72	2.13
36″	.125	.223	.348	.501	.681	.890	1.13	1.43	1.77
42″	.107	.191	.298	.429	.584	.753	.97	1.17	1.52
48″	.094	.167	.261	.376	.511	.668	.85	1.08	1.33

R03210-050 Minimum Wall Reinforcement Weight (PSF)

This table lists the approximate minimum wall reinforcement weights
per S.F. according to the specification of .12% of gross area for
vertical bars and .20% of gross area for horizontal bars.

Location	Wall Thickness	Bar Size	Horizontal Steel Spacing C/C	Sq. In. Req'd per S.F.	Total Wt. per S.F.	Bar Size	Vertical Steel Spacing C/C	Sq. In. Req'd per S.F.	Total Wt. per S.F.	Horizontal & Vertical Steel Total Weight per S.F.
Both Faces	10"	#4	18"	.24	.89#	#3	18"	.14	.50#	1.39#
	12"	#4	16"	.29	1.00	#3	16"	.17	.60	1.60
	14"	#4	14"	.34	1.14	#3	13"	.20	.69	1.84
	16"	#4	12"	.38	1.34	#3	11"	.23	.82	2.16
	18"	#5	17"	.43	1.47	#4	18"	.26	.89	2.36
One Face	6"	#3	9"	.15	.50	#3	18"	.09	.25	.75
	8"	#4	12"	.19	.67	#3	11"	.12	.41	1.08
	10"	#5	15"	.24	.83	#4	16"	.14	.50	1.34

R03210-060 Reinforcing Extras

There are two "base prices" used, the price for bars shipped directly from
the mill and the base price for the bars shipped from the steel fabricator's
shops. The extras for both methods of pricing are listed below and are listed
in dollars per ton for A615 steel.

Extras	Item	From Mill	From Fabricator	Extras	Item	From Mill	From Fabricator
Base Price		**$305**	**$500**				$500 minimum
Size Extras	#3	$100	$102	Quantity Extras	Under 20 tons	$12	$30
	#4	40	50		20-49 tons	—	20
	#5	30	35		50-99 tons	—	15
	#6	25	25		100-300 tons	—	10
	#7 to 11	20	20		Over 300 tons	—	—
	#14	40	40	Bending	Light #2 thru #11	N/A	85
	#18	40	40		Heavy #4 up		44
Grade Extras	Grade 40	—	—	Detailing	Under 50 tons		46
	Grade 60	—	—		50-100 tons		35
	Grade 75	N/A	N/A		150-500 tons		31
					Over 500 tons		21

"Listing only" runs $4 to $5 per ton.

R03210-070 Bend, Place and Tie Reinforcing

See R3210-060 for shop bending costs. Field bending costs are usually higher.

Placing and tying by rodmen for footings and slabs runs from nine hrs.
per ton for heavy bars to fifteen hrs. per ton for light bars. For beams,
columns, and walls, production runs from eight hrs. per ton for heavy bars to
twenty hrs. per ton for light bars. Overall average for typical reinforced
concrete buildings is about fourteen hrs. per ton. These production figures
include placing of accessories and usual inserts. Equipment handling is
necessary for the larger size bars so that installation costs for the very heavy
bars will not decrease proportionately.

For tie wire, figure 5 lbs. 16 ga. black annealed wire at $.85 per lb. for each
ton of bars. Use of commercial accessories improves placing accuracy and
costs of $60 per ton of bars is offset by reduced labor time.

Installation costs for splicing reinforcing bars includes allowance for
equipment to hold the bars in place while splicing as well as necessary
scaffolding for iron workers.

CONCRETE

REFERENCE NOS.

R03210-080 Reinforcing Key Prices

Costs given below are for over 50 tons delivered and bent from fabricators in metropolitan area. Over 500 tons, subtract $11 per ton. Figures are for domestic A615, grade 60. Economic conditions can alter the prices substantially.

City	Bare Costs Per Ton					Costs Incl. Subs O & P		
	Material		Installation		Total per Ton	Material	Installation	Total
	50 Tons Fabricated	Allow for Accessories	Unload, Sort and Pile	Place & Tie	in Place	Incl. 10% Mark-Up	Include Mark-up	per Ton
Atlanta	525	$60	$19	$478	$1,082	$644	$ 590	$1,234
Baltimore	510	60	22	552	1,144	627	717	1,344
Boston	530	60	27	668	1,285	649	910	1,559
Buffalo	500	60	25	623	1,208	616	832	1,448
Chicago	490	60	29	718	1,297	605	995	1,600
Cincinnati	420	60	22	559	1,062	528	726	1,254
Cleveland	510	60	24	606	1,200	627	806	1,433
Columbus	490	60	22	561	1,134	605	729	1,334
Dallas	475	60	17	419	971	589	488	1,077
Denver	500	60	18	457	1,035	616	552	1,168
Detroit	450	60	25	631	1,166	561	847	1,408
Houston	480	60	17	423	980	594	495	1,089
Indianapolis	490	60	22	549	1,121	605	710	1,315
Kansas City	500	60	23	567	1,150	616	741	1,357
Los Angeles	520	60	27	678	1,285	638	926	1,564
Memphis	470	60	18	439	986	583	523	1,106
Milwaukee	490	60	24	606	1,180	605	804	1,409
Minneapolis	525	60	25	626	1,236	644	840	1,484
Nashville	490	60	18	443	1,011	605	529	1,134
New Orleans	475	60	16	409	961	589	474	1,063
New York	530	60	38	954	1,582	649	1,394	2,043
Philadelphia	500	60	27	670	1,256	616	914	1,530
Phoenix	480	60	20	499	1,059	594	626	1,220
Pittsburgh	470	60	24	609	1,163	583	810	1,393
St. Louis	590	60	24	612	1,287	715	815	1,530
San Antonio	465	60	16	410	951	578	472	1,050
San Diego	580	60	27	678	1,345	704	926	1,630
San Francisco	570	60	27	678	1,335	693	925	1,618
Seattle	460	60	24	607	1,151	572	805	1,377
Washington, D.C.	445	60	20	505	1,031	556	637	1,193
Average per ton	500	$60	$23	$580	$1,158	$614	$ 752	$1,363

Note: For field fabrication, add $75 to $100 per ton to shop fabrication costs.

Place and tie costs do not include crane charge.

Bare Material Costs		Total Installed Costs		
Item	Cost per Ton	Description	Bare Costs	Cost Incl. Subs O&P
Base price at mill	$320	Unload, sort & pile, C-5 crew	$ 23	$ 36
Size and length extras	30	Place & tie, 14 hours at $43.05 per hour	580	716
Freight from mill	26			
Warehouse handling & storage	22	Total Installation Cost	$ 603	$ 752
Shearing and shop bending	44			
Drafting, detailing and listing	34	Bare Material Cost	$ 560	
Trucking to job site	24	Material Cost + 10%		$ 616
		Total Installed Cost	$1,163	$1,368
Reinforcing Delivered	$500			
Accessories Delivered	60			
Total Material Delivered	$560			

Engineering or design fees are not included above.

Material and erection costs can be considerably higher than those above for small jobs consisting primarily of smaller bars.

Restrictive union practices can increase field labor costs above those listed above.

R03220-030 Common Stock Styles of Welded Wire Fabric

This table provides some of the basic specifications, sizes, and weights of welded wire fabric used for reinforcing concrete.

	New Designation	Old Designation		Steel Area per Foot				Approximate Weight	
	Spacing — Cross Sectional Area (in.) — (Sq. in. 100)	Spacing — Wire Gauge (in.) — (AS & W)		Longitudinal		Transverse		per 100 S.F.	
				in.	cm	in.	cm	lbs	kg
Rolls	6 x 6 — W1.4 x W1.4	6 x 6 — 10 x 10		.028	.071	.028	.071	21	9.53
	6 x 6 — W2.0 x W2.0	6 x 6 — 8 x 8	1	.040	.102	.040	.102	29	13.15
	6 x 6 — W2.9 x W2.9	6 x 6 — 6 x 6		.058	.147	.058	.147	42	19.05
	6 x 6 — W4.0 x W4.0	6 x 6 — 4 x 4		.080	.203	.080	.203	58	26.91
	4 x 4 — W1.4 x W1.4	4 x 4 — 10 x 10		.042	.107	.042	.107	31	14.06
	4 x 4 — W2.0 x W2.0	4 x 4 — 8 x 8	1	.060	.152	.060	.152	43	19.50
	4 x 4 — W2.9 x W2.9	4 x 4 — 6 x 6		.087	.227	.087	.227	62	28.12
	4 x 4 — W4.0 x W4.0	4 x 4 — 4 x 4		.120	.305	.120	.305	85	38.56
Sheets	6 x 6 — W2.9 x W2.9	6 x 6 — 6 x 6		.058	.147	.058	.147	42	19.05
	6 x 6 — W4.0 x W4.0	6 x 6 — 4 x 4		.080	.203	.080	.203	58	26.31
	6 x 6 — W5.5 x W5.5	6 x 6 — 2 x 2	2	.110	.279	.110	.279	80	36.29
	4 x 4 — W1.4 x W1.4	4 x 4 — 4 x 4		.120	.305	.120	.305	85	38.56

NOTES: 1. Exact W—number size for 8 gauge is W2.1
2. Exact W—number size for 2 gauge is W5.4

CONCRETE 3

REFERENCE NOS.

R03310-010   Proportionate Quantities

The tables below show both quantities per S.F. of floor areas as well as form and reinforcing quantities per C.Y. Unusual structural requirements would increase the ratios below. High strength reinforcing would reduce the steel weights. Figures are for 3000 psi concrete and 60,000 psi reinforcing unless specified otherwise.

Type of Construction	Live Load	Span	Per S.F. of Floor Area				Per C.Y. of Concrete		
			Concrete	Forms	Reinf.	Pans	Forms	Reinf.	Pans
Flat Plate	50 psf	15 Ft.	.46 C.F.	1.06 S.F.	1.71 lb.		62 S.F.	101 lb.	
		20	.63	1.02	2.40		44	104	
		25	.79	1.02	3.03		35	104	
	100	15	.46	1.04	2.14		61	126	
		20	.71	1.02	2.72		39	104	
		25	.83	1.01	3.47		33	113	
Flat Plate (waffle construction) 20″ domes	50	20	.43	1.00	2.10	.84 S.F.	63	135	53 S.F.
		25	.52	1.00	2.90	.89	52	150	46
		30	.64	1.00	3.70	.87	42	155	37
	100	20	.51	1.00	2.30	.84	53	125	45
		25	.64	1.00	3.20	.83	42	135	35
		30	.76	1.00	4.40	.81	36	160	29
Waffle Construction 30″ domes	50	25	.69	1.06	1.83	.68	42	72	40
		30	.74	1.06	2.39	.69	39	87	39
		35	.86	1.05	2.71	.69	33	85	39
		40	.78	1.00	4.80	.68	35	165	40
Flat Slab (two way with drop panels)	50	20	.62	1.03	2.34		45	102	
		25	.77	1.03	2.99		36	105	
		30	.95	1.03	4.09		29	116	
	100	20	.64	1.03	2.83		43	119	
		25	.79	1.03	3.88		35	133	
		30	.96	1.03	4.66		29	131	
	200	20	.73	1.03	3.03		38	112	
		25	.86	1.03	4.23		32	133	
		30	1.06	1.03	5.30		26	135	
One Way Joists 20″ Pans	50	15	.36	1.04	1.40	.93	78	105	70
		20	.42	1.05	1.80	.94	67	120	60
		25	.47	1.05	2.60	.94	60	150	54
	100	15	.38	1.07	1.90	.93	77	140	66
		20	.44	1.08	2.40	.94	67	150	58
		25	.52	1.07	3.50	.94	55	185	49
One Way Joists 8″ x 16″ filler blocks	50	15	.34	1.06	1.80	.81 Ea.	84	145	64 Ea.
		20	.40	1.08	2.20	.82	73	145	55
		25	.46	1.07	3.20	.83	63	190	49
	100	15	.39	1.07	1.90	.81	74	130	56
		20	.46	1.09	2.80	.82	64	160	48
		25	.53	1.10	3.60	.83	56	190	42
One Way Beam & Slab	50	15	.42	1.30	1.73		84	111	
		20	.51	1.28	2.61		68	138	
		25	.64	1.25	2.78		53	117	
	100	15	.42	1.30	1.90		84	122	
		20	.54	1.35	2.69		68	154	
		25	.69	1.37	3.93		54	145	
	200	15	.44	1.31	2.24		80	137	
		20	.58	1.40	3.30		65	163	
		25	.69	1.42	4.89		53	183	
Two Way Beam & Slab	100	15	.47	1.20	2.26		69	130	
		20	.63	1.29	3.06		55	131	
		25	.83	1.33	3.79		43	123	
	200	15	.49	1.25	2.70		41	149	
		20	.66	1.32	4.04		54	165	
		25	.88	1.32	6.08		41	187	

R03310-010 Proportionate Quantities (cont.)

Item	Size	Forms	Reinforcing	Minimum	Maximum
	4000 psi Concrete and 60,000 psi Reinforcing—Form and Reinforcing Quantities per C.Y.				
	10" x 10"	130 S.F.C.A.	#5 to #11	220 lbs.	875 lbs.
	12" x 12"	108	#6 to #14	200	955
	14" x 14"	92	#7 to #14	190	900
	16" x 16"	81	#6 to #14	187	1082
	18" x 18"	72	#6 to #14	170	906
	20" x 20"	65	#7 to #18	150	1080
Columns	22" x 22"	59	#8 to #18	153	902
(square tied)	24" x 24"	54	#8 to #18	164	884
	26" x 26"	50	#9 to #18	169	994
	28" x 28"	46	#9 to #18	147	864
	30" x 30"	43	#10 to #18	146	983
	32" x 32"	40	#10 to #18	175	866
	34" x 34"	38	#10 to #18	157	772
	36" x 36"	36	#10 to #18	175	852
	38" x 38"	34	#10 to #18	158	765
	40" x 40"	32	#10 to #18	143	692

Item	Size	Form	Spiral	Reinforcing	Minimum	Maximum
	12" diameter	34.5 L.F.	190 lbs.	#4 to #11	165 lbs.	1505 lb.
		34.5	190	#14 & #18	—	1100
	14"	25	170	#4 to #11	150	970
		25	170	#14 & #18	800	1000
	16"	19	160	#4 to #11	160	950
		19	160	#14 & #18	605	1080
	18"	15	150	#4 to #11	160	915
		15	150	#14 & #18	480	1075
	20"	12	130	#4 to #11	155	865
		12	130	#14 & #18	385	1020
	22"	10	125	#4 to #11	165	775
		10	125	#14 & #18	320	995
	24"	9	120	#4 to #11	195	800
		9	120	#14 & #18	290	1150
Columns	26"	7.3	100	#4 to #11	200	729
(spirally reinforced)		7.3	100	#14 & #18	235	1035
	28"	6.3	95	#4 to #11	175	700
		6.3	95	#14 & #18	200	1075
	30"	5.5	90	#4 to #11	180	670
		5.5	90	#14 & #18	175	1015
	32"	4.8	85	#4 to #11	185	615
		4.8	85	#14 & #18	155	955
	34"	4.3	80	#4 to #11	180	600
		4.3	80	#14 & #18	170	855
	36"	3.8	75	#4 to #11	165	570
		3.8	75	#14 & #18	155	865
	40"	3.0	70	#4 to #11	165	500
		3.0	70	#14 & #18	145	765

CONCRETE

REFERENCE NOS.

R03310-010 Proportionate Quantities (cont.)

Item	Type	Loading	Height	C.Y./L.F.	Forms/C.Y.	Reinf./C.Y.
Retaining Walls	Cantilever	Level Backfill	4 Ft.	0.2 C.Y.	49 S.F.	35 lbs.
			8	0.5	42	45
			12	0.8	35	70
			16	1.1	32	85
			20	1.6	28	105
		Highway Surcharge	4	0.3	41	35
			8	0.5	36	55
			12	0.8	33	90
			16	1.2	30	120
			20	1.7	27	155
		Railroad Surcharge	4	0.4	28	45
			8	0.8	25	65
			12	1.3	22	90
			16	1.9	20	100
			20	2.6	18	120
	Gravity, with Vertical Face	Level Backfill	4	0.4	37	None
			7	0.6	27	
			10	1.2	20	
		Sloping Backfill	4	0.3	31	
			7	0.8	21	
			10	1.6	15	↓

Live Load in Kips per Linear Foot

	Span	Under 1 Kip		2 to 3 Kips		4 to 5 Kips		6 to 7 Kips	
		Forms	Reinf.	Forms	Reinf.	Forms	Reinf.	Forms	Reinf.
Beams	10 Ft.	—	—	90 S.F.	170 #	85 S.F.	175 #	75 S.F.	185 #
	16	130 S.F.	165 #	85	180	75	180	65	225
	20	110	170	75	185	62	200	51	200
	26	90	170	65	215	62	215	—	—
	30	85	175	60	200	—	—	—	—

Item	Size	Type	Forms per C.Y.	Reinforcing per C.Y.
Spread Footings	Under 1 C.Y.	1,000 psf soil	24 S.F.	44 lbs.
		5,000	24	42
		10,000	24	52
	1 C.Y. to 5 C.Y.	1,000	14	49
		5,000	14	50
		10,000	14	50
	Over 5 C.Y.	1,000	9	54
		5,000	9	52
		10,000	9	56
Pile Caps (30 Ton Concrete Piles)	Under 5 C.Y.	shallow caps	20	65
		medium	20	50
		deep	20	40
	5 C.Y. to 10 C.Y.	shallow	14	55
		medium	15	45
		deep	15	40
	10 C.Y. to 20 C.Y.	shallow	11	60
		medium	11	45
		deep	12	35
	Over 20 C.Y.	shallow	9	60
		medium	9	45
		deep	10	40

R03310-010 Proportionate Quantities (cont.)

Item	Pile Spacing			50 T Pile	100 T Pile	50 T Pile	100 T Pile	
Pile Caps (Steel H Piles)	Under 5 C.Y.	24" O.C.		24 S.F.	24 S.F.	75 lbs.	90 lbs.	
		30"		25	25	80	100	
		36"		24	24	80	110	
	5 C.Y. to 10 C.Y.	24"		15	15	80	110	
		30"		15	15	85	110	
		36"		15	15	75	90	
	Over 10 C.Y.	24"		13	13	85	90	
		30"		11	11	85	95	
		36"		10	10	85	90	

3000 psi Concrete and 60,000 psi Reinforcing — Form and Reinforcing Quantities per C.Y.

	Height	8" Thick		10" Thick		12" Thick		15" Thick	
		Forms	Reinf.	Forms	Reinf.	Forms	Reinf.	Forms	Reinf.
Basement Walls	7 Ft.	81 S.F.	44 lbs.	65 S.F.	45 lbs.	54 S.F.	44 lbs.	41 S.F.	43 lbs.
	8		44		45		44		43
	9		46		45		44		43
	10		57		45		44		43
	12		83		50		52		43
	14		116		65		64		51
	16				86		90		65
	18						106		70

R03310-020 Materials for One C.Y. of Concrete

This is an approximate method of figuring quantities of cement, sand and coarse aggregate for a field mix with waste allowance included.

With crushed gravel as coarse aggregate, to determine barrels of cement required, divide 10 by total mix; that is, for 1:2:4 mix, 10 divided by 7 = 1-3/7 barrels. If the coarse aggregate is crushed stone, use 10-1/2 instead of 10 as given for gravel.

To determine tons of sand required, multiply barrels of cement by parts of sand and then by 0.2; that is, for the 1:2:4 mix, as above, 1-3/7 x 2 x .2 = .57 tons.

Tons of crushed gravel are in the same ratio to tons of sand as parts in the mix, or 4/2 x .57 = 1.14 tons.

1 bag cement = 94#	1 C.Y. sand or crushed gravel = 2700#	1 C.Y. crushed stone = 2575#
4 bags = 1 barrel	1 ton sand or crushed gravel = 20 C.F.	1 ton crushed stone = 21 C.F.

Average carload of cement is 692 bags; of sand or gravel is 56 tons.

Do not stack stored cement over 10 bags high.

R03310-030 Metric Equivalents of Cement Content for Concrete Mixes

94 Pound Bags per Cubic Yard	Kilograms per Cubic Meter	94 Pound Bags per Cubic Yard	Kilograms per Cubic Meter
1.0	55.77	7.0	390.4
1.5	83.65	7.5	418.3
2.0	111.5	8.0	446.2
2.5	139.4	8.5	474.0
3.0	167.3	9.0	501.9
3.5	195.2	9.5	529.8
4.0	223.1	10.0	557.7
4.5	251.0	10.5	585.6
5.0	278.8	11.0	613.5
5.5	306.7	11.5	641.3
6.0	334.6	12.0	669.2
6.5	362.5	12.5	697.1

a. If you know the cement content in pounds per cubic yard, multiply by .5933 to obtain kilograms per cubic meter.

b. If you know the cement content in 94 pound bags per cubic yard, multiply by 55.77 to obtain kilograms per cubic meter.

CONCRETE 3

REFERENCE NOS.

R03310-040 Metric Equivalents of Common Concrete Strengths
(to convert other psi values to megapascals, multiply by 0.006895)

U.S. Values psi	SI Value Megapascals	Non-SI Metric Value kgf/cm²*
2000	14	140
2500	17	175
3000	21	210
3500	24	245
4000	28	280
4500	31	315
5000	34	350
6000	41	420
7000	48	490
8000	55	560
9000	62	630
10,000	69	705

* kilograms force per square centimeter

R03310-050 Quantities of Cement, Sand and Stone for One C.Y. of Concrete per Various Mixes

This table can be used to determine the quantities of the ingredients for smaller quantities of site mixed concrete.

Concrete (C.Y.)	Mix = 1:1:1-3/4			Mix = 1:2:2.25			Mix = 1:2.25:3			Mix = 1:3:4		
	Cement (sacks)	Sand (C.Y.)	Stone (C.Y.)	Cement (sacks)	Sand (C.Y.)	Stone (C.Y.)	Cement (sacks)	Sand (C.Y.)	Stone (C.Y.)	Cement (sacks)	Sand (C.Y.)	Stone (C.Y.)
1	10	.37	.63	7.75	.56	.65	6.25	.52	.70	5	.56	.74
2	20	.74	1.26	15.50	1.12	1.30	12.50	1.04	1.40	10	1.12	1.48
3	30	1.11	1.89	23.25	1.68	1.95	18.75	1.56	2.10	15	1.68	2.22
4	40	1.48	2.52	31.00	2.24	2.60	25.00	2.08	2.80	20	2.24	2.96
5	50	1.85	3.15	38.75	2.80	3.25	31.25	2.60	3.50	25	2.80	3.70
6	60	2.22	3.78	46.50	3.36	3.90	37.50	3.12	4.20	30	3.36	4.44
7	70	2.59	4.41	54.25	3.92	4.55	43.75	3.64	4.90	35	3.92	5.18
8	80	2.96	5.04	62.00	4.48	5.20	50.00	4.16	5.60	40	4.48	5.92
9	90	3.33	5.67	69.75	5.04	5.85	56.25	4.68	6.30	45	5.04	6.66
10	100	3.70	6.30	77.50	5.60	6.50	62.50	5.20	7.00	50	5.60	7.40
11	110	4.07	6.93	85.25	6.16	7.15	68.75	5.72	7.70	55	6.16	8.14
12	120	4.44	7.56	93.00	6.72	7.80	75.00	6.24	8.40	60	6.72	8.88
13	130	4.82	8.20	100.76	7.28	8.46	81.26	6.76	9.10	65	7.28	9.62
14	140	5.18	8.82	108.50	7.84	9.10	87.50	7.28	9.80	70	7.84	10.36
15	150	5.56	9.46	116.26	8.40	9.76	93.76	7.80	10.50	75	8.40	11.10
16	160	5.92	10.08	124.00	8.96	10.40	100.00	8.32	11.20	80	8.96	11.84
17	170	6.30	10.72	131.76	9.52	11.06	106.26	8.84	11.90	85	9.52	12.58
18	180	6.66	11.34	139.50	10.08	11.70	112.50	9.36	12.60	90	10.08	13.32
19	190	7.04	11.98	147.26	10.64	12.36	118.76	9.84	13.30	95	10.64	14.06
20	200	7.40	12.60	155.00	11.20	13.00	125.00	10.40	14.00	100	11.20	14.80
21	210	7.77	13.23	162.75	11.76	13.65	131.25	10.92	14.70	105	11.76	15.54
22	220	8.14	13.86	170.05	12.32	14.30	137.50	11.44	15.40	110	12.32	16.28
23	230	8.51	14.49	178.25	12.88	14.95	143.75	11.96	16.10	115	12.88	17.02
24	240	8.88	15.12	186.00	13.44	15.60	150.00	12.48	16.80	120	13.44	17.76
25	250	9.25	15.75	193.75	14.00	16.25	156.25	13.00	17.50	125	14.00	18.50
26	260	9.64	16.40	201.52	14.56	16.92	162.52	13.52	18.20	130	14.56	19.24
27	270	10.00	17.00	209.26	15.12	17.56	168.76	14.04	18.90	135	15.02	20.00
28	280	10.36	17.64	217.00	15.68	18.20	175.00	14.56	19.60	140	15.68	20.72
29	290	10.74	18.28	224.76	16.24	18.86	181.26	15.08	20.30	145	16.24	21.46

R03310-060 Concrete Material Net Prices

Costs below are C.Y. of concrete delivered; per ton of bulk cement; per bag cement delivered T.L.L.; per ton for stone and sand aggregates loaded at plant (no trucking included) and per 4 C.F. bag for perlite or vermiculite aggregate delivered T.L.L.

City	Ready Mix Concrete Regular Weight		Cement T.L. Lots		Aggregates per Ton Crushed Stone			Vermiculite or Perlite
	3000 psi	5000 psi	Bulk per Ton	Bags per Bag	1-1/2"	3/4"	Sand	4 C.F. Bag
Atlanta	$62.00	$67.00	$74.90	$6.40	$14.70	$15.00	$12.55	$10.35
Baltimore	64.00	69.00	79.00	6.75	14.70	15.00	16.65	8.85
Boston	70.00	75.00	90.70	7.75	11.20	11.50	11.15	9.75
Buffalo	82.00	87.00	90.10	7.70	14.45	14.75	14.00	10.10
Chicago	83.00	88.00	87.75	7.50	12.95	13.25	15.50	8.70
Cincinnati	55.00	60.00	79.00	6.75	8.95	9.25	7.70	10.15
Cleveland	67.00	72.00	88.35	7.55	13.70	14.00	13.60	9.95
Columbus	58.00	63.00	87.15	7.45	9.20	9.50	8.50	10.10
Dallas	64.00	69.00	77.80	6.65	27.70	28.00	19.50	9.80
Denver	64.00	69.00	94.75	8.10	8.05	8.35	21.00	10.20
Detroit	70.00	75.00	86.60	7.40	9.20	9.50	6.75	10.00
Houston	59.00	64.00	85.40	7.30	20.70	21.00	15.50	8.95
Indianapolis	62.00	67.00	81.30	6.95	10.70	11.00	7.00	9.95
Kansas City	62.00	67.00	74.90	6.40	10.95	11.25	8.30	10.20
Los Angeles	59.00	64.00	93.60	8.00	17.20	17.50	9.25	10.40
Memphis	59.00	64.00	79.00	6.75	12.20	12.50	12.00	9.60
Milwaukee	58.00	63.00	87.75	7.50	10.70	11.00	14.25	9.40
Minneapolis	70.00	75.00	86.00	7.35	13.45	13.75	8.00	9.55
Nashville	58.00	63.00	76.05	6.50	9.95	10.25	17.25	9.10
New Orleans	61.00	66.00	79.55	6.80	17.70	18.00	16.50	9.80
New York City	82.00	87.00	90.70	7.75	20.70	21.00	14.50	10.35
Philadelphia	63.00	68.00	86.60	7.40	12.70	13.00	16.25	9.15
Phoenix	62.00	67.00	84.85	7.25	9.20	9.50	11.50	9.70
Pittsburgh	64.00	69.00	81.90	7.00	14.70	15.00	15.35	9.55
St. Louis	51.00	56.00	77.80	6.65	10.95	11.25	10.75	9.80
San Antonio	53.00	58.00	76.05	6.50	10.45	10.75	8.00	8.90
San Diego	70.00	75.00	87.75	7.50	17.20	17.50	21.75	8.95
San Francisco	85.00	90.00	89.50	7.65	19.70	20.00	20.75	9.55
Seattle	61.00	66.00	83.65	7.15	13.20	13.50	13.50	9.95
Washington, D.C.	76.00	81.00	82.50	7.05	16.95	17.25	13.25	10.20
Average	$65.00	$70.00	$84.25	$7.20	$13.80	$14.10	$13.35	$ 9.70

R03310-070 Ready Mix Material Prices

Table below lists national average prices per C.Y. of concrete. Prices in the key cities for different strengths can be closely estimated by factoring against the 3000 psi or 5000 psi price from R03310-060 above or from the City Cost Indexes, cast-in-place concrete material factor.

Strength in psi	Design Mix Nominal Mix	Bags per C.Y.	Heavy Weight Regular	Heavy Weight High Early	Light Weight 110# per C.F.	Light Weight All Light Weight	Admixtures and Special Items Add to Each C.Y. of Concrete for the Following Items:		
2,000	1:3:5	4.5	$61.75	$67.85	$77.20	$ 92.65	Calcium chloride, 1%	$1.75	per C.Y.
2,500	1:2-1/2:4-1/2	5	63.05	69.80	78.80	94.60	" 2%	3.00	per C.Y.
3,000	1:2:4	5.5	65.00	72.45	81.25	97.50	Water reducing agent	.26	per bag
3,500	1:2:3-1/2	6	66.65	74.75	83.30	100.00	Set retarder	.65	per bag
3,750	1:2:3-1/4	6.3	67.60	76.10	84.50	101.40	High early cement	1.35	per bag
4,000	1:2:3	6.5	68.25	77.05	85.30	102.40	White cement	9.70	per bag
4,500	1:2:2-1/2	7	70.20	79.65	87.75	105.30	Pump aid	2.15	per C.Y.
5,000	1:1-1/2:2-1/2	7.5	70.00	80.15	87.50	105.00	Winter concrete	4.75	per C.Y.
	1:1:2	8	74.90	82.40	—	Perlite	Synthetic Fiber Reinforcing	8.50	per C.Y.
	1:4 topping	7.5	71.15	78.25	—	1:6=			
	1:3 topping	8.5	76.40	84.05	—	$ 94.95			
	1:2 topping	11	83.15	91.45	—				

R03310-080   Field Mix Concrete

Presently most building jobs are built with ready mix concrete except for isolated locations and some larger jobs requiring over 10,000 C.Y. where land is readily available for setting up a temporary batch plant.

The most economical mix is a controlled mix using local aggregate proportioned by trial to give the required strength with the least cost of material.

Costs tabulated below are based on a job that requires 10,000 C.Y. of concrete to be placed within an eight month period.

28 Day Strength	3000 psi		2250 psi	
Mix Proportions	**1:2-½:3**		**1:2-¾:4**	
Cement, trucked in bulk @ $4.10 per Cwt.	6-1/4 bags @ 94 lb./bag	$24.75	5 bags @ 94 lb./bag	$19.80
Sand @ $9.45 per ton	.68 tons	9.08	.7 tons	9.35
Stone @ $14.25 per ton, maximum size aggregate 3/4″	.9 tons	12.69	1.02 tons	14.38
Set up plant, foundations, piping, etc.		2.06		2.06
Plant, trucks and equipment rental		7.24		7.24
Labor to mix and transport to forms		13.16		13.16
Supervision		2.86		2.86
Cost per C.Y. FOB Forms		$71.84		$68.83

See R03310-060 for material prices in the major cities.

R03310-090   Placing Ready Mixed Concrete

For ground pours allow for 5% waste when figuring quantities.

Prices in the front of the book assume normal deliveries. If deliveries are made before 8 A.M. or after 5 P.M. or on Saturday afternoons add $25 per C.Y. Large volume discounts are not included in prices in front of book.

For the lower floors without truck access, concrete may be wheeled in rubber tired buggies, conveyer handled, crane handled or pumped. Pumping is economical if there is top steel. Conveyers are more efficient for thick slabs. Concrete pump with an operator can be rented from $650 per day for up to 25 C.Y. to $1,600 per day for a 400 C.Y. pour. Figures include travel time if done at straight time. Pumping lightweight concrete costs an extra $2.50 per C.Y.

At higher floors the rubber tired buggies may be hoisted by a hoisting tower then wheeled to location. Placement by a conveyer is limited to three floors and is best for high volume pours. Pumped concrete is best when building has no crane access. Concrete may be pumped directly as high as thirty-six stories using special pumping techniques. Normal maximum height is about fifteen stories.

Best pumping aggregate is screened and graded bank gravel rather than crushed stone.

Pumping downward is more difficult than pumping upwards. Horizontal distance from pump to pour may increase preparation time prior to pour. Placing by cranes, either mobile, climbing or tower types continues as the most efficient method for high rise concrete buildings.

	Cost per C.Y. for Wheeled Concrete, Dumped Only (Add to appropriate placing cost)							
	10 C.F. Walking Cart				18 C.F. Riding Cart			
Item	Hourly Cost	Wheeled up to 50 ft.	Wheeled up to 150 ft.	Wheeled up to 250 ft.	Hourly Cost	Wheeled up to 50 ft.	Wheeled up to 150 ft.	Wheeled up to 250 ft.
Laborer	$22.85	$5.71	$ 7.63	$10.17	$22.85	$2.29	$2.97	$3.88
.125 Labor foreman	3.11	.78	1.04	1.38	3.11	.31	.40	.53
Concrete cart	6.50	1.63	2.17	2.89	10.40	1.04	1.35	1.77
Total Cost/C.Y.		$8.12	$10.84	$14.44		$3.64	$4.72	$6.18
Hourly production		4 C.Y.				10 C.Y.		

R03310-100   Average C.Y. of Concrete

Rubbing and floor finish not included — 4 uses of forms assumed, 5 story building.

Item	Description	Strength in psi	Ready Mix	Place	Forms	Reinforcing	Total
Beams	10' span	4000	$70.00	$55.88	$300.84	$106.75	$533.47
5 kip/L.F.	25'		70.00	37.25	274.68	131.15	513.08
Beam & Slab, 1 way	15'	4000	70.00	17.19	392.28	56.12	535.59
125 psf Sup. L.	25'		70.00	14.90	252.18	70.84	407.92
Beam & Slab, 2 way	15'	4000	70.00	17.19	328.44	59.80	475.43
125 psf Sup. L.	25'		70.00	14.90	204.68	56.58	346.16
Columns,	16" x 16"	4000	70.00	37.25	370.98	329.68	807.91
square tied	24" x 24"		70.00	24.30	246.78	272.48	613.56
Columns, Tied	16" diameter	4000	70.00	37.25	227.05	315.12	649.42
reinforced	24" diameter		70.00	24.30	153.36	312.00	559.66
Flat Plate,	15' span	4000	70.00	20.32	197.64	57.96	345.92
125 psf Sup. L.	25'		70.00	17.19	106.92	51.98	246.09
Flat Slab with drops,	20'	4000	70.00	20.32	150.07	54.74	295.13
125 psf Sup. L.	30'		70.00	17.19	101.21	60.26	248.66
Grade Wall,	8" thick	3000	65.00	13.66	297.27	19.80	395.73
8' high	15" thick		65.00	11.71	150.47	19.35	246.53
Metal Pan Joists,	15' span	4000	70.00	17.19	265.14	21.15	373.48
125 psf Sup. L.	25' span		70.00	14.90	218.55	36.45	339.90
Pile Caps	under 5 C.Y.	3000	65.00	13.66	60.20	22.36	161.22
"	over 10 C.Y.		65.00	5.72	30.10	20.64	121.46
Slab	4" thick	3500	68.25	11.18	16.37	15.39	111.19
on Grade	6" thick		68.25	7.45	10.68	10.26	96.64
Spread	under 1 C.Y.	3000	65.00	22.36	65.04	24.38	176.78
Footings	over 5 C.Y.		65.00	11.18	24.39	28.62	129.19
Strip	9" x 18" plain	3000	65.00	11.18	81.36	—	157.54
Footings	12" x 36" reinforced		65.00	7.93	40.68	21.20	134.81
Waffle 30" Domes	20' span	4000	70.00	17.19	221.52	64.20	372.91
125 psf Sup. L.	30' span		70.00	14.90	176.08	61.20	322.18

*Placement by direct chute assumed. All others, placement by pump assumed.

When form and reinforcing quantity ratios are available compute the C.Y. costs directly from the unit prices in the front of the book. See also R03310-010 for relative quantities per C.Y. for additional items. Higher strength concrete would change the ratios below. The tables below show typical examples of how the total costs per C.Y. have been derived. Ready mix concrete prices are U.S. average and equipment handling is assumed.

Beams 5 kip/L.F.	10' Span				25' Span			
	Material		Installation		Material		Installation	
4000 psi concrete	1 C.Y.	$ 70.00	1 C.Y.	$ 55.88	1 C.Y.	$ 70.00	1 C.Y.	$ 37.25
Formwork, 4 uses	69 S.F. @ .96	66.24	69 S.F. @ 3.40	234.60	63 S.F. @ .96	60.48	63 S.F.@ 3.40	214.20
Reinforcing steel	175 # @ .28	49.00	175 # @ .33	57.75	215 # @ .28	60.20	215 # @ .33	70.95
Total per C.Y.		$185.24		$348.23		$190.68		$322.40

Beam & Slab, One Way	125 psf, 15' Span				125 psf, 25' Span			
	Material		Installation		Material		Installation	
4000 psi concrete	1 C.Y.	$ 70.00	1 C.Y.	$ 17.19	1 C.Y.	$ 70.00	1 C.Y.	$ 14.90
Formwork, 4 uses	84 S.F. @ 1.01	84.84	84 S.F. @ 3.66	307.44	54 S.F. @ 1.01	54.54	54 S.F. @ 3.66	197.64
Reinforcing steel	122 # @ .28	34.16	122 # @ .18	21.96	154 # @ .28	43.12	154 # @ .18	27.72
Total per C.Y.		$189.00		$346.59		$167.66		$240.26

Beam & Slab, Two Way	125 psf, 15' Span				125 psf, 25' Span			
	Material		Installation		Material		Installation	
4000 psi concrete	1 C.Y.	$ 70.00	1 C.Y.	$ 17.19	1 C.Y.	$ 70.00	1 C.Y.	$ 14.90
Formwork, 4 uses	69 S.F. @ .92	63.48	69 S.F. @ 3.84	264.96	43 S.F. @ .92	39.56	43 S.F. @ 3.84	165.12
Reinforcing steel	130 # @ .28	36.40	130 # @ .18	23.40	123 # @ .28	34.44	123 # @ .18	22.14
Total per C.Y.		$169.88		$305.55		$144.00		$202.16

R03310-100 Average C.Y. of Concrete (cont.)

Columns, Square Tied	16" Square				24" Square			
	Material		Installation		Material		Installation	
4000 psi concrete	1 C.Y.		$ 70.00	1 C.Y.		$ 37.25	1 C.Y.		$ 70.00
Formwork, 4 uses	81 S.F. @ .83	67.23	81 S.F. @ 3.75	303.75	54 S.F. @ .83	44.82	54 S.F. @ 3.74	201.96
Reinforcing steel, avg.	634 # @ .28	177.52	634 # @ .24	152.16	524 # @ .28	146.72	524 # @ .24	125.76
Total per C.Y.		$314.75		$493.16		$261.54		$352.02

Note: Reinforcing of 16" and 24" square columns can vary from 144 lb. to 972 lb. per C.Y.

Columns, Round Tied Reinforced	16" Diameter				24" Diameter			
	Material		Installation		Material		Installation	
4000 psi concrete	1 C.Y.	$ 70.00	1 C.Y.	$ 37.25	1 C.Y.	$ 70.00	1 C.Y.	$ 24.30
Formwork, fiber forms	19 L.F. @ 5.65	107.35	19 L.F. @ 6.30	119.70	9 L.F. @ 10.25	92.25	9 L.F. @ 6.79	61.11
Reinforcing steel, avg.	606 # @ .28	169.68	606 # @ .24	145.44	600 # @ .28	168.00	600 # @ .24	144.00
Ties	70 # @ .56	39.20	70 # @ .35	24.50	18 # @ .56	10.08	18 # @ .35	6.30
Total per C.Y.		$386.23		$326.89		$340.33		$235.71

Note: Reinforcing of 16" and 24" diameter columns vary from 160 lb. to 1150 lb. per C.Y.

Flat Plate	125 psf, 15' Span				125 psf, 25' Span			
	Material		Installation		Material		Installation	
4000 psi concrete	1 C.Y.	$ 70.00	1 C.Y.	$ 20.32	1 C.Y.	$ 70.00	1 C.Y.	$ 17.19
Formwork, 4 uses	61 S.F. @ .80	48.80	61 S.F. @ 2.44	148.84	33 S.F. @ .80	26.40	33 S.F. @ 2.44	80.52
Reinforcing steel	126 # @ .28	35.28	126 # @ .18	22.68	113 # @ .28	31.64	113 # @ .18	20.34
Total per C.Y.		$154.08		$191.84		$128.04		$118.05

Flat Slab with drops	125 psf, 20' Span				125 psf, 30' Span			
	Material		Installation		Material		Installation	
4000 psi concrete	1 C.Y.	$ 70.00	1 C.Y.	$ 20.32	1 C.Y.	$ 70.00	1 C.Y.	$ 17.19
Formwork, 4 uses	43 S.F. @ .98	42.14	43 S.F. @ 2.51	107.93	29 S.F. @ .98	28.42	29 S.F. @ 2.51	72.79
Reinforcing steel	119 # @ .28	33.32	119 # @ .18	21.42	131 # @ .28	36.68	131 # @ .18	23.58
Total per C.Y.		$145.46		$149.67		$135.10		$113.56

Grade Wall, 8' High	8" Thick				15" Thick			
	Material		Installation		Material		Installation	
3000 psi concrete	1 C.Y.	$ 65.00	1 C.Y.	$ 13.66	1 C.Y.	$ 65.00	1 C.Y.	$ 11.71
Formwork, 4 uses	81 S.F. @ .83	67.23	81 S.F. @ 2.84	230.04	41 S.F. @ .83	34.03	41 S.F. @ 2.84	116.44
Reinforcing steel	44 # @ .28	12.32	44 # @ .17	7.48	43 # @ .28	12.04	43 # @ .17	7.31
Total per C.Y.		$144.55		$251.18		$111.07		$135.46

Metal Pan Joists, 30" One Way	125 psf, 15' Span				125 psf, 25' Span			
	Material		Installation		Material		Installation	
4000 psi concrete	1 C.Y.	$ 70.00	1 C.Y.	$ 17.19	1 C.Y.	$ 70.00	1 C.Y.	$ 14.90
Formwork, 4 uses	49 S.F. @ .82	40.18	49 S.F. @ 2.84	139.16	40 S.F. @ .82	32.80	40 S.F. @ 2.84	113.60
Reinforcing steel	47 # @ .28	13.16	47 # @ .17	7.99	81 # @ .28	22.68	81 # @ .17	13.77
30" metal pans	44 S.F. @ 1.55	68.20	44 S.F. @ .40	17.60	37 S.F. @ 1.55	57.35	37 # @ .40	14.80
Total per C.Y.		$191.54		$181.94		$182.83		$157.07

Pile Caps	Under 5 C.Y.				Over 10 C.Y.			
	Material		Installation		Material		Installation	
3000 psi concrete	1.05 C.Y.	$65.00	1 C.Y.	$13.66	1.05 C.Y.	$65.00	1 C.Y.	$ 5.72
Formwork, 4 uses	20 S.F. @ .70	14.00	20 S.F. @ 2.31	46.20	10 S.F. @ .70	7.00	10 S.F. @ 2.31	23.10
Reinforcing steel	52 # @ .28	14.56	52 # @ .15	7.80	48 # @ .28	13.44	48 # @ .15	7.20
Total per C.Y.		$93.56		$67.66		$85.44		$36.02

Slab on Grade	4" Thick				6" Thick			
	Material		Installation		Material		Installation	
3500 psi concrete	1.05 C.Y.	$68.25	1 C.Y.	$11.18	1.05 C.Y.	$68.25	1 C.Y.	$ 7.45
Formwork, 4 uses	9.2 L.F. @ .31	2.85	9.2 L.F. @ 1.47	13.52	6 L.F. @ .31	1.86	6 L.F. @ 1.47	8.82
W.W.Fabric	81 # @ .07	5.67	81 # @ .12	9.72	54 # @ .07	3.78	54 # @ .12	6.48
Total per C.Y.		$76.77		$34.42		$73.89		$22.75

R03310-100 Average C.Y. of Concrete (cont.)

Spread Footings	Under 1 C.Y.						Over 5 C.Y.					
	Material			Installation			Material			Installation		
3000 psi concrete	1.05 C.Y.		$65.00	1.05 C.Y.		$22.36	1.05 C.Y.		$65.00	1 C.Y.		$11.18
Formwork, 4 uses	24 S.F. @	.58	13.92	24 S.F. @	2.13	51.12	9 S.F. @	.58	5.22	9 S.F. @	2.13	19.17
Reinforcing steel	46 # @	.28	12.88	46 # @	.25	11.50	54 # @	.28	15.12	54 # @	.25	13.50
Total per C.Y.			$91.80			$84.98			$85.34			$43.85

Strip Footings	9' x 18" Plain						12" x 36" Reinforced					
	Material			Installation			Material			Installation		
3000 psi concrete	1.05 C.Y.		$65.00	1.05 C.Y.		$11.18	1.05 C.Y.		$65.00	1 C.Y.		$ 7.93
Formwork, 4 uses	36 S.F. @	.44	15.84	36 S.F. @	1.82	65.52	18 S.F. @	.44	7.92	18 S.F. @	1.82	32.76
Reinforcing steel			—			—	40 # @	.28	11.20	40 # @	.25	10.00
Total per C.Y.			$80.84			$76.70			$84.12			$50.69

Waffle, 30" Domes	125 psf, 20' Span						125 psf, 30' Span					
	Material			Installation			Material			Installation		
4000 psi concrete	1 C.Y.		$ 70.00	1 C.Y.		$ 17.19	1 C.Y.		$ 70.00	1 C.Y.		$ 14.90
Formwork, 4 uses	39 S.F. @	.82	31.98	39 S.F. @	2.90	113.10	31 S.F. @	.82	25.42	31 S.F. @	2.90	89.90
Reinforcing steel & mesh	107 # @	.35	37.45	107 # @	.25	26.75	102 # @	.35	35.70	102 # @	.25	25.50
Metal Domes	39 S.F. @	1.55	60.45	39 S.F. @	.41	15.99	31 S.F. @	1.55	48.05	31 S.F. @	.41	12.71
Total per C.Y.			$199.88			$173.03			$179.17			$143.01

CONCRETE 3

REFERENCE NOS.

R03310-120   Lift Slabs

The cost advantage of the lift slab method is due to placing all concrete, reinforcing steel, inserts and electrical conduit at ground level and in reduction of formwork. Minimum economical project size is about 30,000 S.F. Slabs may be tilted for parking garage ramps.

It is now used in all types of buildings and has gone up to 22 stories high in apartment buildings. Current trend is to use post-tensioned flat plate slabs with spans from 22' to 35'. Cylindrical void forms are used when deep slabs are required. One pound of prestressing steel is about equal to seven pounds of conventional reinforcing.

To be considered cured for stressing and lifting, a slab must have attained 75% of design strength. Seven days are usually sufficient with four to five days possible if high early strength cement is used. Slabs can be stacked using

two coats of a non-bonding agent to insure that slabs do not stick to each other. Lifting is done by companies specializing in this work. Lift rate is 5' to 15' per hour with an average of 10' per hour. Total areas up to 33,000 S.F. have been lifted at one time. 24 to 36 jacking columns are common. Most economical bay sizes are 24' to 28' with four to fourteen stories most efficient. Continuous design reduces reinforcing steel cost. Use of post-tensioned slabs allows larger bay sizes. Supplementary reinforcing, post-tensioned tendons, accessories and field labor cost about $2.50 per pound of tendon.

Table below shows the usual range and average S.F. cost of a typical lift slab project that has been designed to take advantage of lift slab techniques. Figures include Subs Overhead and Profit.

Typical Cost per S.F. for Lift Slabs Project Incl. Subs O & P

Item	Description	Typical Range		Average	Sub Total
Concrete Slabs	Edge and bulkhead forms	$ .05	to $ .41	$ .23	$ 5.25
	Reinforcing and post-tensioning steel	$1.60	to $ 2.83	2.22	
	Reinforcing and accessories	$ .06	to $ .15	.11	
	Concrete cast at ground level	$1.55	to $ 2.58	2.07	
	Float or trowel finish	$ .52	to $ .72	.62	
Lifting Slabs	Separating and curing compound	$ .03	to $ .09	.06	2.75
	Lifting collars	$ .26	to $ .57	.42	
	Lifting and welding	$1.34	to $ 3.19	2.27	
Columns	Fabricated columns & accessories	$ .74	to $ 2.16	1.45	1.88
	Set initial stage	$ .05	to $ .25	.15	
	Column splicing	$ .14	to $ .41	.28	
Miscellaneous	Grout plates, patching, bolts, etc.	$ .05	to $ .26	.16	.16
Total in place per S.F.		$6.39	to $13.62	$10.04	$10.04

R03350-130   Granolithic Finish and Base

Description	Granolithic Topping, Mix 1:1:1-1/2				Granolithic Base	
	(Line 03350-300-0850)	1" Topping	(Line 03350-300-0950)	2" Topping	(Line 03350-300-0200)	1" x 5" Straight
Cement @ $7.20 per bag	3.60 bags	$ 25.92	7.20 bags	$ 51.84	1.70 bags	$ 12.24
Sand @ $16.55 per C.Y.	3.60 C.F.	2.21	7.20 C.F.	4.41	1.70 C.F.	1.04
Peastone @ $21.50 Per C.Y.	5.40 C.F.	4.30	10.80 C.F.	8.60	1.85 C.F.	1.47
Clean, Mix, Place forms, and finish: Crew C-10 @ $26.25 per L.H.	4.07 L.H.	106.84	4.80 L.H.	126.00	13.70 L.H.	359.63
Totals	100 S.F.	$139.27	100 S.F.	$190.85	100 L.F.	$374.38

R03350-140   Integral Floor Finish

Mix 1:1:2		(Line 03350-300-0450)	1/2" Thick	(Line 03350-300-0600)	1" Thick
Cement @	$ 7.20 per bag	1.7 bag	$12.24	3.4 bag	$ 24.48
Sand @	$16.55 per C.Y.	.8 C.F.	.49	1.6 C.F.	.98
Gravel @	$20.00 per C.Y.	3.2 C.F.	2.37	6.4 C.F.	4.74
Mix, place and finish using Crew C-10 @	$26.25 per L.H.	2.52 L.H.	66.15	3.21 L.H.	84.26
Total for 100 S.F.			$81.25		$114.46

R03410-030 Prestressed Precast Concrete Structural Units

See also R03410-090 for post-tensioned prestressed concrete.

Type	Location	Depth	Span in Ft.		Live Load Lb. per S.F.	Cost per S.F. Incl. Subs O & P	
						Delivered	Erected
Double Tee	Floor	28 to 34"	60 to 80		50 to 80	$ 5.90 to 8.20	$ 7.10 to 9.85
	Roof	12" to 24"	30 to 50		40	$ 3.95 to 6.20	$ 4.75 to 7.45
	Wall	Width 8'	Up to 55' high		Wind	$4.15 to $ 8.30	$5.00 to $ 9.95
Multiple Tee	Roof	8" to 12"	15 to 40		40	$ 4.15	$ 5.00
	Floor	8" to 12"	15 to 30		100	$ 4.35	$ 5.00
Plank or	Roof or Floor		Roof	Floor	40 for Roof		
		4"	13	12		$ 3.85	$ 4.80
		6"	22	18		4.10	5.35
		8"	26	25		4.35	5.45
		10"	33	29	100 for	4.85	6.05
		12"	42	32	Floor	5.10	6.40
Single Tee	Roof	28"	40			$ 6.90 *	$ 7.95 *
		32"	80		40	8.15 *	9.35 *
		36"	100			10.95 *	12.60 *
		48"	120			11.50 *	13.25 *
AASHO Girder	Bridges	Type 4	100		Highway	$109/L.F.	$164/L.F.
		5	110			145	181
		6	125			181	217
Box Beam	Bridges	15"	40		Highway	$116/L.F.	$174/L.F.
		27"	to			155	194
		33"	100			178	214

*Costs are for 10' wide members; for 8' wide members add $.60 per S.F.

The costs above are based on a project of 10,000 to 20,000 S.F. with a haul distance of 25 to 50 miles.

The majority of precast projects today utilize double tees rather than single tees because of speed and ease of installation. As a result casting beds at manufacturing plants are normally formed for double tees. Single tee projects will therefore require an initial set up charge of approximately $7,500 to be spread over the individual single tee costs. The prices above for single tees includes this cost based on a project size of 15,000 square feet.

For floors, a 2" to 3" topping is field cast over the shapes. For roofs, insulating concrete or rigid insulation is placed over the shapes. Topping is not included in the above costs.

Hauling costs (incl. above) run from $.50 per S.F. for short haul to $1.00 for 50 mile haul. Member lengths up to 40' are standard haul, 40' to 60' require special permits and lengths over 60' must be escorted. Over width and/or over length can add up to 100% on hauling costs.

Multiple tee erection runs between $.65 to $1.80 per S.F. and single tee erection runs between $.75 to $1.85 per S.F. Large heavy members may require two cranes for lifting which would increase these erection costs by about 45%. An eight man erection crew and crane will run about $3,300 to $6,000 per day depending on location and size of crane. The crew can install 12 to 20 double tees, or 45 to 70 quad tees or planks per day.

The cost of supporting beams must be added to the above costs. Simple support beams run from $45 to $110 per L.F. delivered. Inverted tee beams run from $75 to $275 per L.F. delivered. Standard sized columns run $45 to $175 per L.F. delivered.

Grouting of connections must be added to the above. Typical costs are about $25 per connection but can go as high as $50 per connection.

Grouting planks run between $.45 to $.65 per S.F.

Single story buildings, including double tee roof members, supporting columns and girders, but no foundations, cost from $9.00 to $30.00 per S.F. of floor area. Parking garages run from $12.00 to $24.00 per S.F. above the foundations. Optimum parking garage design runs .02 C.Y. per S.F with overall costs for concrete in place running between $540 to $750 per C.Y.

Several system buildings utilizing precast members are available. Heights can go to 22 stories for apartment buildings with costs ranging from $11.50 to $42.00 per S.F. depending on the system, its components, its location and the degree of interior finish supplied. Optimum design ratio is 3 S.F. of surface to 1 S.F. of floor area.

R03410-090   Prestressed Concrete, Post-tensioned

In post-tensioned concrete the steel tendons are tensioned after the concrete has reached about 3/4 of its ultimate strength. The cableways are grouted after tensioning to provide bond between the steel and concrete. If bond is to be prevented, the tendons are coated with a corrosion-preventative grease and wrapped with waterproof paper or plastic. Bonded tendons are usually used when ultimate strength (beams & girders) is a controlling factor.

High strength concrete is used to fully utilize the steel, thereby reducing the size and weight of the member. A plasticizing agent may be added to reduce water content. Maximum size aggregate ranges from 1/2″ to 1-1/2″ depending on the spacing of the tendons.

The types of steel commonly used are bars and strands. Job conditions determine which is best suited. Bars are best for vertical prestresses since they are easy to support. The trend is for steel manufacturers to supply a finished package, cut to length, which reduces field preparation to a minimum.

Bars vary from 3/4″ to 1-3/8″ diameter. Table below gives time in labor-hours per tendon and the labor cost per pound for placing, tensioning and grouting (if required) a 75′ beam. Tendons used in buildings are not usually grouted; tendons for bridges usually are grouted. For strands the table indicates the labor-hours and labor cost per pound for typical prestressed units 100′ long. Simple span beams usually require one end stressing regardless of lengths. Continuous beams are usually stressed from two ends. Long slabs are poured from the center outward and stressed in 75′ increments after the initial 150′ center pour. Prices below do not include subcontractor's overhead and profit.

Labor Hours per Tendon and Labor Costs per Pound of Prestress Steel

Length	100′ Beam		75′ Beam		100′ Slab	
Type Steel	Strand		Bars		Strand	
Diameter	0.5″		3/4″	1-3/8″	0.5″	0.6″
Number	12	24	1	1	1	1
Force in Kips	298	595	42	143	25	35
Preparation & Placing Cables	6.6	10.0	0.7	2.3	0.8	0.8
Stressing Cables	2.4	3.0	0.6	1.3	0.4	0.4
Grouting, if required	3.0	3.5	0.5	1.0		
Total Labor Hours	12.0	16.5	1.8	4.6	1.2	1.2
Prestressing Steel Weights	640#	1280#	115#	380#	53#	74#
Labor cost per lb. Bonded / Non-bonded	$.72 to $.95	$.57 to $.70	$.57 to $.68 / $.50 to $.60	$.43 to $.50 / $.43 to $.55	$.90 to $1.15	$.90 to $1.15

Flat Slab construction — 4000 psi concrete with span to depth ratio between 36 and 44. Two way post-tensioned steel averages 1.0 lb. per S.F. for 24′ to 28′ bays (usually strand) and additional reinforcing steel averages .5 lb. per S.F.

Pan and Joist construction — 4000 psi concrete with span to depth ratio 28 to 30. Post-tensioned steel averages .8 lb. per S.F. and reinforcing steel about 1.0 lb. per S.F. Placing and stressing averages 40 hours per ton of total material.

Beam construction — 4000 to 5000 psi concrete. Steel weights vary greatly. Tendon material cost runs from $1.00 to $2.00 per lb. for grouted and $.90 to $1.25 per lb. for non-grouted strand. Bar costs are from $.90 to $1.45 per lb.

From the chart above placing and stressing cost for grouted tendons runs from $.45 to $.95 per lb; non-grouted placing costs run from $.45 to $1.15 per lb. Labor cost per pound goes down as the size and length of the tendon increases. The primary economic consideration is the cost per kip for the member.

Post-tensioning becomes feasible for beams and girders over 30′ long; for continuous two-way slabs over 20′ clear; also in transferring upper building loads over longer spans at lower levels. Post-tension suppliers will provide engineering services at no cost to the user. Substantial economies are possible by using post-tensioned Lift Slabs. See R03310-120 for Lift Slabs.

R03450-010   Precast Concrete Wall Panels

Panels are either solid or insulated with plain, colored or textured finishes. Transportation is an important cost factor. Prices below are based on delivery within 50 miles of a plant including fabricators' overhead and profit. Engineering data is available from fabricators to assist with construction details. Usual minimum job size for economical use of panels is about 5000 S.F. Small jobs can double the prices below. For large, highly repetitive jobs, deduct up to 15% from the prices below.

Panel Cost and Maximum Size   Base price for panels based on 50 S.F. or larger panels is as follows:

Thickness	Cost per S.F.	Maximum Size	Thickness	Cost per S.F.	Maximum Size
3″	$ 8.05	50 S.F.	6″	$12.20	300 S.F.
4″	8.85	150 S.F.	7″	13.20	300 S.F.
5″	10.60	200 S.F.	8″	13.75	300 S.F.

The above prices are for gray smooth form or board finish one side. Add $1.65 per S.F. for white facing; $8.75 per C.F. for solid white for full thickness. For fluted surface (not broken) add $.50 to $1.25 per S.F. For broken rib finish add $.80 to $1.75 to fluted surface. Add $.35 to $1.35 per S.F. for exposed local aggregate and $1.00 to $4.00 per S.F. for special facing aggregates.

Sandblasting runs $.55 to $1.00 per S.F., and bush hammering runs $1.75 to $3.50 per S.F. Loose hardware (not included above) runs $1.00 to $2.00 per S.F.

2″ thick panels cost about the same as 3″ thick panels and maximum panel size is less. For building panels faced with granite, marble or stone, add the material prices from Division 04400 to the plain panel price above. There is a growing trend toward aggregate facings and broken rib finish rather than plain gray concrete panels.

Composite Panels   Add to above panel prices for core insulation, mesh and shear ties per S.F.

Type	1″ Thick	1-1/2″ Thick	2″ Thick
Fiberglass	$1.84	$2.60	$3.30
Polystyrene (E.P.S. Board)	1.10	1.55	2.00

Erection   Table shows cost ranges for erection including Subcontractor's O & P using a six person crew, crane, operator & oiler.

Panel Size L x H	Area per Panel	Low Rise Hyd. 55 Ton Crane @ $4,682 Daily Cost — Daily Production Range Pieces	Low Rise — Daily Production Range Area	Low Rise — Erection Cost Per Piece	Low Rise — Erection Cost Per S.F.	High Rise — Daily Production Range Pieces	High Rise — Daily Production Range Area	High Rise 55 Ton Crane $4,682 Daily Cost — Piece Cost	High Rise 55 Ton Crane — S.F. Cost	High Rise 90 Ton Crane $5,212 Daily Cost — Piece Cost	High Rise 90 Ton Crane — S.F. Cost	High Rise 150 Ton Crane $5,512 Daily Cost — Piece Cost	High Rise 150 Ton Crane — S.F. Cost
4′ x 4′	16 S.F.	10	160 S.F.	$468	$29.25	9	144 S.F.	$520	$32.51	$ 579	$36.19	$ 612	$38.28
		20	320	234	14.65	18	288	260	16.26	290	18.10	306	19.14
4′ x 8′	32	10	320	468	14.65	9	288	520	16.26	579	18.10	612	19.14
		19	608	246	7.70	17	544	275	8.61	307	9.58	324	10.13
8′ x 8′	64	9	576	520	8.15	8	512	585	9.14	652	10.18	689	10.77
		18	1152	260	4.05	16	1024	293	4.57	326	5.09	345	5.38
10′ x 10′	100	8	800	585	5.85	7	700	669	6.69	745	7.45	787	7.87
		15	1500	312	3.10	14	1400	334	3.34	372	3.72	394	3.94
15′ x 10′	150	7	1050	669	4.45	6	900	—	—	869	5.79	919	6.12
		12	1800	390	2.60	11	1650	—	—	474	3.16	501	3.34
20′ x 10′	200	6	1200	780	3.90	5	1000	—	—	1042	5.21	1102	5.51
		8	1600	585	2.95	7	1400	—	—	745	3.72	787	3.94
30′ x 10′	300	5	1500	936	3.10	4	1200	—	—	1303	4.34	1378	4.59
		7	2100	669	2.25	7	2100	—	—	745	2.48	787	2.62

Total Cost in Place for Low Rise Construction Including Subcontractor's O & P

Description	Gray 4′ x 8′ x 4″	Gray 20′ x 10′ x 6″	White Face 4′ x 8′ x 4″	White Face 20′ x 10′ x 6″	Exposed Aggregate 4′ x 8′ x 4″	Exposed Aggregate 20′ x 10′ x 6″
Panel, steel form, broomed finish	$ 8.85	$12.20	$10.40	$13.75	$10.85	$14.20
Caulking, grout, etc. (runs about $2.50 per L.F.)	.91	.36	.91	.36	.91	.36
Erect, plumb, align (from above)	14.65	3.90	14.65	3.90	14.65	3.90
Total in place per S.F.	$24.41	$16.46	$25.96	$18.01	$26.41	$18.46

No allowance has been made for supporting steel framework. On one story buildings, panels may rest on grade beams and require only wind bracing and fasteners. On multi-story buildings panels can span from column to column and floor to floor. Plastic designed steel framed structures may have large deflections which slow down erection and raise costs.

Large panels are more economical than small panels on a S.F. basis. When figuring areas include all protrusions, returns, etc. Overhangs can triple erection costs. Panels over 45′ have been produced. Larger flat units should be prestressed. Vacuum lifting of smooth finish panels eliminates inserts and can speed erection.

R03470-020   Tilt Up Concrete Panels

The advantage of tilt up construction is in the low cost of forms and the placing of concrete and reinforcing. Panels up to 75' high and 5-1/2" thick have been tilted using strongbacks. Tilt up has been used for one to five story buildings and is well suited for warehouses, stores, offices, schools and residences.

The panels are cast in forms on the floor slab. Most jobs use 5-1/2" thick solid reinforced concrete panels. Sandwich panels with a layer of insulating materials are also used. Where dampness is a factor, lightweight aggregate is used at an added cost of $.50 per square foot. Optimum panel size is 300 to 500 S.F.

Slabs are usually poured with 3000 psi concrete which permits tilting seven days after pouring. Slabs may be stacked on top of each other and are separated from each other by either two coats of bond breaker or a film of polyethylene. Use of high early strength cement allows tilting two days

after a pour. Tilting up is done with a roller outrigger crane with a capacity of at least 1-1/2 times the weight of the panel at the required reach. Exterior precast columns can be set at the same time as the panels; interior precast columns can be set first and the panels clipped directly to them. The use of cast-in-place concrete columns is diminishing due to shrinkage problems. Structural steel columns are sometimes used if crane rails are planned. Panels can be clipped to the columns or lowered between the flanges. Steel channels with anchors may be used as edge forms for the slab. When the panels are lifted the channels form an integral steel column to take structural loads. Roof loads can be carried directly by the panels for wall heights to 14'. For soft ground requiring mats for cranes, add 100% to costs below.

Below are typical costs per S.F. for panels of 300 to 500 S.F. 20' high, not including contractor's overhead and profit.

Item	5-1/2" Thick			7-1/2" Thick		
	Material	Installation	Total	Material	Installation	Total
Prepare pouring surface	$ .02	$ .08	$ .10	$ .02	$ .08	$ .10
Erect, strip side forms	.08	.34	.42	.14	.46	.60
Place concrete, 3000 psi	1.06	.13	1.19	1.44	.46	1.90
Steel trowel finish & curing	.02	.36	.38	.02	.36	.38
Reinforcing, inserts & misc. items	1.02	.59	1.61	1.41	.79	2.20
Panel erection and aligning	—	.73	.73	—	.73	.73
Total per S.F. of Wall	$ 2.20	$ 2.23	$ 4.43	$ 3.03	$ 2.88	$ 5.91
Site precast concrete columns, add	1.10	1.23	2.33	1.06	1.23	2.29
Total per S.F. of Wall	$ 3.30	$ 3.46	$ 6.76	$ 4.09	$ 4.11	$ 8.20
Panels only, per C.Y.	$118.80	$120.42	$239.22	$130.90	$124.42	$255.31

Requirements of local building codes may be a limiting factor and should be checked. Building floor slabs should be poured first and should be a minimum of 5" thick with 100% compaction of soil or 6" thick with less than 100% compaction.

Setting times as fast as nine minutes per panel have been observed, but a safer expectation would be four panels per hour with a crane and a four man setting crew. If crane erects from inside building, some provision must be made to get crane out after walls are erected. Good yarding procedure is important to minimize delays. Equalizing three point lifting beams and self-releasing pick-up hooks speed erection. If panels must be carried to their final location, setting time per panel will be increased and erection costs may fall in the erection cost range of architectural precast wall panels. Placing panels into slots formed in continuous footers will speed erection.

Reinforcing should be with #5 bars with vertical bars on the bottom. If surface is to be sandblasted, stainless steel chairs should be used to prevent rust staining.

Use of a broom finish is popular since the unavoidable surface blemishes are concealed. Many West Coast jobs have used exposed aggregate panels which cost an additional $.50 to $3.60 per S.F. depending on the aggregate and construction method employed. Eastern prices for exposed aggregate tend to be considerably higher. Panel connections run $1.60 to $6.00 per L.F. Precast columns run from three to five times the C.Y. price of the panels only.

R03520-010 Lightweight Concrete

Vermiculite or Perlite come in bags of 4 C.F. under various trade names. Weight is about 8 lbs. per C.F. For insulating roof fill use 1:6 mix. For structural deck use 1:4 mix over gypsum boards, steeltex, steel centering, etc. supported by closely spaced joists or bulb trees. For structural slabs use 1:3:2 vermiculite sand concrete over steeltex, metal lath, steel centering, etc. on joists spaced 2'-0" O.C. for maximum L.L. of 80 P.S.F. Use same mix for slab base fill over steel flooring or regular reinforced concrete slab when tile, terrazzo or other finish is to be laid over.

For slabs on grade use 1:3:2 mix when tile, etc. finish is to be laid over. If radiant heating units are installed use a 1:6 mix for a base. After coils are in place, cover with a regular granolithic finish (mix 1:3:2) to a minimum depth of 1-1/2" over top of units.

Reinforce all slabs with 6 x 6 or 10 x 10 welded wire mesh.

Vermiculite concrete can be purchased ready mixed but the following breakdown is included for field mix. Prices given below are for a one story building and assume 50 C.Y. or more. For less than 50 C.Y. add 10%. For over one story add $3.75 per C.Y. Screed finish cost is included below. Ready mix 1:6 costs $94.95 per C.Y. delivered in truckload lots.

See R03310-070 for prices of ready mix lightweight concrete.

Quantities per C.Y., Field Mix			1:6 Mix Insulating Roof Fill		1:3:2 Mix Lightweight Structural Concrete	
Portland cement @	$ 7.20	per bag	5.0 bags	$ 36.00	6.2 bags	$ 44.64
Vermiculite or Perlite @	9.70	per bag	7.5 bags	72.75		
treated type @	11.50	per bag			4.7 bags	54.05
Sand @	16.55	per C.Y.			12.5 C.F.	7.66
Plant and Water				6.55		6.55
Labor, machine mix, hoist and place, Crew C-8 @	$36.02	per L.H.	1.12 L.H.	40.34	.91 L.H.	32.78
Total in place, per C.Y.				$155.64		$145.68

R04060-100   Cement Mortar (material only)

Type N - 1:1:6 mix by volume. Use everywhere above grade except as noted below.

  - 1:3 mix using conventional masonry cement which saves handling two separate bagged materials.

Type M - 1:1/4:3 mix by volume, or 1 part cement, 1/4 (10% by wt.) lime, 3 parts sand. Use for heavy loads and where earthquakes or hurricanes may occur. Also for reinforced brick, sewers, manholes and everywhere below grade.

Cost and Mix Proportions of Various Types of Mortar

Components	Type Mortar and Mix Proportions by Volume										
	M		S		N		O		K	PM	PL
	1:1:6	1:1/4:3	1/2:1:4	1:1/2:4	1:3	1:1:6	1:3	1:2:9	1:3:12	1:1:6	1:1/2:4
Portland cement @ $7.20 per bag	$ 7.20	$ 7.20	$ 3.60	$ 7.20	—	$ 7.20	—	$ 7.20	$ 7.20	$ 7.20	$ 7.20
Masonry cement @ $5.95 per bag	5.95	—	5.95	—	5.95	—	$5.95	—	—	$ 5.95	—
Lime @ $5.65 per 50 lb. bag	—	1.41	—	2.83	—	5.65	—	11.30	16.95	—	2.83
Masonry sand @ $16.90 per C.Y.*	3.76	1.88	2.50	2.50	1.88	3.76	1.88	5.63	7.51	3.76	2.50
Mixing machine incl. fuel**	1.74	.87	1.16	1.16	.87	1.74	.87	2.60	3.47	1.74	1.16
Total for Materials	$18.65	$11.36	$13.21	$13.69	$8.70	$18.35	$8.70	$26.73	$35.13	$18.65	$13.69
Total C.F.	6	3	4	4	3	6	3	9	12	6	4
Approximate Cost per C.F.	$ 3.11	$ 3.79	$ 3.30	$ 3.42	$2.90	$ 3.06	$2.90	$ 2.97	$ 2.93	$ 3.11	$ 3.42

*Includes 10 mile haul
**Based on a daily rental, 10 C.F., 25 H.P. mixer, mix 200 C.F./Day

Mix Proportions by Volume, Compressive Strength and Cost of Mortar

Where Used	Mortar Type	Allowable Proportions by Volume				Compressive Strength @ 28 days	Cost per Cubic Foot
		Portland Cement	Masonry Cement	Hydrated Lime	Masonry Sand		
Plain Masonry		1	1	—	6		$3.11
	M	1	—	1/4	3	2500 psi	3.79
		1/2	1	—	4		3.30
	S	1	—	1/4 to 1/2	4	1800 psi	3.42
		—	1	—	3		2.90
	N	1	—	1/2 to 1-1/4	6	750 psi	3.06
		—	1	—	3		2.90
	O	1	—	1-1/4 to 2-1/2	9	350 psi	2.97
	K	1	—	2-1/2 to 4	12	75 psi	2.93
Reinforced Masonry	PM	1	1	—	6	2500 psi	3.11
	PL	1	—	1/4 to 1/2	4	2500 psi	3.42

Note: The total aggregate should be between 2.25 to 3 times the sum of the cement and lime used.

The labor cost to mix the mortar is included in the labor cost on brickwork.

Machine mixing is usually specified on jobs of any size. There is a large price saving over hand mixing and mortar is more uniform.

There are two types of mortar color used. Prices in Section 04060 are for the inert additive type with about 100 lbs. per M brick as the typical quantity required. These colors are also available in smaller batch size bags (1 lb. to 15 lb.) which can be placed directly into the mixer without measuring. The other type is premixed and replaces the masonry cement with ranges in price from $5 to $15 per 70 lb. bag. Dark green color has the highest cost.

MASONRY 4

REFERENCE NOS.

R04060-200   Miscellaneous Mortar (material only)

Quantities	Glass Block Mortar		Gypsum Cement Mortar	
White Portland cement at $18.00 per bag	7 bags	$126.00		
Gypsum cement at $11.60 per 80 lb. bag			11.25 bags	$130.50
Lime at $5.65 per 50 lb. bag	280 lbs.	31.64		
Sand at $16.90 per C.Y.*	1 C.Y.	16.90	1 C.Y.	16.90
Mixing machine and fuel		7.81		7.81
Total per C.Y.		$182.35		$155.21
Approximate Total per C.F.		$ 6.75		$ 5.75

* Includes 10 mile haul

R04080-500   Masonry Reinforcing

Horizontal joint reinforcing helps prevent wall cracks where wall movement may occur and in many locations is required by code. Horizontal joint reinforcing is generally not considered to be structural reinforcing and an unreinforced wall may still contain joint reinforcing.

Reinforcing strips come in 10' and 12' lengths and in truss and ladder shapes, with and without drips. Field labor runs between 2.7 to 5.3 hours per 1000 L.F. for wall thicknesses up to 12".

The wire meets ASTM A82 for cold drawn steel wire and the typical size is 9 ga. sides and ties with 3/16" diameter also available. Typical finish is mill galvanized with zinc coating at .10 oz. per S.F. Class I (.40 oz. per S.F.) and Class III (.80 oz per S.F.) are also available, as is hot dipped galvanizing at 1.50 oz. per S.F.

R04210-050   Brick Chimneys

Quantities	16" x 16"		20" x 20"		20" x 24"		20" x 32"	
Brick at $310 per M	28 brick	$ 8.40	37 brick	$11.47	42 brick	$13.02	51 brick	$15.81
Type M mortar at $3.79 per C.F.	.5 C.F.	1.90	.6 C.F.	2.27	1.0 C.F.	3.79	1.3 C.F.	4.93
Flue tile (per foot)	8" x 8"	3.10	12" x 12"	5.75	2 @ 8" x 12"	7.80	2 @ 12" x 12"	11.50
Install tile & brick, crew D-1	.055 day	23.12	.073 day	30.69	.083 day	34.89	.10 day	42.04
Total per V.L.F.		$36.52		$50.18		$59.50		$74.28

Material costs include 3% waste for brick and 25% waste for mortar.

Labor costs are bare costs and do not include contractor's O&P.

Labor for chimney brick using D-1 crew is 31 hours per thousand brick or about $750 per thousand brick. An 8" x 12" flue takes 33 brick and two 8" x 8" flues take 37 brick.

R04210-055   Industrial Chimneys

Foundation requirements in C.Y. of concrete for various sized chimneys.

Size Chimney	2 Ton Soil	3 Ton Soil	Size Chimney	2 Ton Soil	3 Ton Soil	Size Chimney	2 Ton Soil	3 Ton Soil
75' x 3'-0"	13 C.Y.	11 C.Y.	160' x 6'-6"	86 C.Y.	76 C.Y.	300' x 10'-0"	325 C.Y.	245 C.Y.
85' x 5'-6"	19	16	175' x 7'-0"	108	95	350' x 12'-0"	422	320
100' x 5'-0"	24	20	200' x 6'-0"	125	105	400' x 14'-0"	520	400
125' x 5'-6"	43	36	250' x 8'-0"	230	175	500' x 18'-0"	725	575

R04210-100   Economy in Bricklaying

Have adequate supervision. Be sure bricklayers are always supplied with materials so there is no waiting. Place best bricklayers at corners and openings.

Use only screened sand for mortar. Otherwise, labor time will be wasted picking out pebbles. Use seamless metal tubs for mortar as they do not leak or catch the trowel. Locate stack and mortar for easy wheeling.

Have brick delivered for stacking. This makes for faster handling, reduces chipping and breakage, and requires less storage space. Many dealers will deliver select common in 2' x 3' x 4' pallets or face brick packaged. This affords quick handling with a crane or forklift and easy tonging in units of ten, which reduces waste.

Use wider bricks for one wythe wall construction. Keep scaffolding away from wall to allow mortar to fall clear and not stain wall.

On large jobs develop specialized crews for each type of masonry unit.

Consider designing for prefabricated panel construction on high rise projects.

Avoid excessive corners or openings. Each opening adds about 50% to labor cost for area of opening.

Bolting stone panels and using window frames as stops reduces labor costs and speeds up erection.

R04210-120 Common and Face Brick Prices

Prices are based on truckload lot purchases for Common Building Brick and Facing Brick. Prices are per M, (thousand), brick.

City	Brick per M Delivered Common	Face	Mortar 3/8" Joint	Common in 8" Wall Bare Costs	Incl. O & P	Face Brick, 4" Veneer Bare Costs	Incl. O & P	Common in 8" Wall Bare Costs	Incl. O & P	Face Brick, 4" Veneer Bare Costs	Incl. O & P
Atlanta	$200	$275	$38.30 for 8" Wall and $31.50 for 4" Wall	$416	$ 643	$ 500	$ 772	$ 661	$ 912	$ 814	$1,118
Baltimore	255	320		478	738	573	886	779	1,069	934	1,283
Boston	325	500		845	1,305	1,014	1,566	1,218	1,715	1,560	2,167
Buffalo	275	375		711	1,099	854	1,319	1,033	1,453	1,271	1,778
Chicago	280	350		769	1,188	923	1,426	1,096	1,548	1,315	1,857
Cincinnati	245	350		596	921	715	1,105	887	1,241	1,107	1,537
Cleveland	235	325		679	1,049	815	1,259	959	1,357	1,181	1,662
Columbus	250	360		582	899	698	1,079	878	1,224	1,100	1,521
Dallas	225	300		397	613	476	736	667	910	817	1,111
Denver	235	330		473	730	567	876	753	1,039	939	1,285
Detroit	250	300		735	1,136	882	1,363	1,031	1,462	1,223	1,738
Houston	275	300		416	643	500	772	738	997	840	1,146
Indianapolis	265	325		568	878	682	1,053	879	1,220	1,048	1,456
Kansas City	275	325		628	971	754	1,165	950	1,324	1,120	1,568
Los Angeles	255	325		691	1,067	829	1,280	992	1,398	1,195	1,683
Memphis	200	255		391	603	469	724	635	872	763	1,048
Milwaukee	295	390		684	1,057	821	1,269	1,027	1,434	1,254	1,745
Minneapolis	285	410		703	1,087	844	1,304	1,035	1,452	1,298	1,803
Nashville	225	300		410	633	492	760	680	930	832	1,134
New Orleans	210	325		354	547	425	656	609	827	791	1,059
New York City	335	425		963	1,488	1,156	1,785	1,346	1,909	1,625	2,302
Philadelphia	260	345		746	1,152	895	1,383	1,052	1,489	1,282	1,808
Phoenix	325	360		442	683	531	820	815	1,094	933	1,263
Pittsburgh	225	300		610	942	731	1,130	880	1,239	1,072	1,505
St. Louis	245	275		691	1,067	829	1,280	981	1,387	1,143	1,627
San Antonio	250	275		378	584	454	701	674	909	768	1,047
San Diego	290	375		623	963	748	1,155	960	1,334	1,166	1,615
San Francisco	350	375		802	1,240	963	1,488	1,201	1,678	1,381	1,947
Seattle	350	400		688	1,063	826	1,276	1,087	1,502	1,269	1,764
Washington, D.C.	255	325		490	757	588	908	791	1,088	954	1,311
Average	$265	$340		$600	$ 920	$ 720	$1,110	$ 910	$1,270	$1,100	$1,530

Common building brick manufactured according to ASTM C62 and facing brick manufactured according to ASTM C216 are the two standard bricks available for general building use.

Building brick is made in three grades; SW, where high resistance to damage caused by cyclic freezing is required; MW, where moderate resistance to cyclic freezing is needed; and NW, where little resistance to cyclic freezing is needed. Facing brick is made in only the two grades SW and MW. Additionally, facing brick is available in three types; FBS, for general use; FBX, for general use where a higher degree of precision and lower permissible variation in size than FBS is needed; and FBA, for general use to produce characteristic architectural effects resulting from non-uniformity in size and texture of the units.

In figuring above installation costs, a D-8 Crew (with a daily output of 1.5 M) was used for the 4" veneer. A D-8 Crew (with a daily output of 1.8 M) was used for the 8" solid wall.

In figuring the total cost including overhead and profit, an allowance of 10% was added to the sum of the cost of the brick and mortar. Also, 3% breakage was included for both the bare costs and the costs with overhead and profit. If bricks are delivered palletized with 280 to 300 per pallet, or packaged, allow only 1-1/2% for breakage. Then add $10 per M to the cost of brick and deduct two hours helper time. The net result is a savings of $30 to $40 per M in place. Packaged or palletized delivery is practical when

a job is big enough to have a crane or other equipment available to handle a package of brick. This is so on all industrial work but not always true on small commercial buildings.

The prices above are for bricks used in commercial, apartment house or industial construction. If it is possible to obtain the price of the actual brick to be used, it should be done and substituted in the table. The use of buff and gray face is increasing, and there is a continuing trend to the Norman, Roman, Jumbo and SCR brick.

See R04210-500 for brick quantities per S.F. and mortar quantities per M brick. (Average prices for the various sizes are listed in Division 4)

Common red clay brick for backup is not used that often. Concrete block is the most usual backup material with occasional use of sand lime or cement brick. Sand lime cost about $15 per M less than red clay and cement brick are about $5 per M less than red clay. These figures may be substituted in the common brick breakdown for the cost of these items in place, as labor is about the same. Building brick is commonly used in solid walls for strength and as a fire stop.

Brick panels built on the ground and then crane erected to the upper floors have proven to be economical. This allows the work to be done under cover and without scaffolding.

R04210-180   Brick in Place

Table below is for common bond with 3/8" concave joints and includes 3% waste for brick and 25% waste for mortar. Crew costs are bare costs.

Item	8" Common Brick Wall 8" x 2-2/3" x 4"		Select Common Face 8" x 2-2/3" x 4"		Red Face Brick 8" x 2-2/3" x 4"	
1030 brick delivered	$265 per M	$272.95	$310 per M	$ 319.30	$340 per M	$ 350.20
Type N mortar @ $3.06 per C.F.	12.5 C.F.	38.25	10.3 C.F.	31.52	10.3 C.F.	31.52
Installation using indicated crew	Crew D-8 @ .556 Days	599.15	Crew D-8 @ .667 Days	718.76	Crew D-8 @ .667 Days	718.76
Total per M in place		$910.35		$1,069.58		$1,100.48
Total per S.F. of wall	13.5 bricks/S.F.	$ 12.29	6.75 bricks/S.F.	$ 7.22	6.75 bricks/S.F.	$ 7.43

R04210-185   Reinforced Brick in Walls

Table below is for common bond with 3/8" concave joints and includes 3% waste. Standard 4" x 2-2/3" x 8" (nominal) bricks.

Item	8" to 9" Thick Wall		16" to 17" Thick Wall	
1030 brick (select common)	$310 per M	$319.30	$310 per M	$319.30
Type PL mortar @ $3.42 per C.F.	12.5 C.F.	42.63	13.9 C.F.	47.54
Reinforcing bars delivered	50 lb. @ .26 per lb.	14.00	50 lb. @ .26 per lb.	14.00
Installation incl. reinforcing using indicated crew	Crew D-8 @ .517 Days	539.54	Crew D-8 @ .513 Days	552.81
Total per M in place		$915.47		$933.65
Total per S.F. of wall	8" wall, 13.5 brick/S.F.	$ 12.36	16" wall, 27.0 brick/S.F.	$ 25.21

MASONRY 4

REFERENCE NOS.

R04210-500 Brick, Block & Mortar Quantities

Type Brick	Nominal Size (incl. mortar) L H W	Modular Coursing	Number of Brick per S.F.	C.F. of Mortar per M Bricks, Waste Included 3/8" Joint	1/2" Joint	Bond Type	Description	Factor
	Running Bond			**C.F. of Mortar per M Bricks, Waste Included**		**For Other Bonds Standard Size Add to S.F. Quantities in Table to Left**		
	Number of Brick per S.F. of Wall - Single Wythe with 3/8" Joints							
Standard	8 x 2-2/3 x 4	3C=8"	6.75	10.3	12.9	Common	full header every fifth course	+20%
Economy	8 x 4 x 4	1C=4"	4.50	11.4	14.6		full header every sixth course	+16.7%
Engineer	8 x 3-1/5 x 4	5C=16"	5.63	10.6	13.6	English	full header every second course	+50%
Fire	9 x 2-1/2 x 4-1/2	2C=5"	6.40	550 # Fireclay	—	Flemish	alternate headers every course	+33.3%
Jumbo	12 x 4 x 6 or 8	1C=4"	3.00	23.8	30.8		every sixth course	+5.6%
Norman	12 x 2-2/3 x 4	3C=8"	4.50	14.0	17.9	Header = W x H exposed		+100%
Norwegian	12 x 3-1/5 x 4	5C=16"	3.75	14.6	18.6	Rowlock = H x W exposed		+100%
Roman	12 x 2 x 4	2C=4"	6.00	13.4	17.0	Rowlock stretcher = L x W exposed		+33.3%
SCR	12 x 2-2/3 x 6	3C=8"	4.50	21.8	28.0	Soldier = H x L exposed		—
Utility	12 x 4 x 4	1C=4"	3.00	15.4	19.6	Sailor = W x L exposed		-33.3%

Concrete Blocks Nominal Size	Approximate Weight per S.F. Standard	Lightweight	Blocks per 100 S.F.	Mortar per M block Partitions	Back up
2" x 8" x 16"	20 PSF	15 PSF	113	16 C.F.	36 C.F.
4"	30	20		31	51
6"	42	30		46	66
8"	55	38		62	82
10"	70	47		77	97
12"	85	55		92	112

R04210-550 Brick Veneer in Place

Table below is for running bond with 3/8" concave joints and includes 3% waste for brick and 25% waste for mortar.

Item	Buff Face Brick 4" x 2-2/3"x 8"		Red Norman Face Brick 4" x 2-2/3" x 12"		Buff Roman Face Brick 4" x 2" x 12"	
1030 brick delivered	$400 per M	$ 412.00	$680 per M	$ 700.40	$720 per M	$ 741.60
Type N mortar @ $3.06 per C.F.	10.3 C.F.	31.52	14.0 C.F.	42.84	13.4 C.F.	41.00
Installation using indicated crew	Crew D-8 @ .667 days	718.76	Crew D-8 @ .690 days	743.54	Crew D-8 @ .667 days	718.76
Total per M in place		$1,162.28		$1,486.78		$1,501.36
Total per S.F. of wall	6.75 brick/S.F.	$ 7.85	4.50 brick/S.F.	$ 6.69	6.00 brick/S.F.	$ 9.01

R04220-200 Concrete Block

Concrete masonry units, 8″ high x 16″ long, sand aggregate, 3/8 joints for partitions,
tooled joint one side, not including Subs O&P, 113 blocks per 100 S.F.

City	Material				Mortar 3/8″ Joint	Installation		Total Per 100 S.F.	
	Per Block, Delivered		113 Block, Delivered						
	4″ Thick	8″ Thick	4″ Thick	8″ Thick		4″ Thick	8″ Thick	4″ Thick	8″ Thick
Atlanta	$.74	$1.00	$ 83.62	$113.00	$10.72 for 4″	$174.66	$200.14	$269.00	$334.58
Baltimore	.65	.85	73.45	96.05	$21.44 for 8″	200.36	229.60	284.53	347.09
Boston	.75	1.10	84.75	124.30		354.23	405.93	449.70	551.67
Buffalo	.70	1.01	79.10	114.13		298.31	341.85	388.13	477.42
Chicago	.60	.83	67.80	93.79		322.53	369.59	401.05	484.82
Cincinnati	.63	.89	71.19	100.57		250.06	286.54	331.97	408.55
Cleveland	.78	1.01	88.14	114.13		284.74	326.30	383.60	461.87
Columbus	.61	.83	68.93	93.79		244.00	279.60	323.65	394.83
Dallas	.84	1.14	94.92	128.82		166.49	190.79	272.13	341.05
Denver	.89	1.28	100.57	144.64		198.27	227.21	309.56	393.29
Detroit	.75	1.06	84.75	119.78		308.42	353.42	403.89	494.64
Houston	.75	1.03	84.75	116.39		174.60	200.08	270.07	337.91
Indianapolis	.85	1.16	96.05	131.08		238.24	273.00	345.01	425.52
Kansas City	.85	1.08	96.05	122.04		263.48	301.92	370.25	445.40
Los Angeles	.64	.93	72.32	105.09		289.63	331.89	372.67	458.42
Memphis	.73	1.04	82.49	117.52		163.79	187.69	257.00	326.65
Milwaukee	.70	.90	79.10	101.70		287.02	328.90	376.84	452.04
Minneapolis	.85	1.33	96.05	150.29		294.96	338.00	401.73	509.73
Nashville	.77	1.03	87.01	116.39		171.86	196.94	269.59	334.77
New Orleans	.85	1.30	96.05	146.90		148.45	170.11	255.22	338.45
New York City	.85	1.25	96.05	141.25		403.87	462.81	510.64	625.50
Philadelphia	.78	.93	88.14	105.09		312.74	358.38	411.60	484.91
Phoenix	.65	.93	73.45	105.09		185.52	212.60	269.69	339.13
Pittsburgh	.72	.91	81.36	102.83		255.63	292.93	347.71	417.20
St. Louis	.82	1.22	92.66	137.86		289.63	331.89	393.01	491.19
San Antonio	.77	1.00	87.01	113.00		158.51	181.65	256.24	316.09
San Diego	.75	1.02	84.75	115.26		261.39	299.53	356.86	436.23
San Francisco	.90	1.60	101.70	180.80		336.53	385.63	448.95	587.87
Seattle	.88	1.30	99.44	146.90		288.64	330.76	398.80	499.10
Washington D.C.	.66	1.00	74.58	113.00		205.36	235.32	290.66	369.76
Average	$.76	$1.07	$ 85.54	$120.38	▼	$251.06	$287.70	$347.33	$429.52

Cost for 100 S.F. of 8″ x 16″ Concrete Block Partitions to Four Stories High, Tooled Joint One Side						
8″ x 16″ Sand Aggregate	4″ Thick Block		8″ Thick Block		12″ Thick Block	
113 block delivered	$.76 Ea.	$ 85.88	$1.07 Ea.	$120.91	$1.65 Ea.	$186.45
Type N mortar at $3.06 per C.F.	3.5 C.F.	10.71	7.0 C.F.	21.42	10.4 C.F.	31.82
Installation Crew	D-8 .233 days	251.08	D-8 .267 days	287.72	D-9 .294 days	370.79
Total per 100 S.F.		$347.67		$430.05		$589.06
Add for filling cores solid	6.7 C.F.	$114.29	25.8 C.F.	$225.76	42.2 C.F.	$295.42

Cost for 100 S.F. of 8″ x 16″ Concrete Block Backup with Trowel Cut Joints						
8″ x 16″ Sand Aggregate	4″ Thick Block		8″ Thick Block		12″ Thick Block	
113 block delivered	$.76 Ea.	$ 85.88	$1.07 Ea.	$120.91	$1.65 Ea.	$186.45
Type N mortar at $3.06 per C.F.	5.8 C.F.	17.75	9.3 C.F.	28.46	12.7 C.F.	38.86
Installation crew	D-8 .225 days	242.46	D-8 .250 days	269.40	D-9 .270 days	340.52
Total per 100 S.F.		$346.09		$418.77		$565.83

Special block: corner, jamb and head block are same price as ordinary block of same size. Tabulated on the next page are national average prices per block. Labor on specials is about the same as equal sized regular block. Bond beam and 16″ high lintel blocks cost 30% more than regular units of equal size. Lintel blocks are 8″ long and 8″ or 16″ high. Costs in individual cities may be factored from the table above.

Use of motorized mortar spreader box will speed construction of continuous walls. Hollow non-load bearing units are made according to ASTM C129 and hollow load bearing units according to ASTM C90.

MASONRY 4

REFERENCE NOS.

R04220-220 Interlocking Grout Block Walls

Cost per 100 S.F. of 8″ x 16″ Interlocking Grout Block, "Open End" Type						
8″ x 16″ Sand Aggregate	**8″ Thick Block**		**12″ Thick Block**		**16″ Thick Block**	
113 block delivered	$1.60 ea.	$180.80	$2.45 ea.	$276.85	$3.80 ea.	$ 429.40
Type M mortar @ $3.79 per C.F.	7.0 C.F.	26.53	10.4 C.F.	39.42	13.8 C.F.	52.30
Minimum reinf. req.@ $ .28 per lb.						
8″ block #4 @ 24″ horiz.	33.4 lb.	9.35				
32″ vert.	40.0 lb.	11.20				
12″ & 16″ block #5 @ 8″ horiz.			99.7 lb.	27.92	99.7 lb.	27.92
16″ vert.			50.2 lb.	14.06	50.2 lb.	14.06
Type PM mortar @ $3.11 C.F.	25.8 C.F.	80.24	42.2 C.F.	131.24	56.1 C.F.	174.47
Installation Crew D-4 @ $961.90 per day	.408 days	392.46	.455 days	437.66	.541 days	520.39
Total per 100 S.F.		$700.58		$927.15		$1,218.54
1 S.F.		7.01		9.27		12.19

R04270-700 Glass Block

Cost of Blocks Each, Zone 1 Contractor Prices

Nominal Size (Including Mortar)	Truckload or Carload				Less Than Truckload or Carload			
	Regular	Thinline	Essex	Solar Reflective	Regular	Thinline	Essex	Solar Reflective
6″ x 6″	$ 3.50	$ 2.30	—	$ 7.75	$ 3.50	$ 2.60	—	$ 8.75
8″ x 8″	4.50	2.50	$ 5.15	9.50	4.65	3.00	$ 5.25	11.00
Solid 8″ x 8″	24.00	—	—	—	26.00	—	—	—
4″ x 8″	3.00	2.75	—	—	3.25	3.25	—	—
12″ x 12″	10.00	—	—	—	12.00	—	—	—

Size	Per 100 S.F.		Per 1000 Block				
	No. of Block	Mortar ″ Joint	Asphalt Emulsion	Caulk	Expansion Joint	Panel Anchors	Wall Mesh
6″ x 6″	410 ea.	5.0 C.F.	.17 gal.	1.5 gal.	80 L.F.	20 ea.	500 L.F.
8″ x 8″	230	3.6	.33	2.8	140	36	670
12″ x 12″	102	2.3	.67	6.0	312	80	1000
Approximate quantity per 100 S.F.			.07 gal.	0.6 gal.	32 L.F.	9 ea.	51, 68, 102 L.F.

Accessories required for installation — Wall ties: run galvanized double steel mesh full length of joint at $.32 per L.F.— fiberglass expansion joints at sides and top at $.40 per L.F.— silicone caulking one gallon at $50.00 does 95 L.F.— asphalt emulsion one gallon does 600 L.F. at $4.50 per gallon in one gallon lots. If blocks are not set in wall chase use 2′-0″ long wall anchors at $1.50 each at 2′-0″ O.C.

Quantities	Cost per 100 S.F. (Truckload or Carload Price)					
	6″ x 6″ Block		8″ x 8″ Block		12″ x 12″ Block	
Block, delivered	410 @ $3.25	$1,332.50	230 @ $4.10	$ 943.00	102 @ $9.25	$ 943.50
Mortar @ $6.75 per C.F.	5.0 C.F.	33.75	3.6 C.F.	24.30	2.3 C.F.	15.53
Ties, expansion joints, etc.		92.37		92.82		102.00
Crew D-8@ $1,043.60 per day	.690 days	743.54	.465 days	501.08	.417 days	449.36
Total per 100 S.F.		$2,202.16		$1,561.20		$1,510.39

R04430-500 Ashlar Veneer

Quantities			Low Price Stone		High Price Stone	
4″ Stone, random ashlar,	2.5	tons average	$280 per ton	$ 700.00	$375 per ton	$ 937.50
Type N mortar 1:1:6 @	$3.06	C.F.	20 C.F.	61.20	20 C.F.	61.20
50 - 1″ x 1/4″ x 6″ galv. stone anchors @	$1.10	each		55.00		55.00
Crew D-8 @	$1,077.60 per day		.714 days	769.41	.833 days	897.64
Total per 100 S.F.				$1,585.61		$1,951.34

Stone coverage varies from 30 S.F. to 50 S.F. per ton. Mortar quantities include 1″ backing bed.

R04930-100 Cleaning Face Brick

On smooth brick a person can clean 70 S.F. an hour; on rough brick 50 S.F. per hour. Use one gallon muriatic acid to 20 gallons of water for 1000 S.F. Do not use acid solution until wall is at least seven days old, but a mild soap solution may be used after two days. Commercial cleaners cost from $9 to $12 per gallon.

Time has been allowed for clean-up in brick prices.

5 METALS

R05080-310   Coating Structural Steel

On field-welded jobs, the shop-applied primer coat is necessarily omitted. All painting must be done in the field and usually consists of red oxide rust inhibitive paint or an aluminum paint (see Division 09910-650 for paint material costs). The table below shows paint coverage and daily production for field painting.

See Division 05120-680 for hot-dipped galvanizing and for field-applied cold galvanizing and other paints and protective coatings.

See division 05120-680 for steel surface preparation treatments such as wire brushing, pressure washing and sand blasting.

Type Construction	Surface Area per Ton	Coat	One Gallon Covers		In 8 Hrs. Person Covers		Average per Ton Spray	
			Brush	Spray	Brush	Spray	Gallons	Labor-hours
Light Structural	300 S.F. to 500 S.F.	1st	500 S.F.	455 S.F.	640 S.F.	2000 S.F.	0.9 gals.	1.6 L.H.
		2nd	450	410	800	2400	1.0	1.3
		3rd	450	410	960	3200	1.0	1.0
Medium	150 S.F. to 300 S.F.	All	400	365	1600	3200	0.6	0.6
Heavy Structural	50 S.F. to 150 S.F.	1st	400	365	1920	4000	0.2	0.2
		2nd	400	365	2000	4000	0.2	0.2
		3rd	400	365	2000	4000	0.2	0.2
Weighted Average	225 S.F.	All	400	365	1350	3000	0.6	0.6

R05090-510   High Strength Bolts

Common bolts (A307) are usually used in secondary connections (see Division 05090-150).

High strength bolts (A325 and A490) are usually specified for primary connections such as column splices, beam and girder connections to columns, column bracing, connections for supports of operating equipment or of other live loads which produce impact or reversal of stress, and in structures carrying cranes of over 5-ton capacity.

Allow 20 field bolts per ton of steel for a 6 story office building, apartment house or light industrial building. For 6 to 12 stories allow 25 bolts per ton, and above 12 stories, 30 bolts per ton. On power stations, 20 to 25 bolts per ton are needed.

R05090-520   Welded Structural Steel

Usual weight reductions with welded design run 10% to 20% compared with bolted or riveted connections. This amounts to about the same total cost compared with bolted structures since field welding is more expensive than bolts. For normal spans of 18' to 24' figure 6 to 7 connections per ton.

Trusses — For welded trusses add 4% to weight of main members for connections. Up to 15% less steel can be expected in a welded truss compared to one that is shop bolted. Cost of erection is the same whether shop bolted or welded.

General — Typical electrodes for structural steel welding are E6010, E6011, E60T and E70T. Typical buildings vary between 2# to 8# of weld rod per

ton of steel. Buildings utilizing continuous design require about three times as much welding as conventional welded structures. In estimating field erection by welding, it is best to use the average linear feet of weld per ton to arrive at the welding cost per ton. The type, size and position of the weld will have a direct bearing on the cost per linear foot. A typical field welder will deposit 1.8# to 2# of weld rod per hour manually. Using semiautomatic methods can increase production by as much as 50% to 75%. Below is the cost per hour for manual welding.

Welded Structural Steel in Field, per Hour			No Operating Engr.	1/2 Operating Engr.	1 Operating Engr.
Item					
2 lb. weld rod	$1.34	per lb.	$ 2.68	$ 2.68	$ 2.68
Equipment (for welding only)	$210	/40 hrs.	5.25	5.25	5.25
Operating cost @	$5.25	per hour	5.25	5.25	5.25
Welder Foreman 1 hr. @	$34.85	per hour	34.85	34.85	34.85
Operating engineer @	$28.75	per hour	—	14.38	28.75
Total per Welder Hour (Bare Costs)			$48.03	$62.41	$76.78

The welding costs per ton of structural steel will vary from $48 to $307 per ton depending on Union requirements, crew size, design and inspection required.

REFERENCE NOS.

RO5120-210   Structural Steel

1 to 2 Story Building	Bare Costs for 100 Ton Job with High Strength Bolts					Including Subs O&P		
City	Fabricated and Delivered	Unloading and Sorting	Erection Equipment	Field Erection Labor	Total per Ton in Place	Material	Installation	Total
Atlanta	$1,130	$26	$107	$177	$1,440	$1,243	$ 484	$1,727
Baltimore	1,080	32	134	217	1,463	1,188	596	1,784
Boston	1,245	40	170	265	1,720	1,370	736	2,106
Buffalo	1,325	35	129	236	1,725	1,458	631	2,089
Chicago	1,165	43	163	290	1,661	1,282	779	2,061
Cincinnati	1,110	31	115	206	1,462	1,221	554	1,775
Cleveland	1,110	35	115	237	1,497	1,221	616	1,837
Columbus	1,110	32	107	212	1,461	1,221	557	1,778
Dallas	1,220	21	120	139	1,500	1,342	420	1,762
Denver	1,280	23	115	155	1,573	1,408	448	1,856
Detroit	1,250	40	136	265	1,691	1,375	700	2,075
Houston	1,175	21	124	140	1,460	1,293	427	1,720
Indianapolis	1,320	31	107	210	1,668	1,452	552	2,004
Kansas City	1,320	33	143	220	1,716	1,452	613	2,065
Los Angeles	1,420	40	131	265	1,856	1,562	694	2,256
Memphis	1,160	23	124	154	1,461	1,276	456	1,732
Milwaukee	1,220	34	121	228	1,603	1,342	605	1,947
Minneapolis	1,125	37	174	249	1,585	1,238	706	1,944
Nashville	1,285	23	121	151	1,580	1,414	447	1,861
New Orleans	1,270	21	104	140	1,535	1,397	405	1,802
New York City	1,400	62	191	417	2,070	1,540	1,074	2,614
Philadelphia	1,210	44	163	291	1,708	1,331	783	2,114
Phoenix	1,125	28	100	187	1,440	1,238	498	1,736
Pittsburgh	1,220	35	167	236	1,658	1,342	673	2,015
St. Louis	1,295	35	166	236	1,732	1,425	671	2,096
San Antonio	1,135	19	97	131	1,382	1,249	377	1,626
San Diego	1,375	40	132	265	1,812	1,513	695	2,208
San Francisco	1,365	40	142	265	1,812	1,502	706	2,208
Seattle	1,180	35	123	232	1,570	1,298	617	1,915
Washington, DC	1,125	28	149	189	1,491	1,238	555	1,793
U.S. Average	$1,225	$33	$133	$218	$1,609	$1,348	$ 602	$1,950

Adjustments to the Base Price Above	Bare Costs	Incl. Subs O&P
For 3 to 6 story building, add per ton	$ 35	$ 75
For 7 to 15 stories, add per ton	65	100
For over 15 stories, add per ton	125	175
For field welded connections, add per ton	175	250
For multi-story masonry wall bearing construction, add to erection costs	30%	30%

General Average per Ton in Place for A36 Steel (High Strength Steel Base Price May Be Substituted)					
Item	Description	Bare Costs			Incl. Subs O&P
		Itemized	Summary		
Material	Base price	$ 410			
	Extras and delivery to shop	150			
	Drafting	70	$1,225		$1,348
	Shop fabrication & warehouse rehandling	445			
	Shop coat paint	40			
	Trucking to job site	110			
Installation	Unload and shake out, 1.0 hours @ $32.85	33			
	Erect and plumb, 5.0 hours @ $32.85	163	$ 384		$ 602
	Field bolt, 1.7 hours @ $32.85	55			
	Crane & minor erection equipment	133			
	Total per ton in place	$1,609	$1,609		$1,950

5

METALS

R05120-220   Steel Estimating Quantities

One estimate on erection is that a crane can handle 35 to 60 pieces per day. Say the average is 45. With usual sizes of beams, girders, and columns, this would amount to about 20 tons per day. The type of connection greatly affects the speed of erection. Moment connections for continuous design slow down production and increase erection costs.

Short open web bar joists can be set at the rate of 75 to 80 per day, with 50 per day being the average for setting long span joists.

After main members are calculated, add the following for usual allowances: base plates 2% to 3%; column splices 4% to 5%; and miscellaneous details 4% to 5%, for a total of 10% to 13% in addition to main members.

The ratio of column to beam tonnage varies depending on type of steels used, typical spans, story heights and live loads.

It is more economical to keep the column size constant and to vary the strength of the column by using high strength steels. This also saves floor space. Buildings have recently gone as high as ten stories with 8″ high strength columns. For light columns under W8X31 lb. sections, concrete filled steel columns are economical.

High strength steels may be used in columns and beams to save floor space and to meet head room requirements. High strength steels in some sizes sometimes require long lead times.

Round, square and rectangular columns, both plain and concrete filled, are readily available and save floor area, but are higher in cost per pound than rolled columns. For high unbraced columns, tube columns may be less expensive.

Below are average minimum figures for the weights of the structural steel frame for different types of buildings using A36 steel, rolled shapes and simple joints. For economy in domes, rise to span ratio = .13. Open web joist framing systems will reduce weights by 10% to 40%. Composite design can reduce steel weight by up to 25% but additional concrete floor slab thickness may be required. Continuous design can reduce the weights up to 20%. There are many building codes with different live load requirements and different structural requirements, such as hurricane and earthquake loadings which can alter the figures.

*See R13128-310 for Domes and Thin Shell Structures.

Structural Steel Weights per S.F. of Floor Area

Type of Building	No. of Stories	Avg. Spans	L.L. #/S.F.	Lbs. Per S.F.	Type of Building	No. of Stories	Avg. Spans	L.L. #/S.F.	Lbs. Per S.F.
Steel Frame Mfg.	1	20′x20′	40	8	Apartments	2-8	20′x20′	40	8
		30′x30′		13		9-25			14
		40′x40′		18	Office	to 10	Various	80	10
Parking garage	4	Various	80	8.5		20			18
Domes (Schwedler)*	1	200′	30	10		30			26
		300′		15		over 50			35

REFERENCE NOS.

R05120-225 Common Structural Steel Specifications

ASTM A36 is the all-purpose carbon grade steel widely used in building and bridge construction.

The other high-strength steels listed below may each have certain advantages over ASTM A36 stuctural carbon steel, depending on the application. They have proven to be economical choices where, due to lighter members, the reduction of dead load and the associated savings in shipping cost can be significant.

ASTM A588 atmospheric weathering, high-strength low-alloy steels can be used in the bare (uncoated) condition, where exposure to normal atmosphere causes a tightly adherant oxide to form on the surface protecting the steel from further oxidation. ASTM A242 corrosion-resistant, high-strength low-alloy steels have enhanced atmospheric corrosion resistance of at least two times that of carbon structural steels with copper, or four times that of carbon structural steels without copper. The reduction or elimination of maintenance resulting from the use of these steels often offsets their higher initial cost.

Steel Type	ASTM Designation	Minimum Yield Stress in KSI	Shapes Available
Carbon	A36	36	All structural shape groups, and plates & bars up thru 8″ thick
	A529	42	Structural shape group 1, and plates & bars up thru 1/2″ thick
High-Strength Low-Alloy Manganese-Vanadium	A441	40	Plates & bars over 4″ up thru 8″ thick
		42	Structural shape groups 4 & 5, and plates & bars over 1-1/2″ up thru 4″ thick
		46	Structural shape group 3, and plates & bars over 3/4″ up thru 1-1/2″ thick
		50	Structural shape groups 1 & 2, and plates & bars up thru 3/4″ thick
High-Strength Low-Alloy Columbium-Vanadium	A572	42	All structural shape groups, and plates & bars up thru 6″ thick
		50	All structural shape groups, and plates & bars up thru 4″ thick
		60	Structural shape groups 1 & 2, and plates & bars up thru 1-1/4″ thick
		65	Structural shape group 1, and plates & bars up thru 1-1/4″ thick
High-Strength Low-Alloy Columbium-Vanadium	A992	50	All structural shape groups
Corrosion-Resistant High-Strength Low-Alloy	A242	42	Structural shape groups 4 & 5, and plates & bars over 1-1/2″ up thru 4″ thick
		46	Structural shape group 3, and plates & bars over 3/4″ up thru 1-1/2″ thick
		50	Structural shape groups 1 & 2, and plates & bars up thru 3/4″ thick
Weathering High-Strength Low-Alloy	A588	42	Plates & bars over 5″ up thru 8″ thick
		46	Plates & bars over 4″ up thru 5″ thick
		50	All structural shape groups, and plates & bars up thru 4″ thick
Quenched and Tempered Low-Alloy	A852	70	Plates & bars up thru 4″ thick
Quenched and Tempered Alloy	A514	90	Plates & bars over 2-1/2″ up thru 6″ thick
		100	Plates & bars up thru 2-1/2″ thick

R05120-230 High Strength Steels

The mill price of these steels may be higher than A36 carbon steel but their proper use can achieve overall savings thru total reduced weights. For columns with L/r over 100, A36 steel is best; under 100, high strength steels are economical. For heavy columns high strength steels are economical when cover plates are eliminated. There is no economy using high strength steels for clip angles or supports or for beams where deflection governs. Thinner members are more economical than thick.

Below is a table of the high strength steels available and their base price with specification extras. A36 is included for comparison purposes. See also R05120-210 for typical in place costs of A36 steel. The per ton erection and fabricating costs of the high strength steels will be higher than for A36 since the same number of pieces, but less weight, will be installed. See R05120-240 for extras for Jumbo 14″ A36 columns.

Type of Steel	Minimum Yield Stress in KSI	Base	Size Extra		Spec. Extra	Base + Size & Spec. Extra		Size Extra	Spec. Extra	Base + Size Spec Extra
A36 Carbon Structural	36	$410	$0	— $140	—	$410	— $550	$120	—	$530
A529 Carbon Structural	42				—	410	— 550		—	530
A441 Manganese-Vanadium	40 to 50				—	410	— 550		—	530
A992 Columbium-Vanadium	50				—	410	— 550		—	530
A572 Columbiun-Vanadium	42				—	410	— 550		—	530
	50				$40	450	— 590		$45	575
	60				35	445	— 585		40	570
	65				40	450	— 590		50	580
A242 Corrosion-Resistant	42 to 50				—	410	— 550		—	530
A588 Weathering	42 to 50				60	470	— 610		60	590

Table header: **Mill Base Prices and Range of Size and Specification Extras per Ton for Structural Shapes** — **High Strength Low Alloy Steels** | **Special Column Sections W 14 x 455 Thru 805**

R05120-235   Common Steel Sections

The upper portion of this table shows the name, shape, common designation and basic characteristics of commonly used steel sections. The lower portion explains how to read the designations used for the above illustrated common sections.

Shape & Designation	Name & Characteristics	Shape & Designation	Name & Characteristics
W	W Shape Parallel flange surfaces	MC	Miscellaneous Channel Infrequently rolled by some producers
S	American Standard Beam (I Beam) Sloped inner flange	L	Angle Equal or unequal legs, constant thickness
M	Miscellaneous Beams Cannot be classified as W, HP or S; infrequently rolled by some producers	T	Structural Tee Cut from W, M or S on center of web
C	American Standard Channel Sloped inner flange	HP	Bearing Pile Parallel flanges and equal flange and web thickness

Common drawing designations follow:

W Shape
W 18 x 35
— Weight in Pounds per Foot
— Nominal Depth in Inches (Actual 17-3/4″)

American Standard Beam
S 12 x 31.8
— Weight in Pounds per Foot
— Depth in Inches

Miscellaneous Beam
M 8 x 6.5
— Weight in Pounds per Foot
— Depth in Inches

American Standard Channel
C 8 x 11.5
— Weight in Pounds per Foot
— Depth in Inches

Miscellaneous Channel
MC 8 x 22.8
— Weight in Pounds per Foot
— Depth in Inches

Angle
L 6 x 3-1/2 x 3/8
— Length of Long Leg in Inches
— Thickness of Each Leg in Inches
— Length of Other Leg in Inches

Tee Cut from W16 x 100
WT 8 x 50
— Weight in Pounds per Foot
— Nominal Depth in Inches (Actual 8-1/2″)

Tee Cut from S12 x 35
ST 6 x 17.5
— Weight in Pounds per Foot
— Depth in Inches (Actual 6-1/4″)

Tee Cut from M10 x 9
MT 5 x 4.5
— Weight in Pounds per Foot
— Depth in Inches

Bearing Pile
HP 12 x 84
— Weight in Pounds per Foot
— Nominal Depth in Inches (Actual 12-1/4″)

R05120-240   Structural Steel Extras

Principal Extras in Dollars Per Ton

Item quantity — using 5 tons per size as base price. Under 5 tons to 3 tons inclusive add $6 per ton. Under 3 tons to 2 tons inclusive add $11 per ton. Under 2 tons to 1 ton inclusive add $16 per ton. Under 1 ton to 1/2 ton add $55 per ton. Under 1/2 ton add $100 per ton.

Size Extras:

W Shapes: W36 x 393-135, W33 x 354-118, W30 x 326-90, W27 x 217-84, W24 x 176; W21 x 166, W18 x 311-130, W14 x 426-145, W12 x 336-136, add $20; W24 x 162-55, W21 x 147-44, W18 x 119-35, W16 x 100-26, W14 x 132-22, W12 x 120-14, W10 x 112-12, W8 x 67-10, W6 x 25-9, W5 x 19-16, and W4 x 13, no add; W14 x 808-455 add $124. For specification extras see R05120-230.

Miscellaneous Shapes: M14 x 18 to M5 x 18.9 no add. Standard Beams: S24 x 121-80, S20 x 96-66 add $140; S18 x 70 & 54.7, S15 x 50 & 42.9, S12 x 50-31.8, S10 x 35 & 25.4, S8 x 23 & 18.4, S7 x 20 & 15.3 and S6 x 17.25 & 12.5 add $80.

Standard Channels: C15 x 50-33.9, C12 x 30-20.7, C10 x 30-15.3, C9 x 20-13.4, C8 x 18.75-11.5, C7 x 14.75-9.8 add $60.

Miscellaneous Channels: MC18 x 58 to MC13 x 31.8 add $80; MC12 x 50 to MC6 x 18 add $80. Car Building Sections: add $120. Bulb Angles: add $140. Angles Equal & Unequal Leg: add $80.

Cambering: Channels, standard beams, tees & wide flange shapes to 300 lbs./ft. add $60.

Galvanizing under 1 ton, $600; over 20 tons, $500 per ton. For color coating of galvanizing add 40% to prices.

Government Specifications: MIL-S-20166 B, class U, type 1, Grade M-medium add $20; Grade HT-high tensile add $15. American Association of State Highway & Transportation Officials (AASHTO): Without Charpy Impacts, Grade M 188 no add; Grade M 222 add $65; M 223, Gr. 50 add $15.

Cut Lengths: 10' to 20' add $20; 20' to 25' add $20; 25' to 65' no add; over 65' to 90' no add; over 90' add $5.

Milling One or Two Ends: 10 lbs./ft. to 100 lbs./ft., over 10' add $70; over 100 lbs./ft., over 10' add $60.

Handling & Loading: Under 5 tons add $10. Banding or Wiring: add $10. Special loading: add $10. Special marking: add $10.

Special Testing: Bend Tests, $10, Charpy Impact Testing: one set of tests — impact strength values only, $5; one set of tests — impact strength values, lateral expansion, percent shear fracture, $7.

Special Straightening: For tolerances not more restrictive than 50% of standard camber or sweep, $7.

Splitting Beams to Produce Tees: over 15 lbs./ft.-30 lbs./ft., $60, over 30 lbs./ft.-150 lbs./ft. $40, over 150 lbs./ft., $35.

Chemistry: Ladle analysis limits for carbon, manganese, silicon & copper tests run from $10 to $30 per ton.

R05120-245   Installation Time for Structural Steel Building Components

The following tables show the expected average installation times for various structural steel shapes. Table A presents installation times for columns, Table B for beams, Table C for light framing and bolts, and Table D for structural steel for various project types.

Table A		
Description	**Labor-Hours**	**Unit**
Columns		
Steel, Concrete Filled		
3-1/2" Diameter	.933	Ea.
6-5/8" Diameter	1.120	Ea.
Steel Pipe		
3" Diameter	.933	Ea.
8" Diameter	1.120	Ea.
12" Diameter	1.244	Ea.
Structural Tubing		
4" x 4"	.966	Ea.
8" x 8"	1.120	Ea.
12" x 8"	1.167	Ea.
W Shape 2 Tier		
W8 x 31	.052	L.F.
W8 x 67	.057	L.F.
W10 x 45	.054	L.F.
W10 x 112	.058	L.F.
W12 x 50	.054	L.F.
W12 x 190	.061	L.F.
W14 x 74	.057	L.F.
W14 x 176	.061	L.F.

Table B				
Description	**Labor-Hours**	**Unit**	**Labor-Hours**	**Unit**
Beams, W Shape				
W6 x 9	.949	Ea.	.093	L.F.
W10 x 22	1.037	Ea.	.085	L.F.
W12 x 26	1.037	Ea.	.064	L.F.
W14 x 34	1.333	Ea.	.069	L.F.
W16 x 31	1.333	Ea.	.062	L.F.
W18 x 50	2.162	Ea.	.088	L.F.
W21 x 62	2.222	Ea.	.077	L.F.
W24 x 76	2.353	Ea.	.072	L.F.
W27 x 94	2.581	Ea.	.067	L.F.
W30 x 108	2.857	Ea.	.067	L.F.
W33 x 130	3.200	Ea.	.071	L.F.
W36 x 300	3.810	Ea.	.077	L.F.

Table C		
Description	**Labor-Hours**	**Unit**
Light Framing		
Angles 4" and Larger	.055	lbs.
Less than 4"	.091	lbs.
Channels 8" and Larger	.048	lbs.
Less than 8"	.072	lbs.
Cross Bracing Angles	.055	lbs.
Rods	.034	lbs.
Hanging Lintels	.069	lbs.
High Strength Bolts in Place		
3/4" Bolts	.070	Ea.
7/8" Bolts	.076	Ea.

Table D				
Description	**Labor-Hours**	**Unit**	**Labor-Hours**	**Unit**
Apartments, Nursing Homes, etc.				
1-2 Stories	4.211	Piece	7.767	Ton
3-6 Stories	4.444	Piece	7.921	Ton
7-15 Stories	4.923	Piece	9.014	Ton
Over 15 Stories	5.333	Piece	9.209	Ton
Offices, Hospitals, etc.				
1-2 Stories	4.211	Piece	7.767	Ton
3-6 Stories	4.741	Piece	8.889	Ton
7-15 Stories	4.923	Piece	9.014	Ton
Over 15 Stories	5.120	Piece	9.209	Ton
Industrial Buildings				
1 Story	3.478	Piece	6.202	Ton

R05120-250 Subpurlins

Bulb tee subpurlins are structural members designed to support and reinforce a variety of roof deck systems such as precast cement fiber roof deck tiles, monolithic roof deck systems, and gypsum or lightweight concrete over formboard. Other uses include interstitial service ceiling systems, wall panel systems, and joist anchoring in bond beams.

The table below shows bare costs for material only for subpurlins spaced at 32-5/8" O.C., purchased in lots of 10,000 to 40,000 pounds (see Division 05120-140 for pricing on a square foot basis). Maximum span is based on a 3-span condition with a total allowable vertical load of 55 psf.

Type	Bulb Tees, Painted					
	Height	Width	Wt. per L.F.	Sect. Modulus	Max. Span	Cost per L.F.
112	1-1/2"	1-1/2"	1.48 #	.126 in3	5'-6"	$.85
158	1-5/8"	1-9/16"	1.68	.172	6'-4"	.86
168	2"	1-1/2"	1.87	.253	7'-8"	.91
178	2"	1-5/8"	2.15	.324	8'-9"	1.00
218	2-1/8"	2-1/8"	3.19	.520	10'-2"	1.26
228	2-5/16"	2-1/16"	3.87	.736	12'-0"	1.60

METALS 5

REFERENCE NOS.

R05120-810 Dimensions and Weights of Sheet Steel

Gauge No.	Approximate Thickness				Weight		
	Inches (in fractions)	Inches (in decimal parts)		Millimeters	per S.F. in Ounces	per S.F. in Lbs.	per Square Meter in Kg.
	Wrought Iron	Wrought Iron	Steel	Steel			
0000000	1/2"	.5	.4782	12.146	320	20.000	97.650
000000	15/32"	.46875	.4484	11.389	300	18.750	91.550
00000	7/16"	.4375	.4185	10.630	280	17.500	85.440
0000	13/32"	.40625	.3886	9.870	260	16.250	79.330
000	3/8"	.375	.3587	9.111	240	15.000	73.240
00	11/32"	.34375	.3288	8.352	220	13.750	67.130
0	5/16"	.3125	.2989	7.592	200	12.500	61.030
1	9/32"	.28125	.2690	6.833	180	11.250	54.930
2	17/64"	.265625	.2541	6.454	170	10.625	51.880
3	1/4"	.25	.2391	6.073	160	10.000	48.820
4	15/64"	.234375	.2242	5.695	150	9.375	45.770
5	7/32"	.21875	.2092	5.314	140	8.750	42.720
6	13/64"	.203125	.1943	4.935	130	8.125	39.670
7	3/16"	.1875	.1793	4.554	120	7.500	36.320
8	11/64"	.171875	.1644	4.176	110	6.875	33.570
9	5/32"	.15625	.1495	3.797	100	6.250	30.520
10	9/64"	.140625	.1345	3.416	90	5.625	27.460
11	1/8"	.125	.1196	3.038	80	5.000	24.410
12	7/64"	.109375	.1046	2.657	70	4.375	21.360
13	3/32"	.09375	.0897	2.278	60	3.750	18.310
14	5/64"	.078125	.0747	1.897	50	3.125	15.260
15	9/128"	.0713125	.0673	1.709	45	2.813	13.730
16	1/16"	.0625	.0598	1.519	40	2.500	12.210
17	9/160"	.05625	.0538	1.367	36	2.250	10.990
18	1/20"	.05	.0478	1.214	32	2.000	9.765
19	7/160"	.04375	.0418	1.062	28	1.750	8.544
20	3/80"	.0375	.0359	.912	24	1.500	7.324
21	11/320"	.034375	.0329	.836	22	1.375	6.713
22	1/32"	.03125	.0299	.759	20	1.250	6.103
23	9/320"	.028125	.0269	.683	18	1.125	5.490
24	1/40"	.025	.0239	.607	16	1.000	4.882
25	7/320"	.021875	.0209	.531	14	.875	4.272
26	3/160"	.01875	.0179	.455	12	.750	3.662
27	11/640"	.0171875	.0164	.417	11	.688	3.357
28	1/64"	.015625	.0149	.378	10	.625	3.052

R05650-100 Single Track R.R. Siding

Description and Bare Costs	Quantity	Unit Cost	Bare Cost/L.F.	Cost with O&P/L.F.
Rail @ 100 lb/yard	.033 Ton	$ 777.00	$25.64	$ 28.20
Spikes, Plates, and Bolts	.200 CWT	50.00	10.00	11.00
6" x 8" x 8'-6" Treated Timber Ties, 22" O.C.	.550 Ea.	28.50	15.68	17.25
Ballast, 1-1/2" Stone @ .67 Ton/L.F.	.667 Ton	12.50	8.34	9.17
Crew B-14 @ 57 L.F./Day	.018 Day	1,341.00	24.14	36.05
Total Cost in Place			$83.80	$101.67

R05650-200 Single Track, Steel Ties, Concrete Bed

Description and Bare Costs	Quantity	Unit Cost	Bare Cost/L.F.	Cost with O&P/L.F.
Rail, Prime Grade @ 100 lb/yard	.033 Ton	$ 777.00	$ 25.64	$ 28.21
Fasteners and Plates	.200 CWT	50.00	10.00	11.00
6" WF Beams @ 30" O.C. 6'-6" Long	2.600 L.F.	6.20	16.12	17.73
Concrete, 9' wide, 10" thick	.280 C.Y.	76.00	21.28	23.41
Crew B-14 @ 22 L.F./Day	.045 Day	1,341.00	60.35	90.12
Total Cost in Place			$133.39	$170.47

METALS 5

REFERENCE NOS.

R06100-010   Thirty City Lumber Prices

Prices for boards are for #2 or better or sterling, whichever is in best supply. Dimension lumber is "Standard or Better" either Southern Yellow Pine (S.Y.P.), Spruce-Pine-Fir (S.P.F.), Hem-Fir (H.F.) or Douglas Fir (D.F.). The species of lumber used in a geographic area is listed by city. Plyform is 3/4" BB oil sealed fir or S.Y.P. whichever prevails locally, 3/4" CDX is S.Y.P. or Fir.

These are prices at the time of publication and should be checked against the current market price. Relative differences between cities will stay approximately constant.

City	Species	Contractor Purchases per M.B.F. S4S								Contractor Purchases per M.S.F.	
		Dimensions						Boards		3/4" Ext. Plyform	3/4" Thick CDX T&G
		2"x4"	2"x6"	2"x8"	2"x10"	2"x12"	4"x4"	1"x6"	1"x12"		
Atlanta	S.P.F.	$613	$577	$644	$819	$915	$ 824	$ 757	$1,289	$ 900	$ 804
Baltimore	S.P.F.	606	528	642	703	681	943	1000	1500	746	789
Boston	S.P.F.	610	568	630	790	830	1042	1920	1550	1032	831
Buffalo	H.F.	522	553	579	642	650	755	1280	1610	635	515
Chicago	S.P.F.	618	586	614	748	685	690	936	1543	779	774
Cincinnati	S.P.F.	609	683	691	795	882	863	1200	1446	824	904
Cleveland	S.P.F.	684	631	650	892	893	787	984	1910	1030	837
Columbus	S.P.F.	576	722	696	894	908	744	1419	1947	1186	775
Dallas	S.P.F.	784	656	609	690	731	668	728	1029	718	718
Denver	H.F.	642	631	646	766	658	958	771	1131	1196	900
Detroit	S.P.F.	559	589	614	851	886	594	1147	1859	804	889
Houston	S.Y.P.	537	536	536	592	641	802	707	855	985	703
Indianapolis	S.Y.F.	644	615	705	795	835	888	917	1177	825	840
Kansas City	D.F.	600	570	570	645	670	864	1050	1300	785	830
Los Angeles	D.F.	534	536	625	642	654	696	671	1385	690	790
Memphis	S.P.F.	710	654	693	834	770	1068	909	1314	954	1045
Milwaukee	S.P.F.	798	750	862	900	995	842	850	1237	828	859
Minneapolis	S.P.F.	569	545	536	675	754	674	1197	1409	1138	753
Nashville	S.P.F.	619	625	642	804	753	864	831	1543	910	754
New Orleans	S.Y.P.	587	577	561	612	570	732	591	1547	870	717
New York City	S.P.F.	548	522	605	666	577	1044	800	1101	1064	796
Philadelphia	H.F.	586	561	599	704	676	804	1223	1468	749	796
Phoenix	D.F.	624	658	715	838	768	1134	1178	1455	1308	924
Pittsburgh	H.F.	594	624	679	749	780	799	1300	1490	780	830
St. Louis	S.P.F.	496	470	412	438	506	858	910	654	742	691
San Antonio	S.Y.P.	536	531	618	662	737	616	743	712	753	802
San Diego	D.F.	531	522	550	618	588	768	1059	1178	1284	904
San Francisco	D.F.	498	490	487	630	625	840	760	1355	906	937
Seattle	S.P.F.	649	627	673	794	801	817	666	910	800	792
Washington, DC	S.P.F.	577	548	586	752	716	908	819	1210	1126	820
Average		$602	$590	$622	$731	$738	$ 830	$ 977	$1,337	$ 912	$ 811

To convert square feet of surface to board feet, 4% waste included.

S4S Size	Multiply S.F. by	T & G Size	Multiply S.F. by	Flooring Size	Multiply S.F. by
1 x 4	1.18	1 x 4	1.27	25/32" x 2-1/4"	1.37
1 x 6	1.13	1 x 6	1.18	25/32" x 3-1/4"	1.29
1 x 8	1.11	1 x 8	1.14	15/32" x 1-1/2"	1.54
1 x 10	1.09	2 x 6	2.36	1" x 3"	1.28
				1" x 4"	1.24

R06110-030 Lumber Product Material Prices

The price of forest products fluctuates widely from location to location and from season to season depending upon economic conditions. The table below indicates National Average material prices in effect Jan. 1, 2001. The table shows relative differences between various sizes, grades and species. These percentage differentials remain fairly constant even though lumber prices in general may change significantly during the year.

Availability of certain items depends upon geographic location and must be checked prior to firm price bidding.

	National Average Contractor Price, Quantity Purchase					Heavy Timbers, Fir	
	Dimension Lumber, S4S, #2 & Better, KD						
	Species	2"x4"	2"x6"	2"x8"	2"x10"	2"x12"	
Framing Lumber per MBF	Douglas Fir	$ 557	$ 565	$ 602	$ 689	$ 676	3" x 4" thru 3" x 12" $1,123
	Spruce	625	615	649	784	798	4" x 4" thru 4" x 12" 1,280
	Southern Yellow Pine	553	557	584	635	664	6" x 6" thru 6" x 12" 1,930
	Hem-Fir	586	603	639	731	706	8" x 8" thru 8" x 12" 1,983
							10" x 10" and 10" x 12" 2,013

| | S4S "D" Quality or Clear, KD | | | | | S4S # 2 & Better or Sterling, KD | | | | |
	Species	1"x4"	1"x6"	1"x8"	1"x10"	1"x12"	Species	1"x4"	1"x6"	1"x8"	1"x10"	1"x12"
Boards per MBF *See also Cedar Siding	Sugar Pine	$1,435	$1,589	$1,645	$1,960	$2,555	Sugar Pine	$665	$791	$833	$889	$1,092
	Idaho Pine	1,078	1,596	1,526	1,526	2,296	Idaho Pine	812	840	826	854	1,001
	Engleman Spruce	1,260	1,708	1,708	1,778	2,212	Engleman Spruce	518	700	819	749	987
	So. Yellow Pine	1,169	1,477	1,456	1,393	1,953	So. Yellow Pine	406	518	665	728	770
	Ponderosa Pine	1,155	1,400	1,421	1,722	2,009	Ponderosa Pine	504	679	791	721	938
	Redwood, CVG	3,940	3,880	3,750	3,770	5,940						

Flooring per MSF	1" x 4" Vertical grain, Fir "B" & better		$2,400	2-1/4" x 25/32" Maple, select	$2,970
	2-1/4" x 25/32", Oak, clear		3,200	#2 & better	2,700
	Select		3,050	2-1/4" x 33/32" Maple, #2 & better	3,132
	#1 common		2,700	3-1/4" x 33/32" Maple, #2 & better	2,916
	Oak, prefinished, standard & better		3,750	Parquet, unfinished, 5/16", minimum	2,700
	Standard		3,200	Maximum	5,850

Siding per MBF	Clapboard, Cedar, beveled		*Rough sawn, Cedar, T&G, "A" grade 1" x 4"	$2,434
	1/2" x 6" thru 1/2" x 8", clear	$1,442	1" x 6"	3,201
	"A" grade	1,330	"STK" grade, 1" x 6"	1,614
	"B" grade	1,225	Board, "STK" grade, 1" x 8"	1,561
	3/4" x 10" "clear"	2,592	Board & Batten 1" x 12"	1,561
	"A" grade	2,334	Cedar channel siding 1" x 8", #3 & better	$1,183
	Redwood, beveled		Factory stained	1,292
	1/2" x 6" thru 1/2" x 8", vertical grain, clear	1,907	White Pine siding, T&G, rough sawn	$ 637
	3/4" x 10" vertical grain, clear	2,889	Factory stained	837

Shingles per CSF	Red Cedar		White Cedar shingles	
	5X—16" long #1 regular	$ 146	16" long, extra grade (East Coast)	$ 84
	#2	71	Clear, 1st grade (East Coast)	123
	18" long perfections #1	172		
	#2	73	Fire retardant Red Cedar	
	Resquared & Rebutted #1	102	5X — 16" long	$ 251
			18" long perfections	284
	Handsplit shakes, resawn		Handsplit & resawn	
	24" long, 1/2" to 3/4"	141	24" long, 1/2" to 3/4"	241
	18" long, 1/2" to 3/4"	113	18" long, 1/2" to 3/4"	213

R06160-020   Plywood

There are two types of plywood used in construction: interior, which is moisture resistant but not waterproofed, and exterior, which is waterproofed.

The grade of the exterior surface of the plywood sheets is designated by the first letter: A, for smooth surface with patches allowed; B, for solid surface with patches and plugs allowed; C, which may be surface plugged or may have knot holes up to 1″ wide; and D, which is used only for interior type plywood and may have knot holes up to 2-1/2″ wide. "Structural Grade" is specifically designed for engineered applications such as box beams. All CC & DD grades have roof and floor spans marked on them.

Underlayment grade plywood runs from 1/4″ to 1-1/4″ thick. Thicknesses 5/8″ and over have optional tongue and groove joints which eliminates the need for blocking the edges. Underlayment 19/32″ and over may be referred to as Sturd-i-Floor.

The price of plywood can fluctuate widely due to geographic and economic conditions. When one or two local prices are known, the relative prices for other types and sizes may be found by direct factoring of the prices in the table below.

Typical uses for various plywood grades are as follows:

AA-AD Interior — cupboards, shelving, paneling, furniture

BB Plyform — concrete form plywood

CDX — wall and roof sheathing

Structural — box beams, girders, stressed skin panels

AA-AC Exterior — fences, signs, siding, soffits, etc.

Underlayment — base for resilient floor coverings

Overlaid HDO — high density for concrete forms & highway signs

Overlaid MDO — medium density for painting, siding, soffits & signs

303 Siding — exterior siding, textured, striated, embossed, etc.

Grade	Type		4′x8′	Type			4′x8′	4′x10′
	National Average Price in Lots of 10 MSF, per MSF-January 2001							
Sanded Grade	1/4″ Interior AD		$ 476	1/4″ Exterior AC			$ 490	$ 553
	3/8″		532	3/8″			546	561
	1/2″		644	1/2″			658	699
	5/8″		756	5/8″			770	859
	3/4″		1,050	3/4″			840	978
	1″		1,221	1″			1,089	1,126
	1-1/4″		1,464	Exterior AA, add			150	155
	Interior AA, add		150	Exterior AB, add			135	145
Unsanded Grade 4′ x 8′ Sheets				**CD Structural 1**		**Underlayment**		
	5/16″ CDX		$ 428	5/16″, 4′x8′ sheets $258	3/8″,	4′x8′ sheets		$ 588
	3/8″		435	3/8″ 325	1/2″			613
	1/2″		599	1/2″ 441	5/8″T&G			592
	5/8″		712	5/8″ 547	3/4″T&G			678
	3/4″		828	3/4″ 662	1-1/8″ 2-4-1T&G			1,036
	3/4″ T&G		863					
Form Plywood	5/8″ Exterior, oiled BB, plyform		$ 875	5/8″ HDO (overlay 2 sides)				$2,148
	3/4″ Exterior, oiled BB, plyform		987	3/4″ HDO (overlay 2 sides)				2,214
Overlaid 4′x8′ Sheets	Overlay 2 Sides MDO			Overlay 1 Side MDO				
	3/8″ thick		$1,345	3/8″ thick				$1,142
	1/2″		1,576	1/2″				1,316
	5/8″		1,776	5/8″				1,478
	3/4″		2,034	3/4″				1,734
303 Siding	Fir, rough sawn, natural finish, 3/8″ thick		$ 518	Texture 1-11		5/8″ thick, Fir		$ 945
	Redwood		1,796			Redwood		1,890
	Cedar		1,701			Cedar		1,537
	Southern Yellow Pine		418			Southern Yellow		763
Waferboard/O.S.B.	1/4″ sheathing		$ 248	19/32″ T&G				$ 468
	7/16″ sheathing		305	23/32″ T&G				563

For 2 MSF to 10 MSF, add 10%. For less than 2 MSF, add 15%.

R06170-100   Wood Roof Trusses

Loading figures represent live load. An additional load of 10 psf on the top chord and 10 psf on the bottom chord is included in the truss design. Spacing is 24" O.C.

Span in Feet	Cost per Truss for Different Live Loads and Roof Pitches					
	Flat	4 in 12 Pitch		5 in 12 Pitch		8 in 12 Pitch
	40 psf	30 psf	40 psf	30 psf	40 psf	30 psf
20	$ 61	$ 47	$ 49	$ 47	$ 51	$ 49
22	67	50	52	51	54	54
24	73	43	45	44	48	53
26	76	44	46	45	49	61
28	84	55	57	56	60	64
30	106	56	58	57	61	74
32	113	68	70	69	73	111
34	120	99	101	101	105	118
36	127	105	107	107	111	123
38	134	112	114	113	117	132
40	141	114	116	118	122	139

R06430-100   Wood Stair, Residential

One Flight with 8'-6" Story Height, 3'-6" Wide Oak Treads Open One Side, Built in Place				
Item	Quantity	Unit Cost	Bare Costs	Costs Incl. Subs O & P
Treads 10-1/2" x 1-1/16" thick	11 Ea.	$ 27.50	$ 302.50	$ 332.80
Landing tread nosing, rabbeted	1 Ea.	12.50	12.50	13.80
Risers 3/4" thick	12 Ea.	12.40	148.80	163.60
Single end starting step (range $175 to $210)	1 Ea.	193.00	193.00	212.40
Balusters (range $4.50 to $25.00)	22 Ea.	7.75	170.50	187.60
Newels, starting & landing (range $40 to $120)	2 Ea.	73.00	146.00	160.60
Rail starter (range $39 to $190)	1 Ea.	67.00	67.00	73.80
Handrail (range $4.50 to $10.30)	26 L.F.	7.00	182.00	200.20
Cove trim	50 L.F.	.78	39.00	43.00
Rough stringers three - 2 x 12's, 14' long	84 B.F.	.74	62.16	68.40
Carpenter's installation: Bare Cost	36 Hrs.	$ 29.15	$1,049.40	
Incl. Subs O & P		$ 45.60		$1,641.60
	Total per Flight		$2,372.86	$3,097.80

Add for rail return on second floor and for varnishing or other finish. Adjoining walls or landings must be figured separately.

R07110-010   1/2″ Pargeting (rough dampproofing plaster)

1:2-1/2 Mix, 4.5 C.F. Covers 100 S.F., 2 Coats, Waste Included		Regular Portland Cement		Waterproofed Portland Cement	
1.7	lbs. integral waterproofing admixture			$.65 per lb.	$ 1.11
1.7	bags Portland cement	$7.20 per bag	$ 12.24	$7.20 per bag	12.24
4.25	C.F. sand @ $15.20 per C.Y.		2.39		2.39
Labor mix, apply, crew D-1 @ $420.40 per day		.40 days	168.16	.40 days	168.16
	Total Bare Cost per 100 S.F.		$182.79		$183.90

R07310-020   Roof Slate

16″, 18″ and 20″ are standard lengths and slate usually comes in random widths. For standard 3/16″ thickness use 1-1/2″ copper nails. Allow for 3% breakage.

Quantities per Square	Unfading Vermont Colored	Weathering Sea Green	Buckingham, Virginia Black
Slate delivered (incl. punching)	$428.00	$323.00	$470.00
# 30 Felt, 2.5 lbs. copper nails	17.18	17.18	17.18
Slate roofer 4.6 hrs. @ $26.00 per hr.	119.60	119.60	119.60
Total Bare Cost per Square	$564.78	$459.78	$606.78

R07510-020 Built-Up Roofing

Asphalt is available in kegs of 100 lbs. each; coal tar pitch in 560 lb. kegs. Prepared roofing felts are available in a wide range of sizes, weights & characteristics. However, the most commonly used are #15 (432 S.F. per roll, 13 lbs. per square) and #30 (216 S.F. per roll, 27 lbs. per square).

Inter-ply bitumen varies from 24 lbs. per sq. (asphalt) to 30 lbs. per sq. (coal tar) per ply, ± 25%. Flood coat bitumen also varies from 60 lbs. per sq. (asphalt) to 75 lbs. per sq. (coal tar), ± 25%. Expendable equipment (mops, brooms, screeds, etc.) runs about 16% of the bitumen cost. For new, inexperienced crews this factor may be much higher.

Rigid insulation board is typically applied in two layers. The first is mechanically attached to nailable decks or spot or solid mopped to non-nailable decks; the second layer is then spot or solid mopped to the first layer. Membrane application follows the insulation, except in protected membrane roofs, where the membrane goes down first and the insulation on top, followed with ballast (stone or concrete pavers). Insulation and related labor costs are NOT included in Div. 07510-300; they can be found in Div. 07220-700.

Prices shown are bare costs only.

4-Ply Felt on Insulated Deck	Asphalt/Glass Fiber Felt		Coal Tar/Organic Felt	
4 ply #15 felt (1/4 roll per ply)	$3.75 per ply	$ 15.00	$7.50 per ply	$ 30.00
156 lbs. hot asphalt/195 lbs. hot tar	$260 per ton	20.24	$550 per ton	53.63
500 lbs. roofing stone (1/4″ to 1/2″)	$22.25 per ton	5.56	$22.25 per ton	5.56
Installation, crew G-1, @ $1,682.55 per day	.050 days	84.13	.048 days	80.76
Total Bare Cost per Square in-place		$124.93		$169.95

R07550-030 Modified Bitumen Roofing

The cost of modified bitumen roofing is highly dependent on the type of installation that is planned. Installation is based on the type of modifier used in the bitumen. The two most popular modifiers are atactic polypropylene (APP) and styrene butadiene styrene (SBS). The modifiers are added to heated bitumen during the manufacturing process to change its characteristics. A polyethylene, polyester or fiberglass reinforcing sheet is then sandwiched between layers of this bitumen. When completed, the result is a pre-assembled, built-up roof that has increased elasticity and weatherablility. Some manufacturers include a surfacing material such as ceramic or mineral granules, metal particles or sand.

The preferred method of adhering SBS-modified bitumen roofing to the substrate is with hot-mopped asphalt (much the same as built-up roofing). This installation method requires a tar kettle/pot to heat the asphalt, as well as the labor, tools and equipment necessary to distribute and spread the hot asphalt.

The alternative method for applying APP and SBS modified bitumen is as follows. A skilled installer uses a torch to melt a small pool of bitumen off the membrane. This pool must form across the entire roll for proper adhesion. The installer must unroll the roofing at a pace slow enough to melt the bitumen, but fast enough to prevent damage to the rest of the membrane.

Modified bitumen roofing provides the advantages of both built-up and single-ply roofing. Labor costs are reduced over those of built-up roofing because only a single ply is necessary. The elasticity of single-ply roofing is attained with the reinforcing sheet and polymer modifiers. Modifieds have some self-healing characteristics and because of their multi-layer construction, they offer the reliability and safety of built-up roofing.

R07800-030 Firestopping

Firestopping is the sealing of structural, mechanical, electrical and other penetrations through fire-rated assemblies. The basic components of firestop systems are safing insulation and firestop sealant on both sides of wall penetrations and the top side of floor penetrations.

Pipe penetrations are assumed to be through concrete, grout, or joint compound and can be sleeved or unsleeved. Costs for the penetrations and sleeves are not included. An annular space of 1″ is assumed. Escutcheons are not included.

Metallic pipe is assumed to be copper, aluminum, cast iron or similar metallic material. Insulated metallic pipe is assumed to be covered with a thermal insulating jacket of varying thickness and materials.

Non-metallic pipe is assumed to be PVC, CPVC, FR Polypropylene or similar plastic piping material. Intumescent firestop sealant or wrap strips are included. Collars on both sides of wall penetrations and a sheet metal plate on the underside of floor penetrations are included.

Ductwork is assumed to be sheet metal, stainless steel or similar metallic material. Duct penetrations are assumed to be through concrete, grout or joint compound. Costs for penetrations and sleeves are not included. An annular space of 1/2″ is assumed.

Multi-trade openings include costs for sheet metal forms, firestop mortar, wrap strips, collars and sealants as necessary.

Structural penetrations joints are assumed to be 1/2″ or less. CMU walls are assumed to be within 1-1/2″ of metal deck. Drywall walls are assumed to be tight to the underside of metal decking.

Metal panel, glass or curtain wall systems include a spandrel area of 5′ filled with mineral wool foil-faced insulation. Fasteners and stiffeners are included.

R08110-100 Hollow Metal Frames

Table below lists material prices only.

Frame for Opening Size	16 Ga. Frames		16 Ga. UL Frames		16 Ga. Drywall Frames		16 Ga. UL Drywall Frames	
	6-3/4" Deep	8-3/4" Deep	6-3/4" Deep	8-3/4" Deep	7-1/8" Deep	8-1/4" Deep	7-1/8" Deep	8-1/4" Deep
2'-0" x 6'-8"	$ 75	$ 88	$ 82	$ 94	$ 82	$ 89	$ 89	$ 96
2'-6" x 6'-8"	75	88	82	94	82	89	89	96
3'-0" x 7'-0"	77	89	83	96	84	90	90	97
3'-6" x 7'-0"	80	92	86	98	88	94	94	101
4'-0" x 7'-0"	80	92	86	98	88	94	94	101
6'-0" x 7'-0"	94	106	100	112	99	106	105	112
8'-0" x 8'-0"	119	130	126	136	107	126	126	133

For welded frames, add $27.00.
For galvanized frames, add $28.00.

R08110-120 Hollow Metal Doors

Table below lists material prices only, not including hardware or labor.

Door Thickness and Size		Full Flush Doors, 18 Ga.				Flush Fire Doors			
		Hollow Metal		Composite Core		Hollow Metal "B"		Hollow Metal Class "A"	
		Plain	Glazed	Plain	Glazed	20 Ga.	18 Ga.	16 Ga.	14 Ga.
1-3/4"	3'-0" x 6'-8"	$185	$288	$219	$322	$171	$191	$226	$283
	3'-0" x 7'-0"	192	295	226	329	179	198	234	290
	3'-6" x 7'-0"	230	334	266	370	—	236	277	337
	3'-0" x 8'-0"	254	358	288	392	233	261	291	348
	4'-0" x 8'-0"	306	410	342	445	—	312	358	417
1-3/8"	2'-0" x 6'-8"	182	286	—	—	164	189	218	275
	2'-6" x 6'-8"	187	291	—	—	168	194	223	280
	3'-0" x 7'-0"	192	295	—	—	179	198	234	290

R08210-100   Wood Doors

Table below, except where indicated, lists price per door only, not including frame, hardware or labor. For pre-hung exterior door units up to 3' x 7', add $135 per door for wood frame and hardware for types not listed under pre-hung. Pricing is for ten or more doors. Doors are factory trimmed for butts and locksets.

Door Thickness and Size		Flush Type Doors (Interior)					Architectural (1-3/4" Ext., 1-3/8" Int.)					
		Hollow Core		Solid Particle Core			Pine		Fir		Pre-hung	
		Lauan	Birch	Lauan	Birch	Oak	Panel	Glazed	Panel	Glazed	Pine Panel	Flush Birch S. C.
1-3/4"	2'-6" x 6'-8"	$30	$49	$ 64	$ 73 *	$ 78	$314	$359	$205	$248	$427	$181
	3'-0" x 6'-8"	34	55	72	82 *	90	338	379	205	248	450	191
	3'-0" x 7'-0"	43	60	80	88 *	99	380	408	223	265	498	206
	3'-6" x 7'-0"	60	84	101	114 *	123	—	—	—	—	—	338
	4'-0" x 7'-0"	66	89	112	124 *	133	—	—	—	—	—	338
1-3/8"	2'-0" x 6'-8"	24	38	54	67 *	70	112	—	184	—	190	140
	2'-6" x 6'-8"	27	43	60	73 *	78	125	151	197	219	203	148
	3'-0" x 6'-8"	30	49	69	82 *	90	144	165	208	224	222	157
	3'-0" x 7'-0"	39	54	76	88 *	99	192	—	—	—	282	—

*Add to the above for the following birch face door types:

Solid wood stave core, add $35	1 hour label door, add $72	8' high door, add 31%
3/4 hour label door, add $61	1-1/2 hour label door, add $82	

R08210-850   Tin Clad Fire Door

6' x 7' Opening, A Label	Double Sliding Door		Double Swing Door	
Doors, 3 Ply		$ 520.00		$ 520.00
Frame, 8" channel (11.5 lb. per L.F.), installed	275 lb.	101.75	275 lb.	101.75
Track, hangers, hardware	13.75 L.F.	693.00	Straps and hinges	326.00
2 Carpenters @ $29.15 per hour each	16 hrs. total	466.40	16 hrs. total	466.40
Complete in place		$1,781.15		$1,414.15

R08510-100   Steel Sash

Ironworker crew will erect 25 S.F. or 1.3 sash unit per hour, whichever is less.

Mechanic will point 30 L.F. per hour.

Painter will paint 90 S.F. per coat per hour.

Glazier production depends on light size.

Allow 1 lb. special steel sash putty per 16" x 20" light.

DOORS & WINDOWS 8

REFERENCE NOS.

R08550-010 Double Hung Windows - Tilt Wash

Ponderosa pine and vinyl clad sash, exterior primed with double insulated, low E glass.

| | 2'-0" x 3'-0" | | | | 3'-0" x 4'-0" | | | |
Description	Wood		Vinyl Clad		Wood		Vinyl Clad	
Window and frame, 2 lights		$159.90		$212.94		$200.46		$258.96
Removable grilles		14.00		14.00		22.00		22.00
Full screen		16.38		16.38		24.18		24.18
Interior trim set		16.00		16.00		20.00		20.00
Carpenter @ $29.15 per hr.	1.7 hr.	49.56	1.7 hr.	49.56	2 hr.	58.30	2 hr.	58.30
Complete in place		$255.84		$308.88		$324.94		$383.44

Mullions for above windows are about $28 each. Aluminum clad
double-hung windows run about $28.60 per S.F. of glass.

R08700-100 Hinges

All closer equipped doors should have ball bearing hinges. Lead lined or extremely heavy doors require special strength hinges. Usually 1-1/2 pair of hinges are used per door up to 7'-6" high openings. Table below shows typical hinge requirements.

Use Frequency	Type Hinge Required	Type of Opening	Type of Structure
High	Heavy weight	Entrances	Banks, Office buildings, Schools, Stores & Theaters
	ball bearing	Toilet Rooms	Office buildings and Schools
Average	Standard	Entrances	Dwellings
	weight	Corridors	Office buildings and Schools
	ball bearing	Toilet Rooms	Stores
Low	Plain bearing	Interior	Dwellings

| Door Thickness | Weight of Doors in Pounds per Square Foot | | | | |
	White Pine	Oak	Hollow Core	Solid Core	Hollow Metal
1-3/8"	3 psf	6 psf	1-1/2 psf	3-1/2 — 4 psf	6-1/2 psf
1-3/4"	3-1/2	7	2-1/2	4-1/2 — 5-1/4	6-1/2
2-1/4"	4-1/2	9	—	5-1/2 — 6-3/4	6-1/2

R08810-010   Glazing Labor

Glass sizes are estimated by the "united inch" (height + width). Table below shows the number of lights glazed in an eight hour period by the crew size indicated, for glass up to 1/4" thick. Square or nearly square lights are more economical on a S.F. basis. Long slender lights will have a high S.F. installation cost. For insulated glass reduce production by 33%. For 1/2" float glass reduce production by 50%. Production time for glazing with two glaziers per day averages: 1/4" float glass 120 S.F.; 1/2" float glass 55 S.F.; 1/2" insulated glass 95 S.F.; 3/4" insulated glass 75 S.F.

Glazing Method	United Inches per Light							
	40"	60"	80"	100"	135"	165"	200"	240"
Number of Men in Crew	1	1	1	1	2	3	3	4
Industrial sash, putty	60	45	24	15	18	—	—	—
With stops, putty bed	50	36	21	12	16	8	4	3
Wood stops, rubber	40	27	15	9	11	6	3	2
Metal stops, rubber	30	24	14	9	9	6	3	2
Structural glass	10	7	4	3	—	—	—	—
Corrugated glass	12	9	7	4	4	4	3	—
Storefronts	16	15	13	11	7	6	4	4
Skylights, putty glass	60	36	21	12	16	—	—	—
Thiokol set	15	15	11	9	9	6	3	2
Vinyl set, snap on	18	18	13	12	12	7	5	4
Maximum area per light	2.8 S.F.	6.3 S.F.	11.1 S.F.	17.4 S.F.	31.6 S.F.	47 S.F.	69 S.F.	100 S.F.
Daily Bare Crew Cost	$228.40	$228.40	$228.40	$228.40	$456.80	$685.20	$685.20	$913.60

R08810-100   Commercial Window Glass

Description		1/2" Insulated Glass		1/4" Plate Glass	
Glass per S.F.		$10.16	R Value	$ 3.86	R Value
Allow for breakage 10%		1.02	3.00	.39	.93
Glazing compound 1/2 lb. per S.F. @	$1.10 per lb.	.60	Average	.60	Average
Labor, 2 glaziers @	$28.55 per hour each (75 S.F./day)	6.09		6.09	
Total in place, per S.F.		$17.87		$10.94	

DOORS & WINDOWS 8

REFERENCE NOS.

R09205-050   Gypsum Lath

Item	Nailed to Wood Studs			Clipped to Steel Studs		
	Quantities and Bare Cost		Incl. O & P	Quantities and Bare Cost		Incl. O & P
105 S.Y. 3/8″ gypsum lath	$3.78 per S.Y.	$396.90	$436.59	$3.78 per S.Y.	$396.90	$436.59
Fasteners, nails & screws ···	6 lb. @ $1.33/lb.	7.98	8.78	1350 @ $4.26 /C	57.51	63.26
Lather @ $28.20 and $42.10 per hr.	9.4 hours	265.08	395.74	10.7 hours	301.74	450.47
Total per 100 S.Y. in place		$669.96	$841.11		$756.15	$950.32

Regular lath comes in 16″ x 32″ and 16″ x 48″ sheets. Firestop gypsum base comes in 4′ x 8′ sheets. For nailing use 1-1/8″ No. 13 ga. flathead blued nails.

R09205-060   Metal Lath

Painted Diamond Expanded	Nailed to Wood Studs			Screwed to Steel Studs		
	Quantity and Bare Cost		Incl. O & P	Quantity and Bare Cost		Incl. O & P
105 S.Y. 3.4 lb. lath ·-	$2.18 per S.Y.	$228.90	$251.79	$2.18 per S.Y.	$228.90	$251.79
Fasteners, corner beads, etc.		25.69	28.26		45.50	50.05
Lather @ $28.20 and $42.10 per hr.	10.0 hrs.	282.00	421.00	10.7 hrs.	301.74	450.47
Total per 100 S.Y. in place		$536.59	$701.05		$576.14	$752.31

Material prices of other types of lath in Div. 09200 may be substituted in the table above to arrive at their costs in place. For nailing on studs use a 1″ roofing nail with 7/16″ head. For nailing on ceiling use 1-1/2″ No. 11 ga. barbed roofers nail with 7/16″ head for holding power.

R09210-105   Gypsum Plaster

Quantities for 100 S.Y.	2 Coat, 5/8″ Thick		3 Coat, 3/4″ Thick		
	Base	Finish	Scratch	Brown	Finish
	1:3 Mix	2:1 Mix	1:2 Mix	1:3 Mix	2:1 Mix
Gypsum plaster	1300 lb.		1350 lb.	650 lb.	
Sand	1.75 C.Y.		1.85 C.Y.	1.35 C.Y.	
Finish hydrated lime		340 lb.			340 lb.
Gauging plaster		170 lb.			170 lb.

Total, in Place for 100 S.Y. on Walls				2 Coat, 5/8″ Thick			3 Coat, 3/4″ Thick		
				Quantities	Bare Cost	Incl. O & P	Quantities	Bare Cost	Incl. O & P
Gypsum plaster @	$ 13.33 per 80	lb. bag		1300 lb.	$ 216.61	$ 238.27	2000 lb.	$ 333.25	$ 366.58
Finish hydrated lime @	$ 5.65 per 50	lb. bag		340 lb.	38.42	42.26	340 lb.	38.42	42.26
Gauging plaster @	$ 22.26 per 100	lb. bag		170 lb.	37.84	41.62	170 lb.	37.84	41.62
Sand @	$ 16.60 per C.Y.			1.7 C.Y.	28.22	31.04	2.0 C.Y.	33.20	36.52
J-1 crew @	$1,081.70 &	$1,637.70 per day		.87 days	941.08	1,424.80	1.05 days	1135.79	1,719.59
Cleaning, staging, handling, patching				.09 days	94.68	144.46	.10 days	105.21	160.51
Total per 100 S.Y. in place					$1,356.85	$1,922.45		$1,683.71	$2,367.08

R09210-115   Vermiculite or Perlite Plaster

Proportions: Over lath, scratch coat and brown coat, 100# gypsum plaster to 2 C.F. aggregate; over masonry, 100# gypsum plaster to 3 C.F. aggregate.

Quantities for 100 S.Y.				2 Coat, 5/8″ Thick			3 Coat, 3/4″ Thick		
				Quantities	Bare Cost	Incl. O & P	Quantities	Bare Cost	Incl. O & P
Gypsum plaster @	$ 13.33 per 80	lb. bag		1250 lb.	$ 208.28	$ 229.11	2250 lb.	$ 374.91	$ 412.40
Vermiculite or perlite @	$ 13.03 per	bag		7.8 bags	101.63	111.79	11.3 bags	147.24	161.96
Finish hydrated lime @	$ 5.65 per 50	lb. bag		340 lb.	38.42	42.26	340 lb.	38.42	42.26
Gauging plaster @	$ 22.26 per 100	lb. bag		170 lb.	37.84	41.62	170 lb.	37.84	41.62
J-1 crew @	$1,086.20 &	$1,637.70 per day		1.00 days	1086.20	1,637.70	1.25 days	1,357.75	2,047.13
Cleaning, staging, handling, patching				.09 day	95.09	144.46	.10 days	105.66	160.51
Total per 100 S.Y. in place					$1,567.46	$2,206.94		$2,061.82	$2,865.88

9 FINISHES

REFERENCE NOS.

R09220-300 Stucco

Quantities for 100 S.Y. 3 Coats, 1″ Thick		On Wood Frame			On Masonry		
		Quantities	Bare Cost	Incl. O & P	Quantities	Bare Cost	Incl. O & P
Portland cement @	$ 7.20 per bag	29 bags	$ 208.80	$ 229.68	21 bags	$151.20	$ 166.32
Sand @	$15.20 per C.Y.	2.6 C.Y.	39.52	43.47	2 C.Y.	30.40	33.44
Hydrated lime @	$ 5.65 per 50 lb. bag	180 lb.	20.34	22.37	120 lb.	13.56	14.92
3.4lb Metal Lath @	$ 2.32 per S.Y., 3.6#	105 S.Y.	243.60	267.96	—	—	—
Furring nails and jute fiber			14.00	15.40		—	—
Mix and install with crew indicated		J-2 @ .74 days	970.73	1,461.13	J-1 @ .5 days	543.10	818.85
Cleaning, staging, handling, patching		.10 days	125.28	193.21	.10 days	102.72	157.87
Total per 100 S.Y. in place			$1,622.27	$2,233.22		$840.98	$1,191.40

R09250-100 Levels of Gypsum Drywall Finish

In the past, contract documents often used phrases such as "industry standard" and "workmanlike finish" to specify the expected quality of gypsum board wall and ceiling installations. The vagueness of these descriptions led to unacceptable work and disputes.

In order to resolve this problem, four major trade associations concerned with the manufacture, erection, finish and decoration of gypsum board wall and ceiling systems have developed an industry-wide *Recommended Levels of Gypsum Board Finish.*

The finish of gypsum board walls and ceilings for specific final decoration is dependent on a number of factors. A primary consideration is the location of the surface and the degree of decorative treatment desired. Painted and unpainted surfaces in warehouses and other areas where appearance is normally not critical may simply require the taping of wallboard joints and 'spotting' of fastener heads. Blemish-free, smooth, monolithic surfaces often intended for painted and decorated walls and ceilings in habitated structures, ranging from single-family dwellings through monumental buildings, require additional finishing prior to the application of the final decoration.

Other factors to be considered in determining the level of finish of the gypsum board surface are (1) the type of angle of surface illumination (both natural and artificial lighting), and (2) the paint and method of application or the type and finish of wallcovering specified as the final decoration. Critical lighting conditions, gloss paints, and thin wallcoverings require a higher level of gypsum board finish than do heavily textured surfaces which are subsequently painted or surfaces which are to be decorated with heavy grade wallcoverings.

The following descriptions were developed jointly by the Association of the Wall and Ceiling Industries-International (AWCI), Ceiling & Interior Systems Construction Association (CISCA), Gypsum Association (GA), and Painting and Decorating Contractors of America (PDCA) as a guide.

Level 0: No taping, finishing, or accessories required. This level of finish may be useful in temporary construction or whenever the final decoration has not been determined.

Level 1: All joints and interior angles shall have tape set in joint compound. Surface shall be free of excess joint compound. Tool marks and ridges are acceptable. Frequently specified in plenum areas above ceilings, in attics, in areas where the assembly would generally be concealed or in building service corridors, and other areas not normally open to public view.

Level 2: All joints and interior angles shall have tape embedded in joint compound and wiped with a joint knife leaving a thin coating of joint compound over all joints and interior angles. Fastener heads and accessories shall be covered with a coat of joint compound. Surface shall be free of excess joint compound. Tool marks and ridges are acceptable. Joint compound applied over the body of the tape at the time of tape embedment shall be considered a separate coat of joint compound and shall satisfy the conditions of this level. Specified where water-resistant gypsum backing board is used as a substrate for tile; may be specified in garages, warehouse storage, or other similar areas where surface appearance is not of primary concern.

Level 3: All joints and interior angles shall have tape embedded in joint compound and one additional coat of joint compound applied over all joints and interior angles. Fastener heads and accessories shall be covered with two separate coats of joint compound. All joint compound shall be smooth and free of tool marks and ridges. Typically specified in appearance areas which are to receive heavy- or medium-texture (spray or hand applied) finishes before final painting, or where heavy-grade wallcoverings are to be applied as the final decoration. This level of finish is not recommended where smooth painted surfaces or light to medium wallcoverings are specified.

Level 4: All joints and interior angles shall have tape embedded in joint compound and two separate coats of joint compound applied over all flat joints and one separate coat of joint compound applied over interior angles. Fastener heads and accessories shall be covered with three separate coats of joint compound. All joint compound shall be smooth and free of tool marks and ridges. This level should be specified where flat paints, light textures, or wallcoverings are to be applied. In critical lighting areas, flat paints applied over light textures tend to reduce joint photographing. Gloss, semi-gloss, and enamel paints are not recommended over this level of finish. The weight, texture, and sheen level of wallcoverings applied over this level of finish should be carefully evaluated. Joints and fasteners must be adequately concealed if the wallcovering material is lightweight, contains limited pattern, has a gloss finish, or any combination of these finishes is present. Unbacked vinyl wallcoverings are not recommended over this level of finish.

Level 5: All joints and interior angles shall have tape embedded in joint compound and two separate coats of joint compound applied over all flat joints and one separate coat of joint compound applied over interior angles. Fastener heads and accessories shall be covered with three separate coats of joint compound. A thin skim coat of joint compound or a material manufactured especially for this purpose, shall be applied to the entire surface. The surface shall be smooth and free of tool marks and ridges. This level of finish is highly recommended where gloss, semi-gloss, enamel, or nontextured flat paints are specified or where severe lighting conditions occur. This highest quality finish is the most effective method to provide a uniform surface and minimize the possibility of joint photographing and of fasteners showing through the final decoration.

R09400-100   Terrazzo Floor

5000 S.F. 5/8" Terrazzo Topping Quantities for 100 S.F.	Bonded to Concrete 1-1/8" Bed, 1:4 Mix			Not Bonded 2-1/8" Bed and 1/4" Sand		
	Quantities	Bare Cost	Incl. O & P	Quantities	Bare Cost	Incl. O & P
Portland cement @ $7.20 per bag	6 bags	$ 43.20	$ 47.52	8 bags	$ 57.60	$ 63.36
Sand @ $15.20 per C.Y.	10 C.F.	5.63	6.19	20 C.F.	11.26	12.39
Divider strips for 4' square panels, zinc, 14 ga.	55 L.F.	50.60	55.66	55 L.F.	50.60	55.66
Terrazzo fill, domestic aggregates	600 lb.	180.00	198.00	600 lb.	180.00	198.00
15 lb. tarred felt	—	—			2.00	2.20
Mesh 2 x 2 #14 galvanized	—	—			14.75	16.23
Crew J-3 @ $551.90 & $762.75 per day	.77 days	424.96	587.32	.87 days	480.15	663.59
Total per 100 S.F. in place	Bonded	$704.39	$894.69	Not Bonded	$796.36	$1,011.43

2' x 2' panels require 1 L.F. divider strip per S.F.; 6' x 6' panels need .33 L.F. per S.F.

R09658-600   Resilient Flooring and Base

Description	12" x 12" x 3/32" V.C. Tile			4" x 1/8" Vinyl Base		
	Quantities	Bare Cost	Incl. O & P	Quantities	Bare Cost	Incl. O & P
Vinyl composition, tile, standard line	100 S.F.	$112.00	$123.20	100 L.F.	$ 63.00	$ 69.30
Vinyl cement @ $15.10 per gallon	0.8 gallon	12.08	13.29	0.5 gallon	7.55	8.31
Tile layer @ $28.15 and $41.60 per hour	1.6 hrs.	45.04	66.56	2.55 hrs.	71.78	106.08
Total per 100 S.F. in place		$169.12	$203.05	100 L.F.	$142.33	$183.69

R09700-700   Wall Covering

Quantities for 100 S.F.	Medium Price Paper			Expensive Paper		
	Quantities	Bare Cost	Incl. O & P	Quantities	Bare Cost	Incl. O & P
Paper @ $30.00 and $67.00 per double roll	1.6 dbl. rolls	$48.00	$ 52.80	1.6 dbl. rolls	$107.20	$117.92
Wall sizing @ $14.65 per gallon	.25 gallon	3.66	4.03	.25 gallon	3.66	4.03
Vinyl wall paste @ $19.59 per gallon	0.4 gallon	7.84	8.62	0.4 gallon	7.84	8.62
Apply sizing @ $26.25 and $40.00 per hour	0.3 hour	7.88	12.00	0.3 hour	7.88	12.00
Apply paper @ $26.25 and $40.00 per hour	1.2 hours	31.50	48.00	1.5 hours	39.38	60.00
Total including waste allowance per 100 S.F.		$98.88	$125.45		$165.96	$202.57

This is equivalent to about $78.50 and $110.00 per double roll complete in place. Most wallpapers now come in double rolls only. To remove old paper allow 1.3 hours per 100 S.F.

9

FINISHES

REFERENCE NOS.

R09910-100   Paint

Material prices per gallon in 5 gallon lots, up to 25 gallons. For 100 gallons, deduct 10%.

Exterior, Alkyd (oil base)		**Masonry, Exterior**		Rust inhibitor ferrous metal	$23.75
Flat	$23.00	Alkali resistant primer	$19.25	Zinc chromate	20.00
Gloss	22.50	Block filler, epoxy	20.25		
Primer	21.50	Block filler, latex	10.00	**Heavy Duty Coatings**	
		Latex, flat or semi-gloss	19.75	Acrylic urethane	45.25
				Chlorinated rubber	30.00
Exterior, Latex (water base)		**Masonry, Interior**		Coal tar epoxy	34.00
Acrylic stain	19.00	Alkali resistant primer	16.50	Metal pretreatment (polyvinyl butyral)	23.50
Gloss enamel	24.00	Block filler, epoxy	23.25	Polyamide epoxy finish	31.50
Flat	18.25	Block filler, latex	10.25	Polyamide epoxy primer	31.50
Primer	20.00	Floor, alkyd	21.50	Silicone alkyd	32.00
Semi-gloss	23.00	Floor, latex	21.50	2 component solvent based acrylic epoxy	59.50
		Latex, flat acrylic	11.50	2 component solvent based polyester epoxy	88.50
Interior, Alkyd (oil base)		Latex, flat emulsion	11.00	Vinyl	27.00
Enamel undercoater	22.00	Latex, sealer	12.75	Zinc rich primer	94.75
Flat	19.50	Latex, semi-gloss	18.75		
Gloss	26.00			**Special Coatings/Miscellaneous**	
Primer sealer	17.75	**Varnish and Stain**		Aluminum	22.75
Semi-gloss	22.50	Alkyd clear	21.50	Dry fall out, flat	12.25
		Polyurethane, clear	22.00	Fire retardant, intumescent	36.50
		Primer sealer	15.50	Linseed oil	11.00
		Semi-transparent stain	18.50	Shellac	18.75
Interior, Latex (water base)		Solid color stain	18.25	Swimming pool, epoxy or urethane base	36.00
Enamel undercoater	15.75			Swimming pool, rubber base	27.25
Flat	17.00	**Metal Coatings**		Texture paint	11.50
Floor and deck	21.25	Galvanized	25.00	Turpentine	10.75
Gloss	24.00	High heat	49.00	Water repellent 5% silicone	17.75
Primer sealer	17.75	Machinery enamel, alkyd	26.25		
Semi-gloss	20.50	Normal heat	27.00		

R09910-220   Painting

Item	Coat	One Gallon Covers			In 8 Hours a Laborer Covers			Labor-Hours per 100 S.F.		
		Brush	**Roller**	**Spray**	**Brush**	**Roller**	**Spray**	**Brush**	**Roller**	**Spray**
Paint wood siding	prime	250 S.F.	225 S.F.	290 S.F.	1150 S.F.	1300 S.F.	2275 S.F.	.695	.615	.351
	others	270	250	290	1300	1625	2600	.615	.492	.307
Paint exterior trim	prime	400	—	—	650	—	—	1.230	—	—
	1st	475	—	—	800	—	—	1.000	—	—
	2nd	520	—	—	975	—	—	.820	—	—
Paint shingle siding	prime	270	255	300	650	975	1950	1.230	.820	.410
	others	360	340	380	800	1150	2275	1.000	.695	.351
Stain shingle siding	1st	180	170	200	750	1125	2250	1.068	.711	.355
	2nd	270	250	290	900	1325	2600	.888	.603	.307
Paint brick masonry	prime	180	135	160	750	800	1800	1.066	1.000	.444
	1st	270	225	290	815	975	2275	.981	.820	.351
	2nd	340	305	360	815	1150	2925	.981	.695	.273
Paint interior plaster or drywall	prime	400	380	495	1150	2000	3250	.695	.400	.246
	others	450	425	495	1300	2300	4000	.615	.347	.200
Paint interior doors and windows	prime	400	—	—	650	—	—	1.230	—	—
	1st	425	—	—	800	—	—	1.000	—	—
	2nd	450	—	—	975	—	—	.820	—	—

R10505-050   Steel Lockers

Price per Opening, Material Only, Based on 100 Openings, Not Including Locks					
Single Tier	**1-Wide**	**3-Wide**	**Double Tier**	**1-Wide**	**3-Wide**
12" x 12" x 60"	$137.50	$115.00	12" x 12" x 30"	$71.50	$53.50
12" x 15" x 60"	145.00	121.00	12" x 12" x 36"	73.50	57.50
12" x 18" x 60"	155.00	127.00	12" x 15" x 36"	75.00	58.50
12" x 12" x 72"	152.50	130.00	12" x 18" x 36"	77.00	60.00
12" x 15" x 72"	159.00	132.50	15" x 15" x 36"	90.00	75.00
12" x 18" x 72"	167.00	135.00	**Multiple Tier**	**1-Wide**	**3-Wide**
15" x 18" x 72"	180.00	145.00	5-High 12" x 12" x 12"	$30.50	$24.50
18" x 18" x 72"	189.00	160.00	12" x 15" x 12"	31.50	25.00
18" x 21" x 72"	201.00	168.00	15" x 15" x 12"	35.00	30.00
			6-High 12" x 12" x 12"	28.50	23.00
			12" x 15" x 12"	29.50	23.50

R13011-110   Air Supported Structures

Air supported structures are made from fabrics that can be classified into two groups: temporary and permanent. Temporary fabrics include nylon, woven polyethylene, vinyl film, and vinyl coated dacron. These have lifespans that range from five to fifteen plus years, and costs that vary accordingly from $7.50 to $15 per S.F. floor area. This is a package cost for a fabric shell, tension cables, primary and back-up inflation systems and doors. The lower cost structures are used for construction shelters, bulk storage and pond covers. The more expensive are used for recreational structures and warehouses.

Permanent fabrics are teflon coated fiberglass. The package cost runs $35 to $40 per S.F. floor area. The life of this structure is twenty plus years. The high cost limits its application to architectural designed structures which call for a clear span covered area, such as stadiums and convention centers. Both temporary and permanent structures are available in translucent fabrics which eliminates the need for daytime lighting.

Areas to be covered vary from 10,000 S.F. to any area up to 1000 foot wide by any lenght. Height restrictions range from a maximum of 1/2 of width to a minimum of 1/6 of the width. Erection of even the largest of the temporary structures requires no more than a week ($.07 to $.25 per S.F. floor area).

Centrifugal fans provide the inflation necessary to support the structure during application of live loads. Airlocks are usually used at large entrances to prevent loss of static pressure. Some manufacturers employ propeller fans which generate sufficient airflow (30,000 CFM) to eliminate the need for airlocks. These fans may also be automatically controlled to resist high wind conditions, regulate humidity (air changes), and provide cooling and heat.

Insulation can be provided with the addition of a second or even third interior liner, creating a dead air space with an "R" value of four to nine. Some structures allow for the liner to be collapsed into the outer shell to enable the internal heat to melt accumulated snow. For cooling or air conditioning, the exterior face of the liner can be aluminized to reflect the sun's heat. Costs for the liner run about $1.00 to $1.75 per S.F. floor area.

R13128-210   Pre-engineered Steel Buildings

These buildings are manufactured by many companies and normally erected by franchised dealers throughout the U.S. The four basic types are: Rigid Frames, Truss type, Post and Beam and the Sloped Beam type. Most popular roof slope is low pitch of 1" in 12". The minimum economical area of these buildings is about 3000 S.F. of floor area. Bay sizes are usually 20' to 24' but can go as high as 30' with heavier girts and purlins. Eave heights are usually 12' to 24' with 18' to 20' most typical.

Material prices shown in Division 13128-700 are bare costs for the building shell only and do not include floors, foundations, interior finishes or utilities. Costs assume at least three bays of 24' each, a 1" in 12" roof slope, and they are based on 30 psf roof load and 20 psf wind load (wind load is a function of wind speed, building height, and terrain characteristics; this should be determined by a Registered Structural Engineer) and no unusual requirements. Costs include the structural frame, 26 ga. non-insulated colored corrugated or ribbed roofing or siding panels, fasteners, closures, trim and flashing but no allowance for insulation, doors, windows, skylights, gutters or downspouts. Very large projects would generally cost less for materials than the prices shown. For roof panel substitutions, see Section 07410-700; for wall panels, see Section 07460-800.

Conditions at the site, weather, shape and size of the building, and labor availability will affect the erection cost of the building.

13 SPECIAL CONSTRUCTION REFERENCE NOS.

R13128-310 Dome Structures

Steel — The four types are Lamella, Schwedler, Arch and Geodesic. For maximum economy, rise should be about 15 to 20% of diameter. Most common diameters are in the 200' to 300' range. Lamella domes weigh about 5 P.S.F. of floor area less than Schwedler domes. Schwedler dome weight in lbs. per S.F. approaches .046 times the diameter. Domes below 125' diameter weigh .07 times diameter and the cost per ton of steel is higher. Recent costs per ton erected range from $1,800 to $2,800 per ton of steel. See R05120-220 for estimating weights.

Wood — Small domes are of sawn lumber, larger ones are laminated. In larger sizes, triaxial and triangular cost about the same; radial domes cost more. Radial domes are economical in the 60' to 70' diameter range. Most economical range of all types is 80' to 200' diameters. Diameters can run over 400'. Costs above foundations run $32 per S.F. for under 50' diameter. At 77' diameter, radial cost $20 and triaxial cost $23 per S.F. Cost is $14.00 for 120'; $20.00 for 200'; $25.50 for 300' and $33.00 for 400' diameter. Prices include 2" decking and tension tie ring in place.

Plywood — See division 06120-200 for stressed skin and folded plates. Stock prefab geodesic domes are available with diameters from 24' to 60'. Shells cost between $9.00 to $20.00 per S.F. of floor with erection running between $.58 and $2.60 per S.F. Canopies without sides run about $1.20 per S.F. less.

Fiberglass — Aluminum framed translucent sandwich panels with spans from 5' to 45' are commercially available.

Aluminum — Stressed skin aluminum panels form geodesic domes with spans ranging from 82' to 232'. Total in-place cost for the entire range is $35.00 per S.F. of floor. For vinyl faced fiberglass insulation with an R rating of 20, add $10.00 per S.F. of floor. An aluminum space truss, triangulated or nontriangulated, with aluminum or clear acrylic closure panels can be used for clear spans of 40' to 415'. The aluminum panel costs range from $22 to $24 per S.F. floor, plus $5 per S.F. for R 19 bonded thermal and acoustical insulation. The total in-place cost for the acrylic panel is from $70 to $75 per S.F. of floor.

R13128-520 Swimming Pools

Pool prices given per square foot of surface area include pool structure, filter and chlorination equipment where required, pumps, related piping, diving boards, ladders, maintenance kit, skimmer and vacuum system. Decks and electrical service to equipment are not included.

Residential in-ground pool construction can be divided into two categories: vinyl lined and gunite. Vinyl lined pool walls are constructed of different materials including wood, concrete, plastic or metal. The bottom is often graded with sand over which the vinyl liner is installed. Costs are generally in the $16 to $23 per S.F. range. Vermiculite or soil cement bottoms may be substituted for an added cost.

Gunite pool construction is used both in residential and municipal installations. These structures are steel reinforced for strength and finished

with a white cement limestone plaster. Residential costs run from $26 to $38 per S.F. surface. Municipal costs vary from $51 to $77 because plumbing codes require more expensive materials, chlorination equipment and higher filtration rates.

Municipal pools greater than 1,800 S.F. require gutter systems to control waves. This gutter may be formed into the concrete wall. Often a vinyl, stainless steel gutter or gutter and wall system is specified, which will raise the pool cost an additional $60 to $150 per L.F. of gutter installed and up to $290 per L.F. if a gutter and wall system is installed.

Competition pools usually require tile bottoms and sides with contrasting lane striping. Add $12 per S.F. of wall or bottom to be tiled.

R13128-910 Public Garage Costs

Cars	Per Car	Levels	Per Car	Levels	Per Car	Levels	Per S.F.
200 to 400	$ 9,950	3	$10,425	6	$10,225	Surface	$27.50
400 to 600	$10,250	4	$10,425	7	$10,575	2	$28.15
600 to 800	$10,675	5	$10,225	8 to 12	$11,075	3 or 4	$34.40
800 to 1200	$11,075					5 or 6	$33.95
Average	$10,500	Average per Car (310 to 320 S.F. per car)			$10,500	7 or 8	$35.65

The above costs refer to open wall construction. For enclosed structures, costs must be added for sprinkler and ventilation systems.

R13281-120   Asbestos Removal Process

Asbestos removal is accomplished by a specialty contractor who understands the federal and state regulations regarding the handling and disposal of the material. The process of asbestos removal is divided into many individual steps. An accurate estimate can be calculated only after all the steps have been priced.

The steps are generally as follows:

1. Obtain an asbestos abatement plan from an industrial hygienist.
2. Monitor the air quality in and around the removal area and along the path of travel between the removal area and transport area. This establishes the background contamination.
3. Construct a two part decontamination chamber at entrance to removal area.
4. Install a HEPA filter to create a negative pressure in the removal area.
5. Install wall, floor and ceiling protection as required by the plan, usually 2 layers of fireproof 6 mil polyethylene.

6. Industrial hygienist visually inspects work area to verify compliance with plan.
7. Provide temporary supports for conduit and piping affected by the removal process.
8. Proceed with asbestos removal and bagging process. Monitor air quality as described in Step #2. Discontinue operations when contaminate levels exceed applicable standards.
9. Document the legal disposal of materials in accordance with EPA standards.
10. Thoroughly clean removal area including all ledges, crevices and surfaces.
11. Post abatement inspection by industrial hygienist to verify plan compliance.
12. Provide a certificate from a licensed industrial hygienist attesting that contaminate levels are within acceptable standards before returning area to regular use.

R13281-460   Lead Paint Remediation Methods

Lead paint remediation can be accomplished by the following methods.

1. Abrasive blast
2. Chemical stripping
3. Power tool cleaning with vacuum collection system
4. Encapsulation
5. Remove and replace
6. Enclosure

Each of these methods has strengths and weakness depending on the specific circumstances of the project. The following is an overview of each method.

1. **Abrasive blasting** is usually accomplished with sand or recyclable metallic blast. Before work can begin, the area must be contained to ensure the blast material with lead does not escape to the atmosphere. The use of vacuum blast greatly reduces the containment requirements. Lead abatement equipment that may be associated with this work includes a negative air machine. In addition, it is necessary to have an industrial hygienist monitor the project on a continual basis. When the work is complete, the spent blast sand with lead must be disposed of as a hazardous material. If metallic shot was used, the lead is separated from the shot and disposed of as hazardous material. Worker protection includes disposable clothing and respiratory protection.

2. **Chemical stripping** requires strong chemicals be applied to the surface to remove the lead paint. Before the work can begin, the area under/adjacent to the work area must be covered to catch the chemical and removed lead. After the chemical is applied to the painted surface it is usually covered with paper. The chemical is left in place for the specified period, then the paper with lead paint is pulled or scraped off. The process may require several chemical applications. The paper with chemicals and lead paint adhered to it, plus the containment and loose scrapings collected by a HEPA (High Efficiency Particulate Air Filter) vac, must be disposed of as a hazardous material. The chemical stripping process usually requires a neutralizing agent and several wash downs after the paint is removed. Worker protection includes a neoprene or other compatible protective clothing and respiratory protection with face shield. An industrial hygienist is required intermittently during the process.

3. **Power tool cleaning** is accomplished using shrouded needle blasting guns. The shrouding with different end configurations is held up against the surface to be cleaned. The area is blasted with hardened needles and the shroud captures the lead with a HEPA vac and deposits it in a holding tank. An industrial hygienist monitors the project, protective clothing and a respirator is required until air samples prove otherwise. When the work is complete the lead must be disposed of as a hazardous material.

4. **Encapsulation** is a method that leaves the well bonded lead paint in place after the peeling paint has been removed. Before the work can begin, the area under/adjacent to the work must be covered to catch the scrapings. The scraped surface is then washed with a detergent and rinsed. The prepared surface is covered with approximately 10 mils of paint. A reinforcing fabric can also be embedded in the paint covering. The scraped paint and containment must be disposed of as a hazardous material. Workers must wear protective clothing and respirators.

5. **Remove and replace** is an effective way to remove lead paint from windows, gypsum walls and concrete masonry surfaces. The painted materials are removed and new materials are installed. Workers should wear a respirator and tyvek suit. The demolished materials must be disposed of as hazardous waste if it fails the TCLP (Toxicity Characteristic Leachate Process) test.

6. **Enclosure** is the process that permanently seals lead painted materials in place. This process has many applications such as covering lead painted drywall with new drywall, covering exterior construction with tyvek paper then residing, or covering lead painted structural members with aluminum or plastic. The seams on all enclosing materials must be securely sealed. An industrial hygienist monitors the project, and protective clothing and a respirator is required until air samples prove otherwise.

All the processes require clearance monitoring and wipe testing as required by the hygienist.

R13600-610   Solar Heating (Space and Hot Water)

Collectors should face as close to due South as possible, however, variations of up to 20 degrees on either side of true South are acceptable. Local climate and collector type may influence the choice between east or west deviations. Obviously they should be located so they are not shaded from the sun's rays. Incline collectors at a slope of latitude minus 5 degrees for domestic hot water and latitude plus 15 degrees for space heating.

Flat plate collectors consist of a number of components as follows: Insulation to reduce heat loss through the bottom and sides of the collector. The enclosure which contains all the components in this assembly is usually weatherproof and prevents dust, wind and water from coming in contact with the absorber plate. The cover plate usually consists of one or more layers of a variety of glass or plastic and reduces the reradiation by creating an air space which traps the heat between the cover and the absorber plates.

The absorber plate must have a good thermal bond with the fluid passages. The absorber plate is usually metallic and treated with a surface coating which improves absorptivity. Black or dark paints or selective coatings are used for this purpose, and the design of this passage and plate combination helps determine a solar system's effectiveness.

Heat transfer fluid passage tubes are attached above and below or integral with an absorber plate for the purpose of transferring thermal energy from the absorber plate to a heat transfer medium. The heat exchanger is a device for transferring thermal energy from one fluid to another.

Piping and storage tanks should be well insulated to minimize heat losses.

Size domestic water heating storage tanks to hold 20 gallons of water per user, minimum, plus 10 gallons per dishwasher or washing machine. For domestic water heating an optimum collector size is approximately 3/4 square foot of area per gallon of water storage. For space heating of residences and small commercial applications the collector is commonly sized between 30% and 50% of the internal floor area. For space heating of large commercial applications, collector areas less than 30% of the internal floor area can still provide significant heat reductions.

A supplementary heat source is recommended for Northern states for December through February.

The solar energy transmission per square foot of collector surface varies greatly with the material used. Initial cost, heat transmittance and useful life are obviously interrelated.

R14200-100   Freight Elevators

Capacities run from 2,000 lbs. to over 100,000 lbs. with 3,000 lbs. to 10,000 lbs. most common. Travel speeds are generally lower and control less intricate than on passenger elevators. Unit prices in division 14210-200 are for hydraulic and geared elevators.

CONVEYING SYSTEMS 14

REFERENCE NOS.

Conveying Systems | R142 | Elevators

R14200-200 Elevator Selective Costs
See R14200-400 for cost development.

A. Base Unit	Passenger		Freight		Hospital	
	Hydraulic	**Electric**	**Hydraulic**	**Electric**	**Hydraulic**	**Electric**
Capacity	1,500 Lb.	2,000 Lb.	2,000 Lb.	4,000 Lb.	4,000 lb.	4,000 lb.
Speed	100 F.P.M.	200 F.P.M.	100 F.P.M.	200 F.P.M.	100 F.P.M.	200 F.P.M.
#Stops/Travel Ft.	2/12	4/40	2/20	4/40	2/20	4/40
Push Button Oper.	Yes	Yes	Yes	Yes	Yes	Yes
Telephone Box & Wire	"	"	"	"	"	"
Emergency Lighting	"	"	No	No	"	"
Cab	Plastic Lam. Walls	Plastic Lam. Walls	Painted Steel	Painted Steel	Plastic Lam. Walls	Plastic Lam. Walls
Cove Lighting	Yes	Yes	No	No	Yes	Yes
Floor	V.C.T.	V.C.T.	Wood w/Safety Treads	Wood w/Safety Treads	V.C.T.	V.C.T.
Doors, & Speedside Slide	Yes	Yes	Yes	Yes	Yes	Yes
Gates, Manual	No	No	No	No	No	No
Signals, Lighted Buttons	Car and Hall	Car and Hall	Car and Hall	Car and Hall	Car and Hall	Car and Hall
O.H. Geared Machine	N.A.	Yes	N.A.	Yes	N.A.	Yes
Variable Voltage Contr.	"	"	N.A.	"	"	"
Emergency Alarm	Yes	"	Yes	"	Yes	"
Class "A" Loading	N.A.	N.A.	"	"	N.A.	N.A.
Base Cost	$38,260	$84,943	$44,239	$87,854	$49,697	$89,888
B. Capacity Adjustment						
2,000 Lb.	$ 536					
2,500	1,167	$ 2,766	$ 2,298			
3,000	2,957	4,223	3,967			
3,500	5,012	6,018	5,999			
4,000	5,781	6,156	6,420			
4,500	6,988	8,094	7,621		$ 5,827	$ 5,014
5,000	9,758	10,295	10,390	$ 5,064	8,487	6,547
6,000			10,962	8,929		
7,000			17,238	11,955		
8,000			18,785	16,824		
10,000			19,947	20,052		
12,000			24,084	24,486		
16,000			31,405	29,407		
20,000			34,850	32,439		
C. Travel Over Base	$ 345 V.L.F.	$ 222 V.L.F.	$ 345 V.L.F.	$ 222 V.L.F.	$ 345 V.L.F.	$ 222 V.L.F.
D. Additional Stops	$ 3,512 Ea.	$ 5,500 Ea.	$ 3,662 Ea.	$ 5,027 Ea.	$ 6,052 Ea.	$ 6,067 Ea.
E. Speed Adjustment						
100 F.P.M.			$ 728			
125	$ 800		1,382		$ 1,382	
150	1,725		2,616		2,327	
175	3,046		4,102		3,743	
200	4,914				5,462	
Geared 250		$ 2,275		$ 9,691		$ 2,446
4 Flrs. 300		4,683		12,090		4,651
Min. 350		5,558		14,269		5,674
400		7,891		16,134		7,903
Gearless 500		37,075		20,307		35,450
4 Flrs. 600		39,153		22,439		39,154
Min. 700		42,855		26,141		42,745
800		47,224		29,057		47,229
1,000		Spec. Applic.		Spec. Applic.		Spec. Applic.
1,200		"		"		"
F. Other Than Class						
"A" Loading						
"B"			$ 1,714	$ 1,757		
"C-1"			4,299	4,346		
"C-2"			5,147	5,187		
"C-3"			7,075	7,122		

R14200-200 Elevator Selective Costs (cont.)

	Passenger	Freight	Hospital
G. Options			
1. Controls			
Automatic, 2 car group	$3,664		$3,664
3 car group	5,507		5,503
4 car group	8,485		8,497
5 car group	11,312		11,342
6 car group	16,016		16,055
Emergency, fireman service	Yes		Yes
Intercom service	600		600
Selective collective, single car	—		—
Duplex car	3,908		3,908
2. Doors			
Center opening, 1 speed	$1,789		$1,789
2 speed	2,222		2,222
Rear opening-opposite front	4,194		4,194
Side opening, 2 speed	6,159		6,159
Freight, bi-parting	—	$ 5,356	—
Power operated door and gate	—	17,675	—
3. Emergency power switching, automatic	$2,150		$2,150
Manual	432		432
4. Finishes based on 3500# cab			
Ceilings, acrylic panel	$428		
Aluminum egg crate	494		$494
Doors, stainless steel	898 Ea.		898 Ea.
Floors, carpet, class "A" — (Finish flooring by others)	357		—
Epoxy	294		294
Quarry tile	453		455
Slate	632		—
Steel plate	—	$ 712	
Textured rubber	115		115
Walls, plastic laminate	Std.		Std.
Stainless steel	2,575		2,575
Return at door	541		541
Steel plate, 1/4" x 4' high, 14 ga. above	—	$ 1,732	—
Entrance, doors, baked enamel	Std.		Std.
Stainless steel	898 Ea.		898 Ea.
Frames, baked enamel	Std.		Std.
Stainless steel	898 Ea.		898 Ea.
5. Maintenance contract - 12 months	$3,013	$ 2,253	$4,376
6. Signal devices			
Hall lantern, each	$439	$ 439	$439
Position indicator, car or lobby	322	322	322
Add for over three each, per floor	91	91	91
7. Specialties			
High speed, heavy duty door opener	$1,622		$1,622
Variable voltage, O.H. gearless machine	29,224-64,896		29,224-64,896
Basement installed geared machine	$14,400	$14,450	$14,400

R14200-300   Passenger Elevators

Electric elevators are used generally but hydraulic elevators can be used for lifts up to 70' and where large capacities are required. Hydraulic speeds are limited to 200 F.P.M. but cars are self leveling at the stops. On low rises, hydraulic installation runs about 15% less than standard electric types but on higher rises this installation cost advantage is reduced. Maintenance of hydraulic elevators is about the same as electric type but underground portion is not included in the maintenance contract.

In electric elevators there are several control systems available, the choice of which will be based upon elevator use, size, speed and cost criteria. The two types of drives are geared for low speeds and gearless for 450 F.P.M. and over.

The tables on the preceding pages illustrate typical installed costs of the various types of elevators available.

R14200-400   Elevator Cost Development

Requirement: One passenger elevator, five story hydraulic, 2,500 lb. capacity, 12' floor to floor, speed 150 F.P.M., emergency power switching and maintenance contract.

Description	Total Cost
A. Base Elevator, (Hydraulic Passenger)	$38,260
B. Capacity Adjustment (2,500 lb.)	1,167
C. Excess Travel Over Base (4 x 12') = 48' — (12' for Base Unit) = 36' x $345 per V.L.F.	12,420
D. Stops Over Base 5 — (2 for base unit) = 3 x $3,512 Ea.	10,536
E. Speed Adjustment (150 F.P.M.)	1,725
F. Options:	
1. Intercom Service	600
2. Emergency power switching, automatic	2,150
3. Stainless steel entrance doors 5 x $898 Ea.	4,490
4. Maintenance Contract (12 months)	3,013
5. Position indicators 2 x $322	644
Total Cost	$75,005

R14320-100   Escalators

Moving stairs can be used for buildings where 600 or more people are to be carried to the second floor or beyond. Freight cannot be carried on escalators and at least one elevator must be available for this function. Carrying capacity is 5,000 to 8,000 people per hour. Power requirement is 2 to 3 KW per hour and incline angle is 30°.

Table below indicates approximate installed costs per unit, with O & P. Installation outside major cities would increase the costs below, due to mechanics additional travel expense.

Vertical Rise	Stainless Steel Balustrade		Enameled Steel or Glass Balustrade	
	32" Wide	48" Wide	32" Wide	48" Wide
10'	$ 94,307	$ 97,448	$ 88,112	$ 92,729
15'	99,377	102,724	93,647	97,524
20'	109,031	113,140	102,147	106,730
25'	123,375	128,203	115,153	120,282

R14360-200   Moving Ramps and Walks

These are a specialized form of conveyor 3' to 6' wide with capacities of 3,600 to 18,000 persons per hour. Maximum speed is 140 F.P.M. and normal incline is 0° to 15°.

Local codes will determine the maximum angle. A 48" wide, 150' long indoor moving ramp costs between $290,000 to $330,000 per unit installed, including O & P. Outdoor units would require additional weather protection. Approximate cost add is $300 per foot.

14 CONVEYING SYSTEMS

REFERENCE NOS.

R15050-720   Demolition (Selective vs. Removal for Replacement)

Demolition can be divided into two basic categories.

One type of demolition involves the removal of material with no concern for its replacement. The labor-hours to estimate this work are found in Div. 15055 under "Selective Demolition". It is selective in that individual items or all the material installed as a system or trade grouping such as plumbing or heating systems are removed. This may be accomplished by the easiest way possible, such as sawing, torch cutting, or sledge hammer as well as simple unbolting.

The second type of demolition is the removal of some item for repair or replacement. This removal may involve careful draining, opening of unions, disconnecting and tagging of electrical connections, capping of pipes/ducts to prevent entry of debris or leakage of the material contained as well as transport of the item away from its in-place location to a truck/dumpster. An approximation of the time required to accomplish this type of demolition is to use half of the time indicated as necessary to install a new unit. For example; installation of a new pump might be listed as requiring 6 labor-hours so if we had to estimate the removal of the old pump we would allow an additional 3 hours for a total of 9 hours. That is, the complete replacement of a defective pump with a new pump would be estimated to take 9 labor-hours.

R15100-050   Pipe Material Considerations

1. Malleable fittings should be used for gas service.
2. Malleable fittings are used where there are stresses/strains due to expansion and vibration.
3. Cast fittings may be broken as an aid to disassembling of heating lines frozen by long use, temperature and minerals.
4. Cast iron pipe is extensively used for underground and submerged service.
5. Type M (light wall) copper tubing is available in hard temper only and is used for nonpressure and less severe applications than K and L.
6. Type L (medium wall) copper tubing, available hard or soft for interior service.
7. Type K (heavy wall) copper tubing, available in hard or soft temper for use where conditions are severe. For underground and interior service.
8. Hard drawn tubing requires fewer hangers or supports but should not be bent. Silver brazed fittings are recommended, however soft solder is normally used.
9. Type DMV (very light wall) copper tubing designed for drainage, waste and vent plus other non-critical pressure services.

Domestic/Imported Pipe and Fittings Cost

The prices shown in this publication for steel/cast iron pipe and steel, cast iron, malleable iron fittings are based on domestic production sold at the normal trade discounts. The above listed items of foreign manufacture may be available at prices of 1/3 to 1/2 those shown. Some imported items after minor machining or finishing operations are being sold as domestic to further complicate the system.

Caution: Most pipe prices in this book also include a coupling and pipe hangers which for the larger sizes can add significantly to the per meter cost and should be taken into account when comparing "book cost" with quoted supplier's cost.

R15100-420   Plumbing Fixture Installation Time

Item	Rough-In	Set	Total Hours	Item	Rough-In	Set	Total Hours
Bathtub	5	5	10	Shower head only	2	1	3
Bathtub and shower, cast iron	6	6	12	Shower drain	3	1	4
Fire hose reel and cabinet	4	2	6	Shower stall, slate		15	15
Floor drain to 4 inch diameter	3	1	4	Slop sink	5	3	8
Grease trap, single, cast iron	5	3	8	Test 6 fixtures			14
Kitchen gas range		4	4	Urinal, wall	6	2	8
Kitchen sink, single	4	4	8	Urinal, pedestal or floor	6	4	10
Kitchen sink, double	6	6	12	Water closet and tank	4	3	7
Laundry tubs	4	2	6	Water closet and tank, wall hung	5	3	8
Lavatory wall hung	5	3	8	Water heater, 45 gals. gas, automatic	5	2	7
Lavatory pedestal	5	3	8	Water heaters, 65 gals. gas, automatic	5	2	7
Shower and stall	6	4	10	Water heaters, electric, plumbing only	4	2	6

Fixture prices in front of book are based on the cost per fixture set in place. The rough-in cost, which must be added for each fixture, includes carrier, if required, some supply, waste and vent pipe connecting fittings and stops. The lengths of rough-in pipe are nominal runs which would connect to the larger runs and stacks. The supply runs and DWV runs and stacks must be accounted for in separate entries. In the eastern half of the United States it is common for the plumber to carry these to a point 5′ outside the building.

R15100-430   Water Cooler Application

Type of Service	Requirement
Office, School or Hospital	12 persons per gallon per hour
Office, Lobby or Department Store	4 or 5 gallons per hour per fountain
Light manufacturing	7 persons per gallon per hour
Heavy manufacturing	5 persons per gallon per hour
Hot heavy manufacturing	4 persons per gallon per hour
Hotel	.08 gallons per hour per room
Theatre	1 gallon per hour per 100 seats

R15500-035   Heating (42° degrees latitude)

$$\text{Approximate S.F. radiation} = \frac{\text{S.F. sash}}{2} + \frac{\text{S.F. wall + roof} - \text{sash}}{20} + \frac{\text{C.F. building}}{200}$$

R15500-050 Factor for Determining Heat Loss for Various Types of Buildings

General: While the most accurate estimates of heating requirements would naturally be based on detailed information about the building being considered, it is possible to arrive at a reasonable approximation using the following procedure:

1. Calculate the cubic volume of the room or building.
2. Select the appropriate factor from Table 1 below. Note that the factors apply only to inside temperatures listed in the first column and to 0°F outside temperature.

3. If the building has bad north and west exposures, multiply the heat loss factor by 1.1.
4. If the outside design temperature is other than 0°F, multiply the factor from Table 1 by the factor from Table 2.
5. Multiply the cubic volume by the factor selected from Table 1. This will give the estimated BTUH heat loss which must be made up to maintain inside temperature.

Table 1 — Building Type	Conditions	Qualifications	Loss Factor*
Factories & Industrial Plants General Office Areas at 70°F	One Story	Skylight in Roof	6.2
		No Skylight in Roof	5.7
	Multiple Story	Two Story	4.6
		Three Story	4.3
		Four Story	4.1
		Five Story	3.9
		Six Story	3.6
	All Walls Exposed	Flat Roof	6.9
		Heated Space Above	5.2
	One Long Warm Common Wall	Flat Roof	6.3
		Heated Space Above	4.7
	Warm Common Walls on Both Long Sides	Flat Roof	5.8
		Heated Space Above	4.1
Warehouses at 60°F	All Walls Exposed	Skylights in Roof	5.5
		No Skylight in Roof	5.1
		Heated Space Above	4.0
	One Long Warm Common Wall	Skylight in Roof	5.0
		No Skylight in Roof	4.9
		Heated Space Above	3.4
	Warm Common Walls on Both Long Sides	Skylight in Roof	4.7
		No Skylight in Roof	4.4
		Heated Space Above	3.0

*Note: This table tends to be conservative particularly for new buildings designed for minimum energy consumption.

Table 2 — Outside Design Temperature Correction Factor (for Degrees Fahrenheit)									
Outside Design Temperature	50	40	30	20	10	0	-10	-20	-30
Correction Factor	.29	.43	.57	.72	.86	1.00	1.14	1.28	1.43

R15700-020   Air Conditioning Requirements

BTU's per hour per S.F. of floor area and S.F. per ton of air conditioning.

Type of Building	BTU per S.F.	S.F. per Ton	Type of Building	BTU per S.F.	S.F. per Ton	Type of Building	BTU per S.F.	S.F. per Ton
Apartments, Individual	26	450	Dormitory, Rooms	40	300	Libraries	50	240
Corridors	22	550	Corridors	30	400	Low Rise Office, Exterior	38	320
Auditoriums & Theaters	40	300/18*	Dress Shops	43	280	Interior	33	360
Banks	50	240	Drug Stores	80	150	Medical Centers	28	425
Barber Shops	48	250	Factories	40	300	Motels	28	425
Bars & Taverns	133	90	High Rise Office—Ext. Rms.	46	263	Office (small suite)	43	280
Beauty Parlors	66	180	Interior Rooms	37	325	Post Office, Individual Office	42	285
Bowling Alleys	68	175	Hospitals, Core	43	280	Central Area	46	260
Churches	36	330/20*	Perimeter	46	260	Residences	20	600
Cocktail Lounges	68	175	Hotel, Guest Rooms	44	275	Restaurants	60	200
Computer Rooms	141	85	Corridors	30	400	Schools & Colleges	46	260
Dental Offices	52	230	Public Spaces	55	220	Shoe Stores	55	220
Dept. Stores, Basement	34	350	Industrial Plants, Offices	38	320	Shop'g. Ctrs., Supermarkets	34	350
Main Floor	40	300	General Offices	34	350	Retail Stores	48	250
Upper Floor	30	400	Plant Areas	40	300	Specialty	60	200

*Persons per ton
12,000 BTU = 1 ton of air conditioning

R15700-040   Recommended Ventilation Air Changes

Table below lists range of time in minutes per change for various types of facilities.

Assembly Halls	2-10	Dance Halls	2-10	Laundries	1-3
Auditoriums	2-10	Dining Rooms	3-10	Markets	2-10
Bakeries	2-3	Dry Cleaners	1-5	Offices	2-10
Banks	3-10	Factories	2-5	Pool Rooms	2-5
Bars	2-5	Garages	2-10	Recreation Rooms	2-10
Beauty Parlors	2-5	Generator Rooms	2-5	Sales Rooms	2-10
Boiler Rooms	1-5	Gymnasiums	2-10	Theaters	2-8
Bowling Alleys	2-10	Kitchens-Hospitals	2-5	Toilets	2-5
Churches	5-10	Kitchens-Restaurant	1-3	Transformer Rooms	1-5

CFM air required for changes = Volume of room in cubic feet ÷ Minutes per change.

R15810-050 Ductwork

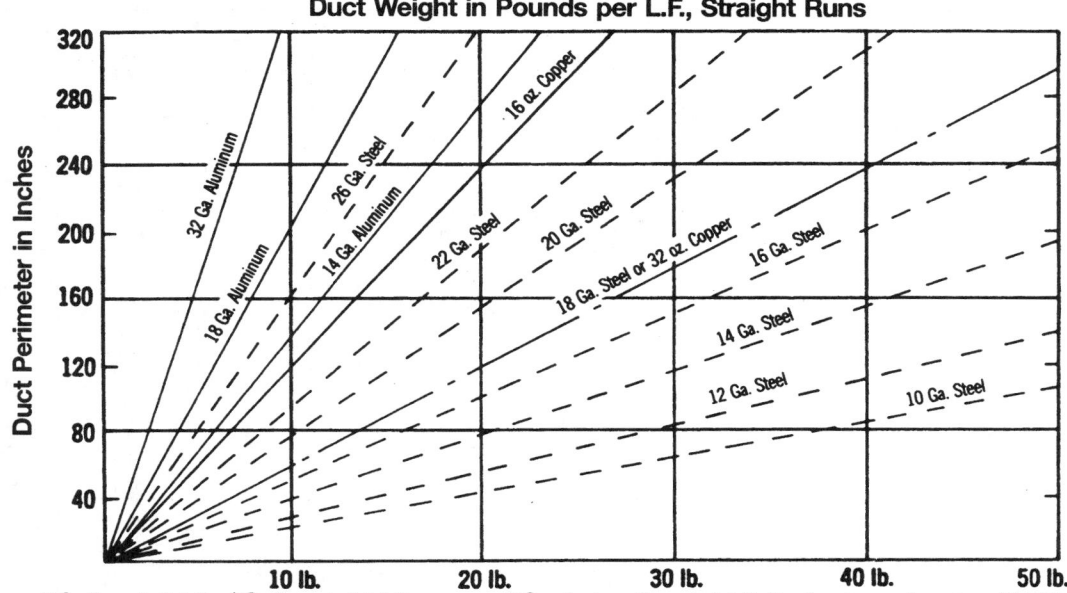

Duct Weight in Pounds per L.F., Straight Runs

Add to the above for fittings; 90° elbow is 3 L.F.; 45° elbow is 2.5 L.F.; offset is 4 L.F.; transition offset is 6 L.F.; square-to-round transition is 4 L.F.; 90° reducing elbow is 5 L.F. For bracing and waste, add 20% to aluminum and copper, 15% to steel.

R16120-910 Minimum Copper and Aluminum Wire Size Allowed for Various Types of Insulation

Amperes	Copper THW THWN or XHHW	Copper THHN XHHW*	Aluminum THW XHHW	Aluminum THHN XHHW*	Amperes	Copper THW THWN or XHHW	Copper THHN XHHW*	Aluminum THW XHHW	Aluminum THHN XHHW*
15A	#14	#14	#12	#12	195	3/0	2/0	250kcmil	4/0
20	#12	#12	#10	#10	200	3/0	3/0	250kcmil	4/0
25	#10	#10	#10	#10	205	4/0	3/0	250kcmil	4/0
30	#10	#10	#8	#8	225	4/0	3/0	300kcmil	250kcmil
40	#8	#8	#8	#8	230	4/0	4/0	300kcmil	250kcmil
45	#8	#8	#6	#8	250	250kcmil	4/0	350kcmil	300kcmil
50	#8	#8	#6	#6	255	250kcmil	4/0	400kcmil	300kcmil
55	#6	#8	#4	#6	260	300kcmil	4/0	400kcmil	350kcmil
60	#6	#6	#4	#6	270	300kcmil	250kcmil	400kcmil	350kcmil
65	#6	#6	#4	#4	280	300kcmil	250kcmil	500kcmil	350kcmil
75	#4	#6	#3	#4	285	300kcmil	250kcmil	500kcmil	400kcmil
85	#4	#4	#2	#3	290	350kcmil	250kcmil	500kcmil	400kcmil
90	#3	#4	#2	#2	305	350kcmil	300kcmil	500kcmil	400kcmil
95	#3	#4	#1	#2	310	350kcmil	300kcmil	500kcmil	500kcmil
100	#3	#3	#1	#2	320	400kcmil	300kcmil	600kcmil	500kcmil
110	#2	#3	1/0	#1	335	400kcmil	350kcmil	600kcmil	500kcmil
115	#2	#2	1/0	#1	340	500kcmil	350kcmil	600kcmil	500kcmil
120	#1	#2	1/0	1/0	350	500kcmil	350kcmil	700kcmil	500kcmil
130	#1	#2	2/0	1/0	375	500kcmil	400kcmil	700kcmil	600kcmil
135	1/0	#1	2/0	1/0	380	500kcmil	400kcmil	750kcmil	600kcmil
150	1/0	#1	3/0	2/0	385	600kcmil	500kcmil	750kcmil	600kcmil
155	2/0	1/0	3/0	3/0	420	600kcmil	500kcmil		700kcmil
170	2/0	1/0	4/0	3/0	430		500kcmil		750kcmil
175	2/0	2/0	4/0	3/0	435		600kcmil		750kcmil
180	3/0	2/0	4/0	4/0	475		600kcmil		

*Dry Locations Only

Notes:
1. Size #14 to 4/0 is in AWG units (American Wire Gauge).
2. Size 250 to 750 is in kcmil units (Thousand Circular Mils).
3. Use next higher ampere value if exact value is not listed in table.
4. For loads that operate continuously increase ampere value by 25% to obtain proper wire size.
5. Refer to Table R16120-905 for the maximum circuit length for the various size wires.
6. Table R16120-910 has been written for estimating purpose only, based on ambient temperature of 30° C (86° F); for ambient temperature other than 30° C (86° F), ampacity correction factors will be applied.

16 ELECTRICAL
REFERENCE NOS.

R16132-210   Conductors in Conduit

Table below lists maximum number of conductors for various sized conduit using THW, TW or THWN insulations.

Copper Wire Size	1/2"			3/4"			1"			1-1/4"			1-1/2"			2"			2-1/2"			3"		3-1/2"		4"	
	TW	THW	THWN	TW	THW	THWN	TW	THW	THWN	TW	THW	THWN	TW	THW	THWN	TW	THW	THWN	TW	THW	THWN	THW	THWN	THW	THWN	THW	THWN
#14	9	6	13	15	10	24	25	16	39	44	29	69	60	40	94	99	65	154	142	93		143		192			
#12	7	4	10	12	8	18	19	13	29	35	24	51	47	32	70	78	53	114	111	76	164	111		157			
#10	5	4	6	9	6	11	15	11	18	26	19	32	36	26	44	60	43	73	85	61	104	95	160	127		163	
#8	2	1	3	4	3	5	7	5	9	12	10	16	17	13	22	28	22	36	40	32	51	49	79	66	106	85	136
#6		1	1		2	4		4	6		7	11		10	15		16	26		23	37	36	57	48	76	62	98
#4		1	1		1	2		3	4		5	7		7	9		12	16		17	22	27	35	36	47	47	60
#3		1	1		1	1		2	3		4	6		6	8		10	13		15	19	23	29	31	39	40	51
#2		1	1		1	1		2	3		4	5		5	7		9	11		13	16	20	25	27	33	34	43
#1					1	1		1	1		3	3		4	5		6	8		9	12	14	18	19	25	25	32
1/0					1	1		1	1		2	3		3	4		5	7		8	10	12	15	16	21	21	27
2/0					1	1		1	1		1	2		3	3		5	6		7	8	10	13	14	17	18	22
3/0					1	1		1	1		1	1		2	3		4	5		6	7	9	11	12	14	15	18
4/0						1		1	1		1	1		1	2		3	4		5	6	7	9	10	12	13	15
250 kcmil								1	1		1	1		1	1		2	3		4	4	6	7	8	10	10	12
300								1	1		1	1		1	1		2	3		3	4	5	6	7	8	9	11
350									1		1	1		1	1		1	2		3	3	4	5	6	7	8	9
400											1	1		1	1		1	1		2	3	4	5	5	6	7	8
500											1	1		1	1		1	1		1	2	3	4	4	5	6	7
600															1		1	1		1	1	3	3	4	4	5	5
700														1	1		1	1		1	1	2	3	3	4	4	5
750														1	1		1	1		1	1	2	2	3	3	4	4

R16220-610 Motors

230/460 Volt A.C., three phase 60 cycle ball bearing squirrel cage
induction motors, NEMA design B Standard Line, including
installation and Subs O & P. (No conduit, wire, or terminations)

Horsepower	Synchronous Speed in RPM	Drip Proof, Class B Insulation 1.15 Service Factor			Totally Enclosed, Class B Insulation, 1.0 or 1.15 Service Factor		
		Motor Only	With Manual Starter	With Magnetic Starter	Motor Only	With Manual Starter	With Magnetic Starter
1	1,200	$ 314	$ 588	$ 613	$ 381	$ 653	$ 683
	1,800	284	558	583	347	623	648
2	1,200	406	678	804	436	708	834
	1,800	318	593	719	396	668	794
	3,600	303	578	704	334	608	734
3	1,200	516	788	914	551	823	949
	1,800	319	593	719	401	673	799
	3,600	341	613	739	341	613	739
5	1,200	601	991	1,105	761	1,151	1,265
	1,800	385	776	890	441	831	945
	3,600	385	776	890	436	826	940
7.5	1,800	528	920	1,370	603	995	1,445
10		622	1010	1,460	712	1100	1,545
15		823	—	1,675	813	—	1,650
20		993	—	2,215	994	—	2,215
25		1,149	—	2,370	1,134	—	2,345
30		1,321	—	2,550	1,296	—	2,525
40		1,880	—	4,265	1,605	—	3,990
50		2,156	—	4,540	1,881	—	4,265
60		2,793	—	7,675	2,293	—	7,175
75		3,165	—	8,050	2,790	—	7,675
100		4,155	—	9,050	3,555	—	8,450
125		4,885	—	16,900	4,310	—	16,300
150		6,410	—	18,400	6,060	—	18,100
200		8,370	—	20,450	7,620	—	19,650

16

ELECTRICAL

REFERENCE NOS.

R17100-100   Square Foot Project Size Modifier

One factor that affects the S.F. cost of a particular building is the size. In general, for buildings built to the same specifications in the same locality, the larger building will have the lower S.F. cost. This is due mainly to the decreasing contribution of the exterior walls plus the economy of scale usually achievable in larger buildings. The Area Conversion Scale shown below will give a factor to convert costs for the typical size building to an adjusted cost for the particular project.

The Square Foot Base Size lists the median costs, most typical project size in our accumulated data and the range in size of the projects.

The Size Factor for your project is determined by dividing your project area in S.F. by the typical project size for the particular Building Type. With this factor, enter the Area Conversion Scale at the appropriate Size Factor and determine the appropriate cost multiplier for your building size.

Example: Determine the cost per S.F. for a 100,000 S.F. Mid-rise apartment building.

$$\frac{\text{Proposed building area} = 100{,}000 \text{ S.F.}}{\text{Typical size from below} = 50{,}000 \text{ S.F.}} = 2.00$$

Enter Area Conversion scale at 2.0, intersect curve, read horizontally the appropriate cost multiplier of .94. Size adjusted cost becomes .94 x $69.50 = $65.35 based on national average costs.

Note: For Size Factors less than .50, the Cost Multiplier is 1.1
      For Size Factors greater than 3.5, the Cost Multiplier is .90

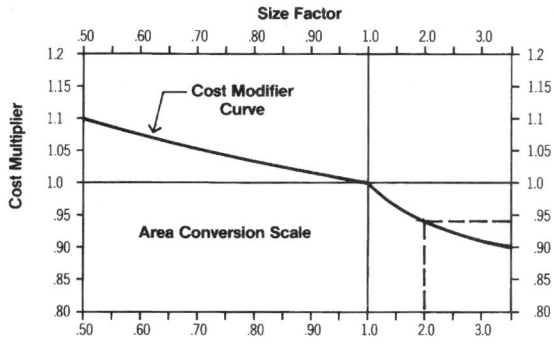

Building Type	Median Cost per S.F.	Typical Size Gross S.F.	Typical Range Gross S.F.	Building Type	Median Cost per S.F.	Typical Size Gross S.F.	Typical Range Gross S.F.
Apartments, Low Rise	$ 55.05	21,000	9,700 - 37,200	Jails	$168.00	40,000	5,500 - 145,000
Apartments, Mid Rise	69.50	50,000	32,000 - 100,000	Libraries	99.15	12,000	7,000 - 31,000
Apartments, High Rise	79.70	145,000	95,000 - 600,000	Medical Clinics	94.80	7,200	4,200 - 15,700
Auditoriums	92.05	25,000	7,600 - 39,000	Medical Offices	89.05	6,000	4,000 - 15,000
Auto Sales	56.95	20,000	10,800 - 28,600	Motels	68.25	40,000	15,800 - 120,000
Banks	123.00	4,200	2,500 - 7,500	Nursing Homes	91.55	23,000	15,000 - 37,000
Churches	83.15	17,000	2,000 - 42,000	Offices, Low Rise	74.30	20,000	5,000 - 80,000
Clubs, Country	82.85	6,500	4,500 - 15,000	Offices, Mid Rise	78.05	120,000	20,000 - 300,000
Clubs, Social	80.65	10,000	6,000 - 13,500	Offices, High Rise	99.85	260,000	120,000 - 800,000
Clubs, YMCA	83.10	28,300	12,800 - 39,400	Police Stations	125.00	10,500	4,000 - 19,000
Colleges (Class)	109.00	50,000	15,000 - 150,000	Post Offices	92.00	12,400	6,800 - 30,000
Colleges (Science Lab)	159.00	45,600	16,600 - 80,000	Power Plants	691.00	7,500	1,000 - 20,000
College (Student Union)	121.00	33,400	16,000 - 85,000	Religious Education	76.25	9,000	6,000 - 12,000
Community Center	86.60	9,400	5,300 - 16,700	Research	130.00	19,000	6,300 - 45,000
Court Houses	118.00	32,400	17,800 - 106,000	Restaurants	112.00	4,400	2,800 - 6,000
Dept. Stores	51.45	90,000	44,000 - 122,000	Retail Stores	54.65	7,200	4,000 - 17,600
Dormitories, Low Rise	88.75	25,000	10,000 - 95,000	Schools, Elementary	79.60	41,000	24,500 - 55,000
Dormitories, Mid Rise	116.00	85,000	20,000 - 200,000	Schools, Jr. High	81.10	92,000	52,000 - 119,000
Factories	49.85	26,400	12,900 - 50,000	Schools, Sr. High	81.10	101,000	50,500 - 175,000
Fire Stations	87.05	5,800	4,000 - 8,700	Schools, Vocational	80.75	37,000	20,500 - 82,000
Fraternity Houses	85.65	12,500	8,200 - 14,800	Sports Arenas	67.70	15,000	5,000 - 40,000
Funeral Homes	95.70	10,000	4,000 - 20,000	Supermarkets	54.85	44,000	12,000 - 60,000
Garages, Commercial	60.80	9,300	5,000 - 13,600	Swimming Pools	127.00	20,000	10,000 - 32,000
Garages, Municipal	77.75	8,300	4,500 - 12,600	Telephone Exchange	147.00	4,500	1,200 - 10,600
Garages, Parking	31.90	163,000	76,400 - 225,300	Theaters	81.20	10,500	8,800 - 17,500
Gymnasiums	80.45	19,200	11,600 - 41,000	Town Halls	89.30	10,800	4,800 - 23,400
Hospitals	152.00	55,000	27,200 - 125,000	Warehouses	36.80	25,000	8,000 - 72,000
House (Elderly)	75.25	37,000	21,000 - 66,000	Warehouse & Office	42.50	25,000	8,000 - 72,000
Housing (Public)	69.70	36,000	14,400 - 74,400				
Ice Rinks	77.40	29,000	27,200 - 33,600				

Change Orders

Change Order Considerations

A Change Order is a written document, usually prepared by the design professional, and signed by the owner, the architect/engineer and the contractor. A change order states the agreement of the parties to: an addition, deletion, or revision in the work; an adjustment in the contract sum, if any; or an adjustment in the contract time, if any. Change orders, or "extras" in the construction process occur after execution of the construction contract and impact architects/engineers, contractors and owners.

Change orders that are properly recognized and managed can ensure orderly, professional and profitable progress for all who are involved in the project. There are many causes for change orders and change order requests. In all cases, change orders or change order requests should be addressed promptly and in a precise and prescribed manner. The following paragraphs include information regarding change order pricing and procedures.

The Causes of Change Orders

Reasons for issuing change orders include:

- Unforeseen field conditions that require a change in the work
- Correction of design discrepancies, errors or omissions in the contract documents
- Owner-requested changes, either by design criteria, scope of work, or project objectives
- Completion date changes for reasons unrelated to the construction process
- Changes in building code interpretations, or other public authority requirements that require a change in the work
- Changes in availability of existing or new materials and products

Procedures

Properly written contract documents must include the correct change order procedures for all parties—owners, design professionals and contractors—to follow in order to avoid costly delays and litigation.

Being "in the right" is not always a sufficient or acceptable defense. The contract provisions requiring notification and documentation must be adhered to within a defined or reasonable time frame.

The appropriate method of handling change orders is by a written proposal and acceptance by all parties involved. Prior to starting work on a project, all parties should identify their authorized agents who may sign and accept change orders, as well as any limits placed on their authority.

Time may be a critical factor when the need for a change arises. For such cases, the contractor might be directed to proceed on a "time and materials" basis, rather than wait for all paperwork to be processed—a delay that could impede progress. In this situation, the contractor must still follow the prescribed change order procedures, including but not limited to, notification and documentation.

All forms used for change orders should be dated and signed by the proper authority. Lack of documentation can be very costly, especially if legal judgments are to be made and if certain field personnel are no longer available. For time and material change orders, the contractor should keep accurate daily records of all labor and material allocated to the change. Forms that can be used to document change order work are available in *Means Forms for Building Construction Professionals*.

Owners or awarding authorities who do considerable and continual building construction (such as the federal government) realize the inevitability of change orders for numerous reasons, both predictable and unpredictable. As a result, the federal government, the American Institute of Architects (AIA), the Engineers Joint Contract Documents Committee (EJCDC) and other contractor, legal and technical organizations have developed standards and procedures to be followed by all parties to achieve contract continuance and timely completion, while being financially fair to all concerned.

In addition to the change order standards put forth by industry associations, there are also many books available on the subject.

Pricing Change Orders

When pricing change orders, regardless of their cause, the most significant factor is *when* the change occurs. The need for a change may be perceived in the field or requested by the architect/engineer *before* any of the actual installation has begun, or may evolve or appear *during* construction when the item of work in question is partially installed. In the latter cases, the original sequence of construction is disrupted, along with all contiguous and supporting systems. Change orders cause the greatest impact when they occur *after* the installation has been completed and must be uncovered, or even replaced. Post-completion changes may be caused by necessary design changes, product failure, or changes in the owner's requirements that are not discovered until the building or the systems begin to function.

Specified procedures of notification and record keeping must be adhered to and enforced regardless of the stage of construction: *before, during,* or *after* installation. Some bidding documents anticipate change orders by requiring that unit prices including overhead and profit percentages—for additional as well as deductible changes—be listed. Generally these unit prices do not fully take into account the ripple effect, or impact on other trades, and should be used for general guidance only.

When pricing change orders, it is important to classify the time frame in which the change occurs. There are two basic time frames for change orders: *pre-installation change orders*, which occur before the start of construction, and *post-installation change orders*, which involve reworking after the original installation. Change orders that occur between these stages may be priced according to the extent of work completed using a combination of techniques developed for pricing *pre-* and *post-installation* changes.

The following factors are the basis for a check list to use when preparing a change order estimate.

Factors To Consider When Pricing Change Orders

As an estimator begins to prepare a change order, the following questions should be reviewed to determine their impact on the final price.

General

- Is the change order work *pre-installation* or *post-installation*?

  Change order work costs vary according to how much of the installation has been completed. Once workers have the project scoped in their mind, even though they have not started, it can be difficult to refocus.

Consequently they may spend more than the normal amount of time understanding the change. Also, modifications to work in place such as trimming or refitting usually take more time than was initially estimated. The greater the amount of work in place, the more reluctant workers are to change it. Psychologically they may resent the change and as a result the rework takes longer than normal. Post-installation change order estimates must include demolition of existing work as required to accomplish the change. If the work is performed at a later time, additional obstacles such as building finishes may be present which must be

protected. Regardless of whether the change occurs pre-installation or post-installation, attempt to isolate the identifiable factors and price them separately. For example, add shipping costs that may be required pre-installation or any demolition required post-installation. Then analyze the potential impact on productivity of psychological and/or learning curve factors and adjust the output rates accordingly. One approach is to break down the typical workday into segments and quantify the impact on each segment. The following chart may be useful as a guide:

	Activities (Productivity) Expressed as Percentages of a Workday		
Task	Means Mechanical Cost Data (for New Construction)	Pre-Installation Change Orders	Post-Installation Change Orders
1. Study plans	3%	6%	6%
2. Material procurement	3%	3%	3%
3. Receiving and storing	3%	3%	3%
4. Mobilization	5%	5%	5%
5. Site movement	5%	5%	8%
6. Layout and marking	8%	10%	12%
7. Actual installation	64%	59%	54%
8. Clean-up	3%	3%	3%
9. Breaks—non-productive	6%	6%	6%
Total	100%	100%	100%

Change Order Installation Efficiency

The labor-hours expressed (for new construction) are based on average installation time, using an efficiency level of approximately 60-65%. For change order situations, adjustments to this efficiency level should reflect the daily labor-hour allocation for that particular occurrence.

If any of the specific percentages expressed in the above chart do not apply to a particular project situation, then those percentage points should be reallocated to the appropriate task(s). Example: Using data for new construction, assume there is no new material being utilized. The percentages for Tasks 2 and 3 would therefore be reallocated to other tasks. If the time required for Tasks 2 and 3 can now be applied to installation, we can add the time allocated for *Material Procurement* and *Receiving and Storing* to the *Actual Installation* time for new construction, thereby increasing the Actual Installation percentage.

This chart shows that, due to reduced productivity, labor costs will be higher than those for new construction by 5% to 15% for pre-installation change orders and by 15% to 25% for post-installation change orders. Each job and change order is unique and must be examined individually. Many factors, covered elsewhere in this section, can each have a significant impact on productivity and change order costs. All such factors should be considered in every case.

- Will the change substantially delay the original completion date?

A significant change in the project may cause the original completion date to be extended. The extended schedule may subject the contractor to new wage rates dictated by relevant labor contracts. Project supervision and other project overhead must also be extended beyond the original completion date. The schedule extension may also put installation into a new weather season. For example, underground piping scheduled for October installation was delayed until January. As a result, frost penetrated the trench area, thereby changing the degree of difficulty of the task. Changes and delays may have a ripple effect throughout the project. This effect must be analyzed and negotiated with the owner.

- What is the net effect of a deduct change order?

In most cases, change orders resulting in a deduction or credit reflect only bare costs. The contractor may retain the overhead and profit based on the original bid.

Materials

- Will you have to pay more or less for the new material, required by the change order, than you paid for the original purchase?

The same material prices or discounts will usually apply to materials purchased for change orders as new construction. In some instances, however, the contractor may forfeit the advantages of competitive pricing for change orders. Consider the following example:

A contractor purchased over $20,000 worth of fan coil units for an installation, and obtained the maximum discount. Some time later it was determined the project required an additional matching unit. The contractor has to purchase this unit from the original supplier to ensure a match. The supplier at this time may not discount the unit because of the small quantity, and the fact that he is no longer in a competitive situation. The impact of quantity on purchase can add between 0% and 25% to material prices and/or subcontractor quotes.

- If materials have been ordered or delivered to the job site, will they be subject to a cancellation charge or restocking fee?

Check with the supplier to determine if ordered materials are subject to a cancellation charge. Delivered materials not used as result of a change order may be subject to a restocking fee if returned to the supplier. Common restocking charges run between 20% and 40%. Also, delivery charges to return the goods to the supplier must be added.

Labor

- How efficient is the existing crew at the actual installation?

Is the same crew that performed the initial work going to do the change order? Possibly the change consists of the installation of a unit identical to one already installed; therefore the change should take less time. Be sure to consider this potential productivity increase and modify the productivity rates accordingly.

- If the crew size is increased, what impact will that have on supervision requirements?

Under most bargaining agreements or management practices, there is a point at which a working foreman is replaced by a nonworking foreman. This replacement increases project overhead by adding a nonproductive worker. If additional workers are added to accelerate the project or to perform changes while maintaining the schedule, be sure to add additional supervision time if warranted. Calculate the hours involved and the additional cost directly if possible.

- What are the other impacts of increased crew size?

The larger the crew, the greater the potential for productivity to decrease. Some of the factors that cause this productivity loss are: overcrowding (producing restrictive conditions in the working space), and possibly a shortage of any special tools and equipment required. Such factors affect not only the crew working on the elements directly involved in the change order, but other crews whose movement may also be hampered.

As the crew increases, check its basic composition for changes by the addition or deletion of apprentices or nonworking foreman and quantify the potential effects of equipment shortages or other logistical factors.

- As new crews, unfamiliar with the project, are brought onto the site, how long will it take them to become oriented to the project requirements?

The orientation time for a new crew to become 100% effective varies with the site and type of project. Orientation is easiest at a new construction site, and most difficult at existing, very restrictive renovation sites. The type of work also affects orientation time. When all elements of the work are exposed, such as concrete or masonry work, orientation is decreased. When the work is concealed or less visible, such as existing electrical systems, orientation takes longer. Usually orientation can be accomplished in one day or less. Costs for added orientation should be itemized and added to the total estimated cost.

- How much actual production can be gained by working overtime?

Short term overtime can be used effectively to accomplish more work in a day. However, as overtime is scheduled to run beyond several weeks, studies have shown marked decreases in output. The following chart shows the effect of long term overtime on worker efficiency. If the anticipated change requires extended overtime to keep the job on schedule, these factors can be used as a guide to predict the impact on time and cost. Add project overhead, particularly supervision, that may also be incurred.

Days per Week	Hours per Day	Production Efficiency					Payroll Cost Factors	
		1 Week	2 Weeks	3 Weeks	4 Weeks	Average 4 Weeks	@ 1-1/2 Times	@ 2 Times
5	8	100%	100%	100%	100%	100%	100%	100%
	9	100	100	95	90	96.25	105.6	111.1
	10	100	95	90	85	91.25	110.0	120.0
	11	95	90	75	65	81.25	113.6	127.3
	12	90	85	70	60	76.25	116.7	133.3
6	8	100	100	95	90	96.25	108.3	116.7
	9	100	95	90	85	92.50	113.0	125.9
	10	95	90	85	80	87.50	116.7	133.3
	11	95	85	70	65	78.75	119.7	139.4
	12	90	80	65	60	73.75	122.2	144.4
7	8	100	95	85	75	88.75	114.3	128.6
	9	95	90	80	70	83.75	118.3	136.5
	10	90	85	75	65	78.75	121.4	142.9
	11	85	80	65	60	72.50	124.0	148.1
	12	85	75	60	55	68.75	126.2	152.4

Effects of Overtime

Caution: Under many labor agreements, Sundays and holidays are paid at a higher premium than the normal overtime rate.

The use of long-term overtime is counterproductive on almost any construction job; that is, the longer the period of overtime, the lower the actual production rate. Numerous studies have been conducted, and while they have resulted in slightly different numbers, all reach the same conclusion. The figure above tabulates the effects of overtime work on efficiency.

As illustrated, there can be a difference between the *actual* payroll cost per hour and the *effective* cost per hour for overtime work. This is due to the reduced production efficiency with the increase in weekly hours beyond 40. This difference between actual and effective cost results from overtime work over a prolonged period. Short-term overtime work does not result in as great a reduction in efficiency, and in such cases, effective cost may not vary significantly from the actual payroll cost. As the total hours per week are increased on a regular basis, more time is lost because of fatigue, lowered morale, and an increased accident rate.

As an example, assume a project where workers are working 6 days a week, 10 hours per day. From the figure above (based on productivity studies), the average effective productive hours over a four-week period are:

$$0.875 \times 60 = 52.5$$

Depending upon the locale and day of week, overtime hours may be paid at time and a half or double time. For time and a half, the overall (average) *actual* payroll cost (including regular and overtime hours) is determined as follows:

$$\frac{40 \text{ reg. hrs.} + (20 \text{ overtime hrs.} \times 1.5)}{60 \text{ hrs.}} = 1.167$$

Based on 60 hours, the payroll cost per hour will be 116.7% of the normal rate at 40 hours per week. However, because the effective production (efficiency) for 60 hours is reduced to the equivalent of 52.5 hours, the effective cost of overtime is calculated as follows:

For time and a half:

$$\frac{40 \text{ reg. hrs.} + (20 \text{ overtime hrs.} \times 1.5)}{52.5 \text{ hrs.}} = 1.33$$

Installed cost will be 133% of the normal rate (for labor).

Thus, when figuring overtime, the actual cost per unit of work will be higher than the apparent overtime payroll dollar increase, due to the reduced productivity of the longer workweek. These efficiency calculations are true only for those cost factors determined by hours worked. Costs that are applied weekly or monthly, such as equipment rentals, will not be similarly affected.

Equipment

- What equipment is required to complete the change order?

  Change orders may require extending the rental period of equipment already on the job site, or the addition of special equipment brought in to accomplish the change work. In either case, the additional rental charges and operator labor charges must be added.

Summary

The preceding considerations and others you deem appropriate should be analyzed and applied to a change order estimate. The impact of each should be quantified and listed on the estimate to form an audit trail.

Change orders that are properly identified, documented, and managed help to ensure the orderly, professional and profitable progress of the work. They also minimize potential claims or disputes at the end of the project.

Crews

Crew No.	Bare Costs Hr.	Bare Costs Daily	Incl. Subs O & P Hr.	Incl. Subs O & P Daily	Cost Per Labor-Hour Bare Costs	Cost Per Labor-Hour Incl. O&P
Crew A-1	Hr.	Daily	Hr.	Daily	Bare Costs	Incl. O&P
1 Building Laborer	$22.85	$182.80	$35.75	$286.00	$22.85	$35.75
1 Gas Eng. Power Tool		64.80		71.30	8.10	8.91
8 L.H., Daily Totals		$247.60		$357.30	$30.95	$44.66
Crew A-1A	Hr.	Daily	Hr.	Daily	Bare Costs	Incl. O&P
1 Skilled Worker	$29.85	$238.80	$46.85	$374.80	$29.85	$46.85
1 Shot Blaster, 20″		146.40		161.05	18.30	20.13
8 L.H., Daily Totals		$385.20		$535.85	$48.15	$66.98
Crew A-2	Hr.	Daily	Hr.	Daily	Bare Costs	Incl. O&P
2 Laborers	$22.85	$365.60	$35.75	$572.00	$23.03	$35.75
1 Truck Driver (light)	23.40	187.20	35.75	286.00		
1 Light Truck, 1.5 Ton		158.00		173.80	6.58	7.24
24 L.H., Daily Totals		$710.80		$1031.80	$29.61	$42.99
Crew A-2A	Hr.	Daily	Hr.	Daily	Bare Costs	Incl. O&P
2 Laborers	$22.85	$365.60	$35.75	$572.00	$23.03	$35.75
1 Truck Driver (light)	23.40	187.20	35.75	286.00		
1 Light Truck, 1.5 Ton		158.00		173.80		
1 Concrete Saw		98.40		108.25	10.68	11.75
24 L.H., Daily Totals		$809.20		$1140.05	$33.71	$47.50
Crew A-3	Hr.	Daily	Hr.	Daily	Bare Costs	Incl. O&P
1 Truck Driver (heavy)	$23.95	$191.60	$36.60	$292.80	$23.95	$36.60
1 Dump Truck, 12 Ton		370.40		407.45	46.30	50.93
8 L.H., Daily Totals		$562.00		$700.25	$70.25	$87.53
Crew A-3A	Hr.	Daily	Hr.	Daily	Bare Costs	Incl. O&P
1 Truck Driver (light)	$23.40	$187.20	$35.75	$286.00	$23.40	$35.75
1 Pickup Truck (4x4)		89.20		98.10	11.15	12.27
8 L.H., Daily Totals		$276.40		$384.10	$34.55	$48.02
Crew A-3B	Hr.	Daily	Hr.	Daily	Bare Costs	Incl. O&P
1 Equip. Oper. (medium)	$30.35	$242.80	$45.95	$367.60	$27.15	$41.28
1 Truck Driver (heavy)	23.95	191.60	36.60	292.80		
1 Dump Truck, 16 Ton		482.80		531.10		
1 F.E. Loader, 3 C.Y.		391.80		431.00	54.66	60.13
16 L.H., Daily Totals		$1309.00		$1622.50	$81.81	$101.41
Crew A-3C	Hr.	Daily	Hr.	Daily	Bare Costs	Incl. O&P
1 Equip. Oper. (light)	$28.75	$230.00	$43.55	$348.40	$28.75	$43.55
1 Wheeled Skid Steer Loader		220.00		242.00	27.50	30.25
8 L.H., Daily Totals		$450.00		$590.40	$56.25	$73.80
Crew A-4	Hr.	Daily	Hr.	Daily	Bare Costs	Incl. O&P
2 Carpenters	$29.15	$466.40	$45.60	$729.60	$28.13	$43.65
1 Painter, Ordinary	26.10	208.80	39.75	318.00		
24 L.H., Daily Totals		$675.20		$1047.60	$28.13	$43.65
Crew A-5	Hr.	Daily	Hr.	Daily	Bare Costs	Incl. O&P
2 Laborers	$22.85	$365.60	$35.75	$572.00	$22.91	$35.75
.25 Truck Driver (light)	23.40	46.80	35.75	71.50		
.25 Light Truck, 1.5 Ton		39.50		43.45	2.19	2.41
18 L.H., Daily Totals		$451.90		$686.95	$25.10	$38.16
Crew A-6	Hr.	Daily	Hr.	Daily	Bare Costs	Incl. O&P
1 Chief Of Party	$34.55	$276.40	$54.75	$438.00	$32.20	$50.80
1 Instrument Man	29.85	238.80	46.85	374.80		
16 L.H., Daily Totals		$515.20		$812.80	$32.20	$50.80

Crew No.	Bare Costs Hr.	Bare Costs Daily	Incl. Subs O & P Hr.	Incl. Subs O & P Daily	Cost Per Labor-Hour Bare Costs	Cost Per Labor-Hour Incl. O&P
Crew A-7	Hr.	Daily	Hr.	Daily	Bare Costs	Incl. O&P
1 Chief Of Party	$34.55	$276.40	$54.75	$438.00	$30.98	$48.30
1 Instrument Man	29.85	238.80	46.85	374.80		
1 Rodman/Chainman	28.55	228.40	43.30	346.40		
24 L.H., Daily Totals		$743.60		$1159.20	$30.98	$48.30
Crew A-8	Hr.	Daily	Hr.	Daily	Bare Costs	Incl. O&P
1 Chief Of Party	$34.55	$276.40	$54.75	$438.00	$30.38	$47.05
1 Instrument Man	29.85	238.80	46.85	374.80		
2 Rodmen/Chainmen	28.55	456.80	43.30	692.80		
32 L.H., Daily Totals		$972.00		$1505.60	$30.38	$47.05
Crew A-9	Hr.	Daily	Hr.	Daily	Bare Costs	Incl. O&P
1 Asbestos Foreman	$32.65	$261.20	$52.30	$418.40	$32.21	$51.60
7 Asbestos Workers	32.15	1800.40	51.50	2884.00		
64 L.H., Daily Totals		$2061.60		$3302.40	$32.21	$51.60
Crew A-10	Hr.	Daily	Hr.	Daily	Bare Costs	Incl. O&P
1 Asbestos Foreman	$32.65	$261.20	$52.30	$418.40	$32.21	$51.60
7 Asbestos Workers	32.15	1800.40	51.50	2884.00		
64 L.H., Daily Totals		$2061.60		$3302.40	$32.21	$51.60
Crew A-10A	Hr.	Daily	Hr.	Daily	Bare Costs	Incl. O&P
1 Asbestos Foreman	$32.65	$261.20	$52.30	$418.40	$32.32	$51.77
2 Asbestos Workers	32.15	514.40	51.50	824.00		
24 L.H., Daily Totals		$775.60		$1242.40	$32.32	$51.77
Crew A-10B	Hr.	Daily	Hr.	Daily	Bare Costs	Incl. O&P
1 Asbestos Foreman	$32.65	$261.20	$52.30	$418.40	$32.28	$51.70
3 Asbestos Workers	32.15	771.60	51.50	1236.00		
32 L.H., Daily Totals		$1032.80		$1654.40	$32.28	$51.70
Crew A-10C	Hr.	Daily	Hr.	Daily	Bare Costs	Incl. O&P
3 Asbestos Workers	$32.15	$771.60	$51.50	$1236.00	$32.15	$51.50
1 Flatbed Truck		158.00		173.80	6.58	7.24
24 L.H., Daily Totals		$929.60		$1409.80	$38.73	$58.74
Crew A-10D	Hr.	Daily	Hr.	Daily	Bare Costs	Incl. O&P
2 Asbestos Workers	$32.15	$514.40	$51.50	$824.00	$30.30	$47.29
1 Equip. Oper. (crane)	31.15	249.20	47.15	377.20		
1 Equip. Oper. Oiler	25.75	206.00	39.00	312.00		
1 Hydraulic Crane, 33 Ton		804.80		885.30	25.15	27.67
32 L.H., Daily Totals		$1774.40		$2398.50	$55.45	$74.96
Crew A-11	Hr.	Daily	Hr.	Daily	Bare Costs	Incl. O&P
1 Asbestos Foreman	$32.65	$261.20	$52.30	$418.40	$32.21	$51.60
7 Asbestos Workers	32.15	1800.40	51.50	2884.00		
2 Chipping Hammers		35.20		38.70	.55	.61
64 L.H., Daily Totals		$2096.80		$3341.10	$32.76	$52.21
Crew A-12	Hr.	Daily	Hr.	Daily	Bare Costs	Incl. O&P
1 Asbestos Foreman	$32.65	$261.20	$52.30	$418.40	$32.21	$51.60
7 Asbestos Workers	32.15	1800.40	51.50	2884.00		
1 Large Prod. Vac. Loader		520.80		572.90	8.14	8.95
64 L.H., Daily Totals		$2582.40		$3875.30	$40.35	$60.55
Crew A-13	Hr.	Daily	Hr.	Daily	Bare Costs	Incl. O&P
1 Equip. Oper. (light)	$28.75	$230.00	$43.55	$348.40	$28.75	$43.55
1 Large Prod. Vac. Loader		520.80		572.90	65.10	71.61
8 L.H., Daily Totals		$750.80		$921.30	$93.85	$115.16

CREWS

588

Crew No.	Bare Costs		Incl. Subs O & P		Cost Per Labor-Hour	
Crew B-1	Hr.	Daily	Hr.	Daily	Bare Costs	Incl. O&P
1 Labor Foreman (outside)	$24.85	$198.80	$38.90	$311.20	$23.52	$36.80
2 Laborers	22.85	365.60	35.75	572.00		
24 L.H., Daily Totals		$564.40		$883.20	$23.52	$36.80
Crew B-2	Hr.	Daily	Hr.	Daily	Bare Costs	Incl. O&P
1 Labor Foreman (outside)	$24.85	$198.80	$38.90	$311.20	$23.25	$36.38
4 Laborers	22.85	731.20	35.75	1144.00		
40 L.H., Daily Totals		$930.00		$1455.20	$23.25	$36.38
Crew B-3	Hr.	Daily	Hr.	Daily	Bare Costs	Incl. O&P
1 Labor Foreman (outside)	$24.85	$198.80	$38.90	$311.20	$24.80	$38.26
2 Laborers	22.85	365.60	35.75	572.00		
1 Equip. Oper. (med.)	30.35	242.80	45.95	367.60		
2 Truck Drivers (heavy)	23.95	383.20	36.60	585.60		
1 F.E. Loader, T.M., 2.5 C.Y.		770.00		847.00		
2 Dump Trucks, 16 Ton		965.60		1062.15	36.16	39.77
48 L.H., Daily Totals		$2926.00		$3745.55	$60.96	$78.03
Crew B-3A	Hr.	Daily	Hr.	Daily	Bare Costs	Incl. O&P
4 Laborers	$22.85	$731.20	$35.75	$1144.00	$24.35	$37.79
1 Equip. Oper. (med.)	30.35	242.80	45.95	367.60		
1 Hyd. Excavator, 1.5 C.Y.		593.20		652.50	14.83	16.31
40 L.H., Daily Totals		$1567.20		$2164.10	$39.18	$54.10
Crew B-3B	Hr.	Daily	Hr.	Daily	Bare Costs	Incl. O&P
2 Laborers	$22.85	$365.60	$35.75	$572.00	$25.00	$38.51
1 Equip. Oper. (med.)	30.35	242.80	45.95	367.60		
1 Truck Drivers (heavy)	23.95	191.60	36.60	292.80		
1 Backhoe Loader, 80 H.P.		228.40		251.25		
1 Dump Trucks, 16 Ton		482.80		531.10	22.23	24.45
32 L.H., Daily Totals		$1511.20		$2014.75	$47.23	$62.96
Crew B-3C	Hr.	Daily	Hr.	Daily	Bare Costs	Incl. O&P
3 Laborers	$22.85	$548.40	$35.75	$858.00	$24.73	$38.30
1 Equip. Oper. (med.)	30.35	242.80	45.95	367.60		
1 F.E. Loader, 3.75 C.Y.		518.80		570.70	16.21	17.83
32 L.H., Daily Totals		$1310.00		$1796.30	$40.94	$56.13
Crew B-4	Hr.	Daily	Hr.	Daily	Bare Costs	Incl. O&P
1 Labor Foreman (outside)	$24.85	$198.80	$38.90	$311.20	$23.37	$36.42
4 Laborers	22.85	731.20	35.75	1144.00		
1 Truck Driver (heavy)	23.95	191.60	36.60	292.80		
1 Tractor, 4 x 2, 195 H.P.		320.40		352.45		
1 Platform Trailer		170.40		187.45	10.23	11.25
48 L.H., Daily Totals		$1612.40		$2287.90	$33.60	$47.67
Crew B-5	Hr.	Daily	Hr.	Daily	Bare Costs	Incl. O&P
1 Labor Foreman (outside)	$24.85	$198.80	$38.90	$311.20	$25.28	$39.11
4 Laborers	22.85	731.20	35.75	1144.00		
2 Equip. Oper. (med.)	30.35	485.60	45.95	735.20		
1 Air Compr. 250 C.F.M.		125.20		137.70		
2 Air Tools & Accessories		39.20		43.10		
2-50 Ft. Air Hoses, 1.5" Dia.		11.80		13.00		
1 F.E. Loader, T.M., 2.5 C.Y.		770.00		847.00	16.90	18.59
56 L.H., Daily Totals		$2361.80		$3231.20	$42.18	$57.70

Crew No.	Bare Costs		Incl. Subs O & P		Cost Per Labor-Hour	
Crew B-5A	Hr.	Daily	Hr.	Daily	Bare Costs	Incl. O&P
1 Foreman	$24.85	$198.80	$38.90	$311.20	$24.94	$38.50
6 Laborers	22.85	1096.80	35.75	1716.00		
2 Equip. Oper. (med.)	30.35	485.60	45.95	735.20		
1 Equip. Oper. (light)	28.75	230.00	43.55	348.40		
2 Truck Drivers (heavy)	23.95	383.20	36.60	585.60		
1 Air Compr. 365 C.F.M.		154.80		170.30		
2 Pavement Breakers		39.20		43.10		
8 Air Hoses w/Coup.,1"		29.20		32.10		
2 Dump Trucks, 12 Ton		740.80		814.90	10.04	11.05
96 L.H., Daily Totals		$3358.40		$4756.80	$34.98	$49.55
Crew B-5B	Hr.	Daily	Hr.	Daily	Bare Costs	Incl. O&P
1 Powderman	$29.85	$238.80	$46.85	$374.80	$27.07	$41.42
2 Equip. Oper. (med.)	30.35	485.60	45.95	735.20		
3 Truck Drivers (heavy)	23.95	574.80	36.60	878.40		
1 F.E. Ldr. 2-1/2 CY		391.80		431.00		
3 Dump Trucks, 16 Ton		1448.40		1593.25		
1 Air Compr. 365 C.F.M.		154.80		170.30	41.56	45.72
48 L.H., Daily Totals		$3294.20		$4182.95	$68.63	$87.14
Crew B-5C	Hr.	Daily	Hr.	Daily	Bare Costs	Incl. O&P
3 Laborers	$22.85	$548.40	$35.75	$858.00	$25.46	$39.07
1 Equip. Oper. (medium)	30.35	242.80	45.95	367.60		
2 Truck Drivers (heavy)	23.95	383.20	36.60	585.60		
1 Equip. Oper. (crane)	31.15	249.20	47.15	377.20		
1 Equip. Oper. Oiler	25.75	206.00	39.00	312.00		
2 Dump Truck, 16 Ton		965.60		1062.15		
1 F.E. Lder, 3.75 C.Y.		990.80		1089.90		
1 Hyd. Crane, 25 Ton		602.00		662.20	39.98	43.97
64 L.H., Daily Totals		$4188.00		$5314.65	$65.44	$83.04
Crew B-6	Hr.	Daily	Hr.	Daily	Bare Costs	Incl. O&P
2 Laborers	$22.85	$365.60	$35.75	$572.00	$24.82	$38.35
1 Equip. Oper. (light)	28.75	230.00	43.55	348.40		
1 Backhoe Loader, 48 H.P.		181.00		199.10	7.54	8.30
24 L.H., Daily Totals		$776.60		$1119.50	$32.36	$46.65
Crew B-6A	Hr.	Daily	Hr.	Daily	Bare Costs	Incl. O&P
.5 Labor Foreman (outside)	$24.85	$99.40	$38.90	$155.60	$26.25	$40.46
1 Laborers	22.85	182.80	35.75	286.00		
1 Equip. Oper. (med.)	30.35	242.80	45.95	367.60		
1 Vacuum Trk.,5000 Gal.		302.20		332.40	15.11	16.62
20 L.H., Daily Totals		$827.20		$1141.60	$41.36	$57.08
Crew B-7	Hr.	Daily	Hr.	Daily	Bare Costs	Incl. O&P
1 Labor Foreman (outside)	$24.85	$198.80	$38.90	$311.20	$24.43	$37.98
4 Laborers	22.85	731.20	35.75	1144.00		
1 Equip. Oper. (med.)	30.35	242.80	45.95	367.60		
1 Chipping Machine		190.60		209.65		
1 F.E. Loader, T.M., 2.5 C.Y.		770.00		847.00		
2 Chain Saws, 36"		86.40		95.05	21.81	23.99
48 L.H., Daily Totals		$2219.80		$2974.50	$46.24	$61.97
Crew B-7A	Hr.	Daily	Hr.	Daily	Bare Costs	Incl. O&P
2 Laborers	$22.85	$365.60	$35.75	$572.00	$24.82	$38.35
1 Equip. Oper. (light)	28.75	230.00	43.55	348.40		
1 Rake w/Tractor		139.70		153.65		
2 Chain Saws, 18"		52.40		57.65	8.00	8.80
24 L.H., Daily Totals		$787.70		$1131.70	$32.82	$47.15

Crew No.	Bare Costs		Incl. Subs O & P		Cost Per Labor-Hour	

Crew B-8

Crew B-8	Hr.	Daily	Hr.	Daily	Bare Costs	Incl. O&P
1 Labor Foreman (outside)	$24.85	$198.80	$38.90	$311.20	$25.61	$39.31
2 Laborers	22.85	365.60	35.75	572.00		
2 Equip. Oper. (med.)	30.35	485.60	45.95	735.20		
1 Equip. Oper. Oiler	25.75	206.00	39.00	312.00		
2 Truck Drivers (heavy)	23.95	383.20	36.60	585.60		
1 Hyd. Crane, 25 Ton		629.60		692.55		
1 F.E. Loader, T.M., 2.5 C.Y.		770.00		847.00		
2 Dump Trucks, 16 Ton		965.60		1062.15	36.96	40.65
64 L.H., Daily Totals		$4004.40		$5117.70	$62.57	$79.96

Crew B-9

Crew B-9	Hr.	Daily	Hr.	Daily	Bare Costs	Incl. O&P
1 Labor Foreman (outside)	$24.85	$198.80	$38.90	$311.20	$23.25	$36.38
4 Laborers	22.85	731.20	35.75	1144.00		
1 Air Compr., 250 C.F.M.		125.20		137.70		
2 Air Tools & Accessories		39.20		43.10		
2-50 Ft. Air Hoses, 1.5" Dia.		11.80		13.00	4.41	4.85
40 L.H., Daily Totals		$1106.20		$1649.00	$27.66	$41.23

Crew B-9A

Crew B-9A	Hr.	Daily	Hr.	Daily	Bare Costs	Incl. O&P
2 Laborers	$22.85	$365.60	$35.75	$572.00	$23.22	$36.03
1 Truck Driver (heavy)	23.95	191.60	36.60	292.80		
1 Water Tanker		184.00		202.40		
1 Tractor		320.40		352.45		
2-50 Ft. Disch. Hoses		12.80		14.10	21.55	23.71
24 L.H., Daily Totals		$1074.40		$1433.75	$44.77	$59.74

Crew B-9B

Crew B-9B	Hr.	Daily	Hr.	Daily	Bare Costs	Incl. O&P
2 Laborers	$22.85	$365.60	$35.75	$572.00	$23.22	$36.03
1 Truck Driver (heavy)	23.95	191.60	36.60	292.80		
2-50 Ft. Disch. Hoses		12.80		14.10		
1 Water Tanker		184.00		202.40		
1 Tractor		320.40		352.45		
1 Pressure Washer		57.40		63.15	23.94	26.34
24 L.H., Daily Totals		$1131.80		$1496.90	$47.16	$62.37

Crew B-9C

Crew B-9C	Hr.	Daily	Hr.	Daily	Bare Costs	Incl. O&P
1 Labor Foreman (outside)	$24.85	$198.80	$38.90	$311.20	$23.25	$36.38
4 Laborers	22.85	731.20	35.75	1144.00		
1 Air Compr., 250 C.F.M.		125.20		137.70		
2-50 Ft. Air Hoses, 1.5" Dia.		11.80		13.00		
2 Breaker, Pavement, 60 lb.		39.20		43.10	4.41	4.85
40 L.H., Daily Totals		$1106.20		$1649.00	$27.66	$41.23

Crew B-10

Crew B-10	Hr.	Daily	Hr.	Daily	Bare Costs	Incl. O&P
1 Equip. Oper. (med.)	$30.35	$242.80	$45.95	$367.60	$27.85	$42.55
.5 Laborer	22.85	91.40	35.75	143.00		
12 L.H., Daily Totals		$334.20		$510.60	$27.85	$42.55

Crew B-10A

Crew B-10A	Hr.	Daily	Hr.	Daily	Bare Costs	Incl. O&P
1 Equip. Oper. (med.)	$30.35	$242.80	$45.95	$367.60	$27.85	$42.55
.5 Laborer	22.85	91.40	35.75	143.00		
1 Roll. Compact., 2K Lbs.		111.00		122.10	9.25	10.18
12 L.H., Daily Totals		$445.20		$632.70	$37.10	$52.73

Crew B-10B

Crew B-10B	Hr.	Daily	Hr.	Daily	Bare Costs	Incl. O&P
1 Equip. Oper. (med.)	$30.35	$242.80	$45.95	$367.60	$27.85	$42.55
.5 Laborer	22.85	91.40	35.75	143.00		
1 Dozer, 200 H.P.		735.00		808.50	61.25	67.38
12 L.H., Daily Totals		$1069.20		$1319.10	$89.10	$109.93

Crew B-10C

Crew B-10C	Hr.	Daily	Hr.	Daily	Bare Costs	Incl. O&P
1 Equip. Oper. (med.)	$30.35	$242.80	$45.95	$367.60	$27.85	$42.55
.5 Laborer	22.85	91.40	35.75	143.00		
1 Dozer, 200 H.P.		735.00		808.50		
1 Vibratory Roller, Towed		168.40		185.25	75.28	82.81
12 L.H., Daily Totals		$1237.60		$1504.35	$103.13	$125.36

Crew B-10D

Crew B-10D	Hr.	Daily	Hr.	Daily	Bare Costs	Incl. O&P
1 Equip. Oper. (med.)	$30.35	$242.80	$45.95	$367.60	$27.85	$42.55
.5 Laborer	22.85	91.40	35.75	143.00		
1 Dozer, 200 H.P.		735.00		808.50		
1 Sheepsft. Roller, Towed		69.80		76.80	67.07	73.77
12 L.H., Daily Totals		$1139.00		$1395.90	$94.92	$116.32

Crew B-10E

Crew B-10E	Hr.	Daily	Hr.	Daily	Bare Costs	Incl. O&P
1 Equip. Oper. (med.)	$30.35	$242.80	$45.95	$367.60	$27.85	$42.55
.5 Laborer	22.85	91.40	35.75	143.00		
1 Tandem Roller, 5 Ton		133.20		146.50	11.10	12.21
12 L.H., Daily Totals		$467.40		$657.10	$38.95	$54.76

Crew B-10F

Crew B-10F	Hr.	Daily	Hr.	Daily	Bare Costs	Incl. O&P
1 Equip. Oper. (med.)	$30.35	$242.80	$45.95	$367.60	$27.85	$42.55
.5 Laborer	22.85	91.40	35.75	143.00		
1 Tandem Roller, 10 Ton		210.40		231.45	17.53	19.29
12 L.H., Daily Totals		$544.60		$742.05	$45.38	$61.84

Crew B-10G

Crew B-10G	Hr.	Daily	Hr.	Daily	Bare Costs	Incl. O&P
1 Equip. Oper. (med.)	$30.35	$242.80	$45.95	$367.60	$27.85	$42.55
.5 Laborer	22.85	91.40	35.75	143.00		
1 Sheepsft. Roll., 130 H.P.		616.00		677.60	51.33	56.47
12 L.H., Daily Totals		$950.20		$1188.20	$79.18	$99.02

Crew B-10H

Crew B-10H	Hr.	Daily	Hr.	Daily	Bare Costs	Incl. O&P
1 Equip. Oper. (med.)	$30.35	$242.80	$45.95	$367.60	$27.85	$42.55
.5 Laborer	22.85	91.40	35.75	143.00		
1 Diaphr. Water Pump, 2"		30.80		33.90		
1-20 Ft. Suction Hose, 2"		6.50		7.15		
2-50 Ft. Disch. Hoses, 2"		10.80		11.90	4.01	4.41
12 L.H., Daily Totals		$382.30		$563.55	$31.86	$46.96

Crew B-10I

Crew B-10I	Hr.	Daily	Hr.	Daily	Bare Costs	Incl. O&P
1 Equip. Oper. (med.)	$30.35	$242.80	$45.95	$367.60	$27.85	$42.55
.5 Laborer	22.85	91.40	35.75	143.00		
1 Diaphr. Water Pump, 4"		62.00		68.20		
1-20 Ft. Suction Hose, 4"		12.50		13.75		
2-50 Ft. Disch. Hoses, 4"		17.00		18.70	7.63	8.39
12 L.H., Daily Totals		$425.70		$611.25	$35.48	$50.94

Crew B-10J

Crew B-10J	Hr.	Daily	Hr.	Daily	Bare Costs	Incl. O&P
1 Equip. Oper. (med.)	$30.35	$242.80	$45.95	$367.60	$27.85	$42.55
.5 Laborer	22.85	91.40	35.75	143.00		
1 Centr. Water Pump, 3"		39.20		43.10		
1-20 Ft. Suction Hose, 3"		9.50		10.45		
2-50 Ft. Disch. Hoses, 3"		12.80		14.10	5.13	5.64
12 L.H., Daily Totals		$395.70		$578.25	$32.98	$48.19

Crew No.	Bare Costs		Incl. Subs O & P		Cost Per Labor-Hour	
Crew B-10K	Hr.	Daily	Hr.	Daily	Bare Costs	Incl. O&P
1 Equip. Oper. (med.)	$30.35	$242.80	$45.95	$367.60	$27.85	$42.55
.5 Laborer	22.85	91.40	35.75	143.00		
1 Centr. Water Pump, 6"		164.40		180.85		
1-20 Ft. Suction Hose, 6"		22.50		24.75		
2-50 Ft. Disch. Hoses, 6"		41.10		45.20	19.00	20.90
12 L.H., Daily Totals		$562.20		$761.40	$46.85	$63.45
Crew B-10L	Hr.	Daily	Hr.	Daily	Bare Costs	Incl. O&P
1 Equip. Oper. (med.)	$30.35	$242.80	$45.95	$367.60	$27.85	$42.55
.5 Laborer	22.85	91.40	35.75	143.00		
1 Dozer, 75 H.P.		266.00		292.60	22.17	24.38
12 L.H., Daily Totals		$600.20		$803.20	$50.02	$66.93
Crew B-10M	Hr.	Daily	Hr.	Daily	Bare Costs	Incl. O&P
1 Equip. Oper. (med.)	$30.35	$242.80	$45.95	$367.60	$27.85	$42.55
.5 Laborer	22.85	91.40	35.75	143.00		
1 Dozer, 300 H.P.		1027.00		1129.70	85.58	94.14
12 L.H., Daily Totals		$1361.20		$1640.30	$113.43	$136.69
Crew B-10N	Hr.	Daily	Hr.	Daily	Bare Costs	Incl. O&P
1 Equip. Oper. (med.)	$30.35	$242.80	$45.95	$367.60	$27.85	$42.55
.5 Laborer	22.85	91.40	35.75	143.00		
1 F.E. Loader, T.M., 1.5 C.Y		307.20		337.90	25.60	28.16
12 L.H., Daily Totals		$641.40		$848.50	$53.45	$70.71
Crew B-10O	Hr.	Daily	Hr.	Daily	Bare Costs	Incl. O&P
1 Equip. Oper. (med.)	$30.35	$242.80	$45.95	$367.60	$27.85	$42.55
.5 Laborer	22.85	91.40	35.75	143.00		
1 F.E. Loader, T.M., 2.25 C.Y.		457.00		502.70	38.08	41.89
12 L.H., Daily Totals		$791.20		$1013.30	$65.93	$84.44
Crew B-10P	Hr.	Daily	Hr.	Daily	Bare Costs	Incl. O&P
1 Equipment Oper. (med.)	$30.35	$242.80	$45.95	$367.60	$27.85	$42.55
.5 Laborer	22.85	91.40	35.75	143.00		
1 F.E. Loader, T.M., 2.5 C.Y.		770.00		847.00	64.17	70.58
12 L.H., Daily Totals		$1104.20		$1357.60	$92.02	$113.13
Crew B-10Q	Hr.	Daily	Hr.	Daily	Bare Costs	Incl. O&P
1 Equipment Oper. (med.)	$30.35	$242.80	$45.95	$367.60	$27.85	$42.55
.5 Laborer	22.85	91.40	35.75	143.00		
1 F.E. Loader, T.M., 5 C.Y.		990.80		1089.90	82.57	90.82
12 L.H., Daily Totals		$1325.00		$1600.50	$110.42	$133.37
Crew B-10R	Hr.	Daily	Hr.	Daily	Bare Costs	Incl. O&P
1 Equipment Oper. (med.)	$30.35	$242.80	$45.95	$367.60	$27.85	$42.55
.5 Laborer	22.85	91.40	35.75	143.00		
1 F.E. Loader, W.M., 1 C.Y.		227.60		250.35	18.97	20.86
12 L.H., Daily Totals		$561.80		$760.95	$46.82	$63.41
Crew B-10S	Hr.	Daily	Hr.	Daily	Bare Costs	Incl. O&P
1 Equip. Oper. (med.)	$30.35	$242.80	$45.95	$367.60	$27.85	$42.55
.5 Laborer	22.85	91.40	35.75	143.00		
1 F.E. Loader, W.M., 1.5 C.Y.		284.40		312.85	23.70	26.07
12 L.H., Daily Totals		$618.60		$823.45	$51.55	$68.62
Crew B-10T	Hr.	Daily	Hr.	Daily	Bare Costs	Incl. O&P
1 Equip. Oper. (med.)	$30.35	$242.80	$45.95	$367.60	$27.85	$42.55
.5 Laborer	22.85	91.40	35.75	143.00		
1 F.E. Loader, W.M.,2.5 C.Y.		391.80		431.00	32.65	35.92
12 L.H., Daily Totals		$726.00		$941.60	$60.50	$78.47

Crew No.	Bare Costs		Incl. Subs O & P		Cost Per Labor-Hour	
Crew B-10U	Hr.	Daily	Hr.	Daily	Bare Costs	Incl. O&P
1 Equip. Oper. (med.)	$30.35	$242.80	$45.95	$367.60	$27.85	$42.55
.5 Laborer	22.85	91.40	35.75	143.00		
1 F.E. Loader, W.M., 5.5 C.Y.		814.60		896.05	67.88	74.67
12 L.H., Daily Totals		$1148.80		$1406.65	$95.73	$117.22
Crew B-10V	Hr.	Daily	Hr.	Daily	Bare Costs	Incl. O&P
1 Equip. Oper. (med.)	$30.35	$242.80	$45.95	$367.60	$27.85	$42.55
.5 Laborer	22.85	91.40	35.75	143.00		
1 Dozer, 700 H.P.		2629.00		2891.90	219.08	240.99
12 L.H., Daily Totals		$2963.20		$3402.50	$246.93	$283.54
Crew B-10W	Hr.	Daily	Hr.	Daily	Bare Costs	Incl. O&P
1 Equip. Oper. (med.)	$30.35	$242.80	$45.95	$367.60	$27.85	$42.55
.5 Laborer	22.85	91.40	35.75	143.00		
1 Dozer, 105 H.P.		399.20		439.10	33.27	36.59
12 L.H., Daily Totals		$733.40		$949.70	$61.12	$79.14
Crew B-10X	Hr.	Daily	Hr.	Daily	Bare Costs	Incl. O&P
1 Equip. Oper. (med.)	$30.35	$242.80	$45.95	$367.60	$27.85	$42.55
.5 Laborer	22.85	91.40	35.75	143.00		
1 Dozer, 410 H.P.		1323.00		1455.30	110.25	121.28
12 L.H., Daily Totals		$1657.20		$1965.90	$138.10	$163.83
Crew B-10Y	Hr.	Daily	Hr.	Daily	Bare Costs	Incl. O&P
1 Equip. Oper. (med.)	$30.35	$242.80	$45.95	$367.60	$27.85	$42.55
.5 Laborer	22.85	91.40	35.75	143.00		
1 Vibratory Drum Roller		357.20		392.90	29.77	32.74
12 L.H., Daily Totals		$691.40		$903.50	$57.62	$75.29
Crew B-11	Hr.	Daily	Hr.	Daily	Bare Costs	Incl. O&P
1 Equipment Oper. (med.)	$30.35	$242.80	$45.95	$367.60	$26.60	$40.85
1 Laborer	22.85	182.80	35.75	286.00		
16 L.H., Daily Totals		$425.60		$653.60	$26.60	$40.85
Crew B-11A	Hr.	Daily	Hr.	Daily	Bare Costs	Incl. O&P
1 Equipment Oper. (med.)	$30.35	$242.80	$45.95	$367.60	$26.60	$40.85
1 Laborer	22.85	182.80	35.75	286.00		
1 Dozer, 200 H.P.		735.00		808.50	45.94	50.53
16 L.H., Daily Totals		$1160.60		$1462.10	$72.54	$91.38
Crew B-11B	Hr.	Daily	Hr.	Daily	Bare Costs	Incl. O&P
1 Equipment Oper. (med.)	$30.35	$242.80	$45.95	$367.60	$26.60	$40.85
1 Laborer	22.85	182.80	35.75	286.00		
1 Dozer, 200 H.P.		735.00		808.50		
1 Air Powered Tamper		21.40		23.55		
1 Air Compr. 365 C.F.M.		154.80		170.30		
2-50 Ft. Air Hoses, 1.5" Dia.		11.80		13.00	57.69	63.46
16 L.H., Daily Totals		$1348.60		$1668.95	$84.29	$104.31
Crew B-11C	Hr.	Daily	Hr.	Daily	Bare Costs	Incl. O&P
1 Equipment Oper. (med.)	$30.35	$242.80	$45.95	$367.60	$26.60	$40.85
1 Laborer	22.85	182.80	35.75	286.00		
1 Backhoe Loader, 48 H.P.		181.00		199.10	11.31	12.44
16 L.H., Daily Totals		$606.60		$852.70	$37.91	$53.29
Crew B-11K	Hr.	Daily	Hr.	Daily	Bare Costs	Incl. O&P
1 Equipment Oper. (med.)	$30.35	$242.80	$45.95	$367.60	$26.60	$40.85
1 Laborer	22.85	182.80	35.75	286.00		
1 Trencher, 8' D., 16" W.		711.40		782.55	44.46	48.91
16 L.H., Daily Totals		$1137.00		$1436.15	$71.06	$89.76

Crew No.	Bare Costs		Incl. Subs O & P		Cost Per Labor-Hour	

Crew B-11L

	Hr.	Daily	Hr.	Daily	Bare Costs	Incl. O&P
1 Equipment Oper. (med.)	$30.35	$242.80	$45.95	$367.60	$26.60	$40.85
1 Laborer	22.85	182.80	35.75	286.00		
1 Grader, 30,000 Lbs.		459.40		505.35	28.71	31.58
16 L.H., Daily Totals		$885.00		$1158.95	$55.31	$72.43

Crew B-11M

	Hr.	Daily	Hr.	Daily	Bare Costs	Incl. O&P
1 Equipment Oper. (med.)	$30.35	$242.80	$45.95	$367.60	$26.60	$40.85
1 Laborer	22.85	182.80	35.75	286.00		
1 Backhoe Loader, 80 H.P.		228.40		251.25	14.28	15.70
16 L.H., Daily Totals		$654.00		$904.85	$40.88	$56.55

Crew B-11N

	Hr.	Daily	Hr.	Daily	Bare Costs	Incl. O&P
1 Labor Foreman	$24.85	$198.80	$38.90	$311.20	$25.47	$38.93
2 Equipment Operators (med.)	30.35	485.60	45.95	735.20		
6 Truck Drivers (hvy.)	23.95	1149.60	36.60	1756.80		
1 F.E. Loader, 5.5 C.Y.		814.60		896.05		
1 Dozer, 400 H.P.		1323.00		1455.30		
6 Off Hwy. Tks. 50 Ton		8796.00		9675.60	151.86	167.04
72 L.H., Daily Totals		$12767.60		$14830.15	$177.33	$205.97

Crew B-11Q

	Hr.	Daily	Hr.	Daily	Bare Costs	Incl. O&P
1 Equipment Operator (med.)	$30.35	$242.80	$45.95	$367.60	$27.85	$42.55
.5 Laborer	22.85	91.40	35.75	143.00		
1 Dozer, 140 H.P.		493.20		542.50	41.10	45.21
12 L.H., Daily Totals		$827.40		$1053.10	$68.95	$87.76

Crew B-11R

	Hr.	Daily	Hr.	Daily	Bare Costs	Incl. O&P
1 Equipment Operator (med.)	$30.35	$242.80	$45.95	$367.60	$27.85	$42.55
.5 Laborer	22.85	91.40	35.75	143.00		
1 Dozer, 215 H.P.		735.00		808.50	61.25	67.38
12 L.H., Daily Totals		$1069.20		$1319.10	$89.10	$109.93

Crew B-11S

	Hr.	Daily	Hr.	Daily	Bare Costs	Incl. O&P
1 Equipment Operator	$30.35	$242.80	$45.95	$367.60	$27.85	$42.55
.5 Laborer	22.85	91.40	35.75	143.00		
1 Dozer, 285 H.P.		1027.00		1129.70	85.58	94.14
12 L.H., Daily Totals		$1361.20		$1640.30	$113.43	$136.69

Crew B-11T

	Hr.	Daily	Hr.	Daily	Bare Costs	Incl. O&P
1 Equipment Operator (med.)	$30.35	$242.80	$45.95	$367.60	$27.85	$42.55
.5 Laborer	22.85	91.40	35.75	143.00		
1 Dozer, 370 H.P.		1323.00		1455.30	110.25	121.28
12 L.H., Daily Totals		$1657.20		$1965.90	$138.10	$163.83

Crew B-11U

	Hr.	Daily	Hr.	Daily	Bare Costs	Incl. O&P
1 Equipment Operator (med.)	$30.35	$242.80	$45.95	$367.60	$27.85	$42.55
.5 Laborer	22.85	91.40	35.75	143.00		
1 Dozer, 520 H.P.		1634.00		1797.40	136.17	149.78
12 L.H., Daily Totals		$1968.20		$2308.00	$164.02	$192.33

Crew B-11V

	Hr.	Daily	Hr.	Daily	Bare Costs	Incl. O&P
3 Laborer	$22.85	$548.40	$35.75	$858.00	$22.85	$35.75
1 Roll. Compact., 2K Lbs.		111.00		122.10	4.63	5.09
24 L.H., Daily Totals		$659.40		$980.10	$27.48	$40.84

Crew B-12

	Hr.	Daily	Hr.	Daily	Bare Costs	Incl. O&P
1 Equip. Oper. (crane)	$31.15	$249.20	$47.15	$377.20	$28.45	$43.08
1 Equip. Oper. Oiler	25.75	206.00	39.00	312.00		
16 L.H., Daily Totals		$455.20		$689.20	$28.45	$43.08

Crew B-12A

	Hr.	Daily	Hr.	Daily	Bare Costs	Incl. O&P
1 Equip. Oper. (crane)	$31.15	$249.20	$47.15	$377.20	$28.45	$43.08
1 Equip. Oper. Oiler	25.75	206.00	39.00	312.00		
1 Hyd. Excavator, 1 C.Y.		490.80		539.90	30.68	33.74
16 L.H., Daily Totals		$946.00		$1229.10	$59.13	$76.82

Crew B-12B

	Hr.	Daily	Hr.	Daily	Bare Costs	Incl. O&P
1 Equip. Oper. (crane)	$31.15	$249.20	$47.15	$377.20	$28.45	$43.08
1 Equip. Oper. Oiler	25.75	206.00	39.00	312.00		
1 Hyd. Excavator, 1.5 C.Y.		593.20		652.50	37.08	40.78
16 L.H., Daily Totals		$1048.40		$1341.70	$65.53	$83.86

Crew B-12C

	Hr.	Daily	Hr.	Daily	Bare Costs	Incl. O&P
1 Equip. Oper. (crane)	$31.15	$249.20	$47.15	$377.20	$28.45	$43.08
1 Equip. Oper. Oiler	25.75	206.00	39.00	312.00		
1 Hyd. Excavator, 2 C.Y.		854.80		940.30	53.43	58.77
16 L.H., Daily Totals		$1310.00		$1629.50	$81.88	$101.85

Crew B-12D

	Hr.	Daily	Hr.	Daily	Bare Costs	Incl. O&P
1 Equip. Oper. (crane)	$31.15	$249.20	$47.15	$377.20	$28.45	$43.08
1 Equip. Oper. Oiler	25.75	206.00	39.00	312.00		
1 Hyd. Excavator, 3.5 C.Y.		1974.00		2171.40	123.38	135.71
16 L.H., Daily Totals		$2429.20		$2860.60	$151.83	$178.79

Crew B-12E

	Hr.	Daily	Hr.	Daily	Bare Costs	Incl. O&P
1 Equip. Oper. (crane)	$31.15	$249.20	$47.15	$377.20	$28.45	$43.08
1 Equip. Oper. Oiler	25.75	206.00	39.00	312.00		
1 Hyd. Excavator, .5 C.Y.		318.40		350.25	19.90	21.89
16 L.H., Daily Totals		$773.60		$1039.45	$48.35	$64.97

Crew B-12F

	Hr.	Daily	Hr.	Daily	Bare Costs	Incl. O&P
1 Equip. Oper. (crane)	$31.15	$249.20	$47.15	$377.20	$28.45	$43.08
1 Equip. Oper. Oiler	25.75	206.00	39.00	312.00		
1 Hyd. Excavator, .75 C.Y.		413.60		454.95	25.85	28.44
16 L.H., Daily Totals		$868.80		$1144.15	$54.30	$71.52

Crew B-12G

	Hr.	Daily	Hr.	Daily	Bare Costs	Incl. O&P
1 Equip. Oper. (crane)	$31.15	$249.20	$47.15	$377.20	$28.45	$43.08
1 Equip. Oper. Oiler	25.75	206.00	39.00	312.00		
1 Power Shovel, .5 C.Y.		357.75		393.50		
1 Clamshell Bucket, .5 C.Y.		48.00		52.80	24.23	26.66
16 L.H., Daily Totals		$860.95		$1135.50	$52.68	$69.74

Crew B-12H

	Hr.	Daily	Hr.	Daily	Bare Costs	Incl. O&P
1 Equip. Oper. (crane)	$31.15	$249.20	$47.15	$377.20	$28.45	$43.08
1 Equip. Oper. Oiler	25.75	206.00	39.00	312.00		
1 Power Shovel, 1 C.Y.		547.20		601.90		
1 Clamshell Bucket, 1 C.Y.		71.00		78.10	38.64	42.50
16 L.H., Daily Totals		$1073.40		$1369.20	$67.09	$85.58

Crew B-12I

	Hr.	Daily	Hr.	Daily	Bare Costs	Incl. O&P
1 Equip. Oper. (crane)	$31.15	$249.20	$47.15	$377.20	$28.45	$43.08
1 Equip. Oper. Oiler	25.75	206.00	39.00	312.00		
1 Power Shovel, .75 C.Y.		473.40		520.75		
1 Dragline Bucket, .75 C.Y.		21.20		23.30	30.91	34.00
16 L.H., Daily Totals		$949.80		$1233.25	$59.36	$77.08

Crew B-12J

Crew No.	Bare Costs Hr.	Daily	Incl. Subs O & P Hr.	Daily	Cost Per Labor-Hour Bare Costs	Incl. O&P
1 Equip. Oper. (crane)	$31.15	$249.20	$47.15	$377.20	$28.45	$43.08
1 Equip. Oper. Oiler	25.75	206.00	39.00	312.00		
1 Gradall, 3 Ton, .5 C.Y.		648.40		713.25	40.53	44.58
16 L.H., Daily Totals		$1103.60		$1402.45	$68.98	$87.66

Crew B-12K

Crew No.	Bare Costs Hr.	Daily	Incl. Subs O & P Hr.	Daily	Cost Per Labor-Hour Bare Costs	Incl. O&P
1 Equip. Oper. (crane)	$31.15	$249.20	$47.15	$377.20	$28.45	$43.08
1 Equip. Oper. Oiler	25.75	206.00	39.00	312.00		
1 Gradall, 3 Ton, 1 C.Y.		774.80		852.30	48.43	53.27
16 L.H., Daily Totals		$1230.00		$1541.50	$76.88	$96.35

Crew B-12L

Crew No.	Bare Costs Hr.	Daily	Incl. Subs O & P Hr.	Daily	Cost Per Labor-Hour Bare Costs	Incl. O&P
1 Equip. Oper. (crane)	$31.15	$249.20	$47.15	$377.20	$28.45	$43.08
1 Equip. Oper. Oiler	25.75	206.00	39.00	312.00		
1 Power Shovel, .5 C.Y.		357.75		393.50		
1 F.E. Attachment, .5 C.Y.		37.00		40.70	23.55	25.90
16 L.H., Daily Totals		$849.95		$1123.40	$52.00	$68.98

Crew B-12M

Crew No.	Bare Costs Hr.	Daily	Incl. Subs O & P Hr.	Daily	Cost Per Labor-Hour Bare Costs	Incl. O&P
1 Equip. Oper. (crane)	$31.15	$249.20	$47.15	$377.20	$28.45	$43.08
1 Equip. Oper. Oiler	25.75	206.00	39.00	312.00		
1 Power Shovel, .75 C.Y.		473.40		520.75		
1 F.E. Attachment, .75 C.Y.		40.00		44.00	32.09	35.30
16 L.H., Daily Totals		$968.60		$1253.95	$60.54	$78.38

Crew B-12N

Crew No.	Bare Costs Hr.	Daily	Incl. Subs O & P Hr.	Daily	Cost Per Labor-Hour Bare Costs	Incl. O&P
1 Equip. Oper. (crane)	$31.15	$249.20	$47.15	$377.20	$28.45	$43.08
1 Equip. Oper. Oiler	25.75	206.00	39.00	312.00		
1 Power Shovel, 1 C.Y.		547.20		601.90		
1 F.E. Attachment, 1 C.Y.		44.40		48.85	36.98	40.67
16 L.H., Daily Totals		$1046.80		$1339.95	$65.43	$83.75

Crew B-12O

Crew No.	Bare Costs Hr.	Daily	Incl. Subs O & P Hr.	Daily	Cost Per Labor-Hour Bare Costs	Incl. O&P
1 Equip. Oper. (crane)	$31.15	$249.20	$47.15	$377.20	$28.45	$43.08
1 Equip. Oper. Oiler	25.75	206.00	39.00	312.00		
1 Power Shovel, 1.5 C.Y.		716.00		787.60		
1 F.E. Attachment, 1.5 C.Y.		134.20		147.60	53.14	58.45
16 L.H., Daily Totals		$1305.40		$1624.40	$81.59	$101.53

Crew B-12P

Crew No.	Bare Costs Hr.	Daily	Incl. Subs O & P Hr.	Daily	Cost Per Labor-Hour Bare Costs	Incl. O&P
1 Equip. Oper. (crane)	$31.15	$249.20	$47.15	$377.20	$28.45	$43.08
1 Equip. Oper. Oiler	25.75	206.00	39.00	312.00		
1 Crawler Crane, 40 Ton		716.00		787.60		
1 Dragline Bucket, 1.5 C.Y.		35.20		38.70	46.95	51.65
16 L.H., Daily Totals		$1206.40		$1515.50	$75.40	$94.73

Crew B-12Q

Crew No.	Bare Costs Hr.	Daily	Incl. Subs O & P Hr.	Daily	Cost Per Labor-Hour Bare Costs	Incl. O&P
1 Equip. Oper. (crane)	$31.15	$249.20	$47.15	$377.20	$28.45	$43.08
1 Equip. Oper. Oiler	25.75	206.00	39.00	312.00		
1 Hyd. Excavator, 5/8 C.Y.		360.00		396.00	22.50	24.75
16 L.H., Daily Totals		$815.20		$1085.20	$50.95	$67.83

Crew B-12R

Crew No.	Bare Costs Hr.	Daily	Incl. Subs O & P Hr.	Daily	Cost Per Labor-Hour Bare Costs	Incl. O&P
1 Equip. Oper. (crane)	$31.15	$249.20	$47.15	$377.20	$28.45	$43.08
1 Equip. Oper. Oiler	25.75	206.00	39.00	312.00		
1 Hyd. Excavator, 1.5 C.Y.		593.20		652.50	37.08	40.78
16 L.H., Daily Totals		$1048.40		$1341.70	$65.53	$83.86

Crew B-12S

Crew No.	Bare Costs Hr.	Daily	Incl. Subs O & P Hr.	Daily	Cost Per Labor-Hour Bare Costs	Incl. O&P
1 Equip. Oper. (crane)	$31.15	$249.20	$47.15	$377.20	$28.45	$43.08
1 Equip. Oper. Oiler	25.75	206.00	39.00	312.00		
1 Hyd. Excavator, 2.5 C.Y.		1557.00		1712.70	97.31	107.04
16 L.H., Daily Totals		$2012.20		$2401.90	$125.76	$150.12

Crew B-12T

Crew No.	Bare Costs Hr.	Daily	Incl. Subs O & P Hr.	Daily	Cost Per Labor-Hour Bare Costs	Incl. O&P
1 Equip. Oper. (crane)	$31.15	$249.20	$47.15	$377.20	$28.45	$43.08
1 Equip. Oper. Oiler	25.75	206.00	39.00	312.00		
1 Crawler Crane, 75 Ton		933.20		1026.50		
1 F.E. Attachment, 3 C.Y.		248.40		273.25	73.85	81.24
16 L.H., Daily Totals		$1636.80		$1988.95	$102.30	$124.32

Crew B-12V

Crew No.	Bare Costs Hr.	Daily	Incl. Subs O & P Hr.	Daily	Cost Per Labor-Hour Bare Costs	Incl. O&P
1 Equip. Oper. (crane)	$31.15	$249.20	$47.15	$377.20	$28.45	$43.08
1 Equip. Oper. Oiler	25.75	206.00	39.00	312.00		
1 Crawler Crane, 75 Ton		933.20		1026.50		
1 Dragline Bucket, 3 C.Y.		74.00		81.40	62.95	69.25
16 L.H., Daily Totals		$1462.40		$1797.10	$91.40	$112.33

Crew B-13

Crew No.	Bare Costs Hr.	Daily	Incl. Subs O & P Hr.	Daily	Cost Per Labor-Hour Bare Costs	Incl. O&P
1 Labor Foreman (outside)	$24.85	$198.80	$38.90	$311.20	$24.74	$38.29
4 Laborers	22.85	731.20	35.75	1144.00		
1 Equip. Oper. (crane)	31.15	249.20	47.15	377.20		
1 Equip. Oper. Oiler	25.75	206.00	39.00	312.00		
1 Hyd. Crane, 25 Ton		629.60		692.55	11.24	12.37
56 L.H., Daily Totals		$2014.80		$2836.95	$35.98	$50.66

Crew B-13A

Crew No.	Bare Costs Hr.	Daily	Incl. Subs O & P Hr.	Daily	Cost Per Labor-Hour Bare Costs	Incl. O&P
1 Foreman	$24.85	$198.80	$38.90	$311.20	$25.59	$39.36
2 Laborers	22.85	365.60	35.75	572.00		
2 Equipment Operator	30.35	485.60	45.95	735.20		
2 Truck Drivers (heavy)	23.95	383.20	36.60	585.60		
1 Crane, 75 Ton		933.20		1026.50		
1 F.E. Lder, 3.75 C.Y.		990.80		1089.90		
2 Dump Trucks, 12 Ton		740.80		814.90	47.59	52.34
56 L.H., Daily Totals		$4098.00		$5135.30	$73.18	$91.70

Crew B-13B

Crew No.	Bare Costs Hr.	Daily	Incl. Subs O & P Hr.	Daily	Cost Per Labor-Hour Bare Costs	Incl. O&P
1 Labor Foreman (outside)	$24.85	$198.80	$38.90	$311.20	$24.74	$38.29
4 Laborers	22.85	731.20	35.75	1144.00		
1 Equip. Oper. (crane)	31.15	249.20	47.15	377.20		
1 Equip. Oper. Oiler	25.75	206.00	39.00	312.00		
1 Hyd. Crane, 55 Ton		901.60		991.75	16.10	17.71
56 L.H., Daily Totals		$2286.80		$3136.15	$40.84	$56.00

Crew B-13C

Crew No.	Bare Costs Hr.	Daily	Incl. Subs O & P Hr.	Daily	Cost Per Labor-Hour Bare Costs	Incl. O&P
1 Labor Foreman (outside)	$24.85	$198.80	$38.90	$311.20	$24.74	$38.29
4 Laborers	22.85	731.20	35.75	1144.00		
1 Equip. Oper. (crane)	31.15	249.20	47.15	377.20		
1 Equip. Oper. Oiler	25.75	206.00	39.00	312.00		
1 Crawler Crane, 100 Ton		1209.00		1329.90	21.59	23.75
56 L.H., Daily Totals		$2594.20		$3474.30	$46.33	$62.04

Crew B-14

Crew No.	Bare Costs Hr.	Daily	Incl. Subs O & P Hr.	Daily	Cost Per Labor-Hour Bare Costs	Incl. O&P
1 Labor Foreman (outside)	$24.85	$198.80	$38.90	$311.20	$24.17	$37.58
4 Laborers	22.85	731.20	35.75	1144.00		
1 Equip. Oper. (light)	28.75	230.00	43.55	348.40		
1 Backhoe Loader, 48 H.P.		181.00		199.10	3.77	4.15
48 L.H., Daily Totals		$1341.00		$2002.70	$27.94	$41.73

Crew No.	Bare Costs		Incl. Subs O & P		Cost Per Labor-Hour	

Crew B-15

Crew B-15	Hr.	Daily	Hr.	Daily	Bare Costs	Incl. O&P
1 Equipment Oper. (med)	$30.35	$242.80	$45.95	$367.60	$25.62	$39.15
.5 Laborer	22.85	91.40	35.75	143.00		
2 Truck Drivers (heavy)	23.95	383.20	36.60	585.60		
2 Dump Trucks, 16 Ton		965.60		1062.15		
1 Dozer, 200 H.P.		735.00		808.50	60.74	66.81
28 L.H., Daily Totals		$2418.00		$2966.85	$86.36	$105.96

Crew B-16	Hr.	Daily	Hr.	Daily	Bare Costs	Incl. O&P
1 Labor Foreman (outside)	$24.85	$198.80	$38.90	$311.20	$23.63	$36.75
2 Laborers	22.85	365.60	35.75	572.00		
1 Truck Driver (heavy)	23.95	191.60	36.60	292.80		
1 Dump Truck, 16 Ton		482.80		531.10	15.09	16.60
32 L.H., Daily Totals		$1238.80		$1707.10	$38.72	$53.35

Crew B-17	Hr.	Daily	Hr.	Daily	Bare Costs	Incl. O&P
2 Laborers	$22.85	$365.60	$35.75	$572.00	$24.60	$37.91
1 Equip. Oper. (light)	28.75	230.00	43.55	348.40		
1 Truck Driver (heavy)	23.95	191.60	36.60	292.80		
1 Backhoe Loader, 48 H.P.		181.00		199.10		
1 Dump Truck, 12 Ton		370.40		407.45	17.23	18.95
32 L.H., Daily Totals		$1338.60		$1819.75	$41.83	$56.86

Crew B-18	Hr.	Daily	Hr.	Daily	Bare Costs	Incl. O&P
1 Labor Foreman (outside)	$24.85	$198.80	$38.90	$311.20	$23.52	$36.80
2 Laborers	22.85	365.60	35.75	572.00		
1 Vibrating Compactor		60.60		66.65	2.53	2.78
24 L.H., Daily Totals		$625.00		$949.85	$26.05	$39.58

Crew B-19	Hr.	Daily	Hr.	Daily	Bare Costs	Incl. O&P
1 Pile Driver Foreman	$30.80	$246.40	$52.40	$419.20	$29.26	$47.71
4 Pile Drivers	28.80	921.60	49.00	1568.00		
2 Equip. Oper. (crane)	31.15	498.40	47.15	754.40		
1 Equip. Oper. Oiler	25.75	206.00	39.00	312.00		
1 Crane, 40 Ton & Access.		716.00		787.60		
60 L.F. Leads, 15K Ft. Lbs.		312.00		343.20		
1 Hammer, 15K Ft. Lbs.		313.40		344.75		
1 Air Compr., 600 C.F.M.		251.00		276.10		
2-50 Ft. Air Hoses, 3" Dia.		34.60		38.05	25.42	27.96
64 L.H., Daily Totals		$3499.40		$4843.30	$54.68	$75.67

Crew B-19A	Hr.	Daily	Hr.	Daily	Bare Costs	Incl. O&P
1 Pile Driver Foreman	$30.80	$246.40	$52.40	$419.20	$29.26	$47.71
4 Pile Drivers	28.80	921.60	49.00	1568.00		
2 Equip. Oper. (crane)	31.15	498.40	47.15	754.40		
1 Equip. Oper. Oiler	25.75	206.00	39.00	312.00		
1 Crawler Crane, 75 Ton		933.20		1026.50		
60 L.F. Leads, 25K Ft. Lbs.		432.00		475.20		
1 Air Compressor, 750 CFM		294.20		323.60		
4-50 Ft. Air Hose, 3" Dia.		69.20		76.10	27.01	29.71
64 L.H., Daily Totals		$3601.00		$4955.00	$56.27	$77.42

Crew B-20	Hr.	Daily	Hr.	Daily	Bare Costs	Incl. O&P
1 Labor Foreman (out)	$24.85	$198.80	$38.90	$311.20	$25.85	$40.50
1 Skilled Worker	29.85	238.80	46.85	374.80		
1 Laborer	22.85	182.80	35.75	286.00		
24 L.H., Daily Totals		$620.40		$972.00	$25.85	$40.50

Crew B-20A	Hr.	Daily	Hr.	Daily	Bare Costs	Incl. O&P
1 Labor Foreman	$24.85	$198.80	$38.90	$311.20	$27.43	$42.06
1 Laborer	22.85	182.80	35.75	286.00		
1 Plumber	34.45	275.60	52.00	416.00		
1 Plumber Apprentice	27.55	220.40	41.60	332.80		
32 L.H., Daily Totals		$877.60		$1346.00	$27.43	$42.06

Crew B-21	Hr.	Daily	Hr.	Daily	Bare Costs	Incl. O&P
1 Labor Foreman (out)	$24.85	$198.80	$38.90	$311.20	$26.61	$41.45
1 Skilled Worker	29.85	238.80	46.85	374.80		
1 Laborer	22.85	182.80	35.75	286.00		
.5 Equip. Oper. (crane)	31.15	124.60	47.15	188.60		
.5 S.P. Crane, 5 Ton		142.00		156.20	5.07	5.58
28 L.H., Daily Totals		$887.00		$1316.80	$31.68	$47.03

Crew B-21A	Hr.	Daily	Hr.	Daily	Bare Costs	Incl. O&P
1 Labor Foreman	$24.85	$198.80	$38.90	$311.20	$28.17	$43.08
1 Laborer	22.85	182.80	35.75	286.00		
1 Plumber	34.45	275.60	52.00	416.00		
1 Plumber Apprentice	27.55	220.40	41.60	332.80		
1 Equip. Oper. (crane)	31.15	249.20	47.15	377.20		
1 S.P. Crane, 12 Ton		425.20		467.70	10.63	11.69
40 L.H., Daily Totals		$1552.00		$2190.90	$38.80	$54.77

Crew B-22	Hr.	Daily	Hr.	Daily	Bare Costs	Incl. O&P
1 Labor Foreman (out)	$24.85	$198.80	$38.90	$311.20	$26.91	$41.83
1 Skilled Worker	29.85	238.80	46.85	374.80		
1 Laborer	22.85	182.80	35.75	286.00		
.75 Equip. Oper. (crane)	31.15	186.90	47.15	282.90		
.75 S.P. Crane, 5 Ton		213.00		234.30	7.10	7.81
30 L.H., Daily Totals		$1020.30		$1489.20	$34.01	$49.64

Crew B-22A	Hr.	Daily	Hr.	Daily	Bare Costs	Incl. O&P
1 Labor Foreman (out)	$24.85	$198.80	$38.90	$311.20	$26.06	$40.55
1 Skilled Worker	29.85	238.80	46.85	374.80		
2 Laborers	22.85	365.60	35.75	572.00		
.75 Equipment Oper. (crane)	31.15	186.90	47.15	282.90		
.75 Crane, 5 Ton		213.00		234.30		
1 Generator, 5 KW		46.90		51.60		
1 Butt Fusion Machine		302.20		332.40	14.79	16.27
38 L.H., Daily Totals		$1552.20		$2159.20	$40.85	$56.82

Crew B-22B	Hr.	Daily	Hr.	Daily	Bare Costs	Incl. O&P
1 Skilled Worker	$29.85	$238.80	$46.85	$374.80	$26.35	$41.30
1 Laborer	22.85	182.80	35.75	286.00		
1 Electro Fusion Machine		118.60		130.45	7.41	8.15
16 L.H., Daily Totals		$540.20		$791.25	$33.76	$49.45

Crew B-23	Hr.	Daily	Hr.	Daily	Bare Costs	Incl. O&P
1 Labor Foreman (outside)	$24.85	$198.80	$38.90	$311.20	$23.25	$36.38
4 Laborers	22.85	731.20	35.75	1144.00		
1 Drill Rig, Wells		1870.00		2057.00		
1 Light Truck, 3 Ton		184.20		202.60	51.36	56.49
40 L.H., Daily Totals		$2984.20		$3714.80	$74.61	$92.87

Crew B-23A	Hr.	Daily	Hr.	Daily	Bare Costs	Incl. O&P
1 Labor Foreman (outside)	$24.85	$198.80	$38.90	$311.20	$26.02	$40.20
1 Laborers	22.85	182.80	35.75	286.00		
1 Equip. Operator (medium)	30.35	242.80	45.95	367.60		
1 Drill Rig, Wells		1870.00		2057.00		
1 Pickup Truck, 3/4 Ton		83.00		91.30	81.38	89.51
24 L.H., Daily Totals		$2577.40		$3113.10	$107.40	$129.71

Crew No.	Bare Costs		Incl. Subs O & P		Cost Per Labor-Hour	

Crew B-23B	Hr.	Daily	Hr.	Daily	Bare Costs	Incl. O&P
1 Labor Foreman (outside)	$24.85	$198.80	$38.90	$311.20	$26.02	$40.20
1 Laborer	22.85	182.80	35.75	286.00		
1 Equip. Operator (medium)	30.35	242.80	45.95	367.60		
1 Drill Rig, Wells		1870.00		2057.00		
1 Pickup Truck, 3/4 Ton		83.00		91.30		
1 Pump, Cntfgl, 6"		164.40		180.85	88.23	97.05
24 L.H., Daily Totals		$2741.80		$3293.95	$114.25	$137.25

Crew B-24	Hr.	Daily	Hr.	Daily	Bare Costs	Incl. O&P
1 Cement Finisher	$27.95	$223.60	$41.55	$332.40	$26.65	$40.97
1 Laborer	22.85	182.80	35.75	286.00		
1 Carpenter	29.15	233.20	45.60	364.80		
24 L.H., Daily Totals		$639.60		$983.20	$26.65	$40.97

Crew B-25	Hr.	Daily	Hr.	Daily	Bare Costs	Incl. O&P
1 Labor Foreman	$24.85	$198.80	$38.90	$311.20	$25.08	$38.82
7 Laborers	22.85	1279.60	35.75	2002.00		
3 Equip. Oper. (med.)	30.35	728.40	45.95	1102.80		
1 Asphalt Paver, 130 H.P		1281.00		1409.10		
1 Tandem Roller, 10 Ton		210.40		231.45		
1 Roller, Pneumatic Wheel		215.60		237.15	19.40	21.34
88 L.H., Daily Totals		$3913.80		$5293.70	$44.48	$60.16

Crew B-25B	Hr.	Daily	Hr.	Daily	Bare Costs	Incl. O&P
1 Labor Foreman	$24.85	$198.80	$38.90	$311.20	$25.52	$39.41
7 Laborers	22.85	1279.60	35.75	2002.00		
4 Equip. Oper. (medium)	30.35	971.20	45.95	1470.40		
1 Asphalt Paver, 130 H.P.		1281.00		1409.10		
2 Rollers, Steel Wheel		420.80		462.90		
1 Roller, Pneumatic Wheel		215.60		237.15	19.97	21.97
96 L.H., Daily Totals		$4367.00		$5892.75	$45.49	$61.38

Crew B-25C	Hr.	Daily	Hr.	Daily	Bare Costs	Incl. O&P
1 Labor Foreman	$24.85	$198.80	$38.90	$311.20	$25.68	$39.67
3 Laborers	22.85	548.40	35.75	858.00		
2 Equip. Oper. (medium)	30.35	485.60	45.95	735.20		
1 Asphalt Paver, 130 H.P.		1281.00		1409.10		
1 Rollers, Steel Wheel		210.40		231.45	31.07	34.18
48 L.H., Daily Totals		$2724.20		$3544.95	$56.75	$73.85

Crew B-26	Hr.	Daily	Hr.	Daily	Bare Costs	Incl. O&P
1 Labor Foreman (outside)	$24.85	$198.80	$38.90	$311.20	$25.76	$40.22
6 Laborers	22.85	1096.80	35.75	1716.00		
2 Equip. Oper. (med.)	30.35	485.60	45.95	735.20		
1 Rodman (reinf.)	32.75	262.00	55.60	444.80		
1 Cement Finisher	27.95	223.60	41.55	332.40		
1 Grader, 30,000 Lbs.		459.40		505.35		
1 Paving Mach. & Equip.		1371.00		1508.10	20.80	22.88
88 L.H., Daily Totals		$4097.20		$5553.05	$46.56	$63.10

Crew B-27	Hr.	Daily	Hr.	Daily	Bare Costs	Incl. O&P
1 Labor Foreman (outside)	$24.85	$198.80	$38.90	$311.20	$23.35	$36.54
3 Laborers	22.85	548.40	35.75	858.00		
1 Berm Machine		144.20		158.60	4.51	4.96
32 L.H., Daily Totals		$891.40		$1327.80	$27.86	$41.50

Crew B-28	Hr.	Daily	Hr.	Daily	Bare Costs	Incl. O&P
2 Carpenters	$29.15	$466.40	$45.60	$729.60	$27.05	$42.32
1 Laborer	22.85	182.80	35.75	286.00		
24 L.H., Daily Totals		$649.20		$1015.60	$27.05	$42.32

Crew B-29	Hr.	Daily	Hr.	Daily	Bare Costs	Incl. O&P
1 Labor Foreman (outside)	$24.85	$198.80	$38.90	$311.20	$24.74	$38.29
4 Laborers	22.85	731.20	35.75	1144.00		
1 Equip. Oper. (crane)	31.15	249.20	47.15	377.20		
1 Equip. Oper. Oiler	25.75	206.00	39.00	312.00		
1 Gradall, 3 Ton, 1/2 C.Y.		648.40		713.25	11.58	12.74
56 L.H., Daily Totals		$2033.60		$2857.65	$36.32	$51.03

Crew B-30	Hr.	Daily	Hr.	Daily	Bare Costs	Incl. O&P
1 Equip. Oper. (med.)	$30.35	$242.80	$45.95	$367.60	$26.08	$39.72
2 Truck Drivers (heavy)	23.95	383.20	36.60	585.60		
1 Hyd. Excavator, 1.5 C.Y.		593.20		652.50		
2 Dump Trucks, 16 Ton		965.60		1062.15	64.95	71.45
24 L.H., Daily Totals		$2184.80		$2667.85	$91.03	$111.17

Crew B-31	Hr.	Daily	Hr.	Daily	Bare Costs	Incl. O&P
1 Labor Foreman (outside)	$24.85	$198.80	$38.90	$311.20	$24.51	$38.35
3 Laborers	22.85	548.40	35.75	858.00		
1 Carpenter	29.15	233.20	45.60	364.80		
1 Air Compr., 250 C.F.M.		125.20		137.70		
1 Sheeting Driver		12.50		13.75		
2-50 Ft. Air Hoses, 1.5" Dia.		11.80		13.00	3.74	4.11
40 L.H., Daily Totals		$1129.90		$1698.45	$28.25	$42.46

Crew B-32	Hr.	Daily	Hr.	Daily	Bare Costs	Incl. O&P
1 Laborer	$22.85	$182.80	$35.75	$286.00	$28.48	$43.40
3 Equip. Oper. (med.)	30.35	728.40	45.95	1102.80		
1 Grader, 30,000 Lbs.		459.40		505.35		
1 Tandem Roller, 10 Ton		210.40		231.45		
1 Dozer, 200 H.P.		735.00		808.50	43.90	48.29
32 L.H., Daily Totals		$2316.00		$2934.10	$72.38	$91.69

Crew B-32A	Hr.	Daily	Hr.	Daily	Bare Costs	Incl. O&P
1 Laborer	$22.85	$182.80	$35.75	$286.00	$27.85	$42.55
2 Equip. Oper. (medium)	30.35	485.60	45.95	735.20		
1 Grader, 30,000 Lbs.		459.40		505.35		
1 Roller, Vibratory, 29,000 Lbs.		451.20		496.30	37.94	41.74
24 L.H., Daily Totals		$1579.00		$2022.85	$65.79	$84.29

Crew B-32B	Hr.	Daily	Hr.	Daily	Bare Costs	Incl. O&P
1 Laborer	$22.85	$182.80	$35.75	$286.00	$27.85	$42.55
2 Equip. Oper. (medium)	30.35	485.60	45.95	735.20		
1 Dozer, 200 H.P.		735.00		808.50		
1 Roller, Vibratory, 29,000 Lbs.		451.20		496.30	49.43	54.37
24 L.H., Daily Totals		$1854.60		$2326.00	$77.28	$96.92

Crew B-32C	Hr.	Daily	Hr.	Daily	Bare Costs	Incl. O&P
1 Labor Foreman	$24.85	$198.80	$38.90	$311.20	$26.93	$41.38
2 Laborers	22.85	365.60	35.75	572.00		
3 Equip. Oper. (medium)	30.35	728.40	45.95	1102.80		
1 Grader, 30,000 Lbs.		459.40		505.35		
1 Roller, Steel Wheel		210.40		231.45		
1 Dozer, 200 H.P.		735.00		808.50	29.27	32.19
48 L.H., Daily Totals		$2697.60		$3531.30	$56.20	$73.57

Crew B-33	Hr.	Daily	Hr.	Daily	Bare Costs	Incl. O&P
1 Equip. Oper. (med.)	$30.35	$242.80	$45.95	$367.60	$28.21	$43.04
.5 Laborer	22.85	91.40	35.75	143.00		
.25 Equip. Oper. (med.)	30.35	60.70	45.95	91.90		
14 L.H., Daily Totals		$394.90		$602.50	$28.21	$43.04

| Crew No. | Bare Costs | | Incl. Subs O & P | | Cost Per Labor-Hour | |

Crew B-33A

Crew B-33A	Hr.	Daily	Hr.	Daily	Bare Costs	Incl. O&P
1 Equip. Oper. (med.)	$30.35	$242.80	$45.95	$367.60	$28.21	$43.04
.5 Laborer	22.85	91.40	35.75	143.00		
.25 Equip. Oper. (med.)	30.35	60.70	45.95	91.90		
1 Scraper, Towed, 7 C.Y.		123.35		135.70		
1.25 Dozer, 300 H.P.		1283.75		1412.15	100.51	110.56
14 L.H., Daily Totals		$1802.00		$2150.35	$128.72	$153.60

Crew B-33B	Hr.	Daily	Hr.	Daily	Bare Costs	Incl. O&P
1 Equip. Oper. (med.)	$30.35	$242.80	$45.95	$367.60	$28.21	$43.04
.5 Laborer	22.85	91.40	35.75	143.00		
.25 Equip. Oper. (med.)	30.35	60.70	45.95	91.90		
1 Scraper, Towed, 10 C.Y.		157.25		173.00		
1.25 Dozer, 300 H.P.		1283.75		1412.15	102.93	113.22
14 L.H., Daily Totals		$1835.90		$2187.65	$131.14	$156.26

Crew B-33C	Hr.	Daily	Hr.	Daily	Bare Costs	Incl. O&P
1 Equip. Oper. (med.)	$30.35	$242.80	$45.95	$367.60	$28.21	$43.04
.5 Laborer	22.85	91.40	35.75	143.00		
.25 Equip. Oper. (med.)	30.35	60.70	45.95	91.90		
1 Scraper, Towed, 12 C.Y.		157.25		173.00		
1.25 Dozer, 300 H.P.		1283.75		1412.15	102.93	113.22
14 L.H., Daily Totals		$1835.90		$2187.65	$131.14	$156.26

Crew B-33D	Hr.	Daily	Hr.	Daily	Bare Costs	Incl. O&P
1 Equip. Oper. (med.)	$30.35	$242.80	$45.95	$367.60	$28.21	$43.04
.5 Laborer	22.85	91.40	35.75	143.00		
.25 Equip. Oper. (med.)	30.35	60.70	45.95	91.90		
1 S.P. Scraper, 14 C.Y.		1597.00		1756.70		
.25 Dozer, 300 H.P.		256.75		282.45	132.41	145.65
14 L.H., Daily Totals		$2248.65		$2641.65	$160.62	$188.69

Crew B-33E	Hr.	Daily	Hr.	Daily	Bare Costs	Incl. O&P
1 Equip. Oper. (med.)	$30.35	$242.80	$45.95	$367.60	$28.21	$43.04
.5 Laborer	22.85	91.40	35.75	143.00		
.25 Equip. Oper. (med.)	30.35	60.70	45.95	91.90		
1 S.P. Scraper, 24 C.Y.		1932.00		2125.20		
.25 Dozer, 300 H.P.		256.75		282.45	156.34	171.97
14 L.H., Daily Totals		$2583.65		$3010.15	$184.55	$215.01

Crew B-33F	Hr.	Daily	Hr.	Daily	Bare Costs	Incl. O&P
1 Equip. Oper. (med.)	$30.35	$242.80	$45.95	$367.60	$28.21	$43.04
.5 Laborer	22.85	91.40	35.75	143.00		
.25 Equip. Oper. (med.)	30.35	60.70	45.95	91.90		
1 Elev. Scraper, 11 C.Y.		668.60		735.45		
.25 Dozer, 300 H.P.		256.75		282.45	66.10	72.71
14 L.H., Daily Totals		$1320.25		$1620.40	$94.31	$115.75

Crew B-33G	Hr.	Daily	Hr.	Daily	Bare Costs	Incl. O&P
1 Equip. Oper. (med.)	$30.35	$242.80	$45.95	$367.60	$28.21	$43.04
.5 Laborer	22.85	91.40	35.75	143.00		
.25 Equip. Oper. (med.)	30.35	60.70	45.95	91.90		
1 Elev. Scraper, 20 C.Y.		1178.00		1295.80		
.25 Dozer, 300 H.P.		256.75		282.45	102.48	112.73
14 L.H., Daily Totals		$1829.65		$2180.75	$130.69	$155.77

| Crew No. | Bare Costs | | Incl. Subs O & P | | Cost Per Labor-Hour | |

Crew B-33H	Hr.	Daily	Hr.	Daily	Bare Costs	Incl. O&P
.25 Laborer	$22.85	$45.70	$35.75	$71.50	$29.06	$44.19
1 Equipment Operator (med.)	30.35	242.80	45.95	367.60		
.2 Equipment Operator (med.)	30.35	48.56	45.95	73.52		
1 Scraper, 32-44 C.Y.		2385.00		2623.50		
.2 Dozer, 298 kw		264.60		291.05	228.41	251.26
11. L.H., Daily Totals		$2986.66		$3427.17	$257.47	$295.45

Crew B-33J	Hr.	Daily	Hr.	Daily	Bare Costs	Incl. O&P
1 Equipment Operator (med.)	$30.35	$242.80	$45.95	$367.60	$30.35	$45.95
1 Scraper 17 C.Y.		1597.00		1756.70	199.63	219.59
8 L.H., Daily Totals		$1839.80		$2124.30	$229.98	$265.54

Crew B-34A	Hr.	Daily	Hr.	Daily	Bare Costs	Incl. O&P
1 Truck Driver (heavy)	$23.95	$191.60	$36.60	$292.80	$23.95	$36.60
1 Dump Truck, 12 Ton		370.40		407.45	46.30	50.93
8 L.H., Daily Totals		$562.00		$700.25	$70.25	$87.53

Crew B-34B	Hr.	Daily	Hr.	Daily	Bare Costs	Incl. O&P
1 Truck Driver (heavy)	$23.95	$191.60	$36.60	$292.80	$23.95	$36.60
1 Dump Truck, 16 Ton		482.80		531.10	60.35	66.39
8 L.H., Daily Totals		$674.40		$823.90	$84.30	$102.99

Crew B-34C	Hr.	Daily	Hr.	Daily	Bare Costs	Incl. O&P
1 Truck Driver (heavy)	$23.95	$191.60	$36.60	$292.80	$23.95	$36.60
1 Truck Tractor, 40 Ton		413.00		454.30		
1 Dump Trailer, 16.5 C.Y.		140.00		154.00	69.13	76.04
8 L.H., Daily Totals		$744.60		$901.10	$93.08	$112.64

Crew B-34D	Hr.	Daily	Hr.	Daily	Bare Costs	Incl. O&P
1 Truck Driver (heavy)	$23.95	$191.60	$36.60	$292.80	$23.95	$36.60
1 Truck Tractor, 40 Ton		413.00		454.30		
1 Dump Trailer, 20 C.Y.		145.60		160.15	69.83	76.81
8 L.H., Daily Totals		$750.20		$907.25	$93.78	$113.41

Crew B-34E	Hr.	Daily	Hr.	Daily	Bare Costs	Incl. O&P
1 Truck Driver (heavy)	$23.95	$191.60	$36.60	$292.80	$23.95	$36.60
1 Truck, Off Hwy., 25 Ton		901.40		991.55	112.68	123.94
8 L.H., Daily Totals		$1093.00		$1284.35	$136.63	$160.54

Crew B-34F	Hr.	Daily	Hr.	Daily	Bare Costs	Incl. O&P
1 Truck Driver (heavy)	$23.95	$191.60	$36.60	$292.80	$23.95	$36.60
1 Truck, Off Hwy., 22 C.Y.		1100.00		1210.00	137.50	151.25
8 L.H., Daily Totals		$1291.60		$1502.80	$161.45	$187.85

Crew B-34G	Hr.	Daily	Hr.	Daily	Bare Costs	Incl. O&P
1 Truck Driver (heavy)	$23.95	$191.60	$36.60	$292.80	$23.95	$36.60
1 Truck, Off Hwy., 34 C.Y.		1466.00		1612.60	183.25	201.58
8 L.H., Daily Totals		$1657.60		$1905.40	$207.20	$238.18

Crew B-34H	Hr.	Daily	Hr.	Daily	Bare Costs	Incl. O&P
1 Truck Driver (heavy)	$23.95	$191.60	$36.60	$292.80	$23.95	$36.60
1 Truck, Off Hwy., 42 C.Y.		1561.00		1717.10	195.13	214.64
8 L.H., Daily Totals		$1752.60		$2009.90	$219.08	$251.24

Crew B-34J	Hr.	Daily	Hr.	Daily	Bare Costs	Incl. O&P
1 Truck Driver (heavy)	$23.95	$191.60	$36.60	$292.80	$23.95	$36.60
1 Truck, Off Hwy., 60 C.Y.		2259.00		2484.90	282.38	310.61
8 L.H., Daily Totals		$2450.60		$2777.70	$306.33	$347.21

Crew No.	Bare Costs		Incl. Subs O & P		Cost Per Labor-Hour	
	Hr.	Daily	Hr.	Daily	Bare Costs	Incl. O&P
Crew B-34K	Hr.	Daily	Hr.	Daily	Bare Costs	Incl. O&P
1 Truck Driver (heavy)	$23.95	$191.60	$36.60	$292.80	$23.95	$36.60
1 Truck Tractor, 240 H.P.		503.60		553.95		
1 Low Bed Trailer		286.60		315.25	98.78	108.65
8 L.H., Daily Totals		$981.80		$1162.00	$122.73	$145.25
Crew B-35	Hr.	Daily	Hr.	Daily	Bare Costs	Incl. O&P
1 Laborer Foreman (out)	$24.85	$198.80	$38.90	$311.20	$28.15	$43.27
1 Skilled Worker	29.85	238.80	46.85	374.80		
1 Welder (plumber)	34.45	275.60	52.00	416.00		
1 Laborer	22.85	182.80	35.75	286.00		
1 Equip. Oper. (crane)	31.15	249.20	47.15	377.20		
1 Equip. Oper. Oiler	25.75	206.00	39.00	312.00		
1 Electric Welding Mach.		100.65		110.70		
1 Hyd. Excavator, .75 C.Y.		413.60		454.95	10.71	11.78
48 L.H., Daily Totals		$1865.45		$2642.85	$38.86	$55.05
Crew B-35A	Hr.	Daily	Hr.	Daily	Bare Costs	Incl. O&P
1 Laborer Foreman (out)	$24.85	$198.80	$38.90	$311.20	$27.39	$42.20
2 Laborers	22.85	365.60	35.75	572.00		
1 Skilled Worker	29.85	238.80	46.85	374.80		
1 Welder (plumber)	34.45	275.60	52.00	416.00		
1 Equip. Oper. (crane)	31.15	249.20	47.15	377.20		
1 Equip. Oper. Oiler	25.75	206.00	39.00	312.00		
1 Welder, 300 amp		84.00		92.40		
1 Crane, 75 Ton		933.20		1026.50	18.16	19.98
56 L.H., Daily Totals		$2551.20		$3482.10	$45.55	$62.18
Crew B-36	Hr.	Daily	Hr.	Daily	Bare Costs	Incl. O&P
1 Labor Foreman (outside)	$24.85	$198.80	$38.90	$311.20	$26.25	$40.46
2 Laborers	22.85	365.60	35.75	572.00		
2 Equip. Oper. (med.)	30.35	485.60	45.95	735.20		
1 Dozer, 200 H.P.		735.00		808.50		
1 Aggregate Spreader		73.00		80.30		
1 Tandem Roller, 10 Ton		210.40		231.45	25.46	28.01
40 L.H., Daily Totals		$2068.40		$2738.65	$51.71	$68.47
Crew B-36A	Hr.	Daily	Hr.	Daily	Bare Costs	Incl. O&P
1 Labor Foreman (outside)	$24.85	$198.80	$38.90	$311.20	$27.42	$42.03
2 Laborers	22.85	365.60	35.75	572.00		
4 Equip. Oper. (med.)	30.35	971.20	45.95	1470.40		
1 Dozer, 200 H.P.		735.00		808.50		
1 Aggregate Spreader		73.00		80.30		
1 Roller, Steel Wheel		210.40		231.45		
1 Roller, Pneumatic Wheel		215.60		237.15	22.04	24.24
56 L.H., Daily Totals		$2769.60		$3711.00	$49.46	$66.27
Crew B-36B	Hr.	Daily	Hr.	Daily	Bare Costs	Incl. O&P
1 Labor Foreman (outside)	$24.85	$198.80	$38.90	$311.20	$26.99	$41.35
2 Laborers	22.85	365.60	35.75	572.00		
4 Equip. Oper. (medium)	30.35	971.20	45.95	1470.40		
1 Truck Driver, Heavy	23.95	191.60	36.60	292.80		
1 Grader, 30,000 Lbs.		459.40		505.35		
1 F.E. Loader, crl, 1.5 C.Y.		358.80		394.70		
1 Dozer, 300 H.P.		1027.00		1129.70		
1 Roller, Vibratory		451.20		496.30		
1 Truck, Tractor, 240 H.P.		503.60		553.95		
1 Water Tanker, 5000 Gal.		184.00		202.40	46.63	51.29
64 L.H., Daily Totals		$4711.20		$5928.80	$73.62	$92.64

Crew No.	Bare Costs		Incl. Subs O & P		Cost Per Labor-Hour	
Crew B-37	Hr.	Daily	Hr.	Daily	Bare Costs	Incl. O&P
1 Labor Foreman (outside)	$24.85	$198.80	$38.90	$311.20	$24.17	$37.58
4 Laborers	22.85	731.20	35.75	1144.00		
1 Equip. Oper. (light)	28.75	230.00	43.55	348.40		
1 Tandem Roller, 5 Ton		133.20		146.50	2.78	3.05
48 L.H., Daily Totals		$1293.20		$1950.10	$26.95	$40.63
Crew B-38	Hr.	Daily	Hr.	Daily	Bare Costs	Incl. O&P
1 Labor Foreman (outside)	$24.85	$198.80	$38.90	$311.20	$25.93	$39.98
2 Laborers	22.85	365.60	35.75	572.00		
1 Equip. Oper. (light)	28.75	230.00	43.55	348.40		
1 Equip. Oper. (medium)	30.35	242.80	45.95	367.60		
1 Backhoe Loader, 48 H.P.		181.00		199.10		
1 Hyd.Hammer, (1200 lb)		190.40		209.45		
1 F.E. Loader (170 H.P.)		518.80		570.70		
1 Pavt. Rem. Bucket		45.60		50.15	23.40	25.73
40 L.H., Daily Totals		$1973.00		$2628.60	$49.33	$65.71
Crew B-39	Hr.	Daily	Hr.	Daily	Bare Costs	Incl. O&P
1 Labor Foreman (outside)	$24.85	$198.80	$38.90	$311.20	$24.17	$37.58
4 Laborers	22.85	731.20	35.75	1144.00		
1 Equip. Oper. (light)	28.75	230.00	43.55	348.40		
1 Air Compr., 250 C.F.M.		125.20		137.70		
2 Air Tools & Accessories		39.20		43.10		
2-50 Ft. Air Hoses, 1.5" Dia.		11.80		13.00	3.67	4.04
48 L.H., Daily Totals		$1336.20		$1997.40	$27.84	$41.62
Crew B-40	Hr.	Daily	Hr.	Daily	Bare Costs	Incl. O&P
1 Pile Driver Foreman (out)	$30.80	$246.40	$52.40	$419.20	$29.26	$47.71
4 Pile Drivers	28.80	921.60	49.00	1568.00		
2 Equip. Oper. (crane)	31.15	498.40	47.15	754.40		
1 Equip. Oper. Oiler	25.75	206.00	39.00	312.00		
1 Crane, 40 Ton		716.00		787.60		
1 Vibratory Hammer & Gen.		1283.00		1411.30	31.23	34.36
64 L.H., Daily Totals		$3871.40		$5252.50	$60.49	$82.07
Crew B-41	Hr.	Daily	Hr.	Daily	Bare Costs	Incl. O&P
1 Labor Foreman (outside)	$24.85	$198.80	$38.90	$311.20	$23.72	$36.99
4 Laborers	22.85	731.20	35.75	1144.00		
.25 Equip. Oper. (crane)	31.15	62.30	47.15	94.30		
.25 Equip. Oper. Oiler	25.75	51.50	39.00	78.00		
.25 Crawler Crane, 40 Ton		179.00		196.90	4.07	4.48
44 L.H., Daily Totals		$1222.80		$1824.40	$27.79	$41.47
Crew B-42	Hr.	Daily	Hr.	Daily	Bare Costs	Incl. O&P
1 Labor Foreman (outside)	$24.85	$198.80	$38.90	$311.20	$25.75	$40.96
4 Laborers	22.85	731.20	35.75	1144.00		
1 Equip. Oper. (crane)	31.15	249.20	47.15	377.20		
1 Equip. Oper. Oiler	25.75	206.00	39.00	312.00		
1 Welder	32.85	262.80	59.60	476.80		
1 Hyd. Crane, 25 Ton		629.60		692.55		
1 Gas Welding Machine		84.00		92.40		
1 Horz. Boring Csg. Mch.		523.20		575.50	19.33	21.26
64 L.H., Daily Totals		$2884.80		$3981.65	$45.08	$62.22
Crew B-43	Hr.	Daily	Hr.	Daily	Bare Costs	Incl. O&P
1 Labor Foreman (outside)	$24.85	$198.80	$38.90	$311.20	$25.05	$38.72
3 Laborers	22.85	548.40	35.75	858.00		
1 Equip. Oper. (crane)	31.15	249.20	47.15	377.20		
1 Equip. Oper. Oiler	25.75	206.00	39.00	312.00		
1 Drill Rig & Augers		1870.00		2057.00	38.96	42.85
48 L.H., Daily Totals		$3072.40		$3915.40	$64.01	$81.57

Crew No.	Bare Costs Hr.	Daily	Incl. Subs O & P Hr.	Daily	Cost Per Labor-Hour Bare Costs	Incl. O&P
Crew B-44	Hr.	Daily	Hr.	Daily	Bare Costs	Incl. O&P
1 Pile Driver Foreman	$30.80	$246.40	$52.40	$419.20	$28.89	$47.31
4 Pile Drivers	28.80	921.60	49.00	1568.00		
2 Equip. Oper. (crane)	31.15	498.40	47.15	754.40		
1 Laborer	22.85	182.80	35.75	286.00		
1 Crane, 40 Ton, & Access.		716.00		787.60		
45 L.F. Leads, 15K Ft. Lbs.		234.00		257.40	14.84	16.33
64 L.H., Daily Totals		$2799.20		$4072.60	$43.73	$63.64
Crew B-45	Hr.	Daily	Hr.	Daily	Bare Costs	Incl. O&P
1 Equip. Oper. (med.)	$30.35	$242.80	$45.95	$367.60	$27.15	$41.28
1 Truck Driver (heavy)	23.95	191.60	36.60	292.80		
1 Dist. Tank Truck, 3K Gal.		328.80		361.70		
1 Tractor, 4 x 2, 250 H.P.		397.60		437.35	45.40	49.94
16 L.H., Daily Totals		$1160.80		$1459.45	$72.55	$91.22
Crew B-46	Hr.	Daily	Hr.	Daily	Bare Costs	Incl. O&P
1 Pile Driver Foreman	$30.80	$246.40	$52.40	$419.20	$26.16	$42.94
2 Pile Drivers	28.80	460.80	49.00	784.00		
3 Laborers	22.85	548.40	35.75	858.00		
1 Chain Saw, 36" Long		43.20		47.50	.90	.99
48 L.H., Daily Totals		$1298.80		$2108.70	$27.06	$43.93
Crew B-47	Hr.	Daily	Hr.	Daily	Bare Costs	Incl. O&P
1 Blast Foreman	$24.85	$198.80	$38.90	$311.20	$25.48	$39.40
1 Driller	22.85	182.80	35.75	286.00		
1 Equip. Oper. (light)	28.75	230.00	43.55	348.40		
1 Crawler Type Drill, 4"		455.60		501.15		
1 Air Compr., 600 C.F.M.		251.00		276.10		
2-50 Ft. Air Hoses, 3" Dia.		34.60		38.05	30.88	33.97
24 L.H., Daily Totals		$1352.80		$1760.90	$56.36	$73.37
Crew B-47A	Hr.	Daily	Hr.	Daily	Bare Costs	Incl. O&P
1 Drilling Foreman	$24.85	$198.80	$38.90	$311.20	$27.25	$41.68
1 Equip. Oper. (heavy)	31.15	249.20	47.15	377.20		
1 Oiler	25.75	206.00	39.00	312.00		
1 Quarry Drill		721.20		793.30	30.05	33.06
24 L.H., Daily Totals		$1375.20		$1793.70	$57.30	$74.74
Crew B-47C	Hr.	Daily	Hr.	Daily	Bare Costs	Incl. O&P
1 Laborer	$22.85	$182.80	$35.75	$286.00	$25.80	$39.65
1 Equip. Oper. (light)	28.75	230.00	43.55	348.40		
1 Air Compressor, 750 CFM		294.20		323.60		
2-50' Air Hose, 3"		34.60		38.05		
1 Air Track Drill, 4"		455.60		501.15	49.03	53.93
16 L.H., Daily Totals		$1197.20		$1497.20	$74.83	$93.58
Crew B-47E	Hr.	Daily	Hr.	Daily	Bare Costs	Incl. O&P
1 Laborer Foreman	$24.85	$198.80	$38.90	$311.20	$23.35	$36.54
3 Laborers	22.85	548.40	35.75	858.00		
1 Truck, Flatbed, 3 Ton		184.20		202.60	5.76	6.33
32 L.H., Daily Totals		$931.40		$1371.80	$29.11	$42.87

Crew No.	Bare Costs Hr.	Daily	Incl. Subs O & P Hr.	Daily	Cost Per Labor-Hour Bare Costs	Incl. O&P
Crew B-48	Hr.	Daily	Hr.	Daily	Bare Costs	Incl. O&P
1 Labor Foreman (outside)	$24.85	$198.80	$38.90	$311.20	$25.58	$39.41
3 Laborers	22.85	548.40	35.75	858.00		
1 Equip. Oper. (crane)	31.15	249.20	47.15	377.20		
1 Equip. Oper. Oiler	25.75	206.00	39.00	312.00		
1 Equip. Oper. (light)	28.75	230.00	43.55	348.40		
1 Centr. Water Pump, 6"		164.40		180.85		
1-20 Ft. Suction Hose, 6"		22.50		24.75		
1-50 Ft. Disch. Hose, 6"		20.55		22.60		
1 Drill Rig & Augers		1870.00		2057.00	37.10	40.81
56 L.H., Daily Totals		$3509.85		$4492.00	$62.68	$80.22
Crew B-49	Hr.	Daily	Hr.	Daily	Bare Costs	Incl. O&P
1 Labor Foreman (outside)	$24.85	$198.80	$38.90	$311.20	$26.69	$41.82
3 Laborers	22.85	548.40	35.75	858.00		
2 Equip. Oper. (crane)	31.15	498.40	47.15	754.40		
2 Equip. Oper. Oilers	25.75	412.00	39.00	624.00		
1 Equip. Oper. (light)	28.75	230.00	43.55	348.40		
2 Pile Drivers	28.80	460.80	49.00	784.00		
1 Hyd. Crane, 25 Ton		629.60		692.55		
1 Centr. Water Pump, 6"		164.40		180.85		
1-20 Ft. Suction Hose, 6"		22.50		24.75		
1-50 Ft. Disch. Hose, 6"		20.55		22.60		
1 Drill Rig & Augers		1870.00		2057.00	30.76	33.84
88 L.H., Daily Totals		$5055.45		$6657.75	$57.45	$75.66
Crew B-50	Hr.	Daily	Hr.	Daily	Bare Costs	Incl. O&P
2 Pile Driver Foremen	$30.80	$492.80	$52.40	$838.40	$27.93	$45.67
6 Pile Drivers	28.80	1382.40	49.00	2352.00		
2 Equip. Oper. (crane)	31.15	498.40	47.15	754.40		
1 Equip. Oper. Oiler	25.75	206.00	39.00	312.00		
3 Laborers	22.85	548.40	35.75	858.00		
1 Crane, 40 Ton		716.00		787.60		
60 L.F. Leads, 15K Ft. Lbs.		312.00		343.20		
1 Hammer, 15K Ft. Lbs.		313.40		344.75		
1 Air Compr., 600 C.F.M.		251.00		276.10		
2-50 Ft. Air Hoses, 3" Dia.		34.60		38.05		
1 Chain Saw, 36" Long		43.20		47.50	14.91	16.40
112 L.H., Daily Totals		$4798.20		$6952.00	$42.84	$62.07
Crew B-51	Hr.	Daily	Hr.	Daily	Bare Costs	Incl. O&P
1 Labor Foreman (outside)	$24.85	$198.80	$38.90	$311.20	$23.28	$36.28
4 Laborers	22.85	731.20	35.75	1144.00		
1 Truck Driver (light)	23.40	187.20	35.75	286.00		
1 Light Truck, 1.5 Ton		158.00		173.80	3.29	3.62
48 L.H., Daily Totals		$1275.20		$1915.00	$26.57	$39.90
Crew B-52	Hr.	Daily	Hr.	Daily	Bare Costs	Incl. O&P
1 Carpenter Foreman	$31.15	$249.20	$48.75	$390.00	$26.91	$41.99
1 Carpenter	29.15	233.20	45.60	364.80		
3 Laborers	22.85	548.40	35.75	858.00		
1 Cement Finisher	27.95	223.60	41.55	332.40		
.5 Rodman (reinf.)	32.75	131.00	55.60	222.40		
.5 Equip. Oper. (med.)	30.35	121.40	45.95	183.80		
.5 F.E. Ldr., T.M., 2.5 C.Y.		385.00		423.50	6.88	7.56
56 L.H., Daily Totals		$1891.80		$2774.90	$33.79	$49.55
Crew B-53	Hr.	Daily	Hr.	Daily	Bare Costs	Incl. O&P
1 Equip. Oper. (light)	$28.75	$230.00	$43.55	$348.40	$28.75	$43.55
1 Trencher, Chain, 12 H.P.		96.80		106.50	12.10	13.31
8 L.H., Daily Totals		$326.80		$454.90	$40.85	$56.86

Crew No.	Bare Costs Hr.	Daily	Incl. Subs O & P Hr.	Daily	Cost Per Labor-Hour Bare Costs	Incl. O&P
Crew B-54	Hr.	Daily	Hr.	Daily	Bare Costs	Incl. O&P
1 Equip. Oper. (light)	$28.75	$230.00	$43.55	$348.40	$28.75	$43.55
1 Trencher, Chain, 40 H.P.		196.40		216.05	24.55	27.01
8 L.H., Daily Totals		$426.40		$564.45	$53.30	$70.56

Crew No.	Hr.	Daily	Hr.	Daily	Bare Costs	Incl. O&P
Crew B-54A	Hr.	Daily	Hr.	Daily	Bare Costs	Incl. O&P
.17 Labor Foreman (outside)	$24.85	$33.80	$38.90	$52.90	$29.55	$44.93
1 Equipment Operator (med.)	30.35	242.80	45.95	367.60		
1 Wheel Trencher, 67 H.P.		424.80		467.30	45.38	49.92
9.36 L.H., Daily Totals		$701.40		$887.80	$74.93	$94.85

Crew No.	Hr.	Daily	Hr.	Daily	Bare Costs	Incl. O&P
Crew B-54B	Hr.	Daily	Hr.	Daily	Bare Costs	Incl. O&P
.25 Labor Foreman (outside)	$24.85	$49.70	$38.90	$77.80	$29.25	$44.54
1 Equipment Operator (med.)	30.35	242.80	45.95	367.60		
1 Wheel Trencher, 150 H.P.		636.80		700.50	63.68	70.05
10 L.H., Daily Totals		$929.30		$1145.90	$92.93	$114.59

Crew No.	Hr.	Daily	Hr.	Daily	Bare Costs	Incl. O&P
Crew B-55	Hr.	Daily	Hr.	Daily	Bare Costs	Incl. O&P
2 Laborers	$22.85	$365.60	$35.75	$572.00	$23.03	$35.75
1 Truck Driver (light)	23.40	187.20	35.75	286.00		
1 Auger, 4" to 36" Dia		519.40		571.35		
1 Flatbed 3 Ton Truck		184.20		202.60	29.32	32.25
24 L.H., Daily Totals		$1256.40		$1631.95	$52.35	$68.00

Crew No.	Hr.	Daily	Hr.	Daily	Bare Costs	Incl. O&P
Crew B-56	Hr.	Daily	Hr.	Daily	Bare Costs	Incl. O&P
1 Laborer	$22.85	$182.80	$35.75	$286.00	$25.80	$39.65
1 Equip. Oper. (light)	28.75	230.00	43.55	348.40		
1 Crawler Type Drill, 4"		455.60		501.15		
1 Air Compr., 600 C.F.M.		251.00		276.10		
1-50 Ft. Air Hose, 3" Dia.		17.30		19.05	45.24	49.77
16 L.H., Daily Totals		$1136.70		$1430.70	$71.04	$89.42

Crew No.	Hr.	Daily	Hr.	Daily	Bare Costs	Incl. O&P
Crew B-57	Hr.	Daily	Hr.	Daily	Bare Costs	Incl. O&P
1 Labor Foreman (outside)	$24.85	$198.80	$38.90	$311.20	$26.03	$40.02
2 Laborers	22.85	365.60	35.75	572.00		
1 Equip. Oper. (crane)	31.15	249.20	47.15	377.20		
1 Equip. Oper. (light)	28.75	230.00	43.55	348.40		
1 Equip. Oper. Oiler	25.75	206.00	39.00	312.00		
1 Power Shovel, 1 C.Y.		547.20		601.90		
1 Clamshell Bucket, 1 C.Y.		71.00		78.10		
1 Centr. Water Pump, 6"		164.40		180.85		
1-20 Ft. Suction Hose, 6"		22.50		24.75		
20-50 Ft. Disch. Hoses, 6"		411.00		452.10	25.34	27.87
48 L.H., Daily Totals		$2465.70		$3258.50	$51.37	$67.89

Crew No.	Hr.	Daily	Hr.	Daily	Bare Costs	Incl. O&P
Crew B-58	Hr.	Daily	Hr.	Daily	Bare Costs	Incl. O&P
2 Laborers	$22.85	$365.60	$35.75	$572.00	$24.82	$38.35
1 Equip. Oper. (light)	28.75	230.00	43.55	348.40		
1 Backhoe Loader, 48 H.P.		181.00		199.10		
1 Small Helicopter, w/pilot		1986.00		2184.60	90.29	99.32
24 L.H., Daily Totals		$2762.60		$3304.10	$115.11	$137.67

Crew No.	Hr.	Daily	Hr.	Daily	Bare Costs	Incl. O&P
Crew B-59	Hr.	Daily	Hr.	Daily	Bare Costs	Incl. O&P
1 Truck Driver (heavy)	$23.95	$191.60	$36.60	$292.80	$23.95	$36.60
1 Truck, 30 Ton		320.40		352.45		
1 Water tank, 5000 Gal.		184.00		202.40	63.05	69.36
8 L.H., Daily Totals		$696.00		$847.65	$87.00	$105.96

Crew No.	Hr.	Daily	Hr.	Daily	Bare Costs	Incl. O&P
Crew B-59A	Hr.	Daily	Hr.	Daily	Bare Costs	Incl. O&P
2 Laborers	$22.85	$365.60	$35.75	$572.00	$23.22	$36.03
1 Truck Driver (heavy)	23.95	191.60	36.60	292.80		
1 Water tank, 5K w/pum		184.00		202.40		
1 Truck, 30 Ton		320.40		352.45	21.02	23.12
24 L.H., Daily Totals		$1061.60		$1419.65	$44.24	$59.15

Crew No.	Hr.	Daily	Hr.	Daily	Bare Costs	Incl. O&P
Crew B-60	Hr.	Daily	Hr.	Daily	Bare Costs	Incl. O&P
1 Labor Foreman (outside)	$24.85	$198.80	$38.90	$311.20	$26.42	$40.52
2 Laborers	22.85	365.60	35.75	572.00		
1 Equip. Oper. (crane)	31.15	249.20	47.15	377.20		
2 Equip. Oper. (light)	28.75	460.00	43.55	696.80		
1 Equip. Oper. Oiler	25.75	206.00	39.00	312.00		
1 Crawler Crane, 40 Ton		716.00		787.60		
45 L.F. Leads, 15K Ft. Lbs.		234.00		257.40		
1 Backhoe Loader, 48 H.P.		181.00		199.10	20.20	22.22
56 L.H., Daily Totals		$2610.60		$3513.30	$46.62	$62.74

Crew No.	Hr.	Daily	Hr.	Daily	Bare Costs	Incl. O&P
Crew B-61	Hr.	Daily	Hr.	Daily	Bare Costs	Incl. O&P
1 Labor Foreman (outside)	$24.85	$198.80	$38.90	$311.20	$24.43	$37.94
3 Laborers	22.85	548.40	35.75	858.00		
1 Equip. Oper. (light)	28.75	230.00	43.55	348.40		
1 Cement Mixer, 2 C.Y.		222.00		244.20		
1 Air Compr., 160 C.F.M.		98.40		108.25	8.01	8.81
40 L.H., Daily Totals		$1297.60		$1870.05	$32.44	$46.75

Crew No.	Hr.	Daily	Hr.	Daily	Bare Costs	Incl. O&P
Crew B-62	Hr.	Daily	Hr.	Daily	Bare Costs	Incl. O&P
2 Laborers	$22.85	$365.60	$35.75	$572.00	$24.82	$38.35
1 Equip. Oper. (light)	28.75	230.00	43.55	348.40		
1 Loader, Skid Steer		114.00		125.40	4.75	5.23
24 L.H., Daily Totals		$709.60		$1045.80	$29.57	$43.58

Crew No.	Hr.	Daily	Hr.	Daily	Bare Costs	Incl. O&P
Crew B-63	Hr.	Daily	Hr.	Daily	Bare Costs	Incl. O&P
4 Laborers	$22.85	$731.20	$35.75	$1144.00	$24.03	$37.31
1 Equip. Oper. (light)	28.75	230.00	43.55	348.40		
1 Loader, Skid Steer		114.00		125.40	2.85	3.14
40 L.H., Daily Totals		$1075.20		$1617.80	$26.88	$40.45

Crew No.	Hr.	Daily	Hr.	Daily	Bare Costs	Incl. O&P
Crew B-64	Hr.	Daily	Hr.	Daily	Bare Costs	Incl. O&P
1 Laborer	$22.85	$182.80	$35.75	$286.00	$23.13	$35.75
1 Truck Driver (light)	23.40	187.20	35.75	286.00		
1 Power Mulcher (small)		124.80		137.30		
1 Light Truck, 1.5 Ton		158.00		173.80	17.68	19.44
16 L.H., Daily Totals		$652.80		$883.10	$40.81	$55.19

Crew No.	Hr.	Daily	Hr.	Daily	Bare Costs	Incl. O&P
Crew B-65	Hr.	Daily	Hr.	Daily	Bare Costs	Incl. O&P
1 Laborer	$22.85	$182.80	$35.75	$286.00	$23.13	$35.75
1 Truck Driver (light)	23.40	187.20	35.75	286.00		
1 Power Mulcher (large)		232.80		256.10		
1 Light Truck, 1.5 Ton		158.00		173.80	24.43	26.87
16 L.H., Daily Totals		$760.80		$1001.90	$47.56	$62.62

Crew No.	Hr.	Daily	Hr.	Daily	Bare Costs	Incl. O&P
Crew B-66	Hr.	Daily	Hr.	Daily	Bare Costs	Incl. O&P
1 Equip. Oper. (light)	$28.75	$230.00	$43.55	$348.40	$28.75	$43.55
1 Backhoe Ldr. w/Attchmt.		168.80		185.70	21.10	23.21
8 L.H., Daily Totals		$398.80		$534.10	$49.85	$66.76

Crew B-67	Hr.	Daily	Hr.	Daily	Bare Costs	Incl. O&P
1 Millwright	$30.55	$244.40	$45.45	$363.60	$29.65	$44.50
1 Equip. Oper. (light)	28.75	230.00	43.55	348.40		
1 Forklift		198.20		218.00	12.39	13.63
16 L.H., Daily Totals		$672.60		$930.00	$42.04	$58.13

Crew B-68	Hr.	Daily	Hr.	Daily	Bare Costs	Incl. O&P
2 Millwrights	$30.55	$488.80	$45.45	$727.20	$29.95	$44.82
1 Equip. Oper. (light)	28.75	230.00	43.55	348.40		
1 Forklift		198.20		218.00	8.26	9.08
24 L.H., Daily Totals		$917.00		$1293.60	$38.21	$53.90

Crew B-69	Hr.	Daily	Hr.	Daily	Bare Costs	Incl. O&P
1 Labor Foreman (outside)	$24.85	$198.80	$38.90	$311.20	$25.05	$38.72
3 Laborers	22.85	548.40	35.75	858.00		
1 Equip Oper. (crane)	31.15	249.20	47.15	377.20		
1 Equip Oper. Oiler	25.75	206.00	39.00	312.00		
1 Truck Crane, 80 Ton		1325.00		1457.50	27.60	30.36
48 L.H., Daily Totals		$2527.40		$3315.90	$52.65	$69.08

Crew B-69A	Hr.	Daily	Hr.	Daily	Bare Costs	Incl. O&P
1 Labor Foreman	$24.85	$198.80	$38.90	$311.20	$25.28	$38.94
3 Laborers	22.85	548.40	35.75	858.00		
1 Equip. Oper. (medium)	30.35	242.80	45.95	367.60		
1 Concrete Finisher	27.95	223.60	41.55	332.40		
1 Curb Paver		444.60		489.05	9.26	10.19
48 L.H., Daily Totals		$1658.20		$2358.25	$34.54	$49.13

Crew B-69B	Hr.	Daily	Hr.	Daily	Bare Costs	Incl. O&P
1 Labor Foreman	$24.85	$198.80	$38.90	$311.20	$25.28	$38.94
3 Laborers	22.85	548.40	35.75	858.00		
1 Equip. Oper. (medium)	30.35	242.80	45.95	367.60		
1 Cement Finisher	27.95	223.60	41.55	332.40		
1 Curb/Gutter Paver		897.60		987.35	18.70	20.57
48 L.H., Daily Totals		$2111.20		$2856.55	$43.98	$59.51

Crew B-70	Hr.	Daily	Hr.	Daily	Bare Costs	Incl. O&P
1 Labor Foreman (outside)	$24.85	$198.80	$38.90	$311.20	$26.35	$40.57
3 Laborers	22.85	548.40	35.75	858.00		
3 Equip. Oper. (med.)	30.35	728.40	45.95	1102.80		
1 Motor Grader, 30,000 Lb.		459.40		505.35		
1 Grader Attach., Ripper		67.20		73.90		
1 Road Sweeper, S.P.		258.00		283.80		
1 F.E. Loader, 1-3/4 C.Y.		284.40		312.85	19.09	21.00
56 L.H., Daily Totals		$2544.60		$3447.90	$45.44	$61.57

Crew B-71	Hr.	Daily	Hr.	Daily	Bare Costs	Incl. O&P
1 Labor Foreman (outside)	$24.85	$198.80	$38.90	$311.20	$26.35	$40.57
3 Laborers	22.85	548.40	35.75	858.00		
3 Equip. Oper. (med.)	30.35	728.40	45.95	1102.80		
1 Pvmt. Profiler, 450 H.P.		3506.00		3856.60		
1 Road Sweeper, S.P.		258.00		283.80		
1 F.E. Loader, 1-3/4 C.Y.		284.40		312.85	72.29	79.52
56 L.H., Daily Totals		$5524.00		$6725.25	$98.64	$120.09

Crew B-72	Hr.	Daily	Hr.	Daily	Bare Costs	Incl. O&P
1 Labor Foreman (outside)	$24.85	$198.80	$38.90	$311.20	$26.85	$41.24
3 Laborers	22.85	548.40	35.75	858.00		
4 Equip. Oper. (med.)	30.35	971.20	45.95	1470.40		
1 Pvmt. Profiler, 450 H.P.		3506.00		3856.60		
1 Hammermill, 250 H.P.		1234.00		1357.40		
1 Windrow Loader		884.00		972.40		
1 Mix Paver 165 H.P.		1428.00		1570.80		
1 Roller, Pneu. Tire, 12 T.		215.60		237.15	113.56	124.91
64 L.H., Daily Totals		$8986.00		$10633.95	$140.41	$166.15

Crew B-73	Hr.	Daily	Hr.	Daily	Bare Costs	Incl. O&P
1 Labor Foreman (outside)	$24.85	$198.80	$38.90	$311.20	$27.79	$42.52
2 Laborers	22.85	365.60	35.75	572.00		
5 Equip. Oper. (med.)	30.35	1214.00	45.95	1838.00		
1 Road Mixer, 310 H.P.		1112.00		1223.20		
1 Roller, Tandem, 12 Ton		210.40		231.45		
1 Hammermill, 250 H.P.		1234.00		1357.40		
1 Motor Grader, 30,000 Lb.		459.40		505.35		
.5 F.E. Loader, 1-3/4 C.Y.		142.20		156.40		
.5 Truck, 30 Ton		160.20		176.20		
.5 Water Tank 5000 Gal.		92.00		101.20	53.28	58.61
64 L.H., Daily Totals		$5188.60		$6472.40	$81.07	$101.13

Crew B-74	Hr.	Daily	Hr.	Daily	Bare Costs	Incl. O&P
1 Labor Foreman (outside)	$24.85	$198.80	$38.90	$311.20	$27.13	$41.46
1 Laborer	22.85	182.80	35.75	286.00		
4 Equip. Oper. (med.)	30.35	971.20	45.95	1470.40		
2 Truck Drivers (heavy)	23.95	383.20	36.60	585.60		
1 Motor Grader, 30,000 Lb.		459.40		505.35		
1 Grader Attach., Ripper		67.20		73.90		
2 Stabilizers, 310 H.P.		1601.60		1761.75		
1 Flatbed Truck, 3 Ton		184.20		202.60		
1 Chem. Spreader, Towed		92.40		101.65		
1 Vibr. Roller, 29,000 Lb.		451.20		496.30		
1 Water Tank 5000 Gal.		184.00		202.40		
1 Truck, 30 Ton		320.40		352.45	52.51	57.76
64 L.H., Daily Totals		$5096.40		$6349.60	$79.64	$99.22

Crew B-75	Hr.	Daily	Hr.	Daily	Bare Costs	Incl. O&P
1 Labor Foreman (outside)	$24.85	$198.80	$38.90	$311.20	$27.58	$42.15
1 Laborer	22.85	182.80	35.75	286.00		
4 Equip. Oper. (med.)	30.35	971.20	45.95	1470.40		
1 Truck Driver (heavy)	23.95	191.60	36.60	292.80		
1 Motor Grader, 30,000 Lb.		459.40		505.35		
1 Grader Attach., Ripper		67.20		73.90		
2 Stabilizers, 310 H.P.		1601.60		1761.75		
1 Dist. Truck, 3000 Gal.		328.80		361.70		
1 Vibr. Roller, 29,000 Lb.		451.20		496.30	51.93	57.13
56 L.H., Daily Totals		$4452.60		$5559.40	$79.51	$99.28

Crew B-76	Hr.	Daily	Hr.	Daily	Bare Costs	Incl. O&P
1 Dock Builder Foreman	$30.80	$246.40	$52.40	$419.20	$29.21	$47.86
5 Dock Builders	28.80	1152.00	49.00	1960.00		
2 Equip. Oper. (crane)	31.15	498.40	47.15	754.40		
1 Equip. Oper. Oiler	25.75	206.00	39.00	312.00		
1 Crawler Crane, 50 Ton		885.80		974.40		
1 Barge, 400 Ton		428.40		471.25		
1 Hammer, 15K Ft. Lbs.		313.40		344.75		
60 L.F. Leads, 15K Ft. Lbs.		312.00		343.20		
1 Air Compr., 600 C.F.M.		251.00		276.10		
2-50 Ft. Air Hoses, 3" Dia.		34.60		38.05	30.91	34.00
72 L.H., Daily Totals		$4328.00		$5893.35	$60.12	$81.86

Crews

Crew No.	Bare Costs		Incl. Subs O & P		Cost Per Labor-Hour	

Crew B-77

	Hr.	Daily	Hr.	Daily	Bare Costs	Incl. O&P
1 Labor Foreman	$24.85	$198.80	$38.90	$311.20	$23.36	$36.38
3 Laborers	22.85	548.40	35.75	858.00		
1 Truck Driver (light)	23.40	187.20	35.75	286.00		
1 Crack Cleaner, 25 H.P.		71.20		78.30		
1 Crack Filler, Trailer Mtd.		142.40		156.65		
1 Flatbed Truck, 3 Ton		184.20		202.60	9.95	10.94
40 L.H., Daily Totals		$1332.20		$1892.75	$33.31	$47.32

Crew B-78

	Hr.	Daily	Hr.	Daily	Bare Costs	Incl. O&P
1 Labor Foreman	$24.85	$198.80	$38.90	$311.20	$23.28	$36.28
4 Laborers	22.85	731.20	35.75	1144.00		
1 Truck Driver (light)	23.40	187.20	35.75	286.00		
1 Paint Striper, S.P.		201.80		222.00		
1 Flatbed Truck, 3 Ton		184.20		202.60		
1 Pickup Truck, 3/4 Ton		83.00		91.30	9.77	10.75
48 L.H., Daily Totals		$1586.20		$2257.10	$33.05	$47.03

Crew B-79

	Hr.	Daily	Hr.	Daily	Bare Costs	Incl. O&P
1 Labor Foreman	$24.85	$198.80	$38.90	$311.20	$23.36	$36.38
3 Laborers	22.85	548.40	35.75	858.00		
1 Truck Driver (light)	23.40	187.20	35.75	286.00		
1 Thermo. Striper, T.M.		390.00		429.00		
1 Flatbed Truck, 3 Ton		184.20		202.60		
2 Pickup Truck, 3/4 Ton		166.00		182.60	18.51	20.36
40 L.H., Daily Totals		$1674.60		$2269.40	$41.87	$56.74

Crew B-80

	Hr.	Daily	Hr.	Daily	Bare Costs	Incl. O&P
1 Labor Foreman	$24.85	$198.80	$38.90	$311.20	$24.96	$38.49
1 Laborer	22.85	182.80	35.75	286.00		
1 Truck Driver (light)	23.40	187.20	35.75	286.00		
1 Equip. Oper. (light)	28.75	230.00	43.55	348.40		
1 Flatbed Truck, 3 Ton		184.20		202.60		
1 Fence Post Auger, T.M.		363.00		399.30	17.10	18.81
32 L.H., Daily Totals		$1346.00		$1833.50	$42.06	$57.30

Crew B-80A

	Hr.	Daily	Hr.	Daily	Bare Costs	Incl. O&P
3 Laborers	$22.85	$548.40	$35.75	$858.00	$22.85	$35.75
1 Flatbed Truck, 3 Ton		184.20		202.60	7.68	8.44
24 L.H., Daily Totals		$732.60		$1060.60	$30.53	$44.19

Crew B-80B

	Hr.	Daily	Hr.	Daily	Bare Costs	Incl. O&P
3 Laborers	$22.85	$548.40	$35.75	$858.00	$24.33	$37.70
1 Equip. Oper. (light)	28.75	230.00	43.55	348.40		
1 Crane, Flatbed Mnt.		222.40		244.65	6.95	7.65
32 L.H., Daily Totals		$1000.80		$1451.05	$31.28	$45.35

Crew B-81

	Hr.	Daily	Hr.	Daily	Bare Costs	Incl. O&P
1 Laborer	$22.85	$182.80	$35.75	$286.00	$25.72	$39.43
1 Equip. Oper. (med.)	30.35	242.80	45.95	367.60		
1 Truck Driver (heavy)	23.95	191.60	36.60	292.80		
1 Hydromulcher, T.M.		263.20		289.50		
1 Tractor Truck, 4x2		320.40		352.45	24.32	26.75
24 L.H., Daily Totals		$1200.80		$1588.35	$50.04	$66.18

Crew B-82

	Hr.	Daily	Hr.	Daily	Bare Costs	Incl. O&P
1 Laborer	$22.85	$182.80	$35.75	$286.00	$25.80	$39.65
1 Equip. Oper. (light)	28.75	230.00	43.55	348.40		
1 Horiz. Borer, 6 H.P.		46.40		51.05	2.90	3.19
16 L.H., Daily Totals		$459.20		$685.45	$28.70	$42.84

Crew B-83

	Hr.	Daily	Hr.	Daily	Bare Costs	Incl. O&P
1 Tugboat Captain	$30.35	$242.80	$45.95	$367.60	$26.60	$40.85
1 Tugboat Hand	22.85	182.80	35.75	286.00		
1 Tugboat, 250 H.P.		466.00		512.60	29.13	32.04
16 L.H., Daily Totals		$891.60		$1166.20	$55.73	$72.89

Crew B-84

	Hr.	Daily	Hr.	Daily	Bare Costs	Incl. O&P
1 Equip. Oper. (med.)	$30.35	$242.80	$45.95	$367.60	$30.35	$45.95
1 Rotary Mower/Tractor		179.20		197.10	22.40	24.64
8 L.H., Daily Totals		$422.00		$564.70	$52.75	$70.59

Crew B-85

	Hr.	Daily	Hr.	Daily	Bare Costs	Incl. O&P
3 Laborers	$22.85	$548.40	$35.75	$858.00	$24.57	$37.96
1 Equip. Oper. (med.)	30.35	242.80	45.95	367.60		
1 Truck Driver (heavy)	23.95	191.60	36.60	292.80		
1 Aerial Lift Truck, 80'		530.80		583.90		
1 Brush Chipper, 130 H.P.		190.60		209.65		
1 Pruning Saw, Rotary		22.00		24.20	18.59	20.44
40 L.H., Daily Totals		$1726.20		$2336.15	$43.16	$58.40

Crew B-86

	Hr.	Daily	Hr.	Daily	Bare Costs	Incl. O&P
1 Equip. Oper. (med.)	$30.35	$242.80	$45.95	$367.60	$30.35	$45.95
1 Stump Chipper, S.P.		166.65		183.30	20.83	22.91
8 L.H., Daily Totals		$409.45		$550.90	$51.18	$68.86

Crew B-86A

	Hr.	Daily	Hr.	Daily	Bare Costs	Incl. O&P
1 Equip. Oper. (medium)	$30.35	$242.80	$45.95	$367.60	$30.35	$45.95
1 Grader, 30,000 Lbs.		459.40		505.35	57.43	63.17
8 L.H., Daily Totals		$702.20		$872.95	$87.78	$109.12

Crew B-86B

	Hr.	Daily	Hr.	Daily	Bare Costs	Incl. O&P
1 Equip. Oper. (medium)	$30.35	$242.80	$45.95	$367.60	$30.35	$45.95
1 Dozer, 200 H.P.		735.00		808.50	91.88	101.06
8 L.H., Daily Totals		$977.80		$1176.10	$122.23	$147.01

Crew B-87

	Hr.	Daily	Hr.	Daily	Bare Costs	Incl. O&P
1 Laborer	$22.85	$182.80	$35.75	$286.00	$28.85	$43.91
4 Equip. Oper. (med.)	30.35	971.20	45.95	1470.40		
2 Feller Bunchers, 50 H.P.		746.00		820.60		
1 Log Chipper, 22" Tree		1789.00		1967.90		
1 Dozer, 105 H.P.		266.00		292.60		
1 Chainsaw, Gas, 36" Long		43.20		47.50	71.11	78.22
40 L.H., Daily Totals		$3998.20		$4885.00	$99.96	$122.13

Crew B-88

	Hr.	Daily	Hr.	Daily	Bare Costs	Incl. O&P
1 Laborer	$22.85	$182.80	$35.75	$286.00	$29.28	$44.49
6 Equip. Oper. (med.)	30.35	1456.80	45.95	2205.60		
2 Feller Bunchers, 50 H.P.		746.00		820.60		
1 Log Chipper, 22" Tree		1789.00		1967.90		
2 Log Skidders, 50 H.P.		1026.80		1129.50		
1 Dozer, 105 H.P.		266.00		292.60		
1 Chainsaw, Gas, 36" Long		43.20		47.50	69.13	76.04
56 L.H., Daily Totals		$5510.60		$6749.70	$98.41	$120.53

Crew B-89

	Hr.	Daily	Hr.	Daily	Bare Costs	Incl. O&P
1 Equip. Oper. (light)	$28.75	$230.00	$43.55	$348.40	$26.08	$39.65
1 Truck Driver (light)	23.40	187.20	35.75	286.00		
1 Truck, Stake Body, 3 Ton		184.20		202.60		
1 Concrete Saw		98.40		108.25		
1 Water Tank, 65 Gal.		13.50		14.85	18.51	20.36
16 L.H., Daily Totals		$713.30		$960.10	$44.59	$60.01

CREWS

Crews

Crew No.	Bare Costs		Incl. Subs O & P		Cost Per Labor-Hour	

Crew B-89A

Crew B-89A	Hr.	Daily	Hr.	Daily	Bare Costs	Incl. O&P
1 Skilled Worker	$29.85	$238.80	$46.85	$374.80	$26.35	$41.30
1 Laborer	22.85	182.80	35.75	286.00		
1 Core Drill (large)		101.45		111.60	6.34	6.97
16 L.H., Daily Totals		$523.05		$772.40	$32.69	$48.27

Crew B-89B

Crew B-89B	Hr.	Daily	Hr.	Daily	Bare Costs	Incl. O&P
1 Equip. Oper. (light)	$28.75	$230.00	$43.55	$348.40	$26.08	$39.65
1 Truck Driver, Light	23.40	187.20	35.75	286.00		
1 Wall Saw, Hydraulic, 10 H.P.		106.05		116.65		
1 Generator, Diesel, 100 KW		211.05		232.15		
1 Water Tank, 65 Gal.		13.50		14.85		
1 Flatbed Truck, 3 Ton		184.20		202.60	32.18	35.39
16 L.H., Daily Totals		$932.00		$1200.65	$58.26	$75.04

Crew B-90

Crew B-90	Hr.	Daily	Hr.	Daily	Bare Costs	Incl. O&P
1 Labor Foreman (outside)	$24.85	$198.80	$38.90	$311.20	$24.85	$38.31
3 Laborers	22.85	548.40	35.75	858.00		
2 Equip. Oper. (light)	28.75	460.00	43.55	696.80		
2 Truck Drivers (heavy)	23.95	383.20	36.60	585.60		
1 Road Mixer, 310 H.P.		1112.00		1223.20		
1 Dist. Truck, 2000 Gal.		314.80		346.30	22.29	24.52
64 L.H., Daily Totals		$3017.20		$4021.10	$47.14	$62.83

Crew B-90A

Crew B-90A	Hr.	Daily	Hr.	Daily	Bare Costs	Incl. O&P
1 Labor Foreman	$24.85	$198.80	$38.90	$311.20	$27.42	$42.03
2 Laborers	22.85	365.60	35.75	572.00		
4 Equip. Oper. (medium)	30.35	971.20	45.95	1470.40		
2 Graders, 30,000 Lbs.		918.80		1010.70		
1 Roller, Steel Wheel		210.40		231.45		
1 Roller, Pneumatic Wheel		215.60		237.15	24.01	26.42
56 L.H., Daily Totals		$2880.40		$3832.90	$51.43	$68.45

Crew B-90B

Crew B-90B	Hr.	Daily	Hr.	Daily	Bare Costs	Incl. O&P
1 Labor Foreman	$24.85	$198.80	$38.90	$311.20	$26.93	$41.38
2 Laborers	22.85	365.60	35.75	572.00		
3 Equip. Oper. (medium)	30.35	728.40	45.95	1102.80		
1 Roller, Steel Wheel		210.40		231.45		
1 Roller, Pneumatic Wheel		215.60		237.15		
1 Road Mixer, 310 H.P.		1112.00		1223.20	32.04	35.25
48 L.H., Daily Totals		$2830.80		$3677.80	$58.97	$76.63

Crew B-91

Crew B-91	Hr.	Daily	Hr.	Daily	Bare Costs	Incl. O&P
1 Labor Foreman (outside)	$24.85	$198.80	$38.90	$311.20	$26.99	$41.35
2 Laborers	22.85	365.60	35.75	572.00		
4 Equip. Oper. (med.)	30.35	971.20	45.95	1470.40		
1 Truck Driver (heavy)	23.95	191.60	36.60	292.80		
1 Dist. Truck, 3000 Gal.		328.80		361.70		
1 Aggreg. Spreader, S.P.		628.60		691.45		
1 Roller, Pneu. Tire, 12 Ton		215.60		237.15		
1 Roller, Steel, 10 Ton		210.40		231.45	21.62	23.78
64 L.H., Daily Totals		$3110.60		$4168.15	$48.61	$65.13

Crew B-92

Crew B-92	Hr.	Daily	Hr.	Daily	Bare Costs	Incl. O&P
1 Labor Foreman (outside)	$24.85	$198.80	$38.90	$311.20	$23.35	$36.54
3 Laborers	22.85	548.40	35.75	858.00		
1 Crack Cleaner, 25 H.P.		71.20		78.30		
1 Air Compressor		78.30		86.15		
1 Tar Kettle, T.M.		37.50		41.25		
1 Flatbed Truck, 3 Ton		184.20		202.60	11.60	12.76
32 L.H., Daily Totals		$1118.40		$1577.50	$34.95	$49.30

Crew B-93

Crew B-93	Hr.	Daily	Hr.	Daily	Bare Costs	Incl. O&P
1 Equip. Oper. (med.)	$30.35	$242.80	$45.95	$367.60	$30.35	$45.95
1 Feller Buncher, 50 H.P.		373.00		410.30	46.63	51.29
8 L.H., Daily Totals		$615.80		$777.90	$76.98	$97.24

Crew B-94A

Crew B-94A	Hr.	Daily	Hr.	Daily	Bare Costs	Incl. O&P
1 Laborer	$22.85	$182.80	$35.75	$286.00	$22.85	$35.75
1 Diaph. Water Pump, 2"		30.80		33.90		
1-20 Ft. Suction Hose, 2"		6.50		7.15		
2-50 Ft. Disch. Hoses, 2"		10.80		11.90	6.01	6.61
8 L.H., Daily Totals		$230.90		$338.95	$28.86	$42.36

Crew B-94B

Crew B-94B	Hr.	Daily	Hr.	Daily	Bare Costs	Incl. O&P
1 Laborer	$22.85	$182.80	$35.75	$286.00	$22.85	$35.75
1 Diaph. Water Pump, 4"		62.00		68.20		
1-20 Ft. Suction Hose, 4"		12.50		13.75		
2-50 Ft. Disch. Hoses, 4"		17.00		18.70	11.44	12.58
8 L.H., Daily Totals		$274.30		$386.65	$34.29	$48.33

Crew B-94C

Crew B-94C	Hr.	Daily	Hr.	Daily	Bare Costs	Incl. O&P
1 Laborer	$22.85	$182.80	$35.75	$286.00	$22.85	$35.75
1 Centr. Water Pump, 3"		39.20		43.10		
1-20 Ft. Suction Hose, 3"		9.50		10.45		
2-50 Ft. Disch. Hoses, 3"		12.80		14.10	7.69	8.46
8 L.H., Daily Totals		$244.30		$353.65	$30.54	$44.21

Crew B-94D

Crew B-94D	Hr.	Daily	Hr.	Daily	Bare Costs	Incl. O&P
1 Laborer	$22.85	$182.80	$35.75	$286.00	$22.85	$35.75
1 Centr. Water Pump, 6"		164.40		180.85		
1-20 Ft. Suction Hose, 6"		22.50		24.75		
2-50 Ft. Disch. Hoses, 6"		41.10		45.20	28.50	31.35
8 L.H., Daily Totals		$410.80		$536.80	$51.35	$67.10

Crew B-95

Crew B-95	Hr.	Daily	Hr.	Daily	Bare Costs	Incl. O&P
1 Equip. Oper. (crane)	$31.15	$249.20	$47.15	$377.20	$27.00	$41.45
1 Laborer	22.85	182.80	35.75	286.00		
16 L.H., Daily Totals		$432.00		$663.20	$27.00	$41.45

Crew B-95A

Crew B-95A	Hr.	Daily	Hr.	Daily	Bare Costs	Incl. O&P
1 Equip. Oper. (crane)	$31.15	$249.20	$47.15	$377.20	$27.00	$41.45
1 Laborer	22.85	182.80	35.75	286.00		
1 Hyd. Excavator, 5/8 C.Y.		360.00		396.00	22.50	24.75
16 L.H., Daily Totals		$792.00		$1059.20	$49.50	$66.20

Crew B-95B

Crew B-95B	Hr.	Daily	Hr.	Daily	Bare Costs	Incl. O&P
1 Equip. Oper. (crane)	$31.15	$249.20	$47.15	$377.20	$27.00	$41.45
1 Laborer	22.85	182.80	35.75	286.00		
1 Hyd. Excavator, 1.5 C.Y.		593.20		652.50	37.08	40.78
16 L.H., Daily Totals		$1025.20		$1315.70	$64.08	$82.23

Crew B-95C

Crew B-95C	Hr.	Daily	Hr.	Daily	Bare Costs	Incl. O&P
1 Equip. Oper. (crane)	$31.15	$249.20	$47.15	$377.20	$27.00	$41.45
1 Laborer	22.85	182.80	35.75	286.00		
1 Hyd. Excavator, 2.5 C.Y.		1557.00		1712.70	97.31	107.04
16 L.H., Daily Totals		$1989.00		$2375.90	$124.31	$148.49

Crew C-1

Crew C-1	Hr.	Daily	Hr.	Daily	Bare Costs	Incl. O&P
3 Carpenters	$29.15	$699.60	$45.60	$1094.40	$27.57	$43.14
1 Laborer	22.85	182.80	35.75	286.00		
32 L.H., Daily Totals		$882.40		$1380.40	$27.57	$43.14

CREWS

Crew C-2

Crew No.	Bare Costs Hr.	Daily	Incl. Subs O & P Hr.	Daily	Cost Per Labor-Hour Bare Costs	Incl. O&P
1 Carpenter Foreman (out)	$31.15	$249.20	$48.75	$390.00	$28.43	$44.48
4 Carpenters	29.15	932.80	45.60	1459.20		
1 Laborer	22.85	182.80	35.75	286.00		
48 L.H., Daily Totals		$1364.80		$2135.20	$28.43	$44.48

Crew C-2A

Crew No.	Bare Costs Hr.	Daily	Incl. Subs O & P Hr.	Daily	Cost Per Labor-Hour Bare Costs	Incl. O&P
1 Carpenter Foreman (out)	$31.15	$249.20	$48.75	$390.00	$28.23	$43.81
3 Carpenters	29.15	699.60	45.60	1094.40		
1 Cement Finisher	27.95	223.60	41.55	332.40		
1 Laborer	22.85	182.80	35.75	286.00		
48 L.H., Daily Totals		$1355.20		$2102.80	$28.23	$43.81

Crew C-3

Crew No.	Bare Costs Hr.	Daily	Incl. Subs O & P Hr.	Daily	Cost Per Labor-Hour Bare Costs	Incl. O&P
1 Rodman Foreman	$34.75	$278.00	$58.95	$471.60	$30.02	$49.55
4 Rodmen (reinf.)	32.75	1048.00	55.60	1779.20		
1 Equip. Oper. (light)	28.75	230.00	43.55	348.40		
2 Laborers	22.85	365.60	35.75	572.00		
3 Stressing Equipment		78.00		85.80		
.5 Grouting Equipment		116.60		128.25	3.04	3.34
64 L.H., Daily Totals		$2116.20		$3385.25	$33.06	$52.89

Crew C-4

Crew No.	Bare Costs Hr.	Daily	Incl. Subs O & P Hr.	Daily	Cost Per Labor-Hour Bare Costs	Incl. O&P
1 Rodman Foreman	$34.75	$278.00	$58.95	$471.60	$33.25	$56.44
3 Rodmen (reinf.)	32.75	786.00	55.60	1334.40		
3 Stressing Equipment		78.00		85.80	2.44	2.68
32 L.H., Daily Totals		$1142.00		$1891.80	$35.69	$59.12

Crew C-5

Crew No.	Bare Costs Hr.	Daily	Incl. Subs O & P Hr.	Daily	Cost Per Labor-Hour Bare Costs	Incl. O&P
1 Rodman Foreman	$34.75	$278.00	$58.95	$471.60	$31.81	$52.50
4 Rodmen (reinf.)	32.75	1048.00	55.60	1779.20		
1 Equip. Oper. (crane)	31.15	249.20	47.15	377.20		
1 Equip. Oper. Oiler	25.75	206.00	39.00	312.00		
1 Hyd. Crane, 25 Ton		629.60		692.55	11.24	12.37
56 L.H., Daily Totals		$2410.80		$3632.55	$43.05	$64.87

Crew C-6

Crew No.	Bare Costs Hr.	Daily	Incl. Subs O & P Hr.	Daily	Cost Per Labor-Hour Bare Costs	Incl. O&P
1 Labor Foreman (outside)	$24.85	$198.80	$38.90	$311.20	$24.03	$37.24
4 Laborers	22.85	731.20	35.75	1144.00		
1 Cement Finisher	27.95	223.60	41.55	332.40		
2 Gas Engine Vibrators		76.00		83.60	1.58	1.74
48 L.H., Daily Totals		$1229.60		$1871.20	$25.61	$38.98

Crew C-7

Crew No.	Bare Costs Hr.	Daily	Incl. Subs O & P Hr.	Daily	Cost Per Labor-Hour Bare Costs	Incl. O&P
1 Labor Foreman (outside)	$24.85	$198.80	$38.90	$311.20	$24.79	$38.24
5 Laborers	22.85	914.00	35.75	1430.00		
1 Cement Finisher	27.95	223.60	41.55	332.40		
1 Equip. Oper. (med.)	30.35	242.80	45.95	367.60		
1 Equip. Oper. (oiler)	25.75	206.00	39.00	312.00		
2 Gas Engine Vibrators		76.00		83.60		
1 Concrete Bucket, 1 C.Y.		27.60		30.35		
1 Hyd. Crane, 55 Ton		901.60		991.75	13.96	15.36
72 L.H., Daily Totals		$2790.40		$3858.90	$38.75	$53.60

Crew C-7A

Crew No.	Bare Costs Hr.	Daily	Incl. Subs O & P Hr.	Daily	Cost Per Labor-Hour Bare Costs	Incl. O&P
1 Labor Foreman (outside)	$24.85	$198.80	$38.90	$311.20	$23.38	$36.36
5 Laborers	22.85	914.00	35.75	1430.00		
2 Truck Driver (Heavy)	23.95	383.20	36.60	585.60		
2 Conc. Transit Mixers		1684.00		1852.40	26.31	28.94
64 L.H., Daily Totals		$3180.00		$4179.20	$49.69	$65.30

Crew C-7B

Crew No.	Bare Costs Hr.	Daily	Incl. Subs O & P Hr.	Daily	Cost Per Labor-Hour Bare Costs	Incl. O&P
1 Labor Foreman (outside)	$24.85	$198.80	$38.90	$311.20	$24.50	$37.98
5 Laborers	22.85	914.00	35.75	1430.00		
1 Equipment Operator (heavy)	31.15	249.20	47.15	377.20		
1 Equipment Oiler	25.75	206.00	39.00	312.00		
1 Conc. Bucket, 2 C.Y.		37.00		40.70		
1 Truck Crane, 165 Ton		1714.00		1885.40	27.36	30.10
64 L.H., Daily Totals		$3319.00		$4356.50	$51.86	$68.08

Crew C-7C

Crew No.	Bare Costs Hr.	Daily	Incl. Subs O & P Hr.	Daily	Cost Per Labor-Hour Bare Costs	Incl. O&P
1 Labor Foreman (outside)	$24.85	$198.80	$38.90	$311.20	$24.98	$38.69
5 Laborers	22.85	914.00	35.75	1430.00		
2 Equipment Operator (medium)	30.35	485.60	45.95	735.20		
2 Wheel Loader, 4 C.Y.		1037.60		1141.35	16.21	17.83
64 L.H., Daily Totals		$2636.00		$3617.75	$41.19	$56.52

Crew C-7D

Crew No.	Bare Costs Hr.	Daily	Incl. Subs O & P Hr.	Daily	Cost Per Labor-Hour Bare Costs	Incl. O&P
1 Labor Foreman (outside)	$24.85	$198.80	$38.90	$311.20	$24.21	$37.66
5 Laborers	22.85	914.00	35.75	1430.00		
1 Equipment Operator (med.)	30.35	242.80	45.95	367.60		
1 Concrete Conveyer		190.00		209.00	3.39	3.73
56 L.H., Daily Totals		$1545.60		$2317.80	$27.60	$41.39

Crew C-8

Crew No.	Bare Costs Hr.	Daily	Incl. Subs O & P Hr.	Daily	Cost Per Labor-Hour Bare Costs	Incl. O&P
1 Labor Foreman (outside)	$24.85	$198.80	$38.90	$311.20	$25.66	$39.31
3 Laborers	22.85	548.40	35.75	858.00		
2 Cement Finishers	27.95	447.20	41.55	664.80		
1 Equip. Oper. (med.)	30.35	242.80	45.95	367.60		
1 Concrete Pump (small)		580.00		638.00	10.36	11.39
56 L.H., Daily Totals		$2017.20		$2839.60	$36.02	$50.70

Crew C-8A

Crew No.	Bare Costs Hr.	Daily	Incl. Subs O & P Hr.	Daily	Cost Per Labor-Hour Bare Costs	Incl. O&P
1 Labor Foreman (outside)	$24.85	$198.80	$38.90	$311.20	$24.88	$38.21
3 Laborers	22.85	548.40	35.75	858.00		
2 Cement Finishers	27.95	447.20	41.55	664.80		
48 L.H., Daily Totals		$1194.40		$1834.00	$24.88	$38.21

Crew C-8B

Crew No.	Bare Costs Hr.	Daily	Incl. Subs O & P Hr.	Daily	Cost Per Labor-Hour Bare Costs	Incl. O&P
1 Labor Foreman (outside)	$24.85	$198.80	$38.90	$311.20	$24.75	$38.42
3 Laborers	22.85	548.40	35.75	858.00		
1 Equipment Operator	30.35	242.80	45.95	367.60		
1 Vibrating Screed		53.90		59.30		
1 Vibratory Roller		451.20		496.30		
1 Dozer, 200 H.P.		735.00		808.50	31.00	34.10
40 L.H., Daily Totals		$2230.10		$2900.90	$55.75	$72.52

Crew C-8C

Crew No.	Bare Costs Hr.	Daily	Incl. Subs O & P Hr.	Daily	Cost Per Labor-Hour Bare Costs	Incl. O&P
1 Labor Foreman (outside)	$24.85	$198.80	$38.90	$311.20	$25.28	$38.94
3 Laborers	22.85	548.40	35.75	858.00		
1 Cement Finisher	27.95	223.60	41.55	332.40		
1 Equipment Operator (med.)	30.35	242.80	45.95	367.60		
1 Shotcrete Rig, 12 CY/hr		341.20		375.30	7.11	7.82
48 L.H., Daily Totals		$1554.80		$2244.50	$32.39	$46.76

Crew C-8D

Crew No.	Bare Costs Hr.	Daily	Incl. Subs O & P Hr.	Daily	Cost Per Labor-Hour Bare Costs	Incl. O&P
1 Labor Foreman (outside)	$24.85	$198.80	$38.90	$311.20	$26.10	$39.94
1 Laborers	22.85	182.80	35.75	286.00		
1 Cement Finisher	27.95	223.60	41.55	332.40		
1 Equipment Operator (light)	28.75	230.00	43.55	348.40		
1 Compressor, 250 CFM		125.20		137.70		
2 Hoses, 1", 50'		7.30		8.05	4.14	4.55
32 L.H., Daily Totals		$967.70		$1423.75	$30.24	$44.49

Crew C-8E

Crew No.	Bare Costs Hr.	Daily	Incl. Subs O & P Hr.	Daily	Cost Per Labor-Hour Bare Costs	Incl. O&P
1 Labor Foreman (outside)	$24.85	$198.80	$38.90	$311.20	$26.10	$39.94
1 Laborers	22.85	182.80	35.75	286.00		
1 Cement Finisher	27.95	223.60	41.55	332.40		
1 Equipment Operator (light)	28.75	230.00	43.55	348.40		
1 Compressor, 250 CFM		125.20		137.70		
2 Hoses, 1", 50'		7.30		8.05		
1 Concrete Pump (small)		580.00		638.00	22.27	24.49
32 L.H., Daily Totals		$1547.70		$2061.75	$48.37	$64.43

Crew C-10

Crew No.	Bare Costs Hr.	Daily	Incl. Subs O & P Hr.	Daily	Cost Per Labor-Hour Bare Costs	Incl. O&P
1 Laborer	$22.85	$182.80	$35.75	$286.00	$26.25	$39.62
2 Cement Finishers	27.95	447.20	41.55	664.80		
24 L.H., Daily Totals		$630.00		$950.80	$26.25	$39.62

Crew C-11

Crew No.	Bare Costs Hr.	Daily	Incl. Subs O & P Hr.	Daily	Cost Per Labor-Hour Bare Costs	Incl. O&P
1 Struc. Steel Foreman	$34.85	$278.80	$63.20	$505.60	$32.09	$56.33
6 Struc. Steel Workers	32.85	1576.80	59.60	2860.80		
1 Equip. Oper. (crane)	31.15	249.20	47.15	377.20		
1 Equip. Oper. Oiler	25.75	206.00	39.00	312.00		
1 Truck Crane, 150 Ton		1478.00		1625.80	20.53	22.58
72 L.H., Daily Totals		$3788.80		$5681.40	$52.62	$78.91

Crew C-12

Crew No.	Bare Costs Hr.	Daily	Incl. Subs O & P Hr.	Daily	Cost Per Labor-Hour Bare Costs	Incl. O&P
1 Carpenter Foreman (out)	$31.15	$249.20	$48.75	$390.00	$28.77	$44.74
3 Carpenters	29.15	699.60	45.60	1094.40		
1 Laborer	22.85	182.80	35.75	286.00		
1 Equip. Oper. (crane)	31.15	249.20	47.15	377.20		
1 Hyd. Crane, 12 Ton		514.80		566.30	10.73	11.80
48 L.H., Daily Totals		$1895.60		$2713.90	$39.50	$56.54

Crew C-13

Crew No.	Bare Costs Hr.	Daily	Incl. Subs O & P Hr.	Daily	Cost Per Labor-Hour Bare Costs	Incl. O&P
1 Struc. Steel Worker	$32.85	$262.80	$59.60	$476.80	$31.62	$54.93
1 Welder	32.85	262.80	59.60	476.80		
1 Carpenter	29.15	233.20	45.60	364.80		
1 Gas Welding Machine		84.00		92.40	3.50	3.85
24 L.H., Daily Totals		$842.80		$1410.80	$35.12	$58.78

Crew C-14

Crew No.	Bare Costs Hr.	Daily	Incl. Subs O & P Hr.	Daily	Cost Per Labor-Hour Bare Costs	Incl. O&P
1 Carpenter Foreman (out)	$31.15	$249.20	$48.75	$390.00	$28.45	$45.08
5 Carpenters	29.15	1166.00	45.60	1824.00		
4 Laborers	22.85	731.20	35.75	1144.00		
4 Rodmen (reinf.)	32.75	1048.00	55.60	1779.20		
2 Cement Finishers	27.95	447.20	41.55	664.80		
1 Equip. Oper. (crane)	31.15	249.20	47.15	377.20		
1 Equip. Oper. Oiler	25.75	206.00	39.00	312.00		
1 Crane, 80 Ton, & Tools		1325.00		1457.50	9.20	10.12
144 L.H., Daily Totals		$5421.80		$7948.70	$37.65	$55.20

Crew C-14A

Crew No.	Bare Costs Hr.	Daily	Incl. Subs O & P Hr.	Daily	Cost Per Labor-Hour Bare Costs	Incl. O&P
1 Carpenter Foreman (out)	$31.15	$249.20	$48.75	$390.00	$29.30	$46.39
16 Carpenters	29.15	3731.20	45.60	5836.80		
4 Rodmen (reinf.)	32.75	1048.00	55.60	1779.20		
2 Laborers	22.85	365.60	35.75	572.00		
1 Cement Finisher	27.95	223.60	41.55	332.40		
1 Equip. Oper. (med.)	30.35	242.80	45.95	367.60		
1 Gas Engine Vibrator		38.00		41.80		
1 Concrete Pump (small)		580.00		638.00	3.09	3.40
200 L.H., Daily Totals		$6478.40		$9957.80	$32.39	$49.79

Crew C-14B

Crew No.	Bare Costs Hr.	Daily	Incl. Subs O & P Hr.	Daily	Cost Per Labor-Hour Bare Costs	Incl. O&P
1 Carpenter Foreman (out)	$31.15	$249.20	$48.75	$390.00	$29.25	$46.20
16 Carpenters	29.15	3731.20	45.60	5836.80		
4 Rodmen (reinf.)	32.75	1048.00	55.60	1779.20		
2 Laborers	22.85	365.60	35.75	572.00		
2 Cement Finishers	27.95	447.20	41.55	664.80		
1 Equip. Oper. (med.)	30.35	242.80	45.95	367.60		
1 Gas Engine Vibrator		38.00		41.80		
1 Concrete Pump (small)		580.00		638.00	2.97	3.27
208 L.H., Daily Totals		$6702.00		$10290.20	$32.22	$49.47

Crew C-14C

Crew No.	Bare Costs Hr.	Daily	Incl. Subs O & P Hr.	Daily	Cost Per Labor-Hour Bare Costs	Incl. O&P
1 Carpenter Foreman (out)	$31.15	$249.20	$48.75	$390.00	$27.92	$44.15
6 Carpenters	29.15	1399.20	45.60	2188.80		
2 Rodmen (reinf.)	32.75	524.00	55.60	889.60		
4 Laborers	22.85	731.20	35.75	1144.00		
1 Cement Finisher	27.95	223.60	41.55	332.40		
1 Gas Engine Vibrator		38.00		41.80	.34	.37
112 L.H., Daily Totals		$3165.20		$4986.60	$28.26	$44.52

Crew C-14D

Crew No.	Bare Costs Hr.	Daily	Incl. Subs O & P Hr.	Daily	Cost Per Labor-Hour Bare Costs	Incl. O&P
1 Carpenter Foreman (out)	$31.15	$249.20	$48.75	$390.00	$29.01	$45.59
18 Carpenters	29.15	4197.60	45.60	6566.40		
2 Rodmen (reinf.)	32.75	524.00	55.60	889.60		
2 Laborers	22.85	365.60	35.75	572.00		
1 Cement Finisher	27.95	223.60	41.55	332.40		
1 Equip. Oper. (med.)	30.35	242.80	45.95	367.60		
1 Gas Engine Vibrator		38.00		41.80		
1 Concrete Pump (small)		580.00		638.00	3.09	3.40
200 L.H., Daily Totals		$6420.80		$9797.80	$32.10	$48.99

Crew C-14E

Crew No.	Bare Costs Hr.	Daily	Incl. Subs O & P Hr.	Daily	Cost Per Labor-Hour Bare Costs	Incl. O&P
1 Carpenter Foreman (out)	$31.15	$249.20	$48.75	$390.00	$28.81	$46.47
2 Carpenters	29.15	466.40	45.60	729.60		
4 Rodmen (reinf.)	32.75	1048.00	55.60	1779.20		
3 Laborers	22.85	548.40	35.75	858.00		
1 Cement Finisher	27.95	223.60	41.55	332.40		
1 Gas Engine Vibrator		38.00		41.80	.43	.48
88 L.H., Daily Totals		$2573.60		$4131.00	$29.24	$46.95

Crew C-14F

Crew No.	Bare Costs Hr.	Daily	Incl. Subs O & P Hr.	Daily	Cost Per Labor-Hour Bare Costs	Incl. O&P
1 Laborer Foreman (out)	$24.85	$198.80	$38.90	$311.20	$26.47	$39.97
2 Laborers	22.85	365.60	35.75	572.00		
6 Cement Finishers	27.95	1341.60	41.55	1994.40		
1 Gas Engine Vibrator		38.00		41.80	.53	.58
72 L.H., Daily Totals		$1944.00		$2919.40	$27.00	$40.55

Crew C-14G

Crew No.	Bare Costs Hr.	Daily	Incl. Subs O & P Hr.	Daily	Cost Per Labor-Hour Bare Costs	Incl. O&P
1 Laborer Foreman (out)	$24.85	$198.80	$38.90	$311.20	$26.05	$39.51
2 Laborers	22.85	365.60	35.75	572.00		
4 Cement Finishers	27.95	894.40	41.55	1329.60		
1 Gas Engine Vibrator		38.00		41.80	.68	.75
56 L.H., Daily Totals		$1496.80		$2254.60	$26.73	$40.26

Crew C-14H

Crew No.	Bare Costs Hr.	Daily	Incl. Subs O & P Hr.	Daily	Cost Per Labor-Hour Bare Costs	Incl. O&P
1 Carpenter Foreman (out)	$31.15	$249.20	$48.75	$390.00	$28.83	$45.48
2 Carpenters	29.15	466.40	45.60	729.60		
1 Rodman (reinf.)	32.75	262.00	55.60	444.80		
1 Laborer	22.85	182.80	35.75	286.00		
1 Cement Finisher	27.95	223.60	41.55	332.40		
1 Gas Engine Vibrator		38.00		41.80	.79	.87
48 L.H., Daily Totals		$1422.00		$2224.60	$29.62	$46.35

Crew No.	Bare Costs		Incl. Subs O & P		Cost Per Labor-Hour	
Crew C-15	Hr.	Daily	Hr.	Daily	Bare Costs	Incl. O&P
1 Carpenter Foreman (out)	$31.15	$249.20	$48.75	$390.00	$27.41	$42.88
2 Carpenters	29.15	466.40	45.60	729.60		
3 Laborers	22.85	548.40	35.75	858.00		
2 Cement Finishers	27.95	447.20	41.55	664.80		
1 Rodman (reinf.)	32.75	262.00	55.60	444.80		
72 L.H., Daily Totals		$1973.20		$3087.20	$27.41	$42.88
Crew C-16	Hr.	Daily	Hr.	Daily	Bare Costs	Incl. O&P
1 Labor Foreman (outside)	$24.85	$198.80	$38.90	$311.20	$27.24	$42.93
3 Laborers	22.85	548.40	35.75	858.00		
2 Cement Finishers	27.95	447.20	41.55	664.80		
1 Equip. Oper. (med.)	30.35	242.80	45.95	367.60		
2 Rodmen (reinf.)	32.75	524.00	55.60	889.60		
1 Concrete Pump (small)		580.00		638.00	8.06	8.86
72 L.H., Daily Totals		$2541.20		$3729.20	$35.30	$51.79
Crew C-17	Hr.	Daily	Hr.	Daily	Bare Costs	Incl. O&P
2 Skilled Worker Foremen	$31.85	$509.60	$50.00	$800.00	$30.25	$47.48
8 Skilled Workers	29.85	1910.40	46.85	2998.40		
80 L.H., Daily Totals		$2420.00		$3798.40	$30.25	$47.48
Crew C-17A	Hr.	Daily	Hr.	Daily	Bare Costs	Incl. O&P
2 Skilled Worker Foremen	$31.85	$509.60	$50.00	$800.00	$30.26	$47.48
8 Skilled Workers	29.85	1910.40	46.85	2998.40		
.125 Equip. Oper. (crane)	31.15	31.15	47.15	47.15		
.125 Crane, 80 Ton, & Tools		165.63		182.20	2.04	2.25
81 L.H., Daily Totals		$2616.78		$4027.75	$32.30	$49.73
Crew C-17B	Hr.	Daily	Hr.	Daily	Bare Costs	Incl. O&P
2 Skilled Worker Foremen	$31.85	$509.60	$50.00	$800.00	$30.27	$47.47
8 Skilled Workers	29.85	1910.40	46.85	2998.40		
.25 Equip. Oper. (crane)	31.15	62.30	47.15	94.30		
.25 Crane, 80 Ton, & Tools		331.25		364.40		
.25 Walk Behind Power Tools		13.25		14.60	4.20	4.62
82 L.H., Daily Totals		$2826.80		$4271.70	$34.47	$52.09
Crew C-17C	Hr.	Daily	Hr.	Daily	Bare Costs	Incl. O&P
2 Skilled Worker Foremen	$31.85	$509.60	$50.00	$800.00	$30.28	$47.47
8 Skilled Workers	29.85	1910.40	46.85	2998.40		
.375 Equip. Oper. (crane)	31.15	93.45	47.15	141.45		
.375 Crane, 80 Ton & Tools		496.88		546.55	5.99	6.59
83 L.H., Daily Totals		$3010.33		$4486.40	$36.27	$54.06
Crew C-17D	Hr.	Daily	Hr.	Daily	Bare Costs	Incl. O&P
2 Skilled Worker Foremen	$31.85	$509.60	$50.00	$800.00	$30.29	$47.46
8 Skilled Workers	29.85	1910.40	46.85	2998.40		
.5 Equip. Oper. (crane)	31.15	124.60	47.15	188.60		
.5 Crane, 80 Ton & Tools		662.50		728.75	7.89	8.68
84 L.H., Daily Totals		$3207.10		$4715.75	$38.18	$56.14
Crew C-17E	Hr.	Daily	Hr.	Daily	Bare Costs	Incl. O&P
2 Skilled Worker Foremen	$31.85	$509.60	$50.00	$800.00	$30.25	$47.48
8 Skilled Workers	29.85	1910.40	46.85	2998.40		
1 Hyd. Jack with Rods		73.25		80.60	.92	1.01
80 L.H., Daily Totals		$2493.25		$3879.00	$31.17	$48.49

Crew No.	Bare Costs		Incl. Subs O & P		Cost Per Labor-Hour	
Crew C-18	Hr.	Daily	Hr.	Daily	Bare Costs	Incl. O&P
.125 Labor Foreman (out)	$24.85	$24.85	$38.90	$38.90	$23.07	$36.10
1 Laborer	22.85	182.80	35.75	286.00		
1 Concrete Cart, 10 C.F.		50.60		55.65	5.62	6.18
9 L.H., Daily Totals		$258.25		$380.55	$28.69	$42.28
Crew C-19	Hr.	Daily	Hr.	Daily	Bare Costs	Incl. O&P
.125 Labor Foreman (out)	$24.85	$24.85	$38.90	$38.90	$23.07	$36.10
1 Laborer	22.85	182.80	35.75	286.00		
1 Concrete Cart, 18 C.F.		76.00		83.60	8.44	9.29
9 L.H., Daily Totals		$283.65		$408.50	$31.51	$45.39
Crew C-20	Hr.	Daily	Hr.	Daily	Bare Costs	Incl. O&P
1 Labor Foreman (outside)	$24.85	$198.80	$38.90	$311.20	$24.68	$38.14
5 Laborers	22.85	914.00	35.75	1430.00		
1 Cement Finisher	27.95	223.60	41.55	332.40		
1 Equip. Oper. (med.)	30.35	242.80	45.95	367.60		
2 Gas Engine Vibrators		76.00		83.60		
1 Concrete Pump (small)		580.00		638.00	10.25	11.28
64 L.H., Daily Totals		$2235.20		$3162.80	$34.93	$49.42
Crew C-21	Hr.	Daily	Hr.	Daily	Bare Costs	Incl. O&P
1 Labor Foreman (outside)	$24.85	$198.80	$38.90	$311.20	$24.68	$38.14
5 Laborers	22.85	914.00	35.75	1430.00		
1 Cement Finisher	27.95	223.60	41.55	332.40		
1 Equip. Oper. (med.)	30.35	242.80	45.95	367.60		
2 Gas Engine Vibrators		76.00		83.60		
1 Concrete Conveyer		190.00		209.00	4.16	4.57
64 L.H., Daily Totals		$1845.20		$2733.80	$28.84	$42.71
Crew C-22	Hr.	Daily	Hr.	Daily	Bare Costs	Incl. O&P
1 Rodman Foreman	$34.75	$278.00	$58.95	$471.60	$32.93	$55.64
4 Rodmen (reinf.)	32.75	1048.00	55.60	1779.20		
.125 Equip. Oper. (crane)	31.15	31.15	47.15	47.15		
.125 Equip. Oper. Oiler	25.75	25.75	39.00	39.00		
.125 Hyd. Crane, 25 Ton		78.70		86.55	1.87	2.06
42 L.H., Daily Totals		$1461.60		$2423.50	$34.80	$57.70
Crew C-23	Hr.	Daily	Hr.	Daily	Bare Costs	Incl. O&P
2 Skilled Worker Foremen	$31.85	$509.60	$50.00	$800.00	$29.97	$46.72
6 Skilled Workers	29.85	1432.80	46.85	2248.80		
1 Equip. Oper. (crane)	31.15	249.20	47.15	377.20		
1 Equip. Oper. Oiler	25.75	206.00	39.00	312.00		
1 Crane, 90 Ton		1290.00		1419.00	16.13	17.74
80 L.H., Daily Totals		$3687.60		$5157.00	$46.10	$64.46
Crew C-24	Hr.	Daily	Hr.	Daily	Bare Costs	Incl. O&P
2 Skilled Worker Foremen	$31.85	$509.60	$50.00	$800.00	$29.97	$46.72
6 Skilled Workers	29.85	1432.80	46.85	2248.80		
1 Equip. Oper. (crane)	31.15	249.20	47.15	377.20		
1 Equip. Oper. Oiler	25.75	206.00	39.00	312.00		
1 Truck Crane, 150 Ton		1478.00		1625.80	18.48	20.32
80 L.H., Daily Totals		$3875.60		$5363.80	$48.45	$67.04
Crew C-25	Hr.	Daily	Hr.	Daily	Bare Costs	Incl. O&P
2 Rodmen (reinf.)	$32.75	$524.00	$55.60	$889.60	$25.93	$44.20
2 Rodmen Helpers	19.10	305.60	32.80	524.80		
32 L.H., Daily Totals		$829.60		$1414.40	$25.93	$44.20

Crew No.	Bare Costs Hr.	Daily	Incl. Subs O & P Hr.	Daily	Cost Per Labor-Hour Bare Costs	Incl. O&P
Crew D-1	Hr.	Daily	Hr.	Daily	Bare Costs	Incl. O&P
1 Bricklayer	$29.60	$236.80	$45.75	$366.00	$26.28	$40.60
1 Bricklayer Helper	22.95	183.60	35.45	283.60		
16 L.H., Daily Totals		$420.40		$649.60	$26.28	$40.60
Crew D-2	Hr.	Daily	Hr.	Daily	Bare Costs	Incl. O&P
3 Bricklayers	$29.60	$710.40	$45.75	$1098.00	$27.14	$41.99
2 Bricklayer Helpers	22.95	367.20	35.45	567.20		
.5 Carpenter	29.15	116.60	45.60	182.40		
44 L.H., Daily Totals		$1194.20		$1847.60	$27.14	$41.99
Crew D-3	Hr.	Daily	Hr.	Daily	Bare Costs	Incl. O&P
3 Bricklayers	$29.60	$710.40	$45.75	$1098.00	$27.05	$41.82
2 Bricklayer Helpers	22.95	367.20	35.45	567.20		
.25 Carpenter	29.15	58.30	45.60	91.20		
42 L.H., Daily Totals		$1135.90		$1756.40	$27.05	$41.82
Crew D-4	Hr.	Daily	Hr.	Daily	Bare Costs	Incl. O&P
1 Bricklayer	$29.60	$236.80	$45.75	$366.00	$26.06	$40.05
2 Bricklayer Helpers	22.95	367.20	35.45	567.20		
1 Equip. Oper. (light)	28.75	230.00	43.55	348.40		
1 Grout Pump, 50 C.F./hr		83.70		92.05		
1 Hoses & Hopper		33.20		36.50		
1 Accessories		11.00		12.10	4.00	4.40
32 L.H., Daily Totals		$961.90		$1422.25	$30.06	$44.45
Crew D-5	Hr.	Daily	Hr.	Daily	Bare Costs	Incl. O&P
1 Bricklayer	$29.60	$236.80	$45.75	$366.00	$29.60	$45.75
8 L.H., Daily Totals		$236.80		$366.00	$29.60	$45.75
Crew D-6	Hr.	Daily	Hr.	Daily	Bare Costs	Incl. O&P
3 Bricklayers	$29.60	$710.40	$45.75	$1098.00	$26.39	$40.80
3 Bricklayer Helpers	22.95	550.80	35.45	850.80		
.25 Carpenter	29.15	58.30	45.60	91.20		
50 L.H., Daily Totals		$1319.50		$2040.00	$26.39	$40.80
Crew D-7	Hr.	Daily	Hr.	Daily	Bare Costs	Incl. O&P
1 Tile Layer	$28.15	$225.20	$41.60	$332.80	$25.43	$37.58
1 Tile Layer Helper	22.70	181.60	33.55	268.40		
16 L.H., Daily Totals		$406.80		$601.20	$25.43	$37.58
Crew D-8	Hr.	Daily	Hr.	Daily	Bare Costs	Incl. O&P
3 Bricklayers	$29.60	$710.40	$45.75	$1098.00	$26.94	$41.63
2 Bricklayer Helpers	22.95	367.20	35.45	567.20		
40 L.H., Daily Totals		$1077.60		$1665.20	$26.94	$41.63
Crew D-9	Hr.	Daily	Hr.	Daily	Bare Costs	Incl. O&P
3 Bricklayers	$29.60	$710.40	$45.75	$1098.00	$26.28	$40.60
3 Bricklayer Helpers	22.95	550.80	35.45	850.80		
48 L.H., Daily Totals		$1261.20		$1948.80	$26.28	$40.60
Crew D-10	Hr.	Daily	Hr.	Daily	Bare Costs	Incl. O&P
1 Bricklayer Foreman	$31.60	$252.80	$48.80	$390.40	$27.65	$42.52
1 Bricklayer	29.60	236.80	45.75	366.00		
2 Bricklayer Helpers	22.95	367.20	35.45	567.20		
1 Equip. Oper. (crane)	31.15	249.20	47.15	377.20		
1 Truck Crane, 12.5 Ton		425.20		467.70	10.63	11.69
40 L.H., Daily Totals		$1531.20		$2168.50	$38.28	$54.21

Crew No.	Bare Costs Hr.	Daily	Incl. Subs O & P Hr.	Daily	Cost Per Labor-Hour Bare Costs	Incl. O&P
Crew D-11	Hr.	Daily	Hr.	Daily	Bare Costs	Incl. O&P
1 Bricklayer Foreman	$31.60	$252.80	$48.80	$390.40	$28.05	$43.33
1 Bricklayer	29.60	236.80	45.75	366.00		
1 Bricklayer Helper	22.95	183.60	35.45	283.60		
24 L.H., Daily Totals		$673.20		$1040.00	$28.05	$43.33
Crew D-12	Hr.	Daily	Hr.	Daily	Bare Costs	Incl. O&P
1 Bricklayer Foreman	$31.60	$252.80	$48.80	$390.40	$26.78	$41.36
1 Bricklayer	29.60	236.80	45.75	366.00		
2 Bricklayer Helpers	22.95	367.20	35.45	567.20		
32 L.H., Daily Totals		$856.80		$1323.60	$26.78	$41.36
Crew D-13	Hr.	Daily	Hr.	Daily	Bare Costs	Incl. O&P
1 Bricklayer Foreman	$31.60	$252.80	$48.80	$390.40	$27.90	$43.03
1 Bricklayer	29.60	236.80	45.75	366.00		
2 Bricklayer Helpers	22.95	367.20	35.45	567.20		
1 Carpenter	29.15	233.20	45.60	364.80		
1 Equip. Oper. (crane)	31.15	249.20	47.15	377.20		
1 Truck Crane, 12.5 Ton		425.20		467.70	8.86	9.74
48 L.H., Daily Totals		$1764.40		$2533.30	$36.76	$52.77
Crew E-1	Hr.	Daily	Hr.	Daily	Bare Costs	Incl. O&P
1 Welder Foreman	$34.85	$278.80	$63.20	$505.60	$32.15	$55.45
1 Welder	32.85	262.80	59.60	476.80		
1 Equip. Oper. (light)	28.75	230.00	43.55	348.40		
1 Gas Welding Machine		84.00		92.40	3.50	3.85
24 L.H., Daily Totals		$855.60		$1423.20	$35.65	$59.30
Crew E-2	Hr.	Daily	Hr.	Daily	Bare Costs	Incl. O&P
1 Struc. Steel Foreman	$34.85	$278.80	$63.20	$505.60	$31.88	$55.39
4 Struc. Steel Workers	32.85	1051.20	59.60	1907.20		
1 Equip. Oper. (crane)	31.15	249.20	47.15	377.20		
1 Equip. Oper. Oiler	25.75	206.00	39.00	312.00		
1 Crane, 90 Ton		1290.00		1419.00	23.04	25.34
56 L.H., Daily Totals		$3075.20		$4521.00	$54.92	$80.73
Crew E-3	Hr.	Daily	Hr.	Daily	Bare Costs	Incl. O&P
1 Struc. Steel Foreman	$34.85	$278.80	$63.20	$505.60	$33.52	$60.80
1 Struc. Steel Worker	32.85	262.80	59.60	476.80		
1 Welder	32.85	262.80	59.60	476.80		
1 Gas Welding Machine		84.00		92.40	3.50	3.85
24 L.H., Daily Totals		$888.40		$1551.60	$37.02	$64.65
Crew E-4	Hr.	Daily	Hr.	Daily	Bare Costs	Incl. O&P
1 Struc. Steel Foreman	$34.85	$278.80	$63.20	$505.60	$33.35	$60.50
3 Struc. Steel Workers	32.85	788.40	59.60	1430.40		
1 Gas Welding Machine		84.00		92.40	2.63	2.89
32 L.H., Daily Totals		$1151.20		$2028.40	$35.98	$63.39
Crew E-5	Hr.	Daily	Hr.	Daily	Bare Costs	Incl. O&P
2 Struc. Steel Foremen	$34.85	$557.60	$63.20	$1011.20	$32.37	$57.02
5 Struc. Steel Workers	32.85	1314.00	59.60	2384.00		
1 Equip. Oper. (crane)	31.15	249.20	47.15	377.20		
1 Welder	32.85	262.80	59.60	476.80		
1 Equip. Oper. Oiler	25.75	206.00	39.00	312.00		
1 Crane, 90 Ton		1290.00		1419.00		
1 Gas Welding Machine		84.00		92.40	17.18	18.89
80 L.H., Daily Totals		$3963.60		$6072.60	$49.55	$75.91

Crew E-6	Hr.	Daily	Hr.	Daily	Bare Costs	Incl. O&P
3 Struc. Steel Foremen	$34.85	$836.40	$63.20	$1516.80	$32.42	$57.21
9 Struc. Steel Workers	32.85	2365.20	59.60	4291.20		
1 Equip. Oper. (crane)	31.15	249.20	47.15	377.20		
1 Welder	32.85	262.80	59.60	476.80		
1 Equip. Oper. Oiler	25.75	206.00	39.00	312.00		
1 Equip. Oper. (light)	28.75	230.00	43.55	348.40		
1 Crane, 90 Ton		1290.00		1419.00		
1 Gas Welding Machine		84.00		92.40		
1 Air Compr., 160 C.F.M.		98.40		108.25		
2 Impact Wrenches		50.40		55.45	11.90	13.09
128 L.H., Daily Totals		$5672.40		$8997.50	$44.32	$70.30

Crew E-7	Hr.	Daily	Hr.	Daily	Bare Costs	Incl. O&P
1 Struc. Steel Foreman	$34.85	$278.80	$63.20	$505.60	$32.37	$57.02
4 Struc. Steel Workers	32.85	1051.20	59.60	1907.20		
1 Equip. Oper. (crane)	31.15	249.20	47.15	377.20		
1 Equip. Oper. Oiler	25.75	206.00	39.00	312.00		
1 Welder Foreman	34.85	278.80	63.20	505.60		
2 Welders	32.85	525.60	59.60	953.60		
1 Crane, 90 Ton		1290.00		1419.00		
2 Gas Welding Machines		168.00		184.80	18.23	20.05
80 L.H., Daily Totals		$4047.60		$6165.00	$50.60	$77.07

Crew E-8	Hr.	Daily	Hr.	Daily	Bare Costs	Incl. O&P
1 Struc. Steel Foreman	$34.85	$278.80	$63.20	$505.60	$32.17	$56.38
4 Struc. Steel Workers	32.85	1051.20	59.60	1907.20		
1 Welder Foreman	34.85	278.80	63.20	505.60		
4 Welders	32.85	1051.20	59.60	1907.20		
1 Equip. Oper. (crane)	31.15	249.20	47.15	377.20		
1 Equip. Oper. Oiler	25.75	206.00	39.00	312.00		
1 Equip. Oper. (light)	28.75	230.00	43.55	348.40		
1 Crane, 90 Ton		1290.00		1419.00		
4 Gas Welding Machines		336.00		369.60	15.63	17.20
104 L.H., Daily Totals		$4971.20		$7651.80	$47.80	$73.58

Crew E-9	Hr.	Daily	Hr.	Daily	Bare Costs	Incl. O&P
2 Struc. Steel Foremen	$34.85	$557.60	$63.20	$1011.20	$32.42	$57.21
5 Struc. Steel Workers	32.85	1314.00	59.60	2384.00		
1 Welder Foreman	34.85	278.80	63.20	505.60		
5 Welders	32.85	1314.00	59.60	2384.00		
1 Equip. Oper. (crane)	31.15	249.20	47.15	377.20		
1 Equip. Oper. Oiler	25.75	206.00	39.00	312.00		
1 Equip. Oper. (light)	28.75	230.00	43.55	348.40		
1 Crane, 90 Ton		1290.00		1419.00		
5 Gas Welding Machines		420.00		462.00	13.36	14.70
128 L.H., Daily Totals		$5859.60		$9203.40	$45.78	$71.91

Crew E-10	Hr.	Daily	Hr.	Daily	Bare Costs	Incl. O&P
1 Welder Foreman	$34.85	$278.80	$63.20	$505.60	$33.85	$61.40
1 Welder	32.85	262.80	59.60	476.80		
4 Gas Welding Machines		336.00		369.60		
1 Truck, 3 Ton		184.20		202.60	32.51	35.76
16 L.H., Daily Totals		$1061.80		$1554.60	$66.36	$97.16

Crew E-11	Hr.	Daily	Hr.	Daily	Bare Costs	Incl. O&P
2 Painters, Struc. Steel	$27.15	$434.40	$50.90	$814.40	$26.48	$45.28
1 Building Laborer	22.85	182.80	35.75	286.00		
1 Equip. Oper. (light)	28.75	230.00	43.55	348.40		
1 Air Compressor 250 C.F.M.		125.20		137.70		
1 Sand Blaster		33.20		36.50		
1 Sand Blasting Accessories		11.00		12.10	5.29	5.82
32 L.H., Daily Totals		$1016.60		$1635.10	$31.77	$51.10

Crew E-12	Hr.	Daily	Hr.	Daily	Bare Costs	Incl. O&P
1 Welder Foreman	$34.85	$278.80	$63.20	$505.60	$31.80	$53.38
1 Equip. Oper. (light)	28.75	230.00	43.55	348.40		
1 Gas Welding Machine		84.00		92.40	5.25	5.78
16 L.H., Daily Totals		$592.80		$946.40	$37.05	$59.16

Crew E-13	Hr.	Daily	Hr.	Daily	Bare Costs	Incl. O&P
1 Welder Foreman	$34.85	$278.80	$63.20	$505.60	$32.82	$56.65
.5 Equip. Oper. (light)	28.75	115.00	43.55	174.20		
1 Gas Welding Machine		84.00		92.40	7.00	7.70
12 L.H., Daily Totals		$477.80		$772.20	$39.82	$64.35

Crew E-14	Hr.	Daily	Hr.	Daily	Bare Costs	Incl. O&P
1 Welder Foreman	$34.85	$278.80	$63.20	$505.60	$34.85	$63.20
1 Gas Welding Machine		84.00		92.40	10.50	11.55
8 L.H., Daily Totals		$362.80		$598.00	$45.35	$74.75

Crew E-16	Hr.	Daily	Hr.	Daily	Bare Costs	Incl. O&P
1 Welder Foreman	$34.85	$278.80	$63.20	$505.60	$33.85	$61.40
1 Welder	32.85	262.80	59.60	476.80		
1 Gas Welding Machine		84.00		92.40	5.25	5.78
16 L.H., Daily Totals		$625.60		$1074.80	$39.10	$67.18

Crew E-17	Hr.	Daily	Hr.	Daily	Bare Costs	Incl. O&P
1 Structural Steel Foreman	$34.85	$278.80	$63.20	$505.60	$33.85	$61.40
1 Structural Steel Worker	32.85	262.80	59.60	476.80		
1 Power Tool		2.90		3.20	.18	.20
16 L.H., Daily Totals		$544.50		$985.60	$34.03	$61.60

Crew E-18	Hr.	Daily	Hr.	Daily	Bare Costs	Incl. O&P
1 Structural Steel Foreman	$34.85	$278.80	$63.20	$505.60	$32.75	$57.59
3 Structural Steel Workers	32.85	788.40	59.60	1430.40		
1 Equipment Operator (med.)	30.35	242.80	45.95	367.60		
1 Crane, 20 Ton		554.80		610.30	13.87	15.26
40 L.H., Daily Totals		$1864.80		$2913.90	$46.62	$72.85

Crew E-19	Hr.	Daily	Hr.	Daily	Bare Costs	Incl. O&P
1 Structural Steel Worker	$32.85	$262.80	$59.60	$476.80	$32.15	$55.45
1 Structural Steel Foreman	34.85	278.80	63.20	505.60		
1 Equip. Oper. (light)	28.75	230.00	43.55	348.40		
1 Power Tool		2.90		3.20		
1 Crane, 20 Ton		554.80		610.30	23.24	25.56
24 L.H., Daily Totals		$1329.30		$1944.30	$55.39	$81.01

Crew E-20	Hr.	Daily	Hr.	Daily	Bare Costs	Incl. O&P
1 Structural Steel Foreman	$34.85	$278.80	$63.20	$505.60	$32.00	$55.92
5 Structural Steel Workers	32.85	1314.00	59.60	2384.00		
1 Equip. Oper. (crane)	31.15	249.20	47.15	377.20		
1 Oiler	25.75	206.00	39.00	312.00		
1 Power Tool		2.90		3.20		
1 Crane, 40 Ton		751.60		826.75	11.79	12.97
64 L.H., Daily Totals		$2802.50		$4408.75	$43.79	$68.89

Crew E-22	Hr.	Daily	Hr.	Daily	Bare Costs	Incl. O&P
1 Skilled Worker Foreman	$31.85	$254.80	$50.00	$400.00	$30.52	$47.90
2 Skilled Worker	29.85	477.60	46.85	749.60		
24 L.H., Daily Totals		$732.40		$1149.60	$30.52	$47.90

Crew E-24

Crew No.	Hr.	Daily	Hr.	Daily	Bare Costs	Incl. O&P
3 Structural Steel Worker	$32.85	$788.40	$59.60	$1430.40	$32.22	$56.19
1 Equipment Operator (medium)	30.35	242.80	45.95	367.60		
1-25 Ton Crane		629.60		692.55	19.68	21.64
32 L.H., Daily Totals		$1660.80		$2490.55	$51.90	$77.83

Crew F-3

Crew No.	Hr.	Daily	Hr.	Daily	Bare Costs	Incl. O&P
4 Carpenters	$29.15	$932.80	$45.60	$1459.20	$29.55	$45.91
1 Equip. Oper. (crane)	31.15	249.20	47.15	377.20		
1 Hyd. Crane, 12 Ton		514.80		566.30	12.87	14.16
40 L.H., Daily Totals		$1696.80		$2402.70	$42.42	$60.07

Crew F-4

Crew No.	Hr.	Daily	Hr.	Daily	Bare Costs	Incl. O&P
4 Carpenters	$29.15	$932.80	$45.60	$1459.20	$28.92	$44.76
1 Equip. Oper. (crane)	31.15	249.20	47.15	377.20		
1 Equip. Oper. Oiler	25.75	206.00	39.00	312.00		
1 Hyd. Crane, 55 Ton		901.60		991.75	18.78	20.66
48 L.H., Daily Totals		$2289.60		$3140.15	$47.70	$65.42

Crew F-5

Crew No.	Hr.	Daily	Hr.	Daily	Bare Costs	Incl. O&P
1 Carpenter Foreman	$31.15	$249.20	$48.75	$390.00	$29.65	$46.39
3 Carpenters	29.15	699.60	45.60	1094.40		
32 L.H., Daily Totals		$948.80		$1484.40	$29.65	$46.39

Crew F-6

Crew No.	Hr.	Daily	Hr.	Daily	Bare Costs	Incl. O&P
2 Carpenters	$29.15	$466.40	$45.60	$729.60	$27.03	$41.97
2 Building Laborers	22.85	365.60	35.75	572.00		
1 Equip. Oper. (crane)	31.15	249.20	47.15	377.20		
1 Hyd. Crane, 12 Ton		514.80		566.30	12.87	14.16
40 L.H., Daily Totals		$1596.00		$2245.10	$39.90	$56.13

Crew F-7

Crew No.	Hr.	Daily	Hr.	Daily	Bare Costs	Incl. O&P
2 Carpenters	$29.15	$466.40	$45.60	$729.60	$26.00	$40.67
2 Building Laborers	22.85	365.60	35.75	572.00		
32 L.H., Daily Totals		$832.00		$1301.60	$26.00	$40.67

Crew G-1

Crew No.	Hr.	Daily	Hr.	Daily	Bare Costs	Incl. O&P
1 Roofer Foreman	$27.70	$221.60	$47.60	$380.80	$24.10	$41.40
4 Roofers, Composition	25.70	822.40	44.15	1412.80		
2 Roofer Helpers	19.10	305.60	32.80	524.80		
1 Application Equipment		181.60		199.75		
1 Tar Kettle/Pot		60.95		67.05		
1 Crew Truck		90.40		99.45	5.95	6.54
56 L.H., Daily Totals		$1682.55		$2684.65	$30.05	$47.94

Crew G-2

Crew No.	Hr.	Daily	Hr.	Daily	Bare Costs	Incl. O&P
1 Plasterer	$27.30	$218.40	$41.80	$334.40	$24.47	$37.72
1 Plasterer Helper	23.25	186.00	35.60	284.80		
1 Building Laborer	22.85	182.80	35.75	286.00		
1 Grouting Equipment		233.20		256.50	9.72	10.69
24 L.H., Daily Totals		$820.40		$1161.70	$34.19	$48.41

Crew G-3

Crew No.	Hr.	Daily	Hr.	Daily	Bare Costs	Incl. O&P
2 Sheet Metal Workers	$33.55	$536.80	$51.80	$828.80	$28.20	$43.78
2 Building Laborers	22.85	365.60	35.75	572.00		
32 L.H., Daily Totals		$902.40		$1400.80	$28.20	$43.78

Crew G-4

Crew No.	Hr.	Daily	Hr.	Daily	Bare Costs	Incl. O&P
1 Labor Foreman (outside)	$24.85	$198.80	$38.90	$311.20	$23.52	$36.80
2 Building Laborers	22.85	365.60	35.75	572.00		
1 Light Truck, 1.5 Ton		158.00		173.80		
1 Air Compr., 160 C.F.M.		98.40		108.25	10.68	11.75
24 L.H., Daily Totals		$820.80		$1165.25	$34.20	$48.55

Crew G-5

Crew No.	Hr.	Daily	Hr.	Daily	Bare Costs	Incl. O&P
1 Roofer Foreman	$27.70	$221.60	$47.60	$380.80	$23.46	$40.30
2 Roofers, Composition	25.70	411.20	44.15	706.40		
2 Roofer Helpers	19.10	305.60	32.80	524.80		
1 Application Equipment		181.60		199.75	4.54	4.99
40 L.H., Daily Totals		$1120.00		$1811.75	$28.00	$45.29

Crew G-6A

Crew No.	Hr.	Daily	Hr.	Daily	Bare Costs	Incl. O&P
2 Roofers Composition	$25.70	$411.20	$44.15	$706.40	$25.70	$44.15
1 Small Compressor		25.60		28.15		
2 Pneumatic Nailers		40.30		44.35	4.12	4.53
16 L.H., Daily Totals		$477.10		$778.90	$29.82	$48.68

Crew G-7

Crew No.	Hr.	Daily	Hr.	Daily	Bare Costs	Incl. O&P
1 Carpenter	$29.15	$233.20	$45.60	$364.80	$29.15	$45.60
1 Small Compressor		25.60		28.15		
1 Pneumatic Nailer		20.15		22.15	5.72	6.29
8 L.H., Daily Totals		$278.95		$415.10	$34.87	$51.89

Crew H-1

Crew No.	Hr.	Daily	Hr.	Daily	Bare Costs	Incl. O&P
2 Glaziers	$28.55	$456.80	$43.30	$692.80	$30.70	$51.45
2 Struc. Steel Workers	32.85	525.60	59.60	953.60		
32 L.H., Daily Totals		$982.40		$1646.40	$30.70	$51.45

Crew H-2

Crew No.	Hr.	Daily	Hr.	Daily	Bare Costs	Incl. O&P
2 Glaziers	$28.55	$456.80	$43.30	$692.80	$26.65	$40.78
1 Building Laborer	22.85	182.80	35.75	286.00		
24 L.H., Daily Totals		$639.60		$978.80	$26.65	$40.78

Crew H-3

Crew No.	Hr.	Daily	Hr.	Daily	Bare Costs	Incl. O&P
1 Glazier	$28.55	$228.40	$43.30	$346.40	$25.35	$39.00
1 Helper	22.15	177.20	34.70	277.60		
16 L.H., Daily Totals		$405.60		$624.00	$25.35	$39.00

Crew J-1

Crew No.	Hr.	Daily	Hr.	Daily	Bare Costs	Incl. O&P
3 Plasterers	$27.30	$655.20	$41.80	$1003.20	$25.68	$39.32
2 Plasterer Helpers	23.25	372.00	35.60	569.60		
1 Mixing Machine, 6 C.F.		59.00		64.90	1.48	1.62
40 L.H., Daily Totals		$1086.20		$1637.70	$27.16	$40.94

Crew J-2

Crew No.	Hr.	Daily	Hr.	Daily	Bare Costs	Incl. O&P
3 Plasterers	$27.30	$655.20	$41.80	$1003.20	$26.10	$39.78
2 Plasterer Helpers	23.25	372.00	35.60	569.60		
1 Lather	28.20	225.60	42.10	336.80		
1 Mixing Machine, 6 C.F.		59.00		64.90	1.23	1.35
48 L.H., Daily Totals		$1311.80		$1974.50	$27.33	$41.13

Crew J-3

Crew No.	Hr.	Daily	Hr.	Daily	Bare Costs	Incl. O&P
1 Terrazzo Worker	$28.30	$226.40	$41.85	$334.80	$25.70	$38.00
1 Terrazzo Helper	23.10	184.80	34.15	273.20		
1 Terrazzo Grinder, Electric		60.50		66.55		
1 Terrazzo Mixer		80.20		88.20	8.79	9.67
16 L.H., Daily Totals		$551.90		$762.75	$34.49	$47.67

CREWS

Crews

Crew No.	Bare Costs Hr.	Bare Costs Daily	Incl. Subs O & P Hr.	Incl. Subs O & P Daily	Cost Per Labor-Hour Bare Costs	Cost Per Labor-Hour Incl. O&P
Crew J-4	Hr.	Daily	Hr.	Daily	Bare Costs	Incl. O&P
1 Tile Layer	$28.15	$225.20	$41.60	$332.80	$25.43	$37.58
1 Tile Layer Helper	22.70	181.60	33.55	268.40		
16 L.H., Daily Totals		$406.80		$601.20	$25.43	$37.58
Crew K-1	Hr.	Daily	Hr.	Daily	Bare Costs	Incl. O&P
1 Carpenter	$29.15	$233.20	$45.60	$364.80	$26.27	$40.67
1 Truck Driver (light)	23.40	187.20	35.75	286.00		
1 Truck w/Power Equip.		184.20		202.60	11.51	12.66
16 L.H., Daily Totals		$604.60		$853.40	$37.78	$53.33
Crew K-2	Hr.	Daily	Hr.	Daily	Bare Costs	Incl. O&P
1 Struc. Steel Foreman	$34.85	$278.80	$63.20	$505.60	$30.37	$52.85
1 Struc. Steel Worker	32.85	262.80	59.60	476.80		
1 Truck Driver (light)	23.40	187.20	35.75	286.00		
1 Truck w/Power Equip.		184.20		202.60	7.68	8.44
24 L.H., Daily Totals		$913.00		$1471.00	$38.05	$61.29
Crew L-1	Hr.	Daily	Hr.	Daily	Bare Costs	Incl. O&P
1 Electrician	$34.30	$274.40	$51.20	$409.60	$34.38	$51.60
1 Plumber	34.45	275.60	52.00	416.00		
16 L.H., Daily Totals		$550.00		$825.60	$34.38	$51.60
Crew L-2	Hr.	Daily	Hr.	Daily	Bare Costs	Incl. O&P
1 Carpenter	$29.15	$233.20	$45.60	$364.80	$25.65	$40.15
1 Carpenter Helper	22.15	177.20	34.70	277.60		
16 L.H., Daily Totals		$410.40		$642.40	$25.65	$40.15
Crew L-3	Hr.	Daily	Hr.	Daily	Bare Costs	Incl. O&P
1 Carpenter	$29.15	$233.20	$45.60	$364.80	$31.54	$48.55
.5 Electrician	34.30	137.20	51.20	204.80		
.5 Sheet Metal Worker	33.55	134.20	51.80	207.20		
16 L.H., Daily Totals		$504.60		$776.80	$31.54	$48.55
Crew L-3A	Hr.	Daily	Hr.	Daily	Bare Costs	Incl. O&P
1 Carpenter Foreman (outside)	$31.15	$249.20	$48.75	$390.00	$31.95	$49.77
.5 Sheet Metal Worker	33.55	134.20	51.80	207.20		
12 L.H., Daily Totals		$383.40		$597.20	$31.95	$49.77
Crew L-4	Hr.	Daily	Hr.	Daily	Bare Costs	Incl. O&P
2 Skilled Workers	$29.85	$477.60	$46.85	$749.60	$27.28	$42.80
1 Helper	22.15	177.20	34.70	277.60		
24 L.H., Daily Totals		$654.80		$1027.20	$27.28	$42.80
Crew L-5	Hr.	Daily	Hr.	Daily	Bare Costs	Incl. O&P
1 Struc. Steel Foreman	$34.85	$278.80	$63.20	$505.60	$32.89	$58.34
5 Struc. Steel Workers	32.85	1314.00	59.60	2384.00		
1 Equip. Oper. (crane)	31.15	249.20	47.15	377.20		
1 Hyd. Crane, 25 Ton		629.60		692.55	11.24	12.37
56 L.H., Daily Totals		$2471.60		$3959.35	$44.13	$70.71
Crew L-5A	Hr.	Daily	Hr.	Daily	Bare Costs	Incl. O&P
1 Structural Steel Foreman	$34.85	$278.80	$63.20	$505.60	$32.92	$57.39
2 Structural Steel Workers	32.85	525.60	59.60	953.60		
1 Equip. Oper. (crane)	31.15	249.20	47.15	377.20		
1 Crane,SP, 25 Ton		602.00		662.20	18.81	20.69
32 L.H., Daily Totals		$1655.60		$2498.60	$51.73	$78.08

Crew No.	Bare Costs Hr.	Bare Costs Daily	Incl. Subs O & P Hr.	Incl. Subs O & P Daily	Cost Per Labor-Hour Bare Costs	Cost Per Labor-Hour Incl. O&P
Crew L-6	Hr.	Daily	Hr.	Daily	Bare Costs	Incl. O&P
1 Plumber	$34.45	$275.60	$52.00	$416.00	$34.40	$51.73
.5 Electrician	34.30	137.20	51.20	204.80		
12 L.H., Daily Totals		$412.80		$620.80	$34.40	$51.73
Crew L-7	Hr.	Daily	Hr.	Daily	Bare Costs	Incl. O&P
2 Carpenters	$29.15	$466.40	$45.60	$729.60	$28.09	$43.59
1 Building Laborer	22.85	182.80	35.75	286.00		
.5 Electrician	34.30	137.20	51.20	204.80		
28 L.H., Daily Totals		$786.40		$1220.40	$28.09	$43.59
Crew L-8	Hr.	Daily	Hr.	Daily	Bare Costs	Incl. O&P
2 Carpenters	$29.15	$466.40	$45.60	$729.60	$30.21	$46.88
.5 Plumber	34.45	137.80	52.00	208.00		
20 L.H., Daily Totals		$604.20		$937.60	$30.21	$46.88
Crew L-9	Hr.	Daily	Hr.	Daily	Bare Costs	Incl. O&P
1 Labor Foreman (inside)	$23.35	$186.80	$36.55	$292.40	$26.46	$42.94
2 Building Laborers	22.85	365.60	35.75	572.00		
1 Struc. Steel Worker	32.85	262.80	59.60	476.80		
.5 Electrician	34.30	137.20	51.20	204.80		
36 L.H., Daily Totals		$952.40		$1546.00	$26.46	$42.94
Crew L-10	Hr.	Daily	Hr.	Daily	Bare Costs	Incl. O&P
1 Structural Steel Foreman	$34.85	$278.80	$63.20	$505.60	$32.95	$56.65
1 Structural Steel Worker	32.85	262.80	59.60	476.80		
1 Equip. Oper. (crane)	31.15	249.20	47.15	377.20		
1 Hyd. Crane, 12 Ton		514.80		566.30	21.45	23.60
24 L.H., Daily Totals		$1305.60		$1925.90	$54.40	$80.25
Crew M-1	Hr.	Daily	Hr.	Daily	Bare Costs	Incl. O&P
3 Elevator Constructors	$35.65	$855.60	$53.80	$1291.20	$33.86	$51.10
1 Elevator Apprentice	28.50	228.00	43.00	344.00		
5 Hand Tools		95.00		104.50	2.97	3.27
32 L.H., Daily Totals		$1178.60		$1739.70	$36.83	$54.37
Crew M-3	Hr.	Daily	Hr.	Daily	Bare Costs	Incl. O&P
1 Electrician Foreman (out)	$36.30	$290.40	$54.20	$433.60	$30.80	$46.64
1 Common Laborer	22.85	182.80	35.75	286.00		
.25 Equipment Operator, Medium	30.35	60.70	45.95	91.90		
1 Elevator Constructor	35.65	285.20	53.80	430.40		
1 Elevator Apprentice	28.50	228.00	43.00	344.00		
.25 Crane, SP, 4 x 4, 20 ton		134.35		147.80	3.95	4.35
34 L.H., Daily Totals		$1181.45		$1733.70	$34.75	$50.99
Crew M-4	Hr.	Daily	Hr.	Daily	Bare Costs	Incl. O&P
1 Electrician Foreman (out)	$36.30	$290.40	$54.20	$433.60	$30.56	$46.29
1 Common Laborer	22.85	182.80	35.75	286.00		
.25 Equipment Operator, Crane	31.15	62.30	47.15	94.30		
.25 Equipment Operator, Oiler	25.75	51.50	39.00	78.00		
1 Elevator Constructor	35.65	285.20	53.80	430.40		
1 Elevator Apprentice	28.50	228.00	43.00	344.00		
.25 Crane, Hyd, SP, 4WD, 40 Ton		218.00		239.80	6.06	6.66
36 L.H., Daily Totals		$1318.20		$1906.10	$36.62	$52.95
Crew Q-1	Hr.	Daily	Hr.	Daily	Bare Costs	Incl. O&P
1 Plumber	$34.45	$275.60	$52.00	$416.00	$31.00	$46.80
1 Plumber Apprentice	27.55	220.40	41.60	332.80		
16 L.H., Daily Totals		$496.00		$748.80	$31.00	$46.80

Crew Q-1C	Hr.	Daily	Hr.	Daily	Bare Costs	Incl. O&P
1 Plumber	$34.45	$275.60	$52.00	$416.00	$30.78	$46.52
1 Plumber Apprentice	27.55	220.40	41.60	332.80		
1 Equip. Oper. (medium)	30.35	242.80	45.95	367.60		
1 Trencher, Chain		711.40		782.55	29.64	32.61
24 L.H., Daily Totals		$1450.20		$1898.95	$60.42	$79.13

Crew Q-2	Hr.	Daily	Hr.	Daily	Bare Costs	Incl. O&P
2 Plumbers	$34.45	$551.20	$52.00	$832.00	$32.15	$48.53
1 Plumber Apprentice	27.55	220.40	41.60	332.80		
24 L.H., Daily Totals		$771.60		$1164.80	$32.15	$48.53

Crew Q-3	Hr.	Daily	Hr.	Daily	Bare Costs	Incl. O&P
1 Plumber Foreman (inside)	$34.95	$279.60	$52.75	$422.00	$32.85	$49.59
2 Plumbers	34.45	551.20	52.00	832.00		
1 Plumber Apprentice	27.55	220.40	41.60	332.80		
32 L.H., Daily Totals		$1051.20		$1586.80	$32.85	$49.59

Crew Q-4	Hr.	Daily	Hr.	Daily	Bare Costs	Incl. O&P
1 Plumber Foreman (inside)	$34.95	$279.60	$52.75	$422.00	$32.85	$49.59
1 Plumber	34.45	275.60	52.00	416.00		
1 Welder (plumber)	34.45	275.60	52.00	416.00		
1 Plumber Apprentice	27.55	220.40	41.60	332.80		
1 Electric Welding Mach.		100.65		110.70	3.15	3.46
32 L.H., Daily Totals		$1151.85		$1697.50	$36.00	$53.05

Crew Q-5	Hr.	Daily	Hr.	Daily	Bare Costs	Incl. O&P
1 Steamfitter	$34.85	$278.80	$52.60	$420.80	$31.38	$47.38
1 Steamfitter Apprentice	27.90	223.20	42.15	337.20		
16 L.H., Daily Totals		$502.00		$758.00	$31.38	$47.38

Crew Q-6	Hr.	Daily	Hr.	Daily	Bare Costs	Incl. O&P
2 Steamfitters	$34.85	$557.60	$52.60	$841.60	$32.53	$49.12
1 Steamfitter Apprentice	27.90	223.20	42.15	337.20		
24 L.H., Daily Totals		$780.80		$1178.80	$32.53	$49.12

Crew Q-7	Hr.	Daily	Hr.	Daily	Bare Costs	Incl. O&P
1 Steamfitter Foreman (inside)	$35.35	$282.80	$53.40	$427.20	$33.24	$50.19
2 Steamfitters	34.85	557.60	52.60	841.60		
1 Steamfitter Apprentice	27.90	223.20	42.15	337.20		
32 L.H., Daily Totals		$1063.60		$1606.00	$33.24	$50.19

Crew Q-8	Hr.	Daily	Hr.	Daily	Bare Costs	Incl. O&P
1 Steamfitter Foreman (inside)	$35.35	$282.80	$53.40	$427.20	$33.24	$50.19
1 Steamfitter	34.85	278.80	52.60	420.80		
1 Welder (steamfitter)	34.85	278.80	52.60	420.80		
1 Steamfitter Apprentice	27.90	223.20	42.15	337.20		
1 Electric Welding Mach.		100.65		110.70	3.15	3.46
32 L.H., Daily Totals		$1164.25		$1716.70	$36.39	$53.65

Crew Q-9	Hr.	Daily	Hr.	Daily	Bare Costs	Incl. O&P
1 Sheet Metal Worker	$33.55	$268.40	$51.80	$414.40	$30.20	$46.63
1 Sheet Metal Apprentice	26.85	214.80	41.45	331.60		
16 L.H., Daily Totals		$483.20		$746.00	$30.20	$46.63

Crew Q-10	Hr.	Daily	Hr.	Daily	Bare Costs	Incl. O&P
2 Sheet Metal Workers	$33.55	$536.80	$51.80	$828.80	$31.32	$48.35
1 Sheet Metal Apprentice	26.85	214.80	41.45	331.60		
24 L.H., Daily Totals		$751.60		$1160.40	$31.32	$48.35

Crew Q-11	Hr.	Daily	Hr.	Daily	Bare Costs	Incl. O&P
1 Sheet Metal Foreman (inside)	$34.05	$272.40	$52.55	$420.40	$32.00	$49.40
2 Sheet Metal Workers	33.55	536.80	51.80	828.80		
1 Sheet Metal Apprentice	26.85	214.80	41.45	331.60		
32 L.H., Daily Totals		$1024.00		$1580.80	$32.00	$49.40

Crew Q-12	Hr.	Daily	Hr.	Daily	Bare Costs	Incl. O&P
1 Sprinkler Installer	$34.45	$275.60	$52.10	$416.80	$31.00	$46.90
1 Sprinkler Apprentice	27.55	220.40	41.70	333.60		
16 L.H., Daily Totals		$496.00		$750.40	$31.00	$46.90

Crew Q-13	Hr.	Daily	Hr.	Daily	Bare Costs	Incl. O&P
1 Sprinkler Foreman (inside)	$34.95	$279.60	$52.90	$423.20	$32.85	$49.70
2 Sprinkler Installers	34.45	551.20	52.10	833.60		
1 Sprinkler Apprentice	27.55	220.40	41.70	333.60		
32 L.H., Daily Totals		$1051.20		$1590.40	$32.85	$49.70

Crew Q-14	Hr.	Daily	Hr.	Daily	Bare Costs	Incl. O&P
1 Asbestos Worker	$32.15	$257.20	$51.50	$412.00	$28.93	$46.33
1 Asbestos Apprentice	25.70	205.60	41.15	329.20		
16 L.H., Daily Totals		$462.80		$741.20	$28.93	$46.33

Crew Q-15	Hr.	Daily	Hr.	Daily	Bare Costs	Incl. O&P
1 Plumber	$34.45	$275.60	$52.00	$416.00	$31.00	$46.80
1 Plumber Apprentice	27.55	220.40	41.60	332.80		
1 Electric Welding Mach.		100.65		110.70	6.29	6.92
16 L.H., Daily Totals		$596.65		$859.50	$37.29	$53.72

Crew Q-16	Hr.	Daily	Hr.	Daily	Bare Costs	Incl. O&P
2 Plumbers	$34.45	$551.20	$52.00	$832.00	$32.15	$48.53
1 Plumber Apprentice	27.55	220.40	41.60	332.80		
1 Electric Welding Mach.		100.65		110.70	4.19	4.61
24 L.H., Daily Totals		$872.25		$1275.50	$36.34	$53.14

Crew Q-17	Hr.	Daily	Hr.	Daily	Bare Costs	Incl. O&P
1 Steamfitter	$34.85	$278.80	$52.60	$420.80	$31.38	$47.38
1 Steamfitter Apprentice	27.90	223.20	42.15	337.20		
1 Electric Welding Mach.		100.65		110.70	6.29	6.92
16 L.H., Daily Totals		$602.65		$868.70	$37.67	$54.30

Crew Q-17A	Hr.	Daily	Hr.	Daily	Bare Costs	Incl. O&P
1 Steamfitter	$34.85	$278.80	$52.60	$420.80	$31.30	$47.30
1 Steamfitter Apprentice	27.90	223.20	42.15	337.20		
1 Equip. Oper. (crane)	31.15	249.20	47.15	377.20		
1 Truck Crane, 12 Ton		514.80		566.30		
1 Electric Welding Mach.		100.65		110.70	25.64	28.21
24 L.H., Daily Totals		$1366.65		$1812.20	$56.94	$75.51

Crew Q-18	Hr.	Daily	Hr.	Daily	Bare Costs	Incl. O&P
2 Steamfitters	$34.85	$557.60	$52.60	$841.60	$32.53	$49.12
1 Steamfitter Apprentice	27.90	223.20	42.15	337.20		
1 Electric Welding Mach.		100.65		110.70	4.19	4.61
24 L.H., Daily Totals		$881.45		$1289.50	$36.72	$53.73

Crew Q-19	Hr.	Daily	Hr.	Daily	Bare Costs	Incl. O&P
1 Steamfitter	$34.85	$278.80	$52.60	$420.80	$32.35	$48.65
1 Steamfitter Apprentice	27.90	223.20	42.15	337.20		
1 Electrician	34.30	274.40	51.20	409.60		
24 L.H., Daily Totals		$776.40		$1167.60	$32.35	$48.65

Crew No.	Bare Costs		Incl. Subs O & P		Cost Per Labor-Hour	
Crew Q-20	Hr.	Daily	Hr.	Daily	Bare Costs	Incl. O&P
1 Sheet Metal Worker	$33.55	$268.40	$51.80	$414.40	$31.02	$47.54
1 Sheet Metal Apprentice	26.85	214.80	41.45	331.60		
.5 Electrician	34.30	137.20	51.20	204.80		
20 L.H., Daily Totals		$620.40		$950.80	$31.02	$47.54
Crew Q-21	Hr.	Daily	Hr.	Daily	Bare Costs	Incl. O&P
2 Steamfitters	$34.85	$557.60	$52.60	$841.60	$32.97	$49.64
1 Steamfitter Apprentice	27.90	223.20	42.15	337.20		
1 Electrician	34.30	274.40	51.20	409.60		
32 L.H., Daily Totals		$1055.20		$1588.40	$32.97	$49.64
Crew Q-22	Hr.	Daily	Hr.	Daily	Bare Costs	Incl. O&P
1 Plumber	$34.45	$275.60	$52.00	$416.00	$31.00	$46.80
1 Plumber Apprentice	27.55	220.40	41.60	332.80		
1 Truck Crane, 12 Ton		514.80		566.30	32.18	35.39
16 L.H., Daily Totals		$1010.80		$1315.10	$63.18	$82.19
Crew Q-22A	Hr.	Daily	Hr.	Daily	Bare Costs	Incl. O&P
1 Plumber	$34.45	$275.60	$52.00	$416.00	$29.00	$44.13
1 Plumber Apprentice	27.55	220.40	41.60	332.80		
1 Laborer	22.85	182.80	35.75	286.00		
1 Equip. Oper. (crane)	31.15	249.20	47.15	377.20		
1 Truck Crane, 12 Ton		514.80		566.30	16.09	17.70
32 L.H., Daily Totals		$1442.80		$1978.30	$45.09	$61.83
Crew Q-23	Hr.	Daily	Hr.	Daily	Bare Costs	Incl. O&P
1 Plumber Foreman	$36.45	$291.60	$55.05	$440.40	$33.75	$51.00
1 Plumber	34.45	275.60	52.00	416.00		
1 Equip. Oper. (medium)	30.35	242.80	45.95	367.60		
1 Power Tools		2.90		3.20		
1 Crane, 20 Ton		554.80		610.30	23.24	25.56
24 L.H., Daily Totals		$1367.70		$1837.50	$56.99	$76.56
Crew R-1	Hr.	Daily	Hr.	Daily	Bare Costs	Incl. O&P
1 Electrician Foreman	$34.80	$278.40	$51.95	$415.60	$30.33	$45.83
3 Electricians	34.30	823.20	51.20	1228.80		
2 Helpers	22.15	354.40	34.70	555.20		
48 L.H., Daily Totals		$1456.00		$2199.60	$30.33	$45.83
Crew R-1A	Hr.	Daily	Hr.	Daily	Bare Costs	Incl. O&P
1 Electrician	$34.30	$274.40	$51.20	$409.60	$28.23	$42.95
1 Helper	22.15	177.20	34.70	277.60		
16 L.H., Daily Totals		$451.60		$687.20	$28.23	$42.95
Crew R-2	Hr.	Daily	Hr.	Daily	Bare Costs	Incl. O&P
1 Electrician Foreman	$34.80	$278.40	$51.95	$415.60	$30.45	$46.01
3 Electricians	34.30	823.20	51.20	1228.80		
2 Helpers	22.15	354.40	34.70	555.20		
1 Equip. Oper. (crane)	31.15	249.20	47.15	377.20		
1 S.P. Crane, 5 Ton		284.00		312.40	5.07	5.58
56 L.H., Daily Totals		$1989.20		$2889.20	$35.52	$51.59
Crew R-3	Hr.	Daily	Hr.	Daily	Bare Costs	Incl. O&P
1 Electrician Foreman	$34.80	$278.40	$51.95	$415.60	$33.87	$50.69
1 Electrician	34.30	274.40	51.20	409.60		
.5 Equip. Oper. (crane)	31.15	124.60	47.15	188.60		
.5 S.P. Crane, 5 Ton		142.00		156.20	7.10	7.81
20 L.H., Daily Totals		$819.40		$1170.00	$40.97	$58.50

Crew No.	Bare Costs		Incl. Subs O & P		Cost Per Labor-Hour	
Crew R-4	Hr.	Daily	Hr.	Daily	Bare Costs	Incl. O&P
1 Struc. Steel Foreman	$34.85	$278.80	$63.20	$505.60	$33.54	$58.64
3 Struc. Steel Workers	32.85	788.40	59.60	1430.40		
1 Electrician	34.30	274.40	51.20	409.60		
1 Gas Welding Machine		84.00		92.40	2.10	2.31
40 L.H., Daily Totals		$1425.60		$2438.00	$35.64	$60.95
Crew R-5	Hr.	Daily	Hr.	Daily	Bare Costs	Incl. O&P
1 Electrician Foreman	$34.80	$278.40	$51.95	$415.60	$29.93	$45.27
4 Electrician Linemen	34.30	1097.60	51.20	1638.40		
2 Electrician Operators	34.30	548.80	51.20	819.20		
4 Electrician Groundmen	22.15	708.80	34.70	1110.40		
1 Crew Truck		90.40		99.45		
1 Tool Van		113.90		125.30		
1 Pickup Truck, 3/4 Ton		83.00		91.30		
.2 Crane, 55 Ton		180.32		198.35		
.2 Crane, 12 Ton		102.96		113.25		
.2 Auger, Truck Mtd.		374.00		411.40		
1 Tractor w/Winch		263.00		289.30	13.72	15.09
88 L.H., Daily Totals		$3841.18		$5311.95	$43.65	$60.36
Crew R-6	Hr.	Daily	Hr.	Daily	Bare Costs	Incl. O&P
1 Electrician Foreman	$34.80	$278.40	$51.95	$415.60	$29.93	$45.27
4 Electrician Linemen	34.30	1097.60	51.20	1638.40		
2 Electrician Operators	34.30	548.80	51.20	819.20		
4 Electrician Groundmen	22.15	708.80	34.70	1110.40		
1 Crew Truck		90.40		99.45		
1 Tool Van		113.90		125.30		
1 Pickup Truck, 3/4 Ton		83.00		91.30		
.2 Crane, 55 Ton		180.32		198.35		
.2 Crane, 12 Ton		102.96		113.25		
.2 Auger, Truck Mtd.		374.00		411.40		
1 Tractor w/Winch		263.00		289.30		
3 Cable Trailers		453.15		498.45		
.5 Tensioning Rig		149.75		164.75		
.5 Cable Pulling Rig		882.00		970.20	30.60	33.66
88 L.H., Daily Totals		$5326.08		$6945.35	$60.53	$78.93
Crew R-7	Hr.	Daily	Hr.	Daily	Bare Costs	Incl. O&P
1 Electrician Foreman	$34.80	$278.40	$51.95	$415.60	$24.26	$37.58
5 Electrician Groundmen	22.15	886.00	34.70	1388.00		
1 Crew Truck		90.40		99.45	1.88	2.07
48 L.H., Daily Totals		$1254.80		$1903.05	$26.14	$39.65
Crew R-8	Hr.	Daily	Hr.	Daily	Bare Costs	Incl. O&P
1 Electrician Foreman	$34.80	$278.40	$51.95	$415.60	$30.33	$45.83
3 Electrician Linemen	34.30	823.20	51.20	1228.80		
2 Electrician Groundmen	22.15	354.40	34.70	555.20		
1 Pickup Truck, 3/4 Ton		83.00		91.30		
1 Crew Truck		90.40		99.45	3.61	3.97
48 L.H., Daily Totals		$1629.40		$2390.35	$33.94	$49.80
Crew R-9	Hr.	Daily	Hr.	Daily	Bare Costs	Incl. O&P
1 Electrician Foreman	$34.80	$278.40	$51.95	$415.60	$28.29	$43.04
1 Electrician Lineman	34.30	274.40	51.20	409.60		
2 Electrician Operators	34.30	548.80	51.20	819.20		
4 Electrician Groundmen	22.15	708.80	34.70	1110.40		
1 Pickup Truck, 3/4 Ton		83.00		91.30		
1 Crew Truck		90.40		99.45	2.71	2.98
64 L.H., Daily Totals		$1983.80		$2945.55	$31.00	$46.02

Crew No.	Bare Costs		Incl. Subs O & P		Cost Per Labor-Hour	
	Hr.	Daily	Hr.	Daily	Bare Costs	Incl. O&P
Crew R-10						
1 Electrician Foreman	$34.80	$278.40	$51.95	$415.60	$32.36	$48.58
4 Electrician Linemen	34.30	1097.60	51.20	1638.40		
1 Electrician Groundman	22.15	177.20	34.70	277.60		
1 Crew Truck		90.40		99.45		
3 Tram Cars		485.70		534.25	12.00	13.20
48 L.H., Daily Totals		$2129.30		$2965.30	$44.36	$61.78
Crew R-11	Hr.	Daily	Hr.	Daily	Bare Costs	Incl. O&P
1 Electrician Foreman	$34.80	$278.40	$51.95	$415.60	$31.00	$46.74
4 Electricians	34.30	1097.60	51.20	1638.40		
1 Helper	22.15	177.20	34.70	277.60		
1 Common Laborer	22.85	182.80	35.75	286.00		
1 Crew Truck		90.40		99.45		
1 Crane, 12 Ton		514.80		566.30	10.81	11.89
56 L.H., Daily Totals		$2341.20		$3283.35	$41.81	$58.63
Crew R-12	Hr.	Daily	Hr.	Daily	Bare Costs	Incl. O&P
1 Carpenter Foreman	$29.65	$237.20	$46.40	$371.20	$27.35	$43.40
4 Carpenters	29.15	932.80	45.60	1459.20		
4 Common Laborers	22.85	731.20	35.75	1144.00		
1 Equip. Oper. (med.)	30.35	242.80	45.95	367.60		
1 Steel Worker	32.85	262.80	59.60	476.80		
1 Dozer, 200 H.P.		735.00		808.50		
1 Pickup Truck, 3/4 Ton		83.00		91.30	9.30	10.23
88 L.H., Daily Totals		$3224.80		$4718.60	$36.65	$53.63
Crew R-13	Hr.	Daily	Hr.	Daily	Bare Costs	Incl. O&P
1 Electrician Foreman	$34.80	$278.40	$51.95	$415.60	$32.43	$48.62
3 Electricians	34.30	823.20	51.20	1228.80		
1 Equipment Operator	31.15	249.20	47.15	377.20		
1 Equipment Oiler	25.75	206.00	39.00	312.00		
.25-1 Hyd. Crane, 33 Ton		201.20		221.30	4.19	4.61
48 L.H., Daily Totals		$1758.00		$2554.90	$36.62	$53.23
Crew R-15	Hr.	Daily	Hr.	Daily	Bare Costs	Incl. O&P
1 Electrician Foreman	$34.80	$278.40	$51.95	$415.60	$33.46	$50.05
4 Electricians	34.30	1097.60	51.20	1638.40		
1 Equipment Operator	28.75	230.00	43.55	348.40		
1 Aerial Lift Truck		211.00		232.10	4.40	4.84
48 L.H., Daily Totals		$1817.00		$2634.50	$37.86	$54.89
Crew R-18	Hr.	Daily	Hr.	Daily	Bare Costs	Incl. O&P
.25 Electrician Foreman	$34.80	$69.60	$51.95	$103.90	$26.86	$41.10
1 Electrician	34.30	274.40	51.20	409.60		
2 Helpers	22.15	354.40	34.70	555.20		
26 L.H., Daily Totals		$698.40		$1068.70	$26.86	$41.10
Crew R-19	Hr.	Daily	Hr.	Daily	Bare Costs	Incl. O&P
.5 Electrician Foreman	$34.80	$139.20	$51.95	$207.80	$34.40	$51.35
2 Electricians	34.30	548.80	51.20	819.20		
20 L.H., Daily Totals		$688.00		$1027.00	$34.40	$51.35
Crew R-21	Hr.	Daily	Hr.	Daily	Bare Costs	Incl. O&P
1 Electrician Foreman	$34.80	$278.40	$51.95	$415.60	$34.33	$51.25
3 Electricians	34.30	823.20	51.20	1228.80		
.1 Equip. Oper. (med.)	30.35	24.28	45.95	36.76		
.1 Hyd. Crane 25 Ton		60.20		66.20	1.84	2.02
32. L.H., Daily Totals		$1186.08		$1747.36	$36.17	$53.27

Crew No.	Bare Costs		Incl. Subs O & P		Cost Per Labor-Hour	
Crew R-22	Hr.	Daily	Hr.	Daily	Bare Costs	Incl. O&P
.66 Electrician Foreman	$34.80	$183.74	$51.95	$274.30	$29.16	$44.22
2 Helpers	22.15	354.40	34.70	555.20		
2 Electricians	34.30	548.80	51.20	819.20		
37.28 L.H., Daily Totals		$1086.94		$1648.70	$29.16	$44.22
Crew R-30	Hr.	Daily	Hr.	Daily	Bare Costs	Incl. O&P
.25 Electricians	$36.30	$72.60	$54.20	$108.40	$27.41	$41.92
1 Electricians	34.30	274.40	51.20	409.60		
2 Laborers, (Semi-Skilled)	22.85	365.60	35.75	572.00		
26 L.H., Daily Totals		$712.60		$1090.00	$27.41	$41.92

CREWS

Historical Cost Indexes

The table below lists both the Means Historical Cost Index based on Jan. 1, 1993 = 100 as well as the computed value of an index based on Jan. 1, 2001 costs. Since the Jan. 1, 2001 figure is estimated, space is left to write in the actual index figures as they become available through either the quarterly "Means Construction Cost Indexes" or as printed in the

"Engineering News-Record." To compute the actual index based on Jan. 1, 2001 = 100, divide the Historical Cost Index for a particular year by the actual Jan. 1, 2001 Construction Cost Index. Space has been left to advance the index figures as the year progresses.

Year	Historical Cost Index Jan. 1, 1993 = 100		Current Index Based on Jan. 1, 2001 = 100		Year	Historical Cost Index Jan. 1, 1993 = 100	Current Index Based on Jan. 1, 2001 = 100		Year	Historical Cost Index Jan. 1, 1993 = 100	Current Index Based on Jan. 1, 2001 = 100	
	Est.	Actual	Est.	Actual		Actual	Est.	Actual		Actual	Est.	Actual
Oct 2001					July 1986	84.2	69.2		July 1968	24.9	20.4	
July 2001					1985	82.6	67.8		1967	23.5	19.3	
April 2001					1984	82.0	67.3		1966	22.7	18.6	
Jan 2001	121.8		100.0	100.0	1983	80.2	65.8		1965	21.7	17.8	
July 2000		120.9	99.3		1982	76.1	62.5		1964	21.2	17.4	
1999		117.6	96.6		1981	70.0	57.5		1963	20.7	17.0	
1998		115.1	94.5		1980	62.9	51.6		1962	20.2	16.6	
1997		112.8	92.6		1979	57.8	47.5		1961	19.8	16.3	
1996		110.2	90.5		1978	53.5	43.9		1960	19.7	16.2	
1995		107.6	88.3		1977	49.5	40.6		1959	19.3	15.8	
1994		104.4	85.7		1976	46.9	38.5		1958	18.8	15.4	
1993		101.7	83.5		1975	44.8	36.8		1957	18.4	15.1	
1992		99.4	81.6		1974	41.4	34.0		1956	17.6	14.4	
1991		96.8	79.5		1973	37.7	31.0		1955	16.6	13.6	
1990		94.3	77.4		1972	34.8	28.6		1954	16.0	13.1	
1989		92.1	75.6		1971	32.1	26.4		1953	15.8	13.0	
1988		89.9	73.8		1970	28.7	23.6		1952	15.4	12.6	
1987		87.7	72.0		1969	26.9	22.1		1951	15.0	12.3	

Adjustments to Costs

The Historical Cost Index can be used to convert National Average building costs at a particular time to the approximate building costs for some other time.

Example:

Estimate and compare construction costs for different years in the same city.

To estimate the National Average construction cost of a building in 1970, knowing that it cost $900,000 in 2001:

INDEX in 1970 = 28.7

INDEX in 2001 = 121.8

Note: The City Cost Indexes for Canada can be used to convert U.S. National averages to local costs in Canadian dollars.

Time Adjustment using the Historical Cost Indexes:

$$\frac{\text{Index for Year A}}{\text{Index for Year B}} \times \text{Cost in Year B} = \text{Cost in Year A}$$

$$\frac{\text{INDEX 1970}}{\text{INDEX 2001}} \times \text{Cost 2001} = \text{Cost 1970}$$

$$\frac{28.7}{121.8} \times \$900,000 = .236 \times \$900,000 = \$212,400$$

The construction cost of the building in 1970 is $212,400.

How to Use the City Cost Indexes

What you should know before you begin

Means City Cost Indexes (CCI) are an extremely useful tool to use when you want to compare costs from city to city and region to region.

This publication contains average construction cost indexes for 719 U.S. and Canadian cities covering over 930 three-digit zip code locations, as listed directly under each city.

Keep in mind that a City Cost Index number is a *percentage ratio* of a specific city's cost to the national average cost of the same item at a stated time period.

In other words, these index figures represent relative construction *factors* (or, if you prefer, multipliers) for Material and Installation costs, as well as the weighted average for Total In Place costs for each CSI MasterFormat division. Installation costs include both labor and equipment rental costs.

The 30 City Average Index is the average of 30 major U.S. cities and serves as a National Average.

Index figures for both material and installation are based on the 30 major city average of 100 and represent the cost relationship as of July 1, 2000. The index for each division is computed from representative material and labor quantities for that division. The weighted average for each city is a weighted total of the components listed above it, but does not include relative productivity between trades or cities.

As changes occur in local material prices, labor rates and equipment rental rates, the impact of these changes should be accurately measured by the change in the City Cost Index for each particular city (as compared to the 30 City Average).

> *Therefore, if you know (or have estimated) building costs in one city today, you can easily convert those costs to expected building costs in another city.*

> *In addition, by using the Historical Cost Index, you can easily convert National Average building costs at a particular time to the approximate building costs for some other time. The City Cost Indexes can then be applied to calculate the costs for a particular city.*

Quick Calculations

Location Adjustment Using the City Cost Indexes:

$$\frac{\text{Index for City A}}{\text{Index for City B}} \times \text{Cost in City B} = \text{Cost in City A}$$

Time Adjustment for the National Average Using the Historical Cost Index:

$$\frac{\text{Index for Year A}}{\text{Index for Year B}} \times \text{Cost in Year B} = \text{Cost in Year A}$$

Adjustment from the National Average:

$$\frac{\text{Index for City A}}{100} \times \text{National Average Cost} = \text{Cost in City A}$$

Since each of the other R.S. Means publications contains many different items, any *one* item multiplied by the particular city index may give incorrect results. However, the larger the number of items compiled, the closer the results should be to actual costs for that particular city.

The City Cost Indexes for Canadian cities are calculated using Canadian material and equipment prices and labor rates, in Canadian dollars. Therefore, indexes for Canadian cities can be used to convert U.S. National Average prices to local costs in Canadian dollars.

How to use this section

1. Compare costs from city to city.

In using the Means Indexes, remember that an index number is not a fixed number but a *ratio:* It's a percentage ratio of a building component's cost at any stated time to the National Average cost of that same component at the same time period. Put in the form of an equation:

$$\frac{\text{Specific City Cost}}{\text{National Average Cost}} \times 100 = \text{City Index Number}$$

Therefore, when making cost comparisons between cities, do not subtract one city's index number from the index number of another city and read the result as a percentage difference. Instead, divide one city's index number by that of the other city. The resulting number may then be used as a multiplier to calculate cost differences from city to city.

The formula used to find cost differences between cities for the purpose of comparison is as follows:

$$\frac{\text{City A Index}}{\text{City B Index}} \times \text{City B Cost (Known)} = \text{City A Cost (Unknown)}$$

In addition, you can use *Means CCI* to calculate and compare costs division by division between cities using the same basic formula. (Just be sure that you're comparing similar divisions.)

2. Compare a specific city's construction costs with the National Average.

When you're studying construction location feasibility, it's advisable to compare a prospective project's cost index with an index of the National Average cost.

For example, divide the weighted average index of construction costs of a specific city by that of the 30 City Average, which = 100.

$$\frac{\text{City Index}}{100} = \% \text{ of National Average}$$

As a result, you get a ratio that indicates the relative cost of construction in that city in comparison with the National Average.

3. Covert U.S. National Average to actual costs in Canadian City.

$$\frac{\text{Index for Canadian City}}{100} \times \text{National Average Cost} = \text{Cost in Canadian City in \$ CAN}$$

614

4. Adjust construction cost data based on a National Average.

When you use a source of construction cost data which is based on a National Average (such as *Means cost data publications*), it is necessary to adjust those costs to a specific location.

$$\frac{\text{City Index}}{100} \times \frac{\text{"Book" Cost Based on}}{\text{National Average Costs}} = \frac{\text{City Cost}}{\text{(Unknown)}}$$

5. When applying the City Cost Indexes to demolition projects, use the appropriate division installation index. For example, for removal of existing doors and windows, use the Division 8 index.

What you might like to know about how we developed the Indexes

To create a reliable index, R.S. Means researched the building type most often constructed in the United States and Canada. Because it was concluded that no one type of building completely represented the building construction industry, nine different types of buildings were combined to create a composite model.

The exact material, labor and equipment quantities are based on detailed analysis of these nine building types, then each quantity is weighted in proportion to expected usage. These various material items, labor hours, and equipment rental rates are thus combined to form a composite building representing as closely as possible the actual usage of materials, labor and equipment used in the North American Building Construction Industry.

The following structures were chosen to make up that composite model:

1. Factory, 1 story
2. Office, 2–4 story
3. Store, Retail
4. Town Hall, 2–3 story
5. High School, 2–3 story
6. Hospital, 4–8 story
7. Garage, Parking
8. Apartment, 1–3 story
9. Hotel/Motel, 2–3 story

For the purposes of ensuring the timeliness of the data, the components of the index for the composite model have been streamlined. They currently consist of:

- specific quantities of 66 commonly used construction materials;
- specific labor-hours for 21 building construction trades; and
- specific days of equipment rental for 6 types of construction equipment (normally used to install the 66 material items by the 21 trades.)

A sophisticated computer program handles the updating of all costs for each city on a quarterly basis. Material and equipment price quotations are gathered quarterly from 719 cities in the United States and Canada. These prices and the latest negotiated labor wage rates for 21 different building trades are used to compile the quarterly update of the City Cost Index.

The 30 major U.S. cities used to calculate the National Average are:

Atlanta, GA	Memphis, TN
Baltimore, MD	Milwaukee, WI
Boston, MA	Minneapolis, MN
Buffalo, NY	Nashville, TN
Chicago, IL	New Orleans, LA
Cincinnati, OH	New York, NY
Cleveland, OH	Philadelphia, PA
Columbus, OH	Phoenix, AZ
Dallas, TX	Pittsburgh, PA
Denver, CO	St. Louis, MO
Detroit, MI	San Antonio, TX
Houston, TX	San Diego, CA
Indianapolis, IN	San Francisco, CA
Kansas City, MO	Seattle, WA
Los Angeles, CA	Washington, DC

F.Y.I.: The CSI MasterFormat Divisions

1. General Requirements
2. Site Work
3. Concrete
4. Masonry
5. Metals
6. Wood & Plastics
7. Thermal & Moisture Protection
8. Doors & Windows
9. Finishes
10. Specialties
11. Equipment
12. Furnishings
13. Special Construction
14. Conveying Systems
15. Mechanical
16. Electrical

The information presented in the CCI is organized according to the Construction Specifications Institute (CSI) MasterFormat.

What the CCI does not indicate

The weighted average for each city is a total of the components listed above weighted to reflect typical usage, but it does *not* include the productivity variations between trades or cities.

In addition, the CCI does not take into consideration factors such as the following:

- managerial efficiency
- competitive conditions
- automation
- restrictive union practices
- unique local requirements
- regional variations due to specific building codes

DIVISION		UNITED STATES 30 CITY AVERAGE			ALABAMA ANNISTON 362			BIRMINGHAM 350-352			BUTLER 369			DECATUR 356			DOTHAN 363		
		MAT.	INST.	TOTAL	MAT.	INST.	TOTAL	MAT.	INST.	TOTAL	MAT.	INST.	TOTAL	MAT.	INST.	TOTAL	MAT.	INST.	TOTAL
02	SITE CONSTRUCTION	100.0	100.0	100.0	94.1	92.7	93.0	88.6	93.8	92.6	108.7	86.4	91.6	86.9	92.5	91.2	106.1	86.4	91.0
03100	CONCRETE FORMS & ACCESSORIES	100.0	100.0	100.0	95.9	41.0	48.5	94.4	77.4	79.7	85.1	54.1	58.3	96.0	57.6	62.9	97.7	53.9	60.0
03200	CONCRETE REINFORCEMENT	100.0	100.0	100.0	92.8	89.9	91.2	92.8	91.0	91.8	103.6	72.0	85.6	92.8	68.8	79.2	103.6	72.0	85.6
03300	CAST-IN-PLACE CONCRETE	100.0	100.0	100.0	91.7	46.9	73.3	93.9	68.1	83.3	89.4	56.4	75.8	91.2	65.1	80.4	89.4	56.4	75.8
03	CONCRETE	100.0	100.0	100.0	93.1	54.3	73.7	89.8	77.7	83.8	94.2	59.9	77.1	88.6	63.9	76.3	93.8	59.8	76.8
04	MASONRY	100.0	100.0	100.0	84.9	39.3	56.8	85.8	72.4	77.5	88.7	41.0	59.3	85.8	58.1	68.8	89.6	41.0	59.7
05	METALS	100.0	100.0	100.0	96.2	92.6	94.9	98.6	95.9	97.6	95.1	85.6	91.7	98.2	86.9	94.1	95.2	85.5	91.7
06	WOOD & PLASTICS	100.0	100.0	100.0	88.3	40.6	63.6	95.3	77.6	86.2	82.6	56.1	68.9	94.4	56.8	75.0	95.7	56.1	75.2
07	THERMAL & MOISTURE PROTECTION	100.0	100.0	100.0	96.7	45.0	72.2	96.8	80.1	88.9	96.7	58.0	78.4	96.5	64.4	81.3	96.8	54.2	76.6
08	DOORS & WINDOWS	100.0	100.0	100.0	94.5	49.5	83.6	98.3	77.9	93.4	94.5	58.0	85.7	98.3	56.3	88.2	94.5	58.0	85.7
09200	PLASTER & GYPSUM BOARD	100.0	100.0	100.0	104.2	39.3	64.5	110.0	77.5	90.1	103.0	55.2	73.8	107.2	56.0	75.9	107.7	55.2	75.6
095,098	CEILINGS & ACOUSTICAL TREATMENT	100.0	100.0	100.0	88.0	39.3	55.8	95.1	77.5	83.5	88.0	55.2	66.4	92.1	56.0	68.3	88.0	55.2	66.4
09600	FLOORING	100.0	100.0	100.0	98.5	43.2	85.1	101.6	60.9	91.7	104.9	34.1	87.7	101.6	63.5	92.4	112.9	41.3	95.5
097,099	WALL FINISHES, PAINTS & COATINGS	100.0	100.0	100.0	92.9	36.1	59.9	92.9	54.9	70.8	92.9	61.2	74.5	92.9	57.2	72.2	92.9	61.2	74.5
09	FINISHES	100.0	100.0	100.0	95.9	40.4	67.6	98.8	71.7	85.0	99.4	50.8	74.6	97.7	58.2	77.5	102.5	52.0	76.8
10-14	TOTAL DIV. 10000-14000	100.0	100.0	100.0	100.0	60.3	91.6	100.0	84.7	96.8	100.0	63.9	92.4	100.0	66.4	92.9	100.0	63.9	92.4
15	MECHANICAL	100.0	100.0	100.0	100.3	45.2	74.8	99.9	72.2	87.1	98.2	48.6	75.3	99.9	58.9	81.0	98.2	48.6	75.2
16	ELECTRICAL	100.0	100.0	100.0	94.0	31.9	51.3	96.3	67.1	76.2	97.2	45.0	61.3	96.7	59.2	70.9	95.3	45.0	60.7
01-16	WEIGHTED AVERAGE	100.0	100.0	100.0	95.9	52.5	74.8	96.6	77.2	87.2	96.6	57.2	77.4	96.3	65.6	81.3	96.9	57.2	77.6

DIVISION		ALABAMA EVERGREEN 364			GADSDEN 359			HUNTSVILLE 357-358			JASPER 355			MOBILE 365-366			MONTGOMERY 360-361		
		MAT.	INST.	TOTAL	MAT.	INST.	TOTAL	MAT.	INST.	TOTAL	MAT.	INST.	TOTAL	MAT.	INST.	TOTAL	MAT.	INST.	TOTAL
02	SITE CONSTRUCTION	109.3	86.6	91.9	92.7	93.0	92.9	86.6	93.0	91.5	92.3	92.8	92.7	97.9	86.8	89.4	98.4	87.3	89.9
03100	CONCRETE FORMS & ACCESSORIES	80.4	55.9	59.2	91.2	52.3	57.6	96.0	57.6	62.9	98.4	43.2	50.8	96.0	60.9	65.7	94.2	55.0	60.4
03200	CONCRETE REINFORCEMENT	104.1	72.0	85.8	101.6	90.4	95.2	92.8	89.2	90.8	92.8	90.1	91.3	95.8	67.2	79.5	95.8	90.0	92.5
03300	CAST-IN-PLACE CONCRETE	89.4	59.2	77.0	91.2	59.9	78.3	88.8	65.3	79.1	101.1	53.6	81.5	93.8	63.3	81.2	95.5	57.0	79.6
03	CONCRETE	94.3	61.7	78.0	93.2	63.8	78.5	87.4	67.7	77.6	96.3	57.6	77.0	90.2	64.4	77.3	90.9	63.9	77.4
04	MASONRY	88.7	46.2	62.6	84.1	48.7	62.3	85.7	58.1	68.7	81.4	42.4	57.5	86.3	58.5	69.2	86.8	40.7	58.5
05	METALS	95.2	85.4	91.7	96.2	94.4	95.6	98.2	93.9	96.7	96.1	93.3	95.1	96.8	86.2	93.0	96.8	93.7	95.7
06	WOOD & PLASTICS	77.9	56.1	66.6	83.2	51.2	66.6	94.4	56.1	74.6	90.6	41.6	65.3	94.4	61.2	77.2	92.3	56.1	73.5
07	THERMAL & MOISTURE PROTECTION	96.7	56.4	77.6	96.6	69.1	83.5	96.6	72.7	85.3	96.6	50.3	74.6	96.6	73.9	85.8	96.3	66.9	82.3
08	DOORS & WINDOWS	94.5	58.0	85.7	94.5	56.5	85.3	98.3	60.4	89.1	94.4	54.9	84.9	98.3	60.3	89.1	98.3	61.9	89.5
09200	PLASTER & GYPSUM BOARD	101.2	55.2	73.1	102.1	50.1	70.3	107.2	55.2	75.4	104.4	40.3	65.2	107.2	60.5	78.6	107.2	55.2	75.4
095,098	CEILINGS & ACOUSTICAL TREATMENT	88.0	55.2	66.4	88.0	50.1	63.0	95.1	55.2	68.8	86.6	40.3	56.0	95.1	60.5	72.3	95.1	55.2	68.8
09600	FLOORING	102.1	34.1	85.6	96.4	54.5	86.2	101.6	52.7	89.8	99.6	41.6	85.6	110.2	66.0	99.5	110.2	34.1	91.8
097,099	WALL FINISHES, PAINTS & COATINGS	92.9	61.2	74.5	92.9	63.0	75.5	92.9	53.8	70.2	92.9	44.3	64.6	92.9	62.3	75.1	92.9	61.2	74.5
09	FINISHES	98.2	52.1	74.7	94.8	52.6	73.3	98.2	55.2	76.3	95.9	42.1	68.4	102.1	61.6	81.5	102.2	50.7	75.9
10-14	TOTAL DIV. 10000-14000	100.0	66.0	92.8	100.0	76.0	94.9	100.0	78.4	95.4	100.0	61.3	91.8	100.0	74.5	94.6	100.0	76.0	94.9
15	MECHANICAL	98.2	51.4	76.5	106.1	51.7	80.9	99.9	54.2	78.8	106.1	63.2	86.2	99.9	67.0	84.7	99.9	48.8	76.3
16	ELECTRICAL	93.0	45.0	60.0	95.7	67.1	76.0	96.7	73.9	81.0	96.0	32.3	52.2	96.7	61.5	72.5	96.3	72.4	79.9
01-16	WEIGHTED AVERAGE	96.1	58.7	77.9	96.9	65.0	81.4	96.2	68.6	82.8	97.4	57.5	77.9	97.1	68.0	83.0	97.2	63.9	81.0

DIVISION		ALABAMA PHENIX CITY 368			SELMA 367			TUSCALOOSA 354			ALASKA ANCHORAGE 995-996			FAIRBANKS 997			JUNEAU 998		
		MAT.	INST.	TOTAL	MAT.	INST.	TOTAL	MAT.	INST.	TOTAL	MAT.	INST.	TOTAL	MAT.	INST.	TOTAL	MAT.	INST.	TOTAL
02	SITE CONSTRUCTION	113.4	87.4	93.5	105.8	87.3	91.6	87.1	92.7	91.4	132.6	135.4	134.8	117.3	135.4	131.2	128.6	135.4	133.8
03100	CONCRETE FORMS & ACCESSORIES	89.8	48.6	54.3	86.6	54.6	59.0	96.0	45.2	52.2	132.5	115.8	118.1	134.1	119.6	121.6	133.8	115.8	118.3
03200	CONCRETE REINFORCEMENT	103.0	97.8	100.0	103.6	89.9	95.8	92.8	90.3	91.4	141.4	106.5	121.5	118.8	106.6	111.8	105.2	106.5	105.9
03300	CAST-IN-PLACE CONCRETE	89.5	57.7	76.4	89.4	57.1	76.1	92.5	54.5	76.8	186.6	115.3	157.2	158.0	115.9	140.6	187.4	115.4	157.7
03	CONCRETE	97.0	62.8	79.9	92.9	63.7	78.3	89.2	58.8	74.0	152.2	113.2	132.7	130.0	115.0	122.5	148.1	113.2	130.6
04	MASONRY	88.7	46.5	62.7	93.3	41.1	61.2	86.0	43.0	59.5	195.5	123.6	151.3	182.8	123.6	146.4	184.8	123.6	147.1
05	METALS	95.0	96.5	95.6	95.0	93.1	94.4	97.3	94.3	96.2	130.0	99.3	119.0	130.1	99.7	119.1	130.3	99.4	119.2
06	WOOD & PLASTICS	87.7	46.7	66.5	84.4	56.1	69.8	94.4	44.5	68.6	123.8	113.8	118.6	124.1	118.5	121.2	123.8	113.8	118.6
07	THERMAL & MOISTURE PROTECTION	97.2	67.6	83.1	96.6	58.0	78.3	96.5	65.4	81.8	199.7	114.1	159.1	195.7	116.4	158.1	196.4	114.1	157.3
08	DOORS & WINDOWS	94.5	58.5	85.8	94.5	61.9	86.6	98.3	59.9	89.0	131.3	107.3	125.6	128.4	110.2	124.0	128.4	107.3	123.3
09200	PLASTER & GYPSUM BOARD	105.1	45.6	68.7	103.8	55.2	74.1	107.2	43.3	68.1	129.9	114.2	120.3	129.9	119.0	123.3	129.9	114.2	120.3
095,098	CEILINGS & ACOUSTICAL TREATMENT	88.0	45.6	60.0	88.0	55.2	66.4	95.1	43.3	60.9	131.7	114.2	120.1	131.7	119.0	123.3	131.7	114.2	120.1
09600	FLOORING	107.9	34.1	90.0	105.8	34.1	88.4	101.6	50.1	89.1	126.3	128.2	126.8	126.4	128.2	126.9	126.3	128.2	126.8
097,099	WALL FINISHES, PAINTS & COATINGS	92.9	61.2	74.5	92.9	61.2	74.5	92.9	52.7	69.5	117.6	110.6	113.5	117.6	116.0	116.7	117.6	110.6	113.5
09	FINISHES	101.0	45.6	72.7	99.5	50.8	74.7	98.2	45.5	71.3	140.1	117.8	128.7	138.0	121.2	129.4	138.7	117.8	128.0
10-14	TOTAL DIV. 10000-14000	100.0	75.2	94.8	100.0	64.0	92.4	100.0	73.0	94.3	100.0	114.8	103.1	100.0	115.5	103.3	100.0	114.8	103.1
15	MECHANICAL	98.2	49.6	75.7	98.2	48.8	75.3	99.9	43.0	73.6	106.4	108.0	107.1	106.4	118.5	112.0	106.4	108.0	107.4
16	ELECTRICAL	96.4	66.9	76.1	94.8	45.0	60.6	96.7	67.1	76.3	161.7	110.5	126.5	164.6	110.5	127.5	164.6	110.5	127.5
01-16	WEIGHTED AVERAGE	97.2	62.9	80.5	96.4	58.7	78.1	96.3	61.1	79.1	134.5	114.1	124.5	130.1	117.0	123.7	132.9	114.2	123.8

COST INDEXES

DIVISION		ALASKA			ARIZONA														
		KETCHIKAN			CHAMBERS			FLAGSTAFF			GLOBE			KINGMAN			MESA/TEMPE		
		999			865			860			855			864			852		
		MAT.	INST.	TOTAL	MAT.	INST.	TOTAL	MAT.	INST.	TOTAL	MAT.	INST.	TOTAL	MAT.	INST.	TOTAL	MAT.	INST.	TOTAL
02	SITE CONSTRUCTION	181.8	135.4	146.3	67.5	99.2	91.8	86.9	99.6	96.7	90.8	99.4	97.4	67.5	99.5	92.0	81.6	99.3	95.1
03100	CONCRETE FORMS & ACCESSORIES	124.5	115.8	117.0	101.6	68.1	72.7	108.9	74.3	79.0	99.5	68.0	72.4	98.7	68.3	72.5	103.6	72.2	76.5
03200	CONCRETE REINFORCEMENT	109.6	106.5	107.9	104.4	66.0	82.5	103.6	80.9	90.7	103.1	71.3	85.0	105.2	71.8	86.2	103.9	77.9	89.0
03300	CAST-IN-PLACE CONCRETE	302.2	115.4	225.2	96.7	73.7	87.2	96.8	84.9	91.9	96.0	73.4	86.7	96.4	73.7	87.1	96.8	76.6	88.4
03	CONCRETE	225.3	113.2	169.2	101.3	69.4	85.4	122.5	78.9	100.7	107.5	70.5	89.0	100.9	70.7	85.8	99.6	74.6	87.1
04	MASONRY	193.7	123.6	150.6	103.6	63.6	79.0	103.1	65.7	80.2	110.6	63.6	81.7	103.6	71.6	83.9	110.7	57.8	78.2
05	METALS	130.1	99.4	119.0	97.7	65.3	86.0	98.1	72.7	88.9	98.0	65.1	87.7	98.2	69.6	87.9	98.3	72.5	89.0
06	WOOD & PLASTICS	114.4	113.8	114.1	102.4	67.3	84.3	109.7	74.1	91.3	97.3	67.4	81.8	98.7	67.3	82.4	101.4	79.1	89.9
07	THERMAL & MOISTURE PROTECTION	200.1	114.1	159.3	109.0	72.3	91.6	111.5	74.9	94.1	107.5	69.5	89.5	108.9	72.3	91.5	106.5	70.1	89.2
08	DOORS & WINDOWS	128.4	107.3	123.3	102.9	65.1	93.8	103.0	74.0	96.0	99.7	67.5	91.9	103.1	67.5	94.5	99.8	74.3	93.6
09200	PLASTER & GYPSUM BOARD	127.3	114.2	119.3	90.8	66.3	75.8	93.2	73.4	81.1	92.5	66.3	76.5	88.5	66.3	74.9	93.8	78.4	84.4
095,098	CEILINGS & ACOUSTICAL TREATMENT	128.6	114.2	119.1	97.9	66.3	77.0	99.2	73.4	82.2	103.3	66.3	78.9	99.2	66.3	77.5	103.3	78.4	86.9
09600	FLOORING	122.7	128.2	124.0	96.5	61.3	87.9	99.0	61.6	89.9	99.9	61.3	90.6	95.5	69.9	89.3	101.4	69.9	93.8
097,099	WALL FINISHES, PAINTS & COATINGS	117.6	110.6	113.5	99.1	58.5	75.5	99.1	58.5	75.5	109.9	58.5	80.0	99.1	58.5	75.5	109.9	62.8	82.5
09	FINISHES	139.3	117.8	128.3	93.8	65.6	79.4	96.8	69.9	83.1	98.3	65.7	81.6	93.4	67.1	80.0	98.2	70.9	84.3
10 - 14	TOTAL DIV. 10000 - 14000	100.0	114.8	103.1	100.0	82.6	96.3	100.0	83.9	96.6	100.0	82.8	96.4	100.0	82.6	96.3	100.0	78.7	95.5
15	MECHANICAL	105.2	108.6	106.8	98.0	79.9	89.7	100.3	82.2	91.9	97.0	69.5	84.3	98.0	81.2	90.3	100.1	73.8	87.9
16	ELECTRICAL	164.6	110.5	127.5	102.1	55.3	69.9	100.4	57.4	70.9	103.4	55.3	70.3	102.1	55.3	69.9	98.1	38.8	57.3
01 - 16	WEIGHTED AVERAGE	144.2	114.2	129.6	98.8	70.8	85.2	102.8	74.8	89.2	100.5	69.4	85.4	98.7	72.7	86.1	99.6	68.7	84.6

DIVISION		ARIZONA												ARKANSAS					
		PHOENIX			PRESCOTT			SHOW LOW			TUCSON			BATESVILLE			CAMDEN		
		850,853			863			859			856 - 857			725			717		
		MAT.	INST.	TOTAL	MAT.	INST.	TOTAL	MAT.	INST.	TOTAL	MAT.	INST.	TOTAL	MAT.	INST.	TOTAL	MAT.	INST.	TOTAL
02	SITE CONSTRUCTION	82.0	100.0	95.8	73.7	99.2	93.3	92.7	99.4	97.8	77.9	99.8	94.7	73.9	83.9	81.5	74.7	83.5	81.4
03100	CONCRETE FORMS & ACCESSORIES	105.0	79.5	83.0	103.4	68.2	73.0	109.3	68.3	73.9	104.4	79.2	82.6	79.2	52.0	55.7	78.8	36.6	42.4
03200	CONCRETE REINFORCEMENT	102.0	81.4	90.3	103.6	82.3	91.5	103.9	66.0	82.3	100.9	80.9	89.5	94.5	53.7	71.3	95.8	29.6	58.0
03300	CAST-IN-PLACE CONCRETE	96.9	84.9	91.9	96.8	73.7	87.2	96.0	73.5	86.8	89.7	84.7	87.6	81.8	51.7	69.4	83.9	38.2	65.0
03	CONCRETE	99.2	81.4	90.3	106.9	72.5	89.7	109.9	69.5	89.7	95.5	81.0	88.3	80.1	53.0	66.5	81.9	37.1	59.5
04	MASONRY	97.5	73.6	82.8	103.6	71.6	83.9	110.6	63.6	81.7	97.5	65.7	77.9	99.3	49.7	68.8	109.6	42.9	68.6
05	METALS	99.6	75.1	90.8	98.1	72.0	88.7	97.8	66.2	86.4	98.9	73.4	89.7	94.8	64.9	84.0	94.8	55.3	80.5
06	WOOD & PLASTICS	102.7	80.9	91.4	104.2	67.3	85.1	107.2	67.4	86.6	102.8	80.9	91.5	79.9	53.6	66.3	79.6	37.9	58.0
07	THERMAL & MOISTURE PROTECTION	106.4	76.8	92.4	109.7	72.3	91.9	107.8	71.5	90.6	107.1	71.3	90.1	96.6	52.6	75.8	96.4	39.8	69.5
08	DOORS & WINDOWS	98.9	77.7	93.8	103.0	69.3	94.9	98.8	65.2	90.7	97.6	77.7	92.8	97.3	49.4	85.7	93.5	32.6	78.8
09200	PLASTER & GYPSUM BOARD	94.3	80.2	85.7	91.5	66.3	76.1	95.3	66.3	77.6	94.5	80.2	85.8	92.5	53.0	68.4	92.5	36.8	58.5
095,098	CEILINGS & ACOUSTICAL TREATMENT	103.3	80.2	88.1	99.2	66.3	77.5	101.9	66.3	78.4	104.7	80.2	88.5	95.5	53.0	67.5	95.5	36.8	56.8
09600	FLOORING	101.8	69.9	94.1	97.3	61.3	88.6	103.4	69.9	95.2	100.9	61.6	91.4	109.2	58.8	97.0	109.1	19.5	87.4
097,099	WALL FINISHES, PAINTS & COATINGS	109.9	70.5	87.0	99.1	58.5	75.5	109.9	58.5	80.0	107.4	58.5	78.9	95.6	51.8	70.1	95.6	40.5	63.5
09	FINISHES	98.4	76.9	87.4	94.9	65.6	80.0	99.7	67.2	83.1	98.1	73.8	85.7	96.9	53.5	74.8	96.9	34.5	65.1
10 - 14	TOTAL DIV. 10000 - 14000	100.0	85.0	96.8	100.0	82.6	96.3	100.0	82.8	96.4	100.0	85.1	96.8	100.0	56.8	90.9	100.0	52.0	89.9
15	MECHANICAL	100.1	82.3	91.8	100.3	71.7	87.1	97.0	81.1	89.6	100.0	76.2	89.0	96.9	49.8	75.1	96.9	38.3	69.8
16	ELECTRICAL	107.2	63.5	77.2	100.0	55.3	69.3	98.7	55.3	68.9	101.6	64.1	75.8	100.1	57.1	70.5	94.3	47.6	62.2
01 - 16	WEIGHTED AVERAGE	99.6	78.4	89.3	100.2	71.2	86.1	100.7	71.3	86.4	98.4	75.8	87.4	94.3	56.9	76.1	94.3	45.9	70.7

DIVISION		ARKANSAS																	
		FAYETTEVILLE			FORT SMITH			HARRISON			HOT SPRINGS			JONESBORO			LITTLE ROCK		
		727			729			726			719			724			720 - 722		
		MAT.	INST.	TOTAL	MAT.	INST.	TOTAL	MAT.	INST.	TOTAL	MAT.	INST.	TOTAL	MAT.	INST.	TOTAL	MAT.	INST.	TOTAL
02	SITE CONSTRUCTION	73.4	83.1	80.8	76.7	83.9	82.2	78.8	83.9	82.7	78.4	83.2	82.1	101.7	99.0	99.6	76.7	83.9	82.2
03100	CONCRETE FORMS & ACCESSORIES	73.7	30.2	36.2	98.7	48.2	55.1	85.0	52.0	56.5	75.5	34.3	39.9	83.1	55.6	59.4	93.0	52.9	58.4
03200	CONCRETE REINFORCEMENT	94.6	25.7	55.3	95.5	72.8	82.6	94.0	53.7	71.0	93.9	28.2	56.4	91.4	54.5	70.4	95.8	71.9	82.2
03300	CAST-IN-PLACE CONCRETE	81.9	40.0	64.6	84.7	52.0	71.2	90.9	51.7	74.7	85.9	37.1	65.8	89.2	63.7	78.7	85.7	52.0	71.8
03	CONCRETE	79.7	34.2	57.0	84.1	55.0	69.5	87.4	53.0	70.2	85.0	35.5	60.2	85.0	60.0	72.5	84.2	56.9	70.6
04	MASONRY	89.4	33.0	54.8	97.0	58.4	73.3	99.5	49.7	68.9	81.1	33.3	51.7	91.3	54.9	68.9	95.2	58.4	72.6
05	METALS	94.8	52.3	79.5	96.6	72.8	88.0	95.7	64.9	84.6	94.8	53.8	80.0	90.9	82.3	87.8	96.2	72.6	87.7
06	WOOD & PLASTICS	74.8	29.7	51.4	100.4	47.3	73.0	86.1	53.6	69.3	76.3	34.3	54.6	83.3	57.0	69.7	96.9	53.6	74.5
07	THERMAL & MOISTURE PROTECTION	97.7	41.4	71.0	98.3	54.5	77.5	97.1	52.6	76.0	96.7	40.8	70.2	108.0	59.3	84.9	96.9	55.1	77.1
08	DOORS & WINDOWS	97.3	27.4	80.4	98.1	50.0	86.5	98.1	49.4	86.3	93.5	32.7	78.8	99.5	54.9	88.8	98.1	54.2	87.5
09200	PLASTER & GYPSUM BOARD	90.4	28.4	52.5	97.6	46.6	66.4	95.5	53.0	69.5	91.7	33.1	55.9	102.1	56.1	74.0	97.6	53.0	70.4
095,098	CEILINGS & ACOUSTICAL TREATMENT	95.5	28.4	51.2	101.1	46.6	65.1	99.5	53.0	68.9	95.5	33.1	54.3	101.7	56.1	71.6	101.1	53.0	69.4
09600	FLOORING	105.5	58.8	94.1	118.7	74.4	107.9	112.6	58.8	99.5	107.4	58.8	95.7	79.3	53.2	73.0	120.0	74.4	108.9
097,099	WALL FINISHES, PAINTS & COATINGS	95.6	29.4	57.1	95.6	67.7	79.4	95.6	51.8	70.1	95.6	43.2	65.1	84.3	60.9	70.7	95.6	51.8	70.1
09	FINISHES	95.5	35.4	64.8	102.0	54.9	78.0	99.5	53.5	76.0	96.5	39.7	67.5	92.6	55.8	73.8	102.4	56.7	79.1
10 - 14	TOTAL DIV. 10000 - 14000	100.0	50.9	89.6	100.0	70.5	93.8	100.0	56.8	90.9	100.0	51.7	89.8	100.0	65.4	92.7	100.0	71.4	94.0
15	MECHANICAL	97.0	33.5	67.6	100.1	50.6	77.2	96.9	49.8	75.1	96.9	39.6	70.4	100.3	50.7	77.3	100.1	57.3	80.3
16	ELECTRICAL	90.0	25.6	45.7	95.6	70.0	78.0	97.7	57.1	69.8	97.9	46.6	62.6	100.7	57.1	70.8	96.7	72.7	80.2
01 - 16	WEIGHTED AVERAGE	92.8	39.5	66.9	96.3	61.6	79.4	95.8	56.9	76.9	93.4	45.3	70.0	95.6	62.5	79.5	96.2	64.0	80.6

		ARKANSAS												CALIFORNIA					
DIVISION		PINE BLUFF			RUSSELLVILLE			TEXARKANA			WEST MEMPHIS			ALHAMBRA			ANAHEIM		
		716			728			718			723			917 - 918			928		
		MAT.	INST.	TOTAL	MAT.	INST.	TOTAL	MAT.	INST.	TOTAL	MAT.	INST.	TOTAL	MAT.	INST.	TOTAL	MAT.	INST.	TOTAL
02	SITE CONSTRUCTION	79.9	83.9	83.0	75.3	83.9	81.9	96.0	84.6	87.3	109.9	99.0	101.6	99.2	108.9	106.6	94.1	110.2	106.5
03100	CONCRETE FORMS & ACCESSORIES	75.0	52.8	55.9	80.3	47.2	51.7	84.1	46.1	51.3	90.2	55.6	60.3	116.3	115.5	115.6	105.2	119.2	117.2
03200	CONCRETE REINFORCEMENT	95.7	71.9	82.2	95.1	55.9	72.7	95.2	52.8	71.0	91.4	54.5	70.4	113.1	117.2	115.4	106.8	117.3	112.8
03300	CAST-IN-PLACE CONCRETE	85.9	52.0	71.9	85.8	51.6	71.7	85.8	49.7	70.9	92.4	63.7	80.6	101.1	111.9	105.6	102.3	116.3	108.1
03	CONCRETE	85.6	56.8	71.2	83.3	51.3	67.3	81.1	49.6	65.4	91.0	60.0	75.5	115.1	113.5	114.3	112.1	116.9	114.5
04	MASONRY	115.0	58.4	80.2	97.0	49.7	67.9	97.1	38.5	61.1	79.6	54.9	64.4	133.1	114.9	121.9	87.8	116.5	105.4
05	METALS	95.4	72.5	87.1	94.8	65.5	84.2	87.7	64.2	79.2	90.2	82.3	87.4	92.9	97.3	94.5	110.5	101.4	107.2
06	WOOD & PLASTICS	75.7	53.6	64.3	81.6	47.3	63.9	85.7	49.4	66.9	90.6	57.0	73.2	102.1	113.7	108.1	99.5	117.7	108.9
07	THERMAL & MOISTURE PROTECTION	96.8	55.1	77.0	98.0	52.0	76.2	97.7	48.5	74.4	108.7	59.3	85.3	106.2	111.5	108.7	121.8	116.7	119.4
08	DOORS & WINDOWS	93.5	54.2	84.0	97.3	46.6	85.0	98.5	47.0	86.1	99.5	54.9	88.8	98.2	112.1	101.6	105.8	115.1	108.1
09200	PLASTER & GYPSUM BOARD	91.2	53.0	67.9	92.5	46.6	64.5	94.2	48.7	66.4	104.2	56.1	74.8	88.7	114.5	104.5	94.8	118.4	109.3
095,098	CEILINGS & ACOUSTICAL TREATMENT	97.0	53.0	68.0	95.5	46.6	63.2	103.8	48.7	67.5	100.2	56.1	71.1	109.7	114.5	112.9	118.1	118.4	118.3
09600	FLOORING	107.2	74.4	99.3	108.8	58.8	96.7	110.1	50.8	95.7	82.3	53.2	75.2	115.5	109.4	114.0	123.1	110.5	120.0
097,099	WALL FINISHES, PAINTS & COATINGS	95.6	51.8	70.1	95.6	51.8	70.1	95.6	42.7	64.8	84.3	60.9	70.7	114.6	114.6	114.6	111.3	116.0	114.0
09	FINISHES	96.8	56.7	76.3	97.0	49.9	73.0	99.8	46.7	72.7	94.1	55.8	74.5	108.4	114.1	111.3	112.9	117.1	115.1
10 - 14	TOTAL DIV. 10000 - 14000	100.0	71.4	94.0	100.0	56.0	90.7	100.0	46.6	88.7	100.0	65.4	92.7	100.0	111.9	102.5	100.0	115.8	103.3
15	MECHANICAL	100.1	53.5	78.5	97.0	43.5	72.2	100.1	44.8	74.5	97.1	50.7	75.7	96.9	111.5	103.6	100.3	114.1	106.7
16	ELECTRICAL	94.5	72.7	79.5	95.6	57.1	69.1	97.7	47.6	63.2	103.4	57.1	71.6	114.9	113.5	114.0	95.0	109.9	105.2
01 - 16	WEIGHTED AVERAGE	95.9	63.3	80.1	94.4	54.9	75.2	94.9	51.5	73.8	95.6	62.5	79.5	104.0	111.2	107.5	104.7	113.0	108.7

		CALIFORNIA																	
DIVISION		BAKERSFIELD			BERKELEY			EUREKA			FRESNO			INGLEWOOD			LONG BEACH		
		932 - 933			947			955			936 - 938			903 - 905			906 - 908		
		MAT.	INST.	TOTAL	MAT.	INST.	TOTAL	MAT.	INST.	TOTAL	MAT.	INST.	TOTAL	MAT.	INST.	TOTAL	MAT.	INST.	TOTAL
02	SITE CONSTRUCTION	98.7	107.1	105.2	120.7	103.9	107.9	109.6	105.8	106.6	100.2	107.2	105.5	83.4	105.9	100.6	90.4	105.9	102.3
03100	CONCRETE FORMS & ACCESSORIES	96.3	118.9	115.8	123.0	133.9	132.4	116.9	120.0	119.6	101.8	121.7	118.9	112.8	115.2	114.9	105.3	115.2	113.9
03200	CONCRETE REINFORCEMENT	106.4	117.1	112.5	96.6	118.0	108.8	103.1	117.9	111.6	106.9	117.1	112.7	108.3	117.3	113.4	107.4	117.2	113.0
03300	CAST-IN-PLACE CONCRETE	97.7	115.1	104.9	131.5	118.0	125.9	106.0	113.6	109.1	106.9	115.7	110.5	82.1	112.1	94.5	93.5	112.1	101.2
03	CONCRETE	109.2	116.2	112.7	124.2	124.2	124.2	123.9	116.3	120.1	114.2	117.7	115.9	101.3	113.5	107.4	111.9	113.5	112.7
04	MASONRY	107.2	113.3	111.0	137.2	125.5	130.0	112.9	126.1	121.0	109.7	112.4	111.4	82.3	115.0	102.4	91.4	115.0	105.9
05	METALS	105.0	100.5	103.4	106.4	105.9	106.2	110.0	101.1	106.8	106.9	101.0	104.8	105.2	98.5	102.8	105.1	98.5	102.7
06	WOOD & PLASTICS	89.1	117.9	104.0	122.0	135.3	128.9	114.2	120.6	117.5	101.4	120.6	111.4	103.9	113.5	108.9	96.2	113.5	105.1
07	THERMAL & MOISTURE PROTECTION	105.9	110.1	107.9	111.5	129.6	120.1	112.9	111.7	112.3	102.3	111.2	106.5	113.9	112.9	113.4	114.1	112.9	113.5
08	DOORS & WINDOWS	104.6	113.4	106.7	108.5	127.6	113.1	105.9	111.6	107.2	104.6	115.3	107.2	94.9	112.0	99.1	94.9	112.0	99.0
09200	PLASTER & GYPSUM BOARD	94.8	118.4	109.3	94.0	136.2	119.8	99.6	121.3	112.9	94.0	121.3	110.7	88.7	114.5	104.5	86.5	114.5	103.6
095,098	CEILINGS & ACOUSTICAL TREATMENT	118.1	118.4	118.3	112.5	136.2	128.1	124.6	121.3	122.4	118.1	121.3	120.2	107.0	114.5	112.0	107.0	114.5	112.0
09600	FLOORING	118.6	73.3	107.6	114.4	120.7	116.0	123.4	125.3	123.9	119.3	143.2	125.1	117.5	109.4	115.5	114.1	109.4	113.0
097,099	WALL FINISHES, PAINTS & COATINGS	114.4	106.0	109.5	118.3	133.2	126.9	113.9	71.1	89.0	113.9	101.7	106.8	108.6	114.6	112.1	108.6	114.6	112.1
09	FINISHES	114.1	109.6	111.8	113.9	132.3	123.3	118.3	116.6	117.4	114.2	123.9	119.2	107.4	113.9	110.7	106.3	113.9	110.2
10 - 14	TOTAL DIV. 10000 - 14000	100.0	130.8	106.5	100.0	136.1	107.6	100.0	132.1	106.8	100.0	133.3	107.0	100.0	111.4	102.4	100.0	111.4	102.4
15	MECHANICAL	100.3	112.7	106.0	97.0	136.4	115.2	97.1	114.9	105.4	100.3	115.1	107.1	97.1	111.4	103.7	97.1	111.4	103.7
16	ELECTRICAL	95.4	94.2	94.6	114.8	130.5	125.6	105.2	98.4	100.5	94.1	99.6	97.9	115.3	113.5	114.1	114.8	113.5	113.9
01 - 16	WEIGHTED AVERAGE	104.1	108.5	106.3	110.2	125.7	117.7	108.5	111.7	110.0	105.2	112.0	108.5	100.6	111.1	105.7	102.4	111.1	106.6

		CALIFORNIA																	
DIVISION		LOS ANGELES			MARYSVILLE			MODESTO			MOJAVE			OAKLAND			OXNARD		
		900 - 902			959			953			935			946			930		
		MAT.	INST.	TOTAL	MAT.	INST.	TOTAL	MAT.	INST.	TOTAL	MAT.	INST.	TOTAL	MAT.	INST.	TOTAL	MAT.	INST.	TOTAL
02	SITE CONSTRUCTION	89.5	109.0	104.5	105.3	106.0	105.9	98.4	106.5	104.6	93.4	106.9	103.7	128.3	104.0	109.7	99.8	104.8	103.6
03100	CONCRETE FORMS & ACCESSORIES	108.8	118.7	117.3	103.0	120.9	118.4	97.5	121.7	118.4	112.1	115.5	115.0	107.7	136.7	132.7	103.1	119.3	117.1
03200	CONCRETE REINFORCEMENT	108.3	117.2	113.4	103.1	117.2	111.1	106.9	117.3	112.8	108.4	117.0	113.3	98.8	118.0	109.8	106.4	117.1	112.5
03300	CAST-IN-PLACE CONCRETE	89.4	113.5	99.3	118.4	114.5	116.8	106.0	115.7	110.0	89.1	116.1	100.2	127.9	118.4	124.0	103.7	115.4	108.5
03	CONCRETE	108.2	115.6	111.9	124.3	116.9	120.6	113.4	117.7	115.6	102.9	115.0	109.0	125.9	125.6	125.7	112.3	116.9	114.6
04	MASONRY	97.8	116.5	109.3	113.8	112.1	112.7	111.7	115.6	114.1	107.6	116.3	112.9	145.5	125.5	133.2	112.4	112.4	112.4
05	METALS	111.2	99.3	106.9	109.3	100.4	106.1	106.5	101.4	104.7	106.3	99.1	103.7	101.7	106.4	103.4	104.4	100.8	103.1
06	WOOD & PLASTICS	99.6	117.3	108.7	99.6	120.6	110.5	93.4	120.6	107.5	104.5	112.1	108.4	106.4	139.1	123.3	98.1	117.9	108.3
07	THERMAL & MOISTURE PROTECTION	114.2	114.6	114.4	112.0	113.5	112.7	111.4	114.3	112.8	106.4	110.5	108.4	111.7	130.0	120.4	111.3	114.1	112.6
08	DOORS & WINDOWS	99.1	114.8	102.9	105.0	115.9	107.6	103.9	116.5	106.9	100.2	110.3	102.7	108.6	129.7	113.7	103.4	115.1	106.3
09200	PLASTER & GYPSUM BOARD	88.9	118.4	106.9	95.1	121.3	111.1	95.7	121.3	111.3	102.4	112.4	108.5	89.1	140.0	120.2	94.8	118.4	109.3
095,098	CEILINGS & ACOUSTICAL TREATMENT	115.2	118.4	117.3	123.2	121.3	121.9	115.0	121.3	119.1	123.2	112.4	116.1	116.9	140.0	132.2	118.1	118.4	118.3
09600	FLOORING	115.7	110.5	114.4	117.9	111.4	116.4	118.6	111.4	116.8	125.8	72.5	112.9	108.8	120.7	111.7	118.6	110.5	116.6
097,099	WALL FINISHES, PAINTS & COATINGS	108.6	114.8	112.2	113.9	114.3	114.1	113.9	94.4	102.5	113.9	98.3	104.8	118.3	133.2	126.9	113.9	109.3	111.2
09	FINISHES	108.5	116.6	112.7	115.1	119.4	117.3	113.5	117.6	115.6	118.2	106.0	112.0	112.6	134.4	123.7	113.9	116.4	115.2
10 - 14	TOTAL DIV. 10000 - 14000	100.0	114.5	103.1	100.0	132.7	106.9	100.0	133.4	107.0	100.0	131.3	106.6	100.0	136.6	107.7	100.0	116.1	103.4
15	MECHANICAL	100.2	114.0	106.6	97.1	113.1	104.5	100.3	115.1	107.1	97.1	114.3	105.1	100.1	136.4	116.9	100.3	114.1	106.7
16	ELECTRICAL	109.8	113.6	112.4	99.5	99.5	99.5	103.4	112.7	109.8	93.6	94.2	94.0	113.6	130.5	125.2	99.2	113.1	108.8
01 - 16	WEIGHTED AVERAGE	104.3	112.9	108.5	107.3	110.8	109.0	105.8	113.8	109.7	102.7	108.2	105.4	110.7	126.3	118.3	105.2	112.4	108.7

CALIFORNIA

DIVISION		PALM SPRINGS 922			PALO ALTO 943			PASADENA 910 - 912			REDDING 960			RICHMOND 948			RIVERSIDE 925		
		MAT.	INST.	TOTAL	MAT.	INST.	TOTAL	MAT.	INST.	TOTAL	MAT.	INST.	TOTAL	MAT.	INST.	TOTAL	MAT.	INST.	TOTAL
02	SITE CONSTRUCTION	85.7	107.3	102.3	115.8	103.9	106.7	95.8	108.6	105.6	105.0	106.0	105.8	127.7	103.9	109.5	92.0	107.9	104.1
03100	CONCRETE FORMS & ACCESSORIES	101.1	115.6	113.6	104.9	134.0	130.0	101.1	115.3	113.4	102.7	120.8	118.3	127.0	136.5	135.2	106.3	119.1	117.3
03200	CONCRETE REINFORCEMENT	108.6	117.0	113.4	96.6	118.2	108.9	114.1	117.2	115.8	103.1	117.2	111.1	96.6	118.0	108.8	105.4	117.1	112.1
03300	CAST-IN-PLACE CONCRETE	93.2	115.0	102.1	111.2	118.1	114.0	95.9	111.7	102.4	117.4	114.5	116.2	127.9	118.3	124.0	101.3	116.3	107.5
03	CONCRETE	104.3	114.7	109.5	111.4	124.3	117.9	109.4	113.3	111.4	123.0	116.8	119.9	127.0	125.4	126.2	111.5	116.8	114.2
04	MASONRY	84.4	112.3	101.6	114.3	129.0	123.3	114.6	114.9	114.8	113.8	112.1	112.7	136.9	125.5	129.6	85.3	113.7	102.8
05	METALS	110.3	99.7	106.5	99.7	106.3	102.1	92.9	96.7	94.3	108.9	100.3	105.8	99.7	105.8	101.9	110.5	101.1	107.1
06	WOOD & PLASTICS	94.2	114.0	104.4	103.6	135.3	120.0	86.5	113.7	100.6	99.2	120.6	110.3	126.7	139.1	133.1	99.5	117.7	108.9
07	THERMAL & MOISTURE PROTECTION	120.4	114.3	117.5	111.1	129.9	120.0	105.6	111.5	108.4	112.0	112.8	112.4	112.1	130.0	120.6	120.8	115.4	118.3
08	DOORS & WINDOWS	102.7	113.0	105.2	108.6	127.8	113.2	98.2	110.7	101.2	106.3	112.5	107.8	108.6	129.7	113.7	105.8	115.1	108.1
09200	PLASTER & GYPSUM BOARD	92.9	114.5	106.1	88.2	136.2	117.6	84.4	114.5	102.8	95.3	121.3	111.2	95.6	140.0	122.8	94.6	118.4	109.2
095,098	CEILINGS & ACOUSTICAL TREATMENT	113.7	114.5	114.2	113.8	136.2	128.6	109.7	114.5	112.9	127.6	121.3	123.4	113.8	140.0	131.1	116.7	118.4	117.8
09600	FLOORING	120.7	104.9	116.9	107.9	120.7	111.0	109.9	109.4	109.7	117.8	111.4	116.3	116.4	120.7	117.5	123.0	110.5	120.0
097,099	WALL FINISHES, PAINTS & COATINGS	111.3	114.6	113.2	118.3	131.4	125.9	114.6	114.6	114.6	113.9	114.3	114.1	118.3	133.2	126.9	111.3	116.0	114.0
09	FINISHES	110.5	113.5	112.0	111.0	132.1	121.7	105.8	114.1	110.0	115.9	119.4	117.7	115.5	134.4	125.2	112.4	117.1	114.8
10 - 14	TOTAL DIV. 10000 - 14000	100.0	112.6	102.7	100.0	136.1	107.6	100.0	111.9	102.5	100.0	132.7	106.9	100.0	136.5	107.7	100.0	115.8	103.3
15	MECHANICAL	97.1	113.3	104.6	97.0	146.2	119.7	96.9	111.5	103.6	100.3	113.1	106.2	97.0	134.4	114.3	100.2	111.5	105.4
16	ELECTRICAL	101.0	105.5	104.1	113.4	137.7	130.1	110.4	113.5	112.6	104.4	99.5	101.0	114.8	121.0	119.0	95.1	105.5	102.2
01 - 16	WEIGHTED AVERAGE	102.3	110.3	106.2	105.5	129.2	117.0	101.3	111.1	106.1	108.3	110.6	109.4	110.0	124.3	116.9	104.3	111.7	107.9

CALIFORNIA

DIVISION		SACRAMENTO 942,956 - 958			SALINAS 939			SAN BERNARDINO 923 - 924			SAN DIEGO 919 - 921			SAN FRANCISCO 940 - 941			SAN JOSE 951		
		MAT.	INST.	TOTAL	MAT.	INST.	TOTAL	MAT.	INST.	TOTAL	MAT.	INST.	TOTAL	MAT.	INST.	TOTAL	MAT.	INST.	TOTAL
02	SITE CONSTRUCTION	95.9	110.5	107.1	116.0	107.1	109.2	71.0	107.4	98.9	100.6	102.1	101.8	130.3	110.5	115.2	136.3	100.4	108.8
03100	CONCRETE FORMS & ACCESSORIES	106.2	121.2	119.2	107.9	122.3	120.3	111.2	115.3	114.7	106.6	113.8	112.8	108.0	137.5	133.4	105.5	136.9	132.6
03200	CONCRETE REINFORCEMENT	99.9	117.2	108.8	106.9	117.9	113.2	105.4	117.1	112.1	110.5	116.9	114.1	112.6	118.4	115.9	103.4	118.3	111.9
03300	CAST-IN-PLACE CONCRETE	111.0	114.8	112.6	102.4	115.0	107.6	69.9	114.5	88.3	105.2	105.0	105.1	127.8	120.1	124.6	123.2	118.8	121.4
03	CONCRETE	117.6	117.1	117.4	125.8	117.8	121.8	81.5	114.4	98.0	116.1	110.5	113.3	127.6	126.6	127.1	122.0	126.0	124.0
04	MASONRY	117.2	112.1	114.1	107.0	123.2	117.0	93.1	111.4	104.4	105.4	110.9	108.7	145.8	130.6	136.4	149.4	129.1	136.9
05	METALS	97.7	100.3	98.6	109.5	102.4	107.0	110.4	99.8	106.6	110.6	100.2	106.8	106.8	107.9	107.2	111.1	108.4	110.2
06	WOOD & PLASTICS	101.1	120.7	111.2	103.8	121.6	113.0	104.4	114.0	109.3	100.1	111.1	105.8	106.4	139.3	123.4	106.0	139.0	123.1
07	THERMAL & MOISTURE PROTECTION	121.3	113.4	117.5	108.1	120.0	113.7	119.2	114.8	117.1	114.7	107.8	111.4	111.7	132.0	121.3	107.9	130.8	118.7
08	DOORS & WINDOWS	120.6	116.5	119.6	104.8	120.3	108.6	102.7	112.3	105.0	104.6	110.9	106.1	111.1	129.3	115.5	95.4	129.7	103.7
09200	PLASTER & GYPSUM BOARD	87.8	121.3	108.2	96.4	122.2	112.2	96.1	114.5	107.4	88.1	111.4	102.4	90.9	140.0	120.9	95.3	140.0	122.6
095,098	CEILINGS & ACOUSTICAL TREATMENT	125.0	121.3	122.5	123.2	122.2	122.5	115.0	114.5	114.7	117.9	111.4	113.6	123.4	140.0	134.4	109.9	140.0	129.8
09600	FLOORING	111.2	111.4	111.3	119.5	120.7	119.8	125.2	105.1	120.3	119.1	109.8	116.8	108.8	120.7	111.7	115.5	120.7	116.8
097,099	WALL FINISHES, PAINTS & COATINGS	116.7	114.3	115.3	113.9	131.4	124.1	111.3	114.6	113.2	111.9	116.0	114.3	118.3	134.1	127.5	115.6	131.4	124.8
09	FINISHES	113.1	119.5	116.4	116.8	123.6	120.2	111.8	113.3	112.5	111.5	113.2	112.4	114.1	134.6	124.6	113.1	134.2	123.9
10 - 14	TOTAL DIV. 10000 - 14000	100.0	132.8	106.9	100.0	132.9	106.9	100.0	112.2	102.6	100.0	115.2	103.2	100.0	137.3	107.9	100.0	136.4	107.7
15	MECHANICAL	100.0	118.2	108.4	97.1	114.3	105.1	97.1	112.9	104.4	100.1	114.1	106.6	100.1	159.3	127.5	100.3	146.3	121.5
16	ELECTRICAL	104.0	100.4	101.5	94.0	116.3	109.4	101.0	108.8	106.4	92.8	93.9	93.6	109.3	140.3	130.6	109.9	137.7	129.0
01 - 16	WEIGHTED AVERAGE	107.5	112.4	109.9	107.1	116.2	111.6	99.8	110.6	105.0	105.6	107.0	106.3	111.9	133.9	122.6	110.2	129.7	119.7

CALIFORNIA

DIVISION		SAN LUIS OBISPO 934			SAN MATEO 944			SAN RAFAEL 949			SANTA ANA 926 - 927			SANTA BARBARA 931			SANTA CRUZ 950		
		MAT.	INST.	TOTAL	MAT.	INST.	TOTAL	MAT.	INST.	TOTAL	MAT.	INST.	TOTAL	MAT.	INST.	TOTAL	MAT.	INST.	TOTAL
02	SITE CONSTRUCTION	107.0	106.7	106.8	124.6	103.9	108.8	109.1	110.4	110.1	83.9	107.4	101.9	100.2	107.2	105.5	136.7	100.3	108.8
03100	CONCRETE FORMS & ACCESSORIES	114.6	115.8	115.7	113.3	136.4	133.2	121.5	136.5	134.5	112.1	115.6	115.1	103.8	119.1	117.0	105.5	122.5	120.2
03200	CONCRETE REINFORCEMENT	108.4	117.1	113.3	96.6	118.1	108.9	97.4	118.2	109.3	109.2	117.1	113.7	106.4	116.9	112.4	120.5	117.9	119.0
03300	CAST-IN-PLACE CONCRETE	110.1	113.9	111.7	123.8	118.3	121.5	144.1	117.1	133.0	89.4	115.0	99.9	103.3	115.2	108.2	122.3	117.5	120.3
03	CONCRETE	122.3	114.4	118.4	122.5	125.4	124.0	149.7	124.8	137.3	101.6	114.7	108.2	112.4	116.3	114.4	123.7	119.1	121.4
04	MASONRY	109.1	112.0	110.9	136.6	128.3	131.5	111.4	129.5	122.5	81.4	112.8	100.7	107.6	109.8	109.0	149.6	123.4	133.5
05	METALS	106.7	99.6	104.2	99.6	105.8	101.8	101.0	102.0	101.4	110.5	99.8	106.7	104.3	100.4	102.9	112.3	107.2	110.5
06	WOOD & PLASTICS	107.0	114.1	110.7	112.3	139.1	126.2	112.9	138.8	126.3	106.5	114.0	110.4	98.1	117.9	108.3	106.0	121.7	114.1
07	THERMAL & MOISTURE PROTECTION	107.8	112.7	110.1	111.7	129.0	119.9	127.8	129.6	128.6	120.9	114.4	117.8	107.0	112.0	109.4	107.9	123.8	115.4
08	DOORS & WINDOWS	102.6	111.4	104.7	108.6	129.2	113.5	119.4	129.5	121.8	101.9	113.0	104.6	104.6	115.1	107.2	97.6	120.4	103.1
09200	PLASTER & GYPSUM BOARD	103.3	114.5	110.2	90.8	140.0	120.9	92.1	140.0	121.4	97.0	114.5	107.7	94.8	118.4	109.3	97.6	122.2	112.6
095,098	CEILINGS & ACOUSTICAL TREATMENT	123.2	114.5	117.5	113.8	140.0	131.1	122.0	140.0	133.9	115.0	114.5	114.7	118.1	118.4	118.3	119.1	122.2	121.2
09600	FLOORING	127.3	99.1	120.4	110.9	110.4	110.8	120.7	131.7	123.4	125.9	108.7	121.7	118.6	99.1	113.8	115.5	120.7	116.8
097,099	WALL FINISHES, PAINTS & COATINGS	113.9	109.3	111.2	118.3	121.2	120.0	113.9	127.1	121.5	111.3	114.6	113.2	113.9	109.3	111.2	115.6	131.4	124.8
09	FINISHES	119.7	112.0	115.7	112.8	130.9	122.1	114.8	135.4	125.3	113.1	114.1	113.6	114.1	114.5	114.3	115.1	123.7	119.5
10 - 14	TOTAL DIV. 10000 - 14000	100.0	129.9	106.3	100.0	136.6	107.7	100.0	135.6	107.5	100.0	112.6	102.7	100.0	116.1	103.4	100.0	133.4	107.0
15	MECHANICAL	97.1	113.4	104.7	97.0	132.6	113.5	96.9	157.6	125.0	97.1	112.2	104.1	100.3	114.1	106.7	100.3	114.4	106.8
16	ELECTRICAL	93.6	107.8	103.4	113.4	135.0	128.2	106.7	107.8	107.4	101.0	109.9	107.1	91.9	106.0	101.6	107.7	116.4	113.7
01 - 16	WEIGHTED AVERAGE	106.2	110.7	108.4	108.7	126.1	117.2	111.9	127.2	119.3	102.1	111.0	106.4	104.4	110.8	107.5	110.9	116.3	113.6

CALIFORNIA / COLORADO

DIVISION		SANTA ROSA 954 MAT.	INST.	TOTAL	STOCKTON 952 MAT.	INST.	TOTAL	SUSANVILLE 961 MAT.	INST.	TOTAL	VALLEJO 945 MAT.	INST.	TOTAL	VAN NUYS 913-916 MAT.	INST.	TOTAL	ALAMOSA 811 MAT.	INST.	TOTAL
02	SITE CONSTRUCTION	98.7	106.6	104.8	98.1	106.4	104.5	112.7	106.1	107.6	92.5	110.7	106.4	114.4	108.6	110.0	140.2	93.6	104.5
03100	CONCRETE FORMS & ACCESSORIES	102.6	136.5	131.8	97.5	121.6	118.3	104.6	120.9	118.6	108.1	136.2	132.3	110.0	115.4	114.6	104.3	56.8	63.3
03200	CONCRETE REINFORCEMENT	104.1	118.3	112.2	106.9	117.3	112.8	103.1	117.2	111.1	98.5	118.2	109.7	114.1	117.2	115.9	109.8	63.6	83.5
03300	CAST-IN-PLACE CONCRETE	116.3	117.4	116.8	103.2	115.6	108.3	106.8	114.5	110.0	114.8	117.1	115.7	101.2	111.7	105.5	107.9	58.5	87.5
03	CONCRETE	124.3	125.0	124.6	112.1	117.7	114.9	126.3	116.9	121.6	119.4	124.7	122.0	127.3	113.3	120.3	120.9	59.5	90.2
04	MASONRY	113.0	130.4	123.7	112.1	115.6	114.2	112.8	112.1	112.4	83.3	129.4	111.6	133.1	114.9	121.9	139.9	63.4	92.9
05	METALS	110.9	104.0	108.4	106.5	101.4	104.7	109.4	100.3	106.2	101.0	102.5	101.5	92.2	96.8	93.8	100.5	76.0	91.6
06	WOOD & PLASTICS	95.7	138.7	117.9	93.4	126.0	110.5	101.3	120.6	111.3	99.6	138.8	119.9	95.5	113.7	104.9	100.3	54.3	76.5
07	THERMAL & MOISTURE PROTECTION	121.5	129.9	125.5	111.4	113.4	112.4	112.9	112.5	112.7	125.6	129.9	127.7	107.2	111.5	109.2	107.1	75.0	91.9
08	DOORS & WINDOWS	103.5	129.0	109.7	103.9	116.5	106.9	106.2	114.9	108.3	122.0	129.0	123.7	98.1	112.1	101.5	94.2	54.1	84.5
09200	PLASTER & GYPSUM BOARD	93.5	140.0	122.0	95.7	121.3	111.3	95.5	121.3	111.2	88.2	140.0	119.9	86.3	114.5	103.6	86.9	52.5	65.9
095,098	CEILINGS & ACOUSTICAL TREATMENT	115.0	140.0	131.5	118.1	121.3	120.2	123.2	121.3	121.9	125.0	140.0	134.9	108.4	114.5	112.4	95.1	52.5	67.0
09600	FLOORING	121.3	120.7	121.1	118.6	111.4	116.8	118.6	111.4	116.8	115.5	120.7	116.8	113.2	109.4	112.3	116.1	83.0	108.0
097,099	WALL FINISHES, PAINTS & COATINGS	111.3	130.1	122.2	113.9	98.9	105.2	113.9	114.3	114.1	114.6	133.2	125.4	114.6	114.6	114.6	122.6	36.3	72.5
09	FINISHES	111.9	133.7	123.0	114.1	118.1	116.1	116.1	119.4	117.8	111.7	134.1	123.1	108.0	114.1	111.1	104.4	58.7	81.1
10-14	TOTAL DIV. 10000-14000	100.0	135.4	107.5	100.0	133.4	107.0	100.0	132.7	106.9	100.0	135.6	107.5	100.0	111.9	102.5	100.0	68.8	93.4
15	MECHANICAL	97.1	159.0	125.8	100.3	114.0	106.6	97.1	113.1	104.5	100.0	130.9	114.3	96.9	110.4	103.1	96.9	65.4	82.4
16	ELECTRICAL	101.5	107.8	105.8	103.4	109.1	107.4	105.0	99.5	101.2	99.8	117.9	112.2	110.4	113.5	112.6	95.3	81.9	86.1
01-16	WEIGHTED AVERAGE	107.2	127.1	116.9	105.7	113.0	109.3	108.4	110.7	109.5	106.0	123.6	114.6	105.3	110.9	108.1	105.1	70.0	88.0

COLORADO

DIVISION		BOULDER 803 MAT.	INST.	TOTAL	COLORADO SPRINGS 808-809 MAT.	INST.	TOTAL	DENVER 800-802 MAT.	INST.	TOTAL	DURANGO 813 MAT.	INST.	TOTAL	FORT COLLINS 805 MAT.	INST.	TOTAL	FORT MORGAN 807 MAT.	INST.	TOTAL
02	SITE CONSTRUCTION	108.7	100.3	102.3	110.1	98.3	101.1	108.4	107.8	107.9	133.0	93.6	102.8	121.3	101.5	106.2	110.5	101.4	103.6
03100	CONCRETE FORMS & ACCESSORIES	113.5	56.0	63.9	93.4	76.2	78.6	103.8	81.3	84.4	117.8	55.9	64.4	103.2	75.1	79.0	115.1	74.9	80.4
03200	CONCRETE REINFORCEMENT	102.7	58.1	77.3	98.9	80.8	88.6	98.4	81.5	88.7	109.8	80.2	92.9	103.7	80.4	90.2	103.7	67.9	83.3
03300	CAST-IN-PLACE CONCRETE	106.6	68.7	91.0	110.8	85.6	100.4	103.7	85.9	96.3	124.1	58.0	96.8	120.4	82.1	104.6	104.6	69.1	90.0
03	CONCRETE	111.7	61.4	86.5	103.8	80.7	92.2	108.3	83.1	95.7	124.2	62.0	93.1	123.0	78.9	101.0	110.2	71.9	91.1
04	MASONRY	103.2	47.7	69.1	108.3	69.4	84.4	107.6	83.3	92.7	126.1	63.4	87.5	121.3	69.1	89.3	119.5	69.1	88.5
05	METALS	100.1	66.8	88.1	101.6	85.9	96.0	105.2	86.8	98.5	100.5	82.6	94.0	101.0	83.6	94.7	99.9	78.0	92.0
06	WOOD & PLASTICS	111.3	56.8	83.1	91.4	76.5	83.7	101.5	82.2	91.5	114.9	53.4	83.1	101.2	76.2	88.3	112.9	76.2	93.9
07	THERMAL & MOISTURE PROTECTION	107.0	66.0	87.6	107.5	81.4	95.1	106.8	84.8	96.4	107.1	68.5	88.8	107.4	76.3	92.6	107.0	76.3	92.4
08	DOORS & WINDOWS	96.6	49.6	85.3	99.2	82.1	95.1	98.6	85.2	95.3	101.5	58.4	91.1	96.6	74.4	91.2	96.6	70.8	90.4
09200	PLASTER & GYPSUM BOARD	99.4	55.6	72.7	89.2	75.7	81.0	97.4	81.9	87.9	92.9	51.6	67.7	96.4	75.7	83.8	99.9	75.7	85.1
095,098	CEILINGS & ACOUSTICAL TREATMENT	90.7	55.6	67.6	97.5	75.7	83.1	96.2	81.9	86.7	95.1	51.6	66.4	90.7	75.7	80.8	90.7	75.7	80.8
09600	FLOORING	117.1	83.0	108.8	111.8	94.1	107.5	112.8	86.6	106.4	121.2	83.0	111.9	112.7	83.0	105.5	117.7	83.0	109.2
097,099	WALL FINISHES, PAINTS & COATINGS	111.9	38.5	69.2	111.9	62.4	83.1	111.9	76.8	91.5	122.6	36.3	72.5	111.9	61.9	82.8	111.9	76.8	91.5
09	FINISHES	102.5	58.7	80.2	100.5	76.9	88.5	101.6	81.5	91.4	106.3	58.2	81.8	101.1	75.2	87.9	102.7	76.9	89.5
10-14	TOTAL DIV. 10000-14000	100.0	65.1	92.6	100.0	85.0	96.8	100.0	85.8	97.0	100.0	68.7	93.4	100.0	71.6	94.0	100.0	71.7	94.0
15	MECHANICAL	97.0	77.4	87.9	100.2	80.9	91.3	100.1	84.7	93.0	96.9	45.8	73.3	100.1	83.3	92.3	97.0	83.0	90.5
16	ELECTRICAL	90.1	70.4	76.6	95.2	85.7	88.7	97.3	90.4	92.6	94.4	75.0	81.1	90.1	70.4	76.6	90.4	89.5	89.8
01-16	WEIGHTED AVERAGE	100.7	68.4	85.0	101.3	82.4	92.1	102.5	87.4	95.2	105.7	65.9	86.3	104.1	79.2	91.9	101.5	81.0	91.5

COLORADO

DIVISION		GLENWOOD SPRINGS 816 MAT.	INST.	TOTAL	GOLDEN 804 MAT.	INST.	TOTAL	GRAND JUNCTION 815 MAT.	INST.	TOTAL	GREELEY 806 MAT.	INST.	TOTAL	MONTROSE 814 MAT.	INST.	TOTAL	PUEBLO 810 MAT.	INST.	TOTAL
02	SITE CONSTRUCTION	150.2	101.0	112.5	125.4	101.8	107.3	131.4	100.1	107.5	106.3	100.3	101.7	143.0	96.5	107.3	122.7	94.9	101.4
03100	CONCRETE FORMS & ACCESSORIES	100.1	66.0	70.7	97.0	75.5	78.4	113.0	51.6	60.0	100.2	55.9	62.0	99.5	52.1	58.6	107.0	76.5	80.7
03200	CONCRETE REINFORCEMENT	107.4	80.1	91.8	103.7	80.0	90.2	108.9	80.2	92.5	102.7	58.1	77.2	107.3	80.2	91.9	101.5	80.7	89.7
03300	CAST-IN-PLACE CONCRETE	107.8	58.4	87.5	104.7	82.2	95.4	119.4	51.2	91.3	100.6	68.7	87.4	107.9	52.2	84.9	107.1	86.3	98.5
03	CONCRETE	126.3	66.7	96.5	122.0	79.0	100.5	120.0	57.8	88.9	105.7	61.3	83.5	116.6	58.3	87.5	108.6	81.1	94.9
04	MASONRY	111.8	59.4	79.6	123.1	59.7	84.1	148.4	56.5	91.9	114.9	47.7	73.6	118.0	56.6	80.3	107.9	67.3	82.9
05	METALS	100.2	83.9	94.3	100.0	83.4	94.0	101.5	81.5	94.3	101.0	66.8	88.6	99.2	82.3	93.1	103.0	86.9	97.2
06	WOOD & PLASTICS	94.7	65.9	79.8	94.8	76.2	85.2	108.6	53.0	79.8	98.1	56.8	76.7	94.2	53.2	73.0	103.0	76.8	89.4
07	THERMAL & MOISTURE PROTECTION	106.8	72.7	90.6	108.1	74.2	92.0	105.5	62.4	85.1	106.5	66.1	87.4	107.1	65.3	87.3	104.9	80.1	93.1
08	DOORS & WINDOWS	100.6	76.3	94.8	96.6	81.9	93.1	101.4	58.2	91.0	96.6	49.6	85.2	101.6	58.3	91.2	95.8	82.2	92.6
09200	PLASTER & GYPSUM BOARD	96.7	64.9	77.3	94.3	75.7	82.9	102.3	51.6	71.3	95.6	55.6	71.1	83.0	51.6	63.8	89.5	75.7	81.1
095,098	CEILINGS & ACOUSTICAL TREATMENT	93.8	64.9	74.7	90.7	75.7	80.8	93.8	51.6	66.0	90.7	55.6	67.6	95.1	51.6	66.4	104.7	75.7	85.6
09600	FLOORING	115.0	76.4	105.7	110.0	83.0	103.4	120.7	83.0	111.5	111.2	83.0	104.4	118.4	68.7	106.3	117.0	86.6	109.6
097,099	WALL FINISHES, PAINTS & COATINGS	122.6	76.8	96.0	111.9	76.8	91.5	122.6	36.3	72.5	111.9	38.5	69.2	122.6	36.3	72.5	122.6	57.8	84.9
09	FINISHES	105.7	68.8	86.9	100.6	76.9	88.5	106.8	55.7	80.7	99.8	58.7	78.8	104.6	52.9	78.2	105.3	75.9	90.3
10-14	TOTAL DIV. 10000-14000	100.0	69.1	93.5	100.0	71.7	94.0	100.0	63.9	92.4	100.0	65.1	92.6	100.0	64.5	92.5	100.0	85.9	97.0
15	MECHANICAL	96.9	81.4	89.7	97.0	83.4	90.7	100.1	40.2	72.4	100.1	77.2	89.5	96.9	40.9	71.0	100.1	79.2	90.4
16	ELECTRICAL	90.6	75.0	79.9	90.4	89.6	89.8	94.0	75.0	80.9	90.1	70.4	76.6	94.0	75.0	80.9	95.3	81.9	86.1
01-16	WEIGHTED AVERAGE	104.9	76.1	90.9	103.3	82.0	92.9	107.1	63.6	85.9	100.9	68.4	85.1	103.9	63.2	84.1	102.6	80.9	92.0

COST INDEXES

City Cost Indexes

		COLORADO			CONNECTICUT														
		SALIDA			BRIDGEPORT			BRISTOL			HARTFORD			MERIDEN			NEW BRITAIN		
	DIVISION	812			066			060			061			064			060		
		MAT.	INST.	TOTAL	MAT.	INST.	TOTAL	MAT.	INST.	TOTAL	MAT.	INST.	TOTAL	MAT.	INST.	TOTAL	MAT.	INST.	TOTAL
02	SITE CONSTRUCTION	132.6	97.3	105.5	107.0	105.4	105.8	106.1	105.4	105.6	106.3	105.4	105.6	105.5	106.3	106.1	106.3	105.4	105.6
03100	CONCRETE FORMS & ACCESSORIES	112.1	56.5	64.1	99.3	102.7	102.3	99.3	108.0	106.8	98.4	108.0	106.6	99.1	108.0	106.8	99.7	108.0	106.9
03200	CONCRETE REINFORCEMENT	106.2	63.7	82.0	111.9	119.7	116.3	111.9	119.6	116.3	111.9	119.6	116.3	111.9	119.6	116.3	111.9	119.6	116.3
03300	CAST-IN-PLACE CONCRETE	123.6	57.7	96.4	105.2	114.5	109.0	98.5	114.4	105.1	98.2	114.4	104.9	94.8	114.4	102.9	100.1	114.4	106.0
03	CONCRETE	118.5	59.1	88.8	110.0	109.9	109.9	106.7	112.1	109.4	106.5	112.1	109.3	104.9	112.1	108.5	107.6	112.1	109.8
04	MASONRY	150.2	65.5	98.1	107.4	115.1	112.2	96.8	115.1	108.1	96.8	115.1	108.1	96.5	115.1	108.0	96.9	115.1	108.1
05	METALS	98.9	75.7	90.6	99.0	112.9	104.0	99.0	112.7	103.9	99.6	112.7	104.3	99.0	112.7	103.9	95.8	112.7	101.9
06	WOOD & PLASTICS	106.9	54.1	79.6	100.9	98.6	99.7	100.9	106.1	103.6	100.9	106.1	103.6	100.9	106.1	103.6	100.9	106.1	103.6
07	THERMAL & MOISTURE PROTECTION	105.7	76.8	92.0	99.4	112.4	105.5	99.5	107.5	103.3	98.3	107.5	102.7	99.5	107.5	103.3	99.5	109.5	104.3
08	DOORS & WINDOWS	94.3	54.0	84.5	110.0	111.7	110.4	110.0	111.0	110.3	110.0	111.0	110.3	112.7	115.8	113.4	110.0	111.0	110.3
09200	PLASTER & GYPSUM BOARD	86.4	52.5	65.7	97.8	97.4	97.5	97.8	105.0	102.2	97.8	105.0	102.2	100.1	105.0	103.1	97.8	105.0	102.2
095,098	CEILINGS & ACOUSTICAL TREATMENT	95.1	52.5	67.0	102.6	97.4	99.1	102.6	105.0	104.2	102.6	105.0	104.2	111.8	105.0	107.3	102.6	105.0	104.2
09600	FLOORING	124.1	68.7	110.6	99.9	109.3	102.2	99.9	109.3	102.2	99.9	109.3	102.2	99.9	109.3	102.2	99.9	109.3	102.2
097,099	WALL FINISHES, PAINTS & COATINGS	122.6	36.3	72.5	95.6	111.5	104.8	95.6	110.7	104.4	95.6	110.7	104.4	95.6	109.6	103.7	95.6	110.7	104.4
09	FINISHES	106.1	55.6	80.3	101.2	103.9	102.6	101.2	108.1	104.8	101.2	108.1	104.7	103.2	108.0	105.7	101.2	108.1	104.8
10 - 14	TOTAL DIV. 10000 - 14000	100.0	68.2	93.3	100.0	112.9	102.7	100.0	113.9	102.9	100.0	113.9	102.9	100.0	113.9	102.9	100.0	113.9	102.9
15	MECHANICAL	96.9	65.4	82.3	99.8	104.6	102.0	99.8	104.5	102.0	99.8	104.5	102.0	96.7	104.5	100.3	99.8	104.5	102.0
16	ELECTRICAL	94.3	81.9	85.8	104.0	103.9	104.0	104.0	105.0	104.7	103.2	105.3	104.7	104.0	94.4	97.4	104.0	105.0	104.2
01 - 16	WEIGHTED AVERAGE	105.1	70.1	88.0	103.3	107.6	105.4	102.3	108.5	105.3	102.2	108.5	105.3	101.9	106.9	104.3	101.9	108.5	105.1

		CONNECTICUT																	
		NEW HAVEN			NEW LONDON			NORWALK			STAMFORD			WATERBURY			WILLIMANTIC		
	DIVISION	065			063			068			069			067			062		
		MAT.	INST.	TOTAL	MAT.	INST.	TOTAL	MAT.	INST.	TOTAL	MAT.	INST.	TOTAL	MAT.	INST.	TOTAL	MAT.	INST.	TOTAL
02	SITE CONSTRUCTION	106.1	106.3	106.3	98.7	106.3	104.5	106.8	105.4	105.8	107.5	105.5	105.9	106.5	105.4	105.7	106.8	105.4	105.8
03100	CONCRETE FORMS & ACCESSORIES	99.1	108.2	106.9	99.1	108.0	106.8	99.3	102.9	102.4	99.3	103.1	102.6	99.3	108.1	106.9	99.3	107.8	106.6
03200	CONCRETE REINFORCEMENT	111.9	119.7	116.3	87.8	119.6	105.9	111.9	119.8	116.4	111.9	119.8	116.4	111.9	119.7	116.3	111.9	119.6	116.3
03300	CAST-IN-PLACE CONCRETE	101.8	118.7	108.8	86.8	118.6	99.9	105.3	119.7	110.2	105.2	119.8	111.2	105.2	114.4	109.0	98.2	114.3	104.9
03	CONCRETE	109.3	113.7	111.5	94.7	113.6	104.1	109.2	111.8	110.5	110.0	111.9	111.0	110.0	112.2	111.1	106.6	112.0	109.3
04	MASONRY	97.0	115.1	108.2	95.6	115.1	107.6	97.2	117.4	109.6	97.3	117.4	109.6	97.3	115.1	108.3	96.7	115.1	108.0
05	METALS	96.0	112.9	102.1	95.8	112.7	101.9	99.0	113.2	104.1	99.0	113.4	104.2	99.0	112.8	104.0	98.8	112.5	103.8
06	WOOD & PLASTICS	100.9	106.1	103.6	100.9	106.1	103.6	100.9	98.6	99.7	100.9	98.6	99.7	100.9	106.1	103.6	100.9	106.1	103.6
07	THERMAL & MOISTURE PROTECTION	99.6	110.1	104.6	99.5	108.1	103.6	99.5	113.7	106.2	99.5	113.7	106.2	99.5	109.5	104.3	99.8	107.5	103.4
08	DOORS & WINDOWS	110.0	115.7	111.4	113.5	110.3	112.7	110.0	111.7	110.4	110.0	111.7	110.4	110.0	115.7	111.4	113.5	111.2	113.0
09200	PLASTER & GYPSUM BOARD	97.8	105.0	102.2	97.8	105.0	102.2	97.8	97.4	97.5	97.8	97.4	97.5	97.8	105.0	102.2	97.8	105.0	102.2
095,098	CEILINGS & ACOUSTICAL TREATMENT	102.6	105.0	104.2	99.5	105.0	103.2	102.6	97.4	99.1	102.6	97.4	99.1	102.6	105.0	104.2	99.5	105.0	103.2
09600	FLOORING	99.9	109.3	102.2	99.9	109.3	102.2	99.9	109.3	102.2	99.9	109.3	102.2	99.9	109.3	102.2	99.9	109.3	102.2
097,099	WALL FINISHES, PAINTS & COATINGS	95.6	104.7	100.8	95.6	110.7	104.4	95.6	111.5	104.8	95.6	111.5	104.8	95.6	109.6	103.7	95.6	109.6	103.7
09	FINISHES	101.3	107.5	104.4	100.2	108.1	104.3	101.2	103.9	102.6	101.3	103.9	102.6	101.1	108.0	104.6	100.8	108.0	104.5
10 - 14	TOTAL DIV. 10000 - 14000	100.0	113.9	102.9	100.0	113.9	102.9	100.0	112.9	102.7	100.0	113.1	102.8	100.0	113.9	102.9	100.0	113.9	102.9
15	MECHANICAL	99.8	104.6	102.0	96.7	104.5	100.3	99.8	104.6	102.0	99.8	104.6	102.0	99.8	104.6	102.0	99.8	97.5	98.7
16	ELECTRICAL	104.0	105.0	104.7	98.7	105.0	103.0	104.0	101.4	102.2	104.0	133.9	124.5	103.2	103.9	103.7	104.0	105.3	104.9
01 - 16	WEIGHTED AVERAGE	102.1	109.0	105.5	99.2	108.7	103.9	102.6	107.7	105.1	102.7	113.2	107.8	102.6	108.5	104.8	102.6	107.1	104.8

		D.C.			DELAWARE									FLORIDA					
		WASHINGTON			DOVER			NEWARK			WILMINGTON			DAYTONA BEACH			FORT LAUDERDALE		
	DIVISION	200 - 205			199			197			198			321			333		
		MAT.	INST.	TOTAL	MAT.	INST.	TOTAL	MAT.	INST.	TOTAL	MAT.	INST.	TOTAL	MAT.	INST.	TOTAL	MAT.	INST.	TOTAL
02	SITE CONSTRUCTION	103.0	90.4	93.4	101.8	113.5	110.7	101.8	113.5	110.7	87.0	113.7	107.5	120.4	87.1	94.9	105.6	73.6	81.1
03100	CONCRETE FORMS & ACCESSORIES	97.0	79.3	81.7	100.6	102.0	101.8	100.6	102.0	101.8	100.4	102.0	101.8	96.6	70.6	74.2	93.9	65.1	69.0
03200	CONCRETE REINFORCEMENT	99.2	93.3	95.8	97.6	96.2	96.8	98.5	96.2	97.2	98.5	96.2	97.2	95.8	89.0	91.9	95.8	80.6	87.1
03300	CAST-IN-PLACE CONCRETE	112.6	85.5	101.4	81.7	91.7	85.8	81.7	91.7	85.8	76.8	91.7	82.9	91.0	74.0	84.0	95.5	69.7	84.8
03	CONCRETE	105.1	85.6	95.4	99.8	98.5	99.2	99.9	98.5	99.2	97.5	98.5	98.0	88.9	76.4	82.7	90.9	71.0	81.0
04	MASONRY	90.2	82.0	85.1	96.5	88.0	91.3	96.5	88.0	91.3	100.7	88.0	92.9	86.7	70.2	76.6	86.9	63.4	72.5
05	METALS	96.9	110.2	101.7	98.2	116.3	104.7	98.2	116.3	104.7	97.8	116.3	104.5	99.1	95.5	97.8	98.5	93.3	96.6
06	WOOD & PLASTICS	94.8	79.8	87.0	104.3	104.1	104.2	104.3	104.1	104.2	104.3	104.1	104.2	95.1	71.9	83.1	90.1	66.8	78.1
07	THERMAL & MOISTURE PROTECTION	94.1	83.6	89.1	99.8	103.7	101.7	100.0	103.7	101.7	99.5	103.7	101.5	96.5	73.6	85.7	96.5	68.6	83.3
08	DOORS & WINDOWS	101.9	85.9	98.0	97.7	104.4	99.3	97.7	104.4	99.3	97.4	104.4	99.1	100.7	69.5	93.2	98.3	65.1	90.3
09200	PLASTER & GYPSUM BOARD	102.3	79.0	88.1	106.1	104.1	104.9	106.1	104.1	104.9	105.9	104.1	104.8	107.2	71.5	85.4	106.7	66.3	82.0
095,098	CEILINGS & ACOUSTICAL TREATMENT	103.8	79.0	87.5	104.0	104.1	104.0	104.0	104.1	104.0	101.1	104.1	103.1	95.1	71.5	79.5	95.1	66.3	76.1
09600	FLOORING	96.3	88.3	94.4	80.5	93.1	83.5	80.5	93.1	83.5	80.3	93.1	83.4	115.9	74.2	105.8	115.9	70.8	105.0
097,099	WALL FINISHES, PAINTS & COATINGS	105.7	92.4	97.9	87.1	99.7	94.4	87.1	99.7	94.4	87.1	99.7	94.4	109.2	87.5	96.6	105.6	60.6	79.4
09	FINISHES	97.0	81.9	89.3	98.1	100.1	99.1	98.1	100.1	99.1	97.6	100.1	98.9	106.9	73.1	89.7	104.9	65.2	84.7
10 - 14	TOTAL DIV. 10000 - 14000	100.0	94.1	98.8	100.0	109.6	102.0	100.0	109.6	102.0	100.0	109.6	102.0	100.0	82.2	96.2	100.0	82.3	96.3
15	MECHANICAL	100.1	89.2	95.0	100.2	106.9	103.3	100.2	106.9	103.3	100.2	106.9	103.3	99.9	70.5	86.3	99.9	68.5	85.4
16	ELECTRICAL	97.4	96.4	96.7	100.1	96.2	97.4	100.1	96.2	97.4	99.8	96.2	97.3	96.7	65.6	75.3	96.7	83.6	87.7
01 - 16	WEIGHTED AVERAGE	99.2	90.1	94.8	99.1	102.7	100.9	99.2	102.7	100.9	98.5	102.8	100.6	98.7	75.0	87.2	97.9	73.5	86.0

FLORIDA

DIVISION		FORT MYERS 339,341			GAINESVILLE 326,344			JACKSONVILLE 320,322			LAKELAND 338			MELBOURNE 329			MIAMI 330 - 332,340		
		MAT.	INST.	TOTAL	MAT.	INST.	TOTAL	MAT.	INST.	TOTAL	MAT.	INST.	TOTAL	MAT.	INST.	TOTAL	MAT.	INST.	TOTAL
02	SITE CONSTRUCTION	117.9	86.8	94.0	131.6	86.4	97.0	120.5	87.5	95.2	120.0	86.5	94.3	128.5	87.3	96.9	105.0	73.5	80.9
03100	CONCRETE FORMS & ACCESSORIES	88.4	55.7	60.2	89.7	58.6	62.9	96.3	59.2	64.3	83.5	55.8	59.6	90.3	72.2	74.7	93.7	65.1	69.1
03200	CONCRETE REINFORCEMENT	96.8	70.0	81.5	101.7	61.8	78.9	95.8	62.4	76.8	99.2	70.4	82.8	96.8	89.1	92.4	95.8	80.6	87.2
03300	CAST-IN-PLACE CONCRETE	99.6	62.5	84.3	104.5	53.7	83.6	91.9	58.6	78.2	101.8	63.6	86.1	105.7	75.9	93.4	93.0	70.1	83.5
03	CONCRETE	91.8	62.5	77.1	99.8	59.2	79.5	89.3	61.3	75.3	93.6	62.9	78.3	98.3	77.8	88.1	89.7	71.2	80.4
04	MASONRY	80.8	50.5	62.2	99.7	47.3	67.5	86.1	56.7	68.0	94.4	58.9	72.6	83.0	73.6	77.2	84.4	63.9	71.8
05	METALS	100.7	87.7	96.0	97.0	83.8	92.2	98.7	85.1	93.8	100.5	87.5	95.8	107.1	95.8	103.0	99.0	93.1	96.9
06	WOOD & PLASTICS	86.8	55.6	70.7	88.2	59.8	73.5	95.1	59.8	76.8	81.6	55.6	68.2	88.6	71.9	80.0	90.1	66.8	78.1
07	THERMAL & MOISTURE PROTECTION	96.3	56.0	77.1	96.9	60.5	79.6	96.8	63.9	81.2	96.2	58.0	78.1	96.8	76.0	86.9	99.5	70.1	85.6
08	DOORS & WINDOWS	99.4	56.1	89.0	98.8	55.6	88.4	100.7	56.3	90.0	99.4	53.5	88.3	99.9	72.9	93.4	98.3	65.7	90.4
09200	PLASTER & GYPSUM BOARD	103.8	54.8	73.8	104.0	59.1	76.5	107.2	59.1	77.8	101.4	54.8	72.9	104.2	71.5	84.2	106.7	66.3	82.0
095,098	CEILINGS & ACOUSTICAL TREATMENT	88.0	54.8	66.1	86.6	59.1	68.4	95.1	59.1	71.3	86.6	54.8	65.6	91.0	71.5	78.2	95.1	66.3	76.1
09600	FLOORING	111.7	48.6	96.4	112.3	41.7	95.2	115.9	58.1	101.9	108.7	61.6	97.3	112.6	74.2	103.3	123.5	71.7	110.9
097,099	WALL FINISHES, PAINTS & COATINGS	109.2	56.5	78.5	109.2	54.4	77.3	109.2	58.4	79.6	109.2	56.5	78.5	109.2	102.4	105.2	105.6	60.6	79.4
09	FINISHES	103.5	53.9	78.2	104.5	54.8	79.1	106.9	58.6	82.3	102.1	56.6	78.9	105.1	75.7	90.1	107.3	65.4	86.0
10 - 14	TOTAL DIV. 10000 - 14000	100.0	75.2	94.8	100.0	79.1	95.6	100.0	73.8	94.5	100.0	75.3	94.8	100.0	83.6	96.5	100.0	82.2	96.2
15	MECHANICAL	98.2	57.4	79.3	99.6	62.6	82.5	99.9	59.3	81.1	98.2	60.3	80.7	99.9	72.5	87.2	99.9	72.2	87.1
16	ELECTRICAL	100.4	48.2	64.5	97.2	49.9	64.7	96.2	70.3	78.4	97.1	55.8	68.7	96.4	72.8	80.2	97.2	78.5	84.4
01 - 16	WEIGHTED AVERAGE	98.2	61.4	80.3	100.2	62.0	81.6	98.7	66.6	83.1	98.8	64.4	82.1	100.8	77.7	89.5	98.1	73.4	86.1

FLORIDA

DIVISION		ORLANDO 327 - 328,347			PANAMA CITY 324			PENSACOLA 325			SARASOTA 342			ST. PETERSBURG 337			TALLAHASSEE 323		
		MAT.	INST.	TOTAL	MAT.	INST.	TOTAL	MAT.	INST.	TOTAL	MAT.	INST.	TOTAL	MAT.	INST.	TOTAL	MAT.	INST.	TOTAL
02	SITE CONSTRUCTION	121.1	86.8	94.8	135.6	84.6	96.6	133.2	86.8	97.7	122.0	86.6	94.9	121.4	86.6	94.7	121.9	86.2	94.6
03100	CONCRETE FORMS & ACCESSORIES	96.4	61.9	66.6	95.2	32.6	41.2	84.7	59.8	63.2	96.6	55.7	61.3	93.7	55.6	60.8	96.3	45.7	52.6
03200	CONCRETE REINFORCEMENT	95.8	84.5	89.4	100.0	61.2	77.9	102.5	61.5	79.1	95.8	70.4	81.3	99.2	70.4	82.8	95.8	61.8	76.4
03300	CAST-IN-PLACE CONCRETE	98.9	73.8	88.6	96.6	39.7	73.1	96.6	62.5	82.5	104.1	63.5	87.4	102.9	63.5	86.7	95.2	55.1	78.7
03	CONCRETE	92.8	71.7	82.3	97.5	42.3	69.9	96.3	62.7	79.5	95.4	62.8	79.1	95.1	62.8	78.9	91.0	54.0	72.5
04	MASONRY	87.3	70.2	76.8	90.9	33.0	55.3	88.1	59.5	70.5	87.6	58.9	70.0	132.4	58.9	87.2	87.6	46.2	62.2
05	METALS	108.4	93.7	103.1	97.4	71.3	88.0	97.3	84.7	92.8	102.1	87.4	96.8	101.1	87.3	96.1	99.0	83.5	93.4
06	WOOD & PLASTICS	95.1	60.6	77.3	93.8	32.8	62.2	82.8	60.6	71.3	95.1	55.6	74.7	92.1	55.6	73.3	95.1	44.1	68.7
07	THERMAL & MOISTURE PROTECTION	96.9	72.5	85.3	97.1	36.1	68.2	96.8	60.5	79.6	96.5	58.0	78.3	96.5	57.0	77.7	97.0	53.4	76.3
08	DOORS & WINDOWS	100.7	61.5	91.2	98.4	30.7	82.0	98.3	57.7	88.5	100.7	52.9	89.1	99.4	53.4	88.3	100.7	47.0	87.7
09200	PLASTER & GYPSUM BOARD	110.0	59.9	79.4	105.7	31.2	60.2	101.8	59.9	76.2	107.2	54.8	75.1	105.3	54.8	74.4	107.2	42.8	67.8
095,098	CEILINGS & ACOUSTICAL TREATMENT	95.1	59.9	71.9	89.7	31.2	51.1	89.7	59.9	70.0	92.1	54.8	67.5	89.7	54.8	66.6	95.1	42.8	60.6
09600	FLOORING	115.9	74.2	105.8	115.3	22.3	92.8	109.5	61.8	97.9	115.9	61.4	102.7	114.3	61.6	101.5	115.9	45.2	98.8
097,099	WALL FINISHES, PAINTS & COATINGS	109.2	67.0	84.7	109.2	29.8	63.1	109.2	67.8	85.1	109.2	56.5	78.5	109.2	56.5	78.5	109.2	48.1	73.6
09	FINISHES	107.3	64.2	85.3	106.6	29.9	67.5	103.9	61.0	82.0	106.3	56.5	80.9	105.1	56.6	80.3	107.0	45.0	75.4
10 - 14	TOTAL DIV. 10000 - 14000	100.0	80.6	95.9	100.0	55.7	90.7	100.0	62.3	92.0	100.0	75.2	94.8	100.0	65.2	92.7	100.0	72.9	94.3
15	MECHANICAL	99.9	65.2	83.9	99.9	30.3	67.7	99.9	60.3	81.6	99.8	57.9	80.5	99.9	60.1	81.5	99.9	48.0	75.9
16	ELECTRICAL	97.3	53.1	66.9	94.9	39.7	57.0	100.4	64.3	75.6	96.7	43.6	60.2	97.1	57.4	69.8	97.3	49.2	64.2
01 - 16	WEIGHTED AVERAGE	100.8	69.5	85.6	99.8	43.6	72.5	99.4	66.1	83.2	100.0	61.8	81.4	102.1	64.3	83.7	99.2	56.2	78.2

FLORIDA / GEORGIA

DIVISION		TAMPA 335 - 336,346			WEST PALM BEACH 334,349			ALBANY 317			ATHENS 306			ATLANTA 300 - 303,399			AUGUSTA 308 - 309		
		MAT.	INST.	TOTAL	MAT.	INST.	TOTAL	MAT.	INST.	TOTAL	MAT.	INST.	TOTAL	MAT.	INST.	TOTAL	MAT.	INST.	TOTAL
02	SITE CONSTRUCTION	121.7	86.6	94.8	102.4	73.6	80.3	105.9	76.4	83.3	115.4	92.9	98.2	110.3	95.2	98.8	106.5	92.8	96.0
03100	CONCRETE FORMS & ACCESSORIES	97.9	55.8	61.6	98.2	64.7	69.3	95.9	49.9	56.2	92.9	48.8	54.8	97.7	79.8	82.2	94.4	60.2	64.9
03200	CONCRETE REINFORCEMENT	95.8	70.4	81.4	98.4	74.8	84.9	95.8	92.2	93.7	106.9	91.1	97.9	102.9	93.8	97.7	108.7	85.2	95.3
03300	CAST-IN-PLACE CONCRETE	100.7	63.6	85.4	90.8	65.1	80.2	97.2	47.4	76.7	99.0	56.1	81.3	99.0	75.2	89.2	93.6	55.8	78.0
03	CONCRETE	93.8	62.9	78.4	88.1	68.2	78.2	91.9	58.7	75.3	97.2	59.9	78.6	94.6	80.6	87.6	90.9	63.7	77.3
04	MASONRY	87.7	58.9	70.0	86.5	56.1	67.8	89.0	37.6	57.4	75.2	64.6	68.7	90.9	72.1	79.3	91.2	47.4	64.3
05	METALS	102.0	87.5	96.8	97.3	90.7	94.9	96.4	92.5	95.0	91.0	77.5	86.1	92.3	81.2	88.3	91.1	74.8	85.2
06	WOOD & PLASTICS	96.7	55.6	75.5	94.4	66.8	80.2	94.4	50.1	71.5	93.9	43.1	67.6	98.6	82.4	90.3	95.4	62.8	78.5
07	THERMAL & MOISTURE PROTECTION	96.8	58.0	78.4	96.2	65.3	81.6	96.6	56.2	77.5	92.3	57.7	75.9	92.4	77.0	85.1	91.8	57.2	75.4
08	DOORS & WINDOWS	100.7	53.7	89.3	97.5	63.8	89.4	98.3	55.5	88.0	94.5	52.0	84.2	98.3	78.9	93.6	94.5	61.2	86.5
09200	PLASTER & GYPSUM BOARD	107.2	54.8	75.1	107.3	66.3	82.2	107.2	49.0	71.6	108.8	41.7	67.8	110.1	82.3	93.1	109.2	62.0	80.3
095,098	CEILINGS & ACOUSTICAL TREATMENT	95.1	54.8	68.5	88.0	66.3	73.7	95.1	49.0	64.7	100.9	41.7	61.8	100.9	82.3	88.6	102.4	62.0	75.7
09600	FLOORING	115.9	61.6	102.7	118.7	59.2	104.2	115.9	37.7	96.9	85.6	68.0	81.3	87.2	72.3	83.6	86.0	48.0	76.8
097,099	WALL FINISHES, PAINTS & COATINGS	109.2	54.5	76.5	105.6	55.9	76.7	105.6	48.1	72.2	94.1	40.1	62.7	94.1	78.2	84.9	94.1	45.7	66.0
09	FINISHES	106.9	56.6	81.3	104.4	62.3	82.9	105.0	46.3	75.0	93.1	50.1	71.2	93.5	78.3	85.7	93.0	56.5	74.4
10 - 14	TOTAL DIV. 10000 - 14000	100.0	75.9	94.9	100.0	82.2	96.2	100.0	73.1	94.3	100.0	64.1	92.4	100.0	82.0	96.2	100.0	69.8	93.6
15	MECHANICAL	99.9	60.3	81.6	98.2	80.0	89.8	99.9	53.4	78.4	97.0	74.5	86.6	100.1	80.3	91.0	100.1	50.6	77.2
16	ELECTRICAL	96.2	57.4	69.5	96.7	62.0	72.8	90.7	66.0	73.8	95.1	75.5	81.7	94.0	84.0	87.1	96.1	54.1	67.2
01 - 16	WEIGHTED AVERAGE	99.9	64.7	82.8	96.8	70.2	83.9	97.5	60.3	79.4	94.6	69.0	82.2	96.4	81.4	89.1	95.2	60.9	78.5

COST INDEXES

City Cost Indexes

COST INDEXES

GEORGIA

DIVISION		COLUMBUS 318 - 319			DALTON 307			GAINESVILLE 305			MACON 310 - 312			SAVANNAH 313 - 314			STATESBORO 304		
		MAT.	INST.	TOTAL	MAT.	INST.	TOTAL	MAT.	INST.	TOTAL	MAT.	INST.	TOTAL	MAT.	INST.	TOTAL	MAT.	INST.	TOTAL
02	SITE CONSTRUCTION	105.8	76.5	83.4	116.4	95.6	100.4	114.4	91.3	96.7	106.6	94.4	97.3	106.4	77.6	84.3	116.5	74.0	83.9
03100	CONCRETE FORMS & ACCESSORIES	97.5	63.8	68.4	82.8	24.3	32.3	97.4	46.2	53.2	94.9	64.5	68.6	95.7	60.1	65.0	75.7	26.2	33.0
03200	CONCRETE REINFORCEMENT	95.8	92.4	93.9	105.0	64.0	81.6	105.8	79.3	90.7	98.2	92.4	94.9	101.5	85.5	92.4	106.7	23.1	59.0
03300	CAST-IN-PLACE CONCRETE	96.8	48.0	76.7	96.2	35.1	71.0	104.0	41.2	78.1	95.5	51.7	77.5	93.8	56.4	78.4	98.8	32.9	71.6
03	CONCRETE	91.8	65.0	78.4	96.0	37.4	66.7	98.9	51.3	75.1	91.3	66.6	79.0	90.9	65.0	78.0	96.3	30.7	63.5
04	MASONRY	88.9	41.4	59.7	78.8	30.0	48.8	86.3	37.8	56.5	103.7	45.2	67.7	92.3	59.0	71.8	77.6	26.1	46.0
05	METALS	96.8	93.1	95.5	93.6	68.3	84.5	90.9	68.5	82.8	91.7	93.5	92.4	97.1	90.9	94.9	96.2	69.3	86.5
06	WOOD & PLASTICS	96.2	69.0	82.1	76.6	23.0	48.9	98.4	43.1	69.8	100.7	67.7	83.6	94.5	59.1	76.2	69.0	25.6	46.6
07	THERMAL & MOISTURE PROTECTION	96.3	59.1	78.7	97.3	31.0	65.8	92.2	45.8	70.2	95.2	63.3	80.1	96.7	59.0	78.9	93.0	28.2	62.3
08	DOORS & WINDOWS	98.3	66.0	90.5	95.6	21.0	77.6	94.5	43.7	82.2	96.7	66.3	89.4	98.3	58.5	88.7	96.4	22.8	78.7
09200	PLASTER & GYPSUM BOARD	107.2	68.5	83.6	94.0	21.0	49.4	110.1	41.7	68.3	114.6	67.2	85.7	107.2	58.4	77.3	95.7	23.7	51.7
095,098	CEILINGS & ACOUSTICAL TREATMENT	95.1	68.5	77.6	113.8	21.0	52.5	100.9	41.7	61.8	87.5	67.2	74.1	95.1	58.4	70.9	110.2	23.7	53.1
09600	FLOORING	115.9	43.9	98.5	86.6	16.3	69.5	87.1	16.3	70.0	90.5	44.3	79.3	115.9	56.6	101.5	100.7	56.6	90.0
097,099	WALL FINISHES, PAINTS & COATINGS	105.6	46.1	71.0	84.8	23.1	48.9	94.1	40.1	62.7	107.2	56.4	77.7	105.6	57.2	77.4	92.6	20.7	50.8
09	FINISHES	104.9	58.4	81.1	100.5	22.1	60.5	93.6	39.5	66.0	91.6	59.7	75.3	105.1	59.0	81.6	103.5	31.2	66.7
10 - 14	TOTAL DIV. 10000 - 14000	100.0	75.4	94.8	100.0	23.0	83.7	100.0	64.1	92.4	100.0	76.9	95.1	100.0	71.5	94.0	100.0	54.8	90.5
15	MECHANICAL	99.9	43.7	73.9	97.1	25.5	64.0	97.0	27.8	65.0	99.9	49.2	76.4	99.9	54.2	78.8	97.3	23.2	63.0
16	ELECTRICAL	92.0	46.7	60.8	102.8	19.1	45.3	95.1	75.5	81.6	90.1	66.2	73.7	93.4	62.7	72.3	95.4	24.0	46.3
01 - 16	WEIGHTED AVERAGE	97.6	58.7	78.7	96.6	36.8	67.5	95.5	53.5	75.1	95.9	65.7	81.2	97.9	64.5	81.7	96.7	35.7	67.0

DIVISION		GEORGIA VALDOSTA 316			WAYCROSS 315			HAWAII HILO 967			HONOLULU 968			STATES & POSS., GUAM 969			IDAHO BOISE 836 - 837		
		MAT.	INST.	TOTAL	MAT.	INST.	TOTAL	MAT.	INST.	TOTAL	MAT.	INST.	TOTAL	MAT.	INST.	TOTAL	MAT.	INST.	TOTAL
02	SITE CONSTRUCTION	116.6	76.8	86.1	113.4	75.0	84.0	123.4	108.2	111.7	127.9	108.2	112.8	161.7	107.4	120.1	82.7	101.5	97.1
03100	CONCRETE FORMS & ACCESSORIES	81.4	51.8	55.9	83.9	33.3	40.3	106.5	150.1	144.1	106.9	150.1	144.2	108.6	57.4	64.5	101.5	87.3	89.3
03200	CONCRETE REINFORCEMENT	101.7	51.0	72.8	101.7	70.0	87.6	107.4	126.7	118.4	106.4	126.7	118.0	689.5	32.0	744.6	100.3	81.6	89.6
03300	CAST-IN-PLACE CONCRETE	95.1	57.1	79.5	107.5	37.7	78.7	197.6	128.9	169.2	190.4	128.9	165.0	171.2	120.1	150.1	101.2	95.3	98.8
03	CONCRETE	95.9	55.4	75.6	100.1	45.2	72.7	159.3	136.7	148.0	155.7	136.7	146.2	345.1	75.5	210.3	104.2	88.8	96.5
04	MASONRY	95.3	53.3	69.5	96.2	33.4	57.6	132.9	133.4	133.2	132.9	133.4	133.2	183.9	40.1	95.5	138.3	83.1	104.4
05	METALS	96.6	79.3	90.4	95.9	85.7	92.2	117.2	110.3	114.7	116.4	110.3	114.2	156.6	85.5	131.0	113.2	81.3	101.7
06	WOOD & PLASTICS	79.3	48.8	63.5	81.8	32.0	56.1	102.4	154.3	129.2	102.2	154.3	129.2	109.9	57.3	82.7	96.3	86.6	91.3
07	THERMAL & MOISTURE PROTECTION	96.4	62.2	80.2	96.1	38.9	69.0	111.6	132.2	121.4	113.7	132.2	122.5	123.1	69.2	97.5	98.1	84.2	91.5
08	DOORS & WINDOWS	93.8	45.2	82.1	93.8	40.8	81.0	103.6	143.5	113.2	109.0	143.5	117.4	103.4	49.6	90.4	95.5	81.2	92.0
09200	PLASTER & GYPSUM BOARD	101.0	47.7	68.4	101.8	30.4	58.2	95.6	156.0	132.5	111.9	156.0	138.9	336.1	41.5	322.5	88.2	86.0	86.9
095,098	CEILINGS & ACOUSTICAL TREATMENT	89.7	47.7	62.0	86.6	30.4	49.6	119.1	156.0	143.5	118.1	156.0	143.1	322.1	41.5	137.0	104.7	86.0	92.3
09600	FLOORING	107.7	45.2	92.5	109.2	37.7	91.9	120.9	131.9	123.6	119.4	131.9	122.5	119.4	39.7	100.1	103.8	65.3	94.5
097,099	WALL FINISHES, PAINTS & COATINGS	105.6	41.7	68.5	105.6	40.1	67.5	114.5	150.0	135.1	113.9	150.0	134.9	113.9	48.0	75.6	108.7	60.3	80.6
09	FINISHES	101.0	48.9	74.4	100.8	33.8	66.6	116.5	148.1	132.6	118.6	148.1	133.6	672.4	53.1	356.5	98.6	80.6	89.4
10 - 14	TOTAL DIV. 10000 - 14000	100.0	70.1	93.7	100.0	56.3	90.8	100.0	129.1	106.2	100.0	129.1	106.2	100.0	120.3	104.3	100.0	84.1	96.7
15	MECHANICAL	99.9	47.5	75.7	97.9	30.1	66.5	100.3	123.6	111.1	100.3	123.6	111.1	103.4	42.4	75.2	100.1	84.8	93.0
16	ELECTRICAL	89.0	36.0	52.5	95.8	65.6	75.0	111.1	129.9	124.1	114.3	129.9	125.1	133.4	38.9	68.5	81.4	80.3	80.6
01 - 16	WEIGHTED AVERAGE	97.4	54.0	76.3	97.9	49.7	74.4	115.9	129.0	122.3	116.6	129.0	122.7	211.9	60.7	138.4	102.1	85.1	93.8

DIVISION		IDAHO COEUR D'ALENE 838			IDAHO FALLS 834			LEWISTON 835			POCATELLO 832			TWIN FALLS 833			ILLINOIS BLOOMINGTON 617		
		MAT.	INST.	TOTAL	MAT.	INST.	TOTAL	MAT.	INST.	TOTAL	MAT.	INST.	TOTAL	MAT.	INST.	TOTAL	MAT.	INST.	TOTAL
02	SITE CONSTRUCTION	82.6	94.3	91.6	80.2	100.2	95.5	88.0	95.2	93.5	84.3	101.5	97.5	91.6	99.6	97.7	88.9	94.2	93.0
03100	CONCRETE FORMS & ACCESSORIES	105.5	45.8	54.0	94.6	42.3	49.5	112.9	76.6	81.6	101.5	87.0	89.0	104.9	41.2	49.9	84.5	107.3	104.2
03200	CONCRETE REINFORCEMENT	113.3	98.3	104.7	107.9	63.7	82.7	113.3	99.0	105.2	100.6	81.1	89.5	109.3	57.0	79.5	102.6	114.2	109.2
03300	CAST-IN-PLACE CONCRETE	105.6	82.9	96.2	92.9	63.5	80.8	109.7	93.0	102.8	100.4	95.1	98.2	103.0	51.0	81.6	94.2	97.9	95.7
03	CONCRETE	112.1	69.5	90.8	96.7	54.8	75.8	116.1	86.6	101.4	103.9	88.6	96.2	113.2	48.7	80.9	92.4	105.5	99.0
04	MASONRY	138.3	63.5	92.3	132.1	37.7	74.1	138.7	91.3	109.5	133.1	74.9	97.4	136.7	46.0	80.9	107.3	102.9	104.6
05	METALS	98.5	87.7	94.6	112.8	72.0	98.1	96.7	89.9	94.3	113.5	80.4	101.6	113.4	68.4	97.2	92.9	111.7	99.7
06	WOOD & PLASTICS	94.5	40.2	66.4	87.3	39.9	62.8	102.0	71.0	86.0	96.3	86.6	91.3	99.7	41.2	69.5	83.7	105.8	95.2
07	THERMAL & MOISTURE PROTECTION	167.9	70.1	121.5	97.6	56.0	77.9	168.2	84.1	128.3	98.3	77.7	88.6	99.4	53.6	77.7	95.8	103.0	99.2
08	DOORS & WINDOWS	115.8	54.6	101.1	98.7	46.4	86.1	115.8	75.3	106.0	95.5	75.6	90.7	98.8	42.0	85.1	92.1	106.3	95.5
09200	PLASTER & GYPSUM BOARD	149.9	38.2	81.7	84.1	37.8	55.8	152.1	70.1	102.0	88.2	86.0	86.9	87.8	39.1	58.1	99.6	105.7	103.3
095,098	CEILINGS & ACOUSTICAL TREATMENT	151.2	38.2	76.7	96.5	37.8	57.8	151.2	70.1	97.7	104.7	86.0	92.3	97.9	39.1	59.1	93.8	105.7	101.6
09600	FLOORING	140.5	69.4	123.3	100.5	65.3	92.0	143.7	95.9	132.1	104.1	65.3	94.7	105.4	65.3	95.7	94.1	105.4	96.8
097,099	WALL FINISHES, PAINTS & COATINGS	136.5	75.5	101.0	108.7	49.9	74.5	136.5	75.5	101.0	108.7	63.2	82.2	108.7	37.2	67.1	91.0	104.1	98.6
09	FINISHES	165.8	51.3	107.4	95.0	46.3	70.1	167.2	79.1	122.3	98.7	80.9	89.6	98.4	44.9	71.1	93.4	106.6	100.2
10 - 14	TOTAL DIV. 10000 - 14000	100.0	70.9	93.8	100.0	58.9	91.3	100.0	92.9	98.5	100.0	84.1	96.7	100.0	57.7	91.1	100.0	101.9	100.4
15	MECHANICAL	102.2	55.8	80.8	102.3	59.0	82.3	101.5	90.7	96.5	100.1	84.7	93.0	100.1	43.0	73.7	97.1	108.2	102.2
16	ELECTRICAL	86.6	44.6	57.7	84.9	79.8	81.4	83.6	89.6	87.7	84.5	79.9	81.3	87.0	37.5	53.0	95.9	94.8	95.1
01 - 16	WEIGHTED AVERAGE	113.4	63.2	89.0	101.3	62.9	82.6	113.7	88.1	101.2	102.1	83.7	93.2	104.2	51.9	78.8	95.2	103.4	99.2

623

ILLINOIS

DIVISION		CARBONDALE 629			CENTRALIA 628			CHAMPAIGN 618 - 619			CHICAGO 606			DECATUR 625			EAST ST. LOUIS 620 - 622		
		MAT.	INST.	TOTAL	MAT.	INST.	TOTAL	MAT.	INST.	TOTAL	MAT.	INST.	TOTAL	MAT.	INST.	TOTAL	MAT.	INST.	TOTAL
02	SITE CONSTRUCTION	98.1	95.2	95.9	98.5	95.8	96.4	98.3	95.4	96.1	86.0	91.0	89.8	82.2	95.3	92.2	100.1	95.8	96.8
03100	CONCRETE FORMS & ACCESSORIES	96.0	100.8	100.2	98.9	103.6	103.0	93.1	105.7	103.9	105.9	130.5	127.1	100.3	104.5	103.9	92.6	109.5	107.2
03200	CONCRETE REINFORCEMENT	102.8	100.9	101.7	102.8	118.2	111.6	102.6	111.2	107.5	94.9	158.7	131.3	96.5	110.4	104.4	102.1	118.2	111.2
03300	CAST-IN-PLACE CONCRETE	88.1	95.7	91.3	88.6	112.0	98.2	109.3	106.7	108.2	103.3	130.2	114.4	96.2	93.2	95.0	90.1	112.3	99.2
03	CONCRETE	84.1	100.2	92.1	84.5	110.3	97.4	104.7	107.3	106.0	100.6	134.6	117.6	93.8	101.9	97.8	85.2	112.9	99.0
04	MASONRY	72.9	98.3	88.5	73.0	109.8	95.6	130.1	102.4	113.0	93.9	131.5	117.0	69.0	101.3	88.9	73.1	110.4	96.0
05	METALS	92.1	115.6	100.6	92.1	124.1	103.7	92.9	109.0	98.7	96.4	123.7	106.3	95.5	108.1	100.0	93.0	123.9	104.1
06	WOOD & PLASTICS	100.3	99.9	100.1	103.5	100.9	100.2	92.6	103.5	98.2	103.3	128.9	116.5	102.6	103.5	103.1	96.8	108.9	103.1
07	THERMAL & MOISTURE PROTECTION	92.0	94.3	93.1	92.1	104.9	98.2	96.6	103.8	100.1	99.3	128.7	113.3	97.0	97.5	97.2	92.0	106.0	98.6
08	DOORS & WINDOWS	88.1	107.1	92.7	88.1	111.8	93.9	92.8	102.6	95.2	104.1	136.4	111.9	99.0	102.4	99.8	88.2	116.1	95.0
09200	PLASTER & GYPSUM BOARD	104.3	99.5	101.4	105.2	100.6	102.4	102.2	103.3	102.8	99.4	129.4	117.7	106.2	103.3	104.4	103.5	108.8	106.7
095,098	CEILINGS & ACOUSTICAL TREATMENT	93.8	99.5	97.6	93.8	100.6	98.3	93.8	103.3	100.0	99.2	129.4	119.1	99.2	103.3	101.9	93.8	108.8	103.7
09600	FLOORING	112.3	87.1	106.2	113.5	76.1	104.4	97.4	99.3	97.9	85.1	126.3	95.1	101.3	96.6	100.2	111.0	61.5	99.0
097,099	WALL FINISHES, PAINTS & COATINGS	99.2	92.9	95.5	99.2	101.7	100.6	91.0	107.6	100.6	80.7	134.4	111.9	91.0	102.0	97.4	99.2	101.7	100.6
09	FINISHES	98.3	96.8	97.5	98.8	98.0	98.4	95.4	104.6	100.1	89.4	129.9	110.1	97.9	103.3	100.6	97.8	99.4	98.6
10 - 14	TOTAL DIV. 10000 - 14000	100.0	103.0	100.6	100.0	104.2	100.9	100.0	101.6	100.3	100.0	123.7	105.0	100.0	101.0	100.2	100.0	105.5	101.2
15	MECHANICAL	97.0	99.2	98.0	97.0	98.4	97.6	97.1	103.1	99.9	100.0	124.5	111.3	100.2	99.6	99.9	100.1	99.8	99.9
16	ELECTRICAL	95.3	101.2	99.4	97.6	101.1	100.0	101.4	93.3	95.9	101.1	130.7	121.4	100.6	83.6	88.9	96.9	102.1	100.5
01 - 16	WEIGHTED AVERAGE	92.4	100.7	96.4	92.8	104.4	98.4	99.1	101.9	100.4	98.2	125.4	111.4	95.9	98.3	97.1	93.5	105.7	99.4

ILLINOIS

DIVISION		EFFINGHAM 624			GALESBURG 614			JOLIET 604			KANKAKEE 609			LA SALLE 613			NORTH SUBURBAN 600 - 603		
		MAT.	INST.	TOTAL	MAT.	INST.	TOTAL	MAT.	INST.	TOTAL	MAT.	INST.	TOTAL	MAT.	INST.	TOTAL	MAT.	INST.	TOTAL
02	SITE CONSTRUCTION	90.1	95.2	94.0	91.3	94.2	93.5	86.0	90.1	89.1	80.6	89.6	87.5	90.8	94.5	93.6	85.2	90.0	88.9
03100	CONCRETE FORMS & ACCESSORIES	106.1	103.6	104.0	93.0	106.8	104.9	106.9	130.7	127.4	97.2	114.3	111.9	112.1	93.1	95.7	105.8	125.1	122.4
03200	CONCRETE REINFORCEMENT	102.6	111.8	107.8	100.1	114.4	108.3	94.9	144.0	122.9	99.1	131.5	117.6	100.9	123.6	113.9	94.9	153.9	128.5
03300	CAST-IN-PLACE CONCRETE	96.0	84.1	91.1	97.0	95.2	96.2	103.2	114.9	108.0	96.3	112.4	102.9	96.9	105.8	100.5	103.3	133.1	115.6
03	CONCRETE	95.1	98.6	96.9	94.9	104.4	99.7	100.6	126.5	113.5	94.8	116.1	105.5	96.3	103.8	100.1	100.6	132.1	116.4
04	MASONRY	76.4	94.5	87.5	107.5	106.8	107.1	95.5	126.4	114.5	93.4	109.5	103.3	107.5	103.5	105.0	93.9	123.7	112.2
05	METALS	92.8	108.6	98.5	92.9	111.5	99.6	94.5	115.2	102.0	94.5	108.9	99.7	93.0	116.0	101.3	95.6	118.4	103.8
06	WOOD & PLASTICS	105.3	103.5	104.4	92.4	106.2	99.5	105.3	131.3	118.7	95.9	115.0	105.7	111.1	87.7	99.0	103.3	123.5	113.7
07	THERMAL & MOISTURE PROTECTION	96.5	96.8	96.6	96.1	101.0	98.4	99.1	125.6	111.7	98.0	115.2	106.2	96.4	98.9	97.6	99.3	121.3	109.7
08	DOORS & WINDOWS	92.7	105.4	95.8	92.1	103.3	94.8	103.9	134.2	111.2	95.3	120.2	101.3	92.1	94.8	93.7	104.0	130.2	110.3
09200	PLASTER & GYPSUM BOARD	105.6	103.3	104.2	102.2	106.0	104.5	97.7	132.0	118.7	95.5	115.1	107.5	107.3	86.9	94.9	99.4	123.9	114.4
095,098	CEILINGS & ACOUSTICAL TREATMENT	93.8	103.3	100.0	93.8	106.0	101.8	99.2	132.0	120.8	99.2	115.1	109.7	93.8	86.9	89.3	99.2	123.9	115.5
09600	FLOORING	102.5	95.6	100.9	97.3	102.0	98.5	84.7	122.0	93.7	81.9	110.1	88.8	104.8	83.8	99.7	85.1	122.0	94.1
097,099	WALL FINISHES, PAINTS & COATINGS	91.0	98.5	95.4	91.0	103.5	98.2	78.4	123.0	104.3	78.4	97.6	89.6	91.0	104.1	98.6	80.7	128.9	108.7
09	FINISHES	97.2	101.9	99.6	95.0	105.8	100.5	88.9	128.7	109.2	87.4	111.1	99.5	98.2	91.1	94.6	89.4	124.6	107.4
10 - 14	TOTAL DIV. 10000 - 14000	100.0	99.9	100.0	100.0	101.6	100.3	100.0	122.7	104.8	100.0	117.1	103.6	100.0	98.7	99.7	100.0	121.8	104.6
15	MECHANICAL	97.1	100.8	98.8	97.1	106.4	101.4	100.2	119.7	109.2	97.1	102.6	99.6	97.1	107.6	101.9	100.0	118.8	108.7
16	ELECTRICAL	97.0	94.9	95.6	97.5	85.1	89.0	100.7	91.9	94.7	92.6	87.0	88.8	92.6	87.0	88.8	99.8	127.3	118.7
01 - 16	WEIGHTED AVERAGE	94.6	99.3	96.9	96.0	101.4	98.6	98.0	115.2	106.4	94.4	104.2	99.2	96.4	99.7	98.0	98.0	120.9	109.1

ILLINOIS

DIVISION		PEORIA 615 - 616			QUINCY 623			ROCKFORD 610 - 611			ROCK ISLAND 612			SOUTH SUBURBAN 605			SPRINGFIELD 626 - 627		
		MAT.	INST.	TOTAL	MAT.	INST.	TOTAL	MAT.	INST.	TOTAL	MAT.	INST.	TOTAL	MAT.	INST.	TOTAL	MAT.	INST.	TOTAL
02	SITE CONSTRUCTION	90.2	94.4	93.4	89.0	95.0	93.6	90.4	94.7	93.7	89.5	93.9	92.9	85.2	90.0	88.9	88.7	95.3	93.8
03100	CONCRETE FORMS & ACCESSORIES	98.4	108.2	106.9	103.0	101.8	101.9	103.2	112.5	111.3	95.4	98.4	98.0	105.8	124.8	122.2	102.6	104.6	104.3
03200	CONCRETE REINFORCEMENT	96.5	114.5	106.7	100.9	98.6	99.6	96.5	141.5	122.2	100.1	115.2	108.7	94.9	154.0	128.6	96.5	110.4	104.4
03300	CAST-IN-PLACE CONCRETE	94.1	105.9	98.9	96.1	96.0	96.1	96.2	104.5	99.6	94.9	101.9	97.8	103.3	125.5	112.5	89.4	100.7	94.1
03	CONCRETE	92.5	108.7	100.6	94.4	99.5	97.0	94.0	115.2	104.6	93.4	103.1	98.2	100.6	129.4	115.0	90.6	104.6	97.6
04	MASONRY	113.0	109.7	111.0	96.0	91.2	93.0	83.9	114.5	102.7	107.3	100.9	103.4	93.9	126.2	113.8	67.7	100.4	87.8
05	METALS	95.5	112.0	101.4	92.9	103.9	96.9	95.5	123.7	105.7	93.0	110.9	99.4	95.6	118.3	103.8	95.5	108.9	100.3
06	WOOD & PLASTICS	102.6	106.0	104.4	102.4	103.5	103.0	102.6	110.1	106.4	94.9	96.2	95.6	103.3	123.5	113.7	102.4	103.5	103.0
07	THERMAL & MOISTURE PROTECTION	96.8	105.2	100.8	96.4	88.9	92.8	96.7	112.8	104.3	96.1	99.3	97.6	99.3	121.1	109.6	96.6	103.5	99.9
08	DOORS & WINDOWS	99.0	106.4	100.8	93.6	99.6	95.1	99.0	116.5	103.2	92.1	98.2	93.6	104.0	128.3	109.9	99.0	102.4	99.8
09200	PLASTER & GYPSUM BOARD	106.2	105.8	106.0	105.2	103.3	104.0	106.2	110.0	108.5	103.0	95.8	98.6	99.4	123.9	114.4	106.2	103.3	104.4
095,098	CEILINGS & ACOUSTICAL TREATMENT	99.2	105.8	103.6	93.8	103.3	100.0	99.2	110.0	106.3	93.8	95.8	95.1	99.2	123.9	115.5	99.2	103.3	101.9
09600	FLOORING	101.3	102.0	101.5	101.3	90.8	98.8	101.3	103.0	101.7	98.5	93.2	97.2	85.1	122.0	94.1	101.5	96.8	100.4
097,099	WALL FINISHES, PAINTS & COATINGS	91.0	96.2	94.0	91.0	63.9	75.2	91.0	111.8	103.1	91.0	103.5	98.2	80.7	123.3	105.5	91.0	101.8	97.3
09	FINISHES	97.8	105.6	101.8	96.7	96.0	96.4	97.8	110.2	104.1	95.4	97.6	96.5	89.4	124.0	107.1	97.9	103.0	100.5
10 - 14	TOTAL DIV. 10000 - 14000	100.0	102.8	100.6	100.0	98.2	99.6	100.0	112.0	102.5	100.0	95.5	99.1	100.0	121.8	104.6	100.0	100.6	100.1
15	MECHANICAL	100.2	105.1	102.4	97.1	102.9	99.8	100.2	106.8	103.2	97.1	105.0	100.7	100.0	115.2	107.1	100.2	99.4	99.8
16	ELECTRICAL	99.5	93.1	95.1	92.8	80.4	84.3	99.5	113.1	108.8	84.7	93.7	90.9	99.8	125.2	117.3	100.5	95.1	96.8
01 - 16	WEIGHTED AVERAGE	98.4	103.6	100.9	95.3	95.4	95.4	97.0	111.2	103.9	94.9	100.2	97.5	98.0	119.6	108.5	95.6	100.6	98.1

INDIANA

DIVISION		ANDERSON 460			BLOOMINGTON 474			COLUMBUS 472			EVANSVILLE 476 - 477			FORT WAYNE 467 - 468			GARY 463 - 464		
		MAT.	INST.	TOTAL	MAT.	INST.	TOTAL	MAT.	INST.	TOTAL	MAT.	INST.	TOTAL	MAT.	INST.	TOTAL	MAT.	INST.	TOTAL
02	SITE CONSTRUCTION	88.0	94.7	93.1	78.5	95.3	91.4	76.0	95.2	90.7	84.0	130.5	119.6	88.8	94.9	93.5	88.6	96.8	94.9
03100	CONCRETE FORMS & ACCESSORIES	91.5	82.2	83.5	103.1	83.4	86.1	92.1	80.0	81.7	91.0	84.1	85.0	91.1	77.1	79.0	92.0	108.3	106.1
03200	CONCRETE REINFORCEMENT	96.8	86.9	91.1	88.8	86.7	87.6	89.2	86.7	87.7	97.3	85.8	90.7	96.8	83.2	89.0	96.8	102.8	100.2
03300	CAST-IN-PLACE CONCRETE	101.7	83.3	94.1	102.7	81.8	94.1	102.2	80.8	93.4	98.1	93.5	96.2	108.0	81.4	97.0	106.2	107.5	106.7
03	CONCRETE	96.7	84.0	90.3	104.2	83.0	93.6	103.1	81.1	92.1	107.0	87.8	97.4	99.7	80.4	90.1	98.9	107.0	102.9
04	MASONRY	92.4	83.6	87.0	92.2	81.9	85.9	92.1	81.9	85.8	88.3	85.8	86.8	89.7	83.2	85.7	93.8	101.9	98.8
05	METALS	102.1	92.7	98.8	97.4	77.4	90.2	97.4	77.2	90.1	90.7	89.6	90.3	102.1	91.0	98.1	102.1	104.1	102.9
06	WOOD & PLASTICS	101.9	82.0	91.6	116.9	82.7	99.2	105.9	78.1	91.5	92.7	82.5	87.4	101.5	75.2	87.9	100.9	109.8	105.5
07	THERMAL & MOISTURE PROTECTION	100.0	82.3	91.6	92.1	86.7	89.5	91.4	85.6	88.7	95.3	88.5	92.1	99.3	86.4	93.2	99.2	104.0	101.4
08	DOORS & WINDOWS	101.9	84.8	97.8	105.5	83.4	100.2	100.8	82.7	96.4	98.0	83.0	94.4	101.9	77.9	96.1	101.8	105.7	102.8
09200	PLASTER & GYPSUM BOARD	106.5	82.0	91.5	105.0	82.9	91.5	101.5	78.2	87.2	101.1	80.8	88.7	102.2	74.9	85.5	103.0	110.7	107.7
095,098	CEILINGS & ACOUSTICAL TREATMENT	93.8	82.0	86.0	83.7	82.9	83.2	83.7	78.2	80.1	95.1	80.8	85.7	93.8	74.9	81.3	93.8	110.7	104.9
09600	FLOORING	87.0	77.4	84.7	102.2	93.7	100.2	96.9	93.7	96.1	95.7	86.6	93.5	87.0	82.6	85.9	87.0	108.4	92.2
097,099	WALL FINISHES, PAINTS & COATINGS	90.9	77.5	83.1	90.2	90.3	90.3	90.2	90.3	90.3	96.5	89.0	92.2	90.9	77.5	83.1	90.9	91.0	91.0
09	FINISHES	91.7	81.0	86.3	96.9	86.1	91.4	94.7	83.4	88.9	96.2	84.9	90.4	90.9	77.7	84.1	91.2	106.7	99.1
10 - 14	TOTAL DIV. 10000 - 14000	100.0	89.2	97.7	100.0	89.3	97.7	100.0	88.7	97.6	100.0	92.3	98.4	100.0	86.5	97.2	100.0	108.4	101.8
15	MECHANICAL	99.8	85.1	93.0	99.8	86.3	93.8	96.6	88.1	92.7	100.0	87.7	94.3	99.8	84.0	92.5	99.8	100.9	100.3
16	ELECTRICAL	81.3	92.8	89.2	101.0	88.4	92.3	99.6	92.7	94.9	95.7	89.6	91.5	81.8	86.7	85.2	88.3	105.6	100.2
01 - 16	WEIGHTED AVERAGE	97.1	87.2	92.3	99.3	85.9	92.8	97.4	86.2	91.9	97.1	91.8	94.6	97.3	84.7	91.1	97.9	103.7	100.7

INDIANA

DIVISION		INDIANAPOLIS 461 - 462			KOKOMO 469			LAFAYETTE 479			LAWRENCEBURG 470			MUNCIE 473			NEW ALBANY 471		
		MAT.	INST.	TOTAL	MAT.	INST.	TOTAL	MAT.	INST.	TOTAL	MAT.	INST.	TOTAL	MAT.	INST.	TOTAL	MAT.	INST.	TOTAL
02	SITE CONSTRUCTION	88.0	98.7	96.2	85.2	94.5	92.3	76.7	95.2	90.9	74.3	116.0	106.3	78.3	95.5	91.5	71.4	100.1	93.3
03100	CONCRETE FORMS & ACCESSORIES	92.0	87.4	88.0	101.4	75.4	79.0	89.1	84.2	84.9	87.7	78.5	79.8	88.5	82.0	82.9	87.1	76.2	77.7
03200	CONCRETE REINFORCEMENT	96.1	86.6	90.7	87.6	86.8	87.1	88.8	83.1	85.6	88.2	82.1	84.7	98.2	86.8	91.7	89.4	84.2	86.4
03300	CAST-IN-PLACE CONCRETE	97.8	87.5	93.6	100.6	86.2	94.7	102.7	85.7	95.7	96.1	79.2	89.1	107.9	82.7	97.5	99.2	74.3	88.9
03	CONCRETE	99.1	86.8	92.9	94.2	82.1	88.1	103.3	84.0	93.7	96.1	80.1	88.1	102.2	83.8	93.0	101.8	77.4	89.6
04	MASONRY	99.6	85.1	90.7	92.1	83.4	86.8	98.6	83.0	89.0	77.4	79.7	78.9	94.3	83.6	87.7	84.5	75.7	79.1
05	METALS	104.1	80.3	95.5	99.1	92.8	96.8	95.9	75.9	88.7	91.9	90.7	91.5	99.0	92.8	96.8	94.3	85.6	91.2
06	WOOD & PLASTICS	99.2	87.5	93.1	112.0	72.6	91.6	102.8	84.4	93.2	91.4	77.3	84.1	103.6	81.8	92.3	93.7	76.4	84.8
07	THERMAL & MOISTURE PROTECTION	98.7	88.1	93.7	99.6	81.7	91.1	91.4	85.8	88.7	91.9	81.5	87.0	93.6	82.6	88.4	86.4	76.3	81.6
08	DOORS & WINDOWS	108.1	87.7	103.1	95.9	79.8	92.0	99.3	85.1	95.9	100.1	79.4	95.1	100.1	84.7	96.4	97.7	79.5	93.3
09200	PLASTER & GYPSUM BOARD	103.0	87.4	93.4	108.5	72.3	86.4	99.2	84.6	90.3	92.8	77.1	83.2	100.0	82.0	89.0	99.4	75.9	85.0
095,098	CEILINGS & ACOUSTICAL TREATMENT	92.4	87.4	89.1	88.3	72.3	77.8	78.3	84.6	82.5	95.1	77.1	83.3	85.1	82.0	83.0	91.0	75.9	81.0
09600	FLOORING	86.8	97.7	89.4	90.9	78.7	88.0	95.7	96.4	95.8	71.0	96.4	77.2	95.1	77.4	90.8	93.9	74.8	89.3
097,099	WALL FINISHES, PAINTS & COATINGS	90.9	90.4	90.6	90.9	76.2	82.4	90.2	88.3	89.1	92.1	80.5	85.4	90.2	77.5	82.8	96.5	71.3	81.9
09	FINISHES	91.2	89.7	90.5	92.2	75.3	83.6	92.9	86.6	89.7	86.9	82.1	84.5	93.8	81.0	87.3	94.8	75.4	84.9
10 - 14	TOTAL DIV. 10000 - 14000	100.0	91.1	98.1	100.0	88.2	97.5	100.0	89.2	97.7	100.0	66.8	93.0	100.0	88.6	97.6	100.0	66.5	92.9
15	MECHANICAL	99.8	91.0	95.7	96.7	87.8	92.6	96.6	85.6	91.5	97.3	83.1	90.7	99.7	85.0	92.9	96.9	74.7	86.6
16	ELECTRICAL	99.0	92.7	94.7	88.6	90.3	89.8	98.7	81.0	86.6	92.6	75.7	81.0	89.4	87.0	87.8	93.2	82.6	85.9
01 - 16	WEIGHTED AVERAGE	100.0	89.6	94.9	95.5	86.0	90.9	97.2	84.6	91.1	93.4	84.3	89.0	97.5	86.3	92.1	95.2	80.1	87.9

INDIANA / IOWA

DIVISION		SOUTH BEND 465 - 466			TERRE HAUTE 478			WASHINGTON 475			BURLINGTON 526			CARROLL 514			CEDAR RAPIDS 522 - 524		
		MAT.	INST.	TOTAL	MAT.	INST.	TOTAL	MAT.	INST.	TOTAL	MAT.	INST.	TOTAL	MAT.	INST.	TOTAL	MAT.	INST.	TOTAL
02	SITE CONSTRUCTION	88.1	95.1	93.4	85.1	130.7	120.0	85.9	129.7	119.5	83.8	95.8	93.0	75.1	95.0	90.3	84.8	94.3	92.1
03100	CONCRETE FORMS & ACCESSORIES	96.8	78.4	80.9	92.6	84.9	86.0	93.4	83.0	84.4	93.7	71.2	74.3	77.6	58.6	61.2	100.9	78.3	81.4
03200	CONCRETE REINFORCEMENT	96.8	79.7	87.0	97.3	84.2	89.8	89.9	75.6	81.8	99.4	81.7	89.3	100.2	60.6	77.6	100.1	82.2	89.9
03300	CAST-IN-PLACE CONCRETE	98.9	86.6	93.8	94.9	88.3	92.2	103.4	93.0	99.1	105.1	53.4	83.8	105.1	67.4	89.5	105.3	83.4	96.3
03	CONCRETE	91.2	83.2	87.2	106.8	86.1	96.4	112.9	85.2	99.1	97.4	67.6	82.5	95.9	62.9	79.4	97.7	81.2	89.5
04	MASONRY	87.1	83.3	84.7	95.2	83.8	88.2	88.4	81.1	83.9	99.6	56.3	73.0	103.3	56.6	74.6	107.3	79.9	90.4
05	METALS	102.1	105.7	103.4	91.4	89.2	90.6	84.2	83.1	83.8	87.4	84.2	86.2	87.4	74.2	82.6	89.6	86.4	88.4
06	WOOD & PLASTICS	102.1	76.8	89.0	95.2	84.5	89.6	95.4	81.9	88.4	97.9	75.2	86.2	81.0	61.3	70.8	105.2	76.6	90.4
07	THERMAL & MOISTURE PROTECTION	98.9	86.9	93.2	95.4	86.6	91.3	95.6	85.8	90.9	96.8	67.7	83.0	97.2	63.1	81.0	98.2	81.0	90.0
08	DOORS & WINDOWS	94.9	78.7	91.0	98.6	85.4	95.4	95.5	83.7	92.6	96.3	70.9	90.1	102.0	55.3	90.7	103.0	79.7	97.4
09200	PLASTER & GYPSUM BOARD	106.1	76.6	88.0	101.1	82.9	89.9	99.4	80.2	87.7	97.9	74.7	83.7	92.7	60.3	72.9	100.4	76.4	85.7
095,098	CEILINGS & ACOUSTICAL TREATMENT	93.8	76.6	82.4	95.1	82.9	87.0	81.5	80.2	80.7	108.5	74.7	86.2	108.5	60.3	76.7	112.6	76.4	88.7
09600	FLOORING	87.0	78.7	85.0	95.7	96.4	95.9	96.9	74.5	91.5	109.3	56.9	96.6	102.2	50.0	89.5	126.4	67.1	112.0
097,099	WALL FINISHES, PAINTS & COATINGS	90.9	83.3	86.5	96.5	84.9	89.8	96.5	89.0	92.2	106.9	100.5	103.2	106.9	47.1	72.1	111.4	77.0	91.4
09	FINISHES	91.7	78.5	84.9	96.2	87.1	91.5	94.0	81.8	87.8	105.6	72.1	88.5	101.6	55.8	78.2	112.6	75.1	93.5
10 - 14	TOTAL DIV. 10000 - 14000	100.0	85.5	96.9	100.0	93.8	98.7	100.0	92.2	98.4	100.0	57.4	91.0	100.0	57.4	91.0	100.0	86.6	97.2
15	MECHANICAL	99.8	81.3	91.3	100.0	85.9	93.5	96.9	87.3	92.4	97.2	81.0	89.7	97.2	62.6	81.2	100.4	86.2	93.8
16	ELECTRICAL	94.2	87.6	89.7	92.9	88.4	89.8	93.8	89.6	90.9	100.0	77.3	84.4	101.1	49.8	65.8	96.2	83.5	87.4
01 - 16	WEIGHTED AVERAGE	96.2	86.2	91.3	97.6	91.2	94.5	95.6	89.9	92.8	96.7	76.2	86.7	96.7	63.0	80.3	99.6	83.5	91.8

City Cost Indexes

IOWA

DIVISION		COUNCIL BLUFFS 515			CRESTON 508			DAVENPORT 527-528			DECORAH 521			DES MOINES 500-503,509			DUBUQUE 520		
		MAT.	INST.	TOTAL	MAT.	INST.	TOTAL	MAT.	INST.	TOTAL	MAT.	INST.	TOTAL	MAT.	INST.	TOTAL	MAT.	INST.	TOTAL
02	SITE CONSTRUCTION	88.1	91.9	91.0	75.0	96.1	91.1	83.6	99.4	95.7	82.6	95.5	92.5	77.1	101.3	95.6	83.0	92.0	89.9
03100	CONCRETE FORMS & ACCESSORIES	76.5	64.7	66.3	78.3	72.4	73.2	100.5	93.6	94.5	90.1	55.5	60.2	102.6	80.7	83.7	78.5	69.5	70.8
03200	CONCRETE REINFORCEMENT	102.2	80.2	89.7	99.6	77.8	87.2	100.1	96.1	97.8	99.4	60.8	77.4	100.1	78.5	87.8	98.7	82.0	89.2
03300	CAST-IN-PLACE CONCRETE	109.6	72.8	94.4	104.8	70.4	90.6	101.5	94.2	98.5	102.2	63.6	86.3	105.7	85.0	97.2	103.1	68.6	88.9
03	CONCRETE	99.4	71.2	85.3	95.8	73.2	84.5	95.8	94.3	95.0	95.3	60.3	77.8	98.0	82.2	90.1	94.0	72.2	83.1
04	MASONRY	107.6	75.0	87.6	103.3	61.4	77.5	106.9	84.7	93.3	122.0	52.6	79.4	101.4	81.8	89.3	108.3	73.5	86.9
05	METALS	94.9	84.9	91.3	87.3	81.9	85.4	89.6	94.9	91.5	87.5	74.1	82.6	89.5	86.8	88.5	88.1	85.5	87.2
06	WOOD & PLASTICS	79.5	62.9	70.9	81.6	76.2	78.8	105.2	92.4	98.6	94.3	56.9	75.0	106.8	79.0	92.4	81.8	67.4	74.3
07	THERMAL & MOISTURE PROTECTION	97.3	68.9	83.8	98.4	66.6	83.3	97.5	88.2	93.1	97.1	53.0	76.2	98.3	78.1	88.7	97.6	71.2	85.1
08	DOORS & WINDOWS	102.0	66.6	93.5	116.0	73.4	105.8	103.0	92.0	100.3	100.1	57.8	89.9	103.0	78.8	97.2	102.0	74.8	95.5
09200	PLASTER & GYPSUM BOARD	92.7	62.2	74.1	92.7	75.7	82.3	100.4	92.4	95.5	97.0	55.8	71.8	97.3	78.6	85.8	93.1	66.9	77.1
095,098	CEILINGS & ACOUSTICAL TREATMENT	108.5	62.2	78.0	108.5	75.7	86.9	112.6	92.4	99.3	108.5	55.8	73.7	111.3	78.6	89.7	108.5	66.9	81.1
09600	FLOORING	101.0	54.8	89.8	102.5	50.0	89.8	112.1	86.4	105.8	108.6	71.0	99.5	111.8	50.0	96.9	115.6	46.7	98.9
097,099	WALL FINISHES, PAINTS & COATINGS	102.5	58.1	76.7	106.9	58.1	78.6	106.9	101.9	104.0	106.9	49.9	73.8	106.9	83.7	93.4	110.1	61.1	81.6
09	FINISHES	101.8	61.1	81.0	101.7	67.0	84.0	107.6	93.0	100.2	105.2	58.0	81.1	106.1	74.5	90.0	107.1	63.3	84.7
10 - 14	TOTAL DIV. 10000 - 14000	100.0	81.5	96.1	100.0	82.8	96.4	100.0	91.8	98.3	100.0	64.4	92.5	100.0	88.3	97.5	100.0	84.0	96.6
15	MECHANICAL	100.4	79.7	90.8	97.2	65.4	82.5	100.4	100.0	100.2	97.2	54.6	77.5	100.4	89.5	95.3	100.4	87.0	94.2
16	ELECTRICAL	104.5	84.9	91.0	92.8	65.0	73.7	93.6	88.4	90.0	96.1	49.6	64.1	96.9	90.1	92.2	102.2	81.9	88.3
01 - 16	WEIGHTED AVERAGE	99.8	77.5	88.9	97.7	71.6	85.0	98.6	93.6	96.1	97.8	60.9	79.9	98.4	86.2	92.5	98.4	79.2	89.1

IOWA

DIVISION		FORT DODGE 505			MASON CITY 504			OTTUMWA 525			SHENANDOAH 516			SIBLEY 512			SIOUX CITY 510 - 511		
		MAT.	INST.	TOTAL	MAT.	INST.	TOTAL	MAT.	INST.	TOTAL	MAT.	INST.	TOTAL	MAT.	INST.	TOTAL	MAT.	INST.	TOTAL
02	SITE CONSTRUCTION	80.1	94.6	91.2	80.2	95.5	91.9	83.7	90.8	89.2	87.0	90.7	89.9	91.6	95.0	94.2	92.5	96.6	95.7
03100	CONCRETE FORMS & ACCESSORIES	79.1	31.8	38.3	85.3	56.0	60.0	87.7	62.2	65.7	78.8	63.2	65.4	79.5	50.3	54.3	100.9	70.2	74.4
03200	CONCRETE REINFORCEMENT	99.6	60.1	77.1	99.4	77.9	87.2	99.4	78.2	87.3	102.2	78.4	88.6	102.2	78.4	81.8	100.1	68.5	82.1
03300	CAST-IN-PLACE CONCRETE	98.3	42.4	75.3	98.3	63.9	84.1	105.8	70.4	91.2	105.9	58.3	86.3	103.8	58.2	85.0	104.4	62.3	87.1
03	CONCRETE	91.3	42.4	66.9	91.7	63.8	77.8	96.9	68.8	82.9	96.9	65.1	81.0	95.9	53.9	74.9	97.3	67.8	82.5
04	MASONRY	101.0	33.2	59.3	115.5	59.6	81.2	105.0	62.9	79.1	107.2	42.9	67.7	126.5	46.8	77.5	101.5	68.1	81.0
05	METALS	87.4	72.7	82.1	87.4	81.7	85.4	87.3	82.6	85.6	94.2	79.6	88.9	87.5	68.7	80.8	89.6	80.1	86.2
06	WOOD & PLASTICS	82.4	29.0	54.8	89.0	56.9	72.4	91.6	62.6	76.6	82.0	69.9	75.7	83.0	50.5	66.2	105.2	70.0	87.0
07	THERMAL & MOISTURE PROTECTION	97.5	38.2	69.3	96.7	58.2	78.4	97.9	66.2	82.8	96.3	52.3	75.4	96.8	58.9	78.8	97.5	64.0	81.6
08	DOORS & WINDOWS	107.9	35.5	90.4	97.3	62.2	88.8	102.0	67.6	93.7	90.6	66.0	84.7	97.7	49.1	86.0	103.0	67.8	94.5
09200	PLASTER & GYPSUM BOARD	93.1	26.9	52.7	95.3	55.8	71.1	96.1	61.9	75.2	93.6	69.5	78.8	93.6	49.2	66.5	100.4	69.3	81.4
095,098	CEILINGS & ACOUSTICAL TREATMENT	108.5	26.9	54.7	108.5	55.8	73.7	108.5	61.9	77.8	108.5	69.5	82.8	108.5	49.2	69.4	112.6	69.3	84.0
09600	FLOORING	104.1	71.0	96.1	106.8	71.0	98.1	119.3	75.5	108.7	101.8	51.6	89.7	103.3	51.2	90.7	112.6	70.7	102.4
097,099	WALL FINISHES, PAINTS & COATINGS	106.9	21.4	57.2	106.9	45.5	71.3	110.1	83.7	94.8	102.5	32.2	61.7	106.9	47.1	72.1	108.2	71.1	86.6
09	FINISHES	103.0	36.7	69.2	104.2	57.5	80.4	108.8	66.2	87.1	102.1	58.5	79.9	103.9	49.8	76.3	108.8	70.4	89.2
10 - 14	TOTAL DIV. 10000 - 14000	100.0	72.1	94.1	100.0	65.5	92.7	100.0	79.3	95.6	100.0	77.8	95.3	100.0	77.5	95.2	100.0	84.2	96.7
15	MECHANICAL	97.2	76.2	87.5	97.2	65.8	82.7	97.2	81.4	89.9	97.2	41.4	71.4	97.2	49.3	75.1	100.4	85.7	93.6
16	ELECTRICAL	103.8	66.2	77.9	102.2	49.6	66.0	99.7	77.3	84.3	96.1	39.4	57.2	96.1	49.8	64.3	96.2	77.9	83.6
01 - 16	WEIGHTED AVERAGE	97.2	59.5	78.8	96.9	65.2	81.4	97.9	75.3	86.9	96.7	57.3	77.5	97.9	57.1	78.0	99.0	77.6	88.6

DIVISION		IOWA						KANSAS											
		SPENCER 513			WATERLOO 506 - 507			BELLEVILLE 669			COLBY 677			DODGE CITY 678			EMPORIA 668		
		MAT.	INST.	TOTAL	MAT.	INST.	TOTAL	MAT.	INST.	TOTAL	MAT.	INST.	TOTAL	MAT.	INST.	TOTAL	MAT.	INST.	TOTAL
02	SITE CONSTRUCTION	91.7	94.9	94.2	84.1	95.9	93.1	106.4	93.2	96.3	103.8	93.2	95.7	105.8	93.2	96.1	96.8	90.7	92.1
03100	CONCRETE FORMS & ACCESSORIES	87.5	49.8	55.0	101.5	56.2	62.4	96.3	50.7	56.9	105.3	50.7	58.2	95.8	50.7	56.9	84.8	46.2	51.5
03200	CONCRETE REINFORCEMENT	102.2	48.7	71.7	100.1	81.9	89.7	104.4	69.7	84.7	107.0	69.7	85.7	104.4	69.7	84.7	103.0	61.3	79.2
03300	CAST-IN-PLACE CONCRETE	103.8	58.0	84.9	105.3	53.6	84.0	114.1	65.8	94.2	109.8	65.8	91.6	111.7	65.8	92.8	110.3	49.8	85.4
03	CONCRETE	96.5	53.6	75.0	97.7	61.1	79.4	111.8	61.1	86.5	109.3	61.1	85.2	110.1	61.1	85.6	104.3	52.0	78.2
04	MASONRY	126.5	46.8	77.6	101.6	62.6	77.6	93.9	50.3	67.1	95.5	50.3	67.8	103.1	50.3	70.7	94.8	49.8	69.1
05	METALS	87.5	68.2	80.5	89.6	85.0	87.9	91.4	86.3	89.5	91.7	86.3	89.7	92.8	86.3	90.4	91.1	82.1	87.9
06	WOOD & PLASTICS	91.5	50.5	70.3	105.9	56.9	80.6	94.8	50.8	72.0	103.3	50.8	76.1	94.2	50.8	71.7	83.7	46.5	64.5
07	THERMAL & MOISTURE PROTECTION	98.1	52.3	76.4	97.1	58.5	78.8	98.0	56.7	78.4	98.0	56.7	78.4	97.9	56.7	78.4	96.1	48.3	73.4
08	DOORS & WINDOWS	112.4	49.1	97.1	98.3	65.8	90.5	98.9	54.7	88.2	98.9	54.7	88.3	98.9	54.7	88.2	96.3	49.6	85.1
09200	PLASTER & GYPSUM BOARD	96.1	49.2	67.5	100.4	55.8	73.1	104.5	48.8	70.5	107.1	48.8	71.5	104.1	48.8	70.3	100.2	44.4	66.1
095,098	CEILINGS & ACOUSTICAL TREATMENT	108.5	49.2	69.4	112.6	55.8	75.1	92.4	48.8	63.7	92.4	48.8	63.7	92.4	48.8	63.7	92.4	44.4	60.7
09600	FLOORING	106.6	51.2	93.1	113.7	71.0	103.4	100.8	59.3	90.8	104.7	59.3	93.7	100.6	59.3	90.6	95.2	55.1	85.5
097,099	WALL FINISHES, PAINTS & COATINGS	106.9	47.1	72.1	108.2	42.2	69.8	91.0	58.6	72.2	91.0	58.6	72.2	91.0	58.6	72.2	91.0	58.6	72.2
09	FINISHES	105.4	49.8	77.0	108.3	57.0	82.1	97.2	52.6	74.4	98.7	52.6	75.2	97.0	52.6	74.4	93.9	48.5	70.8
10 - 14	TOTAL DIV. 10000 - 14000	100.0	49.1	89.2	100.0	78.4	95.4	100.0	60.1	91.6	100.0	60.1	91.6	100.0	60.1	91.6	100.0	54.9	90.5
15	MECHANICAL	97.2	49.3	75.0	100.4	54.8	79.3	97.1	56.8	78.4	97.1	56.8	78.4	100.2	56.8	80.1	97.1	63.2	81.4
16	ELECTRICAL	98.8	49.8	65.1	96.2	64.3	74.2	100.6	60.0	72.7	100.6	60.0	72.7	95.2	60.0	71.0	95.8	78.7	84.1
01 - 16	WEIGHTED AVERAGE	100.2	56.1	78.7	98.2	66.2	82.7	98.8	63.0	81.4	98.9	63.0	81.4	99.6	63.0	81.8	96.8	64.4	81.0

COST INDEXES

KANSAS

DIVISION		FORT SCOTT 667 MAT.	INST.	TOTAL	HAYS 676 MAT.	INST.	TOTAL	HUTCHINSON 675 MAT.	INST.	TOTAL	INDEPENDENCE 673 MAT.	INST.	TOTAL	KANSAS CITY 660-662 MAT.	INST.	TOTAL	LIBERAL 679 MAT.	INST.	TOTAL
02	SITE CONSTRUCTION	93.7	92.3	92.6	109.4	93.2	97.0	86.4	93.5	91.8	107.2	93.6	96.8	86.1	90.4	89.4	109.7	93.5	97.3
03100	CONCRETE FORMS & ACCESSORIES	107.1	66.9	72.4	101.9	50.7	57.7	88.3	35.1	42.4	117.5	35.5	46.7	102.4	90.3	92.0	96.3	34.6	43.1
03200	CONCRETE REINFORCEMENT	102.3	66.6	82.0	104.4	69.7	84.7	104.4	58.1	78.0	103.8	58.0	77.7	99.3	92.9	95.6	105.9	58.0	78.6
03300	CAST-IN-PLACE CONCRETE	102.4	70.5	89.2	86.5	65.8	78.0	80.1	48.4	67.0	112.2	49.1	86.2	87.6	93.1	89.9	86.5	48.2	70.7
03	CONCRETE	100.1	69.3	84.7	100.6	61.1	80.9	83.8	46.1	65.0	111.9	46.6	79.3	92.0	92.4	92.2	102.5	45.9	74.2
04	MASONRY	100.9	57.8	74.4	103.1	50.3	70.7	95.6	48.4	66.6	92.4	49.8	66.2	103.1	88.7	94.3	101.2	48.4	68.8
05	METALS	91.1	85.7	89.1	91.3	86.3	89.5	91.2	82.0	87.8	91.1	81.9	87.8	97.6	100.5	98.6	91.6	81.5	87.9
06	WOOD & PLASTICS	106.5	69.0	87.1	99.9	50.8	74.5	87.0	33.0	59.1	115.0	33.0	72.6	102.4	91.4	96.7	94.8	33.0	62.8
07	THERMAL & MOISTURE PROTECTION	97.2	66.9	82.8	98.4	56.7	78.6	96.6	48.5	73.8	98.1	47.3	74.0	95.6	91.3	93.6	98.5	43.9	72.6
08	DOORS & WINDOWS	96.3	69.1	89.8	98.8	54.7	88.2	98.8	42.2	85.2	96.3	42.2	83.3	97.7	88.5	95.5	98.9	42.2	85.2
09200	PLASTER & GYPSUM BOARD	105.8	67.7	82.5	105.8	48.8	71.0	101.9	30.5	58.2	110.5	30.5	61.6	100.5	90.8	94.6	104.5	30.5	59.3
095,098	CEILINGS & ACOUSTICAL TREATMENT	92.4	67.7	76.1	92.4	48.8	63.7	92.4	30.5	51.5	92.4	30.5	51.5	99.2	90.8	93.7	92.4	30.5	51.5
09600	FLOORING	111.7	59.6	99.1	103.4	59.3	92.7	97.3	59.3	88.1	109.8	59.3	97.5	90.7	63.3	84.0	100.8	59.3	90.8
097,099	WALL FINISHES, PAINTS & COATINGS	93.5	58.6	73.2	91.0	58.6	72.2	91.0	58.6	72.2	91.0	58.6	72.2	99.2	98.5	98.8	91.0	58.6	72.2
09	FINISHES	100.4	64.9	82.3	98.4	52.6	75.1	94.5	40.9	67.1	101.0	41.2	70.5	96.2	86.1	91.0	97.6	40.9	68.7
10 - 14	TOTAL DIV. 10000 - 14000	100.0	71.5	94.0	100.0	60.1	91.6	100.0	55.7	90.7	100.0	56.3	90.8	100.0	90.7	98.0	100.0	55.6	90.6
15	MECHANICAL	97.1	54.6	77.4	97.1	56.8	78.4	97.1	46.4	73.6	97.1	44.6	72.8	100.0	97.1	98.7	97.1	39.2	70.3
16	ELECTRICAL	94.6	78.7	83.7	98.7	60.0	72.1	90.2	71.2	77.1	93.9	78.7	83.5	104.5	78.8	86.8	95.2	47.5	62.4
01 - 16	WEIGHTED AVERAGE	97.1	70.2	84.0	98.1	63.0	81.1	93.7	58.0	76.3	98.6	59.1	79.4	98.0	90.2	94.2	97.9	52.4	75.8

KANSAS / KENTUCKY

DIVISION		SALINA 674 MAT.	INST.	TOTAL	TOPEKA 664-666 MAT.	INST.	TOTAL	WICHITA 670-672 MAT.	INST.	TOTAL	ASHLAND 411-412 MAT.	INST.	TOTAL	BOWLING GREEN 421-422 MAT.	INST.	TOTAL	CAMPTON 413-414 MAT.	INST.	TOTAL
02	SITE CONSTRUCTION	95.6	93.5	93.9	88.4	90.8	90.2	89.7	93.7	92.8	104.9	86.1	90.5	70.8	100.9	93.9	79.6	100.6	95.7
03100	CONCRETE FORMS & ACCESSORIES	90.8	53.4	58.5	101.3	51.6	58.5	98.0	63.6	68.3	82.5	106.1	102.9	82.2	85.3	84.9	84.7	39.5	45.7
03200	CONCRETE REINFORCEMENT	103.8	86.9	94.2	96.5	92.6	94.3	96.5	87.8	91.5	90.7	105.7	99.3	88.1	73.8	79.9	89.0	74.1	80.5
03300	CAST-IN-PLACE CONCRETE	96.9	56.0	80.0	91.3	60.8	78.7	85.8	64.3	76.9	90.3	108.0	97.6	89.6	85.9	88.0	99.9	46.3	77.8
03	CONCRETE	97.5	62.2	79.8	91.4	64.1	77.8	88.4	69.7	79.1	97.0	107.4	102.2	95.3	83.4	89.4	99.4	49.5	74.4
04	MASONRY	117.7	48.4	75.1	96.7	60.6	74.5	91.3	68.9	77.6	93.6	107.0	101.8	95.2	86.2	89.7	93.8	36.2	58.4
05	METALS	92.6	93.4	92.9	95.5	97.4	96.2	95.5	95.2	95.4	93.3	115.1	101.2	94.8	80.8	89.8	94.3	75.6	87.5
06	WOOD & PLASTICS	89.4	54.6	71.4	98.8	48.3	72.7	96.3	62.8	79.0	75.5	104.3	90.4	88.5	82.8	85.6	86.8	38.8	62.0
07	THERMAL & MOISTURE PROTECTION	97.3	61.7	80.4	97.2	72.8	85.6	96.8	71.4	84.8	87.4	101.8	94.2	86.2	84.6	85.4	95.8	48.2	73.2
08	DOORS & WINDOWS	98.8	59.0	89.2	99.0	64.0	90.5	99.0	68.3	91.6	96.0	100.3	97.0	97.7	77.7	92.9	99.3	45.9	86.4
09200	PLASTER & GYPSUM BOARD	102.8	52.8	72.3	106.2	46.3	69.6	106.2	61.3	78.7	69.3	104.4	90.8	97.3	82.5	88.3	97.3	35.8	59.7
095,098	CEILINGS & ACOUSTICAL TREATMENT	92.4	52.8	66.3	99.2	46.3	64.3	99.2	61.3	74.2	83.6	104.4	97.3	91.0	82.5	85.4	91.0	35.8	54.6
09600	FLOORING	98.6	43.3	85.2	102.2	55.1	90.8	101.3	79.4	96.0	76.2	100.4	82.0	91.7	73.1	87.2	93.1	50.8	82.9
097,099	WALL FINISHES, PAINTS & COATINGS	91.0	46.2	64.9	91.0	68.4	77.9	91.0	68.7	78.0	99.3	96.0	97.4	96.5	78.8	86.2	96.5	39.1	63.2
09	FINISHES	95.6	50.0	72.3	98.1	52.2	74.7	97.9	66.6	82.0	81.6	104.0	93.0	93.7	82.2	87.8	94.2	40.8	67.0
10 - 14	TOTAL DIV. 10000 - 14000	100.0	72.7	94.2	100.0	79.5	95.7	100.0	76.8	95.1	100.0	103.6	100.8	100.0	74.5	94.6	100.0	67.4	93.1
15	MECHANICAL	100.2	42.9	73.7	100.2	72.0	87.2	100.2	73.8	88.0	96.7	99.6	98.0	100.2	87.5	94.3	96.9	41.7	71.4
16	ELECTRICAL	94.7	74.2	80.6	101.4	72.2	81.4	99.3	74.2	82.1	89.0	98.1	95.3	93.2	90.4	91.3	88.8	32.9	50.4
01 - 16	WEIGHTED AVERAGE	98.3	63.7	81.5	97.4	71.4	84.8	96.6	75.6	86.4	93.8	101.9	97.7	95.6	86.6	91.2	95.7	50.5	73.7

KENTUCKY

DIVISION		CORBIN 407-409 MAT.	INST.	TOTAL	COVINGTON 410 MAT.	INST.	TOTAL	ELIZABETHTOWN 427 MAT.	INST.	TOTAL	FRANKFORT 406 MAT.	INST.	TOTAL	HAZARD 417-418 MAT.	INST.	TOTAL	HENDERSON 424 MAT.	INST.	TOTAL
02	SITE CONSTRUCTION	76.9	101.1	95.4	75.9	116.7	107.2	66.0	100.4	92.4	77.6	102.7	96.9	77.5	101.1	95.6	74.1	130.6	117.4
03100	CONCRETE FORMS & ACCESSORIES	81.2	39.6	45.3	80.0	87.6	86.5	76.3	82.2	81.3	92.9	69.3	72.6	81.2	39.6	45.3	88.7	84.9	85.4
03200	CONCRETE REINFORCEMENT	88.5	74.1	80.3	87.7	102.3	96.0	88.5	99.1	94.6	89.8	86.7	88.1	89.4	74.1	80.7	88.2	100.8	95.4
03300	CAST-IN-PLACE CONCRETE	94.5	47.0	74.9	95.7	87.7	92.4	81.0	80.5	80.8	94.5	78.4	87.9	96.1	47.0	75.8	79.1	94.1	85.3
03	CONCRETE	94.3	49.8	72.1	97.6	90.7	94.1	87.3	84.9	86.1	95.3	76.2	85.7	95.9	49.8	72.9	92.5	91.1	91.8
04	MASONRY	93.4	36.5	58.4	109.0	95.8	100.9	78.9	81.8	80.7	93.5	65.9	76.5	90.8	36.5	57.4	99.7	97.2	98.2
05	METALS	94.2	76.6	87.9	91.9	98.2	94.2	94.1	91.4	93.1	94.3	86.5	91.5	94.3	76.6	87.9	84.1	94.8	87.9
06	WOOD & PLASTICS	83.2	38.8	60.3	83.7	85.7	84.7	82.7	82.8	82.8	95.2	67.9	81.1	83.2	38.8	60.3	90.6	80.9	85.6
07	THERMAL & MOISTURE PROTECTION	95.4	48.2	73.0	92.2	94.2	93.1	85.8	82.5	84.2	95.6	73.5	85.1	95.6	48.2	73.1	94.9	97.1	95.9
08	DOORS & WINDOWS	98.6	45.9	85.9	101.2	88.5	98.1	97.7	87.3	95.2	97.8	73.6	92.0	99.7	45.9	86.7	95.9	86.6	93.7
09200	PLASTER & GYPSUM BOARD	96.4	35.8	59.4	90.6	85.8	87.7	96.0	82.5	87.8	100.3	65.8	79.2	96.4	35.8	59.4	97.6	79.2	86.4
095,098	CEILINGS & ACOUSTICAL TREATMENT	91.0	35.8	54.6	95.1	85.8	89.0	91.0	82.5	85.4	91.0	65.8	74.4	91.0	35.8	54.6	81.5	79.2	80.0
09600	FLOORING	91.3	50.8	81.5	68.5	99.2	75.9	88.9	77.8	86.2	96.6	62.1	88.2	91.3	50.8	81.5	94.9	92.3	94.3
097,099	WALL FINISHES, PAINTS & COATINGS	96.5	39.1	63.2	92.1	95.2	93.9	96.5	83.8	89.1	96.5	59.1	74.8	96.5	39.1	63.2	96.5	100.7	98.9
09	FINISHES	93.3	40.8	66.5	86.0	90.2	88.1	92.3	81.2	86.6	95.6	66.1	80.6	93.4	40.8	66.6	92.6	87.4	89.9
10 - 14	TOTAL DIV. 10000 - 14000	100.0	67.4	93.1	100.0	93.3	98.6	100.0	87.7	97.4	100.0	82.1	96.2	100.0	67.4	93.1	100.0	92.5	98.4
15	MECHANICAL	96.9	41.7	71.4	97.3	93.2	95.4	97.1	83.5	90.8	100.0	73.8	87.9	96.9	41.7	71.4	97.1	86.0	91.9
16	ELECTRICAL	89.3	33.0	50.6	95.2	85.1	88.2	88.5	90.4	89.8	93.3	72.7	79.1	88.8	33.0	50.4	92.2	89.0	90.0
01 - 16	WEIGHTED AVERAGE	94.7	50.7	73.3	95.6	93.9	94.8	92.2	87.0	89.7	96.1	76.4	86.5	94.9	50.7	73.4	93.1	94.1	93.6

KENTUCKY

DIVISION		LEXINGTON 403 - 405			LOUISVILLE 400 - 402			OWENSBORO 423			PADUCAH 420			PIKEVILLE 415 - 416			SOMERSET 425 - 426		
		MAT.	INST.	TOTAL	MAT.	INST.	TOTAL	MAT.	INST.	TOTAL	MAT.	INST.	TOTAL	MAT.	INST.	TOTAL	MAT.	INST.	TOTAL
02	SITE CONSTRUCTION	78.3	102.9	97.1	67.9	100.4	92.8	83.2	130.4	119.3	77.5	130.4	118.0	115.7	84.5	91.8	70.3	100.6	93.5
03100	CONCRETE FORMS & ACCESSORIES	93.0	73.1	75.8	91.6	82.2	83.5	86.7	75.4	77.0	84.0	84.4	84.4	93.4	69.4	72.7	81.9	39.5	45.3
03200	CONCRETE REINFORCEMENT	97.3	98.1	97.7	97.3	99.1	98.3	88.2	99.4	94.6	88.7	88.5	88.6	91.2	65.1	76.2	88.5	74.1	80.3
03300	CAST-IN-PLACE CONCRETE	96.7	76.0	88.2	93.6	80.6	88.2	92.4	87.8	90.5	84.3	91.9	87.4	99.2	82.6	92.3	79.2	46.3	65.6
03	CONCRETE	97.3	79.1	88.2	95.7	84.9	90.3	104.9	84.5	94.7	97.1	87.9	92.5	111.2	74.8	93.0	82.0	49.5	65.7
04	MASONRY	92.3	56.6	70.3	92.7	81.8	86.0	92.3	61.3	73.3	95.3	81.1	86.6	92.9	65.6	76.1	86.0	36.2	55.4
05	METALS	96.3	90.7	94.3	96.3	91.4	94.5	86.2	92.1	88.3	84.0	89.9	86.1	93.2	93.3	93.2	94.2	75.6	87.5
06	WOOD & PLASTICS	95.2	75.3	84.9	98.2	82.8	90.3	88.4	74.9	81.4	85.8	83.2	84.4	86.4	66.6	76.1	84.0	38.8	60.7
07	THERMAL & MOISTURE PROTECTION	95.8	68.9	83.0	86.4	83.0	84.8	95.3	76.1	86.2	94.9	84.2	89.3	88.3	63.7	76.6	94.8	48.2	72.7
08	DOORS & WINDOWS	98.6	82.9	94.8	98.6	87.3	95.9	95.9	83.3	92.9	95.1	85.6	92.8	96.8	70.0	90.3	98.6	45.9	85.9
09200	PLASTER & GYPSUM BOARD	101.1	73.4	84.1	103.9	82.5	90.8	96.8	73.0	82.3	95.9	81.5	87.1	72.3	65.5	68.1	96.8	35.8	59.5
095,098	CEILINGS & ACOUSTICAL TREATMENT	95.1	73.4	80.8	95.1	82.5	86.8	81.5	73.0	75.9	81.5	81.5	81.5	83.6	65.5	71.6	91.0	35.8	54.6
09600	FLOORING	96.6	50.8	85.5	95.1	77.8	90.9	94.0	73.1	88.9	92.9	73.1	88.1	80.8	60.4	75.9	91.6	50.8	81.7
097,099	WALL FINISHES, PAINTS & COATINGS	96.5	69.5	80.8	96.5	83.8	89.1	96.5	100.7	98.9	96.5	78.4	86.0	99.3	77.4	86.6	96.5	39.1	63.2
09	FINISHES	96.5	68.1	82.1	96.2	81.2	88.6	92.6	77.2	84.7	91.8	81.3	86.4	84.2	68.2	76.0	93.0	40.8	66.4
10 - 14	TOTAL DIV. 10000 - 14000	100.0	92.0	98.3	100.0	92.4	98.4	100.0	94.0	98.7	100.0	84.9	96.8	100.0	72.2	94.1	100.0	67.4	93.1
15	MECHANICAL	100.0	57.3	80.3	100.0	83.5	92.4	100.2	63.0	83.0	97.1	89.5	93.6	96.7	66.8	82.9	97.1	41.7	71.5
16	ELECTRICAL	94.0	60.5	70.9	94.0	90.4	91.5	92.4	89.0	90.0	96.3	89.5	91.7	94.0	58.8	69.8	89.5	32.9	50.6
01 - 16	WEIGHTED AVERAGE	96.9	71.9	84.7	96.1	87.2	91.8	95.5	83.1	89.5	93.6	91.1	92.4	96.7	70.9	84.1	92.6	50.5	72.1

LOUISIANA

DIVISION		ALEXANDRIA 713 - 714			BATON ROUGE 707 - 708			HAMMOND 704			LAFAYETTE 705			LAKE CHARLES 706			MONROE 712		
		MAT.	INST.	TOTAL	MAT.	INST.	TOTAL	MAT.	INST.	TOTAL	MAT.	INST.	TOTAL	MAT.	INST.	TOTAL	MAT.	INST.	TOTAL
02	SITE CONSTRUCTION	104.2	85.4	89.8	114.7	87.0	93.4	115.5	88.5	94.9	115.8	88.4	94.8	116.4	86.7	93.7	104.2	85.2	89.7
03100	CONCRETE FORMS & ACCESSORIES	78.3	50.9	54.7	98.7	56.2	62.0	76.5	62.7	64.6	98.2	47.0	54.0	98.8	57.1	62.8	77.6	51.7	55.3
03200	CONCRETE REINFORCEMENT	97.0	68.2	80.6	98.1	59.2	75.9	96.6	69.5	81.2	98.1	58.6	75.5	98.1	59.0	75.8	96.0	68.3	80.2
03300	CAST-IN-PLACE CONCRETE	97.9	48.9	77.7	88.6	58.8	76.3	89.6	57.8	76.5	89.1	58.0	76.3	93.8	60.5	80.1	97.9	53.8	79.7
03	CONCRETE	90.0	54.6	72.3	93.3	58.5	75.9	92.2	63.0	77.6	93.5	54.1	73.8	95.8	59.5	77.7	89.8	56.6	73.2
04	MASONRY	114.7	50.8	75.4	102.3	60.7	76.7	103.1	60.6	77.0	100.6	48.9	69.8	101.1	61.0	76.5	109.6	52.6	74.6
05	METALS	86.6	76.6	83.0	101.0	72.2	90.6	101.6	77.8	93.0	100.6	71.6	90.1	100.6	72.3	90.4	86.6	76.1	82.8
06	WOOD & PLASTICS	80.0	51.4	65.2	105.8	56.6	80.4	82.5	63.5	72.7	105.8	45.0	74.4	103.7	57.5	79.8	79.1	51.9	65.0
07	THERMAL & MOISTURE PROTECTION	98.3	55.5	78.0	99.3	62.3	81.7	101.4	66.9	85.0	102.2	57.2	80.9	101.9	62.3	83.1	98.2	57.9	79.1
08	DOORS & WINDOWS	100.2	56.9	89.7	104.6	56.7	93.1	100.0	68.5	92.4	104.6	50.4	91.6	104.6	59.0	93.6	100.2	62.0	91.0
09200	PLASTER & GYPSUM BOARD	92.2	50.8	66.9	105.1	56.1	75.1	98.9	63.1	77.0	105.1	44.1	67.8	105.1	56.9	75.7	91.7	51.3	67.0
095,098	CEILINGS & ACOUSTICAL TREATMENT	99.7	50.8	67.4	100.7	56.1	71.3	100.6	63.1	75.9	99.2	44.1	62.9	100.7	56.9	71.8	99.7	51.3	67.8
09600	FLOORING	107.4	58.2	95.5	110.7	70.2	100.9	98.9	70.2	91.9	110.9	52.5	96.7	110.9	61.3	98.9	107.0	50.6	93.3
097,099	WALL FINISHES, PAINTS & COATINGS	95.6	49.0	65.8	97.1	56.2	73.3	97.1	68.0	80.2	97.1	56.2	73.3	97.1	51.8	70.8	95.6	50.6	69.4
09	FINISHES	98.3	51.6	74.5	104.0	58.7	80.9	99.1	64.4	81.4	103.7	47.9	75.2	104.0	57.2	80.1	98.1	50.7	73.9
10 - 14	TOTAL DIV. 10000 - 14000	100.0	84.9	96.8	100.0	73.5	94.4	100.0	75.3	94.8	100.0	71.5	94.0	100.0	73.7	94.5	100.0	70.9	93.9
15	MECHANICAL	100.1	45.3	74.7	100.2	51.6	77.7	97.1	63.8	81.7	100.2	56.6	80.0	100.2	63.6	83.2	100.1	54.6	79.0
16	ELECTRICAL	95.5	55.1	67.7	96.4	60.1	71.4	95.0	59.1	70.3	97.0	71.6	79.5	96.4	63.1	73.5	98.6	59.0	71.4
01 - 16	WEIGHTED AVERAGE	96.9	58.1	78.0	100.7	62.1	81.9	98.7	67.0	83.3	100.8	61.6	81.7	101.0	65.0	83.5	96.8	60.7	79.2

LOUISIANA / MAINE

DIVISION		NEW ORLEANS 700 - 701			SHREVEPORT 710 - 711			THIBODAUX 703			AUGUSTA 043			BANGOR 044			BATH 045		
		MAT.	INST.	TOTAL	MAT.	INST.	TOTAL	MAT.	INST.	TOTAL	MAT.	INST.	TOTAL	MAT.	INST.	TOTAL	MAT.	INST.	TOTAL
02	SITE CONSTRUCTION	118.5	89.1	96.0	102.8	85.1	89.2	118.2	88.5	95.4	87.2	100.9	97.7	87.1	103.2	99.5	85.7	101.3	97.6
03100	CONCRETE FORMS & ACCESSORIES	97.7	64.2	68.8	100.1	54.8	61.0	90.4	63.6	67.3	97.8	39.0	47.0	91.4	90.6	90.7	86.2	43.6	49.5
03200	CONCRETE REINFORCEMENT	98.1	69.6	81.8	95.5	68.2	80.0	96.6	69.5	81.2	91.1	40.9	62.5	91.1	117.9	106.4	90.1	94.8	92.8
03300	CAST-IN-PLACE CONCRETE	92.9	62.5	80.4	96.5	57.9	80.6	96.2	61.9	82.1	81.6	48.9	68.1	81.6	74.4	78.6	81.6	52.3	69.5
03	CONCRETE	95.3	65.3	80.3	90.0	59.3	74.7	97.4	64.8	81.1	100.5	44.5	72.5	99.5	89.3	94.4	99.6	56.0	77.8
04	MASONRY	103.2	61.4	77.5	102.6	47.4	68.7	129.6	61.1	87.5	93.6	43.4	62.7	111.1	63.7	82.0	118.5	41.4	71.1
05	METALS	103.3	78.1	94.2	87.4	75.6	83.2	101.6	77.3	92.8	95.1	75.1	87.9	94.9	86.9	92.0	93.3	59.6	81.2
06	WOOD & PLASTICS	99.5	65.2	80.3	102.6	56.5	78.7	92.1	64.7	77.9	99.8	37.3	67.5	93.1	93.2	93.1	87.7	41.7	63.9
07	THERMAL & MOISTURE PROTECTION	102.7	65.9	85.3	97.4	57.1	78.3	102.9	65.3	85.1	99.8	42.3	72.5	99.6	64.2	82.8	99.6	50.4	76.3
08	DOORS & WINDOWS	103.4	68.7	95.0	98.1	59.7	88.8	105.6	69.2	96.8	106.8	45.3	92.0	106.8	82.1	100.8	106.8	38.5	90.3
09200	PLASTER & GYPSUM BOARD	104.2	64.9	80.2	97.6	56.0	72.2	102.3	64.4	79.1	96.7	34.1	58.4	93.9	91.7	92.6	92.1	38.6	59.4
095,098	CEILINGS & ACOUSTICAL TREATMENT	99.2	64.9	76.6	101.1	56.0	71.4	100.6	64.4	76.7	94.4	34.1	54.6	93.1	91.7	92.2	90.0	38.6	56.1
09600	FLOORING	111.4	60.1	98.9	118.5	53.1	102.6	107.1	64.6	96.8	99.9	50.9	88.0	97.5	50.9	86.2	95.5	50.9	84.7
097,099	WALL FINISHES, PAINTS & COATINGS	99.0	65.9	79.8	95.6	49.0	68.5	99.0	64.4	78.9	95.6	28.2	56.4	95.6	39.0	62.7	95.6	28.8	56.8
09	FINISHES	104.2	63.4	83.4	102.9	53.5	77.7	102.6	63.8	82.8	98.4	39.1	68.2	97.0	78.1	87.3	95.5	42.3	68.3
10 - 14	TOTAL DIV. 10000 - 14000	100.0	75.7	94.9	100.0	71.2	93.9	100.0	75.5	94.8	100.0	64.5	92.5	100.0	87.7	97.4	100.0	65.8	92.8
15	MECHANICAL	100.2	65.4	84.0	100.1	58.2	80.7	97.1	62.4	81.0	99.8	30.8	67.9	99.8	85.0	93.0	96.7	61.8	80.5
16	ELECTRICAL	96.7	67.7	76.8	96.6	69.6	78.1	92.9	67.7	75.6	104.0	86.1	91.7	100.6	86.2	90.7	97.3	36.0	55.1
01 - 16	WEIGHTED AVERAGE	101.4	69.1	85.7	96.9	63.3	80.5	101.9	68.3	85.6	99.5	56.9	78.8	99.8	84.4	92.3	98.8	54.7	77.4

COST INDEXES

MAINE

DIVISION		HOULTON 047			KITTERY 039			LEWISTON 042			MACHIAS 046			PORTLAND 040-041			ROCKLAND 048		
		MAT.	INST.	TOTAL	MAT.	INST.	TOTAL	MAT.	INST.	TOTAL	MAT.	INST.	TOTAL	MAT.	INST.	TOTAL	MAT.	INST.	TOTAL
02	SITE CONSTRUCTION	87.3	101.4	98.1	81.9	100.6	96.3	85.3	103.2	99.0	86.7	101.3	97.9	84.7	103.2	98.9	83.2	100.6	96.5
03100	CONCRETE FORMS & ACCESSORIES	95.7	84.0	85.6	86.8	50.5	55.5	97.9	90.3	91.4	92.2	60.4	64.8	97.1	90.3	91.3	93.4	60.7	65.2
03200	CONCRETE REINFORCEMENT	91.1	117.7	106.2	89.5	52.8	68.6	111.9	117.9	115.3	91.1	80.8	85.2	111.9	117.9	115.3	91.1	80.9	85.2
03300	CAST-IN-PLACE CONCRETE	81.6	56.8	71.4	81.5	57.5	71.6	90.8	74.3	84.0	81.6	58.0	71.9	84.5	74.3	80.3	83.2	58.4	73.0
03	CONCRETE	100.6	80.1	90.4	94.7	54.6	74.6	102.8	89.2	96.0	100.1	63.5	81.8	99.7	89.2	94.4	96.9	63.8	80.3
04	MASONRY	93.6	49.6	66.5	107.4	46.7	70.1	94.7	63.7	75.6	93.6	49.8	66.7	92.6	63.7	74.8	87.3	49.9	64.3
05	METALS	93.6	83.0	89.8	93.2	76.2	87.1	98.1	86.6	94.0	93.6	70.9	85.4	98.2	86.6	94.0	93.4	71.5	85.5
06	WOOD & PLASTICS	97.6	93.2	95.3	88.3	50.1	68.5	99.8	93.2	96.4	94.0	60.5	76.7	99.8	93.2	96.4	95.3	60.5	77.3
07	THERMAL & MOISTURE PROTECTION	99.8	54.4	78.2	99.2	50.1	75.9	99.5	64.2	82.8	99.7	49.2	75.8	99.4	64.2	82.7	99.4	54.1	77.9
08	DOORS & WINDOWS	106.8	82.1	100.9	106.7	54.2	94.1	110.0	82.1	103.3	106.8	54.4	94.2	110.0	82.1	103.3	106.8	54.4	94.1
09200	PLASTER & GYPSUM BOARD	95.8	91.7	93.3	92.1	47.2	64.7	98.2	91.7	94.3	94.5	58.1	72.2	98.2	91.7	94.3	94.7	58.1	72.3
095,098	CEILINGS & ACOUSTICAL TREATMENT	91.4	91.7	91.6	90.0	47.2	61.8	102.6	91.7	95.4	91.4	58.1	69.4	102.6	91.7	95.4	90.0	58.1	68.9
09600	FLOORING	99.0	50.9	87.3	95.8	50.9	84.9	99.9	50.9	88.0	97.9	25.0	80.2	99.9	50.9	88.0	98.2	50.9	86.7
097,099	WALL FINISHES, PAINTS & COATINGS	95.6	39.0	62.7	95.6	39.7	63.1	95.6	39.0	62.7	95.6	29.6	57.2	95.6	39.0	62.7	95.6	39.0	62.7
09	FINISHES	97.4	74.7	85.9	95.2	48.9	71.6	99.8	78.1	88.7	96.9	50.9	73.4	99.9	78.1	88.7	96.5	56.5	76.1
10 - 14	TOTAL DIV. 10000 - 14000	100.0	74.4	94.6	100.0	67.7	93.2	100.0	87.5	97.4	100.0	71.7	94.0	100.0	87.5	97.4	100.0	71.7	94.0
15	MECHANICAL	96.7	53.5	76.7	96.7	53.6	76.8	99.8	85.0	93.0	96.7	55.5	77.6	99.8	85.0	93.0	96.7	55.5	77.7
16	ELECTRICAL	104.0	33.0	55.2	97.3	55.2	68.3	104.0	53.1	69.0	104.0	86.1	91.7	104.2	53.1	69.1	103.9	86.1	91.7
01 - 16	WEIGHTED AVERAGE	98.5	65.3	82.3	97.4	59.7	79.1	100.8	78.7	90.0	98.3	66.8	83.0	100.3	78.7	89.8	97.3	67.6	82.9

DIVISION		MAINE WATERVILLE 049			MARYLAND ANNAPOLIS 214			BALTIMORE 210 - 212			COLLEGE PARK 207 - 208			CUMBERLAND 215			EASTON 216		
		MAT.	INST.	TOTAL	MAT.	INST.	TOTAL	MAT.	INST.	TOTAL	MAT.	INST.	TOTAL	MAT.	INST.	TOTAL	MAT.	INST.	TOTAL
02	SITE CONSTRUCTION	87.4	100.9	97.8	93.6	87.8	89.2	94.5	92.3	92.8	100.7	89.8	92.3	86.7	88.1	87.8	93.1	85.6	87.4
03100	CONCRETE FORMS & ACCESSORIES	85.4	39.0	45.3	101.0	66.2	71.0	101.1	76.2	79.6	79.4	72.4	73.3	89.6	80.8	82.0	86.8	41.8	48.0
03200	CONCRETE REINFORCEMENT	91.1	40.9	62.5	97.2	93.1	94.9	97.2	93.1	94.9	99.2	71.4	83.4	85.9	79.3	82.1	85.1	25.2	51.0
03300	CAST-IN-PLACE CONCRETE	81.6	48.9	68.1	99.0	79.7	91.0	99.0	80.7	91.5	113.6	74.1	97.3	88.5	85.3	87.2	98.2	49.7	78.2
03	CONCRETE	101.2	44.5	72.9	100.4	77.4	88.9	100.4	82.2	91.3	104.7	74.3	89.5	89.6	83.2	86.4	97.3	43.6	70.4
04	MASONRY	105.2	43.4	67.2	88.1	74.6	79.8	88.1	74.6	79.8	103.2	70.8	83.2	85.8	77.7	80.9	99.9	45.4	66.4
05	METALS	93.5	75.1	86.9	95.1	101.8	97.5	95.9	102.6	98.3	92.2	96.4	93.7	94.9	96.0	95.3	95.1	68.5	85.5
06	WOOD & PLASTICS	86.8	37.3	61.2	101.2	63.9	81.9	101.2	77.3	88.8	76.5	73.6	75.0	89.7	80.1	84.7	86.8	42.3	63.8
07	THERMAL & MOISTURE PROTECTION	99.7	42.3	72.5	96.9	79.0	88.4	96.9	80.7	89.2	93.6	78.1	86.3	96.4	83.1	90.1	96.5	49.4	74.2
08	DOORS & WINDOWS	106.8	45.3	92.0	92.3	79.5	89.2	92.3	86.7	91.0	98.3	73.0	92.2	93.5	85.3	91.5	91.6	38.6	78.8
09200	PLASTER & GYPSUM BOARD	91.9	34.1	56.6	100.9	63.6	78.1	100.9	77.2	86.4	94.9	72.6	81.3	97.9	80.3	87.1	97.0	41.2	62.9
095,098	CEILINGS & ACOUSTICAL TREATMENT	91.4	34.1	53.6	89.7	63.6	72.4	89.7	77.2	81.4	97.0	72.6	80.9	89.7	80.3	83.5	89.7	41.2	57.7
09600	FLOORING	95.3	50.9	84.5	91.6	81.7	89.2	91.6	81.7	89.2	88.9	78.2	86.3	87.0	78.3	84.9	86.2	19.4	70.0
097,099	WALL FINISHES, PAINTS & COATINGS	95.6	28.2	56.4	98.2	80.2	87.7	98.2	80.2	87.7	105.7	80.1	90.8	98.2	60.3	76.2	98.2	31.2	59.3
09	FINISHES	95.8	39.1	66.9	91.0	69.3	79.9	91.1	77.1	84.0	92.2	74.1	83.0	88.7	77.8	83.1	88.6	37.6	62.6
10 - 14	TOTAL DIV. 10000 - 14000	100.0	64.5	92.5	100.0	83.3	96.9	100.0	85.5	96.9	100.0	84.2	96.7	100.0	88.5	97.6	100.0	61.7	91.9
15	MECHANICAL	96.7	30.8	66.2	99.9	86.1	93.5	99.9	86.2	93.6	97.0	80.6	89.4	96.8	75.5	87.0	96.8	34.2	67.9
16	ELECTRICAL	103.9	86.1	91.7	100.6	92.5	95.0	101.9	94.5	96.8	96.9	92.4	93.8	98.4	85.7	89.6	97.4	62.0	73.1
01 - 16	WEIGHTED AVERAGE	98.9	56.9	78.5	96.5	83.8	90.3	96.8	86.7	91.9	97.2	82.0	89.8	93.7	82.8	88.4	95.4	51.2	73.9

DIVISION		MARYLAND ELKTON 219			HAGERSTOWN 217			SALISBURY 218			SILVER SPRING 209			WALDORF 206			MASSACHUSETTS BOSTON 020 - 022, 024		
		MAT.	INST.	TOTAL	MAT.	INST.	TOTAL	MAT.	INST.	TOTAL	MAT.	INST.	TOTAL	MAT.	INST.	TOTAL	MAT.	INST.	TOTAL
02	SITE CONSTRUCTION	81.3	86.7	85.5	84.7	88.1	87.3	93.1	85.8	87.5	88.0	82.2	83.6	94.3	82.5	85.2	92.3	110.2	106.0
03100	CONCRETE FORMS & ACCESSORIES	94.8	77.5	79.9	88.4	77.9	79.3	105.3	39.1	48.2	89.1	71.3	73.8	97.9	65.0	69.5	103.9	131.3	127.6
03200	CONCRETE REINFORCEMENT	85.1	74.2	78.9	85.9	79.2	82.1	85.1	74.0	78.8	98.2	81.0	88.4	98.8	73.3	84.3	110.7	141.3	128.1
03300	CAST-IN-PLACE CONCRETE	79.5	58.1	70.7	84.2	66.4	76.9	98.2	48.8	77.8	116.4	77.1	100.2	130.4	70.9	105.9	105.2	142.0	120.4
03	CONCRETE	82.4	70.9	76.6	85.7	75.4	80.6	98.6	50.3	74.4	103.0	76.5	89.8	113.9	70.0	92.0	113.3	136.0	124.6
04	MASONRY	86.5	50.0	64.1	92.3	77.7	83.3	98.9	42.5	64.3	101.6	71.2	82.9	86.1	66.7	74.2	113.9	142.6	131.5
05	METALS	95.1	81.4	90.2	95.0	95.4	95.1	95.1	71.3	86.5	97.9	95.2	96.9	97.9	89.5	94.9	100.9	123.7	109.1
06	WOOD & PLASTICS	94.9	86.2	90.4	88.5	77.1	82.6	105.6	37.4	70.3	84.0	72.4	78.0	92.8	66.6	79.2	104.0	130.6	117.8
07	THERMAL & MOISTURE PROTECTION	96.1	59.9	78.9	96.1	77.0	87.1	96.9	67.1	82.8	94.3	81.8	88.4	95.0	78.3	87.1	100.1	138.1	118.1
08	DOORS & WINDOWS	91.6	70.7	86.6	91.6	78.0	88.3	91.9	32.3	77.5	91.5	74.9	87.5	92.3	65.0	85.7	103.7	131.2	110.3
09200	PLASTER & GYPSUM BOARD	99.2	86.6	91.5	97.5	77.2	85.1	102.2	36.2	61.8	100.1	72.6	83.3	102.7	66.6	80.6	98.2	130.4	117.9
095,098	CEILINGS & ACOUSTICAL TREATMENT	89.7	86.6	87.6	91.2	77.2	81.9	89.7	36.2	54.4	103.8	72.6	80.9	103.8	66.6	79.2	99.5	130.1	119.9
09600	FLOORING	89.0	74.2	85.4	86.7	78.3	84.7	93.3	74.2	88.7	94.6	78.2	90.6	98.5	74.2	92.6	99.7	152.1	112.4
097,099	WALL FINISHES, PAINTS & COATINGS	98.2	87.5	92.0	98.2	47.8	68.9	98.2	35.3	61.7	110.8	80.1	93.0	110.8	82.4	94.3	96.3	139.3	121.2
09	FINISHES	89.3	79.5	84.3	88.7	74.6	81.5	91.7	44.2	67.5	92.3	73.2	82.6	94.3	68.1	80.9	99.0	136.3	118.0
10 - 14	TOTAL DIV. 10000 - 14000	100.0	69.2	93.5	100.0	88.1	97.5	100.0	60.3	91.6	100.0	81.0	96.0	100.0	66.0	92.8	100.0	126.4	105.6
15	MECHANICAL	96.8	75.9	87.1	99.9	85.3	93.2	96.8	51.8	76.0	97.0	83.7	90.8	97.0	81.2	89.7	99.8	122.0	110.1
16	ELECTRICAL	100.6	78.4	85.3	98.0	85.6	89.5	95.3	74.5	81.0	94.3	92.4	93.0	90.3	92.4	91.7	99.1	125.1	116.9
01 - 16	WEIGHTED AVERAGE	92.8	74.5	83.9	94.0	82.7	88.5	95.9	58.5	77.7	96.6	82.1	89.5	97.3	78.3	88.1	102.6	128.0	115.0

MASSACHUSETTS

DIVISION		BROCKTON 023			BUZZARDS BAY 025			FALL RIVER 027			FITCHBURG 014			FRAMINGHAM 017			GREENFIELD 013		
		MAT.	INST.	TOTAL	MAT.	INST.	TOTAL	MAT.	INST.	TOTAL	MAT.	INST.	TOTAL	MAT.	INST.	TOTAL	MAT.	INST.	TOTAL
02	SITE CONSTRUCTION	89.9	106.0	102.3	81.3	106.0	100.2	88.9	106.2	102.1	82.5	105.9	100.4	79.6	105.5	99.5	86.4	105.0	100.6
03100	CONCRETE FORMS & ACCESSORIES	103.5	114.5	113.0	100.3	110.4	109.0	103.5	110.9	109.9	93.2	113.1	110.3	101.7	113.1	111.6	91.1	102.3	100.7
03200	CONCRETE REINFORCEMENT	111.9	141.0	128.5	89.7	124.9	109.8	111.9	128.0	121.1	89.7	136.9	116.6	89.7	140.4	118.6	93.6	119.2	108.2
03300	CAST-IN-PLACE CONCRETE	100.2	135.7	114.8	83.2	138.0	105.8	96.8	138.9	114.2	83.2	127.6	101.5	87.2	118.9	100.3	89.7	110.1	98.1
03	CONCRETE	110.4	126.2	118.3	93.4	122.2	107.8	108.8	123.3	116.0	89.3	121.8	105.5	94.6	119.7	107.2	95.3	107.6	101.5
04	MASONRY	109.5	135.5	125.5	99.8	138.4	123.5	109.2	138.3	127.1	96.0	129.5	116.6	102.7	126.9	117.6	100.4	105.5	103.6
05	METALS	98.0	120.4	106.1	93.1	113.9	100.6	98.0	115.8	104.4	93.0	114.5	100.7	93.0	118.5	102.2	95.3	103.6	98.3
06	WOOD & PLASTICS	103.0	110.8	107.1	99.8	105.8	102.9	103.0	106.2	104.7	95.1	110.0	102.8	102.3	109.6	106.1	93.0	101.3	97.3
07	THERMAL & MOISTURE PROTECTION	99.9	130.9	114.6	99.1	125.0	111.4	99.8	125.1	111.8	99.1	117.8	108.0	99.3	126.2	112.1	99.1	106.3	102.5
08	DOORS & WINDOWS	103.6	120.5	107.7	99.0	111.9	102.1	103.6	112.9	105.9	108.9	119.1	111.3	99.5	119.9	104.4	108.7	105.7	108.0
09200	PLASTER & GYPSUM BOARD	98.2	109.9	105.4	95.1	104.8	101.0	98.2	104.8	102.2	93.9	109.1	103.2	96.0	109.1	104.0	95.2	100.1	98.2
095,098	CEILINGS & ACOUSTICAL TREATMENT	102.6	109.9	107.4	90.0	104.8	99.7	102.6	104.8	104.0	90.0	109.1	102.6	90.0	109.1	102.6	99.5	100.1	99.9
09600	FLOORING	100.2	152.1	112.8	98.8	152.1	111.7	99.9	152.1	112.6	97.5	152.1	110.8	99.2	152.1	112.0	96.7	109.8	99.9
097,099	WALL FINISHES, PAINTS & COATINGS	95.6	125.7	113.1	95.6	125.7	113.1	95.6	125.7	113.1	95.6	125.7	113.1	96.3	125.7	113.4	95.6	94.1	94.7
09	FINISHES	99.7	122.2	111.2	96.0	119.3	107.9	99.6	119.6	109.8	95.5	121.7	108.9	96.2	121.4	109.1	97.4	102.6	100.0
10 - 14	TOTAL DIV. 10000 - 14000	100.0	122.3	104.7	100.0	121.7	104.6	100.0	122.8	104.8	100.0	113.1	102.8	100.0	121.3	104.5	100.0	109.1	101.9
15	MECHANICAL	99.8	101.9	100.8	96.7	102.1	99.2	99.8	102.2	100.9	97.1	100.7	98.8	97.1	107.4	101.8	97.1	97.7	97.4
16	ELECTRICAL	98.7	101.8	100.8	93.9	101.8	99.3	98.1	101.8	100.6	104.8	97.2	99.6	99.0	121.9	114.7	104.8	84.0	90.5
01 - 16	WEIGHTED AVERAGE	101.5	115.0	108.1	95.9	113.2	104.3	101.2	113.6	107.3	97.1	111.5	104.1	96.7	117.2	106.7	98.7	100.1	99.4

MASSACHUSETTS

DIVISION		HYANNIS 026			LAWRENCE 019			LOWELL 018			NEW BEDFORD 027			PITTSFIELD 012			SPRINGFIELD 010 - 011		
		MAT.	INST.	TOTAL	MAT.	INST.	TOTAL	MAT.	INST.	TOTAL	MAT.	INST.	TOTAL	MAT.	INST.	TOTAL	MAT.	INST.	TOTAL
02	SITE CONSTRUCTION	86.6	106.0	101.5	90.7	106.0	102.5	89.8	106.0	102.2	88.6	106.2	102.0	90.9	104.9	101.6	90.1	105.0	101.5
03100	CONCRETE FORMS & ACCESSORIES	93.2	110.4	108.0	103.4	114.5	113.0	99.7	114.5	112.5	103.5	110.9	109.9	99.7	95.1	95.7	99.8	103.0	102.5
03200	CONCRETE REINFORCEMENT	89.7	124.9	109.8	111.0	126.3	119.7	111.9	125.8	119.8	111.9	128.0	121.1	92.9	106.2	100.5	111.9	119.4	116.2
03300	CAST-IN-PLACE CONCRETE	91.3	138.0	110.6	100.4	138.2	116.0	91.8	138.2	110.9	94.0	138.9	112.5	100.1	105.2	102.2	94.0	110.9	101.0
03	CONCRETE	100.4	122.2	111.3	110.4	124.4	117.4	100.9	124.1	112.5	107.4	123.3	115.3	102.6	100.4	101.5	102.0	108.3	105.1
04	MASONRY	108.5	138.4	126.9	108.5	138.4	126.9	94.7	129.5	116.1	109.0	138.3	127.0	95.4	106.4	102.1	94.9	111.4	105.0
05	METALS	94.7	113.9	101.6	95.7	114.8	102.6	95.6	110.9	101.2	98.0	115.8	104.4	95.5	98.3	96.5	98.0	104.1	100.2
06	WOOD & PLASTICS	92.7	105.8	99.5	103.0	110.8	107.1	101.9	110.8	106.5	103.0	106.2	104.7	101.9	92.5	97.0	101.9	101.3	101.6
07	THERMAL & MOISTURE PROTECTION	99.3	125.0	111.5	99.8	132.0	115.1	99.6	128.3	113.2	99.8	125.1	111.8	99.6	104.9	102.1	99.6	108.0	103.6
08	DOORS & WINDOWS	99.7	111.9	102.6	103.6	116.6	106.7	110.0	116.6	111.6	103.6	112.9	105.9	110.0	97.5	107.0	110.0	105.7	109.0
09200	PLASTER & GYPSUM BOARD	93.0	104.8	100.2	98.2	109.9	105.4	98.2	109.9	105.4	98.2	104.8	102.2	98.2	91.0	93.8	98.2	100.1	99.4
095,098	CEILINGS & ACOUSTICAL TREATMENT	93.1	104.8	100.8	102.6	109.9	107.4	102.6	109.9	107.4	102.6	104.8	104.0	102.6	91.0	94.9	102.6	100.1	101.0
09600	FLOORING	96.3	152.1	109.8	99.9	152.1	112.6	99.9	152.1	112.6	99.9	152.1	112.6	100.2	112.2	103.1	99.7	117.3	104.0
097,099	WALL FINISHES, PAINTS & COATINGS	95.6	125.7	113.1	95.6	125.7	113.1	95.6	125.7	113.1	95.6	125.7	113.1	95.6	94.1	94.7	96.8	94.1	95.3
09	FINISHES	95.7	119.3	107.7	99.6	122.2	111.1	99.6	122.2	111.1	99.6	119.6	109.8	99.7	97.8	98.7	99.6	104.5	102.1
10 - 14	TOTAL DIV. 10000 - 14000	100.0	121.7	104.6	100.0	122.4	104.7	100.0	122.4	104.7	100.0	122.8	104.8	100.0	107.7	101.6	100.0	109.7	102.0
15	MECHANICAL	99.8	102.1	100.9	99.8	105.2	102.3	99.8	117.6	108.0	99.8	102.2	100.9	99.8	88.3	94.5	99.8	98.4	99.2
16	ELECTRICAL	93.9	101.8	99.3	103.2	105.9	105.0	104.0	105.8	105.3	99.1	101.8	100.9	104.0	84.0	90.2	104.0	91.6	95.4
01 - 16	WEIGHTED AVERAGE	98.2	113.2	105.5	101.4	115.7	108.4	100.3	116.7	108.2	101.1	113.6	107.2	100.5	95.9	98.3	100.8	102.6	101.6

DIVISION		MASSACHUSETTS WORCESTER 015 - 016			MICHIGAN ANN ARBOR 481			BATTLE CREEK 490			BAY CITY 487			DEARBORN 481			DETROIT 482		
		MAT.	INST.	TOTAL	MAT.	INST.	TOTAL	MAT.	INST.	TOTAL	MAT.	INST.	TOTAL	MAT.	INST.	TOTAL	MAT.	INST.	TOTAL
02	SITE CONSTRUCTION	89.8	105.9	102.2	81.2	93.9	90.9	84.1	88.4	87.4	71.0	93.0	87.8	80.9	94.0	91.0	98.2	95.8	96.4
03100	CONCRETE FORMS & ACCESSORIES	100.3	113.7	111.8	97.1	116.9	114.2	95.0	92.8	93.1	97.2	95.8	96.0	97.0	120.6	117.4	98.8	120.6	117.6
03200	CONCRETE REINFORCEMENT	111.9	137.0	126.2	93.8	119.2	108.3	97.3	93.3	95.0	93.8	118.2	107.7	93.8	119.6	108.5	93.2	119.5	108.2
03300	CAST-IN-PLACE CONCRETE	91.8	132.5	108.6	92.5	122.3	104.8	96.6	111.0	102.6	88.4	102.8	94.4	90.4	124.2	104.3	99.2	124.2	109.5
03	CONCRETE	100.9	123.8	112.4	89.9	119.7	104.8	97.4	98.3	97.8	87.9	103.4	95.7	88.8	122.0	105.4	93.3	120.4	106.8
04	MASONRY	94.7	132.3	117.8	99.2	115.8	109.4	99.3	92.3	95.0	98.8	92.3	94.8	99.0	123.1	113.8	97.9	123.1	113.4
05	METALS	98.0	114.7	104.0	100.2	126.4	109.6	97.5	88.9	94.4	100.8	122.6	108.7	100.3	127.2	110.0	100.8	103.1	101.6
06	WOOD & PLASTICS	102.5	110.8	106.8	93.5	117.1	105.7	95.2	92.0	93.5	93.5	95.8	94.7	93.5	120.3	107.4	95.4	120.3	108.3
07	THERMAL & MOISTURE PROTECTION	99.6	119.3	108.9	94.0	116.4	104.6	91.4	90.5	91.0	92.3	93.8	93.0	93.1	124.8	108.2	91.5	124.8	107.3
08	DOORS & WINDOWS	110.0	119.6	112.3	97.8	113.9	101.7	93.3	84.6	91.2	97.8	100.0	98.3	97.8	115.6	102.1	97.4	115.7	101.8
09200	PLASTER & GYPSUM BOARD	98.2	109.9	105.4	107.9	115.8	112.7	101.1	85.7	91.7	107.9	93.9	99.3	107.9	119.2	114.8	107.9	119.2	114.8
095,098	CEILINGS & ACOUSTICAL TREATMENT	102.6	109.9	107.4	101.1	115.8	110.8	95.1	85.7	88.9	102.6	93.9	96.8	101.1	119.2	113.0	102.6	119.2	113.5
09600	FLOORING	99.9	143.8	110.6	90.4	121.8	98.0	95.3	102.7	97.1	90.1	70.2	85.3	89.9	123.5	98.1	90.1	123.5	98.2
097,099	WALL FINISHES, PAINTS & COATINGS	95.6	116.9	108.0	93.2	117.6	107.4	96.5	89.5	92.5	93.2	90.9	91.3	93.2	119.6	108.5	95.1	119.6	108.5
09	FINISHES	99.6	119.5	109.7	97.3	117.7	107.7	96.0	94.2	95.1	97.2	90.4	93.8	97.2	121.2	109.4	98.3	121.2	110.0
10 - 14	TOTAL DIV. 10000 - 14000	100.0	113.2	102.8	100.0	112.4	102.6	100.0	114.2	103.0	100.0	104.8	101.0	100.0	113.7	102.9	100.0	113.7	102.9
15	MECHANICAL	99.8	100.7	100.2	100.0	104.9	102.3	100.1	84.6	93.0	100.0	95.7	98.0	100.0	115.6	107.2	100.0	115.9	107.4
16	ELECTRICAL	104.0	97.2	99.3	95.2	104.1	101.3	93.3	95.3	94.7	94.6	86.1	88.7	95.2	115.4	109.1	96.5	115.4	109.5
01 - 16	WEIGHTED AVERAGE	100.6	111.9	106.1	97.0	111.1	103.9	96.8	91.8	94.4	96.5	96.7	96.6	96.9	117.0	106.7	98.1	114.8	106.2

MICHIGAN

DIVISION		FLINT 484 - 485			GAYLORD 497			GRAND RAPIDS 493,495			IRON MOUNTAIN 498 - 499			JACKSON 492			KALAMAZOO 491		
		MAT.	INST.	TOTAL	MAT.	INST.	TOTAL	MAT.	INST.	TOTAL	MAT.	INST.	TOTAL	MAT.	INST.	TOTAL	MAT.	INST.	TOTAL
02	SITE CONSTRUCTION	69.6	93.2	87.7	80.4	86.1	84.8	83.8	88.0	87.0	87.4	95.4	93.5	101.5	86.9	90.3	84.4	88.4	87.4
03100	CONCRETE FORMS & ACCESSORIES	98.3	98.9	98.8	92.3	74.8	77.2	95.9	79.0	81.3	87.7	92.1	91.5	89.4	93.6	93.0	95.0	92.2	92.5
03200	CONCRETE REINFORCEMENT	93.8	118.7	108.0	90.6	103.9	98.2	97.3	91.5	94.0	90.3	103.1	97.6	88.0	118.6	105.4	97.3	87.9	91.9
03300	CAST-IN-PLACE CONCRETE	93.1	105.4	98.2	96.4	89.6	93.6	96.9	89.5	93.8	114.1	88.6	103.6	96.3	95.2	95.8	98.6	110.7	103.6
03	CONCRETE	90.3	105.8	98.0	93.7	86.7	90.2	97.6	84.5	91.0	103.9	92.9	98.4	88.3	99.8	94.0	100.8	97.0	98.9
04	MASONRY	99.2	103.7	102.0	111.6	74.7	88.9	96.7	58.9	73.5	96.6	96.1	96.3	90.3	94.1	92.7	99.5	84.7	90.4
05	METALS	100.3	123.7	108.7	99.0	110.4	103.1	97.4	84.9	92.9	98.4	95.8	97.5	99.2	121.5	107.2	97.5	86.0	93.4
06	WOOD & PLASTICS	93.5	97.8	95.7	88.6	72.6	80.3	96.6	79.6	87.8	87.4	91.2	89.4	87.3	94.5	91.0	95.2	92.0	93.5
07	THERMAL & MOISTURE PROTECTION	92.3	99.5	95.7	90.6	72.7	82.1	91.7	67.1	80.1	93.1	88.2	90.8	89.8	99.3	94.3	91.4	88.5	90.1
08	DOORS & WINDOWS	97.8	101.1	98.6	95.0	73.3	89.7	93.3	73.8	88.6	99.9	81.3	95.4	94.0	96.4	94.6	93.3	80.4	90.2
09200	PLASTER & GYPSUM BOARD	107.9	95.9	100.6	103.8	69.6	82.9	101.1	72.9	83.9	69.5	91.5	82.9	102.8	92.2	96.3	101.1	85.7	91.7
095,098	CEILINGS & ACOUSTICAL TREATMENT	101.1	95.9	97.7	92.4	69.6	77.4	95.1	72.9	80.5	92.1	91.5	91.7	93.8	92.2	92.7	95.1	85.7	88.9
09600	FLOORING	90.1	88.3	89.7	88.8	74.0	85.2	95.3	52.1	84.8	107.6	99.6	105.6	87.1	102.0	90.7	95.3	60.4	86.8
097,099	WALL FINISHES, PAINTS & COATINGS	93.2	94.2	93.8	92.1	67.8	78.0	96.5	51.8	70.5	114.9	56.6	81.0	92.1	102.1	97.9	96.5	89.5	92.5
09	FINISHES	96.7	96.0	96.3	96.7	73.3	84.7	96.1	70.6	83.1	97.8	89.7	93.7	97.2	95.9	96.5	96.0	85.5	90.7
10 - 14	TOTAL DIV. 10000 - 14000	100.0	106.4	101.3	100.0	91.0	98.1	100.0	109.8	102.1	100.0	99.5	99.9	100.0	104.0	100.8	100.0	114.1	103.0
15	MECHANICAL	100.0	103.1	101.4	97.0	79.4	88.9	100.0	63.7	83.2	97.0	92.4	94.9	97.0	87.4	92.6	100.0	91.8	96.2
16	ELECTRICAL	95.2	105.3	102.1	89.3	72.7	77.9	93.5	72.6	79.1	99.6	86.4	90.5	95.8	104.0	101.5	93.1	85.0	87.5
01 - 16	WEIGHTED AVERAGE	96.7	103.8	100.1	96.4	81.3	89.1	96.7	74.4	85.9	98.4	91.7	95.2	95.5	97.7	96.6	97.2	89.0	93.2

MICHIGAN / MINNESOTA

DIVISION		LANSING 488 - 489			MUSKEGON 494			ROYAL OAK 480,483			SAGINAW 486			TRAVERSE CITY 496			BEMIDJI 566		
		MAT.	INST.	TOTAL	MAT.	INST.	TOTAL	MAT.	INST.	TOTAL	MAT.	INST.	TOTAL	MAT.	INST.	TOTAL	MAT.	INST.	TOTAL
02	SITE CONSTRUCTION	88.6	93.0	92.0	82.5	88.3	87.0	86.6	93.2	91.7	71.9	92.9	88.0	73.8	94.9	90.0	81.2	98.1	94.1
03100	CONCRETE FORMS & ACCESSORIES	100.7	96.9	97.4	95.9	89.4	90.3	92.4	118.2	114.7	97.1	95.6	95.8	87.4	71.7	73.9	81.4	94.2	92.4
03200	CONCRETE REINFORCEMENT	93.8	118.5	107.9	97.9	92.8	95.0	85.0	117.3	103.4	93.8	118.2	107.7	91.7	73.5	81.3	105.2	107.0	106.2
03300	CAST-IN-PLACE CONCRETE	92.5	102.5	96.6	96.3	108.2	101.2	80.9	110.9	93.3	91.3	102.7	96.0	89.1	78.2	84.6	99.8	97.2	98.7
03	CONCRETE	90.2	103.8	97.0	95.6	95.8	95.7	77.7	114.2	95.9	89.3	103.3	96.3	85.0	75.0	80.0	92.8	98.9	95.8
04	MASONRY	92.7	98.4	96.2	96.5	83.0	88.2	92.7	111.6	104.3	100.6	92.3	95.5	94.7	75.0	82.6	102.0	97.5	99.3
05	METALS	99.5	123.1	108.0	95.6	87.9	92.8	100.0	98.8	99.6	100.3	122.4	108.3	98.3	82.6	92.6	94.6	124.0	105.2
06	WOOD & PLASTICS	96.9	96.8	96.9	92.9	88.7	90.7	89.2	118.7	104.4	93.5	95.8	94.7	87.1	70.0	78.2	73.9	91.2	82.8
07	THERMAL & MOISTURE PROTECTION	93.6	96.8	95.1	90.6	81.5	86.3	91.8	118.4	104.1	92.8	93.8	93.3	92.0	70.3	81.7	98.4	93.5	96.1
08	DOORS & WINDOWS	97.8	100.6	98.4	92.6	87.9	91.4	97.9	114.6	102.0	97.8	100.0	98.8	99.9	65.0	91.5	103.1	118.5	106.8
09200	PLASTER & GYPSUM BOARD	110.7	95.0	101.1	92.3	82.3	86.2	105.9	117.5	113.0	107.9	93.9	99.3	69.5	69.6	69.5	113.7	91.4	100.1
095,098	CEILINGS & ACOUSTICAL TREATMENT	101.1	95.0	97.0	100.6	82.3	88.5	101.2	117.5	111.9	101.1	93.9	96.3	92.1	69.6	77.2	141.8	91.4	108.6
09600	FLOORING	90.4	77.2	87.2	94.4	75.2	89.8	87.5	102.0	91.0	90.4	70.2	85.5	107.5	74.0	99.4	105.5	129.2	111.2
097,099	WALL FINISHES, PAINTS & COATINGS	93.2	89.5	91.1	95.7	75.1	83.8	95.1	117.6	108.2	93.2	90.0	91.3	114.9	67.8	87.6	102.5	86.0	92.9
09	FINISHES	98.2	91.9	95.0	94.9	84.7	89.7	96.3	115.4	106.0	97.1	89.7	93.3	97.1	71.5	84.0	112.3	99.4	105.7
10 - 14	TOTAL DIV. 10000 - 14000	100.0	105.3	101.1	100.0	113.2	102.8	100.0	111.7	102.5	100.0	104.8	101.0	100.0	73.5	94.4	100.0	92.3	98.4
15	MECHANICAL	100.0	94.0	97.2	99.7	94.9	97.5	97.1	108.6	102.4	100.0	95.5	97.9	97.0	70.3	84.6	97.5	101.2	99.2
16	ELECTRICAL	93.9	100.7	98.6	93.4	79.8	84.0	98.6	106.9	104.3	97.6	88.1	91.0	91.8	71.8	78.1	102.7	96.6	98.5
01 - 16	WEIGHTED AVERAGE	96.8	99.8	98.3	95.7	88.5	92.2	94.7	108.5	101.4	96.9	96.8	96.9	94.9	75.2	85.3	98.9	101.5	100.2

MINNESOTA

DIVISION		BRAINERD 564			DETROIT LAKES 565			DULUTH 556 - 558			MANKATO 560			MINNEAPOLIS 553 - 555			ROCHESTER 559		
		MAT.	INST.	TOTAL	MAT.	INST.	TOTAL	MAT.	INST.	TOTAL	MAT.	INST.	TOTAL	MAT.	INST.	TOTAL	MAT.	INST.	TOTAL
02	SITE CONSTRUCTION	82.0	104.3	99.1	79.5	98.6	94.1	82.3	103.3	98.4	79.1	104.2	98.3	82.0	109.3	102.9	81.3	102.5	97.6
03100	CONCRETE FORMS & ACCESSORIES	82.7	91.3	90.1	77.7	81.1	80.7	97.5	121.4	118.1	93.1	102.9	101.5	98.2	139.9	134.2	98.1	109.9	108.3
03200	CONCRETE REINFORCEMENT	104.1	102.5	103.2	105.2	106.9	106.2	95.6	108.1	102.7	101.9	113.1	108.3	95.8	119.4	109.2	95.6	118.2	108.5
03300	CAST-IN-PLACE CONCRETE	108.5	101.9	105.8	96.9	100.6	98.4	109.5	115.1	111.8	99.9	94.1	97.5	107.9	127.3	115.9	105.8	105.0	105.5
03	CONCRETE	96.8	98.5	97.6	90.3	94.3	92.3	96.7	117.2	106.9	92.2	102.8	97.5	97.5	131.7	114.6	94.9	110.6	102.8
04	MASONRY	125.6	104.5	112.6	124.4	104.3	112.0	108.0	127.3	119.9	111.7	116.4	114.6	108.1	137.0	125.8	107.8	105.6	106.3
05	METALS	96.1	123.8	106.1	94.6	123.4	105.0	96.8	125.8	107.2	95.9	128.1	107.5	98.8	133.7	111.4	96.7	130.9	109.0
06	WOOD & PLASTICS	89.1	83.5	86.2	70.1	70.8	70.5	104.2	119.6	112.2	100.2	100.3	100.3	104.7	139.8	122.9	104.7	108.1	106.5
07	THERMAL & MOISTURE PROTECTION	96.7	107.5	101.8	98.2	95.7	97.0	99.0	126.7	112.2	97.2	104.9	100.8	98.9	135.1	116.1	98.8	107.9	103.1
08	DOORS & WINDOWS	89.5	114.3	95.5	103.1	107.5	104.2	101.0	127.7	107.5	94.7	123.3	101.6	102.2	149.4	113.6	101.0	132.3	108.6
09200	PLASTER & GYPSUM BOARD	89.0	83.8	85.9	112.4	70.5	86.8	100.6	121.0	113.1	92.5	101.2	97.8	100.6	141.8	125.7	100.6	109.2	105.9
095,098	CEILINGS & ACOUSTICAL TREATMENT	69.0	83.8	78.8	141.8	70.5	94.7	90.9	121.0	110.8	69.0	101.2	90.2	90.9	141.8	124.5	90.9	109.2	103.0
09600	FLOORING	104.2	129.2	110.3	104.0	123.6	108.7	112.1	129.2	116.2	106.5	129.2	112.0	109.2	118.1	111.4	111.8	92.7	107.2
097,099	WALL FINISHES, PAINTS & COATINGS	98.0	86.0	91.0	102.5	77.6	88.1	99.2	111.2	106.2	106.9	107.0	106.9	106.0	122.4	115.5	101.8	107.0	104.8
09	FINISHES	94.6	96.6	95.6	111.6	87.3	99.2	102.3	122.1	112.4	96.4	108.2	102.4	101.8	135.1	118.8	102.4	106.9	104.7
10 - 14	TOTAL DIV. 10000 - 14000	100.0	89.3	97.7	100.0	92.2	98.3	100.0	110.1	102.1	100.0	101.7	100.4	100.0	116.1	103.4	100.0	105.9	101.2
15	MECHANICAL	96.5	104.8	100.4	97.5	104.5	100.7	99.8	109.1	104.1	96.5	96.6	96.6	99.7	119.5	108.9	99.7	98.8	99.3
16	ELECTRICAL	98.9	104.4	102.7	102.7	57.0	71.3	102.3	104.4	103.8	109.4	94.5	99.2	103.4	101.4	102.0	102.2	94.5	96.9
01 - 16	WEIGHTED AVERAGE	97.1	104.4	100.7	99.7	93.4	96.6	99.6	115.0	107.1	97.3	105.4	101.3	100.1	123.6	111.6	99.3	106.4	102.7

City Cost Indexes

		MINNESOTA																MISSISSIPPI		

DIVISION		SAINT PAUL 550-551			ST. CLOUD 563			THIEF RIVER FALLS 567			WILLMAR 562			WINDOM 561			BILOXI 395		
		MAT.	INST.	TOTAL	MAT.	INST.	TOTAL	MAT.	INST.	TOTAL	MAT.	INST.	TOTAL	MAT.	INST.	TOTAL	MAT.	INST.	TOTAL
02	SITE CONSTRUCTION	84.2	103.7	99.1	77.3	105.3	98.7	79.0	98.0	93.6	77.2	101.9	96.1	71.7	100.7	93.9	107.8	87.1	91.9
03100	CONCRETE FORMS & ACCESSORIES	88.3	132.1	126.1	79.1	108.8	104.7	80.4	93.5	91.7	78.8	73.1	73.9	84.6	68.1	70.4	99.0	52.6	58.9
03200	CONCRETE REINFORCEMENT	92.2	119.3	107.7	103.4	118.7	112.2	107.0	106.9	106.9	102.5	112.4	108.1	102.5	111.6	107.7	95.8	68.7	80.4
03300	CAST-IN-PLACE CONCRETE	108.8	123.7	115.0	95.7	117.9	104.8	95.8	95.0	95.5	97.2	95.7	96.6	84.1	68.9	77.8	105.7	54.0	84.4
03	CONCRETE	98.9	127.1	113.0	88.1	114.8	101.4	90.0	97.8	93.9	88.1	89.9	89.0	79.2	78.3	78.8	96.3	57.9	77.1
04	MASONRY	119.5	137.0	130.2	110.4	116.0	113.9	101.7	97.5	99.1	113.8	93.7	101.4	124.0	68.8	90.1	89.5	47.0	63.4
05	METALS	95.4	133.4	109.1	96.5	133.0	109.7	94.6	123.4	105.0	95.9	121.6	105.2	95.8	120.6	104.8	98.1	87.3	94.2
06	WOOD & PLASTICS	94.5	129.5	112.6	85.2	103.4	94.6	72.8	91.2	82.3	84.8	71.9	78.2	91.1	71.9	81.2	99.0	53.1	75.3
07	THERMAL & MOISTURE PROTECTION	98.7	133.9	115.4	96.8	124.2	109.8	98.2	81.9	90.5	96.6	71.2	84.6	96.7	61.0	79.7	96.5	54.5	76.6
08	DOORS & WINDOWS	98.1	143.8	109.1	94.7	129.7	103.2	103.1	118.5	106.8	92.1	91.6	92.0	96.8	91.6	95.5	98.3	56.2	88.1
09200	PLASTER & GYPSUM BOARD	97.0	131.2	117.9	87.7	104.4	97.9	113.3	91.4	99.9	87.7	71.9	78.0	89.9	71.9	78.9	108.0	52.2	73.9
095,098	CEILINGS & ACOUSTICAL TREATMENT	88.2	131.2	116.6	69.0	104.4	92.3	141.8	91.4	108.6	69.0	71.9	70.9	69.0	71.9	70.9	95.1	52.2	66.8
09600	FLOORING	104.7	118.1	107.9	100.2	129.2	107.3	105.1	129.2	110.9	102.1	56.1	91.0	104.9	49.7	91.5	115.9	49.4	99.8
097,099	WALL FINISHES, PAINTS & COATINGS	106.0	116.8	112.3	106.9	122.4	115.9	102.5	77.6	88.1	102.5	86.0	92.9	102.5	107.0	105.1	105.6	43.7	69.6
09	FINISHES	99.6	128.4	114.3	93.5	113.1	103.5	112.0	98.4	105.1	93.8	70.2	81.7	94.7	68.4	81.3	105.0	50.7	77.3
10-14	TOTAL DIV. 10000-14000	100.0	114.3	103.0	100.0	106.6	101.4	100.0	92.1	98.3	100.0	78.3	95.4	100.0	73.5	94.4	100.0	68.1	93.3
15	MECHANICAL	99.7	119.4	108.9	99.7	110.7	104.8	97.5	100.8	99.0	96.5	96.1	96.4	96.5	80.8	89.3	99.9	63.5	83.1
16	ELECTRICAL	101.3	104.2	103.3	98.9	104.2	102.6	96.1	57.0	69.3	98.9	95.0	96.3	109.4	94.5	99.1	96.7	56.1	68.8
01-16	WEIGHTED AVERAGE	99.5	121.7	110.3	96.2	113.4	104.6	98.0	94.1	96.1	95.3	93.1	94.3	96.1	85.4	90.9	98.9	62.4	81.1

		MISSISSIPPI																		

DIVISION		CLARKSDALE 386			COLUMBUS 397			GREENVILLE 387			GREENWOOD 389			JACKSON 390-392			LAUREL 394		
		MAT.	INST.	TOTAL	MAT.	INST.	TOTAL	MAT.	INST.	TOTAL	MAT.	INST.	TOTAL	MAT.	INST.	TOTAL	MAT.	INST.	TOTAL
02	SITE CONSTRUCTION	105.4	86.1	90.7	107.2	86.5	91.4	112.2	86.8	92.8	109.2	85.9	91.3	104.2	86.8	90.9	113.6	85.1	91.8
03100	CONCRETE FORMS & ACCESSORIES	81.6	23.4	31.4	79.0	37.9	43.6	77.2	43.6	48.2	93.6	25.7	35.0	93.5	49.8	55.8	79.4	29.8	36.6
03200	CONCRETE REINFORCEMENT	103.2	20.8	56.2	102.5	37.6	65.5	103.8	52.9	74.8	103.2	56.4	76.5	95.8	57.4	73.9	103.2	36.9	65.4
03300	CAST-IN-PLACE CONCRETE	103.2	32.0	73.8	107.9	44.4	81.7	106.2	47.3	81.9	110.9	31.9	78.3	103.7	50.2	81.7	105.5	35.7	76.7
03	CONCRETE	93.8	28.6	61.2	97.3	42.4	69.9	98.7	48.7	73.7	100.3	36.1	68.2	94.9	53.3	74.1	99.3	35.6	67.5
04	MASONRY	89.4	25.1	49.9	112.0	29.6	61.4	132.4	44.6	78.4	89.9	23.5	49.1	92.4	44.6	63.0	109.0	30.3	60.6
05	METALS	95.7	66.1	85.0	95.5	73.4	87.5	96.4	80.7	90.8	95.7	78.8	89.6	98.0	82.5	92.4	95.6	71.5	86.9
06	WOOD & PLASTICS	80.1	21.9	50.0	77.5	39.6	57.9	75.6	43.1	58.8	92.8	24.7	57.6	92.8	51.2	71.3	78.4	31.1	54.0
07	THERMAL & MOISTURE PROTECTION	96.1	33.8	66.5	96.2	33.7	66.5	96.5	49.5	74.2	96.6	28.3	64.2	96.2	51.1	74.8	96.3	32.1	65.9
08	DOORS & WINDOWS	97.7	26.4	80.5	97.7	35.6	82.7	97.7	45.8	85.2	97.7	37.0	83.1	98.7	51.3	87.3	94.3	30.8	79.0
09200	PLASTER & GYPSUM BOARD	102.3	20.0	52.0	101.4	38.2	62.8	101.0	41.8	64.8	107.0	22.9	55.6	108.0	50.2	72.7	100.5	29.5	57.1
095,098	CEILINGS & ACOUSTICAL TREATMENT	86.6	20.0	42.7	86.6	38.2	54.7	89.7	41.8	58.1	86.6	22.9	44.6	95.1	50.2	65.5	86.6	29.5	48.9
09600	FLOORING	108.8	28.7	89.4	107.4	24.8	87.4	106.3	42.2	90.8	115.9	25.9	94.1	115.9	48.8	99.7	105.3	23.3	85.4
097,099	WALL FINISHES, PAINTS & COATINGS	105.6	18.4	54.9	105.6	27.1	59.9	105.6	43.1	69.2	105.6	25.1	58.8	105.6	43.1	69.2	105.6	27.1	59.9
09	FINISHES	100.2	23.6	61.1	99.8	34.9	66.7	100.2	43.0	71.0	103.5	25.6	63.7	105.0	48.9	76.4	99.4	29.1	63.5
10-14	TOTAL DIV. 10000-14000	100.0	54.0	90.3	100.0	57.5	91.0	100.0	65.9	92.8	100.0	54.4	90.4	100.0	67.0	93.0	100.0	34.5	86.2
15	MECHANICAL	98.6	23.9	64.0	98.2	32.6	67.9	99.9	43.8	73.9	98.6	25.2	64.6	99.9	43.4	73.8	98.2	27.8	65.7
16	ELECTRICAL	95.6	19.6	43.3	92.6	33.9	52.2	95.6	46.7	62.0	95.6	18.1	42.3	97.2	46.7	62.5	95.0	24.8	46.7
01-16	WEIGHTED AVERAGE	96.9	35.0	66.8	98.3	44.0	71.9	100.5	53.3	77.6	98.4	37.5	68.8	98.7	55.1	77.5	98.3	38.8	69.4

		MISSISSIPPI									MISSOURI								

DIVISION		MCCOMB 396			MERIDIAN 393			TUPELO 388			BOWLING GREEN 633			CAPE GIRARDEAU 637			CHILLICOTHE 646		
		MAT.	INST.	TOTAL	MAT.	INST.	TOTAL	MAT.	INST.	TOTAL	MAT.	INST.	TOTAL	MAT.	INST.	TOTAL	MAT.	INST.	TOTAL
02	SITE CONSTRUCTION	98.9	86.0	89.0	103.1	86.8	90.6	103.4	86.1	90.2	93.1	93.3	93.3	93.9	93.3	93.4	99.4	89.4	91.7
03100	CONCRETE FORMS & ACCESSORIES	79.0	28.5	35.4	75.5	42.3	46.9	77.9	30.3	36.8	93.3	85.8	86.9	83.8	84.5	84.4	91.0	83.8	84.8
03200	CONCRETE REINFORCEMENT	103.8	17.6	54.7	102.5	56.9	76.5	101.0	57.2	76.1	104.7	93.5	98.3	106.0	91.6	97.8	100.8	89.4	94.3
03300	CAST-IN-PLACE CONCRETE	93.6	33.8	68.9	100.2	50.2	79.6	103.2	46.1	79.6	86.0	93.5	89.1	85.1	92.7	88.2	95.0	78.9	88.4
03	CONCRETE	87.1	30.8	59.0	91.4	49.9	70.7	93.3	43.2	68.3	87.0	91.6	89.3	85.9	90.5	88.2	97.6	84.0	90.8
04	MASONRY	114.2	25.1	59.5	89.2	36.4	56.7	121.0	38.6	70.3	119.1	92.0	102.4	114.3	83.0	95.1	103.0	88.7	94.2
05	METALS	95.7	64.5	84.5	96.4	81.7	91.1	95.6	80.8	90.2	92.9	117.3	101.7	93.7	116.1	101.8	92.1	98.2	94.3
06	WOOD & PLASTICS	77.5	29.0	52.4	73.9	41.3	57.0	76.3	29.0	51.8	95.1	85.2	90.0	85.3	84.2	84.7	90.0	86.8	88.3
07	THERMAL & MOISTURE PROTECTION	95.7	31.2	65.1	95.9	48.0	73.2	96.0	42.1	70.4	95.3	95.0	95.2	95.1	86.8	91.2	98.0	82.8	90.8
08	DOORS & WINDOWS	97.7	29.4	81.3	97.7	45.1	85.0	97.7	35.1	82.6	96.6	86.0	94.0	96.6	85.0	93.8	93.2	79.3	89.9
09200	PLASTER & GYPSUM BOARD	101.4	27.3	56.1	100.1	40.0	63.4	101.0	27.3	55.9	101.4	84.3	90.9	98.0	83.3	89.0	104.7	86.0	93.3
095,098	CEILINGS & ACOUSTICAL TREATMENT	86.6	27.3	47.5	89.7	40.0	56.9	86.6	27.3	47.5	92.6	84.3	87.1	92.6	83.3	86.4	95.8	86.0	89.3
09600	FLOORING	107.4	28.7	88.3	105.2	34.3	88.0	106.7	31.6	88.5	103.2	90.1	100.0	99.0	90.1	96.8	94.8	64.7	87.5
097,099	WALL FINISHES, PAINTS & COATINGS	105.6	25.6	59.1	105.6	42.5	68.9	105.6	43.1	69.2	100.8	97.2	98.7	100.8	90.2	94.6	93.2	68.1	78.6
09	FINISHES	99.3	28.6	63.2	99.1	40.2	69.1	99.3	31.5	64.7	95.9	87.2	91.4	94.0	85.5	89.6	98.8	79.6	89.0
10-14	TOTAL DIV. 10000-14000	100.0	54.9	90.5	100.0	65.8	92.8	100.0	55.7	90.6	100.0	82.0	96.2	100.0	81.5	96.1	100.0	78.4	95.4
15	MECHANICAL	98.2	22.3	63.1	99.9	43.4	73.8	98.7	31.3	67.5	97.0	97.7	97.3	100.1	96.9	98.6	97.1	57.7	78.9
16	ELECTRICAL	90.2	22.4	43.6	95.0	61.5	72.0	95.1	30.9	51.0	95.3	87.8	90.1	95.3	113.3	107.7	91.4	51.9	64.2
01-16	WEIGHTED AVERAGE	96.7	36.1	67.2	96.7	54.8	76.3	98.4	44.5	72.2	96.2	93.7	95.0	96.3	96.2	96.2	96.3	75.0	85.9

COST INDEXES

632

MISSOURI

DIVISION		COLUMBIA 652			FLAT RIVER 636			HANNIBAL 634			HARRISONVILLE 647			JEFFERSON CITY 650 - 651			JOPLIN 648		
		MAT.	INST.	TOTAL	MAT.	INST.	TOTAL	MAT.	INST.	TOTAL	MAT.	INST.	TOTAL	MAT.	INST.	TOTAL	MAT.	INST.	TOTAL
02	SITE CONSTRUCTION	98.1	94.5	95.4	95.9	93.4	94.0	90.2	93.0	92.4	90.9	91.6	91.5	100.3	93.9	95.4	99.2	95.9	96.7
03100	CONCRETE FORMS & ACCESSORIES	85.5	76.0	77.3	101.9	85.5	87.8	91.0	83.7	84.7	87.0	93.9	93.0	104.0	71.3	75.8	105.5	69.5	74.4
03200	CONCRETE REINFORCEMENT	100.4	104.4	102.7	106.0	107.9	107.1	104.2	92.0	97.2	100.4	85.3	91.8	99.1	107.3	103.8	104.0	76.6	88.3
03300	CAST-IN-PLACE CONCRETE	86.1	75.1	81.6	88.8	93.9	90.9	81.4	91.4	85.5	97.3	94.1	96.0	90.1	78.3	85.3	102.9	77.6	92.4
03	CONCRETE	81.7	83.0	82.3	89.8	94.4	92.1	83.5	89.7	86.6	94.2	93.3	93.8	85.6	82.6	84.1	97.8	75.0	86.4
04	MASONRY	130.9	75.5	96.9	116.4	84.8	97.0	110.3	88.6	96.9	97.3	91.4	93.7	90.7	75.5	81.4	94.7	61.8	74.5
05	METALS	93.0	120.1	102.8	92.8	122.7	103.6	92.9	116.0	101.2	92.1	104.7	96.6	92.2	121.2	102.6	95.8	94.8	95.4
06	WOOD & PLASTICS	89.4	72.7	80.8	104.2	84.2	93.8	92.8	84.2	88.3	85.2	93.6	89.5	108.9	66.4	86.9	102.7	69.9	85.7
07	THERMAL & MOISTURE PROTECTION	92.2	79.6	86.2	95.6	93.1	94.4	95.1	91.9	93.6	96.8	95.8	96.4	92.4	79.4	86.2	98.5	68.1	84.0
08	DOORS & WINDOWS	93.2	92.9	93.1	96.6	89.4	94.9	96.6	85.0	93.8	93.6	92.2	93.3	89.9	90.3	90.0	94.4	77.6	90.4
09200	PLASTER & GYPSUM BOARD	100.9	71.5	82.9	104.4	83.3	91.5	100.5	83.3	90.0	97.3	93.0	94.7	106.9	65.0	81.3	108.6	68.6	84.2
095,098	CEILINGS & ACOUSTICAL TREATMENT	93.8	71.5	79.1	92.6	83.3	86.4	92.6	83.3	86.4	95.8	93.0	94.0	93.8	65.0	74.8	98.5	68.6	78.8
09600	FLOORING	107.9	75.0	99.9	106.9	90.1	102.9	102.1	90.1	99.2	90.7	90.7	90.7	115.8	75.0	105.9	118.9	60.6	104.8
097,099	WALL FINISHES, PAINTS & COATINGS	99.2	71.5	83.1	100.8	90.2	94.6	100.8	97.2	98.7	97.4	98.5	98.1	99.2	71.5	83.1	92.6	53.3	69.7
09	FINISHES	96.3	73.1	84.5	97.7	85.9	91.7	95.3	85.8	90.4	96.1	93.8	94.9	99.9	69.5	84.4	105.8	65.7	85.3
10 - 14	TOTAL DIV. 10000 - 14000	100.0	95.8	99.1	100.0	82.2	96.2	100.0	80.5	95.9	100.0	94.3	98.8	100.0	95.0	98.9	100.0	86.3	97.1
15	MECHANICAL	100.1	97.8	99.0	97.0	98.1	97.5	97.0	95.8	96.4	97.0	98.1	97.5	100.1	98.2	99.2	100.3	63.2	83.1
16	ELECTRICAL	93.8	85.9	88.4	102.4	113.3	109.9	93.4	87.8	89.5	102.8	103.7	103.4	96.9	85.9	89.3	89.2	69.2	75.4
01 - 16	WEIGHTED AVERAGE	96.4	89.4	93.0	97.3	98.2	97.7	94.9	92.3	93.6	95.8	96.8	96.3	95.0	88.9	92.0	98.0	73.4	86.0

MISSOURI

DIVISION		KANSAS CITY 640 - 641			KIRKSVILLE 635			POPLAR BLUFF 639			ROLLA 654 - 655			SEDALIA 653			SIKESTON 638		
		MAT.	INST.	TOTAL	MAT.	INST.	TOTAL	MAT.	INST.	TOTAL	MAT.	INST.	TOTAL	MAT.	INST.	TOTAL	MAT.	INST.	TOTAL
02	SITE CONSTRUCTION	92.0	94.4	93.9	87.1	89.4	88.9	73.3	93.6	88.8	98.1	93.5	94.6	88.1	90.3	89.8	76.7	93.7	89.8
03100	CONCRETE FORMS & ACCESSORIES	105.0	99.7	100.5	81.6	71.4	72.8	81.5	72.0	73.3	95.8	90.3	91.0	93.1	74.8	77.3	82.9	73.2	74.5
03200	CONCRETE REINFORCEMENT	98.8	105.4	102.6	104.7	85.4	93.7	107.9	85.5	95.1	100.9	69.0	82.7	99.3	88.4	93.1	107.2	85.6	94.9
03300	CAST-IN-PLACE CONCRETE	95.6	96.4	97.2	88.8	79.0	84.8	68.3	76.2	71.5	88.1	79.9	84.8	92.1	78.3	86.4	72.9	79.6	75.7
03	CONCRETE	94.0	101.2	97.6	99.1	78.0	88.5	76.9	77.3	77.1	83.8	84.1	84.0	95.3	79.8	87.6	80.4	79.1	79.7
04	MASONRY	100.1	99.7	99.9	122.4	69.2	89.7	113.9	74.9	89.9	107.0	60.3	78.3	113.3	63.3	82.6	114.0	79.7	92.9
05	METALS	99.2	110.5	103.2	91.2	99.6	94.3	93.7	101.1	96.4	92.1	100.9	95.3	90.3	100.5	94.0	93.6	101.3	96.4
06	WOOD & PLASTICS	102.8	99.4	101.1	79.7	70.7	75.0	78.6	70.7	74.5	100.1	99.7	99.9	93.3	71.5	82.0	79.9	70.7	75.1
07	THERMAL & MOISTURE PROTECTION	97.3	99.8	98.5	99.5	84.1	92.2	98.9	80.6	90.2	92.4	70.8	82.2	96.0	84.0	90.3	99.1	82.3	91.1
08	DOORS & WINDOWS	98.8	100.8	99.3	100.7	76.5	94.9	101.6	69.8	93.9	93.2	80.0	90.0	96.8	79.2	92.6	101.6	69.8	93.9
09200	PLASTER & GYPSUM BOARD	104.0	99.1	101.0	95.7	69.4	79.6	96.2	69.4	79.8	104.3	99.3	101.3	96.7	70.2	80.5	96.7	69.4	80.0
095,098	CEILINGS & ACOUSTICAL TREATMENT	104.0	99.1	100.7	89.8	69.4	76.3	92.6	69.4	77.3	93.8	99.3	97.4	92.4	70.2	77.7	92.6	69.4	77.3
09600	FLOORING	96.8	98.1	97.2	79.7	66.3	76.4	93.7	60.6	85.7	112.2	56.5	98.7	87.2	90.7	88.0	94.4	60.6	86.2
097,099	WALL FINISHES, PAINTS & COATINGS	97.4	104.8	101.7	96.4	53.3	71.3	95.7	70.6	81.2	99.2	85.5	91.3	99.2	98.5	98.8	95.7	70.6	81.2
09	FINISHES	100.6	99.7	100.1	91.7	67.3	79.2	93.5	68.6	80.8	98.3	84.4	91.2	93.4	79.4	86.2	93.9	69.3	81.4
10 - 14	TOTAL DIV. 10000 - 14000	100.0	95.9	99.1	100.0	74.4	94.6	100.0	75.3	94.8	100.0	78.9	95.5	100.0	89.1	97.7	100.0	76.5	95.0
15	MECHANICAL	100.1	99.5	99.8	97.1	93.8	95.5	97.1	94.5	95.9	97.0	89.3	93.4	96.9	91.5	94.4	97.1	96.1	96.6
16	ELECTRICAL	103.4	104.4	104.1	94.1	87.7	89.7	94.2	113.2	107.3	91.2	85.9	87.5	92.6	103.7	100.3	92.8	113.2	106.9
01 - 16	WEIGHTED AVERAGE	99.0	101.1	100.0	97.3	83.6	90.6	94.4	88.8	91.7	94.7	85.2	90.0	95.9	87.6	91.9	94.9	90.0	92.5

MISSOURI / MONTANA

DIVISION		SPRINGFIELD 656 - 658			ST. JOSEPH 644 - 645			ST. LOUIS 630 - 631			BILLINGS 590 - 591			BUTTE 597			GREAT FALLS 594		
		MAT.	INST.	TOTAL	MAT.	INST.	TOTAL	MAT.	INST.	TOTAL	MAT.	INST.	TOTAL	MAT.	INST.	TOTAL	MAT.	INST.	TOTAL
02	SITE CONSTRUCTION	90.6	93.6	92.9	93.4	91.5	91.9	93.3	96.6	95.8	82.7	98.2	94.6	88.6	96.9	95.0	92.1	97.7	96.4
03100	CONCRETE FORMS & ACCESSORIES	103.6	58.6	64.8	104.9	75.2	79.3	101.4	109.2	108.1	94.4	85.7	86.9	80.4	88.5	87.4	100.8	86.3	88.3
03200	CONCRETE REINFORCEMENT	96.5	104.4	101.0	97.6	99.0	98.4	97.0	108.8	103.7	100.1	104.9	102.9	108.6	104.9	106.5	100.1	104.9	102.9
03300	CAST-IN-PLACE CONCRETE	97.4	71.8	86.8	95.6	94.3	95.0	85.1	112.3	96.3	116.3	84.1	103.0	119.7	85.3	105.5	126.5	71.2	103.7
03	CONCRETE	94.6	73.3	83.9	93.8	87.5	90.6	86.0	111.3	98.6	102.6	89.1	95.9	102.3	90.7	96.5	108.1	84.8	96.5
04	MASONRY	86.5	73.8	78.7	99.4	88.2	92.5	96.1	110.6	105.1	122.6	96.2	106.4	121.0	96.9	106.2	124.7	99.5	109.2
05	METALS	96.3	105.0	99.4	97.8	107.1	101.2	96.1	125.3	106.7	98.4	99.4	98.8	97.7	99.1	98.2	98.8	99.2	98.9
06	WOOD & PLASTICS	102.6	54.9	78.0	103.4	71.7	87.0	103.4	107.8	105.7	96.6	86.0	91.1	83.8	91.1	87.6	105.0	86.0	95.2
07	THERMAL & MOISTURE PROTECTION	96.4	73.2	85.4	98.0	88.9	93.7	95.1	105.5	100.1	98.1	87.8	93.2	97.3	86.2	92.0	98.3	86.4	92.7
08	DOORS & WINDOWS	99.0	70.2	92.0	99.5	84.2	95.8	93.6	112.7	98.2	102.7	85.8	98.7	99.3	88.5	96.7	103.0	85.8	98.9
09200	PLASTER & GYPSUM BOARD	106.2	53.1	73.8	109.4	70.5	85.6	104.8	107.7	106.5	100.4	86.1	91.6	93.8	91.4	92.3	100.4	86.1	91.6
095,098	CEILINGS & ACOUSTICAL TREATMENT	99.2	53.1	68.8	102.6	70.5	81.4	96.7	107.7	103.9	112.6	86.1	95.1	109.9	91.4	97.7	112.6	86.1	95.1
09600	FLOORING	110.4	60.6	98.3	99.5	97.1	98.9	106.7	101.6	105.4	110.5	63.1	99.0	102.1	50.2	89.5	110.5	68.1	100.2
097,099	WALL FINISHES, PAINTS & COATINGS	93.5	76.3	83.5	93.2	88.4	90.4	100.8	109.6	105.9	102.5	78.4	88.5	102.5	60.5	78.1	102.5	68.1	82.5
09	FINISHES	101.1	59.3	79.8	101.8	79.5	90.4	98.3	107.5	103.0	106.7	80.4	93.3	102.4	78.3	90.1	106.8	80.6	93.5
10 - 14	TOTAL DIV. 10000 - 14000	100.0	84.1	96.6	100.0	88.6	97.6	100.0	106.3	101.3	100.0	84.7	96.8	100.0	84.8	96.8	100.0	85.6	97.0
15	MECHANICAL	100.2	72.7	87.5	100.3	88.2	94.7	100.1	108.1	103.8	100.4	90.4	95.7	100.4	87.8	94.5	100.4	91.6	96.3
16	ELECTRICAL	100.2	75.0	82.9	102.8	81.5	88.1	99.0	116.5	111.0	95.0	84.6	87.9	106.5	80.7	88.8	94.9	82.3	86.2
01 - 16	WEIGHTED AVERAGE	97.7	76.7	87.5	99.0	87.7	93.5	96.2	110.6	103.2	101.5	89.8	95.8	101.3	88.6	95.1	102.8	89.3	96.2

MONTANA

DIVISION		HAVRE 595			HELENA 596			KALISPELL 599			MILES CITY 593			MISSOULA 598			WOLF POINT 592		
		MAT.	INST.	TOTAL	MAT.	INST.	TOTAL	MAT.	INST.	TOTAL	MAT.	INST.	TOTAL	MAT.	INST.	TOTAL	MAT.	INST.	TOTAL
02	SITE CONSTRUCTION	96.0	97.7	97.3	93.8	97.7	96.8	80.1	96.9	93.0	86.0	97.7	94.9	72.8	96.9	91.3	102.0	97.7	98.7
03100	CONCRETE FORMS & ACCESSORIES	71.7	88.5	86.2	100.9	86.8	88.7	84.8	83.1	83.3	93.6	88.5	89.2	84.8	83.2	83.4	84.5	86.4	86.1
03200	CONCRETE REINFORCEMENT	109.6	100.1	104.1	103.7	99.9	101.5	111.6	109.9	110.6	109.0	100.0	103.9	110.5	110.3	110.4	110.6	100.0	104.6
03300	CAST-IN-PLACE CONCRETE	128.9	80.4	108.9	128.9	83.7	110.3	103.9	81.7	94.8	113.8	80.1	99.9	88.2	81.7	85.5	127.5	74.2	105.5
03	CONCRETE	110.1	88.0	99.1	109.7	88.4	99.1	92.2	88.0	90.1	99.6	88.0	93.8	81.1	88.1	84.6	113.9	85.0	99.4
04	MASONRY	121.9	101.5	109.4	121.9	96.5	106.3	120.1	82.7	97.1	127.4	100.1	110.7	147.4	91.2	112.9	128.5	101.5	111.9
05	METALS	97.6	96.7	97.3	98.0	96.7	97.5	97.4	100.3	98.5	96.9	96.8	96.9	97.8	101.0	99.0	97.0	96.6	96.8
06	WOOD & PLASTICS	74.5	88.3	81.7	105.2	86.0	95.2	88.6	85.7	87.1	95.9	88.3	92.0	88.6	85.7	87.1	86.7	85.7	86.2
07	THERMAL & MOISTURE PROTECTION	97.7	86.7	92.5	98.3	87.7	93.3	96.9	90.1	93.7	97.4	92.0	94.8	96.4	92.8	94.7	98.4	84.8	91.9
08	DOORS & WINDOWS	99.4	85.7	96.1	102.4	84.7	98.2	99.4	87.9	96.6	98.8	85.7	95.7	99.4	87.9	96.6	98.9	84.2	95.3
09200	PLASTER & GYPSUM BOARD	91.2	88.5	89.6	99.9	86.1	91.4	95.5	85.8	89.6	99.6	88.5	92.8	95.5	85.8	89.6	96.6	85.8	90.0
095,098	CEILINGS & ACOUSTICAL TREATMENT	109.9	88.5	95.8	109.9	86.1	94.2	109.9	85.8	94.0	108.5	88.5	95.3	109.9	85.8	94.0	108.5	85.8	93.5
09600	FLOORING	98.5	55.3	88.0	110.5	66.0	99.7	104.0	78.5	97.8	110.2	62.0	98.5	104.0	78.5	97.8	105.9	55.3	93.6
097,099	WALL FINISHES, PAINTS & COATINGS	102.5	67.2	82.0	102.5	75.6	86.8	102.5	68.1	82.5	102.5	63.5	79.8	102.5	68.1	82.5	102.5	63.5	79.8
09	FINISHES	101.3	79.8	90.3	106.3	81.4	93.6	102.9	80.5	91.5	105.5	80.7	92.9	102.5	80.5	91.3	104.6	77.8	90.9
10 - 14	TOTAL DIV. 10000 - 14000	100.0	77.0	95.1	100.0	76.5	95.0	100.0	72.4	94.2	100.0	76.9	95.1	100.0	72.4	94.2	100.0	76.6	95.1
15	MECHANICAL	97.2	92.6	95.1	100.4	90.5	95.8	97.2	82.8	90.6	97.2	92.4	95.0	100.4	82.9	92.3	97.2	92.6	95.1
16	ELECTRICAL	94.9	79.8	84.5	94.9	82.3	86.2	101.5	85.5	90.5	94.9	82.6	86.5	103.1	85.4	90.9	94.9	82.6	86.5
01 - 16	WEIGHTED AVERAGE	100.8	89.2	95.1	102.6	88.9	96.0	98.8	86.8	93.0	100.0	89.7	95.0	99.5	87.8	93.8	102.1	88.8	95.7

NEBRASKA

DIVISION		ALLIANCE 693			COLUMBUS 686			GRAND ISLAND 688			HASTINGS 689			LINCOLN 683 - 685			MCCOOK 690		
		MAT.	INST.	TOTAL	MAT.	INST.	TOTAL	MAT.	INST.	TOTAL	MAT.	INST.	TOTAL	MAT.	INST.	TOTAL	MAT.	INST.	TOTAL
02	SITE CONSTRUCTION	88.6	96.0	94.2	89.0	89.7	89.5	93.1	90.7	91.3	92.4	90.4	90.8	84.2	90.7	89.2	93.2	89.7	90.5
03100	CONCRETE FORMS & ACCESSORIES	89.2	31.1	39.1	100.4	29.0	38.8	99.6	57.3	63.1	104.3	54.4	61.3	105.1	50.2	57.8	96.5	37.4	45.5
03200	CONCRETE REINFORCEMENT	113.6	53.7	79.4	105.6	59.8	79.5	105.0	78.9	90.2	105.0	59.8	79.2	96.5	78.7	86.4	107.0	78.6	90.8
03300	CAST-IN-PLACE CONCRETE	103.7	42.9	78.7	106.2	54.1	84.7	112.4	64.4	92.6	112.4	59.7	90.7	101.5	67.0	87.3	112.4	41.3	83.8
03	CONCRETE	113.2	40.7	76.9	99.8	45.7	72.8	104.2	65.2	84.7	104.6	58.8	81.7	96.7	63.0	79.8	104.3	49.0	76.6
04	MASONRY	107.1	35.2	62.9	113.1	36.4	66.0	104.7	54.5	73.8	113.8	47.7	73.2	94.6	51.8	68.3	102.9	35.2	61.2
05	METALS	101.6	63.0	87.7	91.6	79.4	87.2	92.9	88.0	91.1	91.6	79.8	87.3	95.8	87.6	92.9	91.8	86.2	89.8
06	WOOD & PLASTICS	87.2	29.9	57.6	99.8	26.7	62.0	98.9	53.6	75.5	103.6	53.6	77.7	104.2	44.3	73.2	96.0	37.2	65.6
07	THERMAL & MOISTURE PROTECTION	102.8	41.0	73.5	96.5	37.6	68.6	96.7	63.0	80.7	96.8	54.4	76.7	97.1	55.5	77.4	96.6	41.6	70.5
08	DOORS & WINDOWS	92.7	33.8	78.5	92.5	39.9	79.8	92.5	56.7	83.9	92.5	54.4	83.3	98.1	53.8	87.4	92.6	43.5	80.7
09200	PLASTER & GYPSUM BOARD	98.1	27.4	54.9	103.6	24.0	55.0	103.2	51.7	71.7	104.5	51.7	72.2	106.2	42.1	67.0	102.8	34.8	61.2
095,098	CEILINGS & ACOUSTICAL TREATMENT	113.7	27.4	56.8	92.4	24.0	47.3	92.4	51.7	65.6	92.4	51.7	65.6	99.2	42.1	61.6	92.4	34.8	54.4
09600	FLOORING	99.6	34.5	83.8	99.7	43.8	86.2	99.5	42.1	85.6	101.1	43.8	87.2	101.3	43.8	87.4	98.4	34.5	82.9
097,099	WALL FINISHES, PAINTS & COATINGS	140.5	26.3	74.2	91.0	60.3	73.1	91.0	49.9	67.1	91.0	60.3	73.1	91.0	50.3	67.3	91.0	28.6	54.7
09	FINISHES	100.3	30.6	64.7	96.1	34.0	64.4	96.1	52.4	73.8	96.8	53.0	74.5	98.2	47.4	72.3	95.7	34.9	64.7
10 - 14	TOTAL DIV. 10000 - 14000	100.0	59.7	91.5	100.0	57.2	91.0	100.0	82.3	96.3	100.0	66.1	92.8	100.0	81.1	96.0	100.0	58.6	91.2
15	MECHANICAL	97.0	32.3	67.0	97.1	29.3	65.7	100.2	84.4	92.9	97.1	46.3	73.6	100.2	84.4	92.9	97.1	74.8	86.7
16	ELECTRICAL	94.4	22.1	44.7	93.2	52.5	65.2	91.0	52.5	64.5	90.0	52.5	64.2	100.5	52.5	67.5	97.3	22.1	45.6
01 - 16	WEIGHTED AVERAGE	100.0	41.8	71.7	96.6	48.5	73.2	97.5	68.7	83.5	97.2	58.5	78.4	97.8	67.0	82.8	96.9	53.5	75.8

NEBRASKA / NEVADA

DIVISION		NORFOLK 687			NORTH PLATTE 691			OMAHA 680 - 681			VALENTINE 692			CARSON CITY 897			ELKO 898		
		MAT.	INST.	TOTAL	MAT.	INST.	TOTAL	MAT.	INST.	TOTAL	MAT.	INST.	TOTAL	MAT.	INST.	TOTAL	MAT.	INST.	TOTAL
02	SITE CONSTRUCTION	75.2	89.0	85.8	93.9	90.4	91.2	76.0	89.4	86.2	79.2	92.7	89.5	64.2	102.3	93.4	59.4	101.5	91.6
03100	CONCRETE FORMS & ACCESSORIES	83.9	54.9	58.9	99.5	55.4	61.4	100.1	74.5	78.0	85.2	27.8	35.7	101.1	96.9	97.5	117.2	85.6	89.9
03200	CONCRETE REINFORCEMENT	105.7	68.8	84.7	106.4	78.7	90.6	101.0	80.3	89.2	107.0	48.3	73.6	108.4	117.3	113.5	107.1	84.3	94.1
03300	CAST-IN-PLACE CONCRETE	106.9	66.0	90.0	112.4	60.1	90.9	105.4	75.8	93.2	99.0	50.4	78.9	117.8	94.1	108.0	105.7	87.3	98.1
03	CONCRETE	98.2	62.1	80.1	104.4	63.0	83.7	98.0	76.2	87.1	100.9	41.1	71.0	113.4	99.5	106.5	104.6	86.0	95.3
04	MASONRY	119.5	74.8	92.0	89.9	47.7	64.0	100.4	78.9	87.2	102.0	36.5	61.7	136.3	84.2	104.3	135.4	78.5	100.4
05	METALS	95.7	73.9	87.9	93.1	91.8	92.6	98.4	79.4	91.6	108.8	63.7	92.5	103.9	101.6	103.1	103.1	86.1	97.0
06	WOOD & PLASTICS	81.9	52.8	66.8	98.7	53.6	75.4	99.6	75.6	87.2	82.6	25.9	53.3	95.4	96.7	96.1	112.5	86.5	99.0
07	THERMAL & MOISTURE PROTECTION	94.6	64.7	80.4	96.6	54.5	76.6	92.5	75.2	84.3	95.4	36.8	67.6	104.8	91.6	98.6	104.8	84.5	95.1
08	DOORS & WINDOWS	94.8	55.8	85.4	91.8	62.1	84.6	101.8	70.8	94.3	94.9	32.3	79.8	95.1	105.4	97.6	97.7	86.4	95.0
09200	PLASTER & GYPSUM BOARD	104.4	51.7	72.2	103.5	51.7	71.8	111.9	75.3	89.5	109.8	24.0	57.4	86.9	96.4	92.7	93.4	85.8	88.8
095,098	CEILINGS & ACOUSTICAL TREATMENT	126.6	51.7	77.2	93.8	51.7	66.0	138.8	75.3	96.9	137.0	24.0	62.5	97.9	96.4	96.9	97.9	85.8	89.9
09600	FLOORING	124.8	52.7	107.3	99.5	43.8	86.0	130.2	52.7	111.4	127.6	52.6	109.4	105.2	83.4	99.9	111.5	83.4	104.7
097,099	WALL FINISHES, PAINTS & COATINGS	146.4	60.3	96.3	91.0	60.3	73.1	146.4	60.3	96.3	146.4	40.4	84.8	108.7	93.7	100.0	108.7	93.7	100.0
09	FINISHES	118.7	54.2	85.8	96.4	53.0	74.2	123.9	68.6	95.7	122.8	33.0	77.0	97.0	93.5	95.2	99.7	86.1	92.8
10 - 14	TOTAL DIV. 10000 - 14000	100.0	78.6	95.5	100.0	66.1	92.8	100.0	83.3	96.5	100.0	48.3	89.1	100.0	120.9	104.4	100.0	90.8	98.0
15	MECHANICAL	96.7	62.3	80.8	100.2	82.1	91.8	99.8	83.2	92.2	96.5	28.8	65.2	100.2	96.9	98.7	98.4	92.2	95.5
16	ELECTRICAL	89.2	66.0	73.3	94.3	52.5	65.6	88.3	86.2	86.9	88.1	52.5	63.6	92.7	91.9	92.1	91.8	83.4	86.0
01 - 16	WEIGHTED AVERAGE	99.1	66.9	83.4	96.9	67.3	82.5	100.5	80.1	90.6	100.9	46.0	74.2	102.0	96.5	99.3	100.9	87.7	94.5

DIVISION		NEVADA									NEW HAMPSHIRE								
		ELY			LAS VEGAS			RENO			CHARLESTON			CLAREMONT			CONCORD		
		893			889 - 891			894 - 895			036			037			032 - 033		
		MAT.	INST.	TOTAL	MAT.	INST.	TOTAL	MAT.	INST.	TOTAL	MAT.	INST.	TOTAL	MAT.	INST.	TOTAL	MAT.	INST.	TOTAL
02	SITE CONSTRUCTION	64.9	101.5	92.9	64.3	103.9	94.7	64.6	102.3	93.5	84.3	101.0	97.1	78.4	101.0	95.7	91.0	102.2	99.5
03100	CONCRETE FORMS & ACCESSORIES	105.8	85.8	88.5	97.2	110.0	108.3	101.6	97.0	97.6	84.0	46.2	51.4	91.8	46.2	52.4	85.7	72.6	74.4
03200	CONCRETE REINFORCEMENT	105.9	84.3	93.6	100.1	126.3	115.0	100.1	125.8	114.8	89.5	72.2	79.6	89.5	72.2	79.6	89.5	99.3	95.0
03300	CAST-IN-PLACE CONCRETE	113.5	90.0	103.8	112.1	112.0	112.1	120.0	94.1	109.3	97.6	62.9	83.3	89.7	62.9	78.6	94.8	89.5	92.6
03	CONCRETE	113.7	87.0	100.4	109.3	113.2	111.2	113.5	101.1	107.3	104.5	57.7	81.1	95.9	57.7	76.8	101.1	83.5	92.3
04	MASONRY	140.6	78.5	102.4	130.3	98.5	110.8	136.4	84.2	104.3	90.0	51.3	66.2	89.6	51.3	66.1	94.6	94.9	94.8
05	METALS	103.3	86.3	97.2	104.6	107.5	105.6	104.4	104.8	104.6	93.0	74.7	86.4	93.0	74.7	86.4	93.1	89.3	91.7
06	WOOD & PLASTICS	99.7	86.5	92.8	90.4	108.5	99.8	95.9	96.7	96.3	85.6	45.6	64.9	93.7	45.6	68.8	87.3	67.1	76.8
07	THERMAL & MOISTURE PROTECTION	105.5	86.2	96.4	104.4	102.2	103.3	104.8	91.6	98.6	98.7	54.8	77.9	98.6	54.8	77.8	99.3	96.5	97.9
08	DOORS & WINDOWS	97.7	86.4	95.0	95.5	114.0	99.9	95.5	105.4	97.9	106.7	48.9	92.7	108.0	48.9	93.8	108.0	74.3	99.9
09200	PLASTER & GYPSUM BOARD	90.4	85.8	87.6	87.4	108.6	100.3	88.2	96.4	93.2	90.8	42.6	61.4	93.4	42.6	62.4	91.3	64.8	75.1
095,098	CEILINGS & ACOUSTICAL TREATMENT	97.9	85.8	89.9	104.7	108.6	107.2	104.7	96.4	99.2	90.0	42.6	58.7	90.0	42.6	58.7	90.0	64.8	73.4
09600	FLOORING	109.0	93.3	105.2	105.2	99.3	103.8	105.2	83.4	99.9	94.1	48.0	82.9	96.9	48.0	85.1	94.7	101.9	96.5
097,099	WALL FINISHES, PAINTS & COATINGS	108.7	93.7	100.0	108.7	113.2	111.3	108.7	93.7	100.0	95.6	39.0	62.7	95.6	39.0	62.7	95.6	96.4	96.1
09	FINISHES	98.9	88.1	93.4	98.2	108.0	103.2	98.4	93.5	95.9	93.8	44.9	68.9	94.7	44.9	69.3	94.9	79.5	87.0
10 - 14	TOTAL DIV. 10000 - 14000	100.0	90.8	98.0	100.0	112.6	102.7	100.0	120.9	104.4	100.0	58.9	91.3	100.0	58.9	91.3	100.0	93.6	98.6
15	MECHANICAL	98.4	92.2	95.6	100.2	111.9	105.6	100.2	97.0	98.7	96.7	48.3	74.3	96.7	48.3	74.3	99.8	86.1	93.5
16	ELECTRICAL	91.8	83.4	86.1	94.8	110.2	105.3	92.7	91.9	92.1	99.9	43.7	61.3	99.9	43.7	61.3	104.0	82.3	89.1
01 - 16	WEIGHTED AVERAGE	102.3	88.1	95.4	101.5	108.6	105.0	102.3	97.0	99.7	97.7	56.7	77.8	96.8	56.7	77.3	99.0	86.8	93.1

DIVISION		NEW HAMPSHIRE														NEW JERSEY		
		KEENE			LITTLETON			MANCHESTER			NASHUA			PORTSMOUTH			ATLANTIC CITY		
		034			035			031			030			038			082,084		
		MAT.	INST.	TOTAL	MAT.	INST.	TOTAL	MAT.	INST.	TOTAL	MAT.	INST.	TOTAL	MAT.	INST.	TOTAL	MAT.	INST.	TOTAL
02	SITE CONSTRUCTION	91.6	101.0	98.8	78.4	100.6	95.4	90.0	102.2	99.3	92.1	102.2	99.8	86.2	101.7	98.0	94.9	106.4	103.7
03100	CONCRETE FORMS & ACCESSORIES	89.9	47.5	53.3	102.8	53.4	60.2	99.4	72.6	76.2	99.8	72.6	76.3	85.7	69.5	71.8	111.0	123.8	122.0
03200	CONCRETE REINFORCEMENT	89.5	86.0	87.5	90.3	50.1	67.4	111.9	99.3	104.7	111.9	99.3	104.7	89.5	99.2	95.0	85.3	119.4	104.7
03300	CAST-IN-PLACE CONCRETE	98.1	63.3	83.7	88.0	56.3	74.9	95.1	89.5	92.8	92.8	89.5	91.4	88.0	85.6	87.0	83.2	128.4	101.8
03	CONCRETE	104.3	61.0	82.7	95.4	54.4	74.9	105.1	83.5	94.3	103.9	83.5	93.7	95.1	80.8	88.0	97.8	123.3	110.6
04	MASONRY	95.0	51.3	68.1	102.5	49.6	70.0	96.5	94.9	95.6	96.6	94.9	95.6	91.0	88.4	89.4	98.9	123.1	113.8
05	METALS	93.0	80.8	88.6	93.0	66.0	83.3	98.0	89.3	94.8	98.0	89.3	94.8	94.7	88.0	92.2	92.7	104.4	97.0
06	WOOD & PLASTICS	91.9	45.6	67.9	103.3	52.2	76.9	102.0	67.1	83.9	101.9	67.1	83.9	87.3	67.1	76.8	113.7	123.4	118.7
07	THERMAL & MOISTURE PROTECTION	99.2	57.0	79.2	98.8	60.2	80.5	99.4	96.5	98.0	99.8	96.5	98.2	99.3	97.0	98.2	99.5	122.0	110.2
08	DOORS & WINDOWS	105.0	59.8	94.1	109.1	48.5	94.5	110.0	74.3	101.4	110.0	74.3	101.4	111.0	67.4	100.5	107.6	118.3	110.2
09200	PLASTER & GYPSUM BOARD	93.0	42.6	62.2	102.9	49.5	70.3	98.2	64.8	77.8	98.2	64.8	77.8	91.3	64.8	75.1	100.3	122.9	114.1
095,098	CEILINGS & ACOUSTICAL TREATMENT	90.0	42.6	58.7	90.0	49.5	63.3	102.6	64.8	77.6	102.6	64.8	77.6	93.1	64.8	74.4	90.0	122.9	111.7
09600	FLOORING	96.3	78.7	92.0	106.5	48.0	92.3	100.2	101.9	100.6	99.9	101.9	100.4	94.7	101.9	96.5	104.0	129.2	110.1
097,099	WALL FINISHES, PAINTS & COATINGS	95.6	39.0	62.7	95.6	75.6	83.9	95.6	96.4	96.1	95.6	96.4	96.1	95.6	47.3	67.5	95.6	144.1	123.8
09	FINISHES	95.8	51.2	73.1	99.3	54.4	76.4	99.8	79.5	89.4	100.0	79.5	89.5	95.2	72.2	83.5	99.8	127.3	113.8
10 - 14	TOTAL DIV. 10000 - 14000	100.0	83.6	96.5	100.0	62.2	92.0	100.0	93.6	98.7	100.0	93.6	98.7	100.0	91.0	98.1	100.0	118.1	103.8
15	MECHANICAL	96.7	51.6	75.9	96.7	65.9	82.4	99.8	86.1	93.5	99.8	86.1	93.5	99.8	82.5	91.8	99.6	117.8	108.0
16	ELECTRICAL	99.9	43.7	61.3	101.8	82.2	88.3	104.2	82.3	89.1	104.0	82.3	89.1	100.7	82.3	88.0	95.6	120.3	112.5
01 - 16	WEIGHTED AVERAGE	98.3	60.2	79.7	98.3	66.6	82.9	101.3	86.8	94.2	101.2	86.8	94.2	98.3	83.8	91.3	99.0	118.4	108.5

DIVISION		NEW JERSEY																
		CAMDEN			DOVER			ELIZABETH			HACKENSACK			JERSEY CITY			LONG BRANCH		
		081			078			072			076			073			077		
		MAT.	INST.	TOTAL	MAT.	INST.	TOTAL	MAT.	INST.	TOTAL	MAT.	INST.	TOTAL	MAT.	INST.	TOTAL	MAT.	INST.	TOTAL
02	SITE CONSTRUCTION	95.5	106.3	103.8	106.5	107.0	106.9	110.3	107.0	107.8	107.0	106.8	106.8	95.5	106.8	104.1	100.6	106.9	105.4
03100	CONCRETE FORMS & ACCESSORIES	99.8	123.5	120.2	95.8	117.1	114.1	111.1	125.6	123.6	95.8	126.0	121.8	99.8	126.5	122.9	100.6	124.1	120.8
03200	CONCRETE REINFORCEMENT	111.9	113.5	112.8	86.2	131.4	111.9	86.2	131.2	111.9	86.2	131.3	111.9	111.9	131.4	123.0	86.2	131.2	111.9
03300	CAST-IN-PLACE CONCRETE	80.7	122.0	97.7	103.5	130.7	114.7	88.9	128.7	105.3	101.1	130.5	113.2	80.7	130.8	101.4	89.7	128.1	105.5
03	CONCRETE	98.0	119.9	108.9	105.7	123.6	114.7	101.4	126.7	114.0	103.7	127.5	115.6	98.0	127.6	112.8	103.4	125.5	114.4
04	MASONRY	88.8	123.0	109.8	93.0	125.3	112.9	110.2	125.3	119.5	97.4	125.3	114.6	88.8	125.3	111.3	91.9	123.0	114.9
05	METALS	97.8	102.0	99.3	92.7	112.7	99.9	94.4	111.9	100.7	92.8	112.2	99.8	97.9	109.7	102.2	92.8	107.7	98.2
06	WOOD & PLASTICS	101.9	123.4	113.0	100.9	113.8	107.6	117.6	126.5	122.2	100.9	126.5	114.2	101.9	126.2	114.5	103.1	123.3	113.5
07	THERMAL & MOISTURE PROTECTION	99.2	118.6	108.4	99.8	120.6	109.7	100.1	121.9	110.4	99.5	122.6	110.4	99.2	122.9	110.4	99.4	121.5	109.9
08	DOORS & WINDOWS	110.0	116.6	111.6	113.6	119.7	115.1	111.4	126.6	115.0	110.5	126.6	114.4	110.0	126.8	114.1	105.9	124.3	110.4
09200	PLASTER & GYPSUM BOARD	98.2	122.9	113.3	95.6	113.0	106.2	101.2	126.1	116.4	95.6	126.1	114.2	98.2	125.8	115.1	96.9	122.9	112.8
095,098	CEILINGS & ACOUSTICAL TREATMENT	102.6	122.9	116.0	90.0	113.0	105.2	93.1	126.1	114.9	90.0	126.1	113.8	102.6	125.8	117.9	90.0	122.9	111.7
09600	FLOORING	99.9	123.2	105.6	98.8	118.6	103.6	104.5	66.4	95.3	98.8	66.4	91.0	99.9	133.2	108.0	100.2	129.2	107.2
097,099	WALL FINISHES, PAINTS & COATINGS	95.6	144.1	123.8	95.5	144.2	123.8	95.5	144.2	123.8	95.5	144.2	123.8	95.6	144.2	123.8	95.6	131.0	116.2
09	FINISHES	100.3	126.0	113.4	97.5	119.5	108.7	101.2	116.0	108.7	97.4	116.0	106.9	100.3	129.7	115.3	98.4	125.7	112.3
10 - 14	TOTAL DIV. 10000 - 14000	100.0	118.1	103.8	100.0	98.7	99.7	100.0	99.5	99.9	100.0	99.5	99.9	100.0	100.4	100.1	100.0	99.7	99.9
15	MECHANICAL	99.8	118.3	108.4	99.6	127.8	112.6	99.8	116.5	107.6	99.6	127.8	112.6	99.8	127.8	112.8	99.6	125.5	111.6
16	ELECTRICAL	104.0	120.3	115.2	97.7	118.9	112.3	98.8	115.7	110.4	97.7	133.7	122.4	105.7	133.7	124.9	97.1	113.5	108.4
01 - 16	WEIGHTED AVERAGE	100.1	117.5	108.6	100.5	119.7	109.8	101.7	117.4	109.3	100.1	122.7	111.1	100.3	124.2	111.9	99.7	119.0	109.1

NEW JERSEY

DIVISION		NEWARK 070 - 071			NEW BRUNSWICK 088 - 089			PATERSON 074 - 075			POINT PLEASANT 087			SUMMIT 079			TRENTON 085 - 086		
		MAT.	INST.	TOTAL	MAT.	INST.	TOTAL	MAT.	INST.	TOTAL	MAT.	INST.	TOTAL	MAT.	INST.	TOTAL	MAT.	INST.	TOTAL
02	SITE CONSTRUCTION	114.1	106.7	108.4	108.5	106.9	107.3	108.5	106.7	107.1	110.0	106.9	107.6	107.9	106.8	107.0	96.6	106.9	104.5
03100	CONCRETE FORMS & ACCESSORIES	98.1	126.6	122.7	103.9	123.8	121.1	98.6	126.6	122.8	97.0	126.0	122.0	99.6	125.2	121.6	98.9	124.0	120.6
03200	CONCRETE REINFORCEMENT	111.9	131.4	123.0	86.2	131.2	111.8	111.9	131.4	123.0	86.2	131.2	111.9	86.2	131.2	111.8	111.9	125.1	119.4
03300	CAST-IN-PLACE CONCRETE	90.9	130.8	107.3	102.8	124.8	111.8	102.8	130.7	114.3	102.8	128.1	113.2	85.9	130.3	104.2	90.8	124.8	104.4
03	CONCRETE	102.9	127.9	115.4	116.3	124.3	120.3	108.8	127.9	118.3	115.8	126.4	121.1	97.8	127.0	112.4	102.9	123.3	113.1
04	MASONRY	98.2	125.3	114.9	95.3	123.0	112.4	93.4	125.3	113.0	89.1	123.0	110.0	95.8	125.3	113.9	89.7	122.8	110.1
05	METALS	97.9	112.9	103.3	92.8	108.9	98.6	97.9	112.9	103.3	92.8	109.1	98.7	92.7	111.8	99.6	98.7	107.0	101.7
06	WOOD & PLASTICS	103.8	126.5	115.5	106.6	123.3	115.2	103.8	126.5	115.5	99.2	126.0	113.0	105.0	126.1	115.9	102.0	123.1	112.9
07	THERMAL & MOISTURE PROTECTION	99.5	121.9	110.1	99.9	121.0	109.7	99.9	122.6	110.7	99.6	121.8	110.1	100.4	121.8	110.6	98.1	121.7	109.3
08	DOORS & WINDOWS	116.5	126.6	118.9	101.7	124.2	107.1	116.5	126.6	118.9	103.9	122.6	108.4	119.2	125.7	120.8	110.0	123.6	113.3
09200	PLASTER & GYPSUM BOARD	98.2	126.1	115.3	98.2	122.9	113.3	98.2	126.1	115.3	95.6	125.6	114.0	96.9	125.6	114.5	98.2	122.7	113.2
095,098	CEILINGS & ACOUSTICAL TREATMENT	102.6	126.1	118.1	90.0	122.9	111.7	102.6	126.1	118.1	90.0	125.6	113.5	90.0	125.6	113.5	102.6	122.7	115.8
09600	FLOORING	100.2	133.2	108.2	101.5	86.1	97.8	99.9	133.2	108.0	98.8	129.2	106.2	100.3	66.4	92.1	100.2	123.3	105.8
097,099	WALL FINISHES, PAINTS & COATINGS	95.5	144.2	123.8	95.6	144.2	123.8	95.5	144.2	123.8	95.6	144.1	123.8	95.5	134.5	118.1	95.6	144.2	123.8
09	FINISHES	100.8	129.9	115.7	99.6	119.5	109.8	100.4	129.9	115.5	98.4	128.1	113.9	98.4	114.7	106.7	100.4	125.8	113.3
10 - 14	TOTAL DIV. 10000 - 14000	100.0	100.6	100.1	100.0	99.8	100.0	100.0	100.4	100.1	100.0	100.1	100.0	100.0	99.4	99.9	100.0	117.8	103.8
15	MECHANICAL	99.8	129.1	113.4	99.6	125.5	111.6	99.8	127.9	112.8	99.6	125.6	111.6	99.6	116.5	107.4	99.8	125.4	111.7
16	ELECTRICAL	105.4	121.9	116.8	96.8	122.4	114.4	105.7	118.9	114.8	95.6	113.5	107.9	98.8	108.5	105.5	104.2	127.6	120.3
01 - 16	WEIGHTED AVERAGE	102.8	122.7	112.5	100.8	119.7	110.0	103.1	122.0	112.3	100.4	119.6	109.7	100.6	116.0	108.1	100.9	121.4	110.9

DIVISION		NEW JERSEY VINELAND 080,083			NEW MEXICO														
					ALBUQUERQUE 870 - 872			CARRIZOZO 883			CLOVIS 881			FARMINGTON 874			GALLUP 873		
		MAT.	INST.	TOTAL	MAT.	INST.	TOTAL	MAT.	INST.	TOTAL	MAT.	INST.	TOTAL	MAT.	INST.	TOTAL	MAT.	INST.	TOTAL
02	SITE CONSTRUCTION	99.6	106.3	104.7	83.9	110.1	103.9	105.9	110.1	109.1	92.4	110.1	105.9	89.3	110.1	105.2	98.9	110.1	107.5
03100	CONCRETE FORMS & ACCESSORIES	93.7	123.4	119.3	99.5	73.3	76.9	99.5	73.3	76.9	99.5	73.2	76.8	99.5	73.4	76.9	99.5	73.3	76.9
03200	CONCRETE REINFORCEMENT	85.3	119.2	104.6	100.8	72.3	84.6	108.1	72.3	87.7	109.3	67.0	85.2	110.1	72.3	88.5	105.5	72.3	86.5
03300	CAST-IN-PLACE CONCRETE	89.7	128.2	105.6	110.2	79.5	97.6	102.2	79.5	92.8	102.1	79.5	92.8	110.9	79.6	97.9	104.3	79.5	94.1
03	CONCRETE	102.8	123.1	112.9	108.6	76.4	92.5	124.2	76.4	100.3	111.7	75.3	93.5	112.2	76.4	94.3	119.1	76.4	97.7
04	MASONRY	85.0	119.7	106.4	111.4	74.2	88.5	116.0	74.2	90.3	116.1	74.2	90.3	127.2	74.2	94.6	116.2	74.2	90.3
05	METALS	92.7	103.9	96.7	105.6	92.2	100.8	104.1	92.2	99.8	103.8	89.7	98.7	104.8	92.2	100.3	104.2	92.2	99.8
06	WOOD & PLASTICS	95.8	123.4	110.1	96.3	74.8	85.2	96.3	74.8	85.2	96.3	74.8	85.2	96.3	74.8	85.2	96.3	74.8	85.2
07	THERMAL & MOISTURE PROTECTION	99.0	121.2	109.5	103.6	79.5	92.2	106.5	79.5	93.7	104.8	79.9	93.0	104.6	79.5	92.7	106.0	79.5	93.4
08	DOORS & WINDOWS	103.3	118.2	106.9	95.4	76.1	90.8	94.4	76.1	90.0	94.6	74.5	89.7	98.4	76.1	93.0	98.4	76.1	93.0
09200	PLASTER & GYPSUM BOARD	94.3	122.9	111.8	91.1	73.4	80.3	86.4	73.4	78.5	86.4	73.4	78.5	86.4	73.4	78.5	86.4	73.4	78.5
095,098	CEILINGS & ACOUSTICAL TREATMENT	90.0	122.9	111.7	104.7	73.4	84.1	95.1	73.4	80.8	95.1	73.4	80.8	95.1	73.4	80.8	95.1	73.4	80.8
09600	FLOORING	97.8	123.5	104.0	105.2	72.6	97.3	105.2	72.6	97.3	105.2	72.6	97.3	105.2	72.6	97.3	105.2	72.6	97.3
097,099	WALL FINISHES, PAINTS & COATINGS	95.6	77.7	85.2	108.7	67.2	84.6	108.7	67.2	84.6	108.7	67.2	84.6	108.7	74.8	89.0	108.7	67.2	84.6
09	FINISHES	97.2	118.5	108.1	99.2	72.5	85.6	98.6	72.5	85.3	97.4	72.5	84.7	97.1	73.3	85.0	98.1	72.5	85.0
10 - 14	TOTAL DIV. 10000 - 14000	100.0	118.1	103.8	100.0	82.3	96.3	100.0	82.3	96.3	100.0	82.3	96.3	100.0	82.3	96.3	100.0	82.3	96.3
15	MECHANICAL	99.6	124.2	111.0	100.1	77.5	89.6	98.2	77.5	88.6	98.2	77.2	88.5	100.1	77.5	89.6	98.1	77.5	88.6
16	ELECTRICAL	95.5	120.3	112.5	87.2	77.8	80.8	87.2	77.8	80.8	83.6	77.8	79.6	84.5	77.8	79.9	83.4	77.8	79.6
01 - 16	WEIGHTED AVERAGE	98.0	118.2	107.8	100.6	81.2	91.2	102.7	81.2	92.2	100.3	80.7	90.8	102.0	81.3	91.9	102.0	81.2	91.9

NEW MEXICO

DIVISION		LAS CRUCES 880			LAS VEGAS 877			ROSWELL 882			SANTA FE 875			SOCORRO 878			TRUTH/CONSEQUENCES 879		
		MAT.	INST.	TOTAL	MAT.	INST.	TOTAL	MAT.	INST.	TOTAL	MAT.	INST.	TOTAL	MAT.	INST.	TOTAL	MAT.	INST.	TOTAL
02	SITE CONSTRUCTION	96.0	85.5	88.0	88.5	110.1	105.0	94.2	110.1	106.4	83.1	110.1	103.8	85.5	110.1	104.3	108.2	85.5	90.8
03100	CONCRETE FORMS & ACCESSORIES	96.9	71.3	74.8	99.5	73.3	76.9	99.5	73.3	76.8	99.5	73.3	76.9	99.5	73.3	76.9	96.9	71.5	75.0
03200	CONCRETE REINFORCEMENT	104.0	66.2	82.5	107.2	72.3	87.3	109.3	67.0	85.2	108.1	72.3	87.7	109.3	72.3	88.2	102.7	66.5	82.1
03300	CAST-IN-PLACE CONCRETE	96.4	68.7	85.0	107.8	79.5	96.1	102.1	79.5	92.8	104.2	79.5	94.0	105.7	79.5	94.9	115.8	68.8	96.4
03	CONCRETE	88.5	70.1	79.3	109.3	76.4	92.8	112.7	75.3	94.0	106.5	76.4	91.5	107.9	76.4	92.1	101.5	70.3	85.9
04	MASONRY	111.8	63.8	82.3	116.5	74.2	90.5	127.7	74.2	94.8	116.3	74.2	90.4	116.3	74.2	90.4	114.0	67.8	85.6
05	METALS	98.9	79.7	92.0	103.9	92.2	99.7	104.8	89.8	99.4	104.8	92.2	100.2	104.2	92.2	99.8	98.0	80.1	91.6
06	WOOD & PLASTICS	89.3	73.2	81.0	96.3	74.8	85.2	96.3	74.8	85.2	96.3	74.8	85.2	96.3	74.8	85.2	89.3	73.2	81.0
07	THERMAL & MOISTURE PROTECTION	89.9	70.5	80.7	104.1	79.5	92.4	104.9	79.5	92.8	103.9	79.5	92.3	104.0	79.5	92.4	90.7	71.5	81.6
08	DOORS & WINDOWS	87.6	73.6	84.2	94.6	76.1	90.1	94.4	74.5	89.6	94.5	76.1	90.1	94.4	76.1	90.0	87.6	73.6	84.2
09200	PLASTER & GYPSUM BOARD	88.5	73.4	79.3	86.4	73.4	78.5	86.4	73.4	78.5	86.4	73.4	78.5	86.4	73.4	78.5	88.5	73.4	79.3
095,098	CEILINGS & ACOUSTICAL TREATMENT	99.9	73.4	82.5	95.1	73.4	80.8	95.1	73.4	80.8	95.1	73.4	80.8	95.1	73.4	80.8	99.9	73.4	82.5
09600	FLOORING	138.1	62.6	119.8	105.2	72.6	97.3	105.2	72.6	97.3	105.2	72.6	97.3	105.2	72.6	97.3	138.1	68.9	121.4
097,099	WALL FINISHES, PAINTS & COATINGS	102.1	67.2	81.8	108.7	67.2	84.6	108.7	67.2	84.6	108.7	67.2	84.6	108.7	67.2	84.6	102.1	67.2	81.8
09	FINISHES	114.7	69.2	91.5	97.0	72.5	84.5	97.5	72.5	84.8	96.9	72.5	84.4	96.9	72.5	84.5	115.3	70.5	92.4
10 - 14	TOTAL DIV. 10000 - 14000	100.0	77.6	95.3	100.0	82.3	96.3	100.0	82.3	96.3	100.0	82.3	96.3	100.0	82.3	96.3	100.0	77.7	95.3
15	MECHANICAL	100.4	76.9	89.5	98.1	77.5	88.6	100.1	77.4	89.6	100.1	77.5	89.6	98.1	77.5	88.6	98.1	77.0	88.3
16	ELECTRICAL	85.7	65.7	71.9	87.2	77.8	80.8	85.7	77.8	80.3	87.2	77.8	80.8	84.1	77.8	79.8	90.0	77.8	81.6
01 - 16	WEIGHTED AVERAGE	97.7	72.7	85.6	100.1	81.2	90.9	101.8	80.7	91.6	100.2	81.2	90.9	99.6	81.2	90.6	99.6	75.4	87.8

DIVISION		NEW MEXICO TUCUMCARI 884			NEW YORK ALBANY 120-122			BINGHAMTON 137-139			BRONX 104			BROOKLYN 112			BUFFALO 140-142		
		MAT.	INST.	TOTAL	MAT.	INST.	TOTAL	MAT.	INST.	TOTAL	MAT.	INST.	TOTAL	MAT.	INST.	TOTAL	MAT.	INST.	TOTAL
02	SITE CONSTRUCTION	92.0	110.1	105.8	72.8	107.7	99.5	96.6	90.4	91.8	129.1	128.1	128.3	124.0	131.6	129.8	101.6	93.3	95.2
03100	CONCRETE FORMS & ACCESSORIES	99.5	73.2	76.8	98.4	88.4	89.8	104.3	79.5	82.9	104.2	159.4	151.8	112.2	159.2	152.8	101.7	115.0	113.2
03200	CONCRETE REINFORCEMENT	107.2	67.0	84.3	100.8	87.8	93.4	99.8	87.5	92.8	99.3	178.0	144.2	101.1	178.0	145.0	101.6	103.9	102.9
03300	CAST-IN-PLACE CONCRETE	102.1	79.5	92.8	83.7	104.0	92.1	106.0	92.6	100.5	115.1	161.4	134.2	107.9	160.3	129.5	115.5	120.9	117.8
03	CONCRETE	111.1	75.3	93.2	100.1	95.0	97.6	101.8	88.0	94.9	115.0	161.9	138.4	115.3	161.5	138.4	106.2	114.1	110.1
04	MASONRY	131.4	74.2	96.2	90.6	100.0	96.3	106.5	84.8	93.1	98.8	165.0	139.5	116.5	165.0	146.3	107.2	119.0	114.4
05	METALS	103.8	89.7	98.7	100.1	109.0	103.3	95.2	121.2	104.6	96.8	139.0	112.0	107.1	139.3	118.7	100.0	95.7	98.4
06	WOOD & PLASTICS	96.3	74.8	85.2	100.6	85.8	92.9	110.4	77.0	93.1	107.3	158.0	133.5	114.2	157.9	136.8	103.4	114.9	109.4
07	THERMAL & MOISTURE PROTECTION	104.7	79.5	92.7	91.1	95.1	93.0	100.8	86.8	94.2	106.5	155.4	129.7	105.5	154.6	128.8	100.8	108.6	104.5
08	DOORS & WINDOWS	94.3	74.5	89.5	98.1	82.8	94.4	93.1	77.0	89.2	94.3	159.6	110.1	92.2	159.5	108.4	93.9	106.6	96.9
09200	PLASTER & GYPSUM BOARD	86.4	73.4	78.5	102.4	85.0	91.8	108.1	75.7	88.3	100.5	159.7	136.7	103.9	159.7	138.0	96.7	114.9	107.8
095,098	CEILINGS & ACOUSTICAL TREATMENT	95.1	73.4	80.8	97.9	85.0	89.4	97.9	75.7	83.2	87.4	159.7	135.1	83.0	159.7	133.6	92.2	114.9	107.2
09600	FLOORING	105.2	72.6	97.3	84.8	93.7	87.0	94.6	92.2	94.0	97.4	165.3	113.9	101.2	165.3	116.8	89.9	119.5	97.1
097,099	WALL FINISHES, PAINTS & COATINGS	108.7	67.2	84.6	81.8	82.2	82.0	84.1	79.2	81.3	97.5	150.7	128.4	106.7	150.7	132.3	84.6	118.1	104.1
09	FINISHES	97.4	72.5	84.7	95.6	88.2	91.8	96.1	81.2	88.5	103.4	159.4	132.0	109.5	159.2	134.9	92.7	116.9	105.0
10 - 14	TOTAL DIV. 10000 - 14000	100.0	82.3	96.3	100.0	95.0	98.9	100.0	93.4	98.6	100.0	140.7	108.6	100.0	140.2	108.5	100.0	106.4	101.3
15	MECHANICAL	98.2	77.2	88.5	100.3	92.5	96.7	100.5	87.2	94.4	100.3	156.8	126.4	100.0	160.1	127.8	99.8	97.1	98.6
16	ELECTRICAL	87.2	77.8	80.8	101.9	96.1	97.9	102.8	80.1	87.2	98.0	170.2	147.6	102.4	170.2	149.0	99.5	99.5	99.5
01 - 16	WEIGHTED AVERAGE	101.3	80.7	91.3	97.9	96.3	97.1	99.0	88.2	93.7	102.0	156.0	128.3	105.2	156.9	130.3	99.7	104.8	102.2

DIVISION		NEW YORK ELMIRA 148-149			FAR ROCKAWAY 116			FLUSHING 113			GLENS FALLS 128			HICKSVILLE 115,117,118			JAMAICA 114		
		MAT.	INST.	TOTAL	MAT.	INST.	TOTAL	MAT.	INST.	TOTAL	MAT.	INST.	TOTAL	MAT.	INST.	TOTAL	MAT.	INST.	TOTAL
02	SITE CONSTRUCTION	97.1	89.2	91.1	128.9	131.6	131.0	128.9	131.6	131.0	63.5	107.4	97.1	116.3	131.1	127.7	122.3	131.6	129.4
03100	CONCRETE FORMS & ACCESSORIES	80.8	76.4	77.0	93.7	159.2	150.2	98.8	159.2	150.9	81.6	82.9	82.7	89.0	156.2	147.0	98.8	159.3	151.0
03200	CONCRETE REINFORCEMENT	102.8	89.0	94.9	101.1	178.0	145.0	102.9	178.0	145.7	100.5	86.1	92.2	101.1	177.9	144.9	101.1	178.0	145.0
03300	CAST-IN-PLACE CONCRETE	108.0	93.1	101.9	116.8	160.2	134.7	116.8	160.2	134.7	80.6	100.1	88.6	99.1	156.7	122.8	107.9	160.3	129.5
03	CONCRETE	99.3	87.2	93.3	121.8	161.5	141.6	122.4	161.5	141.9	91.0	90.9	91.0	105.8	158.9	132.3	114.3	161.5	137.9
04	MASONRY	103.6	86.6	93.2	119.6	165.0	147.5	113.5	165.0	145.1	91.6	94.7	93.5	108.8	159.6	140.0	117.9	165.0	146.9
05	METALS	95.7	123.2	105.6	107.1	139.2	118.7	107.1	139.2	118.7	96.7	107.9	100.8	109.8	137.9	119.9	107.1	139.3	118.7
06	WOOD & PLASTICS	83.0	71.8	77.2	95.0	157.9	127.5	100.5	157.9	130.2	83.3	80.2	81.7	90.2	157.9	125.2	100.5	157.9	130.2
07	THERMAL & MOISTURE PROTECTION	101.4	85.6	93.9	105.2	154.2	128.5	105.3	154.6	128.7	89.8	92.4	91.0	104.7	150.4	126.4	105.1	154.6	128.6
08	DOORS & WINDOWS	96.8	74.5	91.4	90.6	159.5	107.2	90.6	158.1	106.9	91.7	79.4	88.8	90.6	159.5	107.2	90.6	159.5	107.2
09200	PLASTER & GYPSUM BOARD	93.8	70.4	79.5	98.8	159.7	136.0	100.5	159.7	136.7	94.0	79.2	85.0	97.5	159.7	135.5	100.5	159.7	136.7
095,098	CEILINGS & ACOUSTICAL TREATMENT	89.5	70.4	76.9	83.0	159.7	133.6	83.0	159.7	133.6	91.2	79.2	83.3	81.5	159.7	133.1	83.0	159.7	133.6
09600	FLOORING	80.3	91.8	83.1	95.6	165.3	112.5	97.3	165.3	113.7	76.7	93.7	80.8	94.3	106.8	97.3	97.3	165.3	113.7
097,099	WALL FINISHES, PAINTS & COATINGS	82.7	80.9	81.7	106.7	150.7	132.3	106.7	150.7	132.3	81.8	82.1	82.0	106.7	145.9	129.5	106.7	150.7	132.3
09	FINISHES	88.3	78.7	83.4	107.3	159.2	133.8	108.1	159.2	134.2	89.7	84.2	86.9	105.6	145.2	125.8	107.7	159.2	134.0
10 - 14	TOTAL DIV. 10000 - 14000	100.0	91.0	98.1	100.0	140.2	108.5	100.0	140.2	108.5	100.0	78.2	95.4	100.0	138.0	108.0	100.0	140.2	108.5
15	MECHANICAL	97.0	88.2	92.9	96.6	160.1	126.0	96.6	160.1	126.0	97.2	87.2	92.6	99.9	145.2	120.8	96.6	160.1	126.0
16	ELECTRICAL	95.8	94.0	94.6	115.7	170.2	153.2	115.7	170.2	153.2	94.6	96.1	95.6	102.4	157.8	140.5	100.7	176.0	152.5
01 - 16	WEIGHTED AVERAGE	96.6	90.3	93.6	105.9	156.9	130.7	105.8	156.9	130.6	93.3	93.0	93.1	102.8	149.1	125.3	103.7	157.9	130.1

DIVISION		NEW YORK JAMESTOWN 147			KINGSTON 124			LONG ISLAND CITY 111			MONTICELLO 127			MOUNT VERNON 105			NEW ROCHELLE 108		
		MAT.	INST.	TOTAL	MAT.	INST.	TOTAL	MAT.	INST.	TOTAL	MAT.	INST.	TOTAL	MAT.	INST.	TOTAL	MAT.	INST.	TOTAL
02	SITE CONSTRUCTION	98.6	89.4	91.5	124.2	129.5	128.3	125.6	131.6	130.2	119.2	129.5	127.0	139.5	126.1	129.3	137.9	126.1	128.9
03100	CONCRETE FORMS & ACCESSORIES	80.9	85.7	85.1	83.4	111.7	107.8	104.7	159.2	151.8	93.0	111.3	108.8	91.1	125.9	121.1	116.7	125.8	124.6
03200	CONCRETE REINFORCEMENT	103.0	99.1	100.8	100.8	130.1	117.5	101.1	178.0	145.0	100.1	127.3	115.6	98.3	176.6	142.9	98.4	176.6	143.0
03300	CAST-IN-PLACE CONCRETE	112.0	96.5	105.6	108.7	116.8	112.1	111.4	160.3	131.6	101.8	116.6	107.9	128.7	128.3	128.5	128.7	128.3	128.5
03	CONCRETE	102.4	91.8	97.1	115.1	116.7	115.9	108.0	161.5	139.7	109.5	115.9	112.7	127.1	135.5	131.3	127.0	135.4	131.2
04	MASONRY	111.6	92.1	99.6	107.5	137.4	125.9	113.5	165.0	145.1	99.6	137.4	122.8	105.1	127.8	119.0	105.1	127.8	119.0
05	METALS	95.7	90.2	93.7	107.1	116.4	110.4	107.1	139.3	118.7	107.0	115.0	109.9	96.6	134.3	110.2	96.9	134.2	110.3
06	WOOD & PLASTICS	82.0	80.2	81.1	84.8	106.4	96.0	106.5	157.9	133.1	95.2	106.4	101.0	94.1	123.2	109.1	121.2	123.2	122.2
07	THERMAL & MOISTURE PROTECTION	100.6	91.4	96.2	107.2	132.8	119.3	105.3	154.6	128.7	106.8	132.5	119.0	108.0	134.5	120.6	108.4	134.5	120.8
08	DOORS & WINDOWS	96.6	86.1	94.1	95.8	120.5	101.8	90.6	159.5	107.2	90.6	119.8	97.7	94.3	140.8	105.5	94.4	139.4	105.2
09200	PLASTER & GYPSUM BOARD	89.6	79.1	83.2	95.1	106.6	102.1	101.8	159.7	137.2	98.5	106.6	103.4	95.9	123.7	112.9	104.6	123.7	116.3
095,098	CEILINGS & ACOUSTICAL TREATMENT	86.8	79.1	81.7	81.7	106.6	98.1	83.0	159.7	133.6	81.7	106.6	98.1	86.1	123.7	110.9	86.1	123.7	110.9
09600	FLOORING	83.0	97.8	86.6	88.3	112.2	94.1	98.9	165.3	115.0	91.3	112.2	96.3	89.2	165.3	107.6	97.0	165.3	113.5
097,099	WALL FINISHES, PAINTS & COATINGS	84.6	85.3	85.0	104.1	150.7	131.2	106.7	150.7	132.3	104.1	106.8	105.7	95.0	150.7	127.4	95.0	150.7	127.4
09	FINISHES	88.2	86.9	87.6	103.6	114.6	109.2	108.6	159.2	134.4	104.8	109.6	107.3	100.4	135.2	118.1	104.0	135.2	119.9
10 - 14	TOTAL DIV. 10000 - 14000	100.0	99.2	99.8	100.0	118.0	103.8	100.0	140.2	108.5	100.0	111.2	102.4	100.0	129.7	106.3	100.0	129.7	106.3
15	MECHANICAL	96.7	92.6	94.8	97.1	114.1	105.0	100.0	160.1	127.8	97.1	110.8	103.5	97.4	128.7	111.8	97.4	128.7	111.8
16	ELECTRICAL	95.1	85.2	88.3	98.9	92.9	94.8	101.6	170.2	148.8	98.9	88.0	91.4	95.5	130.9	119.9	95.5	130.9	119.9
01 - 16	WEIGHTED AVERAGE	97.3	89.7	93.6	103.4	115.7	109.3	104.9	156.9	130.2	101.7	113.2	107.3	102.9	131.5	116.8	103.6	131.4	117.1

COST INDEXES

NEW YORK

DIVISION		NEW YORK 100 - 102			NIAGARA FALLS 143			PLATTSBURGH 129			POUGHKEEPSIE 125 - 126			QUEENS 110			RIVERHEAD 119		
		MAT.	INST.	TOTAL	MAT.	INST.	TOTAL	MAT.	INST.	TOTAL	MAT.	INST.	TOTAL	MAT.	INST.	TOTAL	MAT.	INST.	TOTAL
02	SITE CONSTRUCTION	139.5	128.6	131.1	101.0	91.1	93.5	88.8	103.3	99.9	120.3	129.4	127.3	119.9	131.6	128.9	116.6	131.1	127.7
03100	CONCRETE FORMS & ACCESSORIES	109.7	171.5	163.1	80.8	112.3	108.0	87.7	79.9	81.0	83.4	137.9	130.4	89.2	159.2	149.6	93.6	156.3	147.7
03200	CONCRETE REINFORCEMENT	105.1	181.2	148.5	101.6	103.9	102.9	104.9	87.4	94.9	100.8	127.5	116.0	102.9	178.0	145.7	103.0	177.9	145.7
03300	CAST-IN-PLACE CONCRETE	129.6	163.4	143.5	115.9	121.8	118.3	98.5	98.5	98.5	105.3	117.0	110.1	102.6	160.3	126.4	97.3	156.7	121.8
03	CONCRETE	127.6	168.6	148.1	105.1	113.1	109.1	105.8	87.5	96.7	111.9	127.8	119.8	109.3	161.5	135.4	104.7	159.0	131.8
04	MASONRY	110.9	167.5	145.7	121.3	124.3	123.1	89.0	90.5	89.9	101.6	137.3	123.5	108.0	165.0	143.0	115.7	159.6	142.7
05	METALS	109.5	141.0	120.8	95.7	94.4	95.3	103.4	82.6	95.9	107.1	116.2	110.4	107.1	139.3	118.7	109.8	138.0	120.0
06	WOOD & PLASTICS	112.4	172.6	143.6	81.9	107.8	95.3	90.6	76.1	83.1	84.8	140.8	113.8	90.4	157.9	125.3	94.9	157.9	127.5
07	THERMAL & MOISTURE PROTECTION	107.0	160.6	132.4	100.7	109.6	104.9	98.2	89.7	94.2	107.1	136.7	121.1	104.8	154.6	128.4	104.7	150.4	126.4
08	DOORS & WINDOWS	97.8	168.4	114.8	96.6	99.9	97.4	101.3	77.6	95.6	95.9	138.4	106.1	90.6	159.5	107.2	90.6	159.5	107.2
09200	PLASTER & GYPSUM BOARD	105.8	174.7	147.9	89.6	107.6	100.6	110.7	74.4	88.5	95.1	142.0	123.8	97.5	159.7	135.5	98.8	159.7	136.0
095,098	CEILINGS & ACOUSTICAL TREATMENT	106.5	174.7	151.5	86.8	107.6	100.5	101.9	74.4	83.7	81.7	142.0	121.5	83.0	159.7	133.6	81.5	159.7	133.1
09600	FLOORING	99.0	166.3	115.3	82.8	117.9	91.3	98.7	83.1	94.9	88.3	146.4	102.3	94.3	165.3	111.5	95.6	106.8	98.3
097,099	WALL FINISHES, PAINTS & COATINGS	97.5	151.8	129.1	84.6	111.1	100.0	100.1	78.2	87.4	104.1	106.8	105.7	106.7	150.7	132.3	106.7	150.7	132.3
09	FINISHES	108.8	168.8	139.4	88.3	113.2	101.0	98.5	79.3	88.7	103.5	137.0	120.6	106.0	159.2	133.2	106.1	145.7	126.3
10 - 14	TOTAL DIV. 10000 - 14000	100.0	144.8	109.5	100.0	108.0	101.7	100.0	71.2	93.9	100.0	122.5	104.8	100.0	140.2	108.5	100.0	138.1	108.0
15	MECHANICAL	100.4	163.8	129.7	96.7	108.6	102.2	97.0	87.4	92.5	97.1	115.2	105.5	100.0	160.1	127.8	99.7	145.2	120.8
16	ELECTRICAL	111.1	177.9	157.0	92.8	103.5	100.2	94.0	87.0	89.2	98.9	98.1	98.4	102.4	170.2	149.0	103.6	170.2	149.4
01 - 16	WEIGHTED AVERAGE	108.5	161.9	134.5	98.2	107.0	102.5	99.1	86.9	93.2	102.5	122.2	112.1	103.0	156.9	129.2	103.3	151.3	126.6

NEW YORK

DIVISION		ROCHESTER 144 - 146			SCHENECTADY 123			STATEN ISLAND 103			SUFFERN 109			SYRACUSE 130 - 132			UTICA 133 - 135		
		MAT.	INST.	TOTAL	MAT.	INST.	TOTAL	MAT.	INST.	TOTAL	MAT.	INST.	TOTAL	MAT.	INST.	TOTAL	MAT.	INST.	TOTAL
02	SITE CONSTRUCTION	77.3	107.6	100.5	73.0	107.8	99.6	144.4	128.1	131.9	134.1	126.1	128.0	95.2	107.6	104.7	71.0	106.8	98.4
03100	CONCRETE FORMS & ACCESSORIES	101.4	98.8	99.2	103.8	89.2	91.2	90.5	159.2	149.8	102.7	135.2	130.8	103.1	86.1	88.5	104.3	76.2	80.1
03200	CONCRETE REINFORCEMENT	102.5	89.8	95.2	99.5	87.8	92.8	99.3	178.0	144.2	98.4	130.2	116.6	100.8	86.0	92.3	100.8	83.0	90.6
03300	CAST-IN-PLACE CONCRETE	109.9	105.1	107.9	97.3	105.2	100.6	128.7	161.3	142.1	124.7	123.3	124.1	97.3	95.6	96.6	89.9	95.0	92.0
03	CONCRETE	112.0	100.4	106.2	107.0	95.8	101.4	129.2	161.8	145.5	122.8	129.2	126.0	105.1	90.7	97.9	103.5	85.6	94.6
04	MASONRY	103.1	101.2	101.9	91.2	102.1	97.9	113.6	165.0	145.2	105.7	140.2	126.9	96.6	95.8	96.1	89.9	91.4	90.8
05	METALS	103.3	110.5	105.9	100.1	109.0	103.3	96.8	138.8	112.0	96.8	116.7	104.0	99.9	107.2	102.6	98.2	105.9	101.0
06	WOOD & PLASTICS	99.9	100.0	99.9	107.0	85.8	96.0	92.6	158.0	126.4	106.4	136.1	121.8	107.0	84.0	95.1	107.0	72.2	89.0
07	THERMAL & MOISTURE PROTECTION	97.6	99.0	98.3	91.2	96.0	93.5	106.9	155.4	129.9	108.0	138.5	122.5	99.0	94.2	96.8	91.2	91.5	91.3
08	DOORS & WINDOWS	99.5	93.5	98.0	98.1	82.8	94.4	94.3	159.6	110.1	94.4	136.5	104.5	95.9	79.1	91.9	98.1	73.9	92.3
09200	PLASTER & GYPSUM BOARD	98.0	99.8	99.1	102.4	85.0	91.8	95.7	159.7	134.8	99.8	137.0	122.6	102.4	83.1	90.6	102.4	71.0	83.2
095,098	CEILINGS & ACOUSTICAL TREATMENT	96.5	99.8	98.7	97.9	85.0	89.4	87.4	159.7	135.1	86.1	137.0	119.7	97.9	83.1	88.1	97.9	71.0	80.1
09600	FLOORING	79.7	101.7	85.1	84.8	93.7	87.0	93.1	165.3	110.6	92.8	74.3	88.3	86.4	85.6	86.2	84.8	85.7	85.1
097,099	WALL FINISHES, PAINTS & COATINGS	81.8	105.1	95.4	81.8	82.2	82.0	97.5	150.7	128.4	95.0	110.6	104.0	87.1	86.2	86.6	81.8	86.2	84.4
09	FINISHES	93.9	100.4	97.2	95.3	88.7	91.9	102.4	159.4	131.5	101.8	120.6	111.4	96.7	85.5	91.0	95.3	78.0	86.5
10 - 14	TOTAL DIV. 10000 - 14000	100.0	96.1	99.2	100.0	95.9	99.1	100.0	140.7	108.6	100.0	133.1	107.0	100.0	95.1	99.0	100.0	91.5	98.2
15	MECHANICAL	99.8	92.8	96.6	100.3	93.7	97.2	100.3	143.9	120.5	97.4	129.9	112.4	100.3	89.1	95.1	100.3	88.6	94.9
16	ELECTRICAL	104.5	95.4	98.2	102.3	96.1	98.0	98.0	170.2	147.6	108.6	117.7	114.9	102.3	85.3	90.6	102.2	84.7	90.2
01 - 16	WEIGHTED AVERAGE	101.0	99.4	100.2	98.9	97.0	98.0	104.8	153.5	128.5	103.5	126.7	114.8	99.7	92.2	96.1	98.1	89.3	93.8

NEW YORK / NORTH CAROLINA

DIVISION		WATERTOWN 136			WHITE PLAINS 106			YONKERS 107			ASHEVILLE 287 - 288			CHARLOTTE 281 - 282			DURHAM 277		
		MAT.	INST.	TOTAL	MAT.	INST.	TOTAL	MAT.	INST.	TOTAL	MAT.	INST.	TOTAL	MAT.	INST.	TOTAL	MAT.	INST.	TOTAL
02	SITE CONSTRUCTION	79.5	108.7	101.8	128.5	126.1	126.7	138.9	125.9	129.0	101.3	72.9	79.5	101.6	72.9	79.6	101.3	82.9	87.2
03100	CONCRETE FORMS & ACCESSORIES	83.8	84.0	84.0	110.5	125.7	123.6	109.5	135.7	132.1	93.0	45.4	52.0	101.5	45.5	53.2	95.2	45.7	52.5
03200	CONCRETE REINFORCEMENT	101.4	67.2	81.9	98.4	176.6	143.0	102.3	176.6	144.7	92.7	43.5	64.6	93.1	43.5	64.8	93.1	57.7	72.9
03300	CAST-IN-PLACE CONCRETE	104.7	97.1	101.6	114.1	128.3	120.0	127.8	129.3	128.4	95.7	53.1	78.1	98.1	53.1	79.6	96.0	53.2	78.3
03	CONCRETE	117.1	87.2	102.2	114.6	135.3	125.0	126.6	140.1	133.3	96.9	49.9	73.4	98.1	50.0	74.1	96.6	52.8	74.7
04	MASONRY	91.0	101.1	97.2	105.0	127.8	119.0	110.6	129.8	122.4	77.5	38.9	53.8	79.2	38.9	54.5	77.7	38.9	53.9
05	METALS	98.3	106.7	101.3	99.6	134.1	112.0	106.4	134.2	116.4	93.9	80.4	89.1	95.2	80.4	89.9	95.3	86.1	92.0
06	WOOD & PLASTICS	85.8	79.7	82.6	114.6	123.2	119.0	113.2	135.5	124.7	94.3	46.2	69.4	104.4	46.2	74.3	96.8	46.2	70.6
07	THERMAL & MOISTURE PROTECTION	91.5	95.4	93.3	107.9	134.2	120.4	108.3	138.1	122.4	96.1	46.7	72.7	96.1	47.8	73.2	96.8	47.4	73.3
08	DOORS & WINDOWS	98.1	79.1	93.5	94.4	140.8	105.6	97.9	147.6	109.9	93.1	44.1	81.3	97.1	44.1	84.3	97.1	48.3	85.3
09200	PLASTER & GYPSUM BOARD	96.4	78.7	85.6	102.4	123.7	115.4	105.5	136.4	124.4	100.3	44.3	66.1	105.8	44.3	68.2	105.8	44.3	68.2
095,098	CEILINGS & ACOUSTICAL TREATMENT	97.9	78.7	85.2	86.1	123.7	110.9	105.2	136.4	125.8	88.2	44.3	59.2	92.2	44.3	60.6	92.2	44.3	60.6
09600	FLOORING	77.4	80.9	78.2	95.1	165.3	112.1	94.7	165.3	111.8	92.4	48.1	81.6	95.8	48.1	84.2	96.0	48.1	84.4
097,099	WALL FINISHES, PAINTS & COATINGS	81.8	85.8	84.1	95.0	150.7	127.4	95.0	150.7	127.4	106.5	45.7	71.2	106.5	45.7	71.2	106.5	45.7	71.2
09	FINISHES	92.6	82.8	87.6	102.4	135.2	119.1	106.9	142.9	125.2	92.6	45.8	68.7	95.2	45.8	70.0	95.4	45.8	70.1
10 - 14	TOTAL DIV. 10000 - 14000	100.0	95.8	99.1	100.0	129.7	106.3	100.0	133.3	107.0	100.0	66.7	93.0	100.0	66.7	93.0	100.0	73.5	94.4
15	MECHANICAL	100.3	86.1	93.7	100.5	119.5	109.3	100.5	121.5	110.2	100.1	50.1	77.0	100.1	50.2	77.0	100.1	50.4	77.1
16	ELECTRICAL	102.2	87.1	91.8	95.5	130.9	119.9	108.6	141.0	130.9	99.6	47.7	63.9	99.1	42.8	60.4	97.5	45.6	61.8
01 - 16	WEIGHTED AVERAGE	99.5	91.7	95.7	102.6	129.7	115.8	107.6	134.1	120.5	95.6	53.1	75.0	96.9	52.4	75.2	96.5	55.1	76.4

COST INDEXES

NORTH CAROLINA

DIVISION		ELIZABETH CITY 279			FAYETTEVILLE 283			GASTONIA 280			GREENSBORO 270,272 - 274			HICKORY 286			KINSTON 285		
		MAT.	INST.	TOTAL	MAT.	INST.	TOTAL	MAT.	INST.	TOTAL	MAT.	INST.	TOTAL	MAT.	INST.	TOTAL	MAT.	INST.	TOTAL
02	SITE CONSTRUCTION	106.2	83.8	89.1	99.4	82.9	86.8	101.0	72.9	79.4	101.2	82.9	87.2	100.8	81.8	86.3	99.6	82.6	86.5
03100	CONCRETE FORMS & ACCESSORIES	77.3	29.4	36.0	90.3	45.7	51.9	101.8	45.4	53.1	95.2	45.7	52.5	87.2	28.4	36.5	82.6	28.6	36.0
03200	CONCRETE REINFORCEMENT	92.2	52.5	69.5	92.2	57.7	72.5	93.1	43.5	64.8	93.1	57.6	72.9	92.7	23.7	53.3	92.2	23.7	53.1
03300	CAST-IN-PLACE CONCRETE	96.0	37.9	72.1	92.6	53.2	76.4	93.5	53.1	76.8	95.1	53.2	77.8	95.6	40.6	72.9	92.3	41.8	71.5
03	CONCRETE	96.7	39.3	68.0	94.2	52.8	73.5	95.9	49.9	72.9	96.2	52.7	74.5	96.6	34.6	65.6	93.4	35.2	64.3
04	MASONRY	90.7	31.3	54.2	81.5	38.9	55.4	78.8	38.9	54.3	77.5	38.9	53.8	67.7	31.1	45.2	73.6	31.5	47.7
05	METALS	94.8	82.3	90.3	94.2	86.1	91.3	96.0	80.4	90.4	96.0	86.1	92.4	93.4	73.5	86.2	93.7	75.3	87.1
06	WOOD & PLASTICS	77.7	29.8	52.9	91.1	46.2	67.9	104.4	46.2	74.3	96.8	46.2	70.6	87.5	28.9	57.2	83.0	28.9	55.0
07	THERMAL & MOISTURE PROTECTION	96.0	30.7	65.0	96.4	47.4	73.1	96.4	47.8	73.4	96.8	47.4	73.3	96.4	33.8	66.7	96.2	34.4	66.9
08	DOORS & WINDOWS	94.0	32.3	79.1	93.2	48.3	82.4	97.1	44.1	84.3	97.1	48.3	85.3	93.2	28.0	77.4	93.3	28.4	77.6
09200	PLASTER & GYPSUM BOARD	97.2	26.5	54.0	100.5	44.3	66.2	105.8	44.3	68.2	105.8	44.3	68.2	100.3	26.5	55.2	98.4	26.5	54.4
095,098	CEILINGS & ACOUSTICAL TREATMENT	92.2	26.5	48.9	89.5	44.3	59.7	92.2	44.3	60.6	92.2	44.3	60.6	88.2	26.5	47.5	89.5	26.5	47.9
09600	FLOORING	86.6	18.9	70.2	92.5	48.1	81.7	96.0	33.1	80.7	96.0	48.1	84.4	92.3	17.2	74.1	89.4	25.8	73.9
097,099	WALL FINISHES, PAINTS & COATINGS	106.5	15.5	53.6	106.5	45.7	71.2	106.5	45.7	71.2	106.5	45.7	71.2	106.5	18.3	55.2	106.5	20.1	56.3
09	FINISHES	91.2	25.2	57.5	92.9	45.8	68.8	95.2	43.1	68.7	95.4	45.8	70.1	92.7	24.6	58.0	91.5	26.8	58.5
10 - 14	TOTAL DIV. 10000 - 14000	100.0	72.3	94.1	100.0	73.5	94.4	100.0	66.7	93.0	100.0	66.7	93.0	100.0	61.9	91.9	100.0	68.7	93.4
15	MECHANICAL	97.0	32.5	67.1	100.1	50.4	77.1	100.1	50.2	77.0	100.1	50.4	77.1	97.0	22.3	62.4	97.0	23.2	62.8
16	ELECTRICAL	100.3	35.1	55.5	92.7	45.6	60.3	98.6	42.8	60.2	98.6	45.6	62.1	95.4	35.1	54.0	95.0	35.2	53.9
01 - 16	WEIGHTED AVERAGE	95.8	43.4	70.3	95.0	55.1	75.6	96.7	52.0	75.0	96.6	54.9	76.3	93.9	39.4	67.4	93.7	40.4	67.8

NORTH CAROLINA / NORTH DAKOTA

DIVISION		MURPHY 289			RALEIGH 275 - 276			ROCKY MOUNT 278			WILMINGTON 284			WINSTON-SALEM 271			BISMARCK 585		
		MAT.	INST.	TOTAL	MAT.	INST.	TOTAL	MAT.	INST.	TOTAL	MAT.	INST.	TOTAL	MAT.	INST.	TOTAL	MAT.	INST.	TOTAL
02	SITE CONSTRUCTION	103.1	71.7	79.0	102.4	82.9	87.5	104.5	81.9	87.2	102.3	72.9	79.8	101.6	82.9	87.3	85.1	96.4	93.8
03100	CONCRETE FORMS & ACCESSORIES	102.6	28.4	38.6	98.3	45.7	52.9	85.8	34.0	41.1	94.8	45.7	52.5	96.7	45.5	52.5	93.2	58.2	63.0
03200	CONCRETE REINFORCEMENT	92.2	23.5	53.0	93.1	57.6	72.9	92.2	23.7	53.1	93.4	57.7	73.0	93.1	43.5	64.8	108.6	67.6	85.2
03300	CAST-IN-PLACE CONCRETE	98.9	36.1	73.0	101.5	53.2	81.6	93.9	35.1	69.6	95.3	53.2	77.9	98.2	53.1	79.6	104.9	63.3	87.8
03	CONCRETE	100.1	33.0	66.6	99.6	52.7	76.2	97.7	35.1	66.4	96.8	52.8	74.8	97.8	50.0	73.9	98.0	62.6	80.3
04	MASONRY	69.8	28.3	44.3	84.5	38.9	56.5	73.8	33.4	49.0	67.8	38.9	50.1	77.8	38.9	53.9	107.3	60.5	78.6
05	METALS	93.2	73.1	86.0	95.3	86.1	92.0	93.8	73.3	86.4	94.3	86.1	91.4	95.2	80.5	89.9	95.6	74.5	88.0
06	WOOD & PLASTICS	105.3	28.9	65.8	100.5	46.2	72.4	86.4	35.3	60.0	96.2	46.2	70.3	96.8	46.2	70.6	85.3	54.5	69.4
07	THERMAL & MOISTURE PROTECTION	96.4	36.1	67.8	96.6	46.8	72.9	96.7	32.8	66.4	96.1	47.4	73.0	96.8	47.4	73.3	98.8	59.3	80.1
08	DOORS & WINDOWS	93.1	32.4	78.5	93.9	48.3	82.9	93.3	30.5	78.1	93.3	48.3	82.4	97.1	44.5	84.4	103.4	51.5	90.9
09200	PLASTER & GYPSUM BOARD	105.0	26.5	57.0	108.6	44.3	69.3	99.3	33.1	58.8	101.0	44.3	66.3	105.8	44.3	68.2	117.4	53.6	78.4
095,098	CEILINGS & ACOUSTICAL TREATMENT	88.2	26.5	47.5	92.2	44.3	60.6	89.5	33.1	52.3	89.5	44.3	59.7	92.2	44.3	60.6	143.1	53.6	84.1
09600	FLOORING	96.3	27.5	79.7	96.0	48.1	84.4	90.7	18.2	73.1	93.3	48.1	82.3	96.0	48.1	84.4	111.0	55.3	97.5
097,099	WALL FINISHES, PAINTS & COATINGS	106.5	20.8	56.7	106.5	45.7	71.2	106.5	34.7	64.8	106.5	45.7	71.2	106.5	45.7	71.2	102.5	45.9	69.6
09	FINISHES	94.7	26.7	60.0	95.8	45.8	70.3	92.5	31.5	61.4	93.2	45.8	69.0	95.4	45.8	70.1	115.2	55.8	84.9
10 - 14	TOTAL DIV. 10000 - 14000	100.0	62.0	92.0	100.0	73.5	94.4	100.0	70.5	93.8	100.0	73.5	94.4	100.0	66.7	93.0	100.0	61.2	91.8
15	MECHANICAL	97.0	22.4	62.5	100.1	50.4	77.1	97.0	22.4	62.5	100.1	50.4	77.1	100.1	50.2	77.0	100.6	69.5	86.2
16	ELECTRICAL	101.1	35.1	55.8	98.2	45.6	62.0	103.9	35.1	56.6	99.3	45.6	62.4	98.6	45.6	62.1	96.9	70.8	79.0
01 - 16	WEIGHTED AVERAGE	95.4	38.4	67.6	97.0	55.1	76.6	95.2	40.8	68.7	95.2	54.1	75.2	96.7	53.9	75.9	100.8	68.1	84.9

NORTH DAKOTA

DIVISION		DEVILS LAKE 583			DICKINSON 586			FARGO 580 - 581			GRAND FORKS 582			JAMESTOWN 584			MINOT 587		
		MAT.	INST.	TOTAL	MAT.	INST.	TOTAL	MAT.	INST.	TOTAL	MAT.	INST.	TOTAL	MAT.	INST.	TOTAL	MAT.	INST.	TOTAL
02	SITE CONSTRUCTION	90.2	95.8	94.5	97.2	95.8	96.1	85.1	96.4	93.8	93.0	95.8	95.2	89.2	95.8	94.3	90.7	96.4	95.1
03100	CONCRETE FORMS & ACCESSORIES	102.5	51.8	58.7	84.6	51.8	56.3	93.8	58.9	63.7	89.6	51.9	57.1	86.5	52.0	56.7	84.1	58.0	61.6
03200	CONCRETE REINFORCEMENT	108.6	61.2	81.6	109.8	61.2	82.1	100.1	67.6	81.6	107.0	61.2	80.9	109.3	74.9	89.7	110.7	67.6	86.1
03300	CAST-IN-PLACE CONCRETE	116.0	61.7	93.6	105.0	61.7	87.1	107.4	66.0	90.3	104.9	61.7	87.1	114.5	61.8	92.8	104.9	61.6	87.1
03	CONCRETE	106.8	57.9	82.4	105.6	57.9	81.8	98.2	63.8	81.0	102.8	58.0	80.4	104.8	60.6	82.7	101.3	61.9	81.6
04	MASONRY	113.1	52.9	76.1	115.2	52.9	76.9	107.4	60.1	78.3	107.3	52.9	73.9	125.2	53.0	80.8	107.7	60.6	78.8
05	METALS	95.7	70.9	86.7	95.5	70.9	86.7	95.5	74.5	87.9	95.6	71.0	86.7	95.6	75.8	88.5	95.9	74.3	88.1
06	WOOD & PLASTICS	94.9	50.1	71.7	76.8	50.1	63.0	85.3	55.4	69.8	81.9	50.1	65.5	78.9	50.1	64.0	76.4	54.5	65.1
07	THERMAL & MOISTURE PROTECTION	99.4	55.9	78.8	100.0	55.9	79.1	99.3	60.5	80.9	99.6	55.9	78.9	99.1	55.9	78.6	99.2	59.1	80.2
08	DOORS & WINDOWS	103.5	47.6	90.0	103.4	47.6	90.0	103.4	52.0	91.0	103.4	47.6	90.0	103.4	50.9	90.8	103.6	51.5	91.0
09200	PLASTER & GYPSUM BOARD	120.9	49.1	77.0	114.8	49.1	74.6	117.4	54.5	78.9	116.5	49.1	75.3	115.7	49.1	75.0	114.8	53.6	77.4
095,098	CEILINGS & ACOUSTICAL TREATMENT	143.1	49.1	81.1	143.1	49.1	81.1	143.1	54.5	84.6	143.1	49.1	81.1	143.1	49.1	81.1	143.1	53.6	84.1
09600	FLOORING	115.3	54.5	100.5	106.8	54.5	94.1	110.8	54.5	97.1	109.3	54.5	96.0	107.9	54.5	95.0	106.6	55.5	94.2
097,099	WALL FINISHES, PAINTS & COATINGS	102.5	35.1	63.3	102.5	35.1	63.3	102.5	42.2	67.5	102.5	35.1	63.3	102.5	35.1	63.3	102.5	38.4	65.3
09	FINISHES	117.4	50.1	83.0	114.3	50.1	81.6	115.0	55.7	84.8	115.0	50.1	81.9	114.1	50.1	81.5	113.7	55.0	83.8
10 - 14	TOTAL DIV. 10000 - 14000	100.0	57.7	91.1	100.0	57.7	91.1	100.0	61.2	91.8	100.0	57.8	91.1	100.0	57.7	91.1	100.0	61.2	91.8
15	MECHANICAL	97.5	55.5	78.0	97.5	55.5	78.0	100.6	76.1	89.3	100.6	55.5	79.7	97.5	55.6	78.1	100.6	59.4	81.5
16	ELECTRICAL	96.1	57.3	69.4	110.0	57.3	73.7	96.8	50.9	65.3	101.7	69.4	79.5	96.1	57.3	69.4	106.8	70.8	82.0
01 - 16	WEIGHTED AVERAGE	102.1	60.3	81.7	102.7	60.3	82.1	100.8	66.1	84.0	102.0	62.4	82.7	101.9	61.3	82.1	102.0	65.9	84.4

		NORTH DAKOTA			OHIO														
	DIVISION	WILLISTON			AKRON			ATHENS			CANTON			CHILLICOTHE			CINCINNATI		
		588			442 - 443			457			446 - 447			456			451 - 452		
		MAT.	INST.	TOTAL	MAT.	INST.	TOTAL	MAT.	INST.	TOTAL	MAT.	INST.	TOTAL	MAT.	INST.	TOTAL	MAT.	INST.	TOTAL
02	SITE CONSTRUCTION	91.6	95.8	94.8	102.4	109.4	107.8	92.8	95.2	94.6	102.6	108.4	107.0	81.8	111.4	104.4	78.6	111.0	103.4
03100	CONCRETE FORMS & ACCESSORIES	91.7	51.8	57.3	99.9	102.3	102.0	91.2	73.0	75.5	99.9	90.7	91.9	94.1	98.3	97.7	96.8	90.5	91.3
03200	CONCRETE REINFORCEMENT	111.7	61.2	82.9	99.1	99.7	99.4	90.7	71.1	79.6	99.1	84.3	90.7	88.0	86.3	87.1	93.4	88.9	90.8
03300	CAST-IN-PLACE CONCRETE	104.9	61.7	87.1	101.2	108.9	104.7	107.7	84.7	98.2	102.2	106.8	104.1	97.7	98.0	97.8	90.0	92.5	91.1
03	CONCRETE	102.7	57.9	80.4	100.3	103.2	101.8	104.5	76.3	90.4	100.8	94.2	97.5	98.9	95.7	97.3	93.2	90.9	92.0
04	MASONRY	102.7	52.9	72.1	93.4	103.6	99.7	79.3	76.6	77.6	94.3	93.9	94.0	88.1	98.3	94.3	87.6	98.4	94.2
05	METALS	95.8	70.9	86.8	91.8	83.5	88.8	103.4	68.8	90.9	91.8	76.7	86.4	92.9	87.9	91.1	94.8	89.0	92.7
06	WOOD & PLASTICS	83.8	50.1	66.4	95.2	101.5	98.4	84.1	71.9	77.8	95.2	89.8	92.4	95.0	96.6	95.9	97.7	88.2	92.8
07	THERMAL & MOISTURE PROTECTION	99.5	55.9	78.8	106.4	102.9	104.7	103.9	80.3	92.7	106.9	98.5	102.9	92.4	97.7	94.9	89.9	98.0	93.7
08	DOORS & WINDOWS	103.5	47.6	90.0	107.2	101.1	105.7	97.8	68.7	90.7	101.4	83.1	97.0	91.6	91.2	91.5	97.2	85.8	94.5
09200	PLASTER & GYPSUM BOARD	117.0	49.1	75.5	105.0	100.8	102.4	102.6	70.5	83.0	105.0	88.7	95.0	101.4	96.8	98.6	102.5	88.2	93.7
095,098	CEILINGS & ACOUSTICAL TREATMENT	143.1	49.1	81.1	99.5	100.8	100.4	98.3	70.5	80.0	99.5	88.7	92.4	89.5	96.8	94.3	90.9	88.2	89.1
09600	FLOORING	110.3	54.5	96.8	107.9	102.7	106.6	112.2	82.8	105.1	108.1	88.9	103.4	92.0	87.3	90.9	92.9	103.7	95.5
097,099	WALL FINISHES, PAINTS & COATINGS	102.5	35.1	63.3	103.9	122.1	114.5	105.3	64.2	81.4	103.9	95.0	98.7	101.5	100.7	101.0	101.5	97.5	99.2
09	FINISHES	115.4	50.1	82.1	104.4	104.5	104.5	96.9	73.6	85.0	104.5	90.2	97.2	93.2	96.5	94.9	93.7	93.4	93.6
10 - 14	TOTAL DIV. 10000 - 14000	100.0	57.7	91.1	100.0	102.4	100.5	100.0	77.0	95.2	100.0	92.4	98.4	100.0	96.5	99.3	100.0	91.0	98.1
15	MECHANICAL	97.5	55.5	78.0	100.1	105.3	102.5	96.6	73.3	85.8	100.1	90.4	95.6	97.4	100.2	98.7	99.7	94.6	97.4
16	ELECTRICAL	102.3	57.3	71.3	98.0	93.8	95.1	100.7	69.7	79.4	96.5	97.5	97.2	98.2	93.2	94.7	95.8	87.9	90.4
01 - 16	WEIGHTED AVERAGE	101.2	60.3	81.3	99.8	100.9	100.4	98.4	75.3	87.1	99.2	92.9	96.1	94.9	97.2	96.0	95.3	93.9	94.6

		OHIO																	
	DIVISION	CLEVELAND			COLUMBUS			DAYTON			HAMILTON			LIMA			LORAIN		
		441			430 - 432			453 - 454			450			458			440		
		MAT.	INST.	TOTAL	MAT.	INST.	TOTAL	MAT.	INST.	TOTAL	MAT.	INST.	TOTAL	MAT.	INST.	TOTAL	MAT.	INST.	TOTAL
02	SITE CONSTRUCTION	102.5	109.0	107.5	84.4	100.4	96.6	77.4	111.0	103.1	77.7	111.3	103.4	87.3	96.5	94.3	101.8	108.7	107.1
03100	CONCRETE FORMS & ACCESSORIES	100.0	109.3	108.0	94.4	90.6	91.1	96.7	87.2	88.5	96.7	89.8	90.8	91.1	90.4	90.5	99.9	91.5	92.7
03200	CONCRETE REINFORCEMENT	99.5	100.0	99.8	103.2	88.2	94.7	93.4	85.1	88.6	93.4	88.9	90.8	90.7	84.9	87.4	99.1	99.7	99.5
03300	CAST-IN-PLACE CONCRETE	99.3	118.0	107.0	90.0	98.3	93.4	82.0	92.7	86.4	89.7	91.7	90.6	99.0	101.3	99.9	96.3	98.6	97.3
03	CONCRETE	99.4	109.3	104.4	95.0	92.3	93.6	89.3	88.2	88.7	93.1	90.3	91.7	97.3	92.7	95.0	97.9	94.7	96.3
04	MASONRY	98.0	114.2	108.0	92.7	97.6	95.7	87.0	93.3	90.9	87.5	97.1	93.4	109.2	88.8	96.7	90.2	103.4	98.3
05	METALS	93.2	86.9	90.9	96.3	82.4	91.3	94.1	78.8	88.6	94.2	88.9	92.3	103.4	82.0	95.7	92.3	84.1	89.4
06	WOOD & PLASTICS	94.4	106.7	100.7	95.5	89.2	92.2	99.9	85.8	92.6	97.7	88.2	92.8	84.0	89.4	86.8	95.2	87.9	91.4
07	THERMAL & MOISTURE PROTECTION	105.1	115.9	110.2	101.7	97.9	99.9	95.3	94.0	94.7	92.6	97.5	94.9	105.8	98.5	102.3	106.7	105.4	106.1
08	DOORS & WINDOWS	95.6	104.7	97.8	99.8	87.5	96.8	97.5	84.1	94.2	97.1	85.8	94.3	97.8	78.1	93.0	101.4	94.5	99.7
09200	PLASTER & GYPSUM BOARD	104.3	106.1	105.4	102.9	88.6	94.1	102.5	85.7	92.2	102.5	88.2	93.7	102.6	88.6	94.0	105.0	86.7	93.8
095,098	CEILINGS & ACOUSTICAL TREATMENT	98.2	106.1	103.4	96.5	88.6	91.3	92.4	85.7	88.0	90.9	88.2	89.1	96.8	88.6	91.4	99.5	86.7	91.1
09600	FLOORING	107.6	112.6	108.9	97.1	95.8	96.8	95.4	91.1	94.4	92.9	100.2	94.7	111.5	90.3	106.4	108.1	110.2	108.6
097,099	WALL FINISHES, PAINTS & COATINGS	103.9	122.5	114.7	97.7	100.7	99.4	101.5	95.0	97.7	101.5	89.9	94.8	105.3	89.7	96.3	103.9	122.5	114.7
09	FINISHES	104.1	111.2	107.7	97.9	92.4	95.0	94.7	88.4	91.5	93.6	91.7	92.6	96.1	90.0	93.0	104.5	97.7	101.0
10 - 14	TOTAL DIV. 10000 - 14000	100.0	107.3	101.5	100.0	94.0	98.7	100.0	89.5	97.8	100.0	90.4	98.0	100.0	95.9	99.1	100.0	101.6	100.3
15	MECHANICAL	100.1	109.5	104.5	100.1	96.8	98.6	100.9	90.4	96.0	100.5	93.8	97.4	96.6	92.2	94.6	100.1	95.9	98.1
16	ELECTRICAL	97.1	105.8	103.1	102.1	89.4	93.4	94.5	90.1	91.5	94.5	81.6	85.6	101.2	85.3	90.2	96.5	96.4	96.4
01 - 16	WEIGHTED AVERAGE	98.7	107.3	102.9	97.9	93.1	95.5	95.2	90.9	93.1	95.3	92.3	93.8	99.0	89.7	94.5	98.6	97.2	97.9

		OHIO																	
	DIVISION	MANSFIELD			MARION			SPRINGFIELD			STEUBENVILLE			TOLEDO			YOUNGSTOWN		
		448 - 449			433			455			439			434 - 436			444 - 445		
		MAT.	INST.	TOTAL	MAT.	INST.	TOTAL	MAT.	INST.	TOTAL	MAT.	INST.	TOTAL	MAT.	INST.	TOTAL	MAT.	INST.	TOTAL
02	SITE CONSTRUCTION	98.1	109.3	106.7	80.4	100.5	95.8	78.0	110.0	102.5	120.1	109.7	112.2	83.7	101.4	97.2	102.3	109.4	107.8
03100	CONCRETE FORMS & ACCESSORIES	86.8	90.1	89.7	90.3	84.0	84.9	96.7	88.7	89.8	90.2	95.3	94.6	94.4	103.9	102.6	99.9	92.8	93.7
03200	CONCRETE REINFORCEMENT	90.1	84.4	86.9	95.1	86.1	90.0	93.4	85.0	88.6	92.8	93.1	92.9	103.2	88.4	94.8	99.1	93.3	95.8
03300	CAST-IN-PLACE CONCRETE	93.7	97.0	95.1	82.2	91.0	85.9	86.0	92.2	88.5	89.3	102.3	94.7	90.0	108.0	97.4	100.2	108.6	103.7
03	CONCRETE	92.4	90.6	91.5	87.0	86.3	86.7	91.2	88.7	89.9	91.0	96.3	93.6	94.9	101.8	98.3	99.9	97.5	98.7
04	MASONRY	92.7	97.6	95.7	95.5	87.2	90.4	87.3	92.5	90.5	82.2	98.9	92.5	103.0	101.6	102.1	93.5	99.8	97.4
05	METALS	92.9	77.1	87.2	97.4	78.1	90.4	94.1	78.6	88.5	92.0	80.3	87.8	96.1	86.3	92.6	91.8	81.3	88.0
06	WOOD & PLASTICS	81.8	87.9	85.0	91.3	82.3	86.7	99.9	88.6	94.0	87.5	93.4	90.5	95.5	105.1	100.4	95.2	90.8	92.9
07	THERMAL & MOISTURE PROTECTION	105.9	98.0	102.2	101.0	91.2	96.3	95.3	94.0	94.7	113.7	98.6	106.5	103.6	106.4	105.0	107.0	100.3	103.8
08	DOORS & WINDOWS	100.8	78.1	95.3	96.2	74.0	90.9	97.5	80.2	93.3	97.0	96.1	96.8	99.7	97.6	99.2	101.4	91.7	99.0
09200	PLASTER & GYPSUM BOARD	101.2	86.7	92.3	102.1	81.5	89.5	102.5	88.6	94.0	103.4	92.2	96.5	102.9	105.0	104.1	105.0	89.7	95.6
095,098	CEILINGS & ACOUSTICAL TREATMENT	102.3	86.7	92.0	99.2	81.5	87.5	92.4	88.6	89.9	91.8	92.2	92.0	96.5	105.0	102.1	99.5	89.7	93.0
09600	FLOORING	102.6	101.6	102.4	95.3	91.2	94.3	95.4	91.1	94.4	124.3	100.6	118.5	96.3	74.1	90.9	108.1	95.9	105.1
097,099	WALL FINISHES, PAINTS & COATINGS	103.9	85.3	93.1	97.7	73.1	83.4	101.5	95.0	97.7	114.8	96.6	104.3	97.7	109.4	104.5	103.9	103.0	103.4
09	FINISHES	102.4	91.5	96.8	97.4	83.9	90.5	94.7	89.8	92.2	115.3	96.0	105.5	97.6	98.9	98.3	104.6	93.9	99.1
10 - 14	TOTAL DIV. 10000 - 14000	100.0	95.8	99.1	100.0	86.0	97.0	100.0	89.5	97.8	100.0	99.7	99.9	100.0	98.9	99.8	100.0	99.7	99.9
15	MECHANICAL	97.0	94.9	96.0	97.0	95.8	96.4	100.9	89.9	95.8	97.4	99.1	98.2	100.1	104.2	102.0	100.1	96.3	98.4
16	ELECTRICAL	92.6	91.0	91.5	93.5	91.0	91.8	94.5	89.4	91.0	85.0	104.5	98.4	102.8	98.1	99.6	96.5	92.0	93.4
01 - 16	WEIGHTED AVERAGE	96.7	92.7	94.7	95.3	89.0	92.2	95.4	90.6	93.1	97.2	98.4	97.8	98.5	99.7	99.1	99.0	95.7	97.4

		OHIO			OKLAHOMA													
		ZANESVILLE			ARDMORE			CLINTON			DURANT			ENID			GUYMON		
DIVISION		437 - 438			734			736			747			737			739		
		MAT.	INST.	TOTAL	MAT.	INST.	TOTAL	MAT.	INST.	TOTAL	MAT.	INST.	TOTAL	MAT.	INST.	TOTAL	MAT.	INST.	TOTAL
02	SITE CONSTRUCTION	83.0	101.0	96.8	107.5	90.4	94.4	108.9	88.8	93.5	101.4	88.9	91.8	110.2	89.2	94.1	114.4	88.0	94.2
03100	CONCRETE FORMS & ACCESSORIES	86.4	88.0	87.7	91.3	55.5	60.4	89.7	47.4	53.2	80.4	55.5	59.0	94.3	46.5	53.1	99.4	29.0	38.6
03200	CONCRETE REINFORCEMENT	94.5	86.2	89.8	95.4	84.9	89.4	96.0	84.9	89.7	96.3	68.5	80.5	95.3	84.9	89.4	96.0	40.6	64.4
03300	CAST-IN-PLACE CONCRETE	86.7	91.3	88.6	99.9	54.4	81.1	96.5	54.4	79.1	93.4	54.4	77.3	96.5	57.9	80.6	96.6	35.6	71.4
03	CONCRETE	90.7	88.2	89.4	92.0	60.5	76.2	91.2	56.9	74.1	86.5	57.5	72.0	91.8	57.9	74.8	94.4	34.0	64.2
04	MASONRY	91.5	87.9	89.3	94.3	60.1	73.3	120.6	60.1	83.4	92.9	60.9	73.2	102.0	60.1	76.2	97.8	28.2	55.0
05	METALS	97.4	78.8	90.6	92.2	68.4	83.6	92.3	68.3	83.7	92.3	61.7	81.3	93.4	68.4	84.4	92.7	44.0	75.1
06	WOOD & PLASTICS	87.5	87.2	87.4	93.2	56.1	74.0	91.7	45.2	67.7	82.0	56.1	68.6	96.5	43.9	69.3	101.7	28.6	63.9
07	THERMAL & MOISTURE PROTECTION	101.1	94.9	98.2	98.3	65.9	82.9	98.5	64.8	82.5	97.9	65.0	82.3	98.6	64.6	82.5	99.1	35.0	68.7
08	DOORS & WINDOWS	96.2	86.1	93.8	96.6	64.1	88.7	96.6	58.2	87.3	96.6	59.6	87.6	96.6	57.2	87.1	96.7	31.2	80.9
09200	PLASTER & GYPSUM BOARD	100.8	86.5	92.1	94.8	55.8	71.0	93.9	44.6	63.8	91.3	55.8	69.6	95.2	43.3	63.5	96.3	27.5	54.2
095,098	CEILINGS & ACOUSTICAL TREATMENT	99.2	86.5	90.9	91.4	55.8	67.9	91.4	44.6	60.5	91.4	55.8	67.9	92.9	43.3	60.2	92.7	27.5	49.7
09600	FLOORING	93.3	87.3	91.9	114.9	65.4	102.9	113.1	62.3	100.7	108.4	73.3	99.9	115.6	62.3	102.7	118.2	36.9	98.5
097,099	WALL FINISHES, PAINTS & COATINGS	97.7	63.1	77.6	95.6	66.5	78.7	95.6	66.5	78.7	95.6	66.5	78.7	95.6	66.5	78.7	95.6	23.5	78.7
09	FINISHES	96.7	84.9	90.6	100.1	57.6	78.4	99.5	50.7	74.6	97.2	59.4	77.9	100.9	49.9	74.9	102.2	29.8	65.3
10 - 14	TOTAL DIV. 10000 - 14000	100.0	93.2	98.6	100.0	68.3	93.3	100.0	66.9	93.0	100.0	68.6	93.4	100.0	66.7	93.0	100.0	61.5	91.9
15	MECHANICAL	97.0	86.5	92.1	97.0	69.1	84.1	97.0	69.1	84.1	97.0	69.4	84.2	100.1	69.1	85.8	97.0	33.4	67.5
16	ELECTRICAL	92.4	82.8	85.8	93.3	70.8	77.8	95.0	70.8	78.3	97.7	71.1	79.4	95.0	70.8	78.4	97.7	24.4	47.3
01 - 16	WEIGHTED AVERAGE	95.4	87.2	91.4	96.1	67.6	82.2	97.6	65.7	82.1	95.0	66.7	81.2	97.6	65.7	82.1	97.5	38.0	68.6

		OKLAHOMA																
		LAWTON			MCALESTER			MIAMI			MUSKOGEE			OKLAHOMA CITY			PONCA CITY		
DIVISION		735			745			743			744			730 - 731			746		
		MAT.	INST.	TOTAL	MAT.	INST.	TOTAL	MAT.	INST.	TOTAL	MAT.	INST.	TOTAL	MAT.	INST.	TOTAL	MAT.	INST.	TOTAL
02	SITE CONSTRUCTION	105.5	90.8	94.3	93.4	88.5	89.6	95.9	86.1	88.4	95.9	85.2	87.7	105.8	91.4	94.8	102.4	89.2	92.3
03100	CONCRETE FORMS & ACCESSORIES	98.6	64.1	68.8	77.5	58.3	60.9	94.5	68.8	72.4	100.4	42.2	50.2	100.1	55.0	61.2	88.6	56.1	60.6
03200	CONCRETE REINFORCEMENT	95.5	84.9	89.5	96.0	59.8	75.3	94.6	85.0	89.1	95.3	45.5	66.9	95.5	84.9	89.5	95.3	84.8	89.3
03300	CAST-IN-PLACE CONCRETE	93.4	57.9	78.8	81.8	57.3	71.7	85.8	56.7	73.8	86.9	44.4	69.3	93.4	57.0	78.4	95.9	47.4	75.9
03	CONCRETE	88.4	65.5	76.9	77.6	57.9	67.7	82.2	68.2	75.2	83.8	44.8	64.3	88.5	61.2	74.8	88.7	58.3	73.5
04	MASONRY	97.6	60.1	74.6	110.9	60.6	80.0	96.0	61.8	75.0	110.6	51.0	73.9	99.5	62.7	76.8	86.6	60.9	70.8
05	METALS	95.4	68.5	85.7	92.2	55.0	78.8	92.2	85.2	89.7	93.3	64.4	82.9	95.6	68.4	85.8	92.2	68.1	83.5
06	WOOD & PLASTICS	100.4	67.6	83.4	79.1	60.0	69.7	96.6	73.1	84.4	102.6	43.4	72.0	102.6	54.1	77.5	90.8	56.9	73.3
07	THERMAL & MOISTURE PROTECTION	98.4	67.0	83.5	97.4	66.1	82.5	98.0	68.4	84.0	98.2	51.8	76.2	97.6	66.7	82.9	98.1	64.7	82.3
08	DOORS & WINDOWS	98.1	70.0	91.3	96.6	59.6	87.6	96.6	73.7	91.0	96.5	42.7	83.5	98.1	62.7	89.5	96.6	64.5	88.8
09200	PLASTER & GYPSUM BOARD	97.6	67.6	79.3	90.5	60.8	72.3	95.7	73.2	81.9	96.9	42.6	63.7	97.6	53.7	70.8	93.9	56.7	71.1
095,098	CEILINGS & ACOUSTICAL TREATMENT	101.1	67.6	79.0	91.4	60.8	71.2	91.4	73.2	79.4	92.9	42.6	59.7	101.1	53.7	69.8	91.4	56.7	68.5
09600	FLOORING	118.7	62.3	105.0	107.0	62.3	96.2	116.6	73.3	106.1	119.9	50.2	103.0	118.7	62.3	105.0	112.6	62.3	100.4
097,099	WALL FINISHES, PAINTS & COATINGS	95.6	66.5	78.7	95.6	58.1	73.8	95.6	79.9	86.5	95.6	42.3	64.6	95.6	66.5	78.7	95.6	66.5	78.7
09	FINISHES	103.3	63.7	83.1	96.1	59.1	77.2	99.9	71.1	85.2	101.5	43.9	72.1	103.4	56.4	79.4	99.0	57.7	78.0
10 - 14	TOTAL DIV. 10000 - 14000	100.0	69.8	93.6	100.0	69.3	93.5	100.0	73.9	94.5	100.0	39.2	87.2	100.0	69.1	93.5	100.0	68.8	93.4
15	MECHANICAL	100.1	69.1	85.8	97.0	47.0	73.9	97.0	66.4	82.8	100.1	35.6	70.3	100.1	70.5	86.4	97.0	64.6	82.0
16	ELECTRICAL	97.7	65.1	75.3	95.1	66.6	75.5	97.5	66.7	76.4	94.4	41.9	58.3	96.5	70.8	78.8	94.4	72.2	79.2
01 - 16	WEIGHTED AVERAGE	97.8	68.5	83.6	94.4	61.1	78.2	94.9	71.1	83.3	96.8	48.8	73.4	97.9	68.2	83.4	95.0	66.7	81.2

		OKLAHOMA												OREGON				
		POTEAU			SHAWNEE			TULSA			WOODWARD			BEND			EUGENE		
DIVISION		749			748			740 - 741			738			977			974		
		MAT.	INST.	TOTAL	MAT.	INST.	TOTAL	MAT.	INST.	TOTAL	MAT.	INST.	TOTAL	MAT.	INST.	TOTAL	MAT.	INST.	TOTAL
02	SITE CONSTRUCTION	76.2	84.7	82.7	105.6	88.9	92.8	102.6	86.2	90.0	109.5	88.8	93.6	111.9	106.4	107.7	99.4	106.4	104.8
03100	CONCRETE FORMS & ACCESSORIES	85.6	56.4	60.4	80.2	54.4	57.9	99.5	55.8	61.8	89.9	47.3	53.2	107.8	110.9	110.5	103.2	110.8	109.8
03200	CONCRETE REINFORCEMENT	96.5	84.9	89.9	95.3	65.8	78.5	95.5	84.9	89.5	95.3	84.9	89.4	109.3	105.5	107.1	109.3	105.5	107.1
03300	CAST-IN-PLACE CONCRETE	85.8	56.1	73.6	98.9	53.5	80.2	94.6	56.5	78.9	96.5	54.4	79.1	104.5	109.8	106.7	101.2	109.8	104.8
03	CONCRETE	83.8	62.6	73.2	90.3	56.1	73.2	89.1	62.5	75.8	91.5	56.9	74.2	122.9	109.2	116.0	111.7	109.1	110.4
04	MASONRY	97.0	61.0	74.9	112.2	59.0	79.5	96.8	62.8	75.9	90.8	60.1	71.9	114.5	106.4	109.5	112.3	106.4	108.7
05	METALS	92.2	84.9	89.6	92.2	59.6	80.4	96.0	84.6	91.9	92.4	68.3	83.7	94.2	103.8	97.6	95.1	103.7	98.2
06	WOOD & PLASTICS	87.2	57.1	71.6	81.8	55.8	68.3	101.2	55.7	77.7	91.9	45.1	67.7	102.8	109.8	106.4	98.2	109.8	104.2
07	THERMAL & MOISTURE PROTECTION	98.1	66.1	82.9	98.1	65.5	82.6	98.1	64.9	82.4	98.5	64.8	82.5	112.1	104.3	108.4	111.0	100.7	106.1
08	DOORS & WINDOWS	96.6	65.0	89.0	96.5	55.4	86.6	98.1	63.0	89.6	96.6	58.1	87.3	101.4	112.6	104.1	101.8	112.6	104.4
09200	PLASTER & GYPSUM BOARD	93.1	56.7	70.8	91.3	55.5	69.4	97.6	55.3	71.7	94.2	44.5	63.8	95.9	110.0	104.5	94.8	110.0	104.1
095,098	CEILINGS & ACOUSTICAL TREATMENT	91.4	56.7	68.5	91.4	55.5	67.7	101.1	55.3	70.9	92.7	44.5	60.9	113.7	110.0	111.3	118.1	110.0	112.8
09600	FLOORING	111.7	73.3	102.4	108.3	49.6	94.0	118.5	64.8	105.4	113.1	65.4	101.5	119.0	104.5	115.5	117.1	104.5	114.1
097,099	WALL FINISHES, PAINTS & COATINGS	95.6	66.5	78.7	95.6	52.5	70.5	95.6	62.3	76.3	95.6	66.5	78.7	119.6	73.4	92.8	119.6	82.9	98.3
09	FINISHES	97.3	60.0	78.3	97.3	52.7	74.6	102.8	57.5	79.7	99.9	51.2	75.0	114.7	105.6	110.1	113.9	106.6	110.2
10 - 14	TOTAL DIV. 10000 - 14000	100.0	69.2	93.5	100.0	67.9	93.2	100.0	71.9	94.1	100.0	66.9	93.0	100.0	110.2	102.2	100.0	110.2	102.2
15	MECHANICAL	97.0	65.9	82.6	97.0	68.4	83.7	100.1	62.8	82.8	97.0	69.1	84.1	97.1	112.5	104.2	100.3	112.5	105.9
16	ELECTRICAL	94.6	66.7	75.4	97.9	70.8	79.2	97.7	54.6	68.1	97.5	70.8	79.1	106.3	102.9	104.0	104.2	102.9	103.3
01 - 16	WEIGHTED AVERAGE	94.0	68.0	81.4	96.7	64.9	81.2	97.8	65.3	82.0	96.2	65.8	81.4	105.1	107.3	106.2	103.8	107.3	105.5

City Cost Indexes

OREGON

DIVISION		KLAMATH FALLS 976			MEDFORD 975			PENDLETON 978			PORTLAND 970-972			SALEM 973			VALE 979		
		MAT.	INST.	TOTAL	MAT.	INST.	TOTAL	MAT.	INST.	TOTAL	MAT.	INST.	TOTAL	MAT.	INST.	TOTAL	MAT.	INST.	TOTAL
02	SITE CONSTRUCTION	116.8	106.4	108.8	108.5	106.4	106.9	103.7	98.5	99.7	100.5	106.4	105.0	99.6	106.4	104.8	90.2	98.4	96.5
03100	CONCRETE FORMS & ACCESSORIES	98.7	110.6	108.9	97.5	110.7	108.9	101.0	110.8	109.5	104.8	111.2	110.3	104.7	111.1	110.2	109.5	106.6	107.0
03200	CONCRETE REINFORCEMENT	99.3	96.3	97.6	100.9	105.5	103.5	98.0	105.7	102.4	104.5	105.8	105.2	110.4	105.8	107.8	95.6	105.6	101.3
03300	CAST-IN-PLACE CONCRETE	104.5	107.6	105.8	104.5	109.7	106.6	105.2	109.0	106.8	108.6	109.9	109.2	104.9	109.9	107.0	82.8	107.8	93.2
03	CONCRETE	126.6	106.6	116.6	119.0	109.0	114.0	100.6	108.8	104.7	114.9	109.4	112.1	113.8	109.3	111.6	83.5	106.6	95.0
04	MASONRY	131.6	106.4	116.1	109.1	106.4	107.4	119.7	111.9	114.9	113.6	111.9	112.6	114.3	111.9	112.8	118.0	110.2	113.2
05	METALS	94.2	101.1	96.7	94.7	103.6	97.9	107.6	103.5	106.1	93.8	104.4	97.7	95.7	104.4	98.8	107.4	102.8	105.7
06	WOOD & PLASTICS	93.4	109.8	101.9	92.2	109.8	101.3	96.5	109.9	103.4	100.1	109.8	105.1	100.1	109.8	105.1	105.5	106.0	105.7
07	THERMAL & MOISTURE PROTECTION	112.4	99.7	106.4	111.9	99.7	106.1	99.6	98.2	98.9	110.8	108.3	109.6	110.8	108.3	109.6	98.8	98.3	98.6
08	DOORS & WINDOWS	101.4	111.0	103.7	104.5	112.6	106.5	97.6	112.7	101.2	99.2	112.6	102.4	101.1	112.6	103.9	97.5	105.3	99.4
09200	PLASTER & GYPSUM BOARD	92.9	110.0	103.4	92.4	110.0	103.2	72.4	110.0	95.4	94.0	110.0	103.8	96.0	110.0	104.6	75.4	106.0	94.1
095,098	CEILINGS & ACOUSTICAL TREATMENT	113.7	110.0	111.3	116.7	110.0	112.3	70.3	110.0	96.5	118.1	110.0	112.8	129.0	110.0	116.5	70.3	106.0	93.9
09600	FLOORING	115.4	104.5	112.8	114.7	104.5	112.2	81.1	104.5	86.8	117.1	102.0	113.5	117.1	104.5	114.1	83.5	104.5	88.6
097,099	WALL FINISHES, PAINTS & COATINGS	119.6	70.1	90.9	119.6	70.1	90.9	99.0	89.1	93.3	119.6	82.9	98.3	119.6	82.9	98.3	99.0	73.4	84.1
09	FINISHES	113.5	105.2	109.3	113.1	105.2	109.0	76.1	107.5	92.1	113.8	106.2	109.9	116.0	106.6	111.2	76.5	103.0	90.0
10-14	TOTAL DIV. 10000 - 14000	100.0	110.1	102.1	100.0	110.1	102.1	100.0	110.3	102.2	100.0	110.2	102.2	100.0	110.2	102.2	100.0	109.4	102.0
15	MECHANICAL	97.1	112.4	104.2	100.3	112.5	105.9	97.9	112.3	104.6	100.3	112.5	105.9	100.3	112.5	105.9	97.9	92.2	95.2
16	ELECTRICAL	104.2	93.6	96.9	109.8	93.6	98.6	92.2	98.0	96.2	104.0	112.4	109.8	103.8	102.9	103.2	92.2	81.9	85.1
01-16	WEIGHTED AVERAGE	106.3	104.9	105.6	105.3	105.5	105.4	98.5	106.2	102.2	103.8	109.7	106.7	104.4	108.2	106.2	96.0	98.2	97.1

PENNSYLVANIA

DIVISION		ALLENTOWN 181			ALTOONA 166			BEDFORD 155			BRADFORD 167			BUTLER 160			CHAMBERSBURG 172		
		MAT.	INST.	TOTAL	MAT.	INST.	TOTAL	MAT.	INST.	TOTAL	MAT.	INST.	TOTAL	MAT.	INST.	TOTAL	MAT.	INST.	TOTAL
02	SITE CONSTRUCTION	94.1	107.7	104.6	98.5	107.7	105.6	102.4	107.0	105.9	93.9	108.2	104.8	89.5	108.6	104.1	88.6	105.8	101.8
03100	CONCRETE FORMS & ACCESSORIES	102.9	107.8	107.1	81.8	91.8	90.4	82.6	93.0	91.6	85.3	90.9	90.2	83.8	104.9	102.0	85.3	89.8	89.2
03200	CONCRETE REINFORCEMENT	100.8	108.5	105.2	97.8	98.3	98.1	102.1	88.2	94.2	99.8	98.4	99.0	98.4	106.6	103.1	98.2	93.0	95.3
03300	CAST-IN-PLACE CONCRETE	89.1	99.5	93.4	99.3	92.2	96.4	101.1	92.9	97.7	94.8	93.2	94.1	87.7	101.2	93.3	96.3	91.3	94.2
03	CONCRETE	99.8	106.2	103.0	94.2	94.7	94.4	96.4	93.5	95.0	101.5	94.7	98.1	85.3	105.2	95.3	108.1	92.5	100.3
04	MASONRY	95.0	95.7	95.4	96.8	82.2	87.8	95.0	90.2	92.0	92.7	88.2	89.9	98.8	98.9	98.9	95.3	89.3	91.6
05	METALS	98.1	125.0	107.8	91.8	118.9	101.6	97.6	115.1	103.9	96.1	120.1	104.7	91.5	126.2	104.0	96.0	115.9	103.2
06	WOOD & PLASTICS	107.0	110.5	108.8	81.7	93.1	87.6	83.6	93.2	88.6	88.7	89.0	88.8	83.9	105.8	95.2	92.9	90.5	91.6
07	THERMAL & MOISTURE PROTECTION	99.0	112.1	105.3	97.9	93.2	95.7	94.7	96.8	95.7	98.9	95.4	97.2	97.5	101.7	99.5	97.8	86.7	92.6
08	DOORS & WINDOWS	95.9	108.0	98.8	90.3	101.4	93.0	92.2	99.0	93.9	96.4	97.1	96.6	90.3	111.4	95.4	92.8	90.0	92.1
09200	PLASTER & GYPSUM BOARD	102.4	110.5	107.4	88.8	92.6	91.1	88.2	92.6	90.9	95.7	88.3	91.2	89.7	105.9	99.5	99.2	89.9	93.5
095,098	CEILINGS & ACOUSTICAL TREATMENT	97.9	110.5	106.2	92.4	92.6	92.5	96.8	92.6	94.0	91.2	88.3	89.3	93.9	105.7	101.7	91.2	89.9	90.3
09600	FLOORING	86.4	87.1	86.5	80.7	69.1	77.9	88.1	70.1	83.7	79.9	88.3	81.9	81.6	103.0	86.8	84.0	69.9	80.6
097,099	WALL FINISHES, PAINTS & COATINGS	87.1	102.2	95.9	82.7	104.0	95.1	92.0	104.0	99.0	87.1	88.0	87.6	82.7	103.9	95.0	87.1	88.9	88.1
09	FINISHES	96.7	103.7	100.3	92.1	88.4	90.2	95.1	89.2	92.1	92.4	89.3	90.8	92.3	104.3	98.4	93.6	85.8	89.6
10-14	TOTAL DIV. 10000 - 14000	100.0	103.9	100.8	100.0	100.9	100.2	100.0	102.3	100.5	100.0	102.5	100.5	100.0	105.2	101.1	100.0	94.5	98.8
15	MECHANICAL	100.3	102.7	101.4	99.7	88.3	94.4	96.7	89.7	93.5	97.2	96.9	97.0	96.7	98.0	97.3	97.2	93.7	95.6
16	ELECTRICAL	102.2	89.1	93.2	87.6	102.2	97.6	90.4	102.2	98.5	91.7	102.2	98.9	88.6	95.9	93.6	89.5	81.1	83.7
01-16	WEIGHTED AVERAGE	98.7	103.4	101.0	94.6	96.6	95.6	95.8	97.3	96.5	96.4	99.0	97.7	92.8	104.0	98.2	96.7	92.9	94.9

PENNSYLVANIA

DIVISION		DOYLESTOWN 189			DUBOIS 158			ERIE 164-165			GREENSBURG 156			HARRISBURG 170-171			HAZLETON 182		
		MAT.	INST.	TOTAL	MAT.	INST.	TOTAL	MAT.	INST.	TOTAL	MAT.	INST.	TOTAL	MAT.	INST.	TOTAL	MAT.	INST.	TOTAL
02	SITE CONSTRUCTION	110.2	89.6	94.4	107.7	107.2	107.3	94.9	108.4	105.3	98.2	107.7	105.5	82.8	106.3	100.8	87.3	107.6	102.8
03100	CONCRETE FORMS & ACCESSORIES	80.6	125.2	119.1	81.7	93.3	91.7	101.3	101.9	101.8	91.1	104.9	103.0	94.3	87.0	88.0	77.8	89.9	88.2
03200	CONCRETE REINFORCEMENT	97.4	136.9	119.9	101.4	98.3	99.6	99.8	98.2	98.9	101.4	106.7	104.4	100.8	93.2	96.4	97.9	106.3	102.7
03300	CAST-IN-PLACE CONCRETE	84.2	104.8	92.7	97.5	98.6	98.0	97.7	95.2	96.7	93.9	101.4	97.0	87.4	92.5	89.5	84.2	93.3	87.9
03	CONCRETE	95.0	112.0	107.4	97.4	97.6	97.5	93.2	100.2	96.7	91.6	105.3	98.4	98.2	91.7	95.0	91.4	95.8	93.6
04	MASONRY	97.9	120.6	111.9	95.2	85.0	88.9	88.1	98.4	94.4	106.6	101.1	103.2	92.4	88.5	90.0	106.1	94.5	99.0
05	METALS	95.1	121.1	104.5	97.6	119.6	105.6	91.9	120.8	102.3	97.5	125.8	107.7	99.9	117.6	106.3	97.8	124.0	107.3
06	WOOD & PLASTICS	82.9	126.6	105.5	82.6	93.2	88.1	102.5	102.1	102.3	92.6	105.9	99.5	99.0	85.8	92.2	81.0	88.6	84.9
07	THERMAL & MOISTURE PROTECTION	97.0	125.1	110.3	95.1	97.5	96.2	98.0	100.2	99.1	94.7	103.4	98.8	102.3	105.1	103.6	98.2	105.1	101.5
08	DOORS & WINDOWS	97.6	132.2	106.0	92.2	102.1	94.6	90.4	99.3	92.6	92.2	111.4	96.8	95.9	95.9	95.9	96.6	101.5	97.8
09200	PLASTER & GYPSUM BOARD	88.7	127.1	112.2	87.8	92.6	90.7	96.8	101.9	99.9	91.0	105.7	100.0	102.4	85.0	91.8	94.8	87.9	90.6
095,098	CEILINGS & ACOUSTICAL TREATMENT	95.3	127.1	116.3	96.8	92.6	94.0	97.9	101.9	100.5	95.5	105.7	102.2	97.9	85.0	89.4	98.0	87.9	91.3
09600	FLOORING	70.8	121.9	83.2	87.6	72.6	84.0	87.5	90.4	88.2	92.0	103.0	94.6	86.6	83.2	85.8	77.1	83.0	78.5
097,099	WALL FINISHES, PAINTS & COATINGS	86.5	106.1	97.9	92.0	103.9	98.9	90.9	88.0	89.2	92.0	104.0	99.2	87.1	88.9	88.1	87.1	98.2	93.5
09	FINISHES	86.1	122.7	104.8	95.2	89.6	92.4	96.9	98.3	97.6	96.3	104.4	100.4	95.7	85.8	90.6	92.2	88.5	90.3
10-14	TOTAL DIV. 10000 - 14000	100.0	106.2	101.3	100.0	102.3	100.5	100.0	105.5	101.2	100.0	105.5	101.2	100.0	93.6	98.6	100.0	99.7	99.9
15	MECHANICAL	96.7	122.7	108.7	96.7	89.8	93.5	99.7	98.6	99.2	96.7	93.3	95.2	100.3	93.4	97.1	97.2	91.4	94.5
16	ELECTRICAL	91.6	115.6	108.1	91.3	102.2	98.8	90.0	88.4	88.9	91.3	102.2	98.8	101.3	81.1	87.4	93.1	82.7	85.9
01-16	WEIGHTED AVERAGE	95.4	117.6	106.2	96.2	97.9	97.0	94.8	100.3	97.5	96.0	104.3	100.0	98.1	93.6	95.9	96.0	96.0	96.0

COST INDEXES

642

City Cost Indexes

PENNSYLVANIA

DIVISION		INDIANA 157			JOHNSTOWN 159			KITTANNING 162			LANCASTER 175 - 176			LEHIGH VALLEY 180			MONTROSE 188		
		MAT.	INST.	TOTAL	MAT.	INST.	TOTAL	MAT.	INST.	TOTAL	MAT.	INST.	TOTAL	MAT.	INST.	TOTAL	MAT.	INST.	TOTAL
02	SITE CONSTRUCTION	96.4	107.7	105.0	103.0	107.0	106.1	92.3	108.6	104.8	80.0	106.4	100.2	91.7	107.7	104.0	90.5	107.2	103.3
03100	CONCRETE FORMS & ACCESSORIES	83.5	95.5	93.8	81.7	93.7	92.0	83.8	105.0	102.1	88.0	87.4	87.4	93.8	108.2	106.2	78.9	93.5	91.5
03200	CONCRETE REINFORCEMENT	100.6	106.7	104.1	102.1	106.3	104.5	98.4	106.7	103.2	97.9	93.0	95.1	97.9	108.6	104.0	102.5	106.3	104.7
03300	CAST-IN-PLACE CONCRETE	92.1	101.3	95.9	102.1	94.3	98.9	91.1	98.8	94.3	81.9	93.5	86.7	91.1	99.5	94.6	89.4	94.7	91.5
03	CONCRETE	89.3	101.1	95.2	97.0	97.7	97.4	88.2	104.5	96.3	94.7	92.2	93.4	98.6	106.4	102.5	96.7	97.7	97.2
04	MASONRY	92.0	101.1	97.6	92.7	91.5	91.9	102.2	101.1	101.5	100.9	88.9	93.5	95.1	95.6	95.4	95.0	98.3	97.0
05	METALS	97.6	125.7	107.8	97.6	122.9	106.7	91.6	126.5	104.2	96.0	117.1	103.7	97.8	125.3	107.7	96.2	122.6	105.7
06	WOOD & PLASTICS	84.6	93.2	89.0	82.6	93.2	88.1	83.9	105.8	95.2	95.6	85.8	90.5	97.5	110.5	104.2	82.2	91.9	87.2
07	THERMAL & MOISTURE PROTECTION	94.4	101.5	97.8	94.8	98.5	96.5	97.6	103.8	100.5	97.3	106.2	101.5	98.8	111.0	104.6	98.3	106.3	102.1
08	DOORS & WINDOWS	92.2	104.5	95.2	92.2	103.9	95.0	90.3	111.4	95.4	92.8	90.0	92.1	96.6	113.8	100.8	93.0	103.3	95.5
09200	PLASTER & GYPSUM BOARD	88.7	92.5	91.0	87.5	92.6	90.6	89.7	105.7	99.5	100.0	85.0	90.9	99.6	110.5	106.3	94.0	91.4	92.4
095,098	CEILINGS & ACOUSTICAL TREATMENT	96.8	92.5	94.0	95.5	92.6	93.6	93.9	105.7	101.7	91.2	85.0	87.1	98.0	110.5	106.2	91.2	91.4	91.3
09600	FLOORING	88.5	107.5	93.1	87.6	88.0	87.7	81.6	107.7	87.9	85.0	83.2	84.6	82.8	121.9	92.3	77.7	87.6	80.1
097,099	WALL FINISHES, PAINTS & COATINGS	92.0	104.0	99.0	92.0	104.0	99.0	82.7	104.0	95.1	87.1	87.9	87.6	87.1	102.2	95.9	87.1	98.2	93.5
09	FINISHES	95.0	97.9	96.5	94.6	93.1	93.9	92.4	105.3	99.0	93.6	85.4	89.4	95.0	109.8	102.6	91.2	92.5	91.9
10 - 14	TOTAL DIV. 10000 - 14000	100.0	103.8	100.8	100.0	102.5	100.5	100.0	105.2	101.1	100.0	94.3	98.8	100.0	103.9	100.8	100.0	105.1	100.3
15	MECHANICAL	96.7	92.1	94.6	96.7	90.2	93.7	96.7	100.1	98.2	97.2	94.4	95.9	97.2	102.7	99.7	97.2	93.2	95.3
16	ELECTRICAL	91.3	102.2	98.8	91.3	102.2	98.8	87.6	102.2	97.7	91.9	69.9	76.7	93.1	94.9	94.4	91.7	86.6	88.2
01 - 16	WEIGHTED AVERAGE	94.6	102.2	98.3	95.8	99.4	97.6	93.3	105.7	99.4	95.3	91.7	93.6	96.9	105.4	101.0	95.2	98.1	96.6

PENNSYLVANIA

DIVISION		NEW CASTLE 161			NORRISTOWN 194			OIL CITY 163			PHILADELPHIA 190 - 191			PITTSBURGH 150 - 152			POTTSVILLE 179		
		MAT.	INST.	TOTAL	MAT.	INST.	TOTAL	MAT.	INST.	TOTAL	MAT.	INST.	TOTAL	MAT.	INST.	TOTAL	MAT.	INST.	TOTAL
02	SITE CONSTRUCTION	90.0	108.6	104.2	95.6	96.4	96.2	88.3	108.2	103.6	101.9	95.5	97.0	101.3	110.3	108.2	83.2	106.3	100.9
03100	CONCRETE FORMS & ACCESSORIES	83.8	102.8	100.2	82.0	125.8	119.8	83.8	94.3	92.9	104.0	131.2	127.5	101.2	103.5	103.2	77.1	89.8	88.1
03200	CONCRETE REINFORCEMENT	97.1	100.6	99.1	97.1	131.5	116.7	98.4	100.2	99.4	100.2	123.3	113.3	102.6	107.3	105.2	97.0	100.6	99.1
03300	CAST-IN-PLACE CONCRETE	88.5	101.1	93.7	77.2	120.2	94.9	85.9	96.8	90.9	94.6	124.4	106.9	97.5	101.4	99.1	87.3	95.1	90.5
03	CONCRETE	85.9	103.1	94.5	93.8	124.5	109.1	84.1	97.8	90.9	106.8	126.9	116.8	95.1	104.8	99.9	98.7	95.3	97.0
04	MASONRY	96.5	98.9	98.0	103.0	119.1	112.9	98.1	93.0	95.0	89.9	125.5	111.8	89.2	102.3	97.2	94.7	89.0	91.2
05	METALS	91.6	123.0	102.9	96.9	122.0	105.9	91.6	120.8	102.1	100.1	122.1	108.0	98.6	126.1	108.5	96.2	120.9	105.1
06	WOOD & PLASTICS	83.9	103.6	94.1	85.3	126.5	106.6	83.9	93.1	88.7	107.7	131.3	119.9	103.0	103.7	103.3	84.3	89.5	87.0
07	THERMAL & MOISTURE PROTECTION	97.5	101.5	99.4	99.0	126.4	112.0	97.4	96.7	97.1	100.1	131.1	114.8	95.0	103.5	99.0	97.3	104.2	100.6
08	DOORS & WINDOWS	90.3	105.3	93.9	91.6	130.4	100.9	90.3	95.1	91.5	97.4	134.0	106.2	92.4	111.5	97.0	92.8	100.1	94.6
09200	PLASTER & GYPSUM BOARD	89.7	103.4	98.0	92.8	127.1	113.8	89.7	92.6	91.5	98.8	132.1	119.2	94.3	103.4	99.8	96.2	88.8	91.7
095,098	CEILINGS & ACOUSTICAL TREATMENT	93.9	103.4	100.1	99.9	127.1	117.8	93.9	92.6	93.1	99.9	132.1	121.1	96.8	103.4	101.1	91.2	88.8	89.6
09600	FLOORING	81.6	87.0	82.9	74.6	121.9	86.1	81.6	72.6	79.4	82.3	136.6	95.5	96.5	103.9	98.3	80.7	92.6	83.6
097,099	WALL FINISHES, PAINTS & COATINGS	82.7	103.9	95.0	89.0	133.4	114.8	82.7	103.9	95.0	89.0	138.8	117.9	92.0	116.0	105.9	87.1	72.3	78.5
09	FINISHES	92.3	99.8	96.1	93.3	126.0	110.0	92.2	90.6	91.4	96.9	133.2	115.4	98.6	104.6	101.7	91.8	87.9	89.8
10 - 14	TOTAL DIV. 10000 - 14000	100.0	105.0	101.0	100.0	122.6	104.8	100.0	103.6	100.8	100.0	124.9	105.3	100.0	105.2	101.1	100.0	97.9	99.6
15	MECHANICAL	96.7	97.7	97.1	96.8	122.5	108.7	96.7	96.7	96.7	99.9	124.7	111.4	99.8	100.4	100.1	97.2	90.3	94.0
16	ELECTRICAL	88.6	104.6	99.6	90.3	115.6	107.7	91.2	95.9	94.4	97.5	126.7	117.5	95.0	102.2	100.0	88.8	82.3	84.4
01 - 16	WEIGHTED AVERAGE	92.7	104.0	98.2	95.5	119.5	107.2	92.7	99.0	95.8	99.6	123.9	111.4	97.0	106.0	101.4	95.1	94.5	94.8

PENNSYLVANIA

DIVISION		READING 195 - 196			SCRANTON 184 - 185			STATE COLLEGE 168			STROUDSBURG 183			SUNBURY 178			UNIONTOWN 154		
		MAT.	INST.	TOTAL	MAT.	INST.	TOTAL	MAT.	INST.	TOTAL	MAT.	INST.	TOTAL	MAT.	INST.	TOTAL	MAT.	INST.	TOTAL
02	SITE CONSTRUCTION	99.4	113.5	110.2	94.6	107.7	104.7	85.3	106.6	101.6	89.2	107.0	102.9	93.7	107.4	104.2	96.9	107.7	105.2
03100	CONCRETE FORMS & ACCESSORIES	103.5	93.1	94.6	103.1	93.9	95.1	84.2	92.0	90.9	86.3	106.8	104.0	90.8	85.2	86.0	74.3	104.9	100.7
03200	CONCRETE REINFORCEMENT	98.5	108.2	104.0	100.8	106.5	104.0	99.0	98.6	98.7	101.1	108.5	105.3	99.8	93.2	96.0	101.4	106.7	104.4
03300	CAST-IN-PLACE CONCRETE	69.2	98.8	81.4	93.1	95.3	94.0	89.8	87.3	88.8	87.6	90.4	88.8	95.4	92.0	94.0	92.1	101.3	95.9
03	CONCRETE	94.0	99.5	96.7	101.8	98.2	100.0	102.0	93.1	97.5	95.5	102.5	99.0	102.4	90.8	96.6	88.7	105.2	97.0
04	MASONRY	91.9	91.1	91.4	95.3	100.9	98.8	100.0	87.4	92.2	92.0	98.3	95.9	92.7	88.1	89.9	107.0	101.1	103.4
05	METALS	97.1	124.8	107.1	99.9	124.3	108.7	95.9	119.5	104.4	97.9	123.2	107.0	96.0	117.4	103.7	97.3	125.8	107.6
06	WOOD & PLASTICS	107.7	91.0	99.1	107.0	91.9	99.2	91.7	93.1	92.4	89.8	110.5	100.5	94.5	84.0	89.1	74.9	105.9	91.0
07	THERMAL & MOISTURE PROTECTION	100.1	108.8	104.2	98.9	108.0	103.2	97.6	103.8	100.5	98.5	92.4	95.6	98.7	102.7	100.6	94.3	103.5	98.6
08	DOORS & WINDOWS	97.4	97.4	97.4	95.9	103.3	97.7	92.8	101.4	94.8	96.7	103.3	98.3	92.9	94.9	93.4	92.2	111.4	96.8
09200	PLASTER & GYPSUM BOARD	105.9	90.5	96.5	102.4	91.4	95.7	98.5	92.6	94.9	97.4	110.5	105.4	97.2	83.2	88.6	85.4	105.7	97.8
095,098	CEILINGS & ACOUSTICAL TREATMENT	101.1	90.5	94.1	97.9	91.4	93.6	89.8	92.6	91.7	98.0	110.5	106.2	89.8	83.2	85.4	95.5	105.7	102.2
09600	FLOORING	80.5	85.9	81.8	86.4	93.8	88.2	83.4	75.3	81.5	80.3	77.7	79.7	81.8	64.3	77.6	84.4	96.9	87.4
097,099	WALL FINISHES, PAINTS & COATINGS	87.1	95.1	91.8	87.1	98.2	93.5	87.1	104.0	96.9	87.1	99.4	94.2	87.1	98.2	93.5	92.0	104.2	99.1
09	FINISHES	97.5	91.2	94.3	96.7	93.7	95.2	92.8	89.7	91.3	93.8	101.3	97.6	93.0	82.5	87.7	92.8	103.2	98.1
10 - 14	TOTAL DIV. 10000 - 14000	100.0	101.0	100.2	100.0	101.5	100.3	100.0	94.2	98.8	100.0	99.4	99.9	100.0	96.8	99.3	100.0	105.5	101.2
15	MECHANICAL	100.2	102.6	101.3	100.3	93.2	97.0	97.2	92.8	95.1	97.2	94.9	96.1	97.2	92.9	95.2	96.7	92.1	94.6
16	ELECTRICAL	100.1	81.0	87.0	102.3	86.6	91.5	90.4	102.2	98.5	93.1	130.8	119.0	89.3	84.3	85.9	86.5	102.2	97.3
01 - 16	WEIGHTED AVERAGE	97.9	99.0	98.4	99.2	98.8	99.0	96.1	98.0	97.0	96.0	107.4	101.6	96.0	93.5	94.8	94.7	103.9	99.2

COST INDEXES

		PENNSYLVANIA																
	DIVISION	WASHINGTON			WELLSBORO			WESTCHESTER			WILKES-BARRE			WILLIAMSPORT			YORK		
		153			169			193			186 - 187			177			173 - 174		
		MAT.	INST.	TOTAL	MAT.	INST.	TOTAL	MAT.	INST.	TOTAL	MAT.	INST.	TOTAL	MAT.	INST.	TOTAL	MAT.	INST.	TOTAL
02	SITE CONSTRUCTION	97.0	107.7	105.2	98.1	107.0	104.9	101.7	94.0	95.8	87.1	107.7	102.8	84.3	106.5	101.3	83.5	106.4	101.0
03100	CONCRETE FORMS & ACCESSORIES	83.7	105.1	102.2	84.5	84.4	84.4	91.2	124.0	119.5	89.7	90.5	90.4	86.3	80.7	81.5	81.6	87.5	86.7
03200	CONCRETE REINFORCEMENT	101.4	106.7	104.4	99.0	106.3	103.1	96.1	109.2	103.6	99.8	103.4	101.8	99.0	93.1	95.6	99.8	93.1	96.0
03300	CAST-IN-PLACE CONCRETE	92.1	101.4	95.9	94.1	90.3	92.5	85.4	117.9	98.8	84.2	94.3	88.4	80.7	80.2	80.5	87.7	93.6	90.1
03	CONCRETE	89.4	105.4	97.4	104.4	92.3	98.3	102.5	118.5	110.5	92.5	95.8	94.2	89.0	84.7	86.9	100.0	92.3	96.2
04	MASONRY	93.2	99.7	97.2	99.2	89.9	93.5	98.1	118.7	110.7	107.0	96.5	100.5	85.5	85.0	85.2	93.7	88.9	90.8
05	METALS	97.3	125.7	107.5	96.0	123.2	105.8	96.9	107.2	100.6	96.1	122.5	105.6	96.0	116.8	103.5	97.3	117.5	104.6
06	WOOD & PLASTICS	84.7	105.9	95.7	87.9	84.0	85.9	94.8	126.5	111.2	93.3	88.6	90.9	89.8	80.3	84.9	89.0	85.5	87.2
07	THERMAL & MOISTURE PROTECTION	94.4	103.1	98.6	99.2	101.9	100.5	99.5	123.9	111.1	98.3	106.3	102.1	98.1	101.2	99.6	94.7	106.2	101.6
08	DOORS & WINDOWS	92.1	111.3	96.8	96.4	99.0	97.0	91.6	111.2	96.3	93.0	94.8	93.4	92.9	82.4	90.4	92.8	95.7	93.5
09200	PLASTER & GYPSUM BOARD	88.4	105.7	99.0	95.5	83.2	88.0	95.4	127.1	114.8	97.0	87.9	91.5	96.2	79.4	85.9	97.9	84.7	89.8
095,098	CEILINGS & ACOUSTICAL TREATMENT	95.5	105.7	102.2	89.8	83.2	85.4	99.9	127.1	117.8	91.2	87.9	89.0	91.2	79.4	83.4	89.7	84.7	86.4
09600	FLOORING	88.6	105.2	92.6	79.6	76.9	79.0	78.0	121.9	88.6	81.5	77.3	80.5	80.3	75.3	79.1	82.4	83.2	82.6
097,099	WALL FINISHES, PAINTS & COATINGS	92.0	104.2	99.1	87.1	98.2	93.5	89.0	133.4	114.8	87.1	98.2	93.5	87.1	98.2	93.5	87.1	88.9	88.1
09	FINISHES	94.7	105.1	100.0	92.4	83.5	87.9	95.1	125.2	110.5	92.7	88.4	90.5	92.1	81.0	86.4	92.3	86.2	89.2
10 - 14	TOTAL DIV. 10000 - 14000	100.0	105.5	101.2	100.0	95.9	99.1	100.0	122.4	104.7	100.0	100.5	100.1	100.0	91.3	98.2	100.0	94.3	98.8
15	MECHANICAL	96.7	100.1	98.3	97.2	91.8	94.7	96.8	122.0	108.4	97.2	92.4	94.9	97.2	91.2	94.4	100.3	91.0	95.8
16	ELECTRICAL	90.3	102.2	98.5	91.7	75.7	80.7	90.1	102.4	98.6	93.1	85.2	87.6	90.0	66.5	73.9	91.9	81.1	84.5
01 - 16	WEIGHTED AVERAGE	94.6	105.5	99.9	97.2	92.9	95.1	96.8	113.9	105.1	95.7	96.4	96.0	93.6	88.0	90.9	96.3	94.0	95.2

		PUERTO RICO			RHODE ISLAND						SOUTH CAROLINA								
	DIVISION	SAN JUAN			NEWPORT			PROVIDENCE			AIKEN			BEAUFORT			CHARLESTON		
		009			028			029			298			299			294		
		MAT.	INST.	TOTAL	MAT.	INST.	TOTAL	MAT.	INST.	TOTAL	MAT.	INST.	TOTAL	MAT.	INST.	TOTAL	MAT.	INST.	TOTAL
02	SITE CONSTRUCTION	125.2	94.5	101.7	85.1	105.3	100.6	84.5	105.6	100.6	116.2	81.1	89.3	111.2	81.3	88.3	93.6	82.0	84.7
03100	CONCRETE FORMS & ACCESSORIES	98.9	21.4	32.1	103.5	111.1	110.1	102.5	111.2	110.0	98.6	34.1	43.0	96.5	34.7	43.2	95.2	44.6	51.6
03200	CONCRETE REINFORCEMENT	201.2	14.5	94.7	111.9	119.3	116.1	111.9	119.3	116.1	94.2	13.7	48.3	93.3	35.6	60.4	93.1	65.8	77.6
03300	CAST-IN-PLACE CONCRETE	109.8	36.2	79.4	81.5	118.9	96.9	86.1	118.9	99.6	72.2	36.2	57.3	72.1	46.5	61.6	81.5	55.6	70.8
03	CONCRETE	114.4	26.1	70.2	101.2	114.9	108.1	103.4	114.9	109.2	100.3	33.4	66.9	97.3	41.3	69.3	89.5	54.4	72.0
04	MASONRY	221.3	19.4	97.2	102.0	119.2	112.6	104.3	119.2	113.4	71.2	22.4	41.2	83.4	30.4	50.8	84.7	42.6	58.8
05	METALS	129.6	34.4	95.3	98.0	110.1	102.4	98.0	110.2	102.4	93.4	63.8	82.7	93.5	72.5	85.9	95.2	85.7	91.8
06	WOOD & PLASTICS	94.2	21.1	56.4	102.9	109.1	106.1	102.9	109.1	106.1	100.1	35.1	66.5	98.2	35.1	65.5	96.8	44.1	69.6
07	THERMAL & MOISTURE PROTECTION	168.9	27.1	101.7	99.7	112.4	105.7	98.5	112.4	105.1	97.8	30.7	66.0	97.4	39.2	69.8	96.3	50.5	74.6
08	DOORS & WINDOWS	160.0	18.4	125.8	103.6	111.1	105.4	103.6	111.1	105.4	93.2	30.0	77.9	93.2	35.0	79.2	97.1	46.9	85.0
09200	PLASTER & GYPSUM BOARD	225.4	18.2	98.8	98.2	108.2	104.3	98.2	108.2	104.3	102.0	32.8	59.7	105.5	32.8	61.1	105.8	42.2	66.9
095,098	CEILINGS & ACOUSTICAL TREATMENT	364.2	18.2	135.9	99.5	108.2	105.2	102.6	108.2	106.3	88.2	32.8	51.7	88.2	32.8	51.7	92.2	42.2	59.2
09600	FLOORING	201.6	19.9	157.6	99.9	126.2	106.3	99.9	126.2	106.3	95.0	20.4	76.9	96.5	37.2	82.1	96.0	47.6	84.3
097,099	WALL FINISHES, PAINTS & COATINGS	209.3	18.4	98.3	95.6	121.2	110.5	95.6	121.2	110.5	106.5	31.4	62.8	106.5	31.4	62.8	106.5	46.0	71.3
09	FINISHES	242.3	20.9	129.4	99.1	115.1	107.3	99.5	115.1	107.5	95.8	31.8	63.1	96.4	34.7	65.0	95.6	44.8	69.7
10 - 14	TOTAL DIV. 10000 - 14000	100.0	24.9	84.1	100.0	112.7	102.7	100.0	112.7	102.7	100.0	63.2	92.2	100.0	47.8	89.0	100.0	66.1	92.8
15	MECHANICAL	106.9	18.8	66.1	99.8	102.0	100.9	99.8	102.0	100.9	97.0	37.4	69.4	97.0	31.2	66.5	100.1	52.6	78.1
16	ELECTRICAL	144.8	16.1	56.3	99.1	97.0	97.6	98.6	97.0	97.5	95.5	19.0	42.9	101.3	31.6	53.4	98.5	39.6	58.0
01 - 16	WEIGHTED AVERAGE	143.2	29.0	87.6	99.8	108.1	103.8	100.1	108.1	104.0	95.6	38.6	67.8	96.2	42.5	70.1	95.9	54.6	75.8

		SOUTH CAROLINA															SOUTH DAKOTA		
	DIVISION	COLUMBIA			FLORENCE			GREENVILLE			ROCK HILL			SPARTANBURG			ABERDEEN		
		290 - 292			295			296			297			293			574		
		MAT.	INST.	TOTAL	MAT.	INST.	TOTAL	MAT.	INST.	TOTAL	MAT.	INST.	TOTAL	MAT.	INST.	TOTAL	MAT.	INST.	TOTAL
02	SITE CONSTRUCTION	93.3	82.0	84.6	104.4	82.0	87.2	99.4	81.6	85.8	97.4	81.3	85.0	99.2	81.6	85.7	81.5	95.2	92.0
03100	CONCRETE FORMS & ACCESSORIES	100.6	47.2	54.5	78.9	47.2	51.6	95.1	47.0	53.6	93.0	33.3	41.5	99.3	47.0	54.2	93.5	44.4	51.2
03200	CONCRETE REINFORCEMENT	93.1	65.5	77.4	92.8	65.8	77.4	92.7	46.4	66.3	93.5	22.0	52.8	92.7	46.4	66.3	107.2	57.5	78.9
03300	CAST-IN-PLACE CONCRETE	79.9	51.5	68.2	72.1	55.5	65.3	72.1	55.4	65.2	72.1	40.9	59.2	72.1	55.4	65.2	100.0	55.9	81.9
03	CONCRETE	89.0	54.1	71.6	91.3	55.5	73.4	90.0	51.8	70.9	88.2	36.3	62.2	90.3	51.8	71.1	96.1	52.2	74.2
04	MASONRY	83.7	37.3	55.2	71.2	42.6	53.6	69.3	42.6	52.9	91.1	27.9	52.2	71.2	42.6	53.6	108.5	57.9	77.4
05	METALS	95.2	85.0	91.5	94.2	85.5	91.0	94.0	78.7	88.5	93.5	67.3	84.0	94.0	78.7	88.5	107.4	72.7	94.9
06	WOOD & PLASTICS	103.3	48.0	74.7	79.3	48.0	63.1	96.3	48.0	71.3	94.3	33.9	63.1	101.0	48.0	73.6	96.4	42.1	68.3
07	THERMAL & MOISTURE PROTECTION	96.3	48.4	73.5	96.5	50.9	74.9	96.6	50.9	74.9	96.4	34.2	66.9	96.7	50.9	74.9	97.1	52.4	75.9
08	DOORS & WINDOWS	97.1	49.0	85.5	93.2	49.0	82.5	93.2	44.4	81.4	93.2	31.3	78.2	93.2	44.4	81.4	98.5	45.8	85.8
09200	PLASTER & GYPSUM BOARD	105.8	46.2	69.4	96.7	46.2	65.8	101.2	46.2	67.6	100.7	31.6	58.5	102.4	46.2	68.1	101.7	40.8	64.5
095,098	CEILINGS & ACOUSTICAL TREATMENT	92.2	46.2	61.9	89.5	46.2	60.9	88.2	46.2	60.5	88.2	31.6	50.8	88.2	46.2	60.5	110.8	40.8	64.6
09600	FLOORING	95.8	47.6	84.1	87.0	47.6	77.5	93.6	48.5	82.7	92.7	36.8	79.2	95.3	48.5	83.9	111.4	68.4	100.9
097,099	WALL FINISHES, PAINTS & COATINGS	106.5	46.0	71.3	106.5	46.0	71.3	106.5	46.0	71.3	106.5	31.4	62.8	106.5	46.0	71.3	102.5	40.9	66.7
09	FINISHES	95.5	47.1	70.8	91.7	47.1	68.9	93.9	47.2	70.1	93.4	34.0	63.1	94.7	47.2	70.5	106.7	48.2	76.8
10 - 14	TOTAL DIV. 10000 - 14000	100.0	66.6	93.0	100.0	66.5	92.9	100.0	66.6	92.9	100.0	63.1	92.2	100.0	66.6	92.9	100.0	67.9	93.2
15	MECHANICAL	100.1	44.3	74.3	100.1	44.3	74.3	100.1	44.3	74.3	97.0	22.3	62.4	100.1	44.3	74.3	100.2	41.6	73.1
16	ELECTRICAL	99.6	41.7	59.8	95.4	23.8	46.2	98.9	37.9	57.0	98.9	23.4	47.0	98.9	37.9	57.0	102.5	48.1	65.1
01 - 16	WEIGHTED AVERAGE	95.9	53.2	75.1	94.2	51.0	73.1	94.4	52.0	73.8	94.5	38.0	67.0	94.7	52.0	73.9	101.2	55.7	79.1

City Cost Indexes

SOUTH DAKOTA

DIVISION		MITCHELL 573 MAT.	INST.	TOTAL	MOBRIDGE 576 MAT.	INST.	TOTAL	PIERRE 575 MAT.	INST.	TOTAL	RAPID CITY 577 MAT.	INST.	TOTAL	SIOUX FALLS 570-571 MAT.	INST.	TOTAL	WATERTOWN 572 MAT.	INST.	TOTAL
02	SITE CONSTRUCTION	79.2	95.2	91.5	79.1	95.2	91.5	79.9	95.2	91.6	80.1	94.9	91.5	81.1	97.2	93.4	79.1	95.2	91.4
03100	CONCRETE FORMS & ACCESSORIES	92.4	44.3	50.9	81.0	44.4	49.4	91.7	46.7	52.9	104.8	42.6	51.1	91.7	44.9	51.4	76.5	44.4	48.8
03200	CONCRETE REINFORCEMENT	106.5	57.5	78.5	109.3	57.5	79.7	106.7	64.5	82.6	100.1	64.6	79.9	100.1	65.4	80.3	103.7	57.5	77.3
03300	CAST-IN-PLACE CONCRETE	97.2	55.9	80.2	97.2	55.9	80.2	97.2	51.8	78.4	96.5	48.7	76.8	100.5	56.1	82.2	97.2	55.9	80.2
03	CONCRETE	93.9	52.1	73.0	93.4	52.2	72.8	93.8	53.1	73.5	93.6	50.2	71.9	94.7	54.0	74.3	92.4	52.2	72.3
04	MASONRY	96.0	57.9	72.6	105.8	57.9	76.4	105.8	48.8	70.8	105.9	46.0	69.1	103.0	64.1	79.1	130.2	57.9	85.8
05	METALS	106.6	72.6	94.3	106.8	72.7	94.5	107.3	75.0	95.7	109.4	75.3	97.1	109.9	76.8	98.0	106.6	72.7	94.4
06	WOOD & PLASTICS	95.3	42.1	67.8	83.6	42.1	62.1	94.5	45.5	69.1	105.0	42.6	72.7	94.5	42.1	67.4	79.0	42.1	59.9
07	THERMAL & MOISTURE PROTECTION	96.8	52.4	75.8	96.9	52.4	75.8	97.2	50.3	75.0	97.7	49.2	74.7	97.2	56.0	77.6	96.5	52.4	75.6
08	DOORS & WINDOWS	96.8	45.8	84.5	100.0	45.8	86.9	102.0	49.8	89.4	103.0	48.2	89.8	103.0	47.9	89.7	96.8	45.8	84.5
09200	PLASTER & GYPSUM BOARD	101.0	40.8	64.2	97.4	40.8	62.8	100.6	44.3	66.2	101.6	41.3	64.7	101.6	40.8	64.5	95.4	40.8	62.0
095,098	CEILINGS & ACOUSTICAL TREATMENT	109.4	40.8	64.2	110.8	40.8	64.6	109.4	44.3	66.5	114.9	41.3	66.3	114.9	40.8	66.0	109.4	40.8	64.2
09600	FLOORING	110.8	68.4	100.5	105.3	68.4	96.3	110.5	48.7	95.5	110.5	57.3	97.6	110.5	79.3	102.9	103.4	68.4	94.9
097,099	WALL FINISHES, PAINTS & COATINGS	102.5	40.9	66.7	102.5	40.9	66.7	102.5	40.9	66.7	102.5	40.9	66.7	102.5	40.9	66.7	102.5	40.9	66.7
09	FINISHES	106.1	48.2	76.5	103.9	48.2	75.5	105.9	46.2	75.4	107.1	44.7	75.3	107.1	50.4	78.2	102.8	48.2	74.9
10-14	TOTAL DIV. 10000-14000	100.0	58.8	91.3	100.0	67.9	93.2	100.0	68.4	93.3	100.0	65.7	92.8	100.0	68.0	93.2	100.0	67.9	93.2
15	MECHANICAL	97.1	41.6	71.4	97.1	41.6	71.4	100.2	41.6	73.1	100.2	38.6	71.7	100.2	41.7	73.1	97.1	41.6	71.4
16	ELECTRICAL	100.0	48.1	64.3	102.5	48.1	65.1	96.1	56.4	68.8	96.9	56.4	69.1	95.8	72.1	79.5	98.6	48.1	63.9
01-16	WEIGHTED AVERAGE	98.9	55.5	77.8	99.7	55.7	78.3	100.6	56.5	79.1	101.3	54.9	78.7	101.2	61.6	81.9	100.1	55.7	78.5

TENNESSEE

DIVISION		CHATTANOOGA 373-374 MAT.	INST.	TOTAL	COLUMBIA 384 MAT.	INST.	TOTAL	COOKEVILLE 385 MAT.	INST.	TOTAL	JACKSON 383 MAT.	INST.	TOTAL	JOHNSON CITY 376 MAT.	INST.	TOTAL	KNOXVILLE 377-379 MAT.	INST.	TOTAL
02	SITE CONSTRUCTION	104.9	97.6	99.3	96.7	84.5	87.3	103.6	84.9	89.3	105.0	95.6	97.8	114.5	86.3	92.9	92.0	86.3	87.6
03100	CONCRETE FORMS & ACCESSORIES	95.4	52.5	58.4	77.6	56.7	59.5	77.9	29.1	35.8	86.2	38.0	44.6	79.2	54.7	58.1	94.3	54.8	60.2
03200	CONCRETE REINFORCEMENT	94.0	49.4	68.5	99.4	51.5	72.1	99.4	23.3	56.0	99.7	48.8	70.7	98.0	49.6	70.4	94.0	49.6	68.7
03300	CAST-IN-PLACE CONCRETE	103.0	54.6	83.0	92.0	55.7	77.0	104.2	37.0	76.5	101.7	38.8	75.8	82.8	61.0	73.8	96.7	55.9	79.9
03	CONCRETE	93.9	54.6	74.3	92.4	57.2	74.8	102.2	33.4	67.9	94.0	42.6	68.3	99.2	57.8	78.5	91.0	56.1	73.5
04	MASONRY	96.9	51.8	69.2	110.4	52.1	74.6	105.1	26.0	56.5	110.8	31.1	61.8	107.5	51.6	73.1	74.9	51.6	60.6
05	METALS	97.1	83.1	92.0	93.2	82.7	89.4	93.3	68.7	84.4	95.1	79.7	89.6	94.7	82.8	90.4	97.3	82.9	92.1
06	WOOD & PLASTICS	95.8	53.5	73.9	68.7	64.2	66.4	68.9	30.0	48.8	83.8	40.2	61.3	71.4	56.8	63.8	86.7	56.8	71.2
07	THERMAL & MOISTURE PROTECTION	103.0	54.5	80.0	93.4	52.5	74.0	94.0	33.7	65.4	100.7	40.3	72.0	97.3	55.3	77.4	94.9	54.8	75.8
08	DOORS & WINDOWS	100.7	52.8	89.2	92.9	56.8	84.2	93.0	27.9	77.3	101.7	44.1	87.8	97.0	56.2	87.1	93.7	56.2	84.6
09200	PLASTER & GYPSUM BOARD	95.1	52.7	69.2	99.2	63.6	77.5	99.2	28.4	55.9	98.3	38.9	62.0	104.7	56.0	74.9	110.4	56.0	77.2
095,098	CEILINGS & ACOUSTICAL TREATMENT	93.8	52.7	66.6	83.9	63.6	70.5	83.9	28.4	47.3	95.8	38.9	58.2	85.3	56.0	66.0	90.7	56.0	67.8
09600	FLOORING	99.4	59.1	89.7	89.2	30.7	75.0	89.3	28.6	74.6	90.7	28.6	75.7	92.7	60.8	84.9	98.2	60.8	89.1
097,099	WALL FINISHES, PAINTS & COATINGS	104.9	49.9	72.9	93.8	29.4	56.3	93.8	27.4	55.2	94.4	32.6	58.5	102.8	63.9	80.2	102.8	63.9	80.2
09	FINISHES	97.5	53.5	75.0	95.6	50.5	72.6	96.0	28.9	61.8	95.9	36.3	65.5	98.1	57.0	77.1	92.8	57.0	74.5
10-14	TOTAL DIV. 10000-14000	100.0	65.3	92.7	100.0	62.0	92.0	100.0	28.4	84.9	100.0	58.9	91.3	100.0	68.8	93.4	100.0	68.9	93.4
15	MECHANICAL	100.2	50.7	77.3	98.2	46.4	74.2	98.2	27.2	65.4	100.1	44.8	74.5	99.8	56.1	79.6	99.8	59.8	81.3
16	ELECTRICAL	103.5	63.9	76.3	91.2	33.5	51.5	94.0	25.6	47.0	99.3	36.6	56.2	90.9	39.1	55.3	100.4	62.8	74.5
01-16	WEIGHTED AVERAGE	98.9	62.1	81.0	95.7	54.9	75.9	97.0	37.6	68.1	98.8	49.2	74.7	98.3	58.9	79.1	95.0	63.3	79.6

TENNESSEE / TEXAS

DIVISION		MCKENZIE 382 MAT.	INST.	TOTAL	MEMPHIS 375,380-381 MAT.	INST.	TOTAL	NASHVILLE 370-372 MAT.	INST.	TOTAL	ABILENE 795-796 MAT.	INST.	TOTAL	AMARILLO 790-791 MAT.	INST.	TOTAL	AUSTIN 786-787 MAT.	INST.	TOTAL
02	SITE CONSTRUCTION	102.8	85.1	89.3	98.7	92.1	93.7	95.6	100.3	99.2	103.0	85.1	89.3	103.1	86.1	90.1	88.1	85.9	86.4
03100	CONCRETE FORMS & ACCESSORIES	88.2	28.8	36.9	94.7	62.7	67.1	95.6	68.3	72.0	96.6	48.8	55.3	100.2	58.0	63.8	98.6	62.8	67.7
03200	CONCRETE REINFORCEMENT	100.3	23.0	56.3	92.3	64.2	76.3	95.0	63.1	76.8	95.5	59.9	75.2	95.5	59.5	75.0	94.0	59.9	74.6
03300	CAST-IN-PLACE CONCRETE	102.0	37.5	75.4	95.9	66.5	83.8	91.4	65.5	80.7	98.2	47.6	77.3	101.8	56.0	82.9	91.9	57.9	77.9
03	CONCRETE	101.1	33.4	67.3	89.9	66.2	78.1	89.4	68.0	78.7	90.6	51.5	71.0	92.6	58.4	75.5	82.6	61.1	71.8
04	MASONRY	108.2	42.5	67.8	84.2	62.5	70.8	85.5	64.9	72.9	100.2	53.0	71.2	104.0	47.8	69.4	97.2	53.9	70.6
05	METALS	93.3	70.0	84.9	96.5	93.9	95.6	99.7	91.8	96.9	96.6	70.3	87.1	96.6	70.0	87.0	95.7	69.6	86.3
06	WOOD & PLASTICS	79.9	29.2	53.7	93.4	64.5	78.5	90.9	70.5	80.4	97.2	49.5	72.5	100.4	60.6	79.8	98.2	66.2	81.6
07	THERMAL & MOISTURE PROTECTION	94.1	36.3	66.6	99.1	64.8	82.8	98.4	66.2	83.1	98.3	55.7	78.1	100.4	52.1	77.5	95.2	59.3	78.2
08	DOORS & WINDOWS	93.0	27.7	77.2	98.8	67.2	91.2	96.0	68.9	89.5	93.6	52.2	83.6	93.6	55.4	84.4	95.9	63.7	88.1
09200	PLASTER & GYPSUM BOARD	103.1	27.5	56.8	103.2	63.6	79.0	102.4	70.1	82.7	97.6	48.8	67.8	97.6	60.3	74.8	98.7	66.0	78.7
095,098	CEILINGS & ACOUSTICAL TREATMENT	83.9	27.5	46.7	89.2	63.6	72.3	87.7	70.1	76.1	101.1	48.8	66.6	101.1	60.3	74.2	90.6	66.0	74.3
09600	FLOORING	92.9	58.8	84.7	92.0	54.0	82.8	103.4	73.4	96.1	118.7	64.7	105.6	118.5	52.4	102.4	98.3	60.3	89.0
097,099	WALL FINISHES, PAINTS & COATINGS	93.8	31.2	57.4	93.5	64.8	76.8	109.1	60.2	80.7	94.4	64.6	77.1	94.4	46.1	66.3	95.0	51.8	69.9
09	FINISHES	97.7	34.8	65.6	93.2	60.9	76.7	101.7	68.6	84.8	102.8	53.3	77.6	102.8	55.6	78.8	93.9	61.3	77.3
10-14	TOTAL DIV. 10000-14000	100.0	26.9	84.6	100.0	71.7	94.0	100.0	73.1	94.3	100.0	68.3	93.3	100.0	70.7	93.8	100.0	71.3	93.9
15	MECHANICAL	98.2	24.8	64.3	100.0	66.7	84.6	100.0	66.2	84.4	100.1	43.1	73.7	100.1	59.3	81.2	99.7	67.7	84.9
16	ELECTRICAL	93.6	21.2	43.8	99.1	93.8	95.4	101.6	70.3	80.1	97.7	46.2	62.3	98.7	65.6	75.9	97.1	72.5	80.2
01-16	WEIGHTED AVERAGE	97.3	38.9	68.9	96.3	75.2	86.0	97.4	73.3	85.7	97.7	54.9	76.9	98.4	62.3	80.8	95.1	67.2	81.5

COST INDEXES

645

TEXAS

DIVISION		BEAUMONT 776 - 777			BROWNWOOD 768			BRYAN 778			CHILDRESS 792			CORPUS CHRISTI 783 - 784			DALLAS 752 - 753		
		MAT.	INST.	TOTAL	MAT.	INST.	TOTAL	MAT.	INST.	TOTAL	MAT.	INST.	TOTAL	MAT.	INST.	TOTAL	MAT.	INST.	TOTAL
02	SITE CONSTRUCTION	96.7	87.4	89.6	110.5	84.2	90.3	86.6	88.1	87.7	116.2	84.8	92.1	123.0	81.1	90.9	131.9	82.5	94.1
03100	CONCRETE FORMS & ACCESSORIES	105.9	64.3	70.0	93.9	35.1	43.2	79.6	50.1	54.2	94.2	56.7	61.9	102.4	47.0	54.6	95.4	62.6	67.1
03200	CONCRETE REINFORCEMENT	94.8	54.0	71.6	97.5	31.6	59.9	99.1	60.3	77.0	96.3	50.3	70.1	92.2	57.0	72.1	94.4	61.7	75.7
03300	CAST-IN-PLACE CONCRETE	91.6	64.1	80.2	105.8	43.7	80.2	73.4	71.1	72.4	100.7	54.4	81.6	108.9	53.6	86.1	102.1	62.4	85.7
03	CONCRETE	88.7	63.0	75.9	97.8	38.8	68.3	73.9	60.4	67.2	98.4	55.5	76.9	93.0	53.2	73.1	89.7	64.0	76.8
04	MASONRY	103.3	65.3	80.0	126.7	41.5	74.3	141.1	67.4	95.8	104.2	46.8	69.0	87.9	52.8	66.4	95.9	64.1	76.3
05	METALS	95.9	70.7	86.8	94.8	55.8	80.7	96.2	73.6	88.0	94.6	65.1	84.0	95.2	84.1	91.2	96.5	86.6	92.9
06	WOOD & PLASTICS	107.6	66.1	86.1	94.6	33.9	63.2	74.2	43.9	58.6	95.6	60.6	77.5	109.5	47.1	77.2	99.9	63.9	81.2
07	THERMAL & MOISTURE PROTECTION	100.3	65.9	84.0	98.4	44.4	72.8	94.5	65.7	80.8	99.1	50.6	76.1	97.9	54.1	77.1	93.8	64.6	79.9
08	DOORS & WINDOWS	97.4	59.9	88.3	89.7	34.5	76.4	100.0	52.6	88.5	90.8	54.0	81.9	102.9	47.2	89.5	106.6	60.2	95.4
09200	PLASTER & GYPSUM BOARD	99.9	65.9	79.1	96.4	32.8	57.5	91.7	43.1	62.0	96.4	60.3	74.3	99.7	46.1	66.9	100.8	63.7	78.1
095,098	CEILINGS & ACOUSTICAL TREATMENT	108.4	65.9	80.3	95.5	32.8	54.1	101.2	43.1	62.9	95.5	60.3	72.3	96.0	46.1	63.1	102.1	63.7	76.8
09600	FLOORING	117.3	76.4	107.4	117.2	50.0	100.9	88.0	65.5	82.6	116.1	52.4	100.6	110.4	57.0	97.4	110.5	73.0	101.4
097,099	WALL FINISHES, PAINTS & COATINGS	91.0	62.2	74.3	94.4	37.1	61.1	86.6	70.3	77.2	94.4	49.0	68.0	109.1	46.2	72.6	101.8	60.4	77.7
09	FINISHES	98.7	66.5	82.3	101.6	37.8	69.0	86.1	53.6	69.5	101.8	55.5	78.2	100.3	48.2	73.8	105.7	64.4	84.6
10 - 14	TOTAL DIV. 10000 - 14000	100.0	74.9	94.7	100.0	55.9	90.7	100.0	71.8	94.0	100.0	69.8	93.6	100.0	70.6	93.8	100.0	72.7	94.2
15	MECHANICAL	100.0	65.7	84.1	97.0	36.7	69.1	96.9	74.3	86.4	97.0	58.2	79.0	99.7	56.9	79.9	99.9	65.8	84.1
16	ELECTRICAL	96.6	78.3	84.0	91.2	35.2	52.7	92.6	71.6	78.1	97.7	48.0	63.5	94.0	58.8	69.8	98.9	68.6	78.0
01 - 16	WEIGHTED AVERAGE	97.5	70.1	84.2	98.3	44.3	72.1	95.0	68.7	82.2	97.9	57.9	78.4	98.3	60.0	79.7	100.0	69.1	85.0

TEXAS

DIVISION		DEL RIO 788			DENTON 762			EASTLAND 764			EL PASO 798 - 799,885			FORT WORTH 760 - 761			GALVESTON 775		
		MAT.	INST.	TOTAL	MAT.	INST.	TOTAL	MAT.	INST.	TOTAL	MAT.	INST.	TOTAL	MAT.	INST.	TOTAL	MAT.	INST.	TOTAL
02	SITE CONSTRUCTION	108.8	84.7	90.3	111.2	77.7	85.6	114.0	84.3	91.3	103.5	85.1	89.4	102.8	85.4	89.5	127.5	85.4	95.3
03100	CONCRETE FORMS & ACCESSORIES	90.5	30.9	39.1	105.4	46.5	54.6	97.1	41.4	49.1	97.3	57.5	63.0	99.3	62.2	67.3	90.0	71.5	74.1
03200	CONCRETE REINFORCEMENT	94.0	22.0	52.9	97.2	59.7	75.8	98.2	52.1	71.9	95.5	59.9	75.2	95.5	61.4	76.1	98.8	62.5	78.1
03300	CAST-IN-PLACE CONCRETE	117.3	38.0	84.6	81.8	58.0	72.0	111.9	44.6	84.1	100.5	43.1	76.8	96.5	57.6	80.5	97.4	72.4	87.1
03	CONCRETE	108.0	33.1	70.5	77.3	55.1	66.2	102.5	45.4	74.0	91.8	53.6	72.7	89.9	61.1	75.5	90.3	71.8	81.1
04	MASONRY	103.0	36.3	62.0	134.6	47.6	81.1	99.0	41.7	63.8	99.0	52.3	70.3	95.1	60.3	73.7	98.5	67.4	79.4
05	METALS	94.4	50.4	78.5	94.4	85.5	91.2	94.6	59.1	81.8	96.5	68.7	86.4	96.4	71.4	87.4	97.8	92.1	95.8
06	WOOD & PLASTICS	87.7	31.6	58.7	109.4	47.1	77.2	102.9	42.7	71.7	98.5	62.4	79.8	105.3	63.9	83.9	89.0	72.7	80.5
07	THERMAL & MOISTURE PROTECTION	95.4	36.2	67.3	97.5	53.0	76.4	99.0	45.0	73.4	97.9	58.9	79.4	98.8	60.0	80.4	92.8	68.7	81.4
08	DOORS & WINDOWS	96.7	26.6	79.8	106.4	50.8	93.0	77.7	38.6	68.2	93.6	55.7	84.5	87.1	60.2	80.6	105.4	68.6	96.6
09200	PLASTER & GYPSUM BOARD	96.0	30.3	55.8	100.6	46.2	67.4	96.4	41.8	63.0	97.6	62.1	75.9	97.6	63.7	76.9	96.6	72.5	81.9
095,098	CEILINGS & ACOUSTICAL TREATMENT	87.8	30.3	49.9	106.4	46.2	66.7	95.5	41.8	60.0	101.1	62.1	75.4	101.1	63.7	76.4	104.0	72.5	83.2
09600	FLOORING	95.3	24.0	78.0	109.1	58.4	96.8	152.5	36.0	124.3	118.7	66.7	106.1	153.9	58.4	130.7	103.4	65.5	94.2
097,099	WALL FINISHES, PAINTS & COATINGS	95.0	32.6	58.8	105.7	37.5	66.1	95.6	38.7	62.5	94.4	44.3	65.3	95.6	65.8	78.3	99.6	65.0	79.5
09	FINISHES	93.2	30.5	61.2	98.5	47.3	72.3	113.5	40.6	76.3	102.8	58.5	80.2	114.5	62.0	87.8	96.2	69.8	82.7
10 - 14	TOTAL DIV. 10000 - 14000	100.0	52.8	90.0	100.0	58.2	91.2	100.0	56.6	90.8	100.0	71.3	93.9	100.0	72.7	94.2	100.0	78.3	95.4
15	MECHANICAL	96.5	23.9	62.9	97.0	58.7	79.3	97.0	37.1	69.3	100.1	42.4	73.4	100.1	65.2	84.0	96.8	74.3	86.4
16	ELECTRICAL	97.1	25.0	47.5	93.6	57.0	68.4	91.2	43.8	58.6	96.5	61.7	72.6	96.5	66.3	75.7	95.5	69.2	77.4
01 - 16	WEIGHTED AVERAGE	98.2	37.0	68.4	98.1	59.2	79.2	97.4	47.7	73.2	97.7	58.6	78.7	97.8	66.4	82.6	98.1	74.4	86.5

TEXAS

DIVISION		GIDDINGS 789			GREENVILLE 754			HOUSTON 770 - 772			HUNTSVILLE 773			LAREDO 780			LONGVIEW 756		
		MAT.	INST.	TOTAL	MAT.	INST.	TOTAL	MAT.	INST.	TOTAL	MAT.	INST.	TOTAL	MAT.	INST.	TOTAL	MAT.	INST.	TOTAL
02	SITE CONSTRUCTION	94.9	85.1	87.4	122.6	77.9	88.4	124.5	85.1	94.4	106.9	86.2	91.1	88.2	85.7	86.2	113.8	85.8	92.3
03100	CONCRETE FORMS & ACCESSORIES	88.9	41.5	48.0	84.4	34.6	41.5	92.8	71.6	74.5	89.4	43.4	49.7	90.2	47.1	53.0	78.6	35.8	41.7
03200	CONCRETE REINFORCEMENT	96.9	53.0	71.9	97.2	31.7	59.8	97.5	62.6	77.6	100.4	36.0	63.7	94.0	57.1	73.0	96.4	29.0	57.9
03300	CAST-IN-PLACE CONCRETE	99.4	45.0	76.9	93.0	43.1	72.4	94.4	72.4	85.3	100.9	53.6	81.4	83.9	60.4	74.2	108.1	39.9	80.0
03	CONCRETE	88.6	45.7	67.1	82.9	39.4	61.2	88.0	71.9	80.0	95.8	46.8	71.3	82.2	54.4	68.3	96.4	37.2	66.8
04	MASONRY	110.1	41.6	68.0	141.5	40.3	79.3	98.3	68.8	80.2	140.8	41.9	80.0	96.9	55.3	71.3	138.5	37.2	76.3
05	METALS	93.9	58.9	81.3	94.3	70.4	85.7	100.2	92.3	97.4	96.1	59.9	83.0	96.5	65.2	85.2	87.4	54.2	75.4
06	WOOD & PLASTICS	87.5	42.7	64.4	88.7	33.9	60.3	91.8	72.7	81.9	85.0	45.6	64.6	87.4	46.9	66.5	80.7	36.7	58.0
07	THERMAL & MOISTURE PROTECTION	95.8	45.1	71.7	93.4	45.4	70.6	92.7	69.6	81.7	95.9	46.9	72.7	94.1	57.0	76.5	93.8	39.0	67.8
08	DOORS & WINDOWS	96.0	38.7	82.1	107.4	34.5	89.8	105.7	68.6	96.8	100.0	38.6	85.2	96.5	45.9	84.3	96.5	33.2	81.2
09200	PLASTER & GYPSUM BOARD	94.9	41.8	62.4	97.3	32.8	57.9	98.2	72.5	82.5	95.2	44.8	64.4	96.5	46.1	65.7	93.9	35.9	58.4
095,098	CEILINGS & ACOUSTICAL TREATMENT	86.5	41.8	57.0	99.4	32.8	55.5	108.0	72.5	84.6	101.2	44.8	64.0	90.6	46.1	61.2	95.3	35.9	56.1
09600	FLOORING	94.5	36.0	80.3	105.0	58.4	93.7	104.7	65.5	95.2	91.7	36.0	78.2	95.1	57.0	85.9	112.0	51.4	97.3
097,099	WALL FINISHES, PAINTS & COATINGS	95.0	32.6	58.8	101.8	31.9	61.2	99.6	70.3	82.6	86.6	39.8	59.4	95.0	53.4	70.8	92.9	42.5	63.6
09	FINISHES	91.8	40.4	65.6	102.3	38.5	69.8	103.9	70.4	86.8	88.7	42.1	64.9	92.7	48.9	70.4	108.1	39.5	73.1
10 - 14	TOTAL DIV. 10000 - 14000	100.0	54.7	90.4	100.0	55.2	90.5	100.0	78.3	95.4	100.0	54.7	90.4	100.0	69.5	93.6	100.0	29.9	85.2
15	MECHANICAL	96.6	37.1	69.1	96.8	36.0	68.7	99.9	74.3	88.1	96.9	35.0	68.3	99.7	51.1	77.2	96.7	35.5	68.4
16	ELECTRICAL	92.0	43.8	58.9	93.9	35.2	53.5	98.5	71.6	80.0	92.6	43.0	58.5	97.1	69.0	77.8	96.2	62.5	73.1
01 - 16	WEIGHTED AVERAGE	95.2	47.7	72.1	99.7	45.0	73.1	99.8	75.0	87.7	98.7	47.8	73.9	95.0	59.8	77.8	99.3	47.5	74.1

TEXAS

DIVISION		LUBBOCK 793-794			LUFKIN 759			MCALLEN 785			MCKINNEY 750			MIDLAND 797			ODESSA 797		
		MAT.	INST.	TOTAL	MAT.	INST.	TOTAL	MAT.	INST.	TOTAL	MAT.	INST.	TOTAL	MAT.	INST.	TOTAL	MAT.	INST.	TOTAL
02	SITE CONSTRUCTION	133.7	83.3	95.1	106.8	85.8	90.8	127.9	81.0	92.0	117.4	78.8	87.8	138.2	83.3	96.1	103.0	85.6	89.7
03100	CONCRETE FORMS & ACCESSORIES	98.5	50.6	57.2	82.8	50.5	55.0	100.6	44.1	51.9	83.0	53.3	57.3	103.8	48.6	56.2	96.6	48.5	55.1
03200	CONCRETE REINFORCEMENT	94.8	59.5	74.7	97.9	40.1	65.0	93.6	56.9	72.7	97.2	59.7	75.8	100.6	59.4	77.1	97.7	59.3	75.8
03300	CAST-IN-PLACE CONCRETE	98.4	56.2	81.0	96.8	46.4	76.0	118.4	51.5	90.8	87.2	59.0	75.6	104.5	52.9	83.2	98.2	51.5	78.9
03	CONCRETE	89.4	56.3	72.8	89.2	48.3	68.7	99.0	51.1	75.1	78.6	58.3	68.5	94.6	54.3	74.4	90.8	52.6	71.7
04	MASONRY	99.7	44.1	65.5	109.5	49.1	72.3	101.8	52.8	71.7	151.0	51.8	90.0	117.1	44.2	72.3	100.2	44.2	65.7
05	METALS	100.7	86.3	95.5	94.5	64.0	83.5	94.2	80.9	89.4	94.2	83.6	90.4	99.0	86.0	94.3	96.8	69.3	86.9
06	WOOD & PLASTICS	100.5	52.0	75.4	89.3	52.9	70.4	107.4	43.8	74.5	87.3	53.8	70.0	106.2	49.4	76.8	97.2	49.3	72.4
07	THERMAL & MOISTURE PROTECTION	90.8	54.9	73.8	93.5	50.5	73.1	97.9	51.5	75.9	93.1	58.0	76.5	91.2	51.8	72.5	98.3	50.7	75.7
08	DOORS & WINDOWS	105.7	51.3	92.6	77.3	48.0	70.3	101.5	44.2	87.7	107.3	54.4	94.6	104.7	49.4	91.4	93.6	49.3	82.9
09200	PLASTER & GYPSUM BOARD	98.1	51.2	69.5	95.5	52.5	69.2	98.7	42.7	64.5	96.8	53.4	70.3	99.1	48.6	68.2	97.6	48.6	67.7
095,098	CEILINGS & ACOUSTICAL TREATMENT	103.8	51.2	69.1	89.8	52.5	65.2	93.3	42.7	59.9	99.4	53.4	69.0	98.2	48.6	65.5	101.1	48.6	66.5
09600	FLOORING	109.7	49.6	95.1	151.5	48.1	126.4	109.6	64.7	98.7	104.5	58.4	93.3	111.7	48.9	96.4	118.7	48.9	101.8
097,099	WALL FINISHES, PAINTS & COATINGS	106.4	41.4	68.6	92.9	47.9	66.8	109.1	36.6	67.0	101.8	59.8	77.4	106.4	40.9	68.3	94.4	41.4	63.6
09	FINISHES	104.4	49.0	76.1	119.9	49.9	84.2	99.7	46.8	72.7	101.8	54.7	77.8	104.5	47.4	75.4	102.8	47.4	74.5
10-14	TOTAL DIV. 10000-14000	100.0	69.1	93.5	100.0	70.2	93.7	100.0	69.4	93.5	100.0	60.2	91.6	100.0	70.8	93.8	100.0	70.3	93.7
15	MECHANICAL	99.7	54.2	78.7	96.7	41.5	71.2	96.6	40.1	70.5	96.8	61.0	80.2	96.6	46.4	73.4	100.1	46.4	75.3
16	ELECTRICAL	96.2	56.3	68.8	98.5	60.1	72.1	92.7	44.5	59.5	93.9	68.5	76.5	96.2	52.4	66.1	97.7	52.4	66.6
01-16	WEIGHTED AVERAGE	100.3	59.3	80.4	96.9	55.0	76.5	98.8	53.3	76.7	99.5	63.6	82.1	101.1	56.6	79.4	97.8	55.0	77.0

TEXAS

DIVISION		PALESTINE 758			SAN ANGELO 769			SAN ANTONIO 781-782			TEMPLE 765			TEXARKANA 755			TYLER 757		
		MAT.	INST.	TOTAL	MAT.	INST.	TOTAL	MAT.	INST.	TOTAL	MAT.	INST.	TOTAL	MAT.	INST.	TOTAL	MAT.	INST.	TOTAL
02	SITE CONSTRUCTION	116.4	85.3	92.6	106.2	85.2	90.1	87.7	90.1	89.6	92.7	84.9	86.7	99.8	86.0	89.2	113.2	86.0	92.4
03100	CONCRETE FORMS & ACCESSORIES	71.4	41.3	45.4	94.3	45.7	52.3	90.3	64.6	68.1	100.9	44.1	51.9	92.3	42.6	49.4	85.1	41.3	47.3
03200	CONCRETE REINFORCEMENT	95.6	53.0	71.3	96.8	59.2	75.4	94.0	58.2	73.6	97.8	59.6	76.1	95.5	60.6	75.6	96.4	61.1	76.3
03300	CAST-IN-PLACE CONCRETE	88.4	43.4	69.8	99.8	46.7	79.2	82.3	65.8	75.5	81.8	56.9	71.5	89.1	50.2	73.1	106.2	48.9	82.6
03	CONCRETE	88.6	45.0	66.8	93.1	50.6	71.9	81.4	64.4	72.9	80.0	52.5	66.3	83.3	49.7	66.5	96.0	48.8	72.4
04	MASONRY	103.7	43.6	66.8	123.5	41.9	73.4	96.7	62.3	75.6	133.9	52.4	83.8	154.8	42.1	85.5	145.1	51.1	87.3
05	METALS	94.3	57.7	81.1	94.9	67.2	84.9	97.1	71.0	87.7	94.7	68.4	85.2	87.3	68.1	80.4	94.1	69.2	85.1
06	WOOD & PLASTICS	77.1	42.4	59.2	94.9	47.1	70.2	87.4	65.7	76.2	106.6	42.7	73.5	95.3	41.9	67.7	91.5	39.4	64.6
07	THERMAL & MOISTURE PROTECTION	94.1	47.6	72.0	98.2	48.1	74.4	94.1	69.1	82.2	97.7	53.3	76.7	93.3	49.6	72.6	93.9	53.2	74.6
08	DOORS & WINDOWS	77.3	39.3	68.1	89.8	48.1	79.7	96.5	62.6	88.4	75.6	44.3	68.0	96.5	46.7	84.5	77.2	45.3	69.5
09200	PLASTER & GYPSUM BOARD	91.2	41.8	61.0	96.4	46.4	65.8	96.5	65.4	77.5	97.7	41.8	63.5	98.4	41.2	63.4	95.9	38.7	60.9
095,098	CEILINGS & ACOUSTICAL TREATMENT	89.8	41.8	58.1	95.5	46.4	63.1	90.6	65.4	73.9	95.5	41.8	60.0	93.9	41.2	59.1	89.8	38.7	56.1
09600	FLOORING	140.2	36.0	114.9	117.3	43.7	99.4	95.1	61.3	86.9	155.8	60.0	132.6	122.5	46.5	104.1	153.7	53.3	129.4
097,099	WALL FINISHES, PAINTS & COATINGS	92.9	38.7	61.4	94.4	42.7	64.4	95.0	53.4	70.8	95.6	42.7	64.8	92.9	49.9	67.9	92.9	49.9	67.9
09	FINISHES	116.3	40.0	77.3	101.4	44.7	72.5	92.7	62.6	77.4	113.7	45.9	79.1	111.3	43.3	76.6	121.1	43.3	81.4
10-14	TOTAL DIV. 10000-14000	100.0	56.0	90.7	100.0	67.0	93.0	100.0	74.9	94.7	100.0	56.5	90.8	100.0	66.6	93.0	100.0	66.3	92.9
15	MECHANICAL	96.7	37.1	69.1	97.0	42.2	71.6	99.7	73.3	87.5	97.0	44.2	72.5	96.7	48.3	74.3	96.7	62.2	80.8
16	ELECTRICAL	91.9	49.7	62.9	97.7	41.8	59.3	97.1	69.0	77.8	93.2	66.6	74.9	98.2	57.3	70.1	96.2	59.0	70.7
01-16	WEIGHTED AVERAGE	95.8	48.8	72.9	97.9	51.1	75.2	94.9	70.0	82.8	95.9	56.8	76.9	98.8	54.7	77.4	99.9	58.5	79.8

TEXAS / UTAH

DIVISION		VICTORIA 779			WACO 766-767			WAXAHACHIE 751			WHARTON 774			WICHITA FALLS 763			LOGAN 843		
		MAT.	INST.	TOTAL	MAT.	INST.	TOTAL	MAT.	INST.	TOTAL	MAT.	INST.	TOTAL	MAT.	INST.	TOTAL	MAT.	INST.	TOTAL
02	SITE CONSTRUCTION	133.6	81.7	93.9	101.7	85.4	89.2	120.7	78.6	88.5	142.0	83.6	97.3	102.5	85.1	89.2	96.0	99.8	98.9
03100	CONCRETE FORMS & ACCESSORIES	90.6	51.0	56.5	98.7	48.3	55.2	83.0	58.3	61.7	83.0	46.3	51.3	98.7	50.8	57.4	104.3	68.9	73.8
03200	CONCRETE REINFORCEMENT	93.8	40.2	63.3	95.5	59.7	75.1	97.2	59.9	75.9	98.3	61.7	77.4	95.5	51.6	70.5	100.6	75.7	86.4
03300	CAST-IN-PLACE CONCRETE	109.4	49.4	84.6	88.6	59.6	76.6	92.0	48.0	73.9	112.4	58.6	90.2	94.7	54.4	78.1	93.1	78.1	86.9
03	CONCRETE	97.5	50.9	74.2	86.0	55.4	70.7	81.9	56.7	69.3	101.0	55.7	78.4	89.0	53.4	71.2	112.3	73.7	93.0
04	MASONRY	115.2	49.2	74.6	97.3	56.3	72.1	142.0	53.2	87.4	99.6	43.0	64.8	97.7	54.2	71.0	122.1	72.5	91.6
05	METALS	96.1	84.8	92.0	96.6	70.0	87.0	94.3	83.7	90.5	97.8	87.9	94.3	96.5	70.7	87.2	105.3	78.3	95.6
06	WOOD & PLASTICS	92.7	53.3	72.3	104.1	45.8	74.0	87.3	62.3	74.3	81.8	48.2	64.5	104.1	51.8	77.1	90.1	67.4	78.4
07	THERMAL & MOISTURE PROTECTION	97.3	52.3	76.0	99.0	55.5	78.4	93.3	55.3	75.3	93.2	57.4	76.2	99.0	56.2	78.7	104.5	76.7	91.3
08	DOORS & WINDOWS	105.3	50.3	92.0	87.1	46.0	77.2	107.4	59.0	95.7	105.4	50.1	92.1	87.1	53.3	79.0	90.2	66.5	84.5
09200	PLASTER & GYPSUM BOARD	96.3	52.5	69.6	97.6	45.0	65.5	96.8	62.1	75.6	94.4	47.3	65.6	97.6	51.2	69.3	88.2	66.2	74.8
095,098	CEILINGS & ACOUSTICAL TREATMENT	109.4	52.5	71.9	101.1	45.0	64.1	99.4	62.1	74.8	104.0	47.3	66.6	101.1	51.2	68.2	104.7	66.2	79.3
09600	FLOORING	102.6	48.1	89.4	154.1	45.4	127.8	104.5	48.1	90.8	100.6	36.0	84.9	154.6	66.7	133.3	105.2	72.3	97.2
097,099	WALL FINISHES, PAINTS & COATINGS	99.8	47.9	69.6	95.6	42.7	64.8	101.8	47.9	70.5	99.6	39.8	64.8	97.5	67.7	80.1	108.7	57.7	79.1
09	FINISHES	95.3	50.3	72.3	114.5	46.2	79.7	102.0	55.8	78.5	95.8	43.8	69.3	114.8	55.4	84.5	100.0	67.8	83.6
10-14	TOTAL DIV. 10000-14000	100.0	60.4	91.6	100.0	70.3	93.7	100.0	61.5	91.9	100.0	58.3	91.2	100.0	68.7	93.4	100.0	78.5	95.5
15	MECHANICAL	96.9	41.5	71.3	100.1	62.9	82.9	96.8	59.5	79.5	96.8	34.3	67.9	100.1	52.0	77.9	100.1	74.4	88.2
16	ELECTRICAL	102.9	60.2	73.5	97.7	66.6	76.4	93.8	69.7	77.2	102.2	43.0	61.5	102.6	65.2	76.9	92.7	82.2	85.5
01-16	WEIGHTED AVERAGE	100.4	56.9	79.2	97.6	61.9	80.2	99.5	63.9	82.2	100.3	52.4	77.0	98.3	60.6	80.0	101.8	77.3	89.9

DIVISION		UTAH											VERMONT					
		OGDEN			PRICE			PROVO			SALT LAKE CITY			BELLOWS FALLS			BENNINGTON		
		842,844			845			846 - 847			840 - 841			051			052		
		MAT.	INST.	TOTAL	MAT.	INST.	TOTAL	MAT.	INST.	TOTAL	MAT.	INST.	TOTAL	MAT.	INST.	TOTAL	MAT.	INST.	TOTAL
02	SITE CONSTRUCTION	83.3	99.8	95.9	93.8	96.7	96.0	92.3	97.8	96.5	82.9	99.7	95.8	81.0	99.6	95.2	80.4	99.2	94.8
03100	CONCRETE FORMS & ACCESSORIES	104.3	68.9	73.8	107.4	39.2	48.5	106.1	69.0	74.1	102.9	69.0	73.6	99.7	33.4	42.5	96.6	30.7	39.8
03200	CONCRETE REINFORCEMENT	100.6	75.7	86.4	107.9	75.1	89.2	108.8	75.7	89.9	98.5	75.7	85.5	89.5	65.2	75.6	89.5	87.8	88.5
03300	CAST-IN-PLACE CONCRETE	94.5	78.1	87.8	93.2	54.1	77.1	93.2	78.1	87.0	102.2	78.1	92.3	94.6	50.2	76.3	94.6	41.7	72.7
03	CONCRETE	101.2	73.7	87.4	113.5	52.2	82.9	111.7	73.7	92.7	104.6	73.7	89.2	100.8	46.6	73.7	100.6	46.2	73.4
04	MASONRY	115.3	72.5	89.0	127.5	50.6	80.2	127.6	72.5	93.7	133.9	72.5	96.2	94.8	37.4	59.5	103.2	36.9	62.5
05	METALS	105.7	78.3	95.8	101.9	76.5	92.8	102.7	78.3	93.9	104.5	78.3	95.1	93.2	75.3	86.8	93.2	74.6	86.5
06	WOOD & PLASTICS	90.1	67.4	78.4	93.2	36.8	64.0	92.0	67.4	79.3	90.2	67.4	78.4	101.9	31.2	65.3	98.7	28.6	62.5
07	THERMAL & MOISTURE PROTECTION	102.9	76.1	90.0	107.0	61.4	85.4	107.0	76.7	92.6	106.0	76.7	92.1	98.8	61.0	80.9	98.7	50.9	76.0
08	DOORS & WINDOWS	90.2	66.5	84.5	94.5	48.3	83.4	94.5	66.5	87.8	90.2	66.5	84.5	106.7	43.8	91.5	106.7	39.5	90.5
09200	PLASTER & GYPSUM BOARD	88.2	66.2	74.8	87.6	34.6	55.2	87.1	66.2	74.3	88.2	66.2	74.8	96.4	27.8	54.5	95.1	25.1	52.3
095,098	CEILINGS & ACOUSTICAL TREATMENT	104.7	66.2	79.3	96.5	34.6	55.7	96.5	66.2	76.5	104.7	66.2	79.3	90.0	27.8	48.9	90.0	25.1	47.2
09600	FLOORING	105.2	72.3	97.2	106.4	53.7	93.6	106.0	72.3	97.8	104.8	72.3	96.9	99.9	45.3	86.7	98.7	45.3	85.8
097,099	WALL FINISHES, PAINTS & COATINGS	108.7	57.7	79.1	108.7	57.7	79.1	108.7	67.0	84.5	108.7	67.0	84.5	95.6	19.1	51.1	95.6	17.8	50.4
09	FINISHES	98.9	67.8	83.0	99.3	42.3	70.2	99.0	68.9	83.6	99.2	68.9	83.7	96.3	32.8	63.9	95.7	31.0	62.7
10 - 14	TOTAL DIV. 10000 - 14000	100.0	78.5	95.5	100.0	68.2	93.3	100.0	78.5	95.5	100.0	78.5	95.5	100.0	55.7	90.7	100.0	55.3	90.6
15	MECHANICAL	100.1	74.4	88.2	98.3	49.4	75.7	100.1	74.4	88.2	100.3	74.4	88.3	96.7	39.1	70.1	96.7	19.9	61.2
16	ELECTRICAL	92.7	82.2	85.5	100.4	54.0	68.5	93.2	82.2	85.6	93.6	82.2	85.7	104.0	21.4	47.2	104.0	24.7	49.5
01 - 16	WEIGHTED AVERAGE	99.6	77.3	88.7	102.4	57.6	80.6	102.1	77.2	90.0	101.1	77.4	89.6	98.2	46.6	73.1	98.5	42.6	71.3

DIVISION		VERMONT																
		BRATTLEBORO			BURLINGTON			GUILDHALL			MONTPELIER			RUTLAND			ST. JOHNSBURY		
		053			054			059			056			057			058		
		MAT.	INST.	TOTAL	MAT.	INST.	TOTAL	MAT.	INST.	TOTAL	MAT.	INST.	TOTAL	MAT.	INST.	TOTAL	MAT.	INST.	TOTAL
02	SITE CONSTRUCTION	81.8	99.6	95.4	83.3	101.5	97.3	80.1	100.0	95.3	82.6	101.3	96.9	83.3	101.5	97.3	80.2	99.9	95.3
03100	CONCRETE FORMS & ACCESSORIES	100.0	33.4	42.5	88.5	58.3	62.4	96.2	35.8	44.0	93.3	58.3	63.1	100.2	58.3	64.1	93.3	35.9	43.8
03200	CONCRETE REINFORCEMENT	88.6	87.9	88.2	111.9	66.6	86.1	90.3	42.4	63.0	89.0	66.6	76.2	111.9	66.6	86.1	88.6	65.4	75.4
03300	CAST-IN-PLACE CONCRETE	97.5	50.2	78.0	97.2	64.5	83.7	91.7	57.5	77.6	97.5	64.5	83.9	92.6	64.5	81.0	91.7	57.5	77.6
03	CONCRETE	103.4	50.4	76.9	105.3	62.5	83.9	98.2	45.6	71.9	103.0	62.4	82.7	103.9	62.5	83.2	97.8	49.5	73.7
04	MASONRY	102.5	37.4	62.5	96.3	70.1	80.2	102.8	44.0	66.6	83.9	70.1	75.4	84.0	70.1	75.4	129.9	43.9	77.1
05	METALS	93.2	75.3	86.7	98.6	72.6	89.2	93.2	60.5	81.4	93.2	72.6	85.7	98.0	72.6	88.8	93.2	60.6	81.4
06	WOOD & PLASTICS	102.3	31.2	65.5	88.6	56.9	72.2	96.5	34.1	64.2	91.8	56.9	73.7	102.5	56.9	78.9	91.8	34.1	62.0
07	THERMAL & MOISTURE PROTECTION	98.9	52.4	76.8	99.2	64.0	82.5	98.5	45.6	73.4	98.6	64.0	82.2	99.0	64.0	82.4	98.4	45.7	73.4
08	DOORS & WINDOWS	106.7	43.8	91.5	110.0	52.4	96.1	106.7	34.7	89.4	106.7	52.4	93.6	110.0	52.4	96.1	106.7	34.7	89.4
09200	PLASTER & GYPSUM BOARD	96.4	27.8	54.5	98.2	54.2	71.3	99.9	30.8	57.7	103.8	54.2	73.5	98.2	54.2	71.3	103.8	30.8	59.2
095,098	CEILINGS & ACOUSTICAL TREATMENT	90.0	27.8	48.9	102.6	54.2	70.7	90.0	30.8	51.0	90.0	54.2	66.4	102.6	54.2	70.7	90.0	30.8	51.0
09600	FLOORING	100.1	45.3	86.8	99.9	81.9	95.6	103.5	45.3	89.4	107.5	81.9	101.3	99.9	81.9	95.6	107.5	45.3	92.4
097,099	WALL FINISHES, PAINTS & COATINGS	95.6	19.1	51.1	95.6	46.9	67.3	95.6	31.3	58.2	95.6	46.9	67.3	95.6	46.9	67.3	95.6	31.3	58.2
09	FINISHES	96.4	32.8	64.0	99.1	61.2	79.7	97.9	36.2	66.4	100.0	61.2	80.2	99.0	61.2	79.7	99.8	36.2	67.3
10 - 14	TOTAL DIV. 10000 - 14000	100.0	55.7	90.7	100.0	96.7	99.3	100.0	56.6	90.8	100.0	96.7	99.3	100.0	96.7	99.3	100.0	56.6	90.8
15	MECHANICAL	96.7	39.1	70.1	99.8	60.1	81.4	96.7	48.7	74.5	96.7	60.1	79.8	99.8	60.1	81.4	96.7	48.8	74.5
16	ELECTRICAL	104.0	21.4	47.2	105.2	70.6	81.4	104.0	31.0	53.8	104.0	70.6	81.0	104.0	70.6	81.0	104.0	31.0	53.8
01 - 16	WEIGHTED AVERAGE	99.0	46.9	73.6	101.0	69.2	85.5	98.4	48.9	74.3	98.2	69.1	84.0	100.1	69.2	85.1	100.0	49.5	75.4

DIVISION		VERMONT			VIRGINIA													
		WHITE RIVER JCT.			ALEXANDRIA			ARLINGTON			BRISTOL			CHARLOTTESVILLE			CULPEPER		
		050			223			222			242			229			227		
		MAT.	INST.	TOTAL	MAT.	INST.	TOTAL	MAT.	INST.	TOTAL	MAT.	INST.	TOTAL	MAT.	INST.	TOTAL	MAT.	INST.	TOTAL
02	SITE CONSTRUCTION	84.1	99.5	95.9	112.6	83.8	90.5	123.0	83.4	92.7	106.3	81.6	87.4	110.9	84.5	90.7	111.3	82.9	89.6
03100	CONCRETE FORMS & ACCESSORIES	93.2	30.0	38.7	91.6	73.7	76.1	88.5	72.5	74.7	82.6	38.3	44.4	80.4	46.7	51.3	77.1	66.9	68.3
03200	CONCRETE REINFORCEMENT	89.5	31.5	56.4	82.7	91.3	87.6	93.3	77.9	84.5	93.4	77.7	84.5	92.8	76.3	83.4	93.3	70.8	80.4
03300	CAST-IN-PLACE CONCRETE	97.6	55.2	80.1	99.1	80.9	91.6	96.4	74.9	87.5	96.0	47.4	76.0	99.8	60.3	83.5	98.7	48.5	78.0
03	CONCRETE	105.2	40.3	72.7	96.6	80.6	88.6	104.2	75.5	89.8	100.3	50.9	75.6	100.8	58.9	79.8	97.4	62.6	80.0
04	MASONRY	115.2	36.9	67.1	83.9	70.7	75.7	95.0	68.2	78.6	83.8	36.8	54.9	105.3	50.3	71.5	94.9	41.0	61.8
05	METALS	93.2	75.3	79.5	95.2	97.4	96.0	94.2	92.4	93.5	93.3	87.0	91.0	93.5	91.4	92.8	93.6	88.1	91.6
06	WOOD & PLASTICS	95.1	28.3	60.6	95.7	74.4	84.7	91.3	74.4	82.6	82.8	38.1	59.7	80.4	45.9	62.6	79.0	74.4	76.6
07	THERMAL & MOISTURE PROTECTION	98.9	39.5	70.7	96.5	79.8	88.6	97.2	76.0	87.2	96.7	44.2	71.8	96.2	52.7	75.6	96.4	53.5	76.0
08	DOORS & WINDOWS	106.7	27.2	87.5	97.1	74.9	91.8	95.1	71.9	89.5	98.4	45.6	85.7	96.4	49.5	85.1	96.8	70.6	90.5
09200	PLASTER & GYPSUM BOARD	93.9	24.8	51.7	105.8	73.4	86.0	101.8	73.4	84.5	99.0	36.0	60.5	97.7	43.1	64.3	98.4	73.4	83.1
095,098	CEILINGS & ACOUSTICAL TREATMENT	90.0	24.8	47.0	92.2	73.4	79.8	89.5	73.4	78.9	88.2	36.0	53.7	88.2	43.1	58.4	89.5	73.4	78.9
09600	FLOORING	97.5	45.3	84.9	96.0	80.0	92.1	94.5	80.0	91.0	90.4	40.0	78.2	89.0	47.2	78.9	89.0	79.1	86.6
097,099	WALL FINISHES, PAINTS & COATINGS	95.6	25.0	54.5	117.5	77.8	94.4	117.5	93.3	103.4	106.5	38.8	67.2	106.5	65.0	82.4	117.5	46.4	76.2
09	FINISHES	95.4	31.7	62.9	96.1	74.9	85.3	95.4	76.2	85.6	92.1	37.9	64.5	91.5	47.7	69.2	92.2	68.2	80.0
10 - 14	TOTAL DIV. 10000 - 14000	100.0	55.2	90.5	100.0	86.0	97.0	100.0	85.0	96.8	100.0	69.2	93.5	100.0	80.7	95.9	100.0	68.3	93.3
15	MECHANICAL	96.7	30.5	66.1	100.1	84.6	92.9	100.1	83.2	92.3	97.0	54.8	77.5	97.0	66.1	82.7	97.0	46.2	73.5
16	ELECTRICAL	104.0	33.7	55.7	98.7	93.2	94.9	95.1	90.9	92.2	98.6	36.1	55.6	98.4	69.3	78.4	102.7	58.1	72.0
01 - 16	WEIGHTED AVERAGE	99.8	42.9	72.1	97.3	83.5	90.6	98.4	81.4	90.1	96.2	52.5	74.9	97.3	65.2	81.7	96.7	62.0	79.8

VIRGINIA

DIVISION		FAIRFAX 220 - 221			FARMVILLE 239			FREDERICKSBURG 224 - 225			GRUNDY 246			HARRISONBURG 228			LYNCHBURG 245		
		MAT.	INST.	TOTAL	MAT.	INST.	TOTAL	MAT.	INST.	TOTAL	MAT.	INST.	TOTAL	MAT.	INST.	TOTAL	MAT.	INST.	TOTAL
02	SITE CONSTRUCTION	122.3	83.5	92.6	107.1	84.0	89.4	110.7	83.0	89.5	104.1	81.1	86.5	119.3	83.0	91.5	104.9	81.7	87.2
03100	CONCRETE FORMS & ACCESSORIES	80.8	72.3	73.5	96.3	31.9	40.8	80.8	52.8	56.6	86.5	28.8	36.8	75.7	32.8	38.7	82.6	42.0	47.6
03200	CONCRETE REINFORCEMENT	93.3	88.6	90.6	93.4	57.2	72.8	94.0	90.2	91.8	92.1	57.4	72.3	93.3	70.6	80.4	92.8	77.8	84.2
03300	CAST-IN-PLACE CONCRETE	96.4	74.6	87.4	99.8	52.8	80.4	97.8	54.5	79.9	96.0	42.2	73.8	96.4	68.2	84.7	96.0	53.3	78.4
03	CONCRETE	103.6	77.3	90.5	100.1	45.7	72.9	97.1	62.1	79.6	98.9	40.9	69.9	101.2	54.5	77.8	98.7	54.6	76.7
04	MASONRY	95.0	67.6	78.2	90.4	38.6	58.6	93.5	42.2	61.9	85.2	34.4	54.0	94.4	39.2	60.5	98.7	40.0	62.6
05	METALS	93.6	96.6	94.7	93.5	71.3	85.5	93.6	94.8	94.0	93.3	73.7	86.2	93.5	88.0	91.5	93.4	87.3	91.2
06	WOOD & PLASTICS	82.8	74.4	78.4	98.2	30.6	63.2	82.8	54.0	67.9	86.7	28.1	56.4	77.5	27.0	51.4	82.8	41.5	61.4
07	THERMAL & MOISTURE PROTECTION	97.1	75.8	87.0	96.3	39.6	69.4	96.4	52.4	75.5	96.6	37.4	68.5	96.8	60.0	79.4	96.4	46.0	72.5
08	DOORS & WINDOWS	95.1	74.7	90.2	96.8	30.6	80.8	96.5	63.5	88.5	98.4	29.8	81.9	96.8	44.9	84.3	96.8	47.4	84.9
09200	PLASTER & GYPSUM BOARD	99.3	73.4	83.5	105.0	27.3	57.5	99.3	52.4	70.6	99.9	25.7	54.5	97.7	24.5	52.9	99.0	39.5	62.6
095,098	CEILINGS & ACOUSTICAL TREATMENT	89.5	73.4	78.9	88.2	27.3	48.0	89.5	52.4	65.0	88.2	25.7	46.9	88.2	24.5	46.2	88.2	39.5	56.0
09600	FLOORING	90.7	69.0	85.5	96.0	64.4	88.3	90.7	79.1	87.9	92.0	29.4	76.8	88.5	79.1	86.2	90.4	43.8	79.1
097,099	WALL FINISHES, PAINTS & COATINGS	117.5	81.2	96.4	106.5	41.1	68.5	117.5	46.4	76.2	106.5	38.8	67.2	117.5	50.6	78.6	106.5	38.8	67.2
09	FINISHES	93.7	72.8	83.0	94.7	38.7	66.1	92.9	56.3	74.2	92.6	29.7	60.5	92.3	41.5	66.4	92.0	41.3	66.1
10 - 14	TOTAL DIV. 10000 - 14000	100.0	84.8	96.8	100.0	56.3	90.8	100.0	71.8	94.1	100.0	53.7	90.2	100.0	68.9	93.4	100.0	70.6	93.8
15	MECHANICAL	97.0	83.0	90.5	97.0	32.1	67.0	97.0	77.3	87.9	97.0	32.4	67.1	97.0	47.3	74.0	97.0	65.4	82.4
16	ELECTRICAL	100.4	90.9	93.9	93.9	53.3	66.0	95.5	95.7	95.6	98.6	63.2	74.2	98.9	44.6	61.6	100.3	35.3	55.6
01 - 16	WEIGHTED AVERAGE	97.7	81.6	89.9	96.5	48.3	73.1	96.2	73.1	84.9	96.2	47.7	72.6	97.1	54.1	76.2	96.7	55.8	76.8

VIRGINIA

DIVISION		NEWPORT NEWS 236			NORFOLK 233 - 235			PETERSBURG 238			PORTSMOUTH 237			PULASKI 243			RICHMOND 230 - 232		
		MAT.	INST.	TOTAL	MAT.	INST.	TOTAL	MAT.	INST.	TOTAL	MAT.	INST.	TOTAL	MAT.	INST.	TOTAL	MAT.	INST.	TOTAL
02	SITE CONSTRUCTION	105.2	85.0	89.7	104.4	86.1	90.4	109.1	85.7	91.2	103.6	84.6	89.1	103.5	81.1	86.3	105.8	85.7	90.4
03100	CONCRETE FORMS & ACCESSORIES	95.2	53.7	59.4	100.2	53.8	60.2	86.9	63.0	66.3	81.6	53.7	57.5	86.6	28.8	36.8	96.1	63.0	67.5
03200	CONCRETE REINFORCEMENT	93.1	76.4	83.6	93.1	76.4	83.6	92.8	76.6	83.5	92.8	78.7	84.8	92.1	57.4	72.3	93.1	76.6	83.7
03300	CAST-IN-PLACE CONCRETE	97.0	59.9	81.7	99.8	59.9	83.4	99.8	62.1	84.2	96.0	61.8	81.9	96.0	42.2	73.8	103.1	62.1	86.2
03	CONCRETE	97.1	61.8	79.5	98.9	61.9	80.4	100.8	66.7	83.7	95.7	62.9	79.3	98.9	40.9	69.9	100.2	66.7	83.5
04	MASONRY	86.0	57.9	68.7	93.7	57.9	71.7	97.9	55.8	72.0	90.7	56.2	69.5	81.2	34.4	52.4	82.5	55.8	66.1
05	METALS	95.3	91.6	93.9	94.5	91.7	93.5	93.6	92.2	93.0	94.5	91.5	93.4	93.3	73.7	86.3	95.3	92.2	94.1
06	WOOD & PLASTICS	96.8	54.1	74.7	102.9	54.1	77.7	87.3	65.8	76.2	82.1	54.1	67.6	86.7	28.1	56.4	98.1	65.8	81.4
07	THERMAL & MOISTURE PROTECTION	96.3	53.6	76.0	96.1	53.6	76.0	96.3	56.6	77.4	96.2	53.2	75.8	96.6	37.4	68.5	95.8	56.6	77.2
08	DOORS & WINDOWS	97.1	55.0	87.0	97.1	58.2	87.7	96.5	60.3	87.7	97.2	58.7	87.9	98.5	29.8	81.9	97.1	60.3	88.2
09200	PLASTER & GYPSUM BOARD	105.8	51.6	72.6	105.8	51.6	72.6	100.1	63.6	77.8	98.0	51.6	69.6	99.9	25.7	54.5	105.8	63.6	80.0
095,098	CEILINGS & ACOUSTICAL TREATMENT	92.2	51.6	65.4	92.2	51.6	65.4	89.5	63.6	72.4	92.2	51.6	65.4	88.2	25.7	46.9	92.2	63.6	73.3
09600	FLOORING	96.0	46.6	84.0	95.8	46.6	83.9	91.6	69.3	86.2	88.1	46.6	78.1	92.0	29.4	76.8	95.8	69.3	89.4
097,099	WALL FINISHES, PAINTS & COATINGS	106.5	49.7	73.5	106.5	64.3	82.0	106.5	65.0	82.4	106.5	43.6	69.9	106.5	38.8	67.2	106.5	65.0	82.4
09	FINISHES	95.4	51.4	72.9	95.3	53.1	73.8	92.9	64.6	78.5	91.7	50.7	70.8	92.6	29.7	60.5	95.2	64.6	79.6
10 - 14	TOTAL DIV. 10000 - 14000	100.0	76.7	95.1	100.0	76.8	95.1	100.0	84.2	96.7	100.0	76.8	95.1	100.0	53.7	90.2	100.0	84.2	96.7
15	MECHANICAL	100.1	68.1	85.3	100.1	65.2	83.9	97.0	67.7	83.4	100.1	65.2	83.9	97.0	32.4	67.1	100.1	67.7	85.1
16	ELECTRICAL	98.6	62.7	73.9	98.6	64.7	75.3	98.9	69.3	78.6	95.7	64.7	74.4	98.6	63.2	74.2	99.6	69.3	78.8
01 - 16	WEIGHTED AVERAGE	97.2	66.4	82.2	97.8	66.6	82.6	97.1	70.1	84.0	96.4	66.1	81.6	95.9	47.7	72.4	97.5	70.1	84.2

VIRGINIA / WASHINGTON

DIVISION		ROANOKE 240 - 241			STAUNTON 244			WINCHESTER 226			CLARKSTON 994			EVERETT 982			OLYMPIA 985		
		MAT.	INST.	TOTAL	MAT.	INST.	TOTAL	MAT.	INST.	TOTAL	MAT.	INST.	TOTAL	MAT.	INST.	TOTAL	MAT.	INST.	TOTAL
02	SITE CONSTRUCTION	101.9	81.7	86.4	107.6	84.2	89.7	118.0	82.5	90.8	96.4	90.0	91.5	93.3	118.0	112.2	96.4	118.0	113.0
03100	CONCRETE FORMS & ACCESSORIES	95.0	41.8	49.1	86.2	41.3	47.5	78.8	44.1	48.9	113.3	85.8	89.5	109.7	100.7	102.0	92.5	101.0	99.8
03200	CONCRETE REINFORCEMENT	93.1	77.8	84.4	92.8	57.3	72.6	92.7	87.3	89.6	106.1	92.9	98.6	107.1	95.6	100.6	110.0	95.6	101.8
03300	CAST-IN-PLACE CONCRETE	100.5	53.3	81.0	99.8	53.7	80.8	96.4	66.9	84.2	111.8	93.2	104.1	93.1	105.8	98.3	97.7	108.0	101.9
03	CONCRETE	98.8	54.5	76.7	99.9	50.8	75.3	100.6	62.0	81.3	109.5	89.5	99.5	100.3	100.9	100.6	103.4	101.8	102.6
04	MASONRY	85.6	39.8	57.5	96.4	41.3	62.6	91.5	39.1	59.3	113.8	90.2	99.3	129.6	104.9	114.5	123.2	105.6	112.4
05	METALS	95.1	87.1	92.2	93.5	84.6	90.3	93.6	92.3	93.1	94.1	85.7	91.0	99.3	88.8	95.5	98.9	88.8	95.3
06	WOOD & PLASTICS	96.8	41.5	68.2	86.7	41.5	63.3	80.8	42.3	60.9	103.0	84.6	93.5	111.3	99.0	105.0	92.6	99.0	95.9
07	THERMAL & MOISTURE PROTECTION	96.2	47.5	73.1	96.2	46.9	72.8	97.0	61.4	80.1	169.9	84.2	129.2	107.4	100.5	104.2	107.0	100.7	104.0
08	DOORS & WINDOWS	97.1	47.4	85.1	96.8	44.8	84.2	98.5	56.6	88.4	115.7	86.2	108.5	101.5	97.2	100.5	101.4	97.7	100.5
09200	PLASTER & GYPSUM BOARD	105.8	39.5	65.3	99.9	38.5	62.4	98.8	40.3	63.1	123.8	84.1	99.5	96.8	98.6	97.9	93.4	98.6	96.6
095,098	CEILINGS & ACOUSTICAL TREATMENT	92.2	39.5	57.4	88.2	38.5	55.4	89.5	40.3	57.1	119.1	84.1	96.0	110.9	98.6	102.8	106.5	98.6	101.3
09600	FLOORING	96.0	41.8	82.9	91.4	42.2	79.5	90.0	79.1	87.3	112.2	72.2	102.5	123.6	107.9	119.8	116.0	107.9	114.0
097,099	WALL FINISHES, PAINTS & COATINGS	106.5	38.8	67.2	106.5	32.1	63.2	117.5	32.7	68.2	117.6	86.0	99.2	115.0	91.5	101.3	115.0	91.5	101.3
09	FINISHES	95.2	40.9	67.5	92.4	40.6	66.0	93.1	48.1	70.2	128.6	82.8	105.2	115.9	100.9	108.3	112.2	101.0	106.5
10 - 14	TOTAL DIV. 10000 - 14000	100.0	70.7	93.8	100.0	72.4	94.2	100.0	64.3	92.5	100.0	96.9	99.3	100.0	104.2	100.9	100.0	104.4	100.9
15	MECHANICAL	100.1	47.6	75.8	97.0	41.4	71.3	97.0	72.7	85.7	97.5	89.8	94.0	100.1	105.2	102.5	100.2	102.3	101.2
16	ELECTRICAL	98.6	41.3	59.2	96.6	45.2	61.3	96.2	40.4	57.8	101.5	96.6	98.1	106.3	93.6	97.6	106.0	99.0	101.2
01 - 16	WEIGHTED AVERAGE	97.3	53.4	75.9	96.7	52.4	75.1	97.0	60.9	79.5	107.6	89.6	98.8	104.1	101.4	102.8	103.6	102.0	102.8

WASHINGTON

DIVISION		RICHLAND 993			SEATTLE 980-981,987			SPOKANE 990-992			TACOMA 983-984			VANCOUVER 986			WENATCHEE 988		
		MAT.	INST.	TOTAL	MAT.	INST.	TOTAL	MAT.	INST.	TOTAL	MAT.	INST.	TOTAL	MAT.	INST.	TOTAL	MAT.	INST.	TOTAL
02	SITE CONSTRUCTION	97.2	90.7	92.2	97.3	115.7	111.4	98.0	90.7	92.4	96.1	118.0	112.9	108.8	103.4	104.7	108.2	117.5	115.3
03100	CONCRETE FORMS & ACCESSORIES	113.5	85.6	89.4	92.6	101.2	100.1	122.0	85.7	90.7	92.6	101.0	99.9	97.2	99.9	99.5	99.0	85.9	87.7
03200	CONCRETE REINFORCEMENT	101.1	92.7	96.4	101.1	95.7	98.0	101.8	92.9	96.7	101.1	95.6	98.0	104.0	95.5	99.2	105.3	95.0	99.4
03300	CAST-IN-PLACE CONCRETE	112.1	89.6	102.8	97.7	108.2	102.0	116.1	89.7	105.2	95.7	108.0	100.8	106.9	104.4	105.9	97.7	91.7	95.2
03	CONCRETE	109.2	88.2	98.7	102.3	102.0	102.2	111.7	88.2	99.9	101.3	101.8	101.6	112.9	100.3	106.6	112.1	89.3	100.7
04	MASONRY	113.8	87.2	97.4	123.1	105.6	112.3	115.5	90.2	99.9	123.0	105.6	112.3	124.7	105.7	113.0	125.7	92.5	105.3
05	METALS	93.1	85.4	90.4	100.8	90.9	97.2	92.9	85.7	90.3	100.3	88.8	96.2	98.8	91.5	96.2	98.7	86.4	94.3
06	WOOD & PLASTICS	103.2	84.6	93.6	93.9	99.0	96.5	113.5	84.6	98.5	92.6	99.0	95.9	90.7	98.6	94.7	99.2	83.9	91.3
07	THERMAL & MOISTURE PROTECTION	171.3	84.3	130.0	107.2	101.5	104.5	169.0	84.9	129.1	107.0	101.3	104.3	110.5	97.1	104.1	108.1	85.2	97.2
08	DOORS & WINDOWS	115.7	81.1	107.3	101.7	97.7	100.7	115.4	80.2	106.9	102.1	97.7	101.0	98.5	96.2	98.0	101.7	80.3	96.5
09200	PLASTER & GYPSUM BOARD	123.8	84.1	99.5	91.6	98.6	95.9	126.8	84.1	100.7	94.2	98.6	96.9	95.4	98.6	97.4	95.5	83.1	87.9
095,098	CEILINGS & ACOUSTICAL TREATMENT	122.2	84.1	97.0	112.0	98.6	103.2	122.2	84.1	97.0	113.7	98.6	103.8	122.0	98.6	106.6	106.5	83.1	91.1
09600	FLOORING	112.5	53.0	98.1	115.3	107.9	113.5	116.0	79.7	107.2	116.0	107.9	114.0	121.4	97.6	115.6	119.4	79.7	109.8
097,099	WALL FINISHES, PAINTS & COATINGS	117.6	76.4	93.6	115.0	91.5	101.3	117.6	80.9	96.3	115.0	91.5	101.3	123.1	75.3	95.3	115.0	80.9	95.2
09	FINISHES	129.2	77.8	103.0	112.8	101.0	106.8	130.8	83.8	106.8	113.6	101.0	107.2	114.0	96.6	105.1	114.5	83.6	98.8
10-14	TOTAL DIV. 10000-14000	100.0	92.4	98.4	100.0	104.5	100.9	100.0	92.4	98.4	100.0	104.4	100.9	100.0	99.2	99.8	100.0	99.7	99.9
15	MECHANICAL	100.7	99.9	100.4	100.1	111.8	105.5	100.7	89.8	95.7	100.2	102.3	101.2	100.4	101.4	100.8	97.1	89.7	93.6
16	ELECTRICAL	104.2	96.3	98.8	106.0	105.6	105.7	94.7	88.0	90.1	106.0	99.0	101.2	119.1	108.3	111.6	107.3	89.1	94.8
01-16	WEIGHTED AVERAGE	108.4	90.1	99.5	103.8	104.9	104.4	108.3	87.8	98.3	103.7	102.0	102.9	106.1	101.1	103.7	104.9	91.2	98.3

WASHINGTON / WEST VIRGINIA

DIVISION		YAKIMA 989			BECKLEY 258-259			BLUEFIELD 247-248			BUCKHANNON 262			CHARLESTON 250-253			CLARKSBURG 263-264		
		MAT.	INST.	TOTAL	MAT.	INST.	TOTAL	MAT.	INST.	TOTAL	MAT.	INST.	TOTAL	MAT.	INST.	TOTAL	MAT.	INST.	TOTAL
02	SITE CONSTRUCTION	99.3	117.3	113.1	98.2	85.2	88.3	97.9	85.2	88.2	104.0	84.9	89.3	100.6	86.0	89.4	104.6	84.9	89.5
03100	CONCRETE FORMS & ACCESSORIES	95.1	96.9	96.6	81.2	94.4	92.6	83.0	93.8	92.3	82.1	90.3	89.2	103.5	95.5	96.6	78.8	90.5	88.9
03200	CONCRETE REINFORCEMENT	103.6	94.8	98.6	91.8	85.5	88.2	91.8	72.4	80.7	92.3	97.6	95.3	93.1	85.7	88.8	92.3	93.0	92.7
03300	CAST-IN-PLACE CONCRETE	102.2	90.9	97.6	93.8	108.2	99.8	93.8	108.6	99.9	93.6	95.1	94.2	94.9	108.7	100.6	102.5	95.2	99.5
03	CONCRETE	106.8	93.8	100.3	94.4	98.3	96.4	94.6	95.7	95.1	97.8	94.2	96.0	96.6	99.0	97.8	101.5	93.5	97.5
04	MASONRY	114.9	87.1	97.8	87.0	96.1	92.5	82.9	96.1	91.0	92.9	92.2	92.5	84.4	98.1	92.8	94.4	92.2	93.1
05	METALS	99.2	85.4	94.2	93.5	101.1	96.2	93.5	96.1	94.4	93.6	105.5	97.9	95.3	101.8	97.6	93.6	104.1	97.4
06	WOOD & PLASTICS	95.3	99.0	97.2	82.4	95.5	89.2	84.4	95.5	90.1	83.5	89.5	86.6	106.2	94.9	100.4	79.9	89.5	84.9
07	THERMAL & MOISTURE PROTECTION	107.3	85.5	96.9	96.2	92.6	94.5	96.4	87.9	92.4	96.7	89.1	93.1	96.3	93.0	94.7	96.6	89.1	93.1
08	DOORS & WINDOWS	101.7	85.9	97.9	97.8	86.1	95.0	98.7	83.1	94.9	98.7	85.7	95.6	98.3	85.8	95.3	98.7	90.3	96.7
09200	PLASTER & GYPSUM BOARD	94.3	98.6	96.9	96.8	95.3	95.9	97.3	95.3	96.0	97.5	89.0	92.3	105.8	94.6	99.0	96.7	89.0	92.0
095,098	CEILINGS & ACOUSTICAL TREATMENT	109.6	98.6	102.4	88.2	95.3	92.8	88.2	95.3	92.8	89.5	89.0	89.2	92.2	94.6	93.8	89.5	89.0	89.2
09600	FLOORING	117.3	79.7	108.2	87.5	104.6	91.7	88.1	104.6	92.1	87.8	103.1	91.5	95.8	104.6	97.9	86.6	103.1	90.6
097,099	WALL FINISHES, PAINTS & COATINGS	115.0	80.9	95.2	106.5	56.1	77.2	106.5	56.1	77.2	106.5	93.3	98.8	106.5	100.2	102.8	106.5	93.3	98.8
09	FINISHES	113.5	92.2	102.7	90.4	92.1	91.3	90.7	92.1	91.4	91.2	93.2	92.2	95.4	98.1	96.7	90.6	93.2	91.9
10-14	TOTAL DIV. 10000-14000	100.0	101.5	100.3	100.0	86.3	97.1	100.0	86.2	97.1	100.0	97.7	99.5	100.0	99.4	99.9	100.0	97.7	99.5
15	MECHANICAL	100.2	100.4	100.3	97.0	81.7	89.9	97.0	77.0	87.7	97.0	93.2	95.2	100.1	89.1	95.0	97.0	93.3	95.3
16	ELECTRICAL	110.8	96.3	100.8	92.4	80.8	84.4	96.8	68.1	77.1	99.1	84.5	89.0	98.6	77.9	84.3	99.1	84.5	89.0
01-16	WEIGHTED AVERAGE	104.2	95.9	100.2	94.7	89.2	92.0	95.0	85.1	90.2	96.4	91.7	94.1	97.2	91.6	94.4	96.8	91.7	94.3

WEST VIRGINIA

DIVISION		GASSAWAY 266			HUNTINGTON 255-257			LEWISBURG 249			MARTINSBURG 254			MORGANTOWN 265			PARKERSBURG 261		
		MAT.	INST.	TOTAL	MAT.	INST.	TOTAL	MAT.	INST.	TOTAL	MAT.	INST.	TOTAL	MAT.	INST.	TOTAL	MAT.	INST.	TOTAL
02	SITE CONSTRUCTION	101.5	85.4	89.2	102.1	86.4	90.1	113.6	85.2	91.9	101.7	82.8	87.2	98.8	85.2	88.4	106.6	86.0	90.9
03100	CONCRETE FORMS & ACCESSORIES	81.3	90.6	89.3	95.9	97.8	97.5	79.3	94.1	92.1	81.2	40.0	45.6	79.3	90.5	89.0	84.4	94.2	92.8
03200	CONCRETE REINFORCEMENT	92.3	89.8	90.9	93.1	92.1	92.5	92.3	72.4	81.0	91.8	80.5	85.4	92.3	93.0	92.7	91.8	97.6	95.1
03300	CAST-IN-PLACE CONCRETE	97.9	107.4	101.8	102.3	109.6	105.3	93.9	108.1	99.8	98.3	54.7	80.3	93.5	95.2	94.2	95.6	97.9	96.6
03	CONCRETE	97.9	97.1	97.5	99.8	101.5	100.6	104.5	95.7	100.1	98.0	54.8	76.4	94.2	93.5	93.8	99.8	96.8	98.3
04	MASONRY	95.4	95.6	95.5	85.8	102.1	95.8	84.7	96.1	91.7	89.6	51.4	66.1	111.5	92.2	99.6	74.1	93.7	86.1
05	METALS	93.6	103.3	97.1	95.3	104.5	98.6	93.6	96.4	94.6	93.8	92.8	93.4	93.7	104.1	97.4	94.1	105.7	98.3
06	WOOD & PLASTICS	82.5	89.5	86.2	96.8	96.8	96.8	80.3	95.5	88.2	82.4	36.7	58.7	80.3	89.5	85.1	84.6	92.6	88.8
07	THERMAL & MOISTURE PROTECTION	96.3	91.7	94.1	96.5	94.7	95.6	97.4	92.6	95.1	96.6	61.8	80.1	96.4	89.1	93.0	96.6	90.7	93.8
08	DOORS & WINDOWS	96.6	83.8	93.5	97.1	88.2	95.0	98.7	83.1	94.9	100.0	50.2	88.0	100.1	90.3	97.7	97.7	86.3	95.0
09200	PLASTER & GYPSUM BOARD	97.1	89.0	92.2	105.8	96.5	100.1	96.7	95.3	95.8	97.1	34.5	58.8	96.7	89.0	92.0	99.7	92.2	95.1
095,098	CEILINGS & ACOUSTICAL TREATMENT	89.5	89.0	89.2	92.2	96.5	95.1	89.5	95.3	93.3	89.5	34.5	53.2	89.5	89.0	89.2	89.5	92.2	91.3
09600	FLOORING	87.6	104.6	91.7	95.8	114.2	100.3	86.7	104.6	91.0	87.5	81.3	86.0	86.7	103.1	90.7	91.1	97.9	92.7
097,099	WALL FINISHES, PAINTS & COATINGS	106.5	100.2	102.8	106.5	95.1	99.9	106.5	56.1	77.2	106.5	66.2	83.1	106.5	93.3	98.8	106.5	104.8	105.5
09	FINISHES	90.9	94.3	92.6	95.2	100.9	98.1	91.5	92.1	91.8	90.9	49.3	69.7	90.4	93.2	91.8	92.7	96.0	94.4
10-14	TOTAL DIV. 10000-14000	100.0	97.7	99.5	100.0	100.2	100.1	100.0	86.2	97.1	100.0	69.4	93.5	100.0	95.6	99.1	100.0	99.5	99.9
15	MECHANICAL	97.0	96.4	96.7	100.1	93.0	96.8	97.0	81.6	89.9	97.0	49.1	74.8	97.0	93.3	95.3	100.1	95.8	98.1
16	ELECTRICAL	99.1	79.9	85.9	98.6	90.8	93.2	92.4	68.1	75.7	102.1	36.5	57.0	99.4	84.5	89.1	99.4	97.2	97.8
01-16	WEIGHTED AVERAGE	96.2	92.2	94.2	97.4	96.0	96.7	96.5	86.2	91.5	96.5	56.1	76.8	96.9	91.7	94.4	96.4	95.4	96.0

City Cost Indexes

WEST VIRGINIA / WISCONSIN

	DIVISION	PETERSBURG 268			ROMNEY 267			WHEELING 260			BELOIT 535			EAU CLAIRE 547			GREEN BAY 541-543		
		MAT.	INST.	TOTAL	MAT.	INST.	TOTAL	MAT.	INST.	TOTAL	MAT.	INST.	TOTAL	MAT.	INST.	TOTAL	MAT.	INST.	TOTAL
02	SITE CONSTRUCTION	98.2	85.6	88.6	101.0	85.6	89.2	107.3	85.1	90.3	85.0	104.4	99.9	82.2	102.3	97.6	84.4	98.1	94.9
03100	CONCRETE FORMS & ACCESSORIES	83.4	83.5	83.5	78.2	82.8	82.2	86.6	90.6	90.1	96.4	95.9	96.0	95.9	95.5	95.6	115.7	95.2	98.1
03200	CONCRETE REINFORCEMENT	91.8	88.6	90.0	92.3	77.5	83.9	91.1	93.1	92.2	104.6	108.6	106.9	103.7	99.3	101.2	100.1	91.2	95.0
03300	CAST-IN-PLACE CONCRETE	93.5	93.1	93.3	97.9	90.1	94.7	95.6	101.9	98.2	101.0	97.5	99.5	97.8	92.3	95.5	101.2	97.9	99.8
03	CONCRETE	94.4	88.9	91.6	97.7	85.5	91.6	99.8	95.9	97.8	97.8	98.9	98.4	95.0	95.1	95.1	96.7	95.5	96.1
04	MASONRY	89.3	92.2	91.1	85.0	79.6	81.7	96.1	92.2	93.7	104.6	101.2	102.5	93.6	97.6	96.1	114.5	98.7	104.8
05	METALS	93.7	102.2	96.8	93.7	97.2	95.0	94.2	104.2	97.8	95.5	102.3	97.9	94.0	96.8	95.0	96.6	93.8	95.6
06	WOOD & PLASTICS	84.7	80.6	82.6	79.3	80.6	80.0	86.7	89.5	88.2	108.0	94.6	101.1	106.9	94.5	100.5	122.6	94.5	108.1
07	THERMAL & MOISTURE PROTECTION	96.5	81.1	89.2	96.5	76.7	87.1	96.8	89.9	93.5	95.8	102.1	98.8	96.7	89.7	93.4	99.4	90.1	95.0
08	DOORS & WINDOWS	100.1	80.5	95.4	100.0	78.1	94.7	98.6	90.3	96.6	104.6	100.1	103.5	104.3	91.3	101.2	102.8	87.9	99.2
09200	PLASTER & GYPSUM BOARD	97.5	79.8	86.7	96.2	79.8	86.2	100.1	89.0	93.3	107.3	95.0	99.7	112.5	94.8	101.7	96.4	94.8	95.4
095,098	CEILINGS & ACOUSTICAL TREATMENT	89.5	79.8	83.1	89.5	79.8	83.1	89.5	89.0	89.2	94.8	95.0	94.9	108.5	94.8	99.5	103.5	94.8	97.8
09600	FLOORING	88.5	103.1	92.1	86.4	79.8	84.8	92.0	103.1	94.7	91.9	90.4	91.5	92.6	72.3	87.7	111.5	102.2	109.2
097,099	WALL FINISHES, PAINTS & COATINGS	106.5	66.0	82.9	106.5	66.0	82.9	106.5	93.3	98.8	92.6	92.2	92.4	91.7	80.7	85.3	102.5	72.8	85.3
09	FINISHES	91.1	84.8	87.9	90.4	80.0	85.1	93.0	93.2	93.1	97.9	94.8	96.3	101.1	89.4	95.1	105.0	94.4	99.6
10 - 14	TOTAL DIV. 10000 - 14000	100.0	96.5	99.3	100.0	96.5	99.3	100.0	95.6	99.1	100.0	84.2	96.7	100.0	96.1	99.2	100.0	95.0	98.9
15	MECHANICAL	97.0	97.1	97.0	97.0	96.7	96.8	100.1	93.3	97.0	100.1	95.1	97.0	100.2	90.8	95.1	100.6	90.7	96.0
16	ELECTRICAL	104.8	85.6	91.6	103.5	85.6	91.2	94.6	91.0	92.1	91.4	93.0	92.5	105.0	88.2	93.5	96.1	89.3	91.5
01 - 16	WEIGHTED AVERAGE	96.2	90.1	93.2	96.2	87.2	91.8	97.6	93.1	95.4	98.5	97.5	98.0	98.6	93.3	96.0	100.4	93.3	97.0

WISCONSIN

	DIVISION	KENOSHA 531			LA CROSSE 546			LANCASTER 538			MADISON 537			MILWAUKEE 530,532			NEW RICHMOND 540		
		MAT.	INST.	TOTAL	MAT.	INST.	TOTAL	MAT.	INST.	TOTAL	MAT.	INST.	TOTAL	MAT.	INST.	TOTAL	MAT.	INST.	TOTAL
02	SITE CONSTRUCTION	89.2	101.7	98.8	76.6	102.3	96.2	84.6	103.2	98.8	84.4	105.0	100.2	85.7	93.5	91.7	79.7	103.7	98.1
03100	CONCRETE FORMS & ACCESSORIES	109.9	103.8	104.7	78.6	95.6	93.3	95.4	93.5	93.7	97.1	100.6	100.1	100.0	108.3	107.2	88.4	94.6	93.8
03200	CONCRETE REINFORCEMENT	111.7	96.8	103.2	102.2	89.8	95.1	113.2	71.9	89.7	104.6	90.1	96.4	104.6	97.0	100.3	100.5	99.4	99.9
03300	CAST-IN-PLACE CONCRETE	109.9	100.4	106.0	88.0	91.9	89.6	100.4	84.2	93.7	99.1	98.4	98.8	99.1	104.2	101.2	101.8	98.4	100.4
03	CONCRETE	104.0	101.2	102.6	86.1	93.3	89.7	98.4	86.0	92.2	96.9	97.8	97.4	97.3	103.8	100.6	93.0	96.9	94.9
04	MASONRY	100.4	108.8	105.6	92.8	99.9	97.1	104.6	80.2	89.6	104.5	103.3	103.8	104.4	112.9	109.6	118.4	98.2	106.0
05	METALS	96.7	98.3	97.3	94.0	93.2	93.7	93.5	77.2	87.6	97.0	94.9	96.2	98.6	88.6	95.0	96.5	96.5	96.5
06	WOOD & PLASTICS	117.3	102.6	109.7	88.3	94.5	91.5	107.0	100.2	103.5	108.1	100.2	104.0	111.4	107.3	109.3	95.1	94.2	94.6
07	THERMAL & MOISTURE PROTECTION	96.0	101.9	98.8	95.9	89.5	92.9	95.5	73.5	85.1	95.2	98.0	96.6	94.6	105.1	99.5	96.9	101.0	98.8
08	DOORS & WINDOWS	99.7	101.6	100.1	104.3	85.3	99.7	99.8	82.0	95.5	104.6	97.7	102.9	104.5	104.2	104.4	91.6	88.4	90.9
09200	PLASTER & GYPSUM BOARD	97.4	103.2	100.9	106.3	94.8	99.3	106.0	100.7	102.8	107.3	100.7	103.3	107.3	107.9	107.7	90.8	94.8	93.2
095,098	CEILINGS & ACOUSTICAL TREATMENT	85.8	103.2	97.3	103.1	94.8	97.6	88.0	100.7	96.4	94.8	100.7	98.7	94.8	107.9	103.4	69.0	94.8	86.0
09600	FLOORING	108.5	92.0	104.5	85.3	102.2	89.4	91.2	77.3	87.9	91.9	97.1	93.1	94.6	109.4	98.2	104.2	66.2	95.0
097,099	WALL FINISHES, PAINTS & COATINGS	103.4	96.3	99.3	91.7	80.7	85.3	92.6	92.2	92.4	92.6	92.2	92.4	95.2	104.9	100.8	106.9	80.7	91.7
09	FINISHES	100.9	101.4	101.1	96.5	95.6	96.0	96.2	92.3	94.2	97.8	99.4	98.6	98.9	108.5	103.8	95.4	87.4	91.3
10 - 14	TOTAL DIV. 10000 - 14000	100.0	101.1	100.2	100.0	96.1	99.2	100.0	69.6	93.6	100.0	96.9	99.4	100.0	102.9	100.6	100.0	95.7	99.1
15	MECHANICAL	100.4	98.4	99.5	100.2	91.6	96.2	97.0	63.8	81.6	100.1	94.8	97.6	100.1	99.0	99.6	96.5	90.5	93.7
16	ELECTRICAL	93.3	99.4	97.5	105.4	88.2	93.6	91.4	88.2	89.2	92.1	95.4	94.4	92.9	101.5	98.8	102.7	88.2	92.7
01 - 16	WEIGHTED AVERAGE	99.4	101.0	100.2	96.6	93.5	95.1	96.9	82.5	89.9	98.7	98.0	98.3	99.2	101.6	100.3	96.9	93.6	95.3

WISCONSIN

	DIVISION	OSHKOSH 549			PORTAGE 539			RACINE 534			RHINELANDER 545			SUPERIOR 548			WAUSAU 544		
		MAT.	INST.	TOTAL	MAT.	INST.	TOTAL	MAT.	INST.	TOTAL	MAT.	INST.	TOTAL	MAT.	INST.	TOTAL	MAT.	INST.	TOTAL
02	SITE CONSTRUCTION	77.5	98.3	93.4	76.1	104.6	98.0	84.8	105.5	100.7	88.4	97.0	95.0	76.8	104.3	97.9	73.8	98.2	92.5
03100	CONCRETE FORMS & ACCESSORIES	87.9	90.5	90.2	85.9	100.0	98.1	96.8	103.8	102.9	84.6	91.6	90.6	86.4	97.2	95.7	87.2	95.1	94.0
03200	CONCRETE REINFORCEMENT	100.8	90.9	95.1	114.0	90.1	100.4	104.6	96.8	100.1	102.2	86.8	93.5	101.8	95.0	97.9	102.2	89.8	95.2
03300	CAST-IN-PLACE CONCRETE	93.9	93.9	93.9	86.2	100.7	92.1	99.1	100.0	99.4	106.4	92.3	100.6	96.0	98.1	96.8	87.5	97.8	91.7
03	CONCRETE	88.1	91.9	90.0	86.4	98.4	92.4	96.9	101.1	99.0	100.0	90.8	95.4	87.7	97.1	92.4	83.4	95.1	89.3
04	MASONRY	106.1	94.1	98.7	103.5	101.6	102.4	104.5	108.8	107.1	124.8	90.6	103.8	117.7	102.7	108.5	105.6	98.7	101.4
05	METALS	94.5	91.7	93.5	94.1	95.0	94.4	97.0	98.3	97.5	94.7	85.1	91.2	97.4	95.9	96.8	94.5	93.1	94.0
06	WOOD & PLASTICS	92.9	89.6	91.2	96.5	100.2	98.4	108.4	102.6	105.4	89.5	94.5	92.1	93.0	95.9	94.5	92.1	94.5	93.3
07	THERMAL & MOISTURE PROTECTION	98.0	87.9	93.2	94.7	98.1	96.3	95.8	101.4	98.4	99.0	83.2	91.5	96.5	102.2	99.2	97.7	85.2	91.8
08	DOORS & WINDOWS	97.7	86.4	95.0	100.0	97.7	99.4	104.6	101.6	103.9	97.8	85.7	94.9	91.5	93.3	92.0	98.0	88.7	95.8
09200	PLASTER & GYPSUM BOARD	88.7	89.8	89.4	102.8	100.7	101.5	107.3	103.2	104.8	87.9	94.8	92.1	90.6	96.6	94.2	88.3	94.8	92.3
095,098	CEILINGS & ACOUSTICAL TREATMENT	99.4	89.8	93.1	89.4	100.7	96.8	94.8	103.2	100.3	99.4	94.8	96.4	70.3	96.6	87.6	99.4	94.8	96.4
09600	FLOORING	102.1	82.4	97.3	87.5	108.2	92.5	91.9	92.0	91.9	101.2	102.2	101.4	105.5	108.2	106.2	101.9	102.2	102.0
097,099	WALL FINISHES, PAINTS & COATINGS	102.5	70.0	83.6	92.6	92.2	92.4	92.6	97.0	95.2	102.5	92.0	96.4	98.0	102.0	100.3	102.5	92.0	96.4
09	FINISHES	99.7	86.7	93.1	94.4	101.0	97.8	97.9	101.4	99.7	100.0	94.7	97.3	95.2	99.8	97.6	99.4	96.6	97.9
10 - 14	TOTAL DIV. 10000 - 14000	100.0	88.1	97.5	100.0	96.2	99.2	100.0	101.1	100.2	100.0	80.6	95.9	100.0	98.6	99.7	100.0	95.0	98.9
15	MECHANICAL	97.5	89.7	93.9	97.0	93.6	95.4	100.1	98.4	99.3	97.5	86.5	92.4	96.5	94.6	95.6	97.5	90.8	94.4
16	ELECTRICAL	103.3	88.7	93.3	96.5	95.4	95.8	91.0	99.2	96.7	102.2	87.4	92.0	110.5	101.8	104.5	105.1	87.4	92.9
01 - 16	WEIGHTED AVERAGE	96.7	90.7	93.8	95.2	97.8	96.5	98.6	101.3	99.9	99.5	89.3	94.5	96.8	98.9	97.8	96.1	93.1	94.6

COST INDEXES

651

WYOMING

DIVISION		CASPER 826 MAT.	INST.	TOTAL	CHEYENNE 820 MAT.	INST.	TOTAL	NEWCASTLE 827 MAT.	INST.	TOTAL	RAWLINS 823 MAT.	INST.	TOTAL	RIVERTON 825 MAT.	INST.	TOTAL	ROCK SPRINGS 829-831 MAT.	INST.	TOTAL
02	SITE CONSTRUCTION	84.1	99.2	95.7	84.0	99.2	95.7	84.7	98.8	95.5	101.6	98.8	99.5	94.5	98.9	97.9	87.3	98.8	96.1
03100	CONCRETE FORMS & ACCESSORIES	102.0	50.2	57.3	102.0	50.2	57.3	95.1	35.4	43.6	101.7	35.4	44.5	93.3	41.3	48.4	108.0	35.5	45.4
03200	CONCRETE REINFORCEMENT	107.2	54.2	77.0	100.6	54.4	74.2	108.8	48.8	74.6	108.3	48.8	74.4	109.3	48.9	74.9	109.3	54.0	77.8
03300	CAST-IN-PLACE CONCRETE	104.9	65.0	88.4	104.9	65.0	88.4	105.3	48.9	82.1	105.5	48.9	82.1	105.4	50.2	82.7	105.3	48.9	82.1
03	CONCRETE	106.9	56.9	81.9	106.1	56.9	81.5	106.9	43.8	75.4	121.7	43.8	82.8	115.7	46.9	81.3	107.9	44.8	76.4
04	MASONRY	109.0	45.9	70.2	108.0	48.5	71.4	109.0	37.5	65.0	109.0	37.5	65.0	109.0	40.6	66.9	175.8	37.5	90.8
05	METALS	105.1	66.7	91.2	106.3	66.9	92.1	104.5	63.6	89.7	104.5	63.6	89.7	104.6	63.8	89.9	105.1	65.4	90.8
06	WOOD & PLASTICS	96.8	48.7	71.9	95.8	48.7	71.4	89.7	34.5	61.2	96.6	34.5	64.5	88.0	41.0	63.7	103.7	34.5	67.9
07	THERMAL & MOISTURE PROTECTION	104.5	61.9	84.3	104.5	62.6	84.6	105.0	47.1	77.5	107.4	47.1	78.8	106.4	50.6	79.9	105.2	47.1	77.7
08	DOORS & WINDOWS	94.3	50.0	83.6	95.0	50.0	84.2	101.0	41.1	86.5	100.6	41.1	86.3	100.8	44.6	87.3	101.3	42.4	87.1
09200	PLASTER & GYPSUM BOARD	86.7	46.9	62.3	88.2	46.9	62.9	84.5	32.2	52.6	86.7	32.2	53.4	84.1	38.9	56.5	90.1	32.2	54.7
095,098	CEILINGS & ACOUSTICAL TREATMENT	96.5	46.9	63.7	104.7	46.9	66.5	96.5	32.2	54.1	96.5	32.2	54.1	96.5	38.9	58.5	96.5	32.2	54.1
09600	FLOORING	105.2	49.6	91.7	105.2	72.9	97.4	102.3	48.6	89.3	105.2	48.6	91.4	101.7	48.6	88.8	107.5	48.6	93.2
097,099	WALL FINISHES, PAINTS & COATINGS	108.7	65.7	83.7	108.5	65.7	83.7	108.7	39.9	68.7	108.7	39.9	68.7	108.7	36.6	66.8	108.7	39.9	68.7
09	FINISHES	97.4	50.9	73.7	99.0	55.6	76.9	96.1	37.5	66.2	98.7	37.5	67.5	96.6	41.5	68.5	98.6	37.5	67.4
10-14	TOTAL DIV. 10000-14000	100.0	77.6	95.3	100.0	77.6	95.3	100.0	59.8	91.5	100.0	59.8	91.5	100.0	61.5	91.9	100.0	59.8	91.5
15	MECHANICAL	100.1	69.3	85.9	100.1	52.5	78.1	98.3	37.0	70.0	98.3	37.0	70.0	98.3	47.2	74.7	100.1	37.1	70.9
16	ELECTRICAL	92.6	63.1	72.4	92.6	62.2	71.7	94.2	53.6	66.3	94.2	53.6	66.3	94.2	53.6	66.3	91.6	53.6	65.5
01-16	WEIGHTED AVERAGE	100.3	63.9	82.6	100.6	61.4	81.5	100.5	50.3	76.1	103.3	50.3	77.5	102.0	53.9	78.6	105.3	50.7	78.7

WYOMING / CANADA

DIVISION		SHERIDAN 828 MAT.	INST.	TOTAL	WHEATLAND 822 MAT.	INST.	TOTAL	WORLAND 824 MAT.	INST.	TOTAL	YELLOWSTONE NAT'L PA 821 MAT.	INST.	TOTAL	BARRIE, ONTARIO MAT.	INST.	TOTAL	BATHURST, NEW BRUNSWICK MAT.	INST.	TOTAL
02	SITE CONSTRUCTION	91.6	99.2	97.4	90.7	98.9	97.0	86.0	98.8	95.8	86.1	99.1	96.1	113.3	97.4	101.1	93.0	95.6	95.0
03100	CONCRETE FORMS & ACCESSORIES	93.8	49.9	56.0	97.8	44.3	51.6	97.9	35.5	44.1	97.9	41.0	48.8	120.5	99.6	102.5	92.6	68.6	71.9
03200	CONCRETE REINFORCEMENT	109.3	54.3	78.0	108.8	48.9	74.7	109.3	54.0	77.8	111.3	48.9	75.7	179.6	97.2	132.7	147.8	69.3	103.0
03300	CAST-IN-PLACE CONCRETE	105.4	64.9	88.7	114.9	50.6	88.4	105.3	48.9	82.1	105.3	63.9	88.3	174.7	92.1	140.7	144.0	64.6	111.3
03	CONCRETE	113.4	56.8	85.1	114.8	48.3	81.6	107.2	44.8	76.0	107.4	51.5	79.5	154.3	96.1	125.2	137.0	67.9	102.5
04	MASONRY	109.0	48.7	71.9	109.7	41.6	67.8	109.0	37.5	65.1	109.0	44.4	69.3	153.3	112.2	128.1	143.3	70.6	98.7
05	METALS	104.6	66.7	90.9	104.4	64.0	89.8	104.6	65.4	90.5	105.2	64.0	90.3	106.4	88.9	100.1	101.0	76.0	92.0
06	WOOD & PLASTICS	88.4	48.7	67.9	92.6	44.6	67.8	92.7	34.5	62.6	92.7	38.2	64.5	119.8	98.7	108.9	90.9	68.9	79.5
07	THERMAL & MOISTURE PROTECTION	106.0	62.6	85.4	105.4	52.1	80.1	105.0	47.1	77.6	104.5	54.2	80.6	104.9	99.2	102.2	103.7	68.6	87.1
08	DOORS & WINDOWS	101.2	51.4	89.2	99.6	46.6	86.8	101.2	42.4	87.0	94.5	43.1	82.1	92.1	91.7	92.0	86.3	61.1	80.2
09200	PLASTER & GYPSUM BOARD	84.1	46.9	61.3	85.4	42.7	59.3	85.4	32.2	52.9	85.6	36.0	55.3	168.6	98.8	125.9	194.3	68.0	117.1
095,098	CEILINGS & ACOUSTICAL TREATMENT	96.5	46.9	63.7	96.5	42.7	61.0	96.5	32.2	54.1	97.9	36.0	57.1	102.4	98.8	100.0	103.8	68.0	80.2
09600	FLOORING	101.8	54.6	90.4	103.8	48.6	90.4	103.8	48.6	90.4	103.8	60.0	93.2	132.6	108.8	126.8	114.1	51.2	98.9
097,099	WALL FINISHES, PAINTS & COATINGS	108.7	65.7	83.7	108.7	39.9	68.7	108.7	39.9	68.7	108.7	39.9	68.7	109.9	100.4	104.4	109.2	56.8	78.8
09	FINISHES	96.5	51.9	73.7	97.0	44.1	70.0	96.7	37.5	66.5	97.0	43.2	69.5	124.7	102.0	113.1	121.2	64.2	92.1
10-14	TOTAL DIV. 10000-14000	100.0	77.5	95.3	100.0	75.0	94.7	100.0	59.8	91.5	100.0	67.5	93.1	100.0	84.5	96.7	100.0	72.2	94.1
15	MECHANICAL	98.3	50.5	76.2	98.3	43.8	73.1	98.3	37.1	70.0	98.3	46.7	74.4	102.6	97.2	100.1	102.5	67.2	86.2
16	ELECTRICAL	94.2	53.6	66.3	94.2	53.6	66.3	94.2	53.6	66.3	92.6	53.6	65.8	127.9	98.5	107.7	123.6	74.3	89.7
01-16	WEIGHTED AVERAGE	101.6	59.2	81.0	101.7	54.3	78.7	100.8	50.7	76.4	100.0	55.1	78.2	115.7	98.1	107.2	109.9	72.0	91.5

CANADA

DIVISION		BRANDON, MANITOBA MAT.	INST.	TOTAL	BRANTFORD, ONTARIO MAT.	INST.	TOTAL	CALGARY, ALBERTA MAT.	INST.	TOTAL	CAP-DE-LA-MADELEINE, PQ MAT.	INST.	TOTAL	CHARLESBOURG, QUEBEC MAT.	INST.	TOTAL	CHARLOTTETOWN, PEI MAT.	INST.	TOTAL
02	SITE CONSTRUCTION	110.4	96.3	99.6	112.4	97.9	101.3	107.1	97.4	99.7	90.7	97.8	96.1	90.7	97.8	96.1	104.0	95.0	97.1
03100	CONCRETE FORMS & ACCESSORIES	119.3	79.2	84.7	120.3	108.2	110.9	119.2	80.4	85.7	128.8	96.3	100.7	128.8	96.3	100.7	85.0	62.2	65.3
03200	CONCRETE REINFORCEMENT	161.1	64.8	106.2	174.4	95.6	129.5	161.1	64.3	105.9	147.8	97.5	119.1	147.8	97.5	119.1	147.8	56.8	95.9
03300	CAST-IN-PLACE CONCRETE	162.8	79.3	128.3	170.4	113.9	147.1	162.8	82.8	129.8	137.5	102.8	123.2	137.5	102.8	123.2	166.1	63.5	123.8
03	CONCRETE	139.0	77.1	108.1	151.6	107.5	129.5	146.0	78.8	112.4	132.6	98.6	115.6	132.6	98.6	115.6	154.2	62.4	108.3
04	MASONRY	146.6	75.7	103.0	148.6	117.4	129.4	146.7	81.4	106.5	142.8	97.6	115.1	142.8	97.6	115.1	145.0	68.2	97.8
05	METALS	100.8	82.0	94.0	100.7	96.8	99.3	100.8	83.0	94.4	101.0	94.0	98.5	101.0	94.0	98.5	100.8	71.6	90.3
06	WOOD & PLASTICS	116.0	80.4	97.6	118.2	107.2	112.5	116.2	79.7	97.3	131.0	96.3	113.1	131.0	96.3	113.1	82.2	61.7	71.6
07	THERMAL & MOISTURE PROTECTION	104.3	79.7	92.6	104.5	105.5	105.0	104.3	80.8	93.1	104.5	99.3	102.0	104.5	99.3	102.0	105.0	65.8	86.4
08	DOORS & WINDOWS	92.3	71.7	87.3	91.4	103.0	94.2	92.3	75.6	88.3	92.3	90.4	91.9	92.3	90.4	91.9	94.6	54.4	84.9
09200	PLASTER & GYPSUM BOARD	135.2	79.9	101.4	143.0	107.5	121.3	147.0	79.1	105.5	214.8	96.3	142.4	214.8	96.3	142.4	189.8	60.5	110.8
095,098	CEILINGS & ACOUSTICAL TREATMENT	102.4	79.9	87.6	102.4	107.5	105.8	102.4	79.1	87.0	102.4	96.3	98.4	102.4	96.3	98.4	102.4	60.5	74.8
09600	FLOORING	132.6	76.1	118.9	132.6	108.8	126.8	132.6	83.1	120.6	132.6	109.6	127.0	132.6	109.6	127.0	110.2	68.0	100.0
097,099	WALL FINISHES, PAINTS & COATINGS	109.3	65.9	84.1	109.2	110.3	109.8	109.2	78.1	91.1	109.2	102.6	105.4	109.2	102.6	105.4	109.2	47.2	73.2
09	FINISHES	118.6	77.6	97.7	119.5	109.1	114.2	120.4	81.0	100.3	129.8	99.8	114.5	129.8	99.8	114.5	119.5	62.0	90.1
10-14	TOTAL DIV. 10000-14000	100.0	74.6	94.6	100.0	87.4	97.3	100.0	89.0	97.7	100.0	94.4	98.8	100.0	94.4	98.8	100.0	71.3	93.9
15	MECHANICAL	102.5	81.8	92.9	102.5	100.6	101.6	102.5	73.3	89.0	102.5	89.0	96.3	102.5	89.0	96.3	102.5	61.8	83.7
16	ELECTRICAL	128.8	85.1	98.8	127.0	102.7	110.3	113.7	80.3	90.8	123.6	88.9	99.7	123.6	88.9	99.7	123.6	63.2	82.1
01-16	WEIGHTED AVERAGE	111.9	81.5	97.1	113.5	103.9	108.8	111.8	80.9	96.8	111.3	94.2	103.0	111.3	94.2	103.0	113.1	67.0	90.7

City Cost Indexes

CANADA

DIVISION		CHICOUTIMI, QUEBEC			CORNER BROOK, NFLD			CORNWALL, ONTARIO			DALHOUSIE, NB			DARTMOUTH, NOVA SCOTIA			EDMONTON, ALBERTA		
		MAT.	INST.	TOTAL	MAT.	INST.	TOTAL	MAT.	INST.	TOTAL	MAT.	INST.	TOTAL	MAT.	INST.	TOTAL	MAT.	INST.	TOTAL
02	SITE CONSTRUCTION	89.6	97.8	95.9	112.1	95.5	99.4	110.2	97.4	100.4	93.0	95.6	95.0	96.2	96.8	96.7	108.6	97.4	100.0
03100	CONCRETE FORMS & ACCESSORIES	128.7	96.1	100.6	95.3	65.7	69.7	116.8	99.9	102.2	92.6	68.6	71.9	84.3	76.6	77.7	116.5	80.4	85.3
03200	CONCRETE REINFORCEMENT	111.6	97.5	103.5	147.8	59.1	97.2	174.4	95.3	129.3	147.8	69.3	103.0	147.8	58.8	97.1	161.1	64.3	105.9
03300	CAST-IN-PLACE CONCRETE	131.4	102.7	119.6	179.6	72.7	135.5	153.3	103.9	132.9	144.0	64.6	111.3	178.4	76.2	136.3	163.6	82.8	130.3
03	CONCRETE	125.0	98.5	111.8	165.0	67.7	116.4	142.9	100.3	121.6	137.0	67.9	102.5	151.2	73.8	112.5	146.3	78.8	112.5
04	MASONRY	141.7	97.6	114.6	146.0	69.6	99.0	147.3	107.8	123.0	143.3	70.6	98.7	145.9	78.6	104.6	146.7	81.4	106.6
05	METALS	99.2	93.8	97.3	102.1	76.6	92.9	100.7	95.1	98.7	101.0	76.0	92.0	100.7	79.8	93.2	100.8	83.0	94.4
06	WOOD & PLASTICS	131.0	96.3	113.1	92.4	64.7	78.1	116.0	99.7	107.5	90.9	68.9	79.5	81.8	75.9	78.7	111.9	79.7	95.3
07	THERMAL & MOISTURE PROTECTION	104.5	99.3	102.0	105.9	67.5	87.7	104.2	98.5	101.5	103.7	68.6	87.1	103.0	77.6	90.9	104.2	80.7	93.1
08	DOORS & WINDOWS	91.9	83.3	89.8	98.6	62.0	89.8	92.3	95.8	93.1	86.3	61.1	80.2	82.9	71.0	80.0	92.3	75.6	88.3
09200	PLASTER & GYPSUM BOARD	214.6	96.3	142.3	195.0	63.6	114.7	264.5	99.7	163.8	194.3	68.0	117.1	189.3	75.2	119.6	144.4	79.1	104.5
095,098	CEILINGS & ACOUSTICAL TREATMENT	101.1	96.3	97.9	105.2	63.6	77.7	102.4	99.7	100.6	103.8	68.0	80.2	102.4	75.2	84.4	102.4	79.1	87.0
09600	FLOORING	132.6	109.6	127.0	115.0	61.2	102.0	132.6	107.2	126.4	114.1	51.2	98.9	110.2	72.9	101.1	132.6	83.1	120.6
097,099	WALL FINISHES, PAINTS & COATINGS	109.2	102.6	105.4	109.2	67.0	84.7	109.2	102.7	105.5	109.2	56.8	78.8	109.2	70.6	86.8	109.3	78.1	91.2
09	FINISHES	129.5	99.8	114.3	122.6	64.9	93.2	137.9	102.1	119.6	121.2	64.2	92.1	118.7	75.3	96.6	120.1	81.0	100.2
10 - 14	TOTAL DIV. 10000 - 14000	100.0	94.4	98.8	100.0	72.1	94.1	100.0	84.0	96.6	100.0	72.2	94.1	100.0	73.9	94.5	100.0	84.6	96.8
15	MECHANICAL	102.5	89.0	96.3	102.5	68.6	86.8	102.5	97.9	100.4	102.5	67.2	86.2	102.5	81.8	92.9	102.5	73.3	89.0
16	ELECTRICAL	123.6	88.9	99.7	123.6	69.9	86.7	123.6	99.2	106.8	123.6	74.3	89.7	123.6	78.0	92.3	113.7	80.3	90.8
01 - 16	WEIGHTED AVERAGE	110.0	93.9	102.2	115.9	71.5	94.3	114.1	99.2	106.8	109.9	72.0	91.5	111.0	79.5	95.7	111.8	80.8	96.7

CANADA

DIVISION		FORT MCMURRAY, ALBERTA			FREDERICTON, NB			GATINEAU, QUEBEC			HALIFAX, NOVA SCOTIA			HAMILTON, ONTARIO			KAMLOOPS, BC		
		MAT.	INST.	TOTAL	MAT.	INST.	TOTAL	MAT.	INST.	TOTAL	MAT.	INST.	TOTAL	MAT.	INST.	TOTAL	MAT.	INST.	TOTAL
02	SITE CONSTRUCTION	106.0	97.4	99.4	92.5	95.6	94.9	86.9	97.8	95.2	96.2	96.8	96.7	110.7	97.6	100.7	112.5	98.6	101.9
03100	CONCRETE FORMS & ACCESSORIES	116.5	80.4	85.3	119.1	68.9	75.8	128.8	96.1	100.6	84.3	76.7	77.7	118.6	104.4	106.3	101.9	100.0	100.2
03200	CONCRETE REINFORCEMENT	161.1	64.3	105.9	147.8	69.4	103.1	156.5	97.5	122.9	147.8	59.0	97.2	174.4	97.3	130.4	116.1	97.7	105.6
03300	CAST-IN-PLACE CONCRETE	144.3	82.8	119.0	137.1	64.7	107.2	108.1	102.7	105.9	178.4	78.4	137.1	157.2	106.8	136.4	114.0	104.2	110.0
03	CONCRETE	136.7	78.8	107.8	135.7	68.0	101.8	119.2	98.5	108.9	151.2	74.6	112.9	144.9	103.6	124.3	136.8	100.8	118.8
04	MASONRY	145.2	81.4	106.0	142.8	72.3	99.5	141.5	97.6	114.5	145.9	81.4	106.3	148.4	111.6	125.8	142.2	104.6	119.1
05	METALS	100.8	83.0	94.4	100.5	76.5	91.9	101.0	93.8	98.4	100.7	80.1	93.3	100.9	95.9	99.1	100.1	94.4	98.1
06	WOOD & PLASTICS	111.9	79.7	95.3	120.5	68.9	93.8	131.0	96.3	113.1	81.8	75.9	78.7	117.0	103.8	110.1	94.6	98.6	96.7
07	THERMAL & MOISTURE PROTECTION	104.2	80.7	93.1	104.2	69.8	87.9	104.5	99.3	102.0	103.0	78.3	91.3	104.3	101.6	103.0	104.9	93.5	99.5
08	DOORS & WINDOWS	92.3	75.6	88.3	86.2	59.8	79.9	92.3	85.2	90.6	82.9	71.0	80.0	92.3	99.2	94.0	88.1	95.8	90.0
09200	PLASTER & GYPSUM BOARD	144.4	79.1	104.5	209.6	68.0	123.1	143.8	96.3	114.8	189.3	75.2	119.6	209.2	104.0	144.9	149.1	98.6	118.2
095,098	CEILINGS & ACOUSTICAL TREATMENT	102.4	79.1	87.0	102.4	68.0	79.7	102.4	96.3	98.4	102.4	75.2	84.4	102.4	104.0	103.4	102.4	98.6	99.9
09600	FLOORING	132.6	83.1	120.6	127.7	51.2	109.1	132.6	109.6	127.0	110.2	72.9	101.1	132.6	108.8	126.8	126.9	62.1	111.2
097,099	WALL FINISHES, PAINTS & COATINGS	109.3	78.1	91.2	109.2	72.5	87.9	109.2	102.6	105.4	109.2	70.6	86.8	109.2	110.3	109.8	109.2	92.9	99.7
09	FINISHES	120.1	81.0	100.2	127.7	65.9	96.2	119.0	99.8	109.2	118.7	75.3	96.6	129.5	106.3	117.6	120.2	92.6	106.1
10 - 14	TOTAL DIV. 10000 - 14000	100.0	84.6	96.8	100.0	72.2	94.1	100.0	94.4	98.8	100.0	73.9	94.5	100.0	110.0	102.1	100.0	105.3	101.1
15	MECHANICAL	102.5	73.3	89.0	102.5	76.0	90.2	102.5	89.0	96.3	102.5	81.8	92.9	102.5	102.2	102.4	102.5	92.2	97.8
16	ELECTRICAL	113.7	80.3	90.8	123.1	92.6	102.2	123.6	88.9	99.7	123.6	84.0	96.3	127.0	102.0	109.8	126.6	100.3	108.6
01 - 16	WEIGHTED AVERAGE	110.4	80.8	96.0	110.6	77.2	94.4	108.3	94.0	101.4	111.0	81.0	96.4	113.8	102.8	108.4	110.6	97.3	104.2

CANADA

DIVISION		KINGSTON, ONTARIO			KITCHENER, ONTARIO			LAVAL, QUEBEC			LETHBRIDGE, ALBERTA			LLOYDMINSTER, ALBERTA			LONDON, ONTARIO		
		MAT.	INST.	TOTAL	MAT.	INST.	TOTAL	MAT.	INST.	TOTAL	MAT.	INST.	TOTAL	MAT.	INST.	TOTAL	MAT.	INST.	TOTAL
02	SITE CONSTRUCTION	110.2	97.4	100.4	98.0	97.2	97.4	91.1	97.8	96.2	104.7	97.4	99.1	106.0	97.4	99.4	110.7	97.4	100.5
03100	CONCRETE FORMS & ACCESSORIES	116.8	99.9	102.2	112.3	95.6	97.9	128.8	96.1	100.6	119.2	80.4	85.7	116.5	80.4	85.3	118.5	99.0	101.7
03200	CONCRETE REINFORCEMENT	174.4	95.3	129.3	110.1	97.1	102.7	156.5	97.5	122.9	161.1	64.3	105.9	161.1	64.3	105.9	122.9	95.4	107.2
03300	CAST-IN-PLACE CONCRETE	153.3	103.9	132.9	146.7	86.3	121.8	140.1	102.7	124.7	144.3	82.8	119.0	144.3	82.8	119.0	157.2	104.0	135.3
03	CONCRETE	142.9	100.3	121.6	124.6	92.4	108.5	135.0	98.5	116.8	136.9	78.8	107.9	136.7	78.8	107.8	138.5	100.0	119.2
04	MASONRY	147.3	107.8	123.0	145.8	106.7	121.7	143.8	97.6	115.4	145.2	81.4	106.0	145.2	81.4	106.0	147.6	108.3	123.4
05	METALS	100.7	95.1	98.7	100.7	92.3	97.7	101.0	93.8	98.4	100.8	83.0	94.4	100.8	83.0	94.4	99.2	95.4	97.8
06	WOOD & PLASTICS	116.0	99.8	107.6	110.0	94.4	101.9	131.0	96.3	113.1	116.2	79.7	97.3	111.9	79.7	95.3	117.0	97.7	107.0
07	THERMAL & MOISTURE PROTECTION	104.2	98.0	101.3	102.8	96.4	99.8	104.5	99.3	102.0	104.3	80.8	93.1	104.2	80.7	93.1	104.3	99.4	102.0
08	DOORS & WINDOWS	92.3	93.6	92.6	83.7	90.3	85.3	92.3	85.2	90.6	92.3	75.6	88.3	92.3	75.6	88.3	93.2	94.8	93.6
09200	PLASTER & GYPSUM BOARD	264.5	99.9	163.9	147.7	94.3	115.0	143.8	96.3	114.8	147.0	79.1	105.5	144.4	79.1	104.5	209.2	97.7	141.1
095,098	CEILINGS & ACOUSTICAL TREATMENT	102.4	99.9	100.7	102.4	94.3	97.0	102.4	96.3	98.4	102.4	79.1	87.0	102.4	79.1	87.0	102.4	97.7	99.3
09600	FLOORING	132.6	107.2	126.4	128.2	108.8	123.5	132.6	109.6	127.0	132.6	83.1	120.6	132.6	83.1	120.6	132.6	108.8	126.8
097,099	WALL FINISHES, PAINTS & COATINGS	109.2	104.5	106.5	109.2	100.4	104.1	109.2	102.6	105.4	109.2	78.1	91.1	109.3	78.1	91.2	109.2	110.3	109.8
09	FINISHES	137.9	102.4	119.8	118.1	98.8	108.3	119.0	99.8	109.2	120.4	81.0	100.3	120.1	81.0	100.2	129.5	102.3	115.6
10 - 14	TOTAL DIV. 10000 - 14000	100.0	84.0	96.6	100.0	107.3	101.5	100.0	94.4	98.8	100.0	89.0	97.7	100.0	84.6	96.8	100.0	108.4	101.8
15	MECHANICAL	102.5	98.1	100.5	102.5	97.7	100.3	102.5	89.0	96.3	102.5	73.3	89.0	102.5	73.3	89.0	102.5	98.1	100.5
16	ELECTRICAL	123.6	98.0	106.0	127.0	98.1	107.1	123.6	88.9	99.7	113.7	80.3	90.8	113.7	80.3	90.8	127.0	98.2	107.2
01 - 16	WEIGHTED AVERAGE	114.1	98.9	106.7	108.4	97.4	103.0	110.5	94.0	102.5	110.5	80.9	96.1	110.4	80.8	96.0	112.8	99.7	106.4

CANADA

DIVISION		MEDICINE HAT, ALBERTA			MONCTON, NEW BRUNSWICK			MONTREAL, QUEBEC			MOOSE JAW, SASKATCHEWAN			NEWCASTLE, NB			NEW GLASGOW, NOVA SCOTIA		
		MAT.	INST.	TOTAL	MAT.	INST.	TOTAL	MAT.	INST.	TOTAL	MAT.	INST.	TOTAL	MAT.	INST.	TOTAL	MAT.	INST.	TOTAL
02	SITE CONSTRUCTION	104.7	97.4	99.1	92.3	95.6	94.8	91.1	97.8	96.2	107.9	95.8	98.6	93.0	95.6	95.0	96.2	96.8	96.7
03100	CONCRETE FORMS & ACCESSORIES	119.2	80.4	85.7	92.6	68.6	71.9	128.8	96.1	100.6	97.2	65.9	70.2	92.6	68.6	71.9	84.3	76.6	77.7
03200	CONCRETE REINFORCEMENT	161.1	64.3	105.9	147.8	69.3	103.0	159.2	97.5	124.0	113.7	77.4	93.0	147.8	69.3	103.0	147.8	58.8	97.1
03300	CAST-IN-PLACE CONCRETE	144.3	82.8	119.0	138.7	64.6	108.1	140.1	102.7	124.7	152.8	75.2	120.8	144.0	64.6	111.3	178.4	76.2	136.3
03	CONCRETE	136.9	78.8	107.9	134.4	67.9	101.1	135.3	98.5	116.9	126.8	71.9	99.4	137.0	67.9	102.5	151.2	73.8	112.5
04	MASONRY	145.2	81.4	106.0	142.9	70.6	98.5	143.9	97.6	115.5	145.0	71.8	100.0	143.3	70.6	98.7	145.9	78.6	104.6
05	METALS	100.8	83.0	94.4	101.0	76.0	92.0	101.0	93.8	98.4	98.2	80.3	91.7	101.0	76.0	92.0	100.7	79.8	93.2
06	WOOD & PLASTICS	116.2	79.7	97.3	90.9	68.9	79.5	131.0	96.3	113.1	92.9	64.3	78.1	90.9	68.9	79.5	81.8	75.9	78.7
07	THERMAL & MOISTURE PROTECTION	104.3	80.8	93.1	103.7	68.6	87.1	104.5	99.3	102.1	103.5	71.6	88.4	103.7	68.6	87.1	103.0	77.6	90.9
08	DOORS & WINDOWS	92.3	75.6	88.3	86.3	61.1	80.2	92.3	85.2	90.6	87.2	63.3	81.4	86.3	61.1	80.2	82.9	71.0	80.0
09200	PLASTER & GYPSUM BOARD	147.0	79.1	105.5	194.3	68.0	117.1	143.8	96.3	114.8	122.6	63.2	86.3	194.3	68.0	117.1	189.3	75.2	119.6
095,098	CEILINGS & ACOUSTICAL TREATMENT	102.4	79.1	87.0	103.8	68.0	80.2	102.4	96.3	98.4	99.7	63.2	75.6	103.8	68.0	80.2	102.4	75.2	84.4
09600	FLOORING	132.6	83.1	120.6	114.1	51.2	98.9	132.6	109.6	127.0	120.2	69.2	107.8	114.1	51.2	98.9	110.2	72.9	101.1
097,099	WALL FINISHES, PAINTS & COATINGS	109.2	78.1	91.1	109.2	56.8	78.8	109.2	102.6	105.4	109.2	73.5	88.5	109.2	56.8	78.8	109.2	70.6	86.8
09	FINISHES	120.4	81.0	100.3	121.2	64.2	92.1	119.0	99.8	109.2	112.1	67.0	89.1	121.2	64.2	92.1	118.7	75.3	96.6
10 - 14	TOTAL DIV. 10000 - 14000	100.0	89.0	97.7	100.0	72.2	94.1	100.0	94.4	98.8	100.0	71.6	94.0	100.0	72.2	94.1	100.0	73.9	94.5
15	MECHANICAL	102.5	73.3	89.0	102.5	67.2	86.2	102.5	89.0	96.3	102.5	73.8	89.2	102.5	67.2	86.2	102.5	81.8	92.9
16	ELECTRICAL	113.7	80.3	90.8	123.6	74.3	89.7	123.6	88.9	99.7	128.8	76.1	92.6	123.6	74.3	89.7	123.6	78.0	92.3
01 - 16	WEIGHTED AVERAGE	110.5	80.9	96.1	109.5	72.0	91.3	110.6	94.0	102.5	108.2	75.1	92.1	109.9	72.0	91.5	111.0	79.5	95.7

CANADA

DIVISION		NORTH BAY, ONTARIO			OSHAWA, ONTARIO			OTTAWA, ONTARIO			OWEN SOUND, ONTARIO			PETERBOROUGH, ONTARIO			PORTAGE LA PRAIRIE, MB		
		MAT.	INST.	TOTAL	MAT.	INST.	TOTAL	MAT.	INST.	TOTAL	MAT.	INST.	TOTAL	MAT.	INST.	TOTAL	MAT.	INST.	TOTAL
02	SITE CONSTRUCTION	112.4	97.1	100.7	112.3	97.4	100.9	111.0	97.4	100.6	113.3	97.2	101.0	112.4	97.4	100.9	108.9	96.3	99.3
03100	CONCRETE FORMS & ACCESSORIES	120.3	97.1	100.3	120.3	100.2	102.9	116.8	100.1	102.4	120.5	95.3	98.7	120.3	98.2	101.2	119.3	79.2	84.7
03200	CONCRETE REINFORCEMENT	174.4	94.7	129.0	174.4	98.0	130.8	174.4	95.3	129.3	179.6	97.2	132.6	174.4	95.4	129.3	161.1	64.8	106.2
03300	CAST-IN-PLACE CONCRETE	170.4	90.4	137.4	169.7	92.4	137.8	159.6	104.0	136.6	174.7	86.2	138.2	170.4	92.2	138.2	151.2	79.3	121.5
03	CONCRETE	151.6	94.3	122.9	151.2	96.8	124.0	146.0	100.4	123.2	154.3	92.3	123.3	151.6	95.5	123.5	133.3	77.1	105.2
04	MASONRY	148.6	103.2	120.7	148.5	110.8	125.3	148.6	107.8	123.5	153.3	109.6	126.4	148.6	110.8	125.3	145.7	75.7	102.7
05	METALS	100.7	94.9	98.6	100.7	95.7	98.9	100.9	95.4	98.9	106.4	92.2	101.3	100.7	95.3	98.8	100.8	82.0	94.0
06	WOOD & PLASTICS	118.2	98.1	107.8	118.2	98.7	108.1	116.0	99.7	107.5	119.8	94.4	106.6	118.2	96.6	107.0	116.0	80.4	97.6
07	THERMAL & MOISTURE PROTECTION	104.5	95.9	100.4	104.3	98.8	101.7	104.2	98.5	101.5	104.9	96.8	101.0	104.5	99.4	102.1	104.3	79.7	92.6
08	DOORS & WINDOWS	91.4	93.0	91.8	91.4	96.1	92.6	92.3	95.8	93.1	92.1	90.2	91.6	91.4	95.0	92.3	92.3	71.7	87.3
09200	PLASTER & GYPSUM BOARD	143.0	98.1	115.6	151.6	98.8	119.3	264.5	99.7	163.8	168.6	94.3	123.2	143.0	96.5	114.6	135.2	79.9	101.4
095,098	CEILINGS & ACOUSTICAL TREATMENT	102.4	98.1	99.6	102.4	98.8	100.0	102.4	99.7	100.6	102.4	94.3	97.0	102.4	96.5	98.5	102.4	79.9	87.6
09600	FLOORING	132.6	107.2	126.4	132.6	111.6	127.5	132.6	107.2	126.4	132.6	108.8	126.8	132.6	107.2	126.4	132.6	76.1	118.9
097,099	WALL FINISHES, PAINTS & COATINGS	109.2	101.9	105.0	109.2	120.3	115.7	109.2	102.7	105.5	109.9	100.4	104.4	109.2	104.5	106.5	109.3	65.9	84.1
09	FINISHES	119.5	100.2	109.6	120.7	104.8	112.6	137.9	102.1	119.6	124.7	98.8	111.5	119.5	100.9	110.0	118.6	77.6	97.7
10 - 14	TOTAL DIV. 10000 - 14000	100.0	82.3	96.3	100.0	109.0	101.9	100.0	106.1	101.3	100.0	82.9	96.4	100.0	84.3	96.7	100.0	74.6	94.6
15	MECHANICAL	102.5	95.7	99.4	102.5	99.8	101.3	102.5	98.4	100.6	102.6	95.8	99.5	102.5	99.6	101.2	102.5	81.8	92.9
16	ELECTRICAL	127.0	99.1	107.8	127.0	98.9	107.7	123.6	99.2	106.8	128.9	97.8	107.5	127.0	98.9	107.7	128.8	85.1	98.8
01 - 16	WEIGHTED AVERAGE	113.5	97.0	105.5	113.6	100.3	107.1	114.6	99.9	107.4	115.8	96.6	106.5	113.5	99.0	106.4	111.1	81.5	96.7

CANADA

DIVISION		PRINCE ALBERT, SS			PRINCE GEORGE, BC			QUEBEC, QUEBEC			RED DEER, ALBERTA			REGINA, SASKATCHEWAN			SAINT JOHN, N B		
		MAT.	INST.	TOTAL	MAT.	INST.	TOTAL	MAT.	INST.	TOTAL	MAT.	INST.	TOTAL	MAT.	INST.	TOTAL	MAT.	INST.	TOTAL
02	SITE CONSTRUCTION	103.8	95.9	97.8	119.1	98.6	103.4	92.6	97.8	96.6	104.1	97.4	99.0	109.2	95.8	98.9	93.1	95.6	95.0
03100	CONCRETE FORMS & ACCESSORIES	97.2	65.8	70.1	101.9	100.0	100.2	128.8	96.3	100.7	119.2	80.4	85.7	97.2	65.9	70.2	119.1	68.9	75.8
03200	CONCRETE REINFORCEMENT	118.7	77.4	95.1	116.1	97.7	105.6	147.8	97.5	119.1	161.1	64.3	105.9	113.7	77.4	93.0	147.8	69.4	103.1
03300	CAST-IN-PLACE CONCRETE	145.1	75.2	116.3	164.8	104.2	139.8	151.5	102.8	131.4	139.7	82.8	116.3	162.8	75.2	126.7	141.9	64.7	110.0
03	CONCRETE	123.7	71.8	97.8	161.9	100.8	131.3	139.5	98.6	119.1	134.7	78.8	106.8	131.8	71.9	101.8	138.0	68.0	103.0
04	MASONRY	144.5	71.8	99.8	146.0	104.6	120.5	144.0	97.6	115.5	144.9	81.4	105.8	145.8	72.3	100.6	143.2	72.3	99.6
05	METALS	98.4	80.2	91.8	100.1	94.4	98.1	101.0	94.0	98.5	100.8	83.0	94.4	98.2	80.3	91.7	100.5	76.5	91.9
06	WOOD & PLASTICS	92.9	64.3	78.1	94.6	98.6	96.7	131.0	96.3	113.1	116.2	79.7	97.3	92.9	64.3	78.1	120.5	68.9	93.8
07	THERMAL & MOISTURE PROTECTION	103.4	70.5	87.8	104.9	93.5	99.5	104.5	99.3	102.1	104.3	80.8	93.1	103.5	71.7	88.4	104.2	69.8	87.9
08	DOORS & WINDOWS	85.8	63.3	80.3	88.1	95.8	90.0	92.3	90.4	91.9	92.3	75.6	88.3	87.2	63.3	81.4	86.2	59.8	79.9
09200	PLASTER & GYPSUM BOARD	122.6	63.2	86.3	149.1	98.6	118.2	214.8	96.3	142.4	147.0	79.1	105.5	122.6	63.2	86.3	209.6	68.0	123.1
095,098	CEILINGS & ACOUSTICAL TREATMENT	99.7	63.2	75.6	102.4	98.6	99.9	102.4	96.3	98.4	102.4	79.1	87.0	99.7	63.2	75.6	102.4	68.0	79.7
09600	FLOORING	120.2	69.2	107.8	126.9	62.1	111.2	132.6	109.6	127.0	132.6	83.1	120.6	120.2	69.2	107.8	127.7	51.2	109.1
097,099	WALL FINISHES, PAINTS & COATINGS	109.2	62.7	82.2	109.2	92.9	99.7	109.2	102.6	105.4	109.2	78.1	91.1	109.2	73.5	88.5	109.2	72.5	87.9
09	FINISHES	112.1	65.7	88.5	120.2	92.6	106.1	129.8	99.8	114.5	120.4	81.0	100.3	112.1	67.0	89.1	127.7	65.9	96.2
10 - 14	TOTAL DIV. 10000 - 14000	100.0	71.6	94.0	100.0	105.3	101.1	100.0	94.4	98.8	100.0	89.0	97.7	100.0	71.6	94.0	100.0	72.2	94.1
15	MECHANICAL	102.5	73.8	89.2	102.5	92.2	97.8	102.5	89.0	96.3	102.5	73.3	89.0	102.5	73.8	89.2	102.5	76.0	90.2
16	ELECTRICAL	128.8	76.1	92.6	126.6	100.3	108.6	123.6	88.9	99.7	113.7	80.3	90.8	128.8	76.1	92.6	123.1	92.6	102.2
01 - 16	WEIGHTED AVERAGE	107.6	74.9	91.7	114.1	97.3	106.0	112.3	94.2	103.5	110.2	80.9	96.0	108.9	75.1	92.5	110.9	77.2	94.5

City Cost Indexes

CANADA

DIVISION		SARNIA, ONTARIO			SASKATOON, SASKATCHEWAN			SHERBROOKE, QUEBEC			ST CATHARINES, ONTARIO			ST JOHNS, NEWFOUNDLAND			SUDBURY, ONTARIO		
		MAT.	INST.	TOTAL	MAT.	INST.	TOTAL	MAT.	INST.	TOTAL	MAT.	INST.	TOTAL	MAT.	INST.	TOTAL	MAT.	INST.	TOTAL
02	SITE CONSTRUCTION	110.7	97.5	100.6	104.3	95.9	97.9	91.1	97.8	96.2	98.5	97.2	97.5	112.1	95.5	99.4	98.4	97.1	97.4
03100	CONCRETE FORMS & ACCESSORIES	118.4	106.4	108.0	97.2	65.8	70.1	128.8	96.1	100.6	109.5	97.7	99.3	95.3	65.7	69.7	104.4	97.3	98.3
03200	CONCRETE REINFORCEMENT	122.9	100.6	110.2	118.7	77.4	95.2	156.5	97.5	122.9	111.1	97.2	103.2	147.8	59.1	97.2	112.0	94.8	102.2
03300	CAST-IN-PLACE CONCRETE	157.2	105.6	135.9	149.1	75.2	118.6	140.1	102.7	124.7	140.1	91.1	119.9	179.6	72.7	135.5	140.1	90.4	119.6
03	CONCRETE	138.5	104.7	121.6	125.7	71.8	98.7	135.0	98.5	116.8	121.3	95.0	108.2	165.0	67.7	116.4	121.0	94.4	107.7
04	MASONRY	147.6	113.9	126.9	144.8	72.3	100.2	143.8	97.6	115.4	145.3	103.6	119.6	146.0	69.6	99.0	145.3	103.2	119.4
05	METALS	98.8	97.1	98.2	98.4	80.2	91.8	101.0	93.8	98.4	97.9	92.5	96.0	102.1	76.6	92.9	98.1	95.1	97.0
06	WOOD & PLASTICS	117.0	106.0	111.3	92.9	64.3	78.1	131.0	96.3	113.1	106.8	99.4	103.0	92.4	64.7	78.1	101.4	98.1	99.7
07	THERMAL & MOISTURE PROTECTION	104.3	104.7	104.5	103.4	70.6	87.8	104.5	99.3	102.0	102.7	97.8	100.4	105.9	67.5	87.7	102.7	95.9	99.5
08	DOORS & WINDOWS	93.2	100.2	94.9	85.8	63.3	80.3	92.3	85.2	90.6	83.2	94.9	86.0	98.6	62.0	89.8	84.2	93.0	86.3
09200	PLASTER & GYPSUM BOARD	209.2	106.3	146.3	122.6	63.2	86.3	143.8	96.3	114.8	145.0	99.5	117.2	195.0	63.6	114.7	142.4	98.1	115.3
095,098	CEILINGS & ACOUSTICAL TREATMENT	102.4	106.3	105.0	99.7	63.2	75.6	102.4	96.3	98.4	99.7	99.5	99.6	105.2	63.6	77.7	99.7	98.1	98.6
09600	FLOORING	132.6	113.3	127.9	120.2	69.2	107.8	132.6	109.6	127.0	126.5	108.8	122.2	115.0	61.2	102.0	123.6	107.2	119.6
097,099	WALL FINISHES, PAINTS & COATINGS	109.2	114.6	112.4	109.2	62.7	82.2	109.2	102.6	105.4	109.2	110.3	109.8	109.2	67.0	84.7	109.2	101.9	105.0
09	FINISHES	129.5	109.2	119.2	112.1	65.7	88.5	119.0	99.8	109.2	116.7	101.8	109.1	122.6	64.9	93.2	115.3	100.2	107.6
10 - 14	TOTAL DIV. 10000 - 14000	100.0	86.2	97.1	100.0	71.6	94.0	100.0	94.4	98.8	100.0	81.8	96.2	100.0	72.1	94.1	100.0	106.8	101.4
15	MECHANICAL	102.5	105.5	103.9	102.5	73.8	89.2	102.5	89.0	96.3	102.5	95.8	99.4	102.5	68.6	86.8	102.5	92.6	97.9
16	ELECTRICAL	127.0	106.9	113.2	128.8	76.1	92.6	123.6	88.9	99.7	127.0	99.2	107.9	123.6	69.9	86.7	127.0	99.1	107.8
01 - 16	WEIGHTED AVERAGE	112.7	104.6	108.8	107.8	74.9	91.8	110.5	94.0	102.5	107.3	97.3	102.4	115.9	71.5	94.3	107.2	97.0	102.3

CANADA

DIVISION		SUMMERSIDE, PEI			SYDNEY, NOVA SCOTIA			THUNDER BAY, ONTARIO			TORONTO, ONTARIO			TROIS RIVIERES, QUEBEC			VANCOUVER, B C		
		MAT.	INST.	TOTAL	MAT.	INST.	TOTAL	MAT.	INST.	TOTAL	MAT.	INST.	TOTAL	MAT.	INST.	TOTAL	MAT.	INST.	TOTAL
02	SITE CONSTRUCTION	104.3	95.0	97.2	90.9	96.8	95.4	104.4	97.3	99.0	111.7	98.1	101.2	90.7	97.8	96.1	109.3	98.9	101.4
03100	CONCRETE FORMS & ACCESSORIES	85.0	62.2	65.3	84.3	76.6	77.7	120.1	99.0	101.9	120.3	112.3	113.4	128.8	96.3	100.7	111.0	100.7	102.1
03200	CONCRETE REINFORCEMENT	147.8	56.8	95.9	147.8	58.8	97.1	99.3	96.4	97.6	170.7	101.9	131.5	147.8	97.5	119.1	161.1	97.8	125.0
03300	CAST-IN-PLACE CONCRETE	168.0	63.5	124.9	137.4	76.2	112.2	155.4	104.1	134.2	164.5	114.9	144.0	137.5	102.8	123.2	159.6	104.6	136.9
03	CONCRETE	155.2	62.4	108.8	131.0	73.8	102.4	131.6	100.1	115.8	148.2	110.8	129.5	132.6	98.6	115.6	150.2	101.3	125.7
04	MASONRY	145.1	68.2	97.8	142.8	78.6	103.4	146.2	104.5	120.6	149.0	121.4	132.0	142.8	97.6	115.1	146.4	104.6	120.7
05	METALS	100.8	71.6	90.3	100.7	79.8	93.2	97.3	94.4	96.3	100.9	99.3	100.3	101.0	94.0	98.5	101.1	95.2	99.0
06	WOOD & PLASTICS	82.2	61.7	71.6	81.8	75.9	78.7	118.2	99.9	108.7	118.2	111.2	114.6	131.0	96.3	113.1	103.8	98.6	101.1
07	THERMAL & MOISTURE PROTECTION	105.0	65.8	86.4	103.0	77.6	90.9	103.2	96.9	100.3	104.6	109.9	107.1	104.5	99.3	102.0	104.1	100.9	102.5
08	DOORS & WINDOWS	94.6	54.4	84.9	82.9	71.0	80.0	82.2	94.9	85.3	91.4	106.1	95.0	92.3	90.4	91.9	92.3	96.1	93.2
09200	PLASTER & GYPSUM BOARD	189.8	60.5	110.8	189.3	75.2	119.6	150.8	100.0	119.7	143.0	111.6	123.8	214.8	96.3	142.4	154.8	98.6	120.3
095,098	CEILINGS & ACOUSTICAL TREATMENT	102.4	60.5	74.8	102.4	75.2	84.4	98.3	100.0	99.4	102.4	111.6	108.5	102.4	96.3	98.4	102.4	98.6	99.9
09600	FLOORING	110.2	68.0	100.0	110.2	72.9	101.1	132.6	62.6	115.6	132.6	115.3	128.4	132.6	109.6	127.0	132.6	107.1	126.4
097,099	WALL FINISHES, PAINTS & COATINGS	109.2	47.2	73.2	109.2	70.6	86.8	109.2	104.8	106.7	112.3	120.3	116.9	109.2	102.6	105.4	109.2	116.0	113.2
09	FINISHES	119.5	62.0	90.1	118.7	75.3	96.6	119.6	94.1	106.6	119.7	114.2	116.9	129.8	99.8	114.5	122.1	103.1	112.4
10 - 14	TOTAL DIV. 10000 - 14000	100.0	71.3	93.9	100.0	73.9	94.5	100.0	83.1	96.4	100.0	112.8	102.7	100.0	94.4	98.8	100.0	105.3	101.1
15	MECHANICAL	102.5	61.8	83.7	102.5	81.8	92.9	102.5	96.7	99.8	102.5	108.6	105.3	102.5	89.0	96.3	102.5	100.2	101.5
16	ELECTRICAL	123.6	63.2	82.1	123.6	78.0	92.3	127.0	97.3	106.6	127.0	108.1	114.0	123.6	88.9	99.7	131.0	100.3	109.9
01 - 16	WEIGHTED AVERAGE	113.3	67.0	90.8	108.2	79.5	94.3	109.0	97.2	103.3	113.1	108.9	111.1	111.3	94.2	103.0	113.7	100.5	107.3

CANADA

DIVISION		VICTORIA, B C			WHITEHORSE, YUKON			WINDSOR, ONTARIO			WINNIPEG, MANITOBA			YARMOUTH, NOVA SCOTIA			YELLOWKNIFE, NWT		
		MAT.	INST.	TOTAL	MAT.	INST.	TOTAL	MAT.	INST.	TOTAL	MAT.	INST.	TOTAL	MAT.	INST.	TOTAL	MAT.	INST.	TOTAL
02	SITE CONSTRUCTION	119.1	98.6	103.4	104.8	95.8	97.9	94.3	97.5	96.8	108.4	96.3	99.2	96.2	96.8	96.7	104.8	95.9	98.0
03100	CONCRETE FORMS & ACCESSORIES	101.9	100.0	100.2	97.2	64.0	68.5	120.1	99.7	102.5	119.3	79.2	84.7	84.3	76.6	77.7	97.2	64.2	68.7
03200	CONCRETE REINFORCEMENT	116.1	97.7	105.6	118.7	74.0	93.2	108.8	95.5	101.2	161.1	64.8	106.2	147.8	58.8	97.1	118.7	73.7	93.0
03300	CAST-IN-PLACE CONCRETE	164.8	104.2	139.8	152.8	73.1	119.9	143.5	105.5	127.8	146.7	79.3	118.9	178.4	76.2	136.3	152.8	73.0	119.9
03	CONCRETE	161.9	100.8	131.3	127.5	69.7	98.6	123.4	100.8	112.1	131.1	77.1	104.1	151.2	73.8	112.5	127.5	69.6	98.6
04	MASONRY	146.0	104.6	120.5	145.1	69.1	98.4	145.5	112.3	125.1	145.5	75.7	102.6	145.9	78.6	104.6	145.1	69.0	98.3
05	METALS	100.1	94.4	98.1	98.4	78.7	91.3	97.5	95.8	96.9	100.8	82.0	94.0	100.7	79.8	93.2	98.4	78.5	91.2
06	WOOD & PLASTICS	94.6	98.6	96.7	92.9	62.5	77.2	118.2	98.2	107.8	116.0	80.4	97.6	81.8	75.9	78.7	92.9	62.8	77.3
07	THERMAL & MOISTURE PROTECTION	104.9	93.5	99.5	103.4	68.5	86.8	102.8	101.4	102.1	104.3	79.7	92.6	103.0	77.6	90.9	103.4	68.4	86.8
08	DOORS & WINDOWS	88.1	95.8	90.0	85.8	61.0	79.8	81.9	94.7	85.0	92.3	71.7	87.3	82.9	71.0	80.0	85.8	61.0	79.8
09200	PLASTER & GYPSUM BOARD	149.1	98.6	118.2	122.6	61.4	85.2	150.8	98.2	118.6	135.2	79.9	101.4	189.3	75.2	119.6	122.6	61.6	85.3
095,098	CEILINGS & ACOUSTICAL TREATMENT	102.4	98.6	99.9	99.7	61.4	74.4	98.3	98.2	98.2	102.4	79.9	87.6	102.4	75.2	84.4	99.7	61.6	74.6
09600	FLOORING	126.9	62.1	111.2	120.2	66.2	107.1	132.6	109.6	127.0	132.6	76.1	118.9	110.2	72.9	101.1	120.2	65.9	107.0
097,099	WALL FINISHES, PAINTS & COATINGS	109.2	92.9	99.7	109.2	61.4	81.4	109.2	104.3	106.4	109.3	65.9	84.1	109.2	70.6	86.8	109.2	61.1	81.3
09	FINISHES	120.2	92.6	106.1	112.1	63.7	87.5	119.3	102.3	110.6	118.6	77.6	97.7	118.7	75.3	96.6	112.1	63.8	87.5
10 - 14	TOTAL DIV. 10000 - 14000	100.0	105.3	101.1	100.0	70.3	93.7	100.0	84.6	96.7	100.0	74.6	94.6	100.0	73.9	94.5	100.0	71.3	93.9
15	MECHANICAL	102.5	92.2	97.8	102.5	72.5	88.6	102.5	99.9	101.3	102.5	81.8	92.9	102.5	81.8	92.9	102.5	72.3	88.5
16	ELECTRICAL	126.6	100.3	108.6	128.8	75.0	91.8	127.0	99.6	108.1	128.8	85.1	98.8	123.6	78.0	92.3	128.8	74.7	91.6
01 - 16	WEIGHTED AVERAGE	114.1	97.3	106.0	108.1	73.3	91.2	107.6	100.2	104.0	110.8	81.5	96.5	111.0	79.5	95.7	108.1	73.3	91.1

COST INDEXES

655

Location Factors

Costs shown in *Means cost data publications* are based on National Averages for materials and installation. To adjust these costs to a specific location, simply multiply the base cost by the factor and divide by 100 for that city. The data is arranged alphabetically by state and postal zip code numbers. For a city not listed, use the factor for a nearby city with similar economic characteristics.

STATE/ZIP	CITY	MAT.	INST.	TOTAL
ALABAMA				
350-352	Birmingham	96.6	77.2	87.2
354	Tuscaloosa	96.3	61.1	79.1
355	Jasper	97.4	57.5	77.9
356	Decatur	96.3	65.6	81.3
357-358	Huntsville	96.2	68.6	82.8
359	Gadsden	96.9	65.0	81.4
360-361	Montgomery	97.2	63.9	81.0
362	Anniston	95.9	52.5	74.8
363	Dothan	96.9	57.2	77.6
364	Evergreen	96.1	58.7	77.9
365-366	Mobile	97.1	68.0	83.0
367	Selma	96.4	58.7	78.1
368	Phenix City	97.2	62.9	80.5
369	Butler	96.6	57.2	77.4
ALASKA				
995-996	Anchorage	134.5	114.1	124.5
997	Fairbanks	130.1	117.0	123.7
998	Juneau	132.9	114.2	123.8
999	Ketchikan	144.2	114.2	129.6
ARIZONA				
850,853	Phoenix	99.6	78.4	89.3
852	Mesa/Tempe	99.6	68.7	84.6
855	Globe	100.5	69.4	85.4
856-857	Tucson	98.4	75.8	87.4
859	Show Low	100.7	71.3	86.4
860	Flagstaff	102.8	74.8	89.2
863	Prescott	100.2	71.2	86.1
864	Kingman	98.7	72.7	86.1
865	Chambers	98.8	70.8	85.2
ARKANSAS				
716	Pine Bluff	95.9	63.3	80.1
717	Camden	94.3	45.9	70.7
718	Texarkana	94.9	51.5	73.8
719	Hot Springs	93.4	45.3	70.0
720-722	Little Rock	96.2	64.0	80.6
723	West Memphis	95.6	62.5	79.5
724	Jonesboro	95.6	62.5	79.5
725	Batesville	94.3	56.9	76.1
726	Harrison	95.8	56.9	76.9
727	Fayetteville	92.8	39.5	66.9
728	Russellville	94.4	54.9	75.2
729	Fort Smith	96.3	61.6	79.4
CALIFORNIA				
900-902	Los Angeles	104.3	112.9	108.5
903-905	Inglewood	100.6	111.1	105.7
906-908	Long Beach	102.4	111.1	106.6
910-912	Pasadena	101.3	111.1	106.1
913-916	Van Nuys	105.3	110.9	108.1
917-918	Alhambra	104.0	111.2	107.5
919-921	San Diego	105.6	107.0	106.3
922	Palm Springs	102.3	110.3	106.2
923-924	San Bernardino	99.8	110.6	105.0
925	Riverside	104.3	111.7	107.9
926-927	Santa Ana	102.1	111.0	106.4
928	Anaheim	104.7	113.0	108.7
930	Oxnard	105.2	112.4	108.7
931	Santa Barbara	104.4	110.8	107.5
932-933	Bakersfield	104.1	108.5	106.3
934	San Luis Obispo	106.2	110.7	108.4
935	Mojave	102.7	108.2	105.4
936-938	Fresno	105.2	112.0	108.5
939	Salinas	107.1	116.2	111.6
940-941	San Francisco	111.9	133.9	122.6
942,956-958	Sacramento	107.5	112.4	109.9
943	Palo Alto	105.5	129.2	117.0
944	San Mateo	108.7	126.1	117.2
945	Vallejo	106.0	123.6	114.6
946	Oakland	110.7	126.3	118.3
947	Berkeley	110.2	125.7	117.7
948	Richmond	110.0	124.3	116.9
949	San Rafael	111.9	127.2	119.3
950	Santa Cruz	110.9	116.3	113.6

STATE/ZIP	CITY	MAT.	INST.	TOTAL
CALIFORNIA (CONT'D)				
951	San Jose	110.2	129.7	119.7
952	Stockton	105.7	113.0	109.3
953	Modesto	105.8	113.8	109.7
954	Santa Rosa	107.2	127.1	116.9
955	Eureka	108.5	111.7	110.0
959	Marysville	107.3	110.8	109.0
960	Redding	108.3	110.6	109.4
961	Susanville	108.4	110.7	109.5
COLORADO				
800-802	Denver	102.5	87.4	95.2
803	Boulder	100.7	68.4	85.0
804	Golden	103.3	82.0	92.9
805	Fort Collins	104.1	79.2	91.9
806	Greeley	100.9	68.4	85.1
807	Fort Morgan	101.5	81.0	91.5
808-809	Colorado Springs	101.3	82.4	92.1
810	Pueblo	102.6	80.9	92.0
811	Alamosa	105.1	70.0	88.0
812	Salida	105.1	70.1	88.0
813	Durango	105.7	65.9	86.3
814	Montrose	103.9	63.2	84.1
815	Grand Junction	107.1	63.6	85.9
816	Glenwood Springs	104.9	76.1	90.9
CONNECTICUT				
060	New Britain	101.9	108.5	105.1
061	Hartford	102.2	108.5	105.3
062	Willimantic	102.6	107.1	104.8
063	New London	99.2	108.7	103.9
064	Meriden	101.9	106.9	104.3
065	New Haven	102.1	109.0	105.5
066	Bridgeport	103.3	107.6	105.4
067	Waterbury	102.6	108.5	105.5
068	Norwalk	102.6	107.7	105.1
069	Stamford	102.7	113.2	107.8
D.C.				
200-205	Washington	99.2	90.1	94.8
DELAWARE				
197	Newark	99.2	102.7	100.9
198	Wilmington	98.5	102.8	100.6
199	Dover	99.1	102.7	100.9
FLORIDA				
320,322	Jacksonville	98.7	66.6	83.1
321	Daytona Beach	98.7	75.0	87.2
323	Tallahassee	99.2	56.2	78.2
324	Panama City	99.8	43.6	72.5
325	Pensacola	99.4	66.1	83.2
326,344	Gainesville	100.2	62.0	81.6
327-328,347	Orlando	100.8	69.5	85.6
329	Melbourne	100.8	77.7	89.5
330-332,340	Miami	98.1	73.4	86.1
333	Fort Lauderdale	97.9	73.5	86.0
334,349	West Palm Beach	96.8	70.2	83.9
335-336,346	Tampa	99.9	64.7	82.8
337	St. Petersburg	102.1	64.3	83.7
338	Lakeland	98.8	64.4	82.1
339,341	Fort Myers	98.2	61.4	80.3
342	Sarasota	100.0	61.8	81.4
GEORGIA				
300-303,399	Atlanta	96.4	81.4	89.1
304	Statesboro	96.7	35.7	67.0
305	Gainesville	95.5	53.5	75.1
306	Athens	94.6	69.0	82.2
307	Dalton	96.6	36.8	67.5
308-309	Augusta	95.2	60.9	78.5
310-312	Macon	95.9	65.7	81.2
313-314	Savannah	97.9	64.5	81.7
315	Waycross	97.9	49.7	74.4
316	Valdosta	97.4	54.0	76.3
317	Albany	97.5	60.3	79.4
318-319	Columbus	97.6	58.7	78.7

Location Factors

STATE/ZIP	CITY	MAT.	INST.	TOTAL
HAWAII				
967	Hilo	115.9	129.0	122.3
968	Honolulu	116.6	129.0	122.7
STATES & POSS.				
969	Guam	211.9	60.7	138.4
IDAHO				
832	Pocatello	102.1	83.7	93.2
833	Twin Falls	104.2	51.9	78.8
834	Idaho Falls	101.3	62.9	82.6
835	Lewiston	113.7	88.1	101.2
836-837	Boise	102.1	85.1	93.8
838	Coeur d'Alene	113.4	63.2	89.0
ILLINOIS				
600-603	North Suburban	98.0	120.9	109.1
604	Joliet	98.0	115.2	106.4
605	South Suburban	98.0	119.6	108.5
606	Chicago	98.2	125.4	111.4
609	Kankakee	94.4	104.2	99.2
610-611	Rockford	97.0	111.2	103.9
612	Rock Island	94.9	100.2	97.5
613	La Salle	96.4	99.7	98.0
614	Galesburg	96.0	101.4	98.6
615-616	Peoria	98.4	103.6	100.9
617	Bloomington	95.2	103.4	99.2
618-619	Champaign	99.1	101.9	100.4
620-622	East St. Louis	93.5	105.7	99.4
623	Quincy	95.3	95.4	95.4
624	Effingham	94.6	99.3	96.9
625	Decatur	95.9	98.3	97.1
626-627	Springfield	95.6	100.6	98.1
628	Centralia	92.8	104.4	98.4
629	Carbondale	92.4	100.7	96.4
INDIANA				
460	Anderson	97.1	87.2	92.3
461-462	Indianapolis	100.0	89.6	94.9
463-464	Gary	97.9	103.7	100.7
465-466	South Bend	96.2	86.2	91.3
467-468	Fort Wayne	97.3	84.7	91.1
469	Kokomo	95.5	86.0	90.9
470	Lawrenceburg	93.4	84.3	89.0
471	New Albany	95.2	80.1	87.9
472	Columbus	97.4	86.2	91.9
473	Muncie	97.5	86.3	92.1
474	Bloomington	99.3	85.9	92.8
475	Washington	95.6	89.9	92.8
476-477	Evansville	97.1	91.8	94.6
478	Terre Haute	97.6	91.2	94.5
479	Lafayette	97.2	84.6	91.1
IOWA				
500-503,509	Des Moines	98.4	86.2	92.5
504	Mason City	96.9	65.2	81.4
505	Fort Dodge	97.2	59.5	78.8
506-507	Waterloo	98.2	66.2	82.7
508	Creston	97.7	71.6	85.0
510-511	Sioux City	99.0	77.6	88.6
512	Sibley	97.9	57.1	78.0
513	Spencer	100.2	56.1	78.7
514	Carroll	96.7	63.0	80.3
515	Council Bluffs	99.8	77.5	88.9
516	Shenandoah	96.7	57.3	77.5
520	Dubuque	98.4	79.2	89.1
521	Decorah	97.8	60.9	79.9
522-524	Cedar Rapids	99.6	83.5	91.8
525	Ottumwa	97.9	75.3	86.9
526	Burlington	96.7	76.2	86.7
527-528	Davenport	98.6	93.6	96.1
KANSAS				
660-662	Kansas City	98.0	90.2	94.2
664-666	Topeka	97.4	71.4	84.8
667	Fort Scott	97.1	70.2	84.0
668	Emporia	96.8	64.4	81.0
669	Belleville	98.8	63.0	81.4
670-672	Wichita	96.6	75.6	86.4
673	Independence	98.6	59.1	79.4
674	Salina	98.3	63.7	81.5
675	Hutchinson	93.7	58.0	76.3
676	Hays	98.1	63.0	81.1
677	Colby	98.9	63.0	81.4

STATE/ZIP	CITY	MAT.	INST.	TOTAL
KANSAS (CONT'D)				
678	Dodge City	99.6	63.0	81.8
679	Liberal	97.9	52.4	75.8
KENTUCKY				
400-402	Louisville	96.1	87.2	91.8
403-405	Lexington	96.9	71.9	84.7
406	Frankfort	96.1	76.4	86.5
407-409	Corbin	94.7	50.7	73.3
410	Covington	95.6	93.9	94.8
411-412	Ashland	93.8	101.9	97.7
413-414	Campton	95.7	50.5	73.7
415-416	Pikeville	96.7	70.9	84.1
417-418	Hazard	94.9	50.7	73.4
420	Paducah	93.6	91.1	92.4
421-422	Bowling Green	95.6	86.6	91.2
423	Owensboro	95.5	83.1	89.5
424	Henderson	93.1	94.1	93.6
425-426	Somerset	92.6	50.5	72.1
427	Elizabethtown	92.2	87.0	89.7
LOUISIANA				
700-701	New Orleans	101.4	69.1	85.7
703	Thibodaux	101.9	68.3	85.6
704	Hammond	98.7	67.0	83.3
705	Lafayette	100.8	61.6	81.7
706	Lake Charles	101.0	65.0	83.5
707-708	Baton Rouge	100.7	62.1	81.9
710-711	Shreveport	96.9	63.3	80.5
712	Monroe	96.8	60.7	79.2
713-714	Alexandria	96.9	58.1	78.0
MAINE				
039	Kittery	97.4	59.7	79.1
040-041	Portland	100.3	78.7	89.8
042	Lewiston	100.8	78.7	90.0
043	Augusta	99.5	56.9	78.8
044	Bangor	99.8	84.4	92.3
045	Bath	98.8	54.7	77.4
046	Machias	98.3	66.8	83.0
047	Houlton	98.5	65.3	82.3
048	Rockland	97.3	67.6	82.9
049	Waterville	98.9	56.9	78.5
MARYLAND				
206	Waldorf	97.3	78.3	88.1
207-208	College Park	97.2	82.0	89.8
209	Silver Spring	96.6	82.1	89.5
210-212	Baltimore	96.8	86.7	91.9
214	Annapolis	96.5	83.8	90.3
215	Cumberland	93.7	82.8	88.4
216	Easton	95.4	51.2	73.9
217	Hagerstown	94.0	82.7	88.5
218	Salisbury	95.9	58.5	77.7
219	Elkton	92.8	74.5	83.9
MASSACHUSETTS				
010-011	Springfield	100.8	102.6	101.6
012	Pittsfield	100.5	95.9	98.3
013	Greenfield	98.7	100.1	99.4
014	Fitchburg	97.1	111.5	104.1
015-016	Worcester	100.6	111.9	106.1
017	Framingham	96.7	117.2	106.7
018	Lowell	100.3	116.7	108.2
019	Lawrence	101.4	115.7	108.4
020-022, 024	Boston	102.6	128.0	115.0
023	Brockton	101.5	115.0	108.1
025	Buzzards Bay	95.9	113.2	104.3
026	Hyannis	98.2	113.2	105.5
027	New Bedford	101.1	113.6	107.2
MICHIGAN				
480,483	Royal Oak	94.7	108.5	101.4
481	Ann Arbor	97.0	111.1	103.9
482	Detroit	98.1	114.8	106.2
484-485	Flint	96.7	103.8	100.1
486	Saginaw	96.9	96.8	96.9
487	Bay City	96.5	96.7	96.6
488-489	Lansing	96.8	99.8	98.3
490	Battle Creek	96.8	91.8	94.4
491	Kalamazoo	97.2	89.0	93.2
492	Jackson	95.5	97.7	96.6
493,495	Grand Rapids	96.7	74.4	85.9
494	Muskegon	95.7	88.5	92.2

LOCATION FACTORS

657

STATE/ZIP	CITY	MAT.	INST.	TOTAL		STATE/ZIP	CITY	MAT.	INST.	TOTAL
MICHIGAN (CONT'D)						**NEW HAMPSHIRE (CONT'D)**				
496	Traverse City	94.9	75.2	85.3		032-033	Concord	99.0	86.8	93.1
497	Gaylord	96.4	81.3	89.1		034	Keene	98.3	60.2	79.7
498-499	Iron Mountain	98.4	91.7	95.2		035	Littleton	98.3	66.6	82.9
						036	Charleston	97.7	56.7	77.8
MINNESOTA						037	Claremont	96.8	56.7	77.3
550-551	Saint Paul	99.5	121.7	110.3		038	Portsmouth	98.3	83.8	91.3
553-555	Minneapolis	100.1	123.6	111.6						
556-558	Duluth	99.6	115.0	107.1		**NEW JERSEY**				
559	Rochester	99.3	106.4	102.7		070-071	Newark	102.8	122.7	112.5
560	Mankato	97.3	105.4	101.3		072	Elizabeth	101.7	117.4	109.3
561	Windom	96.1	85.4	90.9		073	Jersey City	100.3	124.2	111.9
562	Willmar	95.3	93.1	94.3		074-075	Paterson	103.1	122.0	112.3
563	St. Cloud	96.2	113.4	104.6		076	Hackensack	100.1	122.7	111.1
564	Brainerd	97.1	104.4	100.7		077	Long Branch	99.7	119.0	109.1
565	Detroit Lakes	99.7	93.4	96.6		078	Dover	100.5	119.7	109.8
566	Bemidji	98.9	101.5	100.2		079	Summit	100.6	116.0	108.1
567	Thief River Falls	98.0	94.1	96.1		080,083	Vineland	98.0	118.2	107.8
						081	Camden	100.1	117.5	108.6
MISSISSIPPI						082,084	Atlantic City	99.0	118.4	108.5
386	Clarksdale	96.9	35.0	66.8		085-086	Trenton	100.9	121.4	110.9
387	Greenville	100.5	53.3	77.6		087	Point Pleasant	100.4	119.6	109.7
388	Tupelo	98.4	44.5	72.2		088-089	New Brunswick	100.8	119.7	110.0
389	Greenwood	98.4	37.5	68.8						
390-392	Jackson	98.7	55.1	77.5		**NEW MEXICO**				
393	Meridian	96.7	54.8	76.3		870-872	Albuquerque	100.6	81.2	91.2
394	Laurel	98.3	38.8	69.4		873	Gallup	102.0	81.2	91.9
395	Biloxi	98.9	62.4	81.1		874	Farmington	102.0	81.3	91.9
396	McComb	96.7	36.1	67.2		875	Santa Fe	100.2	81.2	90.9
397	Columbus	98.3	44.0	71.9		877	Las Vegas	100.1	81.2	90.9
						878	Socorro	99.6	81.2	90.6
MISSOURI						879	Truth/Consequences	99.6	75.4	87.8
630-631	St. Louis	96.2	110.6	103.2		880	Las Cruces	97.7	72.7	85.6
633	Bowling Green	96.2	93.7	95.0		881	Clovis	100.3	80.7	90.8
634	Hannibal	94.9	92.3	93.6		882	Roswell	101.8	80.7	91.6
635	Kirksville	97.3	83.6	90.6		883	Carrizozo	102.7	81.2	92.2
636	Flat River	97.3	98.2	97.7		884	Tucumcari	101.3	80.7	91.3
637	Cape Girardeau	96.3	96.2	96.2						
638	Sikeston	94.9	90.0	92.5		**NEW YORK**				
639	Poplar Bluff	94.4	88.8	91.7		100-102	New York	108.5	161.9	134.5
640-641	Kansas City	99.0	101.1	100.0		103	Staten Island	104.8	153.5	128.5
644-645	St. Joseph	99.0	87.7	93.5		104	Bronx	102.0	156.0	128.3
646	Chillicothe	96.3	75.0	85.9		105	Mount Vernon	102.9	131.5	116.8
647	Harrisonville	95.8	96.8	96.3		106	White Plains	102.6	129.7	115.8
648	Joplin	98.0	73.4	86.0		107	Yonkers	107.6	134.1	120.5
650-651	Jefferson City	95.0	88.9	92.0		108	New Rochelle	103.6	131.4	117.1
652	Columbia	96.4	89.4	93.0		109	Suffern	103.5	126.7	114.8
653	Sedalia	95.9	87.6	91.9		110	Queens	103.0	156.9	129.2
654-655	Rolla	94.7	85.2	90.0		111	Long Island City	104.9	156.9	130.2
656-658	Springfield	97.7	76.7	87.5		112	Brooklyn	105.2	156.9	130.3
						113	Flushing	105.8	156.9	130.6
MONTANA						114	Jamaica	103.7	157.9	130.1
590-591	Billings	101.5	89.8	95.8		115,117,118	Hicksville	102.8	149.1	125.3
592	Wolf Point	102.1	88.8	95.7		116	Far Rockaway	105.9	156.9	130.7
593	Miles City	100.0	89.7	95.0		119	Riverhead	103.3	151.3	126.6
594	Great Falls	102.8	89.3	96.2		120-122	Albany	97.9	96.3	97.1
595	Havre	100.8	89.2	95.1		123	Schenectady	98.9	97.0	98.0
596	Helena	102.6	88.9	96.0		124	Kingston	103.4	115.7	109.3
597	Butte	101.3	88.6	95.1		125-126	Poughkeepsie	102.5	122.2	112.1
598	Missoula	99.5	87.8	93.8		127	Monticello	101.7	113.2	107.3
599	Kalispell	98.8	86.8	93.0		128	Glens Falls	93.3	93.0	93.1
						129	Plattsburgh	99.1	86.9	93.2
NEBRASKA						130-132	Syracuse	99.7	92.2	96.1
680-681	Omaha	100.5	80.1	90.6		133-135	Utica	98.1	89.3	93.8
683-685	Lincoln	97.8	67.0	82.8		136	Watertown	99.5	91.7	95.7
686	Columbus	96.6	48.5	73.2		137-139	Binghamton	99.0	88.2	93.7
687	Norfolk	99.1	66.9	83.4		140-142	Buffalo	99.7	104.8	102.2
688	Grand Island	97.5	68.7	83.5		143	Niagara Falls	98.2	107.0	102.5
689	Hastings	97.2	58.5	78.4		144-146	Rochester	101.0	99.4	100.2
690	Mccook	96.9	53.5	75.8		147	Jamestown	97.3	89.7	93.6
691	North Platte	96.9	67.3	82.5		148-149	Elmira	96.6	90.3	93.6
692	Valentine	100.9	46.0	74.2						
693	Alliance	100.0	41.8	71.7		**NORTH CAROLINA**				
						270,272-274	Greensboro	96.6	54.9	76.3
NEVADA						271	Winston-Salem	96.7	53.9	75.9
889-891	Las Vegas	101.5	108.6	105.0		275-276	Raleigh	97.0	55.1	76.6
893	Ely	102.3	88.1	95.4		277	Durham	96.5	55.1	76.4
894-895	Reno	102.3	97.0	99.7		278	Rocky Mount	95.2	40.8	68.7
897	Carson City	102.0	96.5	99.3		279	Elizabeth City	95.8	43.4	70.3
898	Elko	100.9	87.7	94.5		280	Gastonia	96.7	52.0	75.0
						281-282	Charlotte	96.9	52.4	75.2
NEW HAMPSHIRE						283	Fayetteville	95.0	55.1	75.6
030	Nashua	101.2	86.8	94.2		284	Wilmington	95.2	54.1	75.2
031	Manchester	101.3	86.8	94.2		285	Kinston	93.7	40.4	67.8

STATE/ZIP	CITY	MAT.	INST.	TOTAL
NORTH CAROLINA (CONT'D)				
286	Hickory	93.9	39.4	67.4
287-288	Asheville	95.6	53.1	75.0
289	Murphy	95.4	38.4	67.6
NORTH DAKOTA				
580-581	Fargo	100.8	66.1	84.0
582	Grand Forks	102.0	62.4	82.7
583	Devils Lake	102.1	60.3	81.7
584	Jamestown	101.9	61.3	82.1
585	Bismarck	100.8	68.1	84.9
586	Dickinson	102.7	60.3	82.1
587	Minot	102.0	65.9	84.4
588	Williston	101.2	60.3	81.3
OHIO				
430-432	Columbus	97.9	93.1	95.5
433	Marion	95.3	89.0	92.2
434-436	Toledo	98.5	99.7	99.1
437-438	Zanesville	95.4	87.2	91.4
439	Steubenville	97.2	98.4	97.8
440	Lorain	98.6	97.2	97.9
441	Cleveland	98.7	107.3	102.9
442-443	Akron	99.8	100.9	100.4
444-445	Youngstown	99.0	95.7	97.4
446-447	Canton	99.2	92.9	96.1
448-449	Mansfield	96.7	92.7	94.7
450	Hamilton	95.3	92.3	93.8
451-452	Cincinnati	95.3	93.9	94.6
453-454	Dayton	95.2	90.9	93.1
455	Springfield	95.4	90.6	93.1
456	Chillicothe	94.9	97.2	96.0
457	Athens	98.4	75.3	87.1
458	Lima	99.0	89.7	94.5
OKLAHOMA				
730-731	Oklahoma City	97.9	68.2	83.4
734	Ardmore	96.1	67.6	82.2
735	Lawton	97.8	68.5	83.6
736	Clinton	97.6	65.7	82.1
737	Enid	97.6	65.7	82.1
738	Woodward	96.2	65.8	81.4
739	Guymon	97.5	38.0	68.6
740-741	Tulsa	97.8	65.3	82.0
743	Miami	94.9	71.1	83.3
744	Muskogee	96.8	48.8	73.4
745	Mcalester	94.4	61.1	78.2
746	Ponca City	95.0	66.7	81.2
747	Durant	95.0	66.7	81.2
748	Shawnee	96.7	64.9	81.2
749	Poteau	94.0	68.0	81.4
OREGON				
970-972	Portland	103.8	109.7	106.7
973	Salem	104.4	108.2	106.2
974	Eugene	103.8	107.3	105.5
975	Medford	105.3	105.5	105.4
976	Klamath Falls	106.3	104.9	105.6
977	Bend	105.1	107.3	106.2
978	Pendleton	98.5	106.2	102.2
979	Vale	96.0	98.2	97.1
PENNSYLVANIA				
150-152	Pittsburgh	97.0	106.0	101.4
153	Washington	94.6	105.5	99.9
154	Uniontown	94.7	103.9	99.2
155	Bedford	95.8	97.3	96.5
156	Greensburg	96.0	104.3	100.0
157	Indiana	94.6	102.2	98.3
158	Dubois	96.2	97.9	97.0
159	Johnstown	95.8	99.4	97.6
160	Butler	92.8	104.0	98.2
161	New Castle	92.7	104.0	98.2
162	Kittanning	93.3	105.7	99.4
163	Oil City	92.7	99.0	95.8
164-165	Erie	94.8	100.3	97.5
166	Altoona	94.6	96.6	95.6
167	Bradford	96.4	99.0	97.7
168	State College	96.1	98.0	97.0
169	Wellsboro	97.2	92.9	95.1
170-171	Harrisburg	98.1	93.6	95.9
172	Chambersburg	96.7	92.9	94.9
173-174	York	96.3	94.0	95.2
175-176	Lancaster	95.3	91.7	93.6

STATE/ZIP	CITY	MAT.	INST.	TOTAL
PENNSYLVANIA (CONT'D)				
177	Williamsport	93.6	88.0	90.9
178	Sunbury	96.0	93.5	94.8
179	Pottsville	95.1	94.5	94.8
180	Lehigh Valley	96.9	105.4	101.0
181	Allentown	98.7	103.4	101.0
182	Hazleton	96.0	96.0	96.0
183	Stroudsburg	96.0	107.4	101.6
184-185	Scranton	99.2	98.8	99.0
186-187	Wilkes-Barre	95.7	96.4	96.0
188	Montrose	95.2	98.1	96.6
189	Doylestown	95.4	117.6	106.2
190-191	Philadelphia	99.6	123.9	111.4
193	Westchester	96.8	113.9	105.1
194	Norristown	95.5	119.5	107.2
195-196	Reading	97.9	99.0	98.4
PUERTO RICO				
009	San Juan	143.2	29.0	87.6
RHODE ISLAND				
028	Newport	99.8	108.1	103.8
029	Providence	100.1	108.1	104.0
SOUTH CAROLINA				
290-292	Columbia	95.9	53.2	75.1
293	Spartanburg	94.7	52.0	73.9
294	Charleston	95.9	54.6	75.8
295	Florence	94.2	51.0	73.1
296	Greenville	94.4	52.0	73.8
297	Rock Hill	94.5	38.0	67.0
298	Aiken	95.6	38.6	67.8
299	Beaufort	96.2	42.5	70.1
SOUTH DAKOTA				
570-571	Sioux Falls	101.2	61.6	81.9
572	Watertown	100.1	55.7	78.5
573	Mitchell	98.9	55.5	77.8
574	Aberdeen	101.2	55.7	79.1
575	Pierre	100.6	56.5	79.1
576	Mobridge	99.7	55.7	78.3
577	Rapid City	101.3	54.9	78.7
TENNESSEE				
370-372	Nashville	97.4	73.3	85.7
373-374	Chattanooga	98.9	62.1	81.0
375,380-381	Memphis	96.3	75.2	86.0
376	Johnson City	98.3	58.9	79.1
377-379	Knoxville	95.0	63.3	79.6
382	Mckenzie	97.3	38.9	68.9
383	Jackson	98.8	49.2	74.7
384	Columbia	95.7	54.9	75.9
385	Cookeville	97.0	37.6	68.1
TEXAS				
750	Mckinney	99.5	63.6	82.1
751	Waxahackie	99.5	63.9	82.2
752-753	Dallas	100.0	69.1	85.0
754	Greenville	99.7	45.0	73.1
755	Texarkana	98.8	54.7	77.4
756	Longview	99.3	47.5	74.1
757	Tyler	99.9	58.5	79.8
758	Palestine	95.8	48.8	72.9
759	Lufkin	96.9	55.0	76.5
760-761	Fort Worth	97.8	66.4	82.6
762	Denton	98.1	59.2	79.2
763	Wichita Falls	98.3	60.6	80.0
764	Eastland	97.4	47.7	73.2
765	Temple	95.9	56.8	76.9
766-767	Waco	97.6	61.9	80.2
768	Brownwood	98.3	44.3	72.1
769	San Angelo	97.9	51.1	75.2
770-772	Houston	99.8	75.0	87.7
773	Huntsville	98.7	47.8	73.9
774	Wharton	100.3	52.4	77.0
775	Galveston	98.1	74.4	86.5
776-777	Beaumont	97.5	70.1	84.2
778	Bryan	95.0	68.7	82.2
779	Victoria	100.4	56.9	79.2
780	Laredo	95.0	59.8	77.8
781-782	San Antonio	94.9	70.0	82.8
783-784	Corpus Christi	98.3	60.0	79.7
785	Mc Allen	98.8	53.3	76.7
786-787	Austin	95.1	67.2	81.5

STATE/ZIP	CITY	MAT.	INST.	TOTAL
TEXAS (CONT'D)				
788	Del Rio	98.2	37.0	68.4
789	Giddings	95.2	47.7	72.1
790-791	Amarillo	98.4	62.3	80.8
792	Childress	97.9	57.9	78.4
793-794	Lubbock	100.3	59.3	80.4
795-796	Abilene	97.7	54.9	76.9
797	Midland	101.1	56.6	79.4
798-799,885	El Paso	97.7	58.6	78.7
UTAH				
840-841	Salt Lake City	101.1	77.4	89.6
842,844	Ogden	99.6	77.3	88.7
843	Logan	101.8	77.3	89.9
845	Price	102.4	57.6	80.6
846-847	Provo	102.1	77.2	90.0
VERMONT				
050	White River Jct.	99.8	42.9	72.1
051	Bellows Falls	98.2	46.6	73.1
052	Bennington	98.5	42.6	71.3
053	Brattleboro	99.0	46.9	73.6
054	Burlington	101.0	69.2	85.5
056	Montpelier	98.2	69.1	84.0
057	Rutland	100.1	69.2	85.1
058	St. Johnsbury	100.0	49.5	75.4
059	Guildhall	98.4	48.9	74.3
VIRGINIA				
220-221	Fairfax	97.7	81.6	89.9
222	Arlington	98.4	81.4	90.1
223	Alexandria	97.3	83.5	90.6
224-225	Fredericksburg	96.2	73.1	84.9
226	Winchester	97.0	60.9	79.5
227	Culpeper	96.7	62.0	79.8
228	Harrisonburg	97.1	54.1	76.2
229	Charlottesville	97.3	65.2	81.7
230-232	Richmond	97.5	70.1	84.2
233-235	Norfolk	97.8	66.6	82.6
236	Newport News	97.2	66.4	82.2
237	Portsmouth	96.4	66.1	81.6
238	Petersburg	97.1	70.1	84.0
239	Farmville	96.5	48.3	73.1
240-241	Roanoke	97.3	53.4	75.9
242	Bristol	96.2	52.5	74.9
243	Pulaski	95.9	47.7	72.4
244	Staunton	96.7	52.4	75.1
245	Lynchburg	96.7	55.8	76.8
246	Grundy	96.2	47.7	72.6
WASHINGTON				
980-981,987	Seattle	103.8	104.9	104.4
982	Everett	104.1	101.4	102.8
983-984	Tacoma	103.7	102.0	102.9
985	Olympia	103.6	102.0	102.8
986	Vancouver	106.1	101.1	103.7
988	Wenatchee	104.9	91.2	98.3
989	Yakima	104.2	95.9	100.2
990-992	Spokane	108.3	87.8	98.3
993	Richland	108.4	90.1	99.5
994	Clarkston	107.6	89.6	98.8
WEST VIRGINIA				
247-248	Bluefield	95.0	85.1	90.2
249	Lewisburg	96.5	86.2	91.5
250-253	Charleston	97.2	91.6	94.4
254	Martinsburg	96.5	56.1	76.8
255-257	Huntington	97.4	96.0	96.7
258-259	Beckley	94.7	89.2	92.0
260	Wheeling	97.6	93.1	95.4
261	Parkersburg	96.4	95.4	96.0
262	Buckhannon	96.4	91.7	94.1
263-264	Clarksburg	96.8	91.7	94.3
265	Morgantown	96.9	91.7	94.4
266	Gassaway	96.2	92.2	94.2
267	Romney	96.2	87.2	91.8
268	Petersburg	96.2	90.1	93.2
WISCONSIN				
530,532	Milwaukee	99.2	101.6	100.3
531	Kenosha	99.4	101.0	100.2
534	Racine	98.6	101.3	99.9
535	Beloit	98.5	97.5	98.0
537	Madison	98.7	98.0	98.3

STATE/ZIP	CITY	MAT.	INST.	TOTAL
WISCONSIN (CONT'D)				
538	Lancaster	96.9	82.5	89.9
539	Portage	95.2	97.8	96.5
540	New Richmond	96.9	93.6	95.3
541-543	Green Bay	100.4	93.3	97.0
544	Wausau	96.1	93.1	94.6
545	Rhinelander	99.5	89.3	94.5
546	La Crosse	96.6	93.5	95.1
547	Eau Claire	98.6	93.3	96.0
548	Superior	96.8	98.9	97.8
549	Oshkosh	96.7	90.7	93.8
WYOMING				
820	Cheyenne	100.6	61.4	81.5
821	Yellowstone Nat'l Park	100.0	55.1	78.2
822	Wheatland	101.7	54.3	78.7
823	Rawlins	103.3	50.3	77.5
824	Worland	100.8	50.7	76.4
825	Riverton	102.0	53.9	78.6
826	Casper	100.3	63.9	82.6
827	Newcastle	100.5	50.3	76.1
828	Sheridan	101.6	59.2	81.0
829-831	Rock Springs	105.3	50.7	78.7
CANADIAN FACTORS (reflect Canadian currency)				
ALBERTA				
	Calgary	111.8	80.9	96.8
	Edmonton	111.8	80.8	96.7
	Fort McMurray	110.4	80.8	96.0
	Lethbridge	110.5	80.9	96.1
	Lloydminster	110.4	80.8	96.0
	Medicine Hat	110.5	80.9	96.1
	Red Deer	110.2	80.9	96.0
BRITISH COLUMBIA				
	Kamloops	110.6	97.3	104.2
	Prince George	114.1	97.3	106.0
	Vancouver	113.7	100.5	107.3
	Victoria	114.1	97.3	106.0
MANITOBA				
	Brandon	111.9	81.5	97.1
	Portage la Prairie	111.1	81.5	96.7
	Winnipeg	110.8	81.5	96.5
NEW BRUNSWICK				
	Bathurst	109.9	72.0	91.5
	Dalhousie	109.9	72.0	91.5
	Fredericton	110.6	77.2	94.4
	Moncton	109.5	72.0	91.3
	Newcastle	109.9	72.0	91.5
	Saint John	110.9	77.2	94.5
NEWFOUNDLAND				
	Corner Brook	115.9	71.5	94.3
	St. John's	115.9	71.5	94.3
NORTHWEST TERRITORIES				
	Yellowknife	108.1	73.3	91.1
NOVA SCOTIA				
	Dartmouth	111.0	79.5	95.7
	Halifax	111.0	81.0	96.4
	New Glasgow	111.0	79.5	95.7
	Sydney	108.2	79.5	94.3
	Yarmouth	111.0	79.5	95.7
ONTARIO				
	Barrie	115.7	98.1	107.2
	Brantford	113.5	103.9	108.8
	Cornwall	114.1	99.2	106.8
	Hamilton	113.8	102.8	108.4
	Kingston	114.1	98.9	106.7
	Kitchener	108.4	97.4	103.0
	London	112.8	99.7	106.4
	North Bay	113.5	97.0	105.5
	Oshawa	113.6	100.3	107.1
	Ottawa	114.6	99.9	107.4
	Owen Sound	115.8	96.6	106.5
	Peterborough	113.5	99.0	106.4
	Sarnia	112.7	104.6	108.8
	St. Catharines	107.3	97.3	102.4
	Sudbury	107.2	97.0	102.3

STATE/ZIP	CITY	MAT.	INST.	TOTAL
ONTARIO (CONT'D)				
	Thunder Bay	109.0	97.2	103.3
	Toronto	113.1	108.9	111.1
	Windsor	107.6	100.2	104.0
PRINCE EDWARD ISLAND				
	Charlottetown	113.1	67.0	90.7
	Summerside	113.3	67.0	90.8
QUEBEC				
	Cap-de-la-Madeleine	111.3	94.2	103.0
	Charlesbourg	111.3	94.2	103.0
	Chicoutimi	110.0	93.9	102.2
	Gatineau	108.3	94.0	101.4
	Laval	110.5	94.0	102.5
	Montreal	110.6	94.0	102.5
	Quebec	112.3	94.2	103.5
	Sherbrooke	110.5	94.0	102.5
	Trois Rivieres	111.3	94.2	103.0
SASKATCHEWAN				
	Moose Jaw	108.2	75.1	92.1
	Prince Albert	107.6	74.9	91.7
	Regina	108.9	75.1	92.5
	Saskatoon	107.8	74.9	91.8
YUKON				
	Whitehorse	108.1	73.3	91.2

A	Area Square Feet; Ampere	Cab.	Cabinet	d.f.u.	Drainage Fixture Units
ABS	Acrylonitrile Butadiene Stryrene;	Cair.	Air Tool Laborer	D.H.	Double Hung
	Asbestos Bonded Steel	Calc	Calculated	DHW	Domestic Hot Water
A.C.	Alternating Current;	Cap.	Capacity	Diag.	Diagonal
	Air-Conditioning;	Carp.	Carpenter	Diam.	Diameter
	Asbestos Cement;	C.B.	Circuit Breaker	Distrib.	Distribution
	Plywood Grade A & C	C.C.A.	Chromate Copper Arsenate	Dk.	Deck
A.C.I.	American Concrete Institute	C.C.F.	Hundred Cubic Feet	D.L.	Dead Load; Diesel
AD	Plywood, Grade A & D	cd	Candela	DLH	Deep Long Span Bar Joist
Addit.	Additional	cd/sf	Candela per Square Foot	Do.	Ditto
Adj.	Adjustable	CD	Grade of Plywood Face & Back	Dp.	Depth
af	Audio-frequency	CDX	Plywood, Grade C & D, exterior	D.P.S.T.	Double Pole, Single Throw
A.G.A.	American Gas Association		glue	Dr.	Driver
Agg.	Aggregate	Cefi.	Cement Finisher	Drink.	Drinking
A.H.	Ampere Hours	Cem.	Cement	D.S.	Double Strength
A hr.	Ampere-hour	CF	Hundred Feet	D.S.A.	Double Strength A Grade
A.H.U.	Air Handling Unit	C.F.	Cubic Feet	D.S.B.	Double Strength B Grade
A.I.A.	American Institute of Architects	CFM	Cubic Feet per Minute	Dty.	Duty
AIC	Ampere Interrupting Capacity	c.g.	Center of Gravity	DWV	Drain Waste Vent
Allow.	Allowance	CHW	Chilled Water;	DX	Deluxe White, Direct Expansion
alt.	Altitude		Commercial Hot Water	dyn	Dyne
Alum.	Aluminum	C.I.	Cast Iron	e	Eccentricity
a.m.	Ante Meridiem	C.I.P.	Cast in Place	E	Equipment Only; East
Amp.	Ampere	Circ.	Circuit	Ea.	Each
Anod.	Anodized	C.L.	Carload Lot	E.B.	Encased Burial
Approx.	Approximate	Clab.	Common Laborer	Econ.	Economy
Apt.	Apartment	C.L.F.	Hundred Linear Feet	EDP	Electronic Data Processing
Asb.	Asbestos	CLF	Current Limiting Fuse	EIFS	Exterior Insulation Finish System
A.S.B.C.	American Standard Building Code	CLP	Cross Linked Polyethylene	E.D.R.	Equiv. Direct Radiation
Asbe.	Asbestos Worker	cm	Centimeter	Eq.	Equation
A.S.H.R.A.E.	American Society of Heating,	CMP	Corr. Metal Pipe	Elec.	Electrician; Electrical
	Refrig. & AC Engineers	C.M.U.	Concrete Masonry Unit	Elev.	Elevator; Elevating
A.S.M.E.	American Society of Mechanical	CN	Change Notice	EMT	Electrical Metallic Conduit;
	Engineers	Col.	Column		Thin Wall Conduit
A.S.T.M.	American Society for Testing and	CO_2	Carbon Dioxide	Eng.	Engine, Engineered
	Materials	Comb.	Combination	EPDM	Ethylene Propylene Diene
Attchmt.	Attachment	Compr.	Compressor		Monomer
Avg.	Average	Conc.	Concrete	EPS	Expanded Polystyrene
A.W.G.	American Wire Gauge	Cont.	Continuous; Continued	Eqhv.	Equip. Oper., Heavy
AWWA	American Water Works Assoc.	Corr.	Corrugated	Eqlt.	Equip. Oper., Light
Bbl.	Barrel	Cos	Cosine	Eqmd.	Equip. Oper., Medium
B. & B.	Grade B and Better;	Cot	Cotangent	Eqmm.	Equip. Oper., Master Mechanic
	Balled & Burlapped	Cov.	Cover	Eqol.	Equip. Oper., Oilers
B. & S.	Bell and Spigot	C/P	Cedar on Paneling	Equip.	Equipment
B. & W.	Black and White	CPA	Control Point Adjustment	ERW	Electric Resistance Welded
b.c.c.	Body-centered Cubic	Cplg.	Coupling	E.S.	Energy Saver
B.C.Y.	Bank Cubic Yards	C.P.M.	Critical Path Method	Est.	Estimated
BE	Bevel End	CPVC	Chlorinated Polyvinyl Chloride	esu	Electrostatic Units
B.F.	Board Feet	C.Pr.	Hundred Pair	E.W.	Each Way
Bg. cem.	Bag of Cement	CRC	Cold Rolled Channel	EWT	Entering Water Temperature
BHP	Boiler Horsepower;	Creos.	Creosote	Excav.	Excavation
	Brake Horsepower	Crpt.	Carpet & Linoleum Layer	Exp.	Expansion, Exposure
B.I.	Black Iron	CRT	Cathode-ray Tube	Ext.	Exterior
Bit.; Bitum.	Bituminous	CS	Carbon Steel, Constant Shear Bar	Extru.	Extrusion
Bk.	Backed		Joist	f.	Fiber stress
Bkrs.	Breakers	Csc	Cosecant	F	Fahrenheit; Female; Fill
Bldg.	Building	C.S.F.	Hundred Square Feet	Fab.	Fabricated
Blk.	Block	CSI	Construction Specifications	FBGS	Fiberglass
Bm.	Beam		Institute	F.C.	Footcandles
Boil.	Boilermaker	C.T.	Current Transformer	f.c.c.	Face-centered Cubic
B.P.M.	Blows per Minute	CTS	Copper Tube Size	f'c.	Compressive Stress in Concrete;
BR	Bedroom	Cu	Copper, Cubic		Extreme Compressive Stress
Brg.	Bearing	Cu. Ft.	Cubic Foot	F.E.	Front End
Brhe.	Bricklayer Helper	cw	Continuous Wave	FEP	Fluorinated Ethylene Propylene
Bric.	Bricklayer	C.W.	Cool White; Cold Water		(Teflon)
Brk.	Brick	Cwt.	100 Pounds	F.G.	Flat Grain
Brng.	Bearing	C.W.X.	Cool White Deluxe	F.H.A.	Federal Housing Administration
Brs.	Brass	C.Y.	Cubic Yard (27 cubic feet)	Fig.	Figure
Brz.	Bronze	C.Y./Hr.	Cubic Yard per Hour	Fin.	Finished
Bsn.	Basin	Cyl.	Cylinder	Fixt.	Fixture
Btr.	Better	d	Penny (nail size)	Fl. Oz.	Fluid Ounces
BTU	British Thermal Unit	D	Deep; Depth; Discharge	Flr.	Floor
BTUH	BTU per Hour	Dis.;Disch.	Discharge	F.M.	Frequency Modulation;
B.U.R.	Built-up Roofing	Db.	Decibel		Factory Mutual
BX	Interlocked Armored Cable	Dbl.	Double	Fmg.	Framing
c	Conductivity, Copper Sweat	DC	Direct Current	Fndtn.	Foundation
C	Hundred; Centigrade	DDC	Direct Digital Control	Fori.	Foreman, Inside
C/C	Center to Center, Cedar on Cedar	Demob.	Demobilization	Foro.	Foreman, Outside

Fount.	Fountain	J.I.C.	Joint Industrial Council	M.C.P.	Motor Circuit Protector
FPM	Feet per Minute	K	Thousand; Thousand Pounds;	MD	Medium Duty
FPT	Female Pipe Thread		Heavy Wall Copper Tubing, Kelvin	M.D.O.	Medium Density Overlaid
Fr.	Frame	K.A.H.	Thousand Amp. Hours	Med.	Medium
F.R.	Fire Rating	KCMIL	Thousand Circular Mils	MF	Thousand Feet
FRK	Foil Reinforced Kraft	KD	Knock Down	M.F.B.M.	Thousand Feet Board Measure
FRP	Fiberglass Reinforced Plastic	K.D.A.T.	Kiln Dried After Treatment	Mfg.	Manufacturing
FS	Forged Steel	kg	Kilogram	Mfrs.	Manufacturers
FSC	Cast Body; Cast Switch Box	kG	Kilogauss	mg	Milligram
Ft.	Foot; Feet	kgf	Kilogram Force	MGD	Million Gallons per Day
Ftng.	Fitting	kHz	Kilohertz	MGPH	Thousand Gallons per Hour
Ftg.	Footing	Kip.	1000 Pounds	MH, M.H.	Manhole; Metal Halide; Man-Hour
Ft. Lb.	Foot Pound	KJ	Kiljoule	MHz	Megahertz
Furn.	Furniture	K.L.	Effective Length Factor	Mi.	Mile
FVNR	Full Voltage Non-Reversing	K.L.F.	Kips per Linear Foot	MI	Malleable Iron; Mineral Insulated
FXM	Female by Male	Km	Kilometer	mm	Millimeter
Fy.	Minimum Yield Stress of Steel	K.S.F.	Kips per Square Foot	Mill.	Millwright
g	Gram	K.S.I.	Kips per Square Inch	Min., min.	Minimum, minute
G	Gauss	kV	Kilovolt	Misc.	Miscellaneous
Ga.	Gauge	kVA	Kilovolt Ampere	ml	Milliliter, Mainline
Gal.	Gallon	K.V.A.R.	Kilovar (Reactance)	M.L.F.	Thousand Linear Feet
Gal./Min.	Gallon per Minute	KW	Kilowatt	Mo.	Month
Galv.	Galvanized	KWh	Kilowatt-hour	Mobil.	Mobilization
Gen.	General	L	Labor Only; Length; Long;	Mog.	Mogul Base
G.F.I.	Ground Fault Interrupter		Medium Wall Copper Tubing	MPH	Miles per Hour
Glaz.	Glazier	Lab.	Labor	MPT	Male Pipe Thread
GPD	Gallons per Day	lat	Latitude	MRT	Mile Round Trip
GPH	Gallons per Hour	Lath.	Lather	ms	Millisecond
GPM	Gallons per Minute	Lav.	Lavatory	M.S.F.	Thousand Square Feet
GR	Grade	lb.; #	Pound	Mstz.	Mosaic & Terrazzo Worker
Gran.	Granular	L.B.	Load Bearing; L Conduit Body	M.S.Y.	Thousand Square Yards
Grnd.	Ground	L. & E.	Labor & Equipment	Mtd.	Mounted
H	High; High Strength Bar Joist;	lb./hr.	Pounds per Hour	Mthe.	Mosaic & Terrazzo Helper
	Henry	lb./L.F.	Pounds per Linear Foot	Mtng.	Mounting
H.C.	High Capacity	lbf/sq.in.	Pound-force per Square Inch	Mult.	Multi; Multiply
H.D.	Heavy Duty; High Density	L.C.L.	Less than Carload Lot	M.V.A.	Million Volt Amperes
H.D.O.	High Density Overlaid	Ld.	Load	M.V.A.R.	Million Volt Amperes Reactance
Hdr.	Header	LE	Lead Equivalent	MV	Megavolt
Hdwe.	Hardware	LED	Light Emitting Diode	MW	Megawatt
Help.	Helpers Average	L.F.	Linear Foot	MXM	Male by Male
HEPA	High Efficiency Particulate Air	Lg.	Long; Length; Large	MYD	Thousand Yards
	Filter	L & H	Light and Heat	N	Natural; North
Hg	Mercury	LH	Long Span Bar Joist	nA	Nanoampere
HIC	High Interrupting Capacity	L.H.	Labor Hours	NA	Not Available; Not Applicable
HM	Hollow Metal	L.L.	Live Load	N.B.C.	National Building Code
H.O.	High Output	L.L.D.	Lamp Lumen Depreciation	NC	Normally Closed
Horiz.	Horizontal	L-O-L	Lateralolet	N.E.M.A.	National Electrical Manufacturers
H.P.	Horsepower; High Pressure	lm	Lumen		Assoc.
H.P.F.	High Power Factor	lm/sf	Lumen per Square Foot	NEHB	Bolted Circuit Breaker to 600V.
Hr.	Hour	lm/W	Lumen per Watt	N.L.B.	Non-Load-Bearing
Hrs./Day	Hours per Day	L.O.A.	Length Over All	NM	Non-Metallic Cable
HSC	High Short Circuit	log	Logarithm	nm	Nanometer
Ht.	Height	L.P.	Liquefied Petroleum; Low Pressure	No.	Number
Htg.	Heating	L.P.F.	Low Power Factor	NO	Normally Open
Htrs.	Heaters	LR	Long Radius	N.O.C.	Not Otherwise Classified
HVAC	Heating, Ventilation & Air-	L.S.	Lump Sum	Nose.	Nosing
	Conditioning	Lt.	Light	N.P.T.	National Pipe Thread
Hvy.	Heavy	Lt. Ga.	Light Gauge	NQOD	Combination Plug-on/Bolt on
HW	Hot Water	L.T.L.	Less than Truckload Lot		Circuit Breaker to 240V.
Hyd.;Hydr.	Hydraulic	Lt. Wt.	Lightweight	N.R.C.	Noise Reduction Coefficient
Hz.	Hertz (cycles)	L.V.	Low Voltage	N.R.S.	Non Rising Stem
I.	Moment of Inertia	M	Thousand; Material; Male;	ns	Nanosecond
I.C.	Interrupting Capacity		Light Wall Copper Tubing	nW	Nanowatt
ID	Inside Diameter	M²CA	Meters Squared Contact Area	OB	Opposing Blade
I.D.	Inside Dimension; Identification	m/hr; M.H.	Man-hour	OC	On Center
I.F.	Inside Frosted	mA	Milliampere	OD	Outside Diameter
I.M.C.	Intermediate Metal Conduit	Mach.	Machine	O.D.	Outside Dimension
In.	Inch	Mag. Str.	Magnetic Starter	ODS	Overhead Distribution System
Incan.	Incandescent	Maint.	Maintenance	O.G.	Ogee
Incl.	Included; Including	Marb.	Marble Setter	O.H.	Overhead
Int.	Interior	Mat; Mat'l.	Material	O & P	Overhead and Profit
Inst.	Installation	Max.	Maximum	Oper.	Operator
Insul.	Insulation/Insulated	MBF	Thousand Board Feet	Opng.	Opening
I.P.	Iron Pipe	MBH	Thousand BTU's per hr.	Orna.	Ornamental
I.P.S.	Iron Pipe Size	MC	Metal Clad Cable	OSB	Oriented Strand Board
I.P.T.	Iron Pipe Threaded	M.C.F.	Thousand Cubic Feet	O. S. & Y.	Outside Screw and Yoke
I.W.	Indirect Waste	M.C.F.M.	Thousand Cubic Feet per Minute	Ovhd.	Overhead
J	Joule	M.C.M.	Thousand Circular Mils	OWG	Oil, Water or Gas

Oz.	Ounce	S.	Suction; Single Entrance; South	THHN	Nylon Jacketed Wire
P.	Pole; Applied Load; Projection	SCFM	Standard Cubic Feet per Minute	THW.	Insulated Strand Wire
p.	Page	Scaf.	Scaffold	THWN;	Nylon Jacketed Wire
Pape.	Paperhanger	Sch.; Sched.	Schedule	T.L.	Truckload
P.A.P.R.	Powered Air Purifying Respirator	S.C.R.	Modular Brick	T.M.	Track Mounted
PAR	Weatherproof Reflector	S.D.	Sound Deadening	Tot.	Total
Pc., Pcs.	Piece, Pieces	S.D.R.	Standard Dimension Ratio	T-O-L	Threadolet
P.C.	Portland Cement; Power Connector	S.E.	Surfaced Edge	T.S.	Trigger Start
P.C.F.	Pounds per Cubic Foot	Sel.	Select	Tr.	Trade
P.C.M.	Phase Contract Microscopy	S.E.R.;	Service Entrance Cable	Transf.	Transformer
P.E.	Professional Engineer;	S.E.U.	Service Entrance Cable	Trhv.	Truck Driver, Heavy
	Porcelain Enamel;	S.F.	Square Foot	Trlr	Trailer
	Polyethylene; Plain End	S.F.C.A.	Square Foot Contact Area	Trlt.	Truck Driver, Light
Perf.	Perforated	S.F.G.	Square Foot of Ground	TV	Television
Ph.	Phase	S.F. Hor.	Square Foot Horizontal	T.W.	Thermoplastic Water Resistant
P.I.	Pressure Injected	S.F.R.	Square Feet of Radiation		Wire
Pile.	Pile Driver	S.F. Shlf.	Square Foot of Shelf	UCI	Uniform Construction Index
Pkg.	Package	S4S	Surface 4 Sides	UF	Underground Feeder
Pl.	Plate	Shee.	Sheet Metal Worker	UGND	Underground Feeder
Plah.	Plasterer Helper	Sin.	Sine	U.H.F.	Ultra High Frequency
Plas.	Plasterer	Skwk.	Skilled Worker	U.L.	Underwriters Laboratory
Pluh.	Plumbers Helper	SL	Saran Lined	Unfin.	Unfinished
Plum.	Plumber	S.L.	Slimline	URD	Underground Residential
Ply.	Plywood	Sldr.	Solder		Distribution
p.m.	Post Meridiem	SLH	Super Long Span Bar Joist	US	United States
Pntd.	Painted	S.N.	Solid Neutral	USP	United States Primed
Pord.	Painter, Ordinary	S-O-L	Socketolet	UTP	Unshielded Twisted Pair
pp	Pages	sp	Standpipe	V	Volt
PP; PPL	Polypropylene	S.P.	Static Pressure; Single Pole; Self-	V.A.	Volt Amperes
P.P.M.	Parts per Million		Propelled	V.C.T.	Vinyl Composition Tile
Pr.	Pair	Spri.	Sprinkler Installer	VAV	Variable Air Volume
P.E.S.B.	Pre-engineered Steel Building	spwg	Static Pressure Water Gauge	VC	Veneer Core
Prefab.	Prefabricated	Sq.	Square; 100 Square Feet	Vent.	Ventilation
Prefin.	Prefinished	S.P.D.T.	Single Pole, Double Throw	Vert.	Vertical
Prop.	Propelled	SPF	Spruce Pine Fir	V.F.	Vinyl Faced
PSF; psf	Pounds per Square Foot	S.P.S.T.	Single Pole, Single Throw	V.G.	Vertical Grain
PSI; psi	Pounds per Square Inch	SPT	Standard Pipe Thread	V.H.F.	Very High Frequency
PSIG	Pounds per Square Inch Gauge	Sq. Hd.	Square Head	VHO	Very High Output
PSP	Plastic Sewer Pipe	Sq. In.	Square Inch	Vib.	Vibrating
Pspr.	Painter, Spray	S.S.	Single Strength; Stainless Steel	V.L.F.	Vertical Linear Foot
Psst.	Painter, Structural Steel	S.S.B.	Single Strength B Grade	Vol.	Volume
P.T.	Potential Transformer	sst	Stainless Steel	VRP	Vinyl Reinforced Polyester
P. & T.	Pressure & Temperature	Sswk.	Structural Steel Worker	W	Wire; Watt; Wide; West
Ptd.	Painted	Sswl.	Structural Steel Welder	w/	With
Ptns.	Partitions	St.; Stl.	Steel	W.C.	Water Column; Water Closet
Pu	Ultimate Load	S.T.C.	Sound Transmission Coefficient	W.F.	Wide Flange
PVC	Polyvinyl Chloride	Std.	Standard	W.G.	Water Gauge
Pvmt.	Pavement	STK	Select Tight Knot	Wldg.	Welding
Pwr.	Power	STP	Standard Temperature & Pressure	W. Mile	Wire Mile
Q	Quantity Heat Flow	Stpi.	Steamfitter, Pipefitter	W-O-L	Weldolet
Quan.; Qty.	Quantity	Str.	Strength; Starter; Straight	W.R.	Water Resistant
Q.C.	Quick Coupling	Strd.	Stranded	Wrck.	Wrecker
r	Radius of Gyration	Struct.	Structural	W.S.P.	Water, Steam, Petroleum
R	Resistance	Sty.	Story	WT., Wt.	Weight
R.C.P.	Reinforced Concrete Pipe	Subj.	Subject	WWF	Welded Wire Fabric
Rect.	Rectangle	Subs.	Subcontractors	XFER	Transfer
Reg.	Regular	Surf.	Surface	XFMR	Transformer
Reinf.	Reinforced	Sw.	Switch	XHD	Extra Heavy Duty
Req'd.	Required	Swbd.	Switchboard	XHHW; XLPE	Cross-Linked Polyethylene Wire
Res.	Resistant	S.Y.	Square Yard		Insulation
Resi.	Residential	Syn.	Synthetic	XLP	Cross-linked Polyethylene
Rgh.	Rough	S.Y.P.	Southern Yellow Pine	Y	Wye
RGS	Rigid Galvanized Steel	Sys.	System	yd	Yard
R.H.W.	Rubber, Heat & Water Resistant;	t.	Thickness	yr	Year
	Residential Hot Water	T	Temperature; Ton	Δ	Delta
rms	Root Mean Square	Tan	Tangent	%	Percent
Rnd.	Round	T.C.	Terra Cotta	~	Approximately
Rodm.	Rodman	T & C	Threaded and Coupled	Ø	Phase
Rofc.	Roofer, Composition	T.D.	Temperature Difference	@	At
Rofp.	Roofer, Precast	T.E.M.	Transmission Electron Microscopy	#	Pound; Number
Rohe.	Roofer Helpers (Composition)	TFE	Tetrafluoroethylene (Teflon)	<	Less Than
Rots.	Roofer, Tile & Slate	T. & G.	Tongue & Groove;	>	Greater Than
R.O.W.	Right of Way		Tar & Gravel		
RPM	Revolutions per Minute	Th.; Thk.	Thick		
R.R.	Direct Burial Feeder Conduit	Thn.	Thin		
R.S.	Rapid Start	Thrded	Threaded		
Rsr	Riser	Tilf.	Tile Layer, Floor		
RT	Round Trip	Tilh.	Tile Layer, Helper		

Index

INDEX

Index

Index

CMD Group...

R.S. Means Company, Inc., a CMD Group company, which is a division of Cahners Business Information, the leading provider of construction cost data in North America, supplies comprehensive construction cost guides, related technical publications and educational services.

CMD Group, a leading worldwide provider of total construction information solutions, is comprised of three synergistic product groups crafted to be the complete resource for reliable, timely and actionable project, product and cost data. In North America, CMD Group encompasses:
- Architects' First Source
- Construction Market Data (CMD)
- Manufacturer's Survey Associates (MSA)
- R.S. Means
- CMD Canada
- BIMSA/Mexico
- Worldwide, CMD Group includes Byggfakta Scandinavia (Denmark, Estonia, Finland, Norway and Sweden) and Cordell Building Information Services (Australia).

First Source for Products, available in print, on the Means CostWorks CD, and on the Internet, is a comprehensive product information source. In alliance with The Construction Specifications Institute (CSI) and Thomas Register, Architects' First Source also produces CSI's SPEC-DATA® and MANU-SPEC® as well as CADBlocks.℠ Together, these products offer commercial building product information for the building team at each stage of the construction process.

CMD Exchange, a single electronic community where all members of the construction industry can communicate, collaborate, and conduct business, better, faster, easier.

Construction Market Data provides complete, accurate and timely project information through all stages of construction. Construction Market Data supplies industry data through productive leads, project reports, contact lists, market penetration analysis and sales evaluation reports. Any of these products can pinpoint a county, look at a state, or cover the country. Data is delivered via paper, e-mail or the Internet.

CMD Group Canada serves the Canadian construction market with reliable and comprehensive information services that cover all facets of construction. Core services include: Buildcore, product selection and specification tools available in print and on the Internet; CMD Building Reports, a national construction project lead service; CanaData, statistical and forecasting information; Daily Commercial News, a construction newspaper reporting on news and projects in Ontario; and Journal of Commerce, reporting news in British Columbia and Alberta.

Manufacturers' Survey Associates is a quantity survey and specification service whose experienced estimating staff examines project documents throughout the bidding process and distributes edited information to its clients. Material estimates, edited plans and specifications and distribution of addenda form the heart of the Manufacturers' Survey Associates product line, which is available in print and on CD-ROM.

Clark Reports is the premier provider of industrial construction project data, noted for providing earlier, more complete project information in the planning and pre-planning stages for all segments of industrial and institutional construction.

Byggfakta Scandinavia AB, founded in 1936, is the parent company for the leaders of customized construction market data for Denmark, Estonia, Finland, Norway and Sweden. Each company fully covers the local construction market and provides information across several platforms including subscription, ad-hoc basis, electronically and on paper.

Cordell Building Information Services, with its complete range of project and cost and estimating services, is Australia's specialist in the construction information industry. Cordell provides in-depth and historical information on all aspects of construction projects and estimation, including several customized reports, construction and sales leads, and detailed cost information among others.

For more information, please visit our web site at www.cmdg.com.

CMD Group Corporate Offices
30 Technology Parkway South #100
Norcross, GA 30092-2912
(800) 793-0304
(770) 417-4002 (fax)
info@cmdg.com
www.cmdg.com

Means Project Cost Report

By filling out and returning the Project Description, you can receive a discount of $20.00 off any one of the Means products advertised in the following pages. The cost information required includes all items marked (✔) except those where no costs occurred. The sum of all major items should equal the Total Project Cost.

$20.00 Discount per product for each report you submit.

DISCOUNT PRODUCTS AVAILABLE—FOR U.S. CUSTOMERS ONLY—STRICTLY CONFIDENTIAL

Project Description (No remodeling projects, please.)

✔ Type Building _____

✔ Location _____

Capacity _____

✔ Frame _____

✔ Exterior _____

✔ Basement: full ☐ partial ☐ none ☐ crawl ☐

✔ Height in Stories _____

✔ Total Floor Area _____

Ground Floor Area _____

✔ Volume in C.F. _____

% Air Conditioned _____ Tons _____

Comments _____

Owner _____

Architect _____

General Contractor _____

✔ Bid Date _____

Typical Bay Size _____

✔ Labor Force: _____ % Union _____ % Non-Union

✔ Project Description (Circle one number in each line)
   1. Economy 2. Average 3. Custom 4. Luxury
   1. Square 2. Rectangular 3. Irregular 4. Very Irregular

	✔ **Total Project Cost**			$
A	✔ **General Conditions**			$
B	✔ **Site Work**			$
BS	**Site Clearing & Improvement**			
BE	*Excavation*	(	C.Y.)	
BF	*Caissons & Piling*	(	L.F.)	
BU	*Site Utilities*			
BP	*Roads & Walks Exterior Paving*		S.Y.)	
C	✔ **Concrete**			$
C	*Cast in Place*	(	C.Y.)	
CP	*Precast*	(	S.F.)	
D	✔ **Masonry**			$
DB	*Brick*	(	M)	
DC	*Block*	(	M)	
DT	*Tile*	(	S.F.)	
DS	*Stone*	(	S.F.)	
E	✔ **Metals**			$
ES	*Structural Steel*	(	Tons)	
EM	*Misc. & Ornamental Metals*			
F	✔ **Wood & Plastics**			$
FR	*Rough Carpentry*	(	MBF)	
FF	*Finish Carpentry*			
FM	*Architectural Millwork*			
G	✔ **Thermal & Moisture Protection**			$
GW	*Waterproofing-Dampproofing*	(	S.F.)	
GN	*Insulation*	(	S.F.)	
GR	*Roofing & Flashing*	(	S.F.)	
GM	*Metal Siding/Curtain Wall*	(	S.F.)	
H	✔ **Doors and Windows**			$
HD	*Doors*	(	Ea.)	
HW	*Windows*	(	S.F.)	
HH	*Finish Hardware*			
HG	*Glass & Glazing*	(	S.F.)	
HS	*Storefronts*	(	S.F.)	

J	✔ **Finishes**			$
JL	*Lath & Plaster*	(	S.Y.)	
JD	*Drywall*	(	S.F.)	
JM	*Tile & Marble*	(	S.F.)	
JT	*Terrazzo*	(	S.F.)	
JA	*Acoustical Treatment*	(	S.F.)	
JC	*Carpet*	(	S.Y.)	
JF	*Hard Surface Flooring*	(	S.F.)	
JP	*Painting & Wall Covering*	(	S.F.)	
K	✔ **Specialties**			$
KB	*Bathroom Partitions & Access.*	(	S.F.)	
KF	*Other Partitions*	(	S.F.)	
KL	*Lockers*	(	Ea.)	
L	✔ **Equipment**			$
LK	*Kitchen*			
LS	*School*			
LO	*Other*			
M	✔ **Furnishings**			$
MW	*Window Treatment*			
MS	*Seating*	(	Ea.)	
N	✔ **Special Construction**			$
NA	*Acoustical*	(	S.F.)	
NB	*Prefab. Bldgs.*	(	S.F.)	
NO	*Other*			
P	✔ **Conveying Systems**			$
PE	*Elevators*	(	Ea.)	
PS	*Escalators*	(	Ea.)	
PM	*Material Handling*			
Q	✔ **Mechanical**			$
QP	*Plumbing*	(No. of fixtures	)	
QS	*Fire Protection (Sprinklers)*			
QF	*Fire Protection (Hose Standpipes)*			
QB	*Heating, Ventilating & A.C.*			
QH	*Heating & Ventilating*	(BTU Output	)	
QA	*Air Conditioning*	(	Tons)	
R	✔ **Electrical**			$
RL	*Lighting*	(	S.F.)	
RP	*Power Service*			
RD	*Power Distribution*			
RA	*Alarms*			
RG	*Special Systems*			
S	✔ **Mech./Elec. Combined**			$

Product Name _____

Product Number _____

Your Name _____

Title _____

Company _____

☐ Company

☐ Home Street Address _____

City, State, Zip _____

☐ Please send _____ forms.

Please specify the Means product you wish to receive. Complete the address information as requested and return this form with your check (product cost less $20.00) to address below.

R.S. Means Company, Inc.,
Square Foot Costs Department
P.O. Box 800
Kingston, MA 02364-9988

R.S. Means Company, Inc. . . a tradition of excellence in Construction Cost Information and Services since 1942.

For more information visit Means Web Site at www.rsmeans.com

Table of Contents

Book Selection Guide

The following table provides definitive information on the content of each cost data publication. The number of lines of data provided in each unit price or assemblies division, as well as the number of reference tables and crews is listed for each book. The presence of other elements such as an historical cost index, city cost indexes, square foot models or cross-referenced index is also indicated. You can use the table to help select the Means' book that has the quantity and type of information you most need in your work.

Unit Cost Divisions	Building Construction Costs	Mechanical	Electrical	Repair & Remodel.	Square Foot	Site Work Landsc.	Assemblies	Interior	Concrete Masonry	Open Shop	Heavy Construc.	Resi-dential	Light Commercial	Facil. Construc.	Plumbing	Western Construction Costs
1	1098	586	667	862		1089		491	987	1096	1132	416	621	1612	659	1091
2	3141	1467	509	1881		9149		852	1655	3090	5621	1064	984	5015	1826	3114
3	1516	91	71	768		1321		198	1937	1510	1494	268	233	1378	43	1514
4	871	27	0	688		751		636	1174	853	651	313	396	1124	0	849
5	1857	177	174	955		803		985	667	1824	1056	779	809	1849	95	1841
6	1388	97	84	1314		493		1336	339	1379	612	1532	1473	1411	59	1772
7	1365	180	91	1329		490		546	451	1365	353	805	1036	1357	188	1364
8	1899	60	0	1904		337		1821	726	1880	9	1133	1184	2032	0	1900
9	1650	50	0	1473		188		1746	327	1598	113	1251	1390	1845	50	1644
10	991	58	31	565		217		822	196	995	0	250	467	996	249	991
11	1158	435	213	622		151		917	34	1052	95	116	237	1221	371	1051
12	352	0	0	48		228		1536	30	344	0	72	68	1538	0	343
13	1384	1221	498	587		443		1075	106	1358	302	237	562	2094	1083	1339
14	364	43	0	261		36		330	0	364	40	9	18	362	17	362
15	2510	14742	763	2243		1809		1477	80	2515	2028	1087	1553	12312	10902	2545
16	1517	541	10191	1200		879		1292	62	1535	916	706	1290	9872	481	1459
17	421	0	0	421		0		421	421	460	0	421	421	421	0	421
Totals	23482	19775	13292	17121		18384		16508	9192	23218	14422	10459	12742	46439	16023	23600

Assembly Divisions	Building Construction Costs	Mechanical	Electrical	Repair & Remodel.	Square Foot	Site Work Landsc.	Assemblies	Interior	Concrete Masonry	Open Shop	Heavy Construc.	Resi-dential	Light Commercial	Facil. Construc.	Plumbing	Western Construction Costs
1		0	0	202	131	738	775	0	689		752	841	131	89	0	
2		0	0	40	33	35	48	0	49		0	584	32	0	0	
3		0	0	443	1114	0	3064	228	1245		0	1546	805	174	0	
4		0	0	714	1382	0	3201	255	1273		0	2050	1200	26	0	
5		0	0	288	227	0	459	0	0		0	1081	223	25	0	
6		0	0	1006	843	0	1295	1723	152		0	1077	738	330	0	
7		0	0	42	89	0	179	159	0		0	709	33	71	0	
8		2257	149	998	1689	0	2718	926	0		0	1686	1189	1114	2084	
9		0	1383	355	367	0	1320	306	0		0	238	358	319	0	
10		0	0	0	0	0	0	0	0		0	0	0	0	0	
11		0	0	365	465	0	724	153	0		0	0	466	201	0	
12		501	160	539	84	2392	699	0	698		541	0	84	119	663	
Totals		2758	1692	4992	6424	3165	14482	3750	4106		1293	9812	5259	2468	2747	

Reference Section	Building Construction Costs	Mechanical	Electrical	Repair & Remodel.	Square Foot	Site Work Landsc.	Assemblies	Interior	Concrete Masonry	Open Shop	Heavy Construc.	Resi-dential	Light Commercial	Facil. Construc.	Plumbing	Western Construction Costs
Tables	150	46	84	66	4	84	223	59	83	146	55	49	70	86	49	148
Models					102							32	43			
Crews	408	408	408	389		408		408	408	391	408	391	391	389	408	408
City Cost Indexes	yes	yes	yes	yes	yes	yes	yes	yes	yes	yes	yes	yes	yes	yes	yes	yes
Historical Cost Indexes	yes	yes	yes	yes	yes	yes	yes	yes	yes	yes	yes	no	yes	yes	yes	yes
Index	yes	yes	yes	yes	no	yes	yes	yes	yes	yes	yes	yes	yes	yes	yes	yes

1

Means Building Construction Cost Data 2001

Available in Both Softbound and Looseleaf Editions

The "Bible" of the industry comes in the standard softcover edition or the looseleaf edition.

Many customers enjoy the convenience and flexibility of the looseleaf binder, which increases the usefulness of *Means Building Construction Cost Data 2001* by making it easy to add and remove pages. You can insert your own cost information pages, so everything is in one place. Copying pages for faxing is easier also. Whichever edition you prefer, softbound or the convenient looseleaf edition, you'll get the *DesignBuildIntelligence* newsletter at no extra cost.

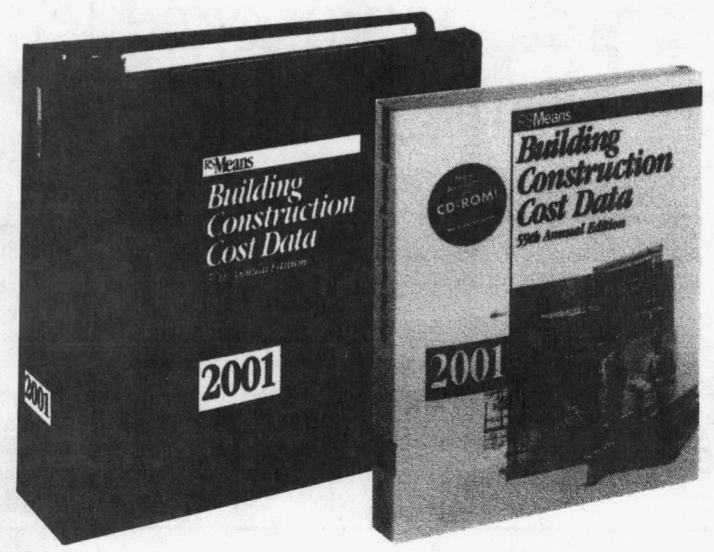

$89.95 per copy, Softbound
Catalog No. 60011

$116.95 per copy, Looseleaf
Catalog No. 61011

Means Building Construction Cost Data 2001

Offers you unchallenged unit price reliability in an easy-to-use arrangement. Whether used for complete, finished estimates or for periodic checks, it supplies more cost facts better and faster than any comparable source. Over 23,000 unit prices for 2001. The City Cost Indexes cover over 930 areas, for indexing to any project location in North America. Order and get the *DesignBuildIntelligence* newsletter sent to you FREE. You'll have year-long access to the Means Estimating **Hotline** FREE with your subscription. Expert assistance when using Means data is just a phone call away.

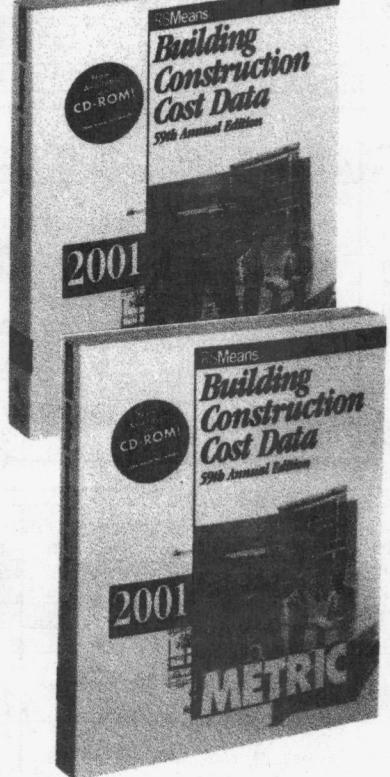

$89.95 per copy
Over 650 pages, illustrated, available Oct. 2000
Catalog No. 60011

Means Building Construction Cost Data 2001

Metric Version

The Federal Government has stated that all federal construction projects must now use metric documentation. The *Metric Version* of *Means Building Construction Cost Data 2001* is presented in metric measurements covering all construction areas. Don't miss out on these billion dollar opportunities. Make the switch to metric today.

$89.95 per copy
Over 650 pages, illustrated, available Nov. 2000
Catalog No. 63011

For more information
visit Means Web Site
at www.rsmeans.com

Annual Cost Guides

Means Mechanical Cost Data 2001

· HVAC · Controls

Total unit and systems price guidance for mechanical construction . . . materials, parts, fittings, and complete labor cost information. Includes prices for piping, heating, air conditioning, ventilation, and all related construction.

Plus new 2001 unit costs for:

· Over 2500 installed HVAC/controls assemblies
· "On Site" Location Factors for over 930 cities and towns in the U.S. and Canada
· Crews, labor and equipment

$89.95 per copy
Over 600 pages, illustrated, available Oct. 2000
Catalog No. 60021

Means Plumbing Cost Data 2001

Comprehensive unit prices and assemblies for plumbing, irrigation systems, commercial and residential fire protection, point-of-use water heaters, and the latest approved materials. This publication and its companion, *Means Mechanical Cost Data*, provide full-range cost estimating coverage for all the mechanical trades.

$89.95 per copy
Over 500 pages, illustrated, available Nov. 2000
Catalog No. 60211

Means Electrical Cost Data 2001

Pricing information for every part of electrical cost planning: More than 15,000 unit and systems costs with design tables; clear specifications and drawings; engineering guides and illustrated estimating procedures; complete labor-hour and materials costs for better scheduling and procurement; the latest electrical products and construction methods.

· A Variety of Special Electrical Systems including Cathodic Protection
· Costs for maintenance, demolition, HVAC/ mechanical, specialties, equipment, and more

$89.95 per copy
Over 450 pages, illustrated, available Oct. 2000
Catalog No. 60031

Means Electrical Change Order Cost Data 2001

You are provided with electrical unit prices exclusively for pricing change orders—based on the recent, direct experience of contractors and suppliers. Analyze and check your own change order estimates against the experience others have had doing the same work. It also covers productivity analysis and change order cost justifications. With useful information for calculating the effects of change orders and dealing with their administration.

$89.95 per copy
Over 450 pages, available Oct. 2000
Catalog No. 60231

Means Facilities Maintenance & Repair Cost Data 2001

Published in a looseleaf format, *Means Facilities Maintenance & Repair Cost Data* gives you a complete system to manage and plan your facility repair and maintenance costs and budget efficiently. Guidelines for auditing a facility and developing an annual maintenance plan. Budgeting is included, along with reference tables on cost and management and information on frequency and productivity of maintenance operations.

The only nationally recognized source of maintenance and repair costs. Developed in cooperation with the Army Corps of Engineers.

$199.95 per copy
Over 600 pages, illustrated, available Dec. 2000
Catalog No. 60301

Means Square Foot Costs 2001

It's Accurate and Easy To Use!

· **Updated 2001 price information,** based on nationwide figures from suppliers, estimators, labor experts and contractors.

· "How-to-Use" Sections, with **clear examples** of commercial, residential, industrial, and institutional structures.

· Realistic graphics, offering true-to-life illustrations of building projects.

· Extensive information on using square foot cost data, including **sample estimates** and **alternate pricing methods.**

$99.95 per copy
Over 450 pages, illustrated, available Oct. 2000
Catalog No. 60051

For more information
visit Means Web Site
at www.rsmeans.com

Annual Cost Guides

Means Repair & Remodeling Cost Data 2001
Commercial/Residential

You can use this valuable tool to estimate commercial and residential renovation and remodeling.

Includes: New costs for hundreds of unique methods, materials and conditions that only come up in repair and remodeling. PLUS:

· Unit costs for over 16,000 construction components
· Installed costs for over 90 assemblies
· Costs for 300+ construction crews
· Over 930 "On Site" localization factors for the U.S. and Canada.

$79.95 per copy
Over 600 pages, illustrated, available Nov. 2000
Catalog No. 60041

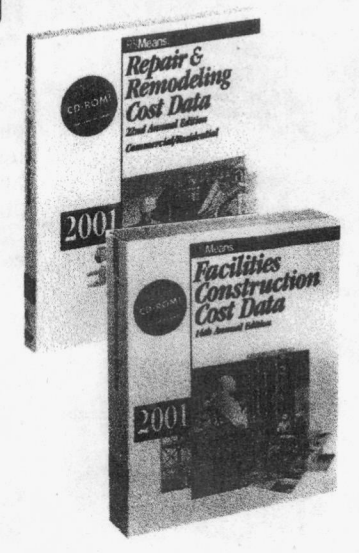

Means Facilities Construction Cost Data 2001

For the maintenance and construction of commercial, industrial, municipal, and institutional properties. Costs are shown for new and remodeling construction and are broken down into materials, labor, equipment, overhead, and profit. Special emphasis is given to sections on mechanical, electrical, furnishings, site work, building maintenance, finish work, and demolition. More than 45,000 unit costs plus assemblies and reference sections are included.

$219.95 per copy
Over 1150 pages, illustrated, available Nov. 2000
Catalog No. 60201

Means Residential Cost Data 2001

Contains square foot costs for 30 basic home models with the look of today—plus hundreds of custom additions and modifications you can quote right off the page. With costs for the 100 residential systems you're most likely to use in the year ahead. Complete with blank estimating forms, sample estimates and step-by-step instructions.

$79.95 per copy
Over 550 pages, illustrated, available Dec. 2000
Catalog No. 60171

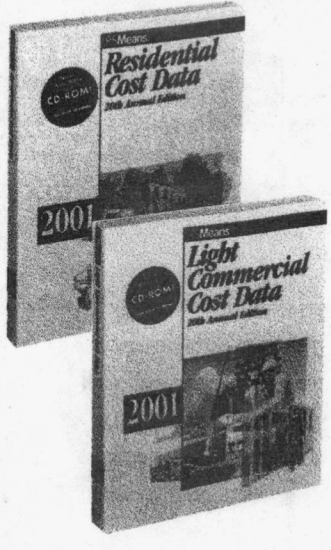

Means Light Commercial Cost Data 2001

Specifically addresses the light commercial market, which is an increasingly specialized niche in the industry. Aids you, the owner/designer/contractor, in preparing all types of estimates, from budgets to detailed bids. Includes new advances in methods and materials. Assemblies section allows you to evaluate alternatives in the early stages of design/planning.

Over 13,000 unit costs for 2001 ensure you have the prices you need... when you need them.

$79.95 per copy
Over 600 pages, illustrated, available Dec. 2000
Catalog No. 60181

Means Assemblies Cost Data 2001

Means Assemblies Cost Data 2001 takes the guesswork out of preliminary or conceptual estimates. Now you don't have to try to calculate the assembled cost by working up individual components costs. We've done all the work for you.

Presents detailed illustrations, descriptions, specifications and costs for every conceivable building assembly—240 types in all—arranged in the easy-to-use UniFormat system. Each illustrated "assembled" cost includes a complete grouping of materials and associated installation costs including the installing contractor's overhead and profit.

$149.95 per copy
Over 550 pages, illustrated, available Oct. 2000
Catalog No. 60061

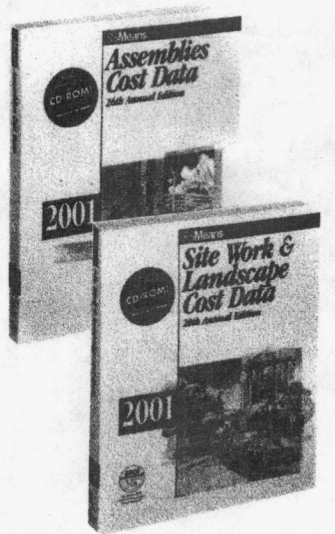

Means Site Work & Landscape Cost Data 2001

Means Site Work & Landscape Cost Data 2001 is organized to assist you in all your estimating needs. Hundreds of fact-filled pages help you make accurate cost estimates efficiently.

Updated for 2001!

· Demolition features—including ceilings, doors, electrical, flooring, HVAC, millwork, plumbing, roofing, walls and windows
· State-of-the-art segmental retaining walls
· Flywheel trenching costs and details
· Updated Wells section
· Thousands of landscape materials, flowers, shrubs and trees

$89.95 per copy
Over 600 pages, illustrated, available Oct. 2000
Catalog No. 60281

For more information
visit Means Web Site
at www.rsmeans.com

Annual Cost Guides

Means Open Shop Building Construction Cost Data 2001

The latest costs for accurate budgeting and estimating of new commercial and residential construction... renovation work... change orders... cost engineering. *Means Open Shop BCCD* will assist you to...
· Develop benchmark prices for change orders
· Plug gaps in preliminary estimates, budgets
· Estimate complex projects
· Substantiate invoices on contracts
· Price ADA-related renovations

$89.95 per copy
Over 650 pages, illustrated, available Nov. 2000
Catalog No. 60151

Means Heavy Construction Cost Data 2001

A comprehensive guide to heavy construction costs. Includes costs for highly specialized projects such as tunnels, dams, highways, airports, and waterways. Information on different labor rates, equipment, and material costs is included. Has unit price costs, systems costs, and numerous reference tables for costs and design. Valuable not only to contractors and civil engineers, but also to government agencies and city/town engineers.

$89.95 per copy
Over 450 pages, illustrated, available Nov. 2000
Catalog No. 60161

Means Building Construction Cost Data 2001
Western Edition

This regional edition provides more precise cost information for western North America. Labor rates are based on union rates from 13 western states and western Canada. Included are western practices and materials not found in our national edition: tilt-up concrete walls, glu-lam structural systems, specialized timber construction, seismic restraints, landscape and irrigation systems.

$89.95 per copy
Over 600 pages, illustrated, available Dec. 2000
Catalog No. 60221

Means Heavy Construction Cost Data 2001
Metric Version

Make sure you have the Means industry standard metric costs for the federal, state, municipal and private marketplace. With thousands of up-to-date metric unit prices in tables by CSI standard divisions. Supplies you with assemblies costs using the metric standard for reliable cost projections in the design stage of your project. Helps you determine sizes, material amounts, and has tips for handling metric estimates.

$89.95 per copy
Over 450 pages, illustrated, available Nov. 2000
Catalog No. 63161

Means Construction Cost Indexes 2001

Who knows what 2001 holds? What materials and labor costs will change unexpectedly? By how much?
· Breakdowns for 305 major cities.
· National averages for 30 key cities.
· Expanded five major city indexes.
· Historical construction cost indexes.

$198.00 per year/$49.50 individual quarters
Catalog No. 60141

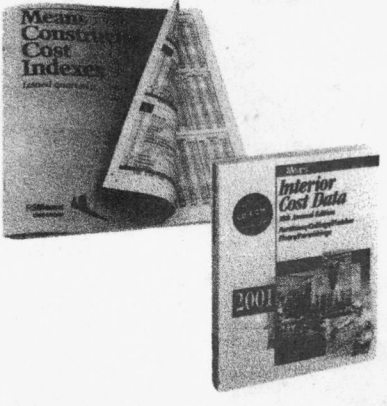

Means Interior Cost Data 2001

Provides you with prices and guidance needed to make accurate interior work estimates. Contains costs on materials, equipment, hardware, custom installations, furnishings, labor costs . . . every cost factor for new and remodel commercial and industrial interior construction, including updated information on office furnishings, plus more than 50 reference tables. For contractors, facility managers, owners.

$89.95 per copy
Over 550 pages, illustrated, available Oct. 2000
Catalog No. 60091

Means Concrete & Masonry Cost Data 2001

Provides you with cost facts for virtually all concrete/masonry estimating needs, from complicated formwork to various sizes and face finishes of brick and block, all in great detail. The comprehensive unit cost section contains more than 8,500 selected entries. Also contains an assemblies cost section, and a detailed reference section which supplements the cost data.

$83.95 per copy
Over 450 pages, illustrated, available Nov. 2000
Catalog No. 60111

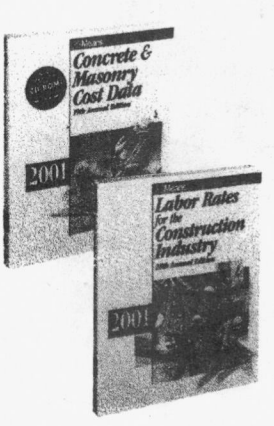

Means Labor Rates for the Construction Industry 2001

Complete information for estimating labor costs, making comparisons and negotiating wage rates by trade for over 300 cities (United States and Canada). With 46 construction trades listed by local union number in each city, and historical wage rates included for comparison. No similar book is available through the trade.

Each city chart lists the county and is alphabetically arranged with handy visual flip tabs for quick reference.

$199.95 per copy
Over 300 pages, available Dec. 2000
Catalog No. 60121

Reference Books

For more information
visit Means Web Site
at www.rsmeans.com

Project Scheduling & Management for Construction

New 2nd Edition

By David R. Pierce, Jr.

A comprehensive, yet easy-to-follow guide to construction project scheduling and control—from vital project management principles through the latest scheduling, tracking, and controlling techniques. The author is a leading authority on scheduling with years of field and teaching experience at leading academic institutions. Spend a few hours with this book and come away with a solid understanding of this essential management topic.

$64.95 per copy
Over 250 pages, illustrated, Hardcover
Catalog No. 67247A

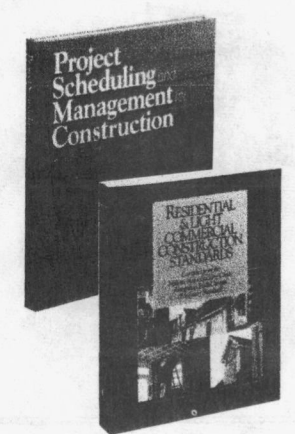

Residential & Light Commercial Construction Standards

A Unique Collection of Industry Standards That Define Quality in Construction

For Contractors & Subcontractors, Owners, Developers, Architects & Engineers, Attorneys & Insurance Personnel

Compiled from the nation's major building codes, professional associations, and product manufacturer institutes, this unique resource enables you to:

• Set a standard for subcontractors and employees
• Protect yourself against defect claims
• Resolve disputes
• Answer client questions with authority

$59.95 per copy
Over 500 pages, illustrated, Softcover
Catalog No. 67322

The Building Professional's Guide to Contract Documents

New 3rd Edition

By Waller S. Poage, AIA, CSI, SAVE

This comprehensive treatment of Contract Documents is an important reference for owners, design professionals, contractors, and students.

• Structure your Documents for Maximum Efficiency
• Understand the Roles and Responsibilities of Construction Professionals
• Improve Methods of Project Delivery

$64.95 per copy, 400 pages
Diagrams and construction forms, Hardcover
Catalog No. 67261A

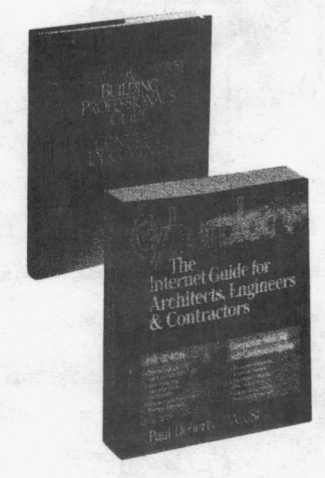

Cyberplaces II: The Internet Guide for AECs & Facility Managers 2nd Edition

By Paul Doherty

With an added section on the New Economy and e-commerce—such as AEC arbitrage, aggregate purchasing, auctions, e-supply chains, and more. Plus the best Knowledge Management and other Internet tools, including PDAs and the newest Web software for scheduling and project management.

The **Web site** keeps you current on the best Internet tools and applications for building design, construction and management—with workshops to put it all into practice.

$59.95 per copy
Over 700 pages, illustrated, Softcover
Catalog No. 67317A

Value Engineering: Practical Applications

... For Design, Construction, Maintenance & Operations

By Alphonse Dell'Isola, PE, leading authority on VE in construction

A tool for immediate application—for engineers, architects, facility managers, owners and contractors. Includes: Making the Case for VE—The Management Briefing, Integrating VE into Planning and Budgeting, Conducting Life Cycle Costing, Integrating VE into the Design Process, Using VE Methodology in Design Review and Consultant Selection, Case Studies, VE Workbook, and a Life Cycle Costing program on disk.

$79.95 per copy
Over 450 pages, illustrated, Hardcover
Catalog No. 67319

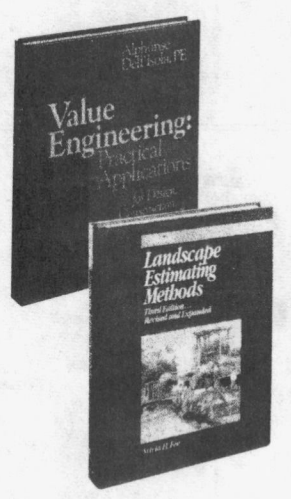

Means Landscape Estimating Methods

3rd Edition

By Sylvia H. Fee

This revised edition offers expert guidance for preparing accurate estimates for new landscape construction and grounds maintenance. Includes a complete project estimate featuring the latest equipment and methods, and **two totally new chapters—Life Cycle Costing and Landscape Maintenance Estimating.**

$62.95 per copy
Over 300 pages, illustrated, Hardcover
Catalog No. 67295A

For more information
visit Means Web Site
at www.rsmeans.com

Reference Books

Preventive Maintenance Guidelines for School Facilities

NEW! By John C. Maciha

This new publication gives you a complete program for school maintenance that ensures: sustained security, safety, property integrity, facility acceptance, user satisfaction, and reasonable ongoing expenditures.

Includes schedules for weekly, monthly, half-yearly and annual maintenance. 3-ring binder with hard copy forms, electronic forms on disk, and laminated wall chart.

$149.95 per copy
Over 150 pages, Hardcover
Catalog No. 67326

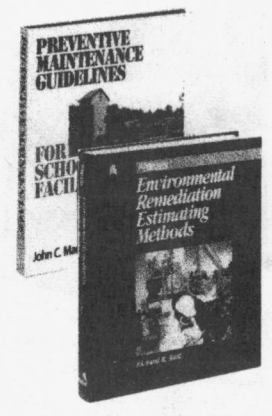

Means Environmental Remediation Estimating Methods By Richard R. Rast

Guidelines for estimating 50 standard remediation technologies. Use it to: prepare preliminary budgets, develop detailed estimates, compare costs and solutions, estimate liability, review quotes, negotiate settlements. A valuable support tool for *Means Environmental Remediation Unit Price* and *Assemblies books.*

$99.95 per copy
Over 600 pages, illustrated, Hardcover
Catalog No. 64777

Means Facilities Maintenance Standards By Roger W. Liska, PE, AIC

Unique features of this one-of-a-kind working guide for facilities maintenance

A working encyclopedia that points the way to solutions to every kind of maintenance and repair dilemma. With a labor-hours section to provide productivity figures for over 180 maintenance tasks. Included are ready-to-use forms, checklists, worksheets and comparisons, as well as analysis of materials systems and remedies for deterioration and wear.

$159.95 per copy, 600 pages, 205 tables, checklists and diagrams, Hardcover
Catalog No. 67246

HVAC: Design Criteria, Options, Selection
Expanded Second Edition

By William H. Rowe III, AIA, PE

Includes Indoor Air Quality, CFC Removal, Energy Efficient Systems and Special Systems by Building Type. Helps you solve a wide range of HVAC system design and selection problems effectively and economically. Gives you clear explanations of the latest ASHRAE standards.

$84.95 per copy
Over 600 pages, illustrated, Hardcover
Catalog No. 67306

The Facilities Manager's Reference

By Harvey H. Kaiser, PhD

The tasks and tools the facility manager needs to accomplish the organization's objectives, and develop individual and staff skills. Includes Facilities and Property Management, Administrative Control, Planning and Operations, Support Services, and a complete building audit with forms and instructions, widely used by facilities managers nationwide.

$86.95 per copy, over 250 pages, with prototype forms and graphics, Hardcover
Catalog No. 67264

Facilities Maintenance Management

By Gregory H. Magee, PE

Now you can get successful management methods and techniques for all aspects of facilities maintenance. This comprehensive reference explains and demonstrates successful management techniques for all aspects of maintenance, repair and improvements for buildings, machinery, equipment and grounds. Plus, guidance for outsourcing and managing internal staffs.

$86.95 per copy
Over 280 pages with illustrations, Hardcover
Catalog No. 67249

Cost Planning & Estimating for Facilities Maintenance

In this unique book, a team of facilities management authorities shares their expertise at:
· Evaluating and budgeting maintenance operations
· Maintaining & repairing key building components
· Applying *Means Facilities Maintenance & Repair Cost Data* to your estimating

With the special maintenance requirements of the 10 major building types.

$82.95 per copy
Over 475 pages, Hardcover
Catalog No. 67314

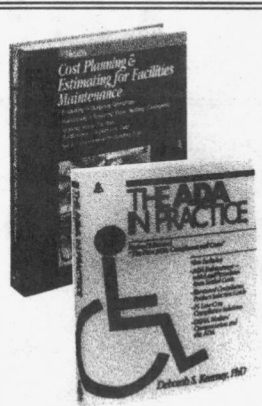

The ADA in Practice

By Deborah S. Kearney, PhD

Helps you meet and budget for the requirements of the Americans with Disabilities Act. Shows how to do the job right by understanding what the law requires, allows, and enforces. Includes a "buyers guide" for 70 ADA-compliant products.

*Winner of IFMA's "Distinguished Author of the Year" award.

See page 9 for another ADA resource.

$72.95 per copy
Over 600 pages, illustrated, Softcover
Catalog No. 67147A

Reference Books

For more information
visit Means Web Site
at www.rsmeans.com

Basics for Builders:
Plan Reading & Material Takeoff
By Wayne J. DelPico
For Residential and Light Commercial Construction

A valuable tool for understanding plans and specs, and accurately calculating material quantities. Step-by-step instructions and takeoff procedures based on a full set of working drawings.

$35.95 per copy
Over 420 pages, Softcover
Catalog No. 67307

Planning & Managing Interior
Projects New 2nd Edition, By Carol E. Farren, CFM

Addresses changes in technology and business, guiding you through commercial design and construction from initial client meetings to post-project administration. Includes: evaluating space requirements, alternative work models, telecommunications and data management, and environmental issues.

$69.95 per copy
Over 400 pages, illustrated, Hardcover
Catalog No. 67245A

Superintending for Contractors:
How to Bring Jobs in On-time, On-Budget
By Paul J. Cook

This book examines the complex role of the superintendent/field project manager, and provides guidelines for the efficient organization of this job. Includes administration of contracts, change orders, purchase orders, and more.

$35.95 per copy
Over 220 pages, illustrated, Softcover
Catalog No. 67233

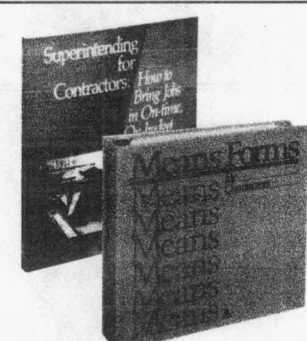

Means Forms for Contractors
For general and specialty contractors

Means editors have created and collected the most needed forms as requested by contractors of various-sized firms and specialties. This book covers all project phases. Includes sample correspondence and personnel administration.
Full-size forms on durable paper for photocopying or reprinting.

$79.95 per copy
Over 400 pages, three-ring binder, more than 80 forms
Catalog No. 67288

Total Productive Facilities
Management
By Richard W. Sievert, Jr.

The best of today's cost and project management, quality, and value engineering principles. Includes Benchmarking, Value Engineering, and Scheduling.

$79.95 per copy
Over 270 pages, illustrated, Hardcover
Catalog No. 67321

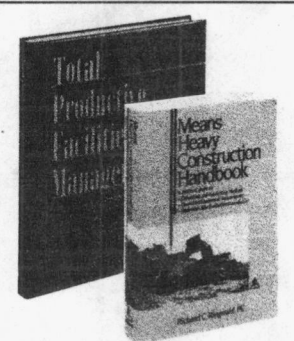

Means Heavy Construction
Handbook

Informed guidance for planning, estimating and performing today's heavy construction projects. Provides expert advice on every aspect of heavy construction work including hazardous waste remediation and estimating. To assist planning, estimating, performing, or overseeing work.

$74.95 per copy
Over 430 pages, illustrated, Hardcover
Catalog No. 67148

Estimating for Contractors:
How to Make Estimates that Win Jobs
By Paul J. Cook

Estimating for Contractors is a reference that will be used over and over, whether to check a specific estimating procedure, or to take a complete course in estimating.

$35.95 per copy
Over 225 pages, illustrated, Softcover
Catalog No. 67160

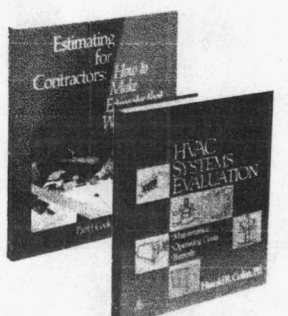

HVAC Systems Evaluation
By Harold R. Colen, PE

You get direct comparisons of how each type of system works, with the relative costs of installation, operation, maintenance and applications by type of building. With requirements for hooking up electrical power to HVAC components. Contains experienced advice for repairing operational problems in existing HVAC systems, ductwork, fans, cooling coils, and much more!

$84.95 per copy
Over 500 pages, illustrated, Hardcover
Catalog No. 67281

Quantity Takeoff for Contractors:
How to Get Accurate Material Counts
By Paul J. Cook

Contractors who are new to material takeoffs or want to be sure they are using the best techniques will find helpful information in this book, organized by CSI MasterFormat division.

Now $17.98 per copy, limited quantity
Over 250 pages, illustrated, Softcover
Catalog No. 67262

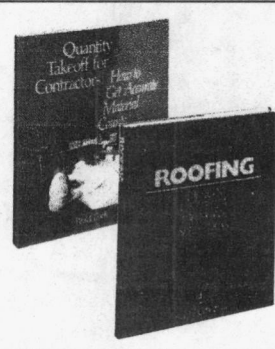

Roofing: Design Criteria,
Options, Selection
By R.D. Herbert, III

This book is required reading for those who specify, install or have to maintain roofing systems. It covers all types of roofing technology and systems. You'll get the facts needed to intelligently evaluate and select both traditional and new roofing systems.

Now $31.48 per copy
Over 225 pages with illustrations, Hardcover
Catalog No. 67253

For more information
visit Means Web Site
at www.rsmeans.com

Reference Books

Means Estimating Handbook

This comprehensive reference covers a full spectrum of technical data for estimating, with information on sizing, productivity, equipment requirements, codes, design standards and engineering factors.
Means Estimating Handbook will help you: evaluate architectural plans and specifications, prepare accurate quantity takeoffs, prepare estimates from conceptual to detailed, and evaluate change orders.

$99.95 per copy
Over 900 pages, Hardcover
Catalog No. 67276

Means Repair and Remodeling Estimating Third Edition

By Edward B. Wetherill & R.S. Means

Focuses on the unique problems of estimating renovations of existing structures. It helps you determine the true costs of remodeling through careful evaluation of architectural details and a site visit. **New section on disaster restoration costs.**

$69.95 per copy
Over 450 pages, illustrated, Hardcover
Catalog No. 67265A

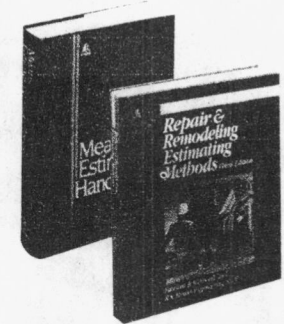

Successful Estimating Methods:
From Concept to Bid
By John D. Bledsoe, PhD, PE

A highly practical, all-in-one guide to the tips and practices of today's successful estimator. Presents techniques for all types of estimates, *and* advanced topics such as life cycle cost analysis, value engineering, and automated estimating.
Estimate spreadsheets available at Means Web site.

$64.95 per copy
Over 300 pages, illustrated, Hardcover
Catalog No. 67287

Means Productivity Standards for Construction

Expanded Edition *(Formerly Man-Hour Standards)*

Here is the working encyclopedia of labor productivity information for construction professionals, with labor requirements for thousands of construction functions in CSI MasterFormat.
Completely updated, with over 3,000 new work items.

$159.95 per copy
Over 800 pages, Hardcover
Catalog No. 67236A

Means Electrical Estimating Methods Second Edition

Expanded version includes sample estimates and cost information in keeping with the latest version of the CSI MasterFormat. Contains new coverage of Fiber Optic and Uninterruptible Power Supply electrical systems, broken down by components and explained in detail. A practical companion to *Means Electrical Cost Data.*

$64.95 per copy
Over 325 pages, Hardcover
Catalog No. 67230A

Means Mechanical Estimating Methods Second Edition

This guide assists you in making a review of plans, specs and bid packages with suggestions for takeoff procedures, listings, substitutions and pre-bid scheduling. Includes suggestions for budgeting labor and equipment usage. Compares materials and construction methods to allow you to select the best option.

$64.95 per copy
Over 350 pages, illustrated, Hardcover
Catalog No. 67294

Means Scheduling Manual
Third Edition
By F. William Horsley

Fast, convenient expertise for keeping your scheduling skills right in step with today's cost-conscious times. Covers bar charts, PERT, precedence and CPM scheduling methods. Now updated to include computer applications.

$64.95 per copy
Over 200 pages, spiral-bound, Softcover
Catalog No. 67291

Maintenance Management Audit

This annual audit program is essential for every organization in need of a proper assessment of its maintenance operation. Downloadable electronic forms from Means Web Site allow managers to identify and correct problems and enhance productivity.

Now $32.48 per copy, limited quantity
125 pages, spiral bound, illustrated, Hardcover
Catalog No. 67299

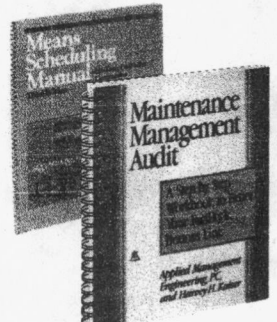

Means Square Foot Estimating Methods Second Edition

By Billy J. Cox and F. William Horsley

Proven techniques for conceptual and design-stage cost planning. Steps you through the square foot cost process, demonstrating faster, better ways to relate the design to the budget. Now updated to the latest version of UniFormat.

$69.95 per copy
Over 300 pages, illustrated, Hardcover
Catalog No. 67145A

Means ADA Compliance Pricing Guide

Gives you detailed cost estimates for budgeting modification projects, including estimates for each of 260 alternates. You get the 75 most commonly needed modifications for ADA compliance, each an assembly estimate with detailed cost breakdown.

$72.95 per copy
Over 350 pages, illustrated, Softcover
Catalog No. 67310

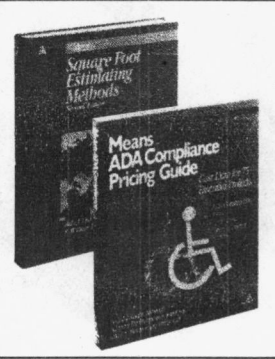

Reference Books

For more information
visit Means Web Site
at www.rsmeans.com

Means Unit Price Estimating Methods
2nd Edition
$59.95 per copy
Catalog No. 67303

Legal Reference for Design & Construction
By Charles R. Heuer, Esq., AIA
Now $54.98 per copy, limited quantity
Catalog No. 67266

Means Plumbing Estimating Methods
New 2nd Edition
By Joseph J. Galeno & Sheldon T. Greene
$59.95 per copy
Catalog No. 67283A

Structural Steel Estimating
By S. Paul Bunea, PhD
Now $39.98 per copy, limited quantity
Catalog No. 67241

Business Management for Contractors
How to Make Profits in Today's Market
By Paul J. Cook
Now $17.98 per copy, limited quantity
Catalog No. 67250

Understanding Legal Aspects of Design/Build
By Timothy R. Twomey, Esq., AIA
$79.95 per copy
Catalog No. 67259

Risk Management for Building Professionals
By Thomas E. Papageorge, RA
Now $29.98 per copy, limited quantity
Catalog No. 67254

Contractor's Business Handbook
By Michael S. Milliner
Now $21.48 per copy, limited quantity
Catalog No. 67255

Basics for Builders: How to Survive and Prosper in Construction
By Thomas N. Frisby
$34.95 per copy
Catalog No. 67273

Successful Interior Projects Through Effective Contract Documents
By Joel Downey & Patricia K. Gilbert
Now $34.98 per copy, limited quantity
Catalog No. 67313

Understanding Building Automation Systems
By Reinhold A. Carlson, PE & Robert Di Giandomenico
$39.98 per copy, limited quantity
Catalog No. 67284

Illustrated Construction Dictionary, Condensed
$59.95 per copy
Catalog No. 67282

Managing Construction Purchasing
By John G. McConville, CCC, CPE
Now $31.48 per copy, limited quantity
Catalog No. 67302

Hazardous Material & Hazardous Waste
By Francis J. Hopcroft, PE, David L. Vitale, M. Ed., & Donald L. Anglehart, Esq.
Now $44.98 per copy, limited quantity
Catalog No. 67258

Fundamentals of the Construction Process
By Kweku K. Bentil, AIC
Now $34.98 per copy, limited quantity
Catalog No. 67260

Construction Delays
By Theodore J. Trauner, Jr., PE, PP
$59.95 per copy
Catalog No. 67278

Basics for Builders: Framing & Rough Carpentry
By Scot Simpson
$24.95 per copy
Catalog No. 67298

Interior Home Improvement Costs
New 7th Edition
$19.95 per copy
Catalog No. 67308B

Exterior Home Improvement Costs
New 7th Edition
$19.95 per copy
Catalog No. 67309B

Concrete Repair and Maintenance Illustrated
By Peter H. Emmons
$69.95 per copy
Catalog No. 67146

How to Estimate with Metric Units
Now $24.98 per copy, limited quantity
Catalog No. 67304

For more information
visit Means Web Site
at www.rsmeans.com

Seminars

Developing Facility Assessment Programs

This two-day program concentrates on the management process required for planning, conducting, and documenting the physical condition and functional adequacy of buildings and other facilities. Regular facilities condition inspections are one of the facility department's most important duties. However, gathering reliable data hinges on the design of the overall program used to identify and gauge deferred maintenance requirements. Knowing where to look . . . and reporting results effectively are the keys. This seminar is designed to give the facility executive essential steps for conducting facilities inspection programs.

Inspection Program Requirements • Where is the deficiency? • What is the nature of the problem? • How can it be remedied? • How much will it cost in labor, equipment and materials? • When should it be accomplished? • Who is best suited to do the work?

Note: Because of its management focus, this course will not address trade practices and procedures.

Repair and Remodeling Estimating

Repair and remodeling work is becoming increasingly competitive as more professionals enter the market. Recycling existing buildings can pose difficult estimating problems. Labor costs, energy use concerns, building codes, and the limitations of working with an existing structure place enormous importance on the development of accurate estimates. Using the exclusive techniques associated with Means' widely acclaimed **Repair & Remodeling Cost Data**, this seminar sorts out and discusses solutions to the problems of building alteration estimating. Attendees will receive two intensive days of eye-opening methods for handling virtually every kind of repair and remodeling situation . . . from demolition and removal to final restoration.

Mechanical and Electrical Estimating

This seminar is tailored to fit the needs of those seeking to develop or improve their skills and to have a better understanding of how mechanical and electrical estimates are prepared during the conceptual, planning, budgeting and bidding stages. Learn how to avoid costly omissions and overlaps between these two interrelated specialties by preparing complete and thorough cost estimates for both trades. Featured are order of magnitude, assemblies, and unit price estimating. In combination with the use of **Means Mechanical Cost Data**, **Means Plumbing Cost Data** and **Means Electrical Cost Data**, this seminar will ensure more accurate and complete Mechanical/Electrical estimates for both unit price and preliminary estimating procedures.

Unit Price Estimating

This seminar shows how today's advanced estimating techniques and cost information sources can be used to develop more reliable unit price estimates for projects of any size. It demonstrates how to organize data, use plans efficiently, and avoid embarrassing errors by using better methods of checking.

You'll get down-to-earth help and easy-to-apply guidance for:

• making maximum use of construction cost information sources
• organizing estimating procedures in order to save time and reduce mistakes
• sorting out and identifying unusual job requirements to improve estimating accuracy.

Square Foot Cost Estimating

Learn how to make better preliminary estimates with a limited amount of budget and design information. You will benefit from examples of a wide range of systems estimates with specifications limited to building use requirements, budget, building codes, and type of building. And yet, with minimal information, you will obtain a remarkable degree of accuracy.

Workshop sessions will provide you with model square foot estimating problems and other skill-building exercises. The exclusive Means building assemblies square foot cost approach shows how to make very reliable estimates using preliminary budget and design information.

Scheduling and Project Management

This seminar helps you successfully establish project priorities, develop realistic schedules, and apply today's advanced management techniques to your construction projects. Hands-on exercises familiarize participants with network approaches such as the Critical Path Method. Special emphasis is placed on cost control, including use of computer-based systems. Through this seminar you'll perfect your scheduling and management skills, ensuring completion of your projects *on time* and *within budget*. Includes hands-on application of **Means Building Construction Cost Data.**

Facilities Maintenance and Repair Estimating

With our Facilities Maintenance and Repair Estimating seminar, you'll learn how to plan, budget, and estimate the cost of ongoing and preventive maintenance and repair for all your buildings and grounds. Based on R.S. Means' groundbreaking cost estimating book, this two-day seminar will show you how to decide to either contract out or retain maintenance and repair work in-house. In addition, you'll learn how to prepare budgets and schedules that help cut down on unplanned and costly emergency repair projects. Facilities Maintenance and Repair Estimating crystallizes what facilities professionals have learned over the years, but never had time to organize or document. This program covers a variety of maintenance and repair projects, from underground storage tank removal, roof repair and maintenance, exterior wall renovations, and energy source conversions, to service upgrades and estimating energy-saving alternatives.

Managing Facilities Construction and Maintenance

In you're involved in new facility construction, renovation or maintenance projects and are concerned about getting quality work done on time and on or below budget, in Means' seminar **Managing Facilities Construction and Maintenance** you'll learn management techniques needed to effectively plan, organize, control and get the most out of your limited facilities resources.

Learn how to develop budgets, reduce expenditures and check productivity. With the knowledge gained in this course, you'll be better prepared to successfully sell accurate project budgets, timing and manpower needs to senior management . . . plus understand how to evaluate the impact of today's facility decisions on tomorrow's budget.

Call 1-800-448-8182 for more information

Seminars

For more information
visit Means Web Site
at www.rsmeans.com

2001 Means Seminar Schedule

Location	Dates
Las Vegas, NV	March 12 - 15
Washington, DC	April 23 - 26
Denver, CO	May 21-24
San Francisco, CA	June 11 - 14
Cape Cod, MA	September TBD
Washington, DC	October 1 - 4
San Diego, CA	October TBD
Atlantic City, NJ	November TBD
Orlando, FL	November 5-8

Note: Call for exact dates and de

Registration Information

Register Early... Save up to $150! Register 30 days before the start date of a seminar and save $150 off your total fee. *Note: This discount can be applied only once per order.*

How to Register Register by phone today! Means toll-free number for making reservations is: **1-800-448-8182.**

Individual Seminar Registration Fee $875 To register by mail, complete the registration form and return with your full fee to: Seminar Division, R.S. Means Company, Inc., 63 Smiths Lane, Kingston, MA 02364.

Federal Government Pricing All Federal Government employees save 25% off regular seminar price. Other promotional discounts cannot be combined with Federal Government discount.

Team Discount Program Two to four seminar registrations: $760 per person—Five or more seminar registrations: $710 per person—Ten or more seminar registrations: Call for pricing.

Consecutive Seminar Offer One individual signing up for two separate courses at the same location during the designated time period pays only $1,400. You get the second course for only $525 (**a 40% discount**). Payment must be received at least ten days prior to seminar dates to confirm attendance.

Refunds Cancellations will be accepted up to ten days prior to the seminar start. There are no refunds for cancellations postmarked later than ten working days prior to the first day of the seminar. A $150 processing fee will be charged for all cancellations. Written notice or telegram is required for all cancellations. Substitutions can be made at any time before the session starts. **No-shows are subject to the full seminar fee.**

AACE Approved Courses The R.S. Means Construction Estimating and Management Seminars described and offered to you here have each been approved for 14 hours (1.4 recertification credits) of credit by the AACE International Certification Board toward meeting the continuing education requirements for re-certification as a Certified Cost Engineer/Certified Cost Consultant.

AIA Continuing Education R.S. Means is registered with the AIA Continuing Education System (AIA/CES) and is committed to developing quality learning activities in accordance with the CES criteria. R.S. Means seminars meet the AIA/CES criteria for Quality Level 2. AIA members will receive (28) learning units (LUs) for each two day R.S. Means Course.

Daily Course Schedule The first day of each seminar session begins at 8:30 A.M. and ends at 4:30 P.M. The second day is 8:00 A.M.–4:00 P.M. Participants are urged to bring a hand-held calculator since many actual problems will be worked out in each session.

Continental Breakfast Your registration includes the cost of a continental breakfast, a morning coffee break, and an afternoon break. These informal segments will allow you to discuss topics of mutual interest with other members of the seminar. (You are free to make your own lunch and dinner arrangements.)

Hotel/Transportation Arrangements R.S. Means has arranged to hold a block of rooms at each hotel hosting a seminar. To take advantage of special group rates when making your reservation be sure to mention that you are attending the Means Seminar. You are of course free to stay at the lodging place of your choice. (**Hotel reservations and transportation arrangements should be made directly by seminar attendees.**)

Important Class sizes are limited, so please register as soon as possible.

Registration Form

Call 1-800-448-8182 x5115/to register or FAX 1-800-632-6732. Visit our web site www.rsmeans.com

Please register the following people for the Means Construction Seminars as shown here. Full payment or deposit is enclosed, and we understand that we must make our own hotel reservations if overnight stays are necessary.

☐ Full payment of $ _____ enclosed.

☐ Bill me

Name of Registrant(s)
(To appear on certificate of completion)

_____

_____

_____

P.O. #: _____

GOVERNMENT AGENCIES MUST SUPPLY PURCHASE ORDER NUMBER

Firm Name _____

Address _____

City/State/Zip _____

Telephone No. _____ Fax No. _____

E-Mail Address _____

Charge our registration(s) to: ☐ MasterCard ☐ VISA ☐ American Express ☐ Discover

Account No. _____ Exp. Date _____

Cardholder's Signature _____

Seminar Name	City	Dates

Please mail check to: R.S. MEANS COMPANY, INC., 63 Smiths Lane, P.O. Box 800, Kingston, MA 02364 USA

Consulting Services Group

Solutions For Your Construction and Facilities Cost Management Problems

We are leaders in the cost engineering field, supporting the unique construction and facilities management costing challenges of clients from the Federal Government, Fortune 1000 Corporations, Building Product Manufacturers, and some of the World's Largest Design and Construction Firms.

Developers of the Dept. of Defense Tri-Services Estimating Database

Recipient of SEARS 1997 Chairman's Award for Innovation

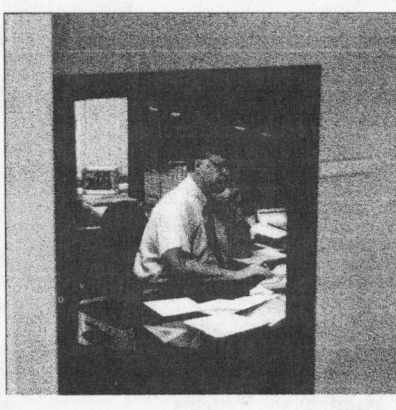

Research...

- **Custom Database Development**—Means expertise in construction cost engineering and database management can be put to work creating customized cost databases and applications.
- **Data Licensing & Integration**—To enhance applications dealing with construction, any segment of Means vast database can be licensed for use, and harnessed in a format compatible with a previously developed proprietary system.
- **Cost Modeling**—Pre-built custom cost models provide organizations that expend countless hours estimating repetitive work with a systematic time-saving estimating solution.
- **Database Auditing & Maintenance**—For clients with in-house data, Means can help organize it, and by linking it with Means database, fill in any gaps that exist and provide necessary updates to maintain current and relevant proprietary cost data.

Estimating...

- **Estimating Service**—Means expertise is available to perform construction cost estimates, as well as to develop baseline schedules and establish management plans for projects of all sizes and types. Conceptual, budget and detailed estimates are available.
- **Benchmarking**—Means can run baseline estimates on existing project estimates. Gauging estimating accuracy and identifying inefficiencies improves the success ratio, precision and productivity of estimates.
- **Project Feasibility Studies**—The Consulting Services Group can assist in the review and clarification of the most sound and practical construction approach in terms of time, cost and use.
- **Litigation Support**—Means is available to provide opinions of value and to supply expert interpretations or testimony in the resolution of construction cost claims, litigation and mediation.

Training...

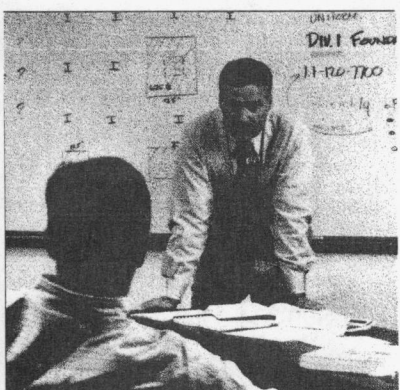

- **Core Curriculum**—Means educational programs, delivered on-site, are designed to sharpen professional skills and to maximize effective use of cost estimating and management tools. On-site training cuts down on travel expenses and time away from the office.
- **Custom Curriculum**—Means can custom-tailor courses to meet the specific needs and requirements of clients. The goal is to simultaneously boost skills and broaden cost estimating and management knowledge while focusing on applications that bring immediate benefits to unique operations, challenges, or markets.
- **Staff Assessments and Development Programs**—In addition to custom curricula, Means can work with a client's Human Resources Department or with individual operating units to create programs consistent with long-term employee development objectives.

**For more information and a copy of our capabilities brochure, please call
1-800-448-8182 and ask for the Consulting Services Group, or reach us at www.rsmeans.com**

MeansData™

CONSTRUCTION COSTS FOR SOFTWARE APPLICATIONS

Your construction estimating software is only as good as your cost data.

Software Integration

A proven construction cost database is a mandatory part of any estimating package. We have linked MeansData™ directly into the industry's leading software applications. The following list of software providers can offer you MeansData™ as an added feature for their estimating systems. Visit them on-line at *www.rsmeans.com/demo/* for more information and free demos. Or call their numbers listed below.

3D International
713-871-7000 budwit@3di.com

ACT
Applied Computer Technologies
Facility Management Software
919-859-1335 patw@srs.net

AEPCO, Inc.
301-670-4642 blueworks@aepco.com

ArenaSoft ESTIMATING
888-370-8806 info@arenasoft.com

Ares Corporation
650-401-7100
sales@arescorporation.com

ASSETWORKS, Inc.
Facility Management Software
800-659-9001 info@assetworks.com

Benchmark, Inc.
800-393-9193 sales@benchmark-inc.com

BSD
Building Systems Design, Inc.
888-273-7638 bsd@bsdsoftlink.com

cManagement
800-945-7093 sales@cmanagement.com

CDCI
Construction Data Controls, Inc.
800-285-3929 sales@cdci.com

CMS
Computerized Micro Solutions
800-255-7407 cms@proest.com

CONAC GROUP
800-663-2338 sales@conac.com

ESTIMATING SYSTEMS, Inc.
800-967-8572 pulsar@capecod.net

G2 Estimator
A Div. of Valli Info. Syst., Inc.
800-657-6312 info@g2estimator.com

GEAC COMMERCIAL SYSTEMS, Inc.
800-554-9865 info@geac.com

GRANTLUN CORPORATION
480-897-7750 support@grantlun.com

HCI SYSTEMS, Inc.
800-750-4424 info@hcisystems.com

IQ BENECO
801-565-1122 mbrown@beneco.com

Lugs International
888-682-5573 info@lugs.com

MC²
Management Computer Controls
800-225-5622 vkeys@mc2-ice.com

PRISM COMPUTER CORPORATION
Facility Management Software
800-774-7622 nalbadri@prismcc.com

PYXIS TECHNOLOGIES
888-841-0004 ldenigris@ebid98.com

QUEST SOLUTIONS, Inc.
800-452-2342 info@questsolutions.com

RICHARDSON ENGINEERING SERVICES, Inc.
480-497-2062 info@resi.net

SANDERS SOFTWARE, Inc.
800-280-9760 hsander@vallnet.com

STN, Inc.
Workline Maintenance Systems
800-321-1969 ask@stn.com

TIMBERLINE SOFTWARE CORP.
800-628-6583
product.info@timberline.com

TMA SYSTEMS, Inc.
Facility Management Software
800-862-1130 sales@tmasys.com

US COST, Inc.
800-372-4003
usc-software@compuserve.com

VERTIGRAPH, Inc.
800-989-4243
info-request@vertigraph.com

WENDLWARE
714-895-7222 sales@corecon.com

WINESTIMATOR, Inc.
800-950-2374 sszabo@winest.com

DemoSource™ One-stop shopping for the latest cost estimating software for just $19.95. This evaluation tool includes product literature and demo diskettes for ten or more estimating systems, all of which link to MeansData™. **Call 1-800-334-3509 to order.**

FOR MORE INFORMATION ON ELECTRONIC PRODUCTS CALL 1-800-448-8182 OR FAX 1-800-632-6732.

MeansData™ is a registered trademark of R.S. Means Co., Inc., *A CMD Group Company.*

14

For more information
visit Means Web Site
at www.rsmeans.com

New Titles

Means Illustrated Construction Dictionary, 3rd Edition

New Updated Edition with interactive CD-ROM

Long regarded as the Industry's finest, the *Means Illustrated Construction Dictionary* is now even better. With the addition of over 1,000 new terms and hundreds of new illustrations, it is the clear choice for the most comprehensive and current information.

The companion CD-ROM that comes with this new edition adds many extra features: larger graphics, expanded definitions, and links to both CSI MasterFormat numbers and product information.

- 19,000 construction words, terms, phrases, symbols, weights, measures, and equivalents
- **1,000 new entries**
- **1,200 helpful illustrations**
- **Contemporary coverage of professional & trade terms**
- **Easy-to-use format, with thumbtabs**

$99.95 per copy
Over 790 pages, illustrated, Hardcover
Catalog No. 67292A

Historic Preservation: Project Planning & Estimating

- *Managing Historic Restoration, Rehabilitation and Preservation Building Projects and*
- *Determining and Controlling Their Costs*

By Swanke Hayden Connell Architects

- Applicable standards and financing
- Site survey and documentation methods
- Protecting finishes and features
- Hazardous materials
- Identifying and qualifying specialty contractors
- Machanical/Electrical systems upgrades
- Restoring old building materials
- How to assemble a reliable, detailed estimate and budget for future maintenance

$99.95 per copy
Over 450 pages, Hardcover
Catalog No. 67323

Facilities Operations & Engineering Reference

An all-in-one technical reference for planning & managing facility projects & solving day-to-day operations problems

Ten major sections address:

- **Management Skills**
- **Economics** (budgeting/cost control, financial analysis, VE, etc.)
- **Civil Engineering & Construction Practices**
- **Maintenance** (detailed staffing guidance and job descriptions, CMMS, planning/scheduling, training, work orders, preventive/predictive maintenance)
- **HVAC & Energy Efficiencies** (optimizing energy use: heating, cooling, lighting, water)
- **Mechanical and Electrical Engineering**
- **Instrumentation & Controls**
- **Environment, Health & Safety**

Produced jointly by R.S. Means and the Association for Facilities Engineering.

$99.95 per copy
Over 700 pages, illustrated, Hardcover
Catalog No. 67318

2001 Order Form

Qty.	Book No.	COST ESTIMATING BOOKS	Unit Price	Total
	60061	Assemblies Cost Data 2001	$149.95	
	60011	Building Construction Cost Data 2001	89.95	
	61011	Building Const. Cost Data–Looseleaf Ed. 2001	116.95	
	63011	Building Const. Cost Data–Metric Version 2001	89.95	
	60221	Building Const. Cost Data–Western Ed. 2001	89.95	
	60111	Concrete & Masonry Cost Data 2001	83.95	
	50141	Construction Cost Indexes 2001	198.00	
	60141A	Construction Cost Index–January 2001	49.50	
	60141B	Construction Cost Index–April 2001	49.50	
	60141C	Construction Cost Index–July 2001	49.50	
	60141D	Construction Cost Index–October 2001	49.50	
	60311	Contr. Pricing Guide: Framing/Carpentry 2001	36.95	
	60331	Contr. Pricing Guide: Resid. Detailed 2001	36.95	
	60321	Contr. Pricing Guide: Resid. Sq. Ft. 2001	39.95	
	64021	ECHOS Assemblies Cost Book 2001	149.95	
	64011	ECHOS Unit Cost Book 2001	99.95	
	54001	ECHOS (Combo set of both books)	214.95	
	60231	Electrical Change Order Cost Data 2001	89.95	
	60031	Electrical Cost Data 2001	89.95	
	60201	Facilities Construction Cost Data 2001	219.95	
	60301	Facilities Maintenance & Repair Cost Data 2001	199.95	
	60161	Heavy Construction Cost Data 2001	89.95	
	63161	Heavy Const. Cost Data–Metric Version 2001	89.95	
	60091	Interior Cost Data 2001	89.95	
	60121	Labor Rates for the Const. Industry 2001	199.95	
	60181	Light Commercial Cost Data 2001	79.95	
	60021	Mechanical Cost Data 2001	89.95	
	60151	Open Shop Building Const. Cost Data 2001	89.95	
	60211	Plumbing Cost Data 2001	89.95	
	60041	Repair and Remodeling Cost Data 2001	79.95	
	60171	Residential Cost Data 2001	79.95	
	60281	Site Work & Landscape Cost Data 2001	89.95	
	60051	Square Foot Costs 2001	99.95	
		REFERENCE BOOKS		
	67147A	ADA in Practice	72.95	
	67310	ADA Pricing Guide	72.95	
	67298	Basics for Builders: Framing & Rough Carpentry	24.95	
	67273	Basics for Builders: How to Survive and Prosper	34.95	
	67307	Basics for Builders: Plan Reading & Takeoff	35.95	
	67261	Bldg. Prof. Guide to Contract Documents–3rd Ed.	64.95	
	67312	Building Spec Homes Profitably	29.95	
	67250	Business Management for Contractors	17.98	
	67146	Concrete Repair & Maintenance Illustrated	69.95	
	67278	Construction Delays	59.95	
	67255	Contractor's Business Handbook	21.48	
	67314	Cost Planning & Est. for Facil. Maint.	82.95	
	67317A	Cyberplaces: The Internet Guide–2nd Ed.	59.95	
	67230A	Electrical Estimating Methods–2nd Ed.	64.95	
	64777	Environmental Remediation Est. Methods	99.95	
	67160	Estimating for Contractors	35.95	
	67276	Estimating Handbook	99.95	
	67249	Facilities Maintenance Management	86.95	

Qty.	Book No.	REFERENCE BOOKS (Cont.)	Unit Price	Total
	67246	Facilities Maintenance Standards	$159.95	
	67264	Facilities Manager's Reference	86.95	
	67318	Facilities Operations & Engineering Reference	99.95	
	67301	Facilities Planning & Relocation	109.95	
	67231	Forms for Building Const. Professional	94.95	
	67288	Forms for Contractors	79.95	
	67260	Fundamentals of the Construction Process	34.98	
	67258	Hazardous Material & Hazardous Waste	44.98	
	67148	Heavy Construction Handbook	74.95	
	67323	Historic Preservation: Proj. Planning & Est.	99.95	
	67308C	Home Improvement Costs–Interior Projects	19.95	
	67309C	Home Improvement Costs–Exterior Projects	19.95	
	67304	How to Estimate with Metric Units	24.98	
	67306	HVAC: Design Criteria, Options, Select.–2nd Ed.	84.95	
	67281	HVAC Systems Evaluation	84.95	
	67282	Illustrated Construction Dictionary, Condensed	59.95	
	67292A	Illustrated Construction Dictionary, w/CD-ROM	99.95	
	67295A	Landscape Estimating–3rd Ed.	62.95	
	67266	Legal Reference for Design & Construction	54.98	
	67299	Maintenance Management Audit	32.48	
	67302	Managing Construction Purchasing	31.48	
	67294	Mechanical Estimating–2nd Ed.	64.95	
	67245A	Planning and Managing Interior Projects–2nd Ed.	69.95	
	67283A	Plumbing Estimating Methods–2nd Ed.	59.95	
	67326	Preventive Maint. Guidelines for School Facil.	149.95	
	67236A	Productivity Standards for Constr.–3rd Ed.	159.95	
	67247A	Project Scheduling & Management for Constr.	64.95	
	67262	Quantity Takeoff for Contractors	17.98	
	67265A	Repair & Remodeling Estimating–3rd Ed.	69.95	
	67322	Residential & Light Commercial Const. Stds.	59.95	
	67254	Risk Management for Building Professionals	29.98	
	67291	Scheduling Manual–3rd Ed.	64.95	
	67145A	Square Foot Estimating Methods–2nd Ed.	69.95	
	67287	Successful Estimating Methods	64.95	
	67313	Successful Interior Projects	34.98	
	67233	Superintending for Contractors	35.95	
	67321	Total Productive Facilities Management	79.95	
	67284	Understanding Building Automation Systems	39.98	
	67259	Understanding Legal Aspects of Design/Build	79.95	
	67303	Unit Price Estimating Methods–2nd Ed.	59.95	
	67319	Value Engineering: Practical Applications	79.95	

MA residents add 5% state sales tax _____

Shipping & Handling** _____

Total (U.S. Funds)* _____

Prices are subject to change and are for U.S. delivery only. *Canadian customers may call for current prices. **Shipping & handling charges: Add 7% of total order for check and credit card payments. Add 9% of total order for invoiced orders.

Send Order To: **ADDV-1001**

Name (Please Print) _____

Company _____

☐ **Company**

☐ **Home**   Address _____

_____

City/State/Zip _____

Phone # _____   P.O. # _____